KT-436-361

THE BRITISH MUSICAL THEATRE

Volume One

THE BRITISH MUSICAL THEATRE

VOLUME I

1865 – 1914

KURT GÄNZL

NEW YORK
OXFORD UNIVERSITY PRESS
1986

First published in 1986 by
THE MACMILLAN PRESS LTD
London, England

Published in 1986 in the United States by
OXFORD UNIVERSITY PRESS INC.
200 Madison Avenue
New York NY 10016

Printed in Great Britain by
Redwood Burn Ltd,
Trowbridge, Wiltshire

Library of Congress Cataloging-in-Publication Data

Gänzl, Kurt.
British musical theatre.
Includes indexes.
1. Musical revue, comedy, etc.—England—London.
I. Title.
MS1731.8.L7G36 1986 782.81'0941 85-29705
ISBN 0-19-520509-X (set)

Prologue

A chronicle must have its boundaries, both in time and in subject matter, and these boundaries should not be entirely arbitrary. This survey of the British light musical theatre limits itself to new and original stage works, that is to say pieces which comprise a text and a score written particularly for the show in question. Under this rule of thumb we do not deal with the ballad operas and burlesques which relied principally on 'borrowed' melodies, nor with the provincial shows which used popular songs and second-hand music hall material for their musical part. Such a criterion is, of course, frequently tested. Musicals of all kinds appear which run closely against the limits set and it has often been necessary to make a decision as to whether a piece with, perhaps, a partly original score or a libretto translated from the French should be included. When such works fit logically into the trends and tradition we are following, they are admitted.

Since we are dealing with the light musical theatre the various forms of opera are excluded. Once again, it is sometimes difficult to draw a line between opera grand, romantic and light. The inclusion of spoken dialogue does not necessarily qualify an opera as 'light', nor does an inherently non-comedic subject necessarily make an opera 'grand'. Quality and intent, two rather insubstantial criteria, seem here to be as important as any. For our purposes we have included the few marginal pieces which were produced in the commercial theatre for a run, as opposed to those which appeared only in the repertoires of the metropolitan opera houses and the touring opera companies.

The light musical theatre show falls into a number of categories under a large variety of contemporary descriptions – most frequently 'comic opera', 'burlesque', 'extravaganza', 'musical comedy' and 'musical farce'. Each of these names was understood to cover a narrowly different type of show, but often the types were apt to overlap; the divisions between them, hazy enough to begin with, were blurred temporarily or broken down definitively as fashions and public tastes took new turnings. But no matter how these joinings and separations of style proceeded, between the most erudite of comic operas and the lowest of burlesques or farces there existed a body of works which were not opera, nor music hall, nor revue, pantomime, oratorio, or concert, but which made up the field of light musical entertainment which has so long been the most popular of all theatrical forms. It is with these shows that this history deals.

This survey begins with the year 1865. There had, of course, been a certain amount of original musical theatre in Britain before that date. The great success of the satiric pasticcio *The Beggar's Opera* in the early eighteenth century had preceded the development of a ballad opera form which had gradually shed its borrowed music for original scores. This genre had produced a number of outstanding and durable works including Dibdin's *The Waterman* and *The Quaker* and Stephen Storace's *No Song, No Supper* which were still included in some repertoires a century and more after their first productions. The years 1830–1865, however, saw Britain entertained basically by two kinds of musical entertainment – the opera and the burlesque.

Opera companies and seasons abounded both in London and the provinces presenting the favourite operas of Bellini, Donizetti, Weber and Mozart to which were added the newest successes of Gounod and Verdi and the highly popular English pieces in which the ballad opera tradition had culminated – the works of Balfe (*Satanella, The Rose of Castile* and, most notably, *The Bohemian Girl*), of Wallace (*Lurline* and *Maritana*), and *The Lily of Killarney* of Julius Benedict. These latter pieces comprised the core of the repertoires of English opera companies for many years. They displayed a degree of achievement not previously reached in Britain in that type of work, and produced a clutch of numbers which became standards – 'I Dreamt that I Dwelt in marble Halls' (*The Bohemian Girl*), 'Scenes that are Brightest' and 'Yes! Let me like a Soldier Fall' from *Maritana* and the glorious 'Eily Mavourneen' (*The Lily of Killarney*). All these pieces, however, were strictly sentimental in content and style, and of a quality which allied them most naturally to the opera companies where they found their home.

Burlesque and its companions 'burletta' and 'extravaganza' existed on a very different footing. It was a feature of the ordinary theatre programme, usually sharing the bill with a farce and a comedietta or a drama, but, in any case, as one-third or even a quarter of an evening's entertainment. The burlesque had come to its first flowering under the management of Eliza Vestris at the Olympic Theatre where James R. Planché produced the first of the long run of pieces which were to make them both famous. *Olympic Revels* made fun of the Greek gods in cleverly-written rhyming couplets, accompanied by music from *La Muette de Portici*, *Der Freischütz* and *William Tell* as well as such popular tunes as 'Highland Laddie' and 'Judy Callaghan'. Its successors were on a similar plan, though Planché subsequently extended his range to make fun of more modern targets, and to move into the field of fairy extravaganza often inspired by French *contes*.

As Vestris progressed from the Olympic to Covent Garden and the Lyceum, the burlesque and extravaganza progressed in public favour. Other writers, notably Gilbert a'Beckett, Talfourd and the Broughs, followed where Planché had led in the way of cultivated and poetic fantasies and clever, humorous conceits and rhymes; and other burlesque stars rose to vie with Vestris and her team without ever excelling them. By 1865, however, the picture was somewhat different. Vestris had died, her successor as 'Queen of Burlesque', Marie Wilton, had taken on the Prince of Wales Theatre and more 'serious' occupations, and Planché had laid down his pen after 176 stage works for a well-earned retirement. The burlesque had degenerated into a broad and facile romp of little or no literary merit, relying heavily on puns and word-twisting and broad clowning for its humour, with its songs sung to hackneyed tunes and its dances repetitious and *rechauffé*.

It was into this relative vacuum of light musical theatre that the British 'musical' tradition was to grow. Starting hesitantly, and both inspired and hindered by the popular French opéra-bouffe and opérette importations, it developed with an enormous vigour so that, within little more than a decade, it had laid the foundations for what would soon become a virtual monopoly of the musical stages of the English-speaking world. This monopoly lasted, with very few intrusions, until the invasion of the waltz strains of Vienna and the syncopated rhythms of America in the years before the Great War.

These volumes follow the development of the British musical, year by year, treating individually each show which was presented in the West End of London as well as a large number of those staged in the suburbs, in the provinces and on the touring circuits. Pieces belonging to the mainstream of the British tradition which were produced initially or entirely outside Britain are also included, though integrally foreign shows, even if they made their first appearance in Britain, are normally not.

Reference Material

The reference sections found at the end of each chapter of this work giving production and cast details have been compiled from the files of *The Era*, *The Stage*, *The Times*, *The New York Dramatic Mirror* and other contemporary newspapers and journals, and the programme collections held by the author, the Theatre Museum at the Victoria and Albert Museum, London, the Performing Arts Research Library of the New York Public Library at Lincoln Center, New York, and others.

Productions: For each show, details of the original production, any other productions prior to London, the original West End production and any subsequent West End revivals are given. Provincial productions and tours subsequent to a West End production are not included. Details of Broadway productions and revivals are also given and, where a show has been played in America but never on Broadway, available details of these productions are also shown. Note is also made of Parisian and Viennese productions. Film, television and videogram performances are listed where traceable.

Touring dates: Tour lists are given in chronological order. Where a date cannot be traced that week is designated by a question mark ?. Split weeks are indicated by a bar /. Dates are indicated by the name of the town only; where only a theatre name is given this refers to a London suburban theatre (Standard, Alexandra, Shakespeare, Parkhurst, Metropole, Grand or Philharmonic, Islington, King's, Hammersmith, Coronet & c.). Dates of more than one week's duration are indicated by a multiplication sign followed by the number of weeks played: × 2, × 3 & c. Where only isolated dates can be traced, these are given.

Cast lists: All traceable cast changes are included and are shown by a bar / whilst performances by principal understudies or alternates are shown in brackets ( ). Cast changes between an out-of-town run and a West End production are shown by a double bar //. Other credits are shown against abbreviated titles as follows: dir = director, md = musical director, ch = choreographer, sc = scenic designer, cos = costume designer, pd = principal dancer, pr = producer, scr = screenplay.

Contents

Volume One

1865–1914

1865–1867

If the British light musical scene of the early 1860s showed little sign of fertility, across the Channel a decidedly vigorous new trend in musical theatre was busily establishing itself under the influence of one of the brightest young composers of all time, Jacques Offenbach, who had just 'invented' the opéra-bouffe. Since his first effort with *Oyayaie ou La Reine des Isles*, the rising star of the French musical had worked up through such delightful oddities as *Ba-ta-Clan* and *Les Deux Aveugles* to the triumph of *Orphée aux Enfers* (1858) and *La Belle Hélène* (1864), landmarks in the history of the French musical and the delight of Paris.

The opéra-bouffe at its best was a combination of extravagantly imaginative plotting and humorously pointed dialogue set to, in Offenbach's case, light and bright music of the highest calibre. The libretti of *Orphée aux Enfers* and *La Belle Hélène* had more than a little in common with the best of British extravaganza, but they were lifted into an altogether different category by the brilliant new music which Offenbach provided for them.

In 1865 came the first attempt to produce something resembling an English opéra-bouffe. The collaborators were the young author, F. C. Burnand, and the musical director of the Royal Strand Theatre, Frank Musgrave, and the production took place under the aegis of Miss Ada Swanborough, the leading lady of that theatre and a member of its managing family. The Swanboroughs had taken over the Strand in 1858 and had featured a policy of burlesque starring Miss Swanborough alongside such great performers as Marie Wilton, Charlotte Saunders, James Bland, Tom Thorne and David James. The burlesques played at the Strand had been in the habitual style, written in rhyming verse, broad in visual and verbal humour and relying on the musical director to perform a 'scissors and paste' exercise to provide a score. The production of the new piece had been immediately preceded by Burnand's *Patient Penelope*, a classical parody, and revivals of Henry Byron's successful *The Maid and the Magpie* (on the opera *La Gazza Ladra*) and *Aladdin or The Wonderful Scamp*. The new opéra-bouffe was itself a burlesque of William Harrison Ainsworth's 1843 novel of the young Henry VIII, *Windsor Castle*, and the treatment which Burnand provided was on the same lines as that given to its predecessors.

Burnand, at the age of 29, was a member of the staff of *Punch* and an experienced and accomplished writer of modern burlesque. He had placed his first piece, *Dido*, with Chatterton at the St James' Theatre when only 23, and his subsequent large output had been chiefly in the burlesque field. His most notable success had been with *Ixion or The Man at the Wheel* which had run 153 performances at the Royalty in 1863. His musical collaborator on *Windsor Castle* had a task very different from the usual. The legend 'the music selected, arranged and composed by. .' attached to the credits of every previous burlesque was self-explanatory. But for *Windsor Castle* the Strand's conductor was required to compose a full original score. Musgrave was a virtual novice in such a field. Burnand later described him:

> Frank Musgrave had no education, musical or otherwise, but he could turn out a catchy popular tune, could score it for a small orchestra, had a keen sense of humour and was a first-class stage manager.

In fact Musgrave's musical output to that date had consisted largely of dance music and arrangements. As 'F.M.' he had arranged several volumes of dances and 'nigger songs' for Booseys (1861–2) and since then had kept up a steady and lucrative flow of Quadrilles, Valses and Polkas, usually based on the themes of other composers.

Windsor Castle was not an extensive work. It lasted some 90 minutes in performance and included thirteen brief musical sections. But when it was produced it was featured as the principal item on the Strand bill and largely publicised, with an emphasis on its novelty:

> The new and original historical opera burlesque
> WINDSOR CASTLE
> with (a novelty in England) entirely new and
> original music by Mr. F. Musgrave.

The story of the piece was a perfect network of love affairs. Pretty Mabel Lyndwood is beloved by the evil forester, Morgan Fenwolf, who has sold his soul to the devilish Herne the Hunter to gain the position of Head Forester and Mabel's hand. But young King Henry notices the lass and his attentions wander from the ambitious Anne Boleyn who is, in her turn, busy shunning the attentions of the lovelorn Thomas Wyatt. At the same time, the Duke of Richmond and the Earl of Surrey are vying for the affections of Anne's lady-in-waiting, The Fair Geraldine, who is rather inclined to the latter in spite of his penchant for writing sonnets for all occasions. The five scenes were full of action. The characters were whisked from the castle to Herne's cave in the depths of the earth and back with all the spectacular accoutrements of popular entertainment:

> 'A Startling Apparition' – 'Great Sensation' – 'An Appalling And Exciting Contest Between Will Somers And Herne The Hunter' – 'Perilous Leap And Escape Of The Jester'
>
> Mabel!
> Morgan!!
> The Ivy!!!
> The Climbing Up The Ivy!!!!
> The Getting Over The Parapet!!!!!
> The Struggle!!!!!!
> The Appearance of Herne!!!!!!!
> The Going Over The Parapet!!!!!!!!
> The Drop!!!!!!!!!

In true burlesque fashion Mabel sings the opening number 'Pretty Dicky Bird' to a stuffed and mechanical canary. She has wrung its neck and had it stuffed so that it will sing to order. The King returns triumphant from the hunt clasping a white rabbit by the ears, and Surrey arrives several stories up at The Fair Geraldine's window claiming to have escaped from prison because he has written a sonnet and must have someone listen to it. Having a short memory, he then proceeds to forget the words:

Oh my Geraldine
No flower was ever seen so toodle-um
You are my lum-ti-toodle-lay
Pretty, pretty Queen
Is rum-ti Geraldine and something seen
More sweet than tiddle-lum in May.

The rhyming couplet dialogue relied heavily on puns, rhymes and word-play. It did not show the elegance or care of the Planché school, aiming more often, in the contemporary fashion, for a quick laugh or a far-fetched verbal effect often only discernible by seeing the lines on paper:

WYATT: (wooing ANNE)
I am not poor, I loved you before Henery
You wouldn't have to live with me in penury
My name at all events has got a handle
ANNE: But to a King a knight can't hold a candle
or
ANNE: What's love? Caprice
A light that burns one minute, then 'twill cease
A flame twixt him and her – a poet's word
WYATT: Yes, by a poet *hymned*, by woman *heard*.

In the end the King is reconciled to Anne, Geraldine to the faithful Richmond, and Mabel, since Fenwolf has been duly claimed by Herne, turns to Wyatt. They have fallen in love at first sight and, in any case, her grandfather, (very) Old Tristram, has finally remembered what he has been trying to say all evening. Mabel is a foundling, and of noble blood. Miss Swanborough had the last word:

Sir T. W.
A good hub'll you
Make me,
Make me.
I'll never trouble you.
Call the 'Charioteer'
Order, Harry, it here
Able
Mabel
To take away![1]
Hold high wassail, oh
Send each vassal, oh
To see
Hen-ree
In Windsor Castle, oh
To be repeated
Every night!

This curtain plea seemingly had good effect, for *Windsor Castle* evoked plenty of interest and was played through till the end of the season to good houses. It could have continued longer but the Swanboroughs had scheduled the theatre for an extensive

[1] This finale was later extended with reprises of the show's 'hits', 'Le Chevalier et sa Belle' and 'Tiddley Wink'

rebuilding programme, so *Windsor Castle* was removed and the collaborators were set to work on a successor.

The production brought interested comment from the press. *The Times* wrote:

> Hitherto one of the chief tasks of the burlesquing dramatist has been to select the popular melodies of the day and to introduce them in the course of his play, and thus many of the tunes which were first made known to the more plebeian section of the public through the music halls have fallen into higher company. From this custom of borrowing melodies Mr. Burnand has departed and his burlesque *Windsor Castle* now played at the Strand Theatre has been fitted throughout with new music composed by Mr. Musgrave, the orchestral director of the establishment. The 'Bouffes Parisiens' of the French capital are his precedent, the notorious success of *Orphée aux Enfers* a few years ago inspiring the hope that a work in which a similar principle was adopted might be fortunate in London. Mr. Musgrave has shown himself equal to the occasion; for his melodies are not only pleasing in themselves but are suitable to that combination of song and grotesque dance which belongs to the very essence of modern burlesque, more especially to that variety of the genus which flourishes at the Strand Theatre.

That variety had some features which made 'the first English opéra-bouffe' a little curious. Its casting was on strictly traditional lines. The 'boy' specialist, Miss Raynham, played Henry VIII, while The Fair Geraldine had her choice between two other travestis, the Misses Hughes (Richmond) and Holt (Surrey). The part of Wyatt was taken by Maria Simpson, and the house 'dame', Tom Thorne, appeared as Anne Boleyn. Thus, almost all the 'male' music was written for soprano or alto and Anne Boleyn sang her French chansonette 'Le Chevalier et sa Belle' in a rusty baritone. This number, which lined up a series of familiar French phrases in a ridiculous conversation, proved one of the highlights of the show:

> Quand gentilhomme (l'Anglais est)
> Demande les pommes de terre
> Partant pour la Syrie
> Et vive Leicester Square

Musgrave's music was well noticed – the solos, the ensembles and the concerted numbers – all of which, in good operatic fashion, proceeded from the action and added to it. His dance music, too, was praised. A ballet in the first scene (The Brush-and-Comb-us Masque) contrasted neatly with an absurd routine of 'bumps and jumps and backfalls' from James and Fenton in their spirited 'Tiddley Wink' number in the second, and some more dignified movements involving the ladies. Before the conclusion of the run Musgrave had signed with the music publishing firm of Metzler & Co., and the music of *Windsor Castle* was saved from the extinction which has befallen so many other musical scores. However, burlesques flowed freely, particularly from Burnand, and *Windsor Castle* was never considered worthy of a revival. Its closure at the end of July, 1865 marked its final performance.

When the Strand re-opened in November, it featured the new Burnand/Musgrave piece, *L'Africaine*. The Burnand version of Meyerbeer's highly popular opera was very different to that currently playing at Covent Garden, although he adhered to the basic story outline and contented himself with ridiculing the characters and their actions. Thus the self-sacrificing negress, Selika (played by Tom Thorne), became 'Missy Dinah' and she and her jealous lover, Nelusko, were metamorphosed into coon-talking nigger minstrels. The Grand Inquisitor became a general buffoon, Donna Anna was a maid mad for the military, and Don Pedro a coxcomb with a passion for attitudinising.

L'Africaine was a more substantial piece than its predecessor. Like *Windsor Castle* it was divided into five scenes, but each scene contained more matter and the musical numbers were more considerable. The tone was, if anything, even more broadly in the tradition of Strand burlesque. The romantic Inez (Miss Swanborough), sings of love:

Under my window my Vasco came
By the light of the trembling moon
Softly he bellowed, 'Dear What'syourname,
I'll sing you a little tune,
My touch and my melody you should hear
As learned from a professor'
A shilling a lesson I paid him dear
To teach me the gay guitar

and, upon seeing Selika in Vasco's arms, cries:

What's that I see?
A pair in a position for a waltz?
One of 'em's Vasco; ergo, Vasco's false!

There was the same insistence on the parody of known works (in addition to the main subject of the burlesque) and the manipulation of the English language. Don Pedro (Miss Raynham), musing on his fate in the Anthropophagian Islands, soliloquises:

To be or not to be a cold collation
(What attitude would suit this situation?)
What attitude! Alas, these black banditti
May roast me on a spit; 'tis true 'ti*s pity.*
Shall I appear in different little lots
Served up by nigger waiters, hot-and-ots?
Posterity to learn my fate may try
And trace me till they find me in a pie
With legs stuck out through the crust as nations gave
High monuments to mark a hero's grave.
Or, in this case, to mark a hero's grav-y
Shed in defence of what he loves – the Navy.
Truss me and bake me; write upon the crust
This is your deed; inside you'll find me trussed!

Jerrold's nautical drama *Black-Eyed Susan* also came in for a good deal of use in Burnand's burlesque of the opera's great ship scene, and parody of the Christy Minstrels provided plenty of low comedy material for Selika and Nelusko. The author got every inch of mileage out of the Cannibal Islands situation, and the word 'cannibal' was twisted every possible way. One number entitled 'I think You would Do for Dinner or Tea' had the refrain:

Cannibal, cannibal, dine and sup,
Can nibble, can nibble, can nibble, can nibble and eat you up

and the Anthropophagian natives made their entrance to a quick burst of 'The Cannibals are Coming'.

On the whole, the book of *L'Africaine* was more ambitious and better executed technically than the earlier work, and the speeches and lyrics showed more care and ingenuity. The rhyming schemes, as always, were purposefully obtrusive. The entrance of the Grand Inquisitor showed them at their most persistent:

PEDRO: Now you may ask who is it a
Casual cursory sort o' visitor
Wonderful phiz it! a
Man might quiz it! a
Girl could kiss it! a
G.I.: More exquisiter
Than I
For why
Cos I am the Grand Inquisitor!
CHOR: Yes, he is the Grand Inquisitor!

and there were the usual topical references (including a particularly popular one to the saucy equestrienne artiste Adah Isaacs Menken) which were kept fresh throughout the run.

Burnand had skilfully arranged his libretto to include all the favourite 'turns' expected of the Strand's stars and Musgrave again supplied music in a suitable vein, burlesquing, in his turn, Christy Minstrels and grand opera in a set of pieces which gave plenty of opportunity for merry singing and dancing. Among the most appreciated numbers were a Drinking Song for the Misses Swanborough, Holt and Johnstone, a quaint duet about 'Geo-gruffy' for Stoyle and Thorne, and an Indian War Song for James (complete with boomerang). *L'Africaine* caught on particularly well and ran through the Christmas and New Year period, closing after three and a half months and eighty-eight performances. Its critical reception was also good. *The Era* claimed Musgrave was 'well entitled to be considered the "Offenbach" of the metropolis', in spite of the fact that it accounted *L'Africaine* inferior musically to *Windsor Castle* and expressed some doubts on the whole principle of original scores:

> We must be allowed to doubt . . the probability of the new extravaganzas produced in succession being able to satisfy the demands of the public so well as the old system of employing the floating street minstrelsy of the day.

In spite of *L'Africaine*'s productive run, the Swanboroughs clearly came to the same conclusion. When the show was withdrawn the policy of 'English opéra-bouffe' was abandoned.

The new piece, *Ivanhoe*, was a return to the old-style pasticcio, and the Strand's brave adventure into a new form was at an end. *L'Africaine* was, however, sufficiently well regarded by its producers to be revived at their theatre in 1876 when it played nearly three months with a cast headed by Edward Terry, Claude Marius[1] and Angelina Claude. Styles in burlesque had changed considerably by that time and there was no longer a travesti Selika, although the young men, the Dons Pedro and Alva, were still played by young ladies, and the work suffered a little from the passing of some of the subjects parodied. Musgrave's music, however, held up well and the *Daily News* was able to report after the first night: 'The songs and breakdowns were all encored'.

But if there was, for the moment, no further interest in pursuing English opéra-bouffe, the French variety was making its presence strongly felt. Hard on the heels of the Strand's *L'Africaine*, *Orphée aux Enfers* arrived in town. Offenbach was already well-known to the English public. His music had been filched liberally by the

[1] Familiarly known as 'Mons' Marius

compilers of burlesques to re-set again and again with fresh lyrics, and almost any theatre showing musical pasticcio included at least one of his melodies in its score. The composer had also paid a brief visit to London's St James' Theatre in 1857 with a group of his short works, but this was the first time that one of his full-length pieces had been presented. As *Orpheus in the Underworld*, in a translation by Planché, it was staged at Her Majesty's, but it was a poor production which did not raise much enthusiasm. In June 1866 *Barbe-Bleu* was given at the Olympic and Burnand's version of *La Belle Hélène* (*Helen, or Taken from the Greek*) at the Adelphi, but in November 1867 Offenbach established himself in the hearts of London society when Charles Lamb Kenney's adaptation of *La Grande Duchesse* was produced at Covent Garden. After six weeks of capacity business the theatre was needed for pantomime, so *La Grande Duchesse* was taken out on tour and during the next few years was instrumental in leading the spread of popularity and influence of the French opéra-bouffe over the whole country, returning from time to time to London to consolidate its triumph.

In those following years Offenbach became the *enfant chéri* of the musical theatre but already in 1867 the whole spectrum of the London theatre, from the most proper to the most popular, was playing his music. While *La Grande Duchesse* was lording it at Covent Garden and the burlesque houses were playing excerpts freely and without fee, a version of *Orpheus* was being given at the Oxford Music Hall and *Ba-ta-Clan* (as *Ching Chow Hi*) was on the programme at Mr German Reed's Gallery of Illustration.

The Gallery of Illustration was the home of a very particular kind of entertainment, mixing comic operetta with drawing-room songs and monologues in a programme which was extremely British and 'correct'. Throughout the nineteenth century little musical pieces dignified by the name of operetta had been widely produced as introductory pieces or fillers for a three- or four-part theatre bill or given amateur or semi-professional performances in private homes and in the many Mechanics' Halls and Corn Exchanges which provided entertainment on a lesser scale. Few of these pieces had shown any great merit or stayed long on the professional stage. Thomas German Reed was to be instrumental in changing that.

Reed had been conductor at the Haymarket Theatre and in 1844 he married the successful actress, Priscilla Horton. Miss Horton had shown an amazing versatility on the stage. At the age of twenty she had played Ariel in Macready's *Tempest* at Covent Garden, and two years later created the role of Georgina Vesey in Bulwer Lytton's *Money* at the Haymarket where she also appeared in a number of major Shakespearian roles. On the other hand, she had played in Purcell's opera *King Arthur* (1842) and in numerous Planché extravaganzas where her deep operatic contralto had been especially appreciated. In 1854 she and her husband compiled a drawing-room entertainment in which Reed accompanied his wife in a series of vocal parodies, and which proved so popular in the provinces that it was decided to bring it to town. The impersonations were complemented by a selection of excerpts from Mrs Reed's past successes and were presented in the genteel atmosphere of St Martin's Hall, Long Acre, as 'Miss Priscilla Horton's Illustrative Gatherings'. These performances were extremely well received and, in 1859, Mr German Reed took larger premises at 14, Regent Street which he christened 'The Gallery of Illustration'. Many people who would not have dreamed of being seen inside a theatre, much less of taking their wives and daughters to one, were happy to be entertained by the refined performances at the German Reed establishment. Theatres in the mid-nineteenth century were by no means the orderly places we know today. Moral turpitude genuinely did lurk everywhere, from the highly suggestive songs and acts of the Music Halls to the prostitutes and pickpockets promenading at the Alhambra, Leicester Square, and many a good Victorian was highly wary of 'the theatre'. The German Reeds' blameless and well-conducted entertainment, therefore, supplied a genuine need. Mrs Reed's solo recitals were gradually expanded to include musical dialogues and short two- and three-handed musical playlets. Original works were commissioned and presented, many with music especially written by German Reed himself and, while the diet was later varied with the occasional French one-acter or pasticcio, the central feature of the Gallery of Illustration soon became the presentation of new English musical comedies, usually of one act.

In 1867 German Reed decided to branch out into more ambitious work. He took a lease on the recently-built St George's Hall in Langham Place and remodelled it as a veritable Opera House. Soon after the opening of *La Grande Duchesse*, 'teaser' advertisements began to appear:

> St George's Opera House, Langham Place, Oxford Circus will open under the direction of Mr German Reed for a short season of comic opera and extravaganza early in December. Further particulars will shortly be announced.

In a few weeks the particulars were forthcoming and, on December 10, 1867 St George's Opera House opened its season. The evening began with a one-act Offenbach piece *Puss in Petticoats* (*La Chatte Metamorphosée en Femme*), a comic four-hander on the theme of metempsychosis, followed by a 'new English comic opera' *The Contrabandista*, and concluding with another Offenbach piece, *Ching Chow Hi*.

The 'new English comic opera' was from the pen of the ubiquitous Burnand. Since his 'opéra-bouffe' ventures with *Windsor Castle* and *L'Africaine* he had scored an enormous hit with his burlesque of *Black-Eyed Susan* which was still playing after twelve months at the Royalty and was eventually to total an incredible 400 consecutive performances. His output had been prodigious. In 1866 he had supplied pieces for half a dozen London theatres and in 1867 he had already written *Olympic Games* for the Olympic, *Mary Turner* for the New Royal Amphitheatre, Holborn, and had adapted Maddison Morton's famous farce *Box and Cox* as a one-act operetta for the society amateur group, the Moray Minstrels, under the title *Cox and Box*. The music of this had been composed by Burnand's Garrick Club confrère, the twenty-five year old Arthur Sullivan.

Arthur Seymour Sullivan had been classically trained at the Royal Academy and Leipzig Conservatorium and had, at this time, very little experience of writing for the stage. His first attempt, an operetta called *The Sapphire Necklace*, had never been staged: his second was *Cox and Box*. He had, however, gained a considerable reputation as a composer of orchestral and vocal works. His *Tempest* music, the cantata *Kenilworth* and the overture *In Memoriam* had resulted in his becoming regarded as one of the most promising of the younger generation of British composers. Sullivan's collaboration with Burnand was continued on *The Contrabandista*.

The story was set in *Fra Diavolo* country, among the bandits of the Continental mountains, and the plot was suitably curious. The chief of the Ladrones has been killed and a new one is to be elected. The two pretenders for the position tie in the election so precedent declares that the post shall go to the first stranger to enter their realm. The new chief will also inherit his predecessor's wife, the bloodthirsty Inez. The fortunate stranger who happens by is Peter Adolphus Grigg, an English photographer out 'pursuing art'. He is proclaimed chief, invested with the Sacred Hat, and betrothed to the fierce chieftainess. But San José, one of the defeated candidates, plots with the lady to remove both his rival, Sancho, and their ineffectual new leader. Sancho overhears and escapes to betray the band, and the Ladrones are just about to wreak their revenge on poor Grigg and Rita, a hostage, when the latter's lover, the Count Vasquez (who has spent the earlier part of the play disguised as an old shepherd to mingle with the banditti and supply the duets) arrives with his soldiery in the nick of time. Everyone is forgiven and they merrily sing the joining of Rita and Vasquez and San José and Inez while Grigg signs off:

> Thanks, noble leader of the Spanish Guard
> If you come to London, there's my card
> Ladrones farewell, good-bye you ugly fellow,
> Now take me back again to Compostello!

With his usual facility, Burnand turned out the libretto in double quick time and the whole piece is said to have been put together in little more than a fortnight. It was divided into two acts and leaned in kind more to the world of Scribe and the French opéra-comique than to that of *The Lily of Killarney* and *Maritana*, or that of opéra-bouffe, French or English. The spoken parts were not extensive and Burnand kept his fancy rather more in check than was usual, so that the tone of the piece was eventually one of lightly mocking melodrama relieved by some not particularly amusing chatter from Grigg. In the lyrics he was occasionally tempted back to the manner of burlesque:

> RITA: The tinkling sheep-bell knells the parting day
> The flocks collect from meadow, hill and moor
> The happy goatherd homeward takes his way
> His wife and children wait him at the door.
> To me the bells send up no cheering tone
> Only the night wind sighs alone.

Likewise, in the first act finale, the presentation of the Sacred Hat bore resemblances to the Sabre ceremonial of *La Grande Duchesse*, and was in its turn rounded off with a pun:

> GRIGG: Of this old hat so old and worn
> The royalty I doubt
> Its regal mark, my friends, is gone
> Behold, its crown is out!

The songs and concerted pieces made up the larger part of the show, and Sullivan's music was a revelation, particularly to that majority not already acquainted with *Cox and Box*. In *The Contrabandista* he showed his particular skill for writing light and humorous theatrical music, both vocal and orchestral. *The Era* commented:

> Mr. Arthur Sullivan's music is melodious and captivating to a degree. The orchestration is smooth and varied besides being technically clever. In the whole treatment of the subject supplied by Mr. Burnand the composer proclaims his true musical instinct. In the concerted music especially Mr. Sullivan displays a light, graceful fancy and a facility of writing nothing less than admirable and *The Contrabandista* taken on its own merits is a triumphant vindication of the fact that musical talent is not denied to the English.

Bell's Life concurred:

> The music is fluent and good, dramatic and characteristic . . the buffo songs are excellent . .'

It was, in fact, a buffo song 'From Rock to Rock' which proved to be the hit of the evening. J. A. Shaw, as the strayed Grigg bumbling his way into the hands of the banditti, had the house in fits of laughter as he pattered:

From rock to rock with many a shock
And bump and thump and many a knock,
I fall and not a soul is near
The trav'ler's lonely path to cheer . .

Among the fourteen musical items the trio 'Dance the Bolero', where Grigg is informed of his 'good luck' by San José and Sancho, and the harmonious quintet 'Hand of Fate' showed Sullivan at his most attractive in a well-balanced score.

Unfortunately, the production left much to be desired. The singers proved to have little acting ability and the actors were unable to cope with the music. Apart from Shaw, who was a decided hit as Grigg, the ladies emerged the best. Arabella Smythe as Rita had an acting role limited to expressing gross anxiety and/or ecstatic delight, but she sang extremely well and the authors consequently wrote in an extra number, 'My Love, we'll meet Again', for her. The young contralto Lucy Franklein as the dramatic Inez coped admirably with the bandit queen's flights of dialogue and largely below-the-stave music to give the best all-round performance, but Thomas Aynsley Cook, fresh from grand opera at Covent Garden, went heavily over the top as San José, and the dashing Vasquez turned out to have next to no voice.

Nevertheless, *The Contrabandista* was agreed to be a success. Reed advertised:

THE CONTRABANDISTA (Enormous success)
F. C. BURNAND
ARTHUR SULLIVAN
FROM ROCK TO ROCK SUNG BY MR. GRIGG
Enthusiastically encored every night
DANCE THE BOLERO Roars of laughter
TIS THE LAW OF THE LADRONES
St. GEORGE'S OPERA HOUSE, Langham-Place,
Oxford Circus

and audiences proved encouraging. But the soprano Madame Leibhardt had been engaged for the latter part of the season and after some two months Reed altered his programme. *Puss in Petticoats* was withdrawn, and *The Contrabandista* and *Ching Chow Hi* were thereafter played alternately alongside Leibhardt's impersonation of Auber's *The Ambassadress.* When the season finally ended in March, *The Contrabandista* had been played 72 times during the fifteen weeks Reed had held the Opera House.

The Contrabandista was never revived in London in its original form but it was played in the provinces a few years later by Frederic Sullivan's company and appeared both in Britain and in the United States in amended versions. In 1894 Richard D'Oyly Carte, deprived of any new Gilbert and Sullivan work, had Burnand and Sullivan disinter their early piece and after extensive revisions and additions it was produced at the Savoy Theatre as *The Chieftain* for a run of 97 performances.

In America the alterations were unauthorised and less tactful. Following the enormous success of *H. M. S. Pinafore* in New York and throughout the United States, American managers were extravagantly anxious to capitalise on the 'craze' for Gilbert and Sullivan. *The Sorcerer* was quickly brought to Broadway, Gilbert's *Engaged* was produced and adulated, and the Philadelphia Church Choir Co. on tour with its superior production of *Pinafore* in 1879 decided to add *The Contrabandista* to their repertoire. In a dire hint of things to come, the libretto was 'Americanised' and some additional music by the company's young conductor, John Philip Sousa, added. Sousa evidently admired the libretto of *The Contrabandista* for he immediately began work on a comic opera of his own, *The Smugglers*, which took Burnand's story, virtually unchanged, as its book. Other companies also staged versions of *The Contrabandista* but it was not played on Broadway.

The Contrabandista was not a piece of the dimensions or stature of Offenbach's *La Grande Duchesse* but it had sufficient merit to achieve a worthwhile run in London. Most importantly, its production had brought an English comic opera before the public which was appreciated and imitated. Between the musical burlesque and the comic opera there were wide fields of light musical theatre to be explored. Musgrave and Sullivan had sketched in the boundaries, and Burnand had given some foundation to his later claim to be regarded as the originator of the British musical. Surprisingly, he had only two more pieces to contribute – the 1897 comic opera *His Majesty* which his diffuse libretto largely helped to kill, and the unsuccessful burlesque *Tra-la-la Tosca* (1890). In a theatrical career which stretched on for many years, Burnand devoted himself principally to burlesque, farce and translations from the French rather than to original musicals. His greatest success came with the aesthetic comedy *The Colonel*, produced at the Prince of Wales Theatre in 1881 for a run of 550 performances. In 1880 he took over the editorship of *Punch*, a prestigious position which he held for twenty-six years. He was knighted in 1902.

1865–1867

0001 **WINDSOR CASTLE an operatic burlesque in five scenes by Francis C. Burnand based on W. Harrison Ainsworth's historical romance of the same name. Music by Frank Musgrave. Produced at the Royal Strand Theatre under the management of Mrs Swanborough 5 June, 1865 for a run of 43 performances closing 26 July, 1865.**

Henry VIII . . . . Miss Raynham
The Duke of Richmond . . . . Fanny Hughes
The Earl of Surrey . . . . Elise Holt
Sir Thomas Boleyn . . . . Mr Collier
Sir Thomas Wyatt . . . . Maria Simpson
Will Somers. . . . . David James
Morgan Fenwolf . . . . J. D. Stoyle
Old Tristram Lyndwood . . . . H. J. Turner
Brian Bowtance . . . . Mr Fredericks
Herne the Hunter. . . . . Charles Fenton
Anne Boleyn . . . . Thomas Thorne
The Fair Geraldine . . . . Louisa Weston
Mabel Lyndwood . . . . Ada Swanborough
The Duke of Shoreditch . . . . Mr Edge
The Duke of Paddington . . . . Mr Sybil
The Duke of Islington . . . . Mr Phillips
The Grand Falconer . . . . Mr White
Launcelot Hyke. . . . . Mr Hunley
Jonzvello . . . . Mr Tenor
Domingo Lamelyn . . . . Mr Webb
Courtiers: Messrs Skinflint, Buncombe, Hookey, Walker &c.
Yeomen of the Guard: Messrs Jeerush, Stinger, Blazey & Slicer
Pds: Emma Gunniss, Helen Gunniss

Dir: F. C. Burnand and Mr Parselle; md: Frank Musgrave; sc: Charles Fenton; cos: S. May and Mrs Richardson

Played with *Short and Sweet* and *Up Stairs and Down Stairs*, replaced 26 June by *Sam's Arrival* and *The Better Half*.

0002 **L'AFRICAINE or The Queen of the Cannibal Islands. An operatic burlesque in five scenes by Francis C. Burnand. Music by Frank Musgrave. Produced at the Royal Strand Theatre under the management of Mrs Swanborough 18 November, 1865 for a run of 88 performances closing 2 March, 1866.**

Vasco da Gama . . . . J. D. Stoyle
Don Pedro . . . . Miss Raynham
Don Diego . . . . H. J. Turner
Don Alva . . . . Elise Holt
The Grand Inquisitor. . . . . Charles Fenton
An Usher . . . . Miss Seycombe/Miss Fairfax
Nelusko . . . . David James

Inez . . . . Ada Swanborough
Anna . . . . Eliza Johnstone
Zelika . . . . Thomas Thorne

Dir: F. C. Burnand and Mr Parselle; md: Frank Musgrave; sc: Charles Fenton; cos: S. May and Mrs Richardson

Played with *Short and Sweet* and *An Alarming Sacrifice*, replaced 27 November by *Nothing Venture, Nothing Win* and *Mrs Green's Snug Little Business*, and 22 January by *Lending a Hand* and *The Artful Dodge*; the latter replaced 4 February by *The Fly and the Web*.

Produced at the Royal Strand Theatre under the management of Mrs Swanborough 15 April, 1876 for a run of 71 performances closing 5 July, 1876.
Edward Terry (VAS), Florence Roberts (PED), H. J. Turner/Harry Carter (DIE), Clara Hodgson (ALVA), Harry Cox (INQ), Claude Marius (NEL), Emmeline Cole (INEZ), Maria Jones (ANNA), Angelina Claude (ZEL)

Dir: W. H. Vernon and Mrs Swanborough; md: Henry Reed; sc: H. P. Hall; cos: Mrs Richardson and M. & Mme Alias

Played with *A Lesson in Love* and *The Rival Othellos*, the former replaced by *His Last Legs*.

0003 **THE CONTRABANDISTA** or The Law of the Ladrones. A comic opera in two acts by Francis C. Burnand. Music by Arthur Sullivan. Produced at St George's Opera House under the management of Thomas German Reed 18 December, 1867. Final performance 27 March, 1868, being a total of 72 performances.

Inez de Roxas . . . . Lucy Franklein
San José . . . . Thomas Aynsley Cook
Mr Grigg . . . . J. A. Shaw
Count Vasquez . . . . Edward Hargrave
Sancho . . . . Mr Neilson
Rita . . . . Arabella Smythe
Spanish Officer . . . . Mr Hodges

Sc: Messrs Cuthbert and W. Telbin Jr

Played with *Puss in Petticoats* (*La Chatte Metamorphosée en Femme*) and *Ching Chow Hi* (*Ba-ta-Clan*). From 15 February the bill consisted of *The Ambassadress* played alternately with *Ching Chow Hi* and *The Contrabandista*, the latter being performed Monday and Wednesday evenings and Friday matinées.

Produced in the United States by Gorman's Philadelphia Church Choir Co. in a revised version with additional music by John Philip Sousa, 1879. Played in repertoire with *H.M.S. Pinafore* on tour.

Played by the London English Opera Co. on tour (U.S.A.) 1979.

Played on tour (U.S.A.) 1880; Geraldine Ulmar (RITA).

Produced in a revised form by Richard D'Oyly Carte at the Savoy Theatre 12 December, 1894 as *The Chieftain*.

Original musical shows produced by Thomas German Reed at St Martin's Hall and the Gallery of Illustration 1855–1867 included:

Holly Lodge	William and Robert Brough
The Enraged Musician	William and Robert Brough
Our Ward's Governess	H. F. Chorley
A Month From Home	William Brough
My Unfinished Opera	William Brough
After the Ball	Edmund Yates
Our Home Circuit	William Brough
Seaside Studies	William Brough

The Card Basket	Shirley Brooks
The Rival Composers	William Brough
The Family Legend	Tom Taylor
The Charming Cottage	Andrew Halliday
The Pyramids	Shirley Brooks
The Bard and his Birthday	William Brough
A Peculiar Family	William Brough
The Yachting Cruise	F. C. Burnand
The Dream in Venice	T. W. Robertson
A Quiet Chateau	Robert Reece/Virginia Gabriel
Love Wins the Way	Finlay Finlayson/Procida Bucalossi
Widows Bewitched	Virginia Gabriel

LOVE'S LIMIT a comic opera in one act by Robert Reece based on *How to Die for Love*. Music by J. E. Mallandaine. Produced at the Royalty Theatre under the management of Fanny Reeve 6 January, 1866 with the burlesque *Prometheus*. Withdrawn 16 February, 1866.

Pierre . . . . Elliot Galer
Cécile . . . . Mme d'Este Finlayson
Susanne . . . . Fanny Reeve
Jabot . . . . Edward Connell
Jacques . . . . Mr Bentley
Max . . . . H. Hayes
Md: J. E. Mallandaine

SYLVIA, the Forest Flower, a comic opera in two acts by Elliot Galer. Music by J. E. Mallandaine. Produced at the Royalty Theatre under the management of Fanny Reeve 17 February, 1866 with *Prometheus*. Withdrawn 16 March, 1866.

Reuben . . . . Edward Connell
Sir Walter Seaton . . . . Elliot Galer
Sylvia . . . . Mme d'Este Finlayson
Ronald. Fanny Reeve
Lord Belmore . . . . H. Hayes
Toby . . . . Mr Bentley
Md: J. E. Mallandaine

Revised and reproduced as *Celia*, 1879.

CONSTANCE by Tom Robertson. Music by Frederic Clay. Produced at the Royal English Opera, Covent Garden by the English Opera Company 23 January, 1865 for a run of 18 performances with *Cinderella*. Withdrawn 8 February, 1865.

Constance . . . . Mlle Martorelle
Rat-ta-taf . . . . Annie Thirlwall
Stanislas. . . . . Henry Corri
Commandant . . . . Thomas Aynsley Cook
Caritz . . . . Charles Lyall
Count Madelinski . . . . Henry Haigh

CASTLE GRIM an opera by G. B. Allen. Produced at the Royalty Theatre under the management of Fanny Reeve 2 September, 1865 with the extravaganza *Prince Amabel*. Withdrawn 21 October, 1865.

FELIX or The Festival of the Roses, a comic opera in two acts by John Oxenford. Music by W. Meyer Lutz. Produced at the Royalty Theatre under the management of Fanny Reeve 28 October, 1865 with *Prince Amabel*. Withdrawn 23 November, 1865.

1868–1869

There was no move to follow up *The Contrabandista* in the months after its production, but neither was there any manager enterprising enough to capitalise on the success of *La Grande Duchesse* by staging another French opéra-bouffe while the public interest was high. It was January 1870 before the Mansell brothers took the initiative of producing Hervé's *Chilpéric* at the Lyceum with suitably happy results.

In the two intervening years the British musical scene made no significant advances. The diet of burlesque and extravaganza peppered with the inevitable performances of *The Bohemian Girl* and *Maritana* continued. German Reed, finding the expenses of a large orchestra (*The Contrabandista* had used forty players) and chorus beyond his means, had returned to the Gallery of Illustration and his small operettas, and it was a number of years before he was tempted to return to St George's Hall. But if the first flame had died down the spark was by no means out, and a number of short English operettas appeared both at the Gallery of Illustration and elsewhere. The most important of these were *Cox and Box* and *Ages Ago*, both produced by the German Reeds in 1869.

Cox and Box had been composed in 1866 or 1867. Arthur Sullivan had been inspired to try something of the kind by seeing a performance of Offenbach's *Les Deux Aveugles* performed by the society amateur group, The Moray Minstrels, and Maddison Morton's famous play was adapted for the purpose by Burnand. The resultant 'triumviretta' was given its maiden performance by the same Moray Minstrels and in public at a charity performance at the Adelphi in May, 1867. Some eighteen months after *The Contrabandista*, the Reeds decided to stage the earlier Burnand/Sullivan piece. *Cox and Box* was produced at the Gallery of Illustration on 29 March, 1869 and proved to be its most successful 'opera da camera' to date. It was played nearly three hundred times over a period of twelve months and subsequently became very popular as a forepiece and as an item for benefit performances. In 1894 it was revived by D'Oyly Carte as a forepiece to *The Chieftain*, and in 1921 it was introduced into the repertoire of the D'Oyly Carte Opera Company where it remained until the company's dissolution.

Its companion piece on its production at the Gallery was the one-act musical *No Cards* written by William S. Gilbert, the music in this case being supplied by Reed. It was Gilbert who was also responsible for the Gallery's next success, *Ages Ago*. He was a young writer and solicitor best known for his contributions to the magazine *Fun*. Under the pen-name 'Bab' he produced a series of comic lyrics which became widely known as 'The Bab Ballads'. Under another pseudonym, F. Latour Tomline, he had also provided burlesques and extravaganzas for several London theatres including, in 1868, the Queen's, the Royalty and the Gaiety. The first of these was *La Vivandière*, a burlesque on Donizetti's *La Fille du Régiment*, which had been first produced by Maria

Simpson in Liverpool the previous year. *The Post* was enthusiastic to a degree:

> We can think of few burlesques which contain so many excellent jokes as this last work of Mr. W. S. Gilbert's, and not one – from those of a'Beckett's or Planché's downwards – which contain better dialogue in a purely literary point of view.

The music, taken from such sources as *La Grande Duchesse, L'Elisir d'Amore* and *La Mariage aux Lanternes* and arranged by the composer and conductor Ferdinand Wallerstein, was of a much higher quality than usual in such shows, and the whole piece had an air of class. It ran in London at the Queen's Theatre for 87 performances. Two months later a burlesque on *The Bohemian Girl* entitled *The Merry Zingara or The Tipsy Gipsy and the Pipsy Wipsy* was staged at the Royalty and in December the third, *Robert the Devil*, based on Meyerbeer's opera, was staged as the opening attraction at the brand new Gaiety Theatre. Both these were noted, like *La Vivandière*, for their lack of vulgarity and the superior level of their dialogue, music and production. In June 1869 Gilbert's next major musical work, *The Pretty Druidess or The Mother, the Maid and the Mistletoe Bough* (a burlesque of Bellini's *Norma*) was produced for the opening of the Charing Cross Theatre in King William Street, and the short piece, *No Cards*, brought him to the Gallery of Illustration.

On November 22 the Reeds presented a new programme. *Cox and Box* retained its place, but *No Cards* was replaced by Gilbert's new operetta, *Ages Ago*. In this, Sir Ebenezer Tare, a former tallow merchant and the dubious occupant of the Castle of Cockaleekie Glen, has forbidden his niece, Rose, to marry the unsuitable Columbus Hebblethwaite. But there is a legend that the original owner of the castle had, ages ago, mortgaged his soul to the devil, and in consequence there is a curse on Cockaleekie by which the rightful heir shall be found only once every hundred years. It is night in the picture gallery of the castle, and the four previous heirs step down from their frames for a confrontation. Morning comes, and they return to their places leaving behind the deeds which announce the heir to be none other than . . . Columbus Hebblethwaite. Confusion to Sir Ebenezer and wedding bells for the new laird and his Rose.

The music to this scenario was written by the young composer Frederic Clay. Born in Paris in 1839[1], he was the son of James Clay, MP for Hull for nearly twenty years but more celebrated as a whist player. Young Clay had begun his career in the Treasury Department before becoming secretary to several cabinet ministers and at one stage being used by Mr Gladstone for confidential missions. However, he had been soundly educated musically and had been composing from an early age. His first efforts, *The Pirates' Isle* (1859) and *Out of Sight* (1860), were performed by amateurs, but in 1862 he supplied the music for Tom Taylor's *Court and Cottage* at Covent Garden and then a short opera called *Constance* for Sir Michael Costa's English Opera Company at the same theatre (23 January 1865). *Constance* was written to a rather 'heavy' libretto by the playwright Tom Robertson who had just been successful with *David Garrick*. It was a tale of love and patriotism set in Poland under the Russians – something of a Polish *Tosca*, but with a happy ending when the hero and heroine are rescued first by a singing vivandière and then by the Polish army. The music, while not evoking any great reaction, was noted as being promising if rather light and, after being performed eighteen times as a curtain-raiser to the Covent Garden pantomime of *Cinderella*, it sank into obscurity.

An inheritance of £16,000 allowed Clay to give up his civil service career and devote

[1] Variously 1840

himself full-time to music, and he thus became the first composer with whom Gilbert developed a working relationship. *Ages Ago* was the first work to come from that partnership and it was a remarkable success, passing even the total of performances amassed at the Gallery of Illustration by *Cox and Box*. Between November 1869 and January 1871 it was performed 360 times. It was subsequently revived, and in 1880 ran for a highly successful six-week season on Broadway. It has not survived into the present-day repertoire as *Cox and Box* did, possibly because Gilbert later re-used the Picture Gallery scene for his more mature work, *Ruddigore*.

A number of other short works appeared during this same period, usually as opening pieces played before the main entertainment of an evening's programme. In this way *Nanette* or Better Late Than Never by W. G. Beale and Henri Drayton (24 August 1868) preceded the drama *Ambition* at the Standard, *Saved by a Song* (E. J. Loder/Col. H. R. Addison) was shown at the Princess's (21 December 1868) and *Coming of Age* (E. L. Hime/Dr J. E. Carpenter) prefaced Gilbert's *Norma* burlesque at the Charing Cross.

At the Gallery of Illustration, Virginia Gabriel produced *Who's the Heir?* to a libretto by her eventual husband, George March. With Miss Gabriel at her accustomed place at the pianoforte, the small cast delivered the slight piece pleasantly. Virginia Gabriel was the epitome of the 'drawing room composer'. Her music was simple, tuneful and correct, and her librettists evolved the slightest tales for her to set. Among her most successful pieces were *Widows Bewitched* (14 August 1865) which ran three months at the Gallery of Illustration and was played frequently thereafter by operetta groups, *A Quiet Chateau* (26 December 1867), and *Lost and Found* (5 February 1870), the plot of which is typical. A Marquise, weary of a horrid husband, runs away and disguises herself as a milkmaid. Her former lover, a painter, falls for the soi-disante milkmaid. While he is painting her portrait she glances at a newspaper and sees that the Marquis is dead. Happy ending. The story is, of course, the merest excuse to string together a series of genteel ballads and ensembles, a field in which Miss Gabriel was decidedly popular. She occasionally tried her hand at more extensive works. Two cantatas, *Evangeline* (1870) and *Dreamland* (1873), were performed at Covent Garden, but *The Lion's Mouth*, a full-length opéra-bouffe to a libretto by Alfred Thompson, produced privately in 1867, was not a success. Her smaller pieces found their own audience and were particularly popular with amateur performers, but Miss Gabriel did not progress to anything more significant.

Of rather more interest, however, is a two-act 'opera da camera', *Dr. Ambrosias, His Secret*, produced at St George's Hall. It received only one private performance, and its interest, in retrospect, lies solely in the fact that this short written-through operatic adaptation of *Tom Noddy's Secret* was composed by a young man called Richard D'Oyly Carte.

1868–1869

COX AND BOX or The Long Lost Brothers. A musical triumviretta in one act by F. C. Burnand based on the farce *Box and Cox* by J. Maddison Morton. Musically interpreted by Arthur Sullivan. Performed at Moray Lodge, Campden Hill in a private performance 27 April, 1867.

John James Cox. . . . . Harold Power
James John Box. . . . . George du Maurier
Mr Bouncer. . . . . John Forster

Performed at the Adelphi Theatre 11 May, 1867 on the occasion of the benefit for the widow and child of the artist C. H. Bennett.
Quintin Twiss (COX), George du Maurier (BOX), Arthur Blunt[1] (BOU)

Produced at the Gallery of Illustration under the management of T. German Reed 29 March, 1869. Withdrawn 26 March, 1870. Played with *No Cards* and subsequently (22 November) with *Ages Ago*.
T. German Reed (COX), Arthur Cecil (BOX), J. Seymour (BOU)

Produced at the Alhambra Theatre 16 October, 1871 and played with the ballets *The Chinese Revel* and *Fête à la Watteau*.
Mr Beverley (BOX), Frederic Sullivan (COX), Mr Carlton (BOU)

Produced in the United States 13 August, 1875.

Performed at St George's Hall for the benefit of Mrs George Buckland, 1884.
Arthur Cecil (BOX), George Grossmith (COX), R. Corney Grain (BOU)

Produced at the Court Theatre under the management of John Clayton and Arthur Cecil 15 April, 1884 with *Dan'l Druce*. Withdrawn 18 April.
Arthur Cecil (BOX), Richard Temple (COX), J. Furneaux Cook (BOU)

Played at a matinée at the Court Theatre under the management of Clayton and Cecil 4 February, 1885.
Arthur Cecil (BOX), E. D. Lyons (COX), J. Furneaux Cook (BOU)

Produced at the Court Theatre under the management of Mrs John Wood and Arthur Chudleigh 25 October, 1888 with *Mamma*. Withdrawn 9 March, 1889.
Arthur Cecil/Deane Brand (BOX), Eric Lewis (COX), William Lugg (BOU). Md: Andrew Levey

Produced at the Savoy Theatre under the management of Richard D'Oyly Carte 31 December, 1894 as a forepiece to *The Chieftain*. Withdrawn 16 March, 1895.
H. Scott Russell (BOX), M. R. Morand (COX), Richard Temple (BOU)

Produced at the Prince's Theatre by the D'Oyly Carte Opera Company 28 November, 1921 and played in repertoire.
Leo Darnton (BOX), Sydney Granville (COX), Daryll Fancourt (BOU)

Subsequently played by the D'Oyly Carte Opera Company in repertoire on tour and in London.

[1] Blunt later took the pseudonym 'Arthur Cecil'.

TV/Video: 1984 Brent Walker Ltd. Pr: Judith de Paul; dir: David Alden; md: Alexander Faris; ch: Terry Gilbert; sc: Allan Cameron; cos: Jenny Beavan
Russell Smythe (BOX), John Fryatt (COX), Alfred Marks (BOU)

NO CARDS a musical piece in one act by W. S. Gilbert. Music by T. German Reed. Produced at the Gallery of Illustration under the management of T. German Reed 29 March, 1869. Played with *Cox and Box*. Withdrawn 21 November, 1869.

Miss Annabella Penrose. . . . . Rosa D'Erina
Mrs Pennythorne . . . . Mrs German Reed
Mr Ellis Dee . . . . T. German Reed
Mr Churchmouse . . . . Arthur Cecil

Produced at St George's Hall 29 March, 1902 with *Charity Begins at Home* and *Tea and Tennis.*

AGES AGO a musical legend in one act by W. S. Gilbert. Music by Frederic Clay. Produced at the Gallery of Illustration under the management of T. German Reed 22 November, 1869 with *Cox and Box*. Played from 28 March 1870 with *Beggar my Neighbour*. *The School Feast* was added to the programme 16 May, 1870. Withdrawn 18 June, 1870.

Ebenezer Tare/Lord Carnaby Poppytop . . . . T. German Reed
Rose/Lady Maud Bohun. Fanny Holland
Angus McTavish/Brown. Edward Connell
Mistress Maggie McMotherly/Dame Cherry Maybud . . . . Mrs German Reed
Sir Aubrey de Beaupre/Columbus Hebblethwaite. . . . . . . Arthur Cecil

Reopened in an abridged form 11 July, 1870 with *Our Island Home* and *The Lady of Lyons.* Withdrawn 13 August.

Produced at St George's Hall 20 April, 1874 with *Charity Begins at Home* and *A Day in Town*, the former replaced by *He's Coming* (12 May). Withdrawn 13 June, 1874.
Alfred Reed (EB), Leonora Braham (ROSE), R. Corney Grain (McT), Mrs German Reed (McM), Stanley Betjeman (COL)

Produced at the Bijou Theatre, New York under the management of John A. McCaull and Charles E. Ford 31 March, 1880 with *Charity Begins at Home*. Withdrawn 15 May, 1880.
Digby V. Bell (EB), Marie Neilini (ROSE), William Herbert (McT), Marie Beauman (McM), William Courtenay (COL). Md: Frederic Clay.

Produced at St George's Hall under the management of Alfred Reed and R. Corney Grain 21 November, 1882 with *Number 204* and *Out of Town*. Withdrawn 17 December. Reopened 26 December with *Our Dolls' House* and *Master Tommy's Theatricals*. Withdrawn 25 February, 1883.

DR. AMBROSIAS, HIS SECRET. An opera da camera in two acts by 'H.B.' founded on T. Haynes Bayley's farce *Tom Noddy's Secret*. Music by Richard D'Oyly Carte. Privately performed at St George's Opera House 8 August, 1868.

Mabel . . . . Jessie Royd
Linda . . . . Adelaide Newton
Philip . . . . Wallace Wells
Captain Ormond. . . . . Denbigh Newton
Dr Ambrosias . . . . M. S. Skeffington

Dir: Richard D'Oyly Carte; piano accompaniment by S. Laville and Lt. W. A. Doorly.

1870

The past two years had brought nothing in the way of a follow-up to *La Grande Duchesse* and *The Contrabandista* but the new season of 1870 was soon to remedy that. The first new production of the year was a work described by its author, W. S. Gilbert, as a 'whimsical allegory', although in effect *The Princess* was a burlesque based on Tennyson's poem of the same name. Before its production the manager of the Olympic Theatre announced that it was to be:

> an attempt to reform a much abused branch of dramatic entertainment – burlesque – not only in the selection of a high class work for the subject, but by treating it with refinement and elegance.

His promises were fulfilled. In this piece Gilbert went above and beyond anything he had previously attempted in the burlesque field. *The Princess* showed him moving well away from the style of burlesque which had now become traditional into one which was imaginatively more free and original. Many of the well-known characteristics remained in one form or another, however. The leading young men's roles in *The Princess* were still played by ladies in tights, a practice Gilbert was later vehemently to reject; the libretto, though not rhyming, still maintained metre and the dialogue was sprinkled with punning lines and contemporary allusions:

ATHO: All is prepared, my liege,
To storm the walls
HILD: Then let the siege commence!
Who leads the serenading party, eh?
OFFICER: Sir Michael Costa[1]
HILD: Good, the light guitars
Fall in at six – the King's own baritones
Led by Sir Santley[2]
OFFICER: He's not knighted, sir!
HILD: He shall be then. They will parade at five.
OFFICER: Who leads the scaling party, sir?
HILD: Of course
The first light tenors, they can highest go.
ATHO: And who shall first climb up the outer wall
And reconnoitre what goes on within?
HILD: Some tenor, fool, who can 'go up to see'!

[1] Sir Michael Costa: conductor and composer
[2] Charles Santley: celebrated baritone. He was later knighted.

The score of *The Princess* was built up from second-hand tunes and the quality of the lyrics was in some degree hamstrung by the necessity of setting them to music conceived for other words. Cyril's song, set to the Laughing Song from Balfe's *Manon Lescaut*, had to have its lyric built around the laughing refrain which stopped any portion of the lyric running longer than three lines before being interrupted by a 'ha ha ha'. Likewise King Hildebrand's song, set to Rossini's 'Largo al Factotum', had to take into consideration the 'la la' sections, and there was, in consequence, little development in the lyric. The most successful part of the work was contained in the book, and Gilbert was later to re-use much of it in *Princess Ida* with fresh lyrics and Sullivan's music to replace the operatic hotch-potch of the original. Some large sections of the dialogue were retained unchanged while other portions were amplified in songs.

The Princess was given a most favourable reception and ran, in tandem with the pathetic drama, *Little Emily*, from January until the middle of April when it was taken off hurriedly to allow the so-called authorised version of the French play *Frou-Frou* to be produced. *Frou-Frou*, a Parisian hit by Meilhac and Halévy, looked like being a big success but it had been pirated by the St James' Theatre and the holders of the 'official permission' were in a hurry to get their version on. They would have done better to have retained *The Princess* as *Frou-Frou* turned out to be a five-week failure.

The other important event of January was the Mansell brothers' Lyceum production of Hervé's *Chilpéric*. For the second time in a month London audiences were presented with a burlesque which was not in the usual ten-syllable rhyming couplets. *Chilpéric*'s dialogue, translated and adapted by Robert Reece, Frederick Marshall and the manager, Richard Mansell, had gone even further than *The Princess* and had neither rhyme nor rhythm but told its tale in prose. It dealt with a light-hearted Ancient British monarch (played by the composer himself) who falls for a shepherdess. The lady, however, is already spoken for, and the king is far more suitably sought by the Princess Galusinda. After a good deal of comical doings the natural order of things wins the day. *Chilpéric* was true opéra-bouffe, a burlesque of grand opera, and it took the British public a little while to come to terms with Hervé's musical comicalities and cheerful operatic parodies. But once they had found the piece's measure, *Chilpéric* quickly became a firm favourite.

It was soon to be followed by others. *Chilpéric* played its last performance on April 9, and on April 16 the Gaiety joined the new trend with the first British production of Offenbach's *La Princesse de Trébizonde* starring J. L. Toole and Nellie Farren. Two days later the Lyceum re-opened with Hervé and Emily Soldene in the former's *Le Petit Faust*. Opéra-bouffe had well and truly arrived. The Standard Theatre jumped on the bandwagon, announcing a 'new British opéra-bouffe', *Guy Fawkes or A New Way to Blow up a King*, for its Easter production. But *Guy Fawkes* turned out to be nothing more than an old-fashioned burlesque. Quite a good one, and rather something in the East End with its Balfe and Offenbach music, but nonetheless, a pasticcio burlesque.

The Standard was not the only theatre to attempt to label its musical compilations opéra-bouffe, but among the new productions which were staged in imitation of Offenbach and Hervé there was a distinct lack of original music. There were plenty of able theatrical musicians around to write ballet music, overtures, arrangements, single numbers or in some cases, like Frank Musgrave, a full score when the occasion demanded, but the challenge was a great one for a theatre which tried to stage an original English work. Their composer had to be able to rival the attractive and literate music of Hervé, or outdo the Offenbach and Balfe scores which the pasticcio writer could plunder so simply and inexpensively for a ready-made popular score.

One composer who had already proved his ability, although on a smaller scale, was Frederic Clay. His collaboration with Gilbert on *Ages Ago* had been a major success and now the two came together again for a more ambitious piece for the Charing Cross Theatre. This was *The Gentleman in Black*, the first original and full-length British musical since *The Contrabandista* nearly two and a half years previously, and markedly different in both character and emphasis. Gilbert's individual and whimsical sense of humour had been made apparent in his ballads and his earlier stage works, and he had shown his ability to draw humorous situations, characters and dialogue from a subject as unlikely as that of *The Princess*. On the other hand he had shown himself equally at home in the more refined atmosphere of The Gallery of Illustration with *No Cards* and *Ages Ago*. *The Gentleman in Black* drew on elements from both styles.

The theme of the 'legend' was the doctrine of metempsychosis – the exchange of minds between two bodies – and the setting was, conventionally, amongst country lads and lasses and horrid potentates. The rustic maiden, Bertha, jokingly accepts the attentions of the ugly Baron Otto von Schlachenstein. Her lover, Hans, is in despair and the mysterious Gentleman in Black comes to his aid. Since each of the two men is jealous of the other, this Gentleman proposes a month's metempsychosis. The possibilities inherent in the exchange and/or alteration of people's natural characteristics and positions was to become one of Gilbert's favourite sources of plot, and he used many different devices to arrive in a situation where it could be exploited, from the spells and love-philtres of *Creatures of Impulse* and *The Sorcerer* to the post-natal mix-ups of *The Gondoliers* and *H.M.S. Pinafore*. In this play, it is the devil himself who exchanges the bodies of Hans and the Baron, leading to all sorts of humorous confusions. The complications thicken when Otto, soon tired of being a peasant, tries to trick his way back into his own body and position before the allotted time:

> Twenty-five years ago the infant son of Baron Rudolf von Schlachenstein was put out to nurse, when two days old, in the family of Hans Gopp, a simple peasant . . . One night – the babes were three weeks old and wonderfully alike – the peasant babe crept from his clothes basket, quietly removed the sleeping baron from his sumptuous cradle, placed the baron's son in the clothes basket and creeping into the baron's cradle covered himself up and went to sleep. The cheat was never discovered! The peasant's son was brought up as the young baron – the young baron as the peasant's son. I was the peasant's son, Hans Gopp, you – YOU – were the babe of Baron von Schlachenstein.

But, confusingly, the Baron's tale turns out to be a fabrication. He is, after all, twenty years older than Hans. The trick finally rebounds on him when the Emperor decides on the abolition of the next ten days and the two men revert to their own bodies. But by Otto's 'confession' Hans is heir to the title and lands of Schlachenstein, and the play ends with the new Baron inviting everyone to his wedding with Bertha.

In contrast to *The Contrabandista*, the book of which had been little more than a framework on which to hang Sullivan's music, *The Gentleman in Black* presented a thoughtful and coherent play, highly individual in plot and style, in which the musical portions played a considerably less prominent part. Most of the numbers were concerted pieces – opening and closing choruses for each act, ensembles, a quintet – and there were only three solos (two ballads for Bertha and a 'whipcrack' song for Grumpff) in the whole hour and a half of the piece's length. Clay's music was, once again, considered charming:

> The music is of a bright sparkling character and has been supplied by Mr. Frederic Clay who has evidently taken Offenbach and Hervé as his models (*Era*)

but the emphasis was clearly on the book. The lyrics, however, do not show any particular merit or ingenuity and suggest that, at this stage, Gilbert, like many of his contemporaries, attached less importance to the content of the musical sections than he was to do later. Bertha's Act II ballad, for example, shows little imagination:

> Ah, once he loved me blindly, all other girls above
> I treated him unkindly and sported with his love
> I smiled on others sweetly and would not tell him why
> I broke his heart completely, a wretched girl am I.

and apart from the gently coy quintet, 'Happy to Do the same for You', none of the numbers contain the glint of humour that might have been expected.

The show was well-received and generally accounted a success but it was performed only twenty-six times before the Charing Cross season was closed and the theatre put up to let. *The Gentleman in Black* was never professionally revived but Gilbert included it in his four-volume edition of plays and it was published posthumously in 1922.

Just before the closure of *The Gentleman in Black* another piece of Gilbert's was produced. The German Reeds decided to take *Ages Ago* out of their bill and, in its place, they presented a new short piece by Gilbert entitled *Our Island Home*. Reed had invited Arthur Sullivan to work with Gilbert on the piece, but the partnership did not come to pass and Reed himself finally supplied the music.

Our Island Home was an unusually imaginative work. Mr and Mrs Reed, Arthur Cecil and Fanny Holland all played themselves. The German Reed company, having set out on the good ship Hot Cross Bun[1] with a tour of *Ages Ago*, are put ashore on a desert island after insisting on performing for the passengers. They divide their island proprietarially into four and exchange goods as seems necessary. This works well until it is discovered that all the food is in Cecil's quarter and he, consequently, becomes a tyrant until he is betrayed by an excessive love for anchovies into swapping his quarter for another where a case of fish-paste has been swept ashore. But worse is at hand. The island is attacked by a marauding pirate chief who, duty bound by his indentures, is about to kill them all when it is revealed that Mr and Mrs Reed are his parents whose stupid nurse accidentally apprenticed him to a pirate instead of a pilot as a child. By adept manipulation of the nautical almanac Cecil proves that the pirate is over 21 and freed from his apprentice obligations, and all ends happily.

The plot provides an interesting link between the earliest and the later works of Gilbert. Whilst the second part of the plot later provided the basis for the story of *The Pirates of Penzance*, the first part shows Gilbert already borrowing from himself. The *Bab Ballads* provided him frequently with ideas and characters upon which he could elaborate in his major operas, and *Our Island Home* is an early example of this self-plagiarism. A ballad called 'Etiquette' tells of two young men cast up on a desert island who divide that island in two and, after the necessities of etiquette are observed, swap oyster for turtle and so forth.

The first performance of *Our Island Home* was threatened with cancellation when the specially ordered costumes failed to turn up. In desperation Mrs Reed thought of her garden nets. A messenger was despatched and returned just in time to allow the castaways to appear draped in nets over some of their own clothes. The 'costumes'

[1] cf. The *Bab Ballads*, 'The Bumboat Woman's Story'

proved so successful that they were retained for the whole run. The show never approached the longevity of *Cox and Box* or *Ages Ago*, but it proved very popular and ran happily to the end of the season.

During the run Fanny Holland was given a benefit performance and she selected another Frederic Clay operetta as the centrepiece of her evening. In 1868 Clay had worked with the 29-year-old writer, B. C. ('Charlie') Stephenson, on a short piece called *The Bold Recruit* for the amateur group 'The Old Stagers' which was performed as part of their cricket week entertainment at the Theatre Royal, Canterbury. With Clay organising affairs from the piano, the little piece scored a decided success and Miss Holland decided to try it as a vehicle for herself in London. And thus yet another name which was to become famous – B. C. Stephenson – added itself to the German Reeds' list of credits.

The final weeks of the year saw what was by far the most ambitious attempt at a full-scale original musical to date. It owed its existence to the energetic manager of the Gaiety Theatre, John Hollingshead, who had already, in only two years of operation, established his theatre as the foremost producer of light musical entertainment in the West End. For his Christmas attraction he decided to present a new musical and the result was *Aladdin II*, written by Alfred Thompson with music by Hervé who was currently taking refuge in London from the Franco-Prussian war.

Thompson E. Jones (Alfred Thompson to the theatrical world) had been a Captain in the Inniskilling Dragoons, but had also studied art in Continental schools and was now largely employed as a journalist. When Hollingshead was organising the staff for his initial Gaiety programme he decided to employ someone to co-ordinate the costume designs instead of allowing, as was usual, the costumiers to provide whatever they felt appropriate. Thompson, whose translation of *L'Escamoteur* (*On the Cards*) was part of the opening entertainment, took on the designing of the wardrobe for *Robert the Devil* and stayed on to design the Gaiety extravaganzas which followed. In spite of the failure of *On the Cards* he was also retained as a writer, being represented by the burlesques *Columbus* and *Linda di Chamouni* and a translation of *Zampa* in the Gaiety's first couple of years. For the production of *Aladdin II* he once again took on the dual role of author and designer.

Aladdin II was variously described as operatic extravaganza, operatic burlesque, opéra-bouffe or as just plain burlesque, but it was clearly a piece in direct line of descent from the old Christmas extravaganzas popularised by Planché. Thompson avoided the tortuous punning and the rhymes and metre of current burlesque and opted for a cultivated but popular prose style which he applied with a good deal of imagination and fancy to this sequel to the famous fairy story. He shifted the location from the China of the original to the picturesque surroundings of Japan, thinly disguised as 'The Effluvial City in the land of Hari-Skari'. There young Aladdin is found working in the toyshop of the magician Ko-kil-ko. The magician is trying to find the Wonderful Lamp of old, and we meet him in his shop rubbing up his latest acquisitions:

(He rubs the lamp and looks around hopefully at the stage trapdoors. Nothing happens)

KO: Not the smallest spirit, black, white or grey, (He takes out another lamp. Same business) No go. This is not calculated to raise one's spirits! Bless you (to audience) I'm forgetting you. Now, you imagine I've been giving new lamps for old ones. I'm no such fool, believe me; since the introduction of gas into Hari-Skari I can buy them for the price of old bottles. Only two lamps this morning, a safety lamp and a

> gig lamp; as innocent of magic as an ambassador of the smell of onions. That makes ninety-three lamps bought since the beginning of the week. My wrist aches with rubbing. No, I shall never find the wonderful lamp without an Aladdin.

He has adopted multitudes of Aladdins to help him find the lamp but, when they have turned out 'duds', he has turned them into dolls which litter his toyshop. The Princess Veloutine chances by the shop and meets the current Aladdin and they fall in love at first sight. But Ko-kil-ko is jealous and he shuts Aladdin up in the cellar where he comes across an old lamp. It is the real thing and the boy turns the horrid magician into a jack-in-a-box. The Princess's father buys the grotesque toy as a gift for his daughter and the mechanical magician and his 'master' are transferred to the royal palace. But Ko-kil-ko still has a powerful magic ring and, when King Ozokerit in a temper throws the lamp into the bath, the royal entourage and Aladdin find themselves at the bottom of the sea while Ko-kil-ko, with the power of the ring, takes on the form and place of the ruler of Hari-Skari. Aladdin and Veloutine try to trick him out of the ring, but they fail and are about to be put to death by the villainous magician when the maid, Karamel, succeeds in stealing the precious ring and saves the day.

The tale was told in lively and amusing dialogue interspersed with a full opéra-bouffe score of twenty-six numbers, and put in the hands of some delightful characters at the head of which were the Aladdin of Nellie Farren and the magician played by J. L. Toole. Johnnie Toole made a veritable feast of his role turning everything into a source of mirth whether plotting to gain the lamp, or burbling sycophantically before the Princess:

VEL: You know me then?
KO: Does not the caterpillar know the bird of paradise? Does not the walrus smile when he sees the Aurora Borealis? Does not the bucket turn pale when he reflects the image of the moon? Give me a screen, Aladdin, this brightness will destroy my sight!

or imitating a very quippy jack-in-a-box:

VEL: (to ALADDIN) You shall wind him up.
KO: They talk of winding me up as if I were a limited company!

or oozing evil over the fate of Aladdin and his Princess:

KO: You shall have your choice of torture. How do you wish to die?
AL: A happy mama in the bosom of her family.
KO: Be serious, I beg. I should suggest fire in preference to the axe . . it is more sensational. I will order it myself. Make the most of your minutes . . stakes for two, well done!

But his best and most popular moment came when, Macbeth-like, he begins to find the position of usurper an uncomfortable one:

KO: I have found the ring, made the genie's acquaintance, played old gooseberry with the reins of government, taken the semblance of the Taicoon, allow myself shrimps and jelly-fish for breakfast and a mild cheroot after dinner, and still I am not happy.

This speech underwent many a change and grew to many times its original length as Toole topically introduced the things which caused him distress, and 'Still I am not happy' became a favourite catch phrase. For many years after Toole could introduce it where he wished and be sure of evoking shouts of laughter and recognition. The song and dance with Miss Farren which followed also gave him plenty of opportunities:

KO: I've everything money can buy
From a minister's vote to a maiden's vow
Yet what they call nobility
Can't be borrowed or bought nohow;
What I ought or ought not to say
At court is my greatest anxiety
The one debt I never can pay
Is the one which I owe to society
For instance, I adore rats smothered in onions, but I dare not ask for my favourite dish. No! What am I expected to order, Remembrancer?
AL: Something like Croquignoles de Bechamel en Papillottes à la Soubise.
KO: Ouf! Now that's a thing I hate! etc.

He was finally seen transmogrified into a huge butterfly by the merciful hero, heading a glamorous Butterfly ballet.

Great though it was, the comic role was not a totally overwhelming one. Nellie Farren had plenty of scope in the title role and she proved a comical foil for Toole while joining in vocal moments both with him and the soprano Constance Loseby (Veloutine). James Stoyle as the forgetful emperor also caused much mirth with his half-remembered quotations to which his Remembrancer (Covent Garden tenor Charles Lyall) was required to provide the tag:

> My duties are confined to recalling vagrant ideas to the preoccupied mind of my august sovereign . . .

Unfortunately the sidekick's memory was even worse than his employer's, and some familiar phrases were topped with unusual endings. Stoyle had one of the show's jolliest numbers, one of a type which was to become very familiar:

OZ: Between you and me I'm a grand Taicoon
I've millions under my thumb
For many there be beneath the moon
Who to cares like mine succumb.
For fleets and armies I tax the land
Though my enemies insist
My standing troops but on paper stand
And my navies don't exist.
On my civil list there is deuce knows who
But I make them pay for the boon
For I put down one and carry two
To the share of the great Taicoon.
When the cry's 'Reform!', I award to a batch
My Order of the Blue Baboon
When they dream of revolt there's the Happy Dispatch
Does the job for the great Taicoon.

Annie Tremaine was a cheeky maid with an odd little song 'The Princess Kalipee', and Edward Perrini a genie bored with his occupation:

NAP: My power's somewhat rusty. I could not throw a flip-flap off this bar to save a dancer's licence who threw off instead some fine vocal pyrotechnics.

Hervé provided suitably light-hearted and 'bouffe' music, and the Gaiety weighed in with the best in production values to make *Aladdin II* a truly spectacular show. Thompson's Japanese costumes caused a sensation. They were a novelty in the London theatre and clever Captain Thompson who had cut and sewn many of them himself had introduced some unusual materials and styles which contributed to something of a Japanese craze in the world of London fashion. The five sets – the magic toyshop, the Princess's swimming bath, the underwater grotto, Ozokerit's chamber and the palace – and the 'special effects' such as the descent of Ozokerit's diving bell into the Kingdom of the Submarines, or the sudden transformation of Ko-kil-ko into the jack-in-a-box (by means of mechanical panels raised from the stage) all added to the remarkable visual effect of the piece.

Aladdin II was the Gaiety's most successful show to date, and it was held on the bill until the following April when Charles Santley had been contracted to return to the theatre, but as soon as the Santley season was over Hollingshead staged a further twelve performances of *Aladdin II*. Toole and his company were then scheduled to go on another of their highly lucrative tours, so *Aladdin II* was taken to the country in repertoire with such favourite Toole vehicles as *Paul Pry, Uncle Dick's Darling, Dot, Bardell v Pickwick* and *Wait and Hope*. Annie Tremaine went too, promoted to the role of Veloutine which she embellished with an extra number, a waltz song 'Oh, how Delightful' composed by the popular ballad-writer James Molloy. When Miss Tremaine returned to London for the next Gaiety musical, *Aladdin II* was dropped from the repertoire, but when Toole himself returned to town the Gaiety was treated once again to a season of *Aladdin II* and another round of 'Still I am not happy'.

The composer of *Aladdin II*, Hervé, was enormously popular in France where the successes of *L'Œil Crevé*, *Le Petit Faust* and *Chilpéric* had put him at the top of his profession. Tempted, no doubt, by this 'rentable' name at the head of the bill, M. Manasse, who had the distinction of having managed the Khedive's Opera House in Cairo, produced *Le Nouvel Aladin* at the Folies-Nouvelles. It is not quite clear why he had renounced his Egyptian post in favour of the uncertainty of Parisian management unless it had something to do with the little episode of a bomb found under the viceroy's box.

The French version of *Aladdin II* opened favourably. It had scenery and costumes painstakingly copied from the splendid Gaiety originals, and its cast included the composer's son, M. Gardel, in the role of the Remembrancer. But after five weeks M. Manasse vanished, leaving a note which said that he had 'gone to Constantinople for some money'. The show was closed and Manasse declared bankrupt. He returned to sell the theatre and within two months of what had seemed a promising opening the costumes for *Aladdin* were auctioned off at a public sale.

1870

0004 **THE GENTLEMAN IN BLACK** a musical legend in two acts by W. S. Gilbert. Music by Frederic Clay. Produced at the Charing Cross Theatre under the management of Emily Fowler 26 May, 1870 for a run of 26 performances closing 24 June, 1870.

Hans Gopp . . . . Emily Fowler
Bertha . . . . Emmeline Cole
The Gentleman in Black . . . . Mr Flockton
Baron Otto von Schlachenstein . . . . . . Edwin Danvers
Grumpff . . . . W. M. Terrott
Baroness von Schlachenstein . . . . Helen Maxse
Schlipps . . . . W. A. Herbert
Maria . . . . Marie Dalton
Gretchen . . . . Rose Roberts
Emma . . . . Miss Wilson
Tintelstein . . . . F. Robson

Md: Theodore Hermann; sc: W. Leitch

Played with *Illusions* and *Captain Smith*. On June 23, for Miss Fowler's benefit, played with *Sarah's Young Man*, *Not so Bad after All* and *Who Speaks First*. On June 24, for Mr Millward's benefit, played with *Illusions* and *The Rough Diamond*.

0005 **ALADDIN II** or An Old Lamp in a New Light. An operatic extravaganza in 5 scenes by Alfred Thompson. Music by Herve. Produced at the Gaiety Theatre under the management of John Hollingshead 23 December, 1870 for a run of 88 performances closing 6 April, 1871. Re-opened May 22, 1871 for a further 12 performances to 3 June, 1871.

Ozokerit* the Lightheaded . . . . J. D. Stoyle
The Remembrancer . . . . Charles Lyall
Ko-kil-ko . . . . J. L. Toole
Aladdin . . . . Nellie Farren
Princess Veloutine . . . . Constance Loseby
Naphtha, the Spirit of the Lamp . . . . . Edward Perrini
Karamel . . . . Annie Tremaine
Chalybea . . . . Lardy Wilson
Principal (Prince) Submarine . . . . . . John Maclean/Rose Coghlan/A. Herbert

Dir: Alfred Thompson, Hervé and Robert Soutar; md: W. Meyer Lutz; ch: C. Carle; sc: Hawes Craven, George Gordon, W. Harford, Mr. Hann; cos: Alfred Thompson

Produced at the Gaiety Theatre at matinées on February 24, 26 & 27, 1872. Opened 9 March for a run of 32 performances closing 26 April, 1872.
John Maclean (OZ), J. G. Taylore (REM), J. L. Toole (KO), Nellie Farren/ Florence Farren (AL), Constance Loseby (VEL), Annie Tremaine (K), Florence Farren/Mlle Clary (NAP), Lardy Wilson (CH), Alma Egerton (PR).

1 Ozokerit was the name of a patent brand of candles

Played with *Uncle Dick's Darling, The Spitalfields Weaver, Birthplace of Podgers, The Hunchback, Our Clerks, Flic, Flec & Floc, Shilly Shally, Mariage aux Lanternes, Les Deux Aveugles* &c in repertoire.

Produced in Paris as *Le Nouvel Aladin* in a version written by the composer 16 December, 1871 at the Folies-Nouvelles.
Marcel (OZ), Gardel (REM), Dailly (KO), Mlle Berthal (AL), Mlle Claudia (VEL)

OUR ISLAND HOME an extravaganza in one act by W. S. Gilbert. Music by T. German Reed. Produced at the Gallery of Illustration under the management of T. German Reed 20 June, 1870. Played from 11 July with *Ages Ago*. Withdrawn 13 August, 1870.

T. German Reed, Mrs German Reed, Fanny Holland and Arthur Cecil played themselves.
Captain Bang . . . . R. Corney Grain

THE BOLD RECRUIT an operetta in one act by B. C. Stephenson. Music by Frederic Clay. Produced at the Theatre Royal, Canterbury by The Old Stagers 4 August, 1868 for one performance.

Gobemouche . . . . Hon. S. Whitehead
Nichette . . . . Fanny Holland
Theophile Pasquin . . . . 'Oliver Twist'
Colin Redingote . . . . 'A. Sharp'
Sergeant Solicoeur . . . . H. Percival
Themistocle . . . . 'John Doe'

Played at the Gallery of Illustration 19 July, 1870 for the benefit of Miss Fanny Holland with *Ages Ago* and *The Lady of Lyons*.
R. Corney Grain (GOB), Fanny Holland (N), Theodore Distin (TH), Arthur Cecil (COL), T. German Reed (SGT). Md: Frederic Clay

QUICK MARCH a comic opera in one act by Henry Leslie and Jno. Allison. Music by Ferdinand Wallerstein. Produced at the New Queen's Theatre 5 February, 1870 with *'Twixt Axe and Crown*. Withdrawn 9 April, 1870.
Cast included Frank Matthews, Ernest Page, George Rignold and Henrietta Hodson.

1871

The first major new work of 1871 did not appear until September but during the previous months London had seen the production of an assortment of imported opéras bouffes and buffe, the most important of which was the English adaptation of Offenbach's *Les Brigands*. Several shorter English works had appeared, the first being Gilbert's *A Sensational Novel* which was the New Year change of programme at the German Reeds. Once again German Reed arranged and composed the music for what was one of Gilbert's most delightful early libretti.

An author, intent on producing one of the multi-volumed novels beloved of the era, has succeeded in getting to the end of his Volume 1, but has got stuck on the second. He calls on the Spirit of Romance for aid and the characters in his book come to life, but they are not at all helpful. They are frankly scornful of what their poor author has in mind for their futures and proceed to behave dreadfully out of character as they act out their own ideas of the succeeding volumes. Had Sullivan or Clay written the score, *A Sensational Novel* might have been exceptional. As it was it ran for more than half the year, right up to the summer break. Considering Gilbert's subsequent record of self-borrowing, it is surprising that he did not in later days return to this whimsical notion and expand it into what might have become a very diverting full-length opera.

His second new work of the year was very different. *Creatures of Impulse*, a 'musical fairy tale' with music by Alberto Randegger, was put on at the Royal Court to make up a bill with his play *Randall's Thumb*. It was a short piece, running less than an hour, and was a dramatic expansion of a sketch which Gilbert had written for the Christmas edition of the previous year's *Graphic*. It told the tale of a strange old lady who lives in an inn where she eats nothing, pays nothing and is generally unprofitable to the landlady who eventually decides the old lady must go. She enlists the aid of the villagers to turn her out, but the old lady is not what she seems. In fact she is a fairy and she enchants each person into a total reversal of character until things are sorted out to her own satisfaction.

It was a merry little piece and Randegger illustrated it with a series of duos and trios in a suitably light vein. After a couple of nights it was evident that the little fairy piece was highly popular and more of a draw than the intended main piece. The programme was reorganised. *Randall's Thumb* was pushed back to open the programme at 7.30 while *Creatures of Impulse* took the evening's central 9.40 spot. Soon after, *Randall's Thumb* was taken off but the shorter piece was retained on the bill through programme changes for fifteen weeks until the season ended and the company headed for Manchester to perform yet another Gilbert piece, *The Palace of Truth*.

Creatures of Impulse was seen again in the West End the following year when a Royal Court Production of a *Zampa* burlesque struck mud, and it was hurried into the bill.

Again, in 1874, it resurfaced at the Vaudeville as a supporting piece and it was played frequently thereafter as a popular part of many bills, sometimes with and sometimes without Randegger's music, and latterly in a shortened version. A century after its production it still held a place in French's catalogue for amateurs.

When Fanny Holland's annual benefit came round she once again persuaded Clay to provide her with an operetta for the Gallery of Illustration. The result was *In Possession*, an unexceptional three-hander built around an unpleasant uncle and a withheld will. It was performed just once, but librettist Robert Reece rescued a number from it for his burlesque of *Ali Baba à la Mode* at the Gaiety the following year.

In August another operetta appeared at the Opéra Comique as an opening piece to Molière's *Le Medecin Malgré Lui.* It was also a short piece – less than an hour – and its plot was as slight as could be. The usual peasant boy and girl and rich lover were involved in a very weak libretto in which the coquette gets her come-uppance and no husband. The music was slightly better than the book but the performance on the opening night was so badly rehearsed that the conductor was compelled to shout out the beat to the inefficient orchestra. The audience gave *Marie* the bird and its composer, Richard D'Oyly Carte, left with it any serious pretensions he might have had as a composer.

With September came the first of the more ambitious pieces of the year. The success of *Aladdin II* had convinced Hollingshead that the creative entente cordiale was an experiment worth pursuing. Consequently he set Thompson to work on another opéra-bouffe on the same lines, this time on the Cinderella theme, in collaboration with Emile Jonas, the composer of the successful opérette, *La Canard à Trois Becs.* The result was *Cinderella the Younger*.

The 'new' Cinderella, Javotte, lives in the town of Pumpernickel with her two horrible sisters, Pamela and Belezza, and her existence is rendered endurable only by the kindliness of her godfather, Peter the Watchman, and Max, whom she knows as the Grand Duke's dancing teacher. But, into the middle of the traditional story which had been shorn of all its 'magical' elements, Thompson introduced two burglars, Dodgerowski and Prigowitz – a comical Macaire and Strop – intent on robbing Javotte's sisters while pretending to make love to them. The two rogues provided a great deal of fun as they pursued their larcenous aims through the show, pursued in their turn by the Night Patrol. Affairs come to a head at the Grand Duke's ball where the robbers attempt to impersonate high police officers and end up arresting the Duke who has disguised himself to get a few peaceful minutes to court Javotte. After much laughter, all ends happily with Javotte becoming the Grand Duchess of Pumpernickel.

J. D. Stoyle and J. G. Taylor had marvellous roles as Dodgerowski and Prigowitz ("My nervous system is so delicate"), disguised as noble lords, as detectives, or acting as hairdressers to the sisters in a low comedy boudoir scene. They shared the comedy with John Maclean as Von Tickelsbach, the 'Hereditary Grand Chamberlain and Prefect of Police', who changes his manner depending on which office he is assuming:

(Von T. kisses Javotte on the shoulder.)

JAV: The Lord Chamberlain seems to forget he is in the presence of the Prefect of Police.

VON: The Lord Chamberlain takes precedence of the Prefect.

JAV: Then turn him out for we don't want the police here!

On his exit he has to pause to see which of the two illustrious gentlemen should go out first.

Annie Tremaine returned to town for *Cinderella* and teamed up with Constance Loseby as the broadly comical ugly sisters, while the *Grande Duchesse* star, Julia Mathews, starred as Javotte. To take the role of the Grand Duke Max, Hollingshead inveigled Mlle Clary away from the Belgian opéra-bouffe company which had been playing at the theatre. When she was sued by the Belgians for breach of contract, the actress went magnificently into court and pleaded that her constitution would not permit her to suffer the channel crossing back to the Continent. She would surely perish of *mal de mer*. She did not perish during rehearsals of *Cinderella* or six performances a week at the Gaiety, and became a valuable member of the company.

Jonas's music included some charming moments. Miss Mathews sang sweetly 'It Isn't much Sleep that I Get' and 'Take back the Ring you gave Me (a heart's a greater prize)' and joined Mlle Clary in a pretty dancing lesson routine. Mlle Clary also took part in the comical side of affairs in a trio with the robbers entitled 'Love the Burglar':

DUKE: Beautiful maid we come to rob
P. & D.: To rob? To rob? Who told you so?
DUKE: We come to rob, we come to steal
P. & D.: To rob? To steal? I tell, you know!
ALL: We come to rob thee of thy rest
To steal thy heart from out its nest
Toc-toc, let me in, I am Love
Toc-toc, must I knock any more
Appear at your window above
Or I shall break in at the door

Also on the buffo side, Von Tickelsbach led a Policeman's song:

Every Prefect of Police will
Out of my book take a leaf
Proper guardians of the peace will
Set a thief to catch a thief
You and I, sir
Are so sly, sir
We've the work of twenty done
In the twinkling of an eye, sir
So we'll drink to Number One.
Yes, we'll drink to Number One, boys
And may we never cease
Our victims to run in, boys
When e'er the cry's 'Police'.

Other favourite forms were equally observed – a Brindisi for the Duke, a 'Legend' for Miss Loseby, and a Rataplan chorus, while the Night Patrol (played by a line of lovely ladies) were featured in a Gendarmes' chorus.

In spite of its excellently devised libretto, *Cinderella the Younger* was not quite up to *Aladdin II*. Although Thompson included plenty of good things in his book, he tended often to physical and verbal grotesqueries more related to burlesque than to the more refined whimsy of the earlier work. Surveying the shoes Dodgerowski and Prigowitz have dropped in their flight, the sisters sigh:

BEL: A memory of the count
PAM: A souvenir of the baron
JAV: A pair of shoe-venirs, I should say!

Jonas, too, was not as adept at musical bouffonnerie as Hervé and, though the cast included many favourite performers, there was no Toole and no Nellie Farren. *Cinderella the Younger* was a clever and attractive piece but it was no hit. It was withdrawn after only four weeks with an announcement that it would be repeated later in the season. The reprise, when it came, was very brief and the Gaiety Company headed by Stoyle and Miss Mathews took to the road with a repertoire entirely French. *Cinderella the Younger* subsequently appeared in Paris under the title *Javotte*, and in Vienna as *Javotte, das neue Aschenbrödel* with some success.

On September 18, the Royalty Theatre re-opened under new management with a revival of *Chilpéric*. W. H. Tilla was engaged for the title role with Augusta Thompson as Fredegonde and Emily Pitt as Galusinda, and the orchestra was under the direction of the lessee himself, the composer J. E. Mallandaine. Mallandaine had been associated with the Royalty several years previously when he had conducted a season for Fanny Reeve in which two of his own works, *Love's Limit* and *Sylvia*, had been included. To these operettas he had since added the duologue *The Haunted Mill* for the singer-manager Elliot Galer and his wife. This, however, was his first venture into management.

Three weeks after his opening, Emily Soldene arrived in town and set up a rival production of *Chilpéric* at the Philharmonic, Islington. She surrounded herself with an excellent cast including her sister Clara Vesey as Fredegonde, Selina Dolaro in her original role of Galusinda and Felix Bury as Landry. The *Chilpéric* season was intended only to hold the fort until *Geneviève de Brabant* was ready but, by the time it was, Mallandaine's production had folded. London preferred to drive to Islington for Soldene and Dolaro than to go to Soho for W. H. Tilla. Mallandaine was not caught unprepared. He already had a new piece in rehearsal, another of his own works, a comic opera entitled *Paquita* or Love in a Frame written to a libretto by Robert Reece whose successful burlesque of *Prometheus* the composer had conducted during his earlier stay at the Royalty.

The libretto was a quaint mixture. The story tells of how one Patricio, an innkeeper, tries to get his daughter Paquita to wed the rich but idiotic Francillo. Paquita is in love with a handsome soldier, Pablos. Under cover of a masquerade dance, Paquita and her ambitious sister Luisita exchange costumes and Francillo, asked to pick his bride, mistakenly nominates Luisita. The angry Patricio locks Paquita up in a 'haunted' picture gallery. Pablos arrives through a secret passage behind one of the portraits to rescue her, followed by Francillo dressed as a ghost with the aim of frightening her into connubial compliance. He is tricked and soundly beaten by Pablos, and the two couples are eventually satisfactorily contracted.

The libretto of *Paquita* was, in effect, two separate operettas. The first covered the masquerade ball and the tricking of Francillo, and came to a light if logical ending; the second was the 'portrait gallery' episode which was loosely tacked on to the first. Not only the plot was unsatisfactory. Reece, so successful in writing literate burlesque, failed to find a style in *Paquita*. He attempted to mix the jokes and puns of burlesque, its topical sallies and political and social jibes, with a lyrical score and graceful song-words. Lively passages of straight and characteristic dialogue were interrupted by word-twistings: '. . . if he'll give me the dollars, I'll give him assent . . .' or by incongruous anachronisms:

> I speculated in the Alexandra Palace Tontine and let the Albert Hall in London to a popular preacher, so I have done pretty well . . . .

and references to stage conventions:

> . . . not so loud, this isn't a melodrama . . .
> . . . nobody ever overhears a private duet in an opera . . .

The audience was confused. They applauded 'a song and chorus in the style of Offenbach' and laughed at the contemporary jokes but, by the time the second act had begun, they were restless and unreceptive and began to object vocally.

Paquita was not a success. *The Era* complained that 'Mr Reece fell below his usual standard of excellence' and that 'he did not seem decided whether he should make the piece comic opera or broad burlesque'. An attempt was made to patch the piece up by increasing the comic element. Reece tacked in additional lines for two subsidiary characters, Guzman and Inez, and re-shaped the piece a little, but there was not sufficient to build on and his efforts were of no avail. After thirteen performances, Mallandaine put *Chilpéric* back on, prefacing it with the dismembered first (and better) act of *Paquita*, but after a further week he closed the theatre and surrendered his tenancy. Some of the music of *Paquita* survived a little and two numbers (the 'Offenbach' song and Paquita's drinking song) were later re-used by Reece in his Gaiety burlesque *Ali Baba à la Mode* (1872).

In the meanwhile the pre-eminence of the French opéra-bouffe was being firmly established. At the Gaiety, Hollingshead staged an English version of *La Belle Hélène*. Although he advertised it as 'for the first time', it had been played in a badly hacked-about version at the Adelphi in 1866, and earlier in 1871 at the Gaiety in French by a touring company. The new translation was by Charles Lamb Kenney and this time the piece caught on with a vengeance. Constance Loseby, in pants as Paris, and Julia Mathews, as Helen of Troy, gave the Offenbach music its proper value and the Gaiety a triumph which *The Era* classed as 'a dramatic event of some importance'.

A few weeks later (November 11) Emily Soldene opened *Geneviève de Brabant* at Islington. It was an even greater success, and Offenbach took command of London. The German opéra-bouffe company at the Opéra Comique had no chance, nor did the British *Paquita*. The time now seemed obvious for a flood of French works in the West End – fully established, tried and acclaimed works which needed only adapting and/or translating. Some of the ablest British writers, with an eye to a quick and sure return, devoted themselves almost exclusively to the trade in hasty adaptations of established foreign material, abandoning the ambition to supply new and original works with unproven scores.

The best of the talent, fortunately, was still interested in creating fresh work, and the next new British piece saw a combination of the major principals from the most notable previous works. Producer John Hollingshead (*Aladdin II* and *Cinderella the Younger*) and designer Thompson staged a new extravaganza, *Thespis* or The Gods Grown Old with libretto by Gilbert (*The Gentleman in Black*) and music by Sullivan (*The Contrabandista*). The combination could not have been bettered at the time and with the casting resources of the Gaiety – Toole, Taylor, the Misses Farren, Loseby, Tremaine, Mlle Clary, and the famous pantomimists the Payne brothers – the promise of *Thespis* was high indeed. For his plot Gilbert chose an amusing premise. The Gods of Olympus have grown old and, when an Athenian theatrical manager and his troupe come to picnic on their mountain, they discover the sorry state of affairs and offer to take the Gods' places while the latter descend to earth and check on things. Needless to say, the actors cause chaos on Olympus and, when the Gods return, are angrily banished back to earth with the dreadful doom: 'You shall all be eminent tragedians whom no one ever goes to see!'

Thespis was a more substantial work than either *The Contrabandista* or *The Gentleman in Black*. Although advertised to run from 9.15 to 11 p.m., it ran nearer to three hours. Some of this difference may be attributed to encores and to ad-libbing and gagging by Toole and the other comics (there were seven of them) but not all. The libretto which survives is palpably incomplete (particularly in the sung portions) but gives us a fair idea of what the show contained. Like *Aladdin II* and *Cinderella the Younger*, it is written in prose rather than in the rhymed and rhythmical form of the old extravaganza but it does, nevertheless, contain a number of the principal features of the seasonal production, not the least being the showy transformation scene, an integral and spectacular part of every pantomime. On this occasion Apollo clears away a preliminary scene full of fog to reveal the heights of Olympus in all their tattered splendour.

Then there was the humour. Gilbert stayed much closer to the type of humour he had used for his livelier burlesques than that with which he had filled the Gallery of Illustration. The later Gilbert would never have presented a number in the fashion in which he directed Toole's best solo, 'I once knew a chap who discharged a function on the North South Eastern Diddlesex Junction,' a song about an over-benevolent railway director who comes to grief through his generosity to his staff:

He followed out his whim with vigour
The shares went down to a nominal figure,
These are the sad results proceeding
From his affable ways and his easy breeding;
The line with its rails and guards and peelers
Was sold for a song to marine store dealers,
The shareholders all are in the work'us
And he sells pipe-lights in the Regent's Circus.

The verse was followed by a chorus in which the full company joined 'screaming, whistling and shouting' while imitating the motion of the train, led by the energetic Fred Payne. Along with his brother, Payne also performed some of the pantomimic antics for which they were famous and an eccentric dance. This was a far cry from the German Reed entertainments or even from *The Gentleman in Black* but, after all, it was Christmas.

Sullivan's music for *Thespis* did not escape criticism. Some of it was thought to be unoriginal but he had not attempted to etiolate his classical training and ability. The *Thespis* music was light and suitable. The most popular number, 'Little Maid of Arcadee', was published as a parlour ballad with Gilbert's slightly cynical lyric sweetened for the occasion. Sullivan claimed in later life that whenever he was stuck for a tune he dug back into *Thespis* and found one. Since the score is no longer extant the assertion cannot be proved, but it is certain that Gilbert lifted the whole of the chorus 'Climbing over rocky Mountains' for *The Pirates of Penzance*, though whether with the same music we cannot be sure.

The two numbers already mentioned were the vocal highlights of *Thespis*, but Nellie Farren also scored with her ditty 'It's the Way of the World' which was encored at the first performance and, doubtless, thereafter:

Oh, I'm the celestial drudge
From morning to night I must stop at it
On errands all day I must trudge
And stick to my work till I drop at it!
In summer I get up at one

(As a good-natured donkey I'm ranked for it)
Then I go and I light up the Sun
And Phoebus Apollo gets thanked for it!
Well, well, it's the way of the world
And will be through all its futurity
Though noodles are baroned and earled
There's nothing for clever obscurity!

In spite of its undoubted quality and the resources it employed, the Boxing Night curtain fell on *Thespis* to the sound of hissing amongst the applause. Gilbert's wit and fancy had been above the heads of some of the audience, and the rather refined music of Sullivan had not been entirely to the taste of the public. It was the Gaiety Theatre and it was Christmas, and a portion of the audience was obviously not content with the lines and tunes that had been put into the mouths of their beloved Toole and Nellie Farren. They had come expecting a good deal more 'fun' or, at least, more obvious fun. It seems, too, that the show had been poorly rehearsed, an amazing thought when one considers Gilbert's known insistence on perfection. But the programme at the Gaiety was heavy and varied, and the performers were inundated with novelties to be learned and staged in a very short time. Gilbert claimed in later years that the whole of *Thespis* was written and produced in four (or variously five) weeks. If this was so, and Gilbert is by no means to be relied on as a factual source where his own shows are concerned, then it is probable that parts of the music, at least, were not delivered to the artists until very late.

Critics were used to this state of affairs at first nights, and were practised at assessing a work even through its première performance. Most of them discerned the value of *Thespis*. *The Sunday Times* called it 'a Christmas novelty par excellence', and *The Era* was categoric:

> . . . the workmanship, both literary and musical, is so admirable that we predict a future of complete success . . . we shall be much disappointed if *Thespis* does not turn out to be, in spite of the first night verdict, the most successful of the Gaiety comic operas.

Hollingshead was not a man to allow a show to continue in poor condition, nor if it were a failure. *Thespis* was rehearsed, cut to a more manageable two hours, polished and run in and, in the end, continued until March, a passable run if less impressive than that of *Aladdin II*. Mlle Clary, who played the 'boy' role of Sparkeion, clearly enjoyed the piece for she chose it as the central item in her benefit performance some six weeks after its closure; but that was to be its last performance. It was mooted for reproduction at the Opéra Comique by Richard D'Oyly Carte for Christmas, 1875, but nothing came of the proposal, and Carte waited instead for a new and original work to produce. In modern times a scholarly attempt has been made to reconstruct the text for performance but the loss of virtually all the music, as well as some of the text and lyrics, makes such an exercise of only relative interest.

1871

0006 **CINDERELLA THE YOUNGER** an opéra-bouffe in three acts by 'Alfred Thompson' (Thompson E. Jones). Music by Emile Jonas. Produced at the Gaiety Theatre under the management of John Hollingshead 23 September, 1871 for a run of 24 performances closing 21 October, 1871, and again from 20 November, 1871 for three performances to 22 November.

Javotte. . . . . Julia Mathews
Grand Duke Max. . . . . Mlle Clary
Dodgerowski . . . . J. D. Stoyle
Prigowitz . . . . J. G. Taylor
Peter, the Watchman . . . . John Furneaux Cook
Von Tickelsbach . . . . John Maclean
Belezza . . . . Constance Loseby
Pamela. Annie Tremaine
Porters. James Dalton, Mr Marshall
with Kate Love, Alma Egerton, Rose Wilson, Misses Angus, Verulam, Herbert, Gordon, A. Villiers, F. Villiers, Hardy, Forster, Cazally, M. Granger, R. Granger, Gresham, Wallace and Butler.
Ballet by W. H. Payne, Fred Payne, Henry Payne, Mlle Esta, Marie Smithers, Lizzie Wright.

Dir: Alfred Thompson & Robert Soutar; md: W. Meyer Lutz; sc: George Gordon & Mr. Harford; cos: Alfred Thompson

Played with *The Serious Family*, then from 15 October with *The Matchmaker* and *Mariage aux Lanternes*.

Produced at the Athénée Theatre, Paris as *Javotte* 22 December, 1871.

Produced in Vienna as *Javotte, das neue Aschenbrödel* 8 November, 1872 and 16 September, 1882.

0007 **PAQUITA** or Love in a Frame. A comic opera in two acts by Robert Reece. Music by J. E. Mallandaine. Produced at the New Royalty Theatre under the management of J. E. Mallandaine 21 October, 1871 for a run of 13 performances to 4 November, 1871.

Paquita . . . . Augusta Thompson
Francillo. . . . . J. A. Shaw
Luisita. Fanny Leng
Patricio . . . . E. Atkins
Pablos . . . . M. Loredan
Inez . . . . Lizzie Russell
Guzman. Oliver Summers
Marcella. . . . . Mrs Johnson

Md: J. E. Mallandaine

0008 **THESPIS** or The Gods Grown Old. An operatic extravaganza in two acts by W. S. Gilbert. Music by Arthur Sullivan. Produced at the Gaiety Theatre under the management of John Hollingshead 26 December, 1871 for a run of 63 performances closing 8 March, 1872.

Thespis . . . . J. L. Toole
Nicemis . . . . Constance Loseby
Daphne . . . . Annie Tremaine
Tipsicon . . . . Robert Soutar
Timidon . . . . Mr Marshall
Stupidas . . . . Fred Payne
Pretteia . . . . Rose Berend
Cymon . . . . Lardy Wilson
Sillimon . . . . J. G. Taylor
Preposteros . . . . Harry Payne
Sparkeion . . . . Mlle Clary
Jupiter . . . . John Maclean
Apollo . . . . Frederic Sullivan
Venus . . . . Annie Jolly
Mercury . . . . Nellie Farren
Mars . . . . Frank Wood
Diana . . . . Mrs H. Leigh
with Alma Egerton, Rose Wilson, Misses Angus, Brown, Chorley and Nicholls.
Dancers: Mlle Esta, Lizzie Wright, Marie Smithers

Dir: W. S. Gilbert; md: W. Meyer Lutz; ch: W. H. Payne; sc: George Gordon; cos: Alfred Thompson

Played with *Dearer than Life*, replaced 20 January by *Ganymede and Galatea* and *Off the Line* and on 26 February by *Paul Pry*.

Played April 28, 1872 at the Gaiety Theatre for the benefit of Mlle Clary with *To Parents and Guardians* and *The Happy Pair*.

A SENSATION(AL) NOVEL in three volumes by W. S. Gilbert. Music by T. German Reed. Produced at the Gallery of Illustration under the management of T. German Reed 30 January, 1871 with *Baden Baden*. Withdrawn 15 July, 1871.

Sir Ruthven Glenaloon/Tom Sittybank . T. German Reed (Alfred Bruce)
Gripper/The Spirit of Romance . . . . . R. Corney Grain
Herbert de Browne . . . . Arthur Cecil
Alice Grey . . . . Fanny Holland
Lady Rockalda . . . . Mrs German Reed

CREATURES OF IMPULSE a musical fairy tale by W. S. Gilbert. Music by Alberto Randegger. A dramatic version of his own sketch *A Story about a Strange Old Lady*. Produced at the Court Theatre under the management of Marie Litton 15 April, 1871 for a run of 91 performances closing 29 July, 1871.

Peter . . . . Maggie Brennan
Pipette . . . . Kate Bishop
The Strange Old Lady . . . . Lucy Franklein
Sergeant Kloogue . . . . W. M. Terrott
Boomblehardt . . . . Edward Righton
Jacques . . . . Charles Parry
Martha . . . . Miss L. Harris
Md: Thaddeus Wells; sc: Brinswood Potts; cos: Misses Cole & Pittock

Played with *Turn him Out* and *Randall's Thumb*, replaced 27 May by *Not at all Jealous* and *Great Expectations*, the former replaced 10 July by *Which is Which*.

Produced in a shortened version at the Court Theatre 20 October 1872. Closed 17 November, 1872. Played with *My Wife's Second Floor* and *A Son of the Soil*, and subsequently with *Amphitryon*.
Lottie Venne (PET), Emily Fowler (PIP), Mrs Stephens (LADY), W. H. Fisher (KL), Edward Righton (BOO), Miss Earnett (MAR)

Produced at the Vaudeville Theatre under the management of David James and Thomas Thorne in an altered version 6 July, 1874. Closed 30 October, 1874. Played with *Old Heads and Young Hearts* and *My Husband's Secret*.
Miss Amalia (PET), Kate Bishop (PIP), C. Richards (LADY), H. R. Teesdale (KL), Edward Righton (BOO), William Lestocq (JAC), Nelly Walters (MAR), Miss Land (JENNY)

IN POSSESSION an operetta in one act by Robert Reece. Music by Frederic Clay. Produced at the Gallery of Illustration for the benefit of Fanny Holland 20 June, 1871.

Fifine . . . . Fanny Holland
Fabian. . . . . Arthur Cecil
Dominique . . . . R. Corney Grain

MARIE an operetta in one act by Richard D'Oyly Carte. Produced at the Opéra Comique under the management of Edward Harris 26 August, 1871 for 5 performances, closing 30 August, 1871.

Marie . . . . Emmeline Cole
The Count . . . . Edward Cotte
Carl . . . . Mr Carlton

Played with *Le Medecin malgré Lui* and the ballet divertissement *La Phrygienne*.

1872

Thespis held the stage at the Gaiety until March when it was succeeded by a season of Toole's plays featuring *Aladdin II*. At the Philharmonic *Geneviève de Brabant* continued, its popularity unabated by the Christmas season, and in March it notched up its hundredth performance without looking likely to come to an end. In March too it was joined by another Offenbach piece, *La Vie Parisienne*, produced at the Holborn Theatre in a very freely adapted version by F. C. Burnand. It was necessarily adapted very thoroughly as the libretto's original series of escapades would scarcely have been acceptable to an English audience. Burnand shifted the locale to London (yet kept the title) and heavily modified not only the characters but the incidents as well. The music, however, was left largely unmolested.

During these months several new short pieces appeared, most notably at the Gallery of Illustration. On February 7 the Reeds replaced the revival of *A Peculiar Family* with a new operetta entitled *Charity Begins at Home*. The libretto had been written by Charlie Stephenson under the pseudonym 'Bolton Rowe' which he used for his amateur acting appearances, while the music had been composed by a former schoolmate of Sullivan's, Alfred Cellier. Cellier was one of two musically talented sons of a French schoolmaster at the Rev. Jackson's Church of England School in the East End. He had spent his early musical days as a chorister at the Chapel Royal but after a spell as an organist he was now following in Sullivan's footsteps as a composer and conductor. *Charity Begins at Home* was his first produced work. Once again German Reed had unerringly selected the most promising talents around. Not only would the novice composer become one of the most important light musicians of the century but his collaboration, begun here, with Stephenson would prove enormously fruitful resulting, fourteen years later, in the writing of *Dorothy*, the longest-running of all nineteenth century musicals. Such things, however, were far in the future when the twenty-six-year-old composer supplied his maiden work to German Reed.

The show's story was simple and well-suited to its purpose. In his parochial position it is the task of Mr Bumpus to look after the local school, the stocks and the village pump and to make sure all are adequately used. But his own daughter is the school's only pupil, there are no criminals, and the pump-water is filthy. To save his post, Bumpus tricks his daughter's suitor into drinking from the pump and getting into the stocks and the young man, in revenge, disguises himself as a Schools Inspector and pays an official visit. Mrs Bumpus and her son, Joe, are dressed up as pupils for the occasion (a scene which provided Mrs German Reed and her son Alfred with good opportunities) but all is eventually discovered and brought to a happy ending. The little piece was received extremely well. *The Era* called it 'a very capital little comic opera' and reckoned 'we never saw a more successful performance at the Gallery of

Illustration'. The same paper considered the music was perhaps not very original but that it was 'admirably adapted for the purpose'. *Bell's Life* asserted that 'success was assured from the outset' which judgement proved to be no exaggeration as not only did the piece run right through to the summer but it was placed on the bill again when the Gallery re-opened after the summer recess. It was later played successfully on Broadway as well as being revived on a number of occasions and proved to be one of the most lasting of the German Reed pieces.

The other new piece which shared the bill with *Charity Begins at Home* between March and October was provided by Burnand and the well-known songwriter James Molloy, best known today for his 'Just a Song at Twilight'. Entitled *My Aunt's Secret* (her secret was that she'd been married to a gambling Marquis who had ruined her), it was little more than an excuse for Mrs Reed and Arthur Cecil to step into different disguises and display their talents for impersonation. In fact the whole cast played at least two characters each. Molloy's music was more than adequate, even the concerted pieces to which he was hardly accustomed, and *My Aunt's Secret* filled very well the spot for which it was designed for six months.

Rather more ambitious was a comic opera presented for a couple of matineés at the Gaiety in April. *The Miller of Millberg* was composed by Wilhelm Meyer Lutz who had taken on the musical direction of the Gaiety following the swift departure of the theatre's original conductor, M. Kettenus. Lutz had a reputation as a distinguished and cultured musician. Since his arrival in Britain in 1850 he had worked as an organist and a conductor and had tried his hand at several light theatrical pieces without any notable success. His career to date had been unremarkable but as the head of the Gaiety orchestral department he was to become the guardian of the growth of that theatre's own particular brand of musical and, galvanised by his surroundings, he would in his sixties produce his own best compositions. *The Miller of Millberg*, however, was a piece of little consequence. The music was lively and melodious but without any distinction which might have ensured its survival. The libretto was described by *The Era* as 'a good deal of useless business'. Two performances comprised its entire life.

A major form of French musical entertainment which had not yet crossed the channel was the unwieldy 'Grand Opéra-Bouffe Féerie' – the overblown extension of the fairytale extravaganza. Paris had seen a number of these highly decorated shows over the past few years: *La Biche au Bois*, *Le Puits qui Chante* and *La Chatte Blanche* being among the more exceptional. These shows, based on tales of féerie, were mounted with unusual splendour and expense, the visual side often being given more attention than the play itself. Their usually simple stories were extended with varied and convoluted episodes designed to give opportunity for elaborate physical displays and special effects. This is not to say that the plays themselves necessarily lacked literary or musical value. On the contrary, some of the finest writers in France devoted their attention to the genre. The latest Parisian success, *Le Roi Carotte*, was, in fact, the work of the eminent playwright Victorien Sardou, with music by Offenbach.

Le Roi Carotte was a blaze of splendid costumes and scenery, but as well as its fairytale story and its trappings also contained some purposeful satire:

> The intention under the guise of extravaganza [is] to ridicule the vulgar pretensions of mob rule at a time when the Second Empire was tottering upon the verge of ruin. (*Era*)

In the story Prince Fridolin sells his ancestral armour to pay for his forthcoming wedding to the 'girl of the period', Princess Cunegonde. But the suits, angered, rise up and predict doom against the Prince for his heresy. He shall be dethroned. The evil fairy Coloquinte puts the curse into action. She brings to life the vegetables of the kitchen garden and the bewitched courtiers swear allegiance to the hideous King Carrot, while Fridolin is expelled. He and his friends wander in exile through a world peopled with strange and colourful people and creatures – Pompeii, the Kingdom of the Insects, The Monkey Island and other such expensively imaginative venues – searching for a power to effect their return. Finally the court revolts against King Carrot and Fridolin is restored.

Le Roi Carotte had been produced in Paris in 1871 and won great popular favour. The Alhambra presented it in London in 1872 in a fairly close translation by H. S. Leigh, and although the political content had been toned down (or maybe because of that) it became very popular. In August it was staged in New York and was equally well received.

This was a field in which the British were truly experienced. The fairy extravaganza had long been popular in Britain and many theatres still preferred it as a Christmas or Easter attraction to the traditional pantomime. It was no wonder, therefore, that the first native Grand Opéra-Bouffe Féerie was not long in putting in an appearance. As it happened, it was under rather unusual circumstances. In January it had been announced that Mr Dion Boucicault, the celebrated actor and author, was to take up the direction of the Covent Garden Theatre for 'a dramatic and spectacular entertainment which will be produced in September next', which would run for a season of seven months, Boucicault himself to be responsible for the book of the proposed 'fairy spectacular', with the music by Offenbach. Before long the revered lessee was in print again:

> I beg to announce that in August next this house will resume its old position as your National Theatre. Covent Garden has been closed to the English drama for the last twenty-five years. I shall endeavour to re-establish it.

Anticipation ran high. Boucicault was a dramatist of high quality. A collaboration between him and Offenbach must surely bring forth something at least as memorable as *Le Roi Carotte* if not even more amazing.

With the financial backing of Lord Londesborough, Boucicault went for the best as he gathered his team together. He persuaded Planché out of retirement to provide the lyrics for *Babil and Bijou*, the dancer/choreographer Leon Espinosa was hired to take charge of the ballets, Captain Thompson was put in charge of designing hundreds of brilliant costumes, and three scenic designers/painters were entrusted with the scenery for the eighteen imaginative locations which Boucicault had incorporated into his scenario.

But as work progressed a blow fell when Offenbach turned down the invitation to compose the score. Boucicault solved the problem by splitting up the musical part, allotting four scenes to Hervé, four to Freddie Clay and the remainder to his conductor, Jules Rivière. Rivière in his turn farmed out some of the tunes, arrangements and orchestrations to his lead violin, de Billemont, and others, for he had the whole musical production to arrange as well as composing original music for certain scenes of a production which involved, perhaps, too many creative stars:

> Sunday midnight
>
> Dear Mons. Planché,
>
> I am glad to inform you that I have done a lot of work today – the score of the Pages

chorus, which I think 'réussi', and a new arrangement with two verses of the Spring chorus. M. Eayres is also busy with the finale of the hut scene, and I should not be surprised if it was a capital piece. Now allow me to point your attention on the fate of that scene, I mean the ending of it. It is quite out of the question to think of having the band and chorus hammering 1 the health to the bride chorus 2 the Brindisi 3 *Espinosa's wretched dance* 4 Eayres' finale – two or three things must disappear and I want you to help me to demolish the lot. Let me repeat you that the Aragonese dance of which [Espinosa] is so fond is the worst piece of music in the world, principally the chorus portion – it is lame in number of bars and will be ineffective by the band – it is ready, therefore it is not for saving my time but only because I am the best judge in the matter and I declare the piece unfit for performance. We shall be laughed at if we play it, this is my firm conviction. I know that I will make an enemy of M. Espinosa if I speak but I cannot help it, and cannot approve the introduction of a piece of music of which I should be perhaps thought the composer – Je veux bien être responsable de mes crimes mais pas de ceux des autres – qu'en pensez-vous? Aidez-moi–
Tout dévoué
Jules Rivière.

By the opening night, however, Boucicault had pulled all the elements of the show together, and *Babil and Bijou* opened to a packed and fashionable house. It was nearly five hours before those who had waited until the end left the theatre after a bewildering display of song, dance and mythological spectacle. But much of the critical reaction was sour. The critics were not deflected by the massed resources of the Covent Garden mechanics and costumiers from complaining about the long-winded and involved story and Boucicault's unattractive dialogue. They called for something of a more classic quality and not merely what they called 'a pantomime without a harlequinade' . . and four months early at that. *The Times* summarised without rancour:

> When the eye is fatigued with gorgeousness the spectator may listen to effective music composed partly by MM. Hervé and Rivière, partly by Mr. Frederic Clay, to some very pretty words by Mr. Planché. The question whether it is a good play is about as irrelevant as the question whether a steamboat is a good windmill. It is a spectacle which, lasting about four hours[1], neither interests by its plot nor affords the least scope for acting. But these deficiencies it has in common with the class to which it belongs and perhaps in the reference made to the revolutionary tendencies of the day there is more point than is to be found in any similar work except *Le Roi Carotte*. Whether the class which stands apart from drama, pantomime and burlesque will long find favour with a public accustomed to these categories only time must decide.

Boucicault had used various established elements of mythological and fairy lore in composing his libretto, and had injected with a determined hand a multiple dose of the same 'anti-mob' creed which Sardou had used in *Le Roi Carotte*. The first scene represented 'A Glade in the Rosewood Forest'. Melusine, the deposed Queen of Fairyland is fleeing before the usurping gnomes, Skepsis and Pragma:

> The working classes in Fairyland have revolted. The populace of gnomes, imps, jins and pixies have driven out my fairy court . .

She confides her royal regalia to the spirits of the Earth, Air and Water before being captured and imprisoned beneath the earth. But the spirits escape with the all-

[1] Most reports indicate that it was nearer 5 hours.

important regalia, and Bijou[1] her baby daughter, is safely got away as well. The second scene turns to the palace of Zanzoozee, and we see how Phassilis (otherwise known as Babil), Prince of Lutetia, is, in his turn, deposed from his throne by a brawling mob led by the demagogic idol, Typocompus. He flees to the forest to his beloved Bijou who is now living there as a peasant girl. But Bijou's birth is revealed and the two lovers set off to find the three items of the regalia and restore it and Melusine to their rightful place and, thus, good order to the world.

The remainder of the show, fourteen scenes, took Babil and Bijou to the bottom of the sea, to the mountains of the moon, through a kitchen garden where the vegetable mob are in revolt against the rule of the flowers, through the air, the water and the earth, until the regalia are regained and Melusine brought back in triumph to Fairyland. Each of these scenes was devised to present the most amazing feats of stage design and machinery. There was a diving bell which took Babil and Bijou to the bottom of the sea where they met the vile King Octopus and his fishy court, usurpers of the kingdom of King Cod under the sea in the image of the gnomes in Fairyland or the vegetables in the Garden of the Four Seasons. There was an aerial gondola which carried the lovers to the moon where a matriarchal society of Amazons has claimed power. There was a huge and glamorous parade, 'The River of Life', depicting the ages of man and his progressive debasement in which the hundreds of cast members poured across the stage in brilliant costumes representative of the various eras of humankind. There were magical effects as Bijou, one by one, used up the magic eggs which brought wishes but shortened her life; Melusine appeared from the belly of the earth encased in a giant ruby; Mistigris, Spirit of the Earth, flew out of a birdcage which expanded in sight of the audience from normal size. There were colourful ballets headed by the French danseuse Henriette d'Or and M. Espinosa, and a dazzling parade of wonderfully armoured and helmeted Moon Amazons headed by the statuesque Helen Barry as the Princess Fortinbrasse. There was no doubt, even among the most disapproving of the critics, that this was the most spectacular show ever presented on the London stage.

But the play itself was not totally without merit. The plot which Boucicault had devised was well-proportioned and suitable for the type of entertainment which he had planned. The dialogue was admittedly rather pompous and lacking in fun, but there is little doubt that it was his overweening advance announcements which undid him with the press. The cognoscenti attacked him on his own criteria. The 'national drama' announcement proved a dreadful error of judgement. Columnists jeeringly referred to it between quotes and the burlesque theatres mocked it frightfully. At the Gaiety, Toole could raise a laugh every night in *Ali Baba à la Mode* by leering in an appropriately grandiose style–'I shall cease this Babble and Bid-you adieu'.

The music for the show was, as it deserved, much more kindly reviewed. For the first act Hervé had provided the charming 'Faces in the Fire', a pretty Bridesmaids' chorus, and a 'Mob' piece to the Planché lyric:

Liberty, Liberty
Everyone now is free
To do what he or she
Chooses to do.

[1] Originally Bee-joo in the same style as Zanzoozee (Sans Souci). The French style was readopted before opening.

Property's robbery
Who has a right to be
Richer than you or me?
I, but not you.

He also rearranged a piece from his recent *Le Trône d'Ecosse* to provide the music for the tenor solo 'To her who Owns my Heart's Devotion'.

Frederic Clay wrote a winning invocation for Mrs Howard Paul in the role of Mistigris ('Wanda, pure Spirit of the Waters') and a 'Museum Song' for King Octopus describing the human exhibits in his aerium as well as some excellent concerted music and, most particularly, a lively march for the River of Life sequence, while Rivière put together music from many sources for the rest of the show including, most successfuly, Semet's 'Gondola Song' for the aerial ship scene and a duet for Mrs Paul and the young contralto Harriet Everard (Omphale) in the Moon scene. But it was one of his own compositions which unexpectedly and violently caught the public fancy and made Rivière a household name.

Jules Rivière was a Frenchman, born in Aix-en-Othe. After being expelled from his seminary he devoted his life to music, first as a violinist, then on a variety of other instruments, as a military bandmaster and finally as a conductor. As an impresario he was less successful and a notable failure in that sphere led him, in 1857, to try his luck in England. Over the next fifteen years he conducted concerts and theatrical performances at the Cremorne Gardens, the Adelphi, the Alhambra and elsewhere, composing incidental and ballet music where required.

For *Babil and Bijou* he composed new music for several sections of the show including the Spring and Summer sections of the Grand Ballet of the Four Seasons. It was the Spring sequence (which he had completed that Sunday midnight before writing to Planché) which became the hit. Twelve young boys dressed as gardeners appeared carrying gardening equipment and bearing a pretty child in a palanquin to sing the chorus 'Spring, gentle Spring':

Spring! Spring! Gentle Spring!
Youngest season of the year,
Hither haste and with thee bring
April with her smile and tear;
Hand in hand with jocund May
Bent on keeping holiday;
With thy daisy diadem
And thy robe of brightest green;
We will welcome thee and them
As ye've ever welcomed been.
Spring! Spring! Gentle Spring!
Youngest season of the year
Life and joy to Nature bring
Nature's darling, haste thee here.

The number, the boys and Rivière became famous overnight and in no time 'Spring, gentle Spring' was heard everywhere, from the politest concerts to the street-corner barrel organs. Having refused a publisher's offer of £20 for the song, Rivière decided to print it himself and it quickly appeared in all manner of forms – as a solo, a duet, a trio for three boys, as a waltz and a set of waltzes, a quadrille, a lancers, and all kinds of marches. The Chevalier de Kontski, a fashionable pianist, arranged it as a fantasia, Mlle Secretin from the Paris Conservatoire and a M. Dubois followed suit, and variations for violin, flute, cornet and other instruments were also prepared. The sheet music printers could not keep up with the demand for the endless incarnations of the hit tune. Eventually, Rivière estimated that his composition brought him some £2,000 in revenues.

Success, however, brought its problems. On several occasions the composer had to go to court to prove his authorship. One woman claimed the manuscript had been stolen from her while she slept on a train, another, a musician's wife, declared that the theme was the work of her late husband. The *Exeter and Plymouth Gazette* published an amazing tale telling how Rivière had stolen the melody from a quadrille by the Austrian composer, Lanner, and was paying the copyright holders 6d a music sheet plus a performance royalty as hush money. The composer sued and won when the paper's 'impeccable London source' dissolved. Rivière's success with 'Spring, gentle Spring' was, unfortunately, an isolated one. Although he continued to write music, including a putative follow-up for the same boys called 'Beautiful Flowers', it was his conducting career which remained the more important. He gave his name to a long and important series of Promenade Concerts both at Covent Garden and throughout Britain and remained a highly respected theatrical musical director for many years.

At first it seemed the unkind comments of the critics might have irreparably harmed the prospects of *Babil and Bijou*. The initial houses were disappointing. But gradually the word-of-mouth spread, for although the amazing staging was a secondary consideration for the press it had an immediate appeal to the public at large. Helped by the oncoming Christmas season, business soon picked up considerably. The writers made some seasonal alterations. Clay and Rivière supplied eight new numbers, new scenery was introduced and the ballets were totally revised to feature Espinosa as a Whirling Dervish, Mlle d'Or as Iris and Emma Gauthier as an Almee Chief. The aerium scene was enlarged to include further 'specimens' and one fairly uncomical scene, in which the henpecked husbands of the Moon Matriarchs went through the motions of role-reversal, was cut to keep the show from overrunning its already enormous length. New costumes were made, and a 'special artist' was incorporated into the Moon scene. This was the Parisian caricaturist Collodion who had been banned from appearing in his home town because his lightning sketches had offended authority. Less touchy, London fully appreciated his act and he became highly popular. Business kept up sufficiently for the show to run out its appointed season until March, soon after which Bijou (Annie Sinclair) retired to a convent and the work itself was consigned to the shelf while Lord Londesborough contemplated a gaping hole in his finances. It had originally been intended that *Babil and Bijou* would be staged as the opening attraction at the new Niblo's Garden in New York but, in the event, deterred perhaps by its critical reception in London and by its unfavourable balance sheets, the theatre preferred to start out with a home-grown spectacle called *Leo and Lotos.* A piece under Boucicault's title later appeared at Howard's Athenaeum in Boston, but the resemblance was very slight. The 'original' *Babil and Bijou* was never seen in the United States.

In a sad epilogue to Boucicault's grand scheme the scenery, costumes and props of *Babil and Bijou* were sold off. First the costumes went. Representatives of the provincial theatres, anxious to pick up some cheap marvels for their forthcoming pantomimes, assembled at Simpson & Putticks, Leicester Square. Only the glorious Amazon armour fetched any price at all. The Theatre Royal, Liverpool purchased the Cupid costumes from 'Spring, gentle Spring' for a mere 9d apiece, the vegetable costumes were knocked down for 10s a half-dozen, and Queen Turtle, who had been the cause of so much mirth, was bundled in with King Octopus and 'sundry fish' at £6 7s 6d. Then it was the turn of the scenery. Under a railway arch on the South Western line, ten double wings of the River of Life which had amazed all London were sold off at £14 10s. The Palace of the Moon did slightly better, but Mr Johnson's spectacular Octopus Cave raised only 8 gns, and a certain Mr Benjamin became the owner of twenty-five working treetops from the Garden of the Four Seasons for a couple of guineas.

The score, too, had re-usable parts. The River of Life pageant turned up in the Manchester Prince's Theatre pantomime, and the Gondola song made it to the Gaiety, interpolated into the extravaganza *The Great Metropolis*. The 'original' *Babil and Bijou* Boys' Chorus stayed together after the close of the show, and Rivière included them in his Promenade Concerts, endlessly singing 'Spring, gentle Spring' which was still to be heard everywhere for a very long time.

Babil and Bijou had been, at best, a qualified success. It had run for 160 performances, it had certainly been the most splendid visual production in living memory with one real hit song, it had been seen and enjoyed by a very large number of people, and was even considered worthy of a revival (though in a substantially altered and shortened version) ten years later at the Alhambra. But there was little doubt that its main attraction had been in its production values rather than in the quality of its book and music, despite the recognised writers who had contributed to its making. It was those same production values, too, which had largely contributed to the impossible costing of the show. The artists' salaries, though many, were insignificant: among the stars tenor Joseph Maas as Babil earned only £12 a week, J. B. Howe £10, and Harry Jones the pantomimist who played Queen Turtle netted £8 and a nickname for life as 'Turtle' Jones. Even Henriette d'Or, the star ballerina, rated only £30 and the great Lionel Brough for the dual job of star comic and stage manager, £40. Supers earned 2s a night and stage children but 6d. Yet *Babil and Bijou* cost Londesborough £30,000. The huge expense of staging a 'Grand Opéra-Bouffe Féerie' made its existence a precarious one to start with, and *Babil and Bijou* had been a financial catastrophe which would be unequalled in half a century. Even in Paris the much praised *Le Roi Carotte* had been reduced to offering seats at half-price to survive. There was doubt, therefore, whether it was viable to pursue the production of such works.

But before *Babil and Bijou* closed at Covent Garden, a second show of the kind had appeared, at the Alhambra. *The Black Crook* was a famous name. In 1866 a phenomenally successful show under that title had been produced at Niblo's in New York. It had music, songs, dances, lavish scenery and a connected story, and is generally quoted as the first important example of an American musical. The tale of how this *Black Crook* came into being is a strange and probably apocryphal one. Two companies, one a second-rate dramatic group playing Niblo's and the other a French ballet company left homeless after the burning of the Winter Gardens, are said to have combined their performances, thus creating a five and a half hour musical. The French company had come to America to perform the ballet of *La Biche au Bois*, a highly successful French opéra-bouffe féerie (1865) by the Cogniard brothers, and it was on that work that the actor/author Harry Paulton and his brother Joseph based their libretto for the Alhambra version of *The Black Crook*.

La Biche au Bois is the source of the basic elements of the modern Sleeping Beauty tale. The Princess Desirée is cursed by the wicked fairy, Black Crook, who has not been invited to the baby's christening. The child shall not look on the daylight for seventeen years. But the jealous Princess Aika, Desirée's rival for the love of Prince Jonquil, has her dragged from her palanquin as she is travelling to Yellowland. Desirée looks on the light and is changed into a fawn. Unwittingly, Jonquil shoots and wounds the animal, but the Princess is saved by her maid, Gabrielle. The story then follows Jonquil and his companions through a series of adventures, first seeking the magic herb which will heal Desirée and restore her to human shape, and then as he is inveigled on by the machinations of the evil fairy and the black Princess. Finally, Dandelion, Jonquil's Chamberlain, gets the herb to Desirée, and Aika, furious, quarrels with Black Crook who blasts the black Princess' flint-steel fortress to pieces and flies away defeated, leaving the lovers to visit the Temple of Hymen for their happy ending.

The libretto was very different from *Babil and Bijou*. It had no satiric intent at all and contented itself with telling its fairy story in the most picturesque and amusing fashion possible. The fairies of the piece spoke their parts in simple rhyming verse, pantomime fashion, while the mortals conversed in plain dialogue and the fun was decidedly basic and tending to the 'low'. The plot rambled cheerfully to allow for the maximum scenic effect and the introduction of characteristic ballets and songs. After the enchantment of Desirée, it all but disappeared under a welter of scenery, comedy and music. Thus, the first scene of the third act opened with a chorus of huntsmen and ended with the trees of the forest moving in across the stage to entrap Jonquil, Dandelion and Gabrielle and the wounded fawn. By the use of a magic ring supplied opportunèly by the Fairy Sapphire, Jonquil turns the wall of trees into a real wall and the companions find themselves in The Wishing Boudoir where all wishes are granted. The stage effects were multiplied as the captives wished up variously a burning fire, a mirror and pieces of furniture. Dandelion wishes for his hat and his cloak to be hung up, and both fly dutifully across the stage to a peg. Gabrielle crossly wishes the over-attentive Chamberlain a hundred miles away and Dandelion disappears down a trapdoor only to be shot back up again when the lady changes her mind . . . 200 miles in just a few seconds! The friends set out for Aesop's Land of Fables to find the magic herb and there they meet a bevy of animals – the lion, the wolf, the monkey, the kangaroo, the donkey – and a Christy Minstrel Aesop. By the way of a parenthesis, attention turns to King Tintinabulum and his ministers Ding Dong and Jingle Jangle who have been captured by Aika's magician Zuzziel, and who go through a comic routine in a seaside set. Next the scene changes to a coral and pearl grotto where Black Crook plots to lure Jonquil from his path. He is waylaid on the Island of Pleasure where merchants sell everything from dreams to kisses and dance a Grand Ballet. The Prince ultimately escapes to the final scene in Aika's fortress for which the Alhambra painters and mechanics had come up with a particularly magnificent set. The most outstanding visual effect, however, was contained in the second act, when Desirée is imprisoned away from daylight in the Hall of a Thousand Tapers. This set was illuminated by a montage of innumerable gas coronas, giving a brilliant but eerie aspect – fraught with danger from the hundreds of open flames.

The second act also contained the best of the music. As in *Babil and Bijou*, the score had been shared. The larger part had been written by Georges Jacobi, the musical director of the Alhambra. Born in Berlin, his musical career had taken him to Paris where he had become conductor of the Bouffes-Parisiens at which theatre his operetta *Mariée depuis Midi* had been produced. He subsequently came to London and to the Alhambra where he stayed for many years and for which he composed almost all his music – songs, short pieces, a good deal of ballet music and the inevitable arrangements of other people's works for the pasticcio extravaganzas staged at the theatre. His music for *The Black Crook* included some attractive pieces – the opening trio 'Moonlight beaming, softly Streaming' for three female voices and the cavatina 'Joy, joy, the dark dread Horrors Flown' (Desirée), while the ballet music showed his exceptional facility with dance measures. The second act music, however, was written by Frederic Clay. Much of it consisted of chorus work, but there was a vengeance scena for the dramatic soprano Cornélie d'Anka as Black Crook, a pretty song for Elisa Savelli as Desirée and, the undoubted hit of the show, a ballad 'Nobody Knows as I Know' sung by Kate Santley (Gabrielle):

GAB: She says she never thinks of young men, and yet she dreams of them. Now, I never dream of them and yet I'm always thinking of them . .

Nobody knows as I know, as I know, as I know,
How fondly the heart can burn
How truly true love return
But men are so shy
Away they'll fly
Their hearts are too faint when we deceive
You say them 'nay'
They've flown away
Never guessing the make-believe
Oh, it's nice to make believe
So nice to make believe
Can't they guess
When 'no' means 'yes'
That's a woman's make-believe.

The Black Crook confirmed the already popular Miss Santley as a star of the first magnitude. Born in Charleston, USA, as Evangelina Estelle Gazina (but also reported born in Germany and emigrated to America at a young age) she had played in the American *Black Crook* on Broadway and had performed in Britain on the halls under the name 'Eva Stella' before breaking into a career in the musical theatre. She had a fine strong voice which she had trained under Viardot Garcia, and a brash and bubbling personality which impressed *The Era's* critic hugely:

> [she] can be merry without being obtrusive, enthusiastic and not vulgar . . . . sings a good song with point and expression, speaks her lines with some sort of intelligence and verve and possesses in a remarkable degree that power which can fill such a huge theatre with welcome expression.

Her role of Gabrielle was a strong soubrette part and she shared a good number of the many humorous scenes with the male comedians, particularly Harry Paulton, the author, as Dandelion. Paulton had supplied a comprehensive role for himself as the blathering Chamberlain of Yellowland. He was in on everything with his daft wordy diatribes and physical and musical foolery. He established a comical relationship with his huge 'little' brother, Buttercup (J. H. Jarvis), and, in the final scene, managed to twist the plot in such a way as to be able to appear disguised as a crocodile.

Like Miss Santley, Paulton was an influential figure in the early years of the British musical, and like her he was not active only as a performer: she contributed as a producing manager, he as a playwright. Born in Wolverhampton in 1842, Paulton had begun as a small-time provincial actor but graduated eventually to larger towns and finally made his London debut in 1867 in *The Lottery Ticket*. He was engaged for the Strand Theatre in 1870 and came to prominence in Farnie's burlesque of *The Idle Prentice*. In collaboration with his brother, Joseph, he made his writing debut with *The*

Three Musket-Dears and a Little One In in 1871. He joined the Alhambra for *Clodhopper's Fortune* in 1872 staying there for six years as chief comedian and sometime author.

More amusement in a show which relied heavily on its broad comic element was provided by Mr Worboys as the Prime Minister of the Kingdom of the Little Bells as he waddled through the show with his nose magicked into a strawberry which was continuously being attacked by marauding wasps, and by Edward Connell as his unfortunate monarch whose forgetfulness had set off the whole business. The show received a more kindly critical reception than *Babil and Bijou*, but with the same reservations:

> Gorgeous, decorated with the rarest taste, glittering with gold and bright with silver, with regiments of Amazons in burnished armour and cohorts of girls in grim funereal costumes of silver and black, with bell scenes and ballet scenes, with summer landscapes and demon glens, with halls glittering with a thousand tapers, with music by the best modern masters, the Alhambra Christmas entertainment is the embodiment of wealth and splendour – but not of fun . . . . The public must not grumble if the eye is pleased more than the ear in the drama of *The Black Crook*. They must not expect to find a dramatic play. They must not grumble if they find it a difficult matter to follow the story. The stage is too huge, the theatre is too large, the undertaking too vast for the careful following of intricate plots, the exhibition of niceties of humour or the delicate rendering of dainty love songs. All the effects must be large and bold at the Alhambra. (*Era*)

The Times noted:

> The dialogue of *The Black Crook* is rather commonplace, and the piece requires immediate and liberal curtailment.

It certainly had a point in its second comment at least, for on opening night the show ran for nearly five hours of non-stop stage display. The point was quickly taken. The show was compressed and shortened, one item in particular being cut – the can-can. Its introduction on the first night had scandalised certain of the audience and the press. *The Times* was severe:

> Any merits the piece may have as a spectacle are neutralised so long as the manager retains the can-can in the performance.

So, along with some other dispensable portions, it went.

As the show ran itself in, the technical side (which had gone somewhat awry on the first night) was smoothed out, new music and dances were added, the comedy became more or less stabilised, and *The Black Crook* was worked up into a very lively show. When *Babil and Bijou* closed the Alhambra management promptly snapped up Collodion, the caricaturist, and incorporated him into their show[1]. *The Era*'s critic, who had shown so many misgivings in his original review in December 1872, returned in April and showed a complete reversal of his opinion of the show:

> What comic opera can boast such facile and melodious composers as Messrs. Frederic Clay and Jacobi who, by their fresh, unaffected harmony save us from repeated doses of Offenbach or his innumerable Parisian imitators? What spectacle

[1] Though not before the vital Prince's Theatre, Manchester, who cornered Collodion for a short engagement immediately following *Babil and Bijou*.

> can distance this beautiful show . . . *The Black Crook* spectacle is the only thing of the kind to be found in London and it is the kind of entertainment that can be visited again and again with interest.

The show eventually extended its run into the middle of August, 1873, easily outstripping the record established by *Babil and Bijou*, closing after 204 performances. Ten years later the Alhambra revived *The Black Crook* in a new and heavily revised version by Harry Paulton. Once again it proved a highly successful piece for the theatre which specialised in spectacular physical productions.

While the larger theatres were running these grandiose and novel entertainments, less ambitious establishments were continuing to produce smaller native works of varying qualities and success. The Vaudeville Theatre produced a benefit for its musical director, Arthur W. Nicholson, part of the programme of which was his own one-act operetta *Love Birds*. The libretto by Conway Edwards was a simple English civil war tale of a country girl who harbours King Charles and excites the jealousy of her lover. It won some very good notices, particularly for its book (an area often especially weak in small operettas), while *The Era* expressed the opinion that 'Mr. Nicholson could write better opéra-bouffe than half the composers who are producing that kind of composition'. This comment did not, apparently, encourage him to do so. Another once-off work was *The Wager*, a two-act piece tried at a Gaiety matinée. The music was by Jacob Kappey, the bandmaster of the Royal Marines at Chatham, and it met with some approval but, hampered by a silly libretto about a baron's bet that he will carry off the prettiest girl in the village, it sank without trace.

At the Gallery of Illustration the German Reeds continued to vary their programme and produced two new pieces. The first was another offering from Gilbert and Clay under the title *Happy Arcadia*. The Arcadians are tired of rustic felicity and when a wandering bogey comes along bringing magic talismans their wishes land them in a strange situation. The highlight of the show was a scene in which, various jealousies having arisen, everyone is simultaneously wishing he were one of the others–and consequently everyone is! And while everyone is someone else they sing:

> If I am she and she is him
> And him is her or me
> Arises then the question grim
> Why, who on earth are we?

–a recognisably Gilbertian lyric incorporating, once again, his favourite theme of change of identity or personality. Both the libretto and music of *Happy Arcadia* were duly praised, and it was deservedly popular.

The other new item was by the Gallery's second current 'team' of Burnand and Molloy who followed up *My Aunt's Secret* with *Very Catching*, a straightforward little piece set on a riverbank and involving a will in a deed-box which is fished up from the river at the appropriate moment. It, too, proved popular and was sufficiently well regarded by Reed to be later selected for revival. While Gilbert's piece represented the highly imaginative and exotic type of work which he was to make his speciality, Burnand's was an example of the simple and very English piece which would survive and occasionally blossom alongside its more ostentatious counterpart.

Although the two spectacular fairy shows were the only full-length British musicals of 1872, British composers contributed by far the larger part of the score for Robert Reece's Gaiety extravaganza *Ali Baba à la Mode*. Instead of plundering Offenbach and the opéra-bouffe for his melodies, Reece turned instead to British works for which he had written the lyrics and lifted numbers from *Paquita*, *In Possession*, *Castle Grim* (G. B. Allen) and *Choknosoff* (Geo. Richardson) as well as George Grossmith's song 'I Am so Volatile' and a vocal waltz of his own composing.

1872

0009 **BABIL AND BIJOU** or The Lost Regalia. A new fantastic music drama in eighteen spectacular scenes divided into five acts, the drama by Dion Boucicault, the lyrical part by J. R. Planché, the music for the first four tableaux composed by Hervé, the music in the fifth to eight tableaux by Frederic Clay, the remaining music composed and selected by Jules Rivière and J.-J. de Billemont. Produced at the Theatre Royal, Covent Garden 29 August, 1872 for a run of 160 performances closing 1 March, 1873. On 3 March, 1873 three acts were played for the benefit of M. Rivière.

Melusine, the fugitive Queen of Fairy-land	Ada Murray[1]/Robertha Erskine
Azurine, the spirit of the air	Alice Phillips
Wanda, the spirit of the water	Edith Bruce/Annie Taylor
Mistigris, the spirit of the earth	Mrs Howard Paul/(Annie Taylor)
Pragma, the Queen of the Gnomes	Mrs John Billington
Skepsis, King of the Gnomes	J. B. Howe
The Spirit of Launcelot, a shepherd boy	Miss M. Edmonds/Julia Vokins
Phassilis (Babil) of Lutetia	Joseph Maas
Orzmarino	Mr Watson/Mr Perry
Pompano	Mr Grainger
Count Chicaforach	Mr Moreland
Befeta	Mr Jackson
Auricomus, an idol worshipped by the court	Lionel Brough (W. M. Terrott)
Typocompus, an idol worshipped by the people	John Wainwright
Hydra, his daughter	Mrs John Billington
Pages	Misses A. Brough and M. Edmonds
Bijou	Annie Sinclair (Mary Pitt)
Mish Mash	H. Massey/Miss Claire
Bruno	Miss G. Claire
Dagmar	Miss Claire/Miss Langford/H. Massey/ R. Tennyson
Zell	Mr Dardy
Olaf	Mr Elliot
Gurth	Mr Lawler
Sunshower	Clara Shelley
H. M. Queen Turtle	Harry Jones/C. Bertram
King Octopus	John Wainwright
Captain Lobster	Mr Gill/Mr Good
Oyster	Mr Dannaville/Mr Elmsley
Walrus	Mr Dardy
Skate	Mr Bush

[1] Miss Murray had formerly been understudy to Adah Isaacs Menken in her infamous portrayal of Mazeppa at Astleys.

Salmon	Mr Gardiner
Ex-King Cod	Mr Elliot
Lord Dundreary	George Temple/Mr Arthur
Prince Cherry	Jessie Anstiss
Princess Rosebud	H. Massey/G. Claire
Geranium	Miss Robson
Otto of Rose	Miss Travers/R. Claire
Queen Bee	Annie Taylor/Julia Vokins
Dragonfly	Miss Meldreth
Squirrel	A. Brough
Pineapple	Mr Curll
Potato	Mr Watson
Cabbage	Mr Webber
Stag Beetle	Miss Manton
Tomato	Mrs Billington
Carrot	Mr Henry
Turnip	Mr Tellon
Beetroot	Mr Cameron
Queen Camellia	Ada Murray/Lytton Grey
Tigerlily	Miss Vivian
Lord Butterfly	Mr Fredericks
Lord Pink	Miss Hervey
Honeysuckle	Miss Poole
Grasshopper	Miss Coleman
Water Lily	Miss Anderson
Heart'sease	Misses Blake and Morgan
Jasmines	Misses Summers and Ames
Fuschias	Misses Nelson and R. Morris
Tulips	Misses Quy and Dot Brougham
Aerolite	J. B. Howe/C. Harrison/Mr Butler
Princess Fortinbrasse	Helen Barry/Robertha Erskine
Lunar Bow	R. Tennyson
Zem Zem	Miss Anderson/Annie Taylor
Kooz Kooz	Clara Shelley/Miss Langford
Omphale	Harriet Everard
Vortex	Jessie Anstiss
Atalanta	H. Massey
Horsa	Miss Coleman
Hero	Miss Berners
Attila	Lytton Grey
Fredegonde	Miss Poole
Gorgona	Miss Ames
Lysandra	Miss Robson
Goneril	Miss Hargreaves
Volscia	Miss Harrington
Bonduca	Miss Temple
Syphax	Miss Travers
Bellona	Miss Vivian
Armida	Miss Quy
Armadilla	Miss Hervey
Galatea	Miss Shelley
King Dodo	Mr Watson/out
Prince Phinnikin	Mr Temple/*out*
Enpekt, Duke of Graymaria	Mr Moreland/*out*
Phoolmeer	Mr Gardiner/*out*
Boolbool	Mr Elliott/*out*

The Wild Men of the Moon: Messrs James, Metcalfe, Williams and Granton.

Pds: Henriette d'Or, Mlle Travaille, Mlle Wichtendahl, Mme Espinosa, Emma Gauthier, Mlle Lavigne, Leon Espinosa, Mlle Roques.

Special artiste	M. Collodion

add Wiri Saltator Vulgaris . . . . Mlle Chenat
Aldemanus . . . . Mr Hanway
Anonyma . . . . Miss Aymott
Scalpus Americanus. . . . . Mr Cutler

Md: Jules Rivière; ch: Leon Espinosa; sc: W. Hann, J. Johnson, and J. Hicks; cos: Alfred Thompson

Produced at the Alhambra Theatre 8 April, 1882 in a largely different version.

0010 **THE BLACK CROOK** a grand opéra-bouffe féerie in four acts founded on *La Biche au Bois*, by Harry and Joseph Paulton. Entirely new music by Georges Jacobi and Frederic Clay. Produced at the Alhambra Theatre under the management of John Baum 23 December, 1872 for a run of 204 performances closing 15 August, 1873.

Black Crook . . . . Cornélie d'Anka/Louise Beverley/Amy Sheridan?
Fairy Sapphire . . . . Marie Barrie/Inez Harland
Fairy Pearl . . . . Alice Hilton
Fairy Coral . . . . Miss Earle
Princess Desirée. . . . . Elisa Savelli/Marie Barrie/Cornélie d'Anka
King Tintinabulum . . . . Edward Connell
Ding Dong . . . . W. Worboys
Queen Orange Hue . . . . Miss Litton/Jessie Anstiss/
Prince Jonquil. . . . . Nita de Castro/Amy Sheridan/Edward Cotte/Frank H. Celli
Gabrielle . . . . Kate Santley/Bella Goodall
Princess Aika . . . . Julia Seaman
Zuzziel . . . . Clavering Power/H. Pritchard
Buttercup . . . . J. H. Jarvis
Jingle Jangle . . . . Edward Cotte/Mr Wray
Dandelion . . . . Harry Paulton
Solfleur . . . . Mr Beverley/J. Marshall
Muley . . . . Mr Valentine
Batiste, a huntsman . . . . T. H. Paul
Marigold . . . . Maud Branscombe
Cowslip . . . . Gertrude[1] Branscombe
Lady Merchaud. . . . . Isabell Harold
Merchant . . . . J. Marshall/Mr. Cattell
Florican . . . . Cissy Somerset
Mohair . . . . Julia Beverley
Tinkle . . . . Amy Clifford
An Officer . . . . Charles Kelleher
Silverstone . . . . Amy Sheridan
Pleasure . . . . Maud Egerton
Gaiety . . . . Helen Hatherley
Vanity . . . . Miss Hamilton
with Robert Sweetman, Isabel Somerset, Blanche Beverley etc.
Pds: Mlles Nana, Pauline Louise, Pepita, Bartoletti, Barratt, M. Bekefey/Bertha Linda.
Special artiste . . . . M. Collodion

Md: Georges Jacobi; ch: M. Hus; sc: Charles Brew, Thomas Rogers and Albert Callcott; cos: Alfred Maltby

Produced in a revised version at the Alhambra Theatre 3 December, 1881.

CHARITY BEGINS AT HOME a musical proverb by 'Bolton Rowe' (B. C. Stephenson). Music by Alfred Cellier. Produced at the Gallery of Illustration under the management of T. German Reed 7 February, 1872 with *King Christmas* and *Home for the Holidays*, the former

[1] The programme shows 'Grace' Branscombe but this is almost certainly Gertrude who, with her sister Maud became more famous as postcard beauties than as actresses.

replaced by *My Aunt's Secret* (March 13) and by *Happy Arcadia* (October 28), the latter by *Five o'Clock Tea* (April 22). Withdrawn 17 August, 1872. Reopened 1 October, 1872, withdrawn 16 November, 1872.

Aloysius Gorringe . . . . Arthur Cecil
Joe Bumpus . . . . Alfred Reed
Mr Bumpus . . . . R. Corney Grain
Susan Bumpus . . . . Fanny Holland
Mrs Bumpus . . . . Mrs German Reed

Produced at St George's Hall 20 April, 1874 with *Ages Ago* and *A Day in Town*. Withdrawn 15 May, 1874.
Arthur Law (ALOY), Alfred Reed (JOE), R. Corney Grain (MR), Leonora Braham (SU), Mrs German Reed (MRS)

Produced at St George's Hall 5 June, 1876 with *A Spanish Bond* and *A Musical Bee*, the former replaced by *The Wicked Duke* (9 June). Withdrawn 22 July, 1876.

Played at St George's Hall 7 February, 1877 for the benefit of John Parry.
Arthur Law (ALOY), Alfred Reed (JOE), R. Corney Grain (MR), Fanny Holland (SU), Mrs German Reed (MRS)

Produced at St George's Hall 21 October, 1878 with *Number 204* and *Mrs Brown*. Withdrawn 4 November, 1878.
Cast as for the Parry benefit.

Produced at St George's Hall 27 May, 1879 with *£100 Reward* and *Our Calico Ball*. Withdrawn 24 June, 1879.

Produced at the Bijou Theatre, New York, under the management of John A. McCaull and Charles E. Ford 31 March, 1880 with *Ages Ago* and subsequently (15 May) with *The Spectre Knight*. Withdrawn 22 May, 1880.
William Herbert (ALOY), Digby V. Bell (JOE), William Courtenay (MR.B), Carrie Burton (SU), Marie Beauman (MRS. B). Md: Alfred Cellier

Produced at St George's Hall 3 October, 1892 with *My Wife's Party*. Withdrawn 5 November, 1892.
Avalon Collard (ALOY), Alfred Reed (JOE), R. Corney Grain (MR), Gertrude Woodall (SU), Fanny Holland (MRS)

Produced at St George's Hall 29 March 1902 with *Tea and Tennis* and *No Cards*, the latter replaced by *Box B*. Withdrawn 20 May, 1902.

MY AUNT'S SECRET by F. C. Burnand. Music by James L. Molloy. Produced at the Gallery of Illustration under the management of T. German Reed 13 March, 1872 with *Charity Begins at Home* and *Home for the Holidays*, the latter replaced by *Five o'Clock Tea* (April 22). Withdrawn 17 August. Reopened 1 October. Withdrawn 26 October, 1872.

Sir Marmaduke Pender/Thomas
Egerton/Signor Amati . . . . Arthur Cecil
Miss Briarly/Miss Lavinia S. Jackson . . Mrs German Reed
Simon Lancaster/Perkins . . . . Alfred Reed
Captain Hurrykin/Mr Chugg . . . . R. Corney Grain
Miss Nelly Chugg/Miller . . . . Fanny Holland

HAPPY ARCADIA in one act by W. S. Gilbert. Music by Frederic Clay. Produced at the Gallery of Illustration under the management of T. German Reed 28 October, 1872 with *Charity Begins at Home* and *Five o'Clock Tea*, the former replaced by *Very Catching* (November 18) and the latter by *All Abroad* (December 16). Withdrawn 2 May, 1873.

Strephon . . . . Arthur Cecil
Chloe . . . . Fanny Holland
Daphne . . . . Mrs German Reed
Colin . . . . Alfred Reed
Astrologos/Lycidas . . . . R. Corney Grain

Produced at St George's Hall 15 July, 1895 under the management of Rutland Barrington with *Soured and Sweetened* and *The Professor*, the former replaced by *The Usual Remedy*. Withdrawn 10 August. Represented 4 November, 1895 with *Daye and Knight* and *Two Blind Beggars*. Withdrawn 30 November, 1895.
Rutland Barrington (ST), Marie Garcia/Chrystal Duncan (CH), Fanny Holland/Emily Cross/Marion German Reed (DAPH), Charles Wibrow (COL), George Traill/Roland Carse (AS), Hilton St Just (LYC)

VERY CATCHING by F. C. Burnand. Music by James L. Molloy. Produced at the Gallery of Illustration under the management of T. German Reed 18 November, 1872 with *Happy Arcadia* and *Five o'Clock Tea*, the latter replaced by *All Abroad* (16 December) and the former by *Mildred's Well* (6 May). Withdrawn 31 July, 1873.

Dora Kettle . . . . Fanny Holland
Mr Dibble. . . . . R. Corney Grain
Mr Dabble . . . . Alfred Reed
Mr Sniggle . . . . Arthur Cecil
Mrs Sniggle . . . . Mrs German Reed

Produced at St George's Hall 7 June, 1875 with *RSVP* and *A Tale of Old China*, the latter replaced by *Eyes or No Eyes* (July 5). Withdrawn 14 August, 1875.

Produced at St George's Hall 14 June, 1880 with *A Flying Visit* and *Our Ascot Party*. Withdrawn 24 July, 1880.

THE MILLER OF MILLBERG a comic opera in one act with original music by W. Meyer Lutz. Performed at a matinée at the Gaiety Theatre under the management of John Hollingshead 13 April, 1872 with *That Blessed Baby* and *Les Deux Aveugles*, and again 20 April, 1872 with *Turning the Tables*.

Raymond . . . . J. L. Toole
Agnes . . . . Constance Loseby
Sebastian . . . . J. G. Taylor
Jacques . . . . Nellie Farren
Margot . . . . Annie Tremaine

LOVE BIRDS an operetta in one act by Conway Edwards. Music by Arthur Nicholson. Performed at the Vaudeville Theatre under the management of David James and Thomas Thorne 19 June, 1872 with *Mrs White* and *Deaf as a Post* for the benefit of Arthur Nicholson.

Ralph Claverton. . . . . Henry Nordblom
Bellows . . . . George Honey
King Charles . . . . H. Elton
Cicely Sweetapple. . . . . Julia Bleadon

THE WAGER a comic opera in two acts with music by Jacob A. Kappey. Produced at the Marine Theatre, Chatham 20 June, 1871. Played at a matinée at the Gaiety Theatre under the management of John Hollingshead 23 November, 1872 with *Debt*.

William . . . . Selwyn Graham
Jeremiah Flip . . . . Edward Connell
Augustus Flip. . . . . Richard Temple
Sir Frederick Languid . . . . James Dalton
John. Mr Cruttwell
Mrs Thomas . . . . Miss Brunella
Mary . . . . Annie Goodall
with Misses Risson, Marshall, Bacon, Hillier, Clifton, Smith, Keller, Lovell and Lister

Md: Jacob A. Kappey

1873

Babil and Bijou closed in March of 1873, leaving *The Black Crook* to dominate the West End musical scene and when that closed in August the stage was clear for the newest French musical hit to sweep all before it. *La Fille de Madame Angot*, written by MM. Clairville, Siraudin and Koning and composed by Charles Lecocq, had opened at the Fantaisies Parisiennes, Brussels, in December and had been a huge success. The production was brought to Britain and staged for a short season at the St James' Theatre with Jeanne d'Albert and Pauline Luigini repeating their original roles, and it was much admired. Lecocq had succeeded in combining the best elements of the old opéra-comique with the spirit of Offenbach to produce a new type of light musical play which would supersede the pure opéra-bouffe and remain the rage of Europe for many years. In October Henry Byron's English version of the piece was staged at the Philharmonic with Julia Mathews and Selina Dolaro in the two prima donna roles and soon, as they had done two years previously for *Geneviève de Brabant*, all London was heading for Islington. In November the Gaiety produced a rival adaptation by H. B. Farnie with Soldene and Annie Sinclair as the leading ladies. It was soon transferred to the Opera Comique to allow the Gaiety's normal programme to continue and the two versions ran side by side until mid-April, 1874, when the Opera Comique began to vary its programme with *Geneviève de Brabant*. A third version was produced for a five-week season at the Globe starring Cornélie d'Anka (May/June), and touring companies were set to capitalise on the greatest success yet for the French musical in Britain. Over the next decade there was scarcely a time when *La Fille de Madame Angot* was not being played somewhere in the British Isles, as it established itself and its genre firmly in the life of the British musical theatre.

The progress, at the moment, of native writers and composers was slower and a step such as that which Lecocq had taken was not yet within their power. They had, to all intents and purposes, rejected the 'Grand Opéra-Bouffe Féerie'. It was quickly seen to be viable only under the peculiar circumstances at the Alhambra and, sensibly, to the Alhambra it was henceforth confined. The few original pieces which were produced during the year on a more realistic scale proved unexceptional.

The young actor, Henry J. Montague, had taken a lease on the Globe Theatre from Lord Newry. Montague had come to the stage from the Sun Fire Office, with dazzling good looks, a black moustache and a colourful style of dress, and after some work with Dion Boucicault he had established himself as 'the first matinée idol'[1] in such roles as Lord Beaufoy in *School* and Jack Wyatt in *Two Roses*. Now, at the age of thirty, he took on the role of actor/manager, and in February presented a curious piece called *Oriana*.

[1] The verdict of H. Chance Newton in 'Cues and Curtain Calls'

Described as 'a romantic legend', *Oriana* was a half-poetic, half-comic piece seemingly inspired by Gilbert's successes with *The Palace of Truth* and *The Wicked World* which had sported with fairyland, and perhaps a little by *Babil and Bijou*. The plot centres around a crippled fairy, Peep, who will be restored to health when King Raymond returns from his wandering ways to the arms of his Queen, Oriana. Peep arms herself with a magic ring which causes the bearer to fall in love with the first person he sees and proceeds to get the King into all sorts of trouble as he falls successively for a milkmaid, the demagogue who is trying to dethrone him, and finally his own reflection. All ends happily, however, when Oriana takes up arms against the demagogue and Raymond comes back to his senses and his wife.

The book for *Oriana* was by the celebrated but erratic James Albery. Albery had had an enormous hit with the play *Two Roses* (1870, Vaudeville), but it was typical of him that he should turn from a triumph with a comedy to a poetic musical in rhyming couplets. It was a turn which the public did not willingly follow. At the end of the first performance the routine cheers were heavily laced with hisses and the piece's prospects looked poor. The newspapers were no kinder. *The London Entr'acte* described *Oriana* as 'three acts of exceedingly mild comedy' and *The Era* concluded 'we fear *Oriana* is not destined to a long life'. They were unanimous, however, in praising the music, the latest composition of Frederic Clay:

> [the play is] so largely supplemented with music that with a little less dialogue and a little more of chorus and song it would in reality take the form of an opera . . [the music is] the best Mr. Clay has written. A ready and graceful vein of melody is noticeable throughout . . (*Era*)

> Some most agreeable music . . . in Mr. Clay's happiest vein and he shows immense progress in his art. (*Bell's Life*)

> [the music is] uniformly excellent and although it savours strongly of Germanic origin, especially in one scene where the opening phrase of Mendelssohn's *Melusine* overture is nearly note for note reproduced, we hail it with delight and proclaim it the highest effort ever made by this young composer. It seems to us that the management of the Globe have erred in not giving better emphasis to the musical side of the question for although we deem it next to an impossibility to make a success of *Oriana* as a pure and simple comedy, we think it quite possible with the bulk of the work given to Mr. Clay that it should have been made remunerative as an opera . . (*Times*)

The largest part of the singing was allotted to Montague himself as King Raymond. Clay had provided him with an attractive air, 'The Moon Fell in Love', sung to a harp accompaniment, and a very strong aria 'I Am weary of my Life', both of which proved so far beyond his vocal abilities that it was unkindly suggested that the attendants should supply ear-trumpets along with the customary opera glasses.

Vigorous attempts were made to save the piece after its unsuccessful opening. Albery went to work on his script, cutting out much of the satiric content and the extravaganza 'business' which slowed down the action and concentrated on emphasising the poetical scenes which had been the most successful. But it was too late. Even though the work was greatly improved it lasted only a few days longer before oblivion.

The season was a disaster for Harry Montague. He fled to America leaving £450 theatre rent unpaid besides other large debts. His leading lady, Rose Massey, followed him and finding herself rejected, brought a breach of promise suit against him. The result was a highly romantic court case but, unlike Oriana, Miss Massey failed to win her point or her man who stayed safely in America where his friend Lester Wallack built him into a highly-paid star in New York. But when the young man died in 1878, and Lord Newry attached his estate for the now nearly $5,000 owing, it was found that Montague had, in spite of his successes, accumulated nothing but debts.

Of almost as good a pedigree, but of little more success, was another fairytale musical produced at the Alexandra Theatre in Camden Town. *The Magic Pearl* had been written by the venerable Edward Fitzball (now in his eighty-first year) some ten years previously for production in Edinburgh, but had been shelved owing to its heavy scenic demands. Fitzball had become famous with a series of dramas and melodramas in the twenties and thirties including *Jonathan Bradford* (1823), *The Floating Beacon* (1824), and *The Pilot* (1825), but his most lasting claim to fame was in the musical field where he supplied the libretti for such works as Balfe's *Siege of Rochelle* and the immortal *Maritana*. From Surrey melodrama to a flimsy bit of make-believe such as *The Magic Pearl* was a long journey and one Fitzball might have been wiser not to take. *The Era* described his book as 'still more hazy than opera librettos in general' – and Fitzball must have felt hazy indeed among the Indian royalty and good and evil spirits around which he concocted the story of a magic jewel which makes its wearer beautiful.

The music for the play had been composed by Thomas Thorpe Pede. Pede had taken the Alexandra Theatre in June to present a short season including *The Lady of Lyons*, *The Hunchback* and his own operetta, *Marguerite*, a little vehicle for soprano Gertrude Ashton and tenor J. W. Turner. After six weeks they had closed down and rumours of trouble were rife. Pede reacted angrily, offering £100 reward for the tracking down of the 'malicious rumours' and, with his 'director', Mme Marion St Claire, promptly re-opened the theatre with *The Magic Pearl*. A good cast of opera singers gave the routine piece a tidy performance, and Mme St Claire as 'The Spirit of the Himalayas' delivered a couple of stationary narrative arias which were presumably her reward for being 'director'.

Two more short pieces of Pede's found their way into the bill in support of *The Magic Pearl*. *A Lesson in Love* and *Moonstruck* also starred Miss Ashton and Turner, and like *Marguerite* were competent little pieces of their kind, if, like all Pede's compositions, rather reminiscent of other people's work. *The Magic Pearl* held the stage at Camden for five weeks, but survived its librettist for Fitzball died on October 27. The Alexandra followed up with a Christmas extravaganza entitled *In the Clouds* for which Pede once again supplied some of the music and which, supplemented by the pantomime, ran through into February of the following year.

Many other composers were also supplying odd numbers for the various extravaganzas around town as managers began to look closer to home for their music. When the Gaiety opened *Don Giovanni in Venice* (11 February 1873) James Molloy, Meyer Lutz and the versatile Robert Reece were all listed among the composers. When Offenbach's *The Bohemians* was produced at the Opera Comique (24 February), dance music by Mallandaine was added to the hotch-potch of Offenbach tunes. Both Clay and Jacobi contributed music to the Alhambra's big extravaganza *Don Juan* to be put alongside the melodies of Lecocq and Offenbach, and wealthy amateur composer and theatre manager W. H. C. Nation, following a formula which he was to continue for many years, interpolated several new songs of his own into *The Daughter of the Danube* (March 3) at the Holborn and no less than nine into *The Last of the Legends* (September 1) at the Charing Cross.

Nation was an eccentric and slightly mysterious character. George Sims described him:

> . . He began to take theatres and produce plays which were sprinkled all over with songs by himself. . In his time he took for periods Sadler's Wells, Astleys, the old Holborn, the Charing Cross and Terry's. The Royalty was his favourite theatre for a time, but his last venture was at the Scala.
>
> The bill of the play during a Nation season was a curiosity. The name of the play and the cast occupied a very small portion of it. The rest of the bill was taken up with large cross-lines giving the names of the 'songs by W. H. C. Nation' introduced into the piece, and after each song mentioned on the programme the name W. H. C. Nation was printed in large type.
>
> The Nation productions were not lavish. The scenery was simple and the dresses would not have been censored by a committee of economy even in wartime.
>
> It was believed at one time that Mr. Nation was in the law, and that he allotted so much money to his theatrical ventures and then retired to make more at his legitimate business. But after his death it was discovered that he was an independent gentleman of very considerable wealth.
>
> There was never much of an audience, but that did not matter. Mr. Nation's happiness consisted in witnessing his own plays and listening to his own songs.
>
> I have seen him sitting in a private box, almost the only person in the front of the house, and when one of his own songs had been sung he would bang the floor of the box with his umbrella and shout 'Encore! Encore!'
>
> Mr. Nation, who was educated at Eton and Oxford, was an amiable and charming old gentleman, but the desire to see his name and his songs starred on the playbill of a West End house was his ruling passion. And in the course of his long and estimable career he must have paid a pretty considerable sum for the privilege . .

The only other complete work to be produced for a London run was, as usual, at the German Reeds'. Burnand provided a slight libretto dealing with romance in an English seaside hotel, entitled *Mildred's Well*, and German Reed set it with his usual slight, pretty music. It held the stage until the Gallery closed its doors on July 31, 1873. It was later to reappear in the German Reed repertoire in the Entertainment's new home at St George's Hall with a certain degree of popularity.

London was not the only centre producing new works, however. Isaac De Frece, the adventurous manager who had done so well at the *Babil and Bijou* sale in snapping up scenery for his Liverpool Theatre Royal, announced the production of a brand new comic opera entitled *Lothair*. Whether London would have quite agreed with his description of 'comic opera' is dubious, for what the architects of the piece – Frank Green, Gaiety stage manager Robert Soutar and Frank Musgrave of *Windsor Castle* fame, now installed at Nottingham as the lessee of the Theatre Royal – had put together was a fairly eclectic work.

The Shah of Persia had recently paid a visit to Britain, so it was to his country that they turned for their colourful location. They introduced, fairly loosely, the obligatory fairy element into a standard plot involving a Shah's daughter and a fisherman who is really a prince. Maurice De Frece, brother of the manager, peppered the script freely with topical and local jokes and Musgrave supplied some original music and songs which were supplemented with such known hits as the Conspirators' Chorus from *La Fille de Madame Angot*. The popular danseuse, Esther Austin, was featured in two picturesque ballets and with Kalulu's charcoal sketches, Professor Wheeler's dissolving scenery and Miss Lottie Cherry's entertainment retained as a supporting programme, the 'musical' was staged as a successor to a two-week season of *Geneviève de Brabant*. *Lothair* was a blatantly parochial and topical piece, strongly cast and vigorously played over an excellent run of six weeks.

De Frece (who had earlier in the year staged a stock revival of Gilbert's *The Gentleman in Black*) continued to encourage indigenous writers and towards the end of the run of *Lothair* he added an operetta *Rustic Roses* to the bill. This piece included original work by the composers Walter Corri and Alfred Lee alongside a selection of Offenbach tunes but it did not have the appeal of the evening's main piece and was discontinued after two weeks.

1873

0011 **ORIANA** a romantic legend in three acts by James Albery. Music by Frederic Clay. Produced at the Globe Theatre under the management of H. J. Montague 16 February, 1873 for a run of 18 performances closing 7 March, 1873.

King Raymond . . . . H. J. Montague
Peep . . . . Carlotta Addison
Moth . . . . Miss Fane
Flamen . . . . E. W. Garden
Solon . . . . Mr Flockton
Oxeye . . . . Mr Compton
Broom . . . . Mr Deane
Senapis . . . . Mr Selby
Queen Oriana . . . . Rose Massey
Chloe . . . . Miss Hughes
Pages . . . . Maud Branscombe, Gertrude Branscombe
Attendants. . . . . Miss Grey, Miss Stansfield

Md: J. T. Haines; sc: T. Grieve & Son; cos: Alfred Maltby

Played with *My Friend Waggles* and *Weather Permitting*, the former replaced on the second night by *Real and Ideal*.

0012 **THE MAGIC PEARL** a comic opera in two acts by Edward Fitzball. Music by Thomas Thorpe Pede. Produced at the Alexandra Theatre, Camden Town, under the management of T. Thorpe Pede 29 September, 1873 for a run of 36 performances closing 8 November, 1873.

Princess Zalouna . . . . Gertrude Ashton
Fadleen, Prince of Delhi . . . . J. W. Turner
Ben Hassan . . . . Edwin Danvers
Nocta . . . . Miss Costin
Aphdal, Spirit of the Himalayas . . . . . Marion St Claire
The Rajah of Delhi . . . . Gordon Wallace/George Marler
Tippoo . . . . George Marler/Gordon Wallace
Palma . . . . Alice Barth
Arcan . . . . Mr Hilston/Mr Clifford
Carchea . . . . Mr Pedder/Mr Hilston
Zanga . . . . Mr Morton
Sahib . . . . H. Harley
Zule . . . . Mr Simpson

Pd: Lillie Lee; dir: T. Thorpe Pede; sc: William Maugham

Played with *The Happiest Days of my Life* and *Les Roses d'Amour*, the former replaced (October 27) by *'Twas I*.

LOTHAIR or Batti-Batti and the Shah-de-doo, a comic opera (later an extravaganza) in three scenes by Frank W. Green and Robert Soutar. Music by Frank Musgrave. Produced at the Theatre Royal, Liverpool under the management of Isaac De Frece 13 October, 1873 for a run of 36 performances closing 22 November, 1873.

The Shah . . . . Haydn Corri
Guardini, a fairy queen . . . . Carrie Braham/Clara Bateman
Batti-Naboobi . . . . Alfred Brennir
Cooki Hash-Bash . . . . Mr Rocketts
Princess Ducksi Daise . . . . Augusta Thompson
Lothair . . . . Fanny Harrison
Deltremini. . . . . Mr Waddom
Dancers: Esther Austin (pd), Little Daisy, Mme Ramsden

Sc: C. Smithers

Played as part of a programme involving Kalulu's charcoal sketches, Professor Wheeler's dissolving photographic scenes, Miss Lottie Cherry's entertainment, and subsequently Harry Jackson, sketches by W. W. Allen, and the operetta *Rustic Roses*.

THE DAUGHTER OF THE DANUBE a new musical and spectacular extravaganza by W. R. Osman, in which are inserted several new songs by W. H. C. Nation. Produced at the Holborn Theatre under the management of W. H. C. Nation 3 March, 1873 and played with *Much Ado About Nothing*.

Baron Humglum . . . . Charles Groves
Von Wurzel . . . . Frank Wood
Rodolphe . . . . Nita de Castro
Prince Teufel . . . . Kate Phillips
The Queen of the Danube . . . . Kitty Fisher
Marguerite . . . . Rose Werner
Topaz . . . . Miss Sabine
Ruby . . . . Miss Travers
Opal. . . . . Miss Cameron
Diamond . . . . Miss Rivers
Emerald . . . . Miss Watkins
Pd: Mlle Roques

Md: W. Corri; ch: William Rowella; sc: Frederick Fenton; cos: Stinchcomb

THE LAST OF THE LEGENDS a new musical and psychological extravaganza by Gilbert a'Beckett into which are inserted several songs by W. H. C. Nation. Produced at the Charing Cross Theatre under the management of W. H. C. Nation 1 September, 1873.

MILDRED'S WELL a romance of the middle ages in one act by F. C. Burnand. Music by T. German Reed. Produced at the Gallery of Illustration under the management of T. German Reed 6 May, 1873 with *Very Catching* and *All Abroad*, the latter replaced by *Our Garden Party*. Withdrawn 31 July, 1873.

Longley/Victor Marden. . . . . R. Corney Grain
Ripton/Sir Angelo Ladbroke . . . . Arthur Cecil
Podder. . . . . Alfred Reed
Miss Byngley . . . . Fanny Holland
Mrs Willington . . . . Mrs German Reed

Produced at St George's Hall 18 October, 1876 with *The Three Tenants* and *A Musical Bee*. Withdrawn 4 November.

MARGUERITE an operetta in one act by T. Thorpe Pede. Produced at the Alexandra Theatre, Camden Town under the management of T. Thorpe Pede 31 May, 1873 for 30 performances to 5 July, 1873. Re-opened 8 November, 1873 for the benefit of Mr Thorpe Pede and played for 43 performances closing December, 1873.

Sir Roland Merton . . . . J. W. Turner/Francis Gaynar
Lady Flora Somerville . . . . Gertrude Ashton
Max . . . . T. J. Montelli
Teresa. . . . . Kate M. Nott
Agatha. . . . . Estelle Emrick/Miss Costin
Sc: C. Perkins

Played with *Friendship* and *A Quiet Family*, subsequently (June 21) with *The Lady of Lyons* and (July 4) *The Hunchback*. Played November 8 with *The Magic Pearl* and *Roses d'Amour* and from 10 with *'Twas I, The Illustrious Stranger* and *A Lesson in Love*, the last being replaced (November 22) by *Moonstruck*. Played from December 8 with *In the Clouds*.

A LESSON IN LOVE an operetta in one act by Robert Reece. Music by T. Thorpe Pede. Produced at the Alexandra Theatre, Camden Town under the management of T. Thorpe Pede 10 November, 1873. Withdrawn 22 November, 1873. Played with *'Twas I*, *Marguerite* and *The Illustrious Stranger*.

Lady d'Arville. . . . . Gertrude Ashton
Lord d'Arville. . . . . J. W. Turner

MOONSTRUCK an operetta in one act by Robert Reece. Music by T. Thorpe Pede. Produced at the Alexandra Theatre, Camden Town, under the management of T. Thorpe Pede 24 November, 1873. Withdrawn 6 December, 1873. Played with *'Twas I*, *Marguerite* and *The Illustrious Stranger*.

Cast: Gertrude Ashton and J. W. Turner

FLEURETTE an operetta in one act by Augustus Taplin. Produced at the Gaiety Theatre under the management of John Hollingshead at a matinée, 1 March, 1873, with *Our Clerks* and *The Spitalfields Weaver*.

Jacques . . . . F. Wood
Fleurette. . . . . Constance Loseby
Marquis Beaurivage. . . . . Frederic Sullivan
Marquise Beaurivage . . . . Alice Cook

DORA'S DREAM an operetta in one act by Arthur Cecil. Music by Alfred Cellier. Produced at the Gallery of Illustration for the benefit of Fanny Holland 3 July, 1873.

Dora. . . . . Fanny Holland
Frederick Fancourt . . . . Arthur Cecil

Played at the Princess's Theatre 5 May, 1876 for the benefit of Pauline Rita with the same cast.

Produced at the Opera Comique under the management of Richard D'Oyly Carte as a forepiece to *The Sorcerer*, 17 November, 1877. Withdrawn 8 February, 1878.

Giulia Warwick (DORA), Richard Temple (FF)

1874

The New Year and Christmas entertainments were dominated, as the latter part of the year had been, by *La Fille de Madame Angot*. Both the Philharmonic and the Opera Comique eschewed special Christmas entertainments and the phenomenally popular show continued its double life in London. New versions continued to appear. The copyright laws declared any foreign work common property and thus, while Byron's and Farnie's adaptations were copyright to them, anyone could and did make an 'original' version of the piece for production. By September six different *Angots* were playing the touring circuits.

The natural consequence of the huge popularity of Lecocq's piece was a spate of 'more of the same'. The most prized capture was that of the now idolised composer's newest piece *Giroflé-Girofla* which was given its première in Brussels in March. The Belgian company arrived at the Opera Comique with their new vehicle on June 6, before it had even appeared in Paris, and an English version was staged at the Philharmonic in October. It was charming and well received but never approached the popularity of its predecessor. The Gaiety also joined in the Lecocq rush with *The Island of Bachelors*, an anodyne version of the previously attacked *Les Cent Vierges*, which played two months.

Offenbach was by no means forgotten. When *Don Juan* closed its career at the Alhambra in May it was replaced with a lavish production of *La Jolie Parfumeuse* (ad. Byron) with the same stars – Kate Santley, Rose Bell and Harry Paulton – which ran for 94 nights between May and September. French was synonymous with good, and every manager wanted his own French musical. Unfortunately there were not enough Lecocq and Offenbach pieces to go round. Some managers spread their efforts a little wider – in August the Opera Comique tried *The Broken Branch* by the lesser known Gaston Serpette – but others were less scrupulous.

A touring manager called Francis Fairlie produced what was ostensibly Offenbach's *Vert-Vert* (1869) at the St James'. In actual fact the music of his piece was taken from six different Offenbach works and the libretto run up in forty-eight hours by Henry Herman and Richard Mansell. The whole bore almost no resemblance to Offenbach's original and can be fairly described as an attempt to deceive the public, who were expecting to see a genuine French opéra-bouffe, with a pot-pourri not even as proficient as many ordinary pasticcio entertainments. The show was hideously bad. *Vanity Fair*'s comment 'the worst orchestra, some of the flattest singing and one of the most indecent dances in London' led Fairlie to sue for libel. He lost, but *Vanity Fair* had unwittingly publicised the element which was to give this shameful travesty of theatre a run: 'one of the most indecent dances in London'. The dance in question was called 'the Riperelle' and the publicity given to it by the papers and by a Lord

Chamberlain's order to lengthen the skirts of the dancers proved just the thing to bring an audience to the St James'.

There was no protest from Offenbach over this massacre of his work, but Charles Lecocq was not to be imposed upon so easily. The next St James' production was entitled *The Black Prince* and billed as 'words by H. B. Farnie, music by Charles Lecocq'. The French composer lashed out in print. He had never written an opera of that name; *The Black Prince* was a fake. And, sure enough, Farnie had been up to the same trick. His 'new' musical was a mixture of unrelated Lecocq music (and a few pieces from elsewhere) pasted together with an 'original' libretto concocted from three French plays. It was terrible, and even the presence in the cast of such favourites as Selina Dolaro and Nellie Bromley could do nothing for it.

Lecocq was not the only French writer to protest at the wholesale pirating of his works and the misuse of his name. Hervé, whose relations with the British theatre had previously been excellent, protested vigorously when the Royal Amphitheatre, Holborn, presented a piece called *Melusine, the Enchantress.* It was a frightful distortion of the French composer's *Les Chevaliers de la Table Ronde* – even the music had been re-orchestrated. When challenged over this last point, the manager coolly replied that the fees for leasing Hervé's proper parts were too high! *Melusine*, like *The Black Prince*, was a salutory disaster and, though pilfering from the French was to continue for many years especially under the aegis of Farnie, nothing quite so barefaced as the crop of 1874 occurred again.

Not all the productions of French musicals in Britain were bad or badly adapted. The best and most successful of the year was the last, the newest from Lecocq, *Les Prés St. Gervais*, produced in London only 14 days after its initial performance. In spite of the dubious reputation gained by French shows through the bastardised productions at the St James', the Criterion management never had a doubtful moment. *Les Prés St. Gervais* was received with total approval by press and public alike and settled in for a run of 132 performances.

This high frequency and popularity of French pieces had the effect of discouraging and squeezing out the native musical which was represented in the West End during the year by only two new pieces, both of partial French parentage. The first was a melodramatic spectacle entitled *The Demon's Bride* which followed *La Jolie Parfumeuse* into the Alhambra in September. It was written by the experienced librettist, Henry J. Byron. Byron was Manchester-born, the son of the British consul to Haiti and a grandson of a cousin of the poet, Lord Byron. He had studied as a doctor and a lawyer, but in 1858 his success with a burlesque of *Fra Diavolo* had led him permanently into the theatre. Like Burnand and Reece he specialised in latter-day burlesque and translations, and during a career of some twenty-six years he produced over a hundred works, the most successful of which was the comedy *Our Boys* (1875) which ran 1,362 performances and established a West End record which lasted forty years.

The Demon's Bride was based on a libretto by the authors of *Giroflé-Girofla*, Leterrier and Vanloo, and it retained a very Gallic character in its new guise. Gipsies have taken over the castle of the Landgrave of Filastenish and when he returns they attempt to scare him away by posing as fiends and pretending the castle is haunted. The gipsy leader, Krock, falls for Hélène, the Landgrave's daughter, and, disguised as a demon, forces her into signing a marriage contract with him as the first act ends. Thereafter, the story degenerated into a mixture of knock-about farce, romantic scenas and ballet. The second act began with a 'grand ballet divertissement', 'The Star of Hope', choreographed by Dewinne and danced by the huge Alhambra troupe headed by Mlle Pitteri. At the end of it, the public were so 'diverted' they had forgotten what little story there was. Another ballet followed in which 'Mlle Sara' took the lead. The can-can had made Sarah Wright's reputation. As Emily Soldene noted:

> The verb 'to kick' had never been so actively conjugated before . . Mlle Sara (who had shorter skirts and longer legs than most girls) to the great delight and satisfaction of herself and all London kicked up her agile heels a little higher than had previously been deemed possible and was equally successful in dusting the floor with her back hair.

But there was a section of public opinion which was violently against the can-can and its 'dreadful obscenity'. The New York Metropolitan had been closed by the police after a display of can-can dancing and the Colonna Quadrille in which Mlle Sara had featured had already been instrumental in the Alhambra's losing its licence in 1870. Perhaps they had been encouraged by the *succès de scandale* of *Vert-Vert*, but, if so, they had misjudged their audience. Mlle Sara's first night performance was greeted by howls and cat-calls. She was quickly announced as 'indisposed' and the dance was withdrawn.

The comedy of *The Demon's Bride* was largely in the hands of Harry Paulton as the diffident Landgrave and Felix Bury (one of the original English gendarmes in *Geneviève de Brabant*) as his daughter's vain and ugly suitor, Baron Ostruck, equipped with the ceaseless catch-phrase 'I was just about to say that'. Messrs Worboys and Fred Clifton added to the comic side of affairs while the gipsies were headed by the darkly impressive Mr Melbourne as the 'Demon' and Rose Bell as a ubiquitous (male) Romany vocalist, and the romantic scenes and numbers were left to Lotty Montal (Hélène) and Lennox Grey (Karl) now promoted from the chorus to principal boy[1].

The music for the piece was by the Alhambra's hard-working musical director, Georges Jacobi. He had achieved some success with his music for *The Black Crook* and had since composed and arranged the music for *Don Juan*. His melodies stood up quite well alongside the borrowed tunes of the best French masters, and he had scored with a lively drinking song 'Sparkling Wine' for Rose Bell in that most recent extravaganza. *The Demon's Bride* contained nothing which achieved the same popularity but Harry Paulton raised encores for a 'Comic Genealogical Ditty' called 'Pass to the Left', and Rose Bell made another drinking song go well. Along with Miss Grey's romanza 'If sleeping Still' these proved the vocal highlights of the evening, but the abundant ballet music once again proved that Jacobi's greatest talent lay in writing dance measures.

Reaction to the show was negative. Both audience and critics found it exceedingly long and diffuse, its book 'dull, uninteresting and very commonplace'. The music fared better and *The Era* remarked:

> Had the libretto contained anything like an intelligible story, the music of Jacobi would have done justice to it.

The Alhambra ballets, as always, retained their drawing power but it soon became evident that the show would not hold out, as had been intended, until Christmas. A revival of *Le Roi Carotte* was hurriedly arranged and *The Demon's Bride* was withdrawn after eight weeks.

[1] Miss Grey had many gentlemen admirers. When she later found herself unable to get work she attempted to 'lean on' each of the more prosperous with gentle threats of 'kiss and tell'. 'A wretch and a blackmailer and a drunkard who died in a workhouse', wrote Clement Scott retrospectively.

The Christmas piece which was scheduled to follow was another Anglo-French creation. Earlier in the year the publishers, Messrs Wood & Co. of Regent Street, had signed the lion of the opéra-bouffe stage, Jacques Offenbach, to compose an original piece to be presented as a Christmas entertainment. For the first and only time in his career, Offenbach was to set a libretto written in English (a language of which he had a ready command) and London would have its very own Offenbach opera. The great composer of opéra-bouffe was no longer the overwhelming star he had been a few years previously. *La Jolie Parfumeuse* in no way compared with *Orphée* or *La Belle Hélène*. The cheerful burlesque style of those earlier days had given way to a more romantic fashion and Offenbach, following where Lecocq so successfully led, was not always so fully at his ease. The subject chosen for his London piece was Dick Whittington which provided plenty of possibilities for the comic excesses the composer handled so well, as did the libretto by H. B. Farnie.[1]

Henry Brougham Farnie was a Scotsman, educated at St. Andrews University and destined for a career as a schoolmaster. He found his way into journalism and was soon trying his hand in that field in London. He became the editor of a little paper put out by the music publishing firm of Cramer called *The Orchestra*, and during this period began writing for the theatre. Among his early works was the libretto for Balfe's operetta *The Sleeping Queen*. His first adaptation from the French was a version of Gounod's *La Reine de Saba* and he achieved his first big success with *Geneviève de Brabant* at the Philharmonic which he followed with versions of virtually all the popular French musical pieces of the day. Farnie was exceptionally facile but, in spite of his many successes both with adaptations and 'original' works, he was almost universally scorned by his peers and the critics as a journeyman cobbler of scripts.

The book of *Whittington* was a curious brew. The traditional story of Dick and Alice Fitzwarren and the killing of the Sultan's rats by Dick's faithful cat was almost totally subordinated to the low comedy element. A large part of the first act involved three idiotic suitors for the hand of Alice – one Scots (The MacPibroch), one Irish (The O'Shamrock) and the third English (FitzFulke). The Fitzwarrens' cook, Dorothy, was also provided with three beaux – the bell-ringer of Bow, the Sergeant of the Watch, and the sea-captain Bobstay. Since these latter were played by W. M. Terrott, Harry Paulton and John Rouse, it was clear they would not be left on the dock-side when the ship carrying the absconding Dick set off for the far-off land of Bambouli at the end of Act I. In fact, most of the second act, set in the traditional foreign climes, was taken up by these three comic worthies. Taken on by the King of Bambouli to run his country, they decide to model it on England.

> Great King, you shall have every modern blessing – rates, taxes, 85 ton guns, vestries, licensing acts and compulsory vaccination . .

There was a burlesque parliamentary scene, and long passages of topical and political jibing, until the Sergeant finally declares:

> Civilisation is marching on with rapid strides. Already you have that truly English bulwark, heavy income tax – and you bask in the sunshine of Schedule D. Then again, look at your social political economy. You now possess strikes and Trade

[1] It has been suggested that Farnie's libretto was, in fact, translated from a French original by Nuitter and Tréfeu. However, comtemporary reports assert that Offenbach set *Whittington* in the English language, although whether Farnie's words were original or translation is unsettled.

> Unions and I am proud to say that your national products are nearly doubling their value . . you pay twice as much for oysters and coals . .

The Bamboulians realise the foreigners have only made things much worse, and it is from this situation that the half-forgotten Whittington saves everyone with his cat-eats-rat act. This sequence was staged with great splendour in a series of five tableaux before the scene returned to London where Alice disposes of her three suitors in favour of Dick, and Dorothy, declaring:

> In the present uncertain state of the church I don't think I would be justified in going into it. And I won't marry a sea-captain until there's a thorough investigation into the loss of the *La Paloma* . .

gives her hand to the Sergeant of the Watch.

Farnie's dialogue veered through variegated styles from the old burlesque punning (which led him to describe Scotland as the place where 'dinners may be described as table d'oats') to the repetitive political pricking of the second act. The libretto of *Whittington* should have followed in the way of Thompson's clever and literate *Aladdin II* and *Cinderella the Younger* scripts, but it lacked both their quality and their genuine humour.

The lack of inspiration in the book and lyrics must have rubbed off on to the composer. He had been given plenty of financial impetus, £1,000 for each of three acts payable act by act as they were handed to the copyist. The score which Woods and Cramers got for their money did not bring them much return. As well as being far from Offenbach's best it was decidedly unsuited to the subject. The familiar London town characters singing French opéra-bouffe couplets were quite incongruous to a British audience. A determinedly English ballad for Lennox Grey, 'The Wind that Blows across the Sea', only served to highlight the essential foreignness of the rest of the score and *The Era* was not alone in complaining that what was needed was an English score – from Clay or from Sullivan – rather than the unremarkable one provided by the master of opéra-bouffe.

One person, however, had done a magnificent job on *Whittington*. Alfred Thompson had really excelled himself with the designs and the Alhambra's reputation for the production of the most gorgeous pieces in town was confirmed with acclamation. The combination of Thompson, Harry Paulton, Kate Santley and the Grand Barbaric Ballet proved sufficient to make *Whittington* into some kind of a success and it became the longest running Christmas entertainment of the season, holding the stage through till the following May when it was replaced by a revival of *Chilpéric*.

Eighteen months later it received a damning obituary in the *Illustrated Sporting & Dramatic News*:

> The most striking proof that Offenbach's powers have decayed was given about a year ago when *Whittington* was produced at the Alhambra Theatre . . . the artistic result was an egregious failure. Only the Great Barbaric Ballet kept it from immediate extinction . . . from a musical point of view *Whittington* was one of the greatest failures in recent times.

The 'decaying' Offenbach was soon to show with *Madame Favart* and *La Fille du Tambour Major* that he was nothing of the sort, but *Whittington* remains one of his least satisfactory works. Nearly twenty years later the piece resurfaced in a splendid production at the Châtelet Theatre in Paris (1893) under the curious title of *Le Chat du Diable* where it had a run of three months.

If the West End of London was largely under the sway of France, further north things were considerably more lively in the field of original enterprises. The Prince's Theatre in Manchester, run by Charles Calvert, had taken on as musical director the young composer/conductor Alfred Cellier who had shown such promise with *Charity Begins at Home*. Under Calvert and Cellier the Prince's was to blossom over the next few years as the foremost producer of new musicals in Britain and, even after the departure of the latter and the sad decline and death of the former[1], Manchester continued to hold a pre-eminent place in inaugurating new shows. The first event of note in 1874 was a revival by Frederic Sullivan of his brother's *The Contrabandista*. It played a fortnight at the Prince's starring Sullivan in the comic role of Grigg, and two further weeks at Birmingham, but went no further. It was followed by the production of two totally new works.

Since her triumph in *The Black Crook* Kate Santley had become a fixture, and a very popular one, at the Alhambra. She had played Helen to Rose Bell's Paris in *La Belle Hélène*, Haidée to Miss Bell's Juan in *Don Juan*, Rose Michon to the Clarinde of Miss Bell in *La Jolie Parfumeuse*, and in the process relations between herself and her co-star had become more than a little strained. During the run of *Don Juan* Miss Santley had successfully prosecuted 'friends of Miss Bell' who had hissed her off the stage before she had spoken one line. The partisans of each lady were as violent as the Tebaldi and Callas camps in the opera world of the 1950s – though Callas and Tebaldi did not, fortunately, appear in the same show in opposing roles.

But Kate Santley had plans that stretched beyond Leicester Square. She was forming her own musical company and for its first presentation she commissioned an original work from Robert Reece and Frederic Clay. The piece was delivered, the itinerary set, and on August 3, 1874 Kate Santley relinquished her role in *La Jolie Parfumeuse* to the Australian singer Lotty Montal and set out for Manchester to prepare the production of *Cattarina* at the Prince's. She had spread her publicity freely and expectations ran high. Was this piece going to be the longed-for English *Angot*? Would it be that definitive work so urgently needed upon which a British musical tradition might be fixed?

On the first night at Manchester, August 17, the house was enthusiastically packed with the best of local society as well as many visitors from London down for the occasion. At the end of the evening, however, reaction was split. Kate, Clay, Reece and the company were applauded to the hilt, but the professionals were less sanguine. It was not the Great British Musical. It was neither particularly original nor, in truth, particularly good. Reece had stuck to the well-worn formula of 'disguised princess meets and marries disguised prince and thwarts evil uncle' and laced it with the usual kind of political and topical references, the whole without much distinction or wit. Clay had, as always, written bright and pretty music but of doubtful lasting value. The reviews were not kind. *The Era* described the story as 'ridiculously improbable' and the libretto as 'not the best Mr. Reece has written'. 'In fact', they added, 'the most effective jokes seem to be those interpolated by the artists which are not in the printed copy.' They conceded that 'a number of the airs can hardly fail to become very popular by reason of their simple and melodious character'.

The story was set in Calabria. A duke's daughter, Cattarina, will inherit her late father's lands and title at the age of 19 if by that time she has married her cousin,

[1] Calvert died in an insane asylum in 1879 aged 51. His superb career as an actor and manager is recounted in his wife's book *68 Years on the Stage*.

Fabian, and established a fitting court in the palace of Pincione. Failing this, the duchy will go to the boy's father. This wicked uncle packs Cattarina off to a 'patent convent' and the boy to 'Leicester Square, near the Palaces of Royalty'. Both escape and meet, unaware of each other's identity, in a village full of peasants where they fall in love. A rejected suitor guesses Cattarina's identity and warns her uncle who complacently reads out the famous will in the market-place, for there are only three days left until Cattarina's nineteenth birthday and his son, he believes, is safely in England. The second act is set in the ducal palace which Cattarina and her rustic friends, now promoted to Ministers and Courtiers, have taken over. When the pretender arrives to claim the duchy he is foiled as Cattarina and 'Anselmo', now revealed as Fabian, are married.

It was a very slight and derivative tale spread thinly over two acts and built largely round set pieces like the long scena in Act 2 in which Cattarina teaches her gauche supporters to behave like courtiers:

> So, so a very fair assumption
> The room looks bright, the dresses far from poor,
> It only wants a trifling show of gumption
> To turn you out as perfect Dames de Cour.

and parades them as ministers. This scene produced some difficulties and a section of the dialogue which punned rather too freely and remarked a little too personally on the actual ministers of the United Kingdom had to be cut:

> You've got a bad temper. You shall be the Home Secretary.
> Why Home Secretary?
> Because he's Cross[1]
> You shall be Lord Chamberlain and pray be careful not to make yourself ridiculous.
> It's difficult in your office.

Freddie Clay added a note to the playwright copy assuring the Lord Chamberlain's office that 'no one of them will be made up to resemble any public personage'. The scene contained many more standard political jibes, including a number in which Cattarina described: 'That's what they do in England'. Exception was also taken to the weak dialogue. Reece, with his background of burlesque, had been tempted into some punning, but mostly his contribution was merely uninteresting. Fortunately J. D. Stoyle and John Wainwright in the two principal comic roles were adept at 'embellishing' their parts and, as the play settled in, much comic business was brought in to decorate their scenes.

The central role of Cattarina was played by Miss Santley and Reece had devised his heroine as what was politely called a 'madcap'. She makes her first appearance explaining:

> I've achieved a wonderful morning's work. I've sent a billet doux from Domenico to Margerita whom he detests fixing a meeting in the wood tonight at ten, I've sent a billet doux from Barbara whom he adores to Domenico fixing a rendez-vous in the wood at ten tonight! Won't there be a scene! That's good enough for a whole day's work but, bless you, I'm indefatigable. I've let loose Patricio's dog and shut

[1] Home Secretary Richard Assheton Cross (Viscount Cross).

> Antonio's up in the larder, I've turned Constantia's hens into the flower garden, I've upset Giacomo's beehives, I've sent a challenge from the Padre to the Bishop, I've dispatched a proposal of marriage from Orlando to Filippina (who means business, I tell you), I've set Crespino's wine tap running and sent him to the end of the village on a fruitless errand, I've changed the labels on Cornelio's draught and embrocation and . . and . . that's all.

Since this objectionable person was played by Miss Santley she soon managed to win her way into the hearts of her audience and proceeded to dominate the entertainment. She flirted and pouted and plotted with her tenor (Selwyn Graham), she danced and she sang songs from the lyrical 'When bright Eyes Shining' and the sentimental 'Farewell, dear simple village Home' to the lively ballad 'It Is so like the Men':

> It is so like the men, you know
> And silly maids believe them so
> They steal our hearts and beg and then
> It is, it is so like the men

More than any other, this number gave Miss Santley the opportunity to use her talent for 'naughty' innuendoes and double entendre, and the roguish glances which had become her trademark at the Alhambra. The song became a firm favourite with audiences and, along with the Ministers' chorus and Anselmo/Fabian's musical ballad:

> There is a hope within our heart
> A gentle and enduring flame
> An anxious calm, a sweet unrest
> A yearning that no tongue can name . .

it was published by the music firm of Boosey & Co. The comic songs were fewer and the most enjoyable was Stoyle's number as the eternally unsuccessful villain:

> It isn't for want of a fight
> No courage nor patience I've needed
> By a hair's breadth or less
> I've approached a success
> But somehow I've never succeeded!

On the whole it was up to Miss Santley to give the audience what they wanted and expected, and on the whole that is what she did. But not everyone was charmed. *The London and Provincial Entr'acte* announced with studied indifference that the production:

> calls for no special comment, saving that the music can scarcely be termed original as it favours being a robbery of opéra-bouffe generally. Messrs. J. D. Stoyle and J. Wainwright deserve more especial praise in the acting. Mr. Graham requires practice. Miss Kate Santley seemed the centre of attraction on account of her name and connection with the Alhambra.

Miss Santley was not one to take such digs passively. From the second night she introduced a few swingeing asides about the press which went down well; then after four weeks in Manchester she proceeded out on a highly profitable tour. It was the first opportunity the provinces had had to see a first-class production of a brand new British comic opera, and the first, since her rise to stardom, to see Miss Santley. To the one and the other they came in large numbers and they left applauding. Every night Kate had to repeat her principal songs two or three times, particularly 'It Is so like the Men'. There was no doubt that she and her show were a great success.

In Dublin the local critic tried to look at the show itself realistically:

> . . without being particularly brilliant or effective either in plot or dialogue the opera is sufficiently comical and amusing to keep the audience in good humour. The music is occasionally very sweet and pretty, but on the whole is not quite so attractive as many of its predecessors in the same class . .

These predecessors had not, of course, had the advantage of Miss Santley whom Dublin audiences cheered just as fulsomely as had the mainlanders. For her second week in Dublin Kate scrapped the little farce, *He's a Lunatic*, which she had been using as a forepiece, and substituted the custom-built Alfred Thompson piece *The Three Conspirators* in which she played four different parts and managed to interpolate her *Black Crook* hit 'Nobody Knows as I Know'. This had the effect of increasing even further the appeal of the evening's entertainment, and *The Three Conspirators* remained on the bill when Kate seized the chance to extend her tour until contractual obligations for the Alhambra's *Whittington* finally forced her temporarily to pack *Cattarina* away.

The next year found the show in the West End. Within a week of the end of *Whittington* a new production of *Cattarina* opened at the Charing Cross Theatre under the auspices of W. R. Field, Esq. With the advantage of four months' continuous run and over a hundred performances in the provinces, *Cattarina* was much better prepared than the usual new West End show. It had been tried, tested, altered and worked up, and the book which had been the object of so much criticism in Manchester had been extensively remodelled. *The Era* changed its tune from 'ridiculously improbable' to 'lively' and had no hard words at all for Reece's contribution. Clay's music was, of course, as charming and attractive as ever, as was the show's star. A stronger supporting cast had been engaged, too. The new tenor Henry Walsham (later to head his own opera company) had a much more virile voice than Selwyn Graham and Edmund Rosenthal made a fine basso Duke. One miscalculation was made in the casting of Alfred Young as Nicolo, and the ever-reliable Charles Kelleher had to be quickly wooed away from Selina Dolaro's Royalty Company to replace him. J. H. Ryley, who was later to achieve considerable fame on the other side of the Atlantic, played the Duke's silly sidekick, Fernando, and the chorus included a sixteen year-old girl who was later to become his wife and, as Madeleine Lucette Ryley, the author of a number of very successful stage plays.

From the start *Cattarina* attracted good houses and the run continued for 75 performances before the actress/manageress headed for the lucrative provinces with a large company and two shows, *Cattarina* and the new Criterion hit *Prés St. Gervais*. In 1876 she again included a few performances of *Cattarina* in her touring repertoire before putting to rest a piece which had served well its purpose as a vehicle for her talents over two good and profitable seasons.

A much more significant work was the Prince's November offering, the first full length musical by Cellier. *The Sultan of Mocha*, produced at Manchester on November 16, 1874, was not presented at the expense of an independent manager, as Miss Santley's *Cattarina* had been, but at that of the theatre itself. Charles A. Calvert, the manager, had made his name as an actor at the town's Theatre Royal and took on the newer theatre when it opened in 1864. There he successfully featured himself and his

American wife in superior Shakespearean productions. Calvert was an adventurous manager and his plays frequently included new and specially commissioned musical scores. His inaugural presentation of *The Tempest* used Arthur Sullivan's incidental music and Sullivan later composed new scores for *Henry VIII* and *The Merchant of Venice*. Frederic Clay supplied special music for Lord Byron's *Sardanapalus* and the theatre's first musical director, Ferdinand Wallerstein, also wrote original pieces for Calvert's productions. In 1873 Calvert hired the young Alfred Cellier as musical director, and at first the composer was limited to individual songs and incidental music, notably for the Christmas pantomime, and arranging such established music as was required. This he had also done previously at the Court Theatre, but his career as an original writer was progressing. Following the success of *Charity Begins at Home* he had been asked to supply a musical for the opening of the new Criterion Theatre. In the event Henry Byron took the theatre and produced his own *An American Lady* and Cellier's participation was limited to the afterpiece *Topsyturveydom* which he composed and conducted. It is probable that some of the music he had prepared for the aborted Criterion musical went into the new piece which he now presented to Calvert to fill the weeks before the 1874/5 pantomime.

The writing of the libretto was entrusted to a Mancunian 'gentleman of some literary attainment'[1] who preferred, for some reason, to remain anonymous. It was rumoured that this was the same person who was engaged in the writing of the subsequent pantomime. Many years later one of the original cast, H. M. Clifford, 'admitted' to being responsible for some of the lyrics, but it is probable these were the numbers which were added after the opening night.

The story of the play was a lively if unsophisticated one. The lovely Dolly is being courted by the wealthy marine store owner 'Admiral' Sneak, but she is not at all partial for she is in love with the handsome sailor, Peter. Her uncle, the grasping Captain Flint, has other and more profitable plans for her than either of these suitors and storms off to sea taking Dolly with him for safe keeping. In Act 2 they are found on the island of Mocha where Peter and the vengeful Sneak, who have followed them, are beached as well. While Captain Flint is selling his slaves Dolly is spied by the amorous Sultan who insists on buying her. She is rescued by the valiant Peter, then recaptured through the villainy of Sneak and condemned to marriage, but the Sultan is tricked finally into wedding the most adoring of his harem (disguised as Dolly) and the lovers are united for the final curtain.

It was a well-designed plot mixing a solidly English story and a Greenwich dock hero and heroine with picturesque locations and exotic characters as well as a strong naval element, the popularity of which had been proven by the huge success of such pieces as *Black-Eyed Susan*. This was a combination which had been well tried both in pantomime and in opera, and transferred to comic opera it was equally acceptable, providing as it did excellent opportunities for song, dance and spectacle.

The dialogue, unfortunately, was not particularly clever. Like Reece, the author of *The Sultan of Mocha* slipped from time to time into the old word-twisting for his humour:

DOLLY: I'm from Greenwich, saving your Tyranny
SULTAN: Greenwich! Ah, Greenwich must be *Dulwich* without its Greenwich fair!
or

[1] (*Era*). The name of Albert Jarret has been attached to the libretto, but whether this is as the original librettist is unsure.

FLINT: It's hard to sell one's niece.
SULTAN: Nothing of the sort, it's *an easy* affair, *an 'eff you* [and if you] don't . . .

but mostly the book was merely a serviceable link, moving the story on between the numbers. Jokes, as such, were few and fairly feeble although Fred Mervin as the oily Sneak, H. M. Clifford (Flint) and Furneaux Cook (Sultan) added business and lines of their own in the approved fashion. But although the libretto had its faults it was strong enough to provide a solid foundation for the best British comic opera score to date.

Cellier's music was scholarly and correct, simply tuneful and fresh sounding, and in no way overtly influenced by the ubiquitous Offenbach and Lecocq. As befitted the work of a man born and raised in Hackney his melodies and his style were purely and staunchly in the English light musical tradition. The score for *The Sultan of Mocha* included a well-balanced variety of musical pieces. There were plentiful choruses including a vigorous Greenwich opening, a stately Chorus of Pensioners, a graceful Odalisques chorus (in which the lyricist rhymed 'Islam' with 'frizzle 'em'), a Sailors' chorus and the highly popular 1st and 3rd act finale in which the seamen declared:

We are sober, we are steady
For the voyage we are ready
To the Tropics or the Mediterranean Sea;
We'll sail away with Peter
And his sweetheart, if we meet her,
Like a lady we will treat her
For a gallant lot are we.

There were frequent duos and trios and a good selection of solos. The heroine was particularly well-supplied. She sang of her lover's return successively in polka time ('Let the Lords of Legislation'), in a more sober ballad ('The Letter') and in a bolero. She sang in 3/8 of 'Women's Rights':

If I could rule all women's hearts
I'd so their spirits fashion
That they should scorn the tyrant sex
And spurn the tender passion.
Tis woman's duty I'll maintain
On love to breathe defiance
To lecture, vote, look wise and talk
Of politics and science.
Talk of propriety
Spread of society
Wide notoriety
This do we crave,
Woman strong-minded
Is not to be blinded
By man when he's minded
To make her his slave.

and more gently, to a 'cello obbligato, the Slumber Song, 'Close, thou gentle sleep, these ever wakeful eyes'.

Peter was equally well equipped with a jolly drinking song ('Pipes and Grog') and two lilting lyrical pieces 'The Yawning Song' and the delightful ballad ''Twas sad when I and Dolly Parted'.

As in *Cattarina* the comic songs were less effective. The lyrics were not exceptionally clever, although the writer showed a determined facility for rhyming in the gruff entrance number for the Sultan:

> Sultan am I
> Not a bit shy
> Look at my eye
> Wary and sly
> And upon my
> Word I defy
> Mighty and high
> Kings far and nigh, etc.

and in the couplets 'The Telescope' where Sneak courts Dolly with a catalogue of his stock:

> Why dream of faithless sailor men
> Say, Dolly, you'll be mine and then
> My yards and spars
> And capstan bars
> My spikes and nails
> And flags and sails
> My ropes and blocks
> And oilskin frocks
> My seamen's kits
> And cheap outfits
> My masts and oars
> And general stores
> My canvass new
> My anchors true
> And all the tackle in my shop
> Shall be your property.

On the whole the score was bright and attractive without leaning to the bubbling frivolity of the most popular French pieces or to the thoroughgoing sentimentality of the earlier English tradition.

On the first night all went well. The audience was enthusiastic and the show seemed destined for success. Robertha Erskine was slightly unhappy in the role of Peter (Cellier had written the role for a tenor, and thereafter a tenor would always play it) and the humorous side of affairs did not go as well as might have been hoped, but the songs were frequently encored and the well-rehearsed production highly effective, with the Sultan's entrance on a real, live camel producing a remarkable effect.

Immediate press reaction was mixed, although *The Sultan of Mocha* came out much better than its predecessor at Manchester. *The Era* was severe on the anonymous libretto, terming it 'feeble' and the plot 'destitute of probability' (a strange criterion for the plot of a comic opera) but the representative of *The London and Provincial Entr'acte* felt differently:

> The new comic opera by Mr. Alfred Cellier. . has been received with enthusiastic tokens of approval. The music bears a marked originality, the libretto is well-written the scenery is charming and the piece is put on the stage in the management's usual excellent style.

The music was generally praised, but there was little doubt that, in spite of its first night reception and its continuing excellent houses, the piece could and would be improved. New jokes and production 'business' were added throughout the run, and an *Era* review of its fourth week noted:

> One or two new airs were introduced on Monday (Dec. 7) the melodies of which will secure for them an equal share of popularity with the other numbers in the opera. Considerable additions in the way of jokes and business have been made by the artists engaged and the piece rattles along in the merriest and smoothest manner.

After five weeks *The Sultan of Mocha* was still drawing remarkably but the Prince's pantomime was set to open so, as originally scheduled, on December 19 the show closed. But it was not long before it was seen again. As soon as the pantomime had finished the directors of the theatre[1] reproduced 'their' lucrative musical for a fortnight until the arrival of Rivière's Promenade Concert Season. Catherine Lewis, fresh from *Les Prés St. Gervais* at the Criterion was engaged for Dolly and the tenor Chatterson who had suffered a run in *The Black Prince* was Peter. Its popularity was confirmed in such style that at the conclusion of the Proms *The Sultan* was brought back yet again.

Manchester had become very proprietorial about Cellier by this time. Every night he was cheered on to his podium at the theatre and local correspondents and newspapers circulated reports of his plans and projects including colourful prospects for *The Sultan of Mocha* which was reported as purchased for London, then for Vienna. . but nothing happened. The following year the now favourite piece was brought out again. But this revival had more interest than those previous for, at last, after all the rumours and efforts, *The Sultan of Mocha* was truly West End bound.

The Prince's had excelled itself with its 1875/6 panto. Alfred Thompson had supplied them with a brand new version of *Aladdin*, Cellier had composed new music, and the first class 'resident' cast had been supplemented by a memorable principal boy in Mrs John Wood. Now in her mid-forties, Mrs Wood was an established star both on Broadway where she had appeared in many musicals, including *The Black Crook*, and in London. In 1869 she had acquired the head-lease of the St James' Theatre and had given a season there, but, finding the twin cares of management and performing too much during a period of tender health, she had sub-let at the end of the season. Now she was quite 'cured' and when she headed back to town in April 1876 she took with her both Manchester's musical and its musical hero, Cellier. On April 8 Horace Wigan's season at the St James' closed, and Mrs Wood resumed working control of her theatre. Nine days later *The Sultan of Mocha* made its London bow. The town had heard of Cellier's provincial success and that of his first major work, and it was awaited with interest.

The libretto which had not pleased originally had, by now, been 'worked in' by the various exponents of the leading roles in a manner which had delighted Manchester, including a barrage of local references. London was not quite so susceptible to such a parochial style. Then again, the piece had been staged in Manchester with great liberality – but Offenbach's *Voyage dans la Lune* had opened in London two nights previously at the Alhambra with all that implied. Mrs Wood's orchestra and chorus of seventy paled somewhat in comparison. Cellier's music, of course, still held up well, but *The Sultan of Mocha* was not quite the outstanding event nor the raging success it had been in the Midlands. It was well noticed, though: *The Entr'acte* commented that it contained 'some capital material' and *The Era* praised Cellier:

[1] Calvert had already departed.

> With regard to the music we may say without hesitation that most of it is entitled to very hearty praise . . Mr. Cellier . . has so much merit of his own that he will be a great acquisition to the ranks of English composers.

and declared that his show had 'every prospect of a long and prosperous career'.

But after 47 performances to only reasonable houses, Mrs Wood decided to withdraw the piece to feature herself in a production of *The Creole*. On Friday, March 2 she gave a benefit for Cellier and presented him with an inscribed baton 'in memoriam' and *The Sultan of Mocha's* West End début was at an end. It continued, however, to appear outside London. Cellier conducted a production at Liverpool the following Christmas and both Liverpool and Manchester staged subsequent revivals. James Meade's Company took it up for an American tour and in 1880 Blanche Roosevelt's Company gave a short season at Broadway's Union Square Theatre.

In 1887, after the monumental success of Cellier's *Dorothy*, there was a new demand for his past works. The most obvious candidate for revival was *The Sultan of Mocha* and the manager who laid down her money and took the chance was Lydia Thompson, more famous for her burlesque companies and the 'Lydia Thompson Blondes'.

In the thirteen years since its original production the art of English libretto writing had progressed somewhat and the book of *The Sultan of Mocha* was clearly in need of an overhaul before it could again be presented in the West End. The actor William Lestocq of the Vaudeville Theatre was the man appointed to the task, with a decidedly cramping brief. All the thirty-three musical portions were to be retained without the alteration or omission of one note or one lyric. The characters' names were to remain the same, but the role of Lucy was to be built up from a six-line part to one running through the whole show. Under these conditions he was to come up with a totally rewritten and reconstructed libretto, and he did a fair job. The story was simplified. Dolly and her friend Lucy are kidnapped by the rascally marine stores owner cum Pirate Chief, Sneak, while Dolly is preparing to elope with her beloved Peter. Sneak takes the girls to Mocha where Dolly is spotted by the Sultan in the slave market and taken home. Peter follows them across the sea disguised as a merchant (and then as a dervish) and, after suitable adventures, rescues Dolly in time for a happy ending.

Miss Thompson had to fight for the rights to the show as Henry Leslie, the producer of *Dorothy*, claimed to have mortgaged the rights to any future works by Cellier. In spite of the 'new' book, *The Sultan of Mocha* was ruled to be an 'old' work and the relevant rights remained with the Manchester producers.

The new production of *The Sultan of Mocha* proved immediately popular. It was gorgeously produced under the tutelage of Charles Harris and its solid virtues were emphasised so successfully that critic Cecil Howard was led to comment:

> It is rather a matter of surprise that the work has not been offered to the public since [the 1876 production] for, like all the composer's music, it is bright and more than tuneful. It certainly never was more perfectly mounted – the result could not be for a moment doubtful.

Violet Cameron starred as Dolly and scored a great personal success, and the composer uncharacteristically allowed her to interpolate a ballad 'Love Ties' written expressly by Tosti for the production. The show was soon playing to packed houses at the Strand Theatre and a second consecutive block-buster for Cellier seemed on the cards. But the initial enthusiasm did not hold up and it closed in January 1888 after a total of 114 performances.

In 1892 it was once again produced in Manchester under the management of J. Pitt

Hardacre and was taken out on a long tour of principal dates including a Christmas season in Liverpool. Nearly twenty years after its first production the piece still proved both enjoyable and profitable. *The Sultan of Mocha*, in spite of all its imperfections, was an important work. It was a true British light or comic opera worthy to be played alongside its French contemporaries while in no way relying on them for inspiration. Within a few years it would be overtaken by more sophisticated libretti and freer, more joyously modern music and orchestrations, but its original popularity was well-deserved and every revival only served to confirm the appeal that this slightly earnest and straightforward composition held.

A number of shorter works made their appearance in the capital during the course of the year, three of them under the German Reed regime. The Reeds had given up their famous Gallery of Illustration in Waterloo Place on the expiry of the lease and shifted their operations to St George's Hall in Langham Place where they had conducted the 1867 season which had included the production of *The Contrabandista*. The new locality gave them the opportunity to play to considerably larger audiences without in any way mortgaging their reputation as the purveyors of nice entertainment.

They began their 1874 season in April with a programme of revivals consisting of *Ages Ago* and *Charity Begins at Home*, complemented by Corney Grain's monologue *A Day in Town (In Fifteen Minutes)*. During the period in which the team had lain relatively idle they had suffered two notable defections. Fanny Holland and Arthur Cecil had both been tempted into the 'real' theatre, the former to appear at the new Criterion Theatre, the latter to the Globe under Montague and then to the Gaiety. To replace Miss Holland, Reed selected the young soprano Leonora Braham who was just beginning the long and brilliant career which was to be hers as a musical leading lady. The amateur tenor Stanley Betjeman took Cecil's roles with more self-confidence than finesse or talent. In May *Charity Begins at Home* was replaced by a new Burnand work, *He's Coming (via Slumborough, Snoozleton and Snoreham)*, set on a railway station and involving its five participants in a large number of characterisations. In June *Ages Ago* was removed (and Betjeman with it) and *Too Many by One* took its place. This little tale of marital mix-ups in an English garden was again by Burnand, but to music of the 22-year-old composer Frederic H. Cowen. Cowen was soon to turn to more serious work and in later years became one of Britain's senior conductors as well as the respected composer of innumerable cantatas, orchestral works, piano pieces, songs and operas. Neither of these two pieces proved as successful as the earlier works, and the Reeds closed their first St George's season on July 18 and did not re-open until Boxing Day when they presented a Gilbert a'Beckett piece called *The Three Tenants*. This was little more than a Scotsified version of *Box and Cox* for which Reed (though Cowen had been originally announced) supplied the music. *Too Many by One* was revived and Corney Grain completed the evening with *The Enchanted Piano*.

The quality of the German Reed product was rather in decline, but the Reeds still had the distinction of having nurtured the best of the musical writers and composers currently on the London scene, and the two most notable short pieces of the year both came from authors and composers who had formerly worked at the Gallery of Illustration. The first of these was *Topsyturveydom* produced for the opening of the Criterion Theatre in March. W. S. Gilbert had let his fancy go with a vengeance on this little piece, and *Bell's Life* described it primly as:

> one of those oddities of dramatic caricature for which its author has acquired a distinctive reputation.

Satis, from the town of Ballotville where everyone is so content there is nothing to do, comes to the land of Topsyturveydom where everything happens in reverse – the people are born old and get progressively younger till they die – and there he falls in love with the Queen's grandmother, a delightful young lady played by Fanny Holland. Many difficulties ensue during his courtship as, of course, the emotions of the people of Topsyturveydom are quite the reverse of normal. The quaintness of the idea gave the scenic artists great rein for imagination – the King's reception room had its chandelier on the floor instead of the ceiling – and the costumier also waxed original, dressing the ladies in matching coloured dresses and wigs. *Topsyturveydom* was played after the evening's main piece, Byron's *An American Lady*, on the inaugural night, but it was later shifted to a better position before the play. Its far-fetched whimsicality proved rather too much for the general public, however, and it failed to win acceptance, being withdrawn after only three weeks.

Robert Reece and Frederic Clay combined for the other principal short piece of the year, a very successful little musical comedy called *Green Old Age*, conceived to star David James and Thomas Thorne, the lessees and stars of the Vaudeville Theatre where a revival of *Two Roses* was being played. It took the place of a revival of *Creatures of Impulse* which, shorn entirely of its music for the occasion, had featured as a supporting piece since July until the production of *Green Old Age* in October.

This time Reece had been a little more chary with his puns and had relied more on situation comedy, and the result was decidedly more popular. The plot was a thin one. Two young wives flirt with two soldiers because they know that their jealous husbands, disguised as veterans, are watching. The story was of little importance except that it gave James and Thorne the opportunity to give very funny impressions of the old men and provided some laughable scenes such as one where the wives, pretending not to recognise their husbands, treat them with old men's medicines. *Bell's Life* described it justly as 'farce of true old English character' and *The Era* as 'half an hour of continuous laughter'. Frederic Clay supplied most of the music but some was by Reece himself.

Less successful was a curious short work, *Potocatapetl*, produced at the Philharmonic on the bill with *La Fille de Madame Angot*. Its plot concerned a cockney photographer caught by brigands to whom he finally turns out to be related . . . a rather obvious steal from *The Contrabandista, Our Island Home et al.* The composer, George Richardson, considered his compositions highly enough to interpolate one of his songs 'Can this be Love' into *Angot* for which he was the conductor, but *Potocatapetl* was not the work of a Lecocq.

1874

0013 **THE DEMON'S BRIDE** or A Legend Of A Lucifer Match. A grand original opéra-bouffe in three acts. Expressly composed for the Alhambra Theatre by Georges Jacobi. The libretto by Leterrier and Vanloo adapted and altered for the English stage by Henry J. Byron. Produced at the Alhambra Theatre under the management of John Baum 7 September 1874 for a run of 48 performances closing 31 October, 1874.

Landgrave Filastenish. . . . . Harry Paulton
Karl . . . . Lennox Grey
Krock . . . . Mr Melbourne
Fil-en-Quatre . . . . H. Parry
Baron Ostruck. . . . . Felix Bury
Japanesh. . . . . T. H. Paul
Bitterbrock . . . . W. Worboys
Sautenbark . . . . Fred Clifton
Picknick . . . . Amy Sheridan
Alga . . . . Rose Bell
Hélène. . . . . Lotty Montal
Wilhelmina . . . . Alice Hilton
Charlotte . . . . Marie Welch
Gretchen . . . . Marie Barrie
Eva . . . . Jennie Howard
Sybill . . . . Inez Harland
Leonora . . . . Clara Risson
Lisbeth . . . . Miss Wright
Conrad . . . . Willie Fredericks
Herman . . . . Miss Amherst
Christian . . . . Miss A. Harman
Pds: M. Dewinne, Mlles Sidonie, Lila, Pitteri, Sara, M. Josset

Md: Georges Jacobi; ch: M. Dewinne; sc: A. Callcott; cos: Alfred Thompson

0014 **WHITTINGTON** Grand opéra-bouffe in three acts by H. B. Farnie. Music by Jacques Offenbach. Produced at the Alhambra Theatre under the management of John Baum 26 December, 1874 for a run of 112 performances closing 7 May, 1875.

Dick Whittington . . . . Kate Santley
Alice Fitzwarren . . . . Julia Mathews
Dorothy, the cook. . . . . Lennox Grey
Alderman Fitzwarren . . . . Charles Heywood
The Bell-ringer of Bow . . . . W. M. Terrott
The Sergeant of the Patrol . . . . Harry Paulton
Captain Bobstay. . . . . John Rouse
Hirvaia, Princess of Bambouli . . . . . . Grace Armytage
The MacPibroch . . . . Mr Swarbreck
The O'Shamrock . . . . Alice Hilton
FitzFulke . . . . Jennie Howard/Inez Harland

King Bambouli XIX	Fred Clifton
The Chief Moonshi	W. Worboys
Colza	Miss Wright
Naphtha	H. Parry
Omawa	Marie Barrie
Taia	Inez Harland/Miss Cecil
Lalaza	Clara Risson
Wyme	Miss Christopher
Thomas, a cat	Master Abrahams
Edward III, King of England	Mr Hutton

Pds: Mlles Pitteri, Pertoldi, Sidonie; M. Dewinne/Betty Rigl

Md: Georges Jacobi; ch: M. Dewinne; sc: A. Callcott; cos: Alfred Thompson

Produced as *Le Chat du Diable* in a translation by Nuitter & Tréfeu at the Châtelet Theatre, Paris, 1893 for a run of 90 performances. With Juliette Darcourt and M. Alexandre.

0015 **CATTARINA** or Friends At Court. A comic opera in two acts by Robert Reece. Music by Frederic Clay. Produced at the Prince's Theatre, Manchester under the management of Kate Santley 17 August, 1874 for 18 performances and thereafter on tour at Birmingham, Leeds, Scarborough, Bradford, Belfast, Dublin, Newcastle-upon-Tyne, Leeds, York and Glasgow to 12 December, 1874, a total of 102 performances.
Played with *He's a Lunatic* replaced (October 26) by *The Three Conspirators.*

Duke Valerio Volcano	J. D. Stoyle/Edwin Danvers
Nicolo	John Wainwright
Anselmo/Fabian	Selwyn Graham
Fernando	Charles Kelleher
Cattarina	Kate Santley
Brigitta	Mary Pitt
Lucia	Blanche Linden
Dorotea	Madge Hatherley
Graziella	Ada Charlton
Linda	Sarah Grundy
Giuliano	Helen Hatherley
Isidoro	Mr Petre
Giuseppe	Mr Harland
Cristoforo	Mr Levisohn
Giovanni	Mr Fraser

Dir: Charles Calvert; md: Frederic Clay; ch: John D'Auban; cos: Alfred Thompson

Produced at the Charing Cross Theatre under the management of W. R. Field 15 May, 1875 for a run of 75 performances closing 9 July, 1875 then toured under the management of Kate Santley in repertoire with *Les Prés St. Gervais* from 26 July to 30 October, 1875.

Duke Valerio Volcano	Edmund Rosenthal/Joseph E. Beyer
Nicolo	Alfred Young/Charles Kelleher
Anselmo/Fabian	Henry Walsham/Gerald Travener
Fernando	J. H. Ryley
Cattarina	Kate Santley
Brigitta	Lillian Adair/Alice Hamilton
Lucia	May Burney
Dorotea	F. Hankinson
Linda	A. Masters
Carlotta	Kate Fellowes
Anina	Madeleine Lucette
Zerlina	L. Masters
Elena	F. d'Arcy
Maritana	Miss Miller/M. Wellington
Letitia	Elsie Vernie/L. Moore
Annetta	Miss Florence

Rosa . . . . E. Gordon
Giuseppe . . . . Eugenie Vernie
Giuliano . . . . Nellie Reed/A. Vaughan
Ministers: A. Knight, H. Deane, Charles Tritton, Fred J. Stimson, C. K. French

Md: Adolphe Lindheim/E. Audibert

Played at the Charing Cross Theatre with *Jeanne du Barry*, replaced June 14 by *A Cure for the Fidgets* and *Les Trois Diables* and on June 27 by *The Young Widow* and *Le Gandin* (Espinosas), the latter discontinued July 2.
Performed on tour with *The Three Conspirators/The Young Widow*.

0016 **THE SULTAN OF MOCHA** a comic opera in three acts by Albert Jarret (?). Music by Alfred Cellier. Produced at the Prince's Theatre, Manchester under the management of Charles Calvert 16 November, 1874 for a season of 30 performances closing 19 December, 1874.

Shallah, the Sultan of Mocha. . . . . . . John Furneaux Cook
Captain Flint . . . . Henry M. Clifford
Admiral Sneak . . . . Frederick Mervin
Peter. . . . . Robertha Erskine
Dolly . . . . Bessie Emmett

Md: Alfred Cellier; sc: T. Grieve and Mr Briggs

Produced at the Prince's Theatre, Manchester 8 March, 1875 for two weeks and again 19 April, 1875 for three weeks ending 8 May.
J. Furneaux Cook (SULT), Henry M. Clifford (FL), Frederick Mervin (SN), Mr Chatterson (PETER), Catherine Lewis/Emily Muir (DOLLY), H. Antoine (FRANK)

Produced at the Prince's Theatre, Manchester 7 March, 1876 for three weeks ending 25 March. Henri Corri (SULT), J. H. Ryley (FL), J. G. Taylor (SN), Alfred Brennir (PETER), Constance Loseby (DOLLY), Marie Williams (ISIDORA). Md: Frederick Stanislaus

Produced in London at St James' Theatre under the management of Mrs John Wood 17 April, 1876 for a run of 47 performances closing 2 June, 1876.

Shallah, the Sultan of Mocha. . . . . . . Henri Corri
The Grand Vizier. . . . . F. Strickland
Lord Chamberlain . . . . George Shelton
Peter. . . . . Alfred Brennir
Admiral Sneak . . . . G. W. Anson
Captain Flint . . . . Edward Connell/J. H. Ryley
Dolly . . . . Constance Loseby
Lucy. . . . . Amy Forrest
Moggy. . . . . Miss Willmore
Frank . . . . G. Paris

Md: Alfred Cellier

Produced in the United States by James A. Meade's Co., San Francisco, 1878.

Produced by Blanche Roosevelt's Company at the Union Square Theatre, New York 14 September, 1880 for a run of 13 performances closing 25 September, 1880.
William Hamilton (SULT), G. B. Snyder (VIZ), Mills Hall (CHAMB), Eugene Clark (PETER), Fred Dixon (SN), Harry Allen (FL), Leonora Braham (DOLLY), Ivy Lepel (LUCY), Pearl Everleigh (MOG), A. Barker (FRANK), Carrie Reynolds (ISIDORA), L. Feitner (EUREKA), G. W. Reynolds (SCRIBE), T. Cuthbert (DANIEL DEADLIGHT), 'L. Sanford' (BOB DUCKETT). 'W. Merton' (BOSEN BILL), 'Tom Bowling' (DAVY JONES), E. Reece (HATCHWAY JIM), Clare Lester (SARAH), Emma Guthrie (JENNY). Md: Alfred Cellier

Produced at the Strand Theatre under the management of Lydia Thompson 21 September, 1887 for a run of 114 performances closing 13 January, 1888. Libretto revised by William Lestocq. Additional song by Paolo Tosti.
Ernest Birch (SULT), Leonard Calvert (VIZ), C. Wrexford/Compton Coutts (CHAMB), Henry Bracy (PETER), Charles Danby/George Walton (SN), Charles H. Kenney/C. A. White (FL), Violet Cameron/Agnes Molteno (DOLLY), Madeleine Shirley/Florence Levey (LUCY), Louis

Batten (FRANK), Florence Melville (ISI), Florence Montgomery (EU), J. Harvey (BILL), Calder O'Byrne (PIRATE CHIEF), Mr Edwards (HEAD SLAVE), Nellie Lisle (JACK), Maud Hunzley (DICK), B. B. Matiste (HARRY), Gladys Carleton/May Gordon/Dot Templeton (WILL), Beatrice Eton/Marie de Braham (JENNY), B. Gordon/Amy Williamson (POLLY), F. England/Florence McIntosh (MADGE), Dot Templeton/Miss Watson/Gladys Carleton (NAN), Florence Levey/(HAIDEE), E. Grant (ZULEIMA), J. O'Mara (ZARA), F. Lloyd (ZOE), Eva Wilton/A. M. Taylor (ZULEIKA), Eulalie Philfair (ZENANA), Lydia Manton (PHOEBE). With Kate Grant, Leslie Melvin, Miriam Waud, Mona Jones, Dorothy Phelps, Kitty Hayes, Misses A. Mill, B. Pleydell, E. Kent, Florence McIntosh/K. Graham, C. Overington, F. Williams, A. Trevor; Messrs G. Leith, R. Holding, J. Cattell, W. Gilbert, J. Lewis, R. W. Smith, C. Campbell, J. Richards, G. W. Parte, A. Partell/J. Hart, J. Russell. Dir: Charles Harris; md: Ralph Horner; ch: Katti Lanner; sc: W. Perkins; cos: Wilhelm

TOPSYTURVEYDOM in two scenes by W. S. Gilbert. Music by Alfred Cellier. Produced at the Criterion Theatre under the management of H. J. Byron 21 March, 1874 with an *An American Lady*. Withdrawn 10 April, 1874.

Satis . . . . John Clarke
King Paratara of Topsyturveydom . . . . Frederic Dewar
Crapolee . . . . E. W. Garden
Wilkins . . . . Mr. Smith
Scrape . . . . Miss Hughes
Tipto . . . . Fanny Holland
Tiddyickle . . . . Dolly Wood
Quop . . . . Miss Montgomery
Crambo . . . . Constance Brabant
Dir: Richard Barker and H. J. Byron; cos: Miss Price

GREEN OLD AGE a musical improbability by Robert Reece. Music by Frederic Clay. Produced at the Vaudeville Theatre under the management of David James and Thomas Thorne as an afterpiece to *Two Roses* 31 October, 1874. Withdrawn 5 December, 1874.

Old Tom . . . . William Lestocq
Old Joe . . . . Mr Hanaford
Mrs Noodle . . . . Kate Bishop
Mrs Poodle . . . . Amy Roselle
Lt. Drummond Fyfe . . . . Nelly Walters
Lt. Mayne Masters . . . . Cicely Richards
Susan . . . . Fanny Lang
Mary . . . . Miss Brittain
Noodle . . . . Thomas Thorne
Poodle . . . . David James
with A. Austin, Mr Howard &c.

HE'S COMING (VIA SLUMBOROUGH, SNOOZLETON & SNOREHAM) by F. C. Burnand. Music by T. German Reed. Produced at St George's Hall under the management of T. German Reed 17 May, 1874 with *Ages Ago* and *A Day in Town*, the former replaced by *Too Many by One* (June 29). Withdrawn 18 July, 1874.

Mrs Wilfred/Miss Furbishaw . . . . Mrs German Reed
Miss Wilfred/Jenny Dimple . . . . Leonora Braham
Shilito Brinkley/Mr Stubbs . . . . Arthur Law
Dashmore/Noah Dunder/Inspector Dunder . . . . Alfred Reed
Hankey Pankeyson/Herbert Segnier/Stodge . . . . R. Corney Grain

TOO MANY BY ONE an operetta in one act by F. C. Burnand. Music by Frederic H. Cowen. Produced at St George's Hall under the management of T. German Reed 29 June, 1874 with *He's Coming* and *A Day in Town*. Withdrawn 18 July, 1874. Revived 26 December, 1874 with *The Three Tenants* and *The Enchanted Piano*. Withdrawn 23 January, 1875.

Mr Hazelagh	Alfred Reed
Ferdinand Browne	R. Corney Grain
Bertha Florinda	Leonora Braham
Dr Gell M.D.	Arthur Law
Florinda Paulena Prior	Mrs German Reed
Edgar Poldoddle	R. Corney Grain

THE THREE TENANTS an entertainment by Gilbert a'Beckett. Music by T. German Reed. Produced at St George's Hall under the management of T. German Reed 26 December, 1874 with *Too Many by One* and *The Enchanted Piano*, the former replaced by *The Ancient Britons* (January 25) and *A Tale of Old China* (April 19), the latter by *RSVP* (April 19). Withdrawn 3 July, 1875.

Peebles	Alfred Reed
Mr Vellum Grope.	Alfred Bishop
Harry Farintosh.	R. Corney Grain
Mrs Fitzfeather	Mrs German Reed
Miss Gwendoline Fitzfeather	Fanny Holland

Produced at St George's Hall 2 October, 1876 with *A Musical Bee* and (from October 18) *Mildred's Well*. Played from 6 November with *Matched and Mated* and *Our Table d'Hôte*. Withdrawn 20 November, 1876.

POTOCATAPETL an operatic piece of extravagance (a musical sketch) by Frederick Robson. Music by George Richardson. Produced at the Philharmonic Theatre, Islington, under the management of Mr Shepherd 4 May, 1874 as a forepiece to *La Fille de Madame Angot*. Withdrawn 4 July, 1874.

Tompkins	John Murray
Marietta	Agnes Lyndhurst
Paulo	Richard Temple
Diego	J. W. Wallace
Juan	Charles Tritton
Manuel	C. Hummerton

Md: George Richardson

1875

Whittington remained popular well into the new year, accompanied by the two new French pieces, *Les Prés St. Gervais* and *Giroflé-Girofla*. At the Strand, Farnie's pasticcio *Loo, or the Party who Took Miss* was on its way to becoming the longest running piece of 1874/5 and Reece's *Ixion Re-Wheeled*, another musical mish-mash, was playing its last weeks at the Opera Comique. The musical flavour of London was still largely French and the new offerings of early 1875 were in the same vein.

The first of these was the most important. *La Périchole* had been presented in Britain before: Hortense Schneider had played it at the Princess's in 1870 in French. It was a slightly risky proposition in English as the plot was based entirely on matters sexual; to the Victorian public it was decidedly 'French' and definitely 'fast'. In February Selina Dolaro appeared as Offenbach's heroine at the Royalty, Dean Street, where she played to large houses for four months before taking the piece out on an equally successful tour. After the summer she returned to the Royalty and continued the run.

The affluence at the Dean Street theatre, however, was not due entirely to Offenbach or to Madame Dolaro, popular though they both undoubtedly were. At the beginning of the run Dolaro and her manager Richard D'Oyly Carte had some difficulty in finding suitable pieces to complete the evening's entertainment. During the first weeks of the engagement they had tried Campbell Clark's *Awaking, A Good Night's Rest* (1837) by the once popular novelist Mrs Charles Gore, and Charles Collette's *Cryptoconchoidsyphonostomata*, before adding to the programme a one act 'dramatic cantata' by the authors of *Thespis*, Messrs Gilbert and Sullivan, in their first collaboration since their Gaiety venture. Its title was *Trial by Jury* and it was an immediate and immense success.

The setting is the courtroom of the Exchequer where court officials and jurymen are assembled to try the case of the heartless Edwin and the abandoned Angelina. Edwin explains to the jury (who are already committed to the cause of the damsel in distress) his change in affections:

But joy incessant palls the sense
And love, unchanged, will cloy
And she became a bore intense
Unto her lovesick boy!
With fitful glimmer burnt my flame
And I grew cold and coy
At last, one morning, I became
Another's lovesick boy

But the jury have little sympathy and when the plaintiff arrives, clad in her wedding dress and surrounded by bridesmaids, the judge and the jury quite lose their hearts. The case is argued vivaciously:

PTF: I love him, I love him with fervour unceasing
I worship and madly adore,
My blind adoration is always increasing
My loss I shall ever deplore!
Oh, see what a blessing, what love and caressing
I've lost, and remember it pray,
When you I'm addressing are busy assessing
The damages Edwin must pay!

But Edwin declares that he would be a drunken husband and beat his wife. The judge proposes getting him drunk to test this statement and, when everyone objects (except the defendant), he flings his books aside and declares he will wed the girl himself. A pair of plaster cherubs descend above them and in a glow of red fire they find the apotheosis of convenient marriage.

The original seed of the idea for *Trial by Jury* had come from a ballad about a breach-of-promise case which Gilbert had written for the humorous magazine *Fun*. He had expanded the idea into a scenario for the opera company of Carl Rosa who had intended to set it musically as a vehicle for his wife, Madame Euphrosyne Parepa Rosa. But in January 1874 Mme Rosa died and the script was returned to Gilbert unset. When D'Oyly Carte suggested that the author might like to combine with Sullivan to supply a short piece to be played with *La Périchole*, Gilbert produced his breach-of-promise libretto. Sullivan liked it, and quickly produced his now famous score.

The popular actress Nellie Bromley was selected to play the leading role of the plaintiff with the composer's brother, Frederic, as the Learned Judge, while Walter Fisher who was playing the leading role of Piquillo in *La Périchole* doubled as the defendant. The success of *Trial by Jury* was never in doubt. *The Era* wrote, catching the appeal of the piece:

> *Trial by Jury* is but a trifle – it pretends to be nothing more – but it is one of those merry bits of extravagance which a great many will go to see and hear, which they will laugh at, and which they will advise their friends to go and see, and therefore its success cannot be doubtful.

Nor was it. D'Oyly Carte suspended his free list and it soon became clear that the little afterpiece was more of an attraction than the main item on the bill, a situation which was not calculated to please 'Dolly' Dolaro who had intended her Périchole to be the centre of attention, and who now found herself decidedly upstaged by *Trial by Jury* and the voluptuous Nellie Bromley. But La Dolaro had an important financial interest in the season as well as a professional one, and she contended herself with being as bewitching a Périchole as her dark attractiveness, excellent voice and the laundered libretto allowed.

Gilbert's libretto was superior to any of his previous efforts. It was concise, modern and satirical without being impossibly whimsical. Having no spoken dialogue it was perforce tightly constructed and allowed of no interpolation or alteration. Both the lyrical portions, such as the Defendant's songs 'Oh, Gentlemen, listen, I Pray' and 'When first my old, old Love I Knew', and the comic showed a great advance in lyrical ingenuity. The comic highlight was undoubtedly the Judge's song:

When I, good friends, was called to the bar
I'd an appetite fresh and hearty,

But I was, as many young barristers are
An impecunious party.
I'd a swallowtail coat of a beautiful blue
A brief which I'd bought of a booby
A couple of shirts and a collar or two
And a ring that looked like a ruby!

in which the learned gentleman describes how he managed to get on in his profession by wedding 'a rich attorney's elderly ugly daughter' of whom he disposed after making his professional mark.

Sullivan had not tried a stage work since *Thespis* apart from some incidental music for the Charles Calvert *Merchant of Venice* and the Gaiety *Merry Wives of Windsor*. He had, however, produced the oratorio *The Light of the World* for Birmingham and a large amount of vocal music both secular and religious. *Trial by Jury* brought him firmly and finally into the world of the musical where, although he would continue composing for the church, the concert and the parlour, he would spend the most significant part of the next twenty-five years. The *Trial by Jury* music confirmed what *Cox and Box* and *Thespis* had suggested – that Sullivan was a composer of light lyric and comic music who could rival Offenbach, Lecocq and any English musician alive.

Trial by Jury was, of course, only a short and relatively slight work and, successful as it undoubtedly was, something a little more substantial needed to be brought forth before the hopes of the British musical could be raised too high. But, following on from the promise of *The Sultan of Mocha*, the delicious little 'dramatic cantata' gave great hope for the immediate future. At the end of her London season Dolaro took *Trial by Jury* on the road in repertoire with *La Périchole* and a hopelessly dismembered version of *La Fille de Madame Angot* which the prima donna had had Frank Desprez mutilate in such a way that her role of Lange was pre-eminent and the co-starring role of Clairette reduced to almost nothing. In October Dolaro returned to town and the same pieces sufficed for a further two months. By now Nellie Bromley had departed and Selina had promoted her friend Linda Verner from the insignificant role of the First Bridesmaid to take over. There had been other cast changes too, but Frederic Sullivan still reigned hilariously supreme as the Learned Judge, and *Trial by Jury* was quickly proved to have lost none of its appeal. Less than a month after its closure at the Royalty it resurfaced at the Opera Comique under the banner of Charles Morton and Emily Soldene, Dolaro's great rival for the title of prima donna buffa suprema. On the first night the little piece was almost the cause of a riot. It was to be played as an afterpiece to Offenbach's *Madame l'Archiduc* in which Soldene co-starred with Kate Santley. The English version of *Madame l'Archiduc* had been entrusted to Farnie and it was, to say the least, wordy. On the first night too the technical side was not as fluent as it might have been. Consequently at 11 pm only two acts had been completed and Morton came on stage to ask the audience to forego *Trial by Jury*. They were not pleased. They had already endured a huge wait between the first and second acts as well as other less scheduled gaps, a band manifestly unfamiliar with its music and a large dose of unadulterated Farnie. 'Play the lot and we'll stay, old man, if it's till two o'clock,' shouted a voice from the gallery to general approbation. But at 11.50 when the main piece ended there was no Gilbert and Sullivan. It was not until the next night that *Trial by Jury* made it on to the Opera Comique stage by which time *Madame l'Archiduc* had been heavily cut.

The Offenbach piece lasted two months, but *Trial by Jury* showed no sign of waning in popularity and was retained while Morton finished off his London season with

Geneviève de Brabant and *La Fille de Madame Angot*. It proved the occasion for Soldene to star her sister[1], Clara Vesey, whom she had nurtured in smaller roles at the Philharmonic, as the Plaintiff and it confirmed the identification of Fred Sullivan with the role of the Judge. Indeed, when Sullivan was taken ill, rather than put his understudy on, the piece was temporarily removed from the bill. Sullivan, however, could not be everywhere, and when *Trial by Jury* was staged simultaneously at Manchester the Judge was played by ex-Gaiety comic J. G. Taylor with another Gaiety star, Constance Loseby, as the Plaintiff. This provincial production was a special one, for Charles Morton had the out-of-town rights sewn up and only Richard D'Oyly Carte, the virtual begetter of the piece, was granted the right to tour a production.

Trial by Jury was now the most desirable supporting piece in London. It was given a major revival at the Strand in 1877 and a less propitious and rather poorly cast one at the Royal Aquarium, Westminster. The managers of the latter house found themselves in court after their production as they had produced it in an area not licensed for dramatic performances. It was hurriedly shifted into the establishment's theatre and played every day as a matinée while the evening bill remained unchanged. By now, outside London, it formed part of the baggage of all the major touring companies and Soldene had taken it as far afield as Australia on her world tour.

A memorable performance was given at Drury Lane for the Compton benefit. An amazing all-star cast was got together, with the jury box crowded with theatrical celebrities, and Miss Rita as the Plaintiff surrounded by a veritable galaxy of famous bridesmaids. In 1898 it was to have an even more incredible performance as part of Nellie Farren's benefit at the same theatre when every star in town crowded on to the stage to pay tribute to their beloved Nellie. On this occasion Gilbert himself took to the boards and appeared in the role of the Associate. D'Oyly Carte revived *Trial by Jury* at the Savoy Theatre as a forepiece to *The Sorcerer* in 1884 and 1898 and with *Pinafore* in 1899, and it remained a part of the repertoire of the D'Oyly Carte companies thereafter, confirming its position as probably the most successful British one-act operetta of all time.

During the original run of *Trial by Jury* Sullivan had another of his short works produced on the London stage. *The Zoo*, written to a libretto by B. C. Stephenson (as 'Bolton Rowe') was produced at the St James' as an afterpiece to Gilbert's farce *Tom Cobb*, and achieved a certain degree of success. It was a farcical tale set in Regent's Park and dealing with a disguised Duke in search of a true and loving wife who gets entangled with the suicide attempt of one Aesculapius Carboys, pharmacist, who has been forbidden by her social-climbing papa to marry his adored Laetitia. Henrietta Hodson made a decided hit in the role of Eliza Smith, the lady behind the refreshment counter who eventually lands the Duke.

The Zoo was, like *Trial by Jury*, sung through, but it was also very much a Gallery of Illustration type piece, not surprising as both writers had worked for the Reeds, whose protegés were now spreading further afield the style which had prospered and developed in Regent St. In fact, the stalwarts of the Gallery would have fitted quite suitably into the roles of *The Zoo*. Sullivan's music was, once again, excellent and attractive, though on this occasion it leaned more broadly towards operatic burlesque than *Trial by Jury*. It was nonetheless a most enjoyable score attached to a libretto which, if it did not reach the literary heights of its predecessor, was nevertheless clever

[1] Clement Scott suggests Clara may have been an illegitimate daughter.

and amusing. *The Zoo* ran for three weeks until the end of Miss Litton's St James' season, and then a further fortnight at the Haymarket where Pauline Markham took over the role of Eliza. In October it re-appeared at the Islington Philharmonic for a season and surfaced once more for a brief run as a forepiece to Grundy's *Crutch and Toothpick* at the Royalty in 1879.

The majority of full-length musicals in 1875 were French. Apart from *La Périchole* and the inevitable revivals of *La Fille de Madame Angot* and *Geneviève de Brabant* there were productions of *Chilpéric* (Alhambra), *Giroflé-Girofla* (Criterion), Vogel's *La Filleule du Roi* (in French), Offenbach's *Les Géorgiennes*, Hervé's *Dagobert* and Lecocq's *Fleur de Thé* as well as a whole season of French pieces from the Coulon company at the Gaiety. In the face of all this there was nothing more original from the British contingent than a handful of pasticcio extravaganzas including revivals of Farnie's popular *Loo* and *Nemesis*.

The most 'original' of the extravaganzas came from the Alhambra where Georges Jacobi supplied a large part of the music for two new spectacles. The first was *Spectresheim*, a Robert Reece 'extravaganza bouffe' based on the old Planché drama *A Romantic Idea*. It was a lively mid-European saga with 'merry music, bustling fun, marvellous special effects, astounding transformations and . . . genuine acting' (*Era*), featuring Harry Paulton as Max Dopplewick alias the Graf von Schlachfeldstein, Kate Santley and Henry Walsham. For its music it borrowed bits of *Pré aux Clercs, Les Prés St. Gervais, Les Bavards* and *Giroflé-Girofla* to put alongside seven Jacobi pieces and odd contributions from G. B. Allen (a quartet), Alfred Lee (a tenor scena for Walsham), W. M. Rooke (opening chorus) and the theatre's new manager, J. A. Cave who supplied a vocal waltz for Kate Santley called 'Queen of my Home'. Jacobi's contribution included a good comic song for Harry Paulton with the unlikely title of 'Chander lolly jam lelly je Bhoy', another, 'Tick-tick', for Marian West and an impressive Enchanted Forest ballet.

Spectresheim was a success, but the Alhambra's Christmas show of *Lord Bateman* was most definitely not. The favourite old ballad story gave plenty of Alhambra-type opportunities but, in spite of ten numbers from the proficient Jacobi backed by writers and composers original and borrowed, the seasonal piece did not catch on at all. Sullivan's ballad 'Once Again' written for Sims Reeves had been 'borrowed' for the contralto Adelaide Newton, and Cave had indulged himself with another showy piece 'The Ocean is the Briton's Home' but neither they nor all the monumentalia of the huge theatre could save *Lord Bateman*. After winning from one critic the amazing epithet for an Alhambra show of 'somewhat dreary' it foundered in six weeks.

But if London was largely sterile, Manchester was not. With their first original work, *Cattarina*, already in London, preparations got under way for a no-expenses-spared production of their very own Alfred Cellier's newest work. It was October before it was ready, and on the fourth of that month all fashionable Manchester assembled, along with many notables from the musical and theatrical world, to witness the first night of *Tower of London*. The orchestra and chorus had been specially augmented for the occasion, an excellent cast engaged and a wonderful new lighting system for the on-stage gaslights had been installed, operated by electricity! But the gas was all that caught light. The audience with all their good will were left dismayed, and the opening of *Tower of London* was an unequivocal flop.

As with The *Sultan of Mocha* the librettist had preferred to remain anonymous. It was just as well, as the blame for the failure of the evening was heaped largely on to his head:

> A weaker or more spiritless attempt at dialogue never found its way into print. Its utter colourlessness is not relieved by a single real joke, though its uniform dulness is disfigured by hysterical attempts at humour which can only be characterised as pitiably silly. (*Era*)

Unfortunately, they were right. The dialogue was boring, laborious and full of pathetic attempts at word-mangling: 'No use asking him to polka, he's too s(h)ottish'; or

GHOST: Swear to immediately arrest all traitors and execute the ringleaders.
BARON: I swear, like Hamlet, register my Oath-ello!

The lyrics, too, were largely characterless. Only once did the show nearly come to life and that was in a low comedy scene in the Tower Armoury in which the beastly Baron is confronted by a gang of ghostly suits of armour:

> We're musty, we're dusty and we're old
> And standing in these passages we've got a fearful cold . . .

But it was sadly reminiscent of and inferior to other scenes of the kind such as that in *Le Roi Carotte*.

Instead of following the path which had been laid in the much-loved *Sultan of Mocha*, *Tower of London* veered towards the old sentimental operas favoured in the early part of the century. The story was unlikely to find favour with the same audience which had laughed and applauded its way through the grotesqueries of *The Sultan* or the bubbly high-jinks of Offenbach or Lecocq. It revolved around one Barbara, daughter of the Tower Governor and her lover, the outlawed Captain Trelawney, who is eventually imprisoned in the Tower by the Baron and is due to be executed until Barbara succeeds (à propos of nothing) in getting a pardon from Queen Bess who happens to be passing; hardly the stuff of a jolly night at the opéra-bouffe or opéra-comique, even if the romantic sections were freely padded out with feeble fooling between the villagers Meg and Robin and the buffoonish gentleman, Toby.

Cellier's music was correspondingly more sober. Several pieces drew great praise, principally the ensembles. The soprano/tenor duets, 'The Meeting' and 'The Parting' were particularly well noted, as was the quintet 'What a wonderful Place is the Tower' in spite of its coy lyric:

> What a wonderful place is the tower
> Where they let people in every hour
> It's the prettiest garden that ever was seen
> With a sweet little block on the green.
> There's jewels and crowns by the score
> And a scavenger's daughter and more
> They've thumbscrews and racks
> And other nick-nacks
> Which you ne'er saw the like of before.

The solos included several straight ballads for Barbara, a drinking song for Robin, a flirting number for Meg and a very un-funny Pedigree song for the Baron who was also given a number bewailing the present state of things called 'Where is old England drifting To?'

> For each roystering boy
> Goes a-seeking of his joy
> At the bottom of a jug of beer

In spite of the long period which he had devoted to *Tower of London*, Cellier had clearly been uneasy. Only the day before the opening he had presented George Fox (Trelawney) with a new song 'Free now, all Danger I defy' which he performed on the first night. But although Fox managed creditably, not all the cast were so conscientious. The dialogue ground to a halt on a number of occasions. Then, too, the soprano Pauline Rita as Barbara was no Kate Santley. She was a rather serious, lofty performer – she would not be thumbing her nose at the critics when the bad notices came in, as they did, unanimously.

Hasty work was done on the libretto, rehearsals were called to sharpen the piece, and J. G. Taylor who was cast as the goonish Toby set to work to jolly up his role with some topical comicalities. He introduced a burlesque lecture into the Armoury scene and salted his lines with the local references which had gone down so well in *Cattarina* and *The Sultan of Mocha*. As the play began to run more smoothly the numbers began to show their genuine musical worth and were frequently encored. When the local papers reviewed the show again a week into its run they found enormous improvement, and by the time *Tower of London* reached the end of its five-week season it had developed into an altogether more entertaining piece. The theatre even announced that it would be revived at a later date, but this was not to be and November 6 was its last performance. The libretto was duly buried, but the score surfaced again over a decade later when part of it was re-used by Cellier for *Doris*, his follow-up to *Dorothy*, which also had its latter part conveniently set in the Tower of London and ended with a Queen's Pardon.

During the year the German Reeds produced four new short pieces. The first of these was *Ancient Britons* which was written by Gilbert a'Beckett and set in London in the year 5005 A.D. A Fijian traveller comes to research some information on the Victorian era and meets the inhabitants of ruined London. This provided the opportunity for a number of satirical jibes at the follies and the fashions of contemporary England. Faute de mieux, Reed, as was becoming his habit, supplied the music for the piece which proved disappointing and unsuitable and lasted only three months.

It was replaced by an F. C. Burnand piece, *A Tale of Old China*, which used the device of a dream set in the scene on an old Chinese teapot. It was more in the line of things expected at the Gallery and did considerably better than its predecessor. In July Gilbert produced his last piece for the Reeds, a very slight piece called *Eyes and No Eyes* which used the same idea as Hans Andersen's 'The Emperor's New Clothes'. Two young girls tease their lovers with a cloak – only he who sees it loves truly. It was nowhere near the calibre of *Ages Ago* and its author's more recent works, and it did not survive long. Its music was by German Reed, but when Joseph Williams came to publish the work it was fitted out with a new score by 'Florian Pascal'.

The final work was another a'Beckett/Reed collaboration, *A Spanish Bond*, telling of a nouveau riche who encounters a fearsome Spaniard while trying to buy his chateau. This gave Corney Grain a great excuse to play up the role of Don Gomez Roderiquez O'Flinnigan (he is really Irish), but one surprise was that there was no role for Mrs German Reed who, for the first time, contented herself with playing in only one part of the bill.

Among the year's curiosities was a production of *The Black Crook* at the Royal Amphitheatre in Liverpool which bore a minimal resemblance to the original even though some of the characters had similar names. The Paultons were given as the authors but a character named 'Parthie' singing 'Il Segreto' and 'Where the Bee Sucks' seems to have had little to do with the Alhambra piece. Harry Paulton's name was attached to another oddity called *Una*, which had music by Lecocq, a libretto specially written by Paulton and was produced by Miss Somerville's Comedy Bouffe Co. on tour. It opened a tour at Worcester's Theatre Royal in April starring Zerlina Zerbini but soon disappeared.

1875

0017 **TOWER OF LONDON** a comic opera in three acts. Music by Alfred Cellier. Produced at the Prince's Theatre, Manchester under the management of G. H. Browne 4 October, 1875 for a run of 30 performances closing 6 November, 1875.

Baron de Montmorency. . . . . John Furneaux Cook
Captain Harold Trelawney . . . . George Fox
Toby . . . . J. G. Taylor
Dick Raddle. . . . . George Shelton
Robin . . . . Charles Carew
Roger . . . . H. N. Antoine
Barbara. . . . . Pauline Rita
Meg . . . . Alice Cook
Ursula. Marie Williams
Sue . . . . Emma Toms
Molly . . . . Miss Grey
First Ghost . . . . Mr Ray

Sc: Walter Hann and W. Young

TRIAL BY JURY a dramatic cantata in one act by W. S. Gilbert. Music by Arthur Sullivan. Produced at the Royalty Theatre under the management of Selina Dolaro 25 March, 1875. Withdrawn 11 June, 1875 and toured in repertoire by Mme Dolaro's company returning to the Royalty 11 October, 1875. Withdrawn 18 December, 1875. Played with *La Périchole*, replaced 29 November by *La Fille de Madame Angot*. This company played three matinées at the Gaiety Theatre 10, 17, & 24 April, 1875.

The Learned Judge . . . . Frederic Sullivan
The Plaintiff . . . . Nellie Bromley/Linda Verner/Rose Stella
The Defendant . . . . Walter H. Fisher/W. Courtenay
Counsel for the Plaintiff . . . . J. Hollingsworth/C. Campbell
Usher . . . . B. R. Pepper/Charles Kelleher/Edward Connell
Foreman of the Jury . . . . Charles Kelleher/C. Campbell/C. Husk/W. S. Penley
First Bridesmaid . . . . Linda Verner/Amy Clifford
add Associate . . . . B. R. Pepper/T. Healey/Mr Cairns

Bridesmaids: Amy Clifford, Julia Beverley, Cissy Durrant, Annie Palmer, Miss Villiers, Miss Lasalle, Miss Lee, Miss Grahame/Julia Barber, Josephine Corri, Laura Carthew, Josephine Russell, Miss Amherst.

Jury: C. Husk, W. S. Penley, Charles Campbell, T. Cheeney, Mr Bradshaw, Mr West, Mr Grundy, Mr Fraser, Mr Marshall, Mr Walsh, T. Healey, Mr Nolan, Mr Plating, Mr Hackworth, G. Paris.

Produced in the United States at the Arch Street Theatre, Philadelphia 22 October, 1875 under the management of Alice Oates.

Produced at the Eagle Theatre, New York 15 November, 1875.

Produced at the Opera Comique under the management of Charles Morton 14 January, 1876 with *Madame l'Archiduc*. Subsequently played with *Geneviève de Brabant* (18 March) and *La Fille de Madame Angot* (3 April). Withdrawn 5 May, 1876.
Frederic Sullivan (JUD), Clara Vesey (PL), Knight Aston (Charles Campbell)/W. G. Bedford (DEF), Charles Campbell/W. G. Bedford (COU), Edward Connell/Charles Kelleher (USH), W. S. Penley (FORE), Amy Clifford (BRI), T. Healey (ASS)

Performed for the Compton benefit at Drury Lane 1 March, 1877.
George Honey (JUD), Pauline Rita (PL), W. H. Cummings (DEF), George Fox (COU), Arthur Cecil (USH); Edgar Bruce, J. Furneaux Cook, Harry Cox, George Grossmith, F. W. Irish, Harry Jackson, John Maclean, Claude Marius, Arthur Matthison, Harry Paulton, E. W. Royce, J. D. Stoyle, J. G. Taylor, William Terriss, J. D. Beveridge, George Barrett, Arthur Bishop, Frederic Darrell, Mr. Everill, James Fernandez, Walter H. Fisher, Henry Hallam, Alfred Maltby, Howard Paul, W. S. Penley, Harold Power, W. H. Vernon, G. Loredan, E. Murray; Carlotta Addison, Kate Bishop, Lucy Buckstone, Camille Dubois, Emily Fowler, Maria Harris, Nellie Harris, Kathleen Irwin, Fanny Josephs, Fannie Leslie, Amy Roselle, Marion Terry, Kate Vaughan, Lottie Venne, Violet Cameron, Ella Dietz, Kate Field, Kate Phillips, Emma Ritta, Rachel Sanger, Emily Cross. Md: Arthur Sullivan.

Produced at the Strand Theatre under the management of Mrs Swanborough 3 March, 1877 with *The Dowager* and *Babes and Beetles*. Withdrawn 26 May, 1877 to be toured as a supporting piece with *Nemesis*. Played from 12 May with *Mammon* and *Toodles*.
J. G. Taylor/George Leitch/Fred Mervin (JUD), Lottie Venne (PL), Claude Marius (DEF), Charles Parry (COU), Harry Cox (USH), W. S. Penley (FORE), Gwynne Williams (BRI)

Produced at the Royal Aquarium, Westminster, 1877.
Mr Fawn (JUD), Kate Rivers (PL), Mr Pearson (DEF), Mr Federici (COU), Charles Kelleher (USH), Mr Talbot (FORE)

Produced at the Opera Comique at a matinée under the management of Richard D'Oyly Carte and then from 23 March, 1878 as an afterpiece to *The Sorcerer*. Withdrawn 24 May, 1878.
George Grossmith (JUD), Lisa Walton (PL), George Power (DEF), Rutland Barrington (COU), Fred Clifton (USH), Frank Talbot (FORE)

Played at the Fifth Avenue Theatre, New York from 24 February, 1879.
Vincent Horgan (JUD), Bianche Corelli (PL), Henri Laurent (DEF), J. H. Burnett (FORE)

Produced at the Carltheater, Vienna as *Im Schwurgericht*, 14 September, 1886.

Performed for the benefit of Amy Roselle at the Lyceum 16 June, 1887.
Rutland Barrington (JUD), Geraldine Ulmar (PL), Henry Bracy (DEF), Richard Temple (COU), R. Lewis (USH). With Fred Leslie, George Barrett, Arthur Roberts, Henry Kemble, Harvey Nicholls, Julian Cross, E. W. Garden, Robert Pateman, William Blakeley, George Giddens, F. Thorne, T. P. Haynes, Egbert Roberts, Herbert Waring; Winifred Emery, Mary Moore, Evelyn Millward, Eva Sothern, Cissy Grahame, Annie Hughes, Helen Forsyth, Grace Huntley, Violet Vanbrugh, Mabel Millett, Annie Rose, Laura Linden. Md: François Cellier.

Produced at the Savoy Theatre under the management of Richard D'Oyly Carte 11 October, 1884 as a forepiece to *The Sorcerer*. Withdrawn 12 March, 1885.
Rutland Barrington (JUD), Florence Dysart (PL), Charles Hildesley/Durward Lely (DEF), Eric Lewis (COU), William Lugg (USH), Arthur Kennett (FORE), Sybil Grey (BRI). Md: François Cellier

Performed for the benefit of Rutland Barrington at the Savoy Theatre 28 May, 1889.
Rutland Barrington (JUD), Lottie Venne (PL), Courtice Pounds (DEF), Alec Marsh (COU), W. H. Denny (USH), Mr Burbank (FORE) with the Savoy Chorus.

Performed for the benefit of Nellie Farren at Drury Lane 17 March, 1898.
Rutland Barrington (JUD), Florence Perry (PL), Courtice Pounds (DEF), Eric Lewis (COU), Walter Passmore (USH), W. S. Gilbert (ASS), Lady Bancroft (ASS. WIFE).
Bridesmaids: Phyllis Broughton, Louie Pounds, Nellie Stewart, Jessie Huddlestone, Aida Jenoure, Ellis Jeffreys, Sybil Carlisle, Grace Palotta, Violet Robinson, Maud Hobson, Ina Repton, Kate Cutler, Emmie Owen, Maggie May, Ruth Vincent, Beatrice Ferrars.
Jury: Henry Lytton, Willie Edouin, Norman Salmond, John Coates, E. J. Lonnen, Richard Green, W. Louis Bradfield, Jones Hewson, W. H. Denny, W. H. Seymour, Mark Kinghorne,

Colin Coop, J. J. Dallas, William Elton, J. Furneaux Cook, H. Scott Russell, Herbert Standing, Arthur Roberts.
Counsel: J. Comyns Carr, C. Haddon Chambers, Sydney Grundy, Lionel Monckton, Edward Rose. With Mary Moore, Lydia Thompson, Charles Wyndham, Kate Santley, Constance Loseby, Marion Hood, Rose Leclerq, Kate Rorke, Carlotta Addison, Fanny Brough, Cornélie d'Anka, Mrs Dion Boucicault, Miss Compton, Florence Young, Helena Dacre, Rosina Brandram, Mrs H. Leigh, Mrs F. H. Macklin, Kate Bishop, Maria Davis, Helen Ferrers, Florence Gerard, Sarah Brooke, Leonora Braham, Irene Vanbrugh, Evelyn Fitzgerald, Beatrice Perry, Miss Nesbitt, Lily Cellier, Louie Henri, Jessie Rose, Daisy Gilpin, Ethel Wilson, Ada Navall, Pattie Reimers, Dorothy Dene, Hetty Dene, Mary C. Mackenzie, Gertrude de Lacy, Valerie de Lacy, Mayer Northcott, Millicent Baker, Laurie Elliston, Marguerite Moyse, Ethel Jackson, Lily Twyman, Annie Russell, Charles J. Fulton, Gillie Farquhar, Nutcombe Gould, James Erskine, W. T. Lovell, Tim Ryley, J. D. Beveridge, Charles Sugden, Dion Boucicault, Cory James, Charles Childerstone, Joseph Ruff, Charles Earldon, Cecil Castle, Avon Hastings, Iago Lewys, Dudley Jepps, Edwin Bryan, J. W. Ivimey, Leonard Russell. Md: François Cellier

Produced at the Savoy Theatre under the management of Richard D'Oyly Carte 22 September, 1898 as a forepiece to *The Sorcerer*. Withdrawn 31 December, 1898.
Henry Lytton (JUD), Isabel Jay (PL), Cory James/Strafford Moss/Harry Frankiss/Albert Gater/Charles Childerstone (DEF), Jones Hewson (COU), Walter Passmore (USH), Leonard Russell (FORE), Mildred Baker (BRI), Charles Childerstone (ASS)

Produced at the Savoy Theatre under the management of Richard D'Oyly Carte 6 June, 1899 as a forepiece to *H.M.S. Pinafore*. Withdrawn 25 November, 1899.
Henry Lytton (W. H. Leon) (JUD), Isabel Jay/Jessie Rose (Gertrude Jerrard) (PL), Charles Childerstone (Leon Graham) (DEF), Leonard Russell (COU), Walter Passmore (USH), Iago Lewys (FORE), Mildred Baker/Madge Moyse (BRI), Albert Gater (ASS)

Subsequently played by the D'Oyly Carte Opera Company on tour and in London in repertoire.

Played at Danzer's Orpheum, Vienna as *Das Brautpaar vor Gericht* 5 October, 1901.

Performed for the benefit of Mr Rignold at the Lyric Theatre, 5 December, 1902.
Rutland Barrington (JUD), Evie Greene (PL), Charles Childerstone (DEF), C. Hayden Coffin (COU), George Grossmith jr (USH), Fred Kaye (FORE), Phyllis Broughton (BRI), Lionel Monckton (ASS); with Olga Beattie-Kingston, Olive Morrell, Mollie Lowell, Gertie Millar, Maie Saqui, Lydia Flopp, Maud Danks, Vera Edwardine; W. Louis Bradfield, Ben Webster, H. B. Warner, Herbert Standing, Max Hecht, William H. Day.

Performed for the benefit of Ellan Terry at the Theatre Royal, Drury Lane, 12 June, 1906.
Rutland Barrington (JUD), Ruth Vincent (PL), Courtice Pounds (DEF), Henry Lytton (COU), Walter Passmore (USH), W. S. Gilbert (ASS) Fanny Brough (ASS. WIFE).
Bridesmaids: Phyllis Broughton, Adrienne Augarde, Amy Augarde, Billie Burke, Kate Cutler, Zena Dare, May de Souza, Agnes Fraser, Aida Jenoure, Mollie Lowell, Olive May, Gertie Millar, Decima Moore, Olive Morrell, Denise Orme, Louie Pounds, Gabrielle Ray.
Jury: Sir F. C. Burnand, Sir Arthur Conan Doyle, Sir Gilbert Parker, Alfred Calmour, J. Comyns Carr, C. Haddon Chambers, Owen Hall, Cosmo Hamilton, Henry Hamilton, Anthony Hope, Cecil Raleigh, Brandon Thomas; with Dion Boucicault, James Fernandez, Sydney Grundy, J. Martin Harvey, Charles Hawtrey, E. S. Willard, Mrs Bernard Beere, Charlotte Granville, Gertrude Kingston, Jessie Millward, Florence St John, Agnes Thomas, Lydia Thompson, Lottie Venne, Genevieve Ward, Mrs John Wood.
With Miss Edouin, Marie Illington, Clara Jecks, Beatrice Lamb, Eweretta Lawrence, Kitty Loftus, Ethel Maynard, Jessie Moore, Tina Murray, Bella Pateman, Elsie Reamer, Cicely Richards, Edith Standen, Gertrude Thornton, Maud Thornton, Gertrude White, Muriel Wylford, Isabelle Agnew, Kate Bishop, Rosina Brandram, Julie Dolaro, Pollie Emery, Miss Emmerton, Vane Featherstone, Helen Ferrers, Basil Hood, Arthur Alexander, W. L. Abingdon, Paul Arthur, J. H. Barnes, Edwin Bryan, Robert Caradoc, Harry Cottell, Alec Davidson, Albert Derrick, William Devereux, A. E. Drinkwater, Carr Evans, Albert Gater, Gloyne, H. G. Gordon, Oliver Grey, Lyn Harding, Rudge Harding, Gilbert Hare, Arthur Hatherton, Bert Hunter, Lawrence Kellie, Mark Kinghorne, Mr Knoblaugh, Herbert Waring, Luigi Lablache, R. Lewis, Iago Lewys, Frank Lincoln, W. T. Lovell, Herbert Mari, Eugene Mayeur, Sydney McAlpine, Norman McKinnel, John Morland, Herbert O'Brien, Robert Pateman, Harry

Paulton, Powis Pinder, Nigel Playfair, Norman Salmond, Edward Sass, George Shelton, Aubrey Smith, Herbert Sparling, William Spray, Ernest Torrence, Sydney Valentine, Hubert Willis.

TV/Video: 1984 Brent Walker Ltd. Pr: Judith de Paul; dir: Wendy Toye; md: Alexander Faris; ch: Terry Gilbert; sc: Allan Cameron; cos: Jenny Beavan
Frankie Howerd (JUD), Kate Flowers (PL), Ryland Davies (DEF), Tom McDonnell (COU), Tom Lawlor (USH), Brian Donlan (FORE), Elise McDougall (BRI)

THE ZOO a musical folly in one act by 'Bolton Rowe' (B. C. Stephenson). Music by Arthur Sullivan. Produced at St James' Theatre under the management of Marie Litton 5 June, 1875 with *A Practical Man* and *Tom Cobb.* Transferred to the Haymarket Theatre under the management of Edgar Bruce, 28 June for two weeks with *Brighton.* Closed 10 July, 1875.

Aesculapius Carboys . . . . Carlos Florentine
Laetitia . . . . Gertrude Ashton
Grinder . . . . Charles Steyne
Thomas Brown . . . . Edgar Bruce
Eliza Smith . . . . Henrietta Hodson/Pauline Markham

Produced at the Philharmonic Theatre, Islington under, the management of J. D. Solomon 2 October, 1875 with *Les Géorgiennes.* Withdrawn 30 October.
Edward Cotte (AC), Agnes Lyndhurst (L), Mr Cullen (G), Richard Temple (TB), Carlotta Zerbini (EL). Dir: Richard Temple

Produced at the Royalty Theatre under the management of Edgar Bruce 14 April, 1879 with *Crutch and Toothpick.* Withdrawn 3 May.
Wilfred Esmond (AC), Viola Dare (L), W. S. Penley (G), Edgar Bruce (TB), Lottie Venne (EL). Md: Edward Solomon

THE ANCIENT BRITONS by Gilbert a'Beckett. Music by T. German Reed. Produced at St George's Hall under the management of T. German Reed 25 January, 1875 with *The Three Tenants* and *A Fairy Tale*, the latter replaced by *The Enchanted Piano.* Withdrawn 17 April.

Imogen . . . . Leonora Braham
Cassivelaunus . . . . R. Corney Grain
Nesta . . . . Fanny Holland
Caractacus. . . . . Alfred Bishop
Boadicea. Mrs German Reed
Baker . . . . Alfred Reed

A TALE OF OLD CHINA by F. C. Burnand. Music by J. L. Molloy. Produced at St George's Hall under the management of T. German Reed 19 April, 1875 with *The Three Tenants* and *RSVP.* Withdrawn 3 July. Reopened 4 October with *Eyes and No Eyes* and *Clever People*, the former replaced (1 November) by *A Spanish Bond.*

Edward Peyton/1st Conspirator. . . . . . R. Corney Grain
The Prince of China . . . . Fanny Holland
Herr Reichenbrunner/Emperor of China. Alfred Reed
2nd Conspirator. . . . . Alfred Bishop
Bertha/Chinese Maid . . . . Leonora Braham
Empress of China. . . . . Mrs German Reed

EYES AND NO EYES or The Art of Seeing by W. S. Gilbert. Music by T. German Reed. Produced at St George's Hall under the management of T. German Reed 5 July, 1875 with *RSVP* and *Very Catching.* Withdrawn 14 August. Reopened 4 October with *Clever People* and *A Tale of Old China.* Withdrawn 30 October.

Cassandre . . . . Alfred Reed
Columbine . . . . Fanny Holland
Clochette . . . . Leonora Braham
Arlequin. Alfred Bishop
Pierrot. . . . . R. Corney Grain
Nicolette. . . . . Mrs German Reed

A SPANISH BOND by Gilbert a'Beckett. Music by T. German Reed. Produced at St George's Hall under the management of T. German Reed 1 November, 1875 with *A Tale of Old China* and *Clever People*, the former replaced by *Our Card Basket* (31 November). Played from 28 February with *An Indian Puzzle* and *Slaves of the Rink*. Withdrawn 4 April, 1876.

Edwin Stubbs . . . . Alfred Reed
Roderiquez O'Flinnigan . . . . R. Corney Grain
Simplicia . . . . Leonora Braham
Mrs Otranto Smith . . . . Fanny Holland

Produced at St George's Hall 5 June, 1876 with *Charity Begins at Home* and *A Musical Bee*. Withdrawn 8 June, 1876.

1876

The 1876 season started poorly. The failure of *Lord Bateman* was echoed by that of the Strand extravaganza *Antarctica*, the only other musical piece in town apart from the seasonal pantomimes. The first new entries were more or less French: a piece by G. M. Layton using the music of Vasseur's *La Timbale d'Argent* and called *The Duke's Daughter*, and Offenbach's *Madame l'Archiduc* which had the advantages of Soldene, Kate Santley and *Trial by Jury* as an afterpiece. The pasticcio extravaganza of *Piff Paff* (from the French *Le Roi Matapa*) and revivals of the Alhambra's *Don Juan* and *La Périchole* at the Charing Cross followed, but were hardly events of great note although they at least brought a little music back into the West End.

The first English piece of the new year opened at the Royalty Theatre, Dean Street, under the management of Mrs Liston on March 25. It had the unpromising title of *Pom*. Both the music and the libretto were credited to the Italian-born composer Procida Bucalossi, by now a long-time British resident and previously the composer of some Italian comic operas as well as several shorter pieces for the English stage.

The story of *Pom* involved a troupe of French opéra-bouffe performers bound for Rio who are shipwrecked on a South Pacific island. The 'governor' of the island, Monsieur Pom, falls for their soprano, Trainette, whom he pursues through various complications involving real and fake Red Indians to the annoyance both of his amorous housekeeper, Angélique, and Trainette's lover, Horace. When the latter, disguised as an Indian Chief, prepares to wed Trainette, Pom concurs, thinking that he has substituted Angélique, but the girls have changed places again and all ends happily.

The work had been unusually well-rehearsed and it was reported that the first night went with 'no hitches, no slips and very little aid from the prompter', but the book was unoriginal and long-winded and in some of the more drawn-out speeches cries of 'dry up' were heard from the gallery. But in the main the reception was fair. The setting gave the opportunity for some picturesque stage pictures and the pleasant and plentiful music helped to mask the fact that the dialogue was totally lacking in imagination and humour. Signor Bucalossi, whatever his musical talents, was no librettist.

Those musical talents received rather a back-hander from *The Era*:

> There is a constant flow of melody which keeps the hearer in an agreeable state of expectation that something very fresh and charming will come presently. Signor Bucalossi is always on the verge of a new idea but although he seldom gets hold of a positively original passage he manages so gracefully with phrases already familiar that few will be hard-hearted enough to find fault.

The Times was less tolerant, and slated the show:

> The only merit which *Pom* possesses is to be found in the music and that

> is a merit for which Signor Bucalossi is not so much responsible as are M. Offenbach, M. Lecocq and sundry other very well-known composers of light and pleasant melodies . . Concerning the legitimacy of the fun we are unable to speak at much length for the same reason that so materially shortened the historian's chapter on snakes in Iceland.

Pom's greatest asset was its prima donna, Pattie Laverne, who was now established amongst the forefront of musical leading ladies and who made the most of her opportunities comic and musical in this production. But, in spite of Miss Laverne, the piece did not catch the public fancy. It was shortened to under an hour and three-quarters and supplemented by a short Bucalossi piece, *Coming Events*. This was a Parliamentary spoof set in the Chamber of the House of Commons containing many allusions to current affairs as well as a thinly veiled caricature of the MP, Dr Kenealy. It ended with a belligerent woman spectator taking over in a Cromwellian fashion as Prime Minister. One of the highlights was a chorus of policemen summoned to eject the presumptive lady. This pair ran in tandem for only a few nights before Mrs Liston gave in and closed down. London's first new musical for over a year was hardly a success. Bucalossi advertised the piece for sale to provincial managements and it was taken up by Richard South who had recently returned to Britain from the Orient and the Antipodes where he had toured extensively at the head of a musical company. South's prima donna, Alice May, abandoned his company on their arrival in Britain and took to opera and, subsequently, the role of Aline in *The Sorcerer*. This left the manager obliged to find a replacement and his choice alighted on Pattie Laverne. When Miss Laverne joined the company to play the Grand Duchess, Clairette etc. her London creation, *Pom*, was added to the repertoire. Duly revamped it succeeded rather more on this occasion and in Liverpool was so popular that the Prince of Wales Theatre was obliged to add some extra rows of stalls to accommodate all the Liverpudlians anxious to see Miss Laverne and hear Bucalossi's music.

The following year South came nearer to town and tried *Pom* at Camden Town's Park Theatre with the co-operation of Marion St Claire who had been instrumental in the staging of *The Magic Pearl*. *The Entr'acte* commented hopefully that 'he will probably catch the Hampstead visitors on their return from the Heath'. But his production was not good enough. Rose Bell made a nice Trainette and George Temple took the role of the Governor effectively. But Joseph Beyer over-indulged himself in over-acting and Henry Hallam's very light tenor did not go down too well. The ballet which had been interpolated for the provinces looked as if that was so and the Park prided itself on not being the provinces. After three weeks *Pom* moved on to Shoreditch and the Standard Theatre where it survived two further weeks before shutting down.

By rights, the piece should now have been decently buried but in April of 1881 a company set out from Liverpool to tour Lecocq's *Le Petit Duc* and Bucalossi's piece was exhumed as a subsidiary item. But the production of *Pom* turned out to be a nightmare. When it was staged at Plymouth it was soon clear that something was wrong. There were internal battles going on amongst the artistes and, apart from that, people didn't seem to know what they were doing. Finally, in the third act, everything fell to pieces. The performers playing Pom and Angélique refused to go on, and in alarm the prima donna, Lizzie Mulholland, rushed on to the stage and started to sing her big number from *Le Petit Duc*. Those of the orchestra with good memories attempted to follow her with predictable results. Miss Mulholland changed song, chaos ensued, and finally the curtain was brought down. The offending performers left and the theatre was closed down until Alice Cook and Edmund Rosenthal could be brought in to continue with a version of *La Fille de Madame Angot*. The tour staggered on under new management with *Pom* remaining a very secondary part of the repertoire until it was finally laid permanently to rest.

In April *The Sultan of Mocha* came to town and settled into its rather disappointing run of 47 performances at the St James'. Given its integral merits it certainly deserved to run at least as long as *Cattarina* with which it compared more than favourably. But it was short on stars and spectacle and did not catch the public imagination as it might have.

As the season of *Madame l'Archiduc* came to an end at the Opera Comique, Kate Santley announced her summer tour plans. She was taking to the road towards the end of June with a repertoire of four French opéras-bouffes plus *Cattarina* and a new work 'especially composed by W. S. Gilbert and Frederic Clay'. Whether *Princess Toto* was 'especially composed' for Miss Santley is a moot point. Gilbert and Clay had been at work on the project for some time. But be that as it may, it was the vigorous Kate who produced the piece and starred herself in the title role.

Toto is a curious character and a great worry to her father, King Portico, who lives in perpetual fear of 'what the surrounding nations will think':

> Toto, bless her, is extremely wilful and obstinate and ridiculously impulsive and romantic. Her head is filled with foolish ideas about gipsies, robbers, actors, pirates, and paving commissioners, Red Indians, auctioneers and outlandish people of that sort. Just now it's the brigand Barberini, the scourge of the neighbourhood. She can think and talk of nothing else, wears a lock of his wig round her neck. You have no idea how she compromises me. Then she has no memory whatever – forgets events that are not ten minutes old . . .

It is upon this lady that the plot turns. Toto has been engaged since childhood to wed Prince Doro but he has vanished, presumed pirated, and Portico has arranged instead for her to marry Prince Caramel:

> A nice, well-behaved young man – plays the flute, does worsted work, wears goloshes and attends spelling-bees[1]

But Caramel is three days late for the wedding when suddenly Doro turns up to claim his bride. Since he's there, Toto takes him and when Caramel arrives he is too late. To win the Princess back he disguises himself as her favourite brigand and tempts her (for she has already forgotten that she is married) to run away with him. But Caramel and his court make poor brigands and Toto is disgusted with their lack of bloodthirstiness, for she is in her romantic element:

> This life suits me down to the ground. I shall live and die a brigand queen!

Doro comes to join the band but Toto has now married Caramel, which puts him out very much. Portico and his ministers come to lure the wayward Princess home:

> Taking advantage of her taste for novelty and disguising ourselves as Red Indians in the hope that the peculiarity of our appearance and the quaintness of our attitudes might fascinate her volatile mind.

Toto is duly fascinated and runs off with them but soon finds that her Indians 'eat

[1] The spelling bee was a current drawing-room 'craze'

caviar and shave with a Mappin's razor' and is sadly disillusioned. Finally she manages to concentrate her dizzy mind on Doro while Caramel must content himself with her lady, the luscious Jelly.

Gilbert's book was the equal of anything the British musical had produced. It was written with a genuine style and wit which was so often blatantly lacking in popular libretti. Admittedly it was rather diffuse. The whole plot rested on the improbable peculiarities of its heroine which served as an excuse to introduce the familiar brigand and Indian disguise scenes for two long acts of singing, dancing and comedy and very little rhyme or reason. But the dialogue and the songs were bright and clever and Miss Santley had a role which displayed her talents fully. The songs were of a high standard. *The Era's* Liverpool critic wrote:

> Mr. Frederic Clay has done his work in a way which is most satisfactory in nearly every respect. Both airs and comic pieces are written with a masterly vigour, considerable originality and appropriate colouring and the instrumentation is certainly not the least attractive portion of the excellent work. The vocal waltz of the first act is quite a gem in its way; the characteristic songs are funny without being vulgar; and the choruses in general have a brightness and artistic colouring about them which fully maintain the reputation of the composer of *Cattarina*, *Oriana* and *Ages Ago* . . . the happy combination of catching music with piquant writing ought to make *Princess Toto* a favourite everywhere.

Among Toto's best pieces were the first act 'Like an Arrow from its Quiver (comes my love to marry me)' and the much more humorous 'The Pig with the Roman Nose' in which she tells a fable to illustrate the folly of not knowing when one is well off. The vain pig tries to make himself notable by having his nose altered:

> His sad ambition proved his ban
> He was sold at once to a peep-show man
> His foolish dreams of glory fled
> He was shown to the mob at a penny a head

Prince Doro also had some attractive songs – a ballad in the opening act:

> Oh, bride of mine, oh, baby wife
> In cradledom demurely plighted,
> Has time dealt kindly with thy life
> Since thou and I were first united?
> Art thou as fair and yet as fond
> As in that stage of preparation?
> Ah, since those days the wizard's wand
> Has worked some wondrous transformation

and the slightly satiric:

> There are brigands in every station
> And robbers in every rank
> Some plunder the wealth of the nation
> Some honestly pillage a bank;
> Some brigands are bubble directors
> And others may wear a fez hat;
> They're out of the reach of inspectors
> But none the less brigands for that

Most of the songs and their lyrics had a straight flavour. Toto's waltz was backed by two further sentimental numbers and a duet with Doro in the same vein, but the liveliness of the piece was in no way impaired. Clay had done his job well.

The first performance was given in the comparative quiet of Nottingham before the principal tour dates were permitted to see it. When they did, the reception was enthusiastic. Kate Santley was greeted nightly with applause, calls, encores and bouquets and the critical reception, if not perfect, was encouraging. Liverpool found that its 'first impressions [were] very favourable', Manchester that it 'abounds in so many merits, musical and literary, that it cannot fail to become extremely popular' whilst Edinburgh, traditionally more reserved, granted it 'amusing dialogue and lively music' as 'a favourable specimen after the model approved at present'. It quickly became popular in the provinces. In Newcastle and Bradford it was played for the full week, and three of the French pieces in the tour's repertoire never got performed at all.

Soon *Princess Toto* was being recast to open at Mrs Swanborough's Strand Theatre. Kate Stanley, of course, retained the star role but the dashing Anglo-Frenchman Claude Marius was to take over as Doro, and the popular comedian Charles Collette, currently touring his highly successful piece *Bounce*, was engaged as Caramel. But troubles soon arose and on September 24 a crisp notice in *The Era* announced that:

> Charles Collette, regarding the part allotted to him in *Princess Toto* . . . as altogether unsuited to him has resigned his engagement at [the Strand] and is now arranging for another tour with *Bounce*.

J. G. Taylor, who had just left the Manchester Prince's Theatre company, was quickly engaged to take over and, with the opening night put back from the Friday to the following Monday, the show was successfully got on. The reviews were appreciative:

> One of the most amusing as it is certainly one of the brightest and most fanciful of pieces (*Daily News*)
>
> If a most charmingly ingenious plot, the most brilliant of dialogues, music full of melodies that dwell in the mind, pretty scenery, quaint dresses and good acting can make a success, then *Princess Toto* is a success indeed (*Echo*)
>
> *Princess Toto* is, I fancy, unsurpassed in London at the present moment (*Punch*)

Quite what went wrong at the Strand Theatre has become obscured by the silence of a century but almost certainly the abrasive personality of *Princess Toto*'s librettist was involved. In any case the show was taken off prematurely after only 48 performances and the Strand returned to burlesque with *Dan'l Tra-Duced, Tinker*, a version of Gilbert's successful play *Dan'l Druce, Blacksmith*. Gilbert obviously had no quarrel with the star of *Princess Toto* for Kate Santley took the show on the road again the following year, but he was clearly displeased with the West End fate of his most important musical to date and continued to work for a revival. The Gaiety's John Hollingshead took up the rights with a contractual promise to produce and *Princess Toto* finally saw the light of day again in 1881, although not at the Gaiety. Hollingshead took the Opera Comique after the departure of D'Oyly Carte for his newly built Savoy Theatre, and followed *Patience* in with a revised version of *Princess Toto*. This time there was a totally different emphasis on the casting. The original choice of Kate Santley had been heavily criticised in some quarters:

> Although this extravaganza has the very grave misfortune to be written for an opéra-bouffe actress and is also wedded to music avowedly written in emulation of the French opéra-bouffe it is in no way to be confounded with the class of productions

> with which of late years under that designation we have been made but too familiar. Although Miss Kate Santley spares no pains in trying to make *Princess Toto* resemble as much as possible those ticklish translations from the French in which at the Alhambra and elsewhere she has so often and so lavishly displayed her exotic charms, the genuinely spiritual quality of Mr Gilbert's libretto cannot be made to wear that kind of mask . . . (*Illustrated Sporting & Dramatic News*)

Although she was hugely popular with the public, Miss Santley was to suffer many sharp attacks from the press over the years on account of her lack of 'spiritual qualities' or rather her excess of physical ones.

For the new *Princess Toto* the casting followed the lines by then established by D'Oyly Carte. The young singer Annette Albu from the Van Biene Opera Company was given the title role and doubtless coped with Clay's often florid music more capably than her predecessor. Richard Temple abandoned his role in *Patience* to play King Portico and George Temple (Jamilek), the original Samuel from *The Pirates of Penzance*, also joined the cast. Alfred Bishop from the German Reed establishment came in to play Caramel, and only the Doro, M. Loredan, had the air of the opéra-bouffe around him. Once again *Princess Toto* was well-received and once again it survived a bare two months before being disappointingly withdrawn. In spite of its obvious qualities it resolutely refused to catch on. An American production featuring Leonora Braham suffered a similar fate and an Australian version with Robert Brough and Annette Ivanova in 1886 proved scarcely enough to establish the show. *Princess Toto* was consigned to the bottom drawer for fifty years until an enterprising stock revival by Sir Barry Jackson's Birmingham Repertory company in 1935.

If Freddie Clay had been disappointed over *Princess Toto*, his reaction to the reception of his other new work, *Don Quixote*, which had opened a week previously at the Alhambra must have been very much worse. *The London and Provincial Entr'acte* had no doubts. It stated quite baldly '*Don Quixote* is not a success'. That was putting it mildly. It was the biggest and most expensive flop, not even excepting *Lord Bateman*, that the Alhambra had had under its present policy, and it lasted only seven weeks before *Le Voyage dans la Lune* was resurrected to fill in until the Christmas production of *Die Fledermaus* was ready to take over.

Clay had suffered from serious libretto trouble. The book had been supplied by Alfred Maltby and Harry Paulton, and the latter also performed the role of Sancho Panza. They gained little credit from it and *The Era* had no doubt why:

> We presume that Mr. Maltby is responsible for the construction of the piece and Mr. Paulton for the dialogue; we imagine so because whenever Mr. Paulton who represented Sancho Panza appears on the scene there is certain to be a very long speech or speeches . .

And, indeed, the title was a little misleading. The opera had become centred around Sancho Panza, the Don himself taking little part but leaving the stage to a standard Alhambra comic version of Sancho, the amorous doings of the lovely Altissidora and Sampson de Caracas, a lot of disguising, and some extravagant doings on the Island of Barataria.

The verdict was unanimous. *Bell's Life* said categorically, 'too much Sancho and not enough Quixote,' and *The London and Provincial Entr'acte* snapped that Paulton

> has been a favourite so long [at the Alhambra] that he thinks they can't have enough of him.

Paulton snapped back, accusing the *Era* critic of personal malice, denying that he had written his own speeches, and defending the quality of the work by saying that no-one wanted Shakespeare at the Alhambra and besides 'the portions which go for nothing are those taken literally from Cervantes'. Not very much had been taken from Cervantes. The Alhambra *Don Quixote* had been developed into a long-winded vehicle for Paulton, Kate Munroe, Loredan and Emma Chambers (as Sancho Panza's daughter, Sanchica), and for the Alhambra ballets and designers. The latter were the most successful, for whatever else *Don Quixote* lacked it was not spectacle. Alfred Maltby had done better with his designs than with his libretto, and also with the ballets he had designed to the choreography of John Lauri. The ballet in the Halls of Chivalry danced by Mlle Pertoldi and the huge corps de ballet was the highlight of the evening. Clay's share in all of this came in for less of a beating. In keeping with the comic treatment his music was light and tuneful, if not his most memorable. Kate Munroe's air 'What is Love?' proved the most popular number, but none of the score survived the precipitate collapse of the whole venture.

Manchester, in the meanwhile, was not to be left out of this sudden burst of indigenous activity, and Tuesday 17 October saw the production at the Prince's of Cellier's newest work, *Nell Gwynne*. Once again the librettist was unannounced but his identity was well-known – it was H. B. Farnie. This being so, there was no chance of the book being original, and it was in fact a re-hash of Moncrieff's play *Rochester* combined with some unpublished pieces of the same author's work.

Cellier had by now been succeeded by Frederick Stanislaus as musical director of the Prince's Theatre, but Manchester still had a special regard for 'their' composer and his new show was produced with every possible accoutrement. Pattie Laverne was hired to impersonate Nell; Alfred Brennir, so well-received in *The Sultan of Mocha*, and the rising young baritone Richard Temple for the leading men; and the orchestra, chorus and staging staff were specially enlarged. But the local critics liked it even less than *Tower of London*, and the London and trade papers were barely more receptive.

Farnie's libretto was actually considerably better than that for *Tower of London*. It had little to do with King Charles and his mistress, and centred on the adventures of two rakish noblemen, Rochester and Buckingham, who set up as landlord and waiter at a country inn to seduce country girls. Rochester has been rusticated for refusing to let the King's mistress, Nell Gwynne, act in his latest play and for expressing low opinions of her acting ability. Buckingham has suffered the King's displeasure for refusing to wed his ward, the Lady Clare, sight unseen. The first prey for the lusty lords is Jessamine, daughter of the miserly Weasel, who is, in her turn, planning to elope with her actor lover, Falcon. Both Buckingham and Rochester insinuate their way into her home disguised as a rat-catcher and a beadle, but find only trouble. More trouble is on the way for them in the shape of Nell and Clare who come in disguise and lead the men on into indiscretion. Nell, disguised as a country Joan, fascinatesRochester with a brilliant Shakespearian recital and some showy vocalising and he proposes to take her to London to displace the untalented Nell Gwynne. Buckingham, meanwhile, is falling in love with Clare. King Charles arrives and the girls declare their identities: Rochester is shamed and Buckingham jilted.

In burlesque fashion, Farnie introduced anachronisms and topicalities on top of the standard repetitive disguises and the popular ghost scene, and if the book showed where it had been cobbled together from several sources it was nevertheless reasonably lively and gave plenty of opportunities to its leading players.

The vocal opportunities, in particular, were many and various. The most popular numbers were Jessamine's Sobbing Song ('He promised to come'), Nell's ballad 'Her Heart'[1] (The slighted maid) and the tenor song for Falcon:

O were I but the morning light
The first to glimmer on the grange
Unto thy dwelling I would fly
Tho' all the world I had to range.

And were thy window hid in rose
Or dark with dewy eglantine
I'd creep among the silent flowers
That so my first beam should be thine

On the comic side, J. H. Ryley as the pompous beadle, Amen Squeak, sang 'On Sundays parish Clerk am I' giving his universal solution to the problems of his post–'I put 'em in the stocks'–and told a pretty moral tale in 'The deluded Bee':

The honey-making season came
Like trumpet-call athwart the hive
And field and garden, hill and lea
With troops of bees were all alive;
And countryward all sped but one
A self-conceited lazy elf
It was the youth's first season so
He thought he'd come out by himself

The self-sufficient bee tries to get honey from the artificial flowers on a lady's hat and comes a cropper. There was a pillory chorus, an old women's chorus, a pawn chorus, a fortune-telling sextette and a Wardrobe and Umbrella Stand duet (Rochester and Buckingham each hidden in one), and many other bright ensembles and solos, including a piece clearly influenced by *Trial by Jury* in which Pattie Laverne sang of 'Breach-of-Promise':

So, so you thought it very fine
To steal a humble heart like mine
You chuckled to yourself and said
Good fun, she's but a low-born maid,
But that is where, my noble rake,
You made a very great mistake
For nowadays, however raw,
All ladies understand the law,
And wipe their tears, prepare for war,
And call on their solicitor!
They are but feeble women.

The show had been set to run four weeks and it ran its course. In spite of the adverse criticisms the Mancunians filled the theatre with very fair audiences and the music became quite popular before the final night. Once again rumours were rife . . the London people had liked it . . it was to go to London . . to Paris . .

In a way the rumours were right for *Nell Gwynne* did eventually make it to London, but in two halves. Farnie withdrew his libretto and presented it in a revised state a few years later to Robert Planquette, by then the darling of the town as the composer of the record-breaking *Les Cloches de Corneville*. The result was another *Nell Gwynne*

[1] cf. *Dorothy* where its melody becomes 'With such a dainty Dame'

presented at the Avenue and Comedy Theatres with a measure of success for 90 performances. Cellier, left with an unattached score, reused some of it in a later work to words by B. C. Stephenson. Under the title of *Dorothy* it appeared in the 1886 season and ran for 931 nights to become the century's most successful musical, smashing the record set a few years earlier by *Les Cloches de Corneville*.

Dan'l Tra-Duced did not prove a success at the Strand and was soon replaced by a new burlesque, the Strand's third British musical of the year after the revival of *L'Africaine* and *Princess Toto*. This piece was a burlesque of Wagner's *The Flying Dutchman* called *The Lying Dutchman* featuring J. G. Taylor in the title role:

> I'm the Lying Dutchman gay
> From my very earliest youth
> I'd a great capacity for mendacity
> I never spoke the truth

It was written pseudonymously by 'Hue and Eye' (Frederick Hay and Arthur Clements), the authors of the burlesque of Gilbert's *Broken Hearts*, *Cracked Heads*, and the original music was supplied by Alfred Lee. Lee was a conductor, arranger and songwriter who had provided some music for the Alhambra's shows, but his principal claim to renown lay in his many popular songs: 'Walking in the Zoo', 'Lounging in the Aq' and the tune to George Leybourne's 'Champagne Charlie'.

The Lying Dutchman was not a good piece. It did not burlesque its supposed subject and was no more than a poorly written mixture of well-tried elements with sixteen unexceptional musical breaks. *The Times* would have none of it:

> .... a purposeless and pointless farrago of nonsense ... Old jokes, and not many even of them, silly songs – let, however, one excellent one sung by M. Marius be excepted – unnecessary dances succeed each other with wearisome rapidity and on the first night of its unfortunate performance every song and dance was repeated whether the audience wished it or no, it really seemed as if the end would never come.

The authors showed their lack of style in an attempt to burlesque Southey's 'An old Man's Comforts' as an advertisement for Captain Coalscuttle's Rag and Bone cart:

> You are smart, Father William, the young man said
> And your hat and your necktie are gay,
> Yet you spend all your time at the Saracen's Head
> Come tell me the reason, I pray.
> In the days of my youth, said the father so grave,
> I took care of my bones and my fat
> And the excellent price Mr. Coalscuttle gave
> Has bought me this necktie and hat.

Lewis Carroll had done it already and rather better.

Mrs Swanborough advertised 'Great Success' but *The Lying Dutchman* was kept afloat only by the fact that it shared the bill with the comedian John S. Clarke 'sustaining in addition to his well-known personations several characters which he has not yet acted in London'.

In a year so productive and progressive in new works a number of shorter works were also presented. The Reeds at St George's Hall tried six new pieces as well as revivals of *Charity Begins at Home*, *The Three Tenants* and *Mildred's Well*. Of the new works Burnand's *Matched and Mated*, a little matrimonial jigsaw, was probably the best, although *The Era* commented:

. . it is hardly equal to some of Mr. Burnand's former entertainments [though] it affords an excellent vehicle to exhibit the talents of the company.

This latter consideration, originally an advantage in the hands of writers of Gilbert's calibre, seemed to have become a liability and an excuse for a lack of originality. The same comment appeared in the lukewarm reviews of each new piece. Gilbert and Arthur a'Beckett gave the company a chance to wish themselves to be pantomime characters in *An Indian Puzzle*, and the elder a'Beckett cast the whole company as amateur actors in *The Wicked Duke*. With his other three productions Reed tried new authors and composers but his old flair seemed to be lacking. Only in the composer Cotsford Dick, writer of the year's final piece, *Our Dolls' House*, did he find a talent of any description.

Of considerably more interest was the début of a little piece called *A Will with a Vengeance* produced as an afterpiece to Boucicault's *Hunted Down* at the Globe Theatre in November. The musical director of that theatre was a 21-year-old named Edward Solomon. His father was a musician and young Solomon had played piano and other instruments in music halls from an early age. He had written a number of pieces of music but this little operetta showed decided promise. It was a comical piece in which the manager, Edgar Bruce, played one Charley Maloni from the Balls Pond Road who is lured to Corsica by a ficticious legacy and finds himself embroiled in a ridiculous vendetta. Solomon provided a dozen musical sections which illustrated it very happily and it earned a certain popularity. Bruce later revived it for a season with Grundy's *Crutch and Toothpick*.

Two other pieces of some interest appeared in the provinces. The first, given by the D'Oyly Carte touring company of *La Fille de Madame Angot,* was a little piece by former Texas cowboy Frank Desprez set to music by 'Mark Lynne' – that is to say, D'Oyly Carte. It found itself a West End berth early in the new year as a forepiece to *Orpheus in the Underworld* at the Royalty under the title *Happy Hampstead* and Desprez, who had met Carte through a fortunate connection with Selina Dolaro, remained with him as secretary and confidant for many years.

The other piece was an operetta entitled *Le Marquis de St. Valéry* composed by 21-year-old Julian Edwards for his sister Fanny's well-known touring concert party. Edwards had previously contributed other little pieces such as *Cornarino's Mistake* (1873) and *May and December* (1875) but *Le Marquis de St. Valéry* was reckoned his best to date. Julian Edwards was Manchester-born and built himself a career as a conductor and small-time composer in Britain before emigrating in 1888 to America where he became a prolific composer of Broadway shows in the nineties and the first decade of the twentieth century. Among the shows he provided for the American stage were *Jupiter* (1892), *Friend Fritz* (1893), *Madeleine* (1895), *The Goddess of Truth*, *Brian Boru* (1896), *The Wedding Day* (1897), *The Jolly Musketeer* (1898), *Dolly Varden*, *When Johnny Comes Marching Home* (1902), *Love's Lottery* (1904), *His Honour the Mayor* (1906), *The Belle of London Town* (1907), *The Motor Girl*, *The Girl and the Wizard* (1909) and *Molly May* (1910).

Dolly Varden was the only one of these to make it back to Britain and it was performed, with less success than in the United States, at the Avenue in 1903. *When Johnny Comes Marching Home*, a patriotic Civil War piece, was probably his best work. Produced in 1902 to a book by his usual librettist, another English exile, Liverpudlian Stanislaus Stange, it caused quite a stir on its original production and was later revived on Broadway.

1876

0018 **POM** a comic opera with book and music by Procida Bucalossi. Produced at the Royalty Theatre under the management of Mrs W. H. Liston 25 March, 1876 for a run of 30 performances closing 29 April, 1876.

Pom . . . . John Rouse
Trainette . . . . Pattie Laverne
Horace. . . . . Knight Aston
Pepinet . . . . Fred Clifton
Laroux . . . . James T. Dalton
Madame Angélique . . . . Annie Goodall
Louisa. . . . . Rhoda Clarke
François . . . . Mr Marshall

Md: E. Goossens; sc: Richard Douglass; cos: Mr & Mrs Samuel May
Played with *Married Bachelors. Coming Events* added to the programme 22 April.

Produced at the Park Theatre, Camden Town by Richard South's Opera Company under the management of Marion St Claire 2 April, 1878 for three weeks. Subsequently played two weeks at the National Standard Theatre closing 25 May, 1878.
George Temple (POM), Rose Bell (TR), Henry Hallam (HOR), Joseph E. Beyer (PEP), Mark Kinghorne (LA), Marie Parselle (ANG), Isabelle Grey (LOU), A. Riches (FR), Harry Templeton (KALU). Md: E. Goossens; ch: M. Dewinne

0019 **PRINCESS TOTO** an English comic opera in three acts by W. S. Gilbert. Music by Frederic Clay. Produced at the Theatre Royal, Nottingham under the management of Kate Santley 26 June, 1876 and toured in repertoire with *Madame l'Archiduc* and *Cattarina* through Birmingham, Liverpool, Manchester, Edinburgh, Newcastle-upon-Tyne and Bradford ending 9 September, 1876.

Princess Toto . . . . Kate Santley
Prince Caramel . . . . Joseph E. Beyer
Prince Doro . . . . E. Loredan
Zapeter . . . . J. H. Ryley
King Portico . . . . John Wainwright
Jelly . . . . Alice Hamilton
Count Floss . . . . B. R. Pepper
Baron Jacquier . . . . W. S. Penley
Jamilek . . . . W. H. Seymour

with Misses M. Temple, L. Masters, M. Jameson, Kate Fellowes, Ryan and Florence Trevallyan

Md: Frederic Clay/Mr Vetter

Produced in London at the Strand Theatre under the management of Mrs Swanborough 2 October, 1876 for a run of 48 performances closing 25 November, 1876.

Princess Toto . . . . Kate Santley
Prince Caramel . . . . J. G. Taylor
Prince Doro . . . . Claude Marius (Herbert Seymour)

Zapeter . . . . W. S. Penley
King Portico . . . . Harry Cox
Jelly . . . . Lottie Venne
Count Floss . . . . W. E. Blatchley
Baron Jacquier . . . . Mr Knight
Jamilek . . . . Charles Otley
Giovanni . . . . F. Cottrell
Divine . . . . G. La Feuillade
Sago . . . . Gwynne Williams
Vermicelli . . . . M. Jameson
Tapioca . . . . Lizzie Coote
Vergilio . . . . T. Cheeney
Paolini . . . . Herbert Seymour
with Messrs Edgar, Andrini, Amphlett, T. Bradshaw; Misses Florence Trevallyan, A. Imms, L. Taylor, K. Neville, E. Neville, M. Brown
Md: Henry E. Reed; ch: John D'Auban; sc: H. P. Hall; cos: Alias and Mrs Reddish

Produced at the Standard Theatre, New York, 13 December, 1879 for a run of 22 performances closing 3 January, 1880.
Leonora Braham (TOTO), Oliver W. Wren (CAR), H. C. Campbell (DORO), William Hamilton (ZAP), H. W. Montgomery (PORT), Verona Jarbeau (JEL), Alfred Holland (FL), H. R. Humphries (JAQ), William A. Paul (JAM), J. A. Oliver (PRISONER), Miss Shandley (DIV), Miss Lawrence (FOLLETTE)

Produced in a revised form at the Opera Comique under the management of John Hollingshead and Richard Barker 15 October, 1881 for a run of 65 performances closing 17 December, 1881. Annette Albu (TOTO), Alfred Bishop (CAR), G. Loredan (DORO), Robert Brough (ZAP), Richard Temple (PORT), Annie Poole/Constance Maitland (JEL), J. Ettinson (FL), Eugene Stepan (JAQ), George Temple (JAM), Harry Chambers (PRISONER), Edith Vane (FOLLETTE). Dir: Richard Barker; md: Frederick Stanislaus; sc: Walter Hann; cos: George Pilotell.

0020 **DON QUIXOTE** a grand comic and spectacular opera in three acts by Harry Paulton and Alfred Maltby. Music by Frederic Clay. Additional music by Georges Jacobi. Produced at the Alhambra Theatre under the management of F. Leader 25 September, 1876 for a run of 42 performances closing 11 November, 1876.

Don Quixote . . . . J. H. Jarvis
Sancho Panza . . . . Harry Paulton
The Duke de Bodego . . . . Edmund Rosenthal
Altissidora . . . . Kate Munroe
Rezio . . . . Lizzie Robson
Clotilde . . . . Eily Beaumont
Sanchica . . . . Emma Chambers
Teresa . . . . Alice Hilton
Duchess de Bodego . . . . Adelaide Newton
Nicholas . . . . Mat Robson
Sampson de Caracas . . . . E. Loredan
Demon Herald . . . . W. G. Ross
Palamesque . . . . R. Marchant
Zerlina . . . . R. Lowe
Anna . . . . Mathilde Wadman
Antinia . . . . Nelly Vane
Drum Major . . . . Mr Russell
Officer . . . . C. Risson
with Messrs Godfrey, Hancock, L. Fontaine, T. Mahoney
Pd: Miss Fisher/Erminia Pertoldi; Dancers: Mlles Sismondi, Richards, Rosa; with The Fiji Flutterers and The Girards.
Dir: Harry Paulton; md: Georges Jacobi; ch: John Lauri; sc: A. Callcott; cos: Alfred Maltby

0021 **NELL GWYNNE** an opera in three acts by H. B. Farnie founded on *Rochester* by Moncrieff.

Music by Alfred Cellier. Produced at the Prince's Theatre, Manchester, 17 October 1876 for a season of 24 performances closing 5 November, 1876.

Buckingham . . . . Richard Temple
Rochester . . . . Alfred Brennir
Nell Gwynne . . . . Pattie Laverne
Lady Clare . . . . Alice Cook
Weasel . . . . John Furneaux Cook
Jessamine . . . . Kathleen Corri
Marjorie . . . . Marie Williams
Talbot . . . . Kate Aubrey
Amen Squeak . . . . J. H. Ryley
Falcon . . . . W. H. Courtenay

0022 **THE LYING DUTCHMAN**, A Phantom Folly. A new and original burlesque in five scenes by 'Hue and Eye' (Frederick Hay and Arthur Clements). Music by Alfred Lee. Produced at the Strand Theatre under the management of Mrs Swanborough 21 December, 1876 for a run of 48 performances closing 17 February, 1877.

Captain Coalscuttle . . . . Harry Cox
François Frenchipani . . . . Claude Marius
Hans von Lie-der-Whopper . . . . J. G. Taylor
Taut . . . . Gwynne Williams/Miss Holmes
Trim . . . . G. La Feuillade
Mizen . . . . W. S. Penley
Coraline Coalscuttle . . . . Lottie Venne
Mopsine . . . . Sallie Turner/Gwynne Williams
Anna Maria . . . . Maria Jones

Md: Henry Reed; sc: H. P. Hall; cos: M. & Mme Alias.

Played with *His Last Legs* and *Keep your Temper*, the former replaced 6 January by *Among the Breakers* and *Toodles.*

AN INDIAN PUZZLE by Gilbert and Arthur a'Beckett. Music by T. German Reed. Produced at St George's Hall under the management of T. German Reed 28 February, 1876 with *Slaves of the Rink* and *A Spanish Bond*, the latter replaced by *Grump's Ménage* (10 April). Withdrawn 3 June, 1876.

Laura . . . . Leonora Braham
Sir Chutney Pepper . . . . Alfred Bishop
Mrs Hollybush . . . . Mrs German Reed
Dick Gordon . . . . R. Corney Grain
Alice . . . . Fanny Holland
Mr Fox . . . . Alfred Reed

GRUMP'S MÉNAGE by John Hermitage. Music by Frederick E. Barnes. Produced at St George's Hall under the management of T. German Reed 10 April, 1876 with *Slaves of the Rink* and *An Indian Puzzle*. Withdrawn 3 June, 1876.

Captain O'Gorman Grump . . . . Alfred Bishop
Adolphus Chesterfield . . . . R. Corney Grain
Fanny Lancaster . . . . Leonora Braham
Mrs Wagstaffe . . . . Mrs German Reed
P. C. 1112 . . . . Alfred Reed

THE WICKED DUKE by Gilbert a'Beckett. Music by T. German Reed. Produced at St George's Hall under the management of T. German Reed 9 June, 1876 with *A Musical Bee* and *Charity Begins at Home*. Withdrawn 22 July. Reopened 2 October with *A Musical Bee* and *The Three Tenants*. Withdrawn 17 October, 1876.

Miss Cynthia Lynch . . . . Mrs German Reed
Augustus Loop Judkins . . . . Alfred Bishop

Olympia Clive. . . . . Fanny Holland
Elsie Travers . . . . Leonora Braham
Shelley Wing . . . . Alfred Reed
Anthony Saffron . . . . R. Corney Grain

MATCHED AND MATED by F. C. Burnand. Music by T. German Reed. Produced at St George's Hall under the management of T. German Reed 6 November, 1876 with *Our Table d'Hôte* and *The Three Tenants*, replaced respectively by *Spring Delights* and *A Puff of Smoke* (21 November), *Our Dolls' House* (December 26), *A Night Surprise* (12 February). Withdrawn 10 March, 1877.

Mrs Barton . . . . Fanny Holland
Sir Maurice Goldeneye . . . . Alfred Bishop
Julia Appleworth . . . . Mrs German Reed
Percy Blythe . . . . R. Corney Grain
Beatrice Kirby . . . . Leonora Braham
Captain Kirby. . . . . Alfred Reed

OUR DOLLS' HOUSE a fairy vision in one peep by William Wye. Music by Cotsford Dick. Produced at St George's Hall under the management of T. German Reed 26 December with *Our Table d'Hôte* and *Matched and Mated*. Withdrawn 10 February, 1877.

Our Lady Doll . . . . Fanny Holland
Our Gentleman Doll . . . . Arthur Law
Our Red Riding Hood . . . . Leonora Braham
Our Wooden Soldier . . . . Alfred Reed
Our Little Bo-Beep . . . . Millie Holland
Our Mr Noah. . . . . Corney Grain

Produced at St George's Hall in a revised version 26 December, 1881 with *Ages Ago* and *Master Tommy's Theatricals*. Withdrawn 28 January, 1882.

Produced at St George's Hall 17 December, 1892 with *All at Sea* and *Boys and Girls*. Withdrawn 14 February, 1893.

A PUFF OF SMOKE by C. J. Rowe. Music by 'Angelina'. Produced at St George's Hall under the management of T. German Reed 21 November, 1876 with *Our Table d'Hôte* and *Matched and Mated*. Withdrawn 23 December, 1877.

Mr Montague . . . . R. Corney Grain
Mrs Montague . . . . Fanny Holland

A WILL WITH A VENGEANCE a comic opera in one act founded on *La Vendetta*. Libretto by Frederick Hay. Music by Edward Solomon. Produced at the Globe Theatre under the management of Edgar Bruce 27 November, 1876 with *Hunted Down* and *The Two Gregories*. Withdrawn 16 December, 1876.

Charley Maloni . . . . Edgar Bruce
Carlo Maloni . . . . Richard Temple
Tedesco . . . . Douglas Cox
Giuseppe . . . . Mr Beveridge
Carina . . . . Rose Cullen
Brigadier . . . . P. Gordon
Md: Edward Solomon; sc: Bruce Smith

Played at the Globe Theatre 15 February, 1877 with *The Invisible Prince* and *The Way of the Wind*.

Produced at the Royalty Theatre under the management of Edgar Bruce 5 May, 1879 as a forepiece to *Crutch and Toothpick*. Withdrawn 31 May.
Fred Solomon/Edgar Bruce (CH), W. S. Penley (CAR), Douglas Cox (TED), Horatio Saker (GIU), F. Desmond (BRIG), Lottie Venne (CAR)

HAPPY HAMPSTEAD a musical pastoral in one act by Frank Desprez. Music by 'Mark Lynne' (Richard D'Oyly Carte). Produced by the D'Oyly Carte Opera Company 3 July, 1876 with *La Fille de Madame Angot* and toured in repertoire.

Costermonger . . . . Walter H. Fisher
Amanda . . . . Bessie Sudlow
with Charles Kelleher, E. G. Osborne, Miss Palmer &c.

Produced at the Royalty Theatre under the management of Kate Santley and Richard D'Oyly Carte 13 January, 1877 with *Orpheus in the Underworld* and *Lischen and Fritzen*. Withdrawn 9 February, 1877.

Costermonger . . . . Walter H. Fisher
Amanda . . . . Rose Cullen
Old Gentleman . . . . J. D. Stoyle
Donkeyherd . . . . Henry Hallam
Policeman . . . . Charles Kelleher
Cook. Ella Collins
Fruit Seller . . . . Mr Amphlett
Pleasure-seekers . . . . A. Imms, Mr. Seymour
Tittlebat-fishers . . . . Blanche Sabine, Louie Verdoni, Violet Melnotte
Donkey-drivers . . . . Messrs Salisbury and Lopresti
Tea-women . . . . Rose Roberts, Maud Digby
Sc: Bruce Smith

LE MARQUIS DE ST. VALÉRY a comic operetta in one act, written and composed by Julian Edwards. Produced at Reading Town Hall by Fanny Edwards' Concert Party 20 January, 1876 and toured in repertoire.

Mlle Muret . . . . Fanny Edwards
Jean du Val . . . . Redfern Hollins
Colombe. . . . . Annie Kinnaird
Dominique . . . . Fred Law
Monsieur Augarde . . . . Campbell Kneale
Pianist: Julian Edwards

1877

The 1877 season in the West End started inauspiciously. The first ten months of the year saw little in the way of successful musical novelties and the most notable productions were, surprisingly, a pair of Gaiety pasticcio burlesques *The Bohemian Gyurl* (117 perfs) and *Little Doctor Faust* (151 perfs). Even the French were having a poor time of it. Their only new representative, a production by Kate Santley of the Paris hit *La Marjolaine* at the Royalty, was dubiously received. The Alhambra followed *Die Fledermaus* with a mediocre revival of *Orpheus in the Underworld* starring Harry Paulton and Kate Munroe, then reverted to Viennese operetta with an unimpressive and unappreciated *King Indigo* (*Indigo und die vierzig Räuber*) (Johann Strauss/ tr. Burnand) which was withdrawn after only seven weeks and replaced by yet another revival of *La Fille de Madame Angot*.

But the season was saved at the eleventh hour by the most successful British musical to date, the first full-length collaboration between Messrs Gilbert and Sullivan and Richard D' Oyly Carte: the comic opera *The Sorcerer*. Since their amazing success with *Trial by Jury*, the triumvirate had been daily expected to come up with a new and equally dazzling popular piece. After all, Carte had already mentioned the existence of a major work in his advertising:

> A Dramatic Cantata by Messrs. Arthur Sullivan and W. S. Gilbert in one act entitled *Trial by Jury* in which Miss Nellie Bromley and Mr. Walter Fisher &c will appear will be produced in a few days. In consequence of the continued success of *La Périchole* the production of Mr. Sullivan's two act opera is postponed.

The rumours had circulated freely. At one stage it was reported that the new and eagerly-awaited work was to be a musical version of *The Wedding March* by F. Latour Tomline (Court, 1873). Tomline was, in fact, Mr W. S. Gilbert and the play was a version of the great farce *Un Chapeau de Paille d'Italie*. Another rumour was that Fred Sullivan had taken the Globe and was to produce the next Gilbert and Sullivan work there, but the elder Sullivan never became a London manager and, indeed, did not survive to see even the first of his brother's great successes. He died on January 18, 1877 after an illness of only a few weeks' duration, at the age of thirty-nine. In fact, at the time when these and other suggestions were current, Gilbert and Sullivan had not begun a new work. Gilbert was trying to make a success out of the unfortunate *Princess Toto*, his final collaboration with Freddie Clay, and Sullivan had been concentrating on the more serious side of his work. It was not until 1877 that work was begun on *The Sorcerer*. Like *Creatures of Impulse*, the libretto was founded on a short story which Gilbert had written for the *Graphic*'s Christmas edition. This story dealt with the Reverend Stanley Gay, curate, who purchases a love-philtre from Messrs Baylis and

Culpepper, Magicians, of St Martin's Lane and causes havoc in his village by his philanthropic distribution of it. Gilbert now elaborated this idea into a two-act musical.

The machinery which was to lead to its production had already been set in motion. The previous year Richard D'Oyly Carte had formed the Comedy Opera Company with the object of presenting the next work of the already successful duo. Carte had already tried his hand in a number of roles in the world of the musical theatre, firstly as a composer (*Dr. Ambrosias*, *Marie*, *Happy Hampstead*), then as an agent and as a manager for Dolaro and Kate Santley in which capacity he had been largely responsible for the production of *Trial by Jury*. Now he was to try himself as an impresario, with the finance of his Comedy Opera Co. behind him, and with the impressive asset of the as yet unwritten Gilbert and Sullivan musical.

The forthcoming production of *The Sorcerer* aroused much speculation as information filtered gradually through to the public of what they were likely to see. Carte announced that he had secured the Opera Comique, scarcely a favourable omen as the old theatre had housed little but flops. Then the opening was announced for October 29, and cancelled. On November 4 a shadow of the character of the new work was given in an advertisement inserted by Carte in *The Era:*

> In announcing the re-opening of this theatre, I wish to address a few words to the public. It is many years since the management of any theatre in London devoted to musical performances has relied for his opening programme entirely on the products of an English author and composer. But the taste of English audiences is turning in this direction and it is a matter of fact that of all the light operas native and foreign that have been given of late years the most remarkably successful has been the little piece *Trial by Jury*, the joint work of our English dramatist, Mr W. S. Gilbert, and our English composer, Mr Arthur Sullivan. In arranging, as I am happy to able to announce that I have done, for a new opera of more important dimensions by the popular author and composer above named, I believe that I have secured an attraction which will at any rate – whatever may be its ultimate result – command the attention of all who are interested in a legitimate lyric performance, a performance which will depend for its success simply on its merits and not on any meretricious displays of costume – or rather absence of costume – or by any objectionable suggestiveness of motive or dialogue. To such a performance I believe many will come who have stayed away from fear of having to sit through hours of dull and unwholesome frivolity . . .. Author, composer, singers and actors are all English. I appeal to the public to come forward and support the undertaking. On them it depends whether it can be made to assume a permanent character or not.

The whole announcement had an unmistakeable air of the German Reeds about it. Carte's professed motives and intentions sounded like an attempt to shift the spirit of The Gallery of Illustration into a 'real' theatre. There was to be no *Babil and Bijou* splendour, no Kate Santley or Harry Paulton, no Emily Soldene or Mlle Sara, no Claude Marius or Toole or Pattie Laverne. Perhaps Carte had lured Priscilla Reed back to the theatre, and maybe Fanny Holland and Corney Grain too.

When the cast of *The Sorcerer* was announced it included none of the established musical stars of the day. Carte could not have Mrs Reed, but he had secured the next best thing–Mrs Howard Paul, née Isabella Featherstone. Mrs Paul had shown a virtuosity equal to that of Mrs Reed as a young woman. She had made a great success as Captain Macheath in *The Beggar's Opera*, she had played Lady Macbeth opposite Phelps and had appeared on a number of occasions as Offenbach's Grande Duchesse.

Like Mrs Reed she had a strong contralto voice and was presently engaged in giving a Drawing Room Entertainment with her American husband which consisted of impersonations and songs in the same style as Priscilla Reed's former act. In place of Fanny Holland the choice of prima donna fell on a young Anglo-Australian, Alice May. Miss May (Mrs G. B. Allen) had only recently returned to Britain after establishing herself in the southern hemisphere. She had played leading roles in India and the Orient on her trip across to England with Richard South's light opera company, and had toured with them in opéra-bouffe on their arrival in Britain. Soon, however, she left the company and made her grand opera début as Marguerite (*Faust*) at Leicester, and before long she had signed for *The Sorcerer*.

The comedy lead of John Wellington Wells, the sorcerer of the title, presented more of a problem. Corney Grain would have been ideal and, of course, had he lived the role would have gone, like all its successors, to Fred Sullivan. Gilbert and Sullivan had a clear idea of what they wanted in this important part and none of their usual comics – Taylor, Penley, Stoyle, Honey – fitted the bill. But earlier in the year Gilbert had staged a production of *Trial by Jury* at the Bijou, Bayswater, where the role of the Judge had been played by George Grossmith, son of the famous piano monologuist and, like his father and John Parry and Grain, a drawing room entertainer. Arthur Cecil reminded the author and the composer of Grossmith and it was on him that their choice fell. After a battle with their directors they had their way and Grossmith was hired. From the world of opera they added Giulia Warwick of the Carl Rosa company and the young tenor George Bentham, formerly a clerk in the war office but now a 'veteran' of Mapleson's Opera Company; while the other principals included twenty-four year old Rutland Barrington, a member of Mrs Paul's troupe for whom she had apparently insisted that a place be found; Harriet Everard (Mrs George Beswick), a 33-year-old contralto (formerly of the Strand Theatre and *Babil and Bijou*) who as 'Miss Everard' would become a D'Oyly Carte stalwart until her tragic early death; and the experienced musical performer Richard Temple who had created the role of Buckingham in Cellier's *Nell Gwynne*. The scenery was ordered from the Reeds' favourite artists, Gordon and Harford, and Miss May's husband, George Allen, composer of the operetta *Castle Grim*, was engaged as conductor.

The Sorcerer was announced, for the second time, for November 12, but it finally opened on the 17th. The evening began with Arthur Cecil and Alfred Cellier's *Dora's Dream* featuring Temple and Miss Warwick in the roles originally written for Cecil himself and Fanny Holland. The tone of the evening was set. The audience was firmly in German Reed-land and, for the first time since *The Contrabandista*, they were to stay there for a genuine full-length musical. It was a success from the start, but this was due largely to the intrinsic merits of the book and score for the first night was a disastrous occasion. George Bentham had almost completely lost his voice, Giulia Warwick had difficulty in keeping in tune and Alice May sang as if she were at Covent Garden, swamping both the auditorium and the music. *The London and Provincial Entr'acte* found that only Temple and Miss Everard of the whole cast kept in tune and that 'the solo singing is of a decidedly indifferent kind'. One of the biggest disappointments was Isabella Paul who, as the gorgonic Lady Sangazure, did not create the impression hoped for, and Grossmith, paralysed with nerves on what was virtually his début, did not do himself or his role justice.

Nevertheless the public were pleased with what they saw: a genuinely clever and witty libretto allied to charming music, a pleasant and enjoyable evening. Had Carte indulged in the nefarious habit of the modern manager he could have decorated the front of the Opera Comique with some superb quotes:

> An elixir of harmless fun . . some of the brightest and most sparkling music ever heard in an English opera. There is not a dull bar in the whole score (*Era*)
>
> Exquisite original music accompanied with musical parodies which are full of humour (*Observer*)

The praise, however, was far from unanimous. *The Entr'acte*, which had criticised the singing so severely, recorded that Sullivan's music was 'if not brilliant always above the commonplace' and seemed, if anything, to have preferred the score of *Dora's Dream*. The London *Figaro* hated the whole thing. It accused Gilbert of being repetitive and lacking in fresh ideas and called the music 'an utterly incongruous mixture of ballads and parodies'. A number of the critics spent a large part of their notice discussing the nature of 'comic opera' and arguing as to whether *The Sorcerer* fitted into that particular box, and complaining that the collaborators hadn't tried to write a *Nozze di Figaro* or a *Fille du Régiment*:

> The only cause for regret is that when Mr W. S. Gilbert and Mr Arthur Sullivan took English comic opera by the hand they did not produce something of a higher grade and more worthy of their individual fame in their respective branches of art.

The story had been skilfully evolved but kept, nevertheless, simple and comprehensible. The young curate of the original story was split in two and became an elderly curate, Dr Daly, and young Alexis Poindextre, son of the local baronet. It is Alexis who, musing on the blessings of love on the day of his betrothal to Aline Sangazure, resolves to treat the whole village to a draught of love-potion so that they too may feel the joys of love. To this end he summons the sorcerer, John Wellington Wells, who provides the potion which Alexis adds to the convivial teapot. In true fairytale fashion the awakening victims fall reciprocally for the first (unmarried) person they see – it is a very proper love-philtre 'compounded on the strictest principles'. But chaos ensues. The baronet falls for his pew-opener; Constance, who adores the curate, finds herself irresistably drawn to the deaf old notary; but worst, Aline, chided by Alexis for refusing to take the potion to reinforce their love, sips it and sees . . Dr Daly! Finally, Lady Sangazure sees Wells, but he has not taken the draught and does not reciprocate. To end the situation Wells declares that the person responsible (either he or Alexis) must sacrifice himself so that all may be restored. He would prefer it to be Alexis 'as we take stock next week, and it would not be fair on the company'. But Aline points out that if all is to be restored, Alexis must be restored to her. The logic is irrefutable, and as all returns to normality, John Wellington Wells sinks into the fiery depths.

It was a basically straightforward plot involving the change-of-identity motif which had already become indispensable to Gilbert, cleverly worked through although not always quite consistent, yet unfailingly humorous. The lyrical predominated in the song-words, but there was much imagination invested in the comic songs, notably Wells' patter song:

> My name is John Wellington Wells
> I'm a dealer in magic and spells
> In blessings and curses
> And ever-filled purses
> In prophecies, witches and knells.
> If you want a proud foe to make tracks

If you'd melt a rich uncle in wax
You've but to look in
On our resident Djinn
Number seventy, Simmery Axe

a duet for Sir Marmaduke and Lady Sangazure, and, above all, in the duet for Wells and the lovesick Lady as she throws herself bodily at his obdurate head:

W: Hate me! I drop my H's–have through life
S: Love me, I'll drop them too!
W: Hate me! I always eat peas with a knife!
S: Love me! I'll eat like you!
W: Hate me! I spend the day at Rosherville!
S: Love me! That joy I'll share!
W: Hate me! I often roll down One Tree Hill!
S: Love me! I'll join you there!
Love me! My prejudices I will drop
W: Hate me! That's not enough!
S: Love me! I'll come and help you in the shop!
W: Hate me! The life is rough!
S: Love me! My grammar I will all foreswear!
W: Hate me! Abjure my lot!
S: Love me! I'll stick sunflowers in my hair!
W: Hate me! They'll suit you not!

The music too, often lyrical, almost classical, was always light and spirited. Never a vulgar burlesque of opera or church music, though frequently echoing both, it was joyously or lugubriously comic as required, though, again, never with the rumbustiousness of the popular song or a Kate Santley point number. It was refined. Gilbert and Sullivan had achieved what Carte had professedly set out to do, produced a full-sized Gallery of Illustration show–witty and merry yet refined and classy. And the new impresario's judgement was quickly confirmed as *The Sorcerer* drew excellent houses for many weeks.

Unfortunately, the few carpers included some of the directors of the Comedy Opera Company. The same people who had criticised the hiring of Grossmith also had ridiculously little faith in Carte. In January when the houses began to thin a little they immediately agitated to close the show. Carte fought back and, on a number of occasions, last nights were advertised only to be withdrawn as business picked up. *The Sorcerer* eventually held its place until May before Carte gave in and withdrew the piece after 175 performances.

During the run Isabella Paul had left. She had never been at the height of her considerable powers as Lady Sangazure and her understudy, Rosina Brandram, had been called on to take over on a number of occasions before Mrs Paul, nervously and vocally exhausted, retired. An unexpected problem arose over the tenor, Bentham, when the Brigade of Guards objected officially to his costume–an exact copy of their uniform. Gilbert treated a tentative approach by the Lord Chamberlain with characteristic bluntness and Bentham kept his clothes. But he too had been a disappointment and when the touring company of *The Sorcerer* was arranged in March he was transferred thence, leaving the role of Alexis to the willowy George Power (later Sir George Power, Bart.). Alice May dropped out to go to the Philharmonic as Drogan in *Geneviève de Brabant* and her husband abandoned his podium to Alfred Cellier, but

Temple, Grossmith, Barrington and Miss Everard maintained their roles throughout the run. Already the nucleus of the Gilbert and Sullivan 'team' was formed.

The Sorcerer remained an intermittent part of the D'Oyly Carte repertoire for many years and was twice revived at the Savoy. It was repeatedly performed throughout the world under the management of Carte and a multitude of others without ever truly being given full membership by acclamation of the eventual Gilbert & Sullivan canon. Its final revival by the D'Oyly Carte Company served to show its enormous virtues as well as the differences which had helped to keep it so unfairly at a distance. For in *The Sorcerer* neither Gilbert nor Sullivan had entirely shaken themselves free of their operatic and burlesque antecedents to settle in to the highly individual style which was to bring them fame. Nevertheless, *The Sorcerer* remains a charming musical which has well deserved its long life.

Two short-lived new pieces made their appearance in the provinces. The musical director of Harry Burnette's touring company, F. W. Allwood, wrote an opéra-bouffe for their repertoire which he called *Haymaking or The Pleasures of Country Life*. It was a burlesque-type piece with a slight pastoral story, a 'grand ballet' and 'an irresistably comic burlesque of the stock melodramatic villain from Mr. Garside' (*Era*). It was played a number of times with a reasonable success in the company's Scottish tour.

The other piece also showed a heavy burlesque influence. *Bluff King Hal* was produced at Cheltenham in April as part of the touring baggage of Harry Lewens' London Opéra-Bouffe Co. which was touring secondary dates with *La Fille de Madame Angot* and *Geneviève de Brabant*. Its story was in the familiar pattern, dealing with lovers' complications among the wayward King Hal, Queen Katherine Parr, Sir Francis Drake and his young lady, and involving Drake and his off-sider being immured in the Tower of London where the girls come in disguise, etc. Affairs are interrupted by a comic but confusing sextet of all Henry's wives before everything is amicably sorted out. Clement O'Neil's book was little more than a vehicle for burlesque comedy and music. It was full of the usual topical and political references and included the currently popular burlesque lecture on anatomy and physics. The music was by the same George Richardson who had tried to 'improve' *Angot* at the Philharmonic. It met with certain approval from *The Era*'s Cheltenham correspondent who described it as having 'some really pretty melodies, thoroughly English in tone'. *Bluff King Hal* was performed at Gloucester, Derby and Rochdale but gradually dropped out of the company's repertoire in favour of the established French pieces.

There was no shortage in the supply of new short works and the Reeds at St George's Hall were, as usual, the chief purveyors. In 1877 they were responsible for six new one-acters, two from Gilbert a'Beckett, two from their own performer, Arthur Law (one under the quickly discarded pen-name of 'West Cromer'), the annual F. C. Burnand and a new version of the Dolls' House idea by William Wye. The first to appear was Law's *A Night Surprise* – a tour de force for Dick Grain as a sleep-walking, cake-stealing operatic composer who, while sleep-walking and cake-stealing gives a full-blown recital of his latest work including singing, dancing and orchestral imitations. Less showy and less successful was a'Beckett's unoriginal *Two Foster Brothers*. Set in a Somerset farm-kitchen, it dealt with a farm-worker and his landlord who are discovered to have been swapped as babies. But neither gets on with his restored position in life, and they happily change back. Even music by Alfred Cellier could not sufficiently redeem the pilfered plot.

For the next offering Reed again supplied the music, to Burnand's script of *Number 204*. The title referred to an hotel room and the plot was a mixture of marital jealousies involving two young couples. It was played up to the summer recess with another Arthur Law piece, *A Happy Bungalow*, which was set in India and centred on the problems of a newly-wed couple lumbered with an auntie and how they plot to get rid of her. This programme was considered to be one of the best since Gallery of Illustration days, but enjoyable though the little pieces may have been, they were still far inferior to those produced previously by Gilbert and Clay and Stephenson and Cellier.

After the summer Reed restaged *A Night Surprise* with *A Happy Bungalow* until their newest piece, *Once in a Century*, was ready to go on. If Gilbert a'Beckett had plundered *The Gentleman in Black* in particular and Gilbert in general for *Two Foster Brothers*, he was even more brazen in his stealing from *Ages Ago* for this play. Curses, lovers, ghosts, plot-line were all taken quite unaltered into the so-called original work. Even the title reflected the span of time stipulated between events in *Ages Ago*. The final new offering was a second Christmas piece from Wye and Cotsford Dick entitled *Our New Dolls' House*. Once again the toys came to life including a new face in the company, Miss Carlotta Carrington.

Other short pieces included *Contempt of Court*, a professed imitation of *Trial by Jury* written by the actor Arthur Matthison and composed by Edward Solomon. In fact the pieces were quite dissimilar. Matthison's plot concerned one Miss Amelia Tarton who wishes to marry a deaf and dumb young man. Her mother forbids her and Amelia takes her parent to court to win her young man. Mama argues that she has little enough control over other sons-in-law, how could she manage one who is deaf and dumb? The Magistrate points out that such a son-in-law could never contradict her and Mrs Tarton is won over. The highlight of the piece was the pantomime performed by Mr Wyatt as he gave his deaf-and-dumb evidence in a caricature of an operatic tenor, but with no voice.

Matthison also wrote another, more whimsical, piece to precede *England in the Days of King Charles II* at Drury Lane. *Barbazon* was a little fairy story about a dukedom of that name. Count Otto comes to win the Lady Dulcinetta and, to test his breeding, dines with the Duke. Absentmindedly he eats his peas with a knife and is condemned. But for his last wish he cleverly demands the eyes of him who saw him err. Since this is the Duke, he is reprieved.

The music for *Barbazon* was by Ferdinand Wallerstein who had been concentrating largely on more grandly operatic pieces and the *Globe* was among many papers to appreciate his contribution:

> . . Mr Wallerstein's music is quaint, fresh, original and melodious and far above the average of such works . .

His best piece was the Duke's song 'The Monarch of all Work':

> 'I'm Duke, I'm King and I'm Parliament too . . '

But *Barbazon* got a frightful reception on its opening night. The general consensus was that the audience had been rather unfair in its eagerness to see the evening's main piece, but *Barbazon* was withdrawn after only a week and replaced by *Sarah's Young Man*. *England in the Days of King Charles II*, which had been a cause of its downfall, lasted only three weeks longer. *Barbazon* resurfaced in Dresden at a later date but was never reproduced in London.

D'Oyly Carte's one-acter *Happy Hampstead* was given its first London performance at the Royalty and Cellier's *Dora's Dream* reached a wider public at the Opera Comique while Julian Edwards made his London début when his newest piece *Dorothy* was performed at the Ladbroke Hall in Notting Hill. *Dorothy*, which had originally been produced in Colchester earlier in the year, was a typical 'country' libretto with the heroine preferring her farmer to a rich husband chosen by her father. It made a second London appearance at the Alexandra Palace in Cattle Show week as part of the entertainment and was later used as a touring forepiece by D'Oyly Carte.

1877

0023 **THE SORCERER** a comic opera in two acts by W. S. Gilbert. Music by Arthur Sullivan. Produced at the Opera Comique under the management of Richard D'Oyly Carte for the Comedy Opera Company 17 November, 1877 for a run of 175 performances closing 24 May, 1878.

Sir Marmaduke Pointdextre	Richard Temple
Alexis	George Bentham/George Power
Dr Daly	Rutland Barrington
Notary	Fred Clifton
John Wellington Wells	George Grossmith
Lady Sangazure	Mrs Howard Paul/Rosina Brandram
Aline	Alice May/Gertrude Cave-Ashton/ Giulia Warwick/Irene Ware
Mrs Partlett	Harriet Everard (Isabelle Muncey)
Constance	Giulia Warwick (Bella Richmond)/ Lisa Walton (Miss Bernard)

Dir: Charles Harris; md: G. B. Allen/Alfred Cellier/Eugene Goossens; ch: John D'Auban; sc: Gordon & Harford

Played at a matinée at the Opera Comique 24 August, 1878.
Richard Temple (MAR), Gerard Coventry (ALEX), Rutland Barrington (DR), Fred Clifton (NOT), George Grossmith (JWW), Rosina Brandram (SANG), Douglas Gordon (AL), Harriet Everard (PAR), Theresa Cummings (CON)

Produced at the Broadway Theatre, New York under the management of Chandos Fulton and George Edgar 21 February, 1879 for a run of 20 performances closing 8 March, 1979.
J. F. Graff (ALEX), W. Horace Lingard (JWW), Matilda Scott (AL), Florence Wood, Annie Boudinot, Minnie Clive, Tom Bullock, W. H. Crompton &c.

Produced at the Lyceum Theatre, New York, by the Philadelphia Arch Street Theatre Company (Campbell's Comic Opera Co.) 10 March, 1879 for a season of two weeks in repertoire with *H.M.S. Pinafore*; cast included Louise Leighton, Nellie Mortimer, Helen Corbyn, J. F. Graff, Charles Dunham, George Gaston, W. Haydon Tilla.

Produced at the Bijou Theatre, New York, under the management of John A. McCaull 16 October, 1882 for a run of 92 performances closing 6 January, 1883.
George Olmi (MAR), Charles J. Campbell (ALEX), Digby V. Bell (DR), George A. Schiller (NOT), John Howson (JWW), Laura Joyce (SANG), Lillian Russell/Madeleine Lucette (AL), Julie de Ruyther (PAR), Madeleine Lucette/Emie Weathersby (CON), A. W. Maflin (BUTTONS)

Produced at the Casino Theatre, New York by John McCaull's Company 17 April, 1883 for a season of three weeks closing 4 May, 1883.

Produced at the Savoy Theatre in a revised version under the management of Richard D'Oyly Carte 11 October, 1884 for a run of 150 performances closing 12 March, 1885.
Richard Temple (MAR), Durward Lely (ALEX), Rutland Barrington (DR), William Lugg (NOT), George Grossmith (JWW), Rosina Brandram (SANG), Leonora Braham (AL), Ada Doree (PAR), Jessie Bond/Alice Davies (CON)

Md: François Cellier; sc: W. Beverley; cos: Auguste, Cater and Co., J. B. Johnstone, Ede & Son, Frank Smith & Co., Hobson & Co.

Produced at the Savoy Theatre under the management of Richard D'Oyly Carte 22 September, 1898 for a run of 102 performances closing 31 December, 1898.
Jones Hewson/Richard Temple (MAR), Robert Evett (ALEX), Henry Lytton (DR), Leonard Russell (NOT), Walter Passmore (JWW), Rosina Brandram (SANG), Ruth Vincent (AL), Ethel McAlpine (PAR), Emmie Owen (CON)

Subsequently played by the D'Oyly Carte Opera Company on tour and in London in repertoire.

TV/Video: 1984 Brent Walker Ltd. Pr: Judith de Paul; dir: Stephen Pimlott; md: Alexander Faris; ch: Terry Gilbert; sc: Allan Cameron; cos: Jenny Beavan
Donald Adams (MAR), Alexander Oliver (ALEX), Clive Revill (JWW), Nuala Willis (SANG), Nan Christie (AL), Enid Hartle (PAR), Janis Kelly (CON)

HAYMAKING or The Pleasures of Country Life, an opéra-bouffe composed by F. W. Allwood. Produced at Kilmarnock under the management of Harry Burnette 16 March, 1877 and toured through Barrow, Whitehaven, Greenock, Dundee &c.
Cast included Lillian Lancaster, Annie Mulvey, Minnie Mulvey, Mrs Charles Pitt, Fred Stanmaur, Fred C. Harcourt, Edward E. Garside, Charles G. Wallace.

BLUFF KING HAL King and Martyr, an opéra-bouffe by Clement O'Neil. Music by George Richardson. Produced at Cheltenham under the management of Harry Lewens 10 April, 1877 and toured in repertoire.

King Hal . . . . Henry Lewens
Wolsey . . . . J. B. Rae
Old Parr. . . . . J. B. Wallace
Kate Parr . . . . E. Adams
Anne Page. . . . . Agnes Lyndhurst
Drake . . . . Fanny Harrison
Marie . . . . Miss Bodson
Sidney. . . . . Henry Gordon

Md: Louis Hermann; cos: M. Alias & Henry Compton

DOROTHY a comic operetta by Julian Edwards. Produced at Colchester under the management of Fanny Edwards 13 January, 1877 and toured in repertoire. Performed at the Ladbroke Hall, Notting Hill 24 September, 1877 and at the Alexandra Palace December, 1877. Original cast included George Challoner, Arthur Rousbey, Alfred Rivers, Fanny Edwards.

London cast:
Mr Cherrytree . . . . Wilfred Esmond
Dorothy . . . . Fanny Edwards
Sidney Darrell . . . . Michael Dwyer
Lubin . . . . Harry Symonds
Phoebe . . . . Annie Kinnaird/Miss Greville

A NIGHT SURPRISE by 'West Cromer' (Arthur Law). Music by T. German Reed. Produced at St George's Hall under the management of T. German Reed 12 February, 1877 with *Matched and Mated* and *Spring Delights*, the former replaced by *Two Foster Brothers* (12 March) and the latter by *Five o'Clock Tea*. Withdrawn 5 May, 1877. Reopened 1 October, 1877 with *A Happy Bungalow* and *At the Seaside*. Withdrawn 13 October, 1877.

Dr Magnet Sharp . . . . Arthur Law
Chubb. . . . . Alfred Reed
Herr Tileoff. . . . . R. Corney Grain
Matilda . . . . Leonora Braham
Muriel Ripley . . . . Fanny Holland

TWO FOSTER BROTHERS by Gilbert a'Beckett. Music by Alfred Cellier. Produced at St George's Hall under the management of T. German Reed 12 March, 1877 with *Spring Delights* and *A Night Surprise*, the former replaced by *Five o'Clock Tea* and subsequently *Edwin and Angelina*, the latter (May 7) by *Number 204*. Withdrawn 9 June, 1877.

James Winzle . . . . Alfred Reed
Thomas Cupid Growl . . . . Arthur Law
Lady Fyddleton. . . . . Mrs German Reed
Margery Primrose. . . . . Leonora Braham
Sir Talbot Towers . . . . R. Corney Grain

NUMBER 204 by F. C. Burnand. Music by T. German Reed. Produced at St George's Hall under the management of T. German Reed 7 May, 1877 with *Edwin and Angelina* and *Two Foster Brothers*. Withdrawn 16 July. Reopened October 15 with *A Happy Bungalow* and *At the Seaside*, the former replaced (November 12) by *Once in a Century*. Withdrawn 20 November.

The cast included Fanny Holland, Leonora Braham, Arthur Law and Alfred Reed.

Produced at St George's Hall October 21, 1878 with *Charity Begins at Home* and *Mrs. Brown*. Withdrawn 4 November, 1878.
Rosa Leo, Fanny Holland, Alfred Reed, Arthur Law.

Produced at St George's Hall November 14, 1881 with *Cherry Tree Farm*, replaced (November 21) by *Ages Ago*. Withdrawn 17 December. Reopened 30 January, 1882. Withdrawn February 25, 1882.

A HAPPY BUNGALOW by Arthur Law. Music by King Hall. Produced at St George's Hall under the management of T. German Reed 11 June, 1877 with *Edwin and Angelina* and *Number 204*. Withdrawn 16 July. Reopened October 1 with *A Night Surprise* and *At the Seaside*, the former replaced (October 15) by *Number 204*. Withdrawn 10 November, 1877.

Ethel Newbound . . . . Fanny Holland
Lady Currie. . . . . Mrs German Reed
Jack Newbound. . . . . Arthur Law
Tom Standbye . . . . R. Corney Grain
Madra. Alfred Reed
Amah . . . . Leonora Braham

ONCE IN A CENTURY by Gilbert a'Beckett. Music by Vivian Bligh. Produced at St George's Hall under the management of T. German Reed 12 November, 1877 with *At the Seaside* and *Number 204*, replaced by *A Musical Almanac* and *Our New Dolls' House* (21 December). Withdrawn 2 February, 1878.

Sir Digby Dimple. . . . . Alfred Reed
Michaelangelo Brown/Sir Bouillon de
Boeuf . . . . Arthur Law
Lilian/The Heiress of Whippingham . . . Fanny Holland
Mrs Butterfligh/Lady Leolanda. . . . . . Mrs German Reed
Baily Young/Humphrey the Headsman . R. Corney Grain

OUR NEW DOLLS' HOUSE by W. Wye. Music by Cotsford Dick. Produced at St George's Hall under the management of T. German Reed 21 December, 1877 with *Once in a Century* and *A Musical Almanac*. Withdrawn 2 February, 1878.

Mlle Pat-a-pouf/Little Red Riding
Hood . . . . Leonora Braham
Japanese Doll/Lady de Montmorency . . Fanny Holland
Admiral Sir Lee Scuppers . . . . Alfred Reed
Noah . . . . R. Corney Grain
China Shepherdess . . . . Carlotta Carrington
Sambo. Arthur Law

BUCKINGHAM a comic opera by Julian Edwards. First produced at Northampton Town Hall 28 December, 1877 and toured as part of Fanny Edwards' entertainment.

Margery . . . . Ethel Pierson
Jonathan. . . . . Harry Symonds
Captain Montrose . . . . Wilfred Esmond
Duke of Buckingham . . . . Michael Dwyer
Lady Ann Fairfax . . . . Fanny Edwards

Md: Julian Edwards

BARBAZON or The Fatal Peas, a very serious and very original opera in one act by Arthur Matthison. Music by Ferdinand Wallerstein. Produced at Drury Lane Theatre under the management of F. B. Chatterton 22 September, 1877 as a forepiece to *England in the Days of King Charles II*. Withdrawn 28 September, 1877.

Duke of Barbazon. . . . . Arthur Matthison
The Lady Dulcinetta . . . . Harriet Coveney
Lord Chamberlain . . . . Edward J. George
Count Otto . . . . Miss Stembridge
Confidentia . . . . Clara Jecks
Grand Steward . . . . Mr Lingham
Commander-in-Chief . . . . Mr Byrne

CONTEMPT OF COURT a romantic cantata in one act by Arthur Matthison. Music by Edward Solomon. Produced at a matinée at the Folly Theatre 5 May, 1877.

Mr Brownlow . . . . W. Forrester
Magistrate. . . . . J. Furneaux Cook
Mrs Tarton . . . . Harriet Coveney
Defendant. . . . . Mr Wyatt
Amelia Tarton . . . . Selina Dolaro

1878

The Alhambra produced an unexceptional 'spectacular fairy musical pantomimic extravaganza' called *Wildfire* as their Christmas attraction for 1877/8, and Kate Santley kept the French flag flying with her production of *La Marjolaine* while the Strand and the Gaiety put their trust in burlesque, the former with a January production of *The Latest Edition of the Red Rover* and the latter with a continuation of their successful *Little Doctor Faust*. But in spite of internal troubles and disputes, the Comedy Opera Company's production of *The Sorcerer* was doing as well as any and beginning to amass itself a good run. While it was running out its career, Gilbert and Sullivan were already preparing its successor, *H.M.S. Pinafore*, a naval satire based on another of Gilbert's *Bab Ballads*, or rather combining elements from a number of them. From 'Captain Reece' the author extracted his female chorus:

> You have a daughter, Captain Reece,
> Ten female cousins and a niece
> A Ma, if what I'm told is true,
> Six sisters and an aunt or two

From 'The Bumboat Woman's Story' he drew another character, Little Buttercup:

> A Bumboat Woman was I, and I faithfully served the ships
> With apples and cakes and fowls and beer and halfpenny dips
> And beef for the generous mess where the officers dine at nights
> And fine fresh peppermint drops for rollicking midshipmites

This particular sexagenarian lady disguised herself as a sailor to follow her beloved Lieutenant Belaye of the Hot Cross Bun to sea, a theme which Gilbert with his developed horror of travesty left to others.[1] In the same poem we meet the gentlemanly crew of the Hot Cross Bun:

> When Jack Tars meet they meet with a "Messmate ho! What cheer?"
> But here on the *Hot Cross Bun* it was "How do you do, my dear?"
> When Jack Tars growl, I believe they growl with a big, big D
> But the strongest oath of the Hot Cross Buns was a mild "Dear me!"
> Yet though they were all well bred, you could scarcely call them slick,
> Whenever a sea was on, they were all extremely sick

This 'gentlemanly' crew turned out to be a swatch of love-sick maidens in disguise, but their well-bred notions of proper speech were kept alive in the transfer to the stage.

[1] cf. *Billee Taylor*, *The Red Hussar* &c.

Elements from 'General John', 'Lt-Col. Flare', 'Little Oliver' and other works filtered through more or less into the new show, and from 'The Baby's Vengeance' came the crux of the story:

> 'Tis now some thirty-seven years ago
> Since first began the plot that I'm revealing
> A fine young woman whom you ought to know
> Lived with her husband down in Drum Lane, Ealing,
> Herself by means of mangling reimbursing
> And now and then (at intervals) wet-nursing.
> Two little babes dwelt in their humble cot
> Her own she slighted. Tempted by a lot
> Of gold and silver regularly sent to her
> She ministered unto the little other
> In the capacity of foster mother.
>
> One day – it was quite early in the week–
> I in my cradle having placed the bantling
> Crept into his! He had not learned to speak . .

This wicked baby bears more resemblance to the baby of *The Gentleman in Black* than to the children of the new *H.M.S. Pinafore*, but Gilbert was losing the outlandish grotesqueries of burlesque and moving into a more probable if still decidedly quaint type of humour. The weird impossibilities of works like *The Gentleman in Black* were no longer good enough – imagination was now tempered with a little more style and genuine wit. The responsibility for the swapping of the babies in *H.M.S. Pinafore* falls upon the foster mother.

The new show was prepared for the same basic cast which had been so successful with *The Sorcerer* – a prima donna, a primo tenore (Power), a comedy role for Grossmith and two strong baritone roles for Temple and Barrington. The second soprano role had been done away with but the two contraltos, Isabella Paul and Harriet Everard, were provided with good characteristic roles as Hebe, cousin to the First Lord of the Admiralty, and as the reformed baby-farmer. A new prima donna was needed and the choice fell on the American soprano Emma Howson. Miss Howson was from a good musical family. She was a niece of the vocalist Mme Albertazzi; her father, Frank Howson, had produced the earliest English and Italian operas in Australia; and her brother John was building an impressive career as a musical performer. Emma had begun her career in opera in San Francisco and had recently made her European début in Malta as Amina in *La Sonnambula*. At the last minute another new cast member was required for Isabella Paul was not well enough to take up her role[1] and a replacement had to be found. The authors, worried, slashed the role of Hebe down to next to nothing and gave what was left of it to Miss Jessie Bond.

Another problem was the title. Gilbert dithered over it till the last minute. His choice was limited by the necessity of rhyming the name of his ship with 'So give three cheers and one cheer more for the Captain of the . . . '. For a while the more obvious *H.M.S. Semaphore* was considered, but on Saturday 25 May at the Opera Comique it was *H.M.S. Pinafore* or The Lass that Loved a Sailor which made its first appearance to a highly appreciative audience and delighted critics. 'A hit, a palpable hit' howled *The Era* – 'the most laughable libretto imaginable' . . 'music so tuneful and a story so

[1] Mrs Paul died in June the following year at the age of 46.

comical and free from the reproaches so justly levelled against most works of the opéra-bouffe class'. Another journal confirmed:

> *H.M.S. Pinafore* is the best light musical composition written in our language since *The Beggar's Opera* – not excepting Sheridan's *Duenna* and Moore's *M.P.* . *Pinafore* has the advantage over *The Beggar's Opera* in that it contains nothing to offend the most fastidious. It has the lightness, the brightness, the airy cleverness, in short all the good qualities of the best French opéra-bouffe with none of the bad . .

Pinafore was, indeed, a happier, more humorous and more tuneful work than any of its predecessors, constructed with great craft by men of outstanding talent. Josephine, daughter of the Captain of H.M.S. Pinafore, is in love with Ralph Rackstraw, a common sailor on her father's vessel, but her father has destined her for the hand of Sir Joseph Porter, K.C.B., First Lord of the Admiralty. Sir Joseph arrives to inspect his fiancée, accompanied by a bevy of sisters, cousins and aunts, and is rather pleased with the bargain, but Josephine is horrified and, abetted by the crew and Sir Joseph's relatives, she prepares to elope with Ralph. Alas, their flight is betrayed by the horrid Dick Deadeye and the Captain stops the lovers as they try to leave the ship. But in his anger he lets slip an exceedingly ill-bred expression. Sir Joseph is horrified and the Captain finds himself condemned to punishment alongside Ralph. But Little Buttercup, the bumboat woman, has a tale to tell. Once she had two little charges:

> Oh, bitter is my cup, however could I do it
> I mixed those children up, and not a creature knew it . .

As a result: 'The well-born babe was Ralph! Your Captain was the other'; so Ralph is promoted to Captain and the Captain reduced to the ranks. Sir Joseph, who has stoutly maintained that 'Love levels all ranks', decides that it does not level them enough for him to ally himself to the child of a foremast-hand. So the new Captain of the Pinafore weds his Josephine whilst Little Buttercup comforts the ex-Captain and Sir Joseph finds true love with his cousin, Hebe.

The plot line, up to its final dénouement, might not have seemed particularly humorous, but Gilbert decked it with clever dialogue and amusing situations in his own inimitable fashion, aided and abetted all along by Sullivan's most joyful music. There were glorious light operatic tunes as Ralph sang of 'A Maiden fair to See' or joined with his beloved in 'Farewell my Own', but Josephine, debating her dilemma in true prima donna fashion, was allowed more than a glimmer of humour:

> On the one hand Papa's luxurious home
> Hung with ancestral armour and old brasses
> Carved oak and tapestry from distant Rome
> Rare 'blue-and-white' Venetian finger-glasses
> Rich oriental rugs, luxurious sofa pillows
> And everything that isn't old, from Gillow's.
> And on the other, a dark and dingy room
> In some back street with stuffy children crying
> Where organs yell, and clacking housewives fume,
> And clothes are hanging out all day a-drying.
> With one cracked looking-glass to see your face in
> And dinner served up in a pudding-basin!

and the 'humble sailor's' love-making also touched a comical note:

RAL: In me there meet a combination of antithetical elements which are at eternal war with one another. Driven hither by objective influences – thither by subjective emotions – wafted one moment into blazing day, by mocking hope – plunged the next into the Cimmerian darkness of tangible despair, I am but a living ganglion of irreconcilable antagonisms. I hope I make myself clear, lady?

JOS: Perfectly. (*aside*) His simple eloquence goes to my heart . .

It was from the mixture of the comical and the nautical that came the show's greatest immediate hits – Captain Corcoran singing 'I Am the Captain of the Pinafore':

Though related to a peer
I can hand, reef and steer
And ship a selvagee
I am never known to quail
At the fury of the gale
And I'm never never sick at sea!
CH: What never?
CAPT: No, never.
CH: What never?
CAPT: Well, hardly ever . .

Sir Joseph telling of his rise from office boy to 'Ruler of the Queen's Nav-ee', and the seamen's rendering of the glee:

A British tar is a soaring soul
As free as a mountain bird
His energetic fist should be ready to resist
A dictatorial word.
His nose should pant and his lip should curl
His cheeks should flame and his brow should furl
His bosom should heave and his heart should glow
And his fist be ever ready for a knock-down blow!

which provoked enormous enthusiasm even if a little of its satiric intent got lost on the way.

In spite of the excellent public and press reaction, *H.M.S. Pinafore* did not immediately leap into sell-out business, and in July and August the directors, once more highly mistrustful, talked of withdrawing the piece. D'Oyly Carte, the authors and the cast all protested. The business had not been that bad. Only two weeks during the hottest period of the year had failed to meet the break figure. The company was making money. But the directors were ultra-nervous. They seemed determined to cut and run while they were ahead. But they were persuaded and/or bullied into continuing when the cast agreed to salary cuts. Then, suddenly, the show really caught on. The hot weather was over, the town began to pour in to the Opera Comique, and the rise in takings reassured the directors.

The sudden boom in the show's fortunes was not due, however, to the weather alone. Sullivan had become conductor of the Covent Garden Promenade Concerts and during one of his concerts he included a fantasia by Hamilton Clarke based on the tunes from *H.M.S. Pinafore*. It was an enormous success, encored several times, and the Covent Garden audiences and their friends began to head for the Opera Comique. The songs quickly became as popular as 'Spring, gentle Spring' in its heyday and everyone was 'polishing up the handle of the big front door' with George Grossmith:

When I was a lad I served a turn
As office boy to an attorney's firm
I cleaned the windows and I swept the floor
And I polished up the handle of the big front door.
I polished up that handle so carefully
That now I am the ruler of the Queen's Navee!

while Captain Corcoran's catchphrase 'What never?' 'Hardly ever' began an irrepressible career through all levels of society. At last there was no doubt that *H.M.S. Pinafore* was a huge, big hit. The hit of the season, even of the century.

But the French musical was not so easily overrun. Up against the first British international hit the French put another brilliant show, Robert Planquette's *Les Cloches de Corneville* which had become a major success in Paris since its production in April, 1877. Publisher Joseph Williams, having heard just one of the piece's enchanting songs – the bell song with its 'Digue-digue-don' refrain – bought *Les Cloches de Corneville* and it made its London appearance at the tiny Folly Theatre (the former Charing Cross) under Alexander Henderson. Kate Munroe created the prima donna role of Serpolette supported by Violet Cameron, Eily Beaumont, John Howson, M. Loredan, W. J. Hill and Shiel Barry as the miser, Gaspard, a role of which he would make almost a whole career. The English libretto was manufactured by Farnie and Reece. This show, one of the greatest of all French musicals, ran uninterruptedly for more than two years (704 performances) at the Folly and later at the larger Globe. It used up no less than six of the top opéra-bouffe prima donnas (Munroe, Emma Chambers, Kathleen Corri, Kate Santley, Lizzie St Quinten and Clara Thompson) as Serpolette and as many tenors as Grenicheux (Loredan, Frederic Darrell, W. H. Woodfield, Knight Aston, Clavering Power and Wilford Morgan) and flooded the provinces with tours that year and for decades to come. Whether *Pinafore* with less managerial strife would have lasted as long is a moot point, but it is probable that the preparation of Carte's next production would have, under any circumstances, ended the piece's London run. In any case the West End was quite large enough to hold two blockbuster musicals and it did so with equally happy results for both.

But at the height of its popularity the Opera Comique shut down. *Pinafore* was performed to a crowded house on Christmas Eve, 1878, and on Boxing Day the doors stayed resolutely closed. The directors of the Comedy Opera Company had miscalculated badly. It looked as if they were going to kill the goose that was laying them so many golden eggs, for *Pinafore* was now taking great sums at the box-office and although it was announced that the theatre would re-open on February 1st with *Pinafore* again, there were few who thought any production could survive such a break in its run. With their customary 'caution', the directors had decided, earlier in the year, that since *The Sorcerer* had dropped in its takings somewhat over the Christmas and January period the previous year, it would be a good idea to close down over that period and use the time to refurbish the theatre. So for five weeks the Opera Comique stayed dark and the holiday theatregoers went elsewhere. Possibly the directors had not expected *Pinafore* to run until Christmas. If it had been running with less extraordinary vigour they would probably have insisted that it be withdrawn. But to compare the holiday potential of an established hit of four and a half months' run with *The Sorcerer*, barely a month into its initial run and plagued with lost voices and nervous backers, was ridiculous. When *Pinafore* resumed on February 1st with its original cast of principals there were a few breaths being held. But not for long. London flooded back to the Opera Comique and the show was safe although some

£2,000 in clear profit had been thrown away by the unnecessary closing. With the show established as a hit, Carte had organised his *Sorcerer* touring company into a two-piece affair, and in September 1878 it went out for a three months' tour of Number 1 Theatres presenting both *The Sorcerer* and *Pinafore*. By the following year the one company had grown into three (the third playing split weeks at up to four different towns) – two of them headed by Sir Joseph Porters who were to become great stars in the non-musical theatre, W. S. Penley and Richard Mansfield.

By this time the metropolitan production was suffering from a titanic behind-the-scenes battle between Carte, Gilbert and Sullivan on the one hand and the majority of the directors of the Comedy Opera Company on the other. The company had originally been formed by D'Oyly Carte to produce *The Sorcerer*. It was he who had, prior to this, leased the Opera Comique from Lord Dunraven (although in the name of his stage director, Richard Barker) before setting up the Comedy Opera Co. to provide the funds to produce first *The Sorcerer* and then *H.M.S. Pinafore*. This exercise had been carried out to the great profit of all, but Carte had suffered much uninformed interference from his directors in the day-to-day management of the shows and was looking forward to the agreed date when he and the Opera Comique could legally be free of the gentlemen of the Comedy Opera Company. Trouble began to brew as the date approached:

> A breeze which has been gently blowing over *H.M.S. Pinafore* lately is likely to burst into a storm. The Directors of the Opera Comique (who it appears are not Directors after July 31, Mr D'Oyly Carte becoming responsible manager) fancy they are the owners of the vessel in question. Messrs Gilbert and Sullivan are under the impression that they are the rightful owners of the craft. Another ship, in all probability, will be built, injunctions will then be applied for and the First Lord of the Admiralty (with his cousins, his sisters and his aunts), the gallant Captain and crew of the *Pinafore* will, perhaps, appear in court as witnesses. It is evident that two Pinafores will not be permitted to float at the same time in London, and no doubt the owners of the one that must sink will use more than one big D. (*Era*)

Carte had gone to America but he had not left his interests unrepresented. Already he and the authors had settled terms for the next opera – not with the money gained from *Pinafore* as most of that had gone to the investors of the Comedy Company, but with the aid of Michael Gunn, erstwhile manager of the Gaiety, Dublin. It was the same Gunn who, with the consent of the directors, Carte installed in his place as manager of the Opera Comique during his absence. No sooner had he sailed than the trouble started. The directors attempted to eject first Gunn, then Carte *in absentia* from the management. They failed, but they had shown their hand.

With Carte still away the *Pinafore* company played what was to be their 374th and last performance under the direction of the Comedy Co., and not a peaceful one. Reports of the evening's events vary, as they did in the subsequent court proceedings, but what is certain is that two of the directors, Messrs Collard Augustus Drake and Edward H. Bayley, accompanied by their lawyer, Cecil Chappell, and what were later described as 'a band of roughs' invaded the back-stage of the Opera Comique during the performance to establish their right to the scenery and effects of the production and, if necessary, to remove them by force. Stage manager Richard Barker refused to submit and the 'hired men' moved into action. The gasmen took up arms to protect their gashouse, where the stage-lighting was controlled, as the bullies tried to plunge the theatre into darkness. This defence was victorious and so the main attack was made under less favourable conditions. Someone, whether by guile or stupidity, called down

'Fire!' from the flies and the audience began to panic. Various cast members tried to calm them with the truth while the stage hands rallied to the buxom Harriet Everard as she laid into the attackers who were finally forced to retreat, beaten, to the cheers of the audience. The show went on. One casualty, however, was Richard Barker, who had been pushed down the stairs. He sued Drake, Bayley and Chappell for assault.

The Comedy Company had lost a battle but the war continued. The very next night a second production of *Pinafore* opened in London at the old Royal Aquarium, rechristened the Imperial Theatre for the occasion. It offered several defectors from D'Oyly Carte's touring companies – Arthur Rousbey, Michael Dwyer, Fanny Edwards – while Isabelle Muncey took the chance of promotion from understudy to the role of Hebe. It also offered Lizzie Mulholland and the grand comic J. G. Taylor (who had already played Sir Joseph in an American version) in the starring roles, and free admission to the Aquarium. Gilbert and Sullivan applied for an injunction to stop the performances. They won, then lost on appeal. The claim to the copyright of the work was in question and the judges carefully opined that there was 'doubt as to the terms of the contract'. After five weeks at the Imperial the new production was switched to the Olympic, just down the road from the Opera Comique. But the public showed a distinct preference for Carte's version, and after another seven weeks, five Josephines and some departures from both script and score[1] the Olympic production folded. Suings and countersuings continued, for the rights to *H.M.S. Pinafore* were clearly going to be of great value.

The value had been much intensified by the show's extraordinary overseas success. America had been quick to pick *Pinafore* up, and it appeared in Boston on 25 November 1878. At the Bush Theatre, San Francisco in a production by Alice Oates' Company, the mangeress starred herself as Ralph Rackstraw. It was announced that 'the lack of good music would be remedied by the interpolation of familiar nautical songs' and, in consequence, Rackstraw rendered 'A Life on the Ocean Wave', Corcoran 'Nancy Lee' and Bill Bobstay 'Rule, Britannia' while the chorus contributed 'The Larboard Watch'. Mrs Oates decided that *Pinafore* did not have a suitable role for her Yorkshire tenor 'Dick' Beverley. A large part christened 'Dick Truck' was bodily interpolated. John T. Ford's company took *H.M.S. Pinafore* to Baltimore and Philadelphia before the first New York production appeared under John Duff's management at the Standard on 15 January 1879. Little more than a week later the Lyceum opened a rival production and in February *The Era*'s US correspondent was able to report that there were twenty-two companies performing various *Pinafores* in the United States. Doubtless there were more. Stock and road companies threw together unlikely productions bearing more or less of a resemblance to the original, interpolating bits of their own repertoire and modern American songs to suit their tastes. The New York productions were normally less haphazard. The original Duff production hung on by virtue of quality but it faced literally dozens of other 'Broadway' versions. There was an all-negro company, a children's version, one with a female impersonator as Buttercup, several with a female Ralph and one, Blanche Corelli's Superb Burlesque Company, cast entirely with women. There was one very successful one composed of church choir singers from Philadelphia. Then there were the inevitable burlesques. Tony Pastor staged *T.P.S. Canal Boat Pinafore* and the San Francisco Minstrels performed a sketch called *No Pinafore* in which all the characters ended up hung from the yardarm.

[1] Wilford Morgan is said to have interpolated the ballad 'My Sweetheart when a Boy' into Act 1.

At the height of the craze there were reported to be more than 150 companies playing *Pinafore* throughout the country, but by November 1879 only the church choir company still held the boards on Broadway until Carte, Gilbert and Sullivan arrived in New York with their own English company and opened at the Fifth Avenue Theatre. They brought two original cast members, Fred Clifton and Jessie Bond, and two expatriate Americans, Blanche Roosevelt (who had been Blanche Tucker in America, Mme Rosavilla in opera, and most famously Mme Macchetta as the *amie* of Guy de Maupassant) who had already sung Josephine at the Opera Comique, and Sgr Broccolini (John Clark from Brooklyn) who had toured with Penley as Dick Deadeye. Thus New York was finally treated to a definitive version of *Pinafore*. Gilbert directed, and on the first night actually took to the stage amongst the chorus to keep things moving. Unfortunately he or someone else deemed it necessary to trick the audience by altering the best-known lines. To hear Captain Corcoran reply to 'What never?' with 'Very seldom' did little but baffle the listeners.

Pinafore's 'correct' version played only four weeks at the Fifth Avenue, for the main purpose of the visit of Carte's company was to present the newest Gilbert and Sullivan show, *The Pirates of Penzance*. Having seen their work destroyed by interpolations, excisions and eccentric performers at absolutely no profit to themselves through the vagaries of the existing copyright laws, the partners determined that their next work should be premièred simultaneously in America and England. So after four weeks the 'real' *Pinafore* was withdrawn.

If *H.M.S. Pinafore* had proved a landmark in Britain where English-language musicals had succeeded in the previous decade in establishing some sort of a nascent tradition, it was a bombshell in America where *Black Crook* type extravaganza, French opéra-bouffe and home-grown vaudeville comprised the staple diet. Here was a consistent, intelligent and humorous libretto set to music of real quality; a work which was an entity in itself where the words and music and plot were actually relevant and even important to one another. If the British musical's first international hit provided a cornerstone for the further development of the genre in Britain, it was virtually the rock on which the next stage of the American tradition based itself.

America was not the only country anxious to get hold of *H.M.S.Pinafore*. Actor-impresario J. C. Williamson made arrangements with Carte for the Australian and New Zealand rights but, not unexpectedly, the gun had been jumped. In New Zealand a certain 'Sgr. Ricciardi' organised a *Pinafore* 'assembled' by himself and set off on a disastrous tour. Houses were good enough, but Ricciardi's accounting was impossible. He left a stream of debts behind him through the South Island and finally, in Wellington, had his scenery seized for debt in the middle of the show. Horace Lingard's company came on behind with a more accurate but equally unauthorised *Pinafore* and Williamson could only sue. Later an 'original' New Zealand musical called *Kianga* appeared with familiar music – it had helped itself not only to chunks of *Pinafore* but of *The Sorcerer* as well.

In Australia Williamson himself appeared as Sir Joseph with his wife, Maggie Moore, as Josephine. But once again they had been beaten to the start by Kelly and Leon's Minstrels, another odd production with a male Buttercup. Their version was successful enough, before being legally banned, for them to write and produce a 'sequel' called *Sir Joseph at Sea*. India and Cuba both witnessed *Pinafores* in 1879, and in 1881 a German-language production titled *Amor am Bord* appeared in Berlin as *H.M.S. Pinafore* spread itself to all corners of the theatrical world.

In London, the piece continued its popular and prosperous run at the Opera

Comique. Josephines came and went. Emma Howson after some 240 performances yielded place to Alice Burville; Elinor Loveday and Duglas Gordon, the touring prima donnas, each had a spell in town as did Blanche Roosevelt; and on December 29, 1879 the prototype herself stepped in. Fanny Holland had left St George's Hall to tour an Entertainment with her husband, Arthur Law, when she was offered the opportunity of appearing at the Opera Comique, and she played out the final months of the run as her only appearance in a Gilbert and Sullivan opera.

Pinafore was a phenomenon: a necessary and fortunate one, coming as it did at a point where a major work was needed to give a base and impetus to the slowly expanding British musical theatre. Its integral value is emphasised by its continued popularity and frequent production a century and more after its first appearance.

In comparison with *Pinafore* any other new British work was bound to look a little pale but, as it happened, the only other new major offering of the year was a distinctly limp piece. Alfred Cellier, now known and celebrated, was still trying to repeat the success of *The Sultan of Mocha* and in his loose connection with the Manchester theatre he joined forces with the new manager of the Prince's and the Theatre Royal, author/designer Alfred Thompson. The two collaborated on a piece called *Belladonna* or The Little Beauty and the Great Beast which was presented in Manchester at the end of April for the usual four-week season, starring Selina Dolaro and the popular music hall comedian Arthur Roberts. It lasted only three. Thompson's book was certainly better than that for *Tower of London* and more whimsical than that for the stolidly English *Nell Gwynne*. It had some flavour of *Princess Toto* about it, but it lacked the stylish charm of Gilbert's piece.

The Era complained 'the plot is weak almost to puerility', and, indeed, it was not of the standard of Thompson's *Aladdin II* or *Cinderella the Younger*. Drearibboi is a miser with eight daughters and sixteen nieces to keep. One of his daughters, the lovely Belladonna, catches the eye of the handsome Prince Lupo, but Lupo is a spoiled and nasty piece of goods with a Mother, and, besides, Belladonna is carelessly engaged to one Juanito whom her father believes to be a wealthy farmer. In fact he is a particularly chauvinistic Brigand Chief and, when their wedding is held up because Juanito's band has waylaid the wretched Padre, he whisks Belladonna off to his lair to use her as a lure for rich tourists. She duly lures, and the captives are her father and Prince Lupo. The heroine drugs the bandits and everyone escapes back to Nonotia. The final scene is in the Palace where the invading brigands are beaten back by the girls of the village led by Belladonna en vivandière. Lupo, who is now a reformed character, keeps his kingdom and wins Belladonna.

There was little in all this to work on, and even the boisterous Roberts could get little fun out of the dialogue and character of Drearibboi. Dolaro, of course, was heavily armed with music – a Spanish number about 'Mercedes', a yodelling chorus, a coy 'You may Play with me just like a Child' and a more lusty 'Who Says we Are the weaker Sex' – but the music was not Cellier's best. *The Era* found it 'lacked the breadth and freedom of *The Sultan of Mocha*' and that the first and last acts both dragged. *The London & Provincial Entr'acte* took a kinder view, finding it:

> an excellent composition in a musical point of view, the scenery excellent and the situations humorous. The libretto written by Alfred Thompson is very creditable.

Events did not confirm his opinion and, though Dolaro spoke of reviving 'her' Cellier opera at a later date, it was not seen again. For once Cellier allowed the score to subside with the book.

The composer was more fortunate with a short work, *The Spectre Knight*, produced at the Opera Comique as a forepiece to both *The Sorcerer* and *H.M.S. Pinafore*. James Albery supplied the libretto which dealt with an impecunious ducal family whose sheltered daughter, Viola, has never seen a man. To the court comes young Otho, disguised as an elderly friar, and he falls in love with Viola. To show her what a young man is, he appears to her in a 'vision' as a ghostly knight. She is charmed, her possessive father less so until he discovers that Otho has put his enemies to flight and restored his exchequer, when all is allowed to end happily.

Cellier had written some highly successful music for the Covent Garden pantomime of 1877/8, and he incorporated some of this into a very attractive score which materially assisted the little piece's success. Metzler & Co. quickly published the music and *The Spectre Knight* was performed frequently thereafter including a brief appearance at Broadway's Bijou Theatre in the Opera di Camera season under John McCaull in 1880.

The Opera Comique used a number of small pieces with *The Sorcerer* and *Pinafore*. Three of these – *Five Hamlets, Beauties on the Beach* and *A Silver Wedding* – were George Grossmith monologues in the manner of his old chats from the piano, but others were more extensive. Grossmith supplied a sketch, *Cups and Saucers*, and Desprez and Cellier a vaudeville called *After All* which told the tale of a man, returning from ten years in Mexico, who encounters a friend who has married his own former beloved who it turns out has become the most frightful shrew. Both were very slight pieces, but both became highly popular and were often used thereafter.

The German Reed establishment had been taken over at the end of the previous year by Alfred Reed and 'Dick' Grain. The policy remained the same and the St George's Hall continued to give the proper and well-performed entertainments for which it was famous. Four new pieces were given during the course of the year, three of which were from F. C. Burnand. *Answer Paid* was yet another little marital plot but the other two works, *Doubleday's Will* and *A Tremendous Mystery*, were more substantial. Each was in two tableaux (a theatre would have called them 'acts') and each held for a time the full length of the programme apart from the few minutes taken up, in the interval, by Corney Grain's little recital.

Doubleday's Will was one of the best St George's Hall pieces. It was based on an eccentric will by which each of the beneficiaries was required to fulfill a very difficult or impossible condition in order to inherit. Everybody dissembles satisfactorily, but gradually things fall apart until they discover that they have *all* broken the conditions so it really doesn't matter. King Hall, now a St George's Hall regular, supplied his usual pretty, forgettable music.

Hall was also responsible for the music to *A Tremendous Mystery* which had for central character a lady novelist played by Priscilla Reed who makes 'a tremendous mystery' out of everything. She is involved in a set of marital jealousies which kept the evening bubbling nicely until eventually a solution is reached. This piece introduced a new young mezzo, Rosa Leo, to fill the vacancy left by the departure of Leonora Braham. Another young singer, Marion Dale, had been brought into the previous production, an Arthur Law piece called *An Artful Automaton*. This was another little love story with a bossy aunt which gave Alfred Reed the chance to imitate a robot. It too had music by Hall.

For their Christmas production St George's Hall reverted to pasticcio, the first time in many years their policy of original musical pieces had not been adhered to. *Enchantment* was a fairy tale piece where Fanny Holland as a Mermaid, Rosa Leo as a parrot and Law, Reed and Bishop as a bear, a bogey and a fox respectively performed nursery songs.

In the provinces a little Frank Musgrave operetta, *Prisoners at the Bar*, presented Alice Cook as a waitress in a railway refreshment bar. Musgrave, who had surrendered the lease to the Nottingham Theatre Royal, was touring his own company with *Giroflé-Girofla* and *La Fille de Madame Angot*, and his operetta was tried at Liverpool as a support piece without exciting much attention or praise.

1878

0024 **BELLADONNA** or The Little Beauty and the Great Beast. An opera in three acts by Alfred Thompson. Music by Alfred Cellier. Produced at the Prince's Theatre, Manchester under the management of Alfred Thompson 27 April, 1878 for a three-week season closing 15 May.

Lupo . . . . Fred Ferrani/Alfred Brennir
Nux . . . . Frederick Marshall
Drearibboi. . . . . Arthur Roberts
Juanito . . . . Sgr Federici
Sergeant. George Shelton
Belladonna . . . . Selina Dolaro
Archduchess of Nonotia . . . . Miss Daly
Elsinore . . . . Lucy Franklein
Graciosa. Eugenie Vernie
Carmela . . . . Elsie Vernie

0025 **H.M.S. PINAFORE** or The Lass That Loved A Sailor. A comic opera in two acts by W. S. Gilbert. Music by Arthur Sullivan. Produced at the Opera Comique under the management of Richard D'Oyly Carte for the Comedy Opera Company 25 May, 1878 for a run of 571 performances closing 20 February, 1880. The theatre was closed between 25 December, 1878 and 1 February, 1879.

Sir Joseph Porter K.C.B. . . . . George Grossmith (Fleming Norton)
Captain Corcoran . . . . Rutland Barrington (Richard Temple)/George Temple
Ralph Rackstraw . . . . George Power/Tom Noel/W. H. Seymour/D'Arcy Ferris
Dick Deadeye . . . . Richard Temple (Frank Talbot)/Frank Thornton
Bill Bobstay . . . . Fred Clifton (F. Bickersteth)/Mr Bosanquet/T. J. Montelli
Bob Beckett . . . . Mr Dymott/C. Ramsay
Josephine . . . . Emma Howson/Alice Burville/Elinor Loveday/Blanche Roosevelt/Duglas Gordon/Fanny Holland (Julia Gwynne) (Alice Mandeville)
Hebe . . . . Jessie Bond/Marian Johnson/Haidee Crofton/Lillian La Rue
Little Buttercup. . . . . Harriet Everard/Rosina Brandram (Emily Cross) (Madge Stavart?)
Sergeant of the Marines . . . . Frank Talbot
Tom Tucker, midshipmite . . . . Mr Fitzaltamont

Md: Alfred Cellier/Mr Berry/François Cellier/Arthur Sullivan; cos: Faustin, Silver & Co., Nathan

Produced at the Boston Museum under the management of R. M. Field 25 November, 1878. Played with *Trial by Jury* from 14 December.

George W. Wilson (JP), James H. Jones (CC), Rose Temple (RR), Ben H. Graham (DD), Joseph S. Haworth (BILL), W. Morris (BOB), Marie Wainwright (JO), Sadie Martinot/Jean Crozier (HE), Lizzie Harold (LB), W. Melbourne (TOM BOWLIN), Little Gertrude (TOM). Md: John Braham

Produced at the Bush Theatre, San Francisco, under the management of Mrs Alice Oates 23 December, 1878.
J. G. Taylor (JP), Edward Connell (CC), Alice Oates (RR), James A. Meade (DD), R. E. Graham (BILL), C. N. Decker (BOB), Lulu Stevens (JO), Agnes Hallock (LB), E. D. Beverley (DICK TRUCK); with Edward Horan, J. McLaughlin, J. Bugby, Mills Hall, J. Clare, A. Godwell, C. Watkins, Hattie Richardson, Pauline Hall, Albertina Hall, Alice Townsend, Ada Dow, Jennie Lanner, Bessie Temple, Miss Sexton.

Produced at Ford's Theatre, Baltimore, under the management of John T. Ford 23 December, 1878. Cast included George Denham (JP), G. S. Young, Mr Garner, F. Pierson, Blanche Chapman (JO), Henrietta Vaders (LB), Belle Mackenzie.

Produced at the Imperial Theatre under the management of the Comedy Opera Company 1 August, 1879. Transferred to the Olympic Theatre 8 September. Withdrawn 25 October, 1879 after a total of 91 performances.
J. G. Taylor/Fleming Norton (JP), Michael Dwyer (CC), Percy Blandford/Wilford Morgan/George Mudie/Frederic Wood (RR), Arthur Rousbey (DD), H. F. Fairweather (BILL), ?/Mr Dymott (BOB), Lizzie Mulholland/Carina Clelland/Emilie Petrelli/Kate Sullivan/Pauline Rita (JO), Isabelle Muncey (HE), Fanny Edwards (LB). Md: Auguste van Biene; sc: Gordon & Harford

Produced at the Standard Theatre, New York, under the management of John C. Duff 15 January, 1879 for a run of 175 performances closing 14 June, 1879.
Thomas Whiffen (JP), Eugene Clarke/Wallace Macreery (CC), Henri Laurent/Alonzo Hatch (RR), William Davidge (DD), Charles Makin (BILL), H. J. Burt (BOB), Eva Mills (JO), Verona Jarbeau (HE), Blanche Galton (LB), J. Wilmot (TOM BOWLIN), Master Henry (TOM). Md: Charles Schiller

Produced at the Lyceum Theatre, New York, under the management of Edward E. Rice 23 January, 1879.
William Forrester (JP), James Vincent (CC), Lizzie Webster (RR), Henry Hunter (DD), Richard Golden (BILL), Venie G. Clancy (JO), Rose Leighton (HE), George Fortescue (LB). Md: Harry Braham

Produced at the Fifth Avenue Theatre, New York, under the management of D. H. Harkins 10 February, 1879.
James Burnett (JP), J. G. Peake (CC), Henri Laurent (RR), James Harton (DD), Van Houten (BILL), Blanche Corelli (JO), Ida Foy (HE), Kate Gurney/Julie de Ruyther (LB). Md: Max Maretzek

Produced at Niblo's Garden, New York 10 February, 1879.
Sol Smith (JP), H. R. Humphries (CC), L. Digby (RR), Harry Chapman (DD), A. B. Barker (BILL), Lisetta Ellani (JO), Emma Mettler (HE), Grace Clare (LB)

Played at Niblo's Garden 1 March, 1879 to 20 March 1879 by the Boston Ideal Company.

Produced at the Broadway Theatre, New York, by Gorman's Philadelphia Church Choir Company 10 March 1879 for a season to 26 April, 1879. Returned 12 May, 1879 for two further weeks and again 10 November, 1879 for three further weeks.
Louis de Lange (JP), A. N. Palmer (CC), M. F. Donovan (RR), G. T. R. Knorr (DD), J. J. Knox (BILL), Emma Howson (JO), E. Cameron (HE), A. V. Rutherford (LB)

Produced at the Fifth Avenue Theatre, New York by the Henri Laurent Opera Co. 7 April, 1879, in repertoire.

Produced at the Globe Theatre, New York 28 April, 1879 by the Coloured Opera Troupe.

Produced at the Germania Theatre, New York 22 March, 1879 in a German version.

Produced at Wallacks Theatre, New York 5 May, 1879 by a juvenile company.

Irene Perry (JP), Miss Ennis (RR), Jerry Cammeyer (CC), Lillian C. Reynolds (JO), Inez de Leon (HE), Maud Elmersdorf (LB)

During the first half of 1879 there were a number of further productions of *H.M.S. Pinafore* in New York including repertoire performances and many very brief runs.

Produced at the Standard Theatre, New York 20 October, 1879 for a season to 15 November, 1879.
Thomas Whiffen (JP), Wallace Macreery (CC), Alonzo Hatch (RR), F. A. Parmental (DD), Alfred Holland (BILL), Eva Mills (JO), Verona Jarbeau (HE), Estelle Mortimer (LB)

Produced at the Fifth Avenue Theatre, New York, under the management of Richard D'Oyly Carte 1 December, 1879 for a season of four weeks.
J. H. Ryley (JP), J. Furneaux Cook (CC), Hugh Talbot (RR), Sgr Broccolini (DD), Fred Clifton (BILL), Mr Cuthbert (BOB), Blanche Roosevelt (Miss Conried) (JO), Jessie Bond (HE), Alice Barnett (LB)

Produced at the Opera Comique under the management of Richard D'Oyly Carte 16 December, 1879 with a company of juveniles. Performed at matinées then, from 21 February 1880, at evening performances. Closed 20 March, 1880.
Edward Pickering (JP), Harry Grattan (CC), Harry Eversfield (RR), William Phillips (DD), Edward Walsh (BILL), Charles Becker (BOB), Emilie Grattan/Blanche Gaston-Murray (JO), Louisa Gilbert (HE), Effie Mason (LB). Md: François Cellier
The juvenile company returned for a further season, 22 December, 1880 to 28 January 1881.

Produced at the Savoy Theatre under the management of Richard D'Oyly Carte 12 November, 1887 for a run of 120 performancs closing 10 March, 1888.
George Grossmith (JP), Rutland Barrington (CC), J. G. Robertson (RR), Richard Temple (DD), Richard Cummings (BILL), Rudolph Lewis (BOB), Geraldine Ulmar/Agnes Wyatt/Rose Hervey (JO), Jessie Bond/Annie Cole/Amy Augarde (HE), Rosina Brandram (LB), Mr Inglis (SGT). Dir: Richard Barker; md: Arthur Sullivan/François Cellier

Produced at the Savoy Theatre under the management of Richard D'Oyly Carte 6 June, 1899 for a run of 174 performances closing 25 November, 1899.
Walter Passmore (JP), Henry Lytton (Iago Lewys) (Leonard Russell) (CC), Robert Evett (Albert Gater) (Charles Childerstone) (RR), Richard Temple (Powis Pinder) (DD), W. H. Leon (BILL), Powis Pinder (BOB), Ruth Vincent (Isabel Jay) (JO), Emmie Owen/Lulu Evans (HE), Rosina Brandram (LB). Md: François Cellier

Produced at the Savoy Theatre under the management of the D'Oyly Carte Opera Company 14 July, 1908 for a run of 61 performances.
C. H. Workman (Henry Lytton) (JP), Rutland Barrington (CC), Henry Herbert (Strafford Moss) (William Davidson) (RR), Henry Lytton (Leicester Tunks) (DD), Leicester Tunks/Leo Sheffield (Fred Drawater) (Sydney Granville) (BILL), Fred Hewett (BOB), Elsie Spain/Dorothy Court (Beatrice Boarer) (JO), Jessie Rose (Beatrice Meredith) (HE), Louie Rene (Ethel Morrison) (LB). Md: François Cellier

Subsequently played by the D'Oyly Carte Opera Company on tour and in London in repertoire.

Produced at the Casino Theatre, New York under the management of Henry E. Dixey 29 May, 1911 for a season of 49 performances ending 8 July, 1911.
Henry E. Dixey (JP), George J. Macfarlane (CC), Arthur Aldridge (RR), de Wolf Hopper (DD), Eugene Cowles (BILL), Harold Crane/Robert Davies (BOB), Louise Gunning (JP), Marie Cahill (HE), Alice Brady (LB), Christine Nielsen (TOM). Dir: Lewis Morton; md: Silvio Hein

Produced at the New York Hippodrome under the management of the Shubert Brothers 9 April, 1914 for a run of 89 performances.
William G. Gordon (JP), Bertram Peacock (CC), John Bardesley (RR), E. Percy Parsons (DD), Eugene Cowles (BILL), Helen Heinemann (JO), Grace Camp (HE), Marie Horgan (LB). Dir: William G. Stewart; md: Manuel Klein/Selli Simonson

Produced at the Century Theatre, New York under the management of Winthrop Ames 6 April, 1926 for a run of 56 performances.
John E. Hazzard (JP), Marion Green (CC), Tom Burke (RR), William Danforth (DD), Charles E. Gallagher (BILL), Chester Bright (BOB), Marguerite Namara (JO), Nydia d'Arnell (HE), Fay Templeton (LB). Dir: Milton Aborn

Produced at the Phoenix Theatre in a production from the Stratford Festival Theatre, Canada 7 September, 1960 for a season of 55 performances to 23 October, 1960.
Eric House (JP), Harry Mossfield (CC), Andrew Downie (RR), Howard Mawson (DD), Igors Gavon (BILL), Vaclovas Verikaitis (BOB), Marion Studholme (JO), Elizabeth Mawson (HE), Irene Byatt (LB). Dir: Tyrone Guthrie; md: Eugene Kismiak

Played in New York by the D'Oyly Carte Opera Company and in various numerous repertory seasons and short productions.

Produced at Her Majesty's Theatre in a production from the Stratford Festival Theatre, Canada 9 February, 1962 under the management of Tennent Productions Ltd. in association with Contemporary Productions (Canada).
Eric House (JP), Harry Mossfield (CC), Andrew Downie (RR), Howell Glynne (DD), Donald Young (BILL), Emyr Green (BOB), Marion Studholme/Anne Edwards (JO), Joan Ryan (HE), Irene Byatt (LB) with Annabelle Adams, Theresia Bester, Elizabeth Bourne, Mary Eley, Anne Edwards, Genevieve Gordon, Gillian Humphries, Ann Pidgeon, Brenda Scaife, Vivienne Stevens, George Ballantine, Brian Beaton, Stafford Dean, Gordon Dobson, Raymond Edwards, Edward Evanko, Robin Haddow, Jeff Hall, David Harris, Robert Jeffrey, Bruce Lochtie, Vernon Midgely, John Sinclair, Bobby Scott-Webster. Dir: Tyrone Guthrie; md: Kenneth Alwyn; ch: Douglas Campbell; sc/cos: Brian Jackson

Produced at the Collegiate Theatre under the management of The Singers Company 22 December, 1981 for a season of 23 performances ending 9 January 1982.
Ronnie Stevens (JP), Alec McCowen (CC), Mike Bulman (RR), Bruce Barry (DD), Andrew Gallacher (BILL), William Snape (BOB), Janis Kelly/Gillian Sullivan (JO), Bronwen Mills (HE), Libby Morris (LB), Suki Turner (TOM TUCKER) with Philip Devonshire, Brad Graham, Richard Pettyfer, William Pool, Paul Whitmarsh, Judith Buckle, Helen Garton, Liza Hobbs, Susan Moore, Catherine Pickering. Dir: Peter Wilson; md: John Owen Edwards/John Alley; ch: Gillian Gregory; cos/sc: Cynthia Savage

Produced at Sadler's Wells Theatre by the New Sadler's Wells Opera Company 4 June, 1984.
Nickolas Grace (JP), Gordon Sandison (CC), Hugh Hetherington (RR), Thomas Lawlor (DD), Martin McEvoy (BILL), Julian Moyle (BOB), Penelope Mackay (JO), Janine Roebuck (HE), Linda Ormiston (LB). Dir: Christopher Renshaw; md: Barry Wordsworth/David Ward; sc/cos: Tim Goodchild.

Film: In 1906 a film and synchronised record set of Iago Lewys singing 'I am the Captain of the Pinafore' was issued by Chronophone Films.

TV/Video: 1984 Brent Walker Ltd. Pr: Judith de Paul; dir: Michael Geliot; md: Alexander Faris; sc: Allan Cameron; cos: Jenny Beavan
Frankie Howerd (JP), Peter Marshall (CC), Michael Bulman (RR), Alan Watt (DD), Meryl Drower (JO), Della Jones (LB)

THE SPECTRE KNIGHT a fanciful operetta by James Albery. Music by Alfred Cellier. Produced at the Opera Comique by the Comedy Opera Co./Richard D'Oyly Carte with *The Sorcerer* 9 February, 1878. Withdrawn March 23. Revived as forepiece to *H.M.S. Pinafore* 28 May, 1878. Withdrawn 10 August, 1878.

The Grand Duke	Fred Clifton
Viola	Giulia Warwick/Laura Clement/ Alice Burville
Lord Chamberlain	Rutland Barrington/Frank Talbot
Otho	Richard Temple
1st Lady-in-waiting	Harriet Everard
2nd Lady-in-waiting	Isabelle Muncey/Rose Hervey

Dir: Charles Harris; sc: Gordon & Harford; cos: Mrs May

Produced at the Bijou Theatre, New York, under the management of Charles E. Ford and John A. McCaull 17 May, 1880 with *Charity Begins at Home*. Withdrawn 22 May.
Carrie Burton (VI), William Courtenay (LC), Digby V. Bell (OTHO), Marie Beauman (1st L), Frank Pierson (STEWARD). Md: Alfred Cellier

ANSWER PAID by F. C. Burnand. Music by Walter Austin. Produced at St George's Hall under the management of Alfred Reed and R. Corney Grain 4 February, 1878 with *A Happy Bungalow* and *A Musical Almanac*. Withdrawn 23 March, 1878.

Mrs Wedderburn . . . . Fanny Holland
Mrs Rosedale . . . . Arthur Law
Kraklyn Pawke . . . . Alfred Reed
Mrs Lysle . . . . Leonora Braham

DOUBLEDAY'S WILL a vaudeville in two tableaux by F. C. Burnand. Music by King Hall. Produced at St George's Hall under the management of Alfred Reed and R. Corney Grain 25 March, 1878 with *A Country House*, the latter replaced 17 June by *The Paris Exhibition*. On July 10 *An Artful Automaton* was added to the bill. Withdrawn 27 July, 1878 and represented 30 September until 19 October, 1878.

Mr Jodleigh/Van der Vetzler . . . . Alfred Reed
Mr Perdie/Willie Doughton . . . . R. Corney Grain
Florence Perdie . . . . Leonora Braham
Mrs Vandeleur . . . . Mrs German Reed
Dawkins/Farmer Hartlebug. . . . . Arthur Law
Mrs Jodleigh . . . . Fanny Holland

AN ARTFUL AUTOMATON by Arthur Law. Music by King Hall. Produced at St George's Hall under the management of Alfred Reed and R. Corney Grain 10 July, 1878 with *Doubleday's Will* and *The Paris Exhibition*. Withdrawn 27 July. Represented 30 September. Withdrawn 19 October, 1878.

Prunella Fosselle . . . . Fanny Holland
Crawley Slide . . . . Alfred Reed
Ariel Flight . . . . Marion Dale
B. A. Lamb . . . . Arthur Law

A TREMENDOUS MYSTERY by F. C. Burnand. Music by King Hall. Produced at St George's Hall under the management of Alfred Reed and R. Corney Grain 5 November, 1878 with *Mrs Brown's Home & Foreign Policy*. *Enchantment* added to the bill 16 December and *Mrs Brown* replaced by *A Trip to Cairo*. Withdrawn 15 March, 1879.

Mrs Capel Beamish . . . . Mrs German Reed
Count Montgireau . . . . Alfred Reed
Tiffleigh Dobson/Major Tofton . . . . . Arthur Law
Hon. Percy Phennick/Jack Henley . . . . Alfred Bishop
Mme de Montgireau . . . . Fanny Holland
Nelly . . . . Rosa Leo

CUPS AND SAUCERS a satirical musical sketch written and composed by George Grossmith. Produced at the Opera Comique with *H.M.S. Pinafore* 12 August, 1878. Withdrawn 20 February, 1880.

General Deelah . . . . Richard Temple/Frank Thornton
Mrs Nankeen Worcester . . . . Emily Cross
Jane . . . . Rose Hervey

AFTER ALL a vaudeville by Frank Desprez. Music by Alfred Cellier. Produced at the Opera Comique under the management of Richard D'Oyly Carte 23 December, 1878 as an afterpiece to *H.M.S. Pinafore*. Played to 20 February, 1880 and then with the juvenile *H.M.S. Pinafore* to 20 March, 1880.

George Pennyfather. . . . . Rutland Barrington/Frank Thornton
Henry Selworthy . . . . Richard Temple/George Temple
Maria . . . . Jessie Bond/Julia Gwynne
The Voice. . . . . J. Harvey

Produced at the Imperial Theatre under the management of the Comedy Opera Co. 1 August,

1879 with *H.M.S. Pinafore.* Transferred to the Olympic Theatre 8 September. Withdrawn 13 September. Re-presented 27 September. Played from 29 October with *Marigold.* Withdrawn 31 November, 1879.
Arthur Rousbey/Percy Blandford/Michael Dwyer/Mr Fairweather (P), George Mudie (S), Lucy Ward/Kate Sullivan/Miss Kinnaird (M)

Played at the Alhambra Theatre 4 March, 1884 for the benefit of William Holland.
Arthur Rousbey (P), George Mudie (S), Miss Mercey (M)

Produced at the Opera Comique 15 November, 1886 with *Our Diva.* Withdrawn 17 December, 1886.
Henry Beaumont (P), Horace Bolini (S), Edie Casson (M)

Produced at the Savoy Theatre under the management of Richard D'Oyly Carte 4 April, 1896 with *The Grand Duke* (to 10 July) and subsequently with *The Mikado.* Withdrawn 8 August, 1896.
C. H. Workman (P), Jones Hewson (S), Emmie Owen (M)

Played at the Haymarket Theatre 16 December, 1896 at a matinée.
Rutland Barrington (P), Jones Hewson (S), Emmie Owen (M)

PRISONERS AT THE BAR an opéra-buffet by C. H. Ross. Music by Frank Musgrave. Produced at the Royal Alexandra Theatre, Liverpool by Frank Musgrave's Company 17 June, 1878 with *Giroflé-Girofla.*

Lord Totters . . . . E. G. Osborne
Lady Totters . . . . Florence Chalgrove
Mr Fogson . . . . C. F. Parry
Selina Elvina . . . . Alice Cook
John Bigge Littlejohn . . . . J. Harry Fischer
The Proprietress . . . . Sallie Turner

Md: Frank Musgrave

1879

The holiday season of 1878/9 presented a variety of musical pieces. Apart from *H.M.S. Pinafore* and *Les Cloches de Corneville*, the two enduring hits of the season, the theatregoer could choose among *Young Fra Diavolo* an entertaining burlesque of the Gaiety brand, the old favourite pasticcio *Nemesis* or later *The Desperate Adventures of the Baby* at the more rumbustious burlesque house, the Strand. For spectacle there was the English version of the féerie *La Poule aux Oeufs d'Or*[1] at the Alhambra and, for those with more 'French' tastes, Kate Santley was back in her theoretically harmless version of *La Marjolaine* at the Royalty.

But 1879 was the year of *Pinafore*. The Opera Comique played through the whole twelve months to full houses, even when the rival *Pinafore* at the Imperial and Olympic Theatres was afloat. No new native work was brought forward to challenge or imitate Gilbert and Sullivan's triumphant success during the year of its dominance. Selina Dolaro announced *Lola*, a new comic opera by Cellier and Thompson, for her season at the Folly to star Nellie Bromley and Lizzie Mulholland, but this piece, which was almost certainly the unfortunate *Belladonna* under a new name, was never produced.

A considerable number of new French works made their London bow in the wake of *Les Cloches de Corneville*. Dolaro eventually tried Maillart's *Les Dragons de Villars* at the Folly, supplementing it with a revival of *La Périchole*. The Alhambra, having had a fair run out of the pasticcio *Venice*, switched to a revival of *La Princesse de Trébizonde* with less success and then to Lecocq's *La Petite Mademoiselle* (Oct 6) starring Harry Paulton and no less than three prime donne, Alice May, Constance Loseby and Emma Chambers, which held until Christmas. The Gaiety briefly tried Nellie Farren in Lecocq's *The Grand Casimir* and the defeated Comedy Opera Company replaced their foundered *Pinafore* with an equally short-lived production of Vasseur's *Marigold* (*Le Droit de Seigneur*). But there was one fresh piece which was to join *Pinafore* and *Les Cloches de Corneville* in the ranks of super successes. The Strand Theatre and its loved-hated scribe, H. B. Farnie, traded their policy of burlesque for one of French musical, and the theatre's 'resident' company headed by Claude Marius and the newly hired prima donna, Florence St John, making her final transition from contralto to soprano in the title role, scored a resounding success with Offenbach's latest hit, *Madame Favart*. *Madame Favart* enjoyed a West End run of 502 performances and established itself as a genuine favourite in the following years with regular tours and revivals. With the Strand thus occupied, burlesque was left to the Gaiety which provided three new

[1] Including music by Bucalossi and Sullivan and with 'new songs, marches and the whole of the original ballet music composed by Georges Jacobi'.

ones, *Pretty Esmeralda* (April 2), *Handsome Hernani* (August 30) and *Robbing Roy* (November 11) as well as a revival of *Young Fra Diavolo.*

Of considerably more interest than these unadventurous jig-saws of rhyme and regurgitated tunes was the appearance of the first American-bred musical in the West End. The Connaught Theatre, Holborn (formerly the Amphitheatre) was barely 'West End' and the piece did not survive long, but 1 November, 1879 remains statistically memorable as the date of America's first incursion into the London musical scene. The piece was *Alcantara*, written by British-born Benjamin E. Woolf and composed by Julius Eichberg. It had been performed in America in 1862 in Boston and subsequently in New York as *The Doctor of Alcantara* and had been quite well received alongside works of good quality. It was an unexpected and isolated piece to have emerged from such an early stage of the development of the musical in America and resembled more than anything a farcical opera buffa done into English. The music was undoubtedly proficient and the Carl Rosa Company deemed it worthy of inclusion in their programme on a number of occasions, but the piece as a whole did not appeal to London and *Alcantara* folded after a brief season.

Although no new British shows had appeared, British writers had not been idle. Gilbert and Sullivan were known to be working on a new piece to be called *The Bold Burglars* which would be:

> a dramatised 'Bab Ballad' in which six burglars, six policemen and six young ladies . . . sing characteristic choruses . .

According to the paragraphists, Gilbert had originally intended the idea for a short piece, but had finally decided to develop it into a full two acts. The idea was, *The Era* affirmed, a satirical one:

> The notion develops a bit of burlesque of Italian opera. It is a mere incident. An old gentleman returns home in the evening with his six daughters from a party. A nice bit of soft music takes them off for the night. Then a big orchestral crash which introduces six burglars. They commence their knavish operations in a mysterious chorus. Lights down. Presently the old gentleman thinks he hears someone stirring, comes on, of course sees nobody, though the burglars are actively at work. The noise is only the sighing of the wind or the gentle evening breeze. The old gentleman and the burglars perform a bit of concerted music and in due course the six ladies enter. The burglars are struck with their beauty, forget their villainous purposes and make love. Chorus of burglars and old gentleman's daughters, whose announcement that they are wards in chancery creates great consternation amongst the bandit lovers. Then there is the policemen's rescue and other humorous conceits of Mr. Gilbert's which I hope and believe will be as funny as anything in the *Pinafore* or *The Sorcerer*.

Frederic Clay seemed to have gone to ground after the indifferent showing of *Don Quixote* and Cellier was giving more time to his conducting duties as well as arranging for productions of his earlier works in America, but the newest young composer, whose name seemed to appear on every second musical playbill, was the precocious 'Teddy' Solomon. After returning from conducting the touring company of *Les Cloches de Corneville* early in the year he was immediately engaged as m.d. at the Criterion and later at the Globe where Kate Santley had taken over as Serpolette in *Les Cloches*. In the meanwhile he had seen his *Will with a Vengeance* revived for a run with the comedy hit *Crutch and Toothpick* at the Royalty, and had been promised a production of his *Bertha, the Betrayer* at the Criterion. During the year he composed and arranged the music for the Folly burlesque of Zola's *L'Assommoir, Another Drink*, and for the Royalty pieces *Venus* and *Balloonacy.*

Another Drink was a rhyming and punning little piece which mocked the moral drama of *Drink* as played in Charles Reade's adaptation at the Princess's. G. W. Anson aped Charles Warner's powerful performance as the alcoholic Coupeau in the company of Selina Dolaro (*vice* Bernhardt) and a ubiquitous teapot laced with alcohol. The original music part of *Another Drink* was small. Solomon's contribution was limited to a few choruses plus a parody of 'Le Roi de Thule' for Dolaro, a song for Anson, 'Nothing like Her', and a 'French' duet performed by the two principals 'à la Comédie Française': that is to say, recited through the music. Linda Verner sang about 'Women's Rights' and there was an intriguing sounding piece called 'Don't Touch the Mangle, Mary Ann'. The burlesque was far beneath the piece it sought to parody and sank quickly.

Venus or The Gods as They Were and not as They Ought to Have Been was an altogether different type of piece, a classical burlesque which mixed Cupid and Psyche with Venus and Adonis and a whole bevy of Olympian characters and events in a merry and popular extravaganza in which the music played a prominent part. Solomon composed and, principally, arranged some twenty pieces for Nelly Bromley (Venus), Alma Stanley (Adonis), Phoebe Don (Mars), Charles Groves (Vulcan) and Marie Williams (Cupid). *Venus* was played with *Crutch and Toothpick* and proved a highly successful accessory for five months.

For its successor, *Balloonacy* or A Flight of Fancy, Solomon wrote eleven original musical pieces – more than half the score. The musical part of this extravagant balloon-journey to an Eastern Isle was generally agreed to be its best feature, but its libretto ensured that its run was limited to six weeks. It was revised and revived later in the year but with no more fortunate a result.

Solomon's final contribution to the year was the whole of the music for the first act of *Rothomago*, the Christmas piece at the Alhambra. Over the past years the Alhambra had varied its Christmas spectaculars from féerie to operetta (*Die Fledermaus*) to extravaganza such as *Wildfire* or the familiar tale of *Whittington*, but the most successful to date had been the French derivative, *The Black Crook*. For the 1879/80 season the same recipe was tried, and the Parisian grand opéra-bouffe féerie *Rothomago* was put into the hands of the master adapter, H. B. Farnie. The music, as with *The Black Crook*, was divided up by the act. Solomon was allotted the first, Procida Bucalossi the second, the French composer Gaston Serpette (*La Branche Cassée* etc) the third, and the conductor Jacobi the fourth with its grand ballet finale.

The story bore a family resemblance to other grand féerie-bouffes, and like them it took every opportunity to involve at any cost the grandiose effects which were the hallmark of the genre. In *Rothomago* or The Magic Watch the principal characters were the Court Sorcerer, Rothomago, his King, Impecunioso XIX and their children, Young Rothomago and the Princess Allegra who are engaged to be married. But the wedding is in trouble because the king can't afford a wedding feast and his useless old magician can't magic one up. But magic, and the first of the major stage effects, are quick to appear. Under the guidance of the nasty fairy, Angostura, the Princess whiles away her waiting at the piano. But at her touch the instrument falls apart and out steps the handsome yokel, Dodo. In the meanwhile Allegra's fiancé, stopping on his way to the wedding to chat up the pretty rustic, Forget-me-not, has lost his magic watch, the benison of future happiness. This is a disaster for king and court. Without the power of the watch they find themselves turned out. The king is reduced to grinding knives and Rothomago becomes a schoolmaster while they search for the watch. But it is Dodo who finds it and, egged on by the bitter Angostura, wishes himself power and riches and Allegra. The rightful royals now proceed to try and regain the vital timepiece with the aid of the nice fairy Anisette by working on Dodo's weaknesses, for every time he forgets to wind the watch at its appointed hour his hold is weakened. The two fairies magic their protegés around from the Forest of the Virgin Snow in Freezeland where Anisette and the Twelve Hours lull Dodo to sleep, to the Gorge of the Lost Footsteps from where they escape in a balloon to Egypt and the Pyramids. Then on to the Land of the Magic Windmills which Angostura changes into a Floating Chinese City and where Rothomago tricks Dodo into losing the last hours from the watch which then returns to its rightful owner, and all ends happily with the temperamental Allegra turning out not to be a *real* Princess after all, but an elfin changeling.

The whole piece was constructed round three major ballets. The first was a 'Grand Vintage Ballet' in the process of which Dodo is tricked into losing an hour while drinking with the merry peasants, the second a Grand Egyptian Ballet and the third the final Grand Ballet Céramique in The Porcelain Palace where the happy finale, for no particular reason, takes place. These ballets composed, respectively, by Bucalossi, Serpette and Jacobi, the illustrated tableaux of the Ages of Man (Solomon) reminiscent of Clay's River of Life in *Babil and Bijou*, and a March of the Mummies were the highlights of the show. No expense was spared. The Egyptian scena even featured real camels and an elephant. The other effects were equally studied. The balloon in which the travellers escaped was constructed so that it became smaller and smaller as it seemingly vanished into the distance. And the piano which disintegrated and reintegrated with Dodo was a prized effect.

Farnie wisely kept his fragmentary book to a minimum. The Alhambra was not the theatre for large speeches or complicated characters or plots. It required broad effects, simple and clear dialogue and a plot that was easy to follow. Of course, there were the stars to attend to. Harry Paulton was used to writing nice big speeches for himself and was liable to provide them if the author did not. Farnie gave him a bulky if irrelevant schoolroom scene where he drew eccentric drawings on a huge slate and gave a comic speech on the latest phenomenon 'Compulsory Education' and contributed to a song on 'Geography' where the chorus listed the 'principal towns of England':

Manchester, Liverpool, Stoke-on-Trent,
Sheffield and London and Margate-in-Kent,
Birmingham, Dublin and Canterbury
Bristol and Glasgow and Clacton-on-Sea,
Barrow-in-Furness, Bath, Brighton and Rugby
Cambridge and Crewe and the junction at Mugby,
Portsmouth and Battersea, Folkestone and Dover
Known on the map as the shortest way over

In the last act he had a scene with the Windmills and disguised himself as a Chinaman for a characteristic routine.

However if the libretto was made up of short and loosely linked episodes, it was made up of a lot of them. On the first night the curtain did not fall till twenty past midnight. Each of the four composers had contributed a deal of music, too, and sadly little of it was exceptional. *The Era* found Bucalossi's portion the most attractive. A ballad for Constance Loseby 'When I had Velvet on my Back', an air 'O Peaceful Vale', for the tenor, Knight Aston, and another for Emma Chambers, a comical 'Knife Grinder' number for the King and the schoolroom and vineyard sections all came from the composer of *Pom*. Solomon, for his part, had possibly been affected by too much arranging – part of his act was a number based on 'Auld Lang Syne' – but he also contributed some pretty dance music including 'The Waltz of the Hours' and a Wedding March and comic numbers for Kelleher and Mlle Julic, the latter advancing petulantly

> 'Tis old and out-of-date today
> This twaddle 'honour and obey'.

The total result was something less like the lofty *Babil and Bijou* or the magical *Black Crook* and dangerously like a song-and-scenery show, but it was given a satisfactory reception and ran out its season to good houses.

Two new works appeared in the provinces during the year for short runs. Both, in fact, opened on October 20, the one at Manchester's Theatre Royal and the other at the Royal Opera House, Leicester. The Manchester offering was *The Lancashire Witches* written by R. T. Gunton with music by Ferderick Stanislaus who had succeeded Alfred Cellier as musical director at the Prince's and who was a highly successful conductor. He had begun his career with the Manley, Corri and Pyne Opera Companies and had subsequently conducted shows in both America and Britain before his appointment at Manchester. Most recently he had been again on the road as a musical director. His composing had previously been limited to small works, but in *The Lancashire Witches* he produced an impressive first musical in the Cellier tradition, thoroughly English in subject, style and execution.

The story of the Lancashire witches of Pendle Hill had been told many times before, most notably in Harrison Ainsworth's novel of the same name. Alizon, the supposed daughter of the witch Mother Demdyke, is in love with Richard Ashton but his wicked father, Sir Ralph, will have none of it and has Demdyke and Alizon banished from the village for witchery. In the meanwhile Hopkins the Witchcatcher and a friend have arrived in town. The friend takes a fancy to the comely widow, Alice, who is in dispute with Sir Ralph over her property rights, and the canny lady recognises that the stranger is King James in disguise out on a 'frolic'.

The second act is set on Pendle Hill where the witches prepare to initiate the unwilling Alizon into their coven. Richard arrives and whisks her away, and the frustrated beldames seize the nearest person to take her place. Unfortunately it is the King who has come out to woo Alice. Hopkins arrives and arrests all the witches including James who, from his captivity, hears Sir Ralph tell of his plans to accuse Alice falsely to get his hands on her land. The King reveals himself and dispenses justice all round, and Alizon (who is really Alice's daughter stolen as a child) and Richard are made happy.

It was a strong and simple plot which gave the opportunity for plenty of traditional comedy of a rather less naive and low quality than was normal. Much of the fun came from the indignities suffered by the disguised King who, as played by Richard Temple, indulged in a thick Scots accent and a jolly number 'On the ither Side of the Tweed' which ended up with a lively Scottish reel. Stanislaus provided the soprano and tenor lovers with some charming light opera solos, but Alice Cook as the merry widow Nutter made a warmly attractive character into a stand-out role as she sang sweetly 'I'm a sad and lonely Widow' and twisted the King's fears of her 'magical powers' in 'Second Sight':

> What then is second sight? 'Tis love

Love draws the clouding veils of sense apart
And soars where eyes of men can never rove
Her second sight is woman's heart.

The show was highly successful in Manchester and ran for its allotted three weeks to excellent houses. *The Era* was most impressed, describing the plot as 'bright and animated', the dialogue as successful in its transitions from 'grave to gay, lively to severe', while the music was adjudged 'high-class yet popular': in fact, all the principal ingredients for a successful musical. Following, intentionally or otherwise, in the footsteps of Cellier, Stanislaus and his librettist had resisted the French opéra-bouffe influence which had invaded works like *Pom* and the féerie aspect with its over-important scenery and costumes and long dance sequences. They had avoided the 'indecent' elements of tights, legs and can-cans, of risqué lines and necklines all of which were widely regarded as necessary accoutrements of success. But Gilbert and Sullivan had laid them aside and triumphed by sheer exuberance of wit and imagination. Cellier had come through by dint of well-engineered simplicity. In *The Lancashire Witches* there was a good element of the same success. The show was performed several times in the Midlands in the years that followed, both in staged performances and as a concert opera, but its popularity was never tried outside its original boundaries and neither of its authors, sadly, was tempted to try his hand at another piece of the same type.

An altogether less substantial piece was the Leicester show *Celia, the Gipsy Girl.* Since his days as a tenor with English Opera and with Fanny Reeve and Mallandaine at the Royalty, Elliot Galer had become manager of the new Royal Opera House in Leicester. It is said that a local banker, Mr Paget, built the theatre to make amends to Galer for having been the cause of a dog-cart accident in which the singer was permanently lamed. Galer and his wife moved in to Paget's own home and for many years thereafter he maintained an active if somewhat curious managership over that theatre and another which he designed and built at Reading. Among Galer's theatre 'rules' were a total ban on smoking and a formal interdiction on non-performers back-stage: both unheard-of restrictions at the time. He also had particular ideas on music. His pantomimes used entirely operatic music and he maintained a large full-time orchestra to accompany the touring companies which formed the bulk of his fare. Occasionally he presented an in-house piece and *Celia* was one of these.

Trouble arose even before the show had opened. Well in advance, Galer had hired Thomas Aynsley Cook to play the leading role, but Cook had a subsequent offer to play five weeks as Dick Deadeye for D'Oyly Carte and, in comparison, twelve performances of Reuben in *Celia* did not seem very important. Not so to Galer who, apart from being the producer, was also the author of the scorned piece. He got an injunction against Cook to prevent him from appearing in *Pinafore* while *Celia* was on, and hoisted Denbigh Newton from the smaller role of Lord Belmore to that of Reuben. With Newton, Edith St John and Galer and his wife starring, *Celia* lasted only six performances, in spite of fair reviews. Cook turned up at the end of the week (with apparently no hard feelings) and appeared in Balfe's *Guy Mannering* as a replacement.

The curtailment of the season was a disappointment for Galer, but there was worse to come. Shortly after the production a letter appeared in the press challenging the originality of the show. *Celia*, it alleged, was a direct pinch from *Sylvia*, a two-act piece by the same author and composer presented at the Royalty in 1866 and published by Metzlers. This was no great piece of detective work. Galer's 'revised' book had been so haphazardly done that the name 'Sylvia' had been left unaltered in several places and the division into the new three acts was quite arbitrary. It was subsequently restored to two by a couple of pen strokes and a shifted interval. Galer hit back. The score was totally new, he claimed, and the book was 'expanded into three acts'. Why shouldn't he use his own old work as the basis for another? He might well have quoted Gilbert as an example. But somehow he seemed to come out of the correspondence the worse. He had unwisely used the all-too-common advertising phrases 'a new and original opera' 'for the first time on any stage'. Any intrinsic merit *Celia* might have possessed was lost in the controversy.

The story of *Sylvia, the Forest Flower/Celia, the Gipsy Girl* (with conveniently equal syllabic construction) was allegedly based on fact. The dashing Captain Seaton, journeying through the forest, meets and falls in love with the gipsy girl, Celia, the darling of her tribe. His host, Lord Belmore, subsequently discovers that Celia is his daughter lost in infancy, and the gipsies render her sadly up to the embraces of Seaton. The three acts were padded out with gipsy jealousies and numerous ballads and choruses of a characteristic nature spread principally among Celia (soprano), Seaton (tenor) and the gipsies Reuben (baritone) and Ronald (mezzo). *Celia* surfaced again the following year at Galer's theatres with Gertrude Cave-Ashton in the title role before being finally put aside.

During the year Reed and Grain provided four new short pieces at St George's Hall. By now, the Gallery company had all but gone. Fanny Holland had married Arthur Law and was touring with an Entertainment they had devised as well as making the occasional foray into the 'real' theatre. Leonora Braham, too, had headed for the brighter lights and her Princess Toto on Broadway was the beginning of a notable career under Gilbert's aegis. Priscilla Reed, after the first piece of the year, joined her husband on the sidelines and, with the death of John Parry, only Alfred Reed and Corney Grain remained active. The casting of the shows and their format became less regular and the old 'repertory' flavour was going.

The first piece was a three-act vaudeville by the a' Beckett brothers called *Grimstone Grange* which centred on a will hidden in an old grange. The heroine's lover dresses as a highwayman to recover it after it has been stolen, and then discovers that he is the heir. *Grimstone Grange* was chiefly remarkable for the facts that it was the first three-part work to be played at St George's Hall and that it marked the effective end of the career of Priscilla Reed. It was followed after a couple of months' run by an Arthur Law trifle *£100 Reward* which also centred on the search for a missing document, this time a marriage certificate which will bring the young lovers together. It was much shorter (being played originally with a revival of the hardy *Charity Begins at Home*) and rather more successful.

Easily the best new offering of the year was *Back from India* contributed by a writer new to the Reed establishment, Henry Pottinger Stephens, with music by the best of their newer composers, Cotsford Dick. Produced in June it was played constantly until March of the following year. The first act, barely original, had a close relationship with *After All.* A gentleman has married the fiancée of a friend in India by pretending that she was unsuitable to be sent out as a bride. On his friend's return he tells him the girl has become a terrible shrew. All threatens to turn out badly when the truth is revealed, but the bacon is saved when the wife's pretty sister turns out to be just the right person to mollify the returned Captain.

In October, *A Pirates' Home* replaced *£100 Reward*. Once again the resemblance to other pieces was notable in a story set on a lighthouse and involving the gentlemen of the cast in piratical disguises in a plot which is resolved by the fishing-up of a pocket-book from the seas. The Christmas piece was *A Christmas Stocking* which turned to the now traditional nursery characters for its inspiration and found little.

When Kate Santley withdrew *La Marjolaine* at the Royalty she replaced it with an unattractive extravaganza, *Little Cinderella*, which was, however, prefaced by an interesting short work in two acts called *Tita in Thibet* written by Frank Desprez. The play was set in the Tibetan town of Lum-ti-foo and brought some very (low) comical situations out of a hitherto unexplored portion of the globe. Tita is the wife of the idol-maker Brum in a land where wives – for obvious economic reasons – are allowed four husbands apiece. Brum foolishly tests his jealous wife with a phony love-letter and she, seeing the trick, resolves to punish him and lines up three more husbands – a Mandarin 2nd Class, a Mandarin 1st Class, and an 'impassioned tea-gardener'. After putting Brum through an actful of deserved misery, Tita tricks two of the suitors into marrying the disguised third (!) and is reconciled with her husband. The role of Tita was tailored for Kate Santley and she played it with all her accustomed gusto leading *The Era* to remark that:

> to those in search of a good and refined evening's entertainment we certainly cannot recommend the Royalty

Tita in Thibet proved to have a quite unexpectedly long life. The following season it was taken up by the eccentric dancer Charles Majilton whose famous touring combination had travelled the world with its lively but definitely provincially-orientated performances of farcical song and dance. Duly revised under the title of *Brum* (A Birmingham Merchant), the 'comic opera' found its rightful place as part of the touring equipment of Majilton's company alongside their long-lived extravaganza *Round the Clock*. Majilton himself was featured in a specially interpolated dance routine. *Brum* proved an excellent accessory for his company and was retained as a prominent and popular part thereof for five seasons. In 1889 it was brought back again featuring a young comedian named Walter Passmore and was played for three more seasons for a grand total of over 2000 performances.

At the Royalty *A Will with a Vengeance* was replaced by a 45-minute operetta called *Nicette* written by Edward Rose, the co-author of *Venus*, with music by Ruggiero Labocetta 'a Portuguese composer'. It proved attractive enough to merit six weeks in support of *Crutch and Toothpick*.

Odoardo Barri, in spite of his name, was British (né Edward Slater). He was a well-known singing teacher and a great personality on the London musical scene for many years. Trained in his early days by the Jesuits, he had begun his life as an oratorio singer in Italy and Spain and had earned his living for some time as a tenor soloist at the Vatican. He fought at Solferino before settling in London and establishing the Odoardo Barri School of Voice Culture which he headed for over fifty years till his death in 1920 at the age of 85. His compositions included a Mass in C for the King of Spain, a small amount of theatre music and some 1,500 songs of which 'The Boys of the old Brigade', 'The Shadow of the Cross' and 'The Good Shepherd' were the best known.

His theatrical effort was a piece called *M.D.* to a script by J. B. Lawreen and Edward Oxenford, best remembered as the writer of the English lyric to 'Funiculi, Funicula'. But it was a show which almost did not eventuate. Barri neglected to seek permission to adapt the story which had provided the basis for his musical. With the score written, the copyright problem arose and the composer fled to his friend Teddy Oxenford with the demand for a quick original libretto to replace the forbidden one. The resultant script told in one act and seventeen numbers the tale of an ancient knight who offers all his wordly goods to whoever will cure him of his gout. Two mannish lady doctors fail and his daughter's lover wins the day and a wife with a liberal prescription of O.D.V. (eau de vie). An interesting cast featured Adelaide Newton and Annie Jolly as the masculine doctors and twenty-six year old Herbert Beerbohm Tree as the gouty gentleman.

1879

26 **ROTHOMAGO** or The Magic Watch. A Grand Christmas Musical Fairy Spectacular in four acts and seventeen tableaux adapted by H. B. Farnie from the French féerie. Music by Edward Solomon (Act 1), Procida Bucalossi (Act 2), Gaston Serpette (Act 3) and Georges Jacobi (Act 4). Produced at the Alhambra Theatre under the management of Charles Morton 22 December, 1879 for a run of 98 performances closing 17 April, 1880.

Rothomago	Harry Paulton
Young Rothomago	Constance Loseby
King Impecunioso XIX.	Louis Kelleher
Surplus	Clavering Power
Dodo	E. J. George
Princess Allegra	Mlle Julic
Fairy Angostura	Annie Bentley
Fairy Anisette	Hetty Tracy
Fracasse	Knight Aston
Frolique	Emma Chambers
Forget-me-not	Rose Stella
Sylph, a page	Carrie Braham
Captain of the bears	Mr Vaughan
Arab devotee	Felix Bury
Scholar	Master F. Marchant
The Twelve Hours, Fairy Godmothers to Young Rothomago:	
Hour of Dawn	Miss Jameson
Hour of Labour	Miss de Lisle
Twilight Hour	Miss Hamilton
Hour of Love	Rose Vere
Breakfast Hour	Miss Veto
Hour of Prayer	Miss Knowles
Hour of the Siesta	Miss Bentley
Midnight Hour	Kate Fellowes
Hour of Pleasure	Miss A. Fellows
Noontide Hour	Miss George
Hour of the Ball	Miss Clifton
Hour of Dinner	Miss Fanchetti

The Grand Vintage Ballet danced by Mlle Theo de Gillert (Champagne), Mlle Rosa (Cognac) with Mlles Anna, Katy, Phillips, Taylor &c.

Memnon, a Grand Egyptian Ballet danced by Mlle Pertoldi (Ibis), Matthews (Ismael), Miss Denevers (Cleopatra), Mlles Anna, Katy, Phillips & Taylor (Priestesses).

Grand Ballet Céramique danced by Mlle Roselli (China), Mlle Rosa (Watteau), Miss Matthews (Geni), Miss Owen (Dresden), Miss Bryan (Sèvres), Miss Braithwaite (Nankin), Miss Coveney (Chelsea) &c.

Md: Georges Jacobi; ch: Mons Bertrand; sc: A. Callcott & F. Lloyds; cos: Wilhelm

27 **THE LANCASHIRE WITCHES** or King James' Frolic. A light opera in three acts by R. T. Gunton. Music by Frederick Stanislaus. Produced at the Theatre Royal, Manchester under the

management of Alfred Thompson 20 October, 1879 for three weeks closing 7 November, 1879.

Alizon . . . . Edith St John
Sir Ralph Ashton . . . . J. Furneaux Cook
Richard Ashton . . . . Henry Hallam
Dame Alice Nutter . . . . Alice Cook
Mother Demdyke . . . . Mrs R. Power
Hopkins . . . . George Leitch
King James I . . . . Richard Temple
Mother Chattox . . . . Bella Cuthbert

Md: John Crook; sc: H. P. Hall & W. B. Spong; cos: Miss Fisher

Produced at the Royal Court Theatre, Liverpool under the management of Capt. R. D. Bainbridge and Mr Duffield 10 September, 1881 for 2 weeks.
Constance Loseby/Gertrude Cave-Ashton (AL), Mlle Mariani (DEM), J. Furneaux Cook (RAL), T. F. Doyle (HOP), W. H. Woodfield/Henry Walsham (RIC), T. Aynsley Cook (KING), Alice Cook (ALICE). Md: John Crook; ch: Emma Toms; sc: H. P. Hall, W. B. Spong & Muir

Produced at the Theatre Royal, Manchester under the management of Captain Richard D. Bainbridge 13 March, 1882 for a two-week season.
Constance Loseby (AL), J. Furneaux Cook (RAL), Fred J. Stimson (HOP), Henry Hallam (RIC), Alice Aynsley Cook (ALICE), Richard Temple (KING)

0028 **CELIA**, The Gipsy Girl. A revised version of *Sylvia, the Forest Flower*. A comic opera in three (later two) acts by Elliot Galer. Music by J. E. Mallandaine. Produced at the Royal Opera House, Leicester under the management of Elliot Galer 20 October, 1879 for six performances to 25 October.

Lord Belmore . . . . Charles Horsman
Reuben . . . . Denbigh Newton
Celia . . . . Carina Clelland
Ronald . . . . Mrs Elliot Galer
Toby . . . . Norman Kirby
Madge . . . . Miss Burdett
Captain Seaton . . . . Elliot Galer

Sc: C. Frampton

Produced at Reading 27 September, 1880 under the management of Charles Durand for a two-week season. Subsequently played at Leicester 8 October sq.
Charles Durand (BEL), Walter Bolton (REU), Gertrude Cave-Ashton (CE), Lucy Franklein (RON), J. McDowell (TOBY), Mlle Mariani (OLIVIA), Dudley Thomas (SEA). Md: J. C. Shepherd; sc: C. Frampton

TITA IN THIBET a comic opera in two acts by Frank Desprez. Produced at the Royalty Theatre under the management of Kate Santley 1 January, 1879 with *Little Cinderella* (*The New Cinderella*). Withdrawn 18 January, 1879.

Tita . . . . Kate Santley
Chinchin . . . . Charles Groves
Brum . . . . Walter H. Fisher
Po Hi . . . . Fred Leslie
Young Hyson . . . . Alma Stanley
The Great Bonze . . . . Charles A. White
The Little Bonze . . . . W. H. Seymour

Revised and reproduced as *Brum*, A Birmingham Merchant, an eccentricity in one act by Charles Majilton and toured by his company in repertoire with *On Business* and *Round the Clock* from 1880.
Louisa Crecy (TITA), Ramsey Danvers (CHIN), Henry D. Burton (BRUM), John Burton (PO), Nelly Milton (HY), Minnie Mulvey (KIO), Angie Russell (GODDESS OF THE TEMPLE), Arthur Blakey (PRIEST OF FO), Nelly Fern (TITA), Wilson Granville (FONG), Edith Cavendish (HONG). Dir/ch: Charles Majilton

GRIMSTONE GRANGE a Tale of Last Century. A vaudeville in three acts by Arthur and Gilbert a'Beckett. Music by King Hall. Produced at St George's Hall under the management of Alfred Reed and R. Corney Grain 17 March, 1879 with *A Trip to China*, replaced by *Our Calico Ball* (23 March). Withdrawn 26 May, 1879.

Mlle Josephine de la Tour . . . . Mrs German Reed
Captain Charles Marjoribanks . . . . . . R. Corney Grain
Copias Wrytte. . . . . Alfred Reed
Alderman Tubkyns . . . . Alfred Bishop
Grizel . . . . Edith Brandon

£100 REWARD by Arthur Law. Music by R. Corney Grain. Produced at St George's Hall under the management of Alfred Reed and R. Corney Grain 27 May, 1879 with *Our Calico Ball* and *Charity Begins at Home*, the latter replaced by *Back from India* 25 June. Withdrawn 26 July, 1879.

Jonathan Mazey. . . . . Alfred Reed
Mrs Butterfield . . . . Lucy Williams
Christopher Lockwood . . . . Alfred Bishop
Frank Maxwell . . . . R. Corney Grain
Evelyn Hope . . . . Edith Brandon

BACK FROM INDIA by Henry Pottinger Stephens. Music by Cotsford Dick. Produced at St George's Hall under the management of Alfred Reed and R. Corney Grain 25 June, 1879 with *Our Calico Ball* and *£100 Reward*. Withdrawn 26 July. Reopened 29 September, withdrawn 20 December. Reopened 26 January, 1880 with *The Pirates' Home* and *Clever People*, replaced respectively by *Castle Botherem* and *Our Table d'Hôte* (16 February). Withdrawn 6 March, 1880.

Captain Rupert Rapier . . . . R. Corney Grain
Rosamond Woodleigh. . . . . Lucy Williams
Abraham Grassleaf . . . . Alfred Reed
Mrs Grassleaf. . . . . Edith Brandon
Jeremiah Diggles . . . . Alfred Bishop

A PIRATES' HOME a vaudeville in one act by Gilbert a'Beckett. Music by Vivian Bligh. Produced at St George's Hall under the management of Alfred Reed and R. Corney Grain 22 October, 1879 with *A Quiet Visit* and *Back From India*. Withdrawn 20 December. Reopened 26 December with *A Christmas Stocking* and *Master Tommy's At Home*. Withdrawn 14 February, 1880.

Lonesome George. . . . . Alfred Reed
Rosie Templeton . . . . Edith Brandon
Digby Straigh . . . . R. Corney Grain
Sir Whipley Creeme . . . . Alfred Bishop
Mrs Player Cardswell. . . . . Lucy Williams

Produced at St George's Hall 4 October, 1880 with *A Flying Visit* and *The London Season*. Withdrawn 18 October, 1880.

A CHRISTMAS STOCKING a fireside fancy by Gilbert a'Beckett. Music by King Hall. Produced at St George's Hall under the management of Alfred Reed and R. Corney Grain 26 December, 1879 with *The Pirates' Home* and *Master Tommy's At Home*. Withdrawn 24 January, 1880.

Little Queenie. . . . . Edith Brandon
Jack-in-the-Box . . . . Alfred Reed
Beadle From Punch & Judy . . . . Alfred Bishop
The Spirit of the Shilling Colour Box . . Lucy Williams
Twelfth Night Prince. . . . . R. Corney Grain

A PAIR OF THEM a musical trifle in one act by Peyton Wrey. Music by W. Meyer Lutz. Produced at the Gaiety Theatre under the management of John Hollingshead 1 March, 1879 at a matinée with *The Serious Family*.

Mr Merryweather . . . . C. Fawcett
Mrs Merryweather . . . . Mathilde Wadman

A GAY CAVALIER an operetta by Ernest Cuthbert. Music by Arthur Nicholson. Produced at the Theatre Royal, Manchester under the management of Sims Reeves 15 September, 1879 and toured in repertoire.

Sir Digby Chick . . . . George Fox
Lady Chick . . . . Emma Howson
Catherine . . . . Lucy Franklein
with . . . . E. Keene

M.D. an operetta by J. B. Lawreen and Edward Oxenford. Music by Odoardo Barri. Produced at the Garrick Theatre under the management of May Bulmer 5 June, 1879.

Dr Mariana Stalker . . . . Adelaide Newton
Dr Betsy Wrackem . . . . Annie Jolly
Clarissa . . . . Fanny Hayward/Annette Ivanova
Sir Benjamin Buffles . . . . H. Beerbohm Tree
Frank . . . . Frederick Russell/Garratt Roche
James Stalker . . . . Horace Wilton

A DRESS REHEARSAL an operetta by George R. Sims. Music by Louis Diehl. Produced at Langham Hall under the management of Lila Clay 30 October, 1879 as part of a programme by Lila Clay's Lady Minstrels.

1880

The 'after-*Pinafore*' period was crucial for the now thoroughly awakened British musical tradition. There were two principal questions: firstly, could Gilbert and Sullivan continue to produce works of the same character and standard, and secondly, and more importantly, could other writers and composers join in, capitalise on the advances made, and bring something of their own to a field which had just brought out its first fully-fledged success? The answers came quickly. By New Year's Eve America knew that Gilbert and Sullivan could undoubtedly carry on in the manner in which they had begun. *The Bold Burglars*, now entitled *The Pirates of Penzance* or Love and Duty (later The Slave of Duty), opened on Broadway on the last night of 1879 to an ecstatic reception. The writers of *Pinafore* had not let their audience down and that audience was duly appreciative.

In fact, they were not the first to see the new piece. For copyright reasons Gilbert, Sullivan and Carte gave the show effectively simultaneous openings in America and Britain, the British performance taking place slightly earlier than its American counterpart. The authors were in America, so music and parts were sent across the Atlantic to Carte's secretary, Helen Lenoir, who organised the British end of the double opening. The Opera Comique company was still going strong with *Pinafore* and, in any case, it seemed hardly wise to pre-empt the forthcoming London season of *The Pirates*, so it was decided that the touring company should have the dubious honour of staging one scratch performance of the new show to secure the U.K. copyright. On 30 December, after one rehearsal, the touring cast of *Pinafore* presented the first-ever performance of *The Pirates of Penzance* to an audience of forty-five people at the seaside town of Paignton. Scenery and costumes were 'done up' to suit. The gentlemen tied handkerchiefs around their heads to signify that they were pirates, and everyone read his or her part and approximated the music. The purpose of the exercise achieved, they then returned to Torquay for a more conventional *Pinafore*.

In the States *The Pirates* created a furore and the other sort of 'pirates' immediately went to work. One thief was none-too-gently ejected from the stalls of the Fifth Avenue Theatre with his blatantly filled shorthand-book confiscated by the management. Others got through the net but Carte and the authors were determined not to be defeated. Carte announced his own touring companies and prepared to sue anyone who showed the intention of staging *The Pirates*. Reputable provincial managers found it easier to deal with the official representatives of the opera than to play it 'the *Pinafore* way'. But all did not run smoothly, and the fault was Carte's. His touring companies were not forthcoming and the provincial managers, waiting impatiently for the latest hit, got annoyed and prepared to break their agreements. One manager in Boston used a legal technicality to prevent the piece being played anywhere in New England after his D'Oyly Carte company failed to turn up.

Then there was the Broadway production. From the start the managers had known they could run at the Fifth Avenue only until the first week of March as the theatre had been booked for another attraction from that date. But Carte temporised. He turned down a Niblo's Garden transfer. Although the theatre had the reputation of being the birthplace of *The Black Crook*, Carte considered it was not a first-class house. March came and, with a huge hit on his hands and tickets still selling at several times their face value on the black market, Carte was obliged to take his production to the Brooklyn Academy of Music where it rusticated until he was able to secure Booth's Theatre and return to Broadway and its profits.

None of this mismanagement was calculated to please Gilbert who made his displeasure felt in his usual forceful way. Another to feel the author's anger was the tenor, Hugh Talbot. Gilbert caught him making 'unauthorised alterations' to his role. Talbot was summarily sacked and an American Frederic brought in until suitable apologies and threats to sue had been made and the unruly tenor was restored.

In spite of Talbot and of Carte's errors of judgement, *The Pirates of Penzance* was a huge success and a glorious confirmation of the talents of Gilbert and Sullivan as the writers of light musical theatre. Gilbert had now settled into a highly individual style of dialogue which he combined with stylish and grotesque plots and comic-strip characters to produce a very particular kind of play, part German Reed entertainment, part comic opera, part burlesque but, above all, his own. Sullivan, too, had succeeded in finding the right style to ally to this creation of Gilbert's: bright and attractive light music with a sufficient backbone of classical and church elements to give it a lasting substance. After three full-length works the manner of the collaboration was set, and received with acclamation.

When *H.M.S. Pinafore* finally furled her sails at the Opera Comique, London was given her first look at the new work and the reaction was every bit as enthusiastic as that of New York. The nucleus of the *Pinafore* team remained and Gilbert had supplied them with suitable roles: for Grossmith the dotty Major General, for Richard Temple a fine burlesque Pirate King, for George Power a primo tenore of reasonable range. Once again, though, a new prima donna was needed and the choice fell on the inexperienced 26-year-old, Marion Hood, who not only had the advantage of being extremely pretty but who auditioned the *Dinorah* 'Shadow Song' for the partners with such aplomb that she was raised straight to leading lady status.

In the contralto department there were graver problems. Harriet Everard, the heroine of the *Pinafore* invasion, was cast as Ruth, the clumsy nursemaid who apprentices her charge to a pirate instead of a pilot 'through being hard of hearing'. But during rehearsals Miss Everard was badly injured when a piece of scenery fell on her and Emily Cross who had appeared in the long running Opera Comique forepiece *After All* was called on at short notice to replace her. With Jessie Bond away playing Edith in New York, new ladies also had to be found for the minor roles. One of these was the very young Lillian La Rue who had taken over as Hebe towards the end of the run of *Pinafore*. Miss La Rue later became prima donna of the Carl Rosa Opera and was seen as Carmen throughout Britain.

Rutland Barrington claims in his autobiography that he was not originally to be included in the company for the *Pirates of Penzance* as the authors considered there was no part for him. Barrington, who had got himself nicely settled during *Pinafore* in the prospect of future stardom, or at least employment, asked if he might have the 'small' role of the lugubrious police sergeant which had probably been intended for Fred Clifton. His request was granted and Barrington stayed with the company to score with one of his very best characterisations.

For the book of *The Pirates of Penzance* Gilbert used his 'Bold Burglars' idea, blending it with the saga of Captain Bang from his earlier piece *Our Island Home.* Frederic, like the Captain, has been bound in error as apprentice to a pirate. Whereas Bang used an astronomical trick to get out of his indentures, poor Frederic is eventually held to his for a similar reason. Being born in a Leap Year, on the twenty-ninth of February, he will not reach the end of his apprenticeship until 1940, for he has a birthday only every four years! Unaware of this he has meanwhile left the pirate band and, through an over-developed sense of duty, vowed himself to the extermination of his old associates at the head of a band of police. He has also vowed himself to Mabel, daughter of Major General Stanley. But Stanley has committed the frightful sin of taking advantage of the susceptibilities of the pirates. To stop his daughters being forced to marry members of the band he has pleaded to being an orphan. As they are all orphans too they have relented. But Frederic, recalled to his indentures by the aforesaid astronomical discovery, is obliged by duty to disabuse the pirates, and 'with catlike tread' they descend to 'wreak a penalty fifty-fold' on the unfortunate Stanley. There is a battle and the pirates triumph, but the Sergeant of Police has a trump card – the name of Queen Victoria! The pirates yield, for 'with all their faults, they love their Queen'. But Ruth has a revelation – the pirates are all noblemen who have Gone Wrong. They are quite eligible matches for General Stanley's daughters after all.

Unlike *Pinafore* which survived almost totally as originally produced, *The Pirates of Penzance* had undergone a number of changes since its original production in Paignton. New songs had been added and others cut out. The Pirates' chorus 'Come, Friends who Plough the Sea' was one notable addition, as was Mabel's famous air 'Poor wandering One' with its chorus of what Arthur Sullivan described as 'barnyard effects':

> Poor Wandering One, though thou hast surely strayed
> Take heart of grace, thy steps retrace
> Poor Wandering One . .

Both these numbers were immediately amongst the most popular, as were Richard Temple's rollicking Pirate King ballad and the comically glum Policemen's Chorus:

> When a felon's not engaged in his employment
> Or maturing his felonious little plan
> His capacity for innocent enjoyment
> Is just as great as any honest man's.
> Our feelings we with difficulty smother
> When constabulary duty's to be done
> Ah! Take one consideration with another
> A policeman's lot is not a happy one.

The tone of *The Pirates of Penzance* was a little less joyous and light-hearted than that of *Pinafore*, probably owing to the nature of the story which was basically a burlesque of melodrama. There was, nevertheless, plenty of humour in such numbers as the Major General's patter-song:

> I am the very model of a modern major general
> I've information vegetable, animal and mineral,

I know the kings of England, and I quote the fights historical
From Marathon to Waterloo in order categorical.
I'm very well acquainted too with matters mathematical
I understand equations, both the simple and quadratical
About bi-nomial theorems I'm teeming with a lot o' news
With many cheerful facts about the square on the hypotenuse

to set alongside the simple vocal lines of the charming duet 'Ah, Leave me not to Pine Alone' and the delightful concerted music of which the unaccompanied 'Hail, Poetry' section proved one of the highlights:

Hail, Poetry, thou heaven-born maid
Thou gildest e'en the pirates' trade
Hail, flowing fount of sentiment
All hail, all hail, Divine Emollient!

The show was full of 'hits', musical and otherwise. London took to *The Pirates of Penzance* with the same fervour it had displayed over *Pinafore* and the show settled into the Opera Comique for a twelve months' run. Its history thereafter was one of uneventful successes. It quickly took its place alongside *Pinafore* in the D'Oyly Carte touring repertoire where it survived a century with undiminished popularity. It was played throughout the world in licensed productions and later by Carte's companies. It was revived at the Savoy by both Carte and, later, his widow. Finally, almost a hundred years after its first production *The Pirates of Penzance* came back to the forefront of the musical theatre with an impetus almost as great as that of its original production.

In 1980 the New York Shakespeare Festival opened a version of the piece at the Open Air Theatre in Central Park with a reorchestrated score and the ostensibly unlikely casting of popular vocalist Linda Ronstadt as Mabel. The rest of the casting was in the same vein. General Stanley's daughters belted out 'Climbing over rocky Mountains' in ringing chest voices, Frederic crooned his way through 'Ah, Is there not one maiden Breast' with maximum effect and an Elvis Presley cadenza, and Gilbert's burlesque pirates tumbled joyously on to the stage to battle with rubber-legged dancing policemen in a farrago of fun. The whole production rang with a comic vigour which Gilbert would have thoroughly appreciated whilst keeping fairly closely to the original text and music.[1] The huge success of the 'new' *Pirates* was continued on Broadway at the Uris and Minskoff Theatres for 787 performances – the longest run achieved by any production anywhere of a Gilbert and Sullivan musical.

In 1982 this latest version of *The Pirates of Penzance* was produced in London, at the Theatre Royal, Drury Lane. It featured Tim Curry, fresh from Broadway success in *Amadeus*, as the Pirate King with George Cole and Pamela Stephenson, both popular television figures, as the Major General and Mabel in a vivacious production which helped to palliate the vocal deficiencies of the top-billed players. In the best tradition of Carte's early days it also introduced some exciting young players in Michael Praed (Frederic), Chris Langham (Sergeant) and Karen Lancaster (Edith/Mabel) as *The Pirates of Penzance* outran its original London season.

A motion picture version starring the principal members of the Central Park cast was filmed in Cornwall in 1982 but the authors would have recognised from *Pinafore*

[1] Josephine's 'Sorry Her Lot' (*Pinafore*) and the patter trio from *Ruddigore* were incongruously inserted to bolster the roles of Mabel and the Pirate King and a piece of the 2nd Act finale, which had been cut by the authors prior to the London production, was restored.

days the spirit in which a simultaneous film, *The Pirate Movie,* appeared from Australia. In the worst traditions of Sgr. Ricciardi and Kelly and Leon and the other 'Down Under' pirates of early days it was a pasticcio of the genuine article and modern interpolations.

Gilbert and Sullivan had assured the continuation of the genre. Now it was important to see if it could expand. Who could follow and compete with the new idols of the British musical theatre? Not unexpectedly it was Edward Solomon who was the first to put forward a new work, a two-act nautical comic opera called *Billee Taylor.* 'Teddy' Solomon had rapidly become one of the 'characters' of the London theatre scene. Jewish, precocious, flamboyant and eccentric to a degree, he was also highly talented and had quickly risen from his unobtrusive position in the orchestra of the Middlesex Music Hall to metropolitan conducting posts and was producing large amounts of worthwhile music which had made him exceedingly well-known and widely considered as the coming man.

Billee Taylor was his first genuine full-length musical and it was written in collaboration with the journalist Henry Pottinger Stephens. Stephens had only recently made his theatre début collaborating with his friend Frank Burnand on the book of *Balloonacy* for the Royalty where Solomon was musical director and had subsequently provided the burlesque *The Corsican Bros. & Co. Ltd* for the Gaiety. *Billee Taylor*, written and composed in six weeks,[1] was his third libretto and his first original musical.

He did not attempt to produce a 'Gilbertian' book. Although there were one or two elements of similarity, he took his story principally from the popular old ballad 'Billy Taylor', the tale of a press-ganged lad followed to sea by his sweetheart. In Stephens' version Billee, a virtuous gardener, is beloved by Arabella Lane, the well-off daughter of 'a self-made knight', but he scorns her for the seemingly modest Charity Girl, Phoebe. The jealous Arabella joins with the schoolmaster, Christopher Crab, and the sea-captain, Flapper, two of Phoebe's admirers, to stop the wedding and Billee is pressed into the navy on his wedding day. In Act 2 we find that Phoebe and her friends, disguised as sailors, have gone to sea in search of him but the determined Arabella has got there first and Billee, now promoted Lieutenant, finds her rank and financial position well suited to his new pretensions. Phoebe, furious, tries to shoot him, but then it is discovered that Lt. Taylor is a fraud and a coward. He is stripped of his honours and disgraced, and to his rank is raised the vigorous Phoebe who settles for a Lieutenancy and a life on the ocean wave.

'Pot' Stephens had done himself proud with his libretto. It was simple, charming and humorous, producing its fun without any obvious effort and without the conscious sophistication of Gilbert's libretti. His characters were delightful. The anti-heroic tenor hero: ' . . the pink of rustic perfection, the incarnation of horticultural morality . . ' who professes to judge everything by its relation to 'virtue' but who is, in reality, a pretty but worthless fraud; the suitably modest charity girl, Phoebe, beneath whose starched pinafore lurks a most unsuitably adventurous and independent spirit; the dismal schoolmaster, Crab, with his longing to be a 'villain': 'I will meditate upon crime, it will refresh me . . ' which always backfires on him. The lusty Captain Flapper with his heavy tack towards every frock in sight, and the determinedly pining Arabella

[1] The first performance was given with incomplete orchestrations and with Auber's *Le Maçon* overture taking the place of the one Solomon had not got round to writing.

Lane who leaves pints of ale in the woodshed to attract her Billee's affection.

The neophyte producer William Edgecumbe Rendle[1] had gathered together a fine cast to fill these roles, headlining Kathleen Corri, a member of the famous musical family and a recent Serpolette (Globe) and Dolly (*Sultan of Mocha*) as Phoebe; Fleming Norton, the Imperial's Sir Joseph Porter, as the lecherous sea captain; Alhambra star Emma Chambers as Arabella; and the favourite comic J. D. Stoyle as the 'Heart of Oak', Ben Barnacle. Solomon provided pretty and suitable music. To what was essentially an old ballad tale he set simple, ballad-like music and succeeded in bringing out several very good songs and one major hit in Ben Barnacle's song 'All on account of Eliza'. This song, described as a 'romance', told of how Ben had gone to sea and become a press-ganger when his Eliza upped and wed another man. James Stoyle put it across with his usual comic skill and 'Eliza' quickly became as popular as any song in town, including anything from *The Pirates of Penzance*:

> The yarn as I am about to spin
> Is all on account of Eliza;
> I'll tell you how I was taken in
> All on account of Eliza;
> She said that she'd ever be true to one
> But she bolted away with a son of a gun!
> So I cut my stick and to sea I run
> All on account of Eliza.

The other principal success of the show was not due entirely to skilful songwriting:

> Everyone should see and hear the ten pretty Charity Girls in *Billee Taylor* at the Imperial. Their song 'We Stick To Our Letters' was the hit of Saturday last (*World*)

Charles Harris, who was turning stage direction into a profession and the chorus into a movable and useful set of individuals, had selected ten very pretty girls for the Charity Girls' song and dance routine and they and it became one of the show's highlights. Crab's song 'The poor wicked Man' describing his attempts to be a villain, Phoebe's ballads 'Yesterday and Tomorrow' and 'The wilful Girl' and Billee's self-satisfied 'The virtuous Gardener' all added notably to the strength of a score that fell away just a little in a second act which, surprisingly, consisted almost entirely of choruses and concerted pieces.

The reaction to *Billee Taylor* was largely appreciative. Some of the newspapers insisted on finding similarities to *Pinafore* and *The Pirates*:

> The most that can be said for the music by Edward Solomon and for the words by Henry Pottinger Stephens is that they both indicated an assiduous study of the works of Messrs Gilbert & Sullivan (*Era Almanac*)

Admittedly there were a few comparable points. A patter song for Arthur Williams as Sir Mincing Lane bore some resemblance to Sir Joseph Porter's famous song:

> Many years ago I made a start
> With nothing as a grocer's boy
> I carried parcels round in a light spring cart

[1] Father of Frank Rendle, lessee of Covent Garden, and Florence, later Lady Augustus Harris. Rendle's own principal claim to fame was as the inventor of puttyless glazing.

And served out pickles and soy
By dint of assiduity and a dextrous hand
I rose a cashier to be
For I always mixed the sugar with sand
And sloe leaves sold for tea
For a self-made man you see in me
Not born of the aristocracy
It's a feather in my cap
That I never cared a rap
How I gathered up the L.S.D.

but most of the numbers leaned more to the style of Cellier than to that of Sullivan and the humour, though occasionally delightfully quirky, was much more straightforward than that of Gilbert. *Billee Taylor* was a piece in a thoroughly British tradition, logically and effectively combining the happiest elements of its predecessors. It was also decidely popular. Even *The Era Almanac* after its dismissal of the work was obliged to admit:

> That the piece lacked originality did not seem to be considered an objection by the patrons, however, as some of the expressions in it soon became nearly as familiar as the much reiterated witticisms of *Pinafore* and *The Pirates of Penzance*.

If some were unwilling to give the piece its due, others saw things differently. *Life* considered:

> Even the Opera Comique must look to its laurels . . nothing more perfect has been put on the stage in the presentation of comic opera than is *Billee Taylor*.

and the noted critic Clement Scott weighed in firmly on the 'pro' side:

> I don't think sufficient justice has been done to *Billee Taylor* which is surely an admirable bit of fooling, bright, witty, capitally danced and sung, and just like good champagne without a headache in it. I advise everyone to go and see *Billee Taylor* to laugh and be amused . . not even at *The Pirates of Penzance* have I seen people enjoy themselves more or go away from the theatre more refreshed and lighthearted. For my own part I should have liked to have heard it all over again . . (*Theatre*)

Unfortunately, *Billee Taylor* was to have a bumpy ride in London. After six weeks the chance was taken to replace the tenor, Rivers, who was putting up a mournfully unconvincing performance in the title-role. Then first Fleming Norton, then Arthur Williams retired and James Stoyle having played Ben on December 30 failed to turn up on New Year's Eve. He was dead. Then it snowed. People stayed away and one performance had to be cancelled. To top it all, relations between the authors and the management were worsening. The score and the American rights had both been sold previous to production, but D'Oyly Carte, sensing a piece of genuine competition, was showing interest in getting in on *Billee Taylor*. The authors were delighted, Rendle less so. The net result was that *Billee Taylor* was withdrawn from the Imperial Theatre, after only three months' run, with houses still running at an excellent level.

Carte had obtained the American rights and arranged with E. E. Rice for a production at the Standard Theatre, New York. Charles Harris was bundled onto the S. S. *Britannic* with the set models and Pilotell's costume designs, and just a fortnight after its London closure *Billee Taylor* opened on Broadway. As in London it was extremely well received, particularly A. W. F. McCollin's 'All on account of Eliza', the Charity Girls' Chorus ('as good as the Policemen's chorus in *The Pirates of Penzance* by which it is evidently suggested'[1]), and the 'Self-Made Knight' of J. H. Ryley, now permanently established in America at the head of D'Oyly Carte's companies. It succeeded excellently in upholding the reputation established for the British musical by *Pinafore* and *The Pirates* and, indeed, in its initial Broadway showing outran its London production, being done at the Standard 104 times consecutively and extending its intended season to its utter limits.

Its popularity soon resulted in Carte having to defend his rights. After the show had become established as a hit, Carte was surprised by the defection of his business manager, Everard M. Stuart. He was more surprised still when Stuart announced his own production of *Billee Taylor* for a Baltimore opening. Carte prepared to sue but then discovered that, although Stuart had pilfered the title and Solomon's by now popular score, he was declaring himself free from copyright restriction on the grounds that he was using a new libretto prepared by a New York journalist, L. P. Richardson.

Billee Taylor became a fast favourite and appeared regularly over the following years both on the touring circuits and for brief seasons on Broadway and in the West End. John Hollingshead had particular faith in it. During the original run his Gaiety company had played the burlesque *The Half-Crown Diamonds* at matinées at the Imperial and, in return, Rendle had sent his company to the Gaiety for three Saturdays with encouraging results. In 1882 Hollingshead revived *Billee Taylor* for a series of matinées which led to an evening run of three weeks and further revivals in 1884 and 1885, the latter of which proved successful enough to warrant a transfer to Hollingshead's new Empire Theatre as a Christmas attraction. The authors brought it back to town yet again the following year at Toole's Theatre with Emily Spiller in breeches as Billee, but in spite of the presence in the cast of Arthur Williams and Harriet Coveney, both of whom had grown considerably in fame since the original production, it was soon removed.

In America it proved even more tenacious. It returned to Broadway for several seasons including an appearance on the Castle Square Opera programme in a double bill with *I Pagliacci* as late as 1898 and was widely produced around the country. In 1882 Howard Vernon introduced the piece to Australian audiences with the young Nellie Stewart as Phoebe and in 1884 a continental tour starring Lillian Russell and Frederic Solomon attempted to introduce Europe to the joys of the English musical with performances of *Billee Taylor* in France, Belgium, Holland and Italy. Touring productions continued in Britain and from 1887 the show was consistently on the road as a part of the juvenile opera companies run by Warwick Grey and Harry Battersby. Although one way and another *Billee Taylor* never got the extended West End run it deserved, it maintained sufficient popularity for D'Oyly Carte to revive it in the provinces as late as 1893.

Two days after the opening of *Billee Taylor* another new work put in a brief appearance, this time in Manchester. Following the example of Cellier and Stanislaus, a third Manchester musical director, John Crook, produced a major musical. Crook had not, to that date, written any work of significance. His compositions had been limited to incidental theatre music and occasional pieces for pantomimes until the successful production of a short piece, *Sage and Onions*, in February. By November he had produced *The King's Dragoons*, a three-act piece, in collaboration with the librettist J. Wilton Jones known principally as the author of the burlesque *Cruel*

[1] *Era* U.S. correspondent

Carmen currently being toured by the Walton Family starring Alice Aynsley Cook. *The King's Dragoons* was a very different kind of work.

Set in 1703, it opened in traditional rustic revelry. The Dragoons are making merry at the tavern run by Mistress Dorothy and, carried away with the occasion, young Robin, her helper, joins up. His sister, Alice, is distraught and the two ladies begin to plot how to get the now reluctant Robin out of his vow. Alice declares that she will wed the man who will take his place and hangs her locket on a bush as a token for him who will go. Edgar, son of the local Marquis and Alice's true love, secretly takes the locket and goes off to war with the Dragoons. When he has served his time, Edgar returns to claim his unknowing bride but the wicked Marquis has got hold of the locket which had been taken from the neck of his son as he lay wounded on the battlefield. The Marquis threatens to wed Alice himself, but Robin succeeds in stealing the locket and Edgar arrives picturesquely at the head of his division to claim his bride.

The piece was amusingly if rather amateurishly written around its old-fashioned and drawn-out French story, and Crook's music was of the ballad-opera type, thus at its most attractive in the solos for Alice ('Home of my Childhood Days'), Dorothy ('The little Drummer Boy') and Edgar's stirring 'My Sweetheart and my King'. The comedy portion of the play, rather slighter than was usual, fell to Fred Stimson as Robin and Furneaux Cook as Sergeant Crowe. Cook's character was written with a touch of warmth and his return as a scarred and grizzled veteran to the inn where he had flirted with the landlady in the early scenes made a surprisingly moving moment amongst the conventional amours of the hero and heroine.

But whereas Stephens and Solomon had combined something of the 'new humour' with their old and English tale and come up with a work which appealed to the public, Jones and Crook had failed to keep abreast of the times and, like *The Lancashire Witches*, their pleasant work rated only a short run in Manchester. It later appeared for several short seasons in the Midlands where its straightforward book and genuine music found a sensible acceptance, but was never tried further afield until it was the object of a successful season in Australia in 1882/3.

In spite of the huge appeal of *The Pirates of Penzance* and the popularity of *Billee Taylor*, the French musical was still holding its own in the West End. *Les Cloches de Corneville* had a five-month run on its second entry, and amongst the new works Varney's *Les Mousquetaires* (au Couvent), Offenbach's *La Fille du Tambour Major* and particularly *Olivette* made their presence felt. *Olivette* introduced the music of Audran to London audiences and followed the 502 performances of *Madame Favart* at the Strand with 466-night run which sealed that theatre's reconversion from burlesque house to bastion of the musical. Only at the Gaiety and the Royalty was burlesque still holding up its head. The musical was 'in' with a vengeance.

The British musical had done well on Broadway. *Pinafore* and *The Pirates* had created a great interest and Alfred Cellier had been there in the middle of it all. He had works of his own to offer and soon Broadway was introduced to them. *Charity Begins at Home* was the first. D'Oyly Carte's American associates John T. Ford and John A. McCaull bought the Broadway Opera House, and opened it on 31 March, refurbished and rechristened the Bijou Theatre, with an all German Reed programme of Cellier's perennial piece and *Ages Ago*. Cellier and Freddie Clay each conducted his own work and the programme went down exceedingly well. Clay returned to Britain and *Ages Ago* was replaced by *The Spectre Knight* which held the second half of the bill until the end of the six week season.

The success of this enterprise tempted McCaull to try more of Cellier's works and, in conjunction with the composer and the soprano Blanche Roosevelt, he announced the preparation of the 'Blanche Roosevelt Opera Co' to present *The Sultan of Mocha*, *Nell Gwynne* and a new work based on Longfellow, *The Mask of Pandora*, with a libretto by B. C. Stephenson. The enterprise was doomed to heavy failure. *The Sultan of Mocha* opened on Broadway in September in the most awful disarray. The principals didn't know their lines and Cellier was forced to carry on audible conversations from the pit with both the stage and the prompter. Leonora Braham as Dolly battled bravely against impossible odds with the experienced Americans William Hamilton and Eugene Clarke doing their best, but they had no chance. Time and again the performance dwindled to a halt in an embarrassing display of inefficiency.

A week later *The Sultan* and the Opera Company withdrew from New York leaving $10,000 and a promise to return with Miss Roosevelt when she should have 'recovered'. *The Sultan*'s Broadway run (if it can be called such) was marred by personal tragedy for its leading lady as well, when Leonora Braham learned that her husband, F. E. Lucy Barnes, had committed suicide in Montreal. *Nell Gwynne* was put back on the shelf and the mysterious *Mask of Pandora* was presumably never written. Cellier's chance for Broadway fame had been squandered irrevocably.

In London a number of good short pieces were produced during the year. Carte staged a Desprez-Cellier one-acter *In the Sulks* which he played as a forepiece to *The Pirates of Penzance* at the Opera Comique and, as an alternative to the long-lived *After All*, in his touring companies. *In the Sulks* was a very slight piece built around a domestic tiff. Mrs Liverby, having made her husband jealous with a trick love-letter, has to get round him so that he will talk to her again. It was a lively piece of nonsense and well-received as an introduction to the main entertainment of the evening. Carte also used two more new short pieces on tour, *Six and Six* written by his touring m.d., P. W. Halton, and *Four by Honours*.

At St George's Hall the best piece of the year was *A Flying Visit*, a curious concoction involving Corney Grain as a tutor sharing his attentions between an aesthetically-bent maid and the more prosaic Thomasina while he discovers which is the better financial prospect. He is finally beaten to the post by his 15 year-old protegé (Alfred Reed). An added ingredient was an impersonation of a Germanic inventor by Alfred Bishop, and the music was written by Grain himself, taking up where Reed had left off under the dearth of suitable good composers.

For the first piece of the of the year he had secured the services of Hamilton Clarke. *Castle Botherem* had the tenants of a derelict Irish castle trying various means to scare away the rightful owners. Arthur Law, no longer with the Reeds, supplied the script. The other two pieces of the year were a'Beckett's *Three Flats* and *A Turquoise Ring*, an improbable French vaudeville play with music by Lionel Benson which nevertheless achieved a certain success. Revivals of *Very Catching* and *A Pirates' Home* completed the programme.

John Crook's one-acter *Sage and Onions* was based on the play *The Goose with the golden Eggs* and involved a goose sent as a present to Miss Clara by her aunt. Her father gives it as a gift to his preferred candidate for the girl's attentions, but the goose is 'off' and that gentleman presents it to his poorer rival. Suddenly it is learned that Auntie had stuffed the goose with banknotes. Frantic efforts to recover it end when Auntie says that she decided to send a cheque at the last minute. Richer by £500, Miss Clara can now choose her preferred husband and does. *Sage and Onions* was a notable first effort by a composer who was to remain busy in the field for many years and score several triumphs.

Edward Solomon wrote a small piece called *Popsy Wopsy* for Kate Lawler's season at the Royalty. Miss Lawler, in the title role, chatted up her would-be-lover's father to get his consent while her theatre-mad brother keeps popping up through a trapdoor in various disguises. It was found most entertaining in spite of the fact that Miss Lawler really couldn't sing.

The 1880 season also saw the first production of a novelty called *Bears not Beasts* written by George Capel, author/composer/actor and currently m.d. of Henry Burton's touring company which was based at the Princess's Theatre, Glasgow. The company presented the operetta in conjunction with the comedy *Turtle Doves* as the bulwark of Burton's touring repertoire for seven years. The story opens with a shipwreck on the island of the Grand Pascha. Petroleum Peck, manager of a menagerie, and Timothy Thompkins make it ashore, but think their wives are lost along with the animals. Only a white bearskin is saved. But the ladies are not lost and run into the Pascha who is mourning the loss of his pet bear. Peck, in the bearskin, is caught as a replacement and delights the potentate with his antics, but the Pascha wants a black bear too, so Thompkins gets in on the act and both men end up in the bear-pit before all is sorted out and they are reunited with their wives. It was a low comedy piece with plenty of fun in it and a few lively songs by H. Round which proved extremely popular in the mainly smaller dates that Burton covered.

1880

0029 **THE PIRATES OF PENZANCE** a comic opera in two acts by W. S. Gilbert. Music by Arthur Sullivan. Performed for the first time at the Bijou Theatre, Paignton, by Richard D'Oyly Carte's touring company 30 December, 1879 for one performance, as a copyright performance.

Major General Stanley	Richard Mansfield
Frederic	Llewellyn Cadwaladr
Pirate King	F. Federici
Samuel	G. J. Lackner
James	John Le Hay
Sergeant of Police.	Fred Billington
Mabel	Emilie Petrelli
Edith	Marian May
Kate.	Lena Monmouth
Isobel	Kate Neville
Ruth.	Fanny Harrison

Produced at the Fifth Avenue Theatre, New York, under the management of Richard D'Oyly Carte 31 December, 1879. Withdrawn 6 March, 1880. Re-opened at the Academy of Music, Brooklyn, 8 March. Re-opened at the Fifth Avenue Theatre 17 May and played there to 5 June, 1880.

Major General Stanley	J. H. Ryley
Frederic.	Hugh Talbot/Wallace Macreery/ Louis Pfau
Pirate King	Sgr. Broccolini
Samuel	J. Furneaux Cook
Sergeant of the Police.	Fred Clifton
Mabel	Blanche Roosevelt/Marie Conron/ Sallie Reber
Edith	Jessie Bond/Miss Lennox
Kate.	Rosina Brandram/Miss Kavanagh
Isobel	Billie Barlow/Miss Lawrence
Ruth.	Alice Barnett/Rosina Brandram

Produced at the Opera Comique under the management of Richard D'Oyly Carte 3 April, 1880 for a run of 363 performances closing 2 April, 1881.

Major General Stanley	George Grossmith (Frank Thornton)
Frederic.	George Power/W. H. Seymour/ Durward Lely
Pirate King	Richard Temple/George Temple
Samuel	George Temple/Edward Lyster (Frank Thornton)
Sergeant of Police.	Rutland Barrington
Mabel	Marion Hood/Ellen Shirley/Emilie Petrelli (Minna Louis)
Edith	Julia Gwynne/Jessie Bond
Kate.	Lillian La Rue/Julia Gwynne/Sybil Grey

Isobel . . . . Neva Bond/Billie Barlow
Ruth. . . . . Emily Cross/Harriet Everard/Alice Barnett

Md: François Cellier/Alfred Cellier; sc: J. O'Connor; cos: Faustin, Alias and Messrs Nathan

Produced at Booth's Theatre, New York 13 September, 1880 by the Boston Ideal Opera Co. for two weeks to 25 September.
Henry C. Barnabee (MG), Tom Karl/W. H. Fessenden (F), Myron Whitney (PK), W. H. MacDonald (SAM), George Frothingham (SGT), Mary Beebe/Marie Stone (M), Clara Merivale (E), Lizzie Burton (K), Miss Mitchell (IS), Adelaide Phillips (R)

Played in New York by the Boston Ideal Co., the Boston Comic Opera Co., the Emilie Melville Co. and J. C. Duff's company in repertoire and short seasons 1881–1891.

Produced at the Savoy Theatre under the management of Richard D'Oyly Carte 23 (?26) December, 1884 with a juvenile cast for a series of matinées ending 14 February, 1885.
Edward Percy (MG), Harry Tebbutt (F), Stephen Adeson (PK), William Pickering (SAM), Charles Adeson (SGT), Elsie Joel (M), Alice Vicat (E), Eva Warren (K), Florence Montrose (IS), Georgia Esmond (R). Dir: Richard Barker; md: François Cellier

Produced at the Savoy Theatre under the management of Richard D'Oyly Carte 17 March, 1888 for a run of 80 performances closing 6 June, 1888.
George Grossmith (MG), J. G. Robertson (F), Richard Temple (PK),Richard Cummings (SAM), Rutland Barrington (SGT), Geraldine Ulmar (M), Jessie Bond (E), Nellie Kavanagh (K), Nellie Lawrence (IS), Rosina Brandram (R). MD: François Cellier

Produced at the Theater an der Wien as *Die Piraten* (Der Sklave seiner Pflicht) 1 March 1889.

Produced at the Savoy Theatre under the management of Mrs D'Oyly Carte 30 June, 1900 for a run of 127 performances closing 5 November, 1900.
Henry Lytton (MG), Robert Evett (F), Jones Hewson (PK), W. H. Leon (SAM), Walter Passmore (SGT), Isabel Jay (M), Lulu Evans (E), Alice Coleman/Louie Pounds (K), Agnes Fraser (IS), Rosina Brandram (R)

Produced at the Savoy Theatre under the management of the D'Oyly Carte Opera Company 1 December, 1908 for a run of 43 performances.
C. H. Workman (MG), Henry Herbert (Ernest Leeming) (F), Henry Lytton (PK), Leo Sheffield (SAM), Rutland Barrington (SGT), Dorothy Court (M), Jessie Rose (E), Beatrice Boarer (K), Ethel Lewis (Doris Rayne) (IS), Louie Rene (R). Md: François Cellier

Subsequently played by the D'Oyly Carte Opera Company on tour and in London in repertoire.

Produced at the Plymouth Theatre, New York under the management of Winthrop Ames 6 December, 1926 for a run of 128 performances.
Ernest Lawford (MG), William Williams (F), John Barclay (PK), J. Humbird Duffey (SAM), William C. Gordon (SGT), Ruth Thomas (M), Dorothy Coulter/Carol Atherton (E), Sybil Sterling (K) Adele Sanderson (I), Paula Langlen (MAUD), Vera Ross (R) with George C. Lehrian, Bert Prival. Dir: Winthrop Ames

Played in New York by the D'Oyly Carte Opera Company and other repertory companies for short seasons.

Produced at the Phoenix Theatre in a production from the Stratford Festival Theatre, Canada 6 September, 1961 for a season of 62 performances closing 22 October, 1961.
Eric House (MG), Andrew Downie (F), Harry Mossfield (PK), Alexander Gray (SAM), Howell Glynne (SGT), Marion Studholme (M), Annabelle Adams (E), Genevieve Gordon (K), Irene Byatt (R). Md: Henri René

Produced at Her Majesty's Theatre in a production from the Stratford Festival Theatre, Canada 15 February, 1962 under the management of Tennent Productions Ltd. in association with Contemporary Productions (Canada).
Eric House (MG), Andrew Downie (F), Harry Mossfield (PK), Donald Young (SAM), Howell Glynne (SGT), Marion Studholme (M), Annabelle Adams (E), Genevieve Gordon (K), Irene Byatt (R) with Theresia Bester, Gillian Humphries, Brenda Scaife, Anne Edwards, Ann Pidgeon, Vivienne Stevens, Mary Eley, Joan Ryan, Elizabeth West. George Ballantine, Gordon Dobson, Emyr Greene, David Harris, Vernon Midgely, Brian Beaton, Edward Evanko, Robin

Haddow, Robert Jeffrey, Bruce Lochtie, Raymond Edwards, John Sinclair, Jeff Hall, Bobby Scott-Webster. Dir: Tyrone Guthrie; md: Kenneth Alwyn; ch: Douglas Campbell; cos/sc: Brian Jackson

Produced at the Delacorte Theatre, New York, under the management of Joseph Papp and the New York Shakespeare Festival 15 July, 1980 for a season of 10 previews and 35 performances ending 31 August, 1980. Opened at the Uris Theatre, New York, 8 January, 1981. Transferred to the Minskoff Theatre 12 August, 1981. Closed 28 November, 1982 after a run of 20 previews and 787 performances.
George Rose/George S. Irving (MG), Rex Smith/Robby Benson/Patrick Cassidy/Peter Noone (F), Kevin Kline/Treat Williams/Garry Sandy/James Belushi (PK), Stephen Hanan/Walter Niehenke (SAM), Tony Azito/David Garrison (SGT), Linda Ronstadt/Maureen McGovern/Karla de Vito/Kathryn Morath/Pam Dawber (M), Alice Playten//Alexandra Korey/Marcie Shaw/Nancy Heiken (E), Marcie Shaw/Laurie Beechman/Bonnie Simmons (K), Wendy Wolfe/Maria Guida (I) with Robin Boudreau, Maria Guida, Nancy Heikin, Audrey Lavine, Bonnie Simmons, Dean Badolato, Brian Bullard, Mark Meudert, Walter Caldwell, Keith David, Tim Flavin, G. Eugene Moose, Joseph Neal, Walter Niehenke, Joe Pichette, Barry Tarallo, Michael Edwin Willson//George Kmeck, Daniel Marcus, Ellis Skeeter Williams, Scott Burkholder, Ray Gill, Phil La Duca. Dir: Wilford Leach; md: William Elliott /Dan Berlinghoff; ch: Graciela Daniele; sc: Wilford Leach and Bob Shaw (and Jack Chandler); cos: Patricia McGourty

Produced at the Theatre Royal, Drury Lane under the management of Michael White 26 May, 1982 for a run of 601 performances closing 29 October, 1983.
George Cole/Ronald Fraser (MG), Michael Praed/Peter Noone/Mike Holoway (F), Tim Curry (Tim Bentinck)/Oliver Tobias (PK), Sylvester McCoy/Kevin Ranson/Andrew Golder (SAM), Chris Langham/Paul Leonard (Peppi Borza) (SGT), Pamela Stephenson (Christina Collier)/Karen Lancaster (Carol Duffy) (Carolyn Allen) (M), Karen Lancaster/Janet Shaw/Carolyn Allen (Nelly Morrison) (E), Bonnie Langford/Sarah Brightman/Teresa Wellard (K), Louise Gold/Anita Pashley (IS), Annie Ross (Sarah Shipton) (R) with Carolyn Allen, Jackie Downey, Gaynor Miles, Janet Shaw/Norma Atallah, Elaine Hallam, Nelly Morrison, Carol Duffy; Timothy Bentinck, Graham Bickley, Keith Binns, Peppi Borza, Ken Caswell, Mark Davis, Kevin Feigherey, Alan Forrester, Andrew Golder, David Hampshire, Paul Hegarty, Simon Howe, Paul Leonard, Clive Packham, Kevin Ranson/Peter Bruce, Ray Hatfield, Gary Huddlestone, Peter Leeper, James Meek, Richie Pitts, Brent Verdon and Christina Collier, John Denton, Mike Holoway, Michael Lessiter, Anita Pashley, Sarah Shipton, William Snape, David Wheldon-Williams, Neil Braithwaite, Teresa Wellard &c. Dir: Wilford Leach; md: Martin Koch/David Firman; ch: Graciela Daniele; sc: Bob Shaw and Wilford Leach; cos: Patricia McGourty

Film: 1982 scr: Wilford Leach; prod: Joseph Papp; dir: Wilford Leach. Original music: William Elliott.
George Rose (MG), Rex Smith (F), Kevin Kline (PK), Linda Ronstadt (M), Angela Lansbury (R). Ch: Graciela Daniele.

Film: The Pirate Movie 1982. Scr: Trevor Farrant; prod: David Joseph, dir: Ken Annikin. Original songs by Terry Britten, Kit Hain, Susan Shifrin and Brian Robertson.
Bill Kerr (MG), Christopher Atkins (F), Ted Hamilton (PK), Garry McDonald (SGT), Kirsty McNichol (M), Maggie Kirkpatrick (R)

TV/Video: 1984 Brent Walker Ltd. Pr: Judith de Paul; dir: Michael Geliot; md: Alexander Faris; ch: Terry Gilbert; sc: Allan Cameron; cos: Jenny Beavan.
Keith Michell(MG), Alexander Oliver (F), Peter Allen (PK), Paul Hudson (SGT), Janis Kelly (M), Kate Flowers (E), Jenny Wren (K), Gillian Knight (R)

0030 **BILLEE TAYLOR** a nautical comic opera in two acts by Henry Pottinger Stephens. Music by Edward Solomon. Produced at the Imperial Theatre under the management of W. Edgecumbe Rendle 30 October, 1880 for a run of 83 performances closing 29 January, 1881.

Captain Felix Flapper. . . . . Fleming Norton/Philip Day
Sir Mincing Lane. . . . . Arthur Williams/J. Furneaux Cook/George Peyton
Ben Barnacle . . . . J. D. Stoyle/Mr Wilson

Christopher Crab . . . . J. A. Arnold
Billee Taylor . . . . Frederic Rivers/Frederic Darrell
Arabella Lane . . . . Emma Chambers
Phoebe Fairleigh . . . . Kathleen Corri
Susan . . . . Edith Vane
Eliza Dabsey . . . . Harriet Coveney
Jane Scraggs . . . . Caroline Ewell
Jumbo . . . . John d'Auban

Charity Girls: Emma Broughton, Minnie Talbot, Kate Talbot, A. Warner, Misses Paget, Clifford/E. Montrose, V. Leslie, Haydn/M. Montrose, West.
with Misses Herbert, E. Montrose, Morris, Gertrude Arthurs, Ellen Vitu, Wakefield, Bessie Leslie, J. Montrose, Palmer, Villiers, Ford, Cole, Birkett, Denham, Roland, Hayman, de Lacy, Pritchard, Lillie Calvert, A. Grey, Ada Ede, K. Warner, Ackland; Messrs Amphlett, Glanville, Nairns, Ackland, Buckstone, Perkins, Woodgate, Zeirs, Taylor, Barker, Fitzsimon, Wilson, Neville, Manley, Knight.
Pds: Mlles Stella and Luna /Emma and Marie D'Auban, John D'Auban, *add* Mr Ross.
Dir: Charles Harris; md: Edward Solomon, ch: John D'Auban; sc: Harry Emden; cos: George Pilotell
During this run *Billee Taylor* was performed at the Gaiety Theatre for matinées on 4, 11 & 18 December, 1880 and a portion of the show was played for the Harcourt Memorial Benefit at Drury Lane 6 December.

Produced at the Standard Theatre, New York, under the management of Richard D'Oyly Carte and E. E. Rice 19 February, 1881 for a run of 104 performances closing 31 May, 1881.
J. H. Ryley (FLAP), W. H. Seymour (ML), A. W. F. McCollin/W. O. Wilkinson (BEN), William Hamilton/Sgr Broccolini (CRAB), Arnold Breedon/Eugene Clarke (BT), Alice Burville/Verona Jarbeau (AR), Carrie Burton/Francesca Guthrie/Verona Jarbeau (PH), Nellie Mortimer/Jennie Hughes (EL), Madeleine Lucette/Rose Chapelle/Emma Guthrie (SU) with Misses Hilliger/Devere, Maynard, Fox, Lawrence, Hall, Delaro, Harrison, Sherwood, Hummell and Cooper (CH G). Pd: The French Twin Sisters/St Felix Sisters; dir: Charles Harris; md: Alfred Cellier/Ernest Meyer; sc: Henry Emden; cos: George Pilotell

Produced at Niblo's Garden, New York, by Richard D'Oyly Carte's Standard Company 6 June, 1881 for two weeks.
J. H. Ryley (FLAP), H. A. Cripps (ML), A. W. F. McCollin (BEN), William Hamilton (CRAB), Eugene Clark (BT), Rachel Sanger (AR), Carrie Burton (PH), Nellie Mortimer (EL), Rose Chapelle (SU).

Played at Booth's Theatre, New York, by the Boston Comic Opera Company 27 March, 1882 for one week.
Cast included Sgr Broccolini, Henri Laurent, William Hamilton, A. W. F. McCollin, T. M. Hengler, James A. Gilbert, Hattie Moore, Verona Jarbeau, Fannie Hall, Rosa Cooke.

Produced at the Gaiety Theatre under the management of John Hollingshead for a series of matinées on 1, 8, 15 and 22 April, 1882.
Philip Day (FLAP), Arthur Williams (ML), E. W. Royce (BEN), J. J. Dallas/James Danvers (CRAB), Frederic Darrell (BT), Emma Chambers (AR), Lizzie St Quinten (PH), Emma Broughton (SU), Harriet Coveney (EL). Md: Edward Solomon

Produced at the Gaiety Theatre under the management of John Hollingshead 17 July, 1882 for a three week season to 5 August.
Tom Squire (FLAP), Arthur Williams (ML), William Elton (BEN), J. J. Dallas (CRAB), Arnold Breedon (BT), Rosie St George (AR), Annie Poole (PH), Emma Broughton (SU), Caroline Ewell (EL), Willie Warde/John D'Auban (JUMBO). Md: Meyer Lutz

Played at the Bijou Theatre, New York, under the management of John A. McCaull 26 August, 1882 for two weeks ending 8 September.
Cast included Carrie Burton (PH), Emie Weatherby, Amy Harvey, Jennie Hughes (EL), Albert Henderson, Charles J. Campbell (BT), A. D. Barker (BEN), Edward Connell (CRAB), Edward Chapman.
Played at the Fifth Avenue Theatre, New York, under the management of James Barton 9 October, 1882 for one week.

W. H. Seymour (FLAP), H. A. Cripps (ML), Harry Brown (BEN), Sgr Broccolini (CRAB), Harry de Lorme (BT), Verona Jarbeau (AR), Marie Jansen (PH), Jennie Hughes (EL), Rose Chappelle (SU).

Produced at the Gaiety Theatre under the management of John Hollingshead for matinées on 15 and 22 November, 1883.
Tom Squire (FLAP), Arthur Williams (ML), William Elton (BEN), J. J. Dallas (CRAB), Arnold Breedon (BT), Alice Aynsley Cook (AR), Lucille Meredith (PH), Grace Pedley (SU), Harriet Coveney (EL). Md: Meyer Lutz.

Played at the Casino Theatre, New York, by E. E. Rice's Gaiety Opera Company 20 June, 1885 for one week.
J. H. Ryley (FLAP), Edward P. Temple (ML), John McWade (BEN), Fred Clifton (CRAB), H. S. Hilliard (BT), Verona Jarbeau (AR), Lillian Russell (PH), Alice Barnett (EI), Josie Hall (SU).

Produced at the Gaiety Theatre under the management of John Hollingshead 31 October, 1885 with *The Vicar of Wide-Awake Field*. Withdrawn 18 December. Transferred to the Empire Theatre opening 21 December with *Hurly Burly*. Withdrawn 2 January, 1886.
Tom Squire/Fred Ferrani (FLAP), J. H. Jarvis (ML), Arthur Roberts/John L. Shine (BEN), George Honey (CRAB), Arnold Breedon (BT), Eva Milner/Rosie St George (Julia St George)/Kate Chard (AR), Marion Hood (Rosie St George)/Agnes de la Porte (PH), Annie Bellwood/Agnes Oliver (SU), Harriet Coveney/Emily Miller (EL), Sylvia Grey (BLACK COOK). Md: Hamilton Clarke/Frederick Stanislaus.

Produced at the Crystal Palace under the management of Henry Pottinger Stephens and William Yardley 27 July, 1886. Transferred to Toole's Theatre 31 July with *Herne The Hunter*. Withdrawn 9 August, 1886.
Arthur Williams (FLAP), E. J. Allnut (ML), Herman de Lange (BEN), Frederic Wood (CRAB), Emily Spiller (BT), Linda Verner (AR), Harriet Vernon (PH), Nellie Bennett (SU), Harriet Coveney (EL), George Reeves/Sylvia Grey (BLACK COOK)

Played at the American Theatre, New York, by the Castle Square Opera Company 11 April, 1898 for two weeks.
Raymond Hitchcock (FLAP), Richard Ridgely (ML), E. N. Knight (BEN), Oscar Girard (CRAB), Jay Taylor (BT), Ruth White (AR), Marie Celeste (PH), Emma King (SU), Bessie Fairbairn (EL)

0031 **THE KING'S DRAGOONS** a comic opera in three acts by J. Wilton Jones. Music by John Crook. Produced at the Theatre Royal, Manchester under the management of Captain Richard D. Bainbridge and Mr Duffield 1 November, 1880 for a two-week season.

Dorothy . . . . Lucy Franklein
Alice. . . . . Gertrude Cave-Ashton
Sergeant Crow . . . . John Furneaux Cook
Edgar . . . . Henry Walsham
The Marquis . . . . Richard Cummings
Robin . . . . Fred J. Stimson

Produced at the Royal Court Theatre, Liverpool under the management of Captain Richard D. Bainbridge and Mr Duffield 24 September, 1881 for a two-week season.
Alice Aynsley Cook (DOR), Gertrude Cave-Ashton/Constance Loseby (AL), J. Furneaux Cook (SGT), Henry Walsham/W. H. Woodfield (ED), Thomas Aynsley Cook (MARQ), T. F. Doyle (ROB). Md: John Crook

IN THE SULKS a vaudeville by Frank Desprez. Music by Alfred Cellier. Produced at the Opera Comique under the management of Richard D'Oyly Carte 21 February, 1880 with *H.M.S. Pinafore* (juvenile). Subsequently played with *The Pirates of Penzance*. Withdrawn 2 April 1881.

Mr Liverby . . . . George Temple
Mrs Liverby . . . . Lillian la Rue/Julia Gwynne
Joseph. Frank Thornton

Produced at the Opera Comique under the management of Richard D'Oyly Carte 25 April, 1881 with *Patience*. Played to 2 May then subsequently with *Patience* at the Savoy Theatre 11–14 October, 1881.

CASTLE BOTHEREM or An Irish Stew, by Arthur Law. Music by Hamilton Clarke. Produced at St George's Hall under the management of Alfred Reed and R. Corney Grain 16 February, 1880 with *Our Table d'Hôte* and *Back from India*, the former succeeded by *Rotten Row* and then *An Ascot Party*, the latter by *Three Flats* (8 March) then *A Flying Visit* (31 May). Withdrawn 12 July, 1880.

Kathleen Dempsey . . . . Edith Brandon
Mrs Dabbler . . . . Miss Hudspeth
Augustus Dabbler. . . . . R. Corney Grain
Larry Dempsey . . . . Alfred Bishop
Phil Doolan . . . . Alfred Reed
Perk . . . . Lucy Williams

THREE FLATS by Arthur a'Beckett. Music by Edouard Marlois. Produced at St. George's Hall under the management of Alfred Reed and R. Corney Grain 8 March, 1880 with *Our Table d'Hôte* and *Castle Botherem*, the former replaced by *Rotten Row*. Withdrawn 29 May, 1880.

Charlie Quicksilver . . . . R. Corney Grain
Titus Brown . . . . Alfred Bishop
Rosie Maybloom . . . . Edith Brandon
Mrs Brown . . . . Miss Hudspeth
Byron Jones . . . . Alfred Reed

A FLYING VISIT by Arthur Law. Music by R. Corney Grain. Produced at St George's Hall under the management of Alfred Reed and R. Corney Grain 31 May, 1880 with *Castle Botherem* and *An Ascot Party*, the former replaced by *Very Catching* (14 July). Withdrawn 24 July. Reopened 4 October with *A Pirates' Home* and *The London Season* replaced by *A Turquoise Ring* (20 October) and *The Haunted Room* respectively. Withdrawn 18 December, 1880.

Thomasina Boycott . . . . Miss Hudspeth
Mr Choker . . . . R. Corney Grain
Hildegarde Schplitter . . . . Edith Brandon
Mr Schplitter . . . . Alfred Bishop
Harold Duff. . . . . Alfred Reed

THE TURQUOISE RING a musical comedietta in one act by W. E. Godfrey and E. W. Craigie. Music by Lionel Benson. Produced at St George's Hall under the management of Alfred Reed and R. Corney Grain 20 October, 1880 with *A Flying Visit* and *The Haunted Room*. Withdrawn 18 December, 1880.

Sir Timothy Turtle. . . . . Alfred Reed
Thibaut . . . . R. Corney Grain
Lady Turtle. . . . . Miss Hudspeth
Pauline . . . . Edith Brandon
Jacques . . . . Alfred Bishop

Produced at St George's Hall 31 January, 1881 with *A Merry Christmas* replaced 28 February by *All At Sea*. Withdrawn 26 March, 1881.

Produced at St George's Hall 23 October, 1882 with *En Route*. Withdrawn 12 December, 1882.

POPSY WOPSY a musical absurdity in one act by Sydney Grundy. Music by Edward Solomon. Produced at the Royalty Theatre under the management of Kate Lawler 4 October, 1880 with *Bow Bells* and *Wild Flowers*. Withdrawn 6 November, 1880.

Old Heavyside . . . . Edward Righton
Young Heavyside . . . . Cecil Raleigh
John Bunyan Wopsy . . . . T. P. Haynes
Popsy Wopsy . . . . Kate Lawler
Betsy . . . . Florence Lavender
Mrs Popsy. . . . . Maggie Brennan
Md: Max Schröter

SAGE AND ONIONS by Alfred Maltby. Based on *The Goose with the Golden Eggs*. Music by John Crook. Produced at the Prince's Theatre, Manchester 12 April, 1880 with *The Sultan of Mocha* and toured.

Clara . . . . Alice May/Ada Melrose
Flockster . . . . Allen Thomas
Bonser. Frederic Wood
Mr Turby. . . . . Fred J. Stimson
Mrs Turby . . . . Juliet Smith

SCHOOL OF (HE)ARTS an operetta by G. R. Walker. Music by Isidore de Solla. Produced at the Park Theatre, Camden Town 27 March, 1880 with *Heart's Delight*, replaced 5 April by *The Maid and the Magpie*. Withdrawn 10 April, 1880.

Miss Brandysnapp . . . . Miss Sutherland
Miss Baggs . . . . Bella Cuthbert
Miss Fair . . . . Stella Brereton
Grace Reems . . . . Daisy Bauer
Rose Marie . . . . Kate Vivian
Charley Atkinson . . . . Charles Cruickshanks
Fred Nolan . . . . J. H. Bucholz
Jim Buttons . . . . Ernest Willmore
Tom Askew . . . . J. E. Emmerson
Miss Bird . . . . Grace Roi
Attentive girl . . . . Miss Strathean
The Captain of the Fire Brigade . . . . Mr Brooklyn

LOVER'S KNOTS by Cunningham Bridgman. Music by Wilfred Bendall. Produced at St George's Hall at a matinée 5 May, 1880 with *The Stepmother*.

Doctor Dilly Dally D.D.D.. . . . . Rutland Barrington
Peter Pentameter . . . . Arthur Oswald
Captain Ormond . . . . Douglas Cox
Mary . . . . Emily Cross
Gabrielle . . . . Miss Purdy

Produced at the Opera Comique with *The Mother-in-law* 31 December, 1881, withdrawn 24 February, 1882.
Robert Brough (DR), George Temple (PP), Richard Temple (CAPT), Constance Maitland (M), Emily Cross (G)

SIX AND SIX an operetta by B. T. Hughes. Music by P. W. Halton. Produced at Hull by the D'Oyly Carte Opera Company 9 August, 1880, and toured in repertoire.

FOUR BY HONOURS a musical absurdity. Produced by the D'Oyly Carte Opera Company and toured.

CHANGE PARTNERS an operetta by Lewis Clifton and J. J. Dilley. Music by Walter Slaughter. Played in repertoire by the Crofton troupe.

BEARS NOT BEASTS a musical extravaganza in one act by George Capel. Music by H. Round. Produced at Booth's Theatre, Ashton-under-Lyne under the management of Henry D. Burton 22 November, 1880 and toured in repertoire.

Petroleum Peck . . . . Henry D. Burton
Timothy Thompkins . . . . Charles E. Stevens/George Capel/
W. L. Harford/Lewis Ward/Fred Benton
The Grand Pascha . . . . Edwin Keens/Wilford Rokeby/
Walter Vernon/C. Harley
Babalam, P. M.. . . . . James Cumberland/Victor Stevens/E. M.
Robson/Fowler Thatcher/Frank Ayrton/
Zolide . . . . Emily Spiller/Daisy Litton/Addie Conyers/
Ada Clare/

Dodo . . . . Grace Huntley/Susie Montague/Louie Lancashire/
Fifi . . . . Nellie Grey/Annie Brophy/

A MERRY CHRISTMAS by Arthur Law. Music by King Hall. Produced at St George's Hall 26 December, 1880. Withdrawn 26 February, 1881.

SANDFORD AND MERTON'S CHRISTMAS PARTY by F. C. Burnand. Music by Alfred Scott-Gatty. Produced at St George's Hall 26 December, 1880. Withdrawn 29 January 1881.
These two pieces were played with Corney Grain's *A Musical Family*.

PRISONERS AT THE BAR an operetta by John Oxenford and Mr Meadows. Produced at the Royalty Theatre under the management of Kate Lawler and played with *Don Juan Jr* and *Stagestruck*.

Alderman Sir Thomas Turtle . . . . . Harry Martell
Algernon Pegg . . . . Frank Wyatt
Tennyson Jones. . . . . Herbert Kelcey
Rosalie. Florence Lavender
Md: Max Schröter

1881

The flow of new musicals into the West End was maintained in 1881. The French contributed *La Belle Normande, La Boulangère, La Petite Mariée, Belle Lurette. Les Voltigeurs de la 32ème* and a disastrous version of Varney's *La Reina des Halles (Gibraltar* or *Mary Rose*) at the Haymarket along with revivals of such established favourites as *Les Cloches de Corneville, Geneviève de Brabant*, and *La Fille du Tambour Major*. However, in spite of the four-month run of Auber's *The Bronze Horse* at the Alhambra, the only truly successful new piece was Audran's *La Mascotte*, which was chosen to open the new Comedy Theatre in Panton Street. Starring Violet Cameron, Lionel Brough and the Frenchman Gaillard it became extremely popular and remained on the stage for a long run. Its 'Turkey Duet', sung by Miss Cameron and Gaillard, became a must for all drawing room duettists and the charming music confirmed the fame of the composer of *Olivette* in London.

British shows were becoming steadily more numerous, and Gilbert and Sullivan's *Patience* proved to be the hit of the year, although of the other pieces produced only Stephens and Solomon's *Claude Duval* succeeded in getting any kind of a metropolitan run alongside revivals of *The Black Crook* and *Princess Toto*.

The new Gilbert and Sullivan work scheduled to replace *The Pirates of Penzance* had originally been intended for production late in 1880, but Gilbert had experienced some difficulty in settling on a subject. His first choice was an expansion of his *Bab Ballad* 'The Rival Curates' which relates how a certain young churchman, Mr Clayton Hooper, who prides himself on his unparalleled mildness, discovers to his horror that the curate of another parish is even milder. By threats of violence he compels his rival to become worldly, and the latter embraces the situation gladly:

For years I've longed for some
Excuse for this revulsion
Now that excuse has come,
I do it on compulsion!

But with two-thirds of the play completed, Gilbert suffered a change of heart. He found himself hampered by his subject. The necessity of respecting things ecclesiastical hamstrung his humour and finally he decided to abandon his original design, retaining only a few elements from 'The Rival Curates' which he built into *Patience*, a satire on the current aesthetic craze as personified by Oscar Wilde and his followers.

Reginald Bunthorne is an Aesthete. Not from genuine persuasion, as he admits:

A languid love for lilies does not blight me
Lank limbs and haggard cheeks do not delight me
I do not care for dirty greens

By any means. I do not long for all one sees
That's Japanese
I am not fond of uttering platitudes
In stained glass attitudes
In short, my mediaevalism's affectation
Born of a morbid love of admiration!

And admiration he has succeeded in gaining, for all the local ladies have forsaken their military lovers to droop and pine at the feet of the fashionable 'poet'. Bunthorne's own particular favourite, however, is the milkmaid, Patience, who is the only one not infected with the mania for mediaevalism and who, indeed, is ignorant of the very nature of 'love', it having been confined in her experience to one great-aunt. One of the lovesick maids explains it to her. Love is a great, unselfish duty. And Patience, who like Frederic in *The Pirates* has exaggerated notions of duty, is horrified to think she has been so selfish as not to have experienced it. She determines to remedy the omission. On to the scene comes Archibald Grosvenor, Patience's childhood sweetheart, grown to beauty and aestheticism, but our heroine determines that to love him would be anything but unselfish and she sadly turns him away. Bunthorne, in the meanwhile, thinking himself spurned by Patience, determines to put himself up for lottery, but Patience rushes in declaring that since she finds him so objectionable she must wed him. The other ladies are in despair but then they discover Grosvenor and quickly transfer their attentions.

Yet somehow no-one is happy. The maidens irritate Grosvenor who only wants Patience: she is perfectly miserable loving Bunthorne who misses the adulation that was once his and finds Patience's duteous devotion totally un-blissful. Finally Bunthorne has had enough and threatens Grosvenor with a nephew's curse unless he becomes commonplace and de-aestheticised. Like the curate, Grosvenor under compulsion yields to what he has secretly longed for all along. He reappears shaven and shorn, upright and dressed in – oh, horror! – primary colours. Since he is no longer 'beautiful' Patience feels duty bound to transfer her affections, and promptly does. But Bunthorne's trick misfires as the other maidens, deciding whatever Grosvenor does must be right, reject aesthetic principles and return to their soldiers. Only plain, 'massive' Jane is left. But the self-effacing Duke of Dunstable has come to choose a bride. In fairness he decides to choose the plainest – Jane. So Bunthorne is left to sigh:

In that case unprecedented
Single I must live and die
I shall have to be contented
With a tulip or lily!

The roles of Bunthorne and Grosvenor were conceived for Grossmith and Barrington who found themselves in central and rather different parts from the previous operas. The tenor role of the Duke of Dunstable was considerably smaller than the previous tenor parts but was taken nevertheless by the company's primo tenore, Durward Lely, who had taken over as Frederic during the run of *The Pirates of Penzance*. Richard Temple as Colonel Calverley, the commander of the rejected brigade of dragoons, had a fine role with two stirring solos.

In this their fourth production, however, the team had to find a fourth new prima donna. The role of Patience, the ingenuous milkmaid, was offered first to Emilie Petrelli who had played both Josephine and Mabel at the Opera Comique and on tour, and was playing Mabel when *The Pirates* gave place to *Patience*. But Miss Petrelli was not impressed. The role of Patience lacked the opportunities for vocal bravura which the earlier roles had contained. It was, she said, a soubrette part and she was not a soubrette, and she defected to the Philharmonic to play in Bazin's *Voyage en Chine*. In her place the triumvirate selected Leonora Braham. Miss Braham had returned from America and taken up her old place at St George's Hall where she had been performing in two little pieces, *All at Sea* and *Many Happy Returns*. *Patience* brought her talents to a wider public which was quick to appreciate them and Leonora Braham remained with the D'Oyly Carte organisation to create the soprano roles in the next four Savoy operas.

The contralto role of the ludicrous Lady Jane was conceived in the mould of Ruth and Lady Sangazure but not, alas, for Harriet Everard. Miss Everard was not well. She had never totally recovered from her accident during the rehearsals of *The Pirates*, and before the run of *Patience* had ended she had succumbed to consumption at the age of 37. In her place Carte engaged the impressive Alice Barnett who had created the role of Ruth in America and later succeeded Miss Everard at the Opera Comique. There were roles for the faithful Misses Bond and Gwynne as rapturous maidens while the third of the principal girls was played by a Miss May Fortescue. This was a name which was to become extremely well-known a couple of years later when the lady was concerned in a much-publicised breach-of-promise suit against Lord Garmoyle. She emerged from it with £10,000 in lieu of a title and a notoriety which was of no little help when she subsequently took the Court Theatre and starred herself in Gilbert's *Dan'l Druce* as preface to a career as a star.

While Gilbert was engaged on his new libretto, however, he was beaten to the post. In February Frank Burnand brought out a play called *The Colonel* which satirised the 'follies of the aesthetic craze' and scored an immense success. He had actually written the play a few months earlier intending it for the Bancrofts, but it had not worked in rehearsal and had been shelved. When Freddie Clay let drop that Gilbert was working on the same theme, Burnand quickly organised a production of *The Colonel* with Edgar Bruce. It caught on amazingly and ran for an eventual 500 nights, by far Burnand's most successful work and the only positive thing born of his intense jealousy of Gilbert. In consequence of *The Colonel*'s popularity, Gilbert and Carte felt it advisable to issue a statement that *Patience* had been written in November (which it had not, being only begun in November after the abandoning of 'The Rival Curates'). But they need not have worried, for *Patience* turned out to be as popular as its predecessors and in no way similar, except in its success, to Burnand's play.

Gilbert's libretto took full advantage of the incongruities of aestheticism:

JANE: (looking at the soldiers' uniforms) Red and yellow! Primary colours! Oh, South Kensington!

DUKE: We didn't design our uniforms, but we don't see how they could be improved.

JANE: No, you wouldn't. Still there *is* a cobwebby grey velvet with a tender bloom like cold gravy, which, made Florentine fourteenth-century, trimmed with Venetian leather and Spanish altar lace, and surmounted with something Japanese – it matters not what – would at least be Early English!

Indeed, the excesses of the topic stirred him into some of his most imaginative lyrics such as in Bunthorne's song:

> If you're anxious for to shine in the high aesthetic line as a man of culture rare,
> You must get up all the germs of the transcendental terms and plant them everywhere.

You must lie upon the daisies and discourse in novel phrases
Of your complicated state of mind.
The meaning doesn't matter if it's only idle chatter
Of a transcendental kind.
And everyone will say,
As you walk your mystic way,
'If this young man expresses himself in terms too deep for me,
Why, what a very singularly deep young man this deep young man must be!'

Sullivan appended a suitably characteristic melody and the song was loudly encored on the first night and often thereafter.

Both Richard Temple's songs were favourites – the stalwart 'When I first Put this Uniform On' detailing the effects of a military appearance on maidens and 'If you Want a Receipt for a popular Mystery' in which he listed the desirable components which go into the character of a dragoon. A comic duet for Jane and Bunthorne outlined the treatment they propose to give Grosvenor to get him to change his appearance, and another for Bunthorne and Grosvenor after the metamorphosis highlighted the differences between the two:

BUN: A Japanese young man
A blue-and-white young man
Francesca da Rimini, niminy, piminy,
Je-ne-sais-quoi young man!
GRO: A Chancery Lane young man
A Somerset House young man
A very delectable, highly respectable,
Threepenny-bus young man!

But the piece which caught the imagination of both critics and audiences was Lady Jane's doleful solo which opened the second act. Seated in a glade the ageing Jane accompanies herself on the violoncello as she soliloquises:

Silvered is the raven hair,
Spreading is the parting straight,
Mottled the complexion fair,
Halting is the youthful gait,
Hollow is the laughter free,
Spectacled the limpid eye,
Little will be left of me in the coming by and by!

The beautiful melody allied to the ludicrous words and the bovine appearance of Miss Barnett produced a comical incongruity which made the song one of the highlights of the evening. Like 'Little Maid of Arcadee' the melody became popular as a salon piece, but the lyric was considered cruel and 'not quite nice', and it was altered to display more conventional sentiments.

The reception for *Patience* was excellent although the new theatrical paper *The Stage*, which had already dismissed *The Pirates of Penzance* as weak and silly, referred to it as 'a very empty trifle'. The charming music suffered a little under the pens of those who still considered Sullivan Britain's prime hope as a 'serious' composer and resented his 'wasting time' in the realms of light music, but they were in a tiny minority and *Patience* ran for twenty months and 578 performances to excellent houses in London as well as in two provincial tours and in overseas productions from Broadway to Sydney to Bombay. The London production played its first 170 performances at the

Opera Comique and during that time Carte was busy building his new headquarters on the Strand, the Savoy Theatre, which was to become the home of his productions henceforth and remain the home of light musical theatre for thirty years. October 10 marked the first performance in the new theatre. Electric light had been installed and Emden was hired to paint more suitable scenery for the now brightly exposed sets. New costumes, too, had to be provided. The transfer was made with the most satisfactory results and it was more than a year before the Savoy required its first new piece.

In view of the lengths to which Gilbert, Sullivan and Carte had gone to protect their copyright in *The Pirates of Penzance*, it was rather surprising that no effort at all was made to ensure that their company would reap its overseas rewards from *Patience*. To general amazement the score and libretto were published by Ditson of Boston and, by United States law, thus became common property. Charles Harris was set to produce the piece for Carte at Broadway's Standard Theatre but there was still plenty of time for rival producers to take advantage of the authors' apparent magnanimity. The first to do so was John Ford who launched a rather bad version of the show in St Louis, and two other producers jumped in to announce Broadway versions which would open before Carte's on 3 October. Other shows took individual numbers and put them into their shows with the result that they were soon well-known, but by the time Harris had prepared the official production a complete *Patience* had still not been seen on Broadway. Although any Gilbert and Sullivan work seemed a licence to make money, there were some grounds for doubt over this one. The aesthetic craze had not yet hit America and what raised so much hilarity in a London wise to the posturings of Wilde and au fait with du Maurier's cartoons of Postlethwaite and Maudle might very well have fallen flat in America. Indeed, Harris' own production of another London hit, *Madame Favart*, opened on Broadway just before *Patience* and melted away in two weeks. But not so *Patience*. Although the Americans were a little bemused to begin with, they quickly caught on to the 'too too' and 'utterly utter' of the 'mediaeval' lingo and the show was an enormous success.

Several of the artists had been brought out from Britain. Arthur Wilkinson, Augusta Roche and Lyn Cadwaladr had all been playing *Pinafore* and *The Pirates* in the provinces, while J. H. Ryley and Alice Burville, both now fixed in New York, had also played for Carte in Britain. Among the Americans were James Barton who opened as Grosvenor and Carrie Burton, the Phoebe of *Billee Taylor*, who took the title role.

After the Standard production had assured *Patience's* popularity other versions tried their luck on Broadway but, as with *Pinafore* and *The Pirates*, none came near the 'official' production either in merit or in length of run. The Booth production under E. E. Rice provided Bunthorne with fifty love-sick maidens instead of the statutory twenty, but moved back to the country after two weeks. The Standard *Patience* gave Gilbert and Sullivan their longest Broadway run to date. By 4 March of 1882 it had been performed 177 times consecutively when the Standard was reminded of its obligation to produce Solomon and Stephens' *Claude Duval*. *Patience* had grossed over $100,000 and was still running to packed houses, however, and finally a compromise was reached. *Patience* was played for four performances a week, Thursday to Saturday, while the remaining dates were given over to *Claude Duval*. But after three weeks of this repertory-style arrangement *Patience* was withdrawn. It later appeared at the Bijou in a new production starring the young and comparatively unknown Lillian Russell who had earlier appeared in a burlesque of *Patience* at Tony Pastor's as the milkmaid, one of the first steps in Miss Russell's climb to her later position as the musical comedy queen of America. Pastor, ironically, found his parody so successful that he temporarily abandoned burlesque and presented *Patience* 'straight' as the piece took its place alongside its great predecessors in public esteem.

D'Oyly Carte had Gilbert and Sullivan, and his friend and associate, Michael Gunn, determined that he too would have 'his' pair of writers. The ubiquitous success of *Billee Taylor* led him naturally to Stephens and Solomon. The pair had already prepared two more musicals both, like the first, based on old English ballads. *Claude Duval*, the gentleman highwayman who danced a minuet with a lady captive, was a well-known English folk-hero, and so was the wandering *Lord Bateman*, already the hero of an Alhambra show and other extravaganzas. Liberal plans were announced for both shows. First one, then the other, was announced to fill the Opera Comique after the departure of *Patience*. Finally *Claude Duval* was promised for the Olympic in August and *Lord Bateman* for the Opera Comique in October under the management of John Hollingshead. But as soon as *Claude Duval* had opened and success seemed assured, Gunn made his move and bought up the rights of all Stephens and Solomon's future and unproduced works, including *Lord Bateman* which he announced to follow *Claude Duval* at the Olympic. So Hollingshead cancelled his season and staged a revival of *Princess Toto*.

Claude Duval had received a good deal of praise. Stephens had developed the tale in three acts. The proscribed Charles Lorrimore is captured by Duval's band, but the highwayman befriends him and, on his behalf, holds up the carriage bearing his beloved Constance and her miserly uncle, Magruder. The charming rogue then dances the famous minuet with Constance in a tableau imitating W. P. Frith's well-known painting in the Royal Academy. But the young lady is being taken to be married to the rich Sir Whiffle Whaffle and when Charles comes secretly to see her he is arrested and only escapes when Duval exchanges cloaks and allows himself to be arrested in his stead. In the final act Duval escapes and proves that Charles is, in fact, the heir to all Magruder's lands. Among the vital papers is a blank 'free pardon' which he duly fills in with his own name to provide a happy ending.

The operatic baritone Frank Celli was hired to play the title role, with Carte's Mabel, Marion Hood, as Constance and his Frederic, George Power, as Charles. From the original cast of *Billee Taylor* Arthur Williams and Harriet Coveney repeated character roles and the composer's brother, Frederick, who had been touring as Ben Barnacle took the role of Duval's ferocious lieutenant Blood-Red Bill. The success of Ben and 'All on account of Eliza' led the writers to attempt to pull off the same coup again and the role of Bill was heavily written-up in spite of the fact that the character was totally incidental to the plot. He was provided with a number called 'William Is sure to be Right' which echoed 'Eliza' and was clearly intended to be the show's 'hit'. Fred Solomon, not the most subtle of performers, gave it with enormous gusto, and 'William' was duly the hit of the night, though it never gained the fame of its model:

> My father and mother would always remark
> William is sure to be right,
> Though my features are fair my ways are all dark
> William is sure to be right.
> No matter though others may make a mistake
> I'm sure to be right for I'm quite wide-awake,
> For while they're eating bread I am sneaking the cake
> William is sure to be right.

William is sure to be right, my boys, William is sure to be right
Though familiarly Bill
I am looked up to still
William is sure to be right

This music-hall style and, indeed, the whole style of Blood-Red Bill were somewhat at odds with the rest of the work. Whereas the more artistic comedy performances of Arthur Williams and Harriet Convey fitted comfortably into the mood of a tale which might have more naturally formed the subject for a ballad opera or even a romantic opera, Blood-Red Bill and Fred Solomon were definitely beyond the pale. *The Era* commented:

> The author, while occasionally treating his subject with cleverness, seems to have been somewhat undecided whether to give up his characters to reckless fun or to make them sentimental and this hovering between two styles has given a certain weakness to the libretto.

Teddy Solomon's contribution was much better noticed than that of his brother:

> The tuneful music of Mr Solomon found great favour from beginning to end. The young composer has not perhaps hit upon quite such catching refrains as are to be found in one or two instances in *Billee Taylor*, but the music as a whole is decidedly superior in quality and again raises the question why, while we have native composers so qualified to write English operas, our authors and managers should run after foreign composers.

The music added a good deal to the popularity of *Claude Duval*, but so also did Blood-Red Bill. The first night performance was greeted with incessant demands for encores and for several weeks Gunn was greeted by the happy sight of customers being turned away from a packed theatre. But after only nine weeks the business had faded right away and he was forced to close. The final performances were given without Celli, Williams and Power and with the play cut down into a new two-act version which D'Oyly Carte had had prepared to send out on tour. The tour went out on Boxing Day with G. Byron Browne in the title role, but by that time Gunn's attempt to rival the Savoy was at an end and the proposed production of *Lord Bateman* was abandoned.

There was still hope for a New York run. After all, America had given a longer season to *Billee Taylor* than had London, and a New York season had already been arranged with Charles Harris repeating his British directing assignment. Unfortunately for the authors, however, their piece was scheduled to follow *Patience* into the Standard and New York audiences at the time had no intention of letting *Patience* go. The date for *Claude Duval* was continually put back until, with the end of the season looming, they were obliged to produce. The company which was playing *Patience* took on the roles in *Claude Duval* which was alternated on the programme with Gilbert and Sullivan's piece. J. H. Ryley scored a triumph as Blood-Red Bill. 'William Is sure to be Right' was encored six times on the opening night, and after three weeks *Claude Duval* was left to run out the remaining weeks of the season on its own until the Hess Acme Company (with a repertoire which included *H.M.S. Pinafore*) arrived to fulfil its booking.

Claude Duval never attained the popularity of *Billee Taylor* and it did not confirm its predecessor's promise in the way that *Patience* and *The Pirates of Penzance* had confirmed *H.M.S. Pinafore* and *The Sorcerer*. Stephens had not developed, as Gilbert had, a suitably individual and attractive style and he had not succeeded in blending the romantic and comic elements with sufficient skill. Solomon had not had an occasion to rise to, and it was notable that the show's 'hit' was the one number which leaned blatantly to the music-hall style. *Claude Duval* was shelved after its initial tour and barely seen again.

Five other new musicals put in brief appearances in London during the year. The first of these was *Lola*, written by the well-liked 'bohemian' writer Frank Marshall. Marshall had entered the theatre in 1870 with a piece called *Mad as a Hatter* at the Lyceum. He had a succès d'estime with *False Shame* produced by Harry Montague at the Globe and then successfully adapted Bronson Howard's *Saratoga* as *Brighton* for the Court Theatre. His first venture into musical spheres was with a five-act grand opera about a Nordic Macbeth entitled *Biorn* produced at the Queen's Theatre in Long Acre. The leading role of Elfrida was played by Mrs Marshall who collected the worst reviews of 1877 for her performance of the pretentious music written by Sgr Lauro Rossi, director of the Royal College of Music in Naples and the perpetrator of several other failed operas. Doubtless encouraged by the successes of Gilbert and Sullivan with the light musical theatre and undeterred by his previous unfortunate connections with Italian composers, Marshall collaborated on the musical *Lola* with Antonio Orsini, a Milanese composer, whose works ranged from grand operas on *Benvenuto Cellini* and *Catherine Howard* to a respected textbook on harmony. Orsini proved rather more competent than his predecessor, but this time Marshall let the side down. In spite of its professed intent his libretto for *Lola* lacked humour and point. Its plot dealt with Alexis, Prince of Baccarato, who, being impecunious, has let out part of his palace as a casino. To his realm come Vere de Vere, a magazine proprietor ('Virtue', price 6d), and Lola, a professional beauty with whom Prince Alexis falls in love, the more so in that she succeeds in winning him some money at his casino. Lola, however, has her own lover, Edgardo, whom Alexis promptly incarcerates as a revolutionary. But Lola escapes the Prince's clutches when Edgardo, disguised as a Spanish Prince, breaks the bank at Baccarato casino, distributes the proceeds to the dissatisfied peasantry, and seizes both the throne and Lola for a happy ending.

In spite of the opportunities provided to satirise, among other things, the 'professional beauty' and the newspaper world, Marshall held back and produced a book which was unobjectionable, certainly, but also largely unentertaining. A few critics found a little to praise in the music, and *The Post* even declared fulsomely that 'the future of the house is made'. It certainly was not, as *Lola* lasted only six laborious weeks in spite of an excellent cast including Elinor Loveday and Harriet Everard from the Opera Comique, Henry Walsham and Edmund Rosenthal.

Lola was, however, a considerably better piece than *Blue and Buff*, a little Liverpudlian musical which found its way, somewhat improbably, to the Haymarket. It had been produced in Liverpool by the local amateur operatic society for three nights in January, then somehow surfaced nine months later in the Bancrofts' theatre, which was hardly renowned for musicals, in tandem with the melodrama *East Lynne*. The libretto dealt with an election campaign and showed the Liberal and Tory candidates each trying to curry votes. The foregone Tory victory is threatened by the late candidature of the mayor's sister, Vinegra Crabb, who has been jilted by the almost victorious Sir Snobley Snooks who is obliged to marry her to carry the day. On its way from Liverpool the script of the exceedingly long one-acter got rather hacked about. The author had decided on cuts and changes but for some obscure reason these ended up in the hands of the stage manager and some bits got put in the wrong places. The production was prepared in one week and the artists on the first night were decidedly under-rehearsed, but they were to have little time to remedy the default as the show was smartly removed after five performances.

The three other shows lasted just one performance apiece in try-out matinées which failed to 'take'. The first was *All in the Downs*, a version of *Black-Eyed Susan* credited to the play's author, Douglas Jerrold. Meyer Lutz provided the music which was scholarly but unsuitable. The eponymous heroine, played by the opera singer Blanche Cole, expressed herself in earnestly florid arias which had little to do with the tone of Jerrold's play. Nevertheless, *All in the Downs* was picked up several years later and toured in repertoire by J. W. Turner's Opera Company.

The second piece was a racing musical called *The Pet of Newmarket* which was put on a few days later at Sadler's Wells. The plot concerned a gambling duke in love with a bookie's daughter. The lass's aristocratic rival, Lady Blanche, bribes a welsher to nobble the duke's jockey, reasoning that if he loses his last bet he will wed her for her fortune. But the plot is overheard and the Duke craftily backs against his own horse. The jockey duly collapses but the heroine leaps into the saddle and wins the race, ruining everything. Then it is discovered that the horse is a ringer and it is disqualified. The disappointed Blanche goes off with the welsher (who turns out to be of noble blood) while the duke and 'The Pet of Newmarket' are happily united. Once again the work went on ill-prepared and badly performed and the contributions of Lizzie Coote and the well-drilled amateur dancers could not save it. The book was poor but the music was even weaker. It was the work of the Belgian-born conductor and composer Camille Vanden Bossche who had thrown up a career in law at the age of 30 and come to Britain to pursue his musical calling. He had worked as a conductor with touring opera and musical companies and also at some of the lesser London theatres, most notably for the Duke's Theatre's spectacular production of *The New Babylon*. As a composer he was less happy. In 1885 he made in ill-judged attempt to revive his musical at Holborn but the production folded in fiasco and Vanden Bossche ended up in court at the behest of his star, Vivienne Dallas, who, along with the rest of the cast, had not been paid.

The most utter failure of all was *The Grand Mogul*, produced at the Royalty, in which Harriet Coveney played an eccentric charwoman and Arthur Williams her long-lost son returned to London disguised as an Eastern potentate to diddle the Lord Mayor (Furneaux Cook) and wed his wealthy daughter (Florence Lavender). It was ill-written, badly rehearsed and staged, and the embarrassed composer/conductor shrieked vainly at an orchestra and chorus which lost both their way and his contradictory beat before the opening number was done. The established stars in the cast muddled on, leaving *The Era* critic to quail:

> We shall never henceforth hear the name of *The Grand Mogul* without a shuddering recollection.

The positive side of affairs represented by *Patience* and, to a lesser degree, *Claude Duval* was reinforced by two revivals – *Princess Toto* at the Opera Comique and the revamped version of *The Black Crook* at the Alhambra. The latter proved an immense success and ran through Christmas and the New Year, closing down finally in April. Harry Paulton's new libretto gave greater prominence to his own role of Dandelion and to that of Gabrielle now played by Lizzie Coote. The Island of Pleasure and Aesop episodes were suppressed and the Wishing Boudoir scene was transformed into a lengthy vehicle for the two comedy stars with the result that the show was still very long indeed. Jacobi and Clay both contributed new songs – particularly for Constance

Loseby who was taking on the title role – and two new ballets, 'The Ballet of the Ferns' and 'The Coral Island Ballet' to feature the Alhambra's huge corps de ballet, but a large part of the work remained untouched and all the old favourites such as 'Nobody Knows as I Know', 'Where can my little Brother Be', 'Break not yet the sweet Illusion' etc were welcomed back with acclamation through a second run of 107 performances.

The greatest contribution to the repertoire of shorter pieces was made by Frank Desprez who had assumed the role of supplier of curtain-raisers to the D'Oyly Carte Companies. While *In the Sulks* went out on tour with the Gilbert and Sullivan operas, he produced *Quite an Adventure* to precede *Claude Duval* at the Olympic and *Mock Turtles* as a forepiece for *Patience* at the Savoy. Desprez's pieces, which he described as vaudevilles, were less substantial than the best of the German Reed fare but quite the thing to put an audience in a lighthearted frame of mind for what was to follow, comprising as they did a slight domestic tale with bright and amusing dialogue and the occasional piece of pretty or comical music supplied in these cases by Teddy Solomon and Eaton Fanning respectively. *Quite an Adventure* concerned a certain Mrs Wallaby who faints on Victoria Station and is aided by a gentleman who puts his latchkey down her back. Unfortunately the lady goes home without retrieving the key and the gentleman is obliged to follow her. In doing so he misses his last train and the lady entertains him until her husband returns. Each man takes the other for a burglar and the expected comicalities ensue until all is cleared up. After its season at the Olympic, Carte retained *Quite an Adventure* as an introductory piece in several of his tours.

Mock Turtles was a hugely successful little piece which told simply and humorously of a bickering married couple who put on a billing-and-cooing act for her visiting mother only to find that they really prefer being nice to each other and fall in love all over again. It was introduced with *Patience* soon after the shift to the Savoy and was played, as was the custom, by the principal understudies for the main piece, in this case Courtice Pounds and Minna Louis as the aptly named Wrangleburys and Rosina Brandram as the mother. It proved so popular that it was retained on the bill when *Iolanthe* succeeded *Patience* and was also given wide play in Carte's provincial companies.

The St George's Hall provided four new pieces during the year, the programme being filled out with revivals of *A Turquoise Ring*, *Number 204* and *Ages Ago* for which last Fred Clay composed a new duet. The new pieces came again from the pen of Arthur Law with the exception of the least successful, *Many Happy Returns*, written by Gilbert a'Beckett and Clement Scott. The best of the new offerings were *Cherry Tree Farm*, a slight marital piece with music by Hamilton Clarke which saw the return to Langham Place of Fanny Holland, and *All at Sea*, another matrimonial puzzle in which Leonora Braham made a temporary come-back for the Reeds.

In the provinces, Fred Solomon tried his hand at composition and produced *The Good Young Man Who . .* which provided a bravura role for himself as a noise-hating gentleman who buys up the instruments of a German band one by one in order to get some peace. It toured with his brother's *Billee Taylor*.

1881

0032 **LOLA** or The Belle of Baccarato. A comic opera in two acts by Frederick Marshall. Music by Antonio Orsini. Produced at the Olympic Theatre under the management of C. Baker 15 January, 1881 for a run of 36 performances closing 1 March, 1881. Played with *The Dowager* and later *My Aunt's Advice*.

Alexis, Prince of Baccarato . . . . Edmund Rosenthal
Bobiski, Chief of Police . . . . M. Bentley
Polonikoff, Lord Chamberlain . . . . . . Henry Lewens
Tigerkoffski, General . . . . Gordon Rae
Edgardo de Toros . . . . Henry Walsham
Reginald Vere de Vere . . . . George deLange
Lord Adolphus . . . . Mr Weathersby
Aunt Priscilla de Montmorency . . . . . Harriet Everard/Emily Cross
Lola de Flores . . . . Elinor Loveday
Lady Lambkin . . . . Alice Mowbray
Hon. Launcelot . . . . Master Jones
Citizen . . . . Mr Mowbray
Sailor . . . . Mr Rylands
Waiter . . . . Mr Williams
Trumpeter . . . . Mr F. Onwyhn/Mr Williams
Reporter . . . . Mr Grundy
Lizette . . . . Cora Saville
Julia . . . . Doreen O'Brien
Emily . . . . Rose Roberts
Citizen . . . . Miss Edrof

Md: Antonio Orsini; ch: John Lauri; sc: W. Perkins; cos: Alias and Swan & Edgar

0033 **PATIENCE** or Bunthorne's Bride. An aesthetic opera in two acts by W. S. Gilbert. Music by Arthur Sullivan. Produced at the Opera Comique under the management of Richard D'Oyly Carte 23 April, 1881. Transferred to the Savoy Theatre 10 October, 1881. Withdrawn 23 November, 1882 after 578 performances.

Colonel Calverley . . . . Richard Temple/Walter Browne (F. Ainsworth)
Major Murgatroyd . . . . Frank Thornton/Arthur Law/Edward Lyster
Lt Duke of Dunstable . . . . Durward Lely
Reginald Bunthorne . . . . George Grossmith/Frank Thornton
Archibald Grosvenor . . . . Rutland Barrington
Bunthorne's Solicitor . . . . George Bowley
Lady Angela . . . . Jessie Bond/Julia Gwynne/Kate Forster
Lady Saphir . . . . Julia Gwynne/Sybil Grey
Lady Ella . . . . May Fortescue/Minna Louis
Lady Jane . . . . Alice Barnett/Rosina Brandram
Patience . . . . Leonora Braham/Ellen Shirley (Minna Louis)

Md: François Cellier; ch: John D'Auban & Harry Emden; sc: John O'Connor; cos: W. S. Gilbert *et al.*

Produced at the Standard Theatre, New York, under the management of Richard D'Oyly Carte 22 September, 1881. From 6 March, 1882 played in repertoire with *Claude Duval*. Withdrawn 23 March, 1882 after a total of 177 performances.
W. T. Carleton/William Hamilton (COL), Arthur Wilkinson (MAJ), Lyn Cadwaladr (D), J. H. Ryley (BUN), James Barton/W. T. Carleton (GRO), William White (SOL), Alice Burville/Janet Edmonson (A), Rose Chapelle (S), Alma Stuart Stanley/Jenny Stone/Marie Hunter (E), Augusta Roche (J), Carrie Burton (PAT). Md: P. W. Halton/Ernest Neyer; sc: Mazzanovich

Performed at Booth's Theatre, New York, by E. E. Rice's Co. 14 November, 1881 for two weeks.
Gustavus Hall (COL), George A. Schiller (MAJ), Henri Laurent (D), A. W. F. McCollin (BUN), Eugene Clarke (GRO), Thomas Sage (SOL), Verona Jarbeau (A), Irene Perry (S), Fannie Hall (E), Rosa Cooke (J), Rose Temple (PAT). Md: Joseph A. Kuhn.

Produced at the Bijou Theatre, New York, under the management of John A. McCaull 5 June, 1882. Transferred to Niblo's Garden. Played at the Bijou Theatre again 9 September, 1882 for 4 weeks.
John E. Nash/Charles Dungan/Joseph S. Greensfelde (C), William Gillow/George Gaston (M), Harry Pepper/Alonzo Hatch/Charles J. Campbell (D), Edward P. Temple/John Howson (BUN), Harry St Maur/Digby V. Bell (GRO), William Ridgeway/Harry Standish (SOL), Marion Lambert/Emma Guthrie/Lily Post (A), Emily Lawrence/Victoria Reynolds/Emie Weathersby (S), G. Bowler/Susie Wiener/Victoria Reynolds (E), Augusta Roche/Laura Joyce (J), Lillian Russell/Lily Post (PAT)

Played at Tony Pastor's Theatre, New York, from 22 May, 1882 to 1 June, 1882.
Henri Laurent (C), Harry Pepper (D), J. H. Rennie (BUN), Alma Stuart Stanley (GRO), May Hill (A), Maggie Duggan (J), Fanny Wentworth (PAT)

Produced at the Carltheatre, Vienna, 28 May, 1887 as *Patience (Dragoner und Dichter)*.

Played for short seasons in repertoire by the Boston Ideal Company, Henry E. Dixey's Company, John McCaull's Company, the Boston Comic Opera Company, the Castle Square Company, etc., 1882–1898.

Produced at the Herald Square Theatre, New York, 13 July, 1896.
W. McLaughlan (COL), Aubrey Boucicault (MAJ), Joseph Sheehan (D), Henry Dixey (BUN), W. T. Carleton (GRO), Sadie Martinot (A), Dorothy Morton (S), Lillian Swain (E), Flora Finlayson (J), Lillian Russell (PAT).

Produced at the Savoy Theatre under the management of Richard D'Oyly Carte 7 November, 1900 for a run of 150 performances closing 20 April, 1901.
Jones Hewson (COL), W. H. Leon (MAJ), Robert Evett (D), Walter Passmore (BUN), Henry Lytton (GRO), H. Carlyle Pritchard (SOL), Blanche Gaston-Murray (A), Lulu Evans (S), Agnes Fraser (E), Rosina Brandram (J), Isabel Jay (PAT)

Produced at the Savoy Theatre under the management of the D'Oyly Carte Opera Company 4 April, 1907 for a run of 51 performances.
Frank Wilson (COL), Richard Andean (MAJ), Harold Wilde (D), C. H. Workman (BUN), John Clulow (GRO), Ronald Greene (SOL), Jessie Rose (Norah McLeod) (A), Marie Wilson (S), Ruby Gray (E), Louie Rene (J), Clara Dow (Dora Eshelby) (PAT). Md: François Cellier

Subsequently played by the D'Oyly Carte Opera Company on tour and in London in repertoire

Produced at the Lyric Theatre, New York, under the management of William Brady and the Shubert brothers 6 May, 1912 for a run of 33 performances to 1 June, 1912.
George J. Macfarlane (C), Eugene Cowles (M), Arthur Aldridge (D), de Wolf Hopper (BUN), Cyril Scott (GRO), George Romain (SOL), Marie Doro (A), Viola Gillette (S), Alice Brady (E), Eva Davenport (J), Christine Nielson (PAT). Dir: William J. Wilson; md: Clarence Rogerson; sc: H. Robert Law; cos: Melville Ellis

Produced at the Provincetown Playhouse, USA, 29 December, 1924 for a run of 104 performances.

Played in New York by the D'Oyly Carte Opera Company and by other companies in repertoire and for short seasons.

Produced by the English National Opera October 9, 1969 at the London Coliseum.

Alan Charles (MAJ), John Delaney (D), Derek Hammond-Stroud (BUN), Emile Belcourt (GRO), Shirley Chapman (A), Pamela Fasso (S), Dorothy Nash (E), Heather Begg (J), Wendy Baldwin (PAT)

Produced at the English National Opera 15 February 1 1984.
Eric Shilling (COL), John Kitchiner (MAJ), Terry Jenkins (D), Derek Hammond-Stroud (BUN), Christopher Booth-Jones (GRO), Maurice Bowen (SOL), Sally Burgess (A), Shelagh Squires (S), Jane Eaglen (E), Anne Collins (J), Patricia O'Neill (PAT) Dir: John Cox; md: Victor Morris; sc: John Stoddart

Played at the Metropolitan Opera House, New York, by the English National Opera touring company in repertoire, 1984.

TV/Video: 1984. Brent Walker Ltd. Pr: Judith de Paul; dir: John Cox; md: Alexander Faris; ch: Terry Gilbert; sc: Allan Cameron; cos: Jenny Beavan
Donald Adams (COL), Roderick Kennedy (MAJ), Terry Jenkins (D), Derek Hammond-Stroud (BUN), John Fryatt (GRO), Shirley Chapman (A), Shelagh Squires (S), Patricia Hay (E), Anne Collins (J), Sandra Dugdale (PAT)

0034 **CLAUDE DUVAL** or Love and Larceny. A romantic comic opera in three acts by Henry Pottinger Stephens. Music by Edward Solomon. Produced at the Olympic Theatre under the management of Michael Gunn 24 August, 1881 for a run of 54 performances closing 20 October, 1881.

Claude Duval . . . . Frank H. Celli (Harold Russell)
Sir Whiffle Whaffle . . . . Arthur Williams (George Peyton)
Charles Lorrimore. . . . . George Power (E. Christy)
Captain Hasleigh . . . . Jack Leumane
Martin Magruder . . . . Charles Ashford
Blood-Red Bill. . . . . Frederic Solomon
Constance . . . . Marion Hood
Mistress Betty . . . . Harriet Coveney
Hodge . . . . Mr Goldie
Podge . . . . H. Cooper Cliffe
Dolly. . . . . Nellie Sanson
Rose . . . . Edith Blande
Boscat . . . . Harold Russell
Prudence. . . . . May Lennox
Kezia. . . . . Violet Dare
Mary. . . . . Daisy Foster
Barbara . . . . Lizzie Beaumont

Dir: Charles Harris, md: Edward Solomon; ch: John D'Auban; sc: Messrs Fox; cos: George Pilotell

Produced at the Standard Theatre, New York, under the management of Richard D'Oyly Carte 6 March, 1882. Played in repertoire with *Patience* for three weeks, and thereafter for five weeks closing 29 April, 1882.
W. T. Carleton (CD), Arthur Wilkinson (WW), Lyn Cadwaladr (CH), William Hamilton (MAG), J. H. Ryley (BILL), J. A. Furey (CAPT), Carrie Burton (CON), Jennie Hughes (BET), Victoria Reynolds (DOL), Marie Hunter (ROSE), F. Dixon (BOSC)
with Clara Allen, Agnes Arlington, Ethel Champney, Annie Dayton, Marie de Noel, Nellie de Vere, Sophie Hummell, Marie Langdon, Eugenie Maynard, Agnes Merrill, Lizzie Miller, Lillie Shandley, Grace Sherwood, Belle Urquhart, Lillie Walters, Clara Wisdom. Dir: Charles Harris; md: P. W. Halton; sc: A. Voegtlin, Hawley; cos: Pilotell

0035 **ALL IN THE DOWNS** a nautical opera in three acts by Douglas Jerrold based on his play, *Black-Eyed Susan*. Music by W. Meyer Lutz. Produced at the Gaiety Theatre under the management of John Hollingshead 5 November, 1881 at a matinée for the benefit of Meyer Lutz.

Black-eyed Susan . . . . Blanche Cole
Captain Crosstree . . . . Michael Dwyer
Jacob Twig . . . . J. J. Dallas

Doggrass	Mr Tempest
Raker	Mr Crook
Quid	Mr Cowlrick
Admiral	Mr Salisbury
Dolly Mayflower	Alice Aynsley Cook
William	J. W. Turner
Gnatbrain	J. Furneaux Cook
Hatchett	Arthur Howell
Seaweed	Mr Friend
Peter	Mr Cruttwell

Dir: Robert Soutar; md: Meyer Lutz; ch: John D'Auban; cos: Mrs May

036 **THE PET OF NEWMARKET** a comic opera in two acts by Herbert Mooney. Music by 'Camille' (Camille Vanden Bossche). Produced at Sadler's Wells Theatre under the management of F. B. Chatterton by the authors at a matinée 12 November, 1881.

Duke of Badminton	William Broughton
Goldraker	Harold Russell
Teddy Martin	Annie Collins
Lady Blanche Fetlock	Nellie Robe
Jimmie Punter	Walter Vernon
Dan Optic	James Bryan
Dicky Bird	Isabel Grey
Nellie	Lizzie Coote

Pds: Mlles Luna & Stella, Fred Evans and the children of the National Training School; ch: Katti Lanner

Produced at the Holborn Theatre 12 December, 1885 under the management of Camille Vanden Bossche for a run of 6 performances. Cast included Vivienne Dallas and Wilford Morgan.

THE GRAND MOGUL a comic opera in two acts by Edward Oxenford. Music by William Meadows. Produced at the Royalty Theatre under the management of Frank Rothsay for one performance at a matinée 22 June, 1881 with *Let Not Your Angry Passions Rise*.

The Great Mogul	Arthur Williams
Silas Boodle	James Neville
Frank Halliday	Walter H. Fisher
Mrs O'Gully	Harriet Coveney
Susan	Jessie Braham
Lord Mayor	J. Furneaux Cook
Dick Dabble	Cecil Raleigh
Colonel Cobb	George Stretton
Gwendoline	Annie Lawler
Grace	Florence Lavender

Md: William Meadows

10a **THE BLACK CROOK** a revised version of the grand opéra-bouffe féerie by Harry Paulton produced at the Alhambra Theatre under the management of Henry Sutton 3 December, 1881 for a run of 107 performances closing 4 April, 1882. Book revised by Harry Paulton. Additional music by Frederic Clay and Georges Jacobi.

Black Crook	Constance Loseby/Kate Sullivan
Gabrielle	Lizzie Coote
Queen Orange Hue	Rose Berend
Princess Desirée	Emilie Petrelli
Queen Aika	Julia Seaman/Florence Bennett
Fairy Sapphire	Kate Sullivan/
Fairy Coral	May Jameison/Jessie Hudson
Fairy Pearl	Louise Beverley
Dandelion	Harry Paulton
Prince Jonquil	Henry Walsham
King Quiribobo	René Longrois

Ding-Dong . . . . W. Hargreaves
Buttercup . . . . J. H. Jarvis
Jingle-Jangle . . . . Louis Kelleher
Zuzziel . . . . Clavering Power
Solfleur . . . . Mr Redmund

Dir: Frank Hall; md: Georges Jacobi; ch: A. Bertrand; sc: Albert Callcott; cos: Wilhelm

ALL AT SEA by Arthur Law. Music by R. Corney Grain. Produced at St George's Hall under the management of Alfred Reed and R. Corney Grain 28 February, 1881 with *A Turquoise Ring* and *Our Institute*, the former replaced by *Many Happy Returns* (28 March). Withdrawn 4 April. Reopened 18 April. Withdrawn 28 May. Reopened 3 October with *Cherry Tree Farm* and *Ye Fancy Fayre 1881*. Withdrawn 12 November, 1881.

Samuel Smallsole . . . . Alfred Reed
May Hawker . . . . Edith Brandon
Lt. Shrapnel Snorter . . . . R. Corney Grain
Belinda Pikestaff . . . . Leonora Braham
Beak Hawker . . . . Alfred Bishop

Produced at St George's Hall 17 December, 1892 with *Our Dolls' House* and *Boys and Girls*. Withdrawn 14 February, 1893.
Avalon Collard (SS), Cecile Brani (MAY), R. Corney Grain (LT), Fanny Holland (BEL), Arthur Helmore (BEAK)

MANY HAPPY RETURNS by Gilbert a'Beckett and Clement Scott. Music by Lionel Benson. Produced at St George's Hall under the management of Alfred Reed and R. Corney Grain 28 March, 1881 with *All at Sea* and *Our Institute*. Withdrawn 4 April. Reopened 18 April. Withdrawn 28 May, 1881.

Marquis de Beauvoisin . . . . R. Corney Grain
Rosalind . . . . Edith Brandon
Professor Septimus Styx . . . . Alfred Bishop
Dr Dundas Daisy . . . . Alfred Reed
Chirruper . . . . Leonora Braham

CHERRY TREE FARM by Arthur Law. Music by Hamilton Clarke. Produced at St George's Hall under the management of Alfred Reed and R. Corney Grain 30 May, 1881 with *Ye Fancy Fayre 1881* and *A Bright Idea*. Withdrawn 23 July. Reopened 3 October with *All At Sea* and *Ye Fancy Fayre 1881*, the latter replaced by *Number 204* (14 November). Withdrawn 19 November, 1881.

Richard Portlock . . . . Alfred Reed
Daisy Springrove . . . . Fanny Holland
Jack Drummond . . . . R. Corney Grain
Mabel Ashton . . . . Edith Brandon
Stephen Springrove . . . . Alfred Bishop

Produced at St George's Hall 6 October, 1884 with *A Terrible Fright* and *Troubles of a Tourist*. Withdrawn 22 November, 1884.

A BRIGHT IDEA by Arthur Law. Music by Arthur Cecil. Produced at St George's Hall under the management of Alfred Reed and R. Corney Grain 30 May, 1881 with *Cherry Tree Farm* and *Ye Fancy Fayre 1881*. Withdrawn 23 July, 1881.

BLUE AND BUFF or The Great Muddleborough Election. A comic opera in one act by E. V. Ward. Music by William L. Frost. First produced January 23–25, 1881, by the Liverpool Amateur Operatic Society at the Bijou Theatre, Liverpool. Subsequently produced at the Theatre Royal, Haymarket, under the management of C. Francis, Esq., in a revised version 5 September, 1881 for a run of 5 performances closing 9 September, 1881. Played with *East Lynne*.

Oylay Crabb, Esq . . . . Eugene Stepan

Pilate Pump, Esq . . . . Eric Lewis
Registrar . . . . Lytton Grey
Vinegra Crabb . . . . Emily Thorne
Mrs Pilate Pump . . . . Lottie Venne
Sir Snobley Snooks . . . . Harry St Maur
Town Crier . . . . Mr Perry
Tory Canvasser . . . . Mr Hunt
Lydia Pump . . . . Rose Doré

QUITE AN ADVENTURE an operetta in one act by Frank Desprez. Music by Edward Solomon. Produced at the Olympic Theatre under the management of Michael Gunn 7 September, 1881 with *Claude Duval*. Withdrawn 29 October, 1881.

Mr Wallaby . . . . Charles Ashford
Mrs Wallaby. . . . . Edith Blande
Mr Fraser . . . . Arthur Williams
Policeman . . . . Fred Solomon

UNCLE SAMUEL an operetta in one act by Arthur Law. Music by George Grossmith. Produced at the Opera Comique under the management of Richard D'Oyly Carte 3 May, 1881 as a forepiece to *Patience*. Withdrawn 8 October, 1881.

Mr Samuel Crow . . . . Frank Thornton
John Bird . . . . Arthur Law
Margery Daw . . . . Rosina Brandram
Jenny Wren . . . . Minna Louis

QUID PRO QUO a vaudeville by Rutland Barrington and Cunningham Bridgman. Music by Wilfred Bendall. Presented at the Opera Comique under the management of John Hollingshead 17 October, 1881 as a forepiece to *Princess Toto*. Withdrawn 17 December, 1881.

Lady Ethel. . . . . Emily Cross
Lord Arthur . . . . George Temple

Produced at the Opera Comique 25 February, 1882 as a forepiece to *The Mother-in-law*. Withdrawn 17 March, 1882.
Emily Cross (ETH), George Temple (ARTH)

MOCK TURTLES a vaudeville by Frank Desprez. Music by Eaton Fanning. Produced at the Savoy Theatre under the management of Richard D' Oyly Carte 15 October, 1881 as a forepiece to *Patience* and subsequently with *Iolanthe*. Withdrawn 30 March, 1883.

Mr Wranglebury . . . . Courtice Pounds/Arthur Law
Mrs Wranglebury . . . . Minna Louis
Mrs Boucher. . . . . Rosina Brandram
Jane . . . . Sybil Grey

GENTLE GERTRUDE of the Infamous Redd Lyon Inn; a musical absurdity in one act (a burlesque melo-drammer) by T. Edgar Pemberton. Music by T. Anderton. Produced at the Alexandra Theatre, Liverpool 21 February, 1881.

Sir Guy de Montfort . . . . Edward Saker
Giles Gowdrodger. . . . . William Hogarth
Mrs Gowdrodger . . . . Pollie Poland
Gertrude. . . . . Mrs Edward Saker

Produced at the Gaiety Theatre under the management of John Hollingshead 14 May, 1884 at a matinée with *Paul Pry*.
George Shelton (GUY), Lionel Brough (GILES), Lydia Thompson (GERT).

Produced at the Novelty Theatre November, 1885, with *Lottie*.
Harry Nicholls (GUY), Henry Parker (GILES), Fanny Robertson (MRS), Lydia Thompson (GERT)

Produced at the Strand Theatre 5 May, 1887 for the benefit of Fannie Leslie.

THE GIRL HE LEFT BEHIND HIM a variety in one act 'from the French of Delacour Daubigny' (George R. Sims). Music by Max Schröter. Produced at the Vaudeville Theatre under the management of Thomas Thorne 29 November, 1881 with *The Half Way House*. Withdrawn 2 February, 1882.

Tom Tarpaulin . . . . J. R. Crauford
Peter Popcorn . . . . Thomas Thorne
Giles Scroggins . . . . William Lestocq
Ned . . . . W. Horne
Polly . . . . Kate Phillips
Sarah Ann . . . . Ella Strathmore
with Messrs Austin, Welch, Marshall; Misses Forrester, Leslie, Vincent, Rudge, Danvers, Briton, Hartland, Burton, Raymond, Hardinge, Truefit

THE GOOD YOUNG MAN WHO . . . an operetta by Frederick Solomon. Produced at Aberdeen 30 May, 1881 by Charles Bernard's *Billee Taylor* Company.

1882

The year 1882 brought a consolidation from the established composers. Sullivan and Solomon both produced new works to books by Gilbert and Stephens, and the prospect of a wider field of successful writers as Bucalossi amongst the composers and Harry Paulton, Walter Parke, H. B. Farnie and Sydney Grundy among the authors all scored in shows with varying degrees of success.

Solomon had two shows staged during the year: *Lord Bateman*, which had been awaiting production since the previous year, and *The Vicar of Bray*, a comic opera written by Sydney Grundy. *Lord Bateman* had already had a strange career. In the aura of the great success of *Billee Taylor* a Solomon/Stephens opera had become prized by managers second only to a Gilbert and Sullivan, and when the work was completed it had been much sought after. It was finally secured, along with *Claude Duval*, by Michael Gunn, and D'Oyly Carte picked up the American rights. But *Lord Bateman* did not appear in 1881. Gunn had announced it to follow *Claude Duval* at the Olympic, but relations between him and the ebullient Mr Solomon were strained and they became even more so as the result of an incident in February when Solomon arranged an orchestral trial of the music at the Savoy. To this rehearsal he invited the press and the cognoscenti of the London musical scene. But nobody asked W. S. Gilbert. Carte being absent in America, Gunn had permitted the use of the Savoy and Gilbert was livid. He descended like Carabosse on the infant princess and forbade the rehearsal at 'his' theatre so that Solomon was obliged to cancel. The composer blamed Gunn and the latter was angry that his privileged relationship with the Savoy had been publicly damaged. Finally John Hollingshead offered the use of the Gaiety and on 21 February the public demonstration of the music for the new show was given. Its intelligibility was marred by the fact that Solomon had not seen fit to hire any singers and, in consequence, took all the roles himself, singing now soprano, now tenor, now basso from his place on the conductor's podium. However, this first known example of what can only be considered as a backers' audition won sufficient approbation. *The Era* predicted that '*Lord Bateman* will be Mr Solomon's best opera' and added prophetically 'should the libretto of Mr Stephens equal the music of Mr Solomon a very decided success is in store for *Lord Bateman*'.

The piece had to wait two months for its first full performance. The Gaiety had produced *Billee Taylor* again and was playing it at matinées each Saturday. After a few weeks it was decided to vary the bill and *Lord Bateman* took its place. It did not fulfil expectations. In the popular tale of Lord Bateman, Stephens had chosen another old English ballad for his subject. The simple story told how the soldiering Lord is captured by an Eastern potentate but is helped to escape by his captor's daughter, Princess Picotee. He swears he will remain single for exactly four years so that, if she will, she may come to him. Bateman returns to England and, as the expiry of the time approaches, prepares unenthusiastically to wed in accordance with his rank. But Picotee arrives just in time for Bateman to renounce his bride-to-be and wed her. These bones were fleshed out with a number of subsidiary characters: the standard Sultan (disguised in act 2 as a conjurer), his Grand Vizier who is of Scottish origin, a semi-villainous lawyer who is uncle to the hero and has an eye to his inheritance, a basso alderman and a termagant Turkish wife. But these added little to the wispy main plot and none was convincingly humorous on its own. The songs produced nothing of the 'Eliza' or 'William' level. A feeble piece for the Vizier McDallah called 'Snappy' was the most obvious concession to the music hall, while there was an attempt to reproduce the Charity Girls' success in *Billee Taylor* with a line-up of ten superfluous Blue Coat Boys which had none of the attraction of its predecessor. Solomon supplied some pretty tunes for the prima donna Lizzie St Quinten (notably the charming ballad 'The Silver Line') and for Frederic Darrell, the star of *Billee Taylor*, who was once again cast as a rather nauseous youth in a libretto which lacked any distinctive character and failed to do anything for the songs.

Reaction to *Lord Bateman* was not totally negative. The music came in for a certain amount of commendation and *Punch* even declared that it was 'the best piece, far and away, that Messrs. Solomon and Stephens have yet done', but *The Era* was more to the point:

> *Lord Bateman* has the worst fault a comic opera could have, its libretto is decidedly dull. There is no invention and no humour in the story, and considering what a capital old ballad it is founded on it is surprising Mr Stephens has not derived greater interest from it. There are a few hits at the topics of the day and these were taken up eagerly by the audience, but the echoes of mirth which they awakened died away immediately and were frequently succeeded by a yawn. The cause of this was the thin and meagre story which instead of helping the composer only hampered him, for in many cases there were really elegant and tuneful airs, choruses and concerted pieces associated with incidents in which nobody could take any interest . . . unless the libretto is condensed and its matter enlivened we fear there will not be a long career for *Lord Bateman*.

There was not. It was repeated the following Saturday and then discontinued. Stephens and Solomon themselves organised a company to tour *Billee Taylor* and announced another to follow with *Lord Bateman*. The first company set off from Brighton nine days after the last Gaiety matinée, but the second was slow to materialise. Then it was announced that the *Billee Taylor* Company would perform *Lord Bateman* in repertoire instead of there being a separate company but when the tour disbanded in Bristol nine weeks later the piece remained unperformed. Carte did not pick up his American option and *Lord Bateman*'s all-time total stayed at two performances. However the authors reaped some little satisfaction when 'The Silver Line' proved a particularly popular ballad for the pantomime season and £30 from this provincial town and £50 from that came in to fill *Lord Bateman*'s empty credit column.

Solomon's second offering proved more to the public taste. The ballad which he chose to elaborate upon this time was that of the Vicar of Bray who changed his faith as expedient:

> In Good King Charles' golden days
> When loyalty no harm meant
> A zealous High Churchman was I
> And so I got preferment.

To teach my flock I never missed
Kings were by God appointed
And lost are those who dare resist
Or touch the Lord's anointed.
And this is the law that I'll maintain
Until my dying day,
That whatsoever King may reign
I'll still be the Vicar of Bray, Sir!

The libretto was supplied by Sydney Grundy, a newcomer to the musical scene but not to theatrical affairs, for he had already made his mark in the straight theatre. Manchester-born, he had qualified and practised as a barrister in his home town for six years while dabbling in journalism on the side before throwing up the law and moving to London with the avowed intent of becoming a dramatist. His first staged work was a one-act piece, *A Little Change*, which he sent unsolicited to Buckstone at the Haymarket and had accepted. His first notable success was with *Mammon*, a translation from the French, produced at the Strand in April 1877, which he followed with further successes in *The Snowball* and *Honour Bound*.

For *The Vicar of Bray* he was obliged to invent a plot, as the liturgical vacillations of the title character hardly provided sufficient material for a full-length show. For this purpose he took up the old tale of Sandford and Merton, already often used on the stage, and combined it with the character of the famous Vicar to compose a story in which the cleric changes his religion for rather more prosaic reasons than his ballad counterpart. The Rev. William Barlow is Low Church. He became Low Church in order to marry his rich wife who, now dead, has left him with one daughter, Dorothy. Dorothy is in love with her father's curate, Henry Sandford, a decidedly priggish young man with a habit of speaking in rounded and polysyllabic periods. The Vicar has other designs for his daughter in the form of Sandford's old schoolmate, Tommy Merton, son of the proprietor of the living of Bray. To get Sandford out of the way the Vicar, on the advice of his confidential family solicitor, Mr Bedford Rowe, turns High Church. Aghast, Sandford flees to become a missionary in the Cassowary Isles. But alas! now that the Vicar and all his students have become 'High' they are doomed to celibacy and the Chorus of Lady Sunday School Teachers is distraught at the loss of their matrimonial prospects. So, too, is Mrs Merton who has had her eye on the Vicar. Tommy Merton is prepared as a husband for Dorothy but suddenly Sandford, whom everyone supposed to have been devoured by cannibals, returns – a decidedly better young man with his rounded periods knocked out of him by the King of the Cassowaries. Dorothy returns to her first love, but her father is adamant. Suddenly the solicitor arrives: the Vicar's High Church propensities have displeased his Bishop who has declared him defrocked, his living to be bestowed on Sandford. There is only one way out. The Vicar becomes 'Low' again. He is now eligible to wed the wealthy Mrs Merton while Henry gets his Dorothy and Tommy goes off with the leading danseuse of the local theatre.

Grundy's dialogue was brisk, smart and a little Gilbertian in flavour as, for instance, when Dorothy introduces Sandford:

DOR: When he was quite a boy, so exemplary was his conduct that he became my father's favourite pupil and when he was ordained papa determined to secure his services for a term of years.

BL: At what rent?

DOR: Fifty pounds per annum.

AG: It isn't very much.

DOR: True. But you must remember that papa covenanted to keep him in good order and preservation, and to deliver him up on the expiry of the term in the same excellent condition in which he found him.

CY: Then it is a repairing lease?

The book of *The Vicar of Bray* had one important characteristic which was most un-Gilbertian. It was set firmly and recognisably in England, and in that it followed *Billee Taylor*, *The Lancashire Witches* and *Claude Duval* rather than the nebulously located *Patience* or Gilbert's Pirates in their Ruritanian 'Penzance'. But the material Grundy had chosen was slight and undramatic, and Solomon showed little of the vigour of his more robust works. The whole tone and quality of *The Vicar of Bray* was light and polite. Even the satire consisted of gentle digs rather than Gilbert's full-bloooded prodding and, though there were some delightful moments in both the book and the songs, the show met with a mixed reception.

After a short while it was withdrawn and Grundy set to work on reconstruction, making considerable alterations in the second act. Some cast changes were made with Emilie Petrelli taking over the role of Dorothy and W. S. Penley replacing Walter Fisher as Sandford, and the piece was tried again. It held on for a satisfactory if uninspiring two months.

In the meanwhile it had come and gone on Broadway. Haphazardly produced at the Fifth Avenue Theatre it had survived only one week. Solomon had personally supervised the production and was piqued at America's failure to recognise his work, but the production had been poor. The cast was weak and even the usually reliable if wooden Welsh tenor Llewellyn Cadwaladr had been a disaster as Sandford. Solomon's only consolation was that the theatre was filled instead with a revival of *Billee Taylor*. Ten years later, during the Gilbert and Sullivan interregnum at the Savoy, D'Oyly Carte scored a notable success with Solomon's *The Nautch Girl* and, as a follow up, he received *The Vicar of Bray* once again, somewhat revised. With a stronger cast led by Rutland Barrington in the title role, Courtice Pounds, Richard Green, Rosina Brandram and the American soprano Leonore Snyder, and the production values of the Savoy organisation behind it, *The Vicar of Bray* caught on rather better and ran for five months before joining the D'Oyly Carte touring repertoire where it remained for several years.

Gilbert and Sullivan were not required to produce a new work until the end of 1882 as *Patience* continued to run strongly throughout the year, and it was not until November that the Savoy was ready to stage a new piece. Once again rumour had been rife. In America, first of all, it was announced that the new work would be set in America and produced in that country. Then a new version of *The Princess* was suggested, then a rewritten *Sorcerer*, until finally it became known that the new piece would be a fairy play entitled variously *The Princess Pearl* or *Perola*. Carte said nothing. He had already planned simultaneous openings in Britain and America and, having suffered badly from thieves again with *Patience*, he was taking no risks. But the new piece was a fairy play, it was being prepared as *Perola* and as far back as February *The Era* had published an almost correct plot synopsis, yet no-one jumped in to try and forestall Gilbert and Sullivan. By now it was proved that it was not just their material but their manner of its treatment that made their great success. On 25 November, 1882 *Iolanthe* was staged within a few hours in both London and New York, and in both places it was immediately hailed as a great success.

The plot concerned the fairy Iolanthe who, against fairy law, had married a mortal and borne him a son. For this she was banished and spent twenty-five years 'on her head at the bottom of a stream' until the Fairy Queen relented and she was pardoned. Her son, Strephon, is in love with Phyllis, a ward-in-chancery for whose hand the whole House of Lords is sighing, but Phyllis prefers the half-fairy shepherd, much to the annoyance of the Lord Chancellor who fancies the girl himself and would marry her if only his applications to himself in his official capacity could be entertained. But Phyllis sees Strephon kissing his mother – such a very young mother – and is heartbroken. She pledges herself to wed a peer, no matter which. Strephon calls on his Fairy Aunts to aid him and the troupe descend upon the peers. Insulted by the Lord Chancellor, the Fairy Queen declares that Strephon shall be a Member of Parliament and every bill he promulgates shall be passed. Chaos reigns and utter horror. In the meantime the Chancellor has succeeded in convincing himself that he is, after all, a suitable husband for Phyllis, which is unfortunate as the lovers have just become reconciled after Strephon has introduced Phyllis to his mother. But Iolanthe puts a stop to the Chancellor's professions of love. Breaking her fairy vows once again, she reveals herself as his wife and Strephon as his son. The Fairy Queen descends. This time Iolanthe has gone too far. But the other fairies step forward: they too have married mortals – the whole House of Lords. The Queen is in a dilemma but the Lord Chancellor, 'an old Equity draughtsman', is equal to the occasion. He alters the fairy law by the addition of one word: 'Every fairy who *don't* marry a mortal is guilty.' The Queen selects a suitably handsome guardsman as a consort and all ends happily.

Once again the staple members of the company were provided with good roles. Grossmith, as the Lord Chancellor, had the merriest of characters and three outstanding songs: 'The Law Is the true Embodiment', 'When I Went to the Bar' and the Nightmare Song, a patter song par excellence giving the details of his Lordship's bad dreams as he dozes racked by unrequited love:

> When you're lying awake with a dismal headache and
> repose is taboo'd by anxiety,
> I conceive you may use any language you choose to
> indulge in, without impropriety;
> For your brain is on fire – the bedclothes conspire
> of usual slumber to plunder you;
> First your counterpane goes and uncovers your toes
> And your sheet slips demurely from under you;
> Then the blanketing tickles – you feel like mixed pickles –
> so terribly sharp is the pricking,
> And you're hot, and you're cross, and you tumble and toss
> till there's nothing twixt you and the ticking,
> Then the bedclothes all creep to the ground in a heap, and
> you pick 'em all up in a tangle;
> Next your pillow resigns and politely declines to remain
> at its usual angle! &c.

Richard Temple found himself, uncharacteristically, cast as a baritone juvenile lead with Leonora Braham as his Phyllis and Jessie Bond, in the title role, rather more prominent than before as his mother. Alice Barnett had a stand-out role as the buxom Fairy Queen, and Barrington and tenor Durward Lely were the two Lords Mountararat and Tolloller who seek Phyllis's hand.

The London opening went well. The first act was applauded and Grossmith's two songs encored. The second produced three further encores. The setting of the Houses of Parliament and the Thames Embankment at night delighted the audience as did the appearance of the leading fairies with little electric lights glistening in their hair. Alice Barnett caused great hilarity with her lovelorn 'O foolish Fay', particularly when she sang:

On fire that glows with heat intense
I turn the hose of common sense
And out it goes at small expense!
We must maintain our fairy law;
That is the main on which to draw–
In that we gain a Captain Shaw!
Oh, Captain Shaw! Type of true love kept under!
Could thy Brigade
With cold cascade
Quench my great love, I wonder!

Captain Shaw, the Commander of the London Fire Brigade and a great social creature, was in the audience and fate (or Carte) had decreed that he should be in the centre of the stalls right where Miss Barnett could see him. She hooted the lines at him with suitable aplomb and brought the house down. But the undoubted hit of the evening came when Grossmith, Barrington and Lely as the three richly dressed lords combined in a trio which John D'Auban had embellished with a comical dance that was utterly grotesque and which the audienced adored:

Nothing venture, nothing win
Blood is thick but water's thin
In for a penny, in for a pound
It's love that makes the world go round.

In spite of all the high spots some of the critics, and the authors, decided that the second act was too long and two songs were quickly cut out. One was Barrington's solo 'De Bellville was Regarded as the Crichton of his Age', a clever lyric in which Gilbert indulged in yet another dig at the arbitrary fashion of selecting peers by birth; the other was a song for Strephon expressing liberal feelings which quite shocked some correspondents and was withdrawn as unfit.

The American production had opened with equal success and was soon playing to an incredible £2,000 per week. J. H. Ryley played Grossmith's role of the Lord Chancellor and scored yet another personal success. But *Iolanthe* did not have the appeal of *Pinafore* or *Patience* for the Americans and by the end of February, after three months, it had run its course. In London, on the other hand, it lasted through the whole of 1883, a total of nearly 400 performances, adding yet another huge success to the Gilbert–Sullivan–D'Oyly Carte list, and following its fellows around the world and into the permanent repertoire.

The other 'home-made' success of the year was *Les Manteaux Noirs* which was produced at the newly-opened Avenue Theatre near Charing Cross Station. The libretto was based on a French opera *Giralda ou La Nouvelle Psyche* by the doyen of French librettists, Eugène Scribe, which had been set to music by Adolphe Adam with moderate success. The French score was discarded and the libretto reorganised by Harry Paulton and Walter Parke until only the very bones of the plot remained. In their version of the story the heroine Girola is betrothed to the loutish miller, Dromez, unwillingly, for she has fallen in love with a mysterious gentlemen, Luis, who rescued her from some ruffians and has since come to serenade her. Dromez is not particularly keen on the girl, who threatens to lead him a dog's life, but he does want her dowry. When an unknown stranger offers him a large sum to give up his place as bridegroom he accepts with alacrity. The disconsolate Girola is unknowingly wedded to the stranger who immediately disappears to take up his place in the service of the Queen Isabel, for that is where he belongs. The Queen has arrived in the village to watch an eclipse but, while she is star-gazing, her lecherous consort determines to pay a late-night call on Girola in the mill where she is spending her wedding night. The central scene of *Les Manteaux Noirs* finds King Philip, his Chamberlain, the miller, and Girola's true love/husband all stalking round the mill in black cloaks and total darkness in a series of farcical confrontations which conclude with the arrival of the Queen. All dissembling is finally put aside and Luis and Girola are revealed as husband and wife, while Dromez collects hush money from everyone involved.

The English authors managed to concoct a lively and comical piece of entertainment from Scribe's situations which was backed up by a score from Procida Bucalossi that suited the old-fashioned and Frenchified character of the piece. The bulk of the music fell to the lot of the prima donna for whom the writers composed such numbers as the pretty air 'I never Could like some Girls Smile', the fandango 'Anita is Sad', the rondo 'Six Months Ago' and the ballad 'The Heart Sighs ever to be Free':

> Love knows not reason, will not be
> Subdued by duty's stern decree
> Lamenting, mourning liberty
> The heart sighs ever to be free!

and to her tenor lover, but the comedians who provided the backbone of the piece also joined in the singing. The most effective of their numbers was a comedy duet for Philip (M. Marius) and his hard-done-by Chancellor (Fred Leslie). The former is trying to serenade Girola while the latter, stuck on a balcony outside and halfway up the mill, bemoans his lot:

> PHIL: I sing love's dulcet, softest lay,
> Tra la la la la la, tra la la la la.
> Beneath the pale and waning moon
> Tra la la la la la, tra la la la la la!
> Inspired by silv'ry lunar ray
> My passions's pent-up pangs allay
> (This dashed thing's out of tune!)
> JOSE: I can't endure this outside berth
> It is the coldest spot on earth
> Without a doubt!
> PHIL: Get out! Get out!
> JOSE: All warmth has from my body fled
> PHIL: Tra la la!
> JOSE: And cold is settling in my head
> A-choo! Oh, dear! A-choo!

Les Manteaux Noirs had the great benefit of being played by a cast headed by the star of *Madame Favart*, Florence St John, and the suave Claude Marius whose popularity only increased when later in the year his wife divorced him for adultery, allowing the two stars to make their off-stage liaison legal. In the years to come they appeared together in a series of musicals at the Avenue and remained the closest of friends even when their marriage came to an end. The rising comedian Fred Leslie scored strongly as the unfortunate Chancellor, and the tenor Bracy confirmed his position amongst the best as Luis. When *The Black Crook* closed at the Alhambra, Harry Paulton hurried across to Charing Cross and took up the role of Dromez which he played to the end of the piece's 190-performance run.

By September the show had embarked on the first of its number one tours and in October, the rights having been snapped up by Carte, it was presented on Broadway as the opening offering in the season which was being staged to lead up to the production of *Iolanthe.* Selina Dolaro took on St John's role, and Carte's best regulars – Richard Mansfield, J. H. Ryley, Arthur Wilkinson and William Carleton – played the four male roles. But the Americans were not as impressed as the patrons of the Avenue and, although the cavortings in the mill were found duly funny, *Les Manteaux Noirs* did not catch on. After a few performances Ryley and Wilkinson decided they would go better in each other's roles and swapped, but the move did nothing to increase the prospects of *Les Manteaux Noirs* which folded after four weeks.

Bucalossi's contribution was considered weak and, in fact, the American correspondent of *The Era*, comparing the work with *Claude Duval*, declared that whereas the latter had been 'all music and no book' this one was 'all book and no music'. This was slightly unfair to Bucalossi, whose simple and old-fashioned style was well-suited to the subject, but the libretto of the piece was clearly its strongest point and played a major role in keeping the show six months at the Avenue. It proved an excellent venture in the provinces and in 1885 made a return visit to the West End with Marion Hood as Girola and the young Letty Lind making her West End musical début as Clorinda. It was continually toured between 1883 and 1886 by T. D. Yorke who featured his wife Alexina Anderson in the leading role, and later by Horace Guy. When its touring potential seemed exhausted it was taken into the repertoire of the Harry Battersby Juvenile Troupe where 16-year-old Florence Baines from Manchester, later to find fame as the comical 'Miss Lancashire Ltd', starred as the soprano Girola. Australia and South Africa both saw *Les Manteaux Noirs*, the former on several occasions, and the piece succeeded in gaining its writers some kind of international recognition on which only Paulton was later able to build.

An altogether larger French influence was to be found in *Rip Van Winkle*, produced at the Comedy Theatre in October. In fact, the only Briton involved among the four creative personnel was the arch-adapter H. B. Farnie who worked on the adaptation of Dion Boucicault's play with the French authors Meilhac and Gille. Robert Planquette, the composer of *Les Cloches de Corneville*, provided the music. *Rip Van Winkle* was specially prepared for the Comedy Theatre, with Fred Leslie in mind for the title role long identified in the straight theatre with the American actor Joseph Jefferson who had toured for many years in the dramatised version of Washington Irving's legend. Planquette was brought from France and, based in the Soho home of his compatriot Charlie Alias, the costumier, he turned out to order some lovely melodies to Farnie's lyrics for the voices of Leslie, prima donna Violet Cameron and the other members of the Comedy company. When he discovered that Leslie had a talent for yodelling, even that became the basis for a song.

Being based on a successful and established drama, *Rip Van Winkle* had the inbuilt advantage of a strong framework of plot and incident. With Farnie involved there were, of course, alterations including a rather 'happier' ending, but the dramatic central tale combined with Planquette's music and the bravura title role came together to produce a show of considerable strength and popularity. It remained at the Comedy Theatre for over a year and confirmed Fred Leslie as a major performer. Unfortunately, financial considerations provoked the star's departure when the show's success was still at its height. Leslie had signed at £25 per week rising to £30 after the show reached its 100th performance. When his contract expired he asked for £40 per week to remain. He was turned down and promptly left the show which had been created for him. His role was taken over by the highly expert J. A. Arnold, but without Leslie the show soon foundered.

Some critics considered that Planquette's score rivalled even his music for *Les Cloches* and, indeed, the score of *Rip Van Winkle* was full of delightful melodies, highlighted by the 'Legend of the Katskills', 'The Letter Song' and the ballad 'Twilight Shadows' all of which fell to Violet Cameron as Mrs Rip, and Rip's enchanting 'These little Heads now Golden' sung with the two little children, Hans and Alice. There was also a highly effective, if eclectic, dream sequence in which Rip conjured up the ghost of Hendrik Hudson and his spectre crew. Hudson gave forth with a basso Sea Song, followed by 'The Ninepins Song' (2nd Lieut), and a serenade for tenor and soprano lieutenants followed by a combination of dances which starred Ada Wilson as the Fay of the Rhine, all ending in a choral finale as the ghosts sing Rip into his twenty years' sleep.

Rip Van Winkle proved popular throughout the world. It was revived in London less than a year after its first season and as late as 1891/2 was brought back to the provinces by the 'cellist/conductor turned actor, Auguste van Biene, as a vehicle for his newly discovered talents. Its greatest and most lasting success came in France where it was produced in 1884 succinctly retitled *Rip!*. The book had been revamped by Ludovic Meilhac, one of the original collaborators, to such an extent that one could scarcely have blamed Farnie for feeling that the Frenchman was taking revenge for his own incessant mutilation of continental libretti.

The alterations did not stop at dialogue and structure. Meilhac eliminated a number of characters and redistributed much of the music. Thus Gretchen's 'Legend of the Katskills' melody was rescored as an air 'Vive la Paresse' for Rip, and was replaced by a new Planquette 'Legend' altogether more dramatic in tone (and not unreminiscent of *Der Fliegende Holländer*) which was also taken over by the hero. Gretchen, rechristened Nelly, made do with a new arrangement of Rip's 'Oh, where's my Girl' which became 'Quel Chagrin, Hélas'. Planquette produced several more new pieces to replace London numbers which were cut out but some, including the whole ballet and most of the dream sequence, were simply removed. The alterations evidently suited the French audiences, for *Rip!* quickly became popular and is generally considered in France as Planquette's best work after the inimitable *Les Cloches de Corneville.*

If *Iolanthe*, *Les Manteaux Noirs*, *Rip Van Winkle* and, to a lesser extent, *The Vicar of Bray* represented the healthy side of the growing British tradition, there was a less happy side of things to be seen – albeit briefly.

One of the worst and most tasteless shows to date was imported from New Zealand. Entitled *The Wreck of the Pinafore* it took the characters of Gilbert's play and wrecked them on a desert island before making whimsy with them. Josephine can't abide Ralph who has turned out to be a hopeless Captain once the ship has put to sea and is obliged to give command back to Corcoran. Buttercup finally admits she lied about mixing up the babies (Corcoran is twenty years older than Ralph) and the Admiral finally gets Josephine to wife as had orginally been intended. And so forth. This exercise had been perpetrated by Horace Lingard during his Australian and New Zealand tour of *Pinafore* and had a smell of sour grapes about it, for Lingard had been taken to court by

J. C. Williamson for his 'pirate' performances. He had escaped by transferring all his property into his wife's name and declaring himself bankrupt, but was forced to leave Australia and New Zealand, after being fined £250 in gold. He took with him his 'new comic opera' and his composer/musical director, a Plymouth-born New Zealander named Isaac Israel who called himself William Luscombe Searelle and who was principally known in New Zealand as a conductor and composer of dance music.

It was Searelle who decided that *The Wreck of the Pinafore* had a future and after its New Zealand and Australian productions (both of which had indifferent success) he produced the piece in America before heading for London. Its opening night at the Opera Comique, the home of the real and original *Pinafore*, was full of incident. One member of the audience was so incensed that he was forcibly ejected by a bouncer to silence his complaints. Then, at the interval, Searelle saw fit to come before the audience and explain proudly that he was not an American but an Englishman and that *The Wreck of the Pinafore* was an English show. The shouts of disapproval continued and the composer/conductor/producer, who had puffed his show wildly before the opening, responded by advertising in *The Times*:

> Received on the first representation with emphatic demonstrations of approval notwithstanding the palpable attempt of an organised opposition to prejudice the production

It was to no avail. *The Wreck of the Pinafore* was withdrawn after four performances and W. Luscombe Searelle moved temporarily out of the London limelight.

Equally disastrous was the production of *Melita*. This piece was an tasteless concoction which mixed four British naval officers, four Parsee maidens and their four fathers in a lengthy now-we-marry-now-we-don't episode which made fun of Indian customs and seemed to find amusing the unattractive officers' stealing away of the girls from their fathers' homes. Juba Kennedy's book was ill-written, banal and objectionable and, in the character of Lt Buzzer with his so-called catchphrase 'I rose from the ranks and my name is Buzzer', produced one of the most repulsive 'comic' roles imaginable. A sample of the author's lyric muse is the farewell solo of the heroine as she sails away from her grieving father:

> Forgive me papa
> I wish you ta-ta
> Your dearest daughter
> Crosses the water
> You cannot come too
> There's no room for you
> So stay there, papa
> I wish you ta-ta.

The music was supplied by one 'Henri Pontet' which was a pseudonym of the popular ballad composer Signor Piccolomini, the son of a Dublin University professor, a grand-nephew of a Cardinal and a relative of the opera singer Maria, Marchesa della Forgnia. In his youth, Piccolomini had fought in the Franco-Prussian War and had been exiled to Algiers for treason. While there, he learnt music from a French priest and developed a talent for light ballad music. It was this type of music which he provided for *Melita* and it was hardly suitable. The production was met by a torrent of scorn. *The Era* called it 'the worst production for many years . . feeble and amateurish . . all the faults but few of the merits . . of modern comic opera'. It faded away after six nights.

The successful revival of *The Black Crook* was instrumental in persuading the Alhambra to resurrect the other British 'spectacle' of the previous decade, *Babil and Bijou.* Their confidence, however, did not go so far as to re-present the piece in its original form and Frank Green was called in to revise Dion Boucicault's book and add to Planché's lyrics. Much of the original score was abandoned in favour of tunes plundered from continental shows including five numbers from Suppé's *Boccaccio* scheduled to make its London bow a fortnight after. The spectacular side was, as always, well attended to even when the show had to be pruned back to allow suburban patrons to see the magnificent final scene and still get home. The production was kept fairly elastic. Consuelo de la Bruyère, the leading ballerina from La Scala,was introduced and Marian, a 16-year-old giantess from Germany, announced as 8ft 2ins tall, was cast as the Queen of the Amazons. She was so admired that, when *Babil and Bijou* was withdrawn after an excellent 167 performances, she and her Amazonian army were interpolated into Johann Strauss' *The Merry War* which followed it into the theatre. But although the new production of *Babil and Bijou* retained the most salient features of the original show, it could scarcely any longer be called an 'original musical' as only a few of the musical pieces from Clay and Jacobi's score remained and their new numbers were lost in a mass of pasticcio.

Boccaccio represented the only positive foreign contribution to the year's West End entertainment with a run of 129 performances at the Comedy Theatre. The French part was limited to revivals of *Madame Favart* and *La Mascotte* and a three-month season of Lecocq's *Manola* (*Le Jour et la Nuit*) at the Strand, while Strauss' *The Merry War* after an unpromising start was burned out of the Alhambra in the total destruction of the impressive Leicester Square house.

At the Olympic a curious American entertainment called *Fun on the Bristol* put its nose into town. It was a musical and comedy hotch-potch of movable parts with songs ranging from selections from *Faust* to Irish ditties and featured the female impersonator John F. Sheridan as the Widow O'Brien. While it was scarcely sophisticated enough for London, it soon succeeded in wearing itself a track around the provinces where its ever-changing 'variety show' nature proved highly popular. Another American piece, *Our Goblins* by William Gill, which had been a succès de ridicule in New York was less fortunate.

In the provinces the influence of the music hall was freely invading the musical play. Unlike *Fun on the Bristol*, the English pieces usually relied wholly or in large part on original songs for their musical portion. A couple of reasonably successful pieces appeared in 1882, the more enduring being a harum-scarum burlesque of Ambroise Thomas' *Mignon* produced by the young comedian Fred Stimson. *Merry Mignon* was in rhyming couplets, littered with word-twistings and dubious puns and as broad as could be. Its robust and unsophisticated humour fell largely to the part of Giarno (Stimson) who was supported in good burlesque style by female juvenile men and a lively fairground setting. The book of *Merry Mignon* was by Wilton Jones who had already done well with a *Carmen* burlesque for Alice Cook, but had also been able to turn his pen to a libretto such as that for *The King's Dragoons.* His partner was the composer of that latter piece, John Crook. The most successful lyrics came from the pen of Stimson himself who provided the show's two most popular pieces, 'Be kind to the Animals' and a topical piece called 'Oh, what a Liar that Boy must Be', both in a blatant music-hall vein. The whole of the show was loosely arranged, allowing for interpolations and alterations to be made as required, and these became numerous as the piece continued its career happily through three seasons.

Romeo the Radical, put together by Charles Percy Emery, transposed some of the events of Shakespeare's play into a political setting and was kept carefully up-to-date with strings of topical allusions and puns. Its advertisement gives some idea of the entertainment it provided:

> Romeo the Radical and Juliet the Jingo or Obstruction and Effect. A Parley-mentory sitting in eight lively debates introducing Harmony without Opposition or Discord and comical motions without suspension, the entire bill being carried with acclamation and without division. Pronounced by the public and press to be superior to any act ever introduced for the benefit of the people. All parts of the house will be open to strangers who will be admitted on payment of the usual fees.

Another touring company, this one organised by the comedian/manager/actor/singer/author/composer Victor Stevens, produced a piece called *Nymphs of the Danube*, a 'grotesque opéra-bouffe' which was based on Wallace's *Lurline*. Stevens supplied the music and George Capel, another former member of H. D. Burton's company, the libretto. Like Stimson's piece it starred its manager in the first of many productions which would make him a much-loved fixture in country theatres for many years.

The provinces also gave birth to a number of more conventional pieces, none of which was destined for a very long life. George Fox and Frederic Wood starred themselves in *The Captain of the Guard*, a fairish musical version of the French play *Le Chevalier de Guet*, through a number of smaller dates whilst Liverpool tried out yet another political musical, *The Chiltern Hundreds*, for the benefit of Edward Saker, manager of the Alexandra Theatre. The first act dealt, like *Blue and Buff*, with a strangely-contested election bound up inexorably with matrimonial propositions while the second detailed some peculiar happenings in the House of Commons. Emily Soldene's company produced an Irish comic opera *The Wicklow Rose* with a script by Reece and a score by G. B. Allen, the original conductor of *The Sorcerer*. It was a mediocre piece featuring the great prima donna as a lass beloved by an outlaw amongst the political shenanigans of Ireland and it did not long hold a place in her repertoire.

The year was the occasion for the production of some particularly durable short pieces. Undoubtedly the most popular was *Mr Guffin's Elopement*, written by Arthur Law and composed by George Grossmith for Johnny Toole. Set in an inn, it introduced its star as a gentleman with intent to elope. A series of complications and discoveries of a farcical nature thwart his intentions and he is finally paired off with the landlady of the inn who is, coincidentally, an old sweetheart of his. Guffin proved an excellent vehicle for Toole but the essence of its popularity was the little show's hit song, 'The Speaker's Eye':

> Mr Peter Jones was a worthy soul
> He represented Slopperton cum Slushing-in-the-Hole
> He had been in the House for thirty years
> And joined the groans and led the cheers
> But though he stuck to his seat like a leach
> He never had made his maiden speech
> All through the day and night he'd try
> But he never could catch the Speaker's Eye!

The song was eventually advertised in larger print than the title of the show and it proved to be one of Toole's most popular numbers. With constant updating it remained, along with the show, in his repertoire for some seasons.

In October the conductress Lila Clay took the Opera Comique theatre with a company composed entirely of women to further the experiment she had begun with her production of Louis Diehl's *The Dress Rehearsal* at the Langham Hall in 1879. She presented a two-part programme consisting of a concert which she called *Something New* and an operetta by Reece and Lutz, *On Condition*. The concert featured Miss Clay with a piano solo, Miss Cora Cardigan on the flute, Miss Birdie Brightling 'the Banjo Queen', a vocal solo with double harp accompaniment by Miss Pauline Feathersby *et al.*, and an American Boot Dance by Emma D'Auban. But the major piece of the evening was the operetta. *On Condition* tells how one Celestine hears that her brother has died, leaving his wealth to a detested aunt and cousins. But to inherit the money they must fulfil a condition. They must publicly perform as pierrots, a form of entertainment which they have always derided and which is Celestine's profession. Greedy for the money, they do so, much to the amusement of Celestine and her brother, far from dead, who has disguised himself as a lawyer to watch his avaricious relatives' discomfort. Although some newspapermen sneered and jibed at Miss Clay's venture, it proved popular enough to permit the company to produce a second operetta in December. This was a piece by Savile Clarke and the young composer Walter Slaughter, appropriately titled *An Adamless Eden*. An Adamless Eden is what a group of ladies 'tired of the tyranny of men' decide to create. They withdraw themselves from male society but Nature, or more particularly feminine nature, lets them down and one by one the leaders of the movement begin to cheat until finally the whole exercise falls apart. The music of the 23-year-old apprentice composer was especially favourably noticed and *An Adamless Eden* proved decidedly successful. It was taken on several provincial tours and was also played by Miss Clay's company in the United States.

At St George's Hall initiative was somewhat lacking and two of the year's productions were revivals of the popular *Number 204* and *The Turquoise Ring*. The first new piece was *The Head of the Poll*, another show following the prevailing trend towards politically-based operettas. It played the full programme and leaned more towards the French farcical vaudeville in its style rather than to the original English operetta style of the Gallery of Illustration. *Nobody's Fault*, written like its predecessor by Arthur Law, centred round a wrongly delivered love-letter and followed the same style. Law, who was now the principal purveyor of entertainments to the Reed establishment, also produced a Christmas piece, *A Strange Host*, which was played in tandem with Gilbert a'Beckett's *That Dreadful Boy*, compiled to allow Alfred Reed to give a stand-out performance in the juvenile title-role.

Amongst the other short pieces the most interesting in retrospect is *Ten Minutes for Refreshment*, a musical sketch written by Richard Mansfield, the D'Oyly Carte comedian. Mansfield was not destined to find fame as a writer but, having abandoned Britain for the United States and Gilbert and Sullivan for more serious stuff, he eventually became the foremost Shakespearian actor of his day on the other side of the Atlantic. The music for the piece was supplied by J. M. (Jimmy) Glover, musical director, composer and raconteur whose genial career was just beginning. The sketch itself was a slight thing about a Colonel who loiters in a railway waiting-room disguised as a porter in order to see how his former actress love is faring. It did well enough as a forepiece at the Olympic and was later revived by Hilda Hilton at the Royalty and at the Empire in 1885 by John Hollingshead.

Liverpool was the birthplace of a comical little piece, *Innocents Abroad* or Going Over to Rome written by the local journalist and playwright J. F. McArdle Sr and dealing with a bunch of British tourists 'doing' the Eternal City. It rushed through some brightly written songs ranging from 'Bumps' (on phrenology), a tambourine nonsense song, an 'Ultra-patriotic song', a ballad 'Do as the Romans Do', an 'Ave Maria' chorus, a music-hall song about a wretched old coat, 'The Goblin Gingham' and a bubbly patter song for the harassed guide:

You've all done St Peter's and rushed through the Vatican
Temple of Vesta, Virginity's home
And so without flattery I aver that I can
Say I have shown you the wonders of Rome

The authors appended two disconnected numbers to their script for ad lib interpolation – an example of the growing elasticity in musical shows.

1882

0037 **MERRY MIGNON** or The Beauty and the Bard. A comic opera (operatic burlesque extravaganza) in 3 scenes by J. Wilton Jones. Music mainly by John Crook. Produced by Fred J. Stimson's touring Company at the Royal Court Theatre, Liverpool 24 April, 1882 and toured.

Semi Breeves, Esq.	R. B. Dale
Sarry Bullivan, Esq.	H. Rutland
Mignon	Florence Smithers/Alice Metcalfe
Filina	Nina Engel
Laertes	Alice Metcalfe/
Wilhelm	Carrie Lee Stoyle/Nellie Hatherley
Carl	Essie Lobel
Enery Hirving, Esq.	Alfred Bankes
Giarno	Fred J. Stimson
Frederick	Jennie Wilton
Gottlieb	Ethel Rosslyn

0038 **LORD BATEMAN** or Picotee's Pledge. A comic opera in 2 acts by Henry Pottinger Stephens. Music by Edward Solomon. Produced at the Gaiety Theatre under the management of John Hollingshead at matinées, 29 April, 1882 and 6 May, 1882.

Ephraim McDallah	Richard Temple
Roderick Rogers	E. W. Royce/James Danvers
Gilbert, Lord Bateman	Frederic Darrell
Amurath CVIII	Arthur Williams
Sir Temple Griffin	T. Aynsley Cook
The Princess Picotee	Lizzie St Quinten
Janet	Rosie St George
Madge	Emma Broughton
Fatima	Miss Sannon
Herald	E. Martin
Ermentrude	Mirabel (?) Harrington
Leila	Harriet Coveney
Selim	Mr Cruttwell
Mesrour	Mr Marshall

with Misses T. Gordon, A. Oliver, Julia St George, E. Holland, G. Claridge, C. Buckingham, T. Roma, M. Meyer, A. Grahame, Minnie Talbot, E. Graham, May, Demondest, Poletti, Milroy &c.

0039 **LES MANTEAUX NOIRS** a comic opera in three acts adapted from *Giralda ou La Nouvelle Psyche* by Walter Parke and Harry Paulton. Music by Procida Bucalossi. Produced at the Avenue Theatre under the management of George Wood 3 June, 1882 for a run of 190 performances closing on 22 December, 1882.

Don Philip of Aragon	Claude Marius (T. G. Warren)
Don Jose de Manilla	Fred Leslie/Henry Ashley
Don Luis de Rosamonte	Henry Bracy

Dromez, the miller . . . . Charles Groves/Harry Paulton
Palomez . . . . Mr Cushing
Nicholas . . . . Charles Ashford
Pedro . . . . Mr Bolder/Albert Sims
Girola . . . . Florence St John (Laura Clement) (Ethel Hughes) (Rosa Hyde)
Isabel . . . . Minnie Byron/Laura Clement
Gomez, a page . . . . Maud Branscombe
Clorinda de Lorenzana . . . . Florence Trevallyan
Samson . . . . Mr Beattie
Manuel . . . . Mr Jackson
Lazarillo . . . . Ethel Hughes
Anna . . . . Louise Percy
Rosina . . . . Miss Mori
Beatrice . . . . Violet Russell
Maria . . . . Miss Louise
Guzman . . . . Annie St Clair

with Misses Bellingham, Collier, Dean, Patti Devros, E. Gower, G. Gordon, Hughes, Mercier, Norman, Powell, Buckingham, F. Pew, Randall, Rivers, Seaton, Delphine, Temple, Vivian, Weathersby, Williams, Dudley; Messrs Barron, Lake, Huntley, Hendon, Ap Tommas, Lovell, Jupp, Sims, Barton. Pds: Mlles Luna & Stella.

Dir: Harry Paulton; md: John S. Hillier; ch: Mrs J. Lauri; sc: Spong & Perkins; cos: Wilhelm

Produced at the Standard Theatre, New York, under the management of Richard D'Oyly Carte 26 September, 1882 for a run of 36 performances closing 27 October. Additional music by Alfred Cellier. Additional lyrics by J. R. Planché.
J. H. Ryley/Arthur Wilkinson (PH), Arthur Wilkinson/J. H. Ryley (JOSE), W. T. Carleton (LUIS), Richard Mansfield (DRO), J. A. Furey (PAL), William Gillow (NIC), Selina Dolaro (GIR), Fanny Edwards (IS), Billie Barlow (GO), Joan Rivers (CLO), William White (MAN), Mina Rowley (LAZ), with Misses de Mongoot, Vickers, Lynne, Allen, Rousbey, Florence, Wisdom, Langley, Forster, Sherwood, Hummel, Weddle, Shandley. Dir: Charles Harris; md: Alfred Cellier; sc: Mazzanovich, Thompson & Goater; cos: Wilhelm

Produced at the Carltheater, Vienna, as *Drei Schwarzmäntel* 14 October, 1882.

Produced at the Avenue Theatre under the management of Violet Melnotte 16 May, 1885 for a run of 25 performances closing 13 June.
Fred Mervin (PH), Frank Wyatt (JOSE), Henry Walsham (LUIS), Charles Groves (DRO), W. H. Rawlings (PAL), J. Ettinson (NIC), C. E. Rose (PED), Marion Hood (GIR), Madge Stavart (IS), Jenny Dawson (GO), Letty Lind (CLO), J. Tompkins (SAM), Ap Tommas (MAN), Ethel Hughes (LAZ), Florence Melville (ANNA), Delia Merton (ROS), Florence Brandon (BEA), Louie Searle (MARIA), Josephine Clare (TERESA), W. Martell (ANTHONY).

0040 **THE VICAR OF BRAY** an English comic opera in two acts by Sydney Grundy. Music by Edward Solomon. Produced at the Globe Theatre 22 July, 1882. Closed 14 August. Revised and represented 2 September. Closed 28 October, 1882 after a total of 69 performances.

Rev. William Barlow . . . . W. J. Hill
Rev. Henry Sandford . . . . Walter H. Fisher/W. S. Penley (R. R. Mason)
Thomas Merton, Esq. . . . . H. Cooper Cliffe
Mr Bedford Rowe . . . . W. S. Penley/Charles Steyne
John Dory . . . . R. R. Mason
Peter Piper . . . . Mr Moreton
Samuel Spicer . . . . Mr Beale
Mrs Merton . . . . Maria Davis
Nelly Bly . . . . Emma D'Auban/Lizzie Coote
Cynthia . . . . Bertie Milner/Catherine Pelling
Agatha . . . . Kate Mortimer
Dorothy . . . . Lizzie Beaumont/Emilie Petrelli

with Messrs Lewis, Althon, Leahy, Hill, Lopresti; Misses Brooke, Hood, Cole, A. Jecks, M.

Jecks, Buckley, Conway, St George, Fairfax, Corri, Wade, Poole, Gilbert.
Dancers: Misses Graham, Kleine, Jennings, Price, Stanhope, Lindenthal, Amy Trevalyan.
Md: J. Hamilton Clarke; sc: Perkins & W. B. Spong; cos: Wilhelm

Produced at the Fifth Avenue Theatre, New York, under the management of James Barton 2 October, 1882 for a run of 6 performances closing 7 October, 1882.
Harry Allen (REV), Lyn Cadwaladr (SAND), George Olmi (MERT), Harry Brown (BED), Jennie Hughes (MRS), Edith Blande (NEL), Marie Jansen (DOR). Sc: John A. Thompson.

Produced at the Savoy Theatre under the management of Richard D'Oyly Carte 28 January, 1892 for a run of 143 performances closing 18 June, 1892.
Rutland Barrington (REV), Courtice Pounds (SAND), Richard Green (Edward A. White) (MERT), W. H. Denny (BED), W. S. Laidlaw (DORY), Bowden Haswell (PP), F. Barrett (SS), J. Wilbraham & Rudolph Lewis (HUNTSMEN), Rosina Brandram (MRS), Mary Duggan (NEL), Louie Rowe/Amy Farrell (CYNTH), Annie Cole (AG), Cora Tinnie/Jose Shalders (BLANCHE), Janet Watts (ROSE), Nellie Kavanagh (GERTRUDE), Leonore Snyder (WINIFRED ex DOROTHY).
Md: François Cellier/Ernest Ford; sc: Perkins & Harker; cos: Percy Anderson; ch: John D'Auban; dir: Charles Harris

041 **THE CAPTAIN OF THE GUARD** a comedy opera in two acts by Frederic Wood adapted from *Le Chevalier de Guet* by Lecroy. Music by George Fox. Produced at the Theatre Royal, Margate 24 July, 1882 and toured.

Madeleine . . . . Josephine Pulham
Viscount François de Lunel . . . . Frederic Wood
The Captain of the Guard . . . . George Fox
Baron de Jarlis . . . . E. J. Henley
Officer . . . . Mr Johnstone
Margot . . . . Isabelle Muncey
Susette . . . . Lucy Franklein
Tobie . . . . Mr Bradshaw

Md: George Arnold

042 **RIP VAN WINKLE** a comic opera in three acts and five tableaux by H. B. Farnie, Ludovic Meilhac and Philippe Gille. Music by Robert Planquette. Produced under the management of Alexander Henderson at the Comedy Theatre 14 October, 1882 for a run of 328 performances closing 27 October, 1883.

Rip van Winkle . . . . Fred Leslie (Louis Kelleher)/J. A. Arnold
Derrick von Hans . . . . W. S. Penley
Peter van Dunk . . . . Louis Kelleher (Maurice de Solla)
Diedrich Knickerbocker . . . . E. Wilmore/Rowland Buckstone/J. B. Rae/ James Francis
Capt. Hugh Rowley . . . . Frederic Darrell/Maurice de Solla/E. T. Steyne/Fred Storey
Nick Vedder/Jan . . . . Lionel Brough
Hans van Slous/1st Lt. . . . . W. S. Rising/Orlando Harley[1]/ Arthur Mavius/Frederic Darrell
Capt. Hendrik Hudson . . . . S. H. Perry
Goblin Steward . . . . Fred Storey/Harry Moore
Gretchen/Alice . . . . Violet Cameron/Agnes Consuelo
Sara/Max/3rd Lt . . . . Clara Graham/Ivy Warner/Vere Carew
Jacintha/2nd Lt. . . . . Constance Lewis/Catherine Gardiner/ Coralie de Vere/Miss Faliero
Katrina . . . . Sadie Martinot/Clara Merivale/Camille Dubois/Camille D'Arville/Gladys Cramer
Little Hardcase . . . . Madge Milton/Annie Vernon/Agnes Lyndon

[1] Harley was sacked for incompetence. He sued and won £250.

Tom Tit/4th Lt/Chicken	Rose Moncrieff
Hans	Effie Mason/Minnie Rayner
Alice	Alice Vicat
Gape	Grace Hawke/May Whitty
Leedle Jan	Master Gallop
Phoebe	Miss Harcourt/Maud Vale
Katchen	Marian Lacy/Jennie Tester/Ida Villers
Meenie	Beatrice St Maur/Madge Marian/ Jennie Tester/ J. Carlton/Maud Bramble
Susanna	Catherine Gardiner/Bessie Bell
Tulipa	Maud deVere/Miss Marsden/Miss deGrey
Annchen	Bessie Bell/E. Dumas/Nellie Lefevre/ Marian Lacy/Bessie Callaway/Miss Mayne/Miss Salisbury
Hermann	Kitty Percival/Alice Hender/Coralie de Vere/Miss Hamilton/Miss Page
Josef	E. Gower/K. Miles/Nellie Lefevre/ A. Clair/ Julie Couteur
Kassar	Minnie Duncan/Miss Pendennis/Louie Searle
Heinrich	Miss Lina/Miss Lester/Dollie Tester/Miss Campbell
Yacob	Marion Howe/M. Russell
Klaus	Clyde Howard/J. Howard
Master Gunner	M. Villa

with Misses Brooks, Long, Clifford, Annie Vernon, Douglas, E. Douglas, May Whitty, Remmington, Sinclair, Grey, Bennett, Ashleigh; Messrs C. Hunt, Harvey, Vaughan, Reeves, Wilkinson, Godfrey, Morgant, Blackburn, Harding, Harriss, Rimbault, Wright, Reid, Steele, Wood, Ford, Sinclair &c.
Pd: Ada Wilson
Dir: H. B. Farnie; md: Auguste van Biene; cos: Faustin & Wilhelm; sc: W. R. Beverley; ch: John D'Auban

Produced at the Theater an der Wien as *Rip Rip* 22 December, 1883.

Produced at the Comedy Theatre 6 September, 1884 for a run of 77 performances closing 20 November, 1884.
Fred Leslie (RIP), Clavering Power (DERR), Louis Kelleher (PET), H. Halley (DIED), Fred Storey (HUGH), Harry Paulton (NICK), Henry Walsham (HANS), Westlake Perry (HUD), Fred Storey (GOB), Berthe Latour (GR), Clara Graham (SARA), C. Gardiner (JAC), Miss Coote (KAT), Agnes Lyndon (LH), Miss Lina (TT), Minnie Rayner (HANS) Alice Vicat (AL), Miss Ridley (GAPE), Miss Howe (YAC), Master Gollop. Chorus included Alice Lethbridge

Produced in Paris at the Théâtre des Folies Dramatiques 11 November 1884 as *Rip!* in a version by Meilhac and Gille.
M. Bremont (RIP), M. Simon-Max (ICHABOD), Mlle Mily-Meyer (KATE), Mme Scalini (NELLY)

Produced at the Théâtre de la Gaîte 18 October, 1894 under the management of M. Debruyère. M. Soulacroix (RIP), M. Dekernel (NICK VEDDER), P. Fugère (ISCHABOD), M. Mauzin (DERRICK), M. Bernard (PICKLY), M. Nivette (Capitaine HUDSON), L. Noel (JAC), Mme Barneart (NELLY), Mariette Sully (KATE), Renée Marcelle (JACINTHE), Fernand Raquet (Little JACK), Suzanne Colin (Little LOWENA)

Produced in the United States at the Standard Theatre, New York under the management of Richard D'Oyly Carte 23 November 1882.
William T. Carleton (RIP), Arthur Rousbey (DERR/HUD), J. H. Ryley (PET), W. H. Seymour (DIE), Arthur Wilkinson (HUGH), Richard Mansfield (NICK), Lyn Cadwaladr (IST/SLOUS), William White (GOBLIN), William Gillow (2ND LT), Theodora Linda da Costa (AL), Maggie Gonzales (HANS), Pollie Gillow (L. JAN), Sallie Reber (KAT), Selina Dolaro (GR), Billie Barlow (TT). Md: Alfred Cellier; sc: G. W. Dayton

43 **MELITA** or The Parsee's Daughter. An opéra-comique in 3 acts by Juba Kennedy. Music by 'Henri Pontet' (Sgr Piccolomini). Produced at the Royalty Theatre under the management of Somers Bellamy 9 December, 1882 for a run of 6 performances closing 16 December, 1882.

Captain Melville . . . . Henry Hallam
Jerbanoo. . . . . Grace Balmaine
Melita . . . . Clare Leslie
Golbanoo . . . . Edith Burgoyne
Lieutenant Seaton. . . . . Walter S. Craven
Lieutenant Buzzer . . . . Frederick Thorne
Aimi . . . . Evelyn May
Jam Set Jee . . . . Edmund Rosenthal
Patrick Maloney. . . . . Edmund D. Lyons
Lieutenant Fitzjames . . . . Robert Hayley
Cursetjee . . . . Fred Clifton
Sarotjee . . . . W. Barron
Merwanjee . . . . F. H. Ellis
Telo . . . . Ivy Warner
Leda. . . . . Lillian Chaplin
Cana. . . . . Miss Emsworth
Nana . . . . Miss Fenton
Police Sergeant . . . . Mr Heyden
Hindoo . . . . Mr Maple
Pds: Mlles Sismondi and Sara

Md: Otto Langey; ch: Henri Dewinne; sc: Albert Callcott; cos: Wilhelm

44 **IOLANTHE** or The Peer And The Peri. A fairy opera in 2 acts by W. S. Gilbert. Music by Arthur Sullivan. Produced at the Savoy Theatre under the management of Richard D'Oyly Carte 25 November, 1882 for a run of 398 performances closing 1 January, 1884.

The Lord Chancellor . . . . George Grossmith
Strephon . . . . Richard Temple
Lord Tolloller. . . . . Durward Lely (Charles Rowan)
Lord Mountararat. . . . . Rutland Barrington
Private Willis . . . . Charles Manners (Charles Ryley)/Warwick Grey
Iolanthe . . . . Jessie Bond (Rosina Brandram)
Phyllis . . . . Leonora Braham (Minna Louis)
The Fairy Queen . . . . Alice Barnett/Rosa Carlingford
Leila. Julia Gwynne/Maud Cathcart (Sybil Grey)
Celia. May Fortescue/Julia Gwynne/M. Hooper (Rose Hervey)/Mina Rowley
Fleta. Sybil Grey (Grace Arnold)

Dir: Gilbert & Sullivan; md: François Cellier; ch: John D'Auban; sc: Henry Emden; cos: Miss Fisher, Messrs Ede, Frank Smith, Moses & Sons, Alias, Auguste.

Produced at the Standard Theatre, New York, under the management of Richard D'Oyly Carte 25 November, 1882 for a run of 105 performances closing 24 February, 1883.
J. H. Ryley (LC), William T. Carleton (STR), Lyn Cadwaladr (TOL), Arthur Wilkinson (MT), Lithgow James (PW), Marie Jansen (IO), Sallie Reber (PH), Augusta Roche (FQ), Mina Rowley (C), Kate Forster (L), Billie Barlow (F), William White (TRAINBEARER). Dir: Charles Harris; md: Alfred Cellier

Produced at the Savoy Theatre under the management of William Greet 7 December, 1901 for a run of 113 performances closing 29 March, 1902.
Walter Passmore (LC), Henry Lytton (STR), Robert Evett (TOL), Powis Pinder (MT), Reginald Crompton (PW), Louie Pounds (IO), Isabel Jay (PH), Rosina Brandram (FQ), Agnes Fraser (C), Isabel Agnew (L), Winifred Hart-Dyke (F). Md: François Cellier

Produced at the Savoy Theatre under the management of the D'Oyly Carte Opera Company 11 June, 1907 for a run of 43 performances closing 23 August, 1907.

C. H. Workman (LC), Richard Green/Henry Lytton (STR), Harold Wilde (TOL), Frank Wilson (MT), Overton Moyle (PW), Jessie Rose (Ernestine Gauthier) (IO), Clara Dow (PH), Louie Rene (FQ), Violette Londa/Ruby Grey (C), Beatrice Meredith/Norah McLeod (L), Violet Frampton (F). Md: François Cellier

Produced at the Savoy Theatre under the management of the D'Oyly Carte Opera Company 19 October, 1908 for 38 performances in repertoire.
C. H. Workman (LC), Henry Lytton (STR), Henry Herbert (TOL), Rutland Barrington (MT), Leo Sheffield (PW), Jessie Rose (IO), Clara Dow/Elsie Spain (PH), Louie Rene (FQ), Dorothy Court (C), Beatrice Boarer (L), Ethel Lewis (F). Md: Francois Cellier

Subsequently played by the D'Oyly Carte Opera Company on tour and in London in repertoire.

Produced at the Casino Theatre, New York, under the management of the Shubert Brothers and William Brady 12 May, 1913 for a run of 40 performances.
De Wolf Hopper (LC), George Macfarlane (STR), Arthur Aldridge (TOL), Arthur Cunningham (MT), John Hendricks (PW), Viola Gillette (IO), Cecil Cunningham (PH), Kate Condon (FQ), Anna Wheaton (C), Louise Barthel (L), Nina Napier (F). Dir: William J. Wilson; md: Frank M. Paret; sc: H. Robert Law; cos: Melville Ellis

Produced at the Plymouth Theatre, New York, under the management of Winthrop Ames 19 April, 1926 for a run of 355 performances.
Ernest Lawford (LC), William Williams (STR), J. Humbird Duffey (TOL), John Barclay (MT), William C. Gordon (PW), Adele Sanderson (IO), Lois Bennett/Kathryn Reece (PH), Vera Ross (FQ), Kathryn Reece/Ruth Marion (C), Sybil Sterling (L), Paula Langlen (F), Bert Prival (TRAINBEARER). Dir: Winthrop Ames; md: Robert Hood Bowers; ch: Louise Gifford; sc/cos: Woodman Thompson

Played in repertoire and short seasons in New York by the D'Oyly Carte Opera Company and others.

Produced at Sadler's Wells Theatre, 24 January, 1962.
Eric Shilling (LC), Julian Moyle (STR), Stanley Bevan (TOL), Denis Dowling (MT), Leon Greene (PW), Patricia Kern (IO), Elizabeth Harwood (PH), Heather Begg (FQ), Elizabeth Robson (C), Cynthia Morey (L), Marjorie Ward (F). Dir: Frank Hauser; md: Alexander Faris

TV/Video: 1984. Brent Walker Ltd. Pr: Judith de Paul; dir: David Pountney; md: Alexander Faris; ch: Terry Gilbert; sc: Allan Cameron; cos: Jenny Beavan
Derek Hammond-Stroud (LC), Alexander Oliver (STR), Thomas Hemsley (MT), Richard van Allan (PW), Beverley Mills (IO), Kate Flowers (PH), Sandra Dugdale (C), Pamela Field (L), Anne Collins (FQ)

THE WRECK OF THE PINAFORE a comic opera in two acts by W. Horace Lingard. Music by W. Luscombe Searelle. First presented at the Princess's Theatre, Dunedin, New Zealand 29 November, 1880. Produced in London at the Opera Comique under the management of Luscombe Searelle 27 May, 1882 for a run of 4 performances, closing on 30 May. Played with *One Touch of Nature*.

Sir Joseph Porter K.C.B. . . . . Gerald Moore
Deadeye Dick . . . . Fred Clifton
Ralph Rackstraw . . . . Arnold Breedon
Little Buttercup . . . . Madge Stavart
Middy . . . . Master Arnold
Josephine . . . . Rosa Leo
Captain Corcoran . . . . J. A. Arnold
Bill Bobstay . . . . George Temple
Hebe . . . . Annie Rose

Md: L. Searelle; sc: Albert Callcott; cos: Alias, Cutler and Mme Duprez

THE WICKLOW ROSE an Irish comic opera by Robert Reece. Music by G. B. Allen. Produced at the Prince's Theatre, Manchester, 3 May, 1882.

Murlough O'Shiel. . . . . Henry Lewens

Terence O'Neil . . . . Henry Nordblom
Andy . . . . Michael Dwyer
Thady . . . . Mr Marshall
Kitty Daly. . . . . Miss Ford
Molly . . . . Alice May
Norah . . . . Emily Soldene
Daly . . . . Mr Horspool
Pergran . . . . Mr Quinton

ROMEO THE RADICAL or Obstruction and Effect, a political comic opera in one act by Charles P. Emery. Produced by Charles P. Emery's Co at the Alexandra Theatre, Walsall 14 August, 1882 and toured in repertoire.

Tybalt Torio . . . . Charles P. Emery
Romeo Irvingo . . . . E. Allen
Peter the Pert . . . . Little Rosey May
Capulet . . . . W. R. Glenney
Juliet Temo . . . . Beatrice Thompson
Nurse Margery . . . . Rose Emery

THE CHILTERN HUNDREDS a comedy opera in two acts by T. Edgar Pemberton. Music by Thomas Anderton. Produced at the Alexandra Theatre, Liverpool, 17 April, 1882.

Christopher Kylcuppe . . . . T. F. Doyle
Col. Carlton Kerr . . . . Edward Saker
First votress. . . . . Miss Kirkpatrick
Returning Officer . . . . Ivan Shirley
Kirby Kirkby . . . . W. H. Woodfield
Mrs Kylcuppe. . . . . Carrie Lee Stoyle
Coralie. . . . . Mrs Saker
Deputy Speaker. . . . . J. Busfield

NYMPHS OF THE DANUBE a burlesque extravaganza in 5 scenes by George Capel. Music by Victor Stevens. Produced at the Theatre Royal, Sunderland under the management of Victor Stevens 31 July, 1882 and toured in repertoire.

Sir Rudolph. . . . . Emily Spiller
Spindlewriggle . . . . Victor Stevens
Baron Poppemorf . . . . George Capel
Count Korfdrop. . . . . E. W. Colman
Heidelstein . . . . W. Gardiner
Krautzen . . . . J. A. E. Halliwell
Coralline. . . . . Marion Huntley
Anenome . . . . Ramsey Danvers
The Lady Fair . . . . Nellie Coombes

MR GUFFIN'S ELOPEMENT a musical farce by Arthur Law. Music by George Grossmith. Produced at the Alexandra Theatre, Liverpool under the management of J. L. Toole 29 September, 1882 and subsequently at Toole's Theatre 7 October, 1882 with *The Upper Crust*. Subsequently played with *Girls And Boys* (from 31 October), *Dot* (8 January, 1883), *Dearer Than Life* (5 February), *Uncle Dick's Darling* (26 February) and *Artful Cards* (9 April). Withdrawn 18 May, 1883.

Benjamin Guffin . . . . J. L. Toole
Mrs Truddle . . . . Eliza Johnstone/Ada Mellon/May Lester/Florence Farr
Miss Crump. . . . . Emily Thorne
Susan . . . . Effie Liston/Isa Marsden/Bella Wallace
C.H.T. Simpson . . . . E. D. Ward
Robert Beate . . . . W. E. Brunton

Performed at the Royal General Theatrical Fund Benefit, 13 March, 1883 by J. L. Toole's Company.

Performed at Toole's Theatre at a matinée 23 June, 1883.

Performed at Sandringham on the occasion of Prince Albert's birthday by J. L. Toole's Company, 1884.

Played at Toole's Theatre at a matinée 5 January, 1884 with *Artful Cards* &c.

Played at Toole's Theatre 5 April, 1885 with *The Upper Crust*.

ON CONDITION an operetta in one act by Robert Reece. Music by W. Meyer Lutz. Produced at the Opera Comique under the management of Lila Clay 19 October, 1882 with the concert *Something New*. Withdrawn 12 December, 1883.

Celestine l'Esparre . . . . Edith Vane/Linda Verner
Paul l'Esparre . . . . Katie Logan/Marie Faudelle
Felix . . . . Alice Aynsley Cook
Millefleurs . . . . Alice Mowbray
The Mayor . . . . Rose Arnoldi
Julia . . . . Clara Douglas
Aurelia . . . . Fanny Howell
Mouse . . . . Emma D'Auban
Jacques . . . . Ada West
Lucien . . . . Dolly Goddard
Louis . . . . Ada Hogarth
Mrs Jarley . . . . Bessie Foote
François . . . . Lizzie Birkett
Babette . . . . Lilly Comyns
Lucie . . . . E. Dumas

Md: Lila Clay; ch: John D'Auban; cos: Lila Clay

AN ADAMLESS EDEN a comic operetta in one act by Savile Clarke. Music by Walter Slaughter. Produced at the Opera Comique under the management of Lila Clay 13 December, 1882 with the concert *Something New*. Withdrawn 3 February, 1883.

Duchess of Breeks . . . . Emily Cross
Sarah Stamps . . . . Emma D'Auban
Lady Mantrap . . . . Cicely Richards
Lady Dorothy Demurrer . . . . Fanny Howell
Algy . . . . Linda Verner
Lady Ruby Wallop . . . . Addie Grey
Fred Blazer . . . . Lizzie Birkett
Mrs Sophie Syntax . . . . Miss Amalia
Peter Blobbs, Esq., ... E. Jonghmans
Lady Minever . . . . Dolly Goddard
Lady Ermine . . . . Miss Henley
Lady Sable . . . . Miss Harris
Reggie . . . . Miss Reba
Lady Gules . . . . Rose Arnoldi/Miss Lee
Perjury Jones . . . . Ada West
Skimmery Hall . . . . Miss Hamilton
Child of the School Board . . . . Tiney Vining

Md: Lila Clay; ch: John D'Auban; cos: Wilhelm

Produced at the Third Avenue Theatre, New York 1 June, 1885.

THE HEAD OF THE POLL in two parts by Arthur Law. Music by Eaton Fanning. Produced at St George's Hall under the management of Alfred Reed and R. Corney Grain 28 February, 1882. *Not At Home* added as an afterpiece March 4. Withdrawn 3 June, 1882.

Mr Upshotte . . . . Alfred Reed
Charles Wardale. . . . . North Home
Colonel Deeplock . . . . R. Corney Grain
Mrs Lovell . . . . Fanny Holland
Arabella Upshotte. . . . . Alice Barth/Edith Brandon

NOBODY'S FAULT by Arthur Law. Music by Hamilton Clarke. Produced at St George's Hall under the management of Alfred Reed and R. Corney Grain 5 June, 1882 with *Small and Early*. Withdrawn 29 July. Represented 9 October. Withdrawn 21 October.

Admiral Sir Louis Bowring. . . . . Alfred Reed
Mary Eden . . . . Edith Brandon
Louis Bowring . . . . North Home
Miss Tozer . . . . Fanny Holland
Joe Dumbledon . . . . R. Corney Grain

Produced at St George's Hall 18 June, 1884 with *Shows of the Season* and *A Terrible Fright*. Withdrawn 26 July, 1884.
Alfred Reed (ADM), Marion Wardroper (MARY), North Home (LOU), Fanny Holland (MISS), R. Corney Grain (JOE)

A STRANGE HOST or A Happy New Year by Arthur Law. Music by King Hall. Produced at St George's Hall under the management of Alfred Reed and R. Corney Grain 13 December, 1882 with *En Route* and *That Dreadful Boy*. Withdrawn 16 December. Reopened 26 December. Withdrawn 6 March, 1883.

Old Year . . . . R. Corney Grain
Miss Gryfield . . . . Fanny Holland
Alice Fairlie . . . . Edith Brandon
Jonas Gryfield. . . . . Alfred Reed
Robert Golding . . . . North Home

THAT DREADFUL BOY by Gilbert a'Beckett. Music by R. Corney Grain. Produced at St George's Hall under the management of Alfred Reed and R. Corney Grain 13 December, 1882 with *En Route* and *A Strange Host*. Withdrawn 16 December. Reopened 26 December. Withdrawn 6 March, 1883.

Johnny Blazer . . . . Alfred Reed
Mr Tracey Bliss. . . . . North Home
Uncle Shattersbury . . . . R. Corney Grain
Mrs Blazer . . . . Edith Brandon
Miss Blazer . . . . Fanny Holland

TEN MINUTES FOR REFRESHMENT a musical sketch by Richard Mansfield. Music by James M. Glover. Produced at the Olympic Theatre under the management of Laura Telbin 14 January, 1882 with *The Member From Slocum*.

Mrs Dorothea Pickering . . . . Harriet Coveney
Colonel Brown . . . . Dalton Somers
Jessie Pickering . . . . Edith Vane
Frank Brown . . . . James Sydney

Produced at the Royalty Theatre under the management of Hilda Hilton 18 February, 1882 with *Pluto* and *The Fast Coach*, the latter replaced by *Meg's Diversion*. Withdrawn 31 March, 1882. Represented 10 April, 1882 with *Sindbad* and *Not Registered*. Withdrawn 10 May, 1882.
Miss Stuart (MRS), Reginald Stockton (COL), Edith Vane (JESSIE), James Sydney/W. Broughton (FR)

Produced at the Empire Theatre under the management of John Hollingshead 28 March, 1885 with *The Lady of the Locket*. Withdrawn 25 July, 1885.
Miss Gaynor (MRS), Henry M. Clifford (COL), Lesley Bell (JESSIE), Charles Ryley (FR)

A STORM IN A TEACUP an operetta with music by Frederic Corder. Produced at the Brighton Aquarium under the management of Alice Barth. Played at the Gaiety Theatre 23 March, 1882 for the benefit of Helen Barry.

Ernest . . . . Faulkener Leigh
Sir Harry Fairweather . . . . Theodore Distin
Waters. . . . . Eric Lewis
Maggie Pie . . . . Kate Leopold
Lady Sylvia Pheasant . . . . Alice Barth

INNOCENTS ABROAD an operetta in one act by J. F. McArdle Sr. Music by W. H. Jude. Produced at the Bijou Opera House, Liverpool 15 May, 1882 and toured in repertoire by Martin & Hiller's Comic Opera Company.

Mr Babbles . . . . Edward Sidney
Frank Felton . . . . W. H. Woodfield
Trent . . . . B. R. Pepper
Titus Timpkinson. . . . . J. Harding
Hilda . . . . Annie Beresford
Marion . . . . Agnes Beresford

Dir: J. F. McArdle Sr; md: W. H. Jude

THE KNIGHT OF THE GARTER an operetta by J. Sheddon Wilson. Music by W. Meyer Lutz. Performed at the Gaiety Theatre 7 December, 1882 for the benefit of Meyer Lutz.

Miss Newton . . . . Alice Aynsley Cook
Mary Ann. . . . . Emma Broughton
Mrs Jones . . . . Miss Webbe
Coppum . . . . J. J. Dallas
Mr Brown. . . . . Mr Cruttwell
Butcher . . . . Mr Crook
Mr Dunn . . . . J. Furneaux Cook
Mr L'Owe. . . . . Henry Walsham

HIS ONLY COAT (Var. MY ONLY COAT) an operetta by J. J. Dallas. Music by Walter Slaughter. Produced at the Gaiety Theatre under the management of John Hollingshead 22 May, 1882 for the benefit of Nellie Farren. Subsequently played with *Aladdin* and then *Little Robin Hood.* Withdrawn 19 October, 1882.

Sparkler . . . . Arthur Williams
Percy Vere . . . . Tom Squire
Bill . . . . J. J. Dallas

A SIMPLE SWEEP a musical absurdity by F. W. Broughton. Music by James F. Downs. Produced 1 March at the Grand, Leeds and subsequently at the Princess's Theatre 26 April, 1882 under the management of Wilson Barrett with *The Lights of London*.

Sir Orange Peel . . . . Charles Coote
Mrs de Vere. . . . . George Barrett
Harold de Vere . . . . Neville Doone
Rosamond . . . . Eugenie Edwards
Miss Lemon Peel . . . . Nellie Palmer
Trusty Minion . . . . Charles Bird

Md: James Weaver

MARIETTE'S WEDDING an operetta by W. E. Morton. Music by Haydn Millars. Produced at the Adelphi Theatre 30 September, 1882 at a matinée with *Chandos*.

Duvalor . . . . Charles Kenningham
Fitzfunc . . . . Fred Kaye
Bishbosh. . . . . G. B. Prior
Roberto . . . . H. Payne
Mariette. . . . . Marian Browning

CONTRARY WINDS an operetta by Frederic Wood. Music by George Fox. Played by George Fox's Co on tour with *The Captain of the Guard.*

Flora . . . . Josephine Pulham
Peter. . . . . Frederic Wood
The Marquis . . . . E. J. Henley

MY LUCK a musical eccentricity by B. T. Hughes. Music by W. Robinson. Played by the D'Oyly Carte Opera Company on tour.

KEVIN'S CHOICE an operetta by Miss Hazelwood and T. A. Wallworth. Played at the Adelphi Theatre 25 March, 1882 for the benefit of Mr Wallworth.

1883

The quick failure of *Melita* and the burning down of the Alhambra meant that only two musicals were playing in the West End of London as the new year began. *Rip Van Winkle* was already well on the way to its hundredth performance and would ultimately outstrip its popular predecessor *La Mascotte* at the Comedy, while at the Savoy *Iolanthe* had also settled in for its expected long season. Apart from the pantomimes, the only other musical entertainments available were at the Opera Comique where Lila Clay and her ladies' troupe were playing *An Adamless Eden* and *Something New* and at Her Majesty's, which housed the burlesque *The Yellow Dwarf*.

The first offerings of the new year were French. Following a five-week revival season of *Olivette* at the Avenue in which Florence St John and Marius repeated their original roles, Offenbach's *Lurette* was staged. His last work, completed a few weeks before his death, it held the stage for 83 performances. On the same night, however, a much more enthusiastic reception was given to a British musical which opened at the Strand. *Cymbia* or The Magic Thimble looked more towards pantomime or the Alhambra for its story and style than to the sophisticated wit of a W. S. Gilbert. Its author, Harry Paulton, had invented a plot centred on a comical King Arthur – the role, of course, tailored to his own abilities – and a shepherdess with a wish-granting thimble which she spends most of the evening losing and finding again to supply the action of the play. He even contrived that in the course of the piece King Arthur should go temporarily mad, giving its author the chance to perform the show's most successful number 'I Am musically Mad' in his particular version of an operatic mad scene:

> A strange kind of humming, a musical strain
> Seems swelling and bursting the bounds of my brain;
> A tune that's forever returning unbid
> As it will, and of which you can never get rid.
> I'm crazy with tune, tho' a bar is to me
> The same as a shake or a clef, and all three
> Might either be, though each to t'other be add
> For I've got them all mix'd: I am musically mad.

The rest of the plot concerned the King's attempts to marry off his three eldest sons to the financially desirable daughters of a Welsh monarch before anyone can discover that the bailiffs are already in his castle. The first act finds them all neatly paired off until the 'madcap' shepherdess upsets everything with her thimble in the second. In the final act she transports the disillusioned Princesses to an 'Adamless Eden' in an enchanted grove. The King and his youngest son, Carrow, with whom Cymbia is in love, turn up and appear, by the magic of the place, as women in the eyes of the ladies.

But Arthur by now has the thimble and his unwitting wishes keep coming true. After a series of scenic effects similar to those of the Wishing Boudoir in *The Black Crook*, the King slips the thimble into Cymbia's pocket and her repentant wishes bring everything to a satisfactory conclusion.

The music for *Cymbia* was written by Florian Pascal, not a fashionable French composer as his name might suggest but a pseudonym of Joseph Williams, the son of one of Britain's leading music publishers and later himself a director of the firm. *Cymbia* was his first full-length stage work and at thirty-three he looked set fair for a promising career but, although he later composed many more works with collaborators of the calibre of Gilbert, 'Pot' Stephens, Walter Parke and Adrian Ross, real success was always to elude him. The music for *Cymbia* was light and attractive enough but generally unremarkable. It was shared principally among the three leading singers, Camille D'Arville (Cymbia), Henry Walsham (Carrow) and Louise Vesalius (Princess Menaa), although Paulton also had a contribution to make in a less lyrical style. *The Era* was enthusiastic:

> It is just what a comic opera should be. There is no excess of sentiment, but just enough to provide the necessary contrast; while for the most part the music is in a merry vein that gratifies the ear completely and fits the libretto as exactly as if author and composer were one. In fact, the music of *Cymbia* flows along with such a sparkling and animated movement that it is only when we pause for a moment to notice some clever effect in the score that we find out how good it is. There are numbers of composers who can write well in a grave and sombre style, but there are few who are naturally gay in style and manner. The libretto is of a thoroughly amusing kind, perhaps a little too diffuse in dialogue; but when we hear an audience kept in a continuous state of hilarity it is not necessary to discuss the matter critically.

and concluded that the show was 'one of the best examples of an English comic opera seen for a long time'. This judgement was not shared by some other critics. *The Stage* found the music 'noisy . . rather than tuneful', the story and the songs 'defective' and the artists poor. They declared that Miss D'Arville could not act, that the Frenchman Gaillard was incomprehensible, Walsham effeminate and Louise Vesalius just plain awful. The management clearly shared this last view as Miss Vesalius promptly disappeared from the cast. The truth of the matter fell somewhere between these two reports. Paulton's libretto in no way compared with his *Manteaux Noirs* effort. *Cymbia* with its minimal plot and magical motivation was like a scaled-down Alhambra script. The effects were broad, the dialogue neither very smart nor very funny, and its heroine verged on the irritating. The music was pleasant – promising perhaps – but little more. The show had a run of seven weeks without looking likely to last longer.

In April the newly-altered Royalty Theatre reopened under the management of the indefatigable Kate Santley and the manageress's first production was a new musical, *The Merry Duchess*, by George Sims and Frederic Clay. This was Clay's first musical since the disappointment of *Princess Toto* and once again he combined his talents with the best of playwrights. George Sims had never ventured into the field of light musical entertainment before. A journalist of stature, he wrote for *The Referee* as 'Dagonet' and had had great successes as a playwright with his comedies *Crutch and Toothpick* (1879) and *The Mother-in-law* (1881) and the dramas *The Lights of London* (1881) and *The Romany Rye* (1882).

For *The Merry Duchess* he adopted an altogether different style in a high-spirited horse racing libretto. The sporting Duchess of Epsom Downs falls in love with Freddy

Bowman[1], the jockey who is to ride her horse in the St Leger, but many vagaries of turf treachery have to be surmounted before both the horse and the course of true love reach their goal. First the villainous Brabazon Sikes, who stands to win £5,000 on a rival horse, forces his wife, Rowena, to drug the Duchess's 'Damozel'. Rowena has sworn to obey at the matrimonial altar, but consoles herself as she sets out that she may give part of her winnings to the poor. She is thwarted in her foul deed, however, by one Captain Walker who is hiding in the stables to avoid being caught making love to Dorothy, the jockey's sister. Since Rowena is disguised in the Duchess' cape, that lady finds herself accused of trying to nobble her own horse. She dares not explain that she forced Rowena to change clothes from jealousy, to test her fears that there was something between Freddy and the suspicious-looking girl. Rowena straightens everything out and we head for St Leger day. Much rides on the result of the race for the Duchess has foolishly bet the 'masher', Lord Johnnie, that she will wed him if her horse fails to win. Under Sikes' influence, Johnnie claims the invincible Freddy to ride his horse and then, when Rowena blackmails the amorous lord into releasing the jockey, Sikes manages to get him locked up for assault. Finally, the race is run, and the last scene brings 'Damozel' home the winner and the Duchess to her Freddy's arms.

Sims' fluent script was bright, active and jokey. At times it skirted the world of burlesque melodrama and it did not shy away from far-fetched verbal effects:

ROWENA: (disguised as a fortune-teller) I see by your hand you have a horse in the Leger.
LORD J: If you can see that in my hand it's a feat of leger-de-main.

as it raced the eventful plot forward. It was packed with allusions to current events – one critic commented 'there was hardly a topic publicly discussed last winter which was not echoed in *The Merry Duchess*' – and the whole tone was one of robust liveliness if hardly of Sims' customary literary excellence. Miss Santley, of course, was strongly featured as Rowena and she and Henry Ashley as Brabazon Sikes were the source of much fun as they tumbled from one disguise to another in their efforts to 'do in' the favourite. The American soprano Kate Munroe appeared as the Duchess and delivered a whipcrack number with great style. The musical side of the show included a good deal of concerted music and a mammoth first act finale which comprised several solos and ensembles and a mock-heroic 'Hymn To Damozel'. None of the individual numbers proved to be real hits, but the tenor ballad 'Love's Messenger' and Miss Santley's song 'The Captive Bird' both won public approval and frequent encores, and Freddy Bowman's tongue-in-cheek 'An English Jockey' provided some satirical fun.

It was soon clear that *The Merry Duchess* was a success and a touring company was quickly put on the road starring Haidee Crofton as the Duchess with Sidney Harcourt and Ruby Stuart as the dopers. While the tour continued the London show flourished and passed its hundredth performance on 6 August, eventually running right through until November for a total of 177 performances. An American production at the Standard Theatre, New York, starred Selina Dolaro alongside the popular favourite Henry E. Dixey (Sikes) and ran there for a healthy two months before touring. The following year it was given an Australian production but, in spite of its lively character,

[1] A not very covert reference to Fred Archer the famous jockey whose affair with the Duchess of Montrose was well-known.

The Merry Duchess had no great lasting substance and did not appear again in the country of its origin.

The next British work to appear in the West End was *Estrella*, the composition of Walter Parke, joint librettist of *Les Manteaux Noirs*, and the forcible New Zealander Luscombe Searelle who had been responsible for *The Wreck of the Pinafore*. It had first been produced at the Prince's Theatre, Manchester, where it met with what can most kindly be described as a mixed reception. *The Era*'s local critic, accustomed to being less harsh than his metropolitan brethren, commented that it was 'scarcely accurate to describe the production as a success'. *The Stage*, on the other hand, which in its third year of existence had already gained a reputation for being scathingly dismissive of the most successful new shows and which had slated many of them from *The Pirates of Penzance* to *The Merry Duchess*, took the opportunity to hail 'a genuine success'.

Parke had developed a reasonable scenario, allegedly based on a French original, of improbable bigamy in Venice which he stretched thinly through three long acts. His innocent heroine (Constance Loseby) is married to the Count Pomposo (Aynsley Cook) in order to balance her family's books. But Pomposo has doubts about his wife's devotion and resolves to test it by staging his own kidnap the day after his wedding. His brother Lorenzo (Arnold Breedon), Estrella's true lover, discovers his plan and has him carried off in earnest before laying claim to his title and his wife. The Count buys his freedom and returns in disguise to spy on proceedings, bringing a letter in his own handwriting proclaiming his own death. Lorenzo and Estrella are happily married and the Count, furious at her falsity, reveals himself and claims her. But he has officially declared himself dead and the lovers refuse to admit his existence. The affair is taken to the Doge's Court and Estrella pleads her case in a scene half *Trial by Jury* and half *Alice in Wonderland*. Unable to disentangle things, the Doge (Robert Brough) judges that all concerned should be sent to Constantinople on bread and water until the settlement of the Eastern question, but, sadly, the characters arrange a more conventional ending among themselves.

The Era noted that the script 'reminded us frequently of scenes connected with other plays we have witnessed' and Searelle's music too was judged more than a little reminiscent of Sullivan, Balfe, and a bevy of foreign composers. The Act I finale was allegedly 'borrowed' from Donizetti while *The Era* accused the composer of pilfering practically note for note an aria from *La Traviata*. Nevertheless, *The Times* found both the book and music 'bright and entertaining' and remarked that the music was 'none the less agreeable for suggesting imitation rather than inspiration on behalf of the composer'. Searelle had provided a substantial score of which one of the high points was a lengthy scena for soprano with flute obbligato which requested the audience (apropos of very little) to 'Listen to the Nightingale' as well as the lyrics for seven of the show's numbers including its most successful piece, 'The Kissing Duet'. He also provided a good deal of the publicity for and push behind the production and a few days after the Manchester performances he brought his show to town. Cut here and changed there, but with the same excellent cast, it surfaced at a matinée at the Gaiety. Improvements were noted but it was hardly expected that *Estrella*'s life would be any further prolonged. However, Francis Fairlie, the embattled manager of the Folies Dramatiques, had just seen his production of Johann Strauss' *Prince Methuselam* turn up its toes after only a few performances and was in need of an attraction to keep his theatre open, so, only three weeks and many bad notices after its original opening, *Estrella* opened at the unfortunate Charing Cross house. Some of the artistes from *Prince Methuselam* had their contracts transferred to the new show–W. S. Rising (Lorenzo) and Phil Day (Doge) joining Aynsley Cook in the starring male roles and Camille Dubois taking over the role of the pert maid, Brigetta. Further work had been done on the show and *The Era* noted that the third opening night had, in fact, gone 'fairly well'. But after four weeks it was withdrawn with an announcement that it would re-open Mr Fairlie's new season in September. In the interim, however, this most dubious of managers decided to call it a day and the lease of the Folies Dramatiques was put up for sale. That was the end of *Estrella*'s London career, but in December she turned up in no less a place than the Standard Theatre, New York with Rising repeating his London assignment alongside Hubert Wilke and Amy Gordon. Having closed down one theatre, this resilient musical proceeded to deal an even worse fate to the next. Three nights after the opening the Standard Theatre burned to the ground, taking with it the sets and costumes for *Estrella*. Since its reception had been less than enthusiastic things might well have been left to rest there, but Parke and Searelle's piece continued to survive. In the years which followed it was seen on tour in Britain, the United States and Canada and in both Australia and New Zealand where it gained a certain popularity.

In spite of its shortcomings *Estrella* had several genuinely humorous moments and it gave some great opportunities to Phil Day as the Doge of Venice. The court scene provided him with a comic tour de force which he was not slow to develop and his brief appearances for the two wedding ceremonies produced some of the funniest lines and business in the piece. It was Day's presence in Australia which kept the piece regularly revived on the Antipodean circuits for several years although Searelle, whose colourful career was soon to develop its managerial side, was also an energetic organiser of productions of his own works and *Estrella* would undoubtedly have had a short life without his inspired hustling.

In July the Gaiety was the scene of the British première of *Virginia and Paul*, the first all-British show to have had its initial run in the United States prior to being produced on home territory. The reason for this inversion of the usual order had been the presence of its composer, Edward Solomon, and his *amie*, the star American soprano Lillian Russell for whom the title role had been conceived, in New York. Still in search of a successor to *Billee Taylor*, Solomon had worked with the same book-writer, 'Pot' Stephens, in producing this derivative story of Mephistophelian doings in Ruritalia. His chief villain, Nicholas de Ville, as his name suggests was a close relation of Goethe and Gounod's Satan, and several other elements of *Faust* were mixed in with a pair of magic rings which made people fall in love with the wrong people and a mixed-up babies twist which owed more than a little to *The Sorcerer* and to *H.M.S. Pinafore*. In fact, Stephens quite cheerfully christened his stout baby-mixing lady Mrs Cowslip. These elements had the effect of bringing more of a burlesque flavour to *Virginia and Paul* than had been evident in the English comic opera style which the collaborators had developed in *Billee Taylor, Claude Duval* and *Lord Bateman*. The plot had the fiendish de Ville separating Paul and Virginia on their wedding day by the means of magic rings which bind him to the local heiress, Lady Magnolia and her to the foundling Robinson Brownjones who has been declared as the long-lost heir to the Marquisate of Smith. De Ville continues his dirty work. A railroad brings prosperity and moral decay to the town and Virginia is persuaded to become a professional beauty. But one Samuel Nubbles, a railway navvy, is unaffected by the powers of darkness for he is the fourteenth son of a fourteenth son, and by the final curtain de Ville is defeated and all are made happy–Mrs Cowslip recognises in Brownjones her true grandson and

Paul is revealed as the heir of Smith. Magnolia takes Brownjones, Mrs Cowslip Nubbles and Virginia is restored to her Paul.

Virginia or Ringing the Changes, as the show was originally called, opened at the Bijou Opera House, New York, on January 8th. Miss Russell, however, was not at the helm. She had succumbed to a bout of ill-health and, while her fans breathlessly followed her convalescence in daily newspaper reports more appropriate to royalty, the singer Lucy Couch took over her role. Her acting ability was, apparently, negligible and she was not received with particular enthusiasm. Neither was the show which ran for an indifferent five weeks before being sent out on the road. Five months later *Virginia and Paul*, as its title had now become to avoid confusion with a recent opera, *Virginia*, by the Welsh composer Joseph Parry, opened at the Gaiety. Once again it met with a half-hearted reception. *The Times* pronounced:

> this work does not meet even the modest requirements of a 'masher' audience . . the story is somewhat sillier than librettos usually are and the music is thin and tuneless.

The Era concurred:

> the subject [is] weaker and the music has a less spontaneous flow [than their previous works].

Lillian Russell, making her British début in the role created for her, was inexplicably hissed on her first entrance but recovered and gave a strong performance as Virginia to general approval although some found her 'deficient in elegance and distinction' and it was quite clear that the queen of the American musical stage was a better singer than actress. *The Era*, however, asserted that she was the best American import in years and, although the verdict was not unanimous, Miss Russell gained a following among all kinds of theatre-goers. There were other features, too, which gave offence to some. *The Times* deplored the introduction of the character of Nubbles:

> Mr W. Elton makes up and acts well as a navvy – a personage whose introduction to the operatic stage it may be hoped will remain the peculiar and distinctive achievement of the present authors.

and others were unhappy about a bathing sequence which featured both the voices and the limbs of Miss Russell and the Gaiety chorus rather too prominently for their liking.

The principal fault of *Virginia and Paul* seemed to be that both the author and composer had tried to throw far too much material into their basic plot. The dialogue was long and long-winded and the hefty score included 35 numbers. There were no less than six solos for the star ranging from English ballads to coloratura fireworks; there were duos, quartettes, quintettes, a decidedly familiar 'Confession' for Mrs Cowslip:

> Just one and twenty years ago
> When bread was high and wages low
> I had a grandson born and so
> Although it filled my heart with woe
> One night amid the falling snow
> I at the Foundling left the lad . . .

and a dismal attempt to follow up 'All on account of Eliza' in a rough ballad for Nubbles:

> I'm a railway navigator yes, and that's just what I am
> Which my Sally didn't love me true
> My surname it is Nubbles and my other name is Sam

Which my Sally didn't love me true
She listened to an officer who wore a coat of red
And talked the sort of lingo which would turn a lass's head
But she isn't Missus Nubbles for she's married him instead
Which my Sally didn't love me true
From an honest tavern waiter
I became a navigator
When my Sally didn't love me true.

Virginia and Paul was no *Billee Taylor*. It lacked the incisiveness and vigour of both the participants' best writing and even Miss Russell and the Stephens and Solomon veterans Arthur Williams and Harriet Coveney couldn't keep it long afloat. After a month it was abruptly withdrawn and Hollingshead returned to his policy of burlesque and popular plays, leaving *Virginia and Paul* to be decently buried.

Through the summer *Iolanthe* still held sway at the Savoy and *Rip Van Winkle* at the Comedy while *The Merry Duchess* provided the British musical with a second representative at the Royalty. It was not until late October that any significant new show came to join them, and it was December before a new British show was produced. Willie Edouin had a disaster with the American farcical musical *A Bunch of Keys* at the Avenue, and a much touted version of *La Vie Parisienne* by Farnie which followed it proved disappointing. But Farnie redeemed himself with his adaptation of Chassaigne's *Falka* (*Le Droit d'Ainesse*) which ran 157 performances at the Comedy in succession to *Rip Van Winkle* to become the only foreign success of the year. *Falka*'s humour and high-quality score ensured that it remained a favourite in Britain for many years. After the withdrawal of *The Merry Duchess*, Kate Santley also turned to the French musical and produced Audran's *Gilette de Narbonne*. It flopped and when drastic surgery failed to cure it Miss Santley removed it without further ado.

The fifth and last new British musical of the year appeared as the opening piece for the rebuilt Alhambra on 3 December. The partnership of George Sims and Freddie Clay which had been so successful with *The Merry Duchess* came together again to supply William Holland with a Christmas piece for his new theatre. If the outrageously extravagant style of the original *Babil and Bijou* had been curbed, the Alhambra still continued with a policy of spectacular entertainment and *The Golden Ring*, with its fairy tale of good and evil mortals and immortals heavily laced with magic, gave full scope for lavish production values. On this occasion they also had a script by one of the finest playwrights of the time with music by one of its most experienced and tuneful composers.

Sims' story found the wandering Prince Florian involved in the battle between the evil Red Fairy, Serpenta, and her White counterpart for Good, Sirene. Serpenta must deliver up the Princess Blanche to her masters within a twelvemonth or be turned forever into a snake. Sirene tries to protect the Princess with the aid of Florian who has fallen in love with her, but the Prince has to fight against many distractions including the usurping of his crown and the gallivanting habits of his future father-in-law before Evil is defeated and the Pythoness descends hissing into the earth clasping her evil earthly minion, the usurper Cleon, in her folds.

The book was much sturdier and more dramatic than most of its Alhambra predecessors, but Sims did not neglect the essential features of an Alhambra show. The opening scene set the key with a gathering of demons on a ghoulish mountaintop to which the Red Queen descended on a fiery car. Flames and trapdoors abounded and ballets and stage-fights kept up the heavy visual element. The scene which evoked special approval was that set in the Fisheries Exhibition. King Calino, Blanche's erring father, has persuaded his wife that he needs a world tour 'for the good of his health' and rushes off, leaving Florian to guard his kingdom. But when Florian needs to return home to deal with his own troubles he has to ask Calino to release him from his guardianship. The King is tracked down in London and the royal family and retinue are whisked thence on a magic yacht by Sirene, suitably disguised as fisherfolk and Spaniards. The scene was principally one of comic foolery which gave J. G. Taylor as the King, Sallie Turner as his wife, Wilfred Esmond and Irene Verona the chance to go through some verbal and physical antics before Serpenta arrives to put an end to the fun.

The libretto of *The Golden Ring* did not lean to burlesque style as *The Merry Duchess* had done. Sims proved that in the field of wordplay it was possible to make jokes with the English language without making a joke of it. His lyrics were straightforward and singable and Clay set them with music which won thorough approval. The piece was reviewed enthusiastically. *The Era* critic wrote:

> Witty, fanciful, poetical, but the wit has no sting, the fancy has no double meaning, the poetry is not sensual. It is as innocent as a nursery tale and as pleasant, reviving the kindly fairy tales of our youth and blending with spirits of good and evil and weird unearthly forms that genial element of everyday life in which Mr G. R. Sims shines more than any author of our day . . . He has been careful not to overload his book with dialogue and his lyrics are as fresh and tuneful as any composer could desire. Of the music of Mr Frederic Clay we can also speak in warm terms of commendation, as we are justified in declaring it to be the most important he has yet composed. Several of the melodies and choruses and the concerted finales and ballet music would not disgrace any opera house in Europe.

The Times concurred, calling it 'an excellent piece of its kind' and finding 'much freshness of treatment in the book and the music', and even *The Stage* nodded approval of 'an attractive piece . . satisfying if not brilliant', saving its real plaudits for the music:

> Mr Frederic Clay has provided some of the most delightful music that has been heard on the light opera stage for some considerable time.

Unfortunately, it was to be the last music Clay would compose. The very next night, while walking home from the theatre with Sims, he collapsed. A blood vessel in his brain had burst and he became paralysed. Although he was to live on for some years, during which his health improved considerably, his career as a composer was over. His best work in the theatrical field had undoubtedly been done in the twelve months preceding his incapacitation and in conjunction with Sims at the beginning of what promised to be an outstanding partnership. Sims would go on to write enormously successful shows with other composers but Clay's contribution to the English musical theatre is often forgotten and he is noted only as an appendage of W. S. Gilbert in *Ages Ago* and *Princess Toto* or as the composer of the popular song 'I'll Sing thee Songs of Araby' which began life as part of a cantata, *Lallah Rookh* (Brighton Festival, 1877). It is worth noting that of the seven full-length musicals which he composed or part-composed, four (*Babil and Bijou*, *The Black Crook*, *The Merry Duchess* and *The Golden Ring*) had initial runs of over 100 performances, while his music for *Oriana* was highly praised and *Ages Ago* and *Princess Toto* both had much to recommend them. *The Golden Ring* continued its run through into March of 1884, a total of 105 performances, a highly satisfactory record for a show basically conceived as a Christmas entertainment.

Outside London only one new full-length show was tried with the production at the Prince of Wales, Liverpool, of a musical by Frederic Solomon. Solomon, brother to the more celebrated Edward, was known as an energetic performer, most particularly for his roles as Blood-Red Bill and Ben Barnacle in his brother's musicals *Claude Duval* and *Billee Taylor*. As a composer, however, he was less capable and his *Captain Kidd* sank without trace. The elder Solomon finally made his home in the United States where, between acting, directing and conducting, he again tried a show score in *King Kalico* (Broadway, 1892) with a result that was equally dismal.

The provincial scene during this last year or two had begun to present a slightly changed aspect. Though the big metropolitan hits continued to be rapturously received, a purely provincial type of original musical was making an appearance. Thus, alongside tours of the four Gilbert and Sullivan shows, *Les Manteaux Noirs, Billee Taylor* and the most popular French pieces (*Les Cloches de Corneville, Madame Favart* &c) there appeared a burlesque/extravaganza type of show of a loosely constructed nature often evolved to fit around the actor-manager leader of the producing troupe. Unlike the old burlesques they were original pieces, true musicals with a full score and a reasonably coherent book.

Fred Stimson, the young comedian, had already produced *Merry Mignon* in the previous season with a certain degree of success and he retained the piece in his 1883 repertoire, giving it a further 160 performances during his long and comprehensive tour which featured in pride of place the comedy *Flint and Steel.* As a further supporting piece he produced an extravaganza, *Tit-Bits*, in which he himself had a hand in the writing and to which the music was once again supplied by John Crook. The story dealt with the two daughters of a poor Turkish tradesman whose father envisages selling them as tit-bits to the Sultan's harem in order to pay his debts. After much colourful run-around (including a ship-wreck) featuring Stimson as the less well-favoured tit-bit, all was wound up into a traditional happy ending. *Tit-Bits* was hardly a sophisticated piece, but as part of a provincial evening's entertainment it proved good value. It preserved a number of the traditions of classical burlesque including the travesty role (Stimson as the maiden Woppittee was joined by three actresses in the principal boy roles), the practice of 'appropriate' names for its characters (e.g. Sultan Ali Mecca Bigphool Offizelf), the rhyming and punning dialogue and frequent full-blooded dance breaks. But instead of leaning on the crutch of old popular songs to keep its audience humming, the new kind of extravaganza relied on a wholly original score which had to make its own mark as an integral part of the show. In the case of *Tit-Bits*, Stimson entrusted the job to a proven composer in Crook.

Another practised provincial manager was following similar lines. H. D. Burton had had wide success with the farce *Turtle Doves* and its musical companion *Bears not Beasts*, both of which he retained in his repertoire for a number of seasons. For this year's tour he added a further musical piece, *The Yellow Boy*, a burlesque of *The Yellow Dwarf*, composed by the same team which had been so successful with *Bears not Beasts.* Emily Duncan, touring with the play *Comrades*, added pasticcio burlesques of *The Miller and his Men* and *Sinbad*, with much of their music composed by Frank Musgrave, while Victor Stevens continued with his *Nymphs of the Danube* and Charles Emery's *Romeo the Radical* notched up a few more performances before his company disbanded in internal wranglings. In spite of the last named piece's announced intention of 'going to town', none of these pieces was intended for a metropolitan audience and none of them would have pleased London, but they were part of a growing genre which would become a popular fixture on the lesser circuits in the years that followed.

The provinces served during the year as an introduction for another phenomenon, this time from America. Miss Minnie Palmer, a diminutive ball of personality, had presented her musical play *My Sweetheart* in America without particular notice. The English provinces felt altogether differently. They were totally enamoured of Miss Palmer who became a firm favourite and remained so for many years. The quality of *My Sweetheart* was less certain. It was a flimsy little love story, partly written in the heavily accented Dutch-American popular in America at the time, which served basically as a vehicle for Miss Palmer, and to a lesser degree her fellow actors, to display their theatrical versatility. The printed copy of *My Sweetheart* notes in introduction:

> The introduced music, songs and business in this drama is, on the part of the performer discretionary and optional. The selection and arrangement is left to the inclination and vocal ability of those concerned.

Such tenets were scarcely a good influence on a musical theatre form which was currently moving towards fully original scores, but *My Sweetheart* with an ever-changing musical content proved to be Britain's most successful transatlantic musical over a number of years and, along with *Fun on the Bristol*, another amorphous pantomimic effort, secured true popularity in the provinces.

The smaller pieces of the year came from the usual sources. At St George's Hall Gilbert a'Beckett contributed *A Mountain Heiress* and Arthur Law *A Treasure Trove* with music by Lionel Benson and Alfred Caldicott respectively. The latter held its place for a large part of the season until replaced by the same team's *A Moss Rose Rent* which proved by far the best new piece of the year for the Reeds. It featured Alfred Reed and Fanny Holland as gipsies paid by the unscrupulous squire (Corney Grain) to frighten the young lovers (North Home and Marion Wardroper) off a property for which the sitting rental is – as the curious title states – one moss rose. *A Moss Rose Rent* proved to be one of the St George's Hall's more successful pieces. George Gear, the establishment's pianist, wrote the music for the year's remaining piece there, *A Water Cure*, and Frank Desprez brought out a new sketch, *A Private Wire*, to precede *Iolanthe* at the Savoy, which followed his habitual light and popular vein.

Of the other little pieces which showed their faces round the country during the year, the most interesting was *The Three Beggars*, an operetta played by the students of the Royal Academy. The chorus included two names soon to become well-known in the professional theatre, Effie Chapuy and W. H. Montgomery, but the largest share of success awaited the composer, M. Edward Belville, recently back in London after studies in Paris. 'Belville' soon dropped the French surname in favour of his original Jakobowski and in less than a year made his West End début with a full-scale musical. Within two years he was world-famous as the composer of *Erminie*.

1883

0045 **CYMBIA** or The Magic Thimble. An English comic opera in three acts by Harry Paulton. Music by 'Florian Pascal' (Joseph Williams). Produced at the Royal Strand Theatre under the management of Mrs Swanborough 24 March, 1883 for a run of 48 performances closing 18 May, 1883.

King Arthur . . . . Harry Paulton
Burbos . . . . F. Gaillard
Bleobber . . . . W. G. Bedford
Redaine . . . . Charles A. White
Carrow . . . . Henry Walsham
Grippinghame . . . . James Francis
Goodyear . . . . Albert Sims
Minna . . . . Miss L'Estrange
Cymbia . . . . Camille d'Arville
Princess Menaa . . . . Louise Vesalius/Mlle Sylvia
Princess Rhaadar . . . . Vere Carew
Princess Penarra . . . . Grace Balmaine
Gurtha . . . . Ruth Avondale
Aethel . . . . Miss Lancaster
Beda . . . . G. La Feuillade
Cadwallader-ap-Cadwallader . . . . G. Weathersby
Ladies-in-waiting: Nellie Vacani, Misses Grey, Ashley, Chaplin, Kent, Wyse, Clair
Pages: Misses Corri, Deacon, Pelham, Vincent, Harcourt, Redcliffe
Shepherdesses: Misses Carlisle, Williams, Lytton, Mercier, West, Challoner, Vernon, Stuart, Beaumont, Normand, Hudspeth
Knights: Messrs Huntley, Barry, Lewis, Sims, Beattie, Gordon
Bards: Messrs Ap Tommas, Tomkins, Leonard, Litton, Bottrell, Child

Dir: Messrs Paulton & Pascal; md: J. FitzGerald; sc: T. E. Ryan; cos: Wilhelm

0046 **THE MERRY DUCHESS** a sporting comic opera in two acts by George R. Sims. Music by Frederic Clay. Produced at the Royalty Theatre under the management of Kate Santley 23 April, 1883 for a run of 177 performances closing 13 November, 1883.

Brabazon Sikes . . . . Henry Ashley/Arthur Williams
Freddy Bowman . . . . W. E. Gregory
Farmer Bowman . . . . J. Furneaux Cook
Sir Lothbury Jones . . . . Fred Kaye
Captain Walker . . . . Henry Hallam
Inspector Green . . . . Bruno Holmes
Alderman Gog . . . . C. Cowlrick/Cecil Crofton
Lord Johnnie . . . . R. Martin/J. Willes
The Duchess of Epsom Downs . . . . . . Kate Munroe
Chloe . . . . Florence Montgomery/Edith Brandon/Florence Rivière
Dorothy Bowman . . . . Annie Rose/Florence Montgomery/Edith Brandon/Miss Huntley

Martin	Miss Randall
Sylvia	Miss Douglas/M. Beaufort
Marian	Miss Hatherley
Ethelfreda	Lucy Weston/Elise McBlain
Rowena	Kate Santley/Edith Brandon

with Misses Cowlrick, Parkhurst, Langley, Downey, Green, Darling, Marsh, Nash, Trevalyan, Beresford, Bell, Hatherley, Herbert, Hillers, Douglass, Rivière, Hardman, Randall, Hastings, Deane, Henri, de Wylde, Huntly, Midleton, Georgie Knowles & Lambert; Messrs Vernon, Burnington, Sheldon, Owen, Lovell, Benson, Hider, Venell, Davenport, Hills, Harold, Ward, Burrows, Robinson, H. B. Fenn, George Vincent.

Dir: Richard Barker; md: Jules Guitton; sc: T. E. Ryan; cos: Auguste, Swan & Edgar, Strachan & Mrs May

Produced at the Standard Theatre, New York under the management of Messrs Brooks & Dickson 8 September, 1883 for a run of 46 performances closing 20 October, 1883.
Harry E. Dixey (BS), John E. Nash (FR), Edward Connell (FAR), W Forrester (LJ), Walter Hampshire (WALK), W. Jones (INSP), William White (GOG), J. Watson (LORD), Selina Dolaro (DUCH), Belle Urquhart (CHL), Jean Delmar (DOR), Fanny Knight (MART), Dickie Delano (SYL), Eva Walton (MARI), Sophie Hummel (ETH), Louise Lester (ROW), G. Wilson (TRAINER), Annie Dayton (HODGE), Addie Davis (JIMMIE). Dir: Richard Barker; md: Ernest Neyer; sc: Geo. Heisler & Wm. Voegtlin; cos: W. Dazian & Sons

047 **ESTRELLA** a comic opera in three acts by Walter Parke. Music by W. Luscombe Searelle. Several lyrics by the composer. First produced at the Prince's Theatre, Manchester 14 May, 1883 for one week. Subsequently played at the Gaiety Theatre at a matinée on 24 May, 1883. Produced at the Folies Dramatiques under the management of Francis Fairlie 6 June, 1883 for a run of 36 performances closing 6 July, 1883.

Manchester/Gaiety:

Count Pomposo di Vesuvio	T. Aynsley Cook
Signor Phylloxera	George Temple
The Doge of Venice	Robert Brough
Signor Lorenzo	Arnold Breedon
Giovanni Tommaso	Herman de Lange
Brigetta	Florence Trevallyan
Tartarella	Sallie Turner
Estrella	Constance Loseby
Giacomo	Edmee Richards
Violetta	Maud Perletti

Md: Luscombe Searelle

Folies Dramatiques:

Count Pomposo di Vesuvio	T. Aynsley Cook
Signor Phylloxera	George Temple
The Doge of Venice	Phillip Day
Signor Lorenzo	W. S. Rising
Giovanni Tommaso	Fred Desmond
Brigetta	Camille Dubois
Tartarella	Sallie Turner
Estrella	Constance Loseby
Giacomo	Edmee Richards
Violetta	Maud Perletti
Enrico	Rose Paton

with Misses Sorell, Laurie, O. Robertson, Con Conway, L. Thompson, Mackiff, Georgie Carre, Ivy Wood, Ida Viller, Franklin, Alice Hender, A. Young, B. Young, Olga, Alice Adair, Ashleigh, Edith East, Lavigne, F. deVere, Violette Gwynne, Powell, Patti Devros, Emma Toms, Georgie Huntley, Alice Selfe, Macnamara, Ida Clifford, Roberts, Marsh, Kate Leslie, Helen Harding, Renee Mortimer, Millie Fenwick, Constance Fenwick, Marion Hindford, Uda Hemblin, Effie Remington, Clara Nicholls, Blanche Dane, Lillie Richards, Violet Robertson &c.

Md: Luscombe Searelle; sc: W. B. Spong, Perkins & Johnson; cos: Alias & Mrs May

Produced at the Standard Theatre, New York under the management of Messrs Brooks & Dickson 11 December, 1883 for a run of 3 performances closing with the destruction of the theatre by fire 14 December, 1883.
Hubert Wilke (POMP), Horace Frail (PH), Edward P. Temple (DOGE), W. S. Rising (LOR), George A. Schiller (GT), Fanny Rice (BR), Jennie Hughes (TART), Amy Gordon (EST), Emma Calif (VI), Kathleen Lynn (PAGE), Polly Winner (NINETTA), Madeleine Dixon (HEN), Mr Slattery (NOTARY). Dir: James C. Scanlan; md: Luscombe Searelle

0048 **VIRGINIA AND PAUL** or Changing the Rings. A comic opera in two acts by H. Pottinger Stephens. Music by Edward Solomon. First produced as *Virginia* or Ringing The Changes at the Bijou Theatre, New York, under the management of John A. McCaull 8 January, 1883. Produced in Britain at the Gaiety Theatre under the management of John Hollingshead 16 July, 1883 for a run of 29 performances closing 17 August, 1883.

Nicholas de Ville . . . . W. H. Hamilton
Paul Plantagenet . . . . Arnold Breedon
Robinson Brownjones . . . . Arthur Williams
Samuel Nubbles. . . . . William Elton
Lady Magnolia . . . . Maud Taylor
Virginia Somerset . . . . Lillian Russell
Mildred . . . . Miss Pedley
Amy . . . . Miss de Wyndale
Alice. . . . . Emma Broughton
Cynthia . . . . Miss Matiste
Sally Cowslip . . . . Harriet Coveney
add A Mysterious Photographer . . . . . Willie Warde
Pds: Willie Warde, Emma D'Auban, Kitty Mason

Dir: Messrs Solomon and Stephens; md: Edward Solomon; cos: Miss Thompson, Swan & Edgar, Hilder & Godbold, Hart, Harris & Co.

Produced at the Bijou Theatre, New York under the management of John McCaull 8 January, 1883 for a run of 40 performances closing 14 February, 1883.
John Howson (deV), Charles J. Campbell (PP), George Olmi (ROB), Digby V. Bell (SAM), A. W. Maflin (SGR. MACARONI), Emie Weathersby (MAG), Lucy Couch/Madeleine Lucette (V), Nelly Howard (MIL), Emma Guthrie (AMY), Victoria Reynolds (AL), Laura Joyce (SC). Md: Jesse Williams

0049 **THE GOLDEN RING** a fairy opera in 3 acts by George R. Sims. Music by Frederic Clay. Produced at the Alhambra Theatre under the management of William Holland 3 December, 1883 for a run of 105 performances closing 22 March, 1884.

King Calino . . . . J. G. Taylor (George Mudie)
Prince Florian of Floridea . . . . F. Gaillard
Carambole. . . . . Wilfred Esmond
Dr Colchicum. . . . . George Mudie
Prince Poppet . . . . Alice Hamilton
Rigmarole . . . . George A. Honey
Cleon . . . . Fred Mervin
Arimanes . . . . T. Aynsley Cook
Admiral of the Fleet . . . . Oscar Hartwell
Herald. . . . . R. Darrell
Captain of the Guard . . . . T. Hodges
Arethusa. . . . . Sallie Turner
Sirene, the White Queen . . . . Constance Loseby
Serpenta, the Red Queen . . . . Adelaide Newton
Casquette . . . . Irene Verona
Sea Nymph . . . . Eily Beaumont
Tribord . . . . Mlle Louie
Joujou . . . . Nellie Vacani
Princess Blanche . . . . Marion Hood (Eily Beaumont)

Dancers: Topsy Elliot, Mlles Sismondi, Pertoldi, Louie; Mlle Consuelo de la Bruyère

Dir: William Holland; md: Jules Rivière; sc: Charles Brookes, Bruce Smith, Albert Callcott; cos: Wilhelm

CAPTAIN KIDD a comic opera in three acts by G. H. Abbott and Frederic Solomon. Produced at the Prince of Wales Theatre, Liverpool by Charles Bernard's *Billee Taylor* Tour Co., 10 September, 1883.

Sir Woolfort Mortimer . . . . George Mudie
Col. Sir John McKenzie R.N. . . . . George Peyton
Captain Henry Clayton R.N. . . . . W. Broughton
Corporal Blinks . . . . Arthur W. Taylor
Ned Buntline . . . . Clara Becque
Tony Blackbeard . . . . J. T. MacMillan
Ray Montbar . . . . F. Williams
Pete Moore . . . . C. H. Bathurst
Giles Chucklehurst . . . . H. Claude
Captain Kidd . . . . Frederic Solomon
Marie Kidd . . . . Adelaide Newton
Floretta Mortimer. . . . . Bertie Milner
Martha Smithers . . . . Carrie Collier
Kitty . . . . Julia St George

TIT-BITS a piece of oriental extravaganza in three scenes by George Lash Gordon and Fred J. Stimson. Music by John Crook. Produced at the Winter Gardens, Blackpool under the management of Fred J. Stimson 25 May, 1883 and toured in repertoire.

Ali Mustapha Lookh . . . . Richard L. Gawthorne
Don Knowyah . . . . Lizzie Olive
Prince Iamreel Mashah . . . . Elise Lewis
Waytah . . . . Alfred Banks
Apnee Papah . . . . Myra Grey
Sultan Ali Mecca Bigphool Offizelf. . . . J. H. Boothe
Bozhfakheer . . . . Thomas Olive
Phlifakheer . . . . Mack Olive
Bhuttons. . . . . Ethel Rosslyn
Donzjhe Naggim . . . . Charlotte Elliot
Poppittee . . . . Nina Engel
Woppittee . . . . Fred J. Stimson

A MOUNTAIN HEIRESS a vaudeville by Gilbert a'Beckett. Music by Lionel Benson. Produced at St George's Hall under the management of Alfred Reed and R. Corney Grain 7 March, 1883 with *En Route*. Subsequently played with *Our Mess*. Withdrawn 4 June, 1883.

Zoe . . . . Marion Wardroper
Benjamin Binns . . . . Alfred Reed
Bicey Kell. . . . . North Home
Mrs Wincher . . . . Fanny Holland
Ralph Probitt . . . . R. Corney Grain

A TREASURE TROVE a comedietta in one act by Arthur Law. Music by Alfred J. Caldicott. Produced at St George's Hall under the management of Alfred Reed and R. Corney Grain 6 June, 1883. Withdrawn 28 July. Reopened 1 October. Played from 22 October with *A Water Cure* and *On the Thames*. Withdrawn 15 December, 1883.

Edward Stoney . . . . Alfred Reed
George Warden . . . . North Home
Flint. . . . . R. Corney Grain
Agnes Franklyn . . . . Marion Wardroper
Mrs Franklyn . . . . Fanny Holland

A WATER CURE by Arnold Felix. Music by George Gear. Produced at St George's Hall under the management of Alfred Reed and R. Corney Grain 22 October, 1883 with *A Treasure Trove* and *On the Thames*, the former replaced by *A Moss Rose Rent* (17 December) and the latter by *Master Tommy's School*. Withdrawn 16 February, 1884.

Robert Curry . . . . North Home
Mrs Flutter . . . . Marion Wardroper
Robert Flutter. . . . . Alfred Reed
Mrs Curry. . . . . Fanny Holland

THE ROYAL WORD a comic opera in one act by Henry Hersee. Music by Isidore de Lara. Produced at the Gaiety Theatre under the management of John Hollingshead 17 April, 1883 at a matinée for the benefit of Miss Vane.

Frank Trevallyan . . . . W. S. Rising
Katherine . . . . Mathilde Wadman
Alfred Tremaine . . . . F. de Lara
King Charles II. . . . . Isidore de Lara

A PRIVATE WIRE a vaudeville by Frank Desprez and Arnold Felix. Music by Percy Reeve. Produced at the Savoy Theatre under the management of Richard D'Oyly Carte 31 March, 1883 as a forepiece to *Iolanthe*. Withdrawn 1 January, 1884.

Mrs Frumpington . . . . Rosina Brandram
Miss Rose Frumpington . . . . Minna Louis
Napoleon Fitz-Stubbs . . . . Eric Lewis
Philip Fitz-Stubbs . . . . Charles Rowan
Mary . . . . Sybil Grey

A MOSS ROSE RENT by Arthur Law. Music by Alfred J. Caldicott. Produced at St. George's Hall under the management of Alfred Reed and R. Corney Grain 17 December, 1883 with *A Water Cure* and *On the Thames*, the former replaced by *A Double Event* (18 February) and the latter successively by *A Little Dinner*, *Master Tommy's School* and *Spring Delights*. Withdrawn 17 May, 1884.

Wisdom Pinfold. . . . . Alfred Reed
Laberina Pinfold . . . . Fanny Holland
Sir Plumly Partridge . . . . R. Corney Grain
Georgie Goldthorpe. . . . . Marion Wardroper
Tom Birkett. . . . . North Home

Produced at St George's Hall 7 November, 1892 with *The Silly Season*. Withdrawn 23 December, 1892.
Alfred Reed (WIS), Fanny Holland (LAB), R. Corney Grain (SIR), Gertrude Woodall (GEO), James Appleton/Avalon Collard (TOM)

THE YELLOW BOY an extravaganza in one act by George Capel. Music by H. Round. Produced at West Hartlepool under the management of H. D. Burton 14 May, 1883 and toured in repertoire.

A LESSON IN MAGIC by T. Malcolm Watson. Music by L. Zavertal. Produced at the Royal Artillery Theatre, Woolwich for two performances, 27 and 28 April, 1883.

Lucille. . . . . Rosa Leo
Bridget . . . . Say Morton
Lord Pactolus . . . . W. S. Rising
Signor Smitherone . . . . A. Cattermole

THE NABOB'S PICKLE an operetta in one act by H. and Frederic Corder. Produced at the Aquarium, Great Yarmouth, by Alice Barth's Opera Co., 9 July, 1883.

Percy Hashmore. . . . . Dudley Thomas
Jack Harding . . . . George Fox

Mr Bangles . . . . Gilbert King
Mrs Trust . . . . Lucy Franklein
Lucinda . . . . Alice Farquharson
Haydee Chinnery . . . . Alice Barth

WHAT AN IDEA an operetta by Knight Summers. Music by H. M. Hubert Terry. Produced at the Brighton Aquarium by Alice Barth's Opera Co., 25 June, 1883.

Thisbe . . . . Alice Barth
Professor Orphatop . . . . Gilbert King
Mandeville de Perkins . . . . Dudley Thomas

SLY AND SHY an operetta by A. R. Phillips. Music by Walter Slaughter. Produced at the Princess Theatre, Edinburgh under the management of W. J. Hill 21 May, 1883 and toured.

MATRIMONY or Six and Six Where Suited.
Produced at the Opera House, Huddersfield by the D'Oyly Carte Opera Co. 14 May, 1883 and toured.

THE SILENT WOMAN
Produced by the D'Oyly Carte Opera Company.

THE THREE BEGGARS by Sinclair Dunn. Music by Edward Belville. Produced at the Royal Academy of Music 28 July, 1883.

Sir Philip Sidney . . . . Sinclair Dunn
Samson . . . . Fuller Allen
Watchman/Doctor . . . . Theo T. Moss
Beggars . . . . W. H. Montgomery, G. A. Bennett, T. Phillips
Servants . . . . Mrs Wilson, Miss Bishop, Effie Chapuy, Mr McLaren

1884

At the beginning of 1884 London's West End prepared for some interesting new musical shows. Although the Alhambra was still playing to good houses with *The Golden Ring* and Chassaigne's popular *Falka* still had another four months of life at the Comedy, *Iolanthe* had come to the end of its long run at the Savoy and was to be replaced by the newest work from Gilbert and Sullivan. At the Avenue Farnie's unrecognisable version of *La Vie Parisienne* was moving into its last weeks, scheduled to give way to an original musical by the prolific Scotsman and his *Rip Van Winkle* colleague, Robert Planquette. London playgoers were also looking forward to the first metropolitan performances of Minnie Palmer's *My Sweetheart* and Kate Santley was to reopen at the Royalty with a new work by B. C. Stephenson and Alfred Cellier entitled *Dorothy*.

As usual, the new Gilbert and Sullivan work had already made the paragraphists' columns well before its production and, for once, they had their facts right. The piece was to take the form of a new version of Gilbert's 1870 burlesque *The Princess*. They also reported that, contrary to the normal in-house policy of casting, the piece would feature London's newest musical star, the American, Lillian Russell, in the title role. Alexander Henderson had already put the prima donna under contract, but he agreed to release her for the role of Ida.

In spite of the failure of *Virginia and Paul*, Miss Russell was quickly accepted as one of the best musical leading ladies available and her services were eagerly sought by managers. But the Savoy was to wait a little longer for its first American prima donna. Miss Russell and Carte had agreed terms (£50 per week) and signed contracts when disagreements arose. It was rumoured that it was Miss Russell's disinclination to rehearse which caused the breach – few theatres were as well and as strictly provided with rehearsals as the Savoy under Gilbert – but the upshot was that the prima donna and *Princess Ida* parted ways with Lillian Russell threatening to sue. Shortly afterwards she was offered the role for the Broadway production, but declined, claiming that she was already engaged for the lead in *The Beggar Student* at the Alhambra. However, she left Britain not long after to tour in *Billee Taylor* on the Continent in the company of her common-law husband, Teddy Solomon, and Marion Hood starred in *The Beggar Student*.

Thus, the Savoy's resident soprano, Leonora Braham, found herself promoted from the smaller role of Psyche to the infinitely more challenging title-role. Ida was far from the soubrette-like Patience or Phyllis which Miss Braham had previously tackled at the Savoy, the role being that of a great lady equipped with some of Sullivan's most dramatic and operatic music and a mouthful of blank verse. In this same image,

Princess Ida differed from all the Gilbert and Sullivan works which had preceded it. It was, in effect, something of a throwback. In using very freely the original text of his Olympic burlesque, *The Princess*, Gilbert necessarily gave a different style to his part than that of his more recent works. But on to the framework of fourteen year-old blank verse he imposed fresh and modern lyrics in his best and most mature style, and the marriage was not an entirely happy one. Alongside the dated word play of the old burlesque:

The youngest there will prove a match for *you*.
With all my heart if she's the prettiest!
Fancy, five hundred matches–all alight!–
That's if I strike them as I hope to do!

She's so confoundedly particular
She'll scarcely suffer Dr Watts's hymns–
And all the animals she owns are 'hers'!

Gilbert placed sophisticated lyrics, both humorous and romantic. Puns and word-torturing had given way, under Gilbert's own leadership and influence, to genuine wit and style in both libretto and lyric writing, and it was no accident that in *Princess Ida* it was the newly-written songs and concerted pieces which stood out, and still do, as the most successful part of the work.

The nature of the *Princess Ida* script presented Sullivan with a challenge. Although the comic lyrics which Gilbert had composed for King Gama (George Grossmith) were of the same kind as those of the preceding operas, and songs like Lady Psyche's 'The Ape and the Lady' clearly belonged to the genre which included such pieces as 'The Magnet and the Churn' (*Patience*), there were new departures. The most striking were in the lyric portions written for the Princess herself– the long, declamatory 'O Goddess Wise':

Oh, goddess wise
That lovest light,
Endow with sight
Their unillumined eyes.

At this my call,
A fervent few
Have come to woo
The rays that from thee fall.

Let fervent words and fervent thoughts be mine,
That I may lead them to thy sacred shrine!

and the equally impressive 'I Built upon a Rock', lyrics which cried out for a dramatic soprano voice and musical writing of some import. Sullivan rose to the task magnificently and produced two superb numbers–numbers which had, however, little in common with 'Poor wandering One' or 'Happy young Heart' and which bore little resemblance to what the devoted Savoy audiences were used to hearing from their idols.

When *Princess Ida* made its appearance at the Savoy it met with a decidedly mixed reception. To *The Era* critic it was another advance in the Savoy procession:

> . . a success as complete as in many previous instances in which the gifted composer and brilliant author have been so delightfully associated . . [it] will enjoy as brilliant a career as *Iolanthe* if indeed her reign be not more extended . . [the music] is his very best, full of grace, fancy, elegance and what is indeed rare in these days, originality.

but *The Stage* felt otherwise:

> . . . . vastly inferior to *H.M.S. Pinafore* and the other works of the same class by these brilliant collaborators.

Inferior or not, there was little doubt that *Princess Ida* did not sit as happily at the Savoy as her predecessors had. Grossmith had been supplied with a fairly characteristic role as King Gama, but one which required him to stay off stage rather longer than either he or the audience would have liked. His patter songs were still there, and he scored clearly with his misanthropic numbers:

> If you give me your attention, I will tell you what I am:
> I'm a genuine philanthropist – all other kinds are sham.
> Each little fault of temper and each social defect
> In my erring fellow-creatures I endeavour to correct.
> To all their little weaknesses I open people's eyes;
> And little plans to snub the self-sufficient I devise;
> I love my fellow-creatures – I do all the good I can–
> Yet everybody says I'm such a disagreeable man!
> And I can't think why!

But Leonora Braham, in spite of her best endeavours, was overweighted with a role not designed for her, and Rutland Barrington was most unhappy with the unsubstantial part of King Hildebrand. Indeed he later attributed the relative failure of *Princess Ida* to that fact that he had been insufficiently prominent. Amongst what was for Gilbert a large cast, the tenor role for Durward Lely was of less character and importance than a Rackstraw, a Frederic or even a Tolloller, and Richard Temple had only a mock-Handelian aria in which to shine. The show had not been tailor-made for the 'home team' and they were less happy in it. *Princess Ida* resulted in the Savoy permanently losing the magnificent Alice Barnett who had been such a majestic Fairy Queen in *Iolanthe*. There was no role for her in the new show, the contralto role went to the younger and more conventionally proportioned Rosina Brandram who henceforth took over as contraltò in residence while Miss Barnett made a career in America and Australia.

But there were a great many members of the public who appreciated the qualities of the newest Gilbert and Sullivan work, and the demand for seats for *Princess Ida* encouraged the Savoy to open bookings an unusual three months ahead. It was nearly ten months before the show began to lose its grip and it was finally closed after a run of 246 performances, a tally which would have constituted a triumph for any other management and writers but remains unjustly considered as a failure in the Gilbert and Sullivan canon.

The American production did prove a comparative failure. John Stetson had even had some thoughts after the split London reaction of not taking up his option on *Princess Ida*, but Carte asserted himself and Frank Thornton was shipped across to reproduce the London staging. With J. H. Ryley (Gama) and Cora Tanner (Ida) starring it was a six week failure – a sad performance in comparison with the triumphs of *H.M.S. Pinafore* and *Patience*. Two British touring companies had been sent out soon after the show's début. They covered the country during 1884, and in 1885 *Princess Ida* was included in two of Carte's repertoire companies where it proved less popular than its fellows and was shelved at the end of that season. It was not until ten years later that *Princess Ida* was finally restored to the D'Oyly Carte repertoire and it was 1919 before it was again seen in the West End.

New works from the pens of Planquette and Farnie and Cellier could be relied upon to attract favourable attention and the next two entries were awaited with interest. The pieces advertised had an unusual background for both *Nell Gwynne* and *Dorothy* had a common parent, the unsuccessful *Nell Gwynne* produced at Manchester's Prince's Theatre in 1876. When that piece failed it was consigned to a bottom drawer where it might have expected to stay, but both collaborators had a higher opinion of their contributions to *Nell Gwynne* than had the public and the critics, and in 1884 both separately decided to disinter it. Farnie, who had had such success working with Planquette on *Rip Van Winkle*, disassociated his libretto from Cellier's music and presented it to the French composer. Cellier, left with a bookful of tunes, turned to his former Gallery of Illustration collaborator 'Charlie' Stephenson who invented a fresh story and a new set of lyrics and turned *Nell Gwynne* into an 'English comedy opera' under the title of *Dorothy*.

Since *Falka* showed no sign of weakening, the new *Nell Gwynne* was scheduled for the Avenue Theatre where *La Vie* was coming to an end, and *Dorothy* was announced to open the Royalty season for Kate Santley. As it happened, only the former appeared. *Dorothy* was shelved in favour of Hervé's *La Cosaque* which ran for just seven weeks. Just how badly Miss Santley's judgement had let her down would become evident a couple of years later.

The composer Planquette, sensible of the esteem in which his work was held in Britain, came from France to direct the rehearsals of *Nell Gwynne* alongside his librettist. Farnie and Henderson had assembled an excellent cast, with Florence St John starring in the all-important title-role, supported by the baritone Michael Dwyer, tenors Henry Walsham and Lyn Cadwaladr and soprano Giulia Warwick on the vocal side, and the comedians Lionel Brough and Arthur Roberts. Roberts, an émigré from the music hall stage, had been easily the most successful element of *La Vie* in his West End musical début and, at thirty-one years of age, was beginning a career in the musical theatre in which he would remain one of the most popular stars for twenty years. The role of the miser, Weasel, in *Nell Gwynne* gave him plenty of opportunities to exercise his talent for impromptu comedy and 'gagging'.

Nell Gwynne opened to general praise. The subject was a popular and attractive one and Farnie had pilfered and stitched well in constructing his lively libretto. Its basis was his Manchester script which had, in turn, been closely modelled on the 1818 play *Rochester or King Charles II's Merry Days* which, again, was taken from the French *L'Exil de Rochester*. *The Stage* commented:

> H. B. Farnie contrived with his usual cleverness to spin a story out of slender materials and to provide amusement by comic imbroglio and mirth-provoking situations

before going on to say: '*Nell Gwynne* is a play of fun and frolic rather than an opera of pretty music'. *The Era* preferred the music, pronouncing it: '. . well worthy of the composer of *Rip Van Winkle* and *Les Cloches de Corneville*. .' but agreeing that Farnie had done his job well in setting 'so interesting a subject' and praised 'his discretion in avoiding all that could shock modern propriety in a story replete with risky matter . . for there is ample amusement in the work and not so much as a tinge of vulgarity in any scene'.

The libretto was one of Farnie's better efforts and, if it did not have the dramatic substance of *Rip Van Winkle*, it nevertheless effectively employed many popular devices for humour and for vocal display. Most of the lyrics of the new *Nell Gwynne* had been freshly written although most of the situations and subjects remained the same. The best of the solos were entirely new as the most notable songs from the old show had appeared in print. Miss St John was given the largest number of these new pieces. Her first entrance came in a pretty rondo:

Only an orange girl
A sort of being courtesy calls human
'Like her fruit', lisp gallants gay
'But fit to press and throw away'.
Ah, alas, my cavaliers for your acumen
Orange girl or player
This you can't gainsay her
Nell is withal a woman.

a form which was repeated in the Act 2 'Rustic Rondo' alongside the waltz song 'First Love' which proved the most successful of Nell's numbers. A patriotic scena called 'The Broken Cavalier' or The Legend of Chelsea Hospital proved rather incongruous, but was topped by another which included an arrangement of 'Greensleeves'.

There were ballads for Buckingham (Dwyer) and Falcon (Walsham), but the most popular piece turned out to be a little song 'The Song of the Clock' sung by Giulia Warwick (Jessamine) as she sat waiting for her lover:

Tic tac, that monotonous tale of time
Tic tac, wearily crooning its ancient rhyme
Tic tac, rather the hourglass with golden sand
Than that still voice and nerveless hand.
Faster, faster, faster, faster, oh what a laggard thou art
Faster, faster faster still than the beats of my heart
Quickly, quickly, quickly, quickly, bring my beloved to my feet
Slowly, slowly, slowly, slowly, mete out the moments sweet

Of comical songs there was a decided lack. Brough had an entrance number which got nowhere near the old 'On Sundays Parish Clerk am I' or 'The Deluded Bee' while Roberts, the singer of comic songs, had practically nothing at all and the soubrette role of Marjorie (Victoria Reynolds) was an acting one. Planquette's contribution to *Nell Gwynne* was patchy. Some pieces were attractive enough in a light romantic style, but the score lacked the distinction of his best works.

When *Falka* closed in April, *Nell Gwynne* was removed to the Comedy Theatre with Florence St John and Roberts continuing in their featured roles. Changes were made, including the introduction of songs and music said to have been part of the original score but not previously performed. The measure was a curious one and smacked of trouble, and, sure enough, after only five weeks at the Comedy *Nell Gwynne* folded. On the final nights the stars did not even appear; the dejected management replaced them with their understudies as Planquette registered his first comparative reverse in London.

If *Nell Gwynne*'s London season was less successful than anticipated, its American sally was a disaster. With Mathilde Cottrelly in the title role and J. H. Ryley playing the new version of the part he had created eight years previously at Manchester, it was a four-week flop at the Casino under the banner of John McCaull. In France it fared barely better. Ordonneau and André's version showed just how little the plot had to do with the historical or even the traditional Nell Gwynne. In their hands the piece became *La Princesse Colombine* for a fortnight's run at the Paris Nouveautés. The piece also appeared in Australia starring Emilie Melville and accomplished a couple of British tours but, in spite of its appreciable points, it failed to register as a success.

The most eagerly awaited offerings of the season had proved somewhat of a disappointment and the non-production of *Dorothy* in April ended any hope of a major hit in the early part of 1884. But the defection of Cellier's work was somewhat palliated by the production of an attractive piece from an unexpected source. The Easter reviews reported from the Globe Theatre the staging by the Gaiety's John Hollingshead and the actor John Shine of a comic opera by 'a new composer and an unknown librettist' entitled *Dick*.

In fact, the writers were not totally unknown, for the composer, Edward Jakobowski, had provided the score for the operetta *The Three Beggars* at the Royal Academy the previous year under the name of Belville and he and his partner, Alfred Murray, had already produced a longer piece called *Little Carmen* which Bella Howard had staged at a matinée at the Globe earlier in the year. *Little Carmen* had been favourably if briefly noted by *The Times* which had commented that it had gained 'more success than usually attends such fugitive experiments' and commended it as 'bright and lively and its topical songs and puns were of a superior order.' Although *Dick* was billed as a comic opera it included many of the characteristics of extravaganza without being in any way a burlesque of the familiar Whittington story. That story was somewhat modified for the occasion.

Alice, the 'romp' of Miss Skeggs' academy, learns that her father, the Alderman Fitzwarren, has picked one of his elderly, wealthy colleagues to be her husband. But she has other ideas for she is in love with the discharged apprentice, Dick. A more forcible suitor, however, is the Emperor of Morocco who has come to England to seek a wife. His courting consists of having Alice carried off by his underling, Jack Joskins, and imprisoned in his African palace until she consents to wed him. Disguised as a servant girl, Dick helps her to escape aided by the imposing Princess Badoura, who has fallen in love with him, and by the turncoat Joskins who hankers after her. To complicate the situation the Aldermen of London arrive disguised as dervishes, but the Emperor discovers all and things look bad for the British contingent when news arrives of a plague of rats in the palace. Dick and his cat exterminate the pests and he is offered the crown of Morocco which he refuses in favour of the position of Lord Mayor of London, conferred on him by the grateful Aldermen. The show was favourably noticed for the most part. *The Era* commented:

> The writing is fairly successful: here and there are to be found some bright speeches, especially when social topics and those in connection with civic matters are broached. The lyrics are all neatly written and some merit higher praise than this . . .

While others were more fulsome:

> It is light, bright and sparkling; it never wearies you for a moment; the story is clear, interesting and free from coarseness; the lyrics are particularly well-written . .
> (*Stage*)

> It is our duty to praise this libretto all round. The dialogue – short, sharp and incisive – has hits which cause explosions of laughter and the lyrics are of a superior quality, sometimes, as in the romance 'Swift pinioned bird' touching the height of genuine poetry . . . Mr Jakobowski . . has the knack of hitting off melodies that an audience can carry away with them, his part-writing indicates musicianship and his rhythmic and harmonic devices are as well as liberally displayed by no means without good results (*Daily Telegraph*)

although *The Times* referred to the libretto as 'singularly dull and heavy':

> a rather wearisomely profuse padding of songs of which most have nothing sufficiently distinctive in words or melody to justify their production on the stage.

Murray's libretto was written in a tone of light, though scarcely scintillating, jokiness. The first appearance of Joskins and the Emperor is typical:

J: Ah, there you are. Late as usual.
E: Late as . . ! Joskins, do you know to whom you are speaking?
J: Perfectly. You are the Emperor of Morocco in disguise! I am Jack Joskins, commander of the one ship which forms your Imperial navy. While incognito in England you agreed under contract to obey me.
E: And under contract you agreed to find me a perfect English wife. You promised to show me the beauties of your country.
J: And I have shown you St Paul's, the Guildhall, the Angel at Islington and the Aldgate Pump.
E: These are not marriageable beauties. We sail for Morocco tonight and I without a wife. You have failed in your contract. It is a rude thing to say, but you have lied to me, Joskins.
J: Emperor, I am an English sailor and, except when at anchor, an English sailor cannot lie. To be sure, I said this morning that I was the President of the Royal Academy which, being a diplomatic expression, was probably not quite accurate. But I have found you a wife in consequence.

Most amusement was gained from the musical numbers – an Aldermen's chorus, 'The Merry Brown', a song in which Fitzwarren related 'How to become rich, or The self-made Fusee Seller', and, most particularly, a dervish trio for Hobbs, Blobbs and Fitzwarren:

It certainly seems a great pity
For a man of renown in the city
To beg like a Turk
Very much out of work
And to sing a ridiculous ditty.

It certainly looks somewhat strange
For an Alderman well known on change
To dress like a fakir
And jump like a shaker
Or poodle afflicted with mange

which, with its accompanying dance, proved the highlight of the evening.

Murray used his subject to drop a good number of topical jibes about the current Municipalities Bill and the Egyptain Question and Dick ended the evening's performance with a rather outspoken number on 'Annexation':

Annexation a plan is to make
The land of your birth a bit bigger
If your skin should be white you can take
Any country that's owned by a nigger . . .

Though to rob a man's house is a crime
Which deserves at least transportation
Yet to filch a whole state at a time
Is right when it's called Annexation.

The exceptionally bulky score also included some pretty songs for Ethel Pierson as

Alice and Camille Dubois as Dick, a music-hall-type number for the Emperor and a sailor song for Joskins as well as a large supply of choruses and ensembles in which the members of the company represented variously schoolgirls, negro slaves and rats.

On its first production *Dick* did not attract very much attention and its season at the Globe was limited to one month during which time Hollingshead brought it to the Gaiety for three Saturday matinées, and then on a flying matinée to Brighton. In August he revived the piece at the Gaiety for a fortnight before taking it on a four-week tour of principal dates, after which it returned to London and settled into its third metropolitan theatre, the newly-built Empire in Leicester Square, for a further month during which time it passed its hundredth performance. It was scarcely a record to compare with that of *Princess Ida* or even with the four score plus consecutive performances in town put up by *Nell Gwynne*, but the certain degree of favour it attained was the more notable for being quite unexpected.

Apart from establishing Murray and Jakobowski as West End writers *Dick* was also notable for the introduction to the musical theatre public of a number of artists who would make good careers in the British musical. There was bubbling little Fannie Leslie who replaced Miss Dubois in the title-role, statuesque Gladys Homfrey (Badoura) and her successor Hetty Chapman, plump Caroline Ewell, the young comedian Harry Monkhouse, little Kate Bellingham and Fanny Robina who took on the part of Dick when the show was produced in Australia. *Dick* was a musical embryonically in the style of the many great hits with which Hollingshead and his successor at the Gaiety, George Edwardes, would delight the world over the following years and its performers were of the kind who would be happily and profitably employed in them.

The Alhambra Theatre had flourished as a very individual institution over the years, delighting London audiences with its hugely spectacular productions. Since its rebuilding in 1883, however, the theatre had been finding it increasingly hard to make ends meet. In spite of the reasonably successful productions of *The Golden Ring* and *The Beggar Student*, William Holland found himself forced to review his policy. When Millöcker's piece closed he gambled on an old favourite and produced a revamped version of Burnard's famous burlesque, *Black-Eyed Susan*. The author enlarged the piece to Alhambran proportions and wrote a complete set of new lyrics which were set to music by Alfred Lee, composer of *The Lying Dutchman*, to supplement the old favourite 'Pretty See-usan, don't Say No' and a new version of Lee's 'Champagne Charlie'. The scenic effects for the show were in true Alhambra tradition. The court-martial scene on board the H.M.S. Phoebus glowed with coloured and feathered admirals as Susan pleaded for her unjustly accused William, and the stage swarmed with life as the famous ballet girls of the Alhambra troupe performed a huge maypole dance and an exercise routine with broadswords. Arthur Roberts as Captain Crosstree, George Honey as the evil Hatchett and Edwin Danvers in his original role as Dame Hatley provided some broad fooling whilst Lizzie Mulholland (Susan) and Bessie Bonehill (William) put over the romantic lines in what was principally an evening for the nostalgic. Burnand's couplets, though largely free of the worst of word-play, lacked any real wit and the songs he and Lee had provided were of no special merit, and although the show was received warmly enough by an audience full of fond memories of 'Pattie' Oliver and Co., it served to keep the Alhambra doors open for rather less than two months. When next those doors opened it was with a Variety programme and the Alhambra spectaculars had become a thing of the past.

The two remaining new offerings of the year were both from Teddy Solomon. The image he had created of himself with *Billee Taylor* and *Claude Duval* had been progressively eroded by the failures of his subsequent works, but the prolific composer was undeterred. With *Polly, the Pet of the Regiment* he departed from his tried and trusted English ballad subjects and also from his old librettists. The new work was written in conjunction with James Mortimer, an American ex-diplomat and journalist who had been set up by his friend, Napoleon III, in the newspaper *The London Figaro* and who was also the author of a good number of plays, mostly taken from the French. *Polly* was a straightforward if rather overwritten pot-pourri of *La Fille du Régiment* and any amount of W. S. Gilbert, designed to give its heroine plenty of chances to be piquant and vocal and its chief comedian a good deal of patter and an equal amount of chatter. It was mounted at the Novelty Theatre with Lillian Russell playing the part of the orphan brought up by a regiment and become their mascot. When the General's sister confesses that Polly is her child the heroine is forced to give up her lowly lover, Private Mangel, but it finally turns out that she is really only a poor soldier's daughter and that Mangel is actually Prince Garnix von Pickelhaube von Mangel Wursley, so all ends happily. The story was a decidedly simple and even unimaginative one, but Mortimer supplied a reasonably efficient book containing some mild military satire and a good deal of arch dialogue which brought approval from most of the critics:

> Mr James Mortimer has told his story with skill and his book is excellently written; it is terse and to the point. . . (*Stage*)
>
> The libretto is smart, lively and well put together [and] not overloaded with dialogue. The action is brisk and the lyrics are sufficiently well-written to amuse the audience and serve the purposes of the composer. (*Era*)

With such as unaccustomed advantage as a praiseworthy libretto, Solomon did not let the side down. He composed a brightly-written score which, while it contained no real hit, provided half a dozen unexceptional ballads for his star, a number in the 'Eliza' vein ('She Was a Cau-, She Was a Shun') for comedian Clarence Sounes, and an amusing piece on intermarriage:

> Old England's laws must be obeyed,
> 'Tis for that purpose they were made
> To govern Englishmen on land and water.
> In disposing of your hand
> You must fully understand
> You're not allowed to marry your sister's daughter

But the most successful moments were provided by the eight pretty girls representing General Bang's daughters:

> We are the General's eight fair daughters,
> Our great beauty all hearts slaughters,
> We're highly educated, it's plain to see,
> We know French, German and the Rule of Three . . .
>
> In the abstruse sciences we've taken a prize
> Philology, conchology, mythology likewise,
> We've very decided predilections
> For logarithms and conic sections

They almost succeeded in rivalling the Charity Girls of *Billee Taylor* as they swarmed around their 'dear Papa' with advice for his forthcoming attack on some African potentate:

You are going to the wars
Dear papa, dear papa, . . .
For your safety have no fear
If you skirmish in the rear,
And you may be made a Peer
Dear Papa.
Plain Bangs does sound so frightful
Debrett is not yet quite full
'Lord Bangs' would be delightful
Papa, dear Papa!

The score was increased by Miss Russell's interpolation of her best number, 'The Silver Line', from *Lord Bateman* which suffered not a whit from being sung by a reasonably English Rose instead of a vaguely Turkish Princess. The music received the approval of the critics:

> .. Mr Solomon has, perhaps, done as good work as in anything he has attempted. We may say at once that *Polly* possesses the elements of popularity in a marked degree (*Era*)
>
> The music is full of catchy tunes and merry fancies . . [it] is by far the best that has emanated from [Mr Solomon's] brain . . . (*Stage*)

After five weeks at the Novelty, *Polly* was transferred to the Empire following the closure of *Dick*. The larger stage permitted the spectacle to be increased and, with the programme completed by the British première of the ballet *Coppelia*, *Polly* held the stage to good houses until it was withdrawn to make way for the production of Solomon's next piece, *Pocahontas*, and sent on tour featuring Clara Merivale as Polly and the provincial comic, Henry Wardroper, as Bangs. Unfortunately the comedian treated the whole show as a vehicle for his personal 'favourite bits from the pantos'. By the time the show had been on the road a few weeks, Mortimer's book was stuffed full of cheap and unsuitable business and routines which did nothing for the show although it appealed to certain elements of the large audiences which *Polly* attracted in a nine-week run through Edinburgh, Paisley, Glasgow, Southport, Bradford and Liverpool. At the end of the tour Hollingshead considered bringing the show back to town and, with Miss Russell now returned to America, he attempted to engage Edith Vane for the leading part. Finally, however, he rejected the plan and *Polly*'s British career terminated in Liverpool.

Miss Russell had, in the meanwhile, taken up the role of Polly Pluckrose at the New York Casino for a limited season of eight weeks. She and Solomon had arrived in America in February to an acid paragraph in *The Era*:

> Lillian Russell and Edward Solomon recently arrived in New York and both are relating tales of their wondrous success in England. The little composer is not liked very well there and as yet the fair Lillian has not been engaged except for three Sunday concerts. She will not enter into any contract unless Solomon is engaged also, and as he demands that his operas shall be produced no manager will accede to his desires.

The Era correspondent was, however, somewhat behind with his story. Within a matter of weeks E. E. Rice's Comic Opera Company had *Polly* in rehearsal with Miss Russell in the title-role and a strong cast featuring the expatriates J. H. Ryley (Bangs) and Alice Barnett (Aunty McAsser). In contrast to the fiasco of *The Vicar of Bray*, *Polly* was meticulously staged and enthusiastically received, quickly booked solid and showing a running profit of £250 week. It ran for seven weeks before being varied with a brief reprise of *Billee Taylor* and was then taken on the road in Miss Russell's repertoire which included Solomon's *Virginia and Paul* along with the staple touring pieces *Maritana*, *The Bohemian Girl*, *Fra Diavolo* and *Carmen*.

The departure of Solomon and his lady from London had been hastened by the failure of his second piece, *Pocahontas* or The Great White Pearl, the libretto for which had been written by Sydney Grundy who had already collaborated with Solomon on *The Vicar of Bray*. It was built around the history of the legendary Indian princess, a role conceived and written for Miss Russell, and had been awaiting production for some time. It had originally been announced for the Opera Comique in the previous March (then sub-titled *The Bear Hunters*) but had never been produced, partly owing to the difficulties caused by Miss Russell who had signed exclusive contracts in the United States. As a result the composer and the prima donna had gone off to Europe with a tour of *Billee Taylor* while the British courts debated the situation. The tour opened in Le Havre and was scheduled to visit France, Belgium, Italy and Switzerland, but the latter part of the tour never took place. Precisely what occurred is difficult to piece together. A good reception in the first French dates led to rumours of a Paris transfer, but as time progressed houses and enthusiasm began to wane. Lillian went 'ill' on a number of occasions and finally she and Teddy abandoned the enterprise and returned to England. A certain Mr Wilson was found to take on the financial responsibility of the tour and the cast was persuaded to set out for Boulogne and the Turin Exhibition. But Mr Wilson's parents had no intention of allowing him to disburse their money on theatricals and he was recalled. The company disintegrated and the penniless actors were left to get home from Switzerland as best they could. When Lillian finally reappeared in the West End it was, in spite of offers including the title role of the Alhambra's *Black-Eyed Susan*, as Polly Pluckrose and she loyally followed up as Solomon's 'Great White Pearl'.

Grundy had supplied a fanciful tale for his libretto, surrounding the 'straight' love-story of John Smith and his Indian princess with four comic characters – the Widow Thompson, Smith's adoring gorgon; Sir Hector Van Trump, a 'Fashionable General' from Rotterdam sent out to disperse the marauding Indians, a General who smacked rather of Sir Joseph Porter as he sang:

> Our lines have fallen in an age when fashion rules the roost
> And he or she is most the rage who's advertised the most
> We've fashionable beauties and we've fashionable beasts
> (For wasn't Jumbo one of them), we've fashionable priests,
> We've fashionable actors and we've fashionable plays
> And fashionable theatres where comic opera plays
> Whilst fashionable actresses electrify the pen
> We've fashionable critics in the very upper ten:
> We've fashionable poets and we've fashionable peers
> We've fashionable scientists and fashionable seers
> We've fashionable barristers who talk a power of fudge
> And we've an extra superfinely fashionable judge
> And tho' I never fired a shot and never mean to try
> A fashionable general am I, I, I!

Then there was a Birmingham commercial salesman, Mr Percival Punsheon Potts, who also expressed himself in patter terms in a song called 'The Political Economist':

> I am not parsimonious
> The adjective's erroneous

And not as ceremonious
As well it might have been.
But possibly it's tentative
And p'raps misrepresentative
Since it is argumentative
If that is what you mean . .

The fourth comedian was the Limerick corporal Flanagan:

If you feel a bit cross and contrary
And itch for an illigant row
There's no place like old Tipperary
For having it out anyhow.
But after it give me Virginny
Because it reminds me of home
Reminds me of dear old Kilkinny
When the cats are all out on the roam . .

There was plenty of fun, for Grundy was at his best in the humorous passages, and the numerous topical references – to politics (particularly Birmingham ones), judicial affairs and immigration (anti-) – which he included pleased the audience. But amongst all this the story got lost. *The Referee*, after accusing the first night house of being 'the worst audience ever played to' was obliged to admit:

> Grundy, who is a clever man and one of our best writers of dialogue has made the same mistake in *Pocahontas* he made in *The Vicar of Bray*. There is no plot, no incident, nothing to interest between the songs and most of the parts are very poor . .

Solomon turned out an adequate score, but one which showed little originality or musical invention to add to the clever lyrics which were the best part of Grundy's contribution. *Pocahontas* was played with a new ballet conceived by M. Bertrand and starring the dancer Alice Holt. Its music was by Adolphe Adam and it was the first opportunity Britain had to see a version of *Giselle*.

The bill did not run. Hayden Coffin in his autobiography speaks of it as having been merely put on as a stopgap until Hollingshead's next show, *The Lady of the Locket*, was ready for production, but it seems that *Pocahontas* was put on principally to please Solomon and Miss Russell and, had it been successful, the producers would have found some way to extend its life. When it quite obviously did not 'take' it was discarded without further ado. Its production marked, on the credit side, the first appearance on any stage of the baritone C. Hayden Coffin. The son of an American dentist who had settled in Britain, Coffin had had some success as an amateur singer and had been promised a leading role in *The Lady of the Locket* by its composer who was by way of being a friend. When that show was postponed and *Pocahontas* staged instead, Hollingshead proposed giving the young singer the role of John Smith. The writers, however, demurred and the operatic baritone, Frank Celli, was given the role with Coffin as understudy. But the understudy had his day when Celli left after the third week and he was called on to make his début for the final six performances, the first in a long and distinguished career.

In the provinces little of note was happening. H. D. Burton's company continued to tour their established repertoire including *Bears not Beasts* and added a burlesque, *The Fire King*, but the *Merry Mignon* tour folded when its manager and star Fred Stimson died of consumption at the age of 27. Lila Clay, having split with her manager, Colonel Caverly, lost her rights to *An Adamless Eden* and formed a new ladies' company to tour a new all-female operetta, *Posterity*. Like its predecessor it passed for being feminist before showing itself to be anything but. Its story was set two hundred years into the future. Ladies have perfect equality and, indeed, are superior to men. An actress is brought to trial for marrying a young male ward-in-chancery; the judge and the barristers are, of course, women. Finally true love and the young man win the day and all ends happily. It was a sparkling little piece which did not forbear to poke fun at the judicial and social happenings of the day, in particular Miss May Fortescue (née Finney) the Savoy chorus girl who had just received £10,000 in breach-of-promise money from the dilatory Lord Garmoyle.

The year's shorter pieces brought forth little of note. At St George's Hall the style had become settled into one of rather unadventurous vaudeville. New pieces included two with music by Corney Grain who suffered a severe illness later in the year and was absent from the bill for some time. His place at the piano was taken by Eric Lewis, George Grossmith's understudy from the Savoy, who gave a little piece called *A Water Picnic* as a complement to Caldicott's operetta *Old Knockles*. At the Novelty, Procida Bucalossi supplied some original music to go with Horace Lennard's burlesque of *Lallah Rookh*, but the piece lasted only a small part of the run of its first half, the play *Nita's First*.

1884

050 **PRINCESS IDA** or Castle Adamant. A respectful operatic perversion in two acts and a prologue of Tennyson's *The Princess* by W. S. Gilbert. Music by Arthur Sullivan. Produced at the Savoy Theatre under the management of Richard D'Oyly Carte 5 January, 1884 for a run of 246 performances closing 16 August, 1884. Re-opened 15 September, 1884. Closed 9 October, 1884.

Princess Ida	Leonora Braham (Kate Chard)
Sacharissa	Sybil Grey
Lady Blanche	Rosina Brandram
Ada	Miss Twyman/Lillian Carr
Melissa	Jessie Bond (Lillian Carr)
Chloe	Miss Heathcote
King Gama	George Grossmith (Eric Lewis)
Hilarion	Henry Bracy
Cyril.	Durward Lely
King Hildebrand	Rutland Barrington
Scynthius	William Lugg
Guron	Warwick Grey
Arac	Richard Temple
Psyche.	Kate Chard
Florian	Charles Ryley (Eric Lewis)

Dir: W. S. Gilbert; md: Arthur Sullivan/François Cellier; sc: Harry Emden and Hawes Craven; cos: Auguste and Miss Fisher

Produced at the Fifth Avenue Theatre, New York, under the management of John Stetson 11 February, 1884 for a run of 48 performances closing 22 March, 1884.
Cora S. Tanner/Mary Beebe (IDA), Eva Barrington (S), Genevieve Reynolds (BL), Clara Primrose (ADA), Hattie Delaro (MEL), Eily Coghlan (CH), J. H. Ryley (GAMA), Wallace Macreery/Charles F. Lang (HIL), W. S. Rising (CY), Sgr Broccolini (HILD), E. J. Cloney (SC), James Early (GU), W. Ainsley Scott (AR), Florence Bemister (PS), Charles F. Lang/Edward P. Temple/Arthur Wilkinson (FLO). Dir: Frank Thornton; md: John Mullaly

Produced at the Fifth Avenue Theatre, New York, under the management of John Stetson 22 November, 1887 for a season of three weeks.
Geraldine Ulmar (IDA), Edith Jennesse (S), Alice Carle (BL), Miss McCann (ADA), Agnes Stone (MEL), Miss Branson (CH), J. W. Herbert (GAMA), Courtice Pounds (HIL), Phil Branson (CY), Sgr Broccolini (HILD), L. W. Raymond (SC), N. S. Burnham (GU), Joseph Fay (AR), Helen Lamont (PS), Stuart Harold (FLO)

Produced at the Shubert Theatre, New York, 13 April, 1925 for a run of 40 performances.

Subsequently played in repertoire in New York by the D'Oyly Carte Opera Company and others.

Subsequently played in repertoire in London and on tour by the D'Oyly Carte Opera Company.

TV/Video: 1984 Brent Walker Ltd. Pr: Judith de Paul; dir/ch: Terry Gilbert; md: Alexander Faris; sc: Allan Cameron; cos: Jenny Beavan

Nan Christie (IDA), Jenny Wren (S), Anne Collins (BL), Claire Powell (MEL), Elise McDougall (CH), Frank Gorshin (GAMA), Laurence Dale (HIL), Bernard Dickerson (CY), Neil Howlett (HILD), Christopher Booth-Jones (SC), Pater Savidge (GU), Tano Rea (AR), Josephine Gordon (PS), Richard Jackson (FLO)

0051 **NELL GWYNNE** A comic opera in three acts by H. B. Farnie. Music by Robert Planquette. Produced at the Avenue Theatre under the management of Alexander Henderson 7 February, 1884. Transferred 28 April, 1884 to the Comedy Theatre. Closed 22 May, 1884 after a total of 86 performances.

Nell Gwynne . . . . Florence St John (Mlle Sylvia)
Clare . . . . Agnes Stone
Jessamine . . . . Giulia Warwick
Marjorie. Victoria Reynolds
Buckingham. . . . . Michael Dwyer/Herbert Standing/ W.H. Hamilton
Rochester . . . . Lyn Cadwaladr
The Beadle . . . . Lionel Brough/Louis Kelleher
Weasel. . . . . Arthur Roberts (C. Hunt)
Talbot. . . . . Cecil Crofton/Vere Carew
Falcon. . . . . Henry Walsham
Hodge. . . . . D. St John/Mr Stewart
Podge . . . . C. Hunt
Peregrine . . . . Agnes Lyndon
Charles II . . . . Augustus Wheatman/D. St John
Prue. . . . . Bessie Bell
Sue . . . . Lily Richards
Roger . . . . Miss J. Clifford
Ned . . . . Miss Deacon
Wat . . . . Miss Yorke
Simon. . . . . Miss Dawson
Robin . . . . Bessie Callaway
Ralph . . . . Minnie Howe
Phoebe . . . . M. Harwood/Miss Vernon
Dorothy. Miss Wentworth
Maud . . . . Miss Heathfield
Lettice. Miss Douglas
Dorcas. Louie Serle
Priscilla . . . . Miss Huntley

with Misses Cecil, de Pothe, Lambert, E. Nicoli, Neilson, Coleman, Vale, d'Oyle, March, Deane, Barnard, Irving, Reid, C. Nicoli, Vere, Seaton, Marsden/Tester, Russell, Kent, Ridley, Duclos, Perrin, de Grey, Gale, Gordon, E. Perren, A. Sylvester, Salisbury, Alice Charteris, Ethel Charteris; Messrs Steward, Withers, Alexander, Rix, Burratt, Valentine, Anglove, Pierce, Risson, Cazzybone, Turmut, Junket, Bacon, Joskin/Morganti, Blackburn, Coleman, Reeves, Felix, Handel, Vaughan.
Dir: H. B. Farnie; md: Georges Jacobi/Rubini A. Rochester; ch: Katti Lanner; sc: T. E. Ryan & W. Grieve; cos: Phil May, Arthur Fredericks, Wilhelm

Produced at the Casino Theatre, New York, under the management of Rudolph Aronson 8 November, 1884 for a run of 38 performances closing 12 December, 1884.
Mathilde Cottrelly (NELL), Laura Joyce Bell (CL), Ida Valerga (JESS) Irene Perry (MARJ), William H. Hamilton (BUCK), Jay Taylor (ROCH) Digby Bell (BEA), J. H. Ryley (WEA), Edward Cameron (TAL), W. H. Fessenden (FALC), J. A. Furey (H), L.C. Schrader (P), Billie Barlow (PERE), Charles Dungan (CH2), Annette Hall (PRUE), Millie Vandenberg (SUE). Md: A. de Novellis.

Produced at the Théâtre des Nouveautés, Paris, as *La Princesse Colombine* 7 December, 1885.

0052 **DICK** a comic opera in two acts by Alfred Murray. Music by Edward Jakobowski. Produced at the Globe Theatre under the mangement of John Hollingshead and J. L. Shine 17 April, 1884. Closed 17 May, 1884 after 29 performances. Played at matinées at the Gaiety Theatre 3, 10, 17 May. Performed at Brighton at a matinée 24 May. Reproduced at the Gaiety Theatre 18 August,

1884 for 18 performances closing 6 September and toured through Manchester, Liverpool, Leeds and Birmingham. Reproduced at the Empire Theatre 6 October, 1884 for 29 performances, closing 7 November, 1884.

Alderman Fitzwarren . . . . John L. Shine/Wilfred E. Shine
Blobbs . . . . F. H. Laye/Harry Monkhouse/Harry Martell
Hobbs . . . . Herman de Lange/Wilfred E. Shine/Harry Martell
Emperor of Morocco . . . . Charles Cartwright/Robert Brough (Charles Mowbray)
Jack Joskins . . . . Charles Lyall/Arthur Williams/F. H. Laye
Landlord . . . . Windham Guise/Harry Martell/Charles Mowbray
Edgar . . . . Hetty Chapman/Miss de Vallence/Katie Seymour
Albert . . . . Kate Bellingham/V. Audrey
Hassan. . . . . Willie Warde/Mr Marryat
Dick . . . . Camille Dubois/Fannie Leslie
Princess Badoura . . . . Gladys Homfrey/Miss Handley/Hetty Chapman
Bulbul . . . . L. Allen/Grace Hope
Zobeide . . . . Violet Leslie/Nellie Carlisle/N. Hope
Fatima. . . . . Alice Holt
Miss Priscilla Skeggs . . . . Caroline Ewell/Bella Cuthbert
Edith . . . . Georgie Grey/Fanny? Robina/Maud Taylor
Maude. . . . . V. Noad/Miss Mowbray
Blanche . . . . Florence Harcourt
Alice Fitzwarren . . . . Ethel Pierson
Ruth. E. Temple

with Misses Gaynor, F. Thomson, Wallis, Norman, Lancaster, Wells, Ida Viller, Faris, du Braham, Lake, C. Graham, Castleton, V. Audrey, Newton, Coleman, L. Thomson, Wilson, F. Franklin, Cavendish, Patti Devros, Price, Langford, D. Ellis, Montague, Poole, Clayton, Nesbit, Grey, Lee, Fern, Murray Carlton, Bessie Leslie, Cromwell, A. St Clair, De Vere, Thomas, Du Cane, E. Graham & c.; Messrs Pentland, Howard, Temple, Botterill, Haslam, Walker, Christie, Stuart, Lake, Parland, Coleman, Le Maistre, Gumpert, Hill, Mori, Elliott, Beckett & c.

Dir: Richard Barker; md: Frederick Stanislaus; ch: Willie Warde/Paul Valentine; cos: Chasemore; sc: Spong & Perkins

053 **BLACK-EYED SUSAN** or The Little Bill That Was Taken Up. A burlesque in two acts by F. C. Burnand. Original music by Alfred Lee. Produced at the Alhambra Theatre under the management of William Holland 2 August, 1884 for a run of 48 performances closing 27 September, 1884.

Captain Crosstree . . . . Arthur Roberts
Lord High Admiral . . . . J. H. Jarvis
Colonel Blazer. . . . . Nellie Douglas
William . . . . Bessie Bonehill (G. LaFeuillade)
Hatchett . . . . George Honey
Raker . . . . T. Hodges
Doggrass . . . . George Mudie
Gnatbrain . . . . Katie Lee
Jacob Twigg . . . . Fred Storey
Blue Peter . . . . Stuart Paget
Admiral of the Blue. . . . . Mr Loraine
Admiral of the Red . . . . H. Husk
Admiral of the Yellow . . . . S. Sinclair
Admiral of the Green . . . . Mr Apsey
Admiral of the Black . . . . Mr Horspool
Midshipmite. . . . . Rose Moncrieff
Limpet . . . . Bertie Venn

Susan . . . . Lizzie Mulholland
Dolly Mayflower . . . . Kate Leamar
Dame Hatley . . . . Edwin Danvers

Pd: Rose Moncrieff, Mlles Pertoldi, Palladino, Topsy Elliot.
Dir: William Holland and F. C. Burnand; md: Georges Jacobi; ch: Hanson; sc: Charles Brooke; cos: Wilhelm

0054 **POLLY** or The Pet of the Regiment. A comic opera in two acts by James Mortimer. Music by Edward Solomon. Produced at the Novelty Theatre under the management of Nellie Harris 4 October, 1884. Transferred to the Empire Theatre 8 November, 1884. Closed 20 December, 1884 after a total run of 69 performances.

General Bangs . . . . Alfred Bishop
Col. Tussell . . . . H. Cooper Cliffe
Captain Drummond. . . . . Maggie Rayson
Captain Jinks . . . . Miss Summerton
Lt. Brazenose . . . . Miss Mowbray
Lt. Daffodil . . . . Kate Bellingham
Sgt Maj Redoubt . . . . Albert Sims
Sgt Pipeclay. . . . . Clarence Sounes/Wilfred E. Shine
Private Mangel . . . . Jack Leumane
Lady McAsser . . . . Susie Vaughan
Baby Bangs . . . . Lesley Bell/Mabel Coates
Sarah Bangs. . . . . Miss Delphine
Susan Bangs. . . . . Maud Bramble
Jane Bangs . . . . Millie? Gerard/E. Temple
Phoebe Bangs . . . . Elise Ward/Miss Havilland
Martha Bangs . . . . Emily Clare/Miss Faliera
Eliza Bangs . . . . Carrie Solomon
Ann Bangs . . . . Miss Brunton/L. Wilson
Cornet Camellia. . . . . Miss Couzins
Polly Pluckrose . . . . Lillian Russell

Dir: Capt A. S. Riddell; md: Edward Solomon; sc: Henry Emden and E. G. Banks; cos: Alias and Harrison Bros.

Produced at the Casino Theatre, New York, under the management of J. C. Scanlan and E. E. Rice 17 April, 1885 for a run of 79 performances closing 20 June, 1885.
J. H. Ryley (GEN), John T. McWade (COL), E. H. Aiken (PIP), H. S. Hilliard (MANG), Alice Barnett (McA), Lulu Campbell (BABY), Josie Hall (SAR), Emma Hanley (SU), Emma Schell (JANE), Annie Lukie (PH), May Bardell (MAR), Agnes Folsome (ANN), Florence Bemister (EL), Lillian Russell (Emma Carson) (P)

0055 **POCAHONTAS** or The Great White Pearl. A comic opera in two acts by Sidney Grundy. Music by Edward Solomon. Produced at the Empire Theatre under the management of John Hollingshead and John L. Shine 26 December, 1884 for a run of 24 performances closing 23 January, 1885.

Pocahontas . . . . Lillian Russell
Mr Percival Punsheon Potts . . . . Henry Ashley
Window Thompson. . . . . Alice Barnett
General Sir Hector Van Trump . . . . . John L. Shine
Corporal O'Flanagan . . . . Robert Brough
Captain John Smith. . . . . Frank H. Celli/C. Hayden Coffin
Ensign. . . . . Nellie Lisle
First Lieutenant. . . . . Kate Bellingham
Second Lieutenant . . . . A. Hill

Dir: Robert Brough and Sidney Grundy; md: Edward Solomon; cos: A. Chasemore; sc: T. W. Grieve, Leolyn Hart, E. G. Banks

Played with *The Pinauderies* and the ballet *Giselle*.

THE UHLANS a comic opera by Ivor Morrison. Music by Mrs C. W. Morrison arranged by Sgr Cellini. Produced at Dublin under the management of Nellie Harris 10 March, 1884.

Rose . . . . Rose Hersee
Marie . . . . Helen Armstrong
Angelique . . . . Effie Morris
Fritz . . . . James W. Turner
Carlowitz . . . . L. A. Rooke
Berthelet St Remy . . . . Charles Lyall
Hon. von Krockery . . . . W.H. Dodd
Lizette. . . . . Clara Hastings
Antoine . . . . Sydney Mooreland
Jacques . . . . W. C. Crofton

Md: Sgr Cellini

LITTLE CARMEN a burlesque by Alfred Murray. Music by Edward Belville (Jakobowski). Produced at the Globe Theatre under the management of Bella Howard at a matinée 7 February, 1884.

Don Jose . . . . Susie Vaughan
Escamillo . . . . E. J. Henley
Micaela . . . . Madeleine Howard
Ilbredbloko . . . . Edgar Granville
Ilfedfello. . . . . Sybil Awdry
Immorales. . . . . Miss Jansen
Frasquita . . . . Miss Gordon
Mercedes . . . . Miss Roma
Pablo . . . . Miss Ross
Gomez. . . . . Miss Handley
Juan . . . . Miss Keith
Diego . . . . Miss Graham
Paquita . . . . Miss Dupré
Inez . . . . Miss Oliver
Carmen . . . . Bella Howard

A DOUBLE EVENT by Arthur Law and Alfred Reed. Music by R. Corney Grain. Produced at St George's Hall under the management of Alfred Reed and R. Corney Grain 18 February, 1884 with *A Moss Rose Rent* and *Spring Delights*, the latter replaced by *A Little Dinner* and the former by *Fairly Puzzled* (19 May). Withdrawn 16 June, 1884.

Timothy Tubs . . . . Alfred Reed
Sally Somers . . . . Marion Wardroper
Mrs Bridget Troutbeck . . . . Fanny Holland
Jack Whiffle . . . . North Home

A TERRIBLE FRIGHT by Arthur Law. Music by R. Corney Grain. Produced at St George's Hall under the management of Alfred Reed and R. Corney Grain 18 June, 1884 with *Nobody's Fault* and *Shows of the Season*. Withdrawn 26 July. Reopened 7 October with *Troubles of a Tourist* and *Cherry Tree Farm*. Withdrawn October 18. Played for a few performances in November.

Jacob Jobling . . . . Alfred Reed
Sarah Filcher . . . . Marion Wardroer
Mrs Bunker Drew . . . . Fanny Holland
Jack Morris . . . . North Home
Gripper . . . . North Home

FAIRLY PUZZLED by Oliver Brand. Music by Hamilton Clarke. Produced at St George's Hall under the management of Alfred Reed and R. Corney Grain 19 May, 1884 with *A Double Event* and *A Little Dinner*. Withdrawn 16 June 1884.

Alfred Partridge . . . . North Home
Bertha Yorke . . . . Marion Wardroper
Sam . . . . Alfred Reed
Professor Cockles . . . . R. Corney Grain
Tabitha . . . . Fanny Holland

OLD KNOCKLES a musical sketch by Eric Lewis. Music by Alfred J. Caldicott. Produced at St George's Hall under the management of Alfred Reed and R. Corney Grain 24 November, 1884 with *Backsheesh*. Played with *A Water Picnic* (Eric Lewis) during the illness of Corney Grain. *A Peculiar Case* was added 8 December. Withdrawn 21 March, 1885.

Sir Miles Allbright . . . . North Home
Maud Coventry . . . . Marion Wardroper
Old Knockles . . . . Alfred Reed
Mr Bellworthy . . . . Charles Allen
Kate Haslewood . . . . Fanny Holland

A PECULIAR CASE a musical triplet by Arthur Law. Music by George Grossmith. Produced at St George's Hall under the management of Alfred Reed and R. Corney Grain 8 December, 1884 with *Old Knockles* and *Backsheesh* replaced respectively by *Hobbies* and *A Vocal Recital* (6 April, 1885). Withdrawn 30 May, 1885.

Valentine Vale . . . . North Home
Dr Spry . . . . Alfred Reed
Mrs Spry . . . . Marion Wardroper

POSTERITY an operatic dissipation in one act by Augustus M. Moore. Music by W. Meyer Lutz. Produced at Newcastle under the management of Lila Clay 10 March, 1884 and toured in repertoire.

Baroness Lady Bairns . . . . E. Jonghmans
Kate Buckingham . . . . Lizzie Coote
Frank Foster . . . . Ethel Cairns
Jack Townsend . . . . Beatrice St Maur/Blanche Sennett
Dick . . . . Ada Hogarth
Dolly . . . . Little Addie Blanche
Jenny Jarvis . . . . Edith Vane
May Filbert . . . . Ada Blanche
Policeman . . . . A. Lorraine
Forewoman of the jury . . . . Julia Egley
Intellectual jurywoman . . . . Miss Hoban
with Misses Hamilton, St Orme/Graham, Henley, Pinder, Rae &c.

1885

The first months of 1885 saw a distinct lack of musicals in the West End. *Pocahontas* closed after its fourth week leaving D'Oyly Carte's revival of *The Sorcerer* as the only British musical in town while the sole foreign representative was a production of Audran's *The Grand Mogul*, passing an unsuccessful season at the Comedy. The feature of this ten year-old piece was a scene where Florence St John sang a number draped with a selection of live snakes, an ordeal which she thankfully had to suffer for only eight weeks.

To fill the gap left by the early removal of *The Grand Mogul*, the Comedy produced a revival of *Barbe-Bleu* and only three weeks later the Gaiety in turn revived its burlesque of *Bluebeard*. The Comedy piece was gone in six weeks and replaced by yet another revival, the perennial pasticcio extravaganza *Nemesis*. The London musical scene had a decided look of déjà-vu. Every musical running in the month of February was a revival. However, better things were in the offing. The long-awaited spectacular of *The Lady of the Locket*[1] was in production and scheduled for a March opening, Gilbert and Sullivan's new Japanese piece was almost ready, and Edward Jakobowski, the composer of *Dick*, was said to be completing two new works, one with Harry Paulton and the other with Alfred Murray.

The first to appear was *The Lady of the Locket*. John Hollingshead had branched out with some success into the new Empire Theatre but, up to date, had filled the house principally with revivals (*Chilpéric*) and transfers (*Polly, Dick*). The unimpressive *Pocahontas* had been produced especially for the theatre, but *The Lady of the Locket* was a work on a different scale. Literally no expense had been spared. The production costs amounted to more than £6,000. The Empire was a large auditorium which needed to be filled with visual effect in the manner of the old Alhambra, and in *The Lady of the Locket* Hollingshead gave London one of the most spectacular productions it had ever seen. The show was a first-timer for its three major creative participants. The composer, William Fullerton, was a young American who had recently finished his musical studies in Leipzig and had come to settle in Britain where he shared the home and the elegant theatrical salon of the designer Percy Anderson who also made his début with the principal costumes for his friend's show. The librettist was Henry Hamilton, a 32-year-old playwright who had been successful with an adaptation of Ouida entitled *Moths* (Globe, 1882) and another from the German, *Our Regiment*, (Vaudeville, 1883), but who was trying his hand for the first time at a musical. As their star the authors chose yet another novice, the baritone Hayden Coffin, who had taken

[1] Prematurely entitled *Venice*.

over from Frank Celli in *Pocahontas*, to play opposite the well-established comedian John Shine and soprano Florence St John.

The Lady of the Locket was set in Venice and followed a familiarly slight outline. The Baron di Bombazina has arranged for his daughter, Francesca, to marry Cosmo, the son of the Doge, but the young people have other ideas and other lovers. The Bombazina heiress eventually wins the right to wed the impecunious but aristocratic Ascanio who has fallen in love with her portrait in a locket, and Cosmo fulfils the hopes of the pretty ballad singer, Stella. Hamilton and Fullerton stretched the usual convolutions of the well-used plot over four hours, twenty-nine musical numbers, and three acts of which the features included a Turkish ballet, a Grand Processional March, a Grand Venetian Ballet and a couple of choruses performed by real live Coldstream Guards. The guardsmen had been knocked into vocal shape by assistant m.d. Jimmy Glover who had suffered a false start when his 'choir' suddenly received orders to sail for the Sudan and the war against the Mahdi. He was obliged to start work all over again with a fresh group of soldiers. The length of the show meant further work for Glover as the conductor, Sgr Dami, found that he could not conduct Act 3 through and still make it down to Covent Garden's New Club for his late evening spot. He took to disappearing in mid-act, leaving Glover holding the baton.

Hamilton's libretto showed no particular originality, but worked its way through its limited plot in what he clearly considered to be musical comedy style with more than a dash of word-play. The reason for Francesca's refusal of Cosmo was given as 'she didn't find the gentleman a Cosmo-polite-un' and the local monetary system was twisted into a reference to 'ducats and drake-ats'. The opening chorus took a typically half-hearted step on the face of the English language:

Oh! yes, we're Venetians ruled by a Doge
A very great person as you may suppoge
With a long white beard and a Roman noge
And a band of music wherever he goge
About the streets of Venice.

The characters were conceived in the standard mould and were well-endowed with songs. Florence St John and Hayden Coffin as the ill-matched pair provided the main vocal contribution. Miss St John sang a waltz song 'Love Is Woman's own Dominion', a romanza 'Love Laughs at Locksmiths' and the rather more frivolous 'I'm such a pretty Girl' while Coffin had a traditional barcarolle and an equally traditional Drinking Song which proved to be the best received number in the show. The two also combined with Henry Bracy (Ascanio), Edith Brandon (Stella) and J. L. Shine (Baron) in a conspirators' chorus:

I've heard that the way to elope (elope)
Is to buy you a ladder of rope (of rope)
By which to descend
With hooks at the end
To catch on the balcony's cope (ny's cope)

Miss Brandon played the rather aggravatingly arch ballad-singer in the popular style and Bracy the limp and lovelorn tenor. The comedy fell to the representatives of the Doge, the forgetful Baron and his fearsome wife (Susie Vaughan). The Doge, christened burlesque-fashion as Talkativo Grandolmanio, was played by Henry Clifford who used the role (which was written entirely in blank verse) to give an imitation of the celebrated barnstorming tragedian Barry Sullivan and to take some sideswipes at Mr Gladstone and his government. With his Council of Ten he sang:

I'm head of a Party united and hearty,
A cabinet crass I combine
From Radical piggy and fossilized Whiggy
Who've only one will and that's mine!
Though hare-brained my chatter, the hours I can patter
You'll reckon by no horloge,
Verbosely sophistic and all egotistic
I am such a deuce of a Doge!

And these are my Council of Ten
All truly remarkable Men!

TEN: General grandifico
Tartar terrifico
Person pacifico
Speaker somnifico
M. D. morbifico
Bard beatifico
Painter prolifico
Lawyer lucifico
Sage scientifico
Quite the magnifico
We are the council of ten.

Shine had a good deal of solo fooling. He detailed the problems of a forgetful Baron in a patter song:

To your welcome unaffected, so entirely unexpected,
I'd a little peroration in reply
But my mind it has deserted and has left me disconcerted
All stranded for a sentence high and dry.
I must own the little failing of a memory unavailing
That lands me in a mess whene'er I speak,
And for saying what I wouldn't to the people that I shouldn't
I've a faculty that's probably unique.

His other principal number, somewhat surprisingly for a show set in Venice, was a coster number:

There once was a gay young coster bloke,
There once was a belted Earl,
Who both, at an inauspicious stroke,
Got spoons on the self-same girl;
The Earl (as a peer) of course was bad
While never a blemish the coster had
And the girl was a downright raving Rad
With notions all a-whirl.

Sing Eastward-ho! Ahoy!
Whitechapel is all my joy!
Sing tripe and trotters and oyster-shell grotters
Fried fish and corduroy! Wey-ho!

Fullerton's music, which was light and pretty and in a vein which followed his classical training, was less easy in this blatantly music-hall atmosphere. There was also a great deal of it, although not as much as the young composer had intended. Director Richard

Barker noticed Fullerton entering the theatre one day with a huge pile of freshly copied music – 'the opening to Act 2, it cost £16 to have it copied'. Barker would have none of it. 'I want eight bars and the curtain up'. And £16 worth of copying retired to a bottom drawer there to join the other excesses of inexperience.

The Lady of the Locket presented Barker with a mammoth staging task and, after protracted rehearsals, he took the unprecedented step of staging six 'previews' to test reaction. These previews were regular performances but they were not advertised. Anyone who was passing and who wished to pay for his seat could come in and watch as Barker put the final touches to his inordinately ambitious show. The immediate reaction to *The Lady of the Locket* was not particularly favourable, but one member of the production team scored an undeniable hit. Percy Anderson's costume designs caused a sensation both with the public and the critics. Anderson had taken full advantage of the Venetian setting and the extensive production budget and the stage was filled with noblemen and grand ladies swathed in individually designed gowns of crimson velvet. But he also introduced one notable innovation. Stage costume to that date had almost invariably consisted of jolly combinations of the brightest of primary colours. Anderson introduced whole sets of designs in delicate and muted shades to enormous effect. He also succeeded, after something of a battle with Barker, in having the unsightly 'trunks' modestly worn by female performers in tights outlawed. Not even the most proper complained.

The Times acclaimed 'a brilliant piece of stage pageantry' and *The Stage* affirmed:

> . . it is seldom that so rich a spectacle is presented on the stage . . . if rich and gorgeous dresses will suffice to make the success of a piece there can be no question that *The Lady of the Locket* will attract all London for many weeks to come.

And, in spite of otherwise indifferent notices, that is precisely what happened. The town came to see the wonderful stage pictures and to hear the new and handsome young baritone whose name had gone quickly round London. Before long the role of Cosmo was duly expanded and the gilded youth of Venice were exhorted in a heroic baritone: 'St George for Merrie England! Charge!' If the effect was even more incongruous than that of Shine kicking up his heels and singing 'Fried fish and corduroy', no-one seemed to mind. The divisions between comic opera, extravaganza and the music halls were steadily breaking down. *The Lady of the Locket* remained at the Empire for four and a half months and only a particularly hot July forced Hollingshead finally to close down when audiences became too thin to give him any chance of pushing the show into the black. The whole production was shunted down to Shoreditch for one last week and then laid to rest.

A few days after its opening *The Lady of the Locket* was presented with a staunch rival for public favour when Carte opened the newest Gilbert and Sullivan work, *The Mikado*, at the Savoy. As usual, rumours about the pair's next work had begun almost as soon as its predecessor had been staged. On this occasion the most persistent tale mongered by the paragraph writers was that Gilbert intended to abandon his own particular style and revert to the old-fashioned sentimentality of Alfred Bunn and the light operas of Balfe and Wallace. When the truth became known it engendered considerable interest. The craze for 'all one sees that's Japanese' was increasing rapidly at the time. The Japanese Gardens at Knightsbridge, staffed by genuine Japanese with 'a cup of tea sixpence,' had been a great success and the fashion which would engulf British middle-class tastes for half a century had firmly taken root. Gilbert was right in there with that fashion.

In an article written for the *New York Tribune* (August 1885) he claimed that the idea for a Japanese piece had come to him when a Japanese sword fell from the wall in his home. Having decided on his subject he then created his characters around the members of his resident company at the Savoy, trying, as he explained, to give each a suitable character which was a little different from those they had played before. The idea of the 'Three Little Maids'–three Japanese schoolgirls–sprang from the fact that the Savoy's three young principal ladies, Leonora Braham, Jessie Bond and Sybil Grey, were rather short. Had one of them been tall the whole concept of the piece might have been different. The part of of Ko-Ko, the comical Lord High Executioner of Titipu, was built around George Grossmith and the large and haughty Pooh-Bah, The Lord High Everything Else, for Barrington, while Richard Temple found himself in the unexpected position of playing the title role. The principal line-up was completed by Durward Lely as a disguised Japanese prince and Rosina Brandram as the most wonderfully dragonistic of all Gilbert's 'heavy' women to date. This time the basic story was not taken from the *Bab Ballads* or any other earlier work. It was an original plot but one which, in spite of its unusual setting, owed more than a little to the world of The Gallery of Illustration.

Nanki-Poo, son of the Mikado of Japan, has fled from court to avoid being wed to an elderly person named Katisha. He meets Yum-Yum, an ingenuous Japanese maiden, and they fall in love, but she is engaged to the local Lord High Executioner. In despair, Nanki-Poo is ready to hang himself, but Ko-Ko has difficulties–it is so long since he executed anyone that his position is to be abolished. Nanki-Poo volunteers to be his victim if he can marry Yum-Yum and enjoy one month of happiness first. When it comes to the point, however, Ko-Ko cannot carry out his duty so the execution is faked and the lovers hurry off. But the Mikado himself arrives and Nanki-Poo's real identity is uncovered leaving Ko-Ko in a frightful spot. The young man must come back to life, but to make it safe for him to do so the wretched Ko-Ko finds himself obliged to wed the horrible Katisha. Then and only then all can end happily.

If the elements were variations on familiar themes, the setting and the amusing characterisations which Gilbert invented served to lift *The Mikado* far above the normal run of libretti. His book and his lyrics produced phrases and songs which became more widely known than those from virtually any other musical piece. To this success Sullivan's contribution was equally notable. The return to a more light-hearted style after the grandeur of *Princess Ida* showed that the composer's ability was as fluent and as characteristic as it was enduring. His melodies for Yum-Yum's song 'The Moon and I' and for Katisha's 'Hearts do not Break' are among his most beautiful lyric compositions. In the show they provided two strangely contrasting moments. The artless Yum-Yum, preparing for her wedding, compares her state to that of the sun and the moon:

The sun, whose rays are all ablaze
With ever-living glory,
Does not deny his majesty–
He scorns to tell a story!
He don't exclaim, 'I blush for shame,
So kindly be indulgent',
But, fierce and bold, in fiery gold,
He glories all effulgent!

I mean to rule the earth, as he the sky–
We really know our worth, the sun and I!

while the bloodthirsty 'heavy' dame turns almost incongruously poetic to bewail the loss of her Nanki Poo:

Hearts do not break!
They sting and ache
For old love's sake,
But do not die,
Though with each breath
They long for death
As witnesseth
The living I!

But there were more and even greater hits in *The Mikado*. George Grossmith, in spite of a disastrously nervy first night performance, was soon scoring hugely with his patter song, 'I've Got a little List':

As some day it may happen that a victim must be found,
I've got a little list, I've got a little list,
Of society offenders who might well be underground,
And who never would be missed, they never would be missed!

He then went on to detail some of the 'offenders'. Gilbert's lyric was highly amusing and could and still does stand without elaboration, but Grossmith's experience as a drawing-room entertainer had fitted him well in the matter of instant impressions and as the song finished its list:

And apologetic statesmen of a compromising kind
Such as What-d'ye-call-him, Thingummy jig and likewise Never-mind,
And 'St-'st-'st and What's-his-name and also You-know-who
The task of filling up the blanks I'd rather leave to you

he left the audience in little doubt as to who was meant, and the number went down wonderfully. Equally successful was Richard Temple's solo as the Mikado – not the huge, impressive personage so often played since in the role but with a 'senile grin and a waddling walk . . . extremely comic' as he sang:

A more humane Mikado never did in Japan exist,
To nobody second, I'm certainly reckoned a true philanthropist.
It is my very humane endeavour to make, to some extent,
Each evil liver a running river of harmless merriment.
My object all sublime I shall achieve in time –
To let the punishment fit the crime –
And make each prisoner pent unwillingly represent
A source of innocent merriment . .

This song barely survived to the opening night. At a late stage in rehearsals Gilbert decided it was not 'going' and decreed that it should be cut out. He was only persuaded by a mass delegation of the chorus to reinstate it. Its reception on the opening night and every night thereafter proved he was right to be persuaded. It was Temple's biggest success in all his long career at the Savoy. Nanki-Poo's 'A wandering Minstrel', Ko-Ko's 'Tit Willow', the 'Three little Maids' from their ladies' seminary, 'The Flowers that Bloom in the Spring' and the by now traditional unaccompanied part song 'Brightly Dawns our Wedding Day' also brought the house down. Never had there been a score quite so full of outstanding numbers.

The vast success of the opening night did not prevent Gilbert and Sullivan from considerable post-production polishing. On the Sunday following the opening a rehearsal was called and some cuts were made in the dialogue. Both the 'Little List' and 'The Moon and I' were moved to more effective places in the show with consequent alterations to the surrounding scenes. In this final form *The Mikado* held the stage at the Savoy for nearly two years (672 performances) and set a new record for a British musical with the longest run ever achieved by any of Gilbert and Sullivan's pieces anywhere in the world.[1]

Although the London production had gone as smoothly and successfully as could have been wished, the American scene was to prove rather more eventful. John Stetson had already taken up the American rights to the piece when, to general surprise, the libretto and score were published in the United States making them, by the law then existing, public domain. Promoters with an eye to a quick profit started arranging *Mikado* companies. One of these was John Duff of the Standard Theatre who had tried to buy the rights in the original auction, but who had baulked at Carte's demand for 60% of the gross with a guarantee of only $500 per week for Duff. The first to get into production was Sydney Rosenfeld who brought out his version in Chicago prior to bringing it to the Union Square Theatre. Injunctions flew and Rosenfeld found himself banned from presenting *The Mikado* until the case could be fully heard. Undeterred, he technically sub-let the theatre to his stage manager and opened on Broadway on 20 July with a very weak show. But the following day he and his manager fled from New York pursued by warrants for their arrest and Broadway's first *Mikado* shut after one performance. Rosenfeld ended up in Ludlow Street jail, but his plight did not prevent productions of the show appearing all over the country. Only two other managers were brave enough to tempt fate on Broadway, the first being Henry Miner, the proprietor of the People's Theatre. Under a milder judgement than Rosenfeld received he lodged a $7500 bond and 'legally' brought out *The Mikado* at the Third Avenue Theatre. On its own this production would not have stirred Carte into action. His audiences would not go down to the East Side for a second-rate version of *The Mikado*. But John Duff and the Standard Theatre was something else, and it soon became evident that Duff was about to move. It is said that Carte discovered Duff's agents in London trying to buy Japanese costumes to imitate those at the Savoy. His reply was to buy up every available kimono and obi in town and to set to work on plans to outwit the American.

Carte had not planned to produce *The Mikado* in New York until October. Duff was heading for an August opening date and this gave Carte a problem, for any efforts he might make to prepare a New York company in London would be quickly spotted and reported to Duff who would be able to launch his show while the London company was on the high seas between England and America. So telling no-one, not even the cast, Carte put into rehearsal what was ostensibly a provincial touring company. Two days before the 'tour' was due to commence the company was told that they were heading for Liverpool, not to open there but to take the S.S. *Aurania* for America, under assumed names and in the deepest secrecy. The secret was well kept, and twelve days after sailing from Liverpool the D'Oyly Carte Company opened at the Fifth Avenue Theatre on Broadway to the consternation of John Duff whose production was far from ready. *The Mikado* was immediately a hit and soon taking £250–£300 night in spite of the fact that Duff managed to open only five nights later with a production which, while

[1] This record survived almost a century until the 1981 *Pirates of Penzance* revival in New York.

it was never as popular as the 'official' version, was by no means a poor one. It included some fine American singers in its cast and starred J. H. Ryley as Ko-Ko but lasted only three months in New York to a profit which can barely have covered the lawyers' fees Duff had had to expend to establish his right to produce. The Carte/Stetson version ran for 250 performances.

The Mikado followed where the other successful Gilbert and Sullivan shows had led, proving particularly popular in Germany, and also made one or two new geographical conquests for the British musical theatre. Over the years it suffered from frequent strange appearances. It was potted for the music halls, translated and altered around many a star and in 1939 made a dual appearance on Broadway in jazz versions, *The Hot Mikado* and *The Swing Mikado*. After the expiry of the Gilbert and Sullivan copyright a further all-black version, *The Black Mikado*, appeared in London, and Ko-Ko and his fellows became fair game for every kind of transmogrification none of which, however, ever approached the original in popularity. As recently as 1983 it was the subject of three revivals in London and a fourth followed in 1984.

While *The Mikado* and *The Lady of the Locket* continued to run through into the unfavourable summer months, they were briefly joined by revivals of *La Mascotte* and *Boccaccio* at the Comedy and by Kate Santley's production of the only new foreign piece of the year, *François the Radical* (*François-les-bas-bleus*), at the Royalty. This piece had been received well in Paris but failed totally in London. The Avenue had more success with a month's reprise of *Les Manteaux Noirs* which had been touring continuously since the end of its initial West End run, but the only new piece to be shown was *Dr D* for which one Andrew Levey leased the Royalty Theatre from Miss Santley.

Dr D was the work of the well-known amateur actor C. P. Colnaghi with music by the ballad and operetta composer Cotsford Dick who had previously had some short works performed by the German Reeds. *Dr D* was in the same vein as these and used the tried and tested plot elements of the Gallery of Illustration. The story was set in a hydropathic establishment run by Dr von Dosemoffen. In order to inherit a fortune, the widowed doctor must find a new wife. His choice falls on an English spinster staying at his Institute. But the lady has received a letter from a young man which she interprets as an offer of marriage. That it indeed is, but it is intended for the doctor's pretty daughter and not for the ageing Miss Lovering. But that lady will not give up her claim or the letter so the Doctor and his daughters lure her to a fairy well in the garden where, disguised, they succeed in frightening her into dropping the letter. All then ends as intended. Although *Dr D* was an adequately written piece of its kind, it was too much the drawing room operetta to be successful in a theatre even of the reasonably intimate proportions of the Royalty. In spite of the concourse of Gilbert and Sullivan veterans Emily Cross, Ethel Pierson and Jack Leumane and the comic talents of Henry Ashley in the title role, it proved too slight to last longer than a few weeks.

In August an interesting new piece appeared at the Gaiety which had featured burlesque as a prominent part of its programme in recent years. F. C. Burnand, Robert Reece and Henry Byron continued to turn out the kind of work they did best and the theatre's musical director, Meyer Lutz, was kept busy arranging music for such pieces as *Handsome Hernani, Robbing Roy* (1879), *The Corsican Bros. & Co. Ltd, The Forty Thieves, The Half-Crown Diamonds* (1880), *Whittington and his Cat, Aladdin* (1881), *Little Robin Hood, Valentine and Orson* (1882), *Bluebeard, Our Cinderella, Ariel* (1883), *Camaralzaman, Our Helen, Der Freyschütz* (1884) and *Mazeppa* (1885). In August of 1885 John Hollingshead's seventeen-year reign at the Gaiety was coming to an end.

Within months illness was to force him effectively to hand over the reins of the theatre which he had created and even at this stage he was having difficulty in coping with the running of the theatre and its new sister, the Empire. Among those who lent him personal as well as professional support were the writers 'Pot' Stephens and William Yardley.

Stephens was well-known as the librettist of *Billee Taylor* &c., but Yardley was less recognised in dramatic circles. The cousin of George Sims, he was a successful journalist for the *Sporting Times* under the nom-de-plume of 'Bill of the Play' and, according to Sims, was also worthy of renown as 'the first man to make a hundred for his Varsity'. Yardley dabbled with more or less success in most branches of the theatre as a writer, a manager and an amateur performer (as William Wye) until his early death in 1900. Between them these two concocted for Hollingshead the libretto for a burlesque based on Goldsmith's *The Vicar of Wakefield*. The choice of subject was influenced by the highly popular revival of W. G. Wills' *Olivia*, an adaptation from Goldsmith's work, currently being given by Irving and Ellen Terry at the Lyceum.

The Vicar of Wide-Awake-Field was in the traditional burlesque pattern. It was in rhyming couplets liberally spotted with linguistic effects:

MOSES: (enters reading a book and is pelted with turnips by two lads)
It's hot for *Moses* when he takes an *airin'*
They nearly drive me wild these hulking boys
That they disturb my *quiets* what *annoys*
This persecution should not be allowed
Although I'm *bullied*, why should I be *cowed* &c

and the numbers and dances were loosely tacked in without too much thought of relevance. The third act opened with Miss Sylvia Grey (Polly) alone on stage, awaiting her lover:

POLLY: Moses is not about. The air is nipping
I'll warm myself while I wait by skipping . .

This was sufficient cue for the performance of a speciality skipping-rope dance.

The Vicar was professedly a 'respectful perversion' and it did stop short of the wilder grotesqueries of some burlesque. Its chief purpose and chief source of fun lay in the performances of Laura Linden and Arthur Roberts in the leading roles. They burlesqued Miss Terry and Irving rather than Goldsmith, and Miss Linden was outstandingly successful in her imitation. Roberts encapsulated his model brilliantly but briefly before lapsing into his own particular and popular style of comedy. The singing of Violet Cameron, the skipping of Miss Grey, a glee, a hunting song and a chorus of (feminine) Bluecoat boys made up a merry ninety minutes. But *The Vicar Of Wide-Awake-Field* differed in one important respect from its Gaiety predecessors. Yardley and Stephens had secured an original score from Florian Pascal, the composer of *Cymbia*. It was attractive, although it did not wholly fulfil the promise of the earlier piece, but the very fact of its existence as the musical part of a burlesque was noteworthy.

The first night did not go smoothly. The piece had not been rehearsed to a high standard and the orchestra occasionally lost its way amongst Pascal's not very efficient orchestrations. Sylvia Grey won the biggest laugh of the night when she skipped forward for her rope dance, tripped, and sat down hard. But, in spite of the hiccoughs, the audience was generally pleased although there were a few dissenting cries at the final curtain. The critics, too, did not agree amongst themselves. While Miss Linden won unanimous praise the work itself got notices ranging from the satisfactory to the impossible. *The Era* qualified *The Vicar of Wide-Awake-Field* as 'a prolonged yawn . . . the dullest entertainment to be found at any theatre in the metropolis' but the public felt otherwise – they enjoyed Roberts and Miss Linden, the word gymnastics and the pretty scenes, songs and dances, and the show was well-received.

In October the farce *Lord Dundreary's Brother Sam* which comprised the other half of the evening's entertainment was taken off, but *The Vicar of Wide-Awake-Field* held its place and was later joined by a revival of Stephens' most successful piece, *Billee Taylor*. Roberts took up the role of Ben Barnacle and regaled the Gaiety with his interpretation of 'All on account of Eliza'. This double bill of musicals proved a decided success but its progress was halted by contractual problems. Arthur Roberts was under contract to Alexander Henderson who had temporarily released him to play the role of Dr Primrose, but Henderson now wanted Roberts back to play in his own production of the burlesque, *Kenilworth*, and claimed that the comedian had not been released to play Ben Barnacle. The Court of Chancery found that Roberts had anyway been given his freedom only until 11 December so on 11 December, after 121 performances, *The Vicar of Wide-Awake-Field* had to be withdrawn. *Billee Taylor*, still as popular as ever, was transferred to the Empire where it ran as a Christmas attraction with John Shine taking over the role of Ben.

However, the Gaiety was already provided with a replacement. This time Stephens and Yardley came up with a full-length burlesque founded on the old English tale of Jack Sheppard and entitled *Little Jack Sheppard*. It was loosely constructed around the bones of the popular tale and, in typical fashion, designed to produce laughter from character, dialogue, lyrics and business rather than from a sustained parody of the original plot. It stayed true to the older burlesque tradition in that it was in rhymed metre and made a certain use of the obligatory forms of word-twisting and punning, but the lyrics to the songs were quite free from these influences and it was noticeable that long sections of the dialogue looked to a more legitimate kind of humour for their effect. Nevertheless, the pun and its allies still sprouted healthily throughout the play and the pit and the gallery joyfully groaned and howled appreciatively at such passages as:

THAMES: Wild and Uncle Rowland trapped me
They caught this poor *kid napping* and *kidnapped* me
Put me on board a ship in half a crack
WIN: A ship! Oh, what a *blow*
THAMES: it was a *smack*.
When out at sea the crew set me, Thames Darrell
Afloat upon the waves within a barrel
WIN: In hopes the *barrel* would turn out your *bier*
THAMES: But I'm *stout*-hearted and I didn't fear
I nearly died of thirst
WIN: Poor boy, alas!
THAMES: Until I caught a fish
WIN: What sort?
THAMES: A Bass! &c.

and one-liners such as:

KNEE: Although she's *Winnie* she can't say me *nay*!

As was usual at the Gaiety, Meyer Lutz was given charge of the music. There had been adverse comments in some quarters over the use of original and unfamiliar music in *The Vicar of Wide-Awake-Field*. The 'Captious Critic' of the *Sporting & Dramatic News* had commented:

> I think . . . original music somewhat out of place in a burlesque. That which Mr Florian Pascal has composed for *The Vicar of Wide-Awake-Field* is pretty but seems to me of the Mahomet's coffin order. It is not quite strong enough for a comic opera and not quite catching enough for a 'respectful perversion'.

But Lutz did not turn back to the selecting and arranging of popular tunes at which he had hitherto proved so adept. Instead he composed a part of the music himself, allotted part to Pascal and turned to several other prominent composers to complete the score. Only two numbers were arranged by Lutz to existing tunes. The final layout ran:

ACT 1: Opening Chorus (LUTZ)
Yokels' Chorus (CORNEY GRAIN)
Duet: 'If you Take into your Head' (PASCAL)
Solo: (Winifred) 'Winifred Wood' (PASCAL)
Solo: (Thames) 'There once Was a Time' (A. CELLIER)
Duet: 'A Fairy Tale' (HAMILTON CLARKE)
Quintet 'Keep the Ball A-Rolling' (LUTZ)
Chorus & March of Janissaries (PASCAL)
Song: (Wild) 'Jonathan Wild' (ARTHUR CECIL)
Song: (Jack) 'Jack's Alive-O' (LUTZ)
Song: (Blueskin) 'True Blue' (LUTZ)
Duo: 'Ri-fol' (LUTZ)
Quartette arr. LUTZ to the air 'Kissing Bridge' by MICHAEL WATSON
Mayday chorus, Morris dance & Finale (CELLIER)

ACT 2: Opening chorus (HAMILTON CLARKE)
Song: (Jack) 'You mustn't believe all you Hear' (LUTZ)
Duo: 'Think what Might Have Been' (LUTZ)
Song: (Thames) 'The Silver Star' (PASCAL)
Trio: 'Leave the whole Business to Me' (LUTZ)
Old Air: "Botany Bay" arr. LUTZ
Finale: LUTZ

ACT 3: Polyglot Duo (All Nations) (LUTZ)
Farewell (LUTZ)
Wedding Chorus (PASCAL)

The Gaiety gathered together an exceptional cast for *Little Jack Sheppard*. In the title role they had their very own Nellie Farren, the greatest of all burlesque 'boys' and the darling of the Gaiety audiences, and opposite her played David James, the famous actor-manager who had been one of 'Our Boys', as Blueskin and Fred Leslie as Jonathan Wild, the evil thieftaker. Leslie had only been made available for this, his Gaiety début, by the quick collapse of his previous show at the Opera Comique. He was secured for *Little Jack Sheppard* before that show had ended and little more than three weeks later opened as the villain of the piece in the theatre which he was to make his home for the rest of his life.

Pretty, proper Marion Hood was the principal girl with the American soprano, Mathilde Wadman, as the romantic Thames Darrell. Miss Wadman, who had not long since been a chorister, had not yet got used to stardom, and was foolish enough on one occasion to come on before the Gaiety audience with her costume decked out with all her finest jewellery. Nellie Farren said nothing to this example of lèse majesté, but the following night she appeared wearing all *her* diamonds which made poor Miss Wadman's collection look decidedly paltry. 'Tillie' got the message and never again tried to upstage Nellie Farren. Harriet Coveney was Jack's mother, Sylvia Grey was Polly Stanmore and one 'Eva Raines' appeared in the tiny part of 'Marvel'. Miss Raines (otherwise Daisy Evelyn Lyster) came to dubious fame in 1951 when her illegitimate eldest son claimed the right to the inheritance of his father, George Fitzwilliam.

Little Jack Sheppard was more successful than any previous Gaiety production. Nellie Farren and Fred Leslie produced a combined tour de force of comic acting and business. Leslie mixed moments of real menace with grotesque dancing and clowning and reduced the audience to helpless laughter simply by cracking his knuckles as he declared:

And yet all the while
I've a manner and style
Which I flatter myself must please;
The things that I say
Bring Barons to bay
And Duchesses down on their knees.
I was ready and smart
With my hand on my heart
And the agony duly piled;
In the popular craze
Of bygone days
I'm Jonathan Oscar Wild.

Miss Farren effortlessly turned the criminal-hero into a lovable scamp, and was regularly encored for her song:

Jack keeps 'em all alive-o
Jack keeps 'em all alive
If there's fun to be had
Why, I am the lad
Jack keeps 'em all alive o!

and she and Leslie brought down the roof with their irrelevant polyglot duet in which they swapped taunting phrases and imitations of various nationalities. David James, in contrast, played Blueskin fairly straight. His best moments came in the extended 'Botany Bay' song and in a clever set of scenes which showed the escape of Jack and Blueskin from Newgate Jail – up a chimney, through a hole in the wall and across the roofs of London in a welter of moving scenery and special effects. He joined with Misses Hood and Wadman in another of the show's vocal high-spots, the trio 'Leave the whole Business to Me'.

Little Jack Sheppard was a combination of fun and song and dance and spectacle in which the Gaiety crowds found their tastes fully gratified and it was given a tremendous reception. Burlesque had received a new boost from the fresh recipe being used at the Gaiety. Like anything at all innovative, it had its critics. *The Stage* questioned:

> We are not very clear in our minds as to whether the piece is burlesque or comic opera . . . however, burlesque or comic opera be it what you will, *Little Jack Sheppard* is a highly entertaining piece of its class and should restore prosperity to the Gaiety.

Whatever it was, it allowed Hollingshead to pass over the management of his theatre in a most healthy condition. The 155 performances of *Little Jack Sheppard* drew the town in huge numbers and the new manager, George Edwardes, only withdrew it to allow the annual season of French plays with Sarah Bernhardt to take its pre-booked place through the summer. *Little Jack Sheppard* was taken to the Islington Grand as a launching pad for an 18-week tour in which Leslie and Miss Farren took their partnership through all the principal towns before returning to prepare their next Gaiety burlesque.

Little Jack Sheppard went round the world. On Broadway it played three successful months at the Bijou where Nat Goodwin starred as Wild opposite 24-year-old Loie Fuller from Illinois who had not yet invented the serpentine dance which would make a star of her. In Australia Fanny Robina took on the title role for Brough and Boucicault and South Africa saw Jenny Dawson and Mark Kinghorne starring with Windham Guise as Blueskin. While new pieces came and went at the Gaiety, *Little Jack Sheppard* continued to prosper. The comedian J. J. Dallas toured it in 1890 and '91 playing the part of Blueskin, with Jacks including the much-travelled Fanny Robina, Florence Forster, Ada Blanche and Kitty Loftus; Loie Fuller starred in a production at the Elephant & Castle and, finally, in 1894 Edwardes brought the show back to the Gaiety. Following the summer season of French plays the 'Guv'nor' needed an attraction to fill in until his new musical comedy was ready for production and he chose to revive *Little Jack Sheppard*. The piece had proved widely successful without its original stars but it was only nine years since the Gaiety had seen Fred Leslie and Nellie Farren take the town to pieces as Wild and Little Jack. Now he was dead and she a semi-invalid and theatre-goers' memories, typically, had idealised their great performances into even greater ones. Casting the show was not easy.

For his new principal boy Edwardes went to the music-halls and tried to engage an up-and-coming performer called Ada Reeve. Miss Reeve professed herself honoured and turned the job down. Like the whole world, she knew what it would be like to follow Nellie Farren at the Gaiety. Braver – or more foolhardy – was another music hall artist, Jessie Preston of The Preston Sisters. The small role of the barmaid, Kitty, was offered to the other half of the act, Georgina, and Jessie Preston went to the Gaiety as Little Jack Sheppard. For Jonathan Wild Edwardes lighted upon a 22-year-old actor named Seymour Hicks who had had considerable success at the Court Theatre with a revue *Under The Clock*. Hicks' wife, Miss Ellaline Terriss, was engaged to play Marian Hood's old role of Winifred Wood. Of the original cast, only Willie Warde and Frank Wood remained in the roles they had created.

The piece was given everything that a Gaiety production implied but it only served to show quite clearly how very much theatrical tastes and styles had altered in a decade. No amount of topical allusion and up-to-dating could give the rhyming couplet dialogue and antique puns the fresh and natural air of a fin de siècle Gaiety libretto. The old songs were just that – old songs, and the new ones which were interpolated included no particular favourites. Charles Danby's rendering of the 'Botany Bay' song was the vocal success of the evening.

Both Miss Preston and Hicks did their best against insuperable odds, but it was significant that Hicks scored the best applause of the night when he left the Fred Leslie interpretation and lines and came on as an anarchistic loafer with (apropos of nothing at all) a routine built up from 'borrowed' American tramp jokes and a boot dance routine. Unhampered by the ghost of Leslie he was able to give a performance and not an imitation and, above all, a 'modern' flavour to the performance.

The Theatre summed up the prevailing attitude:

> If travesties such as this are to please us nowadays they must have more in common with the clever, quaint conceits of Mr Gilbert and Mr 'Adrian Ross' than with the old-fashioned dreariness of Messrs Yardley and Stephens . .

London no longer had the taste for such fare. But, intentionally or not, George Edwardes had set the stage for a coup d'éclat of modern musical comedy at the Gaiety. The contrast between *Little Jack Sheppard* and his next show, *The Shop Girl*, only served to emphasise the modernity and freshness of the new and comparatively natural style of musical comedy which the Gaiety was by then creating. But in 1885 *Little Jack Sheppard* was very new and very much the thing. It was the first in a line of new burlesques which would fill the Gaiety and other metropolitan and provincial houses for nearly ten years until the virtual pretence of consistent parody was dropped and the songs and dances and jokes were incorporated into a different framework under the brand name 'musical comedy'.

It was October before *Erminie*, the first of Jakobowski's new pieces, put in an appearance. It had been secured by the young actress-manager Violet Melnotte for the Comedy Theatre while the American rights had been picked up, almost before the writing had been completed, by John Duff who was determined not to be cut out as he had been over *The Mikado*. The book of *Erminie* was largely the work of Harry Paulton although he shared the writing credit with Claxson Bellamy. In his usual style Paulton had cobbled together well-tried elements, producing a brisk plot centred around two comic thieves: anglicized versions of Robert Macaire and Jacques Strop shorn of their more sinister and satirical purposes.

As the play opens we learn with Erminie de Pontvert that she is intended for marriage to the son of an old family friend, the Vicomte de Brissac. Erminie, who is in love with her father's secretary, Eugene Marcel, dreads the arrival of her unknown bridegroom. On his way to Château Pontvert the Vicomte is waylaid by two escaped convicts, Ravannes and Cadeau, who take his place and present themselves at the Château as de Brissac and friend, intending to take advantage of staying in the place to rifle its contents. When the real Vicomte turns up, the two denounce him as a thieving imposter. The two rogues have some difficulty keeping up their roles as gentlemen and are caught out just before they can make their coup. The freed Vicomte turns out to be the long-lost lover of Eugene's sister, so the marital problems are satisfactorily solved in a happy ending as the two fake nobleman tiptoe off into the sunset.

The book was at its rollicking best when the two picturesque rogues took over the stage and the story. They were a brave pair – Ravannes (Frank Wyatt) the crafty and classy thief whose plans the clumsy, loose-tongued Cadeau (Harry Paulton) is constantly putting in jeopardy with his East End slang and his catch-phrase assertions 'It's my first offence' and 'I can prove a h-alibi'. One of the show's highlights was a ballroom scene in which Cadeau, supposedly a Baron, delights the amazed company with his 'eccentricities' and attracts the amorous attentions of the elderly Princesse de Gramponneur who sees in him (as in everything) the image of her dear late husband. Cadeau entertains everyone with a good giveaway song 'What the Dicky Birds Say' which the noble assembly find charmingly quaint:

> When brought afore his beakship my evidence to give
> I'm allus in a dreadful state
> For fear I'll have to go to a settlement to live
> A penal one is sure to be my fate.
> Now juries ain't very well up to their job
> They, for fear of confinement all day,

Their verdict agree on by spinning a bob;
At least, so the dicky birds say.

The songs provided many popular pieces. Florence St John scored in four numbers: 'When Love is Young', a dream song 'At Midnight on my Pillow Lying', the ballad 'The sighing Swain' and the lullaby 'Dear Mother, in Dreams I see Her', and Paulton joined with Frank Wyatt in a comical duet 'Downy Jailbirds of a Feather':

We're a philanthropic couple, be it known,
Light-fingered, sticking to whate'er we touch;
In the interest of humanity alone
Of wealth relieving those who have too much.
The sour old gent whose worship vile is dross
We hate to see a-wallowing in tin;
It ain't 'cause gain to us to him is loss,
We eases him 'cause avarice is sin.

Downy jailbirds of a feather
We are shifters, we are lifters,
Working skilfully together
Through the wicked world we roam;
Easing many a mortal burden
Kinder coves we never heard on
But a start you'll take our word on
Charity begins at home!

A light, topical number for Edith Vane as Marie emphasised the way the musical play was going. In a piece set in 17th-century France (a legacy from the opéra-comique) the village maiden sang a pretty and pointed number about 'Woman's Dress':

Yes, though fashion often ranges
We are equal to its changes
Though the waist prevailing's high up
Or the skirt accepted short
Alter bonnet, cap or headdress
Tuck or lace confine, or spread dress
Branching pull back, puff or tie up
And improving quick as thought.

Erminie was given a two week try-out at Birmingham and Brighton before making its London début, a virtually unprecedented exercise[1] but one which ensured that the piece was very much better prepared than most for its metropolitan opening. It met immediately with a favourable reception. *The Stage*'s Birmingham correspondent enthused:

> . . if original, bright and melodious music together with a smartly written and humorous libretto go for anything then Birmingham playgoers witnessed the production of one of the best of modern comic operas on Monday last.

Paulton had supplied himself with his best role to date as the merry robber Cadeau and he and Frank Wyatt as his suave partner literally stole the show with their hilarious antics. The pretty singing of Florence St John and Henry Bracy complemented and

[1] *La Mascotte*, which was given a brief trial at Brighton before London, seems to have been the first example of the out-of-town tryout.

contrasted the comedy nicely and the young manageress, who had cast herself in the secondary role of Cerise, was able to watch her show shape up into what seemed like a certain success. Some alterations were nevertheless made on the road into London and two numbers were withdrawn from the rather protracted final part of the second act – the duet 'True Love' and the artificially constructed sextet 'O, Lady Moon'.

After two weeks of polishing in performance, *Erminie* opened at the Comedy Theatre and was warmly received. Both the libretto and the score received high praise and Edward Jakobowski, in only his second full-length show, found himself lionised. The show had been sumptuously staged with its scenic effects enhanced by the use of a revolving stage, a device previously limited to the melodrama theatres, and the audience watched in delight as Spong and Callcott's gorgeous ballroom set revolved into a corridor scene before their eyes. Violet Melnotte's venture into the musical world had caught the public fancy in every possible way. *Erminie* was a hit.

The Era tried to keep its success in perspective:

> *Erminie* is a sketchy opéra-comique and very tastefully is the sketch executed, finished and framed. The difficulty of finding a subject suitable for the libretto of a comic opera is extremely great, the difficulty of finding a composer, English by either blood or residence, who can produce music at all near the standard demanded by a London audience is still greater. By comparison, then, with the work of their British 'compeers' (always excepting, of course, that 'speciality' the Gilbert and Sullivan opera) the result of the labours of Messrs Claxson Bellamy and Harry Paulton and Mr Edward Jakobowski deserves a better fate than to be damned with faint praise. Such an effort deserves to be encouraged in every possible way.

It was encouraged in the best of all possible ways. The public came numerous and appreciative to the Comedy Theatre for 154 nights. The close of its season in London was, however, only the beginning of an amazingly vigorous career for *Erminie*. Its provincial popularity was enormous. The first touring company sent out by Miss Melnotte began with a six weeks' Christmas season at the Princess Theatre in Edinburgh where, in spite of the concurrence of three pantomimes, it proved the hit of the season. From there it toured for 65 weeks to such a reception that in August it was found necessary to put out a second company. This company consisted largely of the original cast who had just taken part in a brief West End revival, and toured only the Number One dates. When this company disbanded, yet another was formed, and then another. All England wanted to see *Erminie*, and not once but several times as multiple return dates at many provincial theatres proved.

Success in Britain was no guarantee of success elsewhere and America's judgements frequently disagreed with those of the London public, but in the case of *Erminie* London's verdict was confirmed with acclaim in New York. John Duff had insufficient faith, for he disposed of the rights and the piece was ultimately produced by Rudolph Aronson at the Casino Theatre with Francis Wilson in the role of Cadeaux (the 'x' seems to have been added as a pronunciation aid). Wilson claims in his 'Life of Himself' that Nat Goodwin purchased the rights of *Erminie* but allowed them to lapse and that they were eventually taken up by Aronson (who had originally refused to buy the show outright for $500) on a rental basis which ultimately earned the British owners $120,000 in fees. However, since Wilson's biography is littered with factual errors, with the truth often turned about to make either a good story or for the greater glory of Wilson, his version of the tale must be approached with care.

Harry Paulton crossed the Atlantic to direct Wilson, W. S. Daboll (Ravannes) and Pauline Hall (Erminie) and the Casino company through what seem to have been rocky rehearsals, but when the night came all was in order and the reaction of the public and the press was unequivocal:

> *Erminie* is the comic opera hit of the season. It will run till the snow flies. (*Daily News*)
>
> A long spell of popularity can safely be predicted (*Commercial Advertiser*)
>
> An exceptionally good libretto (*N.Y. Times*)
>
> *Erminie* is destined to run long and successfully (*Evening Telegram*)
>
> An immediate and unequivocal success . . . there is nothing but praise for *Erminie*; it is a pretty operetta most admirably presented. (*World*)
>
> The Casino made the most pronounced success of its successful career. It is a shout of laughter from beginning to end. (*Morning Journal*)

And they were right. Not only did *Erminie* run till the snow had flown, but until next year's had been and gone as well, giving place only briefly to Violet Cameron's production of *The Commodore*. The Casino public gave the Offenbach piece short shrift and within four weeks *Erminie* was safely reinstalled in 'her' theatre. The ballroom scene proved a triumph and its setting – a fairytale ballroom all painted in shades of pink – became famous; 'Downy Jailbirds' was a huge success and the little lullaby 'Dear Mother, in Dreams I see Her' which had been quietly appreciated in London became all the rage – the hit song of the year and of a good many years to follow:

> Dear mother, in dreams I see her
> With lov'd face sweet and calm,
> And hear her voice
> With love rejoice
> When nestling on her arm.
> I think how she softly press'd me,
> Of the tears in each glistening eye
> As her watch she'd keep
> When she rock'd to sleep
> Her child with this lullaby.
> Bye, bye, drowsiness o'ertaking,
> Pretty little eyelids sleep.
> Bye, bye, watching till thou'rt waking,
> Darling, be thy slumber deep.

On November 6, 1887 the show reached its 500th performance and its record-breaking run was only interrupted in December when its place was taken by a production of Lecocq's *Madelon*. That was soon swept away and a month later *Erminie* was back yet again to run out another five months bringing its metropolitan total to 648 performances and reinforcing the now well-established fame of its principal performers. Wilson and Miss Hall remained in the star roles as *Erminie* continued on through Boston and Philadelphia, until the show which had originally only been intended as a stop-gap at the Casino counted 1256 consecutive performances to its name and had established itself as the favourite piece of a generation of playgoers.

A whole body of mythology built up around *Erminie* and its production, much of it perpetuated by Francis Wilson. Jakobowski was supposed to have written the score for another show and to have swapped it for the 'original' *Erminie* music because of Violet Melnotte's preference for the score of 'the other piece'; 'Downy Jailbirds' was said to have been added for Wilson in America and to have been based on a melody from Planquette's *Voltigeurs de la 32ème* (it is actually named in the original British reviews and appears in the printed English score of 1885); the scenery and the costumes were pieced together from old Aronson shows (yet the pink ballroom was a sensation) and Harry Paulton had declared that the production would be a disaster because he could not prevent 'the many interpellations and the antics of some of the people on the stage, Francis Wilson's in particular. . ' and so forth. Doubtless there was some truth in some of the tales which were 'improved' in the telling, but the truth is buried now in the morass of fictions. *Erminie* returned to Broadway again and again and Francis Wilson made the role of Cadeaux a recurring feature of his career playing in almost every revival right up to the final one at the Park Theatre in 1921.

The composer Jakobowksi, born in London of Polish-Austrian parentage, educated in Vienna and until recently living in Paris, found himself the writer of the biggest hit show in American theatrical history and both he and Paulton became the objects of awed admiration as 'the writers of *Erminie*'. But in spite of frequent visits to America both writers continued, for the meanwhile, to base themselves in Britain and to carry on their careers in the British theatre. Jakobowski's musical technique was solidly based in the European tradition. He had won prizes for harmony and composition at the Vienna Conservatoire and his first writing had been done with the French theatre in mind but he had been sufficiently long back in England to know what 'went' there, and the mixture of light romantic and frankly popular which he allied to the robust and unaffected libretto and lyrics of *Erminie* proved to be just right for both American and English tastes. His easy melodies and the natural dialogue of Paulton and Bellamy were a step away from the rather 'stiff-necked' element in comic opera, and *Erminie*'s effective balance between the comic and the romantic was a model of degree. Coming as it did in the same year as *The Mikado* and *Little Jack Sheppard* it helped establish the British musical firmly and finally in the forefront of the light musical theatre, as it appeared around the world from Australia to Amsterdam and Canada to Vienna.

Amongst these important successes there was still room for failures. November brought one of the most grandiose. The actress Agnes Consuelo announced that she and F. J. Harris were to lease the Opera Comique to present a grand spectacular romantic opera entitled *Fay o'Fire* featuring Mlle Agnes de la Porte from the Leipzig Stadt Theater and a superior cast including Fred Leslie, Henry Walsham, Fred Wood, Marion Grahame and Miss Consuelo herself. As an advertisement, the lyric of the title song was published in advance:

> Through lightning and storm
> In fair woman's form
> On the thunderborne flashes I ride;
> Through hail and through rain
> I dash on again
> And the wings of the wind I bestride.
>
> All men crouch in fear
> When they think I am near
> When they see me, they stay and admire
> They're bound in my chain
> And they serve in my train
> In the train of the Fay o'Fire!

It sounded scarcely like the stuff of musical comedy – more a libretto for a poor man's Weber or Wagner.

The author of this piece was Henry Herman who some eleven years previously had been one of the authors of the disastrous *Vert-Vert*. 'Daddy' Herman was a 'character'. Alsatian by birth, he had been educated to the army and managed to get himself mixed up in the American Civil War. Characteristically, he was on the Confederate side. Equally characteristically he survived, although with the loss of an eye. He made his way to England and into the theatre world, becoming famous overnight when he dreamed up the outline of *The Silver King* for Wilson Barrett. Henry Arthur Jones wrote the play and Barrett ran it for 289 performances at the Princess's Theatre prefatory to a long touring life. The following year Herman supplied the skeleton for W. G. Wills' *Claudian* with which Barrett scored another great success. On this occasion he determined to write a whole play by himself. Edward Jones, musical director at the Princess's Theatre, composed the score and the author advertised the completed work for sale. Miss Consuelo and Harris paid the asking price and took the Opera Comique to stage *Fay o'Fire*.

The plot centred on the title character, a vicious immortal witch. In the year 1385 she falls in love with the young Egobart, chief of a band of minstrels and morris dancers. Egobart, in his turn, is beloved by the Lady Blanche and returns her love. But when he plights his undying troth to her he discovers that it is the disguised witch to whom he has made his eternal vows and Egobart is carried off to her underground lair. In the second act the action has moved on a full five hundred years. The fairy allows Egobart to revisit earth and he finds and marries the direct descendant of his Blanche. The spell of the Fay is broken and she returns to the bowels of the earth alone.

The Tannhauser-like story was told in heavy, quasi-poetic dialogue which fitted poorly with the intentions and pretensions of the composer and the production. The audiences found no fun in Herman's heavy-handed humour and no charm in his 'poetry'. There were howls of disapproval on the first night and small audiences for the fifteen others which preceded its closure. But, although *Fay o'Fire* was an utter failure, it did serve to introduce to the West End public a rising new star in the jeune première role of Lady Blanche. The 19-year-old Marie Tempest (née Etherington) created a great impression with her strong, well-trained voice and her warm acting performance. When *Fay o'Fire* collapsed she was speedily snapped up by Violet Melnotte to succeed Florence St John as Erminie and one of the most distinguished careers of the West End theatre had begun.

Several new works appeared during the year in the provinces. The Prince's Theatre, Manchester, far from its glorious superiority of former years, produced a work by a local parliamentary candidate, C. H. Wharton and a local composer, Alfred Taylor. It was called *The Bachelors* and was set in a wealthy bachelors' club. The members all swear to eschew marriage on pain of ostracism. But the Steward of the club wants his daughter to 'catch' one of them which she eventually does and all the members decide to wed, leaving only their President to remain single (doubtless with a poppy or a lily). It was a fairly dull affair enlivened only by a chorus of landladies describing how they cheat their bachelor boarders.

Of much more interest and of longer duration were two pieces which appeared on the touring circuit in August. Both were of a very different character to the comic opera kind of work currently popular in London. The first was *Chirruper's Fortune* put on the road by Kate Santley and starring her in the title role of Lucy Chirruper, a foundling servant who is finally revealed to be an heiress. The libretto was written by Arthur Law and was an oversized example of his German Reed pieces: thoroughly English, thoroughly proper and including the usual plot and character elements typical of the St

George's Hall in its better days. It was designed largely to show off the talents of the fair manageress who, nevertheless, had the wisdom to surround herself with a strong supporting cast including Mr and Mrs Lionel Rignold (Marie Daltra). *Chirruper's Fortune* had a conglomerate score. Florian Pascal, George Grossmith, Arthur Caldicott, Georges Jacobi and Robert Reece all contributed numbers to Miss Santley's requirements, and others were added to the mobile score as the tour progressed. The piece had been announced for London but, in spite of a reasonably successful tour of major dates, Miss Santley decided against bringing it in.

The other August piece did eventually reach town. *Jack-in-the-Box* was a curious mixture of melodrama, music and variety. Once again it was a show conceived to fit the talents of its manager-star, on this occasion Fannie Leslie, who took the 'pants' title-role in a melodramatic tale set in a circus and littered with skulduggery and pathos. At regular intervals the story was broken into to allow Miss Leslie (and occasionally someone else) to perform a song and/or dance. The whole seemed a rather unsophisticated piece to have come from such august writers as George Sims and the celebrated critic Clement Scott, but they had judged the taste of the British provincial audience to a nicety and *Jack-in-the-Box* was an enormous success. After a sixteen-week tour the show was suspended to permit the fulfillment of Christmas obligations, but it was restaged as soon as possible the following year for a further sixteen weeks in the spring. In August it was sent out yet again and in February of 1887 it arrived at London's Strand Theatre. The taste of the town was not entirely in accord with that of the country, and *The Era* commented sourly that 'the piece varies alternately between the melodramatic absurdities of the old Surrey Theatre and the entertainment at a modern music hall' and that 'Miss Leslie sings, dances, turns catherine wheels until she is tired then comes a brief interval during which a scrap of story is permitted to get itself told' and concluded that 'it would be simple to dispense with the story altogether'. Londoners did not feel quite so supercilious about the show for it played the Strand for three full months before returning to the provinces.

Where *Fay o'Fire* had harboured one budding star in its cast, *Jack-in-the-Box* in its wanderings had two. In the original touring company a small girl made her first appearance on the stage as the Italian boy, Rocco, and *The Era*'s Brighton critic noted on the first night that 'a word of praise is due to little Ada Reeve for her clever dances in the fair scene'. 'Clever' was a word among many more laudatory which would be used over the next decades to describe Ada Reeve in her remarkable career as one of the musical theatre's brightest stars. For the London production Fannie Leslie engaged a young leading man to play the role of Roy Carleton. After a few weeks of the run, however, she agreed to release him when he was offered the jeune premier roles with Forbes Robertson's company – an opportunity which set Lewis Waller on the road to stardom as one of the great actor-managers and matinée idols of his period.

Jack-in-the-Box had a long career and a far-flung one. Carrie Swain took on Miss Leslie's role for the American production and it was successfully played as far afield as Australia while in England it remained on the touring circuits as late as 1897 with Jennie Lee in the star role.

The success of *The Mikado* did not lead to a rush of Oriental shows, but one did appear within six weeks at Toole's Theatre in the repertoire of Johnny Toole. *The Great Taykin* was a medium length piece from Arthur Law with music by the Savoy's Ko-Ko, George Grossmith. It was designed as a vehicle for Toole who starred as a vaguely hen-pecked husband who is discovered by his wife while secretly meeting an ingenuous young lady. To escape detection he disguises himself as a conjurer, The

Great Taykin, and wins redemption by catching his wife flirting with the young lady's guardian. Its Japanese element came from its setting – an English Japanese Tea Garden, along the lines of the one in Knightsbridge, staffed by pretty Japanese East Enders. One of the show's features was a ten-minute conjuring display by a Madame Okita but its principal attractions were Toole and the pretty scenery and girls. It was maintained on the bill through several programme changes and when the London season ended it was played in repertoire on Toole's tour.

A little later another Japanese extravaganza came to town when Willie Edouin brought *The Japs*, which he had been touring, to the Novelty Theatre. The piece existed chiefly to give Edouin, Alice Atherton and Lionel Brough the chance to show off their variegated talents and included the odd song by Meyer Lutz. Half a dozen choruses and a couple of concerted finales completed the musical part. Lionel Brough played an Anglophile Japanese usurper who has introduced into his fief everything English from Grenadier Guards to a London lamp-post, not to mention rates and taxes. There was a revolt and a threatened hari-kiri, a joust and a dénoument featuring an elderly lady who admits that she mixed two babies up. . . . *The Japs* had an inauspicious London opening when the pit and the gallery decided they were not getting their money's worth and started to sing music hall songs and ridicule the actors. The critics were barely kinder – *The Times* marked it as 'a dreary and indeed incomprehensible performance' – but *The Japs* and its stars kept the Novelty Theatre open for two and a half months.

The year's one-act pieces produced nothing new of note. Walter Slaughter's *The Casting Vote* had a brief run at the Prince's but the new German Reed pieces were not up to the standard of their predecessors in spite of the contributions of such proven writers as 'Pot' Stephens, Yardley, Caldicott and Hamilton Clarke.

1885

0056 **THE LADY OF THE LOCKET** A spectacular comic opera in three acts by Henry Hamilton. Music by William Fullerton. Produced at the Empire Theatre under the management of John Hollingshead and J. L. Shine 11 March, 1885 for a run of 120 performances closing 25 July, 1885. Subsequently played at the Standard Theatre, Shoreditch for one week 27 July–1 August, 1885.

Oblivio, Baron di Bombazina . . . . J. L. Shine
Talkativo Grandolmanio, the Doge . . . . H. M. Clifford
Cosmo . . . . C. Hayden Coffin
Ascanio . . . . Henry Bracy/Arthur Mavius
Pietro . . . . Harry Eversfield/Arthur Mavius/Arthur H. Cree
Caesario . . . . Kate Bellingham (Miss Gaynor)/Miss Gordon
Generalissimo Solo Capabili . . . . Mr Risson
Hugo/Gondolier . . . . Charles Ryley
Alastro . . . . Arthur H. Cree/Mr Harcourt
Furioso della Fumo . . . . Mr White
Umbela Pologi . . . . Mr Pink
Kilamani Patienzo . . . . Mr Cattell/Mr Redmond/Mr Walker
Potboilerio Palletto . . . . Tom A. Shale
Sonoro dell'Adjectiva . . . . Mr Percy
Imbroglio Billocosti . . . . Mr Barry
Infinitudo di Twaddleri . . . . Mr Lewis/Mr Jackson/Avalon Collard
Evolutio Protoplasmi . . . . Mr Gregory/Mr Haslam
Ano Bel d'Uffa . . . . Mr Leith
Giovanni . . . . S. Perceval
Cantancarina, Baroness di Bombazina . . Susie Vaughan
Francesca di Bombazina . . . . Florence St John (Kate Bellingham)/Violet Cameron
Stella . . . . Edith Brandon/Kate Bellingham
The Doge's Ethiopian . . . . E. Kirton
Marca . . . . Lesley Bell
Lola . . . . Nellie Lisle/Miss St George/E. Wynne/Miss Rose
Baptista . . . . Agnes Barnett/Miss Gordon/Miss Nelley
Figlia Vecchia . . . . Florence Dawnay
Exquisito . . . . Herbert George

with Misses Mowbray, Gower, Jecks, E. Wilson, Frampton, A. Hill, Leigh, Gaynor, St George, E. Hill, Myln, Solomon, Osman, Villers, Pew, Clive, Lacy, Rowe, Nola, Gordon, Wallis, Richards, L. Wilson, L. Thompson, Rydell, Glen, F. Thompson, McNeil, Conway, Askey, Petipre; Messrs Ellis, Shields, Walker, Rix, Brooks, Edgar.

Dancers: Mlle Sismondi, Misses Brien/Brittu, Voight, Sgra Bessone, Sgra Zauli, Mlle Nita.

Dir: Richard Barker and J. L. Shine; md: A. Dami (J. M. Glover); ch: Paul Valentine; sc: Mr Spong; cos: Percy Anderson & M. Barthe

57 **THE MIKADO** a comic opera in two acts by W. S. Gilbert. Music by Arthur Sullivan. Produced at the Savoy Theatre under the management of Richard D'Oyly Carte 14 March, 1885 for a run of 672 performances closing on 19 January, 1887.

The Mikado of Japan	Richard Temple
Nanki-Poo	Durward Lely (Courtice Pounds)
Ko-Ko	George Grossmith (Eric Lewis)
Pooh-Bah	Rutland Barrington/Frederick Bovill/S. Price
Pish-Tush	Frederick Bovill/Herbert Marchmont/S. Price
Yum-Yum	Leonora Braham/Josephine Findlay
Pitti-Sing	Jessie Bond/Lillian Carr/Annie Cole/Sybil Grey
Peep-Bo	Sybil Grey/
Katisha	Rosina Brandram (Annie Bernard)/Ada Rose
add Go To	Rudolph Lewis/Richard Cummings

Dir: W. S. Gilbert; md: François Cellier; ch: John D'Auban; sc: Hawes Craven; cos: Wilhelm and Liberty's

Produced in the United States at the Museum, Chicago under the management of Sydney Rosenfeld 6 July, 1885 and subsequently at the Union Square Theatre 20 July, 1885 for one performance.
J. W. Herbert (MIK), A. Montegriffo (NP), Roland Reed (KK), Herbert Archer (PB), George H. Broderick (PT), Alice Harrison (YY), Belle Archer (PS), Lizzie Quigley (PB), Emma Mabella Baker (KAT)

Produced at Henry Miner's People's Theatre 10 August, 1885 under the management of Henry Miner and subsequently moved 17 August, 1885 to the Union Square Theatre New York for two weeks to 29 August.
J. W. Herbert (MIK), A. Montegriffo (NP), Roland Reed (KK), Herbert Archer (PB), George H. Broderick (PT), Alice Harrison (YY), Belle Archer (PS), Miss Mollie (PB), Emma Mabella Baker (KAT)

Produced at the Fifth Avenue Theatre, New York, under the management of Richard D'Oyly Carte 19 August, 1885. Transferred to the Standard Theatre 1 February, 1886 to 27 February. Transferred to the Fifth Avenue Theatre 1 March. Closed 17 April, 1886 after a total of 250 performances.
F. Federici (MIK), Courtice Pounds (NP), George Thorne (KK), Fred Billington (PB), Charles Richards/G. Byron Browne (PT), R. H. Edgar (GT), Geraldine Ulmar (YY), Kate Forster (PS), Geraldine St Maur (PB), Elsie Cameron (KAT). Md: P. W. Halton; sc: Harley Merry, H. L. Reed

Produced at the Standard Theatre, New York, under the management of J. C. Duff 20 August, 1885.
William H. Hamilton (MIK), Harry S. Hilliard (NP), J. H. Ryley (KK), Thomas Whiffen (PB), Alonzo Stoddard (PT), Verona Jarbeau (YY), Sallie Williams (PS), Carrie Tutein (PB), Zelda Seguin (KAT). Md: Anthony Reiff

Produced at the Carltheater, Vienna, as *Der Mikado (Ein Tag in Titipu)* 1 September, 1886.

Produced at the Fifth Avenue Theatre, New York, under the management of John Stetson 1 November, 1886 for a season of three weeks to 20 November.
N. S. Burnham (MIK), Courtice Pounds (NP), Joseph W. Herbert (KK), Sgr Broccolini (PB), J. C. Fay (PT), Geraldine Ulmar/Helen Lamont (YY), Agnes Stone (PS), Edith Jenesse (PB), Alice Carle (KAT). Md: John Braham

Produced at the Savoy Theatre, under the management of Richard D'Oyly Carte 7 June, 1888 for a run of 116 performances closing 29 September, 1888.
Richard Temple/Wallace Brownlow (MIK), J. G. Robertson (NP), George Grossmith/John Wilkinson (KK), Rutland Barrington/Henry Le Breton/Charles Gilbert (PB), Richard Cummings (PT), Rudolph Lewis (GT), Rose Hervey/Geraldine Ulmar (YY), Jessie Bond/Annie Cole (PS), Sybil Grey (PB), Rosina Brandram/Madge Christo (KAT). Md: François Cellier

Produced at the Savoy Theatre, under the management of Richard D'Oyly Carte 6 November, 1895 for a run of 127 performances closing 4 March 1896.
R. Scott Fishe/Richard Temple (MIK), Charles Kenningham (NP), Walter Passmore (KK), Rutland Barrington (PB), Jones Hewson (PT), Florence Perry (YY), Jessie Bond (PS), Emmie Owen (PB), Rosina Brandram (KAT). Md: François Cellier
This production was also given six matinée performances during the run of *The Grand Duke* between 27 May and 4 July and returned to the evening bill 11 July, 1896 for a run of a further 226 performances closing 17 February, 1897.
Additional casting: (Jones Hewson) (MIK), (Scott Russell) (NP), (Jones Hewson)/Fred Billingham (PB), (H. G. Gordon) (PT), (Emmie Owen) (YY), (Bessie Bonsall) (PS), Beatrice Perry (PB), (Kate Talby) (KAT)

Produced at the Madison Square Roof Garden, New York, under the management of Messrs Kushibiki and Arni 14 July 1902 for a run of 70 performances.
Nick Burnham (MIK), Grafton Baker (NP), Fred Frear (KK), William Shuster (PB), John Henricks (PT), Grace Meyers (YY), Ursula Marsh (PS), Florence Little (PB), Hattie Arnold (KAT). Dir: Milton Aborn

Produced at the Savoy Theatre under the management of the D'Oyly Carte Opera Company 28 April, 1908 in repertoire for 142 performances.
Henry Lytton (Leicester Tunks) (MIK), Henry Herbert/Strafford Moss (Ernest Leeming) (NP), C. H. Workman (Henry Lytton) (KK), Rutland Barrington (PB), Leicester Tunks/Leo Sheffield (PT), Fred Drawater/Fred Hewett (GT), Clara Dow/Beatrice Boarer/Elsie Spain (YY), Jessie Rose (Beatrice Meredith) (PS), Beatrice Boarer/Maggie Jarvis (PB), Louie Rene (Ethel Morrison) (KAT). Md: François Cellier

Subsequently played by the D'Oyly Carte Opera Company on tour and in London in repertoire.

Produced at the Casino Theatre, New York, under the management of Messrs Shubert and William Brady 30 May, 1910 for a run of 42 performances closing 9 July, 1910.
William Danforth (MIK), Andrew Mack (NP), Jefferson de Angelis (KK), William Pruette (PB), Arthur Cunningham (PT), Fritzi Scheff (YY), Christie MacDonald (PS), Christine Nielson (PB), Josephine Jacobs (KAT)

Produced at the Royale Theatre, New York, under the management of Winthrop Ames 17 September, 1927 for a run of 110 performances.
John Barclay (MIK), William Williams (NP), Fred Wright (KK), William C. Gordon (PB), J. Humbird Duffey (PT), Lois Bennett (YY), S. Suissabell Sterling (PS), Bettina Hall (PB), Vera Ross (KAT). Dir: Winthrop Ames; md: Sepp Morscher; sc/cos: Raymond Sovey

Subsequently played in repertoire and short seasons in New York by the D'Oyly Carte Opera Company and others.

Produced at Sadler's Wells Theatre under the management of Sadler's Wells Opera Company 29 May, 1962.
John Holmes (MIK), David Hillman (NP), Clive Revill (KK), Norman Lumsden (PB), John Heddle Nash (PT), Kenneth Fawcett (GT), Marion Studholme (YY), Gloria Jennings (PS), Dorothy Nash (PB), Jean Allister (KAT). Dir: Douglas Craig; md: David Tod Boyd; sc/cos: Peter Rice

Produced at the Westminster Theatre under the management of Martin Gates and the Musical Theatre Company 28 May, 1979.
Philip Summerscales (Donald Stephenson) (MIK), Neil Jenkins (Michael Bulman) (NP), Martin McEvoy (KK), Thomas Lawlor (Donald Stephenson) (PB), Chris Booth-Jones (PT), Fiona Dobie/Janis Kelly (YY), Alison Truefitt/Carolyn Allen (PS), Rosemary Jenner (PB), Ann Hood/(Judith Buckle)/ (KAT) with Carolyn Allen, Linda d'Arcy, Clive Birch, Judith Buckle, Michael Bulman, Richard Burgess-Ellis, Malcolm Coy, David Eynon, Michael Farran-Lee, Susan Flannery, Eric Gething, Alan Horsfield, Amanda Hughes-Jones, Ben Kelly, Marcia Masters, Paul Napier-Burrows, Wendy Pollock, Jane Roberson, Donald Stephenson, Jillian Summerfield, Celia Tope, Patricia Wheeler. Dir: Ken Hill; md: Jack Forsyth; ch: Olivia Breeze; sc/cos: Sarah-Jane McClelland

Produced at the Cambridge Theatre in a Plymouth Theatre Royal production under the management of Bill Kenwright 28 September, 1982 for a run of 112 performances closing 8

January 1983. Subsequently toured, returning to the Prince of Wales Theatre 16 August, 1983 for a further 32 performances closing 16 September, 1983.
Nicholas Smith (MIK), Gary Lyons/Terry Mitchell (NP), Murray Melvin/Jimmy Thompson (KK), John Hewer/Gareth Jones (Chris Molloy) (PB), Douglas Anderson/Paul Laidlaw (PT), Stella Goodier/Cheryl Taylor (YY), Andrea Levine/Marcia Gresham (PS), Linda-Jean Barry/Judith Street (PB), Eileen Gourlay/Claire Rimmer (Tricia Deighton) (KAT) with Helen Brindle, John Christie, Anna Daventry, Mike Fields, David Farrow, Ronnie Grainge, Marcia Gresham, John Griffiths, Christine Marlborough, Nelly Morrison, Steve O'Hara, Kevin Owers, Alan Radcliffe, Wendy Taylor/Chris Molloy, Anna de Vere, Tricia Deighton, Julie Jupp, Janeen Thom, Elaine Tudor-Williams, Christopher Marlowe, Julian Ochyra, Alan Spencer, Andrew Wightman. Dir: Chris Hayes/Eileen Gourlay; md: Ed Coleman; ch: Michele Hardy/Mike Fields; sc: Sean Cavanagh; cos: Hugh Durrant

Produced at Sadler's Wells Theatre by the New Sadler's Wells Opera Company 27 January, 1983. Revived 19 June, 1984 in repertoire.
Phillip Summerscales/Donald Adams (MIK), Christopher Gillett (NP), Nickolas Grace (KK), Thomas Lawlor (PB), Julian Moyle (PT), Laureen Livingstone/Deborah Rees (YY), Lynn Barber/Yvonne Lea (PS), Jill Washington/Rebecca Caine (PB), Joan Davies (KAT). Dir: Christopher Renshaw; md: Anthony Hose; ch: Carole Todd; sc/cos: Tim Goodchild

THE SWING MIKADO a version of *The Mikado* by Harry Minturn. Music arranged by Gentry Warden. Produced in Chicago and subsequently at the New York Theatre under the management of the Chicago Federal Theatre 1 March, 1939 for a run of 86 performances.
Edward Fraction (MIK), Maurice Cooper (NP), Herman Greene (KK), William Franklin (PB), Lewis White (PT), Gladys Boucree (YY), Frankie Fambro (PS), Mabel Carter (PB), Mabel Walker (KAT). Dir: Harry Minturn; md: Edward Wurtzebach; ch: Sammy Dyer; sc: Clive Rickabaugh; cos: John Pratt

THE HOT MIKADO a version of *The Mikado* by Hassard Short. Topical lyrics by Dave Gregory and William Tracy. Modern musical adaptation by Charles L. Cooke. Produced at the Broadhurst Theatre, New York, under the management of Mike Todd 23 March, 1939 for a run of 85 performances. Subsequently played at the World's Fair.
Bill Robinson (MIK), Bob Parrish (NP), Eddie Green (KK), Maurice Ellis (PB), James A. Lilliard (PT), Gwendolyn Reyde (YY), Frances Brock (PS), Rosetta Le Noire (PB), Rose Brown (KAT) Freddie Robinson (MESSENGER), Vincent Shields (REDCAP). Dir: Hassard Short; md: William Parson; ch: Truly McGee; sc/cos: Nat Karson

THE BLACK MIKADO a version of *The Mikado* with music adapted by George Larnyoh, Eddie Quansah and Janos Bajala. Produced at the Cambridge Theatre under the management of James Verner 24 April, 1975 for a run of 472 performances.
Val Pringle (MIK), Norman Beaton (NP), Derek Griffiths (KK), Michael Denison (PB), Vernon Nesbeth (PT), Patricia Ebigwei (YY), Floella Benjamiyn (PS), Jenny McGusty (PB), Anita Tucker (KAT) with the band Juice. Dir: Braham Murray; ch: Amadeo; sc/cos: Johanna Bryant

TV: NBC-TV (USA) (Bell Telephone Hour) production adapted by Martyn Green, 1960. Dennis King (MIK), Robert Rounseville (NP), Groucho Marx (KK), Stanley Holloway (PB), Barbara Meister (YY), Sharon Randall (PS), Melinda Marx (PB), Helen Traubel (KAT), and the Norman Luboff Choir. Prod: Martyn Green; dir: Norman Campbell; md: Donald Vorhees

TV/Video: 1984 Brent Walker Ltd. Pr: Judith de Paul; dir: Michael Geliot; md: Alexander Faris; ch: Terry Gilbert; sc: Allan Cameron; cos: Jenny Beavan.
William Conrad (MIK), John Stewart (NP), Clive Revill (KK), Stafford Dean (PB), Gordon Sandison (PT), Kate Flowers (YY), Cynthia Buchan (PS), Fiona Dobie (PB), Anne Collins (KAT)

Film: In 1906 Chronophone Films issued a selection of six songs from *The Mikado* on film and synchronised record: 'Behold the Lord High Executioner', 'Tit Willow', 'Three little Maids', 'Here's a how-d'ye Do', 'Were You not to Koko Plighted' and 'The Flowers that Bloom in the Spring' were performed by Albert Gater, James Rouse, George Russell and Marie Grey. In 1907 the same six songs plus 'If you Want to Know who we Are', 'Our great Mikado', 'Miya Sama',

'The Mikado's Song', 'The Criminal Cried' and 'A wandering Minstrel', with a cast featuring George Thorne as Koko, were recorded on the same basis by Walturdaw on Cinematophone Singing Pictures.

Film: 1939. G & S Films. Screenplay: Geoffrey Toye; prod: Geoffrey Toye, Josef Somio; dir: Victor Schertzinger.
John Barclay (MIK), Kenny Baker (NP), Martyn Green (KK), Sydney Granville (PB), Gregory Stroud (PT), Jean Cohn (YY), Elizabeth Paynter (PS), Kathleen Naylor (PB), Constance Willis (KAT)

Film: 1967. British Home Entertainments. Screenplay: uncredited; prod: Anthony Havelock-Allan, John Brabourne; dir: Stuart Burge.
Donald Adams (MIK), Philip Potter (NP), John Reed (KK), Kenneth Sandford (PB), Thomas Lawler (PT), George Cook (GT), Valerie Masterson (YY), Peggy Ann Jones (PS), Pauline Wales (PB), Christene Palmer (KAT)

Film: 1963. *The Cool Mikado*. Screenplay: Michael Winner, Maurice Browning, Lew Schwartz; prod: Harold Baim; dir: Michael Winner.
Stubby Kaye (JUDGE MIKADO/CHARLIE), Kevin Scott (HANK MIKADO), Lionel Blair (NANKI), Frankie Howerd (KOKO), Tommy Cooper (DETECTIVE), Mike and Bernie Winters (MIKE AND BERNIE), Glenn Mason (HARRY), Pete Murray (MAN IN BOUDOIR), Dermot Walsh (ELMER), Jill Mai Meredith (YY), Tsai Chin (PS), Yvonne Shima (PB), Jacqueline Jones (KATIE SHAW).

0058 **DR D** an English comic opera in two acts by C. P. Colnaghi. Music by Cotsford Dick. Produced at the Royalty Theatre under the management of Andrew Levey 30 May, 1885 for a run of 24 performances, closing on 26 June, 1885.

Dr von Dosemoffen . . . . Henry Ashley
Sir Lancelot . . . . Jack Leumane
Fritz . . . . Charles Fisher
Spitz . . . . H. W. Dodd
Kaspar, a page . . . . Miss F. Deane
Postman . . . . Maggie Rayson
Mountain Guide . . . . Nellie Fenton
Belladonna . . . . Amy Florence
Pulsatilla . . . . Cissy Judge
Bryonia . . . . Ethel Pierson
Miss Seraphina Lovering . . . . Emily Cross
with Misses Casaboni, Morrison, Vale, L'Estrange, Austin, Clayton, Schwim, E. Ruskin, Stanhope, Tilly Woolf, Florrie Woolf, Southgate, Douglas, Melvin, Vivian, Lennox Grey, Lambert, Mowbray; Messrs B. Webb, Apsey, Walter Smith, Hunt, A. White, D. Valentine, J. Mahoney, C. P. Leonard, Yates, Belford, G. Moore, W. Hogan & c.

Md: Andrew Levey/Alfred Cellier; cos: Wilhelm; sc: Cuthbert

0059 **ERMINIE** a comic opera in two acts by Claxson Bellamy and Harry Paulton. Music by Edward Jakobowski. First produced at the Grand Theatre, Birmingham 26 October, 1885. Played at Brighton (Nov 2) and opened at the Comedy Theatre under the management of Violet Melnotte 9 November, 1885 for a run of 154 performances closing 3 April, 1886.

Marquis de Pontvert . . . . Fred Mervin
Eugene Marcel . . . . Henry Bracy
Vicomte de Brissac . . . . Horace Bolini
Delaunay . . . . Kate Everleigh/Miss Amalia
Sergeant . . . . A. D. Pierrepoint/Herbert George
Dufois, the landlord . . . . George Marler/Ambrose Collini
Simon, a waiter . . . . J. W. Bradbury/Frank Seymour/Lytton Grey
Henri . . . . Stanley Betjeman
Pierre . . . . Lottie Leigh/Nellie Carlton
Chevalier de Brabazon . . . . Percy Compton/Frank Barsby/C. A. Randolph
Ravannes . . . . Frank Wyatt

Cadeau . . . . Harry Paulton
Cerise Marcel . . . . Violet Melnotte (Marie Huntley)
Javotte. . . . . Kate Munroe
Marie . . . . Edith Vane
Clementine . . . . Delia Merton/Mary Webb
Princesse de Gramponeur. . . . . M. A. Victor
Erminie de Pontvert . . . . Florence St John/Marie Tempest
M. St Brice . . . . Nellie Gordon
M. d'Auvigne . . . . Kitty Graham
M. de Nailles . . . . Marie Huntley
M. de Sangres. . . . . Violet Leigh
Mme St Brice . . . . Lillie Teesdale
Mme de Lage . . . . Ada Maxwell
Mme de Brefchamp. . . . . Ethel Selwyn
Mme de Chateaulin . . . . Millie Gerard
Antoinette . . . . Madge Bruce
Charlotte . . . . Emilie Campbell
Jeanette . . . . Anita Marzan
Mignon . . . . Florence Dudley/Stella Carr
Rosalie. . . . . Carrie Solomon
Niniche . . . . Helen Gwynne
Nanine . . . . Mary Webb/J. Dudley
Fanchette . . . . Sylvia Southgate

with Amy Perrin, E. Pew, Louise Deleau, J. Stanhope, J. Dudley, Frances Stanhope, F. Thornton, Emily Clare, Misses Radcliffe, Vincent, Herbert/Misses Hogarth, Percival, Violet Leigh, Hardinge, Harris, Lillian Edeviean, Maud Vernon, Frances Fletcher, Edith Fletcher, Fannie Pew, Amy Jecks; Messrs Payne, Partell, E. Leahy, Charles Cowlrick, Ambrose Collini, Wigley, O'Connor, Charles Bernhard, T. Vernon, Henry Montague.

Md: Auguste van Biene; cos: Lucien Besche; sc: W. B. Spong and A. Callcott; ch: Mme Bassano

Produced at the Comedy Theatre under the management of Harry Paulton for a limited season of 30 performances, 26 June, 1886 to 30 July, 1886.
Fred Mervin (MARQ), Henry Bracy (EU), Louis C. Batten (VIC), Kate Eversleigh (DEL), H. C. Payne (SGT), Ambrose Collini (DUF), Fred Kaye (SIM), Augustus Cramer (HEN), J. C. Piddock (PI), Percy Compton (CHEV), Frank Wyatt (RAV), Harry Paulton (CAD), Minnie Bell (CER), Violet Melnotte (JAV), Mary Webb (MAR), Delia Merton (CLEM), M. A. Victor (PCESS), Florence St John (ERM); Louise Fletcher, K. Graham, J. Stanhope, Violet Leigh, Edith Fletcher, A. Graham, Miss Rowe, Miss Wynne, Louie Henri, J. Watson, Fannie Pew, Florence Dudley, Carrie Solomon, L. Watson, Lillian Edeviean, Adele Levey, Flora McGregor, Nellie Wilson, Ethel Searle, Messrs E. Leahy, Charles Cowlrick, Henry A. Henri[1], G. R. Luke, G. Sinclair, Arthur Richmond, Henry Johnson, T. Atkins

Produced at the Casino Theatre, New York, under the management of Rudolf Aronson 10 May, 1886. Suspended 2 October, 1886 after 150 performances. Opened at Boston 8 October, 1886. Resumed at the Casino Theatre 15 November, 1886 for a further 362 performances ending 17 September, 1887. Resumed at the Casino Theatre once more 16 January, 1888 for a further 136 performances closing 12 May, 1888.
Carl Irving/J. A. Furey/George Olmi (MARQ), Harry Pepper/Henry Hallam (EU), C. L. Weeks/H. Rolland/B. F. Joslyn (VIC), Rose Beaudet/Alma Varry/Sadie Kirby (DEL), E. Furry/J. Tibbetts (SGT), Murry Woods/Fred Clifton/J. Innes (DUF), A. W. Maflin/Murry Woods (SIM), Max Freeman/Charles Plunkett (CHEV), W. S. Daboll/Mark Smith (RAV), Francis Wilson/Fred Solomon (CAD), Marion Manola/Isabelle Urquhart/Helen Thomas/Kitty Cheatham (CER), Agnes Folsom/Marie Jansen/Georgie Dennin/Fannie Rice (JAV), Victoria Schilling/Sadie Kirby/Josie Sadler/Georgie Dennin (MAR), Jennie Weathersby/Mrs G. C. Germon/Louise Sylvester (PCESS), Pauline Hall/Belle Thorne/Addie Cora Reed (ERM). Md: Jesse Williams; sc: Henry E. Hoyt, T. S. Plaisted; cos: Dazian and Mme Loe

[1] Pseudonym of Henry A. Lytton.

Played at Niblo's Garden, New York, by the Aronson Comic Opera Company 1 April, 1889 for one week.
George H. Broderick (MARQ), Charles J. Campbell (EU), C. F. Weeks (VIC), Edgeworth Starrit (DEL), Henri Leoni (SGT), Ellis Ryse (DUF), Charles Lang (SIM), Richard Cummings (CHEV), Mark Smith (RAV), J. H. Ryley (CAD), Isabelle Urquhart/Anna O'Keefe (CER), Katie Gilbert (JAV), Marie Glover (MAR), Ruth Rose (PCESS), Addie Cora Reed/Isabelle Urquhart (ERM)

Produced at the Casino Theatre, New York, under the management of Rudolf Aronson 20 November, 1889 for a run of 51 performances closing 4 January, 1890.
John E. Brand (MARQ), Charles J. Campbell (EU), Frank Risdale (VIC), Sylvia Gerrish (DEL), Florence Bell (SGT), Ellis Ryse (DUF), A. W. Maflin (SIM), N. S. Burnham (CHEV), Edwin Stevens (RAV), James T. Powers (CAD), Blanche Roberts/Grace Golden (CER), Georgie Dennin (JAV), Emma Lawrence (MAR), Eva Davenport (PCESS), Pauline Hall (ERM). Dir/md: Jesse Williams; sc: Henry E. Hoyt and T. S. Plaisted; cos: Pilotell

Produced at the Carltheater, Vienna as *Erminy* 7 November, 1890.

Produced at the Broadway Theatre, New York, 3 October, 1893 under the management of Francis Wilson for a season (to 16 December, 1893?)
John McWade (MARQ), Harold C. Blake (EU), Propert Carleton (VIC), Bessie Cleveland (DEL), H. A. Cassidy (DUF), Edmund Lawrence (SIM), William Steiger (SGT), Edward P. Temple (CHEV), William Broderick (RAV), Francis Wilson (CAD), Cecile Eissing (CER), Lulu Glaser (JAV), Christie MacDonald (MAR), Jennie Weathersby (PCESS), Amanda Fabris (ERM), E. B. Knight (BENEDICTE). Dir: Richard Barker; md: A.de Novellis; sc: Homer F. Emens, Richard Marston.

Produced at the Bijou Theatre, New York 23 May, 1897 for two weeks ending 5 June, 1897.

Produced at the Casino Theatre, New York, under the management of the Aronson Brothers 23 May, 1898 for a run of 40 performances closing 25 June, 1898.
Arthur Cunningham (MARQ), Clinton Elder (EU), Charles H. Bowers (VIC), Kate Uart (DEL), Joseph Chaille (SGT), Murry Woods (DUF), Edmund Lawrence (SIM), Edward P. Temple (CHEV), Harry E. Dixey (RAV), Francis Wilson (CAD), Celeste Wynn (CER), Lulu Glaser (JAV), Miriam Lawrence (MAR), Jennie Weathersby (PCESS), Pauline Hall (ERM).

Produced at the Casino Theatre, New York, under the management of Francis Wilson 13 May, 1899 for a season of 25 performances to 3 June, 1899.
W. T. Carleton (MARQ), Clinton Elder (EU), Charles H. Bowers (VIC), Mathilde Preville (DEL), Joseph Chaille (SGT), Murry Woods (DUF), Edmund Lawrence (SIM), Max Freeman (CHEV), Thomas Q. Seabrooke (RAV), Francis Wilson (CAD), Josephine Knapp (CER), Lulu Glaser (JAV), Miriam Lawrence (MAR), Jennie Weathersby (PCESS), Lillian Russell (ERM), E. B. Knight (BENEDICTE). Dir: Max Freeman; md: John McGhie; sc: Homer P. Emens, Richard Marston; cos: Percy Anderson

Produced at the Casino Theatre, New York, under the management of Messrs Nixon & Zimmerman 19 October, 1903 for a run of 44 performances closing 28 November, 1903.
Robert Broderick (MARQ), William C. Weedon (EU), J. C. Jackson (VIC), Jessie Bartlett Davies (DEL), Charles Arling (SGT), Patrick Wallace (DUF), William Laverty (SIM), Sgr Perugini (CHEV), William Broderick (RAV), Francis Wilson (CAD), Laura Butler (CER), Madge Lessing (JAV), Lucille Egan (MAR), Jennie Weathersby (PCESS), Marguerite Sylva (ERM), George Dunham (BENEDICTE). Md: John McGhie; sc: Henry E. Hoyt

Played at the Standard Theatre, New York, by the Van den Berg-Conger Comic Opera Company 31 May, 1915 for one week.
Arthur Cunningham (MARQ), Paul Hyde Davies (EU), Charles Drumheller (VIC), Maybelle MacDonald (DEL), Fred Cordes (SGT), Dan Young (DUF), Adele Morrisey (SIM), Frank Bernard (CHEV), Fred Solomon (CAD), Karl Stall (RAV), Dora Kummerfeld (CER), Carrie Reynolds (JAV), Selma Marion (MAR), Alice Gaillard (PCESS), Dorothy Morton (ERM), H. Bell (BEN). Dir: José van den Berg; md: Leo Braun

Produced at the Park Theatre, New York, under the management of Lawrence J. Anhalt 3 January, 1921 for a run of 108 performances.
Francis Lieb (MARQ), Warren Proctor (EU), E. John Kennedy (VIC), Madge Lessing (DEL), John H. Reed (SGT), Richard Malchien (DUF), Adrian Morgan (SIM), Alexander Clark (CHEV),

DeWolf Hopper (RAV), Francis Wilson (CAD), Alice Hanlon (CER), Rosamond Whitende (JAV), Angela Warde (MAR), Jennie Weathersby (PCESS), Irene Williams (ERM). Dir: Charles C. Fais; md: Selli Simonson

60 **FAY O'FIRE** a romantic opera in two acts by Henry Herman. Music by Edward Jones. Produced at the Opera Comique under the management of Agnes Consuelo and F. J. Harris 14 November, 1885 for a run of 16 performances closing 2 December, 1885.

Earl of Landgough/Duke . . . . Fred Leslie
Earl of Cerulam/Marquis . . . . Fred Wood
Wickermark . . . . Charles Manners
Egobart . . . . Henry Walsham
Hendermon . . . . Wilfred Stanyer
Wangar/Dick . . . . Florence Melville
Lady Blanche . . . . Marie Tempest
Ina, the Fay o'Fire . . . . Agnes de la Porte
Flaromen . . . . H. Cooper Cliffe
Lady Allthere . . . . Agnes Consuelo
Lady Minay . . . . Violet Russell
Lady Rosedot . . . . Lilly Comyns
Lucius . . . . Hubert Hall
Ben Burrows . . . . H. M. Clifford
Alice . . . . Marion Grahame
Morris Dancers . . . . Nellie Lisle and Josephine Clare
Henchmen . . . . F. Courtenay and E. St Albyn

Dir: Henry Herman; md: Edward Jones/Alfred Cellier; ch: Paul Valentine; sc: T. E. Ryan; cos: A. Chasemore

61 **THE VICAR OF WIDE-AWAKE-FIELD** or The Miss-Terry-Ous Uncle. A burlesque by H. Pottinger Stephens and William Yardley. Music by Florian Pascal. Produced at the Gaiety under the management of John Hollingshead 8 August, 1885 for a run of 121 performances closing 18 December, 1885.

Dr Primrose . . . . Arthur Roberts
Squire Thornhill . . . . Violet Cameron/Agnes Consuelo/Emily Spiller/Julia St George
Mr Burchell . . . . Tom Squire
Moses . . . . J. H. Jarvis
Farmer Flamborough . . . . A. D. Corri/George Honey
Bill . . . . Miss M. Pearce
Dick . . . . Miss G. Tyler
Leigh . . . . Lesley Bell/Laurie Trevor
Mrs Primrose . . . . Harriet Coveney
Olivia . . . . Laura Linden
Sophia . . . . Agnes Hewitt/Minnie Howe
Polly Flamborough . . . . Sylvia Grey
Gipsy Woman . . . . Maggie Rayson

with Minnie Ross, Lizzie Wilson, Kate Talbot, Emily Robina, Jessie Braham, Edith Beaumont, Birdie Irving, Miss Anderson, Ada Conway, Miss Talbot, Miss Inverson, M. Rowe, A. Rowe, Minnie Sannon, Annie Deacon, Miss Myln, E. Richards, Jessie Bennett, Miss Delaval, Violet Graham, Nellie Webb, Jennie Overington, Eva Milner, M. Nola, Annie Akers, Daisy Graham, Miss Roma, Edith Vancher, Miss Adair, Miss Wilson, Florence Henderson, Miss Blackwood. Tom A. Shale, Messrs Rix, White, Walker, Pink, E. Shale, E. H. Haslem, Barry/Laurie Trevor, D. Ford, C. Howard, N. Lennox, A. Vernon, Alice? Lethbridge, McLewe, Collier, Jerks, Ridley, Young, Webb, Wynne.

Md: Hamilton Clarke; ch: Katti Lanner; sc: E. G. Banks; cos: Mrs May

Played with *Lord Dundreary's Brother Sam*, replaced by *Estranged* (19 Oct) and *Billee Taylor* (31 Oct).

0062 **CHIRRUPER'S FORTUNE** a musical farcical comedy in three acts by Arthur Law. Music by Florian Pascal, Georges Jacobi, George Grossmith, Arthur Caldicott and Robert Reece. Additional songs by S. Hughes. Produced by Kate Santley at the New Theatre Royal, Portsmouth 31 August 1885 and toured through Bath, Bristol, Cheltenham, Manchester, Liverpool, Preston, Sunderland, Newcastle, Edinburgh, Glasgow, ?/Peterborough ending 22 November, 1885.

Horace Buckley . . . . Edwin Shepherd/Robert Courtneidge
Simon Divetail . . . . Allen Thomas
Herbert Noble . . . . Royce Carleton
Sir Temple Trowers . . . . Lionel Rignold
Miss Gimp . . . . Mrs C. H. Stephenson
Rebecca Buckley . . . . Kate Kearney
Mrs Clump . . . . Marie Daltra
Lucy Chirruper . . . . Kate Santley

Md: W. E. Salmon

0063 **LITTLE JACK SHEPPARD** a burlesque operatic melodrama in three acts by H. Pottinger Stephens and William Yardley. Music by W. Meyer Lutz, Florian Pascal, Arthur Cecil, Hamilton Clarke, Henry J. Leslie, Alfred Cellier and R. Corney Grain. Produced at the Gaiety Theatre under the management of John Hollingshead and George Edwardes 26 December, 1885 for a run of 155 performances closing 29 May, 1886.

Jack Sheppard. . . . . Nellie Farren
Thames Darrell . . . . Mathilde Wadman
Blueskin . . . . David James (W. H. Guise)
Jonathan Wild. . . . . Fred Leslie
Sir Rowland Trenchard. . . . . E. J. Odell
Abraham Mendez . . . . Frank Wood
Mr Kneebone . . . . Willie Warde
Mr Wood . . . . W. H. Guise
Captain Cuff . . . . Emily Duncan/Miss Handley
Shetbolt . . . . Miss Ross
Marvel. . . . . Eva Raines
Ireton . . . . Emily Robina
Quilt Arnold . . . . Miss Handley/Florence Melville
Little Gog. . . . . Miss M. Pearce
Little Magog . . . . Miss G. Tyler
Mrs Sheppard. . . . . Harriet Coveney
Winifred Wood . . . . Marion Hood
Edgeworth Bess . . . . Bessie Sanson/Lizzie Wilson (Miss Irvine)
Polly Stanmore . . . . Sylvia Grey
Kitty Kettleby . . . . Eunice Vance
with Florence Henderson, Nellie Webb, Edith Beaumont, Jessie Bennett, Kate Atherton, Jessie Braham, Florence Gayner, Nellie Gayton, Lena Askey, A. Francis, Haidee Moore, Edith Vancher, Florence Doyne, Annie Akers, Alice Bond, Minnie Sannon, Jennie Overington, Minnie Howe, Annie Deacon, M. Nolar, Ada Conway.

Md: W. Meyer Lutz; ch: Willie Warde; sc: Messrs Banks and Spong; cos: A. Chasemore

Produced at the Bijou Theatre, New York, under the management of Messrs Miles and Barton 13 September, 1886 for a season of 101 performances ending 10 December (?), 1886.
Loie Fuller (JACK), Rose Leighton (TD), C. B. Bishop/William Yardley (BLUE), Nat C. Goodwin (JW), E. F. Goodwin (ROW), F. T. Ward (MEND), Frank Currier (KNEE), A. Hart (WOOD), Ida Van Osten (CUFF), Maude Waldemere (SHET), Maude Leicester (IRE), Robert McIntyre (MARV), George F. Campbell (QA), Lillie Craig (GOG), Mabel Craig (MAGOG), Jennie Weathersby (MRS), Addie Cora Reed (WW), Helen Sedgwick (BESS), Lelia Farrell (POL), Mabel Morris (KIT), with Georgie Lincoln, Louise Escott, Carrie Wallace, Adelaide Lee, Barbara Eyre, Lulu Tutein, Sadie Calhoun, Ray Semon, Bessie Semon, Flora Echard, Daisy Temple, Lulu Hesse, Madge Perry, Nora Bagaley, Louise Weldon, Marie Harriott, Laura Wood. Dir: William Yardley and Nat C. Goodwin; md: Gustave Kerker; sc: Harley Merry; cos: Chasemore

Produced at the Gaiety Theatre under the management of George Edwardes 18 August, 1894 for a run of 42 performances, closing 29 September, 1894.
Jessie Preston (JACK), Amy Augarde (TD), Charles Danby (BLUE), Seymour Hicks (JW), William Cheesman (ROW), Frank Wood (MEND), Willie Warde (KNEE), E. W. Royce (WOOD), Ethel Earle/Nora Millington (CUFF), Maude Sutherland (SHET), Carrie Benton (IRE), Kate Cannon (MARV), Lillie Henshawe (QA), Miss Raynor (GOG), Miss Rossell (MAG), Lizzie Collier (MRS), Ellaline Terriss (WW), Violet Monckton/Maude Hill (BESS), Florence Levey (POL), Georgina Preston (KIT). Md: Meyer Lutz; cos: Ida and A. Chasemore; ch: Willie Warde; sc: E. G. Banks and Walter Hann

JACK-IN-THE-BOX a musical variety drama in four acts and eleven scenes by George R. Sims and Clement Scott. Music by W. C. Levey and James Glover. Produced by Fannie Leslie at the Theatre Royal, Brighton 24 August, 1885 and toured to 12 December, 1885.

Jack Merryweather . . . . Fannie Leslie
Milly de Vere . . . . Lillian Gillmore
Richard Moreland. . . . . A. Gow Bentinck
Edward Moreland. . . . . Theo. Balfour
Carlo Toroni . . . . J. A. Arnold
Prof. O'Sullivan. . . . . Harry Parker
Mrs Merryweather . . . . E. Brunton
Sgt. Williams . . . . Malcolm H. Grahame
George Bolton. . . . . A. Meagherson
Roy Carleton . . . . H. J. Lethcourt
Rocco . . . . Little Ada Reeve
Katrina . . . . Kate Leason
Beppo . . . . Charles Reeves
Topley. . . . . Thomas Whitely
Robson . . . . James Rodney
Marconi . . . . A. Sheward
Tonio . . . . Charles Howitt
Mrs Pipkins . . . . Mrs Southby

Produced in Philadelphia 25 January, 1866 and at the Union Square New York 8 February 1886. Carrie Swain (JACK)

Produced at the Strand Theatre under the management of Fannie Leslie 7 February, 1887 for a run of 88 performances closing 7 May, 1887.
Fannie Leslie (JACK), Florence West (MIL), John Beauchamp (RICH), Yorke Stephens/Arthur Estcourt (ED), J. A. Arnold (TOR), Harry Parker (PROF), Sallie Turner (MRS), Malcolm H. Grahame (SGT), W. Thorley/W. J. Manning (BOL), Lewis Waller/Cecil Ward (ROY), Queenie Norman/Blanche Arnold (ROC), Cecil Ward/John A Warden (BEP), A. Sheward (ROB), John A. Warden/E. O. Waller (SHOWMAN), Amy McNeill (KAT). Dir: Charles Harris; md: John Gregory; sc: W. F. Robson; cos: Mrs May, Morris Angel

THE GREAT TAYKIN, A Japanese Mystery. A Japananza in one act by Arthur Law. Music by George Grossmith. Produced at Toole's Theatre under the management of J. L. Toole 30 April, 1885. Withdrawn 6 August, 1885 after 87 performances.

Josiah Gandy . . . . J. L. Toole
Rorti Pal . . . . George Shelton/C. M. Lowne
The Taykin . . . . Watty Brunton
Alfred Glossop . . . . Mr Carlisle
Mrs Gandy . . . . Emily Thorne
Cheeki Sing . . . . Bella Wallis
Col. Turnbull . . . . E. D. Ward
Neu Kut . . . . Wm. Cheesman
Dick Parrot . . . . J. O'Hara
Kitty Appleton . . . . Marie Linden
Winki Sli . . . . Blanche Wolsely
Krikee. . . . . R. Aldridge
Bloko . . . . C. Lidbury

Masha . . . . A. Stanley
Ole Moke . . . . M. Delaney
Bash Bash . . . . J. Samuel
Welsha . . . . L. Barrett
Imy-Imy . . . . Florence Anderson
Tickel-Ing. . . . . Jenny Wise
Chuckee Ching . . . . Amy Norman
Raht Lahcoon . . . . Annie Allen
Rosie Posee . . . . Maude Martell
Kissi Missi . . . . Netty Gray
add Popose . . . . Master Frank Reed

THE JAPS or The Doomed Daimio. A musical extravaganza in 2 acts by Harry Paulton and 'Mostyn Tedde' (Edward Paulton). Music mostly by W. Meyer Lutz. Produced by Willie Edouin at the Prince's Theatre, Bristol 31 August, 1885 and subsequently at the Novelty Theatre 19 September. Withdrawn 1 December.

Lord Sansuki Jappa. . . . . Lionel Brough
Toko . . . . Fred Kaye/Arthur Corney
Campi . . . . Harriet Vernon
The Tycoon. . . . . Frank Wood/Kate Bellingham
Monogashera . . . . Frank Martin
O'Kum . . . . Annie Dacre/Beatrice May
Masakichi . . . . Willis Searle
Yeen. Kate Bellingham/Annie Dacre
Yara . . . . Millie LeCapilaine
Lyza. Alice Atherton
Boobee Jappa . . . . Willie Edouin
Wyar . . . . Kate James
Noga . . . . Emmie Graham
Meemo . . . . Sophie Lingwood
Karaway. . . . . Kate Neville
Hyphon . . . . Amy Trevalyan
Isaka. . . . . E. Dickson
English Policemen . . . . Avis Graham and Florence Lancaster
add Think-In . . . . Frank Wood

Md: Meyer Lutz

THE BACHELORS a comic opera by C. H. M. Wharton. Music by Alfred D. Taylor. Produced at the Prince's Theatre, Manchester 8 June, 1885.

Arthur Singleton . . . . Walter Browne
Sam Sleepy . . . . E. J. Lonnen
Madeleine . . . . Alice Burville
Mrs McNish . . . . Mrs Muddiman
Polly Prettygal . . . . Ada Collins
Harry Benedict . . . . Fred Wood
Hubert Hardup . . . . George Mudie
Belinda . . . . Juliet Smith
Miss McGarth . . . . Miss Forster

Md: Fred Vetter

HOBBIES by William Yardley and Henry Pottinger Stephens. Music by George Gear. Produced at St George's Hall under the management of Alfred Reed and R. Corney Grain 6 April, 1885 with *A Vocal Recital* and *A Peculiar Case*, the latter replaced by *A Night in Wales* (1 June). Withdrawn 27 June, 1885.

Paul Plum . . . . Alfred Reed
Peter Plum . . . . Charles Allen
Miss Plum. . . . . Marion Wardroper

Penelope. Fanny Holland
Reginald. North Home

A NIGHT IN WALES a musical sketch by Herbert Gardner. Music by R. Corney Grain. Produced at St George's Hall under the management of Alfred Reed and R. Corney Grain 1 June, 1885 with *Hobbies* and *A Vocal Recital* replaced respectively by *A Pretty Bequest* (29 June) and *Eton and Harrow*. Withdrawn 18 July, 1885.

M. Boum . . . . Alfred Reed
Roderick Rattleton . . . . North Home
Caradoc Llewellyn . . . . Charles Allen

A PRETTY BEQUEST by T. Malcolm Watson. Music by Hamilton Clarke. Produced at St George's Hall under the management of Alfred Reed and R. Corney Grain 29 June, 1885 with *A Night in Wales* and *Eton and Harrow* the latter replaced by *Election Notes*. Withdrawn 28 November, 1885.

Adolphus Goodyear. . . . . Alfred Reed
Augustus Goodyear. . . . . Charles Allen
Harold Blake . . . . North Home
Miss Hunter . . . . Fanny Holland
Edith Goodyear. . . . . Marion Wardroper/Clara Merivale

IN CUPID'S COURT a musical sketch by T. Malcolm Watson. Music by Alfred J. Caldicott. Produced at St George's Hall under the management of Alfred Reed and R. Corney Grain 30 November, 1885 with *Election Notes*. Withdrawn 6 April, 1886.

Tom Muggeridge . . . . Alfred Reed
Percy Temple . . . . North Home
Joseph Scarlett . . . . Charles Allen
Peggy . . . . Fanny Holland
Ethel Scarlett . . . . Clara Merivale

THE CASTING VOTE an electioneering squib in one bang by Walter Helmore. Music by Walter Slaughter. Produced at the Prince's Theatre 7 October, 1885 with *The Great Pink Pearl*. Withdrawn 2 November, 1885.

Viscount Parlegrand. . . . . Etienne Girardot
O'Donegal. . . . . Stephen Caffrey
Lord Ronald Jawkins . . . . C. Bowland
Emma . . . . Amy Florence
George Gabdhaw . . . . Claude Marius
Miss Forley . . . . Clara Jecks
John Smith . . . . Henry Parry
Thompson. . . . . Sidney Harcourt
MacPherson . . . . George Traill
Lucy Lander . . . . Gabrielle Goldney
French Governess. . . . . Miss Dacre
Lizette. . . . . Miss Laurie
Kitty . . . . Miss Forrest
Waiters: Messrs Strathmore and Ives, Footmen: Messrs H. George and Barker, Flowergirls: Misses Lennox and Thomas.

Md: Walter Slaughter; cos: Lucien Besche

A PROFESSIONAL BEAUTY a musical burletta in three scenes by George Moore. Music by James M. Glover. Produced at the Avenue Theatre under the management of Violet Melnotte 7 April, 1885 as a forepiece to *Tact*. Withdrawn 17 April, 1885.

Mr J. Jackson . . . . Florence Melville
Miss de Winter . . . . Josephine Clare
Mr J. Warde . . . . Alice Greenwood

Lieutenant Phillips . . . . Alice Adair
Miss Leslie . . . . Alice Mori
Mrs Pearce Soapley . . . . Violet Melnotte
Lady Sheeply . . . . Cora Daniels
Mr Adair . . . . Alice Gilbert
Madge Primrose . . . . Letty Lind
Colonel Cooley . . . . Forbes Dawson
Lord Sheeply . . . . E. J. Odell
Captain Pearce Soapley . . . . J. B. Ashley
Miss Lane . . . . Brenda Harper
Flunkey . . . . Frank Marryat

THE NOBLE SAVAGE an operetta by H. and Frederic Corder. Produced at the Brighton Aquarium by the Alice Barth Opera Co., 3 October, 1885 and toured in repertoire.

Spread Eagle . . . . Richard Cummings
Mr Buskin . . . . Michael Dwyer
Manrico Smith . . . . Joseph Pierrepoint
Signorina Vermicelli . . . . Alice Farquharson
Ocean Pearl . . . . Alice Barth

THE GOLDEN WEDDING an operetta by Arthur Sketchey. Music by J. Parry Cole. Produced at the Avenue Theatre under the management of Violet Melnotte 14 March, 1885 as a forepiece to *Tact*.

Michael Marabout . . . . Stanley Betjeman
Madame Marabout . . . . Eugenie de Kervelly

FIVE HUNDRED FRANCS an operetta by Marmaduke Brown. Music by Isidore de Solla. Produced at the Vaudeville Theatre under the management of Florence Grant 6 July, 1885 at a matinée.

1886

The new year opened with all the previous season's hits still running strongly. *The Mikado* was entrenched at the Savoy, *Little Jack Sheppard* at the Gaiety and *Erminie* at the Comedy. The Gaiety's *Billee Taylor* had moved across to the Empire for a few additional performances and Minnie Palmer had returned to town with *My Sweetheart*. An attempted seasonal revival of *The Pet of Newmarket* at the Holborn had folded, however, when the cast realised that the writer/manager Vanden Bossche had no money to pay them since there were no audiences to provide it.

With so many attractive shows running it was quite a while before a new musical was needed for the London stage and, in fact, the first new British musical of the year made its début on the stage of the Union Square Theatre, New York. *Pepita*[1] was British in that it was the work of Captain Alfred Thompson and Teddy Solomon, both at the time trying their fortunes across the Atlantic. To date, those fortunes had been decidedly mixed if not poor. Solomon had had little success since his début with *Billee Taylor*. Of his subsequent works only *Polly* could lay claim to be called successful, but this did not deter him; most of his scores had been let down by indifferent libretti, so on this occasion he tried a collaboration with Thompson, the veteran of *Aladdin II* and *Cinderella the Younger*, who had recently been devoting more time to his designing activities than to writing.

For *Pepita* or The Girl with the Glass Eyes (a somewhat unattractive title) Thompson supplied a story about a Professor with a circus of performing automata in which his daughter (Lillian Russell) takes a part when one of the lady dolls breaks down. She acts out the love scenes with her own lover who has substituted himself for the male doll.

Pepita was well received. The songs were encored vigorously and Miss Russell scored a personal success with her ever-increasing public. The composer's claims for his skills received confirmation in print from *The New York Dramatic Mirror:*

> There can be no doubt in the mind of anyone who is capable of telling good music from bad that, with the single exception of Arthur Sullivan, Edward Solomon is the only English composer who can write comic opera. His music is melodious, sparkling and, when needed, full of a tender strain almost too refined for his subjects but exquisitely charming. Edward Solomon has been handicapped from the start by slipshod books. Had he had a Gilbert to work with he would have been a man of fame and fortune long ago. .

[1] The show performed in Britain as *Pepita* was an English version of Lecocq's *La Princesse des Canaries.*

The show played for over two months, perhaps helped on by a small scandal which seemed to be brewing around Solomon and his wife. The New York *Era* correspondent (who had not liked the show) reported:

> That other piece of trash, *Pepita*, still holds its own pretty well at the Union Square. The difficulty between Mr Solomon and his wife, Miss Russell, is steadily broadening. I noticed the other night that through the whole performance he never looked at her once. She sang so sweetly and he looked as charming as ever as he waved his baton with his usual grace . . .

Rumours blossomed and were chopped down and the little composer gained a certain social notoriety. He had previously gone into print voicing his dissatisfaction with America's reception of his works and himself, and had even in January announced an imminent return to Britain, but the slight warming of the American climate in his respect led him to stay a little longer and to try one more musical.

He collaborated with Charles Hoyt, the American librettist of *A Trip to Chinatown*, on *The Maid and the Moonshiner*, a farcical musical starring Miss Russell and Tony Hart and dealing with the antics of the Moonshiner (Hart) to help his employer win the hand of the Maid (Russell) from the rich plantation boss. It was a two-week failure at the Standard with the blame placed squarely on the faults of the libretto:

> . . . were Hoyt's words only half as good as Solomon's music we should not have to record the failure of *The Maid And The Moonshiner* – a play with no plot, no wit, no fun, no raison d'être. . .   (*N.Y. Dramatic Mirror*)

Teddy Solomon packed his bags and sailed for home leaving his wife, who was under contract to John Duff, in New York and reiterating that there was 'no break up'. His welcome home was not quite what he might have wished: he found himself summoned to Marlborough Street Magistrates Court on a charge of bigamy. When marrying Miss Russell[1], he had neglected to tell her of an 1873 marriage to 15-year-old Jane Isaacs, and of their child born in 1875. Lillian soon heard that her 'husband' had been jailed while he attempted to prove that earlier attempts to free himself from Jane (now a music hall artiste under the name of 'Lily Grey') had been undefended. After nine weeks Jane Solomon withdrew her case and Solomon was released with a stern warning from the judge. He had suffered badly from his spell in prison. Two weeks of rheumatic fever had made him alarmingly weak and his whole world seemed to have collapsed around him. He never regained either his health or his wife and for some time stayed very quiet. Under the circumstances it was not surprising that he made no attempt to get either *Pepita* or *The Maid and the Moonshiner* staged in Britain.

It was May before the first new show appeared in the West End and it was a show which could only be called British in hindsight. *The Lily of Léoville* was written by the French librettist, Félix Rémo, with music by a young Belgian composer, Felix Tilkin, a gold medallist from the Paris Conservatoire making his first venture into the world of the stage musical. The libretto was in the French opéra-comique tradition, dealing with a guardian who tries to marry his rich and pretty ward only to be tricked into tying the knot with an elderly flame suitably disguised for the occasion. The music was light and pretty and also in the French tradition. But, before it received its first production, *The Lily of Léoville* underwent a process of thorough anglicisation. Rémo's book never

[1] Solomon 'officially' married Lillian Russell 10 May 1885. He was charged 30 August 1886.

saw the stage in its original incarnation, for Violet Melnotte, with the support of publisher Charles Willcocks, took *The Lily of Léoville* to follow *Erminie* into the Comedy Theatre. The French libretto was translated and done over by Alfred Murray while the lyrical part was given into the charge of Clement Scott. Scott, famous as the picturesque and often sharp-tongued critic of *The Daily Telegraph*, was also a dramatist. His ventures in that field had been largely translations from the French and the most successful to date had been *Diplomacy* (from Sardou) on which he had collaborated with B. C. Stephenson. His original works had included the extremely popular *Jack-in-the-Box* with George Sims. Tilkin too, had become anglicised. He had moved from Paris to London, at the same time altering his name to 'Ivan Caryll'. As Ivan Caryll he was to have a brilliant career as a composer and conductor of musicals for nearly thirty years before once again changing his national allegiance and crossing the Atlantic to spend his later years in America. At this stage, however, he was unknown and earning a precarious living teaching, writing songs and, latterly, conducting the Comedy Theatre orchestra.

The Lily of Léoville took three acts to tell its all too familiar story, but it had some bright moments on the way. Violet Melnotte had spared no expense on the production and had hired an excellent cast. Agnes de la Porte and George Travener were cast as the cheated heroine and her lover, with Charles Stevens as the villain who forges the will, while the lighter side of affairs fell into the hands of Mary Ann Victor and Miss Melnotte, repeating their *Erminie* characters and, surprisingly, Hayden Coffin as a Bunthorne-like poet:

> Yes, I am a fellow poetic
> A friend of art, a lord of love
> Behold in me a soul aesthetic
> For talent fits me like a glove

given to throwing off doggerel for all occasions, each time capped with the warning 'Copyright'. Walter Andrews added to the fun as a military sergeant who will not hear of disbanding his regiment for he was promised in his cradle that he would one day be a marshal and in his twenty years following the flag he has only risen to sergeant.

Miss Melnotte arranged an out-of-town tryout for *The Lily of Léoville* at the Birmingham Grand and the reception there was encouraging enough. *The Era* correspondent seemed well pleased:

> . . [it] possesses many of the elements which go to make a successful comic opera. In the first place the libretto is piquantly written; there is a considerable amount of ingenuity manifested in the development of the plot; and the music in many parts is of the most delightfully tuneful nature. .

The following week *Erminie* was withdrawn from the Comedy Theatre and *The Lily of Léoville* took its place. Some changes had been made since Birmingham both in script and cast. The tenor Travener had collapsed on dress-rehearsal night and had not been able to play more than the tryout. Henry Bracy, currently playing Eugene Marcel in *Erminie*, hurriedly learned the role and opened with the show a week later. Fred Kaye was also brought in to play the Sergeant.

But London was more choosy than Birmingham:

> The success of *Erminie* raised hopes that a second comic opera by an English author and composer [*sic*] might achieve a similar result at the Comedy Theatre but the proverb *non bis in idem* seems to be applicable in the case of *The Lily of*

> *Léoville*. . . The music is curiously appropriate to the book. It never rises above the commonplace, is seldom ever ear-catching and does not display any deep musical knowledge. It is only fair to admit that the airs it contains, though weak and thin, are refined and melodious – but the style in which the whole is written is too sketchy and light to deserve lengthy criticism. (*Era*)

The general lack of originality and wit in the libretto and a slightly unhappy alliance of styles among the collaborators were against *The Lily of Léoville*, but it was a work which a few years earlier might have comfortably passed several months in a metropolitan house. Now its style and story were passé and its execution insufficiently remarkable to overcome these handicaps. Trying to make a virtue of her show's problem, Miss Melnotte advertised 'the only comic opera in London' (ignoring the presence of *The Mikado* at the Savoy) but after six weeks Ivan Caryll's West End début came to an end. The manageress put on a revival of *Erminie* and, in spite of announcements of revisions, tours in both Britain and France and a return to London's Opera Comique, *The Lily of Léoville* had breathed its last.

The second new offering of the season was also from Alfred Murray who collaborated with Willie Younge on the libretto of *The Palace of Pearl* for the Empire. Libretto, on this occasion, was, however, of only relative importance as *The Palace of Pearl* was staged very much as an old-style Alhambra piece with the emphasis on spectacle and ballet. The Empire had done quite well in that vein with *The Lady of the Locket*, and a version of Jules Verne's *Round the World* with a cast of 400 and real elephants had confirmed the theatre's position as the legitimate successor to the Alhambra. With *The Palace of Pearl* M. Marius, taking up the management of the theatre, aimed to appeal to the same public. He had the financial backing of M. Nicol, proprietor of the Café Royal. It is said that Nicol, anxious to boost his theatrical venture, enquired of a friend how best to set the critics in a favourable frame of mind. The reply came 'feed them' and, in consequence, the famous restaurateur dined a little coven of critics in grand style at his establishment on the first night. Alas for his hospitality, they dined too well and none of them made the performance.

The story was centred on a five-hundred-year-old feud between the dynasties of King Alger and Queen Amaranth over the marvellous Palace of Pearl.

> Till once again on earth is seen
> A living, loving fairy queen
> Till brother can his sister wed
> This hateful feud can ne'er be dead.

The prophecy is fulfilled when Alger and Amaranth fall in love and marry and their respective children, Amor and Alma do the same. The 'Fairy Queen' is improbably found in the guise of the Queen's favourite lady-in-waiting. In the meanwhile many picturesque events intervened, involving the principals, 100 coryphées, 50 orchestral players and 700 costumes in a series of unlikely events of which the principal cleverness was the art required to stitch them together into a plot. At one stage when both Alger and Amaranth have been temporarily deposed by republican revolutions they turn up in a very English inn where they find Amor and Alma at the head of a troupe of strolling players who perform an interpolated burlesque before the plot is allowed to stagger on a little further towards its dénouement. As at the Alhambra, the ballets were a prominent feature of the show. Mlle Luna was featured in a Grand Moorish ballet, and the Lace Ballet choreographed by M. Bertrand to a charming score by Jakobowski proved to be the hit of the evening. The composer of *Erminie* shared the musical creation of *The Palace of Pearl* with the show's musical director, Frederick Stanislaus and, although they had done a satisfactory job, the piece remained first and foremost one of visual appeal, and that of a very high standard:

> [*The Palace of Pearl* with its] splendid ballets, its processions, its songs, chants and dances has evidently given great satisfaction. . . a 'Summer Pantomime' worthy of Old Drury itself. . . (C. Scott)

> every gratification that can be afforded to the eye and, to some extent, to the ear if not to the intellect (*Times*)

> nothing good can be said about the story and the dialogue. . . . a clumsy thread on which to hang pretty melodies and gorgeous scenes. (*Despatch*)

The pretty melodies fell mostly to Tillie Wadman and Grace Huntley as the young lovers, while Charles Cartwright (Alger) and Susie Vaughan (Amaranth) were joined on the comic side by Marius performing under his own management.

The Palace of Pearl was not a happy venture for the popular Anglo-Frenchman. The expensive spectacle never looked like recouping and before long an exchange from the script rang only too true:

PAGE: His Royal Highness the Prince requires an audience.
ALGER: He's not the only person in that plight!

The Palace of Pearl closed after eight weeks and the theatre was returned to its owners for a version of Adam's *Le Postillon de Longjumeau* with Henry Walsham hitting the very high notes of the title role. Jakobowski's Lace Ballet survived the closure, being bought out of the production by the Kiralfy brothers and transported to America to be used in their Niblo's Garden spectaculars.

Following his effort with *The Japs* the previous year, Willie Edouin again came to town and to the Novelty Theatre in 1886, bringing with him a new burlesque constructed for himself and Mrs Edouin (Alice Atherton). *Oliver Grumble* was a piece of considerably more substance than its predecessor. Like most contemporary burlesques it burlesqued nothing, although its title character, a misanthropic rebel, was nominally a perversion of Cromwell and the action included his treacherous dethroning of King Charles, an event which in this case was quickly reversed to make a happy ending. Edouin and Miss Atherton featured as 'The Terrible Twins' who gallivanted chaotically through the action in the same way they had so successfully done in *The Babes*. They were surrounded by a much stronger cast than before. Arthur Williams took the title role and Edith Blande, Emily Spiller, Florence Dysart, Addie Conyers and Charles Stevens had supporting roles.

The libretto for *Oliver Grumble* was written by a young Nottingham journalist, George Dance, the local correspondent of *The Stage*, and marked his début in the musical theatre. He showed a lively imagination and a neat verse style in a piece which cheerfully mixed established styles to suit the individual actors. His word play was of a much milder form than the usual and it made only sporadic appearances in such set pieces as Emily Spiller's opening speech:

> Well, truth to say, we've had a rather tough one
> The gale got up a LILLE bit strong
> Which marred our speed and made the voyage TOULON.
> We should have spread MARSEILLES but it so blew
> We found 'twas NICE-y thing to do.
> At length night came which gave us all the tip

That we should have to sleep on BORDEAUX ship
But on the morn our watchful bosun sung
Cheer up, there's land my lads, we shan't BOULOGNE
And here we are, the better for our cruise
So lets away, we have no time TOULOUSE.

The dialogue was full of bright moments and topical and popular allusions including some to Irish jokes and 'phone tapping (already!).

The musical part of *Oliver Grumble* is nowhere credited, but it seems that the choruses and several of the songs were specially written for the show (perhaps even by Dance himself) while most of the solo spots for Miss Atherton were left for her to fill at her own discretion and she almost certainly included her hit song from *The Japs*, 'Eyes of English Blue' (Lutz). Of the new pieces, Williams' song 'Who wouldn't Grumble at That' was well received and Dance showed the breadth of his compass in a very 'comic opera' song, 'Valour and Discretion':

The soldier engaged in a bloodthirsty war
His trustworthy weapon is anxious to draw
He thinks of his fame and is eager – what for?
VALOUR.
Yet while his brave head is exploding with zeal
He cannot be callous to nature's appeal
Existence is charming and therefore we feel
DISCRETION.
Valour is delightful, yet discretion is essential
But, mark us, this is private and strictly confidential

and a burlesque-style Roundhead conspirators' trio:

By hook or by crook we'll make somehow
An awfully jolly civil row
For when you are short of £SD
There's nothing at all like a mutinee

The whole made for a lively and entertaining evening which kept Edouin busy for five weeks before he headed back into the provinces again where *Oliver Grumble* was exchanged for the play *Turned Up* written by Mark Melford, a young member of his company. *Turned Up* turned out to be a great success and *Oliver Grumble* lost its place in the repertoire.

The next 'musical' to hit town proved to be one of the most inept of all time. *Our Agency* was a 'farcical musical comedy' which arrived at the Avenue in July under the auspices of Mr Burlington Brumell and friends. It was set in a theatrical agent's office and cobbled together some incomprehensible doings, insignificant songs and an extraneous ballet called 'Clito' in the most amateurish way possible. The audience on the first night roared with laughter at its pathetic pretensions. *The Times* christened it 'the completest fiasco seen on the London stage for many years' and its self-important manager/author cut and ran after seven performances.

The first part of the year had come up with nothing to match the triple-headed success of the previous year. Attempts with French pieces fared no better. The brutalised Adam at the Empire was soon gone and Hervé's *Frivoli* at Drury Lane lasted barely a month in spite of a cast led by Marie Tempest, Rose Hersee, Kate Munroe, Victor Stevens, Edith Vane, Henry Walsham and the veteran star of opéra-bouffe, Emily Soldene. The balance sheet for the first part of the year was a negative one and only the Savoy's triumphant *Mikado* lasted through to the autumn.

The next new entry was at the Gaiety. With the burlesque company out on the road in *Little Jack Sheppard* and the annual French play season ended, the Gaiety's new manager George Edwardes changed the mood and brought out, at long last, the much paragraphed 'other half' of the Manchester *Nell Gwyne*, Cellier's *Dorothy*. Some of the old music and some new material had been used in a light operatic piece constructed by Charlie Stephenson with whom Cellier had taken his first steps in *Charity Begins at Home*. The piece had been about for some time and had previously been announced for production by Kate Santley but this time it finally made it to the stage. Marion Hood was kept back from the *Little Jack Sheppard* tour to play the title role and she was joined by Redfern Hollins, Florence Dysart, Furneaux Cook, Hayden Coffin and Arthur Williams to make an exceptionally strong vocal cast.

When *Dorothy* was produced it failed to make the stir that the new burlesque had. *The Times* was unimpressed:

> It was Mr Hollingshead's boast that he had kept the sacred lamp of burlesque burning continually for – we forget how many years. The lamp, as we have had occasion to point out, has for some time been flickering unsteadily. It is at last extinct. Burlesque of the Gaiety pattern, burlesque of scanty wit but still scantier costume, burlesque of the 'cheeky' and slangy order is now a thing of the past.
>
> *Dorothy* . . . is not a burlesque or anything like it, but an extremely genteel comic opera mounted and dressed with an exceptional affectation of propriety. . . . Not a trace of the loudness and vulgarity of the old Gaiety burlesque remains. Gentility reigns supreme and with it unfortunately also a good deal of the refined feebleness and the ineptitude which are the defects of that quality. Neither Mr Stephenson nor Mr Cellier has quite met the requirements of the occasion. The former has provided a disjointed and uninteresting book and the latter a score which although elegant, varied and full of colour, consists almost entirely of concerted pieces . .

It classed Stephenson's book as 'literary carpentry of a clumsy sort', declaring roundly that 'the music is throughout by far the best feature of the piece'. The verdict was almost unanimous:

> . . . . at once gratifying and disappointing. Mr Alfred Cellier has scored splendidly while his co-worker comes out with an ignominious duck's egg . . . the libretto is not worthy of the music . . we can only regret that the piece is so heavily handicapped by Mr Stephenson's book. (*Era*)
>
> the music [is] distinctly good. Almost too good for the subject . . . We fear that Mr George Edwardes has not been fortunate in his choice of a new piece. (*Stage*)
>
> *Dorothy* is a Comedy opera, not comic you observe . . far from it . . Music by Alfred Cellier, words by B. C. Stephenson who, as he seems only partially acquainted with the alphabet of libretto writing, might be called 'A.B.C. Stephenson'. The music is much better than the plot – not that this is saying much . . (*Punch*)

Punch continued its review with its version of the plot:

> The plot depends mainly on the chief characters continually disguising themselves by the simple process – as it appeared to me – of powdering their hair, which of course renders them perfectly unrecognisable until the last Act, when everybody finds out everyone else, and all ends happily. I am sure, speaking for myself, I was quite pleased when it was all over.

The Era summed it up rather less artificially:

> [it] takes three acts to tell how Dorothy . . . and her cousin Lydia Hawthorne

> borrowing from the business of *She Stoops to Conquer*, *The Merchant of Venice* and *She Would and She Would Not* advance towards the matrimonial goal they have vowed to avoid.

In fact, the plot ran as follows. Dorothy Bantam, the squire's daughter, dresses as a country lass to spy on her intended but unknown husband-to-be, and she and her cousin Lydia charm the unwitting Geoffrey Wilder and his friend Harry Sherwood who have come to the country to escape a debt. In their train comes one Lurcher, a sherriff's man intent on serving Wilder with a writ. Wilder decides to trick a loan out of Dorothy's father. He introduces himself into the home of the snobbish Squire disguised as a nobleman and attended by his companion (Sherwood) and his secretary (Lurcher), and there he fakes a robbery. Bantam, whose own fortune has not been touched, is only too glad to recompense his noble guest. In the meanwhile the young gentlemen have begun a flirtation with the daughter and the niece of the house, not recognising them as the same ladies to whom they had vowed eternal fidelity earlier in the day. The girls decide to punish them and, in the name of two ficticious gallants, challenge Wilder and Sherwood to a duel for trifling with the affections of the ladies. Disguised as boys, Dorothy and Lydia come to stage a mock duel and are horrified to see the men preparing to use real bullets. All is saved when the Squire arrives on the scene, having been told the truth by Lurcher, and the girls are glad to marry the men who were willing to risk their lives for them.

Stephenson had done his best to fit a story and lyrics around as much of the *Nell Gwynne* score as he could, but this was scarcely the best way to write a fluent libretto and the effort showed. While the first two acts were attractive enough, some incongruities crept in. The end of Act 2, the discovery of the robbery, had a bevy of ladies in nightdresses in attendance when, to create a finale, morning broke, the hunting horns were heard and on came the scarlet coats and a pack of real hounds to make a flamboyant curtain. The third act eked out the duel situation and the dénoument with a second and a third slice of the rustic wedding with which the show opened and some other vaguely extraneous pieces which, while attractive enough in themselves, diluted the narrative somewhat.

Later, when *Dorothy* became a hit, many learned columnists carefully traced the lineage of the libretto through to Aphra Behn and the Restoration playwrights, but it was little more than a refined and reasonably lively book of no particular originality and the consensus was, slightly unfairly, that while Cellier's music was delightful the accompanying libretto was pretty ordinary.

The piece seemed to have only a moderate chance of survival and Edwardes' attempt to stage a different kind of work at the Gaiety seemed likely to backfire at its very first attempt. If *Dorothy* were to run, clearly something had to be done. Edwardes, Stephenson and the cast came together and alterations on the book were begun. The most urgent matter was to introduce much more fun and humour to lift the piece into its avowed 'comedy' area. Arthur Williams as the bailiff had the leading comedy role, but it was a fairly insignificant one and not particularly robust or funny. He arrived late on the scene and his *Erminie*-like imitation of the manservant in Act 2 gave him only a few opportunities. Williams was not a man to allow things to remain thus and he began, sometimes with and sometimes without the aid or blessing of the author, to elaborate and extend his role. One aspect which Stephenson would not countenance was Williams' interpolation of anachronisms into the period play. When the word 'instalments' appeared in his text the comedian leapt on it and ad libbed 'Instalments? Instalments? What do you take me for? A sewing machine?'. It was determinedly anachronistic but it raised such a huge laugh that the librettist was obliged to let it remain. The over-elaborate third act was trimmed of some of its excess matter and even some of the score, such as Dorothy's 'Snuff Song', was excised. But there was more to the alterations than cuts. One fact which had been commented on by the first night press was that Hayden Coffin as Harry Sherwood had no solo number at all. In view of his ability and his popularity this seemed a decided waste and it was agreed that a song should be added for him. But Alfred Cellier was away in Australia for his health and his brother, François, refused on his behalf to allow any other composer's song to be interpolated into Alfred's score. As an alternative, the Gaiety began to look at earlier songs by the composer and finally, in Chappell's files, they lighted on a ballad entitled 'Old Dreams' written to a poem by the children's writer, Sarah Doudney:

It was but a year ago, love,
In the balmy summer time
That I lingered in the churchyard
Till the bells began to chime.

A catching melody, but totally unsuitable words. Stephenson went to work to provide a new lyric, and Hayden Coffin had his song:

From daylight a hint we might borrow
And prudence might come with the light;
Then why should we wait till tomorrow?
You are queen of my heart tonight.

If Rivière had made a hit with 'Spring, gentle Spring', if Solomon had swept the town with 'Eliza' and Gilbert and Sullivan with any one of a dozen songs, 'Queen of my Heart', with the help of Hayden Coffin's handsome face and ringing baritone, made them all look pale. The very first night the number was put into the show the delighted audience encored it twice. From then until the end of the run there was never a night when Coffin was not required to repeat his song at least once and generally more often. The piece became a sine qua non on parlour pianos and – the ultimate accolade – parodies began to appear: some more and some less tasteful. Dan Leno desisted, at François Cellier's request, from performing a version called 'I'm Queen of the Tarts Tonight'. At the Gaiety it meant nothing to the eager audiences that the little drawing-room ballad was rather out of place in Cellier's score. They liked it very much, and they liked Arthur Williams and his unpredictable fun, as well as the pretty scenery, costumes and chorus. *Dorothy* began to find its feet.

It succeeded in holding its place at the Gaiety until the approach of Christmas. By then the *Little Jack Sheppard* company had finished its tour and was back in town ready to open a new show and the manager was faced with the choice of closing *Dorothy* or transferring it. The Prince of Wales Theatre had just been taken over on a three-year lease by Horace Sedger, so Edwardes arranged with him to begin his lesseeship by taking in the ready-made Gaiety production of *Dorothy*. On 20 December the transfer was effected. But after a short while Edwardes decided to have done with the show and was ready to close when Gaiety accountant Henry Leslie, otherwise an amateur composer who had interpolated songs into several shows, offered to take it on. Edwardes agreed, and for £500 *Dorothy* was sold lock, stock and barrel.

The new impresario had his own ideas, and he was not content to let the show run on unaltered. The first of his actions was the replacement of the two leading artists, Marion Hood and Redfern Hollins. Miss Hood was a tried performer. She had created the role of Mabel in *The Pirates of Penzance* for Gilbert and Sullivan, she had played many burlesque and musical principal girls, always unfailingly ladylike and charming and with a clear, sweet soprano voice. As Dorothy, however, Leslie considered her wrong. Certainly she sang the music delightfully and it was a little hard of *Punch* to say she 'acted spasmodically', but it was her very dignity and ladylike qualities which militated against her. Dorothy needed more spirit. Redfern Hollins was a similar case – a singer, pure and simple. *Punch* had been harder on him . . 'sang, but could not act' . . and he too was replaced. As a tenor Leslie hired the Carl Rosa's Ben Davies and to replace Miss Hood he chose Marie Tempest. After *Fay o' Fire*, *Erminie* and *Frivoli*, the up-and-coming star had taken second billing in Messager's *La Béarnaise* behind Florence St John. *La Béarnaise* was the outgoing tenant at the Prince of Wales as Sedger and *Dorothy* came in, and Leslie snapped Miss Tempest up. Her reading of the role of Dorothy was very different to that given by Miss Hood. Whereas the public had admired the soignée Marion, they loved the joyous and arch Marie. Finally, after more than a hundred performances, *Dorothy* had matured into a hit and a hit of proportions which no-one, even then, could have imagined. Its run eventually extended for 931 performances, eclipsing Gilbert and Sullivan and *Les Cloches de Corneville* and setting a record for a musical which would last for nearly twenty years, making it the longest running musical of the nineteenth century stage. Marie Tempest took over the role of Dorothy at the 133rd performance and played it during the piece's entire career at the Prince of Wales. Others were even more faithful. Hayden Coffin, Harriet Coveney and John Le Hay from the original Gaiety cast remained in their respective roles for the entire thirty months of *Dorothy's* run.

After a while, Henry Leslie began to build himself a theatre on the proceeds of the piece, just as Edgar Bruce had built the Prince of Wales from the profits on *The Colonel.* The site he chose was on Shaftesbury Avenue and the name he chose for his theatre, aptly, was the Lyric. When it was completed Leslie transferred his golden goose there on 17 December, 1888, on the occasion of its 817th performance. Miss Tempest, Coffin and Ben Davies still headed the cast with the role of Lydia taken on by a twenty-year-old newcomer, Amy Augarde, promoted from the chorus. At the Lyric it ran three and a half months longer, finishing its amazing run on 6 April, 1889.

Dorothy toured widely throughout Britain and the English-speaking world and some performers played nothing but *Dorothy* year after year. Lucy Carr-Shaw, sister to the playwright George Bernard, who had understudied the title-role in town made a career of it in the provinces and Marion Cross, Albert Christian, Caroline Ewell, Jerrold Manville and others appeared in the show again and again as first Leslie and then his licencees took it round season after season. In 1892 it came briefly back into town at the new Trafalgar Square Theatre with Florence Dysart, Furneaux Cook and Le Hay all repeating their original parts, and in 1908 a revival was staged at the New Theatre with, twenty years and more after, two of the original cast – Coffin and Williams – playing their original and most famous roles. But in twenty years times and tastes had changed and the piece attracted only in a nostalgic fashion. The moment of magic for *Dorothy* had been and gone.

Almost inevitably, *Dorothy* failed in America. The qualities which had given it its appeal for English audiences were not those appreciated by New York audiences whose tastes ran more to the farcical, the French and *Erminie*. It had a six-week Broadway run with Lillian Russell in the title role and Harry Paulton as Lurcher, coming and going while the London version continued its seemingly unending passage. Australia, on the other hand, took the British attitude and *Dorothy* was immediately successful and frequently revived for many years.

Dorothy was a phenomenon. Its attraction, as often with particularly successful shows, is slightly difficult to pinpoint, but *The Era* critic, commenting on the first transfer, may have come as near to analysing it as can be done. He said, simply:

> . . . good music, well sung, pretty faces, pretty scenery and pretty dresses and a little broad fun and no vulgarity – these are the qualities which have given *Dorothy* its vogue and may prolong its career for an indefinite time.

Its libretto, embellished by Williams' comicalities and smoothed by hundreds of performances, remained a simple and unexceptional piece with a certain dignity but also with some strangely inept moments – the huntsmen and the night-gowns were never rationalised, and the disguises which formed the foundation of the plot remained beyond the suspension of disbelief of many. The music offered charm and melody but, apart from 'Queen of my Heart' no true hits. Dorothy's pretty 'Be wise in Time', the tenor ballad 'With such a dainty Dame' and Phyllis's ballad 'The Time has Come' found their way on to many a drawing-room music-stand and amateur buffos enjoyed singing with Arthur Williams 'I Am the Sheriff's faithful Man', but it was by no means a score which followed hit tune with hit tune. Yet all the elements of the show came together in a way which, as *Erminie* had in America, proved irresistible at the time and place in which they were given and the result was one of the most successful shows in the history of British musical theatre.

Less than three weeks after *Dorothy* began its career at the Gaiety another new musical opened at the Avenue. *Indiana* was the latest Anglo-French collaboration instigated by the irrepressible H. B. Farnie. Farnie had taken an old French piece for the basis of a familiar plot of civil war disguises and deceptions. The American, Indiana Grayfaunt, is engaged to Philip Jervaulx and, in order to see him secretly, she comes to England and disguises herself as a cavalier. But Philip too is in disguise, masquerading as a steward in the house of his cousin, Lady Prue, for he has compromised himself by foolishly delivering a packet from France which contained Jacobite letters. Lady Prue's silly husband is in charge of catching the reprobate, and when he hears of strange cavaliers hiding in the local mill he tracks down these targets who are none other than the disguised Indiana and her maid. In the meantime there has been a good deal of dallying going on with the light Lord Dayrell using the renewal of the lease of the mill to get the miller's pretty young wife up to the Castle. Indiana takes her place and wins not only the errant Dayrell but also the unsuspecting Philip. When Lord Mulberry attacks the mill it is only to find Philip pardoned and in the arms of Indiana and himself undignifiedly dumped in a hopper of flour.

The libretto was rather long-winded and the second act, full of ingenious but not particularly funny romantic convolutions, was stretched out to an inordinate length. But Farnie's writing was a great improvement on much of his earlier work. The dialogue was clear and pointed and organised into an intelligible story in a way he had not always previously managed. The music was written by Edmond Audran who had delighted London with *Olivette* and the delicious *La Mascotte*, but *Indiana* found him less inspired and, although his music was unfailingly pretty, neither it nor Farnie's libretto had enough character to make *Indiana* into a hit. The show was tried for one week in Manchester before opening at the Avenue where it was given a fair reception by the audience and an indifferent one by the critics, and the creative personnel immediately set to work doctoring the book and the songs.

The most successful part of the show had been the comical fooling of Arthur Roberts in the role of the gormless miller, Matt o'the Mill, around whom all the action goes on.

Roberts/Matt was well-featured, but he was given a free hand with his part which grew daily and the Avenue box-office take grew with it. Roberts put across his comic songs with a will and scored hugely with the topical song 'Quite Sufficient' and an interpolated number by John Crook 'The plain Potato' which told the cautionary tale of the vain acorn and the humble potato:

> But ah 'tis not the jacket
> That can make a man of worth
> Nor should an acorn sneer at
> A potato's lowly birth.

In Farnie's lyric the potato is taken off to market to be sold as a truffle while the acorn is gobbled up by a pig.

Even Roberts could not make *Indiana* more than a half-success and it was withdrawn in mid-December to allow the Avenue to present its Christmas attraction, *Robinson Crusoe*, again starring Roberts. The following year it was revived briefly when the Avenue was precipitately forced to end its revival of *Madame Favart* owing to the illness of Florence St John. After a few weeks it was replaced in its turn and taken out on a tour of the principal cities. Simultaneously, Kate Santley took out a second company starring herself and Henry Ashley, but after that season *Indiana* was seen no more. John McCaull tried the piece at Broadway's Star Theatre in the same year but it failed to make any sort of impression on America.

The year's record had been redeemed in no uncertain fashion by *Dorothy*, but it was to be well and truly extended by the year's last production – the Christmas burlesque at the Gaiety. Since its enormous success the previous year, *Little Jack Sheppard* with its starry cast had been selling out on the road in the bigger provincial towns. Now the company was returning to a Gaiety eager for its favourites with a new piece on similar lines, loosely based on Dumas' *The Count of Monte Cristo* and entitled *Monte Cristo Jr*.

Monte Cristo Jr had been written by two members of the staff of the Sunday newspaper *The Referee*, the editor Richard Butler and Henry Chance Newton whose theatrical columns were written under the pen-name of 'Carados'. Newton had begun his connection with the theatre as a young actor before moving to journalism at the age of 21, and subsequently to play writing. George Edwardes accepted their piece and took it up to Bristol to read to the actors who were, in their turn, delighted. The songs were set up and Meyer Lutz organised his composing brigade to prepare their side of the work. Fred Leslie, whose inventiveness had been so prominent a feature of *Little Jack Sheppard*, was in at the beginning this time with ideas for business and for songs and even a tune. 'Chorus to Mr Leslie's Polka' was marked down on Edwardes' music schedule for Act I.

The libretto for *Monte Cristo Jr* was in a different tone to that of *Little Jack Sheppard*. Although it was still in rhyme and metre, it was less strict with both these requirements and the extremities of word-play had vanished. There was the occasional section in a shadow of the old style:

DANTES: And so I took command
MOREL: You?
ALL: You?
DANTES: Why yes, for I'm a regular ripper
There's not much (h)erring in this precious (s)kipper
Though fond of fun on duty I am serious
I ne'er mis-steer my bark to parts mysterious.

and the concessions to rhyming still hampered the dialogue but less than before.

The story vaguely followed Dumas' sensational novel. Young Edmond Dantes has made a number of enemies. There is Fernand, his rival for the hand of the lovely Mercedes, Danglars whom he has officially sanctioned, and the wicked prefect of police, de Villefort, among others. When Dantes foolishly delivers a postcard of an incriminating nature from a source in Ireland they have him seized, at the very moment of his wedding, and thrown into the Château d'If. There he meets the arch-conspirator Noirtier (*vice* the Abbé) and they escape. Dantes finds a fabulous treasure cave and becomes the rich Count of Monte Cristo and sets out to wreak revenge on those who wronged him. On to this inherently 'straight' story the authors built the fun – and two parts in which Nellie Farren and Fred Leslie could repeat their triumphs as Jack and Wild. Nellie, of course, was Dantes and Fred Leslie became Noirtier, the plotter of all plotters, dashing from one disguise to another, turning up everywhere, even doing a costume and make-up change in view of the audience. Agnes de la Porte was the new heroine, replacing Marion Hood who had gone to the Prince of Wales with *Dorothy*, and the new recruits to the team included a buxom American, Fay Templeton, as the unpleasant Fernand, a bouncy English girl called Lottie Collins as a peasant girl, and one Edwin Jesse Lonnen as the police chief.

Monte Cristo Jr was a great hit. Fred Leslie and Nellie Farren had been given some marvellous opportunities and made the most of them. Nellie, dressed in convict costume, and carrying a placard '93' around her neck in burlesque of the drama *Never too late to Mend*, delivered a topical piece called 'Inside', and then joined Leslie in a duet and a grotesque dance which caused a virtual riot before popping into a sack marked 'Washing' to make her escape from the Château. Then, rushing under the stage, she appeared below to be shot at by the guards as she paddled off to safety.

Leslie disguised himself as a Jewish pedlar and eased himself into a brilliant series of impersonations:

> This garb Jew-dicious won't give me away
> It was suggested to me at the play
> So many plays I lately have seen fixed-up
> That somehow in my head they've all got mixed up

and launched into 'Imitations' in the course of which he gave lightning sketches of Toole and Grossmith, Tom Thorne and David James, Harry Paulton, Durward Lely, Arthur Cecil, Rutland Barrington, Edward Terry, Arthur Roberts, Nellie Farren and, finally, of himself. On nights when his repertoire of encore verses was run right through he is said to have parodied twenty-two different stars. He joined with Lonnen in a song and dance declaring 'Tis a glorious Thing to Plot'; he flipped into excellent French for 'Je Suis un grand Detective'; and made fun out of everything that came to hand – his costume, the props, the scenery and even his moustache which was rigged to crawl all over his face until he finally seemed to swallow it.

Fay Templeton half spoke her way through a number called 'I Like it, I Do' which imitated Harry Dixey's hit song 'It's English, you Know', Sylvia Grey performed a variant on her graceful dance, Mlle de la Porte delivered a pretty waltz song and Lottie Collins a more sprightly one, and all the time the lavish scenery and costumes kept on coming. Both public and critics responded most positively. *The Stage* declared it was:

> a distinct advance on anything of the kind that has lately been seen. It is no ordinary show of shapely girls or a repetition of the latest music hall tunes but an entertainment as light, bright, exhilarating and harmless as could be desired. It is of

too fanciful a nature to be classed with ordinary burlesque but all the same it is vastly amusing and commendably clever . . . . an extravaganza of unusual brilliancy of idea and construction which affords ample opportunity for the exhibition of the talents of the actor, and the singer, the dancer, the scenic artist and the costumier.

The Era tried to analyse it:

[it] partakes of the characteristics of melodrama, comedy, comic opera, travestie and one of those boulevard productions known as revue. It is all of these by turns and nothing long but it is a merry and well-compounded mixture nonetheless.

while *The Entr'acte* simply allowed:

. . every credit to the author for his humorous and pointed text, his excellent verses and a pleasant treatment of a fresh subject, to the principals of the company for investing text and 'business' with much importance, and to Mr Lutz for some of the best music that even he has written.

The audiences were not of an analytic turn and they packed the Gaiety for a show which was precisely what they wanted to see. *The Times* reported:

. . deafening volleys of applause, the pit and gallery screaming themselves hoarse with delight . .

But, in spite of its success, *Monte Cristo Jr* was not allowed to play on unchanged. The Gaiety audience was a recurring one and Edwardes believed in keeping the show fresh with additions and alterations. In February of the new year Marion Hood, superseded as Dorothy, returned to take up her old position. A ballad by Tito Mattei was added to the score for her. Fred Leslie also had a new song, but an Irish number for Lonnen about a phony temperance group, 'The Ballyhooly blue Ribbon Army', written by Irishman Robert Martin turned out to be the most popular addition. In no time 'Ballyhooly' became the take-away number of the show.

Whililo, hi ho, let us all enlist, you know
For their ructions and their elements they charm me;
We don't care what we ate, if we drink our whiskey nate,
In the Ballyhooly blue ribbon army.

There was one more alteration in the cast. Fay Templeton had distinct ideas on costumes, which she liked to be rather revealing. The law had other thoughts and she was ordered by the manager to cover up. She refused and Edwardes sacked her. Miss Templeton sued – never a bad thing for an unknown actress's reputation – and lost, which rather took the icing off the publicity. Billie Barlow was promoted to play Fernand.

In April more additions and alterations were made for the 100th performance which was announced as an official 'Second Edition'. Nellie Farren's role was enlarged by a popular piece called 'I'm a jolly little Chap all Round' and 'Inside' was dropped in favour of a medley of her best known songs. Leslie's repertoire of celebrity impersonations had grown and 'Imitations' now featured a notable Hayden Coffin. He had also worked a tremendous amount of 'business' into all sides of his performance. Pretty Letty Lind, who had been 'discovered' by 'Pot' Stephens and written up by him in a *Topical Times* article, was brought in to take on the featured part of Mariette and the lovely Blanche sisters, Ada and Addie, joined the cast as 'Boatswain' and 'Clairette', roles invented to allow them to take part in what was a rather mobile show.

In June the time came to leave the Gaiety to the French play season and *Monte*

Cristo Jr closed after a six-month run. With substantially the same cast it headed for the country, and the provinces once more flocked to see Fred Leslie, Nellie Farren and the new burlesque which ran on until another Christmas hove in sight and it was time to go back to the Gaiety and the next new burlesque. The following year the Gaiety company took *Monte Cristo Jr* and its successor, *Miss Esmeralda,* to Australia and America and both the pieces and the artists scored a great success in spite of attempts at sabotage by an anti-British contingent in New York. *Monte Cristo Jr* played a month at the Standard Theatre before giving way to *Miss Esmeralda,* and the company then toured their two pieces through other US cities.

Another Christmas production was a musical version of *Alice in Wonderland* played for a series of matinées at the Prince of Wales Theatre. Lewis Carroll's famous book was adapted for the stage by Savile Clark and the music was supplied by Walter Slaughter, a pupil of Georges Jacobi, whose principal activity had been as a 'cellist and a pianist in the halls. A large number of the roles were taken by children including, on this first occasion, a certain Miss Mabel Love in the tiny part of 'Rose'. Lewis Carroll himself took an active interest in the production and was personally responsible for the selection of little Phoebe Carlo to represent his Alice for the first time on stage. *Alice in Wonderland* was a remarkable success. Its season was twice extended and it was not taken off until the beginning of March. It was subsequently played at many different London theatres for many different Christmas seasons, the last being as late as 1934.

A number of new shows appeared on the provincial touring circuit during the year and they varied greatly in type, in scale and in degree of success. On the one hand there was a large and spectacular comic opera mounted by Kate Santley for her autumn tour and the grand fairy-tale piece taken out by John Shine; and on the other there was the farcical musical play provided as a vehicle for Harry Monkhouse and the broadly comical opera-melodrama staged by Deane Brand.

Kate Santley's piece was undoubtedly the most ambitious. Having been both performer and manageress for many years, Miss Santley now turned her hand, somewhat nervously she insisted, to writing, and conceived an Indian comic opera which she entitled *Vetah*–Vetah being a charming Indian maiden with the gift of second sight and played by Miss Santley herself. Vetah is beloved by a local fisherman, Nafnez, and returns his love without knowing that he is actually a Prince in disguise. The court of Nafnez' father has come under the influence of one Captain Slope who has been raised to high position and has imbued the Rajah with a taste for all things English. Nafnez, having been sent off to sow his wild oats like an English gentleman, has found Vetah and given up all idea of returning to court. But the Rajah comes to Vetah's tower to consult her as soothsayer and their idyll is discovered, to the fury of the Princess Zamine who is betrothed to the Prince. Nafnez runs away but Vetah is haled off to the Court by the now amorous Rajah. Nafnez comes to save her and with the help of Slope, who turns out to be the heroine's long-lost father, and his Irish chum, Corney, they get away. Pursued by the Rajah they persuade the ambitious Zamine to impersonate Vetah in a marriage ceremony and all ends happily.

Kate Santley's style as a writer varied from the dreadfully arch to the robustly humorous. Her attempts at wordplay were basic and ponderous, her romantic lines littered with 'thee' and 'thou' in a perfect parade of clichés. *The Stage* critic who remarked that her work 'reminded one of the extravaganzas of Planché's days' clearly did not have his mind on the dialogue. The music for the piece was largely by the French composer Firmin Bernicat. But Bernicat had been dead for three years and Miss Santley's connection with him had begun posthumously with her production of his *François-les-bas-bleus* at the Royalty. Quite where she assembled her score for *Vetah* from is not clear, but having done so she handed it to Georges Jacobi to complete and arrange. She had some special material for herself written by Frederick Bowyer which was duly interpolated.

A fine set of Indian scenery – the ruined tower of the White Spirit, the Hall of a Thousand Elephants, the Rajah's Harem – and a cast of lovely young ladies costumed by Wilhelm and choreographed by D'Auban, the whole directed by Richard Barker, produced a more than successful result. Miss Santley was experienced enough to surround herself with the best in creative staff and she also knew her provincial audiences well enough to make her plot and characters uncomplicated. Audiences which were ready to hiss Fred Leslie as the villain of *Little Jack Sheppard* as they would have for the original melodrama were scarcely ready for subtleties. She also knew that every penny spent on the visual side of the production would reap its reward at the box-office, and her Masked Ball and the processional 'Dream of Fair Women' introduced into the second act gave her appreciative audiences a degree of splendour rarely seen outside the very best pantomimes.

Vetah was produced at Portsmouth and toured for sixteen weeks, closing only at the approach of pantomime time. Somewhat surprisingly the tour schedule included Birmingham. Miss Santley had previously had strong words with the theatre management and the newspapers in Birmingham and, sure enough, when the date came up she caused a minor scandal by refusing to appear and putting Amy Grundy on in the title role. The papers attacked her and *The Birmingham Daily Mail* found the incident sufficiently important to devote its leader to 'la belle Kate'. But if Birmingham had reservations about Miss Santley, now a slightly portly maiden at the age of 43[1], the rest of the country did not and *Vetah* succeeded well enough to be taken out again, with some new numbers by Ivan Caryll added to the score, as soon as the pantomimes were over. It played through ten dates between February and May. For the Christmas of 1887 the actress-manager planned to stage a third version of *Vetah* embellished for the occasion with a grand ballet and a harlequinade but the venture was finally abandoned, and *Vetah* was packed away after 156 performances.

The comic opera *Glamour* started out at Edinburgh on the same day that *Vetah* began its career at the other end of the country. It was a whimsical piece with a libretto concocted by H. B. Farnie and the omnipresent Alfred Murray which had already done service as the book of the pasticcio *Piff Paff* or The Magic Armoury staged unsuccessfully at the Criterion in 1876 by Lydia Thompson. For this version new music was composed by William M. Hutchison, best known as the composer of ballads such as 'Dream Faces' and 'Ehren on the Rhine'. Hutchison was a prolific composer of light music of all kinds both under his own name and the pseudonym 'Julian Mount'. Another pseudonym 'William Marshall' covered music publishing activities which included much of his own work.

The plot of *Glamour* showed an impecunious king anxious to marry one of his step-daughters to the rich Prince Glamour but both the girls have lovers and Glamour falls for the shepherdess, Daphne, and determines to get out of his promise. He does this by means of a trial by Magic Armoury – if the magic gun goes off the shooter is proved

[1] or, according to J. M. Glover, 50. But Glover tells a lively tale about Kate and Soldene when *Vetah* visited the latter's theatre at Hastings. Unfortunately, *Vetah* never played Hastings.

unchaste in thought. The Princesses fail the test as does the Queen, who is plotting with the Count Inferno against her husband, and the Countess Allegra, his wife, who is carrying on with the King. Only Daphne passes the test. But the villains add a codicil to the rules reversing the decision and the shepherdess is arrested. All finally turns out well with the aid of a magic humming-bird which traps the Princesses in their amours and the plotters at their plots before the eyes of the horrified king. Daphne turns out to be a long-lost princess and Glamour is able happily to marry her.

The dialogue, in contrast to the new works both authors provided for town during the year, dripped with puns and wordplay of the most extreme kind and relied on the broadest of effects for its humour. The climactic scene had Glamour and his valet impersonating statues to eavesdrop on the King and Allegra and the Queen and Inferno who, under cover of darkness, became involved in a *Manteaux Noirs* series of mistaken identities. There were other notable reminiscences of popular works throughout the show. The score, Hutchison's only attempt at a full-length musical, consisted largely of choruses and songs for the principal tenor Charles Conyers as Glamour and the prima donna, Giulia Warwick (Daphne). The latter had the most felicitous piece, a simple ballad about a country lass and a noble lord called 'He Was Highborn'. Other pieces owed more to tradition – a huntsmen's chorus, a pages' chorus, a conspirators' quintet, a Showman's song and a piece relating 'The Legend of the Guns'.

Glamour toured ten weeks through Number 1 dates with a fine cast headed by the Shine brothers, John and Wilfred. The following season it was brought out again under the banner of Gilbert Tate and taken round for a further two months including a London appearance at the Crystal Palace for one matinée. For this revival Charles Danby replaced Shine as the King and Edith Vane took on the role of Daphne.

Rhoda, also officially called a comic opera, was of a different tone again. It had been thought up by the composer Antonio Mora who had at first tried to write his own libretto. He then enlisted the help of one R. E. Liston and subsequently of the more experienced Walter Parke of *Manteaux Noirs* who turned out the final, playable script which mixed the dramatic and sub-operatic with low comedy and song and dance in an unlikely story set in the South American city of Pavana in the year 1610.

Rhoda, a wealthy heiress, is courted by the nephew of the upstart mayor, Peter Bosco, whom she refuses in favour of the artist, Adolphe Martel. The rejected Valdez has his revenge by borrowing a life-sized automaton from a travelling showman which he dresses in Rhoda's clothes and uses to compromise the artist. Rhoda, hearing her lover swearing eternal love to a supposed other, tries to shoot him and guns down the 'lady'. The second act finds Adolphe in court on trial for the murder of the unknown woman and the kidnap of Rhoda, who has run off with him. When the truth is discovered, Rhoda promises to marry Valdez and gains revenge by tricking him into a marriage with the doll. The villain is made ridiculous before the whole town, and Rhoda and Adolphe are finally united.

Parke's book was lively enough and devoted the whole of its second act to trying to reproduce the success of its author's court scene in *Estrella*. With chief comedian Peter Bosco officiating, interrogating witnesses and suspects through a heavy cold, there was plenty of unsophisticated humour to add to a dash of plot and incident. Mora's music was equally light and derivative, in the style of his previous output of ballads and piano music, rising to its most dramatic in some pieces of the prima donna role, but most successful where most frivolous. The show's best-liked number was a gavotte put across by Agnes Oliver in the soubrette role and called 'Ity Tity':

Love is like a summer's day
Ity Ity Tity, Ity Ity Tity,
Makes the world so bright and gay
Ity Ity Tity, Tra-la-la-la-la!
Someone asked me as his bride
Illy Olly O, Illy Olly O
You may guess what I replied
Illy Olly O, Tra-la-la-la-la

Kate Chard (Mrs Deane Brand and late of the Savoy) took the title-role and did well with a polka in the finale on the 'moth around the flame' theme.

Rhoda's first tour was short but fairly happy and ended with the piece being brought to the Grand at Islington and then into the West End's Comedy Theatre where, once again, it was proved that what went down well in the provinces was not neccessarily to the taste of a London audience. *The Era* remarked that the piece could have been appropriately subtitled 'The Low Comedian Let Loose' and continued:

> A tendency to lay upon the shoulders of the low comedy merchant the principal burden of light opera has been observable of late; but in *Rhoda* a whole act is devoted to developing the peculiarities (and very laughable ones they are too) of Peter Bosco, the mayor of Pavana.

The opening night audience at the Comedy left no doubt as to their opinion, heckling the performers with disparaging comments, and the critics were equally severe with its lack of sophistication. After two weeks the show was closed, but Brand took it to the country 16 months later for a return visit to Northampton and eight new dates. During this run he took a turn at the role of Bosco himself and Millie Vere made a big success of 'Ity Tity'.

A comic opera produced at the Islington Grand as *The Magic Ring* proved a ghastly failure and was quickly done away with; and another, *Atlantis*, tried at a Gaiety matinée suffered an even more summary fate. Gilbert Shirley produced a short tour of *The Countess of Castille* written and composed by himself and it did well enough at a few minor dates on the smaller circuits to be repeated from time to time by its author/star.

One of the most widely toured pieces of the year was a lively show called *Larks* written by Wilton Jones to fit the talents of the comedian Harry Monkhouse. Monkhouse played Dr Theodore Lamb, an organist who is obliged to turn his serious opera into a burlesque to raise money to get his stepson out of a scrape. His wife has religious principles, so he is obliged to keep his 'disgraceful' action from her and spends most of the play avoiding being caught by her in and around the theatre. Monkhouse had many opportunities for disguises and impersonations including a scene where he took to the burlesque stage to escape his pursuing wife. *Larks* was produced in February and toured twenty-three weeks before taking a short break and then resuming with a winter tour. At one stage Monkhouse split his company in two to enable him to fulfil all his November dates, for *Larks* was decidedly popular. It was just the kind of light English comedy which appealed in the provinces and Monkhouse was wise enough to keep it away from town.

The music, principally from Oscar Barrett, Alfred Lee and John Crook, was arranged by Crook who had previously collaborated with Jones on *The King's Dragoons* and *Merry Mignon*. After the pure comic opera style of the first and the traditional burlesque flavour of the second, *Larks* was an example of a third different stream of the British musical, that descended from the drawing room comedy/operetta and the world of the Gallery of Illustration. In the fashion of the day, the low comedian's role was pre-eminent, relegating the romantic and straight vocal element to a subsidiary position. *Larks* was primarily a vehicle for its star. Monkhouse toured his show off and on for nearly two years before leaving it to his leading lady, Ada Clare, while he went on to more metropolitan things. He brought it out again several seasons later for a further tour and in 1899 staged a revised version as *Larks in London.*

Another piece in the same tradition, although with more emphasis on the melodramatic, was *Lovers.* This piece, in the *Jack-in-the-Box* vein, was created by Haldane Crichton and his associates for Crichton's touring company which toured it around principally smaller dates from May till the end of the year. Its story of a melodramatic and scheming lady hypnotist out to get herself a wealthy husband was illustrated musically by George Fox, better known for his vaguely scholarly cantatas and drawing-room music. It was played on similar tours for three seasons.

Shorter pieces were fewer in number now that the days of multiple bills were all but gone. The St George's Hall played through most of the year with an unexceptional piece by Comyns Carr called *A United Pair* which was replaced just before Christmas by the same author's *The Friar,* a little piece in the Gothic vein. The Savoy produced *The Carp*, a little fishing/love story, to precede *The Mikado.* It had a long life, principally due to the success of the main part of the programme rather than to its own merits. It was well-enough thought of, however, to be retained with *Ruddigore* when that piece succeeded at the Savoy. Another long-lived piece was *Blackberries*, a singing, dancing, burlesquing trifle manufactured for Alice Atherton by Mark Melford and played with *Turned Up*. Its music, like Edouin's other shows, was a mixture of original and interpolated pieces under the supervision of Meyer Lutz.

1886

0064 **LARKS** a musical farcical burlesque in three acts by J. Wilton Jones. Music by W. Meyer Lutz, Oscar Barrett, Frederick Stanislaus, John Crook, Alfred Lee. Arranged by John Crook. Produced at the Winter Gardens, Southport under the management of Harry Monkhouse 22 February, 1886 and toured to 7 August. Recommenced 30 August. Company split in two November 6 and reconstituted 13 December. Tour ended 5 March (305 perfs). Recommenced 21 March, 1887 and ended 4 June, 1887. Recommenced 8 August, 1887, ended 3 December, 1887. Recommenced 26 March, 1888 through to 1 December, 1888.

Dr Theodore Lamb . . . . Harry Monkhouse
Hon. Guy Fitzsmythe. . . . . Hebert Stanley/Arthur Lawrence
Charley Dempster. . . . . J. W. Bradbury/Alfred Young/Arthur Lawrence/Vere Matthews
Popshott. . . . . C. P. Amalia/George Lyttleton
Frederick Jinks . . . . J. W. Handley/Herbert Stanley/Alfred Young/Edward Russell/Charles Blight
Timmins . . . . A. Dodd/Hugh Power
Popsy Lee. . . . . Rosie St George/Myra Rosalind/Eleanor Byers/Ada Clare
Mrs Lamb. . . . . Jenny McIntyre/Mrs C. A. Clarke/Marie d'Alvera
Kate Prosper . . . . Ella Sennett Naomi Neilson/Anita Lemaistre/Belle Black/Lena Leicester/Maud Branscombe
Maria . . . . Nellie Bouverie/Kate Neville/Carrie Lee Stoyle/Hetty Chapman/Carrie Ash/Naomi Neilson
Mother of the Gracchi . . . . Edith Orme &c.
Lotty Montmorency . . . . Kate Pinder &c.
Kissie Vivian . . . . Maggie Pinder &c.
Tottie Plantaganet . . . . Emmie Pinder &c.
Polly Leslie . . . . Annie Pinder &c.
Nellie Fitzgerald . . . . Emily Rittur &c.
Lottie Bartlett. . . . . Blanche Percival/Nita Graham
Duncombe . . . . L. James/Otto Culling
Lady Campbell . . . . Katherine Moxon &c.

Md: Alfred Lee

Revised as *Larks in London* with new music by Jacques Greeve and toured by Harry Monkhouse 1899.

0065 **LOVERS** a romantic musical play by W. E. Morton, F. Hugh Herbert and Haldane Crichton. Music by George D. Fox. Produced by Haldane Crichton at the Theatre Royal & Opera House, Cork 5 May, 1886 and toured.

Major Shot . . . . Haldane Crichton
Sir Oswald Denbigh . . . . Alfred A. Wallace/Herbert Barrs

Frank Fairfield . . . . Denbigh Cooper/Fred Maxwell
Capt Leo Broughton . . . . Laurence Corrie/Rupert Woods
Nat Bartelmy . . . . F. Hugh Herbert/Charles Branton
Geoffrey Fairfield . . . . /Fred Hughes
Zanita Tarentelle . . . . Maggie Duggan/Amy Forrest
Violet . . . . Mary Regan
Mrs Hazelton . . . . Agnes Birchenough/Helen Carroll/Lulu Du Cane
Countess de Valmont . . . . Helen Carroll/Lillie Woods

66 **THE LILY OF LÉOVILLE** a comic opera in 3 acts. The original book by Félix Rémo adapted by Alfred Murray. Music by Ivan Caryll. Produced at the Grand Theatre, Birmingham under the management of Violet Melnotte 3 May, 1886. Transferred to the Comedy Theatre 10 May, 1886 for a run of 41 performances closing 25 June, 1886.

Chevalier Georges de Lauvenay . . . . . George W. Travener//Henry Bracy
Coriolon . . . . C. Hayden Coffin
Meridon, a steward . . . . Charles E. Stevens
Sergeant Rataplan . . . . Walter Andrews//Fred Kaye
Lourdad . . . . Lionel Rignold
Lascelles . . . . Charles Ashford
Rigaud, a notary . . . . Ambrose Collini
Jacques, a servant . . . . H. C. Payne
Gabrielle de Léoville . . . . Agnes de la Porte
Turlurette . . . . Violet Melnotte
Mme de la Seche . . . . M. A. Victor
Jacquette . . . . Minnie Byron/Mary Webb
M. Rigault . . . . Maggie Rayson
M. Laferme . . . . Edith Fletcher/Louise Fletcher
M. Pitou . . . . Maudie Vernon
M. Manet . . . . Madge Bruce
M. Champdos . . . . Louise Deleau
M. Foullard . . . . Lillian Edeveian
Mlle Fauvette . . . . Ethel Selwyn
Mlle La Gaillarde . . . . Frances Stanhope
Mlle Cuzon . . . . Mary Webb/
Mlle Chausson . . . . Louise Fletcher/Edith Fletcher
Mlle Manifette . . . . Carrie Solomon
Mlle Cascadette . . . . Kitty Graham
with Fannie G. Pew, Isabel G. Stuart, Adele B. Levey, Alice B. Hartley, Louie G. Searle, Maude S. Moreland, Maggie Barrington, Maude Verney, Francis Mellon, Kate Francis, Laurie Elliston, Flora McGregor, Louie Henri, Minnie Richardson, Violet Leigh, Florence Dudley; Messrs Henry Montague, H. C. Payne, Charles Bernhardt, S. Horsepool, Arthur Richmond, E. Leahy, Charles Cowlrick, J. C. Piddock, Henry A. Henri, J. H. Jupp, G. R. Luke, L. Vernon, G. Sinclair.

Dir: Richard Barker; md: Auguste van Biene; ch: Willie Warde; sc: Bruce Smith; cos: Bianchini and Besche

67 **THE PALACE OF PEARL** a musical spectacular extravaganza in three acts by Alfred Murray and William Younge. Music by Frederick Stanislaus and Edward Jakobowski. Produced at the Empire Theatre under the management of Claude Marius 12 June, 1886 for a run of 48 performances, closing 6 August, 1886.

King Alger XIX . . . . Charles Cartwright/J. J. Dallas
Prince Amor . . . . Grace Huntley
Mentor . . . . Claude Marius
Sinex . . . . A. B. Tapping/Charles Fawcett
Florian . . . . Lizzie? Birkett
Conrad . . . . Isobel Ellison/Florence Levey
Zelos . . . . Stanley Betjeman
Elmos . . . . Emmie Graham

Nifa . . . . Nellie Vacani
Sigismund . . . . Nellie Lisle/J. Hamilton
Trumpeter . . . . Minnie Rayner/W. Stanhope
Roulade . . . . Miss Bell/Miss Ansell
Poeita . . . . Miss Couzins
Raoul . . . . B. E. E. Matiste
Rodolph . . . . Miss Richardson
Queen Amaranth XVIII . . . . Susie Vaughan
Princess Alma . . . . Mathilde Wadman
Tenise . . . . Myron Calice/Arthur A. Bancroft
Elfie . . . . Fanny Wentworth
Fabian . . . . Miss Yonge
Marco . . . . Albert Sims/Mr Simbert?
Sporaz . . . . George Temple/Albert Sims
Almina . . . . Agnes Oliver
Innkeeper . . . . Mr Colman
The Ambassador from the king of Polonia . . E. W. Colman/Mr Courtenay

Pds: Mlles Pertoldi, Luna, Clementine, Johnson, L. Sinclair, Albery, B. Robson, P. Knight, L. Davies, A. Davies.

Dir: Claude Marius and the authors; md: Frederick Stanislaus; sc: W. B. Spong, E. G. Banks, Bruce Smith, Charles C. Brooke, W. Perkins; cos: Lucien Besche, Wilhelm, Mrs S. May

0068 **OUR AGENCY** a farcical musical comedy by Burlington Brumell and W. G. Matchem. Lyrics by Henry Duff. Music by Ernest Trowbridge. Produced at the Avenue Theatre under the management of Messrs Burlington Brumell, Duval & Co. 19 July, 1886 for a run of 7 performances closing 26 July, 1886.

Lt. Benbow . . . . D. E. Mining
Harry Dickerson . . . . H. Reed
Harry Burlington . . . . Frank Oswald
Comte de Torres . . . . Harry Stuart
Mathers . . . . E. Power
Mary Mason . . . . Dot Robins
Emily Winthorne . . . . Lillian Francis
Toby Smart . . . . Julia Lalor Shiel
Mabel Benbow . . . . Cecile Stanhope
Adolphus Boyd . . . . John Tresahar
Mr Sittup . . . . E. Soldene-Powell
Jonathan Finn . . . . Ted Duval
Rev. Theo Aspirus . . . . Percy Rhys
Beatrice Vincent . . . . Ada Dacre
Mrs Higgins . . . . Annie Rose
Servant . . . . Helen Clarence

Ch: Mme Besani

0069 **THE COUNTESS OF CASTILLE** a comic opera by Gilbert Shirley. Produced at the Public Hall, Clacton-on-Sea under the management of Gilbert Shirley 20 August, 1886 and toured through Colchester, North Shields, Grimsby, Walsall &c.

Henri Delacour . . . . Albert Fenton/Christopher Grier/Gilbert Shirley
Cherette . . . . Dora Desmond/Emma Wangeheim
Madame Margot . . . . Miss Dare/Miss Merritt/Martha Wilson
François de Maronville . . . . Gilbert Shirley/Fred Bernard
Zarotte . . . . Miss Davington
Père Bonvin . . . . C. A. Russell
Marie . . . . Miss Conroy/Miss Beaumont
Major Bombonac . . . . Archer A. Ritchie
Fanchette . . . . Martha Wilson/Miss Beaumont/
Md: Mr Herbert

VETAH an Indian comic opera in three acts by Kate Santley. Music by Firmin Bernicat and Georges Jacobi. Special songs by Frederick Bowyer. Produced at the Theatre Royal, Portsmouth, 30 August, 1886, under the management of Kate Santley and toured through Torquay, Plymouth, Cardiff, Bristol, Leicester, Birmingham, Bradford, Manchester, Hanley, Sheffield, Liverpool, Glasgow, Edinburgh and Newcastle ending 11 December, 1886.

Jam Zohreb, Rajah of Jollipore . . . . . . Fred Neebe/Herman de Lange
Prince Nafnez, his nephew . . . . Michael Dwyer
Hamet Abdulerim Abensellan . . . . . . Robert Courtneidge/Marshall Moore
Corney Delaney . . . . Lionel Rignold/J. T. MacMillan
Captain Walker Slope . . . . Henry Ashley/Charles E. Stevens
Serang . . . . James Neville
Mohara, Queen of the Harem . . . . . . Nellie Vacani
Salla . . . . Laura Hansen
Achbar . . . . Madge Avery
Ichandar . . . . Evelyn Darrell
Sareb . . . . Florence Denny (or Dene)
Guitarra, a Spanish beauty . . . . Kate Bellingham
Zedah . . . . Edith Lonsdale
Nilauf . . . . Ida Ferrers
Chereddin . . . . Violet Graham/Lizzie Wilson
Natali . . . . Kate Findlay
Iran . . . . Maud McIntyre/Bertie Clarke
Zilour . . . . Catalina Gomez
Dersa . . . . Violet Hamilton
Orrisa . . . . Rose Graham/Kate Oscar Byrne
Princess Zamine . . . . Edith Blande
Vetah . . . . Kate Santley (Amy Grundy)
with Leonora St Leger (Cidrar), Lillie McIntyre (Durman), Alice Denny (Kansummah), Ida Travers (Dhurge), Violet Masters (Tambi), Carrie Terry (Kitmutghar), Millie Landan (Jindal), Kate Gresham (Peeshkar), Georgie Andover (Mahli), Hope Eversleigh (Moonshee), Stanley Potter (Kotwal), R. Anderson (Subadar), Reginald Fenton (Chuprassie), Arthur Sheffield (Nazzir), Walter Cranbourne (Temadar), Charles McLagan (Havildar), Arthur Farina (Naigue), Granville Harris (Karkim), Henry Melbourne (Pundit)
Md: Sidney Jones, ch: John D'Auban; sc: Richard C. Durant; cos: Wilhelm

071 **GLAMOUR** a comic opera in three acts by H. B. Farnie and Alfred Murray. Music by William M. Hutchison. Produced by John L. Shine at the Theatre Royal, Edinburgh 30 August, 1886 and toured through Aberdeen, Dundee, Birmingham, Bristol x 2, Swansea, Brighton, Edinburgh, Glasgow x 2, ending 13 November, 1886.

King Impecunioso 100th . . . . John L. Shine
Fabian . . . . Victor dde Lore
Hugo . . . . Joseph Wilson
Trip . . . . Fred A. Gaytie
Count Inferno di Penseroso . . . . Wilfred E. Shine
Prince Glamour . . . . Charles Conyers
Angelo . . . . Florence Dawnay
Queen Palmyra Jane . . . . Susie Vaughan
Princess Cynthia . . . . Emilie Holt
Princess Irene . . . . Annie Montelli
Countess Allegra . . . . Augusta? Thompson (Florence Brandon)
Daphne . . . . Giulia Warwick
with a chorus of 30, said to have included J. A. E. Malone
Md: Edward St Quentin

072 **DOROTHY** a comedy opera in three acts by B. C. Stephenson. Music by Alfred Cellier. Produced at the Gaiety Theatre under the management of George Edwardes 25 September, 1886. Transferred to the Prince of Wales Theatre 20 December, 1886. Transferred to the management of Henry J. Leslie. Transferred to the Lyric Theatre 17 December, 1888. Withdrawn 6 April, 1889 after a total of 931 performances.

Dorothy Bantam . . . . Marion Hood (Lucy Carr-Shaw)/Marie Tempest/(Minna Louis)/Effie Chapuy
Lydia Hawthorne . . . . Florence Dysart/Edith Chester/Amy Augarde/Nellie Gayton/Grace Huntley/Minnie Marshall
Phyllis Tuppitt . . . . Florence Lambeth/Minnie Rayner/Lucy Carr-Shaw/(Miss Glenn)/Grace Huntley/Florence Perry/ (E. Chapman?)/Cissie Saumarez
Mrs Privett . . . . Harriet Coveney (Annie Wilson)
Lady Betty . . . . Jenny/McNulty/Florence Beale/ Miss Graham/Florence Neville/ Edith Weston/Birdie Irving
Geoffrey Wilder. . . . . Redfern Hollins/Ben Davies
Harry Sherwood . . . . C. Hayden Coffin (John Peachey)
Squire Bantam . . . . J. Furneaux Cook (John Peachey)/Albert Christian
John Tuppitt . . . . Edward Griffin/Sebastian King/ W. T. Hemsley
Lurcher . . . . Arthur Williams/Fred Emney
Tom Strutt . . . . John Le Hay

Dir: Charles Harris; md: W. Meyer Lutz/Ivan Caryll; ch: Katti Lanner; sc: Walter Hann, W. Perkins, W. B. Spong and E. G. Banks; cos: A. Chasemore/Alias

Produced at the Standard Theatre, New York, under the management of J. C. Duff 5 November, 1887 for a run of 48 performances closing 17 December, 1887.
Lillian Russell (DOR), Agnes Stone (LY), Marie Halton (PH), Rose Leighton (MRS), Eugene Oudin (GW), John E. Brand (HS), William Hamilton (SQ), John E. Nash (JT), Frank Boudinot (TS), Harry Paulton (LUR)

Produced at the Trafalgar Square Theatre under the management of Michael Levenston 26 November, 1892 for a run of 15 performances closing 13 December.
Decima Moore (DOR), Florence Dysart (LY), Lucy Carr-Shaw (PH), M. A. Victor (MRS), Yata Whynier (BET), Joseph Tapley (GW), Leonard Russell (HS), J. Furneaux Cook (SQ), Frank Lacy (JT), John Le Hay (TS), William Elton (LUR). Md: Ernest Ford; ch: John D'Auban; cos: Messrs Harrison

Produced at a special matinée at the Gaiety 28 June, 1897 for the benefit of J. Furneaux Cook.
Marie Tempest (DOR), Florence Dysart (LY), Florence Perry (PH), M. A. Victor (MRS), Florence Neville (BET), Charles Kenningham (GW), C. Hayden Coffin (HS), J. Furneaux Cook (SQ), Sam Hemsley (JT), John Le Hay (TS), Arthur Williams (LUR), Sidney Howard (FOOTMAN), Seymour Hicks (MASTER OF THE HOUNDS), E. J. Lonnen (HUNTSMAN), Arthur Roberts (1st WHIP), Robb Harwood (VICAR) with Lucy Carr-Shaw, Dora Thorne, Marion Cross, Maggie Roberts, Leonard Russell, Cecil Burt, Augustus Cramer, E. Shaw, H. Scott Russell, A. Boucicault, Paul Arthur. Pds: Katie Seymour, Topsy Sinden, Willie Warde, Edmund Payne, Will Bishop. Md: Ivan Caryll

Produced at the New Theatre under the management of Messrs E. D. and J. Maundy-Gregory 21 December, 1908. Transferred to the Waldorf Theatre 4 January, 1909. Withdrawn 6 February, 1909 after a total of 49 performances.
Constance Drever (DOR), Louie Pounds (LY), Coralie Blythe (PH), Emily Spiller (MRS), Betty Hardress (BET), John Bardesley (GW), C. Hayden Coffin (HS), Lempriere Pringle (SQ), F. J. Vigay (JT), Herbert Strathmore (TS), Arthur Williams (LUR) with Misses Maude, Maartens, Ladd, Cloud Bruce, Bryan, Macdonald, Golden, Martini, Dinorben, White, Turner, Phillips, Jesson and Riga, Messrs Cooke, Munro, Bownie, Hayter, Neville, Martin, Rosse, Wright, Stockwell, Dunbar, Reidy. Md: Frederick Rosse; cos: Burkinshaw of Liverpool

0073 **RHODA** a comic opera in 3 acts by Walter Parke. Music by Antonio L. Mora. Produced at the Theatre Royal, Croydon by Deane Brand 27 September, 1886 and toured through Nottingham, Southport, Leicester, Northampton, Islington Grand and then two weeks at the Comedy Theatre from 13 November to 27 November, 1886 (13 performances).

Peter Bosco . . . . Charles H. Kenney
Carlos Valdez . . . . Deane Brand
Baron Poncho . . . . Charles Gilbert/J. B. Ashley
Adolphe Martel . . . . Henry Walsham
Ventro . . . . Harry Martell
Grillo . . . . Percy F. Norton/Charles Norman/Compton Coutts
Rhoda . . . . Kate Chard
Teresa . . . . Agnes Oliver
Nina . . . . Miss Cleveland
Clara . . . . Susie Cohen
Lola . . . . Marian Medus
Sophie . . . . Ellen Mayland
Anna . . . . Kate Grant
A Mechanical Female Figure xxx
with Misses Compton, Wolff, Harcourt, Hanson, Perry, King, Wentworth, Messrs Shaw, Douglas, Luke, Hammond, Cattell, Hopgood, Rainford, Cooper.

Md: Antonio Mora; sc: W. T. Hemsley; cos: Alias and Miss Fisher

74 **INDIANA** a comic opera in three acts by H. B. Farnie. Music by Edmond Audran. Produced at the Comedy Theatre, Manchester 4 October, 1886 and subsequently at the Avenue Theatre 11 October for a run of 70 performances closing 18 December, 1886.

Aubrey, Lord Dayrell . . . . Charles Ryley
Matt o' the Mill . . . . Arthur Roberts
Philip Jervaulx . . . . W. T. Hemsley (Ambrose Collini)
Peter . . . . Sam Wilkinson
Sir Mulberry Mullitt . . . . Henry Ashley
Captain Happe-Hazard . . . . Miss A. Harcourt
Indiana Greyfaunt . . . . Mathilde Wadman (Emmie Graham)
Nan . . . . Mary Duggan/Emmie Graham
Annette . . . . Clara Graham
Maude Cromartie . . . . Ruby McNeill
Lady Prue . . . . Phyllis Broughton (Emmie Graham)
Madge . . . . Jessica Dene
Ruth . . . . Mattie Wynne/R. Dashwood
Belle . . . . Mabel Antony
Winifred . . . . Rita D'Angeli
Lord Turniptop . . . . Ambrose Collini/Benjamin? Bridgeman
1st Keeper . . . . Leon Roche
2nd Keeper . . . . Bruce Blackburn
Cosmo . . . . Lily Richardson
Eric . . . . Connie Edwards
Eben . . . . Emmie Graham
Dickon . . . . Clare Bernard
Giles . . . . Clarence Hunt
with Hettie Harford, Lily Lovell, Teresa Thompson, Bessie Bright, May Ormsby, Cecilia Clarence, Rosy Russell, Constance Cheverton, Marie Shepherd, Clarinda Cleverland, Berlinda Bertram, Eva Evand, Violet Audrey, Annie Harris, Hetty Hamilton, Violet Evelyn, Florence Anstruther, William Withers, Carlo Carpenter, Benjamin Bridgeman[1].

Dir: H. B. Farnie; md: John Crook; sc: T. E. Ryan and F. Storey; cos: Lucien Besche

Produced at the Avenue Theatre 13 June, 1887 for a run of 17 performances closing 1 July, 1887. Ambrose Collini (AUB) Arthur Roberts (MATT), Joseph Tapley (PHIL), Sam Wilkinson (P), Henry Ashley (MM), Mathilde Wadman (IND), Emmie Graham (NAN), Clara Graham (ANN), Ruby McNeill (MAUDE), Phyllis Broughton (PRUE). Md: John Crook

[1] These christian names were printers' or managers' inventions added where, as was usual, only the surnames of choristers were given.

0075 Produced at the Star Theatre, New York, under the management of John A. McCaull 18 January, 1887 for a run of 32 performances closing 15 February. Subsequently toured and reopened in New York at Wallacks Theatre 11 July, 1888 for two weeks ending 23 July. George Olmi/John E. Brand (AUB), Digby V. Bell (MATT), Edwin W. Hoff (PH), H. A. Cripps (PETER), Ellis Ryse/Jefferson De Angelis (MM), Bessie Fairbairn/Julia Heller (HAZ), Lily Post/Marion Manola (IND), Annie Meyers (NAN), Ida Eissing/Grace Seavey (ANN), Adine Drew/Josie Knapp (MAUD), Laura Joyce Bell (PRUE), Celie Eissing/Clara Allen (MADGE), Tolie Pettit (RUTH/BELLE), Belle Jennings (WIN), A. Maina (KEEP), G. Hollingsworth/Lutie Ward (COS), Grace Ward (EBEN), Belle Cavis (DICK), W. F. McLaughlin/Lindsay Morrison (GILES), C. Blanchard/Florence Willey (FOLLIET) C. Daly (LACKEY). Md: Herman Perlet/A. de Novellis; sc: Joseph Clair

ALICE IN WONDERLAND a musical dream play in two acts by H. Savile Clarke. Music by Walter Slaughter. Produced at the Prince of Wales Theatre under the management of Edgar Bruce 23 December, 1886 for a run of 57 matinée performances closing 2 March, 1887.

Alice . . . . Phoebe Carlo
Mad Hatter/Tweedledum . . . . Sidney Harcourt
White RabbitRed King . . . . D. Abrahams
March Hare/Hare . . . . Edgar Norton
Cheshire Cat/Lion . . . . Charles Adeson
Dormouse/Plum Pudding . . . . Dorothy d'Alcourt
Cat/Unicorn . . . . S. Solomon
King of Hearts/White Knight . . . . . . Stephen Adeson
Duchess/Lily . . . . Florence Levey
Queen of Hearts/Red Queen . . . . Mlle Rosa
Jack of Hearts/White Queen . . . . Kitty Abrahams
Cook/White King . . . . Anna Abrahams
Executioner/Carpenter . . . . H. H. H. Cameron
Gryphon/Walrus . . . . Charles Bowland
Tweedledee . . . . John Ettinson
Mock Turtle/Humpty Dumpty . . . . . . William Cheesman
Rose . . . . Mabel Love
Red Knight . . . . C. Kitts
Leg of Mutton . . . . Master Hood
Oyster Ghosts . . . . Isa Bowman, Dot Alberti, Dorothy d'Alcourt

Ch: Mlle Rosa; sc: E. G. Banks; cos: Lucien Besche (from Tenniel)

Produced at the Globe Theatre 26 December, 1888 for a run of matinée performances, closing 9 February 1889.
Isa Bowman (A), Sidney Harcourt (HATTER), T. P. Haynes (TURT/TDEE) Empsie Bowman (DOR) &c.

Produced at the Opera Comique 22 December, 1898 playing twice or thrice daily until 11 March, 1899.
Rose Hersee (A), Alice Barth (RQ/DUCH), Arthur Eliot (HATT), Murray King (GRYPHON/TDEE), William Cheesman (TDUM/TURT), Bert Sinden (JHTS/RED K), H. H. H. Cameron (EX &c) &c.

Produced at the Vaudeville Theatre under the management of Charles Frohman & Gatti 19 December, 1900 for a run of 138 perfs (twice daily) closing 13 April, 1901. (No perfs 1–6 April). Ellaline Terriss (A), Seymour Hicks (HATT), William Cheesman (TURT/TDUM), Murray King (GRYPH/TDEE), Stanley Brett (CATERPILLAR/RED KT), Kathleen Courtenay (MHARE), J. C. Buckstone (KHTS/WALRUS), H.H.H. Cameron (EX &c) &c.

Subsequently played for Christmas seasons 23 Dec 1907 (Apollo), 27 Dec 1909 (Court), 26 Dec 1910 (Savoy), 23 Dec 1913 (Comedy), 26 Dec 1914 (Savoy), 24 Dec 1915 (Duke of York's), 26 Dec. 1916 (Savoy), 26 Dec 1917 (Savoy), 27 Dec 1920 (Victoria Palace), 26 Dec 1921 (Garrick), 26 Dec 1922 (Court), 23 Dec 1927 (Savoy), 22 Dec 1930 (Savoy), 22 Dec 1933 (Duke of York's), 19 Dec 1934 (Duke of York's).

0076 **MONTE CRISTO JR** a burlesque melodrama in three acts by 'Richard Henry' (R. W. Butler

& H. Chance Newton). Music by W. Meyer Lutz, Ivan Caryll, Hamilton Clarke, G. W. Hunt, Henry J. Leslie & Robert Martin. Produced at the Gaiety Theatre under the management of George Edwardes 23 December, 1886 for a run of 166 performances closing on 25 June, 1887.

Edmond Dantes . . . . Nellie Farren (Billie Barlow)
Fernand . . . . Fay Templeton/Billie Barlow/Florence Beale
Mercedes . . . . Agnes de la Porte/Marion Hood (Lizzie Wilson)
Mariette . . . . Lottie Collins/Letty Lind
Albert . . . . Jennie McNulty/Florence Beale
Carconte . . . . Billie Barlow/Nellie Gayton
Valentine . . . . Birdie Irving/Ethel Selwyn
Victorine . . . . Sylvia Grey
Babette . . . . Lizzie Wilson/Emma Broughton
Capt. of Hussars . . . . Florence Beale/Jenny Hylton
Capt. of Guard . . . . Miss Herbert
Noirtier . . . . Fred Leslie (George Stone)
De Villefort . . . . E. J. Lonnen
Danglars . . . . George Honey
Caderousse . . . . George Stone
Morel . . . . W. H. Guise
Old Dantes . . . . Alfred Balfour
Boy at the wheel . . . . Charles Ross
add Boatswain . . . . Ada Blanche
Clairette . . . . Addie Blanche

with Misses Eva Raines, Henderson, Graham, Jecks, Millie Marian, Ada Conway, M. Nola, Dudley, Alice Bond, F. Webb, Minnie Sannon, Wilson, Glynn, N. Howard, Annie Akers, Minnie Howe.
Drummers: Misses Robina, Ross, F. Howard, E. Watson.
Brigands: Misses Nellie Gayton, Florence Doyne, Graves, Annie Deacon, Jessie Bennett, Lena Askey, Mowbray, Rayson.
Gipsies: Misses Ethel Selwyn, Talbot, F. West, Haidee Moore, B. Conway, Stanhope, Nellie Webb, Grey, St Albans.
Waiters: Misses Gilbert and O' Neal.

Dir: Charles Harris; md: W. Meyer Lutz; ch: Dewinne; sc: William Beverley, W. Perkins, E. G. Banks, William Telbin; cos: Percy Anderson

Performed by the Gaiety Co. at matinées April 1888, then toured through Australia and America, opening at the Standard Theatre, New York, 17 November 1888 for a run of 32 performances ending 15 December. Toured and returned to the Standard Theatre for several further performances w/c 27 May, 1889.
Nellie Farren (ED), Fanny Marriott (FER), Marion Hood (MERC), Letty Lind (MAR), Jenny Dawson (ALB), Linda Verner (CARC), Sylvia Grey (VICT), Fred Leslie (NOIR), Charles Danby (VILL), Charles Medwin (DANG), Alfred Balfour (CAD), Fred Storey (MOR) with Misses Gregory, Henderson, Bond, Ryder, Akers, Langton, Belton, Connaught, Holmes, Roe, Bennett, Summerville, Chapman, Manton, Lily MacIntyre, Rollitt, Russell, Moore, Payne, Hilyar, M. MacIntyre, Harrington, L. Davis, A. Davis, E. Raynor, Emily Raynor, Balsh, Barrister, Payne, Josephs, A. Errington, B. Errington, C. Jenkins, Holland, O. Russell, K. Douglas, Defossec, Harrington, B. Whittaker, L. Claire, Wentworth, Collins, Morton, Ogden, Beger, Bell, Wells, George, Bedle, Van Buren, Wadeson, Walters, Riversdale, Douglas. Messrs Nichol, Steolcenburg, Walker, Gross, Silvers, Palmer, Stirling, Johnson, Ridgway, Stern, Roe, Duffhues. Dir: Charles Harris; md: Lovell Phillips/Meyer Lutz; ch: Fred Storey; sc: William Beverley, W. Perkins, E. G. Banks, William Telbin; cos: Percy Anderson

An adapted version was toured in America 1888–1890 under the management of Jennie Kimball.

OLIVER GRUMBLE or The Terrible Twins a burlesque novelty by George Dance. Produced at the Prince of Wales Theatre, Liverpool 15 March, 1886 under the management of Willie Edouin. Opened at the Novelty Theatre 25 March, 1886 for a run of 30 performances closing 1 May, 1886. Played at the Manchester Comedy for 2 weeks, 31 May to 12 June.

King Charles.......................Edith Blande
Prince Rupert.......................Emily Spiller
Lord Fairfax.......................Addie Conyers
Queen Henrietta.......................Florence Dysart
Bridget.......................Nellie Murray
Oliver Grumble.......................Arthur Williams
Old Ireton.......................Sydney Stevens/F. Grove
Rebecca Ireton.......................Emily Dowton
John Hampden.......................Charles E. Stevens
Mr Dee.......................Mark Kinghorne
Sailor.......................Jessie Danvers
Symes.......................Jenny Dawson
Landlord.......................Clotilde Graves
Commander of the Picker...........Alice Greenwood
Harry.......................Willie Edouin
Carrie.......................Alice Atherton
With Nellie Earle, Kate Raleigh, E. Darrell, Connie Seymour, Mabel Herbert, Ada Seymour, Lily Jones, Nellie Lennox, Bella Hill, Marie Shepherd, Amy Gracie, Avis Grahame, Millie Le Capilaine, Louie Trevalyan, C. Gatton, Rosie Laurie, Emmiline Carey, Adelaide Cole, Beattie Howe, Brenda Harper, M. Gray, Gordon Hill, Eric Thorne, W. Oliver, Frank Martin, W. Sharp, T. Brown.
Md: Ralph Horner; cos: Wilhelm

ATLANTIS or The Lost Land a comic opera in three acts by Maurice Dalton and Ernest Genet. Music by T. W. Haddow. Produced at a matinée at the Gaiety Theatre 17 March, 1886.

Prof. Smith.......................Julian Cross
Juliana.......................Mrs Philip Bernard
Tristram.......................Victor de Lore
Elaine.......................Marie Faudelle
Prince Arthur.......................H. Wellesley Smith
Earl Dando.......................C. Hayden Coffin
John Tibbs.......................Walter Sealby
Arnold.......................Ernest Genet
Percival.......................Dorothy Capel
Uther.......................Fred Kaye

PEPITA or The Girl With The Glass Eyes by Alfred Thompson. Music by Edward Solomon. Produced at the Union Square Theatre, New York, under the management of J. M. Hill 16 March, 1886 for a run of 88 performances closing 22 May, 1886.

Pepita.......................Lillian Russell
Professor Pongo.......................Jacques Kruger
Donna Carmansuita.......................Alma Stanley
Curaso.......................Fred Solomon
Pablo.......................Chauncey Olcott
Maraquita.......................Miss Jackson
Giavolo.......................Fred Clifton
Pasquela.......................Lizzie Hughes
Juana.......................Julia Wilson
Juan.......................George Wilkinson
Chiquita.......................Cora Striker

THE MAID AND THE MOONSHINER by Charles Hoyt. Music by Edward Solomon. Produced at the Standard Theatre, New York, under the management of Tony Hart 16 August, 1886 for a run of 15 performances closing 28 August, 1886.

Virginia.......................Lillian Russell
Bourbon Miller.......................John E. Brand
Colonel Peyton.......................James radcliffe
Upton O'Dodge.......................Tony Hart

Captain Beach . . . . Joseph Armand
Captain Barr . . . . George Wilkinson
Captain Sparrow . . . . A. L. Nicholls
Mrs Lee . . . . Emma Delaro
Leonore . . . . Carrie Tutein
Marguerite . . . . Annie Leslie
Violetta . . . . Queenie Vassar
Captain Fahrbach . . . . Frank Boudinot
Rev. Mr Thayer . . . . Fred Solomon
Pomp . . . . John P. Hogan

THE MAGIC RING a comic opera in four acts by Oscar Brand. Music by Immanuel Liebich. Produced at the Grand Theatre, Islington, under the management of Oscar Brand 11 October, 1886 for one week.

Lord Indigo Jones . . . . Julian Cross
Swen . . . . Oscar Brand
Christoph . . . . F. Furtado
Hansen . . . . Alfred Balfour
Eric . . . . William Hillier
Arendt . . . . Hal Forde
Odin . . . . F. Reid-Buchanan
Mother Christine . . . . Stirling Ford
Lisa . . . . Elsie Carew
Hanne . . . . L. de Galton
Hyacynthia . . . . Bertha Foresta
Aquaia . . . . Rhoda Browning

THE GRAND DUKE or Change For A Sovereign. A comic opera by George Lash Gordon. Music by John Gregory. Produced at Dundee under the management of Henry D. Burton 7 August, 1886 and toured in repertoire.

Popemorf . . . . Henry D. Burton
Baron Schoonerlager . . . . Fred Little
General Donderhedsburg . . . . Maitland Marler
Prince Jawboim von Kaklde . . . . Louie Seymour
Kit Kat . . . . Louie Lancashire

A UNITED PAIR by J. Comyns Carr founded on a story by Hugh Conway. Music by Alfred J. Caldicott. Produced at St George's Hall under the management of Alfred Reed and R. Corney Grain 7 April, 1886 with *Amateur Theatricals*, the latter replaced by *Henley Regatta*. Withdrawn 17 July. Reopened 4 October with *Henley Regatta* subsequently replaced by *Taking the Waters*. Withdrawn 14 December, 1886.

Virginia Crackle . . . . Fanny Holland
Benjamin Crackle . . . . Alfred Reed
Ada Norbury . . . . Clara Merivale
Jack Edgeworth . . . . North Home
Sextus Marks . . . . Charles Allen/Sant Matthews

THE FRIAR by J. Comyns Carr. Music by Alfred J. Caldicott. Produced at St George's Hall under the management of Alfred Reed and R. Corney Grain 15 December, 1886 with *Taking the Waters* and subsequently with *Oh, That Boy*. Withdrawn 26 March, 1887.

Lady Isabel . . . . Fanny Holland
Lord Clare . . . . Alfred Reed
Liza . . . . Marion Wardroper
Hubert . . . . North Home
Abbott . . . . Sant Matthews

THE CARP a whimsicality in one act by Frank Desprez. Music by Alfred Cellier. Produced at the Savoy Theatre under the management of Richard D'Oyly Carte 13 February, 1886 as a forepiece to *The Mikado* and subsequently to *Ruddigore*. Withdrawn 5 November, 1887.

Amandus . . . . Charles Hildesley
Amanda . . . . Josephine Findlay
Piscator . . . . Eric Lewis

BLACKBERRIES a musical comedy drama in one act by Mark Melford. Music by W. Meyer Lutz *et al.* Produced at Liverpool under the management of Willie Edouin 14 June, 1886 and toured with *Turned Up*. Produced at the Comedy Theatre 31 July, 1886 with *Turned Up*. Transferred to the Royalty Theatre 11 September. Withdrawn 20 December, 1886.

London cast:
Mr Blendford . . . . Walter Groves
Uncle Jim. . . . . Willie Edouin
Albert Blendford . . . . Morton Selten
Tom Tate. . . . . Lytton Sothern
Redward. . . . . H. Parry
Old Nickle . . . . Harry Penton
Neddar. . . . . Mr Norman
Miss Blendford . . . . Alice Chandos
Edith . . . . Emmeline Dickson
Agnes. . . . . Connie Seymour
Mary . . . . Adelaide Cole
Maud. . . . . Rosie Laurie
Charlie Cott . . . . Alice Atherton

THE GOLDEN PLUME or The Magic Crystal. An extravaganza with music by C. E. Howells. Produced at Workington 30 August, 1886 and toured.

SAPPHO a lyrical romance in one act by Harry Lobb. Music by Walter Slaughter. Produced at a matinée at the Opera Comique 10 February, 1886 for the benefit of the Great Ormond Street Children's Hospital.

Phaon . . . . C. Hayden Coffin
Fauna . . . . Mlle Luna
Daphne . . . . Grace Arnold
Irene . . . . Madge Shirley
Aphrodite . . . . Maud Merrill
Sappho. . . . . Harriet Jay

INNOCENTS ALL ABROAD by Alfred Claude Clarke. Music by John Gregory. Produced by Harry D. Burton's touring company.

MINNA or The Fall From the Cliffs. An operetta by Sutherland Edwards. Music by Isidore de Solla. Produced at the Crystal Palace 20 July, 1886.

1887

The Mikado, *Dorothy* and *Monte Cristo Jr* carried the banner of the British musical into 1887, flanked by the less ambitious but almost as durable *Alice in Wonderland* which was playing matinées to *Dorothy*'s evening performances at the Prince of Wales. The continental musical was represented by a revival of *The Beggar Student* filling in a two-month gap at the Comedy. Both *Our Diva*, a version of Victor Roger's *Josephine Vendue par ses Soeurs*, and *La Béarnaise* had failed to run, making it, with the failure of *Frivoli*, a bad year for the purveyors of French entertainments. The hits of the period were definitely home-grown.

The beginning of the new year, too, seemed similarly favourable. An announcement had already been made of the new Gilbert and Sullivan piece which was to succeed *The Mikado*, and *Ruddygore*, as it was called, was in active rehearsal. That other great hit of 1885, *Erminie*, also had a follow-up on the way. Harry Paulton and Edward Jakobowski had completed a new piece, *Mynheer Jan*, for Violet Melnotte, which was due to test its wings at Birmingham within a matter of weeks prior to coming into town. Also on the West End schedule was Fannie Leslie's exceptionally successful touring production of the musical melodrama *Jack-in-the Box* which was to end its provincial tour in Belfast and come to London's Strand Theatre.

The first offering to appear was *Ruddygore*. As usual, rumours as to its nature had begun almost as soon as its predecessor had been staged. Probably the most ingenious suggestion was one promulgated in America but quickly snapped up by the London gossip writers:

> The next Gilbert and Sullivan opera is being talked about in London. It is whispered that it deals with the Egyptian question and satirises the commercial instinct of Englishmen who hate to annex territory but do so at the rate of 1000 square miles a year. The chorus will be made up of the British army of occupation and Egyptian girls, the leading soprano being an Egyptian girl who is a descendant of a Pharoah princess and so forth.

The same source also suggested that a small part of the new work would be written by an American, in order to secure the US copyright of the work. It was November 22 when Gilbert finally called the company together to read to them the new opera *Ruddygore* or The Witch's Curse, and *The Era* reported authoritatively:

> Mr Temple is to appear as a ghost, Miss Braham as a village girl and Miss Bond as a gipsy who has gone crazy from being crossed in love. As there is only one baritone part in the new opera, Mr Frederick Bovill whose fine voice has been so valuable in the part of Pish Tush in *The Mikado* will be set at liberty. Mr Durward Lely has a capital role, that of a man-of-war's man; and Messrs Grossmith and Barrington have

> two strongly contrasted parts with which they are delighted and in which they are expected to make 'palpable hits' . .

It was clear that 'palpable hits' were going to be more difficult to make than usual, for Gilbert and Sullivan had the heavy task of following themselves. No-one could dare to hope that the magnitude of the success of *The Mikado* would be repeated but every effort was made. Everything was organised with the utmost care and lavishness and £500 worth of costumes were thrown out because it was considered that they resembled too closely some of the Gaiety's *Monte Cristo Jr* clothes. When the new piece opened on January 22 before the usual glittering Savoy first night audience, things went well and at the first interval the collaborators were able to congratulate themselves on another success. In spite of occasional lapses on the part of the performers (particularly Miss Braham and Grossmith) and of the stage management, *Ruddygore* was more than winning through. Gilbert's plot and dialogue were sparkling and characteristically inventive.

The heirs of the baronetcy of Murgatroyd have been cursed down the centuries. Every day the holder of the title must commit a crime or perish in agony. To escape his inheritance Ruthven Murgatroyd has fled to live disguised as a peasant, Robin Oakapple, and is courting the village belle, Rose Maybud. Rose, an orphan found with only a book of etiquette beside her, has taken that book as her bible and lives by its precepts. This leads her to accepting first Robin's foster-brother, Richard, as her fiancé, and then Robin. Richard, who lives by the precept of doing 'what my heart tells me', reveals Robin's identity and wins Rose back. This frees Sir Despard, the present incumbent of the unfortunate title, from his daily crime. Able to be genuinely repentant he marries Mad Margaret whom he had once seduced and abandoned. The second act opens with Robin – now Sir Ruthven – trying to fit himself into his new role, but unable to commit any crime more dastardly than forging his own will or disinheriting the son he doesn't have. His ancestors will not stand for it and, in a scene reminiscent of *Ages Ago*, descend from their portraits and warn Robin/Ruthven that he must carry off a maiden that very day to fulfil his duty. The baronet sends his elderly retainer to do the deed, and that worthy returns with the aged Dame Hannah. Sir Roderic, the most vocal and most recent of the ghosts, is appalled for Hannah was, in his lifetime, his sweetheart. All is resolved when, in a piece of Gilbertian logic, Robin declares that since not to commit a crime daily is, for him, the equivalent of suicide, and since suicide is a crime, then not to commit a crime daily is, in fact, a crime. Therefore all his ancestors have been wrongly condemned and he is no longer Lord of Ruddygore and free to marry Rose.

But although the first act went well on that first night, the second did not. It was found decidedly less witty than the first and the plot, particularly the ending, did not please some of the audience at all. After the light and ridiculous frothiness of *The Mikado*, the melodramatic parody and the almost operatic tenor of some of *Ruddygore* was not what they either wanted or expected. It was the book which came in for the bulk of the criticism. *The Era* found it 'very weak and loosely constructed' and declared:

> The bulk of the second act was frittered away . . . and bolstered up by such worn-out devices as the comic business of the Quaker couple which for many years has done duty at the music halls until audiences grew weary of it . . . Many other expedients to fill up gaps are equally unfortunate and thus the opera must be regarded as a patchwork, pretty enough in places but not 'all of a piece' . .

Most others agreed, and the Sunday *Referee* reported:

> Never has there been a greater consensus of critical opinion than there has been over the demerits of the second act of *Ruddygore* . .

The *Sporting & Dramatic News* highlighted its disappointment, declaring the first act 'one of Mr Gilbert's happiest efforts' and the second as 'containing only one scene of special importance'. This, of course, was the portrait scene which was one of the most splendidly and dramatically staged sequences in the Savoy's history. Even the music did not escape criticism. Some of the audience found pieces such as Richard Temple's splendid 'Ghosts' High Noon' too sombre and operatic, and although *The Daily Telegraph* declared it 'the best [Sir Arthur] has yet contributed to the stage of comic opera' and found plenty to agree with him, *The Era* complained that it was 'far from being as fresh and spontaneous as is his wont' and that 'it too often approaches what is commonplace'. There was, throughout, a lack of unanimity in press and public reaction but, all in all, *Ruddygore* was not the instant hit that had been hoped for.

Gilbert set to work immediately and heavy cuts were made in the 'unsatisfactory' second act, including a revision of the unpopular ending. Some portions of the dialogue were cut out and Grossmith's second act patter song was taken out completely as soon as a new one could be supplied to take its place. So out went:

> For thirty five years I've been sober and wary
> My favourite tipple came straight from the dairy
> I kept guinea pigs and a Belgian canary
> A squirrel, white mice and a small black-and-tan.
> I played on the flute and I drank lemon squashes
> I wore chamois leather, tick boots and macintoshes
> And things that will some day be known as galoshes
> The type of a highly respectable man!

And in came:

> Henceforth all the crimes that I find in the *Times*
> I've promised to perpetrate daily;
> Tomorrow I start with a petrified heart
> On a regular course of Old Bailey.
> There's confidence tricking, bad-coin, pocket picking,
> And several other disgraces
> There's postage stamp prigging, and then thimble rigging
> The three-card delusion at races!
> Oh, a baronet's rank is exceedingly nice
> But the title's uncommonly dear at the price!

The evening's most successful number had been Durward Lely's lively rendering of the jolly 'I Shipped y'see in a Revenue Sloop', but even that brought protest. The *Figaro* correspondent complained that its lyric was insulting to the French when the sailor described his ship's battle with a French frigate:

> But to fight a French fal-lal, it's like hitting of a gal
> It's a lubberly thing to do
> For we, with all our faults, why we're sturdy British salts
> While she's only a Parley-vous, d'ye see?
> A miserable Parley-voo!

However, Gilbert paid no attention to such touchiness, and Lely's song held its place with no alterations.

There were further objections to the title. Gentlemen of the press and of the public who frequented the 'immoral' French comic operas in their original Parisian form, who patronised the burlesque and goodness knows what other establishments, found with their own special brand of hypocrisy that the name chosen by Gilbert and Sullivan for their show was indelicate. After eleven performances the author changed the 'y' to an 'i' and the vocal Mr Grundys were able to congratulate themselves that their modesty had been considered.

The songs from *Ruddigore* were in no way inferior to those of the partners' previous works. In Rose Maybud they had returned to the kind of soubrette heroine which fitted Leonora Braham best. She had a delightful ballad 'If Somebody there Chanced to Be' with which to score early in the piece and took part in three duets including the charming 'I Know a Youth' with Grossmith. Richard Temple had the richly burlesque 'High Noon' and Lely, Rosina Brandram and Jessie Bond were well supplied as well. The comic and patter numbers were the equal of anything Grossmith had ever been given. In the first act he sang:

My boy, you may take it from me
That of all the afflications accursed
With which a man's saddled and hampered and addled
A diffident nature's the worst
Though clever as clever can be
A Crichton of early romance
You must stir it and strump it and blow your own trumpet
Or, trust me, you haven't a chance!

While in the second, in addition to his newly written number, he took part in a superb patter trio with Barrington and Miss Bond:

My eyes are fully open to my awful situation
I shall go at once to Roderic and make him an oration
I shall tell him I've recovered my forgotten moral senses
And I don't care tuppence ha'penny for any consequences
O, I do not want to die by the sword or by the dagger
But a martyr may indulge a little pardonable swagger
And I've got to die tomorrow so it really doesn't matter!

The burlesque element was a strong one. Apart from Temple's Ghost Song there was a burlesque operatic Mad Scene for Jessie Bond while Rosina Brandram's opening 'Legend' had a strong flavour of *Il Trovatore*.

None of the songs from *Ruddigore* survived in the repertoire with the vigour of a 'Poor Wandering One' or a 'Tit Willow' and one reason for this may be the comparative lack of exposure given to *Ruddigore* once its original season had finished. It ran a very healthy 288 performances, closing in November, during which time, and a little after, Carte had two touring companies performing it in the provinces. However, after June 2, 1888 when the second of those companies finished its run at Basingstoke, *Ruddigore* was not seen again professionally on the British stage until 1920. Even the less popular *Princess Ida* had long since found its way back into the provincial repertoire, but *Ruddigore* remained unjustly the black sheep of the Savoy fold for a long time. In New York *Ruddigore* failed to catch the imagination and Carte's imported company played only six weeks at the Standard Theatre.

A fortnight after *Ruddigore*'s opening Fannie Leslie arrived in town with *Jack-in-the-Box* and scored a great personal success although the piece proved a little unsophisticated for the tastes of much of the metropolis. On the same night *Mynheer Jan* was given its first showing in Birmingham. Just as *Erminie* had, this second Paulton-Jakobowski-Melnotte effort was playing an out-of-town try-out, but the resemblances between the two pieces by no means ended there. Paulton had created himself a role in the new show which included all the salient features of his celebrated Cadeau in *Erminie* and he was joined once again by Frank Wyatt as his 'straight man'.

The two played the rebel heroes of a comic saga set in the Spanish occupied Netherlands. 'Mynheer Jan' is the name signed to a set of caricatures aimed at the Spanish governor by their perpetrator Karl (Wyatt), the leader of the rebel 'Daisy Guild'. The same Karl is wooing the Governor's daughter, Camilla, but she has been promised to a Spanish grandee, Don Diego. When Diego arrives to claim her, Karl gets him arrested as the leader of the Guild and disguises his buffoonish sidekick, Hans (Paulton), as the nobleman, following him into the fortress dressed as a servant. Diego escapes and manages to convince the Governor of his identity but Karl is not to be thwarted and, with the aid of Katrine, the Governor's intended, and her lover, the Governor's son Francis, he plots to alienate Diego's affections from Camilla in favour of Katrine. All is solved happily when Karl is conveniently proved to be the son of the Governor's oldest friend and Katrine's step-brother. The young people are suitably paired off and Governor Bombalo contents himself with the attentions of his friend's widow.

The story was more involved than that of *Erminie* and the dialogue and the plotting were less tight, but *Mynheer Jan* included some extremely funny scenes and Jakobowski's music was as attractive as ever. The scene in which Paulton/Hans impersonated the Spanish grandee was probably the most hilarious that the actor/author had ever conceived for himself. Subtly and not so subtly insulting the Governor, deputing his servant (Karl) to publicly make love to Camilla ('why hire someone and then do it yourself?'), flirting with the servant Gretchen, and putting down the apoplectic Bombalo with 'We always do it in Spain', he indulged in a tour de force of comic acting which was every bit as uproarious as its *Erminie* counterpart. In the final act he also caused much mirth when, on the run from Bombalo's troops, he took the place of the scarecrow in the fortress's vegetable patch. Dangling from its pole, his arms blowing dangerously in the breeze, he helped organize affairs in asides to his fellow conspirators while remaining nothing more than a scarecrow to the lurking Diego. He sang a jolly topical song:

All things that are pleasant
In times like the present
Are few and far between
While things that are not so
We have by the lot, so
We grumble not wrongly I ween
For ills are abundant and troubles abound
The joys we delight in unhappily found
Too few and far between

had an equally topical duet, 'Keep your Place', with Wyatt and a nonsensical patter song in his Spanish disguise sequence:

We come from the land where they glory adore
We come from the land of the Toreador
Of powers despotic

Of people quixotic
Of nuts, grapes and fancies,
Of various dances
Fandango, cachuca, gitana, zitella,
Of names Juanita, Inez, Isabella,
Filibuster bravado
Garotte desperado
Sombrero mantilla
Duenna vanilla
Of cigar, cigarettes
And the gay castagnettes!

Wyatt had a much straighter role than in *Erminie* as the dashing 'Mynheer Jan' but it was a very large part and vocally strenuous, including a particularly vigorous high baritone drinking song.

The bulk of the vocal music fell, once again, to the prima donna, in this case the genuinely Dutch Camille D'Arville in the role of Katrine. Her principal numbers were a valse allegretto 'Love's a King', the anecdotal 'Pedro and Inez' and an amusing piece describing how a girl's thoughts can wander when she is on her knees in church. She also joined in duet with the tenor Joseph Tapley as Francis and the two of them had a particularly enjoyable episode in Act 1 where the young man, deputed by his awkward father to woo Katrine in loco parentis, gradually realises that he wishes to make the girl his wife rather than his mother. While Katrine attemps to prod him into an avowal Francis, first obliviously and then manfully, resists the urge to break the code of filial duty until he finally has to admit that the most meaningful of his kisses are bestowed on his own behalf and not as proxy.

Paulton and his brother Edward, his collaborator on the libretto under the pseudonym 'Mostyn Tedde', composed this scene with considerable style and restraint, characteristics not often prominent in the elder Paulton's earlier works, and the result was charming. There were other marks of a more dignified influence including the warm characterisation of the older woman, Donna Tralara, who was in no manner ridiculed in the standard musical play fashion, giving Mme Amadi (formerly Annie Tremaine of the Gaiety) a decidedly sympathetic role to play. Manageress Melnotte had given herself a larger role than previously as the palely determined Camilla, and Mons. Marius as Bombalo and Sidney Harcourt as the put-upon Spaniard had their share of the fun. Poor Kate Munroe, making her last stage appearance at the age of 39, was a bubbling Gretchen. Eight months later, after the birth of a still-born child, the newly-married Kate was dead.

After an enthusiastic reception in Birmingham, *Mynheer Jan* came to the Comedy where it was once again well-received, although generally considered as being inferior to *Erminie*. *The Era* called it 'a bright and lively production above the average of excellence in pieces of its class'. *The Stage* found it 'distinctly amusing' and 'a bright and pleasing entertainment' with 'many music gems', concluding that 'a prosperous career may safely be prophesied'.

But in spite of rewrites, the book was over-complicated and over-written, and the best moments separated from each other by too much involved material. Paulton and Jakobowski were also suffering from the same reaction that Gilbert and Sullivan had faced with *Ruddigore*. They were trying to compete with their own great hit and the public was not inclined to accept anything less or different from them. But *Mynheer Jan* was generally more kindly accepted than *Ruddigore* and a reasonable run seemed ensured, so not a few people were surprised when it was withdrawn after only six weeks. On its merits and its popularity it could have undoubtedly run longer but a split had developed in the management. Paulton and Jakobowski on the one hand and Miss Melnotte on the other were having serious difficulties over financial arrangements and, as a result, the prosperous partnership which had begun so successfuly with *Erminie* was broken up and *Mynheer Jan* removed from the Comedy Theatre. It was expected that the authors would recast and open at another West End theatre, but when the show did reappear it was at Islington's Grand Theatre. Only Paulton and the soprano Camille D'Arville remained of Miss Melnotte's company. Even Frank Wyatt[1] was replaced, breaking a partnership which had looked like becoming something quite special. *Mynheer Jan* played eight weeks round the country before ending its career, but by that time the writers, who had not the strong-minded Violet's business acumen, had relinquished the rights and the tour to the management of Annie Castle and the play's prospects had dissolved in inefficiency and personal bickerings.

Mynheer Jan never made it to Broadway – an amazing omission for the first new work by the writers of the still-running *Erminie*. It was played in America but only outside New York and was never given that thorough re-working and slimming which might have turned it into a really worthwhile piece. Many years later Jakobowski prepared a revised version of the show for publishers Joseph Williams. The libretto was chopped about and the songs swapped around and the 'new' *Mynheer Jan* was hawked around amongst the amateur societies.

The next four West End entries were revivals. *Madame Favart* at the Avenue was removed prematurely when its star, Florence St John, fell ill, and was replaced by a reproduction of *Indiana* which played a brief season before embarking on a seven-date tour. John Sheridan, who had been the original Widow O'Brien in *Fun on the Bristol*, arrived back in Britain to find that 'his' role had been usurped and popularised by others so, wishing to re-establish his proprietorial rights, he got together a company and tried to book the Strand Theatre. The theatre's owners, however, preferred to put their trust in Lydia Thompson who was producing the rewritten version of Cellier's *The Sultan of Mocha*. A good four months' run justified her hopes. Sheridan, having failed to secure the Strand, produced *Fun on the Bristol* at the Gaiety but, having been barred from one theatre by a British musical, he soon found himself shunted from the Gaiety by another. *Miss Esmeralda* took over at Edwardes' theatre and Sheridan moved on to the Opera Comique. In the period open to him between the play season and the return of the main Gaiety company at Christmas, Edwards decided to carry on with the policy of burlesque. There would be no more *Dorothy*s. The autumn piece was a new burlesque of Victor Hugo's *Notre Dame de Paris*.

Miss Esmeralda was declared as written by two unknown writers, A.C. Torr and Horace Mills. In fact, the former was very well known for the pseudonym masked the identity of Fred Leslie. Leslie had provided many ideas for the writers of *Monté Cristo Jr* and had interpolated much of his own into *Little Jack Sheppard*, and now he decided to have a go at constructing a burlesque for himself. But although his brain was fertile in imagining situations and business and comical notions, he needed help with the actual lines and he chose as a collaborator a young 'city gent' who had previously provided a couple of burlesques for Leslie's local theatre, the Royal Artillery at Woolwich. The most recent of these, a little extravaganza called *The Royal Riddle*, had received high praise in an amateur production, but Horace Mills was quite amazed to

[1] Wyatt subsequently became 'Mr Melnotte' – the husband of the energetic Violet.

find himself promoted from a totally amateur status into a collaboration with the famous comedian. He took a holiday from his office and spent two weeks on tour with the Gaiety company while the show was finished, returning to town to see his work into rehearsal at the great Gaiety Theatre. As usual, the larger part of the music came from Meyer Lutz who was, after so many years, suddenly more and more in demand and with more and more success.

The story of *Miss Esmeralda* was a much simplified version of Hugo's classic. The gipsy Esmeralda is loved by both Captain Phoebus and the villainous monk Claude Frollo. Frollo, finding himself rejected, stabs the drunken corporal Gringoire and fixes it so that Esmeralda is accused and jailed. Frollo's revenge seems complete until the lovelorn hunchback Quasimodo reveals the truth and presents Gringoire, very much alive, at Esmeralda's trial.

The seemingly serious story was all but drowned in comic characters and business, song and dance and spectacle. In fact, Leslie had the indignity of being asked practically to rewrite the whole of his second act when the director Charles Harris decided the original version did not contain sufficient opportunities for display. The authors saw such coherence as there was in their story disappear but the plot was a simple and a well-known one and, with Nellie Farren and Fred Leslie about, only the most high-minded critics worried about the details of the story.

But Leslie and Miss Farren could not appear in *Miss Esmeralda*. On opening night they were performing *Monte Cristo Jr* in Sheffield and George Edwardes had created a 'second team' to fill the gap. Marion Hood, E. J. Lonnen, Letty Lind and the Blanche sisters were seconded from the *Monte Cristo* company and brought back to London to take the principal roles, and the important parts of Phoebus and Quasimodo were taken by two performers new to the Gaiety – Fannie Leslie of *Jack-in-the-Box* fame and Frank Thornton, long an understudy to Grossmith at the Savoy but now a leading comedian in his own right. As Leslie had written the role of Frollo for himself, Edwin Lonnen found himself with a part which bristled with possibilities and he was not slow to take advantage of them. Grotesquely dressed with a tall bald pate which moved uncannily and dark, staring eyes he wheeled from the heights of melodrama, as he ad-libbed his way through the forging of Phoebus' love letter (thoughtfully written, in any case, in prose), performing a complicated piece of business with a pin devised for the occasion by Fred Leslie, to a demoniacal dance with the hunchback, to an imitation of an organ grinder (Quasimodo being the monkey), to an Irish ballad à la 'Ballyhooly'. From the moment he walked on the stage declaring:

> Doubtless you'll gather from this gloomy stride
> This scowl which I in vain attempt to hide
> This hang-dog countenance and rolling eye
> That I'm a villain of deepest dye . .

to inform the audience in song and dance: 'I've always been bad since I was a lad' he dominated the proceedings. The vocal highlight of the night was his totally irrelevant Irish ballad in the second act. Robert Martin, who had done so well with 'Ballyhooly' had been given a spot into which to write another in the same strain. 'Killaloe' eclipsed its predecessor, became the feature of the show and confirmed Lonnen as a major new star.

Fannie Leslie and Marion Hood were virtue triumphant but had to work very hard not to be completely overwhelmed by the success of the villain. They had some pretty Meyer Lutz songs, duets and dances in a typical vein, and proved a good foil to the eccentric ghoulishness of Lonnen. The music-hall artist Leo Stormont sang 'The Romany Rye' in the character of the king of the gipsies, and Thornton and George Stone scored with a topical duet which proposed:

What induces a miller to wear a white hat
I give it up – ask me another
What animal mostly resembles a cat
I give it up – ask me another
Suppose we indulge in a topical lay
But first I should like to enquire by the way
What on earth has this song got to do with the play?
I give it up – ask me another

and Letty Lind and little Addie Blanche featured in dancing spots. The principal dance routine came in the show's final scene when justice having been done in a comic melodramatic court scene, all the participants adjourned for a finale in 'Le Jardin de Paris'. The Pyramid Ballet had nothing to do with Egypt, but featured Miss Lind, dressed top to toe in ivory silk and crowned by a pointed white hat dripping with white billiard balls, as a cue-ball. She bounced around the stage in an imitation of a billiard game 'pocketing' one by one the twelve other dancers who, in red cashmere, represented the red balls.

Miss Esmeralda received a mixed critical reception. *The Daily Telegraph* headed the 'pros'. It reported 'extravagant raptures' from the audience and noted that 'in two respects *Miss Esmeralda* is very far superior to its predecessors. The music is of a much higher class than we remember before, some of the choruses and finales being quite as good if not better than are found in ambitious comic opera, and in beauty of design and exquisite blending of colour the stage pictures should attract audiences on their own account.'

Lutz, Lonnen, 'Killaloe' and the scenic and costume artists collected the best notices, and Harris' decision to subjugate the book to the visuals seemed to be justified. However a potential disaster quickly threatened when the music publishers, Ascherberg & Co., stepped in with a demand that 'Killaloe' be cut from the score. Meyer Lutz had sold his score for *Miss Esmeralda* to Ascherberg and his contract with them provided that any interpolations into the score should be from their own lists. They were clearly in the right and Edwardes found himself obliged to cut the show's biggest song hit for several nights while he bought back certain of the rights in the score. It was a lesson learned and thereafter Edwardes himself purchased all publishing rights to music composed for the Gaiety.

Miss Esmeralda ran strongly through until Christmas when the now traditional seasonal change of programme called it to a halt. However, business was still booming so the show was revised and put on, accompanied by a harlequinade, as a matinée piece played by the Gaiety 'B' team with Florence Dysart in the title role. It had been an unfortunate year for Miss Dysart. She had been lined up to have her first starring role opposite Hayden Coffin in *Waldemar, the Robber of the Rhine* which had been scheduled to follow *Dorothy* at the Prince of Wales, but *Dorothy* showed no signs of needing to be followed. William Fullerton, the show's composer, then succumbed to consumption and the show was abandoned. Its authors, Beatty Kingston and Maurice Barrymore (father of the American acting family) took their book to America where it was later produced by Lillian Russell with new music by Charles Puerner. Miss Dysart had the consolation of a leading role at the Gaiety and she made a fine gipsy opposite the Frollo of Lonnen who continued to play his bravura role in the afternoon while taking part in the new show in the evenings. Lonnen also retained the role when *Miss Esmeralda* was taken to the country the following year, but Fred Leslie finally got to grips with the part he had imagined for himself when the Gaiety took the show to Australia and America. The show and the character had undergone considerable changes since their first appearance, but Leslie, as full as ever of new ideas, rewrote and rejigged constantly. The court scene was worked up into a huge tour de force for himself and Nellie Farren. Together they played accused, accuser and all of the witnesses, popping down inside the witness box to emerge each time as a new character. The variations were endless and, of course, Leslie made a meal of 'Killaloe'. *Miss Esmeralda* proved marginally more popular than *Monte Cristo Jr* in the two-play repertoire and it was well received in both countries. It continued to be played in touring productions in Britain for some years, including several tours under the management of actress Madge Rockingham who successively featured the music-hall artist Little Tich and the dwarf Major Tit-Bits as her Quasimodo.

The show which relegated *Miss Esmeralda* to the afternoon slot was *Frankenstein*, a new burlesque by 'Richard Henry' the authors of *Monte Cristo Jr*. This time they had chosen two substantial subjects for their piece – Mary Shelley's novel and the vampire legend – which they combined into an unlikely tale featuring Nellie Farren as Dr Frankenstein, Fred Leslie as her monster and Lonnen and Emily Cross as a pair of vampires. In their version Frankenstein's creation falls in love with Mary Ann, a vampire, who, in her turn is enamoured of another vampire, Visconti. The latter part of the eventful show had the Monster carrying off Tartina, Frankenstein's lady-love, to a ship in the icy northern wastes where the hero could come picturesquely to her rescue on a sled. All ended in a rosy splendour when the sun goddess in the person of Sylvia Grey stepped forward to shine her blessing on the reunited pair.

Meyer Lutz provided the bulk of the music with Robert Martin providing a couple of songs while the 'Moonlight Ballet' was from the pen of William Fullerton. Fred Leslie had doubts about the choice of subject:

> . . the supernatural element pervading it will hamper the comedians considerably . .

he wrote. But the supernatural and almost everything else in the way of plot and storyline disappeared in the perfect glut of scenic effects, costumes, parades and dances, comic songs and comic business, stray ballads and stray jokes. Charles Harris had had his way and *Frankenstein* glittered with spectacular settings and effects. Apart from the 'Moonlight Ballet' there was an umbrella chorus and a 'Grand Parade of the Planets' which belonged more to the Alhambra or the Empire than to burlesque – even to new burlesque.

> We are the stars
> Venus and Mars
> Orion, Saturn, Mercuree
> All leading lights
> Shining o'nights
> Now we come out on a spree

sang the Gaiety ladies as they paraded across the stage in fantastic costumes. There was a very large dance element in the show, but the 43 musical pieces included a wide mixture of numbers which were well shared around amongst the company. Marion Hood, again the heroine, had a couple of straight songs – a vocal waltz and a Spanish song, and the sopranos Camille D'Arville and Florence Dysart as a peripheral military couple contributed several bright numbers. Frank Thornton as the Doctor's assistant had a fair comic number, but the best material fell to the stars. Nellie Farren had a show-stopper in 'It's a funny little Way I've Got', Leslie had a comical number about the Special Police and Martin provided Lonnen with the obligatory Irish song, 'The Dispensary Doctor':

Och boys, there was the doctoring
I was a famous concoctor
If you want amputations
Or such alterations
Tim Molloy's the Dispensary Doctor!

There was an Irish jig and a sailors' chorus, a Spanish waltz and a couple of acrobatic dances for Charlie Ross but the most successful number was Nellie Farren and Fred Leslie's duet 'Seven Ages', a parody on Shakespeare's Seven Ages of Man:

FRANK: When I began life as a baby
They hailed my appearance with joy
The nurse said, o lor', won't he give them what for
Did you ever see such a wonderful boy.
MONSTER: Quite early you took to the bottle
And filled yourself up to the brim
What noises you made, what pranks you played
O wasn't you just an audacious young limb!

Throughout this variety show of song and dance numbers was peppered the comedy. Fred Leslie was full of life and imagination, but the humour of the piece was not as preeminent as in *Monte Cristo Jr* or *Miss Esmeralda*. It was scarcely the fault of the writers whose book was all but submerged in the production detail, but the fun was sometimes struggling to get out. Not that there were not excellent moments. The book gave the Monster/Leslie a sidekick in the shape of Frankenstein's trial model for himself (George Stone). The Monster and the Model provided a good deal of fun, particularly when they stripped down as prize-fighters and indulged in a bout of fisticuffs 'like Jem Smith and Jake Kilrain'. Lonnen fished the most obvious humour from the character of the villainous Visconti, but his female counterpart, Mary Ann, proved less attractive in spite of being played by Emily Cross, the original Ruth of *The Pirates of Penzance*.

Frankenstein, however, suffered a strange fate. On the opening night virtually nothing was successful as very little was given a chance to be heard. The trouble began as soon as the pit was opened and it was discovered that some of the pit places had been done away with to allow the theatre to include a few more lucrative stalls. The pit habitués began a veritable uproar and were not stopped by the rising of the curtain. The very favourites they had come to see became the victims of their distemper, particularly poor Emily Cross who was making her Gaiety début. 'Good old Mary Ann' hooted the pit every time Miss Cross stepped on the stage – enough to totally unnerve a less experienced actress. Also drowned out in the fracas were the first lines sung on the Gaiety stage by a young actor in the small role of the innkeeper:

Come set your glasses clinking
And give your mind to drinking
Go tout for orders here and there
And mind you get the coin

he sang. The young man was Cyril Maude, later the great actor-manager of the Haymarket Theatre, who had been introduced at the Gaiety in the forepiece to *Miss Esmeralda*, the 2-act comedy *Woodcock's Little Game*.

The papers the next day commented largely on the disturbances and had difficulty giving a rational view of the show. But several critics looked dubiously on the new Gaiety emphasis on the spectacular:

> . . . for the sake of the greedy sight-seer, *Frankenstein* became more a showy Christmas spectacular than a coherent work of art . . .
>
> *Frankenstein* is a spectacle rather than a burlesque . . . a congestion of splendour and beauty. But congestion is seasonable at this festive season and it is an ailment which a dose of stage *Eno* will soon put right . .

The *Pall Mall Budget* suggested

> giving Mr Leslie a couple more songs and cutting out some of the dances, a little of the buffoonery and seeing to the absurdities of 'Good Old Mary Ann' . .

In spite of its unpromising début *Frankenstein* survived. It was pulled together and altered in the few places where genuine disapproval had been evident and the disheartened Emily Cross was replaced by Maria Jones. The umbrella dance was cut, the Planets parade sliced in half and some of the book which had got cut and 'forgotten' was restored. Fred Leslie and Nellie Farren swung into their stride and the accustomed laughter and applause came back to the Gaiety to carry *Frankenstein* through 110 performances, until it was time for the company to prepare for its overseas tour. But that was the show's end. It was never toured, never exported or sub-licensed, and the excesses into which it had tried to lead the new burlesque were abandoned.

The remaining offerings of the year were the American play with music *Hans the Boatman* and another Anglo-French affair from H. B. Farnie and Planquette. This time, however, it was not a new work. *The Old Guard* was a reworking of Planquette's 1880 piece *Les Voltigeurs de la 32ème* which had been his first new work after his dazzling début with *Les Cloches de Corneville*. Farnie reconstructed and rewrote the libretto using a certain amount of the original music as well as some new pieces which the composer provided to order. Musical director John Crook gave a severe shaping to the resultant score and added a certain amount of music of his own although he only actually put his name to one song. With Arthur Roberts in another expandable role and Joseph Tapley, Marion Edgecumbe and Phyllis Broughton heading the rest of a large cast, it gathered mediocre reviews but a good degree of popularity and ran out 300 performances at the Avenue, a quick revival, and an exceptionally long touring life. During its tour it had the distinction of marking the stage début of one 'Henri Tempo' in the Arthur Roberts role. 'Tempo' was otherwise the 'cellist/conductor/manager Auguste van Biene. 'Thrown on' one night through the illness of his star he developed a taste for the stage and later tried himself as Rip van Winkle before using his musical talents as the star of the weepie-drama *The Broken Melody* though its run of several thousand performances.

The provincial crop of 1887 included four new works. The first and least successful was *The Royal Watchman* produced in April at the Theatre Royal, Exeter. Its story was in the most durable strain of comic opera plots, dealing with a Swedish prince who, having exchanged clothes with his sergeant, finds himself being courted by plotters against the royal personage, the disguise having rendered him unrecognisable to his own courtiers. The libretto was by twenty-three-year-old William Boosey, later to turn his skills to a different side of the musical theatre, first as a manager and then as a music publisher. The music was by the Nottingham composer Frank Moir. *The Royal Watchman* was toured through three further dates before being put away.

Almost as ephemeral was the latest effort from Walter Parke who was finding it increasingly difficult to repeat the success of *Les Manteaux Noirs*. *Herne's Oak* was a rather dull piece set around Henry VIII and the legend already dealt with in *Windsor Castle*. The music was written by the young Liverpool composer J. C. Bond Andrews. Andrews' bent was really towards more serious music and after this attempt at comic opera he devoted himself principally to grand opera and church music. *Herne's Oak* was received unenthusiastically and Parke reacted indignantly, claiming the work had been sabotaged by lack of rehearsal due to the protracted reconstruction of the Liverpool Prince of Wales Theatre. His protests served little purpose and certainly did not help to keep *Herne's Oak* alive, although it reappeared briefly a couple of years later in the repertoire of Ilma Norina's opera company without notable success.

Nottingham proved more fruitful than Exeter or Liverpool when two local writers, Edgar Wyatt and the theatre's conductor, Alfred Watson, combined to write *Count Tremolio*. It was a Venetian piece which made fair use of Oxenford's 1835 farce *Twice Killed* and contained plenty of opportunities for fun. Pretty Geraldine is to marry the wealthy old Tremolio but her admirer, the young Ernesto, is determined to prevent it. He gains admittance to her guarded rooms hidden in a basket which is sent as a gift to the lady's maid, but the basket is tipped off the window ledge into the canal and it takes a good deal more business before Geraldine is finally 'arrested' at her wedding as a witness to the 'murder' and carried off by the policeman/Ernesto to a more suitable wedding.

Count Tremolio was squarely on the *Erminie* plan – Act 1 set up the situation, Act 2 as much comedy as possible, Act 3 dénouement – with the second act forming the kernel of the entertainment. There were comings and goings at an farcical rate as the hero attempted to get to his beloved. Arriving in the basket he is discovered by Bianca, Geraldine's prudish aunt who is minded to have him for herself. Then he is replaced in the basket by a load of books and mistakenly given a glass of narcotic for wine by Liza, the maid and the old pharmacist, Geraldine's guardian. When the basket tumbles into the water half the household think him drowned, while the other half think him poisoned and have hidden the 'corpse' inside a couch. When he later arises ghost-like from the furniture he causes further chaos. The fun was duly supplemented with some pretty songs for the prima donna and a score which included an unusual 'Legend' on the subject of medication for the doctor, a bright solo 'Tis Love that Makes the World Go Round' for the maid, and a couple of nimble patter songs for James Danvers in the title role.

Count Tremolio received fair notices and took in eleven dates on tour. The following year it was revised and revived under the title *Geraldine* and taken on another and longer tour, and in 1893 it surfaced again under the title of *Fair Geraldine* or A Very Wilful Maid of Venice in the touring repertoire of the Ilma Norina Opera Company.

Since the original British production of *Les Cloches de Corneville* the actor Shiel Barry, who had created the role of the miser Gaspard with such enormous success, had continued to profit from that success by almost continously touring the show. The time had come now for him to vary his repertoire and his managerial partner William Hogarth combined with Walter Parke in a new vehicle for their star. This was *Gipsy Gabriel* which had a plot based on Scott's *Guy Mannering* and was set in seventeenth-century Cornwall. The role of the revengeful gipsy of the title was set up for Barry. The story was again that of the wicked steward and the long-lost heir stolen, in this version, by the gipsy in retaliation for crimes against him supposedly by the child's father but eventually discovered to have been the work of the evil steward, Grimstone. The music for *Gipsy Gabriel* was provided by Florian Pascal, like Parke still in search of a successor to his relatively successful early work, *Cymbia*. *The Stage* found the piece 'pleasing and agreeable . . . without being pretentious'. It contained sufficient humour and sufficient action and pleasant enough songs to give it a fair success and Barry and Hogarth toured it in tandem with the Planquette opera for more than twelve months.

A not very comic opera version of *L'Auberge des Adrets* by the prolific singer/composer George Fox was produced under the title *Macaire* and presented that popular character in a rather less popular way than had Harry Paulton in *Erminie*. *Macaire* made its début at a matinée at the Crystal Palace and was subsequently toured. Two other pieces, *Kittens*, a play evolved for the actress Kate Eversleigh, and *Hunt the Slipper*, a farce produced at Cork, were given extensive tours during the year but, although they included a certain amount of music and songs neither was, strictly speaking, a musical.

The year's shorter pieces were few and unremarkable. The German Reeds produced two pieces, *The Naturalist* and *Tally Ho!*, which did nothing to increase the reputation of the once proud St George's Hall nor to extend their mainly regular audience. At the Prince of Wales a short topical piece called *Jubilation* was produced as a forepiece to *Dorothy*. Its script was by 'Richard Henry', its music the combined effort of the lessee Henry J. Leslie and his conductor Ivan Caryll, and its theme the Queen's jubilee.

1887

0077 **RUDDIGORE** or The Witches' Curse (originally entitled *Ruddygore*). A supernatural comic opera in two acts by W. S. Gilbert. Music by Arthur Sullivan. Produced at the Savoy Theatre under the management of Richard D'Oyly Carte 22 January, 1887 for a run of 288 performances closing 5 November, 1887.

Robin Oakapple	George Grossmith (Henry A. Henri)
Richard Dauntless	Durward Lely
Sir Despard Murgatroyd	Rutland Barrington (S. Price)
Sir Roderic	Richard Temple/Wallace Brownlow (H. Charles)
Old Adam	Rudolph Lewis
Mad Margaret	Jessie Bond/Amy Augarde
Rose Maybud	Leonora Braham/Geraldine Ulmar (Josephine Findlay)/Rose Hervey
Zorah	Josephine Findlay (Aida Jenoure) (Miss Lindsay)
Ruth	Miss Lindsay/Kate Kavanagh (Mabel? Russell)
Dame Hannah	Rosina Brandram/Elsie Cameron/Fanny Edwards/Madge Christo
Sir Rupert	S. Price/
Sir Jasper	H. Charles/
Sir Lionel	Mr. Trevor
Sir Conrad	Mr Burbank
Sir Desmond	Mr Tuer/Mr Shirley
Sir Gilbert	J. Wilbraham
Sir Mervyn	Mr Cox

Dir: Richard Barker; md: François Cellier; ch: John D'Auban; sc: Hawes Craven; cos: Wilhelm

Produced at the Fifth Avenue Theatre, New York under the management of Richard D'Oyly Carte 21 February, 1887 for a run of 53 performances closing 9 April, 1887.
George Thorne (ROB), Courtice Pounds (RICH), Fred Billington (DES), F. Federici (ROD), Leo Kloss (OA), Kate Forster (MM), Geraldine Ulmar (ROSE), Aida Jenoure (ZO), Miss Murray (RUTH), Elsie Cameron (DAME) with Messrs Winterbottom, Poole, Roche, James, Jeffrey, Brand and Huntley. Md: P. W. Halton; sc: H. L. Reid, Hughson Hawley; cos: Wilhelm, Messrs Cater & Co, Mme Leon

This company performed two matinées at the Savoy Theatre, on 9 and 10 February.

Produced at the Cosmopolitan Theatre, New York, under the management of Lawrence J. Anhalt 20 May, 1927 for a run of 19 performances.
Alexander Clark (ROB), Craig Campbell (RICH), William Danforth (DES), Herbert Waterous (ROD), Harvey Howard (OA), Sarah M. Edwards (MM), Violet Carlson (ROSE), Ruth Ramsay (ZO), Juliet Buell (RUTH), Dorothy Pilzer (DAME) with Robert Willard, John Russell, Henry Riebselle, Hugh Sorenson, Noel Harland, Donald Black, Paul Shorran. Dir: Charles Jones; md: Max Hirshfeld; sc: Rollo Wayne

Subsequently played by the D'Oyly Carte Opera Company on tour and in London in repertoire.

Performed in New York in repertoire and short seasons by the D'Oyly Carte Opera Company and others.

TV/Video: 1984 Brent Walker Ltd. Pr: Judith de Paul, dir: Christopher Renshaw; md: Alexander Faris; ch: Terry Gilbert; sc: Allan Cameron; cos: Jenny Beavan
Keith Michell (ROB), John Treleaven (RICH), Vincent Price (DES), Donald Adams (ROD), Paul Hudson (OA), Ann Howard (MM), Norma Burrowes (ROSE), Beryl Korman (ZO), Elise McDougall (RUTH), Johanna Peters (DAME)

0078 **MYNHEER JAN** a comic opera in three acts by Harry Paulton and 'Mostyn Tedde' (Edward Paulton). Music by Edward Jakobowski. Produced under the management of Violet Melnotte at the Grand Theatre, Birmingham 7 February, 1887 for one week before opening at the Comedy Theatre 14 February, 1887 for a run of 35 performances closing 26 March, 1887.

General Bombalo . . . . Claude Marius/Herman de Lange
Francis . . . . Joseph Tapley
Camilla . . . . Violet Melnotte
Donna Tralara . . . . Mme Amadi
Don Diego . . . . Sidney Harcourt
Grenados . . . . Herman de Lange/Charles Ashford
Karl . . . . Frank Wyatt
Hans. Harry Paulton
Conrad . . . . Amy F. Martin
Philippa . . . . Emma Broughton
Gretchen . . . . Kate Munroe (Emma Broughton)/Kate Lawler
Katrina . . . . Camille D'Arville
Brunn . . . . Annie Wilson
Lorenz. . . . . Harrie Price
Pedro . . . . K. Reuss
Ludwig . . . . Mr St Aubyn/Maud Richardson
Carlos . . . . Madge Willoughby
Brotz . . . . H. Bernard
Lopez . . . . Arthur Hendon
Alphonso . . . . Eva Raines/B. E. E. Matiste
Paquita . . . . Alice Lethbridge
with Tessie Graeme, Violet Leigh, Miss Despard, Jessie Douglas, Delphine Gay, Mabel Anthony, Gertrude Tennyson, Annie Teesdale, Maud Franklyn, Ada Hills, B.E.E. Matiste, Lily de Grey, Adeline Bartlett, Mary Clark, Ada Bright, Ruby Osmayne, Isabel Montague, Nellie Gregory, Lillie Gordon, Frances Mara, Lillie Levine, Alice Hartley, Minnie Chene, Lillie Marsden, C. Perrin, Edward Carleton, Wellington Harcourt, Charles Franklyn, Basil Wood, Vincent Culverwell, Charles Bernhardt, Alfred Sutch, Henry Montague, Frank Aldridge, Richard Martin &c.

Dir: Harry Paulton; md: Auguste van Biene; sc: T. E. Ryan; ch: J. Hansen; cos: Lucien Besche

Produced at the Chestnut Street Theatre, Philadelphia, 17 September, 1888 for two weeks.
J. K. Murray (BOMB), Jay Taylor (FR), Alice Vincent (CAM), Clare Wisdom (TRA), E. de Mesa (DIEGO), William T. Carleton (KARL), C. H. Drew (HANS), Clara Lane (KAT)

0079 **THE ROYAL WATCHMAN** a comic opera by William Boosey. Music by Frank L. Moir. Produced at the Theatre Royal, Exeter under the management of Sidney Herberte-Basing 11 April, 1887 and toured through Grimsby, Leicester and Nottingham terminating 7 May, 1887.

Marguerite . . . . Clare Harrington
Pilzou . . . . Charles Ashford
Prince Julian . . . . Henry Lebreton
Philip Stark . . . . Sidney Herberte-Basing
Duke Hildebrand . . . . James Danvers
Gottlieb Stark. . . . . Arthur Walcott
Sergeant of the Guards . . . . J. Brandon Philips

Florian . . . Rita D'Angeli
Mother Kate . . . Bella Fossette
Angelo . . . Delphine Gay
Bertrand . . . Stella Rowe
Marshall Blankenswerd . . . Joseph Wilson
Marchioness Blankenswerd . . . Adee Isacke/Isabelle Muncey
Captain Halt . . . F. A. Barnes

Md: E. Sydney Ward

080 **COUNT TREMOLIO** a comic opera in three acts by Edgar Wyatt. Music by Alfred R. Watson. Produced at Nottingham under the management of Wyatt and Watson 5 September, 1887 and toured through Douglas, Leicester, Darlington, Scarborough, Huddersfield, Stockton, Sunderland, Middlesborough, W. Hartlepool, Sheffield ending 19 November, 1887 (66 performances).

Count Tremolio . . . James Danvers
Dr Figrado . . . Eric Thorne
Rinaldo . . . Lillie Myers
Geraldine . . . Ethel Pierson
Francesca . . . Alice Ware
Ernesto . . . Fred Salcombe
Carl . . . Claude H. Vincent
Bianca . . . Madge Stavart
Liza . . . Kate Braham
Paolo . . . Florence Morton
with Tillie Carpenter, Misses Singelton, Webb, Sherlock, Taylor, Ferrier, Lynn, Devonshire, Dunn, Smithers, Wyatt, Marshall, Simmonds; Messrs Lever, Moore, Slack, Daft, Bromley, Broomhall, Usher, Whitehall, Mavins, Hoyles, Hollamby, Egerton.

Dir: Alfred Watson; md: Alfred Watson; ch: Birdie Wyatt; sc: Harry Potts, Richard Parker; cos: Auguste, Miss Fisher

Toured in a revised version as *Geraldine* or Count Tremolio's Wedding by Hedley & Watson (later Wyatt & Watson) 2 July, 1888 to 20 April, 1889.
J. T. MacMillan/C. Branton/E. Fairlie Fisher/George Traill (COUNT), Fred Salcombe/ Lawrence Mawdore (ERN), Fawcett Lomax/Wm. P. Sheen (DR), F. Reid Buchanan/Allen Morris/F. Sarony/Walter Greyling (CAR), Sarah Dudley/Gertie Virose/Winnie Conyers (RIN), Madge Stavart/Lillie Myers/Emma Rosa/Rosie Pitt (BIA), Ethel Pierson/Poppy Lynne (GER), Kate Neverist/Ada Wallis/Jenny Franklin/Annie Morton (LIZA), Ada Myrtle/Helen Gwynne/L. Norman/Alice Albin (FRAN). Md: Alfred Watson.

Toured in a revised version as *Fair Geraldine* or A Very Wilful Maid of Venice by Ilma Norina's Co. in repertoire from 18 September, 1893.
Gilbert King (COUNT), F. S. Gilbert (ERN), Buchanan Wake (DR), J. J. Donnelly (CAR), Jessie Browning (BIA), Ilma Norina (Reba Henderson)(GER), Mlle Sylvia/Reba Henderson (LIZA), Annie Craig (FRAN), Rosa Lupino (pd)

081 **MACAIRE** a comic opera (romantic opera) written and composed by George Fox. Produced at a matinée at the Crystal Palace 20 September, 1887 and toured from 26 September at Birmingham through Brighton, Manchester, Nottingham, Burnley, Edinburgh x2, Liverpool and Wolverhampton ending 26 November, 1887.

Clementine . . . Mlle Burmeister
Macaire . . . George Fox (Douglas Cox)
Charles . . . H. Sims Reeves
Germeuil . . . Douglas Cox (Edward Muller)
Dumont . . . George Marler
Flon Flon . . . J. C. Belton
Jacques Strop . . . J. G. Taylor
Marie . . . Lucy Franklein
Pierre . . . Fred A. Gaytie

Loupay . . . . Edward Muller
Baton . . . . Mr Bates

Md: John Pew; ch: A. Bertrand

0082 **MISS ESMERALDA** or The Monkey and The Monk, a melodramatic burlesque in three acts by 'A. C. Torr' (Fred Leslie) and Horace Mills. Music by Meyer Lutz. Additional songs by Robert Martin and Frederick Bowyer. Produced at the Gaiety Theatre under the management of George Edwardes 8 October, 1887. Withdrawn 17 December, 1887. Re-produced in a revised version at matinées from 26 December, 1887 and played daily until 7 January 1888: subsequently twice weekly to 28 January and once weekly to 10 March; a total run of 87 performances.

Clopin, King of the Gipsies . . . . Leo Stormont
Claude Frollo . . . . Edwin J. Lonnen
Quasimodo . . . . Frank Thornton
Corporal Gringoire . . . . George Stone
Belvigne, a gipsy . . . . Edward W. Coleman/*out*
Captain Phoebus . . . . Fannie Leslie/Jenny Rogers
Ernest . . . . Ada Blanche (Lena Delphine)/Jenny McNulty
Esmeralda . . . . Marion Hood/Florence Dysart
Madame Gondelarieur . . . . Emily Miller/Linda Verner
Fleur-de-Lis. . . . . Letty Lind/Emma Gwynne
Zillah, a gipsy girl . . . . Addie Blanche/Sylvia Grey/Sybil Grey
Mirzah . . . . Mlle Carmen/*out*
Female Warders. . . . . Maud Richardson
Marie de Braham/Lizzie Wilson
add Lizette . . . . Sylvia Grey
Judge . . . . Charles Ross
The Two Incorrigible Convicts. . . . . . The Two Macs

Dir: Charles Harris; md: Meyer Lutz; ch: John D'Auban; sc: E. Ryan and William Telbin; cos: Percy Anderson

Produced at the Standard Theatre, New York by the Gaiety Theatre Co., 17 December 1888 for a run of 24 performances to 5 January, 1889. Played again from 25 February for a further 31 performances to 23 March and again for several performances in w/c 27 May in repertoire with *Monte Cristo Jr.*
Charles Medwin (CLOP), Fred Leslie (FR), Fred Storey (QU), Charles Danby (GR), Nellie Farren (PH), Fanny Marriott (ERN), Marion Hood (ES), Linda Verner (GOND), Letty Lind (FdL), May Russell (Z), Sylvia Grey (LIZETTE), A. Balfour (JUDGE); with Misses Henderson, Bond, Ryder, Akers, Langton, Belton, Connaught, Holmes, Roe, Summerville, Chapman, Lily MacIntyre, Rollitt, Russell, Moore, Payne, Hilyar, M. MacIntyre, Harrington, L. Davis, A. Davis, E. Raynor, Emily Raynor, Balsh, Barrister, Payne, Josephs, A. Errington, B. Errington, C. Jenkins, Holland, O. Russell, K. Douglas, Harrington, B. Whittaker, L. Claire, Wentworth, Collins, Morton, Ogden, Beger, Bell, George, Bedle, Van Buren, Wadeson, Walters, Riversdale, Douglas; Messrs Nichol, Walker, Gross, Silvers, Palmer, Johnson, Stern, Duffhues. Dir: Walter Raynham; md: Lovell Phillips; ch: Fred Storey

0083 **HERNE'S OAK** or The Rose of Windsor. A comic opera by Walter Parke. Music by J. C. Bond Andrews. Produced at the Prince of Wales Theatre, Liverpool under the management of W. Duck 24 October, 1887 for 2 weeks, then for 1 week at Birmingham (as *Herne the Hunter*).

Henry VIII . . . . Michael Dwyer
Will Somers. . . . . Clarence Hunt
Hubert Sheene . . . . Victor de Lore
Martin Bassett . . . . J. S. R. Page
Captain . . . . Chas. Prescott
Marjorie Bassett. . . . . Kate Lynn
Roger . . . . Miss Ackworth
Herne the Hunter. . . . . F. F. Clive (Charles Prescott)
Earl of Westbourne . . . . James Leverett
Constable . . . . Joseph Burgess

Sailor . . . . David Class
Lady Joan Mandeville . . . . Amy F. Martin
Judith Bassett . . . . Madge Inglis
Ralph . . . . Miss Telford
Gentleman Usher . . . . Mr. Jarman

Played as *The Rose of Windsor* by Ilma Norina's Opera Co., 1889.

0084 **GIPSY GABRIEL** a comic opera by Walter Parke and William Hogarth based on Sir Walter Scott's *Guy Mannering*. Music by Florian Pascal. Produced at the Theatre Royal, Bradford under the management of William Hogarth and Shiel Barry 3 November, 1887 and toured in repertoire with *Les Cloches de Corneville* through Manchester, Newcastle, Darlington/ Dewsbury, Liverpool, Halifax, Rotherham, Dublin, Cork, Limerick/Waterford, Belfast x2, Lancaster/Whitehaven, Glasgow, Edinburgh, Derby, Birmingham, Bath x2, Cardiff, Standard Shoreditch, ?, Crystal Palace/Ealing, ending 5 May, 1888. Resumed 6 August, 1888 to 8 December, 1888.

Colonel Tremaine . . . . George Belmore/Charles Steyne
Harold Penraven . . . . Hilton St Just/Charles Conyers
Mr Quondam . . . . Charles Ashford/Mat Robson
Ritchie Rolleston . . . . William Hogarth
Gabriel . . . . Shiel Barry
Simon Grimstone . . . . John Clulow/Gilbert Shirley
Black Ralph . . . . Leonard Vidal/Harry Melbourne
Constable . . . . Mr Williamson/John Sarle
Timothy Tremaine . . . . Mr Stone/R. Martin
Laura Tremaine. . . . . Amy Grundy/Ethel Murray/Florence Lavender/Adrienne Verity
Tom Polson . . . . Mr Leonard/W. H. Hosgood
Dolly . . . . Marion Erle/Amy Grundy
Mrs Ponsonby. . . . . Mrs Barry/Kate Francis
Margery . . . . Marie Shields
Jenny . . . . Alice Vitu/Florence Black
Mary . . . . Bertha Zaranski
Nancy . . . . Kate Murphy/Florence Mervyn
Lizzie . . . . Ethel Herbert/Cissy Grant
Susan . . . . Minnie Sirling/F. Dare

Pd: Jessie Danvers/Violet Leonard

Md: W. F. Glover/J. Edwin Thompson

0085 **FRANKENSTEIN** or The Vampire's Victim. A burlesque melodrama in three acts by 'Richard Henry' (Richard Butler and H. Chance Newton) Music by Meyer Lutz. Incidental songs by Robert Martin and Frederick Bowyer. Additional music by William Fullerton and G. W. Hunt. Produced at the Gaiety Theatre under the management of George Edwardes 24 December, 1887 for a run of 110 performances closing 27 April, 1888.

Frankenstein . . . . Nellie Farren (Jenny Rogers)
Maraschino . . . . Camille D'Arville/Jenny Rogers
Viva. . . . . Florence Dysart
Tartina. Marion Hood (M. Russell)
Mary Ann. . . . . Emily Cross/Maria Jones)
Stephano . . . . Jenny Rogers (Lena Delphine)/*out*
Risotto . . . . Jenny McNulty (Lena Delphine)
The Monster. . . . . Fred Leslie
Visconti . . . . E. J. Lonnen (E. H. Haslam)
The Model . . . . George Stone
Schwank. . . . . Frank Thornton
Demonico . . . . John D'Auban
Mondelico. . . . . Cyril Maude/*out*
Dotto . . . . Charles Ross

Caramella . . . . Emma Gwynne
Vanilla . . . . Sybil Grey
Tamburina/Goddess of the Sun . . . . Sylvia Grey
add Rosina . . . . Lillian Prince
Lizzina . . . . Letty Lind
Susanna . . . . Lizzie Wilson

Dir: Charles Harris; md: Meyer Lutz; ch: John D'Auban; sc: W. Beverley, Hawes Craven, W. Perkins and E. G. Banks; cos: Percy Anderson

THE NATURALIST by J. Comyns Carr. Music by King Hall. Produced at St George's Hall under the management of Alfred Reed and R. Corney Grain 11 April, 1887 with *Jubilee Notes*. Withdrawn 22 July. Reopened 3 October with *So Quiet*. Withdrawn 8 November, 1887.

Eustace Appleby . . . . J. Duncan Young/Ernest Laris
Sybil Eardley . . . . Kate Tully/Ethel Murray
Dr Christopher Grub . . . . Alfred Reed
Mrs Pomeroy Bliss . . . . Fanny Holland
Captain Braggit . . . . Walter Browne

TALLY HO! by T. Malcolm Watson. Music by Alfred J. Caldicott. Produced at St George's Hall under the management of Alfred Reed and R. Corney Grain 9 November, 1887 with *So Quiet* and subsequently *Our Servants' Ball*. Withdrawn 17 March, 1888.

Edwin Sudbury . . . . Alfred Reed
Harry Vine . . . . Ernest Laris
Joe Bradley . . . . Templar Saxe
Rose Bradley . . . . Kate Tully
Lady Vine . . . . Fanny Holland

Produced at St George's Hall 15 October, 1888 with *John Bull Abroad*. Withdrawn 25 November, 1889.

Produced at St George's Hall 30 May, 1889 with *Brittany Folk* and subsequently *My Aunt's in Town*. Withdrawn 22 June, 1889.

JUBILATION a new musical mixture in one act by 'Richard Henry'. Music by Ivan Caryll and Henry J. Leslie. Produced at the Prince of Wales Theatre under the management of Henry J. Leslie as a forepiece to *Dorothy* 14 May, 1887. Withdrawn 29 March, 1888.

Old Jones . . . . Arthur Williams/John Le Hay
Herkomais Miller . . . . John Le Hay/John Peachey
Young Jones . . . . Edward Griffin/Sebastian King
Julia Ellen . . . . Harriet Coveney/Minnie Rayner
Stragg . . . . Fred Emney/W. Aynsleigh
Araminta Robinson . . . . T. Roma (Miss Lambert)/Jessie Shirley
Ginevra Jones . . . . Birdie Irving[1]/Florence Neville

A SHOWER OF BLACKS a comic operetta in one act by Arthur Shirley and Walter Parke. Music by Ernest Bucalossi. Produced at Terry's Theatre 26 December, 1887 as a forepiece to *The Woman Hater*. Subsequently played with *Sweet Lavender*. Withdrawn 19 April, 1888.

Hippolyte de Bon Bon . . . . Alfred Bishop
Pierre Lenoir . . . . T. P. Haynes
St Juste . . . . W. Calvert/W. Chandler/Sant Matthews
Thérèse du Bois . . . . Amanda Aubrey

KITTENS a musical play in three acts by Fred Lyster. Music by James M. Glover. Produced at Brighton 4 April, 1887 and toured.

[1] later known as Ethel Irving

1888

At the opening of 1888 the West End scene had an old-fashioned look to it. Of the six musicals which were running two, *The Sultan of Mocha* and *H.M.S. Pinafore*, dated from the seventies and a third, *The Old Guard* was an adaptation of an 1880 piece. *Frankenstein* and *Miss Esmeralda*, works from the 'new wave' of burlesque, were based more or less on established pieces of literature, and the sixth, *Dorothy*, now safely housed in the Prince of Wales Theatre, was composed of a book in the old comic opera style and a score much of which was twelve years old. The only other piece with a claim to be called a musical was the American play with music, *Hans the Boatman*, which was fulfilling a brief season at Terry's Theatre before heading for Australia. *Hans the Boatman* was a custom-built piece fitted around the talent of Minnie Palmer's former leading man, Charles Arnold, which had a successful provincial career in later years but which was of little interest to the town.

The year's early productions were not particularly exciting. A French company visited the Royalty with Mary Albert in *La Grande Duchesse, La Mascotte* and *Mam'zelle Nitouche*, all of which were much preferable to the newest import in the line of comic opera, Gustave Michaelis' inane *Babette*, for which Lydia Thompson removed *The Sultan of Mocha* from the Strand. It lasted no time and Miss Thompson who had begun her managerial season so promisingly crashed into failure. The next show to be replaced was the Savoy revival of *H.M.S. Pinafore* which was followed by first a reprise of *The Pirates of Penzance* and then the return of *The Mikado* while D'Oyly Carte awaited his newest offering from Gilbert and Sullivan.

Streak o' Sunshine, a melodramatic effort in the *My Sweetheart* vein, appeared briefly and unprofitably at Sadler's Wells before the first significant piece of the year arrived. Lecocq's *Pepita* had been well tested before its West End début. It had originated in Paris in 1883 as *La Princesse des Canaries*, it had been seen on Broadway as *The Queen's Mate* and in its present adaptation by 'Mostyn Tedde' it had been played more than 700 times in the British provinces. In London it was performed a respectable 102 times at Toole's Theatre before resuming a long and lucrative touring career. With *Pepita* things seemed to take turn for the better. Four weeks later *Carina*, the first new British offering of the year, appeared at the Opera Comique and it too was to succeed in passing the 'magic' 100 performance mark.

Carina had been around for a while. Its libretto had been written several years previously by the venerable Edward Laman Blanchard, dramatist, author, critic and 'the hero of a hundred pantomimes' including 27 consecutive pieces for the flagship of that most popular kind of entertainment, the Theatre Royal, Drury Lane. 'Dear old Blanchard', a revered figure in the world of the theatre, was now 67 and still theatrically active in spite of failing health.

The composer was Miss Julia Woolf, another well-known writer who had been on the musical scene for a long time. Miss Woolf had been a musical prodigy in the early 1850s; a double King's scholar at the Royal Academy when only 15 years old, she had pursued a remarkable academic career winning many prizes. Over the following years she had written a good deal of chamber music, piano works and songs which had proved most acceptable without gaining her any great reputation. She made her theatrical début at Drury Lane with an overture for Chatterton's production of *A Winter's Tale*, but *Carina* was her first attempt at a full-sized lyric work.

Blanchard and Miss Woolf had worked together on a series of songs between 1887/9 and subsequently came together again with more substantial aims. *Carina*, its heroine named after Blanchard's dearly loved wife, was completed as early as 1885 but was not staged and was largely rewritten before being taken up by F. J. Harris who formed a production company with a capital of £5000 and took the Opera Comique to produce it. Fresh rewrites were called for but Blanchard was not well enough to take them on and the task was given to Cunningham V. Bridgman who tactfully revised the libretto and contributed some new lyrics.

Carina was based on the French play *La Guerre Ouverte* which had been 'acted seventy successive nights in Paris on 1786, the longest run then on record'[1]. This ancestry, combined with the classical pedigree of its authors, ensured that *Carina* turned out to be a comic opera of a most correct, artistic and old-fashioned kind. In time honoured fashion General Bobadillo (G. H. Snazelle) who wishes his daughter Carina (Camille D'Arville) to marry a wealthy merchant locks her in her room when she is found to have another lover and other intentions. But the bold Felix de Tornado (Durward Lely) declares that he will carry off the bride before her midnight wedding and he plots with his valet, Cadrillo (E. D. Ward) and the lady's maid, Zara (Josephine Findlay) to bring this about. The valet dresses up as the merchant and delivers a trunk said to hold wedding presents, in which the hero is concealed. He is discovered and turned out but reappears dressed in the clothes of the priest who is to officiate at the wedding. Found out again he is dismissed from the house by the triumphant Bobadillo, and Zara who has helped him is sacked and sent off with him. They leave, but it is Carina dressed in her maid's clothes who is thrown out into the night with her lover, and the wager is won.

The plot and the book were unextraordinary and reminiscent of many others. Blanchard and Bridgman's dialogue and lyrics were workmanlike but lacking in genuine interest and humour, and the music which Miss Woolf added to them was more academic than lyrical. It had strong overtones of the British sentimental operas of earlier days. *The Stage* remarked:

> The composer throughout shows study but little originality. Balfe and Wallace not to speak of other composers are continually recalled by her airs. As a matter of fact some of the ballads are, for this reason, somewhat wearisome.

This was indeed so. The ballad opera simplicity of some of Miss Woolf's melodies verged on the thin and the banal, and her heavy reliance on waltz tunes of the most basic kind was only partly redeemed by some professional orchestration.

The opening night of *Carina* was unfortunate. There were many friends and supporters of the two popular writers out front who were already wedded to the cause

[1] An English version was Mrs Inchbald's *The Midnight Hour*.

of ballad opera in general and *Carina* in particular. Their prolonged reactions (including encores to nearly every number in the first act) created discomfort in the rest of the house and the situation was not improved at the end of the show when Bridgman with doubtless the best of intentions came in front of the curtain to deliver a brief encomium on Blanchard. The small sounds of discontent swelled and Bridgman was shouted off the stage. Miss Woolf, following him on, got a respectful welcome but the evening could scarcely be accounted an all-round success.

The newspaper reviews reflected the split opinions. *The Stage* found 'the plot weak and the libretto feeble' and concluded that 'worse operas than *Carina* have succeeded and better ones have failed'. *The Times* disagreed mildly, calling Blanchard and Bridgman's part 'a very favourable sample of such literary workmanship as is now expended on librettos' and commented on Miss Woolf's: '. . the score is full of melody and imagination . .' though noting that '[she has] little faculty for the expression of humour . . she lingers fondly over her ballads and leaves the fun to develop in the actors' hands'. The hardened devotees of 'legitimate comic opera' were highly enthusiastic. *The Standard* only questioned the show's length and claimed that otherwise:

> [*Carina*] bids fair to be as great a success in its way as Offenbach's *La Grande Duchesse* or Lecocq's *La Fille de Madame Angot* . .

There were enough good quotes for the management to make up a 16 page booklet of them for publicity, but the loud approval of those who deplored the degeneration of the light musical theatre into Gaiety burlesque and an 'extension of the music halls' was not enough to keep the Opera Comique full. *Carina* was an unashamedly old-fashioned piece of a kind of which only the few very best examples still survived and drew houses. Its appeal was decidedly limited and this became quickly evident, but its essentially classical character was not to survive intact for long. The important comedy role of the Irish servant Patricho had been given to Charles Collette, an experienced and fluent comedian with a mind and manner of his own. Collette had tangled with the West End musical before, having walked out on Gilbert over his role in *Princess Toto*. On *Carina* he had no Gilbert to deal with and he quickly set out to 'improve' his part. The audiences received him well and soon he had Miss Woolf setting him a couple of Fred Bowyer lyrics with which to enlarge his part and the comedy content of the show even further. The two songs, 'Spain and Ireland' and 'We Have To', were both duets performed with E. D. Ward. Bowyer's style was not that of Blanchard who noted in his diary for October 16:

> . . hear that they are shovelling this night a lot of rubbish into the opera *Carina* at the Opera Comique . .

The new songs were extremely successful and, although they hardly fitted into the genteel atmosphere of the show as written, they did supply some of the fun that was missing from the libretto. Collette turned 'We Have To' into what was virtually a music-hall turn, full of gags and ad libs with scant regard for the character he was playing or for the play itself:

> How frequently you say you'll not put up with certain things
> But you have to.
> And often times a circumstance much alteration brings
> Then you have to.
> To keep within the limit of the truth we always try

> And form a resolution that we'll never tell a lie
> Till someone asks us how we got that beautiful black eye
> Then we have to!

Its wilder variations sat strangely alongside Blanchard's cultivated verses such as the tenor ballad 'The Halls of Memory':

> Within the halls of memory
> We oft hear, echoing still,
> Some lingering strains of melody
> To which our pulses thrill.
> Then comes a dream of faces fair
> Of voices we know well,
> Linked with the once familiar air
> On which we love to dwell . .

Poor Blanchard, who had been prevented by his health from seeing the show until October 30, confided to his diary:

> First act bright and sparkling enough but the second drags greatly owing to introduced songs.

Collette's two songs were not the only new material. Blanchard's song 'The Hoop of Gold' was cut and the composer ran up a replacement 'O, cruel Love' to a lyric by T. F. Doyle. Doyle also supplied the words to a Wedding Bells Gavotte and Clifton Bingham some banal lines for a rumty-tum aria for the tenor called 'Let me Stay'. The quality was poor but the attraction more immediate. But it was Collette who was the major 'alteration'. *The Era* commented tersely:

> . . in one case the performer has practically written his own role, a method which, cleverly practised, has saved several recent comic operas from extinction; and which though calculated to grieve the judicious certainly amuses the unthinking.

The back reference clearly pointed to Arthur Roberts' efforts on behalf of *The Old Guard*. But Collette was no Roberts either in inventiveness or in performance, nor could he approach the effect of Arthur Williams in *Dorothy* in evolving himself a role around a given character, yet he was undoubtedly funny and the recipe of more and more unbridled low comedy which he practised turned out to be popular enough. The cast was also strengthened by several alterations, particularly the hiring of Leonora Braham who took over the role of Zara from her erstwhile Savoy understudy, Miss Findlay.

Carina kept afloat until the end of its lease of the Opera Comique came in sight. The producing company dissolved itself while Harris looked around for a theatre where the show might be transferred. Finally there was no transfer and *Carina* closed on 12 January, to be put away until August when it was taken on the road for four months. During this tour Blanchard died. *Carina*, along with the year's Drury Lane pantomime, had been his last work for the stage. Miss Woolf made no further forays into the theatre either, and her musical output all but ceased. In spite of its appeal in some quarters it had been the 'modern' interpolations by Collette which had ensured a run for *Carina*. It was clear that the trend of the day was away from the old comic opera style and into something much more free and brighter musically, lower and more topical in humour.

Now was the time when, of all people, Gilbert and Sullivan decided to go against that prevailing trend and bring out a comic opera which not only based its plot on a familiar old English opera story but for which the music was considerably more serious than previously. The critical disappointment over *Ruddigore* had not sent the writers scuttling for cover under a new 'topsy-turvy' piece, nor had it encouraged them to take up any of the subjects imputed to them by the columnists which ranged from 'a piece based on Buffalo Bill's Wild West Show' to 'a Scandinavian opera set during the revolt of the Darlecarlians and the miners of the Falum'. The truth, when it became public, was less unusual than these but it bore already a warning of something different. The new Gilbert and Sullivan piece was to be called *The Tower of London*[1] and was to be set in those surroundings in the reign of Henry VIII. The story selected by Gilbert was fundamentally that of Wallace's still popular *Maritana* in which a blindfold maid is wedded to a man facing execution. Around the central plot, however, Gilbert placed his own characteristic personalities – the poignantly comic jester, Jack Point, for Grossmith; the lugubriously funny jailer for Barrington; the man-hunting dame for Miss Brandram – as well as his own peculiarly stylish dialogue and lyrics so that, different as the new show might be from the pair's earlier collaborations, it was not, as *Carina* had been, a step backwards towards the old sentimental opera. In spite of its plot, in spite of the fact that the librettist headed his book 'a new and original opera' with no sign of the word 'comic', *The Yeomen of the Guard* (as it was re-titled) belonged clearly to the world of the light-hearted musical theatre.

Among the differences between *The Yeomen of the Guard* and its predecessors was the treatment given to the central figure of Jack Point. In Point Gilbert created a character of sincerity and humanity. Lovable as had been Ko-Ko, Little Buttercup and the rest none of them could have been taken seriously for a second. When Major General Stanley and his daughters weep, when Frederic and Mabel part to 'pine alone', when Bunthorne loses his brides, fancy is stimulated but real sympathy is never involved. In *The Yeomen of the Guard* Gilbert clothed his characters in rather more reality and in the case of Jack Point created what was in many respects the most memorable character of the Savoy repertoire. The other roles were less ambitious. Miss Brandram's Dame Carruthers was in the familiar mould, the tenor and soprano roles were shaped to the exigencies of the plot and the music, and Jessie Bond was even told by the author that she wouldn't have to act because her role 'was her'.

The plot begins with Colonel Fairfax falsely condemned for sorcery and imprisoned in the Tower. To defeat the machinations of the greedy relative who has had him condemned, Fairfax asks to marry in his death-cell. The chosen bride is Elsie Maynard, a strolling player, whose partner and lover, Jack Point, is only too pleased to have her go through the charade for a fair price. But Sergeant Meryll, an officer at the Tower and an old friend of Fairfax, helps him to escape and Elsie finds herself the wife of a fugitive instead of the widow of a corpse. Fairfax reappears disguised as Meryll's son and in that guise woos and wins her once she is convinced that her 'husband' is dead. But Fairfax is pardoned and returns to claim his bride and the distraught Elsie finds to her joy that her husband and her lover are one and the same. And poor, rejected Jack falls senseless at his lady's feet as Elsie and Fairfax are happily united.

Sullivan had been delighted when Gilbert presented him with the outline for *The Yeomen of the Guard*. For months after the production of *Ruddigore* the librettist had worked on trying to produce yet another variation on the 'lozenge' plot (as they called it), that favourite notion of Gilbert's since the days of *The Gentleman in Black* and

[1] The title already used for Alfred Cellier's Manchester musical.

Creatures of Impulse where some potion or spell creates a reversal in character and/or position. When *Ruddigore* ended its run, Gilbert was no further forward and it was not until October 1887 that he finally abandoned the 'lozenge' and settled on the *Maritana/Tower of London* outline. While *Pinafore* held the fort he prepared his libretto and, while *The Pirates of Penzance* and *The Mikado* gave the Savoy audiences another taste of their favourites, the score and book of the new piece came together. Presented with lyrics of a frequently more sober kind and with situations and a general atmosphere which reeked neither of topsy-turvydom nor burlesque, Sullivan allowed himself to show a more classical vein in his music without moving outside the idiom which he had created for himself in his earlier works. As the score progressed Gilbert began to have qualms about the amount of 'serious' material, particularly musical, that was going into the show, but after discussion they persevered and when *The Yeomen of the Guard* opened on 3 October, 1888 their judgement was proved right.

The reaction to the show took two forms. The devotees of *The Mikado* and *H.M.S. Pinafore* were not sure that this new departure was quite to their taste. There seemed to be a strong sentimental emphasis at the expense of the fun, particularly the ludicrous kind of fun they had become accustomed to. On the other hand, those devoted to the music, and to predominantly music-based comic operas such as those of Cellier, found the extra significance and substance in the music marked a turning towards a more 'valid' form of light musical entertainment. But, on the whole, audiences simply came, listened and enjoyed. If the Gilbertian 'crackle' was confined on this occasion to a few scenes in what was predominantly a romantic piece there was, nevertheless, a good balance between the fun and the love interest. The question asked by so many after the opening – 'Will the public accept this sort of thing from Gilbert and Sullivan?' – was soon answered. They would. In the meantime the critics had to have their say.

Punch's critic was at his most pretentious and bilious (doubtless with the full support of his ever anti-Gilbertian editor, Mr Burnand) as he attacked Gilbert's contribution while reserving some faint praise for Sullivan. *The Era*, on the other hand, with no axe to grind expressed a mildly confused reaction:

> While the composer is found at his best in this opera, Mr Gilbert's share in it will be regarded with a certain amount of disappointment owing to the absence of the exuberant drollery of the earlier operas.

The Times went further:

> Upon the whole we can agree with the popular verdict – Mr Gilbert is in his way a man of genius, and even at his worst is a head and shoulders above the ordinary librettist. In the present instance he has not written a good play, but his lyrics are suave and good to sing . . .
> Sir Arthur Sullivan's score is fully equal to previous achievements and the success of the piece will no doubt be largely due to it.

The Daily Telegraph and others declared it unequivocally as Sullivan's best score.

Gilbert's fears had been well founded. Although the critics were willing to admire Sullivan's music they were not prepared to grant its due to the libretto which had enabled that music to be set. But the audiences were satisfied enough and the only alteration of consequence which followed the opening night was the cutting of Richard Temple's unnecessary and rather dreary 'A laughing Boy but Yesterday', an action which had been decided on before the first night but had been postponed to allow Temple some sort of a role in the première. Of the songs the most popular was clearly the duet for Point and Elsie, 'I Have a Song to Sing, O!', written in Sullivan's best light-hearted vein to a truly charming and simple verse telling the tale of

> a merryman, moping mum,
> whose soul was sad, and whose glance was glum,
> who sipped no sup, and who craved no crumb,
> as he sighed for the love of a ladye.

The lyric numbers, 'Tis Done, I Am a Bride' (Elsie) and 'Is Life a Boon' and 'Free from his Fetters Grim' (Fairfax), certainly supported the claims of those who declared that Sullivan had surpassed himself. The comic numbers, primarily entrusted to Jack, Wilfred the jailer and the pert Phoebe made less of a sensation. Grossmith had two excellently written patter songs as well as two duets with Wilfred, the second of which, describing the imaginary killing of Fairfax was a triumph of its kind:

> Like a ghost his vigil keeping
> Or a spectre all-appalling
> I beheld a figure creeping
> I should rather call it crawling
> He was creeping
> He was crawling
> He was creeping, creeping
> Crawling

as the two fabricate their tale. Jessie Bond had a gentle ballad with which she opened the show in lieu of the almost obligatory opening chorus, and a vivaciously comic 'Were I thy Bride':

> Were I thy bride,
> Then all the world beside
> Were not too wide
> To hold my wealth of love–
> Were I thy bride!

She abstracts Fairfax's cell keys from the belt of the amorous jailer as she flirts with him before concluding:

> A feather's press
> Were leaden heaviness
> To my caress.
> But then, of course, you see,
> I'm not thy bride!

The Yeomen of the Guard brought other, less intended, innovations. Since *Ruddigore* there had been a number of defections from the company, the most notable being that of Rutland Barrington, a faithful member of the unit since *The Sorcerer* had brought him to prominence. Barrington had decided to go into management on his own account and a few weeks after the production of *The Yeomen* he produced *Brantinghame Hall* at the St James. This four-act drama by Gilbert was a thin, melodramatic weepie of little quality which only brightened when the minor characters appeared to add a touch of Gilbertian facetiousness to the proceedings. Its quick failure hastened Barrington's return to the Savoy, but in the meanwhile he was replaced by W. H. Denny as Wilfred the jailer. The tenor, Durward Lely, had gone too. He had already been replaced by J. G. Robertson for the series of revivals but this was the first première without him for several years. He was now in *Carina* where he was joined by his old Savoy partner

Leonora Braham. Miss Braham had seceded from the Savoy during *Ruddigore* and gone to Australia for health reasons. She had been replaced by the American soprano Geraldine Ulmar to whom the role of Elsie now fell. The tenor was the young and dashing Courtice Pounds, a graduate from the touring companies, who quickly established himself firmly in the town. But amongst the new faces there were still Grossmith and Temple, Miss Brandram and Miss Bond to greet the faithful, until Grossmith took his retirement from the stage in August 1889 leaving Richard Temple as the only member of the original principal cast of *The Sorcerer* still with the company.

The Yeomen of the Guard ran till December 1889, a total of 423 performances, establishing itself firmly in the Gilbert and Sullivan canon. In America reaction was on the same lines as in Britain: initial questions followed by appreciation and good houses for a run of 100 nights. It was also well received in the provinces where the role of Jack Point was taken variously by George Thorne, Cairns James and Henry Lytton. It was Thorne, according to his own claims[1], who introduced in Manchester on 1 Nov, 1888 with Gilbert's blessing the notion that Jack Point should fall not senseless but dead at the final curtain. This interpretation gained currency during Lytton's long tenure of the role in later years, but it was one which did nothing to improve a work which was not intended in any way to be melodrama or a tragedy. *The Yeomen of the Guard* has remained highly popular over the years. On several occasions it has been staged in the moat of the Tower of London, most recently in 1978 for The Festival of London celebrating the ninth centenary of the real life setting of Gilbert's play. The role of Jack was taken by the cockney star, Tommy Steele.

The third new piece of 1888 could not have been less like its two predecessors. *Faust Up-To-Date* was the latest in the line of the immensely popular Gaiety burlesques. Following the closure of *Frankenstein* in April, Edwardes sent his star troupe on tour to Australia and America with *Monte Cristo Jr* and *Miss Esmeralda*, and burlesque at the Gaiety gave way to a series of plays. In October Edwardes prepared to return to the successful policy of burlesque. The subject of the show was the most tried and tested favourite of the burlesque writer, *Faust*, and the authors a team new to the Gaiety, the great George Sims and Henry Pettitt, another well-known playwright whose reputation rested on some outstandingly successful dramas and melodramas. Pettitt, the son of a civil engineer, had found his way into the theatre as advance manager to a circus and later as business manager to a touring opera company. But he soon found his métier as a writer and had already collaborated with Sims on the Adelphi successes *Harbour Lights* (1886) and *In The Ranks* (1883), and with Grundy on *The Bells of Haslemere* (1887) and *The Union Jack* (1888). Here he was venturing for the first time into the world of the musical theatre.

The title selected for the piece, *Faust Up-To-Date*, was an odd one. The expression 'up-to-date', now so common, meant little then to most people. Sims had taken it from the world of commerce – 'Your account up-to-date . .', and in doing so gave it a new meaning and a currency throughout the whole of society. Pettitt and Sims did precisely what their title suggested. They took the familar story and put it in a modern setting amongst people of the period and topical subjects. Marguerite became a barmaid at the Italian Exhibition in Nuremberg. The Old Faust, seeing her, wishes to be young again and Mephistopheles appears to grant his wish – on condition. The now young Faust

[1] In *Secrets of a Savoyard* Lytton made the same claim and Thorne took him publicly to task up to his death in 1922. Later editions of Lytton's book blurred the fact unconvincingly.

courts and wins Marguerite but her brother Valentine spoils the party by having her declared a ward in chancery and calling in the Lord Chancellor to assert his authority. The major features of the story and the opera were retained – Marguerite's jewel scene, the duel between Valentine and Faust where the former falls cursing his rival (in this case in rhyme and with considerable humour), and the imprisonment of the heroine. The whole ended with the rout of Mephistopheles who, returning to claim his own, finds himself thwarted for no one has done anything wrong. Marguerite and Faust have been married by special licence since before the interval, and Valentine is not dead, having been saved when the blade struck the case of his Waterbury watch. The Lord Chancellor, too, is cheated when the lovers escape by balloon from his legal fury as the show ends.

Sims and Pettitt filled their libretto with plenty of good Gaiety fun, smart dialogue (prose and rhyme), the occasional fit of wordplay and plenty of topical allusions and all the expected twists and turns and business which were part of the Gaiety repertoire. They also provided some excellent lyrics to which Meyer Lutz composed his characteristic Gaiety score. From a lively tarantella opening in the splendid setting of the Exhibition grounds the show went from strength to strength through a wide variety of scenes and songs. Florence St John, a knowing Marguerite, gushed over her box of jewels in a parody of Gounod . . 'how awfully, awfully nice!' and joined with a 'cello obbligato in a straight ballad 'The Dawn of Love'. Lonnen as Mephistopheles sang an hilarious 'Little List' number describing his forthcoming victims:

> There are barristers I know of who are eminent QCs
> Who think less about their clients than they do about their fees
> When they've taken say a hundred or a thousand on a brief
> They will let a junior fight it or their client come to grief
> There are members of a vestry not a thousand miles away
> Who waste in wanton gluttony the poor rates that we pay
> There's the smug teetotal lecturer who drinks upon the sly
> I have booked the lot for places and I'll have 'em by-and-by

and, of course, there was the inevitable Irish song from Bob Martin, this time called 'Enniscorthy'. Fanny Robina as Faust burlesqued Gounod's 'Salut, Demeure chaste et Pure', Jenny McNulty (Siebel) sang a pretty ballad 'I Wooed my Love' and George Stone (Valentine) described himself as 'A Soldier Born' among a bevy of bright choruses and dances and plenty of topical references amongst which Sims was not afraid to include the social abuses to which his more serious writings were devoted.[1]

Faust Up-To-Date was more of a genuine burlesque than the other recent Gaiety pieces had been, and it gained a good deal of additional humour from parodying the well known situations and songs of the drama and the opera. The duel became an acrobatic dance, Marguerite's mirror appeared out of the stage, and there was prolonged comedy made from Mephistopheles turning the fair-goers into waxworks around the fountain of wine. There was general agreement that *Faust Up-To-Date* was a step in the right direction and the best of the new burlesques up to date. The combination of humour, song and production values which had been assembled managed even to get over the fact that was no Nellie Farren or Fred Leslie at the head of affairs.

[1] Sims was the author of a number of socially orientated works, notably the forcible 'How The Poor Live'.

The most successful single element in *Faust Up-To-Date* came as a surprise. The gem of the show was, as 'Spring, gentle Spring' had been, hidden in an unexpected place. The opening of the second act included a dance performed by four girls dressed in low-cut frilly blouses, blue skirts and little white aprons, black silk stockings, frothy petticoats and caps. To a catchy tune by Meyer Lutz, Misses Lillian Price, Florence Levey, Eva Greville and Grace Sprague danced a clever routine devised by choreographer John D'Auban which brought the house down. It was recalled twice on the opening night, and thereafter was recalled nightly and frequently as the hit of the show. The tune of the Pas de Quatre became all the rage and its exponents found themselves stars with their portraits on the cover of the sheet music which sold more than all the rest of the show put together.[1]

It had taken Lutz until his 58th year to compose that elusive thing – a hit. He had more than thirty-five years of composing and arranging of his own and other people's music for the 'old' burlesque until the Gaiety and the 'new' burlesque found in him the ideal composer for the mood of the moment. The Pas de Quatre – its tune, its steps and its dancers – were 'up-to-date' and the rage of the town. Its measures were found to fit the steps of the latest dance novelty from America, the Military Schottische or 'Barn Dance' and long after *Faust Up-To-Date* had closed the music of the Pas de Quatre was still played and danced. It was interpolated into other shows and was even reissued in sheet music form in the 1950s for the continued enjoyment of a new generation of music lovers.

It had now become accepted that no light musical show could maintain popularity without regular changes in its musical content and so *Faust Up-To-Date*, in spite of its huge success, was not allowed to stand still. One of the earliest alterations, however, was of another kind. Fanny Robina, an experienced and efficient principal boy, lacked the charm, the star quality to follow in the footsteps of a Farren. Edwardes demoted her to the role of Siebel where she was much better suited and the popular Violet Cameron came in to play the title-role. As the comedians interpolated their own business and laugh-lines, the proportion of prose to verse in the book eased in favour of prose, but the principal alterations were, as always, in the songs. 'Enniscorthy', which did not come up to the popularity of 'Killaloe' or 'Ballyhooly', was replaced first by 'Donegal' and then by 'McCarthy's Widow'; Fred Bowyer wrote a smart lyric capitalising on the way in which the show's title had caught on and Miss Cameron sang of how every masher must be 'Up to Date'. With a recognised vocalist now in the part of Faust, Lutz was called upon to provide more music to that part, but other writers' material was interpolated as well. Teddy Solomon supplied a comic duet for Mephistopheles and Martha (Maria Jones) 'I'm Afraid there is Someone Looking'; Sydney Smith composed a ballad 'For You' for Miss St John whose role had been extended very early by the addition of an opening number and a duet; Albert Chevalier turned out a lyric typical of his own cockney comedy song successes in ''Ave a Glass, won't Yer' and Bob Martin scored with a topical duet for Lonnen and Harry Parker (Lord Chancellor) called 'I Raise no Objection to That', which poked fun at, among other things, 'hit' songs, not excluding Lonnen's own!

MEPH: I hear smoking concerts go on every night
LC: I've no earthly objection to that
MEPH: Songs are always the same and I don't think it right
So I raise an objection to that

[1] Grace Sprague was replaced early in the run by Maud Wilmot who is featured on the music covers leading to the perpetuated error that Miss Wilmot was a member of the original quartette.

'Tom Bowling' some man's almost certain to do
And the 'Queen of My Heart,' can't they give something new?
LC: And that terrible song that they call 'Killaloe!'
MEPH: Come, *I* raise an objection to that!

The changes kept coming and the most popular stayed as *Faust Up-To-Date* played nightly to packed houses, but Edwardes had contracted the theatre out for Abbey and Grau's French play season and at the end of May he found himself with a huge hit on his hands and commitments which obliged him to leave his own theatre. Rather than end the run he moved *Faust Up-To-Date* first to the Islington Grand for two weeks and then to the vacant Globe Theatre until his own theatre was clear again. Just over a month after leaving the Gaiety the show returned and played another four weeks with its popularity unabated. Although the theatre was now free, the company had touring obligations and once again the run looked like ending forcibly. But Edwardes had granted the No. 2 touring rights to the 'cellist/conductor turned impresario, Auguste van Biene, who was preparing to send a company on the road. Van Biene switched direction and on 29 July the new company saw each other for the first time as they filled the vacant Gaiety stage with their *Faust Up-To-Date*. They soon got into the rhythm of things and, while the No. 1 company set out for Liverpool and 14 weeks on the road, the new young comic 'Teddy' Payne,[1] Grace Pedley, Jenny Dawson and Co. took their turns at being stars of the Gaiety. It was a different show in their hands and the variety element, which had been less than usual in the original version, came to the fore. Miss Dawson put in another Albert Chevalier song, 'Suit the Action to the Words', composed by manager van Biene, John Dallas as Valentine added yet another, 'He Knew It' with music by Chevalier's brother, C. Ingle, and low comedy blossomed at the Gaiety until September when van Biene took his company on the road to leave the theatre to the returning Farren/Leslie team with their new burlesque *Ruy Blas and the Blasé Roué*.

Faust Up-To-Date had been the most profitable as well as the most popular of the Gaiety burlesques and it continued to bring in revenue as van Biene toured it constantly and with constant up-to-dating over the next five years. The original Gaiety company took the show on a tour of the United States including two limited stops on Broadway, and in 1892 Lonnen headed Edwardes' company which played *Faust Up-To-Date* in its repertoire in Australia. Kate Santley took a company to Germany with herself as a rather ageing Marguerite who plumped out her part by interpolating the by then more recent Gaiety hit 'Hush, the Bogie' incongruously into the first act finale. The audience were supplied with dual language scripts to follow the performance. In 1892 *Faust Up-To-Date* made a return visit to the Gaiety. Van Biene's touring company, reinforced for the occasion with a few 'names', brought the show in to fill a gap in the programme and played a suitably updated version featuring the original Marguerite, Florence St John, and a pas de quatre headed by Eva Greville, one of the first famous foursome. It ran for two months plus until the regular company had finished its provincial schedule and was ready to return.

All three of the new British productions were still running at the end of the year by which time they had been joined by the long-awaited production of Chassaigne's *Nadgy* at the Avenue. *Nadgy* featured Arthur Roberts alongside Tapley, Dallas, Giulia Warwick and Marie Vanoni, fresh from her triumphs at the Alhambra music hall, and

[1] Payne was a last minute replacement for the intended Mephistopheles, Charles Lamb Kenny, and had only two days' notice of his Gaiety début.

ran for 162 performances. The Strand, back on a policy of pasticcio burlesque, followed *Aladdin* (15 Sept) with *Atalanta* (17 November). In the provinces *Dorothy, Erminie*, Gilbert and Sullivan and *Jack-in-the-Box* remained the staple of the touring British repertoire alongside *Pepita* and the inevitable *Les Cloches de Corneville. Nell Gwynne* and *Les Manteaux Noirs* consolidated their provincial popularity and Shiel Barry continued the *Gipsy Gabriel* experiment although the new piece took decidedly second place to *Les Cloches* in his schedule. Deane Brand took out *Rhoda*, and *Count Tremolio* made a second appearance heavily disguised as *Geraldine*. The new pieces were not particularly notable. Gilbert Tate sent out a tour of *The Punch Bowl*, a comic opera by the learned John Storer, Mus.D., which had been tried without much notice at the Novelty for one matinée the previous June. Billed as 'from the Novelty Theatre, London' it had a two months' tour which included two suburban theatres and the composer's old home town of Scarborough.

Its story had a bored and unpopular monarch fooled into taking a drink which will make him invisible so that he can amuse himself among his subjects. But invisibility brings him nothing but trouble. He hears nothing but ill of himself, he sees his wife flirting with the young men of the court and, worst, he gets nothing to eat. To get the antidote to the 'Royal Brew' he agrees to abdicate, and then discovers that he has never been invisible. Some pretty music of no great weight compensated a little for weak dialogue which the comedian Percy Compton attempted to liven by his own rather unsuitable interpolations. These included two comic songs which sat uncomfortably in the context of a 'comic opera' and did nothing to help the life span of *The Punch Bowl* which was shelved after nine weeks.

An attempt at a musical by three local 'theatricals' at the Manchester Prince's under the title *La Serenata* was a disaster. Into a non-existent plot the author introduced a number of English tourists in Spain whose unoriginal eccentricities were supposed to provide the evening's entertainment. Artists of the calibre of Aynsley Cook, J. G. Taylor and Albert Christian made little sense of it and the odd reasonable number from Cook and Katie Cohen could not make more of *La Serenata* than a two-week mistake.

The third new piece was *Randolph the Reckless*, a jolly extravaganza by Victor Stevens, comedian/writer/manager/composer and all of these with success. For *Randolph* he was author and composer only, leaving the management to another performer, Fritz Rimma and the musical director Hugo Leuze, and the leading transvestite role of Quisbyrina to Edward Sidney as the ugly sister of the heroine, the fair Rosella, who aspires to the hand of Randolph the Reckless in preference to that of Sir Sappy Noodle pressed on her by the Baron Badde.

Randolph was played as an afterpiece to the play *Flint and Steel* with which the late Fred Stimson had had some success. However it soon became clear that it was the extravaganza which was the feature of the very long evening and the play was abandoned and *Randolph* stretched into two acts to fill the whole evening. It was hardly sophisticated entertainment, but it was hilarious and uninhibited broad fun interspersed with some lively popular songs taken from here and there to supplement Stevens's original score, interchangeable at a moment's notice. *Randolph* proved a very popular combination of song and dance and fun and it was toured for a number of seasons, during which time the title role was taken by the music hall artists Vesta Tilley and Lady Mansel, while Josephine Findlay was seen as Rosella and Alice Brookes, later Mrs Victor Stevens and the company's star, made an entry in a small role. One notable short piece made its appearance during the year, *Mrs Jarramie's Genie*, at the Savoy, which kept up that Theatre's reputation for amusing little forepieces.

1888

086 **THE PUNCH BOWL** or The Royal Brew. A comic opera in 2 acts by T. Murray Ford. Music by Dr John Storer. Produced at a matinée at the Novelty Theatre June 18, 1887. Produced by Gilbert Tate at Stratford East 22 March, 1888 and toured through Greenwich, Scarborough, Stockton, Blackburn, Wigan, Burnley, Manchester and Cardiff, ending 19 May 1888.

Prince Blitzen	Henry Ashley/Percy Compton
General the Field Marshal	Walter Marnock
Lord Admiral	Fred Salcombe
Lord Chamberlain	Eric Thorne
Sergeant Forwartz	Charles Mowbray/Gordon Hill
Queen Dowager	Ada Doree
Infant Prince Prima	Dot d'Alcourt
Lady Constance Kissam	Edith Vane
Princess Bertha Blitzen	Maud Vena
Pages to the Queen	Julia Egley, Edith Clifford, Clara d'Alcourt

with Violet Leigh, Nelly Clifton, Annie Lysle, Vera Withers, Edith Northbrook, Louie Hamilton, Edith Russell, Minnie Wolf, Lillie Wolf, Amy Gorden, Julia Gomez, Ella Lewis, Catalina Gomez, Maggie Keith, A. Armstrong. Gordon Hill, Fred C. Bates, Charles Savidge, Arthur Withers, Robert Kempton, Richard Holding.

Dir: Hugh Moss; md: W. W. Meadows

Novelty matinée: Allen Thomas (PR), James Leverett (FM), Charles Conyers (AD), Ambrose Collini (LC), Lillian Adair (DOW), Dot d'Alcourt (IPP), Emmie Graham (CON), Constance Stanhope (BERTHA), Naomi Neilson (PAGE)

087 **CARINA** or Twelve o'Clock. A comic opera in three acts by E. L. Blanchard and Cunningham Bridgman based on *La Guerre Ouverte* ou *Ruse Contre Ruse* by M. Damaniant. Music by Julia Woolf. Additional material by Frederick Bowyer. Produced at the Opera Comique under the management of F. J. Harris 27 September, 1888 for run of 116 performances closing 12 January, 1889.

Don Felix de Tornado	Durward Lely
Cadillo, his servant	E. D. Ward
General Bobadillo del Barcelona	G. H. Snazelle (W. H. Guise)
Olla Podrida	Harry Halley/Arthur Giles
Patricho	Charles Collette
Grimaldo	Eric Thorne/Harry Halley
Sancho	W. H. Guise (Arthur Gill)
Zara	Josephine Findlay/Leonora Braham
Leonina	Ada Doree (Isabel Grey)
Vea	Jessica Dene/Jessie Day
Ella	Flora Wilmos (Fanny Selby)
Zeta	Blanche Murray/Fanny Selby (Grace Lyne)
Panzo	Mary Marden/
Tarella	Alice Lethbridge/Alice Gilbert/Mary Marden

Carina . . . . Camille D'Arville/Annie Lea

Dir: Charles Harris; md: Auguste van Biene/Frederick Stanislaus; sc: T. E. Ryan & William Telbin; cos: Wilhelm

0088 **THE YEOMEN OF THE GUARD** a comic opera in two acts by W. S. Gilbert. Music by Arthur Sullivan. Produced at the Savoy Theatre under the management of Richard D'Oyly Carte 3 October, 1888 for a run of 423 performances closing 30 November, 1889.

Sir Richard Cholmondely. . . . . Wallace Brownlow/Charles Gilbert (George de Pledge)
Colonel Fairfax . . . . Courtice Pounds (Charles Rose) (C. Barrett) (J. Wilbraham)
Sergeant Meryll. . . . . Richard Temple
Leonard . . . . W. R. Shirley (Charles Rose) (C. Barrett) (J. Wilbraham)
Jack Point . . . . George Grossmith/John Wilkinson
Wilfred Shadbolt . . . . W. H. Denny/Charles Gilbert
First Yeoman . . . . J. Wilbraham
Second Yeoman. . . . . A. Medcalf
Third Yeoman . . . . Mr Merton
Fourth Yeoman . . . . Rudolph Lewis
Headsman . . . . H. Richards
First Citizen. . . . . Tom Redmond/Mr Lees
Second Citizen . . . . Mr Boyd
Elsie . . . . Geraldine Ulmar (Rose Hervey)
Phoebe Meryll . . . . Jessie Bond (Annie Cole)
Dame Carruthers . . . . Rosina Brandram/Annie Bernard
Kate . . . . Rose Hervey/Nellie Lawrence/Agnes Wyatt

Dir: Gilbert & Sullivan; md: François Cellier; ch: John D'Auban; sc: Hawes Craven; cos: Percy Anderson

Produced in New York at the Casino Theatre 17 October, 1888 for a run of 100 performances, closing 18 January, 1889.
George Broderick (CHOL), Henry Hallam (FAIR), George Olmi (MER), Charles Renwick (LEO), J. H. Ryley (JP), Fred Solomon (SHAD), Charles Thomas (Y1), J. Priest (Y2), M. J. Thomas (Y3), L. Roach (Y4), H. Adams (HEAD), Edgar Smith (C1), Stanley Starr (C2), Bertha Ricci (EL), Sylvia Gerrish (PH), Isabelle Urquhart (CARR), Kate Uart/Marie Glover (KATE). Dir: Richard Barker; md: Jesse Williams; sc: Thomas Weston; cos: Dazian, Mme Loe

Played in New York by the D'Oyly Carte Opera company and others in repertoire and short seasons.

Produced at the Savoy Theatre under the management of Richard D'Oyly Carte 5 May, 1897. Withdrawn 31 July and reopened 16 August. Withdrawn 20 November, 1897 after a total of 187 performances.
Jones Hewson (CHOL), Charles Kenningham (FAIR), Richard Temple (MER), H. Scott Russell/Cory James (LEO), Walter Passmore (JP), Henry Lytton (Tom Redmond) (SHAD), Cory James/Charles Childerstone (Y1), H. G. Gordon (Y2), Iago Lewys (Y3), C. H. Workman (C1), Edwin Bryan (C2), H. Richards (HEAD), Ilka Palmay (Isabel Jay)/Ruth Vincent (EL), Florence Perry (PH), Rosina Brandram (CARR), Ruth Vincent/Mildred Baker (K). Md: François Cellier

Produced at the Savoy Theatre under the management of the D'Oyly Carte Opera Company 8 December, 1906 in repertoire. Performed 87 times.
Frank Wilson/Alec Johnstone/Leo Sheffield (CHOL), Pacie Ripple/Harold Wilde (FAIR), Overton Moyle (MER), Henry Burnand (Edward Wynn) (LEO), C. H.Workman (JP), John Clulow (SHAD), Frank Beckett (Y1) Leo Sheffield/Donald Ferguson (Y2), Richard Andean (C1), Rowland Williams (C2), H. M. White (HEAD), Lilian Coomber/Clara Dow (Violette Londa) (Marie Wilson) (EL), Jessie Rose (PH), Louie Rene (Ethel Morrison) (CARR), Clara Dow/Marie Wilson/Ruby Gray (K). Md: François Cellier

Produced at the Savoy Theatre under the management of the D'Oyly Carte Opera Company 1 March, 1909 in repertoire. Performed 28 times.
Leo Sheffield (CHOL), Henry Herbert (FAIR), Richard Temple (MER), A. Laurence Legge (LEO), C. H. Workman (JP), Rutland Barrington (SHAD), William Davidson (Y1), Cecil Curtis (Y2), Fred G. Edgar (C1), Sidney Ashcroft/Fred Hewett (C2), Richard Shaw (HEAD), Elsie Spain (EL), Jessie Rose (PH), Louie Rene (CARR), Beatrice Boarer (K). Md: François Cellier

Subsequently played by the D'Oyly Carte Opera Company on tour and in London in repertoire.

Produced at the Tower of London July 9, 1962 for a season.
John Carol Case (CHOL), Thomas Round (FAIR), Bryan Drake (MER), John Wakefield (LEO), John Cameron (JP), Kenneth Sandford (SHAD), Alan Mayall (Y1), Michael Wakeham (Y2), Ian McNeil (C1), Peter Quine (C2), Ann Dowdall (EL) , Anne Pashley (PH), Johanna Peters (CARR), Sylvia Grey (K). Dir: Anthony Besch ; md: L. Leonard; cos/sc: Peter Rice

Produced at the Tower of London 6 July, 1964 for a season ending 18 July, 1964.
John Carol Case (CHOL), Thomas Round/Jack Irons (FAIR), James Atkins (MER), Jack Irons/Ramon Remedios (LEO), John Cameron (JP), Kenneth Sandford (SHAD), John Cheek (Y1), Paul Neal (Y2), Ian McNeil (C1), Charles Grace (C2), Elizabeth Robson/Maureen Keetch (EL), Anita Pashley (PH), Johanna Peters/Jeanette Roach (CARR), Maureen Keetch/Verity Ann Bates (K). Dir: Anthony Besch; md: Lawrence Leonard; sc/cos: Peter Rice

Produced at the Tower of London 11 July, 1966 for a season ending 23 July.
John Gower (CHOL), Nigel Douglas/Dennis Brandt (FAIR), Geoffrey Chard (MER), Dennis Brandt/John Winfield (LEO), Brian Handley (JP), Noel Mangin/Eric Stannard (SHAD), Brian McGuire (Y1), Michael Sim (Y2), Ian McNeil (C1), Charles Grace (C2) Catherine Wilson/Maureen Keetch (EL), Maureen Morelle (PH), Gillian Knight (CARR), Maureen Keetch/Angela Mendham (K). Dir: Anthony Besch; md: Charles Mackerras/David Lloyd-Jones sc/cos: Peter Rice

Produced at the Tower of London on the occasion of the 900th Anniversary of the Tower of London 17 July, 1978 for a season ending 12 August. This performance was reproduced on television by ATV 23 December, 1978 and subsequently issued on video cassette.
Tom McDonnell (CHOL), Terry Jenkins (FAIR), Paul Hudson (MER), David Fieldsend (LEO), Tommy Steele (JP), Dennis Wicks (SHAD), David Bartlett (Y1), Michael Lynch (Y2), Laureen Livingstone (EL), Della Jones (PH), Anne Collins (CARR), Hilary Western (K). Dir: Anthony Besch md: Alexander Faris

Film: In 1907 three pieces from *The Yeomen of the Guard* were issued on film and synchronised record in Walturdaw's Cinematophone Singing Records series: 'Hereupon We're Both Agreed', 'Were I Thy Bride' and the Finale to Act 1.

TV/Video: 1984 Brent Walker Ltd. Pr: Judith de Paul; dir: Anthony Besch; md: Alexander Faris; ch: Terry Gilbert; sc: Allan Cameron; cos: Jenny Beavan
Peter Savidge (CHOL), David Hillman (FAIR), Geoffrey Chard (MER), Michael Bulman (LEO), Joel Grey (JP), Alfred Marks (SHAD), Elizabeth Gale (EL), Claire Powell (PH), Elizabeth Bainbridge (CARR), Beryl Korman (K)

89 **FAUST UP-TO-DATE** a burlesque in two acts by George R. Sims and Henry Pettitt. Music by Meyer Lutz. Produced at the Gaiety Theatre under the management of George Edwardes 30 October, 1888 for a run of 180 performances closing 25 May, 1889. Played for two weeks at the Grand, Islington and then at the Globe Theatre 10 June to 28 June. Returned to the Gaiety Theatre 29 June. Withdrawn 27 July. Toured from 19 August, 1889 through Liverpool, Manchester, Scarborough, Newcastle, Bradford, Leicester, Dublin, Liverpool, Manchester, Edinburgh, Halifax, Birmingham, Islington (Grand) x2 ending 21 November 1889.

Mephistopheles	E. J. Lonnen
Valentine	George Stone (E. H. Haslam)/Charles Danby
Lord Chancellor.	Walter Lonnen/Harry Parker
Old Faust	Harry Parker/E. H. Haslam
Faust	Fanny Robina/Violet Cameron/Maud Hobson/Addie Conyers

Siebel . . . . Jenny McNulty/Fanny Robina (Helen Capet)/Kate Barry/Emily Hughes
Wagner . . . . Emma Broughton/Alice Young
Donner . . . . Alice Young/Maud Hobson
Blitzen. . . . . Hetty Hamer/Leila Wilson
Scwank . . . . Helen Capet/Charlotte Hope
Elsa . . . . Lillian Price
Lisa . . . . Florence Levey
Katrina . . . . Eva Greville
Hilda . . . . Grace Sprague/Maud Wilmot/P. Wilson/P. Knight
Totchen (Vivandière) . . . . Mabel Love/Lydia Manton/Kate Barry
Martha . . . . Maria Jones
Marguerite . . . . Florence St John (Alice Young)/
Waitresses . . . . Emily Robina/Miss Herbert
Minnie Ross
Scheltzer . . . . Charles Ross
pd: Willie Warde

Dir: Charles Harris; md: Meyer Lutz; ch: John D'Auban; sc: T. E. Ryan, E. G. Banks, William Telbin; cos: Percy Anderson

Played at the Gaiety Theatre by Auguste van Biene's Company 29 July, 1889 to 7 September, 1889 and then toured to Southport, Preston, Blackpool, Wolverhampton, Brighton, York, Blackburn,?, Hanley, Nottingham and Northampton ending 23 November. Matinées at Crystal Palace 3 September and Brighton 5 September.
Edmund Payne (MEPH), J. J. Dallas (VAL), George Honey/Eric Thorne (LC), Eric Thorne/E. J. Lovell (OLD), Jenny Dawson (F), Milly Marion/Lily Harold (SIE), Helen Capet (WAG), Miss Arrowsmith/Miss Fedora (DONN), Violet Durkin (BL), Gladys Vane (SCW), Marie Knight/Minnie King (ELSA), Sophie Scotti (LISA), G. Vale/Minnie Knight/Marie King (KAT), Miss Holland (HIL), Grace Leslie (VIV), Ada Doree (MARTHA), Grace Pedley/Nellie Murray/Maud Boyd (MARG), May Raymond & L. Leyton (WAIT), Violet Paget. Md: Edgar Ward

Produced at the Broadway Theatre, New York, by George Edwardes' Gaiety Theatre Company under the direction of Henry E. Abbey & Maurice Grau 11 December 1889 for a run of 43 performances ending 18 January, 1890. Return season played from 21 April to 4 May, 1890.
E. J. Lonnen (MEPH), Charles Danby (VAL), E. H. Haslem (LC), E. Vacotti (OLD), Addie Conyers (F), Katie Barry (SIE), Maude Stone (WAG), Nellie Langton (DON), Gertrude Hillyar (BLITZ), Miss Rutherford (SCW), Lillian Price (ELSA), Florence Levey (LISA), Edith Rayner (KAT), Maud Wilmot (HIL), Mary Stuart (VIV), Maria Jones (MARTHA), Grace Pedley/Florence St John (MARG), Ada Belmore, Josie Wilcox, Gertrude Capel (WAIT), Elsie Everett (SCH), Estelle Rowe (LIESCHEN). Dir: Walter Raynham; md: Lovell Phillips; sc: T. E. Ryan, William Telbin

Played at the Gaiety Theatre by Auguste van Biene's touring company from 11 July, 1892 to 20 August 1892. Played at a matinée at the Crystal Palace 28 July.
Edmund Payne (MEPH), Arthur Williams (VAL), George Honey (LC), Harry C. Barry (OLD), Amy Augarde (F), Kitty Loftus (SIE), Jessie Harrison (WAG), Cissy Fitzgerald (DOWN), Florence Doyne (BLITZ), Winifred Hare (SCW), Alice Batchelor (ELSA), Eva Greville (LISA), Rose Batchelor (KAT), Clara Vinanea (HIL), Etheldine Percy (VIV), Ada Doree (MARTHA), Florence St John (MARG), Harry Phydora (SCH). Dir: J. T. Tanner; md: W. F. Glover

LA SERENATA a comic opera by Luke McHale. Music by Joseph Batchelder and Oliver Gregg. Produced at the Prince's Theatre, Manchester under the management of T. Ramsay 18 June, 1888 for a two-week season ending 30 June.

Colonel Smythe . . . . J. Statham
Mr Simpson. . . . . J. G. Taylor
Captain Santiago . . . . Thomas Aynsley Cook
Mateo . . . . Albert Christian
Paquita . . . . Katie Cohen
Benita . . . . Maud Gwynne

Dona Galatea	Annie Cook
Maraquita	Alice Ford
Mr Jones	Mr Ormerod
Mr Spinner	Mr Clemison
Mr Blackie	Frank Crellin
Mr Rooney	John Allen
Conductor of the Tourist Party	Victor de Lore
Postillion of an indulgence	J. G. Hewson
Screws	Messrs Allen & Incliffe Burton
Sergeant	G.E. Bancroft

RANDOLPH THE RECKLESS an extravaganza (comic opera) written and composed by Victor Stevens. Produced at the Prince of Wales Theatre, Salford 6 August, 1888 under the management of Fritz Rimma and Hugo Leuze and toured.

Quisbyrina	Edward Sidney/Frank Crellin
The Fair Rosella	Lizzie Aubrey
Baron Badde	Tom Redmond/Hal Forde/C. P. Amalia
Blossom	Frank Crellin/
Randolph	Maude Ellison/Maude Stafford
Sir Sappy Noodle	Lottie Wentworth/Maude Stoneham
Grim Grizzle	W. G. Walford
Luke	Clement Ivie
Reuben	Fritz H. Ivie
Giles	Gilbert Arrandale
Margery	Cissie Phillips
Daisy	Lillie Lambe
Albert	Cissy Bristow
Arthur	Polly Bristow
Walter	Lillie Lee
Cherry	Violet Murrielle

MRS JARRAMIE'S GENIE an operetta by Frank Desprez. Music by Alfred and François Cellier. Produced at the Savoy Theatre under the management of Richard D'Oyly Carte 14 February, 1888 as a forepiece to *H.M.S. Pinafore*. Subsequently played with *The Mikado* and *The Yeomen of the Guard*.

Mr Harrington Jarramie	Wallace Brownlow/H. Gordon
Ernest Pepperton	J. Wilbraham
Mrs Harrington Jarramie	Madge Christo/Annie Bernard
Smithers	Charles Gilbert
Bill	Henry Le Breton/Mr. Smith
Jim	A. Medcalf
Daphne	Rose Hervey
Nixon	M. Russell
Ben-Zoh-Leen	John Wilkinson

QUITS a folie musicale in one act by B. T. Hughes. Music by John Crook. Produced at the Avenue Theatre under the management of Henry Watkin 1 October, 1888 as a forepiece to *The Old Guard*. Subsequently played with *Nadgy*, and then with *Lancelot the Lovely*. Withdrawn 4 May, 1889.

Mrs Lamont	Annie Halford
Tuttles	Carrie Coote
Vere Valsingham	Ambrose Collini
Jorkins	Harry Grattan

WANTED, AN HEIR by T. Malcolm Watson. Music by Alfred J. Caldicott. Produced at St George's Hall under the management of Alfred Reed and R. Corney Grain 2 April, 1888 with *Mossoo in London*. Withdrawn 21 July. Reopened 8 October. Withdrawn 13 October, 1888.

John Bigg	Alfred Reed

Mrs Bigg . . . . Fanny Holland
Ned Manson . . . . Ernest Laris
Bertha . . . . Kate Tully
Percy Gunnion . . . . Walter Browne

THE BOSUN'S MATE by Walter Browne. Music by Alfred J. Caldicott. Produced at St George's Hall under the management of Alfred Reed and R. Corney Grain 26 November, 1888 with *John Bull Abroad,* the latter replaced by *A Day's Sport*. Withdrawn 19 March, 1889.

Stephen Pesket . . . . Walter Browne
Lieutenant Jack Hardy . . . . Earnest Laris
Winifred. . . . . Kate Tully
Dorothy Dingle . . . . Fanny Holland
Ben Bouncer . . . . Alfred Reed

1889

The new year found three undoubted hits running strongly: *The Yeomen of the Guard* settling in for the year, *Faust Up-To-Date* for those who preferred something lighter and more eye-catching, and the amazing *Dorothy* in its third theatre and playing to tremendous houses not only in Shaftesbury Avenue but all over the country through its two highly successful touring companies. *Carina* at the Opera Comique had passed its hundredth performance and was heading for its last, while a fifth native work held the Globe stage for matinées – Savile Clarke's version of *Alice in Wonderland* in the second of its many Christmas seasons. Amongst these British pieces only one foreign musical, the Avenue's production of *Nadgy,* survived.

A new Anglo-French piece was the first to swell the ranks of metropolitan musicals in 1889. *Paul Jones* had been first produced at Bolton by Carl Rosa's newly-formed light opera company with which, in conjunction with Horace Sedger of the Prince of Wales Theatre, the impresario hoped to make a successful incursion into the potentially lucrative world of lighter musical entertainment after many years running the country's most notable touring grand opera company. *Paul Jones* was a hybrid piece, being confessedly 'based on' Chivot and Duru's *Surcouf,* a naval comic opera composed by Robert Planquette for the Folies Dramatiques and first performed there in 1887. The English version was in the hands of H. B. Farnie who was attempting to emulate the success he had had in adapting Planquette's earlier *Les Voltigeurs de la 32ème* as *The Old Guard.* With *Surcouf* he had to start with the awkward premise of a French hero and an English villain, Robert Surcouf turning corsair to win the 300.000 francs needed to claim the hand of la belle Yvonne. Farnie, however, while sticking to the broad outline of the story, turned the hero into the Englishman Paul Jones and made his villains Spaniards. Instead of turning pirate, Jones becomes the commander of a Yankee man o'war. Farnie's adaptation was a virtual rewrite, changing the whole atmosphere of the piece. A prologue and three acts (in effect four) became three acts; the dialogue and the characters were re-fashioned to suit 'English tastes' with a heavy injection of sentiment and low humour, less 'big' singing and less Gallic vigour.

Planquette played his part in this transformation. *Rip Van Winkle, Nell Gwynne* and *The Old Guard* had shown him how to please British audiences and he discarded nearly all the score of *Surcouf* to write a whole set of new music which retained only the overture, some pieces of finales and choruses and the odd theme which was cut, re-orchestrated and inserted into a totally different context from its original. He wrote ten new numbers for the Bolton try-out version and, as the inevitable process of alterations and additions began between there and the London opening, added further to that total so that the show which opened in London on 12 January bore only a passing resemblance to the *Surcouf* of Paris 1887. It was, to all intents and purposes, a new work.

The title role of *Paul Jones* was created at Bolton by the baritone Michael Dwyer, but for London Rosa and Sedger hired the American contralto, Agnes Huntingdon. Miss Huntingdon was a striking woman with a warm deep voice and a magnetism which bowled over, among others, George Edwardes who was so amazed by her talent that he made energetic efforts to sign her to a long term contract and began preparations to build an Agnes Huntingdon Theatre in Leicester Square. Although, as it turned out, Edwardes was never to employ Miss Huntingdon the theatre she inspired was finally built and as Daly's Theatre was to house some of Edwardes' and the British musical's greatest successes.

The other principal character in *Paul Jones* was the 35-year-old comedian Harry Monkhouse cast as the comic smuggler Bouillabaisse. His role was one which, as the tradition was now becoming, allowed for 'working up'. Monkhouse was used to that. His past few years had been spent touring his enormously popular musical farce *Larks* around Britain, and *Larks* in true provincial fashion was regularly altered and added to to keep it topical and suitable for its various dates. Monkhouse developed the role of Bouillabaisse into one which differed rather from the reading given by John Wainwright in the touring company. He caused a good deal of mirth through his antics with Albert James in the role of his sidekick, Petit Pierre, and a special number written by the show's conductor, Frederick Stanislaus, was squeezed in to give them an extra chance for fooling.

Paul Jones was an immediate success and Agnes Huntingdon became overnight the toast of the musical stage, but at one point during the second act of the première things had looked for a while as if they might turn out very differently. As so often, a too friendly part of the first night audience was busily encoring every number and the annoyance of the rest of the house finally made itself felt when, after a particularly poor performance by Henry Ashley in the duet 'The Shipping News', the enthusiasts claimed the obligatory encore. A row developed in the audience. Tillie Wadman, who had held up her end of the song fairly well, stood her ground and soon even the rioters felt obliged to recognise her with some applause. Unfortunately the conductor took this concession as a sign to repeat 'The Shipping News', but the audience would have none of Ashley. They allowed Miss Wadman's lines to be heard but each time the comedian opened his mouth there were howls of 'No!' and hissing which drowned him out. It was a bad moment, but the public were won back when Phyllis Broughton flirted her way through the lilt 'He Looked at my Sabots' and danced her pretty bourrée. Miss Wadman warmed things up further with the beautiful prayer 'Before the Altar now I'm Kneeling' and Miss Huntingdon sealed the result with the show's hit, the glorious 'Ever and ever Mine'. The evening was safe and the careers of *Paul Jones* and Agnes Huntingdon assured. The show ran at the Prince of Wales through a full twelve months and over the following years it continually toured. Neither the show nor its star were received with anything like such enthusiasm when *Paul Jones* was staged on Broadway the following year, but it fared quite reasonably during a month's run.

The role of Paul Jones had originally been intended for the baritone of the moment, Hayden Coffin, but Coffin's contract with Henry Leslie had a twelve-month option clause and, just when the singer thought he was free, Leslie decided to take up the option and to use Coffin in his successor to *Dorothy*. In the meanwhile that show continued at the Lyric and it was not until April that the production of *Doris* (as the new piece was finally called after spells as both *Barbara* and *Dorcas*) was staged.

The authors were the same as for *Dorothy* – Charlie Stephenson and Alfred Cellier. Once again the work was based on an earlier Cellier score, this time *Tower of London* which he had produced for Manchester in 1875. The similarities did not end there, for the personnel involved were almost exclusively *Dorothy* veterans. Arthur Williams, Hayden Coffin, Furneaux Cook, John Le Hay and Harriet Coveney were all members of the original *Dorothy* cast; Ben Davies, Effie Chapuy, W. T. Hemsley and Percy Compton had all played in the metropolitan and/or touring versions, and Alice Barnett had been Mrs Privett in Australia. Leslie, who had 'made' *Dorothy*'s success was at the head of affairs and Charlie Harris and Ivan Caryll were once more in charge of the stage and the pit. If success could come by the repetition of a recipe then *Doris* was destined for a very long run. The first performance was greeted by much the same reception as *Dorothy* had been: Cellier's music was given widespread approval and the book and lyrics were found poor and uninteresting.

The subject matter and plot of *Doris* were very slender, dealing with the efforts of Doris and her lover, Martin, and Lady Anne Jerningham to prevent the latter's lover, Sir Philip Carey, from being unjustly executed on Tower Green as a traitor. To achieve their ends and defeat the over-zealously loyalist activities of Doris' father, the foolish Dinniver and then Martin both disguise themselves as the fugitive Sir Philip. All is finally saved when Doris, like her predecessor Barbara in *Tower of London*, arrives with a pardon from the magnanimous off-stage Queen Bess. This rather spare story was stretched over three acts with little in the way of incident or action or of particularly interesting dialogue. Stephenson had consciously made *Doris* a period piece with no concessions to the wider public taste for low comedy and topical jokes and songs, elements which he actively resisted. His stand got him poor notices. *The Stage* called his libretto '. . bare of incident and poor of language'. *The Era* qualified the plot as 'weak', but both agreed that some 'working up', particularly by Arthur Williams as Dinniver, in the same style which had so materially helped *Dorothy*, might do the trick, as Cellier's music was

> . . as tuneful, as artistic in style, as finished and elegant as any [he] has composed . . [he] need not be ashamed to place his score beside that of any foreign composer past or present . .

As in *Dorothy* Cellier had taken some of his old music and had supplemented it with new pieces to make up the score of the show. There were many excellent numbers. Ben Davies (Martin) had a fine tenor song 'I've Sought the Brake and Bracken'[1] and Coffin (Sir Philip) the virile 'Honour Bids me Speed Away'. Furneaux Cook's drinking song 'The Jug of Beer' was encored three times on opening night and regularly thereafter and Arthur Williams's comical post-drinking song 'What Has Become of the Door?' also became deservedly popular:

> What has become of the door?
> It seems that the door is no more.
> It used to be here
> Or at all events near
> Beshrew me! Why didn't I get home before?
> I feel such a buzz in my head
> That I heartily wish I were dead

[1] Later known and much recorded as 'So Fare Thee Well'.

Tomorrow I'll stop
I'll not drink a drop
Oh, why will not somebody put me to bed?
Come, steady lad, stand to your ground
For doors are not easily found
If you chance to be late
You must patiently wait
Till the keyhole has time to get round.

The role of Doris was originally entrusted to the young soprano Annie Lea who had made such a charming début as Carina, but her illness led to it being taken up by the Carl Rosa's Annette Albu, Gilbert's Princess Toto. Miss Albu was attractive if rather unbending in the part and at her best in the vocal sections. Two of her numbers 'Learn to Wait' and the duet 'The Parting' were rearranged pieces from *Tower of London* to which were added another solo, 'Love's Race' and, most successfully, a wistful duet 'If I am Dreaming' sung with Ben Davies.

On the whole, the women's music was not as well done as that for the male principals but the score was a well-balanced and well-written one, put over aptly by the experienced team of singers. What the *Doris* score did not have, however, was a 'Queen of my Heart', the all-important hit song and, surprisingly, no attempt was made to imitate it by the interpolation of a similar ballad for the star baritone. But the indifferent critical reaction which *Doris* provoked did lead to some reassessment. There were heavy cuts made in the long-winded second act, the third was fined down and Williams given his head with the 'gags' which he quite shamelessly lifted from his own and other people's past successes. Then, finally, after two months, Marie Tempest was brought in to bring her very special qualities to the title-role. Cellier supplied her with some fresh numbers but neither 'Let him Sigh' or 'I Thought that Love was Made of Smiles' proved to be the hit which the show so needed. However, the altered version did well enough to stay in residence at the Lyric for seven months and 202 performances, though without ever being a true success. A six-month tour was also well enough received but *Doris* certainly did not, as Henry Leslie had hoped it might, establish Cellier and Stephenson as another Gilbert and Sullivan. It marked, in fact, the end of their partnership from which *Dorothy* survived as the ineradicable landmark. Both writers continued their theatrical careers separately, but never again with anything like the same success.

Leslie, who had begun his producing career so profitably, was now seeing the other side of the coin. He had been lavish in his production of *Doris* – he could afford to be – and his production costs had risen to almost £6,000. The scenery and costumes he provided were superb, the chorus and orchestra almost too large for the theatre, the cast tried, publicly favoured and expensive. He had done everything possible to give the show a chance to be as popular as its elder sister, but the same luck which had made his fortune on *Dorothy* lost him a little of that fortune on *Doris*.

April saw the introduction of unashamed burlesque to the Avenue Theatre. Arthur Roberts had 'made' *The Old Guard*, *Indiana* and most recently what *The Entr'acte* called 'the insipid and unintelligible *Nadgy*' into successes of varying degrees for the Avenue by implanting his own very individual and British low comedy performance into the middle of their opéra-comique scores. Now Roberts and his 'act' had a show built around them instead of vice versa.

The subject of *Lancelot the Lovely* was the Arthurian legend and there was a shiver of disapproval in certain circles where it was felt that, although it was permissible to parody Goethe or Greek mythology or absolutely anything French, to thus attack the 'spirituel' *Idylls of the King* of the Poet Laureate was disrespectful and disreputable. But the authors, 'Richard Henry', newspapermen both and aware of such sentiments, tactfully avoided any direct burlesque of Tennyson as they built up a very basic and rather untraditional story of Camelot centred on a Lancelot who emerged from his lake with all the airs of a contemporary London 'masher' declaring:

> There's nobody knows like us gay Lotharios
> How the fancy female veers
> Some girls, tis said, by the nose are led
> And others are led by the ears;
> Some mash by a smile or their swagger style,
> They may one with the other vie
> Now this is what I do, I merely look them through–
> (*spoken*) And then, in the twinking of an eyebrow, every feminine fraction of the population betrays animation, agitation, trepidation, consternation, determination, intimidation, vexation, vocalisation and–it's all, it's all my eye . .
> I'm the Man With The Mashing Eye, aye, aye,
> To escape me in vain they try, aye, aye . . . &c

In this version of the Arthurian legend Lancelot spends the first act trying to 'mash' Guinevere but, losing out to the King, he carries off the lady to his castle with the aid of a couple of cronies. In the end, in deference to tradition, he is obliged to give her up and content himself with one Vivien who in the guise of the saucy Marie Vanoni has been winking and nodding her way through the show at his side. The entertainment had precious little to do with Lancelot or Arthur or the Knights of the Round Table except to provide a pretty setting and an opportunity for a row of lovely ladies to appear in tabards and tights as the Knights. The authors' attempts to provide some coherent version of their subject could only struggle through the song and dance and antics of the Roberts and Vanoni variety show. But it was not intended to do anything more. The variety paper *Entr'acte* commented approvingly that the writers

> tell their story intelligently and funnily and at the same time they allow Mr. Roberts plenty of margin for parading his droll conceits . .

and another journal recorded:

> [Mr Roberts] gives comic recitations, sings excellent songs, is alert with his business and appears now as a man in a fish tank, now as a proprietor of a Punch & Judy show and now as one of the principals in a boxing match. The authors have given Mr Roberts some funny groundwork and he uses it to great advantage . .

The supporting cast were not so successful. Mlle Vanoni's inalterable style fitted poorly into a burlesque so patently English. The kicks and pouts which had won so much approval at the Alhambra didn't make up for an obvious lack of vocal and acting talent and her *café chantant* song evoked scant enthusiasm. Annie Halford as Guinevere did little with an interpolated number by Milton Wellings, and Joseph Tapley as Tristram gave a straight ballad or two without much distinction basically as relief to the incessant fooling. The best support came from E. D. Ward as a spivvy Merlin:

> I am Merlin the prophet who is never at a loss
> When my wonderful wand I'm twirling
> In all the world from China right away to Charing Cross

There's never a Magician up to Merlin;
You may go to the East
You may go to the West
From Battersea Bridge to Berlin,
You may do your very worst
You may do your level best
But you'll never find another like your Merlin

Lancelot the Lovely was Arthur Roberts' show and there were no apologies for the fact. As the run moved on, the star developed and added to his role and after eleven weeks in town he took the show, now extended into a three-act affair by the addition of a whole act composed of nothing more nor less than a variety programme, on the road for ten weeks until the formation of his own production company brought him back to London again with his first project as actor-manager, the burlesque *The New Corsican Brothers.*

In the meanwhile there had been plenty of further action in the West End. Another April offering was the comic opera *Faddimir* or The Triumph of Orthodoxy which was produced by Lily Linfield for a series of four matinées at the Vaudeville Theatre. *Faddimir* was a curious piece, more like a burlesque with its word-play, its strange disguises and variegated score which included a burlesque on the *Faust Up-To-Date* pas de quatre and the obligatory Irish song ('I'd a Cabin Snug') which sat a little oddly in a piece which was set in Russia and had the Prince Alexis battling against a group of anarchists who have been infuriated by a new law obliging them to wash.

Miss Linfield assembled an outstanding cast for the piece including the famous tenor Sims Reeves and Florence Perry to play the hero and heroine, together with Ada Doree as 'heavy' lady and Eric Thorne, Wilfred Shine and George Temple in the comic roles and *Faddimir* went down a treat with the matinée audiences who were not used to seeing tryouts of this kind with the amount of imagination and vigour which this one possessed. They howled at the comic songs and applauded dialogue and numbers equally and the critical response included some favourable notes:

> . . well written, abounding with pretty sentimental songs and clever topical ones, the dialogue is smart and the music tuneful . . an amusing piece well-acted and it is to be hoped it will find its way into the evening bill at one of the West End theatres.

Even those papers whose appreciation of the show had been qualified found much good in both the writing and the music. *The Times* noted that the show was

> . . obviously a first attempt and bears on its surface evident signs of ignorance of stagecraft . . . the author of the libretto has made the mistake of relying upon his amusing and often clever writing to carry off a story which is silly without being funny . .

but concluded that it was 'cleverly written and full of good points.' However, what pleased at a matinée where the entertainment was habitually rough and unready, was not necessarily the material for an evening's programme and neither Miss Linfield (who had cornered some nice notices for her dancing) nor anyone else felt like taking the risk on what was a bright but rather raw-edged show. In spite of the reservations *Faddimir* was an encouraging début for its librettist, a 29-year-old King's Cambridge scholar and winner of the Chancellor's prize for verse who wrote under the name of 'Arthur Reed'. His full name was Arthur Reed Ropes and his later *nom de plume* was 'Adrian Ross'. As Adrian Ross he became one of the greatest lyricists of the British musical stage in a career lasting more than forty years. The composer, 'Oscar Neville', a fellow Cambridge man, who also gained some good reviews, was also to surface again in a different guise and with scarcely less success as Dr Frank Osmond Carr.

The year's next entry, *Mignonette*, described as a romantic comic opera, had been written by 32-year-old Oswald Brand, thirteen years a stock actor and currently at the Islington Grand with Charles Wilmot. Brand had made many attempts at writing and had managed to get a couple of pieces – *Love and Strategy* (Gaiety matinée) and *My Lady* (Avenue) – tried before making his comic opera début with the transient *The Magic Ring* staged by his own theatre the previous year. The music was by Henry S. Parker, an indefatigable if unexceptional composer of light music who had placed the odd song with Florence St John and Sgr Foli, a fact which he advertised freely, and who had many *morceaux de salon* published by J. B. Cramer. Parker and the tenor J. G. Robertson, who had recently relinquished the star tenor post at the Savoy, went into partnership to present *Mignonette* at the Royalty Theatre.

Brand had written a fulsome story about a misanthropic miser who is transformed into his own good-hearted brother by a 'legendary spirit of the mountains'. Having experienced, in this transformation, the emotions of kindliness and goodness he reforms and allows the play's two young lovers, whose happiness he had previously barred, to be united.

Mignonette opened to a catastrophic reception. The audience at the première grew more and more restless and disillusioned as well-known artists such as Robertson, Lionel Brough and Ada Lincoln struggled their way through the pretentious nonsense. 'We're sorry for you, Lal Brough' a voice cried from the gallery, but less kindliness was shown to the unfortunate author and composer who were unwise enough to show themselves at the final curtain. They were greeted by an avalanche of boos, cries and hisses without precedent. The newspapers were no kinder:

> .. destitute of plot, is foggy to a degree and bereft of interesting dialogue. Moreover the music is of such a nature as to call for little else but rebuke. (*Stage*)
>
> .. utter absence of action, interest and humour . . . *Mignonette* is a hopeless failure (*Era*)
>
> .. feeble .. an incongruous jumble of the supernatural and the farcical .. [the music is] of the drawing room pattern and is so utterly undramatic as to render the librettist little assistance .. (*Graphic*)

What humour the first night had produced had been unwitting. In one particularly dramatic sequence, where the miserly Nicholas is confronted by an apparition of his dead wives, things went totally to pieces owing to the antics of a recalcitrant electric moon.

FRINA: Tis I, thou false one, tremble! Look on me!
NICH: My second spouse, who died of jealousy!
FRINA: Come, let me clasp thee with my bony arm!
NICH: Oh lord, oh lord, this place is getting worse!
WIVES: This place is getting worse, this place is getting worse!
KATRINA: Where would you go? We're tenants of this place.
There! In the moon! See my successor's face!
WIVES: See our successor's face!

At this moment the moon decided to go out. This raised a laugh, but having ruined the big moment the moon then elected to come on again when it should not have and raised an even bigger laugh. Nothing, however, seemed to upset the composer/conductor who audibly sang his music from the pit along with the soloists who were already sufficiently unnerved. Before the show was half way through, the audience began walking out in rows. It was obvious that *Mignonette* was a capital disaster but, in spite of everything, the managers thought their production could be saved. Frederick Bowyer was brought in to provide some new songs, the book was cut and overhauled, the direction reconsidered and some parts of the show restaged, but all in vain. After hanging on grimly for five weeks, *Mignonette* closed and played itself out with a week on home ground at the Grand where it received a less damning reception although *The Era* reported that although the piece 'claimed [to have] undergone certain improvements' they were 'not easily discernable'. Surprisingly, *Mignonette* did not disappear. The following year Robertson and Parker took it out on tour starring Adrienne Verity and Harry Dacre.[1] The show was advertised as a 'gigantic success' for which 'arrangements [were] already pending for its reproduction in London'. 'Not a vapid, light frivolous opera but a sound, sensible, dramatic plot . . as interesting as a drama'. Ten managers from Glasgow to Merthyr Tydvil fell for the line and gave *Mignonette* ten weeks of further life.

After May there were no new pieces until the summer was over. *The Yeomen of the Guard, Paul Jones, Doris* and *Faust Up-To-Date* ran on until the return of the Nellie Farren/Fred Leslie company with a new burlesque, *Ruy Blas and the Blasé Roué* at the Gaiety. As in *Miss Esmeralda*, the moving author of this piece was Fred Leslie, and his collaborator for the occasion was Herbert Clark, a gentleman with whom Leslie, had struck up an acquaintance when Clark had written to him with some unsolicited (but apparently usable) ideas for gags. The actor suggested the subject of Ruy Blas as having excellent opportunities for himself as Don Ceasar and Miss Farren as Ruy, and the two began a strange partnership with ideas, lyrics and scenes going back and forth between Leslie, on tour in America, and Clark at home in London. Lyrics were sent to George Edwardes for distribution to various composers, and when Leslie returned to Britain the two authors rounded off their work, even though the actor was bedridden with gastric trouble in the Cliftonville Hotel, Margate.

When Fred Leslie took to the stage with *Ruy Blas* first in Birmingham and then, eighteen days later, in a triumphant return to the Gaiety, he was at the peak of his career both as an actor and as a creator of comic material. In his version of Victor Hugo's famous story he provided himself with a superb vehicle. The attempts of Ruy, Don Caesar and Donna Cristina to recover the incriminating papers and the jewels of the Queen of Spain served as the slightest of frameworks on which Leslie and Clark hung as many songs, dances and comic scenes as possible, providing as much exposure as possible for the two stars; for the piece's admitted raison d'être was as a showpiece for Fred and Nellie. The book of *Ruy Blas* was unusually written in prose and this allowed for much freer expression at the price of the loss of a few rhyming laughs, and into it the writers wove an astonishing variety of musical and comical pieces.

On opening night at the Gaiety the fans left no doubt in anyone's mind as to their feelings. They had enjoyed *Faust Up-To-Date* hugely, but with *Ruy Blas* they welcomed back Fred and Nellie, and that was quite a different thing. The reception was enormous. As each of their idols appeared on the stage the theatre went wild. Nellie Farren, looking up to the gallery where her most passionate partisans were lodged, saw a banner slung across the house – 'The Boys Welcome Back Their Nellie!'. In return

[1] later to become well known on the halls with 'Daisy Bell' and 'I'll be your Sweetheart'.

she gave them what they wanted to hear:

> Though on some distant shore
> You make friends by the score
> There still is a something you lack
> And which makes you say when
> You are home once again
> I'm glad, very glad to get back!

The Fred and Nellie show took their devotees by storm as they sang, danced and back-chatted their way through a very extended performance, littered with ad libs, pausing only to get their breath back and/or change costume while Sylvia Grey or Letty Lind or Fred Storey performed a dance or Marion Hood a song.

The Gaiety was a far cry from the comic operas of *Dorothy* and *Manteaux Noirs* or the tightly-knit musical comedies of Gilbert and Sullivan, and equally far from the musical melodramas like *Jack-in-the-Box* with their involved plots and almost incidental song-and-dance, from the musical farces and the world of extravaganza. A piece such as *Ruy Blas* had moved even beyond the vagaries of the American variety shows like *Fun on the Bristol* or the touring 'speciality' shows where an act like the Majiltons, the Haytors or the Wardropers built a musical around their own particular variety speciality. At the Gaiety, Fred and Nellie were the 'speciality'. Under their influence and helped by their huge personal popularity, the new burlesque had been born and was prospering under the careful nurturing of George Edwardes. *Ruy Blas* was its biggest triumph up to date.

The 'turns' in the new show were more and better than ever before. If there was no single hit of the magnitude of 'Killaloe' or the Pas de Quatre it might have been merely because there were so many outstanding numbers following one upon the other. Fred Leslie, made up one side Irish, one side Scots, flipped from accent to accent and character to character as he sang the tale of the Irishman and the Scotsman who agree to try each other's national whiskey with unfortunate results:

> Stick to the whiskey you're used to
> Never desert an old blend
> If Irish you drink, take it on till you sink
> Don't risk your life for a friend

He joined with Nellie Farren in a series of duets, one as a pair of music-hall Singing Sisters telling of 'Ma's Advice', (which was to be as silly as possible so that they might marry lords); another, with Nellie dressed as a Salvation Army girl, having a go at the latest news in a topical duo 'I've just had a Wire to Say So'; and a third in a blackface lampoon of the Christy Minstrels in 'Johnny Jones and his Sister Sue'. Each was greeted with delirious joy night after night.

All these pieces were from the stalwart and blossoming Meyer Lutz, but the musical work for *Ruy Blas and the Blasé Roué* had been spread about and a number of other writers were involved in different numbers. The best of these was Fred Leslie's 'Whistling Lullaby' written and composed by Effie I. Canning which remained among the most popular numbers throughout the run as the score was constantly added to and changed through a first and a second edition. A typical programme ran:

1) *Chorus*: 'Lords and ladies of high degree/Hail to our Queen'
2) 'Song of my Heart' (MARION HOOD) F. Henderson/H. Lowe
3) 'Glad to Get Back' (NELLIE FARREN) lyr. Albert Chevalier

4) *Chorus*: 'Private Theatricals'
5) *Polka* (LETTY LIND)
6) 'Razzle Dazzle' (FARREN, LESLIE & DANBY) lyr. Fred. Bowyer
7) *Danse Espagnole* (SYLVIA GREY)
8) *Eccentric dance* (FRED STOREY)
9) 'Ma's Advice' (FARREN & LESLIE)
10) *Pas de deux* (FARREN & LESLIE)
11) *Finale*
12) *Entr'acte* (Spanish dance)
13) 'The Whistling Lullaby' (FRED LESLIE) by Effie I. Canning
14) 'Don't Know' (FARREN & LESLIE) Ed. Solomon/Robert Martin
15) 'The Flower Song' (MARION HOOD)
16) *Gavotte* (pas de huit)
17) *Chorus*: 'Good Night'
18) 'Johnny Jones and his Sister Sue' (FARREN & LESLIE)
19) 'Stick to the Whiskey You're Used To' (LESLIE)
20) 'Nice Boy' (NELLIE FARREN) F. Osmond Carr/Ch. Babbington
21) 'I've just had a Wire to Say So' (FARREN & LESLIE) Lyr. W. J. Sumner and Leslie
22) *Valse chantante* (LETTY LIND)
23) *Pas de quatre* (Blanc et Noir) (FARREN, LESLIE, LIND, STOREY)
24) *Finale* (Sweeps' chorus)
25) *Chorus*: Fan Chorus
26) *Rigadon*
27) *Danse classique* (SYLVIA GREY)
28) 'What Price That?' (NELLIE FARREN) lyr. Albert Chevalier
29) 'Españita' (MARION HOOD) Antonio Mora/Fred Bowyer
30) 'Very Extraordinary, isn't It?' (FRED LESLIE) Solomon/Martin
31) *Pas de deux*
32) *Pas de quatre* (LESLIE, DANBY, NATHAN, STOREY)
33) *March/finale*.

One of Teddy Solomon's numbers, 'Don't Know' was, unusually, second-hand. It was originally written for Solomon's short piece *Penelope*, and from there made its way to both the Her Majesty's pantomime and into *Ruy Blas* where it found easily the most appreciative audience for its music-hall style in something which frankly approached a music-hall programme. Marion Hood's ballads were the only concession to more dignified days and they served principally, as in *Lancelot the Lovely*, as a contrast to the voluminous comedy material.

One of the items in *Ruy Blas* which caused more excitement than its content merited was another Pas de Quatre. John D'Auban, urged on by Leslie, choreographed a burlesque on his own *Faust Up-To-Date* triumph. Instead of the four pretty dancing girls he used Leslie, Charles Danby, Fred Storey and the new boy, Ben Nathan, who appeared in ballet skirts to perform their version of the Pas de Quatre. As if this travesty were not enough, the four men were made up facially to represent Henry Irving, Johnny Toole, Wilson Barrett and Arthur Roberts. It was not a particularly clever routine, but it did well enough until it brought an icy letter from Mr Irving requiring that Leslie's burlesque of him 'in skirts' should cease forthwith. Edwardes gently stirred the storm-in-a-teacup until it had served his publicity purposes and made the dance a feature of the show. Then Fred's make-up, if not his mimicry, quietly disappeared. Irving had by this time marshalled the Lord Chancellor to his aid in an episode which belonged more to the Gaiety's stage than in the court room and which was in no way to the actor's credit.

Ruy Blas and the Blasé Roué, with regular but never major changes to some of its spots, continued at the Gaiety until the middle of July 1890, the longest run yet for a Gaiety burlesque. It could have gone on quite easily, but Edwardes had arranged for the company to take the piece on the usual tour of Britain preparatory to setting off again for Australia, and the London season was duly ended after 282 performances.

No one could realise when the Leslie/Farren company left their theatre to Nat Goodwin and his comedy *Gold Mine* just how long it would be before their favourites would return, and, in fact, that they had seen the last London performance from their beloved Nellie Farren. Nellie suffered from severe rheumatism. On the tour she was occasionally unable to appear and the Australian climate did nothing to help her as it had been hoped it might. Things got worse and at the age of 45 Nellie Farren was forced to abandon the stage which had made her one of the most famous women in London and the musical theatre's greatest and best-loved star.

Ruy Blas survived even without the two stars for whom it had been created. Auguste van Biene, now regular purveyor No. 2 of Gaiety musicals to the provinces, took the show round the country for two years featuring the young actor W. Louis Bradfield in Leslie's role and Ada Blanche, among others, in the part which had been Nellie's. But the American season which had originally been planned did not happen; the Gaiety company and its remaining star stayed at home from now on.

On 22 September Henry Brougham Farnie died. *The Stage*'s obituary concluded:

> Most probably his like will not be seen again. The best interests of the stage compel the admission that it can advantageously be spared.

Over some twenty years the Scotsman had fabricated himself a theatrical career by translating, adapting and pasting together a long and successful series of opéras-bouffes, extravaganzas and musicals of all types as the fashion of the moment dictated. He had worked with the most famous composers of his time, most notably in an unprecedented Anglo-French collaboration with Planquette, Audran and Offenbach, and although his 'original' works with native composers had been less successful he had concocted pasticcio pieces like *Nemesis* which had been the joy of the extravaganza days at the Strand Theatre. His most lasting work, however, was in the English versions of the opéras-bouffes *La Fille de Madame Angot*, *Madame Favart* and *Les Cloches de Corneville* which had been enormously successful and continued to be used even after his death.

The last and posthumously presented work of this champion *bricoleur* opened at the Avenue Theatre four weeks after his death and, ironically, it was a show written in collaboration with a British composer, the well-known piano recitalist and composer Tito Mattei, whose previous stage effort had been with the grand opera *Maria di Gand*. *The Grand Duke* was in the continental opéra-comique style, and its libretto was based on a story published in 1853 in *Blackwood*'s magazine entitled 'The Duke's Dilemma'.

The plot concerned an impecunious Duke who is anxious to put on a good reception for an impending visit from a wealthy Prince whose sister he is hoping to marry. Unfortunately his court has chosen this moment to go on strike, an event which delights the nasty Baron Pippinstir who is pressing the claims of his wealthy ward, the

Margravine of Adelberg, to the position of Grand Duchess. Duke Leopold is saved by the appearance of a company of actors ordered for the entertainment who agree to help by masquerading as courtiers. When the Prince and his sister arrive complications ensue, for Prince Max falls violently for the prima donna of the theatre company whom he takes for a countess. The prima donna's own lover, disguised in his turn as a courtier, revengefully turns his attentions on to the Margravine who is in her turn switching her affections to Max. But Leopold cannot allow the Prince to fall into a mésalliance and he unveils the pretence. Max angrily gathers up his sister and prepares to depart when news comes to say that the Elector is dead and Leopold has succeeded to his position and his fortune. In the face of rank and riches Max can no longer withhold Mina's hand and, surrendering himself to the ambitious Margravine, he allows Leopold to take the princess. The prima donna and her lover return quietly to the status quo.

In spite of its potentially comical plot the libretto of the show did not contain a lot of humour. Farnie, and his partner Alfred Murray, upon whom the bulk of the writing had fallen when Farnie's diabetes had made him incapable, leaned for their topical jokes almost entirely on the vagaries of the recent County Council proceedings which had made the headlines. This token concession to the modern trend in musicals did not prevent the show from being distinctly old-fashioned and it followed awkwardly after the rumbustious burlesque of *Lancelot the Lovely* at the Avenue.

The producer, Mons Marius, met one unexpected hitch just before production when the touring manager Henry Burton claimed the title for his provincial piece of 1886. After a hurried consultation the title was changed to *La Prima Donna,* but it was too late to amend all the printing and first-night customers purchasing copies of the score found the cover and the title-page bearing the legend 'La Prima Donna' whilst the first page heading still read 'The Grand Duke'. The first night went well enough, and *La Prima Donna* was thought pleasant if in no way outstanding. Sgr Mattei's music was generally considered the best part and *The Times* reported:

> The music is very considerably above the level of the plot just as some of the numbers will probably be above most of the frequenters of the theatre. The quartet and finale of the second act are cleverly written as well as tuneful and would not disgrace an entertainment of higher rank. The romance 'Love, Farewell' was perhaps the most successful number of the opera though solos of more or less attractiveness are provided for all the principal characters.

The Era found the music:

> . . bright and tuneful . . that the composer has not made it very elaborate must not be regarded as a fault . . flowing . . well-written for voices . . decidedly pretty melodies and effects.

Easily the most successful piece was a theatrical song 'Behind the Scenes' which was sung/recited by the Franco-Welsh actor Albert Chevalier who had recently turned writer and had supplied several lyrics to the Gaiety Theatre. Chevalier played Ballard, the stage manager of the company of players, and he scored well with his lively presentation of this little piece 'unveiling' the mysteries of the theatres:

> Thus the man who gags on the stage in rags
> Is a star with a prince's pay
> And his lordly grace in the gold and lace
> Is a super on ninepence a day.
> The old dame is played by the youngest maid,

And the heroine in her teens
Has a long-legged son who is twenty-one
And is waiting behind the scenes!

All the world's a stage
That's a fact which means
If you'd know what's what
Go behind the scenes!

His other contribution to the evening's proceedings was a piece called 'Ballard's Budget' in which he described how he would frame a budget if he were Lord Chancellor.

Most of the score consisted of songs and ensembles of a more conventional opéra-comique kind. Tenor Joseph Tapley had the ballad noticed by *The Times* and baritone Alec Marsh and soprano Sara Palma, a débutante from the concert platform, headed the rest of the cast with several romantic pieces each. Mattei's concert background led him to bring his two other principal ladies from that sphere, but neither Amelia Gruhn nor Florence Paltzer adapted as well to the theatre as Miss Palma did, and the second of the two was soon replaced by the more experienced Laura Clement.

La Prima Donna played a fairly unobtrusive two months' season before being replaced for Christmas by a revival of the old burlesque *The Field of the Cloth of Gold* which had been enlivened by a largely new score by John Crook. Farnie's last show lacked, principally, distinction, its music having little originality, its book none, and in an era of highly coloured entertainments it had small chance of a long life. Sixty performances marked the full life-span of Tito Mattei's one and only musical, and left its respected and well-liked composer a disappointed man who never got over what he saw as a total rejection of his work in a field which he had, perhaps, judged it too easy to enter.

Arthur Roberts' follow-up to *Lancelot the Lovely* found him back in town in November, installed at the Royalty Theatre in partnership with his *Lancelot* manager, Henry Watkin, and 'Gus' Harris, and with a new burlesque on *The Corsican Brothers* written for him by Cecil Raleigh. *The New Corsican Brothers* was Raleigh's first attempt at a musical. His previous successes had been won with straight dramas like *The Great Pink Pearl* (1885) and *The Pointsman* (1887). It was also a first for the composer, Walter Slaughter, whose previous full-length works had been confined to matinée bills – the Savile Clarke *Alice in Wonderland* and a try-out of a new piece, *Marjorie*, a few months earlier at the Prince of Wales.

The New Corsican Brothers was engineered to give a tour de force role to the hugely popular Roberts with him playing both of the long-separated twins: Lewis Franks, a junior partner in a tailoring firm, and the Corsican noble Fabien dei Franchi. Their twinship provides them with inexplicable feelings:

My brother lives! My brother lives, I know, but where can my brother be?
The thought goes down with my evening grog to rise with my morning tea.
Is he then a fakir? or a dervish bold? In the far off mild Soudan
Or is he a shaker revivalist or Salvation Army man?
Why when I draw my father's sword do I try to measure tape?
Why when I think of a soldier's grave do I think of mourning crape?
Why when my knife I ought to use do scissors come with ease?
Why when the Captain 'forward' cries do I answer quick – 'Sign, please'?

The brothers are destined to meet. Lewis, disgraced in London for having 'struck a gentleman in his club', takes to sea on a Mediterranean yacht as chaperon to the fiancée of a baronet and finds himself wrecked, all unbeknownst, on his brother's island. After various events and quick changes all is brought to a happy ending in the picturesque setting the Ravine of Revenge. *The New Corsican Brothers* opened to an expectant house on 20 November and was an unmitigated failure.

In spite of some literate and imaginative lyrics from Raleigh and some good music from Slaughter, not to mention all the energy and business which Arthur Roberts could muster, it failed totally to come together. The plot was blamed for incoherence, for non-existence, the subject as unsuitable for the artist and so forth. *The Times* did not seek to analyse but contented itself with stating flatly:

> Rarely has a burlesque been found so flat and profitless . . the curtain fell amid well-merited hissing.

Gus Harris was obliged to admit the show was 'an unmistakeable failure' and the *Entr'acte* kindly suggested that, had he seen it out of town, he might not have wasted his money on bringing it in. Considerable alterations were quickly made and a 'new version' advertised, but *The New Corsican Brothers* still failed to please. It was a sign of the times that one of the few pieces of it which raised any enthusiasm was an arbitrarily inserted music hall scena in the third act which featured 'The Sisters Moonlight' – Roberts was one – singing 'We are belles and we'll marry two titled swells', a ballad 'London after Dark' telling of a Piccadilly tart who stops to buy a hot potato as she hawks her wares, only to find that the pedlar is her father; and finally an impromptu topical song by Roberts:

> I'm going to sing a little song, I hope it will amuse
> And what each verse will be about, I shall leave to you to choose
> But as my 'turn' is rather late I hope you will confine
> Your kind suggestions to events in 1889. .

A specimen of the 'impromptu' verses was:

> The dockers have been out on strike to get another tanner
> Yet all along they acted in a gentlemanly manner
> So, talking of Lord Rosebery I hope he won't resign
> The County Council Chairmanship in 1889.

The alterations continued and finally it was decided that *The New Corsican Brothers* would be reduced to two acts (one totally new) and the resultant piece would be played as half of a programme with the new burlesque which F. C. Burnand was preparing for Roberts based on the currently popular drama of *Tosca*. When *Tra-la-la-Tosca* was staged in the first week of the new year, the much hacked-about *New Corsican Brothers* failed to appear. It had gone out unannounced with the old year after 36 unsatisfactory performances and it was left to its forepiece, *The Opera Cloak*, to fill up the *Tosca* bill.

It was almost five years since Teddy Solomon had last presented a new work to London's audiences. After the dreadful failure of his American musical, *The Maid and the Moonshiner*, Solomon had returned to Britain, bringing with him the score of a new musical with a libretto by 'Pot' Stephens called *The White Sergeant* to which he was adding the final touches. But his life had been made chaotic by his time in jail, his bigamy case, his grave illness, his divorce, and another court appearance, this time for bankruptcy. With liabilities of £1405 and assets of £75 and his copyrights, he was discharged at a dividened of one shilling in the pound. Then another attack of the rheumatic fever which had plagued him in jail weakened him terribly and his artistic output dropped to zero. Early in 1889 he began to write again and produced three short works: *Pickwick*, an operetta on Mrs Bardell's pursuit of its hero; *Penelope*, a musical treatment of Brough and Halliday's 1864 farce *The Area Belle;* and *Tuppins and Co.*, a little piece for Alfred Reed and Corney Grain at St George's Hall. While *Pickwick* was well received at its matinée production and *Tuppins and Co.* ran through the largest part of the year at the German Reed establishment, *Penelope* proved to be the most popular of the three.

The litte farce of *The Area Belle* had had twenty-five years of constant playing and popularity. It told the story of the slavey, Penelope, who takes advantage of her mistress' absence to entertain two 'followers' to food and flirtation before eventually settling her choice on a third. Solomon composed some comical songs for the two suitors, Pitcher and Tosser, some ensembles and pretty music for his leading lady and the resulting operetta was tried out at a matinée where Dan Leno and Rutland Barrington took the parts of the rejected swains. The reaction was enthusiastic and *The Era* declared that Solomon's music 'has given the old piece quite a new claim to popularity'. *Penelope* was picked up as a curtain-raiser for the Comedy Theatre later in the year starring William Lugg and W. S. Penley with Alma Stanley in the title role. Its most successful number, the duet 'Don't Know' which was written for the Comedy production, ended up as a highly popular piece after being introduced into the Gaiety burlesque of *Ruy Blas*.

In the meanwhile, *The White Sergeant* had been completed and sold to Henry Leslie[1] who decided to use it at the Lyric as a successor to *Doris* under the title of *The Red Hussar*. Thus, on 23 November, 1889 London saw the first production of a major Solomon work in Britain since *Pocahontas* in 1884. The plot of *The Red Hussar* bore some resemblance to that of *Billee Taylor*, but had a military setting instead of a naval one. In the tradition of the largest number of Stephens' libretti the story was closely linked to British ballad lore using, on this occasion, the tale of the lass who follows her soldier-love to the front in disguise.

Ralph Rodney believes himself the heir to Avon Manor and conducts his life accordingly. The ambitious Barbara Bellasys is to be his wife but it is unexpectedly revealed that Ralph is not the real heir and Barbara hurriedly rejects him. Distraught, the young man enlists in the nearest regiment, but Kitty Carroll, a ballad singer, who is in love with Ralph, disguises herself as a soldier, following him to war where she distinguishes herself by her valour. Ralph's pretensions to Avon Manor are revived and he is overjoyed. Kitty reveals herself to him and confesses her love but the fickle Barbara has bought him out of the army and reclaimed him. Finally it turns out that it is Kitty who is the mysterious heir and 'The Red Hussar', as she has become known, wins both estate and husband.

Leslie's liberal and well-rehearsed production opened to an excellent reception. *The Era* reported:

> When the curtain fell on *The Red Hussar* at five minutes before twelve on Saturday night last it was quite clear, in spite of a few defects easily to be remedied in

[1] It had also apparently been sold to Solomon's cousin Samuel as *The White Hussar* and elsewhere again as *The Blue Dragoon*. This multiple selling was a habit of Solomon's and helped to account for some of his regular court appearances. Over the years Sam Solomon made continued efforts to get his hands on *The Red Hussar* claiming, at one stage, right of possession as co-author, and he was finally responsible for a touring wartime production of a severely altered version.

> subsequent representations, that the comedy opera of Messrs Stephens and Solomon had passed the ordeal of the first performance not only with credit to all, but we may even say triumphantly . . . The music is decidedly and undoubtedly the best Mr Solomon has composed. As being most suitable to the subject it is one endless flow of tune . . . 'When Life And I' is quite equal to the prettiest melodies of our English composers . . . Bright, merry, genial and tuneful and admirably staged, *The Red Hussar* will be certain to prove attractive for a very long time.

The Times critic was moved by the occasion to pontificate a little before showing his appreciation:

> Recent productions in the branch of music called by the name of comic opera – a term 'soiled with all ignoble use' – have shown, in their music at all events, a tendency to exchange the gay frivolity of an earlier time for a tame and generally very dull respectability of demeanour against which only one charge could be brought – namely, that it failed to amuse. Imagining apparently that the secret of Sir Arthur Sullivan's success in this direction lay merely in his avoidance of vulgarity the composers of these works set themselves to prune away all that was calculated to offend the taste of a Savoy audience, retaining only the conventional 'patter song' for the low comedian. The result, of course, has been to banish almost every trace even of gaiety to say nothing of distinctly musical humour, a quality for which English composers have never been remarkably strong.
>
> The composer of *The Red Hussar*, Mr Edward Solomon, has been influenced far less by such considerations as these than by a healthy admiration for Offenbach tempered by a refinement which, whether natural or acquired, is most welcome. Many pages of his score as, for instance, the delightful refrain of 'Won't you join the army?' and the drummer boys chorus 'Where is the colonel of the regiment' in the finale of the second act – have a frank and spontaneous hilarity that is quite worthy of the composer of *La Grande Duchesse*. This characteristic, together with the constant flow of attractive, if not strikingly original melodies would ensure a successful career even if the music were attached to a far worse libretto than that provided by Mr H. P. Stephens.

Not every newspaper was quite as overwhelmingly enthusiastic as these about *The Red Hussar* (The *Illustrated Sporting & Dramatic News* sniffed that 'there would not be a great deal left in the piece without Miss Marie Tempest . .') but there was no doubt at all that it was a success. At last Solomon and Stephens had produced the work which their public had awaited ever since their excellent début with *Billee Taylor* almost a decade previously.

Stephens had created attractive roles for the Lyric Theatre team. Marie Tempest had her best role yet in the character of Kitty Carroll and her two *Dorothy* leading men, Ben Davies (tenor) and Hayden Coffin (baritone) featured as Ralph Rodney and as Sir Harry Leighton, Barbara's patient lover. For Arthur Williams he devised the role of the comic Corporal Bundy and Florence Dysart was the unpleasant Barbara. All the leading players were equipped with good numbers in a well-integrated score. Ben Davies' song 'When Life and I' came out as the most popular piece and his plaintive 'Guides of the Night' also proved attractive. Hayden Coffin gave two modest ballads 'In the Morning of the Year' and 'Castles in Spain' and Miss Tempest took advantage of the contrast between a marching 'Song of the Regiment', the skittish 'A whimsical Girl Was I' and the waltz songs 'The Glee Maiden' and 'Only Dreams'. The comical side of affairs was less pronounced and Arthur Williams featured the show's only humorous solo in 'Variations':

I intend to sing a song (with variations)
And it shan't be very long (with variations)
It shan't be very strong
And it shan't be very tame
If you shouldn't chance to like it
I'm the only one to blame
And I promise you the verses shall be nearly all the same (with variations)

Stephens' verses stayed strictly within the setting of the show and evoked quite enough humour without the introduction of anachronisms and topical references, while Solomon's orchestration cleverly introduced well-known 18th century musical 'variations' into the song's accompaniment. 'Variations' might not have won the belly laughs of the Gaiety or of an Arthur Roberts number, but it was a good comical piece in the legitimate vein. The score was completed by a selection of straightforward but effective concerted pieces.

The Red Hussar built an advance quickly. The first Saturday's takings amounted to the impressive sum of £325. The show was clearly in for a good run but, if things were going smoothly on Shaftesbury Avenue, there were problems elsewhere. Solomon found himself back in the courts on 13 December. Part of his assets at his bankruptcy had been the unproduced *The White Sergeant*. His receiver now alleged that *The White Sergeant* and *The Red Hussar* were one and the same piece and that the royalties accruing to Solomon from the show belonged in law to his original creditors. By the time the case finally came to court (13 June, 1890, Chancery), *The Red Hussar* had completed a run of 175 performances in the West End and was touring the provinces with Marie Tempest's eternal understudy, Effie Chapuy, as Kitty, while Miss Tempest herself was on her way to New York to star in the Broadway production. Somehow or other Solomon won his case and retained the money and the property, which was just as well for he was soon back in court again being sued for the non-payment of further debts. The show ran through six months at the Lyric without a hitch and an *Era* correspondent paying a return visit in April noted

> . . a spirit and a buoyancy . . such as we have rarely noticed save in the best pieces by one or two of the most popular French composers . .

Williams was fetching multiple encores for 'Variations' and the writer enthused that he

> . . has made everything more whimsical, has enlivened his stage business and given additional smartness and vivacity to every allusion . .

By this time the show was doing without Hayden Coffin who had departed as soon as his hated option had expired, but there had been few other alterations. The character of Barbara had been softened somewhat and the last act of what was a very long show tightened up, but by and large *The Red Hussar* ran through to its final performances much as it had begun.

The American production began under inauspicious circumstances. 'Jack' Leslie had come to grief. The huge success of *Dorothy* must have dulled his accounting senses. He had dropped a good deal of money on his new theatre, but real disaster struck when he took Her Majesty's Theatre for the Christmas of 1889 and poured a ridiculous amount of money into trying to rival Drury Lane with a spectacular *Cinderella* starring Minnie Palmer and Violet Cameron. Original music, fabulous scenery and costumes and an enormous cast meant he was playing with a break figure to challenge *Babil and Bijou* with no possibility of his meeting it. Within weeks the once wealthy producer was back to scratch. He gave up his theatre on a long lease to Horace Sedger and sailed for America with the intention of arranging for a Broadway production of *The Red Hussar* but managers found his terms exorbitant and Leslie was forced to announce that he would produce the show himself with an English cast brought over especially. Eventually Palmer's Theatre took *The Red Hussar* and only Marie Tempest of the British cast was brought over. The play was received with indifference. The humour of 'Pot' Stephens proved once again to be foreign to the American sense of humour and William Gilbert as Bundy ad-libbed American-style jokes to try to salvage some laughs. In spite of a fairly inefficient conductor and chorus the music fared better, but when the curtain came down the applause was all for Marie Tempest.

Her success as Kitty was so great that the original short season planned for *The Red Hussar* had to be extended to one of more than two months before it was taken out on the road. The tour proved to be short-lived, for the demands of the leading role, with its high vocal tessitura and its cadenzas up to D in alt, finally took their toll on Miss Tempest and in Baltimore her voice gave out. *The Red Hussar* company was closed down and Marie headed back to Britain. Leslie stayed in America and news came back that an illness had sent him blind. The £5,000 he had paid out to Izard, Miss Tempest's ex-husband, as co-respondent in their divorce could have assured his comfort. 'Jack' recovered his sight and most of his health but never his fortune or Miss Tempest. His theatrical career was over.

That of *The Red Hussar*, however, continued. It was toured and played in stock and amateur performances in Britain and overseas and was revived at the Liverpool Shakespeare for touring with 'modern allusions added and new topical songs' as late as 1918. The Poluskis produced another version which incorporated a good deal of extraneous music to tour smaller dates in 1919.

The arrival of the new Gilbert and Sullivan piece at the Savoy was preceded by the usual speculation but, instead of asking 'what will be the plot?', this time the question was rather 'what type of work will it be?'. The last three pieces had been so different in character – the whimsical Bab Ballad style of *The Mikado*, the melodramatic burlesque of *Ruddigore*, and the altogether more straight and operatic *The Yeomen of the Guard*. There was no doubt that of these three it had been *The Mikado* which had succeeded most in every way and, although the musical pundits were hoping Sullivan would be given another libretto which would challenge him to extend his musical style further towards the operatic, the general public were as clearly hoping for another *Mikado*.

Nobody except the most devoted opera addict could have been disappointed with what they got. *The Gondoliers* opened at the Savoy on 7 December to a tumultuous reception. As had been hoped, Gilbert had reverted to his 'old' style, employing quaint and ridiculous characters and dialogue in a topsy-turvy story with the whole illustrated by Sullivan's best and brightest music. The story which Gilbert had conceived for the new show was simple and familiar. Long ago the infant King of Barataria was stolen away by the Inquisition to avoid the evil influence of a Wesleyan father, but before his disappearance he had been betrothed to the daughter of the Duke of Plaza-Toro, a Castilian noble. The story opens in Venice where two gondolieri, Marco and Giuseppe, are choosing their brides. No sooner are they married than the Grand Inquisitor arrives on the scene to inform them that one of them is the missing king, and therefore also the husband of Casilda di Plaza-Toro. This latter fact is not mentioned by the careful Inquisitor and the men, putting off their decidedly selfish republican sentiments, set off for the island of Barataria where they are to reign jointly until the question of identity is solved. They attempt to run Barataria on republican principles and encounter the predictable anomaly that 'when everyone is somebody, then no-one's anybody'. Soon their wives arrive and the awful truth is revealed. Neither of them will be a queen and whichever gondolier is the king is an unconscious bigamist! The Plaza-Toro family arrive with Casilda in tow. That young lady is not at all keen on marrying either Marco or Giuseppe as she is in love with her father's private drummer. Her dilemma is resolved when the old crone to whom the stolen baby was farmed out reveals that the real king is Luiz, the 'Private Drum', for whom she substituted her own child in the hour of danger. The gondoliers are reduced to the ranks and Luiz and Casilda are King and Queen of Barataria.

Although many of the elements of the plot were familiar, Gilbert had clothed them in his cleverest dialogue and lyrics, giving them quite a new life. His characters, too, were familiar. The comic penniless nobleman and the dragonistic duchess were standard figures on a nineteenth century cast list, but it is a measure of the success with which Gilbert drew the Duke and Duchess of Plaza-Toro that it is they who remain the archetypes of the long line of such characters. Of course, none of their predecessors had been armed with a number such as that with which Gilbert and Sullivan presented their pair:

Small titles and orders
For mayors and recorders
I get and they're highly delighted
M.P.s baronetted
Sham Colonels gazetted
And second-rate Aldermen knighted.
Foundation Stone laying
I find very paying
It adds a large sum to my makings
At charity dinners
The best of speech spinners
I get ten per cent of the takings . . .
In short, if you'd kindle
The spark of a swindle
Lure simpletons into your clutches
Or hoodwink a debtor
You cannot do better
Than trot out a Duke or a Duchess!

The Duchess of Plaza-Toro was impersonated by Rosina Brandram and the Duke, who may have been a slightly different character had George Grossmith been still with the company, was played by a newcomer to the Savoy – the Ravannes of *Erminie*, Frank Wyatt. Other changes in the company also helped to further the change in the schedule of roles. First and foremost, Rutland Barrington had returned after his unfortunate attempt at management. His 'replacement' W. H. Denny remained, however, while Richard Temple finally severed his long association with the company. Jessie Bond was still there and Courtice Pounds and Geraldine Ulmar were now firmly established in the positions formerly held by Lely and Miss Braham. For the role of Casilda, Carte went outside the company to hire a 17-year-old soprano, Decima Moore, who scored a big success and began an important career.

Sir Arthur Sullivan recorded in his diary after the first night:

> Gilbert and I got a tremendous ovation – we have never had such a brilliant first night.

The papers were inclined to agree:

> Gilbert has never been more whimsical, inconsequential and mock serious . . . Sir Arthur Sullivan has never been lighter and brighter and more transparently tuneful (*Stage*)
>
> *The Gondoliers* is one of the best, if not the best, of the Gilbert and Sullivan operas (*Globe*)
>
> All the qualities by which the music of the former operas has obtained for the series a popularity almost without parallel in musical history are present in the last of the set and the average level of interest and beauty is in this instance higher that usual. Perhaps for that reason no individual song stands out from the rest as prominently as did 'Were I thy Bride' and 'I Have a Song to Sing, O' in its predecessor, but it cannot be doubted that nothing since *The Mikado* has been so good as this new work. (*Times*)

Even *Punch* conceded that *The Gondoliers* deserved to rank in third place behind *The Mikado* and *Pinafore* in the Savoy opus.

The encores on the opening night were plentiful although, with an eye to the clock, rather fewer were granted during the show's second half. Gradually, however, the hits were distilled from the mass of encores: Frank Wyatt's comic solo:

> In enterprise of martial kind when there was any fighting,
> He led his regiment from behind, he found it less exciting,
> But when away his regiment ran, his place was at the fore, O–
> That celebrated, cultivated, underrated warrior, the Duke of Plaza-Toro.

Courtice Pounds' tenor ballad:

> Take a pair of sparkling eyes, hidden, ever and anon,
> In a merciful eclipse–
> Do not heed their mild surprise–having passed the Rubicon,
> Take a pair of rosy lips;
> Take a figure neatly planned–such as admiration whets–
> (Be particular in this);
> Take a tender little hand, fringed with dainty fingerettes,
> Press it–in parenthesis;
> Ah! Take all these, you lucky man–
> Take and keep them, if you can!'

and the lively Cachuca in which the entire Savoy chorus was given an unusual opportunity for a piece of vigorous dancing. Among the ensembles too there were enormously popular pieces, in particular the quintet 'I am a Courtier grave and Serious'. The first night and subsequent success did not leave the authors complacent and a number of small alterations were made as well as one larger one, the cutting of the baritone solo 'Thy wintry Scorn I dearly Prize' sung by Luiz in the first act. For the second show in succession the principal baritone found himself shorn of his only number, although on this occasion it was replaced by a duet which Gilbert evolved from the lyric of the first verse of the excised number and which bore the same sentiment as the song which had been cut. The duet 'Ah, well Beloved' was shared by Brownlow (Luiz) and Decima Moore who had made a decided hit in her role without having any number to herself.

The Savoy production of *The Gondoliers* settled in for an eighteen months' run which laid the foundation of a popularity which continued through countless revivals up to the present day. The American production was less fortunate. Carte had sub-licensed the New York production and enormous advance bookings of up to $7,000 per week must have tempted the management to think their venture was foolproof. They cut corners and presented a production of poor quality with some disgraceful performances which, not unnaturally, got a worse than lukewarm reception. When news of an incipient failure reached Carte he hurriedly put together a nucleus of proven British performers and went at once to America to try to save the situation. He only partly succeeded and *The Gondoliers* lasted 103 performances, a disappointing record given the totals achieved by *H.M.S. Pinafore* and *The Mikado*.

While the West End had been busy producing everything from English comic opera such as *Doris* or the more ballad-opera like *Red Hussar* through opéra-comique (*La Prima Donna*) and Gilbert and Sullivan to burlesque and new burlesque at the Gaiety and the Avenue, the provincial managers stayed principally with the two extremes, the opéra-comique of Ruritanian romance and low comedy and the musical comedy-drama or melodrama. The opéras-comiques had become almost invariably recognisable under their heroines' names. 1889 produced *Delia*, *Geraldine*, *Paola* and *Iduna* as well as a tour of the previous year's *Carina*, with the masculine side represented by *Claudio* and *Belphegor*.

The first and most successful production was *Delia* which appeared at the Bristol Prince's Theatre in March under the auspices of Horace Guy who was touring *Les Manteaux Noirs* with continued success. *Delia* was the first major work from *Les Manteaux Noirs*' composer, Procida Bucalossi, since that initial success. In the intervening years he had pursued an uneventful career as a conductor and as a prolific writer and arranger of light music for a number of publishing houses. The librettist for *Delia* who listed himself as 'F. Soulbieu' was in fact Frank Desprez, sometime right hand to D'Oyly Carte and now a writer for *The Era*[1]. Desprez had supplied a number of useful short pieces to, notably, the Savoy, but *Delia* was his first attempt at a full-length work. It was founded on a libretto by Scribe called *La Frileuse* which had previously formed the basis for a Palgrave Simpson play, *Court Cards*, and dealt with the machinations of a duchess to marry her son to her ward, Delia, for reasons of state. A plot full of misunderstanding, *volte faces* and compromising scenes ends, of course, with young love having its own way. The slight plot was largely concealed in a welter of action and bright dialogue. *The Stage* found it 'amusing and clearly constructed', the dialogue 'interesting and pleasing' and the music 'attractive and bright'. *The Era* recorded that half an hour of the book could be cut without loss but called the show 'an emphatic success'.

Emphatic it might not have been, but a success it certainly was. Desprez and Bucalossi had estimated nicely the temper of the times and of the provinces and had written an accomplished piece which included such popular elements as a vocal gavotte with choreography by Mlle Marie of the Alhambra, a patriotic song, a Convent Bell number for the soprano, a yodelling number for the Prince and the inevitable patter and topical songs. Both these last fell to the lot of George Mudie in the role of Baron von Hornburg. His patter song 'That was the Situation' went down no less well for being reminiscent of Sir Joseph Porter, but more successful and, indeed, the hit of the show was his topical song 'A slight Mistake' in which he pulled out all the stops in the most successful moment of an already distinguished career. 'A slight Mistake' became popular wherever *Delia* went. To keep the song as up-to-the-minute as possible Mudie

[1] In 1893 Desprez became editor of *The Era*, a post which he retained till 1913 when illness forced him into retirement.

and Guy arranged for verses containing local allusions to be prepared ahead of them by contacts on the touring schedule, a ploy which added vastly to the success of the number and the show. *Delia* was worked up well and met with large houses and much enthusiasm, though rarely as much as from the Huddersfield critic who declared 'Messrs Gilbert and Sullivan must look to their laurels . .'

A fourteen-week tour of major centres was followed by a further 18 weeks on the road in the autumn and winter but, in spite of announcements concerning London and America and further tours, *Delia* was not run again. George Mudie and his wife, Adelaide Newton, who played the Duchess were snapped up by Henry Leslie for *The Red Hussar* and *Delia* came to a surprisingly sudden end. Surprising that is, until the truth about Horace Guy's affairs came out. Having started out in 1888 with £4,000 he had succeeded in losing £3,000 of it on his theatrical ventures in 12 months. By the end of 1889 he had not only lost the remainder of his investors' money but had fallen £1,110 into debt. Amongst his mortgaged assets were the production and the rights of *Delia*.

Like *Delia*, *Paola* came from an established background – the writers of *Erminie* and *Mynheer Jan*, the Paulton brothers, Harry and Edward ('Mostyn Tedde'), and the composer Jakobowski. *Paola* was given its original production in America, at the Grand Opera House, Philadelphia in May, with a simultaneous one-nighter being played at the Royalty in Chester to secure the British copyright. The American production arrived on Broadway in August under the auspices of J. C. Duff, but if Duff was looking to repeat the success of *Ermine* he was quickly disappointed. *Paola* stayed only six weeks at the Fifth Avenue Theatre before taking to the road again where it carved itself out a reasonable career. Two companies were still engaged in the American countryside when *Paola* made its real UK debut at the Edinburgh Lyceum in December.

The Paultons' plot was set in Corsica and revolved, naturally, around a vendetta. The two young heirs of the feuding families have been away, but find on their return that they have inherited the leadership of the two sides of the vendetta. In spite of the urgings of their families they refuse to fight, more particularly as one of them has fallen in love with the other's sister, Paola. Their comical efforts to avoid conflict supply the action of a piece which comes to a happy ending when it is discovered that Bragadoccio, the bellicose uncle of Paola, is the official heir to the quarrel, and the young ones go their way leaving him to get on with it.

The authors had written a good, vigorous book which *The Stage* described as 'a smart bit of writing with a sparkle here and there of genuine Gilbertian humour', but *Paola* was a piece which, not unnaturally, looked to the style of *Erminie* and *Les Manteaux Noirs* rather than to the more freely constructed modern works, although the writers did make an attempt to keep up with the times. Alongside their staple romantic numbers they provided the odd piece like Lizzie St Quinten's soubrette number 'How d'ye Do, How d'ye Do' which was more than a little redolent of the Gaiety, and the mixture worked quite well. With a cast headed by Leonora Braham, Charles Groves, Fred Billington and Fanny Harrison, *Paola* proved a highly acceptable entertainment over a six months' provincial tour without progressing to town.

Geraldine, the new version of *Count Tremolio*, ended its reincarnation in split weeks around the north of England in the early months of the year, but even shorter life was granted to *Iduna* produced at Manchester in October. *Iduna* was composed by A. H. Behrend, the grandson of Balfe. Although a respectable composer in his own right with such successful songs 'Auntie' and 'Daddy' he was by no means in Balfe's class. His libretto was by Bristolian Hugh Conway (deceased), and it was set in the nebulous middle European courts so beloved of musical writers. Young Prince Philip is kept in ignorance of the existence of women until his 21st birthday by his despotic father. On the day he is to be informed of the existence of the female of the species, all women under 55 are, as a precaution, banished from the court. Two elderly duchesses try to bribe the Lord Chancellor to convince the young man that they are excellent specimens and most marriageable, but their plan is spoilt by the Princess Iduna who has hidden herself in the castle. After various confrontations the King is made to see the folly of his ways and the youngsters are married while the Lord Chancellor, as a punishment, is condemned to wed both of the Duchesses. *Iduna*'s music was judged reasonably pleasant and its book, principally where the Duchesses were concerned, quite funny, but after showings in Cardiff, Derby and Bristol it was not persevered with.

Another Ruritanian piece staged on a five-week tour was *Claudio*, which had been tried at Portsmouth the previous December and picked up by Joseph Shaw. Its hero (Shaw) was a brigand chief who ends up a Duke's son, its highlights were a masked ball scene and a ballad called 'Goddess of the Night', but its merits were very few. It met with a generally unenthusiastic reception in Nottingham, Wakefield, Bridlington Quay, Grantham, Bath and Cardiff.

Belphegor was a piece on a different plan. It had been prepared for Harry Monkhouse as a successor to the long-running *Larks* by Wilton Jones who had written much of the piece in Denmark where he had gone to work with the composer, Albert Christiansson. It was founded on the 1856 drama *Belphegor the Mountebank* with which Charles Dillon had had such success at the Lyceum. But Monkhouse was now in the West End with the Carl Rosa Light Opera involved in the long runs of first *Paul Jones* and then *Marjorie*, and *Belphegor* was played by Arthur Rousbey when the piece was given a trial run at South Shields in October. The response was not favourable and the Monkhouse company, now headed by its leading lady, Ada Clare, continued to tour *Larks* instead. The following year *Belphegor* was given a production by its hopeful composer in association with Gilbert King who took the main role in a season that opened at the Shopfriars' Hall in Boston, and continued with split weeks in Gainsborough, Yeadon, Workington &c. The first Anglo-Danish musical was not destined for the big time.

Of the musical comedy-dramas which proliferated in the wake of *Jack-in-the-Box*, very few were worthy of any notice or survived very long. Those which were boiled up to fit particular artists or troupes stayed in the repertoire the longest but most were given only short local tours. In 1889 there were several exceptions. *Bright Days*, an Irish piece, written by and starring Horace Wheatley, served him well although the musical element of the piece was so slight as to make it barely a musical play. *Our Babies*, on the other hand, had music by the scholarly George Fox. Easily the most enduring was a melodramatic piece by Hal Collier who had a number of rather third-rate non-musical pieces being hawked around the country. *My Nadine* was advertised and bought by Marie Strachane to star herself in a season. It was a tale of two children stolen by the adventuress Nathalie whose plan to wed their father they are hampering. But the villainess' accomplice shrinks from murdering the children and they return to their father in time to see Nathalie exposed as a charlatan by a former fairground associate. *My Nadine* was rollicking stuff, colourful and fast-moving, with ten numbers and a grande finale. It proved to be just right for the minor circuits and Miss Strachane was able to collect on several seasons as *My Nadine* went on to be toured by Kate

Fedora as *The Swiss Guide* and *André the Mountaineer*.

Among the extravaganzas *Randolph the Reckless* was joined by a nautical piece, *Little Tom Bowling*, toured by its composer Herbert Simpson; *Chickabiddee*, a 'burlesque-extravaganza' of some proportions concocted for the Haytors by Victor Stevens; and *The Fancy Ball* a piece with slightly more plot put out by the Wardropers. All three shows served their creators and stars for more than one season.

As well as its fine crop of new musicals, the year brought out a fair number of short pieces. At St George's Hall, Solomon's *Tuppins and Co.* was preceded by a brief run of *Brittany Folk* and followed by *The Verger*, yet another sketch dealing with an inheritance and a missing document which gave Alfred Reed the opportunity to dress up as the eccentric title character. *The Times* summed up:

> . . [it is] on a par with most of the pieces which have been produced at Mr & Mrs German Reed's entertainment where the audience is very sympathetic and not over exacting . .

John Smith, by the German Reed regulars Arthur Law and Alfred Caldicott had an extended run at the Prince of Wales as a forepiece to *Paul Jones*, and *The Houseboat*, *Love's Trickery* and *Penelope* joined *Mrs Jarramie's Genie* as supporting pieces at principal theatres.

1889

090 **DELIA** a romantic military comic opera in 2 acts by 'F. Soulbieu' (Frank Desprez) taken from *La Frileuse* by Eugène Scribe. Music by Procida Bucalossi. Produced at Bristol under the management of Horace Guy 11 March, 1889 and toured through Cardiff, Birmingham, Brighton, Liverpool, Glasgow, Edinburgh, Newcastle, Dundee, Aberdeen, Sunderland, Manchester, Leeds and Nottingham ending 15 June. Resumed 5 August through Sheffield, Middlesborough, Huddersfield, Halifax, Liverpool, Blackpool, Glasgow, Edinburgh, Newcastle, Huddersfield, Leicester, Derby, Cardiff, Portsmouth, Southampton, Bath, Bristol, Plymouth and Northampton, to 14 December.

Baron von Hornburg . . . . George Mudie
Conrad von Halberstad . . . . Louis C. Batten/William Hillier/Henry Nordblom
Capt. Johann Hendricks . . . . Jennie Wilton/Nelly Cozens/Flo Clive
Prince Max . . . . Lytton Grey
Sergeant . . . . Arthur Kingsley/H. Wellesley Smith/Horace Guy
Marguerite . . . . Bertha Hocheimer/Clare Harrington
Gretchen . . . . Maude Hertie
The Duchess . . . . Adelaide Newton
Princess Delia . . . . Fanny Wentworth/Bertie Milner/Amy Grundy
Lt William Kogh . . . . Blanche Leamington/Violet Leigh

Dir: Claude Marius; md: Procida Bucalossi/Brigata Bucalossi/Augustus T. MacInnes; ch: Mlle Marie; cos: Mrs May

091 **DORIS** a comedy opera in three acts by B. C. Stephenson. Music by Alfred Cellier. Produced at the Lyric Theatre under the management of Henry J. Leslie 20 April, 1889 for a run of 202 performances closing 8 November, 1889.

Doris Shelton . . . . Annie Albu/Marie Tempest (Effie Chapuy)
Lady Anne Jermingham . . . . Amy Augarde (Daisy Raymond) (Hilda Glenn)
Mistress Shelton . . . . Alice Barnett
Dolly Spigott . . . . Effie Chapuy/Hettis Lund
Tabitha . . . . Harriet Coveney
Martin Bolder . . . . Ben Davies (Sydney Tower)
Sir Philip Carey . . . . C. Hayden Coffin
Alderman Shelton . . . . J. Furneaux Cook (Sebastian King)
Crook . . . . John Le Hay (Mr McAdam)
Dormer . . . . W. T. Hemsley
Barnaby Spigott . . . . Percy Compton/Frank Motley Wood
Dinniver . . . . Arthur Williams
Serving Man . . . . B. P. Seare

Dir: Charles Harris; md: Ivan Caryll sc: Hawes Craven, William Telbin, T. E. Ryan; cos: Lucien Besche

0092 **LANCELOT THE LOVELY** or The Idol of the King. A burlesque in two acts by 'Richard Henry'. Music by John Crook. Produced at the Avenue Theatre under the management of Henry Watkin 22 April, 1889 for a run of 66 performances closing 6 July, 1889.

Arthur Pendragon . . . . Alec Marsh
Leodegrance . . . . Ambrose Collini
Merlin . . . . E. D. Ward
Lancelot . . . . Arthur Roberts
Lynette . . . . Carrie Coote
Morgan-le-Fay . . . . Sallie Turner
Gawaine . . . . Hettie Bennett
Geraint . . . . Miss F. Woolf
Enid . . . . Miss Lloyd
Tristram . . . . Joseph Tapley
Gareth . . . . Harry Grattan
Kaye . . . . George Capel
Guinevere . . . . Annie Halford
Iseult . . . . Nelly Woodford
Vivien . . . . Marie Vanoni
Bedivere . . . . Madge Mildren
Elaine . . . . Miss Garthorne

with Lillie Marsden, J. Woolf, Paddy Sinclair, A. Sinclair, T. Thompson, Gladys Garthorne, Adelina Bartlett, Maria Mitchell, Mary Medas, Dora Marlowe, Violet Vizard, Carrie Carlyle, Dorothy Douglas, Beatrice Bertram, Millie Warren, Stanley, Baby Waltham, Clara Carini, Rosy Reynolds, Eva Evand, Edith Edevian, Nelly Norval, Flora Franklyn, Bella Buckland, Maud Maryon, Wilhelmina Woolf, Elfreda Esmond, Selina Shergold, Winnie Wynter; Messrs Betzmann, Bridgeman, Carpenter, Forde, Handel, Hartt, Baldwin, Winterbottom &c.

Dir: Robert Soutar; md: John Crook; ch: Willie Warde; sc: Julian Hicks; cos: J. W. Houghton

0093 **FADDIMIR** or The Triumph of Orthodoxy. A comic opera by 'Arthur Reed' (Arthur Reed Ropes otherwise 'Adrian Ross'). Music by 'Oscar Neville' (F. Osmond Carr). Produced at the Vaudeville Theatre by Lily Linfield 29 April, 1889 for four matinées to 3 May, 1889.

Faddimir the First . . . . Eric Thorne
Prince Alexis . . . . H. Sims Reeves
Baron Krazinski . . . . George Temple
Nitro Glitzerinski . . . . Wilfred E. Shine
Tarakanoff . . . . Joseph Wilson
Lady . . . . Alice Vicat
Sergeant of the Guard . . . . Arthur Hendon
Anna . . . . Lily Linfield
Marie . . . . Florence Perry
Katherina . . . . Ada Doree
Popoff . . . . Malcolm Bell
Christina . . . . Beatrice Perry
Courtier . . . . Mr Metcalfe

Dir: Alfred Lys Baldry; md: 'Oscar Neville'; ch: Lily Linfield; sc: W. Hemsley; cos: Alfred Lys Baldry

0094 **MIGNONETTE** a romantic comic opera in three acts by Oswald Brand. Music by Henry Parker. Produced at the Royalty Theatre under the management of J. G. Robertson and Henry Parker 4 May, 1889 for a run of 31 performances closing 7 June, 1889. Played at a matinée at the Crystal Palace 28 May. Played at the Grand, Islington 17 July for one week.

Nicol Nicholas . . . . Lionel Brough
Vandyke . . . . J. G. Robertson
Alpinor . . . . Henry Pope
Christopher . . . . E. Norris
Mignonette . . . . Ada Lincoln
Annette . . . . Laura Maxwell

Lizette	Agnes Oliver (Louie Wilmot)
Lisl	Rose Deering
Katti	Miss Cole
Frina	B. deLorme
Silverling	Dalton Somers
Adolphus	Edwin Keene
Caspar	Robert Fairbanks
Hans	F. Furtado
Sepp	F. J. Ashby
Martha	Lizzie King
Florette	Louie Wilmot
Lina	Beatrice Eton
Katrina	Eyre Ford

Dir: J. G. Robertson; md: Henry Parker; ch: Harriette D'Auban; sc: W. Hemsley; cos: Lucien Besche

095 **CLAUDIO** a comic opera in two acts by A. V. Thurgood. Music by Thomas Hunter. Produced to register copyright at Portsmouth 1 December, 1888. Produced at Nottingham under the management of J. J. Shaw 5 August, 1889 and toured through Wakefield, Bridlington Quay, Grantham, Bath and Cardiff to 7 September, 1889.

Lady Silvia	Berta Foresta
Prince Florizel	W. G. Bedford
Lady Lucia	Doris Lynne
Jacopo	William Kenwood
Jacquetta	Ethel Blenheim
Count Bimbolo	Willie Drew
Valentine	Florence Terriss
Beppo	Tom Hamilton
Luigi	Pattie Marshall
Peppino	Clifford Leigh
Andrea	Rosie Price
Benedetta	H. V. Fisher
Claudio	Joseph J. Shaw
Jacomo	A. West
Duke Pompatio	Edward Leahy
Captain	William Roe

096 **RUY BLAS AND THE BLASÉ ROUÉ** a burlesque in two acts by 'A. C. Torr' (Fred Leslie) and Herbert F. Clark. Music by W. Meyer Lutz. Additional material by Robert Martin, Edward Solomon, Albert Chevalier, Frederick Bowyer, Antonio Mora, Charles Babbington, F. Osmond Carr, Effie I. Canning, H. Lowe, F. Henderson, William J. Sumner, Bayer, Lovell Phillips, C. Paston Cooper/Henri Loge, Miss Jordan, P. Royle, R. Corney Grain and P. Dresser. Produced at the Grand Theatre, Birmingham under the management of George Edwardes 3 September, 1889 and at the Gaiety Theatre 21 September, 1889. A second edition was produced 10 April 1890. Closed 19 July 1890 after a total of 282 performances.

Ruy Blas	Nellie Farren
Don Caesar de Bazan	Fred Leslie (Fred Storey)
Queen of Spain	Marion Hood/Grace Pedley (Marie Luella) (Julie Couteur)
Donna Elto	Letty Lind (Julie Couteur)
Donna Christina	Sylvia Grey (Eva Greville)
Duchess Agio Uncertaino	Linda Verner
Eiffelez	Alice Young/Flo Henderson
Don Salluste	Charles Danby/George T. Minshull/Dalton Somers (Fred Storey)
Major Domo	Ben Nathan/Maud Hobson/Blanche Massey
Court Physician	Fred Storey (William Benson)

Ceronayez . . . . William Benson/Mr Walker
Tarara . . . . Blanche Massey/*out*
Pages . . . . Grace Wixon, Ada Conway, Lily Harold
with Eva Greville, Lily McIntyre, Maude Maryon, Blanche Massey, Hetty Hamer, Alice Davis, Miss Beresford, Janette Desborough.

Dir: Walter Raynham; md: W. Meyer Lutz; ch: John D'Auban; sc: Walter Hann, T. E. Ryan and W. Perkins; cos: Percy Anderson

0097 **LA PRIMA DONNA** an opéra-comique in three acts by H. B. Farnie and Alfred Murray. Music by Tito Mattei. Produced at the Avenue Theatre under the management of Claude Marius 16 October, 1889 for a run of 60 performances closing 14 December, 1889.

Delia . . . . Sara Palma
Princess Mina . . . . Amelia Gruhn
Ballard. . . . . Albert Chevalier
Prince Maximillian . . . . George Sinclair
Baron Pippinstir. . . . . George Capel
Leopold . . . . Alec Marsh
Duke Sigismund . . . . Harry Grattan
Lebel . . . . Stanley Betjeman
Margravine of Adelberg. . . . . Florence Paltzer/Laura Clement
Foligny . . . . Ida Liston/Florence Lloyd
Pastorale. Maud Brent
Rigolet. . . . . H. Grahame
Anselmo . . . . F. Benwall
Otto . . . . E. Gower
Prince Florival . . . . Joseph Tapley
Ninette . . . . Alice Lethbridge
with Misses Corrie Fay, F. Fairley, H. Fairley, Belle Buckland, Fanny Franklyn, Lilly Reynolds, Mabel Tilley, Winifred Waltham, Amy Wynter, Adelina Bartlett, Florence Lloyd, Rose Warren, Eva Evand, Maud Wallis, Lena Burville, Harriet Harcourt, Wilhelmina Woolf, Geraldine Garcia, Dolly Driscoll, Caroline Corri, Conny Howard, Laura Langton, Delia Lees, Lili Delamere, Vesta Vincent, Katherine Cox, Grace Stanley; Messrs Forde, G. W. Parte, Carpenter, Carter, Laguerre, Winterbottom, Baldwyn, Hart, Blamphin, D. Shallard, Collini.

Dir: Claude Marius; md: John Crook; ch: Willie Warde; sc: Richard Douglass and Fred Storey

0098 **IDUNA** a comic opera in two acts by Hugh Conway. Music by A. H. Behrend. Produced at the Comedy Theatre, Manchester under the management of A. H. Behrend 28 October, 1889 and toured through Cardiff, Bristol and Derby ending 30 November, 1889.

King Almeric I . . . . Tom Paulton
Prince Philip . . . . Frederic Wood
Count Ferdinand . . . . Arthur Marcel
Fintac . . . . Mat Robson
Princess Iduna . . . . Ethel McAlpine
Lady Rosamund. . . . . Ida Liston
Duchess Godiva. . . . . Nora l'Estella
Duchess Grizzle. . . . . Ethel Blenheim
Duchess Ouida . . . . Gertrude McKenzie
Duchess Virginia . . . . May Rosine

Ch: Jessie Noir

0099 **THE NEW CORSICAN BROTHERS** a musical extravaganza in 3 acts by Cecil Raleigh. Music by Walter Slaughter. Produced at the Prince of Wales Theatre, Liverpool 11 November, 1889 for one week and subsequently at the Royalty Theatre under the management of Augustus Harris, Henry Watkin and Arthur Roberts 20 November, 1889 for a run of 36 performances closing 31 December, 1889.

Fabien dei Franchi/Lewis Franks . . . . Arthur Roberts
Sir Alfred Maynard. . . . . Deane Brand

Mr Lanyon Yarns of New York . . . . . Joseph Wilson
Danella Tomato. . . . . John Clulow
Landlord . . . . Augustus Wheatman
First Shopman . . . . Hampton Gordon
Griffo . . . . Miss St Cyr
Carlo . . . . Nellie Woodford
Beppo . . . . Hettie Bennett
Antonio . . . . Guy Fane
Smithi. . . . . Walter Tilbury
Petero . . . . Miss M. Jackson
Jean dei Franchi . . . . Miss R. Allanby
Rioul dei Franchi . . . . Miss C. Lewis
Maude St Azurline . . . . Mimi St Cyr
Mrs Charteris . . . . Amy Liddon
Marita de Lesparre . . . . Edith Kenward
Emily Anstruther . . . . Kate Chard

with Blanche Montague, Paddy St Clare, Gertrude Price, Fannie Merton, Lillie Marsden, Maud Royal, Marie Osman, Francis Denton, Amy Norton, Florence Hooper, Winnie Gwynne, Susie Collingwood, Helen Stewart, Maggie Douglas, Kate Price, Coralie Calvert, Mabel Beaufort, Daisy Lennox, William Gilbert, Robert Mason, James Delaney, John Phillipson, William Lovell, Harry Daniels, Arthur Dodson, &c.

Md: George Byng; ch: M. Lauraine; sc: Julian Hicks & Bruce Smith; cos: J. W. Houghton

0100 **THE RED HUSSAR** a comedy opera in three acts by Henry Pottinger Stephens. Music by Edward Solomon. Produced at the Lyric Theatre under the management of Henry J. Leslie 23 November, 1889 for a run of 175 performances closing on 17 May, 1890.

Ralph Rodney. . . . . Ben Davies
Sir Harry Leighton . . . . C. Hayden Coffin/Alex Marsh/Charles Ryley
Sir Middlesex Masham . . . . Albert Christian (George Willoughby)/ George Mudie
Corporal Bundy. . . . . Arthur Williams (F. L. Scates)
Mr William Byles. . . . . Frank Motley Wood
Private Smith . . . . Sebastian King/John Le Hay
Gaylord . . . . A. Ferrand
Maybud . . . . George Willoughby
Kitty Carroll . . . . Marie Tempest (Maud Holland)
Barbara Bellasys. . . . . Florence Dysart (Dora Thorne)
Daisy . . . . Maud Holland/Edith Briant
Mrs Magpie. . . . . Mrs W. Sidney/Harriet Coveney/Adelaide Newton
Vivandière. . . . . Ellis Jeffreys
Pd: Birdie Irving

Dir: Charles Harris; md: Ivan Caryll; ch: John D'Auban; sc: W. Perkins, A. Callcott, E. G. Banks; cos: Lucien Besche

Produced at Palmer's Theatre, New York, under the management of A. M. Palmer 5 August, 1890 for a run of 78 performances closing 13 October, 1890.
Herndon Morsell (ROD), James Sauvage/Melville Stewart (HARRY), J. W. Handley (MM), William Gilbert/Richard F. Carroll (BUNDY), Joseph C. Fay/Fred Clifton (BYLES),/C. McGovern (GAY), Carl Hartsburg (MAY), Marie Tempest/Maud Hollins (KC), Maud Hollins/(DAISY), Isabelle Urquhart (BB), Fanny Edwards (MRS), Willie Barbier (DRUMMER BOY). Pd: Gussie Coogan, Anna Allen. Dir: John E. Nash; md: Julian Edwards; ch: Rose Becket; sc: W. Perkins, A. Callcott, E. G. Banks

0101 **THE GONDOLIERS** or The King of Barataria. A comic opera in two acts by W. S. Gilbert. Music by Arthur Sullivan. Produced at the Savoy Theatre under the management of Richard D'Oyly Carte 7 December, 1889 for a run of 554 performances closing 20 June, 1891.

Duke of Plaza-Toro. . . . . Frank Wyatt/Cecil Barnard/George Temple

Luiz . . . . Wallace Brownlow/Charles Rose/Helier Le Maistre
Don Alhambra . . . . W. H. Denny/Cecil Barnard/George de Pledge
Marco . . . . Courtice Pounds (Charles Rose)/W. R. Shirley
Giuseppe . . . . Rutland Barrington/W. S. Laidlaw/Duncan Fleet/Wallace Brownlow
Antonio . . . . A. Medcalf
Francesco . . . . Charles Rose/C. Barrett/W. R. Shirley
Giorgio . . . . George de Pledge/
Annibale. J. Wilbraham/P. Burbank
Ottavio . . . . Charles Gilbert/Rudolf Lewis
Casilda . . . . Decima Moore (Cissie Saumarez) (Nellie Lawrence)
Gianetta . . . . Geraldine Ulmar/Carrie Donald/Alice Baldwin/Mina Cleary/Nita Carritte/Maud Holland/Nellie Lawrence/Esther Palliser/Louise Pemberton/Norah Phyllis/Emily Squire/Cissie Saumarez/Amy Sherwin/ Annie Schuberth/Leonore Snyder
Tessa . . . . Jessie Bond/Cissie Saumarez/Annie Cole
Duchess of Plaza-Toro . . . . Rosina Brandram/Elsie Cameron (Annie Bernard) (Agnes Scott)/Kate Forster
Fiametta. Nellie Lawrence/Cissie Saumarez/Agnes Wyatt/Nellie Kavanagh
Vittoria . . . . Annie Cole/Cissie Saumarez/Agnes Wyatt/Norah Phyllis/Jose Shalders/Janet Watts
Giulia . . . . Norah Phyllis/Cissie Saumarez/Agnes Wyatt
Inez . . . . Annie Bernard(Jose Shalders)

Md: François Cellier; sc: Hawes Craven; ch: Willie Warde; cos: Percy Anderson

Produced at the Park Theatre, New York, under the management of Richard D'Oyly Carte 7 January, 1890. Withdrawn 13 February. Reopened at Palmer's Theatre 18 February, 1890. Withdrawn 19 April, 1890 after a total of 103 performances.
George Temple/F. David/J. W. Herbert (DUKE), Arthur Marcel/Helier Le Maistre (LU), J. A. Muir/Fred Billington (DON), Richard Clarke (M), Rutland Barrington/Richard Temple (G), Helier Le Maistre/Mr Rowlands (ANT), Mr McCarthy/Mr Boole (FR), A. Lee/Mr Kavanagh (GIO), Percy Charles (ANN), Agnes Macfarland/Norah Phyllis (CAS), Esther Palliser/Leonore Snyder (GIA), Mary Duggan (TESS), Kate Talby (DUCH), A. Watts/Mattie Geoffrey (FIA), Miss Sadger/Cora Tinnie (VITT), Miss Pyne/A. Watts (GIU), Miss Rochfort/Rose Leighton (INEZ). Md: Jesse Williams; dir: F. A. Leon; sc: Hawes Craven; cos: Percy Anderson

Subsequently played in New York in repertoire and short seasons by the D'Oyly Carte Opera Company and others.

Produced at the Theater an der Wien, Vienna as *Die Gondoliere* 20 September, 1890.

Produced at the Savoy Theatre under the management of Richard D'Oyly Carte 22 March, 1898 for a run of 62 performances closing 21 May, 1898. Restaged 18 July, 1898 for a further 63 performances closing 17 September, 1898.
William Elton (DUKE), Jones Hewson (Cory James) (LUIZ), Walter Passmore (DON), Charles Kenningham/Robert Evett (M), Henry Lytton (Iago Lewys) (G), Leonard Russell (ANT), Cory James (Albert Gater) (FR), H. G. Gordon (GIO), Charles Childerstone (ANN), Ruth Vincent (Isabel Jay) (CAS), Emmie Owen (Ethel Jackson) (Isabel Jay) (GIA), Louie Henri/Blanche Gaston-Murray (TESS), Rosina Brandram (DUCH), Ethel Jackson/Madge Moyse (FIA), Mildred Baker (VITT), Madge Moyse/Lulu Evans (GIU), Jessie Pounds (INEZ). Md: François Cellier

Produced at the Savoy Theatre under the management of the D'Oyly Carte Opera Company 22 January, 1907 in repertoire. Played 75 times.
C. H. Workman (DUKE), Alec Johnstone/Leo Sheffield/Henry Burnand (LUIZ), John Clulow

(Tom Redmond) (DON), Pacie Ripple/Harold Wilde (Strafford Moss) (M), Richard Green/Frank Wilson (G), Overton Moyle (ANT), Henry Burnand/Edward Wynn (FR), Tom Redmond (Henry Burnand) (GIO), Leo Sheffield (ANN), Marie Wilson (CAS), Lillian Coomber (Clara Dow) (Ruby Gray) (GIA), Jessie Rose (Beatrice Meredith) (Violet Frampton) (TESS), Louie Rene (DUCH), Bessel Adams/Violette Londa (FIA), Norah McLeod (VITT), Clara Dow/Winifred Thomas (GIU), Ethel Morrison (INEZ). Md: François Cellier.

Produced at the Savoy Theatre under the management of the D'Oyly Carte Opera Company January 18, 1909 in repertoire. Played 22 times.
C. H. Workman (DUKE), Leo Sheffield (LUIZ), Rutland Barrington (DON), Henry Herbert (A. Laurence Legge) (M), Henry Lytton (G), Fred Hewett (ANT), Ernest Leeman (FR), Cecil Curtis (GIO), A. Laurence Legge (ANN), Dorothy Court (CAS), Elsie Spain (GIA), Jessie Rose (TESS), Louie Rene (DUCH), Ethel Lewis (Josset Legh) (FIA), Beatrice Boarer (VITT), Adrienne Andean (GIU), Amy Royston (INEZ). Md: François Cellier.

Subsequently played by the D'Oyly Carte Opera Company on tour and in London in repertoire.

Produced by Scottish Opera 12 December, 1968.
Ian Wallace (DUKE), John Robertson (LUIZ), William McCue (DON), John Wakefield (M), Ronald Morrison (G), Jill Gomez (CAS), Anne Pashley (GIA), Janet Coster (TESS), Johanna Peters (DUCH). Dir: Joan Cross; md: James Loughran; sc: Jack Notman

Produced by the New Sadler's Wells Opera Company 9 February, 1984 and played in repertoire. John Fryatt (DUKE), Christopher Gillett (LUIZ), Donald Adams (DON), Kim Begley (M), Richard Jackson (G), Michael Fitchew (ANT), Thomas Marandola (FR), Sandra Dugdale (CAS), Laureen Livingstone (GIA), Janine Roebuck (TESS), Joan Davies (DUCH), Rebecca Caine (FIA), Maria Jagusz (VITT), Jane Findlay (INEZ). Dir: Christopher Renshaw; md: Wyn Davies; ch: Michael Corder; sc/cos: Tim Goodchild.

0102 **PAOLA** or The First of the Vendettas, a comic opera in two acts by Harry Paulton and 'Mostyn Tedde' (Edward Paulton). Music by Edward Jakobowski. Performed at the Grand Opera House, Philadelphia and the Royalty Theatre, Chester 10 May, 1889 for copyright purposes.

Produced in New York at the Fifth Avenue Theatre under the management of J. C. Duff 26 August, 1889 for a run of 47 performances closing 5 October 1889.

Bragadoccio . . . . William McLaughlin
Griffo . . . . Fred Clifton
Guglielmo . . . . A. M. Holbrook/W. White
Sapolo . . . . Harry Paulton
Paola . . . . Leonore Snyder
Margarine . . . . Fanny Edwards/Catherine McLaen
Gruello . . . . Clem Herschell
Lucien . . . . Chauncey Olcott
Chilina . . . . Louise Beaudet
Gazzi . . . . Catherine McLaen/Annie Cameron
Martino . . . . Lillian Hawthorne
Anna . . . . Allice Cameron
Maria . . . . Carrie Boelen
Clara . . . . Mittie Atherton/Marion Miller
Bruno . . . . H. Clarke/Ole Norway
Pietro . . . . E. Williams
Bonano . . . . F. Hartberg/J. Weisner

Md: Julian Edwards

Produced in Britain at the Lyceum Theatre, Edinburgh 16 December, 1889 for 3 weeks and toured through Glasgow x3, Stirling, Aberdeen, Dundee, Newcastle, Halifax, Birmingham x2, Cardiff, ?, Southport, Liverpool, Sheffield, Bradford, Manchester x2, Northampton, Brighton, ?, Exeter, Plymouth ending 14 June, 1890.

Bragadoccio . . . . Fred Billington/Sam Finney/Westlake Perry/Mark Kinghorne
Griffo . . . . Sam Finney/Westlake Perry
Guglielmo . . . . Alfred Rolph

Paola . . . . Leonora Braham/Ethel Pierson
Margarine . . . . Fanny Harrison/Marian Medus/Bessie Harrison
Gruello . . . . Foster Courtenay/J. W. Fletcher
Lucien. . . . . Hirwen T. Slack/F. S. Gilbert/Gilbert Porteous
Sapolo . . . . Charles Groves/Charles Lucian/Foster Courtenay/George Thorne
Chilina . . . . Lizzie St Quinten
Gazzi . . . . Carrie Burton
Martino . . . . Vivian Cassell
Anna . . . . Marion Medus
Maria . . . . Frances Mara
Clara . . . . Marguerite Lauraine
Zanetta . . . . Amy Perrin
Fenella . . . . L. Villiers
Trumpeter . . . . Amy Woods
Victor . . . . Miss A. Thompson
Basilio . . . . Alice Stuart
Giacomo. . . . . Miss Erminstone
Humberto . . . . Ethel St Clair
Pietro . . . . Charles Leicester
Bonano . . . . F. Williams

Md: Barter Johns

PAUL JONES a comic opera in three acts by H. B. Farnie based on *Surcouf* by Chivot & Duru. Music by Robert Planquette. Produced at Bolton under the management of Carl Rosa 10 December, 1888 and toured.

Produced at the Prince of Wales Theatre under the management of Carl Rosa and Horace Sedger 12 January 1889 for a run of 370 performances closing 15 January, 1890.

Paul Jones. . . . . Agnes Huntingdon (Miss Emmott Herbert)
Rufino di Martinez . . . . Templar Saxe/George Preston (Tom Shale)
Bicoquet. . . . . Henry Ashley
Don Trocadero . . . . Frank Wyatt/William Cheesman/Arthur Hendon?
Haricot . . . . James Francis/George Temple/Arthur Hendon?
Kestrel . . . . Arthur Hendon/Mr Bottrill/Templar Saxe?
Bouillabaisse. . . . . Harry Monkhouse (Arthur Hendon)
Petit Pierre . . . . Albert James
Yvonne . . . . Mathilde Wadman/(Florence Darley)/Camille d'Arville
Chopinette . . . . Phyllis Broughton
Malaguena. . . . . Kate Cutler/Annie Schuberth/(Florence Darley) Esme Lee
Guava . . . . Mimi St Cyr (Florence Darley)
Captain Octroi . . . . Jeannie Mills/*out*
Delphine . . . . Florence Wilton
1st Lieutenant. . . . . George Preston/
Nichette . . . . Miss Fitzherbert
Mignonne . . . . Miss Forbes/Miss Beresford/Miss Stanley
Estelle . . . . Gladys Knowles/Miss Richards
Ramez . . . . Tom Shale
Don Antonio . . . . Mr Pearce
Jeanne de Kerbec . . . . Miss Stanford
Coralie. . . . . Miss Dashwood/C. Neil
Alva . . . . Minnie Howe/Miss Abbott
Fernando . . . . Miss Gwynne/Miss Mills/Miss Gordon
Mario . . . . Mr Sefton
Goujon . . . . Robert Mason
Don Riboso . . . . Mr Bottrill

Louise de la Forte . . . . Miss Bell/Miss Gwynne
Val de Penna . . . . Miss Douglas/Miss Dewhurst/Miss May
Maroona. . . . . Lillie Levine
Merlan . . . . Mr Feltham
Md: Frederick Stanislaus; ch: John D'Auban; sc: J. Robson and T. E. Ryan; cos: Lucien Besche and Cledat de la Vigerie Bianchini

Produced at the Broadway Theatre, New York, 6 October, 1890.

LITTLE TOM BOWLING a musical nautical comedy by Fisher Simpson. Music by Herbert Simpson. Produced at Gainsborough 5 August, 1889 and toured by Herbert Simpson's Co.

Little Tom Bowling. . . . . Lily Alexander/Maud St John
Captain Howard. . . . . Herbert Newton/Charles G. Vaughan
Jim Todd . . . . Harry Phydora
Harry Vincent. . . . . S. Alexander
Matthew Stokes. . . . . Harry Royce
Jack Windlass . . . . J. W. Pattison
John Plowman . . . . A. Graus
Miss Maitland. . . . . Maud Stewart
Grace Howard . . . . Alice Simpson/Nancy Stirling
Euphy . . . . Maud St John/
with Fanny d'Alroy, Dot d'Alroy, Margaret Watson, Walter Mulvey, George Taylor, A. Illingworth, the Philp trio &c.
Performed at a matinée at Terry's Theatre 19 December, 1889.

MY NADINE or André The Mountaineer. A musical comedy drama in 3 acts by Hal Collier. Music by Jules de Croix. Produced by Marie Strachane at the Exhibition Palace, Folkestone 20 May, 1889 and toured.

Nadine . . . . Marie Strachane/Nellie Meryl
Paul . . . . Julia Mortimer/Louie Scott
Nathalie La Thière . . . . Nora Day/Marie deRoos/Marie Clavering
Rosine. . . . . Nellie Parkinson/Sara Wilson/Florrie Hermann
Louise Temple . . . . Nellie Meryl/Marie Clavering/Louise Esmond
Michael Johannes . . . . John Rouse/M. Bickford
Zack Fiddler . . . . Hal Collier/Mr Carlton/Melville Bickford
Count Vladimir Zarniski . . . . Leo Robson/D. Beattie
André . . . . Harry Tebbutt/Wilfred Barry Lyndon/ Webb Darleigh
Col. Temple. . . . . W. Barry Lyndon
Hector Limpet . . . . Charles Vaughan/Edward Neville
with Nellie Packman, Nellie Stewart, W. N. Gillmore, Arthur Rich &c.

Toured by Kate Fedora as *The Swiss Guide*, 1893.

OUR BABIES a musical comedy-drama by W. E. Morton. Music by George D. Fox. Toured by Alice Morton's Co. (and later in a revised version by Charles Clinton's Co) from West Hartlepool 18 February, 1889.

THE FANCY BALL or The Q. C. or Nubbs, Q. C. An operatic farcical comedy by Henry Wardroper. Music by William W. Meadows. Produced at the Opera House, Ipswich 11 February, 1889 and toured by Henry & Walter Wardroper.

Shifty Flubbs . . . . Henry Wardroper
Alexander . . . . James Rees
Eliza Hamilton . . . . Florence Rivière
Mrs Maria Nubbs. . . . . Wilhelmina Rayne/Miss Bowman
Numbskull Nubbs . . . . Walter Wardroper/C. L. Ludlow
Fanny . . . . Louie Hamilton &c.

A CAPITAL JOKE an operetta in one act by Frederic de Lara. Music by B. Brigata (Bucalossi). Produced by Evelyn Vyron at a matinée at St George's Hall 31 May, 1889 with *Pets.*

Fred Merton (Sunflower) . . . . Frederic de Lara
Lillian Trueblue (Dahlia) . . . . Grace Hardinge
Accompanist: Ernest Bucalossi

BRITTANY FOLK by Walter Frith. Music by Alfred J. Caldicott. Produced at St George's Hall under the management of Alfred Reed and R. Corney Grain 20 March, 1889 with *A Day's Sport* replaced by *Tally Ho!* 30 May. Withdrawn 22 June, 1889.

Ninorch. . . . . Fanny Holland
Tonyk . . . . Walter Browne
Margaridd . . . . Kate Tully
Hon. Tom Kingsbench . . . . Alfred Reed
Riwal . . . . Ernest Laris

THE VERGER a vaudeville in one act by Walter Frith. Music by King Hall. Produced at St George's Hall under the management of Alfred Reed and R. Corney Grain 9 December to 14 December, 1889 and then from 26 December with *A Family Party*. Withdrawn 5 April, 1890.

Margaret Purley . . . . Fanny Holland
Lucy. Kate Tully
Robert Marshall. . . . . J. L. Mackay
Simon Beere . . . . Alfred Reed
Frank Herbert. . . . . Avalon Collard

WARRANTED BURGLARPROOF an operetta in one act by Cunningham Bridgman. Music by Ivan Caryll. Produced at the Lyric Theatre under the management of Henry J. Leslie 2 December, 1889 with *The Red Hussar*. Withdrawn 4 April, 1890.

Mr Theophilus Beeswing . . . . B. P. Seare
Demosthenes Solon Tomkins. . . . . . . Mr Edmunds
Lawkins Delaney Johnson . . . . Sebastian King
Brewster. . . . . F. L. Scates
Sarah . . . . Carrie Fenton
Alice. Edith Briant
Emily . . . . Jessie Braham

LOCKED IN an operetta in one act by Walter Frith. Music by Alfred J. Caldicott. Produced at the Savoy Theatre 28 May, 1889 at a matinée for the benefit of Rutland Barrington with *Petticoat Perfidy* and *Trial by Jury*.

Christopher . . . . Eric Lewis
Miss Antigone Sparkes . . . . Rose Hervey
Sophie Burdell . . . . Jessie Bond

Played at the Comedy Theatre 14 February, 1890 at a matinée with *The Home Feud*. Rutland Barrington (CH), Jane Sullivan (ANT), Jessie Bond (SOPH).

TUPPINS AND CO. an operetta by T. Malcolm Watson. Music by Edward Solomon. Produced at St George's Hall under the management of Alfred Reed and R. Corney Grain 24 June, 1889 with *My Aunt's in Town*, replaced 7 October. Withdrawn 7 December, 1889.

Timothy Tuppins. . . . . Alfred Reed
Stella Tuppins . . . . Fanny Holland
Michael Finnigan . . . . Walter Browne
Harriet Long . . . . Kate Tully
Professor Thyme . . . . J. Duncan Young

JOHN SMITH an operetta in one act by Arthur Law. Music by A. J. Caldicott. Produced by Carl Rosa and Horace Sedger at the Prince of Wales Theatre 28 January, 1889 as a forepiece to

Paul Jones. Withdrawn 15 January, 1890. Subsequently performed with *Marjorie* 20 Jan 1890 to 20 Feb 1890.

John Smith . . . . Albert James
Mrs Strong . . . . Jeannie Mills/Miss May
Tito Palazzo. . . . . Templar Saxe
Mrs Smith . . . . Miss de la Tour
Eliza Smith . . . . Kate Cutler/Annie Schuberth
Office Boy. . . . . Master Callan

PENELOPE a musical version of Brough and Halliday's farce *The Area Belle* arranged by George P. Hawtrey. Music by Edward Solomon. Produced at a matinée at the Comedy Theatre 9 May, 1889.

Pitcher. . . . . Dan Leno
Walker Chalks. . . . . George Hawtrey
Penelope. . . . . Kate Everleigh
Tosser . . . . Rutland Barrington
Mrs Croker . . . . Carlotta Zerbini

Produced at the Strand Theatre 24 September, 1889 as a forepiece to *Aesop's Fables*. Withdrawn 22 October, 1899.
W. S. Penley (PI), William Lugg (T), Reginald Stockton (WC), Carlotta Zerbini (MRS), Alma Stanley (PEN). Md: J. M. Glover

Performed at Maud Brennan's benefit at the Avenue Theatre with the above cast 31 October 1899.

LOVE'S TRICKERY an operetta in one act by Cunningham Bridgman. Music by Ivan Caryll. Produced at the Lyric Theatre under the management of Henry J. Leslie as a forepiece to *Doris* and subsequently to *The Red Hussar* 31 August, 1889. Withdrawn 30 November.

Roland Moss . . . . H. Sims Reeves
Larkyns . . . . John Le Hay/F. L. Scates
Lady Daffodil . . . . Amy Augarde/Hilda Glenn
Lady Leela . . . . Hettis Lund
Count Paulitecknick. . . . . W. T. Hemsley/Sebastian King

PICKWICK a dramatic cantata in one act by F. C. Burnand. Music by Edward Solomon. Produced at the Comedy Theatre at a matinée February, 1889.

Samuel Pickwick . . . . Arthur Cecil
Mrs Bardell . . . . Lottie Venne
Baker . . . . Rutland Barrington
Tommy . . . . Arthur Knight

Produced at the Trafalgar Square Theatre 13 December, 1893 as a forepiece to *Tom, Dick and Harry*. Withdrawn 6 January 1894.
C. P. Little (PICK), Charles H. Hawtrey (BAKER), Jessie Bond (MRS), Master Stratton (TOMMY).

THE HOUSEBOAT an operetta in one act by H. W. Williamson. Music by John Crook. Produced at the Avenue Theatre as a forepiece to *Lancelot the Lovely* 6 May 1889. Withdrawn 6 July, 1889.

Uncle Barbleton. . . . . Harry Grattan
Frank Barbleton. . . . . Ambrose Collini
Effie Greyling . . . . Nellie Woodford
Ethel Manners . . . . Hettie Bennett
Andrew Topham . . . . Leon Bridgeman
Jack Sterling . . . . Mr Ford
Cora Audley. . . . . Miss Garthorne
Nellie Danvers . . . . Mary Glover

1890

After the large number of new works of the previous year, the 1890 season was comparatively quiet. This was due partly to the tenacity of some of the best of the previous year's productions – *The Gondoliers* which occupied the Savoy through the whole of the year, and *The Red Hussar* at the Lyric and *Ruy Blas* at the Gaiety which occupied two of the other principal houses devoted to musicals through the first part of the new year. The first theatre which needed a new show was the Royalty where Arthur Roberts and his colleagues in management were quickly obliged to find a piece to replace the unfortunate *New Corsican Brothers*. They chose another burlesque, this time a rather more topical one, based on Sardou's drama *La Tosca* which was currently playing at the Garrick with Mrs Bernard Beere as its dramatic heroine and which had caused some controversy by its 'indecency'.

In *Tra-la-la Tosca* Frank Burnand turned out a scenario which followed the structure of the play, with the extra step from high drama to rhyming ridicule being easily taken. An example of his ragging of the original can be seen in his treatment of the central scene of the murder of Scarpia where Sardou's heroine followed up her deed by placing a branch of candles by the body in a gesture of respect. Burnand placed the scene in a restaurant. Tosca is bargaining for a train pass for herself and her Mario when the bill is delivered. Folding the paper into a cone she stabs the half-drunken Scarpia, then pauses to put the dish cover over the dead man's head. The Baron returned for the final scene in the guise of manager John Hare of the Garrick Theatre to allow Arthur Roberts to be in on the finale, for Scarpia was the role that the actor-manager had selected for his inimitable treatment.

On the first night that treatment was uncharacteristically poor. To begin with, few copies of the words were available to the audience so many had difficulty in following what was going on but, in any case, Roberts took it into his head largely to ignore the printed script and go off into an orgy of ad libbing. This had the effect of completely unnerving the rest of the cast who had no idea if and when their cues were coming. Margaret Ayrtoun, who played Tosca, was the worst sufferer but she battled on in a fine imitation of Sara Beere which had little to do with what Roberts was up to. *The Stage* queried:

> Why Mr. Arthur Roberts should, on its first production, have seriously endangered the success of a play in which as part proprietor of the theatre he has a special interest will, we suppose, remain a mystery.

It did, although rumours circulated freely of a breach between the members of the ruling syndicate. Augustus Harris, taken unawares by the débacle, wrote to the critics inviting them to come and re-view the piece. Some took up the invitation and *The Daily*

Telegraph was able to report:

> Suddenly a new life has been given to Mr Burnand's clever and amusing burlesque on *La Tosca* and a large audience on Saturday night was delighted with it. The reason is not far to seek. The author's lines are now given as he wrote them, the text is delivered without pause or hesitation, depression has been succeeded by electricity and the favourite actor Mr Arthur Roberts has taken good advice and nerved himself to the attack. The burlesque is now well worth seeing . . .

But problems were not over for *Tra-la-la Tosca*. *The Stage* had noted:

> We cannot but think it a risky undertaking to produce a burlesque of *La Tosca* for audiences who understand it must be limited to those who have seen the original.

This consideration, which was becoming less and less valid in the new burlesques where the subject had become almost incidental to the songs, dances and comedy routines which decorated them, was still a relevant one with the largely unfamiliar story of *Tosca* which Burnand had tackled in an entirely traditional manner.

'Cameradossi', the artist, is a strange socialist who has his paintings ghosted:

> I am a painter of renown
> Ri fol de riddle A.R.A . . .

Angelotti is the fugitive manager of an illegal gaming club (with the occasional Bonapartist line incongrously inserted), Tosca is an ex-street singer and Scarpia a former policeman made good. In the torture scene Mario is subjected to Boulanger's March, Tennyson's 'The Throstle', an amateur impersonation of Henry Irving, a recitation of 'The Boy Stood on the Burning Deck' and the whole of the Parnell Commission Report before Tosca shrieks out the truth of Angelotti's whereabouts in the face of a barrage of puns and acrostics. When Mario re-enters he has been stretched on the rack to an enormous height. The gaolers fold up his 'trick' legs and carry him off. Agnes de la Porte in the hero's role was a long way from her days in German opera. The wordplay in Burnand's libretto was an plentiful as ever. The characters' names were misused unmercifully. 'Mario' suffered references to the opera singer Giuseppe Mario, to music-hall artist Dot Mario, and a bilingual 'Dear Mario, vous êtes mon mari, o!' while there were several variations on the theme 'What made Floria Tosca Wild . .' and an incomprehensible twist on the Marchesa Attavanti which had something to do with uncles. In spite of the excessive 'cleverness', the story was reasonably clear in the first scene but thereafter matters deteriorated somewhat until the final scene which had Cameradossi facing a firing squad of photographers and disappearing through a picture frame. This was all rather puzzling, especially when Scarpia, now transmogrified into Hare, brought back all the principals for the ending.

The musical part of the show had been provided by Florian Pascal and, like the book, it was old-fashioned and unexceptional, earning notices on the lines of 'neat and flowing in style but wanting in brightness and go'. Roberts sang 'I am the bad Baron Scarpia' and 'I am the Man with a wonderful Plan' and indulged in a supper-table duet with Tosca which involved whistling, banjo-playing and tambourine-banging; Angelotti had a song which declared 'I was a Swell' in a well-turned if familiar lyric, but probably the most amusing piece was the little opener sung by Hettie Bennett and Augustus Wheatman:

> In every play
> 'Tis useless to say

There must be someone to begin
Their only use
Is to introduce
The principals who are coming in.
Again they may
Appear in the play
If any scene they can assist
But we must confess
As a rule, unless
They're very good they won't be missed.
So let us try and be very good
I'm sure I can, I'm sure I could
And to make 'em regret when we've left the stage
The little black beadle and the merry page

There is little doubt that a bravura performance by Roberts in a Scarpia role written to display his best capabilities would have saved the show, but Burnand and Pascal had supplied a truly 'old' burlesque which Roberts was attempting to perform with the freedom of the 'new' style of show. The mixture of the two was even more incongruous on this occasion than in *The New Corsican Brothers* and Roberts and the piece were both undoubted failures. After six weeks the show and the partnership folded and Roberts left the Royalty and London for a lengthy provincial tour in another new burlesque, this one on the more traditional subject of Guy Fawkes. Both audiences and character were much more compatible with Roberts' treatment and the star succeeded in getting twenty-nine profitable weeks in top tour dates out of *Guy Fawkes Esq* before returning to town to make the move into modern burlesque in *Joan of Arc* for George Edwardes. *Guy Fawkes Esq* was already a step in that direction. Its book was written in a mixture of rhyme and prose by Fred Leslie and Herbert Clark whose first hit *Ruy Blas and the Blasé Roué* was still running when Roberts took to the road, and it was full of the Gaiety star's clever low comedy ideas.

The story had King James himself involved in the setting up of the Gunpowder plot and signing a warrant for his own execution in the middle of a plethora of plots and counterplots tempered with the usual dash of romance involving young Catesby and Viviana Ratcliff. Guy Fawkes himself was, of course, implicated deeply in both plotting and romancing, ranging from the burlesque of a socialistic harangue:

Friends, countrymen and loafers (sans a job)
How long shall James our homes and houses rob?
Our income tax is eightpence in the pound
We're forced to pay a heavy school board rate
And other people's children educate . . . &c

to the chatting up of the fair Viviana.

Neither Leslie and Clark's ideas nor their careful lyrics earned much respects from Arthur Roberts. Before even the first night the blue pencil had cut out large pieces of the dialogue and most of the specially written songs to be replaced by Roberts' own tried and tired formulae and a few new concoctions. The result was less like *Ruy Blas* and the Gaiety than an old provincial extravaganza or variety musical, but it was one which nevertheless served its star's purpose and did well enough at the box office. By the time he had been on the road a while there was more of Roberts in the show than of Leslie and Clark, and the actor/manager began to resent the £20 per week in royalties going out to the authors. With the intent of saving himself a few pounds he called in the playwright Wilton Jones and commissioned him to write a new *Guy Fawkes* around the Arthur Roberts pieces of *Guy Fawkes Esq* under the title *Guy Fawkes M.P.*

When the new piece was tried out it met with a very poor reception and Roberts returned to his half and half show for the autumn season. But he had not paid Jones his commissioned fee for *Guy Fawkes M.P.*, and the author sued. Roberts insisted that the writer had not done his job – the piece had been unplayable claptrap. He filled the court with big names from the theatre to support his denigration of the text which rebounded on him when it was shown that the most highly criticised 'chestnuts' were the pieces that he himself had insisted on including. His 'original' business was traced back to *The Great Pink Pearl, Erminie, Paul Jones, Falka* &c., and in addition to this public loss of face Roberts lost the case which involved paying out Jones his £100 fee and £5 for train fares.

The most successful burlesque of the year was, as might have been expected, at the Gaiety. The enormous success of the *Miss Esmeralda/Monte Cristo Jr* expedition through the provinces, Australia and America led Edwardes to try the same trip with the even more popular *Ruy Blas* and in July Nellie Farren and Fred Leslie said goodbye to the Gaiety and set out for fourteen weeks on the road. This was to be followed by America, where they were scheduled to open 24 November on Broadway prior to a national tour, and by a full season around Australia, in all eighteen months away from London.

But Broadway was never to get *Ruy Blas*. During the tour both Leslie and Miss Farren were taken ill and Edwardes cancelled the American part of his programme. Both recovered, however, in time to undertake the second part of the plan and the company left for Australia early in 1891. With the 'A' team once more away, Edwardes turned to his second team with a new burlesque prepared by the authors of *Faust Up-To-Date* based on the *Carmen* story. *Carmen Up-To-Data* kept fairly close to the original story, but took the whole of the drama in a whimsically light-hearted spirit. Michaela was changed from the wispy soprano of Bizet's opera into a buxom hussy with a donkey cart, the cynical Escamillo became a pretty girl in tights, an Irish Don José dolled himself up as a thin-blooded masher and his operatically 'ailing' mother was now very much alive – a crafty old soul palming dud coins off on English tourists. Most importantly, the functional role of Captain Zuniga was expanded into a large comico-villainous role for Arthur Williams.

All the elements that were expected in a successor to *Faust Up-To-Date* were there – the inventive humour of Edwin Lonnen and Arthur Williams, the romantic singing of Florence St John as Carmen, the graceful dancing of Letty Lind and the now obligatory pas de quatre. There was no Nellie Farren, but the principal boy role of Escamillo was a comparatively small one which was pleasantly played by Jenny Rogers until Alma Stanley was brought in from playing Daudet's *Struggle for Life* with George Alexander and Genevieve Ward to give a rather different interpretation of the Toreador. *Carmen Up-To-Data* was bright, funny and colourful, its libretto a mixture of light and untortured rhyming passages and more elastic prose sections, its songs some of the best yet to come out of the new burlesque, its dances, settings and costumes all up to the highest Gaiety Theatre standards.

The opening scene in the streets of Seville introduced Zuniga as 'The Villain of the Day', and Lonnen as the Irish hero. A chorus of drummer boys (from Stedman's famous children's choir) and another of picturesque Spanish girls led up to the entrance of 'Jack' St John as a superb Carmen whose operatic greeting 'Well, folks, what do you think of *this*?' evoked the obvious response. The Gaiety's Carmen mixed suitably piquant lines with a handful of Meyer Lutz songs that ranged from the saucy 'Ask me to Marry' to the genuinely romantic 'One who is Life to Me' in a thoroughly winning performance as she set about her seduction of Lonnen's Don José. This José, his head quickly turned, then proceeded to take on the airs of the fashionable masher of the day in order to win the gipsy's favour and also to sing one of the show's most popular numbers, 'The Jolly Boys' Club'. The 'Toreador' entered the scene with another up-to-date piece called 'The Swagger' illustrating the tenet 'You needn't have much money, but you must have style' and the Gaiety quartet danced their newest dance as Spanish damsels to great effect before the first half of the evening's entertainment was done.

The second part took the scene to the smugglers' lair and opened with Letty Lind's 'spot', a number loosely called 'The Gipsy Boy' which involved the farmyard imitations which Miss Lind affected and a lively hornpipe. It had been planned that this should be followed by Lonnen's traditional Irish number and the writers had tentatively mapped out a piece called 'The Irish Muleteer', but Lonnen came up with an altogether different idea for his major spot. The nigger minstrel world had been doing well with the Harrigan/Braham song 'Whist! The Bogie Man!' and Lonnen fancied something of the sort for the 'mysterious' setting of the second act. Sims, Pettit and Lutz worked up a fresh version of the 'bogie' idea and Don José sang and danced his way through their 'Hush, the Bogie' on a shadowy stage to the accompaniment of a *bouche fermée* chorus:

> Hush, hush, hush! here comes the Bogie Man,
> So hide your heads beneath the clothes – he'll take you if he can
> Hush, hush, hush! – and all the children ran –
> So hush-a-bye, my babies dear – here comes the Bogie Man.

'Hush, the Bogie' did all and more that 'Killaloe' had done for Lonnen. The number became the talk of London in no time, and in the end went round the world and into many places and languages which had never heard of *Carmen Up-To-Data*. But first and foremost it set the seal of indubitable success on the show in the way that only a great song hit could. The rest of the show only served to confirm that success. Florence St John scored with 'Within the Maze of Dreams', Williams and Lonnen brought in the latest topics of public interest in the duet 'It will cause Unpleasantness', Letty Lind danced, and a quartet of lady violinists and eight dancing girls contributed their 'turns' until the critical meeting of José and Carmen outside an extravagant bull-ring brought the story into play. In a piece of genuine burlesque José, with the heroine at his mercy, pauses to demand:

> J: Why can't I find some way to quench my rage
> And do a novel murder on the stage?
> A murder in the moonlight, that's the way
> Stabbed in the back . .
> C: That's *London Day by Day*[1]
> J: Well then, I'll try a swifter, neater thing
> I'll chloroform you!
> C: That's *The Silver King*[2]
> J: Then when asleep in bed you'll meet your death
> C: No, that was done by Shakespeare in *Macbeth*

[1] Sims and Pettitt's Adephi drama.
[2] the perennial Henry Arthur Jones drama made famous by Wilson Barrett.

J: A murder with a hairpin then I'll do
C: No, that's in *Theodora* by Sardou

Finally the 'masher' relents and leaves Carmen to her Escamillo and takes the chorus' advice to the young man about town: 'You'd better go home to your mother . .' The critical reaction to *Carmen Up-To-Data* was a largely positive one. The libretto found some critics who asked for more puns and more particular parody, others who asked for none, but the music and the production were everywhere given the highest praise. The public had no reservations at all and came in numbers to see *Carmen Up-To-Data* and Lonnen's 'Hush, the Bogie'.

In the cast list were a couple of interesting names. One was Horace Mills, the erstwhile city man and co-author of *Miss Esmeralda*. Mills had given up his office to join his new friends of the theatre world and made his début in the part of Remendado. Further down the list was the name of Loie Fuller. Miss Fuller had made an unfortunate attempt to 'take' the West End as a star in the play *Caprice* at the Globe. It had been a dreadful flop and she came to the Gaiety to play in the two-handed operetta *His Last Chance* and to understudy Letty Lind whose speciality skirt dance formed the basis for Loie's imminent triumph with the Butterfly Dance. As always there were plenty of changes as the show ran on. When Alma Stanley came in to play Escamillo, new material was put in for her; Sylvia Grey took over as Frasquita and the dancing side of affairs was duly strengthened. Meyer Lutz kept the new songs coming. 'Hush, the Bogie', 'The Jolly Boys' Club' and those pieces relevant to the plot stayed in their places but he wrote half a dozen alternative numbers for Miss St John, dance music for the dancing stars' newest routines, and a ballad 'Only You' to replace Escamillo's more irreverent 'Swagger Song'. Lonnen sang of 'The Recreation Army' and Williams of 'How to Mesmerise 'em' and when W. H. Brockbank and Frank Celli took a turn at a more traditional version of Escamillo several more suitable pieces were provided for that character.

Carmen Up-To-Data filled the Gaiety marvellously. *The Illustrated London News* labelled the show 'one of the most brilliant theatrical successes of the autumn season' and it looked as if, with the usual revisions, the show might last right through until the return of the Farren/Leslie company for Christmas '91. But as the summer season approached there was a sudden fall in takings and it became obvious the show would not hold up so long. After ten months and 248 performances it was withdrawn and sent on tour while the American comedian Nat Goodwin took a turn at the Gaiety with *The Bookmaker*. For the next three years *Carmen Up-To-Data* was toured around Britain under the insignia of the Van Biene Co. while other companies took it through Europe and the Gaiety Company itself, featuring Lonnen, Marion Hood and Robert Courtneidge, played it with great success in Australia during its 1892 tour. But Edwardes had now ceased the practice of sending the company to America and, in consequence, *Carmen Up-To-Data* did not appear on Broadway.

Although the new burlesque was proving more and more popular, the more traditional forms of musical were still present in force. The new metropolitan offerings of 1890 were four in number. Two, *Marjorie* and *Captain Thérèse*, were presented under the banner of the Carl Rosa Light Opera Company at the Prince of Wales Theatre.

Marjorie was the first attempt at a comic opera by the young composer Walter Slaughter whose previous efforts had been confined to operetta and his very successful setting of Savile Clarke's 'authorised version' of *Alice in Wonderland*. His librettists were 'Lewis Clifton' (Clifton Lyne) and Joseph J. Dilley whose previous collaborations had included *Summoned to Court*, and *Tom Pinch* (1881), an adaptation of Dickens' *Martin Chuzzlewit*, but who similarly were making their musical début.

Marjorie was the latest in the *Dorothy/Doris* line of English comedy operas. Its story was set in the thirteenth century – the furthest back in time yet – and told a story based on feudalism. The wealthy serf farmer, Gosric, has bought his freedom from the Earl of Chestermere. Wilfred, Gosric's son, is in love with Marjorie, the daughter of Sir Simon Striveling, an impoverished knight, but when the Earl too falls for the girl he claims the fealty of Wilfred and sends him off to war as Striveling's servant. But his attempts to get Marjorie, in her lover's absence, to the altar are foiled by the ambitious Cicely who disguises herself as Marjorie for the wedding ceremony. The Earl takes an angry revenge, and it is left to Wilfred returning a hero from the wars to set all to rights.

Marjorie first saw the light of day at a matinée in July 1889 when it was tried out by a cast headed by Mathilde Wadman, Joseph Tapley, Frank Celli and Harry Monkhouse. On that occasion it was reckoned a fair success, the music in particular being found pleasing, and the Company scheduled it to follow *Paul Jones* into the Prince of Wales. In the meanwhile the author-poet Robert Buchanan and the composer went to work to revise the piece in the places where it had shown weaknesses. The book was heavily re-written, the dialogue pruned, incidents altered, and more prominence given to the comedy character of Gosric. Several numbers were cut or rearranged and Slaughter composed two new duets for the soprano and tenor to strengthen the score.

He was also required to change the principal tenor role of Wilfred into a contralto so that the Rosa company might star their 'big gun', Agnes Huntingdon. But even for the advantage of Miss Huntingdon's abilities and drawing power, Slaughter was not at all happy about changing his entire score. He contented himself with dropping the highest notes an octave in the ensembles and transposing the solos. Miss Huntingdon was not pleased and on the opening night the audience was stunned to find a prima donna unrecognisable from her triumph in *Paul Jones*. She walked sulkily through her role and a few days later refused point blank to go on. The baritone Tom Shale stepped in to save the day while the management tried to reason with the temperamental star, but to no avail. The music was put back into its original tenor range and Joseph Tapley brought back to sing it. Horace Sedger, determined that Miss Huntingdon should not be allowed to get away with her breach of contract, applied for an injunction to stop her playing anywhere else in Britain until the expiry of the contract and sued for damages. The lady retorted that the role was not a contralto one and was ruining her voice. She was more at a loss to explain why she would not, instead, go out on tour as Paul Jones. However, an out-of-court settlement was arrived at and Miss Huntingdon returned to America with a British company to perform *Paul Jones* for a short season on Broadway and on a national tour.

There were one or two other hiccoughs on the opening night. Although nearly all the alterations were agreed to be improvements, not all of them gained approval. The worst moment came in the final act when Hayden Coffin as the duped Earl tempestuously ordered, one by one, all the other principals off to the dungeons. The repeated sentence and the repeated appearance of a lugubrious jailer to carry it out touched the audience's communal funny-bone and soon they were laughing uproariously. Coffin kept his poise and saved the scene, but the incident nearly caused the show to split up into a fiasco. Many of the audience also found much enjoyment in the lines written into Phyllis Broughton's role making reference to her current real-life position as plaintiff in a breach-of-promise action. Others found the allusions in bad taste and made their feelings felt.

By and large *Marjorie* had a good opening and the reviewers decreed it satisfactory in both libretto and music. Of the numbers the new duet 'Whisper Softly', a spinning chorus and the lively trio 'King of the Rout' were best noticed and Slaughter's music with its 'appropriate old English flavour' and its 'preponderance of dance rhythms' was generally held to represent a better than average first attempt. As the run progressed *Marjorie* was given a further going over. Monkhouse worked up Gosric into an even more prominent character, aided by a new duet with the Jack Point-ish jester, Witgills (Albert James) in the last act. Another interpolation was a song for Hayden Coffin, 'For Love of Thee', which quickly became the musical feature of the show and helped it to settle in for a comfortable six months' run. In the autumn it was sent out on tour starring the 'lady baritone' Miss Emmott Herbert in the title role, and was subsequently played in both Australia and South Africa.

To follow *Marjorie* the Carl Rosa and Sedger commissioned their own Franco-English musical. Having scored such a vast success in their first light opera venture with *Paul Jones* they naturally looked for more of the same and turned to the French composer Planquette. H. B. Farnie had done a thorough job of plundering the Planquette archives for usable pieces, so the partners thought it advisable to have the composer write a totally new work. For the purpose he was teamed with the French librettist Alexandre Bisson whose book and lyrics were subsequently to be put into English by Frank Burnand and Gilbert a'Beckett. At the time of the commission the pride of the Carl Rosa was still Agnes Huntingdon and consequently *Captain Thérèse* featured a young lady who disguises herself for a large part of the action as a soldier. By the time the show was ready for production Miss Huntingdon was lost to the company and the role of Thérèse was allotted to the Canadian mezzo, Attalie Claire.

Captain Thérèse was a competent piece. The music was typically attractive if rather unoriginal; the libretto gave the characters their opportunities even if it smacked of being written to order, as well as being very long and not very funny. The length was soon reduced by forty-five minutes: the humour was left to Harry Monkhouse to work up and Miss Claire, whose performance in the title role had been rather undersized, was replaced by the impeccable Violet Cameron. Hayden Coffin sang of 'A Soldier's Life', Phyllis Broughton joined him for the pretty 'Song of the Butterfly' and displayed once again her dancing and comedic talents, Madame Amadi scored with a number on 'Transmogrification' and Joseph Tapley joined Miss Cameron for the romantic part of the proceedings for a hundred performances plus until *Captain Thérèse* was taken off for the production of the Christmas piece, an adaptation of Thackeray's *The Rose and the Ring* by Savile Clarke and Walter Slaughter. Agnes Huntingdon eventually played the role which had been written for her when *Captain Thérèse* was tried on Broadway in 1892 but after a fortnight she abandoned the show and went back to her staple *Paul Jones*. Paris was barely more welcoming, giving Yvonne Kerlord 26 performances as the soldier heroine in a belated 1901 production.

The most novel work of the year was undoubtedly the third offering, *The Black Rover*, which had the distinction of being the first Australian musical to be presented on the West End stage. The composer/librettist was Luscombe Searelle,[1] already known to London audiences through his *Estrella* and *The Wreck of the Pinafore*. The energetic Searelle had undergone a considerable change of fortune since his last appearance in Britain with *Estrella*. He had formed an opera troupe in Australia with which he toured that country before venturing with it to South Africa. In South Africa

[1] In Australia, the libretto had been credited to a Mr Morley.

gold fever was beginning and Searelle, mindful of what had happened to property prices under similar circumstances in Australia, invested in property in his habitually free-spending manner. On this occasion it made him a fortune, which he spent in buying up South Africa's theatres. Now he was in London with a grandiose scheme to build new theatres throughout South Africa at a vast cost and to give the West End a taste of his *chefs d'oeuvre*, the musicals *Isidora* and *Bobadil*, both of which had been widely played by his company in Australia, New Zealand and South Africa.

Isidora was the first slated for production. In spite of London's experience of *Estrella* and *The Wreck of the Pinafore*, anticipation was high and advance booking quite good. Searelle, with the aid of some well-placed newspaper paragraphs, had re-christened it *The Black Rover* and had emphasised it as 'a daring experiment' full of 'sensation and exciting situations'. He printed quotes from the Australian papers:

> In *Isidora* Mr. Luscombe Searelle has invented an entirely new style of opera, blending, with a master hand, the tunefulness of the French with the dramatic interest of the German school – myth with mirth, melody and mystery . . (*Australasian*)
>
> The first act provoked uproarious laughter. The second act moved the audience to tears with its touching melody and pathos, while the third held the audiences spell-bound with the power of its dramatic situations . . (*Melbourne Argus*)
>
> . . as full of melody as *Maritana* or *The Bohemian Girl* . . (*Melbourne Daily Telegraph*)
>
> unique . . in its story, its music and its scenery . . . (*Sydney Morning Herald*)

and *The Stage* was left to add

> If the opera succeeds it will be one of the biggest hits of the year . .

The book which Searelle had concocted was certainly enterprising. It was set in Cuba and opened with a chorus of negro slaves singing about their homeland. They are silenced by Jacob, the comic German overseer who takes them off for 'pretzels and wine'. We are introduced to Isidora who is the supposed daughter of Patronio, the wealthy owner of the estate. However, Isidora has a strange recurring feeling that she was once on a ship and heard her mother sing this lullaby . . . A wealthy Count is due to arrive to marry Isidora, but she is in love with the fisherman, Felix, and so allows her cousin, Sabina, to change places with her and be courted by the nobleman. In actual fact the man who arrives to do the courting is the count's servant suitably disguised and looking for a rich wife. Next we learn of the legend of the Black Rover, a wicked pirate who once caused the destruction of a ship with all aboard and flung an innocent mother and her child to their deaths. He is condemned to roam the seas until he shall hear once more that lullaby which the mother sang to her child as the ship sank.

The Rover's treasure is said to be hidden under a rock on the island and Felix and Jacob determine to find it despite the legend's threats:

> They who shall dare unearth this gold
> Shall face to face meet the Rover bold
> And be borne on his barque o'er the billows high
> By the Pirate crew who cannot die
> For nought can avail their souls defiled
> But the mother's song to her little child

The Rover materialises and all the principals are carried off to the ghostly ship where they are condemned to walk the plank. As she prepares to die, Isidora starts to sing her dream lullaby and lo! the ship of the Black Rover breaks into pieces and all the pirates vanish. Isidora and her friends escape but she has gone mad and, to add to everyone's troubles, the local slaves have decided to stage a revolution while their masters are in the hands of the pirates. But as the natives approach the shipwrecked party the ghost of the Black Rover arises to protect them

> Back from the grave
> I come to save
> The lives that once I would have slain
> Back from my grave
> Beneath the wave
> My spirit moves on earth again

The natives flee, leaving a now sane Isidora free to marry her Felix while the undisguised Sabina and the servant Guzman discover a mutual passion to add to the happy ending.

The demanding central role of Isidora was set to be played by Mrs Luscombe Searelle, the Sydney-born Blanche Fenton, and the author and his producer, with money no object, surrounded her with the best people available. The Carl Rosa baritone William Ludwig (once a Gaiety chorister) was engaged to sing the Rover at a considerable fee, and the rest of the cast included the well-known comedians Charles Collette and John Le Hay, the soprano Effie Chapuy and the veteran stars of *Les Cloches de Corneville*, Shiel Barry and William Hogarth, the former in the role of a crazed beachcomber and the latter as the heroine's father.

Searelle was undoubtedly a more accomplished composer than a writer. His music was light and tuneful but his ideas often outstripped his talents and the book was a pot-pourri of everything from *The Flying Dutchman* to *Erminie*, in what the *Illustrated Sporting & Dramatic News* called

> a plot for boys . . a story of mystery and adventure of the type 'one penny weekly including coloured plate . .

The score contained a similar range of demands, although the fairly limited orchestration reduced its dramatic potential somewhat. The prima donna and the tenor playing Felix bore a large amount of the more ambitious vocal burden and it was no coincidence that both reached the end of rehearsals in a state of vocal exhaustion and were replaced shortly after the opening. Ludwig justified his fee by making quite a success of the banal 'Rover's Song' and Effie Chapuy was kindly noted for her *Dutchman*-like 'Legend of the Black Rover' but by and large the music was the victim of its own pretensions.

The press reaction to *The Black Rover* was widely divergent. Some emphasised 'brilliant ensembles and marvellous scenic effects' while others lambasted the dialogue as 'weak even for an opera'. Some followed the author's own estimation of his work, others would have none of it. The first night was not a success. The worn-out performances of the stars were not compensated for by the singing of Ludwig and Miss Chapuy and, worst of all, the most touted scenic effect of all, the breaking up of the Rover's ship, failed to materialise. Instead of the spectacular effect which Searelle had taken so much care to publicise, the audience was treated to the sight of the 'drowned' pirates pushing their ship off into the wings, completely destroying the climax of the show.

If the reviews were equivocal, public reaction was not. Cuts, re-casting, revisions, all made no difference and after six weeks *The Black Rover* sank and Searelle set off gaily for New Zealand, promising to return in September to produce *Bobadil* and a revival of *Estrella*. But South Africa and later America were to claim a good deal of his attention and, although *Bobadil*, *Isidora* and *Estrella* were all kept alive by their intrepid creator, Britain had seen the last of his works.

A fourth and more ephemeral piece had had its beginnings in the previous year. *Gretna Green* was the work of Murray Ford and John Storer, the authors of *The Punch Bowl*, here shifting their focus from old-fashioned comic opera to the more recently popular description and style of *Dorothy* in a simplistic comedy opera of the most obvious kind. *Gretna Green* was given a trial run at a matinée in December, 1889 with a fine cast including Leonora Braham, Lyn Cadwaladr and George and Richard Temple, but with insufficient preparation and revision. *The Era* criticised it heavily: 'too much libretto . . lacking in wit . . not comical . . the music is unexceptional . . .' A second performance a week later showed a few improvements but scarcely sufficient, it seemed, to warrant *Gretna Green* being given a full-scale West End production. Nevertheless, the following May the show opened in a revised version at the Opéra-Comique under the management of F. J. Harris. The so-called revisions consisted mainly of the interpolation of a whole new character. Following the example of *Dorothy* and, more particularly, *Carina*, the authors had gone for low comedy as the most likely element to turn their insipid piece into a hit. They hired Charles Collette, allotted him a superfluous character called Peter Pong and gave him his head. Collette did not need such encouragement: in between Storer's ordinary little numbers he shovelled chunks of his touring act: 'stupid jokes and Irishisms totally out of place and wearisome to a degree'; and the result was, predictably, chaotic and unsophisticated. Many of the first-night audience did not bother to see the evening through to its end and the fifteen subsequent performances of *Gretna Green* were played on sufferance. An attempt to set the show up as a touring piece fizzled out and it was quickly forgotten.

The provincial scene of 1890 was even less productive than the metropolitan. The Anglo-Danish *Belphegor* put in a short tour of minor northern dates, a very *Dorothy*-esque piece called *Dolly*, allegedly based on *The Country Girl*, made a brief appearance in the same area, and a comic opera, *Daisy*, the work of the young composer, Henry J. Wood, was tried at Kilburn and Camden, but the only substantial new work premièred out-of-town was staged at Leamington on Boxing Day. It was a 'romantic comedy opera', *Jackeydora*, by the playwright Mark Melford, author of *Turned Up*.

In *Jackeydora* he was trying his hand for the first time at an original musical piece in collaboration with Miss Popsie Rowe, a lady whose main claim to musical fame seemed to be that she was a descendant of Sir George Smart, court musician to William IV. She had studied with Sir Julius Benedict but now worked in the light popular idiom on a modest scale. The libretto was mildly unusual. Egged on by a jealous old flame, the superstitious Sir George Gallipoli has turned out his wife, Evangeline, when, against the omens, she has borne him a daughter, Jackeydora. Evangeline brings up the child apart and in her solitude takes up the practice of white witchcraft. When Jackeydora is ill-treated by her mischief-making schoolmistress, Evangeline takes her revenge by reversing the sex of all those who treat her daughter unkindly and they are only restored when the schoolmistress' treachery is exposed and a repentant Sir George takes back his wife and child. The most prominent role in the piece was the incidental comedy role of Peter Poreboy which Melford created for himself to play. *Jackeydora* was toured briefly and then revised with some new music by Josef Peltzer before being toured again in the autumn with modest success in mostly minor dates.

Very much less substantial but very much longer lived was a seemingly haphazard little omnibus piece called *Cissy* produced at Harrogate by its author, W. H. Dearlove. *Cissy* paired a romantic-dramatic-comic tale of the most obvious kind (its original title was *Love's Devotion*) with an eclectic and movable selection of musical numbers, ranging from a touch of coloratura and mandoline and piano solos to a lady whistler, in an evening of wholly unsophisticated entertainment which proved extremely popular in the smaller (and sometimes not quite so small) provincial theatres and halls through which it was toured year after year after year, becoming something of a phenomenon with its little but insistent success over more than a decade.

Amongst the one-act pieces of the year the most significant was a short piece called *The Gypsies* put on at the Prince of Wales with *Captain Thérèse*. It introduced the public to a new young librettist, 27 year-old Lt Basil Hood, who had written the little operetta in conjunction with Sir Arthur Sullivan's secretary, Wilfred Bendall. His reviews were mixed. *The Era* noted that 'W. S. Gilbert has a faithful and clever disciple' but *The Stage* considered that

> . . [the piece is] closely imitative of the comic opera of Savoy topsy-turveydom, only the imitation does not extend to the merit of the original.

The Gypsies proved well-suited to its supporting purposes and was retained on the programme beyond the withdrawal of *Captain Thérèse*, playing as a filler with de Koven's *Maid Marian*, the successful mime play *L'Enfant Prodigue* and the play *The Planter* over a twelve-month period.

Teddy Solomon produced two new pieces in collaboration with F. C. Burnand. One, *Domestic Economy*, based on the popular comedietta, was played successfully if briefly at the Comedy; the other, *The Tiger*, found the librettist at his worst and was a scandalous flop, being hissed and booed from the St James' stage. Solomon also provided the music for a little sketch by Malcolm Watson entitled *In and Out of Season*. This playlet had been ordered by Kate Santley, on whom the retired life was chafing. Seeing the profits being earned on the drawing room entertainment circuit, she decided to join it and *In and Out of Season* was her vehicle.

At the bastion of the drawing room entertainment, St George's Hall, the German Reed team put on two new pieces from their habitual writers. *Carnival Time* centred around the time-honoured lost will in a bag which, on this occasion, did the rounds of a Spanish carnival. It introduced a few bright characters for, notably, Fanny Holland and Alfred Reed, the two remaining veterans of the old team. *Possession* which replaced it in December was less attractive. *The Times* noticed that it had 'no claim to originality' and 'does not aim at a very high level of excellence', a criticism which was becoming sadly usual at St George's Hall.

1890

0103 **TRA-LA-LA TOSCA** or The High-Toned Soprano and the Villain Bass. A burlesque by F. C. Burnand. Music by Florian Pascal. Additional songs by Messrs Young and Barnett and Wal Pink. Produced at the Royalty Theatre under the management of Arthur Roberts, Henry Watkin and Augustus Harris 9 January, 1890 for a run of 45 performances closing on 22 February, 1890.

The Queen of Naples	Amy Liddon
Floria Tra-la-la Tosca	Margaret Ayrtoun
Baron Scampia Scarpia	Arthur Roberts/(George B. Prior)
Count Mario di Cameradossi	Agnes de la Porte
Caesare Angelotti	Laura Hansen
Spiacroni	George B. Prior/
Jemmi Rino	Hettie Bennett
Bumblini	Augustus Wheatman
Spaghetti	Hampton Gordon
Macaroni	Walter Tilbury
Spermacetti	William Gilbert
Ravioli	James Delaney
Niuncli	Robert Mason
Nianti	William Lovell
Jolinosia	Harry Daniels
Dogerini	Arthur Dodson
Stepito	Guy Fane
Tentoso	Arthur Withers
Marchesa Tutti Tutti/Contessa Anna Cora	Miss Morton
Contessa Lotti Totti/Admiralo Benbo	Maud Royal
Marchesa Nonpica Mesta	Frances Denton
Signor Farfallone	Maggie Douglas
Signorine Connie Moto/Anne Dante/Ada Gio/Ann Diamo	Paddy St Clare
Il Capitano Batti Batti/Marchesa Fan Tutti	Fannie Merton
Signorina Larki Daremo/Generalissimo Trombonio	Lillie Marsden

Md: George Byng; ch: Paul Valentine; sc: Bruce Smith and Julian Hicks; cos: L. & H. Nathan

0104 **MARJORIE** an English comic opera in three acts by 'Lewis Clifton' (Clifton Lyne) and Joseph J. Dilley. Revised by Robert Buchanan. Music by Walter Slaughter. Produced by the Carl Rosa Light Opera Company at a matinée at the Prince of Wales Theatre 18 July, 1889. Re-produced 18 January, 1890 for a run of 193 performances closing 1 August, 1890.

Wilfred	Agnes Huntingdon (Tom Shale)/Joseph Tapley
Cicely	Phyllis Broughton

Lady Alicia . . . . Mme Amadi (Amy Abbott)
Marjorie . . . . Camille D'Arville/Ada Lincoln
Ralf, Earl of Chestermere . . . . C. Hayden Coffin
Sir Simon Striveling . . . . Henry Ashley
Nicholas . . . . Frederick Wood
Witgills . . . . Albert James
Captain . . . . Tom Shale
Martin . . . . Arthur T. Hendon
Gosric . . . . Harry Monkhouse (Arthur Hendon)

Dir: Augustus Harris; md: Frederick Stanislaus; sc: T. E. Ryan; cos: Wilhelm

1889 Matinée: Joseph Tapley (W), Fanny Brough (CIC), Emily Miller (AL), Mathilde Wadman (M), Frank H. Celli (RALF), W. H. Burgon (SIM), Frederick Wood (NICH), Albert James (WIT), Tom Shale (CAPT), Albert Sims (HERALD), Harry Monkhouse (GOS). Dir: C. D. Marius.

105 **GUY FAWKES ESQ** a burlesque in 3 acts by 'A. C. Torr' (Fred Leslie) and Herbert Clark. Lyrics by Doss Chidderdoss. Music by George W. Byng. Produced by Arthur Roberts at Nottingham 7 April, 1890 and toured through Edinburgh, Glasgow, Bristol, Birmingham, Manchester, Southport, Liverpool, Hull, Leeds and Sheffield (21 June). Resumed 26 July at the Gaiety Theatre for one matinée and then through Blackpool, Manchester, Leeds, Douglas, Scarborough, Nottingham, Newcastle, Edinburgh, Glasgow, Liverpool, Standard Theatre, Northampton, Birmingham, Plymouth, Portsmouth, Brighton and Standard Theatre ending 29 November, 1890.

Guy Fawkes . . . . Arthur Roberts (John A. Warden)
Viviana Ratcliff . . . . Amelia Gruhn/Lyddie Edmonds
Ruth Ipgreve . . . . Amy Liddon
Francis Tresham . . . . Grace Wixon/Walter Sealby
Steenie . . . . Ethel Blenheim/Edith Milton
Bates . . . . Constance Groves/Agnes Taylor
Robert Catesby . . . . Fanny Marriot
Angelica . . . . Claire Hepworth/Minnie Thurgate
Lord Mounteagle . . . . Alice Ford
James I . . . . W. H. Rawlins
Badcorn . . . . Sam Wilkinson
Funk . . . . John A. Warden
Sergeant/Trigger . . . . Louie Fay
Policeman . . . . Louise Norman
with Tessie Jones, Emily Williams &c.

Dir: George Capel; md: George W. Byng; cos: Stewart Browne

106 **GRETNA GREEN** a comedy opera in 3 acts by T. Murray Ford. Music by John Storer. Produced at a matinée at the Comedy Theatre, 4 December, 1889. Repeated 11 December in a revised form. Produced at the Opera Comique 22 May, 1890 under the management of F. J. Harris for a run of 16 performances closing 7 June, 1890.

John Bramble . . . . Llewellyn Cadwaladr
Robin Bates . . . . William Hogarth
Host Barnes . . . . Eric Thorne
Phyllis Ferris . . . . Villa Knox
Widow Ferris . . . . Marion Erle
Justice Nettle . . . . H. Gittus Lonsdale/(Maitland Marler)
Peter Pong . . . . Charles Collette
John Paisley . . . . C. Jameson
Ruth Ferris . . . . Leonora Braham
Cicely Barnes . . . . Florence Lonsdale

Dir: Hugh Moss; md: W. F. Glover; sc: E. G. Banks; cos: Mrs. May

1889 Matinées; Llewellyn Cadwaladr (JB), Richard Temple (RB), W. Norman (HOST), Giulia Velmi (PH), Paulina Gear (WIDOW), George Temple (NOBLE), Broughton Black (JP), Leonora

Braham (RUTH), Maud Vena (CIC), Charles Lander (BILL SMART), C. Wotherspoon (DR. PRIG), R. Duval (SIR GYLES DUMPLING), H. Moreton (FARMER GOGG).

0107 **CAPTAIN THÉRÈSE** a comic opera in 3 acts by Alexandre Bisson and F. C. Burnand. Lyrics by F. C. Burnand and Gilbert a'Beckett. Music by Robert Planquette. Produced at the Prince of Wales Theatre under the management of the Carl Rosa Light Opera Co 25 August, 1890 for a run of 104 performances closing 5 December, 1890.

Vicomte Tancrède de la Touche	C. Hayden Coffin
Philip de Bellegarde	Joseph Tapley/Tom Shale
Coupecourt	J. Ettinson
Marquis de Vardeuil	Harry Parker
Captain Boulignac	Tom Shale/Mr Burch
Lieutenant Campastro	Arthur T. Hendon
Major de la Gonfrière	George Marler
Duvet	Harry Monkhouse
Colonel Sombrero	Henry J. Ashley/Leon Roche
Sergeant La Tulipe	A. Thomas
Sergeant Vadeboncoeur	T. Arthur
Marcelline	Phyllis Broughton
Mme la Chanoinesse Herminie	Mme Amadi
Claudine	Florence Darley/Jeanetta Sheene
Mlle Thérèse	Attalie Claire/Violet Cameron

Dir: Charles Harris; md: John Crook; ch: Willie Warde; sc: William Telbin, Perkins, Banks; cos: Mme Auguste, Nathans, Alias

Produced at Union Square Theatre, New York, under the management of Agnes Huntingdon 15 February, 1892 for one performance. Played from 20 February to 28 February, closing after a total of 11 performances.
Eric Thorne (TANC), Clinton Elder (PH), H. Scott Russell (MARQ), J. Hart (BOU), J. Wyn Nickols (CAMP), Karl Mora (GONF), Albert James (DU), Hallen Mostyn (SOMB), Sid Reeves (TUL), John W. Smiley (VADE), Effie Chapuy (MARC), Millie Marsden (HERM), Vinnie Cassell (CL), Agnes Huntingdon (TH), Annetta May (CHAMBERMAID), Joseph Severo (ORDERLY). Dir: Max Freeman; md: Sgr Tomasi; cos: Alias

Produced at the Gaîeté Theatre, Paris, 1 April, 1901 for a run of 26 performances.
Yvonne Kerlord (TH)

0108 **CARMEN UP-TO-DATA** a burlesque in two acts by George Sims and Henry Pettitt. Music by W. Meyer Lutz. Produced at the Shakespeare Theatre, Liverpool under the management of George Edwardes 22 September, 1890 and subsequently at the Gaiety Theatre 4 October, 1890 for a run of 248 performances closing 4 July, 1891. Second edition produced 2 February, 1890.

Carmen	Florence St John (Grace Pedley)
Escamillo	Jenny Dawson/Alma Stanley/(Maud Hobson) (Blanche Massey)/W. H. Brocklebank/Frank H. Celli
Frasquita	Florence Levey/Sylvia Grey/Maud Wilmot/Lillian Price
Michaela	Maria Jones
Alphonse	Katie Barry
Juanita	Maud Wilmot
Inez	Eva Greville/Alice Gilbert
Zorah	Alice Gilbert/Eve Wilson/M. MacIntyre/Adelaide Astor
Morales	Blanche Massey/Grace Wixon/M. Florence Lloyd
Intimidado	Maud Hobson/Day Ford/Miss Maitland/*out*
Larranaga	Grace Wixon/Madge Mildren/Violet Durkin

Mercedes	Letty Lind (Loie Fuller)
Jose	E. J. Lonnen
Dancairo	E. H. Haslem
Lilius Pastia	G. T. Minshull/*out*
Captain Zuniga	Arthur Williams (G. T. Minshull)
Hidalgos	Florence Henderson
	Emily Robina
	Minnie Ross
	Madge Mildren/Lily Harold
Remendado	Horace Mills
Partagas	Hetty Hamer
add Donna Fandango	M. Simmons
Manuelita	Jessie Hassan
Castinetta	Maude Maryon/Lily MacIntyre
Don Antonio	Maud Hobson
Don Roderigo	Blanche Massey
Emanuela	Florence Levey
Donna Pastia	Ethel Gardner
The Violin Quartet	Misses Ashby, Burle, Maud Champion and D'Alcourt/*out*

Dir: Charles Harris; md: Meyer Lutz; ch: John D'Auban; sc: Walter Hann & T. E. Ryan; cos: Percy Anderson

Produced at the Carltheater, Vienna as *Carmen von Heute* 1 September, 1892.

109 **THE ROSE AND THE RING** dramatised by H. Savile Clarke. Music by Walter Slaughter. Produced at the Prince of Wales Theatre under the management of Horace Sedger 20 December, 1890 for a series of matinées ending 31 January, 1891.

Valoroso	Harry Monkhouse (Harry Parker)
Count Hogginarmo	George Marler
Bulbo	John Le Hay
Count Hedzoff	Arthur T. Hendon
Prince Giglio	Violet Cameron
Countess Gruffanuff	Mme Amadi
Angelica	Maud Holland
Tommaso Lorenzo/Count Spinachi	Tom Shale
Glumboso/Padella	William Cheesman
Polly/General Punchikoff	Empsie Bowman
Jenkins Gruffanuff	S. Solomon
Betsinda/Rosalba	Attalie Claire
Queen of Paflagonia	Ada Doree
Fairy Blackstick	Isa Bowman
Jester	R. Bernard

with the Children of Stedman's Choir and D'Auban's School of Dancing

Dir: Charles Harris; md: John Crook; ch: John D'Auban; sc: E. G. Banks; cos: Howell Russell

110 **JACKEYDORA** or The Last Witch. A romantic comedy opera in 3 acts by Mark Melford. Music by Popsie Rowe and Josef Peltzer. Produced at the Theatre Royal, Leamington 26 December, 1890 and toured through Southampton x2, Coventry, Reading, Cambridge to 7 February, 1891.

Kitty Karter	Maude Stoneham
Mother Krail (Evangeline)	Mary Raby
Miranda	Sophie Lingwood
Rosabella Gruff	Florence Silas
Pauline	Madge Johnson
Jackeydora	Rosa Hyde
Sir George Gallipoli	G. C. Stretton
Badger Gruff	Ernest Hilton

Ben Gallipoli . . . . John J. Donnelly
Peter Poreboy . . . . Mark Melford

THE BLACK ROVER a comic opera by W. Luscombe Searelle. Originally produced as *Isidora* in Australia at the Bijou Theatre, Melbourne, 7 July, 1885, with the libretto credited to Mr Morley. Produced in London at the Globe Theatre under the management of George Paget 23 September, 1890 for a run of 40 performances closing 7 November, 1890.

Patronio . . . . William Hogarth
Pedro Guzman . . . . Charles Collette
Felix . . . . Maurice Mancini/Sinclair Dunn/Phillips Tomes
The Black Rover . . . . William Ludwig
Jacob . . . . John Le Hay
Chickanaque . . . . Shiel Barry
Moro . . . . Roydon Erlynne
Annetta . . . . Florence Lloyd
Sabina . . . . Effie Chapuy
Isidora . . . . Blanche Fenton/Giulia Warwick

Negroes/Pirates: Messrs Adams, Aldridge, J. Almonte, G. Almonte, Benwell, Boissonade, A. Bolton, Burry, Buthin, C. Canning, G. Canning, Dear, Fishe, Ford, Grey, Henrihart, Hunt, Judd, Laguerre, Laming, Lowe, Morris, Newman, Owen, C. Romaine, Weston, Winning, Workman.
Planters/Soldiers: Messrs Cairns, Cowes, d'Alberti, Davies, Ellis, Fraser, Hawthorn, Hilsden, Pitts, F. Pritchard, H. Pritchard, Skinner, H. Vernon, Vining, Wadey, Ward, Wood.
Schoolgirls: Misses Benson, Dudleigh, Goodricke, R. Maitland, Montrose, Wentworth; Cocoa girls: Misses Cleaver, A. Maitland, Meredith, Waltham, Stuart; Cotton girls: Misses Chase, Julian, Reynolds, Swannell, Vizard, Wynter; Fruit girls: Misses Adams, Courtenay, Denton, Dipnell Faulkener, O'Connor, Wallis; Negresses: Misses Adare and Deloitte.

Dir: Hugh Moss; md: Luscombe Searelle; ch: Ozmond; sc: W. T. Hemsley; cos: Glindoni

CISSY a musical comedy in three acts by W. H. Dearlove. Music by Jennie Franklin. First produced in a copyright performance at the Town Hall Theatre, Harrogate 11 January, 1890 as *Love's Devotion*. Produced at the same theatre 20 March, 1890 under the management of W. H. Dearlove and toured.

Victor Carlton . . . . Andrew Francis
Gilbert Temple . . . . W. H. Dearlove
Titus Thomas, B.A. . . . . C. H. Paley
Dossy Bowers . . . . C. Davantry
Cissy Vere . . . . Jennie Franklin
Olive Temple . . . . Marie Barrett
Mary . . . . Olivia Sinclair

DOLLY a comic opera by John Bannister based on *The Country Girl*. Music by Josef Peltzer. Produced at Her Majesty's, Carlisle, under the management of Thomas Elsworth 27 October 1890. Also played three nights at Barnsley.

Dolly . . . . Maud Durand
Dick Dashwood . . . . Hugh Carlyle
Squire Clodpole . . . . Henry Kitts
Gussett . . . . Ray Sinnell
Lady Alice . . . . Clara Smith
Lady Frances . . . . Kate Maskell
Lady Lillian . . . . Marion Ayling
Ordnance . . . . Ernest Hilton
Florence . . . . Edith Edgar
Sabretache . . . . Mr Gardner
Hoster . . . . Charles Holden
Punch . . . . Aynsley Fox

Margery . . . . Kate Cohen
Ned Nolledge . . . . Augustus Cramer
Sir Peter Peppercorn . . . . Robert Fairbanks
Seamwell . . . . Minnie Leverentz
Lady May . . . . Vera Baudrant
Lady Bertha . . . . Lilian Edevian
Lady Flora . . . . L. Bolton
Bodice . . . . Evelyn Rivers
Tucker . . . . M. Baudrant
Halberd . . . . Herbert Perretti
Pummell . . . . W. T. Williams
Mantle . . . . Phoebe Josephs

Dir: Thomas Elsworth and John Bannister; md: Josef Peltzer

ALL ABROAD an operetta in one act by Arthur Law. Music by Albert J. Caldicott. Produced at the Prince of Wales Theatre under the management of the Carl Rosa Light Opera Co. 21 February, 1890 as a forepiece to *Marjorie*. Withdrawn 1 August. Represented 26 August with *Captain Thérèse*. Withdrawn 17 October, 1890.

Mr Bunting . . . . Frederick Wood/J. Ettinson
Mrs Bunting . . . . Amy Abbott
Charles . . . . Templar Saxe/Philip Sefton
Winkles . . . . Albert James/W. Burt
Jeannette . . . . Florence Darley

DOMESTIC ECONOMY an operetta by F. C. Burnand. Music by Edward Solomon. Produced at the Comedy Theatre 7 April, 1890 as an afterpiece to *Pink Dominoes*. Withdrawn 3 May, 1890.

Mrs Knagley . . . . Mary Glover
Mrs Whacker . . . . Alice Yorke
Mrs Grumley . . . . Alma Stanley
Boy . . . . S. Solomon
John Grumley . . . . Ells Dagnall
Steward . . . . William Lugg

Md: James M. Glover

THE TIGER an operetta in one act by F. C. Burnand. Music by Edward Solomon. Produced at St James' Theatre under the management of Mrs Langtry 3 May, 1890 with *Esther Sandraz*. Withdrawn 23 May, 1890.

Major Curzon . . . . W. F. Stirling
Jacob Nott . . . . J. G. Taylor
Philip Fuller . . . . C. P. Colnaghi

THE CRUSADER AND THE CRAVEN a mediaeval operetta in one act by W. Allison. Music by Percy Reeve. Produced at the Globe Theatre under the management of George Paget 7 October, 1890 as a forepiece to *The Black Rover*. Withdrawn 7 November, 1890.

Sir Rupert de Malvoisie . . . . William Hogarth
Blondel FitzOsborne . . . . John Le Hay
Dame Alice . . . . Effie Chapuy

THE GYPSIES an operetta in one act by Basil Hood. Music by Wilfred Bendall. Produced at the Prince of Wales Theatre under the management of the Carl Rosa Light Opera Co. 18 October, 1890 as a forepiece to *Captain Thérèse*. Withdrawn 5 December, 1890.

Black Dan . . . . Leon Roche/A. T. Hendon
Albert . . . . Tom Shale/H. Gregory
Percival . . . . Philip Sefton/H. Russell
Zitella . . . . Florence Darley/Ellis Jeffreys

Christine Lightfoot . . . . Amy Abbott/Cissy Cranford

Produced at the Prince of Wales Theatre 9 February, 1891 with *Maid Marian*. Withdrawn 13 April, 1891.

Produced at the Prince of Wales Theatre 15 April, 1891 with *L'Enfant Prodigue*. Withdrawn 7 August, 1891.

THE SENTRY an operetta by Félix Rémo and T. Malcolm Watson. Music by Ivan Caryll. Produced at the Lyric Theatre under the management of Henry J. Leslie 5 April, 1890 as a forepiece to *The Red Hussar*. Withdrawn 17 May, 1890.

Colonel Pettigrew . . . . Frank Wood
Tim O'Brien . . . . John Le Hay
Sergeant Major . . . . F. L. Scates
Peggy . . . . Maud Holland
Polly Burchett. . . . . Ellis Jeffreys
Mrs Pettigrew. . . . . Adelaide Newton

Produced at the Lyric Theatre 20 October, 1890 with *La Cigale*. Withdrawn 3 March, 1891.
George Mudie (COL), E. W. Garden (TIM), Mr Jones (SGT), Annie Schuberth (PEG), Ellis Jeffreys (POLLY), Adelaide Newton (MRS)

Produced at the Lyric Theatre 22 January, 1892 with *The Mountebanks*. Withdrawn 27 June, 1892.
Charles Gilbert/Cecil Burt (COL), Harry Parker/Gilbert Porteous (TIM), Charles Crook (SGT), Jessie Moore (PEG), Ellis Jeffreys/Dora Thorne/Marjorie Field Fisher (POLLY), Florence Melville (MRS)

Produced at the Lyric Theatre 4 November, 1893 with *Little Christopher Columbus*. Withdrawn 28 November, 1893.
Henry Wright (COL), Harry Parker (TIM), Maud Holland (PEG), Dora Thorne (POLLY), Adelaide Newton (MRS)

POSSESSION by Walter Browne. Music by Alfred J. Caldicott. Produced at St George's Hall under the management of Alfred Reed and R. Corney Grain 1 December, 1890 with *Seaside Mania*. Withdrawn 20 December. Reopened 26 December with *At the Pantomime*. Withdrawn 14 March, 1891.

Ella Willoughby. . . . . Kate Tully
Jack Weldon . . . . Avalon Collard
Mrs Lavinia Limpet . . . . Fanny Holland
Thomas Trotter. . . . . Alfred Reed
Samuel Washington Tubbs . . . . J. L. Mackay

Produced at St. George's Hall 28 September, 1891 with *Dinners and Diners*. Withdrawn 4 October, 1891.
Blanche Murray (ELLA), Avalon Collard (JACK), Fanny Holland (MRS), Arthur Wilkinson (TT), Walter Browne (SWT).

CARNIVAL TIME by T. Malcolm Watson. Music by R. Corney Grain. Produced at St George's Hall under the management of Alfred Reed and R. Corney Grain 7 April, 1890 with *Tommy at College*. Withdrawn 19 July. Reopened 29 September with *Seaside Mania*. Withdrawn 29 November, 1890.

Donna Carmen . . . . Fanny Holland
Joyce Somers . . . . Kate Tully
Benjamin Braid . . . . Alfred Reed
Pepito/Gaspard . . . . J. L. Mackay
Charlie Kingsford. . . . . Avalon Collard

HIS LAST CHANCE an operetta in one act by Herbert and Ethel Harraden. Produced at the Gaiety Theatre under the management of George Edwardes 13 October, 1890 with *Carmen Up-To-Data*.

Alice Montrose . . . . Loie Fuller
Charles Chester . . . . G. T. Minshull

Played at the Gaiety Theatre 12 May 1892 as part of a programme for the benefit of Meyer Lutz.
Lizzie St Quinten (A) G. T. Minshull (C)

Produced at the Court Theatre October, 1893 with *The Other Fellow*.
Ellaline Terriss (A), Seymour Hicks (C)

Played subsequently as a supporting piece at the Royalty Theatre and the Princess's Theatre.

PIM POM an operetta by E. T. de Banzie. Produced at the Royal Princess's Theatre, Glasgow 21 February, 1890.

Major Styx . . . . Robert Courtneidge
Millie . . . . Charlotte Hamilton
Theophilus Freshun . . . . Charles Hildesley
Pim-Pom . . . . Agnes Oliver
Simpson . . . . Henry Wright

DAISY a comic opera in two acts by F. Grove Palmer. Music by Henry J. Wood. Produced at the Kilburn Town Hall 1 May, 1890. Revised by Otto Waldon and played 5 November, 1890 at the Royal Park Hall, Camden Town.

MATES an operetta by Walter Browne. Music by Hamilton Clarke. Produced at St George's Hall 27 March, 1890 at a matinée.

1891

Horace Sedger had seen fit to go to France for the score of *Captain Thérèse* and, much more successfully, for *La Cigale* with which he had brought comic opera back to the Lyric Theatre. *La Cigale*, based on La Fontaine's fable 'La Cigale et le Fourmi' by the top Parisian librettists Chivot and Duru, had been set by Edmond Audran, another with a great list of successes behind him including the unforgettable *La Mascotte*. On this occasion, however, Sedger was not prepared to trust the French piece as it stood and he not only had the book heavily revamped by Frank Burnand but employed Ivan Caryll to provide new songs and concerted pieces and to 'arrange' some of Audran's existing music. Caryll's contribution included two songs for the leading tenor as well as a lengthy second act finale and several pieces of orchestral music totalling, in all, nearly a third of the work's musical score. A little gavotte was also supplied by the conductor Lila Clay whose ladies' orchestra was featured on stage. As the show continued on its highly successful way more of Caryll's music was added and *La Cigale*, hybrid though it was, became enormously popular and held the stage right through 1891.

With one of his theatres profitably engaged with a foreign piece, Sedger also went overseas for a new piece for the Prince of Wales to fill the gap left by the disappointing *Captain Thérèse*. After the Christmas season of *The Rose and the Ring* he and the Carl Rosa presented *Maid Marian* by the American writers Harry Bache Smith and Reginald de Koven. Up to now, London had seen very little in the way of American works. *The Doctor of Alcantara* had been the sole representative of the 'comic opera' side, the rest of the trans-Atlantic offerings being dramatic or comic works illustrated with songs and variety turns such as Minnie Palmer's *My Sweetheart* and *My Brother's Sister*, *Hans the Boatman*, *Fun on the Bristol* and *A Trip to Chinatown*, all of which had pleased provincial playgoers far more than those of London.

Maid Marian was a different thing altogether, a fully-developed comic opera. It had been first produced in Boston by the famous Boston Ideal troupe and toured in their repertoire as *Robin Hood* with great success. In London, with its title altered to avoid confusion with pantomimes of the same name, *Maid Marian* played an uneventful three months. Hayden Coffin and American star Marion Manola gave fine performances in the leading roles and two of the songs, 'Brown October Ale' sung by Leonard Russell as Little John and 'Oh, Promise Me' sung by Violet Cameron as Allan a Dale, were highly successful, but *Maid Marian* did not catch the public imagination. The show marked the end of the Carl Rosa Light Opera Company. After the withdrawal of its American piece, the Company was disbanded and the Carl Rosa organisation returned to its original policy of touring grand opera. Horace Sedger continued on his own at the Prince of Wales Theatre where his first solo production was another French work, *Miss Decima*, a transfer from the Criterion. *Miss Decima* was an English version of the 'naughty' Parisian piece *Miss Helyett*. Like *La Cigale* it had a score by Edmond Audran, its book was adapted by Frank Burnand and it had additional music by Ivan Caryll. Although it did not attain the same popularity, *Miss Decima* ran for 191 performances in its heavily bowdlerised English version.

Audran was not alone in keeping the French musical from disappearing from the English stage. André Messager was twice represented in London during the course of the year, firstly with the rather operatic *La Basoche* which D'Oyly Carte presented at his Royal English Opera House as a successor to Sullivan's grand opera *Ivanhoe*. *La Basoche* was a charming piece and was well-received by the critics (except those who insisted that 'English opera' meant opera by English writers and not merely opera in the English language), but it did not run and when it foundered Carte's grandiose scheme foundered with it. Soon his beautiful new opera house was a music hall.

Messager's other work, *Fauvette*, was altogether lighter. Its appearance in London was brief as it had been produced as part of the touring baggage of Horace Lingard's touring company (in repertoire with *The Old Guard* and Lecocq's *Pepita*). For Lingard London was a touring date and *Fauvette* was merely given a short season at the Royalty before continuing round the country. Although the French contribution was considerably more prominent now than it had been for a number of seasons, the new British works were by no means overshadowed. At the Gaiety, George Edwardes continued the run of *Carmen Up-To-Data* and extended his field of action by taking the Opera Comique for a new burlesque of *Joan of Arc*. The receipts for *Carmen* dropped noticeably as the summer approached and it became obvious that it would not hold out until the peripatetic *Ruy Blas* company returned from Australia. Edwardes closed the show and sent it on tour. Two weeks later *Joan of Arc* left the Opera Comique and followed suit. By September the road was overflowing with companies presenting Gaiety burlesques. The two newcomers were accompanied by Auguste van Biene's second *Carmen* company, as well as his productions of *Ruy Blas* and *Faust Up-To-Date*, Rollo Balmain's *Miss Esmeralda*, a second *Joan of Arc* (Odoardo Barri) and a *Little Jack Sheppard* (J. J. Dallas). If *Joan of Arc* was not strictly a Gaiety burlesque it was soon to become one, for once the planned works and redecoration had been done at the Gaiety Theatre, Edwardes opened it with a revised version of the Opera Comique show. It was warmly received and when the overseas company returned with their new piece *Cinder-Ellen Up Too Late* it was still playing to good houses. Edwardes organised a shuffle and transferred his highly successful triple bill programme from the Shaftesbury (on which he had taken a twelve-month lease) and moved *Joan of Arc* into that theatre where it ran out the last weeks of its long life.

Joan of Arc was the work of actor John Shine and 'Adrian Ross', the young author who had written the book and lyrics of *Faddimir* as 'Arthur Reed'. John Shine had a long and successful career in the theatre behind him – fifteen years as an actor, ten of which had been spent in and out of the West End in plays and in musicals such as *Dick*, *Pocahontas*, *The Lady of the Locket* and *Billee Taylor* in leading comedy roles. He had also been active in management including a period in partnership with John Hollingshead during the unsuccessful attempt to run the Empire as a latter day Alhambra, and a disastrous season at the Globe, as well as the running of a number of tours. He was not known as a writer but, having as his collaborator the bright young Arthur Ropes (now and henceforth to be known as Adrian Ross), the actual writing was spared him and his knowledge of the comic opera and burlesque stage was invaluable to his inexperienced partner. The music for the show came from another new name, Dr Frank Osmond Carr, a thirty-three-year old Yorkshireman and Bachelor of

Arts/Doctor of Music graduate from Cambridge. He had used the pseudonym of 'Oscar Neville' in his venture into the less academic side of music as the composer of his Cambridge colleague's *Faddimir*, a collaboration which earned them the commission from Edwardes to work with Shine on *Joan of Arc*. Edwardes put together a consortium to produce the £9,000 required to mount the show and the subscribers included actor William Terriss, agent C. J. Abud, publisher Ascherberg and Messrs H. E. Barnes, E. J. Conlon and C. Campbell as well as Edwardes himself. Shine, who was soon to be declared bankrupt over the *Glass of Fashion* debâcle at the Globe, was not financially involved and was obliged to divest himself of even his author's interest in the show when his affairs came before the courts during the run of the show. Now that he was involved with a show which was a financial success it was too late for him.

The run up to *Joan of Arc* had presented several problems, not the least of which had been the character and casting of the title role. With one company away in Australia and a second involved in *Carmen* at the Gaiety, Edwardes' usual supply of leading ladies had run short. Among his first thoughts was the young Loie Fuller who had taken over from Letty Lind in *Carmen* with some success but Miss Fuller had finished with acting for the moment. She was on her way to becoming 'La Loie', the 'original' and certainly the most celebrated of the serpentine dancers. Alice Atherton (Mrs Willie Edouin), a veteran of the old burlesque, was also considered but the final choice fell upon another experienced performer, Emma Chambers, recently returned from a long spell abroad.

The first night was a rocky affair. Firstly the débutante Florence Monteith, cast in the small featured role of the Duchesse d'Alençon, fell ill and since she was insufficiently covered her part had to be cut out completely for the occasion. John Shine was struck down with laryngitis, but his role being of primary importance he played, although often all but inaudibly. A more serious problem was caused by a 'leak' of the show's content. The press had mentioned that the new show would include some references to the recent labour troubles and several prominent socialists immediately let it be known that they would be on hand for the first night to see what attitude would be taken to their strikes. Neither they nor a partisan portion of the gallery were at all pleased at what *The Era* described as 'an injudicious attempt to make capital out of the great labour question and the right of the British workman to strike when he doesn't get exactly as he wants'. The 'committed' section of the audience forgot that they had, in theory, come to see a show and hissed and howled their way through the last 20 minutes. Another, lesser, controversy concerned the costume worn by Alma Stanley in the boy role of Talbot. Miss Stanley wore black tights, but the costume designer had not added the customary trunks and the effect was, to Victorian eyes, rather startling.

The book which Shine and Ross had evolved was scarcely the story of the historical Maid of Orleans. In fact the authors made a special disclaimer in a preface acknowledging that the well-known characters were merely names upon which to hang the song, dance and comedy material:

> Not her who wrought the great deliverance
> And beat our fathers backward long ago–
> Not her upon our stage we seek to show
> The patriot peasant maid, the soul of France.
> We do but hang our web of song and dance
> Upon the vantage of a name you know
> Bid modern jests through ancient visors flow
> Bid players' fingers wield the knightly lance

In this version Joan is a village maiden of Do-re-mi (a cue for song), whose father is obliged to entertain the impecunious King Charles who is en route with his court to Monte Carlo where he hopes to win back some of the fortune he has spent combating the English. Joan is known for her visions and the King thinks she may be able to 'vision' him a system to break the bank but Joan's vision, less prosaically, leads her to the Great Sword of Charlemagne. She presents it to her lover, de Richemont, Constable of France, and encourages the king to go to war. The second act takes place in the English camp and involves Joan and de Richemont in a set of disguises and songs, while the third represents the execution of Joan. This was where the 'strike' section came in as, with scant regard for history, Joan is saved when all the English, including the headsman, succumb to their national disease and go on strike. Arthur Roberts as de Richemont had a speech where he harangued various groups representing the most perpetual of modern strikers in the fashion of John Burns. The *Pall Mall Gazette* reported:

> The audience listened to it for a while with patience. But the situation was not funny enough, for the disagreeable side of the scene was insisted upon far too strongly. The idea was in no way appropriate. Even in burlesque it seems a little bit pointless to bring on a crowd of characteristic English strikers in the market place at Rouen. There they were, in all their divisions – railway guards, policemen, postmen, 'dockers', colliers, messengers! It was too real, and the humour of it was imperceptible. No wonder then that the scene came to an end amid some very decided hooting and hissing. It was a great pity. The first act of the new piece had not been perfect but it was full of possibilities. The second act, however, had commenced so well that everyone had forgotten the shortcomings of the earlier portions of the piece and prophesied a completely successful ending. And then came this foolish strike scene and spoilt it all! Why was it ever allowed to go into rehearsal? It was absolutely certain to offend the sympathies of at least a quarter of the audience. But it is of no use crying over spilt milk. The scene was played on Saturday night and it sadly discounted the effect of the good work that had gone before. So there is an end of it. Of course the whole episode will be cut out, lock, stock and barrel; and Messrs Shine and Arthur Roberts will between them devise something far better to fill its place. Then *Joan of Arc* will be a different piece altogether.

Others, including *The Times*, found no fault with the scene, only with the noisy element of the audience, but there was no doubt that the whole affair had endangered the success of the show. But there was too much that was good in *Joan of Arc* for it to be sabotaged by such an incident. Arthur Roberts was at his best with the material the writers had provided for him and he scored heavily when he appeared dressed as Stanley to sing 'I Went to find Emin':

> I went to find Emin Pasha and started away for fun
> With a box of weeds and a bag of beads, some tracts and a Maxim gun,
> My friends all said I should come back dead, but I didn't care a pin
> So I ran up a bill and I made my will and I went to find Emin.
> I went to find Emin, I did, I looked for him far and wide,
> I followed him right, I followed him tight and a lot of folks beside
> Away through darkest Africa, though it cost me lots of tin,
> For without a doubt I'd to find him out when I went to find Emin!

The other hit number from the show was 'Round the Town', a coster duet which Roberts and Charles Danby milked for every bit of fun available:

> We're comin' in a sort of disguise
> For it's all to take the English by surprise

We ain't inclined to grumble
At a job 'owever 'umble
For we never minds a hatom what we tries.
Round the town, up and down,
Hanythink to hearn a honest brown
For to get a bit of bread
We will 'old your 'orse's 'ead
Or we'll carry all your baggage – round the town.

The rather 'in' topic of the quarrel between the writers Clement Scott and Sydney Grundy, over which the two gentlemen had expended a good deal of publishers' ink, came in for some particular guying along with other topics of the day. In another section the whole of the court of France, disguised as nigger minstrels, approached the walls of Orleans singing a 'coon' chorus 'De Mountains ob de Moon'. The whole affair was played as a nigger minstrel burlesque with Roberts taking the part of the inevitable male alto with a degree of broad hilarity. Then there was the dancing of Katie Seymour, the cultured singing of Grace Pedley, not to mention Alma Stanley and her tights. Adrian Ross had, however, not caught the normal tone of the new burlesque and his intelligence was apt to shine through a little too much for the average audience. *The Era* remarked:

> We sadly fear that Mr. Adrian Ross – we say nothing about Mr. Shine who probably knows better – is a believer in literary merit in burlesques. His verses are neatly written and some of the ideas in the libretto are dainty and refined – vastly too much so for an entertainment of this sort . .

Preconceptions of what ought and ought not to belong in burlesque (and in other musical theatre pieces) were quickly being eroded. The type of entertainment which Edwardes and his associates were providing had little to do with the classic burlesques of twenty years previously, but the critics, if not the public, anxious to pigeon-hole every new work, insisted on comparing the new with the old, and not all with their tongues so firmly in their cheeks as this *Era* critic. The same gentleman gave more approval to the music, remarking that Carr had 'exactly caught the spirit of burlesque'. Apart from the two hit numbers Roberts had another comic song, 'To that Effect', and Shine, in the role of the king of France, had his turn with 'Otherwise Engaged' as well as joining with Grace Pedley and Linda Verner in a trio on the eternal topic of 'Mother-in-law'. The comedy numbers were the most satisfying and also the most numerous although there was a ration of straight pieces for the heroine.

After the first night it was by no means a foregone conclusion that *Joan of Arc* would be a hit. There was clearly work to be done. Richard Barker, who had been paid the enormous fee of £300 to direct the piece, came together with the authors and the star to popularise the show. A number of basic changes were made. As the *Pall Mall Gazette* had predicted, the whole 'strike' sequence was immediately deleted and a new and less controversial ending tacked on in its place. Emma Chambers, who had proved a jolly but rather unimpressive Joan, was dropped and the Gaiety favourite Marion Hood brought in to play a more seriously slanted character. Roberts, Shine and Danby worked up their respective roles well and it soon became evident that the show was pulling in not only the Gaiety overflow but some of its audience. While *Joan of Arc* grew steadily in popularity, *Carmen Up-To-Data* was beginning to suffer. When *Joan* finally took *Carmen*'s place at the Gaiety it was a very different piece from that which had opened at the Opera Comique. The plot had been tampered with, the dialogue rewritten and up-to-dated everywhere, new business and new burlesques had been added including a take-off of Carré's much admired mime play *L'Enfant Prodigue* currently playing at the Prince of Wales. Roberts was joined in this by M. Marius who had taken over the role of the King from poor Shine, and who was also responsible for directing the new version of the show.

The biggest stir was caused by Roberts' replacement for 'Emin', a number entitled 'Randy Pandy, O'. It was clearly aimed at Lord Randolph Churchill who had left the cabinet after a stormy row with Lord Salisbury and gone off to South Africa for a big-game shoot. There was no doubt as to who was being guyed for his tantrums when Roberts sang:

I'm a regular Randy-Pandy, O
In the deserts dry and sandy O
With my big moustache I'm quite the mash
In the great Mashona-landy, O!

If the public loved it, Lord Randolph did not. His reaction on visiting the show was arctic and, when the song was repeated to him in fun at a party at the Rothschilds, he clearly showed he did not regard it so. Very soon the Gaiety received a communication from the Lord Chancellor requiring the song to be removed and 'Randy-Pandy, O' perforce became 'Jack the Dandy, O' without forfeiting its popularity. 'Round the Town', decorated with a lot of new business, held its place in public favour equally well alongside the new numbers and *Joan of Arc* played a highly successful three months at the Gaiety before moving on to the Shaftesbury and its final weeks. It also had an extensive British tour under the management of the teacher/composer Odoardo Barri and was a feature of the 1892 Gaiety tour to Australia where E. J. Lonnen starred opposite Marion Hood, E. H. Haslem and Robert Courtneidge.

The reason for the departure of *Joan of Arc* from the Gaiety was the production of the new Farren/Leslie show, *Cinder-Ellen Up Too Late*. Fred Leslie, who was also part-author of the piece, had been working on it for some time and had completed his work while on tour in Australia. His collaborators were W. T. Vincent, a long time friend and the author of a number of amateur pieces and, for the music, the increasingly popular Meyer Lutz. As the title indicated the show had been devised particularly for Nellie Farren, giving her a role which would allow her, for once, to get out of breeches and back into the clothes of her own sex. But London was not to have the privilege of seeing Nellie play Cinder-Ellen, a privilege denied to all but the citizens of Sydney and Melbourne where the show was first produced. Walter Raynham, who had travelled with the *Ruy Blas* tour, directed the production for a Melbourne opening followed by a short season in Sydney and Nellie triumphed, but she was already unwell and the sea journey back to Britain and a short continental break did not improve matters.

Cinder-Ellen had to go on without its star and the Gaiety gallery boys had to put away their banners for another day – a day which sadly was never to come. The title role of the new show was taken over by Katie James who had recently stepped in for the leading lady in a straight play and also for Jessie Bond in *The Nautch Girl*. *Cinder-Ellen* was her hardest salvage job yet. Following Nellie Farren was almost impossible.

Leslie and Vincent's story was very un-Perrault. Cinder-Ellen is an heiress who is kept in the dark about her prospects by her family and ill-treated by her two very beautiful sisters (Sylvia Grey and Florence Levey). Prince Belgravia discovers her financial potential and sets forth to woo her but his servant arrives first, wins Cinder-Ellen's heart and elopes with her. The second act finds the lovers in Covent Garden where they are finally caught by the heroine's father and she is sent off to boarding school to be educated into a wife fit for a Prince. The final act was the traditional ball scene which had the servant (Fred Leslie) turning out to be the true Prince and happily winning his Cinder-Ellen.

The whole was stuffed with irrelevancies, songs, dances, burlesques and topicalities in the latest style and staged with great liberality. Fred Leslie reported that the sets, costumes and staging, all made in Melbourne, had cost £3000, and when *Cinder-Ellen* made its début in that city it had shone with the splendour of a Gaiety opening. Both Melbourne and Sydney were delighted with their Gaiety show and Leslie expressed the hope that it might be able to go on in London without any alterations. It was a disappointed hope for, although script and songs reached production fairly intact and the Australian sets and costumes were still in use, that very necessary ingredient, the Ellen of Cinder-Ellen, was missing.

The newspapers agreed after the first night that perhaps this accounted for the lack of 'gaiety' in the show. Unlike Australia, London showed little enthusiasm for the newest Gaiety burlesque. It was not the fault of Katie James whom one particularly disgruntled critic singled out, admitting: '[she] acts no less buoyantly and sings much more tunefully than the absentee'. It was not the fault of Fred Leslie who sang and danced with all his accustomed might, dashed from one disguise to another and performed a hectic tumble down a trick staircase changing appearance in the process from a smart strip-off costume into another of rags. E. J. Lonnen as the Prince and Arthur Williams as the heroine's father fitted less well into their roles than had the elastic-legged and rubber-faced Fred Storey and that very particular comedian, Charles Danby, but they were Lonnen and Williams, two of the most facile comedians in London. Sylvia Grey and Florence Levey led the dances with a Riding Habit pas de deux which was as good as anything previously seen at the Gaiety and there was a pas de quatre featuring the 'big four' of the theatre's line-up, but somehow the mixture lacked the spice and sparkle of previous efforts. Above all, it lacked the one big song hit which had galvanised each of its predecessors.

Leslie had discovered one song which almost made the grade. In Australia he had come upon 'The Mirror Song' written by a local composer, J. A. Robertson, and he had delightedly interpolated it into his role, but 'Bright little Glass' was no rollicking comic song. It was

> . . the romantic pleading of a man who looks in the glass and chides time in a fanciful and fantastic manner, half playful, half serious . . .

ending sighfully:

> You are, when now your face I see
> More heartless than you ever were
> A bitter tale you tell to me
> Of sallow cheeks and scanty hair
> You tell me that my shoulders bend
> The light of youth has left mine eyes
> I cast thee from me, faithless friend.
> Lie there, false heart, no more to rise
> False little friend, hateful to me
> Never again your bright face will I see
> If in my heart long you would reign
> Learn to speak false when the truth gives pain

Lonnen as an excessively 'jolly' Prince sang 'What will you Have to Drink?' (Monckton[1]/Hood), danced a drunken dance and told of 'Teaching McFaddyen to Dance'. Katie James sang Lutz's vivacious 'Make the Best of It' (which rather epitomised her plight) and joined with Leslie in the duet 'So You Are' and another duo in which the two, dressed as costers, made merry with a pile of vegetables and a barrow which moved by itself. But none of these, though all well received and encored, proved the big number which *Cinder-Ellen* needed to give it a boost. The faithful Gaiety audiences came, of course, but Edwardes was aware that the show lacked more than just Nellie Farren. He cut the entire coster/Covent Garden scene, duet, special props and all, the three acts became two and the show was shortened enough to allow the addition of a curtain raiser, *The Lady in Pink*, an operetta by Ethel and Herbert Harraden who had previously provided *His Last Chance* for the theatre. But these alterations proved insufficient and houses weakened, particularly when the premature death of the Duke of Clarence plunged the country into mourning. *Cinder-Ellen* looked as if it would follow the Duke quite quickly, but Edwardes was saved by his own opportunism and one of his former dancing girls.

Miss Lottie Collins had appeared at the Gaiety several years previously in the tiny part of Mariette in *Monte Cristo Jr* before abandoning the theatre for the Mecca of the music halls. Her music-hall career had taken her to America where she had heard and bought a song of doubtful ancestry to add to her repertoire. She had the piece suitably anglicised and arranged by Richard Morton and introduced it at the Tivoli Music Hall on 7 November, 1891 as 'Ta-ra-ra-boom-de-ay[2]'. A demure verse led into an unexpected explosion and into a swirling high-kicking dance as Lottie hit the chorus, and the crowd went wild. The song and its singer were an immediate and amazing hit. The new star went into pantomime as Alice to the Dick Whittington of Millie Hylton at the Grand, Islington, and continued to play the halls with her hit song. The furore did not abate. Edwardes decided Lottie Collins might give the missing lift to *Cinder-Ellen* and engaged her to add one more to her nightly list of turns – the Gaiety. Between the acts Lottie rendered a 'Gaiety version' of 'Ta-ra-ra' which made capital of the song's almost ridiculous vogue and the Gaiety receipts shot up. The £40 per week[3] which Edwardes paid to Miss Collins proved a solid gold investment. Fred Storey came back to his original role as Prince Belgravia and scored as Lonnen never had in a part patently devised for Storey's quaint talents. Charles Danby, too, had returned in place of Williams and *Cinder-Ellen* was suddenly more of a show and, certainly, more of a success. Those who came to see 'Ta-ra-ra' found a show immeasurably better than that which had opened a couple of months previously. It settled in and carried through to the summer before being taken out on tour. Letty Lind, a leading lady at last, was now Cinder-Ellen and a delightful one at that, and she and Leslie and the rest of the company tried out new material here and there around the country until, in October, they were ready to re-open in London with a substantially different show.

The role of Prince Belgravia had become a 'boy' part and Maggie Duggan used it to introduce Millie Hylton's music-hall hit 'The rowdy dowdy Boys' and 'The Man who Broke the Bank at Monte Carlo'. With a 'dancing' Cinder-Ellen in Miss Lind, a new scena, 'Cinder-Ellen's Dream Waltz', was built in along with a simple solo for her not-

[1] a first Gaiety credit for Lionel Monckton.

[2] variously 'boom-de-re' (as in America) and 'boom-de-ray'.

[3] José Collins insists in her autobiography that it was £150. Since Fred Leslie was on £100 this, even to save *Cinder-Ellen*, seems unlikely.

very-large voice, the pretty tale of Oyuchasan, Belle of Japan. The most successful of her new songs, however, was a delightful song and dance duo with Fred Leslie 'I'm in Love with the Man in the Moon'. Leslie sang two new pieces, 'My Cigarette' and his own charming 'Love in the Lowther', a tale of dolls in a toyshop window; Danby sang of 'A beautiful Spot in the Country' and the Big Four danced a Quaker pas de quatre which metamorphosed into a can-can. There was little left of the Melbourne *Cinder-Ellen* beyond the Riding Habit dance, a few choruses and the duet 'So You Are'. The new version proved adequately popular. The casting of Miss Duggan proved a piece of bad judgement and Fred Storey was soon brought back in a specially created role, Lord Leatherhead, to add his inimitable dancing to the programme, but all in all *Cinder-Ellen* seemed to be going well enough. Then, quite unexpectedly, Fred Leslie died. At the age of thirty-seven he succumbed to typhoid. The Gaiety stayed dark on the night of 7 December and when it reopened the next night with Fred's understudy, George Minshull, it was with the unspoken conviction that *Cinder-Ellen*, shorn of both the stars it had been created for, had little life left in it. Ten days later it closed.

The Van Biene touring version starring Louis Bradfield and Kitty Loftus lasted a little longer. It was a severely bastardised version which mixed the best of Leslie and Vincent's work with a heap of pantomime tricks. Harry Phydora and Harry Barry played the dancing sisters, Frances Harrison was a straight Christmas Prince and Tom Ollives was introduced as 'Buttons'. This mélange, every ounce of the authors' originality drowned in 'tradition', deservedly proved much less popular than its predecessors and survived the town version by only a matter of months.

Gaiety burlesque was not the only British work to stand up to the return of the French and the *percée* of the Americans. At the Savoy, the bastion of British comic opera, a new work was required as *The Gondoliers* came to the end of its eighteen months' run but, for the first time since D'Oyly Carte had opened and the theatre with *Patience* nearly ten years previously, it was not to be a Gilbert and Sullivan piece. The stresses and strains which had existed and grown between Gilbert and Sullivan on the one hand and Gilbert and Carte on the other had finally come to a head with Gilbert accusing Carte of unlawfully appropriating money from the profits at the Savoy to pay for improvements – in this case a new foyer carpet – at the theatre. The cracks in the relationship became too large to be papered over and, when Gilbert took legal action over the affair, it was clear that the famous triumvirate could not continue. Whispers of the affair flew round town and *The Stage* (May 9) reported:

> *The Gondoliers* is, I am creditably informed, to be the last of the Gilbert and Sullivan series of comic operas. Mr Gilbert states positively, my informant says, that his collaboration with Sir Arthur Sullivan is at an end. The reasons for this decision . . . are partly personal, but are chiefly concerned, I believe, with the opening of the new theatre in Shaftesbury Avenue by Mr D'Oyly Carte . . .

There was truth in it. Gilbert had little patience with Sullivan's wish to write a grand opera and had refused to have any part in it, while Carte had supplied the lavish new Royal English Opera House for *Ivanhoe* to make its début. But the breach between Gilbert and his partners was no sudden thing. If he had not withdrawn from the collaboration it is quite possible that Sullivan, who was finding it increasingly difficult both to work with Gilbert and to survive with his public attitudes and behaviour, might himself have been forced to end the partnership. Sullivan was not well, and surviving in harness with Gilbert was too much for someone who was ill-equipped, mentally and physically, to take all the stresses it entailed.

Whatever the different reasons, matters came to a head in the 'Carpet Affair', and when *The Gondoliers* came to an end there was no new Gilbert and Sullivan piece to take its place. Carte was obliged to find new authors. The composer to whom he went, probably on the advice of Sullivan, was Teddy Solomon. Solomon had been relatively quiet since *The Red Hussar* although it had been rumoured that he was working with Henry Pettitt on a version of the ballad 'The Bailiff's Daughter of Islington' as a comic opera, and only a few short works had been seen on the stage. Most of these had been written in collaboration with F. C. Burnand, but it was not Burnand who was selected to take the place of Gilbert at the Savoy. That choice fell on the Nottingham writer and journalist, George Dance. Twenty-six years old, Dance's main contribution to the musical theatre to date had been the burlesque extravaganza *Oliver Grumble* written for Willie Edouin and played at the Novelty Theatre in 1886.

Following Gilbert and Sullivan looked like a thankless task. The new collaborators seemed to have very little chance of either popular or critical success but they rose to the challenge in an unexpectedly brave fashion and, when their show *The Nautch Girl* opened at the Savoy, it met with warm acceptance:

> Seldom have the author and composer of a new comic opera had to undergo so severe an ordeal as that awaiting Messrs Dance and Solomon at the Savoy Theatre on Tuesday evening. They were met by difficulties from all sides. They had to challenge comparison with an author and composer who in a long series of productions had reached the highest pinnacle of fame. The Gilbert and Sullivan operas have been unlike all others. From *The Sorcerer* to *The Gondoliers* they have occupied a position positively unique. Mr W. S. Gilbert created an operatic world of his own in which ordinary traditions of life were turned topsy-turvey, and Sir Arthur Sullivan caught the moods of his librettist so perfectly that it seemed impossible to think of a Savoy opera in which their brilliant gifts were not combined. It was therefore the best possible way of getting out of a difficulty that both a new librettist and a new composer should try their hands at a Savoy opera. It was a bold plan but, under such circumstances as Mr D'Oyly Carte was placed in, it was the only one that presented any chance of success. Audiences at the Savoy have been so accustomed to a special kind of production that there was a danger of disappointing them by too abrupt a departure from their former style of opera, and in planning the new work this has been kept in mind. It would have been folly to attempt a direct imitation of Gilbert and Sullivan style. That would have led to certain failure. We may however congratulate all concerned on having steered the Savoy barque through the shoals and quicksands of criticism and public opinion by the production of a comic opera having all the elements of popularity while differing in many important respects from those which have made the theatre so famous . . . . a clear, bright, picturesque and amusing libretto, well laid-out for musical purposes and affording excellent opportunities for brilliant scenic illustration. The composer has happily followed with graceful and flowing melodies well-conceived and having the Eastern character suitable to the subject. Nor is there lacking in the music of Mr Solomon the grotesque humour and quaintness which formed such a captivating feature of the scores of Sir Arthur Sullivan . . . . the attractive libretto [is] graced with pleasing lyrics well adapted for musical purposes by Mr Frank Desprez who has introduced some pleasing touches of sentiment to contrast with the humorous portions. . . . (*Era*)

George Dance had certainly turned out an exceptionally clever libretto. His tale, set in the Indian Ruritania of Chutneypore, had more than a touch of the Gilbertian about it while remaining sufficiently individual.

Indru, son of the Rajah of Chutneypore, has fallen in love with Hollee Beebee, the principal dancer of Baboo Currie's Nautch dance troupe, but being a Brahmin and she of a lower caste, he cannot marry her. Indru has decided to renounce his caste by 'eating a little potted cow' when Beebee explains that she too was once a Brahmin but lost her caste under dubious circumstances:

B: Forty years ago my father, a respected Brahmin, was crossing a river; the boat capsized; a man on the bank threw a rope and hauled him ashore.
I: His life was saved?
B: Yes, but his caste was lost.
I: How so?
B: The man on the bank was a Pariah, and the Court held that the taint of dishonour was communicated from him to my father down the rope.
I: What a pity he didn't slip on a pair of gloves before grasping it.
B: He appealed against the decision, and the case has been pending ever since. We were once a wealthy family but all our possessions have been squandered in Court fees and legal refreshers. It was to pay for Counsel's opinion on a technical point that I took an engagement as a Nautch dancer.
I: Brave girl! But why this endless delay?
B: We have been most unfortunate. First of all one of the Jury died, and they had to go through it all again; then our Counsel took Scarlet Fever—and then, to vary the monotony, the Counsel on the other side took Yellow Fever. Then one of the officials absconded with the brief; then they lost the shorthand notes; and so it has gone on for forty years.

As soon as Indru has renounced his caste the lovers are married. But Beebee's case comes to judgement, she wins and is declared a Brahmin. The law of the land has been broken and their arrest is ordered. Beebee flees with Baboo's troupe which is setting off for a European tour, but Indru is captured and imprisoned. The Rajah himself is a kindly man who suffers from 'an excess of Consanguinity' and has surrounded himself in all the salaried posts of his establishment with cousins of varying degrees. His consanguinity also prevents him from 'shopping' his most hated relative, Pyjama, now Grand Vizier, who once committed the outrage of stealing the diamond eye from Chutneypore's national idol:

> . . [he] sold it to an Englishman who travelled in curios for a London firm. We instantly despatched a High Priest and a couple of Thugs to recover the precious jewel. They pursued it through many vicissitudes, but missed it at every turn. They traced it first to the diamond merchant in Hatton Garden; but the day before they arrived his safe had been broken open and the diamond stolen by a well-to-do burglar who, for better security deposited it at his bankers, whose head cashier promptly absconded with the Idol's eye in his portmanteau to Spain. On the journey the train was robbed by a party of brigands whose leader, a fine, fearless, free-shooting fellow was about to start for the Spanish Exhibition at Earls Court, of which he was to be one of the chief attractions. He ultimately became a lion of the London season and gave the diamond to a Countess whose husband, being dissatisfied with her story that she found it in the folds of her train after a scrimmage at a drawing room at Buckingham Palace, flung it in a rage out of a back bedroom window into a mews where it was picked up and swallowed by an enterprising Cochin China fowl, who was killed next day. It was discovered by the cook in dressing the bird; she gave it to a policeman, who gave it to a housemaid, who gave it to a Life-Guardsman, who gave it to a pretty parlour maid who gave it to a young gentleman just home from Eton against whom she very soon afterwards entered an action for breach of promise. After a vain attempt to convince the court that his letters had been written by a foster brother of whom he was the identical image, the youth fled with the diamond to other

> climes. He was last heard of in the interior of Africa where he has evaded our emissaries and twice escaped being 'rescued' by private expeditions sent out by the English. .

The Rajah's legal system, however, will not allow him to extend consanguinity to the mitigation of Indru's crime, and he condemns his son to death. But the Prince is helped to escape by his 'cousin', Chinna Loofah, who is constantly finding 'affinities' for various gentlemen, the most recent of whom is Indru. In the meanwhile, Pyjama is busy causing trouble. He has left an anonymous letter for Bumbo, the Idol, telling him of Indru's disgrace and demanding that Punka be shorn of his Rajah-hood as a condemned man's father, in favour, of course, of Pyjama himself. Bumbo, who has sat 2000 years on his shelf, comes to life and orders both Punka and Indru to be thrown to the crocodiles. Faced with such an extremity Punka conquers his consanguinity sufficiently to get all the hated 'cousins' included in the order. Only Chinna Loofah who has discovered a mutual 'affinity' with Bumbo is excused. But Currie Baboo has arrived back home with the leftovers of his troupe, including Beebee who wears around her neck a lovely diamond left at a European stage door by an anonymous admirer. It is Bumbo's missing eye and the overjoyed Idol grants her wishes. Indru and Punka are saved, the exposed Pyjama duly punished and Bumbo returns to his shelf complete with his eye and with Chinna Loofah turned to wood beside him on the principle that it is better to be a wooden bride than nobody's bride at all.

The songs included many bright and clever numbers. Frank Desprez provided an 'Idol' song for Bumbo which caused much amusement:

> When a fashionable tenor in a fascinating way
> Unutterably yearning just evades his upper 'A'
> Then ladies of all ages sit and simper, stare and sigh
> And adore his locks luxuriant and deep and rolling eye;
> But as middle age approaches and he takes to singing flat
> And is getting rather bald and unromantically fat
> Then they transfer their devotion to some adolescent elf
> They have found another idol, that one's put upon the shelf

an 'Affinity' song for Chinna Loofah, a song and dance number which included various national dance styles for Baboo Currie and his girls, and above all a duet for Chinna Loofah and Bumbo describing life after marriage. Jessie Bond and W. H. Denny scored the hit of the show as they performed a comic carmagnole singing:

B: I shall flirt and fandangle though people may talk
Both: Vive, vive la liberté
B: Nor my idiosyncracy banefully balk
Both: Vive, vive la liberté
B: I shall find my 'affinities' just where I please
Both: Vive, vive la liberté
B: And if you object, I shall use Ibsenese
Both: Vive, vive la liberté
Vive, vive v'la ce qu'arrive
Vive, vive la liberté

The majority of the lyrics were, however, written by Dance, including a mammoth patter song for Pyjama on avoiding bad luck–

> The secret of my past success is simple in its way
> I carefully avoid unlucky actions night and day

I've never pared my fingernails on Friday in my life
I'd rather cross the river Styx than turn a table knife
I never from my house turned out a black-haired pussy-cat
And when I pass a squint-eyed girl, I always go like that!
And if I see a hunchback pass, I touch him when I'm able
And never since the most innocent days of childhood have I ever so far forgotten myself as to put my boots upon the table

and some very pretty, and much less banal than usual, romantic lyrics for the principal tenor, Indru (Courtice Pounds).

In *The Nautch Girl* Solomon achieved his most finished score. If it lacked something of the youthful vigour of *Billee Taylor* and was sometimes less skilled than parts of *The Red Hussar*, overall it was outstandingly his best effort. He had the enormous advantage for the first time of working with an exceptionally clever book, and lyrics of a bright and modern character, when time and again in the past the critics had taken his works to task for their poor libretti and some very good music had been wasted by the total failure of the books of such shows as *Lord Bateman* and *Virginia and Paul*.

Most of Savoy team were fitted with parts. Jessie Bond, now rising forty, had her best Savoy role as the comical Chinna Loofah and W. H. Denny a jewel of a part as the eyeless Idol. Rutland Barrington returned as the Rajah and Frank Thornton as the mean Vizier while Frank Wyatt swapped the Duke of Plaza-Toro for the cunning leader of the Nautch troupe. *The Gondoliers* had gone through a large number of prime donne after the departure of Geraldine Ulmar (now playing the lead in *La Cigale*), few of whom had played it for very long. It was one of these, the very young American Leonore Snyder, who was chosen as the delicious Hollee Beebee and she proved a good choice to play opposite the romantic Courtice Pounds.

During the course of the run Barrington and Miss Bond, tempted by the fortunes they could see their old colleague Grossmith making on the drawing-room circuit, came out of the cast to try their hand with a similar act. The experiment lasted only a few weeks before they returned to the refuge of *The Nautch Girl*. Otherwise *The Nautch Girl* ran uneventfully and successfully for two hundred performances at the Savoy. It was taken on tour in both that year and the following by Carte's touring companies, and what could have been a severe crisis for the Savoy and for Carte seemed to have been successfully surmounted. Gilbert and Sullivan were missed but it had been shown that the musical theatre and even the Savoy Theatre could survive quite well without them.

In the provinces very little in the way of interesting novelties appeared. Two young writers who would later make a mark produced works with brief lives. In Ireland librettist W. Percy French put on *The Knight of the Road* with music by W. Houston-Collison and at Bradford a piece called *In Summer Days* began a short tour which ended at the Comedy Theatre, Manchester where its composer, Clarence Corri, a member of the famous musical family, was musical director. There were many musicals touring, however. Besides the various Gaiety burlesque tours, there were three D'Oyly Carte companies performing the Gilbert and Sullivan repertoire to which a fourth with *The Nautch Girl* was added in August. Further comic opera was supplied by long-running tours of *Paul Jones*, *The Old Guard* and *Marjorie*. The hardy annuals *Jack-in-the-Box*, *Cissy* and the extravaganza *Randolph the Reckless* maintained their enormous provincial popularity, the last with some enterprising casting when the title role was played first by Vesta Tilley and then by Lady Mansel. The foreign musical was also represented on the road by the inevitable *Les Cloches de Corneville*, *My Sweetheart* and *Falka* as well as more recent pieces like *Pepita* and *Fauvette*, but the accent was heavily on the home product.

Amongst the year's shorter pieces a couple of new names of interest appeared. The 25-year old writer Harry Greenbank provided a libretto for *Captain Billy* which the Savoy's conductor, Frank Cellier set as a forepiece for *The Nautch Girl*, while *The Prancing Girl*, a fairly inept burlesque of Henry Arthur Jones' *The Dancing Girl*, had music by a third Bucalossi, Brigata, the son of the composer of *Les Manteaux Noirs*, who preferred to be known as Sgr Brigata. The greatest success of the year in the one-act field was achieved by a light-hearted little piece called *A Pantomime Rehearsal*, a skittish comedy concerning the antics of a group of society amateurs who decide to produce their own pantomime. The languid, the absurd, the over-enthusiastic and the haughty all came in for their share of the jibes in Cecil Clay's humorous treatment which was interspersed with songs composed by Edward Jones.

Cecil Clay was the brother of the late Frederic Clay, the composer of *Ages Ago* and *Princess Toto*, and he was also closely connected with the theatre through his wife, Rosina, a prominent member of the Vokes family of entertainers. He was an enthusiastic society man of the theatre and it was his idea to develop into a short musical comedy a charade which had evolved during a fashionable gathering at the home of Sir Percy Shelley some seven years previously. He allegedly had the aid of two other devoted amateurs, Eustace and Claude Ponsonby, in the writing of *A Pantomime Rehearsal* which turned out to be a triumph and earned him a perhaps not entirely deserved place in theatrical circles as well as a good deal of money. Jones, the composer, was an experienced London conductor who had spent five years with Wilson Barrett at the Princess's Theatre where his duties had included the composition of incidental music for such substantial pieces as *The Lights of London*, *The Romany Rye*, *The Silver King*, *Claudian*, *Hamlet* and *Hoodman Blind* and later, at the Lyric, for *The Sign of the Cross*, a score which included the hugely popular 'Shepherd of Souls'.

The original cast of *A Pantomime Rehearsal* was a strong one and, as the evident success of the little piece (the backbone of a programme including two short plays as well) grew, so did the stature of its leading ladies who included between times such established stars as Rose Norreys, Carlotta Addison and Phyllis Broughton. The two principal male roles were played by actors who were to find greater fame as writers: Weedon Grossmith, author of *Diary of a Nobody* and Brandon Thomas, soon to be famous for *Charley's Aunt*. The triple bill was first produced at Terry's Theatre and thence transferred by George Edwardes to, successively, the Shaftesbury, Toole's and the Court before being sent out on the road where, at one stage late in 1893, it was being performed by three companies under the aegis of Miss Cissy Graham, all on extended tours. Its life in London was unique: for a one-act musical to run as the feature of a bill for 438 performances in the West End was unprecedented – even *Trial by Jury* had not achieved a like record – and it gave rise to several other attempts to set up bills of small pieces, none of which succeeded. *A Pantomime Rehearsal* continued to survive after its principal run and it surfaced regularly over the years in both professional and amateur productions.

1891

0111 **JOAN OF ARC** a burlesque by J. L. Shine and Adrian Ross. Music by F. Osmond Carr. Produced at the Opera Comique under the management of George Edwardes and Les Entrepreneurs syndicate 17 January, 1891. Withdrawn 17 July after 181 performances and toured through Edinburgh, Liverpool, Birmingham, Bradford, Manchester and Glasgow (September 12). Reopened in a second edition at the Gaiety Theatre 30 September, 1891. Transferred to the Shaftesbury Theatre 22 December, 1891. Closed 15 January, 1892, after a further 106 performances.

Arthur de Richemont	Arthur Roberts
Charles VII	J. L. Shine (J. Ettinson)/Ernest Bantock/Claude Marius/E. J. Lonnen
Jacques d'Arc	Charles Danby/Edward Lewis/Fred Emney
Talbot	Alma Stanley (Ethel Blenheim)/Jenny McNulty/Agnes Hewitt/E. H. Haslam
Fill-up-The-Good.	Ernest Bantock/A. Rolph/E. D. Wardes/ Fred Emney/G. Moore
New York Herald	Ethel Blenheim/Agnes Hewitt/ Beatrice Baum
Mayor of Orleans	G. Moore/A. Rolph/H. Clarke
Joan of Arc	Emma Chambers/Marion Hood/Grace Pedley/Ada Blanche
Marie, Queen of France	Grace Pedley/Florence Monteith/Agnes de la Porte/Florence Dysart
Yolande of Bar	Linda Verner
Catherine of Rochelle	Phyllis Broughton/Alice Lethbridge
Isabelle d'Arc	Louise Gourlay/Maria Jones
Blanche d'Arc	Katie Seymour
Duchess of Alençon.	Florence Monteith/Alice Lethbridge/ E. Julian/Day Ford/Violet Monckton
add French Officer	Lily Harold/Louie Pounds
Aline	Violet Monckton
Dunois	Ruby McNeill/Louie Pounds

Pages &c: Louie Pounds, Ruby McNeill, Miss Fowler, Nita Elwyn, E. Ford, M. Fleury, Miss McAllister, Violet Durkin, Phoebe Carlo, E. Williams, A. Conway, Gertrude Capel, E. Goss, J. Davis, W. Westlake, Ada Bilton, Miss May, R. May, A. Dare, Beatrice Baum, Marion Willcox &c.

Dir: Richard Barker/Claude Marius; md: Frederick Stanislaus; ch: Willie Warde; sc: Harry Emden and Bruce Smith; cos: Percy Anderson

0112 **IN SUMMER DAYS** a comedy opera in three acts by Robert Blatchford. Music by Clarence Corri. Produced at the Theatre Royal, Bradford, under the management of J. Pitt Hardacre 2 March, 1891 and toured through Wolverhampton, Halifax, Nottingham and Manchester x2, ending 18 April, 1891.

M. Jacques	Arthur Watts
Count le Verrier	Charles Hildesley

Pedrillo . . . . Colin Coop
Roland. L. Winning
Gomez. W. Jones/W. B. Stephens
Isabel . . . . Agatha Birch
Lelia. Maggie Forbes Wilson
Chevalier de Tonans . . . . Walker Marnock
Count du Vivier. . . . . T. L. Wyatt
The Brat . . . . M. R. Morand
Reuben . . . . Jas E. Manning
Janet. Miss Turner
Celia. Haidee Crofton
Delia . . . . Effie Chapuy
with the Peri Troupe (Louise Lapham, Maud Hill, Nellie Boyd, Lillie Minette)

Dir: Paul Valentine; md: Clarence Corri; sc: Holmes and D. G. Hall; cos: W. G. Palmer (Wiffly Puncto)

113 **THE NAUTCH GIRL** or The Rajah of Chutneypore. An Indian comic opera in two acts by George Dance. Lyrics by George Dance and Frank Desprez. Music by Edward Solomon. Produced at the Savoy Theatre under the management of Richard D'Oyly Carte 30 June, 1891 for a run of 200 performances closing 16 January, 1892.

Punka, the Rajah . . . . Rutland Barrington/J. J. Dallas/W. S. Penley/W. S. Laidlaw
Indru, his son. . . . . Courtice Pounds
Pyjama, the Grand Vizier. . . . . Frank Thornton
Baboo Currie . . . . Frank Wyatt/Helier Le Maistre/Fred Storey
Bumbo, an Idol . . . . W. H. Denny
Chinna Loofah . . . . Jessie Bond/Kate James/Louie Rowe
Suttee . . . . Cissie Saumarez
Cheetah . . . . Nellie Lawrence/Edith Briant
Hollee Beebee. . . . . Leonore Snyder
Banyan . . . . Louie Rowe/Jose Shalders
Kalee . . . . Annie Cole
Tiffin . . . . Cora Tinnie

Dir: Charles Harris; md: Frank Cellier/Ernest Ford; ch: John D'Auban; sc: T. E. Ryan and Joseph Harker; cos: Percy Anderson

114 **CINDER-ELLEN UP TOO LATE** a burlesque in two acts by 'A. C. Torr' (Fred Leslie) and W. T. Vincent. Music by Meyer Lutz. Additional songs by Lionel Monckton, Georges Jacobi, Sidney Jones, F. Osmond Carr, J. A. Robertson, Walter Slaughter, Leopold Wenzel, Bert Royle and Basil Hood. First produced at the Princess's Theatre, Melbourne 22 August, 1891 by George Edwardes' Gaiety Theatre Co. on tour. Produced in London at the Gaiety Theatre under the management of George Edwardes 24 December, 1891. Withdrawn 9 July, 1892 and toured through Grand Islington, Brighton, Birmingham, Leeds, Liverpool, Manchester, Newcastle, ?, ?, Birmingham and Grand Islington (24 September). Reopened at the Gaiety Theatre in a second edition 1 October, 1892. Closed 17 December, 1892 after 314 performances.

Cinder-Ellen . . . . Katie James/Letty Lind
Linconzina . . . . Sylvia Grey/Adelaide Astor (Maud Wilmot)
Fettalana . . . . Florence Levey/Alice Lethbridge/Katie Seymour/Violet Monckton
Mrs. Kensington Gore . . . . Emily Miller/Maria Jones/Miss Holmes
Miss Longacre . . . . Miss Holmes/*out*
Lord Taplow . . . . Maud Hobson/Florence Lloyd
Lord Eastbourne . . . . Blanche Massey/Ethel Earle
Lord Soho. . . . . Hetty Hamer/Louie Pounds
Lord Whitefriars . . . . Madge Dunville/Florence Henderson/*out*
Sir Peterborough Court. . . . . Maud Boyd/Violet Durkin
Sir Waterloo Bridge. . . . . Janet Norton/Ivy Herzog/Bob Akers/Lilly Harold

Catherina . . . . Lillian Price/*out*
Grazina . . . . Maud Wilmot/Alice Gilbert
Furnivalzina . . . . Violet Monckton/*out*
Griffina . . . . Eva Greville/Emily Robina/Violet Monckton/Bob Robina
Victorina . . . . Lily McIntyre/Topsy Sinden
Templina . . . . Adelaide Astor/Miss Maud
Prince Belgravia . . . . E. J. Lonnen/Fred Storey/Maggie Duggan/Florence Lloyd
Sir Ludgate Hill . . . . Arthur Williams/Charles Danby
Peckham . . . . Mr Harris/Mr Barry
Gnorwood . . . . Mr Walker/E. D. Wardes
Footman . . . . Mr Hill
A Servant . . . . Fred Leslie/G. T. Minshull
Pages . . . . Phoebe Carlo/E. Goss
Claire Solomon/Lillian Sedgewick
add Mrs Bayswater . . . . Kate Welwyn
Lord Blackfriars . . . . Lilly Harold/Miss Farrington
Lord Leatherhead . . . . Fred Storey
Charles Holywell . . . . Arthur Playfair
Miss Ascherbergina . . . . Miss Norina

Dir: Walter Raynham; md: W. Meyer Lutz; ch: Katti Lanner and Willie Warde/Mariette D'Auban; sc: E. G. Banks; cos: Mrs Fisher and Alias/Wilhelm and Hugh Patterson

Australian cast: Nellie Farren (C-E), Sylvia Grey (LINC), Florence Levey (FETT), Miss L. Holmes (MRS), Grace Pedley (TAP), Ethel Blenheim (EAST), Grace Wixon (SOHO), Nita Elwyn (WHITE), Madge Dunville (WB), Janet Norton (TEMPLE COURT), Fred Storey (PCE), Charles Danby (LH), Mr Harris (PECK), Mr Webb (GN), Fred Leslie (SERV). Dir: Walter Raynham; md: Sidney Jones

A PANTOMIME REHEARSAL a musical comedy in one act by Cecil Clay. Music by Edward Jones. Produced at Terry's Theatre under the management of George Edwardes 6 June, 1891 in a triple bill with *A Lancashire Sailor* and *A Commission*. Transferred to the Shaftesbury Theatre 3 August, to Toole's Theatre 19 October and to the Court Theatre 3 December, 1891. Withdrawn 15 October, 1892 after a total of 438 performances. The programme was varied with *Good for Nothing*, *Rosencrantz and Guildenstern* and *The New Sub*.

Jack Deedes . . . . Mr Elliot/C. P. Little
Sir Charles Grandison . . . . A. Danemore/Wilfred Draycott/C. P. Little/Frank Lacy/Mr Maxwell
Lord Arthur Pomeroy . . . . Weedon Grossmith/Compton Coutts
Captain Tom Robinson . . . . Brandon Thomas
Miss Lily Eaton-Belgrave . . . . Laura Linden (Sybil Grey)/Rose Norreys/Phyllis Broughton/Ellaline Terriss
Miss Violet Eaton-Belgrave . . . . Edith Chester/Decima Moore/Sybil Grey
Lady Muriel Beauclerc . . . . Helena Dacre/Beatrice Lamb/Carlotta Addison/Gertrude Kingston
Miss May Russell-Portman . . . . Ruby Tyrrell/May Palfrey
Rose Russell-Portman . . . . Miss Tyrrell/Maude McNaught/Agnes Lorraine
Tomkins . . . . Mr Jolinson/Mr Vaughan
Lady Sloane-Willery . . . . Day Ford/Agnes Lorraine/Lizzie Ruggles
Parker . . . . Lizzie Ruggles

Md: Edward Jones

Produced at the Court Theatre in an expanded form 20 January, 1893 with *The Judge and the Burglar* and *Over the Way*. Withdrawn 25 February.
C. P. Little/Mr Elliot (JACK), Wilfred Draycott (CH), Weedon Grossmith (ARTH), C. H. E. Brookfield (TOM), Ellaline Terriss/Sybil Grey (LILY), Eva Moore (VIO), Irene Rickards (MUR), May Palfrey (MAY), Ethel Wilson (ROSE), Mr Quinton (TOM). Ch: Mme Marie

Produced at the Palace Theatre 15 December, 1913 as part of a variety bill.
Frederic Norton (JACK), Alfred Drayton (CH), Weedon Grossmith (ARTH), Robert Horton (TOM), Gwendoline Brogden (LILY), Dorothy Selbourne (VI), Muriel Barnby (MU), Eileen Temple (MAY), Alice Mosley (ROSE), Duncan Druce (FREDERICK). Dir: C. P. Little and Weedon Grossmith; sc: W. T. Hemsley

Played at Her Majesty's Theatre 17 December, 1918 for the benefit of the King George Actors' Pension Fund.
Kenneth Douglas (JACK), Charles Hawtrey (CH), Weedon Grossmith (ARTH), Robert Horton (TOM), Iris Hoey (LILY), Marjorie Gordon (VI), Ellis Jeffreys (MU), Fay Compton (MAY), Peggy Kurton (ROSE), Mrs Vernon Castle (S-W), Rutland Barrington (TOMK). Dir: Weedon Grossmith

Produced at the Fortune Theatre by the People's Theatre 29 December, 1930 with *A Christmas Carol.*
Ernest Thesiger (JACK), Martin Walker (CH), Sebastian Smith (ARTH), Thomas Weguelin (TOM), Elizabeth Maude (LILY), Pamela Carne (VI), Sydney Fairbrother (MU), Joan Anderson (MAY), Isobel Grant Douglas (ROSE), Richard Hurndall (FOOTMAN), Jean d'Arcy (S-W). Dir: Norman Page

LOVE AND LAW an operetta in one act by Frank Latimer. Music by Ivan Caryll. Produced at the Lyric Theatre under the management of Horace Sedger 4 March, 1891 as a forepiece to *La Cigale*. Withdrawn 12 December, 1891.

Lord Belgravia . . . . Michael Dwyer/John Peachey
Mr Robert Sheepskin . . . . George Mudie
Lady Belgravia . . . . Annie Schuberth
Miss Justinia Taper . . . . Adelaide Newton

Md: Ivan Caryll

KILLIECRUMPER an entertainment in one act by T. Malcom Watson. Music by Edward Solomon. Produced at St George's Hall under the management of Alfred Reed and R. Corney Grain 30 March, 1891 with *Then and Now* replaced by *Dinners and Diners* and then by *The Diary of a Tramp*. Withdrawn 18 July. Reopened 5 October. Withdrawn 17 November, 1891.

Mrs Alexander . . . . Fanny Holland
Commodore Bunnett . . . . Arthur Wilkinson
Killiecrumper . . . . Alfred Reed
Lady Muriel . . . . Isabelle Girardot
Lord Abernethy . . . . Avalon Collard

CAPTAIN BILLY an operetta by Harry Greenbank. Music by François Cellier. Produced at the Savoy Theatre under the management of Richard D'Oyly Carte 24 September, 1891 as a forepiece to *The Nautch Girl*. Withdrawn 16 January, 1892. Represented February 1, 1892 with *The Vicar of Bray*. Withdrawn 18 June, 1892.

Captain Billy . . . . Helier Le Maistre/W. S. Laidlaw
Christopher Jolly . . . . Charles Rose
Samuel Chunk . . . . Rudolph Lewis
Widow Jackson . . . . Rosina Brandram/Agnes Scott
Polly . . . . Decima Morre/Cissie Saumarez/Jessie Moore/Janet Watts/Florence Easton

THE FIFTEENTH OF OCTOBER a farcical military operetta in one act by Vanloo and Leterrier. Music by Georges Jacobi. Produced at the Prince of Wales Theatre 8 August, 1891 as a forepiece to *L'Enfant Prodigue*. Withdrawn 29 October, 1891.

Durandal . . . . Leonard Russell
Capier . . . . George Marler
Larry Owen . . . . Harry Parker
Miss Camille . . . . Cissy Cranford

THE OLD BUREAU an entertainment in in one act by H. M. Paull. Music by Alfred J. Caldicott. Produced at St George's Hall under the management of Alfred Reed and R. Corney Grain 18 November, 1891 with *The Diary of a Tramp* replaced by *A Fancy Dress Ball.* Withdrawn 19 March, 1892.

Lord Tolover . . . . Arthur Wilkinson
Charles Baddely . . . . Avalon Collard
Skipworth . . . . Alfred Reed
Nellie Hobhouse . . . . Nora Maguire
Mrs Hobhouse . . . . Fanny Holland

THE PRANCING GIRL a burlesque in one act of *The Dancing Girl* by Campbell Rae-Brown. Music by B. Brigata (Bucalossi). Produced at the Prince of Wales Theatre under the management of Horace Sedger 26 November, 1891 with *Miss Decima.* Withdrawn 19 December, 1891.

Duke of Gooseberry . . . . Arthur Playfair
Hon. Slaughsy . . . . Tom Shale
David B-Hives . . . . Fred Emery
John Whiskison . . . . Harry Parker
Goldspink . . . . Arthur T. Hendon
Lady Boko . . . . Adelaide Newton
Midget Crake . . . . Natalie Brande/Cissy Cranford
Faith B-Hives . . . . Cissy Cranford/*out*
Priscilla B-Hives . . . . Ellis Jeffreys

1892

The early part of 1892 saw three of the four principal musical theatres in London ready for a change of programme. *The Nautch Girl*, *La Cigale* and *Miss Decima* all came to an end after successful runs and each was replaced by a British musical. At the Savoy, D'Oyly Carte chose another Edward Solomon piece, the eleven year-old *The Vicar of Bray* written with Sydney Grundy and first staged at the Globe Theatre. Since the original production, Grundy had become one of the foremost British playwrights of the time with hit plays of every type from the farcical comedy, both original and from the French, to the romantic play and the high drama, both alone and in collaboration with such other highly rated authors as Henry Pettitt, W. G. Wills and George Sims. His most successful play to date had been *A Pair of Spectacles* (1890), while *The Glass of Fashion, The Bells of Haslemere, The Arabian Nights, The Pompadour, The Union Jack*, *Mamma*, *Fools' Paradise* (originally called *The Mousetrap*), *Esther Sandraz* and *A Village Priest* had all helped to swell his reputation. During the decade since the first production of *The Vicar of Bray*, however, Grundy had only attempted one musical, the short-lived *Pocahontas* in 1884. He now revised his libretto for *The Vicar of Bray* and it was presented at the Savoy in January with Rutland Barrington in the role of the comic Vicar. The piece caught on rather better than it had at the Globe and held the stage until June, after which Carte closed the Savoy down for three months preparatory to producing his next new work in September.

This new work was also from the pen of Sydney Grundy. Since Gilbert had abandoned the Savoy and Sullivan, Carte needed a new librettist to team with the composer. His choice fell on Grundy and he attempted to sign the playwright for a series of comic operas, envisaging a repeat success of the kind he had had with Gilbert and Sullivan. But Grundy would not agree. Although he was quite happy to supply a libretto for Carte and Sullivan, he had no intention of following and being compared with Gilbert. The subject which he selected for his book emphasised this intention. It was the well-known romantic story of Dorothy Vernon, a slight and conventional tale of a puritan girl who elopes with her lover rather than marry the wealthy, sanctimonious husband chosen for her by her father. However, the resulting libretto was not, as the subject might have suggested, one of the old-fashioned sentimental school. Grundy took care to leaven the book with a certain amount of humour. He advanced the time of the story by a century, setting it among the Cavaliers and Roundheads of the Commonwealth days, and from the Puritan followers he made his comedy characters, giving them the satirical and vaguely topical portion of the play which had become so essential to the modern musical. The main part of the book, and more particularly of the music, was of a romantic and lyrical character with a good deal of recitative and much of the operatic about it but, although it was well-written and carefully adjusted to the taste of the time, it was not, in the sense that George Dance's *Nautch Girl* text had been, a Savoy libretto. It was the sort of material which Alfred Cellier of the *Dorothy/Doris* period would have seized upon thankfully, but it was not the kind of work which allowed Sullivan the opportunity to indulge in the musical comicalities of a *Mikado*.

Since *The Gondoliers* Sullivan's musical output had been of a very different nature. Firstly, there had been his grand opera *Ivanhoe* with which Carte had opened the Royal English Opera House, and then, in an equally serious vein, his music for Augustin Daly's production of Tennyson's masque, *The Foresters*. During this same period, Sir Arthur had suffered from a good deal of ill-health, and this too may have had an influence on his treatment of Grundy's far from inherently comic libretto. If Sullivan did not exactly let himself down with the score for *Haddon Hall*, he certainly did not display there the gaiety which had characterised his Gilbert operas. *The Era* was decidedly disappointed:

> The reputation Sir Arthur Sullivan has won by his charming operas and other musical works will not be increased by *Haddon Hall*, which will never take its place with such masterpieces of comic opera as the *Pinafore*, *The Mikado* &c. There is a want of freshness in the music which throughout is somewhat laboured and conventional . . . . for those who expect a companion to the delightful Gilbert and Sullivan combinations of the past, *Haddon Hall* will be a disappointing work. But for this no blame will attach to Mr Sydney Grundy. Few authors of the present day dealing with so slight a subject as the love story of Dorothy Vernon would have succeeded in making so attractive a libretto. The dialogue is smart and witty, and the lyrics admirably suited for musical purposes. Mr Grundy had a difficult task in following such a master of poetry and fun as Mr Gilbert, but he has accomplished his share of the opera in such a manner as to charm the audience and increase his fame as a brilliant and original writer, and he has done this without imitating his predecessor.

But not everyone was so firmly on the side of the librettist and many critics put the blame for the relative lack of success of *Haddon Hall* squarely and unfairly on the librettist who could not escape the inevitable comparisons:

> . . .while meriting praise on the score of clearness and, in some of the patter songs, humour, [the book] falls considerably below the standard of Mr Gilbert's work . . (*Times*)

Grundy maintained a dignified silence apart from one concise open letter:

> Sir – As a humble but sympathetic student of dramatic and musical criticism, may I venture to suggest that a short bill be introduced into Parliament making it a penal offence to supply the Savoy Theatre with a libretto? Having regard to the magnitude of the crime, the punishment – which should of course be capital – might be made at the same time ignominious and painful. Should the libretto be so impertinent as to be successful, I would respectfully suggest 'something lingering with boiling oil in it', if so humble a person as I may be permitted a quotation.
> Yours etc. Sydney Grundy.

Reviews, comparisons and correspondence aside, *Haddon Hall* was, as Grundy suggested, more than adequately successful. Its first night was greeted by a most enthusiastic reception and it continued to play to good houses for over two hundred nights. If the Gilbert and Sullivan die-hards missed the topsy-turvy element to which they had become so attached, there were plenty of light opera lovers who had supported the success of *Dorothy* to take their place.

Unlike *Dorothy*, however, *Haddon Hall* had no outstanding number nor did it have the charismatic presence of Marie Tempest at its centre. Lucille Hill, who had created the dramatic soprano role of Rebecca in *Ivanhoe*, took on the role of Dorothy Vernon supported by a company in which few of the well-known Savoy faces remained. Rutland Barrington was still there to play the Puritan Rupert Vernon with W. H. Denny as his Scots sidekick and Rosina Brandram was cast in the sympathetic but uncomical role of Lady Vernon. Her casting epitomised the different style of *Haddon Hall* as compared to its Savoy predecessors. It fell somewhere between the English grandeur of *Ivanhoe* and the merriment of Gilbert's musicals. It could not attain the popularity of the latter, but proved decidedly more to the public taste than the former during its six and a half months run and subsequent tours.

Following the separation from Gilbert it took Sullivan until September to see his first work staged. Gilbert was very much more quickly off the mark. Following the withdrawal of *La Cigale* at the Lyric, his newest piece, *The Mountebanks*, was produced on 4 January, 1892. On leaving Carte, Gilbert had little option as to which management to approach. As far as musicals went there were, of any stature, only the Gaiety which was deeply involved with a totally different kind of entertainment, and Horace Sedger who controlled the Lyric and the Prince of Wales Theatres where the policy under both his direction and the earlier management of Henry Leslie had always been one of light musical shows. So to Sedger he went.

If Gilbert expected to have everything his own way he was soon disappointed. Having prepared the libretto of *The Mountebanks*, he decided that he wanted it set by Arthur Goring Thomas. Thomas, then aged forty, was a Sussex-born composer who had been destined for a career in the civil service before deciding that music was his preferred sphere. He studied composition in Paris and at the Royal Academy and was at one time a pupil of Sullivan before producing the most notable English grand opera of the last part of the nineteenth century with *Esmeralda* (1883). He never again succeeded in equalling the popularity or quality of that work, although another opera, *Nadeshda*, gained a certain réclame. Thomas announced a move into the lighter sphere of musical theatre when he decided to set a version of Walter Besant's *The Captain of the Fleet* for the Carl Rosa Light Opera Company. After the demise of that wing of the company it was decided that the unfinished work would be performed by the Grand Opera Company instead, but the piece was slow to materialise. The eccentric composer's dilatory nature would not have endeared him to Gilbert but, as it was, Thomas turned down the *Mountebanks* libretto and at Sedger's suggestion it was offered to Alfred Cellier.

Cellier was in a poor state of health during his work on the score for *The Mountebanks* although his unfailingly sparkling music shows no sign of his illness and impending death. He was never to see a performance of *The Mountebanks*. The continuing success of *La Cigale* resulted in its postponement until early 1892, and eight days before the opening the composer died at the age of 47, without finishing the score. He had had a remarkable career from its adventurous and delightful early days with *The Sultan of Mocha* to the record-breaking triumph of *Dorothy*. Apart from these two outstanding pieces only *Doris*, *The Mountebanks* and *Charity Begins at Home* of his relatively small output attained West End runs, but Cellier's bright and artistic musicals earned him a place at the head of the English light opera field and resulted in that type of show winning and maintaining a prominence and popularity which might otherwise have been considerably less.

The Mountebanks was in no way a new departure for Gilbert. Its plot contained many elements which he had made use of in other works over the years and was based on his inevitable 'lozenge' theme which Sullivan had so often rejected since *The Sorcerer*. Uncharacteristically, its story was set in the banditti land which had been the home of so many musicals since and including *The Contrabandista*. Gilbert had visited an imaginary Venice for *The Gondoliers*, a kind of Japan for *The Mikado* and various non-existent parts of Britain for *The Sorcerer*, *Patience* etc., as well as the total Ruritania of *Princess Ida*, but he had never until now gone to that most over-used of locations. However, the liveliness of the author's invention did its best to overcome this initial handicap.

As in *The Sorcerer*, the first act of the piece is spent establishing the characters and their situations before the ending of the act presents them with the 'lozenge' which will change their characters and relationships. In this case the device is a potion which makes everyone be what they are pretending to be, a whimsical notion treated, since this is comic opera, on a physical rather than a metaphysical level.

The principal characters include Arrostino, a brigand chief, and his band who explain:

> Five hundred years ago,
> Our ancestor's next door neighbour
> Had a mother whose brother,
> By some means or other,
> Incurred three months' hard labour.
> This wrongful sentence, though
> On his head he contrived to do it,
> As it tarnished our scutcheon,
> Which ne'er had a touch on,
> We swore mankind should rue it!

The band have come down from their Sicilian mountains to take wives at the rate of one per day from amongst the village maidens. The first, Risotto, has just brought home his Minestra. News arrives that a Duke and Duchess are about to pass by and the inefficient band plot how they may relieve the nobles of their money for:

> I believe we have a vendetta against Dukes and Duchesses? The judge who sentenced the relation of our ancestor's neighbour would have been a Duke if they had created him one.

The bandits decide to disguise themselves as monks and the Duke is to be lured to their abbey by Minestra posing as a wounded old woman.

We now meet Alfredo, a handsome villager, who is in love with Teresa who is in love with no-one but herself as she modestly confesses:

> To be quite candid with you I have often wondered what people see in me to admire. Personally, I have a poor opinion of my attractions. They are not at all what I would have chosen if I had had a voice in the matter. But the conviction that I am a remarkably attractive girl is so generally entertained that, in common modesty, I feel bound to yield to the pressure of popular sentiment and to look upon myself as an ineffective working minority.

Alfredo in his turn is adored by Ultrice, the innkeeper's plain niece, who follows him around everywhere. When the innkeeper decides that he needs to practise his etiquette before the arrival of his noble guests, Ultrice jumps at the chance to impersonate a Duchess with Alfredo as her Duke. A band of mountebanks arrive amongst the locals.

Pietro and his performers Nita and Bartolo have a pair of automata, Hamlet and Ophelia, which they hope to sell to the Duke who is an aficionado of such things, but the dolls have been held up at Customs because they have no passports. Pietro encourages his artistes to take the place of the dolls until they can be hurried to the spot.

Suddenly there is an explosion. The old alchemist who lives on the first floor has finally succeeded in blowing himself up irretrievably and all he leaves behind, apart from the copper ha'pence he has been trying to turn into the rent money, is a bottle of 'magic' potion. Pietro inveigles Nita and Bartolo into taking some of it in order effectively to become the missing dolls. He dilutes it in his winesack and is horrified to see the rest of the company cheerily partaking of the drink. Everyone becomes what he pretends to be. The bandits are now monks, Minestra an old woman, Alfredo and Ultrice are nobles, Nita and Bartolo are clockwork dolls and Teresa, who had sarcastically fainted with love at the 'Duke's' feet, becomes besotted with Alfredo.

The second act presents everyone in his new guise. Pietro can restore all by the simple expedient of burning the label of the bottle, and he is anxious to do so as he pretended the potion was poison to stop the others taking it and he is now dying of the 'poison'. But Ultrice has stolen the label so that she may retain Alfredo and she is only made to relent when Teresa who has gradually gone mad threatens to throw herself off a mountain. The label is burned and all returns to normal as the curtain falls.

The libretto retained some of the Savoy feeling, but it belonged more naturally to Gilbert's pre-Savoy phase, being nearest in theme and construction to *The Gentleman in Black*, *The Palace of Truth* and *Creatures of Impulse*. Plenty of elements familiar from the Savoy pieces did intrude, however. The innocently vain Teresa was closely related to Yum-Yum and Patience, the mock *scène de folie* had already fallen to Mad Margaret, while Alfredo and Ultrice learning how to behave as nobility resembled the Gondoliers being instructed by Plaza-Toro. The device of the automata was one that had been used by other writers (*Rhoda*, *An Artful Automaton*) and, on the whole, *The Mountebanks* did not contain the degree of originality one might have expected of Gilbert. It was as if he had resurrected a fifteen year-old work and modernised it for the occasion. The writing, however, was in his characteristically piquant style and, although the libretto contained nothing to equal the work contained in *The Mikado* or *H.M.S. Pinafore*, it was in no way a disappointment to the critics. *The Stage* devoted three full-length columns to its fulsome review:

> Long before the curtain fell at the Lyric on Monday evening it was fully evident that in *The Mountebanks* Mr Sedger had secured a piece destined to take front rank among successful comic operas . . . . [it is] full of brightness and humour . . . [with a book] which in humour and in ludicrousness is advance of any that has preceded it . . . Though the mainspring of the action may . . . be to some without the charm of novelty, no-one can find fault with the ingenious and laughter-moving detail which the author has evolved in the story or with the polished verse and brilliant wit with which he tells it . .

Cellier came in for a share of the praise. He had written an attractive score which *The Stage* qualified as 'one of the best things, if not the best that he has done'. However, the inherent comicality of Sullivan was missing and Cellier's score was more in the line of his own previous successes than in the lighter and less scholarly manner of the newer composers. Left unfinished on the composer's death the score had been completed by the musical director, Ivan Caryll. He arranged an entr'acte from one of Cellier's themes and an overture from an early orchestral suite of the composer's, but the three numbers which Cellier had not begun to set were omitted from the performance although Gilbert's lyrics were printed in the book of words.

Two numbers earned particular favour; Arrostino's rousing 'High Jerry, Ho!':

The Duke and the Duchess as they travel through the land
With the clips of their whips and their high jerry ho!
Will pass by the rock where that monastery stands,
In a first-class fine-folk fashion,
With their high jerry ho!
Their postilion in vermilion
And the rattle of their cattle,
And their high jerry ho!

hardly a typical Gilbert lyric of the eighties or nineties; and Bartolo and Nita's comic duet as the clockwork dolls 'Put a Penny in the Slot':

If our action's stiff and crude
Do not laugh, because it's rude,
If our gestures promise larks
Do not make unkind remarks
Clockwork figures may be found
Everywhere and all around
Ten to one, if we but knew,
You are clockwork figures too
And the motto of the lot
'Put a penny in the slot'.

which gave opportunities for buffoonery from Harry Monkhouse and Aida Jenoure that savoured more of provincial variety musicals than Gilbertian sophistication.

The Mountebanks caught on well and Sedger sent out three touring companies. In London the grotesqueries of Gilbert and the pretty music of Cellier kept the doors of the Lyric open for eight months until *The Mountebanks* was replaced by *Incognita*, an anglicised version of Lecocq's *Le Coeur et la Main*. This, like *La Cigale*, had been given the Sedger treatment. Herbert Bunning and 'Yvolde' each contributed four pieces to a revamped book by F. C. Burnand and a ninth new piece, a quartet by Hamilton Clarke, made nearly a third of the work (and most of the third act) additional to the French original. It lasted 103 performances.

With *The Mountebanks* Gilbert maintained the run of successes he had established at the Savoy but he was considerably less happy with his second effort. *Haste to the Wedding* was an adaptation of Gilbert's own translation of *Un Chapeau de Paille d'Italie* which had been staged at the Court Theatre in 1873 under the title *The Wedding March*. At that time it had been suggested the piece was to have been a musical one, but in the event it was presented as a pure and simple 'English version'. Nearly twenty years later Gilbert took it up again and added some suitable lyrics to make it into a musical. He chose as his composer not a man of the calibre of Goring Thomas or Cellier, but his old Savoy colleague George Grossmith. Grossmith's experience as a writer of music was limited. He had composed a large amount of material for his own drawing-room entertainments, principally comic songs, duets and sketches, but his theatrical work had been confined to a few short operettas, the most successful being *Cups and Saucers* which had been staged as a forepiece at the Savoy, *Mr. Guffin's Elopement* for Johnny Toole, and *A Peculiar Case* given by the German Reeds in 1884. He had never attempted anything on the scale of *Haste to the Wedding*.

The farce of the Italian straw hat and the difficulties encountered by the young bridegroom whose horse eats the wretched object on his wedding day and obliges him on pain of being compromised to find the offended lady a replica, was a funny and long-lived piece. The sight of poor Woodpecker trailing through London with his provincial wedding party trotting everywhere behind him as he tries to escape an old entanglement and avoid new ones, get married and get the importunate and hatless Leonora out of his house before his bride and her family return, was indeed a humorous one. Whether it needed music was another question. That it did not need the songs it got was barely arguable. Gilbert produced some amusing lyrics, particularly in a song for Bella, the hatshop proprietor and an old flame of the groom, who explains how she lost him:

You offer to take me, one fine day,
To the Naval Exhibition;
You borrow the money from me to pay
The price of our admission.
The rain pours down on my brand-new dress,
And boots of thin prunella.
Do you stand me a hansom? Oh dear, no!
You stand me under a portico,
Like a shabby young fellow, and off you go
To borrow a friend's umbrella!

Like many a music-hall gentleman, Woodpecker returns not, while Bella passes weary months waiting under the portico. Another subsidiary character was supplied with a more Gilbertian number:

DUKE: Oh butcher, oh baker, oh candlestick-maker,
Oh vendors of bacca and snuff–
And you, licensed vittler, and public-house skittler,
And all who sell sticky sweet-stuff–
Ye barbers, and Messrs the Bond Street hair-dressers
(Some shave you, and others do not)–
Ye greasy porkpie-men–ye second-hand flymen–
All people who envy my lot,
Let each of you lift up your voice–
With tabor and cymbal rejoice
That you're not, by some horrible fluke,
A highly-strung sensitive Duke!
An over-devotional
Hyper-chimerical
Extra-hysterical
Wildly aesthetical
Madly phrenetical
Highly-strung sensitive Duke!

But the setting of the lyrics proved rather too much for Grossmith whose musical talent, though tuneful and amusing, was definitely on the small scale. The songs added nothing to the play and indeed, by breaking down the plot and slowing the pell-mell pace of the action, exposed the improbability of the situations. After a first night which evoked some wrathful comments from a disappointed audience, *Haste to the Wedding* survived only twenty-two performances.

Among the cast of *Haste to the Wedding*, which was headed by Frank Wyatt and

Lionel Brough in the roles of the groom and his father-in-law, some small part players were noticed. The composer's son George Grossmith Jr made his stage début in the part of Foodle, kissing cousin to the bride and a constant strain, therefore, to the hero's nerves. Young Grossmith gave a comical performance as the first of the fops and dudes with which he soon went on to make his name at the Gaiety and elsewhere. A Gaiety career was also in the offing for the young actress who played the tiny role of the bride. Lovely Marie Studholme landed her first musical role here after having been in the chorus of *La Cigale* and *The Mountebanks*. The more showy role of the Marchioness of Market Harborough went to another young actress, Ellis Jeffreys, who had started her career in the chorus, at the Savoy in *The Yeomen of the Guard*. She too had been in *La Cigale* as a principal understudy before coming to the Criterion, but her career, unlike her colleague's, would be largely on the straight stage.

If Sullivan without Gilbert and Gilbert without Sullivan had turned in a rather old-fashioned direction they had, by anyone else's standards, produced two worthwhile and successful shows. The comic opera side of affairs received reinforcement from two other plays during the year, one of which was the year's most unexpected success.

Cigarette was described as a 'light romantic opera' and its libretto was built on French opéra-comique lines by the hitherto unknown Barry Montour and E. Warham St Leger, billed as 'author of *Silver Gilt*'. It told how the son and daughter of two long-feuding families fall in love against the feelings of their parents. The Countess de Montrouget threatens to shut up her daughter, Violette, in a convent, while the Marquis de Portale promises to disown his son. The lovers refuse to be daunted and young Claude goes off to join the army while Violette enters the threatened convent. In the second act Claude, who has been wounded, is carried to the village where the convent is situated. He is tended by the vivandière, Cigarette, who has fallen in love with him. When Claude meets Violette again the jealous vivandière rings the convent bell, bringing the Mother Superior and the Countess to the scene to intervene between the lovers. In the final act Claude, for his valour, is presented with lands and a title by the Emperor. They turn out to be the lands and title of his father who has been stripped of his wealth for refusing to recognise the government. Claude returns the family estates to his father, and the elders give in and accept that the feud must end. As Claude and Violette are betrothed the faithful Cigarette returns to the army.

The music for *Cigarette* was written by Aberystwyth's J. Haydn Parry, son of a Penarth family born and educated in the United States. His musical talents had first been noted when an early composition won him a prize at the Liverpool Eistedfodd. Soon after he secured the post of assistant music master at Harrow and the organist's job at the parish church there. His theatrical output had been limited to an operetta entitled *Gwen* produced at the St James' Hall. *Cigarette* was his first attempt at a longer work and, under the patronage of the wealthy Mrs Bennet-Edwardes, it was arranged that it should be given a showing on a professional basis. The piece was rehearsed in London and made its first appearance in Cardiff in August on the occasion of the local Festival. It was received with an approval which prompted those concerned to continue and to try to find it a London showcase. The cast was kept together and *Cigarette* played a couple of weeks in Wales until the removal of *The Mountebanks* at the Lyric gave Mrs Bennet-Edwardes a chance to play it there for a few performances prior to the opening of *Incognita*. Once again it met with a favourable reception, particularly for Parry's score. *The Era* commented:

> Let us at once congratulate the composer upon the cordial and immediate recognition

> of his claims as a musician. . Mr Haydn Parry's music has the qualities to please. It has an endless flow of graceful melody with the dash of sentiment generally popular with English audiences. It is not essentially comic, and that is the reason probably why the composer calls it modestly 'a new light romantic opera'. It is certainly light and romantic but none the less it has claims to be called artistic and it is not often that a composer with no greater experience than Mr Parry succeeeds so well on his first appeal to a London audience . . . Mr Parry has not overweighted the score with ponderous instrumentation . . . He has trusted mainly to melody, and the pleasing songs and concerted pieces are fresh and tuneful . . .

The praise was well-merited. The score of *Cigarette* contained some of the most delightful music heard in London for some time. The soprano and tenor songs were models of the light romantic kind and the ensembles, notably the dramatic second act finale, rang with an almost operatic timbre. The unexceptional book drew strength from its music and from a genuine lack of pretentiousness.

In spite of the fact that *Cigarette* had come to town during the most inauspicious weeks of the year, it attracted good audiences and when the short series of performances at the Lyric was done it was decided to let the show run. Soon *Incognita* was ready to go on and *Cigarette* was still running strongly. Mrs Bennet-Edwardes decided to transfer and took her show across to the Shaftesbury Theatre where it continued for more than two months. When it finally closed at the beginning of the December, the piece which had been intended for two or three representations had totalled no less than 112.

It had, admittedly, reached its final performances in a rather different form to that in which it had begun. No less than half an hour had been cut from the running time during the Shaftesbury season and the comic stars Charles Collette (who also directed) and A. J. Evelyn had manoeuvred their comedy rivalry for the hand of Violette's maid into a prominent position amongst the show's romantic scenes. The cast had been strengthened by the addition of Geraldine Ulmar in the role of Violette and, all in all, *Cigarette* had been worked up from a successful start to an even more successful end. That end was cemented in a suitably happy event when Constance, daughter of the show's 'angel', became Mrs A. J. Evelyn the following April. Somewhat surprisingly *Cigarette* went no further. Talk of an American production proved groundless and a proposed tour did not materialise, but the final balance sheet for the show remained a positive one.

The Baroness was another light piece presented by an equally amateur management but with much less success. It was written and composed by Charles G. Cotsford Dick who had been responsible for the music for *Dr D* (1885) as well as for a number of operettas and songs, notably for the German Reeds. The story he selected was a piece of farcical nonsense concerning a Baron Narcissus who needs to lay his hands on a sum of money to ensure marrying the daughter of a Grand Duke. To this end he tackles a couple of rich uncles telling them, for some reason, that he is already married. The uncles take it into their heads to turn up and Narcissus passes off his intended's married sisters in turn as 'the Baroness'. The uncles take a fancy to the ladies and find themselves imprisoned for flirting. They escape in disguise and in the third act find their way to a palace masked ball where in a series of mix-ups, disguises, mistaken identities they stumble through to a happy dénouement. The piece was conceived basically to allow the two comedians (Lionel Brough and Fred Emney) the usual gamut of opportunities and the leading singers (Charles Conyers and Carl Rosa soprano Agnes Giglio, the daughter of Emily Cross) a series of very slight numbers. Any enduring value *The Baroness* might have had was given no chance to become established. After a fair first week the second found the treasury empty. There were no wages for the cast. They were asked to be patient and duly played the Monday performance but the next day it was evident that the money was not going to be forthcoming and *The Baroness* folded under the weight of public indifference and incompetent management. Amongst the cast in the small role of a bath attendant was the younger Grossmith. His first two roles had been in two of the quickest flops in recent years.

While the comic and romantic opera fields continued to show new and attractive works of no startling originality, there was a certain amount of innovation going on elsewhere. The death of Fred Leslie and the continued incapacity of Nellie Farren were putting at risk the new burlesque tradition for the rise and continued success of which they had been largely responsible. Only Arthur Roberts remained as a star of sufficient range, invention and popularity to fill out a burlesque built around him, and Roberts did not always show the application and integrity which Leslie had devoted to his Gaiety works. The crashes of *The New Corsican Brothers* and *Tra-la-la Tosca* had been redeemed by his great success under the forceful wing of George Edwardes in *Joan of Arc*, but that piece only served to emphasise just how fragile had now become the link between the nominal subject of a burlesque and the entertainment within it. It was only a matter of time before the pretence of parody and its physical decorations were ultimately swept away in a final step towards showing these 'variety show' musicals for what, particularly with a performer like Roberts around, they really were. George Edwardes' 1892 piece at the Prince of Wales took that step. Adrian Ross and James Leader collaborated on the libretto for *In Town* which put Arthur Roberts in the character of one Captain Arthur Coddington (a not very covert reference to the actor's well-known practical 'spooferies') in a modern social and theatrical milieu where the topicalities and comical songs in which he specialised sat much less incongruously than in a classical or burlesque setting.

Coddington is a man-about-town of limited means whose personality is his passport, most particularly among the aristocracy and back-stage at the Ambiguity Theatre, and whose living comes from performing commissions for his aristocratic acquaintances. On this occasion his patron is the young Lord Clanside (Phyllis Broughton) who is anxious to see 'town life' and for whom he arranges a luncheon with some of the girls from the theatre. Deceptions and disguises in the best tradition are necessary to keep Clanside's mother (Maria Davis) in the dark, for the Duchess is intent on keeping a prohibitive eye on the morals of her son, her daughter Gwendoline (Belle Harcourt) and above all her husband (Eric Lewis) whose wandering eye has caused her to sack Gwendoline's governess. But that governess (Florence St John) has now taken to the stage under the name of Kitty Hetherton and is leading lady at the Ambiguity. In the second act all the principals turn up back-stage at the theatre where more complications, disguises and a lot of turns of a more or less relevant nature occur before Kitty's hand is safely bestowed on the jolly Captain.

The setting of *In Town* allowed the producer to dress his actors and chorus in the height of modern fashion (a trend which had already proved popular in *Cinder-Ellen Up Too Late*) and the ladies of the audience could purchase such gowns from the same stores as the glamorous ladies on the stage while the gentlemen were quick to follow the sartorial eccentricities and innovations displayed by the star. The backstage sequences, as a contrast, allowed designer Wilhelm his head with romantic costumes for the show-within-a-show, a burlesque of *Romeo and Juliet*, including gorgeous displays of ancient Greece, the court of France, of Venice and of Tudor England.

In Coddington, Roberts had a character which he could embroider with relative impunity without fear of making plot and setting disintegrate ridiculously, and although his impromptu antics did nothing for the play they did a good deal for his faithful public. His comedy and comic songs combined with Florence St John's special mixture of romantic ballads and warm charm to form the backbone of the entertainment. Osmond Carr's songs for *In Town* gave both stars good opportunities. Roberts introduced himself:

I'm a terrible swell
As is easy to tell
From my dress and my lofty deportment
And I wish to declare
That of qualities rare
I've a large and varied assortment.
I'm at dinners and balls
I'm at theatres and halls
I am never at home for a minute
And a tableau vivant
Will be sure to go wrong
If they haven't inserted me in it!
For I am the chief and the crown
Of the Johnnies who stroll up and down
The affable
Chaffable
Cynical
Finical
Typical man-about-town!

He sang in *café chantant* style of the troubles encountered by 'Milord Sir Smith' on a trip to France, he sang of 'Drinks of the Day':

When you wake with a heavy head
Take a B & S in bed . .

an alcoholic wander through twenty-four hours, and dressed up as a Hibernian Friar Lawrence for a burlesque Scots number 'Friar Larry'. He sang a parody balcony scene 'The Waltz Refrain' with Miss St John and joined Phyllis Broughton and Ernest Bantock in a lively patter trio 'Tarradiddle'. Miss St John had a set of ballads of which the pretty 'Dreamless Rest' proved the most popular. Jenny Rogers as an embryo Coddington – the ambitious theatre callboy – had a comical number which proved extremely effective, Eric Lewis as the Duke bewailed the fact that his heart was decidedly below his station in 'My Propensities Are all the other Way' and lampooned 'The House of Lords', while the Duchess and her daughter discussed the proper style for a girl who would catch a good husband in 'The golden Mean', but much the greater part of the music fell to the two stars who were prominently billed

IN TOWN
in which Mr ARTHUR ROBERTS and Miss FLORENCE ST JOHN
will appear

in concert or music-hall style.

In spite of its ultimate popularity, *In Town* did not meet with critical success. *The Era* was not taken with it at all:

> *In Town* in merely a variety entertainment in disguise. The promise of a plot which is made in the first act results in irritation when the second is reached and is discovered to consist of a series of songs strung together with dialogue which, without Mr Roberts's gags, would be somewhat tedious. . . [The second] act is a mere string of absurd incidents and variety items. There is no action, though there is certainly plenty of 'movement' . . . With respect to the dialogue it is indeed dangerous to attempt to separate the authors' work from that of the principal artist; but from internal evidence we think we may safely say that at least one half of the laughs heard at the Prince of Wales's on Saturday were evoked by the 'gags' of Mr Arthur Roberts. . .Spoken by another person these jokes might, perhaps, fall flat, but Mr Roberts's manner is as amusing as his matter. In this case, he seemed to have actually studied the part written for him. It was for some little time in doubt whether Mr Arthur Roberts was to predominate over the authors, or whether the latter would overcome Mr Roberts. That gentleman at first showed obvious intentions of depicting a personage in Captain Arthur Coddington. By a stretch of the imagination it was possible to conceive an officer in some wonderful Indian regiment as jerky and eccentric as was here represented. But it was soon evident that the shackles of a consistent embroglio were not to be laid on the lively limbs of the popular favourite. The second act of *In Town* was merely a frame and an excuse for Arthur Roberts's songs, jests and droll grimaces. In order that he might have opportunities for repose there were also attempts at character drawing, notably in the case of Shrimp, a call-boy; and a Penley curate was also introduced to make sport; but such tedious trifling was but endured in the absence of the all-popular Arthur. And what thundering, ringing cheers came from his admirers' throats on his entrance! While he was on stage, whether giving an imitation of a French café chantant song, doing a burlesque Irish ditty and dance, or disguising himself in a friar's dress and a long nose, all went well. He was really so funny that it seemed a pity that so much time had to be wasted in the pretence that the second act of *In Town* was part of a play. . ..
>
> The worst of adopting an inartistic and incoherent form is that whatever *is* artistic and rational seems tame and out of place. Miss Florence St John who played a prudent young woman and sang a couple of ballads . . and Mr Eric Lewis who gave a really polished performance as the Duke . . suffered from this fact. The art of their work was 'swamped' in the scramble of irresponsible frivolity.

It is also took exception to the plot, and weighed in with seeming sincerity against the depiction of naughty doings between ladies of the theatrical sorority and gentlemen of means:

> A certain section of the stage and a certain class of playgoer see, apparently, nothing disgusting in the spectacle of a couple of authors, a well-known comedian and a bevy of actresses and dancers uniting to proclaim to the world that the modern burlesque theatre is nothing more nor less than a house of assignation where the aristocratic rake, young or old, finds free entrance for improper purposes and where the penniless 'man-about-town' walks in and out at his pleasure, a regular cock of the farmyard. . . Did we put such statements into plain language we might find ourselves charged with maligning grossly the manager of the only theatre in London now devoted to extravaganza . . Mr George Edwardes himself who assured the authorities that gentlemen were not admitted behind the scenes at the Gaiety Theatre . . . . . Here we have the whole female chorus of the 'Ambiguity Theatre' at the beck and call of a little 'copper captain' who hints pretty plainly that for a consideration he is always ready to add the profession of pander to his other commissionary avocations. He says: 'I can help you, perhaps, if you're one of the chaps who are after some lady or other; She may love you in turn if she ever can learn to regard me as only a brother'. Here too we have Lottie and Lillie quarrelling over the Major and 'jalousing' each other's

> ill-gotten jewels. . . Says one, pointing with her finger to a very handsome diamond brooch, 'I was with your Major last night and he gave me this. I don't think much of him, *you* can have him'. And further, at every touch and turn, we are reminded – as if the spectacle itself were not sufficiently striking – that we are in an atmosphere of vulgar, venal vice. . . . So long as members of the dramatic profession do not mind holding their calling up to public shame and so long as a certain 'fast' section of the playgoing public applaud their efforts in this direction, there is really nothing more to be said. At all events, the public can now see what some actors and actresses think of themselves and their profession. The critic can only be dumb.

These were not considerations likely to deter an audience and the public came in their numbers to see Arthur Roberts and *In Town* which was quickly established as a success.

Roberts, of course, continued to elaborate his role and interpolated, most notably, his own version of Vesta Victoria's music hall hit 'Daddy wouldn't Buy me a Bow-wow' (Joseph Tabrar):

> You ask me why I do not smile, the reason you shall know,
> I had a little birthday once, some thirty years ago,
> I asked my venerable dad to give me no more toys,
> But just a little puppy dog to bite the other boys.
> But oh! (What?)
> Daddy wouldn't buy me a bow-wow! (Wow-wow!)
> Daddy wouldn't buy me a bow-wow! (Wow-wow!)
> He bought a cricket bat.
> I was very proud of that,
> But I'd rather have a bow-wow-wow!

Which soon became swelled with topical verses, whether on the boat race:

> I think that to the most of you it's not exactly news,
> That Cambridge were defeated in the battle of the Blues;
> The crew were very plucky, and they went a famous pace,
> But do you know the reason why they didn't win the race?
> Be-cause. . Oxford got ahead of their bow-wow!
> Oxford got ahead of their bow-wow!
> They'd have won the race in turn,
> If they'd only got their stern
> A bit before their bow-wow-wow!

or the 2000 Guineas:

> I know a certain bookmaker who foolishly declared
> That Isinglass could never win, he was not half prepared.
> He said the ground was far too hard to suit his tender feet
> But though the ground was hard the horse was just as hard to beat
> And . . Isinglass won the two-thow-wow
> The favourite won the two thow-wow

the F. A. Cup, the latest in Parliament or whatever else was the talk of the day. Another successful interpolated number was 'Entre Nous', the music to which was composed by Teddy Solomon. A couple of lyrics were rewritten – the 'House of Lords' piece and the introduction of the chorus ladies were sharpened up and made more witty and less louche – but by and large it was the star role which profited from the additions and alterations.

In Town was still running vigorously at the Prince of Wales when Fred Leslie's death and the subsequent closure of *Cinder-Ellen* left Edwardes in a quandary. The next Gaiety project was to have been a burlesque of *Don Juan* written by Leslie for himself, but unfinished and star-less it had to be shelved. The Gaiety had an embarrassing gap in its programme and Christmas and the New Year holidays were approaching. Edwardes' answer to the problem was a quick switch. He took *In Town* from the Prince of Wales and with a few changes restaged it at the Gaiety where it opened on Boxing Day. To fill the gap at the Prince of Wales he brought in the John Lart/William Boosey production of *Ma Mie Rosette*, another anglicised French piece with music by Paul Lacôme and Ivan Caryll, from the Globe where it had made a promising start. The staff of the Globe, left out of work for Christmas, were taken care of by a charity matinée and Edwardes had both the Gaiety and the Prince of Wales full for the festive season.

In Town flourished at the Gaiety until July when Roberts decided to leave to tour his new burlesque, *A Modern Don Quixote*. Louis Bradfield replaced him as Coddington for the final performances at the Gaiety and on Edwardes' subsequent tour, while John Tresahar headed a second Gaiety company covering other main dates. During the run of the show various 'acts' were interpolated into the running order, emphasising the variety feeling of the piece. The most notable of these were Loie Fuller, and a seventeen year-old impressionist, Cissie Loftus, at the beginning of a fine career both in the halls and, as Cecilia Loftus, as an actress. *In Town* was her first appearance in a theatre. Another youngster, who appeared in 'the programme proper' was nineteen year-old Claire Solomon who was eventually to take over the role of the call boy, Shrimp. Miss Solomon was the daughter of Teddy Solomon, the child whose existence had been brandished in court by her mother, Jane Isaacs, in her bigamy suit against Solomon and Lillian Russell. Under her married name of Claire Romaine she was to have a successful career.

In 1897, *In Town* made a brief reappearance in town at the Garrick, with Bradfield again playing Coddington in a revamped version including a role, 'Juliette Belleville', specially modelled to star the French actress Juliette Nesville. This was the company formed to take *In Town* to America where it duly appeared on Broadway in September but by this time New York had seen *In Town*'s more developed successors and it was judged mediocre fare. At its time, however, it had been a much appreciated entertainment and one which had marked a sufficient variation in Gaiety fare to account for its being, on occasion, called 'the first musical comedy'.

In Town had been Arthur Roberts' third venture of the year. Prior to playing Captain Coddington he had been seen at the Prince of Wales as Captain Crosstree in a version of Jerrold's *Black-Eyed Susan* by Pettitt and Sims called *Blue-Eyed Susan*. *Blue-Eyed Susan* was a compromise work. Its title gave one to believe that it was another of the series of Arthur Roberts burlesques. The programme, however, stated unequivocally that it was 'comic opera'. But Roberts by any other name was Roberts and if the piece was not intended as a burlesque, and the straightish libretto and the preponderance of ballads and sentimental music made it appear that it was not, by the time Roberts had finished elaborating his role it was not markedly different in style from *Joan of Arc* and his other free-wheeling successes. As in *Joan of Arc* the score had been provided by the new young lion, Osmond Carr, who had supplied a highly attractive musical setting. If it was biased more in the direction of light operatic music than in that of the music hall that was only in accord with the professed intentions of the authors.

Blue-Eyed Susan was lavishly staged and strongly cast. The title-role was taken by the Australian prima donna, Nellie Stewart, long a star in her own country and here making her British début, and there was a positive glut of comedians headed by Arthur Williams, Fred Emney, Harry Grattan and the 'American Irishman', Chauncey Olcott. But somehow the mixture was wrong. The audience was not sure whether *Blue-Eyed Susan* was meant to be taken seriously. The story of Black-Eyed Susan had been adhered to, in a rather lighter vein but with none of the trappings of burlesque. Some of the players were playing the well-known roles as they would have played them in a 'straight' *Black-Eyed Susan*, and then there was Arthur Roberts. . . . When the dilemma was seen, the easy way out was taken. The line of least resistance was to go with the star. Both his role and Arthur Williams' were enlarged and officially 'loosened'. New numbers were introduced, notably the comical 'It's Been in the Family for Years' and *Blue-Eyed Susan* settled in at the Prince of Wales for a respectable run of just more than four months.

At the conclusion of the season Roberts went out on tour as Captain Crosstree, but not in *Blue-Eyed Susan*. Whether for artistic or, more likely, financial reasons, he rejected the idea of touring in Sims and Pettitt's show and, with the *Guy Fawkes* débacle in mind, revived instead a five-year-old burlesque *Too Lovely Black-Eyed Susan* by Horace Lennard with music composed and arranged by Oscar Barrett. This piece had been originally tried out at the Crystal Palace and at a matinée at the Strand before being put aside, but Roberts interpolated all the business he had evolved during *Blue-Eyed Susan* and toured it through major dates until he was called back to London for *In Town*. *Blue-Eyed Susan* had to wait a little longer for its provincial season, but it was finally taken out the following year by van Biene with Louis Bradfield in Roberts' role.

The great success of *La Cigale* had led to a new phenomenon in London musical shows, the anglicised or botched French opera which aroused both controversy and audience enthusiasm in turn. Whereas in earlier years considerable liberties had, in the much abused name of decency, been taken with the libretti of French musicals, by and large the music had not been tampered with. Interpolations had been rare or, as with Richardson's assault on *La Fille de Madame Angot*, short-lived. In the latest style of anglicisation as practised by Horace Sedger (and subsequently others) not only was the book subjected to some severe indignities but composers of the quality of Audran and Lecocq saw their music re-arranged, cut and heavily supplemented by numbers and even concerted music by British composers. In the case of *La Cigale*, Ivan Caryll had been responsible for the additions, and in *Ma Mie Rosette* he once again supplied nine of the twenty-six musical pieces. The result was not as satisfactory and, in spite of a shift to the Prince of Wales, the piece, a big success in its original form in Paris, failed to run. *Incognita* at the Lyric was Lecocq improved by Herbert Bunning and 'Yvolde', and the same 'Yvolde' was responsible for some of the additions to Toulmouche's *The Wedding Eve* (*Le Moutier de St Guignole/La Veille des Noces*) with which the new Trafalgar Square Theatre in St Martin's Lane was inaugurated. The principal 'botcher' of *The Wedding Eve* was Ernest Ford, but the result was only convincing enough to win the piece two months' run before *Dorothy* was brought back to take its place.

The one unadulterated French work of the year was Willie Edouin's production of *The Trooper Clairette* at the Opera Comique. It came and went in a month while its Parisian version was still building up a good run at the Folies-Dramatiques. Edward Solomon protested in print about the botching business but, perhaps to his surprise, he was overruled by the French composers, notably Serpette and Lacôme, on whose part he had taken up the cause. They were apparently only too glad to collect the healthy royalties from English productions whether the works presented were much like their originals or no. They murmured unconvincingly about 'the necessity to adapt for English tastes' and *The Era* was unkind enough to suggest that Solomon's concern was more in a wish to subdue opposition to his own work than from artistic integrity. They also implied that Teddy was not averse to composing numbers for interpolation himself when the money was right. Tastes in England had changed since the days when *Les Cloches de Corneville* and *La Mascotte* had carried all before them but revivals of these pieces in their original form were still popular. It was only the new shows which seemed to be considered unpresentable in their full French form. Perhaps the quality was not so high, but whatever the cause 'botching' was to continue and the English went on treating the French musical in the same way that the Americans had and, to an even greater extent, were about to, treat the British musical.

In the provinces a number of new shows of varying types were produced. The one which was to have the longest life was an extravaganza, *Bonnie Boy Blue*, written and composed by Victor Stevens as a replacement for the much-toured *Randolph the Reckless*. The new piece was another bright and fun-filled piece of nonsense with a jolly story, lively songs and dances both original and borrowed, and Stevens himself as Dame at the head of a large cast of comedians and pretty ladies which featured his wife, Alice Brookes, in the title-role. *Bonnie Boy Blue* No. 2 rights were quickly taken up by George Phillips and both managers toured the show widely for several seasons.

Other burlesque/extravaganzas included Chance Newton's *Cartouche & Co*, a burlesque of *Mam'zelle Nitouche* put together for Vesta Tilley with songs by the music-hall songwriter George Le Brunn; *Billy The Buccaneer*; *Shylock* (or The Venus of Venice); and *Dashing Prince Hal* which was to have a respectable career through rewrites and tours under the young actor Huntley Wright as late as 1902.

The comic opera side produced a new piece by the *Delia* team of Procida Bucalossi and Frank Desprez called *Brother George* which was tried out at Portsmouth, Brighton and Manchester with mediocre results. *Brother George* had the unusual feature for a comic opera of having no leading tenor. The whole burden of the male roles lay on four comedians while the music was left to soprano Annie Albu. Its trial run proved unsatisfactory and no proper production materialised.

The star of *Delia*, George Mudie, was enjoying a highly successful stage career but also turned his hand to a little writing from time to time. To the annoyance of Bucalossi's son, Ernest, who had been for some time preparing an opera on the same lines, he brought out a comic opera with music by fellow performer Michael Dwyer based on Planché's *Follies of a Night*. Under the title of *The Duke's Diversion* it was well-enough received on its trial at the Public Hall in West Norwood to earn it extra weeks at Ryde and the Parkhurst Theatre, Holloway. The leading lady, Leonora Braham, assumed control and took the show on a short tour further afield with sufficient success to encourage other managements to pick it up for seasons in the next two years. *The Duke's Diversion* proved there was still an appreciative audience for the kind of 'opera da camera' previously furnished by the German Reed establishment, provided it was tastefully written and well performed.

Another performer turned author was Harry Monkhouse who was partly responsible for the Irish musical comedy *Pat*. Monkhouse and his collaborator George Roberts had originally written the piece for an amateur performance at the Woolwich Barracks but its performance there had been well enough received to justify sending it out on a fully professional tour. Monkhouse himself took a couple of weeks out between the end of *The Mountebanks* and the opening of *Incognita* to play the piece in before handing over the title role to Phil Herman for the rest of a long first run. The music for *Pat* was a collection of pieces supplied by the best composers available – Solomon, Jakobowski, Slaughter, Crook and 'Yvolde' all contributing to the elastic musical part of the show. It went through a number of tours in various versions, latterly under the title of *An Irish Girl* (and her sweetheart Pat) and proved a remunerative piece for Monkhouse as author and manager.

1892 did not produce another *Pantomime Rehearsal* although there were several tidy new short pieces staged during the year. The German Reed establishment produced only one, *The Barley Mow* with music by Corney Grain, the rest of the year being devoted to revivals of *Charity Begins at Home*, *A Moss Rose Rent*, *All at Sea* and *Our Dolls' House*. Hope Temple (the future Mme André Messager) wrote a little piece called *The Wooden Spoon* which was played with *The Wedding Eve*. Basil Hood of the Yorkshire Regiment wrote *Donna Luiza* (The Spanish Duenna) and *The Crossing Sweeper* with Walter Slaughter which, although both pieces had limited lives, represented the beginning of a partnership which was to be one of the most fruitful of coming years.

Another coming man, although his contribution was to be largely in the more serious field, was the nineteen year-old Landon Ronald. Ronald had been working as pianist at the Prince of Wales for the fashionable French mime-play, *L'Enfant Prodigue*, and he worked up a little farcical operetta, *Did You Ring?* to be played with that piece's successor *La Statue du Commandeur*. The new mime was not a success and folded in four weeks, taking Ronald's operetta with it. Ronald's principal fame in later life came as a recording accompanist, a composer and an administrator, which brought him a knighthood in 1922. Although he never composed a full score for a musical play he was responsible, among his more serious compositions, for interpolated numbers in such turn-of-the-century shows as *Little Miss Nobody*, *L'Amour Mouillé* (*Cupid and the Princess*), *Florodora* and *The Silver Slipper*.

Beef Tea was the longest surviving operetta of the year. It was written by young Harry Greenbank and composed by Wilfred Bendall and proved an excellent curtain-raiser, seeing out three principal pieces – *Incognita, The Golden Web* and *The Magic Opal* – at the Lyric.

1892

0115 **THE MOUNTEBANKS** a comic opera in two acts by W. S. Gilbert. Music by Alfred Cellier. Produced at the Lyric Theatre under the management of Horace Sedger 4 January, 1892 for a run of 229 performances closing 5 August, 1892.

Arrostino Annegato . . . . Frank Wyatt (Arthur Playfair)
Giorgio Ravioli . . . . Arthur Playfair/John Moore
Luigi Spaghetti . . . . Charles Gilbert
Alfredo . . . . J. G. Robertson
Bartolo, a clown . . . . Harry Monkhouse
Pietro . . . . Lionel Brough/Cairns James
Elvino di Pasta . . . . J. Furneaux Cook
Risotto . . . . Cecil Burt
Beppo . . . . Gilbert Porteous/Frank Walsh
Teresa . . . . Geraldine Ulmar (Jessie Moore)
Ultrice . . . . Lucille Saunders (Marjorie Field-Fisher)
Nita, a dancing girl . . . . Aida Jenoure (Emmeline Orford)
Minestra . . . . Eva Moore
chorus included Marie Studholme

Md: Ivan Caryll; ch: John D'Auban; sc: T. E. Ryan; cos: Percy Anderson

Produced at the Garden Theatre, New York, under the management of T. Henry French and the Lillian Russell Comic Opera Company 11 January, 1893 for a run of 47 performances closing 27 February, 1893.
Charles Dungan (ARRO), Charles Attwood/John E. Dudley (RAV), Charles Roux (SPAG), C. Hayden Coffin (ALF), Louis Harrison (BART), W. T. Carleton (PIE), James G. Peakes/George Broderick (ELV), John E. Dudley/Henry Hallam (RIS), Russell Malcolm (BEP), A. Bassi (GIUSEPPE), Lillian Russell (TER), Cecilia Pollock/E. Mabella Baker (ULT), Laura Clement (NITA), Ada Dare (MIN). Md: Charles Puerner

0116 **BLUE-EYED SUSAN** a comic opera in 2 acts by Henry Pettitt and George R. Sims. Music by F. Osmond Carr. Produced at the Prince of Wales Theatre under the management of C. J. Abud and William Greet 6 February, 1892 for a run of 132 performances closing 17 June, 1892.

William . . . . Marian Burton/Wallace Brownlow
Doggrass . . . . Arthur Williams/Fred Emney
Gnatbrain . . . . Chauncey Olcott
Raker . . . . Fred Emney/A. Rolph
Hatchett . . . . E. H. Haslam/W. H. Brockbank
Seaweed . . . . Willie Warde
Ben Bobstay . . . . C. Royelle
Quid . . . . A. Rolph/Mr Taylor/Mr Hunt
Jacob Twigge . . . . A. Sneak
German . . . . Mr Hunt/Mr Percival
French . . . . Mr Trott
Russian . . . . Mr Palmer
Spanish . . . . Mr Clarke

Italian . . . . Mr Jackson
Red Admiral . . . . Harry Grattan/
White Admiral . . . . F. Weston/F. Kinsey Peile
Blue Admiral . . . . Ernest Bantock/
Captain Crosstree . . . . Arthur Roberts (Harry Grattan)
Dolly Mayflower . . . . Grace Pedley (Constance Adair)/Phyllis Broughton
Rosy Morn . . . . Katie Seymour
Middy . . . . Katie Barry/Phoebe Carlo
Polly Primrose . . . . Alice Kingsley/Kate Cannon
Violet Bank . . . . Day Ford
Daisy Meadows . . . . Louie Pounds
Lily Lovelorn . . . . Kate Cannon/Mrs Bernstein/*out*
Pansy Blossom . . . . Violet Durkin
May Rose . . . . Miss Collingwood
Blue-Eyed Susan . . . . Nellie Stewart (Maggie Roberts)

Md: Alfred Plumpton; ch: Willie Warde; sc: Joseph Harker and Walter Hann; cos: Percy Anderson

117 **BROTHER GEORGE** a comic opera in 2 acts by Frank Desprez. Music by Procida Bucalossi. Produced at Portsmouth under the management of Willie Drew and B. Brigata (Bucalossi) 16 May, 1892 for one week, followed by one week each in Brighton and Manchester.

Dolly Martin . . . . Annie Albu
Isabella Jane . . . . Ella Stanford
Larry Finigan . . . . Maitland Marler
General Galloper . . . . William Sidney
Tony Oglethorpe . . . . Willie Drew
Lt George Oglethorpe . . . . Guy Drury
Margery . . . . Rose Heilbron
Captain Blizzard Hurricane . . . . Frank Lacy
Pattie Prim . . . . Edith Milton
Adjutant . . . . Ada Seymour
Amelia . . . . Rina Allerton
Bob . . . . W. G. Bedford
Alec . . . . Alice Calcott
Reuben . . . . Florence Dean
Bridget . . . . B. Stanford

Dir: William Sidney; md: B. Brigata (Bucalossi)

•118 **THE DUKE'S DIVERSION** a comedy opera in two acts by George Mudie. Music by Michael Dwyer. Founded on *The Follies of a Night* by J. R. Planché. Produced at the Public Hall, West Norwood 19 and 21 May, 1892, then under the management of Miss Leonora Braham at Ryde (May 23), the Parkhurst Theatre (30 May) and later at Southend (27 June), Folkestone Pier (25 July) and on tour from 8 August, 1892 through Kings Lynn, Aldershot &c.

Duc de Chartres . . . . Michael Dwyer/John Peachey
Duchesse de Chartres . . . . Leonora Braham
Comte de Brissac . . . . George Mudie/C. Akhurst
Mlle Duval . . . . Amy Abbott/Adelaide Newton/Louise Hastings
Pierre Palliot . . . . M. R. Morand/Harry Harron
Sergeant . . . . Fuller Allen
Doctor . . . . A. C. Cantor/George Traill

•119 **DASHING PRINCE HAL** a musical extravaganza (a wildly whimsical drama in tights) in two acts by Walter Thomas. Music by Clarence Corri and Henry W. May. Produced at the Shakespeare Theatre, Liverpool, 20 June 1892 and toured under the management of Frederick Wright.

Prince Hal . . . . Ada Clare
Captain Bacon . . . . Huntley Wright
Dame Quickly . . . . Jessie Francis
Falstaff . . . . Edwin Brett
Henry IV . . . . Bertie Wright
Mary Ellen . . . . Nannie Mead
with Miss E. Custance, Miss E. Holmes, F. Bernardo &c and the Rochelle Ballet Troupe

Produced in a version 'written by Huntley Wright with music by Clarence Corri and Albert Vernon' at Ealing 16 June, 1902.
Cora Duncan (HAL), O. E. Lennon (BACON), Harry F. Wright (QU), Will Smith (FAL), Fowler Thatcher (H4), Connie Leon (MARION) &c.

0120 **HASTE TO THE WEDDING** an operetta in three acts by W. S. Gilbert based on his own adaptation (*The Wedding March*) of Labiche's *Un Chapeau de Paille d'Italie*. Produced at the Criterion Theatre under the management of Charles Wyndham 27 July, 1892 for a run of 22 performances closing 20 August, 1892.

Woodpecker Tapping, a bridegroom . . Frank Wyatt
Mr Maguire, a market gardener . . . . . Lionel Brough
Uncle Bopaddy . . . . William Blakely
Cousin Foodle . . . . George Grossmith jr
The Duke of Turniptopshire . . . . David James
Major General Bunthunder . . . . Sidney Valentine
Cripps, a milliner's book-keeper . . . . . Welton Dale
Wilkinson, a policeman . . . . Percy Brough
Captain Bapp . . . . Frank Atherley
Barns, a family retainer . . . . Fred Bond
Jackson, a valet . . . . W. R. Shirley
The Marchioness of Market Harborough . . . . Ellis Jeffreys
Bella Crackenthorpe, a milliner . . . . . . Sybil Carlisle
Mrs Leonora Bunthunder . . . . Day Ford
Patty Parker, a lady's maid . . . . Haidee Crofton
Anna Maria Maguire . . . . Marie Studholme
with Misses H. Fairlie, E. Fielding. A. McRae, G. Delapoer, Kate Welwyn, Denny Fitzherbert, M. Bell, A. Ford, H. Cornille, E. Burnton, N. Ford, C. Turner, I. Butler & Messrs A. Fowles, E. Shallard, C. Evans, L. Winning, F. Tyler, E. Phillips, A. Jackson, Henry Lebreton, J. Dunn, C. Hood, T. Heslewood, J. Turner, L. Ray.

Md: George Grossmith/Theo Ward; cos: C. H. Fox

0121 **PAT** a musical comedy drama in 3 acts by George Roberts and Harry Monkhouse. Lyrics by Mark Ambient and Frederick Wood. Music by John Crook, Edward Jakobowski, Walter Slaughter, Fred Eplett, 'Yvolde', Edward Solomon, Oscar Barrett and Alfred Lee. First produced by amateurs 16 November, 1891 at Woolwich. Subsequently revised and produced at the Aquarium, Yarmouth 1 August, 1892 and toured under the management of Harry Monkhouse through Newcastle, Manchester, Oldham, Liverpool, Preston, Parkhurst Theatre, Elephant & Castle, Dublin, Belfast, Salford, Blackpool, Walsall, Nottingham, York, Edinburgh and Glasgow ending 26 November. Recommenced 13 March, 1893 at Portsmouth and toured through to 27 May, 1893. Subsequently toured in repertoire with *Larks*.

Pat Fitzpatrick . . . . Harry Monkhouse/Phil Herman/Albert James
Roland Prescott . . . . Charles B. Bedells/Edward Chester
Barney O'Shea . . . . J. R. La Fane/Lloyd Townrow
Plantaganet Ramsdall . . . . Arthur Helmore/William Cuthbert/J. Fraser
Lord Dux . . . . H. R. Trevor
Sgt. O'Reilly . . . . J. Stephens
Constable Flannagan . . . . C. Flood
Rosabel Ray . . . . Alma Stanley/Nellie Lauraine

Mrs Rochester	Margaret Soulby/Augusta Havilland/ Madeleine l'Estrange
Bridget O'Reardon	Jenny McIntyre
Parker	Eleanor Luxmoore/Dora Archer
Nora Anstruther	Ada Clare (Eleanor Luxmoore)/ Edie Casson/Florence Darley
add Jane	Nellie Archer

Md: Alfred Lee/Augustus T. MacInnes

Revised as *An Irish Girl* (and her sweetheart Pat) and presented by Harry Monkhouse on tour 1896/7.

0122 **CIGARETTE** a light romantic opera in three acts. Plot by Barry Montour. Libretto and lyrics by E. Warham St Leger. Music by J. Haydn Parry. First produced at the Theatre Royal, Cardiff 15 August, 1892, then played at Swansea and Newport before opening 7 September, 1892 at the Lyric Theatre under the management of Mrs Bennet-Edwardes. Transferred to the Shaftesbury Theatre 26 September. Withdrawn 3 December, 1892, after a total of 112 performances.

Marquis de Portale	Oswald Yorke
Claude	Joseph O'Mara (Emlyn Jones)
Monsieur Bastian	Neil O'Donovan//Sheridan Lascelles
Sergeant Mouston	Leslie Holland
Gaston	Alfred Warner/Mr Daintree
Justin	Mr Lyons/Mr Fair
Benzoline	A. J. Evelyn
Nicotine	Charles Collette/Cairns James
Violette	Amy Sherwin//Annette Albu (Jessie Bradford)
Cigarette	Florence Bankhardt/Geraldine Ulmar
Comtesse de Montrouget	Hannah Jones/Mme Amadi/Helen Sugden
Babette	May Lawrie
Mme de Vauricourt	Miss Godfrey/Mary Collette?
Lady Superior	Helen Vicary
Mother Lou-Lou	Marion Erle
Julie	Celia Loseby
Clarisse	Jessie Bradford/*out*

Dir: Charles Collette; md: J. Haydn Parry; sc: W. T. Hemsley; cos: Messrs Harrison

0123 **HADDON HALL** a light opera in three acts by Sydney Grundy. Music by Arthur Sullivan. Produced at the Savoy Theatre under the management of R. D'Oyly Carte 24 September, 1892 for a run of 204 performances closing 15 April, 1893.

John Manners	Courtice Pounds/John Macauley/Robert Cunningham (H. R. Blake-Johnson)
Sir George Vernon	Richard Green (H. Crimp)
Oswald	Charles Kenningham
Rupert Vernon	Rutland Barrington (J. Bowden Haswell)
The McKrankie	W. H. Denny
Sing-Song Simeon	Rudolph Lewis/J. Bowden Haswell
Nicodemus Knock-knee	A. Fowles
Kill-Joy Candlemas	W. H. Leon
Barnabas Bellows-to-mend	George de Pledge
Major Domo	Hampton Gordon
Dorothy Vernon	Lucille Hill (Florence Easton)
Lady Vernon	Rosina Brandram
Dorcas	Dorothy Vane
Gertrude	Claribel Hyde
Nance	Nita[1] Cole/May Bell/Emmie Owen

[1] later Annie Cole

Deborah . . . . Florence Easton/Nita Clutterbuck

Dir: Charles Harris; md: François Cellier; ch: John D'Auban; sc: William Telbin, Hawes Craven, Joseph Harker and W. Perkins; cos: Percy Anderson

0124 **THE BARONESS** a comic opera in three acts by C. G. Cotsford Dick. Produced at the Royalty Theatre under the management of Douglas Vernon 5 October, 1892 for a run of 13 performances closing 18 October, 1892.

The Grand Duke . . . . Charles E. Stevens
Baron Narcissus . . . . Charles Conyers
Count Alfonso . . . . William Foxon/Percy Percival
Count Lorenzo . . . . Mr Magrath
Ambrose . . . . Percy Brough
Hamilcar . . . . George Grossmith Jr
Bruno . . . . Fred Emney
Beppo . . . . Lionel Brough
Angelo . . . . Gladys Rees
Rodolfo . . . . Susie Nainby
Marietta . . . . Constance Wallace
Tencredo . . . . Gertrude Hope
Ralooka . . . . Marian Asquith
Isabella . . . . Olga Schuberth
Lauretta . . . . Jessie Moore
Gabrielle . . . . Agnes Giglio

with Violet Dene (pd), Olive Vaughan, Misses Nola, Russell, Campbell, Somerset, Dormer, Taylor, Dickenson, Graham, Greyland, M. Graham, Clifford, Sale, Baudrant, Wilson, Greville, G. Delapoer, Revenscroft, Wetton, O'Connor, Gear, Murray, Leslie, Doherty, Piermont, Norris &c.

Dir: James Tanner; md: Cotsford Dick?; ch: Miss H. Abrahams; sc: Richard C. Durant; cos: C. H. Fox

0125 **IN TOWN** a musical farce in two acts by Adrian Ross and James Leader. Music by F. Osmond Carr. Produced at the Prince of Wales Theatre under the management of George Edwardes 15 October, 1892. Transferred to the Gaiety Theatre 26 December, 1892. Closed 29 July, 1893, after a total of 292 performances and toured from 31 July, 1893 through Brighton, Edinburgh, Glasgow, ?, ?, Birmingham, Manchester and Islington (Grand) x2 ending 30 September, 1893.

Captain Arthur Coddington . . . . Arthur Roberts/W. Louis Bradfield
The Duke of Duffshire . . . . Eric Lewis
Lord Clanside . . . . Phyllis Broughton/Millie Hylton
Lord Alexander Kincaddie . . . . Douglas Patrick/*out*
Rev. Samuel Hopkins . . . . Ernest Bantock/Frederick Vaughan
Benoli . . . . Harry Grattan/Henry N. Wenman/ Ernest Cosham/George Minshull
Hoffman . . . . Fritz Rimma
Fritz . . . . Edgar Frazer/C. Wingrove
Mr Driver . . . . F. Lovell/*out*
Shrimp, a call-boy . . . . Jenny Rogers/Florence Thropp/ Edmund Payne
Bloggins . . . . Frederick Vaughan/Fred Farleigh/ Sidney Watson.
Lady Gwendoline . . . . Belle Harcourt/Kate Cutler/Louie Pounds
Lady Evangeline . . . . Daisy Gilpin/*out*
Flo Fanshawe . . . . Sylvia Grey/Nellie Simmonds
Bob . . . . Maud Hobson/Carrie Benton
Billie . . . . Blanche Massey
Lottie . . . . Hetty Hamer/Florence Henderson
Lillie . . . . Nellie Simmons

Clara . . . . Kate Cannon
The Duchess of Duffshire . . . . Maria Davis
Kitty Hetherton. . . . . Florence St John/Kate Cutler (Louie Pounds)
add Fanny . . . . Florence Lloyd
Molly . . . . Florence Henderson/Ethel Earle
Marie . . . . Louie Pounds/Maud Wilmot
Eva . . . . Topsy Sinden
Letty . . . . Rose Batchelor
Nellie . . . . Violet Dene

Pas de quatre girls: Topsy Sinden, Adelaide Astor, Bob Robina, Violet Dene

Dir: James T. Tanner; md: Sidney Jones/Meyer Lutz/George Byng; ch: Miss H. Abrahams/Mariette D'Auban, sc: William Telbin and E. G. Banks; cos: Wilhelm &c.

The Gaiety No. 2 company played one week at the Gaiety Theatre 31 July, 1893 before touring through to 25 November, 1893. Resumed 5 March, 1894–26 May, 1894.
John Tresahar/Arthur Playfair/W. Louis Bradfield/Bert Gilbert (CODD), George Honey/Eric Thorne/George de la Force/E. Story Gofton (DUKE), Phyllis Broughton/Florence Lloyd (CLAN), Frederick Vaughan/George Mudie (REV), Edgar Frazer/T. Nunn (BENOLI), Wensley Thompson/H. Trant Fischer (HOFF), E. D. Wardes/Guy Fane (FRITZ), Kate Barry/Miss Marsden/Claire Solomon (SHR), Mr Fairfield (BLOG), Belle Harcourt/Jessie Moore (GWEN), Alice Gilbert/Phoebe Carlo/Violet Dene (FLO), Alice Barnett/Maria Davis (DUCH), Cissie Saumarez/Marie Luella/Amy Augarde (KIT) with Violet Durkin, Florence Doyne, Aimée Mills, Maud Vaughan, E. Fowler, M. Crichton, Phoebe Carlo, Ethel Earle, Florence Lloyd, Elsie Dare, Helen Fraser, Margaret Fraser, John Hart, Picton Roxburgh, Sidney Watson &c.

Produced at the Garrick Theatre 9 August, 1897 for two weeks by George Edwardes' American Co. which subsequently opened 6 September at the Knickerbocker Theatre, New York under the management of Al Hayman and Charles Frohman for a run of 40 performances closing 9 October, 1897.
W. Louis Bradfield (CODD), Lawrence Caird (DUKE), Florence Lloyd (CLAN), Leedham Bantock (REV), Fritz Rimma (HOFF), Arthur Hope (BENOLI), Claire Romaine (SHR), E. G. Woodhouse (BLOG), Marie Studholme (GWEN), Rosie Boote (FLO), Minnie Hunt (KITTY), Juliette Nesville (JULIETTE BELLEVILLE), Mrs Edmund Phelps (DUCH), Kitty Adams (LOTTIE), Marjorie Pryor (LILLIE), Lottie Williams (ETHEL), Dora Nelson (ROSE), Violet Trelawney (EDITH), Daisy Jackson (MAY), Norma Whalley (CLARA), Maud Hobson (MAUD)

Dir: J. A. E. Malone; md: Harold Vicars; ch: Willie Warde

SHYLOCK or The Venus of Venice an operatic burlesque in three acts by Montague Turner. Music by H. C. Barry. Produced at the Theatre Royal, Lincoln 1 August, 1892 and toured.

Shylock . . . . John E. Coyle
Mr Antonio Sr . . . . George Wallace
Interrogator . . . . Bruce Bertini
Tokio Chuckeo . . . . Walter Wood
Bassanio . . . . Grace Serata
Salerino . . . . Polly Elcho
Meneta . . . . Lillie Dagmar
Portia . . . . Florence Carlile
Jessica . . . . Ernest Autherley
The McTubal. . . . . Jesmond Johnstone
The Doge . . . . Montague Turner
Hypnotiser . . . . George Gibbens
Gratiano. . . . . Daisy Dalton
Lorenzo . . . . Constance Conway
Donato . . . . Vivenne d'Arcy
Salanio . . . . Doris Melville
Nerissa . . . . Florence Engelmann

BONNIE BOY BLUE a burlesque in three acts written and composed by Victor Stevens.

Produced at Chatham 18 April, 1892 under the management of Victor Stevens and toured.

Dame Diccory . . . . Victor Stevens
Bonnie Boy Blue . . . . Alice Brookes
Lawyer Copall . . . . John A. Warden/W. G. Walford
Squire Longacre . . . . Marius Girard
Archie Lovell . . . . Nellie Spooner/Hetty Senior
Rosy May . . . . Alice Watkins/Daisy Melville
Daisy Druce . . . . Kate Hutton/Kitty Abrahams
Rolland Butter . . . . Emily Spooner/Dorothy Lane
Susan . . . . Jessie Albini
Willie Wimple . . . . /Emily Spooner
Johnny Jones . . . . /Nellie Spooner
Jack Lively . . . . Harry Fischer
Dolly Diccory . . . . Marie Montrose
Molly Minks . . . . Edith Harcourt
Dorkie Dene . . . . Alice Watkins
Mary Mumps . . . . Grace Oxenford
with Louie Norman, Florence Dene, Grace Massey, Eva Harrison, J. Hindle Taylor, Surtees Corrie &c.

Ch: Mme Bassano

CATALINA a comedy opera by H. Woodville. Music by Clement Locknane. Produced at the Town Hall, Kilburn 23 February, 1892.

CARTOUCHE & CO or The Ticket of French Leave. A burlesque by H. Chance Newton. Music by George Le Brunn. Produced at 22 August, 1892 and toured by Vesta Tilley.

THE BARBER a musical comedy by R. Gus Hyde. Music by Arthur Trevalyan and C. W. Cottingham. Produced at the Folkestone Pleasure Gardens 21 March, 1892 and toured by the Maud Musical Comedy Co.

SIR JACK O'LANTERN The Knight of (K)nights or A Curious Curse Curiously Cured. A comic opera in three acts by Arthur H. Ward. Music by Henry Vernon. Produced at the Bijou Theatre and Assembly Rooms, Neath 31 August 1892 and toured by J. A. Hybert in repertoire.

DID YOU RING? an operetta in one act by J. W. Houghton and J. W. Matson. Music by Landon Ronald. Produced at the Prince of Wales Theatre under the management of Horace Sedger 27 June, 1892 with *La Statue du Commandeur*. Withdrawn 23 July, 1892.

Tom . . . . Templar Saxe
Kitty . . . . Amy Farrell
Susan . . . . Katie James

DONNA LUIZA an operetta by Basil Hood. Music by Walter Slaughter. Produced at the Prince of Wales Theatre under the management of Horace Sedger 23 March, 1892 with *Blue-Eyed Susan*. Withdrawn 17 June, 1892.

Luiza . . . . Maggie Roberts
Dolores . . . . Louie Pounds
Maria . . . . Annie Dwelley
Loranza . . . . W. H. Brockbank
Don Alphonso Fandango . . . . J. G. Taylor/F. Weston

THE WOODEN SPOON an operetta in one act by Gilbert Burgess. Music by Hope Temple. Produced at the Trafalgar Square Theatre 26 October, 1892 as a forepiece to *The Wedding Eve*. Withdrawn 12 November, 1892.

Inez . . . . Violet Robinson
Mariana . . . . Millie Vere
Pablo . . . . Leonard Russell

Marquis d'Alvarez . . . . William Philp
Md: Ernest Ford; sc: E. G. Banks

BEEF TEA an operetta in one act by Harry Greenbank. Music by Wilfred Bendall. Produced at the Lyric Theatre under the management of Horace Sedger 22 October, 1892 as a forepiece to *Incognita*. Played subsequently with *The Magic Opal* and *The Golden Web*.

Richard Plum . . . . Charles Gilbert/Charles Crook
Captain Cherry Blossom . . . . Frank A. Walsh/John Moore
Reuben Caldicott . . . . H. Gregory
Mrs Blossom . . . . Lena Monmouth
Lottie . . . . Rose Hamilton

A HUNDRED YEARS AGO an operetta by Alec Nelson. Music by Henry J. Wood. Produced at the Royalty Theatre 16 July, 1892.

Tom Ball . . . . Frederick Bovill
Joe Ball . . . . William Philp
Joe Shortlands . . . . S. Metcalfe
Liz Hindley . . . . Margaret Warren
Alice. . . . . Mary Rough

Played at the Royalty 30 October, 1893 with *Frog*.
Gilbert Davis (TOM), Collwyn Thomas (JOE), Frank Fisher (SHORT), Winifred Ludlam (LIZ), Mabel Archdall (ALICE)

OPPOSITION a debate in one sitting by 'Richard Henry'. Music by Ivan Caryll. Produced at the Lyric Theatre under the management of Horace Sedger 28 June, 1892 as a forepiece to *The Mountebanks*. Withdrawn 5 August, 1892.

Mr Goswell Bloggs . . . . Arthur Playfair
John Jones . . . . Tom Shale
William Brown . . . . Charles Gilbert
Hodge . . . . John Moore
Miss Cornelia Culcher . . . . Dora Thorne
Rose . . . . Emmeline Orford
Susan Nipkins. . . . . Cissy Cranford
Clara . . . . Jessie Moore

THE BARLEY MOW in one act by Walter Frith. Music by R. Corney Grain. Produced at St George's Hall under the management of Alfred Reed and R. Corney Grain 16 April 1892, with *A Fancy Dress Ball*. Withdrawn 21 June, 1892.

Adolphus Fanciter . . . . Alfred Reed
Wideawake Jim . . . . Mr Macmoyse
Rosie . . . . Norah Maguire
Jack . . . . Avalon Collard
Mrs Byrcote. . . . . Fanny Holland
George . . . . Arthur Wilkinson

THE COMPOSER a musical comedietta by Arthur Chapman. Music by J. M. Capel. Produced at the Royal Strand Theatre under the management of Willie Edouin 9 January 1892 with *The New Wing*.

Jack Temple . . . . J. M. Capel
Nellie . . . . Venie Bennett
Mrs Nimblepenny . . . . Lina St Ives

Md: Ernest Bucalossi

OUR FAMILY LEGEND an operetta by Reginald Stockton. Music by Sidney Jones. Produced at the Brighton Aquarium 8 October, 1892.

1893

During 1892 comic opera had prospered well enough in London, largely thanks to the seemingly indestructible Messrs Gilbert and Sullivan, this time separately with Gilbert's *The Mountebanks* and Sullivan's *Haddon Hall*, while *Cigarette* had also unexpectedly added to the success of this more 'respectable' side of light musical entertainment. The early months of '93, however, sounded a warning for the writers and composers of 'traditional' comic opera. In the first part of the year three new works with seemingly impeccable pedigrees and all with some considerable degree of merit failed utterly to gain public approval. They were followed by a comic opera disaster at the Savoy Theatre itself and an unsuccessful revival of that great favourite *La Fille de Madame Angot* at the Criterion. These failures, combined with the disappointment of the Trafalgar Square Theatre's revival of the indestructible *Dorothy*, seemed to point to a general disenchantment with comic opera and its variants, and many an obituary made its way into the trade papers as the failures piled up. The light musical theatre was no less popular than before, but patrons were changing their direction and the younger and near relative of the new burlesque, the variety musical, was solidly making the West End musical stage its own.

The first of the year's musicals to come and to go was *La Rosière*, a Frenchified piece compounded by the comedian Harry Monkhouse. Monkhouse, at the age of 39, had already a fine career as an actor behind him. He had first appeared in a West End musical in *Babil and Bijou* in 1882 and then, after several years of touring his own company with the musical comedy *Larks*, had come back to London as principal comedian for the Carl Rosa Light Opera Company in *Paul Jones*. He remained with the Rosa and then the Lyric Theatre company through a series of shows, punctuated by brief visits to his touring companies which were still playing *Larks* and his new piece, *Pat*, of which he was the part author. *La Rosière* was his second venture into the field of authorship.

The libretto was closely based on the old comedy *Joconde* or The Festival of the Rosière which had been played at the Olympic in 1824 – a very flimsy farce of the *Così fan Tutte* type. Two schoolgirls, Adeline and Hortense, discover that their military lovers are going to test their fidelity by exchanging places and so, disguised as gipsies, they set out to take their revenge on them in time-honoured fashion. Parallel to this tale is that of Jo, the 'romp' of the school and her lover, Pierre, who is pressed for the army. Jo is to be crowned La Rosière (a kind of Gallic May Queen) and when the recalcitrant soldiers flirt with her they find themselves thrown into jail. In the final act they stand trial and Jo makes use of her position to effect their release on her friends' behalf and to secure Pierre for herself.

In spite of the fact that *La Rosière* had already been given a trial run, it was overwritten and its story stretched to an inordinate length. On the opening night, pushed by some rather injudicious encores, the piece ran just short of four hours and when the curtain fell a few minutes before midnight the audience's enthusiasm was mixed with one or two dissatisfied noises. Monkhouse's dialogue was lively enough if not particularly sophisticated, but there was a terrible lot of it and major cuts were needed. The music, composed by Jakobowski, was, on the other hand, agreed to be quite charming. *The Era* noted that it was:

> pleasant and melodious throughout and some of his finales and choruses are full of life and volume . .

going on to say:

> Mr Jakobowski understands the necessity of making comic opera music light, lively and full of marked effects . .

The Times, having dismissed the libretto as 'too trivial to call for serious notice', noted:

> The interest of the performance, however, lies in Mr Jakobowski's light and tuneful music and in the pretty mounting of the opera . .

The general consensus seemed to be that with heavy cutting *La Rosière* might do very well.

But right from the start the piece refused to go. It lacked attractions enough to pull customers away from the bright lights of the Gaiety and the other musical theatres. A couple of ballads from Violet Cameron and J. G. Robertson, some gentle fooling from William Elton, Frank Thornton and Albert James, some pretty 1830s costumes and settings . . all this was mild stuff. The co-manager of the theatre, the American soubrette Marie Halton, injected more of the 'modern style' into her interpretation of the role of Jo, and the dancer Minnie Thurgate contributed an uninhibited gipsy dance which raised the temperature a little but, on the whole, *La Rosière* lacked obvious attractions. Miss Halton and Monkhouse moved into action and the author of the moment, Brandon Thomas, whose *Charley's Aunt* was ruling the roost at the Royalty, was called in to give the kiss of life to the libretto. He began by cutting drastically and melding the three acts of the show into two. He shifted various elements and numbers about in an attempt to inject more 'go' into the show but his attempts were in vain and *La Rosière* died after six weeks.

The unfortunate Monkhouse's production venture was not his only problem. While his short-lived brainchild occupied the stage of the Shaftesbury Theatre, the comedian was appearing in another comic opera further down the Avenue at the Lyric where Horace Sedger had produced *The Magic Opal.* This piece was the work of Isaac Albéniz, pianist to the court of Spain and at 33 years old already a veteran of more than 25 years standing as a concert pianist and an experienced composer, principally of piano music, but also of a few zarzuelas. Albéniz had come to Britain on a concert tour in 1890 and had encountered the wealthy banker Francis Money-Coutts who put him on a retainer as his own private composer. Coutts had ambitions as a librettist and song-writer, and sufficient funds to buy himself the best music going. His choice was Albéniz and the Spanish composer was comfortably contracted. The collaboration was an uneven one. Coutts' more ambitious ideas included an operatic King Arthur trilogy (only the first part, *Merlin*, was completed) and some rather pompous songs, but he also adapted the libretto for Albéniz' most successful stage work, the light opera *Pepita Jimenez* (1896). Albéniz' position with Coutts did not apparently prevent him from writing with other librettists. He supplied a finale for Sedger's production of *Incognita* and in 1892/3 he collaborated with Arthur Law on *The Magic Opal.*

Law's libretto was on traditional lines and a number of the plot elements had done duty on more than a few occasions in the past twenty years. This had never previously proved any bar to success. Plot was the most dispensable of the elements of a musical of the 1880s and early '90s. Good music, clever lyrics and a witty and humorous set of situations and dialogue were much more important. Law's plot, set in a comic opera Greek town, was more than sufficient.

Trabucos, a brigand chief, has fallen in love with the lovely Lolika, adopted daughter of a rich merchant, but Lolika is engaged to marry Alzaga, the son of the town's mayor. Trabucos, not to be denied, kidnaps Alzaga and tries to steal his predecessor's magic opal ring which will make all who touch the wearer fall in love with him or her. But the precious ring is in the town museum and the mayor is intending to give it as a wedding gift to Lolika. Trabucos and his sister Martina make a copy and Martina succeeds in effecting a swap by vamping the mayor into letting her try the genuine ring. When he tries to apprehend her he is struck by the power of the ring and loses his heart. Martina and Trabucos escape to their mountain hideout pursued by the amorous Mayor. In the brigand hideout is an old woman, Olympia, who is in love with the chief. While the rest of the band are rejoicing at the regaining of the ring which will help them to lure rich travellers to be plundered, Olympia plots how to get it for herself in order to attract Trabucos. She succeeds in stealing it but then the Mayor arrives seeking Martina and, touching Olympia, turns his attentions to her. The rest of the principals arrive to rescue Alzaga and the Mayor, and Lolika plots with Olympia to such good measure that the ring is wisely used to bring everything to a happy ending.

The plot had the advantage of introducing a showy comic role for Monkhouse as the infected Mayor as well as good vocal opportunities for the tenor John Child and his prima donna, Aida Jenoure, in the role of Lolika. Law's dialogue was bright and occasionally funny. *The Era* found it most acceptable:

> . . this ingeniously contrived story is embellished by Mr Law with many witty lines and poetical numbers and the book may be praised not only for its interest and humour but for giving excellent opportunities for the composer's skill . .

but the principal attraction of *The Magic Opal* lay in Albéniz' music:

> If bright, tuneful and original music were enough of itself to secure the amount of public recognition that goes to make a success in a modern sense then *The Magic Opal* . . should become familiar as household words . . . . . . Not often in recent years has so good an example of opéra-comique properly so called been presented to the London public. (*Times*)
>
> Those who can appreciate anything better than the thinly orchestrated jingle of the ordinary comic opera composer will revel in the refinement and grace of Senor Albéniz' work . . (*Era*)

The music was of a quality and an individuality which appealed to the critics but the composer had kept within the established traditions of comic opera which his librettist had marked out for him, ranging from the patter duo for Monkhouse and Fred Kaye:

CAR: From my boyhood I was noted for my wonderful sagacity
ARIST: The neighbours were astounded at his youthful perspicacity
CAR: I swallowed information with remarkable avidity
ARIST: And so his head expanded with a marvellous rapidity

through the serenade, the drinking song and the Legend and the usual ration of choruses and ensembles. Among the most successful pieces were the baritone serenade 'Star of my Life' and 'The Legend of the Monastery' both sung by Wallace Brownlow as the brigand chief, the tenor drinking song, a pretty ballad 'Love Sprang from his Couch' for the leading lady and a lively tenor/baritone duet 'The Lady's Mine', although, as *The Times* enthused:

> when every number deserves praise it is hard to single out special features . .

One special feature which the audiences singled out was the performance of Miss Mary Augusta ('May') Yohe from Pennsylvania who was making her London début as Martina. A vivacious little creature of partial Indian extraction with a rough, untrained contralto of minimal range, she put across the song 'Many and many a weary Mile' 'with more emphasis than beauty of tone' but succeeded in winning an important section of the public (principally male) to her cause by sheer personal effect.

After their positive first night and the favourable critical reception the management of the Lyric were satisfied that they had a fair run in prospect, and after four weeks a national tour starring William Cheesman and Annie Schuberth set out from Glasgow with an itinerary of major cities to follow. This did not prevent the managers and authors in London from working on the opening night book and score. May Yohe's success warranted her an extra number, 'Where, oh Where', and the comic element was reinforced by more material for Monkhouse and Kaye. Business at the Lyric was fine and the signs were propitious. But within six weeks *The Magic Opal* had closed.

The touring company continued and they must have been surprised to receive en route a considerably altered libretto and new music with instructions that these were to be put into performance under the new title *The Magic Ring*. Henry Lowenfeld, the 'Kops Ale' tycoon, had decided that *The Magic Opal* was too good to die and he determined to resurrect it. On April 11 the revamped *Magic Ring* opened at the Prince of Wales Theatre with Harry Monkhouse again in the lead and the role of Lolika taken by his erstwhile business partner in *La Rosière*, Marie Halton. The main alteration in the libretto was the total elimination of one principal female role, the functions of 'Martina' and 'Olympia' being rolled into one (again called Martina) and characterised as Trabucos' intended and Queen of the Brigands. Susie Vaughan (aged 40) finally got to play something other than the comic crones which had been her lot for so long and May Yohe was dispensed with. The Olympia episode was cut from the second act and the convolutions of the ring's journey thus reduced. Albéniz introduced some new music and the piece met once again with a decidedly 'pro' critical reaction. It also met once again with complete public indifference and *The Magic Ring* survived no longer in its second incarnation than it had in its first.

In the provinces the *Magic Opal* company, which had become the *Magic Ring* company, completed the fourteen weeks which had been booked for it and was then dissolved. Towards the end of the year Albéniz' piece reappeared one final time, as *La Sortija* in the composer's native country. But Spain had no more time for the Greek bandits and their talisman than had London and the production was a total failure. *The Magic Opal/Ring* was Albéniz' only full contribution to the British stage. After supplying some additional numbers for an unfortunate production of Millöcker's *Der Arme Jonathan*, he moved on to France and Spain where he continued his collaboration with Coutts and finally produced his most famous work, *Iberia*.

To replace the ephemeral *Magic Opal* at the Lyric, Horace Sedger brought into town the Carl Rosa production of Goring Thomas' musical *The Golden Web* which had been commissioned from the composer of *Esmeralda* and *Nadeshda* for the Carl Rosa Light Opera Company. It was originally intended for the Prince of Wales Theatre as a follow up to *Paul Jones* but, since it had no role suitable for the company's new star, Agnes Huntingdon, it was shelved. Goring Thomas continued to rewrite sections of his score while Rosa looked for another spot in which to place it, but his second scheduling of *The Golden Web* hit a new problem. The libretto had been based on Walter Besant's *The Chaplain of the Fleet* and the rights to that piece had been disposed of elsewhere. Once again *The Golden Web* was put aside.

The dissolution of the Carl Rosa Light Opera Company and the deaths of both Thomas and Rosa intervened before *The Golden Web* eventually made its way on to the stage in the repertoire of the organisation's Grand Opera Company. In the meanwhile the original script had undergone considerable changes. Rosa had been dissatisfied with Frederick Corder's treatment of the book and had personally made decisions on the nature of the alterations required. Charlie Stephenson was brought in to do a major rewrite of the libretto whilst retaining Corder's lyrics, most of which Goring Thomas had already set – some in more than one version. On his death Thomas' orchestral score for the 'final' version of *The Golden Web* was far from complete and Rosa hired S. P. Waddington, current holder of the Mendelssohn scholarship, to complete the parts. The conductor, Claude Jacquinot, composed a Four Seasons ballet with which to stretch out the rather short score that Thomas had left and interpolated it into the second act which contained otherwise only an opening chorus, two solos, two duets, and a finale.

If *The Golden Web* was underweighted on the musical side, its length was easily maintained by a profusion of dialogue. The plot of the piece was the story of a Fleet marriage set around the year 1750. Geoffrey Norreys and Amabel Bullion are lovers but she is to marry old Lord Silvertop and her banker father is anxious to keep the penniless Norreys out of the way. Dr Manacle, the Fleet parson, is authorised to pay the young man 5000 guineas to marry someone else. Norreys, in debt and believing Amabel willing to become Lady Silvertop, despairingly agrees and Manacle duly marries him to a hooded lady. After the ceremony they part and the young man sets out alone to earn fortune and fame abroad. In the second act, returned and restored to title and wealth, Norreys seeks out Amabel and protects her from an abduction attempt by the disgruntled Silvertop who is finally tricked into wedding his fiancée's elderly aunt. Amabel then reveals to Geoffrey that she was his hooded bride and all ends happily. The plot was leavened with the antics of Silvertop's servant, Smug, who gets himself into trouble when he dresses as a gentleman and becomes embroiled with the amorous Aunt Pamela.

The Golden Web was put into rehearsal for the 1893 Carl Rosa season and made its first appearance at the Royal Court Theatre in Liverpool with a cast of light opera specialists to which was added the prima donna Alice Esty in the role of Amabel. The show was well received and *The Times* critic sent to Liverpool for the purpose reported:

> . . it is to be hoped this bright and melodious opera will soon find its way into London . .

Horace Sedger, with the Lyric Theatre to fill, took up the suggestion and borrowing the comedians Wilkinson, Laidlaw and Mme Amadi from the Rosa production he put a slightly revised version of *The Golden Web* into preparation. Unfortunately the Grand Opera Co still had need of Alice Esty, so Sedger decided that, rather than run in a new prima donna, he would wait for her to be available. Finally, a fortnight later than intended, *The Golden Web* moved into the Lyric. Once again it was gratified by largely appreciative notices although the libretto was rather unfairly condemned. Stephenson's dialogue was neat and bright and decorated Besant's plot in an attractive if necessarily old-fashioned manner. The writing was altogether superior to that in the libretto of *Dorothy* and was perfectly apt for both the plot and the music.

The music received universal approbation. Dr Manacle's song 'Like a kindly Spider' was particularly well-received:

Like a kindly spider lurking overhead
Ever finer, wider, I my meshes spread
With shuttle swiftly flying wondrous nets I weave
E'en when in them lying none my toils perceive . .

as was Amabel's principal number:

His love is like a naughty child
That none can make obey
Despite the rod the little god
Will always get his way;
We coax him here, we coax him there
We threaten and inveigh
He'll pout and cry, but by and by
We find he's got his way

the duo 'Where is the Lovers' Rest' (Amabel/Norreys), Smug's song 'The tattered Coat' and his comic duet 'Deign to Hear Me' with Aunt Pamela. Perhaps the most successful piece, however, was the gently humorous solo for Mme Amadi (Pamela):

I knew a love song years ago
Ah, well-a-day, 'tis nigh forgot
There were broken hearts in it, I know,
Ah, well-a-day, 'tis the common lot.
There were loves and doves and moon and June
For 'tis thus that lovers make commune.
I forget the words and it had no tune–
Ah, well-a-day . .

In spite of all the encouragements the critics could proffer, however, *The Golden Web* failed utterly to attract. After a fortnight Sedger used the excuse of Holy Week to close down for a week during which time Stephenson and Charles Thomas, the composer's brother, embarked on a major revision. Durward Lely was brought in to take over the rewritten role of Norreys and John and Emma D'Auban were engaged to devise and perform some of their famous dance routines. But all was in vain. The new version played for only two weeks before the worst Easter box-office season in years forced several shows, including *The Golden Web*, to close for good. Alice Esty and the comedians returned to the road company and *The Golden Web* resumed its place alongside *Carmen, Djamileh, Cavalleria Rusticana, Il Trovatore, The Lily of Killarney* and others in the repertoire for a half-dozen further performances, the last of which was at Birmingham in June.

Even the music-hall paper *The Entr'acte* bewailed the passing of a show which had

more good music than is to be found in three of the ordinary operas that get produced at such theatres as the Lyric . .

and decided that it had 'died for the want of nourishing comedy' – that is, low comedy.

But there was clearly more to it than that. *La Rosière, The Magic Opal/Magic Ring* and *The Golden Web* were three competent works by skilled and popular writers and three severe box-office failures. Added to this was the unexpectedly premature passing of the charming *Ma Mie Rosette* which had looked assured of success, and *The Era* was prompted to demand in an editorial:

> Have there been too many comic operas before the public of late? Or is comic opera always a risky venture? Or have not some recent comic operas been sufficiently striking to catch the public ear? . . . several succès d'estime have failed to become succès de box office . . . should they have done better with English titles?

Or was public taste merely changing? If the theatres were empty, the music halls were full to overflowing.

The worst blow of all for the comic opera came when the Savoy, which had never had a box-office failure in all the years since its opening, joined the ranks with the dismal collapse of *Jane Annie*. Carte had got Gilbert and Sullivan working together again, but with the Easter closing of *Haddon Hall* he required something to hold the fort until the new piece by the old masters was ready. In line with his policy of 'first class only' he gathered two of the most interesting young names in contemporary light literature to write his libretto – J. M. Barrie and Arthur Conan Doyle. Both men were at a comparatively early stage in their long and distinguished careers. Barrie, at the age of thirty, had just found theatrical fame with *Walker*, *London* (Toole's, 1892) after having devoted his early literary efforts to the novels *Auld Licht Idylls, A Woman in Thrums* and *The Little Minister*. Conan Doyle had made no mark in the theatre but had already produced three of the Sherlock Holmes volumes which were to ensure his fame, as well as other novels and the play *Foreign Policy*.

The music for *Jane Annie* was provided by Ernest A. Claire Ford. Thirty-five-year-old Ford had been a pupil of Sullivan and later of Lalo in Paris and had a variegated list of composing credits including songs, religious music (among which was a cantata *The Eve of Festa* (1886) to a text by *Punch*'s Mark Lemon), ballet music (*Faust*) and most recently musical theatre, with four numbers for Toulmouche's *The Wedding Eve* and the score for the operetta *Mr Jericho* at the Savoy. He had also been responsible for assisting with the orchestrations of a deal of Sullivan's music as well as for the published arrangements of *Ivanhoe* for which production he had served as musical director. It was Sullivan who convinced Carte to try Ford as a composer.

The combined talents of two of the most imaginative authors of the time might have been expected to produce something of the standard of a Gilbert or a Planché, but *Jane Annie* turned out to be a surprising aberration. Neither the plot nor the dialogue was imaginative or amusing. As in *La Rosière*, the ladies of the piece were schoolgirls and the action evolved around the attempts of one of them, Bab, the standard 'romp of the school' to elope with one of two gentleman friends – quite which of the two she is not sure. Along the line we are asked to be interested in the attempts of Jane Annie, the naughtiest (and most unpleasant) girl in the school, to win the Good Conduct Prize by sneaky means and subsequently to win one of Bab's admirers, for which purpose she resorts to hypnotism. An officious and lascivious Proctor and his old flame, an uninteresting schoolmistress, helped to fill out two acts of irrelevancies including a sporadic attempt at 'satire' of the New Journalism which consisted of bringing on a horde of hyperactive students rushing inexplicably about with cameras and notepads.

The most unusual feature of the libretto was the printed copy which was available to the public. On this occasion it contained, as well as the lines spoken on the stage, copious marginal notes representing the comments and thoughts of the comic page-boy, Caddie, to and through the action. There were also long and carefully written descriptions and stage directions which read like pieces of a prose novel detailing things (such as thoughts) which it was impossible to depict on stage. *The Stage* commented impatiently that it was very peculiar that one had to read the printed libretto to find the humour of the piece, and other papers echoed its opinion that the marginalia were much the best and funniest thing to be found in *Jane Annie*. The piece was almost universally damned, although *The Era* commented hopefully:

> Cases have not been few of late in which the approval of the outside public has completely reversed the decision of the critics . . . *Jane Annie* at the Savoy is just the kind of light, agreeable, frivolous entertainment which pleases the after-dinner patron of the drama. It has the variety of a Gaiety burlesque combined with a refinement which only an author like Mr Barrie–to say nothing of his clever collaborator Mr Conan Doyle–could supply and we should not be surprised to see the opera played for hundreds of nights in spite of the gloomy prognostications . .

The paragraph read more like a press release. *Jane Annie* was not refined or clever and it was nothing like a Gaiety burlesque. If people wanted Gaiety burlesque, *In Town* with an ever-changing programme was available just over the road from the Savoy. The gloomy prognostications were altogether justified and *Jane Annie* was taken off after fifty nights–another, and this time thoroughly deserving, comic opera flop. It did not follow its predecessors into the D'Oyly Carte touring canon and its provincial life was limited to a few weeks' tour with the original cast. The Savoy sadly closed its doors through July, August and September until Gilbert and Sullivan were ready to produce *Utopia (Limited)*.

The prospect of Gilbert, Sullivan and Carte together again was one which the regular Savoy public and many others greeted with delight and almost with relief. When the time arrived for the new piece to be presented, they came in their battalions to be entertained once more by the wit of Gilbert allied to the sparkling melodies of Sullivan. They came and they were not disappointed. At the conclusion of the opening night's performance the audience cheered and cheered when the authors came in front of the curtain, as they had in earlier and happier days. The newspapers came together to applaud the newest Savoy opera. *The Times* declared:

> The latest is also one of the best of the set. Since *The Mikado* indeed it is hard to remember any work of the same hands that is worthy to stand beside the new production for pointed dialogue and easily assimilated music . .

But *Utopia (Limited)* was not of the same quality or, indeed, of the same type as the best of its predecessors. In the interval between *The Gondoliers* and *Utopia (Limited)* a deal of change had come into the lives of the two writers. Gilbert's writing had returned to the less flexible style of translated farce (*Haste to the Wedding*) and early comic opera (*The Mountebanks*) and now, in *Utopia (Limited)*, he produced a brittle and sometimes petulantly satiric libretto from which the joyous bubble and harmless if pointed mockery of earlier works were missing.

The story concerned the Pacific island of Utopia which is ruled by a curious depotism. The King, though paramount (and that is his name), has his autocracy tempered by being subject to the approval of two Wise Men who, should he fail in his fair and just kingly duty are obliged to denounce him to the Public Exploder who must execute him by explosion. Subsequently, to soothe his duly ruffled feelings, the Exploder succeeds to the throne. In Utopia, however, the system has a fault for the

Wise Men have used their position to become an effective oligarchy and are running all sorts of schemes on the side whilst forcing the King to denigrate himself anonymously in press and theatre. The Utopians have another curious idea – to wit, that all that is British is perfect; and, in consequence, the King's eldest daughter has been sent to Girton to obtain an education. She returns, accompanied by the Flowers of Progress, six Britons of various and perfect talents – a Lord Chamberlain, a captain in the Life Guards, a naval captain, a QC who is also an MP, a county councillor and a company promoter called Goldbury. The Flowers of Progress take on the organisation of the island, turning it (and everyone in it) into limited companies each with a capital of eighteenpence. This and their other reforms upset Scaphio and Phantis, the Wise Men, and also the order of things:

> Our pride and boast – the Army and the Navy –
> Have both been reconstructed and remodelled
> Upon so irresistible a basis
> That all neighbouring nations have disarmed –
> And war's impossible! Your County Councillor
> Has passed such drastic sanitary laws
> That all the doctors dwindle, starve, and die!
> The laws, remodelled by Sir Bailey Barre,
> Have quite extinguished crime and litigation:
> The lawyers starve, and all the jails are let
> As model lodgings for the working classes!

The king is puzzled. 'Is everything at a standstill in England? Is there no litigation there? no bankruptcy? no poverty? no squalor? no sickness? no crime?' 'Plenty', cries the Princess and then remembers the thing which makes England what it is – Government by Party! Paramount declares henceforth that Utopia shall have Government by Party – no longer a monarchy (Limited) but a Limited Monarchy, and thus rid itself of its painful perfection. The principal theme was decorated by a slight love story featuring the Princess Zara and her British escort, the Captain Fitzbattleaxe, and the antics of her two sisters who have been brought up to behave with exaggerated propriety by an English governess who is, herself, an attraction to King Paramount.

The general tone of *Utopia (Limited)* was, even in its lighter moments, somewhat bilious. The satiric hits – all important and legitimate ones – were all more direct than usual, less subtle and less humorous. The dialogue was occasionally convoluted and long-winded and purposeful rather than merry. Gilbert's wit and wisdom had failed to adapt to the subject he had chosen and, although his great talent ensured that the libretto of *Utopia (Limited)* was a much better piece of writing than most contemporary musicals, it lacked the spirit of *The Mikado* and *H.M.S. Pinafore* and the topsy turvy comical element which had made them so likeable.

Sullivan, too, had not entirely returned from the styles of *Ivanhoe* and *Haddon Hall* and, in any case, the lyrics with which he was provided did not often give him the opportunities he needed. One, in fact, defeated the composer completely and eventually, it is said, Sullivan composed the music first and Gilbert added fresh lyrics later. The number in question, the finale, was still not found satisfactory and it was replaced by a new one five nights into the run. Perhaps the best numbers which the authors came up with in *Utopia (Limited)* were two which had very little to do with the action and which were loosely inserted into the fabric of the play – King Paramount's song with its echoes of the Bab Ballads:

KING: Of course! Now I see it! Thank you very much. I was sure it had its humorous side, and it was very dull of me not to have seen it before. But, as I said just now, it's a quaint world.

PHAN: Teems with quiet fun.

KING: Yes. Properly considered, what a farce life is, to be sure!

First you're born – and I'll be bound you
Find a dozen strangers round you.
'Hallo,' cries the new-born baby,
'Where's my parents? which may they be?'
Awkward silence – no reply –
Puzzled baby wonders why!
Father rises, bows politely –
Mother smiles (but not too brightly) –
Doctor mumbles like a dumb thing –
Nurse is busy mixing something –
Every symptom tends to show
You're decidedly de trop.

and a comedy tenor song for Fitzbattleaxe:

A tenor, all singers above,
(This doesn't admit of a question),
Should keep himself quiet,
Attend to his diet
And carefully nurse his digestion:
But when he is madly in love
It's certain to tell on his singing –
You can't do chromatics
With proper emphatics
When anguish your bosom is wringing!
When distracted with worries in plenty,
And his pulse is a hundred and twenty,
And his fluttering bosom the slave of mistrust is,
A tenor can't do himself justice.

which had much more the character of a variety number than that of the Savoy in its lyrics but which, suitably enhanced by Sullivan's music, became one of the show's most popular numbers. Also popular was Mr Goldbury's explanation of Company practice, an unlikely and original piece in one of Gilbert's more curious metres:

Some seven men form an Association
(if possible, all Peers and Baronets),
They start off with a public declaration
To what extent they mean to pay their debts.
That's called their Capital: if they are wary
They will not quote it at a sum immense.
The figure's immaterial – it may vary
From eighteen million down to eighteenpence.
I should put it rather low;
The good sense of doing so
Will be evident at once to any debtor,
When it's left to you to say
What amount you mean to pay,
Why, the lower you can put it at, the better.

For the production of *Utopia (Limited)* the triumvirate took the unusual step of giving a public dress-rehearsal the night before the opening. This gave the authors a chance to see how their material would fare, particularly in the hands of the almost entirely new band of performers. Rutland Barrington, Rosina Brandram and W. H. Denny were still there, but most of the cast were tackling their first metropolitan Gilbert and Sullivan show, although some such as Lawrence Gridley and Herbert Ralland had long done service in the touring companies. Totally new, to the Savoy and to the stage, was Gilbert's young protégée, the American soprano Nancy McIntosh who was to play Zara. At the dress rehearsal she was clearly nervous and, like the tenor in the song, certainly did not do herself justice. Since her acting was fairly rudimentary, her performance relied largely on her small but attractive singing voice. When nerves had an adverse effect on that trouble loomed and it was decided that her song 'Youth is a Boon Avowed' should be cut. But the song was Miss McIntosh's big moment and she hurried to Gilbert. It was reinstated for the opening night, but thereafter disappeared.

In spite of the cut, the first act of *Utopia (Limited)* was excessively long – an hour and three-quarters. Of contemporary works allegedly only *Gotterdämmerung* was longer. The newspapers commented on the fact, but did not allow this to mar otherwise glowing reports. Those who felt they could not praise specifically wrote generally but the vicious tone of some of Gilbert's satiric lines had jarred some, most particularly Zara's final speech incongruously delivered by the pretty, fragile Nancy McIntosh:

> Government by party! Introduce that great and glorious element – at once the bulwark and the foundation of England's greatness – and all will be well! No political measures will endure because one party will assuredly undo all that the other party had done; inexperienced civilians will govern your army and your navy; no social reforms will be attempted, because out of vice, squalor and drunkeness no political capital is to be made; and while grouse is to be shot and foxes worried to death, the legislative action of the country will be at a standstill. Then there will be sickness in plenty, endless lawsuits, crowded jails, interminable confusion in the army and navy and, in short, general and unexampled prosperity.

But no-one had come to pick and carp and, after some minor alterations, *Utopia (Limited)* found its place comfortably in the public's favour. In spite of its subsequent lack of popularity, the piece was by no means a failure. It ran for 245 performances, more than any comic opera since *The Gondoliers*, outrunning such pieces as *Doris, Marjorie, The Mountebanks, Haddon Hall* and *The Nautch Girl*, and was received into the D'Oyly Carte touring canon before the end of the year. In 1894 no fewer than four touring companies were playing it round Britain. It was not until 1902 that it disappeared from the repertoire and fell into comparative disregard.

In the meanwhile others were quickly jumping on the Savoy bandwagon. Amongst these was a small-time provincial manager/writer Lloyd Clarance who had secured a piece called *The Island of Utopia*, an extravaganza by Claude Nugent which had one or two features similar to Gilbert's play. Clarance rushed into print with accusations of plagiarism and, finding himself lightly but sternly dismissed, attempted to sell his *Utopia* to the United States possibly in the hope that, at a distance, he might profit from some confusion. The rival *Utopia*, although it held a place for a while in Ben Greet's touring repertoire, failed to make any impression. The Savoy *Utopia* did make it to America where it ran a short season at the Broadway Theatre the following year with a D'Oyly Carte cast.

Utopia (Limited)[1] proved that the year was not totally intolerant of comic opera, but two further colourful failures were still in store. The first of these was a work called *Peterkin* for which a certain Mr Fallen, understood to be an Ipswich businessman, hired the Royalty Theatre from Kate Santley. It had been written by someone who preferred to hide under the pseudonym of George Eliot's hero Will Ladislaw, and the music was from one Signor Camerana.

Peterkin was extensively and enthusiastically advertised but, when it appeared, it was quickly seen that it was not up to professional standards. The story was a weak and old-fashioned concoction set around the Battle of Trafalgar in which the usual wealthy booby disputed with the usual upstanding hero for the hand of the soprano heroine in a welter of amateurish dialogue and florid music whose merits could scarcely be judged because of the demerits of the artists. In spite of the fact that they had been rehearsing for five weeks, some of these were barely ready and others would never have been and clearly owed their leading roles to considerations other than talent. The chorus and the staff had been engaged from genuine professionals and they were disconcerted when, going for their first pay the morning after opening, they found there was no money. Cash was promised and the show went on that night to a full house – surprising in view of the appalling notices. Rumour went round that the piece was to be replaced by *Il Trovatore* and the 'stars' were heard trying the roles. Then new dances and a forepiece for *Peterkin* were put into rehearsal and still the houses were full and still the cast went unpaid. Money was promised from the Saturday box-office but then it was discovered that the full houses were nothing more than the result of energetic papering. Mr Fallen and his manager Mario Moro were nowhere to be found and the box-office receipts would not pay a fraction of what was owing. *Peterkin*'s fifth performance was its last.

The production had a postscript. The Actors' Association was called on but declined to do anything to help the cast who had rehearsed five weeks and played one without pay, or to aid in the prosecution of Fallen and Moro, so a charity matinée was held for the benefit of the actors. In keeping with the tone of the affair it succeeded in making a loss. Finally Mori was brought to justice and was sentenced to twelve months' hard labour, not for his sins against the cast and the public but for fraudulently getting £20 out of a would-be licensee for the refreshment bars in the Royalty.

Financial problems also proved the downfall of *Miami* at the Princess's, although this was a much more legitimate undertaking. John Hollingshead, late of the Gaiety, had taken the Princess's and had had it done up to be a new 'cheap theatre'. His opening attraction was the not-very-comic opera of *Miami*, adapted from the successful melodrama *The Green Bushes* (1845) by J. B. Buckstone. Its story dealt with the Irishman Connor Kennedy who is obliged to flee his native Galway for political reasons, leaving behind his wife and child. He ends up in America, living on the shores of the Mississippi and sharing his life with the beautiful Franco-Indian huntress, Miami. When Kennedy's wife finally comes from Ireland to join him the jealous Miami kills Kennedy and throws herself in the river. In the final act she returns, now a wealthy lady, and restores Kennedy's daughter to her mother before dying nobly.

The show's references were good. The work had been put together by the team responsible for *Cigarette*, Warham St Leger and J. Haydn Parry, with Hollingshead himself working on the adaptation of the book. Violet Cameron was engaged to play the title role supported by a fine cast including the Savoyards Courtice Pounds, Jessie

[1] The parentheses were later discarded.

Bond and Richard Temple. But the opening night was not a success. The elements of the show mixed poorly. St Leger and Parry had tried to turn what was basically a grand opera story into a light opera and their pretty contribution merely sounded trival. Hollingshead had attempted to supply a comic element by playing up two comedy showmen in the American scenes and this, equally, proved a blunder. *Miami* was a grotesque mixture of styles which would please no-one.

The Stage commented:

> *Miami* put off from Sunday to Monday might have advantageously been further postponed . . . some will perhaps declare that it ought to have been postponed *sine die* . .

The troubles were not slow to come. The £2000 capital for the show was exhausted and receipts were poor. At the second week's treasury there was not enough to pay everyone. Hollingshead elected to pay his staff and put the actors and understudies on a promise till Saturday night but the indignant actors were having none of it and Hollingshead was forced to close the theatre. When liability was tested it was discovered that he was only a manager employed by a producing syndicate to give it an attractive 'front'. The members of the syndicate were nowhere to be found. Further trouble arose when a certain W. Sapte, who had collaborated with Parry on a piece called *Marigold Farm* which had been seen at one Opera Comique matinée in February, claimed that the music of *Miami* was largely that composed for *Marigold Farm* which he was currently trying to sell to America. Sapte felt his prospects had been damaged by the failure of *Miami* and the re-use of 'his' music. Since neither *Miami* or *Marigold Farm* would ever be heard of again, Mr Sapte's protests proved of little consequence.

If the balance sheet for the comic opera in London in 1893 was discouraging, that for the new style musical was not. *In Town* held the Gaiety stage until the end of July and in April it was joined by an even more successful piece of a similar kind, *Morocco Bound*, at the Shaftesbury. Following on the initial success of *In Town*, a syndicate was got together with Fred Harris at its head to produce another piece on the same lines. The music and lyrics, as for *In Town*, were provided by Frank Osmond Carr and Adrian Ross while the libretto was the work of Arthur Branscombe. Branscombe was a colourful gentleman whose youth had included a period as a backwoodsman in Australia and a poultry farmworker in Kent but whose most recent efforts had been in the theatre, notably as a press man at the Gaiety.

Harris, following the *In Town* recipe, engaged a cast of new burlesque and variety favourites and mounted the show with great lavishness. After a premature announcement for the unlucky Opera Comique he secured the Shaftesbury and on 13 April *Morocco Bound*, billed as a musical farce, was produced. The first act lived up to the description. It was of the genre of extravagant tomfooleries which had passed under the title in both America and Britain for many years with a story full of fun and incident. The second act consisted largely of a glorified variety show in which the show's stars and various incidental performers could air their talents.

The story which allowed this construction went as follows. An Irish adventurer known as Spoofah Bey is anxious to gain the concession for music halls in Morocco and to finance his venture he and his sister, a phony countess, go to work on the wealthy retired costermonger, Squire Higgins. Their scheme to get him to invest in the British Palace of Varieties is foiled by the arrival of Higgins' down-to-earth brother, Josiah, but by the end of Act One Spoofah has persuaded the Squire to come to stay in his palace in Morocco, and Higgins and his sons Vivian and Dolly, their young ladies Maude and Ethel Sportington, under the chaperonage of their aunt Lady Walkover, the bluff Josiah and his companion bulldog, Miss Rhea Porter, journalist, Miss Eva Sketchley, artist and friends all set sail for Morocco in the Higgins yacht. Spoofah pretends to his guests that the Grand Vizier's palace is his, to the Vizier he explains that his cargo are specimens of the flower of the British Music Hall. By a series of bluffs the guests are inveigled into giving a 'turn' apiece and Spoofah's concession seems safe when all is betrayed by the goofy Lord Percy Pimpleton from the Embassy. The Vizier's fury is calmed by the pretty ladies and all ends good humouredly with Higgins created a Knight of the Red Morocco Boot.

The principal performers were, under this plan, all well supplied with scenes and with song and dance. John L. Shine as Spoofah Bey and Charles Danby as Higgins headed the comic side of affairs, racing through Branscombe's bright and unpretentious dialogue to great advantage. Danby had a grand coster song 'Honest Jim', and Shine sang of 'The grand old Game of Spoof', the topical 'In Morocco' and the great comedy hit of the piece 'The new Home Rule' taking the mickey out of the newly constituted Irish parliament:

> Oh the hear, hear, hear
> And the laughter coming afther
> Sure it nearly shplit the rafther
> And it burst the chandelier
> It was down with the whiskey and down with the rint,
> And that was the beginning of the Irish Parliament.

The two also joined together in a jolly piece in praise of the Music Hall:

> If you go to a swell music hall
> You must sit yourself down in a stall
> With a drink from the bar
> And a shilling cigar
> And a girl who is dressed for the ball
> For it's oh, the music hall
> For it's ah, the music hall
> Through the throne may be abolished
> And the parliament demolished
> Give the Englishman his Music Hall!

which gave them the chance to go into a standard series of topical impersonations of such pieces as Chevalier's 'My old Dutch', Marie Lloyd's latest 'Oh, Mr Porter', Stratton's 'Whistling Coon', Herbert Campbell in 'Up I Came with my little Lot' and simultaneous renderings of two of the year's biggest hits 'The Man who Broke the Bank at Monte Carlo' and '7th Royal Fusiliers'.

The more romantic pieces were less prominent. Violet Cameron had a couple of ballads and Sidney Barraclough as her tenor lover sang of 'A high old Time' and more chastely 'Come, my Own' and 'Light of Love'. Letty Lind in the ingénue role of Maude scored hugely with the duet 'The dancing Girl' which featured a caricature of the skirt dance as badly done by a society amateur:

> An ample skirt you must unfurl
> And learn to be a dancing girl
> So trip and skip and pirouette
> With serpentining whirl

The social pet in every set
It is the Dancing Girl.

and later with a graceful cymbal dance, and brought the house down with a jaunty if slightly inane celebration of 'Marguerite of Monte Carlo'.

The lesser principals joined in the free-for-all of song and dance. Jenny McNulty, a little stouter than in her Gaiety days, belted out a drinking song as the East End Countess, Douglas Munroe as a superannuated butler ground out an appreciation of 'The Style of the hupper Ten' and Colin Coop as the Vizier scored a triumph with his fluid 'Modern Civilization'. Herbert Sparling (Josiah) joined the two comic stars in a trio satirising the sudden overwhelming vogue in society for the music hall:

I feel it is the proper task of civilised humanity
To show the Africans the fruit of British Christianity
They oughtn't to be left to pine in sadness while we revel here
In all the happy influence of Marie Lloyd and Chevalier . .

and won plenty of laughs from his antics with the bulldog and his catchphrase 'Mind the pup!' Some of the biggest laughs were reserved for one of the smallest roles. The part of the silly ass Englishman, Lord Percy Pimpleton, was taken by the younger Grossmith. Goofing around the stage, shunned by all, gasping out *his* catchphrase 'I think you're beastly rude, don't cher know!' George made more than the most of his opportunities. His role grew during rehearsals as Branscombe obligingly tacked in a half page here and another entrance there and after opening night nothing could hold the young comedian. Soon the management were getting a good deal more than their £3 a week's worth as Lord Percy

> introduced impromptu idiotic stories and conundrums every time I came on the stage and when the other comedians tried to shut me up, I indulged in an absurd giggle . .

Grossmith was not the only one to embroider the original text which was elastically enough constructed to allow plenty of alterations and interpolations on the principle of keeping the show fresh and attractive as it moved on towards its hundredth and then its 200th performance.

Morocco Bound caught the mood of the moment precisely. It was jolly, bright, topical, totally digestible and, while figuring to satirise music hall and the current craze, supplied in its parodies material which was sufficiently like the real thing to satisfy the most fashionable craving. Even *The Times* had disapprovingly to admit:

> It does not belong to a very high class but of the class it would be difficult to find a more exhilarating specimen . .

as the public which had shunned *The Magic Opal* and *The Golden Web* filled the Shaftesbury night after night. The show marked a definitive turning point towards a light and easy-going form of musical theatre which would soon lead into what would be loosely classed as 'musical comedy'. It was neither comic opera nor new burlesque, though it borrowed from both and, more notably, straight from the 'halls':

> Nobody can shut his eyes to the revolution which is just just now taking place in the entertainment that is provided at our theatres. At the Gaiety music hall 'turns' are in vogue, the music hall performer is requisitioned at the Vaudeville[1] and no person

[1] the Vaudeville Theatre housed the American song and dance show *A Trip to Chicago*.

> could witness a performance of such a piece as *Morocco Bound* without being convinced of its close relationship to the staple furnished at those establishments associated with the musical glasses.
>
> (*Entr'acte* 19 Aug. 1893)

In true music-hall fashion the 'bill' was changed frequently and after seven months an official second edition saw large alterations made in the show's score. Danby was given a new coster song 'The Coster is the Pet of 'igh Society' and a duet with Letty Lind 'A bit 'Ot'. Miss Lind introduced a comedy song entitled 'The Peer of the Realm' and Colin Coop replaced 'Modern Civilization' with 'An Eastern Legend'. The bulk of the new material went, however, to Shine who supplemented the still popular 'New Home Rule' with 'Calamity's Child', 'Nothing at All' and 'International Flirtation'. Leading ladies came and went and a surprise replacement for Miss Lind came in the shape of 'My Sweetheart', Minnie Palmer, who needless to say brought her own material and interpretation to the role.

As an additional attraction, at one stage the Shaftesbury hired the now internationally famous Loie Fuller to display her serpentine dances at the interval. Miss Fuller was already engaged in a similar capacity at the Gaiety and Fred Harris was not to be outdone. The sharp Miss Fuller who had her own ideas about money had a novel manner of receiving pay. Professing herself unwilling to be a burden on the budget if she did not attract, she declared that she would take no salary at all until the takings had reached the sum of £138 per night (a seemingly arbitrary sum). After that she would take 50% of the gross. Since she was being used in the two most successful musicals in town, Miss Fuller was on to a good thing. But both managements accepted her terms so presumably she was worth her money. Later in the season the Shaftesbury featured Letty Lind between the acts where, according to *The Stage* she 'out-Fullered Fuller'.

As another feature the curtain raiser was replaced by a 'New Musical, Theosophical, Illusory Sketch' by Chance Newton devised for the illusionist Hercat. It was constructed round the characters of Ivanhoe, and Harry Grattan and Marie Studholme, the star understudies for the main piece, assisted. Miss Studholme was subjected to '[the] New and Marvellous Mahatma Illusion REBECCA PRECIPITATED in which Rebecca is invisibly wafted through space from the stake to which she has been securely tied'. Other incidental additions to the show included the 'French duettists' Messrs Fysher and Farkoa, the latter of whom was to become one of the most popular leading men on the London musical stage, the child vocalist Dorothy Hanbury, Marie Cahill from the Gaîté in Paris, and the Parisian Quadrille Dancers, the rage of Paris, with the archly named Nini Patte-en-l'Air at their head.

Morocco Bound saw out 1893 at the Shaftesbury before transferring to the Trafalgar Square to run out the last month of a run of 295 performances. During its London run the show had already been taken into the provinces with, not unexpectedly, great success and Fred Harris continued to tour his golden goose for two further years before handing the Number One dates over to the author, Branscombe, who revised and up-dated his script and took it round for three further years. Number Two tours were licensed and overseas companies produced *Morocco Bound* in Australia, South Africa and on the continent, while the piece remained on the British circuits for many years.

In spite of many successors and imitations, *Morocco Bound* remained genuinely popular. It even returned to London: Branscombe supervised a potted version at the Oxford Music Hall starring Wilfred Shine; John Shine and Charles Danby reappeared at the Comedy Theatre over Christmas 1901/2 in their original roles in a brief revival;

and in 1914 it surfaced once more compressed into a music hall scenario under the title *I've Seen the 'Arem.* All that time it made regular reappearances on the touring lists and Branscombe, who never succeeded in writing another successful show, became known for his inevitable first night (and any other night) conversation, 'When I invented musical comedy . . . .'

The vogue for the so-called 'variety musical', if it needed confirming, had been confirmed, thanks to two well-written, skilfully and expensively staged and cast examples of a type which a decade previously would have been considered suitable only for a provincial audience. Now that musical tastes had become more frivolous, demanding chiefly the comic, the topical, the risqué and the glamorous with the least amount of intellectual content possible, these shows were 'just the ticket'. The so-called 'Naughty Nineties' had a different theatrical taste to the seventies or even the eighties, and they had the time and the means to ensure that their chosen entertainment prospered. And prosper it did through a decade which was to see an unparalleled activity and success in the British musical theatre.

Before the end of the year three variety musicals made their appearance in the West End. Each still sheltered under a remnant of the pretence of being burlesque with their titles including Don Quixote, Christopher Columbus and Don Juan but the plots used little or nothing of those well-known tales. The Prince of Wales Theatre and George Edwardes showed more courage and initiative and took the step into the more vertebrate modern-dress musical comedy with *A Gaiety Girl.* The difference was not enormous but it was significant.

The first of these shows to arrive in town was *A Modern Don Quixote*, the show for which Arthur Roberts had forsaken *In Town.* The libretto was written by George Dance who had been responsible for the excellent book of *The Nautch Girl*, whilst the versatile John Crook supplied the music. The story, described by Dance as 'a musical farcical nondescript', had no relation to Cervantes. An advertising broadsheet gave it:

> The pretty little village of Hogthorpe is in a flutter of excitement. Rosy-cheeked milkmaids hob-nob with buxom widows and love-sick youths discuss the all-prevailing topic with sleek and happy-go-lucky bachelors. The cause of all this anxiety is the long anticipated arrival of the famous Knight of Modern Chivalry, Don Quixote. This worthy, like his eminent namesake, goes about the world assisting distressed maidens and forlorn widows, and it is on their invitation that he has consented to visit Hogthorpe. The men of this benighted village have each sworn a vow of celibacy, and the ladies, in their distress, have petitioned the Don – whose fame as a Matrimonial Revivalist is universal – to come to their assistance. The strains of the local Band announce the hero's approach and in a short time after his arrival the village youths, influenced by his mighty will, have offered their hearts and hands to the poor girls who have waited so long in vain. But here a remarkable event occurs. The Don, who has hitherto regarded love and matrimony from a purely business point of view, suddenly finds himself enamoured of a beauteous maiden, a ward in Chancery, named Maud. He at first weighs over the policy of a matrimonial alliance with some deliberation, but after learning the amount of her dowry, he hesitates no longer, and proposes on the spot. The various couples now return to take the nuptial vow, and the Don, assuming the disguise of a Bishop of Gretna Green – who appears to be touring the provinces with his historic anvil – marries them while they wait. But here his troubles begin. In the excitement of the moment he unites the wrong couples and even marries his own fiancée to another. At this moment too Maud's uncle and guardian enters and, after denouncing him as an impostor orders his niece's arrest. The infuriated villagers turn upon the pseudo-Bishop, but he

mounts his faithful Rosinante – which is in this instance a 'pneumatic safety' and seeks refuge in flight.

We are next shown the interior of Treadmill Castle, which is a prison for first-class misdemeanants. Here Maud is brought by her uncle, who is the governor of the establishment, and he will only set her at liberty on the condition that she marries his son, Algernon. This step is, of course, an illegal one but General Jenkinson claims to be acting under the direction of the Court of Chancery. Love laughs at locksmiths and a knight errant laughs at jailors. A doctor arrives for the purpose of enquiring into the state of Maud's health and, beneath his professional disguise the wily Don is easily recognised. The lovers are thus united. But the length of a doctor's visit is prescribed by custom and after a too brief meeting he is reluctantly compelled to take his departure; but only to return in a few minutes, for when the nurse arrives – a neat and tidy person whom the doctor has recommended – she is no other than the versatile knight in feminine attire. To him the amorous Governor confesses that he has no longer control over the Duchess Maud who is, by order of the Court of Chancery, in a position to marry the man of her choice. A knight who can enter a prison in female attire is surely able to do so as a theatrical manager. They have an Amateur Thespian Club at Treadmill Castle and a professional stage manager is hourly expected. He arrives in the person of Don Quixote not only to conduct the rehearsals of the new opera, but to denounce the Governor as an impostor. With this comes a general reconciliation. All the unhappy marriages are annulled, the prisoners are released and the lovers are united for ever and the repentant Don promises to abandon the somewhat shady profession of Modern Knight Errantry and settle down into solid respectability as an English Country Gentleman . .

The Era sighed:

In the 'good old days' it used to be said that if you wanted a receipt for that popular mystery known to the world as a jolly burlesque, you should take an old story or chapter of history, treat it with humour, and make it grotesque. But all that is altered nowadays. Story and plot are well-nigh discarded. Pretty girls, smart dresses, spicy jokes, songs, dancing and fun are the things. Give your extravaganza the label of some well-known tale or legend, and let the filling-in be anything you like, so long as it is good in its way, and there you are, dontcherknow. On this plan Mr George Dance would seem to have shaped his *Modern Don Quixote*. Cervantes has been laid under contribution for the title but of the incidents in the career of the knight of the rueful countenance there are absolutely none. Any other appellation would have answered equally as well. 'St George and the Dragon', 'Watts' Hymns', 'Brandy and Soda' or anything else would have been equally appropriate and have supplied as ready a clue to the clever and amusing nonsense of which the 'musical farcical play' is compounded . . .

The Don, in this case, is an 'ultra-fashionably-coated, shiny-hatted, lavender-gloved and orchid-buttonholed gentleman, not too particular, up to all sorts of dodges that will pay, honestly or otherwise . . .' – in other words, a not terribly distant relative of *In Town*'s Captain Coddington. The second act took fairly little heed of the fate of the Duchess Maud and was developed into little more than a vehicle for the comic talents of Arthur Roberts and a few lively variety items, but Dance kept the dialogue spitting merrily if inconsequentially along with satirical jabs at the 'first class misdemeanant' system (prisoners who could and did pay for unbelievable luxury during their lawful confinement), the Ward in Chancery system, the all-too-easily satirised foibles of comic opera etc. and just prevented the whole affair degenerating into a shapeless morass of turns comic and musical.

John Crook, now far away from the more ambitious days of *The King's Dragoons*, supplied a score full of lively, well-written and unpretentious numbers from which Roberts's 'The Cat Came Back with the Milkman in the Morning' emerged as the most popular. But the show's writers, while allowing Roberts his head in the kind of role which he required, did not allow him to dominate the show to the exclusion of all else. Edward Coleman was given good opportunities to show off his comic and dancing talents as a modern Sancho Panza, W. H. Denny as the Jailor ('I am a General'), Yata Whynier as Maud ('My Love is a Love Unknown') and soubrette Lizzie Aubrey ('I've lost my Place') all had good numbers and Mabel Love was strongly featured as principal danseuse, giving the show a better overall balance than had been attained in some recent Arthur Roberts' efforts.

A Modern Don Quixote was prepared for a provincial tour and after opening at Nottingham it played ten number one dates before Roberts announced a two-week season at the Strand Theatre under his own management. In the event the show was so well liked during those two weeks that it was deemed worthwhile to postpone further the in-house production of *The Ladykiller* and run *A Modern Don Quixote* one more week. The reaction all round was good:

> a merry piece of nonsense without backbone or sequence reminiscent of endless works that have preceded it, but always affording as its chief end unlimited scope for the fertile humour of Mr Arthur Roberts . . . (*Stage*)
>
> Mr George Dance has written a dialogue not destined, perhaps, to gain him a niche in the temple of literary fame, but full of humour and quite fin de siècle, while all his songs are distinguished by the great merits of being novel, comical and taking. Mr John Crook's music is excellent, and just what it should be. The various airs suit the subjects, and the merry tunes sparkle like bubbles in a champagne glass. Some of his work, also, is almost operatic in character, as witness the finale to the first act, which was marked by a fervour and brilliancy and musicianly ring that brought down the act-drop amid a storm of applause . . (*Era*, Notts)

and even *The Times* conceded

> . . even less story than the variety class of entertainment to which it belongs. On one pretext or another or without any pretext at all Mr Arthur Roberts appears in various characters – now as the blacksmith at Gretna Green, again as an eminent medical man, then as a music hall singer and so on with just sufficiency of song, dance or talking by the other members of the company to allow him a reasonable interval between his turns. The result is amusing enough. Mr Arthur Roberts is a comedian of very considerable resource and his patter dialogue he supplements in the present instance with pure pantomime of a high order representing a gentleman supping at a restaurant and paying his bill and a lady doing up her hair . .

Of course Arthur Roberts was the attraction, but Roberts had failed dreadfully in poor vehicles within recent remory and the efforts of Dance and Crook had as much hand in the success of *A Modern Don Quixote* as had those of their star. At the end of the third week there was still a good deal of future left for the show and Roberts would have liked to continue his actor/manager stint at the Strand in what was undoubtedly a piece which could build up a genuine run, but his contract with George Edwardes required him to go the Gaiety for *Don Juan*. One 'Don' was shelved in favour of another, and *The Ladykiller* finally got on to the Strand stage. Roberts thought well enough of *A Modern Don Quixote*, however, to revive it in a somewhat revised version in 1898 with a French setting, fresh dialogue and additional songs from Paul Rubens, Walter Tilbury and Alfred Morris. It played a short season at the Lyric Theatre and was taken on a two months' tour.

With October came the three remaining and highly successful enterprises of the year. The Lyric, which had abandoned musical fare since the disasters of *The Magic Opal* and *The Golden Web*, returned to its old policy with the production of a 'burlesque opera' by George Sims and Cecil Raleigh entitled *Little Christopher Columbus*. Christopher was an orphan cabin-boy and his principal preoccupation a romance with Miss Guinevere Block, the daughter of the Bacon King of Chicago. Christopher has jumped ship to pursue his amours and is anxiously sought by his Captain, Slammer, who is party to the secret of the boy's birth – he is none other than the long-lost son of the Duke of Veragua and Slammer is intent on making his daughter, Hannah, a Duchess. Little Christopher is also pursued by the law in the form of the Spanish Police Chief, Don Juan, and the Irish detective O'Hoolegan who has been hired by Guinevere's papa to checkmate any marital ideas the boy might have. Block has promised his wife that Guinevere shall have a Duke like all other rich young Americans. Juan and O'Hoolegan are simultaneously pursuing a rival love for the Spanish dancer, Pepita, who is set to sail for the World's Fair in Chicago in order to pay off her family debts. After a series of crosses and double crosses in which Christopher is imprisoned then freed, Pepita, disguised as the boy, is haled aboard the good ship 'Choctaw' which sets sail for America. Aboard the ship also are Guinevere and her father, O'Hoolegan and, bound for the dancing booth at the Fair, little Christopher disguised as Pepita. The second act was set in the grounds of the World's Fair, a fine setting for a Variety concert and for the eventual revelations and reconciliations required to round the evening off happily.

The composer for the show was Ivan Caryll. Since his youthful début with *The Lily of Léoville* Caryll's writing had been limited to little more than hack work, turning out short pieces to order and fill-in and replacement material for Sedger's botched French musicals. His additions to *La Cigale* had contributed largely to its success and his work for *Ma Mie Rosette* had been equally attractive if less long-lived. Now, for the first time, he had the opportunity to compose a full original score for a new English work. It was scarcely the refined continental opéra-comique for which he had been trained, for *Little Christopher Columbus* went as far towards the music hall as any of its predecessors had, but Caryll's indestructible gift for melody and his easy-going and accurate adaptability allowed him to produce a highly apposite and successful score. He had been presented at the outset with one important problem. Sedger had decided to cast in the title role 'that little brown thing', Miss May Yohe, who had aroused so much interest in *The Magic Opal*. Since being written out of that piece Miss Yohe had gone up a step and had appeared as Denise in the Trafalgar Square Theatre's revival of Hervé's *Mamselle Nitouche*, giving her own very particular and vocally truncated version of the role created for Anna Judic. But if May's vocal range was limited, her temperament was not. She stamped, she shrieked, she told *Nitouche*'s young conductor, Henry Wood, that he 'couldn't conduct for nuts' (or something like nuts), she took nights off and finally 'terminated her contract' to be replaced by fellow American Sylvia Gerrish for the last 29 performances. But there was no question that Miss Yohe had something the public liked and she was to be Little Christopher Columbus – she and the whole of her ten tone range. So, with B flat below middle C to a precarious D an octave higher as his field, Ivan Caryll composed the star music for his first all-British show and, against all the odds, he succeeded in coming up with not only the greatest hit Miss Yohe would ever have but a bundle of other tunes which boded great things for the future.

Little Christopher Columbus opened at the Lyric Theatre on 10 October but not with the success anticipated. Edwin Lonnen as O'Hoolegan galloped through disguises as a Turkoman, a magician, a piece of officialdom, a British swell and a coachman as the first act progressed, changing from one to another with gusto–now off-stage, now on–as he pursued Christopher and Pepita through the streets of Seville. Miss Yohe was well enough received in Caryll's charming 'The Land of Love' and the siesta song 'Lazily, Drowsily' in which the composer had prettily manipulated the famous ten tones and Maud Holland did nicely with a coy song in the zoological vein:

A pussy cat sat by a silver stream, Purr . .
Singing away in a dainty dream, Purr . . .
As she sat in the sun and blinked her eye
A pretty goldfish came frisking by
She twitched her mouth in a way feline
And she thought 'how I wish that fish were mine'
Oh, purr. . . .

As soon as that pretty goldfish she saw, Purr . .
The pussy cat lifted her velvet paw, Purr . .
She knew it would be so nice and sweet
But she hadn't the courage to wet her feet
And the little goldfish he whisked his tail
And he winked his eye at the pussy cat's wail,
Oh, purr . . .

There are girls who with fish would like to play, Purr.
And catch for themselves ere they swim away, Purr . .
Our fish floats by with its golden gleam
But we sit and tremble beside the stream
Because like pussy we're frightened so
Of putting our foot in it, don't you know,
Oh, purr . . .

Lonnen was applauded for his Policeman's song 'The Indiarubber Shoe', but the most notable moment of the act was a pas de quatre led by Eva Greville of *Faust Up-To-Date* fame in which the girls appeared in what qualified for the description of 'suggestive costumes'. The offending part of the outfit was apparently the combination of tan (skin-coloured) tights with garters. Garters were bad enough but these garters were worn decidedly high up the leg. . and the dance finished with a turnover. But those who had read their newspapers knew that there was 'worse' to come. Miss May Yohe had been to Paris to study the infamous routines of the Parisian Quadrille dancers Grille d'Egout and La Goulue and she was to perform her version of 'La Chahut' in the first act finale. In the event the boom outdid the actuality. Miss Yohe was no Grille d'Egout. Her 'Chahut' was a tame affair and the pas de quatre remained the scandal of the evening.

In the second act things began to slide. The audience, irritated by the lack of story, began to make uncomfortable noises and only the introduction of the show's most popular songs brought them to order. The first gleam of success came with Lonnen's topical song 'I Pay no Attention to That', then May Yohe contributed a sort of ta-ra-ra hornpipe and a coster dance and followed up by joining Lonnen in the arch duet 'Nummy num num', but things really caught fire when Lonnen rolled on to sing to Caryll's rollicking melody

I am a jolly sort of chap, a favourite everywhere
My pals upon the back I slap and yell out 'Hull-oh there!'

The boys all know when I arrive, there's bound to be a spree
For I always keep the game alive wherever I may be . .
Rumpty tumpty, Rumpty tumpty, that's the song I sing
Everywhere it's Hull-oh there! and youth will have its fling
Oh, spend your cash and cut a dash, no matter who looks green
Rumpty tumpty tiddely umpty, that's the sort I mean!

The song was the hit of the night and when Miss Yohe followed up with the plaintive Plantation Song 'Oh, Honey, my Honey' the evening was well and truly back on course.

When the curtain fell the balance of opinion was in favour of the show running, but satisfaction was by no means universal. Sedger was hissed when he appeared in front of the curtain and the authors did not appear to take their customary first night bows. And the newspapers did not respond well. *The Times* snorted:

> The modern developments of burlesque have reached a point which seems to mark the lowest attainable level of theatrical enterprise and in the class of piece just now in fashion it would be difficult to match *Little Christopher Columbus* . . for unrelieved vacuity. . . . a certain number of fairly good songs, comic and sentimental, but the dialogue is on a level with that of the average amateur charade seasoned with a few puns and topical allusions . . .

and not without justification. The libretto for *Little Christopher Columbus* was an unbelievable lapse on the part of the venerable Sims. The story was flaccid and the dialogue feeble and pointless except when twisted violently in some extraneous direction so as to force in some play on words not worthy of a schoolboy or some vaguely topical reference on the lines of:

Pepita has been engaged to appear at the Chicago Exhibition.
Not in a serpentine skirt?
No. In something much 'Fuller'!.

Lonnen's role was a mere montage of elements from his earlier Gaiety roles with only his personal vigour and a triad of good numbers to see him through and Miss Yohe, working opposite (but barely with) him relied principally on her 'charms' and Caryll's gifts of songs. The script was a watered down burlesque book, a dated piece which threatened to scupper the whole enterprise.

When *Little Christopher Columbus* was taken off just before Christmas to allow some repairs and renovations in the theatre, it would have been a courageous punter who would have taken odds on its reappearance. It had been worked in over its 74 performances, the worst inanities knocked out and its popularity had been slowly but steadily growing, especially with the introduction into the cast of the comedian John F. Sheridan of 'Widow O'Brien' (*Fun on the Bristol*) fame. Sheridan had just returned himself to the good memory of London audiences in *A Trip to Chicago* at the Vaudeville and when that show closed Sedger engaged its star for *Little Christopher Columbus*. The role of 'The Second Mrs Block', a standard heavy lady with vague references to the current drama hit *The Second Mrs Tanqueray*, had originally consisted of a dozen lines allotted to the admirable Adelaide Newton and a number full of Pinero allusions sung by Lonnen which had been cut in rehearsal. In the hands of Sheridan it expanded vigorously into a piece of boisterous low comedy which gave a much needed lift to the second act and to the box office.

On Boxing Day *Little Christopher Columbus* re-opened and it never looked back. The emphasis on the song and dance content increased, the humour was laid on and some of the unnecessary complications of the 'story' ironed out as the script came under heavy rewriting which included a 'second edition' after ten months. Two notable cast changes intervened as the run stretched on. In the title role May Yohe, in an unbelievable switch, gave way to 'The Queen of opéra-bouffe', Florence St John, who was joined by Geraldine Ulmar (Mrs Ivan Caryll) as Genevieve, the two making up an experienced combination of an altogether different vocal value. Occasional attractions were added in what was becoming the accepted fashion. The Parisian dancer 'La Belle Roze' performed a skirt dance with projections on top of a moving and invisible globe and Trevin's Tableaux Vivants also made an appearance between the acts.

After twelve months *Little Christopher Columbus* was still sufficiently well-patronised for Sedger to organise a transfer when his schedule obliged him to stage his new piece, *His Excellency*, at the Lyric. The show which had originally seemed unlikely to run 100 nights ended its run at Terry's Theatre playing ten performances a week until its closure after a run of 421 performances. In October 1894 it was given a production on Broadway, heavily 'botched' to 'suit American tastes', with the American composer Gustave Kerker replacing some of Caryll's music with numbers of his own. Alterations and decorations were made ad libitum but the resultant pot pourri caught on in no small way. *Little Christopher* remained at the Garden Theatre and, subsequently, Palmer's for 264 performances carrying it right through the 1894/5 season before it was taken out for an equally successful tour.

Four days after the original London opening of *Little Christopher Columbus*, George Edwardes opened his newest show at the Prince of Wales. *A Gaiety Girl*, billed as 'a new musical comedy' had been written by a new team: author 'Owen Hall' and composer Sidney Jones[1]. 'Owen Hall' was the pseudonym chosen by solicitor and writer Jimmy Davis, allegedly in reference to his habit of getting into financial trouble. Dublin-born Davis came from a literary family, his sister being the author 'Frank Danby', mother of Gilbert Frankau, but up to now his own literary efforts had been limited to satirical and occasionally risqué journalism. His début as a theatrical writer apparently came about after he had declared to George Edwardes in conversation that he could write a better libretto than that for *In Town*, and Edwardes told him to get on with it[2]. The result was *A Gaiety Girl*. The script was given for its musical setting to lyricist Harry Greenbank and 32 year-old Sidney Jones. Jones was the son of Sidney Jones, m.d. at the Leeds Grand by night and bandmaster of the public band by day, and had begun his career as a clarinettist in his father's orchestra. He left home to join the touring *Fun on the Bristol* company and quickly rose to the position of conductor, subsequently touring with a number of major companies including the Gaiety tour of Australia. His first compositions seem to have been in the way of music for the Vokes family's farce *In Camp*, but he was brought to Edwardes notice as a composer by the song 'Linger longer Loo' which the manager snapped up (and later used most successfully in *Don Juan*) and which convinced him that his young conductor was capable of composing a show of his own.

[1] James Tanner is said to have been responsible for the 'construction' of the piece with 'Owen Hall' providing the dialogue.

[2] J. M. Glover claims that Edwardes saw a production of Charlie Brookfield's *The Poet and the Puppets* at the Criterion into which Charles Hawtrey had introduced four chorus ladies and four dancers. He consequently asked Brookfield to write him a musical play without the customary large chorus and crowd of 'supers'. Brookfield made several abortive attempts before Edwardes accepted Jimmy Davis' challenge.

The book which Owen Hall provided was based on a lightweight plot. The first act, set in 'the cavalry barracks at Winbridge', provided the occasion for the introduction of a set of dapper young officers, three smart young society ladies and their chaperone, and a gaggle of girls from the Gaiety Theatre. Everybody flirts, everybody sings and dances and we discover that the handsome Captain Charles Goldfield is in love with Alma Somerset of the Gaiety and will go so far as to offer to make her his wife. But Alma, conscious of the damage this will do to his prospects, refuses him. The society ladies do their best to excite the matrimonial ambitions of the more eligible officers while their chaperone, a handsome young widow, is seen to be the object of the attentions of the 'Society Judge', Sir Lewis Grey, and the Regimental Chaplain, Montague Brierly. The girls from the theatre, popular with the men, are scorned by the ladies who are not surprised when Alma is accused of stealing a diamond comb. She denies it, but it has been planted in her bag by the French maid, Mina, who is jealous of Goldfield's attentions to her. Alma vows her innocence and leaves the scene in turmoil. In the second act the scene is transposed to the Riviera where all the characters turn up in the middle of Carnival time. The various romances are satisfactorily worked out and Alma's name is cleared.

If the plot seemed slight, Owen Hall fleshed it out with unprecedentedly bright and well-written dialogue. With no Arthur Roberts to cater for, he was able to construct a genuine play in the reasonable hope that it would be performed fairly much as written. The leading roles were shared out more equitably than usual, the characters were allowed some genuine depth and the dialogue was written in a clear and incisive style with no attempts at word-play or blatant popular references. Owen Hall had written neither a burlesque libretto nor a comic opera book but a light dramatic play which more than justified his boast to Edwardes.

Yet *A Gaiety Girl* almost did not appear. With the piece announced and prepared, Edwardes had still failed to clear it with the censor. On its original application it had been turned down – Owen Hall's penchant for personal satire and pointed dialogue had been carried too far. The church, the bar, the army and unmistakeable individuals had all come into the sights of the author's machine-gun pen. It was too much. When the final alterations were made, time was running short and Edwardes was obliged to drive down to Devonshire less than 24 hours before the opening and beard the Licenser of Plays in his home. There he was granted the all-important licence and the first performance of *A Gaiety Girl* was able to go ahead as scheduled.

The reaction to the show was one of unabashed delight. The public found their tastes had been catered for to a nicety and the critics too found it entirely to their liking. The piece did not follow precisely any of the established forms of musical, but it combined the best elements of several of those forms with a simply and sincerely told modern story, literate and even dramatic dialogue, music ranging from the straight ballad to the music-hall ditty, all allied with the impeccable staging and casting for which George Edwardes could be relied upon.

The Era commented:

> [*A Gaiety Girl* is] one of the most curious examples of composite dramatic architecture that we have for some time seen. It is sometimes sentimental drama, sometimes comedy and sometimes downright variety show; but it is always light, bright and enjoyable. The contrast between certain parts of the piece and other portions is almost startling. From the silly folly of 'Jimmy on a Chute' we pass to scenes in which the dialogue is brilliant enough and satirical enough for a comedy of modern life. Line after line goes to its mark; and the audience are as ready to

> appreciate the cleverness as they are to enjoy the frivolity of the entertainment. Set in a different frame, the character of Lady Virginia Forrest, slight as it is, might have brought the author fame, as *A Gaiety Girl* will in all probability produce him – in fees – fortune.

The Times gasped at Hall's audacity:

> . . a comic opera of a somewhat advanced type . . . licence is pushed further than has ever before been attempted in our day . .

in 'amiably but pointedly' ridiculing a judge, a clergyman and the upper echelons of the armed forces, but concluded:

> . . much may be forgiven the anonymous writer for his wit and to the actors for the cleverness of their impersonations . . apart from its questionable characterisation *A Gaiety Girl* is undoubtedly entertaining . . .

The characters in question were Sir Lewis Grey (Eric Lewis) and the Rev. Brierly (Harry Monkhouse), both of whom were depicted in lascivious pursuit of the attractive Lady Virginia (Lottie Venne), a lady with a guilty secret in her past. This secret involves a divorce case in which she and the unknown co-respondent escaped exposure only through the timely death of her husband during the trial. The evidence hinged on a diamond comb – the same comb which is the fulcrum of the play's action – and the judge was none other than Sir Lewis who soon displays himself as not at all what the Pillar of the Divorce Courts ought to be. Heedless of his wife, he is only too keen to make an assignation with Lady Virginia and not at all averse to being petted by a Gaiety girl or two. The Chaplain is a little more honourable. He at least proposes marriage and is willing to claim ownership of the wretched comb to his own disgrace to save Virginia's reputation, but his subsequent attempts to trade on his good deed and his amorous pursuit of a casual skirt do nothing for his cause. Both these gentlemen formed the subject of many caustic throw-away lines and of physical ridicule most particularly when they are both found chatting up the wrong woman (Lady Grey) in a bathing machine, and both find themselves firmly and finally put in their places when Virginia announces her engagement to rich and social Major Barclay.

A good deal of Jones' music and Greenbank's lyrics formed an integral part of the show and its story but this did not prevent them from turning out a delightfully mixed bag of songs and dances. At the head of the show's vocal casting was the handsome baritone Hayden Coffin (Charley), recently returned from touring American with Lillian Russell. He had two attractive ballads in 'Beneath the Skies' and 'Sunshine Above', but he created his biggest hit and, indeed, the hit of the show with an interpolated number written by Henry Hamilton and composed by S. Potter, 'Private Tommy Atkins'. Coffin had originally been unimpressed by the song and by Edwardes' decision to interpolate it into *A Gaiety Girl*. It was not a new song – it had been used without notable success in a military sketch by Charles Arnold of *Hans the Boatman* fame – but Coffin's strong baritone gave the patriotic march song what it needed and very soon the gallery boys were enthusiastically joining in the chorus:

> Tommy, Tommy Atkins you're a good 'un, heart and hand
> You're a credit to your calling and to all your native land
> May your luck be never failing, may your love be ever true
> God bless you, Tommy Atkins, here's your country's love to you!

Harry Monkhouse had a catchy song on music-hall lines for which Harry Greenbank had written both lyric and music. It capitalised on the popularity of Captain Boyton's

Water Show Chute, telling a boy-gets-girl story of what happens when Granny takes young Jimmy for a day at the show:

> Jimmy on the Chute, boys! Won't he have a day?
> Going out with Grandma, Granny's getting gay!
> Down in half a slap-bang, wet from top to toe
> That's the way they 'chute' them at the Water Show!

In contrast, Eric Lewis had a more dignified and traditional patter song:

> I'm a judge of the modern society sort
> And I'm much over-worked with divorces
> But I've always some special attraction in court
> That my name into prominence forces.
> I can sing, I can flirt and 'At Homes' I frequent
> Where the Upper Society crust is
> I'm the Beau of the Bench and by common consent
> I'm the Toff of the High Court of Justice . .

The ladies, too, were well-equipped with numbers. Lottie Venne sang 'I'm a high class Chaperone', Decima Moore in the ingénue role of Rose Brierly whose romance with another officer, Bobby, runs parallel to that of Alma and Charles sang 'It Seems to Me' and the Parisian star of *Ma Mie Rosette*, Juliette Nesville (Mina) had her moment with 'When your Pride has had a Tumble'. Only Maud Hobson, the representative of Alma had, surprisingly, nothing to sing.

In spite of its magnificent reception *A Gaiety Girl* still had a problem to surmount, not with the public who were quick to come in huge numbers to see the new show but with the authorities. The comical depiction of the judge and, more particularly, the Chaplain which had so horrified *The Times* was clearly not to the taste of someone in a high place. One or two of the more obvious personal references had already been cut and the censor had expressed himself satisfied, but now anonymous pressure was brought to bear on the Lord Chamberlain and a demand came to George Edwardes with all the power of that august individual behind it. The character of the Reverend Brierly, the imperfect vicar, was to be suppressed. So, after having been for some weeks a man of the cloth, Harry Monkhouse overnight became Dr Brierly. Although the role was very little altered in substance and still played as a clerical character, propriety and presumably somebody's personal dignity were satisfied.

A Gaiety Girl ran eleven months at the Prince of Wales Theatre before Edwardes took it across to the new Daly's Theatre which had up to then been occupied by Augustin Daly's drama company. A second edition was produced with new songs, new dances and the whole was expanded in scale with an augmented chorus and orchestra. There were also many changes in the cast as a good number of the original performers had left, under Daly's banner, to tour *A Gaiety Girl* around America and Australia starting with a season at Daly's Theatre, New York. Monkhouse, Louis Bradfield and Fred Kaye, all in their original roles, headed the cast with Leedham Bantock promoted to Lewis' role. Maud Hobson and Blanche Massey, the original Alma and Cissy, were promoted respectively to Lady Virginia and Alma for America and the musical director was the young Granville Bantock. *A Gaiety Girl* played 81 performances at the New York Daly's before setting off on its scheduled four-months' tour of the States and a subsequent three-city tour (in repertoire) in Australia.

In London some big names were added to the cast. Rutland Barrington took over as the Reverend/Doctor, the younger Grossmith, a name to reckon with after *Morocco*

Bound, succeeded Kaye as the foppish Major and Letty Lind came in as Alma, remedying the 'no song' situation with 'Dom-dom-domino' and 'The Gaiety Girl and the Soldier'. Among the small roles of the society ladies and the actresses a whole mass of young ladies passed by, some for longer periods some for lesser, whose names would soon find their way to the top of theatre and cinema programmes – Grace Palotta, Constance Collier, Alison Skipworth, Ethel Sydney, Lettice Fairfax and Florence Lloyd. Wherever it went *A Gaiety Girl* was a huge success. *The Era* reported:

> *A Gaiety Girl* has evidently evoked a species of 'cult' similar to that inspired in times past by the earlier operas of Gilbert and Sullivan. There are habitués who have seen the piece over and over again, and there are evidently gallery-boys who know the dialogue by heart. The artists engaged in the performance are all warm favourites and friendly – not to say familiar – cordiality has been substituted for the distance hitherto maintained between the stage and the 'gods'.

Another influence of the music halls.

With *A Gaiety Girl* Edwardes' new writing team had moved away from the hollow shallowness of new burlesque. A straightforward sincerity and a modern style of wit in the writing, served up with music and lyrics of a popular but never debased character and genuine quality, put this show on a different level to those which had gone before – a level which was to become more and more popular until it had completely vanquished the remanants of burlesque and pushed the old style of comic opera into a very small corner indeed.

The original 413 performance run of *A Gaiety Girl* was followed by a comprehensive national tour and, in spite of increasing competition from its successors and imitators, the show was seen on the road up until 1900. In 1899 it made a brief reappearance at Daly's to fill a gap occasioned by Harry Greenbank's death and the consequent unavailability of the new show, *San Toy*. Edwardes paired Lottie Venne in her original role with Rutland Barrington and newer Daly's stars Huntley Wright, Marie Studholme, Scott Russell and Hilda Moody. *The Times* commented:

> [it] wears unexpectedly well and with very little alteration in order to bring the topical allusion up-to-date seems in no way antiquated. From the standpoint of later pieces of its class it seems to be almost over-burdened with plot . . . '

In six years much had happened, but the innate quality of *A Gaiety Girl* assured it a fresh welcome during its stop-gap season.

For the meantime, however, there was still an enthusiastic audience for the new burlesque as purveyed by Arthur Roberts and by the Gaiety, and George Edwardes' next production *Don Juan* was arranged to bring the star and the theatre together once more. *Don Juan* had been the next burlesque in which the late Fred Leslie had planned to star himself, and Edwardes decided to retain the idea, putting Roberts into the role of the servant, Pedrillo, which Leslie had visualised for himself. The material which Leslie had assembled was put into the hands of James Tanner who was to construct the libretto while Adrian Ross and Meyer Lutz went to work on the songs. Tanner had begun his connection with the Gaiety working front-of-house during the van Biene *Faust Up-To-Date* season and had used the opportunity to interest the impresario-musician in his play *The Broken Melody*. Van Biene took the piece up and, starring himself in the role of the disabled cellist, scored an enormous success. Edwardes was quick to invite the author into his own service where he remained as a constructor of libretti and a director to his death in 1915.

The libretto which he evolved on this occasion was not an auspicious first Gaiety effort. *Don Juan* by Fred Leslie and A. N. Other for Fred Leslie and Nellie Farren in their heyday was one thing, *Don Juan* by J. T. Tanner for the equally original Arthur Roberts and Millie Hylton was another, and Tanner was half hamstrung from the start. Nevertheless the story he evolved (which naturally enough bore no debt to Byron) was decidedly weak and unoriginal. Juan and Pedrillo are a pair of men-about-town forever getting into scrapes, amorous and otherwise. Juan falls for Haidee (Cissie Loftus) daughter of the pirate chief, Lambro (Robert Pateman) and he and Pedrillo end up sailing away on the pirate ship with half the town in tow – Pedrillo's beloved Isabella (Louise Montague), Juan's old flame Julia (Sylvia Grey), his mother Inez (Maria Davis) who has taken a fancy to the pirate chief who is keen on Isabella who has ambitions to wed a Sultan, and, since the ship was on a slaving trip, the whole female population of the town taken as tribute for the Sultan of Turkey. The second act takes place on a nebulous island and involves much in-fighting and love-making while the third brings the cast before the Sultan in Constantinople where a great deal of singing and dancing is ordered à la *Morocco Bound* before half those present are sold off by Pedrillo in a mock auction which helps to round things off more or less comprehensibly.

The Era was scathing:

> We have learned to expect something better in an extravaganza libretto than the feeble and shaky scaffolding which Mr James Tanner has supplied for the erection of *Don Juan* . . . we seldom remember an instance of performers being left, as regards action and dialogue, more entirely dependent on their own resources . . . small diversion would be created by this bald plan without the additions made by Mr Adrian Ross who has written some bright and pretty lyrics and Mr Meyer Lutz who has set them to music with his wonted grace and aptitude.

It was the songs and the dances which were, along with the buffoonery of Arthur Roberts, the raison d'être and the saving grace of the show. Millie Hylton, the sister of Letty Lind, playing Juan, was given the Willie Younge/Sidney Jones number 'Linger longer Loo' which had so impressed Edwardes. It quickly impressed the public too and became a long-standing favourite both in Britain and Europe. She also had another very loosely interpolated number written by Mark Ambient and composed by Teddy Solomon. This song, 'Comme Ça', was a topical number with a refrain

> Comme ça, comme ça belongs to bygone age
> Now this style's all the rage
> Both on and off the stage
> Comme ça, comme ça, tra-la-la-la-la . .

which gave her a second stand-out opportunity. Miss Hylton, a great favourite on the halls, was well supplied with numbers with which to forge herself an equal place in the world of musical theatre. She sang two Meyer Lutz songs 'The Ladies of Cadiz' and 'Down on my Luck' and took part in duets with both Haidee and Pedrillo. If Miss Hylton had the best of the numbers, Roberts had the most – and very little was left for anyone else. His principal number in the first scene was 'The Tutor and the Pupil', a scena performed with Miss Hylton where Roberts, in the garb of an Alma Tadema pedagogue, delivered a burlesque lecture. In the second act he performed a number in swimming costume with a bathing machine (shades of *A Gaiety Girl*) under the title 'Bathing', and also performed the comic numbers 'I Want just a Bit for Myself' (Lutz) and 'Some Do it this Way' (Lionel Monckton/Horace Lennard) as well as interpolating Charles K. Harris's Broadway hit 'After the Ball' which had made its first appearance interpolated into *A Trip to Chinatown* and which he had already made use of in *A Modern Don Quixote*. Roberts' version of the famous song was, not unexpectedly, far from a straight one – the lyrics had been given a good going over by Horace Lennard and Roberts's 'business' was his own affair. One of his best moments was the topical duet 'Not a Word' which he performed with the rising young comic Edmund Payne who played the role of the Pirate Chief s lieutenant. Payne and Roberts between them indulged in a tremendous amount of gagging and ad-libbing, striking sparks off each other to such an extent that Roberts later admitted:

> I have galloped hard and taken a few obstacles with all sorts of comedians in my time, but Teddy Payne is the only man who ever made me take up my whip and ride.

'Not a Word' had an unusual development owing to the antics of the two comedians. Roberts, returning to the cast after an attack of lumbago, had forgotten his words and although he managed with help to negotiate the duet (which actually bore some relation to the plot) he was stumped when an encore verse was demanded. The two comics marched with much aplomb to centre stage and the following rousing chorus ensued:

ROBERTS: Oh, they say the British lion
PAYNE: Not a word, not a word
ROBERTS: Oh, they say the British lion
PAYNE: Not a word
ROBERTS: Oh, they say the British lion
Yes, they say the British lion
Oh, they say the British lion
PAYNE: Not a word!

It went down wonderfully and from then on was kept in the show of which, significantly, it proved one of the most popular moments. Roberts also managed to get himself into a burlesque nautical outfit for another bit of business and developed the auction sale in the final act into an ever-changing tour-de-Roberts.

Haidee was played by little Cissie Loftus whose imitations had proved successful at the Gaiety as a filler. In consequence Byron's lovely heroine, in this version, gained her loudest cheers for imitations of Hayden Coffin, the blackface singer Eugene Stratton, *A Gaiety Girl*'s Juliette Nesville and Letty Lind. Miss Lind returned the compliment and the advertisement by inserting, in her turn, into *Morocco Bound* an imitation of Miss Loftus doing her imitation of Miss Lind.

Don Juan did not get a good initial reception. The audience on the first night showed some disapproval and the critics gave it a severe thumping. A more serious protest came from the Turkish Ambassador who objected to the depiction of the so-called 'Sultan of Turkey' and in particular to a scene where Miss Hylton was seen to kick that 'august' gentleman all round the stage. Lord Carrington, the Lord Chamberlain, found himself required to step in once again and the Gaiety was issued with orders to cut the business out. Edwardes took the simpler expedient of changing the character's name to Jabez Pasha (although the name 'Sultan of Turkey' survived in the printed book and score) and, once again, honour was pacified.

Don Juan's popular elements kept the show going for nearly nine months despite the fact that it was one of the weakest of the series of Gaiety burlesques. It was also the last.

Roberts would continue to mix burlesque and the variety musical in his career, but the Gaiety Theatre and George Edwardes were henceforth to devote themselves to musical pieces of the *Gaiety Girl* type rather than to continue in a field of entertainment which had become little more than an extension of the music hall relying on the songs, the costumes and the performers for its popularity.

The final new musical piece of 1893 was a Christmas children's entertainment based on *The Pied Piper* written by the poet Robert Buchanan for the Comedy Theatre for which music was supplied by F. W. Allwood. It played a seven weeks' series of matinées in tandem with a short Burnand/Solomon piece on the old *Sandford and Merton* theme which the composer had already used in his *Vicar of Bray*. In this case Burnand's writing failed to approach that of Grundy in the earlier work and Solomon's music went for nothing.

The most interesting piece presented during the year in the provinces was the 'musical go-as-you-please' produced at the Theatre Royal, Northampton in September under the auspices of H. Cecil Beryl. *The Lady Slavey* had a cheerfully straightforward libretto by George Dance which told the story of the impecunious Major O'Neill and his family of daughters. The matrimonial hopes of the girls and the financial ones of the father have been boosted by the news that Vincent Evelyn, the American tinned tomato millionaire, is staying in the village, is looking for a wife and has been casting his eye in the direction of the O'Neill establishment. In fact he is coming to the house and has announced his intention of chosing a bride. The elder sisters, Maud and Beatrice, prepare themselves for the occasion but the youngest sister, Phyllis, gives up her chances and offers to impersonate a maid or 'slavey' to give the establishment some 'tone', and when a bailiff arrives she uses her charms to persuade him to impersonate a 'Buttons' for the occasion. But Flo Honeydew, an old flame of the Major's, has heard about the rich Yankee and she invites herself to stay, bringing in tow her 'Johnny', Lord Lavender. Flo is a brash and glamorous music-hall star, and the Major is dismayed – Maud and Beatrice no less – but when young Mr Evelyn arrives he expresses his fancy for the soi-disante maid and gives her a ring. Phyllis cannot believe him genuine, and when Flo offers her £5 for the ring she accepts it 'the tradesmen for to pay'. Flo triumphantly declares herself the chosen bride. In Act 2 Evelyn discovers Phyllis' real identity and decides to return the trick. He announces that it is Roberts, the bailiff, who is the real millionaire in disguise – he, Evelyn, is only his secretary. Roberts parades about as 'The Big Boss Dude' while Evelyn successfully woos Phyllis. Roberts orders an entertainment and the variety musical moves into its essential phase before all is revealed and squeezed into a happy ending.

The music for *The Lady Slavey* was a mixture of original pieces composed by John Crook and/or gathered by him from other writers, and current music-hall hits. Edith Rosenthal (Mrs Cecil Beryl) in the role of the music hall singer belted out a version of 'Daisy Bell' whose bicycle built for two had run around the entire country with vigour enough almost to eclipse its predecessor in public favour, 'The Man who Broke the Bank at Monte Carlo'. 'After the Ball' and 'Wotcher' and 'The 7th Royal Fusiliers' all found a place alongside such original pieces as 'Paddy Murphy had a Pig' (composed by the versatile Mrs Beryl), Evelyn's song 'In Friendship's Name' credited to George Dance and Charles Graham as far back as 1891, or Dance and Crook's comic 'Big Boss Dude' for Roberts and some excellent finale writing by Crook.

The Lady Slavey, a modest undertaking, had more than a modest success. Its fourteen-week tour, which terminated in time to allow its cast to take up pantomime engagements (traditionally the most lucrative of the year), turned out to be only the very smallest beginnings for a show which was to have an exceptionally long life during which it would undergo almost total changes to its musical content in productions ranging over all parts of the world over a period of many years.

1893

126 **LA ROSIÈRE** a comic opera in three acts by Harry Monkhouse. Music by Edward Jakobowski. Produced at the Shaftesbury Theatre under the management of Marie Halton and Harry Monkhouse 14 January, 1893 for a run of 41 performances closing 24 February, 1893.

Major Victor Longueville	J. G. Robertson
Captain Henri de l'Espard	Barrington Foote
Pierre Pontois	William Elton
M. Justin Bartenôt	Frank Thornton
Francis Carnex	Albert James
Chief of the Tzigani	C. Jamieson
Adeline Dupret	Violet Cameron
Hortense Ricouard	Lucille Saunders
Mme Marguerite Fontenay	Emily Miller
Annette	Florence Leighton
Julie	Janette Desborough
Barbolet	Elsa Gerard
Victorine	Bertha James
Marie	Lillie? Delamere
Mimi	Louise Brown
Josephine	Marie Halton

Pds: Minnie Thurgate and Rose Wyndham

Dir: Hugh Moss; md: Barter Johns; ch: Sgr Coppi; sc: W. T. Hemsley and Walter Hann; cos: Edel

127 **THE MAGIC OPAL** a light opera in two acts by Arthur Law. Music by Isaac Albéniz. Produced at the Lyric Theatre under the management of Horace Sedger 19 January, 1893 for a run of 44 performances being withdrawn 4 March, 1893.
A revised edition was presented at the Prince of Wales Theatre as *The Magic Ring* 11 April for a run of 37 performances closing 19 May, 1893.

Telemachus Ulysses Carambollas	Harry Monkhouse
Alzaga, his son	John Child//Edwin Wareham
Aristippus	Fred Kaye
Pekito	Tom Shale//Frank Walsh
Trabucos, a bandit chief	Wallace Brownlow//Norman Salmond
Curro, his lieutenant	George Tate//Arthur Watts
Martina	May Yohe//Susie Vaughan
Olympia	Susie Vaughan//*out*
Zoe	Emmeline Orford//Lilian Stanley
Christina	Dora Thorne//Anita Courtenay
Irene	Elena Monmouth//Annie Laurie
Thekla	Rose Hamilton/Maud Michael-Watson
Alethia	Cissy Cranford//*out*
Leila	Dolly Webb//*out*
Lolika	Aida Jenoure//Marie Halton (Miss Abinger)/Annie Schuberth

Pd: Senorita Candida//Mlle Rosa/Mabel Love
with Misses Wood, Rogers, Young, Laubach, Selby, Reynolds, Shawe & Rooke/

Dir: Horace Sedger/Thomas W. Charles; md: Isaac Albeniz/Herbert Bunning; cos: Karl/ Fisher, Mme Auguste & Nathan

Produced in Madrid (trans. Eusebio Sierra) as *La Sortija* November, 1893.

0128 **THE GOLDEN WEB** a comedy opera in 3 acts by Frederick Corder and B. C. Stephenson based on *The Chaplain of the Fleet* by Walter Besant. Music by Arthur Goring Thomas. Produced at the Royal Court Theatre, Liverpool under the management of the Carl Rosa Opera Co. 15 February, 1893 for five performances in repertoire. Revised and represented under the management of Horace Sedger at the Lyric Theatre 11 March, 1893 for a run of 15 performances to 25 March. A revised version reopened 1 April for a further 14 performances closing 15 April, 1893.

Dr Manacle . . . . T. Aynsley Cook//Wallace Brownlow
Lord Silvertop . . . . Lempriere Pringle//Richard Temple
Bullion . . . . C. Campbell//J. Furneaux Cook
Geoffrey Norreys . . . . Edwin Wareham//Tom Shale/Durward Lely
Spindle . . . . W. S. Laidlaw
Smug . . . . Arthur Wilkinson
Mistress Pamela Patch . . . . Mme Amadi
Mrs Scatterwell . . . . F. Shortland//Dora Thorne/Cissy Cranford
Mrs Pounceby. . . . . Minnie Hunt//Emmeline Orford
Amabel . . . . Alice Esty (Dora Thorne)

add pds: John D'Auban, Emma D'Auban

Dir: T. H. Friend/Horace Sedger; md: Herbert Bunning

0129 **MOROCCO BOUND** a musical farcical comedy in two acts by Arthur Branscombe. Lyrics by Adrian Ross. Music by F. Osmond Carr. Produced at the Shaftesbury Theatre under the management of Fred J. Harris 13 April, 1893. Transferred to the Trafalgar Square Theatre 8 January, 1894. Closed 10 February, 1894 after a run of 295 performances.

Spoofah Bey. . . . . John L. Shine (Harry Grattan)
Squire Higgins . . . . Charles Danby/Harry Grattan
Vivian Higgins . . . . Sydney Barraclough/Templar Saxe/ E. H. Haslem
Dolly Higgins . . . . Alfred C. Seymour
Josiah Higgins. . . . . Herbert Sparling
Lord Percy Pimpleton . . . . George Grossmith jr
Sid Fakah . . . . Colin Coop/Richard Temple/ C. Jamieson
Musket . . . . Douglas Munro
Maude Sportington . . . . Letty Lind/Minnie Palmer (Ruby Temple)
Ethel Sportington . . . . Violet Cameron/Florence Dysart/Marie Studholme/Hilda Glenn/Lillian Redfern/Maggie Roberts
Comtesse de la Blague . . . . Jenny McNulty/Marie Studholme (Lizzie Ruggles)
Lady Walkover . . . . Agnes Hewitt
Rhea Porter . . . . Marie Studholme/Maud Henri/Ruby Temple
Eva Sketchley . . . . Eva Westlake/Yata Whynier/Maggie Ripley/Maud Wellington/Blanche Ripley
Nina Featherstone . . . . Yata Whynier/Violet Monckton/Marie Studholme

Hilda Adlette . . . . Ruby Temple/Lizzie Ruggles

with Misses Lyndhurst, Leath/Austin, Adams, Broome, Stone, Stanley, Davis

Dir: Frank Parker; md: Sidney Jones/Carl Kiefert; ch: Mariette D'Auban; sc: E. G. Banks/Walter Hann; cos: Jean Paleologue

Produced at the Comedy Theatre under the management of William Greet 19 December, 1901 for a run of 43 performances closing 1 February, 1902 and toured. Additional lyrics by Claude Askew.

John L. Shine//Walter Westwood (SB), Charles Danby//John Wilkinson (SQ), Frank Barclay//Cyril Dwight-Edwards/Lennox Lochner (VIV), Walter Westwood/Herbert Clark (JOS), Fred Storey (PP), Joseph Wilson/Colin Coop (SID), Mark Joyce/Herbert Clark (MUSK), Kitty Loftus//Adelaide Astor (MAUD), Ethel Clinton//Bessie Graves (ETH), Minnie Blakiston/Millicent Robson (CTESS), Gertrude Aylward//Ethel Holmes (WALK), Lizzie Ruggles/Florence Levey (RHEA), Ethel Crescent (EVA), Hettie Tempest (NINA), Kitty Melrose (HILDA) Millicent Robson/Ella Kitson (ROSE), Maisie Dene (EVELYN) with Nellie Grey, May Carl, Jessie Gunter, Olive Murray, Iris Irwin, Kathleen O'Neil, Omie Bartlett, Addie Kipling, Florrie Vincent, Lillian Bannon, Eunice Desmond, Madge Bryce, Ethel Mayhew, Trixie Ramsden, Marie Gerrard, Winifred Gascoigne; Messrs Courtenay, Wade, Alexander, West, Le May, Allerton, Russell. Dir: Arthur Branscome; md: F. Osmond Carr/Bert Paterson; sc: Selwyn Hart & W. T. Hemsley; cos: Peter Robinson Ltd, Messrs Baruch and Mme Vernon

0130 **JANE ANNIE** or The Good Conduct Prize. A comic opera in two acts by J. M. Barrie and Arthur Conan Doyle. Music by Ernest Ford. Produced at the Savoy Theatre under the management of Richard D'Oyly Carte 13 May, 1893 for a run of 50 performances closing 1 July, 1893. Toured from 24 July at Newcastle through Manchester, Bradford, Birmingham to 26 August, 1893.

Proctor . . . . Rutland Barrington
Sim . . . . Lawrence Gridley
Greg. Walter Passmore
Tom. Charles Kenningham
Jack . . . . R. Scott Fishe
Caddie. Harry Rignold
Miss Sims . . . . Rosina Brandram
Jane Annie . . . . Dorothy Vane
Bab . . . . Decima Moore/Florence Perry
Milly . . . . Florence Perry/Jose Shalders
Rose . . . . Emmie Owen
Meg . . . . Jose Shalders/*out*
Maud . . . . May Bell
Students. J. Bowden Haswell/Herbert Crimp/ Sidwell Jones

Dir: Charles Harris; md: François Cellier/Ernest Ford; ch: John D'Auban; sc: W. Perkins, William Telbin; cos: Wilhelm

0131 **A MODERN DON QUIXOTE** a musical-farcical nondescript [play] in 2 acts by George Dance. Music by John Crook. Produced at the Theatre Royal, Nottingham under the management of Arthur Roberts 17 July, 1893 and toured through Glasgow, Newcastle, Manchester, Southport, Liverpool, Douglas, Leeds (Harrogate mat.), Birmingham, Brighton, terminating at the Strand Theatre 25 September for 21 performances ending 14 October, 1893.

Don Quixote . . . . Arthur Roberts
Sancho Panza . . . . E. W. Coleman (Russell Wallett)
General Jenkinson . . . . W. H. Denny/Arthur Playfair (Russell Wallett)
Hon. Cecil Blake . . . . Lyddie Edmonds/Doris Mountford
Mrs Crumpet . . . . Ada Doree
Maud . . . . Yata Whynier
Mabel . . . . Mabel Love
Louise. . . . . Louie Norman

Lilian . . . . Kitty Burns
Phoebe . . . . Lizzie Aubrey
Percy . . . . Doris Mountford/Alice Rowland/*out*
Algernon . . . . Maud Santley/Florence Dene
Margery. . . . . Florence Hanley
Claude. . . . . Gwendoline North
Farmer Giles . . . . George Gregson/Harold Coulter/ H. Williamson
Jones . . . . Russell Wallett
add Algernon Jenkinson. . . . . Harry Phydora
Nellie . . . . Evelyn Fitzgerald
Bishop of Gretna Green . . . . . . Arthur Jackson

with Violet Crossley, Sophie Moodie, Florence Williams, Lilian Stead, Violet Wyatt, Gwen de Lisle, Madelain Hanbury, Blanche Wellesley, Di Travers, /Alice James, Lionel Whyte, /Gerald Luke, George Paulton, Harold Coulter, Charles Flynn, /Arthur Egerton &c. /Lila Kendal, Ethel Edgecumbe, Ellen Fitzgerald, Stanley Williams, T. Rochfort, Charles Jackson

Dir: Horace Lennard; md: Sydney Ward/G. D. Wright/Ernest Bucalossi; cos: Alias

Produced in a revised version with new songs by Lionel Monckton, Walter Tilbury and Alfred Morris, Paul Rubens, Ernest Vousden and Alfred Murray at the Lyric Theatre under the management of Arthur Roberts 21 May, 1898 for a run of 22 performances ending 18 June, 1898 and toured through Fulham (July 4), ? , Blackpool, Cork, Dublin, Belfast, Edinburgh, Glasgow and Newcastle (September 3) and thereafter in repertoire with *Campano*. Last performance at Brighton, 19 November.

Arthur Roberts (DON Q), Harry Kilburn/Ed Redway (SANCHO), W. H. Denny/J. T. MacMillan (GEN), Frances Balfour (CEC), Elsie Fayne/Amy Singleton (MRS), Millie Legarde/Amy Farrell (MAUD), Rita Darrell (PERCY), Lillian Pollard (ALG), Marie Guest (MARG), Clifford Campbell (FARMER), Albert Weston/Jo Monkhouse (MARMADUKE), Jimmie James (GERALD), Miss Fraser (CHARLES), Violet Crossley (NURSE), Madge Rossell/Rhoda Wyndrum (EVA), Connie Rossell/Marie Lovell (LILIAN), Godwynne Earle/Isa Bowman/Frances Earle (PHOEBE), Miss Wallis (DAISY), Ruta Righton (GLADYS). Md: /Howard Talbot

0132 **PETERKIN** a comic opera in three acts by 'Will Ladislaw'. Music by Sgr L. Camerana. Produced at the Royalty Theatre under the management of G. Fallen and Mario N. Moro 4 September, 1893 for 5 performances closing 8 September.

Matthias Habberjam . . . . Harry Longden
Peter. . . . . Jerrold Manville
Percy Lovel . . . . Thorpe Sheffield
Hector Wellborn . . . . Antonio Medcalf
Lucy Precious. . . . . Adeline Kyle
Mrs Priscilla Precious. . . . . Maud Russell

0133 **THE LADY SLAVEY** a musical go-as-you-please in 2 acts by George Dance. Music by John Crook etc. Produced at the Theatre Royal, Northampton under the management of H. Cecil Beryl 4 September, 1893 and toured through Cheltenham, Bradford, Newcastle, Glasgow, Edinburgh, Liverpool, Hull, Leicester, Sheffield, Bath, Cardiff, Birmingham and Leeds ending 9 December, 1893. Recommenced 26 March, 1894 to 1 December, 1894.

Major O'Neill . . . . James Danvers/Keino Johnston
Roberts . . . . Witty Watty Walton (Stephen Wensley)
Viscount Evelyn. . . . . J. C. Piddock
Lord Lavender . . . . T. W. Volt
Phyllis. . . . . Kitty Loftus
Flo Honeydew . . . . Edith Rosenthal
Maud . . . . Amy Thornton/Rosa Kilner
Beatrice . . . . Florence Wilson/Lily Forsythe
Mlle Pontet . . . . May Metcalf
Mlle Louise . . . . Lola Campbell
Bill . . . . Stephen Wensley

With Evelyn Norgate, Elsie Hull, Phyllis Wardroper, Mabel d'Orsay, May Montague, Nina Montague, Kitty Marion, Rose de Wynter, Minnie Melrose, Edith Stuart, Olga Durham, Florence Cherrington, Frank Worthington, John C. Graves, William Dixon, Lewis Vincent, Stephen Wensley, Ralph Forster; /Nora d'Orsay, Mabel Hensey

Dir: George Dance; md: Ernest Vousden

Toured by William Greet's Co. from 13 August, 1893, from Middlesborough through South Shields, W. Hartlepool, Darlington, Wigan, Preston, Stockport, Blackburn, Ashton-under-Lyne, Chester, Wolverhampton, Bolton, St Helens, Gloucester, Worcester, Walsall, Leamington, Coventry, Doncaster, Jarrow, Stockton, Barrow, Carlisle, Gateshead, Keighley, Crewe, W. Bromwich, St Helens, Bury, Rotherham, Blackburn, Burnley, Lincoln, Warrington, Chester, Sheffield, Eastbourne, ?, Accrington, Preston, Wakefield, Paisley, Aberdeen, Dundee, W. Hartlepool, ?, out four weeks then continued through 1894/5/6/7/8/9/1900/01/02/03/04. Fred Winn/Stephen Caffrey/Wm E. Roberts/H. Arthur Burgoyne/Fred Scates/Harry Walsh &c (MAJ), Fred Walton/Frank Sherlock/H. Arthur Burgoyne/William T. Thompson &c (RBTS), Augustus Cramer/Allen Morris/Frank Morton/Ernest Newnham (EV), Ernest Shand/Charles Leverton/John C. Graves &c (LAV), Dolly Harmer/Howe Carew/Bertha Cadman/Eva Graham/Rosie Loftus Leyton (PH), Daisy Baldry/Madge Lucas/Marion Cross/Flora Hastings/Vera Dunscombe/Clara Jackson/Grace Henderson/Rose Dearing &c (FLO), Susie Nainby/Mabel Nelson/Rose Ewart/Violet Peyton/Eva Graham/Amy Durkin/Jeanne van Dalle (MAUD), Marguerite McLeod/Bertha Cadman/Ada Binning/Nellie King/Lillie Millbank/Maud Madle/Laura Thompson/Rosie Loftus Leyton/Maud Dagmar/Ada Palmer/Laura Clairight/Ethel Ashton &c (BEA), Ethel Webb/Edith Leyland/Rita Quinelle/Louise Stratton/Irene Glanville/Mabel Evelyn &c (PONT), Louie Stafford/Edith Leyland/Rita Quinelle/Constance Jones/Vera Quinelle/Maud Madle (LOU); *add* Bill . . . W. B. Jackson/Walter Rhodes/John Yates &c.
with Rita Quinelle, Vera Quinelle, Madoline Hanbury, Eva Stuart, Madge Evans, Lilly Brammer, Honor Moore, Amy Newman, Ethel Owen, W. E. Roberts, Bernard Vaughan, Fred Dawson, Howard Law, W. B. Jackson, Frank Glynne
Md: /Frank Barrett/Fred W. Southern/George Burnley/Arnold Cooke/Louis Laval

Toured by Charles K. Chute's Co. from 6 August, 1893 into 1894/5/6.

Produced in London at the Avenue Theatre under the management of H. Cecil Beryl 20 October, 1894 in a revised version with new music by John Crook. Additional songs by Joseph & Mary Watson, Henry J. Wood & Joseph Hart, Willie Younge, Charles Graham, Frank S. N. Isitt, Herbert Walther & Alfred Cammeyer, Letty Lind and Adrian Ross. Closed 25 January 1895 after a run of 96 performances.

Major O'Neill . . . . Robert Pateman
Roberts . . . . Charles Danby/J. J. Dallas
Viscount Evelyn. . . . . Henry Beaumont/James Leverett
Lord Lavender . . . . Herbert Sparling
Captain FitzNorris . . . . George Humphrey
Phyllis. May Yohe/Annie Montelli
Flo Honeydew . . . . Jenny McNulty
Maud . . . . Adelaide Astor/Lizzie Ruggles
Beatrice . . . . Blanche Barnett/Beatrice Granville
Mme Pontet. . . . . Miss Elcho
Mme Louise . . . . Irene du Foye
Emma . . . . Phoebe Turner/Miss Desmond
Liza, a flower girl . . . . Miss Maryon/Rita Yorke/Julie Donna

Md: Henry J. Wood; ch: Mariette D'Auban; sc: E. G. Banks; cos: Haywards, Jays, Morris Angel

The revised version toured by H. Cecil Beryl 1894/5/6/7/8/9/1900/01/02/03/04/05/06/07 etc. Keino Johnstone/Harry Kilburn (MAJ), Witty Watty Walton (Fred Walton) (John C. Graves)/William T. Thompson (RBTS), J. C. Piddock (Lewis Vincent)/Harrison Brockbank/Arthur Appleby (EV), T. W. Volt/Herbert Sparling (LAV), Kitty Loftus/Katie Barry/Ada Willoughby/Laura Thompson/Nellie Beryl/Millicent Pyne/Daisy Revelt/Winnie Volt (PH), Edith Rosenthal/Grace Henderson/Queenie Leighton (Kitty Marion)/Violet Raynaur/Rita Presano (FLO), Rosa Kilner/Nellie Beryl/Rosa Bennett/Nelly Palmer (MAUD),

Lily Forsythe/Rose Martin/Eva Gandee/Edith Denton/Ivy Louise (BEA), May Metcalfe Florence Cherrington/Phyllis Wardroper/Nina Montague/Lily Beagle/Kitty Maxwell (PONT), Lola Campbell/Phyllis Wardroper/Nina Montague/Kitty Marion/Florence Cherrington/Mabel Marston/Dora Lyons (LOU), John Wigley/Lewis Vincent/Paul Presano (BILL). Md: Ernest Vousden/Guy Jones/Ashley Richards &c.

A version of this show adapted by George Lederer, Thomas Canary and F. C. McClelland with new music by Gustave Kerker was presented at the Casino Theatre, New York, under the management of Lederer and Canary 3 February, 1896 for a run of 128 performances and subsequently revived 25 April, 1898 for a further 72 performances.

0134 **UTOPIA (LIMITED)** or The Flowers of Progress. A comic opera in two acts by W. S. Gilbert. Music by Arthur Sullivan. Produced at the Savoy Theatre under the management of Richard D'Oyly Carte 7 October, 1893 for a run of 245 performances closing 9 June, 1894.

King Paramount . . . . Rutland Barrington
Scaphio . . . . W. H. Denny (W. H. Leon)
Phantis . . . . John Le Hay
Tarara . . . . Walter Passmore (Clarence Hunt)
Calynx. . . . . J. Bowden Haswell
Lord Dramaleigh . . . . Scott Russell
Captain Fitzbattleaxe . . . . Charles Kenningham
Sir Edward Corcoran . . . . Lawrence Gridley
Mr Goldbury . . . . R. Scott Fishe
Sir Bailey Barre . . . . H. Enes Blackmore
Mr Blushington . . . . Herbert Ralland
Princess Zara . . . . Nancy McIntosh
Princess Nekaya . . . . Emmie Owen
Princess Kalyba . . . . Florence Perry
Lady Sophy . . . . Rosina Brandram (Agnes Scott)
Salata . . . . Edith Johnston
Melene . . . . May Bell (Madeleine Galton)
Phylla . . . . Miss Howell-Hersee/Florence Easton

Dir: Charles Harris; md: François Cellier; cos: Percy Anderson; ch: John D'Auban; sc: Hawes Craven

Produced at the Broadway Theatre, New York 26 March, 1894 for a run of 55 performances closing 12 May, 1894.

J. J. Dallas (PAR), J. W. Hooper (SC), Frank Danby (PH), J. H. Poskitt (TA), Leslie Walker (CAL), Frank Boor (DRAMA), Clinton Elder (FITZ), W. H. Peterkin (CORC), John Coates (GOLD), Eckford Smith (BB), Buchanan Wake (BL), Isabel Reddick (ZARA), Aileen Burke (N), Millicent Pyne (K), Alice Pennington (SAL), Edith Courtenay (MEL), Maisie Turner (PH), Kate Talby (SOPH). Dir: Charles Harris

0135 **LITTLE CHRISTOPHER COLUMBUS** a burlesque opera in two acts by George R. Sims and Cecil Raleigh. Music by Ivan Caryll. Produced at the Lyric Theatre under the management of Horace Sedger 10 October, 1893. After 279 performances a second edition was staged 2 August, 1894, withdrawn 20 October, 1894. Restaged at Terry's Theatre 29 October, 1894. Withdrawn 15 December, 1894, after a total 421 performances.

O'Hoolegan, private detective . . . . . . E. J. Lonnen
Captain Joseph H. Slammer . . . . Harry Parker/W. S. Laidlaw
Mayor of Cadiz . . . . Harry Wright/Roland Carse/
H. Gregory F. Seymour
Don Juan of the Spanish police . . . . . George Tate/Jack Thompson
Silas Block, a millionaire . . . . J. Furneaux Cook
Hotel proprietor. . . . . Roland Carse/Charles Crook
Pedro . . . . Kate Dudley/Marie Wynter/Miss Trevalyan
Sebastian . . . . Vinnie Cassell/*out*
Lopez . . . . Blanche Winter/Marie Wynter/Miss Reike
Vigilant Cutter . . . . Maud Vernon/Dorothy Webb

Head Turk . . . . W. M. Birch
The Second Mrs Block . . . . Adelaide Newton/John F. Sheridan
Hannah Slammer . . . . Maud Leicester/Millie Marsden/ (Elena Monmouth)
Pepita . . . . Eva Moore/Alice Lethbridge/Mabel Love (Maud Fisher)
Guinevere Block . . . . Maud Holland/Effie Clements/Geraldine Ulmar (Maud Michael-Watson)
Chloe Jones . . . . Mimi St Cyr/Gracie Whiteford/Alice Lethbridge/Dorothy Wood
Mercedes . . . . Rose Hamilton/M. Northcote
Penelope. . . . . Gracie Whiteford/Vinnie Cassell
Officer of the Colombian Guard . . . . . Cissie Cranford
Salammbo Smith . . . . Dora Thorne
Mysotes Calhoun . . . . Millie Marsden/A. Maxwell
Little Christopher. . . . . May Yohe (Maud Holland)/Florence St John/Addie Conyers
add Lola. . . . . Cissie Cranford/Maud Maude

Dancers: Alice Gilbert/Blanche Astley/Molly Bonheur, May Gore/Alice Douglas, Edith Gardiner/Florrie Wilson, Eva Greville

Dir: Horace Sedger; md: Ivan Caryll; ch: John D'Auban; sc: Bruce Smith, McCleery; cos: Edel

Produced at the Garden Theatre, New York as *Little Christopher Columbus* (later as *Little Christopher*) under the management of E. E. Rice 15 October, 1894. Transferred to Palmer's Theatre 15 April, 1895. Closed 1 June, 1895 after a total of 264 performances. Additional songs by Gustave Kerker.
George Walton/Charles Bigelow (O'H), Herman Blakemore/J. K. Murray/Edwin Chapman (SLAM), Edwin Chapman/Follett Jocelyn/William Gillow (MAYOR), Edgar Temple/Arthur H. Bell (DON J), James B. Gentry/ Charles Cowles (JOSH HEMINGWAY) replaced by John W. Wilson as WEARY RAGGLES, Alexander Clarke (BEY OF BARATARIA), Henry Leoni (GRAND VIZIER OF BARATARIA), Follett Jocelyn/*out* (HEAD TURK), Lucy Escott (PEDRO), Tillie Richardson/Lula Ward (LOPEZ), Irene Vera (BARATARIAN HERALD), John W. Wilson/*out* (DIEGO), Frankie Bailey (MANUEL), Grace Belasco (RODERIGO), Helen Brackett (SANCHO), Madge Alphabet/Anna Carman (FERNANDEZ), Harry Macdonough (2ND MRS B), Nettie Lyford/Josie Diff (HANN), Mabel Bouton (PEP), Yolande Wallace/Nettie Lyford (GUI), Lila Blow/Pauline Train (MERC), Charles B. Powell (COL G), Helen Bertram/Bessie Bonehill (LCC), Josie Ditt/Lillian Green/Lila Blow (LOLA), Annie Seaberry (CERISCA), Nettie Harrington (ANITA), Mabel Potter (IMOGENE), Bertha Waring (ZULEIKA), Nina Ainscoe (MISS CHRYSANTHEMUM), Sisters Abbott (WAIFS); with the Lyric Theatre Dancing Girls (May Gore, Molly Bonheur, Florence Linton, Marie Linton) and Elena Martinez, Grace Gayler, Pauline Train, Bertha Dowling, Leia Williams, Nettie Burdwin, Mollie Gayler, Kittie Shields, May Hamilton, Bertie Holly, Lula Ward, Loie Riccarti, Lenora Wilson, Neena de Rue, Mabel le Clair, Lillian Green, May Gill, Marjorie Wilburn, Ena Welch, Genevieve Hill, Lizzie Leoni, Catalina Gomez, Louise Lehman, Anna Carman, Estelle Botsford, Lula Farrance, Hetta Beaudet, Julia Lee, Florence Raymond, James Murray, Malcolm E. Russell, Charles Van Dyne, Pierre Young, George C. Miller, F. W. Regas, H. Weitzer, Charles B. Powell, Charles M. Holly, William Gillow, Robert H. McIntyre, Otto D. Lehman, George E. Merrill, William Howard, Ernest de Horn, Jean Dove. Dir: E. E. Rice, George Walton, Tom Terriss; md: Gustave Kerker; sc: Richard Marston, Henry Heinman, H. L. Reid & F. A. Rafter; cos: Edel

0136 **A GAIETY GIRL** a musical comedy in two acts by 'Owen Hall'. Lyrics by Harry Greenbank. Music by Sidney Jones. Produced at the Prince of Wales Theatre under the management of George Edwardes 14 October, 1893. Transferred to Daly's Theatre 10 September, 1894, closing 15 December, 1894, a total of 413 performances.

Charles Goldfield . . . . C. Hayden Coffin (R. C. Stuart)
Major Barclay . . . . Fred Kaye/George Grossmith jr
Bobbie Rivers . . . . W. Louis Bradfield/Laurence Cautley/ Leedham Bantock (R. C. Stuart)/ J. Farren Soutar

Harry Fitzwarren	Leedham Bantock/Reginald Somerville/Donald Hall
Romney Farquhar	Lawrance d'Orsay
Sir Lewis Grey	Eric Lewis (George Mudie)
Lance	Gilbert Porteous (Mr Smith)
Auguste	Fritz Rimma/Charles Eaton
Rev. Montague Brierly	Harry Monkhouse (Leedham Bantock)/ Rutland Barrington/W. H. Rawlins
Rose Brierly	Decima Moore/Kate Cutler (Violet Robinson)
Lady Edytha Aldwyn	Kate Cutler/Louie Pounds/Lettice Fairfax
Miss Gladys Stourton	Marie Studholme/(Sadie Clinton)
Hon. Daisy Ormsbury	Louie Pounds/Ethel Sydney
Lady Grey	Mrs Edmund Phelps/Kate Hodson
Alma Somerset	Maud Hobson (Blanche Massey)/ Marie Studholme/Letty Lind
Cissy Verner	Blanche Massey/Eva Stanford/Alice Davis
Haidee Walton	Ethel Ross-Selwick/Florence Lloyd/ Alison Skipworth/Rose Batchelor/Ada Maitland/Violet Dene/Ethel Selwyn/ Millie Malone/Kitty Adams/Edna Grace
Ethel Hawthorne	Violet Robinson/Alison Skipworth/ Florence Lloyd/Constance Collier
Mina, a French maid	Juliette Nesville/Grace Palotta/Nina Martino
Lady Virginia Forrest	Lottie Venne/Phyllis Broughton/ Aida Jenoure/Sybil Grey/Christine Mayne

with Claire Vannini, Rose Batchelor, Cissy Fitzgerald, Grace Palotta, Florence Lloyd, Nellie Navette, Maggie Gorst, Topsy Sinden &c.

Md: Sidney Jones; sc: Walter Hann & William Telbin; ch: M. Dewinne; cos: Edel

Produced at Daly's Theatre, New York under the management of Augustin Daly 18 September, 1894 for a season of 81 performances ending 24 November, 1894; then toured through Philadelphia, Harlem, Boston, Washington, Brooklyn, Pittsburgh, St Louis, Chicago, Milwaukee and San Francisco to 18 February, 1895.

Charles Ryley (Cecil Hope) (W. Louis Bradfield) (CG), Fred Kaye (MAJ), W. Louis Bradfield (Cecil Hope) (BOB), Arthur Hope (E. G. Woodhouse) (HF), Cecil Hope (Arthur Hope) (RF), E. C. Woodhouse (Mr. Wilbur) (LANCE), Leedham Bantock (W. Louis Bradfield) (SIR), Harry Monkhouse (W. Louis Bradfield) (REV), Fritz Rimma (AUG), Decima Moore (ROSE), Sophie Elliot (GLAD), Blanche Massey (ALMA), Florence Lloyd (CISSY), Marie Yorke/Laura Kearney (ED), Grace Palotta/Madge Rossall (ETH), Juliette Nesville/Grace Palotta (MINA), Maud Hobson (Florence Lloyd) (VIRG), Ethel Selwyn (DAISY), Cissy Fitzgerald/Claire Leighton (HAI), Mrs Edmund Phelps (LADY), Maggie Crossland, Lucy Murray, May Lucas (pds) C. W. Berkeley, Ethel Carlton/Miss Bentley/ Md: Granville Bantock

Produced at Daly's Theatre, New York, under the management of Augustin Daly 7 May, 1895 for a run of 31 performances closing 1 June, 1895.

Leland H. Langley (CG), W. J. Manning (MAJ), Donald Hall (BOB), H. F. Sparks (HF), James Frazer (RF), Mr Bradley (LANCE), Percy Marshall (SIR), Bert Haslem (REV), Mr. Carleton (AUG), Ethel Sydney (ROSE), Miss Beaugarde (GLAD), Elena Flowerdew (ALMA), Margaret Fraser (CISSY), Minnie Sadler (ED), Ethel Craddock (ETH), Nina Martino (MINA), Winifred Dennis (VIRG), Dolly Kirsch (DAISY), Helen Fraser (HAI), May Silvie (LADY), Margaret Fraser, Helen Fraser, Maud Percy (pds), Louise Gomersal (AMY). Md: George Purdy

Produced at Daly's Theatre under the management of George Edwardes 5 June, 1899 for a run of 58 performances closing 2 August 1899.

H. Scott Russell (CG), Fred Kaye/W. J. Manning (MAJ), Ernest Snow (BOB), Donald Hall (HF), Lawrance d'Orsay (RF), Rutland Barrington (SIR), W. J. Manning/Fred Vigay (LANCE), Conway Dixon (VISCOUNT VILARS), Leonard Mackay (GUY BROMHEAD), Akerman May (AUG), Huntley Wright (REV), Hilda Moody (ROSE), Coralie Blythe (ED), Florence Collingbourne (GLAD), Maud Danks/Countess Russell (DAI), Gladys Homfrey (LADY), Marie Studholme (ALMA), Alice Davis (CISSY), Kathleen Francis (HAI), Maidie Hope (ETH), Aileen D'Orme (MINA), Lottie Venne (VIRG), Olive Morrell (LYDIA PENDILION), Topsy Sinden (pd), Maggie Crossland, Kitty Mason (dcrs). Dir: J. A. E. Malone; md: Barter Johns; ch: Willie Warde; sc: W. Hann, E. T. Ryan; cos: Miss Fisher, Louise & Co, Mme Flora Field, 'Vernon', Morris Angel

137 **MIAMI** a melodramatic opera arranged from Buckstone's *The Green Bushes* by John Hollingshead. Lyrics by E. Warham St Leger. Music by J. Haydn Parry. Produced at the Princess's Theatre under the management of John Hollingshead 16 October, 1893 for a run of 11 performances closing 27 October, 1893.

Miami	Violet Cameron
Geraldine	Isabelle Girardot
Tigertail	Clara Jecks
Meg	Mrs B. M. de Solla
Eveleen	May Wallace/Gabrielle Ray
Nelly O'Neil	Jessie Bond
Connor Kennedy	Courtice Pounds
George	Richard Temple
Murtough	Charles Ashford
Dennis	W. S. Osborne
Jack Gong	A. J. Evelyn
Grinnidge	George Barrett

Dir: John Hollingshead, J. Haydn Parry & Mr Edmonds; md: F. Sydney Ward; ch: Paul Valentine; sc: W. T. Hemsley; cos: Comelli

138 **DON JUAN** a burlesque in three acts on Lord Byron's *Don Juan* by James T. Tanner. Lyrics by Adrian Ross. Music by Meyer Lutz. Produced at the Gaiety Theatre under the management of George Edwardes 28 October, 1893 for a run of 221 performances closing 16 June 1894. Played at the Grand Theatre, Islington 18 June for two weeks.

Pedrillo	Arthur Roberts
Lambro, a pirate chief	George Mudie/Robert Pateman
His Lieutenant	Edmund Payne (George Carroll)
Cecco	Willie Warde
The Sultan (Pasha)	E. W. Royce/Colin Coop/George Mudie/ Frederick Vaughan
Haidee	Cissie Loftus (Nita Clavering)/ Lettice Fairfax/Lillian Stanley
Donna Julia	Sylvia Grey/Katie Seymour
Donna Inez	Maria Davis/Lillie Belmore/Maria Jones
Isabella	Louise Montague (Ethel Earle)
Zoe	Katie Seymour/Lettice Fairfax/ Eva Ellerslie/Claire Solomon
Cybele	Topsy Sinden
Don Juan	Millie Hylton (Ethel Earle) (Louise Montague)
add Roderigo	George Carroll
Mercedes	Patty Stanley/*out*

with Ethel Earle/Maud Sutherland, Lily Harold/Lillian Price, Violet Evelyn/, Aimée Mills/Violet Monckton, Florence Henderson, Hetty Hamer/, Kate Connon, Carrie Benton, Constance Collier/, /Annie Vivian,/Nelly Langton,/Violet Durkin/May Lacy

Dir: James T. Tanner; md: Meyer Lutz/F. Sydney Ward; ch: Willie Warde & Mariette D'Auban; sc: E. G. Banks & William Telbin; cos: Wilhelm

0139 **THE PIPER OF HAMELIN** by Robert Buchanan. Music by F. W. Allwood. Produced at the Vaudeville Theatre 20 December, 1893 for a series of matinées ending 8 February, 1894.

The Pied Piper	Frank Wyatt
Conrad the Cooper	Leonard Russell
Major	E. M. Robson
Bummerlang	W. J. Joyce
Sauerkraut	Clarence Hunt
Town Clerk	H. Longden
Town Crier	Frank Walsh
Liza	Lena Ashwell
Martha	Mrs Campbell-Bradley
Hans	Gladys Doree
Deborah	Millicent Pyne
Annchen	Ettie Williams
Frau Hausenfuss	A. O'Brien
Frau Pumpernickel	Neva Bond
Frau Nusscracker	Gertrude Turner
Frau Schmetterling	Blanche White
Frau Dinnerwetter	Maud Jackson

NAUGHTY TITANIA or Mortals Adventure in Fairyland, a burlesque in three acts by Stanley Rogers. Music by Fred Wright and Julian H. Wilson. Produced at Aston Manor under the management of Martin Adeson 7 August, 1893 and toured.

MARIGOLD FARM or The Simple Squire and the Evil Eye. A lyrical play by W. Sapte jr. Music by J. Haydn Parry. Produced at the Opera Comique Theatre for one matinée 7 February, 1893.

FRASQUITA a comic opera in two acts by W. Godfrey. Music by W. Meyer Lutz. Played at the Gaiety Theatre 29 May, 1893 for the benefit of Meyer Lutz.

HIS HIGHNESS a comic opera by John W. Houghton. Music by Auscal Tate and Neill O'Donovan. Played at the Opera Comique 13 June, 1893 at a charity matinée.

MR JERICHO an operetta in one act by Harry Greenbank. Music by Ernest Ford. Produced at the Savoy Theatre under the management of Richard D'Oyly Carte 24 March, 1893 as a forepiece to *Haddon Hall*. Withdrawn 15 April, 1893.

Michael de Vere	George de Pledge
Horace de Vere	Bates Maddison
Mr Jericho	J. Bowden Haswell
Lady Bushey	Agnes Scott
Winifred	Florence Easton/Edith Farrow

SANDFORD & MERTON an operetta in one act by F. C. Burnand. Music by Edward Solomon. Produced at the Vaudeville Theatre 20 December 1893 with *The Piper of Hamelin*. Withdrawn 8 February, 1895.

William Barlow	Lionel Brough
Sandford	Clarence Hunt
Mlle Aurelia	Ada Doree
Nellie	Ethel Norton
Merton	E. M. Robson
Sambo	Leonard Russell
Katie	Olga Garland

BINKS, THE DOWNY PHOTOGRAPHER a musical absurdity in one act. Music by Ernest Bucalossi. Produced at the Strand Theatre 17 October, 1893 with *The Ladykiller*. Withdrawn 17 November, 1893.

Horatio Binks . . . . Willie Edouin
Dickie Chumley. . . . . Gordon Harvey
Bertie Fortescue. . . . . Herbert Ross
Charlie Dodsworth . . . . Cairns James
Chip. . . . . Harry Eversfield
Muggins. . . . . James A. Meade
Ruby Chillington . . . . Alice Atherton
Flossie. . . . . Jenny Dawson
Vesta . . . . Daisy Baldry
Polly. . . . . Amy Gordon
Md: George Byng

Revived for a series of Christmas season matinées at the Strand Theatre. Played with *Best Man Wins*.
Willie Edouin (BINKS), Robson Lambert (DC), Herbert Ross (BF), George Humphrey (CD), Alec Mackenzie (JOHNNIE MONTAGUE), Harry Buss (CHIP), George Giddens (MUGG), Alice Atherton (RUBY), Jenny Dawson (F), Fanny Wentworth (V), Cynthia Brooke (P), R. Pendennis (EMILY), Stella Brandon (MAUDE), Nancy Graeme (CLAUDINE). Md: George Byng.

BOX B a musical trifle by R. Corney Grain. Produced at St George's Hall under the management of Alfred Reed and R. Corney Grain 22 May, 1893 with *Poor Piano* and *Dan'l's Delight*, the former replaced by *Echoes of the Opera*. Withdrawn 8 July. Reopened 9 October with *Piano on Tour* and *An Odd Pair*. Withdrawn 18 November, 1893.

Mr Lumsden . . . . R. Corney Grain
Mrs Hardinge . . . . Fanny Holland
Philippa . . . . Gertrude Chandler
Algie. . . . . Avalon Collard

Revived at St George's Hall 7 April 1902 with *Tea and Tennis* and *Charity Begins at Home*. Withdrawn 20 May.
Roper Lane (L), Leonora Braham (MRS), Tresilian Davy (PH), Avalon Collard (ALG)

DAN'L'S DELIGHT by Archie Armstrong. Music by J. W. Elliot. Produced at St George's Hall under the management of Alfred Reed and R. Corney Grain 1 April, 1893 with *Poor Piano*. *Box B* added 22 May. Withdrawn 8 July 1893.
Cast included Fanny Holland, Gertrude Chandler, Alfred Reed, Avalon Collard, William Lugg.

THE UGLY DUCKLING an operetta in one act by R. Corney Grain. Produced at St George's Hall under the management of Alfred Reed and R. Corney Grain 20 November, 1893 with *Road and Rail* and *An Odd Pair*, the former replaced by *The Parish Pump*. Withdrawn 24 February, 1894.

Adonis Bland . . . . R. Corney Grain
Miss Jones . . . . Fanny Holland
Katie Grant . . . . Gertrude Chandler
Bertie Elliot . . . . Arthur Helmore
Douglas Redde . . . . Avalon Collard

AN ODD PAIR by T. Malcolm Watson. Music by Alfred J. Caldicott. Produced at St George's Hall under the management of Alfred Reed and R. Corney Grain 9 October, 1893 with *Piano on Tour* and *Box B* replaced respectively by *Road and Rail* and *The Ugly Duckling* (20 November). Withdrawn 18 December, 1893.

Marjory . . . . Gertrude Chandler
Ned Fanton . . . . Avalon Collard
Widow Wimpfel. . . . . Fanny Holland
Daniel Dough . . . . Arthur Helmore
David Dough . . . . Alfred Reed

WEATHERWISE an unreality in one act by H. Chance Newton. Music by Ernest Ford. Produced at the Lyric Theatre under the management of Horace Sedger 29 November, 1893 as a forepiece to *Little Christopher Columbus*. Withdrawn 4 July, 1894.

Herodotus Dodderton . . . . Harry Parker/William Bentley/W. S. Laidlaw
Pansy . . . . Maud Holland/Dora Thorne
Tom Yowick . . . . George Tate
Daisy Meadows . . . . Millie Marsden
Harry Grayling . . . . Vernon Drew/Wilbur Gunn

PEGGY'S PLOT an operetta in one act by Somerville Gibney. Music by Walter Slaughter. Produced at St George's Hall under the management of Alfred Reed and R. Corney Grain 20 December, 1893 with *Road and Rail* and *The Ugly Duckling*, the former replaced by *The Parish Pump*. Withdrawn 24 February, 1894. Represented 26 March, 1894 with *Walls have Ears* and *A Funny World*. Withdrawn 29 April 1894.

Peggy Crank . . . . Gertrude Chandler
Richard Crank . . . . Avalon Collard
Miss Popham Featherstone . . . . Fanny Holland
Mr Popham Featherstone . . . . Alfred Reed
Sergeant Pimpernel . . . . Arthur Helmore

THE VENETIAN SINGER an operetta in one act by B. C. Stephenson. Music by Edward Jakobowski. Produced at the Court Theatre under the management of Arthur Chudleigh 25 November, 1893 with *Goodbye* and *Under the Clock*. Withdrawn 8 December, 1893.

Bianca . . . . Agnes Giglio
Paolina . . . . Kate Waldeck Hall
Matteo. . . . . Herbert Thorndike
Gregorio. . . . . Jack Robertson

Md: Edward Jones; ch: Mariette D'Auban; sc: T. W. Hall; cos: Nathan & Co

Subsequently toured as *The Improvisatore*.

THE CROSSING SWEEPER an operetta by Basil Hood. Music by Walter Slaughter. Produced at the Gaiety Theatre under the management of George Edwardes 8 April, 1893 with *In Town*. Withdrawn 29 July, 1893.

Tom. . . . . Florence Lloyd
Bill . . . . Edmund Payne
Nancy . . . . Kate Cutler

THE LASS THAT LOVED A SAILOR an operetta in one act by Neville Doone. Music by J. Bond Andrews.

THE BURGLAR AND THE BISHOP an operetta in one act by Sir J. Jocelyn Campbell. Music by Wellesley Barton.

HELEN OF TROY UP-TO-DATE an extravaganza by J. Wilton Jones. Music by John Crook. Produced as a triple bill by Courtice Pounds' Company at the Pier Theatre, Folkestone 23 May, 1893. The company included Courtice Pounds, W. H. Denny, Augustus Cramer, Isabelle Girardot, John Wilkinson, Millicent Pyne &c.

1894

The fact that the box-office results of the previous year had indicated a decided public preference for the sophisticated variety musical of the *Gaiety Girl* type and the slightly less sophisticated version of the same musical trend embodied in *Morocco Bound* did not lead to a sudden abandonment of other types of musical theatre. Not unnaturally there was a certain amount of jumping on the bandwagon, the most popular model in 1894 being *Morocco Bound* with its simple synthesis of a comical and colourful story and variety songs and turns. Middle Eastern high jinks and a music-hall programme provided the backbone of *Go-Bang, King Kodak* and *Eastward Ho!* while *Jaunty Jane Shore*, *Claude Duval* and *All My Eye-Van-Hoe*, all nominally burlesques, brought the high jinks closer to home without attempting to emulate the superior style of *A Gaiety Girl*. Only George Edwardes followed the path he had opened up with that show when he produced *The Shop Girl* at the Gaiety in November.

The comic opera school, however, still had its word to say. Gilbert and Sullivan as a team had nothing to add to the year's output, but they were responsible respectively for *His Excellency* (Osmond Carr/Gilbert) and *The Chieftain* (Sullivan/Burnand). Another seasoned British comic opera writer, Edward Jakobowski, contributed *The Queen of Brilliants* to Vienna and to London and *The Devil's Deputy* to America, and yet another comic opera, this in the *Billee Taylor* vein, was *Wapping Old Stairs* which introduced the young composer Howard Talbot to the West End. The provincial scene contributed its most enduring work to date when *The Lady Slavey* was produced in London adding another to the band of variety farces in town, while its successor *The Gay Parisienne* began its career in the country, one of many new farcical musical plays and musical comedy-dramas which continued to come from the out-of-town theatres.

With the home product proving so popular, little need was found to import pieces for the light musical theatre. D'Oyly Carte produced an unimpressive Messager piece called *Mirette* which, in spite of all that the Savoy had to offer and in spite of a second run in a revised version, failed to attract. Just how far public taste had swung from such fare was indicated by the 125-performance West End run achieved by *A Trip to Chinatown*, an inane American variety mish-mash which was to find itself a permanent home on the touring circuits for many years to come. Like *The Lady Slavey* and *Morocco Bound*, *A Trip to Chinatown* attracted that class of middle-class Victorians and their ladies who were prevented by ideas of propriety and of safety from patronising the music halls, but who yearned to sample the entertainment given there. With more and more of the content and, indeed, of the performers of the halls being brought into the musical theatre, this section of society could now fulfil its wishes in comparative respectability, and did.

The first new piece to make its appearance was *Wapping Old Stairs* which was given its première in King's Lynn. This was a nautical comic opera written by Stuart Robertson with music by American-born Howard Talbot (né Munkittrick) who had left his native New York to be educated in London. Talbot had studied medicine at King's College but subsequently decided he wanted to make music his career and continued his studies at the Royal College of Music under Sir Hubert Parry. Now, at the age of 29 and settled permanently in Britain, he produced his first major stage work[1]. The King's Lynn try-out was a reasonable success and it was decided to bring *Wapping Old Stairs* to the Vaudeville Theatre. The cast was strengthened by the addition of the Savoy favourites Courtice Pounds and Jessie Bond, Hannah Jones who had been so successful in *Cigarette*, and Avon Saxon, and some six weeks after its initial representation *Wapping Old Stairs* opened in London.

The libretto was professedly based on an old London legend told in Maitland's *London* (1775), telling of a young Wapping man who was falsely accused of murder by a rival in love but who finally returned to clear himself and condemn his guilty accuser to the gibbet. Robertson tried to twist this tale into comic opera shape and came up with the following plot: Mark Mainstay who is to marry the lovely Nancy Joy is drugged by his rival, Captain Crook, and made to believe he has committed a murder, so that he flees. The girls of Wapping persuade their sailor lovers to go and seek him by the Lysistratan tactic of witholding their favours, but Mark is already trying to solve the mystery of the murder himself and is lurking round the neighbourhood disguised as a quack doctor cheering the desolate Nancy with messages and duets at the same time as he hunts for clues. But Mark is no common sailor. He is the nephew of the County Magistrate, Sir Wormwood Scrubbs, and that proud gentleman appears on the scene to apprehend his wayward nephew and have him incarcerated in a lunatic asylum for disgracing the family name by manual labour. Sir Wormwood, however, falls for Nancy Joy and writes her a love letter which he pays the quack doctor to deliver. Mark slyly delivers it to Susan Sinnett, Crook's accomplice, whose head has been turned by reading penny novelettes and who fancies herself as a lady of fiction. Eventually the evil Captain is unmasked and Scrubbs is sentenced to wed the willing Susan while all ends happily for Mark and Nancy and all the other sailor lads and lasses.

The book was rather naive and old-fashioned:

(Sailors attempt to embrace girls who repulse them)

BEN: Steady your hellum there! What! Sheering off your consorts who want to run aside?

DAISY: Yes, keep off.

DICK: Daisy!

DAISY: Dick.

DICK: What d'ye say? Keep off?

DAISY: Yes. Keep off! We want no courting now!

GIRLS: (*sorrowfully*) We want no courting now.

DICK: (*astonished*) No courting?

SAILORS: (*echoing his astonishment*) No courting?

GIRLS: (*emphatically*) No!

BEN: Then what are we ashore for?

DICK: Aye, lad. What indeed? Come, Daisy lass. First you express your admiration for the Mercantile Marine, and then when the Mercantile Marine wishes to

[1] Talbot's staged cantata *A Musical Chess Tournament* to words by the Hon. Albinia Brodrick was produced at the New Theatre, Oxford 28 October, 1892.

give practical expression to its appreciation, you sheer off, and dodge, backing and filling like a ship in stays.

DAISY: Does a ship wear stays, Dick?

DICK: Not exactly. The stays help to wear the ship and keep her trim and taut.

DAISY: Ah, I see! Like a woman! Now I know why a ship is called 'she'.

DICK: Ah! but there's another reason. A ship is called 'she' because the rigging often costs more than the hull! But why treat us like this? We looked forward to a very different welcome!

The songs were rather better and were laid out to allow each of the principal members of the rather small cast to have his or her opportunities, with the principal types of comic opera songs well represented. The widest range of pieces fell to Mark Mainstay who shuttled between the comic patter style in his disguise as the quack:

For every ill of every kind, I've mixtures theriatic,
And can for every trouble find a certain prophylactic;
This cure's as certain as can be for irritant verbosity–
And here's a sov'reign remedy for impecuniosity–
With this and water I assure, taken morning, noon and night
In seven days a perfect cure for over dainty appetite;
When folks to age are sensitive, and grizzle that they're past their prime,
I've here a fine preventitive against a sudden march of time!
While here's a thing that's quite unique, if married men may be believed,
For curing, often in a week, a lover's notions preconceived.
From this I think you'll plainly see, tho' I've not been to college
My mind is an epitome of pharmaceutic knowledge!

to the lyric, in his duets with Nancy Joy.

The rest of the patter music fell to Sir Wormwood:

You'll see by my appearance,
That I brook no interference,
From any lesser magnate of the state!
A pillar of the nation,
I'm proud of my vocation,
A law adoring County Magistrate!

Let a tramp to hunger yield,
Take a turnip from a field,
Just hear me on his villainy dilate!
And he'd better kill a peasant,
Than a partridge or a pheasant,
If brought before this County Magistrate!

He also took part in the show's most successful number, the trio 'Family Pride' with Captain Crook and Susan:

O, Family Pride!
Born of exalted station!
Blue blood to bluer allied
Must maintain your elevation!
So this representative true
Of a line of illustrious dead,
Will defend the superior blue
From the taint of inferior red!

The villain, Crook, made his first appearance in soliloquy:

> Ha! Ha! There they go, fooling with the wenches again! So much the better for me. For while they are so pleasantly occupied they are less likely to suspect that I am not exactly the saintly soul I seem. The consequences of such a suspicion might prove annoying to a sensitive man. But I flatter myself I am too artistic to be found out just yet. Why, I have actually believed in myself on one or two occasions. In public I am a mild mannered moral mariner; in private I review my little peccadilloes and feel proud of 'em – proud with the pride of pre-eminent peculation. That's a pretty phrase. So alluringly alliterative. Not for publication though – oh, dear, no!

to which followed a song 'I Am a Villain double-dyed with Villainy's deepest Tint'.

Ben Brace was given a sea song and a drinking song, Daisy a little ballad 'I Love a Sailor', Molly Joy the 'Spae Wife's Song' and Nancy Joy the bulk of the romantic music. Two of the most appealing numbers, however, were given to Jessie Bond as Susan Sinnett, partly compensating her for a thin and unsympathetic role. In the first she expounded her creed, based on the worst of popular fiction:

'Tis very plain this man of birth and breedin'
Is struck by my superior ettiket
And tip-top air acquired by careful readin'
The ways of high life in the novelette!
In these days of universal eddication
When many a good-looking servant maid is
Raised by marriage to that helevated station
Adorned by peeresses and titled ladies,
Each domestic who like me is blessed by beauty
Should study all the rules of ettiket,
And acquire an air distongway as a duty
By perusin' of the penny novelette!
Yes, each girl of humble station
Should give due consideration
To the matrimonial chances she may get!
And obtain an air of breedin'
With a style 'ho tong' by readin'
Of the Bo-Mongd in the penny novelette!

There you read of 'ousemaids, parlourmaids, and others,
Possessing sylph-like forms and lovely faces,
Pursued by wicked peers, whose moral brothers
Turn up with help in unexpected places!
The baffled rakes repulsed with 'ho-choor' chillin'
The noble brothers they for husbands get,
Then, a haccident the helder villins killin'
They're 'My Ladies' in the penny novelette!
Yes, domestics blest by beauty
Should consider it a duty,
Since by this they see the chances they may get,
To make style and conversation
Fit for that exalted station,
They attain to in the penny novelette!'

> (*reading*) With a look of triumph upon his wickedly handsome face the Earl advanced towards the tremblin' girl when suddenly a figure barred his progress, a strong hand seized him by the throat, and in a voice full of passionate scorn Rupert said:
> MOLLY: (*off stage*) Su-san!

Her second number, as she flies into a fury on being jilted by Sir Wormwood, was on 'The Breach of Promise' theme.

The first night public was kind enough and the young composer and his librettist were given a friendly welcome at the evening's end. They were even gratified by some favourable reviews. *The Globe*, in particular, declared:

> It is years since a prettier work was produced in London. The music is so bright and the opera is so admirably played that it deserves exceptional success

and both *The Telegraph*:

> . . there is scarcely a melody in the opera which may not be singled out for praise

and *The Times*, who labelled the show 'completely successful', joined in congratulating the new composer:

> . . all who can appreciate bright and tuneful music will find plenty of diversion . . . The author of the book . . is at his best in 'patter songs' of the approved type and least happy in dialogue; but its many shortcomings of the words are amply compensated in the music by Mr Howard Talbot which is delightfully fresh and piquant. It is far above the average of such things and from overture to finale there is not a vulgar note nor a point at which the composer's inspiration seems to flag. Like his colleague he is at his best in the 'patter songs' and concerted pieces to which he has contrived new rhythms for his melodies although the verses are for the most part in very hackneyed metres. This freshness of rhythmic invention is perhaps the best point in the work and such numbers as the trio 'O, Family Pride' and the sailors' song with the refrain 'And nobody could do more' to give only two instances out of many are excellent in this respect. In the sentimental numbers the composer is less successful. . . The composer has the power of writing really gay music without using dance measures in season and out of season . . .

But the show was not a complete success. The failings of the libretto were manifest, there was no obvious star in the cast and the songs, though adequate of their kind, were not of the currently popular kind, that is of the music hall. And not all the critics had been as kind as *The Times*. Even *The Era*, traditionally reasonable, had concluded that the only worthwhile things in the show were Jessie Bond and a particularly effective practical moon. When Jessie Bond was claimed for the new Fred Harris show at the Trafalgar Square, the show was already in trouble. Major revisions were scheduled and Courtice Pounds had a new ballad quickly added to his part of the score whilst more serious alterations were carried out. The most important of these was the replacement of the Captain Crook, Henry Bouchier, by the comedian Charles Collette. Collette was given his head in an attempt to bolster the low humour of the piece in the same way he had in *Carina* and as Peter Pong in *Gretna Green*. The dialogue was altered, several new songs were added including a version of Dibdin's famous old ballad of 'Wapping Old Stairs' and Nance Graeme was given a solo skirt dance – a palpable anachronism but a popular and conciliatory step towards the variety musical. Although the second version was agreed to be considerably better than the first, *Wapping Old Stairs* followed in the usual way of patched-up plays and was unable to work up into a success. It closed after only a week. A tour subsequently sent out by Arthur Rousbey proved equally unfortunate, surviving only a few weeks. Howard Talbot's West End début had not been a particularly auspicious one, but at least he had arrived.

The long and successful run of *Morocco Bound* had done well by its producing syndicate, but Fred Harris was anxious to do without his former colleagues in his next venture and he teamed up with C. J. Abud to give the public 'more of the same'. The pair, under the umbrella 'The New Morocco Bound Syndicate', took the Trafalgar Square Theatre to produce a new work by *Morocco Bound's* Adrian Ross and Osmond Carr called *Go-Bang*. *Go-Bang* had nothing to do with nihilists but was the name of a nebulous eastern country ruled over by the Boojam. At least, it would be if anyone knew who the rightful Boojam was. The chief postulant is Dam Row (John Shine as another Eastern potentate) to whom Sir Reddan Tapeleigh KCSI, a diplomat versed in the affairs of Go-Bang, is anxious to wed his daughter, Helen. Helen is not anxious, much preferring Dam Row's secretary, Narain, while the gentleman himself has his oriental eye on Miss Di Dalrymple, principal danseuse of the Vanity Theatre, who is quick to get his signature on a marriage contract. But Dam Row's pretensions to the crown of Go-Bang are shattered when the Golden Idol, which the rightful heir is known to hold, is found in the possession of one Jenkins, an English greengrocer. Jenkins is promptly acclaimed Boojam and everyone heads off to Go-Bang for the coronation. Marital problems, however, raise their head, when Di claims an 'heirs and assigns' clause in her contract making Jenkins her legal betrothed. Neither the grocer's intended Sarah Anne nor the ambitious Sir Reddan are pleased at all and the latter decides that Jenkins will not do at any price. He plots with Dam Row and the venal Wang (representing 'Native Opinion') to get the throne for the old postulant in return for that gentleman's promise to wed the lovely Helen, but after much politicking and foolery it is discovered that the rightful heir is Narain and all ends happily.

Ross had greatly improved as a writer of dialogue since *Faddimir* and the libretto was a neat and literate affair, lacking the rawer and more obvious attractions of *Morocco Bound* but quite colourful enough and full of incident, constructed in such a way as to include all the necessary songs and dance features without recourse to the transparent device of 'ordering an entertainment'. But the storyline was much less important to the paying public than the decoration imposed upon it, and Ross and Osmond Carr (who had already worked together on *Blue-Eyed Susan*, *In Town* and *Joan of Arc* as well as *Morocco Bound*) were well versed in combining their talents in the production of attractive numbers to highlight their cast's abilities.

Letty Lind as the danseuse, Di, was the centrepiece of this show. Since she had added to her qualification as the stage's most proficient and popular dancer by acquiring a tiny but attractive singing voice and a decidedly piquant acting style, her roles had become steadily larger as her popularity increased. In the ingénue role in *Morocco Bound* she had quite eclipsed the romantic leads and in *Go-Bang*, now a very un-ingenuous ingénue, she was quite definitely the leading lady and the main attraction. Her two songs 'Di, Di, Di' and 'The Chinee Dolly', though lyrically far less accomplished than most of the rest of the numbers in the piece, quickly became established as the show's hits and Miss Lind brought the house down as she introduced herself:

I'm a prima ballerina assoluta,
I am famous from St Petersburg to Utah
As the dearest little dancer of today!
When I figure in a ballet operatic
All the gentlemen are ardent and ecstatic,
And this is what I often hear them say–
Fie, Di! Try, Di!
Not to be so shy, Di,
My, Di, why, Di,

Will you not reply, Di?
Charming little dancer,
Only give an answer,
If you do not love me, I shall die, die, die!

'The Chinee Dolly' song was the tale of a Chinese puppet in love with a tin soldier. When the soldier is dropped and broken, she weds instead 'a mandarin with a nodding head'. The number got Miss Lind into a gorgeous oriental costume in which she performed a clever Puppet Dance choreographed by Mariette D'Auban. Dancing was still the star's long suit and she featured a series of imitations of other dancers from Sylvia Grey to Loie Fuller as well as getting in her double-edged 'Lind as Loftus as Lind' impersonation from *Morocco Bound*, but the dancing highlight of *Go-Bang* was a Pierrot pas de deux. In a black spangled ballerina-length skirt Miss Lind danced out a flirtatious pierrot story with Harry Grattan and a cut-out crescent moon which was altogether more charming than some of the brasher routines which coster and quadrille dancing had popularised, and which proved one of the highlights of the evening.

Other *Morocco Bound* favourites were well featured too. Grossmith added 'Augustus Fitzpoop' to his dudes' gallery and put forward claims as a singer for the first time in a number 'See the Military'; Grattan played the comical greengrocer with a mournful song about the effects of his 'Sairey Anne' while Shine as Dam Row cornered the largest supply of comedy songs satirising British double-standards in 'I can't Make it out a Bit':

I heard a tale from an English Earl
In the smokeroom after dinner;
I told that tale to an English girl,
And she thought me a dreadful sinner!
When I sang the ladies an English song
I really was most unlucky–
I had heard it sung to titled throng–
How could I guess there was anything wrong
In 'Give me a cab fare, Ducky!'?

social lion-hunting in 'Society', and just above every current topic from politics to music and theatre in 'The Modern Reformer'. The political and social content of *Go-Bang* was, aided by the subject of the show, rather heavy and the topical aspect was further emphasised in the duet 'A Matter of Detail', the trio 'You're not Supposed to Know' and in Sir Reddan's song 'Red Tape':

Although the British state
Seems going wrong of late,
And danger and calamity are threatening our nation,
No trouble or distress
Our ministers confess
Officially, officially, they have no information!
We can bid our foes defiance,
Though we haven't an alliance,
And we're terribly inferior in military science;
Yet we never fear an enemy of any size or shape,
So long as we are guarded by our good Red Tape!

Jessie Bond (Helen) and Frederick Rosse (Narain) contributed the lesser romantic element.

The show was respectably received on the lines:

> *Go-Bang* shares with *Morocco Bound* the possibilities which have made this class of entertainment popular. It was well received and the author and composer who were called before the curtain at the close may be congratulated on a not unskilful combination of clever lyrics, amusing incidents and well-arranged choruses, tuneful though not very original music and charming costumes. (*Times*)

and it ran fairly smoothly for some five months without ever looking like achieving the popularity of its predecessor.

Once *Go-Bang* was comfortably running, Harris and Abud extended their activities and their ambitions, and took Terry's Theatre to present another variety musical by the third *Morocco Bound* creator, Arthur Branscombe. The same mixture was used – British gentry, a Rurarabian setting (in this case, the Kingdom of Kodakoria), a slight story and a large amount of variety material with more or less relation to the story. The whole was called *King Kodak*.

The Kodak, otherwise former explorer James South, has found gold in Africa and round his mines has built up a 'buffer state' over which he rules and which has grown large enough to be of interest to the world powers. The English connection is to be cemented by the marriage of the Kodak's daughter, Hilda, to the son of Admiral Broadsides. Both the young people are, of course, otherwise engaged. Enter the medical student, Dick Dashaway, who claims to have invented a set of pills which can change people's character, his secret wife and nurse, Dora, a phony cleric, a dud lawyer, one 'Lord Deadbroke' stolen as a child by apes and now being educated to the ways of a British Lord, Jack Broadsides' girl Kitty (a dancer) and Hilda's boy friend, Harry, who are all transported to Kodak where Dick uses his phony pills (he really does it by hypnotism) to get everyone to do a 'turn' before Kitty and Harry are revealed as the long-lost children of the Kodak's exploring partner and the heirs to half the mines of Kodakoria. This makes everything all right and provides a happy ending. The attractions of this bill included the heralded 'return to burlesque' of two old favourites, Edward Terry and Kate Vaughan, the popular comedian Charles Danby of 'Round the Town' fame, and the Sisters Levey (Carlotta, May and Adeline) who were announced to perform an Ostrich Dance which rumour had it was distinctly 'naughty'.

King Kodak was not well received. *The Era* summed it up as

> . . a number of clever people working hard at writing a farce impromptu, industriously endeavouring to remedy the ill-advised attempts of the author to supply a connected plot . .

and concluded

> . . away with literary point and merit, away with feeble political satire, away with everything except the 'variety show', the scenery and the comely and close-clad chorus . .

and commented that, in any case, the variety element needed strengthening.

The play's musical content had been gathered from here and there, with many of the best composers of the day including Slaughter, Crook, Solomon and Monckton contributing numbers to the hotch-potch of entertainment which was not above introducing bits and pieces from old Terry hit shows such as *Bluebeard* to allow room for nostalgia on the one hand and theoretically to give surefire material on the other. Apart from his 'The Best of . . . ' section which, needless to say, was well received, Terry went through several other routines including Monckton's

Irish song 'Mickey Branagan's Party' and another 'I'm a Kodakorian Ruler' which actually bore some relation to the plot.

Miss Vaughan performed several dances in her old style and sang a Teddy Solomon number 'Ah, Men' and another by Gangloff and Plumpton entitled 'Love's Whispers' while the more modern style of dancing was represented by Mabel Love and Eva Levens. There was a clutch of topical numbers which edged in mentions of the current Aunt Sallies – the Jabez Balfour affair and crooked company promoters in general, Home Rule, Ibsen, music halls, the House of Lords, the Maxim gun, lady journalists and socialism. Charles Danby sang a number parodying the habitués of the different English watering places, George de Pledge rendered the inevitable patriotic song 'We've Faith in the old Flag Still' (Monckton) and Lizzie Ruggles joined Danby for a song and dance descriptive of the stages of matrimony, 'Life's Footsteps'. The variety entertainment included a Spanish Dance (Miss Love), a song and dance (Amy Saunders) about 'The Mermaid and the Mate', an Italian ice-cream vendor number (Geo. Giddens), some tableaux vivants and a nurses' routine 'The Hot Cross Bun Brigade' as well as Terry's Irish song and the Ostrich Dance. The 'naughty' Ostrich Dance was not particularly rude. The sisters Levey (daughters of the violinist/pianist Paganini Redivivus, the Liberace of his day) appeared dressed as birds in black and white bodices and little skirts of ostrich feathers, their legs covered by black silk stockings which ended in white silk garters just above the knee. Between the garter and the feathers was, thus, exposed an area of seemingly bare thigh which constituted the 'naughty' bit.

When the first night got a fairly unanimous thumbs down it could not be expected that *King Kodak* would run. Kate Vaughan, professing disenchantment with the new style of musical theatre, soon left and alterations set in. The libretto was revised and the bill enlivened by a lady whistler, a 'French' singer and, finally, in seeming desperation, Loie Fuller in three dances – La Pansie (sic), L'Orchide and La Transparence. These, along with Terry, Danby and the vaguely naughty bits kept *King Kodak* alive for eight weeks before it succumbed, generally unmourned except no doubt by the manufacturers of the Kodak camera who had clearly hoped the free advertisement would continue rather longer and who had shown their appreciation to the librettist and the management by taking a complete panel in the programme to laud their machine:

> . . the greatest friend and companion of the tourist . . used by The Princess of Wales, the German Emperor, the Duke of York and many other members of the Royal Families of Europe; and by travellers such as Nansen and Peary, the Arctic explorers, the latter of whom brought back more than 2000 pictures of Northern life and surroundings, Allen and Sachleben who toured round the world on bicycles; F. Villiers, the celebrated War Correspondent &c&c&c . . .

The product survived rather better than the piece.

King Kodak did surface again, however, in a short tour the following year with a totally rewritten book and the interpolation, as a special attraction, of a lavish series of tableaux vivants terminating with 'Miss Rose Corelli as Britannia'. To stimulate local interest a gossipy paper with contributions from the cast and management was put out in each town as 'The Kodakorian Times', but interest was barely stimulated and the extravaganza, which was what it had now become, toured for only five weeks before its life span was terminated.

Jaunty Jane Shore, which arrived in April at the Strand Theatre, was written by 'Richard Henry' who had supplied such popular material to the Gaiety in its early new burlesque days and, in consequence, it made rather more of a stab at truly burlesquing its subject than was now common. The story of Jane Shore had been well used theatrically. The lady had historically been the mistress of Edward IV and subsequently of the Marquis of Dorset, but was accused of sorcery by Richard III so that he might seize her lands. Thomas More affirmed that her influence with the King was 'never to any man's hurt', but over the years Jane's reputation had suffered somewhat. The principal stage Jane Shores had been Nicholas Rowe's tragedy produced at Drury Lane in 1714 and a W. G. Wills' drama seen at the Princess's in 1876 and 1877. 'Richard Henry' proposed to 'give the lady back her character' and announced:

> Rehabilitation being still fashionable in the higher Historical circles, it has been thought that the time is ripe to give even poor Jane Shore her Whitewashing Day. Hence, instead of the hapless heroine being shown as (according to the Muse of History) she really was, an attempt is here made to present her As She Ought To Have Been. This being thus, it is but fitting that Jane should at the finish be pardoned for what she didn't do. It is hoped that similar forgiveness may be extended to the author for what he has done.

In this 'burlesque' version, Jaunty Jane Shore is the daughter of a licensed victualler engaged to be wed to the pawnbroker Matthew Shore, but beloved of and by the baker, Grist, and admired by most of the rest of the male cast including King Edward, Richard of Gloucester and young Lord Hastings. The plot, such as it was, concerned everybody's attempt to wed and/or bed Jane Shore. The authors mixed verse and prose indiscriminately, riddled the former with word-play and puns of a standard slightly better than usual on the lines:

HAST: This being thus without much aid extraneous
I'll carry off Shore's Jane by my sheer Jane-ious
Her wayside inn-solence I'll swiftly punish
How dare she thus a peerless Peer admunish!
I cannot choose but think that young Jane Shore is
Somewhat tainted with witch-craftiness
It must be so or how in such a Nation
Is barmaid overproof against temptation?

and, in the second act managed to interpolate a good deal of variety material, including a series of tableaux vivants burlesquing the pictures at the Palace and the Empire.

At the centre of all this was the vivacious and popular Alice Atherton in the title role, singing and dancing with her usual prominence everything from a rattling number about 'The British Barmaid' through a mandoline solo to the Laughing Song from Ernest Bucalossi's little piece *Binks, the Downy Photographer* in which she had appeared at the Strand the previous year. The evergreen Harry Paulton appeared as Richard III conceived as a Jekyll and Hyde character based on the 'bad' Richard given us by Shakespeare's version and the 'good' Richard written by Bulwer Lytton, a fancy which caused much amusement even if its literary allusions were not always grasped:

I never can make up my mind
As to which side I'm really inclined
One day I'm willing
To do all the killing
The next day I'm tender, you'll find,

I'm a half and half party
For right and wrong hearty
A mixed sinful saint of a whitey brown kind . .

Eric Lewis as the lecherous King had his best moment with a topical song:

When the East wind doth blow
And the treasury's low
Well, what does a Government do, poor thing?
Why, to keep itself warm
From adversity's storm
It sticks on a tax or p'r'aps two, poor thing!
Now with the Spring Cleaning a new tax will fit
For Midsummer's outings I'll put on a bit
In Autumn I'll tax every bicyclist bold
In Winter I'll tax everyone with a cold . . .

and joined in a comic duet with Paulton, 'Only a Matter of Clothes'. A conspirators' trio and a silent boot dance by Arthur Nelstone were other musical high points of the show.

John Crook, who was responsible for the bulk of the score, straddled the mixture of styles well but *Jaunty Jane Shore* was, on the whole, an unfortunate creation. The classic burlesque element which featured strongly in the first act did not appeal to the same audience as the frankly variety element in the second act, and neither was strong enough to hold the show together alone. The story was hazy and the fact that a straight *Jane Shore* had not been seen in London for a long time rather took the edge off the serious burlesque intention. In the event, *Jaunty Jane Shore* stayed afloat at the Strand for seven weeks with the aid of considerable rewriting and was later taken out on tour featuring Miss Atherton and Fred Emney without winning much praise for anything but its artists.

In the meanwhile the flow of new musicals into the West End continued. In September the American producers Henry Abbey and Maurice Grau of Broadway's Abbey's Theatre brought in *The Queen of Brilliants* for a limited season at the Lyceum en route to America. *Die Brillanten-Königin* by 'Theodore Taube' and Isidore Fuchs with music by Edward Jakobowski had originally been commissioned by Vienna's Carltheater and had been given its first performance there in March. Abbey and Grau had won the subsequent auction for the overseas rights and had commissioned a new English language version for Britain and America. By the time the 'new' version reached the Lyceum stage very little remained of the original. Brandon Thomas, who had been engaged to adapt the libretto, made considerable alterations in the plot and, in fact, retained little more than the central character of Betta, the 'Queen of Brilliants', for which the producers had secured Lillian Russell. The Viennese score was severely chopped about and Jakobowski supplied fourteen new musical numbers to original lyrics by Thomas. As staged in London it was, to all intents and purposes, a new musical. Its story was an exceptionally long-winded one, even for a comic opera. The head of the small Dalmatian township of Borghovecchio, the Count Caprimonte, has the traditional right to make anyone he pleases a Caprimonte and a Count. This has made him extremely useful to Mme Engelstein, proprietress of the matrimonial agency 'The Temple of Hymen' in Vienna, who finds her matches much easier to make when the young gentlemen in question have been ennobled. She brings the young architect Florian Bauer to be suitably raised in rank, but is thwarted when he falls for the local tomboy, Betta. To gain her end Madame has the wild Betta immured in a nunnery, but Betta proves too much of a handful for the nuns and is soon released. Thinking herself deserted by Florian, Betta agrees to the proposition of the local wheeler-dealer Dalla Fontana to join the circus he has inherited. He has a fine set of dazzling jewels amongst his props and needs a beautiful young woman to wear them and star as 'The Queen of Brilliants'. Betta has visions of what fame and fortune might mean and leaves Borghovecchio with the circus. In the final act she returns, rich and famous, to bring prosperity to her home town and her hand to Florian.

Abbey and Grau lavished considerable trouble and £7,000 on the production of *The Queen of Brilliants*. *The Era* marvelled:

> . . so brilliant a spectacle has never been put upon the London stage under the guise of comic opera. How can Messrs Abbey and Grau ever hope to get back their outlay?

But the expense was not limited to the scenic effects and the dresses. A cast of twenty-seven principals were headed by Lillian Russell (at $1,500 per week), the baritone Hubert Wilke as Florian and Annie Meyers as Orsola with the British stars Arthur Williams, W. H. Denny, John Le Hay and Mme Amadi providing the comedy for a try-out of six weeks. Doubtless the producers hoped the initial outlay would be recouped on a successful Broadway season, but their hopes received a severe set-back when *The Queen of Brilliants* received a decidedly mixed reception. While audiences were suitably impressed by the beautiful sets and Comelli's elaborate costumes, they were less enthusiastic about the show.

The *Theatre* summarised . . 'Splendor et praeterea nihil' (splendour, but beyond that . . nothing). It dismissed the music:

> . . the best that can be said is that it is pleasing, fluent and not inappropriate. Of originality it contains hardly a trace . .

and *The Times* concurred:

> . . [he] scarcely ever attempts anything but dance rhythms and even in that restricted area never succeeds in getting hold of an idea that is worth anything . .

An undoubtedly apocryphal conversation quoted in *The Era* expressed the general feeling: a partisan of the composer remarks to a witty fellow 'Don't you think the music is very pretty?' 'Yes', replies the latter, 'I have always thought so'. The composer of *Erminie* seemed, in fact, to be written-out, for although he continued to produce pretty melodies and scores, they remained too reminiscent of his own earlier work to be in themselves memorable.

It was not the score, however, which provoked the principal criticism of the show, but Brandon Thomas' libretto and lyrics:

> Mr Brandon Thomas who has done the book into English has not added to his distinction in this work. He might surely have made the tale more compact and explicit. He might certainly have made the dialogue more amusing . . (*Era*)
>
> . . very feeble, the dialogue is entirely innocent of any sort of humour . . (*Times*)
>
> . . a sad lack of anything like wit or humour . . equally destitute of inspiration are his lyrics in which such monstrous solecisms as the rhyming of 'adoptions' with 'corruptions', 'morning' with 'performing', 'purse' with 'us', 'revel' with 'drivel' are perpetrated . . (*Theatre*)

The author of *Charley's Aunt* was not equally at home in comic opera but he had the aid of Le Hay, Denny and Arthur Williams whose working-up of the role of Lurcher had been one of the determining factors in the success of *Dorothy*. The opening night negotiated, the comedians began to play fast and loose with the dialogue which, if it became less intelligible, certainly became more enjoyable in their hands.

After six weeks, as planned, the London season of *The Queen of Brilliants* closed, and the magnificent scenery and costumes were packaged up for transit to New York where the show opened three weeks later in a largely rewritten version with Digby Bell replacing Arthur Williams as the innkeeper-cum-circus proprietor. Abbey and Grau were never given a moment's hope. After 29 performances the programme was changed to showcase Miss Russell in her perennial success as Offenbach's *Grande Duchesse*.

The Queen of Brilliants was Jakobowski's second work at Abbey's Theatre during the year as he had been responsible for the music for *The Devil's Deputy* produced there by Francis Wilson in September for a run of 72 reasonably successful performances. *The Devil's Deputy* was a slight story of mistaken identity set around an actor who is caught out dressed in a devil's costume. It had originally been intended that Sousa should write the music to Cheever Goodwin's libretto, but financial differences led Wilson to reject him in favour of the man who had done him so proudly with *Erminie*. *The Devil's Deputy* remained in the repertoire in 1895 on a tour of America but was not produced in Britain.

The most successful show of the year to date had been the variety musical *Go-Bang* and the next three entries, two British and one American, were all of that genre and all, likewise, proved popular. The American piece was *A Trip to Chinatown*, a variety farce which had been an enormous success in New York where it set up a long run record for a musical (657 perfs.) which would last nearly thirty years. It had introduced to a wide audience such popular hits as 'After the Ball', 'Reuben and Cynthia' and 'The Bowery', and its ever-changing nature ensured it an enormous popularity all round the country. In London its appeal was less, but it succeeded in running 125 performances at Toole's and the Strand before starting the first of many provincial tours on which it was to become an established favourite.

Claude Duval, which was first produced at Bristol in July and toured before making its London début in September, was the latest in the line of Arthur Roberts burlesques. On this occasion Roberts, under the pseudonym of 'Payne Nunn' (no less apt than Jimmy Davis' 'Owen Hall' in its pecuniary allusion) had taken credit for a share in the libretto, his collaborator and lyricist being Frederick Bowyer, better known for his contributions to the music halls than as a playwright. It was a well put-together piece which bore less relation to the story of the famous highwayman than to *Erminie* and one or two other well-known comic operas. Claude (Roberts) and his lieutenant, Pincher (Chas E. Stevens), come to the home of Sir Phillip Saxmundham (Eric Thorne) disguised as Reginald de Vere and Lord Touchem with the object of stealing the family jewels, an object somewhat tempered by the hero's ardour for the daughter of the house, Miss Marjorie (Florrie Schuberth). Duval steals the jewels but allows them to be retaken as he escapes from the scene by balloon. In the second act the jewels are again threatened by a robbery on the Saxmundhams' coach and the famous scene of the gavotte on the green takes place. In the final part Duval turns up once again at Saxmundham Hall in an attempt to see Marjorie and win her hand. He disguises himself as a barmaid, then a lady guest and finally as Marjorie's unknown bridegroom before carrying off the prize. Affairs throughout are enlivened by a persistent detective, Sherlock Holmes-Spotter (H. O. Clarey) who is constantly on the trail of Duval, and by a Grossmith-type dude, Lord Percy (Fitzroy Morgan).

Although Roberts was strongly featured, he had by now realised the value of having good supporting characters around him and *Claude Duval* was constructed to allow all the principals good material. The libretto was lively with no features except some of the more outrageous effects and disguises to give it the appellation of burlesque. The language was natural and snappy, and Bowyer provided lyrics of a decidedly superior class. The music was from the prolific John Crook and Lionel Monckton. Monckton, a son of the Town Clerk of London and Lady Monckton (an amateur actress of some note) had taken part in theatrical activities at Oxford but was destined for a career in the legal profession. He duly became a member of the bar in 1885 but continued with his theatrical and musical interests and contributed occasional numbers on a professional basis to musical scores such as *Cinder-Ellen Up Too Late* ('What will You Have to Drink?') and *King Kodak*.

In *Claude Duval* he had a larger share of the music which included a number of successful songs. Roberts put over a burlesque French chanson, an almost straight 'Song of the Road', a couple of duets with Florrie Schuberth and a song and dance with Eva Ellerslie as a highway-woman in which they stepped down off a hoarding as a couple of bill-posters, as well as the cautionary 'The Monkey and the Cat' which rounded the evening off:

Let the Tom kiss the Tabby
And the Tabby kiss the Tom
Let the Blackey give the tortoise-shell a pat
When foreigners with cash
Come around upon the mash
Just remember please the Monkey and the Cat

Lady Joan (Amy Liddon), Pincher and Claude had an excellent trio about 'The middle-aged Heart', Clarey a humorous song called 'Spotter on the Track':

Sherlock, Vidoc
Miklejohn and Drascovitch,
Hawksure, Talksure
No chance with me have got.
Slater's ineffective
With this champion detective
Spotter wipes the floor with all the lot!

but the most successful of Bowyer's lyrics was undoubtedly Percy's number 'I Pay another Man to do It':

Since today I am a man
I shall still pursue a plan
Which I've practised most religiously from birth
With much pride I like to brag
That I'll never never fag
When Pater's rich enough to buy the earth.

Off to Oxford I was sent
I returned just as I went
At cards a little fortune I ran through it
Did I attend each class
And study like an ass?
Not me–I paid another man to do it.

Learning's such a bore

A beastly, horrid bore
And the use of it I never could see through it
I played at Nap and Solo
And I won a prize at polo
I mean, I paid another chap to do it . .

As with *Don Quixote*, *Claude Duval* was scheduled for a tour and a short visit to London – three weeks at the Prince of Wales Theatre – but when it arrived its popularity proved such that it was decided to continue the run open-ended. This arrangement involved some shuffling of the other pieces already installed in London. Gilbert's new comic opera, *His Excellency*, which was being prepared for the Prince of Wales was shifted over to the Lyric where *Little Christopher Columbus* was still in possession. That piece was mooted for the Gaiety but, since *The Shop Girl* was virtually ready to go into production there, it was sent for the last part of its run to Terry's.

The success of *Claude Duval* on tour was founded largely on the personal popularity of Arthur Roberts, a grand physical production and the attractive songs of Monckton and Crook. Before the London season, however, an additional precaution was taken by having the hitherto tiny role of Lady Dorcas expanded into a principal soubrette role for Marie Halton. The plot was duly altered and some special material, including two songs 'You've never Seen me here Before' and 'The Magic of Spring', were added for the lady who duly proved the additional attraction intended. *Claude Duval* was kindly greeted by the critics and even more kindly by the public, and its short initial run developed into a season of 142 performances. It continued through into 1895 in a 'New Christmas Edition', being finally withdrawn in February after a very satisfactory career. Interestingly, the piece was sent out the following season on a national tour with Harry C. Barry replacing Roberts in the title-role and proved it could exist quite independently of its star performance.

The third variety musical to come in was *The Lady Slavey* which had been touring with immense popularity since its original provincial production the previous year. The producers had put off a London production on more than one occasion, doubting whether the rather unsophisticated format of the piece would find a public in the West End. *The Lady Slavey* was rather different in character from its contemporaries in the variety musical field. It had the essential set of 'turns' in its second act but it was not set in the lavish Rurarabian context of a *Morocco Bound* or a *Go-Bang* and it had none of the production values lavished on those pieces. It also distanced itself from such shows by having a coherent and forward-going modern story-line and came closest, in reality, to *A Gaiety Girl* without having anything like its style and sophistication in writing, or its budget and casting in production. The producers did their best to remedy these two factors which they feared might prove a bar to West End approval before finally bringing the show in. The book suffered little basic change apart from the introduction of a new character, Captain FitzNorris, a broken-down gentleman fighting to retain his gentility in his employment as second bailiff to the exuberant Roberts. The score, on the other hand, was extensively remodelled and John Crook, who had supplied the principal music for the touring version, put together what was largely a new score for the London production, tailored mostly to the demands of the stars engaged. The cast was headed by the admirable Charles Danby with an outstanding comedy performance as the 'Big Boss Dude' cum Bailiff, while the two leading ladies were both Americans – the popular May Yohe taking the title role and Jenny McNulty playing the ambitious Flo Honeydew.

Miss Yohe made sure she had the larger number of the songs, most notably a sentimental ballad 'Tis Hard to Love and Say Farewell' composed by Frank Isitt, to suit her voice, with a compass of A flat below middle C to the A flat above. The danger of boredom in the resultant basso drone was avoided by affixing to the melody a mobile 'cello obbligato line which virtually made the number into a duet, but also into a decided crowd-pleaser. Crook wrote her a little riding song 'Gee up, Whoa!' but her other two numbers were both interpolations. 'What's a poor Girl to Do', a flirting number, was written by Joseph and Mary Watson:

What's a poor girl to do
I'm sure I can't help it, could you?
To be young and pretty seems almost a pity
But has its advantages too!

and the obligatory Plantation Song, 'The Land of Dreams' was supplied by Herbert Walther and Alfred Cammeyer. She joined in two duets with Danby, the first 'Each Bird and Beast' telling how each variety of animal serenades its loved one, and the other, a topical piece, affirming 'It's a very wise Child that Knows':

It is a wise young child they say
That knows its own Papa,
Yet there are secrets in this world
More wonderful by far
We speculate on this and that
And think we're very smart
Yet who can see the hidden things
Locked up in every heart?

It's a very wise child that knows
Yes, a very wise child that knows
When ladies they at the the-ay-ter call
Wear bonnets and buns in the pit and the stalls
As broad and as wide as the dome of St Paul's–
It's a very wise child that knows!

After further digs at the fashions and customs of the fair sex by Roberts, and the weaknesses of gentlemen by Phyllis, the song launched into a few political sallies:

Why Russia and France although prating of peace
Their powerful navies they yearly increase
And while we permit our shipbuilding to cease
It's a very wise child that knows

If Great Britain's army in action were found
If every man's weapons would prove to be sound
And if there would be enough guns to go round
It's a very wise child that knows . .

as well as having a go at more insular issues such as the decision of the Government to try 'Local Option' on Prohibition, the inevitable Jabez Balfour case, the anti-music hall brigade and that eternal Aunt Sally, the railways:

When a man travels on the South-Eastern railway
From Charing Cross to Cannon Street we will say
If he'll get there that night or some time the next day
It's a very wise child that knows!

The topical allusions of the song proved highly popular and were kept up-to-date as the song lengthened perceptibly during the run.

Charles Danby retained the hit song of the touring show, 'I'm the big Boss Dude from O-hi-o' and the more recent 'The Tears Rolled down his Cheeks' (Crook/Younge), a number in an unashamed music-hall style. The hero was given an interpolated number, 'In Friendship's Name' written three years previously by Dance and Charles Graham, and shared a pretty duet 'Why Love in Secret?' with Blanche Barnett (Mrs Fred Harris) who played one of the sisters. The other sister, Adelaide Astor, was most successful with a peculiar little number 'Dorothy Flop' written by Adrian Ross and composed by her real-life sister, Letty (Rudge) Lind. The subject of the song was a little girl with a fondness for dancing, nicknamed 'Flop' by her father. The real 'Dorothy Flop' was a third Rudge sister, Lydia, who had already taken to the professional stage as Lydia Flopp. Miss Astor performed the childish lyric of the song in a baby-doll fashion and followed up with a skirt dance à la Lind which won great applause. Of the solos only Roberts' song and 'In Friendship's Name' had survived from the original score but much of Crook's concerted music, including Vincent's solo in the first act finale, 'Wanted a Wife for a Millionaire', was retained. The excision of all the old songs and well-known tunes were not to everyone's taste and some claimed the show had been 'injured by changes made to render it palatable to what is supposed to be the hypercritical taste of Londoners'. The flavour of the piece had changed from the rollicking to the vaguely refined and sentimental, and the emphasis had been placed very heavily on the shoulders of Danby and Miss Yohe. The comedian pulled out all the stops as the bailiff in his disguises as, firstly, the footman, getting everything wrong and totally unable to assume the dignity of this kind, and then as the loud and extravagant 'Boss Dude'. Miss Yohe, on the other hand, was not quite right. *The Stage* did not succumb to her much publicised charms and wrote:

> It is easy to understand that much life and frolic would run through the piece were Phyllis played with dash, vigour and humour. Unfortunately these qualities are wanting in Miss Yohe's performance.

Miss Yohe, however, had other things on her mind. She had followed the Gaiety's Connie Gilchrist from the stage into the aristocracy, becoming Lady Francis Hope, heiress to the title of Duchess of Newcastle and to the infamous Hope Diamond. Either that jewel, the traditional bringer of ill fortune, or his own nature had led Sir Francis into trouble for in January of 1895 he was declared bankrupt. He had lost £70,000 on 'theatrical investments' (one of which was doubtless Miss Yohe) and as much again at the gaming tables. A few weeks after this disaster *The Lady Slavey* closed. May did not wait for the last night. She opportunely twisted her ankle and hurried off to Monte Carlo to 'convalesce', with her next contract to star as Dick Whittington safely in her pocket.

The Lady Slavey had survived three months. *The Daily Sketch*'s 'Monocle' reported:

> . . at first failure seemed to be the certain fate of *The Lady Slavey* and it is a striking proof of the vitality of the work that it survived the harsh notices of the critics and cold reception of the first nighters . . . I went on the second night when, as a result of first night criticisms, the piece had been suddenly chopped and changed and, of course, was at its worst; and so, seeing how well it went under the circumstances, I imagine that it may be worked up into a piece that will deservedly outlive some of its rivals .

'Monocle' was right. If the London season had been less than a success, *The Lady Slavey* was still doing barnstorming business in the provinces where three companies toured throughout the autumn. Some numbers from the London production were inserted into the touring versions and the 'new version' of *The Lady Slavey* continued an almost unbroken career around the provincial circuits for fifteen years, becoming, in the process, one of the most played British musicals of all time. As late as 1921 it could still be found in the touring lists.

In 1896 Georger Lederer picked up the piece and staged it at New York's Casino Theatre. New York patrons took more kindly to *The Lady Slavey* than Londoners, but the show which they were seeing was very different. George Dance's libretto had been 'Americanised' and the score 'improved' so completely by Gustave Kerker that not one of Crook's numbers or finales remained. Virginia Earle starred as Phyllis with the extraordinary Dan Daly, soon to be adored in Britain as the hero of *The Belle of New York*, playing a rather different version of Roberts. Flo Honeydew was impersonated by another odd-looking performer in Marie Dressler (her odd looks were later to make a Hollywood fortune) who joined Daly in the hit routine of the American version, an eccentric dance routine called 'The Human Fly'. So little of the original show remained that it could barely be called a British musical. The undistinguished music which Kerker supplied was no better (and often worse) than Crook's and it gained no lasting popularity but as interpreted by Daly and Misses Earle and Dressler it pleased Broadway tastes sufficiently to give *The Lady Slavey* a satisfactory run.

Hard on the heels of *The Lady Slavey* another new musical opened in London – one which was of a completely different character to the simple romping Cinderella tale at the Avenue. *His Excellency* was a George Edwardes production of a W. S. Gilbert piece with music by Dr Osmond Carr which had been rumoured around the town to be an extended travesty of *Hamlet*. The parties involved denied the rumour and, ostensibly to prevent pirating by American agents, made flourishing efforts to keep their story under wraps, even going as far as to take out an ex parte motion against *The Star* newspaper to prevent them publishing the plot and situations of the show before opening night.

On 27 October *His Excellency* opened to a most favourable reception. Gilbert had returned to the world of topsy-turvydom for his plot which was based on the character of a practical-joking governor whose delight in life is to fool all those around him. It is his sad contention that there are no new jokes to be played:

> Quixotic is his enterprise and hopeless his adventure is
> Who seeks for jocularities that haven't yet been said
> The world has joked incessantly for over 50 centuries
> And every joke that's possible has long ago been made.
> I started as a humourist with lots of mental fizziness
> But humour is a drug which it's the fashion to abuse.
> For my stock-in-trade, my fixtures and the goodwill
> of the business
> No reasonable offer am I likely to refuse . . .

Governor Griffenfeld's particular sense of humour involves the building-up and dashing of other people's hopes. He has led the matronly Dame Hecla Courtlandt to believe she is engaged to him, he has led the sculptor Erling and the physician Tortenssen to think they have been raised to prominent positions, and he plays fast and loose with the affections that the two young men have for his daughters who are not at all averse to joining in their father's games. But his fooling is about to get him into trouble. There comes to town a strolling player, one Nils Egilson, who strikes the Governor with the uncanny resemblance he bears to their ruler, the Prince Regent. The Governor thinks it is a capital joke to have the young actor impersonate the Prince and lend credence to his fabrications before blowing up the whole business in everyone's face. Of course Nils really is the Prince Regent in disguise and, in consequence, all Griffenfeld's edicts are royally confirmed – the sculptor and the physician are promoted and married to the Governor's daughters, Dame Hecla is given in marriage to Mats the Syndic who is promoted to Governor, and the Prince himself finds love with a village girl, Christina, while Griffenfeld find the joke against himself, relegated to the common soldiery in the very castle where he was once Governor.

The best of *His Excellency* was in Gilbert's most adept and comical style, the characters were brittle and funny and not too clearly human, his dialogue was smart and neat and his lyrics often in the vein of his past successes. One of the most amusing pieces was a number sung by the Regent bewailing the incessant playing of the National Anthem everywhere he goes:

A King, though he's pestered with cares,
Though, no doubt, he can often trepan them;
But one comes in a shape he can never escape –
The implacable National Anthem!
Though for quiet and rest he may yearn,
It pursues him at every turn –
No chance of forsaking
Its rococo numbers;
They haunt him when waking –
They poison his slumbers!
Like the Banbury Lady, whom everyone knows,
He's cursed with its music wherever he goes!
Though its words but imperfectly rhyme,
And the devil himself couldn't scan them,
With composure polite he endures day and night
That illiterate National Anthem!

The show was not over-burdened with solo numbers and the largest part of the music consisted of concerted pieces. Nancy McIntosh, who had not been particularly successful in *Utopia (Limited)*, was still dear to Gilbert's heart and for her, in the role of Christina, he wrote a fable reminiscent of 'The Magnet and the Churn':

CHR: You know the story of the wilful bee?
ALL: We don't! We never heard it!
ERL: Who was he?
CHR: A hive of bees, as I've heard say,
Said to their Queen one sultry day –
'Please your Majesty's high position,
The hive is full and the weather is warm.
We rather think, with due submission,
The time has come when we ought to swarm?'
Buzz, buzz, buzz, buzz.
Out spake their Queen, and thus spake she –
'This is a matter that rests with me,
Who dares opinion thus to form?
I'll tell you when it is time to swarm!'

Buzz, buzz, buzz, buzz.
Her Majesty wore an angry frown,
In fact Her Majesty's foot was down–
Her Majesty sulked–declined to sup–
In short Her Majesty's back was up.
Buzz, buzz, buzz, buzz,
Her foot was down and her back was up!'

In spite of the Queen's tantrum, one bee decides to swarm, alone:

Pitiful sight it was to see
Respectable elderly high-class bee,
Who kicked the beam at sixteen stone,
Trying his best to swarm alone!

The poor bee makes such a fool of himself that the other bees send him to Coventry:

There, classed with all who misbehave,
Both plausible rogue and noisome knave,
In dismal dumps he lived to own
The folly of trying to swarm alone!

For Jessie Bond, as one of the Governor's daughters, he supplied a song, but others of his cast including Alice Barnett, Ellaline Terriss and John Le Hay found their vocal opportunities confined to ensembles.

The music by Osmond Carr was in his usual efficient and tuneful vein but there was a general regret that the task had not been entrusted to Sullivan for, clever and competent as Carr was, he had not the humour in his turns of musical phrase and orchestration of Gilbert's more illustrious partner. The production was in Edwardes' normal careful and lavish style and the cast featured George Grossmith in his return to the comic opera stage after making himself a small fortune with his Drawing Room entertainment. Rutland Barrington was there too, along with other members of the old Savoy team, and the whole piece had an aura of 'old Savoy' about it. Only Sullivan was lacking. But the show received a wonderful reception on its first night and Gilbert gathered his best notices since *The Gondoliers*:

Mr W. S. Gilbert has added another masterpiece of drollery to those which have made him famous. *His Excellency* has not only a very funny idea as the groundwork of the story but the dialogue and lyrics are full of the author's delightful humour . . . a veritable triumph. (*Era*)

The latest of the Gilbert libretti is whimsical as ever, well-furnished in its peculiar way as ever, and rather more human than usual . . . the memorable Gilbertian opera goes on as before with no diminishment of an unprecedented popular approval. In all the history of the operas no first night aroused a greater enthusiasm. (*Stage*)

Even without any music at all, such a subject, treated as Mr Gilbert treats it, would have been equally sure of good fortune (*Theatre*)

Since the dissolution of the famous Savoy partnership many coalitions have formed, now of Sir Arthur Sullivan with new librettists, now of Mr Gilbert with other composers and again of popular members of the troupe with other authors. Various degrees of success have attended these experiments but none has seemed so likely to succeed permanently because none has been nearly so strong as that which was concerned in the production of *His Excellency* . . . since *The Mikado* Mr Gilbert has given us no book of so satisfactory a kind as far as concerns the construction of the

> plot and the effective manipulation of its threads even if the dialogue seems a little less sparkling than usual . . (*Times*)

> . . one of the brightest, most whimsical and fascinating of the wonderful series that will render the author of the Bab Ballads immortal (*Sketch*)

Osmond Carr's contribution was less enthusiastically received. Comparisons with Sullivan were inevitable:

> Dr Carr is forced into comparison with Sir Arthur Sullivan and it is unfortunate and unfair. Taking his music without any pretence at comparison one finds gaiety, freedom from vulgarity, excellent workmanship and sometimes charming melodic invention. If all were as good as the comic quartet in the second act it would be brilliant. As it stands one may say he has come out of a sharp proof very creditably and almost brilliantly. (*Sketch*)

but not all the reviewers took such a kindly attitude and there was no doubt the skills of the two musicians were just not comparable.

After the crabbedness of *Utopia (Limited)* it was a relief to have Gilbert back in a more relaxed mood and occasionally at his very joyous best but, on the whole, *His Excellency* showed proof of an unfashionable artificiality in its fun and a lack of colour in its story and incidents when looked at alongside such current favourites as *A Gaiety Girl* or *Morocco Bound*. However, it ran for some six months, which was more than satisfactory in a period when the vogue for comic opera was on the wane.

After the London run an American season was staged but, in spite of the personal successes of John Le Hay as the Syndic and Mabel Love as the dancer, Blanca, *His Excellency* never got off the ground in New York and a tour starring Miss Love resulted in a deficit of £4,000 and some acrimonious lawsuits. The Gilbertian style of humour, while it still had many a devotee in London, was all but a thing of the past in New York where variety had taken a much stronger hold and comic opera was expected to be in the *Erminie* mould of low comedy and pretty tunes and faces rather than of genuine wit and literary merit.

Just before the production of *His Excellency* on Broadway, another comic opera by the other member of the Savoy coalition, Sir Arthur Sullivan, had swiftly come and gone in London. This was *The Chieftain*, a revised version of Sullivan's early piece *The Contrabandista*, which D'Oyly Carte mounted in December 1894 at the Savoy. Frank Burnand had largely revised his 1867 libretto. There was an almost totally new second act and the wife of the bemused photographer, Dolly Griggs, was introduced in an attempt to heighten the show's quota of fun. Five of Sullivan's original numbers survived into the new score, including 'From Rock to Rock', the showpiece of the St George's Opera House production, but all the rest was new.

D'Oyly Carte's reasons for staging *The Chieftain* were mainly negative – the failure of *Mirette*, the lack of a new piece from Gilbert and Sullivan – and the public reaction was also mainly negative. The sparkle of Sullivan's music was undeniable, the story was almost droll enough to be a burlesque of the old comic opera style rather than a serious effort at comic opera, and Carte had Florence St John, Rosina Brandram, Courtice Pounds and Walter Passmore to present the material, but *The Chieftain* was little more than a patched-up, old-fashioned curiosity and had very little chance from the start. *The Sketch* noted:

> . . it cannot be asserted that the dialogue and lyrics show Mr Burnand at his best though on the whole they serve their purpose very fairly. . . the music is rather

> curious for what may be called '67 Sullivan and '94 Sullivan are offered almost impartially. Most people will prefer the later vintage . .

Carte kept *The Chieftain* running for three months then cried enough and brought in the Carl Rosa production of *Hansel and Gretel* instead. After that, for the second time in two years, the Savoy Theatre went dark. *The Chieftain* had a mediocre run on Broadway where Francis Wilson took on the role of Grigg, but it never looked like establishing itself there any more than it had in London.

By November eight new musicals had been premièred in the West End since the beginning of the year. *Go-Bang, His Excellency, The Lady Slavey* and *Claude Duval* had all attained some degree of success, *Jaunty Jane Shore* and *The Queen of Brilliants* rather less, and *Wapping Old Stairs* and *King Kodak* were clearly failures. Now, in quick succession, came the disaster and the hit of the season. The disaster came first in the shape of a variety burlesque on Walter Scott's *Ivanhoe*, under the title of *All My Eye-Van-Hoe*, put together by Philip Hayman who had succeeded in getting two wealthy backers to put up £1500 apiece. He persuaded composers of the quality of Solomon, Crook and Talbot to contribute numbers to add to his own compositions and, through John Shine who was to play the leading role, he got artists of the calibre of Phyllis Broughton, Harry Grattan, Agnes Hewitt, Fred Storey and Alice Lethbridge to take part. Messrs Chappell announced the forthcoming publication of the musical score.

The opening night was a fiasco. The artists had no chance at all with the embarrassingly dreadful material and the audience left them in no doubt as to their opinion. 'The nadir of inanity has been reached', groaned *Theatre*. 'A chaotic hotch-potch of stale jokes and trite jests, of forced humour and meaningless fun'. 'The libel laws and my conscience', noted *The Sketch*, 'compel me to declare that some parts of the piece were successful', as it carefully labelled *Eye-Van-Hoe* almost the worst of its kind and reported, 'the whole affair met with substantial disfavour and well deserved it'.

Rewrites were hurriedly announced. The editor of *Fun*, G. T. Johnson, was mooted as rewriter. A new title, *Wink the other Eye-Van-Hoe,* was suggested; a totally new burlesque around the sets and costumes was suggested; the engagement of Edwin Lonnen was rumoured. But *Eye-Van-Hoe* was beyond mortal help and sank into iniquitous oblivion after one week. The gentlemen who had produced the piece could not vanish as easily. Howard Talbot took them to court to pay for the songs that they had commissioned from him for the show – £42. 1s 10d. – Fred Storey summoned them for eight weeks' guaranteed salary at £17 per week. Messrs Perryman and Hand, whose whole capitalisation had already been lost, pleaded no personal liability for the debts of the producing company but were overruled and had to pay up.

The season's hit was no less emphatic. At the Gaiety George Edwardes continued with the kind of entertainment he had begun to purvey so successfully with *A Gaiety Girl.* The combination of a slight and bright modern story, entertaining dialogue, songs and dances by the best light musical writers of the day, and a tasteful and lavish physical production had proved irresistible at the Prince of Wales and Daly's; he now brought the new type of show to the Gaiety, and *The Shop Girl* confirmed the huge appeal of the genre.

The libretto of *The Shop Girl* was prepared by the American playwright Harry Dam. A Californian by birth, Dam had worked principally as a journalist but had succeeded in placing two plays in the West End – *Diamond Deane* at the Vaudeville and

The Silver Shell which the Kendals had played at the Avenue with some success. Dam was also responsible for some of the lyrics, the remainder being supplied by the prolific Adrian Ross while the music was written by Ivan Caryll, supplemented by numbers from young Lionel Monckton, who was beginning a connection with the Gaiety which would last for many years.

The story of *The Shop Girl* was basically familiar. It opens in Mr Hooley's Royal Stores which have become the centre of the search for the missing heiress to a mining fortune. It seems the girl in question has been found in the person of plump and plain shopgirl Ada Smith, and Mr Hooley himself hurries to propose to the unwitting millionairess. Ada, theoretically engaged to the floor-walker Miggles, is delighted and hurriedly gets her 'catch' to the altar. There then arrives from America the millionaire John Brown who had started the search for the missing girl. He explains that there was a misprint in the advertisement and the date of birth given for the young lady was ten years out. This disqualifies Ada from consideration and the real heiress turns out to be pretty Bessie Brent, the 'Shop Girl' of the title, who is now able to marry her medical student, Charlie, the scion of a noble family and hitherto beyond her legitimate aspirations. Hooley is bamboozled while Miggles consoles himself with the beautiful Miss Robinson of Sales.

Dam kept his libretto in the 'new style' – a slight, farcical piece in modern language with all trace of rhyme and wordplay shunted firmly into the lyrical section. The lyrics, too, were comparatively simple and undemanding although, in contrast to the pure variety musical, many bore clear reference to the story in hand. There were, of course, irrelevant and interpolated numbers included for pure entertainment but the piece was a decidedly more homogeneous one than most of its immediate predecessors.

Dam's dialogue was neither particularly clever nor humorous but it had the merit of keeping a brisk rate of action going and introduced a number of very entertaining characters – the impoverished French Count St Vaurien searching to lay his heart at the feet of the missing heiress, if only he can find her first; the socialite Lady Appleby who is interminably collecting for charities but whose 'expenses' include £35 hats so that only 1% of the 'take' is left for distribution to the poor; her quaint-kneed 'financial secretary' and her daughters, Faith, Hope and Charity, who support by their charitable efforts an entire home for young ladies (their own); the girls of the Syndicate Theatre chorus, beauties every one – and every one a foundling with the obligatory strawberry mark[1] of long-lost millionaire's daughters; and the 'Johnnie who trots them round', fatuous, good-hearted, rich Bertie Boyd.

The cast which Edwardes assembled for *The Shop Girl* was an excellent one. Arthur Williams was engaged for the avaricious Hooley with the theatre's new chief comedian, Teddy Payne, as the woebegone Miggles. Maria Davis and Willie Warde of the old brigade of Gaiety players were joined by a group of young players of a type which would become the nucleus of the new Gaiety era – Seymour Hicks and Maud Hill kept on from *Little Jack Sheppard*, George Grossmith Jr now with a 'corner' in goofy Johnnies, Ada Reeve from the music-hall stage, and plump and pleasing Lillie Belmore whose death in 1901 at the age of 29 deprived the musical stage of a potential major star.

Then there were the Gaiety Girls. There had always been Gaiety Girls but now the Girls of the Gaiety Theatre blossomed into something extra special as the gaze of fashionable London fixed itself on them. To the established favourites like Topsy

[1] The strawberry mark proved offensive to some and was withdrawn soon after the opening.

Sinden and Violet Monckton there were added a whole series of beautiful and sometimes talented young ladies who would create a major attraction for the Gaiety for two decades. The Girls of *The Shop Girl* included two youngsters who would make names for themselves in the theatre – 16-year-old Constance Collier already in her third Edwardes show, and 22-year-old Fannie Ward making her first appearance on the British stage after some small roles in America. In *The Shop Girl* she had just one line to speak. The principal cast was completed by another American, Marie Halton, who supplied a little sentimental characterisation to balance the unusual fact that the lovers of the piece, Charlie and Bessie, were not written as the usual love-lorn duet-singing couple but as a lively pair whose dialogue and songs were arch and humorous and bantering but never traditionally romantic. Sentimentality was not in the artillery of Seymour Hicks and Ada Reeve.

One of the most attractive features of the new show was its songs. Probably the most popular was an interpolated number which Seymour Hicks had brought back from America, 'Her golden Hair was Hanging down her Back'. Adrian Ross threw out the original lyric and replaced it with a version of his own:

> There was once a country maiden came to London for a trip,
> And her golden hair was hanging down her back;
> She was weary of the country so she gave her folks the slip,
> And her golden hair was hanging down her back . . . .
> It was once a vivid auburn but her rivals call'd it red,
> So she thought she could be happier with another shade instead,
> And she stole the washing soda and applied it to her head,
> And her golden hair was hanging down her back.
>
> But Oh! Flo, such a change you know!
> When she left the village she was shy;
> But alas! and alack! She's come back
> With a naughty little twinkle in her eye.

Hicks related,

> I was lucky enough to pick up a song in America called 'Her golden Hair was Hanging down her Back' which materially assisted in establishing me at the Gaiety. It had been heard in England before I sang it, but had not succeeded; nor should I have made it the furore it was had I not seen a little sedate woman sing it at a music hall in New York. She rendered it in a most reserved and quiet manner, her very gentleness making all the lines appear to have, if not a double entendre at least the hope, or should I say the fear, that things did not mean quite what they seemed.

In fact, 'Her golden Hair' had been written by the Irish songwriter Felix McGlennon and bought by the English music hall vocalist Alice Leamar who had sung it briefly before it had been pirated to the United States where it found success. Since McGlennon and Miss Leamar officially held rights in the song, Edwardes found himself obliged to pay them royalties throughout the run. His 'free American song' was not as free as Hicks had led him to believe. Along with the Misses Ward and Halton, the United States had made a third contribution to *The Shop Girl* by suggesting one of its principal songs. America also contributed a certain amount of Hicks' dialogue for the young actor, so successful with his 'borrowed' tramp jokes in *Little Jack Sheppard*, was never averse to annexing a good line or even a scene from a fellow artist and he gained quite a reputation for this pilfering in America. In *The Shop Girl* he decorated his role liberally with second-hand gags, many of them transatlantic.

George Grossmith had his best and most successful 'masher' part to date with a Lionel Monckton number to which Grossmith had written the words:

I'm what folks call a 'Johnnie', of the title I am proud,
My manner's always dainty, though my dress a trifle loud,
I've a handsome set of chambers and a balance up at Coutts
But do not shine at anything excepting at the boots.
I've joined the 'Junior Pothouse' and drop in when I am by,
I don't possess much brain, but I have got the latest tie.
When I've done my morning Bond Street crawl, I do the thing in style,
And give the cabbie half-a-crown to drive me half a mile.
For I'm Beautiful, Bountiful Bertie
Best of all the lot!
Beautiful, Bountiful Bertie,
Always on the spot!
Thick with all of the girls you know,
From Flo and Alice to Gertie.
I tell you straight he is up-to-date
Is Beautiful, Bounding Bertie.

Monckton was also responsible (with Adrian Ross) for yet another of the show's hits 'Brown of Colorado' sung by Colin Coop as the struck-it-rich millionaire:

In the steerage of a liner I went out to be a miner,
And in search of gold proceeded for to roam,
I had nothing worth a button, but a little tea and mutton,
And a copy of 'The Miner's Dream of Home'.
So I turn'd the soil and dug it, but I never found a nugget,
And I nearly left the diggings in despair.
When without the slightest warning, why, I struck the reef one morning,
And I left my claim a splendid millionaire!
A splendid millionaire,
Without a single care,
Instead of an unlucky desperado.
I strode into town,
No longer Bunco Brown,
But plutocratic Brown of Colorado!

Caryll scored a big success with his quaint little duet for Miggles and Miss Robinson (Katie Seymour) called 'Love on the Japanese Plan'. Dressed in Japanese costume, they performed the nonsensical little piece to much fluttering of fans and peeping and bobbing, following up with an odd dance routine which brought storms of applause. The Japanese costume was only one of many disguises for Payne: in the second act, set in the colourful surroundings of a Kensington Bazaar, he turned up variously as a pierrot, an ancient Roman and as Hamlet, managing to introduce a good deal of extraneous comedy material at the same time, and delivered a Caryll/Dam song entitled 'The Vegetarian' which was edged blatantly into the script for him. The little man delivered it in an apppopriately music hall style:

It was an evil hour when I met my Mary Ann,
Oh, woe! Woe the day!
She was living with her mother on the vegetable plan,
Yea, verily yea.
She said if I would try it, the cold potato diet,

I'd regulate my liver and become another man.
Though seriously doubting, I took to brussels-sprouting
And now you see what's left of me – a Vegetarian!

Ada Reeve sang skittishly of the experiences of 'The Shop Girl' and knocked reciprocal sparks off Hicks in their unusual dialogue and an anticipatory 'Perambulator Duet'. The lovely Maud Hill described herself as 'The smartest Girl in Town', Marie Halton made a small hit in Caryll's sentimental waltz song 'Over the Hills', and Lillie Belmore was very funny describing her early experiences as 'The Foundling':

Left upon a doorstep at half past nine –
Oh, goodness! it was cold!
Sleeping in a basket tied with twine –
Oh, goodness! it was cold!
Cold, cold, cold as ice.
Oh, goodness! it was cold!

The fun, the songs, the merry story and characters all made a happy whole which, if it had not quite the quality of *A Gaiety Girl* had nevertheless at least that piece's popular appeal. It met with highly favourable reactions all round. *The Stage* commented:

> *The Shop Girl* marks even more emphatically the new school of Gaiety entertainment . . . [it] takes the new order of musical farce a step further and in many respects a step better on its way . .

The Times:

> Judged as a variety entertainment *The Shop Girl* . . might be found wanting; but it aspires to be something other than that, something which might be comic opera if the songs were not of the music hall order and if the cast did not embrace principals who dance a great deal better than they sing . . a hybrid entertainment which may best be described as musical farce but which yields nothing to conventional Gaiety burlesque in the matter of colour, brightness or female interest. *The Shop Girl* is distinguished broadly from the variety entertainment by having a coherent action, not particularly dramatic or amusing in character but boasting at least a beginning, a middle and an end . . the freshness of form which helped so largely to ensure the success of *A Gaiety Girl* is ingeniously reproduced in *The Shop Girl.*

The show became immediately popular and settled into the Gaiety for what was clearly going to be a long run. Edwardes had judged public taste accurately and was now about to reap the reward of 546 performances.

The Shop Girl was still to undergo many and various changes, the earliest occasioned by major changes of cast. The problems began early. On the first night Marie Halton was unable to go on and one of the Girls, Helen Lee, found herself thrust into the limelight for the occasion. No sooner had Miss Halton returned than Teddy Payne was out, unwell. Robert Nainby stepped in, but it soon became clear that the little comedian was seriously ill with typhoid and would not be able to return. A new Miggles was found in the South African actor/manager Frank Wheeler, originally engaged for the small role of Colonel Singleton. The loss of Payne was followed by the departure of Ada Reeve who had no intention of losing her lucrative pantomime engagement. She had a get-out which permitted her to leave in time for the Manchester Comedy Christmas show and she duly departed. Pretty Kate Cutler replaced her, the first in a series of Bessies who would follow in the play's long run.

The musical content also underwent the familiar changes. Bessie's opening song

'The Shop Girl' (Ross/Caryll) was replaced by a Lionel Monckton number on a similar theme, 'The Song of the Shop', and when Ellaline Terriss took over the part she introduced the Fay Templeton coon song 'I want Yer, my Honey', a number by an unknown young composer, Paul Reubens (sic), 'The little Chinchilla' and the most successful of the new pieces, a plantation song 'My Lousiana Lou'. This American-style coon song was written by the Lancashire-born Tom Barrett who styled himself 'Lester Thomas' and, subsequently, 'Leslie Stuart'. Barrett's early career had been spent as a church organist and his first compositions had consisted largely of concert ballads of which 'The Bandolero' popularised by Signor Foli had brought him most prominence. 'Lousiana Lou' was a success of a different kind. It was performed on the halls and published by Francis, Day & Hunter, and was then picked up to be interpolated into *The Shop Girl.* It started the young composer's theatrical career off in the way which it would continue. 'Leslie Stuart' was to have great success both with musicals and with coon songs which he turned out with great facility and skill for, amongst others, Eugene Stratton. 'Lousiana Lou' was not to be as memorable as his 'Lily of Laguna' but it became extremely popular and proved one of the highlights of *The Shop Girl.* Hicks found himself another American number, 'What could the poor Girl Do' (Emilie Alexandra) and Stuart composed him a new song 'The little Mademoiselle'.

With Payne out of the cast and Hicks and Miss Terriss paired in the juvenile leads, the emphasis on the change in the type of performers and their roles became even more pronounced. The lively young pair placed themselves firmly at the centre of affairs in a light romantic comedy performance that fairly twinkled, and though there was still some brisk low comedy to be found in the antics of Williams and Wheeler, the overwhelming burden which had been sustained by the Fred Leslies and the Arthur Roberts in previous shows was significantly reduced. *The Shop Girl* ran on right through 1895 and into 1896 and in April of that year an official second edition was produced. Payne had returned to the cast but *The Shop Girl* seemed to hold a jinx for him for he was soon out again, this time with a broken bone in his leg and a warning against returning to work too soon. Lillie Belmore had left the cast and had been replaced by a new George Edwardes discovery, the equally plump and talented Connie Ediss whom he had spotted on the halls and who was to become one of the most popular Gaiety fixtures and favourites. The show was kept fresh and topical throughout its long run as the public came in droves again and again. Six months after the opening the Gaiety was still turning away business every night, and well before that the shares of the managing company had rocketed to four times their 1894 value. This was theatrical prosperity on a scale unknown since the palmiest days of Fred Leslie and Nellie Farren or the heydey of the Savoy triumvirate.

While the show was still running in London an American production was sent out. Hicks, Grossmith, Connie Ediss, Bertie Wright, Ethel Sydney and a full company crossed the Atlantic and opened at Palmer's Theatre in October of 1895. To general amazement it failed to take and was withdrawn after 72 performances. Many reasons were put forward for its failure. Seymour Hicks blandly suggested the reason might well have been that they had heard his material before – it being all stolen from US comics. Elsewhere it was ingenuously suggested that political differences between Britain and America may have coloured the public's attitude. But America had rejected good and successful shows from Britain before and would do so again in the same way that in both countries inexplicable hits would be created. *The Shop Girl* did not catch on with New York 1895 and that was all there was to it. Australia and South Africa gave the piece a very different reception and it even received the accolade of a French production at the Olympia.

In Britain the show remained popular through the plethora of similar musical farces which followed, and Hicks maintained fondly that it was never bettered. In 1920 it was given a major revival by Hicks and Alfred Butt at the new Gaiety Theatre. The book had been revised and brought up-to-date by Arthur Wimperis, and Herman Darewski had supplied eight new numbers to add to the Jap duet, 'Brown of Colorado', 'Over the Hills' and the other favourite parts of the original score. The most effective of these new pieces was 'The Guards' Brigade' in which the Bessie of the revival, Evelyn Laye, appeared with a full brass band. Other featured members of the revival cast were Alfred Lester (Miggles), Roy Royston (Charlie) and Johnny Danvers (Hooley) while Robert Nainby repeated his original assignment as St Vaurien. Once again *The Shop Girl* proved an out-and-out success and ran for almost twelve months.

Sadly, the production year of 1895 was not to end with the success of *The Shop Girl*. An appalling piece of work arrived on Christmas eve at the Opera Comique. *Eastward Ho!* was a revamped version of a comic opera called *The Caliph* which had been produced by amateurs in Bristol in 1892. This original had been crossed with elements of *The White Cat*, squeezed into the fashionable *Morocco Bound* mould and the result was a peculiar piece about a theatrical troupe in Rurarabia, littered with variety turns. Even the goodwill of Christmas could not save this dismal and unprofessional affair which was quickly dismissed.

The high level of new and attractive productions in the West End over recent years sufficed to keep the provincial theatres well stocked with touring musical attractions. The D'Oyly Carte companies, the inevitable *Dorothy* and the favourite new burlesques were joined on the road by the latest hits – *In Town, A Gaiety Girl, Morocco Bound*. But there was still a place, though largely on the lesser circuits, for provincial-grown extravaganza or burlesque, for the small English operetta and for the musical drama or comedy-drama which had no place in the London theatre but which maintained a certain popularity in the country. Victor Stevens, who had had phenomenal success with his extravaganzas *Randolph the Reckless* and *Bonnie Boy Blue*, came up with a new piece in *The Saucy Sultana* as well as a new version of *Randolph*. Horace Lingard, whose opera company had used *Falka* as one of their staples for a number of years, produced a burlesque version of that piece under the title *Brother Pelican*, while another popular musical, *My Sweetheart*, was parodied in a fairly basic but nevertheless reasonably successful piece called *Laughs*. On a more substantial scale, Horace Lennard produced a musical farce called *Cupid & Co.*, an extravaganza-type piece dealing with the mischief caused when Cupid comes to the present day as a matrimonial agent. The music for *Cupid & Co.* included contributions from Meyer Lutz and Teddy Solomon and featured Russell Wallett, Arthur Roberts' erstwhile understudy, in the leading comic role. It was sufficiently well-liked to justify several small tours.

Alongside these 'new and original' pieces there still existed the old-style pasticcio pieces, most of which now mixed some original music with their collages of familiar tunes. Most of these relied on burlesque books and an extravaganza lay-out – *Crusoe the Cruiser, Robin Hood, Esq.* and *Giddy Miss Carmen* being among the year's newest examples.

The English operetta tradition was represented by a new tour of *The Duke's Diversion* and by an Odoardo Barri tour of his new piece *Our Amateur Theatricals*, a little show obviously modelled on *A Pantomime Rehearsal* but which did not have its predecessor's appeal. Procida Bucalossi, having failed to find again the success of *Les Manteaux Noirs,* switched his attention to light romantic opera and produced an operatic version of Planché's *The Brigand* for Arthur Rousbey's company. *Massaroni,* as it was called, justified only a few performances. The *Jack-in-the-Box* tradition of the dramatic musical play was represented by a 'strong' piece called *Satan's Slave* which stayed alive for several seasons and a couple of less healthy pieces, *The Fight for Freedom* and the Australian show *The Schemer.*

Carl the Clockmaker straddled the comic and the melodramatic. Written by variety comic Harry Starr, it featured himself in the large central role of its comic/pathetic/dramatic tale while still allowing him the opportunity to put over the type of songs he had featured in his early career. *Carl the Clockmaker* was a curious but successful phenomenon, making Starr well known in the provinces as he trouped it and its eventual successors in the genre around the country for the rest of his life.

A totally different proposition to all of these was *The Gay Parisienne,* the latest musical from the pen of George Dance. Following in the footsteps of the same author's *Lady Slavey, The Gay Parisienne* was produced in the provinces, at Northampton, and lined up for a tour of good dates with no intention, or no immediate intention, of running to a London season. Once again Dance came up with a show which was an immediate and significant success. The libretto for his farcical musical was in no way created on the blueprint of *The Lady Slavey* or any of his other pieces. *The Gay Parisienne* took a light, comically ridiculous plot – half old German Reed, half provincial melodrama – stirred in a good dose of genuine humour and a handful of piquant situations to come up with a book which, while no great work of literature, was a perfect basis for a bubbling and undemanding musical of 1894.

Mlle Julie Bon-Bon, the Gay Parisienne, has tricked the well-and-truly married Canon Honeycombe into signing a proposition of marriage and she now arrives at his country parsonage to sue him for breach of promise. By this means she and her accomplice/lover, Adolphe Pompier, intend to stock their bottom drawer at the unworldly Canon's cost. But, in his hasty (and innocent) original encounter with Mlle Bon-Bon, Honeycombe has given her the wrong visiting card and Julie has summonsed his neighbour, Amos Dingle. Dingle once had his life saved by the good Canon and so agrees to take his place in an undefended case for the sake of peace, in spite of the anathema heaped on him by the statuesque Mrs Honeycombe who lends her encouragement to her daughter's lover who has been briefed for the prosecution. Julie arrives and proceeds to bewitch old Major Fossdyke, chairman of the jury, and not unexpectedly wins £10,000 damages. The distraught Canon confesses all and flees to a European spa town where he fakes a report of his death in a mountain accident. But everyone concerned descends on the spa where Honeycombe is hiding disguised as a Scot and after a good deal of coming and going the truth is revealed when Norah Honeycombe's Tom turns the tables on Pompier by blackmailing him over his occupation as a professional spy. Julie gives up her charade and all is allowed to end happily.

The show was illustrated by a lively set of songs, some original, some arranged, the whole written and put together by the show's musical director, Ernest Vousden. *The Gay Parisienne* proved to be an enormously popular touring attraction and, like *The Lady Slavey,* eventually found its way into the West End after a year and a half of pre-London touring during which time it had undergone major changes that built it into a metropolitan and international success.

1894

0140 **WAPPING OLD STAIRS** a comic opera in two acts by Stuart Robertson. Music by Howard Talbot. Produced at the Theatre Royal, King's Lynn 4 January, 1894. Produced at the Vaudeville Theatre under the management of Edward Curtice 17 February, 1894. Withdrawn 17 March after 29 performances, revised and represented 24 March for 6 further performances closing 30 March, 1894.

Sir Wormwood Scrubbs . . . . Herbert Sparling
Captain Crook. . . . . Henry Bouchier/Charles Collette
Dick Fid . . . . Richard Temple/T. P. Haynes
Ben Brace . . . . Avon Saxon
Nancy Joy. . . . . Mary Turner
Molly Joy . . . . Hannah Jones
Daisy Pennant. . . . . Mary Hutton
Mark Mainstay . . . . Courtice Pounds
Susan Sinnett (Susan Swab) . . . . Jessie Bond (Margaret Warren)/ Fanny Marriot
Kate Capstan . . . . Margaret Warren
Betsy Binnacle . . . . L. Stewart
Dolly Hawser . . . . Annie Laurie
Quartermaster. . . . . William Vokes
Nellie Caper. . . . . Miss Lennox
Annie Alport . . . . Amy Bell
Bessie Bouncer . . . . Miss Fane
Pd: Nance Graeme

Dir: Richard Temple; md: Sydney Ward; ch: R. M. Crompton/Mme Marie; sc: R. C. Durant/W. T. Hemsley; cos: W. Clarkson

King's Lynn principal cast as above except Henry Beaumont (MARK), Bert Mayne (BEN), Isobel Marquis (MOLLY), Margaret Warren (SUSAN). Md: Howard Talbot, with the King's Lynn Choral Society.

0141 **GO-BANG** a musical farcical comedy in two acts by Adrian Ross. Music by F. Osmond Carr. Produced by the New Morocco Bound Co. (Fred J. Harris and C. J. Abud) at the Trafalgar Square Theatre 10 March, 1894 for a run of 159 performances closing 24 August, 1894.

Jenkins . . . . Harry Grattan
Sir Reddan Tapeleigh. . . . . Arthur Playfair
Lt the Hon. Augustus Fitzpoop . . . . . George Grossmith Jr
Wang . . . . Sydney Howard/Fred Storey (C. Jamieson)
Narain. . . . . Frederick Rosse/Edgar Stevens
Dam Row . . . . John L. Shine (Arthur Playfair)
Helen Tapeleigh . . . . Jessie Bond (Maggie Roberts)
Lady Fritterleigh . . . . Agnes Hewitt
Sarah Anne . . . . Adelaide Astor
Miss Flo Wedderburn . . . . Ruby Temple/Lydia Flopp
Miss Belle Wedderburn. . . . . Maggie Roberts/Hilda Glenn

Miss Daisy Wedderburn . . . . Maud Lockett
Di Dalrymple . . . . Letty Lind (Adelaide Astor)

Dir: Frank Parker; md: Carl Kiefert; ch: Mariette D'Auban; sc: E. G. Banks & T. E. Ryan; cos: Edel, Stag & Mantle, Swan & Edgar

0142 **JAUNTY JANE SHORE** a burlesque in two acts by 'Richard Henry'. Music by John Crook. Produced by Mackay Robertson at the Royal Strand Theatre 2 April, 1894 for a run of 56 performances closing 19 May, 1894.

Richard, Duke of Gloucester . . . . Harry Paulton
Edward IV . . . . Eric Lewis
Matthew Shore . . . . George Humphrey/Fred Emney
Waterberry . . . . Arthur Nelstone
Catesby . . . . Emmeline Orford/Millie Marion/Lillian Davies
Telefag . . . . Alfred P. Phillips
Dato . . . . Charles Lovell
Grist . . . . Fred Emney/Grace Huntley
Hastings . . . . Grace Huntley/Emmeline Orford
Elizabeth Woodville . . . . Florence Daly
Dame Ursula . . . . Ada Doree
Mary . . . . Carrie Coote
Alicia . . . . Hilda Hanbury
The Young Princes . . . . Nellie & Maggie Bowman
Jaunty Jane Shore . . . . Alice Atherton

Dir: Willie Edouin; md: J. J. Ross/A. Isaacson; sc: Fred Storey; cos: John W. Houghton

0143 **KING KODAK** a topical burlesque extravaganza in two acts by Arthur Branscombe. Music by John Crook, Walter Slaughter, Edward Solomon, Alfred Plumpton, Milton Wellings, Herman von der Fink and Lionel Monckton. Produced at Terry's Theatre under the management of the Burlesque Comedy syndicate (Fred J. Harris and C. J. Abud) 30 April, 1894 for a run of 63 performances closing 30 June, 1894.

James South, the Kodak . . . . Edward Terry
Admiral Sir Wm Broadsides . . . . George Giddens (F. Trott)/George Belmore
Dick Dashaway . . . . Charles Danby/
Mr M. T. Head, chaplain . . . . Compton Coutts/*out*
Hugh E. Foote, attorney . . . . Huntley Wright
Lord Deadbroke . . . . E. H. Kelly
Lt Jack Broadsides . . . . George de Pledge
Charlie Broadsides . . . . Ada Barry
Harry Vernon . . . . Jack Thompson
Sergeant O'Flynn . . . . F. W. Trott/Greene Taylor
Hilda South . . . . Violet Robinson/Blanche Barnett/Emilie Petrelli
Letitia Gushington . . . . Margaret Ayrtoun/Jessie Danvers
Violet . . . . Mabel Love
Lillie . . . . Eva Levens
Dora Nightingale . . . . Lizzie Ruggles
Frankie Dashaway . . . . Amy Saunders
Millie Tarry . . . . Blanche Barnett/Marie Temple
Jennie Rossity . . . . Violet Friend
Eva Nescent . . . . Marie Lascelles
Ella Gant . . . . Irene du Foye
Kitty Seabrooke . . . . Kate Vaughan/Maud Hill
Boleg Nula . . . . W. Edwards
add La Siffleuse . . . . Errol Stanhope
La Petite Parisienne . . . . Nina Martino
Ostrich dance by the Sisters Levey

Dir: Thomas W. Charles; md: John Crook/Ernest Bucalossi; ch: John D'Auban; sc: Walter Hann and E. G. Banks; cos: Mrs Fisher, Mlle Auguste, Alias, Harrison Ltd

0144 **LAUGHS** or Tina and Tony. A travesty on *My Sweetheart* in two acts by Arthur Alexander and A. R. Marshall. Music by C. E. Howells, W. G. Eaton, Scott Folkestone, T. and J. Kent and others. Produced at the Theatre Royal, Edinburgh under the management of Arthur Alexander and Walter Stanton 30 June, 1894 and toured through Liverpool, ?, Nottingham, Sheffield, Birmingham, Walsall, Durham, Sunderland, Newcastle, W. Hartlepool, South Shields, Stockton, Longton, Halifax, Scarborough, Northampton, Cheltenham, Merthyr Tydvil, Rhyl, Birkenhead, Oldham and Bristol (to 8 December) &c.

Tina . . . . Arthur Alexander
Tony Fast . . . . Julia Kent
Katarina Fast . . . . Tina Corri
Pony Cartlett . . . . Joseph B. Montague
Hyam Notwell . . . . Walter Stanton
Dr Codliver . . . . George A. Foote
Farmer Hayseed. . . . . Alfred Ashton
Graphic Tell . . . . Fred Austin
Baby Saveloy . . . . Ben Nutting
Bo-a-Peek . . . . George Ellis
A Dainty Maid . . . . Rosie Clare
Mrs Bullion Fleeter. . . . . Carrie Braham
Mrs Hayseed . . . . Alice Adeson
Dairymaids . . . . Kate Mansfield, Marie Hughes, Ella Tilly, Carrie Anderson
Mr Noah . . . . Mr Woodhead
Mrs Noah . . . . Mr Arkwright
with the Canadian Trio, the Sylphide Ballet Troupe &c.

Dir: Marshall Moore; md: C. E. Howells

0145 **CLAUDE DUVAL** (Blend 1664–1894) an original musical piece in two acts by Frederick Bowyer and 'Payne Nunn' (Arthur Roberts). Music by John Crook and Lionel Monckton. Produced at the Prince's Theatre, Bristol, under the management of Arthur Roberts 23 July, 1894 and toured through Birmingham, Dublin, Glasgow, Edinburgh, Newcastle, Nottingham, Liverpool, Manchester to 22 September. Opened at the Prince of Wales Theatre 25 September, 1894 for a run of 142 performances closing 15 February, 1895.

Claude Duval . . . . Arthur Roberts
Sir Phillip Saxmundham . . . . Eric Thorne/W. H. Denny
Percy . . . . Fitzroy Morgan/E. H. Kelly
Sherlock Holmes-Spotter . . . . H. O. Clarey/James A. Welsh
Pincher (Lord Touchem) . . . . Charles E. Stevens/W. P. Dempsey
Johnny Albany . . . . Georgie Edwards/Carrie Benton
Harry Burlington . . . . Maud Crichton/Poppy Haines/*out*
Gussy Criterion . . . . Ada Peppiate/Edith Stuart
Bertie Grafton. . . . . Marie Burdell/Frances Harrison
Jasper . . . . J. Winterbottom/J. W. Leonard/Leonard Russell/*out*
Simon Wuzzle. . . . . Mr Hayman/Mr Laidman
Lady Joan Saxmundham. . . . . Amy Liddon/Alice Aynsley Cook
Gertie . . . . Eva Ellerslie/Florence Levey
Dolly . . . . Maud Deane/Nellie Arline/Alice Holbrook/Simeta Marsden/Minnie Don/Minnie Davenport
Betty . . . . Miss Thornhill/Kitty Harcourt/Violet Leslie
Letty . . . . Louise Norman/Lily Dickinson/Lillian Farnie/Minnie Davenport/Alice Holbrook

Polly . . . . Ida Young/Ellas Dee/A. Young
Marjorie Saxmundham . . . . Florrie Schuberth/Violet Robinson
Lady Dorcas Chetwynd . . . . Geraldine Wrangham/Marie Halton/Aida Jenoure
add Jeames . . . . Mr Laidman/Mr Danby/Sydney Watson
John . . . . Mr Luke
M. le Maire . . . . H. O. Clarey
Algie Bondstreete . . . . Kate Cannon/Poppie Haines
Lord Lovelace . . . . Leonard Russell

Dir: Arthur Roberts & E. Story Gofton; md: Ernest Allen/Herbert Bunning; ch: Willie Warde; cos: Alias

146 **THE GAY PARISIENNE** A musical comedy in two acts by George Dance. Music by Ernest Vousden. Produced at the Theatre Royal, Northampton under the management of William Greet 1 October, 1894 and toured through Liverpool, Sheffield, Edinburgh, Glasgow, Birmingham, Hanley, Halifax, Manchester and Nottingham, ending 8 December 1894.

Canon Honeycombe . . . . J. T. MacMillan
Mrs Honeycombe . . . . Ada Doree
Norah Honeycombe . . . . Amy Thornton
Major Fossdyke . . . . Fred Mervin
Angela . . . . Winifred Hare
May . . . . Gladys Fontaine
Ethel . . . . Irene Iris
Gladys . . . . Maude Vernon
Amos Dingle . . . . Alfred Fisher
Tom Everleigh . . . . Richard Temple Jr
Algernon P. Ducie . . . . Elwyn Eaton
Hans . . . . George Rayment
Gretchen . . . . Mary Fleming
Johnson . . . . A. Teesdale
Susan . . . . Kate Margarets
Thompson . . . . John Edwards
Fritz . . . . William Vokes
Mary . . . . Violet Dagmar
Miss Edwards . . . . Susie Gerald
Anna . . . . Lilian Elen
Auguste Pompier . . . . Harry C. Barry
Mlle Julie Bon-Bon . . . . Nellie Murray

Md: Ernest Vousden; ch: Mlle Rosa; sc: C. Rider-Noble

Toured by William Greet 1 April–22 June, 1895. Resumed 12 August to 14 December, 1895 then March 9, 1896 ssq.
J. J. Dallas/J. T. MacMillan/G. P. Huntley (HONEY), Carlotta Zerbini/Alice Barth (MRS), Evie Greene/Florence Easton (NORAH), William Morgan/Fred Mervin (MAJ), Eleanor May/Mabel Champion/Vera Dunscombe (ANG), Gladys Fontaine/Annie Ross (MAY), Madge Ross (ETH), Frederick Chant/Frank Sherlock (AMOS), Richard Temple Jr/F. W. Ring/Dick Deville (TOM), Elwyn Eaton/A. Brookes (DUCIE), George Rayment (HANS), Constance Jones (MABEL), Fred Esmond (FRITZ), Gertrude Featherstone (MISS E), Ernest Shand/Edward Lauri (POMP), Nellie Murray (JULIE), Maud Dagmar, Alfred Fisher, James Thain, Beatrice Annesley, Louie Stafford, Susie Eldricks, James Cartwright, J. Archer, W. Walker, Hilda Trevalyan, Lillian Caine, Maud Woods, Edmund Page, Miss St Clair, Jeanne van Dalle, Ethel Ashton, Ada Palmer, Rosa Bennett, Elsie Reeves, Louie Trevalyan, William Boulby &c &c. Md: Ernest Bucalossi

Toured by Wallace Erskine & Charles Macdona 1895/6/7/8.

Produced in London at the Duke of York's Theatre in a revised version with new music by Ivan Caryll and others, under the management of Horace Sedger and the York Dramatic Syndicate 4 April, 1896 for a run of 369 performances closing 28 March, 1897.

Ebenezer Honeycombe . . . . Lionel Rignold
Mrs Honeycombe . . . . Lillie Belmore/Edith Stuart/Helen Kinnaird/M. A. Victor
Nora . . . . Violet Robinson/Edith Courtenay
Mabel, her friend . . . . Marion Dolby/Nellie Gregory/Simeta Marsden
Major Fossdyke . . . . W. H. Denny
Angela . . . . Violet Ellicott
May . . . . Edith Stuart/Violet Foss/Helen Kinnaird/*out*
Ethel . . . . Ethel Carlton/Florence Ellis/May Harrison/May Victor
Gladys . . . . Edith Bartlett
Maud . . . . Edith Mada
Edith . . . . Rose Montgomery/Florrie Glynn/Clare Leighton
Violet . . . . Ivy Herzog/Marjorie Prior/Edith Stuart
Rose . . . . Maud Hoppe
Amos Dingle . . . . Hubert Willis
Tom Eversleigh . . . . Edgar Stevens/Augustus Cramer
Algernon P. Ducie . . . . James Francis/Neville Leese/C. Guildford
Hans . . . . Harry Kilburn/Cecil Burt
Gretchen . . . . Harriet Wood/Edith Milton
Fritz . . . . Mr Garth/Walter Butler
Tiger Tim . . . . Walter Butler/*out*
Anna . . . . Edith Milton/*out*
Auguste Pompier . . . . Frank Wheeler/E. Page
Blatterwater . . . . Akerman May
Percy Tooting . . . . C. Guildford
Cecil Smyth . . . . Philip Leslie/A. Turner/Donald Hall/Henri Leoni/F. Carton
Ruth . . . . Louie Freear/Peggy Pryde
Mlle Julie Bon-Bon . . . . Ada Reeve (Violet Dene) (Clara Thropp)

Dancers: Beatrice Grenville, Nora Neville, Beatrice Young/Violet Dene/E. Millon, Lillie McIntyre

Dir: Horace Sedger; md: Sidney Jones/Maurice Jacobi; ch: V. Chiado/Willie Bishop; sc: E. G. Banks & W. Telbin; cos: A. Comelli

Toured in the London revised version by William Greet 1896/7/8/9/1900/1/2/ &c.

Produced at the Herald Square Theatre, New York, in a revised version as *The Girl From Paris* under the management of E. E. Rice 8 December, 1896 for a run of 266 performances to 10 July, 1897. Suspended and resumed 28 August, 1897 for 33 further performances closing 25 September, 1897.
Charles A. Bigelow/Alexander Clark (HONEY), Phoebe Cohen (MRS), Cheridah Simpson (NORAH), Willis Norton (MAB), Frank Smithson (MAJ), Adele Archer (ANG), Josie Fairbanks/F. Willson/Jessie Banks (MAY), Nina Ainscoe/Dorothy Kendall (ETH), Ida Rock/Arline Potter (GLAD), Anita Willson/Mamie Forbes/Carrie Tutiene (MAUD), May Hamilton (ED), Olivia Astor/Susie Hall (VI), Millie Willson (ROSE), Edward Chapman (AMOS), Charles Dickson/William Armstrong/Benjamin Howard (TOM), Harold Vizard (DUCIE), Louis Mann (HANS), May Lavigne/Ida Rock (GR), Matthew Ott/J. Shuster (FRITZ), Grace Belasco/Lillian Scanlan/Venie Bennett (ANNA), Joseph W. Herbert/W. J. Blaisdell/Nick Long (POMP), Thomas F. Kierns/W. Wallace Black (BLATT), Sydney Tovey/George Courtenay (PT), John Savage/Sydney Tovey (CS), Josephine Hall (RUTH), Clara Lipman (JULIE) Dir: Frank Smithson; md: Herman Perlet; cos: Mme M. I. Dowling

Produced at Wallacks Theatre, under the management of E. E. Rice 17 Jaunary, 1898 for a season of 32 performances to 12 February, 1898.
Fred Lennox (HONEY), Rose Beaudt (MRS), Andree Lorraine (NORAH), Hattie Williams (MAB), William Broderick (MAJ), Mamie Forbes (ANG), Bessie Bonneville (MAY), Mayme Kealty (ETH), Bessie Wilton (GLAD), Mabel Dixey (MAUD), Willie Norton (ED), Harry Earle (AMOS),

Augustus Cramer (TOM), Sydney de Gray (DUCIE), D. L. Don (HANS), Agnes Wadleigh (GR), George F. Campbell (FRITZ), Margaret Trew (ANNA), Thomas F. Kierns (POMP), W. Wallace Black (BLATT), Victor Moore (PT), James Lee (CS), Anna Buckley (RUTH), Georgia Caine (JULIE); pd: Blanche Deyo with Anita Willson, Millie Willson, May Levigne, Helen Whiting, Charles Dickson, Henry Blizard, George Courtney, Sidney Tovey (dcrs). Md: John J. Braham; ch: H. Fletcher Rivers; sc: Frank Rafter and D. Frank Dodge; cos: Mme M. I. Dowling

Played at the Columbus Theatre, New York, 19 December, 1898.

147 **CUPID & CO.** a musical farce in three acts by Horace Lennard. Music by Meyer Lutz, Edward Solomon, Albert Maurice, Herbert Simpson, H. Bemberg, Percy Reeve, Thomas W. Charles &c. Produced at the City Theatre, Sheffield 6 August, 1894 and toured through Manchester, Accrington, Halifax, Birkenhead, Walsall, Birmingham, Richmond/Ealing, Kidderminster,?, Gloucester,?, Cardiff, Plymouth, Croydon, Eastbourne and Leeds ending 1 December, 1894.

John Jupiter Jones . . . . Harry Brayne
Colonel Robinson . . . . Russell Wallett
Perkins . . . . A. G. Spry
Ben Bloggs . . . . Henry Suter
Tipps . . . . James Mahoney
Frank Jones . . . . Louis C. Batten
Bertie Foster . . . . Hettie Cornwallis
Harry Miller . . . . Alexina Glenroy
Charlie Thompson . . . . Linda Lorraine
Willie Long . . . . Jeannie Stokes
June Brown . . . . Sophie Lingwood
Leda. . . . . Ida Glenroy
Mrs Dipper . . . . Emilie Ormesby
Cupid . . . . Maud St John
with Josee Danby, May Trebel, Dot Danby, R. Peele, Nellie Horton, Miss Wallett, Adele Harvey, Mabel Hart, Lettice Sprague &c.

148 **THE QUEEN OF BRILLIANTS** a comic opera in three acts by Brandon Thomas adapted from the German of 'Theodore Taube' (Bohdan Hrdlička) and Isidor Fuchs. Music by Edward Jakobowski. First produced at the Carltheater, Vienna as *Die Brillanten-Königin* 25 March, 1894 in a substantially different version. Produced at the Royal Lyceum Theatre under the management of Henry Abbey and Maurice Grau 8 September, 1894 for a season of 41 performances closing 18 October, 1894.

Florian Bauer . . . . Hubert Wilke
Della Fontana. . . . . Arthur Williams
Lucca Rabbiato . . . . W. H. Denny
Grelotto . . . . John Le Hay
Major Victor Pulvereitzer. . . . . Avon Saxon/Max Eugene
Count Radaman Caprimonte . . . . Owen Westford
Moritz. . . . . Fred Storey
Max . . . . Fred Wright Jr
Beppo . . . . Compton Coutts (Fowler Thatcher)
Andrea . . . . Rupert Lister
Waiter. . . . . Henry George
Fritz. . . . . George Honey
Don Garcia . . . . James Pearson
Footman. . . . . Mr Hendon
Hackney Coachman. . . . . Robert Stevens
Head Gardener . . . . John Evans
Madame Engelstein . . . . Mme Amadi
Emma . . . . Lizzie Ruggles
Orsola . . . . Annie Meyers
Mirandola . . . . Florence Burle
Carola . . . . Sadie Wigley
Fioretta . . . . Lillie Comyns

Minna . . . . Susanne Leonard
Fraulein Kauf . . . . Zoe Gilfillan
Fraulein Schmitt . . . . Jessie Bradford
Betta. . . . . Lillian Russell
Head Matron . . . . Bertha Staunton
Postillions: Misses Lascelles, Dalroy, Doyne, Bond, Matt, Adams
Dancers: Madge Greet, Helen Graeme, Biddy Rees, May Gore, Marion Gordon, Ethel Arundel, Ella Kitson, Gracie Leigh.

Dir: Charles Harris; md: Paul Steindorff; ch: John D'Auban; sc: Hawes Craven, Joseph Harker, W. Perkins; cos: A. Comelli

Produced at Abbey's Theatre, New York, 7 November, 1894 under the management of Messrs Abbey & Grau for a run of 29 performances closing 2 December, 1894. Adapted by H. J. W. Dam.
Hubert Wilke (FLOR), Digby Bell (DELLA), J. G. Taylor (RABB), George Honey (GRE), Sydney Howard (VP), Owen Westford (COUNT), Henry Parry (BEP), George Mackenzie (AND), Wensley Thompson (FR), Theo May (DON), Spencer Kelly (FOOT), James G. Peakes (HACK), George Fournier (GARD), Laura Joyce Bell (MME), Madge Greet (E), Annie Meyers (ORS), Susanne Leonard (MINA), Florence Doyne (MATRON), Lillian Russell (BETTA) Dir: Richard Barker; md: Paul Steindorff; sc: Hawes Craven, Joseph Harker, W. Perkins; cos: A. Comelli

0149 **HIS EXCELLENCY** a comic opera in two acts by W. S. Gilbert. Music by F. Osmond Carr. Produced at the Lyric Theatre under the management of George Edwardes 27 October, 1894 for a run of 161 performances closing 6 April, 1895.

Prince Regent/Nils Egilson . . . . Rutland Barrington (Augustus Cramer)
Governor Griffenfeld . . . . George Grossmith/
Erling . . . . Charles Kenningham
Tortenssen . . . . Augustus Cramer (Mr Burbank)
Mats Munch . . . . John Le Hay
Harold. . . . . Arthur Playfair
A Sentry . . . . George Temple
Officers . . . . Ernest Snow/Fred Garton
Frank Morton
Christina . . . . Nancy McIntosh
Nanna . . . . Jessie Bond/Adeline Vaudrey/Rose Hamilton
Thora . . . . Ellaline Terriss/J. Fane/Aida Jenoure
Dame Courtlandt . . . . Alice Barnett
Blanca . . . . Gertrude Aylward/Augusta Dewsnap
Elsa . . . . May Cross

Dir: W. S. Gilbert; md: Carl Kiefert; ch: John D'Auban; sc: T. E. Ryan; cos: Percy Anderson

Produced at the Broadway Theatre, New York, by George Edwardes' Company under the management of Al Hayman and Charles Frohman 14 October, 1895 for a run of 88 performances.

Julius Steger (PR), Cairns James (GOV), William Philp (ERL), Augustus Cramer (TORT), John Le Hay (MATS), Ernest Snow (HAR), Tim Ryley (SENTRY), C. Clements and J. Jamison (OFF), Nancy McIntosh (CHR), Gertrude Aylward (NAN), Ellaline Terriss (TH). Dir: John Gunn; ch: John D'Auban; sc: Ernst Gros and E. G. Unitt; cos: Percy Anderson

Produced at the Carltheater, Vienna as *Der Gouverneur* 28 December, 1895.

Produced at the Carltheater, Vienna as *Der Herr Gouverneur* 11 April, 1897.

ALL MY EYE-VAN-HOE a burlesque by Philip Hayman. Music by John Crook, Howard Talbot, Philip Hayman, Edward Solomon and others. Produced at the Trafalgar Theatre under the management of the Burlesque and Comedy Syndicate (C. W. Perryman and Major Hand) 31 October, 1894 for a run of 9 performances closing 7 November, 1894.

Ivanhoe . . . . John L. Shine
Will Scarlettina . . . . Harry Grattan

Robert Fitzoof . . . . Fred Storey
Seedie Wreck . . . . Fred Wright Jr
Sir Brandiboy Gilbert. . . . . H. M. Clifford
Prior of Jawfolks Abbey . . . . E. M. Robson
Mithter Ithaacths . . . . James Stevenson
Lady Soft Roe-ina . . . . Maggie Roberts
Prince Johnnie . . . . Harold Eden
Tom-ba . . . . Clara Jecks
Countess of Grundy . . . . Agnes Hewitt
Boilden Oiley Esq. . . . . Bertha Myers
Nell Guitar . . . . Alice Lethbridge
Lady Alicia Fitzworse. . . . . Nita Carlyon
Miss Rebecca Hothouse Peach . . . . . . Phyllis Broughton

Dir: Frank Parker; md: Howard Talbot; ch: Anna Abrahams and Frank Parker; sc: Fred Storey & Mr Warren; cos: Lucien Besche & A. Comelli

151 **THE SHOP GIRL** a musical farce in two acts by H. J. W. Dam. Music by Ivan Caryll. Additional numbers by Adrian Ross and Lionel Monckton. Produced at the Gaiety Theatre under the management of George Edwardes 24 November, 1894 for a run of 546 performances closing 29 May, 1896.

Mr Hooley . . . . Arthur Williams/Charles Danby/George Mudie/Harry Monkhouse
Charles Appleby . . . . Seymour Hicks/Tom Terriss/Lionel Mackinder/George Rollitt
Bertie Boyd . . . . George Grossmith Jr/Fitzroy Morgan/Frank Stayton
Mr Miggles . . . . Edmund Payne (Robert Nainby)/Frank Wheeler/Bertie Wright/Lionel Mackinder
John Brown . . . . Colin Coop (Charles Lane)
Sir George Appleby. . . . . Cairns James/George Honey/(Charles Lane)/Harry Ashford/James Stevenson/George Mudie
Colonel Singleton . . . . Frank Wheeler/Coventry Davis/(George Mudie)/Bertie Wright/W. J. Manning
Count St Vaurien . . . . Robert Nainby
Mr Tweets . . . . Willie Warde (Charles Lane)
Lady Dodo Singleton . . . . (Helen Lee)/Maud Sherman/Marie Halton/Maggie Roberts/Grace Palotta/Amy Augarde
Miss Robinson . . . . Katie Seymour/Lillie Rees/Violet Lloyd
Ada Smith. . . . . Lillie Belmore/Alice Barnett/Hetty Chapman/Connie Ediss
Lady Appleby. . . . . Maria Davis/Annie Dwelley
Faith . . . . Lillie Dickinson/Maud Hoppe/Florence Neville
Hope . . . . Agatha Roze/Marie Yorke/Pattie Stanley
Charity . . . . Lily Johnson/Agatha Roze/Maidie Hope
Maud Plantagenet. . . . . Maud Hill/Adelaide Astor/Constance Collier/M. Glen/Carrie Coote
Eva Tudor . . . . Fannie Ward/Helen Lee/Ethel Sydney/Marie Yorke/Mabel Bouton/Kate Adams
Lillie Stuart. . . . . Maud Sutherland//Marie Yorke/Florence Maitland/Agatha Roze/Kristin Yudall/Maggie Roberts
Ada Wandesforde (Harrison) . . . . (Lillie Henshawe)/Helen Lee/Florence Maitland

Mabel Beresford . . . . Violet Monckton/Florence Maitland/ Louie Coote
Agnes Howard . . . . Louie Coote/*out*
Maggie Jocelyn . . . . Maggie Ripley/Constance Collier/Maggie Roberts
Violet Deveney . . . . Topsy Sinden/Lillie Henshawe
Bessie Brent. . . . . Ada Reeve (Claire Romaine)/Kate Cutler/ Eva Moore (Ethel Sydney)/Ellaline Terriss/Ethel Haydon (Harriet Wood)
add Florence White. . . . . Ada Belton/Topsy Sinden
Sylvia Perry . . . . Maud Hoppe/Maud Sutherland
Max Ollendorf . . . . Fritz Rimma
Show Singer . . . . Bertha Vere
Show Dancer. . . . . Madge Rossall
Birdie Wandesfaude . . . . Maud Sutherland

Dir: James T. Tanner; md: Ivan Caryll; ch: Willie Warde; sc: Johnstone, Walter Hann; cos: Wilhelm

Produced at Palmer's Theatre, New York, under the management of Al Hayman and Charles Frohman 28 October, 1895 for a run of 72 performances.
W. H. Rawlins (HOO), Seymour Hicks/Donald Hall (CA), George Grossmith Jr (BB), Bertie Wright (MIGG), Michael Dwyer (BROWN), Walter McEwan (SIR), George Honey (COL), Herbert Sparling/A. Nilson Fysher/J. Gaillard (StV), Alfred Asher (TW), Annie Albu (DODO), Marie Faucett (MISS), Connie Ediss (ADA), Leslie Greenwood (LADY), May Beaugarde (FAITH), Minnie Sadler (HOPE), Winnie Rose (CHARITY), Adelaide Astor (MAUD), Violet Dene (EVA), Ida Wallace (LIL), Hylda Galton (ADA), Nellie Huxley (MAB), Zara de Larne (FLO), Nellie Langton (BIRD), Violet Durkin (MAG), Annie Vivian (VI), Ethel Sydney (BESS); pd: Dorothy Douglass.
Dir: A. E. Dodson; md: Barter Johns; ch: Willie Warde; sc: Ernst Gross; cos: Wilhelm

Produced at the Olympia Music Hall, Paris, in a version by Maurice Ordonneau 4 June, 1896.
M. Berville (HOULEY), M. Marechal (MIGLES), M. Hurbain (GEORGES APLEBY), M. Danvers (JOHN BROWN), M. Farbel (COMTE D'ESTOCADE), M. Marache (COLONEL), M. Woll (LE SECRETAIRE WILLIAM), M. Gerard (SNOB), Mlle Micheline (BESSIE), Mlle Netty (ADAH), Mlle Deville (MISS ROBINSON), Mlle Manon (MISS STUART), Mlle Ginette (MISS TUDOR), Mlle d'Aurey (MISS WANDESFAUDE)

Md: O. de Lagoanere; ch: Mme Papurello

Produced at the Carltheater, Vienna as *Die Ladensmamsell* 5 February, 1897.

Produced at the Gaiety Theatre in a revised version by Arthur Wimperis with additional numbers by Herman Darewski, Max Darewski and St John Brougham under the management of Alfred Butt and Seymour Hicks 25 March, 1920 for a run of 327 performances closing 1 January, 1921.
Johnny Danvers (HOO), Roy Royston (CA), Fred Hearne (BB), Alfred Lester/Jimmy Godden (MIGG), Leonard Mackay (BROWN), Garnet Wilson (SIR), Frank Attree (COL), Robert Nainby (St V), Ewart Scott (TW), Nancie Lovat (DODO), Mamie Watson (MISS), May Beatty (ADA), Gladys Homfrey (LADY), Kathlyn Holland (CHARITY), Evelyn Laye (BESSIE), Percy Le Fre (MR HUNT), Joseph Grande (MR BLOODGOOD), Joseph Boddy (JOSEPH), Thorpe Bates/Arnold Berkely (HON. BOBBIE BLAKE), Rosie Campbell (TIPLILSKI) with Molly Ramsden, Jessie Lewis/Cyllene Moxon, Isabel Broznan, Sybil Wise, Gladys Marsh, Peggy Lovat/Violet Norton, Gertrude Hayward, Marie Vaughan/Violet Yates, Adeline Roze/Margaret Owen, Valerie Varden, Mabel Heath/Gwen Gilbert, Margery Symons. Pds: Joan Carroll and Barbara Roberts.
Dir: Seymour Hicks; md: Arthur Wood; ch: Willie Warde and Fred Farren; sc: Marc-Henri and Conrad Tritschler; cos: Reville, Margaine Lacroix, Myra Salter, Morris Angel, Mary E. Fisher, John Simmons, Zimmerman, Johns & Bonham, Burkinshaw & Knight &c.

Film: In 1925 the song 'Her golden Hair was Hanging down her Back' from *The Shop Girl* was used as part of Reciprocity Films' 'Milestone Melodies' series. The film was shown while the song was sung live.

0152 **EASTWARD HO!** an operatic burlesque in three acts by C. M. Rodney. Brought up-to-date by Willie Younge. Music by C. E. Howells. Produced originally as *The Caliph* 1 October, 1892 in an amateur production at Bristol. Produced in a revised version as *The Black Cat* at St George's Theatre, Walsall, 31 July, 1893. Produced in a third version at the Opera Comique under the management of H. P. Gatrell and John Donald 24 December, 1894 for a run of 6 performances closing 31 December, 1894.

Reginald Nanty . . . Joseph McBride
Kitty Spangles . . . Jenny Dawson
Julian Ranter . . . Fowler Thatcher
Betterton Burge . . . C. A. White
Gwendoline Brougham . . . Fanny Selby
Rhoda Royal . . . Madge Annesley
Tiny . . . Maudie Brookman
Minnie Pateman . . . Alice Beresford
Bella Vavasour . . . Maude Adams
Inez Brabazon . . . Edith Hoppe
Gladys Fontainbleu . . . Lilian Stead
Vera Fancourt . . . Florence Lavender
Muley Muzpha . . . George de Pledge
Fasti . . . Madge Rockingham
Zeffa . . . Kate Everleigh
Atcha . . . Lillian Morgan
Balradour . . . Rose Bernard
Bebee . . . Lilly Piercey
Beni . . . Charles Baldwin
Mista Murphi . . . Gerald Hoole

with Beatrice Lindenthal, Alma Grosvenor, Alice Barker, Clare Grey, Lucy Cooper, Ada Russell, Madeleine Prince, Minnie Howard, Phyllis Nelson, Miss Angelona, Miss Leslie; Messrs Matthews, Lockwood, Newman, Edward H. Morehen.
Dir: Alfred Ashton; md: C. E. Howells; sc: W. Lowes; cos: Harrison Ltd.

0153 **THE COUNTY COUNCILLOR** a musical variety farce in three acts based on the play by H. Graham. Music by John Crook. Produced under the management of Yorke Stephens and E. W. Garden and toured.

Robert Faddicum . . . E. W. Garden/George de Lara
Dick Wellington . . . Yorke Stephens
William Cripps . . . J. Harold Carson
Detective Inspector Catchpole . . . Joseph B. Montague
Jack Wilding . . . Frank Barclay
Cousin Charlie . . . Eric Stanley
Cabman 648 . . . C. Pennett
Mabel . . . Kate Turner
Kitty . . . Viola Lambert
Maud . . . Beatrice Burton
Edith . . . Dolly Kirsch
Ethel . . . Ethel Maynard
Daisy . . . May Burton
Dolly . . . Carrie Cavanagh
Mrs Perks . . . Nellie Williams
Lottie Singleton . . . Helen Leyton

Md: Ashley Richards; ch: Signor Chopetti; cos: Debenham & Freebody, Alias

003a **THE CHIEFTAIN** a comic opera in two acts. A revised version of *The Contrabandista* by F. C. Burnand. Music by Arthur Sullivan. Produced at the Savoy Theatre, under the management of Richard D'Oyly Carte 12 December, 1894 for a run of 97 performances closing 16 March, 1895. Performed with *Cox and Box* from 31 December.

Count Vasquez de Gonzago . . . Courtice Pounds
Peter Adolphus Grigg . . . Walter Passmore
Ferdinand de Roxas . . . R. Scott Fishe (W. A. Peterkin)
Sancho . . . Richard Temple

Jose	M. R. Morand
Pedro Gomez	H. Scott Russell
Blazzo	J. Bowden Haswell/F. Morrison
Escatero	Powis Pinder
Pedrillo	Master Snelson
Inez de Roxas	Rosina Brandram (Miss Spenser)
Dolly Grigg	Florence Perry
Juanita	Emmie Owen
Maraquita	Edith Johnston
Anna	Ada Newall
Zitella	Beatrice Perry
Nina	Ethel Wilson
Rita	Florence St John

Dir: Charles Harris; md: Frank Cellier; ch: John D'Auban; sc: Joseph Harker; cos: A. Comelli

Produced at Abbey's Theatre, New York under the management of A. H. Canby 9 September 1895 for a run of 54 performances.
Rhys Thomas (VASQ), Francis Wilson (GRIGG), John E. Brand (FERD), Joseph C. Miron (SAN), Edward P. Temple (JO), Peter M. Lang (PG), A. Amadeo (BL), Osborn Clemson (ESC), Bessie Lee/Mabel Major (PED), Lilian Carllsmith (INEZ), Christie MacDonald (DOL), Alice Holbrook (JU), Elena Wright/Agnes Martyne (MAR), Martha Stein (AN), Jeanette Emery (Z), Lulu Glaser (RITA). Dir: Richard Barker; md: A. de Novellis; cos: Percy Anderson

THE DEVIL'S DEPUTY a comic opera by J. Cheever Goodwin. Music by Edward Jakobowski. Produced at Abbey's Theatre, New York under the management of Messrs Abbey and Grau 10 September, 1894 for a run of 72 performances closing 4 November, 1894.

Lorenzo	Rhys Thomas
General Karamatoff	Joseph C. Miron
Melissen	Francis Wilson
Princess Mirane	Adele Ritchie/Amanda Fabris
Elverine	Lulu Glaser
Bob	Christie MacDonald
Mlle Kobolt	Amelia Gardner
Sergeant	Joseph B. Chaille
Bartow	William H. Laverty
Bagatella	Maud Bliss

CARL THE CLOCKMAKER a musical melodrama in four acts by Harry Starr. Produced at the Clarence, Pontypridd under the management of Harry Starr 30 July, 1894 and toured.

Carl Conrad/Dusty Rhodes/Jakey Inkelstein/Fraulein Katrina/Nursey Martha	Harry Starr
Maurice Helmore *alias* Philip Adderly	Charles Harley
Hans Conrad	Raymond Thomas
Arthur Attwood/Weary Raggles	Fred W. Graham
Count Ivan Neikleovitch	Conrad Clarke
Narky Nabbs	Tom G. Warry
Turtle Crawl	G. H. Miles
Tubbs	George Jukes
Bill Bloggs	Bernard Mostyn
Police Sergeant	W. Gossett
Lena Harrigan	Ethel Danbury
Maggie Ryder	Margery Garthorne
Jerusha Jane Picklefinch	Edma Lester
Baby Winnie	Little Dorothy

THE SAUCY SULTANA a burlesque in two acts by Victor Stevens. Music by Victor Stevens and J. C. Shepherd. Produced at Cambridge 26 December, 1894 and toured by Alice E. Percival.

The Sultan of Real Jam Mee . . . . Hugh Seton
The Grand Vizier . . . . Ainslie Burton
Princess Cassandra . . . . Alice Rochfort
Prince Hamiz . . . . Rae Rosenthal
Woppington Whipps . . . . Alice E. Percival
Jeremy Jinks . . . . Whimsical Walter
Hoop Lah . . . . Annie Halford
Zillah . . . . Florence Neville
Zorah . . . . Marian Medus
Haidee . . . . Flo Clive
Zara . . . . Madge Barry

DORCAS a musical comedy by Harry and Edward Paulton. Music by Ernest Woodville, H. Farmer, Edmond Audran &c. Music later credited to Clement Locknane and Watty Hyde. Produced 31 December, 1894 at the Lyceum Theatre, Ipswich and toured by Charles Fisher and Edwin Arthur. (First produced in USA.)

Lord Beauregard . . . . Charles Fisher
Lord Lambourne . . . . Dan Farrough
Meredith . . . . Arthur Burgoyne/John Durant
Jawkins . . . . Fred Langley/J. W. Hooper
James . . . . Charles Mills/Fred Langley
Lubin Mugby . . . . Henry Kitts/C. A. White
Lady Lambourne . . . . Agnes Imlay
Griselda . . . . Emma Victor
Joan . . . . Laurie Wyndham
Margery . . . . Lilian Maude
Dorcas . . . . Edith Marriot/Beatrice Edina
Honoria . . . . Florence Morrison

OUR AMATEUR THEATRICALS a burlesque extravaganza in 2 acts by Harold L. Hillard. Music by Odoardo Barri. Produced at the Theatre Royal, Croydon under the management of Odoardo Barri 23 July, 1894 and toured.

Barnaby Battledore . . . . W. F. Stirling
Tobias Tubbs . . . . Sam Wilkinson
Gordon Dashwood . . . . Harry Phydora
Charles Ogilvie . . . . V. Ostlere
Daisy Braque . . . . Violet Crossley
Kitty Careless . . . . Maud Santley
Barbara Tubbs . . . . Mabel Houghton
Dolly . . . . Florence Neville
Flora . . . . Gladys Wemyss
Ethel . . . . Minnie Hayden
Graham . . . . Lillie Hart
Gertrude . . . . Agnes Fairbarn
Ethel . . . . Olive Gwynne
Letitia Battledore . . . . Florence Terriss

BROTHER PELICAN or Falka's Baby. A burlesque in 2 acts by Alfred Rae and W. H. Dragnil. Music by Giuseppe Operti, Ernest Allen and W. C. Levey. Produced at the Theatre Royal, Belfast, under the management of Horace Lingard 8 February, 1894 and toured in repertoire.

THE WATER BABES a nautical burlesque drama in 3 acts by E. W. Bowles. Music by Merton Clark. Produced at Leamington under the management of Lionel Mackinder and Mr Wingfield 6 August, 1894 and toured.

ROBIN HOOD, ESQ. an operatic burlesque in 2 acts by Stanley Rogers. Music by Henry May. Produced at the Royalty Theatre, Chester under the management of Lester Collingwood 6 August, 1894 and toured.

GIDDY MISS CARMEN a burlesque by 'L. E. Steer' (Sidney Lester). Music by John Crook, Meyer Lutz, Sidney Jones, C. Scott Gatty, James M. Glover, May Ostlere &c. Produced at the Brighton Aquarium under the management of Sidney Lester 27 August, 1894 and toured.

THE HOUSE OF LORDS an operetta in one act by Harry Greenbank. Music by George Byng and Ernest Ford. Produced at the Lyric Theatre under the management of Horace Sedger 6 July, 1894 as a forepiece to *Little Christopher Columbus* (to October 20) and from 29 October with *His Excellency*. Withdrawn 3 November, 1894.

Henry . . . . J. Furneaux Cook
Halifax Finsbury . . . . Wilbur Gunn
Mr Murgatroyd . . . . W. S. Laidlaw/Fred Seymour
Emmeline . . . . Adelaide Newton
Lady Victoria Portobello . . . . Dora Thorne

Produced at the Trafalgar Theatre, under the management of Horace Sedger 21 January, 1895 with *The Taboo*. Withdrawn 26 January.
Charles Crook (H), Vernon Drew (HF), Fred Seymour (MUR), Carrie Fenton (EMM), Maud Maude (VIC)

Produced at the Prince of Wales Theatre, under the management of Henry Lowenfeld 16 March, 1895 with *Gentleman Joe*. Withdrawn 11 April.
J. Furneaux Cook (H), Vernon Drew (HF), Fred Seymour (MUR), Adelaide Newton (EMM), Dora Thorne (VIC). Md: Herbert Bunning

A KNIGHT ERRANT an operetta (romance) in one act by Rutland Barrington. Music by Alfred J. Caldicott. Produced at the Lyric Theatre under the management of George Edwardes 14 November, 1894 with *His Excellency*. Withdrawn 12 January, 1895.

Baron de Boncoeur . . . . Ernest Snow
Lady Ermengard . . . . May Cross
Armand . . . . Marie Alexander
Sir Florian de Gracieux. . . . . William Philp

Md: Carl Kiefert; cos: Percy Anderson

A BIG BANDIT by T. Malcolm Watson. Music by Walter Slaughter. Produced at St George's Hall under the management of Alfred Reed and R. Corney Grain 30 April, 1894 with *A Funny World* and *Walls Have Ears*. Withdrawn 7 July, 1894.

May Dudley. . . . . Gertrude Chandler
Jack Rossiter . . . . Avalon Collard
Rosamund Sitwell. . . . . Fanny Holland
Colonel Chichester Sitwell . . . . R. Corney Grain
Wellington Pitt . . . . Alfred Reed
Pedro . . . . Mr Macmoyse

WALLS HAVE EARS by R. Corney Grain. Produced at St George's Hall under the management of Alfred Reed and R. Corney Grain 26 March, 1894 with *Peggy's Plot* and *A Funny World*, the former replaced by *A Big Bandit* (30 April) then *Missing* (9 July), the latter by *Bond Street*. Withdrawn 21 July. Reopened 8 October. Withdrawn 27 October, 1894.

Mrs Dorrimer. . . . . Fanny Holland
Daisy Marsden . . . . Gertrude Chandler
Peter Power . . . . R. Corney Grain
Paul Pepper . . . . Avalon Collard

MISSING by Somerville Gibney. Music by King Hall. Produced at St George's Hall under the management of Alfred Reed and R. Corney Grain 9 July, 1894 with *Bond Street* and *Walls Have Ears*. Withdrawn 21 July. Reopened 8 October. Played from 29 October with *That Fatal Menu* and *Back in Town*. Withdrawn 15 December, 1894.

Kitty Coetlogan . . . . Gertrude Chandler
Mrs Brocklebank M.D. . . . . Fanny Holland

Hon. Jim Boxer . . . . Avalon Collard
Pilbeam . . . . Alfred Reed

THAT FATAL MENU a musical trifle by R. Corney Grain. Produced at St George's Hall under the management of Alfred Reed and R. Corney Grain 29 October, 1894 with *Back in Town* and *Missing*. Withdrawn 15 December, 1894.

Sophia Smith . . . . Gertrude Chandler
Maria Jones . . . . Fanny Holland
Theophilus Jones . . . . Avalon Collard
Fletcher . . . . R. Corney Grain
Horatio Smith. . . . . J. L. Mackay
Page . . . . Frank Jones

MELODRAMANIA a burletta in three acts by T. Malcolm Watson. Music by Walter Slaughter. Produced at St George's Hall under the management of Alfred Reed and R. Corney Grain 17 December, 1894 with *Uncle Dick*. Later played with *Music à la Mode*. Withdrawn 9 March, 1895.

Sir Rupert Royster . . . . R. Corney Grain
Lady Evelina . . . . Fanny Holland
Mary Truelove . . . . Dora Thornton
Phil Baggs. . . . . Alfred Reed/H. Nye Chart
Frederick Royster. . . . . Avalon Collard
Anthony. . . . . Mr MacMoyse

1895

The early weeks of 1895 saw a wide variety of musical productions running in the West End. The comic operas *His Excellency* and *The Chieftain* represented the traditional side (the one rather more efficiently than the other), *The Shop Girl*, now starring Kate Cutler and Frank Wheeler, was settled in at the beginning of its long career at the head of the field of sophisticated musical farce, whilst *Claude Duval* stood astride the gap separating this new kind of piece from the variety musical pure and simple as epitomised by *The Lady Slavey* which was going into its last weeks at the Avenue.

It was now quite clear that the immediate future of the light musical theatre would belong to the so-called musical comedy in the *Gaiety Girl* and *Shop Girl* mould on the one hand, and on the other, the looser and less sophisticated style of *Morocco Bound*. But in spite of the poor showings of comic opera at the box-office – a trend which even Gilbert and Sullivan, together and separately, could only partly allay – writers continued to create and producers to stage comic opera. Two of the six new pieces presented in the West End in 1895 were comic operas and it was no coincidence that they were also the season's two clear failures.

The first of these was an Anglo-American collaboration entitled *The Taboo* which was presented at the Trafalgar Theatre on 19 January. The libretto and lyrics had been written by the American writer Mason Carnes and the music provided by a Londoner, Miss Ethel Harraden. *The Taboo* was Miss Harraden's first attempt at a full-length work. The daughter of a London and Calcutta agent, she had been sent to study at the Royal Academy where she had some small success as a pianist and writer of ballads. Her stage writing had been limited to a series of insignificant operettas written with her brother, Herbert, the most successful of which was *His Last Chance*, staged as a forepiece at the Gaiety for a good run and later at the Princess's and at the Court where it starred Seymour Hicks and Ellaline Terriss. At thirty-eight years of age, Miss Harraden produced her first full score in *The Taboo*.

The plot evolved by Mr Carnes was based on a curious law of royal succession as practised on the island of Bellmaria. The heir, once he has reached years of discretion, may claim the throne and crown himself king. This being so, Prince Timaru has been kept in ignorance of his age and his rights as his father, King Papkaio, has no wish to abdicate and his mother, Queen Wattatauka, lives in perpetual fear of the law by which it is a crime to be a mother-in-law. This crime is punishable by death or by a vow of eternal silence to which the Queen, as her name suggests, is not eager to submit. But the Prince discovers his 'rights' and chaos, various love affairs and a little war follow before all is cleared up by the legalistic contortions of a convenient English lawyer.

Not far into the opening night it became clear that Horace Sedger had bought a very bad egg. The large audience were soon disenchanted with the unfunny plot and the tinkling tunes and began to vent their feelings upon the unfortunate artists. The worst they saved for the writers who were greeted at the final curtain with hisses and howls which left no-one in doubts as to the ultimate fate of *The Taboo*. The critics added their nails to its coffin:

> From start to finish there is hardly one single number in which even the elements of humour are to be found, the libretto is trivial and pointless to a degree and the music, though occasionally pretty, at its best hardly rises above moderately efficient mediocrity . . (*Times*)
>
> Crude and incoherent . . . the author evidently combines the inexperience of the novice with the incompetency of the ambitious tyro . . . that a manager of Mr. Sedger's knowledge and observation should have been tempted to present it is one of those marvels . . (*Theatre*)
>
> [the author's] method of fun-making is somewhat primitive and sense of humour very strained . . his characters for the most part bore rather than interest and amuse . . (*Stage*)

The Taboo, Mr Carnes and Miss Harraden disappeared permanently from the London theatre scene after one week.

The next new work to be produced was a very different affair and the acme of professionalism. George Edwardes' follow-up to *A Gaiety Girl* at Daly's was awaited with the eagerness and anticipation which a decade earlier had prefaced the opening of a new Gilbert and Sullivan piece. The title and the subject had been objects of interest since the approaching end of *A Gaiety Girl*'s run had become known. Edwardes had engaged the same team of Owen Hall, Harry Greenbank and Sidney Jones to provide libretto, lyrics and music and rumours were soon abroad of the confidence surrounding the production of *A Naughty Girl*, as the piece was to be called. Soon the rumour changed; the confidence was even greater and the title had become *A Woman's Portrait*.

On 2 February Daly's Theatre witnessed the opening of *An Artist's Model* before the most fashionable audience seen at a light musical première in memory. First night tickets had been at a premium for weeks and were said to have changed hands at £5 apiece on the black market. George Edwardes had done everything possible to justify the enthusiasm of his patrons. To the most fashionable writers of the hour he added a splendid physical production and a cast of the most appealing kind. Hayden Coffin and Lottie Venne, who had done so much towards the success of *A Gaiety Girl*, were back again and they were joined by two of the town's most important leading ladies, the ingénue, Letty Lind, and prima donna Marie Tempest in her first British appearance since *The Red Hussar*. The former Savoy star Leonora Braham was featured in a character role and amongst the smaller roles many of the public's *Gaiety Girl* favourites were again in evidence headed by the top 'girls' Marie Studholme, Louie Pounds and Alice Davis. These girls and their companions had already established their own particular followings and, if the girls at Daly's were never given the prominence or the soubriquet of their counterparts at the Gaiety, they were nevertheless popular, much photographed and generally more talented.

The auspices for the opening night of *An Artist's Model* were unimpeachable but the theatrical event of the season turned out to be a little sour and, when the curtain fell at the end of the evening, George Edwardes was a worried man. The piece had run four hours in spite of the fact that two numbers had been cut during the running of the second act, but the audience had begun to register signs of dissatisfaction well before that. There was no doubt where the fault lay. Owen Hall had failed to find that happy mixture of simple plot, attractive characters and bright dialogue with which he had invested *A Gaiety Girl*. The story of *An Artist's Model* was slight but complex, following two vaguely related sets of characters through the artists' world of Paris and an English country house dance. The first plot concerns Adèle and Rudolph, lovers when she was his artist's model but then parted by her marriage for money. She is now a wealthy and merry widow and, very much in the style of a later Merry Widow, returns to her first love after money and pride have got in the way on both sides. Secondly there is the tomboy Daisy Vane, the ward of Sir George St Alban, who gets up to all kinds of 'larks' during which her guardian discovers that the headmistress of her pension is none other than Millie Mostyn with whom he was rather well acquainted when she ran a little hat shop in Sloane Street. Through these stories wander the variegated Cripps family – gauche papa, socially ambitious mama and ingénue daughter – with their different reactions to Gay Paris and the doings of Daisy Vane.

In the first act we are presented with this bevy of characters and situations, and the second act unravels them, giving opportunity at the same time for the little low comedy which the show possessed when the 'lad' Smoggins gets into disguise to fool Sir George that he has been posted to a diplomatic post in Venezuela. It was this second act which proved so sticky in spite of the lavish spectacle produced in the ballroom set and costumes, the former of which had cost an incredible £2500 and had taken so long to make that it arrived in the theatre only after the final rehearsal to be installed just in time for the opening night. The audience was visibly and audibly irritated by long portions of extraneous dialogue and was only restored to a good humour by the music. In many cases, however, irritation won and when the evening ended the piece was the butt of a very mixed response.

Owen Hall suffered the next day at the hands of the critics who, although they recognised that he was attempting to go further towards writing a coherent and intelligent libretto than most of his contemporaries, decided he had failed:

> [Mr Owen Hall] has a caustic pen, a considerable share of boulevardian esprit and fin de siècle irreverence but little aptitude, it would seem, for dramatic concentration or the marshalling of his scenes in telling order . . [the work] will gain greatly if some lively dancing can be substituted for Mr. Owen Hall's reams of vapid dialogue . . (*Times*)

This was slightly unfair on Hall who had publicly admitted that the structure of the piece was not his but had been supplied by James Tanner, the director. *The Theatre* did not care for either of their contributions, noticing in the dialogue ' . . allusions that belong rather to the domain of the smart society paragraphist than to that of the witty epigrammist . .', of the construction '. . a mass of irrelevant details through which the main thread of the story could with difficulty be traced . . ' and concluding that ' . . the only redeeming features were the music, the lyrics and the mounting . . '

The librettist was not entirely to blame for the situation. His original book for *A Naughty Girl*, as its title suggested, had dealt with Daisy Vane, Madame Amélie/Millie Mostyn, Sir George St Alban and their high-jinks and complications in Paris and England. The 'Artist's Model', Adèle, was no part of the story. But George Edwardes had heard of the return of Marie Tempest and he immediately contacted her with an offer to star at Daly's. The fact that his new show had no role for her deterred him not a bit. When she showed willing, he sent Owen Hall's libretto back to its author with instructions for a rewrite which would include a suitable role. Thus *A Naughty Girl* became *An Artist's Model*. Oddly, the Rudolph/Adèle parts of the libretto included most of the best writing in the piece. The scenes between the 'merry widow' and her proud poor artist provided some welcome scenes of genuine characterisation to put alongside the frivolous and shallow banter of the remainder, but they also succeeded in fragmenting the book severely. Hall's much vaunted satirical wit had its moments, but all too often tumbled into unimpressive jibes on the same tired subjects of class and marriage:

> Matrimonial fidelity is like a maid of all work – we only hear of such things among the lower middle classes.
>
> Love is very thin, a little matrimony and it wears out altogether.
>
> A disreputable past is the most popular attribute of the modern woman.
>
> English society is very select and does not care to associate on equal terms with persons of ability and brains.
>
> What has love to do with marriage? We may occasionally marry the person we love but we cannot always love the person we marry.

The characters of the piece included some which were well-conceived and executed. Lottie Venne's Mme Amélie, another 'woman with a past', was not the equal of *A Gaiety Girl*'s Lady Virginia but she had some fine moments and scored superbly with the song 'The Lady Wasn't going that Way':

> It's really hard when times are bad
> And tradesmen unforgiving
> For ladies in Society
> Who haven't any L.S.D.
> To earn an honest living!
> A rough experience I have had
> While friends unkindly mocking,
> Their firm belief would all express
> That nowadays to win success
> One must do something shocking.
>
> But the lady wasn't going that way
> Though they told her impropriety would pay
> So she shut her little eyeses
> To the glitter of the prizes
> And declared she wasn't going that way!

She also featured a humorous piece describing how her pupils are taught the necessities of life – those that will allow them to catch a wealthy husband:

> Oh, my school is most select
> For my pupils don't affect
> All the out-of-date accomplishments of ordinary schools
> If a girl who is good-looking
> Wants to join a class for cooking
> Do you think that I allow it? No! It's quite against the rules!

Bill Blakeley featured as Smoggins, the little studio dogsbody:

> . . from nine to ten I was Judas Iscariot, 10 to 11 a shepherd after Watteau, painted to order for an American, 11 to half past I was a policeman. I had twenty minutes study for the biceps of the village blacksmith and I am now Julius Caesar addressing the senate. It's no catch being odd man in a co-operative studio . .

and made a fistful of the rather obtrusive scene in which he impersonated a foreign office clerk; while Joe Farren Soutar was a slightly less vapid 'Johnnie' than usual, an aristocratic sprig whose artistic appreciation is limited to

> . . two photographs of Mrs Langtry and one of Maud Hobson and an engraving of last year's Derby winner, but I can't count that because the glass is broken . .

Other roles were less well drawn. Letty Lind's Daisy Vane was the standard aggravating 'romp' and was only redeemed by the charm of its interpreter and a particularly popular song 'The gay Tom Tit'. Miss Lind accompanied this zoological fable with a little dance imitative of 'Tom Tit' and 'Jenny Wren' pecking and nodding quaintly but gracefully about the stage to the delight of the audience:

> A tom-tit lived in a tip-top tree
> And a mad little, bad little bird was he
> He'd bachelor tastes, but then – oh dear!
> He'd a gay little way with the girls, I fear

Less attractive but equally arch was 'Daisy with the Dimple' which the star carried off with a twinkling false modesty:

> Yes, the fellows call me Daisy, little Daisy with the dimple
> And they say they are so fond of me because I am so simple
> But they tell me I am sure to learn a lot I don't know now
> And the more I think it over, the more I wonder how!

The show's more serious music was confined to Miss Tempest and Hayden Coffin. The latter had two ballads 'Mine, oh Love, at Last' and 'Is Love a Dream' in his habitual style, while Miss Tempest scored best with a very lively student song:

> On y revient toujours
> Welcome, with hearts grown fonder
> Back to the life that each of us loves best
> For here are home and rest
> When far afield we wander
> Sing comrades all – 'On y revient toujours'!

Several other musical numbers found special approval, including the topical trio for Lottie Venne, Soutar and Eric Lewis entitled 'Antici-tici-pation':

> The felici-lici-tation
> Of antici-tici-pation
> By reality is speedily corrected
> Oscar's epigrams look clever
> Do not analyse them ever
> Or you'll find they're not as smart as you expected.

and a patter song for Lewis, 'The popular Art of the Day', where the unpretentious baronet describes his inability to appreciate Impressionism. His tastes are more limited:

> But Mrs Patrick Campbell, Marie Lloyd and Violet Cameron
> Are framed to much advantage in the corners of my dressing-room
> And when I say I really do not care for the Academy
> I hope I do not shock you for my words are not abruptly meant
> But honestly I much prefer, though doubtless it's too bad of me
> The colour plate presented as a Christmas Extra Supplement

One of the show's most decided favourites, however, was the opening solo 'Gay Bohemia' sung by one of the young artists:

Oh, come and peep when the world's asleep
At Gay Bohemia
And much you'll see that you'll ask of me
Mais qu'est-ce que c'est que ça?
For lots of things we do, you know
Are not precisely comme il faut
But that you'll find is often so
In Gay Bohemia!

Many women in the audience would have been delighted to have been 'not precisely comme il faut' with the singer – the magnificently romantic Turko-Anglo-Frenchman Maurice Farkoa. Farkoa had come to Britain as part of a double act which had appeared as a speciality in *Morocco Bound.* He had subsequently turned his attention to the concert platform before George Edwardes put him into a series of smooth romantic roles which made him adored and famous.

Following the first night reception and the critics' widely expressed reservations, those involved went quickly to work on *An Artist's Model.* By the Monday night's performance large portions of the dialogue had disappeared and more followed. The whole of the considerable role of Archie Pendillon, the love interest tacked in for Daisy, was wiped out within a fortnight and the emphasis tilted towards the more satisfactory Adèle/Rudolph story. Marie Tempest's role was expanded by a bright number 'Give me Love' in the second act, and the full houses began to give more satisfactory responses to the show. But still work went on to make the piece more attractive. The waltz song 'Sei nicht Bös' (Don't Be Cross) from Carl Zeller's *Der Obersteiger* was the newest song in town, so Edwardes annexed it, had Adrian Ross put a new lyric to it, and as 'Music and Laughter' it was added to Jones' score as a duet for Coffin and Miss Tempest until a protest from the owners forced its withdrawal. Within five weeks of its opening *An Artist's Model* was a very different piece to that which had provoked so many unfavourable notices. Large advance bookings and the reputation of Edwardes and his artists had seen the show through a period which might have been fatal under other circumstances. The first six nights showed a net take of nearly £1,800. Now the 'new' *Artist's Model* had been slimmed and massaged into a slick and dazzling show, and word of mouth soon got round to those who had loved *A Gaiety Girl.* From the moment the curtain rose on beautiful Hetty Hamer suitably draped in a scrap of Grecian flimsy, posing on her model's pedestal in front of a purple curtain, to the final whirling ballroom scene with the men in their gaily coloured uniforms and the ladies in fantastically fashioned ball-gowns, the evening was a treat for the eyes, while the ears were well attended to by the new partnership of Tempest and Coffin aided and abetted by Miss Lind, Miss Braham and the fun-making of Lottie Venne, Bill Blakeley and E. M. Robson. The run of *An Artist's Model* continued so strongly that, when Edwardes was obliged to leave Daly's to comply with earlier arrangements to let the theatre to a French play season featuring Bernhardt as *Gismonda* and to Augustin Daly's company with Ada Rehan at its head, he decided to transfer the piece to the Lyric which had recently been vacated by *His Excellency. An Artist's Model* played Saturday night at Daly's, moved out on Sunday and re-opened, ballroom and all, on Shaftesbury Avenue on Tuesday night to a full house and a thunderous reception. When Augustin Daly ended his season in September, Edwardes closed down *An*

Artist's Model at the Lyric, took a fortnight out to rehearse a slightly altered 'new' version, and reopened back at Daly's with success and popularity undiminished. It ran five further months in its original home, only narrowly failing to break the record set by *A Gaiety Girl*.

During the run of over twelve months many cast changes occurred. Letty Lind gave way to one of her sisters, Adelaide Astor, as Daisy, who in turn was succeeded by a third sister, Lydia Flopp. Juliette Nesville was a genuine French Madame Amélie and the veteran Lydia Thompson, once the most famous leading lady of the burlesque theatre and now nearly sixty years of age, took a turn in the same role. The script continued to 'develop' and the score for the second edition at Daly's saw the inclusion of several new songs, although nothing which succeeded in shaking the position of the 'Gay Tom Tit' as the most applauded number of the night. When the Trilby craze hit town with the production of Paul Potter's adaptation of the famous novel at Her Majesty's, Maurice Farkoa was quickly provided with a song on the subject ('Trilby Will be True', words and music by Leslie Stuart).

Farkoa's popularity had already ensured him a larger piece of the action. He had had a rather unsatisfactory military solo from the original score replaced by a lively laughing song[1] and in the second version he was given even more to do, including a duet 'Can this be Love' with Violet Lloyd in the newly written-in role of Maud Cripps. Hayden Coffin had a ballad 'Queen of the Sea and Earth' interpolated in a rather obvious attempt to cash in on his former success with 'Queen of my Heart' but with an added touch of patriotic sentiment. Patriotism was also the key note of the song 'Hands Off' written by Henry Hamilton and Frederick Rosse which the baritone interpolated as relations between Germany and Britain over South Africa grew more tense. The lyric was fairly blunt:

> Let pinchbeck Caesar strut and crow
> Let eagles scream of war
> No jot we bate, no right forego
> We've stood alone before!
> When all the world was just as great
> And we were half our size
> We faced the world in grim debate
> And blacked the bully's eyes!
>
> Hands off Germany! Hands off all!
> Kruger boasts and Kaiser brags, Britons hear the call!
> Back to back the world around, answer with a will
> England for her own, my boys! It's 'Rule Britannia' still!

and the censor took some exception. Unfortunately he was a little late. Coffin tells in his memoirs how the completed song was rushed to the censor by messenger the day it was to be performed. The messenger found that the censor was out shooting and, by the time he had found him and been given the list of alterations required, he had little time to get back to the theatre. He arrived just in time but Edwardes kept him in conversation those few extra minutes needed for Coffin to sing the song. The next night, in due deference to authority, 'pinchbeck Caesar' became, more innocuously,

[1] Farkoa made a large number of gramophone recordings of 'The Laughing Song' in both English and French, the first of which recorded in New York in 1896 seems to have been the first 'original cast' recording from a British musical.

'jealous rivals' and the direct references to Germany, Kruger and the Kaiser were given a less personal form.

Coffin also tells how he interpolated yet another number, this one by 'John Oliver Hobbs' and Frances Allitsen and entitled 'Love is a Bubble' with the rather commonplace comment–

> He [Edwardes] had a reputation for making people work, and what is more, work of their own free will. This he achieved by keeping up a spirit of keen competition among those in his employ. Thus, if a member of the company brought a suitable song from outside, the composer of the opera, conscious of a certain amount of rivalry, was spurred to give of his best . . .

Maybe so, but it was a little strange that almost every 'outside song' brought in was at the suggestion of and for the benefit of Mr Hayden Coffin.

An Artist's Model, by the talents of all concerned, had been worked up from a patchwork of the good and the less good into an enormously clever and popular show which had the vigour to survive two transfers and run almost 400 performances over fourteen months. Its accidental dual nature, as epitomised by its two leading ladies, set the pattern for a series of memorable pieces which the Daly's team of writers would produce for Edwardes' theatre over the years to follow where Miss Lind, Miss Tempest and Hayden Coffin formed the nucleus of a set of stars giving London some of the best light musical shows ever seen in its theatres. In December *An Artist's Model* was produced on Broadway. As in London, it did not receive a wholehearted welcome from the critics, but it survived their reservations once again for a healthy season.

If the eventual success of *An Artist's Model* was briefly in doubt at its opening, that of Arthur Roberts' newest piece *Gentleman Joe* was never challenged. Basil Hood and Walter Slaughter provided the popular comedian with the liveliest and cleverest vehicle of his career in the character of the jolly hansom cabby who finds himself mistaken for an Irish peer, and Roberts made the most of it.

After his smaller attempts with *The Gypsies, Donna Luiza* and *The Crossing Sweeper, Gentleman Joe* was its librettist's first attempt at a full length musical and, when he found himself ordered with his regiment to Burmah before its production, he decided to send in his papers and to devote himself henceforth to the theatre. The younger son of Sir Charles Hood, educated at Wellington and Sandhurst, Hood had spent the ten years since his 19th birthday in the army and had just achieved the rank of Captain. Although his resignation from the army was not finalised for another three years, he had to all intents and purposes given up his planned career to stay with his first show. The plot which he proposed for *Gentleman Joe* was a suitable and elastic one allowing for the interpolations and variations which, with Roberts around, were inevitable. Mrs Ralli-Carr is a 'woman who arranges things'–everything from recommending a dressmaker to arranging a wedding. When the play opens, she is away on a 'business' trip and her servants are having a party. Emma, the 'upper domestic' arrives and tells how she was nearly run over by a cab but the cabby in question has driven her home and she introduces 'Gentleman Joe' to the party. Joe has taken a shine to Emma and she to him, and they agree that they and the whole party will drive down to Margate for a trip the next day. But Mrs Ralli-Carr returns with her protégée Mabel. Mrs Carr is determined to net a rich husband for Mabel but the young lady is pining for a poor Irish peer, Lord Donnybrook, whom Mrs Carr has, in consequence, forbidden the house. The lady also has in tow the four daughters of the nouveau riche patent medicine merchant, Pilkington Jones, and the brash American heiress, Miss Lalage

Potts, for all of whom she is contracted to find titled husbands. In the misunderstandings following this unexpected return, Joe finds himself mistaken for the mysterious Irishman and so, the next day, when he goes to Margate, he finds that Mrs Carr, Miss Potts and all the Pilkington Jones have followed him with matrimonial intentions, and poor Emma thinks that she has been made fun of by a philandering peer. Eventually, after a jaunt around the sands, all is cleared up and Joe gets his Emma whilst Donnybrook, having conveniently inherited, is able to wed his Mabel.

The construction followed the current trend which *The Era* summarised:

> Modern dress opera is, if we may say so, by libretto out of extravaganza. When comic opera and burlesque were almost on their last legs, it occurred to someone to try a 'blend'. The book started with a first act constructed with some care, and apparently leading up to a climacteric second. Fearing, perhaps, that the strain upon the minds of the audience might be too great if he asked them to follow out a second instalment of consecutive narrative, the ingenious author took all his principal personages out of England in his second act and, mermaid-like, the piece tailed off into a variety entertainment, a masquerade or some such gay and harmless frivolity.

but Basil Hood's book for *Gentleman Joe* had two strong points not always characteristic of the genre – a vigorous and carefully written second act and a lively and interesting set of characters to set off the principal comedian's role. Roberts capitalised on this arrangement by surrounding himself with some fine performers.

Apart from the role of Joe, the most prominent part was that of the servant girl, Emma, for which Kitty Loftus, the original *Lady Slavey*, was engaged. Miss Loftus made a hit on her first appearance as she described her accident:

> As I was crossing a crowded street,
> With my skirt held so – above my feet,
> And waving my umbereller thus,
> A-trying to hail a passing 'bus,
> A hansom cab as I'd failed to see
> As near as a toucher ran over me;
> But the driver luckily shouted 'Hi!'
> And pulled up short in a wink of an eye.
>
> Oh my! Oh my! Oh my, my, my!
> I didn't know whether to laugh or cry!
> I'll never forget, if I try till I die,
> What I felt in that there wink of an eye!

and she also scored with a mock cautionary tale 'The Ballad of Miss Prim' describing the horrid fate of that over-modest maid who found herself the subject of a wager between two youths. One wagered that before the week was out he would have seen Miss Prim's stocking, a thing altogether unlikely for, as the maid declared:

> If I raise my skirt as I sometimes must,
> To keep my petticoat out of the dust,
> It shall only be so much above my shoe,
> And not as many young ladies do!

To her horror, she hears at the end of the week that the bet has been won:

> She never asked how the wager was won,
> But she felt there was only one thing to be done.
> With a shriek and a shiver,

To jump in the river,
She ran just as fast as a maiden can run!
O, O, O, poor little Miss Prim!
Her ankle had never been seen by him!
For the stocking that met his masculine eye
Was hung on a clothes-line out to dry!
So ladies who want to escape her fate,
Don't let your modesty be too great!
For O, 'tis so,
Some ladies I know
At innocent matters cry 'Oh, oh, oh!'
And their maidenly modesty out of such
A very small matter may make so much!

'Miss Prim' proved highly popular, and so did another young lady, 'The Lady Bicyclist'.

The role of Mrs Ralli-Carr was taken by Aida Jenoure, another well-liked musical comedy actress who had created the role of Nita in *The Mountebanks*. She, too, had a show-stopper with her song 'A little Commission':

Great confidence by many is placed
In me, as a lady of tact and taste,
And every minute and every hour
I'm assisting my friends to the best of my pow'r–
I am helping my friends in this or in that,
The choice of a husband, a house, or a hat;
And I always intend, till I'm laid on the shelf,
While helping my neighbours to help myself
To what people call a commission–
A small but convenient commission;
For in aiding your neighbours
You're wasting your labours
Unless you can earn a commission!

She also found much fun in 'Put it Down', a number listing the strange things which titled ladies may do with impunity which in anyone of lesser degree might be considered shady or even vulgar.

The romantic leads were taken by the young tenor William Philp (Lord Donnybrook) and the gentle Kate Cutler who left her role in *The Shop Girl* to play Mabel. To their part fell the show's more lyrical music and Philp gained a huge ovation on opening night for his rendering of 'My Heart's Delight', a ballad in the 'Queen of my Heart' vein. Miss Cutler had a pretty but lively song bewailing mercenary instincts in marriage:

And its matrimony! Where's the money?
The penny and shilling and pound,
For love is dead, and it's money instead
That makes the world go round!

and the two came together in the romantic duet 'I Love Thee', which formed a neat contrast to Joe and Emma's cheerful love duet 'Sweethearts' in which that pair illustrated love at different ages, and chorused:

You may think they're a silly pair of sweethearts,
You may laugh at ev'rything they do and say;
But their love is just as true
As the love of me and you,
And they're happy in their own sweet way.

A song which really brought the house down not only on the first night but on every night that followed was the one allotted to the American actress Sadie Jerome in the role of the Yankee heiress, Lalage Potts:

I'm Lalage Potts, of the U.S.A.–
Lalage Potts, that's me!

she sang, with spirit and verve, and a hefty accent on the 'Potts' which soon had the gallery joining in loudly as she declared:

My poppa, who's dead, was a millionaire–
Hiram B. Potts, that's he!
And I'm an heiress fixed up square–
Lalage Potts, that's me!
I'm spying around for an English lord
To marry me quick of his own accord;
But the first that knocks my fancy–wa'al,
If he likes it or not, he'll wed this gal!

The fact that Lalage managed to hook neither the real Duke nor the cabby-Duke, and the fact that the actress involved had a good deal more energy than voice or acting ability, did not detract a jot from the huge popularity which 'Lalage Potts of the U.S.A.' and Sadie Jerome enjoyed.

Many and varied as were the hits brought out by the other members of the cast, the light of Arthur Roberts in the title role was in no way dimmed. He rollicked his way through the role of Joe, and his songs gave away nothing to 'Lalage Potts' or 'The Magic of his Eye'.

O perhaps it's as well as you should know
That wherever you happen to go,
It's a thou to a fiver
You won't see a driver
As dandy as Gentleman Joe!

he affirmed, and the full houses endorsed the sentiment heartily. In 'In my 'Ansom' he described the sights he sees as a cabby–

If you want to go an' study human nature
Why, a cabby's life is very 'ard to beat:
For you're livin' in an open-air theayter
When you're drivin' of your 'ansom in the street;
And I think as I could tell some funny stories
If I took the time and trouble for to blab,
Of the many sorts of fares
As I've studied unawares
A drivin' of my 'ansom cab!

and he joined in duets with Miss Loftus and with W. H. Denny, taking every opportunity to exercise his own brand of popular humour. The role which Hood and

Slaughter had evolved allowed him to work within the script as written without sacrificing any of his comic business, and the critics joined with the public in showering praise on the authors, the star and everyone else involved in transforming the elements necessary to an 'Arthur Roberts show' into a coherent and first-rate musical farce. *The Times* agreed that 'the piece may fairly be described as one of the best of its kind', recording (rather strangely) that 'the house applauded itself hoarse'. *The Stage* commented 'Rarely have we seen a first night audience so unanimous in its approval' and *The Era* noted that:

> Roars of laughter followed each of Mr Roberts' quips and enthusiastic encores demanded the repetition of all his songs . . enthusiasm was the order of the evening.

Gentleman Joe was a well-proportioned, well-organised and well-written show, a complete musical comedy which kept the irrespressible Arthur centre stage at the Prince of Wales for over twelve months.

Much of the show's success was due to the straightforward and literate book and lyrics. Basil Hood used good plain English and stayed well away from any temptation to play games with the language and its construction as so many of his contemporaries and his predecessors had. His song words avoided the complicated inversions used by even the best lyricists to force their lines into rhyming patterns, and he succeeded in producing some of the most natural sounding lyrics on the contemporary stage without sacrificing any of the time honoured rhymes and even employing a certain amount of internal rhyme. With *Gentleman Joe*, Hood placed himself in the forefront of English light musical stage writing, a position which he retained for many years.

In spite of all its excellences, *Gentleman Joe* was not proof against 'improvements'. During the run of the piece Roberts interpolated at will into the scene on Margate Sands. Almost anything could appear there as legitimate seaside entertainment alongside the Nigger Minstrel Troupe which starred 'Uncle Bones' and his eccentric dancing. It was there that Roberts featured a 'risky' song written for him by W. S. Laidlaw and Ella Chapman called 'She Wanted Something to Play With' which proved very successful, but the most substantial addition came in November, just one week after the opening of *Trilby* at the Haymarket, when the Prince of Wales company jumped in with its own version of the play – a short burlesque entitled *A Trilby Triflet* 'with full Organ, cornet and bagpipe accompaniment' in which Roberts played Beerbohm Tree/Svengali and Kitty Loftus was Dorothea Baird/Trilby. It was an enormous success, and *The Times* praised Roberts highly:

> A wonderful imitation alike in make-up, voice and gesture of Mr Tree. Never has Mr Arthur Roberts been more successful in direct caricature.

There were many other lesser additions and variations as Roberts put in whatever gag appealed to him on the spur of the moment. Just how many and how often was displayed one night when the star was off and understudy Eric Thorne stepped in as 'Gentleman Joe'. Thorne had carefully copied down every deviation the variable Arthur had ever made from the script and that night he delivered them all. The curtain came down more than thirty minutes late after a feat which would have stunned even the star himself.

Gentleman Joe was a major hit and deservedly so; it was probably the most effective all-round show among the 'new wave' of musical farces. It remained a popular touring show for many years and was produced around the world, including America (in 1896) where it had an unusually eventful history. The Aronsons and M. B. Curtis were both determined to produce the show on Broadway. Curtis opened out of town with himself in the title role and Aronson, who had taken the trouble to obtain the rights legally, hurried to court to prevent the production from opening in town. Different judgements gave different results, and Curtis' production finally opened at the Fifth Avenue on 5 January. The actor/manager had taken one step towards discretion, however, and Willard Lee was 'Joe' for the occasion. Legal pressures and lack of audiences forced him out after only ten performances, and Aronson was left clear to bring in his version a few weeks later. James T. Powers featured in the 'new' version at the Bijou with Clara Wieland as his Emma, but the battle proved to have been scarcely worth the winning and the American *Joe* in its second incarnation lasted for only a short run.

On the same night that *Gentleman Joe* opened its London run, the Avenue also presented a new musical, *Dandy Dick Whittington.* It was written by the venerable George R. Sims who described it as an opéra-bouffe, and, although it was scarcely that, the now rather old-fashioned term was not inappropriate as *Dandy Dick Whittington* had a good deal of the old-fashioned about it. It had very little to do with the approved story of the Lord Mayor of London but that was to be expected. *Little Christopher Columbus* had had precious little to do with its nominal hero and had made a tidy success for Sims. But things had moved very quickly since that production and plays like *Gentleman Joe*, which treated the English language as an instrument rather than a plaything, were now the vogue. The word-twisting and punning and quaint constructions of burlesque had been put aside. Sims was wise enough to recognise this but the *Dandy Dick Whittington* script had been originally intended for use as a pantomime, with all the traditional elements which that involved and, although the book was on considerably more modern lines than *Little Christopher Columbus* had been, it was not calculated to appeal to those who liked the style of *The Shop Girl* or *A Gaiety Girl.* The response to it was, predictably, mixed. *The Era's* critic was enthusiastic:

> Good acting, good singing, pretty dresses and pretty girls wearing them, good scenery and music of a high class, tuneful and artistic at the same time with a libretto combining the best effects of a brilliant dramatist and first-rate humorist . . *Dandy Dick Whittington* has won a success which must be set down as triumphant. There are no allowances to be made, no defects to be excused.

The Times was more moderate:

> The libretto is fashioned on familiar lines, a plot that fulfils its purpose in providing a series of disconnected situations, a superabundance of topical songs, dances, acrobatic feats, with occasional concerted pieces make up the whole entertainment . . . . Mr Ivan Caryll's music is melodious, fairly free from vulgarity and on the whole shows a higher order of musicianship than some works to which his name has been attached . .

and *The Theatre* just disliked it:

> There is little originality about it and it is certainly not opéra-bouffe. It is devoutly to be hoped that Mr Sims will in future spare his hearers such awful word-twistings as those with which he has burdened his latest stage production . . . The book falls far short of what might have been expected from a writer of Mr Sims' eminence, and were it not for the music, the performers, and the mounting, *Dandy Dick Whittington* would not have had a long life.

The story which Sims had invented to attach to the name of the favourite pantomime here was set in a circus environment. Sir Achilles Fitzwarren is the proprietor of the circus, his wife, Lady Fitzwarren, is the lion-tamer and Dick is the circus apprentice and bareback rider in love with his master's daughter. He is betrayed to Sir Achilles by the jealous clown, Auguste, and is dismissed. The circus is ready to leave for Siam and Dick hitches a ride in the same direction. When Siam is reached further complications ensue involving two acrobats, the one sought by the police and therefore in disguise, the other rightful king of Siam, Koko Gaga, coming, also in disguise, to claim his throne. To complicate affairs further, they are disguised as each other. The wrong acrobat ends up on the throne of Siam, evoking the fury of the real king who imprisons everyone and orders up the boiling oil. Dick, who has in the meanwhile been having a hard time with an amorous Siamese princess, saves the situation by telephoning to England for help and the military arrive in time to set all to rights.

There was much of pantomime and much of burlesque, with the multiplicity of disguises, and all was further confused by Dick being played by a girl and Lady Fitzwarren by a man. The topical element was strong and Sims, while avoiding the excesses of *Little Christopher Columbus*, could not resist a certain amount of word-play. *The Era* quoted one particular quip. Seeing the restaurant bill for his cat's milk and fish Dick remarks:

> Sixpence for waiting on a cat – that's something new in the feeline!

The Era enthused: 'There are plenty of jokes as good as this, and some better'. But it was this very 'feline' joke which the *Theatre* selected as an example of the excruciating nature of the dialogue.

The libretto of *Dandy Dick Whittington* was a fairly competent effort, with more story than some and giving excellent opportunities to both artists and designers. Following closely the recipe of *Little Christopher Columbus*, the leading players were again May Yohe as Dick and the supreme travesty player, John F. Sheridan, who had made a memorable monster of Mrs Block in *Little Christopher*, as the lion-taming, fire-eating Lady Fitzwarren. Henry Wright took the principal comic role of the Irish acrobat, Florence Levey featured a Siamese dance and an acrobatic song and dance with Wright, and the young Australian actress, Ethel Haydon, who would go on to the role of Bessie Brent at the Gaiety when the Avenue Theatre had finished with her, was Alice Fitzwarren.

Ivan Caryll produced a clutch of new songs for Miss Yohe to sing: the lively 'Postilion of Love', the patriotic 'The English Lass' and, in an effort to squeeze in a familiar episode which hardly fitted the new plot 'The Message of the Bells'. Most importantly, there had to be a coon song and Sims and Caryll, who had already collaborated on a number of such efforts under titles like 'De little black Coon', 'My dusky Southern Bride' and 'Way down in Ohio' for the open market, turned out 'De Days ob long Ago' for the occasion:

> Meet me honey, meet me once again
> Kiss me honey, kiss me once again
> Down by de ribber where de quiet waters flow
> Meet me as you met me in the days ob long ago

But none of the star songs was the equal of 'Lazily, Drowsily' or 'Oh, Honey, my Honey' and the score, pleasant but unexceptional, did not contain the hits that *Little*

Christopher Columbus had. Perhaps the most popular number was Henry Wright's song 'I've Played at the Game Before':

In London one night I went out for a walk
I'd played at the game before
A sailor I met and he wanted to talk
He'd played at the game before
He showed me some notes and he said 'Will you drink?'
I buttoned my coat and replied with a wink
Its name is the confidence dodge, I think,
I've played at the game before!

Lady Fitzwarren (to whom 'I love' is pronounced 'Je tame') had a 'New Woman' number 'The Tyrant Man has had his Day', there was a picturesque circus cavalcade with acrobats and a 'Windmill Quadrille' in polite Parisian fashion but, in general, *Dandy Dick Whittington* lacked sufficient features to make it a stayer. It held its place at the Avenue Theatre for four months (almost half of which time Miss Yohe was, for one reason or another, out of the cast) and during its run was given a sub-title, *The Circus Boy*. The original burlesque-like title was considered by the show's partisans as one of the reasons for the less than brilliant business in the later part of the run and, when the show was put out on tour after the conclusion of the Avenue run, the title was altered definitively, according to Greet so that the provincial public might not mistake the show for a pantomime. It had one major tour but was not taken out again.

After four new British musicals, brief appearances were put in by the only new foreign offerings of the year. The first was from America's Miss Hope Booth who had already been responsible for a one-night fiasco called *Little Miss Cute* the previous year. Her new piece, *That Terrible Girl* did little better, and she fled from London after a disastrous first night and outraged reviews. Miss Booth was soon back in America where her next appearance resulted in her being arrested for indecency after appearing at the Casino Theatre in single thickness tights and no trunks. Her performance in court was allegedly much more convincing than that she had given in *That Terrible Girl*.

The second new offering was a French work which as *L'Oncle Celestin* had had a profitable Parisian run for Ordonneau, Kéroul and Audran. It had come to Britain via New York where, under the title of *Uncle Celestin* it had played for eight weeks to a medium reception. For Britain, Meyer Lutz added to Audran's music, the libretto was suitably anglicised and it was staged at the Trafalgar Theatre as *Baron Golosh* with a cast that included E. J. Lonnen, Charles Danby, Harry Paulton, Frank Wyatt, Florence Perry and Alice Lethbridge. After an indifferent reception it was rearranged but to little effect and closed after an unexceptional run.

The British musical was what the public now wanted or, more specifically, the new-style British musical. Cissy Graham, who had done exceptionally well with her touring companies of *A Pantomime Rehearsal* and *A Gaiety Girl*, was one of the first to attempt to climb abroad the latest bandwagon with a new-style musical of her own ordering, *All Abroad*. This piece was moulded on their own latest models by Owen Hall and James Tanner with lyrics supplied by W. H. Risque and music by Frederick Rosse, two names not new to the theatre but new to the authorship of a major show. Risque had worked on the management side, while Rosse had been seen as an actor and vocalist, notably as the young hero of *Go-Bang!*.

All Abroad found Hall and Tanner using a very different type of humour from that of *An Artist's Model.* The show's first act introduces us to the law firm Bowles & Beaver, guardians of one young Connie. Mr Bowles is a music fanatic who spends his and the firm's time rehearsing an opera he has composed, while Mr Beaver is an opportunist who is devoted to finding out whether Connie's elder sister is still alive. If she is not, then Connie is heiress to a large fortune and Beaver intends to wed her to either his son or, if needs be, himself. The second act shifts to a Parisian café concert where, amongst a whole series of farcical episodes, the chanteuse Madame Montesquieu, 'La Chanterelle', turns out to be the missing sister. The show had more the flavour of pure English farcical comedy, relying for much of its humour on visual and physical effects. The wretched Bowles running around Paris with his opera recorded on a phonograph, having it mistaken for a bomb, and suffering, in consequence, both the attentions of the gendarmerie and a thorough dousing was a character straight out of the St George's Hall or an 1880's provincial comedy.

The music consisted of a series of solos, one duet and a couple of trios. The chorus was very little featured and the only concerted piece of importance in the entire show was the first act finale composed by Edgar Ward. The songs were not of great note, but Risque and Rosse turned out one which proved an attraction in 'The Business Girl' in which Minnie Jeffs (Mme Montesquieu) related the rise of a nursemaid through the ranks of the theatre to a coronet. The number was accompained by the manipulation of a trick nursemaid's costume which illustrated the lady's social progress. Ada Reeve, who took over the role of Mme Montesquieu for the London production, described the costume in her autobiography:

> Firstly I let down the top, which became a barmaid's apron-fronted skirt surmounted by a pale blue blouse, then I unhooked it from the waist and swung the drapery behind me, leaving myself in the blue tunic of a chorus girl; finally I unfastened this on one shoulder and passed it round the back, so that it swung free as a long cloak, revealing the tights of a principal boy. On one hip I had a little pale blue cap with a scarlet feather which I pinned to my head to complete the effect . . .

Risque provided a couple of novel lyrics in 'In re the Trespass' in which the law clerk, Capshaw, delivered a summary of a legal document as a song and 'This desirable Residence' (Bowles) which was an acidly amusing piece of land-agent's sales talk set to music, but the remainder of the score was more conventional – some little ballads for Connie, a champagne song for the 'French' lady, shanty for Mr Beaver Jr (the eventual winner of the ward) and some comical bits for Bowles ('The Phonograph') and Beaver ('The Case of obedient Mary').

All Abroad was originally produced at Plymouth and taken on tour with considerable success. During the tour it was seen by Charles Wyndham, proprietor of the Criterion Theatre, who arranged for the show to go into his theatre on the completion of its tour. Although Charles Stevens and the eccentric Horace Mills, of *A Pantomime Rehearsal* fame, retained their roles as Bowles and Beaver, it was thought advisable to strengthen the cast with some names and the two 'Shop Girls', Ada Reeve and Kate Cutler, were engaged for the roles of the 'French' and 'English' sisters respectively. The first night went well and Cissy Graham was cheered from her box to the stage to take a call at the final curtain, but *All Abroad* lacked the style and finesse of the Gaiety and Daly's pieces and some reservations were expressed about its metropolitan prospects. *The Era* reported:

> Owen Hall and James Tanner's libretto contains material of many kinds. There are smartly written lyrics for the literary, humorous ideas for the intelligent, crude farce

> for the groundlings and a certain amount of 'construction' to appease the technical. The work is uneven in merit but it seemed to give general satisfaction on Thursday and though there appeared to be a strong friendly element present, much of the enthusiasm with which *All Abroad* was received may said to have been honestly evoked by the fun and frolic of the curious concoction . . . [it is] just the light, reckless piece of frivolity which suits the present season and if promptly revised and worked up in the weaker places may attain considerable popularity.

Although in no way an outstanding piece, *All Abroad* had more merits than many and its run of three months was a fair reward. It might have continued longer but Wyndham wanted the theatre for his own company and, although the possibility of a transfer was momentarily mooted, Miss Graham decided the pickings were liable to be better in the provinces and so, with the cachet of a West End season behind it, *All Abroad* set out once again on the road.

However, it was to see the West End again early in the new year. The Court Theatre arranged with Miss Graham to produce a new version of the piece with Willie Edouin as Bowles and his daughter May as Connie. A number of the original cast were retained, but Fred Kaye was brought in as Beaver and the Gaiety's Grace Palotta as Mme Montesquieu. Harry Greenbank supplied several new lyrics and the whole piece was reproduced by Edouin himself but the revised version of *All Abroad* did not fare as well as the original had and closed after only three weeks. Miss Grahame continued to profit from the show for another season in the provinces before selling off the rights to future productions.

The final new production of the year was, like the first, a comic opera, but on a much more ambitious scale than *The Taboo*. *The Bric à Brac Will* had been written by the actor turned journalist, S. J. Adair Fitzgerald, and Hugh Moss, an experienced director and man of the theatre, with music by Emilio Pizzi. Pizzi was a 33-year-old Italian who had been long resident in London. He had been a pupil of Ponchielli in Milan, and his musical ambitions had originally been in the operatic sphere where he had succeeded in 1893 in placing an opera, *Gabriella*, with Adelina Patti. The manager, Ernest Lambert (alias Oswald) was a new and enthusiastic and open-handed one. A chorus of 48 and an orchestra of 33 were engaged to do justice to Pizzi's music and singers of the quality of Charles Conyers, Frank Celli and opera singer Kate Drew were signed for the principal roles with the popular comedian 'Johnny' Dallas as the Doge of Venice. Sets and costumes of outstanding splendour were ordered and the production bill rose without difficulty to £6,000.

On the first performance it was quickly evident that there was little novel or interesting about *The Bric à Brac Will*. The only vestige of plot concerned an antique vase, the possession of which entitles the owner to wed the Duke Enrico. Fortunately, by the end, the vase has found its way into the possession of a lady, and more fortunately still the right lady. Fitzgerald's literary talents clearly did not lie in the field of libretto writing. The piece was shapeless and silly, and the reaction to it was solidly unfavourable. *The Times* noted that it was far too long and recommended severe pruning to 'help unravel a plot which at present is terribly vague and unsatisfactory'. It called the music 'pretentious' and 'lacking in any real charm', although admitting that 'without rising anywhere to a very lofty standard [it] is certainly fitted for a vastly better book.' *The Theatre* was even less kind and took particular exception to Fitzgerald's contribution:

> Of Mr Adair Fitzgerald's lyrics it almost seems uncharitable to speak at all. Since the days of the poet Bunn[1] nothing quite so deliciously naive has been seen . . . . Mr Fitzgerald's wit is on a par with his lyrical skill and it is needless therefore to say anything more regarding the quality of the dialogue.

while one witty writer merely said, 'How dare Fitzgerald'.

Something clearly had to be done if the manager were to rescue his expensive venture. Cuts and rewrites were ordered, and new numbers were interpolated freely to the fury of the composer who clearly had a higher opinion of his own work than anyone else did. Kate Drew, who had performed her uninspiring part perfectly adequately, was replaced by Florence St John which gave the evening the special combination of vocal skill and personality that only she possessed, but the chief element which helped to pull *The Bric à Brac Will* out of the morgue was the effort of J. J. Dallas as the Doge of Venice. In the same way in which Phil Day had rescued *Estrella* from utter darkness in the same role, Dallas proceeded to embellish his interpretation with comical bits and pieces and, most effectively, with a hit song 'The nervous Man' for which W. Sapte Jr supplied the lyric:

> How is it that I tremble so
> I with my lion heart?
> How is it that at every noise
> Uneasily I start?
> Fact is I've lately had a shock
> And it's made me – saints preserve us
> For a man who's mostly firm as a rock
> I'm most unaccountably nervous
> Yes, I've recently suffered a terrible shock
> As you know how these things serve us
> I thought I heard Roberto decree
> That Chiara must be married to me
> And it made me so terribly nervous!

The number brought the house out in encores nightly, and Dallas confirmed with another jolly piece 'The Doge with an E':

> Once in the days when I was young
> I used to go the pace, sirs,
> A dandy all the blades among
> Who used to paint the place, sir
> I had sweet maidens fourteen deep
> Who loved me to distraction
> And though of fun I'd such a heap
> Of cash I'd not a fraction.
> For O, I was such a doge
> But I used to spell it D O G
> Though my ways were very bad
> What a lovely time I had
> As a Doge without the E.

[1] Alfred Bunn, the librettist of many musical works (including *The Bohemian Girl*) in the mid-19th century, was noted for his extremely ingenuous sentimentality which led the sophisticates of his later years to refer to him derisively as 'the poet Bunn'.

To make way for these improvements, Dallas' original 'Folly Song' and 'The Things Judges have to Wink At' had to be disposed of. Much of the score (including a number called 'A wandering Minstrel, I') was discarded and Harry Greenbank contributed some more 'in' lyrics, but nothing could save what was instrinsically an old-fashioned and ill-written piece and *The Bric à Brac Will* folded before the New Year. On the last night Dallas set what he claimed as some kind of a record when he gave no fewer than sixteen encores to 'The nervous Man'.

Pizzi remained convinced of the value of his piece and the following November announced that *The Bric à Brac Will* would be toured and then brought back into London in its original version with all the additions and interpolations from the Lyric Theatre cut. However, he failed to find a sufficiently enthusiastic backer to share his project and, mercifully, the piece did not reappear. Pizzi abandoned London a couple of years later and returned to Italy. His subsequent output included an opera with *Madama Butterfly*'s librettist, Luigi Illica, *Rosalba* (1899) and a music drama *Vendetta* (1906) but he kept well clear of the light musical stage where he clearly felt he had been undervalued.

The final event of the year was a revival of *The Mikado* at the Savoy pending the production of the new Gilbert and Sullivan work. The show proved as popular as ever and filled houses for the four months required.

The provincial scene was literally bursting with musical comedy during 1895. Tours of the most popular shows proliferated – *A Gaiety Girl* and *The Lady Slavey* each ran three tours and Carte put out no fewer than four of *His Excellency*. Other favourites like *Little Christopher Columbus* and *Morocco Bound* could still be seen and Carte also supplied a steady diet of Savoy opera. *The Gay Parisienne*, though still awaiting a London showing, had two companies playing in the provinces and it was joined in July by another provincially bred musical of major importance called *The New Barmaid*.

The New Barmaid was in the line of *The Lady Slavey* and *The Gay Parisienne* with which it shared a number of important characteristics. Its plot was straightforward, providing plenty of opportunity for comedy for a set of lively characters, its setting was modern, the songs bright and topical (with thirty-two in the original score) and it was written in an easy and natural style. The authors of the libretto were Frederick Bowyer (already responsible for much of Arthur Roberts' *Claude Duval*) and W. Edward Sprange, while the music, as in *The Lady Slavey*, was by John Crook.

The plot of *The New Barmaid* concerned yet another lost aristocratic child, and also the fortunes of the brothers Bertie and William White, the former an appalling nouveau riche and the latter a waiter at the Owlets Club. It is at this august institution that the first act takes place. Brenda, the retiring barmaid, is planning to make the most of some compromising letters from young Captain Lovebury by suing him for breach of promise, in spite of the fact she is actually married to William. Lovebury's real affections are bestowed on Ethel Joy, the new barmaid of the title. To the club come in turn the awful Bertie and Colonel Claymore whose child is missing. It seems that Brenda is that child and she is taken off to Claymore's home in triumph as the club is raided in a rousing first-act finale. The second act, three years later, shows Claymore regretting his 'found' child. Brenda is lording it dreadfully and spending extravagantly while setting her cap at Lovebury. Bertie White is now a waiter, having gone through his fortune, while William is rich, having made a mint in South Africa. Of course, it is Ethel Joy who is really the missing child and everyone (except Brenda) is delighted when William puts everything straight and Lovebury is able to marry the real Miss Claymore.

The plot was a derivative skeleton upon which to hang Crook's cheerful numbers and a whole lot of fun, principally from the horrid Bertie (Joseph B. Montague) and the jolly William (Arthur Alexander). Several of the numbers became instantly popular and *The New Barmaid* was clearly seen to be just the thing for provincial audiences. It toured principal dates until the new year when it was taken to London's Avenue Theatre for a run. After a good season in town it continued to tour and, like *The Lady Slavey*, became an annual feature of the touring scene for a long period of years.

Another new provincial piece was *The School Girl*, conceived as a vehicle for the little American actress, Minnie Palmer, who had been so overwhelmingly successful with *My Sweetheart*. In spite of her 35 years the diminutive Miss Palmer continued to play very juvenile roles and the role of Little Miss Loo was particularly devised for her by George Manchester (probably a pseudonym for *My Sweetheart* author William Gill). The play was presented in Cardiff and toured with London as its ultimate goal but it never reached town although it was toured successfully for several seasons and also put in a brief appearance on Broadway. As with *My Sweetheart*, Miss Palmer picked songs from where she liked to add to the new material composed by Albert Maurice, and there were frequent changes in the show's musical content. *The School Girl* was not a piece in the modern style, being constructed solely to showcase its star, and its longwinded and silly book was of no significance in what was essentially a one-woman variety show.

The year's shorter pieces included a couple of novelties. At the Opera Comique Nellie Farren went into management with a double bill of comedy and burlesque, the latter in the shape of a parody of the piece of the moment, *Trilby*. *A Model Trilby* was a far-fetched piece of nonsense in the old tradition of burlesque, written by Charlie Brookfield and Bill Yardley with music by Meyer Lutz, in which Svengali succeeds in wrecking the pretty voice of Trilby/Kate Cutler. Miss Cutler's performance of the provocatively titled 'The Altogether' and a barefoot dance by seven chorines stood alongside Robb Harwood's impersonation of Tree/Svengali as the best features of what was essentially a heavy and over-elaborate mixture of rhyme and precious prose. In spite of all the goodwill which the public bore towards Nellie Farren, *A Model Trilby* and its first half *Nannie* were not of sufficient quality to lead the venture to success. The play failed first and was replaced by a James Tanner piece, *Madame*, which proved even worse, and the two pieces were removed unmourned on 1 February after *A Model Trilby* had staggered through two and a half months of performances.

On a smaller scale, husband and wife team Seymour Hicks and Ellaline Terriss combined as authors of a tiny duologue called *Papa's Wife* which Miss Terriss and Arthur Playfair performed as a curtain raiser to *His Excellency*. The musical content of the piece consisted of a song for Miss Terriss, two duets and a dance. It proved quite adequate for its purposes and Hicks and his wife revived it frequently as a forepiece or a benefit item.

1895 was a sad landmark in the history of the shorter musical piece. Although the operetta was now used virtually only as a curtain raiser, and that increasingly rarely, it had, at one stage been a well-considered and much more substantial form. The chief purveyors of all that had been the best in operetta writing had, of course, been Thomas and Priscilla German Reed whose entertainments with John Parry and later with Corney Grain and Alfred German Reed had featured the one-act form so successfully over three decades. Parry and Thomas Reed had passed away, but the German Reed entertainment at St George's Hall had continued in spite of falling attendances occasioned by a change in public taste and moral attitudes but also, unfortunately, by a fall in standards from the early years of the Entertainments when Reed was able to produce works supplied by the very best writers and composers in the country.

Within a period of eight days in March of 1895 the three remaining members of the direction of the German Reed establishment died: Alfred, aged 48, followed two days later by his friend, Grain (50), and less than a week after that by his mother, the famous Priscilla Horton who had begun the whole affair with her Illustrative Gatherings at St Martin's Hall, Long Acre. The English operetta, for which the Gallery of Illustration and later St George's Hall had provided the focal point, had been a considerable influence in the forming of the musical plays and farces of the triumphant turn-of-the-century years. Through years of extravagant comic operas and of overwhelming French influence, of broad and artificial burlesques and almost bookless extravaganzas, the operetta had kept alive the essentially English, modern-dress comical and/or farcical pieces to which musical writers were to return – if in a rather different and less dignified guise. With the deaths of the last of the German Reed team, English operetta, already moribund and having outlived a general popularity, succumbed definitively. There were attempts to continue the tradition at St George's Hall, by Rutland Barrington and the publishers Joseph Williams among others, but no-one could fill the unique position occupied by the Reeds and the hall became the home of different kinds of entertainment, including the famous Promenade Concert series under Sir Henry Wood.

1895 also saw the death of another colourful and important figure of the British musical theatre. 'Teddy' Solomon was conducting rehearsals of *The Taboo* when he was taken ill and, quite unexpectedly, within a few days, at the age of thirty-nine, he died. Solomon had been a prolific composer, never quite as well regarded by the public as he might have been and certainly not as well considered as he thought he should have been. The flamboyant Teddy had lived his life at breakneck speed and his love affairs were the joy of the gossips and the paragraphists. His much publicised bigamous marriage to Lillian Russell had hit the headlines in a way that none of of his shows had; his final marriage to another beautiful actress, Kate Everleigh, had been scarcely noticed. But Solomon's career had gone that way. His greatest theatrical success remained his first, the comic opera *Billee Taylor* composed in 1880 and still, at his death, being currently toured in Britain. Of his other works, some such as *Claude Duval*, *The Red Hussar* and *The Vicar of Bray* had earned some success, but his most complete work and the one which gave him his longest West End run was *The Nautch Girl,* written with George Dance for D'Oyly Carte. Unfortunately the Solomon/Dance alliance was not continued further and over the last years of his life the composer failed to place any of the full-length pieces which he turned out. At his death he left a number of unperformed works of which only a few songs contributed to the musical pot-pourri score of *On the March* would reach a public. Solomon had been principally a composer of light comic opera, but he had proved his ability to compose a popular song in the modern music-hall manner and he should have been able to turn to the new kind of musical comedy writing in the same way as Ivan Caryll and Meyer Lutz had. Sadly, he did not, and his last years saw him limited to interpolating the odd song into other people's scores to no particular effect.

Sir Arthur Sullivan claimed that Solomon was the nearest parallel to Bizet that he could think of in Britain and declared that, had he been given a proper musical education, he might have written the English equivalent of *Carmen*. Lionel Monckton confessedly based himself on Solomon and Sullivan, and he and Jimmy Glover told of copying out the little composer's scores as an educational example in their early days. But Teddy Solomon lingered long only in the minds of his fellow musicians–insufficiently appreciated to the end.

1895

0154 **THE TABOO** a fantastic opera in two acts. Libretto by Mason Carnes. Music by R. Ethel Harraden. First produced in an amateur production at Leamington 22 May, 1894. Produced at the Trafalgar Theatre under the management of Horace Sedger 19 January, 1895 for a run of 7 performances closing 26 January, 1895.

Papkaio . . . . .Harry Paulton
Timaru . . . . .Wilfred Howard
Ranoro . . . . .Kelson Trueman
Bigomoko. . . . . .George Humphrey
Septimus Octopus Sharp. . . . . .Frank Wyatt
Whangahia . . . . .Helena Dalton
Whangathaia . . . . .Maud Maude
Whangayonde . . . . .Bertha Meyers
Wattatauka . . . . .Mme Amadi
Orama . . . . .Lettie Searle
Pateena .Nellie Murray
Kiwi . . . . .Dorothy Wilmot
Vestida de Culteria y Compania . . . . . .Lizzie St Quinten

Md: Barter Johns

0155 **AN ARTIST'S MODEL** a comedy with music in two acts by Owen Hall. Lyrics by Harry Greenbank. Music by Sidney Jones. Additional songs by Joseph & Mary Watson, Paul Lincke, Frederick Rosse and Henry Hamilton. Produced at Daly's Theatre under the management of George Edwardes 2 February, 1895. Transferred to the Lyric Theatre 28 May, 1895. Closed at the Lyric Theatre 6 September, 1895 and reopened in a second edition at Daly's Theatre 28 September, 1895. Closed 28 March, 1896 after a total run of 392 performances.

Adèle . . . . .Marie Tempest (Isabel Reddick) (Alison Skipworth)/Florence Perry/ Louise Beaudet
Lady Barbara Cripps. . . . . .Leonora Braham/Kate Hodson/Ethel Hope/Mrs Edmund Phelps/Maud Hobson?
Lucien .Nina Cadiz/Nellie Curtis/Lydia Flopp
Jessie . . . . .Marie Studholme/Alice Davis
Geraldine. . . . . .Hetty Hamer/Alice Davis
Amy Cripps . . . . .Louie Pounds/Lettice Fairfax/Laura Kearney/Sophie Elliot
Jane. . . . . .Sybil Grey/Alison Skipworth
Miss Manvers (Laura) . . . . .Nellie Gregory
Daisy Vane . . . . .Letty Lind/Marie Studholme/Decima Moore?/Lydia Flopp
Rudolph Blair . . . . .C. Hayden Coffin
Sir George St Alban . . . . .Eric Lewis/E. W. Gardiner/Frank Walsh/ Charles Ryley

Archie Pendillon . . . . Yorke Stephens/*out*
Algernon St Alban . . . . Joe Farren Soutar/Raymond Roze/ Alfred C. Seymour/W. Louis Bradfield
Earl of Thamesmead . . . . Lawrance d'Orsay/R. Jones/Rudge Harding
Carbonnet . . . . Maurice Farkoa
Apthorpe . . . . Gilbert Porteous/Will Bishop
Maddox. . . . . Conway Dixon/Sydney Ellison
James Cripps . . . . E. M. Robson/John Le Hay /Huntley Wright/Leedham Bantock/Fred Wright Jr
Smoggins . . . . William Blakeley/Walter Groves/T. P. Haynes/Harry Monkhouse
Mme Amélie . . . . Lottie Venne/Pattie Browne/ Winifred Dennis/Lydia Thompson/ Juliette Nesville/Sybil Grey
Rose . . . . Kate Cannon
Christine . . . . Alice Davis/*out*
Ruby . . . . Kate Adams
Violet . . . . Lettice Fairfax/*out*
add Mathilde . . . . Ethel Neild/Madge Rossell/Margaret Fraser
Helen. . . . . Lucille Foote
Lucille . . . . Lydia Flopp/*out*
Claire. . . . . Mary Collette/*out*
Lily . . . . Mimi St Cyr
Hatfield . . . . Sydney Ellison/S. Mordy
Yvette . . . . Cossie Shalders
Maud Cripps. . . . . Violet Lloyd
Lena . . . . Lettice Fairfax/*out*

Dir: James T. Tanner; md: Sidney Jones/Carl Kiefert/Leopold Wenzel; ch: John D'Auban/Lefranc; sc: Glendenning & George Lock; cos: Fisher, Redfern, Swan & Edgar, Mme Marie, Jays, Vanité, Scott Son & Claxton, Morris Angel, Arthur Firmin

Produced at the Broadway Theatre, New York under the management of Al Hayman and Charles Frohman 23 December, 1895 for a run of 56 performances.
Nellie Stewart (AD), Gladys Homfrey (LADY), Nina Cadiz (LUCIEN), Cissie Neil (JES), Alison Skipworth (GER), Louie Pounds (AMY), Marie Studholme (DAISY), John Coates (RUD), Percy Marshall (StA), Harry Eversfield (ALG), Lawrance d'Orsay (EARL), Maurice Farkoa (CARB), Gilbert Porteous (AP), Frank Lambert (MADD), E. Lovat Frazer (HATFIELD), Fred Wright Jr (CRIPPS), E. W. Garden (SM), Christine Mayne (AM), Minnie Cathcart (ROSE), Lillie Pounds (VI), Amy Reimer (RUBY), Alice Nixon (MATH), Madge Greet (LUC), Elsie Dare (CL), Lucy Golding (MAUD), Lucy Nixon (LENA). Dir: Sydney Ellison

0156 **GENTLEMAN JOE**, The Hansom Cabby. A musical farce in two acts by Basil Hood. Music by Walter Slaughter. Produced at the Prince of Wales Theatre by Henry Lowenfeld 2 March, 1895, for a run of 391 performances closing 28 March, 1896.

Gentleman Joe . . . . Arthur Roberts (Eric Thorne)
Lord Donnybrook . . . . William E. Philp (Wilfred Wynnstay)/Roland Cunningham
Mr Hughie Jaqueson . . . . Evelyn Vernon
Mr Ralli-Carr . . . . E. H. Kelly/St John Hamund
William, a page boy . . . . Clara Jecks
Dawson . . . . Eric Thorne/Walter Brooke
James, a footman. . . . . Picton Roxburgh/Philip Yorke
Mr Pilkington Jones . . . . W. H. Denny
Mrs Ralli-Carr . . . . Aida Jenoure/Phyllis Broughton

Hon Mabel Kavanagh . . . . Kate Cutler/Lettie Searle/Audrey Ford
Miss Lalage Potts . . . . Sadie Jerome (Violet Neville)
Miss Pilkington Jones . . . . Carrie Benton/May Adair/Florence Linton
Ada Pilkington Jones . . . . Ellas Dee (Attie Chester)/Kate Herman
Lucy Pilkington Jones . . . . Audrey Ford (Winnie Carl) (Susie Reimers)/Christine Salisbury
Amy Pilkington Jones . . . . Eva Ellerslie
Emma . . . . Kitty Loftus (Ellas Dee)
Photographer . . . . Walter F. Brooke
Postman . . . . G. Danby/S. Mantell/Ernest A. Thiel
Cook . . . . Annie Wilson/Adelaide Newton

with May Adair, Ethel Arundel, Molly Bawn, Freda Coventry, Phyllis Crewe, Lilly Clifden, Milly Coles, Emmie Fairfax, Dora Fenwick, Florence Gordon, Mina Goss, Lucille Grahame, Poppy Haines, Ethele Hawthorne, Simeta Marsden, Ray Maynotte, Maggie McIntosh, Minnie Ross, Aimée Rowe, Daisy Russell, Jenny Smart, Christine Salisbury, Ruby Stewart, Hamilton Sandford, Florence Turner, Hester Vincent, Florence Coles

Dir: Hugh Moss; md: Herbert Bunning; ch: Willie Warde; sc: T. E. Ryan & Joseph Harker; cos: Swan & Edgar &c.

From 7 November–27 March the burlesque *A Trilby Triflet* was interpolated, with the following cast:
Svengali: Arthur Roberts; Trilby: Kitty Loftus; Taffy: Philip Yorke; The Laird: W. H. Denny; Little Billie: Clara Jecks; Gecko: Eric Thorne.

Produced at Henry C. Miner's Fifth Avenue Theatre under the management of Henry Miner and M. B. Curtis 6 January, 1896 for a run of 10 performances.
M. B. Curtis/Willard Lee (JOE), Henry Hallam (DONNY), Arthur Pacie (HJ), Joseph C. Fay (R-C), Eugene B. Sanger (WM), Gus Bruno (DAW), John W. Lawes (JAS), George K. Fortescue (PJ), Carrie Roma (MRS R-C), Laura Moore (MABEL), Adelaide Worth (LALAGE), Leonora Cousens (MISS), Viola Fortescue (ADA), Marina Godoy (LUCY), Ida M. Godbold (AMY), Annie Meyers (EMMA), A. W. Maflin (PHOTO), Paul Dana (POST), Lillian Knowles (COOK), Louis Miller (IKEY), Wesley Johnstone (POLICEMAN), Charles F. Lang (FAKIR), Harry Brooks (CIOGLAS), L. H. Croxson (DUKE MARRIOTTE), Bergh Morrison (TOMMY ATKINS), Hillyer Burr (CHEF), William Dunbar (BAKER), Phila May (DICKIE STOCK), Camille Dagmar (DAN ELUDGES) Minnie Carleton (HAL FRANKS), Ione Newhall (ADOLPHUS LINN), Ena Welsh (NANETTE), Bertha King (IRENE), Grace Benedict (SLAVEY), Alberte True (HEAD NURSE), Myretta Waite (CHAMBERMAID), Leila Williams (GOVERNESS). Dir: Willard Lee

Produced at the Bijou Theatre, New York, under the management of Rudolph Aronson 30 January, 1896 for a run of 48 performances closing 29 February, 1896.
James T. Powers (JOE), David Torrance (DONNY), V. M. DeSilke (HJ), Louis de Lange (R-C), Dorothy Usher (WM), William Cullington (DAW), Arthur T. Foster (JAS), George K. Fortescue (PJ), Grace Huntington (MRS R-C), Ada Brooks (MABEL), Florence Irwin (LALAGE), Grace Belasco (MISS), Josie Allen (ADA), Fannie Briscoe (LUCY), Mabel Montgomery (AMY), Clara Wieland (EMMA), G. H. Brooks (PHOTO), Brownie Wells (COOK), May Levigne (TOM), Edna Lyle (GEORGE), Stella Alexander (LEONARD), Millie Rollins (HENRY). Dir: Richard Barker; md: Herman Perlet; ch: Rose Becket; sc: Elmer E. Swart, Arthur Voegtlin; cos: Miss Siedel

0157 **DANDY DICK WHITTINGTON** an opéra-bouffe in three acts by George R. Sims. Music by Ivan Caryll. Produced at the Avenue Theatre under the management of William Greet 2 March, 1895 for a run of 122 performances closing 9 July, 1895.

Sir Achilles Fitzwarren . . . . A. J. Evelyn
Lady Fitzwarren . . . . John F. Sheridan
Captain Fairfax . . . . James Barr/James Leverett/Roland Cunningham
Larry O'Brannagan . . . . Henry Wright/Frank Smithson
Koko Gaga . . . . Robert Pateman
Auguste . . . . Frederick Vaughan
Tom . . . . Harold Paterson
Phra Maha . . . . Henry N. Wenman

Alice Fitzwarren . . . . Ethel Haydon
Lola, Queen of the Arena . . . . Bertha Meyers
Sa Dee, Princess of Siam . . . . Gracie Whiteford
Willasee. . . . . Florence Levey
Nuntahtari . . . . Ellen Goss
Chantawee . . . . Maude Fisher/Lily MacIntyre
Jenny . . . . Irene Du Foye
Zoe . . . . Lydia Lisle
Nina . . . . Miss Morgan
Susan . . . . Miss Elcho
Song Kla . . . . J. McBride
Phung Tha . . . . E. Shale
Chanta Buree. . . . . Mr Wilkes
See Papat . . . . Mr Davies
Dick Whittington. . . . . May Yohe/Millie Hylton/Marie Alexander
Head Groom . . . . E. Plumpton
Dancers: Ethel Ashton, Rosa Bennett, Jeanne van Dalle, Ada Palmer/Nellie Palmer, Addie Witts, Rosa Schenk

Dir: Frank Parker; md: Landon Ronald/Victor Champion; ch: Willie Warde; sc: T. E. Ryan; cos: Edel

Toured by William Greet as *The Circus Boy*.

0158 **ALL ABROAD** a musical farce in two acts by Owen Hall and James T. Tanner. Lyrics by W. H. Risque. Music by Frederick Rosse. Additional music by George Capel, Edgar Ward and J. Philp. Produced under the management of Cissy Graham at Portsmouth 1 April, 1895 and toured through Hastings, Eastbourne, Manchester, Liverpool, Glasgow, Newcastle, etc (?). Opened at the Criterion Theatre under the management of Charles Wyndham 8 August for a run of 87 performances closing 2 November. Played Grand Theatre, Islington 4 November, then toured.

Mr Bowles . . . . Charles E. Stevens
Mr Beaver . . . . Horace Mills
Baron Fontenay . . . . Fred Emney/Herman de Lange/Alfred Maltby
Ernest. John Coates
Capshaw . . . . Lionel Rae/L. Johnson
Maurice Meurice . . . . Fred Rolph/C. P. Little/H. O. Clarey
Skeggs . . . . George Carroll
Charlie Feltop . . . . Charles Thorbourn/*out*
Riggie Andale . . . . Gerald Luke/R. Lister
Henry Hanshaw . . . . Percy Ashley/*out*
Boots . . . . Harry Norton/*out*
Connie . . . . Isa Bowman/Kate Cutler/May Edouin
Mme Montesquieu . . . . Minnie Jeffs/Ada Reeve
Chloe Feltop . . . . Mabel Love/Millie Thorne/*out*
Beatrice Vyse . . . . Gwynneth Boleyn/*out*
Eva Esdale . . . . Kathleen Seton/*out*
Nora Drummond. . . . . Helen Gallon/*out*
Aline Carthorpe . . . . Florence Angeloni/*out*
Edith Wyber . . . . Violet Grazia/*out*
May Aster . . . . Mildred Balfour/Lena Brophy/Edna Grace
Dora Dexter . . . . Emilie Price/*out*
Dancer . . . . Gertrude Briscoe
add Blanche Leonide . . . . Pierina Amella
Adolphe . . . . L. Johnson/Lionel Rae
Gendarme . . . . Cecil Frere
Jack Smythe . . . . Fred Garton
Tim Eltham . . . . R. Lister

The London cast also included the dancers Rosa (*sic*) Boote, Olive Dalmour, Rose Martin, Pattie Thornhill & William Vokes, with Louise Lister, Daisy Gilpin, May Romney, Lydia Lisle, Florence Cameron, Ada Maxwell, Maud Michael-Watson, Marguerite Osland, Bessie Pelissier, Rose Heilbron,/Magdalene Lockie,/Marjorie Clark; Messrs H. Linwood, Charles Crook, L. Wennesley, E. Calverwell, W. G. Sheehan, L. Winning/A. Luke.

Md: Carl Kiefert; cos: Redmayne, Alias, Pitts & Richards, Grace Watkin, Mme Eroom, Thomas Giles & Co., Morris Angel.

Produced at the Court Theatre under the management of Arthur Chudleigh 2 January, 1896 for a run of 21 performances closing 23 January, 1896.
Willie Edouin (BOW), Fred Kaye (BEA), David James (FONT), Templar Saxe (ERN), Lionel Rae (CAP), Charles Sugden (MM), L. Johnson (AD), George Elliston (SK), Cecil Frere (POLICEMAN), Charles Mills (JACK), May Edouin (CON), Miss Blaney (BESSIE), Daisy Bryer (LOTTY), Maude Trautner (AMY), Edna Grace (GLADYS), Ethel Borlase (YVETTE), Grace Palotta (MME); with Jenny Holland, Olive Dalmour, Miss Murray, Maud Wilmot (Dancers), Marguerite Osland, Bessie Pelissier, Lydia Lisle, Helena Waverley, Maud Michael-Watson, Mary Leonard, Sybil Awdry, Augusta Dewsnap; Misses Waldorf, Walpole, Christian, Mori & Darlington; Messrs Eric Phillips, H. Brereton, H. W. Mortimer, Wilson, C. R. Stewart, J. Brand.
Dir: Willie Edouin; md: Carl Kiefert

0159 **THE NEW BARMAID** a musical play in two acts by Frederick Bowyer and W. Edward Sprange. Music by John Crook. Produced at the Opera House, Southport, under the management of Alexander Loftus and Francis Howard 1 July, 1895 and toured through Blackpool, Douglas, Nottingham, Manchester, Oldham, Brighton, Metropole, Pavilion, Kilburn, Preston, Birmingham, Liverpool, Burnley, Aberdeen x2, Sheffield, Leicester, Walsall,?, Halifax, Middlesborough, Hull, to 7 December. Recommenced 26 December at Cheltenham through Worcester,?, Hastings, Eastbourne, Reading, Northampton, Coventry, Cambridge/-, Walsall, Wolverhapton, Derby, Rochdale, Huddersfield, Oxford, Bath, Parkhurst, Aldershot, Richmond, Reading, Southampton, Jersey, Guernsey/Bournemouth, Hastings, Folkestone, Salford, ?, Lincoln, Grimsby, Scarborough, S. Shields, Darlington, Stockton, Harrogate, Bolton, Warrington, Wigan, Crewe, Ashton-under-Lyne, Birkenhead, Chester, Blackburn,?, Ipswich, Gateshead, S. Shields, Jarrow, Chorley, Stalybridge, Keighley, to 5 December; recommenced 23 December at Buxton and continued. The tour became Alexander Loftus & Ernest Oswald's, later Eade Montefiore's and then Mrs J. W. Gordon's. On 6 April, 1896 Alexander Loftus sent out a renewed company from Sheffield which ran to 27 June, then 20 July to 28 November, 1896 continuing into 1897. A No. 1 tour under the management of Austin Fryers began 25 May, 1896 at Kidderminster, and a second No. 1 tour under the same management in September, 1896, both continuing into 1897.

Captain Lovebury . . . . Wilfred Howard/Wilberforce Franklin/ J. Orde Knox/
Lt. Bradley . . . . Victor M. Seymour/C. Douglas/ Hugh Glendon/Mary Thorne/
Col. Claymore . . . . C. L. Wilford/James E. Thompson/ Alexander Romanes/Samuel Laing/Charlie Douglas/Hugh Seton/
Bertie White . . . . Joseph B. Montague/W. Groves Watson/Cecil Lawrence/A. E. Chapman/Alfred Donohoe
William White . . . . Arthur Alexander/Alexander Loftus/ James Stevenson
M. Bonsor . . . . Harold Coulter/Maurice Drew/Harry J. Butler
Gussie . . . . Michael Dure/H. Perry/Hetty Montefiore/Marie Fontaine/May Linden/Marie Baines
Inspector Hart . . . . F. J. Walton/Alexander Romanes
Club Porter. . . . . Henry Bishop/Mr Wilson &c.
Lady Moulton . . . . Florence Lynn/Annie Brophy
Dora . . . . Julia Kent/Lizzie Aubrey/Maude

	Bowden/Bertie Clyde/Hetty Montefiore/ Rachel Lowe
Mabel	Marjorie Johnson/Maude Langton/ Phemie Barnes/
Tommy	Edith Denton/Bertie Clyde/Marie Fontaine
Brenda Louth	Reika Ronalds/Ida St George/Hetty Montefiore/Marie Loreth
Ethel Joy	Amy Augarde/Ethel Tinsley/Mary Thorne/Agnes de la Porte/Florence Baines/Nannie Meade

with Marjorie Johnson, Elsie Johnson, Lily Johnson, Ethel Tinsley, Ada Peppiate, Gertrude Thomas, Josephine Young, Elinor St Louin, Estelle Dudley, Rosie Claire/Lily Piercy, Violet Raymaur, Dorothy Manners, Constance Arnott, Grace Charlton, Georgie Beaufort, Alice Anstey, Mabel Ferrar, Maud Ferrar, Alice Russell, Beatrice Ashton, H. Neville, Mr Glendon, Mr Bangs, Mr Wilson, Florence White (pd), Ruby Hallier, Nora Cecil, Wentworth Young

Md: J. C. Shepherd/Augustus T. MacInnes

The new Howard & Loftus tour starred Wilfred Howard (CAPT), Charles Rowan/Fitzroy Morgan (LT), Hugh Seton/Charles Esdale/Charles Rowan (COL), Joseph B. Montague/Stratton Mills (BW), Willie Scott/Alexander Loftus (WW), George Paulton/Walter McEwan (BONS), Minna Louis (LADY), Dolly Harmer (DORA), M. Grantham/Evelyn Graham/Cornelie Charles/Ada Seymour/? Evelyn Grantham (BRENDA), Amy Augarde (EJ)

Austin Fryers' No. 1 tour starred Harold Perry/Austin Fryers (CAPT), Edward Crofton/E. Langley (LT), A. Steffens Hardy/H. J. Broughton (COL), J. G. Taylor/Forsyth Bruce/C. H. Kenny (BW), Edgar Dereve/Harry S. Dacre/Harold Perry (WW), James FitzJames (BONS), Phyllis Desley/Marion Howard (LADY), Amy Grundy (DORA), Jenny Beauville/Reika Ronalds/Sophie Scotti (BRENDA), Ilma Norina (EJ). Md: Henry Vernon

Produced at the Avenue Theatre under the management of Francis Howard and Alexander Loftus 12 February, 1896. Transferred to the Opera Comique after 120 performances in a new edition 8 June, 1896. Closed 3 July, 1896 after a total of 138 performances.

Captain Lovebury	Harrison Brockbank
Lt. Bradley	Charles Rowan/Fitzroy Morgan/Jack Thompson
Col. Claymore	C. L. Wilford
Bertie White	J. J. Dallas/Joseph B. Montague
William White	John L. Shine/E. J. Lonnen/Arthur Alexander
M. Bonsor	Ells Dagnall/Walter McEwan
Gussie Laverstoke	Jack Thompson/Mr Seymour
Inspector Hart	Mr Brandreth
Club Porter	Mr Carling
Lady Moulton	Maria Saker
Dora	Lottie Collins (Maud Bowden)/ Jennie Rogers/Lillian Menelly
Mabel	Edith Denton
Brenda Louth	Maggie Hunt
Ethel Joy	Agnes de la Porte/Lottie Collins/Jenny Rogers
Tommy	Agnes Ingreville/Mr Rawden
Kitty	Ethel Gain
Laura	Marie Alexander/Agnes Ingreville
add Alice	Lillian Menelly/*out*

Pds: Edith Denton, George Elliston with Misses Singlehurst, Alexander, Trevor, Graves, Gain, May Butler, Douglas, Wilson, Leslie, Ross, Franks, Carlisle, Reed, Phillimore, J. Butler, Hamilton, Clair, Beaufort, Leigh, Jessop, Meikle, Tremaine, Temple, Leslie, L. Wilson, Percy; Messrs Gillett, Winning, B. Wensley, Seymour, L. Wensley, Stanislaus, Mignot, Rawdon, Pearce, Bentley, Charles, Williams, Cane and Bruce.

Dir: George Capel; md: Ernest Bucalossi/Howard Talbot; ch: Will Bishop & John D'Auban; sc: W. T. Hemsley; cos: Comelli &c.

1160 **THE BRIC À BRAC WILL** a comic opera in 3 acts by S. J. Adair Fitzgerald and Hugh Moss. Additional lyrics by Harry Greenbank and W. Sapte Jr. Music by Emilio Pizzi. Produced at the Lyric Theatre under the management of Ernest Oswald 28 October, 1895 for a run of 62 performances closing 28 December, 1895.

Duke Enrico Lantazaro . . . . Charles Conyers
Antonio . . . . Frank Wyatt
Paolo . . . . Harrison Brockbank
The Doge of Venice . . . . J. J. Dallas
Barnaba . . . . E. W. Royce
Roberto . . . . Frank H. Celli
Beppo . . . . Stanley Patterson
Mudillo . . . . Watty Brunton Jr
Watchman . . . . Horn Conyers
Chiara . . . . Susie Vaughan/Phoebe Cohen
Lisette . . . . Fanny Marriot
Sylvia . . . . Kate Drew/Florence St John

with Louise Forrester, Nancie Ellison, Nellie Yorke, Winifred Davies, Ada Lennox, Beatrice Bailey, Edith Merton, Marie Romanes, Ada Allen, Lillian Stead, Honorine Schofield, Agnes Matz, Gertrude Lonsdale, Heloise Osland, Bessie Alleyne, Ada Maxwell, Cordelia Knight, Alice Ancliffe, Amy Douglas, Emily Greene, Phoebe Cohen, Mabel Grey, Agnes Verney, Madelaine da Costa; Messrs H. E. Garrod, Edward Shale, R. Beresford, T. France, G. Wells, J. W. Birtley, P. H. Kingsbury, T. T. Moss, C. Flynn, T. Carling, T. J. Montelli, Alexander Romanes, P. Percival, G. Phillips, E. Rosoman, J. Rix, H. Dorien, R. Davies, G. Scholefield, H. Trevor.

Dancers: Mable Tilson/,Ada Wilkinson/,Phyllis Desmond, Rose Doris/,Kate Doris/,Connie Desmond, Cissie King, Amy Ward, Dollie Cook, Lillie Wilkinson, Jessie Collier, Kate Wyndham, Alice Tyler.

Dir: Hugh Moss; md: Arthur E. Godfrey; ch: Kate Paradise; sc: W. T. Hemsley and Bruce Smith; cos: Karl

A VILLAGE VENUS or The Merry Mashing Major, a military musical comedy in two acts by Victor Stevens. Additional music and lyrics by Carl Kiefert, E. Boyd-Jones, Harry Dacre and Felix Leaman. Produced at the Grand Theatre, Nottingham under the management of Herbert Shelley 5 August, 1895 and toured in repertoire.

Major Muddle . . . . Victor Stevens
Bertie Glendon . . . . Herbert Shelley
Tom Froth . . . . Mr Royce/John Wilkinson
Inspector Grab . . . . A. G. Spry
Isobel . . . . Helene Pillans/Rhoda Larkin
Winifred . . . . Maud Chichester
Aunt Tabitha . . . . Bessie Glover
Lady Beattie May . . . . Olive Varley
Hon. Kate Osborne . . . . Katie Frane
Hon. Ethel Herbert . . . . Bessie Shirley
Lady Starkey . . . . Maud Trevalyan/Alice Boundy
Marmaduke . . . . Rhoda Larkin
Lord Dampshire . . . . C. Ronald Bantock
Archie Fitzraymond . . . . Spenser Kelly
Simon the Cellarman . . . . F. Dudman Bromwich
Daisy Bell . . . . Florence Trevalion
Dorothy Dean . . . . Miss Gordon
Annie Rooney . . . . Gertrude Grey
Ta ra ra boom de ay . . . . Grace Mortimer
Trooper Buckley . . . . Twyford Jones
Trooper Cavendish . . . . Daniel Roach
Trooper Murphy . . . . Bob Strangeways
Trooper Riley . . . . Alf Riley

with the Boundy-Glen Continental Quartet

Dir: Victor Stevens; md: Felix Leaman; sc: E. G. Banks; cos: Derry & Toms etc.

A MODEL TRILBY or A Day Or Two After Du Maurier. A burlesque in one act by C. H. E. Brookfield and William Yardley. Music by W. Meyer Lutz. Produced at the Opera Comique under the management of Nellie Farren 16 November, 1895 with *Nannie* and subsequently with *Madame* (7 December). Withdrawn 1 February, 1896.

Svengali. .Robb Harwood
Taffy . . . . .Joe Farren Soutar
Jacko . . . . .Fred Storey/Mr Horniman
The Laird . . . . .C. P. Little
Little Billee. . . . . .George Antley
Thomas Bagot . . . . .E. H. Kelly
Durien . . . . .Eric Lewis
Trilby. . . . . .Kate Cutler
Mme Vinard . . . . .Helen Vicary/F. Montgomery
Mrs Bagot . . . . .Mary Stuart
Musette. . . . . .Greville Moore
Mimi . . . . .Eva Hamblin
Zouzou .Millie le Capilaine
Dodor. .May Romney
add The Stranger. . . . . .E. Scott
with Madge Greet/Maud Lindo/Maude Rundell, Lillian Hubbard, Nora Neville, Rose Vera, Marie Lovel, Beatrice Dunbar, Marie Beevor.

Dir: James T. Tanner; md: W. Meyer Lutz; ch: Willie Warde; sc: E. G. Banks; cos: A. & Ida Chasemore

GIDDY GALATEA an operatic trifle in one act by Henry Edlin. Music by Edward Jones. Produced at the Duke of York's Theatre as a forepiece to *Her Advocate* 15 November, 1895. Withdrawn 30 November.

Galatea Green . . . . .Minnie Thurgate
Phidias Phixum. . . . . .Forbes Dawson
Pygmalion Potts . . . . .T. P. Haynes
Daphne Potts. . . . . .Annie Dwelley

A NEAR SHAVE a musical farce in one act by George D. Day. Music by Edward Jones. Produced at the Court Theatre 6 May, 1895 as a forepiece to *Vanity Fair*. Withdrawn 27 July. Restaged 23 September. Withdrawn 1 November, 1895.

Ebenezer Addleshaw . . . . .G. W. Anson/William Wyes/H. N. Ray
Josiah Giggins . . . . .H. O. Clarey
Arabella Pettifer . . . . .Emmeline Orford/Blanche Wolsely

Md: Edward Jones

Played at a matinée at Terry's Theatre 13 June.

PAPA'S WIFE a musical dualogue by Seymour Hicks and F. C. Phillips. Music by Ellaline Terriss. Produced at the Lyric Theatre 26 January, 1895. Revived 23 February, 1895 as a forepiece to *His Excellency*.

Kate Wetherby . . . . .Ellaline Terriss
Gerald Singleton . . . . .Arthur Playfair
William. . . . . .Frank Morton

THE NEWEST WOMAN a musical comedietta by H. Chance Newton. Music by Georges Jacobi. Produced at the Avenue Theatre 4 April, 1895 at a matinée.

THE TWENTIETH CENTURY GIRL or The Weaker Vessel. A musical comedy by Claude Trevalyan. Produced at the Theatre Royal, Norwich 26 December, 1895 and toured by R. B. Caverley's Company with *An Adamless Eden*.

LOVE AND WAR a nautical comic opera in 3 acts by Lawrence Olde. Lyrics by Lawrence Olde and Basil Gotto. Music by Evan Kefe. Produced at Portsmouth under the management of E. H. Lockwood 17 June, 1895 and toured.

Admiral Hornblower . . . . .Harry Halley
Prince de St Bris . . . . .Windham Guise
Colonel Sir Everett Lascelles . . . . . . .Walter Ashley
Captain Sinclair Lascelles . . . . .John Coates
Vicomte Rigaud . . . . .L. Wensley
Phelum O'Tiger . . . . .Dan Fitzgerald
Bottle Bill. . . . . .Hampton Gordon
Lady Lascelles . . . . .Sophie Harris
Jessie Hornblower . . . . .Josephine Findlay
Princess de St Bris . . . . .Pierina Amella
Maraquita .Nellie Cozens
Fanchette .Susie Nainby
Mrs Jenkins . . . . .Dora Birkett
Kitty . . . . .Edith Hunter

THE PROFESSOR a musical duologue by Rutland Barrington. Music by Edward Solomon. Produced at St George's Hall under the management of Henry Reed 15 July, 1895 with *Happy Arcadia* and *Soured and Sweetened*, the latter replaced by *The Usual Remedy*. Withdrawn 10 August, 1895.

Professor Wünderbaren . . . . .Rutland Barrington
Lady Gladys Mudfordshire . . . . .Elsie Cross

BOBBO an operetta by Adrian Ross and James T. Tanner. Music by F. Osmond Carr. Produced at the Prince's Theatre, Manchester under the management of Cissy Graham 12 September, 1895 and toured in a triple bill with *A Pantomime Rehearsal* and *Faithful Jeames*.

Mlle Adèle . . . . .Maud Boyd
Tavernier .Mr Gregory

BUTTERCUP AND DAISY a musical comedy in 3 acts by George Dance based on his play of the same name. Music by Arthur Richards &c. Produced at Kilburn 9 September, 1895.

QWONG HI a farcical comedy (musical oriental skit) by Fenton Mackay. Songs by John Crook and J. A. McWeeney &c. Produced at Bristol under the management of Willie Edouin 1 April, 1895.
Subsequently produced at Terry's Theatre under the management of Willie Edouin in an enlarged version 27 June, 1895 and at the Avenue Theatre 25 July, 1895.

THE TOURIST or Here, There And Everywhere by Montague Turner and W. E. Sprange. Lyrics by Sylvia Carvalho. Music by Thomas Hunter. Produced at the Prince's Theatre, Portsmouth 5 November, 1895.

1896

The year 1896 brought a veritable explosion of new British musicals onto both the West End and provincial scenes. Sixteen new pieces – fifteen home-grown and one foreign, *The Little Genius* from Austria – made their appearance in London, and as many again were produced for the provincial and touring circuits. Musical comedy in its various forms was decidedly the theatrical genre of the moment. By now, the lightly structured modern music, spectacle and laughter pieces favoured by George Edwardes had relegated the comic opera and burlesque forms into an almost total oblivion, taking from them such elements as they pleased to decorate the amalgam of ballad and music-hall song, of glamour and comedy, that was the modern musical.

At the turn of the year Daly's, the Gaiety and the Prince of Wales, the three bastions of the musical play, were still occupied by their established hits, *An Artist's Model, The Shop Girl* and *Gentleman Joe*, while D'Oyly Carte's revival of *The Mikado* at the Savoy, although a stop-gap, was satisfying the lovers of comic opera. After the Court Theatre's unfortunate revival of *All Abroad* had quickly come and gone, the first débutante of the year (at the Avenue Theatre) was *The New Barmaid* which had been designed and composed as a provincial touring piece. Its first tour the previous year had proved so successful that its owners, Francis Howard and Alexander Loftus, had decided it was worth a London run. In spite of the show's impressive record to date, they were by no means assured in advance of success, and London's disappointing reaction to that enormous country favourite, *The Lady Slavey*, stood as a recent warning. *The Lady Slavey* had undergone severe surgery before being exposed to West End audiences but the managers and authors of *The New Barmaid*, in contrast, decided to retain their piece as it had been shown to the provinces. A little 'scandalous' publicity was used to heighten interest, as the first act was set in one of those dubious 'mixed' clubs to which theoretically no gentleman belonged and of which many a naughty tale was told. The act ended with the raiding of the club by police, a fact which added no little spice to the expectations of the lascivious.

If those who came with a debauched intent were disappointed in that expectation, they did find, however, plenty to give them genuine amusement. *The New Barmaid* was by no means a sophisticated piece. Its story was slight and the lively libretto anything but a literary masterpiece, but it had several important assets, the most conspicuous being a simple yet attractive plot, a lively and rollicking set of music-hall songs, and some highly accomplished people to put them over. Perhaps the greatest interest was aroused by the casting of Lottie Collins in the prominent, though peripheral, role of Dora, a lady journalist. Since the days when she had slayed the gilded youth of London with 'Ta-ra-ra-Boom-de-Ay!', Miss Collins had spent much of her time in America and confined her appearances in Britain to the variety stage. Now she returned to the

London musical theatre, and brought the house down with her performance of 'The Lady Journalist':

Since everyone to write a book most anxious seems to be,
Just follow my instructions to gain fame and £sd;
You use a mental Kodak and minutely photograph
Every section of society, its morals and its chaff!
Be tersely analytical, nor ever be afraid
To diagnose the darkest side, and call a spade a spade.
Use plenty of French epigrams, they have such power to charm,
With dashes and asterisks where the situation's warm.

With my pencil and my pocket-book
I'm ready for the fray,
And I make a note of everything
That comes along my way.
What's that? Down it goes!
It never must be missed,
It's naughty but it's copy for
The Lady Journalist!

If anyone offends you or askance at you may look,
You can have a lovely vengeance, for just put 'em in your book;
All their little peccadilloes you can greatly magnify,
And only thinly veil the names of people you descry.
As for plot, it doesn't matter, it is best to be without,
You should always leave your readers in a state of mental doubt.
Never mind if critics slate you and exclaim 'unfit to read',
Everyone is sure to buy you, you're certain to succeed!

Miss Collins had lost none of her popularity, and her presence in the cast was a large plus for the production.

The romantic side of the plot involving the two barmaids and the fickle Captain Lovebury took very much second place to the comic episodes in which the brothers, Bertie and William White, were involved. The fall of the obnoxious Bertie and the simultaneous rise of patient William from club porter to diamond millionaire gave much scope for attractive fooling and the comedians J. J. Dallas and J. L. Shine took every advantage of them. Dallas, in particular, was fortunate in being supplied with an outstanding number in the topical song 'A little Bit of Sugar for the Bird' which took a look at some of the tempting things of town to the accompaniment of the quaint refrain:

Sweet-sweet, tweet-tweet,
Isn't it a funny thing . . .

This song proved to be an enormous hit, Dallas' second consecutive 'strike' after 'The nervous Man' in *The Bric à Brac Will.* In fact, shortly after the run of *The New Barmaid* began, Dallas advertised that he had equalled his own 'record' (established by the former song) by having to give sixteen encore verses of 'A little Bit of Sugar' at one evening performance. Sixteen was rather unusual, but it was true that never a night passed where three or four extra verses at the very least were not demanded. Eventually the song became so widely popular that the management began to advertise its title as a subtitle to the play. To add to these two favourite pieces there was a whole line of other songs to which the audience responded more than favourably – Dallas and Shine's singing of the brotherly duo 'Mother was the Mother of us Both', 'A Bicycle Marriage', 'Love's old Song', 'Oh, the River', 'Mashonaland', 'Just Bread and Cheese and Kisses' and 'The waning Year' all bore witness to John Crook's ability to write both a rousing popular chorus song and a pretty, light sentimental ballad.

Another feature of *The New Barmaid* was the speciality dances for which Will Bishop and the endlessly inventive John D'Auban contributed the choreography. The highlight was a Black and White pas de deux danced by George Elliston and Edith Denton. Miss Denton gave the scandal-seekers a little of what they had come for with a vigorous series of splits and high kicks which were not universally approved. *The Era* reported that '[she] raised her leg in a perpendicular position by her head . . [which was] voted vulgar and unpleasant'. In general, however, the newspaper reaction to the show was largely appreciative. *The Times* reported:

> The piece achieved a more than respectable first night success. [It is] one of those nondescript productions which can hardly be said to owe their being to any particular author or authors . . . it is, properly speaking, a variety entertainment . . the story is lost sight of and its incidentals which, in the hand mainly of Miss Lottie Collins as a Lady Journalist and Mr Dallas as an elderly 'masher', are of the liveliest description . .

The Era commented:

> In our notice of *The New Barmaid* at the Theatre Metropole, Camberwell, we remarked that it contained all the elements of popularity – plenty of variety, good comic and topical songs, and pretty melody. Merit is relative, and what may please audiences in the provinces and in the suburbs may not be quite so well suited to the more fastidious tastes of the West End; but there is much in the musical play . . . that is calculated to amuse any audience. The wit may not be very refined nor the music particularly 'catchy', but there is a sufficiency of fun of a certain order and the melodies, if they do not bear the stamp of distinct originality are agreeable and effective.

The Stage referred, rather harshly, to the 'thinness of the plot and the poor quality of the book' but declared 'the chief person to gain kudos from *The New Barmaid* is Mr John Crook whose music is consistently tuneful, sparkling and, save for two or three meretricious effects, exceedingly artistically done'.

Clearly, *The New Barmaid* was not set for a triumph on *Gentleman Joe* lines, but Miss Collins, Dallas and those songs – in particular 'A little Bit of Sugar for the Bird' – proved attractive enough to pull in a certain type of patron for long enough to make the London season a success.

One result of the success of the two featured artists was the almost total drowning of the central plot concerning the lady of the title, Miss Ethel Joy, and her rivalries with her predecessor. *The Stage* summarised caustically:

> . . few people will care a jot whether Brenda Louth, the Old Barmaid at the club, or Ethel Joy, the New Barmaid, is the long-lost daughter of that not unfamiliar Anglo-Indian Colonel or which of them succeeds in marrying so insipid a young officer of the Guards . . .

The role of Ethel Joy had originally been planned as the female lead and on tour the vivacious Amy Augarde had succeeded, in the face of less overwhelming competition from her fellow players, in keeping the equilibrium of the piece tilted towards the romantic heart of the story. With Lottie Collins engaged for Dora, Loftus and Howard recognised the need to find a prima donna capable of holding her own in the title role. The answer seemed obvious for they had to hand the Queen of Comic Opera herself,

Florence St John. Miss St John had been signed as part of the rescue operation on *The Bric à Brac Will* in which she had duly played the lead for the dying weeks of its run. But the manager, Ernest Oswald, now an investor in *The New Barmaid*, had signed his prima donna somewhat optimistically for a sixteen weeks' contract at the mighty salary of £100 per week, that optimism tempered by a clause in the contract stating that in the event of *The Bric à Brac Will* folding prematurely the engagement could be transferred to another similar production under the same management. Loftus presented Miss St John with the role of Ethel Joy, and the star promptly refused to consider it. Loftus countered by refusing her the £100 per week and the lady countered with a writ claiming that *The New Barmaid* could in no way be considered 'similar' to Pizzi's grandiose comic opera and the contract was thus invalid. Tempers calmed and the matter was settled out of court. Miss St John got her money and Loftus got Agnes de la Porte as Ethel Joy.

Miss de la Porte was an excellent artist but she could not lift the story of Ethel Joy into prominence in the way that was needed. The problem was solved after a month's run when Agnes de la Porte was seconded for the highly successful provincial tour and her part was taken over by Lottie Collins. The role of Dora reverted to its original size and style and *The New Barmaid* took on more of the appearance of a coherent play. Ethel Joy was now, of course, quite a different character for Lottie Collins brought to the role her own style and her own material, including an Alfred Carpenter/Eustace Baynes number; 'Just on the Tip of my Tongue' which she performed to great effect.

After four months at the Avenue, however, *The New Barmaid* was given notice to quit as Sir Augustus Harris required the theatre for his production of Eugen von Taund's *Der Wunderknabe* (*The Little Genius*). Loftus and Howard had to decide whether a transfer was justified. They had lost J. J. Dallas who had gone out to join his own production of *One of the Girls*, but they still had Lottie Collins and E. J. Lonnen who had taken over Shine's role to head their bill. With their faith firmly pinned on Miss Collins they announced a bold transfer to the unpopular Opera Comique. It was a decision which proved unwise and expensive. Lonnen refused to go into a 'second-class theatre', so both principal comics had to be replaced and, although Arthur Alexander and Joseph Montague resumed the roles they had created with credit, they did not have the same drawing power. Lottie Collins soon sensed the way things were going and she too departed, leaving Lillian Menelly, who had started the show in the chorus, to step up to share the billing with Jenny Rogers. *The New Barmaid* was falling to pieces, and after only 18 performances in its new home it closed its London season.

Miss Collins, in the meanwhile, had sent her husband to America to treat with Charles Frohman for an American *New Barmaid* production, but his efforts were in vain and Broadway was never to see Lottie's return to the stage. In May, 1896, with two hugely successful tours still on the road, the owners sold off the small town rights to Austin Fryers who thereafter sent additional companies regularly round the country circuits until *The New Barmaid* came to be one of the all-time top touring pieces, rivalling *The Gay Parisienne* and even *The Lady Slavey* in the number of tours sent out and their length. In 1904–5 Loftus ran one company for 90 consecutive weeks, reconstituting it after a short break for a further 40 weeks.

The next musical to arrive in town was as different as could be from *The New Barmaid*. *Shamus O'Brien* was described by its author as a romantic comic opera but there was little enough about it to which the word 'comic' could be accurately applied. The piece was the work of two Irishmen, the American-Irish playwright and journalist George Jessop, and the Cambridge-Irish composer, organist and conductor Charles

Villiers Stanford. Jessop had previously made his career is San Francisco where he had worked as a journalist while writing for the theatre such pieces as the comedy *Mademoiselle* for Aimée and the Irish drama *Mavourneen* for Scanlan. Having inherited an estate in Ireland he abandoned America and came to settle there, and *Shamus O'Brien* was the first text he provided for the British stage.

For his book he took the principal incidents from Joseph Sheridan Le Fanu's well-known poem of love and betrayal in the Irish bogs. The 'rebel', Shamus, is betrayed to the English by Mike Murphy who then tries to buy the love of O'Brien's wife, Nora, with promises of his release. Eventually O'Brien evades his captors and Mike is killed trying to prevent his escape. Set amongst the picturesque scenery and traditions of Ireland, *Shamus O'Brien*'s libretto capitalised on such colourful features as the legend of the banshees but, on the whole, Jessop's contribution lacked substance. In the first act Shamus is seen luring the English across the bogs before he is captured, while his wife's sister Kitty flirts with the English captain, and there is a good deal of singing both patriotic and folk; while the second act has little more than the trial and escape of Shamus to sustain it among more flirting and more song. But if the incidents of *Shamus O'Brien* were few and basic, Jessop nevertheless succeeded in creating a bright and varied set of characters and found much that was attractive in dialogue and lyric to put into their mouths. Unusually, he took the trouble to investigate the characters of his 'bad' characters and was at great pains to have the English captain express distaste for the job he is obliged to do and his dislike of the informer, Mike. Mike himself is shown as twisted and soured by jealousy. As a dramatic piece, however, *Shamus O'Brien* suffered irreparably from a lack of content which had been imposed on the writer by his choice of source.

Shamus O'Brien was a new departure for its composer, 43-year-old Stanford. His principal work was in a much more classical vein, whether for church, orchestra or stage. His 1884 opera *The Canterbury Pilgrims* had been widely praised, *The Veiled Prophet* and *Savonarola* had been serious musical attempts far removed from the stage of the Opera Comique, and his work as organist at Trinity College, Cambridge, as conductor of the Bach Choir and later on with the Leeds Philharmonic and Festival gained him a serious reputation and a knighthood. His scholarship gave substance to the little Irish melodies of *Shamus O'Brien*, finding it a ready acceptance among music lovers, but he wisely refrained from allowing the music to become heavy or academic or the scoring too weighty and, even in the frankly emotional and dramatic moments of the story, the piece was never allowed to echo grand opera or melodrama. The opening chorus was enough to warn the audience they were not in for a modern musical comedy or even a comic opera in the *Manteaux Noirs* line:

> Too soon, faith, we'll know
> Whence is comin' the blow
> The murder, the terror, the pillage
> They will hunt him wid dogs
> Through the mountains and bogs
> Our darlint, the pride of our village . .

and from that moment the light and the tragic were deftly mixed. The most attractive of the light numbers fell to the part of Kitty and the English Captain Trevor, and all were on virtually the same subject:

> Where is the man who is comin' to marry me?
> Where is the gossoon that is eager to court?

Time runs a-wastin' the longer I tarry me
Age comes so surely and youth is so short.

The patriotic numbers were the share of the baritone Shamus:

I've sharpened the sword for the sake of ould Erin
I carried a pike when she called on her sons
I ran the risk then, and I will not be fearin'
The enemy's gallows no more than his guns . .

while the heavier moments were the lot of the distraught Nora who, having heard the banshee's wail, is convinced that it foretells the death of her husband:

A grave yawns cold
In the churchyard mould
A low, dark bed for the bold and bright
It opened wide
On the mountain side
The first night ever the banshee cried.
No child or scion
Of the great O'Brien
But the banshee keens when she knows him dyin'.
One night a sigh
The next a cry–
With the third wail surely a man must die.
The sound comes clear
To the tortured ear
Of her the doomed one has loved most dear.
Twice through the gloom
Have I heard the doom
Wailin' like women before the tomb.
If once more I
Hear that awful cry
I'll know my Shamus is called to die.

But Nora is the best-loved not only of Shamus but also of the wretched Mike, and it is his death the banshee cries for.

To cast *Shamus O'Brien* a call was made to the students of the Royal College of Music and the result was outstanding. The young baritone, Denis O'Sullivan, took the title role with another Irishman, Joseph O'Mara, as Mike. But the greatest find amongst the cast was the young contralto, Louise Kirkby Lunn, who was selected to play Nora. At the end of the season of *Shamus* Miss Lunn was snapped up by the Carl Rosa Opera Company and went on to an international operatic career.

Critical reaction to the piece was predictably favourable. *The Times* declared its hand in its opening paragraph:

> Now that the lighter forms of comic opera have for the most part become merged in dreary imitations of the music halls, it is not unlikely that public interest many revive in opéra-comique of the higher class . .

before going on to praise the show at much greater length than usual for any piece, and in particular a musical one:

> . . the old plan of dividing one thrilling 'situation' from another by means of comic scenes is quite discarded. While there are here no low comedians who are responsible

> for the 'relief', each of the characters is represented as possessing a sense of the humorous as well as the pathetic side of things. The sources of laughter and tears are never far apart . . . . . The workmanship of the libretto is admirable, the dialogue being direct, concise and natural yet brimming over with genuine Irish humour, while the lyrics have plenty of point and charm as well as feeling for rhythmic variety . . . . An interesting story told in dialogue that is bright and to the point and music which while it delights the musician by its refinement contains nothing that can seem abstruse to persons of ordinary intelligence . . .

Not all the critics were quite as rhapsodic. Some found the book too diffuse and lacking in incident. *The Stage* suggested the dialogue should be cut by half, whilst others found the music too reminiscent and folksy (it actually employed two well-known airs, 'Father O'Flynn' and the march 'The Glory of the West'). *Shamus O'Brien* was, however, the best example of its kind to have been produced in the English language since the days of Balfe, Wallace and Benedict, and for the public which interested itself in such works it was an undisputed success. For the patrons of the Gaiety and the Prince of Wales it offered little attraction, but there were plenty of more serious-minded music-lovers around to keep the Opera Comique in business for 86 performances before the piece was taken out into the provinces where it gained an equivalent reception and success. In January 1897 it was given an American production at New York's Broadway Theatre where it survived a respectable two months, and it later appeared in Germany. Thereafter it received occasional performances and in the last days of Joseph O'Mara's touring opera company in the mid-20s *Shamus O'Brien* formed part of the repertoire of that company. In 1930 it was broadcast by the BBC.

At the Savoy, the revival of *The Mikado* was doing extremely well but the new Gilbert and Sullivan musical was ready and, in consequence, the older piece was withdrawn. The days were past when the subject and plot of the newest Savoy opera constituted the hottest piece of gossip amongst the cognoscenti and a scoop for the best-placed and first-in columnist. As the new piece arrived it was known to be called *The Grand Duke* and was rumoured, in one paper, to contain some bits of *Thespis*. When *The Grand Duke* appeared on 7 March the basis of the rumour was clear; resemblances to the very first of the Gilbert/Sullivan works were there, not textually but in style and subject. The principal model was nearer in time, in Tito Mattei and H. B. Farnie's comic opera *The Prima Donna*, itself based on the *Blackwood's* magazine story 'The Duke's Dilemma'. Gilbert had used for his starting point the same tale of a troupe of players installed at a ducal court and, taking Farnie's original title *The Grand Duke*, grafted on to the basic situation conceits of his own.

In Gilbert's *Grand Duke* the actors, far from being in league with the Grand Duke, are plotting to dethrone him and have formed a conspiracy, the secret sign of which is the eating of a sausage roll. But there is a clash between two of the players – the manager Ernest Dummkopf and the comedian Ludwig who has accidentally exposed their plan to the Duke's private detective. They resolve their differences by means of a statutory duel – whoever draws the lower card is by the law of the land statutorily dead – and Ludwig is left 'alive' to confess to the Duke the conspiracy and the 'death' of its instigator. But Ludwig sees his own way to the ducal seat, and persuades the Duke, who knows that the law runs out the next day, to allow himself to be 'killed' so that he will miss the genuine assassination attempt. Having accomplished this, Ludwig promptly takes his throne and re-enacts the vital law for another hundred years. But further problems arise. Ludwig is married to the soubrette, Lisa, but the leading lady,

Julia, insists that he must honour her contract which gives leading roles to her. In this case the lead is the role of the Grand Duchess. But the elderly Baroness of Krakenfeldt has a prior claim – she was engaged to be married to the Grand Duke. Ludwig has to admit three 'wives'. Finally the Princess of Monte Carlo turns up and proves to have been betrothed to the Grand Duke in infancy. She has twenty years' prior claim. Ludwig is in a most polygamic position when it is suddenly discovered that he has no rights at all to the ducal seat. The ace with which he won his duels is, by the law of the land, the lowest and not the highest card in the park. He is 'dead', and the Duke and Ernest Dummkopf are 'alive'. They claim their respective positions, the Princess and Julia, whilst Lisa happily contents herself with Ludwig's 'corpse'.

The libretto was not what one might have expected from the author of *Pinafore*, *Patience* and *The Mikado*, but rather from that of *Thespis* and *The Gentleman in Black*, both of which were echoed in the conceit whereby a real relationship must give way to one artificially set up. Gilbert's plot was indubitably ingenious in a manner which showed its early origins, but his dialogue lacked the sparkle of his principal works and many of the lyrics were, by his standards, commonplace. The very first solo, describing the Conspiracy of the Sausage Roll, was prosaic and unfortunate and, although it was duly encored on the first night, it set an awkward tone for the rest of the evening. The libretto had the disadvantage, too, of consisting of three separate parts – the actors and their relationships, the whim of the statutory duel, and the comic succession of Ludwig's wives. It was this last, when the rather heavy and uncomical atmosphere of the Germanic court scenes had been escaped, which succeeded the best as Florence Perry, Ilka von Palmay, Rosina Brandram and Emmie Owen in turn claimed the bridegroom.

Casting had been a consideration for Gilbert in his construction of *The Grand Duke*. The unprecedented prominance of the role of Ludwig was due to his desire to give outstanding opportunities to Rutland Barrington, now the only original member of the Savoy team remaining. He took less care with the role of the Baroness for that other Savoy veteran, Rosina Brandram, and neither Richard Temple nor Jessie Bond would have been particularly keen on the roles of the Prince and Princess of Monte Carlo. In the event, Temple and Miss Bond seceded from the Savoy and the final version of the roles were truncated ones with their songs eliminated. The other principal who needed to be accommodated was the Savoy's new prima donna, the Countess Eugene Kinsky, professionally known as Ilka von Palmay and a successful performer in her native Hungary where she had performed in Gilbert and Sullivan, notably as a travesti Nanki-Poo in *The Mikado*. It was Gilbert's whim to have Miss Palmay with her middle European accented English play the British actress, Julia Jellicoe, while the rest of the cast played the Germans in perfect English. It was an imaginative idea, but one which added little to the production.

As prima donna, the lady needed to be provided with numbers and Gilbert and Sullivan provided 'The Grand Duke's Bride' (more than a little reminiscent of Phoebe's 'Were I thy Bride' from *The Yeomen of the Guard*) as Julia tells how she would play the role of Grand Duchess:

> With many a winsome smile I'd witch and woo
> With gay and girlish guile I'd frenzy you
> I'd madden you with my caressing
> Like turtle, her first love confessing,
> That it was 'mock' no mortal would be guessing
> With so much winsome wile I'd witch and woo . .

She also had a very straight solo 'Broken every Promise Plighted' and shared in a number of other pieces, notably a scene with Ludwig where she was able to show off her versatility, describing how she would play the jealous wife:

> I have a rival! Frenzy-thrilled
> I find you both together!
> My heart stands still – with a horror chilled
> Hard as the millstone nether!
> Then softly, slyly, snaily, snaky
> Crawly, creepy, quaily, quaky,
> I track her on her homeward way
> As panther tracks ill-fated prey &c . .

The jealously is succeeded by remorse in twelve lines, a mad scene in eight, of all of which Julia declares:

> This calls for the resources of a high class art
> And satisfies my notion of a first rate part.

The role of Julia evidently became too much of a 'first rate part' for Mme von Palmay as she soon found herself obliged to leave the matinée performances to Florence Perry and, later, Carla Dagmar. The elevation of Miss Perry to the prima donna role gave opportunity to the young soprano, Ruth Vincent, to stand in as Lisa for the matinées. Soon Miss Vincent would herself take prima donna status among the best comic opera performers of the time.

As well as the dramatic and lyrical sections of *The Grand Duke* there were the patter songs for Walter Passmore as the Duke, and for Barrington. Passmore was very poorly served. His principal number was a sad piece, 'When you Find you're a broken-down Crittur', which described the malaise of low-living:

> When your lips are all smeary – like tallow
> And your tongue is decidedly yellow
> And a pint of warm oil in your swallow
> And a pound of tin-tack in your chest
> When you're down in the mouth with the vapours
> And all over your new Morris papers
> Black beetles are cutting their capers
> And crawly things never at rest . .

It was a very poor relation of the *Iolanthe* nightmare song and even the facile Passmore could not work it up into much. Another solo lampooning court ceremonial was much more popular but largely through its accompanying 'business' where a snuff box was passed comically through a line of chamberlains. Barrington fared little better. His 'Sausage Roll' song was an aberration, and his other first act number 'Ten Minutes since I met a Chap', describing how he had unwittingly given away the conspiracy (and in which the sausage roll put in yet another appearance) was equally unattractive. His most substantial number found him installed as Grand Duke, declaiming:

> At the outset I may mention it's my sovereign intention
> To revive the classic memories of Athens at its best,
> For the company possesses all the necessary dresses
> And a course of quiet cramming will supply us with the rest.

The song continues to etiolate knowledge – including some Greek quotes – until Ludwig is obliged to admit that: 'This show of learning is the fruit of steady cram.' It was loosely attached to the plot, but gave a glimpse of Gilbert's true technique and imagination:

> In the period Socratic every dining room was Attic
> (Which suggests an architecture of a topsy-turvy kind),
> There they'd satisfy their thirst on a recherché cold ariston
> Which is what they called their lunch – and so may you, if you're inclined.

It was not only Gilbert who seemed to have strayed from the paths of his best works. Sullivan, too, seemed to be trying to find the delightful lightness and grotesquery of his former contributions. Much of the score seemed almost like self-parody and the best parts were undoubtedly in the most straightforwardly 'vocal' numbers. It was significant that Chappell & Co. selected for single publication only Julia's 'Broken every Promise Plighted', Lisa's uncomplicated ballad 'Take Care of Him' and the inexplicably popular Herald's song – a curious mixture of *Lohengrin* and *The Gondoliers*.

There was considerable trouble over the script during production and the problems had not been solved by opening night. After a mixed reaction at the première, Gilbert decided on further alterations. Some of the earlier changes had been, to say the least, injudicious and those that followed seemed equally so. The far more enjoyable second act was sliced about, resulting in the banishing of Rosina Brandram's Brindisi (her only solo), the Prince's Roulette Song, an amusing parody of the café chantant, and some of the final patter scene, cutting down the bright and lively side of *The Grand Duke* and angling the show even further on to the Barrington/von Palmay axis, to patter and to ballad. These ill-timed cuts did not improve the show or its popularity. In spite of kindly and nostalgic comments from much of the press, *The Grand Duke* failed to build an audience and its life span at the Savoy was limited to four months. The Gilbert and Sullivan partnership which had given so much to the light musical theatre of Britain and of the whole of the world was at an end and, sadly, it ended not with a bang but a whimper, and with the least successful of all their works. But the partnership had come to a timely end for the best days of comic opera were over. Revivals of their past triumphs would fill theatres to overflowing for many years to come but the conjunction of manager, author, composer and public which had existed so fruitfully over the years was now dissolved; each had altered and would now go his separate way, as they had in truth begun to do long before the curtain fell on July 10, 1896, the last night of the least of the Savoy operas.

The place of comic opera had been well and truly filled, however, by the thriving musical comedy and its near relation the variety musical, and a prime example of this new favourite quickly found its way into town on the heels of *The Grand Duke*. *The Gay Parisienne* was following in the footsteps of *The Lady Slavey* and *The New Barmaid*, having extensively and successfully toured around the provinces for eighteen months before coming into town. Like those two pieces it was in the 'provincial' style – full of comedy and music-hall type songs: bright, tuneful, funny and fairly unsophisticated. But Horace Sedger and his associates had the examples of *The Lady Slavey* and *The New Barmaid* before them, and it was decided that *The Gay Parisienne* in its present version would not do for the West End. Major alterations in both the book and the score were decided upon, although it was settled that the plot should not be changed. The libretto changes were chiefly to accommodate the stars whom the management had secured. The key role of Mlle Julie Bon-Bon had been very effectively played on tour by Nellie Murray, but Miss Murray was persuaded to renounce her option for London to allow the management to feature a truly 'drawing' star name. Cissie Loftus was first approached to star at the Duke of York's but, in the end, the ebullient Ada Reeve was engaged to play alongside Frank Wheeler, who abandoned the role of Miggles in *The Shop Girl* to take on that of Auguste Pompier, with several talented comedians – Lionel Rignold, Lillie Belmore, W. H. Denny and a new discovery of George Dance's, a munchkin-like girl called Louie Freear. To feature Miss Freear, Dance wrote in a new role, Ruth, the foundling cockney slavey. New music was then needed to give Ruth a chance to shine but, before long, it was decided to go further and to throw out the entire Ernest Vousden score. Ivan Caryll was commissioned to write sixteen new numbers, some to the existing lyrics and others to fresh words by Dance. Such a major rewrite meant the show was now a very different piece.

The first act plot was only slightly altered, still following, as in the original, the story of Julie and Pompier's successful attempt to defraud Ebenezer Honeycombe and Amos Dingle through their phony breach-of-promise case. The second act, however, involving the loosely constructed high-jinks in the German spa town of Shoffenburgen, with Honeycombe disguised as a Scot and all the other characters involved in their own particular complications, allowed for almost any degree of alteration and its opening night state was by no means the last it would have. Even on that vital occasion things were still in a state of flux and several numbers which had been printed in the book of words were not performed, but what remained proved enough to please. Ivan Caryll's music was in his best and most tuneful style and all the principals had plenty of chances to shine. Ada Reeve, as a piquant Frenchwoman, scored instantly in her first duo with Wheeler:

J: I'm all the way from Gay Paree, Mam'selle Julie Bon-Bon.
A: And I am Monsieur Pompier, un p'tit garçon.
J: I pack my, what-you-call, my box and visit Angleterre.
A: And I am Mam'selle's chaperon, so trespassers beware!
J: I come to teach a lesson to you naughty Englishmen.
A: She comes to have une grande revanche, la belle Parisienne.
Ma chère Julie!
J: Mon cher Auguste!
BOTH: Phew!
Bonjour, bonjour Madame. Bonjour, bonjour Monsieur
How do you do? Comment vous portez-vous?
I throw to you a kiss – a real one, not a sham
A tout le monde, brunette et blonde, Messieurs, Mesdames!

at the conclusion of which the two danced a comic routine which involved Wheeler playing leapfrog over his partner's back. Miss Reeve also scored with an interpolated American number by Thomas and Andrew Mack, a plantation song called 'Sambo', accompanied by a characteristic dance.

In a different vein, another popular piece fell to W. H. Denny as the blustery major who is entranced by Julie into giving the court verdict in her favour. He describes himself:

I'am proud to say that I am one
Of the Battersea Butterfly Shooters;
As Volunteers we take the bun,
Do the Battersea Butterfly Shooters.
And every Saturday we meet,

And don our uniforms so neat,
And then parade along each street,
To give the darling girls a treat.
Shoulder arms! Forward! By your right!
The drummer whacks the big, big drum–
The Battersea Butterfly Shooters come;
And as we step with martial dash,
The cornets roar and cymbals crash!
The girls all run to see the show;
They kiss their dainty fingers–so!
And wave their hands and cry 'Bravo'
As we go marching by!

The Gay Parisienne was noticeably broader than the fashionable Gaiety and Daly's musicals. Its plot and action were wildly farcical and its humour much more basic, but this did not displease a good number of people and it quickly became clear that the show was as big a success in London as it had been in the provinces. *The Gay Parisienne* occupied the Duke of York's for over a year. In December, Louie Freear had to leave the cast as she was signed for pantomime. The owners of *The Gay Parisienne* by now had two touring companies coining money on the road and there was no way they were going to allow Miss Freear to ruin their market by using their and her hit song in a pantomime. Permission was asked and duly refused. But Louie Freear was not to be defeated. She ordered a song from writer–composer Harry Pleon and her pantomime audiences found themselves informed:

Sit back! Hold tight! Mary's going to sing!
She's going to try again to crack her throat.
It stops the birds a-singing
And it sets the bells a-ringing,
Sister Mary Jane's top note.

But the triumph of the show and the hit song of the night came from an unexpected quarter–unexpected, that is, to those who weren't in the know. Little Louie Freear became a star overnight with her playing of the role of the quaint slavey and her singing of the number especially fabricated for her, 'Sister Mary Jane's Top Note'. The song had started life at the Moore and Burgess Minstrels where its lyric, written by Frederick Bowyer, had attracted Dance's attention. He secured the song and turned it over to Ivan Caryll for fresh music as a vehicle for Miss Freear. Bowyer thus provided the biggest song hit of the season for a show in opposition to his own *The New Barmaid:*

You've heard about my sister Mary Jane's top note,
Well, I'm sorry to inform you that it's cracked;
She was singing at a hall and tried to get it off her chest,
It was a dismal frost, and she was sacked.
So now she's took to dancing, with her slippers full of feet
In the front row of the ballet she's the pick;
It ain't so much her dancing that upsets our apple cart
But it's the nasty 'orrid way she's learned to kick!

All the house is upside down now, everybody's got the sick,
Mother's got the hump, father's off his chump, and the old dutch
clock won't tick.
Mary Jane she kicks like thunder, she'll kick us all to
somewhere quick,

Everything's broke up, from the mangle to the pup,
With SISTER MARY JANE'S HIGH KICK!

Even the departure of Miss Freear could not dim the by then well-established popularity of *The Gay Parisienne*. There had been many changes, of course, to keep the show fresh and varied. 'First and Third', a duet which had featured in the original score, found its way back into the show along with a new duo for Ruth and the Major called 'Upon the Stage let's have a Fling' which also proved well-chosen. The show was produced in America by E. E. Rice during December as *The Girl From Paris* and there, too, it proved a hit, settling in for a run of 265 performances at the Herald Square Theatre. One of the additional numbers composed for the U.S. version was 'The harmless little Girlie with the downcast Eyes' by 'Hugh Morton' (Charles S. McLellan) and Gustave Kerker, which proved attractive enough to warrant interpolation into the London version. Another American song 'Swingin' on de golden Gate' by Paul Barnes also found its way in, but all the favourite numbers, the backbone of the show, retained their place. *The Gay Parisienne* maintained a remarkable popularity through its run and on the occasion of its 300th performance a thousand people had to be turned away from the Duke of York's. Forty police were needed to control the queues and crowds, and the management were obliged to open the gallery doors at 6 pm to ease the pressure. When the show was finally withdrawn, it continued to tour widely and incessantly over a period of many years and joined *The Lady Slavey* and *The New Barmaid* as the third of the trio of popular musicals which were fixtures in the provinces over the next decade.

A week after the opening of *The Gay Parisienne*, Arthur Roberts produced his successor to *Gentleman Joe* at the Prince of Wales. Somewhat surprisingly, in view of his propensity for ignoring his writers' dialogue, Roberts had taken the trouble to secure as librettist the well-known author of *Three Men in a Boat*, Jerome K. Jerome. Now in his mid-thirties, Jerome had still to make a mark on the theatrical scene in spite of a few attempts. For Roberts he composed a story called *Biarritz* for which Adrian Ross supplied the lyrics and Dr Osmond Carr the music.

The plot of *Biarritz* was a convoluted affair involving the buffoonish son of a hotel magnate sent out to Biarritz to investigate troubles in the family hotel there. As the idiotic John Jenkins, Roberts gallivanted through a series of misfortunes and disguises coming in contact variously with Janet, the pretty hotel cashier, and her boyfriend who have been trying to run down the place so they may buy it, with a diamond king whose daughter has run away with a friend of his, and with his own fiancée, the music-hall singer, Tessie Carew, who eyes his attentions to Janet with grave suspicion. In the second act, at the obligatory masquerade ball, the plot subsided in a morass of song, dance, costume and burlesques of scenes from other shows.

Jerome's idea of what a musical book should be had clearly been modelled on some of Roberts' poorer previous efforts. His dialogue did nothing for his reputation, although quite how much of it was his and how much was Roberts' by the time opening night arrived cannot be judged. The lyrics which Ross had provided were also surprisingly sub-standard and Carr's music showed a worrying lack of imagination. Of the whole score, only two songs gained much approval – Roberts' numbers 'The General of the Umtiados' in which he included some fairly inept references to Forbes Robertson's *For the Crown* at the Adelphi, and a saucy song called 'The Farmer's Daughter' in which the singer, having picked up an innocent-looking maid, finds she is angling to cost him his fortune and freedom.

Kitty Loftus sang and danced her way through an inane number called 'My Partner':

I'am a jolly little folly
And my lover's name is Dolly
He's the very nicest Johnnie of the fancy fête
He the sort that all the girls adore
Just a stick and nothing more
My pretty little partner up-to-date!

whilst Sadie Jerome was cast as a superfluous American journalist, Niagara G. Wackett, and declared:

I'm a child of the great Democracy
Out of the wild and woolly west,
In European aristocracy
Taking contemptuous interest

with the refrain:

If you've anything worth a show
Guess I'll learn it before I go
For I am Niagara Wackett
and I WANT TO KNOW!

But Niagara Wackett was no Lalage Potts and *Biarritz* was no *Gentleman Joe*. At the end of the evening the opening night audience reserved their limited cheers for the adored Roberts and gave a hearty booing to the piece. The gallery and pit called loudly for the authors in order that they might express their displeasure, but Jerome, Ross and Carr wisely stayed out of sight. This verdict was confirmed by the papers. *The Times* asserted:

> There is almost everywhere an absence of pointed wit and real humour in the dialogue, while the vocal numbers rarely rise to a level above the commonplace . .

No-one disagreed, although some critics hedged their bets on the fact that with Arthur Roberts it was just possible, by judicious cutting and interpolations, the piece might be worked up. Roberts certainly gave it a try. The script was hacked about freely and the feebly copied Niagara G. Wackett axed completely. A song was ordered from Ella Chapman and W. S. Laidlaw, the composers of 'She wanted Something to Play with', and inserted as 'Another Fellow'. Another piece from the young writer Edgar Wallace set by Lionel Monckton, 'A Sort of a Kind of a . . ' joined it, then one from 'Daddy wouldn't Buy Me a Bow-Wow' writer, Joseph Tabrar, called 'Just the Same as Dolly Does' and a typical Roberts piece called 'A funny, peculiar Feeling'. Roberts stepped up the ad-libbing and topical references. The day the Prince of Wales' horse Persimmon won the Derby, Roberts was ready with a new verse:

We're pleased to find the Prince of Wales the Derby won today
We all join in the mighty shout of hip hip hip hooray
And now a little tip I'll give – it's not one of my jokes
I'm told that Thais on Friday next is sure to win the Oaks

Roberts' tip went down the drain as Rickaby piloted home Lord Derby's Canterbury Pilgrim, and not long after *Biarritz* went in the same direction, never having succeeded in surmounting the initial handicap of an impossible book and undistinguished songs.

By now five new musicals had reached the London stage, not one of which had been a George Edwardes show. With *An Artist's Model* at Daly's and *The Shop Girl* at the Gaiety, Edwardes had no need of a new production. But, finally, in March he decided to withdraw *An Artist's Model* and to produce the new Japanese piece which the *Artist's Model* team of Owen Hall, Harry Greenbank and Sidney Jones had prepared. Much care had been taken over the preparation of *Happy Japan* or *The Geisha* (the title was still in the balance) and lessons had been learned from the experience of *An Artist's Model*, the first of which was that a complicated plot was both an unnecessary and undesirable thing and that a multiplicity of plots was even worse. Consequently, for *The Geisha* (as it was eventually called), one straightforward plot with a beginning, a middle and an end and a picturesque location was evolved and adhered to.

The choice of Japan as a setting was a happy one (the success of *The Mikado* had already borne witness to it) and gave Edwardes opportunities for magnificent spectacle. He had gone into the scenic side of affairs with great seriousness, aiming to have everything as attractive yet as authentic as possible, and to this end had even called in the services of one Mr Diosy, Vice-Chairman of the Japan Society, and went to the lengths of obtaining a real Japanese gramophone record to help Jones with the authenticity of a song for Letty Lind. Then, too, Daly's was kept dark for nearly a month to allow stage preparations for the new show to go forward undisturbed – an unprecedentedly expensive way of proceeding. But when the piece was finally produced, on April 25, all the pains and financial risks proved to have been worthwhile. The first night audience gave the show the kind of reception that authors and managers dream of, and the newspapers were no less enthusiastic. Even *The Times* was bound to report:

> There can be no two opinions as to the distinct and emphatic success obtained by *The Geisha* . . nor was the success greater than the piece deserved. One has come to associate these collaborations with flimsy works of a too familiar type in which 'the play' was the last thing dreamed of, all semblance of connected story being sacrificed for the benefit of individual singers and dancers, and although in *The Geisha* the majority of the songs have little or no connexion with the plot, there yet remains a plot, perhaps of a rather attenuated kind. The efforts of both authors and composer to produce a piece of a higher order of artistic merit are deserving of great praise and it seems well within the bounds of possibility that these writers may develop from the ashes of the glorified variety show a form of dramatic entertainment similar in most respect to the real light opera – a consummation devoutly to be wished. Certainly *The Geisha* is a marked improvement, musically and dramatically, upon all of its predecessors. It is humorous without eternally transgressing the laws of decency, clever without being forced and silly, and extremely beautiful from the spectacular point . . . The dialogue is often smart and many of the lines are quite happy, while musically Mr Jones has never previously reached so lofty a standard. The scoring is generally very refined and skilful and more than once it rises to a high level of excellence . .

What *The Times* and all the other writers who constantly bewailed the lack of 'real light opera' failed consistently to recognise was that the public were not, in great numbers, interested in seeing 'real light opera'. *The Geisha* with its felicitous blend of songs and pretty ballads provided, musically, precisely what they wanted to hear, and the story – attractive and simple and providing plenty of opportunity for their favourites to make them laugh – was also aimed at just the right level. Like *Dorothy* before it and like many others after it, *The Geisha* arrived at the right moment with the right characteristics and a degree of excellence in the writing and the execution which made it an immediate major hit. The framework which Owen Hall had provided was sensibly slight and sufficient, and cleverly written. The smart society tone which had pervaded *A Gaiety Girl* and *An Artist's Model* was largely abandoned and the dialogue of *The Geisha* was much more natural and uncomplicated.

O Mimosa San is the most popular Geisha in the tea house of Ten Thousand Joys owned by the Chinaman, Wun-Hi, and at present her services (quite innocent ones, for Mr Hall's geishas are no more than singing waitresses with a good deal of time on their hands) are much in demand by the navy's Reggie Fairfax. This disturbs Lady Constance Wynne, who is friendly with Reggie's fiancée, Molly, and it also disturbs the Marquis Imari, the local potentate, who has decided to wed Mimosa himself. Mimosa, though she conscientiously entertains and even flirts with the handsome sailor to earn her living, has, however, a young Japanese lover of her own, the Captain Katana. Imari orders that Mimosa shall be prepared to marry him, but seeing her with Fairfax furiously orders Wun-Hi's establishment to be broken up and his girls' indentures put up for auction. At the auction, however, he is outbid for Mimosa by Lady Constance who intends to keep her out of the hands of both Fairfax and Imari, and the Marquis relieves his disappointment by buying up the next girl on offer who turns out to be none other than madcap Molly, who has decided it would be fun to try life as a geisha and ends up being carried off to marry him. The second act finds the preparations for the wedding under way, and Molly's friends under the guidance of Mimosa set out to rescue her. The geisha disguises herself as a fortune-teller to gain access to Molly's room and she engineers a change of place between Molly and the willing Juliette, the French interpreter from chez Wun-Hi. The wedding ceremony goes ahead and all ends happily.

The story was heavily unoriginal and bore, in a large part, a striking resemblance to *The Sultan of Mocha*, but Hall succeeded in telling it with a freshness and simplicity which made it new and he filled it with delightful characters tailored to fit the Daly's stars – Marie Tempest, Letty Lind, Huntley Wright, Hayden Coffin, Harry Monkhouse and Juliette Nesville – and opportunities for the young ladies of the house to be displayed in attractive Japanese costumes. For those stars and their characters Sidney Jones and Harry Greenbank provided the vital musical part of their roles.

The title role of O Mimosa San was created for Marie Tempest, allowing her gently to run the gamut of moods and styles from the coyly flirting to the serenely human, from despairing to plotting to loving. If the part was a little deficient in humour it was never heavy and Miss Tempest encompassed its extremes stylishly. She was equipped with a variety of songs, beginning with the delicious little fable of the 'Amorous Goldfish':

A goldfish swam in a big glass bowl
As dear little goldfish do
But she loved with the whole of her heart and soul
An officer brave from the ocean wave
And she thought that he loved her too.

Her small insides he daily fed
With crumbs of the best digestive bread,
'This kind attention proves', said she,
'How exceedingly fond he is of me!'

And she thought, 'It's fit-fit-fitter

He should love my glit-glit-glitter
Than his heart give away to the butterflies gay
Or the birds that twit-twit-twitter!'

Alas for the goldfish, her officer finds himself a young lady and quite forgets the little fish and her breadcrumbs, and finally tragedy strikes:

Until at last some careless soul
With a smash knocked over the big glass bowl
And there on the carpet dead and cold
Lay the poor little fish in her frock of gold . .

In contrast to this and to the coy 'Teach me how to Kiss' duet with Fairfax, was the lovely 'A Geisha's Life' which Miss Tempest invested with a considerable amount of pathos without allowing it to ever become too serious:

A gėisha's life imagination tints
With all the charming colours of the rose
And people won't believe her when she hints
Its beauties are not quite what they suppose . .

A further solo was given by Mimosa disguised as the sorceress, describing how she will make the Marquis' bride love him so that he may escape the dreadful fate of loveless wedded life. This song, 'Love, Love', with its waltz refrain exploited the leading lady's range and flexibility and proved a third popular piece of her.

Edwardes took great care that the roles for Miss Tempest and Letty Lind should be of equal prominence. Neither of them could claim to be assoluta at Daly's and, by the vagaries of the plot, both could claim in *The Geisha* the title role, yet because of the differences in their style there was no direct competition. In the part of the high-spirited English girl, Molly Seamore, Miss Lind found her personality well-suited and she revelled in the scene where Molly, disguised as the geisha 'Roli-Poli', shows off her accomplishments at the auction sale with the 'Japanese' song 'Chon Kina', extolling her own charms and virtues as a geisha. After her huge success with 'The gay Tom Tit' in *An Artist's Model* it was expected that Jones and Greenbank should supply Miss Lind with a new zoological-moral song, no matter how irrelevant. After tomtit came parrot and 'The Interfering Parrot' proved another huge success for the star with its tale of nasty Polly and how he causes trouble between two newly-wed canaries who disturb him with their billing and cooing. Decrying husbands in general, and her new one in particular, to the canary wife, Polly sees strife born in the little ménage and soon the two are off to Mr Justice Owl for a judical separation while:

Polly winked his eye and Polly gave a sigh
And Polly bought a special 'Sun'
He read the full report of what occurred in court
And chuckled at the mischief done.
Then going off to bed
Contentedly he said
Thank goodness that's all right
I'll get some sleep tonight
A thing I cannot do
When lovers bill and coo
They won't annoy a soul
Poor Polly! Scratch a Poll!

Animals seemed to suit Miss Lind, for she was even more successful with an interpolated Lionel Monckton number 'I'll Wish Him a polite Good-day'. Greenbank composed two separate sets of lyrics for this song. The first was conceived to fit the action when Molly finds herself sold, through her foolishness, to the Marquis:

> Poor little maiden who loves a bit of fun
> Learns her propensity to rue
> Just look at me! What a pretty thing I've done!
> Here's a delightful how-de-do!
> A precious pickle I'm in!
> Foolish little Molly
> Punished for your folly
> A wooden monkey climbing
> Isn't on a stick like you!

The other version, made up for the sheet music market, told the tale of a toy monkey on a stick who goes out vainly to show off and only succeeds in getting drenched in the rain, run down by a bicycle and ends up paying for his pride in the rubbish bin. Both versions, however, caught on with the refrain:

> Click, click!
> I'm a monkey on a stick

Soon the show song was being announced as 'The toy Monkey' and the sheet music selling by the thousand.

If there was a weakness in the score of *The Geisha* it was in the songs allotted to the popular baritone, Hayden Coffin, as Fairfax. Jones and Greenbank did not bring up a new 'Queen of my Heart' or 'Tommy Atkins' though they followed the formulae with a sentimental ballad 'Star of my Soul' with a nicely swinging tune. A rather straight song called 'Chivalry' did not go at all and was later cut from the show. Lionel Monckton's second contribution to the show, a simple naval piece called 'Jack's the Boy', proved in the end to be the hero's best opportunity.

In the comedy role of the Chinese tea-house keeper, Huntley Wright came through with flying colours, making a meal of his home-made Chinese lingo, oriental malapropisms and vigorous visual comedy and of the most enduring number in the whole piece 'Chin Chin Chinaman':

> Chin chin Chinaman Muchee muchee sad!
> Me afraid Allo trade Wellee wellee bad!
> Noee joke, Brokee broke, Makee shuttee shop!
> Chin chin Chinaman Chop, chop, chop!

Harry Monkhouse as the pompous Marquis and Maud Hobson as the do-gooding Lady Constance had good acting roles with little singing, but Juliette Nesville had her own specially written role as the ambitious French girl and a delightful number 'If that's not Love':

> To win the man that's won my heart
> There's nothing I wouldn't do
> I'd wear a frock that wasn't smart
> An unbecoming chapeau too
> If square-cut shoes should please his taste
> Then no more pointed toes for me
> And thirty inches round the waist I'd cheerfully consent to be
> And if that's not love – what is?

However, Jones and Greenbank had done more than just write a selection of choice characteristic numbers for their stars. There was a good deal of ensemble and concerted music and one piece which drew special attention and favour from the critics was a short madrigalian section in the first act finale. The Lamentation Chorus and the Japanese March in the second act were also cleverly done and the lively concerted number 'We're Going to Call on the Marquis' was a frequent object of encores.

With such excellent material and such excellent artists, Edwardes had only to add his usual splendid production values and care for detail for success to be inevitable. After its tremendous first night reception *The Geisha* settled in for a run which was to extend over more than two uninterrupted years, setting a 760 performance record for a George Edwardes show, second only to *Dorothy*'s amazing run, and establishing itself as one of the greatest of stage musicals.

The success of *The Geisha* did not prevent the usual ration of alterations during the run. Edwardes kept his piece in trim with constant rehearsals and amendments both to the piece and to the cast. Coffin's 'Chivalry' number soon went, a quartet 'What will the Marquis Do?' was added and, most notably, the James Philp/Harry Greenbank number 'The Jewel of Asia' was interpolated for Marie Tempest. A few years later Miss Tempest recorded this song which remains the only original cast record from *The Geisha*. Napoleon Lambelet supplied a laughing song 'I can't Refrain from Laughing' which took its place in the show for a while, but the majority of the additions were supplied by the show's original writers. Amongst these were a quartet for four sailors, 'Jolly young Jacks', 'The Wedding', 'It's Coming off Today' and, in another attempt to find a song for Coffin, a ballad called 'Molly Mine'. Other later productions saw the interpolation of special numbers by particular leading artists but, the larger part of the score being so popular, such interpolations did not usually involve the cutting of any of the established score.

The Geisha was toured season after season for many years, mostly under the powerful Morell and Mouillot banner, and it returned to London on a number of occasions after its first triumphant run. In 1906 Edwardes brought it back to Daly's with the American May de Souza as Mimosa and Marie Studholme as Molly and with Huntley Wright's brother, Fred, taking his role of Wun-Hi. In 1931 it was again seen at Daly's and in 1934 at the Garrick.

Overseas, too, *The Geisha* had a remarkable career. On Broadway[1] it was produced by Augustin Daly at his own theatre but, in spite of a great reception, it had to be withdrawn after six weeks to allow Ada Rehan to take in her pre-booked production of *Henry IV*. The company was taken out of town and returned when the house was free but before long it was obliged to head for the country again to permit another pre-booking to be fulfilled. It speaks well of *The Geisha*'s popularity that it survived this treatment with the vigour of an *Erminie* and continued around New York and America for several years, notching up over 200 nights on Broadway in the process.

The show established itself as one of the most internationally popular of all British musicals and was played liberally in all the usual corners of the Empire as well as in some of the less likely parts of South America, in Germany, Hungary, Scandinavia, Russia, Australia, Czechoslavakia, Switzerland, Latvia, Italy, Spain and in France where the book apparently caused some problems which required major rewrites – a fate which had befallen many a 'naughty' French libretto in Britain but which hardly

[1] The original Broadway cast included amongst its chorus the 18-year-old-dancer, Isadora Duncan.

seemed justified (on those grounds, at least) in the case of *The Geisha*. It was also performed by a company in St Petersburg having been put together from memory by comedian George Graves and Richard Temple who had, at one stage or another, appeared in it. Even more curiously, it was performed by an enterprising Signora in Italy as a one-woman show. Quite how she managed the ensembles is not related. In both Italy and Germany *The Geisha* gained a solid reputation and a place in the standard repertoire. Both countries have also produced gramophone recordings of the show although it has never been recorded in the original English.

The Geisha, following on the heels of *A Gaiety Girl* and *An Artist's Model*, consolidated the creation of a middle-of-the-road light musical theatre, shunning on the one hand the more serious aspects of romantic and light opera and, on the other, the rumbustious vulgarities and musical rhythms of the music hall and the variety musical. It was light, bright and attractive entertainment for public who came repeatedly to see it and its successors at Daly's over the following years.

The next new piece in the West End was, again, in direct contrast. *On the March* had been produced by the energetic Cissy Graham at Sheffield and was a musical comedy adaptation of the vaudeville *In Camp* with which the celebrated Vokes family of pantomimists had had an enormous success throughout the country in the 'eighties. The entertainment centred round the efforts of some young army officers to arrange an amateur performance of *Faust*. Three ladies who are guests of the Colonel are mistaken for the professional actresses who have been hired to play opposite the theatrical soldiers, and until the Colonel turns up confusion reigns after which all is settled happily. That the story had more than a passing resemblance to Miss Graham's earlier touring success *A Pantomime Rehearsal* was no coincidence, for one of the co-authors of *On the March* was Cecil Clay, the writer of that popular one-acter. Clay was also the widower of Rosina Vokes who had died in 1894 at the age of 39, followed soon after by her sister, Victoria, the last of the four famous brothers and sisters, all of whom had died young. It was Victoria who was officially credited with the authorship of *In Camp*, so some surprise was felt when, just before the West End opening of *On the March*, Bella Moore, daughter of G. W. Moore of Ministrels fame and the widow of Fred Vokes, claimed for herself the rights to the original play as 'the only thing poor Fred left'. The timing of her allegation was impeccable, but Miss Graham was made of stern stuff and *On the March* duly made an unencumbered West End bow, after five weeks' No. 1 touring, at the Prince of Wales Theatre, filling the gap unexpectedly left by the failure of *Biarritz*.

On the March was credited to three librettists, Bill Yardley, Charlie Stephenson and Clay, a combination which seemed excessive given the slight and ready-made nature of its plot and dialogue. As a musical it brought the variety musical down to its barest bones with the gentlemen and the ladies' maid contributing the comedy, the ladies the pretty music, and everyone as many and as varied 'turns' as they pleased. The music for the piece was again from three different writers of whom two were already dead. Cecil Clay had delved into his brother Frederic's chest to find some numbers to add to the last commissioned compositions of poor Teddy Solomon, with John Crook, foremost composer of the variety musical, filling in the rest. Of course there was plenty of latitude for interpolations of which perhaps the most curious was a piece which led the audience through its verse and then, as it seemed ready to launch into its refrain, simply stated 'No Chorus'.

The cast of *On the March* was headed on the comedy side by the American variety comic Thomas E. Murray, one half of the double act of Murray and Murphy. *On the*

March was his British début and he played the role of Fitzallerton Scroggs, the put-upon theatre manager, originally created by Fred Vokes. Murray, a highly original comedian to English eyes, extended his role with his own specialities and did very well. The ladies' maid, Maggie (which role Victoria Vokes had written for herself) was taken by the well-loved Alice Atherton who danced, joked and sang through the evening in her usual vivacious way. She interpolated an American number into the score, a song called 'I've been Hoo-dooed' – an expression which more than one newspaper found it tactfully necessary to define.

The versatile Charlie Brookfield proved himself equally able as an actor and a writer as the humorous Lieutenant with his catch phrase 'What I ask myself is this . . . '; the soprano Maud Boyd and the baritone Templar Saxe provided the ballad music; and a beautiful débutante, Miss Augusta Walters, provided the principal glamour supported by a large line-up of attractive young people. A show which had originally been intended only as a touring piece, *On the March* scarcely had the qualities for metropolitan success but both audiences and critics seem to have accepted it at its face value, as a very simple variety farce, and made allowances for its sudden precipitation into the West End as a stopgap for the Prince of Wales management. The notices were quite kindly and the show held up for eleven weeks in Coventry Street before it left the theatre once more to Arthur Roberts and resumed its tour.

Preparing London shows in the provinces had become accepted practice over recent years but it was not a fashion which George Edwardes had ever followed. His Gaiety and Daly's pieces had always opened cold in town. For his successor to *The Shop Girl*, however, Edwardes resorted to the provincial try-out and his new Tanner/Ross/Osmond Carr musical was produced at Birmingham's Theatre Royal and given seven weeks' touring to prepare it for London. This was not an arbitrary move. It was undertaken because *The Clergyman's Daughter* was not merely a carbon copy of the *Shop Girl* formula, but an attempt to invest the musical with a substantial plot, a story as interesting and coherent as a straight play, while retaining the song, dance and spectacle which were the essential features of a Gaiety musical.

The clergyman of the title is the Rev. Arthur Mildreth who is determined that his children shall have the best in life, to which end he has saved a deal of money and obtained for his son a commission in the Guards. But the young Theo has sown his wild oats rather extravagantly and fallen into debt. His sister May would help him but her nest-egg is nowhere near enough so she hopefully invests it in some peculiar mining shares to try to raise the money. Theo's father cannot help him as his bank has failed, and the boy is obliged to seek his fortune and redeem himself in South Africa. In the second act we meet the swindling financier, van Fontein, who has been the cause of Theo's downfall. He is touting around a black African 'Prince', to the delight of the socialite Mayor of the town and his equally credulous wife. But the villain is unmasked with the help of the comical stock-jobber, Alex McGregor, the financial situation is saved by the opportune blossoming of May's mining shares, and all ends happily.

The reaction to Edwardes' and Tanner's initiative seemed promising. *The Stage*, reviewing the Birmingham première, commented that the show had:

> . . . an interesting, coherent, and at times really moving story . . . Mr Tanner knows exactly how to treat his subject so that the attention of the audience is not apt to wander. Bathos is never allowed to enter the serious side of his story while the farcical element is kept well in view.

This latter was certainly true for Tanner had created excellent roles for his principal comedians. John Le Hay, fresh from his Broadway triumph in *His Excellency*, played the Jewish bucket shop keeper, Alex McGregor (alias Moses Aaron, 'but it gives the customers confidence'), who, unusually, courts and wins the virtuous Rebecca von Fontein between his comic moments. His performance was given an added edge by the fact that he played McGregor as an impersonation of Jimmy Davis (librettist 'Owen Hall'), reproducing not only the author's speech and mannerisms but even going so far as to make himself up as a passable imitation. The swindler, the jumped-up Mayor and his wife (played by Connie Ediss) and the dusky 'Prince of Bashangoland' all added further to the fun.

The Clergyman's Daughter went down extremely well in the provinces and the seven weeks on the road were profitably used in polishing the piece preparatory to its production at the Gaiety where *The Shop Girl* was about to end its run. The improvements en route included the complete cutting of one of the lesser comedy roles (Admiral Bargrave, played by Carte veteran Cairns James) as well as the simplification of some of the plot elements which had been rather overladen with stock-market jargon and jokes. The tour ended and the piece, with its title suspended as unsatisfactory, went into rehearsal at the Gaiety. Edwardes had intended the light romantic leads of May and Theo for his top team of Ellaline Terriss and Seymour Hicks, but Hicks found the role unsuitable and declined to play it. Edwardes promoted the actor Paul Arthur who had been intended for the second juvenile role of Lord Barum (May's romantic interest) temporarily to take Hicks' place but angrily ensured, by having the contract reaffirmed in court, that Hicks appeared nowhere else until Edwardes could use him again. Lawrence d'Orsay took over as Barum until Louis Bradfield was engaged to take over the Hicks role. Arthur then stepped back into his own part and Edwardes had a new role written into *The Geisha* for the now unemployed Lawrence d'Orsay. Mrs Hicks, on the other hand, was perfectly suited with the ingénue role of May. Others of the Gaiety favourites from the *Shop Girl* cast were brought in to replace the touring stars and, as *My Girl*, the new show opened at the Gaiety on 13 July to a largely enthusiastic reception.

The next day *The Times* commented:

> The 'variety piece' into which the once flourishing amusement of comic opera has degenerated seems now to have reached a turning point none too soon and the success of *My Girl* . . . may have the happy result of popularising a more sane type of piece with fashionable audiences . . .

continuing:

> The new production by Mr J. T. Tanner is called a domestic musical play and may be described as an attempt to combine domestic comedy of a very old-fashioned kind with the quasi-musical entertainment now in vogue. The result of the amalgamation is not altogether happy from either a dramatic or a musical point of view, but everything must have a beginning and later experiments may succeed better in respect of construction . . .

Others were not quite so consistent in their reactions. Critics who had long and loudly bewailed the lack of plot and of 'play' in recent musicals, suddenly objected to having their Gaiety fare diluted with vaguely serious dialogue or anything else which might necessitate a degree of concentration. *The Era* considered that thirty minutes of the dialogue needed to be cut out and that they should be taken from 'the serious interest, the love-making and the financial intrigue', going on to complain:

> There is at present far too much intrigue in Mr James T. Tanner's book. On a sultry summer's evening it is irritating to be asked to remember a number of facts about banks with unlimited liability and the different prices of shares; and it is impossible to be thrilled to the core by the misfortunes of a spendthrift hero and a speculative heroine when the rush of our excitement has to halt to permit the introduction of a pas de trois or a South African nigger ditty. Let musical plays be musical plays and Adelphi dramas dramas of the Adelphi. We go to the Gaiety to be amused . .

There was little doubt that *The Era* expressed the opinion of the majority of playgoers – of Gaiety playgoers, at least. The mixture of dramatic plot and a light musical score did not suit them as well as the old combination. The theorists who had cried so long against the semi-plotless musical found that their demand for a thoroughly worked-out and reasonably involved plot in a light musical piece was, in practice, not a popular innovation. Fears that the Jewish community might object to the characters of McGregor, van Fontein and Rebecca were allayed by an excellent notice in the *Jewish Chronicle* and *The Era*, having expressed its reservations, went on to assure its readers that:

> there is an abundance of the diverting and the delightful in the entertainment . . song after song and dance after dance were encored . . with a little judicious curtailment and revision *My Girl* might be made as successful as most pieces of the class to which it belongs . .

Since the piece had overrun considerably on opening night, some revisions and curtailments were clearly in order and they were duly made, but Edwardes suddenly lost confidence in the staying power of *My Girl* and promptly set Tanner to work on another new musical based on the Austrian play *Eine tolle Nacht* which he had recently purchased. In the meanwhile, however, *My Girl* did nothing but prosper for, as *The Era* had agreed, it was indeed an entertainment full of good things. Although the score of Ross and Carr did not produce a major hit number, there was plenty of clever and attractive material, the most effective of which was probably Connie Ediss' number as the social-climbing Mayoress dreaming of 'When my Husband is Sir Tom':

> I'll have brilliant garden parties
> If it's not too hot
> For I'm sure that Sarah Bernhardt is
> Coming like a shot,
> And a meeting I'll devise her
> That will pleasantly surprise her
> I'll invite the German Kaiser
> When he sails his yacht.
> Come to tea
> Sarah B!
> When my husband is Sir Tom, pom, pom, pom.
> None shall take the biscuit from
> The extremely high and mighty Lady Tom, pom, pom.

Adrian Ross' lyrics were of his merriest and unusually frequently relevant. May sang, with refreshing candour:

> Preachers say that gold's a curse
> You will find it the reverse
> If you've money in your purse . .

Van Fontein recounted how

I've made my pile
In splendid style
By every wile
That's mercantile . .

and the stock-jobber led a trio vaunting 'Stocks and Shares':

When a weary weeping widow finds her income falling short
Which is risky,
When a gallant half-pay Colonel has to dock his pint of port
Take to whiskey!
When a clergyman has children who are causes of expense
And would like to make a trifle, but he can't imagine whence
Then he needn't mope and maunder in his lonely moated grange
Let him try the Stock Exchange – the Stock and Share Exchange

as well as describing the reasons for his tactful change of name:

It seemed to bring the speculative clergy to a stop
When they struck upon the name of Sammy Moses.

There were plenty of topicalities too. The lady cyclist was given her most expert lyrical treatment:

Female votaries
Of our coteries
Not like vicars' daughters fair
On their bicycles
Cool as icicles
Clad in knickers take the air.

along with the music hall craze:

Not for opera
Cares a copper a
Dame of fashion nowadays,
Ibsen's rank arrays
Mrs Tanquerays
Plot or passion, nothing pays . .
Though a Duse calls
Yet the music halls
Thronging thickly we attend
Those at any rate
Are degenerate
Suit our sickly age's end.

Water rates, the Boers, breach of promise and the lady journalist all got a verse of 'A Thing I cannot Explain' while society crazes (golf in, tennis and croquet out & c) were reviewed in 'The Form at a Glance'. Others were less directly satirical. Theo's song about 'The Grenadiers' emphasised principally their abilities in non-martial fields:

There's cricket and polo
And poker and solo
And other diversions with cards,
There is potting at Hurlingham doves
And racing that everyone loves
With raking in ponies from bookies and cronies
And losing to ladies in gloves . .

The vicar sang of fond memories of days as a 'varsity oarsman and a useful marriage got a tart rebuff:

LADY B: I've found you a lover
So rich and rare
His mansion will cover a West End Square
He's rich as a Barney
BEA: He's rude as a bear
And lacking in grammar and h's and hair!

It was very much more substantial stuff than the usual musical score. There were no catchy dance tunes equipped with lyrics which barely mattered, no trite love-songs full of standard sentiments, no music hall rum-ti-tum and suggestiveness: it was the score for a modern musical play of a certain ambition. That some of the Gaiety audience were happier with the dance tunes, the love songs and a few sniggers was inevitable, but there were plenty who appreciated the worth of *My Girl*, its songs and its play.

It soon became evident that Edwardes' haste to get a new piece prepared had been a little pessimistic. *My Girl*, without setting the Strand on fire, had caught on quite nicely and, although its popularity never looked like approaching that of *The Shop Girl*, it was nevertheless attracting plentiful audiences to the Gaiety. After six months, however, Edwardes decided that he would have to close the show. He had already announced *The Circus Girl* once and postponed it when *My Girl* showed no sign of weakening, and now he had promised the new show for Christmas and felt he could not postpone again. But *My Girl* was still running strongly and he decided it was worthwhile transferring it to the Garrick to continue its run. Thus, on 1 December, *My Girl* migrated to a new home where, with a cast now devoid of nearly all its stars, it played out the last weeks of its run. The show was subsequently seen in the provinces over five touring seasons and in South Africa as late as 1903 with considerable success.

Horse-racing drama and comedy-drama had always been popular in the British theatre and the race track had served as the background for one successful musical in Sims and Clay's *The Merry Duchess*. A new piece in a similar vein turned up in the 1896 season under the management of Alexander Loftus. *Newmarket* was the work of Mrs Frank Taylor, an author who as Emily Coffin had supplied Willie Edouin with two plays, *Run Wild* (1888) and *No Credit* (1892) during his period at the Strand. In Mrs Taylor's libretto the crooked jockey Charley Fenn and a devious American bookmaker known as Colonel Singleton are responsible for the ruin of the young Lord Kempton when they conspire to 'pull' the horse 'Snapshot' on which the racing peer's last hopes rest. Kempton's fiancée, Lady Windsor, and his trainer Tom Snaffle, raise enough money to back Tom's horse 'Poppy' in the China Cup for which it is apparently unbeatable but they are unable to find a jockey and it seems that Tom's daughter (also called Poppy) will have to take the ride. But Billy Price, a jockey fleeing from an unpleasant contract in France, turns up pursued by a French detective and agrees to get up on the horse only to be beaten by the double-dealing Fenn and 'Snapshot' in a close finish. But just when all looks grim, 'Snapshot' is disqualified for interference, and all ends happily.

The play had been constructed around and for the benefit of Willie Edouin, and the popular comedian was heavily featured as the honest-Joe trainer as was his daughter, May, in the role of his stage-daughter, Poppy. Edouin filled his role with the little peculiarities for which he was famous and introduced a couple of catch phrases . . 'It's hereditary' and ' . . . cake?', which were calculated to catch on. May Edouin sang prettily through John Crook's 'The Pedigree' and 'The Dream'. Sadie Jerome had also been hired for *Newmarket* and to fit her Mrs Taylor introduced into the first act a superfluous couple, Sir William and Lady Ascotte, he a phlegmatic aristocrat and she a music-hall lady married above her station. They had a few scenes of fairly poor repartee and Miss Jerome did her turn by performing two weak songs 'My Society Music Hall' and a dubious piece called 'Little Mrs Brown'. Once again, as in *Biarritz*, the role was not strong enough to support Miss Jerome's talents.

J. M. Capel's satirical song 'Say I've Nothing to Do' was one of the better numbers of an undistinguished score, and his trio 'Fal Lal' for the Edouins and Littledale Power proved, along with John Crook's 'Brass Band' quartet, the best received piece in the show. *Newmarket* originally saw the light of day at the Prince's Theatre in Manchester in June and arrived in town exactly two months later to play the Opera Comique. In the meantime it had been re-cast, re-jigged and theoretically improved, but quite what happened on its opening night in London is a little difficult to fathom. *The Times* evidently had a good evening, unless he was merely trying to help manageress Nellie Farren who had taken over the ailing Opera Comique Theatre. He reported:

> After the succession of scarcely-disguised variety entertainments which have lately been seen at so many theatres it is refreshing to find in Mrs Frank Taylor's 'original racing comedy with music' a work that has at least a fairly dramatic plot sufficient to sustain interest for 3 acts. In *Newmarket* the music hall element is not altogether absent, but it is chiefly confined to the first act and the piece would undoubtedly prove more effective if this part of the play were shortened and compressed, especially as the act as it stands is much the weakest and least satisfactory of the three. Without being very original or very well worked-out in its details, the story of *Newmarket* improves as the play goes on, and the last act, with its exciting scene on Newmarket Heath is so good as to atone for some of the dull moments of the opening . . . . The whole piece is well-mounted and was received with marked favour, the applause at the end being prolonged until the authoress had bowed her acknowledgements from a box.

The Stage seemed to have seen a different show. It described the second act as 'long and often uninteresting', dismissed the third (which had begun at 11 p.m.) as 'like every racing drama' and complained that the first act had used up all the best material. It also reported that Mrs Taylor had failed to appear in the face of satirical cries of 'author' at the final curtain. *The Era* inclined to the *Stage* version:

> . . the weakest part of the show is the last act . . . this act should be bolstered up with attractive variety items like those so freely introduced in the former part of the play. Lightness, brightness and gaiety are lavishly expended in the former part of the play . .

The Times had evidently gone wanting to see a racing comedy-drama, *The Stage* and *The Era* for a variety musical. What Mrs Taylor and her confederates on the musical and lyrical side had provided was just what they professed to provide – a racing play with incidental songs and dances dotted through it. Unfortunately the standard of the work was not what it might have been and, though the mixture was one which might just do well enough on the road, it was not going to please either the *Times* or the *Era* audiences in its present half-play, half-musical state. *Newmarket* lasted out 58 mediocre performances at the Opera Comique before taking to the road again. Edouin brought it out to tour a second time in 1897, as the role of Snaffle evidently appealed to him, but although it did fair business *Newmarket* was not equipped to become a favourite.

Just five days after *Newmarket* another new musical appeared on the reviewers' pads.

> . . Yet one more has been added to the long list of nondescript pieces which have so largely occupied the bills of many West End theatres during the last few years. To judge by its reception last night there seems to be no reason to doubt that *Monte Carlo* will be any less successful than any of its predecessors. It contains all that experience has shown to be the requisites of popularity in such entertainments. A plot which is so slight as to be practically non-existent, any number of bright songs and dances, a cast which includes artists who have made their reputations in better works and, last but not least, a strong infusion of music hall songs: these are the elements out of which a successful musical comedy is concocted, and in the new piece at the Avenue they are put together with sufficient skill to make a fortunate result almost a foregone conclusion. (*Times*)

Even *The Times*, while heaping its customary scorn on the lighter forms of musical entertainment, felt bound to admit that *Monte Carlo* seemed to have 'got it right', and it seemed that Henry Dana and H. J. Wilde had made a good choice for their venture into musical comedy at the Avenue. The pedigree of their show was excellent. It had a book and lyrics (the former under a pseudonym) by Harry Greenbank, the Daly's Theatre lyricist who had been responsible for the bulk of the songs in *A Gaiety Girl, An Artist's Model* and *The Geisha*, and the music was from the pen of one of the most promising young composers about, Howard Talbot, who had come upon the scene with *Wapping Old Stairs* a few years previously.

The story they had concocted employed the usual ingredients of money and marriage and the usual picturesque setting. Mrs Carthew, an ex-actress of some success and substantial means, has moored her yacht at Monte Carlo for the season, bringing with her her daughter, Dorothy. Mrs Carthew and her money are pursued by General Boomerang of the army on one hand and Sir Benjamin Currie MP on the other, while Dorothy has a truer and more disinterested lover in the dashing Fred Dorian. Also in Monte Carlo is the fly Professor Lorrimer who is 'agenting' for his daughters, the Sisters Gelatine, serios upon the West End stage, and their disapproved-of sister, known on the East End halls as Little Jemima. While biding their time over Mrs Carthew and Dorothy, the high-placed gentlemen are quite content to dally with the theatrical ladies. Owing to a misunderstanding over a letter, Fred and Dorothy quarrel and the young man dashes off to take the shilling. Mrs Carthew is, simultaneously, having even worse problems, for the waiter at the Hotel de Par turns out to be none other than James, her husband, whom she married when he was an acrobat and she a struggling performer, and whom she thought dead. He is not, but he is about to marry the French girl, Suzanne. At a second act party on board the yacht, the Silver Swan, all is disentangled. Mrs Carthew and James come together again, young Fred returns from Egypt covered in glory to claim his Dorothy, whilst the army and the Commons content themselves with the Sisters Gelatine, and Suzanne gets the whole male chorus.

The plot of the first act all but vanished in the second, returning in time for the ritual winding-up at the end of the show. The advances in dramatic form made by *An Artist's Model, My Girl* and *The Geisha* were ignored in the construction of *Monte Carlo* which turned quite gleefully and unashamedly to the *Morocco Bound* tradition of the variety musical, whilst using songs that were far superior on the whole to the normal run of variety show numbers. The hit of the opening night, however, was made by a distinctly music-hall song, 'I'm Jemima', sung by Lalor Shiel as the diminutive East End trouper. Miss Shiel, a grand-niece of the politician, Lalor Shiel, had made a career in child's roles in melodrama, as principal boy in pantomime and, on occasionally, on the halls. Her last roles had been as Lucien in *An Artist's Model* on tour and as one of the sisters in a production of *The Lady Slavey*. With *Monte Carlo*, and with Louie Freear having made munchkins all the rage, she landed the role of Jemima, and became a favourite with her quaint antics and her singing of:

I'm the pet of the 'alls
I'm Jemima
And they whistles and calls
For Jemima!

Every night, 'owever late,
They escorts me 'ome in state
You should see the crowds that wait
For Jemima!
Hi boys, ho boys, 'ave you seen Jemima?
She's the sort of girl to knock you flat!
With 'er fascinatin' figger
In a rig that's quite de rigger
And a cocky little feather in 'er 'at!

It was hardly a classic lyric, but Talbot's driving tune and Miss Shiel's broad Cockney delivery (she came from Canada via Cork) helped to make it the high point of the evening. Jemima had another number telling the tale of one 'Miss Priscilla Pip', and joined in a duet with Charles Rock as Sir Benjamin describing the superfluous antics of 'The dancing Dean' who transfers his talent to the stage:

The people flocked to see
Determined not to miss it
Till his Bishop heard
Of the sight absurd
And went in the pit to hiss it.

But so entranced was he
With the pas de doo's devices
That the next day saw
A pas de traw
Announced at special prices!

Sing tooral looral lay!
Oh, didn't that performance pay
The bishop stout, the ballerine,
And the truly rooral-looral Dean!

The audience's taste for a saucy song was further catered for by the Sisters Gelatine, played by a genuine sister act from the variety stage, May and Venie, the Belfry Sisters. There is Gertie who claims:

. . as everyone knows
I can stand on my toes
For a quarter of an hour without a murmur

and Bertie who in her turn informs us:

. . my feet, if you should care,
I can fling in the air
To an altitude that's perfectly astounding

before assuring us catchily that they are:

The haughty little, naughty little
Know-you-didn't-ought-y little
Pretty little, witty little
Sisters Gelatine.

Bertie also delivered a coy music-hall ditty entitled 'If only I Knew the Way', detailing all the things she would do if she did. Comedy songs abounded. General Boomerang had a typical piece about the problem of having a warhorse which *would* lead you into the thick of the battle, Lottie Venne as Mrs Carthew was successful with an arch warning to the flirt 'Very careful if you Please' and joined in a trio with Suzanne and Dorothy concerning 'The Duties of a Ladies' Maid'. The role of Suzanne was taken by Emmie Owen, who had recently been promoted leading lady at the Savoy, and who had a couple of good duets with her intended (E. W. Garden). The first, 'The Use of French' described the indispensable French expressions used in day-to-day English:

Britannia rules the waves, it's true,
But what would you poor Britons do
Without the festive, ever-restive
Too suggestive Parley-vous?

and the second, accompanied by a dance routine, a clever little tale of romance and jealousy: he is a yellow-book poet, she blue with loneliness, the result is a jealous green. The romantic representatives of Dorothy and Dorian, Kate Cutler and Richard Green, had a large share in the score, and the romantic numbers compared very favourably with most recent specimens of the kind. Green scored with a pretty ballad, 'I only Know I Love Thee':

Though earth and air
Are bright and fair
Around thee and above thee
I only see
My world in thee
I only know I love thee

and a patriotic song, 'The scarlet Coat', and joined with Kate Cutler in a fine duet 'Along the Way where Lovers Go', while the lady scored best with the romantic 'The Land of Heart's Desire'. The musical plan of *Monte Carlo* was a very full one and, indeed, at the last moment two interpolated numbers by Reginald Somerville which had been printed in the first-night script were cut out. *Monte Carlo* was the work of a lyric-writer and it was no coincidence that its songs formed the strongest and most important part of the show, while the fortunate choice of Talbot as a composer emphasised their effectiveness.

But the opening night success of *Monte Carlo* did not satisfy those concerned with the show, and over the weeks that followed many new numbers were tried out, some from Greenbank and Talbot, others from outside. 'Miss Priscilla Pip' was eliminated, as were a 'Roses red and White' duet, the Paolo Giorza number 'Out of Fashion' and a piece which Greenbank had composed for Robb Harwood called 'Pirate Peter'. Somerville's 'For the Safety of the Public' was given a try, and another Giorza number, 'A distinguished Visitor', was tried for Eric Lewis. One of the best of the outside numbers was a pathetic little piece written by the actor Leedham Bantock and composed by his conductor brother, Granville, called 'Who'll give a Penny to the Monkey?'. Harry Greenbank had another go at proving himself a composer with a number about balding, 'The Thinning of the Thatch' and Garden was given a cautionary tale, 'A Tale of a Restaurong', but the best of the new pieces were John Crook/Harry Nicholls' 'I'm Doing very well Indeed' for Harwood and a Felix McGlennon piece, 'Fiddle-de-diddle-de-Dee' for Lalor Shiel. Seldom had a piece gone through so much in the way of alteration after a seemingly positive opening.

Audiences looked to be good, and the general consensus was that *Monte Carlo* would run on for a long season. But after ten weeks Dana and Wilde announced that their lease of the Avenue had terminated. *Monte Carlo* could not stay at the Avenue and it was not considered practicable to transfer. To the general surprise what had seemed a surefire success, if not even a hit, fizzled out prematurely and there was an end of it. Quite what the truth behind the affair was it is impossible to guess. 'Terminated lease' was often a euphemism for 'terminated cash resources', but unless someone had done his sums very poorly *Monte Carlo* must surely have been running at better than break-even figures. And then there were the residual rights.

Those rights were picked up. Wallace Erskine toured two companies the following spring playing *Monte Carlo* in the provinces and it also achieved an American production under the management of E. E. Rice. But there again the show fell on unfavourable circumstances. The numerous successes recently achieved on Broadway by British musicals had clearly annoyed one important section of the American public – the press. *Monte Carlo* arrived just in time to take the brunt of their views. The American correspondent of *The Era* reported:

> One of the 39 articles of the American constitution, as New York journalists understand it, is that humour is exclusively an American product. Accordingly all the stock phrases about 'deadly British humour' that the average New York space writer repeats with the regularity of a well-trained parrot were trotted out once more and *Monte Carlo* was damned either with faint praise or unreservedly.

before giving his own version of the facts:

> I saw the play last Friday night (March 25) after it had been 'Americanised' which is merely their way of saying that a number of 'specialities' as they are called in America, had been introduced into the second act. I heard, as I have often heard before, the 'dreary London jokes', on which the newspapers' contumely had been heaped unmercifully, laughed at as heartily as if they had had 'Made in America' stamped on them . . The poor misguided audience evidently didn't know the difference . . . There was a full house and although the play had been variously described as 'British and dull to a degree', 'a weird British product' and as 'having only a few amusing moments', the laughter and applause were continuous . .

Word of mouth, however, did not save *Monte Carlo*'s Broadway season. It was barely surprising, for the second act in particular now resembled a country music hall performance. One of the 'specialities' introduced a 'humorous' version of the song 'On the Banks of the Wabash' enlivened by the use of a couple of prop. moons and the throwing of hay on to the stage at 'appropriate' moments in the lyrics. There were a series of biograph pictures showing views of Havana harbour, the battleship Maine (cheers), its sinking (hisses), General Wyler and various other patriotic motifs; an animated music-sheet and an imitation of the striptease trapeze artist Charmion from

Koster and Bial's Music Hall. These 'acts' were announced, in true music-hall fashion, as changeable weekly. Although the bulk of the original score survived, the existing music-hall element of *Monte Carlo* was utterly submerged which, since the Sisters Gelatine were apparently played by two American ladies giving impressions of Bessie Bellwood, was probably just as well. The result of the whole was, in the words of *The Era* man, 'a hideous mimicry'. Rice withdrew what for history's sake goes down as the run of Harry Greenbank's *Monte Carlo* after a very short run, some $10,000 the poorer.

If *Monte Carlo* deserved better than its fate, London's next new entry assuredly did not. *Lord Tom Noddy* had a pedigree equal to that of its predecessor, being written by two top writers, George Dance and Frank Osmond Carr. It also had the advantage of a provincial run-in of eight weeks since its original April production in Bradford. But *Lord Tom Noddy*'s central fault was not one which could be amended by a little touching-up and a few interpolations, for it lay in the conception of the piece as a whole and in a matter of taste. The show took the prevailing craze for diminutive heroes and heroines too far, and it centred its story around the music hall entertainer Little Tich with a clumsiness and display of bad taste which was truly offensive. The story which the usually impeccable Dance created round his star was a peculiarly unpleasant one in which every character, the 'hero' not excepted, motivated by pecuniary greed, spend their time searching for the inevitable missing heir. The only exception to this avaricious rule is the pretty nurse, Phoebe, and it is she who, not unexpectedly, gets the 'little man' who has turned out to be the lost beneficiary.

The piece's chief source of humour lay in emphasising the inches or lack of them of 'Tom Noddy', most particularly in contrasting him with the chief 'baddies', Colonel and Miss Ben Nevis as played by the gigantic Picton Roxburgh (a great favourite as a pantomime giant) and Annie Esmond. The character of 'Tom Noddy' was not particularly sympathetic:

> I'd an ancestral home old and rich
> A library fit for a sage
> And family portraits all of which
> I sold on my coming-of-age.
> My taste is for fast-trotting gees
> And bow-wows that worry and kill
> And dens where you sit at your ease
> And witness a jolly good mill
> And clubs where a supper is served
> With Cliquot and Moet and Pom
> And rarebits and devils – the king of the revels
> Is 'Good Old Tom'

As *The Sketch* commented:

> You will see from the ballad what his Lordship is like, and perhaps be a little surprised that such a person is the hero of the piece and that one is supposed to take a friendly interest in him, and rejoice that the love affairs of this debauched homunculus with a beautiful young girl end in marriage – it must be borne in mind that throughout the book Lord Tom is represented as a dwarf.

After the original Bradford production, under the personal supervision of Dance himself, there were some major alterations. One role, Mlle Bébé de Sans Souci, was cut out and replaced by an English role to allow Katie James to come into the show for town. But the piece stood or fell almost entirely on the performance of Little Tich and the audience's taste for him. Unfortunately the material with which he had been provided was not up to the best standard of either author or composer and there was less and less applause from the London first-night audience as the evening progressed. At the final curtain the response was more than mixed, as was the subsequent press reaction. *The Sketch* had no doubts:

> *Lord Tom Noddy* is contemptible stuff . . . Mr Dance shows quite a remarkable lack of inventiveness and little judgement in his borrowings . . a lamentable desecration of the theatre . . a perversion of the functions of the stage . .

It goes without saying that the *Sketch* critic did not like 'Little Tich'. But *The Times*, which felt less horror at what the *Sketch* called 'a freak show', could still find little good to say about the piece:

> It would be rash to say that *Lord Tom Noddy* is the worst of its class, for experience has shown that this kind of piece is capable of so much alteration that what at a first performance seems hopelessly feeble may be worked up into a popular if not an artistic success . . .. Flimsy construction and general vagueness which characterise the plot of *Lord Tom Noddy* almost exceed the licence allowable to authors of musical comedies . . the music which Mr Carr has written for this foolish piece will not rank with his most successful efforts . . many of the numbers in the later part of the work met with chilling silence . .

With indifferent if not downright bad material and a star who proved to have limited appeal for the theatre public, *Lord Tom Noddy* could scarcely expect to survive, and after two months it folded in London and crept back to the provinces. Little Tich stubbornly took the show out again briefly in the spring of 1897 and again, at slightly more length, in the autumn before it was put aside for good.

The London season did, however, put forward one positive aspect by bringing into prominence Miss Mabel Love, who scored a personal success in the role of Nurse Phoebe. Miss Love had made a huge triumph in America in the role of Blanca in *His Excellency*, and London playgoers now saw her in her first major West End role in which she sang and danced her way into the hearts of her audiences with 'I am a sweet Hospital Nurse'. Along with the interpolated 'Rhoda on a Roadster' (Willie Younge/Harnett) sung by Sidney Harcourt, Miss Love took the chief musical honours of the show. The principal dancing credit went to one Miss Goss, a lady with a busy schedule as she began her evening at the Lyric dancing the Heathen Dance in *The Sign of the Cross* before coming up the road to the Garrick to give a rather less pagan piece in *Lord Tom Noddy*.

The next new show to follow, *The White Silk Dress*, was also written around its star, once again the irrepressible Arthur Roberts, returning to the Prince of Wales with a successor to *Gentleman Joe* and *Biarritz*. His latest vehicle had been written by Henry J. W. Dam, the author of the libretto to *The Shop Girl*, and Dam had encountered the well-known difficulties of working with the egocentric comedian. During rehearsals he found his dialogue being virtually thrown out of the window to accommodate Roberts' ad-libbing, but he also found that there was no point in complaining – there was no controlling the popular comedian. The book which Dam was trying to protect was scarcely a scintillating affair. It was an old-fashioned episode concerning a missing will. A lady has died and left her wealth unexpectedly away from her logical heirs. But it is discovered that there may be a second will, hidden in the pocket of a certain white silk dress. The action of the play concerns the farcical chase after the dress with the 'briefless barrister', Jack Hammersley, played by Roberts, at the head of the chase.

After a succession of songs and disguises have been gone through it turns out that the lady of the will is not dead at all, but merely wanted to see the reactions of her 'loved ones'. Jack (who has acted mercenarily throughout and uttered not a few rude comments about her) is, for some reason, adjudged to have performed most satisfactorily and becomes the heir of a third will.

The musical portion of the show consisted of a section of songs composed by the show's conductor, George Byng, the actor-turned-composer Reginald Somerville and Alick McLean, composer of the prize-winning opera *Petruchio*, with Byng providing the few concerted pieces. None of the numbers was in any way exceptional and the show itself disappointed even Roberts' most ardent fans. At the fall of the curtain on opening night *The Stage* reported 'it was difficult to say in the babel of sound if the ayes or the noes had it'. But the ayes were clearly for Roberts and the noes were for the piece. Even though the show would have doubtless worked up fairly well by the natural Roberts process, the lesson of *Biarritz* encouraged him to more radical action. After seven weeks' run the show was given a wholesale face-lift. Entire scenes were scrapped and replaced, changing the plot and action of the piece considerably; new business was introduced and eleven fresh numbers were put into the score including 'He Wants some More' from Roberts' trusted Chapman and Laidlaw and an effective piece called 'The Trombone Man' for Kitty Loftus. Cast changes were made too. Decima Moore and the veteran Furneaux Cook, both more accustomed to comic opera than the vagaries of an Arthur Roberts' production, were replaced by Stella Gastelle and Isidore Marcil, while Charles Rock, who had just closed in *Monte Carlo*, was brought in for Eric Thorne. Several other actors found that rewrites had eliminated their roles altogether. *The White Silk Dress* was more firmly focused on its star than ever. But the improvements were, apparently, just that and *The Daily Telegraph* reported: 'New songs and business have worked marvels for *The White Silk Dress*'. They certainly provided sufficient impetus to ensure that the show did not suffer the undignified fate of *Biarritz* and, although it was several classes below what Roberts had achieved in *Gentleman Joe*, it survived, largely on its star's reputation and energy, for a highly respectable 132 performances before being removed to allow the production of Lowenfeld's new French import, *La Poupée*.

The Belle of Cairo was a third consecutive 'vehicle' to open in London when it was produced at the Court Theatre on October 10, the 'Belle' in question being May Yohe who had earlier that year presented herself at the same theatre in a revival of *Mamselle Nitouche*. *The Belle of Cairo* had been prepared for her by F. Kinsey Peile and was staged under the aegis of a syndicate set up for the purpose and to supply the necessary £5,000.

Peile, born of Indian Army stock at Allahabad, had been in the Welsh Regiment before turning to acting at the age of 30 and making his début in a tiny role in *Blue-Eyed Susan*. The book for *The Belle of Cairo* was his first produced stage work, written in conjunction with the dramatist Cecil Raleigh whose previous venture into the field of musicals had been with *Little Christopher Columbus*, Miss Yohe's original London success. *The Belle of Cairo* was an unambitious and unimaginative piece with a small if relatively coherent story, illustrated by a number of rather amateurish and blatantly imitative songs. Its principal attraction seems to have been its choice of Egypt as a locale.

The Times commented:

> It is hardly so loose in construction as the go-as-you-please performances of Mr

> Roberts. On the other hand it depends much more upon its accessories of song and dance than upon its story, which indeed is primitive, and it may be regarded as one of the numerous forms of the variety entertainment.

The Era was less kind:

> The musical play is undergoing the usual penalty of general demand; it is degenerating in quality. From an artistic point of view the incoherent 'go-as-you-please' character of the entertainment has put it out of court; but we have pardoned slip-shod construction and the irrelevant introduction of songs and dances for the sake of smartness of observation, mordant wit, and above all, for the diverting nature of the variety entertainment. *The Belle of Cairo* . . is like the vapid liquor which is drawn from the apples in the cider-making counties after the juice of the fruit has been exhausted by the press. Its plot is feeble, its humour is feeble, the voice of the leading lady is feeble. It is emphatically poor stuff; and, really, the best thing in the entertainment is the dancing of the low comedian.

The 'primitive' plot was just that, consisting of over-familiar elements, the principal of which finds the lady of the title, Nephthys, who is betrothed to Duval Bey (owner of a gambling casino, but once a member of the civil service) following her real sweetheart, the gallant Sir Gilbert Fane of the 21st Cavalry, to the front in the war against the dervishes, disguised as a boy servant. Her pursuing relatives track her down, but a simple change of clothes with the obliging Lady Molly Rosemere (who, with her family, also appear tracking various partners through the desert battlefields) serves to confound the Egyptians and bring the plot to what is apparently its logical ending.

The role of Nephthys was created for Miss Yohe and its chief advantage, according to *The Times*, was that it allowed her to get into boy's clothes. It also, most unfortunately, required her to act and, worst of all, sing. She had never had much of a voice but by now it had almost disappeared and Kinsey Peile, in asking her to reach an E natural, was taking a risk which Ivan Caryll had not been game to take in the lady's heyday. He took an even greater risk in providing her with three big solos and a duet ranging from the romantic 'The Hour of Prayer' to a curious patriotic number 'The Gordon Boys' praising military training for orphans, to a zoological song, 'The Hoo Poo Bird'. This last told the tale of Mr and Mrs Hoo Poo who live happily among the reeds of the Nile until shot down by a British sportsman. In the final verse, stuffed, on his mantelpiece in Bloomsbury Square, the Hoo Poos sing their ghostly love song as of yore. It did not, apparently, have any particular moral but it was a simple and amusing enough song which, needless to say, suffered somewhat at the hands of its exponent.

There was some applause for a blatantly patriotic effort 'An Englishman's Duty' as rendered by the baritone John Peachey:

> An Englishman must march to glory
> An Englishman must thrash the foe
> Each Englishman repeats the story
> As Englishmen have done, you know,
> No Englishman knows when he's beaten
> Each Englishman does all he can
> From days of Rugby, Harrow and of Eton
> An English boy's an Englishman!

The score included Peile identikits of all the most popular types of numbers. To add to the patriotic and the zoological there was a picturesque piece called 'Good old Cairo' which served, reprised, as a finale; there was the comic with a piece about 'The Carpet

Seller of Cairo'; several ballads for the sentimental; and that sine qua non, the suggestive. Peile's chief effort in this direction proved distasteful, not to say transparent:

Betsy Jane she had a dimple
Pretty little maid
She only showed it when she smiled
The artful little jade.
A charm within that dimple lay
She prized it very highly
She well knew how to make it pay
She dimpled it so slyly

Betsy Jane, of course, ended up with a millionaire because she 'prized her dimple highly'. But not for long, for she was quickly cut from the score. This scarcely mattered at there were two other songs, both interpolations, which told an almost identical tale; 'Henrietta, have you Met Her' (Walter Ford/J. W. Bratton) and 'Such a timid little Thing' (Percy Gaunt).

To get a little capable singing into the show, a sub-plot had been constructed concerning a romance between Lady Molly's father and Nephthys' aunt-in-law. This latter role was taken by the 1870's prima donna Giulia Warwick, whilst another former opera singer, Michael Dwyer, was seen as Nephthys' father. The principal comedy was provided by a comic servant, James, played by clever Arthur Nelstone whose eccentric dancing *The Era* had appreciated.

There was no doubt that *The Belle of Cairo* was a total failure from the word go. Miss Yohe, however, perservered for two months before announcing that her show would be withdrawn for revisions. The Court closed on the Saturday with the re-opening advertised for Tuesday coming, but when that day arrived the theatre remained mercifully closed. However, the revised version was eventually to see the light. The experienced H. Chance Newton prepared a very different book with the peripheral Stallabrass family exorcised from the script and a gaggle of exaggerated Americans taking their place. A bundle of other excess characters vanished and new songs and 'business' were tacked in amongst the remnants of Peile's work. The new version came out at the Grand Theatre, Birmingham in November of 1901 and was sent on tour with Jessie Huddlestone starring as Nephthys. But the tour collapsed en route when insufficient funds were forthcoming from the box-office to pay the cast, and the management were taken to court by the angry star. Amazingly, *The Belle of Cairo* resurfaced again the following year and in 1903 was taken on a tour by Charles Wibrow, the original 'Earl of Bulcester'. It was by now a shapeless mass of interpolations and was finally laid to rest after a persistent but wholly unsuccessful career.

This succession of dubious star vehicles was varied in December by the production of the new George Edwardes' show at the Gaiety. Edwardes had seen Freund and Marinstädt's play *Eine tolle Nacht* in Vienna and had been taken by the central incident set in a circus ring viewed from backstage. He bought the British rights to the piece and handed it to James Tanner to use as the core for a circus musical. Tanner duly obliged by constructing a Gaiety piece, *The Circus Girl*, in which two scenes were 'suggested by an incident in *Eine tolle Nacht*'.

The experience of *My Girl* led Tanner to moderate the convolutions of his plot and he centred the whole business of the evening on a set of English ladies and gentlemen in Paris who get mixed up with the affairs of a peripatetic circus. Dora Wemyss, fresh out of school and intended for the Hon. Reginald Gower, falls for Dick Capel whom she takes for a member of the circus. Reginald, arrived in Paris with Dora's parents, has meanwhile taken a fancy to La Favorita, the circus girl. Before the respective pairs can finally get together we pass through lively scenes on the boulevards of Paris, at the Café Régence, in the circus ring and finally in the Commissariat of Police where the whole company ends up after a series of adventures including the shooting of Dora's flirtatious father from a circus cannon. In the end all is happily resolved under the twinkling lights of the Artists' Ball. Through these variegated scenes of 'la vie Parisienne' passed the whole equipage of Gaiety stars in the cheerful roles that the choice of subject allowed, all well supplied with songs and dances from the best composers and lyricists of the light musical stage.

The opening night of *The Circus Girl* was a triumph. The box-office on the Monday morning was inundated with requests for tickets and an unprecedented amount was taken in advance bookings in the one day. Edwardes had lined up an outstanding set of stars for the production. Ellaline Terriss, now established as the Gaiety's leading lady, took the role of Dora and her husband Seymour Hicks returned to the fold to play her lover, Dick. The Australian, Ethel Haydon, who had also appeared in *My Girl*, added to the romantic side as La Favorita, with Maurice Farkoa as a dashing French Vicomte Gaston. The comedy side was overwhelmingly catered for with Harry Monkhouse as the philandering Sir Titus and Arthur Williams as the ringmaster representing the older generation alongside Maria Davis, in her umpteenth Gaiety show, as Lady Wemyss. Edmund Payne as a little bartender and Katie Seymour as his Lucille who will marry him if he fights the Terrible Turk, Toothick Pasha, the circus strongman, were another delightful comedy team and Connie Ediss as the fat and jealous lady wife of the ringmaster consolidated her place as a Gaiety favourite with a hilarious performance. Stalwarts such as Robert Nainby, Bertie Wright, Leslie Holland, Colin Coop (of 'Brown of Colorado' fame) and William Powell were all there in lively minor roles.

The costumes, the dances and the scenery, were executed with the Gaiety's impeccable taste and lavish hand but, like all others of its type, *The Circus Girl* was bound to stand or fall on its fun and its songs, and in both these areas it proved infallible. Ellaline Terriss scored a major hit with a Lionel Monckton number 'A simple little String', which described the uses of a bit of string – firstly to keep baoy in her highchair, then, as a child, to play tricks with a penny tied to a string and, finally, as a woman:

Now I am a woman and expect to be a wife
I will not lead the customary miserable life
My husband shall be safe at home as happy as a king
And if he ever tries to roam, I'll try a bit of string!

Just a little bit of string, such a tiny little thing
Shall I tell you what the string may be?
Make him put his slippers on, and be sure his boots are gone
And you've got him on a string, you see.

while Connie Ediss topped even her 'Sir Tom' number from *My Girl* with another Monckton number describing 'The Way to Treat a Lady'. Abandoned by her husband amongst the throng of the Artists' Ball she sang:

I think that it's behaving very shabby
For any man to say unpleasant things

Because I've had some trouble with a cabby
Who went and said I'd broke his blessed springs.
I haven't ate enough to keep a baby
One gets so hungry at a fancy ball
And there my husband dashes off a-drinking brandy smashes
Oh, it's not the way to treat a wife at all!

Though I never care to make a fuss
Unless a thing is positively shady
I've a woman's heart that feels
When I cannot get my meals
That it's not the proper way to treat a lady!

before going on to other unfortunate episodes related to her size – abandoned at a cricket match, being 'reduced' by the massage system or having to wear a bathing suit and declaring:

I decline to wear a dress
Made of half a yard or less
For I think it's hardly decent for a lady!

Edmund Payne and Katie Seymour scored with two typical duets with dances – 'Clowns' (Monckton) and 'Professions' (Caryll) – which detailed the possible jobs the couple might take when married, each suggestion being foiled by the little man's jealousy of the men his wife might meet in the process. Payne and Seymour made their numbers more than just ordinary song and dance pieces, interpolating series of impersonations and eccentric movements in an almost burlesque style, but one which thoroughly pleased the audiences.

Imitations formed part of the artillery of Hicks and Miss Terriss as well. In their first act duet, 'In the Ring', they managed to show off their versatility in a selection of extended circus mimes – a juggling routine to Fahrbach's *En Forêt Polka*, an acrobatic performance, an equestrienne display to Waldteufel's *Vision Valse* and a performing dog section to close. Hicks had a pretty number with a chorus of girls and umbrellas called 'A wet Day' (Monckton) but was less successful with Ivan Caryll's 'She never Did the same Thing Twice'. He described:

On the first night I sang a song called 'She never Did the same Thing Twice'. It was a very ordinary song, and before I had got half way through the second verse a boy in the gallery called out to me 'Seymour'. I looked up, and he said 'Granted'. I said 'Eh?'. He said 'Granted, old boy' and, bowing politely, I took the hint, finished as quickly as I could, and never sang the song again.

Maurice Farkoa, now a firm favourite with the ladies, had two songs, one celebrating 'Wine, Women and Song' and the other a charming little Parisian tale 'Now that you Know your Way' in which he invested a tra-la-la reprise with all the varying significances in the world:

When strolling down the boulevard that's near the Opera
Tra la la la la la la la la la – Tra la la la la la!
I met a pretty maiden without her dear Mama
Tra la la la la la la la la la – Tra la la la la la!
She dropped her dainty parasol and much to her distress
Somebody came and trod on the frame and smashed it more or less
I said I'd get it mended if she'd tell me her address
Tra la la la la la la la la la – Tra la la la la la!

She answered me so prettily
You go to the left and keep on straight
Then first to the right and through a gate
Up seven steps and past a lane
Down a flight of stairs again!
You turn to the right, count twenty-five
And round by a court and a carriage drive
Fourteenth floor is where I stay
So now you know your way!

But when the young man has bought a new parasol and followed the tortuous instructions to their end, he finds that the lady has had her parasol mended by another gentleman and he is given short shrift.

The choicest comic piece of the night fell to Teddy Payne with his barman's song, describing his aptitude for his trade:

Supposing you should suffer from depression that is chronic
If only you will trust yourself to me
I'll fix you up directly with a pick-me-up or tonic
However out of spirits you may be
Perhaps your little trouble is a 4 a.m. o'clock tale
Returning from a Covent Garden ball
Be sure that I'll supply you with a 'Morning Glory' cocktail
And mix a 'Tom & Jerry' when you call!
Champagne, Cocktail, Saratoga, Cooler
Gin Sling, Negus, Sherry Sangaree
Mixtures that are Yankee ones
Are all hanky-panky ones
Name your symptoms, leave the rest to me!

The Circus Girl was brimful of good songs, bright dialogue and genuine fun, the whole performed by a cast of the most loved musical artists in the country, and it duly established itself as a solid hit for all those concerned, including Gaiety Board Chairman 'Walter Palings' (otherwise Pallant) who got himself a share of the book credit along the way. The run of the show extended right through 1897 and finally terminated after a fifteen months' season with some claiming it as the best Gaiety show yet. An American production, at Daly's Theatre, confirmed the piece's virtues, being one of the hits of the 1897 Broadway season with a run of 172 performances, in spite of the bedevilment of a hot summer which forced a temporary closure at the height of the show's popularity.

West End producers had been unusually busy during the year, but new provincial offerings were no less numerous. Several of the year's metropolitan pieces owed their origins to provincial productions and, of the crop of 1896, four pieces bred out-of-town made it to the West End theatre. Three, *Lord Tom Noddy, On The March* and *The Clergyman's Daughter/My Girl* transferred during the year, the fourth, the Basil Hood/Walter Slaughter collaboration *The French Maid* had a little longer to wait. The Hood/Slaughter combination had been so immensely successful with *Gentleman Joe* that it was logical they should continue to work together. The result was *The French Maid* produced at Bath in April under the management of Milton Bode who had been so very happy with his extended tours of *Gentleman Joe*. The new piece opened with every semblance of success and was given a nine-weeks' tour followed by a nineteen weeks' run in the autumn, all with most positive results. These tempted Bode to try for

London and the following year, while its lucrative tours continued, *The French Maid* opened in London.

This was by far the most superior piece that the provinces threw up during the year, but two other works which were to have provincial careers spanning a good number of years also made their first appearance. One of these, the farcical musical *Skipped by the Light of the Moon*, was even seen briefly in the West End in 1899 in a very heavily revised version under the title *A Good Time*.

The history of *Skipped by the Light of the Moon* was a long one and extended over a fair part of the globe. Its origins were in the George Sims farce *A Gay City*, commissioned from the distinguished author/journalist in 1881 by Charles Majilton for his family troupe and toured by them around the country with great success for many years. The musical content of the piece was apparently first introduced in America. Two gentlemen had visited the touring company of *A Gay City* at Her Majesty's Theatre, Carlisle and, sitting each night in the front row with their hats on their laps, had bit by bit inscribed the whole piece on to a pile of visiting cards which, completed, were dropped into the strategic hats and thus left the theatre headed for the other side of the Atlantic. As *Skipped by the Light of the Moon*, the resultant show was toured continually in America over a period of some ten years. Early on in its career, it was also introduced to Australia where it gained equal popularity.

The nature of the piece and of its musical sections were such that numbers could be inserted or altered or dropped at will, and new and currently popular songs were freely introduced for longer or shorter periods during the show's meanderings. The comedian George Walton secured the British rights and produced it at Reading in August, 1896, beginning a series of tours which was to last for many years. The plot and large pieces of Sims' original dialogue either remained or had been restored, and from time to time he was given a book credit on programmes, but the music was an odd collection. Some of the pieces were new for the occasion, others had been collected through time, and some were frankly pilfered – quite how much is no longer easy to establish – but the music credit was given to Australia's George Pack and to Henry W. May, the musical director of Walton's company, and the lyrics were said to have been written by Percy Marshall. The Reading performance is known to have included Ivan Caryll's 'Down in the O-hi-O', R. G. Knowles' 'On the Benches in the Park', 'Don't I wish that I was Young', 'Then the Band Began to Play', 'Only a little Paper Parcel' and 'A Chambermaid at a Country Hotel'.

The story of *A Gay City* was of the type justifiably known as 'screaming farce'. Obadiah Dingle and Felix Crackle off for a spree at Brighton (though theoretically in the Isle of Wight) have the misfortune to encounter their own wives at the seaside resort and all sorts of merriment develops as the men get mistaken for rogues, a baby gets mislaid, and a blundering detective makes everything worse until dénouement time. The play had proved the joy of the touring circuits a decade previously and the musical proved that it had lost none of its charm. A thorough updating by Walton ensured that the piece stayed sparklingly topical as the newest version of Sims' farce pursued a happy and lucrative career.

Another piece of extravagant nonsense which survived under the same precepts was the latest creation of Victor Stevens, author of the long-lived *Randoph the Reckless* and *Bonnie Boy Blue*. Stevens had done less well with his more recent pieces, *The Saucy Sultana* and *A Village Venus*, and decided to change direction. Abandoning the pantomime-extravaganza style of these earlier pieces he opted for the currently popular mode of musical comedy in *A Merry Madcap*. This piece had no pretensions to being a

Shop Girl or a *Geisha*; Stevens knew his limitations and his small-town audiences. He also knew the practicalities of touring and *A Merry Madcap* had a principal cast of just eight to enact its domestic comedy story. The story centred on a touring actor-manager, Compton Chambers, who is producing a new play while lodging with a certain Mrs Armstrong. That lady's daughter ends up going on when the leading lady walks out and also ends up falling for the play's backer, young Archie Frampton. The play is threatened when Archie's inheritance is claimed by another relative, then saved when Mrs Armstrong's long-lost brother Joe turns up with a new-found fortune. Complications come and go but Kitty ends up rich and famous and married to Archie (who hasn't lost his money), while Chambers is ensnared by Mrs Armstrong whose brother Joe *has* lost all his. The story had enough ups and downs for a half-dozen shows but Stevens peopled it with simple, recognisable and likeable characters and illustrated it with a stock of lyrics and tunes in the same vein, many written by the multitalented author himself, others commissioned from fellow authors and composers.

The première of *A Merry Madcap* was an odd affair. After a try-out at Grantham on 30 July, it was officially opened on 3 August in two places. The A Company, starring Stevens himself as Chambers, performed at Nottingham, whilst the B Company, under J. Herman Dickson, a long-time tourer of Stevens' pieces, made its début at Ealing. Both companies did well until the Christmas period dispersed their components for the pickings of the pantomime season, but they were soon reconstituted in the new year and *A Merry Madcap*, in an ever-changing form, played its way through the smaller dates for a number of seasons.

The rest of the new provincial offerings were less haphazard and mobile in structure than *Skipped by the Light of the Moon* and *A Merry Madcap* and they were correspondingly less durable. Several of them, however, came from well-known writers and composers.

One of the Girls was an attempt by the comedian J. J. Dallas to concoct a successful touring musical. He took a handful of popular plot ingredients – a foundling who is an heiress, a comical American detective &c – and placed the action in a girls' school to allow for the maximum display of short skirts. To this he added a set of songs from such well-known composers as Sidney Jones, Meyer Lutz and John Crook, and a Christy Minstrel type of variety entertainment for the second act, before topping the whole with a girly title and sending it out on the road under his own management. The formula might have seemed a good one but *One of the Girls* had a rather half-hearted effect. When a date at the Metropole, Camberwell, brought the piece near to town, Dallas decided the time had come to abandon his plum role in *The New Barmaid* and get out on the road to add lustre to his own investment. After Camberwell he broke the play's season and brought it back in the autumn with a few revisions and a noticeably strengthened cast but without any special success.

Belinda was a musical comedy from the Basil Hood/Walter Slaughter combination of the minute, but it lacked almost everything that their two previous stylish efforts had had. The story of a waspish widow with her gaggle of daughters chasing a millionaire was tiresomely old-hat and the chief comic character, a leech called 'The O'Flannagan' who preys on Mr Millionaire Smith and his money to the extent of almost driving him to suicide, had too much of a nasty flavour to be truly enjoyable. Slaughter's pretty tunes were not enough to liven this misconceived affair and *Belinda*'s six weeks' try-out tour proved to be its entire life.

Much happier was a Bucalossi family affair entitled *En Route*. Ernest and Procida Bucalossi were responsible for the score of this piece while Brigata took on the producing. The book was by Reigate's Cecil Maxwell and the lyrics by Procida's erstwhile *Manteaux Noirs* collaborator, Walter Parke, who in many attempts since had never approached that first winner. *En Route* made a brave attempt:

> The plot is interesting and developed with more care than many of the musical pieces of the same description which have seen the light; but the most attractive force in *En Route* is the music . . (*Era*)
>
> Slight though Cecil Maxwell's plot may be, it serves its purpose pretty well and altogether *En Route* forms a very bright and lively entertainment . . (*Stage*)

The action of the show was set on board an ocean liner, the SS *Planet*, among whose passengers are John T. Smythe, a retired egg merchant, his parvenue wife and two daughters. One of these, Ethel, is beloved of young Ted Stanford, but Mamma has her eye on a grander passenger for her daughter, the Count Gustave de Montpelier. But Ted is not poor for he has been given a fabulous ruby by a grateful Indian whose life he has saved, and the Count, alas, is no Count but a heavily disguised international jewel thief. Stealing the keys of Ted's box from his drunken Irish servant, Montpelier makes off with the jewel and poor Pat finds himself accused. He runs away and is believed to have fallen overboard, but he returns in the nick of time in the disguise of an Italian detective and sorts everything out, to the discomfort of the 'Count' and the foolish Mrs Smythe.

Brigata hired the Savoy's comedian Walter Passmore to direct *En Route* and the experienced comic Sam Wilkinson to take the leading laughter role of Pat. The juvenile leads were given to Richard Temple Jr, son of that other Savoy stalwart, and pretty, talented Evie Greene, soon to be one of London's leading musical ladies. A short preliminary tour was adjudged a positive success, and Brigata announced preparations for a major tour and began making preliminary advances towards West End theatres. But, for reasons now unfathomable, his ambitious plans evaporated and the SS *Planet* and all on board her sank without trace. After the disappointment of *Delia*, Procida Bucalossi once again saw a worthwhile piece mismanaged out of a possible success.

Sport or The Queen's Bounty had a lien of parentage with *The New Barmaid*, being partly from the pen of W. Edward Sprange, but there the resemblance stopped. It had neither the interest nor the liveliness of the earlier piece, and the music by touring conductor Thomas Hunter could not compare with that of John Crook. The show was, again, a light English comedy-drama and took its title from the fact that Act 1 was set at the Cowes Regatta and Act 2 at Kempton Racetrack. The action concerned impecunious Lord Glentowers and his three sons – a major, a lieutenant and a vicar – each of whom proposes to the American heiress, Rosetta Mississippi, who finally marries their father. At the same time they foil the villainous Ronald Freize who has designs on Miss Aide Glentowers and the intention to ruin her lover. There was plenty of action, including the usual crooked jockey episode with our hero leaping to saddle on the cheated horse to win the race.

Sport was produced at Plymouth and sent out on tour, but half a dozen weeks into the tour it became evident that the producer, Mr Tuck, and his associates were having book-balancing problems. When the show arrived at the Parkhurst Theatre, Holloway, the two prime donne, Cissie Saumarez and Emma Chambers, both ladies of some reputation, had not been paid and had had enough of their Mr Tuck. They refused to go on. Understudies were summoned, but at the end of that week *Sport* folded and was only heard of again when Miss Saumarez successfully took poor, silly Tuck to court to claim her unpaid wages.

Inez, the Dancing Girl was altogether less ambitious and less disastrous. It was an old-fashioned comic opera written and composed by Wallace Pringle and staged by Miss Geraldine Verner who starred as the eponymous Inez while Pringle conducted affairs from the pit. It had an unpretentious tour of No 2 and No 3 dates before being sold to another management to feature an ambitious prima donna who failed to materialise.

Another comic opera, *Toledo*, was produced by Austin Fryers' *New Barmaid* company on its minor towns' tour. It was more opera than comic and, although it received a reasonable hearing on the occasions when the company presented it as a variation to their main piece, it became evident that takings dropped on *Toledo* nights and *The New Barmaid* was soon back on full weeks.

The William Hogarth touring company, which had lived for so many years off *Les Cloches de Corneville*, was responsible for the production of a third comic opera, this one of more sizeable pretensions and put together by two well-known theatrical figures, 'Pot' Stephens and composer Florian Pascal. Stephens threw everything he could into the plot of *The Black Squire*. There was an unrightful heir, a lost daughter, a Rosière prize-giving, an exchanging of costumes and much in the way of mistaken identity in a busy story of dark doings in deepest Cornwall. Pascal provided his usual pretty and undramatic music but, like *Toledo*, *The Black Squire* soon proved less popular than the repertoire's main piece and was little performed.

Another comedian-turned-manager was the old Alhambra favourite J. G. Taylor. Taylor was touring in Fryers' *New Barmaid* company when he picked up a piece called *Le Bal Masqué* by conductor Henry Vernon, m.d. of the *New Barmaid* company. Taylor, Vernon and the company's other comedian, Edgar Dereve, seceded from Fryers' troupe and produced the show under the title *The President* at Maidenhead. It was an outrageously silly piece about a Captain who takes over the Presidency of a banana republic and the consequent comic opera problems of government and ladies which pursue him to his just deserts. It lasted less than a month through Bilston, Reading, Kidderminster and Wrexham.

More successful was *Sunny Florida*, a variety piece with a story concerning a villain and a 'woman with a past' who attempt to trick the heroine out of her inheritance. The plot was minimal and the chief raison d'être of the show was to give its author-composer-star Edward Marris a chance to display his comic versatility. It toured six weeks up to Christmas, popped up again the following year as *The Armenian Girl*, and then went into cold storage to emerge again several years later, re-written, as *Somebody's Sweetheart*, finally to find a secure place on the minor circuits for a great number of seasons.

The surprise of the season, though, was undoubtedly *Playing the Game*. A lively though not particularly innovative little farce put together by song-writer and 'personality', Willie Younge, it was intended for a couple of showings at London's Strand Theatre for the enjoyment of its author and the husband and wife team of Deane Brand and Kate Chard. The story dealt with the penniless Earl Penruddock who lets his house overlooking Kempton Racetrack to an American pork-packing millionaire for the season. Since there are no servants, Penruddock and his family dress up and make a frightful hash of their menial duties. Dinner is approaching and nothing is cooked and the Penruddocks have to use all sorts of tricks to postpone the meal, aided and abetted by their friend, Lady Nesta Danby, who has come for the racing. The pork-packer gets bread and cheese, a party and concert develop, and all ends happily when Lady Nesta's horse wins the big race and makes everyone rich.

The music of the show consisted of a couple of songs for Miss Chard and a bundle of ensembles. But the production of *Playing the Game*, in which the author under the pseudonym 'Rupert Rusden' took to the stage, collected some unexpectedly good notices. *The Era* called it:

> . . a pleasant surprise . . excellent entertainment of its kind and, in its way . . we can see *Playing the Game* earning a good deal of money at suitable places in London or the provinces . .

while *The Stage* allowed that it was 'a harmless and generally amusing piece of fooling'. In the worst month of the year (June) at an 'unlucky' theatre (the Strand) without a real star the little show made a little success. With its musical content strengthened to popular dimensions, the show went out for an eleven-week tour which it had never intended and which did very nicely for its unpretentious producer.

The ladies' company headed by Lila Clay which had been so successful in the past with *An Adamless Eden, On Condition* and the concert *Something New*, was reconstituted at Christmas under the banner of its old manager, R. B. Caverley, whose breach with Lila had been healed under the prospect of mutual benefits. They decided to tour a new piece and Claude Trevalyan was commissioned to write *The Twentieth Century Girl* to be ready in less than a month. Trevalyan obliged, and the Lila Clay Co. opened at Norwich on Boxing Day with their new show. A five-month tour had been planned but after just six weeks it became only too clear that *The Twentieth Century Girl* did not have the merit or the appeal of its predecessors. Caverley quickly revived *An Adamless Eden*, but after less than three months the tour folded with recriminations on all sides and Trevalyan suing loudly for his commission fee and royalties on the 'dud' he had provided. When the case had been settled Caverley was 19 guineas further in the red.

The use of short operettas as forepieces was gradually being discontinued, but the Savoy clung to the old fashion and produced *Weather or No* by Adrian Ross, W. Beach and Luard Selby as a curtain-raiser to *The Mikado*. It was a slight 30-minute piece about a flirtation between the little man and the little lady on a weatherhouse and served its purpose adequately. It later turned up, somewhat oddly, at Berlin's Thalia Theatre as *Der Wetterhauschen*.

1896

0161 **SHAMUS O'BRIEN** A Story Of Ireland 100 Years Ago. A romantic comic opera in two acts and three tableaux founded on the celebrated poem by Joseph Sheridan Le Fanu. Libretto by George H. Jessop. Music by Charles Villiers Stanford. Produced at the Opera Comique under the management of the Shamus O'Brien Opera Co. (Jessop, Stanford & Messrs Boosey & Co.), 2 March, 1896 for a run of 82 performances closing 23 May, 1896.

Shamus O'Brien. . . . . Denis O'Sullivan
Captain Trevor . . . . William H. Stevens
Mike Murphy. . . . . Joseph O'Mara
Father O'Flynn . . . . Charles Magrath
Sergeant Cox . . . . Frank Fisher
Lynch, the piper . . . . Mr Garoghan
Little Paudeen . . . . Master Ross
Nora O'Brien . . . . Kirkby Lunn
Peggy . . . . Winifred Ludlam
Kitty O'Toole. . . . . Maggie Davies/Edith Montgomery

Dir: Augustus Harris; md: Henry J. Wood; ch: R. M. Crompton; sc: Joseph Harker and Robert Caney; cos: Comelli

Produced in the repertoire of the Beecham Opera Company and played at Her Majesty's Theatre 24 May, 1910.
Albert Archdeacon (SH), John Bardesley (TR), Joseph O'Mara (MIKE), Robert Radford (O'F), Reginald Scrope-Quintin (COX), Edith Evans/Muriel Terry (NORA), Carrie Tubb (PEG), Caroline Hatchard (KITTY). Md: Hamish MacCunn

Produced at the Broadway Theatre, New York, under the management of Messrs Cowdery & Duff 5 January, 1897 for a run of 56 performances.
Denis O'Sullivan (SH), Reginald Roberts (TR), Joseph O'Mara (MIKE), A. G. Cunningham (O'F), Walter Leland (COX), P. Touhey (LYNCH), Master Henry (PAUDEEN), Annie Roberts (NORA), Helen Marvin (PEG), Lucy Carr-Shaw (KITTY), Augusta Schiller (BANSHEE). Md: S. P. Waddington; ch: Ed. Murphy

0162 **THE GRAND DUKE** or The Statutory Duel a comic opera in 2 acts by W. S. Gilbert. Music by Arthur Sullivan. Produced at the Savoy Theatre under the management of Richard D'Oyly Carte 7 March, 1896 for a run of 123 performances closing 10 July, 1896.

Grand Duke Rudolph. . . . . Walter Passmore
Ernest Dummkopf . . . . Charles Kenningham
Ludwig . . . . Rutland Barrington
Dr Tannhäuser . . . . H. Scott Russell
Prince of Monte Carlo . . . . R. Scott Fishe
Viscount Mentone . . . . E. Carleton/Basil Wood
Ben Hashbaz . . . . C. H. Workman
Herald. . . . . Jones Hewson
Princess of Monte Carlo . . . . Emmie Owen
Baroness von Krakenfeldt. . . . . Rosina Brandram

Julia Jellicoe. . . . . Ilka von Palmay (Florence Perry) (Carla Dagmar)
Lisa . . . . Florence Perry (Ruth Vincent)
Olga . . . . Mildred Baker
Gretchen . . . . Ruth Vincent
Bertha . . . . Jessie Rose
Martha . . . . Beatrice Perry
Elsa . . . . Ethel Wilson

Dir: Charles Harris; md: François Cellier; ch: John D'Auban; sc: W. Harford; cos: Percy Anderson

163 **ONE OF THE GIRLS** a musical comedy in two acts by Herbert Darnley and 'S. A. Llad' (J. J. Dallas). Music by John Crook, Sidney Jones and Meyer Lutz. Produced at Birmingham under the management of J. J. Dallas 9 March, 1896 and toured through Chester, Halifax, Newcastle, Middlesborough, Blackpool, Burnley, Preston, Cardiff, Bath, Portsmouth, Hastings, Metropole, ending 6 June. Tour recommenced 20 August at Ealing under the management of Brigata Bucalossi and Alfred Beaumont and toured through Leicester, Wolverhampton, Derby, Walsall, Sheffield, Southport, Longton, York, Hull, Bradford, Oldham, Stockton, Newcastle, Glasgow and Edinburgh ending 5 December, 1896.

Jabez Crouch . . . . J. Harold Carson/Arthur Ring
Sammy Daddle . . . . Wattie Allen/J. J. Dallas
Harry Russell . . . . M. Munro/Richard Temple Jr/Charles Crawford
Bertie Winks . . . . George Elliston/Harry Phydora/Bertie Ross
Simon C. Gull . . . . Alfred Aubyn/Walter Lonnen
Thomas . . . . G. Willis/Frank Fuller
Cecil Blake . . . . Arthur Haytor/
George Clare . . . . Bertie Ross/Will Goodwin
Charley Vane . . . . Lynn Howard/R. Mansell Fane
Ernest Morton . . . . Frank Lewis/J. J. Allen
Percy Clarke . . . . W. Goodwin/Lyddon Phillips
Walter Wade . . . . F. Worthington/Reginald G. Vernon
Toby Grubb . . . . Frank Manning/William Walton
Miss Taplow . . . . Bessie Armytage/A. Thomas
Sally Lunn . . . . Dora Gregory/Pattie Prescott
Mary . . . . Dorothy Woodville/Kate Butler
Gerty Larks . . . . Maude Elliston/Nellie Dallas
Daisy Pink . . . . Bessie Alleyne
Marie Fitzgeorge . . . . Millie Morrell/Marie Rovers
Ella Riddell . . . . B. Frampton/Mabel Frampton
Lilly Roslin . . . . E. Byrne/
Phoebe Riddell . . . . Mabel Frampton/Blanche Frampton
Marie Good . . . . Verna Reed/Laura Carlton
Eva Rosedale . . . . Nellie Owen/Clara Webber
Vera Martin . . . . Rea Bruce/
Dora Gray. . . . . Mary Duggan
add Alice Rose . . . . Lily Verdno
Blanche Ivy. . . . . Madge Wilson
Maud Evesley . . . . Mabel Tomlinson
Jack Graham . . . . Wattie Allen

164 **THE FRENCH MAID** a musical comedy in two acts by Basil Hood. Music by Walter Slaughter. Produced at the Theatre Royal, Bath, under the management of Milton Bode 4 April, 1896 and toured through Cheltenham, Bath?, Plymouth, Metropole, Portsmouth, Hastings, Oxford and Standard, to 6 June. Recommenced July 27 at Brighton through Cheltenham, Bristol, Birmingham, Belfast, Nottingham, Hull, Yarmouth, Halifax, Huddersfield, Dewsbury, Hanley, Carlisle, Southport, Newcastle, Liverpool, Bolton, Manchester and Metropole, to 5

December, 1896. Continued in 1897 (January 4–June 12; August 22–December 4), 1898 (December 27, 1897–June 4, 1898; 18 July–3 December, 1898), 1899 (26 December, 1898–27 May, 1899; 7 August–2 December, 1899), &c.

Admiral Sir Hercules Hawser . . . . . . H. O. Clarey/Frank Morrison/J. Harold Carson
General Sir Drummond Fife . . . . Charles Thorburn/Frank Couch/Fred Twitchen/Wallace Stranack/
Lt Harry Fife . . . . Spenser Kelly/Fred Twitchen/ J. J. Fitzgibbon/Allen Turner/Robert Perris/Clifford Morgan/
Maharajah of Punkapore . . . . Percy Percival/Wilson Pemberton/Colet Dare
Paul Lecuire . . . . Arthur Watts/Colet Dare/Harry P. Gribben/
Monsieur Camembert. . . . . Murray King/Marmaduke Langdale/ Walter Westwood/Cecil Wilford/Alfred E. Wyn/
Charles Brown . . . . Windham Guise/Murry King/Bert Gilbert/Harry C. Barry/A. E. Chapman/ Arthur Reynolds
Jack Brown . . . . Joseph Wilson/Arthur Ring/Herbert Shelley/Fred Twitchen
Alphonse . . . . C. Tallent/L. Weinogradow
Dorothy Travers . . . . Louie Pounds/Mary Thorne/Nancy Pounds/Marion Ayling/Ethel Negretti
Lady Hawser . . . . Caroline Ewell
Madame Camembert . . . . Lillie Pounds/Beatrice Goodchild/ Helen McCullough/Mabel Mellor/Elaine Spearing
Suzette . . . . Andrée Corday/Jenny Owen/Madge Crichton/ Bella Bashall/Florence North/Clarissa Talbot

Pd: Blanche Vaudon/Grace Sprague/Sisters Righton
with Helen Beresford, Janet Delmar, Enid Dane, Florence Hardy, Frances Neville, Julia Bohers, Saccha Johnson, Millie Wetton, Nellie Godfrey, Dora Watson, Florence North, Lizzie Appleby, A. H. Loupresti, Alec Murray, Richard Dare, Fred Twitchen, Alfred Vine, L. Weinogradow, C. Stewart, James Dolling, William Cook &c/ Gladys Leigh, Eva Douglas, Alice Kean, Cissie Manders, Maud Marriot, Belle Vivian, Beatrice Lister, Bertha Drayton, Adelia Rivers, Lisa Nelson, Emmie Cobb, W. G. Woodward, John Wilson, Basil Astley, Hugh Carlisle, Joe Shaw, George Weenly, Tom Norbury

Dir: Frank Parker; md: Ernest Vousden/Guy Jones/Sydney Shaw/Frank Seddon; ch: Will Bishop; sc: C. Rider Noble; cos: Morris Angel, John Hooper, Stagg & Mantle &c.

Produced in London at Terry's Theatre under the management of W. H. Griffiths 24 April, 1897. Transferred to the Vaudeville Theatre 12 February, 1898. Withdrawn 6 August, 1898 after a total run of 480 performances.

Admiral Sir Hercules Hawser . . . . . . H. O. Clarey
General Sir Drummond Fife . . . . Windham Guise/Barton de Solla/George Mudie
Lieutenant Harry Fife . . . . Richard Green
Paul Lecuire . . . . Herbert Standing/Windham Guise
Monsieur Camembert. . . . . Eric Lewis/George Mudie
Maharajah of Punkapore . . . . Percy Percival
Charles Brown . . . . Murray King
Jack Brown . . . . Joseph Wilson/Hugh Metcalfe
Alphonse . . . . J. W. MacDonald
Dorothy Travers . . . . Louie Pounds
Lady Hawser . . . . Kate Talby/Alice Barth

Violet Travers . . . . Hilda Jeffries
Madame Camembert . . . . Lillie Pounds
Suzette . . . . Kate Cutler/Kitty Loftus

with L. Williams, M. Taylor, V. Taylor, L. Valda, D. Thomas, E. Borlace, J. Taylor, Miss Mercie, Ada Peppiate, J. Armstrong, A. Josephs, Miss Curtice, L. Winning; Messrs Garrod, Oades, Vine, Garton, Sterling, George, Barrington. Pds: Blanche Vaudon, Rose Batchelor/Miss Greville, Bert Sinden, Mr Vine/G. E. Shepheard, *add* Edward Sillward.

Dir: Frank Parker; md: Maurice Jacobi; ch: Will Bishop; sc: E. G. Banks; cos: Lucien Besche

Produced at the Herald Square Theatre, New York, under the managemet of E. E. Rice 27 September, 1897 for a run of 175 performances closing 19 February, 1898.
John Gourlay/Edd Redway (HH), Edward S. Wenworth (DRUMM), William Armstrong (HARRY), Henry Norman (PAUL), George Honey (CAM), Henry Leoni (MAH), Charles A. Bigelow (CH), Hallen Mostyn (JACK), Charles E. Sturgis/J. Grant (ALPH/WILLIE SPLINT), Anna Robinson/Lucille Flaven (DOR), Eva Davenport (LADY), Yolande Wallace (MME), Marguerite Sylva/Ollie Redpath (SUZ), Leonora Ginto (MARIE), Florence Wells (JEANETTE), Saharet (pd), with Maud Sohlke, Frances Wilson, Mazie Follette, May Bradley, Carol Glover, Mollie Gaylor, Minnie Gaylor, Carrie May, Gypsey Grant, Fannie Burkhardt, Millie Tait, Beatrice Tait, Alma Desmond, Dorothy Kendall, Maud Chandler, Gabrielle de Thien, Florence Dressler, Netta Scarsez, Edna Lyle, Fannie Bradley, Margie Wade, Josie Winner, Violet Carlstadt, Bertha Dowling. Dir: Frederick A. Leon; md: Herman Perlet; ch: Augustus Sohlke; sc: Frank Rafter and D. Frank Dodge; cos: Mme M. I. Dowling

Played at the Herald Square Theatre under the management of E. E. Rice 12 September, 1898 for three weeks to 1 October, 1898.

Film: In 1907 a film and synchronised record set of 'The Twin Duet' was issued by Chronophone Films.

165 **LORD TOM NODDY** a musical piece in two acts by George Dance. Composed by F. Osmond Carr. Produced at Bradford under the management of George Dance 6 April, 1896 and toured through Leeds, Edinburgh, Newcastle, Glasgow, Liverpool, Birmingham, Manchester and Oxford to June 6, 1896. Opened at the Garrick Theatre 15 September 1896 for a run of 62 performances closing 14 November, 1896.

Lord Tom Noddy. . . . . Little Tich
Magnum. . . . . F. D. Pengelly//Cecil Frere
Colonel Ben Nevis . . . . Picton Roxburgh
Miss Ben Nevis . . . . Annie Esmond//Gladys Ffolliott
Solomon Van Delle . . . . Harry C. Barry
Lt Crowshaw . . . . C. Baring//George Paulton
Marion Forsyth . . . . Dolly Doyle//Sybil Arundale
Constance Forsyth . . . . Maude Vernon//Katie Leechman
Angela. . . . . Violet Friend
Maud . . . . Dora Nelson
Ethel . . . . Maud Trautner
Florrie. . . . . Maidie Hope
Beatrice . . . . Olive Dalmour
Marguerite . . . . Germaine de Marco
May . . . . Edna Grace
Gladys. . . . . Edith Singlehurst
Augustus A. Jackson . . . . Maurice Mancini//Sidney Harcourt
Mlle Bébé de Sans Souci . . . . Nina Martino//*out*
Nurse Phoebe . . . . Mabel Love
add Hopkinson . . . . Henry Elliston
Polly Primrose . . . . Kate James

Pd: Miss Goss
Dir: George Dance; md: Barter Johns; ch: Will Bishop; sc: W. Harford and Harry Emden; cos: Comelli

166 **BIARRITZ** a musical farce by Jerome K. Jerome. Music by F. Osmond Carr. Produced at the

Prince of Wales Theatre under the management of Arthur Roberts 11 April, 1896 for a run of 71 performances closing on 20 June, 1896. The title was altered 9 May to *John Jenkins in Biarritz*.

John J. Jenkins . . . . Arthur Roberts
Johannes. . . . . Fred Kaye/Albert Sealy
General Tomassino . . . . Eric Thorne
Rodney Kemp. . . . . Roland Cunningham/Augustus Cramer
Duke of Melton Mowbray . . . . Algernon Newark
Bishop of Newmarket (Dr Arlistreete) . . L. F. Chapuy
Gendarme . . . . Walker Marnock
Honourable Johnnie. . . . . Harold Eden
Tessie Carew . . . . Phyllis Broughton
Mr Charlie Bargus . . . . Millie Hylton
Babette . . . . Pierette Amella
Enriqua . . . . Ellas Dee/Attie Chester
Duchess of Melton Mowbray. . . . . . . Harrie Doreen/Sadie Jerome
Mrs Carew . . . . Adelaide Newton
Florence. . . . . Eva Ellerslie
Jane . . . . Julia Kent
Elizabeth . . . . Carrie Benton
Niagara G. Wackett. . . . . Sadie Jerome/*out*
Janet. Kitty Loftus
Alphonse . . . . Attie Chester/Christine Salisbury
Louis . . . . Christine Salisbury/Freda Coventry
Michel. . . . . Nellie Alwyn
Antoine . . . . Fanny Harris
Louise. . . . . Florence Linton
Annette . . . . Lucille Graham
Jeanne. . . . . Mary Turner
Marie . . . . Florrie Schuberth

Md: Herbert Bunning; sc: R. C. McCleery; cos: Sarah Meyer & A. Morhange

0167 **MY GIRL** a domestic musical play in 2 acts by James T. Tanner. Lyrics by Adrian Ross. Music by F. Osmond Carr. Produced at the Theatre Royal, Birmingham, under the management of George Edwardes as *The Clergyman's Daughter* 13 April, 1896 and toured through Manchester, Southport, Liverpool, Hull, Newcastle, Sheffield to 30 May, 1896. Produced at the Gaiety Theatre under the management of George Edwardes 13 July, 1896. Transferred to the Garrick Theatre 1 December. Closed 16 January 1897 after a total of 183 performances.

Rev. Arthur Mildreth. . . . . Charles Ryley
Theo Mildreth . . . . Ernest Snow//Paul Arthur/W. Louis Bradfield
Alexander McGregor . . . . John Le Hay
Dr Tertius Huxtable . . . . H. J. Carvill//Fred Kaye/Robert Nainby?
Lord Barum. . . . . Paul Arthur//Lawrance d'Orsay/Paul Arthur
Leopold van Fontein . . . . Martin Adeson//W. H. Rawlins
Saunders . . . . Leslie Holland/William H. Powell/Tom Terriss
Mayor of Porthampton . . . . Percy Paul//Colin Coop/Tim Ryley/Robert Nainby
Admiral Bargrave . . . . Cairns James//*out*
Pinkle . . . . Tim Ryley//*out*
John Fahee . . . . W. Downes
Lady Bargrave . . . . Marie Winter//Maria Davis/Emily Spiller/Christine Mayne/Madge Langton
Beatrix Barum. . . . . Ethel Sydney//Ethel Haydon/Ethel Sydney/Mabel Warren/Sybil Carlisle/Florence Dysart

Rebecca van Fontein . . . . Marie Montrose/Nelly Murray
Phoebe Toodge . . . . Ada Willoughby//Katie Seymour/Grace Palotta/Blanche Astley/Lillian Menelly
Melissa Banks . . . . Madge Alexander//Ethel Sydney/Florence Lloyd/Retta Villis/Florence Dysart/Christine Mayne
The Mayoress . . . . Connie Ediss/Lillie Belmore
Dorothy . . . . Kate Adams/Maud Santley/Sophie Elliott
Mary . . . . Ada Maitland/Edith Singlehurst/Retta Villis
Miss Veriner . . . . Florence Lloyd/Margaret Fraser/Lucille Graham/Annie Vivian
Mrs Porkinson . . . . Grace Palotta/Mabel Warren/Retta Villis/Lucille Graham
May Mildreth . . . . Kate Cutler//Ellaline Terriss/Ethel Sydney/Isa Bowman
add Miss Cholmondely . . . . Annie Vivian/*out*
Weeks . . . . Willie Warde/Alfred Asher

Md: John H. Korte/Barter Johns; ch: Willie Warde; sc: Walter Hann and William Telbin; cos: Wilhelm

0168 **THE GEISHA** A Story of A Tea House. A Japanese musical play in two acts by Owen Hall. Lyrics by Harry Greenbank. Music by Sidney Jones. Additional songs by Lionel Monckton and James Philp. Produced at Daly's Theatre under the management of George Edwardes 25 April, 1896 for a run of 760 performances closing 28 May, 1898.

O Mimosa San . . . . Marie Tempest (Elise Cook) (Maggie May) (Jessica Lait) (Hilda Moody)
Juliette Diamant . . . . Juliette Nesville/Mary Fawcett/Elsie Cross/Mabel Duncan
Nami . . . . Kristine Yudall/Florence Collingbourne/Rhoda Windrum/Florence Rooke/Christine McGill
O Kiku San . . . . Emelie Hervé/Mary Fawcett/Maggie May/Florence Lauri/Jessica Lait/Florence Collingbourne/Gertie Carlow
O Hana San . . . . Mary Fawcett/Elise Cook/Christine McGill/Mary Collette/Maggie May/Eva Clark/Gertie Carlow
O Kinkoto San . . . . Elise Cook/Maggie May/Gertrude Palmer/Grace Arundale/Mary Collette/Marguerite Roche
Komurasaki San . . . . Mary Collette/Toby Claude/Marguerite Roche/Emelie Hervé
Lady Constance Wynne . . . . Maud Hobson/Gladys Homfrey/Lucy Golding
Marie Worthington . . . . Blanche Massey/Lucille Graham/Marie Yorke
Ethel Hurst . . . . Hetty Hamer/Lucy Golding/Maie Saqui
Mabel Grant . . . . Alice Davis
Louie Plumpton . . . . Margaret Fraser/Kate Cannon
Molly Seamore . . . . Letty Lind (Violet Lloyd) (Emilie Hervé
Reginald Fairfax . . . . C. Hayden Coffin (John Coates) (Conway Dixon)
Dick Cunningham . . . . W. Louis Bradfield/Ernest Snow/Joe Farren Soutar (Donald Hall)
Arthur Cuddy . . . . Leedham Bantock/Donald Hall/Conway Dixon/E. L. Fraser/Edmund Sherras
George Grimston . . . . Sydney Ellison/E. L. Fraser/*out*

Tommy Stanley . . . . Lydia Flopp/Fanny Dango/Nellie Curtis
Captain Katana . . . . William Philp/Frank Boor/Percy Mordy/Maurice Farkoa/H. Scott Russell
Takemine . . . . Frederick Rosse/Colin Coop (Mr Williams)
Wun-Hi . . . . Huntley Wright/Fred Wright Jr/Bertie Wright
Marquis Imari . . . . Harry Monkhouse/Rutland Barrington/ W. H. Rawlins
add Miss Marchant . . . . Kate Cannon
Miss Foster . . . . Marie Yorke/Mabel Tempest
Miss Waters . . . . Olive Morell
Gerald St Pancras . . . . Lawrance d'Orsay/H. Scott Russell/ Donald Hall/Arthur Appleby

Md: Sidney Jones/Leopold Wenzel/Ernest Ford/Victor Champion; ch: Willie Warde; sc: William Telbin; cos: Percy Anderson

Produced at Daly's Theatre, New York, under the management of Augustin Daly 9 September, 1896. Suspended several times and closed 23 April, 1897 after a total of 161 performances.
Dorothy Morton/Nancy McIntosh (MIM), Helma Nelson (JUL), Sarina Alexe/Grace Rutter (NAMI), Mabel Thompson (KIKU), Lila Convere (HANA), Mabelle Gillman (KINK), Maud Carter/Gertrude Bennett (KOMUR), Marie St John/Pauline French (CON), Pauline French/Gerda Wissner (MARIE), Gerda Wissner/Carolyn Stephenson (ETH), Maym Kelso/Helen Underhill (DOROTHY SWEET), Annette Spencer/Anne Hathaway (MABEL), Violet Lloyd/Virginia Earle (MOLLY), Van Rensslaer Wheeler/Philip Tomes (REG), Herbert Gresham (DICK), George Lesoir (ARTHUR), Henry Gunson/Frederic Truesdell (GRIM), Alice Winston/Clara Emory (TOMMY), Neal McKay (KAT), Robert Shepherd (TAKE), William Samson (WUN), Edwin Stevens (IM), Eric Scott/Charles Bates (StP), William Hazelton/Damon Lyons (A BUYER) with Lena Lorraine, Anee Caverly, Claire St Clair, Alethe Craig, Isadora Duncan, Belle d'Arcy, Elsie Bennett, Clara Hollywood, Lillian Lipyeat, Mabel Strickland, Margarete Whiticar, Ellen Mortimer, Maud Vincent, Marion Marshall, Lottie Moore, Marjie Carl, Eugene Taylor, Alice Burke, Marguerite Barre. Dir: Herbert Gresham; md: William Withers; ch: Willie Warde; sc: William Telbin; cos: Percy Anderson

Produced at Daly's Theatre, New York, under the management of Augustin Daly 8 November, 1897 for a season of three weeks to 27 November. Returned 27 December, 1897 for one week, a total of 32 performances.
Nancy McIntosh (MIM), Virginia Earle (MOLLY), Julius Stieger (REG), Cyril Scott (DICK), James T. Powers (WUN)

Produced at the Carltheater, Vienna, 16 November, 1897.

Produced at Daly's Theatre, New York, under the management of Augustin Daly 21 March, 1898 for a run of 22 performances closing 9 April, 1898.
Marguerite Lemon (MIM), Helma Nelson (JUL), Belle Harper (NAMI), Sandol Milliken (KIKU), Bessy Ryan (HANA), Marion Stuart (KINK), Marie Murphy (KOMUR), Ethel Hornick (CON), Beatrice Morgan (MARIE), Virginia Navarro (ETH), Corinne Parker (DOROTHY), Louise Draper (MABEL), Mabelle Gillman (MOLLY), Frank Rushworth (REG), Cyril Scott (DICK), Charles Bates (ARTHUR), Frederic Truesdell (GRIM), Lillian Coleman (TOMMY), Neal McKay (KAT), George Wharnock (TAKE), James T. Powers (WUN), Joseph Herbert (IM), Eric Scott (StP) with Ida Hawley, Belle d'Arcy, Lena Lorraine, Margaret Hoyt, Miss Ashton, Miss Mills, Francis Gordon, Carolyn Gordon, Miss Carrington, Miss Carlisle, Miss Clements, Marguerite Barre. Md: Sebastian Hiller; sc: W. Telbin

Produced in Paris at the Atheneé Comique in a version by Charles Clairville, A. Mars and Jacques Le Maire 8 March, 1898 for a run of 4 performances.
Jeanne Petit (O MIMOSA), Augustine Le Riche (ZOE PANACHE), Mlle Sorano (NAMI), Jeanne Calve (CONSTANCE), Miriam Manuel (NELLY SEYMOUR), Mlle Liliane (MABEL), Mlle Verdant (MARY), Mlle de Luxille (ETHEL), Perrin (REGINALD), La Renaudie (DICK), Duvelleroy (ARTHUR), Froment (GEORGES), Mdlle de Montbrion (TOMMY), Barron (KATANA), Diemat (TAKEMINE), Gayon Jr (MAC-CHOU-LI), Jannin (IMARI)

Produced at the Théâtre du Moulin Rouge, Paris, 1906.

Produced at Daly's Theatre under the management of George Edwardes 18 June, 1906 for a run of 60 performances closing 16 August, 1906.
May de Souza/Nora Brocklebank (MIM), Mariette Sully (JUL), Kathleen Severn/Dorothea Clarke (NAMI), Thelma Ray/Nora Guy (KIKU), Iris Hoey/Miss McGlory (HANA), Daisy Stratton (KINK), Alice Hatton (KOMUR), Watt Tanner (CON), Gertrude Glyn/Maud Hamerton (MARIE), Nina Sevening/Dorothy Dunbar (ETHEL), Angy Edwardine/Beatrice Dunbar (WATERS), Grace Pinder (MABEL), Marie Studholme (MOLLY), Robert Evett (REG), W. Louis Bradfield (DICK), Valentine O' Connor (GRIM), Gordon Cleather (BRONVILLE), Edith Fink (TOMMY), Talleur Andrews/H. Scott Russell (KAT), Norman Greene (TAKE), Fred Wright Jr (WUN), George Graves/Fred Kaye (IM), Willie Warde (WO-MI). Dir: J. A. E. Malone; md: Barter Johns; ch: Willie Warde; sc: Alfred Craven, Joseph Harker; cos: Miss Fisher, Mrs Patrick, Mme Field, Morris Angel

Produced at the 44th Street Theatre, New York, under the management of Arthur Hammerstein and Messrs Shubert 27 March, 1913 for a season of 52 performances.
Alice Zeppili (MIM), Georgia Caine (JUL), Irene Cassini (NAMI), Alice Baldwin (KIKU), Zetta Metchik (HANA), Olga Harting (KINK), Edith Thayer (KOMUR), Pauline Hall (CON), Grace Bradford (MARIE), Florence Topham (ETH), Jane Burdett (MABEL), Lina Arbanell (MOLLY), Carl Gantvoort (REG), Charles King (DICK), Bert Young (ARTHUR), Cecil Renard (TOMMY), Frank Pollock (KAT), George Williams (TAKE), James T. Powers (WUN), Edwin Stevens (IM) with Eugene Roder, Anna Ailson, Amelia Rose, Susanne Douglas, Nellie Ford, Vilma Roberts, Elsie Waller, Grace Williams, Marion Thompson, Bernice McLaughlin, Janne Daws, Blanche Netta, Ruby Lewis, Ethel Merrillies, Emily Saunders, Marjorie Cummer, Jessie Lewis, Elizabeth West, Lily Norton, Blanche Barnes, Gladys Coleman, May Whitney, Nellie Chick, Austina Mason, Helena Baird, Louise Chanfrau, Marie Heutte, Nell Jenkins, Alberta Masters, Alice Evanston, Hortense Ireland, Lucy Todd, Ted Sullivan, Arthur Spencer, Robert Harberson, Fred Bradbury, Nat Webster, A. H. McCurdy, Harry Sulkin, Irving Lanti, Tony Sachs, Harry Hanft, Al Lefkowitz, Arthur Wilson, Max Dorfman, Jack Howard, Harry Sachs, N. Agnini, Sol Singlust, Arthur Stapleton, Frank Wayne, Eugene Podget, S. Annisman, W. Wagman, Harry Erschof, Ed Wheelahan. Dir: Arthur Hammerstein; cos: Melville Ellis

Produced at the Gaîeté-Lyrique, Paris, 1920.

Produced at Daly's Theatre under the management of J. Bannister Howard 1 June, 1931 for a run of 48 performances closing 11 July. Played again from 14 September, 1931 for two weeks to 26 September.
Rose Hignell/Sylvia Pickering (MIM), Reita Nugent/Violet Deane/Eva Scott Thompson (JUL), Alison Maclaren/Rosamund Ross (NAMI), Sylvia Pickering/Violet Dean (O SIMANI SAN), Rosamund Ross/Hazel Glenn (KIKU), Juliette Jose/Marie Conan (HANA), Eve Lynett/Ann Angela (KINK), Violet Dean/Rosamund Ross (KOMUR), Stephanie Stephens (CON), Glae Carrodus/Marjorie Kershaw (MARIE), Eva Scott-Thompson/Eva Evelyn/Essie Brett (ETHEL), Margaret Watson/Jeanette Burnell (MABEL), Essie Brett/Enid Steele (LOUIE), Lorna Hubbard/Noreen Hamilton (MOLLY), Donald Mather/Barry McKay (REG), Dudley Rolph/Ronald Hall (DICK), Bruce Anderson/William Marshall (ARTHUR BRONVILLE), John Coast/Charles Clapham (GRIM), Pat Moloney (TOMMY), John Newton (KAT), Ian Rodney/Stanley Tustain (TAKE), George Lane/Percy Le Fre (WUN), Leo Sheffield (IM). Dir: Frederick G. Lloyd; md: Leonard Hornsey

Produced at the Erlanger Theatre, New York, by the Civic Light Opera Company 5 October, 1931 for a season of 16 performances.
Hizi Koyke (MIM), Ethel Clark (JUL), Theo van Tassel (NAMI), Doris Delehante (KIKU), Margaret Walker (HANA), Olga Schumaker (KINK), Mary Moss (KOMUR), Ann Carey (CON), Cyrilla Tuite (MARIE), Irene Hubert (ETH), Kathryn Curl (MABEL), Mary Rysz (LOUIE), Rella Winn (MOLLY), Roy Cropper (REG), Sano Marco (DICK), S. Otis Holwerk (ARTHUR), August Loring (GRIM), Milton Tully (KAT), Edward Orchard (TAKE), James T. Powers (WUN), Detmar Poppin (IM), Siegfried Langer (CHARLES BAKER), Sigmund Glukoff (VERNON JOHNSON) with Francis Baldwin, Sylvia Gans, Dorothy Watson, Vera Miller, Marie Dolan, Frances Moore, Mary Adeline Moss, Frances Baviello, Dorothy Duncan, Therese Hyle, June Yorkin, Walter Franklin, Lloyd Ericssen, Rudy Glaisek, Serge Ury, Mario Pickler, Thomas Green. Dir: Milton Aborn

Produced at the Garrick Theatre under the management of John Southern 24 April, 1934 for a season of 39 performances closing 26 May.
Rose Hignell (MIM), Hylda Wray (JUL), Diana Wong (NAMI), Adah Thorp (KIKU), Joan Collier (HANA), Rosalie Dyer (KINK), Marie Conan (KOMURA), Winifred Nathan (CON), Monica Stanley (MARIE), Eileen Brand (ETHEL), Kitty Attfield (MABEL), Beryl Fellowes (LOUIE), Bertha Riccardo (MOLLY), E. Dudley Stevens (REG), Walter Bird (DICK), Adrian Burgon (GRIM), Lawrence Tabor (BRONVILLE), Brian Blades (TOMMY), Webster Millar (KAT), Cecil Brierley (TAKE), Percy Le Fre (WUN), Leo Sheffield (IM) with Elsie Maynard, Millicent Collins, Iris May, Paula Chesterton, Ruby Woodhouse, Ada Collins, May Hewitt, Sybil Darling, Kathleen Knox, Dorothy Moyne, Ann Beverley, Ruby St Clair, Lily Aldis, May de Lys, Joan Wilson; V. Driver, W. Stuart, W. Tinkler, W. Colvin, T. Clarke, H. Collins, A. G. Willard, H. Rake, P. Hanlon, Pat Barrow. Dir: Frederick G. Lloyd; md: Leonard Hornsey; ch: Alison Maclaren; sc: Grantham; cos: B. J. Simmons & Co.

Film: Two scenes from *The Geisha* were filmed by R. W. Paul in 1897 (silent) and in 1909 Warwick Cinephonic Films issued a film and synchronised record set of 'The Kissing Duet'.

0169 **ON THE MARCH** a musical comedy in two acts by William Yardley, B. C. Stephenson and Cecil Clay based on *In Camp* by Victoria Vokes. Music by John Crook, Edward Solomon and Frederic Clay. Produced at the Theatre Royal, Sheffield, under the management of Cissy Graham 18 May, 1896 and toured through Glasgow, Edinburgh, Newcastle x2, to 20 June. Opened at the Prince of Wales Theatre 22 June, 1896 for a run of 77 performances closing 5 September. Opened at Stratford East 7 September and toured again through Manchester, Leeds, Aberdeen, Dundee, Glasgow, Belfast, Dublin, Liverpool, Birmingham, Edinburgh, Cheltenham and Bristol ending 5 December.

Fitzallerton Scroggs	Thomas E. Murray
Colonel McAllister	Cecil Ramsay/Stratton Mills
Captain Felix McAllister	Templar Saxe/George Sinclair
Lt Jack Ferris	H. Nye Chart//Charles H. E. Brookfield/Stuart Champion
Sergeant Struggles	Horace Mills/W. Searle
Corporal Rush	George Ellison//Cecil Frere/George Sinclair/George L. Wilson
Captain King	George L. Wilson/H. Rosse
Edith de Bang	Frances Earle//Maud Boyd/Frances Earle/Maggie Roberts/Winifred Hare
Florence Pringle	Rhoda Windrum//Frances Earle/ Florrie Schuberth/Winifred Hare/ B. Eldon
Elfrida Molyneaux	Bab Morgan//Augusta Walters/Mary Thorne
Maggie Welland	Alice Atherton/Madge Merry
Polly	Attie Chester
Sarah Tubbs	Gladys Carswell
Mary Ann Grass	Kate Herman
Jane Tuppet	Lucille Grahame
Martha Scrooge	Christine Salisbury
Jenny Scrooge	D. Russel
Marie	Ethel Borlase/Miss Melton
Musette	B. Benson

Dancers: Misses Martin, Rundell; George Elliston
with Misses Clifden, Barker, Humphreys, J. Salisbury, Mary Turner, Linton, Melton, Rosa, Douglas, Stirling, Boyce, Wood, Dexter, Pruce, Haines, Hargreaves, Seymour, Faulkener, Maurice, Spencer, Margot; Messrs Atkins, Drew, Jameson, Seymour, Wilfred Wynnstay, A. Luke, Pennington, Gregory, Brooke, Tyler and Rose.
Dir: Frank Parker; md: George Byng; ch: Will Bishop; sc: Bruce Smith; cos: Jays Ltd., Mme Marie, Watkin, Alias

0170 **PLAYING THE GAME** a musical farcical comedy in 3 acts by Willie Younge and Arthur Flaxman. Music by Fred Eplett. Additional music by Edward Jones. Produced at the Strand Theatre under the management of Deane Brand 12 June, 1896 for 5 performances. Subsequently toured from 3 August at Llandudno/Shrewsbury through Aberystwyth, Birmingham, Coventry, Manchester, Bridlington/Harrogate, W. Hartlepool, S. Shields, Middlesborough, York and Scarborough ending 17 October, 1896.

Earl Penruddock . . . . J. S. Blythe/William Lugg
Countess Penruddock . . . . Marion Sterling
Lord Peter Penruddock . . . . J. W. Bradbury
Lady Amy Penruddock . . . . Violet Darrell
Col. Michael O'Clancey. . . . . 'Rupert Rusden' (i.e. Willie Younge)
Mrs O'Clancey . . . . Nellie Newton/Julia Temple
Emmerson O'Clancey . . . . Deane Brand
Lady Nesta Danby . . . . Kate Chard

Dir: Deane Brand; md: Fred Eplett

0171 **SPORT** or The Queen's Bounty. A musical comedy in two acts by Montague Turner and W. Edward Sprange. Music by Thomas Hunter. Produced at the Theatre Royal, Plymouth, under the management of Mr Tuck 30 March, 1896 and toured through Ryde, Leamington/ Cambridge, Northampton, Darlington, Liverpool, Woolwich and the Parkhurst ending 23 May, 1896.

Hon. Aide Glentowers . . . . Cissie Saumarez (Alice Ancliff)
Letitia Hardinge . . . . Evelyn Vaudrey
Rosetta Mississippi . . . . Emma Chambers (Marie Ford)
Cissy Forrester . . . . Nina Engel
Felicity Beauclerc . . . . Alice Ancliff
Florence Merry . . . . Hetty Cornwallis
Alicia Winter . . . . Ida Lawrence
Doris Harford . . . . Violet Clarence
Lord Glentowers . . . . Arthur Rodney/Leslie Walker
Major Cecil Hallam . . . . Charles Wilson/Guy Logan
Lt. Harvey Hallam . . . . Newton Pearce
Ronald Freize . . . . Reginald Garland
Arthur Braithwaite . . . . Harry Brayne
Rev. Robert Hallam. . . . . George T. Minshull
Tommy Aldgate. . . . . J. E. Nightingale
Nabbs . . . . C. A. Russell
Morningside. . . . . Gertrude Parker
Sergeant Vigilant . . . . Edgar Reed/Edgar Force
Telegraph Boy . . . . Miss Ford/'E. X. Press'
with Louie Newman (pd) and the Ariel Troupe

Md: Arnold Cooke; sc: John Turner

0172 **NEWMARKET** a racing comedy with music in three acts by Mrs Frank Taylor. Lyrics by Ernest Boyd-Jones. Music by John Crook, J. M. Capel, Alfred Plumpton & c. Additional lyrics by J. A. McWeeny. Produced at the Prince's Theatre, Manchester, under the management of Alexander Loftus 22 June, 1896. Opened at the Opera Comique 22 August, 1896 for a run of 58 performances closing on 17 October, 1896. Played the Metropole, Camberwell 9 November, then toured through Oxford, Brighton &c.

Lord Kempton . . . . Joseph E. Pearce//Wilfred Forster
Colonel Stockbridge. . . . . St John Hamund//Forbes Dawson/ Aubrey Fitzgerald
Tom Snaffle . . . . Willie Edouin
Ronald Mayver . . . . Fred Featherstone/Charles Stuart/Sydney Cosby
M. Brisson . . . . Laurence Caird/J. Brabourne
Ferdie Craddock . . . . Grisbrook Waller//Kenneth Altamont
Charlie Fenn . . . . Greene Taylor//George A. Seager

Jemmy Smart	Harry Norton//Littledale Power
Billy Price	George Curtiss//Bryant Rashlie/Greene Taylor
Nap Jones	Edwin Saxon//Paul Boswell/Frederic Topham
Bob Cordyce	George Gregory/F. Lenoir
Clerk of the Scales	Reginald Forbes//Victor M. Seymour/ L. C. Dudley
Poppy Snaffle	May Edouin
Lady Ascotte	Sadie Jerome/Alison Skipworth
Lady Windsor	Kate Sergeantson/Florence Harwood
Lady Sandown	Lilas Meredith//J. Butler/Miss Dillon
Mrs Nap Jones	Grace Pyne//Greene Taylor
Mrs Charles Fenn	Daisy Bryer//Winnie Carl
add Sir William Ascotte	Aubrey Fitzgerald/George Humphrey
Dick Groundsell	George Curtiss
Tim Crop	Harry Wynne
Miss Alexandra Parkes	Louie Stafford/Miss Bentham
Kitty	Virginia Boswell
Maggie	Rose Hamilton
Sam Bale	Frederic Topham/Paul Boswell
Grace Beresford	Daisy Bryer

Md: Ernest Woodville; sc: E. G. Banks; ch: R. M. Crompton

0173 **INEZ, THE DANCING GIRL** a comic opera in three acts written and composed by Wallace Pringle. Produced at Stafford 3 August, 1896 under the management of Geraldine Verner and toured through Bacup, Darlington, Gainsborough, Doncaster, Mexborough, Dudley, Macclesfield/Wrexham and Llandudno to 3 October, 1896.

Don Georgio Pedrillo	Charles Herman
Andrea Valetti	J. S. Radford
Giuseppe Tasca	Kenyon Lyle
Petito	William Marsden
Donna Camilla Sylvia	Lucy Cantley/Hetty Senior
Lizette	Mabel Hoare
Inez Malasquez	Geraldine Verner
Natalie	Doris Leslie
Angelica	Kitty Douglas
Lucia	Cissie Brandon
Maretta	Jeannie Jerome
Violetta	Norah Pemberton
Stella	Iris Irwin

with Daisy Danvers (pd)

Md: Wallace Pringle; ch: Daisy Lord

0174 **MONTE CARLO** a musical comedy by 'Sydney Carlton' (Harry Greenbank). Lyrics by Harry Greenbank. Music by Howard Talbot. Produced at the Avenue Theatre under the management of Henry Dana and H. J. Wilde 27 August, 1896 for a run of 76 performances closing 6 November, 1896.

Sir Benjamin Currie	Charles Rock
General Frederick Boomerang	Eric Lewis
Fred Dorian	Richard Green
James	E. W. Garden
Harry Verinder	A. Vane Tempest
Professor Lorrimer	Robb Harwood
Belmont	Guy Fane
Standring	C. L. Wilford
Captain Rossiter	William H. Kemble
Croupier	Roland Carse

François . . . . Edward Espinosa
Dorothy Carthew . . . . Kate Cutler/May Metcalf
Mrs Carthew . . . . Lottie Venne/Aida Jenoure
Gertie Gelatine . . . . May Belfry
Bertie Gelatine . . . . Venie Belfry
Ethel Boomerang . . . . Hettis Lund
Little Jemima . . . . Lalor Shiel
Midshipman. . . . . Kitty Abrahams
Suzanne . . . . Emmie Owen

with Misses Gaumore, Kavanagh, Carlton, Cross, Gain, Dannett, Sefton, Baun, Boyce, Winter, Hensey, Cooper, Stirling, Millbank, d'Albertson, Peppiate, Stuart, Wood, Stafford, Dennett and Bond; Messrs Vaughan, Roberts, Fitzgerald, Brook, Arnold, Wigley, Headsworth, Pearson and Melville.

Dir: Fred Mervin; md: Howard Talbot; ch: Edward Espinosa; sc: Bruce Smith and W. T. Hemsley; cos: Marshall & Snelgrove, Pitts & Richards, Stagg & Mantle, Redferns

Produced at Herald Square Theatre, New York, under the management of E. E. Rice 21 March, 1898 for a run of 48 performances closing 1 May, 1898. Additional music by E. E. Rice and Herman Perlet.

Thomas F. Kearns (BENJ), Frank Smithson (GEN), Augustus Cramer (FRED), Alexander Clark (JAS), Sidney de Grey (HARRY), Edward Chapman (PROF), Edward Thomas (BEL), Frank H. Crane (STAND), Neil McNeill (CAPT), James Grant (FR), Marguerite Sylva (DOR), Jeannie Winston/Phoebe Coyne (MRS), Sadie Kirby (GERT), Marie Cahill (BERT), Helene Tuesart (ETH), Josie Sadler (JEM), Susie Brown (MID), Gerome Edwardy (SUZ), Edward Thomas (1st SAILOR), Frank H. Crane (2nd SAILOR) with Mazie Trew, Ethel Cameron, Gypsey Grant, Frances Wilson, Susan Brown, Kittie Burton, Bessie Bonneville, Mollie Gaylor, Jessie Banks, Nonie Dore, June Jackson, Millie Tait, Lena Dykstra, Agnes Wadleigh, Nina Ainscoe, Minnie Gaylor, Maude Terriss, Marie Lachere, Florence Dressler, Agnes Elliott, Bessie Wilton, Grace Pierrepont, Sophie Brochard, Carrie May; Messrs Dunn, Savage, Amodeo, McBride, Tesson, Cameron, Thomas, Hill, Shuster, Crane, Vernon, Aiken, Mears, Terry. Md: Herman Perlet; sc: Frank Rafter &c; ch: H. Marchetti; cos: Mrs M. I. Dowling

75 **EN ROUTE** a musical comedy in two acts by Cecil Maxwell. Lyrics by Walter Parke. Music by Ernest Bucalossi. Additional numbers by Procida Bucalossi and Roland Carse. Copyright performance 14 May, 1895. Produced at the Parkhurst Theatre under the management of Brigata Bucalossi 21 September, 1896 and toured to Stratford East, Walsall and Sheffield ending 17 October, 1896.

John T. Smythe. . . . . A. E. Chapman
Colonel Curryman . . . . Herbert Shelley
Comte Gustave de Montpelier . . . . . . E. Webster Lawson
Ted Stanford . . . . Richard Temple Jr
Bertie Langdale . . . . J. Willes Irwin
Orton . . . . Reginald Clayton
Captain Johnson . . . . E. Ernest Boyd
Third Officer . . . . Walter Gibbens
Pat Cafferty . . . . Sam Wilkinson
Mrs J. T. Smythe. . . . . Minnie Clifford
Ethel . . . . Evie Greene
Gracie . . . . Emilie Wade
Bella Stellarina . . . . Stella May
Lizzie . . . . Ada Lee
Lottie . . . . Margot Frewin
Daisy . . . . Hilda Henley
Maud . . . . Geraldine Nelson
Alice. . . . . Alice Ancliffe

Pd: Alice Douglas
Dir: Walter Passmore; md: Ernest Bucalossi; ch: Edouard Espinosa; sc: Richard Douglass

76 **THE WHITE SILK DRESS** a musical farce in two acts by Henry J. W. Dam. Music by Alick McLean, Reginald Somerville and George Byng. Produced at the Prince of Wales Theatre

3 October, 1896 for a run of 132 performances closing 19 February, 1897. From 24 November a revised version was played.

Jack Hammersley . . . . Arthur Roberts
Sir James Turner . . . . Eric Thorne/Charles Rock
Lord Macready . . . . E. H. Kelly/Harold Eden
Major Penyon . . . . J. Furneaux Cook/Isidore Marcil
Professor Beasley . . . . Walter Uridge/Laurence Caird
Charles Hammersley . . . . Harold Eden/*out*
Angus McWhirter. . . . . George Traill/*out*
Skinderson . . . . William Cheesman
Bolingbroke . . . . L. F. Chapuy/Eric Thorne
Office Boy . . . . Harry Rignold
Mary Turner . . . . Decima Moore/Lucille Graham/Stella Gastelle
Mrs Pennington. . . . . Ellas Dee
Lady from Algiers . . . . Mrs E. H. Brooke/*out*
Lady Turner . . . . Miss M. Singleton
Miss Talbot . . . . Eva Ellerslie
Miss Essex . . . . Pierette Amella/Ida Heath
Edith Hammersley . . . . Carrie Benton
Mrs Bailey . . . . Kitty Loftus
Bellamy . . . . Laurence Caird/Arthur T. Hendon

Pd: Ida Heath
Dir: Hugh Moss; md: George Byng; sc: W. T. Hemsley

0177 **BELINDA** a musical comedy in two acts by B. C. Stephenson and Basil Hood. Music by Walter Slaughter. Produced at the Prince's, Manchester under the management of W. H. Griffiths 5 October, 1896 and toured through Halifax, Newcastle, Glasgow, Edinburgh and Sheffield, ending 14 November, 1896.

Mr Smith . . . . E. M. Robson
Mr Shepherd . . . . Avalon Collard
The O'Flannagan . . . . Forbes Dawson
Mr Wapshott . . . . Fred Emney
Timmins . . . . R. R. Lawrence
Oluf Nielsen . . . . George Marshall
Mrs Wapshott. . . . . Emily Cross
Belinda . . . . Isabelle Girardot
Matilda . . . . Dorothy Foote
Laura . . . . Kate O'Connor
Flora . . . . Violet Walford
Dora. Belle Rosa
Nora. N. Gravelstein

Sc: Bruce Smith and W. T. Hemsley; cos: Harrison & Co.

0178 **THE BELLE OF CAIRO** a play with music in 2 acts by Cecil Raleigh and F. Kinsey Peile. Music and lyrics by F. Kinsey Peile. Produced at the Court Theatre under the management of Arthur Chudleigh and May Yohe 10 October, 1896 for a run of 71 performances closing 19 December, 1896.

Earl of Bulcester . . . . Charles Wibrow
Lady Ermintrude . . . . Milly Thorne
Susan Smith . . . . Maud Wilmot
Lady Molly Rosemere . . . . Ethel Earle (Miss Bliss)
Mr Stallabrass. . . . . Victor M. Seymour
Maud Stallabrass . . . . Miss Rieke
Martha Stallabrass . . . . Miss Loraine
Mary Stallabrass . . . . Miss Bliss
James Parker . . . . Arthur Nelstone
Cooks' Guide . . . . F. D. Pengelly

Mr Patching . . . . H. V. Surrey
Mrs Patching . . . . Grace Dudley
Luigi . . . . Mr Horniman
Duval Bey. Eugene Mayeur
Sir Gilbert Fane . . . . John Peachey
Major Trevor . . . . Philip Leslie
Lt Marchmont . . . . E. V. Tarver
Surgeon Captain Cree . . . . Mr Roy
Al Ibrahim . . . . Michael Dwyer
Barbara . . . . Giulia Warwick
Nephthys . . . . May Yohe
add Lady Betty . . . . Olive O'Hara
Corporal Said. . . . . Ulysses Grant

Md: Carl Kiefert; ch: Arthur Nelstone; sc: Harry Emden; cos: Percy Anderson

Produced in a revised version by H. Newton Chance at the Grand Theatre, Birmingham under the management of Charles Wibrow 25 November, 1901 and toured.
Rose Martin (SUSAN), Madge Mavis (MOL), C. A. White (DUVAL), Allen Turner (GILB), E. W. Maule Cole (TREVOR), Charles Terry (MARCH), J. J. Reidy (CREE), Maud Nelson (BAR), Jessie Huddlestone (NEPH), Arthur Watts (WASHINGTON QUINCY QUEERPOINT PORGAN), Millicent Athol (VERMONTINA), Rose Temple (MASSACHUSSATTA), Eva Dare (MARIE). Md: J. A. Robertson

0179 **THE BLACK SQUIRE** or Where There's A Will There's A Way. A comic opera in three acts by Henry Pottinger Stephens. Music by Florian Pascal. Produced at Torquay under the management of William Hogarth 5 November, 1896 and played in repertoire with the Hogarth Company's production of *Les Cloches de Corneville* on tour.

Philip Bolsover . . . . William Hogarth
Algernon Bolsover . . . . Walter Cranbourne
Rupert Rattlebrayne . . . . Richard Martin
Septimus P. Chipmunk . . . . E. W. Royce
Portland Bill . . . . Harry Melbourne
Kitch . . . . Wilfred Henry
Mrs Baytree. . . . . Rose Wilmot
Dora. . . . . Annie Halford
Daphne . . . . Ernestine Walter
Cherry. . . . . Mimi Davenport
Cissy . . . . Adela Harvey
Patty. . . . . Rose Marks

0180 **THE CIRCUS GIRL** a musical play in two acts by James T. Tanner and 'Walter Palings' (Walter Pallant). Lyrics by Harry Greenbank and Adrian Ross. Music by Ivan Caryll. Additional numbers by Lionel Monckton. Produced at the Gaiety Theatre under the management of George Edwardes 5 December, 1896 for a run of 494 performances closing 7 May, 1898.

Sir Titus Wemyss. . . . . Harry Monkhouse/Ells Dagnall
Dick Capel . . . . Seymour Hicks/W. Louis Bradfield (W. H. Powell)
Drivelli . . . . Arthur Williams (Charles Lane)/C. Roper Lane?
Hon. Reginald Gower. . . . . Lionel Mackinder/W. Louis Bradfield
Albertoni . . . . Colin Coop
Vicomte Gaston. . . . . Maurice Farkoa/W. H. Powell/Robert Selby
Commissaire of Police . . . . Robert Nainby
Auguste . . . . Willie Warde
Adolphe . . . . Bertie Wright/Alfred Asher/E. W. Coleman/Harry Phydora
Toothick Pasha . . . . Arthur Hope/Fernley Swift/Herbert Clayton/Milroy Cooper

Rudolph . . . . E. D. Wardes/Percy Lockner
Café Proprietor . . . . Leslie Holland/W. H. Powell/E. D. Sellward/Charles Lane
Flobert . . . . Robert Selby/George Farrow/Herbert Clayton
Cocher. . . . . John Brooke?/W. F. Brooke/R. Douglas
Sergeant de Ville . . . . Fred Ring/Charles Lane/W. J. Manning
Valliand . . . . W. H. Powell/Fred Ring/Charles Lane/H. Bernhard
Biggs . . . . Edmund Payne/Horace Mills
Lucille. . . . . Katie Seymour (Madge Greet) (Coralie Blythe) (Florence Lauri)
La Favorita . . . . Ethel Haydon/Frances Earle/Maidie Hope/Elise Cook/Alison Skipworth?
Mme Drivelli . . . . Connie Ediss
Lady Diana Wemyss . . . . Maria Davis/Annie Dwelley
Marie . . . . Grace Palotta/Mabel Duncan/Nina Cadiz
Louise . . . . Lily Johnston/Marjorie Glenn/Maud Wilmot/Maud Lovell/Alice Betelle
Liane . . . . Louie Coote
Emilie . . . . Alice Betelle/Madge Greet/Maud Wilmot/Maie Saqui
Juliette . . . . Maidie Hope/Rose Brady/Madge Greet/Florence Percival/Edith Denton/Sophie Elliott/Rose Brady/Florrie Schuberth/Maie Saqui
Marquise de Millefleurs. . . . . Kathleen Francis/Marjorie Pryor/Kate Adams/Rose Brady/Ada Maitland/Rosie Boote
Comtesse d'Epernay . . . . Ada Maitland/Mabel Duncan/Birdie Sutherland/Margherita Kowska/Edith Johnston/Norma Whalley
Mlle Rose Gompson . . . . Alice Neilson/Margaret Fraser/Frances Earle/Mabel Warren/*out*
Dora Wemyss . . . . Ellaline Terriss/(Lily Johnston) Ethel Haydon/Grace Dudley
add Marie Beauville. . . . . Maie Saqui/Mabel Duncan/Dora Duley

Quartet: Margaret Fraser, Ethel Neild, Lottie Williams, Madge Greet/Rosie Boote, Edith Denton

Md: Ivan Caryll; ch: Willie Warde; sc: T. Ryan and W. Telbin; cos: Comelli

Produced at Daly's Theatre, New York, under the management of Augustin Daly 23 April, 1897. Suspended 26 June, 1897 after 75 performances and reopened 16 August, 1897. Closed 6 November, 1897 after a further 97 performances, a total of 172 performances.
Herbert Gresham (TITUS), Cyril Scott (DICK), Samuel Edwards (DRIV), Eric Scott (REG), Douglas Flint (ALB), George Miller/Neil McCay (VIC), Augustus Cook (COMM), Richard Hanford (AUG), Randolph Roberts/Hobart Bosworth (TOOTH), Pierre Young/Algernon Aspland (RUD), Deane Pratt/John Mourphy (CAFE), Abner Symmons (FLO), Richard Quilter (CO), George Heath/David Fingleton/Mr Dean (SGT), Tom Hadaway/Hans Roberts (VAL), James T. Power (BIGGS), Mary Young/Blanche Astley (LU), Nancy McIntosh (LA), Catherine Lewis/Marie Sanger (MRS), Effie Germon (DI), Helma Nelson (MARIE), Beatrice Morgan/Mabelle Gilman (LOU), Grace Rutter/Gerda Wissner/Carolyn Gordon (LI), Edith Miller/Corrine Parker (EM), Margaret Hoyt/Corinne Parker (JU), Matilde Preville/Lila Convere (COMT), Rose Davies (MARQ), Bessie Ashbaugh (GOM), Virginia Earle (DORA), Ruth Holt/Gertrude Bennett (MME DE GROUCHY). Dir: J. A. E. Malone; md: Paul Steindorff; ch: Marwig; sc: Ernest Gros, Henry E. Hoyt; cos: Comelli

Produced at Daly's Theatre, New York, under the management of Augustin Daly 2 May, 1898 for a run of 40 performances closing 4 June, 1898.

Herbert Gresham (TITUS), Cyril Scott (DICK), James Herbert (DRIV), Eric Scott (REG), Douglas Flint (ALB), Neal McCay (VIC), George Lesoir (COMM), William Gilbert (AUG), Randolph Roberts (TOOTH), Frederic Truesdale (RUD), Mr Stanley (CAFE), Mr Taylor (FLO), Mr Regis (CO), Mr Kelly (SGT), Mr Smith (VAL), James T. Powers (BIGGS), Mabelle Gillman (LU), Irene Perry (LA), Catherine Lewis (MRS), Ethel Hornick (DI), Carolyn Gordon (MARIE), Matilde Preville (LOU), Marion Carlton (LI), Rosa Vera (EM), Margaret Ashton (JU), Edith Hutchings (MARQ), Grace Rutter (COMT), Violet Goodall (GOM), Virginia Earle (DORA), Francesca Gordon (GROU). Md: Sebastian Hiller; ch: Marwig; sc: Ernest Gros, Henry E. Hoyt; cos: Comelli

Produced at the Theater Krenn, Vienna, 31 January, 1902 as *Das Circusmädel.*

TOLEDO a comic opera in 2 acts by Oliver Brand. Music by Leonard Gautier. Produced at Plymouth under the management of Austin Fryers 12 November, 1896 and played in repertoire with Fryer's touring production of *The New Barmaid.*

Don Pedro de Cabanos . . . . Llewellyn Cadwaladr
Prince Alva de Taragona . . . . Austin Fryers/Charles H. Kenny
Don Mosquito . . . . Wilfred Langley
Dingo . . . . Harold Perry
Juan Ribo . . . . James FitzJames
Ali Hassan. . . . . H. J. Broughton
Ben Ba . . . . Hugh Glendon
Ben Bu . . . . R. Ferris
Moorish soldier . . . . W. Lister
Pepita . . . . Amy Grundy
Azmora . . . . Nancy Manners
Zuleika . . . . Maude Langton
Maraquita . . . . M. Grist
Clarita . . . . F. Greville
Donna Manilla . . . . Marian Howard
Princess Irene . . . . Ilma Norina

Pd: Elva Dearen
Md: Leonard Gautier; ch: Katti Lanner

THE PRESIDENT or The Republic Of Tucatan. A musical comedy in two acts by John M. Fisher and Edgar Larner. Music by Henry Vernon. Produced at Maidenhead under the management of J. G. Taylor 19 October, 1896 and toured through Bilston, Reading, Kidderminster/Wrexham, to 14 November, 1896.

Captain Briggs . . . . J. G. Taylor
Diaz Dasco . . . . George Handel
Mortimer Pye Smith . . . . Edgar Devere
General Alvarado . . . . A. Bernard
Lt Pimco Narino . . . . F. Farrington
Sandoval. . . . . Harding Davis
Duero . . . . Guy Cavendish
Garay . . . . A. B. Williams
Lopez . . . . John M. Davis
Benjamin Dilley. . . . . A. Best
Don Olid . . . . James James
Robert Owen . . . . Vincent Clarke
Li Kwod . . . . J. M. Feiley
Li Kwise . . . . C. Whatmon
Inez . . . . Florence Baines
Kitty . . . . Marie Baines
Corello . . . . Nellie Douglas
Avario . . . . Bessie Douglas
Lilono . . . . Alice Reed
Rosa . . . . May James
Maria . . . . V. Leslie

Pd: Florrie White

A MERRY MADCAP a musical domestic comedy in two acts written and composed by Victor Stevens. Lyrics partly by Albert Birch. Additional music by Carl Kiefert, F. V. St Clair and Charles Deane. Produced at Ealing under the management of J. Herman Dickson 3 August, 1896 and toured simultaneously by that company and a second company under the management of Victor Stevens.

Dickson cast

Kitty Armstrong	Maud Denny
Mrs Armstrong	Annie Bernard
Joe Jaffrey	E. A. White
Compton Chambers	Albert E. Good
Archie Frampton	Arthur Leyshon
Charlie Waggs	A. G. Spry
Selina Sparks	Louie Cleveland

Stevens cast

Kitty Armstrong	Ada Willoughby/Lottie Brooks
Mrs Armstrong	Nora Millington
Joe Jaffrey	Arthur Deane
Compton Chambers	Victor Stevens
Archie Frampton	George Willoughby
Charlie Waggs	Fred Eastman
Selina Sparks	Clara Jecks

SKIPPED BY THE LIGHT OF THE MOON a musical farcical comedy adapted from George R. Sims' play *A Gay City*. Lyrics by Percy Marshall. Music by George Pack and Henry W. May. Additional music by Ivan Caryll, H. Carson, H. Trotère, O. Verne, F. L. Moir, A. H. Behrend &c. First produced in America and subsequently in Australia. First produced in Britain under the management of George Walton in an up-to-date version at Reading 24 August, 1896 and toured. Produced in London 27 April, 1899 under the title *A Good Time*.

SUNNY FLORIDA a musical comedy in two acts by Edward Hilldyard Marris. Music by Marris and Augustus T. MacInnes. Produced at the Royal Court Theatre, Warrington under the management of E. H. Marris 2 November, 1896. Reproduced as *The Armenian Girl* 2 August, 1897 and subsequently as *Somebody's Sweetheart* and toured.

WEATHER OR NO by Adrian Ross and W. Beach. Music by Luard Selby. Produced at the Savoy Theatre under the management of Richard D'Oyly Carte 10 August, 1896 with *The Mikado*. Withdrawn 17 February 1897.

She	Emmie Owen
He	H. Scott Russell

1897

After the amazing West End rate of the previous year, 1897 proved rather less prolific in the production of new musicals. This was not a tendency, but largely the effect of the success of several of the previous year's crop. The two Edwardes' musical theatres, the Gaiety and Daly's, were tied up and would remain so throughout the year with his 1896 hits *The Circus Girl* and *The Geisha*, and 1897 saw no new George Edwardes' production. At the Duke of York's *The Gay Parisienne* also continued its run through the early part of the year.

The season's first new offering was an unfortunate and briefly-lived one. *Man About Town* appeared on the second day of the year at the Avenue Theatre and survived only three weeks in spite of a cast which included such proven favourites as Edwin Lonnen, Alice Lethbridge and Alma Stanley, the last seemingly arisen from the dead as London newspapers had carried appreciative obituaries of her the previous year when she had been taken ill in America. The authors of *Man About Town* hid behind the pseudonym of 'Huan Mee' (You and Me) and on the first night they should have been glad to take advantage of their anonymity as hoots and howls of disapproval arose from the gallery well before the final curtain. Composer Alfred Carpenter, presenting his first West End score, was unwise enough to take a call in the company of one of his authors at the evening's end. The friendly element in the audience could not disguise the hostility of the remainder.

The story of *Man About Town* was familiar in essence, bearing a notable resemblance to, most particularly, Harry Monkhouse's still touring musical *Larks*. Frank Ennesleigh has done a version of French writer Henri Lavelle's comic opera and spends his time (or so he tells his wife) hawking it round theatrical managements. But, in reality, that time is being spent in dalliance with the actress Gwendoline Grova. His bluff seems to have been called when Mrs Ennesleigh, unbeknown to her husband, succeeds in selling his script to the very theatre where Miss Grova is employed and, furthermore, finds herself offered the starring role by the smooth and flirty manager, Lucius Light. The second act, set in a Shaftesbury Avenue hairdressing salon, went through the inevitable series of disguises, overhearings and flirtings involving Lavelle, Miss Grova and the hairdresser before all was finally tied up neatly with Frank returning chastened to the matrimonial home. The newspaper verdicts were no kinder than that of the first night public. *The Era* stated flatly:

> Very little can be said in praise of . . *Man About Town*. It is involved without being ingenious and frivolous without being amusing . . the artists struggled bravely with the book they had to interpret . .

The music fared little better than the libretto, *The Times* noting merely that it was:

'. . rather characterless and calls for little comment'. An unfortunate touch in this largely ineffectual piece was a number in which the 'failings' of the comic opera genre were detailed:

There's a class of play much patronised, it's frequently the rage
And it's often unintentionally humorous,
For of all those incongruities displayed upon the stage
Those revealed in comic opera are most numerous.
All the stories are perplexing, and the book is often 'rot'
But the artistes seldom speak it, since as frequently as not
They are too intent on gagging to develop any plot
It's always done that way in comic opera.

When they first ring up the curtain on that rustic village green
Where the peasants promenade with regularity,
In their dresses fresh from Paris they're invariably seen
All indulging in most meaningless hilarity.
Then to cheerful tripping music of the pizzicato sort
Comes a maid dispensing liquor – for you never see it bought
And she pours out several gallons from a jug that holds a quart,
It's a miracle performed in comic opera.

When the heroine steps on the scene, the chorus clusters round
She is up-to-date or very puritanical
And a patch of silver moonlight that's been shining on the ground
Gets up and follows her with jerk mechanical.
Then the peasants stroll into the inn, perhaps they seek more beer.
It can only hold a couple, but three dozen disappear,
And the maiden sings a ballad because no-one's there to hear
She likes the stage alone in comic opera.

If the song itself was amusing enough, its presence in this particular play smacked of glasshouses and stone-throwing. *Man About Town* gave up the ghost, after unsuccessful efforts had been made to enliven it with new material and business, on January 23rd, the first piece to come and the first to go in 1897.

'Huan Mee' might ridicule the comic opera and its conventions but the genre provided within its framework the opportunity for much fun and much attractive and popular music, song and dance and its continuing validity as a form was soon reaffirmed, not on this occasion by a British work but by the first profitable French import for some time. *La Poupée* was a Maurice Ordonneau piece on well-established lines, the principal motif being the substitution of a live girl for an automaton doll, the same as used so many years previously in *La Princesse de Trébizonde* and since incorporated in *Coppélia*, *Les Contes d'Hoffmann* and such British pieces as *Rhoda*, *Pepita*, *The Mountebanks* and *An Artful Automaton*.

La Poupée had been produced the previous year at the Gaîté in Paris where it had had a successful run of 121 performances. During that time it had been vetted by George Edwardes and most of the other principal London musical producers and rejected as unsuitable for London's present frame of mind. The only one who disagreed was Henry Lowenfeld who saw the piece as a possible vehicle for Arthur Roberts in the role of the comical doll-maker and who, in spite of Roberts' misgivings, bought the rights for a London production. When the time came to replace *The White Silk Dress* the unabashed Lowenfeld, ignoring the warning cries of his colleagues, scheduled *La Poupée*. Roberts, by now, had been talked out of the piece. He surrendered his interest and refused to take the role intended for him. In his place, Lowenfeld hired Willie Edouin who was preparing to go on the road with *Newmarket*. *La Poupée* in its English version (adapted by Arthur Sturgess, and with some notable alterations made to the score by George Byng) was a huge surprise to those theoretically 'in the know'. From the first it was an enormous hit, proving that the market for comic opera was still there when the combination of good fun and good music was right. *La Poupée* compiled a first run of 576 performances, becoming Edmond Audran's most successful piece of all time, seventeen years after *La Mascotte* had first brought him to the notice of the British public.

British comic opera had given its latest offering four nights previously at the Savoy, but without comparable result. With the Gilbert/Sullivan alliance definitely ended, D'Oyly Carte was forced to tap new sources for his original works and, on this occasion, he turned to F. C. Burnand, finally giving that august gentleman the opportunity to prove that he and not Gilbert should have had the chance to work with Sullivan through the years. Burnand allied himself with one of his *Punch* contributors, Rudolph C. Lehmann, journalist and Liberal MP (but rather more famous for having coached the boating teams of Cambridge and Harvard), to produce *His Majesty* or The Court of Vingolia, only his second full-length original musical since *The Contrabandista* thirty years previously. But Burnand did not, even now, have the privilege of working with Sullivan again. The composer had other projects to hand and the man eventually selected was the equally respected, if less popularly celebrated, Sir Alexander Mackenzie, principal of the Royal Academy of Music. Mackenzie was an Edinburgh man who had begun his career as a concert violinist and music teacher before making his mark as a conductor and composer. His works to date had been in the more serious fields – *La Belle Dame Sans Merci* and *The Scottish Rhapsodies* for orchestra, songs, instrumental pieces, cantatas *The Bridge*, *Jason* and *The Story of Said*, operas *The Rose of Sharon* and most notably *Columba*. *His Majesty* was, at the age of 40, his first and only venture into the field of the musical, and it showed just what he might have achieved had he, like Sullivan, taken to the lighter form more consistently.

Mackenzie's music on its own, however, was not enough to make a Savoy opera and *His Majesty* finally laid the F. C. Burnand ghost. Writing with every ounce of Gilbertian style he could muster, the editor of *Punch* amassed a diffuse morass of libretto and lyrics which required a six-page synopsis in the book of words to cover all its meanderings. The plot itself was exiguous in the extreme and traditionally reminiscent, being the age-old story of the King who falls in love with the woodsmaiden, even though he is betrothed to an unknown foreign princess. The maiden eventually turns out to be that very princess in disguise. This basic story was heavily elaborated with comic characters and subordinate singing roles and a very great deal of dialogue. So much, indeed, that the first act, on opening night, ran for one hour and fifty minutes.

But the first disaster of *His Majesty*'s career had occurred even before the show's opening. During the rehearsal period the show's director, Charles Harris, died. Harris was 42 years old, the son of the celebrated actor-manager Augustus Glossop Harris and a younger brother of producer Sir Augustus Harris. His sisters Ellen (Mrs Horace Sedger) and Maria were both actresses and Charles took naturally to the theatre as a way of life when very young. By the time he was 22 he was engaged as stage manager for Carte, and he co-operated on the original staging of *The Sorcerer* and *H.M.S. Pinafore* in the days before Gilbert took it solely on himself to direct his own pieces. After a brilliant world-wide career, Harris had returned to the Savoy to direct *The*

Nautch Girl, *The Vicar of Bray*, *Haddon Hall*, *Jane Annie* and *The Chieftain*, as well as taking a hand in *Utopia (Limited)*, *The Grand Duke* and the recent Gilbert and Sullivan revivals, and he had become established as the outstanding stager of musical plays of the nineteenth century. When he first made his appearance on the scene as a stage manager in the early '70s, the preparation of plays was a fairly haphazard affair, the staging as often as not being worked out by the actors and more particularly by the stars with practical help from the stage manager. It was Harris who first, and often alone, managed to concentrate authority for the physical staging of a musical into the hands of the so-called stage manager. His task was no doubt facilitated by the relatively starless nature of the D'Oyly Carte Company of early days but, with his reputation confirmed world-wide by his staging of *H.M.S. Pinafore*, he had little difficulty in maintaining the position which he had created for himself as 'Stage Director'. The position subsequently became separated from the day-to-day running position of stage manager and, as Stage Director, Charles Harris remained the undisputed number one of the musical theatre until his early death.

The second disaster occurred on the show's opening night and it concerned the other survivor of the Carte Opera Comique days, George Grossmith. *His Majesty* had been much talked of and 'boomed' in the press before its presentation, and one of the most talked of points was Carte's coup in enticing George Grossmith, the star of the Savoy in its heyday, to make a return to the stage in the role of the quaint and lovelorn monarch of the title. Grossmith had been a nervous and unwilling convert to the comic opera stage in the first place, although it had finally made his name and fortune, and on his return after a lapse of years he was even more nervous, but although the inducements offered by Carte had overcome his considerable reticence, they had not overcome his nerves. His first-night performance was appalling and even the faithful public and the well-disposed press had to admit that the star's jittery and forgetful rendering of an admittedly inadequate role had made a fiasco of the evening.

The role was a curious one, combining as it did the dual functions of comedian and hero, with songs ranging from a patter-song satire on the Kaiser:

> In the arts I was a dabbler, for I dipped in Hedda Gabler
> And emerged with the aroma of a quintessential brain,
> And I drew cartoons historic with a meaning allegoric
> You can buy them in the city, twopence coloured, penny plain.
> Then I taught my friends to grovel at a sketchy little novel
> Which I wrote to put the novels of the ancients on the shelf
> And without a word of proem I made up an epic poem
> And composed a three act opera and acted it myself.
> Thus, let all the nations know it, I am a painter, playwright, poet,
> I'm the father of my country and that country's greatest son
> When I'm sad my subjects falter, but when circumstances alter
> I can always set them laughing with what I consider fun.
> When compared to King or Kaiser I am greater, better, wiser,
> I'm to all my brother sovereigns as infinity to naught,
> Yet my character's the oddest, for I'm so supremely modest
> That I know I never value all my merits as I ought!

to duets with the heroine, Felice, impersonated by Ilka Palmay (by now she had dropped the 'von') which required a very different feeling. Grossmith got totally and embarrassingly lost, and so did *His Majesty*. The newspaper reaction was reluctantly unfavourable. *The Times*:

> *His Majesty* . . . must have been a surprise to those who, from the fact of Mr Burnand's experience as a librettist of comic opera and Sir Alexander Mackenzie's inexperience in this class of composition expected to find a brilliant book weighed down by music of too ambitious and serious a type. The exact opposite is the case: the book for which Mr Burnand and R. C. Lehmann are jointly responsible lacks the all-important quality of animation, the dialogue is rarely redeemed by a happy thought and the confused plot is hardly ever interesting. If the piece should prove definitely unsuccessful – and its extremely ambiguous reception by a very tolerant pit and gallery promises no certain career of prosperity – it will not be the fault of the music which is neither commonplace nor abstruse but appropriate throughout, musicianly and very often marked by distinction as well as humour.

The Era had no doubts:

> There will be an imperative necessity for wholesale curtailment in the book of the opera, and a few omissions will have to be made from the score.

The first alteration was the most necessary. After four performances, poor Grossmith declared illness and departed. His understudy, Herbert Workman, took over the leading role until Henry Lytton, till then little seen in the West End, came in to give the imperative star performance in the star role. The book was duly condensed but the piece could not be saved. *His Majesty* had to be admitted a failure and closed after 61 performances. It was interpolated briefly into the repertoire of two D'Oyly Carte touring companies but not long persevered with.

If *His Majesty* had provided a talking point before its production, it received nothing like the publicity devoted to the next show to open in London. In 1896 a traveller in Armenia attended the theatre in Pera. The traveller, vocalist A. Nilsson Fysher, was taken with the show, a musical entitled *Leblebidii Itor-itor Agha* written by Nalian and composed by Tigran Tchoughadjan, which had caused a sensation in Pera and ran an incredible 165 performances before it was belatedly closed by the authorities because of its political references. Fysher brought the show back to London with him and sold it to A. H. Chamberlyn who then set about forming a syndicate with a capital of £10,000 for its production. Immediately 'The Armenian Opera' was paragraphed and talked about everywhere.

Seymour Hicks was hired to do an English version of *The Yashmak*, as the show was to be called, and under his 'adapting' the book of the Armenian piece quickly disappeared as its dramatic plot was trivialised into a series of standard musical comedy scenes. Tchoughadjan's music was discarded and a plethora of new pieces ordered under the management of the Corfiot composer Napoleon Lambelet. Lambelet had made his theatrical début with the comic opera *'E Pardarmena* in Athens in 1890 before settling in London where he had worked as m.d. for several theatres whilst composing songs and incidental music for the stage. *The Yashmak* was his first substantial English work, although much of the score was in the nature of either interpolations or arrangements, and rather less than half was the original work of the credited composer.

The Yashmak finally opened on 31 March, 1897, almost a year after the first paragraph had announced it, and it proved to be, to all intents and purposes, a totally new show. *The Times* noted:

> From the occasional occurrence of certain melodramatic incidents and other signs it may be surmised that the form in which *The Yashmak* now appears is not that in which it was cast at first.

The new *Yashmak* quite obviously owed more to currently popular British shows than to its putative Armenian source. Its locale harked back to *The Sultan of Mocha*, for the Ottoman Empire of Messrs Hicks and Cecil Raleigh was as one with the fictional Mocha or Go-Bang, with the Morocco of *Morocco Bound* or the Cairo of *The Belle of Cairo*, and its characters were equally familiar – the Hotel Proprietor, the chirpy caddy, the impoverished aristocratic hero and the bevy of girls from the Gaiety Theatre, now as large a part of stage fiction as their genuine counterparts were of stage fact.

The story in which all these characters became enmeshed was no more Armenian than they. The theatre ladies, on tour in the Ottoman Empire, are kidnapped by the officious Bustapha Pasha for the harem of his master, the Sultan. Our hero and our comedian, disguised, go to their rescue. In the second act, the Sultan, who has learned of Bustapha's misdeeds in the provinces, decides to sentence him to death, but our hero has come to town disguised as that beastly potentate to accomplish his mission of duty. There is a duel between Bustapha the fake and the Sultan's English adviser (a seeming remnant of *Leblebidii* & c) before all is settled conveniently and a variety entertainment can intervene.

Everything was done to try to appeal to the popular taste. A common denominator of proved elements provided the plan for *The Yashmak* – both its book and its score. Plantation songs were popular: *The Yashmak* picked up three of them including one by Fay Templeton and another by E. E. Rice; an imitation of the kinematograph had been successful in *My Girl*: *The Yashmak* piled on the effect to such an extent in Kitty Loftus' song about 'Dainty Dora' that *The Times* complained that it was 'almost as trying to the sight as the real thing'. A patter song, 'I'm a Monarch with original Ideas', a song about the music halls, 'That's how They do it on the Halls', a dash of smut and, of course, a 'naughty dance'. 'La Danse du Bain', doubtless named in French to add piquancy, turned out to be an ordinarily competent John D'Auban affair danced in pink trunks and flesh-coloured tights on top of a bit of under-lit glass.

With so much crammed in, the first performance of *The Yashmak*, not unexpectedly, ran for a little under four hours. But faults in the writing were less noticeable because it had been carefully prepared and was unusually capably performed for a first night, at a time when the tendency was still to produce as quickly as possible and to touch up and renovate at leisure. Nevertheless, reaction was mixed. To those who had expected something original, interesting and exotic, *The Yashmak* was a disappointment. To those to whom 'more of the same' was what they liked, it provided a good evening's entertainment. *The Times* was disappointed:

> Upon the well-worn framework first used in *Morocco Bound* and with the aid of the central situation of *The Geisha* a new production has been arranged . . . . there is a good deal of smart dialogue of a refreshingly quaint kind, and the effect of the whole is lively though it is . . far too long . . the music may best be described as pasticcio . . not only are there many numbers in the score which are familiar to every player, but those portions which are professedly original convey suggestions of older composers . . .

The Era had little time for it:

> The sanguine and erratic Mr Micawber is described in 'David Copperfield' as always waiting for something to turn up. This was the attitude of the audience during the greater part of the first performance of *The Yashmak* . . . and that attitude was patiently though despairingly preserved until about half past eleven when the long expected bit of fun arrived, in the shape of an amusing skit on the Blondi-Fregoli

> business[1] done by Mr John Le Hay and Miss Kitty Loftus . . . .
> Should any new numbers be added to the score, they will doubtless be more tuneful than some of the music composed and arranged by Mr Napoleon Lambelet . . . Lengthy description . . is precluded by the fact that there is very little to describe . . It is useless to engage clever artistes if you give them parts of which they can make little or nothing and songs which are neither 'catchy' nor melodious.

On the other hand, *The Stage* correspondent was delighted with everything:

> . . [it] contained so many good things, it was such a brilliant spectacle and the whole was carried through with such zeal, intelligence and spirit that the onlookers praised everything, leaving the authors the responsibility of making the necessary excisions to reduce the piece to orthodox dimensions. Very rarely has an exceptionally lengthy piece gone with corresponding smoothness of interpretation and evenness of public approval . . . Honest fun abounds. For tuneful 'swing' and 'go' the music bears comparison with that of any piece of its kind yet produced in the metropolis, whilst graceful instrumentation of sundry airs and choruses affords evidence that Mr Lambelet could offer workmanship of a quality that would be rather out of place in a musical play . .

The initial reaction to *The Yashmak* reflected fairly its future appeal. It was a competent and characteristic entertainment put on the stage in a businesslike way; as further attractions, there were the comic talents of Le Hay, Kitty Loftus and Fred Emney, the dancing of pretty Mabel Love and talented Topsy Sinden and her 'Bathmaidens', and the vocal values of Charles Ryley and, most especially, Aileen d'Orme, fresh from the Paris Conservatoire where she had studied with Melba's teacher, Mme Marchesi, here making her stage début. But there was also in the piece much that was mediocre and unoriginal which efficient staging and performance could not wholly mask.

Having been indecisively launched, *The Yashmak* soon began to suffer its share of disasters. Firstly, poor Charles Ryley collapsed one night during the show and within weeks he was dead. Then the actress Maggie Roberts, whose role had been cut, sued the management and in June, Aileen d'Orme suddenly left the show. Composer and man-of-the-town Jimmy Glover was called in to liven up affairs with a regular 'second edition' and *The Yashmak* struggled through to its hundredth performance with wedding bells ringing for composer Lambelet and chorine Dora Temple. The show finally succumbed after four months. The recipe had not totally failed, but it had not succeded either, and the management had shown more doggedness than sense.

When the show ended Chamberlyn, the brothers McKean and the Leadenhall Street advertising agents, Blumbergs, found their company dissolved in disarray and both Chamberlyn and the hapless McKeans ended up in the bankruptcy courts. Only the wretched Eastern traveller seemed to have come out of the affair with a profit, and for all that had been retained of his 'discovery', his fee could well have been saved.

One additional factor which probably contributed to the limited life of *The Yashmak* was the arrival hard on its heels in the West End of *The French Maid* which had all the popular elements of *The Yashmak*, but which was also relatively new, fresh and original. *The French Maid* had already 45 weeks of touring behind it, having been produced at Bath as long ago as April, 1896, and toured almost continuously since with

[1] an Italian protean act

outstanding success. The path from the provinces to the metropolis had by now been well beaten by *The Lady Slavey*, *The New Barmaid* and *The Gay Parisienne*, and *The French Maid* followed in their successful steps and, indeed, outstripped them all by running in the West End for some sixteen months while continuing all that time to tour under the flourishing banner of Milton Bode.

The French Maid was from the *Gentleman Joe* team of Basil Hood and Walter Slaughter. When Arthur Roberts preferred to go to Jerome K. Jerome and Henry Dam for his new pieces, the partners had set to work on a piece for Bode, the provincial manager of *Gentleman Joe*, and the result was *The French Maid*. During its provincial peregrinations the opportunity had been taken to fine down the show's dialogue and business and to replace some of the musical numbers, so that it appeared in London in a fully tried and tested form. Unlike *The Lady Slavey* and *The Gay Parisienne* it did not require wholesale alterations to make it acceptable to a London audience, for Hood and Slaughter had not bowed to provincial traditions to make their piece a hit outside London. *The French Maid* was a strong and thoroughly well-written piece.

It was brought in with a large part of its original cast intact, including nearly all the stars – Louie Pounds and her sister Lillie, Joseph Wilson, Murray King, Windham Guise and H. O. Clarey. The original leading baritone, however, had to be replaced as young Spenser Kelly who had created the role had lost a leg in a railway accident during the tour. His place was taken by another promising young singer, Richard Green. The other major alteration to the cast was in the title role. It had been created by a genuine Frenchwoman, Miss Andrée Corday, but after the initial tour Miss Corday had been snapped up by George Edwardes to play the French role created by Juliette Nesville in *The Geisha*. For the 1897 tour, Bode replaced her with a fifteen-year-old Scarborough girl, Madge Crichton, making her first appearance on stage. It would not be many years before little Miss Crichton would establish herself as a West End leading lady but, for the present, the managing syndicate decided to play safe and the ubiquitous Kate Cutler took over the role of Suzette.

The plot of *The French Maid* was adequately insignificant, dealing with little more than the various flirtations of its title character. Suzette has many admirers, including a jealous gendarme, Paul Lecuire, and Charles Brown, a waiter at the hotel where she works. They are concerned by her impending choice of escort to the forthcoming bal masqué. But things are further complicated by various visitors to the hotel who also fall for the pretty maid's charms – an Indian Prince, his attaché and Jack Brown, an English soldier and twin brother to the waiter. In traditional French style Suzette strings them all along, causing havoc in the lives of all concerned, including the aristocratic Admiral and Lady Hawser, their niece Dorothy and her lover, Harry, who get involved in a second act full of jealousy, disguises and misunderstandings until all is disentangled and a chastened Suzanne goes back to her faithful gendarme.

If the plot was insubstantial it had the advantage of being described in the dialogue of Basil Hood, one of the best purveyors of snappy lines and crisp and attractive lyrics available, and it delighted so many of the critics that they appeared not to notice the lack of significant incident in their reviews. *The Era* went so far as to say that ' . . the plot is ingenious, but slightly complicated' but *The Stage* countered:

> . . [Basil Hood] deserves less credit for the plot which has the demerits of being at once attenuated and complicated than for the witty and pointed dialogue, the graceful turning of the lyrics and a whimsical playing upon words in the comic ditties that reminds us, in common with other writers, of his celebrated namesake, the elder Tom Hood.

The Stage was not the only paper to compare Hood's abilities to those of his illustrious ancestor. The promise which had blossomed in *Gentleman Joe* had certainly been confirmed in *The French Maid*. The music written by Walter Slaughter was also pretty and apt. Slaughter had shown his versatility in *Marjorie*, *Gentleman Joe* and *Alice in Wonderland*, three very different kinds of production from each of which he had emerged with credit. For *The French Maid* he used a wholesome and skilful popular style which was entirely compatible with Hood's writing and which led to the production of a bouquet of attractive and well-received numbers.

In the title role, Kate Cutler scored with a saucy polka, ' The Femme de Chambre', and joined with Joseph Wilson, as Jack, in the duet 'I'll Lead You such a Dance'. Wilson, who had the role of his career in *The French Maid* (although he had played Tony in *My Sweetheart* some 500 times), had a rousing number 'The jolly British Sailor' which gained great favour:

When quite a little chap a-sitting on my mother's lap
She told me of a silly superstition
That when eating cherry tart
You should set the stones apart
To tell your future calling and position.
And they said I'd come to grief as a ploughboy or a thief
An apothecary, tinker or a tailor,
But they told a thumping lie, for I mean to live and die
In the navy, as a jolly British Sailor!

and the very funny 'I've 'er Portrait next my 'Eart' which brought the house down every night, and which bears quoting in full:

I ain't no famous 'ero
Of 'alf an 'undred fights
But just an honest sailor
According to my lights
But there ain't no bluejacket
Nor yet no KCB
As proud as I'm because I knows
My Liza's proud o' me!

I've 'er portrait next my 'eart, dressed up so spry and smart
In 'er jacket trimmed with artificial fur,
And it makes a sailor feel a sorter prouder of 'isself
To be loved by a gal like 'er.

One day, as I remembers
I says to Mary Ann
'How is it you can love me
A common sailorman?'
And Emily, she creeps closer
And I well nigh sobs with pride
When she says, 'It ain't the coat I loves,
But the 'eart what beats inside!'

I've 'er portrait in my breast, all dressed up in 'er best
With feathered 'at and yellow neckercher
And it makes a sailor feel a sorter prouder of 'isself
To be loved by a gal like 'er.

So when my heart is 'eavy
And when my 'eart is down

I turns and thinks of Nancy
As lives in Portsmouth town,
And it makes me inches taller,
And straighter in the back,
To think 'ow I love Mary
And 'ow Mary loves 'er Jack!

I've 'er portrait in my breast, tho' I allows, if I am pressed
It ain't like her, for the face is all a blur
But it makes a sailor feel a sorter prouder of 'isself
To be loved by a gal like 'er.

The love you bears a sweetheart
It seems a sorter charm
And it 'olds a sailor steady
And keeps 'im out of 'arm.
And the only time the bullets
Fell around me, thick as 'ail
'Twas my Sarah's love as kept me up
Alive to tell the tale

I'd 'er portrait in my breast, with a bundle of the rest
Of the gals as I had arst to be my wife
And arf way through them photergraphs a bullet spent isself
So I feels as they saved my life!

As the other brother, Charles, Murray King came in for some good songs too. 'Do not Jump at your Conclusions' described how things (as Gilbert remarked) are 'seldom what they seem', 'A Bit too Far' bewailed the modern trend towards women 'wearing the pants' both literally and figuratively, and 'That is a curious Way' echoed to the refrain 'A bloke may be no-one to-day but he'll find himself someone tomorrow'.

Hood composed a pseudo-Gilbertian patter-song for H. O. Clarey as the haughty but flirtatious Admiral Sir Hercules Hawser:

It's ever my endeavour that I never, never, never
May do anything, at any time, whatever or at all
That can lower my position, or alter my condition
As a stern and solemn, Nelson's column sort of Admiral . .

and another, even more popular, 'I'm an Admiral' in which that lofty gentleman hypocritically declares his intention of improving the morals of the British sailor. The romantic music of *The French Maid* was the part of Louie Pounds and Richard Green as the young lovers, most successfully in a charming duet 'You can Read it in my Eyes' which was provided with an unusually logical and progressive lyric for a straightforward love song.

Other numbers included a Gendarmes' Chorus (more than a little reminiscent of French opéra-bouffe, but undoubtedly intentionally so), Richard Green's 'Britannia's Sons' which *The Stage* selected as being particularly worthy of mention as one of the best patriotic ballads about, a song for Eric Lewis as the hotelier Camembert 'Je ne Comprends pas' which satirised the hypocrisy of the Englishman – Mrs Grundy at home and a dirty old man in France – and a waltz song for the Gendarme about his 'Pretty Suzette'. But the song which scored the greatest success of all was 'The Twin Duet' for the two brothers, Jack and Charles, in which they declared their different characters with another dash of Hood word-play:

So you'll agree
That I and he (my brother)
Are opposite
And not a bit
Like each and one another

The London opening of *The French Maid* was an unqualified success. At the end of the show the delighted audience were showered with streamers and confetti from the stage as they applauded the newest hit in town. The papers were unanimous:

> As bright, lively and agreeable entertainment as has been witnessed for some time (*Stage*)
>
> . . one of the brightest and most melodious and most effective [pieces] that have been seen and heard on the English stage for a very long time . . (*Truth*)
>
> . . a fresher, brighter piece has not been seen for many a day – the mixture is piquant and palatable in a high degree, especially as, with a spicy French element it happens to contain a considerable Jack Tar flavouring . . (*Times*)

Suzette, the French Maid, settled in for a 480-performance run in the West End. During the run it was transferred to the Vaudeville Theatre after having given Edward Terry's little theatre the greatest success it had known in its ten years of existence. The show's metropolitan popularity was more than equalled by its provincial record. Like its predecessors – *The Lady Slavey*, *The Gay Parisienne* and *The New Barmaid* – it became a regular feature of the major touring circuits for many years.

The French Maid also became part of the repertoire of companies in Australia, South Africa and further afield, and its American production, starring Marguerite Sylva, was one of the hits of the 1897/8 Broadway season at the Herald Square Theatre where it ran for a respectable 175 performances. Hood and Slaughter had now provided London with two of the best shows of recent years, and their next contribution could be looked forward to with considerable eagerness. It was not long to appear.

In August, Arthur Roberts, rusticated by the immovable *La Poupée* at 'his' Prince of Wales London base, opened a tour of his new musical. He had placed his faith once again in the authors who had supplied him with his top role of 'Gentleman Joe', and Hood and Slaughter repeated the same formula, casting their star this time as a Lifeguardsman with a 'mash' on a pretty nursemaid, and constructed a piece which gave Roberts frequent opportunity for all the drolleries and quick-change impressions for which he was famous.

The story of *Dandy Dan the Lifeguardsman* bore a strong constitutional resemblance to *Gentleman Joe*. 'Dandy Dan' Smith of Her Majesty's Lifeguards meets the pretty nursemaid, Mary, in Hyde Park and proceeds to 'mash' her, to the chagrin of Mary's regular beau, Robert White, a policeman. Onto the scene comes the socialite Lady Catherine Wheeler, a lady of rank who has married a commoner who is 'something in the city':

He makes a hundred thousand a year
Though I don't know how he does it
But if you'll excuse the expression I use
I do know how to 'buzz' it!

Lady Catherine mistakes her maid's acquaintance for an aristocratic sprig named Roderick Ptarmigan and, consequently, in Act 2, 'Dandy Dan' finds himself in the lady's Park Lane salon among her society guests. But the real Roderick turns up and

Lady Catherine realises that she has an impostor amongst her valuables. The police, in the form of the jilted White, are called in and havoc ensues as Dan appears in a variety of disguises – as a waiter, an earl, a society masher – and plays various pranks including persuading the beefy retainers of the Earl of Capercailzie that White has come to arrest their beloved master, which results in the 'twa Hielanders' falling furiously on the unfortunate policeman. As a master-stroke, Dan persuades the Inspector of Police to change clothes with him to enable that representative of the law to gather stealthy information. With the real Inspector locked in a back room, Dan proceeds to impersonate him, treating the aristocracy with an overweening manner which horrifies them until they realise it has all been a trick and find it in their hearts to forgive the 'lovable rogue'.

The part fitted Roberts wonderfully and, of course, he immediately set to to embroider it with his own popular brand of business and humour. The construction of the piece duly suffered, but the public cared not a jot for the construction; they wanted Roberts and Roberts they got. If they had heard and seen an awful lot of it before, no-one seemed to care. By the time the show reached London, more than three months later, the programme bore the slightly ominous legend – 'Produced by Mr George Capel under the direction of the Author, Composer and Mr Arthur Roberts'.

Roberts took the Lyric Theatre for his season, having decided to present himself in what looked like being his surest success since *Gentleman Joe*. He opened to a great reception – for himself, but the show was not looked on with nearly so much favour as *Joe* had been. *The Times* wrote:

> [Dandy Dan] may best be described as a rechauffé of some former performances by Mr Arthur Roberts, such as *Gentleman Joe* and his parody of Signor Fregoli . . . There was certainly more than one mauvais quart d'heure, and a dull quarter of an hour in a piece in which the fun must be fast and furious is a very serious affair . .

While exempting Roberts himself from criticism it continued:

> Directly he departs [from the stage] there is a Cimmerian darkness so far as regards both fun and lucidity . .

and promptly followed its review with another, three times as long, raving over the Savoy revival of *La Grande Duchesse*.

The Era took a similar attitude:

> People will condone the absence of plot and pardon the wildest improbabilities for the sake of one surpassingly funny creation. And Mr Arthur Roberts as Dandy Dan *is* immensely funny – funnier even than in *Gentleman Joe*. The adored peculiarities again come into play effectively, the mobile eyeballs turn and roll, the sharp staccato enunciation is crisp and comical, the 'tricksy' oddities and quaint, jerky gags prove irresistibly laughter-evoking, and the result is success . . . without Mr Roberts as the Lifeguardsman the public would not tolerate for a moment the slipshod arrangement and the straggling story of Mr Basil Hood's libretto. The musical numbers are commendable, and Mr Walter Slaughter's music is some of the most spirited he has ever written but, after all, the chief attraction of *Dandy Dan* is Mr Arthur Roberts, and to his exertions the success of the evening on Saturday was almost entirely due.

What the critics overlooked or chose to ignore was that many of the flaws in the construction and the shape of *Dandy Dan* were by no means the fault of the talented and craftsmanlike Hood, but of their beloved Roberts whose interpolations, arbitrary excisions and blatant ignoring of the written book made a nonsense of the libretto. What had been needed – what was always needed for Roberts – was a character upon which he could build and an outline of plot within which he could cavort. That had been, by the critics' own admission, brilliantly provided. The public agreed. They clearly preferred Roberts as Dandy Dan to his John Jenkins in *Biarritz* or the unimaginative lawyer of *The White Silk Dress*, and they came in good numbers for five months before *Dandy Dan* once again took to the road, a success but scarcely on the scale that might have been hoped for. *Dandy Dan* was a spectacular vehicle for Roberts, but it was not the equal in merit of *Gentleman Joe* or *The French Maid*. For it to have been so, under the conditions, would have been almost impossible. Roberts was too big and too strong for any semblance of balance to be maintained. That it *had* been maintained in *Gentleman Joe* was one of nature's little miracles, and it was a miracle that was not about to occur twice. Phyllis Broughton and 'Bill' Denny, the only other recognisable 'names' in the cast, fell in with the star's manner, and allowed themselves to be largely eclipsed in the 'one-man show'.

The score of *Dandy Dan* was more than adequate, but there was nothing in it to threaten the string of clever, tuneful pieces the collaborators had turned out for *The French Maid*. Roberts himself had the title song:

> My name it is Dan Smith
> I'm known to all my pals
> For my taking ways
> Which are quite the craze
> With the London servant girls . .

which he later went on to elucidate in an almost unpleasant but, nevertheless successful and popular, number 'The Magic of my Eye', in which Hood betrayed his Gilbertian origins amongst some rather banal sentiments:

> The different expressions I'll apply
> From the 'stern-and-stop-the-traffic'
> To the innocent seraphic
> Sort of 'Good-young-man-who-died' look in my eye

or

> In a trice I entice
> Her to slip out after teatime on the sly
> With the 'How-I'd-like-to-kiss-you'
> Sort of 'Mother-wouldn't-miss-you'
> 'Only-girl-I-ever-loved' look in my eye.

Each of the other principals was allowed one number. Miss Broughton had a brisk song describing how 'Society takes its cue from Lady Catherine Wheeler'; little Isa Bowman as the nursemaid gave a bashful waltz 'I'm your Sweetheart today'; Denny (the policeman) had a minuet based on the conceit 'Cupid is a Cracksman', Blake Adams as the Scots Earl had a routine patter song about a Scot too mean even to buy whisky, and Steve Blamphin as an incidental sailor in Hyde Park dragged in the obligatory patriotic ballad 'I'm just a common Sailor Man' (but Old England's good enough for me).

Probably the best piece in the show was a bright little trio sung by Dan, Mary and Robert White each describing 'My little Game', but this was later joined by a sprightly topical song, 'Someone ought to Speak to Millie Simpson', composed by Howard Talbot, which was interpolated with good effect.

Sadly, the promise of *Gentleman Joe*, *The French Maid* and *Dandy Dan* to lead to a long collaboration to vie with the most popular was not realised. *Dandy Dan* was not the last piece that Basil Hood and Walter Slaughter would write together, it was not even their last West End presentation, but it was their last true success as a partnership. Both continued to have eminent and prosperous careers, Hood first with Sir Arthur Sullivan (for whom he abandoned the coalition with Slaughter) and later with Edward German; Slaughter with, most notably, Seymour Hicks before a premature death in 1908.

The only other new British piece to open in the West End during 1897 was the unfortunate *The Maid of Athens*. It was a musical piece written by H. Chance Newton, formerly one half of the successful burlesque combination 'Richard Henry', and by 'Charles Edmund' (C. E Pearson), with music by Frank Osmond Carr and five extra lyrics by Adrian Ross. *The Maid of Athens* was a sadly misconceived piece. Although pieces like *Morocco Bound* remained popular in the country, the variety musical as such had effectively given way to musical plays of the Daly's/*Geisha* light comic opera type and the Gaiety/*Circus Girl* brand of musical comedy. To string together a series of blatantly music-hall numbers with a few vestiges of plot was not a recipe for success in 1897, particularly when it was not done very well. Newton and Pearson's plot was a farcical mishmash of the most unlikely kind which *The Era* attempted to unravel:

> . . a rich Irishman, named the O'Grady, is troubled with delusions to the effect that he is being followed and watched by enemies. Lord Alfred FitzClarence, a little 'masher' has disguised himself as a footman in order to be near Topsy St Leger, a dancer, who is staying at Vexhill-on-sea. There is a young lady named Ina, and with this Ina, a young man called Seymour is in love. Seymour, while staying at a hotel has accidentally entered the bedroom of the O'Grady and has nearly strangled him. This incident, however, is purely episodic. The O'Grady with unaccountable idiocy, mistakes Seymour for a doctor; and the young man writes the wealthy Irishman a prescription which turns out to be poisonous. The O'Grady has secured for himself a lordly pleasure house where everything is ancient Greek and has filled it with girls in classic costumes, slightly altered to suit the tastes of the modern young man. The principal personages are invited to this place, and there FitzClarence falls in love with a dark-haired damsel called Iphigenia, Topsy St Leger pairing off with the O'Grady. There is an underplot in which the attempts of a French speculator called De Belvidere to purchase, beneath its real value, from Seymour a gold mine in South Africa are – apparently – frustrated by a blunder in the delivery of some letters. The Frenchman after making undesirable advances to Ina is obliged, in order to escape the jealous wrath of Seymour, to disguise himself as a statue, and stand upon a pedestal with a chalked face. The personages in this musical play, indeed, seem to have a mania for disguising themselves. Seymour and his friend Marlow appear dressed as Pierrots, the O'Grady is a perfect chameleon for changes of attire and even the elderly beau, Major Treherne, masquerades in a dressing gown and pyjamas while his inamorata Ambrosia is seen in a light and becoming negligée of which she is unnecessarily ashamed . . .

As in *The Yashmak*, though with considerably less talent, an attempt had been made to formulate a musical success out of a bundle of popular elements. It had been overdone and badly done, particularly in regard to its ridiculously involved and inconsequential book.

The songs and the variety pieces were of little moment and what was arguably one of the show's better pieces came horribly to grief on the first night when E. J. Lonnen, battling his way through the role of the impossible Irishman, got lost in the middle of his 'The Socialistic Club of Tipperary' and finished up cutting half the number. He managed to remember all of 'An Odd-ditty' and was rewarded with sympathetic calls for an encore. Louise Beaudet (Topsy) and Claire Romaine, daughter of the late Teddy Solomon, as Ina had music-hall numbers, the former 'A timid little Maid' and the latter 'If you Please' and 'I am so Careful', all of which were more or less on the same tired old theme to which they added little in the way of novelty. A friendly first night audience could do little to disguise the failings of *The Maid of Athens* and the piece was quickly doomed, sped on its way by such comments as:

> . . the first act is dull and pointless and some of the music reminds one too strongly of other composers . . . (*Times*)

> [The] obnoxious plot of *The Maid of Athens* was like a skeleton at a feast – a regular wet blanket . . . the mental strain caused by the attempt to understand the elusive 'story' absorbed much of the vitality needed for the enjoyment of the songs and dances . . (*Era*)

> Unmitigated drivel . . . [the libretto is] made up merely of the lyrics, detached portions of dialogue and a bewildering mass of business . . . Mr Osmond Carr in his music shows some loss of his wonted cunning . . (*Stage*)

Poor Carr, it seemed, was quite written-out. His earlier successes had been recently over-shadowed by a larger number of failures. He had become heavily derivative – not least from himself – and many of the nearly thirty numbers which he provided for *The Maid of Athens* were unprofitable attempts to reproduce what might most politely be called examples of popular genres. The coon song 'Lubly little Dinah', the patriotic 'Noble Volunteers' and the bevy of coy little female numbers had all been done so often so much better. *The Maid of Athens* staggered on for a month at the Opera Comique and passed on, remaining memorable for just one thing – the West End début in a proper speaking (and singing) role, the rather small title role, of a nineteen-year-old ex-Gaiety Girl, Miss Constance Collier. It was her last musical role. Soon afterwards she joined George Alexander and headed on towards Beerbohm Tree, Shakespeare and an international acting career.

The West End had the chance of seeing productions of two old favourites during the year. Carte revived the well-loved *Yeomen of the Guard* after the failure of *His Majesty*. Walter Passmore took the coveted role of Jack Point whilst Henry Lytton was cast as the basso Wilfred Shadbolt. The piece proved as popular as ever and played nearly 200 performances until Carte's new version of Offenbach's *La Grande Duchesse* was ready to go on the stage. This production, featuring Florence St John, was not, however, the success anticipated, running for barely a hundred performances.

Its short stay served to prove that the taste for opéra-bouffe, as the century neared its end, was no longer what it had been thirty years previously. The right French musical could still be very popular – *La Poupée* was the living proof – but opéra-bouffe was no longer so, even at its very best. A production of Lecocq's *La Petite Mariée*, adapted by Harry Greenbank and with some Lionel Monckton numbers added, fared even less well than the Offenbach when it was staged at the Shaftesbury Theatre as *The Scarlet Feather*. It was more than twenty years since London had first seen *La Petite Mariée* and it quickly showed that it had no particular wish to see it again.

American comic opera fared no better. The Shaftesbury production of the highly successful Broadway piece *The Wizard of the Nile*, the second show of young composer Victor Herbert, failed to catch on and another U.S. success, *Lost, Stolen or Strayed* (later *A Day in Paris*) by Woolson Morse and Cheever Goodwin was no more fortunate. The latter, a piece in the American musical farce tradition, followed *The Gay Parisienne* into the Duke of York's. It was anglicised with new numbers by Sidney Jones, Leslie Stuart, Arthur Godfrey and Herbert Darnley and the effect was much the same as with the 'botched' British works in America – a tidy mess. Louie Freear was brought in as a last, desperate effort to court popularity, but even she could do nothing to save the show.

There was also a very brief revival of *In Town* which played two weeks at the Garrick en route to America. The nostalgic saw a fine company headed by Louis Bradfield, Minnie Hunt, Juliette Nesville and Claire Romaine go through a revised version of the old favourite. Among the small parts were two young ladies who would later be much more noticed: Marie Studholme and Rosie Boote.

The volume of West End production was, perforce, down on the previous year but a more lively rate of new shows was maintained in the provinces. Two kinds were now being produced on the country circuits. Firstly, the staple diet of the traditional only-for-out-of-town fare – the musical variety farces and extravaganzas, the comedy dramas and almost-melodramas with music; and secondly, the try-outs, the plays hopefully headed for something bigger and better than an autumn tour around a dozen dates. The big successes of *The Lady Slavey*, *The New Barmaid*, *The Gay Parisienne* and now *The French Maid* were encouraging more and more managements to test their West End fare on tour before submitting it to London; to try over their material, change it where necessary and run in the whole to a less critical audience instead of risking a show, often half-prepared, before the public and critical judgement of London first. The rate of failures and bankruptcies amongst would-be (and sometimes extremely amateurish) managements in West End theatres, added to the rising cost of productions on the scale and of the standard to which producers like Edwardes had now accustomed playgoers, was also having a cautionary effect. In consequence, 1897 saw works from such top writers as Hood and Slaughter, James Tanner and Adrian Ross, George Dance, Arthur Sturgess and Jimmy Glover, start their lives – some long, some short – outside London.

The first important novelty was *The Ballet Girl*, produced at Wolverhampton's Grand Theatre in March. This had a libretto by the Gaiety's James Tanner, lyrics by Adrian Ross, and music by the conductor Carl Kiefert. Kiefert, formerly a 'cellist, had come to Britain in the '80s to play at Drury Lane as a member of the Saxe-Meiningen Company, and he had remained. His excellent musical education and flair for orchestrations and arrangements swiftly made him popular with composers and publishers alike, and Kiefert became the regular orchestrator for Lionel Monckton, Osmond Carr and, eventually, practically all the big names of the British musical theatre as well as the most sought-after of dance music arrangers amongst publishers. As a result, all the principal theatre orchestras took on the same 'Kiefert sound' – fine, correct and occasionally imaginative, but the same – and the arrangements of piano and orchestral sheet music leaned the same way. In the field of original composition he was less well known, and *The Ballet Girl* represented his first attempt at a musical theatre score of his own, a score which was stiffened by three additional songs by Leslie Stuart and a fourth from Luard Selby.

Set in Holland and in Paris, the piece centred on the penniless Earl of Kilbeggan who proposes to the wrong girl and finds himself in the usual kind of trouble. He has intended to pay court to Nita Vanderkoop, an American heiress, but, being misled by a monogrammed suitcase, actually lays his heart at the feet of the danseuse Violette who is being secretly courted by his own son. Nita, in her turn, is in love with the young artist Reuben who lodges with her Dutch peasant aunt. Misunderstandings abound all the way from Heerenbergen to the Folies Theatre in Paris where the Earl discovers his awful error. By threats of breach of promise (somewhat recalling *The Gay Parisienne*) the Earl is made to consent to Violette's marriage with his son whilst Reuben's pictures win success and Nita's father's business fails, allowing the prerequisites for their union to be fulfilled.

Although its opening performance ran for over three and a half hours, *The Ballet Girl* was well received at Wolverhampton where the local *Era* critic commented:

> The libretto is very well written, the lyrics are clever and can hardly fail to become popular, and the music is fresh, exhilarating and fascinating. It is safe to predict success for the new musical comedy.

while *The Stage* praised Ross's contribution as ' . . exceptionally witty, appropriate and clever'. *The Ballet Girl* toured thirteen weeks with considerable success and the producer was able to sell off the secondary rights for the autumn to the indefatigable touring management of Wallace Erskine who played the show right through to December in the smaller southern dates whilst H. H. Barclay, the original producer, continued to travel his company around the major dates. But *The Ballet Girl*, perhaps wisely, was never given a London production. It was undoubtedly better than many pieces which did play the West End but it lacked, finally, the necessary distinction. The show did, however, make it to Broadway, Edward Rice having picked up the rights early on. It was staged at New York's Manhattan Theatre with Rice taking care not to attract the wrong audience:

> *The Ballet Girl* is not a ballet, but a pretty love story with tendrils of affection shooting out from the parent stalk in every direction and entwining its principal personages.

The American version of *The Ballet Girl* had been subject to the usual textual interference, the more particularly in this case owing to the musical talents of its producer, the composer of *Evangeline* and *Adonis*. Rice substituted a number of his own songs for some of Kiefert's without succeeding in making the show a success. It spent some time on the road, rather less on Broadway, and faded away leaving its producer $20,000 poorer.

A much longer lived piece, which was to confine its whole long life to the British provinces, was George Dance's newest musical *The New Mephistopheles*, written to a score by the original *Gay Parisienne* composer, Ernest Vousden. The Faust legend had been treated again and again by burlesque writers, most successfully in *Faust Up-To-Date*, but Dance had his finger unerringly on the pulse of public taste and the entertainment he devised was rightly calculated to appeal to the contemporary provincial public. In his version 'Faust' became one Captain Meredith who has been parted from his beloved, a village girl called Dolly, by shocked relatives. To his aid comes Mr Mephistopheles who offers to help him on the condition that he does not offer marriage to Dolly until a specified time is up. In the meanwhile, the disconsolate girl is being assiduously courted by two strange gentlemen, Lord Hummingtop and Major Bantam. They are, in fact, married men, but their wives have long presumed them dead as they went up in a balloon one day, attempting to reach the moon, and have never been heard of since. Meredith, by his pact, is obliged to woo his sweetheart without declaring his honourable intentions, and Lord Hummingtop, in consequence, is doing better, particularly when some jewels Mephisto has magicked up for the

Captain are mistaken by Dolly as a gift from his lordship. All is resolved when the balloonists' wives suddenly turn up, and Mephisto is double-crossed when Meredith inherits a fortune, allowing him to dispense with the demon's services and to marry his Dolly.

This rather less than startling tale was clothed in the best George Dance dialogue and illustrated with all sorts of songs, so that when it was produced at the Grand Threatre, Leeds, at the end of March under the banner of *Lady Slavey* tour manager William Greet, it received a magnificent reception. The representatives of firms seeking pieces for America were rumoured to have started making offers before the second act had even begun! Its notices confirmed its reception, and *The New Mephistopheles* set out on an eleven weeks' tour with four hours of excellent entertainment. Greet soon found that *The New Mephisto* (as it was later named) was, rightly placed, as lucrative a touring piece as *The Lady Slavey.*

Odd Man Out was a curious English farcical piece masterminded by the actor A. G. Spry, who was responsible for producing the show in which he also took the leading role and supplied some of the songs. The book was the work of the prolific Montague Turner in collaboration with Frank Dix and it dealt with an eccentric gentleman named Dauphin Dottyon who had once been unfairly immured in an asylum for his peculiarities. Dottyon's sister has returned from South Africa bringing in tow a diamond millionaire who has come to find his nephew, bearing a fistful of diamonds. That nephew has been in jail but he now turns up at the Dottyon house. He gains the eccentric's favour by pretending to be a little odd himself and finally succeeds in stealing the diamonds which he is not aware are intended for him anyway. After many vagaries all is sorted out at the obligatory fancy dress ball.

The piece looked set for an unfortunate start when the company's publicity manager, preparing the Nottingham opening, was arrested for stencilling advertising slogans on the city streets, but he was released in time to see *Odd Man Out* score a reasonable success. Spry (in the role of the devious nephew), Harry Brayne, Will Clements and the tiny Major Tit-Bits provided enough fun to see the piece healthily through a 27-week tour in largely secondary dates.

Another well-received production was *Regina B.A.* or The King's Sweetheart, launched in Birmingham in August by John Tiller. The libretto, by Arthur Sturgess, told of a flirtatious King who is obliged to marry by his strait-laced parliament. His queen is to be chosen by a test of wisdom, that being the quality which the MPs consider pre-eminently important in someone else's wife and a queen. The entries include a bundle from the Academy of Miss Seraphine Plummer. But Miss Plummer has regal ambitions and pilfers for herself the paper of her prize pupil, Lucie, and gets herself proclaimed the winner, to the horror of the King who recognises in Lucie the girl with whom he has fallen in love during one of his jaunts in disguise. To add further confusion it is then discovered that the Prime Minister is Miss Plummer's long-lost husband. There is a coup d'état by a demagogue who is then challenged for the right to rule by most of the piece's characters until one of Miss Plummer's teachers exposes her as a cheat, Lucie gets her prize and her King gets back his kingdom.

The songs for *Regina B.A.* were provided by 'Jimmy' Glover. Glover had been around for some time as a conductor, raconteur, bon viveur and composer of songs and incidental music. With *Regina B.A.* he proved himself up to supplying a full score of a certain merit. The show's title for its first run had been chosen by competition – the prize £5 – but after a two-month autumn season that title was rejected in favour of the sub-title, *The King's Sweetheart*, and in 1898 a second, reasonably successful, tour was put out under the new name.

Basil Hood and Walter Slaughter had been remarkably successful in their partnership. Only their 1896 try-out of *Belinda* had failed to make a mark, but *The Duchess of Dijon* produced at Portsmouth in September proved to be one of their less happy collaborations. Hood had produced a complicated plot which he called 'comic opera', Slaughter had tried to go along with him and the result was an uneasy piece which ran through a mixed tour of No. 1 and No. 2 dates to moderate enthusiasm for two and a half months.

The other new touring pieces varied widely in kind and in degree of success. With bicycling the latest craze it was small wonder that a 'bicycling musical' should soon make its appearance. Wrangles over use of the title *The Bicycle Girl* inevitably occurred with Gore Ouseley's company finally winning the battle. Billie Barlow played a bicycling mistress at a girls' school who succeeds in preventing the school's heiress from making an ass of herself over a roguish and already married Lieutenant. The highlight of the piece was the heroine's race on her bike to the station to foil the villain. It was well staged with a strong cast including Horace Mills as a pageboy with a taste for salacious literature and the D'Oyly Carte veterans Llewellyn Cadwaladr and Millie Vere in prominent roles, but in spite of a good reception, a nine weeks' tour was the sum of its life.

Another cycling musical, *The Lady Cyclist*, was produced by Edward Graham Falcon's *Gentleman Joe* touring company. Its basic premise was a swap of clothes between Jack and his ward-in-chancery lass, Dolly, whilst on a cycling tour. He returns to her school while she suffers the indignities of being pursued by the law for having eloped with herself on a bicycle. In spite of some reasonably cultivated music by George Fox, it came nowhere near the standard of its competitor.

Kitty, an old-fashioned comic opera by Henry Parker, Guildhall professor and the composer of the appalling *Mignonette*, written to a libretto by Walter Parke, appeared at Cheltenham in August and proved somewhat less offensive than its predecessor. It was toured in both 1897 and 1898 on a modest scale.

The comic opera genre was, for the most part, ignored by provincial producers. Musical comedy was the safe bet of the day, although by no means foolproof, two attempts going badly astray. Milton Bode's *The American Belle* written by actor Hugh Seton and composed by m.d. Sydney Ward set out from Cheltenham with a cast headed by comedians Charles Stevens and Arthur Alexander and singers Maurice Mancini and Cissie Saumarez. They ran through some good dates without much distinction, and fizzled out after eight weeks. *The Armenian Girl*, which was *Sunny Florida* with its name changed in an attempt to capitalise on the publicity generated by *The Yashmak*, was produced in Manchester but saw few other dates.

There were some unusual shows on the road. *The Kangaroo Girl* was a version of the 1890 Avenue Theatre hit *Dr Bill* with music by Oscar Barrett who sent it through a small tour; but a sporty piece called *The Indian Prince* involving Mabel Ingham as a housemaid-cum-bareback rider did very much better. Miss Ingham rode the horse of the title to victory through burlesque, racing folk, foreign potentates and villains in a saga of marital and gambling coups which did very nicely on the smaller circuits. So did *Lord Dunnohoo* which involved its star, Harry Roxbury, in a perfect riot of disguises (most of them female) and ended up with a scene in the Moulin Rouge. Produced at Aldershot in July, it ran through a good number of touring weeks and was brought back again the following year for a further run.

Horace Lingard produced his much-heralded *A Theatrical Duchess* under the title of *The Chorus Girl* and included it in the repertoire of his *Old Guard/Pepita* company. He was too ill on the show's first night to play the role created for him, and had little chance thereafter. *The Chorus Girl* proved nowhere near as attractive as *The Old Guard* or *Pepita* and was soon dropped.

A blatant attempt at bandwagon-jumping was perpetrated by Austin Fryers, the proliferator of minor *New Barmaid* tours and dramatic critic of the *St Pauls*. Fryers was actually an Irishman named W. E. Clery whom Jimmy Glover once described as 'living in an atmosphere more heavily charged with writs than any other man I know.' He specialised in theatrical opportunism, mostly with unfortunate results. On this occasion he announced his new musical as *The Geisha Girl* and immediately received the expected trumpetings from Daly's. Having got the publicity he was after, he avoided court action by altering his title to *The Japanese Girl* before opening at Plymouth. *The Era* critic pointedly commented: 'There is very little fear of this piece being mistaken for the other' but *The Japanese Girl* was successful enough in its own way and served Fryers for some time.

That most unsophisticated of all types, the musical-comedy-drama, still survived and 1897 saw further examples added to the old cobbled-together favourites like *Cissy* and *Our Sailor Lad* which were annually redecorated and trotted out in the Mechanics' Halls and Institutes and small town theatres. One of the new pieces, *Lady Satan*, serves to show the content of this kind of highly-coloured show.

Its prologue introduces the audience to the Russian adventuress, Isola. Smarting under an amorous rejection from Lt Reggie Rutherford, she plots with the local Burmese to kidnap Dora, the object of Reggie's affections, and also to steal the fabulous Diamond of Doom with which she hopes to buy Rutherford's love. She succeeds in purloining the jewel and strangles her accomplice in the process, hiding his corpse in the altar of the jewel-room. Her minions arrive with the captured Dora but their leader finds the hidden corpse. It is his father! He swears revenge but Isola guns down the rebel as Reggie arrives in his ship to rescue his beloved.

The principal part of the play then begins, in Britain. Dora is unhappily married to Captain Clive who is more interested in Olga (none other than Isola disguised). The lady continues her evil deeds. She stabs her long-lost husband Ivan when he arrives on the scene, using his own sword-stick, and then gets Clive to hypnotise Dora into admitting the deed, but the victim recovers. More ways are tried to rid the world of the hapless Dora. She is tied before a rock-drill; she is confined to a madhouse where she is stripped, whipped and branded; she is whisked off to Russia – all the time followed and rescued by the vengeful Ivan, the loyal Reggie and the two comics Zachariah Touchit and Adolphus Butterbun, all disguised as circus performers. At the Moscow carnival they meet their enemies. Olga strangles the long-suffering Ivan and is arrested while Clive takes poison and Dora (or what is left of her) finally tumbles into Reggie's arms.

It was pure and simple melodrama with plenty of very low comedy and a series of musical numbers, though these lowered the tension somewhat since they required, on one occasion, villainess and heroine momentarily to drop their animosity and perform a song and dance duo before returning to mortal combat. It was barnstorming stuff of riotous inconsistency, but it had its place.

In spite of the volume of provincial production, only one piece of the crop of '97 apart from *Dandy Dan* eventually made the transfer to the West End. This was another star vehicle, Albert Chevalier's *The Land of Nod* produced at Lincoln in March and toured thereafter for 29 weeks. As with Roberts' piece, it rested principally on the talents and appeal of its author and principal performer as a comic singer and impersonator. It was well received on tour but survived only one week in town in September, 1898. The popularity of Chevalier as a performer failed to outweigh the old-fashioned book and the fairly ordinary music of his conductor/accompanist and general right-hand man, West-country musician Alfred West, who was once described as 'an extraordinary pianist with a left hand like a full band' but who was less remarkable as a composer.

1897

0181 **MAN ABOUT TOWN** a musical farce in three acts by 'Huan Mee'. Music by Alfred Carpenter. Produced at the Avenue Theatre under the management of F. J. Harris 2 January, 1897 for a run of 18 performances closing 23 January, 1897.

Frank Ennesleigh . . . . E. J. Lonnen
Ralph Fenton . . . . Charles Cherry
Lucius Light . . . . Ells Dagnall
Henri Lavelle . . . . Sidney Howard
Robert Jansen . . . . Littledale Power
Gwendoline Grova . . . . Alma Stanley
Edith . . . . May Edouin
Kate Derwent . . . . Grace Hamond
Nora Ennesleigh . . . . Alice Lethbridge
with Alice Cox

Dir: Fred W. Sidney; ch: John D'Auban; sc: Leolyn Hart

0182 **HIS MAJESTY** or The Court of Vignolia. A comic opera in two acts by F. C. Burnand and Rudolph C. Lehmann. Additional lyrics by Adrian Ross. Music by Sir Alexander C. Mackenzie. Produced at the Savoy Theatre under the management of Richard D'Oyly Carte 20 February, 1897 for a run of 61 performances closing 24 April, 1897.

Ferdinand V, King of Vingolia . . . . . . George Grossmith (C. H. Workman)/Henry A. Lytton
Count Cosmo . . . . H. Scott Russell
Baron Vincentius . . . . Jones Hewson
Prince Max of Baluria . . . . Charles Kenningham
Mopolio VII, King of Osturia . . . . . . Fred Billington
Borodel . . . . Walter Passmore
Baron Michael . . . . Charles Earldon
Herr Schnippentrimmer . . . . Edwin Bryan
Chevalier Klarkstein de Frise . . . . H. Charles
Adam, a woodman . . . . C. H. Workman/
Princess Lucilla Chloris . . . . Florence Perry
Felice . . . . Ilka von Palmay
Duchess Gonzara . . . . Miss Macaulay
Dame Gertrude . . . . Bessie Bonsall
Helena . . . . Jessie Rose
Dorothea . . . . Ruth Vincent
Claudina . . . . Mildred Baker

Dir: Charles Harris; md: François Cellier; ch: John D'Auban; sc: W. Harford; cos: Percy Anderson

0183 **THE BALLET GIRL** a musical comedy in two acts by James T. Tanner. Lyrics by Adrian Ross. Music by Carl Kiefert. Additional songs by Leslie Stuart and Luard Selby. Produced at the Grand Theatre, Wolverhampton, under the management of H. H. Barclay 15 March, 1897 and toured through Blackpool, Newcastle, Southport,?, Liverpool, Manchester, Bradford, Leeds, Hull, Grimsby, Birmingham, Oxford to 12 June. Resumed 2 August at Brixton. Played to 4 December. Resumed 7 March, 1898 through to 4 June, 1898. A second company toured simultaneously from 2 August, 1898 (York) to 4 December (Stoke) and again 7 March-4 June, 1898.

Reuben van Eyt . . . . Hugh Enes Blackmore
Lord Comarthy . . . . James Lindsay
Earl of Kilbeggan . . . . Fitzroy Morgan/Frank Lacy/E. W. Maule Cole
Eugene Taradelle . . . . Gilbert Porteous/Fred Dark/John Humphries
Kotsdoppen/Baton Blanc . . . . John A. Howitt
Perch . . . . George L. Wilson/Frank Lincoln
Floots . . . . Bernard Arthur
Lisa . . . . Ethel Lethe/Tessa Snelson
Frieda . . . . Fanny Harris/Sadie Wigley
B'lindy . . . . Nellie Sheffield/Marie Alexander/Marie Dainton
Violette . . . . Violet Dene
Nita Vanderkoop . . . . Alys Rees/Maud Denny/Mary Middleton
Vrouw Schomberg . . . . Kate Osborne/Polly Marsh
Pd: E. W. Royce
with May Lynn, Eva Penys, Nellie St John, Mabel Scott, Florence Cudlipp, Mamie Stanley, Lillian Wellesley, Maggie Crawford, Violet Leslie, Kitty Cuznor, Jessie MacCaulay, Amy Selby, Kate Sabine, George Parte, Howard Lingham, Keith Hudson, Leonard Leslie, George Edwards, L. Thomas.

Dir/ch: E. W. Royce; md: George Arnold; sc: Fred Storey; cos: Comelli

Produced by E. E. Rice at the Manhattan Theatre, New York 21 December, 1897 for a run of 31 performances, closing 5 February, 1898.
David H. Lythgoe (REUBEN), Charles Arthur (LORD), Thomas Ricketts (EARL), Edouard Jose (EUG), Snitz Edwards (KOPS), Fred Solomon (BB), Christopher Bruno (PERCH), Charles Seagrave (FL), Dorothy Merlyn (VIZIER), Lillian Cooley (GRETCHEN), Violet Potter (MINNA), Marie Hilton (BEDALIA), Arline Crater (VI), Louise Willis-Hepner (NITA), Christine Blessing (VROUW), Irene Vera (FRITZ) with Marjorie Relyea, Lila Haynes, Gabriella de Thein, Vashti Earl, Violet Potter, Maud Emmerson, May Hamilton, Gladys Kensington, Lillian Kensington, Caroline Rhodes, Emma Guthrie, Mabel Belton, Nettie Scarsez, Rose Flores, Clarice Middleton, Phyllis Baranco, Suzie Hale, Mazie Follette &c.

Dir: James T. Tanner and Frederic A. Leon; md: ?; sc: Frank Rafter, Hugh L. Reid; cos: W. A. Barnes

0184 **THE BICYCLE GIRL** a musical bicycle comedy in three acts by Charles Osborne and E. M. Stuart. Additional lyrics by Hugh Seton. Music by Orlando Powell. Additional songs by Edgar Ward and Arnold Cooke. Produced at Nottingham under the management of Gore Ouseley 29 March, 1897 and toured through Sheffield, Newcastle, Edinburgh, Oldham, Belfast, Glasgow, Liverpool, Hanley and Manchester, terminating 5 June, 1897.

Atalanta Granville. . . . . Billie Barlow
Hippolyta Brown . . . . Vere Gerald
Mrs d'Erskine. . . . . Millie Vere
Camilla d'Erskine . . . . Minnie Blanchard
Joanna Sharp . . . . Lillian Redfern
Sub-Professor Brophy . . . . Flo Pritchard
Sophia Austen. . . . . Winifred Chase
Major Haliwell . . . . Hugh Seton
Lt Everton . . . . Llewellyn Cadwaladr
Lt Burton . . . . Jack Cole
Tramp. . . . . James McAnney
Policeman . . . . Charles Stuart

Alphonso Burke . . . . Horace Mills
Dir: John Morton; md: Edgar Ward; sc: Richard Durrant

0185 **THE NEW MEPHISTOPHELES** a musical comedy in two acts by George Dance. Music by Ernest Vousden. Produced at the Grand Theatre, Leeds, under the management of William Greet 29 March, 1897 and toured through Derby, Glasgow, Newcastle, Edinburgh, Liverpool, Birmingham, Southport, Wolverhampton, Manchester and Bradford to 5 June. Recommenced at Oldham 2 August through Blackpool, Leicester, Huddersfield, Halifax, Brighton, Manchester, Hull, Walsall, Brixton, Bristol, Cardiff, Southport, Liverpool, Bradford, Leeds and Sheffield to 27 November, 1897 &c.

Mr Mephistopheles . . . . W. T. Thompson
Captain Meredith . . . . George Sinclair
Tom Harker. . . . . Mr Ellis
Lord Hummingtop . . . . Stratton Mills
Major Bantam. . . . . H. O. Clarey
Paul . . . . Guy Drury
Dick Pilgrim . . . . Henry Wright
Mrs Gertie Gentle . . . . Rose Dearing
Mrs Connie Gentle . . . . Kate Guest
Mrs Prudie Gentle . . . . Anita Guest
Blanche . . . . Violette E. Bessell
Blanchette . . . . Laura Thompson
Nichette . . . . Violet Friend
Becky . . . . Ruby Hallier
Dolly . . . . Nellie Murray

0186 **THE YASHMAK** a musical play in two acts by Seymour Hicks and Cecil Raleigh. Music by Napoleon Lambelet. Additional lyrics by Roland Carse and Alfred J. Morris. Additional songs by Ellaline Terriss, Clement Scott & J. M. Glover, Leslie Stuart, Francis J. Bryant, Fay Templeton, George Rosey, Hattie Marshall, A. R. Marshall & Herman Finck, Percy Gaunt, Percy Pinkerton, H. Nevin, Richard Temple Jr and E. E. Rice. Produced at the Shaftesbury Theatre under the management of A. H. Chamberlyn and Theatrical Enterprises Ltd 31 March, 1897 for a run of 121 performances closing 30 July, 1897.

Smudge . . . . John Le Hay
Owen Moore . . . . Lionel Mackinder (J. G. Wigley)
Hon. Fitzroy Lende. . . . . Lawrance d'Orsay
Mr Dingley . . . . Fred Emney
Sir Andrew Drummond . . . . Charles Ryley/H. Scott Russell
Bustapha Pasha . . . . Ells Dagnall
The Sultan of Shelack . . . . Arthur Nelstone
The Vizier. . . . . Sidney Howard
Dr Cathcart . . . . J. G. Wigley
Captain Murad . . . . H. Foster/Birdie Sutherland
Mr Marshall . . . . George Humphrey
Zillah . . . . Aileen d'Orme/Marguerite Cornille
Mary Montressor de Courcey . . . . . . Mabel Love
Dot Sinclair . . . . Marie Yorke/M. Thorne
Violet Delmere . . . . Edith Johnston
Noormahal . . . . Topsy Sinden (pd)
Balroubadour . . . . Maggie Ripley/Eleanor May
Hetty . . . . E. Maurice
Florrie. . . . . Helene Sevier
Corrie . . . . Dora Temple
Irene . . . . M. Temple
Connie. . . . . Blanche Wallace
Gwendoline . . . . Miss Nelson
Mabel . . . . Miss Wallis
Captain Hassan . . . . Miss Dudley

Captain Calid . . . . Georgie Lennard
Captain Ali . . . . Miss Budd
Zorah . . . . Eleanor May/*out*
Lalah . . . . Miss Davenant
Medora . . . . Miss Cameron
Haidee. Miss Erskine
Dora Selwyn . . . . Kitty Loftus
Dancers: Miss Rundle, Miss Corke, Miss Dalmour, Susie Raymonde, *add* Elsie Dare
add Sultan's Guard . . . . Birdie Sutherland

Dir: Horace Sedger; md: Napoleon Lambelet; ch: John D'Auban; sc: W. T. Hemsley, William Telbin; cos: Robert Crafter

0187 **THE AMERICAN BELLE** a musical play in two acts by Hugh Seton. Music by F. Sydney Ward. Produced at the Opera House, Cheltenham, under the management of Milton Bode 19 April, 1897 and toured through Bath, Oxford, Croydon, Metropole, Bristol, Birmingham and Hastings, to 12 June.

Dick Beaumont . . . . Charles E. Stevens
Shakespeare Middleman . . . . Arthur Alexander
Lord Pomeroy. . . . . H. G. Dupres
Hon. Gussie Granby . . . . Harold Eden
Bertie Brown . . . . O. E. Lennon
Mr Peter . . . . Walter Westwood
Jack Dunne . . . . Maurice Mancini
Prudence Beaumont. . . . . Cissie Saumarez
Sadie Clay. . . . . Jenny Owen
Gertrude Youngbody . . . . Clarissa Talbot
Hannah . . . . Marie Campbell
Araminta Youngbody . . . . Laura Leighton/Dorcas Crosbie
Charles . . . . Frank Couch

0188 **ODD MAN OUT** a musical farce in three acts by Montague Turner and Frank Dix. Lyrics by Will L. Clement. Music by Thomas Hunter and Sidney Shaw. Special numbers by George Le Brunn and A. G. Spry. Produced at Nottingham under the management of A. G. Spry and Mr Burlinson 19 April, 1897 and toured through Oxford, Walsall, Halifax, Cambridge, Leamington, Cheltenham, Torquay, Bournemouth, *out* x2, Hastings, Bury, Rochdale, *out*, Gloucester, Dewsbury, Longton, Wigan, Warrington, Hebburn, Belfast, Cork, Greenock, Carlisle, South Shields, Stockton-on-Tees, Bishop Auckland, Preston and Wednesbury to 13 November.

Douglas Daring . . . . A. G. Spry
Dauphin Dottyon . . . . Harry Brayne
John Patrick O'Plodder . . . . Will L. Clements (John Lisbourne)
Robbins . . . . Cecil Webb/B. S. Monti
Hubert Dottyon. . . . . Karl Mora
Matilda Dottyon . . . . Isabel Grey/Laura Coyne/Jessie Warner
Florence Kingsley. . . . . Amy Long
Anna Maria Puddikins . . . . Bella Bashall/Freda Winchester
Peeps, a page boy . . . . Major Tit-Bits
Lilian Daring . . . . Millicent Marsden
Police Inspector. . . . . F. H. Bardsley/Charles Silver
Md: Henry Younge/J. H. Yorke

0189 **THE LAND OF NOD** a musical play in two acts by Albert Chevalier. Music by Alfred H. West. Produced under the management of ? Albert Chevalier at Lincoln 24 May, 1897 and toured through Halifax, Blackpool, Eastbourne, Hastings/Dover, Brighton, Bournemouth/Exeter, Swansea, Cheltenham, Llandudno, Southport, Buxton, Stafford/? Burton-on-Trent/Chester, Shrewsbury/Harrogate, Leamington, ?, ?, ?, Preston, Kidderminster/Longton, Oldham, Worcester/Loughborough, Gloucester, Wolverhampton, Hanley, Sheffield and Derby to 18 December.

Professor Peter Pinder	Albert Chevalier
Raha Ramjah	Julian Cross
Dr Goodwin	Isidore Marcil
Geoffrey Goodwin	G. King Morgan
Simon Sims	Ernest Spalding
Inspector	F. Barlow/F. Leighton
Mrs Pinder	Amy Singleton
Nellie Pinder	Daisy Baldry/Cissie Bell
Nadoura	Florence Darley

Pd: Constance Mori
with Messrs Beaumont, Cook, Dillon, Garland, Kirkley, F. Leighton, Metcalfe, Verity; Misses Cissie Bell, Brunton, Claremont, Florence, Hamilton, Norman, Regnier, Wilton, Barnett.

Dir: Albert Chevalier and Fred Edwards; md: Alfred H. West; ch: Espinosa; cos: Messrs Harrison, Miss Phillips

Produced at the Royalty Theatre under the management of W. H. Dawes and the St Martin's Syndicate 24 September, 1898 for a run of 6 performances closing 29 September, 1898. Albert Chevalier (PETER), Julian Cross (RAHA), Herbert Linwood (GEOFFREY), Homer Lind (DR), Harry Brett (SIM), Wilfred Howard (PC), Madge Talbot (MRS), Lettice Fairfax (NELLIE), Violet Robinson (NAD), with Jennie Holland, Edith Milton and Constance Mori. Md: Alfred H. West

0190 **THE MAID OF ATHENS** a musical play in three acts by 'Charles Edmund' (C. E. Pearson) and H. Chance Newton. Music by F. Osmond Carr. Produced at the Opera Comique under the management of F. Osmond Carr and Reginald Livesey 3 June, 1897 for a run of 27 performances closing 3 July, 1897.

The O'Grady	E. J. Lonnen
Major Treherne	William Elton
Seymour	Charles Weir
Marlow	Percy Brough/Gilbert Vincent
O'Rigger	Edward Morehen
Lord Alfred FitzClarence	Cecil Ramsay
Branks	St John Hamund
Sergeant	W. C. Newton
De Belvidere	Fred Storey
Ambrosia	Cicely Richards
Ina	Claire Romaine
Chloris	Ettie Williams
Hebe	Lily Forsythe
Medea	Esmé Gordon
Daphne	Dolly Douglas
Merope	Florence Wilson
The Maid of Athens	Constance Collier
Topsy St Leger	Louise Beaudet

Dir: Frank Parker; ch: Will Bishop; sc: Charles Rider Noble; cos: Lucien Besche

0191 **THE JAPANESE GIRL** a Japanese musical comedy in two acts by Austin Fryers. Music by Charles J. Lacock. Produced at the Theatre Royal, Plymouth under the management of Austin Fryers 26 June, 1897 and toured 1897/8.

O Cri-Kee	J. G. Taylor Jr/Robey Ferris/Walter Lonnen
Capt. Richard Lastre	Ernest Theil/Harold Perry/Llewellyn Cadwaladr
Hon. Arthur Bonanza	Alfred Terris/Wilfred Langley/J. G. Taylor Jr
Ap-Hee	Robert Ferris/Charles Brook/Charles Jackson

Charlie Ogilvie . . . William Bayfields/Reginald Eyre/Harold Perry
Colonel Robertson . . . Harry Lyle
Reggie Verne . . . Tom Stuart
Kik-Hee . . . Charles Lewis
O-Jo . . . Richard Power/Maud Leslie
Lilli-O-Mi . . . Rita Ravensberg/Madge Victoria/Clara Weber
Tappi-O-Ki . . . Dulcie Murielle/Ethel Lockwood/Marie Deighton
Lady Ensford . . . Edith Matt/Florence Nightingale
Gracie Darling . . . Maude Marsden
Edith Dear . . . Mary Fleetwood
Amy Love . . . Ruby Lyndhurst
O To-to San . . . Elva Dearen

Md: W. W. Meadowes

0192 **LORD DUNNOHOO**, The Society Pet. A musical comedy in three acts by Roy Redgrave. Lyrics by Montague Turner. Music by G. Oastlere Walker. Produced at Aldershot under the management of Harry Roxbury and F. Marriot Watson 5 July, 1897 and toured through Hanley, Halifax, Wolverhampton, Woolwich &c.

Lord Dunnohoo . . . Harry Roxbury/Victor Gouriet
Prince Wotsitawlaboutski . . . Roy Redgrave/Henry E. Hambro
Major Titus Blazes . . . W. G. Walford
Dick Thredgold . . . Reginald Garland/E. Wensley Russell/F. Roberts
Shamus O'Shaughnessy . . . Ernest Jerome
Belladonna Blazes . . . Ida Glenroy/Nellie Sheffield
Mirable Blazes . . . Florence Carlile
Lady Poppinjay . . . Judith Kyrle/Carrie Anderson
Molly Murphy . . . Aggie Fenton
Kathleen . . . Laura Gordon
Bridget . . . E. McBain
Grisette . . . E. Wilson
Jeames . . . S. Marks
Pompom . . . Elsie Vane
Eileen . . . G. Boundy

Md: B. Draeger

0193 **THE KANGAROO GIRL** a musical version of *Dr Bill*, a farce by Hamilton Aide adapted from the French of Albert Carré. Music by Oscar Barrett. Produced at the Pleasure Gardens, Folkestone, under the management of Oscar Barrett 12 July, 1897 and toured through Metropole, Ryde, Glasgow, Sheffield &c.

Dr Bill . . . J. R. Crauford
Mr Firman . . . George Raiemond
George Webster . . . Edward Morehen
Mr Horton . . . Francis Hawley
Mrs Horton . . . Nellie Ganthony
Mrs Firman . . . Pattie Bell
Mrs Brown . . . May Cross
Jennie Firman . . . Kate Dudley
Ellen . . . E. Price
Kate Fauntleroy . . . Florrie Harrison

0194 **THE INDIAN PRINCE** a musical sporting comedy by T. Gilbert Perry. Music by Harry Richardson. Produced at the Grand Theatre, Walsall, 26 July, 1897 by Cissie Ward's Company, and toured.

Horatio Childs . . . . T. Gilbert Perry
Thistles . . . . Bob Crosby
Mr Stubbs . . . . A. B. Ly
Captain Hertage. . . . . Baxter Watson
Ernest Travis . . . . Elwyn Eaton
Ted Perkins . . . . d'Arcy Salter
Potts. . . . . W. Osborne
Charcoal. . . . . Kofi O. Kakra
Edith . . . . Madge Christie
Florence St Clair . . . . Hettie Stevenson
Maud Montgomery . . . . Ruth Stanley
Eliza. . . . . Mabel Ingham
Primrose. Etta Turner
with the Holland Sisters

0195 **REGINA B.A.** or the King's Sweetheart. A comic opera in two acts by Arthur Sturgess. Music by James M. Glover. Produced at the Grand Theatre, Birmingham, under the management of John Tiller 2 August, 1897 and toured to 9 October. Resumed 7 March, 1898 to June 25 as *The King's Sweetheart.*

Valorous. Wilson Sheffield/Charles Angelo
Populo. . . . . Fred Eastman
Rupert Brazenose . . . . Malcolm Scott/Horace Barri
Dommer. Sidney Vincent
Chambertin . . . . Fred Emney/Charles Raymonde/ J. W. Handley
Notary. . . . . George Fearnley
Clarice. . . . . Mary Dolman/Daisy Mines
Marie . . . . Edie Fenchester/Miss Hartman
Rose . . . . Eileen Moore
Miss Seraphine Plummer . . . . Alice Aynsley Cook
Lucie . . . . Decima Moore/Elise Cook/Eone Delrita
with Maggie Crossland, May Lucas, Ennie Franks, Nellie Cort/Ethel Neild, Letty Williams, R. Morley, E. Fogler

Md: Joseph Skuse/J. C. Shepherd/George Arnold

0196 **KITTY** or The Farmer's Daughter. A comic opera by Walter Parke and Henry Parker. Produced at the Opera House, Cheltenham, under the management of George B. Philipps 30 August, 1897 and toured.

General Sir George Jungle . . . . J. W. Brighten
Sir Timothy Beaumont . . . . A. P. Kaye/Arthur Leyshon/A. Neil
Captain Lionel Norman. . . . . Harry G. Tebbutt/Carl Sobieski/ J. J. Donnelly
Cummerbund . . . . George Danvers Jr
John Mayfield. . . . . Rudolph Lewis/J. Furneaux Cook/ Hugh Seton
Sgt Peter Pike. . . . . James Leverett/George W. Traverner
Nicodemus Ketchum . . . . Albert James/J. J. Dallas
Robert. . . . . H. Arthur
James . . . . Lewis Levy
Thomas . . . . R. Brown/Mr Soult/Frank Roberts/ H. Fuller
Lady Jungle. . . . . Ada Maskell/Lindsay Grey/Nellie Taylor
Augusta Beaumont . . . . Barry Eldon
Mrs Heeltap. . . . . Kate Bellingham
Kitty . . . . Julia Daphne/Stella St Audrie
Waiter . . . . Mr Cleaver

Md: /H. E. Wellings/Edgar Haines

197 **THE LITTLE DUCHESS** a coster opera in 2 acts by Captain F. W. Marshall and Frederick Mouillot. Music by Frank Congden. Produced by Morell and Mouillot at Stockton-on-Tees 9 September, 1897 and toured in repertoire with *The Shop Girl* 1897/8.

Duke of Pada . . . . Alec Derwent/Vincent Flexmore/ Charles Cameron
Henry Hawkins . . . . Stephen Adeson
Roberts . . . . Russell Wallett
Crackett . . . . H. Wellesley Smith
Soapy . . . . Tom Fancourt/Jennie Rubie
Bunny . . . . James O. Russell
Leary . . . . Harry Wright
Harley St Thomas . . . . A. Macfarlane
Signor Samsonia . . . . Mr Habijam
Duchess of Pada . . . . Nellie Clifton/Topsy Sinden
Nora Crackett . . . . Carrie Kavanagh/Isabelle Girardot/Lillian Digges
Sweeney Sal . . . . Clara Clifton
May Rivers . . . . Nellie Wallett
Jeames . . . . Charles D. Cleveland
Liza Burge . . . . Violet Leigh

with Violet Friend/Miss Gerard, Mildred Webber/Beatrice Palmer, Lulu Lang, Edith Thornley, Nina Carlisle/Miss Gilbert, Ethel Hubert, Gertrude Grey/Miss Piercey/Helene Stanway,/M. Russell

Md: Aynsley Fox

198 **DANDY DAN THE LIFEGUARDSMAN** a musical comedy in two acts by Basil Hood. Music by Walter Slaughter. Produced at Belfast under the management of Arthur Roberts 23 August, 1897 and toured through Liverpool, Southport, Aberdeen, Dundee, Glasgow, Newcastle, Manchester, Halifax, Leeds, Nottingham, *out*, Blackpool and Dublin, terminating 27 November. Opened at the Lyric Theatre under the same management 4 December, 1897 for a run of 166 performances closing 19 May, 1898. A second edition with the addition of the sketch 'Much Ado About Something, or Beerbohm Tree-lawney of the Wells' by H. Chance Newton was performed from 16 April, 1898.

Dandy Dan . . . . Arthur Roberts (George E. Bellamy)
Earl of Capercailzie . . . . Blake Adams
Roderick Ptarmigan . . . . Frank Barclay
Robert White . . . . Harry Kilburn//W. H. Denny
Mr Wheeler . . . . Arnold Lucy/Grisbrook Waller//Arnold Lucy
Ben Smith . . . . Leon Roche/James Parkinson//Steve Blamphin
Trumpeter Tom . . . . Eva Ellerslie//Rose Seymour/Lydia West
Donald . . . . F. Cremlin
Colin . . . . George E. Bellamy
James . . . . George A. Highland/Alex Stuart/Owen Harris
Henry . . . . Inez de Warr//Maud Mason/Miss Guest
Inspector Grigg . . . . Felix Forster//William Birch
Drummer Jones . . . . Elsie Fanshawe//Elsie Lanoma/ Miss Drake
Lady Margaret Ptarmigan . . . . Kate Erskine
Lady Cicely Ptarmigan . . . . Gladys Byrd//Mabel Hensey
Lady Letty Ptarmigan . . . . Frances Balfour
Mrs Smith . . . . Rose Vernon Paget//Jane Grey
Lady Bulwarke . . . . Helen Bradshaw//Ella Essington
Hon. Madeleine Lee-Scupper . . . . . . Maud Rundle//Hilda Trevernor
Hon. Muriel Lee-Scupper . . . . Kitty Mason//Violet Foulton/Muriel Johnson

Kate . . . . Hilda Crosse
Barbara . . . . Violet Dalrymple
Mary . . . . Isa Bowman
Lady Catherine Wheeler . . . . Aida Jenoure//Phyllis Broughton (Muriel Johnson)
add Lady Mabel Ptarmigan. . . . . Maud Stanley

Dancers: Edith Stuart, May Stuart, Albert Weston
with Sybil Champion, Vie Linde, Reggie Raymonde, Adela Clyde, Lily Nisbett, Ethel Caryl, Rita Darrell, Amy Pennington, May Karl, Lilian Champion, Gladys Gordon, Neva Bond, Alice Benzon, Violet Berkeley, Vena Risenbaum, Edith Singlehurst, Jenny Lindsay, Dora Langroyd, B. Waugh, L. Pleydell, V. Mitchell, Gladys Cromwell, William Birch, Lloyd Edgar, A. Hayden, R. Bates, Thomas Sheridan, James Lane, Edward Sykes, W. E. Bentley, Austin Churton, Bert Hearn, J. B. Fraser, J. Mather.

Dir: George Capel, Arthur Roberts and Walter Slaughter; md: Howard Talbot; ch: Will Bishop; sc: T. E. Ryan and W. B. Spong

0199 **THE DUCHESS OF DIJON** a comic opera in two acts by Basil Hood. Music by Walter Slaughter. Produced at Portsmouth under the management of Charles Clark 20 September, 1897 and toured through Worcester, Northampton, Nottingham, Sheffield, Colchester/Ipswich, Metropole, Liverpool, Birmingham, Leamington/Oxford and Newcastle, terminating 4 December, 1897.

The Prince of Parma . . . . Tom Redmond
Duke of Dijon. . . . . George Mudie
Baratanza . . . . D. Harold Lythgoe
Valentine . . . . Cecil Stephenson
Jacques . . . . Mat Robson
Mons Pouffon . . . . Willis Searle
Marco . . . . M. Paltzer
Beppo . . . . Leslie Conroy
Peppo . . . . Henry Norton
The Duchess of Dijon . . . . Rita Ravensberg
Clementine . . . . Gertrude Jerrard
Cerise . . . . Annie Roberts
Bon-Bon. . . . . Lily Hall Caine
Marie . . . . Lilyan Lait
Hortense. . . . . Rachel Lowe
Lisette. Marion Bell
Pierre . . . . Hugh Metcalfe

Dir: Frank Parker; md: Rowland Wood; ch: Will Bishop; sc: E. G. Banks; cos: Lucien Besche

THE LADY CYCLIST or A Bicycle Belle. A musical comedy in two acts by St Aubyn Miller. Music by George D. Fox. Produced by Edward Graham Falcon at the Town Hall, Luton, 24 April, 1897 and played in repertoire with *Gentleman Joe* on tour.

Colonel Slashington. . . . . Fred Danvers
Harold Merryweather. . . . . Fred Clifford
Titus Flipkin . . . . Fred Lyne
Dolly Bessington . . . . Marie Rainbird
Florrie Templeton . . . . Elvira Lyne
Miss Arabella Snap . . . . Kate Doyle
Kate Silverthorne. . . . . A. Wingfield
Topsy Howard . . . . L. Wingfield
Jack Stephney. . . . . Charles Cranston
Mr Juniper Tallow . . . . Geo Daniels
Parker . . . . E. Lowe
Mutton . . . . G. Mason
Clara Westfield . . . . Lucie Fitzroy
Emma Flipkin. . . . . Winnie Latham

Susan Bunthing . . . . L. Latham
Bessie Banks . . . . M. Wingfield

Md: George D. Fox

TURPIN À LA MODE a musical burlesque play by G. P. Huntley and George Grey (i.e. Graves). Music by Harry C. Barry. Produced at the Royalty Theatre, Chester, 5 April, 1897 and toured.

LADY SATAN a musical comedy-drama in 4 acts by William P. Sheen. Produced at Openshaw under the management of Sydney Vereker 28 June, 1897 and toured.

STIRRING TIMES a romantic musical play by Frank H. Celli and Brian Daly. Music by F. Sydney Ward. Produced at Southport under the management of Hardie and Von Leer 2 August, 1897 and toured.

OLD SARAH an operetta in one act by Harry Greenbank. Music by François Cellier. Produced at the Savoy Theatre 17 June, 1897 with *The Yeomen of the Guard*. Withdrawn 31 July. Restaged 16 August, withdrawn 20 November. Subsequently played with *The Grand Duchess* from 10 December.

Rt. Hon. Claud Newcastle . . . . Jones Hewson
Archibald Jones . . . . Charles Childerstone
Simon . . . . C. H. Workman
Margery . . . . Jessie Rose
Old Sarah . . . . Louie Henri

THE CHORUS GIRL Produced at Portsmouth under the management of Horace Lingard 28 June, 1897 and toured in repertoire.

JUNO or A Night's Folly. By George Roberts. Music by J. S. Baker. Produced under the management of Maud Vena and toured.

1898

The opening months of 1898 saw no new entries in the musical field, for none was needed. *The Geisha* and *The Circus Girl* were both still running strongly in their second year and *Dandy Dan the Lifeguardsman* at the Lyric and the latest Savoy revival, *The Sorcerer*, were also still popular. *The French Maid* was heading for its first anniversary and transferred to the Vaudeville in February when Edward Terry reclaimed his theatre for his own production of *The White Knight*. Unlike many other pieces, it remained unaffected in popularity by the move and continued its run for more than six months in its new home. *The Sorcerer* was the first show to be withdrawn, being replaced in March by another Gilbert and Sullivan revival, this time of *The Gondoliers* which was to fill in until the new work awaited from Sir Arthur Sullivan was ready.

In the meanwhile, however, other new shows were in the pipeline. Edwardes was preparing replacements for both of his hits and Arthur Roberts was lining up a successor to *Dandy Dan*, but before any of these could reach the stage they found their success pre-empted by a most unlikely candidate, an American musical. There had been successful American pieces in Britain before, but these had been largely provincial pieces of the variety type such as *Fun on the Bristol* and *A Trip to Chicago* or musical comedy-dramas like *My Sweetheart* or *Hans the Boatman*, all with sentiments and music of a basic and low-brow kind. The new piece was of a different class altogether – it was a genuine musical, and it had been brought integrally from New York with a full American cast and chorus – a novelty for the West End and an almost insanely risky venture for producer George Musgrove. *The Belle of New York* arrived at the Shaftesbury Theatre billed as the Casino Theatre Company's 'greatest success', a rather misleading claim since the show's life on Broadway had been limited to an unenthusiastic 56 performances. But in London it caught on well and truly, though why cannot be fully explained, for it was in no way an exceptional piece. Its music, by the prolific and derivative Gustave Kerker, was pretty and occasionally, as in the title song 'She is the Belle of New York', very catchy. Its book by 'Hugh Morton' (C. S. McLellan) was routine. Had a stop-gap show not been needed for the Shaftesbury, *The Belle of New York* might have joined the pile of Broadway flops and never been seen again, the fate of most of Kerker's pieces, but one of those strange twists of theatrical fate and quirks of public taste turned in the show's favour.

Its most obvious advantages were twofold and both feminine. In the role of Violet, the Salvation Army lassie of the title, was featured a young American performer called Edna May and with her the London public fell wholeheartedly in love. They also fell for the Casino Theatre chorus line, a collection of buxom, bouncing and vigorous young women as different as could be from the superior and elegant 'girls' of the Gaiety or of Daly's. These transatlantic girls, bursting with obvious health, didn't stroll, pose and daintily step, they worked, and London flocked to see them fling themselves into the vigorous routines of the American light musical theatre.

The performers of the Casino must be given the largest credit for turning *The Belle of New York* into a success which in a two-year, 697-performance run at the Shaftesbury, set the show in orbit round the provinces and the world for decades to come. It was to reappear on several occasions in London but, in spite of its continued popularity, it remained an isolated phenomenon. The occasional American piece appeared in London during the next ten years, but two subsequent Kerker/McLellan pieces, *An American Beauty* and *The Girl from up There* put on for Edna May, gained less success than in their land of origin. *The Belle of New York* was the smash hit of its own moment, a novelty for the London public, which appeared like most other huge hits at precisely the moment it was needed.

The end of May saw the new season's anticipated crop of West End musicals begin to put in its appearance, starting on the twenty-first with a double opening at the Lyric and the Gaiety.

The Lyric Theatre had taken off *Dandy Dan* and Arthur Roberts brought back the George Dance/John Crook *A Modern Don Quixote* which he had produced in 1893 at the Strand. This version was considerably different. The whole of the second act had been re-written, new songs provided and much of the old score discarded, although the more successful pieces like 'The Echo Song' and 'I'm the Bishop of Gretna Green' were retained. Of the new pieces Lionel Monckton's 'Rumpity Scrumpity' for Godwynne Earle (Phoebe), Paul Rubens's 'There's just a Something Missing', and the Alfred Morris/Walter Tilbury 'That's not the Sort of Girl I'd Care About', all did well, but the show remained little more than a tour de force for its star as he gambolled along from one unlikely disguise to another, impersonating the Bishop of Gretna Green, a lady nurse, a French hairdresser and so forth to the evident delight of his partisans of whom there were still very many. But *A Modern Don Quixote* even in its 1898 version was a decidedly unsophisticated piece and, in spite of its star's attractions to London playgoers, it was clearly a much better proposition for the paying provinces, where it went after four weeks at the Lyric.

The life-span of the new Gaiety piece was in marked contrast. *The Circus Girl* had been an enormous success, but with its successor, *A Runaway Girl*, Edwardes managed to outstrip the former show in both popularity and longevity. It was the most successful and, arguably, the best of the Gaiety musicals to date.

George Edwardes was unable to persuade Seymour Hicks to return to his place as jeune premier of the Gaiety. That versatile and ambitious young star had other plans for himself as an actor, but he did offer to provide the libretto for the next Gaiety show. That Edwardes agreed to this after the public and critical reaction to the young man's previous book-writing effort with *The Yashmak* showed his faith in Hicks' abilities. But then, of course, the would-be author was the husband of the Gaiety's invaluable star, Ellaline Terriss.

For *A Runaway Girl* Hicks collaborated with Harry Nicholls, another actor, best known at Drury Lane and the Adelphi for his comic performances over some fifteen years. Nicholls had already found success as a writer allied to William Lestocq on the long-running *Jane* (1890). The plot which they concocted had little chance to spread itself too widely since its authors were required, as Gilbert had been at the Savoy, to include 'typical' roles for the theatre's leading players – Miss Terriss, Louis Bradfield (*vice* Hicks himself), the comedians Harry Monkhouse, Edmund Payne and Connie Ediss – as well as providing opportunities for the displays of the dancing soubrette,

Katie Seymour, and her girls and the various other talents of the less prominent but no less important and well-loved Gaiety habitués such as Willie Warde, Robert Nainby, Fred Kaye and Ethel Haydon.

A Runaway Girl was set in Corsica where an English girl, Winifred Grey, is being educated in a convent. Having discovered that she is to be wed sight unseen to a nephew of the elderly aristocrat, Lord Coodle, she runs away from the school and joins a band of wandering minstrels. During their travels she meets and falls in love with Guy Stanley who also joins up with the band. But we are in Corsica. The minstrels are not quite what they seem and they attempt to extract a large sum of money from Guy as the price of having joined their 'secret society'. Unable to pay, Guy flees to Venice with Winifred, one Flipper, a servant of the Coodles, and Lady Coodle's maid, Alice. The bandits track them down and Flipper, who has stood security for Guy, is ordered to kill him. Flipper and Alice get away disguised as nigger minstrels and all is set to rights when the Coodles turn up and it is discovered that Guy is the very nephew Winifred was to be betrothed to anyway and everyone can go back to relatively safe England.

The plot was liberally interlaced with songs, dances and jokes of the most popular kind for all the show's principals and the authors devised some amusing characters for them to play. Harry Monkhouse was cast as an unctuous lay brother, Tamarind, whose passion in life is Carmenita, a buxom member of the 'minstrel' band, impersonated by Connie Ediss. But Carmenita is also not all she seems, for in spite of her name and a penchant for Spanish dancing which she exhibits in the burlesque song and dance 'Barcelona':

> Vive Cadiz, though we don't know where it is
> Vive Navarre which is just about as far . .

she is, in fact, a native of the Blackfriars Road with delusions of grandeur. The role gave Connie something to get her teeth into, and Lionel Monckton provided her with a number, 'Society', which she turned into one of the hits of the show and of her career as she bewailed her lowly birth and detailed what she could have been with the 'right' father. The third verse went almost too far:

> O, I love Society, Real Society, Real Society,
> I'd ride on horses with long white tails
> If my Papa were . . . the Prince of Wales!

Report had it that the gentleman referred to was not amused, but nothing was said and the line remained.

The role of Flipper, the cocky little manservant, was in the traditional line of Teddy Payne parts – Shrimp, the perky call-boy of *In Town* was never quite forgotten. The *Shop Girl* formula which had proved repeatedly successful was turned out once again and 'Love on the Japanese Plan' was paralleled by 'Piccaninnies' in which Payne and Katie Seymour (as Alice) once more scored a hit with a quaint song and dance routine, this time in blackface and deep south tatters and with more than a touch of that old Gaiety hit 'Hush, the Bogie':

> When de twilight's fallin' and de stars a-peepin' out
> When de night begins, when de night begins
> Is de time our mammy says de bogeyman's about
> And de gobelins! And de gobelins!
> And when de little piccaninnies softly creep around
> Dat's what makes 'em hold dere breath

'Cos dey's almost scared to death
Startin' when de shadows move an' feared of every sound
'Cos dey know dere's goblins lurkin' in de wood
Behind de trees where dey abound . . .

In the romantic leads, Ellaline Terriss and Louis Bradfield had the kind of roles which Miss Terriss and her husband had largely created. No longer were the young lovers represented as heartfelt, earnest and rather 'soppy', but played with sprightliness and vigour. They no longer sang soulful ballads and duets but bright and often humorous numbers. Miss Terriss in the title role had the largest share of the score – no less than four solo numbers including 'The sly Cigarette' in which the unlikely refrain:

Oh, sly cigarette, o fie, cigarette
Why did you teach me to love you so
When I have to pretend that I don't, you know?

set to a lilting Lionel Monckton waltz tune provided the occasion for a ladies' song and dance feature. Rather more appropriate were two Ivan Caryll numbers. 'I'm only a poor little singing Girl' and 'Beautiful Venice', but it was left to the clever Monckton to supply Ellaline with her most popular song of the piece – 'The Boy Guessed Right', another light and almost childish song for which he provided both the lyric and the music:

There once was a little boy who went to school
And he was an aggravating lad
He smashed every window and he broke every rule
His behaviour was really very bad.
So the master invited him to come one day
For a private little interview
And he welcomed Master Jack
With his hand behind his back
Saying 'Guess what I've got for you?'

And the boy guessed right, the very first time,
Very first time, very first time,
He guessed right away it was not a cricket bat
I wonder how he came to think of that?

Miss Terriss also joined with Bradfield in an interpolated duet by Alfred D. Cammeyer called 'No-one in the World', while the hero sang a Lionel Monckton number 'Not the Sort of Girl I care About'. The strong baritone music, including a romantic waltz song in praise of Corsica, 'My Kingdom', and a vigorous saltarello in the Water Fête scene in Venice, was entrusted to John Coates as the leader of the minstrel-brigands. As with the bulk of the concerted music and the more traditional numbers, both these pieces were from the pen of Ivan Caryll.

The writers had managed to include all the other favourite Gaiety actors and actresses in the action by the simple device of introducing a party of itinerant Cooks' tourists led by courier Harry Phydora and including the Italian Signor Paloni (Nainby), Count and Fraulein Ehrenbreitstein von der Hohe (Fritz Rimma and Grace Palotta), Sir William Hake (Fred Wright) and his daughters (Marie Fawcett and Emilie Hervé), the Hon. Bobby Barclay (Lawrance d'Orsay), Mr Creel (Willie Warde) and Dorothy Stanley (Ethel Haydon). Their octet 'Follow the Man from Cooks' provided a free advertisement:

Oh, follow the man from Cooks
The wonderful man from Cooks
And whether your stay be short or long
He'll shew you the sights, he can't go wrong
Oh, follow the man from Cooks
The wonderful man from Cooks
It's twenty to one
You have plenty of fun
So follow the man from Cooks

The final verse was less enthusiastic:

Weary and lame at the end of the day
Bother the man from Cooks
Worried to death, you will probably say,
'Bother the man from Cooks'
Hurried along when you wanted to stop
Loaded with half the contents of a shop
Bustled about till you're ready to drop
Bother the man from Cooks!

That number was by Lionel Monckton and it was he who was to contribute the most enduring number in the score, a military piece written for Ethel Haydon as the second ingénue, Dorothy, and entitled 'Soldiers in the Park' with its martial chorus:

Oh, listen to the band
How merrily they play
Oh, don't you think it's grand
Hear everybody say
Oh, listen to the band
Who doesn't love to hark
To the shout of 'Here they come'
And the banging of the drum
Oh, listen to the soldiers in the park!

The number was to become identified with the actress Grace Palotta who was promoted to the role of Dorothy later in the run and who made herself famous with 'Soldiers in the Park'. In a later incarnation the song became the signature tune of bandleader Jack Hylton, ensuring its recognition by another generation of lovers of a catchy tune.

A Runaway Girl was full of good things – fun, songs and dances – and its reception was immediately overwhelming. *The Era* predicted '. . it will not be surprising if *A Runaway Girl* repeats – or even exceeds – the successes of its predecessors' and it was right. Even *The Times*, given to sighing for comic opera and disdaining the lighter musical theatre, admitted:

> Nothing is more likely to give the coup de grâce to the 'variety show' that has too long engrossed many of our cleverest actors and authors than such a return to the healthier methods of operetta as is exhibited in *A Runaway Girl*. . . [The authors have evolved] a perfectly reasonable plot for their amusing piece and not merely a peg on which a number of irrelevant performances can be hung. If they sometimes yield to the conventionalities that have become established in recent years they keep their main thread in view throughout and it may be said at once that many less carefully constructed pieces have before assumed the more ambitious title of 'comic opera' . .

A Runaway Girl was not comic opera. If it had been, it would probably have been noticeably less successful. It was an outstandingly lively, tuneful and spectacular Gaiety entertainment:

> The animation of the stage seems almost incessant. Picture succeeds picture and revel revel. The scene is an enchantment of pretty faces, a kaleidoscope of rich colours and at times a very complex affair of chorus and dance marvellously well carried out. Light, sparkling to look at, brilliantly changeful of aspect, *A Runaway Girl* bids for remarkable success in these respects. The music helps it liberally with tunes and rhythms. The tunes may not be very new and the rhythms may show no great ingenuity of resource – the score indeed is rather a patchwork thing. But the music is put together in a way to appeal readily to unexacting ears, and one or two of the numbers such as 'The Boy Guessed Right' and 'The Soldiers In The Park' are, of their sort, palpable hits. Add a tower of strength in the company . . . (*Stage*)

In spite of the show's immediate enormous popularity, Edwardes continued with alterations and additions throughout the run of the piece, as *A Runaway Girl* saw out not only 1898 but also 1899 and took the Gaiety Theatre through into the twentieth century. Much as the Gaiety regulars loved the shows George Edwardes gave them, they liked, on their tenth, twentieth or thirtieth visit to a piece to find some novelties, whether it be in scenery, costumes, numbers or pretty faces, and since Edwardes had a huge wealth of talent at his disposal it was not difficult for him to supply these changes. New songs were frequent enough, and some of them turned out to be extremely popular. Ellaline Terriss interpolated the 'Leslie Mayne' (Lionel Monckton) song 'When little Pigs Begin to Fly' in September, and it was immediately successful, the more so when she and the author began to decorate it with topical allusions. Connie Ediss interpolated 'What makes Pussy Jump' and, more successfully, the humorous 'I thought it my Duty to say So' and Louis Bradfield introduced 'She Picked Me out a nice One'.

At one stage the whole second act was remodelled, the party of Cook's tourists suffered regular alterations and/or subtractions, and finally an official 'second version' was produced, but all through its 593-performance run *A Runaway Girl* maintained a popularity unmatched by any of its predecessors.

It was not only in Britain that the piece proved popular. Augustin Daly took it to Broadway where it received an excellent production at his theatre with James T. Powers, Virginia Earle, Mabelle Gillman. Cyril Scott and Paula Edwards at the head of affairs. Daly took care to reproduce the piece as closely as was possible to the original book and to Malone's Gaiety production. His care paid dividends, and one paper commented:

> London's latest musical comedy would in other hands have been transplanted, adapted, localised, Americanised, swathed in stars and stripes and distorted beyond all recognition . .

But *A Runaway Girl* was not, and the benefits were obvious. When the show finished its fourteen weeks at Daly's it had averaged a weekly take of $10,000. This was too good to relinquish, but Ada Rehan was once again booked into the theatre, so Daly transferred to the Fifth Avenue Theatre where *A Runaway Girl* ran blithely on to total over 200 performances. Australia also took strongly to the Gaiety's latest triumph and the show repeated its original success throughout the English-speaking countries of both hemispheres.

A week after the première of *A Runaway Girl*, D'Oyly Carte opened his new Arthur Sullivan musical, *The Beauty Stone*. Savoy habitués, who had just re-seen *The*

Gondoliers, were now presented with what its authors called a 'Romantic Musical Drama'. The word comic was glaringly absent. And rightly so, for there was nothing comical about *The Beauty Stone*. Sir Arthur Sullivan had spent much time during his collaboration with Gilbert trying to avoid his partner's re-use of the so-called 'lozenge' motif by which people are changed, usually magically, from one form or personality into another. It was ironic, then, that his first collaboration with that foremost of British playwrights, Arthur Wing Pinero, venturing here with the cachet of Sullivan's collaboration into the musical field, should have been based on that very theme.

Laine, a crippled peasant girl, is tired of life, for her ugliness has prevented love from entering her life. The Devil gives her 'the Beauty Stone' and by its effect she becomes beloved of the Flemish Lord of Mirlemont. But when Lord Philip has left for the wars the Stone passes first into the hands of Laine's father, who becomes young and handsome, and finally into those of Philip's scheming ex-mistress, the Arab Saida. Rejoicing, Saida awaits Philip's homecoming, but when he returns he is blind and seeks for companionship the once more crippled Laine whom he had known so beautiful. Saida is outwitted and so is Satan to whom the Stone, as always, returns.

Sullivan's feeling had been right. Powerful talismans were a bore. Treated with the skill and acerbic humour of a Gilbert they could be made palatable as in *The Sorcerer*, *Creatures of Impulse* and *The Gentleman in Black*; dressed up with much splendour and low humour they could get by in such pantomime-like pieces as *Cymbia* or *The Golden Ring*. Dealt with in the earnest and poetic fashion which Pinero employed for his libretto, the theme became dull and inapposite. The book of *The Beauty Stone* had no sparkle. It was not a Savoy libretto and, worse, it was not a libretto for Arthur Sullivan for it made his music seem almost trivial and his music made it seem ponderous and pretentious. Some attractive pieces, such as Laine's prayer:

> Dear Mother Mary
> Unto thee I bring a poor maid's prayer
> I am a crooked, wan, misshapen thing
> And may not dare
> To lift mine eyes to thine . .

emerged from the exercise, but the net result of the combination of the writers' talents was very disappointing. As had been proved before, notably with *Jane Annie*, and would be again, the most noteworthy authors are not necessarily the most suitable writers for light musical entertainment. In this case the distinguished playwright and the barely less distinguished poet and author, Comyns Carr, who was responsible for the lyrical portion of *The Beauty Stone*, did not prove to be a suitable catalyst to the genius of Arthur Sullivan. Their musical lasted for only fifty performances before *The Gondoliers* was resurrected and the Savoy became its cheerful self once again.

With the end of May, 1898, came the end of the run of *The Geisha*. It had filled Daly's for over two years and the time had finally come to replace it. Edwardes was faced with the eternal problem of the manager of an outsize hit – how to follow that hit. The formula he used was undoubtedly the best one: more of the same wrapped up in an entirely different package. Thus, from nineteenth century Japan, Owen Hall, Harry Greenbank and Sidney Jones turned their attention to ancient Rome and the year AD 90: equally picturesque, equally flexible as regards custom and humour, and as far from nineteenth-century Japan as could be. But inside the decoration the contents were to be the same. As with *A Runaway Girl* there were resident stars to be written for, for the Daly's galaxy was just as popular and just as powerful in box-office terms as its Gaiety counterpart, and a Daly's show without Marie Tempest, Letty Lind, Hayden Coffin and Huntley Wright would have been gravely weakened in its appeal. It was no trouble for the ingenious Hall to fabricate a newish plot and a set of characters to suit the stars of *The Geisha*, and the result was *A Greek Slave*, produced by George Edwardes at Daly's on 8 June, 1898.

Huntley Wright was cast as Heliodorus, a wily Persian soothsayer patronised by the wealthy matrons of Imperial Rome for the odd prophecy on the prospects of their love life. He is assisted in his charlatanism by his daughter Maia (Marie Tempest) who pretends to have the gifts of an oracle and who utters incomprehensible prophecies at a suitable price. Among their servants is one Archias, a talented sculptor (Scott Russell) whose most recent achievement is a statue of Eros, God of Love, for which his fellow slave Diomed (Hayden Coffin) has acted as model. With Diomed Maia has fallen in love. The princess Antonia (Hilda Moody) comes to the soothsayer in disguise and Maia, egged on by the Prefect Pomponius (Rutland Barrington) who has been spurned by the princess, plans a humiliating trick. She announces to the princess that the God of Love himself has fallen in love with her. The statue is brought forth, and Heliodorus prepares to 'bring it to life'. Diomed is substituted and serenades the princess. But Heliodorus is planning a double-cross. He disapproves of his daughter's fancy for a slave and when the séance is over and Maia has intended that Antonia should walk off with the statue, Heliodorus arranges that the real Diomed falls to the princess. But it does her little good. The slave, in his luxurious new surroundings, pines for Maia, and all Antonia's love-making goes for nothing. Pomponius, who was anxious to see his marble lady wasting her affection on a marble statue, is furious at the social slight involved and Heliodorus finds himself in hot water. Eventually, in the middle of the Roman Saturnalia, all is cleared up and the correct pairs of lovers are united.

A Greek Slave was a less obviously comical affair than its predecessors. Rutland Barrington's role gave him little opportunity to consolidate his 'second career' and the humorous moments were left largely in the hands of Huntley Wright with Letty Lind as a pert lady's maid. The music was less tripping and bright and more ambitious, although Sidney Jones' score was peppered with enough Lionel Monckton songs to keep the balance tipped in the direction of popular taste. Even though they had George Edwardes and Monckton in common, Daly's fare and that of the Gaiety were getting further apart. The advance towards a more substantial kind of piece was, not unexpectedly, largely appreciated by the critics:

> From the point of view of the musical critic, the score of *A Greek Slave* is far and away the best that Mr Sidney Jones has ever written. From the point of view of the literary critic Messrs Harry Greenbank and Adrian Ross's lyrics are the most admirable of their many versiculations. And from the point of view of the ordinary individual with eyes to see and the intelligence to appreciate glorious colour, graceful form and the flavour of antiquity, Mr George Edwardes's mounting of *A Greek Slave* is a thing to be seen – once seen it is certain to be immensely and enthusiastically admired by the lovers of high art and good music (*Era*)

> As the first of the two new Edwardes pieces was an advance in taste, prettiness and charm, so the second is an advance in beauty and form. The actual plot of *A Greek Slave* may not be a very brilliant affair but it is at the least a dramatic groundwork. The go-as-you-please humour of *Artist's Models* and *Geishas* with music ad captandum vulgus are exchanged for a story with a beginning, a middle and an end, set out with some approach to the dimensions of grand opera and strengthened by a pictorial treatment more direct, more consistent and altogether more pleasing in its

> artistic principles than the mere display that has largely held its own against everything else. *A Greek Slave* may at present move rather slowly as a whole but the movement if slow is fascinating. It could hardly be otherwise, if only for the succession of lovely pictures in which the action is taken from point to point or for the steady flow of Sidney Jones' most skilful strains, as apt and clever in the nimblest of the lines of Harry Greenbank and Adrian Ross as in the more ambitious numbers and finely scored concerted pieces. Scene and music alone, in short, will make the fortune of *A Greek Slave*. But the piece has abundant other recommendations for favour, chief among them the remarkable ability with which it is acted, sung and – it is only fair to add – danced . . (*Stage*)

Not everyone was quite so laudatory. *The Times* found fault, not only with the piece, but with the performers:

> The somewhat limited resources of certain members of the company and the physical or vocal qualifications of others necessitate the introduction of one characteristic or another without consideration for such matters as the logical sequence of the plot upon which the piece is supposed to be based.

The vocal writing in *A Greek Slave* was certainly more demanding than usual. Jones took full advantage of Miss Tempest's power and range and went so far as to demand a high C from his tenor, Scott Russell, in his 'Revels' number. But the tone was kept suitably un-operatic by the unpretentious lyrics and the tunefulness of the melodies. In one song, however, the right flavour was not achieved. It was a song for which, significantly, Ross and Greenbank were not responsible, as the lyric for Hayden Coffin's first act song, 'Freedom' was supplied by Henry Hamilton:

> Content? It were to say my manhood nay,
> My soul were slave to find my fetters light;
> To me they mar the glory of the day,
> They mock the soft nepenthe of the night.
> Creation fair with freedom cries my wrong,
> Free is the wind, unfettered is the wave;
> It breaks my heart to hear the wild bird's song
> That doth but sing of freedom to the slave.
>
> Let me be free, 'tis all the world and more to me
> Free as the boundless heav'n above
> To dare, to do, to live, to love.
> Be mine the freeman's hand and soul,
> My fate to conquer and control;
> I cry, as cry the blind to see,
> Let me be free, let me be free!

The song was to find much popularity with baritone singers both professional and amateur, for it had the ringing tones of the drawing room about it. Jones had set Hamilton's archaic words with a gloriously operatic melody which was far too ambitious in its context. Fortunately, it was surrounded by much in a more suitable tone. Marie Tempest scored with 'The lost Pleiad', telling the story of a prodigal star-maiden:

> 'Twas a pretty little maiden in a garden grey and old,
> Where the apple-trees were laden with the magic fruit of gold;
> But she strayed behind the portal of the Garden of the Sun,
> And she flirted with a mortal, which she oughtn't to have done!

For a giant was her father and a goddess was her mother,
She was Merope or Sterope – the one or else the other;
And the man was not the equal, though presentable and rich,
Of Merope or Sterope – I don't remember which.

Merope (or Sterope) is ostracised, until the Dog-star courts her and brings her back to light, and together they produce the Milky Way. This piece proved an apt contrast to Miss Tempest's more romantic pieces with Coffin and her sentimental show ballad 'The Golden Isle'.

Amongst the other lighter pieces, Huntley Wright gave a number 'The Wizard' describing how he became one:

I lived in desert Eastern lands
A mass of lions mixed with sands,
Which danced eccentric sarabands
When blown on by a blizzard.
My lodging was a ruined tomb,
A shelter from the wild simoom,
And there in ghastly, ghoulish gloom,
I learned to be a Wizard.
So now I am a marvel of a Mage,
The wonders of the future I can gauge,
A forecaster of disaster like the Master Zoroaster,
I'm the mightiest magician of the age!

and, even more popularly, the stuttering song 'I'm Nervous' which he accompanied by an eccentric dance. The bulk of the lighter music, however, fell to the ever-popular Letty Lind who detailed the part of her life that was 'Confidential' and admitted 'I would rather Like to Try' in the first act before going on, in the second, to deliver the now expected zoological number. After the Gay Tomtit and the Interfering Parrot things came down to ground level for what was probably the best of the series, 'A Frog he Lived in a Pond'. Adrian Ross had clearly dipped into his classical background for this most Aristophanic-sounding of numbers:

A frog he lived in a pond, O!
He warbled a plaintive rondo
Of brek-ke-ke-kex ko-ax
The other frogs thought it was splendid
Applauding him when he ended
With brek-ke-ke-kex ko-ax

The mixture of styles in *A Greek Slave* was highly attractive and it was made more so by the addition, a few weeks after the opening, of a new number for the rather underparted Rutland Barrington entitled 'I Want to be Popular', composed by Lionel Monckton:

A person who holds an official position
Your pity may very well claim
The praises of men are his only ambition
And yet he gets nothing but blame,
Some order in council I think of indicting
To make me a favourite strong
If I tie up the dogs to prevent them from biting
O, shall I be popular long?

For I want to be popular, popular,
Worshipped by women and men
If my edicts embrace
Any hounds of the chase
O, shall I be popular then?

The song proved an excellent vehicle for topical references, and it grew and grew as the grim Pomponius thought up new measures which he might take, only to find they would not make him liked at all. The Dreyfus case was grist to the lyricist's mill, and the Czar and M. de Rougemont and many other prominent figures found themselves being used to make Pomponius popular.

But although *A Greek Slave* had, seemingly, got everything as right as possible, it never achieved the popularity of *The Geisha*. It held the stage at Daly's for twelve months, and went into a second edition with the usual ration of new songs and new dances, but in spite of all its virtues it never caught on in the way that its predecessor had. Perhaps audiences were not enchanted by ancient Rome in the way they were by Japanoiserie, perhaps it was a case of reaction after such an immense success immediately before, but *A Greek Slave* remained a splendid and profitable piece without becoming a true hit. It was long and widely toured and even revived by Jimmy White in 1926 with José Collins as Maia in a full-scale production which, partly due to its stars' inefficiencies, was not brought back to Daly's. However, it failed in America where its Herald Square production in 1899 lasted only 29 performances and seems unfairly destined in the long run to be remembered for not equalling *The Geisha*.

August and September brought into the West End a series of pieces which had originated out of town. The first of these was a musical called *Bilberry of Tilbury* which had been produced in Northampton by Cecil Beryl and taken on tour. The book was by George Day (the husband of Lily Hall Caine and the author of a few dramatic trifles) and Silvanus Dauncey with Guy Jones, the brother of Sidney, supplying the music. The plot was a farcical one, involving an actress, Stella Dashwood, whose sideline is the running of a ladies' detective agency. One of her customers is the Duchess of Adstock who hires her to track down the actress with whom she believes her son has become all but inextricably entwined. That actress is actually Stella herself, but she is unaware of the fact as her lover has courted her under a false name. Realising that something is up, the young man has a friend pose as 'Lord Bilberry' and Stella expends her energies tracking down the wrong man, alarming the Duchess with her colourful reports for, not only is the false Bilberry married, but he is also carrying on with one of Stella's colleagues, Sadie Pinkhose. In the end, of course, everything is resolved happily.

Bilberry of Tilbury was a perfectly competent little piece constructed with a provincial tour in view but, part way through that tour, Beryl was offered the chance to put it into the Criterion Theatre. Cancelling his tour dates, he transferred the show into London where it had a reasonable reception for four weeks before returning to the road. It was not particularly suited to the West End. Its humour was broad and rather obvious; its songs – and some of its performances – had more of the music hall spirit than appealed to the Gaiety or the Lyric audiences; and the little Criterion Theatre was not really the place to hold some of the 'large' performances of Beryl's cast. Yet it was by no means a failure and fulfilled its function of filling the theatre's vacant weeks without disgrace. It was happier, however, back in the provinces and, with the cachet of its London season, was brought back for a second round in 1899 under the title *The Lady Detective* starring Madge Merry, Joseph B. Montague, Rosie St George and featuring a young actress named Gertie Millar in the role of Sadie Pinkhose.

A considerably more substantial piece of work was *The Dandy Fifth*, a comic opera version of the French vaudeville *Un Fils de Famille* which had already made several appearances under various titles on the London stage, the most recent and successful being the Court Theatre production *The Queen's Shilling* (1879) which had been revived in the same year at the St James' with John Hare, Mrs Gaston Murray and the Kendals and again in 1885 with the same cast. The musical version was devised by George Sims, who had proved his aptitude at writing for the provinces with pieces such as *A Gay City/Skipped by the Light of the Moon*, and the music was composed by the musical director of the Manchester Theatre Royal, Clarence Collingwood Corri. Corri was a member of the most distinguished musical family, being a great-grandson of the Italian composer Domenico Corri (1746–1825), a grandson, son and brother of composers and conductors, including the Old Vic conductor Charles M. Corri and a second cousin to singers Haydn and Henri Corri. *The Dandy Fifth* was his most notable achievement as a composer.

The story, as Sims adapted it to suit the tastes of his public, told of Dick Darville, private soldier, who rescues his General's daughter Kate from unwelcome attentions contracted while running about in peasant disguise. Their acquaintance is carried further, arousing the jealousy of Kate's suitor, Colonel Slasherton, and Dick finds himself embroiled in a duel. When the Colonel discovers that his rival is a private in his own regiment he plans revenge by court martial, but Dick's fortunes have been restored and he has been bought out of the army so the Colonel's revenge is left unsatisfied as Dick and Kate are made happy.

The piece was written for the well-known touring management of Hardie and Von Leer who were making their first foray into musical production with it. They were joined for the occasion by a third partner, Frank A. Gordyn. The show was mounted at the Prince of Wales Theatre, Birmingham, and before the first performance had even been staged it had received its first good notice – from the Lord Chamberlain. As was required, the script had been sent for his approval before presentation and a reply came back:

> Dear Sir – My best congratulations to everyone concerned. It is really quite refreshing to read a comic libretto which is amusing, consistent and witty, without an objectionable word from start to finish. My friend G. R. Sims has discovered how to please the greatest number and offend none.
> Yours truly, G. A. Redford.

The Lord Chamberlain proved a good judge, for *The Dandy Fifth* received a tremendous reception on its first performance and its popularity with provincial audiences quickly became quite exceptional. Under these circumstances, Hardie, Von Leer and Gordyn decided to try a London season, and the Duke of York's Theatre was taken for an eight-week period in August and September. Since the touring company was to continue its profitable path around the country, it was necessary to find some new stars, including someone to take on the role of the barmaid, Polly Green, created by Frances Earle and currently being played on tour by Minnie Jeffs.

It was Corri who brought to Hardie a young lady named Manette Yvere who had been playing a spot at the Palace at £7 per week. A Frenchwoman, Miss Yvere had lived fifteen years in Britain, the last three of them pursuing a stage career. Her most recent credit, prior to the Palace, had been a music-hall tour of South Africa. She was hired at £5 per week and, along with Scott Russell, released from *A Greek Slave* to play the hero, and with Ruth Davenport, wife of Charles Wilson, manager of the Alhambra, and several principals from the road show, went into rehearsal.

As rehearsals progressed it became clear that Mlle Yvere would not do, and after the public dress-rehearsal it was decided she must go. Minnie Jeffs was brought hurriedly down from Oldham to take over while Mlle Yvere did the only thing a lady could do. She sued. The case did not come to court until *The Dandy Fifth* had been and gone, but when it did it proved nearly as good an entertainment as the show itself. The lady read aloud from the script in court to prove that she had no French accent and was quite capable of playing a British barmaid, and the reasons for ever hiring her became more and more obscure (or obvious) as the defence shrank from saying categorically that she was actually no good. Sims himself took the stand to testify that she was totally unsuitable as a barmaid, before going on faint-heartedly to compliment the lady upon her possibilities in other roles. He might have saved his breath. As usual, the Westminster County Court found for the plaintiff. At £30 damages the producers were well rid of her. But to the end nobody explained satisfactorily why she had been hired in the first place.

This managerial faux pas was rather typical of the London production of *The Dandy Fifth* and a much greater mistake was soon to come to light: the eight weeks' rental contract. For *The Dandy Fifth*, in spite of opening in the middle of a heatwave and the sudden replacement of Corri's 'discovery', was, if by no means a stand-up hit, an undoubted success. *The Times* reported:

> [*The Dandy Fifth*] is the sort of piece which appeals to audiences that are pleased by plenty of humour of a rather obvious description, by dresses that are chiefly remarkable for their singular gaudiness and by music which is more tuneful and catchy than original. In writing for this class of theatre-goers, Mr Sims evidently knows just the kind of dialogue and verse which is required, and the delight with which *The Dandy Fifth* was received by the occupants of the gallery of the Duke of York's Theatre . . . proved that his appeal to the tastes of the 'gods' was based on an intimate knowledge of the wants of his audience. For more sophisticated playgoers the libretto does not afford much that will give satisfaction, but August is not a month in which to be too critical, and Mr Sims may easily be forgiven for the artlessness of some of his 'lyrics' and the commonplace flavour which pervades some of his dialogue. The music of *The Dandy Fifth* is by Mr Clarence Corri. Though not very original it displays plenty of vigour and a ready command of tune . . . influence of Offenbach . . . the catchy nature of the tunes appealed strongly to the audience and encores sometimes double and treble were the order of the evening . . . a very favourable reception . . . if first night approval counts for anything it should be assured a satisfactory career.

In other words, it was an evening of boisterous good fun, and the gallery and the pit were not alone in appreciating this, even at 80 degrees in the shade. *The Era* praised the 'good clean story' uninterrupted by variety entertainment, adding 'the music is bright and melodious and Mr Sims' lyrics are excellent'.

The Times critic was right, of course. *The Dandy Fifth* was not an entertainment designed for the sophisticate or the avant-garde; both book and songs had a wider appeal. Edward Lewis as a cockney Trooper Brown found willing encores for his ditty 'The Sprig o'Horringe Blossom':

> Of my 'eart the present owner is a dainty little doner
> But she treats it like a kitten treats a cork upon the floor.
> Though I worship 'er beauty I'm neglectin' of my duty

An' my clothes are 'anging on me as they never 'ung before.
O Polly!
But there ain't a heart in Hengland, or a King upon 'is throne
As I'd change my 'appy lot with if I'd got you for my own
If the ring was on your finger and I'd paid the parson's fee
And you'd stuck the horringe blossom in your hauburn hair for me
All a-blowin' and a-growin'
The sprig o'horringe blossom in your maiden hair for me.

and Scott Russell's patriotic 'Toast of the Dandy Fifth' swung along merrily with its refrain:

The flag that waves o'er us
The hearts that adore us
The heroes of England who sleep 'neath the green
The flag that we sigh for
The land that we'd die for
The lass that we love, and our lady the queen.

But it was to the lot of Harry Cole, as Sergeant-Major Milligan, that fell the choicest piece – another military number called 'Tommy's Tournament' or, as it became known during the long life which it was to have, 'A little British Army goes a * long way!'

So come you foreign soldiers, And we don't care who you are,
The Uhlans of the Kaiser, Or the Cossacks of the Czar,
Our Army may be little, But you've learnt before today,
A little British Army goes a * long way!

But it wasn't going any distance in London, for in spite of frantic efforts on the part of the producers to find another London home for their show as the end of the eight weeks approached, *The Dandy Fifth* was forced to shut down on 8 October. The best Hardie, Von Leer and Gordyn had been able to manage was to book the piece into a number of suburban theatres a week at a time, so the London company spent the remainder of the year on tour whilst the producers devoted themselves to doing battle with Mlle Yvere. London's loss was the provinces' gain. *The Dandy Fifth* became a huge money-spinner for the triumvirate and joined the list of inveterate touring pieces. 'A little British Army' went on going a long way for many, many years.

The next town entry was the newest in the Basil Hood/Walter Slaughter series. The writers of *Gentleman Joe*, *The French Maid* and *Dandy Dan* had somewhat changed direction with their new piece which they advisedly christened an extravaganza. *Her Royal Highness* was virtually a return to the style of Planché. It was by no means musical comedy in the style of the Gaiety or of Daly's, nor was it 'comic opera'. Its reliance on a fairy-tale story of supra-Gilbertian proportions, on pantomime spectacle and on the qualities of pure charm and attractiveness, clever words and catchy music placed it squarely in the genre of the old extravaganza, as its authors had rightly suggested.

The scene of the show is the Palace of King Fou-Fou, a monarch whose credo is 'Liberty, frivolity and jollity'. His daughter is to marry and a number of princes come to sue for her hand although Fou-Fou has already decided that she will choose Rollo, the richest. Rollo is not pleased by this reason and vows to woo and win the Princess Petula incognito, even though love is outlawed in that land as far too serious. The other princes are even less pleased, and combine to declare war on Fou-Fou. The alarmed King throws Petula out and she seizes the opportunity to run off with the attractive Rollo. The second act takes place in Rollo's kingdom where Fou-Fou and his exiled court have been shipwrecked. With the help of a bored War Captain, Fou-Fou lays claim to the kingdom while Rollo and Petula are wandering around as players – but finally all is set to right and Petula and Fou-Fou find that Rollo and the princess's own true love are the king of the country and one and the same person.

Her Royal Highness was given a run-in at Bournemouth and the auguries seemed fair. *The Era* correspondent enthused:

> The entertainment evidently aims at combining the lightness and frivolity of [musical comedy] with the legitimate dramatic form and musical value of [comic opera], the result being a bright, funny and eminently picturesque concoction with a style of its own, a style which we believe we shall be right in conjecturing will supply a long-felt want in light musical plays. The charms and fascinations of Mr. Slaughter's most refined and scholarly but lively and piquant musical setting and the clever and sparkling wit of Mr Basil Hood's dialogue and lyrics . . . &c

Certainly Hood and Slaughter were in good form. Hood indulged himself delightfully:

> I played the role with heart and soul
> Of a lover of the sea
> At first I thought I'd caught the role
> But then the roll caught me.
>
> I sang a song, but it went wrong
> So take advice from me
> And never start a sailor song
> Till you are on the quay.
>
> The coast was getting out of range
> We'd left the land behind
> At first I didn't mind the change
> And then I changed my mind.
>
> The gale increased – its icy breath
> Froze every thought of mirth
> At first I prayed to meet my death
> Then asked to see my berth.
>
> The vessel kicked us like a horse
> And bruised us with the shocks
> They were not equine blows, of course,
> It was the equi-nox
>
> But when we struck a rock the shock
> Gave me a moment's ease,
> I'd rather seize upon a rock
> Than rock upon the seas.

but he indulged himself in a fashion which reeked more of the 1870s or even of the 1860s than of the West End and fin de siècle.

The London opening split the critics. *The Times* man waxed even more eloquently lyrical than had *The Era* in Bournemouth as he claimed *Her Royal Highness* the equal of *The French Maid*, describing it as

> an abundance of song, dance, quip and crank, general extravagance, bright costume and lively music . . .

The Era, however, had changed its critic and its mind. As well staged as it might be, *Her Royal Highness*, it asserted, was an old-fashioned pantomime, out of season and out of its time. The latter opinion prevailed. The piece lasted only seven weeks and bankrupted its backer, the actor W. P. Warren Smith, who lost his entire £2500 investment. It was a sad episode in the Slaughter/Hood collaboration which had produced so much that was of the first quality.

Little Miss Nobody, which was produced at the Lyric on 18 September, can justifiably be described as a 'sleeper'. The first production of an unknown producer, 31-year-old Tom Buffen Davis – a former solicitor who had turned to the theatre and had at one time been manager of the Queen's Theatre, Birmingham – it was written by the author of *The County Councillor*, H. Graham, and its music was largely the work of Arthur E. Godfrey, better known as a composer of drawing-room ballads. Its track record prior to London was one copyright performance arranged by Yorke Stephens at the Cheltenham Opera House on the previous 5 March.

For the West End version, Stephens and Davis assembled a good cast: Kate Cutler[1], Cairns James, Lionel Mackinder and the old favourite 'Lal' Brough, the Gaiety's Maria Davis and the popular provincial performers Fred Eastman and Frank Lacy. Stephens himself was to play the show's hero. The first night was a total success. 'Everything seemed to go on wheels', recorded *The Times*, 'and the success of the piece was never in doubt for a moment.' *Little Miss Nobody* came from the blue and ran for two hundred performances.

> *Little Miss Nobody* has the advantage of an intelligible and amusing plot and music that is tuneful without being common-place. It was received last night with a degree of rapture which only those who have had to endure some of the more recent specimens of musical comedy presented to the metropolis can understand . . . ingenious and diverting . . . the play is interspersed with some pretty dances which form a pleasant relief to the wildly farcical incidents of the plot . . .
> (*Times*)
>
> One of the brightest and liveliest musical comedies . . . for a long time . . . Amusing story . . . Fresh lyrics . . . the great merit of Mr Graham's book is its coherence and the careful construction of its plot . . . the music is fresh, gay and spirited . . .
> (*Era*)

The outline of *Little Miss Nobody* was constructed on *Erminie* lines, involving a pretty Scottish love story concerning the noble Guy Cheviot and the governess, Elsie Crockett ('Little Miss Nobody'), and a farcical piece of masquerade which finds the ill-bred money-lender, Christopher Potter, and three common music-hall 'artistes', the sisters Triplet, passing themselves off as the Earl of Cripplegate and daughters. Lady Cheviot makes a fool of herself over the false Earl, and the real nobleman when he arrives is subjected to all kinds of indignities before the truth is disentangled.

The role of Elsie gave Kate Cutler, who had stepped in and out of most of the best jeune première roles in recent years, her most winning role of all and she proved to be a hugely attractive draw alongside the comicalities of Eastman and the 'dragon' of Maria Davis. Mabel Tempest, sister to Marie, played a small role. The songs were numerous and bright and, although none was truly exceptional, a couple became popular, notably a jolly piece called 'The Gay Excursionist':

[1] Florence Perry was originally hired for the show's title role with Miss Cutler top-billed in the role of Trixie Triplet. Miss Perry's late withdrawal led to Miss Cutler being switched and Gracie Leigh getting her London début as Trixie.

It's safe to bet that you've often met The Gay Excursionist
And some I fear are disposed to sneer at The Gay Excursionist
His two-guinea suit is a picture to view
And a rainbow encircles his hat
He wears tan shoes of a daffodil hue
And a thunder and lightning cravat.
But the ladies can't resist The Gay Excursionist!
He trots them out in twos and threes
And stands them eighteenpenny teas
And they love to travel upon the knees of The Gay Excursionist

This song gained much of its popularity from being put over by a young lady unknown to the London public at large, Miss Gracie Leigh. As a result of her performance she was quickly contracted by George Edwardes under whose management she continued her rise to popularity, fame and a prominent place in the forefront of British musical stars.

Also popular was a number added to the score soon after the opening and sung by Lionel Mackinder (or George Grossmith during Mackinder's absence after an accident). It was written by the young Paul Rubens and called 'Trixie of Upper Tooting', and it claimed:

Trixie is a terror, Trixie is a Turk,
Trixie set the neighbourhood a-hooting
When she came to stay
All the curates went away
For Trixie was the talk of Upper Tooting

In fact, Trixie comes out as a fairly unpleasant little person, but the bouncy tune obviously outweighed the lyric. Credit for that lyric was surprisingly claimed by Ada Reeve for whom the song became a music-hall standard. She wrote:

> It was one Saturday night at the Lyric Club in Coventry Street, where we used often to foregather after the show. In a private room Evie Green, Louis Bradfield, Paul Rubens and I were having a sing-song. Paul was a very prolific composer and lyric-writer who could knock off a song in just a few minutes while tinkling the piano after supper. On this particular evening Paul at the piano began a tune that sounded promising. I made him finish it there and then. Together he and I wrote the words . . 'Trixie of Upper Tooting'. Paul orchestrated it next day; on Monday morning I rehearsed it, and at night made a little sensation with the song, which proved my biggest 'hit' for many years.

'Trixie' was by no means the only addition to the score. Landon Ronald supplied an extra number for Kate Cutler in the 'Hush, the Bogie' vein under the title 'Ghosts' and the brothers Rubens (Paul and stockbroker Walter) wrote her another, more appropriate, called 'Wee little Bit of a Thing like That' which allowed for topical allusions. Gracie Leigh's success won her another number, also by Rubens, called 'We'll just Sit Out' in which she described various types of men and their reasons for wanting to sit out rather than to dance. Fanny Dango, as her little sister, was given the moral tale of 'Mary Ann' and the two joined with Dora Dent in another Rubens' song, 'The People all Come to See Us'.

The success of the piece was reflected in the quality of the cast changes. John Le Hay took over as Potter, George Grossmith deputised for Mackinder and John Coates replaced Stephens in the role of Guy. This was somewhat of a waste as the role had been conceived as a non-singing one. Arthur Godfrey promptly provided two baritone solos, the lilting 'Highland Sport' and a waltz ballad 'Why should we Part' for the former opera singer. Some novelties were also introduced, and for a while La Loie Fuller could be seen as part of the night's entertainment, performing a set of five serpentine dances. The volume of the piece became quite considerable without producing any numbers or features of particular distinction, but *Little Miss Nobody* was a jolly Highland winner, and ran for six months surrounded by success with the only shadow cast by the sad death of little Mabel Tempest at the age of 24.

Little Miss Nobody was hardly the stuff of Broadway fare, so it was no surprise that, in spite of its West End run, it did not make it to New York. But Charles Frohman tried. He had picked up the rights even before the show had made its London début and, in fact, the Broad Street Theatre in Philadelphia welcomed *Little Miss Nobody* with Ethel Jackson in the title-role nine days prior to the West End première. It was a quick failure and all thoughts of Broadway vanished, but Miss Jackson, plucked from the lower echelons of the D'Oyly Carte Opera Company to give the show a fashionably English star, stayed on in America to become grist to the mills of the gossip writers and Broadway's original *Merry Widow*. *Little Miss Nobody* had a full and successful touring career in Britain as well as several other, more fruitful, overseas productions and proved, in sum, an unexpected windfall for all concerned.

The happy fate of *Little Miss Nobody* was not in store for the next West End arrival. Albert Chevalier brought in his hypnotism piece, *The Land of Nod*, which he had toured the previous year. It had been heavily remodelled and alterations were going on up to the last moment with numbers being cut and replaced. This affected no-one but the star, as the piece was little more than a vehicle for the popular Chevalier to display his talents for comic singing and impersonation. The public preferred to see him on the halls, and *The Land of Nod*'s run at the Royalty lasted just one week, at a loss of £2,500, sealing the fate of the syndicate which had been set up to produce it – ingeniously set up, so it seemed, for its principals Michael Levenston and Arthur Laurillard were apparently able to make a profit even out of this disaster. Not so the syndicate.

Chevalier later brought out a reduced version of *The Land of Nod* under the title of *The Dream of his Life* and played it as an item on concert-bills, its first appearance being at Eastbourne's Devonshire Park Theatre on 8 April, 1907.

The Belle of New York had started the year well for the foreign musical, but other extra-Britannic pieces fared much less happily. A production of Charles Hoyt's *A Stranger in New York* at the Duke of York's folded quickly and in September two further imports failed to make an impression. The first of these was *The Royal Star* for which the book was accredited to Francis Richardson and to Maurice Ordonneau, author of so many brilliant French opérettes including *La Poupée*. In *The Royal Star* (the title refers to a theatre and the lady *en vedette* there) he was unrecognisable. The music was by the Argentine-born, Paris-educated, Lisbon-based composer Justin Clérice who had promised much with his early work but failed disastrously to confirm in this show. Lowenfeld, who had seen in the piece a possible successor to *La Poupée* which had made him a fortune, closed *The Royal Star* before Christmas and restaged *La Poupée*.

Of much better quality was *Topsy-Turvey Hotel*, the *L'Auberge du Tohu-Bohu* of Victor Roger, also to a book by Ordonneau, which had run over 200 performances at the Folies Dramatiques in 1897. For its London version, seven of the twenty-three numbers were supplied by Lionel Monckton with Napoleon Lambelet/Ronald Carse, music hall artist Harry Fragson and A. Stanislaus each providing one. Like many other good quality French works before it, *L'Auberge du Tohu-Bohu* was butchered to suit what was considered to be the British taste. After what seemed a promising opening, the result was found to be to the taste of too few and the piece foundered after little more than two months.

The final new piece of the year came again from the provinces. When Arthur Roberts went out on tour in *A Modern Don Quixote* he began the preparation of his next show. It was to be based on a French play by Henri de Gorsse and Georges Elwall, the English libretto being prepared by George Day with Adrian Ross supplying the lyrics and Edward Jakobowski the music. *Campano* or The Wandering Minstrel (the sub-title was later changed to the burlesque-ish 'Change of a Tenor') was produced at the Leeds Grand in September and took the place of *Don Quixote* on Roberts' tour.

The plot of the piece had Roberts as a raffish soldier who, caught in a compromising position with a married lady, declares himself to be the famous tenor, Campano, rehearsing a scene for the next day's performance. His own young lady, to teach him a lesson, summons the real Campano from Paris, hoping in the meanwhile to see her lover make an ass of himself in the opera. But when Campano arrives he turns out to be a friend of the rogue who ends up having the last libidinous laugh on all. The piece was less of a one-man show than was normal with a Roberts production and, while this may not have appealed to his fans, it certainly made for a better proportioned show. *Campano* was worked in round the provinces and Roberts began to look out for a West End house for his new piece. But even for him an empty theatre could not be found and he was obliged to await the collapse of *Topsy-Turvey Hotel* at the Comedy Theatre before he could come into the West End just before Christmas.

In the meanwhile changes had been made to the show, for the most part metamorphosing what had been a French opérette libretto into an Arthur Roberts vehicle. The plot was changed. Roberts became an English aristocrat instead of a French soldier, the offended Ligereau became a chemistry professor and the lady compromised in the kissing scene was no longer his wife but his daughter and, finally, his niece. The unhappy fiancée became a standard 'old flame' – Celeste, a music hall singer of the El Dorado – and the finale now resulted in the Englishman being happily united with his little indiscretion and Celeste silenced by the arrival of her husband. Many of the original cast were retained for town, though some found their roles vastly altered or even omitted. A new tenor had to be found to play the role of the veritable Campano, since Henry Walsham, the hero of so many opéras-bouffes and early musicals, had taken to his bed after the fourth night on tour and died soon after. But the day of production drew near and Roberts still had no Celeste. A chance meeting in the street with Ada Reeve solved that problem and Ada found herself with songs to learn, but no script. Her scenes were with the star and therefore unscripted. Arthur Roberts had no intention of following any author's book and Ada, too, would be expected to ad lib the scenes.

Milord Sir Smith, as the piece had now been retitled, was staged on 15 December and received a very moderate reception despite the furious gagging of Roberts and Miss Reeve. The original plot had been pulled down to its very barest bones and these reset and decorated with barely relevant business. In spite of the refined and pretty music supplied by Jakobowski, the effect was one of disorganised music-hall high-jinks. Affairs were scarcely helped when, come Christmas, Ada Reeve announced that she would have to leave to fulfil a prior engagement at the Palace. Without Ada there would be no show – even Roberts could see that. He went to discuss the situation with Charles Morton at the Palace and came to an agreement that he would reconstruct the story of

Milord Sir Smith in such a way that Ada could be offstage long enough to allow her to nip from Panton Street up to Cambridge Circus, do her 'turn' at the Palace, and hurry back to complete the show at the Comedy. With the help of a hansom cab (six minutes from one stage door to the other), this arrangement continued through the admittedly short run of Roberts' piece and on into the next Comedy show for which Ada Reeve was also retained.

In true go-as-you-please manner, the principals inserted their numbers of the moment – irrelevant as they were – into the show. Roberts did best with a topical number by George Rollitt, 'She'd never Been in Pantomime Before', while Ada introduced her 'Love me a little, Sue' with which she had already scored on her Australian tour, and when things needed a bit of bucking up Roberts pulled out the same card he had used with *Dandy Dan* in its dying days – he interpolated a chunk of old-fashioned burlesque into the second act, quite impervious to the fact that *The Three Musketeers* bore absolutely no relation at all to *Campano* (or what was left of it) or to *Milord Sir Smith* such as it was.

By the time the show was withdrawn in March what had, in the provinces, been a reasonable attempt at a musical, had descended into a two-handed virtuoso variety turn which belonged perhaps in a music hall but scarcely in a theatre. Ada Reeve in her autobiography refers to *Milord Sir Smith* as a success. For her, no doubt, it was. With her salary at the Comedy and that at the Palace, she was picking up the very tidy sum of £100 per week. For the rest of the world, the show was an unfortunate exercise.

The provinces were producing more and more musicals which were eventually to turn up in London, but there were plenty of others which confined their activities to the out-of-town sphere with varying degrees of success. The first to appear was a piece called *Black and White*, written by the successful dramatist Mark Melford of *Turned Up* fame. Melford's only previous attempt at a musical had been with the interesting *Jackeydora*, but *Black and White* was a more conventional piece on English farce lines, bearing a strong resemblance to F. W. Sidney's comedy *A Loving Legacy* which was itself to be turned into a musical by its author later in the year. The story was a strong, detailed one, as befitted a writer of Melford's class, and the piece could doubtless have stood as a straight farce without music. However, John Crook's music proved an added attraction and *Black and White* had a very successful tour.

Its story concerned a young lady who is left in the guardianship of her father's friend while her father, remarried, is in India with his new wife and daughter. Thérèse is handsomely provided for by her absent father, and her guardian plans that she should wed his son who is wooing her assiduously. But Thérèse's father calls for her – it is the turn of the even more richly endowed half-sister to spend time in England. The greedy young lover immediately changes allegiance and renounces Thérèse but is horrified when Verona arrives to find that she is coloured. Father and son trick an ambitious money-lender into marrying Verona's maid instead of the heiress and they think that they have won the day when Thérèse's father is found to have died, leaving his 'treasure' to his friend. That 'treasure' turns out to be the old man's coloured wife, Treasurina, and she arrives accompanied by her Indian gentleman friend who has inherited the money. An amicable swap is made – the Indian couple marry and the greedy Rooks, somewhat unfairly, get the money, while Verona and Thérèse take the young men of their choice.

The Stage was most impressed and wrote up the play as 'wholesome, brilliant and full of fun. . . . the music is pretty and appropriate, some of the numbers being re-demanded several times'. *Black and White* proved successful enough to run through two good tours in 1898 after which producer Alexander Loftus incorporated it into a tandem with *The New Barmaid* for the 1899 season.

Among the cast of the original *Black and White* tour Loftus hired a 29-year-old actor from London to play the role of Lord Rook. George Arliss had been on the stage more than ten years without making very much impression and *Black and White* was scarcely able to give a boost to his so far unremarkable career. It did, however, provide him with a wife in Florence Montgomery who played a small role as the Indian maid and whom he married the following year. Arliss's future fame in the theatre and in the cinema did not capitalise on his small experience of the musical theatre.

The ABC or *Flossie the Frivolous* was put together by the old partnership of 'Richard Henry' as a vehicle for the music-hall star Marie Lloyd. Its outline bore more than a passing resemblance to *The Shop Girl*. Flossie (Miss Lloyd) is an assistant in the ABC Stores and is in love with the actor Macklin McGarrick. Her colleague, Lenore, is in love with Marmaduke, a disguised Earl. It is announced that Flossie is an heiress and Macklin altruistically renounces his claim to her, but then it is found to be a mistake – it is Lenore who is the daughter of the Lord of the Manor. She is instated, but at a charity bazaar held at her new home a box is found containing the true identity of the heir. The child was a boy and that boy is . . . McGarrick!

The plot was immaterial. The show existed to give Marie Lloyd the opportunity to display her talents in a long list of numbers and some clever dialogue and, in that, it succeeded well enough. The songs for the show were a lively lot, ranging from Miss Lloyd's 'A Bicycle Belle', 'I am an ABC Girl' and 'I certainly Expected Something more than That!' to the quartet 'London's all right when you're Used to It' and an amusing ditty for Fanny Harris called 'She Was only a little Girl (and he was a big, big man)'. Several of them were the work of the brother of Leedham Bantock, the Daly's and Gaiety actor who had turned director for this occasion. The young composer used the acronym of 'Graban', though as Sir Granville Bantock he was better known later for more serious music and as professor of music at Birmingham University.

The tour of *ABC* was brief. Although it was tailored well to its purpose, that purpose was not a particularly valid one. Miss Lloyd could shine more brightly and more freely in the halls in her own most attractive character – there was no need for her to assume another – and her devotees were frankly more interested in seeing Marie than in seeing Flossie, no matter how frivolous. The experiment was not repeated and the show was laid to rest after eight weeks.

Billy was another piece on similar lines, featuring Little Tich in a successor to *Lord Tom Noddy*, this time under his own management. Tich starred as the Hon. Billy Vavasour, a penniless scion of the nobility at grips with the horrid Soap King, Augustus Cadell, for the love of the beautiful General's daughter, Ethel. Billy eventually achieves fame by thwarting the evil Cadell and riding the General's racehorse to victory in time-honoured fashion to win both earldom and girl.

Although the show was a vehicle for Tich, the star and his writers had the wisdom to build a consistent if fairly unoriginal plot with worthwhile characters which enabled Tich to call on such performers as Joe Farren Soutar, Evie Greene, Richard Temple and Alice Barnett in sizeable supporting roles. This helped the show materially and, in particular strengthened its vocal element. The giant Picton Roxburgh repeated his *Tom Noddy* function of making Tich look even more dwarf-like than ever. *Billy* was a piece in better taste than *Lord Tom Noddy*. Although Tich's size was emphasised by the use of such actors as Roxburgh and Miss Barnett, it was not constantly harped upon as it had been in the former piece and the romantic element was not allowed to appear so grotesque. However, Tich wisely kept the piece away from the West End and its critics and passed, instead, a very healthy eight months in the provinces with it.

With Adrian Ross and Dr Carr involved in its making, *Billy*, although not a West End show, had a metropolitan pedigree, and the same could be said for *The Transit of Venus* produced by the country's most prolific touring management, H. H. Morell and Frederick Mouillot. The book of *The Transit of Venus* was by the Gaiety's James T. Tanner, author of *My Girl* and *The Circus Girl*, the lyrics again by Ross, and the music by *The Yashmak* composer Napoleon Lambelet.

The Transit of Venus was a complicated affair set in the Austrian Alps town of Bad Eggstein. It involved the Count Stefan (really a girl, but brought up as a boy to inherit the title and its wealth) and the 'rightful' heir – another Count Stefan – in a series of mix-ups as both, in their turn, are interned, as a girl, in a school, or as a man in the army. The whole was set against a background of an astronomy meeting (thus the title), military manoeuvres and school fun with the inevitable happy ending.

A good deal of work was expended on the show. Tanner's book was intricate and Adrian Ross went to the extent of composing nine different sets of simultaneous lyrics for the first act finale of the show and its nine solo characters – rather wasted labour since none of them, in consequence, could be heard or understood. Lambelet's music, too, was more substantial than his contribution to *The Yashmak*. The production was well received on its opening. The standard of craftsmanship of these experienced and talented writers met with an approval which might not have been so wholehearted had the piece opened in London where a little more than mere skilfulness might have been expected.

The Era's Leeds correspondent was, however, more than satisfied:

> The librettist has succeeded in putting together a number of amusing and humorous incidents which cannot fail to be appreciated and throughout the whole production there was ample evidence of the ability and the knowledge of construction of the author. The lyrics are by Mr Adrian Ross who has introduced some quaint songs which are certain to become popular, judging from the manner in which they were received on the opening night. The music of Mr Napoleon Lambelet throughout the comedy is of a light, airy and melodious description and it contains numerous brilliant passages and the orchestra is very good indeed.

The Transit of Venus progressed on an eighteen weeks' tour for Morell and Mouillot during which it was greeted with the same muted enthusiasm. Those concerned judged this insufficient to justify continuing with the piece and it was laid aside.

Basil Hood and Walter Slaughter continued their partnership to produce a musical comedy to fit the talents of another music-hall star, Dan Leno. Leno had been signed for a stage musical nearly two years previously by the enterprising producer, Milton Bode, who then commissioned a vehicle to display his star. The resulting show was produced in August of 1898 at the Fulham Grand under the title of *Orlando Dando, the Volunteer*. The plot centred on the character of the hairdresser, Orlando Dando, and was a traditional series of disguises and mistaken identities as Orlando vies with his assistant, Thomas, for the love of the maid, Susan, and also gets mixed up in the love affairs of (a) Captain Hamilton and rich Gladys who is disguised as a flower girl and (b) the real flower girl, Nancy, and her boyfriend Bill, as the action ranges from barbershop to convent to the Volunteer Camp on Hampstead Heath.

Hood kept the fun going, Slaughter illustrated it all with some pretty enough songs, and with Harry Barry taking the role intended for Leno it was successful enough on its Fulham début for Bode to send that company out on the road and to form a second company to star Leno when the little man's schedule reached its pre-booked place. Leno was only able to spare his producer six weeks before the lucrative and all-important pantomime season began, but he was pleased enough with 'his' *Orlando Dando* to go out in it again the following year at greater length. The piece did not add greatly to the reputations of its authors or its star but was sufficiently successful at the box-office to allow Bode to more than recoup the £125 per week he was paying Leno.

Lottie Collins had already been successful in the musical theatre with her performance in *The New Barmaid*, and the authors of that highly popular piece attempted a repeat performance by supplying her with the role of Nelly Catchpole, the Queen of the Circus, in a new musical *The White Blackbird*. The character was a fairly incidental one in a plot which combined the most well-worn of musical comedy characters and incidents: Sir Armand Fleet, a retired tradesman, chasing after the rich, elderly soap-boiler's daughter who prefers, in the end, the low comedian; the eager Mrs Somerton and her three marriageable daughters; the missing heir, in this case Charlie Glare, a society pierrot ('The White Blackbird'), who is being pursued by the comic lawyer-detective; and so forth.

Miss Collins cavorted through a series of scenes and song and dance routines including 'Queen of the haute Ecole', 'The lone little Widow', 'That's how it's Done' and a 'tickling duet' with the stalwart William Lugg, while Thomas E. Murray in the chief comic role held up his end of the proceedings with equal vigour. After some weeks on tour, however, Miss Collins decided she had had enough of *The White Blackbird* and returned to the halls, leaving the role of Nelly to Madge Merry and taking a large part of the show's appeal with her. The tour ran on to a final total of fifteen weeks to a reduced audience.

The music of *The White Blackbird* was the work of the 31-year-old organist and choirmaster John W. Ivimey, sometime music master at Wellington and Harrow and a keen composer of light stage music but much more fame awaited the conductor of the show, James Tate, composer in later years of the unforgettable 'A Bachelor Gay'and the unnamed half of the husband and wife variety team 'Clarice Mayne and That'. Currently, however, he was Mr Lottie Collins and stepfather to her young daughters José, Cleo and Lucia.

More successful and much more enduring was George Dance's latest piece, *The Gay Grisette*, set to music by *Ballet Girl* composer, Carl Kiefert. *The Gay Grisette* was taken up as the inaugural production of the Provincial Managers' Syndicate under the direction of the young manager of the Manchester Prince's, Robert Courtneidge, and was produced with notable success at Bradford. It was a lively and amusing piece in Dance's best rollicking style involving Babette, a Colonel's niece, disguised as a grisette and her amours with the philandering Captain Jack. The inevitable lawyer and inheritance intervened as the plot galloped from France to Hungary through litterings of the popular types of songs and jokes, all of which were unerringly engineered to appeal to the provincial audiences which Dance knew so well.

The Gay Grisette was to have a good, long career around the touring circuits with Claire Romaine, Marie Montrose, Nell Gwynne and Alice Chasemore taking turns at heading the bill through several seasons, but Courtneidge and his partners resisted the temptation to try the show in London's West End. It went down excellently at Camberwell, but the Strand would very likely have found it a little 'provincial'. The initial tour of *The Gay Grisette* provided the opportunity for a young would-be comedian to take his first steps towards fame when Courtneidge replaced the departing Arthur Ricketts in the small role of Janos with the inexperienced 22-year-old George

Graves. Graves did well enough to find himself promoted to the larger role of the heroine's father in the following year's tour and a famous career as an 'elderly' comic was launched.

Like *The Gay Grisette*, *The Skirt Dancer* was a musical of limited ambitions, and like Dance's piece it more than fulfilled them. It was a jokey little story concocted by the actor George Ridgewell and Fenton Mackay, author of the successful farce *The J. P.* The music was from the well-known ballad composer 'H. Trotère' (né Harry Trotter) whose most notable work to date had been the inescapable 'In old Madrid'. The plot presented a patent pill manufacturer and a Captain involved in a guilty relationship with the 'naughty' lady of the title and relied on a series of farcical disguises and mistakes to bring things to a happy ending. Its lack of originality was adequately compensated for by its brightness and 'go'. *The Era* commented:

> A sprightly composition from a musical standpoint with smart dialogue and not much to speak of in the shape of plot. It is by no means deficient, however, in humour though of a somewhat boisterous type, and the piece runs with a rollicking vigour which is characteristic throughout. The audience is carried on breathlessly through a couple of acts from one droll situation to another, and the fun, if fast and furious, is undoubtedly genuine. The music includes some passages that will abide in the memory and the composer of 'In old Madrid', 'Asthore' and other well-known songs has not diminished his repute by the lyrics of *The Skirt Dancer*. Mr. Trotère has known how to captivate the public and in the present instance some of the work is worthy of being placed in line with his former successes.

It proved to be another highly popular piece on the touring circuits and its life was extended over three seasons. It also made a fine career in Australia where it was presented by George Stephenson and was played there for a number of years.

Amongst the other more successful productions were Fred Sidney's adaptation of his own comedy *A Loving Legacy* with music by the well-known teacher and sometime impresario, Odoardo Barri, which toured spring and autumn under the title of *The Terrible Turk*. Like *Black and White* it involved a middle eastern inheritance which turned out, in this case, not to be just one coloured lady but a whole harem. Our hero solved the embarrassing problem which resulted by putting them out to work as dancers in the music halls.

Otto the Outcast was a wildly melodramatic-pathetic-comic concoction set in the streets of Paris by its author-producer-star Harry Starr who had already become a fixture on the B-tour circuits with his *Carl the Clockmaker*. This startling hotch-potch of song, joke, emotion and breakdown proved as successful as its equally amazing predecessor and kept Starr touring non-stop for a number of years.

Jacko was another eclectic amalgam of comic elements and new and old songs manufactured to the lowest common denominator. It was full of farcical action, endless disguises and bred specifically for the B and C houses. It was energetically enough done to spin out its life through several seasons of unambitious and profitable performances.

One of the Family was a rather more solid and original piece of the same genre produced at Boscombe where, according to *The Era*, 'its ludicrous situations and amusing episodes kept the house in a roar.' It, too, was blessed with a good life on the smaller circuits and even took in some of the larger dates such as Glasgow, West Hartlepool, Carlisle, Stockton and York.

A certain degree of success also attended a piece described as 'comic opera', a venture into the world of the musical theatre by the West Country novelist, the Reverend Sabine Baring Gould, and adapted from his novel *The Red Spider*. Lucy Carr-Shaw, fresh from her American success in *Shamus O'Brien*, played the role of Honor Luxmore, affectionately known as 'The Red Spider' in an eighteenth-century tale of love, legacies and crooked lawyers set to music by the Scots composer Learmont Drysdale. It toured seventeen weeks, including several in Scotland.

Less fortunate was an oriental piece, *The Celestials*, for which Osmond Carr provided the score for a good team headed by J. J. Dallas, Katie Barry and John Wilkinson. It was a limp Chinese edition of 'Prince-falls-in-love-with-poor-girl-who-is-actually-his-betrothed-in-disguise' which even the efforts of its talented cast could not rescue. Finally, Arthur Law and George Byng provided a new and typical vehicle for Minnie Palmer as *The Showman's Sweetheart* which performed its function adequately without being in any way remarkable. It survived rather longer, however, than an ambitious light opera called *The Puritan Girl* which saw the light of day at Taunton in April and subsequently had a short tour.

1898

0200 **BLACK AND WHITE** a musical farcical comedy in two acts by Mark Melford. Additional lyrics by W. Sapte Jr. [Later credited to Sapte, Herbert Cottesmore and H. Trevor.] Music by John Crook. Produced at the Prince of Wales Theatre, Southampton under the management of Alexander Loftus 3 January, 1898 and toured through Jersey, Bournemouth, Oldham, Leamington/Cambridge, ?, Norwich, Kingston/?, Southend & c. Recommenced 1 August.

Lord Rook	George Arliss
Christopher	Frank Lacy/Alexander Loftus
Sir Charles Aldergate	Philip Sefton/James Leverett
Thomas Hodgekell	James Stephenson/W. Groves Watson
Mr Grinsell	Walter Rimer/Harry Rovert
Rivers	J. Franks/Thomas H. Wilson
Coolovatch	H. B. Brandreth/Harold Cotter/Percy Brough
Nanna Squiff Herse Potam	Herbert Cottesmore/George Moore
Thérèse	Bertha Cadman
Verona Carew	Alice Carlton/Lilian W. Stanley/Mary Milton
Lady Lydia	Minna Louis
Kulikullucka	Thomas H. Wilson/John Lisbourne
Madame Carew	Adeline Montagu
Deenalooloo	Florence Montgomery
Matilda	Harrie Brookes/Mary Graeme
Countess of Tabbycorn	Miss Maitland
Lady Alton	Grace Gilbert

with Lily Hassal, J. Selby

Dir: Willie Edouin; md: E. Valenza

0201 **THE ABC** or Flossie the Frivolous. A musical comedy in two acts by 'Richard Henry'. Music by 'Graban' (Granville Bantock), Gustave Chandoir *et al.* Produced at the Grand Theatre, Wolverhampton 21 March, 1898 and toured through Dublin, Newcastle, ?, Sheffield, Leeds, Stratford East and the Metropole terminating 14 May.

Christopher Booklet	Francis Hawley
Marmaduke Hyde	Frank Lacy
Macklin McGarrick	A. G. Spry
Valpy Valumy	Charles H. Kenney
Spadger	W. T. Thompson
Lord of the Manor	W. E. Pennington
Lenore Mayville	Margaret Warren
Jessamina	Marie Wright
Dotlina	Fanny Harris
Mrs Booklet	Adeline Montagu
Flossie Furbelow	Marie Lloyd

Dancers: Dollie Bell, Kate Bell

Dir: Leedham Bantock and Charles H. Kenney; md: Frank E. Tours; ch: Edouard Espinosa; sc: W. T. Hemsley

0202 **THE SKIRT DANCER** a musical comedy in two acts by George Ridgewell and Fenton Mackay (later credited to Ernest Mansell). Music by 'H. Trotère' (Harry Trotter). Produced at the Royal Artillery Theatre, Woolwich under the management of George Ridgewell 28 March, 1898 and toured through Bristol, Reading, Swindon, Merthyr Tydvil, Wakefield, Stoke, Walsall, Gloucester, Dudley to 4 June. Re-opened 27 June at Fulham, toured through Folkestone, Dover, Lowestoft, ?, Middlesborough, Oldham, Nottingham, Bury, Lincoln, Barnsley, West Hartlepool, Bishop Auckland, Newcastle, Scarborough, Halifax, Gateshead, York, Longton, Ashton-under-Lyne, Peterborough/Ipswich, Cambridge/Ealing, Swindon, Parkhurst and the Shakespeare ending 24 December. Recommenced two weeks later and toured on through 1899 and into 1900.

Lt Frank Mildmay . . . . George Ridgewell/Harry Marsden/ Harry G. Tebbutt
Sir Benjamin Mapleton . . . . Charles Seguin/Fred A. Ellis/W. H. Powell
Captain Bunting. . . . . James Grant/Fred Smythe/A. Lichfield Owen/George P. Ascot/ George Groves
Teddy . . . . Thomas C. Wray/Gus Oxley/Phil Smith
Lord Harry Parkton . . . . J. Sebastian Smith/Gordon Chasemore
James . . . . William Seguin/T. Norton
Waiter . . . . Ernest Mansell/Gus Mansell/Fred Storrie
Reginald . . . . Lennox Chandler
Gendarme . . . . Ralph Courtice/Frank Sutton/William Gardner
Gardner . . . . Fred Smythe
Butler . . . . A. E. Bird/W. Ramsden
Lady Parkton . . . . Marion Cross/Lindsay Grey/Lillian Shelbourne
Lady Charlotte Dene . . . . Nora Carewe
Mabel Mapleson . . . . Jean Douglas Wilson/Corney Daphne/ Nellie Knight/Eileen Guilbert/Marie Beaufort/Lucie Fitzroy/Edith Loveday
Mary . . . . Hilda Bretton/Winnie Davies/Maud Wright/Alice Markham
Jane . . . . Chrissie Ralland/Winnie Davies/Violet Clarence
Sarah . . . . May Wright/Alice Courtenay/Madge Godfrey & c
Lady Wimbledon . . . . Mabel Harrison & c
Lady Hyde Parker . . . . Edith Dixon/May Lyn/Mary Graeme & c
Lady Whiteford . . . . Lindsey Grey/Nana Shaw & c
Lady Beverley. . . . . Alice Markham/Alice Courtenay & c
Mary Dorcas . . . . Rose Berkley & c
Eva Bayswater. . . . . Rose Dixon/Alice Markham & c

Md: Rowland Wood/Albert Bartlett; ch: Will Bishop; sc: Bruce Smith; cos: Morris Angel

A large number of added characters included
Casino Manager. . . . . Ernest Mansell/Fred Storrie & c
Police Commissioner . . . . William Seguin/Frank Sutton & c
La Belle Fleurette. . . . . Gwennie Harcourt/Dot Harvey & c

0203 **THAT TERRIBLE TURK** (and his Loving Legacy). A musical comedy in three acts by Fred W. Sidney adapted from his own play *A Loving Legacy*. Lyrics by Eardley Turner. Music by Odoardo Barri. Produced at the Shakespeare Theatre, Clapham, under the management of Odoardo Barri 4 April, 1898 and toured through Plymouth, Torquay, Ipswich, Greenwich, ?, Blackpool, Newcastle, ? to 4 June & c.

Nicholas Babley . . . . Stephen Russell
Harry Henderson . . . . Vernon Cowper/Charles Mills
James Lovebird . . . . Frederic Jacques/Harry Fischer
Terence . . . . Charles E. Warne/George Antley
Mohammed el Rustemi . . . . W. F. Stirling/H. G. Dupres
Selim . . . . Leonard Norman
Hafiz . . . . Raymond Wood
Abdallah. . . . . Ernest Holyoake
Kitty Rorke . . . . Marie Campbell/Adele Rose/Alice Carlton
Mrs Amelia Rorke . . . . Minnie Rayner/Alice Aynsley Cook
Mabel Babley . . . . Annie Montelli/Alice Carlton/Olive Gwynne
Marie . . . . Bella Bashall

Pd: Lydia Neilson

with Olive Gwynne/Florrie Curitte, Annie Vivian, Alice Vane, Marion Mayne, Nellie Pemberton, Martha Crae, Lillie Fortescue, Alice Fortescue, Florence Elvey/Nellie Herbert,/Kitty Chandos

Dir: Frank Wyatt; md: Arnold Cooke

0204 **THE TRANSIT OF VENUS** a musical comedy in two acts by James T. Tanner. Lyrics by Adrian Ross. Music by Napoleon Lambelet. Produced at Dublin under the management of Frederick Morell and H. H. Mouillot 9 April, 1898 and toured through Edinburgh, Glasgow, Newcastle, Southport, Liverpool, Brighton and Oxford to 4 June. Recommenced 1 August at Eastbourne through Portsmouth, Swansea, Bristol, Manchester, Sunderland, Sheffield, Dublin, Crouch End and Brixton terminating 8 October.

Ninon . . . . Aida Jenoure/Cissie Saumarez
Stefanie . . . . Marie Montrose
Jack Alleyn . . . . Charles Mills/Russell Wallett/Reddick Anderson
Sir Jocelyn Parke . . . . Tom J. Redmond/James Francis
Captain Franz. Roland Cunningham
Herr Pumpernickel . . . . John F. McArdle
Graf Otto von Gluckenstein . . . . Daley Cooper
Count Stefan . . . . Edwin H. Wynne
Koppel . . . . Ralph Forster/Wilton T. Selby
Schloppel . . . . Harold L. Gordon/George T. Edwardes
Sergeant Blitz . . . . George Williams/A. J. Nicholls
Lili . . . . Ethel Netherton
Miss Parallax . . . . Marie Wynter
Bessie . . . . Eagleton Laurie/Mimi Davenport
Jessie . . . . Violet Capel/May Hallett
Cissie . . . . Connie Dyke/Muriel Seaton
Frissie . . . . Lillie Earle/Rene Lombard
First Girton Girl . . . . Ethel Clarke
Schoolmistress . . . . Miss Desmond

with Misses Langley, Davies, Pennington, Firth, Nelson, Weston, Bartlett, Brooke, Adams, Charlton, Derwent, Seaton, Clarke &c.

Dir: F. Leslie Moreton; md: Frank Barrett; sc: Harry Sydney; cos: Hal Crafter

0205 **ONE OF THE FAMILY** a musical and farcical comedy in three acts by George Capel and Fred Benton. Lyrics by Frank Dix and Frank Ayrton. Music by Henry W. May and Arnold Cooke. Produced at the Grand Theatre, Boscombe under the management of Henry Eglinton and Fred J. Little 9 April, 1898 and toured.

Captain Lightfoot . . . . Cyril Summers/James Francis/George Kendal
Terry O'Flannagan . . . . Willie Scott/Henry Eglinton
Bartelmey Crowe . . . . Harry Brayne
Hon. Herbert Berkely . . . . Frank Withers

Matthias Maggs . . . . Jack Bull/Henry Eglinton
Jeames. . . . . P. H. Brodie
Mrs Seymour . . . . Hetty Cornwallis
Emily Fanshawe. . . . . Rosie Ewart/Julia Daphne
Kate Denny. . . . . Madeleine Duval/Laura Walker
Mary . . . . May Seaton
Ruth Ann . . . . Ella Seaton
Jane . . . . Alice Cross
Martha . . . . Daisy Bernard
Susan Hopkins . . . . Dolly Harmer/Lalor Shiel

0206 **BILLY** a musical comedy in two acts by G. Cooper and Adrian Ross. Lyrics by Adrian Ross. Music by F. Osmond Carr. Produced at the Tyne Theatre and Opera House, Newcastle, under the management of Little Tich and W. H. Dawes 11 April, 1898 and toured through Hull, Bradford, Leeds, Sheffield, ?, Glasgow, Blackpool, Manchester, Nottingham and Leicester (June 25). Recommenced August 8 at Blackpool through Southport, Stoke Newington, ?, Deptford, Brighton, Scarborough Newcastle, Derby, Liverpool, Fulham, Birmingham, Halifax, Hanley, Manchester, Bolton, ?, and Stratford East to 3 December.

Hon. Billy Vavasour . . . . .Little Tich
Reggie Neville . . . . .Joe Farren Soutar
General Sir Richard Neville . . . . .Richard Temple Jr/George Paulton
Augustus Cadell. . . . . Herbert Sparling
'Enery . . . . Picton Roxburgh
Bourne . . . . George Paulton/B. Monti
Corporal Ganby. . . . . Harry Elliston
Wiggens . . . . J. H. Bishop
Ethel Neville . . . . Evie Greene/Kate Erskine
Lady Amy Kempton . . . . Gladys Carswell/Miss Price/Lillie Comyns
Harriet Trevor . . . . Aggie Morris
Becky Blisset . . . . Alice Barnett/Avis Graham

Md: Ernest Woodville; ch: Edouard Espinosa and Little Tich

0207 **THE DANDY FIFTH** an English military comic opera in three acts by George R. Sims based on *The Queen's Shilling* by G. W. Godfrey, being an adaptation of *Un Fils de Famille* by Bayard and De Belville. Music by Clarence C. Corri. Produced at the Prince of Wales Theatre, Birmingham under the management of Hardie, Von Leer and Frank A. Gordyn 11 April, 1898 and toured through Portsmouth, Plymouth, Hanley, Wolverhampton, Newcastle, Southport, Manchester and Croydon, to 11 June. Recommenced 1 August at Liverpool through Douglas, Oldham, Sheffield, Blackpool, Newcastle, Belfast, Glasgow, Edinburgh, Sunderland, Northampton, Southampton, Exeter, Plymouth, Brighton, Yarmouth, Wakefield, Bradford, Stoke Newington, Kingston, ?, Newcastle, continuing into 1899 &c.

Dick Darville . . . . Arthur Appleby (Austin Boyd)/Frank Barclay
Colonel Slasherton . . . . Leonard Calvert/Truman Towers/Cecil Fowler/Philip Sefton
Sgt-Major Millington . . . . Harry Cole/Harry Kilburn
Trooper Brown . . . . Edward Lewis/M. R. Morand/George Delaforce
Trooper Jones. . . . . Cameron Carr/Jack Crichton/Howard Law/P. Maitland
Trooper Robinson . . . . Frank Robey/Cameron Carr
Sir Victor Vavasour. . . . . Austin Boyd/Charles G. Cautley/Cecil Curtis/George Ross
Polly Green . . . . Frances Earle/Minnie Jeffs/Zoe Gilfillan/Maud Terry/Ruth Grosvenor/M. Sadie
Kate Lorrimer . . . . Ruth Davenport/Hebe Bliss/Maggie Roberts/Zoe Gilfillan

Mme von Blitzen . . . . Marie Hassell/Ada Murray/Annie Dwelley
Antoinette . . . . Hebe Bliss/L. Vernon/Mary Middleton/ Zoe Gilfillan/Pauline Hague/ Jessie Wilton
Footman . . . . L. Alan Wright

Dir: Frank Parker; md: Clarence Corri/Charles W. Johnson; ch: Will Bishop; sc: T. Holmes; cos: Lucien Besche

Produced at the Duke of York's Theatre under the management of Hardie, Von Leer and Gordyn 16 August, 1898 for an eight-week season to 8 October and then toured through Portsmouth, Metropole, ?, ?, Deptford, Birmingham, Lyric Hammersmith, Ipswich, Stratford East and the Shakespeare to 17 December.

Dick Darville . . . . H. Scott Russell
Colonel Slasherton . . . . Cecil Morton York
Sgt-Major Millington . . . . Harry Cole
Trooper Brown . . . . Edward Lewis
Trooper Jones . . . . P. Howard Sturgess
Trooper Robinson . . . . Reginald Cooper
Sir Victor Vavasour . . . . Guy Fane/Philip Sefton
Polly Green . . . . Minnie Jeffs/Eva Hamblin
Kate Lorrimer . . . . Ruth Davenport
Madame von Blitzen . . . . Ada Murray/Marie Hassall
Antoinette . . . . Jessica Lait
Miss d'Alroy . . . . Re Stephanie

with Ree Ansell, Jessie Castleton, Geraldine Wrangham, Heloise Osland, Marguerite Osland, Madge Churchill, Zara Barone, Rachel Stephanie, Una Palmer, Eva Grant, Celia Loseby, Eva Bernard, Alice Kean, Nellie Glen, Alice Calcott, Cissy Calcott, Verna Reed. James Buckland, Alfred Warner, Frank Lewis, E. Buckland, J. Newcome, J. Ivanhoe, J. d'Auvergne Edwards, H. Freeman, G. Cruttwell, Luigi Quadri, Atheling Farrar, Phil Sturgess, E. L. Carter, Howard Law, R. Coward.

Dir: Frank Parker; md: Clarence Corri; ch: Will Bishop; sc: T. Holmes; cos: Lucien Besche

208 **BILBERRY OF TILBURY** a musical farce in three acts by Silvanus Dauncey and George D. Day. Lyrics by George D. Day. Music by Guy Jones. Produced at Northampton under the management of H. Cecil Beryl 18 April, 1898 and toured through Nottingham, Derby, Manchester, Bradford, Hull, Leeds, Leicester, Birmingham, Bristol, Plymouth, Portsmouth, Brighton, Brixton, *out*, Liverpool. Opened at the Criterion Theatre 8 August, 1898 for four weeks (24 performances) before continuing the tour from Oldham (5 September) through Burnley, Huddersfield and Halifax ending 1 October, 1898.

Lord Bilberry . . . . Templar Saxe
Duke of Adstock . . . . W. J. Manning
Robert Sparrow . . . . Ernest Shand/W. T. Thompson
Adolphe Friquet . . . . Eugene Mayeur
Bertie Melton . . . . Stratton Mills
Hon. George Pipperton . . . . George Wilson
Jimmy Fanshaw . . . . Courtenay Wyley
Captain . . . . Ernest Grafton
Steward . . . . W. P. Cameron
Hallkeeper . . . . W. Fullbrook
Callboy . . . . Frances Lytton
Stella Dashwood . . . . Violet Lloyd (Margaret Warren)/ Frances Earle
Sadie Pinkhose . . . . Jennie Owen/Nell Gwynne
Priscilla Sparrow . . . . Carlotta Zerbini
Duchess of Adstock . . . . Amy Augarde
Mabel . . . . May Norton
Susie . . . . Lucy Lawrence

Gerty	Marjorie Garthorne
Amy	Alice James
Florrie	Mabel Mitchell

Dir: E. T. Steyne; md: Guy Jones; ch: Edouard Espinosa; cos: Comelli

Toured subsequently as *The Lady Detective*.

0209 **A RUNAWAY GIRL** a musical play in two acts by Seymour Hicks and Harry Nicholls. Lyrics by Aubrey Hopwood and Harry Greenbank. Music by Ivan Caryll and Lionel Monckton. Produced at the Gaiety Theatre under the management of George Edwardes 21 May, 1898 for a run of 593 performances, closing 12 January 1900 (closed from 28 July to 9 September 1899).

Brother Tamarind	Harry Monkhouse/G. P. Huntley/ William Wyes
Guy Stanley	W. Louis Bradfield
Lord Coodle	Fred Kaye/William Wyes/Alfred Asher/ G. P. Huntley
Hon. Bobby Barclay	Lawrance d'Orsay
Mr Creel	Willie Warde/Alfred Asher
Sir William Hake	Fred Wright/Alf Donohoe/Harry Phydora
Santa Cruz	Robert Selby/E. D. Wardes
Boccaccio	Mr Percival
Doloroso	A. F. Cramer
Leonello	John Coates/Robert Selby/Jack Thompson
Pietro Pascara	Edward O'Neill
Gendarmes	Leslie Holland/C. Baring/L. Deschamps W. H. Powell/S. Barry
Waiter	Walter F. Brooke/Alfred Asher/ Mr Watson
Flipper	Edmund Payne
Signor Paloni	Robert Nainby/*out*
Count Ehrenbreitstein von der Hohe	Fritz Rimma/*out*
Cooks' Agent	Harry Phydora/C. Roper Lane/*out*
Alice	Katie Seymour
Dorothy Stanley	Ethel Haydon/Grace Palotta
Lady Coodle	Madge Talbot/Kate Talby/Watt Tanner/ Maud Hobson
Agatha	Margaret Fraser/Marie Shields/ Lottie Rees
Mrs Creel	Maidie Hope/Rosie Boote/Dora Duley/ Norma Whalley
Serving maid	Marguerite Roche/Marie Fawcett/Lottie Rees/Ada Carter
Marietta	Rosie Boote/Lilian Gregory
Margherita (Flower Girl)	Cissie Vaughan
Winifred Grey	Ellaline Terriss/Coralie Blythe/ Violet Lloyd
Carmenita	Connie Ediss (Marie Shields)
Fraulein Ehrenbreitstein von der Hohe	Grace Palotta/*out*
The Misses Hake	Marie Fawcett/Fanny Dango/*out* Emilie Hervé/Florence Lauri/*out*
add Stella d'Aubigny	Margaret Fraser
Sir Arthur Haslock	Harry Phydora

Dancers: Margaret Fraser, Madge Greet/Miss Duncan, Kitty Mason/Maie Saqui, Rosie Boote with Norma Whalley, Miss Maitland, Coote, Pryor, Duncan, Dora Duley, Ada Carter, Emilie Hervé, Miss Lowell.

Dir: J. A. E. Malone; md: Ivan Caryll; ch: Willie Warde; sc: Joseph Harker and T. E. Ryan; cos: Wilhelm

Produced at Daly's Theatre, New York, under the management of Augustin Daly 31 August, 1898. Transferred to the Fifth Avenue Theatre 21 November, 1898. Closed 25 February, 1899 after a total of 216 performances.
Herbert Gresham/Frank Celli (TAM), Cyril Scott (GUY), Wilfred Clarke/Harold Vizard (COO), Eric Scott/Robert Kelly (BOB), Thomas Hadaway (CREEL), Paul McAllister/Lionel Hogarth (HAKE), Frank Regis (SC), Charles Bates (BOCC), Percy Smith (DOL), Arthur Donaldson (LEO), George Lesoir (PP), Randolph Roberts (GEND), Frank Evans (GEND), John Taylor/James Castle (WAITER), James T. Powers (FLIPPER), Henry Stanley (PAL), Mabel Gillman (AL), Yvette Violette/Adele Rafter/Adele Ritchie (DOR), Catherine Lewis (LADY), Gerda Wisner/Carolyn Gordon (MRS C), Blanche Carlisle (AG), Virginia Earle (WIN), Paula Edwardes/Elsa Ryan (CARM), Belle Harper (EHR), Marian Stuart/Marion Carlton (MARTHA), Beatrice Morgan (DOLLY), Mabelle Thompson/Frances Gordon (MAUDE), Violet Goodall (GRACE), Edith Hutchins (BERTIE), Rosa Vera/Cecilia Garrick (JESSIE), Edna Hunter/Marie Murphy/Ida Hawley/Adele Rafter (GEORGIE), Hazel Pughsley (EVA) with Carolyn Gordon, Frances Gordon, Elsa Ryan, Edna Archer, Ida Hawley, Florence Smyth, Louise Kitteridge, Grace Garrick, Edith Terry, Adelaide Phillips, Katherine Clinton, Hilda Henning, Ida Hobson, Alice Mills, Beatrice Clements, Marie Murphy, Winifred Wolcott, Victoria Stone. Dir/ch: Herbert Gresham; md: Sebastian Hiller; sc: Henry E. Hoyt; cos: Wilhelm, Dazian

Produced at the Theater an der Wien, Vienna as *Ein durchgegagnes Mädel* 2 April, 1899.

Produced at Daly's Theatre, New York under the management of Daniel Frohman 23 April, 1900 for a run of 40 performances closing 2 June, 1900.
John L. Weber (TAM), Van Rensslaer Wheeler (GUY), Maurice Abby (COO), Charles Ruthven Smith (BOB), Spottiswood Aitken (CREEL), Frank Regis (SC), Robert M. O'Neil (BOCC), Joseph Caito (DOL), Arthur Cunningham (LEO), George Lesoir (PP), Messrs Roerke & Symonds (GEND), William J. Welch (WAITER), James T. Powers (FLIPPER), Henry Stanley (PAL), Rachel Booth (AL), May Baker (DOR), Carrie Locke (LADY), Carolyn Gordon (MRS C), Mamie Walsh (AG), Marie Celeste (WIN), Paula Edwardes (CARM), Jane Schenk (EHR), Ollie Craig (MARTHA), Frances Tyson (PEARL), Beth Marr (MAUD), Isobel Hall (GRACE), Jeanette Ivel (BERTIE), Eleanor Burton (JESSIE), Almira Forrest (GEORGIE), Babe Stanley (EVA). Dir: B. D. Stevens and Edwin H. Price

0210 **THE BEAUTY STONE** a romantic musical drama in three acts by Arthur Wing Pinero and J. Comyns Carr. Music by Arthur Sullivan. Produced at the Savoy Theatre under the management of Richard D'Oyly Carte 28 May, 1898 for a run of 50 performances closing 16 July, 1898.

Philip . . . . George Devoll
Guntran . . . . Edward Isham
Simon Limal . . . . Henry A. Lytton
Nicholas Dircke . . . . Jones Hewson
Peppin . . . . D'Arcy Kelway
Seneschal . . . . Leonard Russell
Lad of the Town . . . . Charles Childerstone
Baldwyn . . . . J. W. Foster
Lord of Serault . . . . Cory James
Lord of Verlaines . . . . Hampton Gordon
Lord of St Sauveur . . . . Joe Ruff
The Devil . . . . Walter Passmore
Laine . . . . Ruth Vincent
Joan . . . . Rosina Brandram
Jacqueline . . . . Emmie Owen
Loyze . . . . Madge Moyse
Isabeau . . . . Minnie Pryce
Barbe . . . . Ethel Jackson
Shrewish Girl . . . . Mildred Baker
Matron . . . . Ethel Wilson
Saida . . . . Pauline Joran

Dir: Pinero, Carr and Sullivan; md: François Cellier; ch: John D'Auban; sc: William Telbin; cos: Percy Anderson

0211 **A GREEK SLAVE** a musical comedy in two acts by Owen Hall. Lyrics by Harry Greenbank and Adrian Ross. Music by Sidney Jones. Additional music by Lionel Monckton. Produced at Daly's Theatre under the management of George Edwardes 8 June, 1898 for a run of 349 performances closing 2 June, 1899.

Maia . . . . Marie Tempest (Maggie Roberts)/ Maud Boyd/Florence Collingbourne/ Ruth Davenport
Antonia . . . . Hilda Moody/Minnie Hunt (Margaret Ruby)/Olive Morrell
Melanopis . . . . Gladys Homfrey
Nepia . . . . Elizabeth Kirby
Circe . . . . Maggie May/Florence Jamieson/ Coralie Blythe/Jessica Lait
Licinea . . . . Elise Cook/Florence Collingbourne/ Maggie Roberts/Margaret Ruby/ Maud Le Hay/E. Barker
Flavia . . . . Olive Morell/E. Barker
Tullia . . . . Margaret Ruby/Kathleen Francis
Cornelia . . . . Alice Davis
Iris . . . . Letty Lind (Coralie Blythe)/Florence Collingbourne/Violet Lloyd
Diomed . . . . C. Hayden Coffin (Harrison Brockbank) (Conway Dixon)
Heliodorus . . . . Huntley Wright (Frank Holt) (Horace Mills)
Archias . . . . H. Scott Russell/Donald Hall/Ernest Snow
Manlius . . . . Charles Magrath/W. T. Andrews/D. Forrest Scott
Lollius . . . . A. L. Giubara/Frank Boor/Conway Dixon/ Sebastian King/Leonard Mackay
Curius . . . . Donald Hall (Sebastian King)
Marcus Pomponius . . . . Rutland Barrington (Cadwaladr King) (Akerman May)
Pd: Topsy Sinden/Rose Batchelor/Madge Rossall
add Timon . . . . Llewellyn Cadwaladr

Dir: J. A. E. Malone; md: Sidney Jones/Barter Johns; ch: Willie Warde; sc: Joseph Harker & T. E. Ryan; cos: Percy Anderson

Produced at Herald Square Theatre, New York, under the management of Fred C. Whitney 28 November, 1899 for a run of 29 performances.
Dorothy Morton (MAIA), Kate Michelena (ANT), Marion Sanger (MEL), Ethel Brougham (CIRC), Inez Rae (LI), Adine Bouvier (FL), Mittie Atherton (T), Minnie Halsey (COR), Minnie Ashley (IRIS), Hugh Chilvers (DIO), Richard Carle (HEL), Albert A. Parr (ARCH), W. H. Thompson (MAN), Ole Norman (LOLL), William Maitland (SILIUS), Arthur Stanford (CUR), Herbert Sparling (MP)

Produced at the Theater an der Wien, Vienna as *Der Griechische Sklave* 16 December, 1899.

0212 **(THE) RED SPIDER** a romantic comic opera in three acts by Sabine Baring Gould from his novel of the same title. Music by Learmont Drysdale. Produced at the Marina Theatre, Lowestoft 25 July, 1898 and toured through Ipswich, Swansea, Leamington, Exeter, Plymouth, Norwich, Reading, Walsall, Barnsley, Llandudno, Liverpool, Edinburgh, Paisley, Inverness, Aberdeen, Dundee and Coatbridge ending 26 November, 1898.

Lawyer Langford . . . . Leslie Walker
Larry Langford . . . . Frank Pemberton/Faithful Pearce
Sam Voadun . . . . J. D. Newton
Oliver Luxmore . . . . A. Pennington
Charles Luxmore . . . . Vernon Cowper/Robert Hyett

Honor Luxmore . . . . Lucy Carr-Shaw/Elaine Gryce
Stout . . . . E. Carleton/Richard Martin
Kate . . . . Alys Rees
Mrs Veale . . . . Jessie Browning
Pd: Daisy Le Hay
with May Wood, Florrie Curette, Tissie Nelson, Beatrice Shirley, Alice Hartley, Maria Barras, Freda Bevan, Fanny Lawton, Tillie Hardwick, Ada Hargreaves, Hettie Jennings, Gertrude Andrews, Rose Bramble, Mabel Ward, Dorothy Bevan, Gwendoline Bevan; A. Henfrey, M. O'Connor, C. Birney E. Mills, E. Carleton, John Aldrid, T. Warick, Mr English, Henry Watson.

Dir: Richard Temple; md: Learmont Drysdale/Walter Scott; ch: Will Bishop

213 **THE WHITE BLACKBIRD** by Frederick Bowyer and W. Edward Sprange. Music by John W. Ivimey. Produced at Croydon 1 August, 1898 and toured through Grand, Stratford East, Metropole, Brighton, Deptford, Liverpool, Oldham, Manchester, Dublin, Belfast, Salford, Hull, Edinburgh and Glasgow ending 12 November, 1898.

Nelly Catchpole . . . . Lottie Collins/Madge Merry
Charlie Glare . . . . Sidney Barraclough
Sir Armand Fleet . . . . William Lugg/A. D. Adams
Aubrey Pearce . . . . Edward Morehen
Algie Aldgate . . . . Marius Girard/Fowler Thatcher
Septimus Tweedale . . . . J. W. Henson
Dick Dreadnought . . . . G. W. Parte
Tom Weller . . . . Mr Leslie
Harry Bliss . . . . Mr Turner
Freddie Larcom . . . . Thomas E. Murray
Alphonse . . . . Guy Barrett
Duckett . . . . C. W. Bestic
Mrs Somerton . . . . Mary Denver
May . . . . Violet Friend/Alice Carlton
Juno . . . . Phyllis d'Aubigny
Julia . . . . Dora Nelson
Tilly . . . . Florrie Harmon
Lady Margate . . . . Katherine King
Dulcie . . . . Miss Sutherland
Hilda Fleet . . . . Miss Ruggles/Madeleine Rees
Dancers: Maud d'Albertson, M. Rossmore, Miss Difanger, the Sisters Righton

Dir: Alfred Davenport; md: James Tate; sc: J. Pritchard Barrett

214 **THE GAY GRISETTE** a musical farce in 2 acts by George Dance. Music by Carl Kiefert. Produced at the Theatre Royal, Bradford under the management of Robert Courtneidge and the Provincial Theatre Managers Syndicate 1 August, 1898 and toured through Leeds, Bristol, Birmingham, Liverpool, Hull, Sheffield, Nottingham, Bolton, Newcastle, Edinburgh, Glasgow, Manchester, Belfast, Dublin, Oldham, Salford, Wolverhampton and the Metropole to 10 December, 1898. Recommenced at Eccles 27 February, 1899 and toured through Grimsby, Huddersfield, Halifax, Blackburn, Sunderland, West Hartlepool, Middlesborough, Bury, Rochdale, Derby, Oldham, Manchester to 27 May, then from 2 August at the Metropole through Portsmouth, Bristol, Dublin, Blackpool, Sheffield, Hull, Leeds, Bradford, Liverpool, Manchester, Birmingham, Glasgow, Aberdeen, Dundee, Nottingham to 25 November, 1899 &c.

Captain Jack Landis . . . . Ernest Shand/Colin Mackay
Blossom . . . . Percy Clifton/George L. Montague/ E. Statham Staples
Rev. Amos Basingstoke . . . . Fred Emney/George Bastow
Colonel Pompompom . . . . Laurence Caird/George Grey[1]

[1] George Graves

Mr O'Hooley . . . . Maitland Dicker/Walter Groves/Sidney Sterling
Janos . . . . Arthur Ricketts/George Grey
Sultan Sahara . . . . Fred Winn/Maitland Dicker
Marco . . . . J. Ambrose Green/S. Graham
Lena. . . . . Addie Conyers/Violet Bessell/Nannie Meade
Miss Basingstoke . . . . Marie Hassall/Marie Anderson
Princess Lulu . . . . Amy Height (Kate Turner)/Ruby Hallier
Mabel . . . . Violet Irving/Edith Fenchester/ May Pattison
Florrie. Rosa Ravensburg/Dora Tully
Edie . . . . Edith Broad/Miss Hare
Vera . . . . Vera Dunscombe/Dolly Daintree/ Miss Leonard
Marie . . . . Louie Stafford/Miss Hague
Babette . . . . Claire Romaine/Marie Montrose/Nell Gwynne

Pd: Connie Dyke and Lillie Earle

Dir: Robert Courtneidge; md: Ernest Vousden; sc: W. R. Coleman and Conrad Tritschler; cos: Howard Russell

0215 **ORLANDO DANDO**, The Volunteer. A musical comedy in two acts by Basil Hood. Music by Walter Slaughter. Produced by Milton Bode at the Grand Theatre, Fulham, 1 August, 1898 and toured through Hastings, Plymouth, Brighton, Metropole, Eastbourne, Southport, Scarborough, Oldham, Hanley, Wolverhampton, Sheffield, Ipswich/Cambridge, Oxford, Dalston and the Shakespeare to November 19, 1898.

Orlando Dando . . . . Harry C. Barry
Thomas Turnbull. . . . . Walter Groves
Marquis of Mulberry . . . . Stuart Edgar
Packer . . . . F. W. Inwood/Edward Lohet
Gen. Turnham Green . . . . Kyrle Thornton
Sir Gregory Gargoyle. . . . . Arnold Lucy
Captain Hamilton. . . . . Dillon Shallard
Jack Beresford. . . . . Broughton Black
Crawley . . . . Alfred Lester
Bill . . . . Colin Mackay
Policeman . . . . Charles Stuart
Jonathan Q. Jefferson . . . . Edwin Brett
Gladys Jefferson. . . . . Annie Roberts
Susan Trimmer . . . . Emmeline Orford
Marie Gargoyle . . . . Kate Bishop
Betty Gargoyle . . . . Jessie Barlee
Nancy . . . . Leah Lauri
Bella Bellew . . . . Bertha Woolcote
Maud . . . . Clara Vanoni

pds: Ethel Neild, Gracie Wright, Ethel Forster/Ada Murray

Md: Walter Slaughter/Henry W. May

Milton Bode's Dan Leno Company opened 31 October, 1898 at Newcastle and toured through Liverpool, Glasgow, Birmingham, Manchester and Deptford ending 10 December, 1898. Dan Leno (OD), Johnny Danvers (TT), Edward Jephson (MARQ), Charles Thornton (GEN), E. Maule Cole (SIR), Vernon Cowper (CAPT), Charles Mills (JACK), J. G. Shuter (CRAW), James Grant (BILL), Herbert Shelley (JQJ), Elaine Gryce (GLAD), Lillie Young (SU), Alice Mansfield (MAR), Isabel Vernon (BET), Clarissa Talbot (NAN), Emily Ward (BELLA), Louie Guilford (MAUD). Pds: Maggie Crossland, May Lucas, Emmie Franks, Nellie Cort.

0216 **THE CELESTIALS** or The Flowery Land. A musical Chinese play by Charles Harrie Abbott. Lyrics by John D. Houghton. Music by F. Osmond Carr. Produced at Her Majesty's Opera House, Blackpool, 1 August, 1898 and toured through Cheltenham, Margate, Liverpool, Darlington &c.

Algernon de Bogus . . . . J. J. Dallas (Cliff Brooke)
The Tee-to-Tum . . . . H. M. Imano
Sham-Poo . . . . John Wilkinson
Prince Quahn . . . . George Sinclair
Tae Tae . . . . Katie Barry
Peek-A-Bo . . . . Gertrude Aylward
Ah Lin . . . . Marie Lucille
Norman Bluett . . . . Algernon Newark
Bob Pilado . . . . Archie Selwyn
Nancy Pilado . . . . Lydia Nelson

217 **HER ROYAL HIGHNESS** an extravaganza in two acts by Basil Hood. Music by Walter Slaughter. Produced at Bournemouth under the management of W. P. Warren Smith 22 August, 1898. Produced in London at the Vaudeville Theatre 3 September for a run of 56 performances, closing 28 October, 1898.

Rollo . . . . Louie Pounds
Fou-Fou . . . . Murray King
Court Clown . . . . W. H. Denny
Eric . . . . Frank Barclay
Bodega . . . . H. O. Clarey
Lieutenant . . . . Hugh Metcalfe
Sergeant . . . . H. M. Clifford
Footman . . . . Percy Percival
Showman . . . . William Wyes
Professional Fool . . . . W. P. Warren Smith
Prince Caramel . . . . Dorothy Foote
Captain of the Lifeguards . . . . Poppy Haines
Lord Chamberlain . . . . Bert Sinden
Court Photographer . . . . William Vokes
Mechanical Soldiers . . . . Windham Guise
George Bellamy
Ancient Mariner . . . . Ben Stirling
Citranella . . . . Mollie Lowell
Queen Placida . . . . Lillie Pounds
Showman's wife . . . . Alice Barth
Princess Petula . . . . Kitty Loftus
Solicitor . . . . O. Steggall
with Blanche Vaudon, Edith Denton, Beatrice Grenville, Miss Lennard

Dir: Frank Partner; md: Maurice Jacobi; sc: T. E. Ryan; ch: Will Bishop; cos: Lucien Besche

218 **THE SHOWMAN'S SWEETHEART** a musical comedy in three acts by Arthur Law. Lyrics by Arthur Law and Guy Eden. Music by George Byng. Produced at the Queen's Theatre, Crouch End, 29 August, 1898 and toured through Margate, Folkestone, Sheffield, Hull, Manchester, Nottingham & c, ending at Newcastle 10 December.

Sir Joseph Strudwick . . . . F. Joynsen Powell
Spencer Charteris . . . . Clarence Hague
Dick Seymour . . . . Phillips Tomes
Bowler . . . . George Robinson
Ben Odger . . . . Austen Hurgon
Joseph Hawker . . . . James Skea
Miss Sophia Strudwick . . . . Maude Marlowe
Miss Nora Strudwick . . . . Nora Benson
Maggie . . . . Adelaide Aylmer
Carrie . . . . Nellie Groome
Nellie . . . . Mai Daintry
Lottie . . . . Ethel Lyndale
Jennie . . . . Minnie Desmond
Kittie . . . . Nellie Harlon
Lizzie . . . . Kittie Chalmers

Pollie . . . . Mabel Murray
Belle Hawker . . . . Minnie Palmer

0219 **MILORD SIR SMITH** a musical comedy in two acts adapted from the French of Henri de Gorsse and Georges Elwall by George D. Day and Adrian Ross. Music by Edward Jakobowski. Produced under the title *Campano* at the Grand Theatre, Leeds, under the management of Arthur Roberts 8 September, 1898 and toured through Leeds, Manchester, Liverpool, Bradford, Sheffield, Leicester, Belfast, Hull, Nottingham[1], Birmingham[1], and Brighton[1] terminating 19 November. Opened in a revised version at the Comedy Theatre 15 December, 1898 for a run of 82 performances closing 4 March, 1899.

Sir Robert Smith, Bart . . . . Arthur Roberts
M. Ligereau. . . . . Robert Nainby
M. Poribelle. . . . . J. T. MacMillan
Major MacLachlan . . . . Charles Wibrow
O'Reilly . . . . John W. Braithwaite
Philoxène Bosse . . . . Watty Brunton Jr/Algernon Newark
Piccolo. . . . . H. Enes Blackmore
Campano . . . . Alfred Fisher
Celeste. . . . . Ada Reeve
Angélique . . . . Ethel Sydney
Mlle Tournesol . . . . Alice Aynsley Cook
Ninette . . . . Alice Betelle/Bessie Pelissier
Madame Poribelle. . . . . Marguerite Aubert/May Clifton/ Ethel Bartlett
Edmée . . . . Ida Winton
Fifine . . . . Bessie Pelissier/Ada Wood
Geneviève . . . . Kate Worth
Henriette . . . . Enid St Maur
with Misses Abbot, Milton, Bartlett, Irvine, Benson, Mabel Wallis, Lillyan Lait, May Karl, Gertie Singlehurst, Marie Kenrick, Emily Mori, Chiddie Mori, Terry Frazieur, Gertrude James, Addie Burney, Ida Heron, Poppy Melville, Lillian Holmes, Gerty Muir, Belle Lytham, Olive May; Messrs J. Winterbottom, T. J. Lane, Albert Hayzen, A. Churton, Tom Sheridan, G. Sykes, J. Pridmore, W. Gillette.

Md: Howard Talbot

From January 25 was introduced 'a drama in six compressed tabloids' entitled *The Tree Dumas-Skiteers* written by Adrian Ross with music by Augustus Barratt.

D'Artagnan and others . . . . Arthur Roberts
Hothouse . . . . T. Sheridan
Pothouse. . . . . Charles Braithwaite
Bonifacieux/Landlord . . . . J. T. MacMillan
Louis XIII/Duke of Buckingham . . . . Robert Nainby
Arrymiss. . . . . Alfred Fisher
Roquefort . . . . Tom Birch
Planchet . . . . H. Huddlestone
The Stranger . . . . Algernon Newark
Richelieu . . . . Ells Dagnall
The Queen . . . . Alice Aynsley Cook
Constance Gabrielle. . . . . Kate Worth
'Mi Lidy' . . . . Ada Reeve

The original cast of *Campano* on tour was:

De Maviettes . . . . Arthur Roberts
M. Ligereau. . . . . Ferdinand Gosschalk/Stratton Mills
Poribelle. . . . . J. T. MacMillan

[1] Performed in repertoire with *A Modern Don Quixote*.

Piccolo	Augustus Cramer
D'Escarpin	Jo Monkhouse
Campano	Henry Walsham/
Baptiste	Walter McEwan
Landurin	A. Hayzen
Mme Ligereau	Maud Hobson/Frances Earle
Ninette	Annie Halford/Amy Farrell
Mme Poribelle	Mary Webb
Mlle Tournesol	Kate Osborne/Amy Singleton
Suzette	Lillian Pollard
Margot	Sybil Champion
Clairette	Lillian Champion
Josephine	Marie Guest
Captain Gigot	Tom Birch
Sous-Lt Philibert	Austin Churlton
Celeste	Juliette Nesville/Amy Augarde
Alphonse	Ed Reddway

0220 **LITTLE MISS NOBODY** a musical comedy in two acts by H. Graham. Music by Arthur E. Godfrey. Additional music by Landon Ronald. Added songs by Paul and Walter Rubens. Produced at the Lyric Theatre under the management of Tom B. Davis 14 September, 1898 for a run of 200 performances closing 18 March, 1899.

The Earl of Cripplegate	Cairns James
Guy Cheviot	Yorke Stephens/John Coates/Francis Stewart
Gussie Stilton	Lionel Mackinder/George Grossmith Jr/ Ernest Lambart
Dominie Crockett	Lionel Brough
Christopher Potter	Fred Eastman/John Le Hay/William Elton
Dandy Triplet	Frank Lacy/Robb Harwood
Jock Jameison	Ernest Hendrie
Lady Cheviot Stilton	Maria Davis
Violet	Alice de Winton/Daphne Powell
Lady Gwendoline	Lois Everard/Ida Yeoland
Lady Geraldine	Nellie Evelyn/Miss Singlehurst
Lady Marjoline	Mabel Tempest/Hilda Stephens/Miss Halliday
Maggie	Helen Leyton
Tiny Triplet	Lydia West/Fanny Dango/Marie Barnett
Tootsie Triplet	Dora Dent
Trixie Triplet	Gracie Leigh
Elsie Crockett	Kate Cutler (Alice Burke)

Pd: Darine Kerry
Dancers: Lily MacIntyre, Maud Rundell, Florence Wilson, Lucy Murray, May Lynn, Ethel Maynard, L. Pulvermacher/Beatrice Grenville, Gladys Horwell, Fanny Dango, Daisy Jackson.

Dir: Yorke Stephens; md: Landon Ronald; ch: John D'Auban; sc: Warings; cos: Percy Anderson

Produced at the Broad Street Theatre, Philadelphia under the management of Charles Frohman and Al Hanby 5 September, 1898 for two weeks.
Cast included Ethel Jackson (ELSIE), Jessie Merrilees, Minnie de Ren, Agnes Paul, Beatrice Vaughan, Sara Miskel, Nettie Neville, Frances Dennison, Lettie Bryan, Josephine Stevens, Fritz Williams, William Sampson, Charles Plunkett, Robert Cotton, Edwin Hanford, Thomas Ricketts.

Film: (silent) Carlton Productions 1923. Screenplay/Director: Wilfred Noy
Alfred Clark (EARL), John Stuart (GUY), Donald Searle (GUS), Sydney Paxton (DOM), Ben Field (CHR), Aubrey Fitzgerald (JOCK), Eva Westlake (LADYC), Gladys Jennings (VI), Flora le Breton (MISS NOBODY), James Reardon (MANAGER)

OTTO THE OUTCAST or The Bird-Seller Of Paris. A musical comedy-drama by Harry Starr. Produced at the Grand Theatre, Nelson under the management of Harry Starr 4 April, 1898 and toured.

Roderigue d'Estalier/Dr Coquedille/ Prince Ranjani	T. Greenwood Croft
Marquis Marcel de la Porte	Conrad Clerke
Augustine Carotte	F. W. Graham
Daddy Bruneau	David Beattie
Hungry Adolphe	Eric C. Merrie
Bosquet the Barker	Walter Dunlo
Father Friseau	W. Gossett
Monsieur Dubourgh	Bernard Mostyn
Jacques Sillon	Carlson Hill
Wally the Waster	George Jukes
Corinne Jarbeau	Christine Bonneville
Marchioness d'Anvilliers	Madge Blundell
Madame de Chaumont	Rose Rayne
Susette	Edna Lester
Lara	Ethel Danbury
Otto	Harry Starr

1899

Three British musicals, *A Runaway Girl*, *A Greek Slave* and *Little Miss Nobody* carried through into 1899 accompanied by a seasonal revival of *Alice in Wonderland* at the Opera Comique. The revival of France's *La Poupée* was still there running into its final weeks at the Prince of Wales, and *The Belle of New York* represented the United States at the Shaftesbury.

Both *A Runaway Girl* and *The Belle of New York* were to survive the full year and pass into the twentieth century and, in consequence, no new pieces were needed for either the Gaiety or the Shaftesbury. But the other theatres were at some time obliged to look for new material. For the first half of the year these were mostly either revivals or foreign-bred pieces.

Tom Davis, who had made such a notable début as a producer with *Little Miss Nobody*, closed his successful season at the Lyric in March, continuing, however, to collect considerable revenues from two companies touring his popular piece. But Davis had now taken a long lease of the Lyric and was obliged to find a new show to take over where *Little Miss Nobody* had left off. French musicals had, with the success of *La Poupée*, once again become interesting to London managers and it was to the French that Davis turned to produce a version of Prével and Liorat's *L'Amour Mouillé* with music by Louis Varney. In contemporary fashion he had the piece anglicised with additional numbers by Landon Ronald and Paul and Walter Rubens and he equipped it with his best *Little Miss Nobody* cast – Kate Cutler, John Le Hay, Fred Eastman, Cairns James – with the addition of the young provincial singer/actress, Evie Greene. Miss Greene made a personal hit but the show did not. In spite of a belated anglicisation of the title to *Cupid and the Princess* and some heavy publicity, it closed after only seven weeks.

Having failed with the French, Davis followed up with an American piece, John Philip Sousa's Broadway success *El Capitan* with its original star, De Wolf Hopper, the great American singing comedian. This was somewhat more successful and stayed on until Davis had his pièce de résistance ready for production, the first stage musical from the hugely successful songwriter, Leslie Stuart. When Stuart's *Florodora* opened in November, *El Capitan* was moved to the Comedy to finish its respectable 140-performance run.

Another foreign piece which came to grief was *The Coquette* which was chosen by Henry Lowenfeld to follow his stop-gap revival of *La Poupée*. The nationality of *The Coquette* is slightly difficult to define, but it may best be categorised as Portuguese, for it was in Lisbon's Theatre Trinidad that its prototype had first been staged in 1887 under the title *O Moliero d'Alcala* (*The Miller of Alcala*). Its music was by Justin Clérice who had also been responsible for the score of Lowenfeld's previous failure, *The Royal Star*, and the English version of the piece had been prepared by Henry (*Shop Girl*) Dam and songwriter Clifton Bingham. It was, for all that it had been Clérice's very first performed work, clearly a better piece than *The Royal Star*, but on the first night the Prince of Wales' gallery found it quite unpalatable and hissed and hooted its disapproval. Lowenfeld was furious and marched onto the stage to challenge the demonstrators with allegations that they were a paid claque. An angry dialogue blew up between manager, gallery and an interfering journalist in the stalls, and Lowenfeld finally stalked off. A little more than a month later, in spite of the fact that *The Coquette* was doing quite reasonable business, Lowenfeld withdrew it and sold his lease on the Prince of Wales Theatre, disgusted by the apparently unreasoning vagaries of the theatre world which had made him, and then lost him, a fortune.

Another attempt at anglicisation was made at the Savoy. D'Oyly Carte laid hands on the French opérette *L'Étoile* written by Leterrier and Vanloo with music by Chabrier, performed originally at Paris' Bouffes-Parisiens in 1877/8. Since those days, *L'Étoile* had been americanised by Cheever Goodwin and Woolson Morse as *The Merry Monarch* and presented at New York's Broadway Theatre (1890) in a production by Carte's director, Richard Barker. It had lasted less than two months. However, Carte, doubtless with Barker's encouragement, decided on an English version. Charlie Brookfield, Adrian Ross and Aubrey Hopwood had a go at the book and lyrics, taking from the French original and the American adaptation at will, while Ivan Caryll set to work on an almost completely new score. Finally, Mrs D'Oyly Carte herself organised the enormous amount of material into a presentable shape and length and, on 7 January 1899, the resulting piece opened at the Savoy under the title *The Lucky Star*.

The outlines of Leterrier and Vanloo's story had managed to survive. King Ouf is about to execute the boy Lazuli when it is discovered that the lad has been born under the same star-sign as the King and that their fates are linked. For the rest of the evening Ouf goes to great lengths to keep Lazuli alive and happy, even to the extent of naming him as his heir and his son-in-law, 'safe' in the knowledge that the heir is destined to predecease the King by a day.

The new show gave Chabrier no billing and not without reason, for of all his charming music only a portion of one finale remained. Ivan Caryll's new music was in a different, more contemporary and popular vein, but it was not entirely appreciated by the critics and *The Times* demanded, understandably, why, if Carte wished to produce *L'Étoile*, he had not retained Chabrier's highly attractive original score. With all the 'contributions' which had been made by the team responsible for *The Lucky Star*, the resulting piece was virtually a new musical and it was one which, while it did not attract wholehearted approval from press and audience, had sufficient pleasing features to ensure that it kept running where *Jane Annie* and *The Beauty Stone* had not. It was clear, however, that the show as produced would not do and the collaborators were obliged immediately to introduce some major revisions. When the *Times* critic returned to see the second version of *The Lucky Star* some two months later he found that considerable alterations had been made, large rewrites in the dialogue and five new numbers being not the least of them, and he was moved to note:

> Few comic operas run any length of time without some doctoring. Fewer are so successfully doctored as *The Lucky Star* which is now not only one of the prettiest but also one of the best and pleasantest pieces in town.

It was not only the text which had been revised to such effect. The show's comic content had been enhanced by the addition to the cast of Fred Wright Jr in the key role of the Astrologer, Siroco. Wright's low comedy proved an effective contrast to the more traditional Savoy fooling of Walter Passmore. The dance content of the show was also increased and Katie Vesey was brought in to be featured as a solo dancer. But *The Lucky Star*, for all its attractions, was not destined to re-found the fortunes of the Savoy. It had a respectable run of 143 performances after which it was replaced by a revival of *H.M.S. Pinafore* which added another 174 performances to that old favourite's score before Carte's newest offering, *The Rose of Persia*, was ready to take over in November.

The Lucky Star and *The Coquette* both had an international pedigree, and both had come to Britain after overseas productions. *The Prince of Borneo* had equally international origins but it was to see daylight, albeit briefly, for the first time on the West End stage. Its libretto was officially credited to the Anglo-American comedian and writer, Joseph Herbert, and seems to have been a version of the play *The Man from Borneo* by actor-manager Frank Wheeler, played the previous year in South Africa. Herbert was not without references. As a performer he had starred on Broadway opposite Marie Tempest in *The Algerian*, in Victor Herbert's *The Fortune Teller* and a host of British musicals; as an author he had been responsible for the burlesques *Thrilby* in which he had also starred and *The Geezer*, a parody of *The Geisha* which had been staged at the new Weber and Field's Music Hall. His book for *The Prince of Borneo* betrayed his burlesque background with its heavy humour but, in this case, he did not parody the traditions and conventions of the musical but rather collected them all together and cobbled them into a plot using all the timeworn disguise/mistaken identity/love and marriage themes of the contemporary musical farce.

In The *Prince of Borneo*, the heroine, Nadine, has been engaged since birth to her cousin, Nicholas Kromeski, but having grown up she is in love with the handsome Paul. Kromeski, in the meanwhile, has gone to Borneo and taken a wife. In order that all shall evolve for the best, Kromeski and Paul exchange identities. Mixed in with this plot is another involving Kromeski's native servant who is disguised as the prince of the title, and yet another involving the ex-actress Madame Samovar who is anxious to disconnect herself from a nude painting for which she posed in the days before becoming respectable. A mole on her knee, however, proves rather damning. The plot, or plots, were by current standards rather over-complicated and reminiscent of provincial farce-melodrama, too many of their elements having been seen too recently and frequently in such pieces as *The Ballet Girl*. The bulk of the music for *The Prince of Borneo* was composed by the British composer, Edward Jones, but the show provided the opportunity for the co-lessee of the Strand Theatre, Anglo-American George H. Broadhurst, who had already used his theatre as a home for his latest plays *Why Smith Left Home* and *Whatever Happened to Jones*, to dabble in composition and he contributed several songs of his own to the score. The show failed to make an impression. *The Times* dismissed it as: 'not the best entertainment of its kind we have seen, but it is by no means the worst . .' whilst *The Era* found it too sentimental and insufficiently funny. The opening night audience were less pleased. They gave the show a poor reception, not the least because of what *The Stage* called:

> not too tasteful jokes and dialogue and the most unpleasant and objectionable song introduced by Miss Cissie Fitzgerald whose 'wink' so popular across the Atlantic is happily not likely to be appreciated at so high a figure in London.

Wheeler, Herbert and Broadhurst had erred in judging the moral taste of the London turn-of-the-century audience whose 'naughtiness' was then, as since, grossly over-rated. Cissie Fitzgerald, who had scored a huge hit with a 'Winking' song in America (where the music-hall euphemisms had much the same meanings as in London) had none of the scabrous finesse of a Marie Lloyd and her 'turn' in *The Prince of Borneo* was unpleasantly out of place. Miss Fitzgerald was also the centre of the piece of business concerning the delicately situated mole which was 'plot', laboriously insisted on throughout the show. Harry Dam, another American, had introduced a similar element (a strawberry mark) into his book for *The Shop Girl.* It had aroused an angry reaction from audience and critics, and had been quickly removed from the libretto. In this case it was the unappreciated Miss Fitzgerald who was removed, mole and all, and the tried and true, popular and unsuggestive Phyllis Broughton took over the role of Madame Samovar. But *The Prince of Borneo* was not salvageable. After four weeks plus it was removed and, though it made an appearance on the touring schedules of the following year under Frank Wheeler's management, its unfortunate life had to all intents and purposes finished.

Among the carnage of the first ten months of 1899 there were also a couple of more genuinely native pieces, both opening in the final days of April.

Late in 1898 a slightly dubious gentleman by the name of Arthur Eliot had taken a lease on the poor old Opera Comique, now far from its glorious days of *The Sorcerer*, *H.M.S. Pinafore*, *The Pirates of Penzance* and *Patience*. Eliot, who had been through the bankruptcy courts only three years previously, had been dabbling in a venture known as The Dental Therapeutic Company which devoted itself to the manufacture of false teeth. But he had theatrical ambitions, and at Christmas he took a year's lease on the younger of the 'Rickety Twins' to produce a revival of the Walter Slaughter/Savile Clarke version of *Alice in Wonderland.* It was an enormous success, playing thrice daily for part of its season to accommodate the demand for seats. Eliot took for himself the plum role of the Mad Hatter while his wife played the Queen of Hearts and the White Queen.

At the end of the season, which continued till March in tandem with *The Brixton Burglary*, Eliot had made as his share an amazing £2,000 profit. The theatre was obviously a better investment than false teeth. He looked around for something else to fill his theatre and lit upon a burlesque piece called *Great Caesar* which had been written by the younger Grossmith as a possible vehicle for himself, with Arthur Roberts as Caesar. Eliot fancied himself in the role intended for the more famous Arthur, and made preparations to produce *Great Caesar* at the Opera Comique with Grossmith as Antony and the lovely Ethel Ross-Selwick as Cleopatra. But it was not to be.

The recent closings of *Little Miss Nobody* and *Milord Sir Smith* had left some rather more reputable managements and performers free–including Arthur Roberts. It seems to have been Grossmith who persuaded Eliot to let *Great Caesar* go in favour of Yorke Stephens who had taken the Comedy Theatre and was prepared to engage Roberts. Undoubtedly Eliot profited financially from his magnanimity but he was left without a play for the Opera Comique. His choice fell upon that most successful and long-lived of touring shows, *Skipped by the Light of the Moon*, whose peripatetic career had embraced thousands of performances all over the world and, notably, under the aegis of the Walton family, in the British provinces. *Skipped by the Light of the Moon* was being prepared for another year's touring but Eliot summoned it instead to the Opera Comique. There was no question of ousting the Walton brothers from the leading roles of Crackle and Dingle, so Eliot contended himself with jollying up the minor role of P.C. XL for himself, while his wife did rather better with the role of Mrs

Crackle. The score of *Skipped* had, as was common in that kind of variety musical, always been a fairly chimeric thing. Numbers came and went and the present version bore little resemblance musically to the version seen at Reading in 1896 on the occasion of its first British production. The present score ranged from 'Dancing in the Light of the Moon' through 'Not with *Those* on', 'If any of them Looked at me' and 'There's Something about the English after All' to a 'Pitter Patter' trio, a lullaby and a duet about 'Tact'.

Under the new title of *A Good Time*, the old piece opened on 27 April. But it was not West End fare. In spite of its out-of-town credentials, or perhaps because of them, Londoners found it crude and unsophisticated. Its knockabout antics and variety turns were not for them. One journal summed it up in its one word review: 'No.' *A Good Time* closed after three weeks and the Opera Comique sat sad and empty until it was pulled down a few years later to make way for the development of the Aldwych. Arthur Eliot's adventure was over. He had not enough left to pay the rent on 'his' theatre and he ended up back in the bankruptcy courts.

Two days after the opening of *A Good Time*, *Great Caesar* opened at the Comedy. Stephens had not succeeded in booking Roberts to play Caesar and had turned instead to the star of *La Poupée*, Willie Edouin. The much loved Willie had signed along with Louie Freear to sail to New York to take the lead in *The Man in the Moon*, a new spectacular piece from the pens of Liverpudlian/American Stanislaus Stange and Louis Harrison, but Stephens induced him to break his contract and take the role of Julius Caesar. Author Grossmith would play Mark Antony and as Cleopatra – a far cry from thoughts of the dignified Miss Ross-Selwick – he cast Ada Reeve who was still doing her nightly hop and skip between the Comedy and the Palace music hall.

Great Caesar was a throwback. It was billed as burlesque and it bowed to all the traditions and conventions of that all-but-forgotten genre. It was written in rhyming couplets – small wonder the ad-libbing Roberts had turned it down – and tried to make humorous capital out of the use of ancient Roman anachronisms, a form of 'wit' by now in well-merited disrepute. It did not, in the manner of the best of the older burlesques, carefully caricature its subject but like the later works had little beyond its characters' names to relate it to its professed model. In Grossmith's version of Shakespeare's play, Caesar manages to escape the murder plot of Brutus and Cassius when the conspirators mistakenly stab a mummy brought to him as a gift from Cleopatra. He goes underground and surfaces in disguise as the manager of the Coliseum where most of the principal characters subsequently turn up as offerings to the lions. Finally virtue (Caesar and family) triumphs over evil (the rest).

> 'So silly that one cannot help laughing at it' . . fortunately for *Great Caesar* it was in this tolerant attitude that the majority of the audience received the new burlesque on Saturday evening. A few of them evidently expected something more than schoolboy humour and rough and tumble pantomime but their sounds of dissatisfaction were drowned by approving voices . . . the authors have had to eke out their small halfpennyworth of wit with a great deal of the ordinary stuff of musical farce. But they have between them invented some really comic business and with Mr Willie Edouin to help it out, *Great Caesar* is, at any rate, funny enough to make people laugh (*Times*)

> There is much that is trivial, 'slangy', puerile, tedious . . there are also laughable things and clever things, and very suitable music by Paul and Walter Rubens, the songs, the dances the dresses and assuredly not least the general talents of the company are sources of strength to the whole . . (*Stage*)

> . . completely out-of-date . . . the authors of *Great Caesar* were most tedious . . . when they observed some of the traditions of that dead and buried form of entertainment . . . many very dull moments . . . superfluity of pointless dialogue . . . groans and hisses . . . (*Era*)

It was long, often juvenile and tedious, but it also had Willie Edouin and it had Ada Reeve and within quite a short time under their influence *Great Caesar* underwent more than a few changes. The dialogue was slashed to get the piece down to under three hours' playing time, and then cut some more. The scene set in the arena of the Coliseum became a variety free-for-all and Willie Edouin introduced into it a bare-back circus act and comic dance which went down well, whilst Ada Reeve introduced some comic business with that novel invention, the Edison phonograph, to add to her music-hall numbers and her love scenes with Grossmith. Her tale of the production of these last scenes points out a problem at the heart of *Great Caesar*: the author/actor wanted the Antony and Cleopatra scenes played straight. The lady took one glance at her partner's goggle eyes and knobbly knees and firmly decided otherwise.

The public, in spite of Willie and Ada and others of a good cast, also decided otherwise. They were not interested in *Great Caesar*. It ran for two expensive months before being relegated to the provincial circuits £1200 in the red. Willie must have eyed ruefully the 192-performance Broadway run of *The Man in the Moon*, and sighed at Louie Freear's outstanding success therein. Ada Reeve had no such regrets. Her nightly double stand might be over, but she had in her pocket a contract for Daly's theatre and was headed back to work under the banner of George Edwardes as lead soubrette in his new Chinese piece, *San Toy*.

When, after a year's run, it became necessary to replace *A Greek Slave* at Daly's, the new show *San Toy* had not been completed. The Daly's triumvirate which had reigned so successfully had already been broken, for Owen Hall was not writing the book for the new piece. That had been submitted by the writer and critic Edward A. Morton, a long time journalist and most famous as 'Mordred' of *The Referee*. Morton (né Eleaza Aaron Moses) was the author of 'Travellers Tales' and had been previously represented on the London stage by the one-act play *Miss Impudence* at Terry's in 1892.

On 26 February the old coalition was shattered beyond repair when Harry Greenbank, aged only 33, died of consumption at his new home in Boscombe where he had gone with his family some twelve months previously for the benefits of the sea air. During his short career Greenbank had provided many of the happiest and most popular lyrics of the British musical stage, and had ranked with Adrian Ross at the head of their profession as writers of lyrics for the new-style British musical. Greenbank had been responsible for *A Gaiety Girl*, *An Artist's Model*, *A Greek Slave*, *The Circus Girl*, *A Runaway Girl*–so many hit shows with so many hit songs–as well as for the book and lyrics of the ill-treated *Monte Carlo*, and he had been instrumental in the development of the Daly's musical to its high standard of workmanship and popularity, most memorably seen in *The Geisha*. His epitaph came from the hand of his colleague, Ross:

> Under the shadow of the wings of death,
> He gave us laughter for our leisure time,
> Shaping with failing and and ebbing breath
> His stainless humour into faultless rhyme.
> He met the looming menace of the grave
> Year after year; and when it came to fall,
> He passed into the dimness, bright and brave,
> A dearer friend to some, a friend to all.

And it was Ross who took over the songs of *San Toy* where his friend had left off.

A revival of *A Gaiety Girl* did service as a stop-gap before the theatre was closed for the stage rehearsals of *San Toy* which opened in October and changed the fortunes of the year as the first of three 1899 hits – two palpable (*San Toy* and *Florodora*) and one d'éstime (*The Rose of Persia*).

But the course of *San Toy* to its first night was not destined to run smoothly. The death of Greenbank was followed by the defection, in rehearsal, of one of the show's stars. Edwardes had always managed to maintain the balance of power between Marie Tempest and Letty Lind at Daly's. Miss Lind having departed, he had brought in Ada Reeve and that balance was upset. Miss Reeve considered herself engaged as chief soubrette, and the role which Morton had constructed for Marie Tempest – the title role of a girl disguised as a boy – was, in Miss Reeve's opinion, the chief soubrette role. Edwardes did not believe that Ada's voice was equal to the demands or the tessitura of the songs . . . . and, anyway, this was Daly's and the role was Miss Tempest's. Miss Reeve was cast as the maid, Dudley.

The atmosphere between the two prime donne grew stiffer during rehearsals. On one occasion, as Miss Tempest prepared for a solo, she noticed Ada still on the stage and pointed out sweetly that the script read 'Exeunt Omnes'. Ada pointed out equally sweetly that she was not Omnes, she was Dudley. Omnes meant the chorus, and until the script said 'Exit Dudley' she would remain where she was. Needless to say, Miss Tempest was not slow to score back. It was Ada, with the lesser role, who finally cried enough and quit the show, and Gracie Leigh, who had been touring for Edwardes in *The Merry-Go-Round*, got the role of Dudley.

By the time the opening night was reached the troubles seemed over. Everything went perfectly and *San Toy* was immediately and obviously a huge hit. The recipe had been got wholly right this time. Ancient Rome abandoned, a return had been made to the picturesque Orient – China instead of *The Geisha*'s Japan, although the pictorial differences were minimal – and the same combination of English officer and native lady were set at the centre of the plot.

San Toy is the daughter of a mandarin but she has been raised as a boy to evade the consequences of a law drafting young ladies into a female regiment serving the Emperor. Her femininity is no secret, however, to Captain Bobby Preston, her naval lover, nor to Fo Hop his would-be Chinese rival. An elopement is forestalled by a new law drafting the sons of mandarins into the army. Rather than be called up, San Toy admits her sex and is put into the ladies' corps where she attracts the amorous attentions of the Emperor. But the stars conveniently decree that he should wed Wun Lung, a large perpetual corporal of the female guard, so San Toy is left free to wed her Bobby. The plot was decidedly reminiscent of James Tanner's *Transit of Venus*, but that was of small importance as Morton's libretto, or what remained of it after swingeing alterations in rehearsal, had become a grand tale with a bevy of suitable characters and lively and amusing situations and dialogue.

Rutland Barrington, who had been rather under-parted in *A Greek Slave*, fared better in the role of Yen How, the father of the heroine and the possessor of a Chinese harem of six little wives:

YEN HOW: Oh, my name is Yen How, I'm a mandarin great,
And this is my famous umbrella of state
And these are the robes that my office contrives
And these, if you please, are my six little wives.
WIVES: Yes, we are his six little wives
Kow tow, kow tow to the great Yen How

And wish him the longest of lives
With his one little, two little, three little
Four little, five little, six little wives!

Barrington scored enormously as he related how various failings might compel him, one by one, to get rid of his wives and, in the last verse, with all gone, to start all over again with a fresh half dozen. Even more popular was his second number, 'I Mean to Introduce it into China', a variation on the *Utopia (Limited)* theme:

I used to think a Chinaman
Was twenty times a finer man
As any born of European nations:
Our manners were superior
To anything exterior
And had been so for many generations.
But now there's not a doubt of it
That China will be out of it
Unless we can effect a vast improvement
We'll copy the variety
Of Western high society
And I will be the leader of the movement.
So we'll imitate the styles
Of the blessed British Isles
Though the reason isn't easy to divine-ah!
But they do it in the West
So of course it must be best
And I mean to introduce it into China!

The verses mixed the satiric and the social with the blatantly patriotic (fuelled by the growing Boer war) and Barrington had his biggest hit since his Savoy days.

Huntley Wright repeated his *Geisha* impersonation of a comic Chinee, and once again succeeded in bringing down the house, notably with his song 'Chinee Soje-Man' (Chinese Soldierman) in which the simple Chinese soldier is compared to the British, the French, the German and the Boer equivalent, all in the almost incomprehensible Chinee lingo Wright had developed and which his audiences could obviously understand quite easily:

Blitish sojeman in led
Lady's muffee topside head
Always dlilling, getting shilling
Evly day with beef and bread.
Chinee soje cuttee dash
Longee pigtail and moustache
Captain collar piecee dollar
Sojeman get copper cash
Oh, Chinee sojeman
He wavee piecee fan
He shoutee hip holaay for Empelor
Him beatee bigee dlum
Make eveythingee hum
When Chinee soje marchee out to war

The same pidgin was used for two duets with Gracie Leigh who had the female comedy largely to herself as well as two Lionel Monckton numbers, the unexceptional 'Ladies'

Maid' and the much more sprightly 'Rhoda and her Pagoda', telling how Miss Rhoda Rye sets up a Chinese tea-house in the Strand built like a pagoda. She succeeds in attracting society to her shop and, inevitably, hooks herself a stray duke.

In the romantic roles, Marie Tempest and Hayden Coffin were well supplied with typical and attractive ballads and duets. Coffin was given one of his prettiest songs of recent years with 'Love has Come from Lotus Land', while Miss Tempest had the charming 'The Petals of the Plum Tree' and the zoological (*pace* Letty Lind), 'The Butterfly'. Their duet 'A.B.C.' was rather reminiscent of, among others, the kissing duet from *The Geisha* but, like the many other elements which the two pieces shared, fared none the worse for that.

In many respects, however, *San Toy* was quite different from its predecessor. The opening scene of the show was surprising in its seriousness. In it San Toy's old nurse, Chu, is shown being led to the suttee pyre after the death of her husband. Changing her mind about such a death, she escapes her attendants and seeks sanctuary at the door of Sir Bingo Preston, the British consul. But for having been preceded by a lovely opening chorus, the scene could have belonged to a very different type of show. With that scene, Morton set a background of sincerity for the frivolities which were to follow and established the theme of the disparity of Eastern and Western cultures and customs upon which his work, like *The Geisha*, was based. If, thereafter, the libretto became thinner and less well-constructed with regard to the elaboration of the plot and the theme, it was only to allow the other elements of the musical – the song, the dance and the spectacle – to take their rightful place. The combination was clearly in the right measure for popular success and the triumph of *San Toy* was never for a moment in doubt. In typical Edwardes' style, all the production values were beautifully maintained and the minor roles in the show were cast with a caring precision which clearly made an effect. It is interesting to note how some of the lesser players of *San Toy* stuck in the memories of reminiscers:

> Two items will surely never be forgotten by those who saw them – the Pas Seul danced by that fine artiste, Topsy Sinden, in the second act, and the inimitably funny walk of the diminutive Fred Kaye . . . (D. Forbes Winslow)

> A minor memory is Akerman May's astonishing make-up as Sing-Hi, President of the Board of Ceremonies. The aged Chinaman was there to the fingernails, and the strange collection of curios which the actor made to complete his portrait included the thumb ring of white jade, the tortoise-shell spectacles complete with case, and the Cantonese fan and tassel . . After fifty years one can remember Sing-Hi, and this without the least recollection of any song, dance or jest, if the part of Sing-Hi was thus dowered[1] (Ernest Short)

San Toy was not all stars. And it showed that, amazingly, a good enough piece could run at Daly's even without that fixture of the theatre, Letty Lind. And without Marie Tempest.

San Toy was to suffer many changes throughout its two-years plus run, but none so violent as the first: the defection of Marie Tempest from Daly's and from the musical stage. Ostensibly this disaster for the musical theatre was sparked by a disagreement over a costume. In her role as the disguised San Toy Miss Tempest was required to wear a pair of Chinese trousers. After having worn them for a few weeks, she got, or was given, the idea that she would look better in trunks. Edwardes dismissed the idea. *San*

[1] It wasn't. It was barely a speaking role.

Toy was not a pantomime or a burlesque. Miss Tempest's answer was to take a pair of scissors and make the alteration herself. There was an explosion, an ultimatum, and much publicity: 'Trunks v Trousers. Tempest non-suited' before the prima donna stormed out with the run of the show only a few weeks old. Thus, Marie Susan Etherington, *dit* Tempest, possibly the greatest singing actress the British musical had and has known, walked out of the genre of which she was one of the shining stars and into the straight theatre where she made herself a star all over again. Miss Tempest had been eyeing the non-musical theatre for some time and there is little doubt that the costume fracas was engineered as a means of breaking her contract with Edwardes when another long run at Daly's looked sure. Her loss was a grievous one, but it was not a mortal wound for *San Toy*. Florence Collingbourne, who had been playing the role of Yen How's number one wife, was promoted to the leading role, gave a stunning performance, and audiences still crammed Daly's nightly, Tempest or no Tempest.

One who took quick advantage of the star's departure was Hayden Coffin. He appropriated for himself her best number 'The Petals of the Plum Tree', leaving Miss Collingbourne with a rather depleted title-role. He also enhanced his role by interpolating his *Gaiety Girl* blockbuster 'Tommy Atkins' with topical references to the Boer War added in new patriotic verses. Other artists interpolated, too, as the run of *San Toy* wore on. One of the more drastic novelties was a burlesque of the Japanese tragedienne Sadi-Yacco which Huntley Wright and Ethel Irving (the new Dudley) slipped in. Edwardes was not impressed with its incongruity and had it quickly removed.

In time-honoured fashion fresh songs continued to be tried and they came from many different sources. Huntley Wright tried a new song by the young Paul Rubens 'Me Gettee outee velly Quick', but there was a perfect avalanche of new songs in the wake of a major cast change when Ada Reeve finally took over the part which she thought she should have had all along, during a spell when both Florence Collingbourne and her cover, Maggie May, were indisposed. After having proved to Edwardes that she could sing the part as it was written, she then set about changing it to suit her more ebullient interpretation of the role. 'It's nice to Be a Boy Sometimes' she sang, before launching into 'All I Want is a little Bit of Fun' in which she crowed:

To old Sing-Hi I'll go on the sly
And pull at his pigtail plait
I'll stick some pins in the mandarins
Oh, what will they say to that?

Oh, I'm the girl to set the place awhirl
By shocking and surprising everyone
This life's a trifle slow, and I want to make things go
For I'm so fond of a little bit of fun!

It was more West Hartlepool than O Mimosa San. It was a song Marie Tempest would never have sung and it belonged neither in the show nor in the theatre, but Ada made it go for her, as she made another Lionel Monckton piece called 'Somebody' go. But there was one reason why both songs had a place at Daly's – their lyrics were by twenty-three year-old Percy Greenbank, younger brother to the regretted Harry, who had only recently made his theatrical début with a contribution to the Gaiety show *The Messenger Boy*, starting him on a career which, in a lifespan almost three times the length of his brother's, would take him in his turn to the foremost position in the musical theatre.

The Times had predicted in its review that *San Toy* would be a second *Geisha*, and it was right. At Daly's it even outran its famous predecessor by a couple of weeks while its New York season was, if slightly shorter, equally successful. Like *The Geisha* it found its way around the world, even beyond the usual limits of the English-speaking world, and everywhere it went it was popular.

The triumph of *San Toy* was quickly followed by a second great hit, this time for Tom Davis. After his initial success with *Little Miss Nobody*, he had been less fortunate with *L'Amour Mouillé* and less financially rewarded with *El Capitan*, but towards the end of the year he was ready with his prize piece, the show which every other London manager would have liked to secure, the first full-length musical by Leslie Stuart, the well-known composer of such top songs as 'Lily of Laguna', 'Soldiers of the Queen', 'Little Dolly Daydream', Lousiana Lou, 'The Bandolero', 'Trilby will be True' and a host of others. 'Leslie Stuart' was the pen-name of Tom A. Barrett, a Southport man who had become well-known in the concert and musical theatre fields through his exceptionally clever and popular songs and by his promotions. In his early days Stuart had put on series of concerts in Manchester and he had claimed the distinction of being the first impresario to introduce Paderewski to British audiences. His own skill at the piano had made him something of a prodigy, but it was as a composer that he made his career and his greatest mark. His first full-length show, *Florodora*, was produced by Davis at the Lyric on 11 November, 1899 and it made him world famous.[1]

The book for *Florodora* was by the omnipresent Owen Hall with lyrics written by the young and largely untried actor/lyricist Ernest Boyd-Jones and by the up and coming Paul Rubens whose own first score, for *Great Caesar*, had gone down with that unfortunate show.

Florodora had a picturesque setting – an imaginary island in the Philippines where millionaire Cyrus W. Gilfain produces the popular 'Florodora' perfume. Gilfain is seen to be paying noticeable and inexplicable attentions to one of his working girls, Dolores, and it emerges that she is, in fact, the rightful owner of the perfumery which had been her father's. But she is not interested in Gilfain, for her heart is set on the handsome overseer Frank Abercoed whom Gilfain has earmarked for his own daughter, Angela. Angela, however, has other ideas. Into this mélange of amours and non-amours comes Anthony Tweedlepunch – showman, phrenologist, hypnotist, palmist and of a suspicious mind. Gilfain allays his 'suspicions' with a sizeable cash payment and Tweedlepunch proceeds to hold a series of phrenological sessions to prove that Dolores is 'suited' to Cyrus W. and Angela to Abercoed. Abercoed refuses to be spoken for in such a manner and sets off back to his family seat in Wales. But Gilfain has bought up the castle of the impoverished Welsh earldom and has installed himself there. Abercoed, Dolores and Tweedlepunch gain entry in disguise and scare the villain into a confession of his misdeeds so that all is set right.

Subsidiary to this story was the character of Lady Holyrood, a snappy society lady, who was to become the most prominent female character in the piece. This role had not originally existed but was added in rehearsal to permit the hiring of Ada Reeve. Miss Reeve had not long 'resigned' from the original *San Toy* when she was approached by Jimmy Davis (Owen Hall) who asked her if she would like to play in his new show at the Lyric. Not unnaturally, Ada enquired what the part was. Davis cheerfully replied that

[1] It is said that for the score of *Florodora* Stuart re-used a number of tunes which he had originally composed for the pantomimes at the Prince's Theatre, Manchester.

she could take her pick for there was no part . . he would write one in. Thus was born the star role of Lady Holyrood, and Ada Reeve joined Willie Edouin (Tweedlepunch), Charles E. Stevens (Cyrus), Kate Cutler (Angela), Evie Greene (Dolores) and the American baritone, Melville Stewart (Abercoed), in the star line-up for *Florodora.*

Things looked well on opening night. Leslie Stuart was given three cheers from the gallery before a note had been played as he made his way to his place on the conductor's rostrum. And they continued well:

> . . . tempestuous laughter [greeted] nearly every sally and topical allusion in Owen Hall's book, full of that writer's mordant humour and insolently audacious cynicism . . . (*Stage*)

The songs went down well too, particularly Ada Reeve's numbers. The first was 'Tact':

> Tact, tact, take it for a fact,
> Just try it and you'll find it will invariably act
> P'r'aps they told you in your youth
> That there's nothing like the truth
> But it really can't compare with tact!

in which she took the odd dig at society manners and shams, slightly daring in one or two places:

> The Academy you view
> If you've really fond of art, of course you don't.
> Then a pianist you know
> And you promise you will go
> To his concerts: if you're musical, you won't.
> Then a gorgeous gown you buy
> The price is cut so high
> Well, considering the gown is cut so low,
> For the lady of today
> Hasn't got a heart they say
> But she's got a neck – and that she means to show!
> Tact, tact, take it for a fact
> Her dining dress has no support and yet it seems to act
> And her costume at a ball
> Is not 'material' at all
> It's enough if she has diamonds – and tact!

The lyric was the work of Paul Rubens who supplied both words and music for Miss Reeve's other song 'I've an Inkling', in the same slightly saucy vein, which also went down particularly well. Kate Cutler was rather more refined with the beautiful, melodious 'The Fellow who Might' while the romantic leads, Evie Greene and Melville Stewart, had two particularly attractive ballads, 'The silver Star of Love' and 'In the Shade of the Palm' respectively. But *The Times* noticed:

> Perhaps the most ingenious number is a so-called concerted piece in which a little scene of courtship is gone through by six couples at once; strange to say, this number 'Are There Any More At Home Like You' made a great hit . . . .

'Are there any more at Home like You' soon became better known as 'Tell me, pretty Maiden'. The number with its quaintly wandering tune and its gently promenading routine was performed by a double sextette of young men and young ladies in attractive modern walking clothes:

HE: Tell me, pretty maiden are there any more at home like you?
SHE: There are a few, kind sir,
But simple girls and proper too . . .

'Tell me, pretty Maiden' quickly became the focal point of the show. It achieved the dimension of popularity which the *Faust Up-To-Date* pas de quatre had achieved in its day. Stuart jokingly gave his recipe to a journal:

> For the business, take one memory of Christy Minstrels, let it simmer in the brain for twenty years. Add slowly, for the music, an organist's practice in arranging Gregorian chants for a Roman Catholic church. Mix well and serve with half-a-dozen pretty girls and an equal number of well-dressed men . . .

It was as simple as that but its success was incredible. To have been a member of the 'original *Florodora* sextette' gained a special cachet and in consequence there were suddenly a lot of claimants for that honour. Among the twelve genuine participants, however, was one name which would become better known in another capacity – first as a manager, but notably as a playwright and novelist – Roy Horniman, the author of *Idols*. The ladies included Jane May, sister of the more famous Edna, and Nina Sevening making her adult theatre début at the beginning of a fine career, musical and straight, on both sides of the Atlantic.

There was no doubt, right from the start, that Davis and his writers had a great success on their hands. They had more than that, for *Florodora* turned out to be one of the most international of all hits, succeeding even in Paris where *The Geisha* had failed and triumphing in New York where its 501-performance run made it the fourth longest running musical in Broadway history (after *Erminie*, *A Trip to Chinatown* and *Adonis*). At the Lyric, *Florodora* ran for seventeen months, through many ups and downs and alterations but little fluctuation from the highest box-office figures.

One of the show's first alterations was the sacking of the baritone Melville Stewart. *The Era* had described him as 'handsome, earnest and manly', noting that he 'has a good voice and sings his solos with admirable expressiveness'. But that view was not shared by the management. Stewart was dropped in favour of Sydney Barraclough. The American, wounded in his amour propre, took the most popular recourse of the day and sued, gaining a settlement of 12 weeks' wages (£300). Ada Reeve was out almost as soon as she was in, having previously committed herself to *Aladdin* at Bristol, but as soon as she was free she returned to the role which had been custom-built for her. The success of *Florodora* prompted a number of stars to come in as replacements. Louis Bradfield took over as Arthur Donegal in March and brought with him two fresh numbers: 'He didn't Like the Look of it at All' and the Frank Clement/Leslie Stuart 'I Want to be a Military Man' extolling the virtues of the man in khaki, yet another number prompted by the Boer War and the consequent focus on the army. There was a bevy of new songs in both halls and theatres devoted to the new 'khaki'; there were khaki quadrilles, khaki waltzes, and Marie Lloyd sang the patriotic virtues of 'The Girl in the khaki Dress'; but Bradfield topped them all:

Now as this is from the stable
I hope you'll keep it dark
But the straightest of tips I had
From Tattersalls today.
And I hear that all the racecourses
Right down to Kempton Park
Will be laid with khaki turf without delay.

And all the jockeys you will see
Will ride a khaki gee
And the starter will look smarter in the sober tan;
And the vague impression's growing
That the Prince of Wales is going
To the races dressed in khaki
Like a Military Man!

Willie Edouin could no longer regret having stayed at home and missed *The Man in the Moon*. He triumphed absolutely as the silly little phrenologist in *Florodora* before going on to repeat the role on Broadway. When he went, his replacements were de luxe – first Fred Eastman and then Harry Monkhouse. These replacements had little effect on the show's content but the substitution of Evie Greene by the 'queen of comic opera', Florence St John, brought the interpolation of several new songs: 'He Loves me, He Loves me Not', the Ivan Caryll number 'The Island of Love', 'Such a Don' and the duet 'When we Are on the Stage' (with Edouin) all found their way into the show for the benefit of the new prima donna.

During its lifetime *Florodora* became the receptacle for any number of exterior songs, but the original London score contained virtually all the hits – and hits indeed they were. Tom Davis had a huge money-spinner on his hands and his contentment could not be marred even when his production company was sued by a dissatisfied shareholder who considered his 'cut' insufficient from what was known to be a big success. This Mr Horlock had the producer brought to court for dissipating the profits of the show in expenses and running costs, and failure to win did not prevent him from continuing his harassment as Davis poured money back into *Florodora* for new costumes and scenery to keep the piece as bright and interesting throughout its run as it had been on the opening night. By the time the London run was done, *Florodora* was already a fixture in the provinces and it had very many years of successful life there as well as two revivals in town in 1915 and 1931, both under the management of Bannister Howard. The first of these featured Evie Greene in her original role, with the composer's daughter, May Leslie Stuart, as Lady Holyrood, and two new songs, 'Jack and Jill' and 'Beautiful garden Girl'. It spent a short season in London before going to the provinces. The second starred George Graves as Tweedlepunch and Dorothy Ward as Lady Holyrood, and reverted to the original score adulterated only by 'topical lyrics by Arthur Klein'.

In America the show, and particularly 'Tell Me, pretty Maiden', created an even greater furore than it had done in London in spite of some half-hearted or even carping reviews. The original *Florodora* girls became celebrities, and many celebrities went out of their way to claim to have been one of the six originals. Agnes Wayburn, Margaret Walker, Marie L. Wilson, Daisy Greene, Marjorie Relyea and Vaughan Texsmith were hit by the full glare of publicity, but nothing like that attracted by replacements Frances Belmont who became Lady Ashburton in 1906, Nan Patterson who, a jury finally decided, did *not* kill her lover and lovely Evelyn Nesbit. Miss Nesbit became Mrs Harry K. Thaw and a very wealthy woman, and it was her betrayed husband who one evening in that same year gunned down his wife's lover in his seat at a packed Madison Square Garden. *Florodora* became a theatrical and social phenomenon on Broadway as its run stretched on through one full year and into a second, and from the Casino Theatre to the New York Theatre until the five hundredth performance had been reached. The following night *Florodora* closed, but forty-eight hours later another production with a cast of no less than 250 performers leaped in to replace the new rival for the long-run crown of *Erminie*, and for six further weeks Broadway retained *Florodora* at the Winter Garden. In 1905 the show returned to Broadway once more and in 1920 the Shuberts mounted a major revival at the Century Theatre. The score was decorated with the hit songs from *Havana* ('Hello, People') and *The Belle of Mayfair* ('Come to St. George's') and *Florodora* scored again under the billing 'the greatest musical comedy ever staged'. In 1981 the show was seen in New York once more in a production off-off-Broadway by the Bandwagon company.

Florodora companies proliferated not only in Britain and the States but all over the world. Grace Palotta and George Lauri broke box-office and long-run records in Australia with a series of 210 performances in Melbourne and Sydney; Mabel Nelson and Frank Danby headed a triumphant production in South Africa; and the Bouffes-Parisiens in Paris welcomed a fine cast and an energetic chorus for a six weeks' run with the same enthusiasm as London had shown for the Casino girls of *The Belle of New York*. In the tradition of *H.M.S. Pinafore*, *The Pirates of Penzance* and *The Geisha*, *Florodora* joined the select list of true world hit musicals of the nineteenth century.

The great successes of *San Toy* and *Florodora* were followed by a third. Things had not gone well for D'Oyly Carte and the Savoy Theatre since the dissolution of the Gilbert and Sullivan partnership. Although revivals of former glories had succeeded in keeping the theatre ticking over, the new ventures had not been successful. *The Rose of Persia* was. Sir Arthur Sullivan had found himself a new librettist: a man of the theatre and an experienced lyricist, with a series of established hit shows and songs behind him and with an intellect and wit of the highest degree – Basil Hood. For *The Rose of Persia*, Hood turned away from the hansom cabbies and the volunteer barbers with which he had gained such a wide popularity and took a much more 'Savoy' line.

His story contained the usual elements of disguise and mistaken identity, with a veiled marriage and royalty promenading through the outside world incognito. It even used the favourite Gilbertian lozenge trick, in this case an hallucinogen called 'bhang', to make things not what they seemed. However, Hood put the familiar elements together deftly in the surroundings of the court of the Persian Sultan, and supplied the whole with a gallery of delightful characters and a deliciously clever final twist, as well as dialogue and lyrics of a very superior standard which lifted *The Rose of Persia* well above the level of the other recent new works at the Savoy. Hassan is a rich eccentric who holds open house to the halt and the lame of the town. One evening his impromptu guests include a group of dancing girls who are actually the Sultana Rose-in-Bloom and her maidens in disguise. Problems ensue when the Sultan turns up. Hassan, foreseeing his immediate execution, resolves to go under the influence and doses himself heavily with bhang before telling the Sultan that he, Hassan, is his and any man's equal. The Sultan arranges to play a joke on Hassan. When he recovers from his drug he is made to believe that he truly is the Sultan. Hassan's wives are also taken in, and his No. 1 wife, the dragonistic Dancing Sunbeam, all her social ambitions finally realised, eagerly declares herself Sultana. The real Sultana, however, is in trouble. Her little nocturnal escapade has been discovered and the Sultan declares that she shall be divorced and married off to the poor story-teller Yussuf who is presently sighing for the slavegirl, Heart's Desire. These instructions misfire when Dancing Sunbeam insists that 'Sultana' means her and, to her chagrin, finds herself divorced from her 'Sultan' and wed to the frantic Yussuf. But Heart's Desire 'confesses' that it was she, wearing the Sultana's signet ring, who had visited Hassan from whom she was getting a wondrous story with which she was accustomed to regale the Sultana. The Sultan says that he will hear the story, and when it is finished both Hassan and Heart's Desire shall be executed. He also insists that the story shall have a happy ending. So Hassan tells his tale:

> There once was a small street Arab,
> And his little name was Tom;
> And he lived in Gutter-Persia
> Where such Arabs all come from:
> And like little Gutter-Persians
> (Ev'ryone and one and all),
> His spirits were elastic
> As an india-rubber ball.
> And all day long he sang a song,
> A merry little ditty as he danced a cellar-flap;
> 'The life I lead is all I need,
> And I know no better' – the lucky little chap!
>
> Now among the bricks and mortar
> Did his little lifetime pass;
> He had never seen a flower
> Nor a single blade of grass;
> But one day he found a daisy,
> And he thought that simple thing
> Was a wondrous flow'r from heaven,
> And he took it to the King!
> He meant no wrong, but through the throng
> He struggled to the Sultan, and laid it on his lap
> (That simple weed – he did, indeed),
> For he knew no better – the foolish little chap!
>
> But the Sultan gravely thanked him,
> Saying 'Would that I had eyes
> To see a simple daisy
> As a gift of Paradise!
> I will not now reward thee,
> Or exchange thy humble lot –
> For riches would but rob thee
> Of a wealth that I have not!'
> So all day long he sang his song
> That merry little ditty as he danced a cellar-flap!
> 'The life I lead is all I need!'
> For he knew no better – the lucky little chap!

The Sultan inquires– 'Is the story finished?' to which Hassan answers:

> That is only the beginning, O King. That little boy was myself and the Sultan was your father – and the story I have been telling to the slave, which she has been telling to the Sultana, is the story of my own life – and, O king, this is the point: you have yourself commanded that the story, which is my life, is to have a happy ending.

The Sultan admits himself tricked, and reprieves Hassan and Heart's Desire, but takes the edge off the smiling merchant's triumph by reuniting him with the gruesome Dancing Sunbeam as the curtain falls.

The roles in *The Rose of Persia* were designed for the members of the Savoy Company. Henry Lytton was the Sultan, Walter Passmore the merchant, Rosina Brandram the awful No. 1 wife and Robert Evett took the tenor role of Yussuf. Louie

Pounds, Emmie Owen and Isabel Jay had nice lesser roles. The principal soprano role of the Sultana, Rose-in-Bloom, was taken by the American soprano Ellen Beach Yaw, celebrated for her phenomenal upper register, a quality not normally needed in a Savoy leading lady. Sullivan duly tailored the soprano music to suit her, including the use of a top F in alt. in her solo 'Beneath my Lattice'. The music was, of course, a feature of *The Rose of Persia*. It was not the music of *The Mikado* or *The Gondoliers*, but it did not depart so far from the Savoy idiom as had *The Beauty Stone*. It was light in character but highly accomplished and, if it lacked somewhat the jokey quality of some of the earlier works, it retained a dignity which had humour always just beneath the surface and combined with Hood's lyrics to produce songs of romantic beauty and comic joyfulness with equal ease.

The former style was epitomised in Yussuf's ballad:

Our tale is told,
And now is growing old!
For fate, who holds the book
Of childhood, youth, and age,
Her finger now doth crook
To turn another page.

Try to forget –
Although a soft regret
Like some poor faded roseleaf lie
(To mark the place)
Within the book where thou and I
Have read one passage full of grace!

The desert's wide –
And we must mount and ride!
Each with a caravan
That's laden with our sighs;
To barter, if we can,
Our loads in Paradise.

Try to forget!
Our caravans have met
Amid the burning desert space,
Where thou and I
Have rested in a shady place
A little while, and then passed by!

A far cry from the normal romantic lyric of the musical with its banal and often trite expressions and conceits, and yet the same lyricist could come up with songs of *French Maid* cleverness such as Hassan's 'Something in the City' in which the merchant could declare:

A prophet I'd never been made at home
But I made one in the city . .

and

Now there's many a millionaire may thank
The facts that I'm disclosing,
For his riches and imposing rank
Have sprung from rank imposing

Hood's command of language and his use of it brought forth a respect and feeling from

Sullivan which set him at his highest level in the writing of the music. Only when he attempted to accommodate the unusual attributes of Miss Beach Yaw did Sullivan let himself down, for top Fs in alt. do not fall easily into melodic light music. In the event, both Miss Beach Yaw and the high notes were to last a very short time.

The Rose of Persia received a good old-fashioned Savoy first-night triumph as the audience recognised the happy conjunction of exceptionally literate words and accomplished and attractive music. The show was a clear success. But even such a success could only stretch its run to a season of 220 performances. A decade previously it would probably have run two or three times as long, but the larger audiences now were for pieces of *A Runaway Girl* or *The Geisha* or *Florodora* kind, and the 'comic opera' style of musical, although still having an appreciable audience, was no longer as popular as in the days of *H.M.S. Pinafore* or *Les Manteaux Noirs* or *Dorothy*.

Nevertheless, *The Rose of Persia* stayed seven months at the Savoy. Miss Beach Yaw stayed only a few weeks. She had not been a good idea. Her understudy, Isabel Jay, was promoted from the small role of Blush-of-the-morning to take over the role (shorn of its top notes) and she proved a delightful prima donna. The new combination of Hood and Sullivan looked to be one which could carry on successfully the great Savoy tradition, and *The Rose of Persia* it was hoped, would be only the first of a new series of Savoy operas. The pair quickly settled down to work on the successor to *The Rose of Persia*, but the death of Sullivan intervened before the completion of *The Emerald Isle*, leaving *The Rose of Persia* as the only example of what might have been one of the great collaborations of the British musical theatre.

The limitations imposed by the kind of audiences to which it appealed meant that *The Rose of Persia* did not compile a long run in any of its productions. New York, in particular, clearly preferred Weber and Fields' music hall to what seemed to them to be an old-fashioned light opera and the show's run on Broadway was brief, while a 1935 London revival in the wake of the successful return of *Merrie England* did not catch on in the same way that German's piece did.

A good number of new pieces appeared in the provinces during the year, only one of which, H. Cecil Beryl's production of George Dance's *A Chinese Honeymoon*, would have any future. The remainder were of little moment although several were taken on quite extensive tours. *The American Heiress* was the work of Arthur Branscombe (*Morocco Bound*) and George Day (*Bilberry of Tilbury*), with music from a whole host of composers. It had a futuristic (1941) setting in which the American philanthropiste Mrs Miranda Q. Strongmynde gathers around her as servants the relicts of the abolished House of Lords, in order to mate the best example of the ex-aristocracy with her niece. But her selection, Lord Stonyhurst, is in love with her other niece, a Parisian chanteuse. After many incidents, including a sculling race with a stake of £2 million decreed by the International Arbitration Committee to settle by proxy a difference between Germany and the U.K. (and which our hero wins for the red, white and blue) all is set to rights.

The role of Lord Stonyhurst appealed to the Chevalier Scovel who had become something of a celebrity with his success in *La Cigale*. He took a half share in the piece and, having seen it tour fairly well with the baritone John Peachey in the lead, he had the music altered to fit his tenor range and took *The American Heiress* out for a second term in the autumn. Like *The Rose of Persia*, it began its career with an American prima donna, Madame Roma 'The Californian Nightingale', and separated fairly quickly from its star to the profit of her understudy. Unlike *The Rose of Persia*, the show's career ended with 1899.

Tours were also produced of *Miss Chiquita* and *In Gay Piccadilly*, two new pieces from the pens of the *Dandy Fifth* team of George Sims and Clarence Corri. Neither was in the same class as the military piece. *Miss Chiquita* had plenty of fun and some good lyrics grafted on to a thin story of thwarted love and disguises, bigamy and misunderstandings with a slight Spanish flavour. It had a three-and-a-part months' tour with the very young Madge Crichton in the title-role. Sims thought well enough of the piece to attempt to revise and revive it in 1907 under the title of *Dancing Girl of Spain* but the second version fared no better than the first.

In Gay Piccadilly was conceived for Dan Leno and had a book in the *Skipped by the Light of the Moon* vein which had been brought off so successfully by Sims on the former occasion. It had two 'detectives' tracking around after the various halves of a pair of married couples, thus providing for the maximum in the way of disguises and knockabout farce. It played itself out in nine dates before Leno went off to his pantomime.

Perhaps the most disappointing piece of the year was a George Edwardes' tour of a new Seymour Hicks musical *The Merry-Go-Round*. This combination which, not unnaturally, aroused high hopes, had originally conceived the show under the title *The Seven Ages* and had Shakespeare coming down from his pedestal to lead the characters through the Seven Ages of Man. There was, in fact, little or no plot and *The Merry-Go-Round* was less a musical than a collection of vaguely related songs and dances linked by a tenuous theme. Some of the songs were reasonably attractive – a Brandon Thomas number 'Peekin' froo de Moon' was probably the most successful – but, in general, *The Merry-Go-Round* was a poor piece. An example of its 'farcical dialogue' quoted at the time gives sufficient idea:

A: Life would be worth living but for one's little troubles.
B: How many have you?
A: Two.
B: Were they born in wedlock?
A: No. One in Limehouse. One in Poplar.

Had it turned up a few years later, *The Merry-Go-Round* would undoubtedly have thrown aside all pretence of a plot and unashamedly have called itself a revue which in essence, it was, if rather a poor one. In spite of a cast of stars – Joseph Wilson, Gracie Leigh, Lionel Mackinder, Frank Wheeler, Frances Earle, Hetty Chapman – *The Merry-Go-Round* had a life of only eight weeks. Revue was not an unknown form in Britain. Planché had dabbled with it as far back as 1825 and Hicks himself had written the short *Under the Clock* for the Court Theatre triple bill in 1893 but it was more popularly, at this stage, a French form. But apart from *The Merry-Go-Round*, 1899 saw two other pieces which were more interesting and more honest about their genre. *Pot Pourri* described itself accurately as 'revue'; it interpolated skits, songs, dances and all sorts of material into a framework consisting primarily of a light burlesque of the play *The Great Ruby*. It had a decided, if limited, success both on tour and in a short season at the Avenue Theatre. *A Dream of Whitaker's Almanack*, presented at the Crystal Palace (initially indoors, but later al fresco) also called itself 'revue' and it threw in a bit of everything– ballets, a burlesque opera, a burlesque play, and a cast of stars– the whole encapsulated in the ingenious story of a group of people shipwrecked on the island where lives the Spirit who collects the information for Whitaker's Almanack. This enabled the year's events to be neatly 'revued'.

Smaller tours included the farcical piece *The Joking Girl* starring Bertie Leslie (most of the time) as a naughty schoolgirl who mis-delivers love-letters and sits back to watch the chaos caused; *The Principal Boy* in which Nellie Cozens interfered in the love-lives of the fellow members of her 'digs'; and a semi-pasticcio piece by the Paultons called *The Dear Girls* in which the farce was rather more important than the music, even though some of the latter was the original work of Clement Locknane.

All these had longer runs than the eight pre-Christmas weeks which were the allotted first span of *A Chinese Honeymoon* and its unambitious production. This was a comical little East-misunderstands-West piece thrown together in four weeks by George Dance during a stay at Birchington-on-Sea. The music had been added by Howard Talbot, still seeking an unfairly elusive success, and the whole put tidily on to the stage at Hanley with a competent cast headed by comedian W. T. Thompson, Lionel Rignold and his wife, Marie Daltra, and Florence Wilton. It attracted little attention. *The Era* gave an outline of the plot before adding briskly:

> Mr Talbot's music is particularly catchy and the overture was loudly applauded. The songs are smart and likely to catch on. The play is well mounted and admirably dressed.

A Chinese Honeymoon, destined to become the longest running West End show of the Victorian and Edwardian eras, had made its modest beginning.

1899

0221 **THE LUCKY STAR** a comic opera in three acts founded on and adapted from *L'Étoile*, an opéra-bouffe by Leterrier and Vanloo with music by Alexis-Emmanuel Chabrier and an American version thereof by Cheever Goodwin and Woolson Morse entitled *The Merry Monarch*. New English dialogue by Charles H. Brookfield. Lyrics by Adrian Ross and Aubrey Hopwood, the whole revised and assembled by Helen Lenoir (Mrs D'Oyly Carte), with new music by Ivan Caryll. Produced at the Savoy Theatre under the management of Richard D'Oyly Carte 7 January, 1899 for a run of 143 performances closing 31 May, 1899.

King Ouf I . . . . Walter Passmore
Baron Tabasco . . . . Henry A. Lytton
Siroco . . . . Sydney Paxton/Fred Wright Jr
Kedas . . . . Frank Manning/Henry Claff
Tapioca . . . . Robert Evett
Cancan . . . . Leonard Russell
Chamberlain. . . . . Charles Childerstone
Possumus . . . . Master William Pardue
Hocacus . . . . Master Clito Clifford
Princess Laoula . . . . Ruth Vincent (Jessie Rose)
Aloes . . . . Isabel Jay
Oasis . . . . Jessie Rose
Asphodel . . . . Madge Moyse
Zinnia . . . . Mildred Baker
Lazuli . . . . Emmie Owen
add Adza . . . . Katie Vesey

Dir: Richard Barker; md: François Cellier; ch: Willie Warde; sc: T. E. Ryan and W. Harford; cos: Percy Anderson

0222 **THE AMERICAN HEIRESS** a musical play in two acts by Arthur Branscombe and George D. Day. Music by Herbert Simpson, Guy Jones, Edward Dean, Frank Lambert and Sydney Shaw. Produced at the Grand Theatre, Birmingham 3 April, 1899 and toured through Plymouth, Cheltenham, Kingston, Fulham, Metropole, Hanley and Sheffield to 27 May. Resumed Newcastle 7 August and toured through Edinburgh, Glasgow, ?, Aberdeen, Dundee, Liverpool, Oldham, Chester, Derby, Blackpool, Belfast, Oldham, Cork, Halifax, Ipswich to 25 November, 1899.

Lord Stonyhurst . . . . John Peachey/Chevalier Scovel
Lieutenant O'Reilley . . . . Herbert Shelley/George Bastow/C. E. Vernon
Col. Hiram P. Windbag . . . . Harry Meynott
Hon. James Fitz James/Fritz von der Hausen . . . . Walter Westwood
Jack Grap . . . . Harry Denvil
Donald . . . . Geordie Taylor
Gripper . . . . A. Shiron

Stuart McNab	Horace Lingard/J. T. MacMillan
Sadie Brooklyn	Rose Nesbit/Rita Leslie
Mrs Miranda Q. Strongmynde	Alice Aynsley Cook
Marie	Alice Brookes/Hettie Lane
Lady Janet Gaybody	Roy Lytton/Poppy Haynes
Mamie Wayhupp	Poppy Haynes/
Fay Cashmore	Dora Card
Dolly deMure	Violet Gordon
Lola Silverton	Kitty Upton
Flora MacDonald	Hettie Lane/
Cora Brooklyn	Mme Roma/Marie Outram/Mme Morel
Phoebe Owen	Marie Outram

Md: B. J. Paterson; sc: Pritchard Barrett; cos: Worth, Mme Vernon

0223 **THE MERRY-GO-ROUND** a musical farce (an up-to-date musical play) in two acts by Seymour Hicks. Lyrics by Aubrey Hopwood. Music by W. Meyer Lutz. Additional songs by Robert Martin, Ellaline Terriss, Brandon Thomas, Harry Hunter and Edmund Forman. Produced at the Coronet Theatre under the management of George Edwardes 24 April, 1899 and toured through Nottingham, Birmingham, ?, Fulham, Liverpool, Manchester ending 10 June, 1899.

Charlie Dalrymple	Lionel Mackinder
Algy Scott	Joseph Wilson
Toby Prescott	Sydney Harcourt
Horace Dale	Leslie Holland
William Shakespeare	Martin Adeson
Winch	Frank Wheeler
Norah	Frances Earle
Lydia	Ethel Palliser
Molly	Florence Lloyd
Mary	Gracie Leigh
Anne, the cook	Hetty Chapman

with a chorus of 40.

Dir: J. A. E. Malone; md: Guy Jones; ch: Will Bishop; cos: Harrison

0224 **GREAT CAESAR** a burlesque in two acts by George Grossmith Jr and Paul A. Rubens. Music by Paul and Walter Rubens. Additional lyrics by Harold Ellis. Produced at the Comedy Theatre under the management of Yorke Stephens 29 April, 1899 for a run of 56 performances closing 23 June, 1899.

Julius Caesar	Willie Edouin
Brutus	Leon Roche
Casca	William Cheesman
Cassius	Arthur Hatherton
Trebonius	Laurence R. Grossmith
Cinna	Tim Ryley
Cicero	Fred Emney
Nubian Dancer	Edouard Espinosa
Fourteenth Citizen	Mr Rowe
1st Soldier	Mr Hill
One of the crowd	E. Barratt
Marc Antony	George Grossmith Jr
Lucia	Decima Moore
Calpurnia	Nellie Christie
Nicippe	Jenny Owen
Alsatia	Lydia Flopp
Octavius	Mary Thorne
Claudia	Looloo Halliday
Dardania	Nellie Evelyn

Barine . . . . Greene Taylor
Slave . . . . Edie Neilson
Cleopatra . . . . Ada Reeve/Jenny Owen
add Mercurius. . . . . Lydia West
Dancers: Misses L. Greenaway, A. Greenaway, Marie Lovell, King, Lea Espinosa
with Misses Braham, Charlton, Foot, Graham, Groves, Galton, Lind, Langdon, Lewis, Milton, Owen, Ravesburg, Seymour, Taylor, Nevill; Messrs Ashley, Garton, Gregory, Garrod, Ivermeski, Robinson, Sykes, Vine.

Dir: Horace Sedger; md: Howard Talbot; ch: Edouard Espinosa; sc: E. G. Banks; cos: Comelli

225 **THE PRINCIPAL BOY** a musical comedy in three acts by Guy d'Lanor. Music by Arnold Cooke. Produced at the Lyric Theatre, Liverpool 5 June, 1899 and toured through Bedford, Reading, Swindon, Boscombe &c.

Harry Golightly . . . . Percy Knight
'Arry . . . . James Grant
Theodore Tipton . . . . Joseph E. Nightingale
Robert Nettlefold . . . . E. Fancourt
Harcourt Lavender . . . . E. R. Beaumont
Herr Johann Bach. . . . . G. I. Hale
Bilker . . . . Sydney Harcourt
Victor Redmayne . . . . Joseph Robins
Jackson . . . . Tom Green
Julie Nettlefold . . . . May Pratt
Mrs Jane Tipton . . . . Nellie Birchenough
Julie . . . . Peggie Lennie
Doris Tipton . . . . Maude Prenton
Millie St Aubyn. . . . . Nellie Cozens

226 **MISS CHIQUITA** a musical comedy in two acts by George R. Sims. Music by Clarence Corri. Produced at the Prince of Wales Theatre, Birmingham, under the management of Milton Bode 7 August, 1899 and toured through Coronet, Deptford, Brixton, Wolverhampton, Blackpool, Hull, Sheffield, Stratford East, Fulham, Ipswich/Cambridge, Oxford, Plymouth, Portsmouth, Brighton, Shakespeare ending 25 November, 1899.

Terence McGinty. . . . . Harry Cole
D'Arcy Davis . . . . George Graves
Don Julian Alvarez . . . . Michael Dwyer
Sir Jeremiah Joyce . . . . Campbell Bishop
Don Carlos Alvarez . . . . Percy Percival/John J. Daly
Jack Davis. . . . . Jack Crichton/Ansell Gifford
Pedro . . . . J. Jordan
Gonzales. . . . . Tom Grove/E. Courtenay Grattan
Guitarez. . . . . John J. Daly/Tom Grove
Reverend Alonzo Joyce . . . . A. E. Chapman/Jack Crichton
Roderigo. . . . . William Bayfield
M. Pierre . . . . Mr Brookfield
Mr Green . . . . J. P. Flint
Mr Jones . . . . James Barclay
Marie Montressor. . . . . Marian Ayling
Lola . . . . Alice Calcott/Beatrice Ross
Manuelita . . . . Jessie Kosiminski/May Norton
Lizette. . . . . Blanch Ayling
Mercedes . . . . Edie Dennett/Marie Wilson
Dolores . . . . J. James
Chiquita Joyce . . . . Madge Crichton/Jennie Owen

Dir: Frank Parker; md: Frank Seddon; ch: Edouard Espinosa; sc: Royal County Theatre, Reading; cos: Herbert Norris

Produced in a revised version as *Dancing Girl of Spain*, 1907.

0227 **THE PRINCE OF BORNEO** an operatic farce in two acts by Joseph W. Herbert. Music by Edward Jones. Additional numbers by George H. Broadhurst. Produced at the Strand Theatre under the management of Frank Wheeler and Broadhurst Brothers 5 October, 1899 for a run of 31 performances closing 4 November, 1899.

General Samovar . . . . Martin Adeson
Nicholas Kromeski . . . . Roland Cunningham
Santuzzi . . . . Robert Nainby
Krasch. Wilton Heriot
Paul Bennett . . . . Richard Temple Jr
Chickoree . . . . Frank Wheeler
Madame Samovar . . . . Cissie Fitzgerald/Phyllis Broughton
Countess Nitsky. . . . . Alice Aynsley Cook
Nadine . . . . Nora Maguire
Henriette . . . . Maisie Turner

Dancers: Lea Espinosa, Blanche Garford, Marie Lovell

Dir/ch: Frank Wheeler; md: George Arnold; sc: Philip Howden; cos: J. A. Harrison & Co and Mme Louise

0228 **IN GAY PICCADILLY** a musical farce in 2 acts by George R. Sims. Music by Clarence Corri. Produced at the Theatre Royal, Glasgow, under the management of Milton Bode, October 9, 1899 and toured through Edinburgh, Newcastle, Sheffield, Birmingham, Manchester, Liverpool, Stoke Newington, Deptford ending 9 December.

Aubrey Honeybun . . . . Dan Leno
Ebenezer Tinkletop . . . . Johnnie Danvers
Lord Dudeville . . . . Charles Thorburn
Guy Brabazon. . . . . George Sinclair
Montague Miggs . . . . Tim Ryley
Bertie Grey . . . . George Hudson
Charlie Vere. . . . . Edward Griffin
Algy Phipps . . . . John Daniels
Attendant . . . . T. Hill
Lady Dudeville . . . . Florence Darley
Lady Molly Wildgoose . . . . Beatrice Willey
Mrs Honeybun . . . . Emily Stevens
Gladys Ada . . . . Adie Boyne
Daisy Delamere/Dolly Flopp . . . . Lillie Young
Cissie Potts . . . . E. Graham
Ruby Green. . . . . P. Peppiate
Pd: Rita Barrington
Md: Arnold Cooke; ch: Edouard Espinosa; sc: S. King Alexander

0229 **A CHINESE HONEYMOON** a musical comedy in two acts by George Dance. Music by Howard Talbot. Produced at the Theatre Royal, Hanley, under the management of H. Cecil Beryl 16 October, 1899 and toured through Newcastle, Hull, Sheffield, Manchester, Birmingham, Liverpool and Bradford ending 9 December. Resumed 9 March, 1900 at Wolverhampton and toured through Middlesborough, Oldham, Rochdale, Derby, Sunderland, Halifax, Cheltenham and Leicester to 12 May. Resumed under the management of George Dance 27 August at Lincoln and toured through Darlington, Scarborough, Blackburn, Bury, Wakefield, Harrogate, Ashton, Stockport, West Hartlepool, Southport, Preston, Oldham, Wigan, Aston to 7 December, 1900. Resumed 7 January, 1901 at Lincoln and toured through Crewe, Cambridge, Northampton, Halifax, Dewsbury, York, ?, ?, Sunderland, Middlesborough, Jarrow, ?, Hanley, Edinburgh, Glasgow, Newcastle and Great Grimsby to 11 May, 1901. Recommenced 9 September, 1901 at Torquay and toured during London run.

Hang Chow . . . . W. T. Thompson/Fred Winn/W. H. Kirby Leonard May Tom Redmond
Chippee Chop. . . . . Richard Saker/Picton Roxburgh/Frank Sutton

Hi Lung . . . . Herbert Bouchier/Herbert Walsh/G. A. Seager
Mr Pineapple . . . . Lionel Rignold/J. T. MacMillan
Tom Hatherton . . . . Stephen Adeson/George Taylor/Charles F. Howard
Soo Soo . . . . Violet Dene/Isabel Dillon/Annie Roberts
Yen-Yen . . . . May d'Orsi/Nellie Clyde/Nellie Glen/ Gertrude Moxie
Sing-Sing . . . . Marion Bayard/Kate Turner/Violet Dickens
Mrs Pineapple . . . . Florence Wilton/Fanny Wright/Violet Raymaur
Florrie . . . . Adela Clyde/Nellie Glen
Violet . . . . Lillian Champion/Mabel Vendome
Fi-fi . . . . Kate Howell/Lillie Vernon/Lillie Soutter
Mrs Brown . . . . Marie Daltra/Elsie Carew/Lillie Alliston/Gertrude Claridge

Md: Edwin Thornton; sc: S. King Alexander

Opened in London at the Strand Theatre under the management of Frank Curzon 5 October, 1901 for a run of 1075 performances closing 23 May, 1904. Additional music for the London version written by Ivan Caryll, Ernest Woodville, Ernest Vousden with lyrics by Alfred Murray, Harry Greenbank and J. Adams.

Hang Chow . . . . Picton Roxburgh/Harry A. Gribben
Chippee Chop . . . . Ernest Boyd-Jones/Edward Shale
Hi Lung . . . . Percy Clifton
Tom Hatherton . . . . Leslie Stiles/Joe Farren Soutar (Frank Crimp)
Mr Pineapple . . . . Lionel Rignold/Arthur Williams/J. T. MacMillan
Violet . . . . Blanche Thorpe/Eleanor May/Gladys Ward/Marie Clements/Frances Balfour/ Miss Jameson/Maud Burton
Florrie . . . . Fay Wentworth/Alice Beaugarde
Millie . . . . Rosie Edwardes/N. McGrath/Rhoda Cecil/Hilda Galton
Gertie . . . . Florence Burdett/Rita Ravensburgh/ Pheemie Barnes/Edith Neville/Florence Randle
Mrs Brown . . . . M. A. Victor/Jennie Lowes/Marie Daltra
Yen-Yen . . . . Jessica Lait/Empsie Bowman/Mabelle George
Sing-Sing . . . . Fanny Wright
Mimi . . . . Madge Temple/Jennie Lowes/Bertha Seaton
Soo Soo . . . . Beatrice Edwards/Lily Elsie/Kate Cutler/Mabel Nelson
Mrs Pineapple . . . . Ellas Dee (Fanny Wright)/Marie Dainton/Gracie Leigh
Fi-fi . . . . Louie Freear (Nellie Marler)/Hilda Trevalyan (Gwennie Harcourt)
add Dolly . . . . May Cassel
Winnie . . . . Bertha Culpin

with F. Rooke, D. Sylverton, Hilda Galton, I. Jay, G. May, M. Burton, May Cassell, Bertha Culpin &c.
Dir: George Wilson; md: Ernest Vousden; ch: Will Bishop and Fred Farren; sc: Philip Howden and Walter Hann; cos: Comelli

Produced at the Casino Theatre, New York, under the management of Sam S. Shubert and Messrs Nixon and Zimmerman 2 June, 1902 for a run of 356 performances closing 18 April,

1903. Interpolated numbers by Robert B. Smith and William Jerome, and Melville Ellis. Edwin Stevens (HANG), William Burgess (CHIP), William Pruette (HI), Van Rensselaer Wheeler (TOM), Thomas Q. Seabrooke (MR. P) Aline Potter (VI), Aline Redmond (FL), Eleanor Burns (MILL), Genevieve Whitlock (GERT), Helen Dixey (BEATRICE), Mae Fellon (MARGARET), Sylvia Lisle (FRANCES), Nonie Dore (GWENDOLIN), Annie Yeamans (MRS B), Nella Webb (YEN), Edith Barr (SING), Aimee Angeles (MIMI), Amelia F. Stone (SOO), Adele Ritchie (MRS P), Katie Barry (FIFI), Adelaide Phillips (NETTIE). Dir: Gerald Coventry; md: Herman Perlet; sc: Frank Dodge; cos: Mme Caroline Siedle, Lord & Taylor

Produced at the Prince of Wales Theatre under the management of Frank Curzon 28 January, 1915 for a run of 36 performances closing 27 February, 1915.
Edward Sass (HANG), Kevan Bernard (CHIP), Arthur Hatherton (HI), Lawrence Robbins (TOM), Arthur Wellesley (MR. P), M. Dawson, Heather Featherstone, I. Goulston, V. Leicester (BRIDESMAIDS), Marie Daltra (MRS B), Clarisse Batchelor and Ida Evelyn (MAIDS OF HONOUR), Edith Streeter (MIMI), Carda Walker (SOO), Marie George (MRS P), Dorothy Minto (FIFI). Dir: Frank Curzon; md: Ernest Vousden; ch: Fred Farren; sc: Leolyn Hart

0230 SAN TOY or The Emperor's Own. A Chinese musical comedy in 2 acts by Edward A. Morton. Lyrics by Harry Greenbank and Adrian Ross. Music by Sidney Jones. Additional music by Lionel Monckton. Produced at Daly's Theatre under the management of George Edwardes 21 October, 1899 for a run of 778 performances, ending 14 December, 1901 (closed 22 January-4 February 1901).

Captain Bobby Preston . . . . C. Hayden Coffin (William E. Philp)
Yen How . . . . Rutland Barrington/W. H. Rawlins/ (Colin Coop) (Fred Vigay)
Sir Bingo Preston . . . . Fred Kaye/W. J. Manning
Sing Hi . . . . Colin Coop/Akerman May
Lt Harvey Tucker . . . . Lionel Mackinder/W. Louis Bradfield/ Donald Hall/A. Hickman/Ernest Snow/ Cecil Castle
Fo Hop . . . . H. Scott Russell
Fang. J. T. Maclean/*out*
Hu Pi . . . . S. Arrigoni/J. Murphy
Li Hi . . . . T. H. David
Li Lo . . . . Fred Vigay
The Emperor . . . . Akerman May/Colin Coop/Leedham Bantock/William Wyes
Li . . . . Huntley Wright/Bertie Wright
Poppy Preston. . . . . Hilda Moody/Minnie Hunt/Maidie Hope/ Olive Morrell
Dudley . . . . Gracie Leigh/Ethel Irving (Marie Fawcett)
Chu . . . . May Buckley/Louie Collier/Lizzie Ruggles/ Florence Jameison
Wun Lung . . . . Gladys Homfrey
Ko Fan . . . . Maidie Hope/Mildred Howell/Annie Purcell/Valerie de Lacey
The Wives: Yung Shi . . . . Florence Collingbourne/Aileen d'Orme/ Pearl Lyndon/Leah Lauri/Maud Darrell
Me Koui . . . . Marie Fawcett/Millicent Vernon/Leah Lauri
Siou . . . . Marguerite Roche/O. Hughes/Emilie Hervé
Shuey Pin Sing . . . . . . Florence Allen/Maggie May/May Snowdon/Madge Vincent
Li Kiang . . . . Ethel Hope/Madge Vincent/Maud Darrell/ Florence Allen/Maxwell Hope/Leah Lauri/Maggie May/ Miss Callen
Hu Yu. . . . . Mary Collette
Trixie . . . . Topsy Sinden/Coralie Blythe/Kitty Mason
Mrs Harley Streeter . . . . Alice Davis/Molly Lowell/Vera Edwardine/Dora Field

Hon. Mrs Hay Stackpole . . . . Kathleen Francis
Miss Mary Lambkin . . . . Ada Carter/Miss Charteris/Nellie Seymour/St Clair Innes
Lady Pickleton . . . . Hilda Coral/Dorothy Field/Vera Edwardine/Olga Beatty Kingston
San Toy . . . . Marie Tempest/Florence Collingbourne/Maggie May/Ada Reeve (Alice Davis) (Louie Collier)
add Wai Ho . . . . J. Murphy/S. Arrigoni
Mo Ti . . . . Sebastian King
Rose Tucker . . . . Margaret Fraser/Olive Morrell/Blanche Massey/Nellie Seymour/Vera Edwardine
Officer . . . . Valerie de Lacey/Mildred Howell/Lilian Spencer

Dir: J. A. E. Malone; md: Barter Johns; ch: Willie Warde; sc: Hawes Craven and Joseph Harker; cos: Percy Anderson

Produced at Daly's Theatre, New York, under the management of Daniel Frohman 1 October, 1900 for a run of 65 performances closing 24 November, 1900. Reproduced at Daly's Theatre 4 March, 1901 for a further 103 performances to 1 June, 1901.
Melville Stewart (BP), George K. Fortescue (YH), Wilfred Clarke (SIR), J. L. Weber/Joseph Cauto (SING), Henry Girard (HAR), Joseph Goodrowe (FO), Joseph Cauto/William Wallace (HU), W. W. Scott/A. Gillis (LH), George A. Roarke (LL), Sarony Lambert (EMP), James T. Powers (LI), Flora Zabelle/Helen Royton (POP), Minnie Ashley/Carolyn Gordon (DUD), Jean Newcombe (WUN), Isobel Hall (KO), Elgie Bowen (YUNG), Marie Welch (ME), Nora Lambert (SIOU), Jeanette Palmer (SHUEY), Mary Kier (LI K), Elsie Thorne (HU), Carolyn Gordon/Nora Lambert (TRX), Virginia Streeter (HAR), Stella Krum (HAY), Marie Celeste/Flora Zabelle (ST), Robert M. O'Neil (WAI HO), Frances Gordon (ROSE). Dir: B. D. Stevens and Edwin Price; ch: Willie Warde; sc: Ernest Gros, Henry E. Hoyt

Produced at Daly's Theatre, London, 7 April, 1902 for a season of 32 performances closing 3 May, 1902.

Produced at Daly's Theatre, New York, 17 April 1905 for a season of 24 performances closing 6 May, 1905.

Produced at the Carltheater, Vienna as *San Toy (Der Kaisers Garde)* 9 November, 1900.

Produced at Daly's Theatre, under the management of J. Bannister Howard 22 February, 1932 for a run of 32 performances closing 19 March, 1932.
Donald Mather (BP), Leo Sheffield (YH), Harry Hilliard (SIR), Frank Foster (SING), Walter Bird (HAR), Arthur Digney (FO), Henry Hale (HU), Reginald Matthews (LH), Alex Thomas (LL), Conway Dixon (EMP), Frederick Bentley (LI), Brenda Clether (POP), Rita Page (DUD), Marie Conan (CHU), Susanne Patterson (WUN), Molly Francis (KO), Rosalind Dyer (YUNG), Elma Slee (SIOU), Eileen Lorme (SHUEY), Molly O'Day (LI K), Ivy Oliver (HU), Jean Colin (ST), Fred Drawater (AH WEN), Francis Bergin (WAI HO). Dir: Frederick G. Lloyd

Film: (silent) 1900. An excerpt from *San Toy* featuring Marie Tempest, Coffin, Wright and Barrington was issued by Mutoscope & Biograph.

FLORODORA a musical comedy in 2 acts by Owen Hall. Lyrics by Ernest Boyd-Jones and Paul Rubens. Music by Leslie Stuart. Produced at the Lyric Theatre under the management of Tom B. Davis 11 November, 1899 for a run of 455 performances closing 30 March, 1901.

Cyrus W. Gilfain . . . . Charles E. Stevens
Frank Abercoed . . . . Melville Stewart/Sydney Barraclough/Leonard Russell/Donald Hall
Leandro . . . . Frank Holt
Captain Arthur Donegal . . . . Edgar Stevens/W. Louis Bradfield (Roy Horniman)
Tennyson Sims . . . . Roy Horniman/Lewis Hooper
Ernest Pym . . . . Ernest Lambart/Harry B. Burcher/Charles Hanbury

Max Applebaum . . . . Alfred Barron/Ben Nathan
Reginald Langdale . . . . Frank Haskoll
Paul Crogan. . . . . Sydney Mannering
John Scott. . . . . Frank Walsh
Anthony Tweedlepunch . . . . Willie Edouin/Fred Eastman/Harry Monkhouse (Ben Nathan)
Dolores . . . . Evie Greene/Florence St John/Lena Maitland
Valleda . . . . Nancy Girling (Miss Neville)/Blanche Carlow
Inez . . . . Lydia West/Hilda Jacobson
Jose . . . . Lily MacIntyre/Lucile Murray/E. Neville
Juanita. . . . . Fanny Dango/Maud Rundell/Blanche Carlow
Violante . . . . Blanche Carlow/*out*
Calista . . . . Beatrice Grenville
Angela Gilfain. . . . . Kate Cutler/Nina Sevening/Decima Moore
Daisy Chain. . . . . Edith Housley/Lillie Lane
Mamie Rowe . . . . Jane May/Dorothy Dale/Nellie Harcourt/Dora Sevening
Lucy Ling. . . . . Nora Moore
Cynthia Belmont . . . . Beryl Somerset/Dorothy Dale
Lottie Chalmers. . . . . Nellie Harcourt/Rose Dixon
Claire Fitzclarence . . . . Nina Sevening/Dora Sevening
Lady Holyrood . . . . Ada Reeve/Pattie Browne (Edith Housley)/Phyllis Rankin
add Esperanza. . . . . Nellie Lawrence/Lily MacIntyre
Milistra . . . . Madge Greet

Dir/ch: Sydney Ellison; md: Carl Kiefert; sc: Julia Hicks; cos: Comelli

Produced at the Casino Theatre, New York, under the management of John C. Fisher and Thomas W. Ryley 12 November, 1900 for a run of 379 performances to 12 October, 1901. Transferred to the New York theatre 14 October, 1901 for a further 122 performances closing 25 January, 1902 after a total of 501 performances.
R. E. Graham/W. T. Carleton (CY), Sydney Deane/W. T. Carleton (AB), Nace Bonville (LEA), Cyril Scott (DON), Frederick Edwardes/George deLong/D. W. Mott (TS), Lewis Hooper/T. E. Whitbread/Joseph S. Colt (PYM), C. C. Robinson/Edward Gore (MAX), James A. Kiernan/Karl Stall/T. E. Whitbread (LANG), Charles R. Adams/Thomas A. Kiernan (CROGAN), Roy Lauer (SCOTT), Willie Edouin/Philip H. Ryley/W. J. Ferguson/James A. Kiernan (Nace Bonville) (TW), Fannie Johnstone/Helen Redmond/Guelma L. Baker/Bertha Waltzinger (DOL), Guelma L. Baker/Esther Hull/Susan Drake/Florence Gammage/Francis Tyson (VALL), Lillian Warde/Florence Gammage/Francis Tyson (MONA), Geraldine Bruce (INEZ), Olive Wethered/Sadie Lauer (JOSE), Vivian Austin/Isabelle Carroll (JUA), Dottie Fox/Evelyn Nesbit/Aline Potter (VIO), Julia Gray/Emma Thompson (CAL), May Edouin/Guelma L. Baker/Janette Lowrie (ANG), Margaret Walker/Maybelle Courtenay/Dessa Gibson/Marjorie Relyea/Frances Belmont (DAI), Vaughan Texsmith/Challis Wynter/Susan D. Drake/Edna Goodrich (MAMIE), Marie L. Wilson/Alice Toland/Daisy Green/Minnie Edwardes (LU), Marjorie Relyea/Florence Clemons/Kathryn Sears (CYNTH), Agnes Wayburn/Kathyrn Sears/Clarita Vidal (LOT), Daisy Greene/Elaine van Selover/Susan Drake/Gertrude Douglas/Molly Mayne (CL), Edna Wallace Hopper/Grace Dudley (HOLY), Elaine van Selover/May Hopkins/Sadie Emmons/Ethel M. Harrison (ESTELLE LAMONT). Dir: Lewis Hooper; md: Arthur Weld; sc: Moses & Hamilton

Produced at the Winter Garden Theatre, New York 27 January, 1902 for a run of 48 performances closing 8 March, 1902.
Albert Hart (CY), Sydney Barraclough (AB), Thomas Q. Seabrooke (TW), Dorothy Morton (DOL), Toby Claude (ANG), Virginia Earle (HOLY)

Produced in Paris at the Bouffes-Parisiens in a version by Adrian Vely 1903.
Cast included Paulette Darty, Mlle Dziri, Mlle Ginette, Simon-Max, Jannin, Lucien Prad, Fernal, Roze, Piccaluga (?). Dir: Sydney Ellison

Produced at the Broadway Theatre, New York under the management of John C. Fisher and Thomas Ryley 27 March, 1905 for a run of 32 performances closing 22 April, 1905.
Henry V. Donnelly (CY), Joseph Phillips (AB), Thomas A. Kiernan (LEA), Cyril Scott (DON), Edward Gore (TS), George P. Smith (PYM), D. C. Mott (MAX), James Hughes (LANG), Ralph Williams (CROGAN), Jack Standing (SCOTT), L. Hazeltine (WM), Philip H. Ryley (TW), Maud Lambert (DOL) Lillie Collins (VALL), Lillie Lanton (INEZ), Madeleine Anderton (JOSE), Jennie Bolger (JUA), Maud Crossland (VIO), Maggie Taylor (CALL), Elsa Ryan (ANG), Gertrude Douglass (DAI), Elsa Kennart (MAMIE) Gladys Lockwood (LU), Almeda Porter (CYNTH), Loucile Egan (LOTTIE), Kathleen Dealey (CL), Adele Ritchie (HOLY), Harriet Merrit (ESP), Sallie Lomas (MONTA).

Produced at the Lyric Theatre, under the management of J. Bannister Howard 20 February, 1915 for a run of 62 performances. Transferred to the Aldwych 19 April for a further 28 performances closing 8 May.
H. Scott Russell (CY), Jamieson Dodds (AB), G. H. Asquin (LEA), Herbert St John (DON), James Wright (TS), Dudley Maurice (PYM), James Wright (PAUL GROZON), Cyril Bell (J. TUDON), Fred Dent (S. GIBBONS), Mr Sandbrook (LAGO), Billy Reynolds (MONS LE BLANC), Edward Lewis/Ben Nathan (TW), Evie Greene (DOL), Euphan Maclaren (VALL), Kitty Bell (INEZ), Connie Hazelden (JOSE), Anita Louis (JU), Gracie Baker (VIO) Dorothy Clifford (CAL), Josephine Ellis/Julia James (ANG), Marie Clements (DAI), Margaret Mitchell (LU), Miss Harcourt (CYN), Violet Bruce (LOT), Violet Heath (CL), Olive Royston (XENIA), Mr Desmond (FOOTMAN), May Leslie Stuart/Clara Beck (HOLY) with Amy Preston, Esme Manette, Marion Robinson, Mia Syvelin, Marie Glier, Violet Heath. Dir: Stanley White; md: Leslie Stuart/B. J. Paterson; sc: England & Wallis; cos: B. J. Simmons, Johns Ltd., Mrs Phillips, Cubitt, Thelma, Geo. Seddon & c.

Produced at Daly's Theatre, under the management of J. Bannister Howard 29 July, 1931 for a run of 52 performances closing 12 September. 'Topical lyrics by Arthur Klein'.
Charles Stone (CY), Geoffrey Davis (AB), George Bellamy (LEA), Dudley Rolph (DON), Bruce Anderson (TS), Edward Laing (PYM), B. Reynolds (SMITH), Kenneth Mackay (LANG), J. Ind (CROGAN), A. Richardson (SCOTT), George Graves (TW), Violet Code (DOL), Alison Maclaren (VALL), Fanny Charles (INEZ), Terry Leloir (JO), Daisy Dalziel (JU), Sylvia Page (VIO), Betty Martin (CAL), Glae Carrodus (GLORIA), Lorna Hubbard (ANG), Iris May (DAI), Eva Scott-Thompson/Jane Colne (MAMIE), Josephine Messum (LU), Pamela Drake (CYN), Jean Anita (LOT), Irene Hunter (CLAIRE), Dorothy Ward (HOLY); *add* Eva Scott-Thompson (TYPIST) with B. Bartram, Eileen Brand, Babette Branksmere, Doreen Coburn, Nina Butland, P. Grey, M. Langford, L. Lyon, G. Manning, B. Martin, E. Pole-Harvey, P. Stevens, I. Strong, L. Warne. J. Ashford, Francis Bergin, Austin Camp, T. George, J. Hardy, Mr McBeen. Dir: Frederick G. Lloyd; md: Leonard Hornsey; ch: Alison Maclaren; sc: Grantham & Co.; cos: B. J. Simmons & Co. etc.

Produced at the Century Theatre, New York, under the management of J. J. Shubert 5 April, 1920 for a run of 150 performances.
John T. Murray (CY), Walter Woolf (AB), Nace Bonville (LEA), Harry Fender (DON), Lucius Metz (TS), Minor McLain (PYM), Lewis Christy (ALLEN), George Ellison (LANG), William Lillite (CROGAN), Allen C. Jenkins (SCOTT), George Hassell (TW), Eleanor Painter (DOL), Muriel de Forrest (VALL), Isabelle Rodriguez (JUA), Marie Wells (MARAQUITA), Perle Germonde (PAQUITA), Margot Kelly (ANG), Muriel Lodge (DAI), Dama Sykes (CLAIRE), Dorothy Leeds (BERENICE), Fay Evelyn (MABEL), Beatrice Swanson (LUCILLE), Marcella Swanson (ALICE), Christie MacDonald (HOLY) with Billy Andrews, Bernice Dewey, Margaret Grace, Adelina Thomason, Blue Cloud, Betty Dair, Elizabeth Darling, Beatrice Darling, Jacqueline Logan, Rheba Stewart, Helen O'Day, Bunny Stewart, Hannah Krum, Helen Weber, Dorothy Johnson, Gypsy Mooney, Ellen Este, Hilda Wright, Madelene Laurell, Margaret Adair, Edna Rodet, Natalie Graves, Olive Channing, Frances Dunlap, Anna Berg, Peggy Holmes, Estelle Langner, Imelda La Morte, Leila van Holk, Helen Sovrani, Betty Palmer, Ethel Loris, Ruth Hervey, Elizabeth Walsh, Camilla Lyon, Eleanor Grover, Idamae Oderlin, Elaine Hall, June Kellard, Helen Adams, Mona Mode, Trixie Stegman; Messrs Conroy, Miller, Harvey, Christy O'Donnell, Packard, Dillon, Tillett, Steele, Johnson. Dir: Lewis Morton; md: Oscar Radin; ch: Allen K. Foster and Lewis Hooper; sc: Watson Barrett; cos: Cora MacGeachy &c.

Produced off-off-Broadway 20 February, 1981 by Bandwagon.

0232 **THE ROSE OF PERSIA** or The Story Teller and The Slave. A comic opera by Basil Hood. Music by Arthur Sullivan. Produced at the Savoy Theatre under the management of Richard D'Oyly Carte 29 November, 1899 for a run of 213 (220?) performances closing 28 June, 1900.

The Sultan Mahmoud . . . . Henry A. Lytton.
Hassan. Walter Passmore
Yussuf. Robert Evett
Abdallah. . . . . George Ridgewell/Jones Hewson
The Grand Vizier. . . . . W. H. Leon
The Physician-in-Chief. . . . . Charles Childerstone
The Royal Executioner . . . . Reginald Crompton
Soldier of the Guard . . . . Powis Pinder
Sultana Zubedyah. . . . . Ellen Beach Yaw/Isabel Jay/Agnes Fraser
Scent-of-Lilies . . . . Jessie Rose/Gertrude Jerrard?/Decima Moore
Heart's Desire. . . . . Louie Pounds
Honey of Life. . . . . Emmie Owen
Dancing Sunbeam . . . . Rosina Brandram (Jessie Pounds)
Blush-of-the-Morning. . . . . Isabel Jay/Agnes Fraser/Norah Maguire
Oasis-in-the-Desert . . . . Madge Moyse
Song-of-Nightingale . . . . Rose Rosslyn
Moon-upon-the-Waters. . . . . Jessie Pounds
Whisper-of-the-West-Wind. . . . . Gertrude Jerrard/Nell (or Nina) Richardson

Dir: Richard Barker; md: François Cellier; ch: Willie Warde; cos: Percy Anderson; sc: W. Harford

Produced at Daly's Theatre, New York, under the management of Richard D'Oyly Carte 6 September, 1900 for a run of 25 performances closing 29 September, 1900.
Charles Angelo (SULT), John Le Hay (HASS), Sidney Bracy (YUS), Herbert Clayton (ABD), Stuart Hyatt (VIZ), John Doran (PHYS), Arthur Barry (EX), Ruth Vincent (ZUB), Hettie Lund (SCENT), Isabel Dillon (HD), Hilda Stephens (HON), Amy Martin (DANC), Mary Conyhgham (BLUSH), Doris Latour (OASIS), Hetty Herzfeld (MOON), Marguerite Trew (SONG), Nell Meissener (WHISP)

Produced at the Prince's Theatre, under the management of R. Claud Jenkins 28 February, 1935 for a run of 25 performances closing 23 March, 1935.
Eddie Garr (SULT), Joseph Spree (HASS), Robert Naylor (Y), Franklyn Kelsey (AB), Leonard Russell (VIZ), Philip Merritt (PHYS), Norman Greene (EX), Helene Raye (ZUB), Marie Layne (SCENT), Desiree Ellinger (HD), Carlita Ackroyd (HONEY), Amy Augarde (DS), Lilian Keyes (BLUSH), Esme Dunning Moore (CYPRESS), Nancy Evans (SONG), Marita Tate (MOON), Arabella Tulloch (WHISPER), Daphne de Witt (OASIS). Dir: William J. Wilson; md: Sydney Baynes.

SOMEBODY'S SWEETHEART a musical comedy-drama in 3 acts. A revised version of *Sunny Florida/The Armenian Girl* by Edward H. Marris. Music 'arranged' by Charles W. Johnson. Produced at West Hartlepool under the management of Warwick Major 15 July, 1899 and toured.

THE JOKING GIRL a musical farcical comedy in one scene, by Robert A. Williams. Music by J. Capel Woodruffe. Produced at the Albert Theatre, Gainsborough, 9 March, 1899 and toured. Dates included Goole, West Hartlepool, Macclesfield, Darwen, Ramsgate, Margate, Bury St Edmunds, Southend, Eastbourne, Walsall, Aldershot, Rhyl, Lytham, Neath &c.

Robert McNaughty . . . . Charles Usher
Bob Maxwell . . . . Fred Parr
Sergeant Stout . . . . E. Stevens
P. C. Onions . . . . Alfred Pierce
P. C. Whiskey. . . . . Lionel Allen
Tommy Christmas . . . . W. Edwardes
Brutus Fitzlollipop de Romeo . . . . . Dray Robinson
Painty . . . . M. Todd
Asylum Attendant. . . . . Mr Smith

Aunt Chimpanzee	Lillie Mowbray
Jemima Pry	Maggie Mowbray
Nancy	Blanche la Rose
Lillie Fielding	Maud Howarth
Maggie Fielding	Elsie Capel/Bertie Leslie
Mons. de Poppe	Alfred Austin

1900

The first year of the new century was a quiet one for new musical productions. They were scarcely neeeded. The triumph of *San Toy* and the popularity of *Florodora* meant that both Daly's and the Lyric were occupied throughout the year while at the Shaftesbury *The Belle of New York* gave way to a series of American pieces. None of these succeeded in even approaching the popularity of their illustrious sister, and Sousa's *A Mystical Miss* (*The Charlatan*) with De Wolf Hopper and *An American Beauty* starring Edna May both disappeared in a couple of months. *The Casino Girl,* produced in July with Mabelle Gillman in the title role did better and ran on through the remainder of the year. Another American venture, *A Parlour Match*, tried at Terry's, was the work of Charles Hoyt who had been so successful with *A Trip to Chinatown*. Hoyt was now in an asylum and, shortly after the West End production of his 1896 piece, he died. *A Parlour Match* had already closed.

The British musicals in town fared rather better. *San Toy* and *Florodora* were impressive throughout the year at the head of the hit shows and the Savoy, after the close of *The Rose of Persia* produced fine revivals of first *The Pirates of Penzance* (127 perfs) and then *Patience* (150 perfs). At the Gaiety, *A Runaway Girl* finally closed out its long and happy run, and George Edwardes produced the next of his unfailingly prosperous modern-dress hits by the house team of James Tanner, Lionel Monckton, Ivan Caryll, Adrian Ross, Percy Greenbank and, on this occasion, Alfred Murray. This new piece was set to be called *The Messenger Girl* and, according to various reports, was to star Evie Greene or Florence Lloyd in its title role. But when it opened its run on 3 February, to a tumultuous reception, the new show was called *The Messenger Boy*: the series of 'Girl' musicals at the Gaiety had come to an end.

The shift of emphasis in the title reflected the changes in the Gaiety's team of actors. The most notable recent defection had been that of the theatre's leading lady, Ellaline Terriss, who was soon to appear with her husband in a series of musicals specially constructed for them under the management of Charles Frohman. Miss Terriss was replaced in the principal girl's role by Violet Lloyd, but Miss Lloyd was obliged to concede the top female billing to Katie Seymour whose established partnership with Teddy Payne had become one of the features of the Gaiety musical since their comic Orientalisms in 'Love on the Japanese Plan' in *The Shop Girl*. It was Payne whose now unchallenged pre-eminence at the theatre earned him the title role of *The Messenger Boy*. Violet Lloyd and Lionel Mackinder were featured in the light romantic leads, formerly reserved for the Hicks family, but the comedy side of the piece clearly took the upper hand in a cast which included the inimitable Connie Ediss and the well-known comic Harry Nicholls as the 'boy's' parents; Fred Wright Jr; and, in a welcome return, E. J. Lonnen as the inevitable Eastern potentate.

The libretto of *The Messenger Boy* was an advance on most of its contemporaries in the realm of light musical plays. James Tanner had already shown, notably in *My Girl*, a greater predilection for plot and construction in the book of a musical than most librettists. In the case of *The Messenger Boy* Tanner and Murray's book proved to be just the thing for the Gaiety's patrons. Light and jolly, farcical in parts without falling into grotesque rough and tumble, it provided its leading players with all the right opportunities while keeping to its simple but suitable and effective storyline.

There are two rivals for the hand of the lovely Nora. The favoured one is Clive Radnor, the other is wily Tudor Pyke. Nora accepts Clive's offer of marriage and the young man sets off post-haste for Egypt to get the consent of her father, Lord Punchestown. But the wicked Pyke has other ideas. He holds a promissory note of Clive's which he determines to get to Punchestown to ruin his rival's chances. He employs the messenger boy, Tommy Bang, to carry the vital paper to Egypt, overwhelmed with dire threats should anyone relieve him of the 'evidence'. Tommy sets off for Egypt, but Pyke suddenly discovers he has given him the wrong piece of paper – the boy is carrying a compromising letter written by . . . Lady Punchestown! Pyke sets off to stop the messenger. Nora, who has discovered the plot also chases after Tommy but the intrepid messenger boy, aided and abetted by Lady Punchestown's maid, Rosa, succeeds through various tricks and disguises in eluding all his pursuers. Eventually all ends well. Nora and her Clive are united, Pyke is discomfited, and Tommy and Rosa tied in final-curtain matrimony.

The elements of the libretto were in the best tradition of the British farcical musical but, in this case, they were put together with an exceptional degree of style and economy, and with the extraneous material strictly controlled. Of course there were subplots. Connie Ediss as Mrs Bang recognises in the magazine photo of 'Hooker Pasha' her long-lost husband and promptly joins the exodus to Egypt, and Willie Warde as the archeologist, Phunkwitz, provides an opportunity for Tommy and Rosa to escape disguised as the mummies he is transporting; but the book was basically sound and *The Era* went so far as to claim:

> *The Messenger Boy* bids fair to be the most successful of the whole of the very popular series of musical plays . . . due to its ingenious and interesting plot . .

The songs and the dances were, as always, of the utmost importance, and *The Messenger Boy* maintained the standards of it predecessors. Teddy Payne scored in the first act with the show's title song:

> I am a smart little sort of a chap
> Very obliging and active
> Notice my uniform, buttons and cap,
> Neat, but extremely attractive;
> Though rather small you will find that I know
> Plenty of dodges and wrinkles
> All over London I rush to and fro
> No matter where – I am ready to go
> Soon as the telephone tinkles.
>
> I'm the Messenger Boy
> With my jaunty air
> And my cheeky stare
> I'm the lad you ought to employ
> Quite a model Messenger Boy.

and joined in a duet with Katie Seymour (Rosa) called 'Aspirations' in which they dreamed of the things they would like to be – a policeman, a soldier, a fireman and so forth. A concerted piece making fun of the much-maligned Bradshaw's Guidebooks also went well, as did a coy little duet for Nora and Clive called 'Ask Papa'.

In the second part of the first act it was Connie Ediss who hit the bullseye with a comical song written by Adrian Ross and Lionel Monckton and titled 'In the Wash':

You talk about detectives in a story
That guess whatever people say or do
I think that Sherlock Holmes in all his glory
Might ask the humble laundress for a clue.
If any crime is hard to disentangle
You get a washerwoman in the box
For when she's put a party through the mangle
She knows him, from his dickey to his socks.

O, I found things out when I did a bit of washing
A man may say he's wealthy, but I know that's bosh.
I can tell he's got no dollars
By the edges of his collars
For it all comes out in the wash, wash, wash!

In the second act, Fred Wright Jr had a sprightly number 'Captain Potts', Payne and Miss Seymour brought down the house with their 'Mummies' song and dance, Connie Ediss scored again with 'Comme çi, Comme ça' and Violet Lloyd had a follow-up to 'Soldiers in the Park' with the patriotic 'When the Boys Come Home once More'. But, as on so many similar occasions, it was a minor character who stole the limelight with the show's 'hit' song. Little Rosie Boote had progressed from the chorus and the touring companies finally to be given a featured spot in *The Messenger Boy*. In the tiny role of Isabel Blyth she caused the rafters to ring as the audience erupted before:

Maisie is a daisy
Maisie is a dear
For the boys are mad about her
And they can't get on without her
And they all cry 'whoops' when Maisie's coming near
Maisie doesn't mind it
Maisie lets them stare
Other girls are so uncertain
When they do a bit of flirtin'
But Maisie gets right there!

Soon the whole town was singing about 'Maisie' but Rosie Boote's first solo at the Gaiety was also her last, for she left the cast of *The Messenger Boy* early in 1901 to become the Marchioness of Headfort, following Connie Gilchrist from the Gaiety boards to the peerage.

There was no doubt, right from the start, that *The Messenger Boy* would carry on the now traditional success of the Gaiety musicals. *The Times* enthused:

> If ever a piece was launched upon a run with every promise of future success, *The Messenger Boy* produced on Saturday night was so launched .

The excellence of the framework and the book was everywhere commented on, and the songs were not denied their fair share of the praise. Edwardes' typically stylish and extravagant staging also met with due compliment:

> Success unqualified . . . . a brighter and more exhilarating entertainment would be difficult to conceive . . (*Stage*)

And so *The Messenger Boy* took up residence at the Gaiety for the next sixteen months and its popularity remained high throughout.

In the fashion of the time, constant alterations were made to keep the piece novel. Numerous new songs were introduced, although the biggest favourites such as 'Maisie', 'In the Wash' and 'The Messenger Boy' all held their places. Even the concerted pieces were replaced, but the major alteration was the complete restructuring of the second act for the so-called 'second edition' of the show. From their Egyptian happy ending, the whole cast were diverted to the Paris Exhibition for a supplementary scene involving a new set of numbers. Payne and Katie Seymour had a new duet written by Paul Rubens and Ivan Caryll to replace the 'Mummies' routine, Connie Ediss dropped 'Comme çi, Comme ça' and related instead 'How I saw the CIV':

> You talk about your Paris shows
> You should have come with me
> When Mrs Brown and I we went to meet the CIV
> We'd heard about the khaki boys returning from afar
> So I says, 'Martha, let's be there' and she said, 'Right you are'
>
> Oh, the volunteers, the lovely CIV
> They're the boys that all the gals come out to see
> I bought a little Union Jack and so did Mrs Brown
> And off we went to welcome back the lads of London town . .

Paul Rubens and John Stromberg contributed a parody on the now famous 'Tell me, pretty Maiden' double sextette which was performed by Marie Studholme (now playing Nora), Rosie Boote, Maie Saqui, Fred Wright, Lonnen and Payne:

> MEN: Tell us, pretty ladies, don't you think that we are rather neat?
> GIRLS: You're not so bad, young sirs, but smarter boys we often meet
> MEN: Most people can't resist us–we're so captivating, don't you know
> GIRLS: It's awfully kind of you to say that, for it interests us so

A new duet for Wright and Payne, 'A little Bit further On', a fresh song for Mackinder, 'A perfectly peaceful Person' (Rubens), and a Melville Ellis number 'I'm Tired of being Respectable' for Wright all made appearances, but the basis of the piece remained the same, and its popularity did not falter. The rest of its life, in the tradition of its fellow Gaiety shows, followed on naturally. Broadway was treated to a 129-performance run with James T. Powers in the Teddy Payne role, and Australia, South Africa and the British provinces all gave *The Messenger Boy* a warm reception. The Gaiety musical was at the peak of its popularity all around the English-speaking world.

Success did not, however, attend the only other new British entry of the year, a misconceived piece called *The Gay Pretenders*. It was produced at the Globe Theatre in November with a libretto by George Grossmith Jr and music by Claud Nugent, the 33-year-old son of Sir Edmund Nugent of West Harling Hall, Thetford, and a newcomer to the West End musical.

Originally described as 'a burlesque extravaganza' it later changed its soubriquet to 'comic opera', but in fact it was half an old-fashioned historical burlesque and half a mass of ill-defined intentions. Familiar characters abounded – Henry VII of England,

Prince Harry, Perkin Warbeck, Lambert Simnel – in a curious tale of disguises and of jumpings on-and-off the throne of England. On this occasion Grossmith did not have, as in *Great Caesar,* the assistance of Willie Edouin and Ada Reeve but he did have, nevertheless, a good cast around him. In spite of the fiasco of *His Excellency,* he had persuaded his father to come out on to the stage again as the pretender-turned-falconer, Lambert Simnel. His old Savoy colleague, Richard Temple, was Henry VII and the vocal side of affairs was further enriched by the casting of John Coates as Perkin Warbeck. Grossmith himself took on the part of the Prince while the female team was headed by no less a favourite than Letty Lind in the role of Clotilde.

But the material with which they had to work was too much even for a cast such as this. *The Times* took no half measures in its review, describing the piece as 'an entertainment of the most incongruous description . .' with 'perfectly commonplace' music, and reported that its reception had been 'ambiguous'. *The Stage* complained that it was

> a bad specimen of semi-historical burlesque . . . half seriously treated and interesting as far as it goes . . . eked out by topical banalities in the way of allusions to current matters and comic ditties that seem to have strayed out of the realms of musical comedy . . . the result is by no means satisfactory for, just as the audience is really taking heed of the personages with names familiar to all schoolboys, attention is distracted by some stupid 'quip' or dull 'turn' in the very worst manner of the new school.

This particular reviewer was a little too keen to pigeonhole the various 'species' of musical play, and his displeasure at the 'mixing of styles' was scarcely a valid criticism, but the fact remained that Grossmith's attempt to mix old burlesque with modern methods and material was not well enough done to justify itself. His wit was decidedly feeble, and his fancies far too stretched. One number, a quartet called 'Propaganda' was constructed around the tortured line: 'He's a very proper goose, and we're a propaganda' which had very little relation to the rest of the song. Another song rejoiced in the chorus:

> I'm sorry I've seen Pauline
> For my love became fearfully keen
> So keen, my Queen, I ween, she has always been
> And yet I'm sorry I've seen Pauline.

which made 'Maisie the Daisy' seem like literature. Anguished rhymes abounded (such as 'halidom' and 'balletdom' which was probably intended to be humorous) and complex conceits such as the founding of a number for Lady Katherine Gordon on a card game:

> Behold, you see the KING before your face
> Of stepping on the throne within an ACE
> With an army of a hundred thousand men
> Ably represented here by TEN.
> Such advantage no opponent disregards
> Though the HAND, its seems, still misses two more CARDS.
> Will you help the situation, sir, to save
> By supposing for the while you are the KNAVE.
> With the matter we will now proceed to DEAL
> On the issue rests his fortune, woe or weal
> When Fate who is the DEALER quickly jumps

To the obvious conclusion HEARTS ARE TRUMPS
And proceeds, amidst the all-appalling hush
To lay upon the board a ROYAL FLUSH
Which without my help you never would have seen
For I graciously consent to be THE QUEEN

It can be little coincidence that Jeanne Douste, hired to create this role, left the show fairly promptly. The show itself hung on through Christmas and folded soon after. Its young composer survived his West End début by only a few months and died at the age of 34, in April of 1901.

If London had, in this year, little call for new musical pieces, the provinces kept up their vigorous flow of fresh productions. Alongside tours of the long-lived *The Lady Slavey, Dorothy* and *The New Barmaid*, such perennial favourites as *The French Maid, The Dandy Fifth* and *Gentleman Joe* and multiple companies of the newer hits such as *The Geisha, Florodora* and *A Runaway Girl,* there appeared a good collection of new musicals. Of these, the two most important were *Kitty Grey* and *H.M.S. Irresponsible,* two widely different pieces both destined to turn up in the West End the following year alongside *A Chinese Honeymoon* which was touring its second year without having, as yet, been tried in the metropolis.

Kitty Grey was produced under the management of George Edwardes. It was a version of Hennequin and Mars' successful French play *Les Fêtards*[1] which Edwardes had presented at the Vaudeville Theatre earlier in the year in a non-musical version by J. Smyth Piggott, starring W. L. Abingdon, Miriam Clements and Ellis Jeffries at the head of a cast which also included a number of well-known musical performers: Cairns James, Fritz Rimma, Cecil Frere, C. P. Little, 'Bob' Robina and Lillie Belmore. It had received notice as being slightly scandalous and held the stage for 107 performances without becoming particularly popular. A musical version was soon in the air. First it was announced that Lederer would be setting one up for the Shaftesbury Theatre under the title *The Night Owls,* but Edwardes put his team to work on the Vaudeville version: Ross, Rubens, Monckton, Talbot and Augustus Barratt all contributed, and the musical *Kitty Grey* opened at Bristol a mere nineteen days after the closure of the play's Vaudeville season. Some of the cast – notably Lillie Belmore – retained their roles from the straight production, but the leading roles were taken by Harry Monkhouse as the King of Illyria, Ethel Sydney and Evie Greene, with Maurice Farkoa, G. P. Huntley and Mabel Love in supporting roles.

Kitty Grey was very different to the prevailing kind of musical. The play had been but little tampered with and the result was a particularly strong libretto – virtually a play with music – which was decorated with not too many numbers of the prettiest and most popular kind from Edwardes' workshop. The songs enhanced the appeal of the play, the play provided a solid setting for the songs, and the result was altogether positive; *Kitty Grey* toured through the latter months of the year with great success. During the tour Harry Monkhouse came out of the leading role to take over as Tweedlepunch in *Florodora* and was replaced by the show's 'without songs' King, W. L. Abingdon, and a further cast change saw the departure of the always troublesome Mabel Love who decided her role was not worthy of her talents. But *Kitty Grey* was unaffected as it shaped up for a West End run which finally took place in September of the following year through to April of 1902.

[1] *Les Fêtards* with music by Victor Roger was successfully played at the Palais Royal, Paris, in 1897.

H.M.S. Irresponsible (or, variously, *The Cruise of the H.M.S. Irresponsible*) had little in common with *Kitty Grey*. Its book was as amorphous, flexible and incoherent as could be and its star was Arthur Roberts. The plot, telling how a party of travellers wrecked on a Greek Island are captured by bandits, had the lofty Captain Chepstow obliged for his safety to change identities with the lowly Jim Slingsby. Jim escapes and finds himself in command of the Captain's ship. After the first act, the plot more or less dissolved into a welter of songs, dances and 'turns'. The character of Jim, and the basic situation of the little common man placed in the shoes of his social superior, appealed to Roberts and his audiences, however, and *H.M.S. Irresponsible* became one of his favourite touring vehicles. His best number in the piece was a George Rollitt song called 'Topsy Turvy' which remained a feature through constant changes in the score as the show was toured round the country before its West End début. It opened at London's Strand Theatre the following May for a good season of five months.

Lolo or The End Of The World was an attempt at a comic opera by Arthur Sturgess and Jimmy Glover, the authors of *Regina B.A.* It was a whimsical tale of an evil magician, Presto, set on a tropical isle. Presto has forecast the end of the world by explosion as a way of forcing the heroine, Lolo, to marry him. In spite of the arrival of the British marines, the first act ends with Lolo refusing to give in and Presto faking the blowing-up of the island. In Act 2, the islanders have fled to England, where Presto tries to blackmail them with compromising letters rescued from the 'catastrophe'. Good eventually triumphs, and everyone can return to their island home. In spite of the occasional pretty number, *Lolo* was scarcely a success. It was revised and revived in 1902 without notably improving itself or its record.

Also in the comic opera vein was a piece called *The Wonder Worker* produced at Fulham. It was not a success. *The Stage* described it as:

> . . a slender plot devoid of dramatic situations and wit, but few interesting incidents framed a theme which in spite of some clever and well-written lyrics set to tuneful, sparkling and lively music, failed to rivet the attention . .

The 'tuneful, sparkling and lively music' was the work of Albert W. Ketèlbey, whose name survived to posterity largely as the composer of 'In a Monastery Garden' and 'In a Persian Market'.

Some of the more unpretentious of the provincial musicals of 1900 were destined to have much longer lives. *His Majesty's Guests*, *The Dandy Doctor*, *The Squatter's Daughter* and *Schwenk, the Dreamer* all survived through a number of seasons on the smaller touring circuits without ever threatening to break into the Number One touring dates or the metropolitan scene. *His Majesty's Guests* was produced by the Fred Karno troupe and was constructed from two of the troupe's sketches, *Jail Birds* and a skit on the 'New Woman', with songs and dances composed by Herbert Darnley, writer of such songs as 'Mrs Kelly' and 'The Beefeater' for Dan Leno, to all of which was added a fair lashing of variety turns. A musical comedy element was added by importing several popular artists from the provincial musical stage: Walter Groves, Dolly Harmer and Bessie Allayne all featured in the original production. *His Majesty's Guests*, described as a 'musical pantomimic farce', proved very popular with its provincial and suburban audiences and was reproduced for several seasons.

The Dandy Doctor was the work of Edward Marris, and involved most of the traditional elements of musical low comedy: disguises, dissimulations, mistaken identities, and a good deal of money and romance, the whole ending up with a carnival on Brighton pier. It was bright and smart, constantly changing and continued to be appreciated on the smallest circuits for several years.

The Squatter's Daughter was a mixture of far-fetched melodrama and variety entertainment. It was based on the familiar tale of the wicked villain and the wealthy maid, set, in this case, in the romantically distant land of Australia. Its format was devised to allow the interpolation of some songs and dances by one 'Sparrow' Harris, plus anything and everything from a tumbling act to the showing of 'cinematograph pictures'. This last-named effect came to grief on the first night and the *Stage* critic wrote that the best thing in the show was the Cragg Family acrobatic act in the final scene. Nevertheless, *The Squatter's Daughter* did perfectly well in its first tour and was revived the following year under the more dashing title of *Dare-Devil Dorothy* for the first of a long series of annual tours over the ensuing decade.

Schwenk, the Dreamer was the latest in the series of musical comedy-dramas concocted by Harry Starr for his own display. He had been most successful with *Carl the Clockmaker* and *Otto the Outcast*, and *Schwenk* proved to be almost as popular. It was a version of the Rip van Winkle legend with Starr featured in the title-role of Schwenk/Rip in what he called a 'romantic comedy opera'. One of the interpolated numbers, 'Swinging on the Gate', gained a certain degree of popularity.

1900

0233 **THE MESSENGER BOY** a musical play in two acts by James T. Tanner and Alfred Murray. Lyrics by Adrian Ross and Percy Greenbank. Music by Lionel Monckton and Ivan Caryll. Produced at the Gaiety Theatre under the management of George Edwardes 3 February, 1900 for a run of 429 performances closing 8 June, 1901. The Gaiety Theatre was closed between 29 July and 1 September 1900.

Hooker Pasha . . . . Harry Nicholls/Harry Monkhouse/George Grossmith Jr?
Cosmos Bey . . . . E. J. Lonnen
Clive Radnor . . . . Lionel Mackinder
Captain Pott. . . . . Fred Wright Jr
Professor Phunkwitz . . . . Willie Warde/Edward Redway
Comte le Fleury. . . . . Robert Nainby/A. Nilson Fysher
Tudor Pyke . . . . John Tresahar (Julian Royce)
Lord Punchestown . . . . William Wyes/Spenser Barry/Ellis Ogilvie/Arthur Hatherton
Captain Naylor . . . . Harry Grattan
Mr Gascoigne. . . . . Arthur Hatherton/Ellis Ogilvie
Purser . . . . Jack Thompson
Mr Trotter . . . . F. Standen/Arthur Hatherton/Frank Greene/F. Carrol
Tommy Bang . . . . Edmund Payne
Nora. . . . . Violet Lloyd/Marie Studholme
Daisy Dapple . . . . Grace Palotta/Katie Vesey/*out*
Mrs Bang . . . . Connie Ediss/Claire Romaine (May Lucas)
Lady Punchestown . . . . Maud Hobson/Gladys Homfrey/Maie Saqui
Isabel Blyth . . . . Rosie Boote/Maidie Hope/Coralie Blythe
Lady Winifred . . . . Margaret Fraser
Cecilia Gower . . . . Maie Saqui/Kate Mason
Rosa . . . . Katie Seymour
Society Ladies: Hetty Hamer, Ada Maitland, Florence Lauri, Connie Rossell, F. Langtyre, K. Warren/Doris Beresford, Sara Miskel, F. Gillian, F. Lawrence, G. MacKenzie
Pd: Kitty Mason
add Stubbs . . . . Frank Greene/'A Standen'
Dorothy Marjoribanks . . . . Katie Vesey/*out*
Selim . . . . E. D. Wardes
with Mabel Warren, Muriel Cusins, Cissie Vaughan

Dir: J. A. E. Malone; md: Ivan Caryll; ch: Willie Warde; sc: Joseph Harker & T. E. Ryan; cos: Wilhelm

Produced at Daly's Theatre, New York, under the management of Messrs Nixon & Zimmerman 16 September, 1901 for a run of 129 performances closing 4 January, 1902.

George Honey (HOOK), Paul Nicholson (COS), John P. Park (CLIVE), Harry Kelly (POTT), Tom Hadaway (PHUNK), George de Long (FL), George Health/Charles Giblyn (PYKE), Harold C. Crane (PUNCH), John P. Kennedy (NAY), Herbert Darley (TROT/PURS), Armand Cortes (STUBBS) James T. Powers (BANG), Georgia Caine (NORA), May Robson (MRS), Jobyna Howland (LADY), Flora Zabelle (IS), Hattie Waters (WIN), Agnes Wayburn (CG), Helen Chichester (DOR), Miss Fanchonette (PEPITA), Rachel Booth (ROSA); with Abner Seymour, George Pullman, J. W. Styles, Florence Redmond, Bertha Hunter, Agnes Blake Wadleigh, Caroline Lock, Sally McNeil, Louis Murry, Dene Woodruff, Jeanette Stanhope. Dir: Herbert Gresham; md: Louis F. Gottschalk; sc: Joseph Harker; cos: F. Richard Anderson

0234 **THE SQUATTER'S DAUGHTER** a romantic musical comedy-drama in three acts by Wilfred Carr. Music by Sparrow Harris. Produced at the Opera House, Coventry, under the management of J. W. Cordiner 5 March, 1900 and toured. Dates included Worcester, Longton, Ashton-under-Lyne, Stockport, Salford, Nottingham, Woolwich &c.

Lt Harold Vivian . . . . Thomas Kennard
Captain Dudley . . . . Tom Grove
Featherstone Haugh. . . . . Wilfred Carr
Smith . . . . F. W. Wibert
Hawkins. . . . . Henry Staveley
Jacko . . . . Ronald Blair
Silas Crump. . . . . Edward Kipling
Judith . . . . Fanny Humber
Ruth Montrose . . . . Nellie Arline
Mabel Montrose . . . . Kathleen Gerrard

Later played as *Dare-Devil Dorothy*, a musical comedy novelty in 3 acts. Music by K. Ernest Irving.

0235 **THE DANDY DOCTOR** a musical something-to-laugh-at in three acts by Edward Marris. Music by 'Dudley Powell' (Dudley Jepps). Produced at the Avenue Theatre, Sunderland, under the management of James Francis and Harry Poole 26 March, 1900 and toured. Dates included Oldham, Coventry, Liverpool, Leeds, Blackburn, Wakefield, Burnley, Preston, Eccles, Southport, Accrington, Wigan, Salford, Balham, Huddersfield &c.

Melchisadeck Brown . . . . James Francis
Colonel Pendred . . . . Owen Dacroy
Arthur Vandyke. . . . . Harry Marsden
Bertie Bolingbroke . . . . O. E. Lennon
Henson . . . . Alfred Sewell
William Basham. . . . . Alec Keith
James Straight . . . . Edmund Brown
John James Murphy PC III . . . . William Morgan
Penniless Pursey . . . . Harry Herbert
Mrs Vandyke . . . . Annie Johnson
Jane, 'The General'. . . . . Florence Smithers
Ivy Pendred. . . . . Sallie Lomas
B. A. D. Patient. . . . . 'Mr Drycoff'
with the Tyneside Trio and The American Beauties.

0236 **H. M. S. IRRESPONSIBLE (THE CRUISE OF)** a musical play in 2 acts by J. F. Cornish. Music by George Byng. Additional lyrics by Bennett Scott and George Rollitt. Produced at the Royalty Theatre, Chester under the management of Arthur Roberts 2 August, 1900 and toured through Dublin, Belfast, Preston, Southport, Douglas, Blackpool, Bolton, Liverpool, Edinburgh, Glasgow, Manchester, Sheffield, Leeds, Bradford, Halifax, ?, Broadway, Kennington, Coronet, Standard, Folkestone, Hastings, Balham, Southampton, Kingston, Kennington, Croydon, Cheltenham, Stratford East, Liverpool, Hanley, Huddersfield, Oldham, Crouch End, Brighton, Portsmouth, Fulham, Blackpool/Cambridge, Bournemouth, Alexandra, Nottingham, Sheffield, to 25 May, 1901.

Bob Chaffers	W. H. Denny/Charles Goold/Keino Johnston
Ibrahim	J. G. Birtles/S. Haydon/Fred Keen
Ruffino Raffaelo	Edward Story-Gofton/Harold Eden/Fritz Rimma
Cheeko	Dan Thomas/E. Thomas?/J. M. Hayden
Dragoman	A. Dampier/A. Birtles/Walter Burton
Admiral Sir Vigers Maxim	Percy Clifton
Lt Angus Anderson	Robert Selby
Captain Grimsby Chepstow	Maitland Dicker
Chevalier Luigi Vollavento	Dan Thomas/A. Dampier
Harold Dundas	S. Haydon/D. S. Jeffrey
Horatio Nelson	Ruby Celeste/Mabel Fairfax
Jim Slingsby	Arthur Roberts
Hon. Gwendoline Lovitt	Nelly Cozens/Clarissa Talbot/Heloise Osland
Olive Chepstow	Clarissa Talbot/Josephine Le Barte
Miss Diane de Montgomerie	Norah Cecil/Hilda Stephens/Ruby Celeste
Victoria Chaffers	Queenie Leighton/Kitty Loftus/Georgie Martin
Bosun	W. Morgan/Tom Bennett
The Bey of Smyrna	Frank Cochrane/George Davis

with Gertrude Paterson, L. Hodson, Maud Cameron, Davis Shirley, Violet Lanoma, Beatrice Cross, Victoria Vokes, Maud de la Porte, Alice Vivian, Georgie Gray, Misses Norman, Onslow and Stanley; Messrs Cochrane, Lewis, Jones, Hayden, Huddlestone, George Watson, Walter Lester, James Pridmore, Gordon Brown, Henry James, Walter Keates, Arthur Webster, Alec Nisbet, D. Aquila, Andrew Grey, Harry Newlands.

Dir: E. Story-Gofton; md: Augustus Bingham; ch: Mme Rosa; sc: Fred Storey; cos: J. A. Harrison & Co.

Produced at the Strand Theatre, under the management of Arthur Roberts in a revised version 27 May, 1901. Transferred to the Globe Theatre 29 July, 1901. Closed 26 October, 1901 after a run of 165 performances.

Bob Chaffers	W. H. Denny/Fred Grove
Ibrahim	Allen Leslie/*out*
Ruffino Raffaelo	Fritz Rimma/Harry Collier
Cheeko	J. M. Hayden/Fred Storey/O. E. Lennon
Dragoman	Harold Wilrowe
Admiral Sir Vigers Maxim	Percy Clifton/William Wyes
Lt Angus Anderson	Robert Selby
Captain Grimsby Chepstow	Maitland Dicker
Harold Dundas	D. S. Jeffrey
Horatio Nelson	Ruby Celeste
Jim Slingsby	Arthur Roberts
Olive Gwendoline Lovitt	Florence Perry/Gladys White/Jessie Barlee/Alys Rees[1]/Josephine Le Barte[1]
Mabel Chepstow	Georgie Martin/*out*
Lady Clarehaven	Josephine Le Barte/*out*
Eva Anderson	Heloise Osland/*out*
Miss Diane de Montgomerie	Ruby Verdi/Grace Arundale/*out*
Victoria Chaffers	Kate Cutler/Phyllis Broughton
Bosun	Edward Allen/George Watson
The Bey of Smyrna	Frank Cochrane/J. Jordon
add Collingwood Drake	Georgie Martin
Muriel de Montgomerie	Mabel Frenyear

with Gertrude Paterson, Victoria Vokes, Mabel Lanoma, Beatrice Sealby, Dorothy Dene, Violet

[1] as 'Olive Chepstow'.

Cross, May Karl, Nina Franklin, Marcelle Chevalier, Florence Townsend, Amy Laurence, Eva George, Annie James, Fanny d'Arcy, Lucy Fuller, Mabel Harrison, Amy Clarkson; Messrs Lane, Wilson Jones, Garland, J. Jordon, Martin, Thompson, Newlands, Huddlestone, Polldan, Taylor, Devonport.

Dir: Arthur Roberts; md: Augustus Bingham; sc: Fred Story; cos: Harrison & Co., Mme Vernon

KITTY GREY a musical comedy in 3 acts adapted by J. Smyth Piggott from *Les Fêtards* by MM. Mars and Hennequin. Music by Lionel Monckton, Howard Talbot, Victor Roger and Augustus T. Barratt. Produced at Bristol under the management of George Edwardes 27 August, 1900 and toured through Bradford, Glasgow, Edinburgh, Newcastle, Sheffield, Blackpool, Kennington, Portsmouth, Brighton, Manchester, Dublin, Liverpool, Nottingham, Birmingham to 8 December. Resumed 11 March 1901 through Kennington, Leeds, Manchester, Blackpool, Bradford, Liverpool, Glasgow, Edinburgh, Newcastle, Sheffield, Bristol, Birmingham, Shakespeare to 8 June, &c.

The King of Illyria	Harry Monkhouse/W. L. Abingdon/J. F. McArdle
Lord Plantagenet	G. P. Huntley/George Grossmith Jr
Baron de Tregue (Sir John Binfield)	Maurice Farkoa/Sydney Barraclough
Comte de Trenitz	Arthur T. Hendon/Ralph Foster
Pontbichet	A. Nilson Fysher/Maurice Carlton
Khonody	Fritz Rimma/*out*
Jollit	G. Carey/*out*
Slater	Mr Taylor/*out*
Fritz	Mr Stephenson/Norman Greene
Carl	John Donald
Herr Strum	A. W. Clark/*out*
Eugene	A. Thomas/W. Lloyd
Joseph	Robert Rivers/A. Roberts
Waiter	W. Lloyd/Robert Rivers
Sadie Poulson	Mabel Love/Nancy Hervyn/Winifred Leon
Mrs Bright	Lillie Belmore/Hetty Chapman/Millie Hylton
Pamela	Norah Strome
Carmen	Effie Rivière/Sybil Lonsdale
Chambermaid	B. Love
Baroness de Tregue (Lady Binfield)	Ethel Sydney
Kitty Grey	Evie Greene
add Mayor of Biarritz	A. E. Rees

with Misses Forde, Beresford, Daisy Le Hay, Dorothy Cameron, Pheemie Barnes, Nancy Hervyn, Wells and Sybil Lonsdale/Maude Dagmar, A. Maynard, Erica Mostyn, May Dewar, Maude Christie, C. Scott, Elsie Duncan, D. Claire.

Dir: J. A. E. Malone; md: Howard Talbot/George Saker; ch: Willie Warde/Will Bishop; sc: W. Spong; cos: Auguste & Cie., Peter Robinson, Miss Fisher

Produced at the Apollo Theatre, under the management of George Edwardes and Charles Frohman 7 September, 1901 for a run of 220 performances closing 19 April, 1902. Music now credited to Monckton, Talbot, Barratt, Paul Rubens and Bernard Rolt.

The King of Illyria	Charles Angelo
Lord Plantagenet	G. P. Huntley
Baron de Tregue	Maurice Farkoa (G. F. Stephenson)/ Roland Cunningham
Comte de Trenitz	Arthur T. Hendon/Wensley Thompson
Pontbichet	A. Nilson Fysher
Fritz	Robert St George
Carl	E. Wolseley
Eugene	Granville Barker/George Bickmore
Joseph	Sydney Honey
Robert	Mr Grain

Sadie . . . . Eva Kelly
Mrs Bright . . . . Gladys Homfrey/Hetty Chapman
Pamela. . . . . Miss Raynor
Carmen . . . . Alice Charteris
Baroness de Tregue. . . . . Edna May (Hilda Jeffreys)
Kitty Grey . . . . Evie Greene (Bertha Palliser)/ Ada Reeve

with Bertha Palliser, May Karl, Christine Lawrence, Jane May, Sybil Lonsdale, Queenie Dudley, Kitty Gordon/Mathilde Duncan, Norah Strome, Sara Miskel, Effie Rivière, Madge Greet, Harriet Bradford, Alice Charteris
add Mayor of Biarritz. . . . . Gilbert Laye

Dir: J. A. E. Malone; md: Howard Talbot; ch: Will Bishop; sc: W. B. Spong; cos: Jays, Peter Robinson

Produced at the New Amsterdam Theatre, New York, under the management of Charles Frohman 25 January, 1909 for a run of 50 performances closing 6 March, 1909.
Charles Angelo (KING), G. P. Huntley (EARL OF DULSTON), F. Pope Stamper (SIR JOHN), Frank Perfitt (TREN), Francis Gaillard (PONT), Robert Corray (FR), Percy Corray (CARL), Percival Knight (JOS), Eva Kelly (SADIE), Valli Valli (LADY B), Barbara Huntley (MME PONTBICHET)

Film: In 1906 a film and synchronised record set of the interpolated number 'Strolling Home with Angeline' sung by Joe Mack was issued by Chronophone Films.

0238 **LOLO** or The End of The World (later or The False Oracle) a comic opera in two acts by Arthur Sturgess. Music by James M. Glover. Produced at the Prince's Theatre, Manchester, under the management of C. P. Levilly 8 September, 1900 and toured through Oldham, Bristol, Cardiff, Bolton, Nottingham, Hanley x2, Brighton x2, Metropole and Alexandra x2 latterly in repertoire with *La Poupée*, ending 8 December, 1900.

Bobo. Roland Cunningham
James Jones . . . . St John Hamund
Rev. Tobias Trummel . . . . John Morley
Captain Jacko . . . . Fred Seymour
Rumbo . . . . Fred Hobbs
Presto . . . . Eric Thorne
Martha . . . . Madge Avery
Lady Harriet . . . . Kitty Cavendish
Zaidee . . . . Kathleen Gerrard
Lucy. Florence Linton
Lolo . . . . Stella Gastelle

Dir: Walter Summers

Revised and represented as *Loloh* 24 June 1901.

0239 **THE WONDER WORKER** a comic opera in two acts by Edward Cadman. Music by Albert W. Ketèlbey. Produced at the Grand Theatre, Fulham, under the management of Edgar and F. Sydney Ward 8 October, 1900 and toured.

Sir John Forrester . . . . Tom Grove
Guy Forrester. . . . . John M. Hay
Sir Walter Shirley. . . . . Philip Lincey
Bertram . . . . Ernest Spalding
Captain of the Guard . . . . Stuart Ethell
Felton . . . . S. Spears
Longstaff . . . . E. Church
Blades . . . . George Hudson
Jack-in-the-Green. . . . . Edward Montelli
Master Bunsay . . . . Edwin Keene
Queen Elizabeth. . . . . Annie Bernard
Marjorie. . . . . Faith Laborde
Hilda . . . . Connie Leon

Elsa . . . . Nellie Harper
Mary . . . . Ethel Thorne
Pattie . . . . Kittie Denton
Sallie . . . . Dora Weber
Eleanor . . . . Lottie Siegenberg

024 **THE GAY PRETENDERS** a comic opera (variously a burlesque extravaganza) in two acts by George Grossmith Jr. Music by Claud Nugent. Additional numbers by Walter Rubens. Produced at the Globe Theatre under the management of Yorke Stephens and George Grossmith Jr 10 November, 1900 for a run of 49 performances, closing 29 December, 1900.

Henry VII. . . . . Richard Temple
Prince Harry . . . . George Grossmith Jr
Earl of Oxford . . . . Frank Wyatt/Fred Winn/Frank Lister
Perkin Warbeck. . . . . John Coates
Herald. . . . . Fritz Rimma/A. Garcia
Sir Privy Purse . . . . Cecil Ramsay
Lord Truax . . . . W. H. Palmer
Master of Ayr. . . . . C. Pickford
Knight of Cork . . . . H. George
First Falconer. . . . . R. Auberies
Lambert Simnel. . . . . George Grossmith
Lady Katherine Gordon . . . . Jeanne Douste/Annie Purcell
Margaret, Duchess of Burgundy . . . . Agnes de la Porte
Comtesse de Beaune Fleury . . . . Ethel Clinton
Mary, the Lady Jolliffe . . . . Adelaide Astor
Hon. Sylvia Hollinsworth. . . . . Daisy Denvil
Mistress Clarissa Wilbraham . . . . . . Bertie Farrar
Venus . . . . May Joyce
Juno . . . . Miss Ritchie
Pallas Athena . . . . Miss Burrage
Columbia . . . . Don Kersley
Maids . . . . Misses Western and Marion Pierrepoint
Clotilde . . . . Letty Lind
Dancers: Misses Kitson, Jackson, Farrell, Bernard

Dir: George Grossmith Jr & Fred Winn; md: Frederick Rosse; ch: John D'Auban; sc: H. Drury; cos: Percy Anderson

HIS MAJESTY'S GUESTS a musical pantomimic farce in three acts by Herbert Darnley. Produced by Fred Karno's Company at the Prince of Wales, Kennington, 26 March, 1900 and toured through Folkestone, Richmond, Hanley, Wigan, Oldham, Halifax, Bury, Derby &c.

P. C. Lightning . . . . Walter Groves
Lord Hoodoo . . . . John Henderson
Sam Potts . . . . Lew Maskell
Bunker . . . . Fred Whittaker
Reverend Mr Minto . . . . Harry Oxberry
Warden Lockem . . . . W. Ritchie
Mr Dazzle. . . . . Bert d'Arcy
Mr Miffen. . . . . George Craig
Dolly . . . . Bessie Allayne
Mrs Miffen . . . . Winifred Wilmer
Miss Manley . . . . Ada Maskell
Selina . . . . George Ross
Lady Laura . . . . Ada Minister
Lady Lena . . . . Lily Gossling
Lady Lily . . . . Amy Minister
Lady Louise. . . . . Lucy Walden
Maud . . . . Dolly Harmer
Dir: Herbert Darnley; md: Alfred C. Toone; sc: Francis Bull

THE REGISTRY OFFICE a comic opera by Eleanor Farjeon. Music by Herbert Farjeon. Produced at the St George's Hall 29 June, 1900 by the operatic class of the Royal Academy of Music.

HIGH JINKS or Fun on the Sands. A farcical musical terpsichorial burletta by J. Hickory Wood. Music by James M. Glover. Produced by John Tiller 1900 and toured.

LITTLE LADY LOO a musical comedy in three acts by W. H. Dearlove. Music by Sydney Shaw. Produced at the Opera House, Harrogate 10 May, 1900 and toured.

PUNCH AND JUDY a romantic musical comedy-drama by Arthur Law. Music by George Byng and Arthur Meredyth. Produced at the Theatre Royal, Croydon 25 June, 1900 and toured.

1901

The early months of 1901 saw the West End flourishing with musical hits – *The Messenger Boy* at the Gaiety, *San Toy* at Daly's, *Florodora* at the Lyric, the revival of *Patience* at the Savoy, and the seasonal *Alice in Wonderland*, produced for Christmas at the Vaudeville, which kept up its twice-daily schedule right through to April. The sole foreign representative was Smith and Englander's *The Casino Girl* at the Shaftesbury which, although not up to any of the current native pieces, was the most successful of the wave of American shows following *The Belle of New York*.

The musical theatre was now even more diverse in its successful parts that it had been before. Alongside each other there existed several very different types of musical shows, ranging from light opera to music hall in their music and from carefully-prepared comedy, drama and satire to crude and often ad lib jokes in their spoken part. 1901 saw representatives of every kind of musical staged in the West End – extravaganza, comic opera, Gaiety musical comedy, the play with songs, the simple variety musical and, persisting in the wake of *The Belle of New York*, a mini-series of American pieces cast in the same energetic mould. The public was given a full choice and marked out its areas of preference in an unmistakeable way.

The first offering of the year opened on New Year's Day at Terry's Theatre. It was billed as an 'extravaganza' and entitled *The Thirty Thieves*. Based on the old tale of the Forty Thieves, brought up to date, it was cast in the shape of something between an extravaganza and a comic opera by W. H. Risque, the lyricist of *All Abroad*, with music written by Edward Jones who had been responsible for the songs of *The Prince of Borneo*. The producer of *The Thirty Thieves* was E. H. Bull, once a touring manager for D'Oyly Carte and most recently manager of the Grand Theatre, Wolverhampton, who took a short lease on Terry's Theatre to stage his first venture into West End production. The show's opening was not unpromising. *The Era* commented that it was 'an ingenious and not unsuccessful attempt to turn the well-worn legend of the forty thieves into a comedy with music . .' whilst *The Times*, though critical of the show's length and some of its costumes, concluded that it was 'by no means a bad example of its class' and noted that it was 'a success'.

In fact, *The Thirty Thieves* had much going for it. Risque had provided a lively book and lyrics which Edward Jones had set in an unpretentious but attractive style. Both comedy and music were well-served, especially as Bull had hired a small but effective cast including the D'Oyly Carte leading lady, Florence Perry, for the female lead and a handful of strong comedians including Charles Groves as the rascally mayor, Aubrey Fitzgerald as his comic secretary, Ells Dagnall as the aged woodcutter, and the vigorous Australian comedienne, Pattie Browne.

The first days of the run seemed to Bull to justify taking out an extension of his lease at

Terry's, but the show's future was doomed by the death of Queen Victoria on 22 January, 1901. The shutters went up throughout the West End and it was nearly a fortnight before the principal theatres could be relit. Business did not pick up, and after three weeks Bull was obliged to cut his losses and close.

It was an unfortunate ending for a show with many attractive elements, particularly as far as the songs were concerned. Florence Perry had been successful with two delightful numbers, 'I'm Going to be a Lady' and 'The vanishing Lady'. The first was on a familiar theme:

> I've always known a lowly sphere and the poorest circumstances
> But something's happened lately like things happen on the stage
> It's like the fairy tales you hear, the wildest of romances
> For I've heard of something greatly to my advantage!
> And I'm going to be a lady, a proper kind of lady
> With everything belonging to the very highest rank
> With diamond rings and brooches
> And with bicycles and coaches
> And a great big fortune in the bank!

whilst 'The vanishing Lady' was the tale of a lady with a horse and pair and 'an address in a very good square' who gets credit up and down Bond Street and Piccadilly before disappearing, leaving the rental of both house and equipage unpaid and a string of much wiser shopkeepers throughout W1:

> The moral is funny
> To live without money
> You've only to make a good show!

Modern social comment abounded, although without any particular sting. Ells Dagnall had a number which poked fun at the topical song:

> Sing a song of nonsense, everything in turn
> Four and twenty verses, what a lot to learn!
> One for every subject underneath the sun
> Won't you all be joyful when it's done-done-done!

before taking on the current subjects of bicycling ladies, soldiers and housemaids, greedy lawyers etc. W. R. Shirley as the hero also had a number ridiculing the conventions of the musical theatre, asserting 'there's always time for that' whether it be an aria for the villain who has just declared fearfully 'I must away' or a solo dance for the heroine when left alone in despair. The concerted music, too, was attractive. *The Times* picked out for special mention the septet 'There's Thunder in the Air'. Altogether, *The Thirty Thieves* would seem to have been worthy of a slightly better fate.

As it was, Bull organised a tour with Florence Perry and Shirley retaining their original roles and with a cast strengthened by the addition of such provincial favourites as J. C. Piddock of *Lady Slavey* fame, Charles Goold, C. A. White and Lyddie Edmonds, and with the ex-Mohawk Minstrel, Johnnie Schofield, taking on the plum part of the Secretary. He inserted a jolly new number 'You never can Tell' into his role, which helped to give the piece the right flavour for two years of provincial dates. In its later incarnations *The Thirty Thieves* operated under the less seasonal title *Miss Mariana* and was described as 'comic opera'. It had, in fact, been intended to call the piece *Mariana*, but that plan had been scotched by Mrs Patrick Campbell's announcement of an imminent revival of Jose Etchegaray's play of the same name at the

Royalty. The addition of 'Miss' made the subsequent alteration possible, but also meant that Boosey & Co were obliged to overstamp their entire stock of scores with 'Miss Mariana or' above the title, *The Thirty Thieves*. The book was heavily revised for a 1904 production in Swindon as the show passed from the professional into the amateur repertoire.

The next three productions in the West End were all of American origin. The first, at the Apollo, was *The Belle of Bohemia* written by Harry B. Smith and Ludwig Englander who had been responsible for *The Casino Girl*. It was a piece very much in the 'new' American musical style and was based on the *Comedy of Errors*' two Dromios idea. It had failed (55 performances) in New York, as a follow-up to *The Casino Girl*, and it fared little better in London where it survived for ten and a half weeks with a cast basically from America and including Richard Carle, Marie George and, in lesser roles, Edna May's husband, Fred Titus (Hooligan) and sister-in-law, Sylvia Thomas (Mamie). England's Marie Dainton received the best notices in the role of Paquita.

Little more successful was the production of Victor Herbert's *The Fortune Teller* at the Shaftesbury which also arrived intact with its American stars Alice Neilsen, Frank Rushworth and Joseph Herbert and the impressive Canadian basso, Eugene Cowles. *The Fortune Teller* met with a mixed reception from both audience and critics. *The Era* called it 'a triumph', but *The Times* remarked that '. . were it to depend upon its merits as a play, its life would probably be very short. .' Alice Neilsen, Cowles and the general vivacity of the performers could not disguise the fact that the show lacked quality and above all originality in its libretto. It featured the 'polite lunatic' character which had been popularised by *The Belle of New York* but which was now becoming a bore, and there was little in it to justify a run longer than the 88 performances it achieved.

The third import was from the *Belle of New York* team of 'Morton' and Kerker and featured their star, Edna May. It was a peculiar piece which opened with the heroine being released from a block of ice in which she has been imprisoned for some five hundred years, after which she sets out in search of a golden chalice without which she must perish in ninety days. On her trip *The Girl from up There* encounters the rest of the cast. It ran 102 performances to complete a hat-trick of trans-Atlantic nonentities. The success of *The Belle of New York* had been in its novelty. The pieces in a similar idiom which followed did not improve upon it and public interest lapsed quickly.

Much more of interest to a large section of the theatre-going public was a new Savoy opera. *The Rose of Persia* had awakened hopes of a fruitful collaboration between Sir Arthur Sullivan and his new librettist, Captain Hood, and expectation ran high over their newest venture, *The Emerald Isle*, a comic opera with an Irish setting. But, with the musical setting of the piece only half completed, Arthur Sullivan died. D'Oyly Carte had the task of finding another composer capable of completing the score from the sketches left. Rumours were rife. First Ernest Ford, the composer of *Jane Annie*, was mooted, then François Cellier, the long time musical director of the Savoy and composer of a number of smaller pieces, but Carte's final choice fell on a 39-year-old composer who had never, in fact, written a musical of any sort. German Edward Jones – professionally known simply as 'Edward German' – had made his theatrical mark to date supplying incidental music for plays, particularly for Shakespearian productions. He had begun in 1889 with music for Richard Mansfield's *Richard III* at the Globe, before writing the still well-known dance music for Irving's 1892 *Henry VIII* at the Lyceum. Among his other scores were those for Beerbohm Tree's *The Tempest* (1893, Haymarket), the Forbes Robertson/Mrs Patrick Campbell *Romeo and Juliet* (1895, Lyceum) and George Alexander's *As You Like It* at the St James'. His works also included symphonies and other orchestral pieces and a certain amount of vocal music.

His task with *The Emerald Isle* was an unenviable one. Sullivan had completed only two numbers in full score. The remainder of the first act was well sketched, as were certain parts of the second but, for the rest, German was obliged to provide typical music and orchestrations, maintaining quality without showing unsuitable originality. He accepted the task, and fell to work.

By the time *The Emerald Isle* was ready to open, further tragedy had struck the Savoy with the death of its founder and moving spirit Richard D'Oyly Carte. It had been Carte who had consolidated the exceptional partnership between Gilbert and Sullivan and who had been responsible for the production, at a continually high standard, of all their works from *The Sorcerer* to *The Grand Duke*, not only at his own Savoy Theatre built by and for the British comic opera repertoire, but all over the world. He was the guiding force and the catalyst in the creation of a series of works which have survived longer and more strongly than any other series of light musical pieces anywhere in the world. But although his fame and reputation rest on his association with and his work for Gilbert and Sullivan and their repertoire, and the company which so long bore his name, it must not be forgotten that he encouraged and produced works by numerous other writers and composers at the Savoy, on tour, and overseas. *The Nautch Girl*, *The Vicar of Bray*, *Billee Taylor*, *Haddon Hall* and *Les Manteaux Noirs* are just some of the British works which owed all or parts of their career to Carte.

The production of *The Emerald Isle* was taken over by his wife, Helen, and duly opened on 27 April in an atmosphere of goodwill. Everyone wanted the piece to be a success and the critics reacted accordingly:

> . . delightful music, humorous dialogue and the ablest interpretation render it one of the most acceptable entertainments yet offered at the Savoy . . . (*Stage*)
>
> . . refinement, beauty, grace, humour and complete freedom from offence . . . [the music] free, fanciful and scholarly . . . . the libretto is an agreeable compromise between what the French call opéra-comique and the ironic humour brought into fashion by W. S. Gilbert . . (*Era*)
>
> The most delightful opera we have seen since *The Gondoliers* . . (*Daily Mail*)

The Times had slightly more reservations:

> If the invention of a multitude of humorous details and funny verbal quips, if not precisely witty points of dialogue, could be accepted as a satisfactory substitute for a connected plot, then Captain Hood's libretto must rank very highly among things of the kind. But the genre of Savoy opera has not yet become assimilated to the type of American variety operetta and those who recall the finest specimens of the Gilbertain libretto will find it difficult to accept the second act of the new piece as it now stands . .

In fact, the second act of *The Emerald Isle*, and a good deal of the first as well, were decidedly short on plot. The piece began strongly. A jolly spoof-Irish chorus written by Sullivan introduces the hero, Terence O'Brien, an Irish patriot who, as he claims in song, is 'descended from Brian Boru'. But, alas, he speaks with an English accent, having been brought up in 'the luxurious lap of London'. He is not alone, however. All his countrymen now speak with an English accent for the English Viceroy has been giving elocution lessons in the infant schools:

> Now every Irish boy
> And all colleens and lasses

Professors teach
The saxon speech
At elocution classes!
And all who don't employ
The purest English accent
Are as a rule
To infant school
Incontinently back sent!

and now

. . . there's not a man nor a colleen here that could dance an Irish jig correctly, and say 'Begorra' at the end of it with any conviction.

To the village comes one Professor Bunn, 'Mesmerist, Ventriloquist, Humorist and General Illusionist, Shakespearian Reciter, Character Impersonator and Professor of Elocution. Children's Parties a Speciality'. He has been employed by the Lord Lieutenant for his re-education programme but offers to change sides and re-teach the Irish how to be precisely that:

If you wish to appear as an Irish type
(Presuming, that is, you are not one)
You'll stick the stem of a stumpy pipe
In your hat-band, if you've got one
Then no doubt you're aware you must colour your hair
An impossible shade of red
While a cudgel you'll twist with a turn of your wrist
Being careful to duck your head
Or your own shillelagh unhappily may accidentally knock you down
With a fearful crack on the comical back of your typically Irish crown
If you manage, instead of the back of your head, to belabour the floor like that
And shout 'Whirroo', bedad, you'll do!
You're the popular type of Pat.

Terence is anxious to meet up with his sweetheart, Rosie, who is, unfortunately, none other than the daughter of the Lord Lieutenant. As he explains:

This lady and I met in London before we understood the incongruities of our positions. We fell in love and have never yet succeeded in falling out.

'Twas in Hyde Park beside the Row
That she and I first met
Against the rails I pressed my suit
Although the paint was wet.
I said 'Love me and I'll love you'
She could not answer 'no'
For she was one, and I was two,
That day in Rotten Row.

It is arranged that Terence shall hide out in the reputedly haunted caves of Carric-Cleena, and that Rosie shall come to him there. But Bunn notifies the Lord Lieutenant of their plans, and the Irish are obliged to find a subterfuge to keep the redcoats away. They decide that Molly, one of their number, shall appear as the fairy, Cleena, and Bunn as an ancient who has been held captive by her for fifty years, and thus they shall scare away the superstitious Devonshire soldiers. The first act ends with them bringing their trick off successfully.

The second act carries on in much the same vein. Bunn goes through his paces, Terence and Rosie pursue their romance and Molly carries on with the hereditary 'blind' fiddler, Pat Murphy, who dares not confess his perfect sight for fear of losing her sympathy and love. When the Lord Lieutenant descends upon them all, Bunn succeeds in saving the 'rebels' by proclaiming:

> If we had guessed (as we ought to have guessed) that you, being a scion of a noble English house, had so much American blood in your composition, we should not have rebelled against you. America is the friend of Ireland. You are an English nobleman. Therefore you are, nowadays, more than half American. Therefore you are our friend. . .

It was not the most ingeniously attractive ending, nor one which Gilbert would have considered as sufficiently witty or effective. But there was much in *The Emerald Isle* which was more than a little reminiscent of Gilbert. The characters of the Lord Lieutenant, his wife, and their chaplain, Dr Fiddle, D.D., bear a strong family resemblance to the Plaza-Toros:

> L.L.: I am the Lord Lieutenant and
> It's well that you should understand
> I am the highest in the land
> The Lord Lieutenant of Ireland.
> CTESS: And I, his wife, of high degree
> Enhance my husband's dignity.
> FIDDLE: And I'm his private chaplain who
> To some extent enhance it too.

while the Lord Lieutenant's solo, too, is strongly in the Savoy tradition:

> At an early stage of life
> I said, I'll choose a wife
> But where shall I find the particular girl
> Who is fit to be knit to a noble earl
> Such a very particular
> Perpendicular
> Noble earl as I?

The viceregal pair communicate in blank verse:

> I am
> The only king, or representative
> Of royalty (outside the characters
> Of Shakespeare's plays) who makes a special point
> Of talking in blank verse, and who insists
> That every member of his family
> And household shall converse in blank verse too

a trick used by Gilbert as far back as *Our Island Home* in his early Gallery of Illustration days. The principal patter song for Bunn also has very obvious parentage:

> Oh, the age in which we're living strikes a man of any sense
> As an age of make-believe, of imitation and pretence
> And it's gradually growing more impossible to see
> The difference between what people are – and seem to be!
> Our ladies grow more youthful now, the longer they're alive
> And reduce their ages annually after thirty-five

(But for such miscalculations they will always make amends
By liberally adding to the ages of their friends).
And if Æsop wrote his fables
In the present year of grace
He perhaps would turn the tables
On the tortoise in the race
For which goes quicker on ahead, and stays the faster there
The imitation tortoise-shell, or imitation hair?

However, Basil Hood's genuine skill in both lyrics and dialogue did no little credit to the established forms, and the Savoy hardies found it no strain to take in his Gilbertian pieces and fancies which were duly mixed with pieces of a more 'popular' type, such as the song 'The little wooden Soldier' which was more reminiscent of Daly's than of the Savoy:

There once was a little soldier
Who was made of wood
He always did his duty
And he proudly stood
Very bravely at attention
As a soldier should.

Rat-a-plan, rat-a-plan, rat-a-plan!
He was always very ready to receive hard knocks
He and all his wooden brothers, in the same big box
Where their master chose to put them
They would stand like rocks
Rat-a-plan, rat-a-plan, rat-a-plan,
Rat-a-plan, rat-a-plan, rat-a-plan, rat-a-plan!
He did his duty, just like a man,
But kindly remember, if you can,
He was only a wooden soldier.

As for the music, there was general agreement that Sullivan's pieces were as good as ever, and that Edward German had done his part of the work with an undeniable taste and skill. If the show produced no 'hits' comparable with those of *The Mikado* or *H.M.S. Pinafore*, it nevertheless was quite as attractive as some of Gilbert and Sullivan's lesser works. And in the obvious comparison with C. V. Stanford's *Shamus O'Brien* it held its own. The music was of a totally different kind, and *The Emerald Isle* made no pretence at the genuine Irish-ness of the more serious piece. Its Irishmen were comic opera Irishmen, belonging to that land where they might equally well have been dubbed French peasants or Spanish bandits, and where the ridiculous Bunn was as much at home as his predecessor the ridiculous Griggs had been amongst the banditti of *The Contrabandista* so many years previously. *The Emerald Isle* ran over twice as long as the more ambitious *Shamus O'Brien*. It continued through until early November, no mean record at a time when the lighter forms of musical comedy were all the rage.

An American production was staged by the Shuberts at Broadway's Herald Square Theatre in 1902 with Jefferson de Angelis taking the role of Bunn, played in London by Walter Passmore, but in spite of some excellent reviews it did not catch on. The vogue for the type had quite passed in America. However, *The Emerald Isle* remained popular in England, being toured by D'Oyly Carte's companies in 1902 before entering on a long career with amateurs and choral societies for whom a special version of the score was arranged. The comic opera which, it had seemed, would to all intents and purposes die with Arthur Sullivan, still had a word or two to say thanks to Carte's last discovery – Edward German. In *The Emerald Isle* the two composers overlapped in a work of considerable wit, charm and attractiveness which was to be a prelude to even better things from the new team of German and Basil Hood.

On the heels of the comic opera came three shows which were very different: two modern musical comedies, to succeed *The Messenger Boy* at the Gaiety and *Florodora* at the Lyric, and the third a cheerfully blatant example of the much-criticised variety musical. Arthur Roberts had successfully toured his new vehicle *H.M.S. Irresponsible* since August of the previous year and now he brought it into town, to the Strand Theatre. It had gone through many changes since its original production and for the London season further changes were made.

During the tour the musical content had been varied: Bennett Scott's 'La, la, la' and Scott MacKenzie's 'After you with That' had been interpolated as featured numbers and the female cast had been constantly changed about, with at one period Clarissa Talbot and Alice E. Percival alternating the role of 'Gwendoline' half-weeks about. For London the feminine roles were severely altered. 'Olive Chepstow' became 'Mabel', with some of her original role being combined with that of 'Gwendoline' into a featured role for Florence Perry christened 'Olive Gwendoline Lovitt'. Georgie Martin was transferred from the leading part of 'Victoria' to the remnant 'Mabel' to make room for a 'name', in the shape of Kate Cutler. A new role 'Lady Clarehaven' was dreamed up for Josephine Le Barte, while Heloise Osland, the most recent touring 'Gwendoline', became 'Eva Anderson'. They had less to do, but it did not really matter, for the show was Arthur Roberts, its raison d'être and its all-consuming star; he was everything and anything his large and worshipping public expected him to be in 'an Arthur Roberts show'. He fooled his way through the slight and tacked-together story in a fashion which truly deserved the epithet 'inimitable': he sang, he danced, he disguised himself continuously in a virtuoso performance which left the subordinate characters as just that. It was the kind of show and of performance which, in other hands, would have had little or no chance of success, and which could barely expect to receive favourable notices from a discerning critic. *The Times* launched its first night notice with the warning that '*H.M.S. Irresponsible* scarcely comes with the scope of serious criticism' before attempting just that, focusing, naturally, most of its attention on Roberts:

> . . [he] afforded abundant amusement to an amiable bank holiday audience by his foolish blunders and his scarcely less foolish attempts to escape from his uncomfortable position. That Mr Roberts is a comedian of an alert and facile invention no-one would deny, but it is a pity that he so often condescends to employ methods of doubtful taste. There are many pieces of 'business' in *H.M.S. Irresponsible* . . . which are not amusing at all, merely disgusting. . . At the same time there is a good deal of harmless fun in the piece which, indeed, would not be a bad one of its kind if it were not spun out to an inordinate length by superfluous songs and dances. .

The Stage had no very high opinion of the show:

> There is nothing very briliant or clever about the libretto. . the music or the lyrics. . . . the variety entertainment that takes place on board the ship in Act 2 is no better and no worse than that introduced years ago into *Morocco Bound*. .

Morocco Bound and its famous variety entertainment had, of course, been widely praised and enjoyed in its time. There was no doubt that *H.M.S. Irresponsible*, somewhat in the image of its star, belonged to a slightly earlier era, but about the merits of that star *The Stage* had no doubts, not even the quibbles expressed by *The Times*:

> . . We have rarely seen this popular comedian more genuinely amusing than he was in the burlesque proposal of marriage or in the parody of a speech delivered by a pompous chairman of a semi-public meeting. Again, he was wonderfully funny, whilst keeping clear of all offence, in poor Slingsby's attack of mal de mer, the proceedings on deck being indeed most hilarious throughout; his disguises as a blundering first stoker and as a glib waiter at a Smyrna cafe were both capitally done and vastly amusing, though possibly a little near the border line was the imitation, in dumb show, of course, of a lady very carefully and slowly undressing, literally from head to foot, whilst preparing to emerge from a bathing machine. . . .

On the musical side Roberts did best with 'Sounds all Right' and the show's most notable song, George Rollitt's 'Topsy Turvy', and combined with Kate Cutler in two duets, 'The Motor Car' and 'The Letter'.

The other members of the cast, who were given few chances to shine in the play, did at least have a vocal contribution to make. Kate Cutler sang about 'Little Popsy', soprano Florence Perry sang of 'Love's Surprises' and the 'Cuckoo', Georgie Martin had a chanty 'On the Briny', and Ruby Verdi commented on the 'Same Thing' and told the tale of 'Silly Milly'. The gentlemen were, of course, more limited in their opportunities, although Maitland Dicker had a good comedy number in 'Lunatic Queries' and Percy Clifton, as the Admiral, gave forth with 'There's no such Word as Can't in the British Navy'. Between the songs and dances and Roberts' impersonations and ad-libs, the story limped on unheeded to its end.

In July, with the piece still doing good business, Roberts' lease at the Strand came to an end and he decided that *H.M.S. Irresponsible* had enough life left in it to justify a transfer to the Globe, where it ran until the end of October before Roberts prepared to take it out on the road again. By this time the show had undergone many more changes, particularly with regard to the already much sliced-about ladies' roles. Now 'Olive Chepstow' had gone back to being 'Olive Chepstow' and was played by Alys Rees for whom the Sam Richards number 'Love Me as long as I live' had been interpolated. 'Victoria' had been taken over by Roberts' favourite leading lady, Phyllis Broughton, and all the other female roles had been cut out. Georgie Martin found her fidelity to the show rewarded by a third character change, this time into a boy, as the midshipman 'Collingwood Drake'.

At the end of the London run Roberts took the piece out on an extended tour. *H.M.S. Irresponsible* proved a happy vehicle for its star, and the role of Jim Slingsby, if not as well-moulded or as genuinely clever as those of Gentleman Joe or Dandy Dan, nevertheless provided him with three good tours and a London season. The role of Victoria proved more troublesome when an epilogue to his London transfer found him sued by his *Gentleman Joe* co-star, Kitty Loftus, to whom he had promised the lead in the new piece following her willingness to do the pre-London tour. Prolonged court proceedings found Roberts the loser and then the winner as Miss Loftus' character became distinctly greyed by the evidence with the result, finally, that the seemingly deserved judgement for £250 damages was quashed on appeal.

Leslie Stuart's first attempt at a musical with *Florodora* had been a gigantic success and there was no question of Tom Davis looking anywhere else for a successor to that piece. Owen Hall was once again to be the librettist and W. H. Risque, who had produced the neat lyrics of *The Thirty Thieves*, was given the task of providing Stuart with words. *The Silver Slipper* was the result of this collaboration and it opened at the Lyric Theatre on June 1.

The Silver Slipper had particular and familiar requirements to fulfil. To appeal to the public acquired by *Florodora* it had to retain the elements which had contributed to that piece's popularity, yet it needed to be sufficiently different to be interesting and attractively new all over again. Hall had made his priorities public in an interview with the *Western Mercury*:

> Mr 'Hall' attaches first importance to atmosphere – that is, to the selection of a picturesque spot – and he thinks the planet Venus idea will prove good in that respect. Then he casts about to determine the central figure in the play, knowing how much depends on the leading actress and her part suiting each other. As regards *The Silver Slipper*, Mr Hall's next thought was to arrange for skilful contrast in manners and dress between Europeans and aborigines. The plot is the fourth consideration.

'The planet Venus idea' was the basis of Hall's book, and around that setting he contrived a piece which allowed him to contrast his leading Venusian lady (Winifred Hare) with earthlings of both the British and Parisian varieties. That the plot was subordinate to these other considerations was fairly clear, and it was neither particularly original nor interesting in spite of a vigorous opening. In fact it had uncomfortable reminiscences of many former pieces from Gilbert's *The Wicked World* and *Pygmalion and Galatea* to the very recent *The Girl from up There*, a title which, indeed, might have more aptly described the action of *The Silver Slipper* than its original North Pole plot.

A Venusian maiden, Stella, has longings to find out what man is like – Venus being an 'Adamless Eden'. Mischievously, she lets her satin slipper tumble down to earth and is banished from Venus to recover it. The slipper falls into the garden of Sir Victor Shallamar where it is found by his niece, Wrenne, daughter of the book-making shyster, Samuel Twanks. Stella, arriving on earth, proceeds to wreak havoc as she learns the art of flirtation and finds out just what men are like. Finally she tires of Earth life and takes herself and her slipper back to Venus.

As in *Florodora*, Hall had dressed his story in smart society dialogue and stuffed it with plenty of topical allusions and comicalities carefully moulded to the characters of his principal comedians, Willie Edouin as Twanks and Connie Ediss as the cockney housekeeper, Bella Jimper. On the musical side, too, Stuart had followed the *Florodora* formula, sometimes alarmingly closely. The famous sextet was virtually copied in its most obvious equivalent 'Come, little Girl and Tell me Truly'. The double sextet featured once again six pretty girls in pink – severe pale pink bengaline with lovely silver embroidery – and three-cornered hats with pink and black ostrich feathers showered with silver, carrying tall black canes, while the gentlemen relinquished their frock coats for brown coats and cream waistcoats to sing:

MEN: What would you do when you reached the moon
And you found no man there after all?
GIRLS: I'd never conclude on a long solitude
When a girl is always waiting
And continues titivating
There'll be men in the air after all
MEN: Quite so
But what do you think he would tell you when he finds you
For, of course, you're the first girl that he's seen.

GIRLS: I know what he'd say
MEN: Little girl
GIRLS: In the usual way
MEN: Little girl, 'I'd never love another one –
GIRLS: So long as you're the only one
MEN: You are the first I've seen'
GIRLS: And then –
MEN: So, come, little girl and tell me truly if you love me
GIRLS: (You are my solitary girl up here)
MEN: Don't have a fear, dear, I will be near you, always near,
GIRLS: (So long as the moon shines on none but you)

The lyric gave the effect of having been fitted in rather curiously to Leslie Stuart's unusual rhythms. He had, in fact, written it himself with more care for syncopation than sense. Nevertheless, it happily recalled 'Tell me, pretty Maiden' to a comfortably reminiscent audience who duly applauded it well. The sextet was not the only successful *Florodora* number to be repeated. The 'Inkling' song got another going over with a pretty piece called 'A Glimpse-impse-impse' which included the verse:

I peeped into a theatre and saw a splendid show
The stage was full of handsome ladies standing in a row
There were lovers, there were villains, there were comic gentlemen
But what the piece was all about, well, every now and then
I got just a glimpse-impse-impse
The tiniest glimpse-impse-impse
There was some kind of something, I hardly know what
But it couldn't be fairly described as a plot
It was only a glimpse-impse-impse.

It is only fair to add that the other verses were considerably cleverer but, as in *The Thirty Thieves*, the self-mockery seemed a little too close to home to be safe.

The introduction of Connie Ediss as the main female humourist brought a natural change in the comic register from *Florodora*. Stuart provided her with two typical 'Connie' numbers, 'Good Behaviour' and 'Class', the second of which was to prove the popular song of the show as London's favourite singing comedienne galumphed through the numerous verses:

There's a boarding house over the way
And it isn't obtrusively gay
They call it a 'pension' – the term is a French 'un
The lodgers are 'guests', though they pay.
Hymn tunes all Sunday they play
And for dinner they dress every day
And William the waiter can make a pertater
Go round amongst twenty, they say.

But it's class, class, class
Every guest has a fine finger glass
You should see them manouevre to get the hors d'oeuvre
And subsequent dishes that pass.
They water with care the vin ordinaire
To make it look more in the glass
But they've wined and they've dined
And they feel so refined
And it's class, class, class.

There were other 'typical' numbers: a 'Hayden Coffin' song for the society duettist, Henri Leoni, in the romantic role of Louis Tiraupigeon, called 'Two Eyes of Blue'; a point number, 'She Didn't Know enough about the Game' for the manly Louis Bradfield; and a travesti song 'If I were a Girl Instead' for Wrenne (Coralie Blythe) who for some unexplained reason (which may have been that *San Toy* had just re-emphasised the appeal of travesti) started off the show in boy's clothes. Stuart had certainly repeated the formulae which had been so popular in his former piece and which were expected from him any following work, but the score of *The Silver Slipper* was not without invention. One feature was a choral 'Invocation to Venus' written for three-part female chorus and soprano solo which demanded a good deal of its soloist, on this occasion Miss Mimi Margotine.

In all, the opening night sported twenty-five numbers, all bar one (a concerted piece called 'Go Home with Nursey' written by Landon Ronald) the work of Leslie Stuart. That opening night was by no means an unqualified success. In fact, it was scarcely a success at all. The show ran, in spite of a strict 'no encores' policy, from 8 until 11.30, and had not the last scene included some of the best and most appreciated numbers of the evening – 'Class', 'Four and Twenty little Men', 'Two Eyes of Blue' and 'She Didn't Know enough about the Game' – the mixed reception given to *The Silver Slipper* at its final curtain might have been markedly less favourable. One newspaper estimated the audience as being 'three fifths for', another dismissed the negative responses as being from 'the usual element in the gallery', but there was no doubting that the piece was not right. The numbers, especially 'Class', 'Good Behaviour' and the Invocation had gone down well, though there were clearly one or two too many of them, and Connie Ediss, Louis Bradfield and Willie Edouin were as clever and as popular as ever, even if the two men had not been given sufficient, in their public's eyes, to do in the show. But others involved had been less appreciated. Winifred Hare, fresh from a big success in the Coronet pantomime, was no Ada Reeve. She had talent but apparently little charm; Coralie Blythe, in a role of her own after so many understudies at the Gaiety, made a poor boy and did not manage to bring off her 'Tupp'ny Show' number in Act 2. Nancy Girling, promoted from the sextet, flopped in the role of Brenda, and Leoni, while making a predictably competent job of his song, looked and acted decidedly spare through the other three hours of the show.

The audience took exception not only to the straggly plot but to some of Owen Hall's well-known cracks. Topical, smart, racy dialogue had been the popular trademark of Hall's writing ever since *A Gaiety Girl* but he could, on occasions, badly misjudge his audience's limits and sympathies. Hisses and boos greeted an ill-tempered dig at French justice à propos the Dreyfus case: 'You can't expect justice here – you're in France now!' and a jibe at *The Belle of New York* and its sisters: 'The public likes a noise – that's why American entertainments succeed.' He was on safer ground with Government contractors and other political targets but some of his lines, particularly those given to Connie Ediss, were very near to being in bad taste. That lady, however, got one of the best laughs of the night when she declared uncontroversially: 'The greatest discovery of the age is the man who invented the flat-bottomed soda-water bottle!' Willie Edouin had some excellent comic moments both in his dialogue – shared, at one stage, by a non-existent pet dog called 'Billy' – and in actions such as a ridiculous skipping-rope dance, but he knew well enough to steer clear of anything in dubious taste. Hall had also erred in attempting to introduce a certain amount of genuine feeling into the story of the embittered old astronomer who refuses to receive his niece and son-in-law and, again, into the relationship between Twanks and his daughter. It was an ill-judged attempt which the audience refused to accept and a scene in which Edouin confessed to Miss Blythe his failings as a father came badly unstuck before an unsympathetic audience.

The reviews, not surprisingly, were generally unpromising. The inevitable comparisons with *Florodora* were almost unanimously in that show's favour, although *The Topical Times* which had perversely loathed *Florodora* concluded that *The Silver Slipper* was better and, therefore, bound to last for less of a run. The book and dialogue were generally criticised and the songs, though admitted as good, were often chided as too reminiscent of Stuart's other work. The management was not slow to take action. Within a few nights the book had been severely pruned. The offending lines were removed and others were smartened up. Neither were the songs spared. Out went the quartette 'Toys' which had passed virtually unnoticed, out went several other pieces and, eventually, out went Bradfield's number, 'My Studio'. Soon, as a result, the show was running shorter and more smoothly and, since the faithful of *Florodora* had ensured an advance of several thousand pounds, Davis was able to ride out the crisis period with virtually full houses until the reputation of the revitalised show had spread. Noticing the subsequent good houses and enthusiastic reactions, *The Illustrated Sporting & Dramatic News* decided:

> The fact is that the journalistic standard for this sort of piece is always very spasmodic and is sometimes placed altogether too high; the critics ask for more than the playgoer does and the playgoer after all does not wish to be educated, but to be amused. . .

The public were amused by *The Silver Slipper* for six and a half months at the Lyric; nowhere near the record of *Florodora*, but a fair run. The 'improvement' process continued throughout that time. Landon Ronald supplied a new duet called 'Riding' for Edouin and Connie Ediss, Winifred Hare was given a new Leslie Stuart number, 'If you must Sigh', and the principal composer also brought in new songs for Bradfield ('The detrimental Man' and 'Fun on a Motor') and a duet for him and Miss Blythe ('Ping Pong'), but in the popularity stakes it was always 'Class' which scored – six encores per night being often demanded from Connie Ediss. Another piece which had gone unnoticed on the opening night was also contributing encores – a Parisian café dance sequence in which the ladies, dressed in yellow, danced with waiters in a routine which included the use of trick tables which lifted up and remained suspended between the couples as they danced.

In 1902 *The Silver Slipper* was produced on Broadway. The book had been 'adapted' by Clay Greene, but only in the comedy parts where a certain amount of americanising was necessary to suit the roles of Twanks (now christened Henry Bismarck Hensches) and Bella to comedian Sam Bernard and Josie Sadler. The score too had undergone some changes. The conductor of the piece, Arthur Weld, introduced some pieces of his own, the ballad 'If Hearts but Knew', a duet and a *valse lente* for the ballet, and Stuart produced some fresh material as well. Another character which suffered some change was that of the Queen of Venus, which was expanded into a prima donna role and put in the hands of the English soprano, Mai de Villiers. *The Silver Slipper* tried out at Newhaven and from there Miss de Villiers cabled Stuart in London:

> SILVER SLIPPER GREAT SUCCESS. I ALSO. MAI.

The following week, Mai must have felt less jubilant. On Broadway, the piece received mixed notices, and the *Daily News* remarked:

> Mai de Villiers as Venus was fine to see, as long as she did not walk or sing. One or two songs she sings might just as well be lent to somebody else or just put in the cellar. .

and the *Morning Telegraph* reported that 'Mdlle Mai de Villiers, the imported soprano, did not find favour. . ' that the 'Invocation of Venus' was 'ridiculously noisy' and that there was: 'a decided suspicion of numerous screeches where the composer had intended clear top notes.' *The New York American* declared that 'the nocturnal miaulings of enraged tabbies were harmony' compared to 'that Invocation'. But *The Daily News*, if it did not care for Mai, declared the show itself 'a find of the first water' and selected as the evening's high point the 'champagne dance' – the French café routine which had passed by the first night critics in London. It was not the only paper to do so. William Laffan headlined in the *Evening Sun* with:

> SIX ENGLISH DANCERS SAVE 'THE SILVER SLIPPER' AT THE BROADWAY . . . Manager Fisher has made a gorgeous production in which the now Historical Sextet Ladies are Snowed under by Six English Girls in a Champagne dance Which was Most Intoxicating. .

The World agreed . . 'The dancing of a sextet of English girls . . is the backbone of *The Silver Slipper* . . .' and the *New York Herald* also headlined:

> Sextet the Hit of 'Silver Slipper' . . But This Time it's a Dancing Sextet, not a Vocal as in 'Florodora'

The Mail and Express described the number:

> . . An hour later [after the vocal sextet] the new double sextet introduced itself surprisingly. Six slim and limber girls ran into sight. They wore yellow gowns that were soft, swishy and mighty rakish. No doubt there are terms to convey the character of these frocks more clearly to the understanding of female readers, but the writer is not conversant with the subject. He knows for sure, though, that there was deviltry in every flip and flap of those skirts. The companion men were disguised as restaurant waiters. This was not a double sextette of singers. No member of it opened a mouth except to grin. The girls were dancers. The men were subsidiary aids. Together they gave a pantomime representation of beverages being ordered, served and drunk. .

The Sun takes up the description:

> . . they quickly fixed our attention by kicking, whirling and fairly dancing their clothes off in mad gaiety. . The six creatures danced about in French deviltry until six men joined them with a sympathetic skip of agile friskness. They were not half as smart as the sextet men . . but we liked them much better. They were as animated as jumping jacks, and the fact that each carried a little table did not interfere a little bit with their agility. When the men finally put the tables on the ground, the girls took their feet up. They rested their legs on the table, and when the waiters went from them they touched the bells gracefully with their toes to call them back. After that they danced some more and kicked the bells again, and kept the whole thing up everlastingly not because their gaiety was insatiable but because the audience wouldn't let them go. They lost hats and underskirts and still the spectators yelled for more. The success of 'The Silver Slipper' was made in that dance.

And so it proved. *The Silver Slipper* played for 165 performances at the Broadway, and the 'champagne' dance was cheered wildly and nightly while three of the famous *Florodora* girls – Marjorie Relyea 'who sued a man for something or other', Margaret

Walker 'the first chorus-girl stockbroker' and Daisy Greene 'whose dark beauty has assisted cigarettes to a sale by posing in picture advertisements' – stood by. Others from that sextette such as Clarita Vidal and Susie Drake also featured in the cast, but this time the limelight was off them. The unexpected heroines of *The Silver Slipper* were Dolly Corke (not long since in the failing *The Thirty Thieves* in London), Beatrice Grenville (from the original London cast of *Florodora*), Sallie Lomas, Rose Martin, Maggie Taylor and Lillie Lawton. If the Americans had been given the credit for bringing 'snap' to the West End with *The Belle of New York*, England had now repaid Broadway in style.

The Silver Slipper appeared later in Germany, at Berlin's Neues Königs Opern Theater, where it shared the weekly bill with Strauss' *Zigeunerbaron* and Millöcker's *Bettelstudent*, a fine honour for a piece which had received so little praise on its first production.

George Edwardes, at the Gaiety, had more experience than the Lyric Theatre team in producing what the public wanted. He also had a magnificient team of performers, constantly reinforced from his touring companies, to whom the material created by his writers could be entrusted safely. And those writers were the very best. The credits for the new piece, *The Toreador*, were virtually the same as those for the previous Gaiety triumph, *The Messenger Boy*: Ivan Caryll and Lionel Monckton for the music, James T. Tanner for the book (assisted this time by comedian/writer Harry Nicholls) and, for the lyrics, the ever-fertile Adrian Ross and twenty-three-year-old Percy Greenbank who had made his Gaiety début with his words for *The Messenger Boy* and was on his way to becoming a valued part of that theatre's creative team. Born in London, in 1878, Percy had originally been intended for the law but, following in his famous brother's steps, he had turned to writing as a contributor to such journals as *Punch*, *The Sketch* and *Tatler*. In *The Messenger Boy* and *San Toy* he was given the opportunity to provide some lyrics and he rose swiftly thereafter to a position as one of the most prolific and popular lyricists of the British theatre in a career of some thirty years before retiring soon after the age of fifty to spend his last forty years in comparative silence.

For *The Toreador*, Tanner built a brisk and comical story around Teddy Payne in his usual character of a diminutive 'tiger' who, on this occasion, gets mixed up with a Carlist conspiracy in Spain. Like Owen Hall, Tanner contrived a picturesque locale for his plot – for *The Messenger Boy* it had been Egypt and Paris, for *The Toreador* it was to be the often-favoured Biarritz and Villaya in Spain – and for his stars. The Gaiety's list of stars had changed of late, although Teddy Payne was still there, Lionel Mackinder and Marie Studholme were gently establishing themselves as successors to Hicks and Ellaline Terriss, and the faithful Robert Nainby, Harry Grattan, Willie Warde and Fred Wright provided a solid phalanx of experienced campaigners. But, even since *The Messenger Boy*, Connie Ediss had been lost, albeit temporarily, to the Lyric, Rosie Boote to the aristocracy, Grace Palotta to Australia, Katie Seymour to marriage, and both Harry Monkhouse and E. J. Lonnen to premature death. However, Edwardes was rarely at a loss in casting. He re-engaged George Grossmith who had not appeared at the Gaiety since *The Shop Girl*, brought Florence Collingbourne from her newfound stardom in *San Toy* at Daly's, promoted the imposing Claire Romaine to the 'Connie' role, and brought in from the tour of *The Messenger Boy* an impish-faced but experienced actress to whom Lionel Monckton had taken a great fancy, for the role which would normally have gone to Rosie Boote. Her name was Gertie Millar and she would be as great a star as the Gaiety had ever known.

In the opening scenes the characters gather in Biarritz. There is the buxom widow,

Mrs Malton Hoppings (Claire Romaine) engaged to be married to the dashing Spanish toreador, Carajola (Herbert Clayton, promoted from chorus and bits to his first genuine principal role), much to the fury of her other admirer, the wild-animal dealer Pettifer (Fred Wright). There is the ward-in-chancery, Dora Selby (Marie Studholme) called to Biarritz to meet her husband-to-be, Augustus Traill (Lionel Mackinder). But Dora does not like the idea of being so arbitrarily paired off, and plans a deception. She pretends she is already married and brings along her 'husband' – her girl friend, Nancy (Florence Collingbourne) in disguise. To Biarritz, too, comes the little 'tiger' Sammy Grigg, in answer to a newspaper advertisement placed by Pettifer for a real tiger for his zoo. When Grigg arrives and discovers his error he is left broke and at a loose end, but he soon finds himself embroiled in the romantic affairs of all the other members of the cast as well as in a flirtation of his own with the perky florist, Susan (Violet Lloyd). Soon he finds trouble. The vivacious Donna Teresa (Queenie Leighton, fresh from Arthur Roberts' *H.M.S. Irresponsible*) kids him into a toreador disguise to help her cross the frontier into Spain, and little Sammy finds himself caught up in a Carlist plot, carrying a bomb which is liable to explode at any minute, as well as the target of the jealousy of the irrational Pettifer who has a bull ring full of particularly wild bulls which Sammy seems destined to have to face, thanks to his disguise. Eventually all is resolved and everyone, including the fatuous man-about-town, Archie (George Grossmith), paired off into a happy Spanish ending.

The plot might not have had the merit of novelty, but it was bright, straightforward and fluid, with humour and songs in the best Gaiety manner. At the head of these were the obligatory Teddy Payne duets. With Katie Seymour gone, he now shared these numbers with Violet Lloyd and together they sang 'If ever I Marry', detailing the difficulties of marriage to a celebrity, and a comical 'Punch and Judy' piece, and Payne also joined in an amusing trio with Grossmith and Mackinder entitled 'Blanks':

> Oh, memory's a funny thing indeed
> When incidents occur
> Over which you would prefer
> In the future, so to speak, to draw a curtain.
> If creditors for settlement should press
> One needn't stop to listen to their chatter
> Just tell them you regret
> That you can't recall their debt
> For your mind is quite a blank upon the matter.

The solo numbers were well spread about: Clayton had a vigorous 'Toreador's Song', Queenie Leighton a tempting 'O Senor Pray', and Harry Grattan as the Governor of Villaya and Maidie Hope as La Belle Bolero both had songs, but the most successful pieces were those written for Grossmith, Wright, Miss Collingbourne, Miss Romaine and a little number for Gertie Millar called 'Keep off the Grass' in which she coyly warned:

> Hi, little boys, hi, little boys, hi!
> Take care now!
> Keep off the grass, keep off the grass,
> Conduct like this I won't pardon.
> Play at your ease, but, if you please,
> Keep off the grass in the garden!

Like 'Maisie', 'Keep off the Grass' was a huge success, but so also was a number written for George Grossmith by Paul Rubens in which he gave the archetypal description of the young and foolish man-about-town whom he represented so often and so well:

I'm an awfully simple fellow
As I'm sure you'll all agree
And I really don't know what
My various friends can see in me.
My acquaintances are endless
And their names I quite forget
For one half I only know by sight
And the rest I've never met.

But everybody's awfully good to me, don't you know,
I'm just about as spoilt as I can be, don't you know,
If I go out, say, to Princes and alone I chance to dine
Why, it's ten to one I meet some dear old Oxford friend of mine
Well, not only does he join me, but he orders all the wine,
Everybody's awfully good to me . .

Grossmith composed the lyric himself for his other solo 'Archie' which told the tale of:

Sir Archie was a subaltern who sallied to the south
A sword about his waist, a cigarette inside his mouth
He got some cuts and scratches and was mentioned in despatches
For he always takes a chance whenever he sees one.
He left some girls behind him 'cause he couldn't take them too
He tried to get permission, but they thought it wouldn't do
So he did his share of duty and returned to home and beauty
If there is a gallant officer, well, he's one!

Archie, Archie, he's in town again
The idol of the ladies and the envied of the men
He doesn't really care a jot
If a girl is dark or fair or what
For they all look beautiful to Archie!

The sartorial elegance which the role allowed him to affect, and the dashing style of his own lyrics appealed much more to Grossmith than some of the silly-ass parts he had been playing, and 'Sir Archie' gave him a place at the Gaiety which he would retain. Florence Collingbourne sang a pretty number called 'The Language of the Flowers', in a panama hat and knickerbockers, which advised young men to 'say it with flowers' as a flower is no proof in a breach-of-promise case. After *The Toreador*, Miss Collingbourne retired to matrimony where she was finally able to get out of male attire. For Claire Romaine, the authors composed a 'heavy lady' number called 'I'm Romantic', but Miss Romaine interpolated a Harry B. Smith song called 'Maud' which proved to be her best opportunity.

The Toreador was staged with all the Gaiety's accustomed style and splendour, but to the first-night audience *The Toreador* was more than just another Gaiety musical . . it was the last Gaiety musical. By now, it was common knowledge that the theatre was condemned. The plans for the widening of the Strand and the construction of the Aldwych entailed the demolition of a number of buildings and the Gaiety Theatre was one. The authorities had provided a new and, in many ways, better site on which a new Gaiety Theatre could and was going to be constructed and where, hopefully, things would carry on as always, but Gaiety faithfuls recognised that it could never be exactly as before and to them the première of *The Toreador* was the last Gaiety first night. It could not have gone better. Number after number was cheered and encored. And it was not just the occasion – the critics were in agreement. *The Times* declared:

> In the long list of Gaiety successes it is difficult to recall under the present or the former régime any work so heartily to be commended as *The Toreador* . .

The Stage called it . . 'a fitting conclusion to thirty-three years of merry entertainment . .' concluding that '. . the new play should outlast the numbered days of the old Gaiety . .' The plot could scarcely expect accolades, but *The Times* summed up the general reaction:

> A piece which presents Mr Edmund Payne in the character of an English tiger disguised as a Spanish matador with his arms full of Carlist bombs which may explode at any moment, can surely dispense with anything in the shape of plot, or of unity of style.

The Toreador was to turn out to be the most successful of all of the Gaiety's shows. As was forecast, it actually did last out the theatre's life, closing down, after 675 performances, on July 4, 1903, the last night of the old Gaiety.

During its run much happened, most notably the rise to stardom of Gertie Millar. Gertie caught on with the Gaiety fans straightaway and her role began subtly and then not so subtly to expand. A new Lionel Monckton number was written for her and she sang of how 'Captivating Cora makes the Bride look small'. A third number, written by Paul Rubens, 'I'm not a simple little Girl', further expanded the part of the little bridesmaid.

Another role which expanded was that of Mrs Malton Hoppings. Trouble began with the popularity of the song 'Maud'. The Gaiety authors objected to Miss Romaine inserting her American song into the show and insisted with all the power of their position that it be removed. But Miss Romaine's husband, Edgar, weighed in and Edwardes allowed 'Maud' to remain until Miss Romaine went. She never appeared at the Gaiety again. The departure of Claire Romaine brought the return of Connie Ediss, back from *The Silver Slipper*. Connie lit into 'I'm Romantic' with a vengeance and then proceeded to give the Gaiety her version of how 'She Lay Low' (Rubens), of 'Books' (Bernard Rolt) and of 'Fairy fingered Fanny' as the role took on the ample proportions due to her star status.

Many other numbers came and went during the two years in which *The Toreador* held the Gaiety stage, and many actors and actresses too, but the end in sight seemed very close when a new piece, *The Linkman*, was introduced into the programme following the main entertainment. Devised by Grossmith, it reviewed the past glories of the theatre. A short scene at the stage door of the Gaiety introduced members of the company in a selection of pieces from the hit Gaiety shows of the past, from the burlesques of *Miss Esmeralda, Monte Cristo Jr, The Forty Thieves, Faust Up-To-Date*, up to the most recently ended show, *The Messenger Boy*.

On the last night, this particular part of the show was extended. Only the second act of *The Toreador* was given, and *The Linkman* featured some of the theatre's greatest stars in their original roles – Florence St John as Marguerite in *Faust Up-To-Date*, Ethel Haydon as La Favorita (*Circus Girl*), Letty Lind as Donna Elto and Charles Danby as Salluste in *Ruy Blas*, Arthur Williams (Hooley) and Seymour Hicks (Charlie) in *The Shop Girl* and Louis Bradfield as Guy (*Runaway Girl*) alongside the new members of the Gaiety company. Many other stars, past and present, appeared on the Gaiety stage that night: Constance Loseby, Lionel Brough, Jennie Lee, Richard

Temple and the only remaining member of the famous old-time Gaiety foursome, E. W. Royce. All brought back memories of shows that seemed a lifetime ago. The old and the new Gaiety met as the theatre's newest star, Gertie Millar, danced Kate Vaughan's Morgiana from *The Forty Thieves*. Kate had passed away a few months earlier in South Africa. But the evening was not a sad one. *The Toreador* was gone, the Gaiety was gone, but on the corner of the Aldwych the new Gaiety was rising, and George Edwardes had still many delights in store for the British musical public.

Of course the success of *The Toreador* was by no means limited to the Gaiety or to London. It took over the usual touring circuits and appeared in all the usual overseas dates, including a successful Paris season at the Moulin Rouge, another at Vienna's Theater an der Wien and a Broadway run at the Knickerbocker Theatre where it remained for 121 performances with Francis Wilson starring as Sammy. In the unfortunate way of Broadway, the show was 'Americanised' and, in this case, 'Wilsonised', but enough of the fun and the original score (there was only one interpolated song) survived to keep the show alive and attractive for a thoroughly respectable season.

Having got *The Toreador* comfortably settled at the Gaiety, Edwardes switched his attention to another property, *Kitty Grey*, which had been running with outstanding success in the provinces since its production at Bristol in August of the previous year. *Kitty Grey* was not a typical Edwardes' musical. Its origins meant that it had a particularly strong plot, and characters and action which had been devised to operate within the construction of a Palais Royal farce. The alterations which had been made to turn *Kitty Grey* into a musical took it some way from *Les Fêtards*, but not too far from the play which had been seen at the Vaudeville. The songs were incidental and not too numerous – nineteen musical pieces including two opening choruses and three finales – and the staging, while fully worked-out and attractive, did not encompass the more exuberant and colourful extremes of, say, *The Messenger Boy*. Nevertheless, the adjuncts of the musical did serve to change what had been a fair but scarcely world-beating play into a more than respectable light musical success.

The story of *Kitty Grey* centred on Lord and Lady Binfield, the former a warm-blooded gentleman of fashion, the latter a respectable, not to say puritanical, wife. The prudishness of Lady Binfield has led her husband to seek consolation in the arms of the actress, Kitty Grey. When she discovers her husband's infidelity, Lady Binfield follows him to London and finally confronts Kitty in her dressing room, more hurt than angry. Kitty counsels her to more easy-going ways and more inviting manners if she wishes to hold her husband. The next visitor to Kitty's dressing room is the amorous King of Illyria who is very taken with Lady Binfield who introduces herself as the actress's cousin. He leads both Kitty and the disguised Lady Binfield off to supper where he lavishes his attentions and a pearl necklace on the married lady while her husband looks on unwittingly. Alarmed at the response she has elicited with her innocent flirting, Lady Binfield again enlists Kitty's help and the necklace ends up round the neck of the chirpy Mrs Bright, a former flame of the rumbustious King. Sir John, learning the mysterious lady's identity, is jealous enough to return to his wife who has now learned new ways and will not let him wander again.

The musical version of the piece had opened with Evie Greene featured in the starring role of Kitty and with Ethel Sydney and Maurice Farkoa as the couple whom she helps to happiness. But to cast Farkoa as an English baronet was out of the question and, since his value to the piece was obviously more important than sticking to the play, affairs were rationalised by altering the nationality of his character. Sir John became M.

le Baron de Tregue. Harry Monkhouse was featured as the King and Lillie Belmore repeated her 'straight' performance as Mrs Bright with George P. Huntley in the comic role of Lord Plantagenet.

Edwardes had contracted to take the Apollo Theatre from Henry Lowenfeld and had announced the forthcoming production there of *Three Little Maids*, the first full work by the up-and-coming Paul Rubens, with Evie Greene, Edna May and Ada Reeve starring in the triple title-role. But, seeing the success Miss Greene was having with *Kitty Grey*, he changed his mind. *Three Little Maids* was shelved and *Kitty Grey* was brought in to the Apollo instead. Part, at least, of the original plan was adhered to for Miss Greene was joined at the head of the bill by Edna May in the role of the puritanical Baroness de Tregue. Ada Reeve had no cause for care as Edwardes had placed her neatly into *San Toy* where she was having a merry time rewriting the title role.

George Huntley was brought in from the touring company to repeat his role in town, but the other stars had sadly to be replaced for during the tour both Harry Monkhouse (aged 47) and Lillie Belmore (only 29) had died. Charles Angelo, who had taken over from Monkhouse, took on the role of the King and Gladys Homfrey, the Dragon of Daly's, came in as Mrs Bright. The Baron, of course, was the smooth Maurice Farkoa who brought his nationality with him: as soon as he departed the touring show, M. le Baron was able, in the person of Roland Cunningham, once more to become Sir John. In spite of the short time between tour and town, there were some very necessary rewrites to be done. In the original, the role of Lady Binfield/Baronne de Tregue was decidely subsidiary to that of Kitty Grey, but now La Baronne was Edna May. Paul Rubens was put to work on some extra songs and Edna's role grew in the days before the London opening.

When the show opened at the Apollo, Misses Greene and May had the most prominent parts. Kitty sang a little number about make-up called 'The Powder Puff' composed by Augustus Barratt, a lilting Howard Talbot song relating the sad tale of 'Mademoiselle Pirouette' and a piece by Paul Rubens asserting 'Kitty's not Built that Way'. The Baroness responded with the more heartfelt 'Trust Me' and 'Give back your Heart to Me' which Rubens had supplied for her and the andante religioso 'Look Aloft' (Barratt). But probably the most successful of the show's songs was a silly little piece by Lionel Monckton called 'Little Zo-Zo' which survived from the touring score to be sung by Gladys Homfrey:

> When I was young as you girls are
> I was famous as a circus star
> Shouts resounding hailed me bounding
> Through the circle or above the bar.
> I could captivate a foreign king
> And he promised any mortal thing
> Diamond brooches, four-horse coaches
> All his property except a ring!
> Zo-Zo, Zo-Zo, I was little Zo-Zo &c.

The songs were pretty but relatively insignificant. The emphasis in *Kitty Grey* was, unusually, on its story and the characters of its principal protaganists.

The show was generally agreed to be a success. The verdict of the provinces was heartily confirmed and the Apollo regularly well filled. When Evie Greene fell ill and was forced to leave the role of Kitty, Edwardes acted with typical bravado and brought in the third 'little maid', shifting Ada Reeve from Daly's to take on the part of the sympathetic and worldly-wise actress. Instead of the show's attraction being lessened it was, if anything, increased. Edna May and Ada Reeve on the same bill was a rare treat.

In her autobiography, Miss Reeve asserts that the role of Kitty was her favourite musical comedy part and, indeed, it was a gem. The mixture of strong and sympathetic acting and lively song and dance was one that could only appeal to any actress. But it was hard work too; at one stage, after a strong scene, she was required to go into a dance which included high kicks wearing a full-length dress with a train. Miss Reeve also tells how she dealt with the inevitable Johnnies who sent her importuning notes. In one scene played in her 'dressing room' she was required to read out fatuous notes sent by supposed admirers. Into this scene she inserted the real notes which had been sent to her, Ada:

> My dear Miss (Grey), I suppose you get so many of these letters that this is but another to add to your collection. I come night after night to see you. Won't you just give me a smile? I have a white gardenia in my buttonhole, and am sitting in seat No. 14 Row B . .

Dutifully in character, Ada turned her gaze directly onto seat 14, Row B, smiled magnificently, and then, as the action required, tore the letter into tiny pieces and deposited them in the waste basket.

New numbers were introduced in consequence of the cast change – one for Ada ('Why?' by Rubens) and, therefore, one for Edna ('Just Seventeen' by Bernard Rolt), but the most interesting additions to the score came when *Kitty Grey* made a belated New York bow in 1909 with Julia Sanderson as Kitty. 'Just good Friends 'and 'If a Girl wants You' were written by the twenty-three-year-old Jerome Kern. They did not help the show to succeed, but then New York had already had its version of *Les Fêtards* nine years previously with Harry B. Smith and Ludwig Englander's *The Rounders* at the Casino and it, too, had failed to run in spite of a cast featuring Mabelle Gillman, Phyllis Rankin, Dan Daly and Thomas Q. Seabrooke.

Kitty Grey's London run was a marked success – seven and a half months and 220 performances – and all that while touring companies proliferated in the provinces and overseas versions lined up to follow in the success of the production. The decision to musicalise his unexceptional play had proved another example of Edwardes' uncanny theatrical wisdom, one more winner to add to his string of musical successes.

A Chinese Honeymoon had been making itself exceptionally popular in the provinces. Its original eight weeks' tour had been quickly followed, in March of 1900, by a second featuring Picton Roxburgh as the fearsome Emperor and his wife, Fanny Wright, as Mrs Pineapple. In August, Dance took the management of the play into his own very efficient hands and launched a fourteen-weeks' north of England season, which recommenced in January of 1901 to highly appreciative audiences in eighteen further dates. The demand for *A Chinese Honeymoon* was such that Dance announced that two full companies would tour the piece in the autumn. But the show's success in the provinces had prompted Frank Curzon, lessee of the Royal Strand Theatre, to take an interest and he bought the London rights with a view to an autumn production. He also signed up little Louie Freear, who had been such a hit in Dance's *Gay Parisienne*, to take a part in the show. With a West End production in sight, Dance decided to divest himself of his responsibilities to further provincial tours of *A Chinese Honeymoon* and offered the touring rights to Milton Bode for nothing more than the cost of the scenery and the costumes, with his sole remaining right to be his author's royalties. Bode declined to take an interest and so George Dance retained a property which was to become, over the next decade and more, one of the most lucrative of all time.

In the meanwhile he was busy. The hiring of Louie Freear for the Strand necessitated the building-up or in of a role for her. It was decided the small role of Fi-fi, the waitress, could be worked up into a part which had suitable emphasis on the qualities that had made her so successful in *The Gay Parisienne*, and Dance set to work on some low comedy and rousing music-hall type songs. So, duly expanded, Frank Curzon's production of George Dance and Howard Talbot's *A Chinese Honeymoon* opened 5 October, 1901 at the Royal Strand Theatre where it was received with enthusiastic laughter and applause. If it did not seem like an instant hit, there was clear evidence that it would enjoy a run in the metropolis.

The Times found much to commend:

> [it] differs from most of the other works of the same class by possessing very distinct signs of a plot which not only begins with the rise of the curtain but is actually followed out to the close of the second and final act. One cannot but welcome this sign of a reaction. Of late, musical comedies have grown more and more plotless till they have reached a climax in the latest importations from America which have come to be nothing but a series of music-hall turns strung together with short passages of pointless dialogue . . . [the music is] bright, attractive and well-written, though this again contains reminiscences of the Savoy, it is in his choruses that he is most successful, and it is certainly refreshing to find some good part-writing in a modern comic opera for it is rare enough at the present time . .

To call *A Chinese Honeymoon* comic opera and to compare it to Savoy opera was, perhaps, taking matters a little too far and the piece a little too seriously, but *The Times* was right: Dance's play had a beginning, a good number of middles, and an end. In the new 'Louie Freear version', the plot had been slightly altered, allowing her to be not entirely incidental to the story which now ran:

Tom Hatherton is in love with a pretty Chinese singing girl and has resigned his post in the army to stay in China to woo her. He spends his spare time flirting with the little waitress, Fi-fi, who, alas, takes him all too seriously. Unknown to Tom, however, his true love, Soo Soo, is actually the daughter of the Emperor, Hang Chow. That potentate is, in his turn, in search of a new wife and he has sent off his Lord High Admiral, Hi Lung, armed with an Imperial photograph to find a girl who will love him for himself and not for his position. As the play opens, Hi Lung is returning, disconsolate. He has not found any maid for whom the Imperial features hold any charm. Arriving at the same time are the newly-wed Mr and Mrs Pineapple who are taking their honeymoon in China. They are accompained by Mrs Pineapple's four little bridesmaids whom she has brought along to keep an eye on her newly acquired husband. The bridesmaids are equipped with whistles with which to sound the alarm should Mr Pineapple give them, or any other lady, the slightest provocation. The honeymooners have a tiff and the trouble begins. Mr Pineapple goes off flirting to his heart's delight and gets himself into a fix by kissing Soo Soo. By the law of the land, anyone who kisses a member of the royal family must marry them on the spot and, in spite of the fact that he has just been married once, Mr Pineapple finds himself going through the whole thing again with an equally unwilling Soo Soo. Mrs Pineapple has also got herself into trouble. She has been rounded up, along with Fi-fi and other local ladies, to be presented to the Emperor as a candidate for his heart, hand and throne. But while the Emperor dallies with Mrs Pineapple, her poor husband is getting even more deeply into trouble. The Emperor, since he has no wife, has engaged an 'official mother-in-law' to keep an eye on his daughter's new husband. This venerable lady turns out to be Pineapple's old housekeeper, Mrs Brown, with whom, in his bachelor days, he had played fast and loose. This dragonistic lady takes her opportunity for revenge. But Soo Soo, decidedly unhappy, turns to trickery and takes a Chinese sleeping drug to feign death. Pineapple now finds himself obliged to perform a royal suttee, but the heart-broken Tom steps in to take his place. The arrival of the British Ambassador prevents disaster: the lovers are united, the Pineapples reconciled and the Emperor promotes Mrs Brown from proxy wife to the real thing, while poor Fi-fi is left to make do.

The dialogue was in Dance's very best typical style: light, bright and by no means highbrow, but unfailingly funny to both stalls and gallery, though *The Stage* commented:

> . . lyrics and dialogue rarely rise above the requirements or comprehension of Matthew Arnold's 'average sensual man' . .

The songs, too, were delightful. Like Dance's dialogue, Louie Freear levelled all ranks, giving the stalls a touch of the still frowned upon music halls in her comic elfin delivery of a bundle of numbers. The first was 'The twiddley Bits' composed for the occasion by Ernie Woodville in which Fi-fi related the story of her attachment to her piano teacher:

> . . and oh! The twiddley bits he used to play
> When all alone with me
> Popping around whenever he found the opportunity
> And oh! The twiddley bits he used to play
> It almost gave me fits
> My heart was won
> And the deed was done
> With his dear little twiddley bits.

In the second act she gave double measure, and brought the house to cheers with each of two songs. The first was Dance's own piece 'I Want to be a Lidy' and the second was Talbot's 'Martha Spanks the grand Pianner' into which little Louie swung with a style reminiscent of the famous 'Sister Mary Jane's high Note' as she described her 'musical' family who insisted, apparently, on playing their family orchestra in all the most embarrassing places:

> Martha spanks the grand pianner, Father whacks the drum
> Mother, in a soulful manner, blows the tootle-tum
> Charlie swings the concertina, Bob goes fiddle-dee-dee
> But I'm a brick, for I waggle the stick, with a one-two-three!

It was good, unclean music-hall stuff, and everyone loved it. But there was more to Howard Talbot's score than music-hall songs, and Louie Freear did not by any means have all the choice numbers. The show opened with a tea-house chorus and solo leading into a chorus of welcome for the returning Hi Lung who replied with a little piece describing his unfortunate journey. The refrain ran:

> It's roly-poly, roly-poly
> O'er the sea once more
> Here and there and everywhere
> Where the angry billows roar,
> Some Admirals at court have pals
> And quit the sea when young
> But it's roly-poly and nothing else
> For Admiral Hi Lung!

This piece proved a very lively and useful opening for the show. It was followed by Soo Soo's pretty solo, 'A Paper Fan', in which the princess relates how a little paper fan was given to a Chinese princess so that artful half-display might make her more successful in wooing than an open face. For the Emperor's entrance Dance devised an 'increasing' song, such as he had used for the Rajah Punka in *The Nautch Girl* as the potentate declared, finally:

This is the marriage settlement
That gives my bride and her descent
The charge of the overflowing purse
Without which life would be a curse
That induces the smile so soft and sleek
That proves a nature mild and meek
That illumines the warm and gushing heart
That yearns to play a loving part
That goes with the hand that seeks a mate
The hand of a wealthy potentate
That very delectable
Highly respectable
Emperor Hang Chow.

The Pineapples introduce themselves in a sextet (with the omnipresent bridesmaids), 'The Chinese Honeymoon', before Mrs Pineapple sings another Talbot song which was to become extremely popular, describing 'The à la Girl':

The à la girl is an English girl
With lots of à la ways
She gets her frocks at Brixton
But they're fashioned à la Jays.
She's awfully fond of diamonds
And she wears them all she can
Though, just between ourselves, they're made
À la Parisian!
Oh, the à la girl is a knowing girl
With heaps of à la talk
And when she strolls down Regent Street
She's got an à la walk
There's an à la twinkle in her eye
She wears an à la curl
And she loves a dash with an à la mash
Does the à la English girl

The American, Scottish and Parisian girls come in for similar treatment in the other verses.

A waltz duet, 'Roses red and White', for Tom and Soo Soo provided a romantic element before a curious interpolated piece 'Nursery Rhymes' by Ernest Vousden. 'The twiddley Bits' brought back humour before a long finale (25 printed pages) in which the unfortunate Pineapple is wedded to Soo Soo. The second act opened with a chorus of Soo Soo's maidens, followed by a bright waltz 'Laughter is Queen Tonight' for the Princess who returns, after 'I Want to be a Lidy', to add an element of the Gaiety with an Ivan Caryll song called 'Dolly with the Dimple on her Chin'. Pineapple then introduced an ingenious piece with a patter recitative:

(sung) I dreamed a dream the other night
I thought that I had flown
Into a land where all was bright
And troubles were unknown
And man was lord and master there
And held the upper hand
And woman was a small affair
Throughout that happy land.

(patter) For there a man went out when he liked, and came home when he liked and his wife never asked any questions but stayed at home and minded her own business and darned his stockings and stitched on his buttons and put some braid on the bottom of his trousers when they were beginning to get whiskers on them and she never asked him to buy her a new bonnet but stitched a few flowers on her old one and made it do and when the baby was cutting its teeth she didn't expect him to get up in the middle of the night and warm its Ridges food and take it in his arms and trot it up and down the corridor in his naked feet on the cold linoleum . .

(sung) In that happy, happy land.

An octet around the word 'pat' followed, of which the conclusion was that a pat of butter, a pat repartee and the pat of the rain cannot compare with a pat on the back.

Mrs Brown was welcomed with a choral fanfare and Tom Hatherton contributed a soulful ballad entitled 'But Yesterday' for the sentimental, before an odd duet (Mrs Pineapple and Hi Lung) called 'Tit Bits from the Plays' in which current plays and songs were reviewed . . favourably of course. This bit of free advertising proved amusing to audiences who liked to hear familiar topics tackled on the stage. 'Click Click' was a little duet for the Emperor and Fi-fi, describing the satisfactory conclusion reached by the man who could not find a wife. He had an automaton made which he could turn off when she got tiresome. 'Penelope' was a topical sextet based on the long-suffering Mrs Odysseus, with the chorus:

Penelope was a patient one
She swore she'd wait until
(A matinée hat is not higher than that)[1]
And Penelope's waiting still

It was not the most popular piece in the score, and later disappeared. The final number was left, of course, to Louie Freear, and Martha spanked the grand pianner to lead up to the brief finale which brought affairs to a close.

The combination of the romantic, the robustly comic and the picturesque, the music hall, the musical comedy and the comic opera was a well-made one. The ingredients had been mixed in just the right proportions and quality. *A Chinese Honeymoon* appealed to both the West End and the East End, and the Strand Theatre was well filled for an unprecedented 1075 performances, clearly out-running *Dorothy* to become the longest-running musical up to that time and the first musical anywhere to run for more than 1000 consecutive performances.

Louie Freear held on to her role of Fi-fi for two years before relinquishing it to Hilda Trevalyan, who was by no means daunted by the succession. The Irish actress, Ellas Dee, however, left the role of Mrs Pineapple very soon after opening night, and was succeeded by Marie Dainton playing opposite Lionel Rignold, the only member of the

[1] This line varied in each refrain.

original cast to repeat his role in the West End until his wife, Marie Daltra, succeeded to her original role of Mrs Brown. Many of the stars remained with the show for very long periods, but the quota of well-known names on the cast list increased as the success of the piece became established: Arthur Williams took over a stretch as Pineapple, Joe Farren Soutar played Tom, Gracie Leigh was Mrs Pineapple and Kate Cutler Soo Soo. And as the show entered on its third year, a young lady made her London debut as Mrs Pineapple – pretty Lily Elsie, soon to find fame as 'The Merry Widow'. Provincial tours went out year after year, and one of these found another star of the future promoted from the chorus to play a very young Mrs Pineapple: Lottie Collins' daughter, José.

A Chinese Honeymoon, unlike so many other outsize London hits, was quick to prove itself a major success all around the world. It was taken to New York by the budding young producer Sam Shubert and staged at the Casino Theatre, a few days after Shubert had managed to prise that theatre from the hands of its former owners, the Sires brothers. On the stage on which *Erminie* and *Florodora* had set up their American long-run records, *A Chinese Honeymoon*, with Katie Barry featured as Fi-fi and Thomas Q. Seabrooke and Adele Ritchie as the Pineapples, kept the new Shubert flag flying for a whole year before going on the road in a multiple set of companies, one of which stayed around the environs of New York for another twelve months. By and large, Dance's script was not badly mauled in its Atlantic crossing, but Talbot's score suffered the inevitable 'popular' interpolations one of which, a ditty called 'Mr Dooley' by Jean Schwartz, became exceptionally popular.

In Australia, May Beatty, Edward Lauri and J. C. Piddock headed a highly successful George Musgrove production which also featured English expatriates Foster Courtenay, W. R. Shirley and Henry Hallam. It set up a 165-performance record at Melbourne's Princess Theatre and covered Australia and New Zealand at length. George Walton reaped the benefits of securing the South African rights and, in 1903, a German version opened in Hamburg. *A Chinese Honeymoon* made its way through Austria, Hungary and South America; Maurice Bandmann, the indefatigable Oriental touring manager, took it on a tour of the Mediterranean; Henry Dallas presented it in Hong Kong and even in China; and, all the time the profits from the London production escalated towards the magic £100,000 mark, with other record-breaking figures appearing on every side as it took its place in theatrical history as one of the greatest musical successes of all time.

The euphoric current record of the British musical theatre was not, however, proof against failure. To join the prevailing circuit of success, a certain degree of talent and organisation was needed, as well as a good show. None of these qualities were found in the year's next entry. Arthur Eliot, of *A Good Time* notoriety, had re-surfaced and there was apparently no legal bar to his dabbling once more in things theatrical. Eliot formed a company called Lyric Trusts Ltd with a nominal capital of £5000 and issued shares to the value of £2257. A ten-week lease was taken on the Globe Theatre and the piece announced was *Hidenseek* or The Romance of A Ring with book and lyrics largely by Arthur Eliot and music by Carl Kiefert, Scott-Gatty and the Gaiety veteran, Meyer Lutz, who had also been hired as conductor. An excellent cast was assembled – John Le Hay, Alice Lethbridge, John Peachey, J. C. Piddock and Americans Edward Abeles and Erminie Earle – and the musical play duly opened on 10 December.

Eliot's book was a mixture of burlesque and comic opera and straightforward plagiarism. The central character was a curious detective called Peter Pike, modelled on Sherlock Holmes who was currently being represented by William Gillette at the

Lyceum. Abeles played a miser who bore considerable resemblance to his counterpart in *Les Cloches de Corneville*, Tim Ryley played an Eastern King with 'seven little wives' who was a direct steal from *San Toy*, and so it went on. The whole action was set on a comic opera island with the unlikely name of Hidenseek, from whence the title.

The show's opening was not encouraging and the audience greeted the first night not even with vociferous disapproval but in silent indifference. The papers made up for their lack of expression. *The Times* noted curtly that it was 'entirely devoid of any vestige of a story', and *The Stage* continued:

> . . as the feebly punning title might have led one to expect *Hidenseek* proves to be one of the most indifferent go-as-you-please pieces performed in London for some time. Its construction is marvellously bad; a myriad of reminiscences of other plays of various classes surrounding the thin thread of plot that winds its devious way throughout the action in such a manner as almost to defy disentanglement . . .

There were talented performers, there were some fairly attractive pieces of music, but *Hidenseek* was never going to survive on those. The theatre took a two-day break over Christmas and Eliot announced a revised version to be performed after the holiday, but it was obvious the ship was sinking. When the resumption took place, John Le Hay had departed. The next day Edward Abeles also took his leave. Arthur Eliot, whose ambitions had never been limited to producing and/or writing, took to the stage himself in the leading role but soon the position was no longer tenable. *Hidenseek* was taken off. A short tour of Scotland and the North ended with the scenery and dresses being sold off for £300, and the loss to the shareholders of £2619.

The scene over Christmas was very different from that of the previous year. The hit shows of the previous year were gone, and London passed the festive period with *A Chinese Honeymoon, Kitty Grey* and *The Toreador*. These were joined by a revival of *The Belle of New York* which had been put on to replace a fourth American failure, *The Whirl of the Town*, with which the New Century (Adelphi) Theatre had re-opened; *Iolanthe*; and a revival of the time-honoured *Morocco Bound* at the Comedy. To these were added the seasonal pieces, an insignificant trifle at the Royalty called *The Swineherd and the Princess* (Carl St Amory/Alfred England and Avalon Collard) and an altogether more important one at the Vaudeville where Charles Frohman and the Hicks family were installed. Their new piece had been written by Seymour Hicks with lyrics by Aubrey Hopwood and Charles H. Taylor and music by Walter Slaughter who had already been so successful with his *Alice in Wonderland* as a seasonal show. It was called *Bluebell in Fairyland* and it told of a little girl, Bluebell, who is transported into fairyland where she goes on a search for the Sleeping King to restore him to his throne, usurped by 'The Reigning King'.

Bluebell was an immediate and spectacular success. *The Times* qualified it as 'very dainty and charming', the music as 'bright and tuneful' and the libretto as 'full of humour'. The scenery was 'very beautiful indeed' and the cast, headed by Ellaline Terriss in the title role and Hicks as the Sleeping King, was a strong and attractive one being made up, as in *Alice*, partly of adults and partly of children. Other notices were even more enthusiastic:

> One of the prettiest and brightest [plays] ever presented for the verdict of juveniles . . (*Era*)
>
> One of the most charming juvenile plays of recent years . . the story is delightfully unreal and irresponsible and while containing many delights for the young contains

> also many quips of a mildly satiric nature to inspire the appreciation of grown-ups . . (*Stage*)

In fact, *Bluebell in Fairyland* was a pretty and innocent fairy play, with plenty of straightforward fun, the variety element, such an increasing feature of pantomime, almost entirely absent. The Christmas atmosphere was enhanced by a display of magic lantern slides between the acts, and the whole charming evening was one which could not fail to appeal to the tasteful and innocent of all ages. Neither was its appeal limited to the season of goodwill, for *Bluebell* continued on to packed houses after the festivities had long ceased, running through Easter for a total run of nearly 300 performances. The songs of *Bluebell* were suitably light and were, in the main, simplified versions of musical comedy songs. The current mania for one-word titles was well in evidence in the comedy numbers: 'Maxims', 'Games', and the topical element was gently maintained in 'Amusements' in which Bluebell and her little crossing sweeper friend, Dicky, enumerated and imitated some of the town's entertainments in much the same way as Louie Freear and Percy Clifton did in *A Chinese Honeymoon*. The piece was also heavily interlaced with dances, the most successful of which was a will o'the wisp routine by little Dorothy Frostick, and which included an Autumn Leaves Dance, a Dutch Sabot Dance, a Yacht Dance, a gavotte, a polka and a number of song-and-dance pieces.

The take-away hits of the show, however, came from two interpolated numbers by William H. Penn – 'The Honeysuckle and the Bee' and 'The Sunflower and the Sun', both sung by Ellaline Terriss and both made on the same plan:

> You are my sunny, sunny sunflower, sweet and shy
> I'd like to be a sunny sunbeam from the sky
> Turn, turn your pretty face to me and say you'll be true
> And I'll be the sunny, sunny sun that shines for you.

and

> You are my honey, honeysuckle, I am the bee
> I'd like to sip the honey sweet from those red lips, you see
> I love you dearly, dearly and I hope you will love me
> You are my honey, honeysuckle, I am the bee

Both were enormous successes and went quickly round the country and the world.

After its closure in London, the touring rights to *Bluebell* were taken by Murray King, one of the company's principal comedians, and the following Christmas it was revived at Liverpool's Prince of Wales Theatre with Mabel Love in the title role. Stanley Brett, the brother of Seymour Hicks, who had originally played the bad King, now took over Hicks' role and several of the children from the Vaudeville company made the trip to Liverpool for the repeat season. *Bluebell* became a perennial Christmas favourite. Hicks and Miss Terriss repeated it at the Aldwych in 1905, and it played a further season of 105 performances at the Princes in 1916. In later years it played seasons at the Alhambra, the Metropolitan Music Hall, the Aldwych, the Chelsea Palace, three times at the Scala, and in 1937 at the People's Palace, and many a notable actor has a credit for *Bluebell in Fairyland* hidden away in the early notes of his career.

During 1901, new musicals were equally prolific in the cities outside London, though, of the nine new musicals produced, none reached the standards required for a metropolitan production. The best of the year's crop were the earliest: *The Southern Belle, The Ladies' Paradise* and *The Fisher Girl. The Southern Belle* was billed as an 'American musical comedy' although there was little or no attempt in it to imitate *The*

Belle of New York style. It was as American as *San Toy* was Chinese. It was an unsophisticated piece with a simple story: Lieutenant Truebody arrives on his wealthy uncle's ranch on his return from war, pining for the pretty nurse who nursed him when he was wounded. But rich Uncle Tobias has the heiress Otis Truely in mind for his nephew. The second act combined a variety entertainment with the opportunity for the comic servant to impersonate Otis in *Charley's Aunt* fashion and for Nurse Amy and her friend to impersonate soldiers before Amy is shown to be Otis and vice versa and all can end happily.

The author of the show preferred to hide himself in anonymity, but the music of *The Southern Belle* came from the experienced pen of Osmond Carr. His score included examples of all the most popular kinds of songs of the period (and of earlier periods), and the American location permitted, with rather more logic than usual, the introduction of the coon song 'Lubly Dinah' which was probably the show's most popular number. *The Southern Belle* ran through a twelve-town tour without ever looking like extending its life any further.

An even better pedigree was behind *The Ladies' Paradise*. Its book was by Dance, its music by Caryll and it opened its career as *A Chinese Honeymoon* had done at the enterprising Hanley Theatre. But *The Ladies' Paradise* did not have the brightness nor the character of its predecessor. Its story and characters lacked the interest of the more successful piece. Instead of staying in the conventional locales of musical comedy, Dance shifted his play to France and into an atmosphere of comic opera and vaudeville. The singing star, Mlle Antoinette, known as Sans Souci, has a number of admirers: Samuel Peashooter, the American sausage king, M. Camembert, her author, and a young artist who is really the English Lord Allington in disguise. Naturally, her preference is for the last named. In order to resolve the situation 'fairly' she decides to raffle herself amongst the three, after having fixed it so that Allington shall win. But Peashooter bribes her maid to re-fix the result and, to the horror of the lovers, wins the prize. In an ambitious section of the show, Dance had the young lord's mother pleading with the singer not to ruin the reputation and life of her son, and Antoinette vowing to do so, but before the final curtain love had found its own way to unite the two.

In spite of its drawbacks, *The Ladies' Paradise* had compensations. The libretto, being by Dance, was full of lively and amusing things. *The Era* called the author 'the master of libretto writing', qualifying his book as 'cleverly contrived' and 'very smart'. *The Stage* agreed:

> . . the libretto is very smart and the music is bright and decidedly catchy. The story is well-conceived and well worked-out . . .

In fact, taken piece by piece, there was not an awful lot that one could find wrong with the show and *The Era* even went so far as to sum it up as' . . one of the brightest and most amusing pieces of its kind . . of late.' But its career was limited to only eight weeks in Britain. During that time, however, it was taken by the American impresario Alfred Aarons and in September of the same year opened on Broadway in no less a place than the Metropolitan Opera House, with the honour of being the first musical comedy ever to play there. Aarons had imported Templar Saxe and Lydia West from Britain for principal roles and twelve English chorus ladies for the front line of the ballet. On the same ship came Richard Carle, returning to America after an unfortunate West End experience. Carle was also booked for *The Ladies' Paradise* and was bringing with him a musical written in conjunction with Walter Slaughter, *Little Miss Modesty*, for which he was hoping to find a market.

Aarons soon found he had over-reached himself. There were money problems before the opening and even more after the show failed to attract favourable notice. It closed down after only fourteen performances. Carle was left to howl for $3,000 in unpaid salary, Dave Lewis for $4,500 and Lydia West and Templar Saxe found themselves stranded with $900 and $500 wages owing to them. *The Ladies' Paradise* quickly sank into oblivion, except for a few of its pretty songs which, individually, found a publisher. One of these propounded a theme which has turned up since in both British and Americans shows – 'She never did the same Thing Twice'.

The Fisher Girl was quite a different kind of work. It was written and composed by Oscar Brand and William Gliddon, the chef d'orchestre of the Grand Theatre, Islington, and it was to all intents and purposes an attempt to render the *Flying Dutchman* tale in comic opera terms in the same way as Planquette had tackled *Rip Van Winkle*. It was a sound piece of work without any great inspiration and it proved interesting and amusing enough to sustain two 1901 tours through some good dates with a company which featured J. M. Jones as Vanderdecken, the sterling baritone voice of Frank Land, sopranos Agnes Molteno and Lottie Siegenberg and the comedy of Edward Kipling, and was brought back again in 1903 for a further spring run.

Another attempt to turn a classic work into a comic opera was Herbert Shelley's musical *Melnotte* based on the famous play *The Lady of Lyons*. Bulwer Lytton's five-act play was condensed into two; or, rather, the original play was decapitated so that the action virtually began at the beginning of the original Act 3, omitting much of the courtship of the haughty Pauline by the disguised Claude Melnotte, an operation which left the plot rather incomprehensible to the uninitiated. However, Frank Tours' music was attractive and the familiar tale retained some of the merits which had made it a classic. A tour was sent out, surrounded by some fancy advertising, under the name of another Lytton – the Savoy comedian Henry A. Lytton. In fact, he was not involved in the financing of the tour but had agreed to lend his name to the product to make it more marketable. *Melnotte* was announced for a major tour opening at the Coronet, but the finances of the producing syndicate melted away and they decided to abandon. Poor Lytton, whose name alone had been splashed all over the prospectus for the show, decided that his reputation was more valuable to him than his bank account and personally subsidised the piece which staggered through the eight weeks that had been booked, before being interred. Lytton told of a friend whom he had asked to check the show on the road to see why it was not 'going'. The meaningful reply came back: 'Harry, I've never done you a bad turn. I've seen it once'.

A little better was a lively piece produced at Birmingham under the auspices of Yorke Stephens and composer Basil Davies and entitled *The Gay Cadets*. Its conventional story dealt with a Pasha's daughter, Cara Luna, at school in England, who falls for a young man from the neighbouring cadet college. In the second act the action was shifted to Egypt where the comedy was supplied by two English housemaids pursuing with intent a comic Irish Highlander, by a musical comedy Sultan, and a leery Major from the Cadet Corps. It was all good fun and the songs were suitably reminiscent of the hits of the day: 'The typical, topical Topper', 'Seven little Girlies are We', 'Dear old Country, how We love Her', 'Love and I' &c. *The Gay Cadets* was written to the fashion and, if its quality was rather second-rate, the critics still found time to give a word of praise to the young composer. From Birmingham, the piece toured fairly successfully with Phyllis Rankin starred as Cara Luna and a strong cast including Edward Thirlby, Charles E. Stevens, Alice Aynsley Cook, Lydia Flopp, Roland Cunningham and Henry Wright. In 1902 it was sent out again with Decima Moore in the lead and with Donald Hall as her hero, while Johnnie Schofield, W. H. Denny, Keino Johnston, Rose Martin, Elsie Carew and Grace Vicat provided the comedy.

Carmita was a simple piece co-written by Walter Parke and Arthur Shirley. The music was by English-born Jesse Williams who had been musical director of the Moore and Burgess Minstrels but was better known as the long time conductor at the Casino Theatre, New York. The piece on which they collaborated was of the romantic comedy opera type. It told a familiar story of disguises: in this case an English lord feigns poverty and tests and tames his new wife, the aptly named Miss Turbellino, in a kind of musical *Taming of the Shrew*. The tour was set up by John Rogers for his protegée Mlle Corinne, a plain and youngish lady with a good singing voice who had played Little Buttercup in the original children's *Pinafore* in America. She had been lined up by George Edwardes as a possible take-over for *San Toy*, but he did not use her and *Carmita* proved nothing like an equivalent vehicle.

F. Kinsey Peile's *Bebe* had Kitty Loftus playing a skating instructress from Niagara attempting to pose her way into a fortune as the missing niece of an Earl. The role gave Miss Loftus a few chances as she declared 'There may not be much of me, but what there is is highly inflammable', but little for anyone else and *Bebe*'s life was limited to one tour. *Sunny Switzerland* was a curious concoction – a tale of fortunes, soldiers and grasping guardians reminiscent of the French comic operas of half a century earlier. Its author tried to introduce some of the methods and styles of modern musical comedy into his fossilised story, but the result was an awkward mixture of mediocre quality which had a short life.

What Became of Totman? was an altogether more successful piece compiled by the actor Augustus Hammond and the conductor Arnold Cooke which also reached back in time for its plot, this time to the old provincial farces. Young Jack, sent to do a Miles Standish for his uncle, marries the girl and tells the uncle she was old, fat and ugly. The uncle turns up and takes it that the boy's landlady is the lady in question before the second act wanders off to deal with the consequences of a night out taken by the lady's real husband. The show had a first career of small dates but did very much better in a second incarnation, much altered, as *What Became of Mrs Racket?*, when toured by actor-manager Charles Stone.

A Ladies' Maid was another unpretentious piece which won itself a good span on the touring circuits. Maid and mistress swapped places to test an unknown fiancé in a lively enough set of variations on standard jokes and tunes by Ernest Hastings and C. A. Lord. It toured, with Lilian Beszant in the title-role, for more than a year on its first round including several appearances in the London suburbs.

There was very little demand remaining for smaller pieces now that the tradition for the forepiece was all but forgotten, but occasionally one turned up for a special occasion and 1901 saw two of these played briefly at the Savoy. The first was *Ib and Little Christina*. It had originally been written as a play by Basil Hood for Martin Harvey at the Prince of Wales, but Franco Leoni added some charming music and the resulting operetta was performed for two weeks in November between the closure of *The Emerald Isle* and a new revival of *Iolanthe*. The other half of the programme was another little piece, *The Willow Pattern*, based loosely on the picture shown on the china. *Ib* proved attractive enough to warrant reproduction by George Edwardes and publication.

1901

0241 **THE THIRTY THIEVES** (later *Miss Mariana* or) a musical extravaganza in two acts by W. H. Risque. Music by Edward Jones. Produced at Terry's Theatre under the management of E. H. Bull 1 January, 1901 for a run of 42 performances closing 23 February, 1901 (closed 22 January to 4 February owing to the death of Queen Victoria).

Lord Mayor . . . . Charles Graves
Secretary . . . . Aubrey Fitzgerald
Captain . . . . Sidney Howard
Appy . . . . Ells Dagnall
Sonny . . . . W. R. Shirley
Mariana . . . . Florence Perry
Rhoda . . . . Pattie Browne
Dancing girls . . . . Susie Nainby, Dolly Corke

Dir: W. H. Risque; md: Edward Jones/George A. Arnold; sc: W. Harford; ch: R. M. Crompton; cos: J. A. Harrison & Co.

0242 **THE SOUTHERN BELLE** an American musical comedy in two acts. Music by F. Osmond Carr. Produced at the Empire Theatre, Southend-on-Sea under the management of Hugh Carson 7 March and toured through Halifax, Cheltenham, Southampton, Hastings, Jersey, Margate, Southend, Kingston, Brighton, Brixton and Harwich/Cambridge, ending 1 June.

Tobias U. Truepenny. . . . . Vernon Cowper
Lt A. Truepenny . . . . Frank Grans/Ernest Attwell
Mr Parkins . . . . Charles Wakeman
Horatio Blaythwaite. . . . . Algernon Newark
Tom Spurritt . . . . Dalton Somers
Otis Truely/Nurse Amy . . . . Lillian Hubbard/Alys Rees
Kitty Willoughby . . . . Freda Coventry
Mabel Raymond . . . . Mabel South
Ruth Raker . . . . Annie Halford

with Ethel Raymond, Lillian Murray, Dolly Harcourt, Kitty Parry, Ada Robinson, Clarissa Lovelace, Madge Earle, Lillian Quartano, Frida Bevan, Gladys d'Esterre, Evelyn Eck, Stella Brandon, Madge Raynor, Alice Vane; Messrs Brandon, Birtles, O'Connor, Ballard, Verity, Linton, Edwards, Edgington, Gregory.

Dir: Hugh Moss; md: T. P. Sutton; ch: Leon Espinosa; sc: Stanes Prem; cos: J. A. Harrison & Co.

0243 **THE LADIES' PARADISE** a musical play in two acts by George Dance. Music by Ivan Caryll. Produced at the Theatre Royal, Hanley, under the management of George Dance 11 March, 1901 and toured through Northampton, Halifax, *out*, Belfast, Darlington, Middlesborough, Sunderland and Lincoln, to 11 May.

Mlle Antoinette . . . . Rita Presano
Mons. Pomade . . . . Arthur E. Stigant
Sarah . . . . Millie Ward
Pincher . . . . Phil Smith

Marie . . . . Isabelle Dillon
Lisa . . . . Violet Gordon
Adele . . . . Linda Hanbury
Duke of Beaumont . . . . Kenneth Altamont
Duchess of Beaumont. . . . . Edith Matt
Lord Allington . . . . Hal Forde Jr
Mons. Camembert . . . . Charles Adeson
Samuel Peashooter . . . . Harry Kilburn
Maud . . . . Elsa Brethingham
Anastasia . . . . Marie Wright

Dir: Arthur E. Stigant; md: Ernest Vousden; sc: W. T. Hemsley; cos: Morris Angel/Mme Vernon

Produced at the Metropolitan Opera House, New York, under the management of Alfred A. Aarons 16 September, 1901 for a run of 14 performances closing 28 September, 1901.
Queenie Vassar (ANT), John Hyams (POM/MULLINS), Ethele Gordon (SAR), Richard Carle (PINCH), Lydia West (MAR), Caroline Huestis (LISA), Kathryn Pearl (AD), Alexander Clark (DUKE), Phoebe Coyne (DUCH), Templar Saxe (AL), Dave Lewis (CAM), Louis Wesley (SAM), Lucille Verna Burnham (MAUD), Josephine Hall (ANA). Pd: La Tortajada; with Florence Relda, Jessie Jordan, Frances Wilson, Reine Davise, Maud Barnard, Nonie Dore, June Dale, Sylvia Star, Minnie Fisher, Anna Leslie, Pearl Henri. Dir: William Parry

0244 **THE EMERALD ISLE** or The Caves Of Carric-Cleena. A comic opera in 2 acts by Basil Hood. Music by Arthur Sullivan and Edward German. Produced at the Savoy Theatre under the management of Mrs D'Oyly Carte 27 April, 1901 for a run of 205 performances closing 9 November, 1901. During the run of the show the management was assumed by William Greet.

Pat Murphy . . . . Henry A. Lytton
Professor Bunn . . . . Walter Passmore (Robert Rous)
Black Dan . . . . W. H. Leon
Sergeant Pincher . . . . Reginald Crompton/Rudolf Lewis
Dr Fiddle D.D. . . . . Robert Rous
Terence O'Brien . . . . Robert Evett/Joseph Boddy
Perry . . . . Powis Pinder/Charles Childerstone
Earl of Newtown . . . . Jones Hewson/Powis Pinder
Mickie O'Hara . . . . Charles Earldon
Countess of Newtown. . . . . Rosina Brandram
Lady Rosie Pippin . . . . Isabel Jay/Agnes Fraser
Susan . . . . Blanche Gaston-Murray
Kathleen. . . . . Agnes Fraser (Madge Moyse)/Mildred Baker
Molly O'Grady . . . . Louie Pounds
Nora. . . . . Lulu Evans/Winifred Hart-Dyke

with Misses G. Thornton, M. Thornton, Rose Rosslyn, Bond, Paull, Isabel Agnew, St Clair, Lesle, Richardson, Hope, Davies, De Lacy, Alice Coleman, Marriott, Vivian, Murray, Madge Moyse, Seymour, Newall, De Mervale, Quarry, Jessie Pounds; Messrs Lewis Campion, Gordon, Gater, Arthur Boielle, Graystone, Bryan, Iago Lewys, Ritte, Owen, Marlyn, Joseph Boddy, Wood, Hildreth, Lewis, Alexander, Herbert.

Dir: Richard Barker; md: François Cellier ; ch: John D'Auban; sc: W. Harford; cos: Percy Anderson

Produced at Herald Square Theatre, New York, by the Jefferson de Angelis Opera Company under the management of R. H. Burnside 1 September, 1902 for a run of 50 performances closing 18 October, 1902.
Bernard Sullivan (PAT), Jefferson de Angelis (BUNN), Lester Reeves (DAN), Frank Belcher (PINCHER), F. Stuart Hyatt (FIDDLE), John Dudley (TER), Frederick K. Logan (PERRY), Charles Dungan (EARL), C. V. Clark (MICK), Amelia Fields (CTESS), Josephine Knapp (R), Edna Burd (SU), Lois Garneau (KATH), Kate Condon (MOL), Norma Bell (NORA)

0245 **THE FISHER GIRL**, a Romance of the Flying Dutchman. A musical play in 2 acts by Oscar Brand. Music by William T. Gliddon. Produced at the Theatre Royal, Hanley under the management of Harry S. Parker 27 May, 1901 and toured through Nottingham, Liverpool, Southampton, Margate, Brighton, Peckham, Hastings to 20 July, then from Reading (September 16) through Grand Islington, Eccles, Norwich, Ipswich, Balham, Jersey, Southend, Ealing, Dublin, Aberdeen, Dundee, Bradford, to 14 December &c.

Vanderdecken . . . . J. M. Jones
Steersman . . . . Frank Land
Bosun . . . . Harlow Saker
Mate. . . . . James Fletch
Sailor . . . . W. Woodhouse
Mynheer Jan Stofel . . . . Frank W. Couch
Nickel . . . . Charles Baldwin/Arthur Gallimore
Baron Finkelstein . . . . Edward Kipling
Klaus . . . . A. G. Poulton/Stockall Ward
Kasper. . . . . Frank Land
Philip . . . . Arthur Martin
Hendrick . . . . Charles Fisher/Colin Bryce
Hans. . . . . George Marshall
Leedle Jan. . . . . Louis Phillips
Frau Jan. . . . . Alma Evelyne/Nell Gilmore
Elsbeth . . . . Agnes Molteno
Hannah . . . . Lottie Siegenberg
Lena. . . . . Miss de Silva
Lisa . . . . Louie Edwardes
Bella (pd) . . . . Beatrice Harold

with the Sisters Felicia, Misses Georgina Jeanes, Kitty Norman, Olive Clive, Ivy Norman, Saunders, Russell, Courtenay, Vernon, Grove, Sullivan, Hart, Gibbs, Norres, Adale Wynn, Southby, Belmore, Wilmot, Chesterton, McDonald; Messrs Dawson, McLaughlan, Crofton, Clarkson, Marshall, Bedford, Harny, Cullen, Wilmer, Fredericks, Kirby.

Dir: J. M. Jones; md: Albert Bartlett/Haydn James; sc: George R. Hemsley; cos: Robert Crafter and Baruch

0246 **THE SILVER SLIPPER** a new modern extravaganza in 2 acts by Owen Hall. Lyrics by W. H. Risque. Additional lyrics by Leslie Stuart, Charles H. Taylor and George Rollitt. Music by Leslie Stuart. Produced at the Lyric Theatre under the management of Tom B. Davis 1 June, 1901 for a run of 197 performances closing 14 December, 1901.

Sir Victor Shallamar . . . . Ells Dagnall
Louis Tiraupigeon . . . . Henri Leoni
Douglas Wharton . . . . Charles S. Kitts/Edward Shale
Harry Hepworth . . . . Roy Horniman
Roland Western . . . . Sydney Mannering/Arthur Raymond
Claud Croucher . . . . Harry B. Burcher
Fred Rawlins . . . . Frank Walsh
Noel Gatsford . . . . Murri Moncrieff/Charles Hanbury/Charles Crawford/Edward Shale/Walter Mead/Allan Pollock
Berkeley Shallamar . . . . W. Louis Bradfield
Snax. . . . . William Cheesman
Crushall . . . . Frank Holt
Samuel Twanks . . . . Willie Edouin
Wrenne . . . . Coralie Blythe
Brenda Shallamar . . . . Nancy Girling/Fanny Dango/Ilma Montagu
Miss Bella Jimper . . . . Connie Ediss (Nellie Cozens)
Cynthia Grey . . . . Edith Housley/
Ella Hatfield. . . . . Lydia West/Monica Sayer
Maisie Rhodes . . . . Dora Nelson/Norah Rich
Jenny Vereker. . . . . Nellie Harcourt
Mary Astell . . . . Nina Sevening/Dora Sevening

Minnie Lomas . . . . Nora Moore/Gertie Singlehurst/Dora Sevening
Millicent Ward . . . . Fanny Dango/Daisy Holly
Mme Suzette . . . . Edith Neville/Kathleen Alleyne/Mimi Margotine
Letty Villiers . . . . Dorothy Dale
Judicia. . . . . Agnes de la Porte
Gillian. . . . . Mollie Lowell/Nora Moore
Avoria . . . . Augusta Walters/Beatrice Grenville
Curia . . . . Grace Evelyn/*out*
Queen of Venus. . . . . Mimi Margotine/Kathleen Alleyne/Grace Evelyn
Echo. . . . . Edith Lofthouse
Foreman of the Jury . . . . Lena Maitland
Usher . . . . Nellie Pryce/May Clifton
Minna . . . . Dora Langroyd
Stella . . . . Winifred Hare (Mollie Lowell)
add Winnie Beaufort . . . . Rose Dixon
Gendarme . . . . Alfred Webb/Charles Wingrove
Servant . . . . Nellie Pryce

Parisian Café Dance by Fanny Dango, Beatrice Grenville, Lucy Murray, Madge Greet, Dora Dent, Lilian Brendall, Charles Wingrove, Walter Mead, Edward Shale, Messrs Frazer, Dolphin and Headsworth.

Dir: Sydney Ellison; md: Landon Ronald/I. A. de Orellana; sc: Julian Hicks; cos: Comelli

Produced in the USA at the Hyperion Theatre, Newhaven, Conn., 21 October, 1902 for four performances and subsequently at the Broadway Theatre, New York, under the management of John C. Fisher 27 October, 1902 for a run of 165 performances closing 14 March, 1903. The book re-arranged by Clay M. Greene. Additional music by Arthur Weld.
Snitz Edwards (SIR V), Mackenzie Gordon (DONALD GREGOR), A. B. Furlong (DOUG), B. H. Burt (ALGERNON HEPWORTH), Harry B. Burcher (ROL), Fred Walsh? (CLAUD), W. H. Pringle (FRED), Jack Taylor (HARRY POWLER), Cyril Scott (BERK), Sam Bernard (HENRY BISMARCK HENSCHES), Edna Wallace-Hopper (WRENNE), Susan Drake (BRENDA), Josie Sadler (BELLA), Edith Blair (CYN), Maud Thomas (ELLA), Louise Lonsdale (MAISIE BROOKES), Sadie Hollister (JEN), Clarita Vidal (MARY), Francis Hill (MIN), Clarita Vidal (SUZ), Daisy Greene (JUD), Gertrude Douglas (CLEO), Margaret Walker (DIONE), Marie Allen (IRA), Alice Toland (ASTRIA), Marjorie Relyea (LYDIA), Mai de Villiers (QUEEN), Helen Royton (STELLA), J. Ardisonne (DUVAL), Rebecca Kaufmann (DOLLY)
The Champagne dance by Sallie Lomas, Dolly Corke, Beatrice Grenville, Rose Martin, Maggie Taylor, Lillie Lawton with Messrs Hoey, Marsden-Robinson, Hodson and Hirschberger.
Dir: James Francis & Harry B. Burcher; md: Arthur Weld

0247 **WHAT BECAME OF TOTMAN?** a musical farce by Augustus Hammond. Music by Arnold Cooke. Produced at the Globe Theatre, Deal under the management of J. E. Nightingale 3 June, 1901, and toured through Dover, Canterbury, Reading &c.

Bertie Totman . . . . Colin Mackay
Jack Fitzroy . . . . Charles Adeson
Obadiah Diggs . . . . J. E. Nightingale
James Barton . . . . Augustus Hammond
Baring . . . . F. T. Ford
Potts. . . . . Joe Robins/O. J. Bosher
Mrs Totman . . . . Grace Wixon
Kitty . . . . Marion Vyner
Mary Nugent . . . . May Joyce
Tootsy Wootsy . . . . The Baby
Dora Fitzroy . . . . Maude Prenton

Md: Arnold Cooke

Revised and revived as *What Became of Mrs Racket?*, 1904.

0248 **(IN) SUNNY SWITZERLAND** a musical comedy in two acts with music by J. A. Robertson. Produced at the Empire Theatre, Southend under the management of Lewis Sealy 3 June, 1901, and toured through Greenwich &c.

Hans Bietman . . . . Alfred Donohoe
Fritz Arnheim . . . . Templar Saxe
Carl Geisler . . . . Lewis Sealy
Max . . . . Horace Corbyn
Agostino . . . . Laurence H. Stevenson
Stefano . . . . Harry Ashley
Gustav . . . . F. W. Hartley
Lizette . . . . Rhoda Windrum
Louise . . . . Violet de Beaufort
Minette . . . . Dorothy Lee
Francette . . . . Ida Chichester
Janette . . . . Gracie Hawes
Marguerite . . . . Marie Andrews
Babette . . . . Amy Young
Marie . . . . Violet Young
Henriette . . . . Poppie Haines

Md: Ernest Vousden
Played with *A Heathen Goddess*, a musical farcical comedy in one act.

0249 **THE TOREADOR** a musical play in two acts by James T. Tanner and Harry Nicholls. Lyrics by Adrian Ross and Percy Greenbank. Music by Ivan Caryll and Lionel Monckton. Produced at the Gaiety Theatre under the management of George Edwardes 17 June, 1901 for a run of 675 performances closing 4 July, 1903. A revised version was staged 3 April, 1902. The theatre was closed 25 July–4 September, 1902.

Augustus Traill . . . . Lionel Mackinder/Arthur Hatherton
Pettifer . . . . Fred Wright Jr/Bert Sinden/Duncan Kaye
Sir Archibald Slackitt . . . . George Grossmith Jr
Rinaldo . . . . Robert Nainby
Governor of Villaya . . . . Harry Grattan
Bandmaster . . . . Willie Warde/Gordon Begg/Will Bishop
Carajola . . . . Herbert Clayton
Mr Probitt . . . . Arthur Hatherton/Gordon Begg
Moreno . . . . Sydney Bracy/Frank Lincoln/Kevin Gunn/George Gregory
Waiter . . . . Frank Green/Spencer Barry
Sammy Grigg . . . . Edmund Payne
Dora Selby . . . . Marie Studholme/Hilda Jeffreys/Millie Legarde/Adrienne Augarde/Gertie Millar
Susan . . . . Violet Lloyd
Mrs Malton Hoppings . . . . Claire Romaine/Connie Ediss/Pattie Browne/Ada Clare
Donna Teresa . . . . Queenie Leighton/Maidie Hope/Hilda Jacobson/Norma Whalley
La Belle Bolero . . . . Maidie Hope/Hilda Jacobson/*out*
Cora Bellamy . . . . Gertie Millar/Minnie Baker (Gabrielle Ray)
Ethel Marshall . . . . Maie Saqui/Marguerite Grey
Isabelle . . . . Sybil Arundale/*out*
Inez . . . . Kitty Mason/*out*
Nancy Staunton . . . . Florence Collingbourne/Eva Kelly/Florence Allen/Madge Vincent/Ethel Sydney/Maude Darrell
add Porter . . . . J. Grande

Violet Newman. . . . . Minnie Baker/Olive May/Daisy Holly
Maud Steward . . . . Hilda Jeffreys/Kitty Mason

with Hilda Coral, Gaynor Rowland, Kitty Mason, Minnie Baker, Olive May, Florence Warde, Doris Beresford, Madge Vincent, Florence Allen, Hilda Jeffreys, Evelyn Corri, Sara Miskel, Florence Alleyne, Nellie Pryor/Maude Darrell, Georgie Reed, Lucille Graham, Daisy Holly, Blanche Carlow, Winifred Carruthers, Marie Fawcett, Daisy Roche, Millicent Vernon, Doris Dewar, Lydia West, Winifred Le Barte, Rosie Brady, Ethel Negretti, Nancy Langtyre, Emilie Hervé, B. Tattersall, Marguerite Grey, Constance Lait, Daisy Denvil, N. Lait, K. Vincent, Elise Cook, Maude Odell, Florence Nielson, Nonie Graham, Millie Field, Louie Haines, Maud Percival, Hilda Guiver, Irene Florence, M. Duncan &c. Dir: J. A. E. Malone; md: Howard Talbot/Ivan Caryll; sc: Joseph Harker and Hawes Craven; ch: Willie Warde; cos: Wilhelm

Played with the compilation *The Linkman* from 21 February, 1903.

Produced at the Knickerbocker Theatre, New York, under the management of Messrs Nixon Zimmerman 6 January, 1902 for a run of 121 performances closing 3 May, 1902.
Melville Ellis (TR), William Blaisdell (PETT), Joseph Coyne (ARCH), Robert A. Evans (RIN), Edward Gore (GOV), H. G. Haynes/W. H. Thompson (BAND), William Broderick (CAR), Joseph Fay (PROB), Harry L. Wallace (MOR), Francis Wilson (GRIGG), Adele Ritchie (DORA), Queenie Vassar (SU), Maud Raymond (MRS), Jennie Hawley (DONNA), Christie MacDonald (NANCY) with Sadie Peters, Mabel Redfern, Stella Krum, Helen Chichester, Belle Chamberlain, Sylvia Lisle, Emma Millard, Eleanor Brudell, Marjorie Relyea, Hermione Hazelton, Margot Hobart, Lucille Verna, Maude Furniss, Margaret McDonald, Nonie Dore, Essie Lyons, Lillian Wallace, Elizabeth Innes. Dir: Herbert Gresham; md: Louis F. Gottschalk; sc: Ernest Gros; cos: Wilhelm & F. Richard Anderson

Produced at the Theater an der Wien, Vienna, 19 September, 1903.

Produced at the Moulin Rouge, Paris, 1904.

250 **THE GAY CADETS** a musical comedy in two acts and 4 scenes by Norman Prescott and J. Thomson. Lyrics by Percy Greenbank and Harold Simpson. Music by Basil Davis. Additional numbers by Charles Braun and Bernard Johnson. Produced at the Prince of Wales Theatre, Birmingham, under the management of Basil Davis and Yorke Stephens 24 June, 1901 and toured. Toured from Hastings (17 March 1902) through ?, Fulham, Sheffield, Hull, Manchester, Nottingham, Derby, Edinburgh, Glasgow, Newcastle, Birmingham, Richmond, Metropole, Shakespeare, ending 28 July.

Cara Luna. . . . . Phyllis Rankin/Decima Moore
Edna. Alice Powell/Nell Richardson
Sultan of Badmash . . . . Charles E. Stevens/Johnnie Schofield
Felix Paletot. . . . . Albert Le Fre
Sergeant Slick. . . . . Henry Wright/Keino Johnston
Major-General Sir Tipton
Tallbois KCB . . . . Edward Thirlby/W. H. Denny
El Kopje . . . . Lewis Vincent/R. King
Phil Almond . . . . Roland Cunningham/Donald Hall
Sarah Slade . . . . Alice Aynsley Cook/Elsie Carew
Dora. Lydia Flopp/Rose Martin
Nora. Adelaide Astor/Grace Vicat/Edith Adeson
Johnny Mount . . . . Henry Claff
Lt Col. Kempton . . . . Walter Wright
Brown & Co. . . . . W. D. Brodie
Damietta . . . . C. W. Standing
Viva . . . . Maida Wynstey
Phyllis. . . . . Nellie Ferguson
Connie. . . . . Ethel Mack
Ada . . . . Kitty Sylvestra
Hilda . . . . Florence Wakeman
Violet . . . . Nell Hope

Dir: E. T. Steyne/Warwick Major; md: Basil Davis/Ashley Richards

0251 **MELNOTTE** or The Gardener's Bride, a comic opera in 2 acts by Herbert Shelley. Lyrics by Arthur Anderson. Music by Frank E. Tours. Produced at the Coronet Theatre under the management of Henry Lytton 30 September, 1901 and toured through Brixton, Walsall, Bradford, Blackpool, Portsmouth, x?, Dublin?.

Claude Melnotte . . . . Conway Dixon
Pauline . . . . Josephine Cazabon (Bertha Liebman)
Colonel Damas . . . . F. Percival Stevens
Beauseant . . . . Standley Wade
Glavis . . . . J. Harold Carson
Gaspar. . . . . A. G. Poulton
Besançon . . . . Victor Stevens
M. Deschapelles. . . . . Bertie Roos
Augustus Le Beau . . . . William Rokeby
Major Loubet . . . . Simms Bull
Captain Genvais. . . . . Frank Hulburd
Widow Melnotte . . . . Leonora Braham
Marie . . . . Lila Lillian Stanley
Madame Deschapelles . . . . Carina McAllister
Lisette. . . . . May Taverner
Marcelle. . . . . Bertha Liebman
Ninon . . . . Katherine Perard
Margot . . . . Constance Porter
Estelle . . . . Daisie Desmond
Clarisse . . . . Elsa Westerleigh
Julie . . . . Mabel Neville

Pd: Hettie Lane
Dir: Victor Stevens; md: Learmont Drysdale; sc: Leolyn Hart

0252 **CARMITA** a comic opera by Arthur Shirley and Walter Parke. Music by Jesse Williams. Produced at the Victoria, Broughton, Salford, under the management of John H. Rogers 7 October, 1901 and toured. Played at Kennington 28 October.

Lord FitzHarold . . . . Pacie Ripple
Balthazar . . . . John Bidding
Paderesco . . . . Fred A. Ellis
Tim O'Toole . . . . E. C. Matthews
Ambrosio . . . . Vernon Cowper
Serpentino. . . . . William Vokes
Isachar . . . . Joseph Seghlioni
Martin/Porter . . . . J. W. Jordan
Pedro . . . . John Purdy
Lola . . . . Kate Kavanagh
Rita . . . . Maude Dickson
Zelosa . . . . Madge Westerleigh
Teresa. . . . . May Florence
Carmita Turbellino . . . . Mlle Corinne de Briou

Dir/md: Jesse Williams

0253 **BEBE** a musical play in 3 acts by F. Kinsey Peile and Harold Ellis. Lyrics and music by F. Kinsey Peile. Produced at the Empire Theatre, Southend, 21 October, 1901 and toured through Metropole, Worthing/Oxford &c.

Earl of Swindon. . . . . Arthur Jackson
Hon. Claude Stronginthearm . . . . Albert Gran
Viscount Spiers . . . . Philip Leslie
Charlie Vavasour . . . . Kenneth Altamont
Joe Chumley . . . . Maurice Douglas
Waiter. . . . . Harry Paulton Jr
Detective . . . . Mr Wilson

Demetrius Gobankin . . . . Dalton Somers
Lady Elizabeth Paddington . . . . Sophie Lingwood
Diana Vavasour . . . . Katherine Brook
May Waites . . . . Mary Ruby
Hermione . . . . Violet Royal
Celestine. . . . . Miss de la Marsh
Gretchen . . . . Maud Noel
Adelina . . . . Miss Wynnsty
Eulalie. . . . . Nellie Noel
Bebe. . . . . Kitty Loftus

Dir: Willie Edouin; md: Walter Meadows

254 **HIDENSEEK** or The Romance of a Ring. A musical play in three acts by Arthur Eliot and Edward Granville. Lyrics by Arthur Eliot. Music by Carl Kiefert, C. Scott-Gatty and Meyer Lutz. Produced at the Globe Theatre under the management of Arthur Eliot and Lyric Trusts Ltd. 10 December, 1901 for a run of 50 performances closing 25 January, 1902.

King Ping Pong VIII . . . . Tim Ryley
Prince Timdot . . . . John C. Piddock
Nicholas. . . . . John Peachey
Medoc, the miser . . . . Edward S. Abeles/A. G. Poulton
Dr Watteau . . . . Louis Mercanton
Sergeant Macrelle. . . . . A. G. Poulton/Donald Rayne
ADC VC CIC PTO ETC . . . . Lennox Lochner
Hankuff . . . . H. M. Imano
PomPom. . . . . Ernest Pope
Peter Pike . . . . John Le Hay/Arthur Eliot
Linnette . . . . Josephine Cazabon/Edith Neville
Jo Jo. . . . . Birdie Sutherland
Glissarde . . . . Alice Lethbridge
JuJube. . . . . Alice Selwyn/Isabel Clare
Honeydew. . . . . Aimee Cozens/Gertrude Page
Goldflake . . . . Edith Neville/Lilian Holmes
Caramel . . . . Blanche Doyle/Mary Carlisle
Nougat . . . . Clare Seymour/Ella Kitson
Cachou . . . . Irene Allen/Jean Ritchie
Chiffon . . . . Ada Rodney/Irene Allen
Lottie . . . . Maude Rossell
Maudie . . . . Madge Rossell
Vivandières . . . . A. and L. Grist
Fleurette. . . . . Erminie Earle

Dir: Frank Wyatt; md: Meyer Lutz/Arnold Cooke; ch: Will Bishop; sc: Hemsley & Fred Storey; cos: Comelli

•255 **BLUEBELL IN FAIRYLAND** a musical dream play in 2 acts by Seymour Hicks. Lyrics by Aubrey Hopwood and Charles H. Taylor. Music by Walter Slaughter. Produced at the Vaudeville Theatre under the management of Charles Frohman 18 December, 1901 for a run of 294 performances ending 26 June, 1902.

Dicky . . . . Seymour Hicks
Mr Joplin . . . . J. C. Buckstone
Will . . . . Murray King
Wont . . . . Sydney Harcourt
Policeman I. C. . . . . Stanley Brett
An Organ Grinder . . . . Frank Carroll
Peter the Cat . . . . George Hersee
Slim the Cat . . . . Clarice Errani
Mrs Hearty . . . . Florence Lloyd
Mab . . . . Phyllis Dare
Winnie . . . . Winifred Hall

A Rich Lady . . . . Blanche Thorpe
Meg . . . . Kathleen Courtney
First Bootblack . . . . Alfred Sawyer
Bluebell . . . . Ellaline Terriss (Gertrude Glyn)
The Water Lily . . . . Gwendoline Brogden
The Spirit of the Cup . . . . Margaret Fraser
Will o'the Wisp . . . . Dorothy Frostick
Yellow Dwarf . . . . Charles Trevor
Chamberlain. . . . . Lilian Burns
Herald. . . . . Hilda Antony
The Fish . . . . Stanley Crisp Jr
The Kite . . . . Fred Sullivan
The Thrush. . . . . Philip Hedges
The Beetle . . . . Henry Gatehouse
Maids . . . . Genee Heywood, Edith Heslewood
Fairies. . . . . Katie May, Moira Hersee, Eileen Moore
Rich Child . . . . Mary Bradbrook/Ivy Thorpe
A Doll. . . . . Molly Moore
The Black Rabbit . . . . W. Hall
Bess . . . . Gertrude Glyn
Babs. . . . . Nellie Lonnen
Dolly . . . . Florence Hersee
Annie . . . . Sylvia Storey
Dutch Sabot Girls . . . . E. Windsor, D. Paver
Sparrow . . . . Frank Jervis

Dir: Seymour Hicks; md: Walter Slaughter; ch: Willie Warde; sc: W. Harford; cos: Wilhelm

Produced at the Aldwych Theatre under the management of Charles Frohman 23 December, 1905.
Seymour Hicks (DICKY), J. C. Buckstone (JOP), Murray King (WILL), Bert Sinden (WONT), Reginald Crompton (PC), John Clifford (PETER), Sydney Fairbrother (MRS H), Decima Brooke (MAB), Florry Arnold (W), Ethel Grace (RICH), Ellaline Terriss (BLUE), Dorothy Frostick (WILL O) Frank Carrol (YELLOW), Molly Lowell (GOOD FAIRY), Reginald Kenneth (OBERON), Maudie Darrell (FRENCH DOLL), Topsy Sinden (SAILOR), Barbara Deane (BABY), Ralph Moore (DOVE) with Pauline Francis, Claire Rickards, Hilda Harris, Eva Carrington, Enid Leslie, Lily MacIntyre, Sylvia Storey, Nell Carter, Maud St Quentin, Kitty Melrose, Marion Lindsay, May Gates, Julia James, Evelyn Gwynne. Dir/ch: Edward Royce; md: Carl Kiefert; sc: W. Harford; cos: Wilhelm

Produced at the Prince's Theatre, under the management of Seymour Hicks and Ellaline Terriss 2 December, 1916 for a run of 106 performances. Additional numbers by Herman Darewski and Clifford Grey.
Seymour Hicks (DICKY), J. C. Buckstone (JOP), Johnny Danvers (WILL), Fred Farren (WONT), J. J. Hooker (PC), Patrick Healey-Kay[1] (PETER), Sylvia Acham (SLIM/FOX), Mollie Lowell (MRS H), Vera Foster (MAB), Rita Page (W), Grace Newcombe (RICH), Winifred Strain (MEG), Jack Renshaw (BBK), Ellaline Terriss (BLUE), Alice Coombs (WLILY), Rita Glynde (WILL O), Jack Renshaw (YELLOW), Mignon Morenza (FISH), Gladys Deane (KITE), Jack Belford (THRUSH), Nora Strobel (BEET), May Taverner, Phyllis Sidney (MAIDS), Gladys Cowell, Renee Sutton, Dorothy Ardley (FAIRIES), Dorothy Eagle (DOLL/COCK SPARROW), Doris Palmer (BLK R), Harry Harrison (DOVE), Charles Cecil (BULL), Montague Criddle (OWL), Ena Claremont (GOOSE); Emma Holderness (pd) with Cissie Lennard, Estelle Cleverley, Isobel Borznan, Cynthia Greaves, Evelyn Puxton, Carnworth Lockhart, Nora Robinson, Lesley Birks, Monica Noyes, Violet Marley.

Dir: Seymour Hicks; md: Allan Grey; ch: Adeline Genée; sc/cos: George de Feure

Produced for Christmas seasons in London 24 December, 1917 at the Alhambra, 26 December, 1923 at the Aldwych, 26 December, 1927, 1935 and 1936 at the Scala. Produced at the Metropolitan Music Hall 29 December, 1919, at the Chelsea Palace 23 December, 1925 and at the People's Palace 27 December, 1937.

[1] later Anton Dolin

0256 **A LADIES' MAID** a musical piece in two acts by C. A. Lord. Music by Ernest Hastings. Produced at the New Theatre, Cambridge, under the management of Ernest Carpenter and Haldane Crichton 26 December, 1901 and toured through Leigh, Gloucester, Swindon, Wolverhampton, Oldham, Blackburn, Balham, Aldershot, Dover, Deal, Folkestone, Woolwich, ?, Norwich, ?, Kings Lynn, Peckham, Newport, Merthyr, Chatham, Aston, Smethwick, Yarmouth, Hastings, Ramsgate, Folkestone, Margate, Eastbourne, Portsmouth, Southampton, Jersey, Llandudno, ?, ?, ?,/Gainsborough, Broughton, Warrington, Kettering, Oxford, Goole, Southport, Grimsby, Salford, Blyth, Blackpool, Barrow, Widnes, St Helens, Stoke, Aberdare, Swansea, Farnworth, ?, Swindon, ?, ?, Walthamstow, to 7 February 1903 &c.

Josiah Biffin	Frank Hemming/Larry Clements
Charlie Marchmont	Campbell Goldsmid/Edward Overington
Samuel Spriggs	Charles T. Challoner/Harry Herbert
Mr Bentence	George Marshall
Hon Augustus Puphpayst	Leslie Cathie/Harry Wren
Pietro Conti	Oliver Rogers/Dan Lydon
Sergeant Tomkins	G. Buckley
Antonio	Charles Fisher/Gale St John
Luiz	Ivor Llewellyn/Percival Hughes/Frank St John
Alison Grey	Marion Yeulett/Flo Gordon
Minnie Taylor	Lilian Beszant
May Marmosette	Sadie Seymour/Ida Cunard
Miss Vavasour	Nina Bernard/Ida Bell
Miss Montmorency	Irene Stuart/Violet Carlyle
Miss Plantagenet	Babs Stuart/Grace Edwards
Miss de Courcey	Mona Spearing
Nina	Edna Grace/Edie Hylton
Mariette	Blanche Grace/Kitty Lingard
Lizette	May Howard/Marie Serle
Mizandi	Daisy Thorneycroft/Ethel Serle

with the Royal Welsh Glee Singers (W. Gamble, C. Fisher, I. Llewellyn, P. Hughes)

IB AND LITTLE CHRISTINA a musical play by Basil Hood. Music by Franco Leoni. Produced at the Savoy Theatre, under the management of William Greet 14 November, 1901 for a season of 16 performances closing 29 November. Played with *The Willow Pattern*.

Ib's father	Henry A. Lytton
Little Ib	Laurence Emery
Gipsy Woman	Isabel Jay
Christina	Louie Pounds
Henrik	H. Thorndike
Little Christina	Ela Q. May
Ib	Robert Evett
John	Powis Pinder

Dir: Basil Hood; md: Franco Leoni/François Cellier; sc: W. Harford

Produced at Daly's Theatre under the management of George Edwardes 11 January, 1904. Transferred to the Lyric Theatre 19 January, 1904. Withdrawn 27 February, 1904. Played at a series of matinées with *The Outpost*.
Ivor Foster (FATHER), Louise Douste (L.IB), Susan Strong (GIPSY), Edna Thornton (CHR), Gordon Cleather (H), Ela Q. May (L.C.), Ben Davies (IB), Charles Bennett (J).

THE WILLOW PATTERN a musical play by Basil Hood. Music by Cecil Cook. Produced at the Savoy Theatre under the management of William Greet 14 November, 1901 for a season of 16 performances closing 29 November, 1901. Played with *Ib and Little Christina*.

Ah Mee	Agnes Fraser
So Hi	Reginald Crompton
Wee Ping	Rosina Brandram
Hi Ito	Powis Pinder

So Lo . . . . Robert Rous
Ping Pong . . . . Walter Passmore
Fee Fi . . . . Blanche Gaston-Murray
Tee Thing. . . . . Jessie Pounds
Fo Fum . . . . W. H. Leon

Dir: Basil Hood and Richard Barker; md: François Cellier; sc: W. Harford

YOU AND I a musical farce in one act by Seymour Hicks. Lyrics by Aubrey Hopwood. Music by Walter Slaughter. Produced at the Vaudeville Theatre under the management of Messrs A. and S. Gatti and Charles Frohman 24 April, 1901 with *Sweet and Twenty*.

Hon. Herbert Fitzallan . . . . Stanley Brett/George Mudie
Sandy McPherson. . . . . J. C. Buckstone
Miss Middleton . . . . Gracie Leigh
Mary . . . . Florence Lloyd

Md: Walter Slaughter; ch: Will Bishop; cos: Jays Ltd, Mrs Arthur Patrick &c.

1902

The musical scene was a bright one at the beginning of 1902. The public's money had had its effect on producers and the shows that were running bore witness to what people wanted to see: *The Toreador*, *A Chinese Honeymoon*, *Kitty Grey*, *Bluebell in Fairyland* – fun, romance and, above all, lively songs and dances. The *Belle of New York* syndrome had been purged, at considerable financial loss to those producers who had thought they were jumping on a profitable American bandwagon and, as the taste for things French had not consolidated after *La Poupée*, the home-made musical reigned unchallenged and supreme. In 1902 every new piece produced in the West End and out of town was British; in the provinces the foreign musical was represented only by such old favourites as *Les Cloches de Corneville*, *Olivette* and, of course, *The Belle of New York*.

The first new piece presented in London was at Daly's. *San Toy* had closed its record-breaking just before Christmas as the longest running piece George Edwardes would ever produce[1], and January brought the re-opening of the theatre with its newest work, *A Country Girl*. Daly's had always specialised in the romantic, spectacular, semi-comic opera style of musical, using as an essential part of its attraction the most picturesque and extravagant settings – *The Geisha* had taken us to Japan, *A Greek Slave* to ancient Rome, *San Toy* to China, *An Artist's Model* to Paris – with enormous success. It was a matter for some surprise, therefore, when shortly after the opening of *San Toy* Edwardes announced to the *Daily Mail* that a change of policy was in view. 'The days of musical plays in modern dress are coming to an end,' he declared. 'It is difficult to keep on making them interesting,' and went on to say that the next Daly's piece would look back to the earlier French opéra-bouffe or comic opera style. *A Country Girl* was thus awaited with some trepidation. But the two years of *San Toy's* run apparently gave Edwardes time for reflection, and when *A Country Girl* appeared it was seen to owe more to the Gaiety musical than to either opéra-bouffe or opéra-comique. Certainly it was not in direct line from *The Geisha* or *San Toy*. To begin with, it was set in Devonshire which, while pretty enough, was hardly as exotic as the East or as far-fetched as ancient Rome. It was also the work of a new Daly's team. Sidney Jones and Owen Hall had been deployed elsewhere, Harry Greenbank was dead, and the grand triumvirate had been replaced by what was essentially the Gaiety team, James Tanner, Adrian Ross and composer Lionel Monckton. This new triumvirate knew better than to produce a *Toreador* or a *Messenger Boy* for Daly's; the audience there had its tastes and expectations which were as established and unbending as those of a Savoy

[1] *Dorothy*, which ran longer, did not do so under Edwardes' management.

or a Gaiety audience. And, equally, they had the Daly's team of stars to suit. Marie Tempest and Letty Lind might have moved on, but there were still Hayden Coffin, Rutland Barrington and Huntley Wright who needed to be treated in the same manner by their writers as Teddy Payne at the Gaiety or Rosina Brandram at the Savoy.

So, in spite of Edwardes' pronouncement, *A Country Girl* was set in Britain and in modern dress but there was little else about it that was modern. The plot was a mixture of the principal elements of English farce and musical comedy of the last few decades and the characters were straight from the stockpot of those same pieces, but around those well-used elements Tanner wove a bright set of situations and some cheerful dialogue and he and his colleagues suited their stars' abilities and specialities to a nicety so that *A Country Girl* turned out to be a very pretty thing indeed.

Its tale is set in Devon at election time. Sir Joseph Verity, the tenant of the manor, is anxious that his son, Douglas, should be elected to Parliament, but Douglas is more interested in dallying with Nan, the village flirt. The villagers have as little time for Douglas as he for politics and much prefer the impoverished owner of the manor, Geoffrey Challoner, who opportunely arrives home from sea at that moment. He has in tow his servant Barry, a Rajah, and an Indian Princess. The Rajah is actually Mr Quinton Raikes who supposedly fell off a mountain in India a couple of years previously and, by the inexorable law of musical comedy, his large society wife also happens to be in that particular part of Devonshire when he arrives. The Princess has conceived a passion for Geoffrey which Barry, with his eye on the main chance and her fortune, encourages, but Geoffrey is faithful to his old love, Marjorie Joy, the Country Girl. Unknown to him, however, Marjorie has become rich and famous as a singer while he has been at sea, but she returns to the village *à la paysanne*, and meets Geoffrey who dares not ask for her hand as he has no money and no prospects and intends to return to sea. Barry, in the meanwhile, is working on getting Geoffrey elected and also on wheedling £8000 out of old Verity for a tin mine which is Geoffrey's sole and rather useless asset. But the first act ends in dismay when Marjorie Joy sees Geoffrey kissing old friend Nan and leaves town as the Princess stakes her claim. In the second act the whole village has removed to London to the home of Lord Anchester where a ball is in progress and to that ball come all the principal characters including Barry dressed, for no well explained reason, as an elderly lady and, later, as an Indian. The plot, as usual, dissolves into a series of songs and dances, of comical scenes and flirtations, culminating in the natural happy ending.

What made *A Country Girl* a success, where so many musical plays of a similar ilk had been damned by critics and public alike, was its quality in the writing and in the moulding of each role around the actor concerned – particularly in the case of Huntley Wright who, in the part of Barry, was able to take the show by the scruff of its neck and shake it into fits of laughter. And, of course, the quality of Lionel Monckton's songs.

The Times' opening night comments included:

> There is no plot strictly so-called. The play is composed of the usual string of scenes, all of which are effective because all are so extremely well done . . . *A Country Girl* has a very good skeleton – at least as good as most of its predecessors, which in the course of time will be so well clothed that it will be galvanised into life . .

It certainly needed the 'course of time' as, on its first night, *A Country Girl* was far from ready. At the time when the curtain should have gone up, an apologetic Edwardes came before the curtain and announced there had been an accident to the scenery and that there would be a delay. In fact the scene painters were still working furiously on the second act set. The curtain rose a half-hour late, and even then things did not go as smoothly as they might. There was a plethora of material, both spoken and sung, to be got through and the cast was evidently not as well-rehearsed as was Edwardes' custom. The late start and the odd hang-up meant that it was necessary to cut a large slice of the second act, including four numbers, during the running, but the audience still found plenty to amuse and attract them and some of the numbers were received with an enthusiasm which brought the show to a standstill. The most popular was a little duet performed by Wright and Ethel Irving as his seamstress sweetheart, 'Two little Chicks', written and composed by Paul Rubens:

BARRY: Two little chicks
Lived in a farmyard
Happy as chicks can be
SOPHIE: She was a Dorking
Proudly stalking
Only a bantam was he!
BARRY: He was a most superior bantam
And he adored her true
SOPHIE: But she was proud
And cried aloud
Now what in the world are you?
BARRY: Cluck
SOPHIE: Cluck
Chick, chick, chick, chick
You're a very free chick
Wait a little bit, said she
BARRY: Give me one kiss, said the little he-chick
What is more he kissed her too.
SOPHIE: Let me be, chick,
Said the little she-chick
BARRY: Cock-a-doodle doo!

but the whole of Lionel Monckton's score was full of popular pieces. Evie Greene in the role of the piquant Nan was particularly well provided for with the delightful 'Try again, Johnny':

Try again, Johnny, try again, do
Fair village maids are the right sort for you
Lasses in London set the heart awhirl
But they're not half so fetching as a Devonshire girl.

to one of Lionel Monckton's prettiest and most enduring tunes. 'Molly the Marchioness' was another catching piece in which Nan told the cautionary tale of Molly Gurney from Little Witticombe who married a lord from London:

So Molly married the Marquis
What a thing to do
He said, like a shot, 'You'll be mine, eh what?'
And gave her a kiss or two.
She turned red as a poppy
And whispered, 'Oh, thank you, yes
It will be so proper
When I'm tip-topper
As Molly the Marchioness!'

Huntley Wright was provided with excellent material. In 'Yo Ho, little Girls' he described the unromantic truths of the sailor's life:

Yo ho, little girls, yo ho
That's so, little girls, that's so
For it sounds all right in a sailor song
But you soon find out that it all goes wrong
Heave ahead, my hearties,
And if you want to know
I'll spin you a yarn, ahead and astern,
Yo ho, little girls, yo ho!

and, in the second act, disguised as the elderly 'Edna', he talked about his friend 'Mrs Brown of Notting Hill':

She loves to tell your fortune
By the tea leaves in your cup
And if she doesn't like you
I believe she makes it up
She knows everybody's income
And everybody's past
And she knows what Mrs Tomlinson
Is going to call her last . .

while inviting everyone to tea with 'Me and Mrs Brown'.

Hayden Coffin, of course, was not lacking in suitably showy pieces. Monckton and Ross wrote him a stirring patriotic 'In the King's Name . . Stand!' and Percy Greenbank contributed the lyric for a sentimental ballad 'My own little Girl'. As usual, Coffin managed to interpolate an irrelevant number for himself – on this occasion an arrangement of 'A Sailor's Life' which did not ever reach the popularity of 'Tommy Atkins' or its successors and was later replaced. Much more successful was a pretty duet for Geoffrey and Marjorie Joy called 'Boy and Girl' recalling childhood joys.

The role of Marjorie Joy was taken by a new leading lady, Lillian Eldee, the daughter of Nellie Bromley who had been the original Angelina in *Trial by Jury*. Her vocal contribution to the show was the Paul Rubens number 'Coo', ostensibly the song which hero and heroine had sung together as children. The lyric was, at the best, puerile:

Hark to the sound of coo . .
Calling for me and you, for me and you,
Whether through darkest storms we go
Or under skies of blue
Nothing shall sever
I shall for ever
Be true to my coo . .

and it provoked the odd disdainful comment. At one stage the editor of *The Era* used it as the example of the fatuous degeneracy of the musical comedy song. But, somehow, it went down perfectly well in the show.

Considerably more substantial was the lovely 'Under the Deodar' sung by Maggie May in the role of the Indian Princess, and the rhythmic 'Rajah of Bhong' in which that august person and the Princess were introduced to Devon in the fashion of so many a comic potentate from the Mikado of Japan to the Monarch of Pynka Pong to the Emperor Hang Chow. Rutland Barrington, as Quinton Raikes alias the Rajah of Bhong, had his best moment in a rather Gilbertian patter waltz called 'Peace, Peace' in which

Adrian Ross managed to include some jibes against the legal profession, the newspapers, the modern woman, Rudyard Kipling and other eternal targets. Tanner, too, had his targets and the book, although by no means an Owen Hall barrage of society chatter and barbed-wire satire, had its points to make on its meanderings through its tiny story. The episode which raised most amusement was Barry's parody of a recent declaration by Lord Rosebery concerning the running of Parliament like a business venture.

A Country Girl was quickly worked into shape. Cuts in the book and also of one or two numbers (an unnoticed piece called 'Soldiers' was the first to go) brought it down to a more manageable size, and the marvellous series of songs and dances and the fun generated by Wright, Barrington, Ethel Irving and co., had audiences filling Daly's to such an extent that the show held the stage there for more than two years. One hiccup in its triumphal progress occurred when Edwardes found himself summoned to court by Augustus M. Moore who claimed that he was author of the original book of the show. Moore was the brother-in-law of Lionel Monckton and had ambitions as a librettist. Monckton had introduced him to 'The Guv'nor' and Edwardes had read some of Moore's work, including a scenario based on *Charles O'Malley, the Irish Dragoon.* This last was an idea which appealed to Edwardes who offered to buy the scenario. Moore refused: he wanted to write the libretto and work on a royalty. Edwardes agreed, but insisted that he work with the experienced and literate James Tanner. When Moore produced his work it was not of an acceptable standard. Edwardes paid the man £100 and rejected it, and finally abandoned the whole idea when *The Emerald Isle* came in with an Irish theme. Moore now claimed that Tanner and Edwardes had taken 'ideas' for *A Country Girl* from his book. In spite of clear evidence to the contrary, the court found for the plaintiff, though it limited his damages to £100.

During its London run the show underwent the usual quota of changes. Many new numbers were introduced, particularly into the loosely constructed second act, but the show maintained its essential shape as well as all its principal pieces. *A Country Girl* became and remained an exceptionally popular show. It had in no way been the return to opéra-bouffe or comique which Edwardes had suggested and, if anything, it helped to prove that the well-made modern-dress musical play, particularly when supplied with songs by such as Monckton and Ross, was anything but finished. It was precisely what the London public of 1902 wanted, and what Edwardes was so very good and experienced in giving them.

A Country Girl proved immensely popular on tour, equalling even the phenomenal record of *The Geisha*, and was revived in the West End as early as 1914 with Gertie Millar as Nan and Bill Berry as Barry when it added another 173 performances to its record. In 1931 it returned once again to Daly's, starring Dorothy Ward (Nan) and Dudley Rolph (Barry) as part of J. Bannister Howard's series of revivals of the glories of the Edwardes era. The American Daly's was quick to follow up the London success and *A Country Girl* opened in New York in September for a 115-performance run. Paris gave a fine welcome to a French production at L'Olympia starring Max Dearly and Mariette Sully and the show went round the world as one of the most popular of all George Edwardes' contributions to the musical theatre.

At the Savoy, in contrast to the situation at Daly's, managerial continuity had been broken. During the run of *The Emerald Isle*, Mrs D'Oyly Carte had passed control of the theatre to the highly experienced William Greet. An era had ended. Greet, however, determined to keep to the tradition of high-class English comic opera at the Savoy. He had no Gilbert and no Sullivan, but Captain Basil Hood had proved himself a worthy successor to the former in *The Rose of Persia* and *The Emerald Isle*, and the latter work had also succeeded in throwing up the most obvious heir to Sullivan's mantle in Edward German. It was Hood and German who, in the natural course of things, provided Greet with his new piece for the Savoy.

They, too, selected an English setting, but the scene and the era could scarcely have been more different. While *A Country Girl* operated in rural Devon and a London ballroom in the young twentieth century, *Merrie England* was set in the England of Queen Elizabeth I, on the banks of the Thames and in Windsor forest, and dealt with the fictional amours of the Virgin Queen, Sir Walter Raleigh and the Earl of Essex. Basil Hood's libretto was even shorter on basic plot than *The Emerald Isle*, as it turned wholly on the jealousy of the Queen upon finding that Raleigh, for whom she has some feeling, is in love with her lady, Bessie Throckmorton. She plans to poison Bessie, but is shamed from her petty designs by a faked apparition of Herne the Hunter engineered by Essex, the 'witch' Jill-all-alone and her forester lover. Raleigh is left to wed Bessie, and the ambitious Essex consoles his monarch. On to this framework Hood grafted a characteristic set of Savoy roles: the comic actor-playwright Walter Wilkins for Walter Passmore, his sidekick Simkins (Mark Kinghorne), the wise witch (Louie Pounds), the spiteful village May Queen (Joan Keddie), the brother Foresters, Long Tom and Big Ben (Torrence and Crompton) while Rosina Brandram, Henry Lytton and Robert Evett starred as the Queen, Raleigh and Essex. The Savoy's newest star was Agnes Fraser, promoted to take the soprano role of Bessie Throckmorton.

The sixteenth century setting inspired Hood to a somewhat antiquated style. Puns, wordplay, extended similes, conceits and metaphors and an enormous amount of thee-ing and thou-ing permeate the libretto of *Merrie England*. If it occasionally bears the flavour of *The Yeomen of the Guard* it seems more often akin to the burlesques and comic operas of the 1870s, although Hood's skill as a writer ensures that some kind of action entertainingly carries the piece forward from number to ensemble to a little piece of plot.

The Stage expressed the thought:

> . . [the dialogue] is for the most part as smart as his lyrics and in many places he indulges in quaint turns of expression that may be regarded as satirical of the forms of speech current at the period of the supposed action . .

The Times enjoyed that style:

> Not even Mr Gilbert himself has succeeded more neatly in the 'Paronomasia play 'po' words' than Captain Hood. Technically there is abundance in common between the systems of both librettists. But whereas Mr Gilbert wove the intricate web of his quips around at least the thread of a definite story, Captain Hood presents a series of pictures – very pretty and very lively pictures – which, though ultimately connected with each other, have together no very intimate connection with anything in particular beyond what is naturally inferred from describing England as 'Merrie' and sundry references to Robin Hood and Maid Marion . .

In short, where Gilbert put humour in plot, dialogue and lyrics, Hood here confined his wit to the lyrics. He did not even shy away from including the occasional set piece, such as a recitation for Wilkins disputing the gloomy plots of Shakespeare and describing what *Romeo and Juliet* might have been like had he written it:

> A was the Angel he met at the ball
> B was her beauty apparent to all

C is for Capulet (name which she bore)
D the disguise which young Romeo bore
E for the Ease of his elegant pose
F the fandango they danced on their toes
G the guitar which he played by and by
H for her handkerchief dropped in reply
I am young Romeo, breathing his love
J is for Juliet sitting above
K the last kiss as apart they are torn
L by the Lark who's the herald of morn
M is the moon that's preparing to set
N is the Nurse calling 'Come, Juliet'
O is the ejaculation she sighed
P because promised as Paris's bride
Q are the quarrels that quickly ensued
R are the rapiers drawn in the feud
S for the sentence pronounced by the 'Dook'
T for the Tragical Turn events took
U is the unhappy end of the play
V is the version which I'll write some day
W Shakespeare's an X-llent writer
But Wise Editors will say, my version's brighter!

The musical part of the play saw the flowering of all the attractive qualities which German had shown in *The Emerald Isle.* In the concerted writing he was, as might have been expected, scholarly and yet imaginative; 'In England, merrie England', 'Love is Meant to Make us Glad' and 'When Cupid first this old World Trod' were all ensembles which attracted immediate attention, and the opening choruses and finales also made great use of choral writing. However, it is the solo numbers from *Merrie England* which have ensured its continuing popularity through the years both with the public and with generations of singers. Strangely, it was not the 'bon-bons' of the score which originally appealed most to the critics. *The Times* noted the tenor drinking song 'Every Jack must Have his Jill' as the outstanding solo of the evening, yet that number has not survived with the popularity of Sir Walter Raleigh's other solo, 'The English Rose':

Dan Cupid hath a garden
Where women are the flowers
And lovers' laughs and lovers' tears
The sunshine and the showers.
But, oh, the fairest blossom
That in that garden grows
The fairest queen, it is, I ween
The perfect English Rose . .

Essex's patriotic ballad 'The Yeomen of England' was another case in point. Although well-received, it did not win an acclaim consistent with its later enduring success. Possibly it was not helped by the essentially character performance of Henry Lytton, cast as the vigorously baritone Earl. Certainly, when made popular by the phonograph and the voice of Peter Dawson, amongst others, 'The Yeomen of England' became a world-wide standard.

The female songs were no less outstanding. Bessie Throckmorton had a brilliant waltz song 'Oh, who shall Say that Love Is Cruel' and a contrasting ballad 'She Had a

Letter from her Love', Queen Elizabeth the impressive 'O, peaceful England' which allowed the Savoy contralto a rare opportunity for strong legato singing (indeed, the role of Queen Elizabeth was one of very few where Rosina Brandram was not required to be grotesque), and Jill-all-alone two excellent numbers.

The comic element was slightly less memorable; the comedy songs being amusing enough but without the merit of the lyrical numbers. In fact Chappell, the publishers, issued a special version of the score for concert performance from which the role of Wilkins, and his songs, were totally omitted. Wilkins had plenty of opportunities. At the end of Act I, having been thrown into the river he emerges bedraggled to find himself in front of the Queen. He explains:

> . . 'twas a quaint conceit of mine to be thrown into the river that I might afterwards emerge in the character of Father Thames, who I now represent. As Father Thames I stand before you as Ambassador for King Neptune to offer unto beauteous England the dignity and title of Mistress of the Sea!

and he continued into song, describing how Neptune sent out to discover 'The Mistress of the Sea':

> The Sturgeon and the Stickleback
> The Porpoise and the Conger Eel
> The Whiting and the Octopus
> The Shark, the Mullet and the Smelt
> The Brill, Anchovy, Sprat and Plaice
> The Whale, the Winkle and the Whelk
> The fish that coil, the fish that fly,
> The fish you boil, the fish you fry,
> The Turbot and the Mackerel
> The Lobster in the lobster shell
> The Sole, the Whiting and the Jell –
> Y fish and more than I can tell
> Whose names I cannot speak nor spell
> In fact, in fact, in fact all fish fishmongers sell
> And all they do not sell as well
> In short, all fishes that do dwell
> Where Neptune bids them be
> Away did swim, to find for him the mistress of the Sea.

Wilkins also sang of 'The big brass Band', explained that 'That's where I and Shakespeare Disagree', and mused on 'Imagination' which gave Hood a chance to use all the twists and turns of speech so dear to him:

> The imaginary invalid who fancies she is ill
> After reading the advertisement of someone's patent pill
> Will hurry to her doctor, whom she counts a perfect dear
> (For his practice makes him perfect and I don't know what a year)
> For the doctor is in luck and heavy fees will never lack
> Whom the ladies call a duck and other doctors call a quack
> And the honour of the medical profession as you'll see
> With imaginative patients is a matter of degree!

It was not only songs which German supplied for *Merrie England*, for the show was much more liberally sprinkled with dances than usual. The qualities evident in his *Henry VIII* and *Nell Gwynne* dances were again apparent, and the dance and chorus music added much to the score of *Merrie England*.

In spite of its undoubted merits, *Merrie England* did not receive the uproarious reception one might have expected. Here was a work with a libretto full of fun, a straightforward plot, and a score which harboured as many hit numbers as the best Gilbert and Sullivan works, yet it was greeted with pleasure rather than with enthusiasm and, like *Shamus O'Brien* a few years previously, did not manage to stay on the stage for as long as it deserved. Both works clearly belonged to a genre for which the public was now more limited. *Merrie England*, to be sure, had a somewhat broader comic basis than *Shamus O'Brien*: further away from light opera than Stanford's piece had been it was without the special quirkiness of Gilbert and of Sullivan, while retaining a certain amount of their tone but to have been a great stage success, *Merrie England* should probably have come fifteen or even twenty years earlier.

That it deserved success is evident from its longevity. But in 1902 Greet decided four months had seen out the piece's London potential. He sublet the Savoy and took *Merrie England* on tour with its Savoy cast, a rare opportunity for the provinces to see Rosina Brandram, Walter Passmore and Co. After four further months on the road he returned to the Savoy and *Merrie England* re-opened on November 24 to play through the Christmas season for another 57 performances.

This disappointing first run was redeemed in later years. In 1934 *Merrie England* was revived at the Prince's Theatre by R. Claud Jenkins with the famous Scots tenor Joe Hislop as Raleigh and contralto Enid Cruickshank as Elizabeth. The role of Bessie was played by Nancy Fraser, daughter of the original Bessie, Agnes Fraser, and Walter Passmore. It played 187 performances. In 1944 it was revived at the Winter Garden starring Walter Midgley, Reginald Gibbs and Victoria Campbell with a young Charles Hawtrey as Wilkins, but *Merrie England* finally got its due public recognition the following year when it was again revived at the Prince's, this time by Jack Waller, in a revised three-act version by Edward Knoblock. Knoblock's adaptation involved some fairly wholesale cutting of the book, including the creation of a whole swathe of new characters and the reprehensible elimination of Jill-all-alone, the May Queen and Simkins. Two ballets and a hornpipe were interpolated, the woodsmen's duet became 'We're Gentlemen at Arms', and 'The big brass Band' and 'Where the Deer do Lie' were notable song casualties. The production did, however, have the advantage of some fine singing from such as Heddle Nash (Raleigh) and Dennis Noble (Essex) and it ran for a full year of 365 performances.

In 1960 yet another revised version by Denis Arundell appeared at Sadler's Wells. It restored much which had been cut by Knoblock but still found it necessary to 'improve' Hood's libretto. One tangible result of this production was the issue of an excellent double disc gramophone recording of the show which complements the still frequent amateur productions to keep *Merrie England* before the public until its return to the professional repertoire.

In May, the long-expected *Three Little Maids* made its bow at the Apollo Theatre. It had originally been mooted more than a year previously as a vehicle for Edna May, Ada Reeve and Evie Greene but had been postponed when Edwardes brought *Kitty Grey* in from the provinces. Now it was to have its turn and 27-year-old Paul Rubens, who had contributed so many successful songs to other people's shows by way of additional material, was finally to have a show of his own, and very much his own for, apart from being responsible for the bulk of the lyrics and music, he was also author of the libretto.

Rubens had been around the London musical theatre scene for a number of years, although until *Three Little Maids* his only attempt at a full musical piece had been *The Great Caesar*, the ill-fated burlesque on which he had collaborated with his brother

Walter. They came of a well-off society family; their father, Victor, was a successful stockbroker and Walter (who confined his musical talents to a dilettante level) followed in the same profession. The family lived in Kensington Palace Gardens and Paul was educated at Winchester and Oxford where he took to amateur acting and composing pieces for OUDS. He had no musical education at all and was unable to score even the simplest of harmonies, but his university theatrical adventures determined him to throw up a projected legal career in favour of the stage.

He was 19 when 'The little Chinchilla', interpolated into *The Shop Girl*, introduced him to the London theatre, and his musical contributions to *Dandy Dan*, *Little Miss Nobody*, *A Modern Don Quixote*, *Milord Sir Smith*, *L'Amour Mouillé* and *Florodora*, as well as the incidental music to Tree's 1901 production of *Twelfth Night* at Her Majesty's, led him to his first full show success with *Three Little Maids*. During the same period he also tried himself as a dramatic writer and his play, *The Young Mr Yarde*, written in collaboration with Harold Ellis and produced at Buxton in 1898, was staged at the Royalty Theatre by George and Weedon Grossmith, although with little success. Rubens later collaborated on other straight plays but he devoted his attention mainly to the libretti for his own musical comedies through an enormously busy career which contained many successes but also too much routine and facile work.

The postponment of *Three Little Maids* had meant a change in Edwardes' plans. Evie Greene was now safely ensconced in *A Country Girl*, so the third little maid was re-written to order for Ethel Sydney then, finally, for Hilda Moody. During the rehearsal period Ada Reeve fell ill. Opening night was put back but it soon became evident that Ada was going to be out for quite a while. Twenty-year old Madge Crichton, daughter of manager Haldane Crichton and a provincial leading lady since the age of 15, was called in. The role was pared down so as not to offend the status of the Misses May and Moody, and the revised show hurried on to the stage.

Quite what was expected had once again been put in doubt by early managerial announcements. Edwardes had given out that the new work would be a 'light opera of delicate texture' in the spirit of the old German Reed pieces. Since that announcement, a revival of the German Reed repertoire at St George's Hall had failed to attract. *Charity Begins at Home*, *Box B*, Gilbert's *No Cards* and the monologues of Griffith Humphreys were not what the London of 1902 looked for in entertainment. But there was, in any case, little likelihood of a resemblance between *Three Little Maids* and the work of Cellier, Burnand or Charlie Stephenson. Paul Rubens' rather basic lyric and musical styles were well-known and they bore little or no similarity to those of the educated and well-mannered German Reed establishment. But *Three Little Maids* did differ from the prevailing kind of light musical entertainment. It was constructed and written with an almost naive simplicity in both its book and its songs, providing a not unpleasant contrast to the multi-coloured pieces of the Gaiety and the Lyric. In fact, as *The Stage* commented, its content was 'not substantial enough to be beaten out over three acts'.

The story was as light as could be: three society ladies and their beaux visit the country where three rural maidens succeed in artlessly detaching the men from the ladies. In the second act, they repeat the process in town, where they have taken jobs as waitresses in a tea room, and in the third they consolidate their triumph in the drawing room of a fashionable house. Rubens' dialogue was light and snappy without being in any way complicated or witty, and each time a scene looked like fading into nothingness, he simply threw in a song: one of the catchy little pieces with which he had made his name. The quality of the songs in *Three Little Maids* varied enormously, but Rubens had the happy knack of making a trivial phrase catch on and pieces which made 'Coo' sound sophisticated became, in his hands, the stuff of the popular song. For the show's concerted music, however, he turned to Howard Talbot for the composition of most of the opening and closing music for each act and the sextet 'Suppose we Have a Breakdown'. He also interpolated a song by his brother Walter, 'I'm only the Caddie', for little George Carroll. But the largest part of the score was his own, including the best and the worst. The best included an unharmonised sextet for the six ladies called 'The Town and Country Mouse', a little cakewalk for the three waitresses entitled 'The Tea and Cake Walk', and a song for George Huntley on George Grossmith lines, 'Algy's simply awfully good at Algebra':

You must have met a friend of mine called Algy, that's his name
He sups out at the Carlton all the week.
He's an awfully clever scholar, and his Euclid's deuced fine
And his algebra is simply magnifique.
Of course, he don't know much about the world and girls and all
But his mathematics nobody can beat
If you want to know how much you owe, he'll tell you like a shot
He's a fearfully sort of useful chap to meet.
Oh, Algy's simply awfully good at algebra
He's really awfully smart
Knows everything by heart
He sits on Boards of Companies
At least, he don't sit long
He goes away and hopes the wretched thing is going strong
But when he meets the shareholders, he knows at once what's wrong
'Cos Algy's simply awfully good at algebra!

Algy's sense of mathematics became more improbable as the verses progressed.

Some of the songs were exceptionally naive in their lyrics and, alongside the wit of Basil Hood, the attempts at word-play seemed extremely poor. Rubens also moved from time to time into the risqué, the coarse and the vehement, creating some amazing and incomprehensible contrasts which were both unsuitable and in bad taste. This was a habit of which, in his long and successful career, he was never entirely to rid himself. Hilda's number 'She Was a Miller's Daughter' described a young lady's bored rejection of a suitor, until that suitor forgets himself and 'said one risqué word, quite by mistake' at which the maiden cries 'Hurrah' and becomes extremely forward:

She was a miller's daughter
And lived beside a mill
Though there were flies on the water
Yet she was 'flyer' still . .

Sung with total innocence by Hilda Moody, its meaning was certainly not lost. Madge Crichton's tirade against 'Men' was also fairly tasteless, without the redeeming feature of genuine cleverness:

You men are a terrible bore
Why were you ever invented?
They ought to have stopped you before;
Your stupidity's unprecedented
How did you come to exist?
Were you meant as an up-to-date toy?
I assure you you'd not have been missed
If you'd only been drowned when a boy

Only in its last verse did it turn to say 'we do rather like you'. If some of the numbers lacked judgement, others were just plain bad, including another number for Madge Crichton (and intended for Ada Reeve), 'Sal', for which the lyric ran:

I'm sure you've never seen a gal like my gal, Sal
Because there's never been a gal like my gal, Sal
She's not the ordinary kind
Of stupid gal you always find
Just talk to her and see, but mind
She's my gal, Sal.
Sal, Sal, you're so original
You never do or say a thing like any other gal
You can't look lovely, cause you aren't
But you're a gal, you're a pal
In fact, you're Sal, plain Sal.

A case of simplicity being something less than a virtue. With all its faults, *Three Little Maids* prospered. The words 'simple', 'easily intelligible', 'slight but pleasant' which had typified the reactions of the critics were taken as commendation and, as Edwardes smartened the piece up, it grew into a highly popular show. The three little maids and their equally attractive beaux – Farkoa, Huntley and handsome Bertram Wallis in his first West End lead – aided and abetted by Lottie Venne, tiny George Carroll and the three fine 'city ladies' waltzed carefully through the unsubstantial froth of the show, skating over its lesser parts to provide a pleasant undemanding evening.

Into the run, Edna May left the cast to go into the provinces with the show, with Coralie Blythe and Alice Davis as her two 'sisters' and, soon after, *Three Little Maids* transferred to the Prince of Wales. Then Ada Reeve returned and with her came trouble. Ada asked for her part to be enlarged, Edwardes refused, and once more the pair parted company. But that was not the end of the affair. Ada, with a blithe disregard of copyright, began singing the song 'Men' at the Palace music hall. Edwardes and Rubens took out a court order to prevent her and the sparks began to fly. Ada claimed that the song had been written by her some time before *Three Little Maids*, in conjunction with Rubens 'the way we write all my songs', and she produced the manuscript of the song with Rubens' pencilled inscription 'here is your song' across the top. The court was unmoved and Ada was ordered to stop singing 'Men'.

Madge Crichton took up the role of Ada again and with Miss Moody and Delia Mason (as Edna) completed what became almost a year's run for *Three Little Maids*. The show became a firm favourite on the touring circuits and in 1903 was presented on Broadway for a season of 130 performances at Daly's Theatre. Unlike *A Country Girl* and *Merrie England* it was not the stuff of which revivals are made, but its success had been an indubitable one, not only in London but wherever it had been put on the stage.

The most unlikely entry of the year was a piece called *Naughty Nancy* which booked in to the hallows of the Savoy Theatre when Greet took *Merrie England* on the road. It had first made an appearance at Southend in March under the banner of the popular singing actress, Kitty Loftus, but it had failed to gain much in the way of attention beyond some enthusiasm for the lively Miss Loftus' own performance. It was toured to Blackpool and Liverpool and closed in Margate after its fourth week to be 'rewritten and re-constructed', as common a euphemism for abandonment as was ever heard. But *Naughty Nancy* did resurface, some four months later, duly rewritten and once again featuring Kitty Loftus as actress-manager, not only in the West End but at the Savoy. Attached to the piece were a number of unfamiliar names: Oliver Bath, Walter

Davidson and Ralph E. Lyon. The last-named turned out to be a schoolmaster from Malvern College; Davidson, who was apparently responsible for the largest part of the 25-number score, was a small-time composer from Oxford best known for a series of drawing-room pieces called 'Songs for Smokers'. Oliver Bath was the pseudonym of Viscount Tiverton who had, in his time, written a few sketches and short plays but who was here making his first attempt at a full-length musical. The name which was familiar, of course, was that of Kitty Loftus, and *Naughty Nancy* was a true-bred vehicle for her as the 'romp' of the school in love with a nobleman and mixed up in the doings of an uncle sought by the police (who ends up in women's clothes) and the love-life of a number of other people.

The Era noted:

> The piece is cleverly contrived and arranged and shows Miss Kitty Loftus in her merriest and most 'rollicking' mood; and, with the popular comedienne as the centre of attraction, the piece was rattled through at a pace which gave little time for thought or analysis. Neither is, indeed, deserved by the smart and sketchy concoction . . . Triumph was assured by the exertions of Miss Kitty Loftus who as the rebellious Nancy frisked, flirted and frolicked in the most exhilarating and amusing manner, and carried the piece along by sheer good spirits and jollity . .

The Stage, too, had some slight praise:

> . . [the dialogue and lyrics] without being remarkably witty or brilliant, reveal a facile pen . . . tuneful and tripping music . . but one or two numbers have the ring of the average music hall refrain . .

This last qualification might have done something to deter the normal Savoy audience but it was not likely to turn away the followers of Miss Loftus and, indeed, *Naughty Nancy* prospered well enough for its star to extend her season through until the time Greet required his theatre for the return of *Merrie England*. Negotiations for a transfer to Terry's Theatre fell through and *Naughty Nancy* closed its West End season preparatory to going back on tour.

It had been a piece in true variety musical style – the Kitty Loftus show – but Miss Loftus had, nevertheless, surrounded herself with capable performers such as Gladys Homfrey, Cairns James, Charles E. Stevens, Eva Kelly and tenor John M. Hay, and she had not been so foolish, Viscount or no Viscount, as to lumber herself with impossible material. The songs Davidson and his collaborators gave her provided her plenty of varied opportunities to display her skills whether as an up-to-date dude (in 'What, What?'), in a burlesque operatic duet, imitating a policeman as she sang about 'The splendid Force' or describing to her audience the points of 'A Ladies' Orchestra'. One of her most successful songs was an extended version of Henry Leigh's 'Uncle John' verses from 'Carols of Cockayne':

> I never loved a dear gazelle
> Because, you know, I never tried
> But if I had, I know full well
> The thing would certainly have died.
>
> Yet I have loved rich Uncle John
> I've loved him long, I've loved him well
> But Uncle John goes living on
> Ah! would he were a dear gazelle . . .

The other members of the cast also had their opportunities. Charles Stevens found plenty of fun in his 'drag' scenes, particularly when getting into a mistaken identity crisis with his own wife (Gladys Homfrey); Cairns James, back at the Savoy under rather different circumstances, had a comical song, and John Hay sang a tenor ballad which the rather over-enthusiastic *Era* critic described:

> Mr John M. Hay sent the house into raptures by his melodious and expressive delivery of an intense and thrilling ballad, the nature of which may be imagined from the refrain:
>
> Ah, do not leave me
> Ah, do not grieve me
> Life is not life when my darling's away
> Now I have found thee
> Grieve me tomorrow, but love me today!
>
> This song, which is called 'Thou art my world' should become a favourite with amateur emotionalists in private life, as the depth of feeling which may be thrown into its appeal is almost infinite . .

Naughty Nancy's metropolitan success led Kitty Loftus to formulate ambitious plans for her show and at one stage she announced that three companies would be sent out to play the show round the provinces through 1903. But the show virtually was Miss Loftus; she realised in time that she could not split herself in three and only one company was actually sent out, the following year. But the show had proved a point – one which Miss Loftus was anxious to make after her long and acrimonious lawsuit with Arthur Roberts who had refused to take her into town as his co-star in *H.M.S. Irresponsible.* She was a more than viable West End star in her own right and she had a successful season at the Savoy Theatre to underline the fact. She had lost the lawsuit but she had proved the point at issue in her favour. *Naughty Nancy*, having served its purpose, was shelved and Miss Loftus gave up the cares of management for those of stardom.

Lawsuits were clearly the order of the day but the year's last new entry, *The Girl from Kays*, must have set some kind of a record by being the subject of a court case before its libretto was even written. Its author, Owen Hall, had announced that this new show at the Apollo would be entitled *The Girl from Jay's* and immediately found himself summonsed by Jays Ltd, the Bond Street millinery firm. Far from being pleased at the publicity, they feared that their exclusive image might be smirched by a possible association with the events in an Owen Hall play. The author altered his shop's name to 'Kays', but nobody was fooled, and the touchy proprietors must have felt regretful when the show became an enormous hit on both sides of the Atlantic.

The libretto of *The Girl from Kays* was professedly based on a French farcical original, but that original was never credited and it would seem that the show's style was about all that Hall had borrowed from the French[1]. It could scarcely have been the story which was amazingly flimsy, a trend which, following on from *Three Little Maids*, seemed to be coming regrettably popular. In this case, the entire plot was based on one kiss. Or maybe two. Young Harry has just married his Nora, and they are waiting to leave on their honeymoon when Nora's new hat arrives. The hat is brought by Winnie, the girl from Kays, who turns out to be an old friend of Harry's. But as she is giving him a congratulatory kiss, Nora and her family arrive and take the whole thing very much

[1] Gandillot's *La Marieé Recalcitrante* may have been the source in question. The author subsequently sued for unauthorised adaptation but lost.

amiss. The honeymoon is off on a bad tack – she in room 27 and he in room 42. Finally, of course, Nora realises that her jealousy is unjustified, but in the meanwhile there have been two more acts of fun and games, though hardly of plot. Mixed up in the proceedings were a bevy of bridesmaids and Kays' shopgirls, the obligatory noodle (the Hon Percy Fitzthistle), the staff of the honeymoon hotel, the bride's relations and, above all, an American millionaire with a taste for feminine beauty and especially for Winnie. The American millionaire had become a stock comic character of the British musical over a period of years but, in 'Mr Hoggenheimer of Park Lane', *The Girl from Kays* produced the great example of the species. As played by Willie Edouin, 'Piggy' Hoggenheimer proved the outstanding feature of the show.

The rather facile target of the 'commercial' millionaire (in this case one which resembled rather too closely a genuine specimen of the genre, Sir Alfred Rothschild, who had like 'Piggy' built himself a large home in Park Lane) was not the only one to which Owen Hall devoted his attentions in *The Girl from Kays*. He was dealing with the London of the here and now, and he let his wit and his spite run rife in a more unbridled fashion than ever before, prompting *The Stage* to comment:

> Jimmy Davis has never displayed his cynical humour more uncompromisingly than in the present work which abounds in barbed thrusts against classes and institutions regarding which he feels but moderately friendly feelings . .

If the pretentions of the nouveaux riches bore the main brunt of his attacks, he also had words for the worst classes of slippery businessmen, for the Salvation Army and for the self-styled lady who 'lives at the virtuous end of Regent Street' of whom his 'heroine' was an example. However, protest came, not from these, but from quite another quarter. When *The Girl from Kays* opened, the bridesmaids of Nora and Harry had each been prettily christened with the name of an Anglican bishopric – Miss Ebor, Miss Ely, Miss Cantuar, Miss Sarum. The Archbishop, having apparently no more wish for publicity than Jay's Ltd had made a polite complaint and the bridesmaids became, more prosaically, Misses Racine, Hildesley, Mayen and Leslie.

The musical portion of *The Girl from Kays* was pretty much of a hotch-potch. The principal musical credit was variously attributed to Ivan Caryll and to Cecil Cook but even these two, between them, were responsible for only a part of what was, in any case, a decidedly reduced score. Apart from its opening choruses and finales, which were of a fairly basic kind, the score of *The Girl from Kays* was simply a series of solo numbers with only a couple of duets as diversion. The songs were incidental enough to the action to allow for a fairly free exchange and during the run of the show numbers came and went with rather more frequency than was now current in a musical play.

Of the original score, perhaps the best piece was the charming waltz song written by Lionel Monckton and Adrian Ross in which the overwrought bride sobs out her woe to her father:

> Ah, ah, ah, I know at last his black pa-past
> Ah, ah, ah, sad is my heart, we must pa-part
> Ah, ah, ah, I cannot pardon him, I know
> That's so, Papa! That's so, Papa! Papa, that's so!

The hero's 'I Don't Care' sung at the end of the second act:

> Women are extraordinary beings
> Upon my word, I don't know what to think
> At one time they're annoyed because we husbands are *too* fond of them,

At other times they're furious if we wink.
I've got into a pretty piece of trouble
I don't know what to do or what to say,
I don't know whether p'raps I'd better stay at home and drown myself
Or go and have some lunch and run away.
I don't care!
Let her get into a temper if she likes to. Blow it!
Curse it!
If that wretched Uncle Theodore should get to know it!
Oh! I don't care!

was an example of the best of Paul Rubens, as was a later addition, 'The Glass Song', which was interpolated to give Aubrey Fitzgerald as Fitzthistle something to sing. Howard Talbot wrote a coon song to showcase the American actress Ella Snyder ('Smiling Sambo') which did quite well, and Caryll produced a very pretty duet, 'Semi-detached', for Nora and Harry, as well as Winnie's triumph song 'Mrs Hoggenheimer' as she bears off her little millionaire.

On the whole the score was subordinate to the book, or rather to the dialogue and the characters. Reaction was varied. *The Stage* spoke of the 'preposterous story' and the 'generally odious' characters. *The Times* merely sighed 'that wretched kiss', remarked that the second act was 'somewhat tedious' and criticised the bad taste of the song 'She Was a nice Girl – Once' which was duly cut. *The Era*, on the other hand, spoke of the 'well-constructed and brilliant book', the 'smart and occasionally saucy dialogue', the 'tripping and gaily jingling numbers' and the 'tasteful and expensive costumes'. The public quickly decided *The Era* was right. If the piece was a little saucy, well and good. Smart dialogue, pretty clothes and lively music went a good way to making a success, and there was no doubt that was precisely what *The Girl from Kays* was.

A large portion of the credit for success fell to Max Hoggenheimer. Odious he may have been with his 'Rude? I'm not rude, I'm rich', but he was also very funny, and at the end of the piece one was left feeling almost sorry for the vulgar little rich man who had landed himself with the go-getting girl from Kays. That role fell to Ethel Irving, moving on from soubrette roles at Daly's to a title role of her own and sharing the star billing with Edouin, Kate Cutler as the offended bride, Letty Lind as her maid and Kitty Gordon as a singing shopgirl, while Louis Bradfield was featured as the hero.

Hoggenheimer's adventures kept London entertained for well over a year at the Apollo and later the Comedy Theatres, but the expenses entailed in the production found the net result at the end of the run to be a deficit of some £20,000. A comparable run with such a loss was unheard of, outdoing even the massive losses of *Babil and Bijou.*

A series of successful tours helped to set the balance right, and the show was sent soaring into profit by the amazing reception of its American production. British shows, whilst highly popular in America, had not always been appreciated there proportionately to their London reception and run. On Broadway *The Silver Slipper*, for example, could outrun *A Country Girl* or *The Toreador*, *Erminie* was still unchallenged and *The Gay Parisienne* still ranked among the top half dozen imports. More often than not, these anomalies were not caused only by differences in taste or by a fortunate adaptation but by some 'catching' element, some craze, such as the double sextet in *Florodora* or the Champagne dance in *The Silver Slipper*. In *The Girl from Kays* there was Hoggenheimer. Far from taking offence at the satirical depiction of their upstart countryman, the Americans took Sam Bernard's performance as the Park Lane millionaire to their hearts and he and *The Girl from Kays* became the hit of the Broadway season of 1903/4. The show opened in November and held the stage at the Herald Square Theatre for 205 performances. Even then, Sam Bernard was not ready to let the character of Hoggenheimer go and in 1906 Charles Frohman staged a specially-written vehicle, *The Rich Mr Hoggenheimer*, at Wallacks, for which Harry B. Smith had concocted a series of knock-abouts and disguises that had little to do with *The Girl from Kays*. Nevertheless, Bernard's impersonation of the character again won loud praise and a huge public following and *The Rich Mr Hoggenheimer* had a run of 187 performances. But still Broadway had not seen the last of the Sam/Piggy combination. In 1914 at the Shubert he turned up in a re-vamped version of *The Girl from Kays* under the title of *The Belle from Bond Street*. The show had been revised almost out of recognition and this time the luck of the Hoggenheimers ran out: in spite of a cast featuring, among others, Gaby Deslys and the interpolation of the popular 'Who Paid the Rent for Mrs Rip van Winkle' borrowed from Al Jolson and *The Honeymoon Express*, the show crashed in just a few weeks. *The Belle from Bond Street* was re-exported to London where it had a brief unsuccessful run at the Adelphi.

Another British piece which turned up on Broadway in the 1903/4 season was *An English Daisy*. It had begun its career in Britain under the title *My Best Girl*, and had been intended as a follow-up for *The Silver Slipper* at the Lyric Theatre. But the management of the Lyric decided to take the transfer of the revival of *The Belle of New York* from the New Century (Adelphi) and *An English Daisy* had to wait until August 1902 to get a production, under the auspices of touring manager Milton Bode, at the rather less classy Royal County Theatre, Reading. From there it was taken on a tour. It had a libretto by Seymour Hicks with music composed by Walter Slaughter and seemed to be an attempt to follow on where the composer had left off in his fruitful collaboration with Basil Hood. The plot followed three sets of love affairs: that of a gay lieutenant with, on the one hand, his true love, an English flowergirl who is really a wealthy lass in disguise, and on the other with Celestine, the belle of Ostend; the standard comic affair of the 'buttons' and maid; and the courting of the wealthy Lavinia Squib by a couple of destitute Yankees. The highlight of the show was a whole set of high jinks around a marriage ceremony held in a lion's cage.

There were reminiscences of *The French Maid*, *The Circus Girl* and many other pieces, but the songs and dances were sufficiently sprightly to make the whole thing go fairly well. The first act was well received but the second was rather extenuated, leaving *The Stage to* complain:

> . . the fun, it must be confessed, palls somewhat at times and a few of the second act passages are dragged out unduly.

The Era concurred, but added:

> There is plenty of good material, and with a little strengthening and condensation the interest might be well-sustained throughout the piece.

Alterations were duly made as *An English Daisy* continued its tour, and the show proved an adequate provincial attraction. The starring comedy role of the Yankee 'Hiram Out' was taken by Thomas E. Murray who paired with Will Spray to provide the show's laughter quota, and they were joined, in the title role, by a fifteen year-old girl whose only professional stage experience to date had been in pantomime. *The Era* reported: 'Miss Zena Dare made a taking heroine. She acted and sang very prettily and had a well-deserved ovation.'

In 1903 *An English Daisy* was taken out again with Murray once more in the role of Hiram and Lucie Caine as Daisy. However, it seemed clear by now that the show was not a West End prospect and it must have been a pleasant surprise for the proprietors when the American Edgar Smith, as eager for British product as any other New York manager, took the show for Broadway. Having duly 'substituted up-to-date American humour for the original English drollery' and having had 'the score strengthened by A. N. Norden with new numbers by Maud Nugent and Messrs Schwartz, Edwards and Jerome', Smith opened what remained of *An English Daisy* in Boston. After six weeks' run-in there it came in to New York's Casino Theatre equipped with a cast of 125 and a list of stars headed by Christie MacDonald, Truly Shattuck, Charles Bigelow, George A. Beane and Templar Saxe, but the underweight and overproduced variety show folded after only a brief run.

Another British provincial musical which failed to make it to the West End, yet found itself a spot, albeit briefly, on Broadway was *Mr Wix of Wickham*. Herbert Darnley's musical comedy was set up by Milton Bode as a vehicle for Dan Leno whom he had previously toured with success in *Orlando Dando*. Mr Wilfred Wix is an ordinary little man who finds himself mistaken for the missing descendant of a Duke. The play had a South African setting and had Wix fighting off a native attack, getting arrested for being a.w.o.l., court-martialled, and finally acquitted by a jury of ladies. He had a scene in which he contrived to leave himself dangling from a punt-pole on a South African river and another into which he managed to introduce his famous Lancashire clog dance. In fact the show was little more than a three-hour parade of the many talents of its star. It proved an adequate vehicle and was taken up by William Walton for himself and his South African company, and by E. E. Rice for a Broadway production. It did not succeed in New York but was notable for the fact that several new numbers which were added to the score came from the pen of a nineteen year-old New Yorker placing his first songs in a Broadway show: Jerome D. Kern.

By far the most successful provincial production of the year was a new Sidney Jones musical, *My Lady Molly*. Having left the Daly's combination, Jones had combined with G. H. Jessop, who had been so successful with the libretto to *Shamus O'Brien*, and the two produced *My Lady Molly* which they described as a 'comedy opera', the same soubriquet which had been attached to *Dorothy* and its kind. The description was justified in *My Lady Molly*, for Jones turned to a much more Cellier-like kind of composition than he had generally provided for Daly's. The score was heavy with broadly-written ensemble numbers and dignified ballads. In the same way, while Jessop's book by no means ignored the comedy element, his tale of marriages, disguises and rapier-fights in mid-eighteenth century England was a far cry from modern musical comedy pieces and even from the more substantial Daly's pieces. *My Lady Molly* was produced in Brighton in August, under the management of its composer, and taken on tour. It proved immensely popular and in March of 1903 it found its way to the West End and further success.

The West End was the hopeful title of the newest George Dance musical, written in conjunction with the actor George Arliss. Dance produced *The West End* at Norwich and took it on tour but it did not prove one of his more notable efforts. Its story was centred on the intriguing Duchess of Delamere who tramples over her old friend and financial saviour, Colonel Carruthers, and his daughter, Madeleine, in a strenuous effort to marry off her daughters, the ladies Isabelle and Clementine. There was more than a touch of *Three Little Maids* in the make-up of the piece which also included the standard private detective hired, in this case, by the equally standard rich American

(Southern variety). The ending, of course, had little Miss Carruthers snatching the marital prize from under the nose of the Ladies Delamere.

Dance's unfailingly bright dialogue and well-judged sense of theatre ensured that *The West End* pleased its audiences, but its derivative nature showed everywhere and nowhere more obviously than in its songs which had distinct echoes of recent hits: 'The Country Mouse' (*Three Little Maids* 'The Town and Country Mouse'), 'The Blue Belgravian Band' (*A Country Girl* 'The Pink Hungarian Band'), 'The Spider and the Fly' (Daly's Theatre). The lyrics for *The West End* were by Ernest Boyd-Jones, a member of Dance's *A Chinese Honeymoon* company. He had made a promising start with some words for *Florodora*, but his career ended suddenly with his premature death in 1904 at the age of 34. The music was the work of Edward Jones, still writing capable tunes without ever managing to break through with a truly successful show.

A more successful and much less ambitious piece was the farcical musical comedy *Runaways* produced by the touring actor-manager John Gerant. It was an unpretentious show, more farce than musical, although it was illustrated by a set of cheerful enough incidental songs composed by Knight Pearce, the company's conductor. Nominally, it was the work of one 'Jacob Sugarman' which looks as if it must have been a portmanteau name for two of the company's actors, Henry S. Ugar and Frederick Mantell, and possibly of Gerant himself as the 'Jacob'. It told the story of one Jack Hastings who, having compromised his widowed status by staying out all night lost in the fog with plain Clorinda Tuppy, finds himself faced with marital demands. The fly Clorinda knows that there is a lawyer looking for Jack to tell him 'something to his advantage'. Jack and his daughter Edith flee, pursued by Father and Miss Tuppy and others. After interludes in disguises, a mix-up with a detective looking for a robber, and the finding of a true love apiece, Jack and Edith escape into a happy ending.

Runaways was good old-fashioned farce-comedy and it went down as such. Pearce decorated it aptly with examples of the latest (and some less recent) song crazes – a cake-walk, a clog dance, a German (!) coon song &c – allowing the actors to pause in the helter-skelter action and knockabout fun to introduce a little variety into the proceedings. It was an enjoyable piece of nonsense and did Gerant proud when, after a good tour in 1902, it was brought back for a second tour in 1903.

There were several small-scale musicals presented for short tours during the year, including *The Golddiggers*, *The Marriage Market*, *A Father of 90* and *The Variety Girl*, but none was particularly good or successful. *The Golddiggers* (or Matrimony Mania) had a goldfields landlord turned matrimonial agent trying to sell new wives to the miners. All concerned are confounded when the real wives turn up, along with an old flame of the instigator. The show was produced at Balham with a strong cast, but some fairish music by author-composer Walter Wadham Petre was the best it had to offer and, though it did duty for a second season in 1906, it was agreed to be a fairly poor piece.

The Marriage Market was an equally ineffective piece with music by the Chevalier Legrand, produced in Jersey in March. Its matter was related to its title, but it had a very much longer life than *The Golddiggers*, in two tours – spring and autumn – through a couple of dozen secondary dates. *A Father of 90* (a mormon gentleman) was a plotless affair set in Egypt, concocted to allow the Darnley brothers, Herbert (the author) and Albert, to go through as many antics as possible to justify what they advertised as 'salaries more than those paid to some entire companies'.

The Variety Girl emanated from Ireland. It starred Witty Watty Walton as a menagerie proprietor, Frank Berham as a comic sleuth and Cassie Corelli as the 'Variety Girl' of the title. It was a mild melodrama – a far cry from the gnashing and rending days of *Jack-in-the-Box* – full of low comedy and vaguely centred on the search for a missing baby. The songs, written by *H.M.S. Irresponsible* composer George Byng, were principally of the music-hall variety: 'I can't Tame Martha Jane', 'Amy the Gamey', 'The little Bit of Blue', 'If I were Top of the Bill', 'Oh, how Embarrassing' &c. *The Variety Girl* had one short tour of little note.

The London suburbs provided a couple of interesting revivals during the year, but neither was precisely a triumph. Victor Lloyd-Bostock and Leslie Roy Cathie staged a revival of Huntley Wright's old extravaganza *Dashing Prince Hal* with music by Clarence Corri of *Dandy Fifth* fame and the company's m.d., Albert Vernon. In true extravaganza fashion it was not above borrowing the latest hits and, amongst the original material, up popped Ellaline Terriss' *Bluebell* hit 'The Sunflower and the Sun'. The fame subsequently earned by its author as an actor did nothing for the limp dialogue and structure of the show, and the mock-Tudor extravaganza failed. At Balham, Kinsey Peile's revised *Belle of Cairo* also went in for interpolations (including Rose Temple's 'My Moonlight Loo') as it tried again, and in vain, for success.

The Christmas period brought its usual crop of seasonal pieces of which the most notable was a version of Charles Kingsley's *The Water Babies*, written by actor Rutland Barrington and composed by Frederick Rosse. It played a successful season at the Garrick Theatre and was brought back for a second run the following year.

1902

0257 **A COUNTRY GIRL** or Town and Country. A musical play by James T. Tanner. Lyrics by Adrian Ross. Additional lyrics by Percy Greenbank. Music by Lionel Monckton. Additional numbers by Paul Rubens. Produced at Daly's Theatre under the management of George Edwardes 18 January, 1902 for a run of 729 performances closing 30 January, 1904.

Geoffrey Challoner	C. Hayden Coffin (Conway Dixon)
Quinton Raikes (The Rajah)	Rutland Barrington
Sir Joseph Verity	Fred Kaye (Fred Vigay)
Douglas Verity	Leedham Bantock/Gilbert Porteous
Granfer Mummery	Willie Warde
Lord Anchester	Akerman May
Lord Grassmere	Bertram Wallis/S. Gotto/Conway Dixon
Major Vicat	Alfred Hickman/E. D. Wardes
Sir Charles Cortelyon	Cecil Castle/S. Gotto
Tzanticheff (Herr Toutscha)	Fred Vigay (H. D. Pink)
Rube Fairway	Sebastian King
Barry	Huntley Wright/Frank Danby/Roland Henry
Marjorie Joy	Lilian Eldee/(Annie Purcell)/Olive Morrell/(M. Moore)/Isabel Jay
Princess Mehelaneh	Maggie May/Aileen d'Orme/Elise Cooke/Pearl Lyndon/Emma Boccardo/ Ida Worsley/Octavia Barry
Madame Sophie	Ethel Irving/Gracie Leigh (Mabel Hirst)
Mrs Quinton Raikes	Beryl Faber/Vera Edwardine
Nurse	Mrs Edmund Phelps/Valerie de Lacey/ Ethel Webster
Miss Carruthers	Topsy Sinden/Florence Warde
Captain of the Golden Hussars	Olive Morrell/*out*
Lady Anchester	Vera Edwardine/Olga Beatty-Kingston/ May Cranfield/Hallowell Morton
Miss Powyscourt	Nina Sevening/Hilda Coral/Olive Morrell
Lady Arnott	Olga Beatty-Kingston/Nina Sevening/ Pearl Lyndon/Hilda Coral/Mabel Hirst
Miss Courtlands	Dora Field/May Cranfield
Miss Ecroys	Mabel Hirst/Daisy Le Hay
Indian Attendants	Mary Collette/Alice d'Orme, May Snowdon/Ida Worsley
Nan	Evie Greene (Valerie de Lacey) (M. Moore) Olive Morrell
add Miss Egerton	Olive Morrell/Hilda Coral
Comte D'Aurignac	Charles Angelo

Dir: J. A. E. Malone; md: Barter Johns; ch: Willie Warde; sc: Hawes Craven and Joseph Harker; cos: Percy Anderson

Produced at Daly's Theatre, New York, under the management of J. C. Duff 22 September, 1902 for a run of 115 performances closing 27 December, 1902.
Melville Stewart (GC), Hallen Mostyn (QUINT), Harold Vizard (JO), Paul Nicholson (DOUG), Clarence Harvey (GRANFER), W. E. Philp (ANCH), Lawrence Earle (GRASS), W. H. Smith (VICAT), Jefferson Egan (CORT), Robert Chawner (TZ), N. C. Shaw (RUBE), William Norris (BARRY), Grace Freeman (MJ), Genevieve Finlay (PCESS), Minnie Ashley (SOPHIE), Adine Bouvier (MRS QR), Marion Singer (NURSE), Blanche Deyo (MISS C), Isobel Delmont (LADY A), Helen Sherwood (MISS P), Isobel Yates (ARNOTT), Grace Gresham (MISS COURT), Julia Millard (MISS E), Helen Marvin (NAN) with Alice Campbell, Susie Kelleher, Lena Wright, Leila Benton. Md: Alfred R. Moulton; ch: Blanche Deyo; sc: Walter Burridge, Henry E. Hoyt; cos: Percy Anderson

Produced at L'Olympia, Paris under the management of the Brothers Isola, 1904.

Produced at Herald Square Theatre, New York by the Steward-Grey Musical Company 29 May, 1911 for a run of 33 performances closing 24 June, 1911.
Melville Stewart (GC), Robert Elliot (QR), George E. Mack (JO), Donald Hall (DOUG), A. W. Fleming (GRANFER), Cyril Chadwick (ANCH), A. L. Clark (GRASS), W. L. Doyle (VICAT), Charles Kamp (CORT), F. Von Gottfried (TULZER), J. A. Bingham (RUBE), John Slavin (BARRY), Grace Freeman (MJ), Genevieve Finlay (PCESS), Laura Jaffray (SOPH), Ada Sterling (MRS QR), Anna Bell (ARNOTT), Florence Burdett (NAN), with Teresa Bryant, May Wesley, Edna Houch, Madge Gest, Ada Holt, Florence Burnham, Florence Farnham. Md: Anton Heindel

Produced at Daly's Theatre under the management of George Edwardes 28 October, 1914 for a run of 173 performances closing 27 March, 1915.
Robert Michaelis (GC), F. S. Burroughs/Leedham Bantock (QUINT), Tom Walls (JO), Pop Cory/Vernon Davidson (DOUG), Willie Warde (GRANFER), Austin Camp (ANCH), Arthur Wellesley (GRASS), Frank Perfitt (PETER GURNEY), Fred Vigay (RUBE), Cecil Fletcher (CORT), Edward Arundell and Ford Hamilton (ATTDTS), W. H. Berry (BARRY), Nellie Taylor/Lilian Burgis (MJ), Mabel Sealby (Connie St Clair) (SOPHIE), Melisande d'Egville/Clara Butterworth (PCESS), Phyllys Le Grand (MRS QR), Kate Welch (NURSE), Elise Craven (MISS C), Modesta Daly (LADY A), Isobel Hatchard (LADY CYNTHIA ABBEY), Elsie Spencer (MISS E), Connie Stuart (MISS COURT), Doreen Langton and Stella Riga (ATTDTS), Gertie Millar (NAN). Dir: Edward Royce; md: Merlin Morgan; sc: Alfred Terraine; cos: Comelli

Produced at Daly's Theatre under the management of J. Bannister Howard 29 September, 1931 for a run of 56 performances closing 14 November, 1931.
Roy Mitchell (GC), Griffith Moss (QUINT), George Bellamy (JO), Cedric Percival (DOUG), Fred Drawater (GRANFER), Conway Dixon (ANCH), Bruce Anderson (GRASS), W. Reynolds (WIND), A. Jarratt (VICAT), B. Kanelm (CORT), Austin Camp (RUBE), Dudley Rolph (BARRY), Ann Burgess (MJ), Eva Scott-Thompson (PCESS), Lorna Hubbard (SOPHIE), Stephanie Stephens (MRS QR), Iris May (NURSE), Babette Branksmere (MISS C), Eileen Brand (MISS ANSTRUTHER), Doreen Coburn (LADY A), Nina Butland (MISS P), Glae Carrodus (ARNOTT), Billie Benzie (MISS COURT), Joan Panter (MISS E), Dorothy Ward (NAN), Alison Maclaren (pd); with Jean Anita, Y. Anning, D. Caine, Daisy Dalziel, Pamela Dranek, P. Gray, C. Hill, M. Langford, M. Lynn, L. Lyon, Josephine Messum, K. Patterson, E. Pole Harvey, P. Rhys, Barbara Silverius, P. Stephens, I. Strong, C. Terry, J. Anstey, A. Baskerville, Francis Bergain, J. Hardy, J. Ind, Kenneth McKay, D. Walker, J. Willoughby. Dir: Frederick G. Lloyd; md: Leonard Hornsey; ch: Alison Maclaren; sc: Grantham & Co; cos: B. J. Simmons & Co

0258 **NAUGHTY NANCY** a musical comedy in two acts by 'Oliver Bath' (Viscount Tiverton). Lyrics by George W. Preston and 'Oliver Bath'. Music by Ralph E. Lyon and Walter Davidson. Additional music by George W. Preston. Produced at the Empire Theatre, Southend, under the management of Kitty Loftus 31 March, 1902 and toured through Blackpool, Liverpool and Margate closing 26 April. Rewritten and reproduced at the Savoy Theatre under the management of Kitty Loftus 8 September, 1902 for a run of 77 performances, closing 22 November, 1902.

Josiah Sliggs . . . . John Le Hay
Viscount Valentine . . . . Garnet Wilson/Ronald Thomas
Gilette Sherlock. . . . . James Frayling
Inspector . . . . Harry Denvil

Servant . . . . T. W. Graham
Martha Sliggs . . . . Caroline Ewell
Miss Pringle. . . . . Davies Webster
Nancy . . . . Kitty Loftus
Maisie . . . . Ellen Darling/Nellie Ward
Alice. Mabel Grace
Kitty . . . . Dolly Robertson
Maude. May Canisford
Jessie . . . . Ethel Vincent
Evelyn. . . . . Dora Rivers
add Tomkins . . . . Ernest Heathcote
Mrs Groggins. . . . . Jane Burdett

Savoy cast:

Josiah Sliggs . . . . Charles E. Stevens
Viscount Valentine . . . . Kenneth Douglas/Charles Hanbury
Earl of Aycon . . . . Cairns James
Maurice Le Strange. . . . . John M. Hay
Michael Molloy . . . . John T. Macallum
Waiter. . . . . J.W. Brighten
Tailor . . . . Harry Davis
Martha Sliggs . . . . Gladys Homfrey
Lady Barbara Dawn . . . . Mollie Lowell
Nephele Noggs . . . . Eva Kelly/Claire Rickards
Miss Pringle. . . . . Davies Webster
Nancy . . . . Kitty Loftus
Maisie . . . . Olive Loftus Leyton
Alice. Susie Raymonde/Miss Travers
Emily . . . . Ethel Kenyon
Beatrice . . . . Heloise Osland/*out*
Belinda . . . . Nellie Black
Violet . . . . Maisie Lowell
add Rosalind . . . . Louie Edmonds
Dancers: Susie Raymonde, Marie Lowell, Lily Brendall, Mea Winifred, Maud Rundell

Dir: Cairns James; md: T. Silver/D. Nabarro; ch: Charles Wilson and Fred Farren; sc: Walter Hann; cos: Peter Robinson, John Shore & Co

ɔ259 **THE MARRIAGE MARKET** a musical comedy in three acts by Frederick Jarman. Music by the Chevalier Legrand. Produced at the Opera House, Jersey 31 March, 1902 and toured through ?, Weymouth, Torquay, Bournemouth, Swindon, Worcester, Leamington, to 31 May. From 28 July through Aldershot, Oxford, Dublin, Belfast, Crewe, Liverpool, Hebburn, South Shields, Lancaster, Darlington, Eccles, Blackpool, Harrogate/York, Goole/Gainsborough, to 1 November.

Russell. . . . . Bertram Gates/Johnny Chippendale
Marion Smithers . . . . Maidie Scott/Edith Burman
Daisy . . . . Gertrude Sage
Carl Darrell . . . . Robert Hyett
Leonard . . . . Hugh Jarman/B. Wade
Auguste Merlinggarde . . . . W. Mowbray Harle
Hoeation Parum. . . . . Frederick Jarman/C. J. Barber
Max Rosenburg . . . . Alfred Wood/Bertram Gates
Fanny . . . . Edith Burman/Lily Craig
Susan . . . . Florence Hanlon/J. Morelli
Kate. E. Darsley
Zenobia . . . . Maud Steffany/Isa Culmer/Ray Roberts
Dorothy . . . . Ray Roberts/Mattie Everitt
Celeste. . . . . Gertrude Dickson

Md: Jean Desormes

•260 **MERRIE ENGLAND** a comic opera in two acts by Basil Hood. Music by Edward German.

Produced at the Savoy Theatre under the management of William Greet 2 April, 1902 for a run of 120 performances closing 30 July, 1902. Toured through dates including Glasgow (22 September), Newcastle, ?, Kennington, Leeds, Hull, Bradford, Sheffield and the Alexandra, to 22 November. Reopened at the Savoy Theatre 24 November, 1902 for a further 56 performances, closing 17 January, 1902.

The Earl of Essex. . . . . Henry A. Lytton
Sir Walter Raleigh . . . . Robert Evett/H. Manfred Russell
Walter Wilkins . . . . Walter Passmore
Silas Simkins . . . . Mark Kinghorne/M. R. Morand
Long Tom . . . . Ernest Torrence
Big Ben . . . . Reginald Crompton
The Fool . . . . George Mudie Jr
The Butcher . . . . Powis Pinder
The Baker. . . . . Joseph Boddy
The Tinker . . . . Rudolph Lewis
The Tailor . . . . Robert Rous
A Lord . . . . Charles Childerstone
Soldier. . . . . Lewis Campion/Charles Earldon
Pages . . . . Roy Lorraine/Lawrence Emerey/
Ela Q. May/*out*
Queen Elizabeth I. . . . . Rosina Brandram
Bessie Throckmorton . . . . Agnes Fraser (Isabel Agnew)
Jill-all-alone . . . . Louie Pounds
May Queen . . . . Joan Keddie/Olive Rae
Marjorie. . . . . Winifred Hart-Dyke
Kate. . . . . Alice Coleman/Lena Leibrandt
Lady-in-waiting . . . . Rose Rosslyn

Dancers: Poppie Wilkinson, Lena Leibrandt/C. Sidna, Edith Standen

Dir: Basil Hood; md: Edward German/Hamish MacCunn; ch: E. W. Royce Jr; sc: W. Harford; cos: Percy Anderson

Produced at the Prince's Theatre under the management of R. Claud Jenkins 6 September, 1934 for a run of 187 performances closing 16 Feb, 1935.
Edgar Owen (ESSEX), Joseph Hislop (Philip Merritt) (RAL), W. S. Percy (WW), Bertram Dench (SS), Denis Hoey (TOM), Norman Greene (BEN), Andrew Emm Jr (FOOL), Frank Watts (BUTCH), Wensley Russell (BAK), Norman Astridge (TIN), Phillip Merritt (TAI), Leonard Granville (LORD), Clelia Matania & Peggy Hart (PAGES), Enid Cruickshank (Mary Freeman) (QEI), Nancy Fraser (BESS), Rosalinde Fuller (JILL), Muriel Page (MAY), Mary Freeman (KATE), Felicity O'Dell (LIW), with Ann Blair, Helen Callaghan, Joan Collier, Doris Colston, Sibyl Darling, Rosalie Dyer, Dorothy Fox, Sheila Gray, Gladys Holmes, Dorothy Ivimey, Norah Moore, Violet Nicholls, Jessica Roland, Barbara Silverius, Grace Webb, Madge Wickham; Gerald Aintree, Gordon Crocker, Frank Dawson, Edward Earle, David Evans, Harry Foster, Ernest Freeman, Herbert Garry, Walter Gummow, Stuart Harding, Ernest Ludlow, Trenholme Macbenn, Reg Matthews, Wynford Morse, Andrew Reid, Marie Petersen, Winnie Dyer, Dorothy Hardy, Joan Marion, Audrey Robbins, Olga Schwiller; Carlito Ackroyd and John Thorpe (pds). Dir: William J. Wilson; md: Herman Finck; sc: Leolyn Hart; cos: B. J. Simmons & Co.

Produced at the Winter Garden under the management of Reginald Fogwell & Will Hammer 19 October, 1944 for a run of 52 performances closing, 2 December, 1944.
Reginald Gibbs (ESSEX), Walter Midgley (RAL), Charles Hawtrey (WW), Frank S. Henry (SS), Edward Dykes (TOM), Tom Pile (BEN), Duncan Sim (BUTCH), Lionel Endersby (BAK), Tom Clark (TIN), Leonard Mackrill (TAI), Dudley Ash (LORD), Jean Langford & Joan Valentine (PAGES), Gladys Palmer (QEI), Eugenie Castle (MAY), Victoria Campbell (BESS), Constance Stocker (JILL), Elsie Ford (KATE), Joan Eyre (LIW), Norman Newcombe (FOOL), Betty Bucknell (pd). Dir: Harry Knight; md: Herbert Lodge; ch: Alison Maclaren; sc: Cape; cos: B. J. Simmons & Co.

Produced at the Prince's Theatre under the management of Jack Waller in a revised version with the libretto adapted by Edward Knoblock 6 September, 1945 for a run of 365 performances closing 20 July, 1946.

Dennis Noble (ESSEX), Heddle Nash (RAL), Morris Sweden (WW), Richard Melton (TOM), John Gough (BEN), Linda Grey (QEI), Anna Jeans (BESSIE), Chic Elliot (MAY), Joyce Neale (LIW), Edna Clement (JANE), Alan Rolfe (DICK), Monti de Lyle (DON FERNANDO), Conway Dixon (SHAKESPEARE/A CITIZEN), Howard Fry (SERGEANT PORTER KEYS), Betty Geary (LADY MARY GRAY), Douglas Stewart (LORD BURGHLEY), Bernard Verrey (JONSON), Cyril Dossor (DEKKER), Harry Gawler (HEYWOOD), Bade Powell (SCRIBE), May Joyce, Claire Maxwell, Mavis Heath (COURT LADIES), with Elvira Cavatorta, Wynne Elias, Doris Crusett, Rosemary Linda, May Joyce, Doris Palm, Vera Compton, Doris Siese, June Milland, Marion Leonard, Rita Kaye, Joan Weston, Angus Calder, Ronald Woodhouse, William O'Connor, Harry Lacy, Jack Reidy, Maurice Diamond, Cliff Clifford, Frank Markham, Gerry Bailey, Derrick Claye, Shaughan Doyle, Harold King. Dir: William Mollison; md: Jan Hurst; ch: Pauline Grant; sc: Edward Delaney; cos: Elizabeth Fanshawe

Played at the London Coliseum by the National Light Opera Company under the management of Ralph Reader for a season of 15 performances from 23 January to 3 February, 1951.
William Dickie (ESSEX), Kenneth Macdonald (RAL), C. Denier Warren (WW), Douglas Thomson (SS), Godfrey Tiffen (TOM), Bernard Dudley (BEN), Noel Kenward (BUTCH), David Byerley (BAK), Peter Hember (TINK), John Green (TAI), Roger Avon (LORD/FOOL), Joan Wood (QEI), Vera Christie (BESS), Linda Hagan (JILL), Gladys Cooper (MAY), Eileen Carey (KATE), Patricia Schofield (MARJ). Dir: Ralph Reader

Produced at the Sadler's Wells Theatre in a revised version by Dennis Arundell by the Sadler's Wells Opera Company 10 August 1960.
John Hargreaves (ESSEX), John Carolan (RAL), Denis Dowling/John Holmes (WW), Alfred Oldridge (SS), Leon Greene (TOM), Lawrence Folley (BEN), Stanley Bevan (BUTCH), Eric Stannard (BAK), Peter Tracey (TINK), John Fryatt (TAI), Peter Firman (CAPTAIN OF THE GUARD), Arthur Gomez (DR RODERIGO LOPEZ), Anna Pollak (QEI), Joan Stuart (BESS), Ava June (MAY), Graham Curnow (FRANCIS BACON), Patricia Kern/Sylvia Rowlands (JILL) with Carl Abrahamson, Bryan Clifford, Paul Janssen, Arthur Thelwell, Gillian Ashby, Diana Chadwick, Lydia Conway, Beryl Cornish, Georgina Holley, June Johnstone, Norma Kubel, Patricia McCarry, Betty McClelland, Cynthia Morey, Barbara Walmsley, Marjorie Ward, Anne Caswell, Teresa Duckworth, Mirri Fuller, Mary Gilmore, Jean Manning, Janet Mays, Elizabeth Naylor, Gay Roberts, Jane Whitehead, Mildred Wood, John Darnley, James Higgins, Elvet Hughes, Valerio Martinez, Alan Morrell, Jon Weaving, Stanley Beedle, William Cuthbertson, Basil Hemming, Gwilym Lloyd, William McGovern, Carmelino Satariano, Douglas Stark. Dir: Dennis Arundell; md: John Robertson/John Barker; ch: Andrée Howard; sc/cos: Peter Rice

0261 **THREE LITTLE MAIDS** a musical play in three acts written and composed by Paul Rubens. Additional music by Howard Talbot. Additional lyrics by Percy Greenbank. Produced at the Apollo Theatre under the management of George Edwardes and Charles Frohman 20 May, 1902. Transferred to the Prince of Wales Theatre 8 September, 1902. Withdrawn 25 April 1903 after a total run of 348 performances.

Ada Branscombe . . . . Madge Crichton/Ada Reeve (Ruby Ray)
Hilda Branscombe . . . . Hilda Moody/Lydia Flopp
Edna Branscombe. . . . . Edna May/Delia Mason (Hilda Jeffreys)
Lady St Mallory . . . . Lottie Venne (Barbara Huntley)
Lady Rosemary Beaulieu . . . . Millie Legarde/Norma Whalley/Muriel Kennedy/Sara Miskel
Venetia Grafton. . . . . Betty Belknap/Eva Kelly/Evelyn Bond/Sara Miskel
Lady Marjorie Crichton . . . . Ruby Ray/Muriel Kennedy
Miss Deare . . . . Sybil Grey
Miss Crane . . . . Hilda Jeffreys/Mildred Baker
Miss Price. . . . . Jane May/Lydia Flopp/Ethel Grace
Reverend Branscombe . . . . John Beauchamp
Cupid . . . . George Carroll
Brian Molyneux. . . . . Bertram Wallis/J. L. Mackay/Alec Marsh
M. de L'Orme . . . . Maurice Farkoa/Jacques Volnys/Charles Angelo
Lord Cheyne . . . . G. P. Huntley/Laurence Grossmith

Hon. Bobbie Windsor. . . . . Madge Vincent
Miss Effie Thames . . . . Effie Rivers/Sara Miskel
with Muriel Kennedy, Mary Fraser, May Coverick, Kathleen Grey, Evelyn Bond, Mildred Baker, Kellie Seymour, Sara Miskel, Bertha Palliser, Ethel Grace, R. St George, E. Wolseley, J. Walsh, A. Anderson.

Md: Howard Talbot; ch: Willie Warde; sc: Hawes Craven & Joseph Harker; cos: Wilhelm

Produced at Daly's Theatre, New York, under the management of Charles Frohman and George Edwardes 1 September, 1903. Transferred to the Garden Theatre 16 November after 86 performances for a further 43 performances, closing 26 December, 1903 after a total of 129 performances.
Madge Crichton (ADA), Elsa Ryan/Maggie May (HIL), Delia Mason (ED), Maud Hobson (MALL), Vera Edwardine (BEAU), Eva Kelly/Etta Daincourt (VEN), Kathleen Warren (CRI), Barbara Huntley (DEARE), Vera Vallis (CRANE), Marie West (PRICE), R. St George (REV), George Carroll (CU), J. Edward Fraser (BRI), Maurice Farkoa (DEL'O), G. P. Huntley (CH) with Gertrude Kuzelle, Etta Daincourt, Misses Brooks, Watts, Tunison, Maurice, Robinson, Thorne, Vallis, Callan, Gordon, Wright, Sandford, Lucie; Messrs Armstrong, Lipson, Finley, Alston, Ozab, Weaver, Cutter, Featherstone. Md: Frank E. Tours

Revised and revived as *The Miller's Daughters*, 1916.

0262 **THE GOLDDIGGERS** or Matrimony Mania. A comedy opera in 3 acts by Walter Wadham Petre. Produced at the Duchess Theatre, Balham, under the management of Augustus Bingham 9 June, 1902 and toured?.

Suza . . . . Coralie Blythe
Mrs Buckle . . . . Alice Aynsley Cook
Mildred . . . . Minnie Hunt
Terence Rainsford . . . . Harrison Brockbank
Hon. Sir Joseph Pickles. . . . . George Mudie Jr
Alphonse, Comte de Beaumont. . . . . . Harry C. Barry
Billy . . . . Tom Redmond
Jacob Henry Bregwood . . . . M. R. Morand
Registrar. . . . . D. M. Miller
Violet . . . . Amy Venese
Deborah. . . . . Ada Rodney
with Dolly Douglas

Revised and revived as *The Golddiggers* or The Girls From Utah at Bath 16 April, 1906.

0263 **MR WIX OF WICKHAM** a musical comedy in two acts by Herbert Darnley. Music by Frank Seddon, George Everard, Frank E. Tours and Herbert Darnley. Produced at the Borough Theatre, Stratford East, under the management of Milton Bode and toured.

Duke of Tadminster . . . . Standley Wade
Tom Howard . . . . Michael Dwyer
John Smyth . . . . Arthur Bishop
Mr Banks M.P. . . . . J. Harold Carson
Mr Potter . . . . George Blunt
Mr Dodd . . . . E. W. Maule Cole
Shamus O'Scoot . . . . Laurence Caird
Wilfrid Wix . . . . Dan Leno
Lady Betty . . . . Grace Taylor
Mme Marie . . . . Jennie Armstrong
Maud Benton . . . . Georgina Leno
Mrs O'Scoot . . . . Amy Fanchette

Md: John Weaver

Produced in a version with book and lyrics by John Wagner and music by Herbert Darnley, George Everard and Jerome D. Kern at the Bijou Theatre, New York, under the management of E. E. Rice 19 September, 1904 for a run of 41 performances closing 22 October, 1904.
Sidney de Grey (DUKE), David Lythgow (TOM), Julian Dalton Eltinge (JOHN), Arthur Wooley

(BANKS), Douglas Flint (POT), Andrew O'Neill (DODD), Frank Lalor (SHAM), Harry Corson Clark (WIX), Thelma Fair (BET), Laura Guerite (MME), Alice Maude Poole (MAUD), Catherine J. Hayes (MRS O'S), Fred Waters (JINKS), Milt Pollock (DRINKAWELDRY), Frances Wilson (SUSAN), Cecile Mayer (TOTTIE), David Abraham (FROLICSOME KANGAROO) with Violet Holbrook, Marion Stokes, Frankie Loeb, Lillian MacCeney, Ocia Thompson, Mabel Douglas, Mildred Tate, Lucille Monroe, Adelaide Ackland, Helen Ryley, Wally Vaughn, Trixie Orient, Ethel Filmore, Sybil Ellwood, Mabel Gilmore, Ethel Gilmore, Kate Young, Maude Stanley, Elise Yale, Meredith S. Brown, Joseph Levere, Fred Smythe, William Mowry, Jackie Sullivan, Fred Lalor, Walter Garfield, Frank White, Jack Howell, Herman Noble. Dir: Tom Ricketts

264 **RUNAWAYS** a musical farce in three acts by 'Jacob Sugarman'. Music by F. Knight Pearce. Produced at the Artillery Theatre, Woolwich, under the management of John Gerant 28 July, 1902 and toured through Longton, Bedford, Deal, Margate, Dudley, Gloucester, Nuneaton, Hastings, Great Grimsby, Southend, Ipswich, Windsor, Peterborough, Luton, Colchester, Dover, Ramsgate, Alexandra, to 6 December. Toured from 3 August, 1903 at Longton through Darwen, Bishop Auckland, York, Burton, Broughton, Oxford, Cambridge, Dover, Eastbourne, Croydon, Stafford Barrow, Leigh, Peterborough, Bedford, Chester, Crouch End, ?, ?, Gainsborough, ?, Seaham Harbour, Workington/Whitehaven, Swindon to 23 January, 1904.

Jack Hastings . . . . John Gerant

Angus Tuppy . . . . Frank Dix

Archie Bounder . . . . Frederick Sandy

Nicodemus Bibb . . . . Ernest St John

Tom Welsh . . . . Henry S. Ugar

Norman Rivington . . . . Frederick Mantell/Philip Sefton

Tippett . . . . Graham Morrison

Bill Bunkum . . . . Percy Gold

Ted Mooney . . . . Bertie Fullalove

PC CXIV . . . . Horace Glendenning

Piffles . . . . Albert Plant

Oscar Winkle . . . . Fred Dent

Edith Hastings . . . . Zoe Davis

Rosie Dimple . . . . Dorothy Payne

Millicent Rivington . . . . Doris Lorraine

Clorinda Tuppy . . . . Kate Vivian

Mrs Bounder . . . . Nellie P. Dent

Angelina Pim . . . . Cecilia Byron

Hypatia Smith . . . . Violet Lingard

Alexandra Pew . . . . Edith Maynard

Md: F. Knight Pearce

265 **AN ENGLISH DAISY** a musical comedy in two acts by Seymour Hicks. Music by Walter Slaughter. Produced at the Royal County Theatre, Kingston under the management of Milton Bode 11 August, 1902 and toured through ?, ?, Sheffield, Nottingham, Stoke Newington, Hanley, Hull, Newcastle, Birmingham, Coronet, Camden, Stratford East, Kennington, Dalston, to 22 November. Toured again from 7 September, 1903 at Manchester through Newcastle, Hull, Nottingham, Metropole, Grand, Oxford, Birmingham, Shakespeare, Dalston and Liverpool, ending 21 November, 1903.

Hiram Out . . . . Thomas E. Murray

Daniel Grab . . . . Will Spray/W. Harman

Lt Charles Lambton . . . . Charles F. Hanbury/Walter Crimp

Major Bickersdyke . . . . J. E. Nightingale

Lt Dick Pepler . . . . Ronald Thomas/Louis Stanislaus

Lt Tom Brown . . . . Fred Twitchen

Monsieur Jacques . . . . J. D. Newton/W. J. Rippon

Alf . . . . Fred Groves

Bert . . . . Alfred Sawyer

Joe Tents . . . . Harry Gregory/H. Dalton

Devine . . . . Louis Stanislaus/Charles Benson/ J. Harrison
Comte Dubois . . . . Arnold Lucy
Henri . . . . George Hudson
Gustave . . . . Vernon Edgar
Adolphe . . . . A. Thompson/Ronald Thomas
Waiter . . . . A. Segheloni
Gendarme . . . . G. L. Bokenham
Daisy Maitland . . . . Zena Dare/Lucie Caine
Lady Lauderdale . . . . Violet Ley
Lavinia Squib . . . . Marie Hassell
Mdlle Celestine . . . . Mary Thorne
Mdlle Cherie . . . . Margaret Fraser
Josephine . . . . Lillian Burns
Clotilde . . . . Genee Hayward
Lucille . . . . Nita Clarence
Henriette . . . . Maude Prenton
Madame Jacques . . . . Margaret Rotah
Lady Winifred . . . . Blanche Thorpe
Lady Marjorie . . . . Marjorie Glenn
Lady Mabel . . . . Hilda Antony

with M. Cunningham, Vic Charlton, Eva Dagmar, L. Herbert, L. Donizetti, Marian Keith, Gertrude Luiche, Grace Mackay, A. Murray, Beatrice Ross, G. Beaumont, Charles Benson, L. Gardner, G. Tomkins.

Dir: Seymour Hicks; md: Thomas M. Tunbridge; ch: Willie Warde; cos: Langston & Sons, Maytum & Courtenay, Morris Angel

Produced in the United States in a revised version by Edgar Smith with additional music by A. N. Norden, Maud Nugent, Jean Schwartz, Gus Edwards and William Jerome. Produced under the management of Edgar Smith at the Casino Theatre, New York 18 January, 1904 for a run of 41 performances closing 20 February, 1904.
Fred Lennox (HIRAM), Charles A. Bigelow (GRAB), Templar Saxe (CH), George A. Beane (MAJOR), George P. Smith (DICK), Alfred Truschler (TOM), Louis Wesley (BERT), Frank Hammond (TENTS), Henri Leoni (DU), Franc V. Le Mone (HEN), Osborne Clemson (GUST), Arthur Stanford (AD), J. C. Newell (WAI), Frank Lalor (BLIFFKINS), Christie MacDonald (DAISY), Jean Newcombe (LADY), Kitty Baldwin (LAV), Truly Shattuck (CEL), Nora Sarony (CH), Lillian Maure (JO), Emily Sanford (CLO), Helen Wilmer (LU), Clara Belle Jerome (HEN), Carrie B. Munroe (WIN), Lillian Marshall (MAR), Jane Tyrrell (MAB). Dir: Ben Teal

0266 **MY LADY MOLLY** a comedy opera in two acts by G. H. Jessop. Additional lyrics by Percy Greenbank and Charles H. Taylor. Music by Sidney Jones. Produced at the Theatre Royal, Brighton under the management of Sidney Jones 11 August, 1902 and toured. Dates included Leeds, Belfast, Blackpool, Hull, Newcastle, Nottingham, Bristol &c.

Lady Molly Martingale . . . . Sybil Arundale
Alice Coverdale . . . . Decima Moore
Hester . . . . Mabel Allen
Mdlle Mirabeau . . . . Andrée Corday
Captain Harry Romney . . . . Richard Green
Lionel Bland . . . . Walter Hyde
Sir Miles Coverdale . . . . Charles F. Cooke
Mickey O'Dowd . . . . Bert Gilbert
Landlord of the Inn . . . . H. M. Imano
Head Groom . . . . William Waite
Rev Silas Wapshott . . . . Walter Wright
Judge Romney . . . . Cecil Howard
Housekeeper . . . . Dorothy Cameron
Alison . . . . Grace Arundale
Lucy . . . . Rose Batchelor
Martin . . . . O. H. McKiernan
Roger . . . . E. L. Carter

with Sallie Morrison, May Carlton, Kathleen Mackay, Adelaide Russell, Madge Rivers, Lily Ward, Ethel Verdi, Marie West, Gertie Russell, Nora Deane, Connie Ross, Kitty Rawlinson, Katherine Comber, Lizzie Elliston, Ruby Pond, Freda Stanley, Helen King, Linda Bretland, Bert Drewett, E. Iram Fay, M. Florence, Harold Cashel, Philip Somers, W. J. Mundy, T. J. Bariseale, Dixon Blackburn, T. W. Reynolds, S. Brookes.

Dir: Sydney Ellison; md: Sidney Jones/H. G. Baker; sc: Walter Hann and Joseph Harker

Produced at Terry's Theatre under the management of Frederick Mouillot 14 March, 1903 for a run of 342 performances closing 16 January, 1904.

Lady Molly Martingale . . . . Sybil Arundale/Florence Perry (Margaret Parker)
Alice Coverdale . . . . Decima Moore
Hester . . . . Gaynor Rowlands/Kathleen Mackay
Mdlle Mirabeau. . . . . Andrée Corday
Captain Harry Romney . . . . Richard Green (William Waite)
Lionel Bland . . . . Walter Hyde (Mr Hedsworth) (Bert Drewett)
Sir Miles Coverdale. . . . . Arthur Winckworth
Mickey O'Dowd . . . . Bert Gilbert/(John T. MacCallum)
Reuben Oates . . . . John T. MacCallum (William Waite)
Head Groom . . . . William Waite/C. J. Evans/George Hubbard
Judge Romney . . . . Gilbert Laye
Housekeeper. . . . . Margaret Parker
Alison . . . . Madge Greet
Lucy. . . . . Susie Nainby
Martin. Dixon Blackburn/C. J. Evans/Sam Carleton
Roger . . . . Leonard James

with Gladys McGarry, Lily Kenyon, Emilie Wade, Irene du Foye, Lily Ward, Helen King, Norah Deane, Connie Ross, Lizzie Elliston, Ethel Verdi, Norah Stagg, Ruby Pond, Freda Stanley, Robina Palmer, Nellie Davis, Katherine Comber/Pansy Elliot, Daisy Watson, May Middleton, Kathleen McKay, Bert Drewett, Walter Wright, F. C. Prickett, James Saker, F. Heybank, G. H. Hunt, C. J. Evans.

Dir: Sydney Ellison; md: Arthur Wood; sc: Joseph Harker and Walter Johnson; cos: Alias

Produced at Daly's Theatre, New York, under the management of Charles Frohman 5 January, 1904 for a run of 15 performances closing 16 January, 1904.
Vesta Tilley (MOLLY), Adele Ritchie (AL), Alice Judson (HE), Anna Boyd (MDLLE), Sidney Deane (HR), Ray Youngman (LI), David Torrence (MILES), Richard F. Carroll (MICK), Luke Martin (LAND), Edward Chapell (HG), John Henderson (JUDGE), Oriska Worden (HOUSE), Belle Robinson (AL), Amy Lesser (LU), E. Matthews (MART), W. J. Morgan (OWEN), Francis Motley (HEAD WAITER)

0267 **THE VARIETY GIRL** a musical farcical comedy in two acts by Chris Davis. Lyrics by Albert E. Ellis. Music by George Byng. Produced at the Opera House, Cork, under the management of F. T. Newell 1 September, 1902 and toured through Belfast, ?, ?, ?, Oldham &c.

David Martin . . . . Witty Watty Walton
Robert Sniff. . . . . Frank Berham
Harry Warmum . . . . Charles A. White
Charles Bliss . . . . Sydney Mannering
Willie Bungle . . . . W. P. Dempsey
Mrs Crier . . . . Stella St Audrie
Maria Wilkins. . . . . Lucie Fitzroy
Mrs David Martin . . . . Denny Fitzherbert
Marie . . . . Ida Yeo
Suzette . . . . Dora Harrison
Vivette. . . . . Cassie Corelli

Dir: George Highland; sc: E. H. Lyneham; cos: H. C. Russell, Miller & Smith

0268 **THE WEST END** or The Doings of the Smart Set. A musical comedy in three acts by George Dance and George Arliss. Lyrics by Ernest Boyd-Jones. Music by Edward Jones. Produced at the Theatre Royal, Norwich 29 September, 1902 and toured through Ipswich, Folkestone, Lincoln, Wakefield, Crewe, Coventry, Stockton, West Hartlepool, Derby, to 6 December.

The Duchess of Delamere . . . . Annie Esmond
Lady Isabelle . . . . Cissie Vaughan
Lady Clementine . . . . Dulcie Garland
Colonel Carruthers . . . . Harry Phillips
Madeleine Carruthers . . . . Nellie Dale
Hon Percy Blythe . . . . Leslie Holland
Algy Marmaduke . . . . Lawrence Winning
Sir Anthony Poppleton . . . . Charles P. Challoner
Mumble . . . . Henry Woodville
Smith . . . . Charles Peck
Mabel . . . . Maisie Stather
Lord Romney . . . . E. Scrope Quinton
Horrocks . . . . Helier Le Maistre
Mme Soufflet . . . . Madge Merry
Edith Ponsonby . . . . Gladys Ward

0269 **A FATHER OF 90** a musical comedy in three acts by Wal Pink and Herbert Darnley. Music by Herbert Darnley. Produced at the Eden Theatre, Brighton 29 September, 1902 and toured through ?, Leeds, Bradford, Liverpool, Glasgow x2, Newcastle, Gateshead, Elephant & Castle, to 6 December.

Lord Bob Gillon/The Hon. Jon . . . . . Herbert Darnley
Rhames . . . . Albert Darnley
Earl of Winterby . . . . Thomas Kennard
Maggie McKie . . . . Bertie Ross
Mrs Pepperano . . . . Kathleen Gerard
Lady Barbara . . . . Elsa Brethingham
Don Pharzo . . . . E. Purser
Mrs Thomas Mifkin . . . . Violet Temple
Martin . . . . Cissie Dawes
Russell White . . . . J. T. Tees
Jabez Dedder . . . . George Thompson
Captain Cosmos . . . . William Jordon
Junoli . . . . Harry Mellor
Ghazi . . . . E. Johnston
Alinoz . . . . B. Clark
Paulas . . . . Fred Wilson
Hiram . . . . J. Gardner
Martha . . . . Daisy Weston
Hester . . . . Maud Nowlam
Marcy . . . . Gertrude Cecil
Nancy . . . . Doris Dickens
Marjorie . . . . Louie Mavis
Alphonse . . . . Arthur Behan

0270 **THE GIRL FROM KAYS** a musical play in 3 acts by Owen Hall, said to be based on *La Mariée Recalcitrante* by Gandillot. Lyrics by Adrian Ross and Claude Aveling. Music by Ivan Caryll and Cecil Cook. Additional numbers by Paul Rubens, Lionel Monckton, Howard Talbot, Bernard Rolt, Edward Jones, Meyer Lutz, Kitty Ashmead, Charles H. Tayor and A. D. Cammeyer. Produced at the Apollo Theatre under the management of George Edwardes 15 November, 1902. Transferred to the Comedy Theatre 14 December, 1903. Closed 23 January, 1904 after a run of 432 performances.

Norah Chalmers. . . . . Kate Cutler (Ruth Lincoln)
Ellen. Letty Lind/Carrie Moore (Edith Neville)
Mrs Chalmers . . . . Marie Illington/Lottie Venne/Sybil Grey

Nancy Lowley. . . . . Ella Snyder/Marion Winchester
Hilda French . . . . Miss Graham/Delia Beresford/N. Lincoln/ Marie Billing/Joan Keddie
Mary Methuen . . . . Kitty Gordon/Cecil Engleheart/Maude Darrell
Mabel McDonald/White . . . . Nellie Souray/Madge Temple/Annie Vivian/Lucille Graham
Ella Winton/Wyly. . . . . Vashti Earle/Hilda Jeffreys
Maud Ebor/Racine . . . . Evelyn Corri/Hilda Jeffreys/Edith Neville
Gertrude Sarum/Hildesley . . . . Rosie Chadwick/Edith Wakefield/May Blaney/Jessie Broughton
Olive Manton/Whitney . . . . Edith Neville/Vashti Earle
Joan Ely/Mayen. . . . . Irene Allen/Ruth Saville/Marie Dupuis
Rhoda Cantuar/Leslie. . . . . Delia Beresford/Jessie Broughton/Eileen Douglas
Jane . . . . Kitty Ashmead/Lydia Flopp/Kate Leigh
Winnie Harborough. . . . . Ethel Irving/Millie Legarde
Harry Gordon. . . . . W. Louis Bradfield/Robert Michaelis
Theodore Quench QC. . . . . William Cheesman
Hon Percy Fitzthistle. . . . . Aubrey Fitzgerald
Mr Chalmers . . . . E. W. Garden/Lytton Grey
Joseph. . . . . Fred Emney/William Wyes/Helier Le Maistre
Pepper. . . . . Master Bottomley/Fred Payne
Archie Pembridge. . . . . Jack Thompson
Frank . . . . Ernest Lambart/Richard Kavanagh
Waiter. . . . . William Payne
Cora Paget . . . . Georgie Read/Annie Vivian
Clara Buller. . . . . Florence Nielson
Scavvin . . . . E. Fence
Max Hoggenheimer. . . . . Willie Edouin
add Marie Butler . . . . Susie Vining

Md: Edward Jones; ch: Willie Warde; sc: Joseph Harker & W. B. Spong; cos: Wilhelm

Produced at the Herald Square Theatre, New York, under the management of Charles Frohman and George Edwardes 2 November, 1903 for a run of 205 performances.
Kathryn Hutchinson/Grace Freeman (NORAH), Grace Dudley (ELLEN), Carrie Lee Stoyle/Maude Granger (MRS), Mary Nash/Marie Doro (NANCY), Mae Gilman/Harriet Burt/Elsie Barry (HILDA), Teddie Ducoe/Leonore Harris (MARY), Francis Duff/Vera Cameron (MABEL), Laura Baird/Margaret Malcolm (ELLA), Sylvia Beecher/Olive Ullrich (MAUD), Helen Walton/Lillian Seville/Carrie Thompson (GERT), Louis MacNamara/Belva von Kersley/Lillie Heckler (OL), Pearl Ben Yusef/Mabel Clarke/May Reinheimer (JOAN), Marie Kellar/Teddie Ducoe (RH), Lulu Le Sage/Blanche Wood (JANE), Hattie Williams (WINNIE), George Howard/Harry Davenport (HG), Arthur Elliott/Homer Granville (QU), Ernest Lambart (PERCY), George R. Sprague (CH), George Honey/Winchel Smith (JO), Frank McCullough/Ernie Heusel, Joseph J. Horowitz (PEP), Maurice Lavigne (ARCH), Paul Decker (FR), Blanche Brooks/Carrie Thompson/Sadie Peters (CORA), Carrie Thompson/Blanche Brooks/Elsie Ferguson (CLARA), Sam Bernard (MAX). Md: Maurice Levi; sc: Unit & Emens and Ernest Gros; cos: Mrs Robert Osborn

Produced at Herald Square Theatre, New York, 18 August, 1904 for 18 performances closing 3 September, 1904.

A revised version of *The Girl From Kays* was produced as *The Belle of Bond Street* at the Shubert Theatre, New York and the Adelphi Theatre, London in 1914.

0271 **THE WATER BABIES** a musical play adapted by Rutland Barrington from the book by Charles Kingsley. Music by Frederick Rosse. Additional music by Alfred Cellier and Albert Fox. Produced at the Garrick Theatre under the management of Arthur Bourchier 18 December, 1902 for a season of 100 performances ending 28 February, 1903.

Tom . . . . Nellie Bowman
Dame . . . . Edith Miller
Nurse . . . . Kate Bishop
Mother Carey . . . . Freda Bramleigh
Ellie . . . . Norah Moir
Sir John Harthover . . . . Ian Maclaren
Grimes . . . . Webb Darleigh
Frozen Sailor . . . . Michael Santley
Blunderbuss . . . . Thomas Crook
Six . . . . Fred Neeri
Trucheons . . . . Messrs Atkins, Webster, Evans, Moss, Santley
Queen of the Fairies (
Mrs Doasyouwouldbedoneby (Marion Draughn
Mrs Bedonebyasyoudid (
Otter . . . . 'Walter Hunte'
Lobster . . . . Edward Rigby
Napoleon the Poodle . . . . Master Fickin
Beauty the Pug . . . . Master Restall
Rough the Terrier . . . . Master Taylor
Water Babies . . . . Mary Collette, Madge Titheradge, Elsie Skillin
Fairies . . . . Florence Hersee, Moira Hersee, M. Bright Morris

pd: Madge Titheradge
with Misses L. Deane, Johnson, Wartenburgh, Scott, Raven, Makeham, Weyman, Rosaire, Batchelor; Masters Green, Bemrose, Scholler, Abbott, Kelly. Prologue sung by Constance Courtenay.

Md: Frederick Rosse; ch: Fred Farren; sc: E. G. Banks; cos: Robert Crafter &c.

Produced at the Garrick Theatre 22 December, 1903. Withdrawn 20 January, 1904.

NANA a musical stage society play by Brian Daly. Music by Herbert Simpson, John Crook and Henry May. Produced at the Grand Theatre, Birmingham under the management of C. W. Somerset 5 May, 1902.
Cast included Frank H. Celli, Wilfred Shine and Mlle Mars.

THE DRESSMAKER a musical adaptation of *Coralie et Cie* by Adeline Votieri. Lyrics by Richard Elton. Music by Denham Harrison. Produced at the Grand Theatre, Islington, under the management of James Tate 7 April, 1902.
Cast included Lottie Collins.

A GENTLEMAN OF THE ROAD an operetta in one act by Eleanor and Herbert Farjeon. Produced at a matinée at St George's Hall 22 July, 1902.

1903

In spite of the fact that three of the principal musical theatres held their previous year's shows right through 1903, the year saw the production of a large batch of new shows. *A Chinese Honeymoon* was now a fixture at the Strand, *A Country Girl* was prospering at Daly's and the Apollo had *The Girl from Kays* firmly entrenched for the full twelve months; but it was not long before replacements were needed for *Merrie England* at the Savoy, where William Greet was now back in control, and for *Three Little Maids* at the Prince of Wales.

Merrie England was followed by another work from the pair who looked like becoming the new Gilbert and Sullivan of the British musical, Basil Hood and Edward German. Their latest show was a return to fairy realms although, on this occasion, Hood concentrated more on the mortals in whose lives the fairies enjoy interfering and in Shakespeare's comedian, Puck.

A Princess of Kensington was set in Kensington Gardens where there is immortal trouble brewing. The Fairy Prince, Azuriel, has been suffering from jealousy for a thousand years over the love shared by the lovely fairy Kenna and the mortal Prince Albion. Although Albion is well and truly dead, the mischievous Puck has cosseted Azuriel's jealousy through the centuries and one day the latter determines that he shall see Albion safely married off to a maiden of his own kind – that very day. To calm the angry fairy, Puck and Kenna have to produce a false wedding. For their false Albion they light on one William Jelf, a sailor from the H.M.S. Albion, and to provide a bride Puck disguises himself as Sir James Jellicoe, revokes his acceptance of the young Lieutenant Brook Green as a husband for his daughter Joy, and hands her over to Jelf for the necessary nuptials. Complications ensue with the arrival on the scene of Mr Reddish and his daughter, Nell, to whom Jelf is actually engaged. Reddish is anxious to get Nell off his hands as she is a 'reformer' and has turned his pub into a coffee house, to the disgust of his cronies. Neither of them is any more pleased than the other mortals at the turn events have taken. Further complications ensue before Azuriel is finally convinced that Albion is no longer a threat and the fairies can return to fairyland, Joy to her lieutenant and Nell to the side of one of her father's friends who, she decides, needs the benefits of her reforming zeal. William Jelf goes back to sea, a highly relieved bachelor.

Hood's previous Savoy ventures *The Rose of Persia*, *The Emerald Isle* and *Merrie England* had all had picturesque settings, but with *A Princess of Kensington* he was, in spite of the fairies, returning to the here and now which he had handled so well in *The French Maid* and *Dandy Dan*. But in neither of these earlier pieces had he attempted to inject very much plot amongst the bevy of jolly characters. In contrast here, he invented a series of complications for his players that was little less than bewildering as people –

or, rather, fairies–took on each other's forms or appearances to entangle matters further and further. Nevertheless, he kept up the bright and bantering dialogue for which he was now celebrated and which *The Times* described as 'genuine fun and liveliness that is not quite wit and not quite humour, but something by itself', and provided a set of lyrics that were almost more Hood than Hood. *The Stage* found the construction of the piece unwieldy:

> . . the leading idea is so good it is a pity Captain Basil Hood encumbered it with so much superfluous incident . . [there is] too much story for two acts . . everything seems to have been sacrificed to the oddities of Puck . .

but agreed that

> . . against the spasmodic and jerky action must be set the exceedingly humorous dialogue and neat lyrics . . . were the dramatic construction as satisfactory as the dialogue, the book of *A Princess of Kensington* would rank among the best ever written for the Savoy. .

Indeed, some of the lyrics were very attractive. A pretty tenor ballad for Lt Brook Green saw Hood at his most poetic:

> My heart a ship at anchor lies
> Upon the azure of thine eyes
> Whose rippling glances come and go
> To toss my heart from weal to woe;
> Oh! if one tear would rise for me
> 'Twould be a pearl from that fair sea!
> And such a jewel I would prize
> Beyond the hope of Paradise.
> Then drive my heart all tempest-tossed
> On that dark shore where souls are lost
> But grudge me not that merchandise
> One little tear from thy sweet eyes.
> Yet if my heart lie broken there
> Wrecked by the maelstrom of despair
> The favouring zephyr of thy sighs
> May drive it back where haven lies

while a jolly trio 'Love in a Cottage' had Puck describing the 'joys' of poverty to Green and Joy in a fashion by *French Maid* out of Savoy:

> But you'll have to cook your dinners yourself
> Do you know what that will mean?
> It will mean that you will find that you somehow fail
> With the soup, which you meant to be thick ox-tail
> For it comes out thin and extremely pale
> And you give the potatoes a hopeless prod
> But they won't get soft; and the fish, a cod
> May taste very nice, but it looks so odd
> As (being a slippery sort of fish)
> It fell on the fender off the dish
> Not quite what a first-rate cook would wish.
> And it's boiled too little or boiled too long
> (You're not sure which, but there's something wrong)
> And the joint has acquired the usual sin
> Of a burnt outside and a raw within

And as for the pudding, you're free from doubt
How that will turn out: for it won't turn out
Or your fingers fumble the steaming string
And when you undo it, the cloth will cling
And the pudding appears like a shapeless mass
That's been out in the rain all night in the grass

There were other reminiscences of the earlier Savoy, such as a ballad 'The Cloud and the Mountain' which bore a strong family resemblance to 'The Magnet and the Churn' (*Patience*), but there were also plentiful echoes of musical comedy and a particularly large dose of patriotic songs. The quality of the work was not altogether even. In a song for Joy, 'He Was a simple Sailor Man', Hood stretched his felicity for word play into contortions worthy of the most agile of the mid-nineteenth century burlesque writers with such passages as:

Give me a lock of hair, he cried,
Choose what you will, said she
She knew he could not pick that lock
While she stood on the quay

but the larger part of the words of *A Princess of Kensington* was in the best Hood style.

German had done his part of the work well. His concerted pieces – the finales, an excellent sextet, the bridal music (which *The Times* considered to possess 'a breadth of theme that has scarcely been observed on this stage since the days of the Greek chorus in *The Grand Duke*'), and the opening fairy music for soprano (Peaseblossom) and chorus – all found him at his finest level. If the music lacked some of the rumbustiousness of the *Merrie England* score, that was largely due to the choice of subject. The solos, too, produced some good pieces of which the best was probably the tenor ballad, but none of them stood out or survived as their predecessors from *Merrie England* had. One piece, however, did and lived on with the best of the songs from the Savoy canon: a male voice quartet for Jelf (Henry Lytton) and his three companions (Charles Childerstone, Rudolph Lewis and Powis Pinder). *The Times* picked it out for attention while noting:

. . the tune is obviously based on a well-known Welsh ballad, while there is a strong suggestion of 'Widdicombe Fair' in its structure.

'Four Jolly Sailormen' was soon the equal in popularity of both the 'well-known ballad' and 'Widdicombe Fair'.

We're four jolly sailormen come up from the sea
There's Bill Blake, Will Weatherley, Jem Johnson and me . .'

A Princess of Kensington gave plenty of chances to the leading lights of the Savoy company. Walter Passmore, in particular, had a true starring role as Puck, but both Lytton as the put-upon sailor and Robert Evett as the cut-out lieutenant also had excellent roles, and M. R. Morand had some very funny moments as the policeman whose body is taken over by Azuriel. Louie Pounds made a sweet Joy Jellicoe and Rosina Brandram, in what was to be her last role at the Savoy, was cast as the bossy Nell. German supplied some demanding music for his three sopranos: the new prima donna, Agnes Fraser, as Kenna; Constance Drever as Peaseblossom; and Olive Rae as Titania. But prior to the opening Miss Fraser fell ill and Constance Drever, her understudy, was sent on to play the leading soprano part which she did with enormous success, particularly in view of the fact that *A Princess of Kensington* was her first appearance on any stage. When Miss Fraser returned, Miss Drever went back to the smaller role.

A Princess of Kensington was well received by the hard core Savoyards but its appeal was limited by its curious and complicated second act and its essentially highbrow flavour. It stayed at the Savoy for four months before Greet decided to remove it and, as with *Merrie England*, he took *A Princess of Kensington* on the road with its original cast. But it did not prove nearly as popular as its predecessor and part way through the tour *Merrie England* was added to the company's repertoire.

Greet gave up his lease on the Savoy and Mrs D'Oyly Carte set about refurbishing the theatre prior to seeking a new lessee. The Savoy remained dark for nine months and when it re-opened it was no longer as the home of British comic opera. With *A Princess of Kensington* that tradition came to an end. The company which Greet had taken over from D'Oyly Carte stayed with him through the tour until he brought them back to town in *The Earl and the Girl*, an unashamedly modern piece which had little in common with the works to which they had become accustomed over the years. *A Princess of Kensington* made its way to Broadway where it was produced in August of the same year with James T. Powers featured as Jelf. Several members of the British cast appeared again in the American version but the presentation was not particularly successful.

Like *Merrie England* and *The Emerald Isle*, *A Princess of Kensington* remained popular with musical groups and amateurs through the medium of its eminently singable music, and a specially published concert edition allowed the songs to be displayed shorn of some of the excess of the plot. Unfortunately, it was the swansong of the Hood/German collaboration from which so much had been expected. With the demise of the Savoy dynasty, the two who had almost succeeded in keeping it alive parted ways, each to gain further fame with other partners in very different careers.

The relative lack of success of *A Princess of Kensington* cannot be blamed merely upon public indifference to a piece which relied mainly on the light or comic opera strain for its tone and its music, for the Savoy show was followed in by another piece which also had strong leanings towards the more scholarly forms that had fallen largely into disuse. *My Lady Molly* was Sidney Jones' most seriously written piece to date, and it had been enormously successful in the provinces since its original production in Brighton in August of the previous year. Frederick Mouillot, who had taken the piece up, took a lease on Terry's Theatre which had not housed a musical success since *The French Maid* in 1896, and transferred the show in with the majority of its touring cast headed by Sybil Arundale in the title role.

The show's provincial success had already led to its being taken up by overseas managements and on 14 March, 1903, *My Lady Molly* not only made its début in London's West End but also opened a South African engagement in Johannesburg with the Gaiety's lovely Katie Seymour in the lead. Both Miss Seymour, who was prima donna of the Mouillot touring company, and *My Lady Molly* made an immense hit in South Africa, but the London production did even better. It received a rapturous reception on its opening night and the critics were delighted. *The Times* considered the authors had been far too modest: *My Lady Molly*, it thought, should have been boldly called a 'comic opera' 'with *Dorothy* and *La Fille de Madame Angot* and the operas of the Savoy'. The fact that *Dorothy*, like *My Lady Molly*, had been described as 'comedy opera' seems to have escaped the reviewer's notice, but the notion was clear enough. Jessop and Jones had produced a piece of a kind and quality for which the critics of the dramatic papers had sighed for nearly a decade: a genre which they insisted upon calling 'genuine comic opera'. George Edwardes had insisted that there was a returning market for it; the journalists who regarded the Gaiety musical, most unfairly, as a rather degenerate younger step-cousin, had continually called for its renaissance; and *My Lady Molly* proved that there was indeed a market for it if authors could hit the right note.

The story of *My Lady Molly* was entrenched in the tradition of the British comedy opera. Sir Miles Coverdale has arranged for his daughter, Alice, to wed Captain Harry Romney in spite of the fact that Alice has a favoured lover of her own choice. But when Harry is on his way to meet his future wife he quarrels with his manservant, Mickey, and Mickey stalks off taking with him his ex-master's bag containing clothes and papers. At the inn at Coverdale he meets Lady Molly Martingale who, in past years, has turned down marriage offers from Romney a dozen times. Now, hearing the news of his impending marriage, she realises that she would like him to ask a thirteenth time. Mickey and Molly form a conspiracy, and Molly dresses up in Romney's clothes and presents herself to the Coverdales in his place. When the real Harry turns up he is treated as an impostor and a highwayman. Alice realises that her 'fiancé' is a woman in disguise and when Molly reveals the motives for her subterfuge Alice is glad to join the plot. After many a complication, including a duel between the real and the false Harrys, the logical happy ending is reached. The plot was conventional, to say the least, and had obvious parentage in *Erminie* and *Dorothy*, but Jessop's skill in simple and straightforward dialogue and in keeping a strong and unencumbered plotline going forward once again earned him widespread praise. *The Times*, which gave the whole show an outstanding notice, pointed particularly to Jessop's contribution:

> . . Mr G. H. Jessop has provided not merely a peg to hang 'numbers' on, but a real plot and a neat one, and his pretty little intrigue, if not actually the main business of the evening, is closely followed throughout. To put it plainly, while most entertainments of the kind suggest that the book was written to fit the music and the lyrics, *My Lady Molly* – with the exception of a feeble ending to the first act – suggests that the music and lyrics . . . were written to fit the book. The result is a single and charming whole, not a piece of patchwork . . . [there is] nothing perhaps . . that is marked by noticeable originality, but it is all very neatly put and straight to the point; and if there are no witty things that compel quotation, the dialogue is full of humour.

Jessop's style was as far as could be from the incisive one-liners and satirical moues favoured by Owen Hall and his kind, just as *My Lady Molly* was as far from the Gaiety style as it was from the arch and educated wit of the Savoy. If such a style did not have a universal appeal, there were still plenty of people who agreed with *The Times* critic:

> If there is still a taste in town for genuine and really excellent comic opera, there is *My Lady Molly* to satisfy it.

On the musical side, Sidney Jones succeeded in turning his hand from the style he had developed so brilliantly at Daly's to one more in keeping with the character of the libretto with which he had been provided, and he too received the accolade of *The Times*:

> Mr Jones' music is all that such music should be – and a little more. It is bright without cheapness, tuneful without trickery, never merely catchy and exceptionally well orchestrated. It has the true dramatic quality . . .

The musical pieces were well integrated into the story and only the incidental sub-plot of a flirtation between Mickey O'Dowd and the French governess Mlle Mirabeau produced anything like a standard 'lift out' number. None of the songs was to gain particular popularity as a single but there were a number of very attractive pieces in the score. Perhaps not unexpectedly, given the author's origins, the best numbers seemed to be those written for the Irish manservant. His first act solo 'Ballinasloe' proved one of the show's comic high points:

> Ye sarve a man for sivin years and follow him about
> One day ye take too many beers an' then 'Ye're drunk, get out!'
> Ye dress yer Captain up for mess and mix his stingo bowl
> Tell lies for him ye can't confess, enough to lose yer soul
> Ye shut the dure upon the duns and let the ladies in
> Ye know which knocks more times than once, an' that's a deadly sin
> Ye pick him up when he's upset, advise him when in doubt
> An' some fine day, here's what ye get: 'Ye're drunk me man, get out'
> Och, me father was born in Ballinasloe, an' me mother was one of the Sheridans
> An' this was the lesson they taught me to know
> That sarvice is not an inheritance.

Another of Mickey's numbers, 'Don't Whistle so Loud' was also a favourite:

> There's times when the world is a beautiful place
> Wid never an ache or a trouble
> I'd swagger along wid a smile on me face
> An' me two cheeks as round as a bubble.
> But just when I'm dressed in me Sunday clothes
> There's something comes or there's something goes
> An' clane out o' joint goes me noble nose
> An' I feel that me years is double.
> An' that is the moment the divil appears
> An' whispers his divilment into me ears
> Don't whistle so loud, get away from the crowd,
> Ye've nothin' to boast about, Mickey O'Dowd'

There was also no lack of charming songs and sentimental ballads in *My Lady Molly*, nor of strong and deeply scored ensembles and concerted pieces. Lady Molly had a delightful song 'Oh, I'll Greet him soft and low' and Alice a quaint and pointed ballad detailing the adventures of a 'Merry mediaeval Maid' who was locked in her room on bread and water by a preventive father, but escaped:

> But her gallant lover was ever true
> And to him her faith was pinned, oh
> So one night she climbed down a rope he threw
> To her second story window

There were many opportunities for vigorous singing from the male members of the cast as well, but all in all the impression left by the score was, as with the libretto, of a well-made and integrated whole without particularly pointed or commercial parts.

My Lady Molly turned out to be the greatest 'comedy opera' success of many years. It ran for almost twelve months, until Mouillot's lease on Terry's expired. Towards the end of the run the demand for tickets was still sufficiently high for the management to lay on four matinées a week but there was no question of a transfer and, after 342 performances, the London season closed. Its success in England continued when it was toured again the following year, and the South African production was followed by an equally well-received Australian one starring Florence Young as Molly and George Lauri as O'Dowd.

Early in 1904, *My Lady Molly* appeared on Broadway. She had suffered a little on the crossing and also in the casting, for Jessop's gentle eighteenth-century maid was played by the variety star Vesta Tilley[1] whose principal qualification for the role seemed to be her experience in appearing in male attire. Into Jones' neatly self-contained score she interpolated her own material, singing about 'The Seaside Sultan' and 'Algy' who had absolutely nothing to do with either the eighteenth century or Lady Molly Martingale. Her performance, however illogical, appealed to America and her notices were stunning; not so those for the piece, or what remained of it, and *My Lady Molly* U.S.A. version survived a sadly short time.

Sidney Jones' career had been one of uninterrupted success and *My Lady Molly* proved that he could heighten his style most adeptly, but in the season's next offering he tried a variation in another direction. *The Medal and the Maid* had a book by Owen Hall and lyrics by the suddenly ubiquitous Charles H. Taylor. Jones had worked with Hall many times previously on the Daly's series, *An Artist's Model*, *A Greek Slave*, *A Gaiety Girl* and *The Geisha*, but *The Medal and the Maid* was intended for the Lyric Theatre and, although it retained a certain amount of the flavour of the Daly's hits, it was designed much more in the line of the lighter and more frivolous works which had gained popularity at the Gaiety and the Lyric – an area into which Jones had not previously ventured.

The story was not one of Owen Hall's more fortunate inventions. As the tale unwound it seemed that scarcely anyone was who they were pretending to be. The two heroines of the piece, Josephine the flowergirl and Merva the heiress, have exchanged clothes and the identifying medal of the title. Josephine has gone to school in Merva's clothes, while Merva finds herself pursued by the police for having stabbed a man. The school in question is run by one Miss Ventnor who has secured as 'stars' for her prize-giving ceremony the 'aristocratic' Mrs Habbicombe (actually a well-off second-hand clothes dealer) and her low friend Pentweazle who masquerades as a gentleman of letters. Lovers and lawyers pursue the two girls and, for some reason, everyone turns up on a mythical island, gets captured by brigands and then, as even *Play Pictorial* was bound to admit in its advertising review: 'we cannot pretend to unravel the rest of the story. It unwinds from a tangle into a tangle . . ' though apparently all ends happily.

The harum-scarum plot served, in fact, merely to tack together some attractive and/or funny scenes. The most successful of these was the depiction of Miss Ventnor's academy where her pupils were introduced:

> Now Gladys there is devoted to Poetry. She is going to write all the songs for the next dog show. Sarah Sevenoaks there is of the parsimonious, saving disposition: she wouldn't even contribute to my last bi-annual birthday present: she will marry a City millionaire, see if she doesn't. And then there is Maudie. When she was quite a baby she had a box of toy soldiers, and always broke the officers. She's destined to become a Gaiety girl . .

and Miss Ventnor explained her school's curriculum:

> Well, first, instead of reading books
> A girl is made to pass

[1] Ethel Levey played the role in the American première in Boston but was superseded for Broadway.

A course of fascinating looks
Before a looking glass . .

She learns here how to neatly bait
Her matrimonial hook
To play at bridge, to speculate
And how to make a book . .

We teach her dodges to renew
Her beauty or a bill
And how to drive a motor through
Good form without a spill.
In fact, that in society
Some one she may become
That is the end and aim you see
Of my curriculum.

The pupils of the academy have a particular reward for accomplishment – an extra frill on their petticoats:

The ten-frill girl is our show girl when titled parents call
The nine sees bachelor guardians and has a Girton drawl
The eight plays classical music to serious families
The seven and six talk church work to reverend dignities
We thus descend to the girl with one, and I think that's all, but stop!
We've a no-frill girl whose dear Papa is an Archbishop.

The annual prize giving is conducted by Pentweazle in the same vein:

To Miss Ilma Malden, for the composition of the best dinner menu for two persons served in a private room in the merry month of May . . Bacon's Moral Essays

while he muses on the commendable things in life in 'She Ought to get a Prize for That'.

The lengthy school episode was, however, more like a sketch and, in fact, the whole show had very much the feeling of a variety entertainment. Little Daisy Jerome from the U.S.A., who had already had experience of the variety stage including a recent appearance at London's Palace, sang a neat little number called 'Katie Had a Kodak' which she put across with practised point:

Katie had a suitor
Gushing as could be
Everything he said to her
Excepting 'Marry me',
Katie thought it useful
Before she cooked her hare
To catch him with her Kodak
Well – somewhat unaware.

Click! went the Kodak
That young man she took
While he kissed her fondly
In a shady nook
Placed it nice and handy, then,
Leaning on his chest,
Katie kicked the button
And the Kodak did the rest!

Comedian James E. Sullivan played the school music teacher and sang a couple of songs including a burlesque of the 'Vanderdecken' story, while the much loved 'Telephone Girl' of a few years back, Ada Blanche, returned to the West End with a George Rollitt song tinged with risqué in which she averred 'The Lady wasn't Taking any Fruit'. The variety element was tempered by some rather more substantial music. As Merva and Josephine, the soprano Ruth Vincent and the French dramatic mezzo Sylvia Sablanc joined in a florid 3/4 duet 'Come, kind Gentlemen' and both ladies were well endowed the solos. Miss Vincent had two melodies, 'Free' and 'If Girls had Wings' and Mlle Sablanc sang a flower song and a Mignon-esque ballad 'Home of my Childhood'. The 'straight' men, too, had their vocal moments, particularly the baritone, Norman Salmond, who played the brigand chief with a rousing number 'The philosophic Brigand', but another singer who was later to find renown, Frederick Ranalow, had nothing to sing except a Paul Rubens/Sidney Jones duet which found Rubens at his most coyly suggestive and tiresome. After passing by a young man with disdain when meeting him in public, a girl meets him again in a quiet lane:

> He said to her, 'Sweet maiden, may I snatch but one short kiss'.
> She said to him 'What is that, sir? I'm a simple country miss'
> The consequence was he showed her, and not one word said she
> And the world said nothing at all, because the world didn't happen to see'.

But even in such an accomplished cast the show had only one star, for the part of Miss Ventnor was taken by Ada Reeve. Ada had the best numbers and she worked them with a vengeance, but on the very first night of the show disaster struck. A freshly painted dressing room affected Ada's throat and by the end of the evening she was voiceless. On the second night Daisy Jerome had to go on for her, reading from the script. She got by but the show, which needed every bit of strength it could get, was not helped. Mediocre notices hadn't helped either. They had expressed general frustration with the plot, and while there was praise for the staging and for some individual performances they were scarcely ticket-selling reviews.

It was decided that the comic content needed increasing and Mlle Sablanc's 'Home of my Childhood' was jettisoned along with a good deal of the 'story' and much of the romantic 'business'; but then, as if things were not difficult enough already, Ada Reeve decided to leave the leaky ship to go into management in her own account. *The Medal and the Maid* was taken off and given a major overhaul. The original score of 29 numbers was reduced further, particularly the serious music. Even 'The philosophic Brigand' went and Salmond's role, one way and another, was cut to an unrecognisable wisp. Ada Blanche was promoted to the role of Miss Ventnor and veteran comic opera star Lizzie St Quinten came in to fill the gap. James Sullivan, who had failed to make anything out of the unimpressive role of the music master, had abandoned his role to Robb Harwood. Now producer Davis engaged Ells Dagnall who had scored so well for him in *The Silver Slipper* in the hope that he could lift the comic side of the show. The revised version opened three weeks later and it was immediately evident that the problems of the piece had not been solved. *The Medal and the Maid* lasted only four further weeks before Davis threw in his hand.

The show had been a salutory example of how a musical built, in theory, to a winning formula by the best hands in the business could still fail. Hall had gone too far in his casual and eclectic construction:

> To take an hour and a half in expounding a plot which, in the end of the piece is destined to be completely disregarded would not appear to be a sound principle of dramatic construction . . . philosophical spectators will be thankful that that the

> various quite uninteresting threads of such a plot as that of *The Medal and the Maid* are not thoroughly followed out since the process would spin out the piece to the crack of doom . . (*Times*)

and Jones had proven quite clearly that his talent lay much more certainly in the direction of such works as *My Lady Molly* and *The Geisha*. The same critic who had showered praise on those works could only comment sourly of the *Medal and the Maid* score:

> [Jones'] knack of turning out catchy tunes of no special merit has seldom been better illustrated . . . the necessity of writing down to the level of his public has been too strong . .

That there was music of value in the show is undoubted – the soprano/mezzo waltz duet is a most attractive piece – but the varying range of styles used showed up the weaknesses in the armour of both composer and librettist. *The Medal and the Maid* was a misfire.

Davis persisted with the piece on the touring circuits in spite of its London failure, and an optimistic Broadway production was staged in January 1904, just a few days after the opening of *My Lady Molly* in New York. It caused some slight interest, largely due to the interpolation of the 'Simian Love Song', 'In Zanzibar', sung by Emma Carus to the accompaniment of six whistlers situated in the gallery and with the assistance of a dozen damsels in grey performing a Monkey Dance. But even this artistic creation proved insufficient to sustain the show and it folded quite quickly. The final blow to the production budget came after the London closure. Teresa Terry Anderson, who had rated three frills in the line-up of Miss Ventnor's pupils, showed an acumen beyond that rating when she sued the management, claiming that an accident which she had suffered on the stage was due to the management's supplying her with ill-fitting shoes. In spite of the fact that it was almost certainly her own inept dancing which had been at fault, Miss Anderson won a sympathetic £125 and *The Medal and the Maid* dwindled even further into the red.

Charles Taylor, the lyricist of *The Medal and the Maid*, was also part of the team on the next and much more successful musical brought into the West End. *The School Girl* was Leslie Stuart's third musical, written to a text supplied by the veteran dramatist, Henry Hamilton (billed in thick type) and the Brighton-born American journalist and playwright Paul M. Potter (in thin type) the author of *The Conquerors* and the stage adaptor of *Under Two Flags* and *Trilby* making an unusual foray into the world of the musical.

Its framework was a little story about a convent lass who runs away from school to help prevent a girlfriend from having to marry an elderly knight instead of her artist lover. The intrepid child turns up in Paris, at the Open Stock Market, where she is mistaken for the new typist and finds herself privy to the secrets of a swindler who is floating a bogus mine. She uses her information to save her father, her friend's father and a bevy of American chorines from financial ruin before the action moves on to an Artists' Ball where the plot dissolves into a series of amatory goings-on which end in true love being triumphant.

The authors managed to strike a happy note with some lightly frivolous dialogue and a set of amusing characters. The heroine, Miss Lilian Leigh, being played by Edna May, had little need to be more than sweet and appealing but Hamilton and Potter produced three good comic roles to interlock around her: Sir Ormesby St Leger (George Huntley), the half-unwilling prospective bridegroom:

> I'm far too boyish to get married. I can't settle down. I should simply fret. I think that marriage is the first step to bigamy.

who goes round draped in a quintet of American chorus girls for whom he is inclined to do 'little favours'; General Marchmont (George Graves, in his first London role), the frolicsome father of the intended bride; and Tubby Bedford, another Englishman, out to make his fortune on the Paris stock market (James Blakely). Amongst the three of them they produced an enormous amount of fun whilst the young lovers (Marie Studholme and Reginald Somerville) fossicked for a clear path to their ultimate union.

Leslie Stuart provided an eclectic but successful score. In the opening scene, set in the convent, he provided an almost light operatic song, 'When I Was a Girl like You' for the wistfully nostalgic Mother Superior. In order that it should have its vocal due, Edwardes and Frohman lured back to the stage the former first lady of the musical stage, Violet Cameron, now 40 and not seen in a musical since the disaster of *Miami*. Her voice was now lower and broader in quality and she gave considerable weight to Stuart's charming song, helping to get the show off on the right foot. Edna May, performing what the *New York Sun* described as 'her great act–How to Sing without a Voice', put over 'The Daughters of the Guard' and lovely Marie Studholme with marginally more serviceable vocal equipment, sang of being 'The Honeymoon Girl'. The whole of the prologue was, due to its setting, written entirely for female voices but with the start of the Stock Exchange sequences the tone of the piece altered completely. From the delicate tones of the opening scene it moved into fast and furious action with the villainous Overend and his fake mine. The quintet of American girls performed a routine only slightly reminiscent of 'Tell me, pretty Maiden' and Huntley put over a fair piece about a telephone called 'Belinda on the Line', but the most successful songs were 'Looking for a Needle in a Haystack' in which Blakely described the adventures of a country lass whose aunt has advised her that trying to find a man who had never kissed a girl before was like &c., and Edna May advising her beaux to 'Call around Again' in a week or two if the flame of their ardour hasn't guttered out. But the show's hit came in the shape of a semi-coon song in the masquerade ball sequence when one of the American girls stepped out to sing catchily:

> Mamie, I've a little canoe
> Room for me, my Mamie, and you
> I'll paddle along and rock you in my cradle
> Mamie, you'll have nothing to do,
> And when I've told my worries to you
> Then we might canoodle, Mamie, we two

The young lady who sang 'My little Canoe' was making her first West End appearance after a couple of provincial pantomimes. She was 17 years old and her name was Billie Burke, destined for fame on both stage and screen on both sides of the Atlantic and marriage to the impresario Florenz Ziegfeld. With Leslie Stuart's little song that career began with a true hit.

The School Girl's combination of melody and fun proved an attractive one and the piece held the stage at the Prince of Wales through nearly twelve months and many cast changes. George Grossmith and Arthur Roberts both took a spell at the delightful role of Sir Ormesby although the latter, saddled with two other comics in good roles, took it to pieces and remade it to suit his own ego. In his reminiscences, Roberts claims that *The School Girl* was in bad financial straits when he joined the cast, and quotes a note left for him by his predecessor in the role:

> I hereby will and bequeath to Arthur Roberts an uncomfortable dressing room, some dirty grease paints and a part out of which I could never make anything. George Grossmith.

Roberts implies that the 'infusion of humour' which he introduced into the show, with the aid of George Graves, was the saving grace of *The School Girl.* There is no doubt that he altered the show, interpolating much of the ad lib foolery for which he was famous, plus an extraneous number 'Now They've Got into the London Way' (Bateman/M. Scott), his provincial leading lady, Ruby Celeste, and a whole burlesque section on Belasco and Long's play *The Darling of the Gods* currently playing Her Majesty's. This piece of nonsense was forced into the ball scene to allow Roberts to cavort around as a burlesque Jap and sing a specially written song 'Under the Beerbohm Tree'. Quite whether these 'improvements' were responsible for the show's survival or hastened its end is open to doubt, but *The School Girl* proved to be the last opportunity London would have to see Arthur Roberts as primo comico in a musical. At the age of 51 and after twenty years in the musical theatre he turned his attention to the halls where his undeniable if unruly talents were well suited and where he spent the largest part of his remaining career.

If George Grossmith had truly claimed he was unable to make anything out of the role of Sir Ormesby, he must have been stunned at the reaction in America to his performance as that whimsical knight. After the closure of *The School Girl* in London, a company was arranged to take the show to America. It was to be Edna May's triumphant return to the city and the theatre where she had begun life as a chorus girl, and the newspapers made much of the fact. She had not been seen in New York since the unimpressive *Girl from up There* but this time she was coming in an established show and the anticipation was high. Britain sent her some fine support: Grossmith, Fred Wright and James Blakely as the comic trio, Talleur Andrews and Mildred Baker (the original understudies) promoted to hero and Mother Superior, and a fine collection of 'girls' headed by Lulu Valli, Constance Hyem, and Jane – the 'other' Miss May.

After a pre-season in Boston's Colonial Theatre, *The School Girl* opened at the Casino and was received with a huge enthusiasm. But while there was a warm welcome home for their very own Edna May and a more than respectable regard for the dignified and beautiful English girls, it was the trio of comedians who stole the public's hearts and the reviews, and in particular George Grossmith. The American critics welcomed, too, the relatively civilised dramatic construction of *The School Girl* as a pleasant relief from the low-brow thrown-together efforts that too many of their native suppliers had been producing in recent months. The show was not the same as that which had opened in London nor as that which had closed in London. The wrecking perpetrated by Arthur Roberts had been made good but there were four Paul Rubens numbers which had not been there in the original all-Leslie Stuart score. As was Rubens' wont they ranged from the catchy and popular to the pretty awful – one of the most startling was a 'Japanese medley' which ended with a version of Auld Lang Syne. Howard Talbot, too, had contributed a song 'One of the Boys' with which Fred Wright made great play. Edna May's original three songs had grown to five en route for she had cannily appropriated 'My little Canoe' for herself in the American version and succeeded, as Billie Burke had done, in making it the song hit of the show. All the best elements of the London show, however, survived through a 120-performance run which fulfilled hopes and expectations.

The next two contributions to West End musical entertainment were both from America, and were of widely differing characteristics. The first was *In Dahomey*, the first all-negro musical, with lyrics by the esteemed poet Paul Dunbar and music by Will Marion Cook, a pupil of Dvořák. In America it had failed to attract, folding after 53 performances, but London enjoyed the unfamiliar antics of its lively leading men, Bert Williams and George Walker, and *In Dahomey* stayed at the Shaftesbury from mid-May through to Boxing Day.

Less fortunate was the Shubert brothers' production of *Dolly Varden* which had run well at New York's Herald Square Theatre (154 perfs) in 1901. It was the work of two expatriate Englishmen long settled in the United States, Julian Edwards and Stanislaus Stange. Both were exceptionally prolific if not highly talented, but *Dolly Varden* had proved one of their happier collaborations. It had very little to do with its professed heroine, being more of a mish-mash of several old English pieces including *The Country Girl*, and its lack of genuine wit or original plot and its unexceptional music ensured that London paid it little attention. Accusations of anti-Americanism were loudly levelled at all and sundry by producer Sam Shubert which, considering the actual nationality of the writers and the concurrent success of *In Dahomey*, made him look fairly silly.

The next home-grown contribution was not forthcoming until October when the withdrawal of *The Medal and the Maid* left the Lyric Theatre vacant. George Edwardes stepped in, where Tom Davis had failed, with what he called a 'romantic light opera'. After *A Princess of Kensington* and *My Lady Molly*, the West End was to be taken one step further towards that elusive genre so beloved of the critics and in which Edwardes clearly genuinely placed some hope for the future.

The new show was an adaptation by Henry Hamilton of the Madame Sans-Gêne story, and it took the unusual step of introducing a serious portrait of Napoléon Bonaparte (non-singing) to the musical stage. The musical portion of the show was the work of Ivan Caryll, returning to the style of his earliest days and *The Lily of Léoville* in a score which allowed of no collaborators or interpolations. *The Duchess of Dantzic* was a brave experiment on the part of the Edwardes management. It leaned closer to light opera than any recent work of substance, and its book included passages of straight drama which were more like grand opera libretto or even plain drama to set alongside Caryll's tuneful light operatic music.

The Times complained that the work did not stand up as an artistic whole, claiming that the first act was comic opera, the second 'began at the Gaiety and ended at the Lyceum', while the third was drama, pure and simple. *The Era*, on the other hand, while recognising the various elements, did not find them necessarily incongruous and remarked that it was 'a grand opera story set to light opera music and a very effective and agreeable mixture it is . .' Both were right. The mixture was a curious and unusual one. The show began with some buffoonish business, bad jokey lines and poor puns but rose to highly effective dramatic scenes in its later stages, and the whole was illustrated with some of Caryll's best and most pleasant music. The mixture could succeed brilliantly or fail dismally – it all depended on the public taste for such things. The first night public had no doubt as to its reaction. There were one or two faint boos from the highest echelons of the house, but the general reception was thoroughly positive and *The Duchess of Dantzic* was pronounced a success by acclaim. The critics, too, were largely pleased. In spite of its reservations about the libretto, *The Times* resumed: 'On the whole, the rules must go to the wall. *The Duchess of Dantzic* is amorphous but enjoyable . .' *The Stage* called it 'as brilliant and artistic a show as has been seen for some time' and *The Era* staunchly declared that it was 'good all round . . good in book, good in music, good in acting and singing and in mounting superb . .' But, most importantly, the public liked George Edwardes' newest concoction, and they patronised the Lyric Theatre for the eight months of the run of *The Duchess of Dantzic*.

The story of Madame Sans-Gêne was originally the work of French playwright Victorien Sardou. It had been first seen in Paris in 1893 and adapted for the English stage by Comyns Carr to play at the Lyceum in 1897, 1898 and again in 1901. Catherine 'Sans-Gêne' Upscher is a laundress in pre-Bonapartian Paris who marries an up-and-coming soldier. One of her clients is a poor lieutenant named Bonaparte who cannot pay his bill. Catherine takes in the child of an aristocrat who has been hounded and killed in the revolution, and she brings him up as her own child. In the second act Lefèbvre, the husband of 'Sans-Gêne', is seen to have risen to a high post in the new government but his wife is not welcomed at court because of her untutored manners. Napoléon, who is considering divorcing Josephine, decides to kill two birds with one stone: he will test the ground for his own divorce by getting rid of his friend's embarrassing wife. He orders Lefèbvre to divorce Catherine and to marry his Imperial ward, Renée de St Mezarde. Lefèbvre refuses, as does Renée who is in love with Catherine's foster-son, Adhémar. Adhémar, in his turn, speaks rashly of Napoléon's tyranny and finds himself condemned to death, but the Emperor agrees to pardon him if Lefèbvre and Catherine will consent to divorce. In the play's climactic scene, Catherine forces herself into the Imperial presence and reminds Napoléon of his early days, of his poverty and his idealism. She presents to him the unpaid laundry bills from the days when neither of them was anybody and he remembers the kindness of the laundress who offered him help and money when he was in need. The Emperor relents: Adhémar is pardoned and permitted to wed Renée, and Lefèbvre, now created the Duke of Dantzic, and his loving wife fall into each other's arms.

Hamilton was far more at home in the dramatic scenes than the frivolous ones, but he introduced humour into his story through the character of Papillon, a pedlar risen to be couturier to the Empress, and in the bitcheries of the parvenue sisters of Napoléon in their constant and unavailing attempts to put down the sharp-tongued Catherine. The nature of the piece did not make for a series of hit songs. Much of the score consisted of choruses and ensembles and each of the three acts included a finale, of which the first two were of some considerable scope. However, Lefèbvre's drinking song 'Wine of France' made an acceptable solo as did the patriotic song 'Noblesse Oblige'. In the second act, Adhémar had a vigorous love song with the waltz refrain 'Love and ever Love' and a pretty duet with Renée called 'The Legend Olden' and, on the lighter side, Papillon had a comical number 'The Milliner Monarch':

Then let the sex acclaim
Their arbiter serene
Who lends to blue and yellow too
And every hue a glamour new
Let fashion waft his fame
From Paris to Pekin
Who forms the taste and moulds the waist
Of the Empress Josephine

Hamilton was inclined to be florid and occasionally awkward in his unaccustomed role as lyricist, but he hit the right note with 'The Mirror Song' sung at the opening of the third act by the disconsolate Catherine, seated at her dressing table:

Mirror in thy glass we see
All the little life of man:

Childhood with unthinking glee
Crows to view itself in thee
Youth with happy hope aflush
Blithe beholds its bloom and blush;
Middle age must take thy mocks
Gathering lines and thinning locks,
Count with smiles that might be tears
All the havoc of the years,
Silvered age with wrinkled front
Needs must heed thy counsel blunt,
Lesson out of thee there looks
More than speaks from reverend books,
Thee to clay-cold lips we hold
All in vain, the tale is told
Mirror, mirror! Schooled by thee
Of what shadow stuff are we.
We, who o'er thy polished glass
Flit like phantoms in a dream
Sigh for poor humanity
Murmur, 'all is vanity'.

and combined with his composer perfectly in a superb sobbing trio 'A real good Cry'. There was no doubt that the music of *The Duchess of Dantzic* was appreciated. Caryll, who had been dismissed by many in recent times as a writer of tasty trifles for mass consumption, proved that his ability was in no way lessened: the composer of *The Lily of Léoville*, *Ma Mie Rosette* and *La Cigale* had been well-educated and was a writer of considerable light operatic talent, and *The Duchess of Dantzic* proved it:

> Ivan Caryll has never written pleasanter music . . (*Times*)

> Ivan Caryll's music too is excellent, bright, exhilarating, sometimes Offenbachian in its sparkle and entrain and with the concerted pieces and ensembles worked up with musicianly skill . . (*Stage*)

Much of the weight of the show fell on the shoulders of the actress playing the title-role, and the star chosen was not most obviously suited to the role.[1] Evie Greene's vocal ability was by no means in doubt but her acting talents seemed more suited to the saucy Nan of *A Country Girl* or, at best, to a Kitty Grey, than to the warm-blooded earthiness of Madame Sans-Gêne. But, if she did not turn out precisely to be a revelation, Miss Greene nevertheless made a more than satisfactory job of the role and was particularly appreciated in her strong scenes with Holbrook Blinn as Napoléon. Both Lefèbvre and Bethune were capably taken by vocalists Denis O'Sullivan and Lawrence Rea, but Clare Greet had to be brought in at the last moment to take over the role of the ladies' maid, Lisette, when Carrie Moore, for whom the role had been intended, had to be diverted to *The Girl from Kays, vice* Letty Lind. Since Miss Greet was an actress rather than a singer, Lisette's number 'Little Blanche Marie' was cut out and it later found its way into *The Orchid* at the Gaiety before finally returning to the score where it belonged. By its very nature, the show suffered little alteration during its comfortably successful run. A new song for Catherine in the least tightly constructed Act 2 ('My

[1] Hamilton and Caryll had written *The Duchess of Dantzic* as early as 1897 with Florence St John in mind. Ilka Palmay also claimed it was offered to her.

Sabots') and a number for pretty little Adrienne Augarde as Renée called 'Le petit Caporal' were the only additions.

The Duchess of Dantzic's metropolitan career was a good one and its provincial popularity proved, perhaps a little surprisingly, to be even greater. Evie Greene spent some time touring in the role which she had made particularly her own before heading Edwardes' English company to Daly's Theatre, New York, where she was again joined by Blinn, Rea and Adrienne Augarde with Lempriere Pringle as Lefebvre, for a three months' run and a highly successful tour which, nevertheless cost Edwardes a loss of some £10,000. Elsewhere, *The Duchess of Dantzic* also succeeded well, being taken through the usual English-speaking dates from Australia to the Orient without Evie Greene but with more than adequate results. In 1932 it made a brief return to London as part of Bannister Howard's Daly's Theatre season of revivals with Dorothy Ward and Frank Cellier in the lead roles, and in 1943 it was the subject of a major touring revival by Tom Arnold and Bernard Delfont starring Fay Compton, Kenneth Kent, Teddie St Denis, Charles Heslop and Reginald Gibbs. Edwardes had not been afraid to test his theories on the changing tastes of the public with regard to musical entertainments. Over the past couple of years *Kitty Grey*, *Three Little Maids* and, now, *The Duchess of Dantzic* had all varied considerably from what had been the solid norm of light musical productions. They had each, in their own way, been successes, but *A Country Girl* and *The Toreador* had proved that, while variety was a pleasant thing, the established genres as typified by the Edwardes' productions at the Gaiety and at Daly's were still the most popular favourites of all.

Only ten days after the opening of *The Duchess of Dantzic*, Edwardes had on his hands a very much more significant opening – that of the new Gaiety Theatre. It remained to be seen whether the atmosphere of the old and dearly loved Gaiety could be transferred to its successor down the road. Edwardes had done everything he could: the new theatre was as beautiful and as lavishly furnished as could be, and the link with the old house was emphasised by full-length panels in the crush bar depicting the great female stars of the old Gaiety – Nellie Farren, Letty Lind, Ellaline Terriss, Sylvia Grey, Kate Vaughan and, doubtless because of her elevation to the peerage, Connie Gilchrist, who had never taken a leading role on the stage. A further link was provided by the piece with which Edwardes opened the new theatre, for *The Orchid* was well and truly in the line of Gaiety musical comedies as his public had come to know and love them, and it brought them their favourite Gaiety stars – George Grossmith, Lionel Mackinder, Connie Ediss, Teddy Payne, Gertie Millar, Fred Wright and, of course, the girls headed by the gorgeous Olive May. By the end of that all-important evening, the new Gaiety had taken up where the old had left off. It was a wonderful success and so, almost incidentally, was *The Orchid*.

The new show had been prepared by the Gaiety team of Tanner, Ross, Greenbank, Monckton and Caryll, and set half in an English horticultural college and half in the sunny gaiety of Nice. The plot concerned the efforts of Aubrey Chesterton, British Minister of Commerce, and the explosive Count Raoul de Cassignat of the Quai d'Orsay to get their respective hands on a particularly rare orchid. Two of the flowers in question turn up; one brought back from the depths of Peru by Zaccary, a professional orchid hunter, and the other grown in the grounds of the Countess of Barwick's Horticultural College by its little gardener-in-chief, Meakin. After the destruction of his own flower, Zaccary gets hold of Meakin's bloom which, pursued by all, ends up decorating the hat of one Miss Twining (of a matrimonial turn). Also involved in the proceedings are two pairs of young lovers who have been quietly married in Paris but who, owing to the absent-mindedness of the registrar, have been certificated as paired off each with the wrong mate.

The libretto bounced along without too much serious reference to a connected plot, the orchid itself serving neatly to link up the various scenes and incidents. One of the most comical pieces was a duel scene in which the Count (Robert Nainby), all whiskers and smoking nostrils and backed by two extremely funny 'seconds', pitted himself against little Meakin for the possession of the famous flower. Since Meakin was played by Teddy Payne, the result was humorous in the extreme. Meakin's idea of combat clothes turned out to be an oversized suit of chain mail and his preferred weapon a sword so large he could scarcely lift it as he threw in a touch of *La Grande Duchesse*–'Voici le sabre de mon père!'–and prepared for battle.

There were other topical and burlesque elements, too. Harry Grattan as Chesterton came on dressed like Joseph Chamberlain, even to the eyeglass. When 'Chesterton' turned out to be a rather indiscreet fellow, fond of taking tea with pretty Gabrielle Ray ('Don't forget you promised to choose an evening dress for me') as his secretary, there were protests. Tanner replied naively:

> . . it is true that Mr Aubrey Chesterton sings songs and drinks tea in Bond Street with his pretty lady secretary but I don't know that that can be called undignified in a Cabinet Minister . .

In fact, the little secretary turned out to be one of the big attractions of *The Orchid.* 'Gabs' Ray had a tiny voice and limited acting ability, but she was a delightful dancer and her face and figure made her one of the most popular 'postcard girls' of all time. *The Orchid* was not her first appearance as she had been seen in *The Toreador* and *The Girl from Kays* quite recently, but now she had her own little role and, like Rosie Boote with 'Maisie', she made quite a mark. Her song and dance routine to Bernard Rolt's 'Rose-a-Rubie' enchanted the Gaiety, as, indeed, did the entire evening. Tanner had excelled himself. He had limited his book to just the degree of plot now expected by a Gaiety audience (and it seemed to be gradually shrinking) and the song-writers, without too much care as to what the book was about, had supplied a jolly selection of numbers with which to break up the comedy and the little bits of romance.

The brightest and most popular of these songs fell to Gertie Millar, the leading lady of the new Gaiety. She sang delicately of 'Little Mary':

> There's a certain little lady who's already known to fame
> As little Mary, as little Mary,
> Though she may not be romantic, yet it's such a pretty name
> Is little Mary, is little Mary.
> Now, I want you all to know her when I mention her again
> But exactly who she is, it isn't easy to explain,
> Let me merely say that baby often has a tiny pain
> In little Mary.
> Mary, Mary, dainty little Mary
> She's a fickle but a fascinating fairy
> So if baby boy should cry
> And you want to find out why
> Please enquire of little Mary.

Little Mary, of course, was not a person. She was a euphemism. A few weeks earlier, J. M. Barrie's 'uncomfortable play' *Little Mary* had opened at Wyndhams. The heroine's name signified 'stomach' or 'belly', words not mentioned in polite Edwardian circles, and the reaction to the play was mildy outraged, helping it no doubt to its run of over 200 performances. The Gaiety, never slow to jump on any passing bandwagon, brought out its own 'Little Mary' right away and found equal success. It was very difficult to take exception to Gertie Millar no matter what she was singing, and besides, the Gaiety audiences were fond of an upper-class version of the music hall, where the euphemism polite or otherwise was an integral part of the entertainment.

Gertie also sang 'Come along with Me' (to the Zoo, dear) and joined with Fred Wright in clogs and shawl to sing about a subject very close to home in a Lionel Monckton song 'Liza Ann':

Liza Ann is a neat young lass and she's working up at Briggs' mill
Every morning at six o'clock you can see her walking up the hill
There she goes with her turned-up nose and her dinner in a nice tin can
Oh, you'll all of you be mad when you see another lad is a-takin' out Liza Ann

There were other lively numbers, too. Harry Grattan described himself and his life (dressed, of course, as Chamberlain) in 'Pushful':

Tho my former friends at present
Are sarcastic and unpleasant
When they see that I am going in to win,
I ignore their aimless chatter
For I know it doesn't matter
And I stand up for the Empire, thick and thin.
I'm denounced in song and sermons
By the French or by the Germans
For my monstrous Mephistophelian aims,
But I let them go on writing
For I find when two are fighting
It's not the one who wins that calls the names

Pushful, pushful, I'm so very pushful,
First I land the bird in hand
And then I bag the bushful;
If the foes of Britain makes a sudden disappearance
That is all the product of my pushful perseverance.

Connie Ediss, in a great white crinoline and frightful blonde curls, sang of herself in 'Fancy Dress' as Joan of Arc and Josephine and 'Elizabeth Queen of Scots, when Oliver Cromwell shot her', of 'Advertisements' and joined in a comical duet with Payne called 'Fancies' with an unusual chorus:

Life is a pudding, love is a plum
Into my brain
Now and again
Fancies like this will come
Often I wonder, hour after hour,
When with my thumb
I pull out the plum
Will it be sweet or sour?

Lionel Mackinder and Ethel Sydney, as one of the mis-matched pairs of jeunes premiers sang a doleful duet:

JO: Though rudeness as a general thing I very much deplore
You'll pardon me for mentioning that I find you such a bore

RO: I feel the same, but didn't see how I could tell you so before
Ah me, alack-a-day, alas!

and George Grossmith and Payne came together dressed as tramps to give their opinions of 'The Unemployed':

When will justice be done in England
Why don't they allow us to earn our bread,
It ain't much enjoyment
To ask for employment
And only get work instead

Grossmith himself supplied the pointed and highly appreciated lyric for the song but his real triumph came with 'Bedelia', a song which he had 'borrowed' from Broadway's *The Jersey Lily*. It had been an interpolation there as well, tacked into de Koven's less than inspired score by its young writers Jean Schwartz and William Jerome who had already been responsible for other such hugely successful interpolations as 'Rip van Winkle was a lucky Man' (*The Sleeping Beauty and the Beast* (USA)/*The Cherry Girl* (GB) and 'Mister Dooley' (*A Chinese Honeymoon* (USA)/Ernest Shand and George Grossmith[1] (GB). In *The Jersey Lily*, 'Bedelia' was sung by Blanche Ring and when the show folded after a three-week run it was largely due to her that it survived to carry on a life as a popular song. In Grossmith's rewritten version, Bedelia became a little theatre-goer for whom he sighs, but who has eyes only for the romantic lead:

Bedelia, I'm going to steal yer
Bedelia, you are my queen
I'll be your Hayden Coffin
If you'll be my Evie Greene.
Say something sweet, Bedelia
Your voice I want to hear
Oh, Bedelia, -elia, -elia
I've made up my mind to steal yer, steal yer, steal yer
Bedelia dear

In Britain, 'Bedelia' became as much attached to Grossmith as it had been to Miss Ring in the States.

The Orchid followed comfortably in the long line of Gaiety successes. It occupied the new theatre for a run of 559 performances before following its predecessors around the British provinces and the rest of the world. For America, it was produced by the Shubert brothers. Joseph Herbert of *Prince of Borneo* notoriety was given the opportunity to 'nationalise' the show, and Eddie Foy, its comic star, emerged after the rewrite as 'Artie Choke' to lead basically the same orchid-chase through its out-of-town run-in. It was not a trouble free one. Foy became incensed by the popularity being gained by his feminine co-star, Trixie Friganza, and demanded that her role be reduced. Miss Friganza, understandably, objected and Foy staged a 'her-or-me' scene which ended with news of the lady's dismissal. But when *The Orchid* reached Broadway, Miss Friganza was still there and, as Foy must have feared, she made a personal triumph. But Foy did well enough himself. The role of Meakin/Artie Choke was a prime one and it had been whooped-up with suitable American songs such as 'He

[1] Shand made a great success with the song on the halls and Grossmith introduced it at the Gaiety, seemingly during the run of *The Toreador*.

Goes to Church on Sundays' (Bryan/Goetz) which enabled him to try to hold his own 'against' the lady. In spite of the infighting, *The Orchid* was a great success and achieved a run of 178 performances in New York before setting out for the rest of the country. The Shuberts, delighted with their success, announced great plans for *The Orchid* including a return to the West End with Foy and Miss Friganza prepared to challenge Payne and Connie Ediss on their home ground. But Foy refused the trip and, as it turned out that George Edwardes had Trixie Friganza under contract for any British appearances, the whole scheme collapsed.

1903 was a prolific year for Ivan Caryll. He had already produced *The Duchess of Dantzic* and had a share in *The Orchid* and, in December he was responsible for the music for two further shows, both written in conjunction with Seymour Hicks. The first of these was *The Earl and the Girl* (prematurely publicised as both *The Dog Tamer* and *The Only Girl*) which was chosen by William Greet as the piece to start off his ex-Savoy company in a new West End season at the Adelphi Theatre.

Hicks' story was of a suitably well-used character. Jim Cheese, a dog trainer, cannot pay his hotel bill and wishes he were someone else. Dick Wargrave has got engaged to £3m heiress Elphin Haye and has heard that her fearsome uncle, A. Bunker Bliss, is after him and he, too, wishes he were, at least ostensibly, someone else. In good musical comedy fashion, the two swap identities with the complicity of their respective young ladies. But other people are after Dick as well: an English solicitor and an American attorney with the news that he has inherited the Earldom of Stole. In the circumstances it is Jim Cheese who receives both the brickbats of Bunker Bliss and the coronet. Therewith everyone repairs to the increasingly popular second act location of Nice where the sorting-out motions are gone through.

Hicks' book was bright and entertaining and not offensively original, while Caryll brought himself back to a style which suited the words with which he was supplied – drawing-room ballad music for the Fred Weatherley lyrics, rather more lively and up-to-date sounds for George Grossmith, and a photofit musical comedy style for Percy Greenbank. It was perfectly adequate music, even if one had the feeling that it had all been heard before, but the public knew what it wanted and seemingly could not have enough of such things. On opening night the ex-Savoy company found their venture into the less lofty echelons of the musical West End greeted with what *The Era* noted as 'a wildly triumphant reception'.

There was, of course, the novelty of seeing the well-known Savoy favourites making their first stab at the conventional characters of the modern-dress musical. Walter Passmore as the common little dog trainer impersonating a fellow being an Earl made the most of the opportunities for fun offered by the role and managed quite well without the witty lines of a Gilbert or a Hood. M. R. Morand had a volatile role as the American solicitor, but Lytton, Evett, Agnes Fraser and Louie Pounds were strait-jacketed into the mildly humorous Hicks/Terriss juvenile mould which gave them considerably less in the way of character than heretofore. Such roles relied very largely on charm. There were some additions to the company. John C. Dixon had what was virtually a repeat of his role in Hugh Morton's *Glittering Gloria* as the fire-eating Yankee uncle. Florence Lloyd played Cheese's chirpy girl friend, the everlasting Phyllis Broughton had a small part as the heroine's aunt, while the massive Helen Kinnaird played the circus strong woman, Mrs Shimmering Black, who 'once sustained a platform with ten men on it, and two of them Canadians'.

The notices were what might be called mixed. *The Times* regretted that the Savoy team had been reduced to such fare which it called 'pointless, often tasteless

. . . . . and never new'. *The Stage* merely found it: 'nothing remarkable . . . safe without being divertingly funny' the lyrics 'no better than any other' and the music nothing more than 'pleasant and familiar'. Critical indifference did not, however, extend to *The Era* which so often proved a better guide to public taste than its more academic brethren. It enthused:

> Mr Seymour Hicks has carried the science of libretto writing to the pitch of perfection. Seldom have we seen a piece of this kind which went with so much snap and smartness from the moment that the curtain rose to the time when it descended amidst a tumult of ecstatic applause. *The Earl and the Girl* positively bristles with 'business'. Every inch of the canvas has been worked over by the assiduous 'producer', every instant some fresh item of gesture or action or ingenious contrivance is, so to speak, sprung upon our delighted and astonished senses . . . . then there is the comedy thread of the entertainment – the humorous idea worked out sufficiently – to supply the opportunities to a consummate comedian; and also the sensuous charm of sentimental verse and amorous melody, the exhilarating dances and the crisp, witty dialogue and, to all this, a running accompaniment of verses by various 'eminent hands' and the music of a composer than whom no-one knows better how to please the ear of the gay after-dinner playgoer . . . a marvellously piquant combination . . .

There was also an expensive and lavish production with some eye-catching effects to please the public taste for such things. In one scene eight girls were lowered from the flies on swings which were wreathed in garlands of electric lights to be swung out into the audience by the chorus men. It was delightful, stunning, and cost nearly £1,000. Another electrical effect was even more costly. In the café scene the girls danced on tables in shoes designed to make an electrical connection each time they tapped the table top. The scene was rehearsed strenuously, but what seemed such a brilliant idea in conception proved unreliable in practice, and the piece and its £1,200 worth of equipment were scrapped before opening night.

The score of *The Earl and the Girl* introduced a wide variety of types of songs including, of course, all the most popular of the moment: the patriotic song ('The Grenadiers'), the drawing-room ballad ('Thou Art my Rose'), the European rhythms ('By the Shores of the Mediterranean'), the Payne/ Seymour duet ('Celebrities') and even a colourable 'Tell me, pretty Maiden' called 'Little Ladies in Distress'. It was not, however, in spite of its attractive features, a score which bristled with hits, and piquancy was added by the interpolation of, at first one, and then several other established American hit tunes. The pilfering of trans-Atlantic songs had been going on for some time with Hicks and Grossmith among the chief practitioners of the trade. In *The Earl and the Girl* it became a rather overwhelming thing, if an understandable one, since the clear hit of the rather ambivalent first night had been an American ditty sung by Agnes Fraser and Henry Lytton dressed as war veterans – 'My cosy corner Girl' written by Charles Noel Douglas and composed by John Bratton:

> In my cosy corner shady
> Where I sit with my darling lady
> With her dear little hand in mine
> And gaze into her eyes divine.
> Ah! my cosy corner pillow
> Beats the moonlight, stream or billow
> And my head's in a whirl
> As I kiss each curl
> Of my cosy-corner girl

The most sophisticated song of the year it certainly was not. Lyrically it was in the class of 'Coo' and its kind, but it was in its own way decidedly catchy and caught the public favour. Its success led to the introduction of further extraneous numbers. The popular song 'Sammy' which had been introduced in the Broadway show *The Wizard of Oz* and by Blanche Ring in the short-lived *The Lovebirds* in London was appropriated for Louie Pounds, and the lively 'In Zanzibar' which, with its Monkey Dance, had been put into *The Medal and the Maid* on Broadway, was put in for Agnes Fraser and chorus. Once again, the lyric was scarcely literature:

> My little Chimpanzee, you're all this world to me
> A branch I'll find for thee in my own family tree.
> No monkeyshine for me, a wedding fine there'll be
> In high society Zanzibar

but, once again, it was bright and extremely popular.

Another Bratton song, 'He Was a Sailor', took its turn in the show as well but not all the interpolations were from Broadway even if, on this occasion, most of the best ones were. The musical director, Hamish MacCunn, contributed music for a solo dance 'L'Entente Cordiale' for Winifred Hart-Dyke, there was an Owl Song 'To Hoo? To You' with electrical effects for Louie Pounds, a tenor Gondola Song by Ernest Bucalossi for Robert Evett, a new duet 'The Patchwork Garden' (J. Airlie Dix/Edward Bateman & Paul Mill) for Passmore and Florence Lloyd, and 'a culinary ballad' for Agnes Fraser during which she made a pudding. And so it went on, with the show degenerating into more and more of a variety programme as time went by. However, the solid experience of the Savoy players in book shows served to help keep the show under control as it ran through twelve months of popularity which survived even a transfer to the Lyric Theatre after nine months.

In America, where it was produced under the Shubert banner, the show underwent even more additions and alterations. The Shuberts had inveigled Eddie Foy from the Erlanger stable to star as Jim Cheese and they opened the show at their new Philadelphia Lyric before bringing it to the Casino where it had a healthy 148-performance run. Amongst the songs interpolated for Broadway were Nat Martin's 'I Want a Man Made to order for Me' sung by Zelma Rawlston and a Jerome Kern swing song for Georgia Caine, 'How'd you Like to Spoon with Me?' which became the young composer's first genuine hit. It made its way thereafter into a number of other shows including the London production of *Show Boat* (1928) leading to its appearance as recently as 1971 in the latest and longest-running revival of that piece at the Adelphi, original home of *The Earl and the Girl*, where it was performed with spoons accompaniment by Jan Hunt. None of Ivan Caryll's numbers had an equivalent success, but the ensemble of the British and the American elements produced an appealing flavour which gave *The Earl and the Girl* in its varying forms a long and successful career not only in the West End and on Broadway but in Australia, where James Sheridan starred himself alongside Maud Amber and Winifred Blake, and all round that portion of the world where the lighter forms of musical were known as entertainment.

In 1914/15 Bannister Howard's company played *The Earl and the Girl* for three successful months in the West End prior to taking it on the road. Phyllis Broughton and Florence Lloyd repeated their original roles and Ellaline Terriss took a turn in the ingénue role of Elphin Haye when the show shifted from the Aldwych to the Lyric to end its town run. Miss Terriss interpolated her *Circus Girl* success, 'A little Bit of

String', and Irving Berlin's 'I Want to Go back to Michigan' joined 'Cosy Corner Girl' and 'In Zanzibar' to enlarge the American portion of the score. Extra matinées were staged to accommodate the demand for tickets and *The Earl and the Girl* proved one of the most successful of the large crop of musical comedy revivals of the early wartime period.

The second Hicks /Caryll piece was *The Cherry Girl*, produced for Christmas at the Vaudeville in a patent attempt to reproduce the success of *Bluebell in Fairyland*. Pansy lives in an attic and on the roof above live the pierrots, black and white ones, bad and good. Pansy bears a likeness to the Queen and, on changing clothes with her, finds herself pursued amorously by a black and a white pierrot. Drama ensues as a magic talisman is introduced into the proceedings and everyone is suddenly in eighteenth-century England until it is time to tie up the ends.

If the plot was fairly incomprehensible, the details were attractive and the mood was one of the Christmas fairy play of old. There were numerous dances, including a special one for little Dorothy Frostick who had made such a success as the Will o' the Wisp in *Bluebell*, there were glorious costumes and scenery and pretty music and, of course, once again as in *Bluebell* there were Hicks himself (as the White Pierrot) and Ellaline Terriss as the Queen. As in *The Earl and the Girl*, Ivan Caryll had written a pretty if unexceptional score, the best pieces of which were a little song 'Naughty just for Once' for Miss Terriss and a ballad, 'Telephone to the Moon', for Hicks.

But Hicks' success with American songs in the earlier show sent him quite indiscriminately in pursuit of more and nearly the whole second act was compiled of pieces gathered from one extraneous composer or another. Bratton was again represented, this time by the Chinese Coon Song 'My little Hong Kong Baby', and Jerome and Schwartz, the writers of 'Bedelia', were represented by 'Rip van Winkle Was a lucky Man', already proven on Broadway. There was a 'Dixie Land Cakewalk' from Chauncey Haines, and, in fact, in the second act alone, Miss Terriss sang four American songs as well as Bernard Rolt's 'Miss Innocence'. This did not leave much room for the show's nominal composer, but he did manage to squeeze in one number of his own for Hicks and another for the former D'Oyly Carte tenor Courtice Pounds, no longer a matinée idol but a distinctly rotund comic, plus the pleasing song 'The Coming of Dawn' sung by unknown newcomer Barbara Deane.

As the mélange of *The Earl and the Girl* had pleased, so too did that of *The Cherry Girl* with its unusual mixture of fairy play extravaganza and American music hall which recalled the flavour of the early Alhambra pieces without, of course, attempting to attain their extravagance of staging. *The Cherry Girl* paid no heed to the end of the festive season but continued on for six months at the Vaudeville on a heavy schedule of matinées and proved, while never challenging *Bluebell*, to be extremely popular.

It was not entirely popular, however, with the manufacturers of the well-known beef extract, Bovril. Courtice Pounds had a line referring to his lost horses – 'Alas, they are all Bovril now . . . ' – which had them quivering with horror. They leapt into print with complaints and Pounds altered the line to 'beef extract', which fooled no-one and the protests continued until the line was cut. But *The Cherry Girl* was easily the most profitable of the Christmas musicals of 1903.

At the Adelphi an attractive version of *Little Hans Andersen* was clearly second in favour, although its intrinsic merits were probably greater. It introduced three of the famous children's author's most popular tales – The Emperor's New Clothes, The Little Mermaid and The Tinder Box – worked into an ingenious framework whereby the Dream Fairy, Ole-Luk-Oie, takes the child Hans from his bed and leads him through the stories he will write down later in his life. The book, by Basil Hood, was charmingly adapted and Walter Slaughter, his partner from earlier days, supplied some songs of the kind which he had proved in *Alice in Wonderland* that he could measure so well to the juvenile and not-so-juvenile taste. The whole was a much more integrated and better-written piece than its rival at the Vaudeville, though it lacked the up-to-date gloss provided by the music-hall interpolations of the latter, and, for the star seekers, where the Vaudeville had Hicks and Miss Terriss, the Adelphi had Walter Passmore as the Emperor, Louie Pounds, Henry Lytton, Robert Evett and, as the highlight of the show, Rosina Brandram giving all her power and vigour to Slaughter's beautiful 'Song of the Sea Witch'. Four weeks proved a sufficient run for the piece, however, before the cast abandoned the heavy schedule of playing *Hans* in the afternoon and *The Earl and the Girl* at night.

A less successful enterprise was a new version of part of the Alice story, *Alice Through the Looking Glass* at the New Theatre. It was a curiously hybrid entertainment combining elements of Carroll's tale and his dialogue with 'original' pieces, some rather unimpressive bits of music, and some odds and ends of music hall as Tweedledum and Tweedledee gave forth with football jokes and the White Knight paused in his story to give a series of impressions. The list of Christmas pieces was completed by a revival of the previous year's Rutland Barrington *Water Babies* at the Garrick.

The year's provincial productions did not bring forth any pieces of notable scope. There were plenty of West End hits to tour and, apart from the try-out run of the comic opera *Amorelle (1798)* at Kennington, the new musicals were all minor pieces of the loosely constructed go-as-you-please style. They served the purpose for which they were created as a series of more or less amusing episodes interspersed with light popular music, colour and dancing which pleased the taste of, often, the smaller provincial dates with ambitions to go no further. Among the list there were several with interesting features. *Bill Adams*, for example, had Arthur Roberts. Herbert Shelley and Reginald Bacchus, aided no doubt by the star himself, had conceived as the comedian's newest vehicle the character of a blustering but likeable braggart of the Napoleonic campaigns. Their scenario gave Roberts the chance to masquerade in turn as Wellington, Napoleon, a German-French agent's clerk and a lady clairvoyante as he became mixed up not only in war and romance but also with a Rajah carrying a fake gem, thieves who are trying to steal that gem, an American millionaire, etc. It also provided him with long solo 'spots' and the chance for set pieces full of smart quips and topical hits. *The Era* referred to it as:

> an entertainment of the old Arthur Wood or John Parry type with intervals for song and speech by other performers . . .[1]

Bill Adams was pretty much a one-man show and fine artists such as Alice Aynsley Cook, Louise Beaudet, Robert Selby and others had precious little to do.

Although the piece was paragraphed as heading for a London season, it was abandoned by Roberts after only half-a-dozen dates. He played Dandy Dan for the remainder of his tour and Bill Adams never made it to the West End. It surfaced quite successfully in Australia a couple of years later under the banner of George Stephenson with Edward Lauri in Roberts' role, May Garstang and May Beatty as his leading ladies, and Sydney businessman Harold H. Reeves in the romantic lead; and

[1] G. H. Snazelle's solo show as Bill Adams had once been very popular on the drawing-room circuits.

reappeared in Britain in a shorter version in 1912 to be tried as a music-hall show.

Another Reginald Bacchus piece was *The Rose of the Riviera* written in conjunction with George Sheldon and composed by Osmond Carr. It consisted of much the same kind of farcical material, though this time the setting was the French Riviera and the 'hero' one Elisha Briskett who gets into trouble with the police for photographing the fort at Nice when he is actually snapping a stray bathing belle. With the aid of pretty Milly he disguises himself as an aristocratic guest who is expected at her hotel and the foreseeable high jinks ensue during which Briskett varies his disguise (including a period as a Duchess), gets involved in a duel, a motor car race and the inevitable masked ball before all is worked out and Milly lands herself the real aristocrat. Harry Dent and Isa Bowman led the merriment but, in spite of keeping on the rounds for a while, *The Rose of the Riviera* proved no money-spinner, bankrupting its author-producer George Sheldon to the tune of £12,000.

However, it also turned up in Australia with the Stephenson company where it proved a popular vehicle for Edward Lauri and May Beatty in repertoire with *Bill Adams* and *The Skirt Dancer*. Its variety show construction left plenty of room for interpolations of which the stars took full advantage. Lauri introduced his speciality comedy sketches, and the latest song hits such as 'My cosy corner Girl' were interpolated at will.

All At Sea was the work of 'Mostyn Tedde' – Edward Paulton writing under his given name. It, too, was a farcical musical although it had a reasonably solid plot dealing with yet another ambitious lady trying to marry off her daughters advantageously, and yet another jewel theft involving false jewels. In fact, nearly everything in Paulton's tale turned out fake – the lady is not a society widow, the girls are not her daughters and most of the rest of the cast are someone other than they claim to be. It had some bright music by Wilfred Arthur and accomplished a good tour with a strong cast.

The other pieces were less substantial. *Jack's Sweetheart* was a mixture of melodrama, comedy, old tunes and new dealings with a French spy and some secret plans heinously planted on our hero. Written and staged in four days when another play disintegrated in rehearsal, it toured the very smallest circuits continuously for more than two years. *The Cruise of the Calabar* saw a hundred ladies tricked on to a Marriage Ship bound for South Australia and had for its main distinction a Walter Slaughter song, 'The Maiden and the Saint'; and *Percy, the Ladykiller*, true to its title, dealt with the farcical amours of one Percy Gamble from a houseboat on the Thames to the Scottish highlands. Johnnie Schofield in the title role was aided by Georgie Corlass as a Louie Freear-type slavey in creating enough business to stuff out a fairly plotless piece. The year's total was made up by *That Terrible Tomboy* who was Maidie Scott; the extravaganza *The Isle of Champagne*; *The Sultan of Ranogoo* which spent most of its short life in a reduced version on music-hall bills; and the 'romantic comic opera' *Cupid in a Convent* which had a Blondel-like character searching for his lost love who has been imprisoned in a convent.

Two interesting productions appeared during the year in America which had a bearing on the British scene. One was the new musical *Winsome Winnie* written by the *Erminie* team of Harry Paulton and Edward Jakobowski. It was first played at the Academy of Music in Baltimore before being brought to Broadway where it had a short and fairly unhappy life. On the way, the original book and score had been 'improved' by Frederick Ranken and Gustave Kerker, so that virtually nothing of Jakobowski's score remained to be damned by the New York critics. The other event was a surprise. That wheeler-dealer supreme, Luscombe Searelle, turned up in Boston where he arranged a production of his old work *Bobadil.* In his normal flamboyant style he arranged for a simultaneous copyright production to be staged at the Bijou Theatre in Teddington so that America and Britian were treated to *Bobadil* on the same night. After fair reviews, however, the American *Bobadil* withered away in four weeks and the Bijou performance remained the work's only British performance.

1903

0272 **A PRINCESS OF KENSINGTON** a comic opera in two acts by Basil Hood. Music by Edward German. Produced at the Savoy Theatre under the management of William Greet 22 January, 1903 for a run of 115 performances closing 16 May, 1903.

Sir James Jellicoe	Arthur Boielle
Lt Brook Green	Robert Evett
Puck	Walter Passmore
William Jelf	Henry A. Lytton
Bill Blake	Powis Pinder
Will Weatherley	Charles Childerstone
Jem Johnson	Rudolph Lewis
Yapp, a policeman	M. R. Morand
Mr Reddish	Reginald Crompton
Old Ben	George Mudie Jr
James Doubleday	Edwin Bryan
Oberon	Alec Fraser
Azuriel	Ernest Torrence
Recruiting Sergeant	F. Percival Stevens
Joy Jellicoe	Louie Pounds
Nell Reddish	Rosina Brandram/Ray Vivian
Titania	Olive Rae
Butterfly	Winifred Hart-Dyke
Moth	Maude Thornton
Cobweb	Nancy Pounds
Dragonfly	Lily Bircham
Peaseblossom	(Isabel Agnew) (Maude Thornton)/ Constance Drever
Lady Jellicoe	Cora Lingard
Kenna	Constance Drever/Agnes Fraser (Isabel Agnew)

Dancers: Poppie Wilkinson, Lily Bircham, Winifred Hart-Dyke,/Edith Standen, Edward Royce.

Dir: Basil Hood; md: Hamish MacCunn; ch: Edward Royce; sc: W. Harford; cos: Percy Anderson

Produced at the Broadway Theatre, New York, under the management of John C. Fisher 31 August, 1903 for a run of 41 performances closing 3 October, 1903.
George B. Jackson (JJ), Richie Ling (BG), William Stephens (PUCK), James T. Powers (JELF), Fred Huntley (BILL), Bernard Tieman (WILL), P. J. Worthington (JIM), Walter S. Craven (YAPP), Stanley H. Forde (REDD), George Mudie Jr (BEN), C. H. Hillman (DOUB), Jack Taylor (OB), Edward Martindell (AZ), Thomas Shannon (SGT), Cecil Engelheart (JOY), Amelia Fields (NELL), Pauline Fredricks (TIT), Lily Bircham (BUTT), Leila Williams (MOTH), Elsie Gibbons (COB), Nellie Emerald (DRAG), Estelle Ward (PEASE), Pauline de la Paz (MUSTARDSEED), Angela May (LADY), Dora de Fillipe (KENNA), Loyd Hoey (ZEPHYRUS). Dir: Cyril Scott; md: J. Sebastian Hiller; cos: Alias, Mme Friesinger

Film: In 1907 Walturdaw issued a film and synchronised record of 'Four Jolly Sailormen' from *A Princess of Kensington* on their Cinematophone Singing Pictures and in 1908 Warwick Cinephonic Films issued the same song on the same basis.

0273 **BILL ADAMS, THE HERO OF WATERLOO** a musical play in 2 acts by Herbert Shelley and Reginald Bacchus. Music by Stephen Philpott. Additional material by Mark Mason and Herman Finck. Produced at the Theatre Royal, Eastbourne under the management of Arthur Roberts 26 February, 1903 and toured through Brighton, Portsmouth, Cardiff, Nottingham, Stoke Newington, to 4 April.

Bill Adams . . . . Arthur Roberts
General Sir Bingo Barr . . . . Maitland Dicker
Cornet, Duke of Brighton . . . . Robert Selby
Caesar Q. Anthony . . . . Arthur G. Poulton
Captain Brussell-Sprout . . . . Harold Eden
Lightning . . . . Charles Goold
Rajah . . . . Fritz Rimma
O'Malley . . . . J. Harold Carson
Farrier. Herbert Clark
Lady Bingo Barr . . . . Alice Aynsley Cook
Mimette. . . . . Louise Beaudet
Mamie Anthony. . . . . Mary Thorne
Captain Ffolliott . . . . Nellie Gray
Cornet le Breton . . . . Frances Fowler
Marguerite . . . . Lili Leverne
Julie. . . . . Edith Duncker
Camille . . . . Maud Selwyn
Mathilde. . . . . Stella Melrose
Louise. Kathleen Dennis
Marie . . . . May Hylton
Jeanne. Mabel Thornton
Clotilde . . . . Gipsy Touzen
Lucette . . . . Jane Howard Reynolds
Margot . . . . Ruby Celeste

Md: H. Shaw; sc: Julian Hicks

Produced in a revised version 22 April, 1912 at Crouch End Hippodrome and toured.

0274 **THE MEDAL AND THE MAID** a musical comedy in two acts by Owen Hall. Lyrics by Charles H. Taylor. Additional lyrics by Paul Rubens, George Rollitt and H. Fordwych. Music by Sidney Jones. Produced at the Lyric Theatre under the management of Tom B. Davis 25 April, 1903. Withdrawn 25 July, 1903 and re-presented in a revised version 15 August, 1903. Withdrawn 12 September, 1903 after a total of 98 performances.

Merva Sunningdale . . . . Ruth Vincent
Josephine . . . . Sylvia Sablanc
Mrs Habbicombe . . . . Ada Blanche/Lizzie St Quinten
Miss Ventnor . . . . Ada Reeve/Ada Blanche (Daisy Jerome)
Elsie Habbicombe. . . . . Daisy Jerome
Maud Hersham . . . . Gurney Delaporte/Mabel Gregory
Sarah Sevenoaks . . . . Madge Vincent
Ilma Malden . . . . Mea Winifred/Grace Arundale
Gladys Combe . . . . Grace Arundale/Mea Winifred
Mona Vale . . . . Monica Sayer
Ada Bray . . . . Teresa Terry Anderson/Edith Henderson
Antoinette. . . . . Fanny Dango/Lucie Murray
Violette . . . . Lucie Murray/Phyllis Desmond
Rosa. . . . . Lillian Brendall/Lucie Murray
Tita . . . . Violet Dene/*out*
Conchita. . . . . Dora Dent/Violet Dene
Marie . . . . Eileen Douglas/Dora Dent

Druscilla Parker . . . . Dorothy Temblett
Admiral Lord Belton . . . . Laurence Caird/Colin Coop
Darien . . . . Norman Salmond
Simon Pentweazle . . . . J. Robert Hale
Allen Blythe R.N . . . . Frederick Ranalow
Lionel Habbicombe . . . . Tom Terriss
Sergeant . . . . Colin Coop/M. Sterling Mackinlay
Blakeley . . . . M. Sterling Mackinlay/*out*
Grant . . . . Philip H. Bracy
Melville . . . . H. E. Garden
Kingsley . . . . Lennox Lochner
Wheeler . . . . Cecil Cameron
Levanter . . . . James E. Sullivan (Robb Harwood) (Laurence Caird)/Ells Dagnall

with Misses Boielle, Gregory, Huxley, Lorraine, Gertrude Kuzelle, Knowlton, La Bare, Seton, Tims, Harrington &c.

Dir: Sydney Ellison; md: Guy Jones; sc: Walter Hann, T. E. Ryan; cos: Comelli

Produced at the Broadway Theatre, New York, under the management of John C. Fisher and Thomas Ryley 11 January 1904 for a run of 41 performances closing 20 February, 1904. Ruth Vincent (MERVA), Cecil Engelheart (JO), Emma Carus (MRS), Georgia Caine (VENT), Edna McClure (EL), Charlotte Leslay (MAUD), Carla Byron (SARAH), Laura Stone (ILMA), Bessie Denham (GL), Nettie Vester (MONA), Virginia Sargent (ADA), Beatrice Walsh (LILLIAN), Lillian Rice (VIOLET), Grace Wilson (DAISY), Lou Wheelan (THE NO FRILL GIRL), Lily Collins (ANT), Sadie Raymond (VI), Lelia Benton (ROSA), Edith Girvin (TI), Avita Sanchez (CON), May Willard (MA), Ita Kamph (JEANETTE), Mary Lachere (CORA), W. T. Carleton (AD), Stanley H. Forde (DAR), James T. Powers (PENT), W. P. Carleton (ALLEN), Tom Terriss (LI), Frank D. Nelson (SGT), Harry Pyke (BL), Leon de Lisle (GR), M. M. Johnson (MEL), Lawrence Howell (KING), Nat K. Cafferty (WH), Frank Garfield (GATACRE), Ignacio Martinetti (LEV), George Jackson (JUNGO), McCoy Sisters (KODAK GIRLS), Mary Clayton, Mildred Devere, Martha Garver, Gladys Lockwood, Susan Parker, Grace Vaughn. Md: Arthur Weld

0275 **THE SCHOOL GIRL** a musical play in 2 acts by Henry Hamilton and Paul Potter. Lyrics by Charles H. Taylor. Music by Leslie Stuart. Produced at the Prince of Wales Theatre under the management of George Edwardes and Charles Frohman 9 May, 1903 for a run of 333 performances closing 4 April, 1903.

Lilian Leigh . . . . Edna May/Ethel Sydney
Mother Superior . . . . Violet Cameron (Mildred Baker)
Marianne . . . . Marianne Caldwell
Mamie Reckfeller . . . . Billie Burke/Adrienne Augarde/Lulu Valli/Miss Carleton
Norma Rochester . . . . Norma Whalley/Ruby Ray/Jane May
Yolande . . . . Maude Percival
Violette . . . . Pauline Chase
Mimi . . . . Ethel Negretti/Minnie Baker
Saeefreda . . . . Clarita Vidal
Miss Yost . . . . Lulu Valli/Violet Grey/Ida Worsley
Mrs Marchmont . . . . Barbara Huntley/Eva Kelly/Susie Wilkes
Kate Medhurst . . . . Mildred Baker
Jessie Campbell . . . . Mary Fraser
Evelyn Somers . . . . Evelyn Bond
Mabel Kingston . . . . Alice Coleman
Cicely Marchmont . . . . Marie Studholme/Annie Purcell/ Doris Stocker/Lulu Valli/Deborah Volar
Edgar Verney . . . . Reginald Somerville/J. Edward Fraser/W. Talleur Andrews
Tubby Bedford . . . . James Blakeley/Leedham Bantock

Peter Overend . . . . J. A. Warden/John Tresahar
Corner . . . . Gilbert Porteous/Richard Kavanagh
General Marchmont . . . . George Graves/O. B. Clarence
Jacques de Crevert . . . . Frank Walsh
George Sylvester . . . . Charles Hampden
Adolphe Delaporte . . . . Murri Moncrieff
Fifine . . . . Mamie Stewart/*out*
Jack Merrion . . . . W. Talleur Andrews/*out*
Sir Ormesby St Leger . . . . G. P. Huntley/George Grossmith Jr/ Arthur Roberts/Dallas Welford
add Louise . . . . Ruby Celeste
La Rosière . . . . Edith Fink
Mary Jones . . . . Claire Pridelle

with Misses C. Marsden, Ada Webster, M. Graham, Hilda Scott, Ida Worsley, M. Harvey, Stella de Marney, A. Dawson; Edgar Wolseley, F. Hatton, G. Gotto, E. Williams, Bourne, H. Borrett, H. Goodwin, F. Garton.

Md: Leslie Stuart/Carl Kiefert; ch: Willie Warde; sc: Hawes Craven and Joseph Harker; cos: Percy Anderson

Produced at Daly's Theatre, New York, under the management of Charles Frohman 1 September 1904. Transferred to Herald Square Theatre 24 October, 1904 after 54 performances, and played for a further 66 performances closing 24 December, 1904 after a total of 120 performances.

Edna May (LL), Mildred Baker (MOTHER), Clara Braithwaite (MAR), Lulu Valli (MAMIE), Jane May (NOR), Vivian Vowles (YO), Ivy Louise (VI), Dorothy Dunbar (MI), Barbara Dunbar (LOUISE), Madge Greet (MARGOT), Lakme Darcier (SAE), Virginia Staunton (YOST), Mrs Watt Tanner (MRS), Jeannette Paterson (KATE), Queena Sanford (JESS), Eithel Kelly (EV), Joyce Thorn (MAB), Constance Hyem (CIC), W. Talleur Andrews (ED), Robert Minster (OV), W. R. Shirley (COR), Fred Wright Jr (GEN), Fred Ozab (J), Harry Hudson (G), Murri Moncrieff (AD), Jerome Hayes (MERR), James Blakeley (TUBBY), George Grossmith Jr/Fred Wright Jr (ORM).
Dir: J. A. E. Malone; md: William T. Francis; sc: Ernest Gros

0276 **ALL AT SEA** a musical comedy in 2 acts by Edward Paulton. Music by Wilfred Arthur. First performed at Llandudno 21 to 23 May, 1903 and officially produced under the management of Alexander Keith at the Prince of Wales Theatre, Liverpool 25 May, 1903 and toured through Cheltenham, Cambridge/Bedford, Kingston, Birmingham, ?, ?, ?, ?, ?, Sheffield, Glasgow, Edinburgh, Newcastle, Burnley, Peckham, Newport, ?, ?, ?, Brighton, Eastbourne, ?, Swindon, to 7 November.

Endell S. Bounce . . . . Harry Phydora
Hector Orme . . . . Jack Walters/Ernest Spalding
Dot Dimpleton . . . . Julia Kent
Lord Eustace Willoughby . . . . Victor Stevens/Edward Lowe
Mrs Delamore . . . . Lila More/Daisy Baldry
Willis Letgow . . . . Cyril Harcourt/Elliot Skinner
Wintergreen . . . . Adele Roze/Muriel Langley/Ada Desmond
Caramel . . . . Daisy Sylverton/Edie Adeson
Jujube . . . . Addie Lennard/Ella Willmer
Lady Bouverie . . . . May Karl/Marion Warren
Adolph . . . . H. Glyn/Edgar Wilson
Lord Angus McPhilibeg . . . . G. P. Polson/John Richter
Captain . . . . Fred Bell
Baron Spoof . . . . Herbert Landeck
Count Augustino Spaghetti . . . . C. D. Cleveland/Frank Attree
Count Forloff . . . . Lawrence Winnigh
Herbert Jackson . . . . Conison Carr/Arthur Hickman
add Auguste . . . . Maurice O'Connell
Max . . . . E. David

Dir: Alexander Keith, md: James W. Tate

0277 **THE ROSE OF THE RIVIERA** a musical comedy in two acts by Reginald Bacchus and George Sheldon. Music by F. Osmond Carr. Produced at the Eden Theatre, Brighton, under the management of George Sheldon 25 May, 1903 and toured through dates including Reading, Glasgow, Newcastle, Hull, Leeds, Leicester, Eastbourne, Gateshead, Newcastle, Aberdeen, Dundee, to 10 October.

Elisha Briskett. . . . . Harry Dent
M. Erol . . . . Sidney Dooley/Harold Eden
Telly Graph. . . . . J. C. Bland
Don Pedro Muria . . . . Will Letters
M. Maurel . . . . George Howard
Duke of Clapham . . . . Philip Brooklyn
Duchess of Clapham . . . . Ada Maskell
Lord Balham . . . . Charles F. Cooke/Eric Dalvere
Mathilde. . . . . Janet Morel
Jaquette . . . . Fanny Harris
Bostinia Hubb. . . . . Ada Binning/Poppy Lytton
Susan Frisco . . . . Mabel Latimer
Therese . . . . Florrie Drew
Miss Algebra . . . . Madge Allen
Molly . . . . Gertie Tullet
Lily . . . . Dora Haydon
Edna. . . . . Zara Knesborg
May . . . . Poppy Lytton/
Milly Daventry . . . . Isa Bowman

Md: George Sheldon; sc: Fred Storey

0278 **PERCY, THE LADYKILLER** (later THE LADYKILLER) a musical farce in four acts by J. Hickory Wood. Music by Frank Leo. Produced at Tunbridge Wells under the management of Messrs Austin and Major 25 May, 1903 and toured through Leamington, Bath, ?, Kennington, Peckham to 4 July.

Percy Gamble. . . . . Johnnie Schofield
William Jellicoe . . . . Arthur Ricketts
Smiles . . . . J. W. Wilkinson
Alexander . . . . John Dobson
Jack Bateman . . . . Frederick Jacques
Reggie Bateman . . . . Arthur Foote
Connie Fleet . . . . Nellie Johnston
Kate. . . . . Minnie Rayner
Molly May . . . . Molly Cameron
Daisy May . . . . Senga Ripley
Polly. . . . . Georgie Corlass

with Claud Jones, C. W. Hoddy, W. Anderson, J. E. Corlass, Harry J. Butler/S. McNeil, Edward May, C. Kilburn, Louie Evelyn, Cissie Evelyn, Evelyn Arnold, Maud Goodman, Harriet Tidd, Violet Laxton, Nina Grey, Beattie Lawler.

0279 **AMORELLE (1810)** a comic opera in three acts by Barton White. Lyrics by Ernest Boyd-Jones. Music by Gaston Serpette. Produced at Kennington as *Amorelle (1798)* under the management of C. P. Levilly 8 June, 1903 for one week. Subsequently toured by C. P. Levilly from 21 December, 1903 at Manchester x5 through Hull, Sheffield, Dublin, Nottingham, Southampton, Liverpool, Oldham, Derby, Edinburgh, Aberdeen, Dundee, Glasgow, Middlesborough, Birmingham, Hanley, Bolton, Marlborough, Kennington and Alexandra terminating 4 June, 1904.

	Kennington	*Tour*
Dr Napoleon Bonaparte Crow . .	Willie Edouin	Eric Thorne
Dotard	Eric Thorne	Fred Seymour/Walter Standish
Comte de Cideaux	St John Hamund	Robert Fairbanks
François	Robert Michaelis	John Morley
Boissey	Fred Seymour	George Paulton

Lupin	Gerald Clifford	Gerald Clifford
Alphonse	Fred Edwards	Maurice Carlton
Nikko	Leon Simkin	Leon Simkin (as Van Kemfersdam)
Jules	Roland Cunningham	Sydney Barraclough/Leslie Stiles
Marina	Madge Avery	Madge Avery
Lesbia	May Edouin	Daisy Le Hay/Kitty Cavendish
Jeanette	Kitty Cavendish	May Bradbury
Cossette	Frances Manners	
Pepita	Annie Courtenay	
Amorelle	Stella Gastelle	Stella Gastelle
The Mayor	Vernon Reid	Vernon Reid
Max	A. Cunningham	
Coachman	J. Leroni	J. Leroni
Jacques	Arthur Owens	
Notary	Seymour Richards	
Yvonne	Rose Lytton	
Karl	Bert Rolfe	Md: Harry Rushworth

Produced at the Comedy Theatre, under the management of Frank Curzon 18 February, 1904 for a run of 28 performances closing 19 March, 1904.

Dr Napoleon Bonaparte Crow	Willie Edouin
Dotard	Charles Wibrow
Comte de Cideaux	Evelyn Vernon
François	F. Pope Stamper
Boissey	Charles R. Walenn
Lupin	Sidney Bracy
Alphonse	Roland Bottomley
Nikko	Leon Simkin
Harpagon	Alfred Ibberson
Jules	Sydney Barraclough
Marina	Claire Romaine
Lesbia	Kitty Cavendish/Daisy Le Hay
Jeanette	Lillian Hubbard
Cossette	Ruth Savile
Pepita	M. Seymour Hodges
Amorelle	Mabelle Gillman
The Mayor	S. Millen
Max	E. J. Evans
M. de Launay	Robert Vincent
Coachman	Hewson Elliott
Madame Ribot	D. Miller
Babette	Miss Van Bergen
Favole	Miss Bach
Gendarmes	Messrs Willis and Longden

Md: Ernest Bucalossi, ch: Fred Farren; sc: W. B. Spong; cos: Arthur Fredericks.

0280 **THE DUCHESS OF DANTZIC** a romantic light opera in three acts by Henry Hamilton. Music by Ivan Caryll. Produced at the Lyric Theatre under the management of George Edwardes 17 October, 1903 for a run of 236 performances closing 17 October, 1904.

Catherine Upscher	Evie Greene/Kitty Gordon/Elizabeth Firth
Lisette	Clare Greet/Billie Burke/Monica Sayer
Jeanne	Dorothy Temblett/Irene Edwards
Mathilde	Mea Winifred
Jacqueline	Monica Sayer/N. Johnston
Thérèse	May Glenn/Marjorie Grey
Louise	Isabelle Gray/A. Marchand
Babette	E. Labare
Marianne	Pearl Hope

Bethune/Adhémar . . . . Lawrence Rea/Leonard Mackay
Regnier/d'Alegre . . . . Philip H. Bracy
Napoléon Bonaparte . . . . Holbrook Blinn
François Lefèbvre . . . . Denis O'Sullivan
Sergeant Flageot . . . . A. J. Evelyn
Gildon/Chanteloup . . . . Frank Greene/Mr Kelvin
Papillon . . . . Courtice Pounds/Fred Wright Jr/Henry J. Ford
Empress Josephine . . . . Beatrice Parke/Elizabeth Kirby/ Mabel Lorrell/Eleanor Souray
Caroline Murat . . . . Kitty Gordon/Florence Snell
Pauline Borghese . . . . Violet Elliot/Elizabeth Firth/Evelyn Tyser/ B. Dudley
Renée de St Mezarde . . . . Adrienne Augarde/Cissie Vaughan
Comtesse de la Borde . . . . Rose Rosslyn/*out*
Mme de Beauffremont . . . . Mabel Lorrell/Mabel Clifton
Mme de Chatel . . . . Mina Green
Mme de Lagrange . . . . Florence Snell/*out*
Comte de Narbonne . . . . Barry Neame
Comte de Laborde . . . . Claude Dampier
M. de Flahault . . . . Ford Hamilton
M. de Montmorenci . . . . Cecil Cameron
with Ethel Dunbar etc.

Dir: Robert Courtneidge; md: Carl Kiefert; sc: Joseph Harker; ch: Willie Warde; cos: Percy Anderson

Produced at Daly's Theatre, New York, under the management of George Edwardes 14 January, 1905 for a run of 93 performances closing 15 April, 1905
Evie Greene (CATH), May Francis (LIZ), Helena Byrne (MATH/CTESS), Evelyn Cottee (JACQ/CHATEL), Ethel Forsyth (TH/BEAUFF), Agnes Matz (LOU/LAGRANGE), Lawrence Rea (BETH/ADH), Philip H. Bracy (REG/D'A), Holbrook Blinn (NAP), Lempriere Pringle (LEFEB), A. J. Evelyn (SGT), Frank Greene (GILD/CHANT), Courtice Pounds (PAP), Olga Beatty-Kingston/ Grace Heyer (EMPR), Elizabeth Firth (CARO), Mary Grant (PAUL), Adrienne Augarde (RENÉE), Ridgewell Cullum (NARB), Martin Hayden (LAB), Cecil Cameron (MONT). Dir: Holbrook Blinn; md: Barter Johns; ch: Willie Warde; sc: Thomas Mangan; cos: Percy Anderson

Produced at Daly's Theatre under the management of J. Bannister Howard 26 April, 1932 for a run of 31 performances closing 21 May.
Dorothy Ward (CATH), Wilma Vanne (LIZ), Walter Bird (BETH/ADH), Frank Cellier (NAP), Franklyn Tilton (LEFEB), Charles Stone (PAP), Jean Stirling (EMPR), Nancy Fraser (RENÉE), Lily Lapidus (CARO), Winifred Williamson (PAUL). Dir: Frederick G. Lloyd.

0281 **THE ORCHID** a musical play in two acts by James T. Tanner. Lyrics by Adrian Ross and Percy Greenbank. Music by Ivan Caryll and Lionel Monckton. Produced at the Gaiety Theatre under the management of George Edwardes 28 October, 1903 for a run of 559 performances closing 24 May, 1905.

Hon. Violet Anstruther . . . . Gertie Millar/Gertrude Glyn
Caroline Twining . . . . Connie Ediss
Zelie Rumbert . . . . Hilda Jacobson/Bertha Palliser/Gaynor Rowlands/May Cranfield
Thisbe . . . . Gabrielle Ray/Maude Percival/ Gertrude Glyn/Lulu Valli
Countess Anstruther . . . . Phyllis Blair
Billy . . . . Lydia West/Iris Innes/*out*
Lady Warden . . . . Gladys Aylward
Josephine Zaccary . . . . Ethel Sydney/Marie Studholme/Ida Lytton
Hon Guy Scrymgeour . . . . George Grossmith Jr/Charles A. Brown
Dr Ronald Fausset . . . . Lionel Mackinder
Mr Aubrey Chesterton . . . . Harry Grattan
Comte Raoul de Cassignat . . . . Robert Nainby

Zaccary . . . . Fred Wright Jr/James E. Sullivan/Bert Sinden
M. Frontenbras . . . . George Gregory/Will Spray
M. Merignac . . . . Charles A. Brown/Henry Taylor
Registrar. Arthur Hatherton/George Chapman
Master of Ceremonies. . . . . Will Bishop/J. W. Birtley
M. d'Auville . . . . H. Lewis
Meakin . . . . Edmund Payne
add Koskiusko . . . . Bert Sinden
Josephine Joy. . . . . Ethel Oliver

with Kitty Mason, Blanche Carlow, Doris Beresford, Olive May, Daisy Holly, Florence Warde, Daisy Denvil, Winifred Carruthers, Marguerite Grey, Winifred Labarte, Doris Dewar/Madge Rossmore, Florence Dudley, Minnie Baker, Gertrude Glyn, Ida Heath, Gwen Livingstone, Edith Neville, Nancy Mansell, Ethel Christine, Leone Roy, Lydia West, Lucie Murray, Maude Percival

Dir: Sydney Ellison, md: Ivan Caryll/Leopold Wenzel; sc: Hawes Craven and Joseph Harker; cos: Wilhelm

Produced at Herald Square Theatre, New York, under the management of Lee and Sam Shubert 8 April, 1907 for 163 performances. Transferred to the Casino Theatre 2 September, 1907. Closed after 15 further performances 14 September, 1907, a total of 178 performances. Amelia Stone (VI), Trixie Friganza (CARO), Laura Guerite (ZE), Maude Fulton (TH), Jean Newcombe (CTESS), Doris Cameron (LADY), Irene Franklin (JOS), Roy Atwell (GUY), Melville Ellis (RON), George C. Boniface Jr (AUB), William Rock (ZACC), Eddie Foy (ARTIE CHOKE), Barrington Foote (REGISTRAR), Marietta di Dio (MASKER), Estelle Coffin (ANNETTE), Urla Rottger (FLEURETTE), Margaretta Masi (CLARICE), Beatrice Walsh (JEANETTE), Mabel Weeks (MARIE), Louise Perry (LIZETTE), Arthur Warren (MC), Barrington Foote (BEAUCLASSE), William Moore (COMMISSAIRE), Mr Neilson (COCHER), R. L. McAndrews (GENDARME), George Pullman (ICE CREAM VENDOR), J. C. Newell (MARCHAND D'NEZ). Pd: La Petite Adelaide with Misses A. Ford, F. Royce Elton, Calvert, Pouts, Holmes, Merrilees, M. Ford, Foster, Franklin, Fairfax, Barthold, Brennan, Doherty, Armstrong, Nile, Skeer, Warren, Cameron, Snyder, Archer, Beckwith, Melles, Creagh, Verinde, Brown, Lorraine, Spencer. Messrs Prady, Lyman, King, Kirtland, Smith, McCann, Rose, Clemens, Moore, Beem, Toland. Dir: Frank Smithson; md: Alexander Spencer; ch: William Rock

0282 **THE EARL AND THE GIRL** a musical comedy in 2 acts by Seymour Hicks. Lyrics by Percy Greenbank. Music by Ivan Caryll. Produced at the Adelphi Theatre under the management of William Greet 10 December, 1903. Transferred to the Lyric Theatre September 12, 1904. Closed December 17, 1904 after a total run of 371 performances.

Jim Cheese . . . . Walter Passmore
Dick Wargrave . . . . Henry A. Lytton
Hon Crewe Boodle . . . . Robert Evett/Gwyllym Allwyn
A. Bunker Bliss . . . . John C. Dixon/Ernest Torrence
Downham . . . . M. R. Morand
Mr Talk. . . . . Frank Elliston
Mr Hazell . . . . Reginald Crompton
Dudley Cranbourne. . . . . Powis Pinder
George Bellamy . . . . Charles Childerstone
Hugh Wallender . . . . Alec Fraser
Rossiter . . . . Ernest Torrence/Rudolph Lewis
George . . . . Rudolph Lewis/*out*
Charles . . . . J. Gordon
Elphin Haye. . . . . Agnes Fraser/
Liza Shoddam. . . . . Florence Lloyd
Mrs Shimmering Black . . . . Helen Kinnaird/Glayds Fontaine/Annie Esmond
Daisy Fallowfield . . . . Louie Pounds/Maud Aston
Virginia Bliss . . . . Phyllis Broughton
Lady Gussie. . . . . Lena Leibrandt/Mary Fraser

Lady Violet	Olive Rae
Lady Gwendoline	Gertrude Thornton
Lady Ethel	Edith Standen
Lady Muriel	Winifred Hart-Dyke
Hon Birdie Harold	Florrie Sutherland
Hon. I.O. Ewe	Miss Hammerton
Miss Astorbilt	Miss Taylor/Maud Aston/Aime Grey
Miss D. Licht	Miss Glenn/Cissie Vaughan/Dawn Aston
Hon. Mrs de Brett	Miss Williams/Marjorie Grey
Miss T. Gordon	Rosie Edwardes
Miss Bertha Late	Miss Rickards
Miss R. Rollo	Miss Francis
P. R. Brighton	Miss Ohmead/Miss Whitmore
Miss L. Montez	Lily MacIntyre
Violet Rose	Jessie Beresford/Clara Taylor/Enid Leslie
Miss Ventnor	Miss Harris

Dir: Seymour Hicks; md: Hamish MacCunn; ch: E. Royce Jr; cos: Comelli; sc: W. Harford

Produced at the Casino Theatre, New York, under the management of Sam and Lee Shubert 4 November, 1905 for a run of 148 performances closing 10 March, 1906.
Eddie Foy (JIM), Victor Morley (DICK), Templar Saxe (CREWE), J. Bernard Dyllyn (BUNK), W. H. Armstrong (DOWN), W. H. Denny (HAZ), John Peachey (DUD), Dudley E. Oatman/Harold Hendee (BEL), Alan Campbell (GEORGE), Georgia Caine (EL), Zelma Rawlston (LIZ), Amelia Summerville (SB), Nellie McCoy/Lillian Lawton (DAI), Violet Holls (VIR), Louise de Rigney (G), Ruth Langdon (V), Jane Hall/Estelle Coffin (GW), Violet Adams (E), Edna Jeans (MU), Ione Kerr/Katherine Hyland (MAUD), Beatrice Adams (GER), Enid Forde (MILLICENT), May Lewis (GLADYS), Grace Walton (MARGUERITE) Lillian Rice (ANITA), Angie Wiemers (INEZ), Ralph Williams (CHARLES), Bert Boyce (ROSSITER) with Misses Hall, Langdon, Highland, B. Adams, Forde, Lewis, V. Adams, Walton, Chandler, Clayton, Stanley, Ayer, M. Alexander, Watson, L. Alexander, Taylor, Raymond, Gibbons, Howard, Heath, Traves, Rice, Weimers, Zimmerman, de la Paz, Heckler, Fitzgerald, Wellington, Myres, Courtenay, Aroval; Messrs Campbell, Goodman, Weick, Zerger, La Doux, Boyce, Oatman, Harder, Marshall, Handee, Strauss, Pyke, Lanning, Dennison. Dir: R. H. Burnside

Produced at the Aldwych Theatre, under the management of J. Bannister Howard 4 November, 1914. Transferred to the Lyric Theatre 26 December, 1914. Closed 6 February, 1915 after a total of 107 performances.
Bert Beswick (JIM), Haddon Cave/Charles Childerstone/Basil Foster (DICK), Montague Syrett/H. Scott Russell/Talleur Andrews (CREWE), James Prior/John Clulow (BUNK), Frank W. Cane/M. R. Morand (DOW), Mark Henry (TALK), Alf E. Passmore/Charles Wakeman (HAZ), Harry Hilliard (DUD), D. Maurice (BEL), C. Bell (WAL), Ernest Trimmingham (BLACKSMITH), J. Freeman/Ernest Trimmingham (ROS), J. Boys (GEO), G. Franks (CHAS). Dorothy Monkman/Ellaline Terriss (EL), Florence Lloyd (LIZ), Helen Langton (SB), Cressie Leonard/Edith Drayson (DAI), Phyllis Broughton (VIR), Mia Syvelin (G), Daisy Grainger (V), Esme Manette (GW), Marjorie Gresham/Audley Thorpe (E), Nancy Hamley (M), Marie Glier (ROSEDALE), Miss Denman (BH), Miss Cookson (IOU), Dorothy Way/Daisy Barker (ASTOR), Margaret Mitchell (LICHT), Sonia Raye/Lily Brice (deB), Violet Heath (TG), Nikki Amor/Amy Harcourt (BL), Doris Lemon (PRB), Marie Clements (RR), Gracie Baker (LM), Bessie Middleton (VR), Therese Blan (V), Euphan Maclaren (pd), Audley Thorpe/Miss Ellaby/Marjorie Gresham and Paula Desborough (pd). Dir: H. B. Brandreth; md: Thomas Parker; sc: W. Harford; cos: B. J. Simmons & Co.

Film: In 1907 Walturdaw issued 'My Cosy Corner Girl' from *The Earl and the Girl* on film and synchronised record in the Cinematophone Singing Pictures series.

0283 **THE CHERRY GIRL** a musical play in two acts by Seymour Hicks. Lyrics by Aubrey Hopwood. Music by Ivan Caryll. Produced at the Vaudeville Theatre under the management of Messrs A. & S. Gatti and Charles Frohman 21 December, 1903 for a run of 215 performances closing on 25 June, 1904.

Moonshine/Happy Joe . . . . Seymour Hicks
Starlight/Squire . . . . Courtice Pounds/Stanley Brett
Bow/Grabb . . . . Stanley Brett/Charles Trevor
Scrape/Snatches. . . . . Murray King
Esau/White Surrey/Hecuba. . . . . Edward Sillward
Snowball . . . . George Hersee/Louis Victor
Watchman. . . . . Philip Ritte
Pansy . . . . Constance Hyem/Hilda Antony/ Claire Marsden
Night/Tip-toe. . . . . Kate Vesey
Sylvia/Millicent . . . . Carmen Hill
Morning. . . . . Hilda Antony/Lillian Burns
Dimples . . . . Winnie Hall/Rosie Campbell
Mlle Pas Bas . . . . Dorothy Frostick
Josephine . . . . Gladys Archbutt
Rainbow. . . . . Nancy Buckland
Chamberlain. . . . . Eva Carrington
Maids of Honour . . . . Blanche Thorpe
Lillian Hewetson/Ida Lytton
Heralds . . . . J. Bewlay
Charles Phillips
Queen . . . . Ellaline Terriss/Constance Hyem
Rose of the Riviera . . . . Albert Valchera
Robin Roy. . . . . Frank Carroll/Mortie Campbell
Robin Me . . . . Robert Wilkes
Robin Anyone. . . . . William Hay/Mortie Campbell
Ikestein . . . . Charles Trevor/Philip Ritte/Frank Carroll
Spirit of Dawn . . . . Barbara Deane
Sunbeam . . . . Nellie Lonnen
Clotilde . . . . Phyllis Canton/*out*
Country Belles . . . . Claire Marsden/Ida Lytton
Lillian Burns/Genee Hayward
Flower. . . . . Jessie Lonnen
Truth . . . . Decima Brooke

with Dora Glennie, Edith Lee, Genee Hayward, Muriel Wood, Rosie Campbell, Ida Lytton, Misses Travers, Clare, Melville, Barkman, Sarony.

Md: Howard Carr; ch: Willie Warde; sc: W. Harford and R. McCleery; cos: Wilhelm

0284 **ALICE THROUGH THE LOOKING GLASS** a fairy play in two acts adapted from Lewis Carroll's book by 'Y. Knott'. Music by Walter Tilbury. Produced at the New Theatre under the management of John Donaldson 22 December, 1903 for a season of 60 performances to 29 January, 1904.

Alice. Maidie Andrews
White Queen . . . . Constance Courtenay
Red Queen . . . . Rose Temple
White King . . . . Tim Ryley
Man in White Paper . . . . Algernon Newark
Tweedledum . . . . Dallas Welford
Tweedledee . . . . Lennox Pawle
Humpty Dumpty . . . . Willie Atom
The Goat . . . . H. Romaine
Guard . . . . James Lewis
Spirit of Fairy Revels. . . . . Haidee Hemsley
The Beetle . . . . H. Ballinger
Tiger Lily. . . . . Daisy Cathcart
The Violet. . . . . Mabel Martin
Red Rose . . . . Hilda Moss

Queen of the Fairies . . . . Winnie Crisp
Seaweed . . . . Alexandrina Vercisi

Dir: George Grossmith Jr; md: Augustus Bingham; ch: W. Ozmond; sc: Messrs Banks; cos: Robert Crofter

0285 **LITTLE HANS ANDERSEN** a fairy play in two acts and seven scenes by Basil Hood. Music by Walter Slaughter. Produced at the Adelphi Theatre under the management of William Greet 23 December, 1903 for a series of 27 matinées ending 22 January, 1904.

Little Hans Andersen . . . . Roy Lorraine
His Father. . . . . Powis Pinder
His Mother . . . . H. Kirkpatrick
Karen of the Red Shoes . . . . Winifred Hart-Dyke
Ole-Luk-Oie . . . . M. R. Morand
The Emperor who Loved New Clothes. . Walter Passmore
The Prince with the Magic Pipe . . . . . Robert Evett
The Royal Footman . . . . Reginald Crompton
The Royal Butler . . . . Ernest Torrence
The Royal Valet . . . . Mr Herbert
The Lord Chamberlain . . . . Mr Cullin
The Court Physician . . . . Arthur Boielle
The Royal Governess . . . . Alice Barth
The Two Professors . . . . Edwin Bryan and Mr Holloway
The Head Housemaid . . . . Lena Leibrandt
Chief Swineherd . . . . Charles Earldon
The Princess who was Kissed by a Swineherd . . . . Louie Pounds
The Prince who was Wrecked . . . . . . Alec Fraser
The Princess whom he Married . . . . . Olive Rae
The Little Mermaid . . . . Edith Standen
The Merman . . . . Powis Pinder
The Sea Witch . . . . Rosina Brandram
A Real Soldier. . . . . Henry A. Lytton
Two Wooden Soldiers . . . . Reginald Crompton and Ernest Torrence
The King of the Copper Castle . . . . . Richard Temple
The Queen . . . . Rosina Brandram
The Prime Minister. . . . . Charles Childerstone
The Three Big Dogs . . . . Messrs Cullin, Edwin Bryan and Charles Earldon
The Witch . . . . Rudolph Lewis
The Mayor . . . . Frank Elliston
The Princess who Married the Soldier . . Agnes Fraser

Dir: Basil Hood; md: Hamish MacCunn; ch: E. W. Royce Jr; sc: W. Harford

47a **WHAT BECAME OF MRS RACKET?** a revised version of *What Became of Totman?* by Charles Townsend and Charles Dixon. Produced at the Royal Artillery Theatre, Woolwich 22 June, 1903 under the management of C. R. Stone and toured.

Obadiah Dawson . . . . C. R. Stone
Timothy Totman . . . . Jack Haines/Gerald Wyatt
Robert Racket. . . . . Harry Herbert/Edward Raymond
Mr Dalroy. . . . . Aidan Lovett/Edward Oxlee
Hobson . . . . S. Junior
Mrs Racket . . . . Edith Madelle
Mrs Totman . . . . Emily Kelsey
Buttons . . . . Winifred Maye
Katy. Daisy Stone
with Jennie and Alice Temple and Letitia Flopp

THE SPORTING GIRL a musical play in three acts by T. Gilbert Perry. Music by Alfred Sugden. Produced at Elswick under the management of Perry and Stanton 7 November, 1903 and toured.

JACK'S SWEETHEART a musical comedy in three acts by J. Fletcher Sansome. Music by A. Leopold and A. Sheldrake. Produced at Workington 2 February, 1903 under the management of Sansome & Silvester and toured.

THE CRUISE OF THE CALABAR a musical comedy by Percy and Arthur Milton. Lyrics by Milton Rosmer and Henry Louther. Music by Walter Slaughter *et al.* Produced at the Royal Court Theatre, Warrington by the Milton Rays 3 August, 1903 and toured.

CUPID IN A CONVENT a romantic comic opera in three acts by Edward Martin Seymour. Music by Mario di Capri. Produced at the Theatre Royal, Croydon, 17 August, 1903 and toured.

THAT TERRIBLE TOMBOY a musical comedy in two acts by Alfred Wood. Music by Chevalier Legrand. Produced at the Theatre Royal, Windsor, under the management of Alfred Wood 9 March, 1903 and toured.

THE ISLE OF CHAMPAGNE a musical comedy by T. Gilbert Perry. Music by Alfred Sugden. Produced at the Duchess Theatre, Balham, under the management of R. C. Buchanan 19 January, 1903 and toured.

1904

The turn of the year saw no less than ten musicals running in London theatres, nine of which were successes and all British. The tenth was the unfortunate production of Hugo Felix's *Madame Sherry* of which great things had been expected, but which folded in April with a large deficit, leaving the 'libraries' with £6,000 worth of valueless tickets which they had taken in advance. *The Earl and the Girl*, *A Chinese Honeymoon*, *The Cherry Girl*, *The Girl from Kays*, *The School Girl*, *My Lady Molly*, *The Orchid*, *The Duchess of Dantzic* and *A Country Girl* were all highly successful.

The first addition of the new year was at the Savoy. William Greet had relinquished his lease of the theatre and Mrs D'Oyly Carte had found a new lessee, Mr J. H. Leigh, who had taken on a twenty-year lease. He immediately sublet the Savoy to Edward Laurillard for the production of a new musical, *The Lovebirds*, written by George Grossmith Jr. The music was by Raymond Roze, son of the famous prima donna Marie Roze. Not yet thirty, he had already been responsible for a good deal of theatrical music including incidental music for several of Tree's productions at Her Majesty's but this was his first stage musical.

The Lovebirds was a strange little concoction. The story begins in the idyllic surroundings of the riverside home of Alex and Gracie, the lovebirds of the title. They explain:

> In our connubialities there never was a hitch
> And someday we shall both go forth to claim the Dunmow Flitch
> We never go visiting or entertain a guest
> We don't want any cuckoos' eggs in our own nest . .

Their self-contained contentment is broken in upon by the arrival of a dude-y acquaintance, Sir Billie Duffield, and then by the whole cast of the Venus Theatre dressed as Pink Pierrots. The leading lady of the troupe, Effie Doublehurst, flirts with Alex and then claims a kiss which, unfortunately, is seen by Gracie who rushes out and heads for the wicked city. After two further acts of what was little more than a variety entertainment, the status quo is restored.

The show started with an considerable disadvantage in its theatre. It was impossible that the audience and the critics should not remember the glories of the Savoy under D'Oyly Carte and Greet and, in spite of the evidence of *Naughty Nancy*, a piece of the confessedly variety type would have had to be another *Morocco Bound* to hold its own. *The Lovebirds*, notwithstanding some goodish music, was of nothing like that quality. On the first night the gallery booed the piece at the final curtain and *The Times*' critic admitted that he felt like joining in with them, although his motives seemed to be largely based on feeling 'what we have lost'. He commented acidly:

> [Mr Grossmith's libretto] pleased his patrons hugely and in a week or two, when it has begun to play a little closer, it will be like several variety entertainments rolled into one . .

To the music he paid slightly more heed:

> now and then he becomes really interesting . . . our impression throughout was that when Mr Roze thought no-one would be listening, he put in something he enjoyed writing . . his numbers have just a touch of unlikeness to other people's . .

The songs were, however, not sufficiently interesting to sustain the feeble story and the larger part of the responsibility for keeping the entertainment going fell upon the artists. Alex and Gracie were played by Bertram Wallis and Kate Cutler ('a soothing tint of freshness in a great deal of blare and noise'). The baritone role had originally been intended for Sydney Brough, but in the last stages of rehearsal Brough's voice broke down, Wallis was called upon, and the opening postponed until he had been rehearsed. The principal light roles were both taken by Americans, comedian George Fuller Golden and the diminutive Blanche Ring, and Louise Raymond, Maude Darrell, Lawrence Grossmith and Fred Leslie Jr all had solos to add to the programme. Grossmith had one of the more attractive numbers, 'Backwater Bertha':

> Backwater! Backwater! They oughter have taught her
> The proper way to steer a boat
> As her ideas were most remote.
> Backwater! Backwater! Now mind how you go.
> Oh dear, oh dear, she's in the weir
> Backwater Bertha, wo!

and Miss Raymond sang a piece lauding the properties of crème de menthe:

> Crème de menthe, crème de menthe,
> You're a little green fairy so gay
> And you're just twice as nice
> When they fill you with ice
> For it can't take the fire of desire away.
> Oh, how I want a little sip from those dear lips
> Oh say not nay
> Oh, my sweet peppermint with your emerald glint
> Crème de menthe, crème de menthe frappé!

Maude Darrell told of the flirtations of 'The Programme Girl' with the audience and Blanche Ring ended proceedings with a humming and ooh-aahing coon song, 'The silent Coon'. There was also a parody number which took off pieces from 'Little Mary' to 'Hiawatha' and Kate Cutler indulged in the currently inescapable burlesque of Lena Ashwell's Japanese maiden in *The Darling of the Gods*.

The opening night reception meant almost certain failure for *The Lovebirds*, but the next day saw some major alterations in an attempt to save the show. Golden and Miss Ring ransacked their repertoires and interpolated their own business and songs, leaving the show with very little pretension to belong anywhere but a music hall. Grossmith and Arthur Longley introduced American songs and *The Lovebirds* managed to keep going. If the piece had not caught on, Blanche Ring had. She had attracted a young and exuberant male audience all of her own who returned to the show night after night to hear her sing her song 'Sammy'. Their excesses became quite alarming. One night two of them leapt from a stage box to join the actress in her famous number, another night there was lowered from a box, to which she pointedly sang the song each night, a bull terrier pup with its pedigree tied to its collar, dangling from the end of a fishing line! But even Blanche Ring and 'Sammy' were not sufficient to make ends meet at the Savoy and, after ten weeks, *The Lovebirds* folded.

If its life was short it was, nevertheless, double that of the next entry, an Anglo-French collaboration called *Amorelle (1810)*. This piece was written by Barton White with lyrics by Ernest Boyd-Jones, who was still playing in *A Chinese Honeymoon* at the Strand. The music was by the French composer, Gaston Serpette, best known in Britain for his first musical *The Broken Branch*, the more recent *The Telephone Girl* and many opérettes in his home country including *Le Carnet du Diable*, *Le Capitole* and *La Dot de Brigitte*.

Amorelle was a piece in the old-fashioned whimsical comic-opera style. Jules and François are ostensibly twin brothers and both are after the hand of lovely Lesbia. It is decided that whichever shall return at the end of a given time with the most money shall win the lady. François takes little heed; his answer to the wager is to borrow enough money from a money-lender on the day appointed to allow him to win the contest. But Jules sets out to earn his fortune with the quack Doctor Napoleon Bonaparte Crow as his aide. They are wrecked on an island of happy-go-lucky people whom Jules galvanises into a prosperous wine-producing community. Their wine is named after a pretty inhabitant, Amorelle. The wine is bought by the Emperor, assuring the fortune of Jules who arrives just in time to win the hand of Lesbia. The plot was decorated with considerable detail. The 'twins' turn out to be nothing of the kind, François being proved rich and aristocratic and Jules poor and lowly, until a Gilbertian baby-swap is revealed. Amorelle turns out to be Jules' long-lost sister and Dr Crow receives the attentions of a lady of comic opera proportions who is looking for 'someone to cherish', and so forth.

Amorelle was first tried out in 1903 at Kennington, under the title *Amorelle (1798)*, where Willie Edouin assembled a strong cast and took a week off from playing Hoggenheimer in *The Girl from Kays* to star as Dr Crow. The reaction was positive and a tour was set up by C. P. Levilly which opened in Manchester at Christmas, staying there for five weeks to excellent houses before moving on through other major dates where its popularity was confirmed. The piece was picked up by Frank Curzon and produced in London in February, but there it inspired only indifference. *The Times* commented that it: 'aims at the level of *My Lady Molly* and [does] not quite reach it . .' and continued:

> . . we liked it very much to begin with – up to about the middle of the second act, and if we saw it again after a good deal of it has been cut out, we should probably like it all . . .

The Stage agreed: 'its action drags somewhat and there are many portions that could be profitably cut . .' Amongst the four hours of material there were some attractive pieces; the American Mabelle Gillman in the title role had a pretty ballad, 'I don't Cry for the Moon':

> But what care I for luxury or state
> The rich may sigh and sorrow reach the great
> True friends have I, my wants are few,
> So I don't cry for the moon, would you?

Claire Romaine as the amorous Marina caused much amusement with 'I would Woo Thee':

My love will only cease
When burglars love police
When the world's upsetting and all are getting mad and madder
When a hog can sail a yacht
When ice is served up hot
Then I'll be untrue, my Crow, to you and die a shadder.

and Charles Wibrow had a plot number 'Twas a nasty Night' which went down well. Willie Edouin, as the Tweedlepunch-ish Dr Crow, had a balloon song 'You Fly sky High', but the role was by no means the equal of the *Florodora* one, not indeed of his more recent Hoggenheimer.

Amorelle never looked like becoming a West End success. Three weeks or so into the run Ernest Boyd-Jones died suddenly and four days later the show followed suit after one of the shortest runs in recent years. But, in spite of its collapse in London, *Amorelle* continued to find a certain degree of popularity out of town and Levilly ran it right through into 1906 with two concurrent companies playing a good part of 1904/5.

After two failures, the West End was ready for a new hit and it was not long coming. At Daly's, the run of *A Country Girl* had ended and George Edwardes produced in its place a piece with a Sinhalese setting, variously mooted as *Delightful Ceylon*, *Sunny Ceylon* and *The Singhalis* but finally christened *The Cingalee* or Sunny Ceylon. In spite of his former declarations and the slightly different path taken by *A Country Girl*, *The Cingalee* was very much in the established groove of Edwardes' earlier Daly's musicals. It had been written by the *Country Girl* team of Tanner, Ross, Greenbank, and Monckton and it involved many of the established Daly's stars: Coffin, Wright, Barrington, Fred Kaye, Willie Warde, Gracie Leigh *et al* as well as two new leading ladies, Isabel Jay, who had come into *A Country Girl* as a take-over, and the star of *My Lady Molly*, Sybil Arundale.

The plot was a standard one, by Daly's out of *Florodora*. Harry Vereker, the owner of a Sinhalese tea-plantation, wishes to wed Nanoya, one of his workers. She, however, cannot follow her inclinations having been married at four years old to the potentate of Boobhamba. To avoid this marriage she has fled, disguised, from her position as the owner of the very plantation on which she now works, and Harry has been conned into 'buying' it by a rascally lawyer, Chambuddy Ram. But the High Commissioner orders that Nanoya must be found and Ram is accused of hiding her. He is also accused of the theft of a famous black pearl and ordered to produce both at once. The pearl turns up with one Peggy Sabine, engaged as governess for Harry's wife-to-be. Peggy has won it in a gambling game in London. Ram sets out to get hold of both Peggy and the jewel, not to mention Nanoya. Things are made easy for him when Harry buys the pearl as a gift for Nanoya and Ram easily delivers both parts of his commission up to the judiciary. In the second act Nanoya is freed from the unhappy early marriage by the combined efforts of everybody. Boombhamba has a harem in which every wife wears a different colour as an aid to identification. Since there is only one colour missing from his rainbow he can have only one wife more. At the crucial moment he spots one he prefers to Nanoya, who is sent packing back to her Harry's arms.

It was safe and uninspired, and *The Times* was prompted, with good cause, to comment:

> . . all the clever people who concoct these entertainments are obviously suffering from lack of stimulus. They are in a comfortable, smooth-running rut. They know exactly what to do and how to do it and the result is that their very respectable talent never develops new strength and they repeat themselves again and again . . .

This was precisely the case. The return from Devon pastures to the mysterious and colourful East meant a return to the world so successfully shown in *The Geisha* and *San Toy*. It also meant a return to the types – now stereotypes – developed in those shows: Rutland Barrington as his umpteenth Pasha figure; Hayden Coffin not, for once, in uniform, but playing much the same role as always; Huntley Wright as a close relation of Wun Hi in black-face; and the whole, yet again, resting on the confrontation of the British and the Eastern ways of life.

If the libretto was predictable, the music and the songs were a little less so. Lionel Monckton was as reliable as always although, in this case, supplied with some less than inspiring lyrics by Greenbank and Ross whose enormous output seemed to be affecting their standards. Paul Rubens supplied additional material but he was no Sidney Jones as a musician and his lyrics often suffered from lapses of skill and taste. His original contribution to *The Cingalee* was limited, but by the time the piece had run for a while there were no fewer than seven of Rubens' songs in the score which, while they did not affect the popularity of the piece, certainly lowered the standard.

The score did not produce any hits. Monckton supplied an attractive quartet called 'True Love' (later replaced by a Rubens song) as well as two straightforward ballads for Coffin, 'Pearl of sweet Ceylon' and 'My dear little Cingalee' to unimaginative lyrics. Isabel Jay's song in Act 1 proved quite popular although it must have been difficult for the lady to keep a straight face while singing 'My heart's at your feet (pick it up, pick it up)', and Miss Arundale had a pretty ballad 'My cinnamon Tree'. Rubens also wrote a song for her called 'Sloe Eyes' to a fairly anodyne lyric, but he concentrated principally on numbers for the comic Chambuddy Ram and Peggy. The most successful of these was 'The wonderful English Pot' describing the manners of an English gentleman with an irritating kind of inverted snobbery and a decided lack of imagination. The same old jokes and topics were rolled out in an attempt to inculcate some humour by making Chambuddy Ram into a kind of Indian Malaprop. In a duet the two comedians imitated 'Monkeys' with much fooling to cover some more very routine lyrics. But both 'The wonderful English Pot' and 'Monkeys' appealed to the audience just as much as the more worthy work of Monckton and, in consequence, Rubens was given his head with 'Make a Fuss of Me', 'She's all Right', 'You and I and I and You', a piece called 'Gollywogs' which could never exist nowadays:

> Once a gollywog loved a dolly-wog
> (wog, wog, wog, wog) . .

and 'Something's devilish Wrong', another number for Chambuddy Ram which simply repeated the rather limp satire of the other songs.

The Cingalee showed that imitation was not an inexhaustible recipe for artistic success nor generally for a commercial one. Edwardes knew, however, just how much depended on his performers and on the lavish style with which his productions were staged. He spent £14,000 in putting the new piece on the stage, of which an amazing £500 was spent on artificial flowers to decorate the opening set of the tea plantation. The expense was justified. The scene on the rising of the opening curtain was one of the most beautiful in memory and those that followed were barely less splendid. Another feature was the special dancing: devil dances copied from Cingalese originals by Loku Banda and the ever-present Willie Warde, Parahara (Festival) Dances by the 'Sisters Amaranth', and in contrast the indispensable solo for Topsy Sinden on more familiar lines. At the end of the first night there was no doubt that *The Cingalee*, in spite of its defects, was another success for Edwardes and for Daly's.

During its run, it underwent considerable re-writing. Louis Bradfield joined the cast and the role of best-friend Bobby was written up for him and a Lionel Monckton/Adrian Ross song, 'The Ladies' added. Numbers were added or changed with a frequency unusual in a Daly's show, but at one stage the whole production looked like collapsing through a totally non-artistic consideration. Doubtless inspired by the at least partial success of the plaintiff in the *Country Girl* case, an Indian army officer, one Captain Fraser, sued Edwardes for plagiarising his play *Hanjahan*. Fraser had been introduced to Edwardes by Hayden Coffin and had read his play to 'the Guv'nor'. Edwardes had been largely unimpressed but Fraser was unwilling to change a word of his 'masterpiece', though finally consenting to work with Tanner before returning to India.

The parallels between *Hanjahan* and *The Cingalee* were minimal and Jimmy Davis, Charlie Brookfield and Lionel Monckton were among the distinguished expert witnesses who took the stand to swear that there was 'no substantial similarity' . . after all, musical comedy libretti were all pretty much alike. But, even more ludicrously than in the *Country Girl* case, the decision was given in favour of the plaintiff, with £3,000 in damages. Edwardes appealed, but finally settled with Fraser out of court for £2,000 with no admission of liability.

The Cingalee had a twelve months' run; good by normal standards, but less than any other Daly's musical except the underrated *A Greek Slave*, confirming George Edwardes in his opinion that a new type of show must be found for that theatre. In America *The Cingalee*, not surprisingly, failed to repeat the success won there by its predecessors. With a cast headed by Blanche Deyo, Melville Stewart and Martha Carine it stayed only a short season at Daly's, New York.

So the great series of Daly's musicals which had begun with *A Gaiety Girl* and *An Artist's Model* came to an end with *The Cingalee*, and it was many years before another British musical would play there. Edwardes' search for a suitable class product for his theatre now led him away from the famous 'team' and towards the ready-made successes of Europe.

The next new London entries of 1904 were foreign works. A revival of *La Poupée* went into the Prince of Wales after the withdrawal of *The School Girl* and filled in there for a couple of months, but much more worthy of notice was the arrival of two new shows. The first was probably the best of the American imports to date, Frank Pixley and Gustave Luders' *The Prince of Pilsen*, a lively if lightweight piece of considerably more charm and less raw spirits and buffoonery than many of its compatriots. It did not succeed in becoming a genuine hit in Britain, although it outran its American production (143 perfs) by totalling a very respectable 160 nights. One of the show's most popular features was a young member of its cast, Miss Camille Clifford. Miss Clifford, a Broadway chorine, had been the winner of a lucrative contest organised to find a 'Miss New York' as conceived by the artist Charles Dana Gibson and, as 'The Gibson Girl' she paraded wordlessly across the stage in *The Prince of Pilsen* for the delectation of the London public who took enthusiastically to her amazing figure and posture and pretty face. When the *Prince of Pilsen* company left to return to the U.S.A., Miss Clifford stayed behind to consolidate her 'stardom' as 'The Gibson Girl' on the halls.

Much more successful and more relevant to events to come was the new production at the Apollo. The Apollo was in trouble with the collapse of *Madame Sherry*, and the 'libraries' were in even deeper trouble. The theatre offered to suspend their liability if they could find a new piece and get it mounted at the theatre to replace the deceased show. The agencies got to work and discovered *Véronique*, a musical which had been produced at a matinée by Murray Carson with the backing of Lady de Grey and her brother, H. V. Higgins. It was a French piece, translated by Henry Hamilton with the lyrics done by the late Lilian Eldee of *A Country Girl* fame and, although the music was by the respected French composer André Messager, it had failed to find a commercial producer, leaving the Higginses to get it staged as a mark of respect towards Messager with whom they were closely linked at Covent Garden. *Véronique* was hastened into the empty theatre and, almost before anyone realised it, was established as a huge success – the biggest foreign success in Britain since *La Poupée*. It ran for 495 performances and the 'Swing Song', 'Trot here, Trot There' and its other delightful tunes became deserved favourites.

When it had seemed that only the British could produce musicals of quality, suddenly both America and France had weighed in with really attractive examples of their art. The blossoming of the American musical in Britain was still a long way off, but *Véronique*'s triumph marked the beginning of a new continental revival on the scale of the opéra-bouffe invasion of thirty years previously which was to help eventually to end the great era of British dominance in the light musical theatre. For the moment, however, that British musical tradition was still very much on top. The next two entries were both British hits and one of them, indeed, would comprehensively outrun *Véronique*.

The pedigree of *Sergeant Brue* was a strange one. Frank Curzon had built up a very special and heterogenous audience at the Strand Theatre during the huge run of *A Chinese Honeymoon*. He needed to retain that audience with his next show, striking the same cheerful unpretentious note that had characterised *A Chinese Honeymoon* and that was a task which would not be easy, particularly now that George Dance had laid down his pen for the more exacting task of management. But *A Chinese Honeymoon* had made Curzon unbelieveably wealthy. He could afford to go to the top, and he did. Owen Hall was commissioned as librettist for the new show. The lyricist was the journalist, pantomime-writer and author J. Hickory Wood and the composer – no Lionel Monckton, Ivan Caryll or Howard Talbot – but the lady composer of popular drawing room and concert songs, Elizabeth Frederika Lehmann.

Liza Lehmann was the daughter of the painter, Rudolf Lehmann, and had been brought up among the fashionable and famous of London. A lady of many accomplishments, she had a career as a concert soprano before turning her attention to composing. In 1896 she came to notice by writing the song cycle 'In a Persian Garden' which she followed with two further works, 'In Memoriam' (based on Tennyson's poem) and the nursery songs 'The Daisy Chain' which increased her reputation. Curzon brought her to the stage for the first time as the composer of *Sergeant Brue*. If the combination of Hall, Wood and Miss Lehmann seemed an unlikely one it was, nevertheless, a highly intelligent one and the result of the collaboration was better than anyone – except, doubtless, Curzon – could have hoped. Owen Hall excelled himself. He produced a hilarious plot which kept going through all three acts of the piece yet allowed room for all the important turns and numbers which Wood and Miss Lehmann supplied.

The plot of *Sergeant Brue* centred on the efforts of that diffident policeman, who has been made Sergeant 'because I saw a man stop a horse in the street', to get himself promoted to Inspector and become eligible for a large legacy dependent on the promotion. He enlists the help of Crookie Scrubbs, burglar, to fake an arrest 'in flagrante delicto' but merely succeeds in getting himself arrested and almost fired from the force. All ends happily when he accidentally catches the influential magistrate in charge of his case playing an illegal gambling game in Brue's own house. A touch of blackmail and Brue gets his Inspectorship, his fortune and the hand of the penniless but extravagant Lady Bickenhall after whom he has yearned since the day he saw her in Piccadilly 'and turned all the traffic into Berkeley Square to let you pass'. Brue was played by Willie Edouin, back on the right track after his disastrous flirtation with comic opera in *Amorelle*. It was a character which fitted him admirably and which rated with his Tweedlepunch and his Hoggenheimer amongst the most joyful characterisations of the era. He was brilliantly supported by two excellent acting performances from Arthur Williams, in his best role for years as the thick-headed Crookie Scrubbs, and Ethel Irving as the vivacious and enterprising Lady Bickenhall. Two sets of young lovers were added to provide the more conventional romantic moments – the younger members of the Brue family played by Joe Farren Soutar and Olive Morrell, and their respective lovers, Sydney Barraclough and the young Zena Dare.

Miss Lehmann's score was a more than passable imitation of a popular musical score. *The Stage* commented:

> [she has been] forced to descend to the conventions of cakewalks and coon songs; but where her sense of musical humour has had free play she has shown a vein of pretty fantasy and a clever balancing of the romantic with the prosaic . .

while *The Times* affirmed that she had been 'very clever at catching the manner', continuing:

> . . the prophetic ear heard the barrel organ even in the overture and, as the piece went on, it became continually harder to remember that it was the composer of 'The Daisy Chain' who was the composer of *Sergeant Brue* . .

But Miss Lehmann had not had things all her own way. Perhaps the most successful number from *Sergeant Brue* never saw the opening night. 'If I Built the World for You' was a little piece intended for Zena Dare which was cut out in rehearsal as being insufficiently 'bright'. Some time later, however, Miss Lehmann needed a song for the soprano, Louise Dale, to sing in concert: Arthur Boosey rejected the piece she proffered as being too serious and Miss Lehmann ironically commented, 'Ah, you want something like this,' and tinkled out the despised 'If I Built the World for You'. To her surprise, Boosey replied that it was indeed what he wanted, and Louise Dale went on to make a considerable success with the song. It was not only cuts that the composer found herself forced to endure. To her fury, she found that the management intended to sprinkle her score, in the manner of the day, with popular songs from America. She protested loudly before discovering that she was contractually unable to do anything about the dilution of her score, and she had to watch James Tate, Ernest Vousden and musical director Frederick Rosse all put in their tuppence worth of music alongside the imported numbers 'The sweetest Girl in Dixie' by James O'Dea, the writer of 'Sammy', and 'Under a Panama' by his compatriot Vincent Bryan of 'Tammany' fame, and J. B. Mullen. During the show's run, which was a long and successful one, as revisions and replacements were required, Miss Lehmann made sure she was at hand to supply the majority of new songs herself.

Sergeant Brue was well received on its opening night. Curzon and his writers had caught the required flavour and their audience was duly appreciative:

> They ask for the kind of fun that is sometimes known as 'good, honest fun' of the

> rough and tumble order that makes no demands on the brain for its comprehension, and they ask for the kind of music that best fits such fun, rollicking, rattling stuff for the most part with here and there a dash of highly sugared sentiment, the whole as imitative and as outworn as you please so long as there are plenty of good, catchy tunes and plenty of drums . . (*Times*)

Subtlety of expression was not required. *Sergeant Brue* moved well away from the older comic opera form into what was virtually a music-hall musical: a series of bright point numbers and ballads interspersed with humorous sketches. Owen Hall's plot was sufficiently amusing to give a reasonable shape to the string of material, and he had created characters which raised the piece above the level of the normal variety or farce musical. Of its kind *Sergeant Brue* was a well-written example, beautifully cast and staged by Curzon. First and foremost in its popular elements came Willie Edouin clowning his way through the title role with practised skill, superbly supported by Williams and Miss Irving. On the vocal side, the most popular songs were 'The twopenny Tube' in which Joe Soutar and Zena Dare described how they fell in love in Shepherd's Bush tube station with the porter constantly interrupting with cries of 'next stop', and 'So did Eve' in which Soutar sang of the fair sex:

> Girls of today are but daughters of Eve, Mother Eve,
> They cause all the trouble, men say, I believe, so did Eve.
> Oh, why do men blame them for using their power
> When they bring such nice apples for man to devour
> Though they know all the time that the apples are sour, so did Eve.
>
> Daughters of Eve, daughters of Eve,
> Like their fair ancestors
> London or Manchester
> Girls go out strolling without Papa's leave, so did Eve.

Ethel Irving was well supplied with melody, whether describing herself as 'My Lady Busy' to a humming 'busy-bee' accompaniment:

> The work that I get through in a day
> Is sufficient to make you dizzy
> I've meetings her and meetings there
> And new societies everywhere
> Wherever I go, I take the chair
> For I am My Lady Busy.

or musing on the insensitivities of men in 'Hey ho, Men Come and Go' or on the ludicrous nature of the modern musical comedy in one of those masochistic songs in which the genre seemed to specialise. The lyric for this particular piece was by a 29-year-old accountant turned songwriter from Manchester, George Arthurs, at the beginning of what was to be a long and successful career in which he would produce rather better lines than:

> My income undoubtedly sparse is
> So I think that the best I can do
> Is in one of those musical farces
> To endeavour to make my début.
> I, of course, should commence in the chorus
> Though the lyrics might come as a shock,
> In a sweet rustic spot
> I would sing Tommy Rot
> In the latest Parisian frock . .

The number did, however, give Ethel Irving the chance to parody the styles of the chorus girl, the jeune première and the saucy chanteuse to good effect and it did not take a very up-to-date person to catch the reference when she gazed up into the stage box and sang:

> Freddy, my darling Freddy, we'll be as happy as we can be
> Freddy, come closer, Freddy, I'll marry you if you won't marry me

But although the songs of *Sergeant Brue* were well-received, there was none amongst them which caught on in the way that the burlesqued 'Sammy' had.

There was plenty to look at in *Sergeant Brue* in spite of its unpromising settings in a hairdressing salon and a law court. The final scene was set in a Berkeley Square house where Brue, in true *Artist's Model* fashion, throws a masquerade ball – in this case a Great Zoological Party in which all the guests arrive wearing animal costumes. It was designed with great élan and some extravagance, and also the odd error. One part of the Party consisted of a song 'Fido Was a Poodle' in which Hilda Trevalyan, in one of the skivvy roles at which she ranked second only to Louie Freear, performed a dance dressed as a white poodle. She jumped through a series of hoops surrounded by a bevy of chorines dressed as black poodles in a routine which was too silly for words and which was soon cut out. What remained was altogether better and more attractive stuff.

If *Sergeant Brue* lacked something of the colour and the universal appeal of *A Chinese Honeymoon*, it nevertheless settled in quickly at the Strand and showed every sign of becoming an established success. But Owen Hall was not content. He had forced Curzon to agree that the piece should be transferred to a 'first class theatre' as soon as was possible and thus, after only four weeks, the Strand's new success was taken off and re-staged at the Prince of Wales Theatre where it remained for five months until Curzon, in spite of Hall's protests, moved it back to the Strand when George Edwardes needed the Prince of Wales. *Sergeant Brue* wound up its metropolitan career with a final three months in its original home, coming in with a total of 280 performances which, under less muddling circumstances, might have been increased.

In April 1905, *Sergeant Brue* was staged at Broadway's Knickerbocker Theatre with Frank Daniels in the title role. Amongst the cast was Blanche Ring who had re-crossed the Atlantic and who, characteristically supplied the hit song which had been missing in London in the shape of Jerome and Schwartz's 'My Irish Molly, O'. But *Sergeant Brue* failed to catch on and its run was limited to a disappointing 93 performances. It was more successful in its other overseas productions, however, and in Britain it pursued a long and happy provincial career.

During the run of *The Cherry Girl* at the Vaudeville, Seymour Hicks began the preparation of a new vehicle for his wife and himself with which, eventually, to replace the long-running Christmas show. The idea of doing an up-dated musical version of the Cinderella story was apparently suggested to him by the playwright, Captain Robert Mansell, and Hicks himself prepared a libretto, *The Catch of the Season*, on those lines with the collaboration of Cosmo Hamilton, the young author of several minor plays, and the 24-year-old composer Herbert Edgar Haines. Haines was the son of the well-known Alfred Haines, m.d. at the Prince's, Manchester, and it was in that theatre that young Haines had placed his first stage music – some ballet pieces for Robert Courtneidge – at the age of 17. He subsequently became a conductor himself and joined George Edwardes' tours for four years before coming to London to conduct *Three Little Maids* at the Prince of Wales. His score for *The Catch of the Season* was a scale of work quite new to him.

The plans for the new musical suffered a major setback when it was discovered that its intended star, Mrs Seymour Hicks, was pregnant and Hicks was faced with deciding between postponing the production which had all but been created around her and trying to find a replacement for such an important and demanding part. He decided upon the latter course and remembered the very young ingénue star of his 1902 touring show *An English Daisy* who was presently playing in *Sergeant Brue*. Arrangements were made for her to be released from her role at the Prince of Wales and Zena Dare came to the Vaudeville to take on the role of the season as Cinderella of 1904. She was supported by the strong Vaudeville company, Seymour Hicks himself as her leading man, his brother Stanley Brett, the experienced actress Rosina Filippi and the outfit's latest singing find, Barbara Deane, but the chief weight of the huge and costly production was placed squarely on the shoulders of its eighteen-year-old leading lady.

Hicks and Hamilton had told their story with a sure hand. The nature of the piece which they had constructed, in accordance with the version of the story that has the Prince (here the Duke of St Jermyns) visiting and getting to know his Cinderella (now Angela) before the episode at the ball, necessitated a considerable emphasis on the love story of its principals, but the authors managed to avoid an atmosphere of excess sentimentality, with the aid of such characters as the comic page-boy, Bucket, whose love for Angela from his very young years made a light-hearted contrast to the central love story. The ugly sisters of legend were turned into the Hon Sophia and the Hon Honoria Bedford, two magnificently statuesque beauties of a slightly acidulous turn, while the Fairy Godmother was metamorphosed into Lady Caterham, aunt to the unhappy Angela, who turns up from Paris at the traditional moment bearing in her train a bevy of French dressmakers to replace the usual mice in the manufacture of ball-gown and glass slippers which turn Angela into 'Molly O'Halloran from County Clare'.

The Prince's friend was not 'Dandini' but 'Lord Dundreary' in which role Sam Sothern gave a passable imitation of the unforgettable character created 43 years previously by his late father in *Our American Cousin*; but the most notable addition was an innovation – the comical Mr William Gibson, father of nine daughters:

They were all alike, one end was curls
And the other end all black stocking . .

Like the now famous Camille Clifford, the Misses Gibson followed the fashion sketched by Charles Dana Gibson and became 'the Gibson Girls', the acme of fashion:

We've become the great attraction of the season
You ask us the reason?
We'll tell you why.

We discovered when a public place we entered
On us was centred
The public eye.
So, seeing we were proving a sensation
We thought we might become a bigger one
By walking in single file
In the Dana Gibson style
So we tried it, and the trick was done.

We realise the pictures, tall and divinely fair,
By society invited, we go everywhere,
We've copied every detail, dress, stately walk and curls
And everybody calls us 'Dana Gibson Girls'.

The 'Gibson Girls' were soon indeed the great attraction of the season: pretty, dark-eyed Kathleen Dawn, aristocratic Lily Mills, quaint Kate Vesey, tall and calm Marie Ashton and perky Elsie Kay, all towering over their stage Papa and parading the most beautiful clothes ever seen on the stage of the Vaudeville Theatre. Perhaps the most noticeable of all the 'Gibson Girls' was a later addition to the ranks, Eva Carrington. Nearly six feet tall and with a figure in proportion, Miss Carrington was the only Gibson Girl to be dressed in black, and she stood out accordingly. Eva Carrington had appeared in several shows under Seymour Hicks since her début in *Alice in Wonderland* but her Gibson Girl appearance was her most outstanding – and also her last as, before *The Catch of the Season* had finished its run, she had joined the ranks of the showgirl peeresses as Lady de Clifford.

The girls' costumes were a particular feature of the show. They had been the object of considerable pre-publicity by their creator Lady Duff Gordon who, through her firm, Mme Lucile of 23 Hanover Square, had been the provider of what were described as 'emotionalised costumes'. The range of colours in the gowns was said to be representative of the various phases of love from 'the passion of love' to 'the climax of love'. Lady Duff Gordon held a special preview of the dresses at her showroom before the opening of *The Catch of the Season* and they attracted a good deal of attention not only by their beauty but by the way they were displayed – the mannequins unprecedentedly moving about rather than posing immobile. A few weeks after opening night, the Gibson Girl line-up received the ultimate fillip. *The Prince of Pilsen* had closed and, on October 1, the American company sailed for home: but one member stayed behind with a contract in hand to appear in *The Catch of the Season* in the role of 'Miss Sylvia Gibson' – the prototype, Camille Clifford. In *The Prince of Pilsen* she had had nothing to do except walk across the stage and look magnificent, but Frohman and Hicks were more daring. 'Miss Sylvia' was given some lines and allowed to introduce a song specially composed for her by Hugh Rumbold and Frank Compton in which she declared:

> Sylvia is the Gibson Girl who goes out walking every day
> All the people come to see her walking slowly down Broadway
> As she comes strolling down she sets their hearts in a whirl
> She's the cutest little pearl, Sylvia, the Gibson Girl . .

In spite of the song and even though Miss Clifford had no voice whatsoever, 'Sylvia' became one of the show's most popular features and audiences flocked to see the New Yorker and her figure display themselves on the stage.

Opening night had no Camille Clifford but there were quite enough attractions to secure *The Catch of the Season* a thorough success. If Zena Dare could not quite make the public forget the expected Ellaline Terriss, she nevertheless had a talent and a charm of her own which combined most appealingly with Seymour Hicks' romantic Duke and, if the Gibson Girls were not the genuine article, Lily Mills, Kathleen Dawn, Irene Allen and their associates had enough charm and style and a wardrobe to stagger any audience. The low comedy element in *The Catch of the Season* was less prominent than in most of its contemporaries, but there was still plenty of fun to mix with the story and the sentiment which Hicks and Hamilton had blended so judiciously, although the comic business was not allowed to detract from the central story.

The musical portion, on the other hand, was rather less carefully integrated. Many of the songs bore little reference to the tale of Cinderella/Angela, and the ensemble music was limited to an opening chorus and finale for each of the two acts, an entrance piece for the Gibson Girls, another for Angela's arrival at the ball and a duet for the lovers. The basic score consisted of thirteen solo songs, a total which was constantly varied with additions and replacements during the run of the show. Of the original first-night material undoubtedly the most popular piece was Hicks' solo, the vigorous march 'The Church Parade', a song in the 'Soldiers in the Park' tradition with an insubstantial lyric but a good deal of 'swing'. Zena Dare also gained a warm reception with a little Irish song 'Molly O'Halloran' written by Evelyn Baker who had joined Haines in supplying the bulk of the music for the show. It was as lightweight as Ernest Bucalossi's waltz-song 'Butterfly', sung by Frank Wilson (and later Barbara Deane) while the Gibson Girls, equipped with large pink cushions, attempted to catch toy butterflies in little golden nets. Altogether more clever were two songs for Hilda Jacobson (Honoria), a mock ballad 'Cigarette' and a humorous number called 'The Charms on my Chain' in which the 'ugly' sister recalls her memories:

When I look at these trophies, I'm filled, be it said
With a feeling akin to alarm
For they tell how the years and the lovers have sped
Since the first of them gave me a charm.
It is here, and a generous lover was he
For his heart, like his waistcoat, was big;
He was fonder indeed of his dinner than me,
And he gave me this little gold pig.

He gave me this charm for my chain
And I never shall see him again
He sleeps by the waters of Marienbad
And his memory lives in the dinners we had
And this little gold pig on my chain.

Later in the run changes brought in a whole volume of new material, including the inevitable American 'pops', as the leading role changed hands with regularity. Zena Dare left the show at Christmas for a previous engagement in *Beauty and the Beast* at Bristol, and was replaced by pretty Maie Ash from the chorus who held the fort until Ellaline Terriss had given birth and was fit to return to active duty. The role of Angela did not make Miss Ash a star, but it brought her into the ruling family for she became the wife of Stanley Brett, brother and understudy to Hicks. Later, when Hicks and Miss Terriss took *The Catch of the Season* on the road, Brett took over as St Jermyns at the Vaudeville and Zena Dare's younger sister, Phyllis, who had played for Hicks as a child in *Bluebell*, became a fifteen year-old Angela. The run continued for nearly two very successful years, during which time Madge Crichton joined the galaxy of Angelas before the show closed finally after 621 performances.

But *The Catch of the Season* was not immune to the current fashion for ridiculous lawsuits, and one was brought by a Ethel Lucy Karri Thomas. Miss Karri, as she called herself, had been hired to play one of the Gibson Girls at a salary of £3 per week. After three weeks of the run, she had been given a fortnight's notice. She sued, claiming that, as an actress, she was automatically on a run-of-the-play contract. The point of law at stake was 'Was a Gibson Girl – that is to say a 'showgirl' – an actress, or was she a member of the chorus and therefore subject to a fortnight's notice?' The differentiation between principals and chorus had hitherto been a simple one, but the arrival of this new class of creatures, required to do little but wear clothes and walk beautifully, was causing a problem. Miss Karri claimed to be an actress, since she had lines to speak. She had to say 'I'm a perfect wonder at spotting winners and I hardly ever lose at bridge' and later, 'Dear old Hyde Park'. The defence brought Hayden Coffin and Robert Courtneidge into court to declare that a 'showgirl' (a term which the judge found particularly offensive) was only a chorus lady who couldn't dance or sing, but to no avail. Miss Karri won £3 a week for every week *The Catch of the Season* had run (less £32 which she had managed to earn in the meantime), took the money and disappeared, leaving Courtneidge and other managers angrily declaring that in future they would put everyone except their stars on two weeks' notice.

The success of *The Catch of the Season* did not end with London's run. It was toured through Britain and played throughout the Empire with all the success a well-made piece deserves. Edna May appeared as Angela on Broadway in a heavily altered and less well-made version and scored successes with Luke Forwood's 'My little Buttercup' and the role of Angela. Joe Farren Soutar was her Duke and amongst the interpolations in the musical part were three Jerome Kern songs, 'Raining', 'Edna May's Irish Song' and 'Won't you Kiss me once before I Go'[1]. In 1917 *The Catch of the Season* was brought back for a short run in the West End, at the Prince's, where Hicks took up his old role opposite Isobel Elsom as Angela for 84 performances. It was, as might have been expected from Hicks, a 'revised' version. There were new songs by Herman Darewski, Adrian Ross and Clifford Grey including a sentimental war number 'Someone is Waiting over There' and the latest dance craze was satisfied by Fred Farren and Irene Magley in 'The Faust Rag', but all the favourite elements of the original production were still there and proved just as popular as the more up-to-date additions.

Since March, the West End had seen nothing but successes: *The Cingalee*, *Véronique*, *Sergeant Brue*, *The Catch of the Season*. Even *The Prince of Pilsen* had found some of the success it deserved. The balance was surely waiting to be redressed. It soon was, through the medium of an ill-advised and amateurish attempt to restore old-style English comic opera to the West End with a piece called *Ladyland*. *Ladyland* was written by the enthusiastic old Etonian Eustace ('Scroby') Ponsonby. Formerly a Guardsman, briefly an actor and songwriter, Ponsonby was a popular and ubiquitous devotee of the theatre, an asset to any first night on account of his loud laugh which regularly and quickly pointed all the laugh lines to the less quick-witted members of the audience. After some unfortunate efforts he eventually found himself a niche in the world he loved as a play-reader for Grossmith and Malone. The music of *Ladyland* was by the ballad writer Frank Lambert.

As its title suggests, the show was set in a pseudo-Gilbertian colony ruled over by The Great Lady, and the plot hinged on the marriage of that lady to one of her subjects, a necessary prerequisite to her retaining her position. Her rival, Alma Molyneux, seeks to trick her into wedding a foreigner and thus forfeiting her place. Ponsonby omitted nothing in the compilation of his book. He drew on all the popular elements of other people's burlesques, comic operas and opéras-bouffes for his material and glued it all together with modern musical comedy turns and such essential effects as the cake-walk. The dialogue alternated between old-fashioned burlesque punning and such jokes as:

> You are Roy's alter ego
> I feel more like a hard-boiled ego

[1] the chorus of French Gibson Girls (the Broadway Mr. Gibson had two sets of daughters, local and Parisienne) included Mlle. Elise Delisia – the twenty year-old Alice Delysia.

No mean cast was got together to present this piece of well-intentioned rubbish. Ethel Irving was Alma, Aline May from the San Carlo Opera Company was brought in to play The Great Lady, and Geraldine Ulmar was lured back from profitable retirement as a voice teacher for a smaller role. Richard Green, John Tresahar and the Gaiety veteran Windham Guise headed the male cast with the comedian Austin Melford in the role of an astronautical Professor Puddle. No-one knew what to do with the material. Ethel Irving took the only way out and sent the whole thing up. This succeeded in raising a few laughs, but there was nothing more to be done. The first-night reaction was surprisingly mild considering the pitiful value of the entertainment offered:

> The audience was mirthful but merciful and contented itself with gently 'guying' the more absurd details of the entertainment (*Era*)

That same paper had no doubts about the show's merits:

> The dominant note of the production of *Ladyland* at the Avenue Theatre on Monday was one of pathos. It was sad to see so much liberal expenditure, hard work and ability entirely wasted. The book of the piece is 'simply impossible'. There is an elaboration of dullness in it which only aggravates its inanity. It is absolutely deficient in humour; and some of it is completely incomprehensible . . .

Ladyland staggered on through Christmas and expired on Boxing Day.

After the success of *Three Little Maids*, it was no surprise to see George Edwardes line up another Paul Rubens musical for the Prince of Wales. *Lady Madcap* was ready in time for Christmas, and opened at the Coventry Street house following the removal of *Sergeant Brue* back to the Strand. Rubens had again written book, lyrics and music although, in the book, he accepted the accredited collaboration of Colonel Newnham-Davis and, in the lyrics, of Percy Greenbank.

Newnham-Davis was a new figure to the musical theatre. Now fifty years old, he had made his career in the army, firstly with the 'Buffs' in the Zulu Wars and in Griqueland and, later, as an intelligence officer in China and Malaya. He subsequently turned to journalism, becoming assistant editor and dramatic critic of *The Sporting Times*, to novel-writing, and produced several books on food including *Dinners and Diners* and *The Gourmet's Guide*. His influence on the erratic Rubens in *Lady Madcap* does not seem to have been very considerable.

Once again the English countryside, or that strange version of it beloved of the stage, served as a setting as it had for *Three Little Maids* and, once again, what plot the piece had was concerned with the working out of a clutch of frivolous love affairs. The central character, the 'Lady Madcap' of the title, is Lady Betty Claridge whose favourite pastimes seem to be getting her own way and playing stupid tricks on those who try to make her behave, thus apparently qualifying as 'a jolly romp'. She fakes a telegram to send her father hastening to London so that she may use his home to entertain a unit of hussars and flirt with one Trooper Smith. Trooper Smith, incidentally, is made to pose as a butler and Lady Betty disguises herself as a maid while good friend Gwenny pretends to be *her* and attracts the attentions of (a) a French count and b) two *Erminie* type impostors who arrive at the party in response to an advertisement for a millionaire husband placed in *The Morning Post* by Betty. This in spite of the fact that she despises millionaires, except, of course, when Trooper Smith turns out to be one in disguise which reconciles the ill-used father and makes everything All Right. The fact that it would have been All Right without three and a bit hours of the arch Lady Betty's antics was not intended to occur to the audience.

The libretto of *Lady Madcap* was largely Paul Rubens at his worst and the songs varied wildly in merit with the sudden lapses of taste which consistently marred Rubens' work. On the first night the audience took exception on several occasions to his suggestiveness and showed their disapproval in booing both the dialogue and lyrics. The offending parts were not permitted to remain long. But there was also much which had the popular ring and *The Times* critic noticed that

> some of the tunes were being whistled and sung by parts of the audience before even the curtain fell . . .

And, indeed, it was the songs which were the hard core of *Lady Madcap*. The twenty-five musical numbers were, this time, without exception the work of Rubens and many contained the simple, catching qualities which made his songs so popular with the public. Put over by such established *Three Little Maids* favourites as Maurice Farkoa and Delia Mason, or by perky Eva Sandford or by lovely Adrienne Augarde in the title role, they soon became favourites.

It was Farkoa who had the hit of the show. He 'wore a pale mauve suit and a diamond ring and was voted fascinating' as the French Count courting the pretended Lady Betty. Although he was now in his forties and tending to a certain *embonpoint*, Farkoa's attraction remained and in *Lady Madcap* he scored with a little ballad with a twist in its tail which declared:

> I like you in velvet, I love you in plush
> In satin you're just like your own lovely blush
> You're charming in silk, or a plain woollen shawl
> But you're simply delightful in anything at all . .

The 'anything' was, naturally, sung with a pause and a clear indication of 'nothing'. Delia Mason, as Gwenny, had two pretty numbers, 'Pretty Primrose' and 'Who? who? Who?' and Eva Sandford as the maid, Susan, sang humorously of 'Nerves' as well as declaring 'I don't Seem to Want you when you're with Me' and complaining of 'The Missis':

> Who is it who comes downstairs
> The Missis, the Missis,
> Catching you quite unawares
> In friendly tête-à-têtes . .

Two others of the more popular numbers fell to the lot of the leading lady who sang a rather unoriginal song about a 'Scarlet Uniform' in a brisk 4/4, and an inane piece called 'Her little Dog':

> He loved her little dog, so don't you see
> He really must have loved her equally
> But when he sent that dog a collarette
> Why do that? said she
> Don't spoil my little dog, just spoil me . .

surrounded by chorus ladies miming little dogs in their arms. Equally inane was a number for Leedham Bantock called 'The Beetle and the Boot' which took musical comedy anthropomorphism rather too far in detailing the love of a beetle for a boot which finally turns and squashes it.

The comedy of the piece was well cared for, with G. P. Huntley in the role of the ill-treated 'Trooper Smith' alias Oroya Brown (millionaire) being backed up by George

Carroll, Bantock, and Aubrey Fitzgerald and Fred Emney as the two familiar crooks who introduce themselves irrelevantly into the story. Indeed, *Lady Madcap* was truly stewed to order, with a bevy of old and obvious elements included. *The Stage* pointedly commented on the fact in the light of Edwardes' previous declarations:

> [Mr Edwardes] evidently decided on none of the reversions to comic opera or innovations in the direction of comedic treatment already much hinted at . . . [The book] has the simplest and most obvious ingredients of fun . . . and the music is in the nature of modest accompaniment with plenty of tuneful chorus work and sentimental and comic songs of a well-approved pattern.

But this seemed to be precisely what a certain public wanted. *Lady Madcap* was pronounced a success, and it ran.

By September 1905 it was seen that the piece needed a new injection of life and a 'second version' was staged. Maurice Farkoa dropped in French versions of Blanche Ring's hits 'Bedelia' and 'Sammy', and some new music was added for Zena Dare who had taken over the role of Lady Betty, before *Lady Madcap* finally closed in November after a year's run – a highly successful commercial enterprise.

Given the success gained in the export of *Three Little Maids*, it was natural that *Lady Madcap* should also set out on the Broadway trail. The results were sadly different. *Lady Madcap* was Americanised by Edward Paulton and R. H. Burnside, who had just had a Broadway success with *The Tourists*, and was re-christened *My Lady's Maid*. Madge Crichton (Betty), Delia Mason and George Carroll from the London cast were imported to emphasise the *Three Little Maids* connection. G. P. Huntley did not go on this occasion, and a young American comedian who had hitherto specialised in silly-ass roles took the part of Trooper Smith. Joseph Coyne was taking his first step towards becoming a straight-ish leading man, a course which was to culminate in the role of Danilo in London's *Merry Widow*. But neither Coyne nor the 'three little maids' could save *My Lady's Maid*:

> MR JOE COYNE AND
> THREE LITTLE MAIDS
>
> ---
>
> They are about all that is worth
> while in production known as 'My Lady's Maid'
>
> ---
>
> DULL NIGHT AT THE CASINO
>
> ---
>
> Misses Madge Crichton, Delia Mason and Elsa Ryan
> assist the Star in Saving Piece from Utter Failure
>
> (*NY Herald*)

In fact they did not succeed and the show was quickly gone.

The final musical offering of 1904 in London was a curious piece. The Irish-American vocalist, Denis O'Sullivan, who had become popular in *Shamus O'Brien* and *The Duchess of Dantzic*, needed a vehicle in which to tour. His wife, under the pen-name of 'Patrick Bidwell', put together a piece called *Peggy Machree* for the purpose. *Peggy Machree* had a story in the vein of *Martha* or *The Marriage Market* and told of a young lady who goes through what she thinks is a mock marriage only to find she is truly married. Many years later the two meet again and fall in love, only to discover that they are already man and wife.

For the musical part of the show, O'Sullivan went to Dr Michele Esposito who arranged a selection of popular Irish airs which the star and his wife had selected and topped them off with a little original music. Thus the piece had very much the flavour of an early nineteenth century ballad opera. The O'Sullivans called it a 'romantic comedy with music' which was a fair enough description. *Peggy Machree* was produced at Grimsby in November and began to tour with great success. When producer Charles Hamilton had an opportunity of five weeks at London's Wyndhams Theatre before the production there of *The Lady of Leeds*, he quickly took it. The reaction was remarkable, particularly from the critics who found in the piece some of the elements which they had missed in such pieces as *Lady Madcap* or *The Catch of the Season*:

> [it is] one of those disappointing pieces that just miss being, if not first rate, let us say good second rate. It is a genuine little comic opera, spirited and amusing for the most part and lightly touched here and there with pleasant pathos; the music is at least not the music we are all mortally tired of and, better still, there is no mere comedy part, no actor who is supposed to make us laugh at all cost . . the fun of the thing is in the piece itself, not in the accessories . . . (*Times*)

With Marie Dainton (ex-Mrs Pineapple of *A Chinese Honeymoon*) as his Peggy, O'Sullivan ran out a highly popular five weeks before taking *Peggy Machree* back on the road. The show's musical content was varied at will both with traditional Irish songs and with original modern material, and it continued to serve its purpose as a vehicle for its star until his untimely death at the age of 39 in 1908 whilst touring in America.

The Christmas entertainments for the 1904/5 season brought one new offering in *Little Black Sambo and Little White Barbara* adapted by Rutland Barrington as a follow-up to his *Water Babies* which had filled the Garrick so well for the past two seasons. This mélange of the two popular children's 'Dumpy' books proved less attractive than the earlier piece.

The provincial circuits were reasonably prolific in new works over the year. Easily the most notable was *The Blue Moon* which was brought out at Northampton in February and subsequently toured by a syndicate including Gaiety director J. A. E. Malone and actor-turned-manager Robert Courtneidge. It was announced that after the eight weeks' tour *The Blue Moon* would be taken into London but, in the event, it was some eighteen months before the show made its London début. It was extremely well received on its production although *The Era*'s Northampton correspondent noted:

> . . there is originality in the piece, but it would be folly to close one's eyes to the similarities of incidents and characters that have done duty before both in *San Toy* and *The Geisha* . .

going on to report, however, that

> nearly the whole of the eighteen numbers [had to be] repeated and, in some instances, again and again . .

Those numbers, provided by Howard Talbot, Percy Greenbank and the inexhaustible Paul Rubens, effectively padded out the familiar story of the oriental singing girl and her British Navy lover and the comic high jinks which surrounded their path to wedded bliss. A feature of the original production was the debut of nineteen-year-old soprano Florence Smithson. The daughter of a provincial theatre manager, Miss Smithson had been on the stage since childhood, most recently in a touring opera company where her brilliant light soprano had been heard in Donizetti's *Daughter of the Regiment*, as Marguerite in *Faust* and, less obviously, as Carmen. As the Indian singing girl, Chandra Nil, she entered the world of musical comedy and created a sensation which was to be repeated when *The Blue Moon* in a new and revised form finally found its way to London.

A more established star was the feature of another new musical, *Winnie Brooke, Widow*, produced at Boscombe in April. Ada Reeve had decided to go into management on her own account and, to this end, she produced this musical version of *The Brotherhood*, a play written by the Daily Telegraph drama critic, Malcolm Watson, a former purveyor to the German Reeds. For her purposes, Miss Reeve added a selection of music – old, new, borrowed and sometimes a shade of blue. The story of the play dealt with the breaking-up of a coterie of gentlemen who have formed a misogynistic brotherhood by the wiles of one Winnie Brooke, widow. That role, of course, was taken by Miss Reeve who interpolated into it all her most attractive and popular 'turns'. In the tried and true fashion of provincial musicals, the second act party scene provided the opportunity to introduce a virtual variety show in which Winnie Brooke is prevailed upon to give her 'celebrated impersonation of Miss Ada Reeve', allowing the star to give the audience a few of the 'pearls' of her repertoire, notably the song 'Only a Penny' which she had created as long ago as 1898 in *The French Maid* in Australia.

Winnie Brooke, Widow was an effective enough showcase for Miss Reeve and she restaged it in the provinces at a later date but, in the meanwhile, Frank Curzon decided to bring it into the Criterion. However he decided that he preferred the play without the music and, in consequence, *Winnie Brooke, Widow* opened in London denuded of its variety show. It was not a success and Miss Reeve promptly put the musical bits back, added a few new ones, and took the whole thing back on the road where it belonged. Later, during the war, she brought it out once again, revised and retitled *A Modern Eve*, and used it as a theatre and music-hall vehicle which was briefly seen in London during an engagement at the Palace Theatre.

The remainder of the provincial novelties were works of considerably less pretension, whether in the comic opera vein like the carefully written *The King's Diamond* at Kingston or *The Island of Pharos* which was picked up for a professional tour from an amateur production in Chelsea; or in the more conventional musical comedy cum variety mould, such as *The Girl from Japan*, a jolly piece dealing with disguise, inheritance and love in a broken-down hotel run by a ladies' band and their bailiff. Composed and produced by its conductor, Colet Dare, it ran the smaller circuits for several years.

More ephemeral were Frank Danby's production of *Where's Uncle?* which had the cast members chasing after an amnesiac geologist to music by Clement Locknane; *Little Lady Loo*, an attempt by the authors of *Cissy* to provide a replacement for their seemingly immortal C-circuit musical comedy-drama; *The Girl from Corsica*, Victor Stevens' shot at revamping a hopelessly confused 1903 libretto into a passable vehicle for himself; and *Miss Mischief*, the story of yet another 'jolly romp' written by Reginald Bacchus with music by one-time West End star composer Osmond Carr, now reduced to supplying tunes for third rate touring combinations.

The touring scene continued healthy, with the latest town hits as always coming to join such perennials as *The New Barmaid*, *The Dandy Fifth*, *The Lady Slavey*, *The Gay Parisienne*, *The New Mephisto*, *The Geisha* and its Daly's compatriots and *Gentleman Joe* on the one hand, and the odd provincial hardies such as *Somebody's Sweetheart* (ex-

Sunny Florida), the Karno Company's *His Majesty's Guests* potpourri, *Daredevil Dorothy* (ex-*The Squatter's Daughter*) and Harry Starr's *Otto the Outcast* and *Carl the Clockmaker*, on the other. Few of the new provincial shows succeeded in coming up to any of the new West End favourites or those hardy annuals in quality or popularity.

1904

0286 **THE LOVEBIRDS** a musical comedy in three acts by George Grossmith Jr. Additional lyrics by Percy Greenbank. Music by Raymond Roze. Produced at the Savoy Theatre under the management of Edward Laurillard 10 February, 1904 for a run of 75 performances closing 23 April, 1904.

Alec Rockingham . . . . Bertram Wallis
Hon. H. Wilson West. . . . . Dennis Eadie
Sir Billie Duffield . . . . Lawrence Grossmith
Lord Southmolton . . . . Arthur Longley
Templar Fane. . . . . Mervyn Dene/Reginald De Veuille/ Gwillym Wigley
Maharajah of Mohook . . . . Fred Leslie Jr
Plummey . . . . Fred A. Ellis
Brooks. Phil Carlton
Gondolier . . . . M. Sterling Mackinlay/Paul de la Henty
Butler . . . . H. G. Hunt
Fireman . . . . Rowland Williams
Cellist . . . . C. Phillip
Courtenay Q. Borroprop . . . . George Fuller Golden
Effie Doublehurst . . . . Blanche Ring
Fatima Wilson West . . . . Lottie Venne/Audrey Ford
Lillie de Jones. . . . . Louise Raymond/Fanny Dango
Maie. . . . . Aimée Grey
Bertha . . . . Maude Darrell
Principal Dancer . . . . Connie Powell
Phyllis. . . . . Noel Neville/Fanny Jeffreys
Princess Getoutski . . . . Marie Ball
Lady Linnett . . . . Nellie Seymour
Miss Nightingale . . . . Addie Marze
Miss Flossie Flamingo . . . . Lillian Lake
Hon. Sybil Spoonbill . . . . Dot Roberts/Hilda Jeffreys
A type of English beauty . . . . Edith Neville
Miss Starling . . . . A. Cousins
Grace Rockingham . . . . Kate Cutler
with Doris Kennedy, Lucie Murray, Maud Burton, Susie Nainby, Marion Bradford, Ruby Travers, Rosa Bennett

Dir: Will Bishop; md: Raymond Roze; ch: Will Bishop; sc: Banks and Hemsley; cos: Comelli

0287 **THE BLUE MOON** a musical comedy in two acts by Harold Ellis. Lyrics by Percy Greenbank and Paul Rubens. Music by Howard Talbot and Paul Rubens. Produced at Northampton under the management of Robert Courtneidge, Arthur Hart and J. A. E. Malone 29 February, 1904 and toured.

Major Vivian Callabone. . . . . Alfred Clarke
Captain Jack Ormsby . . . . Vernon Davidson
Bobbie Scott . . . . Fred Allandale

Moolraj . . . . E. Statham Staples
Private Charles Taylor . . . . Frank Couch
Chief Juggler . . . . Edmund Sayers
Hon. Archie May . . . . Robert Carados
Clive Mansfield . . . . James Martin
M. Sharitcharki . . . . W. Biddlecombe
Nizam of Karikar . . . . Arthur Soames
Millicent Leroy . . . . Daisie Wallace
Chua . . . . Millie Vere
Miss Lovelhill . . . . Lydia Naylor
Miss Sparrow . . . . Mabel Lavelle
Hon. Evelyn Ormsby . . . . Ella Blume
Lady Augusta Brabazon . . . . Ethel Delaporte/Helen Langson
Chandra Nil . . . . Florence Smithson

Dir: Robert Courtneidge; md: Howard Carr/Guy Jones; sc: Joseph Harker

Produced in London in a revised version by Alexander M. Thompson at the Lyric Theatre under the management of Robert Courtneidge 28 August, 1905 for a run of 182 performances closing 24 February, 1906.

Major Vivian Callabone . . . . Courtice Pounds
Captain Jack Ormsby . . . . Harold Thorley/Herbert Clayton (Harry Cottell)
Bobbie Scott . . . . Fred Allandale
Moolraj . . . . Willie Edouin
Private Charles Taylor . . . . Walter Passmore/Bert Gilbert
Prince Bahadur of Sanatsinjhi . . . . . . Clarence Blakiston
Hon. Archie May . . . . Gwyn Alwyn
Clive Mansfield . . . . Ernest Crampton Bryant
Leslie Arbuthnot . . . . Harry Cottell
Lady Brabasham . . . . Eleanor Souray/Ruth Mackay
Evelyn Ormsby . . . . Billie Burke/
Chandra Nil . . . . Florence Smithson
Millicent Leroy . . . . Carrie Moore/Violet Lloyd
Miss Lovelhill . . . . Rose Begarnie/Queenie Finnis
Oma . . . . Ruth Savile
Chua . . . . Aimee Parkerson
Miss Lillian Moore . . . . Ella Blume
Captain Calthorpe . . . . Vincent Clive
Abdul . . . . Mr Tipler
Miss Sparrow . . . . Gertrude Kuzelle
Bhinga . . . . Hattie Herbert

Dir: Robert Courtneidge; md: Hamish MacCunn; ch: Fred Farren; sc: R. McCleery and Stafford Hall; cos: Wilhelm

Produced at the Casino Theatre, New York, under the management of the Shubert Company 3 November, 1906 for a run of 76 performances closing 5 January, 1907.
Edward M. Favor (CALL), Frank Rushworth/Templar Saxe (JACK), Dick Temple (BOB), Philip H. Ryley (MOOL), James T. Powers (CH), Arthur Donaldson (PRINCE), Louis Franklin (ARCH), Arthur Bell (CLIVE), Willie Cohan/Joseph West/Frank Lasalle (LESLIE), Edith Sinclair (LADY), Coralie Blythe/Grace La Rue/Ida Hawley (EV), Ethel Jackson (CHANDRA), Clara Palmer (MILL), Marion Mosby/Kathryn Robinson (LOVE), Marjorie Nevin (OMA), Lucy Jane Johnstone (CHUA), Myrtle Cosgrove (LILL), Donald Archer (AB), Ada B. Gordon (BINGO), Blanche Wilmot (CUPID), Fred Bond/Richard Knollenberg (HAFIZ) with Max Sharpe, O. W. Risley, John Kuester, Clarence Satchell, Edna Snyder, Lola May, Leona Courtenay, Gertrude Barnes, Loreen Boardman and the English Pony Ballet (Elizabeth Hawman, Seppie McNeil, Louise Hawman, Ada Robertson, Dorothy Marlow, Beatrice Liddell); pd: La Petite Adelaide. Dir: Frank Smithson; sc: Ernest Albert, Emens, Unitt & Wickes; cos: Wilhelm

0288 **THE GIRL FROM JAPAN** a musical comedy in two acts by Wilfred Carr. Music by Colet Dare. Produced at the Theatre Royal, Dover under the management of Colet Dare 29 February,

1904 and toured through ?, Eastbourne, Oldham, Leeds, Accrington, York, South Shields, Birmingham, Brighton, Ealing, Margate to 28 May; then under the management of Frederick Philpotts from 29 August through Peterborough, Lincoln, Dewsbury, Derby, Bedford/Luton, ?/Eastbourne, Swindon, Shrewsbury, Crouch End, Southampton, Dudley, Windsor, Newport, Margate to 3 December, then from 6 February 1905 Folkestone, Canterbury/Walmer, Colchester, King's Hammersmith, ?, Hastings, Bournemouth, Oxford, Nottingham, Ipswich, Birmingham, Lincoln, Sunderland, South Shields, Harrogate, Buxton, Hull, Sheffield, Bradford, Manchester to 17 June, 1905, &c.

Lord Allenbury . . . . S. Lockridge
Sir Mulberry Flippington. . . . . Wilfred Carr/Alfred Wood
General Baugh . . . . Percy Baverstock
Rev. John Smith . . . . Colet Dare/Tom E. Sinclair
Bingle . . . . J. W. Hooper/Charles L. Ludlow
Chuckerabuddy . . . . Mr Grimshaw/*out*
Hans Creton . . . . H. Benson
Countess de la Rue . . . . Bessie Deane
Polly Perkins . . . . Nellie Jackson
Lady Flippington . . . . Nellie Parker Dent
Marjorie . . . . Doris Dew/*out*
Maud . . . . Nellie Arline/Maidie Scott
Violet Meadows . . . . Nellie Valentine

with Ethel Beechey, Eva Beechey, Kitty Pauline, Effie Rydon, Geraldine Marjoribanks, Dorothy Webb, Nellie Varden, Gertrude Foster, Alice Martin; pds: Violet and Lillie English

Dir: Fred C. Dew; md: Colet Dare

0289 **THE CINGALEE** or Sunny Ceylon. A musical play by James Tanner. Lyrics by Adrian Ross and Percy Greenbank. Music by Lionel Monckton. Additional dialogue, music and lyrics by Paul Rubens. Produced at Daly's Theatre under the management of George Edwardes 5 March, 1904 for a run of 365 performances closing 11 March, 1905.

Harry Vereker . . . . C. Hayden Coffin/W. Louis Bradfield/(Conway Dixon)/Gordon Cleather
Boobhamba . . . . Rutland Barrington (Charles Jameison)(Colin Coop)/Leedham Bantock
Sir Peter Loftus . . . . Fred Kaye/W. J. Manning
Myamgah . . . . Willie Warde/S. Arrigoni
Bobby Warren . . . . Henry J. Ford/W. Louis Bradfield/Arthur Hope/James Blakeley
Dick Bosanquet . . . . Conway Dixon
Jack Clinton . . . . Norman Greene/Archie Anderson/Henry J. Ford/Jack Thompson
Freddie Lowther . . . . Arthur Hope/F. J. Blackman/Henry J. Ford/Jack Thompson/E. D. Wardes
Willie Wilson . . . . Joseph Boddy
Captain of the Guard . . . . Archie Anderson/Norman Greene
Attendant . . . . F. J. Blackman/Jerome Murphy
Chambuddy Ram . . . . Huntley Wright/Henry J. Ford
Nanoya . . . . Sybil Arundale (Ivy Moore)/Florence Smithson
Peggy Sabine . . . . Gracie Leigh/Eva Sandford/Mabel Hirst
Naitooma . . . . Carrie Moore/Mabel Russell/Alice D'Orme
Sattambi . . . . Alice D'Orme/Dorothy Gould
Mychellah . . . . Freda Vivian/Winifred Macey
Soomo/Coorowe . . . . Alice Hatton/Doris Severn/Edith Fink/Kathleen Severn/Nancy Duncan
Angy Loftus . . . . Doris Stocker/Rhoda Gordon
Miss Pinkerton . . . . Nina Sevening/Alice Oppitz
Fraulein Weiner . . . . Mary Fraser/Patience Seymour/Topsy Sinden
Mlle Chic . . . . Mabel Hirst/Vera Edwardine/Dora Thorne

Signorina Tasso . . . . Joan Keddie/Topsy Sinden/Kitty Mason/Patience Seymour/Mabel Allen
Lady Patricia Vane . . . . Isabel Jay/Anna Hickish
Parahara dances by the Sisters Amaranth. Devil dancing by Loku Banda and Willie Warde; pd: Topsy Sinden/Kitty Mason

Dir: J. A. E. Malone; md: Barter Johns; ch: Willie Warde; sc: Hawes Craven; cos: Percy Anderson

Produced at Daly's Theatre, New York, under the management of John C. Duff 24 October, 1904 for a run of 33 performances closing 19 November, 1904.
Melville Stewart (HV), Hallen Mostyn (BOO), Harold Vizard (SIR), Charles Wallace (MY), George Lesoir (BW), Lionel Hogarth (DICK), George Featherstone (JACK), Jordon Osborne (FRED), Edward Gore (CAPT), Paul Pancer (ATTDT), William Norris (CHAM), Genevieve Finlay (NAN), Blanche Deyo (PEG), Julia Millard (NAI), Kathleen Warren (SAT), Noel Gordon (MYCH), Dorothy Bertrand (COO), May Hengler (ANG), Flora Hengler (MOLLY LOFTUS), Viola Kellogg (MISS P), Amy Forsslund (MISS WERNER), May Hopkins (MISS VERNON), Myrtle McGrain (MISS CLEMENTS), Martha Carine (PAT); pds: The Eddies. Dir: Lewis Hooper; md: Louis Gottschalk; sc: John Young; cos: Percy Anderson

0290 **THE HOUP-LA GIRL** or The Queen of The Ring. A musical comedy by George Sheldon. Music by Antonius Baker. Produced under the management of Henry Johnston 1904 and toured.

La Belle Rosière . . . . Evelyn Hughes/Margaret Wilson
Lieutenant Lambton . . . . Francis Hope/Lancelot Usher
Prince of Felsenberg . . . . Jack Durant/Thomas Wyndham
Frank Saville . . . . Frank Stather/Jack Durnat
Matilda Birkins . . . . Bella Fossette
Major Daffney Davenport . . . . Eric Dalvere
Olga, Duchess of Stadt . . . . Miss Harland
Isobel . . . . Maggie Fraser
Dick . . . . Edith Haley
with the Rosie Rice Quartet.

Md: George Sheldon; sc: Leolyn Hart

0291 **WINNIE BROOKE, WIDOW** a comedy with music in 3 acts by Malcolm Watson and Herbert Fordwych. Lyrics by Herbert Fordwych. Music by J. A. Robertson, Howard Talbot, Herman Finck and F. Osmond Carr. Additional lyrics by Adrian Ross and Eustace Baynes. Produced at the Grand Theatre, Boscombe, under the management of Ada Reeve 2 April, 1904 and toured through Portsmouth, Plymouth, Edinburgh, Glasgow, Dublin, Liverpool, Bristol, Manchester, Birmingham to 4 June; then from 10 October through Eastbourne, Kennington, Peckham, Bournemouth . . . , Huddersfield, ?, ?, Bolton, Southport. . . . Portsmouth, Northampton, Manchester, Wolverhampton, Edinburgh, Glasgow, Newcastle, Leeds, Belfast, Dublin, ?, Hull, Hereford/Worcester, Birmingham, Liverpool, Bristol, Coronet, Camden to 10 June 1905, &c.

Dudley Mayne . . . . Henry Vibart/Charles Weir/Frank Elliott
Rev. Elihu Garside . . . . Robb Harwood/James Stephenson/Frederick Tyrrell/Stephen Adeson
Julian Croft . . . . Leon Ashton Jarry
Montague Brent. . . . . Arthur Lewis/J. F. McArdle/John Gerant/Stephen Adeson/Harry Halley
Reggie Frampton . . . . Ernest Stephens/Edgar Stephens
Hercules. . . . . Burt Fordie/Edward Rigby/Donald Prince-Evans/J. D. Newton
Toby Blossom. . . . . George Traill/Frederick B. Sharp/Ulick Burke/Frederick Tyrrell
Thorp . . . . Herbert Johnson/*out*
Gracie Frampton . . . . Amy Betteley/Lucie Caine/Cecile Beresford/Mabel Murray/Janet Neville

Nora Caswell . . . . Doris Lind/Ruth Hazelwood
Mrs Garside. . . . . Janet Hodson/Alice Lawrance
Hannah . . . . Barbara Scott-Kerr/Mrs Charles Maltby
Eustasia Honoria Eglantine Brown . . . . Drusilla Wills
Ethel Carter. . . . . Maude Bowden/Florence Leigh
Rose Cathcart. . . . . Clement Scott/Freda Stanley
Gladys Binfield . . . . Kitty Clinton
Daisy Denton . . . . Maude Marriott/*out*
Kitty Thorpe (Maude) . . . . Ethel Claremont/Lucienne Meard
Eva Thompson . . . . Rita Rhylle/*out*
Henalee . . . . Walter Rignold/*out*
Winnie Brooke . . . . Ada Reeve

Dir: Wilfred Cotton; md: J. A. Robertson; sc: Robson; cos: Jays, Regali and Hyman & Sons

Revised and revived as *A Modern Eve*, 1916.

0292 **THE GIRL FROM CORSICA** a musical comedy in 2 acts by Mark Allerton. Revised by Victor Stevens. Additional lyrics by James Wilcock and San Rey. Music by Harry T. Dickerson. Additional numbers by Albert Vernon, Victor Stevens and F. V. St Clair. Produced at Peterborough under the management of G. E. V. Russell 12 May, 1904 and toured through Norwich, Sunderland, Edinburgh, St Helens, Southport to 18 June.

Maimoun . . . . Leicester Tunks
Alexis . . . . Cyril Harcourt
Rinaldo . . . . Cliff Appleby
Fletici . . . . Frank Dilne
Gazando. . . . . D. McAndrew
French Attaché . . . . Louis Stanislaus
Lusania . . . . Nellie Grant
Lord Gilbert Poole . . . . Archie Selwyn
Hon. Augustus Devereux . . . . Arthur Linton
Henri Marcliand Bombatier . . . . D. Denard
Sam Spindler . . . . Victor Stevens
Lady Deborah Poole . . . . Maud Gwynne
Muriel Devereux . . . . Beatrice Poole
Lily White . . . . Connie Leon
Lady Bisley . . . . Edith Lamont
Evelina Hartopp. . . . . Nina Cathie
with Cissie Trent, The Strolling Singers and the Cliquot Troupe

Md: Albert Vernon

0293 **WHERE'S UNCLE** a musical comedy in three acts by F. D. Foster. Music by Clement Locknane. Additional material by Dudley Smith, E. Field-Fisher and Harold Vicars. Produced at the Lyceum Theatre, Sheffield under the management of Frank Danby 16 May, 1904 and toured through Hull, Manchester, ?, ?, ?, Edinburgh, Glasgow, Stratford East.

Gibson Gallivant . . . . Frank Danby
Capt Archie Graham . . . . T. W. Volt/Charles Adeson
Lt Roy Neilson . . . . Rhys Thomas
Sgt Angus McNab . . . . Milroy Cooper
Stephens. . . . . Albert Hayman/Fred Dornan
Mark N. Slatem. . . . . Jocelyn Hope/Stephen Adeson
Professor Robert Stone-Hunter. . . . . . Gus Darrell?/Gus Danby
Mrs Stone-Hunter . . . . Elsie Carew
Winnie Graham. . . . . Mabel Russell/Miss Carruthers
Madge Barlow. . . . . Lily Fortescue/Rose Brady
Mrs Cummings . . . . Nellie Bouverie/Kathleen Grey
Dorothy Saltem . . . . Minnie Hunt

0294 **THE KING'S DIAMOND** a comic opera in three acts by Charles Hanbury. Music by

Meredith Ball. Produced at the Royal County Theatre, Kingston under the management of Peter Davey 23 May, 1904 and toured through Kennington and Coronet to 11 June.

King Charles II . . . . George Mudie
Earl of Rochester . . . . François Cellier Jr
Lord Fortescue . . . . Ernest Mozart
Frank Hardy . . . . Cyril Dane
Roger Dunscombe . . . . Charles Hanbury/Alfred G. Poulton
Martin Fosbrooke . . . . Elliott Ball
Oldson Fosbrooke . . . . Joseph A. Brill
Elinor Fortescue . . . . Beatrice Edwardes
Phoebe Larkin . . . . M. Sadie
Dorothy . . . . Ernestine Desborough
Sybil . . . . Marie Westcott
Alice Hardy . . . . Winifred Hare

Dir: Charles Hanbury; md: Meredith Ball; sc: G. Miller

0295 **SERGEANT BRUE** a musical farce in three acts by Owen Hall. Lyrics by J. Hickory Wood. Music by Liza Lehmann. Additional music by James Tate, and Ernest Vousden. Produced at the Strand Theatre under the management of Frank Curzon 14 June, 1904. Transferred to the Prince of Wales Theatre 11 July, 1904. Returned to the Strand Theatre 5 December, 1904 and closed there 24 February, 1905 after a total of 280 performances.

Sergeant Brue . . . . Willie Edouin (Arthur Laceby)
Michael Brue . . . . Joe Farren Soutar (Percy Rogers)
Aurora Brue . . . . Olive Morrell (Kitty Ashmead)/Madge Lessing/Alice Hollander
Daisy . . . . Hilda Trevalyan/Ruth Savile/Jessica Lait
Mabel Widgett . . . . Zena Dare/Nina Wood/Jeannie MacDonald
Vivienne Russell . . . . Nellie Seymour
Louise Clair . . . . Kitty Ashmead
Sir Fergus Traherne . . . . Frederick Lewis
Gerald Traherne . . . . Sydney Barraclough/Arthur Appleby
Matthew Habbishom . . . . Edward Kipling
Inspector Gorringe . . . . Arthur Laceby/Lennox Lochner/S. Brooke
Erskine Murray . . . . Jack Thompson
Captain Bay . . . . S. Brooke/Lennox Lochner/Michael Santley
Mr Crank . . . . Gilbert Porteous/Arthur Laceby
Crookie Scrubbs . . . . Arthur Williams
Lady Bickenhall . . . . Ethel Irving (Valerie De Lacey)/Millie Legarde
Arriet . . . . Valerie De Lacey
Mr Lambe . . . . P. Leslie
add Eva Graham . . . . Monica Sayer/Dorothy Drew

with Violet Loraine, Zilla Gray, Monica Sayer, Lily Mills, Nina Wood, Gwen Anthony, Phyllis Allen, G. Franklin, Ryder Glyn, H. Warren, Edward Shale, Percy Rogers, Reginald De Veuille, R. Lechner, Lennox Lochner, F. Powys Bates, Mr Salmon/Helen Holland

Md: Frederick Rosse/Ernest Vousden; sc: Julian Hicks; cos: Nathans and Morris Angel

Produced at the Knickerbocker Theatre, New York, under the management of Charles Dillingham 24 April, 1905, for 71 performances to 1 July. Suspended and resumed 14 August, 1905 for 21 further performances closing 2 September, 1905 after a total of 93 performances. Frank Daniels (BRUE), Alfred Hickman (MI), Sallie Fisher (AU), Clara Belle Jerome (DAI), Constance Eastman (MAB), Elphie Snowden (VIV), Mary Clayton/Miriam Norris (LOU), Myrtle McGrain (FLORENCE), Irene Cameron (NELLIE), Claire Leslie/Millie Cook (DOLLIE), Aileen Goodwin/Maud Leroy (CISSIE), Della Connor (MADGE), Greta Burdick (OLIVE), Walter Percival (GER), Nace Bonville/Henry Goodman (HABB), James Reaney (INSP), David Bennett (CAPT), Gilbert Clayton/Charles H. Drew (CRANK), Harry McDonough (CROOK), Blanche Ring (BICK), Lawrence Wheat/Nace Bonville (LAMB), George Lestocq (PERCY PROCTOR), Louis

Fitzroy (HADDON WALLIS), Ida Gabrielle (DOT), Sally Daly (PIPPINS), Leavitt James (BILL NOKES), Leslie Mayo (BRIDGET), Maisie Follett (AMY KNIGHT). Dir: Herbert Gresham; md: Wally Hydes; sc: Richard Marston; cos: F. Richard Anderson

0296 **THE ISLAND OF PHAROS** a comic opera in two acts by William Caine. Music by Osborne Roberts. First produced by amateurs at the Chelsea Town Hall May 18-20, 1904. Produced professionally at the Theatre Royal, Plymouth under the management of Augustus Bingham and Glynn Osborne 11 July, 1904 and toured through Blackpool, York, Middlesborough, Birmingham, Ramsgate, to 20 August.

Earl of Erinscorthy . . . . Arthur Wilmot
William Sykes . . . . Daley Cooper
Henry Sykes . . . . Maitland Dicker
Lord Alfred Yeovil . . . . A. S. Barber
Mr Reginald Powys . . . . Frank Loudon
Sir John Kerr . . . . Leonard Russell
Agathos . . . . Greville Hayes
Captain of the Yacht . . . . Horace Corbyn
Daphnis . . . . Albert Wortley Drewitt
Lady Gladys Lovering . . . . Cissie Vaughan
Lady Mabel Hogan . . . . Bella Graves
Lady Henrietta Hogan . . . . Ada Rodney
Antigone . . . . May Clifton
Chloe . . . . May Brooke
The Arch Nymph . . . . B. Luscombe
Md: Chevalier Legrand

0297 **THE GIRL FROM BOND STREET** a musical comedy by Roland Oliver. Music by Louis La Rondelle. Produced at the Central Theatre, Northwich under the management of Woodbridge and La Rondelle 5 September, 1904 and toured through Stafford, Workington, Stanley &c.

Lucy Harvey . . . . Violet Varcoe
Lady Fielding . . . . Bella Bartlett
Lottie Harvey . . . . Lillian Beszant
Lady Tremayne . . . . Nellie Scott
Mrs Harvey . . . . Phyllis Manners
Lord Herbert Seacombe . . . . J. W. Woodbridge
George Fielding . . . . Stenson Liddiard
Archie Maynard . . . . George Watts
Mickey Mulvaney . . . . Fred A. Ellis

0298 **THE CATCH OF THE SEASON** a musical comedy in two acts by Seymour Hicks and Cosmo Hamilton. Lyrics by Charles H. Taylor. Music by Herbert E. Haines and Evelyn Baker. Produced at the Vaudeville Theatre under the management of Messrs A. & S. Gatti and Charles Frohman 9 September, 1904 for a run of 621 performances closing 17 February, 1906.

Duke of St Jermyns . . . . Seymour Hicks/Stanley Brett
Lord Dundreary . . . . Sam Sothern (Vere Smith)
Higham Montague . . . . Stanley Brett/Charles Troode
Lord Yatton . . . . Cecil Kinnaird/Philip Desborough
Sir John Crystal . . . . Charles Daly
Mr William Gibson . . . . Compton Coutts
Captain Rushpool . . . . Mervyn Dene
Mr Frank Wilson . . . . Frank Wilson/*out*
Almeric Montpelier . . . . Philip Desborough/Vere Smith/Albert Wortley Drewitt/Wescombe Penney
Bucket . . . . Albert Valchera
Duchess of St Jermyns . . . . Ruby Ray
Lady Crystal . . . . Mollie Lowell/Ethel Matthews
Hon. Sophia Bedford . . . . Ethel Matthews/Louie Pounds/Hilda Jeffreys/Olive Morrell

Hon. Honoria Bedford . . . . Hilda Jacobson/Florence Lloyd/Miss Sothern?/Gladys Ward/Hilda Jeffries
Princess Schowenhöhe-Hohenschowen . . Lily Maynier
Miss Enid Gibson. . . . . Kate Vesey/Hilda Jeffreys/Elsie Kay
Miss Snyder Caw . . . . Barbara Deane/Ethel Bryan
Clotilde . . . . Helene Blanche/Andrée Corday/Irena Langlois
Lady Caterham . . . . Rosina Filippi/Mrs S. Sothern
Footmen. . . . . William Jefferson/Cecil Tresilian/Charles J. Evans/H. N. Mason
Angela. Zena Dare/Ellaline Terriss/Maie Ash/ Alice Russon/(Stella De Marney)/Phyllis Dare/Madge Crichton
add Sylvia Gibson. . . . . Camille Clifford
Corrie Fay . . . . Winifred Hart-Dyke
Lady Dorking . . . . Alice M. Cox

The Gibson Girls: Hilda Jeffreys, Lily Mills, Marie Ashton, G. Ethel Karri, Elsie Kay, Kathleen Dawn, Irene Allen, Marion Cecil, Barbara Roberts/Lillian Burns, Eva Carrington, Hilda Harris, Alexandra Carlisle, Miss Gates, E. Coodrich, Maie Ash, Irene Florence, Amy Kaye, Kitty Melrose, Morris Clarke, D. Graham, Hilda Hammerton, Mollie Wallbran, Dorothy Hanbury, Nancy Malone, Irene Desmond, Pauline Francis, Claire Rickards, Enid Leslie, Rosamund Bury, Ethel Mills, Millicent Vernon, Dora Poole, Nell Hope, Margery Douglas, Vera Anderson, Daisy Cordell
Bridesmaids: Winnie Hall, Chrissie Bell, Winnie Geoghegan, Alice Dubarry,/Mirabel Hillier, Miss Hope, A. Hillier, B. Hiller, Crissie Stevens
with Lily Eyton, Edith Lee, Munro Ross, Ida Mann, Stella DeMarney, Clara Webber, Lily Maynier, Maie Ash, Eva Carrington, Jennie Bateman, Elsie Melville, Genee Hayward, P. Shawe, Molly Wallbran, Alice M. Cox, Constance Guilbert, Dora Quarry, Nellie Lawrence, Dora Glennie, Kitty Hyde, Crissie Bell, L. Webster; Messrs Rowlands Williams, Michael Henry, H. Wescombe Penney, Albert Wortley Drewitt, W. H. L. Ralph/A. Wigley, C. A. Bowes, M. Head, Idris Jenkins

Dir: Seymour Hicks; md: Carl Kiefert/Edward Jones; sc: W. Harford; cos: Luçile Ltd

Produced at Daly's Theatre, New York, under the management of Charles Frohman 28 August, 1905 for a run of 93 performances closing 25 November, 1905.
Joe Farren Soutar (DUKE), Fred Kaye/George Frothingham (MONT), Bert Sinden (YATT), W. L. Branscombe (CRYSTAL), Fred Wright Jr (GIBSON), Frank Norman (RUSH), Talleur Andrews (HIMSELF), Jack H. Millar (ALM), Louis Victor (BUCK), Mrs J. P. West (DUCH), Annie Esmond (LADY CR), Jane May/Dora Sevening (SO), Margaret Fraser (HON), Madge Greet (HOH), Dora Sevening/Mabel Reid (CLOT), Maud Milton (LADY CAT), Edna May (ANGELA), Vivian Graham (BADMINTON), John F. O'Sullivan (W. M. DORKING), Vivean Vowles (ERMINTRUDE DORKING), Lillian Purns (LOUISE D'ORSAY) with Dorothy Zimmerman, Elaine Barry, Eithel Kelly, Dorothy Reynolds, Edna Sidney, Alys Hardy, Muriel St Quinten, Queenie Pete, Violet Conrad, Evelyn Powys, Helen Morrison, Sylvia Eagan, Elise Delisia, Suzanne Maud, Martha Dufrene, Suzanne Mallot, Angele Lerida, Germaine de Valeral, Marguerite de Manges, Suzanne la Page

Dir: Ben Teal; md: William T. Francis; sc: Ernest Gros; cos: Ward

Produced at the Sommer Theatre, Vienna, 15 July 1913 and at the Theater an der Wien 25 December, 1913 as *Die Ballkönigen*.

Produced at the Prince's Theatre 17 February, 1917 for a run of 84 performances closing 28 April, 1917.
Seymour Hicks (DUKE), Stafford Dickens (DUN), Montague Criddle (HIGH), Johnny Danvers (YAT), J. C. Buckstone (SIR), Fred Farren (GIB), Charles Cecil, M. Bacci, Charles McConnell (BUCKET), Hilda Dick (DUCH), Mollie Lowell (LADY), Modesta Daly (SOPH), Alice O'Brien (HON), Josset Ellis, Germaine Arnoux, Mary Rorke (CATE), Isobel Elsom (ANG), Enid Sass (SYL). Md: Cuthbert Clarke; ch: Fred Farren; sc: George R. Hemsley

Film: In 1907 Walturdaw issued a film and synchronised record of 'The Church Parade' from *The Catch of the Season* on its Cinematophone Singing Pictures.

0299 **MISS MISCHIEF** a musical comedy by Reginald Bacchus. Music by F. Osmond Carr. Produced at the West London Theatre under the management of Godfrey Lamplugh 30 October 1904 and toured. Dates included Chester, Walsall, Leicester, Sheffield, Great Grimsby, Coventry, Margate, Eastbourne, Hull, Glasgow, Southport &c.

Private Harris V.C. . . . . Fred Eastman
Admiral Sir Hannibal Bethune . . . . . . T. E. Conover
Captain Jack Bethune . . . . Cecil Curtiss
Hiram Q. Peg . . . . J. C. Bland
Lord Percy Fitzsherry . . . . A. H. Liet/G. H. Sidh
Count von Himmelblau . . . . J. T. Green
Jules . . . . W. Lane
Graf von Gruber . . . . Miss Reichenberg
Furst von Ahrensheimer . . . . Miss Rene
Matilda . . . . Zara Kriesberg
Arabella . . . . Poppy Lytton
Priscilla . . . . Miss Desmond
Virginia . . . . Mdlle Thelma
Frau Schmuttz . . . . Ellen Douglas
Lady Orrery . . . . Eileen Guilbert
Mary Ann Smith . . . . Annie Francess
Kitty Malone . . . . Evelyn Hughes

Md: Chevalier Legrand

0300 **LADYLAND** a comic opera in two acts and three scenes by Eustace Ponsonby. Music by Frank Lambert. Produced at the Avenue Theatre under the management of H. J. Grant-Seymour 12 December, 1904 for a run of 15 performances closing 26 December 1904.

Professor Puddle . . . . Austin Melford
Harry Sartorys . . . . Richard Green
Sir George Pembroke . . . . John Tresahar
Peter . . . . Alfred Mansfield
Max Moggins . . . . Windham Guise
Roy . . . . George Giddens
Geraldine . . . . Aline May
Jane Jingle . . . . Geraldine Ulmar
Charity . . . . Gurney Delaporte
Nina Weasel . . . . Nancy Girling
Susan . . . . Margaret Cooper
Sally . . . . Kitty Lindley
Junona . . . . Nonie Trefusis
Alma Molyneux . . . . Ethel Irving
with Blanche Love, Gertrude Livingstone, Dora Dent, Rita Ravensburg, Madge Tinsley, Nellie Lee, Irene Vere, Lillian Wakefield, &c., Dennis Creeden, Harold Allen, J. P. McMullen, Hew Walker, Alexander Sinclair, Robert Long, E. Dini, F. Stirling, Fred Locking, Stanley Ross, Paul de la Hanty, C. E. Pierpoint.

Dir: Ells Dagnall; md: François Cellier; ch: Paul Valentine; sc: W. Harford and Bruce Smith; cos: Robert Crafter

0301 **THE SCILLY GIRL** a musical comedy by Athol Mayhew. Music by William Neale. Produced at the Grand Theatre, Woolwich under the management of Frank Nelson 12 December, 1904 and toured through Bishop Auckland &c for five weeks. Revised and represented 27 February 1905 and toured under the management of Frank Nelson and Charles Cautley.

Cecil Trevalyan . . . . Charles Cautley
Hon. Adolphus Delaware . . . . H. E. Garden
Bertie Carruthers . . . . J. W. Davis
Hughie Fallowfield . . . . T. Nichols
Capt. Johnnie Walker . . . . H. Lewis
Duke of Ayrshire . . . . Robert Rivers

Hiero . . . . Alf Donohoe
Mr Wheeler . . . . Milroy Cooper
Muriel . . . . Bessie Pelissier
Patty Pepperjoy . . . . Dorothy Vernon
Duchess of Ayrshire . . . . Susie Oak
Lady Spooner . . . . Miss Duncan
Hon. Mrs Wormun . . . . Dot Danby
Trixie Martingale . . . . Kitty Wyndham
Mrs Jack Bridges . . . . Miss Pope
Mme Endora . . . . Ella Kitson
Miss Katherine Wheeler . . . . Miss Blondin

0302 **LADY MADCAP** a musical play in two acts by Paul Rubens and Colonel N. Newnham-Davis. Lyrics by Paul Rubens and Percy Greenbank. Music by Paul Rubens. Produced at the Prince of Wales Theatre under the management of George Edwardes 17 December, 1904. An official second edition was produced on 16 September, 1905. Closed 25 November, 1905 after a run of 354 performances.

Major Blatherswaite . . . . Dennis Eadie
Comte St Hubert . . . . Maurice Farkoa/Leo Mars
Bill 'Stony' Stratford . . . . Aubrey Fitzgerald/Paul Arthur/J. Robert Hale/Fred Leslie Jr
Posh Jenkins . . . . Fred Emney
Colonel Layton . . . . Leedham Bantock
Captain Harrington . . . . J. Edward Fraser/Gordon Cleather
Lt Somerset . . . . Spenser Trevor/
Lord Framlingham . . . . Herbert Sparling
Corporal Ham . . . . George Carroll
Palmer . . . . R. St George
Old Huntsman . . . . Richard Kavanagh/Charles Crook
Trooper Smith . . . . G. P. Huntley (Spenser Trevor)
Gwenny Holden . . . . Delia Mason/Nina Sevening/Patience Seymour/Lily Elsie
Susan . . . . Eva Sandford/Mabel Russell/Gabrielle Ray/Ethel Oliver/Maude Darling
Mrs Layton . . . . Nellie Massey/Maud Hobson/Blanche Massey/Kathleen Warren
Lady Betty Claridge . . . . Adrienne Augarde/(Alice Hatton)/Madge Crichton/Zena Dare/Marie Studholme

with Misses M. Shaw, N. Munro, D. Dombey, N. Wakefield, F. Wakefield, Kathleen Warren, M. Maxwell, Wood, A. Grandville, Alice Coleman, Molly McIntyre, Sylvia Storey, Nancy Rich, Patience Seymour, Hilda Hammerton, F. Thornton, M. Webster &c; Messrs Hamworth, Palmer, Frank Walsh, Scott Melville, Borritt, Barrington, Blackman, Hamilton, Cooper, Perfitt

Dir: J. A. E. Malone; md: Frank E. Tours; ch: Willie Warde; sc: Hawes Craven and Joseph Harker; cos: Percy Anderson

Produced at the Casino Theatre, New York, under the management of Sam and Lee Shubert as *My Lady's Maid* 20 September, 1906 for a run of 44 performances closing 27 October, 1906. Libretto revised by Edward Paulton, R. H. Burnside and Percy Greenbank.
Claude Flemming (MAJOR), Henry Bergman (COUNT MANUELO DE COLONNA), R. E. Graham (BILL), Walter E. Perkins (POSH), Joseph Maylon (LAYT), Frank Rushworth (HARR), John Dudley (SOM), Charles W. Dungan (FRAM), George Carroll (HAM), Nicholas Burnham (PALMER), Prince Miller (OLD), Joseph Coyne (SMITH), Delia Mason (GW), Edith Blair (LAYTON), Elsa Ryan (SU), Madge Crichton (BETTY)

0303 **LITTLE BLACK SAMBO AND LITTLE WHITE BARBARA** a musical medley in 2 acts adapted from the 'Dumpy' books by Rutland Barrington. Music by Wilfred Bendall and Frederick Rosse. Produced at the Garrick Theatre under the management of Arthur Bourchier 21 December, 1904 for a series of matinées ending 3 February, 1905.

Little Black Sambo . . . . Nellie Bowman
Pompey . . . . Frank Lawton
Plantagenet . . . . Webb Darleigh
Black Jumbo . . . . Edward Rigby
Dr Funnyman. . . . . Leonard Calvert
Jake . . . . Frank Lacey
Shere Khan . . . . John Crooke
Shere Khant . . . . Fred Neeri
Khant Shere . . . . D. Imbert
Shere Shant . . . . Thomas Lipton
Bruin . . . . A. B. Allen
P. C. White . . . . D. Stewart
Liza . . . . Madge Titheradge
Little White Barbara . . . . Iris Hawkins
Mammy Mumbo . . . . Kate Bishop
Aunt Dosy . . . . Lena Halliday
Aunt Posy . . . . Caroline Ewell
Topsy . . . . Ida Valli
Ching-a-ling. . . . . Pat Collinge
The Ten Little Niggers: Gladys Makeham, Kathleen Cooke, Daisy Connell, Nellie Cowdrey, Queenie Preston, Doris McIntyre, Zeta Russell, Dorothy Weyman, Master Cross, Master Morris.
Darkies: Lottie Stockman, Marie Löhr, Violet McIntyre, Winnie Brooke, Eve Titheradge, Gertrude Wykes, Maude Buchanan, Elsa Skilling, West Collins, Gladys Godfrey, Constance Godfrey, Gertrude Lang, Misses Glynne, Parry, Greville-Moore, Mills, Villis, White; H. W. Webster, H. Kemp, T. Moss, T. J. Bourne, H. Garrod.

Dir: Arthur Bourchier and Alexander Stuart; md: Howard Carr; ch: Fred Farren; sc: W. Harford; cos: Simmons & Son and Miss C. L. Fox

THE DUCHESS OF SILLIE CRANKIE or The Earl And The Cheery Girl or Cingularlee Entangled Honeymoon. Libretto by Herbert Fordwych. Lyrics by Herbert Fordwych and Arthur Wimperis. Music by George W. Byng. Additional music by H. G. Pelissier. Produced at Terry's Theatre under the management of Kitty Loftus and played with *A Maid From School.*

Kitty, Duchess of Sillie Crankie . . . . Kitty Loftus
Marie . . . . Murielle Langley
Cora . . . . Ruth Argent
Four Ladies With One Line Each . . . . Daisy Hamilton
Miss Wakeman
Miss Gordon
Miss North
Duke of Sillie Crankie . . . . Edgar Ashley Marvin
Professor Pinman-Through . . . . Dallas Welford
A Footman . . . . Victor Bridges
Another Footman . . . . Arthur Jackson
Pretty D. Smart. . . . . Morris Harvey
Md: Louis Laval; sc: J. T. Bull; cos: John Hyman & Co.

1905

The opening of the new year saw the West End bursting with flourishing musicals. *The Orchid* at the Gaiety had run through the whole of the previous year and had still five months left in it whilst *The Cingalee* (Daly's) and France's *Véronique* (Apollo), *Sergeant Brue* (back at the Strand), *The Catch of the Season* (Vaudeville), *Lady Madcap* (Prince of Wales), *Peggy Machree* (Wyndhams) and the children's show *Little Black Sambo and Little White Barbara* (Garrick) all continued through into the new year. These last two pieces were on limited runs, but all the others had achieved considerable success and *The Catch of the Season* was to remain at the Vaudeville right through the year and into 1906.

To this array of hits the first addition came only five days into the new year. The Lyric Theatre had not hosted a musical in twelve months, but now William Greet brought back the company who had played there in *The Earl and the Girl* with a new piece by the creators of *The Catch of the Season*, Seymour Hicks, Charles Taylor, Herbert Haines and Evelyn Baker, under the title *The Talk of the Town*.

The Talk of the Town took what had become known as 'musical comedy' to its furthest degree yet. The plot outline was so exiguous as to be virtually non-existent, and what there was of it was as well-used and as familiar as could be, serving merely to introduce a number of standard personalities – hero, heroine, comic bailiff, long-lost wife – to perform a series of humorous scenes and gorgeously staged numbers. The pretence of fitting the numbers logically into the libretto, even by the transparent device of staging a concert in the middle of the second act like *Morocco Bound*, was all but abandoned and *The Talk of the Town* was largely a selection of pretty songs and dances, elaborately dressed and designed, linked by impersonations and sketches from, principally, the leading comedians.

Reggie Drummond has gone through his fortune and is to be sold up. The bailiff arrives and installs himself while the principal creditors, two very Jewish gentlemen, also make themselves prominent. Hope comes for Reggie in the form of a missive from his friend, Hambledon, who will lend him sufficient cash to tide him over. But, alas, Hambledon is delayed a week by the delights of Paris and Reggie's creditors press, so a masquerade is decided upon. Snipe, the bailiff, will impersonate Hambledon with the Jews as his Indian servants. Snipe, of course, gets himself into all sorts of scrapes in the process of the ensuing act and all is happily resolved when it is discovered that Hambledon does not have any money anyway, the rightful heir to his fortune being Ellaline Lewin who is . . Reggie's sweetheart.

The character of Jerry Snipe, the little bailiff, was evolved for Walter Passmore and the vagaries of the action gave him the opportunity of posing as a fine lieutenant of the hussars (something his height would clearly have barred him from in real life) and as an elderly lady, be-wigged and be-laced, as well as the lugubrious little bailiff with his rheumy wife and five little 'uns. Henry Lytton and Agnes Fraser completed the Savoy 'heart' of the company as the romantic interest, while M. R. Morand was joined by Stanley Brett as the Jewish Brothers English. Other featured artists incorporated more or less loosely into the story were Maudie Darrell as 'Madame Modiste' (otherwise Miss Biff) and her brother, Harry, a middle-weight boxing champ played by Daly's character actor, Akerman May, Olive Morrell as an irrelevant gipsy, Reginald Crompton as a Scottish soldier-servant and Robert Evett as a tenor Lieutenant/Duke.

Reaction was widely divergent:

> Tasteful *The Talk of the Town* may not always be, but it is never dull. It is a success . . a triumph – of the animated, the incessant. Mr Seymour Hicks begins with a whirl – with a dancing and gyrating crowd to which contingent after contingent adds number and bustle and noise; and not for a moment is the stage still afterwards. His extraordinary fortissimo opening Mr Hicks does not maintain – it would not be in human energy to do that; but the 'goey' quality of the whole . . . . is sufficiently prodigious. Fortunately Mr Hicks is full of ideas. All is not mere movement nor all loudness vocal and otherwise. Mr Hicks has an abundance of fun, a store of ingenuities and devices at the heart of his commotions. Fortunately, also, he has lively and tuneful music and unusually well turned 'lyrics' at his call . . . innumerable lovely dresses, innumerable pretty faces and even the element of surprise . . . it is not the plot that matters, but the scenes, the songs, the dances, the drolleries; in these important features Mr Hicks could scarcely be better served than he is . . . . (*Stage*)
>
> *The Talk of the Town* has louder music, more and gaudier dresses, more frequent bewildering changes of scene and subject and less coherence than any musical comedy in London . . . the music, with the exception of one or two numbers, is noise and jingle, the comedy only exists because Mr Passmore is there to make us laugh (*Times*)

Public reaction seemed equally undecided. It was not that they wanted comic opera, the wit and construction of a Gilbert or a Hood or the music of a Sullivan or a Cellier or a German. After all, they were quite happy with the hotch-potch content of such shows as *Lady Madcap*. They had shown a huge appreciation of the same writers' *Catch of the Season* but, in this case, the authors had failed to bring out the same charm they had milked from the 'Cinderella' story and no £8,000 production budget could hide the fact.

Amongst the dizzy whirl of song, dance and scenery there were pretty and popular things to be found, however. In the second act, in a sequence which particularly aroused the ire of the advocates of coherence in musicals, the standing set of the Modiste's Regent Street shop opened up to reveal a Lapland sunset scene and a bevy of ladies in furry suits, pompons and muffs from whom an ermine-swathed Olive Morrell stepped forth to sing:

> My little Laplander
> Nobody could be grander
> Your bright eyes I can see
> Wherever I may be.
> My little Laplander
> Don't say you're to go – oh, no,
> A heart beats true and warm for you
> In the land of snow

At the end of the song the scene returned to Regent Street, but not for long before down from the flies floated seven pretty swings, their ropes twisted with artificial flowers and electric light bulbs, and another extraneous routine ensued.

Although Haines and Miss Baker were again responsible for the show's basic score, *The Talk of the Town* incorporated many interpolated numbers. If the most popular of these was C. W. Murphy's 'Laplander' song, there were also others which did well enough. The conductor, Hamish MacCunn, was the composer of a rather more substantial ballad 'Two Eyes' for tenor Robert Evett, while J. Airlie Dix, composer of the famous ballad 'The Trumpeter', contributed a song for Passmore and his 'family' called 'Me and my little Brood'. Sydney Fairbrother as the bedraggled Mrs Snipe scored a personal success in her first musical appearance and put across an Evelyn Baker number 'The nice young Man (who whistled down the lane)' with great aplomb. Also in the popular vein was an Edward Carey ballad 'My Ellaline' for Lytton while the heroine's namesake, Mrs Hicks, was represented as a composer by a little song for the Brothers English and Haines himself supplied a Dutch number, 'Tina Schwartz', which had Maudie Darrell and the girls in caps and clogs.

In spite of its attractive individual parts and its £4,000 worth of dresses, *The Talk of the Town* did not live up to its title. It drew a certain public but it would not become a paying success. Maybe there was a real reaction against its lack of substance, its hollow showiness, but, whatever the reason, when Martin Harvey claimed the theatre for his production of *Hamlet*, the previously announced transfer of *The Talk of the Town* did not take place. After exactly one hundred performances it closed amid many dark prophecies as to the future of the 'musical comedy'.

The next two home-made pieces seen in London did nothing to refute that gloomy prognostication. The first was a musical intended for the provinces which authors and management saw fit to produce at the West London Theatre and send cannily into Terry's Theatre for eight performances to allow them to take it on the road loudly billed as 'direct from Terry's Theatre, London'. *The Officers' Mess* (and how they get out of it) was a piece in the tradition of *In Camp* and *The Pantomime Rehearsal* which based its fun on being 'back-stage' and placing in theatrical circumstances several aristocratic amateurs, stirring up the whole lot with a comedy theatre-manager, adding a few slightly naughty bits and a lot of gay songs and dances to produce what was little more, essentially, than a variety show. It included a bit of 'something for everyone' from a Hayden Coffin ballad (this one called 'Come Weal, Come Woe') and a coon song and dance to a 'Ladies' Maid' type number and so forth. It was an unpretentious and mediocre piece which had its own area of appeal, but not in the West End. *The Times* summarised:

> We have seen worse musical comedies which were intended for London . . . [it] aims at noisy, rattling nonsense and achieves it. It is absurd and impossible and stupid, quite without wit, ill-rehearsed and but moderately well-acted, sometimes vulgar and always noisy; but at least it does not stand still . . . we can imagine it going with a roar in certain towns, it seems hardly worthwhile to produce it in the Strand . . .

However, *The Officers' Mess* did produce one not negligible element. The production was directed by a thirty-year-old actor called Alfred Lester who decided, once the piece had set out on tour, to enliven it with a 'turn' of his own. He interpolated a scene for himself in the guise of a comic scene-shifter, in which he performed a humorous re-telling of the *Hamlet* story. It brought the house down and, when *The Officers' Mess* ended its short life, Lester was hired to reproduce his potted Shakespeare at the Palace Theatre music hall. There he came to the notice of George Edwardes who quickly signed him for the Gaiety and the start of a great career.

The second entry was of barely longer duration. The trouble was that *Miss Wingrove*, unlike *The Officers' Mess*, had been built to last and was Frank Curzon's new bet for the Strand Theatre where *A Chinese Honeymoon* and *Sergeant Brue* had done so marvellously well. The show's pedigree was good: the book and lyrics were by the talented W. H. Risque, the music by Howard Talbot, and Arthur Williams, Joe Farren Soutar and Millie Legarde headed the cast. A young lady named Violet Loraine was selected for the comedy role of Cora, but was replaced during rehearsals by the more experienced provincial leading lady, Simeta Marsden.

Miss Wingrove, having postponed its opening for a week, made its bow on May 4. It closed nine days and eleven performances later. It was by no means an incompetent piece and, in fact, *The Times*, which made no allowances at all when musical comedy was to be criticised, was less harsh on *Miss Wingrove* than it had been on very many of its successful brethren:

> Some of it is quite amusing, some of it very dull, some of it is well-acted, some of it very ill; there are stupid things and clever things in the book and the music maintains an inoffensive level of insignificance . . . it is not at all unlikely that *Miss Wingrove* will settle down for a long run . .

Its main crime would seem to have been a pleasant mediocrity: a lack of any outstanding or catching features. Its story was the bitterly tired old love-money-disguise and will combination. Sonia and Frank are to inherit if they marry each other, and the play follows the various attempts to aid or hinder them by interested parties, as well as Sonia Wingrove's changing of places with another lady to 'test' her prospective groom. There was little originality in either story or dialogue and, although Risque was happier in his more normal capacity as a lyric writer, even the songs were not sufficiently interesting to win more than an indifferent reaction from the public.

These two failures bore out the current prophecies of the imminent death of musical comedy, that is to say of the type of 'medley' show which relied little on plot and leaned almost totally on its songs, dances, dresses, scenery, pretty girls and the abilities of its performers – particularly the leading comedian. Burlesque had followed the same path. The repetition of the same subject and plots, the same jokes, the same routines in scarcely varying patterns had led to a staleness which led, in turn, to public indifference and the gradual total demise of the genre.

Had the newer kind of musical show now outlived its life-span and degenerated into the same uninventive and repetitious spectacle? There were many who believed so, particularly those critics who had never ceased to bewail the passing of the comic opera with its higher standards of classical artistic integrity and who considered most modern musicals trivial and vulgar. Yet these same critics were not satisfied even with comic opera, they criticised the French for being salacious and long-winded and allowed only Gilbert and Sullivan any credit among English writers:

> Except the Savoy pieces we have nothing we can point to as English comic opera. The genius of the nation does not lie in that direction. Our efforts in it lack point and fun and charm, often they are feeble, silly and clumsy, nearly always they are obviously pieced together, the songs patched roughly on to the dialogue with no result of singleness and continuity. For lightness of touch we show feebleness, for fancy folly, for grace affectation, distinction we lack altogether. As we cannot produce it, so we do

> not care for it. When it is imported from abroad we will not look at it unless it is adulterated to our taste with low comedians and dancers. But that is not perhaps entirely the fault of the public who have been 'warned off' light opera by their experience of home-made things in the past. And so, Gilbert and Sullivan stand together alone . . .

What this artistic snob of *The Times* and his allies ignored was the fact that the public enjoyed low comedians and dancers equally as much as they enjoyed the Gilbert and Sullivan and the Offenbach so beloved of the cognoscenti. The success of the Gaiety and Daly's and the variety and medley musicals of two decades bore witness to this. *A Chinese Honeymoon*, *The Geisha* and *The Toreador* were and had been as popular as any of the Savoy operas and had attracted the public for very much longer than such excellent and cultivated works as *The Rose of Persia* or *Merrie England*. Could it be true, then, that audiences were now about to desert the kind of entertainment which they had patronised so fervently for so many years?

Even George Edwardes who had had such a large share in the creation and establishment of the new kind of musical had been having doubts for some time. He had been persistently making statements affirming that a change of public taste would mean a new kind of show would have to appear and, more importantly, his chief artisans were also showing signs of being at the end of their tether in what was now the traditional style of show. Which of the two considerations was the genuine one, which the more important can never be known but the result was that Edwardes, the central figure of the British light musical theatre, turned away from the commissioning of new British works and went instead to the continent from where he could take proven works of a high standard which, incidentally, bore with them no threat of litigation.

The first of these made its appearance at Daly's following the withdrawal of *The Cingalee*. From France, Edwardes brought in a production of André Messager's *Les P'tites Michu* first staged at the Bouffes-Parisiens in 1897. *Les P'tites Michu* did not have the most original of plots, but it had the advantage of a most delightful, educated and melodious score by the composer of *Véronique* and also the virtue, by English standards, of having a 'polite' story which could be translated without the destructive hatchetting which befell so many French works being prepared for the British stage. *Les P'tites Michu*, the first foreign musical to be presented at Daly's, started off the theatre's new 'overseas' era most promisingly. It ran for more than double the length of its original Paris season, holding the stage for over twelve months.

With one bastion of the British musical now holding a French work, and *Véronique* still maintaining its place at the Apollo, the native musical received another blow when Edwardes announced that the successor to *The Orchid* at the Gaiety would be an adaptation of the French farce *Le Coquin de Printemps*. This was, however, a different style of show altogether to *Les P'tites Michu*. It was a 'regulation Palais Royal piece': full of innuendo, indiscretion and, indeed, was based entirely on sex, in a style which was in no way acceptable for the English stage. The adaptation of the piece was confided to George Grossmith who carefully dismembered the original, removing unsuitable portions to avoid any offence and leave room for musical numbers. What was left was a sufficiently amusing and not too diffuse libretto. This was the first time that a modern Gaiety musical had been based on an existing work rather than composed especially for the purpose, and the fact that *Coquin de Printemps* had already proved a successful play was of great assistance in making the broad outline of *The Spring Chicken* more solid than many of its contemporaries.

The story was, necessarily, simple. Gustave Babori, a Parisian lawyer, is a model of propriety through three seasons of the year, but at the approach of spring he becomes a *coquin de printemps* (a term rather inadequately rendered by 'Spring Chicken') and his fancy turns to other things than his work, and to other ladies than his pretty English wife, Dulcie. This spring, the object of his 'affections' is the Baroness Papouche, estranged wife of his client the Baron whom he is representing in their divorce. On the scene arrive Dulcie's parents, Mr and Mrs Girdle, with their remaining children. Mr Girdle is inclined to sympathise with Babori as he, too, has a wandering eye and is given to taking weekend trips to Paris to escape the monstrous Mrs Girdle; but the ladies get together and plot to catch their errant husbands out. After various tricks and business all ends happily when the Baroness repulses the lawyer's advances and returns to her husband, leaving Babori to go back to his Dulcie.

The little plot was, in true Gaiety style, all but smothered in songs, dances and comedy provided as usual by Lionel Monckton, Ivan Caryll, Adrian Ross and Percy Greenbank, but many of their songs were neatly fitted into the story and well-suited to their characters so that, instead of distracting from the story of the piece, they actually enhanced it. This shift towards a more coherent nature, which had been similarly evident in *Les P'tites Michu*, did not seem to dismay the Gaiety audience. *The Spring Chicken* was received rapturously on its first night and for over a year thereafter, and the critical response was equally warm even if the gentlemen of the press failed to agree on the nature of the piece and why they liked it:

> Once more have the usual ingredients required for the forming of the pasticcio known as musical comedy been compounded with skill and the accustomed happy effect. There are pretty scenes and beautiful dresses of great taste and infinite variety; Mr Caryll has once more contributed tuneful strains and Mr Monckton truly musicianly work: the dances are as effective as possible; and amid a labyrinth of topical sallies and variety business there meanders a shred of plot . . (*Stage*)

The Times pursued its favourite topic:

> Is musical comedy dead? There were moments during the first part of *The Spring Chicken* when musical comedy seemed to be very much alive. But, since nobody has yet defined what it is or was (its definition was, in fact, that it could not be defined) we may agree that it is dead and go to laugh at the new Gaiety piece without a suspicion that the funeral baked meats are coldly furnishing forth the new entertainment. *The Spring Chicken* is a farce; farce with 'numbers'; a good farce, and well stuffed with good things. It is when we come to ask ourselves whether a farce is the better for stuffing that we hesitate. As pure farce the thing would go with a rattle. The inclusion of the 'numbers' makes the first act drag a little . . . and interrupts the course of the story in the second act . . . But then these interrupting numbers are some of them so funny that we must confess to having laughed heartily at a play which, though not very far removed in detail from the old musical comedy is, at any rate, a most amusing piece of frivolity . . . . . as usual at the Gaiety the success of the piece depends very largely on the players; but they have in *The Spring Chicken* on the whole more and better material to work on than they are usually allowed . .

The Spring Chicken was, indeed, a superior piece. It leaned just closely enough towards the coherence of comic opera to please those to whom such traits were important while, at the same time, it sacrificed none of the jollity and spectacle of its Gaiety predecessors.

The characters of the original story gave plenty of scope to the Gaiety stars. Grossmith had a fine role as the 'frisky' avocat, Babori, while Teddy Payne and Connie Ediss were an unbeatable comic team as the British in-laws supported strongly by

Harry Grattan as the elderly Baron and demure Kate Cutler as his beautiful wife. Gertie Millar, Olive Morell and Lionel Mackinder provided the juvenile romantic interests while the host of faithful supporting players lead by Robert Nainby and Arthur Hatherton provided the usual selection of happy character sketches.

But, although the framework that Grossmith had provided was unusually stout and filled with enjoyable scenes, it was still the songs, the dances and the spectacle which fleshed out the show. The spectacle, as always at the Gaiety, was well attended to. Keeping inside the story, a startling transformation scene was achieved in the first act when the sombre and severe offices of the lawyer awaken with him to the first feelings of spring. From out of the corners of the set burst forth sprays of flowers, turning the stage into a positive bower as Babori became *le coquin de printemps*. In the second act, the inn of 'The Crimson Butterfly' and the final artists' studio setting were equally magnificently provided by the doyen of scene painters, Joseph Harker.

The songs, too, were excellent:

> The really important point – the supply of suitable songs – has been attended to with striking ability. The 'spirit of spring' seems to have inspired Mr Ivan Caryll and Mr Lionel Monckton and the best numbers in their score are full of jilting, lilting exuberance. . . . The score of *The Spring Chicken* indeed reminds us, in a way, of some of the best of the old French 'vaudevilles' so instinct is it with daintiness, with espiègलerie, and with crisp vivacity and musical tact . . (*Era*)

Among the high points were a duet for Grossmith and Payne 'Under and over Forty':

> Over, under, which is it I wonder, which you would rather be
> Is this your whim, to be old like him, or a gay young dog like me?
> A youth so slim, who is just like him, or a deep old dog like me?

and another for Payne and Gertie Millar where 'The Delights of London' are described by the errant Mr Girdle as he tries to persuade the country lass to take a trip with him. 'The Delights of London' gave the starring pair an opportunity for much joyous fooling as they burlesqued various scenes of London life: the tea shop, with Payne as a troublesome customer; the omnibus with the comic imitating a flirtatious driver; or again as a grenadier flirting with Miss Millar as a nursemaid. The popular comedian was well served as he also had an Ivan Caryll song 'Not so very Old' and shared a quartet with his wife and two children entitled 'The British Tourist' in which Percy Greenbank neatly encapsulated some of the more ghastly attributes of the British abroad:

> Experience has taught us that it's much the better plan
> When very far away we have to roam,
> To try and carry with us all the comforts that we can
> In order to remind ourselves of home.
> Papa had the 'Daily Mail'
> Mamma had a new 'Home Chat'
> The little ones had 'Sketchy Bits' to gaze and wonder at . .
>
> We filled up the compartment with our luggage and wraps
> Which made the other passengers complain
> I think that they were overcome with jealousy perhaps
> To see us having dinner in the train.
> Papa had a big bath bun
> Mamma had a stale pork pie
> The little ones had peppermints to eat upon the sly.

With plenty of things like these
So happy indeed were we
The British tourist
And his wife
And all his fam-i-lee . .

And so, this British entourage arrive in Paris, where Mrs Girdle voices her thoughts in a comical Adrian Ross/Monckton piece 'I don't Know, but I Guess' which was stretched to many verses in the hands of Connie Ediss:

I don't say that husbands are all of them bad
But I don't put much trust in them
I've pretty good eyes, as I've always had
And never let people throw dust in them.
My husband comes over to Paris, says he,
On business, alone, just for one day
He never tells me what his business may be
Or why it is done on a Sunday!

I found in his pocket a bill for a hat
And what do you think is the meaning of that?

Well, well, how can I tell
I'm not Sherlock Holmes, I confess,
But I heard him repeat
In his sleep 'Marguerite'
And of course, I don't know – but I guess!

With her plump and pointed style, Connie scored a huge success.

If this material reeked a little of the music hall, there were also pieces of a more sedate nature. The Baron introduced himself Pasha-like as 'One of the old Noblesse', Grossmith described his metamorphosis musically in 'Coquin de Printemps' and there were attractive ballads for Olive Morrell ('The Moon of May') and Kate Cutler, who was making her last appearance as a leading lady after seventeen years in the musical theatre[1] ('The very first Time').

Gertie Millar's material was a thing apart. It was totally provided by Lionel Monckton, now her husband, who wrote both the music and, under the pen-name of 'Leslie Mayne', the lyrics for all her songs. There was a coy little piece 'I've Come along to Paris' in Act I and a rather more topical one, 'The cordial Understanding', in which the Entente Cordiale was reduced to the level of an Anglo-French flirtation. Neither song was outstanding, though both had charm and the assistance of Miss Millar's piquant delivery. Her most successful solo was undoubtedly 'Alice Sat by the Fire'. Monckton and Miss Millar had done well with the song 'Little Mary', based on J. M. Barrie's play-title, in *The Orchid* so it was scarcely illogical for them to use Barrie's newest dramatic success as the topic for a number for *The Spring Chicken*. The song, once again written and composed by Monckton, was a kind of cautionary tale about a young lady who had a talent for sitting down well: first by the fire, then on a gentleman's knee, and finally on an errant husband's head.

Another blatantly inserted piece was less fortunate. Grossmith determined to have his tuppenceworth to say on the perennial issue of the 'National Theatre' which was

[1] After a long career in the straight theatre Kate Cutler returned to the musical stage in her late fifties as a character performer.

currently to the fore again and which was scorned by the majority of theatre managers. Grossmith took a hitch in the story and came on stage dressed as Shakespeare to sing his own lyric to 'The National Theatre':

The drama of Britain is limping
Outside of Jericho's Walls
Of all they've bereft us
There's nothing now left us
For Shakespeare is going on the halls.
The day of the National Theatre
Enthusiasts tell us is near
There's hope for tomorrow
Today all our sorrow
We'll drown in a bumper of beer

Beer, beer, beautiful Beerbohm
How does your academy do?
If you a way can see
Find me a vacancy
Then I'll play Caliban too.
How's your pretty miss Viola?
Fair and so charming is she
A very short time
It will take her to climb
To the top of the Beerbohm Tree

It was not a very good song. Most of the jokes, particularly the overworked Beerbohm Tree gags, had been used an infinite number of times before and mentions of the familiar names of George Alexander, Cyril Maude, Pinero, Barrie and Sydney Grundy were not sufficient to arouse enthusiasm by recognition. On the first night, however, Grossmith was well prepared with encore verses which he doggedly gave one by one with scant regard to his play, though more sparingly later.

There was never a doubt, however, that *The Spring Chicken* was the next in the line of Gaiety Theatre triumphs, and it settled in for a very successful run of over twelve months. During the run the inevitable interpolations into Caryll and Monckton's score were perpetrated and the relative homogeneity of the original piece was gradually eroded as such irrelevant pieces as 'Rotterdam' (featuring a chorus of Dutch boys), 'Laura's Latest' and 'Emmy Lou Went in for Extras', both by Philip Braham, 'Yes and No', 'I Made them Jump', 'Lucky little Lucy', 'The Macshiste', 'Regent Street', 'Paris Frissons' and 'The Orange Garden' made their appearance. Jerome Kern's song 'Rosalie' had, at least, the name of one of the principal characters. But, if the show became gradually more like an evening of variety and less like the musical play it had begun as, it never wavered in its popularity. *The Spring Chicken* firmly consolidated the position of the Gaiety company in its new home. It did the usual international rounds covered by a Gaiety musical and in 1906 was produced on Broadway by the American star Richard Carle. Being a musical writer and composer himself, Carle had to 'Americanise' and 'improve' the show so that the version presented on Broadway was scarcely that played at the Gaiety. However, Carle did very nicely in the role created by Teddy Payne in London, and Victor Morley as the sprightly lawyer and Emma Janvier, who scored the hit of the night with 'I don't Know, but I Guess', supported him superbly. When Forbes Robertson's season at the New Amsterdam collapsed, Carle took *The Spring Chicken* from Daly's into the New Amsterdam where it continued its successful run until the star and his company had to move their show on to a pre-booked season in Chicago.

If the successes of *The Little Michus* and *The Spring Chicken* following hard upon the triumph *Véronique* seemed to herald a change in the character of public taste in popular musical theatre, the status quo was, at least partially, maintained by the year's three remaining entries, *The Blue Moon*, *The White Chrysanthemum* and *Mr Popple* (*of Ippleton*). These three pieces were all very different and represented, roughly, the three principal divisions of contemporary British musicals. *The Blue Moon*, which had been produced and toured already the previous year, was a piece of the *Geisha/San Toy* genre which had now been heavily rewritten into a song and dance and variety piece; *The White Chrysanthemum* had leanings to comic opera and took much of its inspiration from the Daly's shows; while *Mr Popple* was musical farce, pure and simple. All three were to have reasonable runs – 182, 179 and 173 performances respectively – but none could be considered to have succeeded outstandingly, particularly when compared with similar pieces of recent years: *Three Little Maids* (348), *The Girl from Kays* (432), *My Lady Molly* (342), *The School Girl* (333), *Sergeant Brue* (280) or *Lady Madcap* (354). George Edwardes had recently gone on record announcing the end of long runs – 'killed by the increased number of new attractions' – but his own productions of *The Little Michus* and *The Spring Chicken* were there to disprove this. There had to be another reason why shows which were not of a lesser standard than many of their longer running predecessors, now only managed what could be considered moderate runs. Perhaps the surefeit of similar musical entertainments over the past years had dulled the public's appetite for anything but the very best and most catching of musical pieces, or perhaps an injection of something new and original was needed.

The Blue Moon was brought into town by Robert Courtneidge. During the time which had elapsed since the end of the original tour the author, Harold Ellis, had died and Alexander M. Thompson was brought in to revise the libretto for London tastes. Thompson, who had considerable journalistic experience, had recently worked with Richard Mansell on a new libretto of *Chilpéric* for the Coronet Theatre and had been associated with Courtneidge on a number of pantomimes. He almost entirely rewrote *The Blue Moon* and the composers supplied so much in the way of new music and songs that the piece as presented at the Lyric Theatre bore only a passing resemblance to the original. Courtneidge engaged a very strong cast including two of the most popular comedians in the country, Walter Passmore and Willie Edouin, for whom Thompson worked up respectively the comic roles of the private soldier, Charlie Taylor, and of Moolraj (idol-maker, juggler and marriage-broker). The former D'Oyly Carte idol, Courtice Pounds, was cast as the portly Major Callabone, Fred Allandale being the only member of the original cast to retain his role as the hero's best friend Bobbie. For his leading ladies, Courtneidge secured the popular Ida Rene, Billie Burke and Carrie Moore but the last-minute forfeit of Miss Rene left him in need of a new Chandra Nil. He decided to go back to his touring starlet and, through this lucky chance, Florence Smithson made her London début and became a star.

When *The Blue Moon* opened at the Lyric it was seen to have been transformed into a regular variety musical. *The Times* commented sarcastically on the fragments of plot inserted between the tunes and added:

> The only things that matter now are the 'turns'. Are they bright and pretty? Are Mr Edouin and Mr Passmore funny? Are the dresses splendid, the music soothing or exciting and the ladies beautiful?

but found itself forced to admit: 'We can answer all these questions in the affirmative . .' *The Stage* likewise declared:

> *The Blue Moon* ought to prove attractive to thorough-going supporters of musical comedy . .

The Era was more enthusiastic, calling it

> . . One of the most consistently bright and unflaggingly vivacious entertainments of the stage to have been seen in London for some time . .

but added that 'in spite of its remarkable briskness' it was half an hour too long.

The best pieces from the original show had been preserved, including the two songs with which Florence Smithson had made her mark in the touring version. If the Talbot/Greenbank song 'Little blue Moon' was the more artistic, Rubens' 'The Poplar and the Rainbow' was just as popular. Miss Smithson made a personal hit with these songs and even *The Times* was moved to remark:

> One quiet and pleasing note in all the rattle and crash was struck by Miss Florence Smithson who plays the part of the singing girl, Chandra Nil. Her voice is a little thin, but beautifully clear and, if she will be careful to avoid the suspicion of imitating Miss Gertie Millar, she will do well.

Miss Smithson, in the event, proved to possess a talent of quite a different kind from Miss Millar and did much more than merely 'well'. Howard Talbot and Greenbank produced some fine ensemble pieces, in particular a stirring first act finale in which hero Jack proclaims his love for the native singing girl only to be dragged away by horrified relations while Chandra Nil is told that she will be married to the Prince of Kharikar.

Talbot was also responsible for a galloping number for the Major which capitalised on Courtice Pounds' unusual (for a 'father') singing voice, and 'The Major's a Man for all That' took him up to a ringing top G in true comic opera style. Pounds was too good to leave with one number and Paul Rubens turned out two more, one singing the praises of the 'Burmah Girl' and another detailing the exploits of the Major who got his own way with all the ladies by using his 'high top G'. For some reason, and it may have been rhyme, G was the note selected although the high note in the song was, in fact, an A.

Pounds and Miss Smithson took care of the more sophisticated part of the music, but Rubens supplied plenty of other pieces for Passmore, for Carrie Moore (as his ladies'-maid love) and for Billie Burke, which closely followed the prototypes of the day. The 'National Theatre' number from *The Spring Chicken* and its many predecessors were followed in a duet called 'Entertainments' in which Passmore and Miss Moore gave their version of London's theatrical scene. They included a burlesque on the Swing Song and 'Trot here, Trot There' from *Véronique*, jibes at the new Coliseum show and its hit song 'Goodbye, little Girl', a take-off of Maskelyne and Cooks and another of the pygmy show at the Hippodrome. This last went down particularly well, leading *The Era* to remark, somewhat gallingly for the rest of the show, that

> *The Blue Moon* will be remembered as the piece in which Mr Walter Passmore and Miss Carrie Moore were so funny as pygmys . .

The bevy of fictional young ladies with peculiar habits so popular in songs of the day gained reinforcement from one 'Rosie' whose attribute was

She didn't mind
She didn't care
She didn't stamp
Or tear her hair
She didn't scream
Or try to go
She didn't mind . . .
She didn't know.

What she mostly didn't know was good behaviour, and though Carrie Moore did quite well with 'Rosie' she never attained the popularity of 'Little Mary' or 'Alice' (who sat by the fire). The soubrette was happier with an arch little piece called 'Shopping'. Billie Burke had a pretty but unexceptional love ditty called 'Sometimes' (I think you love me) and a flippant 'Silly Billy', neither of which looked like coming up to 'My little Canoe'.

The mixture was fairly judicious, with a little something for all, and it seemed likely to catch on. Immediately after the opening some song cuts were made (including 'Silly Billy') to bring the show down to a sensible size and some of the other less attractive material was gradually weeded out, leaving *The Blue Moon* looking to have all the qualities of a normal long-running show. But, in the event, it lasted only a disappointing six months. The following year, after a successful US tour, it was produced on Broadway where it had another reasonable run with James T. Powers taking on Passmore's role as the comical Charlie. Once again, the libretto and score suffered in the exporting, and Powers' dictates resulted in every other role except his own being cut to a minimum, including such large and musical ones as Courtice Pounds' Major. Interpolations included novelties like 'The English Pony Ballet' salvaged from Julian Edwards' *His Honor the Mayor* which had recently expired at the New York, and a bookful of new songs included 'Don't you Think it's Time to Marry' (Gus Edwards/Burkhardt) and, even more incongruously Goetz and Gilroy's 'Don't Go in the Lion's Cage Tonight' as well as a British song 'When Love comes Knocking at the Door'. This last had been managed through a new agency set up in New York to try to reverse the current trend by getting songs from English publishers into American shows. Along with Wilkie Bard's 'Let me Sing' which was inserted into *Sergeant Brue*, this number was one of their first successes. *The Blue Moon* did less well in New York than it had on tour and achieved a respectable rather than a notable season before leaving town again.

The White Chrysanthemum, which opened in the West End three days after *The Blue Moon*, had a number of similarities to it. The story was set in the orient and involved the habitual picturesque choruses of sailors and oriental ladies and like *The Blue Moon* its composer was Howard Talbot. Here, however, Talbot had written the whole of the score, which assumed a rather different kind of work from that in which he had shared the music with Paul Rubens.

The White Chrysanthemum had some unusual features, the first being that it had a principal cast of only seven performers. Frank Curzon, who had taken up the piece for production, engaged Savoy stars Isabel Jay, Rutland Barrington, Henry Lytton and M. R. Morand to whom he added the American soubrette Marie George, comedienne Gracie Leigh and Lawrence Grossmith. The remainder of the cast consisted of six Japanese maidens and six sailors of the Admiral's escort who served as a mini-chorus. *Florodora* had furthered the Gaiety practice of taking a select 'A' team from the chorus and featuring them; *The White Chrysanthemum* went a step further and kept the double sextet, but did without the chorus.

This unusual musical was to find an unusual home. The little Criterion Theatre in Piccadilly Circus was better known as the home of light comedy, and previous attempts to stage musicals such as *All Abroad* and *Bilberry of Tilbury* there had been exceptions which had not been notably successful. But *The White Chrysanthemum*, carefully named by its authors 'a lyrical comedy in three acts', fitted neatly into the pretty little house. The authors of the piece were Leedham Bantock, better known for his series of acting roles under George Edwardes' management, and a newcomer, Arthur Anderson, and their story was an excessively simple one. Sybil Cunningham has followed the man she loves, Reggie Armitage R.N., out to the east where he has chastely set her up in a little house pending his father's permission to marry. But his father has arranged that Reggie shall wed an American heiress, Cornelia Vanderdecken, and he arrives with her in tow. Sybil attempts to hide herself, disguised as a Japanese girl, and it requires all the wiles of her friend, Betty, and Reggie's servant Sin Chong to achieve the happy ending with Sybil and Reggie united, the old Admiral tied up to Betty and the perky American in the arms of Reggie's Best Friend.

The songs for the show were nicely varied. Making full use of his limited resources, Talbot interspersed the solo numbers with a number of duets, a quintet and a sextet and a couple of jolly ensembles as well as an accompanied recitation for variety. He was at his best when he stayed within the educated style of writing at which he was most adept and which also blended best with Arthur Anderson's very literate lyrics. 'The Butterfly and the Flower' for Isabel Jay in the first act was superior to the run of such songs, and if some of the others were slightly reminiscent of early Daly's Theatre or even of the Savoy they, nevertheless, had a sufficient integral merit. The play opened quite simply with Sybil, reclining in her hammock, singing of 'The Love of a Maid for a Man':

It was just an old world village near an English country town
It was just at eve in autumn when the leaves are showing brown
And the maiden stood a-waiting for her lover to confess
Till he breathed a whispered 'Will you? and she softly answered 'Yes'.
It's only a story, a little love story,
And that is the way it began
And it tells of the love of a man for a maid
And the love of a maid for a man

The maiden follows her lover when he must go away on duty:

So the scene of the story, the little love story
Is set in the land of Japan
And it tells of the love of a man for a maid
And the love of a maid for a man

And the scene for the show was set.

Anderson's lyric talent was displayed in a different fashion in an amusing song for Lawrence Grossmith as 'Chippy', wondering how he should propose:

I've never been in love before and do not know the way
In which the modern lover should propose.
I've witnessed declarations by the heroes at the play
But they were only acting, I suppose.
And yet, it can't be difficult to bring the thing to pass
For almost every single man I meet

No matter if he's clever or a brainless sort of ass
Has always got a woman at his feet.

So I wonder, yes, I wonder how it's done
I should like to know the proper thing to say,
Should I frankly ask the question
Or convey it by suggestion
Or invent some more dramatic kind of way?

Upon which he contemplates proposing in the fashion of Faust or Lohengrin.

A clever topical song for Rutland Barrington 'The latest News' even contrived to get in mentions of some of Barrington's famous past roles in a verse devoted to the Japanese War:

It is pleasant to know that the Japanese War
Has come to a peaceful conclusion
And though Russia would seem in the treaty to score
It really is quite a delusion.
For the gallant Mikado has checked her bravado
And crushed her on sea and on land
And now in arranging the terms they're exchanging
He deals with a generous hand.

Really? Truly? Can it be so?
Even indemnity will he forego?
Money to him is as nothing to Peace
It's one of the wonders that never will cease
Had he a Pooh Bah at hand to advise
That Peace in the Valley of Bhong would be wise?

Another lively number for Henry Lytton, 'You can't Please everybody Always', included some clever lines, whilst a charming song for Sybil, 'O wandering Breeze', only let itself down by constantly rhyming 'breeze' with 'trees'.

Unfortunately, the character of the American Cornelia seemed to lay strictures on the author and composer. Whenever she appeared they felt obliged to provide suitably 'modern' material and, in consequence, there stood out as misfits such pieces as the coon song 'Mammy's Piccaninny' (of which Marie George thought highly enough to put it on gramophone record) and an under-par point number 'The only Pebble on the Beach':

Fie boy! My boy! You're a perfect peach
Sailors' hanky-panky
Doesn't suit a yankee
You must practise everything I preach
For I've got to be the only pebble on the beach.

which justified itself only by the ingenious rhyme which Anderson uncovered for the familiar word 'schoolgirl' attempted many many times before but never with such adroitness as:

I'm not an easily-persuaded-as-a-rule girl
Though at times exceptions there may be
I'm not a simple, unsophisticated schoolgirl &c

But the height of imitative banality was reached in what one can only hope was intended as a satirical duet for Cornelia and Chippy of which the chorus ran:

I'll be your popsy-wopsy-woo
My little kootsy-kootsy-koo
I'll be your squeezy-weezy
Do all I can to pleasey
My pipsy-wipsy, popsy-wopsy-woo

Fortunately, most of *The White Chrysanthemum* was rather better and, charmingly designed and staged, it proved to be a successful evening. The Savoy artists were well suited, with Morand finally having a role worthy of his talents as the comic Chinaman, while Millie Legarde (who had had to take over from Gracie Leigh) made a charming partner for the flirtations of the white-haired Barrington. The Savoy element was increased when Louie Pounds relieved Marie George of the role of Cornelia and pruned it of some of its excesses.

A further novelty of *The White Chrysanthemum* was that, in spite of being in three acts, it was a decidedly short piece. The curtain did not go up until 8.30 p.m., hopefully in time to catch the after-dinner trade. In its early days it seemed the gamble had come off: its popularity was enormous and the theatre, which had not counted on playing a mid-week matinée, found itself obliged to include a Wednesday afternoon show and still had to turn people away. The initial fervour faded after a while, but the mini-musical stayed at the Criterion for nearly six months before being withdrawn and sent out to begin a touring career of several years.

Given the success of the two recent Messager musicals it was no surprise, on the closure of *Véronique*, to see the Apollo billed to produce another French piece, the 1903 Théâtre des Variétés hit *Le Sire de Vergy* by Robert de Flers and Gaston de Cavailler, with music by Claude Terrasse. It was an unusual choice as its libretto was in quite a different vein from those of *Véronique* and *The Little Michus*. It was a rumbustious, farcical Chaucerian tale of sexual liaisons, beginning with a ménage à trois and romping from one outrageous incident to another. The British version, of course, was watered down in an adaptation by Arthur Sturgess and the result was a disaster. Even Terrasse's delightful music allied to the anodine words of the English *The Gay Lord Vergy* could do nothing for the piece which closed its doors in confusion and disappointment after only seven performances. The show was quite untransferable to the English stage, given the moral strictures of the times, and its production was a gross error of managerial judgement.

The final British entry of the year was Paul Rubens' *Mr Popple (of Ippleton)*. In *Mr Popple*, Rubens took a new turn. Abandoning the coy English style of *Three Little Maids* and *Lady Madcap*, he turned to musical farce, the old French vaudeville style, with a piece which was farcical play first and musical entertainment second. *Mr Popple* was a different and much more agreeable Paul Rubens work. The story was simple and neatly worked out around its star performers, G. P. Huntley and Ethel Irving.

Freddy Popple (Huntley) is a country fellow of a certain naivety:

> People laugh at me because I've only been to London three times. I know a chap who has never been to Ippleton at all.

He prefers the country and would rather chase rabbits than ladies, but on this occasion he has been obliged to come up to the big city and he bumbles his way into the Piccadilly Hotel only to find that there is no room available. To his rescue comes the beautiful actress, La Boléro (Irving) who lives in the hotel and who has an apartment which she will lend to Freddy. The apartment has been rented for her by two amorous gentlemen, each of whom is paying the whole rent and is unaware of the other's existence. But since this is London and not Paris, La Boléro has never used the apartment. Her fancies have been taken by another Mr Popple, Freddy's sophisticated brother Norman, but he has left her and La Boléro resolves to have her revenge by taking up with his country brother.

In the apartment, in the second act, much action ensues – the two gentleman lessees arrive followed by their wives, not to mention a bevy of actresses, friends of La Boléro, and the fun is fast and furious until the actress, to get out of a spot, declares that Freddy is her husband. The final act, set at a motor carnival, sees everything sorted out. Boléro weds an old admirer, the erring husbands are reconciled to their wives and good old Freddy catches the first train back to Ippleton and the rabbits.

The role of Freddy Popple provided George Huntley with perhaps the best part he had had. The gentle, kindly male version of the popular 'country mouse' was endearing character and Huntley made the most of him. Ethel Irving, returning to musicals after a series of straight roles, had a showy yet warm part as the glamorous actress and, between them, in spite of some excellent lesser performances in good minor roles, they dominated the evening's entertainment. *Mr Popple* was received with great enthusiasm at its première, but the critical reaction was variable. *The Times* dug into the author-composer:

> It is not a production on which we can congratulate Mr Rubens though we have little doubt that it will have a satisfactory run; and we cannot help thinking Mr Rubens could, if he would, do better work than this. There was a hope at one time that the smartness he showed in writing songs and lyrics might ripen into wit. Perhaps the public has hampered his development by enjoying his early efforts too much. His smartness remains smartness – very often in this play it is the smartness of the schoolboy and the city man combined – and his facility in spinning tunes remains facility.

and *The Stage* ventured that:

> Mr Rubens has not equalled the catchiness of most of his former music in some . . of the sixteen or seventeen numbers in the three long acts and though the plot opens brightly enough, it is not well carried out . . . as essentially 'modern', flippant and saucy, almost verging on suggestion as his previous writings . .

Although these criticisms were at least partly justifiable, they seemed rather harsh after the comparative mildness shown towards *Lady Madcap*, a decidedly inferior piece to *Mr Popple* and one in which all the criticisms here levelled at Rubens were doubly justified. In *Mr Popple*, Rubens had shown consistently better taste both in his dialogue and his lyrics. He had managed mostly to be risqué without being vulgar and he had turned out some delightful lyrics which avoided the banality and tastelessness of so many of his previous songs. One of the joys of the evening was to hear Huntley singing of 'Rabbits':

> I've heard about the Carlton
> The Cecil and Savoy
> And the rest of all your swagger London habits.
> I'm an awful fool with women
> Well, our vicar says I'm shy,
> Yet, d'you know I'm not the least bit shy with rabbits!

whilst Ethel Irving brought down the house with a rousing café chantant number 'Oh, la, la la!' in a direct contrast to a charmingly simple little piece 'You dear, sweet, stupid old Thing' which she addressed to Freddy in the second act:

I'm awfully fond of you
And I can't tell you why – can you?
For you seem to like me too
And I can't tell why – can you?
You're not good-looking, are you?
You can't dance and you can't sing
But I like you very much
You're such a dear, sweet, clumsy old thing:

Also popular was a semi-parlando piece 'A Question of Bait' which dealt with the question of what to put 'on one's hook' to catch the right kind of spouse.

To the funny lines, the pretty songs and the star performances there was added a further attraction in the shape of 'The Scarlet Runners', six pretty actresses all costumed in bright red silk, and another in the form of spectacular scenery, particularly for the motor carnival scene which was based on the Kursaal at Bexhill-on-Sea. The attractions of *Mr Popple* served to keep it running merrily at the Apollo until the arrival of Robert Courtneidge and *The Dairymaids* forced it out. The piece was still doing well enough to make a transfer worthwhile and Tom Davis shifted *Mr Popple* into the Shaftesbury. Unfortunately the roof of the Shaftesbury was giving grave worries to the City Council and it was not long before they insisted that the theatre should be closed. *Mr Popple* was not strong enough to last out another transfer and Davis called it a day.

Mr Popple went to the provinces with success and had a fair run of overseas performances but it was ten years before it made its way to Broadway and then in a sad shape. Freddy Popple, in the person of Lawrence Grossmith, had very little of his original adventures left and, under the 'revising' of Jerome Kern and Guy Bolton, most of the score and the dialogue was totally new. Even the title had disappeared. The piece was now called *Nobody Home*. It had a 135-performance run in the little Princess Theatre without causing a great deal of interest.

To close 1905 in the West End, Seymour Hicks and Ellaline Terriss appeared at the newly completed Aldwych Theatre in a successful revival of their Vaudeville Theatre hit *Bluebell in Fairyland*, revised and with four new scenes added.

The year in the provinces produced several worthwhile pieces. The most successful was undoubtedly the Scottish musical *A Trip to the Highlands*, a cheerful medley of song, dance and humour presented at the new Grand Theatre, Edinburgh under the enterprising management of Eade Montefiore. It was an unpretentious piece written by the most popular of local pantomime writers, Fred Locke, with songs by the theatre's musical director, E. T. de Banzie, intended to fill in four weeks at the theatre in April.

The plot was minimal. A pair of young runaway lovers, pursued by relatives and a detective, end up in the picturesque highland setting of Oban Bay amongst the usual combination of disguises, mistakes, flirtations and musical numbers. A troupe of twelve 'Gibson Girls', another of twelve dancers and a cast including *Chinese Honeymoon* stalwarts Picton Roxburgh and his wife, Fanny Wright, little Isa Bowman and provincial veterans Nellie Cozens and Harry Fischer breezed through some typical numbers: 'Mademoiselle New York', 'Japanese Maid', 'Style', 'Love in a Cottage', 'Girls' and, more topically 'I've never Been to London Before', with a little local colour added by 'The Princes Street Parade' and versions of 'Robin Adair' and 'Comin' through the Rye' to make up a lively evening; and, amid general surprise, *A Trip to the Highlands* turned out to be hit of the Edinburgh season. It was taken to Glasgow, to Manchester, to London's Marlborough Theatre, Holloway, and then back again to

Edinburgh for a return season where up to £100 per week in profits went to swell the limited coffers of the Edinburgh Grand Theatre which hastily formed itself into a limited company with the announced intention of producing original musicals for home-town and touring. And all the while the first all-Scots musical kept on touring with a good degree of success. Before its first year's activities had finished a second year was already booked as the piece marched on into 1906 and 1907 as a great little money-maker.

The Golden Girl saw the shining hope of British comic opera, Basil Hood, returning to his earlier *Gentleman Joe/French Maid* style with a rollicking made-for-the-provinces piece in which a lawyer's clerk is prevailed upon to play the part of a married man in order to protect 'Mrs Robinson' who is, in fact, a single and very rich young lady desirous of warding off unwanted suitors. Although not in the class of those very popular early works it had plenty of vigour and fun and an accomplished if rather reminiscent score by former Savoy conductor Hamish MacCunn. MacCunn's previous works had been in a more serious vein including such pieces as 'The Land of the Mountain and the Flood' and 'Lord Ullin's Daughter' and the operas *Jeannie Deans* (1894) and *Diarmid* (1897) for the Carl Rosa Opera Company of which he had, for a time, been conductor. Spectacle was well cared for in *The Golden Girl* with the introduction of three Japanese princesses and feminine illustrations to the songs 'The Fashion Plate of 1834', 'The Beauty Parade' and the first act finale 'There Goes the Golden Girl'. The show was successfully toured through major dates in 1905 without being brought into the metropolis for which it was clearly not suited.

Following on from *Winnie Brooke, Widow*, Ada Reeve made a second venture into touring management with a musical based on Frank Barrett's story, *A Set of Rogues.* This was an eighteenth-century romance about a strolling player girl, Moll Dawson, who poses as a missing heiress. The role of Moll was one which allowed Miss Reeve to run the gamut from the poor player-girl to the warm-hearted lady of the final scenes. The piece was put together by Miss Reeve's husband Wilfred Cotton and was staged at the Prince's, Manchester, without a title, a competition being announced to find the name under which it would continue. The rather unimaginative winner was *The Adventures of Moll.*

In spite of the enthusiasm engendered by the star's performance, it was evident that the play was not sufficiently well constructed and it was withdrawn and revised. New songs were added with lyrics by Percy French and music by the company's m.d., J. A. Robertson; the prize-winning title was discarded and as *Moll the Rogue* the resulting revision was staged at Cheltenham in September. Once again it did little for anyone and was soon put away[1] in favour of more *Winnie Brooke, Widow.*

More promising was an unpretentious piece called *The Gipsy Girl* written and composed by Claude Arundale, brother to actresses Sybil (of *My Lady Molly* and *Cingalee* fame) and Grace, and an architect by profession. Frederick Mouillot took up his little show and, with the two Arundale sisters featured in the leading roles, sent it on a short tour. In its original state *The Gipsy Girl* ran an unwieldy three hours and forty minutes, but the piece was well-received by provincial audiences despite this and its lack of originality. The story was the traditional comic opera one of the lost child, reared by gipsies, and finally returned to home, fortune and lover; and the dialogue and the music were both conceived in a style suitable to that subject. Sybil Arundale in the

[1] In her autobiography Miss Reeve gives a different and incorrect history of this piece.

title role gave the show a boost which may have led its connections to expect a little too much of it for, when it was eventually decided to produce *The Gipsy Girl* in the West End in 1907, even its star did not prove proof against failure.

A much more uncomfortable failure attended a show instigated by the lessee-manager of the Maidenhead Theatre, Edgar Dereve. Dereve had tried his hand at writing on several occasions and his latest effort was a piece called *A Gay Girl* which leaned heavily on the *Morocco Bound* tradition as one Monsieur Slashoni (played by Dereve) supplied entertainments for an Eastern potentate. A few weeks after its initial production, *A Gay Girl* opened at Swindon's Queen's Theatre. During the first act, the audience began to show its discontent at the standard of the entertainment and, half way through the second act, the angry theatre manager let down the curtain. The aggrieved audience were offered free tickets for a variety show later in the week when a collection was taken up for the actors stranded by the collapse of *A Gay Girl*. The piece was never seen again.

One of the most durable of the provincial pieces of 1905 was a farce with a pot-pourri of songs entitled *Miss Lancashire Ltd.* written by Sydney Sydney and produced at Croydon in September. It starred Florence Baines as Mary-Ellen, a parlourmaid who changes place with an heiress, and proved to be a popular entertainment on the smaller provincial circuits. Miss Baines held onto the role for many years and toured it with special success in Australia and New Zealand.

The Treasure Island, a comic opera of the most obvious kind, was also sent on tour by its author Peter Eland who had produced it at Bradford's Theatre Royal. It dealt with a treasure hunt amid cannibal isles and its high point was the staging of an eclipse. It had a company of 45, a wages bill of £60 per week, and its takings at one Monday's performance amounted to £9 7s 6d. In fifteen weeks on the road it lost £500 and cured Mr Eland's theatrical optimism.

1905

0304 **THE TALK OF THE TOWN** a musical comedy in two acts by Seymour Hicks. Lyrics by Charles H. Taylor. Music by Herbert E. Haines. Additional music by Evelyn Baker and Hamish MacCunn. Produced at the Lyric Theatre under the management of William Greet 5 January, 1905 for a run of 100 performances closing 15 April, 1905.

Jerry Snipe . . . . Walter Passmore
Lt Reggie Drummond . . . . Henry A. Lytton
Lt the Duke of Topford . . . . Robert Evett/Charles Childerstone
Lt Dordell. . . . . Powis Pinder
Lt Raglan . . . . Charles Childerstone/*out*
Lt Logan . . . . Robert McGrath
Lt St George . . . . Vernon Davidson
Lt Donnethorn . . . . Ernest Arundale
Col Sir Charles Nightingale . . . . . . Tom Graves/Arthur Boielle
Lt Richard Hambledon . . . . Arthur Harrold
'Arry Biff . . . . Akerman May
Private Belsey . . . . Reginald Crompton
Ernest English . . . . M. R. Morand
Frank English . . . . Stanley Brett/Tom Graves
Cyril Slipp . . . . Arthur Boielle/G. Boielle
J. Ochletree Ott . . . . Frank Elliston
Footman. J. Gordon
Gwendoline Snipe . . . . Edith Jurman
Imogen Snipe . . . . Alice Valchera
Jack . . . . P. Healey
Bert . . . . J. Healey
La Pa Doo . . . . Ernest Torrence
Juddy Wuddy Ah . . . . Rudolph Lewis
Madame Modiste . . . . Maude Darrell/Cissie Vaughan
Ellaline Lewin. . . . . Agnes Fraser
Lady Nightingale . . . . Annie Esmond
Marjorie Nightingale . . . . Gertrude Thornton
Mabel Nightingale . . . . Lydia West
Geraldine Evelyn Snipe. . . . . Sydney Fairbrother
June . . . . Olive Morrell

The Vaudeville Girls: Claire Rickard, Lily McIntyre, Hilda Hammerton, Miss Gibson, Rosie Edwardes, Vashti Earle, Florrie Sutherland, Pauline Francis, Margaret Leslie
pd: Winifred Hart-Dyke
with Miss H. Barton, Cissie Vaughan, G. Boielle, Dora Quarry, Edith Standen & c.

Dir: Seymour Hicks; md: Hamish MacCunn; ch: Edward Royce Jr; sc: Hawes Craven; cos: Percy Anderson

0305 **A TRIP TO THE HIGHLANDS** a Scottish musical play by Fred Locke. Music by E. T. de Banzie. Additional numbers by W. Scott Phipp, Maitland Malcolm, J. G. Aitken *et al.* Produced at the Grand Theatre, Edinburgh, under the management of Eade Montefiore 3 April, 1905 for four weeks and toured through . . . Manchester, Marlborough, Leeds, ?, Middlesborough, Edinburgh x3, to July 15; Bristol (21 Aug), Cheltenham, Sheffield, Glasgow, ?, Perth, Aberdeen, Dundee, Coatbridge, Kircaldy/Falkirk, Aberdeen to 4 November &c ending 25 November &c.

Rt Hon. Viscount Lackington . . . . . . Picton Roxburgh/Herbert Cottesmore
Hon. Frederick Lackington . . . . Sam Walsh/Arthur Poole
Sir Septimus Brown-Windsor . . . . . . Harry Fischer
Araminta Brown-Windsor . . . . Nellie Cozens/Mary Norton
Winnie Brown-Windsor. . . . . Isa Bowman
Fanny Flounce . . . . Lulu Evans
MacMutchkin of that Ilk . . . . Wal Croft
Flora . . . . Florence Moore/Kate Sherry
Jane . . . . Cissie Locke
Dexter. . . . . Arthur Poole/Fred Rolph
Timmins . . . . William Rokeby
Charley Chatterton . . . . Fanny Wright/Florence Moore
Miss Lottie Langley . . . . Muriel George/Lothian West
The Gibson Girls: Clara Stanton, Jane Maclean, Julie Stanley, Aurelie de Loriere, Dorothy Loton, Belle Hamilton, Lillian Ward, Lothian West, Kitty Elmore, Rhoda Clighton, Grace Mackay, Gladys Taverner, Dorothy Mayhew; with the Collins troupe of dancers and the Fiori del Monti quartette

Sc: Edmund Swift

0306 **THE OFFICERS' MESS** (And How They Get Out Of It) a military musical comedy in three acts by Cyril Hurst. Music by Mark Strong. Additional numbers by Emily Beatrice Gadsdon. Produced at the West London Theatre under the management of W. Penrhyn Foster and E. P. Clift 3 April, 1905. Played at Terry's Theatre from 10 April, 1905 for 8 performances, then toured from 1 May at the Grand, Woolwich. Dates included Eastbourne/Cheltenham, Peckham, Ipswich, Colchester, Chatham and Fulham.

Major General Sir Albert de Beaune . . . Stephen Hanworth/Jerrold Manville
Captain the Hon. Claude Melville . . . . Roland Bottomley
Antonio Wilkins. . . . . Walter Rignold
Rienzi Poorpoori . . . . L. Poynter
Thomas Rugg . . . . T. E. Conover
Sybil Carruthers . . . . Gladys Huxley/Joan Yelland
Lady Constantia de Beaune. . . . . Grace Heywood
Rose Smith . . . . Hilda Corelli/M. Sadie
Timothy Tiptop/Jack . . . . May Hart
add Scene-shifter . . . . Alfred Lester
with Freda Vaughan, Elvira Trevalyan, Nita Alexander, Hilda Geoghegan, Maude Vyvian, Jessie Collins, Ivy Stanmore, May Stanmore, Rita Holdsworth, Ada Bernan, May Florence, Cissie Burton, Tom Cook, Guy Marsh, George Parte, Charles Cartwright, George Goodwin, J. H. J. Jeffrey, C. D. Thomas, V. Jackson, S. Jackson, H. Chappell, Cyril Kitson
Dancers: Elsie Perrin, Ethel Perrin, Florence Stevenson, Eveleen Hartford, Lillian Hartford, May Lawrence, Nellie Lawrence, Dollie de Veney

Dir: Alfred Lester; md: Mark Strong; ch: Tina Alston; sc: Edmund Swift

0307 **MISS WINGROVE** a musical play in two acts by W. H. Risque. Music by Howard Talbot. Produced at the Strand Theatre under the management of Frank Curzon and Austen Hurgon 4 May, 1905 for a run of 11 performances closing 13 May, 1905.

Frank Leyland . . . . Joe Farren Soutar
Hon Basil Chesterton . . . . G. M. Graham
Count Polo . . . . Holman Clark
Registrar of Marriages . . . . Windham Guise
Clerk to the Registrar. . . . . B. Ansell
Danilo . . . . Arthur Grover
Alberto . . . . Austen Hurgon
Topping. . . . . Arthur Williams

Kitty Merton . . . . Mabel Nelson
Cora . . . . Simeta Marsden
Lucia . . . . Maisie Stather
Santa . . . . Verna Reed
Zana . . . . F. Randall
Camillo . . . . Iago Lewys
Miss Sonia Wingrove . . . . Millie Legarde
with Misses Curzon, Reynolds, Vincent, Edmunds, Moore, Langton, Macey, Flower, Stewart, Adele Lewis, Hammerstein, Thunder, Halden, Enid Lewis, Harrison, Newcombe, Morrison, Janes, Leigh; Messrs Duff, Vigney, J. P. McMullen, Franklin, Radcliff, Moss.

Dir: Austen Hurgon and Frank Curzon; md: Frederick Rosse; sc: Hemsley & Julian Hicks; cos: Karl

0308 **THE GIPSY GIRL** a musical comedy in two acts by Claude Arundale. Additional lyrics by Follett Thorpe. Produced at Liverpool under the management of Frederick Mouillot 15 May, 1905 and toured through Manchester, Dublin, Belfast, Birmingham, to 19 June.

Colonel Charlton . . . . Walter Balfour
Freddie . . . . George H. Liot
Canon Willoby . . . . Broughton Black
Jack Willoby . . . . Gordon Cleather
Augustus Short . . . . J. T. MacCallum
Pedro . . . . Esme Percy
Harlequin . . . . J. M. Jones
Horatio Victorious . . . . Fred Eastman
Grace Willoby. . . . . Gladys Fontaine
Marion Willoby . . . . Grace Arundale
Evangeline Short . . . . Zoe Gilfillan
Florette . . . . Andrée Corday
Waitress . . . . Mina de Silva
Katrina . . . . Sybil Arundale

Md: Chevalier Legrand

Produced in London in a revised version with additional numbers by Claude Arundale and Tom Heffernan at a matinée at the Waldorf theatre 8 January, 1907.

Produced at the Waldorf Theatre under the management of Benbrick Blanchard 22 March, 1907 for a run of 30 performances closing 20 April, 1907.

Colonel Charlton . . . . Leonard Russell
Freddy . . . . Aubrey Fitzgerald
Professor Willoby . . . . Percy Clifton
Jack Willoby . . . . Gordon Cleather
Augustus Short . . . . John M. Hay
Pedro . . . . Reginald Dane
Horatio Victorious . . . . Fred Eastman
Inspector . . . . Joseph Bruce
Policeman . . . . Vincent Earne
Farmer . . . . George Stone
Grace Willoby. . . . . Annie Esmond
Marion Willoby . . . . Grace Arundale
Evangeline Josephine Short. . . . . . . Kittie Davis (Emily Faulkener)
Florette . . . . Andrée Corday
Waitress . . . . Kitty Mackay
Katrina . . . . Sybil Arundale
with Llorien Hamilton, Eileen Cecil, Ella Lorraine, Ada Gilbride, Violet Kennerley, Gladys Greville, E. Baker-Ker, Warwick Wellington, E. Cooper Willis, Laurence Wensley, Basil Mercer, Gordon Leslie

Dir: Harry Bishop; md: Arthur Wood; cos: Hugo Baruch, Hanover Dress Co. & Fred W. Clarke

0309 **THE SPRING CHICKEN** a musical play in two acts adapted by George Grossmith Jr from *Le*

Coquin de Printemps by Adolf Jaime & Duval. Additional lyrics by Adrian Ross and Percy Greenbank. Music by Ivan Caryll and Lionel Monckton. Produced at the Gaiety Theatre under the management of George Edwardes 30 May, 1905 for a run of 401 performances closing 6 July, 1906. New edition produced 22 March, 1906.

Gustave Babori . . . . George Grossmith Jr/Charles A. Brown
Boniface . . . . Lionel Mackinder /Henry A. Lytton
Baron Papouche . . . . Harry Grattan
Félix . . . . Robert Nainby/Leigh Ellis
Stephen-Henry . . . . Will Spray
Proprietor of the 'Crimson Butterfly'. . . Arthur Hatherton
Alexis . . . . George Gregory/Bert d'Arcy
Waiter . . . . Leigh Ellis/J. W. Birtley
Ferdinand . . . . Harry Taylor
Napoléon . . . . Master Cross
Joseph Boniface . . . . Charles A. Brown/George Chapman
Inspector . . . . R. Tremayne
Mr Girdle . . . . Edmund Payne
Mrs Girdle . . . . Connie Ediss/Gertrude Aylward
Baroness Papouche . . . . Kate Cutler (Fanny Dango)
Dulcie Babori . . . . Olive Morrell/Ethel Oliver
Emmy-Lou . . . . Olive May/Nellie Lonnen
La Modiste (La Belle Cissi) . . . . Isabelle Lidster/Marion Winchester
Sylvana . . . . Gaynor Rowlands/Yvonne Moel
Thérèse . . . . Gertrude Glyn/Jean Aylwin
Henriette . . . . Marguerite Grey/Evelyn Beresford/ Ethel Forsyth
Yvonne . . . . Kitty Mason
Yvette . . . . Fanny Dango/Clara Pitt/Edith Loe
Celeste. . . . . Ethel Oliver/Florence Warde/Vera Harland
Rosalie. . . . . Gertie Millar (Gertrude Glyn)
add Marianne . . . . Minnie Baker
Georgette . . . . Daisy Holly

with Doris Beresford, Daisy Holly, Lulu Valli, Addie Baker, Minnie Baker, Edith Neville, Doris Dewar/Ethel Forsyth, Gladys Desmond, Clara Pitt

Dir: Sidney Elliston; md: Ivan Caryll; cos: Wilhelm; sc: Walter Hann and Joseph Harker

Produced at Daly's Theatre, New York, under the management of Richard Carle 8 October, 1906 for 66 performances to 1 October. Resumed 10 October at the New Amsterdam Theatre for 25 further performances closing 29 December, 1906 after a total of 91 performances. 'Americanised by Richard Carle'.
Victor Morley (BAB), Richard Ridgely (BON), Sylvain Langlois (PAP), Arthur Conrad (S–H), Horace Whitaker (PROP), J. N. Roseland (ALEX), W. R. Paschal (FERDINAND), C. H. Beardsley (PIERRE), James Yates (HENRI), H.A. Smith (JOS), J. H. Purcell (INSP), Richard Carle (GIRDLE), Emma Janvier (MRS G), Adele Rowland (BAR), May Bouton (DUL), Amy Dale (EMMY), Frankie Douglas (SILVIE), Burleigh Murray (TH), Gertrude Gibbens (CLARICE), Violet Handy (SYBELE), Florence Averell (CELESTE), Helen St John (TESSA), Blanche Deyo (LA BELLE SISSI), Bessie McCoy (ROSALIE), Leila Smith (PAGE), Vivian Rushmore (MODEL), Lois Fennel (DUTCH BOY) with Misses Barrell, Alain, O'Donnell, Sanchez, Capron, Lorena, Bennett, Windsor, Ashland, West, Cullom, Boley, Valori, Mansfield, Warner, Crandall, Leonard, D'Arville, Smith, Raymond, Fisher. Md: Frank Pallma

Produced at Daly's Theatre, New York, 1 April, 1907 for a run of 24 performances closing 20 April, 1907.

0310 **MOLL, THE ROGUE** (The Adventures of Moll) a romantic musical comedy by Wilfred Cotton adapted from Frank Barrett's novel *A Set of Rogues*. Lyrics by Percy French. Music by J. A. Robertson. Produced at Manchester under the management of Ada Reeve 14 June, 1905. Revised by Frank Barrett and T. H. Read and re-presented at the Opera House, Cheltenham 27 September, 1905 under the title *Moll, the Rogue*.

	Manchester cast	Cheltenham cast
Host of the Bell Inn	Harry Halley	Philip Somers
Simon Sourby	Frederick Tyrrell	Frederick Tyrrell
Don Sanchez	Frederick Annerley	Leon Ashton-Jarry
Mohand	Leon Ashton-Jarry	Harry Welchman
Kit Sutton	T. P. Haynes	Stephen Adeson
Jack Dawson	John A. Warden	Harry Halley
Moll Dawson	Ada Reeve	Ada Reeve
Mrs Marjory Butterby	Alice Aynsley Cook	Alice Lawrence
Peter	Mr Price Evans	J. D. Newton
Susan Butterby	Kitty Clinton	Kitty Clinton
Richard Godwyn	Herbert Clayton	Douglas Vigors
Walter Fare	R. S. Lindon	H. West
Mistress Hector Bumpkin	Mrs Charles Maltby	Lucy Beaumont
Sir Geoffrey	Harry Eversleigh	E. Edwards
Sir Jasper	F. S. Lumley	E. Neville
Miss Wilder	Drusilla Wills	Ruth Hazelwood
Abimelech Bagshot	Ulick Burke	Cyrus P. Cliff
Rebecca Bagshot	Amy Lawrence	Janet Neville
Lady Godwyn	Freda Stanley	Mrs Charles Maltby

Md: J. A. Robertson

0311 **THE GOLDEN GIRL** a musical comedy in two acts by Basil Hood. Music by Hamish MacCunn. Produced at the Prince of Wales, Birmingham, under the management of H. Cecil Beryl 5 August, 1905, and toured through Sheffield, Bradford, Leeds, Hull, Dublin, Manchester, Hanley, Portsmouth, Brighton, Cheltenham, Northampton, Leicester, Sunderland, Edinburgh, Newcastle and Glasgow to 9 December.

Charles Beverley	E. H. Kelly
Matthew Gabbage	Martin Adeson
Lord Derwent Waters	Conway Dixon
Prince Ji-Ji	Gilbert Laye
Horace	Bert Lloyd
Reggie Pepperton	Powis Pinder
Lady Virginia Waters	Nellie Beryl
Miss Dobson	Nellie Bouverie
Lady Broadstairs	Helen Kirkpatrick
Mrs Bobbie Lancaster	Gertrude Sinclair
Mrs Dalrymple	May Gray
Clara Tempest	Beatrice Jackson
Princess To-to	Julie Dolaro
Princess Ta-ta	Winifred Volt
Princess Tu-tu	Dora Dolaro
Lottie Lightfoot	Queenie Finnis
Porteress	Annie Hathaway
The Pretty Mrs Robinson	Louie Pounds

with Florence Marston, Violet Cashmere, Edith Broad, Kate Johnstone, Joyce Thon, Daisy Athelstan, Gladys Anderson, Kate Rossell, Elsie Sinclair, Jennie Danvers, Queenie Hawthorne, May Jackson, Harry Leslie, J. Graham, J. C. Nevill, William Russell, Richard Webster, Michael Watson, Emlyn David, Hugh Bevan, Henry Smith

Md: Edwin Thornton

0312 **THE TREASURE ISLAND** a comic opera by Peter Eland. Music by Vincent Exley. Additional music by Ralph Illingworth and Crashaw Crabtree. Produced at the Theatre Royal, Bradford, under the management of Peter Eland 7 August, 1905, and toured through Hull, Leeds, Rochdale, Ashton, Dewsbury, Cheltenham, Swindon, ?, Sheffield, ?, ?, Darlington, Lincoln, Crewe, Bolton to 2 December.

Ralph Revill	E. H. Bertram
Jack Jocelyn	Theodore Jones

Septimus Smart	Johnnie Clegg/J. C. Bland
Sheridan Shakespeare Smith	Jo Monkhouse/Scott Battye
Mr Gathergold	Edward Raymond
King Umbo-Grumbo	W. A. Buckstone/Ashton Foster
Lord Chamberlain	Scott Battye
Dicky Mizzenmast	Harry Oswald
Bill Bonniface	Mr Ridley
Princess	Jenny Whitehead
Bella Bonniface	Rosie Kearns
Maud	Ethel Rainforth
Millicent	Edith Maynard/May Fallowfield

Md: Vincent Exley

0313 **THE WHITE CHRYSANTHEMUM** a lyrical comedy in three acts by Leedham Bantock and Arthur Anderson. Lyrics by Arthur Anderson. Music by Howard Talbot. Produced at the Criterion Theatre under the management of Frank Curzon 31 August, 1905 for a run of 179 performances closing 10 February, 1906.

Admiral Sir Horatio Armitage KCB	Rutland Barrington
Lt Reginald Armitage	Henry A. Lytton
Lt Chippendale Bennett	Lawrence Grossmith
Sin Chong	M. R. Morand
Cornelia Vanderdecken	Marie George/Louie Pounds
Betty Kenyon	Millie Legarde/Daisy Le Hay
Sybil Cunningham	Isabel Jay
Jinrickshah men	Messrs Arnold & Thomas
Tokiwa	Leila Leibrandt/Ethel Callanan
Kokomoye	Claire Pridelle/Lillian Graham
Zaye	Ethel Callanan/Miss Ellis/Maisie Stather
O Kiko	Dorothy Brunt
Kawoyo	Miss Vernon/Miss Weatherley/Doris Trevor
Konami	Miss Maguire/Joyce Temple
H. Nelson	John Clulow
F. Drake	Edward? Shale/Reginald? Cooper
C. Columbus	Mr Brooke/Herbert Hulcup
T. Bowling	Reginald? Cooper/Mr Ashley
P. Jones	Herbert Hulcup/Mr Ward
M. Frobisher	Mr Ashley/Mr Ricketts
add Midshipman Easy	Claire Pridelle

Dir: Austen Hurgon; md: Roland Macurtha/Howard Talbot; sc: W. T. Hemsley; cos: Karl

0314 **MR POPPLE (OF IPPLETON)** a comedy with music in three acts by Paul Rubens. Music by Paul Rubens. Produced at the Apollo Theatre under the management of Tom B. Davis 14 November, 1905. Transferred to the Shaftesbury Theatre under the management of Paul Rubens 17 March, 1906. Closed 5 May, 1906, after a total of 173 performances.

Freddy Popple	G. P. Huntley (Morris Harvey)
Norman Popple	Kenneth Douglas/Bertram Steer
George Hennay	William Cheesman
Henry Doring	Harold Eden
Jacques Kenyon	Leon Rennay/J. Edward Fraser/Robert Michaelis
Lord Downe	Erskine Lang/St John Ronaldson
Pat Fenton	Gregory Scott
Hon. Kerr Buretta	Charles Hampden
Alfred	Frank Perfitt
Maurice	Morris Harvey
John	S. Hughes
William	Berridge Fraser

Platt	Lionel Victor
Mrs Doring	Marie Illingworth
Mrs Hennay	Grace Dudley
Violet Brinton	Olive Hood/Nancy Malone/Violet Lloyd
Gladys	Violet Englefield
Rosie	Nancy Malone/Gladys Ivery
Catherine	Mollie Ventry/Miss Wakefield
Marie	Sara Sydney
Clytie	Addie Marze
Mabel	Vivienne Evans
Louise	Coralie Blythe/Lydia Flopp/Eva Kelly
La Boléro	Ethel Irving (Violet Englefield)

with Gladys Ivery, Misses Delva, Kelly, Clare, Romney, Vaal, O'Ferrall, Inbawk,/Gwendoline Brogden, Maidement, Michae; Messrs Ronaldson, Romer, Hampden, Warren, Digues, Hay, Walsh

Dir: E. T. Steyne; md: I.A. de Orellana; sc: Joseph Harker & Julian Hicks; cos: Percy Anderson

Produced in the United States in a heavily altered version as *Nobody Home*.

MISS LANCASHIRE LTD. a farce with music in two acts by Sydney Sydney. Produced at Croydon 4 September, 1905 and toured.

A GAY GIRL a musical comedy in two acts by Edgar Dereve. Music by Giuseppe Leone. Produced at the Grand Theatre, Maidenhead under the management of Edgar Dereve 1 May, 1905 and toured.

1906

The early months of 1906 saw the disappearance of a large number of the previous year's shows. In February *The Catch of the Season*, *The Blue Moon* and *The White Chrysanthemum* all closed and *Mr Popple* shifted to the Shaftesbury where the state of the roof indicated that it would not stay long before the County Council and the Lord Chamberlain closed the theatre for repairs. *The Little Michus* and *The Spring Chicken*, the two George Edwardes pieces, still had a few months left.

There was no lack of new shows, however, to fill the places of those departing, and Edwardes was first into the breach with a new Owen Hall/Ivan Caryll piece for the Prince of Wales. *The Little Cherub* was, according to the author, partly based on Henri Meilhac's *Decoré*, played by Réjane at the New Royalty, but the elements which Hall had lifted from the French piece in fact formed a tiny sub-plot in the doings of the new musical. The principal story concerned the four daughters of the Earl of Sanctobury who are putting on a play. To improve their amateur dramatics they invite Molly Montrose, the professional star of the play 'The Little Cherub', to come to coach them. Their austere father is appalled both at the play and at Miss Montrose but he agrees, finally, to go along when the lady invites him to Dunbridge to see her play for himself and to dine with her after to discuss it. Alas for the Earl, his daughters turn up at the same restaurant. They see their Papa surrounded by a bevy of show ladies and blackmail is the order of the day: the girls use the lever to have their own way over the play (amongst other things) whilst the Earl makes Molly Lady Sanctobury.

The basic story was enlivened with multiple sub-plots including the *Decoré* one involving Algy, an asinine friend of the girls, who rescues what he believes to be a drowning man from the river (the man is, in fact, a long-distance swimmer chasing a record) and becomes an unjustified hero. Since, on the occasion, he is in the company of the Ladies Congress he is taken for their father which leads to further complications, with the genuine Earl being dragged off to the police station as an impostor.

Almost the entire score for *The Little Cherub* came from Ivan Caryll,which gave it more homogeneity than most musical scores on display in London. *The Times* passed it off as:

> . . tuneful, commonplace, agreeable, rising now and then to the level of [the song] 'Experience' . . . but for the most part making no impression whatsoever.

but the theatre papers were much more enthusiastic:

> Mr Ivan Caryll has seldom written a brighter and more ear-catching score and many of his tunes – if not the words to which they are set – 'Experience' and 'The Supper Girl' for example – seem sure of an extra-theatre popularity (*Stage*)

. . Mr Caryll is in his best form, his music having all those bright and sparkling qualities which usually distinguish his work. (*Era*)

But, if Caryll was at his most tuneful, Adrian Ross had succumbed in many of the solo numbers to the dreary archness so prevalent in modern songs, relying on the same palely suggestive atmosphere and tired rhyming which had become all too familiar. And yet the public, or sufficient of it, never seemed to tire of such pieces. The song 'Experience' sung by Evie Greene was an example, becoming the most popular in the show, with its tale of a girl sent to market by her aunt and waylaid by a young man in the lane:

Said he, my dear
Your shoe, I fear
Will trip you on your face
I see the lace
Coming down, will you
Let me tie up your shoe?
Said I, young man
I'd say you can
But auntie told me I
Must not reply
She has such good sense
For she's had Experience

A 'walk in the woods' is agreed and the lass arrives home to her aunt minus the marketing:

Said I, Dear Aunt
I fear I can't
Quite tell you where I've been
And what I've seen
But in consequence
I've had Experience

Another popular piece, an interpolation by Frank Tours, was on a similarly outworn theme: the getting of a rich husband. Its lyric was also by Ross, and Gabrielle Ray sang the song 'Cupid's Rifle Range' describing how Cupid has put away his bow and arrow and taken up a rifle:

There's a stock-and-share man
Bull-and-bear man
Some say his ways are shady
Good for diamond brooches
Motor coaches
He'll do . . or can I change
There's a Marquis splendid
Well-descended
Fair game for any lady
To hit him right'll
Win a title
He's my prize on Cupid's rifle range

The number was decorated prettily as the attractive pin-up favourite dressed in a short tunic and buskins, wings and a wreath, knocked down toy gentlemen on a little rifle-range, while half a dozen miniature Cupids danced about her.

In similar vein, Maurice Farkoa as an incidental amorous Rajah flirted with Molly in a duet offering her a 'String of Pearls', with an Alderman's wife in an 'Invitation to the Waltz' and with the whole chorus in 'It's the Girls' as well as having a mildly suggestive number 'The Supper Girl' which glorified the girl who will go to supper as opposed to those straight-laced ladies who will only accept invitations for luncheon or tea. Rendered in the sleek Farkoa manner, each one was well received by the ladies. A new dimension was added to the 'tomboy' number in another Frank Tours song for which C. H. Bovill had written the lyric. Zena Dare described how 'I should so Love to be a Boy' and, accompanied by Gabs Ray, Lily Elsie and Grace Pindar, went through a pantomime of various boyish games – swimming, riding, rowing and finally football – this last ending with Miss Dare kicking a football into the auditorium (or, rather, into a certain private box – *cash oblige*).

Most of the humorous work fell to the representatives of the servants. George Carroll and Elsie Clare had an amusing number, 'Couples', where they described and pictured various types of people at a dance, and an unknown young man making his first appearance on the stage, W. H. (Bill) Berry, scored with a neat piece called 'The Gentleman's Gentleman' and later appeared in Grecian garb to sing 'I wasn't Engaged for That':

> Although it's no part of my duty
> I even consented to go
> Assisting the rank and the beauty
> Who get up this amateur show,
> But classical poses
> And garlands of roses
> Are hard on a man that's fat
> Your Wallers and Trees
> May show off their knees
> I wasn't engaged for that!

which stretched itself to many verses, taking swipes at the L. C. C. and its steamers:

> Said he: we get wages
> For stopping at stages
> That never a soul is at
> But me and my mates
> Are paid by the rates
> They'll have to be raised for that!

the new government and Cabinet and any other topical subject that came up.

Politics, of course, was not always a subject that pleased a theatre audience. On the first night, with election results coming through hourly, the gallery made its feelings noisily felt when an attempt was made to introduce some references and results and the cries of 'No Politics!' brought back memories of old days at the Savoy and elsewhere. There were other things, too, on that opening night to which the audience took exception, such as Lily Elsie's number 'Baby Bayswater' which was of the standard coyly rude kind, and unsuited to her. Nevertheless, the opening night went pretty well and the contents of the show and artists engaged in it seemed to guarantee a fairly good run. But something resolutely refused to go right, and *The Little Cherub* did not 'work up' into the kind of success to which the management was accustomed. After some superficial additions and alterations had failed, Fred Kaye was taken out and replaced in the role of the Earl by Willie Edouin. The role of Sanctobury had never turned out as the showy central comic role that had been planned, and Kaye had failed to liven it up with the necessary individual contributions of a chief funny man. For Edouin, Hall rewrote the part, making it larger and so much more important, that the curtain time had to be put back from 8.15 p.m. to 8 o'clock to accommodate the extra material. Maurice Farkoa had been in and out of his role of the uxorious Rajah of Talcutta and it was decided to replace him with the more manly Louis Bradfield while Colin Coop was added in the role of the ambitious Alderman Briggs. But still *The Little Cherub* did not move as hoped, and finally, after 114 ever-changing performances, Edwardes took the show off and returned it to the author for a major rewrite. Caryll produced six new numbers, six 'outside' pieces from Frank Tours and Jerome D. Kern were added and, one week later, the Prince of Wales Theatre reopened with *A Girl on the Stage*.

The piece had undergone considerable alterations. Much of the suggestive business had been dropped; the Rajah had suffered a complete character change; and a new character, the Earl's dashing son (Lionel Mackinder), had been added to give the affair of a Sanctobury with Molly an air of decency. No longer did she cavort mercenarily with the father but, instead, sighed romantically with the son. The favourite numbers including 'Experience' were retained and, if the new ones included no hits, they were, at least, pleasant. Lily Elsie had been released along with Grace Pindar – the Earl had now only two daughters – and there were many other cast changes, most notably in the leading role where Evie Greene had been replaced by Ruth Vincent, returned from America and making her first appearance in the West End since *Véronique*. Unfortunately, however, on the first night of *A Girl on the Stage* as Miss Vincent stepped forward to sing the new song 'Love and Laughter' she crumpled to the floor in a dead faint. After she had been removed, the play continued but the audience was relieved to see Miss Vincent reappear, albeit unsteadily, to give the last few lines of her role, and she received an enormous ovation at the end of the evening.

There was general agreement that *A Girl on the Stage* was a better piece than *The Little Cherub* had been but it still refused to draw and, after four weeks, Edwardes called it a day and removed the show for good. But success was ultimately in store for *The Little Cherub*. A version of it which combined the plot of the second London version with the title of the first plus some of the original score and the usual stack of American interpolations from Kern, Schwartz *et al.* made an appearance at Broadway's Criterion Theatre with Hattie Williams, star of the previous year's *The Rollicking Girl*, giving her version of Molly Montrose. Joe Coyne turned down the role of Algy for reasons of billing and James Blakeley was imported from England to co-star.

The production caught on and, in contrast to the London show, each time it seemed to have run its course, it rallied strongly enough to be retained. Its proposed limited run on Broadway was to have been followed by a three months' Christmas season in Boston but its popularity resulted in its staying in New York for a run of 169 performances before setting out on a lengthy tour. In the following August, the company even returned to Broadway and the Criterion for a further three weeks' season prior to the opening of *The Dairymaids*. Then, with Miss Williams and Coyne still starring, it headed out for a further long inter-state tour. In Britain, by this time, *The Little Cherub* had long played its last performance, and thus joined the select list of British musicals to have suceeded in America after failure or relative failure on the home market.

The closure of *Bluebell* at the Aldwych prefaced the opening of the newest of the Charles Frohman/Seymour Hicks shows. *The Catch of the Season* team of Cosmo Hamilton, Charles H. Taylor and Herbert Haines joined again with Hicks to produce a new Hicks/Terriss vehicle, *The Beauty of Bath*, which opened in March to great acclaim. *The Beauty of Bath* had a number of advantages which endeared it to the professional critics and raised it artistically above the level of many of its contemporaries. Firstly, it was largely based on a minor classic of the English stage, Tom Robertson's *David Garrick*, which had first been presented at the Haymarket in 1864 with E. A. Sothern in the title role and had since been frequently revived. Around the principal events of *David Garrick*, Hicks and Hamilton constructed a set of subordinate characters and details suited to the established favourites of the Aldwych company, but the central plot was not too obscured by trimmings.

Neither were there too many musical numbers and dances, which allowed the libretto to be decidedly stronger and less diffuse than usual and to contain some good solid 'dramatic' portions. In the first act only three songs and a duet were used to supplement the obligatory opening chorus and finale and a small piece of entrance music. In the second act, the writers faltered rather, or perhaps the managerial side of Hicks triumphed over the author, and a certain amount of superfluous business was inserted, occasionally to the detriment of the story. The fourteen musical numbers, however, as Hicks had no doubt foreseen, proved mostly only to add to the public's enjoyment. *The Beauty of Bath* thus had a strong and theatrical plot with the focus on its two central characters, which kept it away from the amorphous collection of sketches and showgirls that the same management and writers had descended to with *The Talk of the Town. The Times* wrote:

> Up to the end of the first act we thought Mr Seymour Hicks' new musical play the best we had ever seen . . . . pretty dresses, more than usually pretty ladies . . but in spite of the trimmings, moving directly and strongly forward and containing at least one convincing and admirable scene between Alington and his mother . . . Now if the play had gone on in that manner we should have been able to congratulate all concerned not only on a financial success (they are sure of it as it is) but on something nearer to artistic success than any musical play has achieved yet.

Hicks' and Hamilton's version of the *David Garrick* plot had Miss Betty Silverthorne (the Beauty of the title) up from Bath for a visit to the Mascot Theatre where she has become enamoured of the celebrated actor, Mr Beverley. But Mr Beverley has a double, one Lt Richard Alington R.N., and this young man has fallen in love with Betty from a picture sent to him at sea by his mother. Dick returns from ten years at sea and meets Betty in the foyer of the theatre where she mistakes him for the actor. Betty's guardian is not at all happy with his ward's infatuation with an actor and persuades Alington (mistaking him, likewise, for Beverley) to feign drunkenness at a ball, thereby disgusting Betty into giving up her illusions. In the second act we see Dick carrying out the plan, but Betty has long since discovered his real identity and by the end of the act happily declares that he is the man for her.

Hicks and his wife were cast as Dick and Betty and the 'amazing likeness' was solved by casting Hicks' brother, Stanley Brett, to whom he bore quite a physical similarity, as Beverley. Rosina Filippi was the hero's mother and Sydney Fairbrother, who had made such an impression in *The Talk of the Town*, was written in as Mrs Goodge, an ex-landlady of Beverley's who nourishes for him a more than maternal passion. Young Albert Valchera who had sighed so comically after Ellaline Terriss in *The Catch of the Season* played her son, Lemon Goodge (so-called because he 'loves being squeezed'), the programme boy at the theatre, sighing this time after the glamorous actress Miss Truly St Cyr (Maudie Darrell) who is engaged to the witless Lord Quorn (Lawrence

Caird) who says little but, 'Oh, you *are*, you know you are!'. Lord Quorn was provided with a sister, Dorothy, in order to give Barbara Deane an opportunity to sing her now obligatory solos. In succession to the Gibson Girls and the Vaudeville Girls, there were the Bath Buns, twelve lovely young ladies, the adoptive daughters of Sir Timothy Bun of Bath (Murray King), who paraded very decoratively through the play looking for husbands and enlivening the stage.

The opening of *The Beauty of Bath* is set in a theatre foyer and, on the rise of the curtain, the audience hear the final notes of the show inside before the fashionable audience chatter into view:

How delightful – simply ripping – most amusing little play
And the scenery and the dresses cost a trifle I should say
Really charming, altogether very, very, very, very, very, very funny
Pretty faces in the chorus, must have spent a lot of money &c . .
We're Johnny up from Aldershot and Bertie from the Bar
And Sammy from the Stock Exchange, and critics too we are
The men who do the music and the chaps who write the play
Know well they have to please us or the thing will never pay,
So where they steal their melodies or get their rotten rhymes
It really doesn't matter, if they're well up with the times
Throw in a lot of pretty girls and dresses up to par
And we'll come up from Aldershot, the City and the Bar . .

Also at the play are Sir Timothy and Lady Bun and their brood of 'Ready Maids'. Sir Timothy explains how, being of a proudly prolific family and yet childless, he sought to amend matters by adopting a dozen children. However, in picking out the babes he neglected to check the sexes and has, consequently, ended up with twelve daughters all of the same, now marriageable, age:

Here I am with my little family, stop! stop! stop!
If you don't see what you want in the window, walk inside the shop
All girls, large assortment, fashionable shapes and shades
So come into the Matrimonial Mart and ask for the Ready Maids

Barbara Deane welcomed the heroine with a fine waltz song 'The Beauty of Bath', before that lady told, in a lyric verging on the saccharine, of 'When a little Girl's in Love'. The nearest thing in the show to low comedy came in an operatic burlesque duo between the lovesick Mrs Goodge and her lovesick Lemon:

Laugh on, light-hearted Gower Street,
Smile, giddy Gordon Square,
The shadows fall on our street
Ah, little do you care.
Eat, drink and make you merry,
For us, eternally,
The accent's on the 'bury'
The bloom's off Blooms-bur-y!

In the second act, the songs became less relevant as the Fancy Ball dissolved into the usual string of numbers. Ellaline Terriss sang, to great approval, of 'Things you never Learn at School' which succeeded in being gently humorous without being sniggery and of how 'By gentle Means you'll Get your Way', and joined in a duet in wigs and spectacles, in a manner reminiscent of 'My cosy Corner Girl', playing on playing-card terminology in 'Bridge'. Barbara Deane sang another waltz song ('Look in your Heart and you'll See') and Valchera another comical piece called 'George's Love Affairs' describing how a hungry lad called George swapped his girl friends for a different tradesman's daughter each time his appetite changed. Needless to say, he took great care to marry a doctor's daughter. The music to this jolly number was the work of the young singer/composer Frederic Norton.

Hicks had an amusing 'stir-it-and-strump-it' march song 'The social Drum' and a totally irrelevant one lauding 'Our Brum chum, popular, perky Joe' (Mr Joseph Chamberlain) who was credited with all sorts of exploits:

He plays for Aston Villa just by way of keeping fit
He runs the mile in four fifteen and wrestles Hackenschmidt
He sleeps a couple of hours a week and works right round the clock
He wrote 'The Master Christian' and 'Stop yer ticklin', Jock' . .

This unsuitable piece was an interpolated number by Jerome D. Kern and a 25-year-old journalist from Guildford, Pelham G. Wodehouse. It went a long way to destroying the good work done in building a coherent show and proved once again that Hicks was willing to sacrifice almost anything to his penchant for introducing extraneous material for himself into his shows.

The Wodehouse/Kern partnership, in collaboration with F. Clifford Harris, also provided a song for Bert Sinden called 'The Frolic of the Breeze' which the agile dancer performed with eight ladies in frilly crinolines and the inevitable parasols. Sinden shared the show's dancing honours with his daughter Topsy, now a twenty-seven year-old veteran of dozens of musicals which she would soon abandon to become principal dancer at the Empire, following in the footsteps of Adeline Genée. On this occasion, Miss Sinden played a broadly Zummerzet ladies' maid, and delivered a duet with Bert 'Where do you Come from, my pretty Maid' in which she repelled the advances of a London swell:

HE: What is your fortune, my pretty maid?
SHE: Zummerzet sense, and plenty too
Eyes to see, and sense to tell
That you be a Lunnon swell
Wit to fit and just a view
Of a clean pair of heels for chaps like you!

But the picturesque highlight of the show was, as so often, made by the Girls. The setting for the second act ball was cleverly arranged so that a large picture placed at the head of the stairs framed each person making their entrance and, across those stairs was presented a parade of Famous Beauties. Wearing specially-made dresses by Wilhelm which reproduced famous paintings there came the Gainsborough Duchess of Devonshire, Perdita, Mrs Siddons, a Greuze, Reynolds' Mrs Carnac, Nelly O'Brien, Boucher's Madame de Pompadour and the gorgeous Sylvia Storey as Romney's Lady Hamilton. The parade was a huge success and wildly applauded.

The first night reaction to *The Beauty of Bath* was more than enthusiastic and the critics, too, were pleased though mostly agreeing with *The Times* that the second act was overfull of irrelevancies. *The Stage* decided that this was because of too much music and suggested cutting the 'Mr Chamberlain' number and a concerted piece about a 'Flying Machine', the lyric to which sounds all too up-to-date:

Leave town at noon, in Greece alight
See all there is to see,
Aboard and munch a hasty lunch

Ten minutes in Pompeii.
A rapid flight, a lightning sight,
Of Egypt and the Rand
An hour in Spain
Then France again
And six o'clock in the Strand.

but the critic concluded:

> [there is] not so much matter introduced à propos des bottes as has been the case with some of the Seymour Hicks pieces and, as the new musical play is sumptuously staged and beautifully dressed, and as the plot though seemingly intricate is not difficult to follow, *The Beauty of Bath* should enjoy a prosperous career.

His prediction was correct, and the box-office was quickly overwhelmed, but his good advice was not taken. Far from cutting down on the second act's musical content, Hicks soon began to enlarge it. In the time-honoured fashion of *The Lady Slavey, Morocco Bound et al.*, the act became the vessel for all kinds of material. As well as new numbers there were some old ones as Barbara Deane inserted 'Down at the old Bull and Bush' and 'Stop yer Ticklin', Jock', and there was even a whole scena in which members of the cast burlesqued theatrical personalities: Lawrence Caird came on as Nero, the role in which Beerbohm Tree was currently making a stir in Stephen Philips' 'poetical drama' of the same name; Stanley Brett and Murray King paraded about as Sandow Girls from *The Dairymaids*; Maudie Darrell was Edna May in *The Belle of New York* and Sydney Fairbrother gave such a lifelike impression of Camille Clifford's Gibson Girl that one foreign royal visitor was convinced, years later, he had seen the real thing. Young Valchera added his bit as the author Hall Caine, presently triumphant with *The Bondsman*.

The additional songs included one by a new young composer, 23-year-old Herman Darewski, elder brother of the musical prodigy, Max. Darewski had placed one or two pieces previously. Eva Sandford and Winifred Hare had both used his work, but 'My little Hyacinth' was the first of his songs which had made it into a West End show. It had originally been bought by John Tiller and John Huddlestone for their song and dance spectacular at the Winter Gardens, Blackpool, and it was there that Hicks heard it and arranged to 'borrow' it for *The Beauty of Bath*, where Ellaline Terriss sang it with considerable success.

When Charles Frohman's new Hicks Theatre was completed, the production of *The Beauty of Bath* was taken from the Aldwych and transferred there to be the new house's opening piece. It made its second bow on Boxing Day of 1906 and it ran out the final weeks of its 287-performance run in the theatre named for its star and guiding genius before being taken out for a twelve weeks' provincial tour to leave the theatre free for the newest of the Hicks/Frohman musicals, *My Darling*. There was a brief reappearance when a juvenile company headed by Albert Valchera was seen in a mini-version of the show at the Hicks in February, but *The Beauty of Bath* confined the rest of its career to the provinces.

It was nearly two years since a Leslie Stuart piece had been seen in London. Not since *The School Girl* had the composer of *Florodora* given a new work to the West End, so expectations were aroused by the announcement of a new Charles Frohman production for which Stuart was to write the score, and in which Edna May, currently making a great success as Angela in *The Catch of the Season* on Broadway, was to star. Capitalising on its heroine's past glory, the show was to be called *The Belle of Mayfair*.

A new element seemed to be entering into the construction of musical plays: the basing of the libretto on an established work. This, of course, was nothing novel but the consistency with which authors were now seeking out proven dramatic pieces to provide the bones for their musicals was noticeable. *The Girl from Kays* and *The Spring Chicken* had both been based more or less on French originals, *The Catch of the Season* had followed the Cinderella story, *The Beauty of Bath* had relied on *David Garrick* and *The Little Cherub* at least partially on Meilhac's *Decoré*. *The Belle of Mayfair* followed the trend – it was to be a modern retelling of *Romeo and Juliet* set in the most fashionable of London districts.

Juliet and her family became the Chaldicotts, Sir John and Lady Chaldicott and their daughter Julia, a nouveau riche family for whom the more lofty Mount Highgates (Montagues) have a healthy disdain. But their son Raymond (Romeo) falls in love with the unsuitable Julia and vice versa. Their parents attempt to keep them apart and the Comte de Perrier (Paris) is proposed as Julia's official suitor, but Raymond arrives at the second act ball disguised as the leader of a Bashi-Bazouk band and plots to elope with his beloved. Tragedy being scarcely an apt ending for a musical, the parents had to give in so that all can end happily.

The original idea of the parallel came from Basil Hood who collaborated on the libretto with author and wit Charles Brookfield. Close analogies were worked out and amongst the characters Friar Lawrence became 'Dr Marmaduke Lawrence', Bishop of Brighton, Tybalt became 'Captain Theobald', Mercutio 'Hugh Meredith' and even Rosalind, Romeo's unseen former love, put in an appearance as Lady Rosaline Rockesley. However, by the time *The Belle of Mayfair* reached the stage of the Vaudeville Theatre, many hands had had a go at the story and songs, and most of Hood's well-laid designs had been eroded. Some of the planned literary parodies remained, in particular one of Mercutio's Queen Mab speech where the Fairy Queen travelled by motor bus, which was unanimously voted the best bit of writing in the entire show.

Clever writing, however, was not the producer's primary aim and the outlines of *The Belle of Mayfair* finally bore less of a resemblance to *Romeo and Juliet* than did its cast list. Even that had been diluted by the addition of special characters for Louie Pounds as a 'fairy godmother' wife of the German Prince who sponsors Julia at court, and for Camille Clifford, featured as the American wife of an English Duke. Many of the numbers, too, bore little reference to the story, but the plot, if no more an elaborate modernisation of the classic story, was coherent enough. It was illustrated by Leslie Stuart's songs, staged with the splendid resources and staff of Charles Frohman, and played by Edna May, a strong cast and a bevy of beauties. *The Belle of Mayfair* had all the ingredients of success.

Charles Frohman telegraphed to the composer on the first night: ALL I ASK IS THAT THEY APPRECIATE WHAT YOU HAVE DONE AS I DO. His hopes were fulfilled for, if the book of the new show proved occasionally uninspired and lacking in humour, the songs brought the house down. Number after number had the audience calling for encores as they carried the show to a rousing finale after which the composer was called again and again before the curtain. Stuart had supplied a judicious mélange of gentle ballads, point numbers and lively production numbers all in his best and most catchy style which was acclaimed by audience and critics alike. Perhaps the best received piece of all was a lively quartet sung by Misses May and Pounds and Messrs Soutar and Courtice Pounds and called 'Come to St George's'. It was nominated 'the hit of the season' by several newspapers, in spite of the fact that one reckoned it rather reminiscent of *Carmen* and another found that it had traces of 'Down at the old Bull and Bush'!

Won't you come to St George's
To see how love forges
His chain, chain, chain?
Don't you endeavour to sever the fetters
It's all in vain . .

There were plenty of other hits: Louie Pounds delivered two delightful ballads with huge success: a Basil Hood song 'Said I to Myself' where she described how she had married for love in spite of the rejection of society, and a number written by George Arthurs, 'The weeping Willow Wept'. This latter was much less lugubrious than its title suggested and told of a little flirtation with a painful ending. 'The weeping Willow' was one of those songs which had nothing to do with anything, introduced into the action by Miss Pounds interjecting into a conversation, 'Ah, no wonder the weeping willow wept' and heading into her number which was, nevertheless, a delightful piece and very well received.

In fact, Miss Pounds' performance as the 'fairy godmother' proved one of the evening's high points. At the final curtain on opening night when the public had duly cheered and called the composer (and, pointedly, not the librettists), and welcomed back Edna May for a series of umpteen curtsies, the gallery decided it was time they got what they really wanted. 'Louie!' they called out. 'Louie!' 'Pounds!' and, as the stalls gradually emptied, they called on and on until, some twenty minutes after the end of the show, the Pounds, brother and sister, took a call to a cheering 'gods'. For the other personal success of the evening had been for Courtice Pounds. Now established firmly as a character actor but undiminished in voice, he played Mercutio-Meredith and, apart from his modified Mab speech, had two songs which proved as popular as those given by his sister. 'What will the World Say' was a philosophic little waltz song by Basil Hood:

Youth's as old as time
Yet loves a lilting rhyme
He is no fair weather friend to pass you by
Let the world go round
Whither it be bound
And we'll go on our journey together, my youth and I

which, apart from its intrinsic merit, cleverly illustrated the character of the warm-hearted bachelor. More lively was 'Hello, Come along, Girls', a typical Leslie Stuart piece with which he stopped the show in the second act.

But, of course, the star of the show was Edna May, slightly older and plumper, but still as sweet and soulful as ever, leading the *Referee* to comment: 'Nobody, I'm sure, was ever so innocent as Edna May looks'. She still had very little voice and a limited quota of vivacity, but that was nothing new and she got the expected enthusiastic reception. Stuart had supplied her liberally with numbers: an entrance piece called 'In gay Mayfair' in which, accompanied by six young men in flannels and blazers, she bemoaned the injustice of the marriage customs of the social élite; a charming love song 'Where you Go, will I Go' (Hood) with a *bouche fermée* accompaniment, and a lively song called 'Play the Game' with the message:

Play the game if you can
Little maid, little man,
So somebody used to say
And don't make too much noise, my dears,
For shouting doesn't pay.
And never forget the lesson
You learned as girls and boys
The winner isn't always the one that makes most noise!

in which she sketched some rather unconvincing business with a toy sword. But her most successful number was an incongrously irrelevant piece called 'In Montezuma'. In the middle of the ballroom, in her gorgeous white court dress, the star was suddenly surrounded by chorines disguised as Red Indians as she sang what might be called a Red Indian coon song:

In Montezuma, they say, when I build my little cave
Far up in the mountain, I'll try to save
A corner, just a little corner.
You'll rule this place
And this little fellow too
In Montezuma there's nothing too good for you

which never failed to arouse a set of encores.

And still the hit numbers came: a brisk duet for the cockney maid, Pincott (the new version of Juliet's nurse), and a footman called 'My little Girl is a shy little Girl' set the second act swinging along, and Joe Soutar as the rather underwritten Romeo of the piece sang 'What Makes a Woman' as he decorated a tailor's dummy with feminine accoutrements to answer his own question. In the final verse, the dummy was replaced by a live woman. For further entertainment, Sam Walsh gave a sympathetic 'I Am a military Man' (William Caine). Stuart had also written a charming number for Camille Clifford called 'I'm a Duchess' but, unfortunately, Miss Clifford's voice was as small as her waist (a publicised 14 inches). She really was better seen and not heard, and her number simply did not take off. The concerted music for the show was particularly successful. Apart from 'Come to St George's', Stuart supplied a delightful quintet 'We've Come from Court' and a rollicking piece called 'I Know a Girl' sung by Soutar, Pounds, Walsh and Charles Angelo at the end of the second act. Even the liverish *Evening News* critic, who professed to having loathed the show, described this last piece as 'a hit'. And the first act finale, a piece noticed as being in 'an almost comic opera vein', was also loaded with praises.

The Belle of Mayfair's musical content was clearly overall the strongest of its kind for some time and its attractions were such that any weaknesses in the libretto were safely papered over. The newspapers which headlined 'Return of Edna May' went on to reserve their praise chiefly for the score and for the Pounds family, but none (except the blatantly anti-Frohman *Winning Post*, which began . . 'Mr Charles Frohman 'presents' another failure' and spent its first paragraph in vituperation) expressed the slightest doubts about the prospects of *The Belle of Mayfair*. It was an out and out hit.

But the show was to be plagued with ructions. The first came directly after the opening. Captain Basil Hood withdrew his name from the libretto credit and it was replaced, to the consternation of the musical comedy world and of the critics, by that of Cosmo Hamilton who had not been mentioned anywhere on the original billing. The arrangement between Hood and Frohman was reputedly amicable, and the Captain's name remained attached to the individual lyrics for which he was responsible, but the position of Hamilton in the whole affair raised many a questioning eyebrow. Presumably Hood's original intentions had been sufficiently destroyed in rehearsal by person or persons unknown for him to wish to disclaim the final result.

However, the show ran profitably through to September before real drama struck. The root cause of the trouble was the position occupied in the show by Camille Clifford. After her sensational appearance in *The Prince of Pilsen* and all through her equally popular performances in *The Catch of the Season* and *The Belle of Mayfair*, Miss Clifford had attracted a huge amount of attention and numberless proposals of marriage. Now, finally, she accepted one, and from no less a person than the Hon Henry Lyndhurst Bruce, heir to Lord Aberdare. If 'The Gibson Girl' had been the object of public curiosity before, this made her doubly so and the box-office at *The Belle of Mayfair* soared as all and sundry came to see her. The producers were not slow to capitalise on the windfall publicity: Camille's minimal role was increased by a new number written by Leslie Stiles and Stuart called 'Why do they Call me a Gibson Girl?' and her name began to appear in the commercial advertising.

It was a placard which finally did the damage, outside the theatre announcing in large letters, as if for a variety show: 'MISS CLIFFORD WILL APPEAR TONIGHT POSITIVELY AT 10.10'. Edna May promptly resigned, and battle lines were drawn: Frohman supported his star, Stephano Gatti, his co-producer, refused to knuckle under to Miss May. Under these pressures the Frohman-Gatti alliance broke down irrevocably and Miss May departed, leaving her understudy, Ethel Newman, to take over the mammoth role of Julia. Miss Clifford stayed, however, sang the 'Gibson Girl' number and the town crowded in to see her. Miss May went to Paris, in spite of all the blandishments of the music hall managers and their cheque books, leaving Frohman to announce her return early in the new year in the starring role of a new musical especially written for her by Charles McLellan, author of *The Belle of New York*.

In the meanwhile, a new leading lady was needed for *The Belle of Mayfair* and the choice finally fell on young Phyllis Dare. Since her stint as Angela in *The Catch of the Season*, Phyllis had returned to her schooling. Now, dramatically, her father drove to collect her from her convent to take her back to London and to stardom at the Vaudeville Theatre. The show's troubles, however, were still not over. Ethel Newman, who had filled the breach so valiantly during Miss May's absence, bore a grudge. She had played the part adequately 37 times during the interregnum and found it hard to accept that it was not to be hers for the rest of the run. Without any justification she sued, and the jury awarded her £100 damages which, considering that she was on £4 per week plus £1 a performance, was a considerable amount. The Gatti estate appealed and the decision was reversed, on the ground that Miss Newman had never had a take-over clause in her contract.

Leslie Stuart composed a new song for Phyllis Dare called 'I'll Wait for You, little Girlie', the role was rewritten to suit her more vivacious personality and she filled it delightfully until Christmas when she departed to fulfil a pantomime contract and was, in turn, replaced by Billie Burke for whom further rewrites were worked in. In February, the whole show was revised in a 'new version', and the run eventually lasted for well over a year: when the London season closed it had had an excellent 416 performances.

Thomas Ryley, who with John C. Fisher had made a fortune out of *Florodora* in America, was quickly into action with the American production of *The Belle of Mayfair*. The book, which had been considerably altered since its first showing, was now further 'adapted' and spiced up with American jokes, but Leslie Stuart's score was maintained, as *Florodora* had been, untouched and intact. The resulting piece was staged by Ryley at Rochester preparatory to bringing it to Broadway, but the American production also had its problems, and they began even before the show had been put into rehearsal. Sitting in the audience for the opening night of the new musical *My Lady's Maid* (the Americanised *Lady Madcap*), Ryley had been horrified to hear from the stage the strains of 'Come to St George's' . .

> . . He took a languid interest in the proceedings until the orchestra struck up the opening bars of a song that appeared in the programme as 'Flirtation'. Before the first verse was half over, Mr Ryley was beating it up the aisle like a volunteer fireman on his way to the engine-house. By the time the chorus was finished, Mr Ryley had corralled all the Shuberts, the Shubert managers, the Shubert press agents and Shubert lawyers in the lobby and was reading them an improved version of the riot act. 'Robbery', shouted Mr Ryley, 'Piracy! Assistance! Help! Murder! Thieves! Grafters! you stole that song. That is the song hit of *The Belle of Mayfair* . . . Your bum authors have swiped the music and words bodily. All you've changed is the title. Nothing so cruel has happened since the kidnapping of Charlie Ross. Here is me coming into Daly's with *The Belle of Mayfair* in two months and you abduct the song hit of my piece that I pay good money for.'
>
> The Shuberts acted as if they were from Missouri instead of from Syracuse. They wanted to be shown. Mr Ryley offered to sing the rest of the song to prove that he knew it but, happily, this was averted. However, Mr Ryley was unable to convince the Shuberts.. . .
>
> Mr Ryley got busy today. Through his counsel. . he got an injunction [which] will be served today if Mr Ryley can find any of the Shuberts. .

Ryley need not have worried. The collapse of *My Lady's Maid* was a herald to the total success of *The Belle of Mayfair*. The book had been strengthened and the musical score proved quite as popular as it had been in London. 'Come to St George's' was the hit that Ryley had hoped – 'it's going to be *the* song of the season' proclaimed the *Evening Mail* – while Miss Valeska Suratt in the Camille Clifford role was encored six times for the 'Gibson Girl' song and the men's 'I know a Girl' was brought back three times. Christie MacDonald as Julia, Irene Bentley as the Princess and Miss Suratt shot into stardom as Leslie Stuart received the accolades of press and public:

> Not since another composer waved his magic baton and showed us the glowing musical qualities of the score of *Véronique* . . had we been more regaled by the numbers of a production than we were last evening . . . . *The Belle of Mayfair* made a sharp, decisive and tuneful hit last night and, what is important nowadays in a musical comedy, there was not a whimper nor a dress nor a note that descended to the level of banality . . . (*Daily News*)

The Belle of Mayfair settled happily in on Broadway as a genuine hit and stayed there for 140 performances before moving on into the country.

Just three days after the first night of *The Belle of Mayfair* at the Vaudeville, another new musical opened in London, this one at the Apollo Theatre, chasing out the still viable *Mr Popple* to the Shaftesbury Theatre. The piece was Robert Courtneidge's follow-up to *The Blue Moon* and, like that piece, it used the team of Alexander Thompson, Paul Rubens and Frank Tours with the addition, in the lyric-writing department, of Arthur Wimperis, a 29-year-old former black-and-white artist who had recently taken to writing song words. *The Dairymaids* was Wimperis' first full stage assignment.

As the fashion of the moment was to announce your work as 'based' on something, whether it was or not, Courtneidge let it out that his new musical was to be based on *Measure for Measure*. With Hicks announcing almost simultaneously that his next piece would be a version of *As You Like It*, it seemed that Shakespeare was in for a wholesale plucking. However, when *The Dairymaids* appeared, even the most ardent of Shakespearian defenders would have been pressed to notice much of Angelo and Isabella in the gently misanthropic relationship between Lady Brudenell (Phyllis Broughton) and the Irish Dr O'Byrne (Ambrose Manning). In fact, *The Dairymaids* was so insubstantial, dramatically, that it bore little resemblance to anything at all. It did not attempt, as *The Blue Moon* had done, to set up an old-fashioned plot and then decorate it heavily with song and dance: it merely introduced its characters and let them perform.

But those characters, played by the new set of Courtneidge stars, were most attractive. Winifred (Agnes Fraser) and Peggy (Carrie Moore) are the 'Dairymaids' of the title. In fact, they are nothing of the sort, but are merely going through the motions on a model dairy farm run by Lady Brudenell (Phyllis Broughton) who has ideas on The Forming of the Youthful Mind. While the good lady is away, her nephews Sam (Walter Passmore) and Frank (Horace Land) arrive and begin to dally with the heroines. In the other corner, the servant Joe Mivens (Dan Rolyat) is making his advances to the pert maid (Gracie Leigh). Now Lady Brudenell arrives home, bringing with her a fourth pair of sweethearts – her ward, Hélène (Florence Smithson) and Captain Leverton (Frank Greene) – and angrily returns her errant protegées to the confines of Miss Penelope Pyechase's boarding school. After a brief glimpse at the shipboard quarters of the nautical nephews, the scene moves to the gymnasium of the school where the lads arrive disguised as schoolgirls to indulge in more fun, more love making, songs and dances until all is sorted out matrimonially.

Fun, songs and dances were quite plainly the aim of *The Dairymaids* and they were of the simplest and most basic kind. Paul Rubens provided some neat, straightforward songs which did not depend entirely on coy references to innocent lassies being 'undone' or being 'wiser' than they seemed or marrying for money, although Agnes Fraser was given one number to sing which explained why that tiresome 'maiden' stood on 'The Country Stile':

As Marjorie stood in her graceful pose
A youth from town
Just come down
Caught a glimpse of her dainty hose
And a hint of her understanding . .

and Gracie Leigh gave out with 'Mary from the Dairy', the tale of a very unpleasant-sounding young person who kept a 'dairy' in Bond Street and who knew 'half the men in town' but tipped up her plate to get the gravy. Frank E. Tours supplied the concerted music for the show and also contributed three charming coloratura ballads for Florence Smithson which were easily the show's best melodies and for which Arthur Wimperis provided the slightly flowery lyrics. As for the fun, Courtneidge and Thompson provided some fine moments which were developed into even better ones by the comical wizardry of Walter Passmore, Gracie Leigh and Dan Rolyat, an ex-Karno comic making his first London appearance. Whether wrestling with a wheelbarrow, battling unsuccessfully with a gymnasium punch-ball or sliding down stairs with a frightening agility, this acrobatic little new comedian kept things very much alive.

The verdict of the critics on *The Dairymaids* was not over-enthusiastic:

> Dull waltz and polka rhythms prevail and indistinctive tunes which will make up conveniently into sets of 'lancers' for the season . . . . The play itself begins well but deteriorates . . . as the whole plot lies in the fact that the young officers make love to the dairymaids, and they do this in the first act, it is not surprising that the second act drags somewhat. It is, in fact, just a medley of scenes, some amusing, some boresome with irrelevant songs, topical allusions and other devices scattered here and there to keep the play alive. (*Times*)

One of those 'other devices', however, was probably what turned *The Dairymaids* from a fairly successful variety musical into a very successful and long-lived piece.

Gibson Girls, Vaudeville Girls and Bath Buns had, to varying extents, captured the public's imagination. *The Dairymaids* introduced The Sandow Girls. After a vigorous gymnasium scene of swinging chorines in blue skirts and stockings and bloomers, and after a couple of pretty songs for Misses Fraser and Leigh, on to the stage came bubbly Carrie Moore accompanied by four young and lovely ladies to sing the virtues of the 'healthy English girl' as typified in the advertisements for Sandow's physique equipment. Wielding tiny dumbbells and with backs arched to out-Gibson the Gibson Girls, the five ladies became the hit of the show as they sang:

> Oh, the Sandow, Sandow Girl
> She is smooth and slim and supple,
> And compared with any couple
> Of other girls
> The Sandow, Sandow Girl
> Is a priceless, peerless pearl,
> Even Sandow, I think
> Would be frightened to wink
> At his Sandow Girl

One of those little Sandow Girls was Miss Dorothy Ward, rising sixteen years old and appearing for the first time in London at the beginning of a career which would see her become a leading lady and one of the most famous pantomime principal boys of all time.

The low comedy in *The Dairymaids* was much more prominent than the public had, of late, been used to. The Frohman/Hicks school of musicals used no truly low comedian, and the Gaiety had only Teddy Payne and Connie Ediss to fool about in the old-fashioned way, but in the Apollo's new show the low comedy was once again frank and straightforward. Passmore and Rolyat gallivanted broadly as unconvincing young ladies and Passmore regaled his fellow 'pupils' with two of Rubens' better pieces, 'In Dover Street' where he impishly sent up the Ladies' Clubs into which ladies work so hard to be admitted so that they can keep all their friends out:

> In Dover Street, In Dover Street
> Is the snug little club where we often meet
> When to some smart 'at home' we have been all day
> Laced up in a pair of (I'd rather not say)
> Well, it's such a relief to pop in on our way
> We can take off our boots in Dover Street

and 'The Sea Serpent' where he danced about pursued by a snake of young ladies imitating the dreaded 'Serpent'.

Among the other features were a number for Agnes Fraser poking fun at the Child Phenomenon syndrome ('The little Stranger') with four small girls dressed up to burlesque the most recent 'prodigy' play currently at the Criterion; and a fall-about song and dance for Passmore and Rolyat on the subject of 'Poaching'. The comedy was leavened with some sentimentality and good singing (both largely from Miss Smithson) and the combination proved to be very much to the taste of a large part of the public.

The Dairymaids played right through until the run-up to Christmas when, with Carrie Moore, Dan Rolyat and Walter Passmore all engaged for pantomime and therefore obliged to leave the show, Courtneidge preferred to take the piece off rather than attempt major re-casting. Its public gave it a noisy farewell. At the final curtain young men in the audience pelted Carrie Moore, Phyllis Broughton and Gracie Leigh with flowers and, finding their supplies of blooms exhausted, rushed out and replenished their artillery with vegetables! At which the management found it advisable to bring the curtain down and leave it down.

In May of 1908 it was back, however, at the new Queen's Theatre, in a substantially revised version starring Phyllis Dare, Fred Leslie, Statham Staples and Florence Lloyd with Dan Rolyat and Florence Smithson from the original cast. Rolyat was lucky to be there. A few weeks previously, on tour with *The Dairymaids* in Manchester, he had over-reached himself in the gymnasium scene while leaping from a high balcony to catch a swinging rope. Missing the rope, he tumbled some fifteen feet to the floor but, amazingly, was unhurt. The favourite pieces from the original *Dairymaids* were retained for the revival: 'Poaching', 'The little Stranger', 'The Sea Serpent' (now appropriated by Rolyat) and, naturally, 'The Sandow Girl', but a good number of new pieces were added: 'Boy Blue' and 'Lazyland' for Florence Smithson, 'Put me into Trousers' and 'The long, long Lane' for Phyllis Dare, 'Elizabeth' (Leslie), 'Votes for the Women' (Staples) and two pieces by Jerome Kern retained from the bundle he had written for the New York production, 'I'd Like to Meet your Father' and 'The Hay Ride'. There was also a topical song 'How's it all Going to End' which proved a vehicle for up-to-date references and verses.

When Maud Allen swooped onto the Palace Theatre stage to thrill the town with her Dance of the Seven Veils, *The Dairymaids* was quick to take up the idea and soon there was a verse to the topical song which featured six miniature dancing Salomes. 'The little Stranger', too, was updated with references to the latest crazes: *The Merry Widow*, 'Dutch-ism' and the eternal matinée hat which Courtneidge had taken the unprecedented step of forbidding by an edict printed on the back of the theatre tickets.

By this time *The Dairymaids* had gone round the world. Fred Leslie, George Lauri and Fanny Dango had toplined in a highly successful Australian production, and the ever-present Edwardes/Wheeler Co. had presented it in South Africa. It had also done well on Broadway where, with half a dozen Jerome Kern songs tacked on and with Huntley Wright starring, it played 86 times before setting out on an extensive national tour. In 1915 it made a third, brief West End appearance when it was brought into the Aldwych Theatre for eighteen performances but its appeal had, by that time, largely become a nostalgic one.

The much-touted 'death of musical comedy' was not particularly evident. The new pieces of the year had not varied greatly in general style from their many predecessors in spite of the half-hearted introduction of established works as the bases for libretti or the occasional achievement of a complete score from one composer. Following the success of *Les P'tites Michu* there had been no attempt to head towards a style reminiscent of the French, and the authors of *The White Chrysanthemum* which had touched here and there on a more coherent style were now to produce, as their next work, an out-and-out 'musical comedy'.

The Girl behind the Counter, as its name suggests, was in the true tradition of all the other 'Girl' musicals from *A Gaiety Girl* to *The Girl from Kays*. Like the latter, it was set in a department store; like the former, the plot (or part of the plot) hinged on a theft; like innumerable others its second act took place at a fancy ball; and like every single one it consisted largely of a series of love affairs all duly disentangled for the final scene.

Frank Curzon took Wyndham's Theatre for the production of his new piece, and it opened just a week after *The Dairymaids* to an enthusiastic reception and pleased critical comment:

> A most diverting and dainty production . . . It is very cleverly put together, authors, composers and lyricists having combined their forces most judiciously. There are some 'great favourites' amongst the artists in the cast and each of these has to do just what he or she can do best. And it has not been found necessary, in order to amuse, to introduce an unsavoury subject or a doubtful detail. The fun is as harmless as it is humorous and as clean as it is clever . . (*Era*)

> Whatever virtue is in musical comedy *The Girl behind the Counter* seems to possess . . . it bears all the stamp of its class, though in some cases there is some successful combining of voices in something like a real ensemble. This is so especially in the duets, of which the best is the really dainty flower duet 'Won't you buy' in Act 1 and the quartet in Act 2 'We won't say a word to a soul' which is reminiscent of Sullivan's most successful numbers. But for such things the public cares little. With Hayden Coffin and Isabel Jay to sing love songs together, Mr Laurence Grossmith to act an altogether impossible comic dandy and with other low comedy characters to make good fun or bad fun, as the case may be, nothing else save brilliant dresses and excellent staging, which were both abundantly supplied, seemed necessary to enjoyment. (*Times*)

The Times was right. Bantock, Anderson and Talbot had known just how to provide the right mixture of materials for the right performers. They had done their concocting with skill and taste if, perhaps, less orginality than might have been wished, but the result was a happy and a prosperous one.

The story of *The Girl behind the Counter* is that of Winnie Willoughby. Her mother wishes her to marry the frightful 'Johnnie', Viscount Gushington, but Winnie has other ideas. Among her ideas is a fancy to play at shop-girl and she persuades Millie Mostyn, manageress of the Maison Duval, to let her take on the flower stall at that establishment. Who should be her first customer but Hayden Coffin (that is to say, Charlie Chetwynd) recently and richly returned from the goldfields of Africa. But trouble is afoot. Winnie has been keeping her eyes on Charlie instead of on her till and it is found that £10 is missing. 'The Girl behind the Counter' is sent packing. In the second act, at a Fancy Ball, Winnie sets out to prove her innocence and to get her father's approval of Charlie as a mate. She achieves both: the real culprit in the affair of the £10 note is the shop boy, Adolphus Dudd, who wanted the cash to impress his sweetheart at the ball; and Winnie's papa is caught being flirtatious with Ninette, an employee of the Maison Duval, which puts him in no position to refuse his consent to Winnie.

At the head of affairs were the romantic stars of the town, Coffin and Isabel Jay. Coffin was no longer the jeune premier of *Dorothy* days but, at 44 years of age, he maintained a remarkably fine figure (a slight tendency to the barrel-chest notwithstanding) and the fashionable manly air of one who knows he is adored by a million women. He also retained the ringing baritone voice which had been the other half of his fortune and which was put to good use by the authors of *The Girl behind the Counter* in a stirring ballad called 'In the Land where the best Man Wins'. The song proved an unqualified hit as, with his sleeves rolled back and his jacket flung to the floor, he sang:

> A land there is o'er the ocean wide
> 'Tis a land of great endeavour
> Where lust and greed unbridled ride
> And kin from kindred sever
> 'Tis a land of fever, rich in gold,
> Where pluck and grit are needed
> Where health is bartered, honour sold,
> And love goes by unheeded!
>
> And it's dig, dig, dig in the daytime
> And it's take your rest at night
> And it's pray, pray, pray
> That at last you may
> Find the red, red gold in sight &c

The Era sighed:

> The event of the evening was the return of Mr Hayden Coffin in finer form than ever, acting with a gracious ease and a manly energy which delighted everybody and singing in splendid style. Mr Anderson and Mr Talbot gave Mr Coffin an excellent opportunity in the spirited song 'In the Land where the best Man Wins' and Mr Coffin rose to the occasion con amore, rendering the verses with a vigour and earnestness that electrified the house and won an unanimous and enthusiastic encore. Quite in the romantic and sentimental tone of Mr Coffin's earlier impersonations was the ballad by Mr Arthur Anderson and Mr Augustus Barratt called 'Someday' and the singer treated it with all the necessary refinement and taste. Mr Coffin's performance of the part was a complete success and, both in the free-and-easy attire of the returned adventurer and in the becoming grey costume of a Spanish student in the masquerade. Mr Coffin looked a 'perfect picture'. He was in excellent voice and his acting was an agreeable mixture of delicacy and determination.

Alongside him, twenty-six year old Isabel Jay was by no means overshadowed. Refined but unaffected, and the possessor of a true and genuine leading soprano voice, she too had been well-served by the writers who had given her a vivacious number in 'I Mean to Marry a Man':

> I want no scented, extravagant dandy
> Who brags of his vices and debts
> Dines every evening on coffee and brandy
> And sups on perfumed cigarettes.
> I must have a leader, a maker of history
> One who intends to, and can,
> Courage and grit in him,
> Honesty writ in him,
> I mean to marry a man!

with which she 'brought down the house in a chorus of applause'. It was interesting that both the 'hit' songs of *The Girl behind the Counter* were songs expressing virtuous and admirable sentiments, and as far from the giggly suggestiveness of certain popular songsmiths as could be.

But if both those songs fitted neatly and carefully into the plot and character structure of the show, there were plenty of other pieces which could barely make the same claim. With the end of the first act and the beginning of the Fancy Ball, the 'concert' began and the costumes of the characters for the ball often provided the excuse for the themes of the songs. Coralie Blythe and Horace Mills came on dressed as a Kate Greenaway pair – she in puff sleeves, bonnet and muff and he in a Little Boy Blue outfit with turned-down collar and turned-back cuffs, high breeches and buttoned shoes – to sing 'The Greenaway Girl'; J. P. McArdle, fittingly rigged out, sang of Sir Walter Raleigh; Marie Dainton was thoroughly French in 'Ze Enterpraising Frenchman'; and the comics from Grossmith, McArdle and Mills to George Barrett as an excruciating Baron's Court waiter and Akerman May as a heavy German commissionaire all drew plenty of humour from their characters and their situations to keep things lively between the numbers. It was a musical of the most characteristic sort written with more style and less vulgarity than many and boasting two great stars and two very popular songs. It seemed set for a long run. Yet, on September 1 after a run of only 141 performances it closed, having simply run out of audience. 'More of the same' even of above average quality was no longer a recipe for success. The show was left to continue into the provinces where Hayden Coffin took the unusual step of playing his original role, something which he had never done since becoming a star.

The Girl behind the Counter had to wait for real success until it reached Broadway. In October the following year it was produced at the Herald Square Theatre by Lew Fields for whom it proved a much happier venture than his first English musical, *An English Daisy*, which had flopped so badly three years previously. The book had been severely 'got at' since London. Edgar Smith had done it over thoroughly and Fields starred as 'Henry Schniff', stepfather to Winnie, who helps (instead of hindering as Sir Wilkie Willoughby had done) our heroine to the hand of Charlie Chetwynd (now a Nice American Boy) instead of the effete and English Lord Gushington. Mrs Schniff was played by Connie Ediss and the show was a festival of low comedy, 'turns' and songs original and, more often, interpolated including the pretty 'Glow-worm' song lifted from Paul Lincke's *Lysistrata* and the Paul West/Herman Wade song 'I Want to be Loved like a leading Lady'. Fields kept *The Girl behind the Counter* running for precisely double the number of performances of its London version. It remained on Broadway for 282 performances and was even brought back in 1916 in a revised version to give Fields another turn at the role of 'Schniff'.

So far, the West End year had brought five new pieces and all five had been more or less in the 'moribund' musical comedy vein. But, as writers and producers searched for the 'coming' formula, the remaining months of 1906 brought out some very different entertainment including several pieces designated as 'comic opera'. The first of these, produced at the Royalty Theatre, was an extraordinary concoction. The English-born comedian-vocalist-cum-songwriter Harry Fragson (né Potts) was an outstanding and highly popular artist in his natural habitat, the Paris music halls, and the 29-year-old Chicago soprano May de Souza was an attractive and promising performer. Around them Fragson, with the help of Cosmo Hamilton and the eager amateur Eustace Ponsonby, responsible two seasons earlier for the fiasco of *Ladyland*, boiled up a good old-fashioned comic opera under the title *Castles in Spain*. As a starting point they used the famous Spanish zarzuela *La Gran Via* from which they lifted seven songs to which were added several new pieces by Fragson and Ponsonby, a harum-scarum plot and some serviceable dialogue compiled by all concerned.

Fragson, who had recently come to the notice of British audiences as Dandini in the Drury Lane pantomime, was not an experienced actor but rather an all-round entertainer. Here he cast himself as a strangely fey French count, a role in which his fanciful peculiarities were cleverly used and accented. Miss de Souza was an American schoolgirl who ends up, quite innocently, at his apartment while running away from school. The two become entangled with the business of recovering a bundle of compromising letters from a Spanish singer on behalf of her father who, when all has been successfully realised, happily joins the two in obligatory wedlock.

Gaston Meyer, who took on the production of the piece, evidently had little enough faith in it. It opened at the Royalty on 18 April with Coquelin *aîné* and Réjane already confirmed to follow it in on 23 May with their season of French plays. But, in a modest way, *Castles in Spain* proved a surprise. Fragson and his songs and his fun-making were received by London with interest and a good deal of praise. Miss de Souza found favour too and the show brought forth such gently surprised comments as: '[it] only needed a better libretto for its complete success' (*Stage*).

Castles in Spain duly ran out its month at the Royalty to good houses by which time Meyer had decided that a transfer to Terry's Theatre was worthwhile. Fragson put in three new numbers and announced that he and Miss de Souza would take the show on the road when their season ended and tour it until they returned to Drury Lane for pantomime. On June 9 the piece notched up its fiftieth performance, but then disaster struck, in the guise of George Edwardes. *The Little Michus* was finishing at Daly's and Edwardes had decided to follow it with a revival of *The Geisha* while preparing his next musical, Hugo Felix's *Les Merveilleuses*. For Marie Tempest's old role of Mimosa San he decided to approach May de Souza and on June 18 the young American opened at Daly's in the starring role of the greatest of its musicals. Ten days later *Castles in Spain* closed. In spite of the valiant efforts of understudy Noel Neville the piece had apparently lost too much with Miss de Souza's departure. The show came off, the tour was off and Fragson went to the Tivoli to share the bill with Vesta Victoria, Harry Tate, soprano Elise Cook *et al.*

Altogether less effective was *Petronella*, another 'Spanish' piece in a determinedly old-fashioned, and less original and sprightly, manner. It was set against the background of a Carlist uprising, larded with puns and light music by its author Montague Turner and composer William Gliddon, and avowedly meant for provincial cosumption. Before its tour it was presented eight times at the Great Queen Street Theatre which was none other than the poor old Novelty/Folies Dramatiques under yet another name. Although not the disaster which that theatre had so often witnessed, it was scarcely a piece to enthuse about. Its story of cloaked disguises and love matches professed to have somthing to do with the forthcoming marriage of King Alfonso of Spain and the Princess Ena, but that was difficult to detect. A fair cast gave some fairish numbers in a manner which was not calculated to set Great Queen Street alight and a Louie Freear-type comedienne brought in a touch of the halls with some standard 'skivvy' songs and business. Wigan's Marie Ault was destined for many better things than *Petronella* which, in the event, toured briefly and unobtrusively.

A third and altogether more substantial and ambitious attempt in the direction of 'comic opera' soon followed. On June 20, George Edwardes presented the first new Sidney Jones musical in London since *The Medal and the Maid* more than three years previously. Once again, as with his most successful pieces, *The Geisha* and *San Toy*,

Jones was working on an oriental theme. Charles Brookfield had taken the winning Parisian farce *La Troisième Lune* written by 'Fred' de Grésac and Paul Ferrier and had transformed it into a neat and suitable libretto which, after being prematurely titled *The Third Moon* and *The Chinese Bride*, made its appearance at the Prince of Wales Theatre as *See See*.

See See was set in Pekin. A group of particularly favoured young ladies known as The Priceless Pearls is in love, all except the most beautiful and the most wise, See See, who, in spite of the riches and fame poured upon her, is discontented:

I am a flake of the snow on the mountain
Perfect and pure and pale
Never to fall in the flow of a fountain
Down to the pleasant vale
Throned in a loneliness splendid and bitter
High on the peak afar
Queen of the hills in the moonbeam I glitter
Bright as a frozen star.

Sun of desire with eye of fire, look down on me
Till I melt and flow
To the brook below
That runs to the boundless sea
From the height above
To the land of love
I hurry fast
To join the mirth
Of the merry earth
I shall live, I shall love at last

But she is soon to be embroiled in the doings of the world. Two old friends, Hoang and Cheoo, have betrothed their children in infancy and the time has now come for them to marry. But Lee, daughter of Hoang, is in love with the coolie Hang-Kee, and her fiancé, Yen, has fallen for a portrait of See See. So a plot is hatched. The Cheoos and the Hoangs have not set eyes on each other since those far-off schooldays, so it is decided that Hang-Kee and the fortune-teller Mai-Yai shall impersonate the Hoangs and that See See shall go in the palanquin in place of Lee to the wedding ceremony. Their plan is, in the *David Garrick* fashion, to be so vulgar and disgusting that the Cheoos will call off the wedding in horror. But Cheoo is an easy-going fellow and the plan fails. See See finds herself wed to Yen in reality and he, unveiling his bride, is overjoyed to find that his wife is the lady of his dreams. See See is not so pleased. But Yen sets out to tame the imperious lady who soon returns his love and since it conveniently turns out that See See is actually the long-lost child of Hoang's former wife, the bargain is not broken.

Although it included many of the standard ploys of the genre – the veiled wedding, the lost child, the love-by-portrait, the *David Garrick* trick – *See See* was a more mature piece than many. Such elements as the introduction of the *Taming of the Shrew* idea after the wedding, where an old comic opera would have ended, gave a depth to its construction and its principal characters which was unusual in such a piece. Indeed, *See See* was peopled by a group of quite delightful characters, played by a particularly strong cast.

At the hub of affairs came Huntley Wright as the comical coolie, Hang-Kee. Although the character inevitably owed something to Wun Hi (*Geisha*) and Li (*San*

Toy), it gave Wright even more opportunities than those two great roles had. Firstly, there was a whole series of disguises: in the first instance, in order to gain entrance to See See's palace, he masquerades as a Viceroy and as a gardener, and finally gets in hidden in a packing case; later, of course, he impersonates Hoang, and in that disguise he gave the song which became the highlight of the show, a clever piece by Adrian Ross called 'British Slavery':

There's an island I've heard of from travellers
That lies in the barbarous West,
Where it's dark all the daytime and freezes in Maytime
And rains pretty much all the rest.
Though it's doubted by critics and cavillers
Yet unless our informants are Knaves,
The accounts they have written concerning Great Britain
Are proof that its people are slaves!
Free, free is the happy Chinee
But there on that Isle in the waves
You must wear a tall hat
Which is something like that
And the wearers are certainly slaves . .

In fact, Wright took an unusually large part of the vocal responsibility in the show. In the first act he had a lightly topical song called 'Good and Bad' and another where, as the Viceroy, he delivered a sub-Gilbertian piece detailing his rise to his supposed position:

When I became a Mandarin
Employed in our finances
The revenues came rolling in
At a rate beyond romances;
If any wealthy man was shy
Of paying double taxes
I would hang him by his pigtail high
His toes on red-hot axes.
Then rather than annoy
All men would pay with joy
And that is why, see,
I'm a spicy
Gay young Viceroy

He joined in a trio with Amy Augarde (Mai-Yai) and Lily Elsie as they chastise him with bamboo canes for his deception ('The Bamboo') and in a duet with Adrienne Augarde (Lee) plotting to avoid the hated wedding ('If We lay our Heads Together'). In the second act he had a very funny duet with Cheoo ('Bill' Berry) called 'Some People never Take a Hint' in which the kindly fellow fails to react to the coolie's attempt to disgust him, and another with Gabs Ray where, dressed in large paper costumes, they sang a charming little number called 'Chinese Lanterns' describing the courtship of two paper lanterns:

Come, lazy wind and blow us stronger
Bring the lovers heart to heart
We cannot bear it any longer
If we have to dance apart.

Down came the wind and blowing, blowing,
Wildly swung the lamps about
Just as they met in rapture glowing
Chinese lanterns both went out!

The fact that Miss Ray was supposed to be playing the role of a boy did not seem to matter.

If Wright had the lion's share of the comedy, he was by no means alone in that sphere. As the Cheoo family, Bill Berry with Lilian Hewitson, Sybil Grey and Lena Maitland as his unprepossessing wives, provided much fun and Fred Emney and Kitty Hanson as the genuine family Hoang were also there in support. In the title-role 21-year-old Denise Orme (ex-Smither) who had been promoted from the chorus of *The Little Michus* made a welcome addition to the ranks of singing leading ladies. She had several pretty numbers: 'My Birthday', 'The Girl with the drooping Eye', 'Won't he Be Surprised', but none succeeded so well as the reconciliation duet 'Doves' with which she and Maurice Farkoa (Yen) brought the plot to its conclusion. Gabs Ray, as the boy attendant So-Hei, made a success with a silly little song about 'Chinese Dolls' but danced attractively and succeeded in looking nothing at all like a boy, while Lily Elsie once again had a rather ungrateful part as Humming Bird, with her sole opportunity coming in a short introductory solo 'See See', but she contributed largely to the glamour of the production as did Adrienne Augarde singing charmingly if irrelevantly about 'Butterflies'.

A welcome return to the British musical was that of Miss Augarde's aunt Amy, 'The New Barmaid', who had recently been playing in *The Little Michus* and who here gave a wonderfully enjoyable performance as the dragonistic fortune-teller with her tea-leaf readings and one of the show's most popular songs, the legend of 'Chang Ho', the queen of the silver moon, who falls in love with a star. Prevented by the gods from pursuing her love, she spends her time in bringing mortal lovers to grief so that she shall not weep alone.

Brookfield had cut *La Troisième Lune* severely to reduce it to libretto proportions, but the songwriters had re-inflated the whole considerably and *The Times* found the result rather over-rich:

> . . a pretty and amusing comic opera overloaded with splendours. There are too many people and too many colours in the chorus, too many songs and too many verses in most of them, too many tunes and too many instruments in the orchestra, too many jokes and too little wit . .

but it conceded that *See See* was the most ambitious of all Jones' works to date, not excepting *My Lady Molly*, and concluded:

> On the whole we liked *See See* very well: we should have liked it much better if it had been less lavish and less long.

But *The Times* was in a minority and more people agreed with *The Stage* which declared:

> *See See* must take worthy rank in the long list of Mr George Edwardes' achievements as a production of considerable charm and beauty . .

and the public were delighted to have it.

But *See See*'s career at the Prince of Wales lasted only a disappointing five months. It was respectable but insufficient and served to confirm the only average runs of other good pieces like *The White Chrysanthemum*, *Mr Popple* and *The Girl behind the Counter*.

Were the pundits right? Had the audience for the musical shrunk? Or was Edwardes right: was it just a case of too much competition? Neither argument seemed satisfactory. It was still quite possible to have a long run: *The Catch of the Season* (621p) had done it. *The Little Michus* and *The Spring Chicken* had both topped 400 performances and *The Belle of Mayfair* was in the process of doing so, while *The Dairymaids* could undoubtedly have run as long had it stayed at the Apollo. And yet this list of winning shows was a very eclectic one: no formula for the 'popular musical' emerged. As for competition, there had been just as many and successful musicals running at the same time on many previous occasions. The whole question was a puzzle, and any manager venturing an untried comic opera into the West End looked certain to come to grief.

Yet the next entry, at the New Theatre, was just such a one. Producer Louis Calvert, lessee of the Broadway Theatre, New Cross, presented a comic opera by Frederick Fenn, drama critic of the *Daily Graphic* and the author of several unremarkable forepieces and a couple of provincial comedies, with music by an unknown 31-year-old musician, Philip Michael Faraday. *Amasis*, billed as 'an Egyptian comic opera' took no half measures. Unlike *See See* it made no concession to the variety element of the modern musical comedy but stuck to the form and style of works such as those of the Gilbert and Sullivan canon. Yet it gave no impression of being merely a pale imitation of those already revered works. Against all odds, *Amasis* turned out to be both an artistic and a popular success.

The story of the play was based on the ancient Egyptian worship of the cat. Prince Anhotep has come to Egypt to marry the Princess Amasis. Disturbed in the small hours in his writing of a love poem, by the caterwauling of a feline, he drops a brick on the wretched animal's head only to find that the punishment for such an action is death. Cheiro, a poor scribe who is in love with the princess from afar, attempts to save his beloved's bridegroom by confessing to the 'crime' himself, but he is saved from execution by Amasis who has read in an old book of lore that a condemned man may be saved by the petition of a maiden. The jealous chief embalmer, Ptolemy, who has striven to bring about Anhotep's death so that he may inherit his wealth, is mummified in his own patent embalming machine and the wedding goes ahead as planned with Cheiro sadly inscribing the tale on his obelisk as the play closes in merrymaking.

Amasis achieved a very attractive blend of the comic, the sentimental and the spectacular which combined with an undeniable quality made the show immediately popular. The first-night audience responded wildly and the box office was quickly besieged. The piece played nightly to full houses and eventually a second matinée had to be added to the weekly schedule as well. The critics, too, welcomed the show. Having cried so long for more comic opera, they were clearly pleased that one of a reputable standard had come along:

> Before we can make any progress [in reviving the lost art of comic opera] we have to shear away all the vulgar and foolish accretions of musical comedy which have set a false standard to public taste . . . [Mr Fenn] has left out what we have long craved to see left out, the irrelevant episodes, the vulgar display, the senseless distortions of musical comedy and given us a comic opera which, if not very funny nor very witty nor very graceful, is a thing of recognisable structure with a beginning, a middle and an end. Only once has he made a concession to popular taste in a topical song for Mr Rutland Barrington. We take pleasure in recording that the topical song was a failure . . (*Times*)

> Freshness and originality are distinguishing qualities in *Amasis* which specially recommended it in these days of conventional musical pieces. It is a comic opera with

> a book worth considering, a book which the author has endeavoured to endow with some of the whimsical grace of the kind made popular by Mr W. S. Gilbert, while the music is that of a man with musicianly ideas. (*Stage*)

The book, indeed, followed its main story through tidily, the sub-plots were limited to a man-hunting manoeuvre by the princess's maid and the various antics of Sebak, the comical Keeper of the Crocodiles with his pet animal, Lilian (a clever prop which Lauri de Frece made balance lumps of sugar on its nose) and with an octet of local ladies.

The dialogue was consistently amusing with the occasional bon mot:

PHAROAH: I am sorry he cannot marry my daughter. Murderers, I have always noticed, make excellent husbands. They find an outlet for their superfluous energies on other people, and are most humane and considerate in their home life.

On the musical side, Faraday was easily at his best in the romantic numbers. Ruth Vincent, in the title role, had three most attractive songs: 'Little Princess, Look Up', on her first entrance:

> Last night the moon beamed on me and cried
> Little Princesss, look up,
> Do you know why I shine with a radiance fine
> Little Princess, look up;
> Oh, my love is the Sun, the great Sky King
> And we answer with a love unwavering
> Little Queen of the Earth, be happy as I
> Laugh, for the Prince, your sun, is nigh
> Laugh and look up! Look up! Look up!
> Little Princess, look up.

the dismayed 'The Morning's heartless Sun' and 'Long, long Ago' in which she claimed the sparing of Cheiro's life: but it was to the latter that the gem of the evening fell – a plaintive tenor ballad, 'I Prayed for Life', his reaction to the news of his princess's wedding to Anhotep:

> I prayed for life, a little life, and now –
> Come Death!

On the comical side, Rutland Barrington was rather more successful with his topical song than *The Times* was willing to admit, but did better with a more suitable number, 'A lovely Woman', in which he admitted amours with Cleopatra and Helen of Troy who

> Though a beautiful toy
> Is a doll that may lead you a dance
> Still, she did not consent
> And to Paris she went
> But it wasn't the Paris in France!

There was also a song for the evil Ptolemy describing his calling ('Ptolemy Ltd. Fils et Cie.') and a funny piece in which Sebak described his house-hunting efforts on behalf of the engaged pair which, of course, took the opportunity to jibe at modern tastes:

> I thought undecorated stone was just a shade prosaic
> So I've had Sir William Richmond down to dab it with mosaic . .

The ensembles of the piece were well and often amusingly written. The first act finale, with Anhotep being dragged away to his fate to the ringing tones of a Ramfis-like high priest, had some effective moments as the chorus clamoured:

Oh, fool to smite a hallowed cat
Was it worthwhile to die for that?

and Anhotep cast his farewell curse on the feline race:

I curse their fur, it shall drop off in patches
I curse their claws, they'll poison scratches
I curse their tempers, they'll grow up like Diogenes
I curse their wooing and all their little progenies;
I curse their brains, they'll get congestion,
I curse their food, they'll have indigestion,
I curse their home life, I curse their morals
Their eyes shall be scratched out in frequent quarrels
I curse each whisker, I curse each tail
They shall sing out of tune, their voices fail
I curse their living, and to humour all those popular fallacies
It is my curse that each shall suffer nine deaths from paralysis

A quartet in the second act, in spite of its title of 'Death', also contained some humorous moments.

On the whole *Amasis*, though occasionally patchy, was a good piece with a definite public appeal. Its popularity stayed high as Fenn worked on his libretto to capitalise on the show's most successful elements. The role of the Pharoah, for example, which had been entrusted to Rutland Barrington (looking larger than ever and hilariously idiotic under a long, ringletted wig) had been confined to the second act. It was quickly extended and a new number 'Twas such a forceful Argument' which told of his rise from 'operatic captain' to the throne, was introduced for him. A solo dance was interpolated and the ubiquitous Winifred Hart-Dyke engaged to perform it. The atmosphere was euphoric at the New Theatre. Rumour had it that Fenn and Faraday were signing to write a series of comic operas for Calvert and, inevitably, there were comparisons with Gilbert and Sullivan. But when November came, *Amasis* hit a problem. Its unexpected success had meant that it had run right through to the theatre's prior booking with Julia Neilson and Fred Terry. Now it had to move. The white hope of the comic opera pundits transferred to the Criterion and the bubble burst. After four weeks in its new home the show closed.

Things were then revealed to be in a very bad state. In the current fashion, Fenn was being plagued by not one but two opportunistic plagiarism suits. The first had appeared very early. Immediately after the opening, one W. Gunn Gwennet (otherwise Wilhelm Hermann Scholz) had written to the papers claiming similarities with his own (unperformed, of course) 1897 piece *The Son of the Sun*. He contented himself with the mild remark that this letter merely wished to place facts on record so that he should not be accused in his turn of plagiarism in the event of a production of his show. This was a not infrequent and reasonably harmless ploy to gain publicity for an unproduced show, but Fenn reacted wildly with threats of lawyers. He was in more trouble, however, with a Mr Pritchard. Fenn had been foolish enough to pay Mr Pritchard some money at some stage, either for services or for hush. When *Amasis* turned out to be successful, Pritchard grabbed for 'his' piece of the cake and the *Amasis* company found itself obliged to settle for a substantial sum. The law suits rolled on, followed by appeals and the result was that the net financial position on *Amasis*, instead of being a moderate profit, was eventually declared as a loss of some £6500, including £1400 of Fenn's own money. It was a sad end to an operation which had given so many signs of hope and promise, and it left its effects on the show which never proceeded, as it should have, to further productions but which was severely left alone after just one season's touring.

With *The Spring Chicken*, George Edwardes had made something of a change to the fare offered at the Gaiety. The change had not made any appreciable difference to the success of the theatre – with a run of 401 performances, *The Spring Chicken* had been a deserved favourite for over a year – but, with its withdrawal, the pattern was again altered, and this time more drastically. Since the triumphant introduction of *The Shop Girl*, the Gaiety had presented an unequalled series of hits, all basically in the same modern-dress mould: now, the new piece was to be something very different, 'a partial return to burlesque', and the subject that of the earliest of Gaiety musicals, the Aladdin story. Edwardes had been intimating a change in such a direction over recent months:

> Goodbye to a hero in a frock coat, goodbye to a heroine in an accordion-pleated frock. The public is sick of 'em and so am I.

he had announced on the production of *See See*. Now he was putting his conviction into practice. But was a return to burlesque the answer?

The architects of the piece included the usual Gaiety purveyors: Ross, Greenbank, Grossmith, Monckton and Caryll, with the chief of plotmakers, James Tanner, and W. H. Risque providing the libretto. The bill was worthy of a Drury Lane pantomime with May de Souza as Aladdin and Gertie Millar as her Princess. But a pantomime in September? And at the Gaiety? The answers all round were 'no'. The casting changed first. Miss Millar was now to be the hero. Then the Gaiety's favourite star was forced to withdraw when her husband fell ill, and Lily Elsie was brought into the title role with Adrienne Augarde as her 'principal girl'. And *The New Aladdin* was nothing at all like a Drury Lane panto. Neither was it much like a burlesque. In spite of its settings and its décor, *The New Aladdin* was very much like a normal musical comedy of the day.

In the first act 'Lally', a modern day Aladdin, finds a ring in his Uncle Ebenezer's curio shop. The ring has a genie, and Lally and his companions are whisked off to far Cathay where the hero meets his Princess and finds the magic lamp of Aladdin. The second act brings all the principals to the 'Ideal London' wished for by Lally, where Uncle Ebenezer and various other villains attempt to get hold of the lamp, a process confused by the introduction of an imitation lamp (with an imitation genie). Amongst as much song and dance as could be fitted in, all ended as it should.

Initial reaction was not encouraging. For the first time in memory, boos were heard from the gallery on a Gaiety first night and, although there had been much good and attractive material in the night's entertainment, the general reaction was 'thumbs down' for the piece as a whole and for its conception. Edwardes had called the piece a 'musical extravaganza', but *The Stage* noted:

> [it is] really a mixture of refined pantomime and musical comedy in which each form of entertainment loses its individuality . .

before concluding that '*The New Aladdin* is a weak, disappointing piece'. *The Times* analysed it differently:

> It is not a burlesque, it is not an extravaganza, it is a musical comedy. That is to say that possessing a bright first act of some merit and promise, it has a shapeless, tedious, senseless second act; a collection of music-hall turns put together in a way any manager of a music hall would despise . .

before pontificating on the shortcomings of musical comedy second acts in general. Whatever *The New Aladdin* was, the combined talents of the Gaiety stars could not rescue it from disaster, and even the most faithful of Gaiety devotees had to admit that it was neither what they expected nor wanted from 'their' theatre.

The most popular parts of the entertainment succeeded well enough. Connie Ediss was the Genie of the Ring – a very substantial genie – who was hilarious as she sighed over little Teddy Payne:

I want to be mortal, I want to stop on earth
At present I'm nothing but vapour and mist
I want to be loved and I want to be kissed . .

George Grossmith as the Genie of the Lamp (a role which had somehow grown so large that it threatened to swamp the main protaganists of the story) pulled out all his usual stops and did particularly well with a number satirising the new 'hygienic' craze for openwork blouses and sea air, 'The no Hat Brigade', in which he wondered, 'I wonder what they'll leave off next?' Teddy Payne headed the comic team, backed up by Arthur Hatherton, Robert Nainby and Harry Grattan and a new addition to the Gaiety team in Alfred Lester, the comic scene-shifter of *An Officers' Mess.* It was Lester who had the biggest personal success of the night in the role of a London policeman lost in the new and unfamiliar 'Ideal London'.

Another newcomer also made an impression. George Grossmith had seen a young French girl in Paris and had persuaded Edwardes that he should engage her for the Gaiety. The role of Fossette, a French maid, was written in to *The New Aladdin* but it did nothing for Mlle Gaby Deslys, and a new role was prepared. As 'The Charm of Paris' she arrived in 'The Ideal London' to give that town its final touch of perfection. She sang a couple of numbers in Franglais and was well received. To replace her in the role of the maid, Jean Aylwin was taken from the chorus. Jean, who had understudied Gertie Millar in *The Spring Chicken*, was a tall 21-year-old from Hawick with a broad accent which she attempted to cover up with broken English. She had joined the chorus at the Gaiety for *The Orchid* but now was promoted to a full role for the first time.

The New Aladdin was allowed to run for two months before Edwardes had it totally revamped. Gertie Millar had now become available again so Lily Elsie was removed and Miss Millar brought in to take over a title role which was greatly increased in size. Four fresh numbers, none of which had anything to do with Aladdins new or otherwise, were interpolated for the star to sing. In 'Grandmama' she appeared in a crinoline and bonnet with a chorus of little girls to sing about 'naughty, naughty Grandmama' who ran off to Gretna Green to wed Grandpapa and had lots of children:

All just like their dear Papa
So he was assured by Grandmama

It was scarcely Ross and Monckton at their best, but in spite (or maybe because) of its silly lyric it proved perfectly popular. No less so was a childish piece called 'Bedtime at the Zoo' with Miss Millar dressed in a dashing cowboy outfit with boots and sombrero crooning:

Sleep well, Miss Orang Outang,
Goodnight, Kangaroo,
When another day is breaking
You will all of you be waking
In the Zoo

For 'Down where the Vegetables Grow' the star changed into a smart coster suit with pearly buttons and, joined by Teddy Payne, declared: 'We're only 'umble costers and uneddicated chaps' while the fourth song had words and music by Monckton and asserted: 'That's the sort of chap I like to know'.

The show was now even more of an irrelevant variety show than any of its predecessors, and new numbers were stuffed in liberally in an attempt to find something successful. Connie Ediss did best with a topical waltz song called 'In the Strand' which did a tour of that famous street taking in as many personal references as possible:

You'll see Mr Asche who cuts quite a dash
His knees are so sweetly antique . . &c

Marie Lloyd, Little Tich and the Follies at the Tivoli all got their mention and there was a whole verse devoted to the *Belle of Mayfair* scandal:

And if you would gaze
On musical plays
There's lots of variety there
Each month pretty well
They get a new Belle
To reel in the peal of Mayfair
You'll notice a score
Of cars at the door
Or more, as a general rule,
To take off one girl
To marry an earl
And bring back another from school

The verse ended with the prediction

And I bet we shall get
Billie Burke in Debrett
When she's playing along the Strand

a prediction which was to remain unfulfilled as Miss Burke became 'only' Mrs Florenz Ziegfeld.

The two newcomers who had succeeded so well were given songs. Jean Aylwin gave up all pretence at being French: her character was now called 'Maggie' and finally, with no pretence at anything at all, simply 'Jeannie'. She became the braw Scots lassie she really was and made a big success with the song 'Dougal' and constant references to her 'big, braw Hielander'. Alfred Lester was made more prominent with a song called 'The gentle Constable'. In its new form, the *New Aladdin* variety show proved acceptable enough to run for five months, but it made a heavy loss and the formula was not one that Edwardes would ever repeat.

Edwardes also drew a short straw with his new Daly's production. Following the success of *Les P'tites Michu*, he kept faith with European sources and staged his own continental musical *Les Merveilleuses* with music by Hugo Felix, composer of *Madame Sherry*. *Les Merveilleuses*, in spite of some wonderful Directoire costumes, a book by Sardou anglicised by Basil Hood, and a stunning leading performance by Evie Greene, did not catch on as it might have and despite a title change to the more seductive *The Lady Dandies* survived for only 196 performances, far below Daly's usual high tally.

The final new piece of the year took the seeming trend towards comic opera even further. The baritone David Bispham, who had made an international career in grand opera since his début in D'Oyly Carte's *La Basoche*, picked up a new musical based on Goldsmith's *The Vicar of Wakefield* which he determined to present in London featuring himself in the title role. This piece had been composed by Liza Lehmann in the wake of her success with *Sergeant Brue* to a libretto by the poet and writer Laurence Housman who had previously been represented on the stage by *Bethlehem* (1902) and *Prunella* written with Granville Barker for the Court Theatre (1904) where it had recently been revived.

Unfortunately the two writers, both highly respected in their own field, had little understanding of the light musical theatre and the compromises it demanded in a collaboration. Housman's adaptation, rather than focusing on one particular section of Goldsmith's book as W. G. Wills had so successfully done with *Olivia*, taken from the same source, tried to cover all the book's principal events and the result was a very long libretto indeed. Madame Lehmann, too, after the unsettling experience of seeing her *Sergeant Brue* score added to by foreign hands, provided a very full score. She not only set all the lyrics provided by Housman but added some of her own, some pieces of Goldsmith and such traditional pieces as 'It was a Lover and his Lass' and 'Drink to me only with thine Eyes'. The end result was twenty-eight musical pieces plus incidental music. *The Vicar of Wakefield*, as written, was inordinately long and clearly something was going to have to be cut if and when it was produced on the stage. That moment arrived when Bispham took up the rights and put the piece into rehearsal for an opening at the Prince's, Manchester, and troubles soon arose. Rehearsals brought out the show's impracticalities and the cutting process duly began. Most of what went was book, although the young lead tenor, John McCormack, also departed when he proved too inexperienced and too Irish to cope with the role of Squire Thornhill. By the time the dress-rehearsal arrived, *The Vicar of Wakefield* had been pruned to more reasonable proportions (though it was now rather over-weighted with music) and Walter Hyde had been brought in to play Thornhill. Housman, who had been absent during rehearsals, arrived for the occasion and was furious when he saw what had been done to his libretto. He threatened to stop the performance from proceeding, he threatened lawsuits and finally demanded that his name be removed from what remained of his book, leaving himself credited only as the show's lyricist.

So it was under rather strained circumstances that *The Vicar of Wakefield* opened in Manchester but, in spite of everything, it was warmly and appreciatively received and duly headed for London and the Prince of Wales Theatre with discord in attendance. The first night brought that discord to a head. Housman, seated in a box, audibly ridiculed the show and Frank Curzon had him ejected from the theatre in the middle of the entertainment.

> Quoth the author 'My play's in a mess
> Don't tell me it's such a success,
> You have cut it about
> And you've had me thrown out
> And now you have told all the press'

ran a subsequent lampoon which was all the more telling in that *The Vicar of Wakefield* was, judged on its own pretensions, a kind of success. Mme Lehmann, who had been the initiator of the whole project and who had stuck to her score grimly throughout the alterations and cuttings of the Manchester period, gained some excellent reviews:

> Never has Mme Lehmann produced more successful work . . . delighting all hearers with melodies that are as fresh and spontaneous as folk songs and marked for the most part by a good deal of character . . (*Times*)

David Bispham was, as he had known he would be, well suited by the role of Dr

Primrose and he had one of Mme Lehmann's best songs, a setting of the 'Elegy on a mad Dog' in which he declared to an extended cadenza:

> The man recovered of the bite
> The dog it was that died!

For London, Isabel Jay took on the role of Olivia in what proved an excellent piece of casting. She sang several ballads in the style which suited her so well and performed the character with such dramatic ability that *The Times* was moved to compare her interpretation with that given by Ellen Terry in the straight play. Indeed, whether singing Goldsmith's 'When lovely Woman stoops to Folly' or Housman's duet 'Rose and Lily' or Miss Lehmann's slightly limp lyrics to 'Tomorrow' or 'Prince Charming', or playing the sympathetic scenes the part allotted her, Miss Jay made a quite outstanding impression. The two stars were strongly supported by a fine cast including Hyde with his fine operatic tenor and Savoy veteran Richard Temple, now nearing 60, as the basso 'Mr Burchell'.

The Vicar of Wakefield was an artistic opéra-comique or light opera with some elegant song-writing to recommend it but there was little time for it to act as a barometer of public taste or to point up the degree of profitability of such works in a period of changing tastes. The internal wranglings which had dogged it through its production proved too much and, after little more than a month, Bispham closed the show and returned to the operatic stage.

The provincial year of 1906 was not particularly rich in new shows. The first attempt was the production at Edinburgh of a new Scottish musical on the lines of *A Trip to the Highlands*. Harry Fischer, who had taken over the Grand Theatre from Eade Montefiore, continued with his predecessor's announced policy and brought out *The Scottish Bluebells* by David James with music by Osmond Carr. The new piece was set in West Princes Street and the fancy fair in Waverley Market and introduced some fairly standard characters: a 'Johnny', a 'Willie Edouin' comic, an Irish comic and, of course, a Scots comic and ran them through a series of sketches and numbers which made up the reasonably bright story of the piece. *The Scottish Bluebells* won some popularity but never looked like repeating the success of its predecessor and when the time came to send it on the road it was decided, instead, to revert to the proven *Trip to the Highlands*.

Fred Locke, the author of that last named piece, brought out for 1906 a 'musical farcical absurdity' which he called *Lucky Liza*. It leaned heavily towards the 'variety show' type of musical with its numbers and routines joined up by a slight story about a missing heiress. Its touring life was limited to Scotland. Fred Paul produced at Worthing a piece called *The Lord of the Last* which followed a whole heap of amorous entanglements to their conclusion to the accompaniment of some catchy if unoriginal songs – the inevitable coon song, patriotic songs, a 'stage' song, waltzes &c – by Denham Harrison and Percival Knight. Harry Starr, borrowing from the historical Borgia tale, produced *The Unseen Power* which in no way rivalled his perennial breadwinners *Otto the Outcast* and *Carl the Clockmaker*.

The short musical piece had made something of a comeback with the relaxing of the laws regarding plays in the music halls. The Hippodrome produced regular spectacular pieces such as 'The Earthquake' and 'The Flood' which relied more on their scenic than their human element and which were supplied with music by Clarence Corri, the composer of *The Dandy Fifth*. Other halls joined in with every possible kind of musical play and playlet. At the Tivoli, Arthur Roberts and Ruby Celeste appeared in an unamshamedly old-fashioned burlesque entitled *Robin Waller A. O. F. or The Maid of the Mill-ard By* (Lewis Waller was appearing in *Robin Hood* at the Lyric) written by Herbert Shelley and composed by Ernest Bucalossi. M. R. Morand and Millie Hylton starred as Nero and Poppaea in *S'Nero or a Roman Bank Holiday* at the Coliseum, burlesquing Tree's production of Stephen Philips' *Nero*. The authors in this case were Chris Davis and two other refugees from the musical comedy, Roland Carse and Walter Slaughter. On the same programme, Florence St John appeared in a little piece called *My Milliner's Bill*. Roberts , too, had his crack at Nero at the Oxford with Ruby Celeste as 'Agrippineapple' in *Naughty Nero* written by Adrian Ross and composed by Augustus Barrett, and Little Tich did his version of Robin Hood at the Pavilion in *Cock Robin Hood* (Wal Pink/W. B. Baker).

At the Tivoli, the 'Follies' entertainment of H. G. Pélissier had expanded from one item on the programme to a large part of the evening's entertainment. Their repertoire included a heavy larding of burlesque and pieces such as *The Bustler of Bath or The Crash Without Reason* parodied the Seymour Hicks musicals. Pélissier himself played Hicks and Lewis Sydney impersonated Camille Clifford. Even George Edwardes joined in the new trend and produced a piece by Americans R. H. Burnside and Gustave Kerker called *Very Grand Opera or Burning to Sing* at the Empire.

Burlesque had found itself a new home and was thriving. But it was not only burlesque which was to be found in the music halls. The most impressive piece of the variety year was billed as a 'revue' although in fact it was basically a satirical sketch illustrated with topical songs. It was called *Venus 1906* and was written for the Empire by George Grossmith with music composed and arranged by the American composer, Constance Tippett. The framework for the piece was a challenge laid down to Venus by a Gibson Girl. The 'Judgement' is held in an English court and the Gibson Girl wins. Venus is furious and turns Britain back to prehistoric times. The cast included Sybil Arundale (singing 'The Picture Postcard Girl'), Elizabeth Firth, Harry Grattan and Bill Berry who poked fun at the unwashed supporters of the new Labour Party in a Jerome Kern song 'The Leader of the Labour Party'.

At the Coliseum 'revue' was also billed with Thomas E. Murray and Louis Bradfield compèring a satirical entertainment. Elsewhere there were mini-musicals like *The Belle of India* (Hackney Empire), *Omar Seer, the Mysterious Millionaire* (Balham, Islington) and Joseph Tabrar's *The Elopement of the Parson's Daughter*, as well as more seriously conceived pieces. Napoleon Lambelet's operetta *Fenella* was played at the Coliseum, and Emilio Pizzi, composer of *The Bric à Brac Will*, had *The Magic Eye of Egypt* played at the New Cross Empire and *Betta the Gipsy* staged by Edith Mellor for Alice Esty at the same time that his opera *The Vendetta* was being produced at the Opera House in Cologne.

But the oddest piece of the year was left to the theatre. The indefatigable dilettante W. H. C. Nation took Terry's Theatre for a season and staged a chopped-down version of the old farce *He's Much to Blame* along with a 'musical and satirical play' called *Yellow Fog Island*, put together by Arthur Sturgess with songs, of course, by W. H. C. Nation. *Yellow Fog Island* was a fiasco. It was ill-rehearsed, the orchestra was a shambles and the material they had to play quite dreadful. The newspapers sighed:

> If jokes of a certain kind ever die of extreme old age, then the life of *Yellow Fog Island* cannot be very long . . (*Times*)

> A mixture of dull satire and indifferent pantomime . . . clumsily laboured, heavy-handed journeyman work (*Stage*)

Nation, blithely unconcerned, advertised his songs and went into the theatre every night to hear them sung while his admittedly large financial resources paid the price. Sturgess revised the piece and after twenty nights the farce was replaced by another piece which allowed the insertion of three more of Mr Nation's numbers. The manager/composer advertised his show with newspaper quotations to the effect 'Mr Nation carries fearlessly on . .' and invented his own:

> UNCONVENTIONAL IDEA. FEARLESS REMARKS. JESTS WHICH ARE SPIRITUELS NOT COARSE TURPITUDES. SONGS WITH A PURPOSE. MUSIC WORTH HEARING.

And he carried on with minimal houses to the end of his announced season.

1906

0315 **THE LITTLE CHERUB** a musical play in three acts by Owen Hall. Lyrics by Adrian Ross. Music by Ivan Caryll. Additional lyrics by George Grossmith Jr, W. H. Risque. Additional music by Paul Rubens and Frank E. Tours. Produced at the Prince of Wales Theatre under the management of George Edwardes 13 January, 1906 for a run of 114 performances closing 28 April, 1906. Revised and reproduced at the same theatre under the title *The Girl on the Stage* 5 May, 1906 for a further 29 performances closing 2 June, 1906. Additional songs by Frank E. Tours and Jerome D. Kern.

Earl of Sanctobury	Fred Kaye/Willie Edouin	Willie Edouin
Algernon Southdown	Lennox Pawle	Lennox Pawle
Shingle	W. H. Berry	W. H. Berry
Ethelbert	George Carroll	George Carroll
Capt. Hereward	Spenser Trevor	Spenser Trevor
Mr Grimble	Henry Adens/ Valentine O'Connor/ Ralph Roberts	Ralph Roberts
Alderman Briggs	Edmund Cooper/Colin Coop	Colin Coop
Crumm	Fred J. Blackman	Fred J. Blackman
Sir George Monteith	Ford Hamilton/ Edmund Cooper	Edmund Cooper
Interpreter	Valentine O'Connor/*out*	
Bricks	Arthur Hope/*out*	
The Rajah of Talcutta (Grand Duke of Bakavia)	Maurice Farkoa (Charles Angelo)/ Edouard Garceau/ W. Louis Bradfield	W. Louis Bradfield
Lady Isobel Congress	Zena Dare/Ida Lytton	Zena Dare
Lady Dorothy Congress	Gabrielle Ray	Gabrielle Ray
Lady Agnes Congress	Lily Elsie	
Lady Rosa Congress	Grace Pindar	
Mrs Briggs	Ida Lytton/Kitty Hanson	Kitty Hanson
Letty	Elise Clerc	Doris Dean
Cuckoo Van Blane	Mildred de Vere/ Marion Erskine	Marion Erskine
Kitty Cranbourne	Hilda Coral	Hilda Coral
Florence/Maudi Rochester	Stella Hammerstein/ Dorothy Dunbar	Dorothy Dunbar
Mabel/Baby Ducross	Daisy Denville/Mabel Munro	Mabel Munro
Mary/Gertie Macclesfield	Amy Webster	Amy Webster

Olive Mandeville	Blanche Thorpe	Blanche Thorpe
Molly Montrose.	Evie Greene/Alice Oppitz	Ruth Vincent
add Lord Congress		Lionel Mackinder

Dir: J. A. E. Malone; md: Frank E. Tours; ch: Willie Warde (& Sydney Ellison); sc: W. Telbin and Joseph Harker; cos: Percy Anderson

Produced at the Criterion Theatre, New York, under the management of Charles Frohman 6 August, 1906 for a run of 169 performances closing 5 January, 1907
Henry V. Donnelly/Tom Wise/Sam Edwards (SANCT), James Blakeley (ALG), Will West (SHING), Sol Solomon/John Mayon (ETH), Charles Gibson/Martin Haydon (HERE), Charles Frischer/Charles Gibson (GRIM), Martin Haydon/Richard Chawner (BRIGGS), J. Rider Glyn/John F. Rogers (CRU), H. F. Hendee (SIR), Bertram Wallis/Andrew Higginson (LORD C), Corinne Francis/May Narden (IS), Mabel Hollins (DOR), Winona Winter (AG), Lucy Monroe/Grace Field (RO), Trixie Jennery/Beth Stone (LIZA), Adelaide Kornau/Emily Francis (BRIGGS), Eithel Kelly/Dorothy Zimmerman (CUCK), May Maloney/Elsa Reinhardt (KIT), Helen Dudley/Eithel Kelly (MAUD), Grace Madison/Clara Pitt (MAE), Virginia Harms/Grace Kimball (MARY), Stella Hansen/Edna Sidney (OL), Hattie Williams (MOLLY). Dir: Ben Teal; md: Clarence West; sc: Ernest Gros; cos: Mrs Robert Osborn, Pascaud of Paris

0316 **THE BEAUTY OF BATH** a musical play in two acts by Seymour Hicks and Cosmo Hamilton. Lyrics by Charles H. Taylor. Music by Herbert E. Haines. Additional music by Frederic Norton and Jerome D. Kern. Produced at the Aldwych Theatre under the management of Charles Frohman 19 March, 1906. Transferred to Hicks Theatre 27 December, 1906 and closed 23 January, 1907 after a total of 287 performances.

Hon. Betty Silverthorne	Ellaline Terriss/Zena Dare (Mabel Sealby)
Lt. Richard Alington	Seymour Hicks/Stanley Brett
Sir Timothy Bun	Murray King
Lady Bun	Mollie Lowell/Marguerite Leslie/Florence Lloyd
Mrs Goodge.	Sydney Fairbrother
Lemon Goodge	Albert Valchera
Mr Beverley.	Stanley Brett/Tom Terriss
Hon. Charles Templeton	Reginald Kenneth/Cecil Curtis/ McNaughton Duncan
Earl of Orpington.	E. W. Royce
Viscount Bellingham	William Lugg
Tattersall Spink.	Bert Sinden/Will Bishop
Hon. Dorothy Quorn	Barbara Deane
Countess of Chandon	Georgie Read/*out*
Countess of Orpington	Vera Morris/Hilda Antony
Countess Thérèse Rosemere	Renée de Montel
Lady Delbeck	Marguerite Leslie/Marion Lindsay/Mabel Sealby
Mrs Alington	Rosina Filippi/Mollie Lowell
Miss Truly St Cyr	Maudi Darrell/Mabel Sealby
Jane Topit.	Topsy Sinden
Hot Bun.	May Gates
Iced Bun	Lillie McIntyre/Ruby Kennedy
Spice Bun	Kitty Melrose
Plum Bun	Claire Rickards
Rice Bun	Hilda Harris/Madeleine Morton
Crumb Bun	Marion Lindsay
Penny Bun	Pauline Francis
Youngest Bun	Agnes Hodgkinson/Margot Erskine
Currant Bun	Enid Leslie
Cross Bun	Mabel Watson
Seed Bun	Mabel Ellis

Home-made Bun . . . . Elsie Kay
add Lord Quorn . . . . Laurence Caird
Hon. Mortimer Gorst . . . . Cecil Kinnaird/H. Plunket/Mervyn Dene

Dir: Seymour Hicks; md: Carl Kiefert; ch: Edward Royce; sc: Walter Hann; cos: Wilhelm

Played by a juvenile company 11 February, 1907.
Marjorie West (B), Albert Valchera (RA), Reginald George (SIR), Doris MacIntyre (LADY B/JANE), Ivy Sawyer (MRS G), Connie Bethel (LEMON), Ethel Evans (BEV), Isidore Phillips (CHAS/GORST), Archie McCaig (ORP), Charles Swanson (BELL), Elsie Sawyer (TS), Florence Arnold (DOR), Euphan MacLaren (MRS A), Hetty Bullen (TRULY), Roy Jeffries (QU) with Kathleen Crook, Connie Walters, Winifred Barnes, Dorritt MacLaren, Ivy Knight, Alexandra Vercisi, Beatrice Hillier, Doris Chisholm. Md: Mr Harnack

0317 **THE SCOTTISH BLUEBELLS** a musical comedy by David James. Music by F. Osmond Carr. Produced at the Grand Theatre, Edinburgh, under the management of Harry Fischer 31 March, 1906.

Ex-Bailie Maie . . . . Peter D. Berningham
Montague Migg . . . . Leon Simkin
Hon. Bobby . . . . Harry Stuart
Prince Izan . . . . Clifford Morgan
Rory . . . . Dan O'Connor
Hamish . . . . Alec Stewart
Guy Chalmers . . . . Arthur Stewart
Guy Chalmers . . . . Arthur Cartwright
Mrs Elspeth . . . . Kate Sherry
Jennie . . . . Kitty Clinton
Maggie . . . . Delia Cherry
Mrs Melton Mowbray . . . . Elsie Steadman
Mrs Washington Potts . . . . Edythe Carlyle
Kersty . . . . May Anderson
Maisie Maie . . . . Hettie Gale
Gordon Mackay . . . . C. Fitzsimons
Ronald Gray . . . . Arthur Wade
Allan Mack . . . . Albert Ferriss
Rob McKenzie . . . . Jack Cookson
Ewan Currie . . . . T. W. Kingston
Donald Menzies . . . . Percy Madgwick

sc: J. F. McLellan & Edmund Swift; cos: Mrs Nerney

0318 **THE BELLE OF MAYFAIR** a musical comedy in two acts by Basil Hood and Charles H. E. Brookfield (later billed as Cosmo Hamilton and C. H. E. Brookfield). Music by Leslie Stuart. Produced at the Vaudeville Theatre under the management of Messrs A. & S. Gatti and Charles Frohman 11 April, 1906. A new version produced 8 February, 1907 and closed 13 April, 1907 after a total run of 416 performances.

Earl of Mount Highgate . . . . Sam Walsh
Hon. Raymond Finchley . . . . Joe Farren Soutar
Sir John Chaldicott . . . . Arthur Williams
Hugh Meredith . . . . Courtice Pounds
Comte de Perrier . . . . Charles Angelo
Dr Marmaduke Lawrence . . . . Charles Troode
Captain Theobald . . . . Mervyn Dene/Philip Desborough
Captain Goodyer . . . . Philip Desborough/*out*
Bandmaster . . . . Tom A. Shale/*out*
Simpson . . . . W. Pringle/Cecil Clayton
Gregory/Perkins . . . . Normal Ridley/Cecil Tresilian
François . . . . Murri Moncrieff
Bramley . . . . C. A. Cameron/H. Wescombe-Penney/Fred Rawlins

Bagstock . . . . John Blankley
H.S.H. Princess Carl of Ehrenbreitstein . Louie Pounds
Countess of Mount Highgate . . . . Irene Desmond
Lady Chaldicott . . . . Maud Boyd/Alice M. Cox
Lady Rosaline Rockesley . . . . Ruby Ray
Lady Violet Gussow . . . . Jane May/Dora Denton
Lady Jay . . . . Hilda Hammerton/Rose Levey
Lady Paquin . . . . Kitty Harold
Lady Louise . . . . Dora Glennie
Lady Lucille . . . . Maud Hobson/Mabel Seymour/Gertrude Kuzelle
Lady Peter Robinson . . . . Kitty Dale/Dora Sevening/Rose Levey
Lady Hayward . . . . Florence Randle/Maud Millais
Lady Swan . . . . Ivy Desmond/Crissie Bell/Gladys Cooper/Bertha Hope
Lady Edgar . . . . Helen Colville
Duchess of Dunmow (Miss Diana P. Cholmondley) . . . . Camille Clifford
Pincott . . . . Lillian Digges
Sophie . . . . Stella de Marney
Miss Corrie Fay . . . . Vivien Vowles/Vera Crichton
Julia Chaldicott . . . . Edna May (Ethel Newman)/Phyllis Dare/Billie Burke
add Gentleman Jack . . . . Sydney Mannering
Marianne . . . . Gertrude Hope
Bobbie . . . . Barbara Roberts

with Margaret Long, Agnes Marchant, Gladys Anderson, Connie Ross, Lily Maynier, Munro Ross, Florence Manton, Ethel Leigh, Daisy de Levante, Alice M. Cox, Dora Denton, Winifred Godard, Vera Crichton, Nessie Walker, Phyllis Gibbons, Dorothy Monkman, Phyllis Monkman, Marjorie Villis, Dorothy Brunt, Winifred Hall/Regina Gratz, Mabel Bailey; Messrs Mendy Wigley, Cecil Tresilian, Michael Henry, J. Martin, Pearce Robinson, H. Wescombe-Penney, Blair Headsworth, E. Crampton Bryant/Claud Glyn
Characters in the Harlequinade: Arthur Williams (CLOWN), Joe Farren Soutar (HARLEQUIN), Charles Angelo (SWELL), Louie Pounds (FAIRY PRINCESS), Billie Burke (COLUMBINE), Sam Walsh (PANTALOON), Courtice Pounds (POLICEMAN), Ruby Ray (MLLE AMORETTE), Camille Clifford (LA POMPADOUR).

Dir: Herbert Cottesmore; md: Edward Jones; ch: Fred Farren; sc: W. Harford; cos: Jays Ltd, Paquin, Hawkes & Co., B. J. Simmons & Co./Mme Phillips, Mme Hayward, Miss Fisher, J. A. Harrison

Produced at Daly's Theatre, New York, under the management of Thomas W. Ryley 3 December, 1906 for a run of 140 performances closing 30 March 1907.
Harry B. Burcher (EARL), Van Rensselaer Wheeler (RAY), Richard F. Carroll (SIR J), Jack Gardner (HUGH), Ignacio Martinetti (PERRIER), Cyril Offage (GOODYER), J. Costellanos (BAND), Frank W. Shea (SIMP), W. Freeman (BRAM), J. Louis Mintz (SIR GEORGE CHEETHAM), Irene Bentley (PCESS), Honore French (CTESS), Jennie Opie (LADY C), Annabelle Whitford (VIO), Valeska Suratt (DUCHESS), May Hobson (JAY), Elinora Pendleton (PAQ), Margaret Rutledge (LOU), Hattie Forsythe (LUC), Stella Beardsley (PR), Clare Lascelles (HAY), Elizabeth Whitney (SWAN), Rose Beatrice Winter (EDG), Bessie Clayton (PINC), Helen Cullinan (SOPH), Christie MacDonald (JULIA); with Florence Gardner, Eula Mannering, Beaula Martin, Caroline Lee, Palmyre Monnett, Lillian Earle, Beatrix Tuite-Dalton, Sadie Miner, Bessie Penn, Alice Tallant, Alice Knowlson, Myrtle Lawton, Florence Saville, Viola Bowers, Gene Cole, Maud Falkland, Dorothy Hutchinson, Edith Barr, Effie Wheeler, Ethel Davis, Grace Russell, Rose Eaton, Ethel Vivian; Joseph Parsons, Pierre Young, Harry Husk, Walter Grover, William Griffin, Arthur Nestor, Trestell Ayres, J. Sidney, Richard Davis, Harry Hoffman, J. Davis.

Film: in 1906 Chronophone Films issued a film and synchronised record of 'In Montezuma' from *The Belle of Mayfair* and in 1907 a further extract was issued by the same firm.

0319 **THE DAIRYMAIDS** a farcical musical play in two acts and three scenes, by Alexander M. Thompson and Robert Courtneidge. Lyrics by Paul A. Rubens and Arthur Wimperis. Music by

Paul A. Rubens and Frank E. Tours. Produced at the Apollo Theatre under the management of Robert Courtneidge 14 April, 1906 for a run of 239 performances closing 8 December, 1906

Lady Brudenell . . . . Phyllis Broughton
Sam Brudenell . . . . Walter Passmore/E. Statham Staples
Frank Brudenell. . . . . Horace Lane
Capt. Fred Leverton . . . . Frank Green (Harry Cottell)/Alec Fraser
Dr O'Byrne . . . . Ambrose Manning
Joe Mivens . . . . Dan Rolyat/W. L. Rignold
Tim Capus . . . . F. W. Bowes
Lt. Brereton. . . . . Rupert Mar
Jack Biffen . . . . Harry Cottell/Edgar Ward
Todgers . . . . Carr Evans
Peggy . . . . Carrie Moore/Winnie Volt/Vere Vere
Winifred. . . . . Agnes Fraser/Rhoda Gordon
Hélène. . . . . Florence Smithson/Mabel Green
Miss Penelope Pyechase . . . . Carlotta Zerbini
Eliza. . . . . Gracie Leigh
Daisy . . . . Gertrude Kuzelle/Muriel Varna
Betty . . . . Dorothy Ward
Joan . . . . Alice Coleman
Jenny . . . . Winnie Volt/
Nancy . . . . Louie Lochner/Olive Wade
Rosie . . . . Beryl Vaudrey/Alys Read
Gertie . . . . Gertie Sinclair/Bertha Russell
Bessie . . . . Kittie Sparrow
The Sandow Girls: Dorothy Ward, Gertrude Kuzelle, Minna Moore, Bessie Maddox/Mabel Medrow, Rosemary Collis, Gertie Sinclair

Dir: Robert Courtneidge; md: Arthur Wood; ch: Harry Grattan; sc: Conrad Tritschler & R. McCleery; cos: Wilhelm

Produced at the Criterion Theatre, New York, under the management of Charles Frohman 26 August, 1907 for a run of 86 performances closing 16 November, 1907.
Ruby Ray (LADY), George Gregory (SAM), Langford Kirby (FRANK), Donald Hall (FRED), Eugene O'Rourke (O'B), Huntley Wright (JOE), Julia Sanderson (PEG), Bessie De Voie (WIN), Thelma Raye (HEL), Emily Francis (PYE), Flossie Hope (EL), Beatrice McKay (DAI), Hazel Neason (BET), Florence Wilson (JOAN), Freida Weigold (JEN), Wilma Wood (NAN), Dorothy Gibson (RO), May Gerson (GERT), Isabelle Meyers (BESS), Edna Dodsworth (MAG), Minna Martrit (CEILIA), Rose Leslie, Hatty Lorraine, Maude Leroy, Enid Gibson, Grace Lindsay, Lillian LeRoy, Ray Gilmore, Maud Thomas (SANDOW GIRLS). Dir: A. E. Dodson; md: William T. Francis; ch: Ad. Newberger; sc: Ernest Gros; cos: Mrs Osborn, Dazian

Produced at the Queen's Theatre under the management of Robert Courtneidge 5 May, 1908 for a run of 83 performances closing 18 July, 1908.
Phyllis Broughton (LADY), E. Statham Staples (SAM), Fred Leslie Jr (FRANK), Ambrose Manning (O'B), F. Percival (TIM), A. Wyndham (LT), Dan Rolyat (JOE), Carr Evans (TODGERS), Phyllis Dare (PEG), Florence Smithson (WIN), Gladys Ivery (HELENE), Marie Daltra (PYECHASE), Florence Lloyd (ELIZA), Dorothy Laine (HYDE), Maisie Sinclair (CHEYNE), Edythe Burnand (KNIGHTSBRIDGE)

Produced at the Aldwych Theatre under the management of J. Bannister Howard 22 May, 1915 for a run of 18 performances closing 5 June.
Alice Venning (LADY), Coningsby Brierley (SAM), Herbert St John (FRANK), Robert Ayrton (O'B), John Sandbrook (TIM), Charles P. Hughes (LT), Edwin Dodds (JOE), Fred Dent (TODGERS), Clara Beck (PEG), Edith Drayson (WIN), Gabrielle Gordon (HELENA), Rose Edouin (PYE), Edie Martin (ELIZA), Josephine Ellis (HYDE), Marjorie Burgess (CHEYNE) with Amy Preston, Babs Christopher, Millicent Healy, Lily Bell, Doris Woodroffe, Marie Glier, Grace Warrell, Ruby Vincent, Barbara Hall, Lena Reeves, Noreen Craigie, Joan Coulthurst. Dir: Robert MacDonald; md: B. J. Paterson

0320 **THE GIRL BEHIND THE COUNTER** a farcical musical play (musical comedy) in two acts by Leedham Bantock and Arthur Anderson. Lyrics by Arthur Anderson. Music by Howard

Talbot. Additional lyrics by Percy Greenbank. Additional music by J. St A. Johnson and Augustus Barrett. Produced at Wyndham's Theatre under the management of Frank Curzon 21 April, 1906 for a run of 141 performances closing 1 September, 1906.

Charlie Chetwynd. . . . . C. Hayden Coffin (Donald Hall)
Gen Sir Wilkie Willoughby. . . . . J. F. McArdle
Lady Willoughby . . . . Violet Crossley
Millie Mostyn. . . . . Violet Englefield
Viscount Gushington . . . . Lawrence Grossmith/G. Davy Burnaby
Monsieur Duval. . . . . Fred Allandale
Ninette . . . . Marie Dainton/Annie Mars
Susie . . . . Coralie Blythe/Kathleen Courtenay
Rudolph. . . . . Akerman May
Adolphus Dudd. . . . . Horace Mills/Lionel Victor
Waiter. . . . . George Barrett
Alice. Jenny Buckle/Helen Rose
Mildred . . . . Evelyn Powys
Olive . . . . Violet Vassilla
Phyllis. . . . . Constance Guilbert
Poppie Waring . . . . Dorothy Reynolds
Lottie Vernon. . . . . Nancy Malone
Rosie Marshall . . . . Mollie Ventry
Lillie Lovegrove. . . . . Lily Mills
Kitty Debenham . . . . Dolly Beaufey/Dolly Grey
Hettie Hudson . . . . Kitty Hives
Jack Spenser . . . . Reginald Cooper
Harold Vane . . . . Fred Maguire/Geoffrey Allsopp
Cyril Scott . . . . Barry Neame
Frank Mason. . . . . Walter Dolphin
Harry Thornton. . . . . H. B. Clarke
Gerald Miles . . . . Edmund Hollick
Winnie Willoughby. . . . . Isabel Jay
add Joseph . . . . A. E. E. Edwards

Dir: Frank Curzon and Austen Hurgon; md: Howard Talbot/Howard Carr/Louis Hillier; sc: Julian Hicks; cos: Karl

Produced at Herald Square Theatre, New York, under the management of Sam and Lee Shubert 1 October, 1907 for a run of 282 performances. Freely adapted and reconstructed by Edgar Smith.
Joseph Ratliff (CH), Lew Fields (HENRY SCHNIFF), Connie Ediss (MRS SCHNIFF), Louise Dresser (MILLIE), Denman Maley (GUSH), George Beban (DUV), Lotta Faust (NIN), Topsy Siegrist (SU), William Rock (DUDLEY CHEATHAM), Vernon Castle (JOHN BLOBBS), Edith Ethel McBride (MRS WHITTINGTON), Lottie Fremond (MRS CROSSLEY-SHOPPINGTON), Patsy Mitchell (MAGGIE), Hubert Neville (LORD RUMBOLD), Vernon Castle (HON AUBREY BATTERSEA) with Beatrice Liddell, Ada Robertson, Dorothy Marlowe, Louise Hawman, Seppie McNeil, Elizabeth Hawman, Vincent Cooper, Elsa Reinhardt, Mae Allen, Claire Casscles, Helen Turner, Marion Whitney, Nan Brennan, Viola Hopkins, Mildred Gibson, Julia Mills, Jane Grant, Frances Harris, Ruth Humphries, Helen Scott, Winifred Vaughan, Ida Doerge, Anna C. Wilson, Reina Swift, Lillian Raymond, Ethel Millard, Bettine Le Fevre, Madge Robertson, Stella Bowe, Molly Mack, Lillian Devere, Daisy Carson, Erminie Clark, Josephine Harriman, Jack Strause, J. J. Younge, Joseph Torpey, Richard Fanning, Sebastian Cassie, Charles Mitchell, Radford D'Orsay, John Reinhardt, J. J. MacDonald, A. Van Sant. Dir: Julian Mitchell & J. C. Huffman; md: William E. MacQuinn; sc: Arthur Voegtlin; cos: Eaves & Castel-Bert, Matthews, Mme Lubin, Lord & Taylor, Ritche, Harndon & Co, Mme Ripley &c.

0321 **PETRONELLA** or A Royal Romance. A Spanish comic opera in two acts by Montague Turner. Music by W. T. Gliddon. Additional lyrics by Miss Stafford M. Smith. Produced at the Great Queen Street Theatre under the management of Harold Payne 26 May, 1906 for a season of 8 performances and toured.

Captain Philippe Bravadura. . . . . Harold Payne
Duc de Caceida . . . . Fred Hill
Don Sebastian Salutia . . . . Harry Gribben
Marquis Circumvita. . . . . Alfred H. Majilton
Sergeant Bodega . . . . Broughton Black
Corporal Posada. . . . . Ivor Harvey
Salvados. . . . . W. Benson
Queen Casilda. . . . . Alice Rene
Petronella . . . . Zoe Gilfillan
Inez . . . . Aline Goldsmith
Paquita . . . . Rosina Effingham
Balasco . . . . M. Byron
Dolores . . . . Netta Neville
Loretta . . . . Adela Crispin
Step-Annie Floretta Dossano . . . . Marie Ault
with the Four Arosas and Beatrice Ford (pd)

Dir: Harold Payne; md: Sydney Payne; ch: Beatrice Ford; sc: Egertons; cos: Henrique Valdez

0322 SEE SEE a Chinese comic opera in two acts by Charles H. E. Brookfield adapted from *La Troisième Lune* by Frédérique de Grésac and Paul Ferrier. Lyrics by Adrian Ross. Music by Sidney Jones. Additional material by Frank E. Tours and Percy Greenbank. Produced at the Prince of Wales Theatre under the management of George Edwardes 20 June, 1906 for a run of 152 performances closing 17 November, 1906.

See See . . . . Denise Orme (Jessie Hill)/Deborah Volar
Yen . . . . Maurice Farkoa (Albert Wortley Drewitt)
Cheoo . . . . W. H. Berry/John Humphries
Hoang . . . . Fred Emney /Gus Oxley
M. Mascotte . . . . Ralph Roberts/*out*
Hi-Tee . . . . Fred J. Blackman/H. Leslie
Sing-Song . . . . Francis Rayne
Tie-Pin . . . . H. E. Pearce/E. D. Wardes
So-Long . . . . Philip H. Bracy
Hang-Kee . . . . Huntley Wright
Lee . . . . Adrienne Augarde/Alice Hatton
Poo-See . . . . Lena Maitland/Kitty Hanson/Bella Newstead
Miao-Yao . . . . Sybil Grey
Shoo-Shoo . . . . Lilian Hewitson
Mrs Hoang . . . . Kitty Hanson/Mrs Watt Tanner
Mai-Yai . . . . Amy Augarde
Humming Bird . . . . Lily Elsie/Mabel Russell (Shelley Calton)
So-Hei. . . . . Gabrielle Ray (Mabel Russell)
Silky Lips . . . . Shelley Calton (Claire Marsden)
Sea of Jade . . . . Doris Dean
Sly Smile . . . . Dora Langham
Forbidden Fruit. . . . . Mabel Russell/Blanche Astley
add Tin-Kang. . . . . Gertrude Thornton

Dir: Sydney Ellison; md: Frank E. Tours; sc: Joseph Harker and Hawes Craven; cos: Mrs Freed & B. J. Simmons

0323 AMASIS an Egyptian Princess. A comic opera in two acts by Frederick Fenn. Music by Philip Michael Faraday. Produced at the New Theatre under the management of Louis Calvert 9 August, 1906. Transferred to the Criterion Theatre 31 December, 1906. Closed 6 February, 1906 after a total run of 200 performances.

Amasis IX, Pharoah of Egypt . . . . . . Rutland Barrington
Prince Anhotep . . . . Roland Cunningham
Cheiro. . . . . Whitworth Mitton (H. Scott Russell)

Nebenchari . . . . Norman Salmond
Ptolemy Theopompus Allakama . . . . . Herbert Ross/Reginald White
Sebak . . . . Lauri De Frece
Psamtik . . . . Frank Perfitt
Zopyrus . . . . G. MacKarness/*out*
Town Crier . . . . Leonard Calvert
2nd High Priest . . . . F. Aubrey Millward/G. Swinhoe
Expert Witnesses . . . . Berridge Fraser
John Clulow
C. Gregory/G. MacKarness
W. Derwent
Natis . . . . Madge Vincent
Qeressa . . . . Maisie Stather/Winnie O'Connor/Dorothy Aylmer
Anna . . . . Emmie Santer
Atossa . . . . Marion Marler
Ladice . . . . Evelyn Beresford
Kleis. . . . . Ethel Grahame
Tachot. . . . . Gladys Erskine
Ranofre . . . . Kathleen McKay/*out*
Rhodopis . . . . Max Hinton/Winifred Macey
Nitetis. . . . . Paula St Clair
Kassa . . . . Poppet McNally/Phyllys La Grand/*out*
Princess Amasis . . . . Ruth Vincent
Mummy Guards: Messrs Skinner, Stedman, Wingfield, Brodie, d'Anville, Marsland
Priests: Messrs Johnson, Hoscroft, Bennett, Birts
add pd: Winifred Hart-Dyke
with Misses Birbeck, Reeves, Winifred Macey, West, Dunbar, Hodges, Morrison, Gardner, Wentworth, Maynard, Moore/Luton, Gerard; Messrs Digues, Brook, Ferguson, Harberd, Wingrove, G. Swinhoe, Ashley, Walsh, Hopwood/Ashdowne, Vincent
Md: Jan van Heuvel; sc: Clement Barnes/Hugh Freemantle; cos: Tom Heslewood & F. M. Kelly

0324 **THE NEW ALADDIN** a musical extravaganza in two acts by James T. Tanner and W. H. Risque. Lyrics by Adrian Ross, Percy Greenbank, W. H. Risque and George Grossmith Jr. Music by Ivan Caryll and Lionel Monckton. Additional music by Frank E. Tours. Produced at the Gaiety Theatre under the management of George Edwardes 29 September, 1906. New version produced 24 November, 1906. Closed 27 April, 1907 after a total run of 203 performances.

General Ratz . . . . Robert Nainby
Genie of the Lamp . . . . George Grossmith Jr
Cadi . . . . Arthur Hatherton
Ebenezer . . . . Harry Grattan/John A. Warden /J. W. Birtley
The Lost Constable. . . . . Alfred Lester
The Ideal Man . . . . Charles Brown
Billy Pauncefort. . . . . Eustace Burnaby
Reggie Tighe . . . . J. R. Sinclair
Tony Cavendish. . . . . S. Hansworth
Tippin. . . . . Edmund Payne
Lally. . . . . Lily Elsie/Gertie Millar
The Princess . . . . Adrienne Augarde
Laolah. . . . . Olive May
Fossette (Maggie) (Je(a)nnie). . . . . . . Jean Aylwin
Mrs Tippin . . . . Winifred Dennis/*out*
Winnie Fairfax . . . . Kitty Mason
Flo Carteret . . . . Dot Beresford
Di Tollemache . . . . Enid Leonhardt
Kit Lomax . . . . Tessie Hackney
Vi Cortelyon . . . . Gladys Desmond

May Warrener . . . . Florence Lindley
Nan Jocelyn . . . . Violet Walker
Madge Oliphant . . . . Edna Loftus
Millie Farquhar . . . . Minnie Baker
Charm of Paris . . . . Gaby Deslys/Kitty Lindley
Spirit of the Ring . . . . Connie Ediss/Ruth Argent/Watt Tanner
add Little Grandmama . . . . Nora Nagle
Bertie Mortimer . . . . Marion Draughn
with Gladys Saqui, Clara Farren, May Flower, Lily Collier/Rosie Bennett, Kitty Lindley, Edith Lee

Md: Ivan Caryll; ch: Harry Grattan; sc: Joseph & Philip Harker and Hawes Craven; cos: Wilhelm

0325 **THE VICAR OF WAKEFIELD** a light romantic opera in three acts based on Oliver Goldsmith's novel of the same name. Lyrics by Laurence Housman. Music by Liza Lehmann. First produced under the management of David Bispham at the Prince's Theatre, Manchester 14 November, 1906. Opened at the Prince of Wales Theatre, London 12 December, 1906 for a run of 37 performances, closing 18 January, 1907.

Dr Primrose . . . . David Bispham
Mrs Primrose . . . . Mrs Theodore Wright
Sophia . . . . Edith Clegg/Kathleen Maureen
Squire Thornhill . . . . Walter Hyde
Moses . . . . Arthur Eldred
Dick . . . . Gordon Travis
Bill . . . . Elfin Arthur
'Mr Burchell' . . . . Richard Temple
Mr Jenkinson . . . . Charles Oram Lander/Arthur Willerby
Farmer Williams . . . . Powis Pinder
Lady Blarney . . . . Amy Martin
Gipsy . . . . Bella Wallis
Harvester . . . . Percy Bates
Dan o'the Mill . . . . W. Ford-Hamilton
Gossip . . . . Beatrice Jeffreys
Sally . . . . Phyllis Taylor
Miss Carolina Wilhelmina Amelia
Skeggs . . . . Valerie de Lacey
Olivia . . . . Violette Londa//Isabel Jay
Villagers . . . . March Harding, Theo Moss
Dir: Hugh Moss; md: Hamish MacCunn; sc: Joseph Harker, W. T. Hemsley, Harry Potts; cos: Nathan's

0326 **TWO NAUGHTY BOYS** a musical fairy play in two acts by George Grossmith Jr based on *Max und Moritz* by Wilhelm Busch and Palmer Cox. Lyrics by Percy Greenbank. Music by Constance Tippett. Additional material by C. H. Bovill and Philip Braham. Produced at the Gaiety Theatre under the management of George Edwardes 8 January, 1906 for a series of matinées ending 27 January.

Max . . . . Edmund Payne
Moritz . . . . Will Spray
Schoolmaster . . . . Arthur Hatherton
Hans . . . . G. Franklin
Farmer's boy . . . . Lewis Grande
Lulu the donkey . . . . The Almontes
Fritz the dog . . . . E. Hallom
Granny Bauer . . . . Kate Bishop
Widow Bolt . . . . Kitty Hanson
Agnes . . . . Ida Valli
Grizel . . . . Alice Hatton

Gretchen . . . . Coralie Blythe
Brownie King . . . . Roy Lorraine
Old Brownie . . . . Walter Cross
Bogey . . . . D. A. Steele
Daffydowndilly . . . . Doris Stocker
Dir: Sydney Ellison

THE LORD OF THE LAST a musical farce in two acts by Fred Ellis. Music by Percival Knight and Denham Harrison. Produced at Worthing under the management of Fred Paul 23 August, 1906 and toured.

PRINCE PRETENDER or Borroedene. A musical by 'Patrick Bidwell' produced at the Lyceum Theatre, Sheffield, 7 September, 1906.

THE CORNISH GIRL a romantic opera in two acts by Edward C. Arden. Music by Julian H. Wilson and Clement Locknane. Produced at the Pleasure Gardens, Folkestone 12 November, 1906.

LUCKY LIZA a farcical musical play in three acts by Fred Locke. Produced at Paisley 7 May, 1906.

THE DANDY DUKE a musical piece in two acts by Vere Smith. Lyrics by D. Eardley Wilmot, Stephen Eaton and Vere Smith. Produced at the Theatre Royal, Brighton, under the management of Vere Smith and Mervyn Trevor 17 December, 1906.

AN EXILE FROM HOME a conventional tragical musical absurdity in one act by Malcolm Watson. Music by Percy Fletcher and R. Hess. Produced at the Savoy Theatre under the management of Lena Ashwell as a forepiece to *The Shulamite* 12 June, 1906. Withdrawn 26 June.

Sgr Giulielmo Baillini. . . . . Edward Sass
Harry Merton . . . . Reynolds Dennison
Beppo . . . . Thomas Paunceforth
Miss Sarah Bulby . . . . Mrs De Solla
Marjorie Wren . . . . Evelyn d'Alroy

YELLOW FOG ISLAND a musical and satirical play in two acts by Arthur Sturgess. Music composed and arranged by Napoleon Lambelet with songs imitated from the French by W. H. C. Nation. Produced at Terry's Theatre under the management of the W. H. C. Nation 29 September, 1906 on a bill with *He's Much to Blame*, the latter replaced by *A Restless Night*. Withdrawn 30 November.

Dysma. . . . . Campbell Bishop
Sir Precedent Poskine. . . . . Robson Paige
Simkins . . . . A. B. Imeson
Rolls. . . . . Elise Cook
Princess Lucy . . . . Maie Ash
Dolly . . . . Gladys Archbutt
Dame Madge . . . . Alice Barth
Norah . . . . Iredale Hope
with Eleanor Harwood, Adelina Balfe, Daisy Nunn
Md: Napoleon Lambelet; sc: Cecil E. Hicks; cos: Hymans

1907

The survivors of 1906 did not run far into the new year. *The Vicar of Wakefield* and the seasonal revival of *Alice in Wonderland* both shut down in January, soon followed by *Amasis*. In April, *The Beauty of Bath*, *The Belle of Mayfair* and *The New Aladdin* completed their runs and left the scene to the new season's offerings.

The first of these was Charles Frohman's new vehicle for the popular Edna May. Frohman had stood by Miss May after her exit from the cast of *The Belle of Mayfair* and he had organised the preparation of a new show for her. *The Belle of New York* was still basically what Miss May was remembered for and as it was decided to follow the same pattern for the new piece, Frohman engaged Charles McLellan who, as 'Hugh Morton', had scripted *The Belle of New York*, and paired him with composer Ivan Caryll. Between them, they came up with a show which they called *Nelly Neil.*

In *Nelly Neil*, Miss May, instead of being a sweet Salvation Army lassie was a sweet little Socialist, rallying every available man to her cause and successfully defeating the enemy in the form of the anarchist Princess Rasslova, who is plotting to blow up the bank owned by the father of rich young Billy Ricketts, the inamorata of Nelly Neil whom she will wed in pomp and splendour (conveniently forgetting the simple Socialist life) at the piece's end.

Being constructed for and around Edna May, the show also consisted largely of her, although surrounded by a numerous cast, very few of whose characters were developed to any degree and a number of whom were more than a little reminiscent of the characters of *The Belle of New York*. The eccentric hero, Billy Ricketts, had some amusing moments in the hands of the American actor, Joe Coyne, here making his British début, and Kitty Gordon as the vigorous Rasslova, Ells Dagnall as a mildly comic detective and Gertrude Lester as 'The Hon. Muriel Vickery' had moments, albeit rather brief ones, but performers of the quality of J. J. Dallas, Robb Harwood and Mollie Lowell were reduced to little more than looking on. The raison d'être of *Nelly Neil* was its star, and the show was duly prepared and presented in such a way as to show her to every advantage. In the choice of Socialism as his heroine's main characteristic, however, McLellan got himself in something of a muddle. It was rather difficult to make his heroine adhere to her professed principles, yet give her the necessary qualities of sweetness and archness as well as a happy ending with a suitably rich and prosperous capitalist.

We first meet Nellie expounding her creed in a song called 'The Millennium' which was clearly intended to be the 'Follow On' of the new show:

> I've carried the word of warning all along Park Lane
> I haven't converted them yet but I shall try again

My Socialist creed won't charm them in a minute
But I think I'm getting them interested in it
For one millionaire I lately went to see
Was rather inclined to give his wealth to me.
Oh, I sing of the Park Lane magnates
Renouncing their ill-earned gold
And weary of strife
Seeking sweet simple life
With the lambs in my Socialist fold.
Oh, I sing of the bright day coming
Of the day that has almost come
When they'll all avoid wealth
As a state of ill-health
I sing the Millennium!

She doesn't seem to be able to convince anyone by explanation or argument, but she gathers a fair-sized following by the exercise of her personal charms. Having enraptured the gilded youth of London, she turns her attention to their titled elders:

Now, don't be merely Dukes and Earls
That surely must be dreary
It wears you out
And fills you with gout
And makes you excessively thin or stout
And everyone round you weary.
You can't be happy like you are,
So don't be like it any longer.
Come out and be entirely free
And don't be afraid to dance with me
It'll make your hearts beat stronger . .

By the end of the act everyone is off in her wake to Countess Rokeby's 'Simplicity Farm' where she leads her disciples in the 'simple life'. But Nelly confesses:

Perhaps you have suspected I'm a sort of Suffragette
Because I want to set the people free
But really I'm like every other girl you've ever met
And in my heart I only want to be:
Just something pretty, pretty, pretty like a song &c

and soon she is singing love songs with rich Billy, telling him:

All life for me and you
Is now, now, now!

In the third act Nellie leads her band in a display of Socialistic strength to the Savoy Hotel. They are all picturesquely and richly dressed, in a repetition of the famous *Belle of New York* sequence, in marvellous military uniforms which Nellie explains:

This uniform I wear
I hasten to declare
Is not to be construed by you as symbolising strife,
This military cut
Is rather dashing but
It's part of my conception of the sweetly simple life.
To have the public notice me is highly necessary
And nothing else will catch them like a touch of military . .

and she continues:

I've thought the matter out
And feel no sort of doubt
That even in the Simple Life one's costume means a lot
And I confess that I
Can see no reason why
The soldiers should wear the pretty clothes while Socialists should not . .

The law arrives but, most unfairly, it is the relatively consistent Princess Rasslova who is arrested and Nelly gets her Billy while everyone joins in the chorus:

Back, back to the land! . .

before launching into a reprise of an odd paean to the British public schoolboy which Nelly had introduced in the second act:

Oh nothing could be finer
Than little Smith minor
When he gets his flannels on
He is quite the ticket
When he's off for cricket
See him and your heart is gone.
I have got a lover
Very far above a
Lover in a book or play,
Breezy little cool boy
Jolly English schoolboy
You're the one I love today!

The Stage puzzled over the politics and principles of the piece:

. . one wonders if he (McLellan) intended to contrast the ideal Socialism in its most simple and visionary form with the warped Socialism of unreasoning and bloody anarchy . .

and concluded only that Nelly's beliefs were 'uncertain and insincere'. Most, however, accepted the whole subject with a suitable smile, accepted its incongruities and the fact that Edna May was nice and the heroine even if she did say silly things, and left it at that. Unfortunately it was not just that the character of Nelly was dubiously conceived; worse, there was nothing in the material of Miss May's role which allowed her anything like the opportunities of *The Belle of New York*. The show's two best numbers, in fact, fell to subordinate characters. Joe Coyne, having already scored neatly with a quaint piece called 'What's the Use of Going to Bed' did even better with 'Such a Bore' in which he complained at being rusticated by his doctor as a cure for 'what ails him':

Oh I'm going in for grapenuts and wheaten
Farina, for sago and soothing semolina,
I'm going in for afternoon siestas, as resters,
And the only game I'll play is philopena;
Oh, I found that life was easy
But it soon became so breezy
I developed what the doctors called the higgly-pigs
So now I've got to rusticate
And regulate my gusty gait
Or else I'll get an awful case of jiggly-jigs

Coyne's illustration of the jiggly-jigs won him warm applause. Princess Rasslova had her otherwise thankless role redeemed by two good numbers, the pensive 'Cigarette Song' and a Tzigane number 'Take the Road' in which she, in her turn, roused her followers to duty. This latter proved particularly successful.

To stage *Nelly Neil*, Frohman was obliged to shift *The Beauty of Bath* to the new Hicks Theatre, and Edna May had what was to be her last London opening night on January 10 at the Aldwych Theatre to a warm and welcoming reception:

> [the show was] received with favour; indeed with rather more favour than its intrinsic merits deserved (*Stage*)
>
> a thoroughly comfortable evening with no shock of novelty to disturb digestion . . . old stories and old tunes in a new guise . . (*Times*)

Although *Nelly Neil* had little of the new and interesting about it, it was staged with Frohman's customary elegance and lavishness and, with Edna May at the head of affairs, it seemed likely that the show would have a fair run. But it quickly became evident that Miss May alone could not keep *Nelly Neil* afloat. After fifty performances it was thought necessary to make some swingeing alterations to the show. New songs and new dance routines were interpolated into the ailing musical and the role of the comic detective, Nordheim, was rewritten and expanded into a large and featured comedy role for Fred Wright who was brought in to replace Ells Dagnall. The sisters Lurlina and Verbena Tizzle who had been introduced in imitation of the Portuguese twins in *The Belle of New York* were cut along with their inept duet:

> Oh here come the chiccy sisters Tizzle
> Dressed like a perfect pair of queens
> Life had become a dreary drizzle
> But now they have taught us what it means!

The libretto was tightened up, more comedy was introduced everywhere and the whole piece was made less sprawling and less concentrated upon its star.

The new songs included two for Fred Wright, 'Demon', a number reminiscent of the old 'Hush, the Bogie', and 'Jane the Suffragette' which imitated a recent Tom Costello music-hall hit, while Joe Coyne sang 'They never Would be Missed', another of the self-destructive numbers which authors insisted on including in musicals, this one mocking the various kinds of songs habitually included in modern shows. But, in spite of all remodelling, the writing was on the wall for *Nelly Neil*. Edna May had become engaged and would be quitting the theatre for married life as Mrs Oscar Lewisohn. Had the show been worth saving, Frohman might have recast: after all, *The Belle of Mayfair* had been just as successful with Phyllis Dare and Billie Burke as it had been with Miss May, but *Nelly Neil* was not in the same class as Leslie Stuart's piece and, when Edna May went, so too did *Nelly Neil* after a total of 107 performances. As a farewell gesture, or perhaps to bolster the unimpressive audiences with a few *Belle of New York* fans, Edna May interpolated her old hit 'Follow On' into the show for the last few performances and went out of the London theatrical scene on the same song with which she had entered it nearly a decade previously.

The next opening was at the Savoy where Mrs D'Oyly Carte continued her newest season of Gilbert and Sullivan revivals, succeeding *The Yeomen of the Guard* with *The Gondoliers*. During the year she also brought back *Patience*, but a revival of *The Mikado* was blocked from high up. It was feared it might offend the Japanese Prince Fushimi who was visiting Britain. The ban caused a furore: questions were asked in the House of

Commons and Mr Gladstone himself became involved in the controversy but, finally, *The Mikado* was not produced. To select a replacement, Mrs D'Oyly Carte canvassed her audience and the result came out 1. *Iolanthe* 2. *H.M.S. Pinafore* 3. *Princess Ida* 4. *Pirates of Penzance* 5. *The Sorcerer*, so that *Iolanthe* was produced as the third item of the season.

The third January opening was at the Prince of Wales where the newest Paul Rubens piece was produced by Frank Curzon. *Miss Hook of Holland* had been a long while in coming to fruition. It had originally been planned for the previous year but ill-health, from which he suffered continually, prevented Rubens from completing his show. Finally, it was deemed necessary to bring in a collaborator and the choice fell on Austen Hurgon. Hurgon had been an actor and had appeared in the musical *Miss Wingrove* at the Strand before turning to directing. As a writer he had been responsible the previous year for the play *The Impossible Trio* but his work on the script of *Miss Hook* turned out to be only the first in a long series of musical libretti.

The collaboration was a well-judged one for the book of *Miss Hook of Holland* proved to be altogether more likeable than Rubens' previous efforts. The dreadful sniggeryness which had permeated parts of *Three Little Maids*, *Lady Madcap* and even occasionally *Mr Popple* had been avoided; *Miss Hook* was able to amuse and entertain by its story, its characters and its lines rather than by coy sallies of innuendo or dollops of bad taste. Its story was in the regular vein. Sally Hook is beloved by two gentlemen, the bandmaster Van Vuyt and the dashing Captain Adrian Papp: she returns the feelings of the former. But Sally's father is the owner of the distillery which makes its fortune from the liqueur 'Cream of the Sky' and one day he carelessly loses the paper with the precious recipe written on it. The loafer Slinks finds the paper and sells it to Papp who tries to use it to further his suit with Sally. But Sally is not to be outwitted, and all ends as it should.

The characters of the show were also in the usual mould, though Dutch. G. P. Huntley gave London its first taste of the 'old man' characters he had impersonated so successfully in the provinces at the beginning of his career with a delightful interpretation of the erratic Mr Hook, bumbling his way through his bottles and kegs; Isabel Jay's Sally was a clogged version of most of the other young heroines she had played; whilst Walter Hyde and Herbert Clayton were suitably handsome and vocal pretenders for her hand. Gracie Leigh provided her 'comic maid' and George Barrett as the loafer supplied the usual unctuous comedy element. Refreshingly, however, there were no 'Girls' – Gibson, Sandow or whatever. The chorus was quite simply a chorus.

In choosing Holland for their setting the authors had thought in terms of a fanciful and picturesque production with public appeal, and the simple, careful story and the fun which Hurgon and Rubens embroidered on to that background produced just the right effect. Fortunately, too, Rubens, in spite of his illness, turned out for *Miss Hook* some of his best songs which he chose, in a self-deprecating manner which was no doubt not very sincere, to bill as 'jingles and tunes', with the book being described as 'chatter'.

The success of *Miss Hook of Holland* was never in doubt. Even when the first night opening act ran for two hours, the audience remained entranced and delighted. *The Times* commented acidly:

> Expectations founded on a long course of musical comedies were disappointed and very pleasantly disappointed . .

before going on to deliver some grudging praise:

> Chatter, jingles and tunes without a doubt, a plot with one great improbability

making a gap right through it, the usual restless care to be constantly introducing new and irrelevant episodes, as if in mistrust of the interest of the plot; chatter instead of dialogue, jingles and tunes instead of music; all these old faults were present. But other things not usually present were noticeable – a lightness of touch, a humour not all due to the eccentricities or mannerisms of the players; and certain things usually present were absent – sickly, drawling sentiment and luscious display. The very jingles and tunes had something fresh and clean and gay about them, something that seemed (though indeed it may have been reflected from the book and the action) to mark them off from the 'usual thing'.

The Stage, in line with most other critics, was much less chary of its praise and called *Miss Hook*

one of the brightest, merriest and most enjoyable of light musical entertainments presented for some years past.

The show quickly settled itself into the Prince of Wales Theatre and soon Paul Rubens' songs were a firm part of the town's favourites and things Dutch were all the rage. The hits of the show were many, from Gracie Leigh's delightfully comical 'Flying Dutchman' song:

You've heard of the Flying Dutchman
The story is sad but true
If you'd seen his wife
You'd have flown for your life,
So no wonder the Dutchman flew!

and her saucy counting-up of the petticoats she had been given by her boyfriends in 'A pink Petty from Peter':

I've a little pink petty from Peter
And a little blue petty from John
And I've one green and yellow
From some other fellow
And one that I haven't got on.
I've one made of lovely red flannel
That came from an Amsterdam store
If I meet a new friend
Where on earth will it end
I shall never get in at the door!

to the gentler rhythms of 'Fly away Kite', a charming waltz song for Isabel Jay, or 'The sleepy Canal' in which she joined with tenor Walter Hyde and the chorus.

Harry Grattan had a topical number called 'Harwich to Hook' which opened with two jolly verses before turning into a catalogue of recent events, and he also joined with Gracie Leigh in the merry duet 'Pop, pop, pop!' and with Huntley and Barrett in 'A little Bit of Cheese'. Gwendoline Brogden scored with 'The Cigar he Brought Her', a little Dutch love-story, and Herbert Clayton had a rousing patriotic piece called 'Soldiers of the Netherlands'. 'Tra la la', 'Little Miss wooden Shoes', 'Love is a Carnival', 'The House that Hook Built', 'Bottles' – nearly every number in the show earned huge applause and high music sales. *Miss Hook of Holland* was a genuine hit in which Paul Rubens had finally married success and quality.

With the uneventfulness of a true success, the piece ran on through the whole of 1907 and into 1908, being joined over the Christmas period by a juvenile production playing matinées in which Ida Valli (Mr Hook), Maggie Jarvis (Sally), Clarisse Batchelor

(Papp), Peggy Bethel (Mina) and Archie McCaig as Van Eck were featured. McCaig and Miss Bethel later joined the adult cast and there were a number of other cast changes when Isabel Jay headed a company to Manchester to play *Miss Hook* there over Christmas instead of the usual pantomime. One of the take-overs was Maurice Farkoa who had several new numbers added to the score when he took up the role of the bandmaster.

In December, *Miss Hook* opened on Broadway after Reginald de Koven's attempt to pre-empt it with *The Girls of Holland* had been a dire failure. In spite of out-of-town troubles which included the sacking of comics Al Leech (Hook) and Hallen Mostyn (Slinks) and an ill-prepared first night, the show confirmed its London success and, with Tom Wise and Will West replacing the departed stars and Christie MacDonald scoring a personal success as Sally, it ran at the Criterion for 119 performances before heading for Chicago for the summer. The following year the show continued its world-wide success in Australia where its popularity necessitated a revival before the year was out. Following its initial London run, *Miss Hook* was toured constantly in Britain and reappeared in the West End in 1914, for a further 62 performances at the Prince of Wales, and again as part of J. Bannister Howard's Daly's season of past glories in 1932.

The next so-called musical in town was barely a show. It had a career of one night, on the occasion of the music hall strike, when a mish-mash of music, comedy and variety was squeezed into the framework of a *Morocco Bound* story and christened *A Night with the Stars*. The cast and orchestra were members of the 'National Alliance' who were refusing to appear under the aegis of the music-hall managers and this was their attempt to present a rival attraction themselves. But what stars there were at the Scala Theatre on that one night were mainly in the audience rather than on the stage, lending moral support rather than exposing themselves in the aptly-named 'hotch-potch' put together for the occasion by John F. Preston ('Max Goldberg').

The next offering in the realm of genuine musical theatre was from Seymour Hicks' stable and it followed *The Beauty of Bath* into the Hicks Theatre. As was only right, the new theatre had been launched on Hicks and Miss Terriss but, at the closure of *The Beauty of Bath*, the stars decided to take that piece on a twelve weeks' tour of principal towns so that the new piece at the theatre was opened without them. Hicks was represented, however, by the libretto of *My Darling* for which his *Beauty of Bath* collaborators Charles Taylor, Herbert Haines and Evelyn Baker again provided the songs.

My Darling turned out to be an unimpressive combination of too-familiar elements: on the one hand the *Pink Dominos* couple, each out on the loose in Paris, and inevitably fated to come up against each other; on the other the pure young convent maiden in love with the aristocractic scion who is threatened by some compromising letters written to an old flame. There was also one over-bibulous tenor for whom our hero agrees to deputise with disastrous consequences, that tenor's fiancée, the now obligatory 'sentimental' scene, which made in all an undistinguished piece with echoes of *Campano*, *The New Barmaid*, *Castles in Spain* and all the earlier Hicks musicals. Repetition was everywhere: Marie Studholme as Joy Blossom was obliged to give an imitation of Ellaline Terriss (for whom the role had undoubtedly been originally intended) while Henry Lytton had the unenviable task of replacing Hicks. Archie McCaig was the 'new' Albert Valchera, Helen Kinnaird was Mrs Pomeroy P. Green instead of Mrs Shimmering Black, and the Butterflies line-up of showgirls was just the next in succession to the 'Bath Buns', the 'Gibson Girls' *et al.* Armand Kalisz had the Farkoa part, Clare Greet 'was' Connie Ediss but Barbara Deane who stayed at home was lucky enough to play herself with nothing else to do but sing prettily.

With *My Darling*, Hicks had gone to the well once too often. *The Times* wrote:

> *My Darling* on its 'play' side suggests all the farces we have ever seen and on its 'musical' side all the musical comedies we have ever seen . .

and only the singing of Alice Hollander and Barbara Deane and an impression done by Cyril Clensy and Gladys Marsden appealed to him: 'They are good enough for any of the leading music halls . .' he commented disagreeably. The big scene of the show between the old flame Sylvaine of the Follies and Joy Blossom, in which the young girl impresses the hardened demi-mondaine by her sincerity and her love for Jack and leads the actress to give up the damaging letters for the price of a chaste kiss from the pure maid, should have been the dramatic highlight of the evening. But in spite of the efforts of Miss Studholme and the fine actress Beryl Faber it could barely raise itself above the welter of old material. Nor was the music particularly notable. A couple of interpolated numbers, 'Hats off to the King' sung patriotically by Henry Lytton and 'The shady Side of Bond Street' featuring Kalisz did well and Barbara Deane sang an appealing piece called 'Songs my Mother Sang' in which she again succeeded in bringing in pieces of popular songs such as 'Home, sweet Home' and 'Killarney'. Herbert Haines composed a number called 'The Glowworm' for Joy Blossom but it came nowhere near Lincke's now famous piece in quality, and out of an ordinary score probably his most successful piece was a lively café song for Alice Hollander called 'Zip, zip, zip!' which she performed with eight dancing waiters.

It had been rumoured before the production of *My Darling* that it was merely a stopgap to keep the theatre open during the absence of Hicks and his wife; the show was to hold the fort until their return and then tour. Hicks denied the story: *My Darling* was being produced for a West End run. When the piece closed hastily after only seven weeks the old rumour arose again, but there can be little doubt that it was not the truth, and that the show had been intended to run. Hicks and Miss Terriss had no new vehicle in which to return to their theatre and it was not until September that they were able to come back with a fresh show. *My Darling* was replaced with the play *Brewster's Millions* and went out hopefully into the provinces for the rest of its natural life.

The next new entry was no more successful, though it was very different in character. *The Gipsy Girl* had already been tried out in the provinces after its original production in Liverpool in 1905, with some small success. Its author/composer Claude Arundale arranged for it to be showcased at a matinée at the Waldorf Theatre and it was subsequently taken up by a gentleman named Benbrick Blanchard who formed a company, Musical Productions Ltd., with the object of presenting a commercial run of the show at the Waldorf.

The Gipsy Girl opened on 22 March. Blanchard had assembled a fine cast including the author's sisters, Sybil and Grace, Fred Eastman, Leonard Russell, Gordon Cleather, John Hay, Andrée Corday and Annie Esmond, and Arundale had done some considerable work on his libretto, but the West End production of *The Gipsy Girl* emerged as a very second-rate rehash of *The Bohemian Girl*.

> No-one in the play and no part of the play could arouse a spark of interest. From beginning to end it was well-meaning and dull. There was nothing really bad in it and nothing really good, nothing really funny, nothing really pretty, nothing really at all. We have seen far worse productions and found them more interesting. To be moved to dislike is better than to be left absolutely cold. (*Times*)

> . . there is no occasion to say anything severe about an agreeable and unpretentious

> work [which] may prove attractive enough to hold its own as an entertainment in the West End (*Stage*)

The show was competent and correct but it had very little in the way of special attractions for the public beyond the performance of Sybil Arundale in the title role. As the gipsy, Katrina (who, of course, turns out to be the well-bred child of the Squire stolen in infancy), Miss Arundale set out to confirm the popularity she had won in *My Lady Molly* and *The Cingalee*, and her brother tried to give her all the opportunities necessary. She appeared, as she had so successfully done in *My Lady Molly*, disguised as a particularly fine boy to sing 'If only I'd been Born a Boy', she sang a more traditional number in skirts 'Sing on, little Gipsy Maid', and followed up with a song yearning for 'The ideal Lover', she appeared in a ballerina outfit to dance a classical piece and less grandly clad to perform a Polish mazurka while all the time furthering the story of love and revenge which led up to her discovery of a family and a husband.

Fred Eastman supplied traditional comedy as a travelling showman, Aubrey Fitzgerald repeated his standard 'dude' and Gordon Cleather was the romantic baritone hero with a ballad entitled 'Love Is a golden Crown'. Andrée Corday trotted out her 'French maid' and tenor John M. Hay as mine host rendered 'The home-brewed Ale' while sister Grace Arundale was a soubrette singing of being 'On the Shelf'. *The Gipsy Girl* was quickly and obviously in trouble. The amateurish management of Benbrick Blanchard had done its sums badly and poor houses soon led to cash flow problems. The producer announced that the show was to be withdrawn after its fourth week and sent out on the road where it would be largely re-written before returning to London in a second edition. Bookings were made, with the tour set to start at Kennington immediately after the London closing, but when the fourth week's treasury call arrived it arrived empty handed. Blanchard asked his cast to wait twenty-four hours for their salary but some were suspicious, having already had experience of their producer's money methods. As 'Blanchard's Amusements Association' he was taking a 10% agent's fee from the artists he had cast in the show! Aubrey Fitzgerald demanded that he be paid in cash as, under the circumstances, the management's cheque did not seem very attractive, but Blanchard turned up on the following night with a cheque. Fitzgerald refused to go on for the second act until cash was produced and, in the end, his understudy completed the performance – the last performance in London or anywhere else of *The Gipsy Girl*. Blanchard's Musical Productions went into receivership and the proposed tour vanished into thin air. The Kennington Theatre hurriedly brought in *Our Boys* to fill the gap and *The Gipsy Girl* was laid to rest.

With the successful productions of *The Gay Grisette*, *The Blue Moon* and *The Dairymaids*, Robert Courtneidge had become a producer to be reckoned with. His next venture, however, was a step in a very different direction to that which he had taken with his earlier shows. In collaboration with his *Dairymaids* co-author Alexander Thompson, he prepared an adaptation of Henry Fielding's great novel *Tom Jones* which he had set with songs by Charles Taylor and Edward German – altogether a different level of endeavour to the frankly farcical tone taken in, most particularly, *The Dairymaids*.

Tom Jones had been the subject of a number of previous stage musicals and plays, the most successful of which had undoubtedly been Robert Buchanan's 1886 play *Sophia* which had played over twelve months at the Vaudeville Theatre. The earliest musical adaptation had been in French, but an English *Tom Jones* by Joseph Reed had been unsuccessfully produced at Covent Garden in the eighteenth century and Thomas Dibdin, with a piece written for the Surrey, had been among those who, with more or less success, had followed his example. 1907 marked the second centenary of the birth of Fielding and it also marked the production of the best conceived and most successful musical version of his most famous work.

Courtneidge's *Tom Jones* started with much in its favour. Edward German, so successful with his other 'English' music, was an ideal choice to set this most English of picaresque romances, and Charles Taylor's abilities as a lyric writer were unquestioned. It remained to be seen, however, how Courtneidge and Thompson would tackle the task of making a suitable libretto out of the huge bulk of Fielding's masterpiece. In the event their approach to the matter was sensible. Subsidiary events and characters were omitted and the main thread of the romantic tale of Tom and Sophia, including his lapse with Lady Bellaston, was retained as the backbone of the plot. In order to introduce a sufficient low comedy interest, they rewrote the character of the schoolmaster/barber Benjamin Partridge as a principal comedian in the same way that Charlie Stephenson had introduced the comical Lurcher into the romantic story of *Dorothy* to give the required relief. Local and period colour were added plentifully so that the resulting piece made no pretence at being a full representation of Fielding's *Tom Jones* but retained the essentials of the adventure and the lusty flavouring of the book while packaging it neatly into a three-act comic opera form in the happy tradition of *Dorothy*.

Tom Jones was given its initial showing out of London, at the Prince's Theatre in Manchester which had been the cradle of so many important early musicals of the British tradition. Its quality was immediately evident, its performance excellent, and it was clear that Courtneidge had produced a musical of a particularly high standard of construction and musicianship, the legitimate heir of the old light opera tradition marked by *The Bohemian Girl* and *Maritana*, modified by Cellier into a more light-hearted being, and now stabilised into a play of romantic, comic and musical values of the highest degree. *Tom Jones* opened at the Apollo Theatre in London little more than a fortnight later and the verdict of Manchester was confirmed. *The Times*, while complaining that the show had little to do with Fielding, expressed its thanks that at least *Tom Jones* was not musical comedy and then promptly compared it to *The Tales of Hoffmann*. *The Stage* was more forthcoming:

> . . interesting and delightful from beginning to end . . avoided the danger of being too 'literary' . . . selects the incidents best suited to comic opera treatment . . [the lyrics are] of an order of merit which is all too seldom encountered in modern musical plays . . . [German] fully maintained his reputation as a weaver of dainty old English melodies and dance . . . a score of general excellence . .

The opening night audience was delighted with the piece and the stars of the show were called in front of the curtain again and again, not only at the final curtain but between the acts. The cast was headed by two most popular singers in Hayden Coffin (Tom) and Ruth Vincent (Sophia) and these two in particular were liberally provided with the very best of German. Sophia had the evening's undoubted popular hit in the form of a brilliant waltz song, a soprano showpiece which has remained loved and sung ever since:

> For tonight, for tonight,
> Let me dream out my dream of delight
> Tra-la-la Tra-la-la-la-la-la-la
> And purchase of sorrow a moment's respite

She also showed her skills in a less taxing 'Love Makes the Heart a Garden Fair' and 'By Night and Day' while Coffin sang of 'A little foundling Boy' and 'If Love's Content' and the two joined effectively for the charming duet 'For aye my Love' leading into a first act finale which rose to almost operatic levels.

To balance the romantic scenes, there was plenty of fun. Dan Rolyat as the strange-kneed Partridge declared himself:

Benjamin Partridge, a person of parts,
Versed in the healing and medical arts
Fortune or weather prepared to foretell
Doctor, adviser and barber as well.
Come and I'll shave you and if you are ill
Blister and bleed you and throw in a pill
Bring you back cheap from the edge of the grave
The closer you're fisted, the closer the shave!

and then brought down the house with his impromptu antics in search of his pet leech, Lizzie, escaped from her jar in the inn at Upton. Lizzie's perambulations grew as the run progressed until she found her way definitively into the show's script.

Carrie Moore, as Sophia's maid, Honour, contributed a soubrette performance of unusual excellence and scored with a little song describing what a girl did 'all for a green ribbon to tie in her hair'. There were other excellent pieces, from Squire Western's 'On a January Morning in Summersetshire' to Gregory's 'Gurt Uncle Jan Tappit' and some fine ensembles. The critics were almost unanimous in nominating the first act madrigal 'Here's a Paradox for Lovers' as the most musically successful piece in the show, but there was equal popular approval for the lusty rendering of 'The Barley Mow' in which Jay Laurier and Carrie Moore at the head of a Somerset quartet declared:

We'll drink to the Barley Mow
In a ocean, a river,
An 'ogs'ead, a gallon jar
A quart pot, a pint pot
A nipperkin, a pipperkin,
Under a green bow

Honour, Partridge and Gregory also had a merry 'Laughing Trio' in the second act and later a trio, 'Say a well-worn Saw'.

Armed with such a battery of winning songs and ensembles and a brisk and lively book, *Tom Jones* rolled along to excellent effect in the hands of its carefully-chosen cast – a cast amongst which, in tiny roles, stand out three names destined for greater things: Dorothy Ward as 'Etoff', Harry Welchman as 'an officer' and 15-year-old Cicely Courtneidge making her début as 'Rosie Lucas'.

In spite of its excellent reviews and its popularity, *Tom Jones* was not to remain unaltered. Apart from the ravages wrought on the script by 'Lizzie the Leech' there were additions and alterations made to the score. On the night of the hundredth performance, Ruth Vincent introduced a new number, one that was destined to become as famous and popular as the waltz song:

I'll wear a petticoat of muslin said Dream o'Day Jill
And a great gilded coach shall carry me to a church on the hill
When somebody comes to marry me
A gentleman great of noble estate
At the church on the hill, said Dream o'Day Jill
Heigh ho, heigh ho, for nobody less shall marry me . .

To add even further to the show's musical gems there was a vivacious new number for Carrie Moore:

> As all the maids and I one day
> Were in the meadow a-making hay
> There came, the lane tit-tuppin' down
> A gentleman fine from London town.
> And, oh! he looked at me,
> He looked askance at me!
> I felt my cheeks go flaming red
> I didn't have eyes in the back of my head
> But I knew that he looked
> I knew that he looked
> I knew that he looked at me!

Both these songs were to lyrics by Charles Taylor who, with *Tom Jones*, had achieved his best work since Courtneidge had chivvied him out of the silk trade and into the world of the theatre a decade earlier. But they were, sadly, to be his last songs for, on June 27, at the age of 47 he died. Taylor had come late to the theatre and had begun by supplying topical verses for Courtneidge's Manchester pantomimes. Coming to London, he was soon writing lyrics for the best houses and his credits included work for *The Silver Slipper*, *The Medal and the Maid*, *The School Girl*, *The Catch of the Season*, *The Talk of the Town*, *My Darling* and, finally, *Tom Jones* which contains his most enduring work, not the least his last song, 'Dream o'Day Jill'.

Accolades for the show continued. After that century performance *The Era* wrote:

> The success of *Tom Jones* has shown once again, as B. C. Stephenson and Alfred Cellier showed us in *Dorothy*, that English comic opera has no need to be founded on adapted French libretti when there is such excellent material to be found in our English authors . . . we are reminded of the best days of the Savoy . . .

But, inexplicably, after ten more performances, *Tom Jones* was removed from the Apollo and sent out on tour. Ruth Vincent, Dan Rolyat and Carrie Moore retained their London roles with Harry Welchman taking over as Tom with a new number 'We redcoat Soldiers Serve the King'. It was announced that the show would tour, as *Merrie England* had, returning to town in the following spring for a further season. But when the spring came, Courtneidge preferred to revive *The Dairymaids* and *Tom Jones* was not seen again.

In the meanwhile it had been produced on Broadway where it had been received with the same critical approbation it had received in London. *The Era*'s American correspondent wrote:

> The taste of New York in the matter of light, sane and sensible musical entertainment is now undergoing a conclusive test. If audiences want good, ringing, refreshing opera intermingled with graceful, imaginative and romantic fiction, it has Robert Courtneidge and Edward German's *Tom Jones* at the Astor Theatre. If, on the other hand, they want horse-collar humour, slap-stick comedy and cheap variety acts they can be accommodated in half a dozen other playhouses along Broadway.

If New York was indeed up for testing, then it failed the test. Van Rensselaer Wheeler and Louise Gunning lasted at the Astor Theatre for only a short season while much less substantial works than *Tom Jones*[1] prospered around them. *Tom Jones* never had a run

[1] An interesting interpolation into the score for New York was the *Merrie England* 'King Neptune' number, previously unheard there and sung by comedy star William Norris as Partridge.

of the proportions earned by a number of the lighter works of its time but, unlike nearly all of them, it remained popular with performers and audiences alike for many years. In any other country it would have been taken permanently into the repertoire of the national opera or light opera theatre but in Britain it owes its continued life largely to amateur and concert societies and to the countless sopranos who enjoy so well singing the Waltz Song or 'Dream o'Day Jill'.

Another attempt at light opera followed *Tom Jones* into London at only a fortnight's distance. *Lady Tatters* had a slightly less distinguished pedigree. It was a free adaptation of the novel *A Set of Rogues* (which had already been used for Ada Reeve's *Moll, the Rogue*) done by Herbert Leonard, manager of the Prince's Theatre, Poplar, and the occasional author of dramas such as *On Active Service* for the Surrey Theatre. The lyrics were by Roland Carse and the music by Walter Slaughter, attempting in this to return to the more educated style of his early work, *Marjorie*.

Lady Tatters had a copyright performance at the Marlborough Theatre, after which it was taken up by the actor Ells Dagnall who arranged to produce it at the Shaftesbury Theatre in association with Norman J. Norman and Charles E. Hamilton. A strong cast was gathered together including the ex-Savoyards Courtice and Louie Pounds and Walter Passmore with the American actress Claudia Lasell taking the title role of the showgirl who masquerades as a dead Lady in order to set that lady's affairs to rights. The creative side was well cared for too: Espinosa for the dances, Comelli designing the costumes, Herbert Cottesmore directing the stage but, although it was of a higher quality than *The Gipsy Girl*, *Lady Tatters* suffered a similar fate as a victim of public indifference.

The critics joined the apathy, *The Times* noting:

> It would be very easy to be angry with *Lady Tatters*, with its author, its lyricist (especially perhaps its lyricist with his horrible rhymes), its composer, its producer, most of its players, its chorus and its orchestra (which was usually at loggerheads with the chorus and the players). But it is not worth the powder and shot.

The cast did their best to enliven the show sufficiently to make it popular. Walter Passmore as the grotesque Seth Lewys embroidered his role ('I'm a terror when I'm roused, but I'm a heavy sleeper') and made great capital out of the search for a dog to join him in his principal number 'The Fiddler and the Dog'. The dog was required to bark at certain places in the music and Passmore insisted that a machine was no good, he must have a live dog. One was finally found and the number duly performed:

> A fiddler fiddled fast and slow
> Yet he fiddled no air
> He fiddled high, he fiddled low
> But why, I'm not aware.
> He had an old decrepit dog
> Which had no hair nowhere
> The fiddle of all air was bare
> The dog was bare of hair.

The fiddler tries hair restorer on the beast until:

> The fiddler couldn't bear the dog
> It looked so like a bear

and the barber is called in. He shaves the dog so much that only its bark is finally left and the fiddler curiously plods on:

With a fiddle that's without a tune
And a bark without a dog!

After the indifferent opening Slaughter tried to make the show more attractive with new songs for Marie George, Passmore, Courtice Pounds and Miss Lasell, bringing the show's total to a hefty 27 numbers, and some major alterations were made to the book. *The Era*, taking a second look at the piece, surprisingly recanted and judged that 'it is now one of the brightest attractions in town' but the show still failed to arouse public interest and *Lady Tatters* folded after its eightieth performance.

The withdrawal of *The New Aladdin* at the Gaiety left the company's exchequer severely damaged. The attempt at a change in policy had not been at all well received and, with the next show, George Edwardes was quick to return to something more like the established Gaiety style. *The Girls of Gottenberg* was written by George Grossmith and L. E. Berman and was based on a recent incident in Germany where a cobbler from the village of Koepenick had succeeded in making the German hierarchy look extremely silly by masquerading as a high-up official for some considerable time before being found out.

It was decided to base a role for Teddy Payne on the German cobbler and the authors came up with Max Moddelkopf – barber, army deserter and valet to the Prince Otto of Saxe-Hilversum (George Grossmith) the commander of the Blue Hussars. The occasion for Moddelkopf to put on his false feathers is an amatory one. The Blue Hussars are quartered in Rottenberg which lives up to its name for them by having a population which includes only one girl. They are looking forward to being transferred to Gottenberg where there is a ladies' university. But when orders come through it is the rival Red Hussars who have been given the desired posting and evasive action has to be taken. The envoy bringing the grim news is disposed of and little Max takes his place to order the Blue Hussars to Gottenberg. Once they are there he proceeds, in his new character, to issue all sorts of alarming orders and to make love to the daughter of the Burgomaster. Otto also gets himself involved in a love affair with the innkeeper's pretty daughter who fortunately turns out to be his destined fiancée who has swapped places with the village girl for a change of air. By the end of the evening everyone is suitably paired off.

If the setting, in deepest Prussia rather than the Strand or Paris, was rather unusual for a Gaiety musical, the material which went into the make-up of the piece was as traditionally varied as always. The Gaiety stars Payne, Grossmith and Miss Millar were given plenty of opportunities and the other regulars and the newcomers all had their due places and pieces. The songs supplied by the resident team of Caryll and Monckton to lyrics by Adrian Ross and Basil Hood did not include any overriding hits, but *The Girls of Gottenberg* introduced several numbers which won their fair share of popularity. The best-liked features of the evening were a Lionel Monckton duet in which Payne and Miss Millar sang the tale of 'Two little Sausages':

Once in the window of a ham and beef shop
Two little sausages sat
One was a lady and the other was a gentleman
Sausages are like that.
He fell a victim to her simple charm
And her form he would have embraced
But a sausage, you see, never has any arm
And the lady hadn't got any waist!

and Grossmith's rendering of his own number 'Otto of the Roses' (music by Monckton):

> Oh, the girls all call me Otto
> They know my heart never closes
> If you don't like what you've got, oh
> Pick another from the grotto
> Is the motto
> Of Otto of the Roses.

There were plenty of other good-humoured moments: Max Moddelkopf describing himself as 'The special Envoy', the large American Violet Hall (in loco Connie Ediss) singing of 'Tina Strauss', the fooling of Arthur Hatherton as the half-blind innkeeper who does not notice his daughter's substitution, and, of course, Gertie Millar singing, dancing and amusing if not noticeably well supplied with top rate songs. Basil Hood's 'Berlin on the Spree' provided her with an attractive finale and there was some mirth in the Wagnerian parodies of 'Rhinegold' but Hood fell far below his best standards with a tasteless piece of nonsense called 'The titsy bitsy Girl' which proved, nevertheless, perfectly popular. Lionel Monckton, too, failed to improve on the tired old flirting theme in a piece called 'A Glass of Beer', but Miss Millar's appeal shone clear through the more mediocre material and even *The Times* was moved to remark loftily that 'Miss Gertie Millar showed that her resources are not so limited as previous performances seemed to show'. May de Souza as the aristocrat disguised as a peasant gave a couple of numbers in an accomplished fashion and Jean Aylwin, elevated to principal status after her success in *The New Aladdin*, sang of 'The Girls of Gottenberg', covering her Scots accent with a thick Prussian one.

Whatever its shortcomings, *The Girls of Gottenberg* clearly had public appeal. It was received rapturously by the Gaiety theatre-goers on a triumphant first night – the Gaiety was back giving its customers something like they wanted to see and they were grateful for it. The critics, too, were mostly pleased with the new show although *The Times* commented irrelevantly that the play wasn't as funny as the real incident, without suggesting how the real incident might have been fitted on to the Gaiety stage. *The Era* assured:

> *The Girls of Gottenberg* is one of the prettiest and pleasantest musical plays that have ever been done at the Gaiety. The book is based on a really comic 'notion'; the lyrics are smartly and neatly written; and the piece is cast with admirable judgement and liberality . .

and *The Stage*:

> A bustling piece of almost pantomimic fun . . . too farcical to have any sting of satire . . it is for amusement . .

Pretty it certainly was. Apart from the delightful scenery and the colourful military and peasant costumes, there was a line-up of feminine beauty which even the Gaiety itself would have found it hard to equal at any other period of its existence, including such girls as Gladys Cooper, Julia James, Olive May, Edith Lee and the gloriously graceful Kitty Mason whose dancing of the new two-step with Robert Hale was one of the highlights of the evening. And it was certainly pleasant: easy on the ear and on the eye in the true Gaiety tradition with only the occasional topical note or sketched impression to lend a very gentle bite to the proceedings.

At one stage *The Girls of Gottenberg* even gained the dubious honour of being burlesqued on the London stage. H. G. Pélissier's *Follies* at the Tivoli were rising steadily into prominence and their variety programme began to include parodies of current shows. Two of the chosen shows were *The Girls of Gottenberg* and *The Merry Widow*, both from the George Edwardes stable. Pélissier was unwise enough to use music from those shows in his burlesques and Edwardes quickly brought an injunction to prevent 'his' music being thus pirated, which forced *The Follies* to back down. The show quickly settled in and continued to delight London as it began to appear in theatres all round the world. Before Christmas it had opened in South Africa (with Foster Courtenay as Max) in Australia (starring Fanny Dango and George Lauri) and in India where Bandmann's voracious touring company was becoming noticeably quick with its reproductions of the latest London shows.

For the British Christmas, Edwardes decided to send *The Girls of Gottenberg* to the Prince's, Manchester for a season and so, while Coralie Blythe took over in London, Gertie Millar headed a company of eighty to provide a little opposition for *Miss Hook of Holland* at the Manchester Gaiety. The show had, by then, undergone the usual additions and alterations in its score. The two hundredth performance was marked by the addition of four new numbers including 'A common little Girl' for Gertie Millar, a diabolo trio for Payne, Grossmith and Miss Millar, and the topical song 'In Jericho'. In America it was to suffer even further at the hands of the 'improvers' after which it enjoyed a reasonably successful run at Broadway's Knickerbocker Theatre in 1908. It closed at the Gaiety after 303 performances but continued to be a favourite touring piece for many years. In August 1908 it was briefly seen in the West End again when the No.1 touring company featuring Payne and the music hall comedienne Happy Fanny Fields played two weeks at the Adelphi before beginning their national tour, and it also gained the unusual distinction of being produced in Paris, which normally shunned the musical productions of the British stage. In October 1912, *The Girls of Gottenberg* under the title of *Les Jolies Filles de Gottenberg* was staged at the Théâtre du Moulin Rouge in the wake of Monckton's Parisian triumph with *The Quaker Girl*. Although it could not challenge the success of its stable-mate, Timmory and de Marsan's adaptation achieved an honourable record for a British musical in France.

The next London production of 1907 proved to be one of the most important for some time, though it was not a British musical. Edwardes had experimented at Daly's with the French operette and the home-made continental musical; now he had bought an Austrian piece, *Die lustige Witwe*, which, translated into a new and anglicised version by Edward Morton and/or Basil Hood (both eventually claimed and disclaimed the libretto), he presented at Daly's on 8 June as *The Merry Widow*. Lehár's gloriously lighthearted melodies, pretty Lily Elsie (at last cast suitably) and the fertile comedy of George Graves all contributed to make the new show into a huge and deserved success. London witnessed once more the éclat which had characterised the arrival from abroad of *La Grande Duchesse* and *The Belle of New York*, and *The Merry Widow* started a vogue amongst producers for the Viennese musical in the same way that *La Grande Duchesse* had opened up the field for the opéra-bouffe.

The home-grown musical had had virtually everything its own way – give or take a *Véronique* or a *La Poupée* – since the last of the great French opéras-bouffes had run its course two decades earlier. Now Lehár in particular and Viennese music in general was staking a claim in the theatres of London. It would not be, like *The Belle of New York* had been, a flash in the stylistic pan, a novelty without a follow-up. The Viennese musical would be around, filling houses, for some years to come although none would ever equal *The Merry Widow* either in brilliance or in success. *The Merry Widow* was to stay at Daly's for over two years, 778 performances, setting a record which had been bettered up to that time only by *Dorothy* and *A Chinese Honeymoon*, and making itself a memorable and enduring place in the history of the musical theatre.

There was no further new piece seen in London until August when Frank Curzon produced a new Howard Talbot musical at the Apollo. The libretto for *The Three Kisses* was by Leedham Bantock who had headed in the direction of comic opera with *The White Chrysanthemum*. For the new piece he allied himself with lyricist Percy Greenbank in the place of Arthur Anderson but the partnership did not prove to be as fortunate as the earlier combination.

The plot which the authors chose was a creaky one based on the old 'family curse' theme and set in sunny Italy where such things are known operatically to flourish. Into their story of Neapolitan nonsense Bantock and Greenbank tried to insert as much modern entertainment as possible. There were songs and dances, a motor car imitation, a skit on the fashionable thought-reading act, the Zancigs and indeed in the second act more pantomime than musical theatre. The music, too, ranged widely from such numbers as 'When Nelly Came to Naples' which the unfortunate Ethel Irving was obliged to tackle, to the more lyrical 'Life's a Song' or 'The Neapolitan Boat Song', both of which Talbot's publishers printed while declining to put out the full score. Walter Passmore found himself in a second flop after *Lady Tatters*, this time playing an old man in a wheelchair, and Ethel Irving, who had already suffered *Ladyland*, was the Contessa di Ravolgi – but only for one month. In fact it was fortunate for Miss Irving that the piece ran no longer as its failure permitted her to take up the title role in W. Somerset Maugham's *Lady Frederick* which secured her the greatest success of her career.

The Three Kisses was an ill-conceived and poorly written piece from which no-one gained any credit, and was a rare lapse of judgement on the part of Frank Curzon. *The Times* could only say:

> The worst thing about *The Three Kisses* is not its absurdities nor its rough and heavy fun. It is the total lack of the lyric spirit, of fancy or delicacy, of atmosphere and grace . .

and of its scenic acme, the eruption of Vesuvius, which closed Act I:

> [it] reminded us of lighted advertisements that flash up, change colour and go out in Piccadilly or Tottenham Court Road . . .

Alterations were not even seriously attempted. After one month *The Three Kisses* was shuttered at the Apollo and only the rather indiscriminate Bandmann took it up to inflict upon the Far East.

London had not seen Seymour Hicks and Ellaline Terriss since they had gone into the country with *The Beauty of Bath*, and their return to the Aldwych in September was keenly awaited. The piece which Hicks had written to replace the ill-fated *My Darling* was set in Scotland and entitled *The Gay Gordons*. The lyrics for the new show had been written by Arthur Wimperis and it had been intended to entrust the musical part to Hicks' musical director, Frank Tours, but Tours demurred, preferring to limit himself to a couple of interpolated numbers, and eventually the bulk of the score was given over to Guy Jones, brother of the more famous Sidney.

In true Hicks tradition, *The Gay Gordons* relied very heavily on its two principals, and was built entirely around their relationship in what was essentially a commonplace story but one which was told with a great deal of charm. Mrs McLeod has fostered the

[1] a fashionable thought reading act.

young Angus but, now that he is grown, she realises he is in fact the lost heir to the Earl of Meltrose and she secretly sets to work to establish that fact. Angus has fallen in love with Mrs McLeod's 'help', Peggy, who is really the daughter of an American millionaire who has changed clothes with the daughter of a Punch and Judy man in search of true and untitled love. Circumstances bring together and part the lovers for two and a half hours of song, dance and sentiment until they are united and titled at the final curtain.

The Gay Gordons was rather more dependent upon its scenes, both sentimental and comic, than most of the preceding Hicks musicals. There were few choruses and the songs and production numbers were kept carefully in their place and were not allowed to intrude too far into the piece nor to stop its forward motion. The dialogue found Hicks at his unpredictable best. Whereas the crucial scene of *My Darling* had failed to come off, in *The Gay Gordons* he managed to build up his important moments with a simple skill which put them suitably into relief. There were also no 'Bath Buns', no 'Gibson Girls': the delightful, though now rather hackneyed, showgirl convention was given a welcome rest.

The Times puzzled as to what the piece ought to be called. It eschewed 'play' because of the songs, refused 'musical comedy' because of the lack of choruses and of lavish display and finally settled on 'play with music' which it described as 'boisterous fun tempered with domestic passion . . ' *The Era*, too, stressed the strength of the book:

> Mr Seymour Hicks is a magician who is able to put new vitality into musical plays and to laugh at the forebodings of quidnuncs fond of proclaiming the inanities of the form of theatrical production of which – whatever its failings – the public are far from being tired. The usual complaints tabulated are want of plot, lack of sustained dramatic interest, flabbiness of dialogue, and absence of coherence; but these faults cannot be charged to *The Gay Gordons* produced on Wednesday with all the pleasant accompaniments of success; for in the latest production there is a capital story, a plethora of sentiment, not a little pathos and a pretty touch of romance that might go to the making of a first class comedy. Indeed, at times one becomes so interested in the development of the character and the sundry happenings that the introduction of a topical song is to be regarded as a banality not to be tolerated.

The score was not insignificant, but varied in quality and style as Jones tried to cover as many of the popular forms of musical comedy song as possible. He was most successful with a beautiful opening chorus, 'The Dawn', written for soprano solo and chorus and for which the singer Georgina Delmar, a former Carmen from the Carl Rosa, was specially engaged; and with a pretty ballad called 'White Heather' for Barbara Deane who, as was now traditional in a Hicks/Terriss musical, was added as a character quite superfluous to the action simply to sing a brace of the ballads of which she made a speciality. On this occasion her second song, 'Wonderful Night', was written by Frank Tours, and Miss Deane used her limpid soprano to good effect in both pieces.

Another feature of Jones' score was the second act opening, a strong baritone solo and chorus called 'Here's a Health to the Graeme'. In a lighter vein he supplied a tune to a rather tasteless lyric by C. H. Bovill, 'Flies around the Honeypot', in which Zena Dare as the Punch and Judy girl disguised as the heiress brushes off what she sees as mercenary advances, but was much happier with a series of songs for Miss Terriss: 'Daddy, Do', 'See-saw' and 'You, you, You'. Miss Terriss' most successful song, however, was 'Humpty and Dumpty', an interpolated number written by the young Herman Darewski who had been responsible for 'My little Hyacinth'.

Humpty and Dumpty were just boy and girl
Humpty called Dumpty his peach and his pearl
She seemed to like it – he risked an embrace
Dumpty responded by smacking his face.
Humpty was merely the average man
Dumpty a girl on the usual plan
She ran away, very shocked, so he thought
But Dumpty took very good care she was caught.

In the same vein the song follows their marriage, his misbehaviour and the arrival of a little third, Tumpty. If the lyric sounded precious it was nevertheless set to a clever tune by the young composer and Miss Terriss played it simply and charmingly with the aid of two knotted handkerchiefs to represent the protaganists.

The Gay Gordons was by no means all romance and sentiment. Fred Emney and Sydney Fairbrother provoked much hilarity as the Punch and Judy stall-keepers ('there's too much competition in show business these days, what with Bernard Shaw and Hall Caine') and A. W. Baskcomb was their comically asinine assistant, while Will Bishop as an eccentric Highland corporal swirled his kilts effectively in a very odd Highland dance. But the show's best moments came in the scenes between Angus and Peggy and a touching dialogue between Mrs McLeod (Rosina Filippi) and Angus, a parallel to the successful scene between the same two performers in *The Beauty of Bath*, but none the less effective for that.

In spite of a few inexplicable boos from the gallery, *The Gay Gordons* received an excellent first-night reception. The disappointment of *My Darling* could be put aside and the Hicks-Terriss team was firmly re-established in London for another good run – 229 performances. During the run the score was given the usual reinforcement of new and sometimes extraneous music, including 'Lucia' by the American songwriter Manuel Klein and a French chanson rewritten by Arthur Wimperis as 'Come along, little Girls', but its strength remained in its scenes rather than in the decorations supplied by the songs and dances.

Like *The Girls of Gottenberg* and *Miss Hook of Holland*, *The Gay Gordons* was booked for an outside season at Christmas and Zena Dare and Stanley Brett headed to Scotland for a good holiday season. The London production continued on through to April and *The Gay Gordons* subsequently toured widely and successfully both in Britain and through the Empire.

It had been a year of wide contrasts in the West End – big, though widely differing new successes such as *The Merry Widow*, *Miss Hook of Holland*, *The Girls of Gottenberg* and *Tom Jones* and extremely short-lived failures, most of which had been ill-judged attempts to capture some of the flavour of light or comic opera which German mastered in *Tom Jones*.

In the provinces there was less that was new. The perennial favourities still toured regularly: *The Gay Parisienne*, *The Toreador*, *The New Barmaid*, *The Lady Slavey*, *A Chinese Honeymoon*, *San Toy*, with the special provincial phenomena such as Harry Starr, still leading his *Otto the Outcast* company through long engagements, or Cordiner and Swinerd's *Dare-Devil Dorothy*, mixed with companies presenting the newest town hits, sometimes three and four companies at a time. The new pieces brought forth little of significance. Clarence Corri sent out his old show *Miss Chiquita* in a revised version as *Dancing Girl of Spâin* and a musicalised version of the farce *After the Ball* was produced as *The Pick of the Bunch* for the smaller circuits, ending eventually in the music halls.

At Cardiff, in May, a new musical called *The Maid and the Motor Man* made an appearance. It had a book by J. Hickory Wood and its music was the work of the music teacher and ballad composer Alessandro Romilli. Italian-born but long resident in Britain, Romilli had been conductor at a number of theatres but his greatest achievement had been as an accompanist notably, on one occasion, for Patti. This, his first musical score, was supplemented by numbers from the show's conductor, Ernest Bucalossi. The story was of a chauffeur in love with his master's daughter. Caught in an amatory situation, he is sacked and flees to America where he strikes oil, returning in time to save his former master from disaster and to claim his beloved's hand.

A company of sixty was directed by the provincial veteran Victor Stevens and the result was sufficiently satisfactory to allow the piece to be sent out again (having been musically done over by Bucalossi who now got the major music credit) with an altogether more ambitious cast including Aubrey Fitzgerald, Ruth Lincoln, M. R. Morand, Albert Valchera and Lulu Valli.

The Scarlet Patrol, produced at Kingston, was written by the actor St John Hamund with music by Owen Trevine. It had a flavour of *An Adamless Eden* or *Ladyland* about it as it dealt with a certain Miss Amazon North, leader of a feminist group, who finds she can only retain her inheritance, a south sea island, if she marries a certain young lord. Since her lawyer stands to inherit if she fails to fulfil, skulduggery takes place ending with Miss North and an army of ladies taking over the island. As police (The Scarlet Patrol) they have their difficulties (and two comic trial scenes), but our heroine has meanwhile fallen for a young journalist and she renounces her island for him – but, lo! he is the very young lord she has been willed to marry and all can end happily. The songs were in the modern mould and passed muster well enough to allow *The Scarlet Patrol* to have a respectable tour.

The Young Lieutenant, which was produced at the Woolwich Artillery was an unambitious mixture of love scenes, nautical scenes and comical scenes involving middle-aged love and jolly servants. Its plot was minimal and its songs and dances unremarkable and it was happy with a minor tour under the guidance of Mrs Annie Hughes.

To supplement the ever-faithful *Dandy Doctor*, Edward Marris produced a new piece called *The Gentleman Jockey* which was first staged in Guernsey before being taken on the road. It dealt with the efforts of the unworthy Frank Snakeworth to do down the 'Gentleman Jockey' of the title. On the eve of the all-important race, the villain has Sir Francis arrested for dangerous motor car driving and it is left to his faithful trainer, Grayson, to ride the horse to victory. The highlight of the piece was the actual race shown on the Bioscope. *The Gentleman Jockey* proved a well-made successor to Marris' earlier pieces and provided him with a good minor touring regular for some years.

Another reasonable tour was undertaken by *The Pet of the Embassy* which had originally been produced by amateurs in Bootle. It was taken up for a professional production starring Witty Watty Walton and reproduced at Eccles from where it toured extensively. One of the take-overs in the cast was a young actor named Ralph Lynn, later to become famous as a comic performer, particularly in the Aldwych farces. *The Pet of the Embassy* was in the traditional farcical style, involving long-lost husbands, mixed-up portmanteaux and mistaken kisses, but principally it supplied a good leading comic part in 'John William Bung', the midshipman who manages during the course of affairs to end up disguised variously as a golf caddie, a Chinaman and His Excellency the Ambassador. Walton was seen to particular advantage in a number entitled 'Would you Like to Hear the Truth about the Matter' which left an imaginable amount of space for improvisation.

A further provincial piece which found itself some audience was *Such a Nice Girl*, produced at Worthing. The authors ingenuously disarmed criticism with a programme note:

> The authors of *Such A Nice Girl* claim no great originality either in their dialogue or plot, it being their intention to provide a bright and amusing entertainment and they leave it to the public to judge whether the method of obtaining hearty laughter justifies the means . . .

Their little tale of high-jinks and disguises in Brighton proved satisfactory to their provincial audiences, and an eighteen-week tour was the result. The piece was revised in 1908 as *The New Girl*.

Short pieces had become, by now, almost entirely the property of the music halls, although during 1907 an operetta entitled *The King's Hat* was produced at the Coronet Theatre with a cast including Rutland Barrington and Blanche Fenton (Mrs Luscombe Searelle). It played part of a bill with the well known *Faithful James* and a potted version of *La Mascotte*. Barrington was the author of another little piece called *His Escape* with music by H. M. Higgs which was featured at the same theatre the following week. Elsewhere there were few surprises. Emilio Pizzi's scena *Betta the Gipsy* was played at Collins' Music Hall, and at the Hippodrome W. H. Risque and Carl Kiefert combined in a 'farcical Dutch sketch' (*Miss Hook* had started a vogue for things Dutch everywhere) called *Zuyder Zee* which featured in its cast Tom Shale, Bert Gilbert and Nipper Lupino Lane. Blackpool also went Dutch with a piece called *By the Zuyder Zee*. Another well-known name appeared on the bill at Devonshire Park when Marjorie Slaughter, daughter of Walter, provided the music for a little piece called *The Constable and the Pictures* which starred Agnes Fraser and M. R. Morand.

Joseph Tabrar composed *The Factory Belle* for the Standard, Pimlico; George Sheldon wrote *The Maid of the Adriatic* for the Hulme Hippodrome, Manchester. The new musical sketches were many and varied in style and in quality, and they borrowed from every sphere of the musical theatre both for their material and for their interpreters. Perhaps the most unusual incident of the musical theatre year, however, was a Gilbert and Sullivan performance given by George Thorne 'and other Savoy favourites'. It was a recording made by the Walturdaw Company of simultaneous film and sound which allowed the audience to watch Thorne and his companions performing songs and dances from *The Mikado*; surely the earliest film of a British musical.

The demise of the so-called musical comedy in that form best-known at the Gaiety, Daly's, the Lyric and the Prince of Wales had now long been a talking point, but 1907 marked an irreversible change in its prospects with the death of Jimmy Davis, or 'Owen Hall' as he was known to countless theatre-goers. Since his abrupt and innovative entry into the musical theatre with *A Gaiety Girl* in 1893, 'Owen Hall' had made himself a particular place at the head of the brigade of authors of musical comedies. Copied by many, he was never equalled at his own type of bright society libretti littered with bons mots, beautiful people and occasionally over-daring satire. He had been cheered and banned, critically lauded and scorned in turn; he had made several fortunes and prodigally spent them all and one more besides in a career where the next big success was never far behind the odd comparative failure and which produced so many classics of the light musical theatre – from *A Gaiety Girl* through *An*

Artist's Model, The Geisha, A Greek Slave, Florodora, The Silver Slipper, The Girl from Kays, The Medal and the Maid (his only big failure) and *Sergeant Brue* to his last work, *The Little Cherub.*

In fact, the deaths in 1907 included many featured players from the early days of the British musical. As well as Hall and Charles Taylor there went the two great eccentrics Luscombe Searelle (*Estrella* &c) and Richard Mansell; Richard Mansfield, Gilbert and Sullivan comic turned tragedian; 76-year-old Mary Ann Victor, the wonderful Princesse in *Erminie*; Mrs Phelps from *A Gaiety Girl*; Rosina Brandram of the Savoy; Emily Thorne; Charles Goold; Groves Watson who had toured so long as Lurcher in *Dorothy* after originally going out as cover to the romantic lead; William Cheesman; little Carrie Coote (now Lady Pearce); provincial actor-manager Henry Dundas who had trouped *Jack-in-a-Box* so long; and Alhambra dancer Erminia Pertoldi: so many artists who had contributed their part to the building of the dominating light musical tradition of the English stage and who disappeared now as, after nearly three decades, that tradition itself was beginning to be questioned by its makers and purveyors.

1907

0327 **NELLY NEIL** a musical play in three acts by C. M. S. McLellan. Music by Ivan Caryll. Produced at the Aldwych Theatre under the management of Charles Frohman 10 January, 1907 for a run of 107 performances closing 27 April, 1907.

Billy Ricketts	Joseph Coyne
Nordheim (alias Donetti)	Ells Dagnall/Fred Wright Jr
Duke of Tysmoke	Herbert Sparling/C. Roper Lane
Viscount Larktenbigh	Langford Kirby
Duke of Penge	A. T. Gullifer
Earl Bursley	Harry Warren
Mr Tizzle	J. J. Dallas
Captain Neil	Robb Harwood
Orloff	Akerman May
Smith Minimus	Stewart Fortescue
Simcoe	Frank Walsh
Gustave	William Jefferson
Inspector	Ernest Crampton/C. Roper Lane/David Davies
Bank Messenger	Derrick Knowles
Princess Rasslova	Kitty Gordon (Gertrude Lester)
Countess of Rokeby	Mollie Lowell
Lady Dulcie Oddling	Edith Neville
Mrs Neil	Mary Brough
Hon. Muriel Vickery	Gertrude Lester
Lady Theo Thistle	Kathleen Warren
Lady Noreen Jenks	Manon Margotine
Lady Mollie Brent	Louie Lynton
Lurlina Tizzle	Ethel Allandale/*out*
Verbena Tizzle	Amie Payne/*out*
Crystal Kibblewhite	Gertrude Thornton
Gwendoline Geeks	Gerty Latchford
Phoebe Hacker	Flossie Hope
Gloriana Tribb	Carrie Bowman
Myrtle Dimity	Maude Morrison
Maud Arklight	Flora Prince
Isabel Nestle	Elfrieda Salber
Chloris Van Quiver	Margaret Dalrymple
Timmy Tucker	Estelle Christy
Preciosa Patterson	Grace Kimball
Nelly Neil	Edna May

with Beatrice Grenville, Ethel Badham, Lena Leibrandt, Edith Kelly, Dolly Corke, Lilian Jeffries,/Amie Payne

Dir: Sydney Ellison; md: W. T. Francis; sc: Hugo Baruch, Walter Johnstone, W. Helmsley; cos: Percy Anderson

0328 **MISS HOOK OF HOLLAND** a Dutch musical incident in two acts by Paul Rubens and Austen Hurgon. Music and lyrics by Paul Rubens. Produced at the Prince of Wales Theatre under the management of Frank Curzon 31 January, 1907 for a run of 462 performances, closing 4 April, 1908.

Mr Hook . . . . G. P. Huntley (Morris Harvey)/George Giddens
Simon Slinks . . . . George Barrett
Van Vuyt . . . . Walter Hyde/F. Pope Stamper/Maurice Farkoa (Berridge Fraser)
Captain Adrian Papp . . . . Herbert Clayton
Ludwig Schnapps. . . . . Harry Grattan/Fred Allandale/William Pringle
Lt de Coop . . . . Basil S. Foster/Herbert Hulcup
Old Policeman . . . . Morris Harvey/Eliot Skinner
Mina . . . . Gracie Leigh (Peggy Bethel)/Joan Penrose
Freda Voos . . . . Gwendoline Brogden
Gretchen . . . . Eva Kelly/Joan Penrose
Miss Voos. . . . . Phoebe Mercer
Clara Voos . . . . Gladys Ivery
Old Market Woman . . . . Alice Coleman
Thekla. . . . . Maisie Stather
Hendrik Draek . . . . Ralph Holland
Hans Maas . . . . Berridge Fraser
Van Eck. A. E. E. Edwards
Sally. . . . . Isabel Jay/Elsie Spain
add Van Jo . . . . Archie McCaig
Greta . . . . Joan Penrose/Peggy Bethel

Dir: Austen Hurgon; md: Ignatius A. de Orellana; sc: Joseph Harker & Walter Hann; cos: Karl

A version of *Miss Hook of Holland* was staged with a juvenile cast at a matinée 9 May, 1907 and subsequently for a series of matinées over the Christmas period.
Ida Valli (HOOK), Charles Swanson (SL), Ethel Lawson (VUYT), Clarisse Batchelor (PAPP), Decima Brooke (SCHN), Pearl Aufrere (COOP), Winnie Browne (PC), Peggy Bethel (MINA), Winifred Mason (FREDA), Gerty Murray (GR), Mabel Lawson (CLARA), Bertha Roberts (MKT), Marjorie Gummerson (RIEKA), Philip Phillips (DRAEK), Albert Keats (MAAS), Archie McCaig (ECK), Maggie Jarvis (SALLY), Olive Marchand (GRETA). Dir: Austen Hurgon; md: I. A. de Orellana; sc: Joseph Harker & Walter Hann

Produced at the Sommer Theatre, Vienna, 22 June, 1907.

Produced at the Criterion Theatre, New York, under the management of Charles Frohman 31 December, 1907 for a run of 119 performances closing 11 April, 1908.
Tom Wise (HOOK), Will West (SL), John McCloskey (VUYT), Bertram Wallis (PAPP), Richard L. Lee (SCHN), Glen White (COOP), Tom Collins (PC), Georgia Caine (MINA), Catherine Cooper (FREDA), Florence Nash (GR), Marion Little (CLARA), Eleanor Mansfield (MKT), Gunnis David (ECK), Christie MacDonald (SALLY). Md: William T. Francis; sc: Unit Wickes; cos: Dazian

Produced at the Prince of Wales Theatre under the management of Frank Curzon 27 October, 1914 for a run of 53 performances closing 19 December, 1914.
Alfred Wellesley (HOOK), Dan Rolyat (Fred Lyne)/George Barrett (SL), F. Pope Stamper (VUYT), J. C. Dalglish (PAPP), Charles Stone (SCHN), Reginald Matthews (COOP), Kevan Bernard (PC), Gracie Leigh (MINA), Claire Lynch (FREDA), Peggy Bethel (GR), Eileen Lawler (CLARA), Ida Evelyn (MKT), Edith Streeter (TH), L. F. Russell (DRAEK), Iago Lewys (MAAS), Bertie White/Arthur Bailey (ECK), Phyllis Dare (SALLY), Heather Featherstone (GRETA). Dir: Austen Hurgon; md: I. A. de Orellana; sc: J. A. Fraser; cos: B. J. Simmons.

Produced at Daly's Theatre under the management of J. Bannister Howard 24 March, 1932 for a run of 28 performances closing 16 April.
Mark Lester (HOOK), Hal Bryan (SL), Harold Kimberley (VUYT), Robert Layton (PAPP), Walter Bird (SCHN), Jenny Dean (MINA), Marie Conan (FREDA), Sadie Tremayne (MKT), John Denis (ECK), Jean Colin (SALLY), Alison MacLaren (GRETA). Dir: Frederick G. Lloyd

0329 **MY DARLING** a musical play in two acts by Seymour Hicks and Herbert E. Haines. Lyrics by Charles H. Taylor. Music by Herbert E. Haines. Additional numbers by Evelyn Baker. Additional lyrics by P. G. Wodehouse. Produced at the Hicks Theatre under the management of Charles Frohman 2 March, 1907 for a run of 71 performances, closing 25 April, 1907.

Joy Blossom . . . . Marie Studholme
Hon Jack Hylton . . . . Henry Lytton
Sir Arthur Jagg . . . . Will Bishop
Sir Henry Heldon. . . . . J. F. McArdle
Oddy . . . . Tom Graves
Mrs Pomeroy P. Green . . . . Helen Kinnaird
Squib . . . . Archie McCaig
Slow. . . . . Charles Caffery
Maurice Le Blanc. . . . . Armand Kalisz
Daphne Bell. . . . . Barbara Deane
Lady Heldon . . . . Clare Greet/Alice Barth
Sylvaine of the Follies . . . . Beryl Faber
Gabriel Reeve. . . . . Alice Hollander
Hon. Mutty Farrell . . . . Mervyn Dene
The MacSporran . . . . Charles Childerstone
Hon. Charles Dimsdale. . . . . George Castles
Lt Taff Davies . . . . Kenneth MacLaine
Alphonse . . . . Jack Thompson
Adolphe . . . . Alfred Lloyd
Achille. . . . . Alfred Haines
Sir Charles Aldershot . . . . Cyril Clensy
Lisette. . . . . Ethel Nash
Hon. Miss Gram O'Phone . . . . Gladys Marsden
Miss Edinburgh. . . . . Sylvia Storey
Miss Newcastle . . . . Rena Goldie
Miss Liverpool . . . . Kitty Melrose
Miss Dublin. . . . . Dorothy Roberts
Miss Llanfaerfechan . . . . Lydia West
Miss Birmingham. . . . . Elsie Kay
Miss Brighton. . . . . Birdie Sutherland
Miss Bristol . . . . Vashti Earle
Miss Sheffield. . . . . Doris Stocker
Miss Leicester. . . . . Dini Graham
Miss Manchester . . . . Claire Rickards
Miss London . . . . May Gates
Mlle Andaro . . . . Marguerite Leslie
Auguste . . . . Harold Borrett

pd: Will Bishop
with Dolly Parnell &c

Dir: Seymour Hicks; md: Herbert Haines; ch: Edward Royce; sc: R. C. McCleery and Walter Hann; cos: Comelli

0330 **TOM JONES** a comic opera in three acts founded on the novel by Henry Fielding. Libretto by Alexander M. Thompson and Robert Courtneidge. Lyrics by Charles H. Taylor. Music by Edward German. Produced at the Prince's Theatre, Manchester 30 March, 1907 and subsequently at the Apollo Theatre under the management of Robert Courtneidge 17 April, 1907 for a run of 110 performances closing 3 August, 1907.

Tom Jones . . . . C. Hayden Coffin
Sophia. Ruth Vincent
Lady Bellaston . . . . Dora Rignold
Honour . . . . Carrie Moore
Betty . . . . Mabel Newcome
Peggy . . . . Fay Temple

Gregory . . . . Jay Laurier
Dobbin . . . . Reginald Crompton
Grizzle . . . . Walter L. Rignold
Allworthy . . . . John Morley
Squire Western . . . . Ambrose Manning
Blifil . . . . Arthur Soames
Benjamin Partridge . . . . Dan Rolyat
Etoff . . . . Dorothy Ward
Squire Cloddy . . . . Harry Cottell
Pimlott . . . . D. Percival
Tony . . . . W. Biddlecombe
An officer . . . . Harry Welchman
Highwaymen . . . . Messrs Melville & Derrick
Postboy . . . . Mr Woodin
Waiter . . . . Carr Evans
Colonel Hamstead . . . . Rupert Mar
Tom Edwardes . . . . Mr Manners/Victor Tollemache
Colonel Wilcox . . . . Mr Dalmuir
Miss Western . . . . Marie Daltra
Hostess . . . . Florence Parfrey
Bessie Wiseacre . . . . Minnie Green
Letty Wheatcroft . . . . Annie Heenan
Rosie Lucas . . . . Cicely Courtneidge
Susan . . . . Maud Thornton

Dir: Robert Courtneidge; md: Hamish MacCunn; ch: Harry Grattan; sc: Stafford Hall & Conrad Tritschler; cos: Wilhelm

Produced at the Astor Theatre, New York, under the management of Henry W. Savage 11 November, 1907 for a run of 65 performances, closing 4 January, 1908.
Van Rensselaer Wheeler (TOM), Louise Gunning (SOPH), Laura Butler (BEL), Gertrude Quinlan (HON), Evelyn Smith (BETTY), Anna Hall (PEGGY), John Bunning (GREG), Henry Turpin (DOB), Bernard Gorcy (GRIZ), Albert Pellaton (ALL), Henry Norman (WEST), Vaughan Trevor (BL), William Norris (PART), Madge Marston (ET), E. P. Foster (CL), E. W. Bowman (PIM), E. A. Clark (TONY), Percy Parsons (OFF), E. J. Oden & T. D. Crittenden (HWYMN), William Herman (POST), John Frolisch (WAIT), Banning Willis (COL), Charles Kingsland (TOME), John Hassan (WILC), Florence Burdett (HOST), Marjorie Fairbanks (BES), Odette Bordeaux (LET), Louise Meyers (ROSIE), Lucy Tonge (SU); with Misses Norton, Lang, Aubrey, Bownes, Carroll, Crantzell, von der Muehlen, Peters, J. Standish, Stoner, Vernon, Weeks, Blanchard, Curtis, Leslie, Rankin, Smith, M. Standish, Messrs Fay, Fougerard, Pearson, Kearns, Supraner, Edwards, Hammond, Fenton, Terry. Dir: Robert Courtneidge; md: Herman Perlet; ch: Dave Marion; sc: Walter Burridge; cos: Mme Herman

0331 **THE PET OF THE EMBASSY** a musical play in two acts by Albert E. Wilson and Sidney F. Bailey. Produced by C. Hamilton Baines and H. Keates Hales at Eccles 30 March, 1907 and toured. Dates included Preston, Bolton, Newcastle, Sunderland then from 19 August Leicester, Manchester, Dudley, Merthyr, Swindon,?, Birmingham,?, Glasgow,?, Greenock &c.

John William Burg . . . . Witty Watty Walton/Walter Champney
Eric Brown . . . . Robert Hyett/Laurence Wensley
Palatine Brown . . . . Harry Fischer
Hon. Percy Bravington . . . . T. Sinclair Holden/Ralph Lynn
Hilda Graham . . . . Ethel Dunford/Beatrice Rowe
Dorothy Stanley . . . . Florence Watson/Ida Ernest
Mrs Pamela Bury . . . . Julia Bassett
Maud . . . . Trilby Collier/Marjorie Crofton/Winifred Ray
Eva d'Alwy . . . . Lily Duncker
Doris May . . . . Ethel Duncker
Carnation Grant . . . . Tilley Davies
Phyllis Haye . . . . Winifred Ray

Camille Ford . . . . Grace Mackay
Edna Grand . . . . Winifred Waring
François . . . . J. H. Weekes
Ali . . . . Guy Blythe

Md: Albert E. Wilson; sc: John Turner; cos: Mme Neroy; Affleck & Brown; W. A. Hulma & Sons

0332 **THE PICK OF THE BUNCH** a musical comedy in two acts adapted from *After the Ball* by Charles Carey. Lyrics by H. Buckstone Clair. Music by Louis Laval and Harry W. Wellmon. Produced at the Royal County Theatre, Kingston 8 April, 1907 and toured. Dates included Burnley, Glasgow, Sunderland, Consett, Blackpool, Barrow, Pembroke Dock, Boston &c.

Haliwell Menit . . . . Charles Carey
Colonel Joseph Menit . . . . H. Buckstone Clair
Nancy . . . . M. Sadie
Martin . . . . Algernon W. Lee
Dick Seymour . . . . Harold Wantage
Nellie Mather . . . . Madge Christopher
Ruth Gay . . . . Eva Ellis
Wilhelmina . . . . Nellie James
Alice . . . . Gladys Glynn
Joan . . . . Sybil Glynn
Mary . . . . Mabette May
Minette . . . . Elsie May
Gladys Paule . . . . Minnie Seymour
Ida Downe . . . . Loudolph Barrett
Stella Austin . . . . Clair Barrington
Julia Green . . . . Madge Lacey
Ethel Fancourt . . . . Mabel Colman
Nancy Cliffe . . . . Eunice Euston
Nora Fossel . . . . Elaine Gray
Freda Holmes . . . . Babs Christopher
Jack Nesby . . . . Harold Clemence
Thomas . . . . W. Millard
Charlie Austin . . . . Charles Swinburne
James . . . . Bertram Gunnel
Tiny Tim . . . . Little Tom Lewis

0333 **LADY TATTERS** a romantic light opera in three acts by Herbert Leonard. Lyrics by Roland Carse. Music by Walter Slaughter. Played for one stage rights performance at the Marlborough Theatre 31 August, 1906. Produced at the Shaftesbury Theatre under the management of Ells Dagnall 1 May, 1907 for a run of 80 performances closing 20 July, 1907.

King Charles II . . . . Sidney Brough
Lord Rochester . . . . Herbert Sparling
Earl Ludlow . . . . Oscar Adye
Captain Walter Somerville . . . . Ivor Foster
Sergeant Tom Gurney . . . . Johnny Danvers
Matthew Scraby . . . . Powis Pinder
Landlord Simon . . . . Algernon Newark
Seth Lewys . . . . Walter Passmore
Dick Harrold . . . . Courtice Pounds
Poll Merrie . . . . Marie George
Isabel Scraby . . . . Louie Pounds
Tatters . . . . Claudia Lasell

Dir: Herbert Cottesmore; md: Leonard Hornsey; ch: Edouard Espinosa; sc: Bruce Smith, Harry Potts, W. Raphael; cos: Comelli

0334 **THE GIRLS OF GOTTENBERG** a musical play in two acts by George Grossmith Jr and L. E. Berman. Lyrics by Adrian Ross and Basil Hood. Music by Ivan Caryll and Lionel Monckton.

Produced at the Gaiety Theatre under the management of George Edwardes 15 May, 1907 for a run of 303 performances closing 28 March, 1908.

Prince Otto of Saxe-Hilversum	George Grossmith Jr/Lionel Mackinder/ Lawrence Grossmith
Sergeant Brittlbottl	Robert Nainby/Theo Leonard
General the Margrave of Saxe-Nierstein	Eustace Burnaby/H. E. Garden/Fred J. Blackman/F. Raynham
Colonel Finkhausen	A. J. Evelyn
Fritz	T. C. Maxwell
Herman	Harold Thorley/J. Redmond
Franz	Somers Bellamy/Augustus Cramer
Karl	George Grundy/Henry Vincent
Albrecht	J. Robert Hale/W. Louis Bradfield
Burgomaster	George Miller/Harry Cane
Kannenbier	Arthur Hatherton
Adolf	Charles Brown/P. De la Hanty
Policeman	Fred J. Blackman/Robert Burns/ H. E. Garden
Waiters	Messrs Grande and Hill
Corporal Riethen	J. R. Sinclair
Private Schmidt	S. Hansworth/J. Redmond/H. Raymond
Max Moddelkopf	Edmund Payne
Elsa	May de Souza/Thelma Raye/Enid Leonhardt (Gladys Cooper)/ Cissie Murray/Dolly Castles
Clementine	Violet Halls
Lucille	Olive May
Kathie	Kitty Mason/Topsy Sinden
Hana	Edith Lee/Edith Kelly
Hilda	Kitty Lindley
Minna	Jean Aylwin/Gladys Cooper/Mary Fraser
Freda	Olive Wade/Crissie Bell
Anna	Mary Hobson/May Charteris/Dora Fraser
Eva	Gladys Cooper/Frances Kapstowne/ Connie Stuart/Blanche Browne
Lina	Julia James/Cissie Murray/Dora Fraser
Katrina	Kitty Hanson
Barbara Briefmark	Enid Leonhardt/Marie Dean
Betti Bernkastler	Tessie Hackney/Gladys Desmond
Mitzi	Gertie Millar/Coralie Blythe/Mabel Russell (Enid Leonhardt)
add Gretchen	Florence Tomes/Florence Phillips

with May Charteris, Cissie Murray, Dora Fraser, Blanche Browne, Connie Stuart, Gertrude Wykes, Lily Shepherd, Margaret Webster, Irene Warren, Pattie Wells, Marie Dean, Kitty Lindley, Edith Lee, May Laroni, May Savory etc.

Dir: J. A. E. Malone; md: Ivan Caryll; ch: Fred Farren; sc: Alfred Terraine and Joseph & Phil Harker; cos: Percy Anderson

Played at the Adelphi Theatre by George Edwardes' touring company 10 August, 1908 for two weeks.

Lawrence Grossmith (OTTO), Fred Payne (BRIT), Jocelyn Hope (GEN), Arnold Lucy (FINK), Ernest Arundel (FRITZ), Arthur Whitehead (HER), Lawrence Robbins (FRANZ), Ellis Holland (KARL), Fred Allandale (ALB), Douglas Munro (BURG), A. Chantrene (KANN), Charles Brown/Louis Deaver (AD), D. Logum (PC), W. Garret & D. Goodbar (WAITERS), H. Glyn (CORP), Edmund Payne (MAX), Thelma Raye (ELSA), Maisie Gay (CLEM), Florence Phillips (LUC), Dora Dent (FR), Peggy Paton (AN), Kitty Sparrow (EVA), Nancy Rich (LINA), Florence Melville (KAT), May Weston (BAR), Ethel Wilson (BET), Happy Fanny Fields (MITZI). Dir: Edward Royce; md: Philip Braham

Produced at the Knickerbocker Theatre, New York, under the management of Charles Frohman, 1 September, 1908 for a run of 103 performances closing 28 November, 1908.

Lionel Mackinder (OTTO), John E. Hazzard (BRIT), Ross Clifford (GEN), Ernest Cossart (FINK), Overton Moyle (FRITZ), Warwick Wellington (HER), Ridgwell Cullum (FRANZ), Henry Vincent (CARL), Leslie Gaze/Wallace McCutcheon (ALB), Edward Garvie (BURG), Sarony Lambert (KANN), R. R. Neill (AD), Theodore Walters (PC), Messrs Grant & Leech (WAITERS), Guy Maingy (CORP), Decimus Williams (SCH), James Blakeley (MAX), May Naudain (ELSA), Louise Dresser (CLEM), Edith Kelly (LUC), Hazel Neason (K), Grace Riopel (HANA), Ethel Vivian (HILD), Mabel Hollins (MIN), Clara Pitt (FRE), Molly McGrath (AN), Mary Lee (EVA), Adelaide Kornau (LINA), Louise Brunelle (KAT), Grace Walsh (BAR), Esther Robinson (BET), Gertie Millar (MITZI). Dir: J. A. E. Malone; md: W. T. Francis

Produced in Paris as *Les Jolies Filles de Gottenberg*.

0335 **THE YOUNG LIEUTENANT** a musical comedy by Herbert Dawson and A. F. Allen Towers. Music by R. A. Smith. Produced at the Royal Artillery Theatre, Woolwich under the management of Annie Hughes 20 May, 1907 and toured through Croydon, King's Hammersmith, Bexhill-on-Sea, Hastings, etc. to 22 June, and from 5 August Peterborough, Wakefield, Burnley, Kilmarnock/Kircaldy, Ayr/Clydebank, Dumfries/Hawick, Berwick/Durham, Glossop, Oxford, St Leonards-on-Sea, Southend, Bedford, Bury St Edmunds/Goole, Ilkley/Yeadon, Scunthorpe, Hereford, Dudley, Kidderminster, Aldershot, to 14 December.

Admiral Sir Stoke Newington . . . . . . Campbell Bishop/Edwin Sykes
1st Lt Charles Langhurst . . . . Wilfred Norman/Leslie Hawkins
2nd Lt Reginald Greenlane . . . . E. B. Davis
3rd Lt Harry Summers . . . . Douglas Phillips/Leslie Austin/Sexton Granville
Duke of Bowminster . . . . Llewellyn C. Hughes
Bill Barnacle . . . . Richard Cummings/Steane Louch
Jack Plane . . . . George Robertson
Bob Bruiser . . . . Bert Burton
Jem Fellowes . . . . A. E. Drinkwater Jr
Dick Bouncer . . . . Fred Payne/Harry Walsh
Dowager Lady Harlington . . . . Madeleine Stone/Katie Kyrle
Lady Winifred Archer . . . . Madge Davies
Lady Evelyn Archer . . . . Madge Ferwin/Dorothy Waldron
Mother Price . . . . Maud Esdaile/Marion Lewis
Marjorie Playfair . . . . Kathleen Emmett/Maggie Robertson
Kitty Green . . . . Violet Campbell
Nellie Brown . . . . Nellie Braham
Polly Price . . . . Nellie Wigley/Hettie Gale
pd: Dorothy Shaw
Md: Alex Humphreys

0336 **THE MAID AND THE MOTOR MAN** a musical comedy in 2 acts by J. Hickory Wood. Music by Alessandro Romilli. Additional music by Ernest Bucalossi. Produced at the New Theatre, Cardiff under the management of John Hart 27 May, 1907 and toured. Dates included Leeds, Glasgow, Edinburgh, Birmingham, Hull, Sheffield, Liverpool, Bradford &c.

Hon. Dudley Newark . . . . Horace Mills/Aubrey Fitzgerald
Sir John Warrington . . . . Colin Coop/Percy Yorke
Alys Warrington . . . . Sylvia May/Ruth Lincoln
Mrs Shepperton . . . . Winifred Morice
Suzanne Shepperton . . . . Olive Eveline/Daisy Stratton/Sylvia May
Lady Newark . . . . Hebe Bliss
Dick Hastings . . . . Edmund Sherras/Cyril Thompson
Jack Bolter . . . . Willie Manning/William Stevens/M. R. Morand
William Binns . . . . Alfred Clarke/Harry Nicholls
Percy Sly . . . . George Carroll/Paul Phillips/Albert Valchera

Kate Wicks . . . . Lulu Valli
Martha Pottle . . . . Annie Ainsley/Irene Verona/ Florence Parfrey
add Robert Gregory. . . . . Ivan Capell
Tom . . . . Jocelyn Hope
Jane. . . . . Olive Crellin
Silas. . . . . H. Jocelyn

Dir: Victor Stevens; md: Harry Rushworth/Ernest Bucalossi/R. Sedgewick; sc: R. C. Oldham and D. G. Hall; cos: Mrs Skinner and Beaty Brothers

0337 **SUCH A NICE GIRL** a musical comedy by Frank Stanmore (and Percy Nash). Music by E. Paschal. Produced at Worthing under the management of Cowper Smith and Douglas Payne 1 July, 1907 and toured through 18 dates including Bexhill-on-Sea, Shrewsbury, Weston-super-Mare, Nuneaton, Scarborough/Whitby, Lincoln and Burton-on-Trent to January, 1908; and from 17 February, 1908 through Chester, Dudley, Cheltenham, Saltley, Widnes, Wolverhampton, Keighley, Bedford, Sunderland, Stafford, Luton, Peterborough/King's Lynn, Farnworth, Middlesborough, Oldham, Leicester and Preston to 13 June.

Bertie Holbrook . . . . Frank Stanmore/Ralph Lynn
Harry Harrow. . . . . Frank Tennant/Edgar McIntyre
Brown . . . . Douglas Payne/Kenneth Black Jr
William . . . . Fred Clarke
Colonel Bullitt V. C. . . . . Arthur Poole/Mark Lester/Douglas Payne/E. Warburton-Gamble
Cerise . . . . Maude Percival/Dot Carey/Margaret Cathcart/Ivy Leighton
Little Flossie . . . . Gladys Anderson/Beatrice Sutherland
Martha Grimn . . . . Nellie Clarence/Amy Fanchette/ Ethel Lodge/Victoria Douglas
Ida Downe . . . . Marjorie Battis
Violet Powder. . . . . Ada Smart
Rhoda Dendrum . . . . Lilian Lilford
Pattie de Foie Gras . . . . Constance Lilford
Hilda Colman . . . . Nell Richardson/Rosa Bennett
P. C. Fogg . . . . C. Daniels
Penelope. . . . . Ruth Pope

Md: W. Scott Phipp/Leo Croke/W. Penley Jr/Julian Rutt

0338 **THE THREE KISSES** a musical production in 2 acts by Leedham Bantock and Percy Greenbank. Lyrics by Percy Greenbank. Music by Howard Talbot. Produced at the Apollo Theatre under the management of Frank Curzon 21 August, 1907 for a run of 32 performances closing 21 September, 1907.

Garibaldi Pimpernello . . . . Walter Passmore
Sir Cuthbert Bellamy . . . . Charles Angelo
Andrea . . . . Walter Hyde
Contessa di Ravolgi . . . . Ethel Irving
Harry Trevor . . . . Lionel Mackinder
Ethel Trevor . . . . Coralie Blythe
Crump. William Pringle
Mr Gobbins. . . . . Albert Le Fre
Chi Chi . . . . Willie Warde
Roderico. . . . . R. Carr
Beppo . . . . Iago Lewys
Camillo . . . . C. Hood
Nicolini . . . . Murri Moncrieff
Elvira . . . . Max Hinton
Zenone . . . . Millie Collier
Teresa . . . . Kitty Gordon
Marietta . . . . Caroline Hatchard

Philippina . . . . Edith Streeter
Lisetta . . . . Alice Hatton

Dir: Austen Hurgon; md: Howard Talbot; sc: Joseph Harker; cos: Karl

339 **THE SCARLET PATROL** a musical comedy in three acts by St John Hamund. Music by Owen Trevine. Produced at the Royal County Theatre, Kingston 26 August, 1907 and toured. Dates included Croydon, Fulham, Derby &c.

Lord Robert Cumberland . . . . J. S. Durant
Phineas Fogey . . . . St John Hamund
Nicholas Quiller . . . . Arthur Stigant
Inspector Jury . . . . Leonard Russell
Mr Cooper . . . . Fred Rolph/E. Percy Rogers
Johnny . . . . J. H. Bishop
Cecil . . . . Joseph Bruce
Algernon . . . . Leo Minster
Freddy . . . . W. E. Gulson
Monty . . . . Day Chester
Maurice . . . . H. Pinnock
Ferdinand . . . . E. A. Bennett
Claude . . . . C. H. Stowell
Desmond . . . . Max Wakeman
Amazon North . . . . Reydon Dallas
Ernestine . . . . Florence Linton
Myra Myrtle . . . . Elise Cook
Maud . . . . Kathleen Kinross
Sybil . . . . Lucy Kipling/Florence Baseley
Edith . . . . Cissie Woolgar/Lucy Kipling
Daisy . . . . Hettie Leslie
Ethel . . . . Hilda Rennards
Miriam . . . . Mamie Russell
Susan . . . . Doris Cammell
Joyce . . . . Mollie McGuigan
Little girl . . . . Nellie Lamport

Dir: Herbert Cottesmore; md: Mark Strong; sc: George Miller

340 **THE GAY GORDONS** a play with music in two acts by Seymour Hicks. Lyrics by Arthur Wimperis. Music by Guy Jones. Additional lyrics by P. G. Wodehouse, Walter Davidson, Henry Hamilton and C. H. Bovill. Additional music by Frank E. Tours and Walter Davidson. Produced at the Aldwych Theatre under the management of Charles Frohman 11 September, 1907 for a run of 229 performances closing 11 April, 1908.

Angus Graeme . . . . Seymour Hicks (Stanley Brett)
Nervy Nat . . . . Fred Emney
Edmund Siddons . . . . A. W. Baskcomb/Lawrence Baskcomb (or G. Baskcomb)
Andrew Quainton . . . . William Lugg
John Smith . . . . Laurence Caird
Viscount Belstairs . . . . Kenneth MacLaine/J. C. Woolley/Crampton Bryant
Marquis of Dalesbury . . . . Cecil Kinnaird/Mervyn Dene
Lord Elmington . . . . Arthur Royd
Lord Mertsham . . . . Mervyn Dene/Paul Plunket/Arthur Florence/Frank Lincoln
Archibald Speedy . . . . J. C. Buckstone
Corporal . . . . Will Bishop
Janet McCleod . . . . Rosina Filippi/Mary Brough/(Eugenie Vernie)/Maud Milton
Victoria Siddons . . . . Zena Dare/Maudi Darrell/(Nellie Lonnen)/Maie Ash

Charlotte Siddons . . . . Sydney Fairbrother
Mary McCleod . . . . Barbara Deane/Daisy Williams/Doris Stocker/Dorothy Laine
Lady Millicent Graeme . . . . Katie Butler/Nellie Lonnen/Maie Ash
Lady Graeme of Lockalt . . . . Vera Morris/Rosie Chesney
Peasant woman . . . . Georgina Delmar
Peggy Quainton . . . . Ellaline Terriss/Maie Ash
with Aimée Dixon, Pauline Francis, May Gates, Rena Goldie, Hilda Harris, Elsie Kay, May Kennedy, Ruby Kennedy, Dorrie Keppel, Marion Lindsay, Claire Rickards, Doris Stocker, Sylvia Storey, Mabel Watson, Kitty Beresford/Madge Hodgkinson, Dorothy Laine, Alice du Barri, Lillian Burns, Jennie Bateman, Mollie Ventry, Millie Field, Lilian Rankin, Miss Boielle, Miss Burrows

Dir: Seymour Hicks; md: Frank E. Tours; ch: Edward Royce; sc: R. McCleery and Philip Howden; cos: Wilhelm

0341 **THE GENTLEMAN JOCKEY** a musical play in three acts by Edward H. Marris. Music by George Ess &c. Produced at St Julian's Theatre, Guernsey under the management of Edward H. Marris 18 October, 1907 and toured.

Sir Francis Granmere . . . . Cecil W. Parke
David Grayson . . . . Percy Maitland/Helier Le Maistre
Frank Snakeworth . . . . Frank Gala/Walter B. Nugent
Archie Fitzherbert . . . . C. R. King/Leonard Dalrymple
P. C. Blodgers . . . . George Brentwood
Uriah Grant . . . . Fred Parker/Victor Rowland
P. S. Barrowby . . . . Arthur Herries
Dr Potter . . . . James Green
Jenny Jarvis . . . . May Norris/Gertie Reid
Moore . . . . Violet Laurel
Bellamy . . . . Norah Palliser
Mary Grayson . . . . Dora Hargreaves
Lady Kitty . . . . Maisie Gerrard/Lillian Drake
Poppy Grayson . . . . Norah Melton/Ethel Ward
Tommy . . . . Stanley Jefferson

0226a **THE DANCING GIRL(S) OF SPAIN** a revised version of *Miss Chiquita* by George R. Sims. Music by Clarence Corri. Produced at the Theatre Royal, Hull, under the management of Haldane Crichton and Clarence Corri 24 June, 1907 and toured. Dates included Aberystwyth, Scarborough, Southport, Loughborough/Cambridge, Ipswich, Tunbridge Wells/Eastbourne, Hastings, Merthyr, Dundee, Dunfermline &c.

Don Julian Alvarez . . . . W. H. Austin/Lawrence Emery/Lauri Dixon
Sir Jeremiah Joyce . . . . George Danvers
Rev. Alonzo Joyce . . . . Jack Crichton
Terence McGinty . . . . George Delaforce/George Beverley
D'Arcy Davis . . . . Edgar Dereve/Phil Hartley/Will Smith
Jack Davis . . . . Johnny Schofield Jr
Don Carlos Alvarez . . . . Donald Edward
Guitarez . . . . Arthur White
Interpreter . . . . Edward Durant
Roderigo . . . . James Falson
Miss Chiquita Joyce . . . . Dolly Varden/Eva Kelland/Bessie Frank
Miss Marie Montressor . . . . Gertrude Fawcett/Pauline Hague/Violet Leslie
Lola . . . . Kitty Lambert
Juanita . . . . Millie Neal
Mercedes . . . . Gertie Jackson
Manuelita . . . . Sadie Thompson

Md: Clarence Corri

A NIGHT WITH THE STARS an up-to-date musical comedy hotch-potch by Max Goldberg (John F. Preston). Presented by the 'National Alliance' at the Scala Theatre 11 February, 1907.

Ali Ben Hassan	Bert Byrne
O'Sullivan Pasha	John F. Preston
Dick Darrell.	Hal Forde
Bill Breezy	Nannie Goldman
Mustapha	Harry J. Worth
Sherlock Holmes	Carl Lynn
Tommy Twinkle	Harry Liddle
Polly Twinkle	Claire Romaine
Mabel Musgrove	Maud Walsh
Indian Slave.	'Spot'
George Robey	Dion Wade
Joe Elvin	Charles Austin
Victoria Monks	Clarice Mayne
Baikis	Evelyn Vaudrey
Gulnare	Florence Darrell
Amina	Florence Harcourt
Enid	Lillian Leonard
Kassi Kassi	Marie Preston

with Ada Colley, Marie Kendal, Whit Cunliffe, Edgar Romaine, Michael Braham

1908

The light musical theatre headed into 1908 in an attractive and healthy state. Four musicals, all hits, held the stage in the West End: *The Merry Widow* at Daly's and three British pieces, *Miss Hook of Holland* (Prince of Wales), *The Girls of Gottenberg* (Gaiety) and *The Gay Gordons* (Aldwych). Each of these last named had still several months of metropolitan life left, so the first new musical of the year was not needed for some time.

The first entry was a foreign show – the only one of the year. Encouraged by the success of *The Merry Widow*, George Edwardes had bought the rights to Oscar Straus' Viennese hit *Ein Walzertraum* and had had it arranged for presentation at the Hicks Theatre. It was hoped that *A Waltz Dream*, as it was called, would be another hit on the scale of *The Merry Widow* and the big guns were brought in accordingly: Gertie Millar, George Grossmith, Arthur Williams, Robert Evett – a mixture of the Gaiety's and Daly's most popular artists. An American version of the show was already running successfully at the Broadway Theatre, New York, and the omens looked excellent but, in spite of Straus' delightful score and the production values which Edwardes gave the show, *A Waltz Dream* never looked likely to imitate the success of its predecessor. It stayed at the Hicks Theatre for a respectable 136 performances without ever becoming truly popular. Its integral lack of comedy and a rather routine book may have been partly to blame but, whatever the reason, the show did not catch the fancy of the 1908 theatre public. A second attempt, in 1911 at Daly's, with a rewritten book by Basil Hood, notched up a further 111 performances but still without turning *A Waltz Dream* into a real success.

The first new British pieces came in April. *Miss Hook of Holland* and *The Girls of Gottenberg* had come to the end of their runs and the Prince of Wales and the Gaiety both produced new shows. The overwhelming success of *Miss Hook of Holland* naturally prompted Frank Curzon to search for more of the same fare, and the *Miss Hook* team of Paul Rubens and Austen Hurgon were commissioned to prepare the follow-up to their 1907 hit.

The milieu chosen for the new piece was the French Riviera, the fictional town of St Leo which seems to have been not too far from Menton. The picturesque setting of *Miss Hook* had been an important ingredient in its success and, with Dutchism now worked to death, the French Riviera seemed a suitable alternative. Often used for second acts, it had not yet been thoroughly worked over as a full setting for a musical. The emphasis to be taken was shown in the primitive choice of title: *The Land of Flowers*. In the event, the more alliterative title of *My Mimosa Maid* was chosen, and the new Rubens/Hurgon musical opened on 21 April to an excellent first night reception:

> If the reception accorded . . . on its opening night can be taken as a guide, the piece will prove a worthy follower to its predecessor. (*Stage*)

The papers found the new show clearly enjoyable:

> Mr Paul Rubens is as light and vivacious as ever . . . the piece is undeniably fresh, pretty and tuneful . . . the connecting tissue or 'chatter' as (Rubens) and Mr Hurgon modestly describe it on the programme, appeared in parts a little long-drawn but never seemed to be received impatiently by the house. The 'jingles and tunes' – any substitute is to be welcomed for the use of the term 'lyrics' – tintinabulate for the most part very pleasingly, there is plenty of variety, if none of the words are particularly clever or original . . . the gay medley went with much vivacity and had the merit of improving towards the end . . (*Times*)

> The dialogue is fairly witty, but is excelled in this respect by some of the lyrics . . (*Stage*)

Not precisely raves, but reviews which indicated that *My Mimosa Maid* had more than a little entertainment value.

The story had been evolved around the principal stars of the *Miss Hook* company. George Huntley was Victor Guilbert, a chimney sweep, who falls in love with the lovely Paulette, 'head girl on a Mimosa plantation' (Isabel Jay). She also falls for him but both are silent. Then Victor wins the *gros lot* in the big Riviera lottery. He gives up his job and decks himself out in fashionable finery to attempt to woo his Paulette under an assumed name and character. But he is unsuccessful, for she is still pining for the vanished sweep. Finally, Victor returns to his old ways and his real persona and he and Paulette are happily and richly united.

The other favourite Curzon performers were loosely inserted into this little tale. Maurice Farkoa was a café proprietor, the rival of Victor for Paulette's affections, George Barrett Victor's comical brother who inherits the sweeping business when Victor becomes 'Count Victor'; Gracie Leigh was a funny flower girl, Eva Kelly (Mrs Huntley) the dowager proprietress of the Mimosa plantation and F. Pope Stamper a military person with a suitable song. But *My Mimosa Maid* was, above all, a vehicle for Huntley. The authors had not been persuaded to follow up their happy inspiration of making him an older man in *Miss Hook*, and for the new show he returned to being a comic-romantic leading man as in *Three Little Maids* or *Lady Madcap*. But now the size of the role had grown even greater and, particularly in Act 1, he was scarcely off the stage. Switching with facility and great effect from the sentimental to the humorous, he dominated the stage, whether making gentle love to Isabel Jay or hilariously describing a chimney sweep's first bath.

But if Huntley's role was the overwhelming one dramatically, the music was largely divided between Miss Jay and Farkoa and, in consequence, the score was a little more lyrical than others of Rubens' works. Isabel Jay had a pretty set of numbers: 'Somebody else I Love', 'The Land of Flowers', and 'Rippling Waterfall' which she sang to the accompaniment of an off-stage chorus and a tinkling music box in the orchestra:

> Rippling, rippling waterfall
> Your murmur never ceases,
> All day long your restless song
> With melody increases.
> Life for you is endless May,
> The birds sing as you call,

Sun and bubbles fill the day
Of rippling waterfall . .

Farkoa was a little less well-supplied, although the song 'Stay as You Are' proved quite well-liked and an irrelevant piece about 'The twopenny Tube' ('When I first went to London . .') gave him a chance to be surrounded by the female chorus. His best piece was 'My absolutely Quite':

If you can't be my 'one and only'
Be my 'sometimes, please' to me,
I would be your 'nearly always'
Or your 'almost sure to be',
Should you be my 'next to nothing'
I would be your 'p'raps I might'
Oh! why can't you be my 'one and only absolutely quite'.

The comic numbers were not neglected, with Gracie Leigh there to sing 'The Cobbler Stuck to his Last' and the highly enjoyable 'I've Got an ugly Uncle':

I've got an ugly uncle
He's very useful too
On Saturday I get my wages
And on Monday he pulls me through.
All of the nice things I've had
Some time have gone to him
Why, for more than seven years our enamelled tin bath
Has been 'staying' with Uncle Jim!

'Uncle Jim' was a common euphemism for the pawnshop.

Eva Kelly and her daughters (Clarisse Batchelor and Gertie Murray) sang humorously about 'Young Persons' and Charles McNaughton mused on 'When I'm a Millionaire' but there were also, a little surprisingly from Rubens, a number of ensembles and concerted pieces, which enabled Hurgon (in his directorial capacity) to keep the stage bustling with colour and movement. *The Times* commented:

> The liveliness of the piece was kept up by relays of brightly costumed choruses including Zouaves, hospital nurses, flowerpickers, schoolgirls and other slightly heterogenous classes of southerners who undeniably warded off stagnation, but were occasionally too vociferous for the size of the house . .

My Mimosa Maid certainly had all the requisites, if not to challenge *Miss Hook*, then at least to have a most successful run. But it was not to be. The public which had flocked to see the previous piece did not flock to its successor, and although it was undeniably a better piece than some of Rubens' earlier and more successful works, it lasted less than three months. There was no real explanation for the failure. Better plays had fared worse and many worse ones had been successful. Curzon asked no questions, but simply withdrew a show which would not take on. It was given a tour through 1908/9 and was then packed away.

George Edwardes had been investigating the changing public taste for some time. He had failed with twentieth century pseudo-burlesque in the shape of *The New Aladdin*, he had triumphed with European operetta in *The Merry Widow* then had the verdict reversed with *A Waltz Dream*, while *The Girls of Gottenberg* had proved that there was still a wide taste for the sort of fare generally purveyed by the Gaiety, even with (or especially with) a little more backbone than before.

His new piece at that theatre had more than just extra backbone. *Havana* was an altogether more ambitious piece than anything recently seen at the Gaiety. It was far from being a song and dance and variety show based on the town's favourite stars, it was less frivolous and musically more substantial than the Gaiety habitués were used to, but George Edwardes was following his own forecasts and *Havana* was evidence of them. It has been suggested that *Havana* had originally been intended for the more up-market Daly's Theatre and that only the long run of *The Merry Widow* and a contractual obligation to produce led Edwardes to stage the piece at the Gaiety, but this is very unlikely. The town's greatest and most prolific presenter of musical shows was experimenting – as he had with *The Merry Widow* or with *The New Aladdin* or so many years before with *In Town*, *A Gaiety Girl* and *The Shop Girl*. The musical show of what Edwardes labelled a more 'comic opera' variety was his bet for the next turn in public fancy and *Havana* was intended to fill that, as yet unstated, need.

The libretto for the new show was credited to George Grossmith and the young writer Graham Hill. Its composer, Leslie Stuart, had little doubt to whom the major credit belonged: in a presentation copy of the score which he dedicated to Hill, Grossmith's name was struck heavily through with black ink. The story of the piece was set, as the title indicated, in Cuba. Consuelo, niece to the capital's mayor, is to marry his son, Don Adolfo. On the day leading up to their betrothal the two agree that they may have a day free in which to flirt as they please before they are committed to each other. Consuelo's choice falls on Jackson Villiers of the steam yacht Jaunty Jane, and she proceeds to woo him heavily with the result that the two fall truly and mutually in love. The course of true love is interrupted by many an incident and misunderstanding: Villers' yacht is taken variously for a privateer and a gun-runner and he for an 'enemy of Cuba', Adolfo finds himself kidnapped by the crew of the 'Jaunty Jane' and conspiracy is (or seems to be) rife. In the end, as must be, the lovers come together while Adolfo finds consolation elsewhere. The comedy was provided by Villiers' shipmates, the bosun Nix and the 'boy' Reginald Brown. On an earlier visit to Havana, some seven years previously, Nix carelessly married a little cigar-seller before sailing on. Now he is cornered by the fearsome Isabelita and claimed as her husband. Eventually it is discovered that his bride was the pretty Anita and all ends well.

This Gaiety show had not, for once, been compiled around a given set of stars. There was no 'Gertie Millar role' and, anyway, Gertie was across at the Hicks in *A Waltz Dream* before heading for New York to star in *The Girls of Gottenberg*. The leading role of Consuelo, which would have been well outside Miss Millar's vocal range, was taken by Evie Greene who had both the looks and the voice for it. The aquiline baritone Leonard Mackay was her hero and Lawrence Grossmith took the role of Adolfo (which had probably been intended for author George). Alfred Lester and Bill Berry, transferred from *The Merry Widow*, supplied the comedy aided and abetted by the greatest gorgon of them all, Gladys Homfrey, knocking sixty now and hilarious as the monstrous Isabelita. In the minor roles some of the Gaiety usuals remained: Arthur Hatherton was the Mayor, Jean Aylwin the cigar-seller, and Kitty Mason, Olive May and Kitty Hanson were featured but, by and large, the changes in cast reflected the change in style. *Havana* was a piece of a kind and a quality designed to appeal to more than the diehards of the Gaiety gallery and the after-dinner members of its stalls and boxes.

It was Leslie Stuart's first new score since *The Belle of Mayfair*, two years previously, and he showed that he had lost none of his ability to produce tuneful and catchy songs full of rhythmic ingenuity. For *Havana* he also composed concerted pieces of considerable scope – an octet, a sextet, a quartet and finales to the first and second acts which stretched to 35 and 45 pages of the printed vocal score respectively. The solo songs were of a pretty variety, but the favourite was agreed to be Evie Greene's number 'Little Miquette', whose charming lilt gained it instant popularity:

Little Miquette, you mustn't forget
Was French and extremely pretty
And she lived in the plain of dry Champagne
For there was her native city.
She was so fair, the gentlemen there
Came courting her by the dozen
But she didn't find them suit her mind
Not even her favourite cousin . .

The vain little Epernaise falls instead for a flighty American who goes off and leaves her. Miss Greene also lauded the beauties of Cuba in 'I'm a Cuban Girl' and ended with a waltz ballad 'Waiting for Me'.

Bill Berry, one of the best singing comedians about, had his share of the musical action and scored well with the mock pirate song 'Filibuster Brown':

For I'm wiry, fiery Fili-filibuster Brown
The demon of the Dover Strait, the terror of Canning Town,
The Captains all quake, they get in a fluster
They're white as chalk if you should talk of Brown,
Of Mr Brown, of Reggie Brown the Filibuster, that's me!

a topical song 'How did the Bird Know That' and in duets with Jean Aylwin ('The Slopes of Denmark Hill') and Lester ('According how You Are'). Lester – less of a singer than a comedian – built up his role in the comic direction and left the singing to Berry, but he did have a duet with Jean Aylwin in which they parodied the *Merry Widow* waltz with certain effect. The rest of the songs were spread freely among the other members of the cast and produced some of the show's best moments. The statuesque contralto Jessie Broughton, from the chorus, sang a Creole song called 'Zara' which showed Stuart's rhythmic mastery at its best; J. Robert Hale in a smallish role sang the attractive 'A little supper Table for Two' and joined with Jean Aylwin, Mabel Russell and Berry in a comical quartet:

If you see a little bag
Lying out upon a flag
In the street
Be discreet
Never steal it!
If you meet a lobster tin
In a dust-collecting bin
That has got
Rather hot
When you feel it,
If you spot a cigarette
Someone happened to forget
Then beware
Leave it there
Never smoke it.
And a Barcelona nut
That is roosting in a rut

On the road
May explode
If you poke it!
IT'S A BOMB!

Leonard Mackay, as the hero, sang, to one of Adrian Ross's less inspired lyrics 'And then that Cigar Went Out' but compensated with his ringing voice for any deficiencies in the words; Jean Aylwin sang of 'My Husband' who'd been missing seven years – a state of affairs she seemed to find quite satisfactory; Mabel Russell in frills and ribbons sang 'Down in Pensacola'; while Lawrence Grossmith had a ten-little-niggers type piece 'Hello, People!' played with half a dozen girls in a skip, and a rather less attractive telephone song, 'Cupid's Telephone'. It is interesting that the numbers which emerged as the most attractive were those which had relevance to the plot and the characters, while those like 'Cupid's Telephone' which were of the patently 'movable' variety were less inspired.

The score of *Havana* had one very particular advantage. In spite of its variety, it was the work of one man and thus had an integrity which was often missing from the multi-authored scores so frequently found in the current musical theatre. Stuart had always fought against the practise of interpolation and collaboration and his scores had always benefited from the resultant homogeneity. *Havana* proved his point, and reaction to the play's production was largely favourable. *The Stage* reported:

> [*Havana*] is a great stride forward for the Gaiety. Mr Edwardes has made something like a clean sweep of the comic shreds and patches of what must now be accounted the old style of Gaiety pieces. How ready the public was for the change, Saturday evening showed. *Havana* gave Mr Edwardes the most successful first night that he has ever had at the Gaiety . . . . Hour after hour the piece went on, from eight o'clock until Sunday morning came, but the audience laughed and applauded and remained. Save in the stalls, the house was crowded at the last as when the curtain first went up.

Some others were, predictably, less extravagant. Some regretted the absence of certain favourite stars, others of the Caryll/Monckton style of piece, but *The Times* came up with a surprising complaint:

> . . . too long, too loud, and too lavish and too loose-limbed . . . . It starts with a blaze and a rattle and ends with a rattle and a blaze; and even in the second act during part of which one can look at the scene without blinking, the rattle goes on though the blaze is subdued . . . [our] pleasantest recollections are of the quieter moments . . . . it is a pity that the Gaiety cannot contrive us more such moments out of all the wealth of colour and sound and female beauty which it continues to throw higgle-piggle in crude masses at our bewildered eyes . . . it was not a meal but a gorge . .

It was not a complaint with which many of the audience would have agreed. Amongst the 'blaze and rattle' however, *The Times* found time to praise the comedy of Lester and Berry, the singing of Mackay, and Stuart's music – with particular praise for 'Zara' and 'It's a Bomb'.

When the smoke had cleared it was evident that *Havana* was a success, if not on the scale of *A Country Girl* or *The Toreador* or even of *The Girls of Gottenberg*. At the annual shareholders' meeting of the Gaiety Company, Edwardes was able to announce that the financial deficit created by *A New Aladdin* had been wiped out and, by the time the show was taken off after some seven and a half months and 221 performances, things were well back into the black again at the Gaiety.

Additions and alterations during the run were, as customary with a Stuart show, kept to a minimum although the role of Diego de la Concha was revised and enlarged when Courtice Pounds took over from Edward O'Neill. Further alterations were necessary when Evie Greene was forced to leave the show because of ill health. Gertrude Lester and the lovely Enid Leonhardt filled the gap until Miss Leonhardt in her turn left to become Mrs David Wellesley Bell and May de Souza was brought in. A new duet for Miss de Souza and Pounds was added for the occasion. Another who left *Havana* to get married was the beautiful Gaiety Girl Sylvia Storey who was added to the ranks of Gaiety peeresses as the Countess Poulett.

Within months of its withdrawal from the Gaiety, *Havana* went round the world. In America it caused a sensation in its out-of-town try-out in Philadelphia. James Powers had rearranged the script to give himself, as Nix, all the best bits of the other comic roles as well as his own, and he used them to good enough advantage to conceal the shortcomings of his prima donna 'Mlle Courtenay from the Opéra Comique, Paris'. But Leslie Stuart's music caused the greatest furore and the music shops were inundated with customers. *The Stage* correspondent reported:

> It took the audience by storm and there is not the least doubt that it will prove as huge a moneymaker as did *Florodora* . .

The Shuberts hurried the show into Broadway's Casino Theatre, replacing the unfortunate Mlle Courtenay en route, and *Havana* opened on 11 February, 1909 to a fine reception:

> . . one of the biggest successes lately produced on this side of the Atlantic . . (*Stage* correspondent)

Powers and the Shuberts had a hit on their hands. The first-named promptly cancelled his holiday cottage at Stratford-on-Avon in preparation for an extended run and the latter chalked up a joyful mark in their continuing battle against the rival Klaw/Erlanger combine. The more exaggerated expectations for *Havana* on Broadway turned out to be disappointed but it had, nevertheless, a fine run of 236 performances and added to Leslie Stuart's excellent record on American shores. It opened in quick succession in Australia, starring Florence Young, Victor Gouriet, Reginald Roberts and Andrew Higginson with Susie Vaughan as Isabelita, and in South Africa, while in Britain it was sent into the provinces to consolidate its worthy record with the young Dorothy Ward starring as Consuelo. Edwardes' judgement had been at least partly vindicated. *Havana* was a good solid success. Not, perhaps, a triumph – particularly by Gaiety standards – but a thoroughly artistic and enjoyable show which found a large and appreciative audience in each country where it played.

In the meanwhile there were revivals around. *The Mikado* now being totally cleared, Mrs D'Oyly Carte brought it back into the repertoire at the Savoy where it was seen to have lost none of its old popularity and at the Queen's Robert Courtneidge reproduced *The Dairymaids* starring Phyllis Dare who varied her diet by playing Juliet at a matinée of *Romeo and Juliet* during the run.

But there was not long to wait for the new next piece. Less than three weeks after the opening of *Havana*, another new musical hit town, this one at the Apollo Theatre. *Butterflies* was the latest managerial venture of the popular singer, Ada Reeve. Her previous attempts had not been notably successful. Neither *Winnie Brooke, Widow* nor

Moll, the Rogue had lived up to expectations but this latest property looked to have much stronger prospects.

The libretto was the work of William J. Locke, architect-turned-writer who had already been successful with the novels *The Morals of Marcus Ordayne* (1905) and *The Beloved Vagabond* (1906) and their dramatic versions, the former of which as *The Morals of Marcus* had played 197 performances at the Garrick in 1907 and the latter had been produced just three months previously at Her Majesty's with every sign of success. *Butterflies* was a musical version of a third play, *The Palace of Puck*, which had been produced at the Haymarket by Frederick Harrison for a disappointing run of only six weeks. It had been remarked at the time that the piece might serve better as the basis for a musical and, under Miss Reeve's management, the author's adaptation of his own play with songs by T. H. Read and J. A. Robertson, Miss Reeve's conductor, was produced at the Tyne Theatre in Newcastle. After three weeks it was brought into the Apollo where it opened to a curious critical reception:

> instead of the rapidity and fluidity of the play we have songs, dances, displays of clothes, concerted pieces, everything – except a patriotic song . . (*Times*)

> an incongruous mixture of the elements of odd fantasy, noisy farce and emotional sentimentalism . . . in the process of transformation [from a play] much of the original fancy, poetry, wit and imagination seem to have evaporated . . (*Stage*)

But they had not liked the play – or had they forgotten? – and it had run only six weeks. The musical, in spite of these unfavourable comparisons, ran six months in town before being taken round the country as an undeniable success.

No one could complain of *Butterflies* that it lacked plot. In fact, it went even further and had – almost alarmingly – what its author called a 'philosophic purpose':

> I took three honest suburban people, father, mother and daughter who, from the circumstances of their training and environment had been blind to the sweet and beautiful things of the world. The chief blindness lay in the father and mother who had married and lived together in the dull, prosaic British way, without realising their own or each other's inner qualities that make for life. I put them suddenly in a gay, fantastic environment, 'The Palace of Puck', where, everything being all the time sweet and clean, they should find a complete upsetting of all the conventions that had stood for them as ideals. I postulated these coincidences: each of the Podmores should recognise an old acquaintance in the 'Palace of Puck'. I arranged that, with Puck's control, there should be three love stories. The young man without a penny should quickly teach the little girl that she 'would sooner have Peter without a penny than a world full of pennies without Peter'. Rhodanthe, the witch, should teach Podmore that he was a man, with a man's strength and gallantness and capacity for passion. Max, the dreamer, should teach Mrs Podmore the poetry, sweetness and tenderness of life. When their lesson was complete I made Puck contrive to bring them together in a dramatic explanation during which they should witness the elopement of their daughter with Peter. My object then was to shew that Podmore realised in Mrs Podmore all the woman that he had seen in Rhodanthe, Mrs Podmore all the man that she had seen in Max, that the little girl's love story should open their eyes to the beauty of love and to the years they had wasted, and that they should go away into the world, hand-in-hand together, lovers at last, to lead a new and happy existence in the real Fairyland . .

'Puck' in this context is one Mr Widgery Blake, a charming and whimsical gentleman of means living in a château in France where he has surrounded himself with a happy Bohemian crowd including the vivacious model, Rhodanthe, and her lover, Max. Into this gay setting come the prosaic and blinkered Podmores and Rhodanthe and Max, having quarrelled, each take it upon themselves to flirt with a Podmore until each of the loosened-up spouses is ready to run away with his or her new lover. At the crucial rendezvous, however, they find . . . each other, and they watch in silence, together, as their daughter Elsie elopes with her 'unsuitable' young man. Reunited and with a new awareness of each other, they leave the 'Palace of Puck' and the reconciled Max and Rhodanthe.

For the musical version the play was retained by and large within its original outlines. The jeune première role of Elsie was enlarged and the role of the chauffeur, Yarker, was written-up as a principal low comic role and, for obvious reasons, Max became a professional vocalist instead of a poet but the essence of the piece and its content remained unaltered.

The two most important roles were, of course, those of 'Puck' and Rhodanthe, created at the Haymarket by H. V. Esmond and Miriam Clements, and here Rhodanthe became the property of the manageress. The role gave Miss Reeve the opportunity to display her considerable talents as an actress as well as to put over a series of numbers of which the most worthily popular was undoubtedly 'Morals' (Walter Davidson/T. H. Read) which declared 'In each tale of our youth is a great moral truth' and illustrated:

From Bo-Peep and her sheep let us strive to derive
A lesson for rich and for poorish,
From the way she mislaid all her flock I'm afraid
That Bo-Peep was a bit amateurish.
To return to her mutton she first resolved but on
Reflection abandoned her chase,
For she said, they're no loss, they'll turn up in due course
With their tails in the usual place.

Sisters, sisters, is it not true?
Have we not here a lesson for you?
Try to imagine that you are Bo-Peep
Likewise consider your husband a sheep.
If you should find him addicted to roam
Leave him alone and in time he'll come home
And like Bo-Peep's sheep you'll find he'll not fail
When he comes to bring with him a beautiful tale!

The final verse had scathing references to some recent childish squabblings in Parliament which elicited the odd cry of 'No Politics' on the opening night, but this clever song, put over with enormous panache by Miss Reeve, proved a big success. She had a couple of numbers in a more lyrical vein which proved less to the public liking than a lively duet with little Lauri de Frece called 'A Lesson from the French' in which the lady tried to teach the cockney chauffeur to woo *comme il faut*. Originally she also had a fairish piece called 'Lapland' (not the country, but a gentleman's knee), but by the time London had been reached that piece had been handed down to her understudy, Jessie Lonnen (daughter of E. J.) in the small role of 'Myra'.

As 'Puck', Miss Reeve engaged the Daly's leading man W. Louis Bradfield whose amazingly youthful charm and strong voice suited him admirably to the role. He made a success with a song called 'The Girl with the Clocks':

Ask her to dine, she'll decline 'Never met you',
Says she can't without her aunt,

Take her aunt, and she'll let you.
For the girl's only mocking,
She's got clocking on her stocking,
So she does know the time of day!

although his other material was probably better. One of his songs, 'The Palace of Puck', had a lyric written jointly by Read and Percy French, and French was also responsible for the words to a bright trio 'Three blind Mice' in which Puck, Rhodanthe and Max tell what they intend to do with the three 'blind' Podmores:

Mice, mice, take our advice
Come when the cat's away,
We'll open your eyes, we Butterflies,
To a life that is always gay!

Max was played by another Daly's hero, Hayden Coffin, equipped with a couple of characteristic ballads and a fine suit of clothes. One of the ballads saw Coffin at his favourite pastime of interpolating his own choice of song. On this occasion he fancied a French piece called 'Où est Koko?'. Koko was a dog. This had nothing at all to do with *Butterflies* and/or Max Riadore, but the song duly found its way into the score with its music rearranged by Robertson and a completely new lyric written by Arthur Anderson – nothing to do with dogs – entitled 'Life'. The rest of the cast was equally well-chosen, and ranged from such rising stars as the young comic Lauri de Frece, who had been so praised in *Amasis*, 23-year-old Iris Hoey in her first leading role as Elsie, and the promising tenor John Bardesley, to veterans like Willie Warde, Fred Edwardes and Stella St Audrie.

Although the dramatic and musical sides of *Butterflies* were both good and strong, the visual part was by no means neglected. The third act was set at a 'Butterfly Ball' which gave the costume designer the opportunity to dress his chorus ladies in the most fantastic creations. During the run of the piece it was decided to introduce a special Butterfly pas seul into this scene and a particularly gorgeous dress was created for the solo dancer. The lady hired, however, refused to wear the garment. Miss Reeve relates:

> This was a case where the dress was more important than the dancer. It was a semi-Oriental costume with a skirt of transparent black gauze and a bodice joined to it by ropes of pearls through which a few inches of bare flesh showed at the sides. Nowadays, of course, no one would think twice about wearing it, but in 1908 it was quite daring . . .

There were four dancers in the show, hired to perform a can-can number which was one of the show's most successful spots:

> I saw the blonde dancer, whom I had already noted as the best of the can-can girls, looking at me with wistful eagerness. 'Would you like to try it, Phyllis?' I suggested . .

And so Phyllis Monkman stepped from the chorus to become the principal dancer in *Butterflies* and, in time honoured fashion, never looked back.

After the opening night and its equivocal reactions, Miss Reeve boldly announced that *Butterflies* would play the Apollo until mid-November when it would be sent on tour. 217 performances later November duly arrived and *Butterflies* was still playing to good business, but the previous commitments Miss Reeve had made obliged her to quit the Apollo and take the show on the road. In spite of the defections of Bradfield and Coffin and the departure of Miss Reeve herself to her all-important pantomime, the show found itself an appreciative provincial audience but, although thoughts of a return to the West End were mooted, it did not appear again in London.

Butterflies showed, as *Kitty Grey* had, that a shift of emphasis from the accoutrements of the musical show–its songs, dances and splendid staging–to a strong and intelligent libretto which used the expected elements of fun and glamour only to enhance the play and its characters, was one which was viable and even popular.

For some time, Frank Curzon had been nurturing a young writer, Frederick Lonsdale, as yet unproduced, who had brought him a play and a musical, both of which he had liked. The musical he had sent to Adrian Ross and Sidney Jones to set and *King of Cadonia* was the result. The collapse of *My Mimosa Maid* left the Prince of Wales Theatre unexpectedly empty, and *King of Cadonia* was quickly scheduled for production to fill the gap. Curzon also put his farce *The Early Worm* into rehearsal for Wyndham's Theatre, but it was the musical which had the distinction of being the first Lonsdale piece to appear on the London stage and it was an immediate and undisputed success.

The story was familiar enough. Two young scions of neighbouring dynasties are to marry but they object to such a peremptory bethrothal and each runs away in disguise. In disguise, they meet fall in love and wed tidily. Lonsdale's version fleshed out these ancient bones with a fanciful situation in which the people of Cadonia, swayed by republican and/or anarchistic feelings, have a habit of getting rid of their kings. The present young king is closely guarded, not the least on behalf of the nervous Duke of Alasia, next in line for the throne and not at all eager for the job. It is this Duke's daughter, Marie, whom the government has selected to marry the King, and it is from this situation that the young people escape. King Alexis falls in with the band of conspirators responsible for the quick turnover in kings and becomes respected by them so that when, with Marie at his side, he is revealed as the King of Cadonia, rebellion ceases and all ends happily. *The Stage* commented:

> The author–Mr Frederick Lonsdale–a comparatively new man–has not, it is true, happened upon a pre-eminently fresh idea for his central theme, but as a decidedly accomplished writer for the stage he has proved (as so many accomplished writers have proved before him) that the whole art of the matter lies rather in its treatment than in the theme itself. His first act is an admirably constructed piece of work and, as first acts should, it arouses considerable interest in what is to come: whilst of the second act, which is more humorous than its predecessor, it may be said that it fully satisfies one's expectations . .

and even *The Times* admitted: 'The author, new we believe to this kind of work, makes the most of his none too striking story.'

The basic story of Alexis, Marie and the conspirators was well embroidered with comical characters and situations. Huntley Wright had what the *Play Pictorial* considered his best and most original role since *The Geisha* as the jittery Duke of Alasia. Made Regent after the disappearance of Alexis, he dispenses honours and rewards in the pursuit of popularity and support while all the time quailing before his formidable wife (Amy Martin) who scares him just as much as being King does. Heading the female side of the comedy was Wright's old Daly's colleague, Gracie Leigh, firmly installed as resident comedienne at the Prince of Wales and playing, once again, the comedy maid with even more opportunities than before.

The central roles featured Isabel Jay and the baritone Bertram Wallis, recently returned from playing *The Little Cherub* and *Miss Hook* in America and making his first

West End appearance since *Love Birds*. The pair made a handsome and vocally exciting combination. They were also fortunate in having some of the best dialogue and songs which had appeared in the British musical theatre for some time. Adrian Ross had risen to his best standards for *King of Cadonia* and Sidney Jones had caught exactly the right level of musical composition for what looked like developing into the new style of musical: like *Havana* less frivolous, less go-as-you-please, like *Butterflies* with a coherent and properly worked-out storyline: not comic opera, not musical comedy, but something neatly and intelligently constructed in between. It was a field into which Jones, with his years of experience in the early Daly's musicals, fitted comfortably and naturally and, in consequence, the fabric of *King of Cadonia* was a superior and well-knit one.

The bulk of the music fell to the four stars, with Miss Jay and Wallis exceptionally well-treated. Miss Jay sang the waltz song 'The Wind of Love' and the pretty 'The Man I Marry' with enormous success, while Wallis described the business of royalty as 'Over-rated' before bringing the house down in the second act with the stalwart 'There's a King in the Land Today':

So the people still may say
As the parties pass away
Be they up or down, we have still the Crown,
There's a King in the land today!

The two were also featured in a set of particularly well-written duets: 'The Lady of the Castle in the Air' in which the King describes how he would find his Queen . . if, that is, he were a King, 'The Woman and the Man' and later 'Love and Duty', as well as a pretty scena in which Marie sketches a portrait of the man she has just met and fallen in love with while Alexis listens from behind a tree.

On the humorous side, Huntley Wright's patter song 'Do not Hesitate to Shoot' earned a nightly encore. It was a piece in the vein of Gilbert's 'Little List' number in which the Duke enumerated to his soldiers all the dangerous and annoying types of people on whom they were expected to fire at first sight:

In these days of deadly danger any monarch has to fear
If he finds a doubtful stranger inconveniently near
So I mean to be protected by the marksmen of my guards
Who can pot a man suspected at about four hundred yards.
Do not hesitate to shoot! Do not hesitate to shoot!
If he's carrying a coconut or other massive fruit
For it may be full of dynamite, or possibly may not,
You can see when he is shot. You can see when he is shot!
And the one who gets him first is made a sergeant on the spot
So of course he should be shot.
Shot.

The proscribed list included bad bridge players, large slow ladies in ticket queues and people who hum the music inaccurately at the opera. From time to time the list was expanded. Wright had another song in which he enumerated 'Things that I Know I could Do' in preference to being King, and he shared a comic duet with Gracie Leigh in which, preparing to flee from a conspiratorial attack, they discuss 'Disguises'. The number gave them the chance to do imitations of Indian, Scottish and Italian performers in various verses.

'Disguises' had a lyric by Arthur Wimperis, as did the most successful of Gracie Leigh's three numbers 'Situations':

Lots of mistresses I've had
Some were good and some were bad
And others knew no better, I suppose,
But I've always had my way
And my wages to the day
And I've always had to earn 'em, heaven knows.
Now when service first I took
I was asked to help the cook
Which I stooped to, being only a beginner,
And my mistress said one day
Where's that bit of mutton, eh
Which I ordered to be 'eated up for dinner?
Well, I hope I know my place,
But I told her to her face
You should give your aitch more careful aspiration
Eat it up, you said to me,
So I ate it up, you see,
So I had to get another situation

The first night of the new musical was a marked success:

> at the conclusion there was a scene of much enthusiasm, all the principals being called, together with the author, the composer and the producers . .

King of Cadonia was safely launched on a twelve months' West End run and Freddie Lonsdale on a notable career. In the following August it was produced in Australia starring Herbert Clayton as Alexis, and by September three companies were out in the British provinces with Conway Dixon, Roland Cunningham and J. Warren Foster at their heads. For an American production, however, it was necessary to wait until 1910 when the show was presented at the New York Daly's in a version in which it had been thought necessary to pepper Sidney Jones' well-proportioned score with inappropriate Jerome Kern interpolations. Not surprisingly, the incongruous result lasted only two weeks.

To succeed *A Waltz Dream* at the Hicks, Charles Frohman produced a musical from a surprising source. G. P. Huntley had turned his hand to writing and collaborated with baritone Herbert Clayton on the book of a piece called *The Honourable Phil* which dealt with the amorous escapades of the dashing French Lieutenant Jules de Valery (Clayton) and his quaint, aristocratic friend Captain the Hon. Phil Giffard (Huntley) on the Breton island of St Angelo. The objects of their amours were, respectively, the talented Denise Orme, who contributed not only singing and dancing but also a violin obbligato to her lover's second act solo and the music for her own song 'Drifting', and the delicious American soubrette, Julia Sanderson, Broadway star of *The Dairymaids*. Of story there was virtually none. Jules, for reasons unexplained, conducts his wooing of the lovely Marie disguised as a boatman, and the principal plot line seemed to concern the efforts of the nouveau riche Marinet (O. B. Clarence), Marie's father, to avoid customs duty on his cigars. *The Honourable Phil* was a return to the virtually plotless song and dance amalgams of earlier years but its song and dance were not sufficiently memorable to justify its existence.

The music for the show was largely written by the young concert pianist, Harold Samuel, better known for his Steinway Hall recitals and other such 'proper' activities. He had trained in Vienna and had turned out a number of platform songs as a composer but this was his first attempt in the light musical theatre. Unfortunately many of the lyrics with which he was provided were of a mediocre standard and his music was neither original nor catching enough to redeem them. *The Honourable Phil* was a vaguely agreeable piece of nothingness. It was not even a tour de force for Huntley whose character, in spite of being the title name, was quite irrelevant to the action, and who shared the comedy of the show with Clarence and with Horace Mills as the valet, Buckle, who had the show's two best numbers:'A Gentleman's Gentleman' and an interpolated piece by Herbert Haines and Douglas Townshend, 'I'm a raging, ramping, roaring Vesuvius'.

A complaisant first night reception was followed by lukewarm reviews:

> [it] does not cause the continuous roars of laughter which it will doubtless evoke when it has been, as we say, properly worked up .... though the men may work and the ladies sing and dance their hardest, and though the music is bright and sufficiently tuneful *The Honourable Phil* does not, as a musical comedy, quite seem to justify the popularity of that branch of the dramatic art, which is one of the signs of our times . . (*Times*)

> . . musical comedy of the most conventional kind . . . the author and the composer, though they bring fresh energies to their work are content to keep to the beaten track. Here and there the music of Mr Harold Samuel shows qualities of some little distinction especially of fancy and delicacy – but they are not well-sustained . . [he] has certainly had little help from the various writers of the lyrics . . . the piece on the whole is commonplace. (*Stage*)

The public seemed to agree. In spite of the presence in the cast of Huntley and of a lovely new Broadway star, their reaction was largely one of indifference. Frohman did not wait long. He set up an American season of *Kitty Grey* for his contracted stars and, as soon as he was ready, closed down *The Honourable Phil* and exported Huntley and Miss Sanderson to the other side of the Atlantic. The show had lasted, on sufferance, just a little more than two months.

Rather more success awaited Tom Davis' newest venture at the Queen's. For *The Belle of Brittany* he reunited the successful architects of *The White Chrysanthemum* and *The Girl Behind the Counter*, librettist Leedham Bantock and composer Howard Talbot. Bantock had shown, both in *The White Chrysanthemum* and in the less well-judged *The Three Kisses,* a tendency towards a modern type of comic opera libretto, and the successes of *Havana* and *King of Cadonia*, not to mention *The Merry Widow*, showed evidence that this type of book was now to be preferred to the lax and more trivial outlines once popular.

In a collaboration with P. J. Barrow, Bantock took the full comic opera turn back to the meadows of Brittany and a plot concerning the love of Raymond, son of an impoverished nobleman, for the miller's daughter Babette. Raymond's father, the Marquis, wants his son to marry profitably to save the family estate and has chosen his ward, Mlle Denise de la Vire, to supply that need. Speed is of the essence, as the Marquis has mortgaged his estate and is about to be foreclosed on. But the holder of the mortgage is none other than Poquelin, the miller and the father of Babette, and he, too, is anxious to stop the Raymond/Babette affair for he has arranged to affiance his daughter to the famous chef Baptiste Boubillion. Things look bad but the situation is saved when the all-important deeds to the estate fall into the hands of old Jacques, the clarionet player, who uses them to bring things to a happy conclusion.

The setting may have been 'comic opera' and the plot, resting as it did on little more than a series of love matches and the oldest *deus ex machina* in the business, the vital document, scarcely had much sophistication to it, but *The Belle of Brittany* did not turn out to have an oldfashioned air. The authors had the first sine qua non of the modern musical in their picturesque setting: the daffodil fields of Brittany provided a glorious stage picture. They had a straightforward and comprehensible story which, if old, they had treated in a modern way and decorated with attractive characters, pretty songs and dances and a good deal of wholesome fun, the whole being done in a gently pleasant fashion which did not dazzle but could never offend. *The Times* reaction seemed confused:

> *The Belle of Brittany* is rather difficult to describe. It is rather pretty and rather funny and rather bright. It was rather well produced and not much more than rather well played and so it was rather well received and will probably be rather successful. It has the faults of its class in only a mild degree. It is not frankly absurd nor absolutely trivial, neither the colours nor the music give one a headache, it keeps pretty close to such plot as it has. But the fact is that both plot and music are rather feeble for those who like comic opera while for those who like musical comedy, first nights are only the infancy of what will grow out of knowledge as the months run by.

The Stage also tried unsuccessfully to pigeon-hole the show:

> . . the suggestion is one of comic opera. But comic opera *The Belle of Brittany* can scarcely be called. The book . . in not consistent enough . . . the music not strong enough. [It is a] conventional musical comedy score, clever of its kind, tuneful and cheerful, getting very well its effect of the moment, but with little colour, without the distinction of a big and characteristic work . .

What, in fact, the authors and composer had created with *The Belle of Brittany* was an attractive and cultivated modern musical. Taking some of the settings and styles of the older comic operas they had used them in a piece which used also the musical and lyrical styles of 1908. Greenbank and Barrow introduced a sufficiently modern flavour without being too out of keeping with the eighteenth century French setting. Talbot's music, too, was in no way a reproduction of Auber or Bucalossi or Jakobowski. It was in the same light vein which had characterised his greatest successes from *A Chinese Honeymoon* to *The White Chrysanthemum*, but it was never unsuitable or at odds with the contribution of the writers.

Ruth Vincent sang charmingly of 'Daffodil Time in Brittany', of 'The Dawn of Love' and of 'My Wedding Morn' and joined with the baritone Lawrence Rea in describing what occurred by the 'Stepping Stones'. He, in his turn, declared 'I'm not a Marrying Man' before being converted to 'The Kingdom of a Woman's Heart'. Less romantically, Maudie Darrell, as the pert maid Toinette, declared herself 'A Bit of the very best Brittany' and joined the comical chef (Walter Passmore) to sing about 'Two giddy Goats' and of their dreams for 'A little Café'. There was a quintet describing 'The Old Château' which sounded mightily like the Château de Corneville and a number called 'The Ingle Nook' which rather resembled the 'Cosy Corner' of *The Earl and the Girl*, while Lily Iris, making her musical comedy début, scored with a song on the well-used theme of 'Little Country Mice'. None of the ideas used for the songs of the show were particularly startling or new, but it was all attractive material.

Passmore, as the Parisian chef intended for Babette but finally happier with her maid, had some excellent moments. His entrance number described him as 'The King of the Kitchen'.

> As chef of a swell Parisian hotel
> I have studied the human inside
> And I make it my boast

That I rule the roast
Not to mention the boiled and the fried.
Each night I don my warpaint, cap and apron white as snow,
And deftly mix an omelette or a custard
But if the eggs aren't fresh, my wrath is like the oven's glow
And I pepper the assistants round me mustered!

I'm the King of the Kitchen, Prince of all the pots and pans
Commander-in-chief of the barons of beef
And Lord of the flavoury
Entrée and savoury
I'm famous for my grills
And even cutlets put on frills
When they're served by the great Baptiste &c

and it was supplemented by some humorous scenes and a 'Hush, the Bogie' number called 'In the Oven' where naughty children are threatened with being popped in the frying pan:

Look, look, look, here comes cook,
He's got a great big oven down below . .

The chief comic role was that of the Marquis, taken by George Graves who was now famous as Baron Popoff of *The Merry Widow* and the creator of the Gazeeka and of Hetty the Hen.[1] He did not add to his mythical menagerie in *The Belle of Brittany* but, nonetheless, he enlarged and worked-up his part to a formidable extent until, along with the singing of Ruth Vincent and the stunning scenery, the performance of 'the Marquis' was one of the principal features of the show.

The remainder of the show was also given a working up, a number of new pieces being added within a few weeks of the opening. The first and most winning was a number for Maudie Darrell which proved to be her best piece in the show:

When Monsieur the Marquis
Wakes up each morning early,
He rings the bell for me
In temper somewhat surly;
A nice hot cup of tea
I bring in just to cheer him,
He's better tempered, you will find,
As soon as I pull up the blind
For he likes Toinette to be near him!
Oh, I'm not a ladies' maid
Fetching frock and fan
I much prefer the plan
Of waiting on a man
Good wages I am paid
But none too good, you see,
For I'm indispensable to Monsieur le Marquis

Marie Horne turned out another reminiscence of *Les Cloches de Corneville* with a bell song for Ruth Vincent, and George Graves, of course, had fresh material as well.

[1] Graves had padded and popularised his roles in *The Little Michus* and *The Merry Widow* with the antics of these ad-libbed animals.

The Belle of Brittany was not a hit. As *The Times* had predicted it fell into the category of 'rather'. It had a respectable run of 147 performances and was duly appreciated by those who did not look for the extremes of light opera or frivolous variety musicals. Its charm and warmth did not prove to be sufficiently positive virtues to make it a major success. It had aimed for that 'centre field' which *Havana* and *King of Cadonia* had pointed as the coming style, but it had not done so with enough panache and emphasis for the taste of the large theatre public. One who clearly did have faith in its virtues was George Graves for he and Maud Boyd (the original Mme Poquelin) headed a cast which took *The Belle of Brittany* into the country the following year where it found a willing public.

In 1909 it also found its way to Broadway. After an encouraging opening in Washington it came in to Daly's Theatre. Unavoidably, it had been tampered with since London but the new material, including three songs by Harold Atteridge and Henry Carroll, did not destroy the show's essential gentle charm and Elsa Ryan's rendering of 'A Bit of the very best Brittany', Winnie O' Connor's 'Daffodil Time' and the little duet 'Stepping Stones' combined with an hilarious portrayal of the Marquis from comedian Frank Daniels to win the show a warm reception. *The Era's* American correspondent hailed it as being 'like the good old days of English musical comedy', but *The Belle of Brittany* survived only 40 performances on Broadway: the good old days clearly had a limited appeal.

The production of *The Belle of Brittany* rather took the wind out of the sails of one Mr Henry R. Smith, partner of Sheppard at the Lyceum, who had taken on the Waldorf Theatre which had been unsuccessful and neglected in recent months. Though only three years old, the Shuberts' theatre was already in need of restoring to life and Smith proposed to do this with a musical called *Miss Blossom of Brittany* by Sutton Vane and Edward Jones. Tom Davis' production effectively put paid to that plan and Smith announced instead a new musical called *The Antelope*. This was to be a musical version of Hippolyte Raymond and Paul Burani's celebrated vaudeville *Le Cabinet Pimperlin* (1878) adapted by Adrian Ross with music by the Viennese composer of *Madame Sherry* and *Les Merveilleuses*, Hugo Felix, who was now living in London.

Le Cabinet Pimperlin had, in fact, already been set to music some years previously by no less a composer than Hervé and his opérette had been played at the Atheneée-Comique in 1897 after the composer's death. *The Antelope*, which was produced on 28 November, proved to be rather less satisfactory. The basic story of *Le Cabinet Pimperlin* was that of a marriage agency which insures its customers against the evils of elopement – thus the English title 'The Anti-Elope' or 'Antelope' which was the trading name of the agency. To prevent the payment of an indemnity, the owner of the bureau sets his own wife to captivate a young man who looks like eloping with the wife of one of his customers.

The original English production of the play at the Vaudeville in 1886 had seemed somewhat indecent. Twenty years on and treated as a musical it seemed innocuous enough and also rather long drawn-out with the single comic premise barely serving as a core to a full evening of farcical entertainment. Adrian Ross had taken on the dual task of libretto and lyrics but he could not instil enough wit and sparkle to bring the old farce to life. *The Stage* referred to the 'by no means brilliant dialogue' and the 'injudicious political allusions' but the *Era* disagreed and judged it 'a bright, lively and amusing libretto which only wants vigorous and judicious cutting to be quite acceptable'. Either way, the book of the show as it stood was not right.

Hugo Felix wrote some attractive music with no particular individuality. The nearest thing to a successful song turned out to be a dramatic piece for little Maudi Thornton as a drummer boy – a musical version of Kipling's 'The Drums of the Fore and Aft'. It was generally agreed, however, that the music was the best feature of the new show which really had little else to recommend it.

Although the cast included stars of the magnitude of Florence Lloyd, Fred Emney, Fred Wright, Kitty Gordon and Joe Farren Soutar, in retrospect the most interesting member of the company was the young singer who took the role of Iris, the jeune première. A few weeks previously, José Collins had been singing 'My Cuban Girl' and mugging her way through 'Looking for the Limelight' at the Oxford Music Hall; in *The Antelope* she had her first West End principal role, though only for three weeks.

The repercussions did not come to an end quite as quickly, owing to Smith's means of financing his production. By representing himself as already having subscribers for a large part of his capitalisation, Smith had persuaded George Dance to invest £3000. In fact, Smith's company held just £50 and Dance's money was soon spent. The cheated Dance sued for fraud and was granted a decision for the return of his entire investment.

The revival season was continued at the Savoy. Mrs D'Oyly Carte followed *The Mikado* with *H.M.S. Pinafore* and *Iolanthe* and December brought back *The Pirates of Penzance*. It also saw the return of the still popular *Dorothy*. This latest revival was sparked by Hayden Coffin and the tenor John Coates who set on foot a tour of the major provincial and suburban theatres in September and achieved notable popularity. A short period being available at the New Theatre, the brothers Maundy-Gregory decided to bring the production to town with a strengthened cast for a two-week period. *The Times* critic who constantly bewailed the 'noise and glare' of modern musicals was nostalgically ecstatic:

> The pleasantest feeling of all is the conviction that *Dorothy* completely deserved all the admiration we lavished on it . .

The revival overran its intended stay, remaining at the New till February and finishing its run at the Waldorf.

The final new piece of 1908 was a children's Christmas play written by the author/illustrator W. Graham Robertson, with music by Frederic Norton. *Pinkie and the Fairies* had been published in illustrated dramatic form before its stage production was arranged by Beerbohm Tree as a seasonal piece at Her Majesty's Theatre. It was undoubtedly one of the most successful of the musical fairy plays which had been produced over the years. Unlike the even more popular (and more commercial) *Bluebell in Fairyland* it did not look to the world of the musical comedy for inspiration, but was simply a work of poetic fantasy, illustrated with songs in a suitable vein rather than with echoes of the Gaiety or the music halls.

In the story, two children, Pinkie and Tommy, and their teenage cousin Molly visit a fairy party where they meet various storybook characters. Molly has been sent to the country to prevent her making an unsuitable marriage, but with the help of the children and the fairies love conquers all and even goes so far as to unbend the starchy Aunts Caroline and Imogen. The story was told in an elegant and whimsical fashion with admittedly quite a few allusions which would have been above the head of all but the most precocious child; but it was unfailingly charming and amusing.

Song and dance held a reasonably prominent place in the show, from delicate fairy rhymes and music to poetic little ballads, some parody processional music announcing the arrival of the aunts, and a mock aria in which Aunt Caroline sang of the past and present in culinary terms:

Cold is the joint so warm of yore
Hashed is the mutton of yesterday. Ah me, ah me.
And the elderly egg that has gone astray
Is never the egg that it was before. Ah me, ah me.
For breakfast and lunch and tea
It's hey for the dinner that's cleared away
Then ho! for the dinner to be!

Robertson's poetic background came to the fore in such pieces as the Sleeping Beauty's song:

As I leaned over the Slumber Well
Where the wild white poppies grow
The heart from my bosom slipped and fell
Into the depths below.
And the waters cool of that healing pool
So stilled the throb and pain
That my heart sank deep in the Wells of Sleep
And never came up again.

Tree had the resources to give an exceptionally strong cast to the piece. Amongst the adults, Ellen Terry and Augusta Havilland played the Aunts with Frederick Volpe as Uncle Gregory, while the younger members of the cast included 18-year-old Marie Löhr as a garrulous society Cinderella, 24-year-old Viola Tree as the somniac Sleeping Beauty and Stella Patrick Campbell as Molly. Fifteen year-old Iris Hawkins was Pinkie, a role in which she could still be seen on tour ten years later, and Philip Tonge, another experienced child, was Tommy. There were many lesser known children in the cast as well. One who attracted much pre-publicity was Elise Craven, a ten year-old pupil of choreographer Elise Clerc who was booked to play the Queen of the Fairies; she had a shining success and went on to make a career as a dancer. An even more notable career awaited the 11-year-old who, also making her first stage appearance, played the tiny part of a fairy herald. *The Era* noted: 'Miss Hermione Gingold [was] acceptable as the Fairy Herald'. *Pinkie and the Fairies* was a most attractive piece:

a very choice entertainment for children, all grace and elegance and dainty rather than boisterous fun . . Mr Norton's music is all suavity . . (*Times*)

The piece ran through the Christmas season with such success that Tree produced it again for Christmas the following year. The cast was not quite as starry this time but Edward Terry, Baroness van Hutten, Gwendoline Brogden and May Leslie Stuart, daughter of composer Stuart, were prominent additions to remnants of the original team. *Pinkie* was seen on a number of occasions in the provinces and became a perennially popular piece with both professionals and amateurs.

Provincial productions had ceased in recent years to provide West End material of the calibre of *The Gay Parisienne*, *The French Maid* and *The Lady Slavey*, but pieces were still being produced out of town which were capable of running up good records on the touring circuits without taking the ultimate, and often unwise, step of testing themselves in town.

1908 brought two such pieces. The first was produced at the Theatre Royal, Lincoln, in May and was entitled *The Flower Girl*. The libretto and the music were both the work of William Gliddon, the composer of the ambitious *Fisher Girl* and the less fortunate *Petronella*. Its plot was straightforwardly familiar. Joe Wheeler, a busman, once found an abandoned baby and he brought her up along side his own son, Billy. Little Lily is now 20 and a Piccadilly flower girl and engaged to Billy. Joe loses his job with the introduction of the motor bus and becomes instead a private detective. His first job is for the swell Reginald Rackett and his aristocratic French relations, the de Racquets, who are searching for their little lost niece. By the end of the play this is discovered to be Lily who achieves the aim of all musical comedy heroines by becoming rich, aristocratic and married.

The show leaned on a strong patriotic element, exemplified in Lily's rendering of the stirring 'The Rose of England' with massed chorus. It also used most of the established and popular musical elements: a topical trio ('A Twinkle in the Eye'), the girlie song ('Oh, you Girls' – sung by Reginald in good Grossmith style with a quartet of dancing girls), the romantic ballad ('All the World Loves a Lover'), the comic song ('One of the Force' for Joe) and so forth. The book was slight and bright and of the songs *The Stage* noted:

> [there is an] abundance of bright numbers, of the lyrical merit it can be said that they are neither better nor worse than average, while the music is always catchy and is sure to please the popular ear.

And it did. *The Flower Girl*, under the management of C. M. Bestic, was sent on tour. It ran right through the hot summer months when the touring scene was almost empty and it continued through to Christmas when it was announced that it would end only to allow its artists to take up their pantomime engagements. But there was still a demand and, in the end, *The Flower Girl* extended its marathon tour right through the holiday period and into 1909. Even the death of Bestic in March of that year did not stop *The Flower Girl* carrying on its way. It was brought out for a further tour in 1910 and, at the end of the year, a revised version, rewritten and staged by George Unwin was put on the road under the title *The Missing Maid*. It was given a brief tour in 1911 and, in 1912, was unwisely ventured in a metropolitan appearance when it was produced at a matinée at the Court Theatre. It achieved no success, putting a final stop to the show's drawn-out career.

The Gay Deceivers was another provincial success. It was produced at Margate in June with no creative credits given, although it was rumoured that it was the work of two authors already well-known and, indeed, with work currently on display in the West End. It had the familiar 'arranged marriage' plot and a good deal of mistaken identity and flirtation and comedy and its second act was topically set at the Franco-British Exhibition currently running at Shepherds Bush. It was well-received on its production:

> a number of funny situations, some of the dialogue, too, is decidedly smart. There are a capital set of songs . . .

and was sent on tour with a West End opening announced for October. October came and went and *The Gay Deceivers* showed no sign of appearing in London. However, it had done well enough on its trial run to warrant another more extended tour.

The remainder of the provincial output included two variations on the Cinderella story. The first (prematurely titled *A Hielan' Cinderella*) was produced at the King's Theatre in Hammersmith by George MacKarness as *The Girl from over the Border*. In it, Prince Carl, a student, is in love with Stella, the star of the local pantomime *Cinderella*. In order to avoid seeing a deputation from the Highland laird, Wee

McGregor, he changes clothes with his friend Dandy. In a dream (which comprised the main body of the show) he sees the story of Cinderella before wakening to a happy ending when Stella turns out be the daughter of the Wee McGregor who is being proposed for his bride.

The show was strongly cast: George Carroll and Bertie Wright headed the comedy with T. W. Volt, the Lord Lavender of more than a decade of *Lady Slavey* companies, as Dandy. Leslie Stiles played the romantic Prince and Gay Silviani was principal girl. West End dancing star Winifred Hart-Dyke was featured, and provincial stalwarts Nellie Bouverie and Amy Fanchette were not-so-ugly sisters. The piece was reasonably well received, but short-lived.

The second *Cinderella* was on a less ambitious scale. *The Belle of the Ball* was a piece of a frankly pantomime flavour, although it clothed the Cinderella story in comic opera characters. The fairy godmother became a broad male comedy role and he engineered the tale's denouement at the Squire's Ball where the heroine nets her groom. Comedian Johnnie Schofield as 'Timothy Timmins' had the central role and a few of the songs written by *Trip to the Highlands* composer E. T. de Banzie and baritone-cum-composer Michael Dwyer. These were largely destined for Gertrude Melville as Poppy, the modern Cinderella and Robert Hyett as her Squire. There were echoes of other and earlier successes in such titles as 'A true blue British Girl', 'Over in Monkeyland', 'Pretty little heather Bell', 'Cupid Is a Tyrant' and the coon song (not yet dead) 'Kiss me, Honey'. *The Belle of the Ball* toured some good dates in the provinces and in the London suburbs.

The only other piece of any substance to appear was a second anonymous piece called *A Merry Maid*. It was a cheerful mixture of favourite elements: beginning in Ireland with a simple country heiress being wooed by a knowledgeable lawyer, it skated happily through a ball, a trip to the Riviera, a yachting escapade and some burlesque-like humour on its way to a happy ending. The show could not manage the same.

1908

0342 **MY MIMOSA MAID** a Riviera musical incident in two acts. Chatter by Paul A. Rubens and Austen Hurgon. Jingles and tunes by Paul A. Rubens. Produced at the Prince of Wales Theatre under the management of Frank Curzon 21 April, 1908 for a run of 83 performances closing 11 July, 1908.

Victor Guilbert	G. P. Huntley
Max Guilbert	George Barrett
Bock	Charles McNaughton
Boy	Archie McCaig
M. Emile Gerrard	Maurice Farkoa
Groue	Windham Guise
Captain Louis du Laurier	F. Pope Stamper
Lt Jean Courmandet	Harold A. Deacon
Lt Baptiste d'Eranger	Charles Hillman
Lt Raoul St André	H. F. R. Lightfoot
Boss	Cecil Burt
Cigarette Seller	Cecil Curtis
Popitte	Gracie Leigh
Mme de Pilaine	Eva Kelly
Granny	Joan Penrose
Marie	Clarisse Batchelor/Peggy Bethel
Antoinette	Gertie Murray
Paulette	Isabel Jay

with Queenie Merrall &c

Dir: Austen Hurgon; md: Ignatius A. de Orellana; sc: Hawes Craven and Walter Hann; cos: Karl

0343 **BUTTERFLIES** a musical play in three acts founded on *The Palace of Puck* by William J. Locke. Lyrics by T. H. Read and Arthur Anderson. Music by J. A. Robertson. Produced at the Tyne Theatre, Newcastle, under the management of Ada Reeve 20 April, 1908 and toured through Glasgow and Manchester. Opened at the Apollo Theatre 12 May, 1908 for a run of 217 performances closing 14 November, 1908.

Salome	Gladys Soman
Paul	Willie Warde/Alfred Selby
Peter	Kenna Lawson/Roy Sydney/J. Mansell Stringer
Gilbert	John Bardesley/Walter Hyde
Lalage	Lucie Caine
Myra	Jessie Lonnen (Hilda Vining)
Yarker	Lauri de Frece
Christopher Podmore	Fred Edwards/George Giddens
Elsie Podmore	Iris Hoey
Nora Podmore	Stella St Audrie
Widgery Blake	W. Louis Bradfield
Max Riadore	C. Hayden Coffin/Frank Wilson

Rhodanthe. Ada Reeve (Jessie Lonnen)
add Alfonso . . . . J. Mansell Stringer/*out*
Parisiennes: Phyllis Monkman/Miss Worth, Misses Glynne, Brock and Gordon
Parisians: Messrs Giron, Edwarde, Alfred Selby, Rubins
with Olive Cherry, Gwendoline Hay, Hilda Vining, Mabel Maartens, Florence Nobbs, Gladys Purnell, Flora McDonald, Alice Sands, Verona Phyllis, Raynor Golden, Ella Carlisle, Hilda Saxe, May Foster, Maisie Sainsby, Marguerite Penfold, Lassem

Md: J. A. Robertson; ch: Willie Warde; sc: Joseph Harker; cos: 'Crow'

0344 HAVANA a musical comedy in three acts by George Grossmith Jr and Graham Hill. Lyrics by Adrian Ross. Additional lyrics by George Arthurs. Music by Leslie Stuart. Produced at the Gaiety Theatre, under the management of George Edwardes 25 April, 1908 for a run of 221 performances closing 12 December, 1908.

Jackson Villiers . . . . Leonard Mackay/T. C. Maxwell
Hon. Frank Charteris. . . . . J. Robert Hale
Hilario. T. C. Maxwell/Harry B. Burcher
Alejandro . . . . Ernest Mahar
Antonio . . . . Barry Lupino
Bombito del Campo . . . . Arthur Hatherton
Don Adolfo . . . . Lawrence Grossmith
Diego de la Concha . . . . Edward O'Neill/Courtice Pounds/Alec Fraser
Customs House Officer . . . . Lewis Grande
Sentry . . . . J. R. Sinclair/F. Raynham
Nix . . . . Alfred Lester (George Gregory)
Reginald Brown . . . . W. H. Berry (Somers Bellamy)
Anita . . . . Jean Aylwin
Isabelita . . . . Gladys Homfrey/Gladys Fontaine
Maraquita . . . . Kitty Mason
Tita . . . . Olive May (Sylvia Storey)
Pepita . . . . Mabel Russell
Lolita . . . . Adelina Balfe
Mamie. Barbara Dunbar
Teresa. Enid Leonhardt/Marie Dean
Lola . . . . Florence Phillips/Moya Mannering
Zara . . . . Jessie Broughton
Isolda . . . . Senorita Tortola Valencia/*out*
Signora Verriotti . . . . Kitty Hansen (Ruth Argent)
Consuelo . . . . Evie Greene (Gertrude Lester) (Enid Leonhardt) May de Souza
add Piccaninny . . . . Nora Nagle
Touring newspaper beauties: Gladys Cooper, Julia James, Frances Kapstowne, Daisy Williams, Connie Stuart, Kitty Lindley, Crissie Bell, Phyllis Barker
Ladies of Havana: Enid Leslie, Gladys Desmond, Claire Rickards, Eileen Caulfield, Pauline Francis, Sylvia Storey, Pattie Wells/Irene Warren, Gertrude Wykes
Gentlemen of Havana: Harry B. Burcher, Alec Fraser, W. Raymond, J. Redmond, Cecil Cameron, Sidney Lyndon

Dir: Edward Royce; md: Carl Kiefert; ch: Edward Royce; sc: Joseph Harker and Alfred Terraine; cos: Percy Anderson

Produced at the Casino Theatre, New York, in a revised version by James T. Powers under the management of Sam & Lee Shubert 11 February, 1909 for 177 performances to 10 July, 1909. Resumed 8 August, 1909 for a further 59 performances closing 25 September, 1909 after a total of 236 performances.
Joseph Phillips (J. DE PEYSTER JACKSON), William Phillips (FRANK VAN DUSEN), Ernest Hare (HIL), Ted Sullivan (ALE), Glen Conner (ENRIGO), Harold Vizard (BOMB), Ernest Lambart (ADOL), William Pruette (DI), Eugene Roder (SENTRY), James T. Powers (NIX), Percy Ames (REG), Clara Palmer (ANITA), Eva Davenport (IS), Mabel Weeks (TITA), Daisy Green (PEP), Viola Kellogg (LOL), Violet Gerrard/Adelaide Rosini (MA), Geraldine Malone (TER), Edith

Decker (CONSUELO), Edith Kelly (GLADYS), Bertram Grassby/J. Donald Archer (RODERIGO), Joseph Galton (SR. PATIGO/SOLDARO), Milburry Ryder (OFFICER), Little Lillie Fuehrer (CHIQUITA), Master Robbie Fuehrer (SAMMY Jr/CHIQUITO), Harry Sulkin (JUAN); with Caroline Green, Dolly Filly, Erminie Clark, Elsa Croxton, Cecilia Mayo, Irene Hawley, Julia Mills, Emily Monti, B. Ryan, Gladys Alexander, Janet North, Freda Braun, Helen Broderick, Marion Hartman, Elise Raymond, Adelaide Rossmi, Suzette Gordon, Isabelle Daintry, Mildred Bright, Lorraine Bright, Mary Murrilo, Patsy O'Connor, Libbey Diamond, Mona Sartoris, Hazel Williams, Dorothy Sayce, Ruth Elton, Irma Dixon, Jeanne McPherson, Miss Holmes, Isobel Cannar, Sylvia Loti, Mildred Dupree, Nathalie Harvey, Harold Nelson, Jack Brese, Harold Watson, Arthur McSorley, George Allison, Jean Roeder, Arthur Whitman, Harry McDonough, Philip Haring, Albert Massour, Jack Leonard, George Skillman, Alexander Groves. Dir: Ned Wayburn; md: Clarence Rogerson; sc: Arthur Voegtlin

0345 **THE FLOWER GIRL** a musical play in two acts. Book, lyrics and music by William T. Gliddon. Produced at the Theatre Royal, Lincoln, under the management of Charles M. Bestic 14 May, 1908 and toured through Smethwick, Hull, Brighton, Longton, Newcastle, Glasgow, Edinburgh, Scarborough, Llandudno, Birkenhead, Oldham, Southport, Rochdale, Birmingham, ?, Preston, Cheltenham, Broughton, Dewsbury, St Helens, South Shields, Wakefield, Aberdeen, Dundee, Newcastle, Edinburgh, Glasgow, Nuneaton, Croydon, Woolwich, Shakespeare, Worthing to 26 December, then from 18 January 1909 Eastbourne &c.

Lily	Lily Brammer/Dorothy Firmin/Kitty Hyde
Joe Wheeler	Martin Adeson/John McCullum
Billy (later Johnny) Wheeler	Walter Purvis/Alfred Donohoe
Johnny (later Hon. Billy)	B. Currie/Robert H. Howard/Robert Craig
Reginald Rackett	Edward Kipling/Norman Bowyer/Louis du Cane
Alphonse de Raquet	Henry Adnes
Lisette de Raquet	Florence Wilton/Lillian Drahn
Miss Spankard (later Greenwhill)	Jennie Holmes/Ella Brettingham
Jessie	Cissie King
Kate	Phyllis Leslie
Dot	Kitty Hyde/
Policeman	Louis Stanislaus/P. Prujean
Mr Bunker	Arthur Carter
Bertie	Tom Squire/F. Williams
Maisie Flirtington	Lucy Kipling/Townley Lawrence

Dir: F. Norris Martin; md: William T. Gliddon/William Neale

Revised and reproduced under the title *The Missing Maid* in a version by George Unwin with lyrics by George de Lara and additional music by Jacques Henri. Produced at Swindon 26 December, 1910 and toured. This version was presented at a matinée at the Court Theatre 16 March, 1912, with the following cast:
Ferne Rogers (LIL), Harry Benet (JOE), D. Price-Evans (WH), E. Floyd Gwynne (HON), Reggie Gray (RR), Ernest Lindsay (AL), Dora Sawyer (LIS), Rose Temple (LADY GREENHILL), E.Shannon (PC), Walter West (NEVAH PARKER), Charles Ashley (HON ARTHUR FOPPINGTON), Marie Montague (JIMMY), Gladys Vernon (LADY MAMIE TEARAWAY), Kathleen O'Neil (HON MAUDE RHODES), Ethel Harper (LILY SINCLAIR), Maud Tresilian (HILDA DE LANGE). Dir: George Unwin; md: Percy Elliot

0346 **THE GAY DECEIVERS** a musical absurdity in 2 acts by Mark Lester and others. Produced at Margate under the management of George Waters 22 June, 1908 and subsequently toured by Frank Stanmore and then Leslie Hawkins and Joseph Hindle. Dates included Ramsgate, Sheerness, Eastbourne, Aldershot, Brighton, Leicester, Widnes &c.

Colonel Dewar	George Delaforce/Arthur Dennis/Charles Leverton
Lt Frank Dewar	Guy Williams /Douglas Phillips/Eric Langham
Major Kurrie	Clive Currie/J. W. Bradbury
Lord Reggie Muddleton	Frank Stanmore/Leslie Hawkins

Pinch . . . . . J. W. Woodington
Monsieur Giraffe . . . . . Pat Eden
P. C. Parker . . . . . Will Capers
Joseph . . . . . Mark Lester
Mrs Dewar . . . . . Kate Chard
Winnie Winter . . . . . Cicely Stuky/Dora Lane
Dora Darling (Dartney) . . . . . Dorothy Chard/Gertrude Palmer
Rosie . . . . . Pauline Primm/Hettie Gale
with Miss Goss, Brenda Guider, Nellie Day, Violet Darling, Maud Leslie, Mlle de Taillebois
Md: E. Ramsay

0347 **THE BELLE OF THE BALL** a musical play in 3 acts by A. Norden. Music by E. T. de Banzie and Michael Dwyer. Produced at the Opera House, Southport under the management of Violet Osmund and Alexander Loftus 27 July, 1908 and toured. Dates included Edinburgh, Glasgow, Hull, Oldham, Birmingham, Broughton, Luton, Peckham, Eastbourne &c.

Sir Francis Lake . . . . . Robert Hyett
Bobbie Fletcher . . . . . Llewellyn C. Hughes/Johnny Schofield Jr
Farmer Jones . . . . . James Chippendale/Charles Adeson
James Forster . . . . . E. W. Chewd
William . . . . . Jack Hale
Timothy Timkins . . . . . Johnnie Schofield
Showman Jack . . . . . Frank Collins/E. H. Bertram
Footman . . . . . E. Osborne
Queenie Trevor . . . . . Maud Terry/Florence Watson
Lucy . . . . . Vera Grafton
Alice . . . . . Mary Earle/Ethel Bertram
Mary . . . . . Corona L'Estrange
Red Riding Hood . . . . . Clara Casey/Rosie Wade
San Toi . . . . . May Hawthorne
Poppy . . . . . Gertrude Melville
Irene . . . . . Miss Cartwright/Gwennyth Penrhyn
Marie . . . . . Sydney Penrhyn
add Gussie Maitland . . . . . Llewellyn C. Hughes
Md: W. Stephenson

0348 **KING OF CADONIA** a musical play in two acts by Frederick Lonsdale. Lyrics by Adrian Ross. Music by Sidney Jones. Produced at the Prince of Wales Theatre under the management of Frank Curzon 3 September, 1908 for a run of 333 performances closing 30 July 1909.

Duke of Alasia . . . . . Huntley Wright/E. Statham Staples
Alexis, King of Cadonia . . . . . Bertram Wallis
General Bonski . . . . . Roland Cunningham
Captain Laski . . . . . F. Pope Stamper/Reginald Kenneth/ (Fred W. Ring)/Cameron Carr
Lieutenant Jules . . . . . Harold A. Deacon
Lieutenant Saloff . . . . . Cameron Carr/Fred W. Ring
Panix . . . . . Arthur Laceby
Laborde . . . . . Akerman May
Bran . . . . . George Barrett/James Blakeley
Militza . . . . . Gracie Leigh/Joan Penrose
Stephanie . . . . . Peggy Bethel
Natine . . . . . Queenie Merrall/Marian Marler
Wanda . . . . . Gladys Beech
Ottaline . . . . . Claire Lynch
Fridoline . . . . . Gladys Anderson
Duchess of Alasia . . . . . Amy Martin
Princess Marie . . . . . Isabel Jay (Marian Marler)
with Misses Allen, Milner, Davison, Meredith &c
Dir: Sydney Ellison; md: Ignatius A. de Orellana; sc: Hawes Craven; cos: Karl

Produced at Daly's Theatre, New York, under the management of Messrs Shubert 10 January, 1910 for a run of 16 performances, closing 22 January, 1910. Additional songs by M. E. Rourke and Jerome Kern.
William Norris (DUKE), Robert Dempster (ALEX), Albert Gran (BON), Melville Stewart (LAS), Donald Buchanan (JU), William Davis (SAL), D. L. Don (PAN), St Clair Bayfield (LAB), William Danforth (BR), Clara Palmer (MIL), Mabel Weeks (ST), Addie Marze (NAT), Edna Broderick (WAN), Carolyn Armstrong (OTT), Bessie Tannehill (DUCH), Marguerite Clarke (M), Vincent Dusenberry (BARBER); with Misses Richards, Gordon, Ryan, Langhorn, Grant, Sargent, V. Rose, Hamilton, Weston, Howard, Walters, Williams, A. Rose, Booth, E. Wheeler, Hines, Daily, Virginia, D. d'Irinyl, Wheeler, Forbes, Summers, Baron, St John, Winters, McKeon, Flint, Addison, Banta, Ryan, Hempstone, Silver, Stewart, Sheldon, Clifford, Addison, Deveraux; Messrs Wells, Giles, Mayer, Brandell, Bingham, Somerville, Dusen, Kingsley, Ford, Warwick, Dodge, Spears, Tedret, Feiner, Carter, Johnston, Searl, Andres, Sleck, Pierce, Alston, Wellikens, Ryan, E. Gran. Dir: Joseph Herbert; md: Hugo Bryk; sc: Arthur Voegtlin; cos: Melville Ellis

0349 **THE HONOURABLE PHIL** (The Hon'ble Phil) in two acts by G. P. Huntley and Herbert Clayton. Lyrics by Harold Lawson. Additional lyrics by Bertrand Davis and Claude Aveling. Music by Harold Samuel. Additional numbers by Ralph Nairn. Produced at the Hicks Theatre under the management of Charles Frohman 3 October, 1908 for a run of 71 performances closing 12 December, 1908.

Capt. the Hon. Phil Giffard	G. P. Huntley
Capt. Jules de Valery	Herbert Clayton
Maurice Montpensier	Charles Brown
Monsieur Marinet	O. B. Clarence
Buckle	Horace Mills/Ralph Roberts
Cournot	Charles Seguin
Dubois	Hubert Willis/T. M. Hickton
Homard	T. M. Hickton/Frank Stedman
Jerome	Frank Perfitt
Gascon	Carlton Brough
Gobert	J. Herbert
Courriol	Herbert Hulcup
Marie	Denise Orme
Didine	Eva Kelly
Brigette	Elsie Spain/Ethel Negretti
Mme Lascelles	Barbara Huntley
Annette	Nellie Francis
Fleurette	Dorothy Dunbar/Lily Collier
Fanchette	Alice Kay
Mauricette	Tessie Hackney
Josephine	Ella Brandon
Marcelle	Violet Wyatt
Eugenie	Barbara Allen
Clarice	Winifred Harris/*out*
Julie	(Mary) Douglas Frere
Henriette	Nancy Reeve
Louise	Nellie Brownlee
Babette	Nell Clapton
Suzanne	Julia Sanderson

with Dorothea Grey, Marie West, Ruby Luton &c

Dir: Austen Hurgon; md: Herbert E. Haines; sc: James A. Hicks; cos: Comelli

0350 **THE BELLE OF BRITTANY** a musical play in two acts by Leedham Bantock and P. J. Barrow. Lyrics by Percy Greenbank. Music by Howard Talbot. Additional numbers by Marie Horne. Produced at the Queen's Theatre under the management of Tom B. Davis 24 October, 1904 for a run of 147 performances closing 20 March, 1909.

Marquis de St Gautier	George Graves

Raymond de St Gautier . . . . Lawrence Rea (Harry Leslie)
Comte Victoire de Casserole . . . . Davy Burnaby
Poquelin. M. R. Morand
Old Jacques . . . . E. W. Royce sr/Royston Keith
Pierre . . . . Frank Melville
Bertrand. Vere Matthews
Eugene . . . . John Montague
Philippe . . . . Harry Leslie
Vivien . . . . Hamlyn Hamling
Baptiste Boubillion . . . . Walter Passmore
Toinette. Maudi Darrell (Jessie Fraser)
Mlle Denise de la Vire . . . . Lily Iris/Millie Legarde (May Hackney)
Madame Poquelin. . . . . Maud Boyd (Poppet McNally)
Lucille. . . . . Blanche Stocker
Miquette . . . . Cora Carey/Doris Beresford
Adele . . . . Alice Hatton
Mirette . . . . Blanche Carlow/Claire Pridelle
Christine . . . . Minnie Baker
Rosalie. . . . . Gladys Saqui/Maisie Stather
Babette . . . . Ruth Vincent
add Margot . . . . Jessie Fraser
Claire . . . . Emmie Santer

with Poppet McNally, Miss Russell, Miss Temple, Ida Sydney, Marie Desmond, Lucy Davis, Emmie Santer

Dir: Sydney Ellison; md: Howard Talbot; sc: Julian Hicks, J. Harbour; cos: Percy Anderson

Produced at Daly's Theatre, New York, under the management of Sam & Lee Shubert 8 November, 1909 for a run of 72 performances closing 8 January, 1910.
Frank Daniels (MARQ), Frank Rushworth/Hubert Neville (RAY), George M. Graham (VIC), Harry Crandall (POQ), Joseph A. Bingham (OLD), Hubert Neville/(BERT), Story Chipman (EU), Homer Potts (PH), Jack Laughlin (VIV), Martin Brown (BAPT), Elsa Ryan (TOI), Daisy Dumont (DEN), Frances Kennedy (MME), Evelyn Mitchell (LU), Dorothy Perry (MI), May Hopkins (AD), Helen Paine (MIR), Helen Albert (CHR), Elsa Harris (RO), Christine Neilson (BAB), Clara Schroeder (COLITTE), Josephine Brandell (MALINE); with Tracy Elbert, Camille Truesdale, Louise Elton, Blanche Huntingdon, Sidney Jacouver, Dixie Compton, Mudge Harman, May Hopkins, Helen Mackey. Dir: Frank Smithson; md: Clarence Rogerson; cos: Melville Ellis

0351 **THE ANTELOPE** a musical comedy in three acts by Adrian Ross adapted from *Le Cabinet Pimperlin* by Hippolyte Raymond and Paul Burani. Lyrics by Adrian Ross. Music by Hugo Felix. Produced at the Waldorf Theatre under the management of Henry R. Smith 28 November, 1908 for a run of 22 performances closing 19 December, 1908.

Bennett Barker . . . . Fred Wright Jr
Hon. Guy Daubeney . . . . Joe Farren Soutar
Joe Derrick . . . . Fred Emney
Montague Mosenstein . . . . John Brabourne/Windham Guise
Loisl Huber. . . . . Jack Cannot (Murri Moncrieff)
Vincent Clive . . . . Charles R. Rose
Gerald Grosvenor. . . . . Arthur Grover
Peter. . . . . Maudie Thornton (Lily Maxwell)
Araminta Mosenstein . . . . Hilda Stewart
Gwendoline Barker . . . . Florence Lloyd
Iris Fenton . . . . José Collins
Gladys. Vivienne West
Stella Smithson . . . . Beatrice Read
Theodora Thompson . . . . Ethel Oliver
Celia Corinth . . . . Lily Mills
Violet Vivian . . . . Dorothy Monkman
Camilla Claude . . . . Nancy Hervyn
Speranza Derrick . . . . Kitty Gordon

Delia de Vere . . . . Lily Maxwell
with Misses Ashcroft, Madeley, Darrell, Dale, Lillington, Levine, de Lacey, Dolaro, Lee, Muret, Ismay, Mann, Grey, Kipling, Bland, Bride, Barbour, O'Brien, Germaine, Gosling, Herbert and Hartopp; Messrs Hugh Cross, A. Harris, Richard Long, Andrew Paice, Murri Moncrieff, Baker Ker, Robert Hine, E. Martin, H. Wingrove, Alec Turnbull

Dir: Herbert Cottesmore; md: Hugo Felix; ch: Fred Farren; sc: W. F. Hemsley & H. Brook; cos: Percy Anderson

0352 **PINKIE AND THE FAIRIES** a fairy play in three acts by W. Graham Robertson. Music by Frederic Norton. Produced at Her Majesty's Theatre under the management of H. Beerbohm Tree 19 December, 1908 for a season of 73 performances closing 13 February, 1909.

Aunt Imogen . . . . Ellen Terry (Edith Craig)
Aunt Caroline . . . . Augusta Havilland
Uncle Gregory . . . . Frederick Volpe
Molly . . . . Stella Patrick Campbell
Pinkie . . . . Iris Hawkins
Tommy . . . . Philip Tonge
Elf Pickle . . . . Sidney Sherwood
Elf Whisper . . . . Marjorie Duggan/Marjorie Burgess
Elf Twinkle . . . . Kathleen Yorke
Herald . . . . Hermione Gingold
Prince Frog . . . . William Parke
Cinderella . . . . Marie Löhr
Sleeping Beauty . . . . Viola Tree
Beauty . . . . Winifred Beech
The Beast . . . . Walter Creighton
Jack the Giant Killer . . . . Francis Walker/*out*
Jack of the Beanstalk . . . . Frank Varna/*out*
Queen of the Fairies . . . . Elise Craven
Mr Irons . . . . Mr Smithson
The Cat . . . . Norman Page
The Butcher . . . . Henry Mather
Daffodil . . . . Kathleen Starling

Dir: Herbert Beerbohm Tree; md: Adolf Schmid; ch: Elise Clerc; sc: Joseph Harker; cos: Dion Clayton Calthrop

Produced at Her Majesty's Theatre under the management of H. Beerbohm Tree 16 December, 1909 for a season ending 22 January, 1910.
Baroness von Hutten (IM), Augusta Havilland (CAR), Edward Terry (GREG), Hilda Antony (MOLLY), Iris Hawkins (PINK), Philip Tonge (TOM), Patty Jacobs (PICK), Mimi Crawford (WHISP), Olga Hope (TW), Charles Burford Hampden (HER), Robert Chalton (FROG), Gwennie Brogden (CIND), Millicent Field (SLEEP), May Leslie Stuart (BEA), Walter Creighton (BEAST), Florrie Lewis (QUEEN), Doreen Wayliss (DICK WHITTINGTON), J. Wessen (CAT), A. Wessen (PUSS-IN-BOOTS), Isabel Jones (DAFFODIL), Mr Smithson (MR IRONS), J. Oliver (TELEGRAPH BOY), H. Brown (MR BUNNY). Dir: H. Beerbohm Tree; ch: Elise Clerc; sc: Joseph Harker; cos: Dion Clayton Calthrop

THE GIRL FROM OVER THE BORDER a musical extravaganza by Marshall Moore. Additional lyrics by Roland Carse. Music by Clement Locknane and M. J. Lawrence. Produced at the King's Theatre, Hammersmith, under the management of George MacKarness 18 May, 1908.

Prince Carl . . . . Leslie Stiles
Dandy Pearsop . . . . T. W. Volt
Tubby Wiggles . . . . Bertie Wright
The Wee McGregor . . . . George Carroll
Sandy MacAlpine . . . . Cecil Frere
A Student . . . . Herbert Standing Jr
Lady Dorothy Clancarty . . . . Winifred Hart-Dyke

Lady Joan Campbell . . . . Marion Marler
Margaret Helen . . . . Gladys Ffolliot
Jeannie . . . . Nellie Bouverie
Jessie . . . . Amy Fanchette
Mary McAlpine . . . . Norah Walker
Stella . . . . Gay Silviani
Dir: Marshall Moore

A WELSH SUNSET a musical piece in one act by Frederick Fenn. Music by Philip Michael Faraday. Produced at the Savoy under the management of Mrs D'Oyly Carte as a forepiece to *H.M.S. Pinafore* 15 July, 1908. Subsequently played with *H.M.S. Pinafore* and *The Pirates of Penzance* in repertoire.

Jenny Jones . . . . Beatrice Meredith
Griffith Dowd . . . . Stafford Moss
Mrs Jones . . . . Ethel Morrison
Mary Fewlass . . . . Mabel Graham
Nancy Raine . . . . Beatrice Boarer
Gwennie Davis . . . . Bertha Lewis
Owen Rhys . . . . Leo Sheffield
John Lloyd . . . . Sydney Granville
Morgan Llewellyn . . . . Allen Morris

PIERETTE'S BIRTHDAY an episode with music by Colin Neil Rose. Music by Clement Locknane. Produced at the New Theatre 24 June, 1908 and subsequently at the Haymarket Theatre under the management of Frederick Harrison as a forepiece to *Lady Frederick*.

Pierette . . . . Elaine Inescourt
Pierrot . . . . Robert Cunningham
Harlequin . . . . Reginald Eyre

1909

The opening weeks of 1909 offered a representative mixture of musical shows in the West End. On the one hand there were the 'old' represented by Mrs D'Oyly Carte's repertoire season of Gilbert and Sullivan at the Savoy and by the revival of *Dorothy*, now transferred to the Waldorf in the wake of the failure of *The Antelope*; on the other there were the 'new', *King of Cadonia*, *The Belle of Brittany*; and the 'borrowed', the only foreign representative, the seemingly inexhaustible *Merry Widow* at Daly's now starring J.F. McArdle and Emmy Wehlen. Alongside these ran Beerbohm Tree's fairy play *Pinkie and the Fairies* and a W.H.C. Nation 'vanity' production: *The Kingdom of Kennaquhir*.

It was not a situation which was to last for long. The producers of *Dorothy*, having ambitiously announced a whole season of old comic operas for the Waldorf, closed down suddenly. They had been losing money and, with Hayden Coffin announcing his departure to the banner of Seymour Hicks, they saw themselves about to lose an important part of their attraction. The 'famous continental artist' boasted to replace him did not have time to be named: the notice for *Dorothy* was posted. The last advertised performance did not even take place. After the Saturday matinée a number of the staff and orchestra scented money troubles and demanded to be paid immediately. The Maundy-Gregorys raked up enough cash to satisfy their staff and asked the orchestra to wait until the end of the evening performance. They refused. The queues outside the popular parts of the theatre had to be sent away and the Waldorf Theatre remained closed. It was a sad ending to the last West End production of one of the best loved and most successful British musicals of all time. But the succession had already been assured. Two weeks previously the first new show of 1909 had opened at the Gaiety and *Our Miss Gibbs* was about to lift itself into that charmed circle of alltime greats alongside *Dorothy* and its fellows.

With *Our Miss Gibbs* it might have been argued that the Gaiety was taking a half-pace backwards from the slightly more substantial textures of *Havana* or even of *The Girls of Gottenberg*. The elements of its plot, taken separately, were not particularly fresh. Once again the heroine was a shop girl, once again courted by an earl in disguise who, yet once again, was supposed to be paying his attentions to a more suitable young lady. As usual there was the 'funny little man' and the dragon mother, the crusty earl and the society dude, as well as the inevitable bevy of pretty, well-dressed girls and smart gentlemen, and the whole was mixed by the same team of writers who for so long had served up the Gaiety product – Tanner, Ross, Greenbank, Monckton and Caryll.

The book was announced as being by 'Cryptos', a pseudonym for all the lyricists and composers with Tanner at their helm, and the book which they concocted held so many well-used pieces of subject matter that it must have been long odds against their coming up with anything fresh and original but, yet once again, it was proved that the manner of the treatment was more important then the basic framework. The writing and composing co-operative of *Our Miss Gibbs* hit upon a set of characters, a style and setting and tone which were sufficiently different from previous shows and attractive in themselves and, with all their efforts combined, they produced what was, arguably, the best and most enduring of all the Gaiety musicals. *The Times* tried to pinpoint the characteristics which marked it out:

> . . [it] is the least boisterous and glaring piece that the Gaiety has produced: and it is one of the brightest, merriest and most amusing . . . . we cannot expect realism, of course, or verisimilitude, but there was more of them than usual . . . . . We have never seen the Gaiety favourites so free from their familiar tricks and we have never seen Miss Millar or Mr Payne so amusing. The former has gained enormously in point and deftness of late and tricks have nothing to do with the success of her Mary Gibbs. Mr Payne we suspect never made so little of his lisp and his elastic face and so much of his genuine drollery . .

The creative team had, indeed, evolved delightful versions of the stars' characters. Gertie Millar was Mary Gibbs, a Yorkshire lass come to town and working as a shop girl in 'Garrods' where she sells candy. All the local hooray Henrys are making themselves sick on sweets as they come to ogle and sigh over the no-nonsense Miss Gibbs who disapproves thoroughly of their attempts at 'sophisticated' familiarity: 'Why do they call me 'Mary' when my name's Miss Gibbs?' Miss Gibbs has given her heart to a young bank clerk who is, in reality, Lord Eynsford. When she discovers this deception, she concludes promptly that 'he never meant to marry me' and dumps him on the spot.

Teddy Payne played Timothy, Mary's cousin, down from Yorkshire to play second euphonium for the town band in the big contest at the Crystal Palace. Timothy is a real country cousin and his adventures in the big city make Mr Popple of Ippleton's look like a quiet Sunday outing. The little man manages to get himself mixed up in crime when he mistakenly picks up a bag belonging to the Hon. Hughie Pierrepoint, an enthusiastic amateur criminal. The bag contains the Ascot Gold Cup which Pierrepoint has just managed to steal.

The second act takes place at the Franco-British Exhibition at the White City. Little Timothy is in a sweat over his 'crime' and imagines that the police bloodhounds are after him. He disguises himself as an entrant in the big marathon race and staggers into the stadium to be mistakenly acclaimed the winner. Finally, the cup is recovered and restored to its owner who happens to be young Eynsford's father, by now so charmed by Mary Gibbs that he is more than happy that she should become his daughter-in-law.

George Grossmith had a superb role as the would-be 'Raffles' of London. He described in song the plight of the budding criminal whom no one will take seriously:

> Though I'm a man of noble birth
> I'm trying all the time
> To win renown throughout the earth
> By daring deeds of crime!
> But when for deeds that I have done
> I'm brought before the beak
> He doesn't even make a pun
> And will not let me speak,
> For when he hears my name

He always says the same:
It's Hughie, just Hughie, I knew he was Hughie
There are few
Such as Hugh
In the zoo!
Not two all through Who's Who &c

Hughie's attentions are sharply distracted from the indifferent Miss Gibbs when he meets Lady Betty Thanet. Lady Betty (played by Denise Orme, without her violin) is the young lady designed by her Mama as a wife for Eynsford. But Betty reads modern fiction and has other ideas:

Parents do not understand it
When their daughter, on the spot,
Loves a pirate or a bandit
So they tell her she must not!
Then come tears and fears and hopes
Till the girl at last elopes
Most confiding, softly sliding,
Down a ladder made of ropes!
It's romance and the chance of a life
When a bandit makes you his wife
It's the height of delight to be dear
To a bold and a bad buccaneer.
Though his cause all the laws may condemn
I declare that I care not for them
If I could discover such a thrilling lover
I would jump at the chance of romance!

Her 'advanced' ideas make the criminally-inclined Hughie just her cup of tea: what bliss to be married to a burglar!

Jean Aylwin was allowed to lapse back into her ineradicable Scots as a Scots-French modiste, Gladys Homfrey added to her gallery of fearsome mothers, Maisie Gay (who had been noticed as Clementine in the tour of *The Girls of Gottenberg*) made her Gaiety début as 'an impecunious woman of fashion', while Robert Hale had a juicy part as the professional crook, Slithers, who is Hughie's 'tutor'.

Indisputably one of the most important assets of *Our Miss Gibbs* was its score. *The Stage* commented:

Seldom, indeed, has a musical piece owed more to its songs . . songs sentimental, songs fanciful, songs funny, songs pantomimic . . (and) scarcely a solo sung without a background of pretty faces.

And from the welter of grand material one number, in particular, stood out. It had been composed by Lionel Monckton for his wife, and Miss Millar made of 'Moonstruck' the biggest hit to come out of the Gaiety Theatre for many a year:

Moon, Moon, aggravating moon
Why do you tease me so?

The number was introduced into the White City scene, with Gertie Millar dressed as a dark blue pierrot, surrounded by Gaiety Girls as pale blue pierrots, singing and dancing her most famous song in the 'moonlight' of the theatre lamps. In a heartier mood she sang of Yorkshire – of its common sense compared to the posturings of the town:

A cockney will say in superior tone
That he reckons he knows all there is to be known
If he goes on a journey he puts on such airs
And spends a lot more than it costs him in fares
He'll tip a chap sixpence to carry the bag
Simply because it's a fag.
But we never do that in Yorkshire
A chap takes a ticket, excursion, third class
He won't call a porter – he's not such an ass
He tips himself sixpence and pockets the brass,
Sixpence is sixpence in Yorkshire

and she brought the house to cheers and encores with a little duet with Teddy Payne, where they described 'Our Farm':

It's a nice little farm and you won't do any harm
If you come and have a tumble in the hay,
We've a cow you would applaud and we always call her Maud
'Cos she comes into the garden every day.
We've a spade and a hoe and some turnips in a row
Which are doing very nicely in the showers
And we now intend to keep just half a brace of sheep
Oh! you'd love a little farm like ours

The pair revolved solemnly, she turning sedately under his arm at the end of each verse, singing

. . . [Miss Millar] without a single squeak and [Mr Payne] with barely a single grimace.

There were plenty of other high spots in the score. J. Edward Fraser sang of 'My Yorkshire Lassie' and Jean Aylwin described the different effects one can make with 'Hats'. One chorus saw the White City populace performing a routine in bath chairs, another featured Olive May, Rose Begarnie and Adeline Balfe as three bright Irish girls, and a third had a chorus of Dudes declaiming:

A fashionable band of brothers are we – you see
What everyone has done the others must do – it too
Our clothes and our hats are made to match – they show it
We have one bill for all the batch – and we owe it.
For we're correct in every respect
And you note the effect!
In day-time or at night-time
The right thing at the right time,
We mayn't be great in intellect
But we are so correct

One slightly false note was struck on the opening night by a song which Grossmith had imported from America and interpolated into the score. Edwardes hadn't thought much of it and had allegedly refused to pay Grossmith more than £5 for his English version of the lyric, but the song went in and it stayed in despite a mixed reception at the first performance. Edwardes was right, it fitted poorly into the score: it was precisely what *Our Miss Gibbs* succeeded in not being – boisterous and inane. *The Times* noticed it as 'a noisy saltz song warranted to run in one's head till it aches' while *The Stage* predicted that it had a future on the street corner. They were right too. 'Yip! I-addy! I-ay' had come to stay and not only in the long run on the street corner.

Our Miss Gibbs lasted for 636 performances, outrunning all but *The Toreador* of the Gaiety musicals, and that without the advantage of the latter's second edition and the sentimental additive of *The Linkman*. It remained and remains the best loved of all the Gaiety shows. Charles Frohman staged a version on Broadway which featured former Edwardes chorus girl Pauline Chase (known largely now for *Peter Pan*) in the title role and Fred Wright Jr as Timothy. It was loaded with the usual Jerome Kern ditties and lasted only 57 performances at the Knickerbocker Theatre, another great Broadway casualty – and in excellent company as such – which nevertheless was played all around the rest of the world for many years and remained a favourite on the British touring circuits for a very long time. But with it another era of Gaiety history came to an end, as the team which had written so many hit shows for the theatre was about to be broken up. Before a new show was needed for the Gaiety, Ivan Caryll had decided to pursue his career in America. He had come to Britain with the comic opera *The Lily of Léoville* as long ago as 1886, and had since shown an extraordinary versatility in French opérette (*La Cigale*, *Ma Mie Rosette*), new burlesque (*Little Christopher Columbus*), the Gaiety musical comedy or even provincial theatre. From 'Lazily, Drowsily' for the small vocal range of May Yohe to the cultured and delicious *Duchess of Dantzic* Ivan Caryll had covered the whole gamut of the light musical theatre and he left behind him on his departure a string of hit credits without equal.

His leaving did not mark the end of his composing career, nor did it mean that no more of his works would be seen in London. Two of his first four New York efforts in conjunction with Charles McLellan made it back to the West End after successful runs on Broadway (*The Pink Lady* and *Oh! Oh! Delphine*) and in 1919 he returned to London for two new shows, the highly successful *Kissing Time* and a last show for the Gaiety, *The Kiss Call*, in which he worked once more with Adrian Ross and Percy Greenbank and with the failing George Huntley. But a new generation of writers was by that time on the move. The libretto was by Fred Thompson, virtually unknown when Caryll left Britain and now in the forefront of librettists. And sharing the lyric credit with the old collaborators was a young writer called Clifford Grey. Evelyn Laye, Austin Melford, Binnie Hale, Stanley Lupino – so many new names appeared on the programme where so many familiar ones had been before. *The Kiss Call* was Caryll's last London show. He died in America on November 29, 1921 at the age of 60 and his last Broadway show, *The Hotel Mouse*, was produced posthumously.[1]

But Ivan Caryll was not the only old retainer to depart from the Gaiety with *Our Miss Gibbs*. His long time partner, Lionel Monckton, was also moving on, for George Edwardes had signed Leslie Stuart to provide the music for the next two Gaiety musicals, presumably intending to follow the direction established in *Havana*. There was no chance of Monckton establishing with him the mutually advantageous

[1] Ivan Caryll supplied the scores for the following pieces written and produced in America between 1911 and 1922: *Marriage à la Carte, The Pink Lady, Oh! Oh! Delphine, The Little Café*, (*The Belle of Bond Street*/revision of *The Girl from Kays*), *Chin Chin, Papa's Darling, Jack o'Lantern, The Girl behind the Gun, The Canary, Tip Top, The Hotel Mouse.*

partnership he had had with Caryll, since Stuart brooked no interpolations and collaborated with no one. And, in any case, by the time the Gaiety was finished with *Our Miss Gibbs*, Monckton had *The Arcadians* and *The Quaker Girl* under his belt and was reigning supreme over the London musical theatre from another vantage point. The centre of affairs had moved from the Gaiety Theatre. Gertie Millar, too, made her exit from the Gaiety with *Our Miss Gibbs*. Like her husband, her career was far from done, but the Gaiety episode was over.

A few weeks after the first performance of *Our Miss Gibbs*, the newest Hicks/Terriss musical opened in London under the aegis of Charles Frohman. It was their first new show since *The Gay Gordons* in 1907 and, once again, the winds of change were evident for *The Dashing Little Duke* marked a complete change of formula from that which Hicks had built up through *The Catch of the Season*, *The Beauty of Bath*, *My Darling* and *The Gay Gordons*. Like *Butterflies* and *The Antelope*, the new piece was based on an established straight play, in this case a piece called *A Court Scandal* in which Hicks had played the lead at the Court and Garrick Theatres in 1899. *A Court Scandal* was, in its turn, an adaptation of the French play *Les Premières Armes de Richelieu*, a piece which had much in common with such excellent French musicals as *Le Petit Duc* and *Les Mousquétaires au Couvent*.

The principal character was the very young Duc de Richelieu who has been married to the haughty Diane de Noailles but who, according to the marriage contract, may not see his wife except in the presence of her mother for twelve months. The young man rebels at being treated like a child and boasts unwisely of the favours shown to him by the Duchess of Burgoyne. That lady, furious, retorts by making him a wedding gift of sugar-plums in front of the whole court, reducing him in their eyes to a cocky child instead of the man he is trying so hard to become. The wily Chevalier de Matignon who is in love with Diane has obtained her promise to give in to him if it is proved that her husband has been unfaithful. To this end, de Matignon persaudes Richelieu to write compromising letters to ladies of the court but the young Duke discovers the Chevalier's treachery and challenges him to a duel. As the duel approaches, Diane discovers that her feelings for her young husband have blossomed into love and, when he defeats Matignon, all ends happily.

The music for *The Dashing Little Duke* gave the conductor/composer Frank E. Tours, his first opportunity to write a full West End score. He had, over the years, contributed individual numbers to many pieces, including *The Dairymaids*, *The Little Cherub*, *See See* and *The New Aladdin* as well as the score for the unsuccessful *Melnotte* whilst carrying out his principal function as a musical director and now, at the age of thirty, he tried his skill in a more ambitious field. *The Dashing Little Duke* had more of the feel of *The Duchess of Dantzic* or *Cigarette* about it than of such as *The Dairymaids* or *The New Aladdin*. This was emphasised by the fact that the role of young Richelieu was to be taken not by Hicks, but by Miss Terriss – a thing scarcely seen in the West End since the days of Agnes Huntingdon and the last Gaiety burlesques.

Hicks in fact did not appear in the show but he gathered a fine cast together to support his wife. Matignon was played by the doyen of baritones (still only 46), Hayden Coffin, Diane was taken by Elizabeth Firth who had been featured in *The Duchess of Dantzic* and who had most recently created the role of Nathalie in *The Merry Widow*, Coralie Blythe was the maid, Césarine, and Courtice and Louie Pounds were featured as the Abbé de la Touche, a bonhomous clergyman, and as the Duchess of Burgoyne.

The Dashing Little Duke was given a week's run-in at Nottingham and, in spite of its unexpected style, proved most successful. Miss Terriss scored a huge personal success and on the first night was called before the curtain no less than twenty-two times. The show came into London on an optimistic note and there again it met with every sign of favour:

> [it is] . . something infinitely in advance of [musical comedy] . . which may be enjoyed to the full by those who can appreciate what is best in music and drama . . [Seymour Hicks has been faithful to the original] with the happiest of results. Its plot, though light in texture and simple in design is, nevertheless, a real plot and one of sustaining interest, and its characters are all of them real, living characters whose sayings and doings are always . . well in the picture. Added to these most desirable qualities are the delightful musical score of Frank E. Tours, the deftly turned lyrics of Adrian Ross, the artistically designed costumes of Percy Anderson and the magnificent scenery of Joseph Harker and the combined result is certainly one of the best musical plays seen in the metropolis for many a long day, and one for which it is safe to predict a lengthy and prosperous career (*Stage*)

The show was not completely free from the influence of the earlier Hicks musicals. Hicks himself was responsible for the staging and it was impossible for him to resist employing some of the known and popular pieces of business of yore – particularly those more or less expected of Miss Terriss. But the show, by and large, was different. It had an atmosphere of light and bubbling enjoyment running through it, but was almost entirely devoid of low comedy, apart from a few moments from Sam Walsh and Florence Wood as a vulgar Baron and Baroness, and the 'girls', so prominent as a rule in a Seymour Hicks show, were kept in the background[1]. The music, too, was largely in a sentimental vein so that a topical song from Miss Terriss called 'Five little Pigs', with political allusions and no relevance at all, was rather out of keeping.

Probably the most popular song was 'Lizette' sung by Courtice Pounds in which the ageing Abbé ruefully regrets the girl he met by the well when he was a young soldier:

> It is long since the day we met, Lizette,
> And by now you have wed another
> And the little ones run to your knee, maybe,
> And they beg for a kiss from mother.
> And the girls have eyes I have known, your own,
> With the look that I loved when I met Lizette.
>
> Lizette, Lizette, I will not fret
> That my life is lonely, in vain regret,
> Though your fireside gleams
> In the land of dreams
> Yet to me it is only a dream, Lizette

but Elizabeth Firth was also provided with some most attractive pieces: the scornful 'Boy', 'The Sun Dial' and a dramatic waltz song 'Love and Pride'. Miss Terriss' music was in a lighter vein and not as well put together, although her interpretation of the numbers inevitably ensured encores for 'Nobody Cares for Me' and 'A little married Man'. Coffin was rather routinely supplied with a piece reminiscently called 'Rose of the World' and a rakish number called 'Women'. He had his best moments in duets, one with Miss Firth ('The Mirror of the Moon') in which he tries to persuade her to desert the Duke, and another called 'A good Story', a well-conceived laughing duo for

[1] The dozen featured chorines of *The Dashing Little Duke* played courtly ladies.

Matignon and the Abbé in which the former scorns and the latter defends the Duke's relationship with his wife.

After a promising start, however, it was not long before *The Dashing Little Duke* ran into trouble. Miss Terriss found the role of Richelieu too demanding and, in a unique move, Hicks stepped in to play the matinées for her. Ellen Terry's daughter, Edith Craig, had played for her at matinées of *Pinkie and the Fairies* over Christmas, but a husband and wife sharing a role? The change did not affect the box office but before too long Miss Terriss felt able to resume a full schedule.

Perceptibly, however, the piece began to lose its character. George Barrett left *King of Cadonia* and took over the role of the Baron de Bellechasse which grew, consequently, in size and in low comedy. Julia Sanderson, who had returned to her native America after *The Honorable Phil* to play *Kitty Grey*, came back to London and took over the role of Césarine. That superfluous role promptly expanded to include, amongst other things, three new numbers by Jerome Kern! Then Miss Terriss flagged again, and again Hicks came to the rescue; and finally it was announced, after little more than three months of performances, that the show was to be withdrawn. It was later put out to tour with Miss Terriss in her original role in an effort to recoup something of the five-figure deficit which the London run had provoked, but it was an effort in vain.

The next new London venture was one from America. Miss Marie Dressler arrived in town with a brace of Maurice Levi/Edgar Smith pieces, *Philpoena* and *The Collegettes*, and opened with them at the Aldwych to a perfectly disastrous reception. After ten performances Miss Dressler decamped, declaring 'Shylock must have been an Englishman' and 'How you British hate Americans!'. She left behind debts of £5,000, an unpaid cast and bankruptcy proceedings for, she claimed, she had 'mortgaged everything' for the cast. The same cast must have been interested to read not long after that Miss Dressler was on the West Coast of the United States 'looking after her mining interests'. In the event, George Graves arranged a benefit for the duped actors and Marie Dressler joined the list of 'bogus managers'.

The Belle of Brittany had done sufficiently well for Tom Davis to serve up more of the same for his next production. Bantock, Barrow and Percy Greenbank as writers were teamed for *A Persian Princess* with Sidney Jones (instead of Howard Talbot) and once again the leading artists were nominated as George Graves and Ruth Vincent. The new piece used the formula of 'Prince falls in love with girl, actually his betrothed in disguise' in a slightly varied way.

Prince Omar, elected to be the next King of Persia in preference to his brother Hassan, is intended to wed the Princess Yolene. On her way to meet him, Yolene escapes from her royal father and arrives, disguised, in the slave market where she sees Omar misbehaving and making remarks about women. The bereft King, in the meanwhile, has persuaded the soubrette Zingarie to pretend to be his missing daughter. Zingarie is exposed, but Hassan has noticed his brother's affection for a supposed slave girl and inveigles him into a wedding with her, thinking thus to secure Yolene and the throne for himself. The marriage done, Hassan finds that he has been his own undoing and Yolene, forgiving Omar's youthful follies, condescends to a happy ending.

Ruth Vincent was Yolene, Noel Fleming (the son of tenor Barton McGuckin) made his stage début as Omar, Carrie Moore (the 'Sandow Girl') was Zingarie, Clarence Blakiston played Hassan and George Graves took on the expandable role of Omar's father, King Khayyam. In a role rather reminiscent of Sebak in *Amasis*, the comedian

Horace Mills played Swaak, the keeper of the royal camel. The keeper of the royal camel lives under the threat of the Death of A Thousand Pecks (by pelicans) should anything befall the precious beast and, of course, poor 'Alfred' passes away (to the accompaniment of an amusing dirge), poisoned by the dastardly Hassan. 'Alfred' was played by a genuine Bactrian camel who quite stole the show as he paraded across the stage in full-length trappings, decked out in white plumes with bright red flowers tucked behind his ears and looking out soulfully at the audience.

But 'Alfred' and the singing of Ruth Vincent and the ad libs of George Graves and his allied comedians were scarcely sufficient to make a show. In spite of a warm enough first night reception it was soon evident that *A Persian Princess* would not do. Bantock and Barrow had failed to achieve that sparkle that *Amasis* had glowed with, even though they had imitated that piece in a number of ways. Sidney Jones had scarcely done himself justice with the music, although the lyrics which a clearly off-form Greenbank had provided were hardly inspiring. One pretty song for Ruth Vincent ('The Juniper Tree') did not make up for the tired conceits and arch words in such pieces as 'When I Am King', 'The Doctor, the Patient and the Nurse' or 'Come to Persia' (For a jolly day and a holiday, Persia's quite the spot!'). An 'Insomnia' patter song for Mills reeked of *Iolanthe*'s Nightmare Song and Miss Vincent's 'big' number 'The Land of Heart's Content' spent a good deal of its lyric on 'Ah', as she negotiated what were becoming her obligatory (and lengthening) coloratura passages. But perhaps the most inane of all was a truly frightful number, 'The Doggies and the Bone', in which Carrie Moore likened herself to the morsel and her admirers to the canines:

> Such a lot of hungry doggies watching round a tasty bone
> If I tried to go
> You'd pounce on me so
> And you're six to one, you know

The Stage ventured half-heartedly that it ' . . should do as well as *The Belle of Brittany*' and praised Sydney Ellison's production and the

> . . heliotrope and various shades of red figuring prominently in the beautiful colour scheme formed by the dresses designed by Percy Anderson

and a number of critics noted, with amazement, that the second act was actually stronger than the first. The first act, however, was abysmal.

Attempts were made to patch the worst spots. Graves was given an extra scene in which he conducted a long inquest on the death of Alfred. In a performance reminiscent of Phil Day's Doge in *Estrella* he made great play of addressing the court and the jury. Pieces which had not 'gone' were cut, and wholesale alterations were practised throughout. Fleming, who had 'failed to stay', was replaced by John Bardesley. But *A Persian Princess* was beyond saving. It lasted a bare two months at the Queen's Theatre before it was withdrawn on 3 July and announced for the provinces. But when touring time came in September, Ruth Vincent went to the country as Véronique and *A Persian Princess* was forgotten.

Robert Courtneidge had not brought out a new musical since *Tom Jones* but he had not been idle. His revival of *The Dairymaids* had been seen in town and his touring operations had continued extensively while his most recent venture had been the production of the Adelphi Theatre pantomime of 1908/9 in which Dan Rolyat had starred as Baron Hardup. By April, however, Courtneidge was ready with another new musical: *The Arcadians.*

The original idea for *The Arcadians* came from the eccentric little playwright Mark Ambient who thought up the piece's central situation in which a Londoner is accidentally introduced into Arcadia where he learns of Truth and Beauty and subsequently leads the Arcadians to Britain to see how those virtues can be made to prosper there. Ambient had had little experience with the musical stage. His most successful pieces had been for the Royalty Theatre – the comedies *Oh, Susannah!* (1897) and *A Little Ray of Sunshine* (1898), both in collaboration. His one venture into the musical had been the adaptation of Audran's *L'Oncle Celestin* into *Baron Golosh* for the Trafalgar Square Theatre in 1895.

Ambient found himself unequal to turning his idea into a full-grown show, so he consulted Courtneidge and the manager's writing partner, Alexander Thompson, and eventually a fuller story was evolved and written, principally by Thompson. The play opens in Arcadia, that perfect land forgotten by Time, who explains to the inhabitants:

Since the days before the flood
When the world was mainly mud
Where the mammoth met the mighty mastodon,
I've been saddled with the berth
Of policeman to the earth
I'm the man who keeps creation moving on.
But I've had so much to do
That I'd quite forgotten you
Yes, I've skipped you as a schoolboy skips a page
So I fear you're in arrears
Just about three thousand years
For with you I see it's still the golden age.

Things are quite perfect in Arcadia: the joys of life are untainted by falsehood, jealousy and all the other fashionable British characteristics. Into this perfect world comes James Smith, a London caterer. He has been flying his aeroplane over the North Pole when it crashes and down he comes amongst the amazed natives. The Arcadians interrogate the strange creature but, to their horror, he is caught telling a Lie. Quickly, he is bundled into the Well of Truth and he emerges as 'Simplicitas', a true Arcadian. But now it is decided that the Arcadians will seek out this dreadful London and bring back truth and virtue to it. Headed by Sombra and Astrophel, they set out:

To all and each
Where sin is rife
We go to teach
The simple life,
To banish lies
The wrong to right,
To darkened eyes
To bring the light
So shall they be
In true accord
With Arcady
Where love is lord

The Arcadians arrive in England at Askwood race-course on the day of the big race. Jack Meadows, a young man-about-town, needs his bad-tempered horse 'The Deuce' to win to restore his fortunes but, in the meantime, he is spending more time flirting with the pretty Irish girl, Eileen Kavanagh. The only jockey who can be found to ride the unpopular 'Deuce' is lugubrious Peter Doody but he is obliged to give up the mount when the horse takes a bite out of him. Sombra, the Arcadian, speaks to the horse to find out why he is so miserable and, cheered up, with Simplicitas on his back, 'The Deuce' wins the race.

In the final act we see Simplicitas at the head of a tea room which he has set up on Arcadian principles but which has become fashionable and a mockery of all the Arcadians stand for:

Cheer for Simplicitas, cheer!
Tell him Belgravia's here
Eagerly clamouring
Shouting and hammering
Waiting for him to appear.
Tell him we won't go away
Go to our hero and say
We of the smart set
Have all got our hearts set
On seeing our hero today

Distraught at this outcome, the Arcadians resolve to leave the hopeless city and return home. Simplicitas becomes plain James Smith once more – a richer and more successful Smith with a chain of hotels – and Jack and Eileen are left happy as Sombra and her friends depart from London forever.

The libretto was an excellent one:

> The spirit of Planché hovers over the book in which there is also something of Gilbertian topsy-turveydom and it is all very delightful, exhilarating, picturesque and a very riot of drollery (*Era*)

It mixed fantasy and originality with known musical comedy elements in a delightful fashion, scoring best when the fantastic was in ascendancy and perhaps a little less well in the final act where Courtneidge was at pains to introduce what was little more than a series of numbers. That they were numbers of extraordinary excellence ensured, however, that *The Arcadians* never flagged for an instant. After *Our Miss Gibbs*, 1909 had produced a second and even greater hit and one which would endure many decades.

Much light musical theatre is, by its very nature, an ephemeral thing. The songs and music which survive are liable to be those of comic opera or of the music hall. But Monckton and Talbot provided a score for *The Arcadians* from which half a dozen numbers passed into the popular canon where they have stayed for three-quarters of a century. The strongest musical impact was made by the songs which were written for Sombra, in the person of the 'Welsh nightingale', Florence Smithson, who at last had a role worthy of her talents and of her incredible light coloratura soprano. She sang 'Arcady Is always Young' (Monckton), 'Light Is my Heart' (Talbot) and, above all, 'The Pipes of Pan' (Monckton):

So follow, follow, follow,
The merry, merry pipes of Pan
The magic reed that charms at need
The heart of maid and man.
Away, away, they seem to say
And catch us if you can,
Come, follow, follow, where they lead
The merry, merry pipes of Pan

The Times reported quite simply:

> Mr Monckton and Mr Talbot both surpassed themselves in writing songs for [Miss Smithson] to sing . . .

But the evening held other great musical moments of a very different kind. Alfred Lester was cast as the gloomy jockey, Doody. It was a role which exactly suited him, although it was not a large one, but Courtneidge felt that the £10 a week he was paying for the Gaiety comic was excessive. He could not see the humour in Lester and his one song and, it is said, on opening night there was a letter of notice awaiting the comedian on his dressing table. But Lester went out and eclipsed even the memory of his 'Lost Policeman' (*New Aladdin*) with an hilarious performance, bringing down the house as he sang glumly:

> I've gotta motter
> Always merry and bright
> Look around and you will find
> Every cloud is silver lined.
> The sun will shine
> Although the sky's a grey one,
> I've often said to myself, I've said,
> Cheer up, cully, you'll soon be dead,
> A short life and a gay one!

The next morning Courtneidge had to negotiate a new contract with the comedian at £30 per week.

Talbot composed the catchy tune for Doody's song, while Monckton turned out an equally attractive one for Eileen Kavanagh's opening song. Phyllis Dare had a charming role, but nothing in it was more charming than 'The Girl with the Brogue':

> Ah, now, stop your philanderin'
> You can't capture the rogue!
> She's heard your blarney
> From Clare to Killarney
> The dear little girl with the bit of a brogue

She also had two show-stopping duets with Harry Welchman (Jack): 'Charming Weather' and 'Half past Two'. Even the minor characters were equipped with hit songs. May Kinder as Sombra's sister opened the final act with another rousing piece which became very popular:

> I like London, I like town
> I cannot understand why people run it down
> Although it does the wicked things
> And leaves the good things undone
> I'm very, very fond of London

and a little fellow called Nelson Keys, making his West End début, sang 'Back your Fancy' to open the race-course scene. When Keys had been given the role of 'Bobby' it had consisted of one line and 'Back your Fancy' had been a quartet. But Monckton was dissatisfied with the piece and was considering cutting it altogether until Keys pleaded for a chance to sing it as a solo. His audition pleased enough for 'Back your Fancy' to be left in the show where it proved a great success. *The Arcadians* also included some of the most attractive ensemble work heard for some long time. Talbot's 'The Joy of

Life', and the quintet 'Truth Is so Beautiful' were both outstanding pieces and the choruses were as bright and pretty as could be.

The third element which went to make up the show's huge success was Courtneidge's direction and production which *The Times* picked out for special praise:

> . . The first and second acts were unusual and well above the common level of musical pieces. And the authors, who must be congratulated on their share, were aided to a certain extent by the musicians especially . . where Miss Smithson's part was concerned, but more by the producer, Mr Courtneidge. The whole production showed ingenuity, care, and to some extent originality so that familiar elements took on an unfamiliar look, and new things had their full effect. And certainly the close of that second Act was hugely exciting . . . [the race meeting] was one of the most exciting scenes ever contributed to this kind of piece . .

The race meeting scene was a mass of colour and avant-garde fashion. Courtneidge filled the stage with ladies in new model dresses from the Maison Courtenay of Albemarle Street, bright, modern and sometimes outrageous confections which were changed regularly to provide a truly up-to-date fashion parade for the audience. The spectacle of these colourful ladies, and their elegant gentlemen in Doherty and Yell's best morning suits, lined up across the front of stage, breathlessly following the progress of the Gold Cup through their glasses as it galloped by somewhere across the front of the dress circle, was a brilliant piece of direction and one which other shows, in later years, did not shrink from copying. And 'The Deuce' with Dan Rolyat clinging to his back, parading victoriously across the stage to bring the second act to an uproarious close, was a sight which remained long in playgoers' memories.

The Shaftesbury Theatre had its greatest hit of all time. The record of *The Belle of New York* was properly effaced as *The Arcadians* held the stage for two years and three months while companies proliferated all over the world with equal and unqualified success. Only *A Chinese Honeymoon* and *Dorothy* of musicals had ever run longer in London's West End, and even they could not equal the length and breadth of the subsequent popularity of *The Arcadians*.

In spite of the huge and instantaneous success obtained by the show, the script and score were still subject to alteration after the opening. The most notable addition was an extra number for Dan Rolyat who had scored a real triumph as 'Simplicitas'. In the last act he was given a Lionel Monckton song which was quickly added to the show's hits:

> All down Piccadilly -dilly -dilly -dilly
> Down by the park
> You'll see ladies running after little Willie
> Till it gets dark . .

Sombra's 'Light Is my Heart' gave way to the even more successful 'Come to Arcady' and Jack's second act number 'Fickle Fortune' was replaced by 'The only Girl Alive' which proved more suitable for Harry Welchman. Welchman had been most unfortunate for his first West End lead. Just before opening night he fell ill and the first performance was played by his understudy, Harry Pearce. Welchman was soon back in the cast, however, and played Jack Meadows throughout the run, establishing himself as the heir apparent to Hayden Coffin.

On the show's second anniversary there was a further crop of additions to the score. Welchman sang a new ballad 'Love will Win'; Cicely Courtneidge, one of the seventeen Chryseas of the run, sang 'I'll be a Sister to You'; and Nelson Keys exhorted 'Have a

Bit on with Me' and joined Rolyat and Welchman in a trio about 'Little George Washington'. Harry Ray joined the cast to perform a two-step routine with Maudi Thornton to the music of 'Oh, do the Two-step'. But none of these late additions proved superior to the parts of the existing score and they did not survive into the show's definitive version.

Before the end of the year, *The Arcadians* had been played as far afield as Bombay and had begun its American career at the Forrest Theatre in Philadelphia. After three weeks out of town it arrived on Broadway where it proved, once again, a great success and settled in for a run of 193 performances at the Liberty Theatre. The role of Sombra was taken by the English soprano Ethel Cadman who had been playing *A Waltz Dream* in the provinces, whilst Julia Sanderson, having done nothing for *The Dashing Little Duke*, took on the much more suitable role of Eileen Kavanagh. And in the warmly comical role of Mrs James Smith was Connie Ediss, now three years resident in America. *The Arcadians* travelled through all the usual countries and venues with enormous success as well as returning briefly to London in 1915 for a revival season starring Cicely Courtneidge and Jack Hulbert, and became a lasting feature of the British touring circuits for more than thirty years before becoming the property of amateur groups. In 1984 a professional revival by Britain's most enterprising provincial musical house, the Northcott Theatre in Exeter, brought *The Arcadians* to a new and delighted generation of theatre-goers and critics. Director Stewart Trotter brought out the very best of the fun from a libretto which showed itself to have stood the test of time in a manner characterised by only the most classic of books, and discovered a beautiful young soprano, Gaynor Miles, to lead the company through the multiple highlights of the score with a brilliance worthy of Florence Smithson herself. The national newspapers descended on Exeter to return full of praise for this 'Edwardian time-capsule packed with enchantment' and its delicious production – a production which must surely lead to others for what may be considered as the most complete of all British pre-war musicals.

When *King of Cadonia* had completed its highly successful stay at the Prince of Wales Theatre, Frank Curzon turned back to Paul Rubens for his new show. Austen Hurgon had moved on and this time Rubens was entirely responsible for the book, music and lyrics. The titles *The Great Danes* with its burlesque flavour and *The Bell Founder* having been finally rejected, the Prince of Wales show opened as *Dear Little Denmark*, a title well in the tradition of *Miss Hook of Holland* and *My Mimosa Maid*. But *Dear Little Denmark*, although it had inevitable similarities to its predecessors, also had considerable differences. Rubens was quite willing and fairly able to move with the times, and the success of *King of Cadonia* and the general leaning towards a more 'comic opera' type of plot, setting and characters had not been lost on him. The story of *Dear Little Denmark* bore unmistakeable resemblances to the comic operas of the later years of the 19th century and its locality and characters gave it a fair flavour of such pieces as Gilbert's *His Excellency*. There, however, the resemblance ended, for Rubens' talents did not lie in the same direction as those of Sidney Jones or of Osmond Carr, and his lyrics – his 'jingles' as he was pleased to call them – had absolutely nothing Gilbertian in them.

The story of *Dear Little Denmark* concerned a Danish duke (James Blakeley) cursed with hereditary gout. The gout can be kept at bay while a certain peal of bells is ringing, but the bells require mending and the bell founder, Conrad (Bertram Wallis), is too busy courting the lovely Christine (Isabel Jay) to tend to them. Conrad ends up in prison, is rescued by Christine disguised as a soldier and, eventually, in spite of the machinations of one Hans Hansen (Huntley Wright) who wants his place, mends the bells, cures the duke and marries Christine.

It was a very slight framework which Rubens duly decorated with the expected comedy (for Blakeley, Wright and Gracie Leigh) and romantic numbers (for Wallis and Miss Jay). Gracie Leigh, in fact, came out of it the best. She took the part of Ophelia the maid, described as 'a native of Jutland'. The English equivalent of Jutland was seemingly Yorkshire and Ophelia was played as a comical Miss Gibbs – Paul Rubens was never chary of a bandwagon. She had a number of merry songs: one describing 'Gout', another declaring 'I've Come down from the North' and a third about 'Reading, Riting and 'Rithmetic'; she shared a humming duet and led a sextet which pilfered a song title straight from *Our Miss Gibbs*, calling itself 'Hats'. In retrospect, some of Rubens' other song titles have the ring of familiarity: 'Copenhagen', 'The Land of Love', 'Do, re, mi'.

The numbers for Wallis and Miss Jay, however, did not have the distinction of *King of Cadonia* pieces which were still so fresh in the public mind although Wallis' song 'The Great Danes' had some success. The title referred to the Duke's special bodyguard for which Curzon hired a group of particularly imposing male choristers who appeared on the stage at every possible turn and caused a deal of amusement.

The reaction to the show was medium. It was generally rated somewhere between *Miss Hook of Holland* and *My Mimosa Maid*, which was perhaps a little unfair to the latter. *The Times* concluded

> The plot is thin, even for a musical comedy, but it includes good material for post-prandial laughter . . . this, after all, is only unpretentious musical comedy chatter, jingles and tunes, and very agreeable of its kind.

Paul Rubens' self-deprecatory description had disarmed more than one critic, but *The Times* did take exception to a vulgar scene of 'doctors' between Huntley Wright and a group of girls. Amazingly, it also took a violent fancy to a short scene between Conrad and Christine in Act 2 which it compared to Bernard Shaw and 'the Court Theatre three or four years ago . . '. Any resemblance between Shaw and Rubens really took a good deal of seeing. That it should be *The Times*, with its constantly scornful attitude towards light musical theatre, which postulated it was even more surprising. *Dear Little Denmark* was a very slight piece, but enough after-dinner listeners and Gracie Leigh or Isabel Jay fans appreciated it to allow it a three and a half months' run.

September and October saw two new Viennese musicals in London. The triumph of Austria's *The Merry Widow* was still to be truly confirmed by other shows but its success, like that of *The Belle of New York*, was bringing similar pieces in its wake. George Edwardes put his faith in Leo Fall's *The Dollar Princess* as a tenant for Daly's, and the Strand Theatre also bet on Fall with a production of *The Merry Peasant* (*Der Fidele Bauer*). *The Dollar Princess* gave Edwardes the confirmation he required – his new policy was the right one – and Lily Elsie and Joe Coyne repeated their earlier success in the new show which stayed in the West End for 428 performances. The Strand was not so lucky. Their 'improved' version of *Der Fidele Bauer* lasted only 71 performances. Viennese operetta was 'in', but not anywhere and not indiscriminately.

A few days after the opening of *The Dollar Princess* a new British musical opened at the Savoy. Mrs D'Oyly Carte had relinquished the management of the theatre during the run of *The Yeomen of the Guard* in favour of the company's leading comedian Herbert Workman and, in September, the new manager decided to produce something other than the regular Gilbert and Sullivan revivals at his theatre. The piece which he chose was a rather ambitious 'romantic comic opera' called *The Mountaineers* written by Guy Eden with music by Reginald Somerville. Somerville had appeared in several musicals as an actor and singer but he was also a well-trained musician and composer. He had shown undoubted signs of talent in shorter works such as *The Prentice Pillar*, but *The Mountaineers* was a show on an altogether different scale.

Its story was basically a sentimental one. Clarice, daughter of Pierre, a customs house man, has two lovers: Fritz, the burly villager, and Conrad, refined and rich. To choose between them, Clarice has recourse to the old custom whereby she will take whichever brings her the first sprig of edelweiss which grows only on the top of the highest of the neighbouring mountains. Conrad eagerly sets off, but the mountain-wise Fritz sees a storm coming and holds back. Conrad is trapped in the storm and old Pierre begs Fritz to go to his rival's rescue. The mountaineer brings Conrad back alive and, in the third act, the latter repays him by taking his place in an army call-up and leaving Clarice to him. The comedy was provided by Pierre and by Miss Spinifex, an English spinster whom he spends his time wooing.

The show's first performance received a warm reception from the Savoy audience but the notices were mixed. *The Mountaineers* was an old-fashioned piece which had aligned itself awkwardly on a course between comic opera and grand opera without really achieving the best of either. There was much that was good in it, particularly in the best of Somerville's melodies such as 'The Legend of the Edelweiss' and the 'Sleep Song' written for Elsie Spain as Clarice, but too much militated against it for it to have a long run.

Its leading characters were poorly drawn. Both Fritz and Clarice had a rather unpleasant air about them – he a stiff-necked opportunist, she a senseless and heartless coquette – which prevented the sentimental side of the story from being in any way affecting. Poor Conrad (whose only failing seemed to be that he was well-bred and well-off) was a much more sympathetic character who seemd unduly hard done by. The role of Pierre, taken by Workman himself, was peripheral and sometimes intrusive upon the main thread of the story but it did provide welcome relief. The show's main disadvantage, however, was its genre – one with a limited public – and its failure to achieve any sort of distinction in its words and music. *The Times* commented:

> Beyond a tendency in both author and composer to confine themselves too closely to a few rhythms there is no great fault to be found with it. It commits no offences against sense or taste, but it forms one of those instances of respectable mediocrity which are more difficult to describe than many less meritorious works. This does not mean that it is dull or 'not worth going to see', on the contrary, it provides a very pleasant, pretty, amusing entertainment . . .

Workman recognised the need to change the show's character if it were to succeed. Like so many before him, he leaned on the comic part of the show. Arthur Wimperis was brought in to write a topical song for the manager, and another new number for Jessie Rose called, reminiscently, 'On the Shelf' was interpolated. The dialogue was revamped and the piece generally popularised. And, as in virtually every preceding case, all the additions and alterations made not one whit of improvement to a show which, from its conception, can hardly have entertained the prospect of a long commercial run. *The Mountaineers* closed after 61 performances, leaving some slight regrets that the promise it contained could not have been better fulfilled.

The Mountaineers was replaced at the Savoy on 15 December by another new work, this time from a much more experienced set of writers – W. S. Gilbert and Edward

German. *Fallen Fairies* was a musical version of Gilbert's own play *The Wicked World* which had originally been produced at the Haymarket in 1873 with Kendal, Buckstone, Mrs Kendal, Miss Litton and Amy Roselle and had run there for an excellent 154 performances. Gilbert's adaptation was largely limited to inserting lyrics into the body of the play which he reduced from three acts to two, omitting some of the more intricate and characteristic sub-plots including 'a good deal of unnecessary business about a ring and a potion'. What remained was an artfully constructed fable about the perils of human love.

Fairyland is a cloud, floating above the earth to which the fairies have never descended. But two of them, Phyllon and Ethais, are commanded to go down to earth to receive a 'priceless gift'. During their absence it is possible 'by some half forgotten law' for their mortal counterparts to be summoned to Fairyland and, in spite of the dreadful opinion that the fairies hold of mankind, they are led by curiosity to call up the mortal Phyllon and Ethais. The result is disastrous. Mortal passions are aroused in the fairies which result in hatred and jealousy and the deposition of their Queen before the absent pair return, and the mortals are forced back to earth. The fairy messengers have brought back the 'priceless gift' – it is 'love'. From now on, the fairies will be able to love as mortals do. Horrified, Fairyland rejects the gift and returns gratefully to its former ways.

Edward German composed some highly attractive music to rather uninspired Gilbert lyrics, some of which duplicated the dialogue and almost all of which went to prove that *The Wicked World* had no real need for a musical setting, no matter how proficient. The finished work, with its wordy blank verse dialogue and its bitter tone, did not resemble the other lyrical works of Gilbert at all. The misanthropy of *Fallen Fairies* did not have the satiric twinkle of a King Gama, it was harsh and genuine, and even the purposefully comic episodes involving Lutin, the esquire of the mortal knights, did little to lighten the prevailing atmosphere of grey jealousy and recrimination. Gilbert had advisedly billed the piece as 'opera' – it was certainly no comic opera. The lack of humour spilled over into the preparations for the piece as well. Gilbert, who had directed the show with his customary forcefulness, had laid about him with many a hard word and had even loudly criticised the sets designed by Joseph Harker, the doyen of scene painters and the designer of *H.M.S. Pinafore*.

The first night of *Fallen Fairies*, suitably decked with devotees, went splendidly. The audience liked what they heard and the piece had been spectacularly produced. The sight of the 18-stone Australian ex-stockman, Claude Flemming, and the six-foot, 15-stone Leo Sheffield doing battle with 42-inch broadswords made a quite extraordinary effect. But the appeal of *Fallen Fairies* was very limited. Audiences had radically changed their preferences since the days of *The Wicked World* and Gilbert himself had effectively 'finished off' his own particular brand of literary fairy with *Iolanthe*. The plaintively locquacious Selene and the vituperative and long-winded Darine were, in spite of anything Nancy McIntosh and Maidie Hope could do, old-fashioned wordmongers and, in this case, notemongers, who aroused little interest or passion. In spite of its undoubted qualities, *Fallen Fairies* suffered from the same failings as the less expert *The Mountaineers* and it suffered from them rather more severely.

Some alterations were attempted. Amy Evers replaced Miss McIntosh as Selene and was given a new number written by German and Gilbert, but, when Workman interpolated an outside piece 'Love Rules the World', Gilbert rushed petulantly to court for an injunction. Finally, the song stayed but with 'by permission of Mr W. S.

Gilbert' noted in the programme. But not for long. *Fallen Fairies* played through Christmas to the new year and folded at the end of January after 51 performances.

Very few new productions emerged from the provincial scene in 1909. The most considerable of these was a choc-a-bloc piece called *The Lily of Bermuda* which began its career at Manchester's Theatre Royal with an advance announcement of a short tour of principal towns while heading for London.

The Lily of Bermuda showed its serious intentions by hiring John Bardesley, the up-and-coming tenor of the moment, as its leading man and Georgina Delmar as 'Lily' and surrounding them with an enoromous cast representing practically every stereotype of the past years in musical comedy: the crusty colonel (Arthur Hare), the brash millionaire (E. M. Robson), the dashing lieutenant (J. Burlington Rigg), the American belle (Olive May), the suffragette (Beatrice Park), the dude (Arthur Longley), the dragon (Marie Burdell), the lascivious Frenchman (Henry Adnes) and threw in a gispy fortune-teller and a coloured comic for good measure. Of plot there was little, except that it led its hero (who spent a good deal of the evening inexplicably masked and cloaked) into the arms of heiress Lily at the final curtain after the depredations of a certain flower which, in the tradition hawked from *A Midsummer's Night's Dream* to *Oriana* to *Cymbia* and countless others, makes whoever shall see it bloom fall in love with the first person he/she sees. *The Lily of Bermuda* duly completed the 'short tour' but did not appear in London.

The Purple Emperor, on the other hand, opened in London at the King's Theatre, Hammersmith, where it was tried by Alexander Leighton's company which were there touring *A Chinese Honeymoon*. It received a 'polite' reception and was not persevered with. More enduring, and on a less ambitious plane, was a piece called *The Cruise of the Constance* produced at the Theatre Royal, Worthing in June. It, too, brought together a familiar set of characters, aboard a yacht: a rich widow, her niece with her (comic) maid, and her lover, an adventurer, a Swiss admiral – and embroiled them in a case of stolen diamonds. Needing to marry in twenty-four hours to inherit a fortune, the hero elopes with his lady on the island of Malta which provided a suitably pretty setting for the second act. Some lively songs and plenty of topicality kept the 'Constance' afloat for several unpretentious tours both under its original title and later as *The Girl on the Boat*.

1909

0353 **OUR MISS GIBBS** a musical play in two acts by 'Cryptos' and James T. Tanner. Lyrics by Adrian Ross and Percy Greenbank. Music by Ivan Caryll and Lionel Monckton. Produced at the Gaiety Theatre under the management of George Edwardes 23 January, 1909 for a run of 636 performances closing 3 December, 1910.

Hon. Hughie Pierrepoint	George Grossmith Jr/Frank Hector
The Earl of St Ives	O. B. Clarence/Arnold Lucy
Slithers	Robert Hale
Mr Toplady	Arthur Hatherton/Harry B. Burcher
Lord Eynsford	J. Edward Fraser
Mr Beavis	J. A. Evelyn
Taxi Cabby	F. Payne
Mr Amalfy	Harry B. Burcher/George Grundy
Timothy Gibbs	Edmund Payne (Willie Stevens)
Lady Elizabeth Thanet	Denise Orme/Gladys Cooper/Olive May/ Julia James/Blanche Browne/Enid Leslie
Madame Jeanne	Jean Aylwin/Marjorie Napier/Ruth Argent/Nancy More/Dora Sevening
Duchess of Minster	Gladys Homfrey
Mrs Farquhar	Maisie Gay
Clarita	Kitty Mason/*out*
Nora	Olive May/Mabel Russell/Marie Mitchell/*out*
Sheilah	Adeline Balfe/Mabel Russell/Julia James/Alice Hatton/*out*
Kathleen	Rose Begarnie/Alice Pollard/Edith Standen/*out*
Lady Connie	Gladys Cooper/Gertrude Thornton/Amy Webster
Lady Sybil	Julia James/Blanche Stocker
Lady Trixie	Enid Leslie/Grace Slater
Lady Angela	Crissie Bell/Muriel Gibb/Blanche Stocker
Lady Muriel	Suzanne Selbourne/Dorothy Selbourne
Lady Gwen	Gertie Thornton/Phyllis Barber/Moya Mannering/Gertie Murray
Mary Gibbs	Gertie Millar (Rose Begarnie) (Olive May) (Enid Leslie)
add Pageboy	S. Fortescue
Youri	W. Richardson
Soshi	Marie Mitchell
Fan-Fan	Alice Hatton
Si-Klop	Edith Standen
Lady Beryl	Gertie Murray
Lady Edith	Connie Stuart

Lady Jane. . . . . Lena Leibrandt
Lady Nora . . . . Chloe O'Hara

with Madge Melbourne, Ida Barnard, Rhona Dalvy, Joe Howard, Gladys Carrington, Pattie Wells, Irene Warren, Shirley Power, Pauline Francis, Nancy More, Marjorie Michie, Marjorie Napier, Ruby Kennedy, Ruth Argent, Gertrude Birch, Marie Dean, George Grundy, E. Camp, Alec Fraser, Cecil Cameron, Sidney Lyndon, J. Redmond/Nellie Hodson, Babs Taylor, Millicent Field, Ruby Artrey, Pauline Twemlow, May Flower, Olive Tempest, May Kennedy, Maud Percival, Gertrude Allen, Clara Taylor, Jessie Fraser, Violet Heath, F. W. Pedgrift.
Ju-jitsu dance by Maud Percival, Peggy Franklin, Dora Broughton, Florrie Arnold

Dir: E. W. Royce Jr; md: Ivan Caryll/Carl Kiefert; sc: Joseph Harker; cos: Comelli

Produced at the Knickerbocker Theatre, New York, under the management of Charles Frohman 29 August, 1910 for a run of 57 performances. Closing 22 October, 1910.
Ernest Lambart (HU), Ernest A. Elton (EARL), Bert Leslie (SL), Arthur Laceby (TOP), Craufurd Kent (LORD), Reginald Sheldrick (BEA), Victor Le Roy (CAB), Gilbert Coleman (AM), Fred Wright Jr (TIM), Julia James (ELIZ), Jean Aylwin (JEA), Daisy Belmore (DUCH), Mollie Lowell (MRS), Kitty Mason (CL), Ethel Wheeler (N), Marion Mosby (SH), Gertrude Vanderbilt (K), Clara Pitt (CON), Margaret McKenzie (SY), Henrietta Pellard (TR), Freda Barun (AN), Margaret Von Keese (MU), Bert Rice (GW), Pauline Chase (MARY) with Ethel Kelly, Helen Morrison, Doris Cameron, Irene Claire, Bessie Frewen, Sara Carr, Madelain de Boeuf, Adel Kornan, Anna Kuehl, Maybelle Dean, Helen Dixon, Natalie Dana, Lillian Smalley, Nancy Butler, Florence Plunkett, Montacuse Melmen, Lillian Francis, Mary E. Martin, Madge Robinson, Della Dolson, Lillian Shepherd, Dorothy Castle, Lethea Grey, Dorothy Courtney, Mona Sartoris, Nellie Stewart, Louise Louis, Julie Newell, Edith Warren, Edna Dana, Glory Gray, Lillian Stair, Edward Leech, Roger Davis, H. Edelman, Oliver Sterling, Ralph O'Brien, Eddie Morris.
Dir: Thomas Reynolds; md: W. T. Francis; cos: Lord & Taylor, Dazian &c.

Film: (silent) In 1909 a film excerpt of some ten minutes in length featuring George Grossmith, Edmund Payne and Madge Melbourne (Mary) was issued by Gaumont.

0354 **THE DASHING LITTLE DUKE** a play with music in three acts by Seymour Hicks. Lyrics by Adrian Ross. Music by Frank E. Tours. Produced at the Theatre Royal, Nottingham, under the management of Charles Frohman 8 February, 1909 and subsequently at the Hicks Theatre 17 February, 1909 for a run of 101 performances closing 28 May, 1909.

Chevalier de Matignon . . . . C. Hayden Coffin
Baron de Bellechasse . . . . Sam Walsh/George Barrett
Lt Armand de Soliveau. . . . . Frank Wilson
Dubois . . . . Lawrence Caird
Merlac. Fred Vigay
Lepas . . . . M. Protti
Moulinet . . . . Hughes Croise
Fleury. Charles Le Galley
Canif . . . . Roland Chester
Abbé de la Touche . . . . Courtice Pounds
Duchesse de Bourgoyne . . . . Louie Pounds
Duchesse de Noailles . . . . Maud Milton
Diane de Noailles. . . . . Elizabeth Firth/Coralie Blythe
Césarine de la Noce. . . . . Coralie Blythe/Dorothy Monkman/Julia Sanderson
Baronne de Bellechasse . . . . Florence Wood
Mlle Geneviève Fauvepré. . . . . May Kennedy
Mlle Juliette de Lanbriet . . . . Doris Stocker
Mlle Antoinette de Preselles . . . . . . Rena Goldie
Mlle Marie de Mortemer . . . . Marie Brenda
Mlle Celestine de Gaillet . . . . Carina Cliff
Mlle Clarie de Viennez . . . . Mabel Watson
Mlle Madeleine de Maugars . . . . Rosie Chesney
Mlle Violette de Vaux . . . . Dini Graham
Mlle Cécile du Grand Vivier . . . . Nelli Pryor

Mlle Elise de Gontaut . . . . Millicent Field
Mlle Hélène de Laundal . . . . Gwendoline d'Arcy
Mlle Thérèse de Belair . . . . Eileen Chisholm
Duc de Richelieu . . . . Ellaline Terriss/Seymour Hicks
add Officer of Dragoons . . . . Harry Frankiss

Dir: Seymour Hicks; md: Frank E. Tours; ch: Fred Farren; sc: Joseph Harker; cos: Percy Anderson

0355 **A PERSIAN PRINCESS** an oriental musical play in two acts by Leedham Bantock and P. J. Barrow. Lyrics by Percy Greenbank. Music by Sidney Jones. Additional music by Marie Horne. Produced at the Queen's Theatre under the management of Tom B. Davis 27 April, 1909 for a run of 68 performances closing 3 July, 1909.

King Khayyam . . . . George Graves
Prince Hassan . . . . Clarence Blakiston
Prince Omar . . . . Noel Fleming/John Bardsley
King Khafilah . . . . M. R. Morand
Swaak . . . . Horace Mills
Amm Zaid . . . . John Morley
El Tabloid . . . . Aubrey Fitzgerald
Akbar . . . . J. Warren Foster
Mustapha . . . . Sydney Bracey
Wunbarest . . . . John Lawson
Tubarest . . . . Richard Attwood
Khomunkaud . . . . James Haughton
Dhiskord . . . . James Bernard
Mpoani . . . . Lionel Braham/Arthur Jenner
Mpogo . . . . Willie Hartill
Zingarie . . . . Carrie Moore
Lady Ayala . . . . Lily Iris
Ujujube . . . . Vivien Talleur
Selim . . . . George Burns
Zoraida . . . . Jessie Lonnen
Meranda . . . . Ethel Negretti
Nurmahl . . . . Gladys Herries
Marzipan . . . . Doris Beresford
Zobeide . . . . Emmie Santer
Fuljan . . . . Tessie Hackney
Lulu . . . . Beatrice Harrington
Kya-la . . . . Isabel Agnew
Khissme . . . . Minnie Baker
Zen-Zen . . . . Alice Hatton
Mai-i . . . . Moya Mannering
Dou-Dou . . . . Hilda Stewart
Ylopia . . . . Lucy Davies
Goulnal . . . . Maggie Jarvis
King Khafilah . . . . M. R. Morand
Princess Yolene . . . . Ruth Vincent

Dir: Sydney Ellison; md: Carl Kiefert; sc: Alfred Terraine & Joseph Harker; cos: Percy Anderson

0356 **THE ARCADIANS** a fantastic musical play in three acts by Mark Ambient and Alexander M. Thompson. Lyrics by Arthur Wimperis. Music by Lionel Monckton and Howard Talbot. Produced at the Shaftesbury Theatre under the management of Robert Courtneidge 28 April, 1909 for a run of 809 performances closing 29 July, 1911.

James Smith/Simplicitas . . . . Dan Rolyat/Vincent Earne/Dan Agar
Peter Doody . . . . Alfred Lester/George Hestor
Jack Meadows . . . . (Harry Pearce) Harry Welchman
Bobby . . . . Nelson Keys

Sir George Paddock	Akerman May
Percy Marsh	Deane Percival/Harry E. Ray
Reggie	Charles Chamier/Frank Haylett/Victor Tollemache
Sir Timothy Ryan	Charles Strood/Victor Tollemache
Harry Desmond	George Masters/E. Stanmore/E. Matthews/ F. W. Hearne
James Withers	Walter L. Rignold/*out*
Hooter	Arthur Johnston/*out*
Time	George Elton
Mrs Smith	Ada Blanche
Lady Barclay	Violet Graham/Muriel Varna
Lucy Selwyn	Muriel Hastings
Marion	Mary Berys/Muriel Varna/Eveline Laune
Beatrice	Violet Walker/Daisy Athelstan
Amaryllis	Billie Sinclair/M. Sinclair?
Daphne	M. Lawson/Lillie Nanton
Dryope	Dorothy Laine/Violet Morene
Eileen Kavanagh	Phyllis Dare/Cicely Courtneidge/ Frances Kapstowne/Nellie Taylor/
Chrysea	May Kinder/Gladys Silvani/Cicely Courtneidge/Maggie Jarvis/Maie Ash/ Moya Mannering/Maudi Thornton/ Nellie Taylor/
Astrophel	Harry Pearce/Charles Chamier
Strephon	Charles Charteris/Vere Matthews/ E. Stanmore
Damoetas	S. Oliver/Lewis Oliver?
Sombra	Florence Smithson (Ethel Lawson)
add Psyche	R. Gould/Kathleen Alleyne
Hon. Maud Barclay	Maggie Jarvis/Esther Robinson/Barbara Roberts/Julia de Vere/Blanche Tomlin/Margaret Swallow

Dir: Robert Courtneidge; md: Howard Talbot/Arthur Wood; ch: Harry Grattan; sc: Conrad Tritschler; R. C. McCleery, Stafford Hall and W. Holmes; cos: Wilhelm

Produced at the Liberty Theatre, New York, under the management of Charles Frohman 17 January, 1910. Transferred to the Knickerbocker Theatre 16 May, 1910. Closed 2 July 1910, after a total of 193 performances.
Frank Moulan (SIMP), Percival Knight (DOO), Alan Mudie (JACK), Alfred Kappeler (BOBBY), Lawrence Grant (SIR), John Paulton (PERCY), H. H. Meyer (REG), E. H. Lyle (TIM), Tom Collins (HARRY), Sam Collins (JAS), J. Gunnis Davis (TIME), Connie Ediss (MRS), Eithel Kelly/Vivian Blackburn (BAR), Esther Brunette (LUCY), Grace Studiford (MAR), Josephine Howard (BEA), Jane Hall (AM), Marion Mosby (DAPH), Julia Sanderson (EIL), Audrey Maple (CHR), Stanley Jessup (AST), H. H. Meyer (STR), John O'Hanlon (DAM), Ethel Cadman (SOMB), Eleanor Pendleton (MAUD), Eithel Kelly (LADY JIM), with Viola Clark, Gertrude Fursman, Beatrice Burrows, Carol Oty, Muriel Parker, Lucile Parsons, Frances Ceratt, Bessie Nelligan, Jeanette Lewis, Ruth Mason, Connie de Tournie, Ethel Vivian, Alice Randolph, Elise Kimber, Antoinette Le Comte, Mary Pendleton, Mae d'Arcy, Cherry Gildea, Gypsy Dale, Helen Edwards, Mollie Alexander, Jeanette Singer, Myrtle Lawton, Millie Murray, Irene von Muller, Josephine Angela, Leslie Zannere, Helen Wheeler, Mollie Lorraine, Irene Hopping. Dir: Thomas Reynolds; md: Watty Hydes; sc: Homer Emens; cos: Wilhelm, Lord & Taylor &c.

Produced at the Wiener Stadttheater, Vienna as *Die Arkadier* 24 February, 1911.

Produced at L'Olympia, Paris in a version by Charles Quinel and Max Dearly as *Les Arcadiens*, 3 April, 1913.

Produced at the Shaftesbury Theatre under the management of Robert Courtneidge 20 May, 1915 for a run of 31 performances closing 19 June.
Dan Agar (SIMP), Alfred Lester (DOO), Harry Welchman (JACK), Jack Hulbert (BOBBY),

Ambrose Manning (SIR), Harce Percival (REG), Charlton Morton (TIM), Edgar Stanmore (HARRY), George Elton (TIME), Gwen Clifford (MRS), Ivy Louise (LADY), Louie Lochner (LUCY), Doris Vinson (MAR), Leslie Graham (BEA), Gretchen Yates (AM), Madge Compton (DAPH), Phyllis Smith (DRY), Cicely Courtneidge (EIL), Hetta Kelly (CHR), Harry E. Pearce/Nelson Hancock (AST), Harold Clemence (STR), Kathleen Hayes (DAM), Hope Charteris (SOMB), Lena Miller (PS), Mabel Munro (MAUD). Dir: Robert Courtneidge; md: Arthur Wood; sc: Conard Tritschler, T. Holmes, R. C. McCleery; cos: Wilhelm.

Film: (silent) 1927, Gaumont. Pr: Maurice Eley, Victor Saville & Gareth Gundrey. Dir: Victor Saville
Ben Blue (SIMP), Gibb McLaughlin (DOO), John Longden (JACK), Humberstone Wright (SIR), Jeanne de Casalis (MRS), Vesta Sylva (EIL), Nancy Rigg (CHR), Doris Bransgrove (SOMB), Cyril McLaglen (THE CROOK) with Teddy Brown, Ivor Vintor, Lola & Luis, Tracey & Haye, Balliol & Merton, the Donovan Sisters, the Tiller Girls, and the twelve Arcadian nymphs.

0357 **THE CRUISE OF THE CONSTANCE** a comedy with music in two acts. Music and lyrics by Cyril Winchcombe. Libretto by Violet Hatherley. Produced at the Theatre Royal, Worthing, under the management of Harry Lumley 10 June, 1909 and toured.

Sir Walter Wesleydale . . . . Frederick Hobbs
Captain . . . . Powis Pinder
Admiral Weber . . . . John Wigley
Mr Edward Harvey . . . . Lewis Wigley
Mike. . . . . James Dooling
Stephano . . . . J. J. Jordon
Ezekiel Pott . . . . Charles E. Paton
Clementa . . . . Ethel Quarrie
Hetty Smith. . . . . Phillis Shale
Gabrielle Glenister . . . . Jack Martyn
Phyllis Claire . . . . Mona Ray
Zena Fadyn . . . . Maime Stuart
Gertie Flower . . . . Ivy Holmes
Bella. . . . . May Garstang
Mrs Hope . . . . Florence Parfrey

Reproduced at Brixton 10 October, 1910 as *The Girl on the Boat*.

0358 **DEAR LITTLE DENMARK** a Danish musical incident in two acts. Book, music and lyrics (chatter, jingles and tunes) by Paul Rubens. Produced at the Prince of Wales Theatre under the management of Frank Curzon 1 September, 1909 for a run of 109 performances closing 18 December, 1909.

Duke Ernest von Rassmussen . . . . . . James Blakeley
Karl . . . . C. Morton Horne
Conrad Petersen. . . . . Bertram Wallis
Simon Jorgensen . . . . John Clulow
Jonas Jensen . . . . A. W. Baskcomb/Ralph Holland
Sergeant Ohlis . . . . Fred W. Ring
Chamberlain. . . . . Warwick Wellington
Robins. . . . . J. Dornan
Town Crier . . . . Iago Lewys
Neils. . . . . J. B. Fraser
Hans Hansen . . . . Huntley Wright
Ophelia . . . . Gracie Leigh/Joan Penrose
Xandra . . . . Hazel Dawn
Adeline . . . . Peggy Bethel/Phyllis Monkman
Elsa . . . . Phyllis Monkman
Christine . . . . Isabel Jay
Ballet Dancers. . . . . Daisy Fisher, Claire Lynch, Gladys Beech, Winnie Erskine, Nancy Rich, Kitty Sparrow

with Leila Griffen &c

Dir: Frank Curzon; md: Ignatius A. de Orellana; ch: Fred Farren; sc: Bruce Smith; cos: C. Karl

0359 **THE MOUNTAINEERS** a romantic comic opera in three acts by Guy Eden and Reginald Somerville. Lyrics by Guy Eden. Music by Reginald Somerville. Produced at the Savoy Theatre under the management of C. Herbert Workman 29 September, 1909 for a run of 61 performances closing 27 November, 1909.

Pierre	C. H. Workman (Sydney Ashcroft)
Fritz	Claude Flemming
Conrad	Laurence Legge
Gustave	Reginald Lawrence
Sergeant Frederico	Frank Perfitt
Louis	A. Wellton Fordham
François	Sydney Ashcroft
A Priest	A. Everette
Citizen	D. Fergusson
Clarice	Elsie Spain
Annette	Jessie Rose
Miss Spinifex	Kate Forster
Yvonne	Ruby Gray
Armandine	Mabel Burnege
Celestine	Gladys Lancaster
Noélie	Hilda Vining
Yvette	Josset Legh
Prudence	Marjorie Dawes
Bridesmaids	Fay Temple, Giovanno Botto

Dir: Sydney Ellison; md: Reginald Somerville; sc: Raphael; cos: Percy Anderson

0360 **THE LILY OF BERMUDA** a colonial comedy with music in two acts by Duse Mohamed and Ernest Trimmingham. Lyrics by Hinton Jones. Music by Mark Strong and Harry M. Wellmon. Produced at the Theatre Royal, Manchester, 8 November, 1909 and toured.

Lt Sir Geoffrey Hilton	John Bardesley
Lt-Col. the Earl of Lang	Arthur Hare
Allen Ginter	E. M. Robson
Lt Jack Ward	J. Burlington Rigg
Lord Anglosax	Arthur Longley
Monsieur Leon	Henry Adnes
Colonel Clarance	Holliday Attley
Major Hon. John Westinghouse	John Orchill
Capt. Lord Catterage	William Guilbert
Adjt Viscount Nuneaton	Luis Heron
Lt Henry Seacombe	Hayden Scott
Major Lord Derwentwater	Mr McKiernan
Capt. William Hennessy	Baron Heron
Adjt de Rothe	W. C. Hoddy
Lt Sir Herbert Field	M. Courtney
Walter Woods	Robert Rivers
Joe Tucker	Charley White
Bill Smith	Frank Attree
Hon. Lionel Roberts	Peter Grata
Viscount St Germin	Edgar Driver
Henry Arthur Brown	Ernest Grata
Lord Hugh Park	Agnes Ellis
Cecil Pearce	Lucy Lingard
William Clarke-Nelson	Ada Eshelby
Claribel Dreadnaught	Beatrice Park
The Dowager Duchess of Margate	Marie Burdell

Miss Montague of Chicago	Olive May
Yama Zora	Violet Campbell
Lily Ginter	Georgina Delmar

with Beatrice Rowe, Muriel Johnston, Marguerite Penfold, Eva Brickwell, Dorothy Desmonde, Nora Dene, Dorothy Ewins, Mabel Maartens, Georgie Forrester, Hilda Saxe, Nellie Beacon, Lena Brickwell

0361 **FALLEN FAIRIES** an opera in two acts by W. S. Gilbert adapted from his play *The Wicked World*. Music by Edward German. Produced at the Savoy Theatre under the management of C. Herbert Workman 15 December, 1909 for a run of 51 performances closing 29 January, 1910.

Ethais	Claude Flemming
Phyllon	Leo Sheffield
Lutin	C. H. Workman
Selene	Nancy McIntosh/Amy Evers
Darine	Maidie Hope
Zayda	Jessie Rose
Locrine	Ethel Morrison
Neodie	Alice Cox
Fleta	Marjorie Dawes
Zara	Mabel Burnege
Leila	Ruby Gray
Cora	Rita Otway
Maia	Gladys Lancaster
Chloris	Miriam Lycett
Ina	Isabel Agnew

Dir: W. S. Gilbert; md: Edward German/Hamish MacCunn; ch: John D'Auban; sc: Joseph Harker; cos: Percy Anderson

THE PURPLE EMPEROR a musical comedy in two acts by T. Crutchley. Lyrics by T. C. and C. Austin. Music by H. Austin. Produced at the King's Theatre, Hammersmith by Alexander Leighton's Co. 6 December, 1909.

Constantine Jakes	Charles McNaughton
Major Domo	Rudolph Kloss
Lt Leonard Kestrain	Roland Bottomley
Sub-Lt Clinton	Norman C. Bennett
Sub-Lt Gerald Jones	Reginald Hartley
Sub-Lt McLean	William Pringle
Reginald Vincent	Maie Sydney
Christine Carlington	Gladys Ivery
Danny Bedford	Winnie Browne
Ethel Huntingdon	Gladys Erskine
Kitty Green	Grace Courtley
Lavinia Brown	Phyllis Manners

1910

The new year began with the three big hits of 1909 (*The Arcadians*, *Our Miss Gibbs* and *The Dollar Princess*) holding the centre of the stage. But there was plenty of space alongside them, for *Dear Little Denmark* had faded away on December 18 and the disappointing *The Merry Peasant* on New Year's Day, leaving only the short-lived *Fallen Fairies* and the Christmas revivals of *Pinkie* and *Alice in Wonderland* to otherwise represent the musical theatre.

However, in the first four months of the year there were four new British pieces offered in the West End: all very different and achieving varying degrees of success. The first was an unmitigated flop. *Captain Kidd* had seemingly impeccable lineage and credits. It was a Seymour Hicks production adapted by its producer from the successful American farce *The Dictator* (1904) with lyrics by Adrian Ross and music by Leslie Stuart, and it brought Hicks back to co-star with his equally popular wife for the first time in London since *The Gay Gordons*. For his return to musical comedy, Hicks had prepared himself a full-scale starring vehicle. The original play had been vigorously slimmed of incident and 'extraneous matter' and the gaps filled with song, with Hicks in the character of the dashing young Viscount Albany, otherwise 'Captain Kidd'.

Albany has had an altercation with a New York cabbie and, as in *Wapping Old Stairs*, has fled believing himself a murderer. He is bound for South America on the S. S. Bolivar when he meets pretty Lucy Sheridan, bound for the same place and for marriage with a Reverend Arthur Bostick. Also bound on that journey is Colonel Bowie, consul-elect for their destination of Porto Banos. When they arrive, the town is in revolt and Bowie's ally has been 'removed' by the noisy revolutionary, Santos Campos. Since Albany has qualms about staying on the ship, due to the attentions of a certain detective, he agrees to change places with Bowie and goes ashore as consul. After many complications he settles Santos Campos and the country by hiring a private army and claims Lucy as his wife.

Neither Ross nor Stuart were up to their usual level in *Captain Kidd*. Stuart had abandoned the promise of *Havana* for reminiscent tunes and Ross showed little originality in his choice of topics. Miss Terriss sang of 'Yucatan' and 'A Honeymoon in Peru' and somewhere called 'Um-te-ay' which brought back memories of Gaiety burlesque, while Hicks insisted 'You could Do Wonders with Me' to 'The only Girl I ever Loved' and Hilda Guiver as a Latin lady assured everyone that she was 'The Star of Panama'. One of the more successful pieces of the evening was a modest number for Aggie, the stewardess, called 'My Affinity' where she described the sort of men she wants to meet. It was sung in the Louie Freear manner by a young actress called Ivy St Helier making her début in the West End, and she 'brought down the house with her high note'.

However, *Captain Kidd* rested squarely on the back of its hero and its heroine, particularly the former, and the reactions to his performance were uncharacteristically varied:

> The success of the play is assured by the dominating personality and immense popularity of Mr Seymour Hicks who is the spoilt child of his particular public and is allowed by them unlimited licence. He keeps the house in intermittent laughter while he is on the stage: and so deliciously absurd are his 'gags' and jokes, so buoyantly audacious are his sallies, and he has such a complete faith in himself and trust in his audience, that he proves entirely irresistable. He gets the utmost out of his songs, notably the one about the only girl he ever loved. But it is the never-ceasing activity, the unfailing good humour of Mr Hicks that wins the day (*Era*)

> In pieces of this sort he is always three parts himself to one part the character he is supposed to represent. Last night the proportion was nine to one. Mr Hicks was not only rattled but ragged – there is no other word for it. He dropped unauthorised asides right and left, he addressed the audience frequently, though hurriedly, in his own person, he imitated his brother players and his brother artistes of the variety stage. And the delight he took in it all was infectious . . (*Times*)

The Times, nevertheless, concluded:

> . . of course, *Captain Kidd* will be a great success, with these two popular favourites . . . one of them at her best and the other at his maddest and merriest . .

Quite clearly the artist, or rather the artists, outweighed the material in importance. As in the most self-indulgent of Arthur Roberts' pieces (and there were quite a few parallels with *H.M.S. Irresponsible*), *Captain Kidd* was a vehicle pure and simple, but unfortunately its star could not rise above his commonplace material and his undisciplined performance. *Captain Kidd* closed in disarray after just one month to such total indifference that even the music of Leslie Stuart was not taken up by his publishers. Wyndham hurriedly brought in Monckton Hoffe's *The Little Damozel* for an altogether more professional and happy run, and *Captain Kidd* was put in storage until October when it was sent on the road with Roland Bottomley and Maie Ash in the leading roles. It failed again, and the once high-flying Hicks family found themselves deep in debt. It had all gone wrong, and they were obliged to turn from the theatre and their own productions to lucrative spots on the music halls to set themselves to rights. Hicks had totally failed in *Captain Kidd* to capture the new feeling in musical comedy. It was not sufficient now merely to present a group of characters and a situation and then fill up the evening with song and dance in any old manner; a higher level of coherence was required.

One who had grasped the right style immediately and securely was Frederick Lonsdale, author of *King of Cadonia* which had done so well for Frank Curzon. Its follow-up from Curzon's regular, Paul Rubens, had been less successful, so this time Curzon decided to pair Rubens with young Lonsdale, who produced a libretto in substantially the same vein as *King of Cadonia* with the central character altered to a female one: *The Balkan Princess*.

Princess Stephanie of Balaria sits upon a slightly shaky Balkan throne. To secure the succession, Parliament demands that she should marry, and presents her with the choice of the six wealthiest lords in the land. Five rush to be considered but the sixth, the Grand Duke Sergius, refuses. He has an hereditary objection to the ruling family and writes antagonistic articles for the newspapers about the present Princess. But Stephanie refuses the five suitors and decides to go out into the world for the week remaining before her decision, to try to find out what love is. She finds out in the 'Bohemian Restaurant' where she meets Sergius. Unaware of each other's identity, they fall in love. But disaster strikes when Sergius gives a toast, 'Down with the Princess Stephanie'. Royalty displaces womanhood, and Stephanie commands that the traitor be arrested. Sergius is taken to the palace but before the piece has ended he has exchanged his prison chains for those of wedlock. For Stephanie abdicates rather than marry any of the remaining five lords and Sergius, recognising her greatness of spirit, abandons his feud, tears up the abdication document, and takes his place at her side.

The central roles of Stephanie and Sergius supplied strong, dramatic parts for Isabel Jay and Bertram Wallis, similar to those in *King of Cadonia*, but these were carefully balanced with the comic element supplied by James Blakeley, Mabel Sealby (in the 'Gracie Leigh' role), Charles Brown and Lauri de Frece. The last two were comical villains, direct descendants of Cadeau and Ravennes. Max Hein (Brown) has kidnapped one of the five dukes and has come in his place, disguised, with the intention of stealing the crown jewels. He brings with him the professional burglar, Blatz (de Frece) who turns out to be more interested in the 'char', Magda (Miss Sealby)–or, rather, in the insurance money she stands to gain from the disappearance of her former husband. That husband, of course, is very much alive and is working as a waiter at the 'Bohemian Restaurant'. He was played with lively gloom and pessimism by Jimmy Blakeley. Alfred Lester's success as Doody in *The Arcadians* had made the lugubrious good coin.

It was a strong, forward-moving script full of incident and lively dialogue and it deserved better musical illustration. Paul Rubens was no Sidney Jones, and *The Balkan Princess* score was a patchy affair. Much of the trouble lay in the lyrics. There was a joint credit–Rubens sharing with Arthur Wimperis–and none of the numbers was singly credited, but the merit of the lyrics varied alarmingly and the style of each writer showed through quite clearly.

There were some good comic numbers. Mabel Sealby described her 'calling':

Now when I char, I char
With all my heart and soul
In every cranny and chink I grope
My motto is 'While there's life, there's soap'.
Why, I char the black off the coal!
For charring is an art
I've got a first prize for floors
And in spite of my having the Housemaid's Hip
I won the Bulgarian championship
For scrubbing the paint off doors . . &c

the two 'poetical' burglars theirs:

When the moon comes stealing
Through the branches of the old oak trees
Yes, stealing with the evening breeze
And floods the night with silver light
It's then a sort of feeling
Comes a-stealing
Over every man
To go a-stealing, stealing,
Stealing
Everything he can!

and Henri the waiter his in the suitably downhearted 'It's a hard life'. The romantic numbers were less successful. Isabel Jay's ballads 'Wonderful World' and 'Dreaming' were undistinguished and the numbers allotted to Wallis were frankly poor. In one he had yet another go at the most over-used theme of all:

Oh, you dear delightful women
Why, I simply love you all . .

while the other was an heroic march which was only made so with the aid of Wallis' bearing and baritone:

A man may be born to the purple
Or be born to the pick and the spade
It may be his fate
To rule in state
Or follow a humble trade.
He may live in a cot or a castle
In the court or a caravan,
It's naught to me
What a man may be
As long as a man's a MAN!

The Times dismissed it as 'silly nonsense' and the audiences were equally unenthusiastic. A small consolation came in the form of a bright duet for the two principals. Having just met and enjoyed themselves, they decide 'Don't Let's Meet Again' and spoil a lovely memory.

But there was more than enough in *The Balkan Princess* that was good – even very good – to make it a success. *The Times* noted

> Saturday's audience came determined to make a success of the new musical play, but before long the affair was taken out of their hands as *The Balkan Princess* did the work for itself. In shape it is the best musical comedy of recent years; its story is almost reasonable and quite interesting and its music is above average level of these things . . . *The Balkan Princess* is not a gem of light opera, but it is not a music hall entertainment disguised. There has been an unmistakeable attempt to fit the music and the plot and the fun and the display into a single scheme. A good deal of it is nonsense, but . . . very little of it is silly nonsense; much of it is good and interesting sense . .

The dramatic ending to the second act, with the Princess' revelation of her true identity and the arrest of Sergius, was a particularly strong and effective part of the show, as was the final scene between Stephanie and Sergius. The libretto was excellent stuff and was largely responsible for the show's success and certainly for its acclamation by several critics as the best musical for some time.

It had a six months' run in London and by the end of the year it had made appearances from India to Australia to the King's Theatre in Buda-Pesth and everywhere to an excellent reception. Early in 1911 it made its American début at New Haven before opening three weeks later at the ageing Herald Square Theatre in New York where it proved a welcome success for the hard-pressed management, running through 111 performances with Louise Gunning and Robert Warwick in the starring roles. In Britain it took enthusiastically to the touring circuits where it was still to be occasionally found as late as the 1930s, playing twice nightly.

At the Savoy, C. H. Workman pressed on with his plan of producing new musicals in a resolutely old-fashioned style. After *The Mountaineers* and the disaster of *Fallen*

Fairies he came up with a third new piece, *Two Merry Monarchs*, written by Arthur Anderson, whose work had been seen to advantage in *The White Chrysanthemum*, *The Girl behind the Counter* and *Butterflies*, and George Levy. The music for the piece was by the Welsh conductor and composer, Orlando Morgan.

Two Merry Monarchs was determinedly 'comic opera', more Savoy than the Savoy. Its plot was thoroughly whimsical. King Paul of Esperanto is 942 years old, because he has an elixir of perpetual life. His longevity has caused him to outlive all the other monarchs except King Utops of Utopia whose downfall he is now plotting. His ingenious murder plan consists of giving his previously immunised daughter a deadly poison and then marrying her to Utops. When they kiss, as surely they must, Utops will be poisoned. Unfortunately, the betrothal kiss is interrupted by the Princess' lover, Charmis. He is the head of the police and kissing is forbidden in Esperanto except by licence. The licence that Utops has taken out is a liquor licence. When the kiss finally does occur, however, Utops does not drop down dead. He, too, has drunk the famous elixir – he was Paul's assistant in the days of its discovery! There is no room for two immortal kings and it is decided to fight a curious duel. Two beakers are filled, one with a fluid which will annul the elixir and make its drinker mortal again. The two kings drink and both become mortal. Charmis has played them false. Since the two monarchs are now excessively aged, Princess Cynthia steps onto the throne with Charmis at her side, which is a happy ending.

The libretto was complicated and often confusing, and without the genuine wit required for its kind, particularly when presented at the Savoy. Morgan's music gained some approval but, as *The Era* admitted:

> [it] has the very welcome merits of dash, sound and spirit, and is, for that reason, exhilarating; but it does not contain many of those haunting melodies which are hummed and whistled 'after the opera is over'. It is, however light, bright and pleasing and there is plenty of emphatic and rousing appeal in the concerted pieces and choruses.

The piece was rather de-centred by the fact that the principal role was the comic one of Rolandyl, Postmaster General and Assessor of Taxes, played by Workman. Although Rolandyl had little to do with the plot he was in charge of the stage for long periods of business and song, including the clever 'You Won't Want a Licence for That' which enumerated some current licensing laws including the 'Children in the theatre' one:

> If an actress is passé and plays the soubrette
> Well, you won't have a licence for that,
> She may even have reached second childhood and yet
> You won't need a licence for that;
> But supposing a manager wants to engage
> Someone graceful and slim for the part of a page
> And he chooses a child that is just under age,
> Well, he must have a licence for that!

It was deservedly popular and well-received, but it soon became clear that *Two Merry Monarchs* was not going to succeed at the Savoy. Marie Brema's matinées of Gluck's *Orpheus and Eurydice* drew some extra money but Workman was soon obliged to throw in his hand. He surrendered the lease of the Savoy and ended his career as actor-manager.

However, director Austen Hurgon was sufficiently confident to pick up the piece for an attempt at a low-price season at the Strand (as the unfortunate Waldorf had now been renamed) and, a week after its closure at the Savoy, the show reopened in Aldwych. Most of the cast were the same, but Hurgon had secured the services of Hayden Coffin for Prince Charmis and, to replace Workman, he put forward a new comedian, 'discovered after a huge search', whom he got paragraphed as a 'rising star'. The 'new' comedian billed as 'Smith' turned out to be Philip Smith, a successful provincial musical comic. Neither Coffin nor 'Smith' nor the 5/– top ticket succeeded in lifting *Two Merry Monarchs* to success and the death of King Edward VII, which obliged the theatre to close for a week, did not help matters. After the third playing week Hurgon had to give up, and it was not until later in the year with a tour of his show that he was able to recoup some of his losses.

The burlesque and variety entertainment of *The Follies* having closed its long and successful season at the Apollo Theatre, Alexander Henderson, son of the great Victorian manager, took it to try his hand at management with a musical piece called *The Islander*. The composer of *The Islander* was Philip Michael Faraday who had succeeded so outstandingly on his first attempt with *Amasis*. On this occasion however he had a different librettist, Major Frank Marshall instead of Frederick Fenn, and the change was not for the better. Marshall had little of Fenn's imagination and verbal skill, and the plot on which he chose to build his book was a one-joke skeleton reminiscent of early provincial variety musicals.

Captain Alderson Jarrett is sent with a warship to take an island in the Persian Gulf. The Pasha of the island turns out to be a Scotsman who cannily sells him the island which has, apparently, never been anything but British anyway. The rest of the action was supplied by a series of fairly obvious love affairs with Kitty the heroine turning out to be the Pasha's daughter and so forth.

Much of the lyrical part of the show had a familiar ring: the Captain's song 'I'm Captain of one of Her Majesty's Ships', a chorus and song for Kitty, 'The orphan Ward' and a chorus 'Hark, the Luncheon Bell is Ringing' all bore the unmistakeable mark of the Savoy, without the necessary ingenuity of execution. The composer had little chance with such material or with such traditional models as 'Maid o'Mine' or 'Jack the Handyman'. His best numbers came with a little duo 'The Globe Trotters' describing the agonies of doing the Grand Tour, and a simple ballad for Kitty called 'I love Someone'.

More ingenuity seemed to have been spent on the show's incidentals than on its content. A programme note for the setting gave the location of Act 2 as – 'Somewhere in the Persian Gulf. 51°32′ North Latitude, 0°5′12″West Longitude'. The educated realised at once that the reference was that of the Adelphi Theatre. Then there was the 'vaporiser' which was turned on into the auditorium. '[it] dispenses over the audience spring Oriental breezes of a thoroughly Occidental character' reported *The Times*, unimpressed. There was another novelty in the intermezzo. Faraday wrote his solo line for the saxophone – 'the first occasion on which that instrument has figured in musical comedy', which, at least, was a novelty with some artistic merit.

However, this strangely unsophisticated piece had its good points, which gained it a warm first night welcome and a healthy subsequent run. Faraday's music was strong enough to survive many of the feeble lyrics, there was Elsie Spain as a charming leading lady and there was also Neil Kenyon, who was making his stage début in a musical. His reputation had been made on the halls and in pantomime, and what he brought to *The Islander* was a comedy which was not the traditional low comedy but lively Scots humour with which to invest the role of the Scottish Pasha and make it a starring vehicle for his talents. He seized upon his number 'The Caledonian Chiel' and elicited laughter with the most time-worn jokes about kilts and the most obvious double entendres:

> But it's oh, for the bonnet and the kilt
> It's hey hoitch, there's nothing like the kilt,
> Aye, but everybody knows
> That you canna wear these clothes
> Unless ye're like ma-sel',
> Properly built.

The good points kept *The Islander* afloat for 114 performances during which time it was duly added to and worked up. Kenyon turned 'The Caledonian Chiel' into a topical song; others were added, one of which, 'I Feel so Lonely', was by a young songwriter called Bert Lee, making an early appearance in the British musical theatre where he would later become a familiar name. At the end of the run of *The Islander*, a new version of *The Follies* returned to the Apollo and added another 521 performances to the 571 chalked up on their first run.

The London public was given a brief reminder of one of the best native light operas of the fin de siècle period when Thomas Beecham included Stanford and Jessop's *Shamus O'Brien* in his season of light opera at Her Majesty's. It joined *A Village Romeo and Juliet* as the only full-length British works performed, although a new short piece – a one act 'opéra-comique' called *A Summer Night* by G. H. Clutsam was produced on July 23.

After four new British pieces, it was the turn of the continental ones. George Edwardes came first with Fall's *Die Geschiedene Frau* as *The Girl in the Train* with Phyllis Dare as the eponymous Gonda van der Loo. It played at the Vaudeville for nearly a year, but F. C. Whitney fared even better with his version of Oscar Straus' *The Chocolate Soldier* at the Lyric Theatre. Ex-Liverpudlian Stanislaus Stange, after a long series of mostly undistinguished shows in America, finally set a seal on his fame with the immortal words:

> Come, come, I love you only
> Come, hero mine!

and Constance Drever sang to her 'hero' for a round 500 nights.

It looked as if 1910 were to be the year of the Viennese. Continental light music theatre seemed about to overrun the native product, but that was to count without Lionel Monckton and his colleagues. On 5 November a rocket went up from George Edwardes at the Adelphi Theatre as the year's most successful musical opened its doors – *The Quaker Girl*. The Adelphi had not hitherto been regarded much as a musical theatre. *The Whirl of the Town* had failed there in 1901 and *The Earl and the Girl* had succeeded in 1903/4, but now it was brought into the sphere of influence of George Edwardes and it began a career as a home of light musical entertainment which, with few deviations, it has maintained ever since. The new policy got off to a marvellous start with *The Quaker Girl*. *The Era* commented:

> [it] promises to be as successful as any of Mr Edwardes' productions at the Gaiety or Daly's. The piece has all the requisites for success which should be possessed by a piece of its class, and there is no reason why, after its baptism of comic opera – for the piece approached that genre in many ways – the Adelphi should not become a home of light, pretty, frivolous entertainment.

And, indeed, that described *The Quaker Girl* well. It blended the light frivolity of the

Gaiety musical with the comic opera style and backbone of a *Dorothy* in a manner which exactly caught the spirit of the moment. It made no concessions to Ruritania or to the Viennese operetta. It was solidly English and in the English comic opera tradition while having all the most attractive decorations of that tradition and of musical comedy.

This happy blend was emphasised by the combination of artists whom Edwardes chose for the piece. Gertie Millar came from *Our Miss Gibbs* to take the title role, playing opposite Joe Coyne, the darling of Daly's *Merry Widow* and *Dollar Princess*; Gracie Leigh deserted the Prince of Wales to play another in her line of comic maidservants; and Elsie Spain, ex of the D'Oyly Carte, was brought in from the defunct *The Islander*. To this star line-up were added Hayden Coffin, the comedian Jimmy Blakeley (star of *The Balkan Princess*), Edwardes' latest singing 'find' Miss Phyllys Le Grand, the large comedienne Mlle Caumont, Herbert Ross (who had once played Laertes for Benson) and Ada Reeve's dancing discovery, Phyllis Monkman.

It was an amazing cast, but it did not outshine its material, for James Tanner had evolved a charmingly lively story for *The Quaker Girl* which Greenbank, Ross and Monckton had illustrated with songs worthy to rank with those they had provided for *Our Miss Gibbs*. In Act 1, Prudence Pym, the Quaker Girl (Gertie Millar) is befriended by the Bonapartiste Princesse Mathilde (Elsie Spain) who is marrying Captain Charteris (Hayden Coffin) during her exile in Britain. At the wedding celebrations, Prudence is persuaded to try a glass of champagne and, caught in the act, is rejected by her Quaker elders. But Prudence's Quaker garb has caught the eye of Mathilde's friend Madame Blum, a Parisian couturier (Mlle Caumont) who sees in it the inspiration for a new mode, and so sweeps Prudence off across the Channel. Mathilde, disguised as a servant girl, comes too in order to be near Charteris who has had to return to France, and Phoebe (Gracie Leigh) and her Jeremiah (Blakeley), another back-sliding Quaker, also make the trip, so that Act 2 is set at the Maison Blum where Prudence's Quaker style has become the rage of Paris. She is also the subject of much admiration from the local men, particularly Prince Carlo (George Carvey), an aristocratic wolf, which causes some trouble with her friend, Tony (Joe Coyne) who has fallen in love with her himself.

Tony's past is very much in evidence in the shape of the French actress Diane (Miss Le Grand) who is furiously jealous and attempts to discredit Tony in Prudence's eyes by giving her a bundle of his old love letters. In the meanwhile, the authorities have discovered that Mathilde is in Paris and the Chief of Police is near to tracking her down. Carlo is prepared to denounce her but Prudence saves the situation by agreeing to partner the Prince to that evening's ball. At the ball, Prudence returns the bundle of letters to their owner – the Minister of State, Duhamel. Diane has given her the wrong packet of billets doux. In gratitude, Duhamel declares that Mathilde is, by her marriage, now British and that she is outside the jurisdiction of the Police Chief. It is only left for Prudence to get her Tony before all ends happily.

Tanner's book was better proportioned than most, partly due to the fact that he was no longer required to provide an overwhelming star comic role, and the songs which filled it were without exception charming. As always, Lionel Monckton provided his wife with some delightful pieces. She was perfectly fitted in the role of Prudence and scored enormously with the title song in which she bewailed:

All the world is very grey
For there's not a Quaker lad who will come to me and say . .
Thee loves me and me loves thee
None to woo a maiden and to take her
Nobody seems to care about me
Life is very dull for a Quaker!

Another piece for which Monckton provided both music and lyrics was 'Ah, Oui!' in which Prudence outlined the trouble a lack of French could get you into, but the most appealing of all was the lilting 'Tony from America' which Miss Millar sang and danced with all her most attractive graces.

The outstanding numbers were well shared out. Elsie Spain opened the show with a waltz song fit to challenge the best of Viennese in 'Time', Joe Coyne, spared too much solo singing, shared some pretty duets with Miss Millar of which the most attractive was probably 'The bad Boy and the good Girl', and Gracie Leigh and Jimmy Blakeley joined in the comical 'Mr Jeremiah, Esquire'. The undoubted hit of the show, however, fell to George Carvey as the lascivious Carlo as he exhorted everyone at the end of Act 2 to 'Come to the Ball':

Come with me, come to the ball
Music and merriment call.
Golden and gay are the lamps above,
Every tune is a song of love

The Quaker Girl outran both *The Girl in the Train* and *The Chocolate Soldier*, staying at the Adelphi for 536 performances, during which time it established itself as a thoroughgoing favourite. A few changes were made to the score – Lionel Monckton added 'My little grey Bonnet' for Gertie Millar and Gracie Leigh got a Hugo Felix song called 'Or Thereabouts', both of which proved popular. *The Quaker Girl* had a triumphant career wherever it went. Edwardes had a company on the road before the end of the year with Alice Collard and Louis Bradfield starring alongside Jessie Lonnen (Phoebe), Maisie Gay (Mme Blum), Kathleen Courtenay (Mathilde), Basil Foster (Charteris) and the veterans Irene Verona, Robert Nainby and William Lugg.

The following May *The Quaker Girl* achieved the virtually impossible by going to Paris, to the Châtelet Theatre no less, with a George Edwardes cast and securing a veritable triumph. The French had shown little interest or enthusiasm over the years for English language shows. They had rejected everything from *Billee Taylor* to *The Geisha* and given a good but limited welcome to such as *Florodora* and *The Toreador*. Up to now, *A Country Girl* had been the most appreciated, but Monckton, Ross, Greenbank and Tanner were to break their own 'record'. The visitors, headed by Phyllis Dare and Joe Coyne supported by Carvey from the original cast and Foster, Nainby and Lugg from the tour, were hugely appreciated. So great, indeed, was the success of *The Quaker Girl* that a French language version was subsequently prepared by Paul Ferrier and Charles Quinel and as *La Petite Quaker* it opened at the Olympia in 1913 when the success won by the English company was more than confirmed. *La Petite Quaker* continued its triumphant way into the French provinces and even returned to Paris in 1920 in a revival at the Ba-ta-Clan.

In October 1911 *The Quaker Girl* opened in the United States, at the Apollo, Atlantic City. Three weeks later it came to Broadway's Park Theatre and once again it proved a triumph with Ina Claire and Clifton Crawford at the head of a cast including such fine English performers as Maisie Gay, Lawrence Rea and F. Pope Stamper. The American production notched up 246 Broadway performances and was in every way a success.

The Quaker Girl maintained a popularity with performers and with audiences throughout the English-speaking world for many years. In 1934 it was again produced in the West End, at the Garrick Theatre, and in 1944 Emile Littler staged a version at the London Coliseum with the libretto revised by the producer himself. Celia Lipton starred as Prudence, Billy Milton was Tony and Ivy St Helier played Mme Blum. The production held on until flying bombs forced the Coliseum to close and it was then taken out on tour, returning to town with a substantially unaltered cast in February, 1945 to continue its run at the Stoll Theatre.

The only other new piece of the year in London was a rather unimpressive musical called *The Pigeon House*, which appeared briefly at the Court Theatre in September. Written by 'Eric Hope', it was based on a story by Molly Elliot Seawell and had been staged as a straight play as far back as 1901. The enterprising Hope was responsible not only for the play, the music and the lyrics, but he also took the leading role and directed. Some of the support needed to get *The Pigeon House* staged was undoubtedly provided by 'Hope', since he was in fact the Earl of Yarmouth. The show's plot involved two necklaces – one real and one paste – and the story served, in essence, to bring a flighty husband back to his wife. It was staged initially at Cardiff after which it was toured before coming to London where it was judged on its merits and found wanting.

The touring circuits were as full of musical entertainment as ever. Old favourites such as *The Cingalee, Florodora, The Geisha* and *A Greek Slave* played alongside multiple companies of the latest hits and the 'phenomena' of the provinces among which *The New Barmaid* and *Dare-devil Dorothy* continued their seemingly inexhaustible lives. Newer contributions, however, were few. New versions of *The Flower Girl* (*The Missing Maid*) and *The Cruise of the Constance* (*The Girl on the Boat*) were tried, but the only new piece of any pretension was a Liverpool show called *Chasing Cynthia*, largely the work of Frank Stanmore, which was well-publicised if nothing else. Before it had even reached the stage it had been announced for a first class tour culminating in a West End engagement. While it rehearsed it was loudly put about that America was after it and, soon after, that it had been sold not only for the U.S.A. but for India.

When it actually opened in October, at the Winter Gardens in Bootle, it turned out to be the veriest of variety musicals based on a thin plot concerning two men courting one girl. The 'first class tour' proceeded from Bootle to Lancaster, Derby, Tidworth, Weymouth, Worthing, Hastings &c and the management was obliged to advertise to fill an empty week, although even this was turned to publicity with the boast that 19 applications had been received. *Chasing Cynthia* continued its doddle around the country with no let-up in its extravagant puffing. It was to go to France, business was extraordinary &c &c. What was not advertised was that a good deal of *Chasing Cynthia* was secondhand material patched together in a third-rate variety show. Nevertheless, the piece served well enough in suitable surroundings and it returned the following year for another series of scarcely prestigious dates.

A less loud-mouthed piece which did rather better on the small circuits was *Miss Plaster – of Paris*, a little farcical musical produced at New Brighton in March. It was a made-to-order piece by Henry Osmund and Henry Wardroper which they toured several times with success.

Christmas brought *Alice in Wonderland* back to the West End, *Pinkie and the Fairies* to the suburbs and *Colin in Fairyland*, a new entertainment based on George MacDonald's 'The Carasoyn', to Glasgow's Royalty Theatre while the big hits – *Our Miss Gibbs, The Dollar Princess, The Arcadians, The Chocolate Soldier, The Girl in the Train* and *The Quaker Girl* played on to full houses in a period of almost unprecedented prosperity in the musical theatre, British and continental, in London and in Britain.

1910

0362 **CAPTAIN KIDD** a musical play in 3 acts adapted by Seymour Hicks from Richard Harding Davis' play *The Dictator*. Lyrics by Adrian Ross. Music by Leslie Stuart. Additional lyrics by George Arthurs. Produced at Wyndham's Theatre under the management of Frank Curzon 12 January, 1910 for a run of 34 performances closing 12 February, 1910.

Viscount Albany . . . . Seymour Hicks
Simpson . . . . Hugh E. Wright
Dick Hyne . . . . Evelyn Beerbohm
Col. John T. Bowie . . . . John Clulow
Duffy . . . . Fred Lewis
Rev. Arthur Bostick . . . . Cyril Ashford
General Santos Campos . . . . Frank Wilson
Samuel Codman . . . . Fred Vigay
Dr Vasquez . . . . J. J. Hooker
Lieutenant Perry . . . . Charles Bradley
Colonel Garcia . . . . Frank Aimes
Lieutenant Manuel . . . . F. F. Holt
Teresa Glond . . . . Rosie Chesney
May Pole . . . . May Kennedy
Grace Hufnagle . . . . Doris Stocker
Rosie Flipmaguilder . . . . Marie Brenda
Amy Striapolo . . . . Carina Cliff
Lady Friedenhamar . . . . Laurie Opperman
Anne Tigue . . . . Nellie Pryor
Olga Comoff . . . . Nancie Freyne
Emmie Palorompius . . . . Asta Fleming
Sarita . . . . Florence Thurston
Mrs John T. Bowie . . . . Sylvia Buckley
Senorita Juanita Arguilla . . . . Hilda Guiver
Aggie Shrubb . . . . Ivy St Helier
Madame Ducrot . . . . Mollie Lowell
Lucy Sheridan . . . . Ellaline Terriss

Dir: Seymour Hicks; md: Frank E. Tours; ch: Fred Farren; sc: Joseph Harker; cos: Karl

0363 **THE BALKAN PRINCESS** a musical play in 3 acts by Frederick Lonsdale and Frank Curzon. Lyrics by Paul Rubens and Arthur Wimperis. Music by Paul Rubens. Produced at the Prince of Wales Theatre under the management of Frank Curzon 19 February, 1910 for a run of 176 performances closing 19 August, 1910.

Grand Duke Sergius . . . . Bertram Wallis
Captain Boethy . . . . William Lugg
Captain Radomir . . . . Ridgewell Cullum
Lieutenant Varna . . . . C. Morton Horne
Max Hein . . . . Charles Brown
Blatz . . . . Lauri de Frece

Lounger . . . . Norman A. Blumé
Emil . . . . Peter Blunt
Herman . . . . Barry Neame
Henri . . . . James Blakeley
Magda . . . . Mabel Sealby
Olga . . . . Hazel Dawn
Sylvia . . . . Mabel Green
Paula . . . . Margaret Ismay
Tessa . . . . Madge Kirkham
Carmen . . . . Peggy Lorraine
Margarita . . . . Babs Capelle
Teresa . . . . Stephanie Beresford
Cashiers . . . . Marjorie Blythe, Alethea Allardyce
Princess Stephanie . . . . Isabel Jay/Florence Wray
Nobles: Herbert Sharp, Harry Leslie, John Hamilton, Hugh Weybrance, Vincent Lawson

Dir: Frank Curzon; md: Ignatius A. de Orellana; ch: Fred Farren; sc: Joseph Harker and Hugo Baruch & Co; cos: Percy Anderson

Produced at Herald Square Theatre under the management of Sam and Lee Shubert 9 February, 1911. Transferred to the Casino Theatre 27 February, 1911 after 21 performances for a further 90 performances closing 13 May, 1911 after a total of 111 performances.
Robert Warwick (SERG), J. H. Pratt/W. T. Carleton (BOE), Kenneth Hunter (RAD), Fritz Macklyn (VAR), Percy Ames (HEIN), Teddy Webb (BLATZ), Harold de Becker/Charles Yorkshire (LOU), Harry Llewellyn (EMIL), Robert Milliken (HER), Herbert Corthell (HEN), May Boley (MAGDA), Alice Brady (OLGA), Vida Whitmore (SOFIA), Rose Firestone (PAULA), Bobby B. Nicholls (TESSA), Carmen Romero (CAR), Daisy James (MARG), Peggy Merritt (TER), Sylvia Clark (CASH), Louise Gunning/Christine Nielsen (STEPH) with Olin Howard, S. Keen, Irving Finn, Millie Bright, Grace Kimball, Mabel Ferry, Nanon Welch, Len Litchfield. Dir: William J. Wilson; md: John McGhie; cos: Melville Ellis

0364 **TWO MERRY MONARCHS** a musical play in two acts by Arthur Anderson and George Levy. Lyrics by Arthur Anderson and Hartley Carrick. Music by Orlando Morgan. Produced at the Savoy Theatre under the management of C. H. Workman 10 March, 1910 for a run of 43 performances closing 23 April. Reopened at the Strand Theatre under the management of Austen Hurgon 30 April, 1910 for a further 4 performances, closing 4 May, 1910 &c.

Rolandyl. C. H. Workman/'Smith'
King Paul of Esperanto . . . . Robert Whyte Jr
King Utops of Utopia . . . . Lennox Pawle
Prince Charmis . . . . Ronald Cunningham/C. Hayden Coffin
Helvanoise. Leslie Stiles
Mandamus . . . . Neville George
Head Flunkey . . . . Francis Pater
Princess Cynthia . . . . Daisy Le Hay
Iris . . . . Alma Barber
Caroline . . . . Mayne Young/Lily Mills
Dorothy . . . . Aileen Peel
Hermia . . . . Maire West/Ella Daincourt
Gretchen . . . . Laurie Opperman/Josset Legh
Jean . . . . Joan Adair
Carmenita . . . . Betty Heaps
Celeste. Adeline Waterlow
Trumpeters . . . . Messrs Brown and French
add Prince Frederic . . . . Fred Vigay
with Edward Arundell, Arthur Bourne, Rix Curtis, George Gregson, Jack Hulcup, Frank Melville, Leslie Owen, Harold Slade, Henry Saunders, Alexander Sinclair, Walter Scollick, Fred Tooze, Frank Walsh; Violet Beryl, Gwladys Clarke, Mona Campbell, Ella Daincourt, Belle Fairley, Ruby Gray, Norah Gourlay, Dolly Germaine, Ray Golden, Yvonne Ingram, Josset Legh, Vivien Maxwell, Eveline Pearce, Elsie Reamer, Kathleen Severn, Ruth Trafford, Fay Temple, Maidee Tomlinson, Ivy Vernon, Dora Woodruffe

Dir: Austen Hurgon; md: Thomas Silver/Leonard Hornsey; sc: Alfred Terraine and R. C. McCleery; cos: Percy Anderson

0365 **MISS PLASTER–OF PARIS** a musical comedy in 3 acts by Henry L. Osmond and Henry Wardroper. Produced at the Pier Pavilion, New Brighton, under the management of Henry L. Osmond 14 March, 1910 and toured. Dates included West Stanley, Falkirk, Crook, Ashington, Stockton, Leith, Ayr, Methill, Coatbridge, Belfast, Sutton-in-Ashfield, Mansfield, Dinnington, Leigh, Todmorden, Manchester, Accrington, Bargoed &c.

Numbskull Nubbs/Oliver Cromwell/Widow McKay . . . . Charles Tolcher/John McElroy
Tom Flubbs. . . . . Wilfred E. Brandon/Frank Bellamy
Alexander . . . . Harry E. Ray
Medea Hamilton . . . . Winifred Chalmers
Margery Mayfair . . . . Ida Conroy
Mizpah Mills . . . . May Wyatt
Gertie Downes . . . . Gertie Brace
Lottie Golightly. . . . . Edith Leslie
Polly Slapcabbage. . . . . Mabel Hall
Tina All Mark . . . . Madge Franks
Mrs Nubbs . . . . Sid Dean
Eliza Plaster. . . . . Celestine Brandon/Nellie Harcourt
The Berlin Troupe

Md: Fred R. Wyatt

0366 **THE ISLANDER** a musical comedy in two acts by Major Frank Marshall. Music by Philip Michael Faraday. Produced at the Apollo Theatre under the management of Alexander Henderson 23 April, 1910 for a run of 114 performances closing 6 August.

Captain Alderson Jarrett . . . . Sam Walsh
Lt d'Arcy Langton . . . . Fred Allandale
Lt Reginald Hume . . . . Laurence Legge
Midshipman Jackson Maulever. . . . . . Bobby Andrews
Captain Grant. . . . . Wilfred Seagram
Lt Bailly. . . . . Otto Alexander
Lt Fergusson . . . . Montague Syrett
Lady Birkenhead . . . . Ethel Morrison
Wilhelmina . . . . Mary Dibley
Georgina . . . . Elaine Inescourt/*out*
Kitty McIan . . . . Elsie Spain
Sir William Pickerton. . . . . Laurence Caird/Fred Kaye
Mirza Makh Ali Khan . . . . Neil Kenyon
Hakim Sirdar . . . . Reginald Lawrence
Mahmoud . . . . Master P. Heron
Boatswain . . . . Caryll Storrs/Murri Moncrieff
Quartermaster. . . . . Murri Moncrieff/Mr May
Steward . . . . William Guilbert
Kurbadar . . . . Harry Danby
Hon. Gwendoline Cholmondely . . . . . Stephanie Bell
Princess Haidee . . . . Mabel Burnege
Sister Katharine. . . . . Lesley Everell
Zeeba . . . . Edris Coombs
with Isabel Lidster, Vivian Carter, Dahlia Gordon, Rita Otway, Lilian Cooper, S. Bellew, Hilda Harris, Miss Lindley, Miss Rich; pds: S. Bell, Sybil Warren

Dir: Harry Grattan; md: J. van Heuvel; sc: Bruce Smith; cos: Karl

0367 **THE PIGEON HOUSE** a comedy with music in three acts by 'Eric Hope', from a story by Molly Elliot Seawell. Lyrics by 'Eric Hope' (the Earl of Yarmouth). Music by 'Eric Hope' with additional numbers by Hugh Wright, W. B. Parker and Archie Sullivan. Produced at Cardiff

New Theatre under the management of 'Eric Hope' 27 June, 1910 and toured. Recommenced 5 September, 1910 at Plymouth, then Cheltenham; played at the Court Theatre under the same management from 19 September, 1910 for a season of two weeks, then returned to touring.

Paul Bouchard . . . . O. E. Lennon/A. J. Nicholls/Ivan Berlyn
Victor de Meneval . . . . Eric Hope
Major Fallières . . . . A. Welton Fordham/Ernest Arundale/John T. MacCallam
Dr Delcasse . . . . H. Chubb/E. Herbert
Pierre . . . . Trefor Davies/A. J. Nickolls
François . . . . F. J. Schroter/A. Walker
Jacques . . . . Lionel Lindsay/Coram Smart
Vicomte de Chantecler . . . . Dan G. Thomas/Haddon Cave
Concierge . . . . B. Frank/T. Dillon
Destoque . . . . F. W. Serrington/*out*
Caron . . . . P. M. Rogers/*out*
Mme Vernet . . . . Olive May/Jane Eyre
Mlle Celeste Bouchard . . . . Snead Davies/Amy Fanchette
Elise . . . . Julia Sylvester/Mary Hay
Duchesse de Grand Marnier . . . . Queenie Watts/*out*
Princess X. . . . . Millicent Jones/*out*
Aglaia . . . . Violet Dene
Olga . . . . D. Griffiths/Edith Gray
Louise . . . . Ida Duncan/Elsie Eyre
Pepita . . . . E. Loffler/F. Garthorne
Léontine de Merval. . . . . Thelma Raye/Iris Hoey/Dorothy Moulton
add Gendarmes . . . . Alfred Lee, Percy West

with (Court Theatre): Norah Bennett, Ida Chichester, Ethel Kenyon, Dorothy Moulton, Lil Leslie, Elsie Miller, Elsie Sanderson, Marion Hargrave, Rosa Irene, A. Downes, A. Grahame, Ronald Grahame, George Rodney, George Henri, C. S. Austin

Dir: Eric Hope[1]; md: Christopher Wilson; cos: Hanover Dress Co. and T. Holt

0368 **CHASING CYNTHIA** a musical comedy in two acts by Frank Stanmore. Produced at the Winter Gardens, Bootle, under the management of Charles C. Ommaney 3 October, 1910 and toured. Dates included Worthing, Chatham, Sheerness, Deal/Herne Bay, Bedford, Woolwich, Dalston, &c.

Billy Bootle . . . . Frank Stanmore
Colonel Chutney . . . . Arthur Poole
Dobson . . . . Mark Lester
T. Axee . . . . Arthur Henderson
Drowsy . . . . Thomas Beckett
Fifi . . . . Gladys Beech
Miss Finch . . . . Adie Boyne
Cynthia . . . . Gurney Delaporte
Trixie . . . . Roma Lewis
Babs . . . . Babs Kendal
Queenie . . . . Lily Leonhardt
Fluffy . . . . Lucy Carrington
Kiddie. . . . . Muriel Valerie
Freda . . . . Edna Earle

0369 **THE QUAKER GIRL** a musical play in three acts by James T. Tanner. Lyrics by Adrian Ross and Percy Greenbank. Music by Lionel Monckton. Produced at the Adelphi Theatre under the management of George Edwardes 5 November, 1910 for a run of 536 performances closing on 11 May, 1912.

[1] (Court Theatre programme states 'produced by Edwin Bryan')

Captain Charteris . . . . C. Hayden Coffin
Jeremiah. . . . . James Blakeley
Monsieur Duhamel . . . . Herbert Ross
Prince Carlo. . . . . George Carvey/Leonard Mackay
Monsieur Larose . . . . D. J. Williams
Nathaniel Pym . . . . Henry Kitts
William . . . . E. H. Wynne
Jarge. . . . . George Bellamy
Tony Chute . . . . Joseph Coyne
Phoebe . . . . Gracie Leigh/Luna Love
Princess Mathilde. . . . . Elsie Spain
Diane . . . . Phyllys Le Grand/Irene Warren/Alice Hamilton/Gina Palerme
Madame Blum . . . . Mlle Caumont/Maisie Gay
Mrs Lukyn . . . . Luna Love/Miss Featherstone
Rachel Pym . . . . Jennie Rickards
Toinette. Gina Palerme/Claire Lynch/Germaine France
Gaby . . . . Irene Warren/Gladys Wray/Marie West/Chrissie Bell/Kitty Melrose
Cleo . . . . Kitty Melrose/Gipsy O'Brien/Chrissie Bell
Liane . . . . Mabel Duncan/Betty Heaps/Leila Griffin
Louise. . . . . Marie West/Dora Fraser
Prudence . . . . Gertie Millar (Kitty Melrose)/Phyllys Le Grand

Pds: Phyllis Monkman, Addy Hine, Oscar Odee

Dir: J. A. E. Malone; md; Carl Kiefert; ch: Willie Warde; sc: Joseph Harker, Paquereau and Alfred Terraine; cos: Percy Anderson, Mme Alexandra &c.

Produced at the Park Theatre, New York, under the management of Henry B. Harris 23 October, 1911 for a run of 246 performances, closing 18 May, 1912.
F. Pope Stamper (CH), Percival Knight (JER), Edward Martyn (DU), Lawrence Rea/Hamilton Earle (PCE), Arthur Klein (LAR), Lawrence Eddinger (NATH), Harold Thomas (WM), Fred Tooze (JARGE), Clifton Crawford (TONY), May Vokes (PH), Natalie Alt (PCESS), Olga Petrova (DIANE), Maisie Gay (BLUM), Nellie McHenry (LUKYN), Eleanor Shedden (RACH), Viola Clark (TOI), Stella Beardsley (G), Blanche Malli (C), Gertrude Fayot (LI), Alice Chase (LOU), Ina Claire (PRU), Elaine Hall (DORCAS), Irma Bertrand (PHYLLIS), Marge Wallace (MARGUERITE), Nora McClory (MIMI), Florence Grant (FIFI), Belle Delmar (SUZANNE), Myrtle McCloud (MICHELINE), A. W. Metcalfe (COMMISSIONAIRE); with Dolly Shimmin, Thelma Belmont, Gertrude Williams, Irene Hopping, Florence Deshon, Minnie Higgins, Charlotte Graham, Sophia Ralph, Ethel Dunn, Laura Harland, Helen Merest, Ida Hall, Gertrude Fursman, Hazel Proctor, Mae Borden, Marie Pendleton, Ada Proctor, Mae Mortimer, Adelaide Murray, Billie Grant, Ruth Mason, Dolly Sterling, Bessie Bell, Clara Heath, Theresa Morton, Martin Cox, R. Denny, Curtis Dunham Jr, Herbert Hall, C. H. Kittridge, J. R. Newell, G. Pullman, Byron Russell, Gus Schult, Frank Snyder, M. Stephen, R. Walton, F. Wells, A. Willis, Jeff Worden, Harry Montgomery, Charles Morgan, Henry Betts, Henry Harrison; pds: Oscar Odee, Hazel Clements. Dir: J. A. E. Malone; md: Augustus Barratt; sc: H. Robert Law; cos: Maison Blum, Mrs Field, Lucile

Produced in Paris at the Châtelet Theatre, 1911 by the Adelphi Theatre company.

Produced in Paris at L'Olympia, 1913.
Henri Arbell (CH), M. Dorville (JER), M. Pré (DU), M. Leoni (PCE), Harry Mass (TONY), Miss Lawler (PH), Mdlle Rosni-Derys (PCESS), Alice Delysia (DIANE), Marie Thery (BLUM), Alice O'Brien (PRU)

Produced at the Ba-ta-Clan Theatre, Paris, under the management of Mme Rasini, 1920.
Harry Arbell (CH), M. Moriss (JER), M. Castelli (PCE), M. Zidner (TONY), Odette Darthys (PH), Jane de Poumayrac (PCESS), Mary Thery (BLUM), Jeanne St Bonnet (PRU)

Produced at the Garrick Theatre under the management of John Southern 28 May, 1934. Closed

7 June. Reopened at the Winter Garden Theatre under the management of a cast co-operative 18 June, closed 23 June.
Walter Bird (CH), Percy Le Fre (JER), C. Jervis Walters (DU/NATH), Noel Leyland (PCE), George Bellamy (LAR), Adrian Ross (WM), John Mullins (JARGE), Eric Fawcett (TONY), Bertha Riccardo (PH), Gwynneth Lascelles (PCESS), Enid Lowe (DIANE), Winifred Nathan (BLUM), Ida Hall (LUKYN), Jennie Richards (RACH), Marie Conan (TOI), Lorna Hubbard (PRU) with E. Aubrey, O. Williams, M. Lynn, S. Sydney, H. Marion, J. Leyton, M. Hindes, J. Torode, C. Tennant, M. O'Day, N. Butland, B. Smith, P. Gaunt, I. May, R. Dyer, J. Collier B. Fellowes, K. Attfield, K. Knox, V. Joyce; Messrs W. Tinkler, K. Bayter, H. Collins, H. Howarth, R. Matthews, A. Donovan, T. Fenwick, D. Thomson, D. Walker, H. Rake, W. Colvin. Dir: Frederick G. Lloyd; md: Arthur Wood; ch: Alison MacLaren; sc: Grantham; cos: B. J. Simmonds.

Produced in a revised version by Emile Littler at the London Coliseum, under the management of Emile Littler 25 May, 1944. Closed 8 July, 1944 and toured returning to London at the Stoll Theatre 8 February, 1945. Withdrawn 7 April, 1945.
Pat McGrath (CH), Hal Bryan (JER), Stanley Drewitt/Frank Wignall (DU), Dunn/Jack Mayer (PCE), Dimitri Vetter (LAR/JARGE), Dewey Gibson/Roy Neilson (NATH), Will Henry (WM), Billy Milton (TONY), April Ross (PH), Joy Hayden/Odette Field/Joy O'Neill (PCESS), Peggy Livesey/Brenda de Banzie (DIANE), Ivy St Helier (BLUM), Marcelle Turner/Gwen Harris (LUKYN), Lucille Dale (RACH), Jasmine Dee (TOI),Celia Lipton (PRU), Enid Meredith (MARY), Sheila Poet/Peggy O'Neill and Gladys Cowper (PAGES), John Stock and Harold Farrar (GENDARMES); pd: Pamela Foster. Dir: Emile Littler; md: Tom Lewis; ch: Phyllis Blakston; sc/cos: Doris Zinkeisen.

1911

The musical theatre in London moved into 1911 in a superbly vigorous state. The previous season's crop of hits had produced a degree of prosperity which boded well for future prospects. It remained to be seen whether the relay could be safely taken over by equally brilliant new shows, both home-grown and foreign, during 1911.

The first effort proved a comparative failure. George Edwardes, who still had faith in *A Waltz Dream*, revived the Oscar Straus piece in a newly revised version by Basil Hood at Daly's as a successor to *The Dollar Princess*, but the public only reconfirmed its comparative rejection of it and Edwardes was obliged to admit defeat. He withdrew the revival after 111 performances and turned back to Franz Lehár for *The Count of Luxembourg* which opened at Daly's in April to a very much more gratifying reception and a run of almost twelve months. *The Count of Luxembourg* was, however, the only success among the pieces imported into Britain during the year.

Fred C. Whitney, who had struck it rich with *The Chocolate Soldier*, attempted to set up the Waldorf/Strand Theatre which he had taken over as a musical house playing continental operetta. His first production there was a version of Felix Albini's *Baron Trenck*. Willner and Bodansky's book had been done into English by Henry Blossom and Frederick Schrader and a fine cast headed by Walter Hyde, Rutland Barrington, Walter Passmore and prima donna Caroline Hatchard more than did justice to Albini's ambitious score but, in spite of some excellent reviews and many subsequent attempts at 'popularising' the show with alterations and additions, it folded after only 43 performances. When Whitney later tried it in New York it proved even more unfortunate.

For his next attempt in the theatre, which he had renamed the Whitney Theatre, he took a proven success in the Harry B. and Robert Smith adaptation of Heinrich Reinhardt's *Die Sprudelfee* which, as *The Spring Maid*, had run for 194 performances at New York's Liberty Theatre in the first part of the year. It proved rather less to the taste of Londoners. Whitney's production ran just two months and put an end to the experiment of the 'Whitney Theatre'.

Even more unfortunate was an attempt to bring Belgian musical theatre to London in the shape of a piece called *The Love Mills* (Les Moulins qui Chantent) written by Franz Fonson and Fernand Wicheler, the authors of the play *The Marriage of Mdlle. Beulemans*, and with music by Arthur van Oost. The English version by Leslie Stiles, starring himself and Nan Stuart lasted a meagre 24 performances at the Globe.

An undignified fate also awaited the much more worthy *Castles in the Air*, a version of Paul Lincke's *Frau Luna*, which was played at the Scala Theatre in tandem with a lecture on and demonstration of 'Kinemacolour'. It proved the less popular half of the programme and found itself edged out in favour of coloured pictures of 'Our Farmyard Friends', 'Picturesque North Wales', some time-lapse photography and a dramatic piece called 'The Rebel's Daughter, an Episode of the Peninsular War'.

The final weeks of the year saw two revivals of past continental glories when new versions of *Orphée aux Enfers* and *Die Fledermaus* were staged, the former by Tree at Her Majesty's, the latter on the profits of *The Chocolate Soldier* by Philip Michael Faraday at the Lyric where it lasted some four months.

The British pieces of the year fared rather better. With *The Quaker Girl* entrenched at the Adelphi, *The Chocolate Soldier* at the Lyric and *The Count of Luxembourg* at Daly's for the greater part of the year only a relatively small number of new shows were needed and, in fact, only three British musicals put in a first appearance in the period in question – a far cry from the hectic production rate of a decade earlier.

But the public's attitude to the theatre had taken a turn. It demanded something more now, something special and individual in its shows, and was no longer content to give applause and attention to the over-familiar and the repetitive. Shows which were poorly written or badly rehearsed and staged with insufficient style and lavishness no longer lingered on to be 'worked up' – they closed in a matter of weeks. A show needed to be more than just 'good' to succeed, it needed to be very good, interesting, and with positive virtues which would attract a public grown altogether less indulgent. Mounting production costs also made it less easy for the smaller producer to venture into the staging of musical plays in competition with Edwardes, Frohman, Courtneidge or Whitney. When it cost £3,000 merely to outfit the ladies' chorus there was little chance of a repetition of the advent of Tom Davies and *Little Miss Nobody*. The new shows came from Edwardes (*Peggy* at the Gaiety), Robert Courtneidge (*The Mousmé* at the Shaftesbury) and from a brave group called the Bonita syndicate which took the Queen's Theatre to stage a musical of that name under the aegis of Granville Barker.

Peggy was the first to arrive, the first of the 'new regime' musicals at the Gaiety under the contract which Edwardes had signed with Leslie Stuart. The libretto for the new show was taken, in line with the current fashion, from the French play *L'Amorçage* by Xanroff and Guérin and was the work of George Grossmith, a Grossmith with a brief very different to the normal Gaiety one. The book of *Peggy* had still to supply roles for Teddy Payne and for Grossmith himself, but there was no Gertie Millar for the title role. When Gertie's contract for the Gaiety had expired with the closure of *Our Miss Gibbs*, the theatre's favourite female star since Nellie Farren had decided to follow her husband. Monckton had, over the years, provided his wife with the songs which had made her name and her fame: when Leslie Stuart was made chief composer to the Gaiety and Monckton moved elsewhere in the scheme of things, Mrs Monckton went too – the gain of the Adelphi Theatre and Monckton's *The Quaker Girl* was the Gaiety's loss. But Grossmith knew the likes and dislikes of the Gaiety public and the libretto which he produced for *Peggy* was staunchly in the style which the theatre-goers he knew so well expected. He fulfilled his task neatly and efficiently, providing a good outline on which the business of the evening might hang and filling it with plenty of opportunities for Payne, himself and the new Gaiety leading lady, Phyllis Dare, whose latest appearance had been under Edwardes' management at the Vaudeville in *The Girl in the Train*.

Leslie Stuart set the lyrics of C. H. Bovill (here in his first major show) to a series of typically clever and attractive tunes, varying his well-known rhythmic tricks with a leaven of waltz tunes, and the result was a well-made Gaiety Theatre musical comedy which may have lacked the distinction of an *Our Miss Gibbs* but which was, nevertheless, a thoroughly proficient and worthy work.

Edwardes postponed *Peggy* until the General Election ('always a bad time for theatres') was over and opened the Gaiety doors again on March 4 with a highly successful first night.

> Mr George Edwardes has again provided an Aladdin's feast of dainty songs and dances together with wit and general sparkle set amid beautiful surroundings with his accustomed generosity . . Leslie Stuart has provided some of his most melodious and characteristic music and the splendid scenery by Joseph Harker together with the beautiful costumes designed by Comelli are also things to be remembered for many a day . . . . . The story that runs through the play is a distinctly good one. That it is allowed to become but faintly evident during the course of the second act is also a circumstance which may well be overlooked since here, as elsewhere, it amply serves its purpose . . . with the inevitable 'pulling together' process *Peggy* should settle down into a long run at the Gaiety. (*Stage*)
>
> There has never been a more artistic production at the Gaiety than that of *Peggy* which took place there on Saturday last. Mr George Grossmith Jr has founded his libretto on Xanroff and Guérin's *L'Amorçage* which yields a story decidedly superior to the ordinary musical play libretto. It has indeed quite a philosophical 'pivot' . . . . the music of *Peggy* contains some of the most dainty melodies that Mr. Leslie Stuart has ever written and the lyrics by C. H. Bovill have all the desirable 'lilt' and neatness of phrase . . . it is safe to prophesy that *Peggy* will be a success (*Era*)

The basic premise of the play was, as its French title implied, a question of 'bait'. In order to win the pretty manicurist Peggy from her funny little hairdresser fiancé, the Hon. James Bendoyle employs the science of 'ground bait'. He arranges a plot by which Peggy will be showered with luxuries for a certain period – then the supply will be cut off and, having got used to having nice things, the young lady will supposedly see the advantages of marrying the wealthy Bendoyle in preference to the foolish Albert Umbles. To carry out his plan, Bendoyle hires the impecunious Auberon Blow to impersonate an Uncle of Albert's who is returning from South America loaded with cash which he is only too eager to throw about in the direction of the little man and his fiancée. But his plan is wrecked when the real uncle turns up, when Auberon falls in love with Peggy and when Umbles transfers his affections to a French dancer. Peggy, in the event, returns Auberon's affections and Bendoyle is finally made more than happy by pretty Doris, the daughter of the real rich uncle.

The role of Auberon gave Grossmith the opportunity he longed for, to play not only the comical dandy which was his accepted persona but also the romantic hero who gets the girl. It also gave him plenty of opportunity for broad fun in his impression of the rich uncle from South America. The variety of the role was reflected in the songs which he was given to sing: as the penniless fellow he sang hopefully 'Tomorrow's my big Day', as the phony Uncle he indulged in a humorous duet with Payne called 'I Beg your Pardon', and he joined romantically with Phyllis Dare in 'You're the one Girl I'm Looking For'.

The bulk of the comedy was, of course, the province of Teddy Payne who found much he could use in the antics of the little hairdresser. He had a good deal of business with the tools of the hairdressing trade, he indulged in a mock balcony scene with Peggy:

Oh Juliet, Juliet
Night winds blow uncommonly coolly yet
Under your window I sing like a star
Although I am suffering from slight catarrh

and, in the second act when the whole company had decamped to the French seaside town of Friville, he made much of a pair of striped bathers and some lost trousers, performed a turn as a ventriloquist's dummy and a duet with Olive May as a Pierrot and a Pierette as well as joining Grossmith in the comical 'I Beg your Pardon'.

Phyllis Dare had a good deal to do as well, but it was all sweet and straightforward stuff and her best moments came in Leslie Stuart's charming waltz songs 'Come to Friville' and 'Ladies Beware'. In the latter piece, which proved to be one of the show's most effective numbers, she cautioned the chorus ladies to beware of the man who turns down the lights:

Beware of the man who knows the different tunes the band will play
Beware, his heart will change to every tune the band will play

to the accompaniment of the obbligato violin of Walter de Groot. In the second act, which developed in the traditional way with little more to do than to sort out the various love affairs, Gabrielle Ray put in an appearance as the French danseuse. She contrived to get into a French schoolboy outfit to sing 'Go away, little Girl, Go back to School' and into an attractive bathing dress to join Phyllis Dare and Olive May in a bathing trio. There was also a dance, 'Fascination', for Miss May and J. Robert Hale as Bendoyle, the Pierrot scena, duets romantic and comic, and a quaint sextet called 'Be a Lady all the Time'.

The most successful routine of the show, however, fell to Olive May who performed a song called 'The Lass with the Lasso'. She sang:

A lass with a lasso
Should know how to throw
Discover your lover
Then after him you go.
You track him, and when you've found him
You simply throw your lasso round him
And I will bet I get him
Every time with my lasso.

and accompanied the words with suitable actions as she lassoed a fine set of uniformed gentlemen.

It was all good Gaiety stuff, and went down decidedly well. If Gertie Millar and the rather more insouciant melodies of Lionel Monckton and Ivan Caryll were a little missed, there was a pleasantly, almost gravely, pretty feeling about the love scenes of *Peggy* which had been missing at the Gaiety since the transformation of the leading lady into a light comedienne. Teddy Payne, on the other hand, was still Teddy Payne and the newest Gaiety girls yielded nothing to their predecessors in the way of charm, particularly in those pink bathing dresses.

George Edwardes was able to report to his annual directors' meeting that, even though the financial year had included the end of the run of *Our Miss Gibbs* and a period 'dark', the balance for the year was not far below that of the previous comparable period. The overseas rights of *Peggy* had all been sold 'advantageously', the piece was running strongly and smoothly, and the Gaiety company declared a 20% dividend.

Peggy ran on through the summer and Edwardes kept the show fresh and bright with the usual alterations and additions. Hale got a new song called 'Where are the Girls I used to Know' which gave rise to a 'Dream Parade' of the pretty ladies of his amorous past, and Grossmith was particularly happy in a new number called 'Mr Edison':

Mr Edison, you're unique
At Patents supreme.
Every moment of the week
You give us some new scheme.
Every up-to-date invention
Seems to come from you
So won't you please give your attention
To human beings too?

which allowed him to introduce some up-to-date topics as he pleaded with 'Mr Edison' to invent remedies for cabinet ministers, the harem skirt (the latest craze in fashion), the War Office, explorers and, of course, suffragettes.

But *Peggy* began to sag at the box-office rather earlier than a Gaiety show should, and Edwardes was obliged to look for a strong remedy. *Peggy* rested very much on the shoulders of Payne, Grossmith and Miss Dare and it was decided to strengthen the appeal of the show by a healthy infusion of new star blood. To that end, a new role was written in and Connie Ediss, recently returned to Edwardes from America, was transferred from *The Girl in the Train* to lift *Peggy* back on to the right tracks. She was equipped with two fine songs, one on a racing topic:

I like to have a little bit on
A little bit on a gee.
Not much, you know,
A sovereign or so,
That's really a lot for me.
They said 'Your horse has run off the course
'The opposite way he's gone.'
'Then,' I said, 'You must pay
For I backed him each way
When I put my little bit on.'

and a mildly topical piece 'Which he didn't Expect from a Lady' in which she, too, had a go at the ubiquitous harem pants:

I've got a skirt that's a harem
Really, you know, it's a pair.
I've got the figure to wear 'em
Still, it does make people stare.
Boarding a bus to Belgravia
Halfway upstairs I had got
When the conductor's behaviour
Made me come over all hot.
He sez 'Madam,' sez he,
'E sez to me
'What's those I see?' he sez:
So I made a reply
Which he didn't expect from a Lady!

Both these songs were written by Arthur Wimperis and composed by Philip Braham, not Leslie Stuart. And 'Mr Edison' was from Paul Rubens. Edwardes had clearly decided that the usual inviolability of a Stuart score was not for him. And he had also decided not to take up the second show which he had contracted from Stuart. He had already announced that the successor to *Peggy*, when it was required, would be composed by Rubens.

The advent of Connie Ediss was not enough to turn the respectable run of *Peggy* into one more in line with the usual Gaiety musical. When the requisite results were not forthcoming within a reasonable time Edwardes withdrew the show, just before Christmas, after a run of 270 performances. The previous week, the Broadway production at the Casino Theatre had failed to catch the critical and public favour and it was left to the provincial touring company put out by George Dance with Roma June, Phil Smith and Alfred Field Fisher at its head to continue to fly the flag for what was to be the last Leslie Stuart musical, playing its way around the country alongside his first and most famous, *Florodora*, now twelve years old and still a feature of the provincial circuits.

At forty-five years of age Leslie Stuart had finished with the theatre. In a career dominated by that first crowning success with *Florodora* he had written only eight musicals – to *Florodora*, *The Silver Slipper*, *The School Girl*, *The Belle of Mayfair*, *Havana*, *Captain Kidd* and *Peggy* was added the American show *The Slim Princess* which had been staged in New York earlier in 1911 without notable success. But that career had placed Stuart immediately and prominently among the talented élite of the world's most successful light musical and theatrical composers, and there he must stay. Three-quarters of a century later he is probably as well remembered for 'Lily of Laguna', 'Little Dolly Daydream' and 'Soldiers of the Queen' as for 'Tell me, pretty Maiden' and the rest of *Florodora* and for his work in establishing the basis for the existing rules and laws on international music copyright, but in his life – a life often wasted by personal excesses – he was a formidable musical figure who made a major contribution to the British musical theatre.

Peggy had not been able to follow up the huge success of *Our Miss Gibbs* and it was difficult to see what could possibly follow the even greater triumph of *The Arcadians*. Robert Courtneidge faced up to the problem by bringing together the same creative team – himself and Alexander Thompson, Arthur Wimperis and Percy Greenbank, Howard Talbot and Lionel Monckton, to work on the new piece for the Shaftesbury Theatre. The location of the show was settled as Japan, already so successful as a setting for *The Mikado* and *The Geisha*, and Talbot set off for the Orient to gather some genuine local colour. Courtneidge and Thompson evolved a book which would allow suitable opportunities for the Courtneidge stars – Florence Smithson, Cicely Courtneidge, Harry Welchman, Dan Rolyat, Nelson Keys – and Conrad Tritschler set to work on the complicated scenic demands.

The Mousmé was given every attention that Courtneidge could lavish upon it. It was going to be the most glamorous, lavish, stunning piece of light musical theatre ever seen in the West End and, in consequence, the most expensive. When it opened on September 9 at the Shaftesbury it was quite evident where the money and effort had gone: the show was indeed stunning and it received a resounding reception from an amazed première audience. The critical opinion came swiftly in its favour:

> . . a musical comedy with a plot that develops on sound dramatic lines. It lasts beyond the first act. It is carried on in the second. It ends with the third. Such a novel feature alone should make *The Mousmé* a success. But that is not the only factor that

> makes for popularity. There are others. For example, a magnificent mise-en-scène, ear-tickling music, genuine vocalists and comedians who are comic. Surely that is enough for one evening's entertainment (*Play Pictorial*)
>
> . . the great success attained by *The Arcadians* inclined one to doubt the probability of the same high excellence being attained by its successor, but in the Japanese play *The Mousmé* . . a worthy follower has been found. A charming story . . [the] lyrics are prettily and pleasantly set . . a little judicious cutting may have to be done as the piece on Saturday was not ended at 11.30 but, this effected, the success of *The Mousmé* is undoubtedly assured . . (*Era*)
>
> It is one's pleasant duty once more to record the whole-hearted and emphatic success of a Robert Courtneidge production as well as to predict for it a long and prosperous career at the Shaftesbury. *The Mousmé* is perhaps a shade below *The Arcadians* in general artistic merit but, as regards sheer spectacular beauty of form and colouring, sweetness of melody and comic and sentimental interest it is certainly a most worthy successor to that remarkably successful musical comedy . . . . of the artistic charm of its music and of the directness of its popular appeal there can be no possible doubt . . (*Stage*)

The story of *The Mousmé* is that of O Hana San and her lover Captain Fujiwara and their attempts to get married in spite of the evil machinations of one Captain Yamaki. When, through Yamaki's influence, Fujiwara is threatened with disgrace over a gambling debt, Hana unbeknown sells herself as a Geisha to a Tokio tea-house to raise the money, allowing him to take his place again in the army. When the army returns, Yamaki has gained much glory – but unrightfully, for the real hero of the campaign was Fujiwara and this will be revealed in the enquiry which is forthcoming. But the cunning Yamaki gets hold of Hana's indentures and, to free her, Fujiwara agrees not to give his vital evidence, a deed which will disgrace him for ever. As the hour of the enquiry arrives, a frightful earthquake hits Tokio, and Yamaki and all the evil of the story are buried in its debris and the hero and heroine saved for a happy ending. The principal story was lightened by the parallel fluctuations of the love affair of Hana's sister, Miyo, and her particular officer and by the antics of the comical fortune teller, Suki, husband of the tea-house owner, Mitsu.

It was all cleanly and cleverly worked out on the best established principles with enough extra emphasis given to the more serious central story to make the piece of rather more weight than the standard musical comedy, but with plenty of humour to provide the setting for the main characters and their love stories.

The music did not show much influence of Talbot's overseas trip. In fact, he had found that Japanese music was strictly unsuited to the demands of the West End Theatre. 'There is only one Japanese national instrument,' he noted, 'the samisen, and since the Japanese have no notion of harmony the result is that orchestras consist simply of a large number of samisens all playing in unison'. Nevertheless, he claimed to have worked into his songs the occasional genuine Japanese phrase, and to have transcribed and harmonised one dance tune. Whatever the influences, both he and Monckton had come up with some lovely pieces, particularly for Florence Smithson in the role of O Hana San.

Monckton composed an ingenuous ballad called 'I Know nothing of Life' and a vertiginous 'Temple Bell Song' which rendered nothing to Delibes' *Lakmé* song and which the soloist negotiated with a beauty and ease up to its final high D, while Talbot used his eastern experience in a delightful piece called 'My Samisen':

Many songs a little maiden sings
To her samisen,
While her heart is throbbing like the strings
Of her samisen,
Gladly I sang when love was near
Murmuring softly in my ear
Setting my cheeks aglow
As I bent low
O'er my samisen

which went one better and encompassed Miss Smithson's E in alt. The petite dark beauty of the star, added to her amazing voice and style, made her performance a highly memorable one which contrasted nicely with the cheerful soubrette of Cicely Courtneidge singing of being an 'Honourable Jappy Bride':

Some day I may be most tip-top married little lady
Oh, my, won't I have my way in everything I do?
I'll find nice kind high-class six foot amicable bridegroom
So it's no use thinking of a silly little boy like you!

or, later, a 'Little Japanese Mama' and joining with Nelson Keys in a commentary on 'Foreign Customs' – amatory ones, of course. Dan Rolyat had an amusing role as Suki 'of the Japanese Phrenological Institute' and his songs also proved popular as he declared:

I'll tell your fortune while you wait
Whatever your position
And bargains I'll negotiate
At ten per cent commission

or described his 'adventures', having returned from the wars when all thought him dead:

I've faced some dangers terrible
I've met with horrors grim
I've been pursued and hacked and hewed
And sundered limb from limb.
I've been blown up with dynamite
And pirates captured me
They stuck hot needles in my ears
They stabbed me through and through with spears
And pushed me in the sea!
But now I'm home again in Tokio
Adventures grim and gory
Have covered me with glory
While shot and shell around me fell
I chuckled soft and low
'What a terrible tale I'll have to tell in Toki-oki-o!

He was supported, as in *The Arcadians*, by Ada Blanche as his large wife, the lady of the tea-house. Harry Welchman as the hero of the piece had no solo song, but he joined in an effective duet with Miss Smithson in the first act and also contributed enormously to the glamour of the piece by his robust singing and his exceptionally picturesque appearance in the (presumed) uniform of the Japanese army.

One of the real heroes of *The Mousmé* was Conrad Tritschler who was responsible for the scenery and mechanics of the show. The first act setting simply dripped with gorgeous cherry blossom, the tea-house of Mitsu was draped with quantities of wistaria and Chinese lanterns, and was ingeniously constructed so as to tumble safely yet impressively to the ground in many pieces as the second act ended with the spectacular destruction of Tokio by earthquake. The earthquake scene from *The Mousmé* was still talked about by playgoers decades later.

It was clear that Courtneidge had another success on his hands. The American rights for the show were snapped up by Henry Savage and the producer announced that three touring companies would take the show on the road before the end of the year. In the meanwhile, the first night script was trimmed down to a more reasonable length and the show worked itself in to large and enthusiastic houses. *The Mousmé* ran for 209 nights and closed with a deficit of £20,000. The expense of the production and of its maintenance had left Courtneidge with an enormously high weekly break figure which the show was unable always to meet and, in the tradition of so many expensive spectacular musicals from *Babil and Bijou* down, it failed to survive and prosper in spite of its undoubted quality and drawing power. The touring companies which took *The Mousmé* to the provinces provided a rather less extravagant version of the show, but its future turned out to be limited by its inherent excesses and most of the markets opened up to Courtneidge by *The Arcadians* preferred not to take up his new show. The lesson of *The Mousmé* was one Courtneidge did not forget. Never again did he attempt a piece on such a scale – or one with such demanding financial conditions.

The news that a group known as 'the Bonita Syndicate' had taken the Queen's Theatre to present a comic opera by an unknown author and composer would have been apt to send many theatrical hands flying up in horror had it not been for one remarkable circumstance: *Bonita*, a comic opera in a prologue and two acts by Wadham Peacock with music by Harold Fraser-Simson was announced to be directed by no less a luminary than Harley Granville Barker, actor, playwright, director and co-manager of the Court Theatre where he had been responsible for the staging of many important new dramatic works including *Man and Superman*, *The Doctor's Dilemma*, *You Never Can Tell* and prestigious revivals of Ibsen and Euripides. During the weeks of rehearsal the composer was discreetly paragraphed, but almost the entire press interest was centred on Barker, on his methods and on his attempts to invest 'even' a comic opera with the values of a modern drama. When the director explained character and motivation to amazed chorus girls it swiftly found its way into the newspapers. Quite why the distinguished man of the theatre wished to be involved with *Bonita*, of all musicals, it is difficult to understand. The unknown Scots composer had, admittedly, written some pretty songs – some were even more than just pretty – but the author had provided a perfectly ridiculous story reminiscent of the alarming excesses of Luscombe Searelle in *The Black Rover* or Henry Herman in *The Fay o' Fire*. The characters were impossible and the plot virtually non-existent, consisting merely of the attempts of a hero and a comical villain to gain the hand of the eponymous heroine. This duel was stretched out to two acts and twenty-eight musical pieces by a handful of other love affairs (attempted and actual) of little moment and a lot of business around a shrine where the victor of the contest for the maid's hand is decided by a test of fire. But far from any heroic action being involved, the test consists of each man putting a flower into the flame, and whichever flower does not burn is the winner. The villain douses one flower in paraffin, then gets the wrong one and has to be content with marrying a mezzo-soprano who has been sighing after him since the beginning of the second act.

The whole thing was prefaced by a Dramatic Prologue in which the great-grandparents of the two lovers were seen in a tender farewell scene with him dying in her arms in the wars.

Bonita was an alarming mixture of styles ranging from the pathetic drama in its prologue through old-fashioned comic opera, through pure burlesque – almost pantomime in the character of its villain – to modern musical comedy and it could never have been a success with the talents of a dozen Granville Barkers lavished on it. Nevertheless, it was undoubtedly his presence at the show's helm which caused a guardedly polite tone in some of the criticisms:

> *Bonita* . . contains many features which tend towards the success of a piece of this description . . . Little can be said in over-praise of the able production by Mr Granville Barker, the careful attention paid to detail, and the clever touches that bespeak the master hand of the artist . . (*Era*)

> Mr Barker is, of course, a modern of moderns in drama and literature and it is not surprising to find that the dominating feature in the production is one of modernity. [But] . . there is no hint in it of that impressionism, post or otherwise, which so often conceals or seeks to conceal bad art. Rather may one call it a kind of theatrical equivalent of that clear-sighted hard cut literature which is having so great an influence upon the thought and art of the day and which . . it is not unreasonable to suppose has had so notable effect on the best German productions . . . as regards the opera itself it is at once easy to describe and rather difficult to classify, although one should hasten to say that the book is interesting and the musical score refined and melodious. There is a melodramatic prologue, for instance, followed by a couple of acts which contain in them not only comic opera features but also elements here and there of burlesque and fantasy and musical comedy. The prologue could certainly be dispensed with altogether and a discordant note thereby removed . . the book itself could be strengthened with some advantage . . (*Stage*)

> . . it is too long and the second act straggles . . but it is easy to see why Mr Granville Barker thought it worth producing. There is a graceful humour and a sense of burlesque about Mr Wadham Peacock's idea which I found very refreshing: he makes fun of villains and heroes and heroines in a quiet, literary way which is continuously amusing and he manages to keep the whole thing on just the right plane of paradoxical absurdity. Mr Fraser-Simson, too, has written some very attractive choral work and a waltz which is really graceful and though not so happy in his setting of the songs, his orchestration is often ingenious and original . . . the chorus is handled with an originality which does credit to Mr. Barker's art as a stage manager (*Sketch*)

> . . the production shows clear evidence of Mr Barker's genius and untiring industry while Mr Harold Fraser-Simson, the new composer, becomes a personage to be reckoned with in the musical world (*Bystander*)

The best element in *Bonita* was its music. Fraser-Simson, a Scots composer in his mid-thirties, hitherto unknown in the West End, had come up with some good pieces in a number of styles. His duet and soprano solo for the ancestors in the prologue were written in a strong and direct fashion and there was a nice waltz song called 'Long Ago' for the heroine which told the tale of a Moorish maiden and a Christian knight in a fairly flimsy lyric. The tenor hero sang whimsically of 'A Subaltern's Heart', the pining mezzo made capital of 'Old Boots':

> Why does a cynic world
> Treat age with flouts and jeering
> Why are these insults hurled

Or years a butt for sneering?
You don't despise old wine
Old friends demand affection
Old boots are, I opine,
Your chiefest predilection.
Old boots, sublime old boots,
Oh why do poets sing
Of almost everything
Except old boots

and, in the face of all the evidence, the villain declared:

I am not a comic villain of the musical variety
With a mantle, a sombrero and a long black moustache
With a nose that's slightly tinted with the hues of inebriety
And a voice which, when on business, may be qualified as harsh

There were a number of competent ensembles and a fetching dance routine ('We are very Blithe and Merry') choreographed by Espinosa, but *Bonita* was a compôte of styles and lack-of-styles which never seemed to know what it was trying to do – if anything – and Barker's attempts to impose some sort of coherent pattern on it, and to treat it as a realistic piece, was perhaps good for the dramatic training of the chorus girls but achieved little more. It struggled hopelessly through 46 performances at the Queen's Theatre and expired.

The best British composers contributed three 'American' musicals during 1911. Alongside Leslie Stuart's *The Slim Princess* appeared two pieces by the now expatriate Ivan Caryll, *Marriage à la Carte* which had a run of some 50 performances at the Casino and *The Pink Lady*, like the former to a book by McLellan, and based on the French play *Le Satyre*, which proved a major success with a run of 316 performances at the New Amsterdam. *The Pink Lady* crossed the Atlantic in the following year to play a season at the Globe but did less well in Britain.

The provinces had almost completely dried up as a source of musical shows of scope or ambition. The only pieces which aimed for any kind of run or tour in 1911 were *Lady Lavender*, a three-act piece with music by Clarence Corri, and a comedy vehicle *That Chauffeur Chap*, produced at Belfast in April.

Lady Lavender, billed as a 'musical play', was a rumbustious piece of provincial hokum involving a missing heir, fortunes, swindlers and lawyers in the usual set of love affairs, trickeries and low comedy all leading up to the usual wedding scene when the swindlers have been routed and a lot of songs and dances sung and danced. Clarence Corri, far from the days of his triumph with *The Dandy Fifth*, supplied some routine music to decorate the piece which was produced at Manchester and taken out by Haldane Crichton for a patchy but well-sustained tour from June through to the end of the year and into 1912. In 1915 it reappeared in a much cut and altered version as *Sweetheart Mine* for a further small tour.

That Chauffeur Chap was the latest of the Edward Marris pieces which featured its author in the title role and his co-manager, comedian Arthur Rigby, in the other leading part of a 'non-stop laugh with music'. It played several months in the provinces and a couple of weeks in the London suburbs, and reappeared in 1913 slimmed down as *Mum's the Word* to end its days in the music halls. Rigby was also behind the production at the Shakespeare Theatre in Clapham of a fanciful piece called *The Sky Skipper* of which he was also composer and, in conjunction with *That Chauffeur Chap*'s lyricist Arthur Ellis, co-author. *The Sky Skipper* was a heavily farcical musical dealing with some stolen aeroplane plans and it had Rigby disguised as 'Gertie Guzzlegravy of Paris' chasing the villainous inventor who is trying to do him out of his deceased father's invention. The show played one week at Clapham but was not persevered with.

In June, two other new musicals were tried out in outer London when C. St John Denton, the managing director of Denton, Bode and McKenzie, and the representative in London for the Australian management of Clarke and Meynell, staged two new pieces at Kennington. The first of these was *The Algerian Girl* written by the authors of the Australian success *Bill Adams*: Herbert Shelley, currently appearing on the Moss circuit with his protean act 'The Royal Highwayman', and Stephen Philpot. It was a broadly old-fashioned piece revolving round the efforts of one Casarita to avoid becoming the 51st wife of The Bey in forfeit for a debt. The comedian William Cromwell, star of Clarke and Meynell's last Melbourne season, featured in the comic lead and Florence Beech, recently returned from musical repertoire in the East, was Casarita, while The Bey was impersonated by no less than Colin ('Brown of Colorado') Coop. The piece had a fairish reception and was hopefully puffed by its author:

> Mr Herbert Shelley and Stephen Philpot's new musical comedy having caught the taste of both the managers, public and press, negotiations are in progress for its reproductions in Australia, America and the West End of London this autumn . .

In the meanwhile, Denton continued with a week of *The King's Bride*, an even more solidly provincial piece with little in the way of modern flavour to it. Cromwell, Coop and Miss Beech were joined by Jessie Lonnen for the hurriedly staged occasion. Shelley's hopeful announcements came to nothing and he was reduced to seeing Miss Beech disappear back to India bearing his piece and *The King's Bride* as fodder for the ever-hungry Maurice Bandmann and his touring company. *The Algerian Girl*'s only subsequent British appearance was a week of twice-nightlys in a cut-down version at the Crouch End Hippodrome the following year, a venture which had no future, but *The King's Bride* finally came to the West End in 1918 in a revised version under the title *Violette*.

1911

0370 **PEGGY** a musical play in two acts by George Grossmith Jr based on *L'Amorçage* by Xanroff & Guérin. Lyrics by C. H. Bovill. Music by Leslie Stuart. Produced at the Gaiety Theatre under the management of George Edwardes 4 March, 1911 for a run of 270 performances closing 16 December, 1911.

Auberon Blow . . . . George Grossmith Jr
Hon. James Bendoyle . . . . J. Robert Hale
Montagu Bartle . . . . Herbert Jarman
Aristide Picot . . . . Arthur Hatherton/Frank Hector
Phonso . . . . Ernest Mahar
Marquis of Didsbury . . . . Guy Struthers/*out*
Emil . . . . Harry B. Burcher
Albert Umbles . . . . Edmund Payne
Polly Polino . . . . Gabrielle Ray (Gladys Guy)/Avice Kelham?
Doris Bartle . . . . Olive May
Diamond . . . . Enid Leslie/Coralie Blythe/
Avice Kelham/Maude Percival
Lady Florence Alister . . . . Nancy More
Mrs Ware-Wills . . . . Ruby Kennedy
Miss Vooch of Cincinnati . . . . Madge Melbourne
Jinnie . . . . Dorothy Selbourne
Ethel . . . . Blanche Stocker
Cecile . . . . Marie Mitchell/Florrie Arnold
Rosie . . . . Gertrude Thornton
Maud . . . . Connie Stuart
Nini . . . . Gladys Ffolliott
Jeannette . . . . S. Bourcard
Peggy Barrison . . . . Phyllis Dare
add Lady Snoop . . . . Connie Ediss
Lt Paul Shields . . . . George Grundy
Bertie . . . . S. Fortescue
Violet . . . . Peggy Franklin

with Elsie Collier, Gladys Guy, Babs Taylor &c

Dir/ch: Edward Royce; md: Leopold Wenzel; sc: Joseph Harker; cos: Comelli

Produced at the Casino Theatre, New York, under the management of Thomas W. Ryley 7 December, 1911 for a run of 37 performances closing 6 January, 1912.
Charles Brown (AUB), Joe Farren Soutar (BEND), John W. Ransome (MONT), Jules Charmette (ARI/PHON), Tom Dingle (MARQ/RASTUS), A. Hylton Allen (EMIL), Harry Fisher (CECIL, CARRUTHERS), Louise Alexander (POL), Vida Whitmore (DORIS), Esther Bissett (DI), Rose Winter (LADY), Margaret Rutledge (VOOCH), Alva York (LADY SNOOP), Elise Hamilton (DOLLY), Maud Brown (RUBY), Blanche West (NINI), Renée Kelly (PEGGY), Florence Walton (JEANETTE); pds: Mons Maurice, Madeleine d'Harville. Dir: Ned Wayburn

0371 **THAT CHAUFFEUR CHAP** a musical play in two acts by Edward Marris. Lyrics by Albert E. Ellis. Music by Arthur Rigby. Produced at the Opera House, Belfast, under the management of Messrs Marris and Rigby 17 April, 1911 and toured through dates including Dublin, Cork, Tunbridge Wells, Southampton, Leicester &c.

James Dickens . . . . Phil Lester/P. L. Julian
Archie Framland . . . . Arthur Rigby/W. Wilson Blake/Owen Stirling
Major Wellington Bluff. . . . . Louis du Cane/Phil Lester
Jim Stent . . . . Edward Marris/Jack McKenzie
Mr Tailby. . . . . George Power
Inspector Birch . . . . H. Morris/Fred Kirtland
Fagin . . . . Fred Rigby
Mrs Dickens . . . . Emily Stevens/Grace Lester
Mrs Stent . . . . Gwen Clifford
Poppy Preston. . . . . Gertrude Morrow
Mary . . . . Josephine Hilton/Alice Williams
Mildred Dickens . . . . Madge Prior
Iris Dickens. . . . . Vera Crackles
Todd . . . . Tom Payne

with Cecilia Morris, Kitty Morris, Lily Hoden, Vi Reher, Violet Lindsay, Vere Grace, K. Holmes, James Goddard, Frank Rex, Arthur Greenwood, Fred Bradford

Md: W. Harvey Pélissier

Revised and produced in an abridged form as *Mum's the Word*, 1913.

0372 **LADY LAVENDER** a musical comedy in three acts by Henry Edlin. Music by Clarence Corri. Produced at the Theatre Royal, Manchester, under the management of Haldane Crichton 19 June, 1911 and toured through Coventry, New Brighton, Morecambe, Belfast, Matlock, Bath, Weymouth, Rugby, Newcastle, Wigan, ?, ?, Cambridge, Birkenhead, Oldham, and other dates including Woolwich, Doncaster, Oxford, Blackburn, Hastings &c.

Tommy Turmutt . . . . Jack Crichton/Hylton Warde
Billy Brandon . . . . Frank Barclay
Jim Grimes . . . . George Delaforce
Furnival Deedes. . . . . W. Besley Beltram/Jack Crichton/Stanley Liston
Capt. Bernard Fortescue . . . . Leonard S. Harrison/Dannell Greene
Hon. Algernon Albemarle . . . . Hylton Warde/Scott Cullen/Stanley Liston/Hubert Connorton
P. C. Packham . . . . Stanley Liston/Richmond Somerville
James . . . . Richmond Somerville/*out*
Hon. Josephine Fairfax . . . . Isa Bowman
Countess Cora. . . . . Valerie Crespin/Getrude Harrison
Lady Vera Vavasour . . . . Dorothy Doveton/Renée Rees
Duchess of Dichwater . . . . Kathleen Cotter
Marchioness of Muddshire . . . . Edie Burton
Baroness von Bilke . . . . Annie Bunce
Mollie Mopps. . . . . Nancy Sheridan
Pollie Popps. . . . . Nellie Sheridan
Dolly Dopps . . . . Doris Wheatley
Florry Flopps . . . . Nellie Graham
Lavender Hill. . . . . Maude Ray/Mona Hersee

Md: Clarence Corri

Revised and produced as *Sweetheart Mine*, 1915.

0373 **THE MOUSMÉ** a musical play in three acts by Robert Courtneidge and Alexander M. Thompson. Lyrics by Arthur Wimperis and Percy Greenbank. Music by Howard Talbot and Lionel Monckton. Produced at the Shaftesbury Theatre under the management of Robert Courtneidge 9 September 1911 for a run of 209 performances closing 23 March, 1912.

General Okubo . . . . George Elton

Captain Yamaki . . . . Eric Maturin
Captain Fujiwara . . . . Harry Welchman
Lt Makei . . . . Nelson Keys
Lt Ito . . . . Conningsby Brierley/Victor Tollemache
Hashimoto. . . . . George Hestor
Kieke . . . . Alfred H. Majilton
Tanaka . . . . Harry Ray
Suki . . . . Dan Rolyat
Miyo Ko San . . . . Cicely Courtneidge
Mitsu . . . . Ada Blanche
Little Pine Tree. . . . . Sheila Hayes
Little Wisteria. . . . . Gladys Miles
Little Willow . . . . Violet Morene
Little Chrysanthemum . . . . May Etheridge
Plum Blossom. . . . . Cissie Debenham
Miss Purity . . . . Leslie Graham
Miss Snow . . . . Evelyn Laurie
Miss Crane . . . . Louie Lochner
Miss Silver . . . . Muriel Varna
Miss Spring . . . . Hetty Kelly
Miss Bamboo . . . . Lily Nanton/Maisie Sinclair
Miss Brightness . . . . Hope Charteris
Old Woman . . . . Dorothy Garth
Kanskei . . . . F. W. Hearne
Jiubei . . . . Arthur Stroud
Seifu. . . . . Bert Stanmore
O Hana San. . . . . Florence Smithson (Hope Charteris)
with Campbell Bishop, C. Victor Tollemache

Dir: Robert Courtneidge; md: Arthur Wood; ch: Espinosa and Alfred H. Majilton; sc: Conrad Tritschler; cos: Wilhelm

0374 **BONITA** a comic opera in a prologue and two acts by Wadham Peacock. Music by Harold Fraser-Simson. Produced at the Queen's Theatre under the management of the Bonita Syndicate 22 September, 1911 for a run of 42 performances closing 3 November, 1911.

Lt Philip Mannerton/Lt Arthur
  Mannerton . . . . Walter Wheatley
Margarida/Bonita . . . . Clara Evelyn
Sergeant Jones . . . . Cyril Vernon
Private Capper . . . . Robert Connolly
Mariana . . . . Thelma Raye
Joaquim . . . . Charles Maude
Rosa . . . . Minna Deacon
Teresa . . . . Billie Sinclair
Perpetua. Edith Clegg
Thomaz . . . . Frederick Volpe
Frederico . . . . Lionel Mackinder
Pedro . . . . Mark Lester
Sergeant of the Vermilion Lancers . . . . Eric Roper
Brother Domingo . . . . Gordon Yates
The Vermilion Lancers: Messrs Brady, Robert Connolly, Garton, Larkin, Mason, Pollard, Slade, Tait-Knight, Underwood, York.
with Messrs Elliott, Fenwick, Gage, Horscroft, Lillie, Mepstead, Murray, Prescott, Sedgely, Strachan, Ward, Wyatt; Misses Ashton, Bliss, Clare, Constance, Davies, Diggins, Du Cane, Ida Evelyn, Finucane, Hanton, Herbert, Hart, Horne, Irish, La Bare, Lewis, Masters, Montague, Morel, Sears, Vickers, Wells
Dancers: Misses Burde, Denton, Harrison, Nicholls, Nainby; Mr Hall

Dir: Granville Barker; md: S. P. Waddington/Howard Carr; ch: Espinosa; sc/cos: Norman Wilkinson

0375 **THE NEW CLOWN** the play by H. M. Paull adapted to musical comedy purposes by Charles C. Ommaney. Music by Tom Wood. Produced at the Palace Theatre, Rugby, under the management of Charles C. Ommaney 26 December, 1911 and toured through Kirkcaldy, Luton, Cambridge, Walmer, Hastings, Folkestone, Eastbourne, Sheerness, Weymouth, Tidmouth/Salisbury, Birkenhead, Buxton/Grantham, Lincoln/King's Lynn, Leeds, Manchester Junction and Longsight to 27 April, 1912.

Lord Cyril Garston . . . . Victor Kerr
Captain Jack Trent . . . . Frank Nugent/Charles C. Ommaney
Joe Dixon . . . . George Barran
Jesse Lamb . . . . Jack Hellier/Frank Nugent/Monty Goodwin
Tom Baker . . . . George Byrne
Billy . . . . Alfred Lawrence
Hezekiah Pennyquick . . . . Monty Goodwin/Frank Nugent
Fred . . . . Gerald Smithers
Figgis . . . . Frank Searle
Policeman . . . . Reginald Hollingdale
Tommy . . . . Babs Kendal
Winnie Chesterton . . . . Marie Moss
Maud Chesterton . . . . Violet Leslie
Trixie . . . . Betty Norton
Fifi . . . . Pearl d'Alroy
Babs . . . . Nora Gunter
Cheeky . . . . Dolly Manners
Queenie . . . . Violet Delver
Fluffy . . . . Ena Wilson
Rosie . . . . Dulcie Dalmer/Kitty Avey
with Marjorie Lark, Winnie Harrison, Winnie Morgan, Hilda Gresham

THE ALGERIAN GIRL by Herbert Shelley. Music by Stephen Philpot. Produced at the Kennington Theatre under the management of C. St John Denton 5 June, 1911 for one week.

The Bey . . . . Colin Coop
Arthur Brooklyn . . . . Leslie Gaze
Bob Robinson . . . . Mark Lester
Mataro . . . . Alfred de Manby
Hippolyte Bresson . . . . Myles Clifton
Hassock . . . . Powell Eastbury
Beppo . . . . F. Williams
Benjamin Biggs . . . . William Cromwell
Casarita . . . . Florence Beech
Marjorie Ayrshire . . . . Mabel Graham
Lady Ayrshire. . . . . Edith Cruickshanks
Bon Bon. . . . . Connie Emerald
Dir: William Clark; md: J. Wilson; sc: W. D. Hobbs

THE KING'S BRIDE a comic opera in two acts by Norman Slee. Music by John Ansell. Produced at the Kennington Theatre under the management of C. St John Denton 19 July, 1911 for one week.

Maximilian IX . . . . Mark Lester
Prince Rudolph . . . . E. J. Marsden
Count Franz Elfenbein . . . . Leslie Gaze
Count von Blumenkohl . . . . Myles Clifton
Sergeant Dolch . . . . Colin Coop
Konrad Blitz . . . . Powell Eastbury
Hugo Backer . . . . Oscar Layton
Baron Pepstein . . . . William Cromwell
Lady Mynette. . . . . Florence Beech

Avis von Senzburg	Jessie Lonnen
Princess Frizelda	Edith Jeffries
Kathie	Connie Emerald
Ellaine	Patty Moore

Dir: William Clarke; md: John Ansell

Revised and produced as *Violette*, 1918.

THE SKY SKIPPER a musical comedy in two acts by Albert E. Ellis and Arthur Rigby. Lyrics by Arthur E. Ellis and E. W. Rogers. Music by Arthur Rigby. Produced at the Shakespeare Theatre, Clapham, under the management of Arthur Rigby 27 November, 1911 for one week.

Richard Rowton	Jack McKenzie
Jack Gordon	Arthur Rigby
Sam Slapp	Charles E. Paton
Robert Reddison	Teddy Rutland
Timothy	Ernie Weslo
Emperor of Amoros	Michael Mahoney
Winnie	Claire Barrington
Selina	Gwen Clifford
Mimi	Laurie Potter
Sauci	Vi Reher

1912

In the past few years there had been sure, if in some ways slow-moving, changes in the British musical theatre. The previously unchallenged supremacy of the British musical comedy had found itself eroded by competition not just from isolated foreign hits like *The Belle of New York*, *Véronique* or *La Poupée* but by the persistent tradition of the Viennese musical. The huge success of *The Merry Widow* had spawned a considerable public and producing interest and had led to such successful productions as *The Dollar Princess*, *The Girl in the Train*, *The Chocolate Soldier* and *The Count of Luxembourg* to set alongside the native triumphs of *Our Miss Gibbs*, *The Quaker Girl* and *The Arcadians*. Franz Lehár, Oscar Straus and Leo Fall were new names to most of the British public, but the popularity of their works now challenged the best of British composers.

The ranks of the native musicians were thinner now than they had been a decade previously: Caryll had gone to America, German was finished with the theatre, Slaughter had died and Leslie Stuart was in the doldrums and the bankruptcy courts. Philip Michael Faraday, who had seemed the white hope of the comic opera after *Amasis* was too busy with the Lyric Theatre and his new role as a producer, Sidney Jones had gone very quiet in the field since *The Persian Princess* disaster and it was left to Lionel Monckton, composer or co-composer of all the three great hits of the past couple of years, to head the remnants of the famous 'old band' with Howard Talbot and Paul Rubens in support. New younger composers were not appearing to fill the gaps; Herman Darewski, Harold Fraser-Simson, Philip Braham, Reginald Somerville and G. H. Clutsam had all put in their word, but a producer – a George Edwardes or a Robert Courtneidge – looking for a writer did not have the obvious choices of a few years earlier.

Another important change in affairs was the new approach being taken by the music halls, particularly the major halls and the circuits. Over a number of years the traditional variety programme of the music halls had been loosened to include sketches, then musical sketches, little burlesques, potted shows and, finally, full-blown short musical comedies and operettas. The traditional preserve of the theatres was now being shared by the halls, the best of which were capable of producing a piece like Leo Fall's one-act operetta *The Eternal Waltz* which had proved the centrepiece of the entertainment at Sir Edward Moss's Hippodrome in 1911/12 before being taken on to the Moss' Empires circuit.

The halls were also capable of producing 'revue'. With the aid of a compère or commère, a number of performers and acts were loosely slotted into a framework consisting of a series of tenuously-linked scenas full of song, dance and scenic effect – a musical without characters, without story, but with all the visual, musical comical and topical elements it liked. It did not necessarily, in the French fashion, review anything, but this new kind of variety show consisting of a half a dozen or more little shows and a cast which did not change week by week, nevertheless retained the title of 'revue'.

1912 saw both the Viennese musical and the new style music-hall entertainments at an important stage: the former at its most ubiquitous and yet at the beginning, already, of its end; the latter at the beginning of its beginning, catapulted into public favour by a group of hugely popular and long-running shows.

While two *Merry Widow* companies, four *Count of Luxembourgs*, three *Chocolate Soldiers*, two *Girl in the Trains*, two *Waltz Dreams* and a *Dollar Princess* worked their way around the country, each of the most successful musical producers in the country brought new continental works into town. George Edwardes had two: one for Daly's (*Gipsy Love*) and one for the Adelphi (*Autumn Manoeuvres*) where Lionel Monckton had lately reigned unchallenged; Robert Courtneidge staged Alexander Thompson's version of Leo Fall's *Der Liebe Augustin* as *Princess Caprice* at the Shaftesbury where he had made a fortune with Talbot and Monckton's *Arcadians* and lost much of it again with their *Mousmé*; and Michael Faraday turned to Germany and Jean Gilbert's *Die Keusche Suzanne* which he played at the Lyric as *The Girl in the Taxi*. The Coliseum management went one further and actually commissioned Oscar Straus, composer of *The Chocolate Soldier*, to write a piece for them, and *The Dancing Viennese* made up the total of the year's continental shows. They were backed by a whole clutch of smaller pieces, many specially commissioned, in the music halls. De Courville at Moss' Empires ordered *The Blue House* from Emmerich Kálmán and *Arms and the Girl* from Richard Fall, brother to the 'red hot' Leo whose *Brüderlein Fein* was played at the Coliseum as *Darby and Joan*; Heinrich Reinhardt's *The Daring of Diane* played the Tivoli and its circuit; Paul Lincke contributed *The H'arum Lily* to the Pavilion; and so it went on.

Nearly everywhere success shone. The critics were delighted with 'the rise in the standard of composition' and the public was pleased by the charm and beauty and novelty of the new pieces. *Gipsy Love* ran a fair 299 performances at Daly's, *Princess Caprice* satisfied with 265 and *The Girl in the Taxi* became the year's most successful piece with a run of 385 performances. But Adelphi audiences gave only a moderate welcome to Kálmán's *Ein Herbstmanöver* which Edwardes removed after 75 performances and *The Dancing Viennese* proved even less attractive.

Revue, too, claimed success, firstly with the Empire show *Everybody's Doing It* (named for the Irving Berlin song with which Ida Crispi and Robert Hale scored so well) – ninety minutes of song, dance, impersonations, burlesque &c which shared the bill with Lydia Kyasht and Fred Farren's ballets of *New York* or *The Water Nymph*; then with *Kill that Fly* (also named for a number); and finally, and most resoundingly, with the full-length *Hullo, Ragtime!* which put the seal both on the popularity of the new syncopated rhythms which had been creeping across the Atlantic since the beginning of the year and on the new British large-scale revue form.

Hullo, Ragtime! was the brainchild of Albert de Courville, assistant to Sir Edward Moss of Moss' Empires. He combined elements of the American and French 'revue' with his own ideas of mass entertainment – the spectacular, the topical, the glamorous – and brought together the cast: Shirley Kellogg, Ethel Levey and comic Willie Solar from the U.S.A., Australia's O.P. Heggie, comedy actress Dorothy Minto, Cyril Clensy from musical comedy, dancers Bonita and Lew Hearn with the already famous 'Hitchy Koo' to perform, Jerry Kirby, Checkers von Hampton and Maud Tiffany. He hired Louis Hirsch, American composer of *He Came from Milwaukee*, *The Whirl of Society* and *The Passing Show of 1912* to provide songs like 'How do You do, Miss Ragtime' and 'The Wedding Glide'. He even wheedled a sizeable sketch burlesquing censorship from J. M. Barrie, and tailored all his gatherings together into a bright, modern and fast-moving entertainment which made the Gaiety musicals seem almost langorous and the Viennese shows something from a different world.

Against this rising tide of alternative entertainment, only George Edwardes kept faith with the product which had served him so well and so long. Viennese musicals might do for Daly's, but the Gaiety was an altogether different thing and the Gaiety remained British. Paul Rubens, Cecil Raleigh (absent from the world of the musical since *The Yashmak*) and Arthur Wimperis got the contract for the Gaiety's successor to *Peggy*. And, when *Autumn Manoeuvres* failed to catch on at the Adelphi, Edwardes was ready with a new Lionel Monckton musical to follow where *The Quaker Girl* had led. But that was it: the whole of the year brought forth only two new British musicals in the West End, both from the faithful purveyors of many years.

Both of them were successes. Not great hits, and neither outstripped the twelve months' run of *The Girl in the Taxi* or approached the most famous of their predecessors in durability, but *The Sunshine Girl* at the Gaiety held on for 336 performances and Monckton's *The Dancing Mistress* notched up 242 at the Adelphi. In spite of all the novelties, the audience for the type of entertainment supplied over the more recent years by Edwardes and his writers and artists was still a large and enthusiastic one, and there were many who still preferred Monckton to Fall and Rubens to Kálmán and both to ragtime.

The Sunshine Girl brought Paul Rubens to the Gaiety to supply a show for his beloved Phyllis Dare, Grossmith, Teddy Payne, and Connie Ediss, now reinstalled at the home of her greatest triumphs. He was joined for the libretto by Cecil Raleigh, the author of *Little Christopher Columbus*, *The Belle of Cairo* and *The Yashmak*, whose last fifteen years had been devoted to supplying a series of very successful dramas – *The White Heather*, *The Great Ruby*, *Hearts Are Trumps*, *The Sins of Society*, *Marriages of Mayfair*, *The Whip* &c – to Drury Lane. The lyric credit he shared with Wimperis, the lyricist of *The Arcadians* with whom he had previously worked on *The Balkan Princess* for Curzon. It was a team new to the Gaiety but the piece they produced turned out to be well and truly in the established mould. If anything it was more Gaiety than the Gaiety. It took no French original for its basis as *Peggy* had, it harked back to the days of minimal plot and maximum star exposure with a story which was as old-fashioned and unconvincing as could be and which existed only to display the theatre's favourite stars in a series of songs and dances and scenas. Quite what the contribution of Raleigh, a well-known playwright, consisted of is difficult to fathom, but he had never been at his dramatic best with his efforts in the musical world and *The Sunshine Girl* was no exception.

The story had Phyllis Dare as Delia Dale, a worker in the 'Sunshine' soap factory at Port Sunshine (a very thinly disguised version of Port Sunlight), in love with Vernon Blundell, one of her workmates. But Vernon is really the heir to the whole place who, by the terms of his inheritance, has to go five years without getting engaged or married. He wants to be loved for himself and not his position, so he gets his friend Lord Bicester (Grossmith) to pose as head of the establishment while he continues as a humble workman. Bicester, however, is recognised by his fiancée, Lady Rosabelle and by the ex-cabby Floot (Payne) and his wife Brenda (Miss Ediss). The complications that follow provided fine opportunities for comedy to Payne, Grossmith and Miss

Ediss and plenty of songs for Miss Dare, in a well-ordered, well-aimed piece of entertainment which more than fulfilled the need of its patrons. *The Times* wrote:

> No one goes to the Gaiety for the play. We all go to enjoy the Gaiety company disporting themselves – Mr George Grossmith Jr wearing his clothes, Mr Edmund Payne twisting his face, Miss Olive May moving her limbs, Miss Connie Ediss speaking her mind and Miss Phyllis Dare (or whoever the ingénue of the moment may be) looking pretty. And the greatest merit of *The Sunshine Girl* is that it sends us away feeling that we should like to see more of all these and of Mr George Barrett and Mr Robert Nainby and clever Miss Mabel Sealby and Miss Violet Essex, the new singer with the fine voice, and Mr Basil Foster, the gallant but rather obscure hero. We have a strong impression that Mr George Grossmith's clothes were not so various and beautiful as usual, though to be sure he wore them with all his usual art; that Mr Edmund Payne ought to have had a bombardon or something equally ridiculous to play with. We are quite certain that he and Mr Grossmith will play about together more elaborately before a week is over: and we are quite sure that we want at least twice as much as we got of Miss Olive May. The explanation of this ingratitude is probably nothing more than the coherence and swiftness of the piece as a whole. It is long but there is no tedium in it. . . . But the coherence and movement of the piece do not lie in its plot. They are the result of artfulness on the part of Mr Paul Rubens and whoever else put the thing together. Each item comes so well after the one before and leads so well into the one that comes after that it seems gone – encores and all – before it has begun. We have never known a gayer evening in the gay and absurd world behind the footlights of the Gaiety . .

Absurd and gay indeed it was, as *The Sunshine Girl* ran from one rousing chorus to another and from one laugh to another through the delightful scenery, dresses and girls which the Gaiety provided.

From the moment the first curtain rose on 'Port Sunshine' and its chorus of soap-making ladies, headed by pretty Mabel Sealby telling them all to 'Get a Move On' in a lively song and dance, the pace of the evening was never allowed to slacken as the love affair of Delia and Vernon was obliterated under an avalanche of Rubens' most characteristic material. Among the most successful moments of the evening were a handful of those naively naughty numbers which had made Rubens' name. Grossmith sang to Miss Dare that she was:

> Too delicious in the grey light
> In the shy light of the twilight
> Quite delightful in the daylight
> But a darling in the dark

and warned:

> Little girl, little girl, mind how you go,
> Supper is jolly
> But possibly folly,
> Twelve thirty – hullo!
> Twopenny tube is safer but slow,
> Taxi is quicker but oh dear, no
> So, little girl, mind how you go

and Miss Dare retaliated with:

> Take me for a game of golf
> Take me for a walk

Take me for
A turn round the floor
Or a tiny little talk.
Take me out to supper
And when you've turned my dizzy head
Oh, please ring the bell
At my charming hotel
And take me up to. . my mother for she's waiting up for me!

Olive May had an unexceptional piece about 'Miss Blush' who blushed at everything except when no one was looking. But there was much more enjoyment to be had in the quartet (Payne, Grossmith, Misses Sealby and Ediss) 'The Butler':

When there's a party held upstairs
One of those upper ten affairs
William the butler hears it all
Whispers it around the servants hall
Somebody told a tale last night
(Ladies were not about)
All of us heard that tale all right
How did the thing leak out? Well . . .
The butler told the footman
The footman told the cook
The cook repeated, I'm much afraid,
The whole caboodle to the parlourmaid
The 'tweeny shed a tear
Oh, wouldn't you like to know, ho, ho,
What did the butler hear?

or in Teddy Payne describing 'The Science of Being Lazy', Grossmith on 'The other Chap', or the one and only Connie Ediss singing of 'Brighton':

Oh, when I leave my own back garden
I don't look for Baden Baden
I've travelled once or twice
To Monte and to Nice
But Brighton's nice enough for me!

or, uproariously, of how, 'I've Been to the Durbar':

Didn't we have a spree!
They say that I tickled the Rajahs
But they all tickled me!

There was time for Miss Dare and Foster to sing, at the start of Act I, about 'Lovers' before he virtually disappeared from the show along with the plot; there was a pretty waltz song specially inserted to show off the young singer Violet Essex whom Edwardes had plucked from the concert stage and the recording studio; there was a unison octet of businessmen (Rubens still ran shy of writing part music) and a make-up ballad 'A tiny Touch' for the heroine who also danced a 'new dance from South America' with Grossmith to the strains of 'In the Argentine' as everything rolled happily along to the final curtain.

The show's first night was an undoubted success and good notices followed:

Yet another 'Gaiety Girl' has made her début and we seek for new superlatives with which to describe her. Soap and sunshine both seem to have contributed to the bright

> charm and the fresh appearance of her appearance. The plot of the piece is of the slightest, but is often lost sight of in the pleasure created by the tuneful songs and dainty dances which are linked together with a slight thread of sometimes inconsequent but always humorous dialogue . . The music as a whole is light, tuneful and pretty and the lyrics are smart and up to the mark. (*Era*)

with only an odd demurring voice:

> An obvious first night success was made before a typical Gaiety audience . . . Unfortunately the seemingly promising and interesting plot with an apparently substantial basis of Raleighality which started amidst [the] sumptuously artistic and characteristically Edwardian setting went all to pieces early in the long second act formed more or less of clever and diverting variety episodes . . . and it was dragged in again just before the end. The versatile Cecilian genius has received further livening up from the effervescent sparkle of Paul Rubens, some of whose lyrics partake of the quality best expressed by the good, old long-recognised term of 'saucy'. In the composing of the music the prolific Mr Rubens has kept successfully enough to his own pattern, his bright and ticklingly tuneful strains having about them a certain sameness that produces a somewhat cloying effect long before a score of them (quite a dozen encored) have been heard. Hence, in Act 2, *The Sunshine Girl* loses any pretentions to be considered a coherent and well-made musical piece that it might have had. (*Stage*)

Both notices were right. *The Sunshine Girl* had a libretto which was better ignored and included as much of the worst of Rubens as of the best, but it had the bright and breezy, picturesque and comical attributes which made a Gaiety piece what it was and it went down decidedly well. In August, when the Gaiety Company's annual meeting was held, Edwardes was able to report that

> the present piece was very much stronger than the last and the rest of the world had apparently thought so too, for in America it had been sold well to Mr Frohman and good terms had also been obtained in Australia and elsewhere . .

and the show ran on uneventfully through the year with the minimum in the way of alterations (Mabel Sealby's success earned her a duet with Payne about 'Two Nuts') until February of the following year, by which time two touring companies were purveying the show in the provinces and Broadway had acclaimed it as a success.

For Broadway, of course, it had been altered. Inevitably, the book had been 'Americanised' and Rubens' score had been supplemented with the inescapable Jerome Kern songs. But *The Sunshine Girl* was still largely the piece which had played the Gaiety and Eva Davenport's version of 'I've Been to the Durbar' went for as much in the success of the show as the dancing of Vernon Castle (in the Grossmith role) and Irene Castle, the comedy of Joseph Cawthorn or sweet Julia Sanderson in the title role. The 'new dance from South America' performed by Castle and Miss Sanderson proved particularly popular and the 'tango' joined ragtime as one of the crazes of the moment as *The Sunshine Girl* danced its way through 181 performances at New York's Knickerbocker Theatre.

For *The Dancing Mistress*, George Edwardes reassembled the creators of *The Quaker Girl* – Tanner, Greenbank, Ross and Monckton – for the benefit of stars Gertie Millar and Joe Coyne. The Monckton/Miss Millar combination had never failed him except in the unsalvageable *New Aladdin*, and Coyne was the darling of the musical comedy world, adored for his Count Danilo and his 'Tony from America'. Both had been perfectly served in *The Quaker Girl* and Edwardes wished only to repeat that happy consensus. The new piece was duly in the same mould with Miss Millar being cast as a dance teacher from a ladies' finishing school and Coyne as an aviator in a plot which visited Brighton, Oberwald and a London hotel in plenty of delightful songs and dances and magnificent sets and dresses.

The Times commented:

> The ingenuity of the makers of musical comedy is wonderful. Moving within very narrow limits they seem to be able to make innumerable changes. Their problem is to find names and parts for a small number of well-known players and sometimes, as in *The Dancing Mistress*, they actually succeed in getting a story which can fit them all in, give them plenty of opportunities of being themselves and yet have an air of novelty. A girls' school and a winter hotel in Switzerland are new, so far as we know, in musical comedy and we doubt whether Miss Gertie Millar has ever before been a dancing mistress, Mr Coyne an airman or Miss Gracie Leigh a Scot and so, though *The Dancing Mistress* is a musical play of the very familiar English type, there is something fresh about it . .

James Tanner's story had some useful twists and turns, if not so much in the way of new plot elements:

> . . the story, as it goes along on its, at present, much too leisurely course does seem to give good opportunities to Miss Gertie Millar and Mr Joseph Coyne, plenty to Mr Blakeley and that very downright comedian Mlle Caumont and not quite enough to Miss Gracie Leigh . . the things that will stay in the memory are Mr Coyne in a rage, Miss Gracie Leigh mixed up in her skis, Mlle Caumont after being searched by a customs officer and several little dances and songs.

The 'opportunities' were of rather more significance than the plot which took Miss Millar and her teaching colleagues Mlle Touchet, M. Tonelli and Jeannie McTavish (of the tuck shop) gallivanting across Europe in the wake of aviator Coyne &c. in a bundle of good familiar stuff which had the additional merit of allowing Joseph Harker loose on a perfectly splendid snow and sunshine setting for Act 2 and Lionel Monckton and his lyricists plenty of chances for more or less relevant numbers.

The score for *The Dancing Mistress* did not boast any songs to equal the hits of *The Quaker Girl* or *The Arcadians.* It was Monckton at his most typical, at his most unfailingly, lightheartedly skilful, but none of the songs proved to have the lasting value which had characterised the gems of his last few scores. Gertie Millar explained herself in a pretty title song:

> For if you want to be gay
> That is the very best way
> It's my experience, so I am not romancing
> You do a pirouette light
> And things come round again right
> For life goes merrily, if you keep on dancing

and did very well with 'Dance, little Snowflake':

> Dance, little snowflake,
> While the moon is glistening
> No one can hear you
> For there's no one who's listening
> Dance, little snowflake
> Till the moonlight is done
> But remember you will melt away
> If you dance in the sun

as well as joining Coyne in a couple of duets of which 'If I were to Dance like You' was the more successful with its accompanying dancing and skating interlude. Gracie Leigh affirmed 'I'm Havin' a richt guid Time', Blakeley described 'A little Flutter', Gina Palerme sang of being 'The Parisienne' and there were several good ensembles ('Cantering', 'What is wrong with London', 'Keep Cool'), but the favourite pieces from the show turned out to be the dance 'The Porcupine Patrol' introduced into the first act finale and the waltz song 'When You are in Love' sung by George Carvey:

> When you are in love
> All the world is fair
> Hearts are light with laughter gay
> Roses, roses all the way,
> There is not a cloud
> In the blue above
> Ah! life's a golden dream
> When you are in love.

It was scarcely vintage Greenbank, but its catching waltz tune ensured its success.

The Dancing Mistress never looked like breaking any records, but it received a warm welcome and an appreciative reaction from both its first-night audience and the critics:

> . . another success at the Adelphi with this bright and pleasant musical comedy (*Era*)
>
> Mr George Edwardes, as is his invariable wont, has again 'gone one better' in providing his public with a regular embarrassment of riches. Indeed, it is difficult to recall to mind any like production within recent years which surpasses it for sheer lavishness of display in the matter of dainty costumes and gorgeous scenery and when such highly desirable qualities as these are associated with an always melodious and characteristic score by Lionel Monckton and smooth running lyrics by Adrian Ross and Percy Greenbank it is easy to predict the use of house full boards for some considerable time to come . . (*Stage*)

Perhaps the visual side of *The Dancing Mistress* came out the best. Monckton's music was not rated everywhere as highly as it might have been:

> Mr Lionel Monckton's tunes call for no special comment, but they fulfil the purpose of *The Dancing Mistress.* (*Times*)

and the book came in for some caustic comments, but the summing-up was everywhere the same: *The Dancing Mistress* was a success and would run, which it did.

Two months after its opening, Edwardes had Dora Fraser and Louis Bradfield heading the first touring company out for Christmas in Glasgow and George Dance's No. 2 company smartly followed it. At the same time things were prospering to such an extent at the Adelphi that Edwardes was obliged to squeeze in extra rows of seats in the stalls to help ease the demand for tickets. New songs made their way into the score, and two of them 'Every Woman' (Gertie Millar) and 'Somehow, Somewhere' proved welcome adjuncts. The show ran on vigorously until Edwardes deemed it necessary to withdraw Gertie Millar from the cast to take up the lead in the latest Daly's piece *The Marriage Market*. Phyllis Dare was brought in to replace her but *The Dancing Mistress* seemed to have run through its audience and it closed soon after. The following year it appeared in Australia with a cast headed by a number of familiar names: Grace Palotta, Billie Barlow, Leslie Holland, Blanche Browne, Jack Cannot and Frank Greene; and it was duly snapped up and appreciated on the Oriental circuits but was not picked up for America and its London run of 242 performances rated it only a relative success in the face of Monckton's previous triumphs.

Alongside the Continental and British musicals of the year, two American pieces appeared. One was Tom Davis' production of Gustave Kerker's *Grass Widows* at the Apollo which proved an utter failure, lasting only 50 performances in spite of all Constance Drever and Alfred Lester could do. The other was *The Pink Lady*, an attempt to import Ivan Caryll's American success into Britain. It came equipped with its American production and cast and installed itself at the Globe Theatre where it excited considerable public and critical interest. Unfortunately, someone had done his sums badly and it turned out that even the excellent houses which the piece attracted were not enough to secure the weekly break figure. After four months the over-paid Americans were sent home and *The Pink Lady* sent on tour with a less improbable budget.

The provinces again produced little of worth. The last worthwhile provincial successes were now well in the past and writers who might otherwise have turned out good material for fresh touring musicals were now doing the much less demanding work required by the music halls. Musical sketches, short musical plays, burlesques, pantomime pieces and revues large and small occupied the attentions of most available composers and writers and what new pieces did appear were, on the whole, unambitious works set up to showcase a particular actor-manager on the small circuits.

In this vein Charles Ommaney took up the role of Jack Trent in his own adaptation of the successful play *The New Clown* by H. M. Paull, and Isa Bowman starred as Winnie Wimple in a concoction of her own called *The Girl in the Picture* which she kept on the road in minor dates for a good long tour. A slightly more up-market piece on the same lines was *The Boy Scout*, a comedy with music written by Arthur Branscombe for soubrette Marie George who turned producer and took out a company starring herself and Hayden Coffin. Coffin donned naval uniform for the umpteenth time and Miss George impersonated a Baron's daughter for six weeks in dates which owed more to the popularity of the stars than to Branscombe's bit of nonsense. At the end of the year it appeared on a lesser scale with its title altered to *Merry Miss Mischief* and its expensive stars replaced by Charles Childerstone and Hilda Moss for a further tour.

1912

0376 **THE SUNSHINE GIRL** a musical play in two acts by Paul Rubens and Cecil Raleigh. Lyrics by Paul Rubens and Arthur Wimperis. Music by Paul Rubens. Produced at the Gaiety Theatre under the management of George Edwardes 24 February, 1912 for a run of 336 performances closing 15 February, 1913.

Lord Bicester . . . . George Grossmith Jr
Vernon Blundell. . . . . Basil Foster
Commodore Barker . . . . George Barrett
Hodson . . . . Tom Walls
Stepnyak . . . . Robert Nainby
Dever . . . . Willie Stephens/W. Jackson
Whitley . . . . George Grundy
Telfridge . . . . Joseph Grande
Garing. . . . . Spencer Lloyd
Williams. Oswald Collins
Nelgrove. Garry Lynch
Clarence. Fred Raynham
Floot . . . . Edmund Payne
Lady Rosabelle Merrydew . . . . Olive May/Gwendoline Brogden/Crissie Bell
Marie Silvaine. . . . . Mabel Sealby
Emmeline . . . . Violet Essex
Lady Mary . . . . Irene Warren/Gladys Squier
May . . . . Blanche Stocker
Sybil. . . . . Avice Kelham/Barbara Dunbar
Lucy. . . . . Elsie Collier
Kit. . . . . Marie Mitchell/Ethel Lawson
Lily . . . . Olive Wade/Judith Nelmes
Miss Molyneux . . . . Gladys Wray
Hon Miss Grey . . . . Pattie Wells/Violet Norton
Brenda Blacker . . . . Connie Ediss
Delia Dale. . . . . Phyllis Dare (Ethel Lawson)
Major Lascelles . . . . Arthur Wellesley
Bobbie McLeod. . . . . G. Comyn
Policemen . . . . Charles Russ and James Redmond
Sailor . . . . Austin Camp
Daisy . . . . Kitty Lindley/*out*
Violet . . . . Florence Reade
Lady Clare . . . . Dorothy Fane/Patience Seymour
Miss Rivers . . . . Ethel Lawson/Daisy Waller
Miss Pontifex . . . . Gertie Birch/Kitty Lindley
Miss Meadows . . . . Marjorie Michie/*out*
add Miss Clive . . . . Mollie Gordon
Beryl . . . . Connie Stuart
Mary . . . . Gladys Squier

Dir: J. A. E. Malone; md: Leopold Wenzel; ch: Willie Warde; sc: Alfred Terraine and Joseph Harker; cos: Comelli

Produced at the Knickerbocker Theatre, New York, under the management of Charles Frohman 3 February, 1913. Suspended 21 June, 1913. Resumed 1 September, 1913. Closed 20 September 1913 after a total of 181 performances.
Vernon Castle (LORD), Alan Mudie (VB), E. Soldene Powell (HUDSON), J. J. Horwitz (STEP), Joseph Tullar (DEV), Edward C. Yeager (WHIT), Russell Griswold (WMS), Joseph Cawthorn (SCHLUMP), Eileen Kearney (ROS), Flossie Hope (MS), Flossie Deshon (KATE), Eleanor Rasmussen (ALICE), Irene Hopping (SYBIL), Constance Hunt (VIOLET), Dorothy Berry (LILY), Eva Davenport (BB), Julia Sanderson (DORA DALE), Tom Lewis (STEVE DALEY), Edwin Stone (WEARS), Robert Hickey (BOBBY McLEOD), James O'Neill (SIR WALTER RAEBURN), Ruth Thorpe (LADY MARY), Raymond Sabater (LASCELLES), Dickson Elliott (BOGGS), Harry Law (SNELL), Lew Leroy & William Francis (PCS), Charles L. McGee & Owen Jones (FLUNKEYS). Dir: J. A. E. Malone; md: Augustus Barratt; sc: Homer Emens, Ernest Albert; cos: Lord & Taylor, Russell Uniform Co.

0377 **THE BOY SCOUT** a comedy with music in three acts by Arthur Branscombe and George Fearnley. Produced at the Theatre Royal, Birmingham, under the management of Marie George 20 May, 1912 and toured through Liverpool, Manchester, Leeds, Edinburgh and Glasgow, to 30 June.

Lt Richard Meredith . . . . C. Hayden Coffin//Charles Childerstone
Percy Fitzwinney . . . . Herbert Sparling
Baron Deschamps. . . . . Evelyn Vernon
Rivers . . . . Fred Trott
Old Joe . . . . Cecil A. Collins//James Loman
Suli . . . . D. McArthur
Gwendoline Amesbury . . . . Mildred Cottell//Wynne Wheeley
Rose Boyton. . . . . Margery Grey
Mrs Meredith. . . . . Grace Lester
Claire . . . . Ivy Knight
Suzanne . . . . Violet Welford
Paul/Pauline. . . . . Marie George//Hilda Moss
Md: J. R. Bingley

0378 **THE GIRL IN THE PICTURE** a musical comedy by Isa Bowman. Music by Harry Richardson. Produced at Deal under the management of Isa Bowman 2 September, 1912 and toured.

Frank Fortescue. . . . . Frank Barclay
Sammy Smears . . . . Hylton Warde
Esme Hantier . . . . Gregory Scott
John Matthews . . . . Besley Beltram
Hilton Hardmere . . . . Tom Squire
Waiter. . . . . George Holmes
Marjorie Matthews . . . . Vera Davis
Mrs Wimple . . . . Kitty Kirwan
Vera . . . . Kitty Carlisle
Nina. . . . . Nora Harrison
Grace . . . . Peggy Phyle
Lucy. . . . . Wynne Bronte
Marie . . . . Jessie Compton
Leonard . . . . Arnold Dean
Edward . . . . Hubert Graham
Fisher . . . . Graham Ross
Winnie Wimple . . . . Isa Bowman
Sc: Ernest Howard & Philip Howden

0379 **THE DANCING MISTRESS** a musical play in three acts by James T. Tanner. Lyrics by Adrian Ross and Percy Greenbank. Music by Lionel Monckton. Produced at the Adelphi Theatre under the management of George Edwardes 19 October, 1912 for a run of 242 performances closing 21 June, 1913.

Widdicombe . . . . James Blakeley
Lord Lyndale . . . . F. Pope Stamper/Nicholas Hannen/ Harold E. Pearce
Dubois . . . . D. J. Williams
Baron Montalba . . . . Georges Carvey/Harold Latham
Berchili . . . . Ivan Berlyn
Signor Tonelli . . . . Eliot Skinner
Monsieur Rosenblum . . . . Ernest A. Douglas/Alfred Beers
Teddy Cavanagh . . . . Joseph Coyne
Jeannie McTavish . . . . Gracie Leigh
Mlle Virginie Touchet . . . . Mlle Caumont
Bella Peach . . . . Elsie Spain
Miss Pindrop . . . . Agnes Thomas/Jeannie Thomas?
Lady Margrave . . . . Maud Cressall/Lilian Hadley
Lili . . . . Gina Palerme/Gertrude White
Nancy Joyce . . . . Gertie Millar/Phyllis Dare
Customs Officer . . . . H. Tyndall

with Ruby Kennedy, Ann Cleaver, Gertrude White, Leila Griffin, Lilian Hadley, Dorothy Devere, Yvonne Fitzroy, Heather Featherstone, Isobel Elsom, Kathleen Vincent, Gipsy O'Brien, Claire Lynch, Betty Olgar, Flora Allen, Nora Wadeley, Maude Aston, Bessy Millard, Gladys Ivery/Lilian Harvey, Trixie Hillier, Gladys Kurton, Maud Harris, Kitty Kent, Marjorie Hume, Chloe O'Hara, Dorothy Laine.

Dir: J. A. E. Malone; md: Carl Kiefert; ch: Fred Farren; sc: Alfred Terraine and Joseph Harker; cos: Comelli

THE COLOMBO GIRL a musical comedy. Toured under the management of J. W. Cordiner and Harry Richardson.

1913

The face of light musical entertainment in London's West End had undergone major changes in a comparatively short time. The coming of revue, of the Viennese musical, of ragtime and the tango, and the simultaneous passing of many of the great old guard of British writers had combined to leave the West End theatre in a decidedly parti-coloured state. 1913 saw productions of all kinds staged, and successes and failures occurred in every genre as public taste spread itself freely about and made up its mind on value rather than in accord with any popular fashion.

Thus, *Hullo, Ragtime!* ran through the year in London, took to the road, and finally transferred to the Palladium to leave the Hippodrome to its equally triumphant younger sister *Hullo, Tango!*; Louis Hirsch and J. R. Johnson's *Come over Here*, built on similar lines, prospered at the London Opera House and *Keep Smiling* continued the Alhambra's successful conversion to revue, while half a dozen other new revues came and went unprofitably. While George Edwardes' version of Victor Jacobi's *The Marriage Market* settled itself in at Daly's for a run of over a year and *The Girl on the Film* at the Gaiety for 232 performances, Michael Faraday's production of Oscar Straus' pretty new *Love and Laughter* collapsed after only 65 nights and Edmund Eysler's hit piece *Der Lachende Ehemann* failed twice – as *The Laughing Husband* at the New and as *The Girl who Didn't* at the Lyric, also under Faraday's management.

America partly atoned for the failure of *Grass Widows* and the mismanagement of *The Pink Lady* with the newest Ivan Caryll musical *Oh! Oh! Delphine*, imported by Robert Courtneidge for the Shaftesbury Theatre. An adaptation of the French farce *Villa Primrose* by Charles McLellan, it had had a fine Broadway run and stayed a respectable 174 performances in London before taking to the road. *The Pink Lady* and *Oh! Oh! Delphine* made Ivan Caryll's departure all the more regrettable at such a tentative time in the British musical world, for both pieces had musical scores of a delightfully eclectic nature. Caryll had adapted himself to the modern taste in music in a way that Lionel Monckton and Paul Rubens never could or would, and it looked as though America would have a long and enjoyable line of Caryll musicals to send back to Britain in future years when, failing some new talent, England would have little to send in return.

In the meanwhile, however, the 'old brigade' of the British musical produced two new pieces which put up highly satisfactory showings. Robert Courtneidge's production of *The Pearl Girl* at the Shaftesbury largely outran its predecessor, *Oh! Oh! Delphine*, and ended the year second only to *The Marriage Market* and Gertie Millar among new musical plays, whilst Edwardes' new Adelphi musical *The Girl from Utah*, which teamed Jones and Rubens with the resident authors, clocked up 195 performances before going on to success in America.

The Pearl Girl was Basil Hood's first original West End musical for more than ten years. Since *A Princess of Kensington* he had devoted himself to the adaptation of Edwardes' continental pieces with libretti and/or lyrics for *Les Merveilleuses*, *The Merry Widow*, *The Count of Luxembourg*, *A Waltz Dream*, *The Dollar Princess* and *Gipsy Love*, with only the provincial *The Golden Girl* (1905) as an original effort. This latest musical was also to be his last but there was no shadow of impending end over the bright and imaginative libretto of *The Pearl Girl*.

The choice of pearls as a subject for a musical comedy was a fortunate one. Fortuitous, surely, too, as Hood was not noted as a fast worker. For some two months pearls had been making big headlines owing to a glamorous and highly publicised jewel robbery. No-one was ignorant of the drama surrounding the theft of the fabulous pearl necklace which jeweller Max Meyer had sent to Paris in the hope of a sale at £150,000 – the price of a battleship. From July to early September the 'Pearl Necklace Case' had been featured regularly in the headlines as stories were told and retold about it and about the four members of the jewellery trade arrested as having substituted lumps of sugar for the necklace as it travelled from Paris by registered mail. The colour of the drama only increased when a piano-back maker on his way to work picked up a matchbox wrapped in brown paper in St Paul's Road, Islington, and found it to contain the missing jewels. Then, while the courtroom drama of the trial was at its height, a Mrs Edward Brockledon Fielden of Condover Hall and Dobroyd Castle brought pearls to the fore again when her 77-pearl necklace, lost five years previously, turned up behind a heater in a Buxton hotel. Decidedly, pearls were news, and two weeks after this second incident Basil Hood's new show opened.

The Pearl Girl was a musical built unashamedly on the traditional model. Its principal elements were disguise, love and low comedy, but Hood had combined these three basic 'necessities' into a book of unusual coherence and logic. The fabulously wealthy Madame Alvarez has come to London for the season, bringing with her a fortune in pearls. Hearing of a plot to steal her jewels, she resolves to have a duplicate set made and she visits Messrs Palmyra Pearls to order them. Mr Jecks, the director of Palmyra, is overjoyed, for Mme Alvarez' pearls are sure to be the talking point of the season, but his jubilation is cut short when the lady decides suddenly to return to the Argentine in pursuit of a handsome naval officer and cancels her order. Leaving a large sum of money with the company's lady secretary to pay her bills, Mme Alvarez vanishes from the London scene. Then the secretary has a bright idea: no one in London has yet seen the millionairess so why should not she, Miranda Peploe, 'do the season' as Mme Alvarez, wearing the Palmyra pearls and gaining the firm priceless publicity? Supported by Mr Jecks (disguised as her Spanish uncle), Miranda Peploe/Alvarez is launched with great éclat upon London society and in society she finds true love in the form of the young Duke of Trent. Jecks, too, finds his fate in the arms of the wealthy if parvenue Mrs Baxter-Browne, and a third love affair, between Lady Betty Biddulph and the Duke's agent, Robert Jaffray, helps to fill out the play's latter scenes up to the inevitable dénouement.

There was plenty of incidental comedy as well: Alfred Lester, lugubrious and lovelorn, moping faithfully along behind Miranda like a shopworn Buttons; Lauri de Frece as the 'Spanish nobleman' and Ada Blanche as the vulgar nouveau riche contributed some lively moments; and the love affair of Lady Betty (Cicely Courtneidge) and Jaffray (Jack Hulbert, newly plucked from his Cambridge revue) was of the most light-hearted variety. But Iris Hoey and Harry Welchman as Miranda and Trent kept the central story well to the fore in what was, apart from a rather long lead-up to the dénouement, a particularly well-constructed libretto.

The show's first night was splendidly received in spite of a section in the gallery who had also booed *Oh! Oh! Delphine* and whose motives seemed to be not entirely artistic. The show's notices were as favourable as its reception:

> Mr Robert Courtneidge has scored a great and unqualified success. Not only does the play possess a coherent, interesting plot, neat dialogue and exceptionally pretty lyrics by Captain Basil Hood; tuneful, sparkling music by Messrs Hugo Felix and Howard Talbot; exquisite scenery by Messrs Conrad Tritschler and R. C. McCleery; it is also one of the most magnificently dressed plays that have been seen on the London stage . . *The Pearl Girl* is likely to win the enthusiastic applause of a huge audience for a long time to come . . (*Era*)

> Our thanks are due to Mr Courtneidge for demonstrating that even a musical comedy is improved by the semblance of a story . . . *The Pearl Girl* will certainly add to Mr Courtneidge's list of successes as a thoroughly enjoyable evening's entertainment . . (*Times*)

> *The Pearl Girl* is a good example of the best type of musical play. It has a pleasing sufficiency of plot, and its sentimental and comic interest is well up to the standard the public expects at theatres under the management of those who devote themselves especially to the lighter form of the theatrical art. (*Play Pictorial*)

The music of *The Pearl Girl* was the work of Howard Talbot and Hugo Felix, composer of *Les Merveilleuses* and the unfortunate *The Antelope*. The result was:

> . . much charming music, alternately in the old English style and humorous in the case of Mr Talbot and bright, piquant and sometimes whimsical and always cleverly scored as far as concerned [Mr Felix] . . (*Stage*)

but there was nothing in the show to equal Talbot's work in *The Arcadians*, the best numbers being an amusing song for Alfred Lester called 'Ow I loves Yer' (Talbot), a lively duo for Hulbert and Miss Courtneidge in which she declares:

> I sum up young men and their characters when
> I have seen what they do at the zoo

and he responds:

> I never alarm a llama
> The tiger at me never squirms
> And I seldom get cross with rhinoceros
> I am gentle with all pachyderms

and a comic song for Victor Tollemache as a gossip columnist:

> Then you see that a duchess is down
> With a common catarrhal affection
> She is ill with the 'flu, so, it happens, are you
> What an aristocratic connection

The newly popular tango was de rigueur and Felix duly obliged with a piece called 'Over There!' which got the whole company up performing the latest dance hit.

While the songs and dances of *The Pearl Girl* provided a highly satisfactory part of the entertainment, there were really no outstanding pieces to take away. What many of the audience would have dearly loved to take away were the costumes. Even in the lavish shows of George Edwardes there had rarely been clothes on the stage like the clothes for *The Pearl Girl*:

> It is no exaggeration to say that every costume is a creation worthy to stand alone under a big glass case in the showrooms of the famous dressmakers whose names appear on the programme. To view them en masse worn by the graceful, lovely girls of the Shaftesbury chorus is enough to take away the breath of the average woman . . (*Era*)

The green and sulphur hunting ensembles of the opening scene (Phillips & Son, 58 Regent St) were highlighted by the white piqué riding habit worn by Joan Hay – the heart of a costume hailed by *Play Pictorial* as 'a masterpiece'. The mannequins of the 'Maison Palmyra' dripped with pearls from the house of Tecla over dresses from Martial Armand & Cie (of Place Vendôme and 125 Bond St), while Marjorie Maxwell as the genuine Madame Alvarez featured a huge leopardskin muff and a crested hat in a black and white outfit from Maison Lewis of Regent Street. The outdoor scene at 'Hurlelagh' gave the cue for a perfect torrent of fashionable clothes: Cicely Courtneidge in white satin and gemstones; Iris Hoey in a lovely confection of white brocade and lace striped and tied in orange, a crossover skirt with an accordion-pleated tunic and sleeves, topped by black and white osprey feathers on a perky black hat and a huge string of pearls; Dorothea Temple in green satin and black lace ornamented with jet; and all the men in polo gear specially made by Turnbull and Asser of Jermyn Street. The costume credits ran on and on – Reville and Rossiter of Hanover Square, Davies, Jamieson & Wood of Maddox Street, Gamba for shoes, Clarkson for wigs, Salter and Sons of Aldershot for the polo sticks. *The Pearl Girl* was a many-handed triumph of dressing and design.

Its combination of a lively and sensible story, pretty music, superb design and a delightful cast which included so many of the new generation proved a sufficiently winning one to turn *The Pearl Girl* into a successful show. It remained at the Shaftesbury from September through to May of the following year, a run of 254 performances and it later toured most successfully with Iris Hoey, who had forsaken her role in London for 'personal reasons' and the part of the Queen of France in *The King's Wooing*, again starring as Miranda Peploe. Without becoming anything like a major hit, this pleasant and well-produced show proved itself a pretty, amiable attraction and altogether more to its producer's benefit than the oversplendid *Mousmé* or the imported *Oh! Oh! Delphine*.

Like *The Pearl Girl*, *The Girl from Utah*, which was staged at the Adelphi in succession to *The Dancing Mistress*, dealt with a popular subject. Mormons had become the latest butt of theatrical disapproval in succession to Puritans and Quakers and upper-class rakes, and a rash of Mormon plays had appeared under titles such as *At the Mercy of the Mormons*, a heavy drama which was doing fairly well in the provinces, or the less violent but equally dramatic *His Mormon Wife* or Her Life in Utah.

James Tanner built his book for the new Edwardes musical around the 'Girl from Utah', little Miss Una Trance, who is fleeing from her home and Mormonism after her father's decision to 'seal' her to a particularly gruesome inhabitant of Salt Lake City. In her flight, Una meets willing helpers: Lord Amersham (Alfred de Manby) and his fiancée Dora (Phyllis Dare), the actor Sandy Blair (Joseph Coyne), the odd little ham-and-beef shop man, Trimmit (Teddy Payne) and his intended, Clancy (Gracie Leigh) who is Dora's maid. Matters become melodramatic when the dreaded polygamist lures Una and half the chorus of the Folly Theatre to his dwelling in Brixton, whilst the police are on the wrong track chasing poor Trimmit who has accidentally picked up the Mormon's hat in a restaurant. But the amateur detectives are on the right scent, following a trail of blue confetti which Una has dropped in her wake. Finally Trimmit, disguised as a fireman, scrambles up the fire escape to effect the rescue and, with the action of the piece over, everyone repairs to the Arts Ball for the winding up of the love affairs and ten of the show's twenty-four numbers.

It was a libretto which, with its premature ending and its virtual variety show of a final scene, was not likely to appeal to the critics, but there were sufficient features in *The Girl from Utah* to counterbalance this and to please both them and the audiences enough to make the show a success. Firstly, there was the return to the stage and to George Edwardes' management of Teddy Payne who had left the Gaiety to become a producer on his own behalf. Tanner and Rubens (who had a credit for 'collaboration' on the dialogue) had given him a grand role with all the opportunities for impersonation and disguise which had characterised his best Gaiety roles and a genuine plot reason for going through the antics provided. Rubens also turned him out a jolly little song:

> If you come to Brixton there are lots of sights to see
> There's the Bon Marché and the Public Baths and then there's me,
> And all the way to Brixton the people flock in shoals
> To just get a peep at my little face among the sausage rolls.
> Stop at my little shop, if you're passing Brixton way
> There I am
> A-hacking at the ham
> And slicing at the beef all day,
> My pork pies
> Take a prize
> And my sausages are finer still;
> So mind you stop
> At my little shop
> At the bottom of Brixton Hill!

as well as a burlesque Russian dance, a lively song and dance piece called 'Out of It!' with Gracie Leigh, and a comical number 'We're Getting on very Well' with Phyllis Dare. Miss Dare and the ex-opera baritone de Manby had some nice material as well, in particular Miss Dare's pretty waltz ballad to one of Rubens' most attractive lyrics:

> Only to you, only for you,
> I gave a little kiss one day,
> You gave that little kiss away,
> She gave it to
> Some man I knew
> So I've got the little kiss again
> That I gave to you

Gracie Leigh, Irish this time, sang 'Nothin', nothin' at All' and was as comical as always, and Joe Coyne was dashing and charming and whimsical to such an extent that the *Era* largely declared 'he has never done anything better than his Sandy Blair', but the other triumph of the show came in the shape of the little ingénue Edwardes had imported from America. Ina Claire had played Prudence in *The Quaker Girl* on Broadway with great success; in *The Girl from Utah* she took London as well. The 19-year-old Miss Claire proved a real hit on all counts as she sang and danced her way through the piece's title role to the final curtain in the arms of Joe Coyne. 'Where do you think I've come from' she questioned as she entered upon Sidney Jones' charming title song, and when she ended:

Now I'm here in England, I would like to stay
I don't want to go back to Utah!

the house was in total agreement. She sang from her prison window:

I hear you calling me
In the street outside
What a pity the window
Doesn't open wide!
I hear you calling
Don't be crazy, dear
'Stead of standing there a-calling
Why don't you call right here?

joined with Coyne in Sidney Jones' Kissing Duet:

However clocks may chime
Surely the hour is plain
For it's half-past-Kissing Time
Time to kiss again!

and there was only one answer when she sang:

Would you follow me through Europe or through Asia
Would you follow me to Spain or Timbucktoo . .

The Girl from Utah seemed bound for success:

. . . calculated to outrival in almost every particular the sustained popularity of the many 'Girls' that have preceded it (*Stage*)

Yet another signal success to be scored to the credit of Mr George Edwardes and his versatile band of writers and musical composers (*Era*)

although *the Times* found it was:

. . not quite so entertaining as some of its predecessors . . somehow the production lacks that stamp of individuality which counts for so much . .

and objected to the fizzling-out of the plot in the latter stages.

It was successful, though not as much as such a 'Gaiety-type' musical, equipped with all the attributes and artists of that favourite theatre, might have been a few years earlier, but it still ran for 195 performances at the Adelphi which, if less than *The Dancing Mistress* and much less than *The Quaker Girl*, was distinctly superior to Edwardes' other Adelphi venture, *Autumn Manoeuvres*.

It may have been the subject of the piece and its obvious American associations which caused Charles Frohman to take *The Girl from Utah* for Broadway when he had ignored *The Dancing Mistress*, but he staged it at the Knickerbocker Theatre in August of the following year with Julia Sanderson starring as Una. As usual, the libretto had been 'improved' and the score peppered, this time heavily, with extraneous songs by Jerome Kern. But this time one of the changes made the difference. For although most of the interpolations were no better (nor sometimes even as good) as the original score, there was one song which was of the stuff that memories are made of. When Julia Sanderson stepped forward on that opening night in New York and sang:

And when I told them how wonderful you are
They didn't believe me, they didn't believe me . .

the botchings of a decade of Kern/Frohman British musicals could be forgiven in one wonderful song.

There is no doubt that 'They Didn't Believe Me' contributed to *The Girl from Utah*'s 120-performance run on Broadway, to its success around America and its eventual return to New York. More than that, it marked, as much as one song can, the coming-of-age of Jerome Kern and the real beginning of what he would mean to the budding American musical theatre. The success of *The Girl from Utah* on Broadway was as much America's success as it was Britain's: Edwardes, Tanner and Co had provided the springboard for the best of America's young talent.

There was a third British musical staged in 1913 but it did not come from the established purveyors of such affairs. Bolstered by the success of *Hullo, Ragtime!* and by his satisfactory organising of the short operettas such as *Arms and the Girl* and *The Eternal Waltz* for the Hippodrome, Albert de Courville announced that he would produce a musical comedy at the Prince of Wales. *Are You There?* was to be written by himself and his *Hullo, Ragtime!* collaborator Max Pemberton, and the music would be by Ruggiero Leoncavallo, the celebrated composer of *I Pagliacci* and, more recently, of the operetta *I Zingari* for de Courville at the Hippodrome.

The piece was widely paragraphed as de Courville set about gathering together the elements of his show. Shirley Kellogg (now Mrs de Courville) was billed to star, with the American comedian Billy Arlington imported to supply the humour. American dance director Ned Wayburn, the director and/or choreographer of more than forty Broadway musicals over a dozen years, was brought across to stage the show and it was given out that six and a half miles of wire and 3500 light bulbs would be employed to create the scene of the London Telephone Exchange where the first part of the piece's action was set.

Pemberton cried off, so de Courville proceeded to write the show's libretto alone, leaving the lyrical part to the successful young writer Edgar Wallace. Then Wayburn arrived and put the resulting piece into rehearsal, and the clashes began. The director had not worked in London before although he had directed *Havana* and *Peggy* on Broadway, and his idea of what should be expected of chorus girls was something new to the elegant young ladies engaged for *Are You There?*'s front line. The first shock came when Wayburn sacked several who could not do his dance steps. *The Era* reported:

> The rehearsals for *Are You There?*, the first night of which is fixed for October 30 at the Prince of Wales, have reached a stage where only those immediately concerned with the production will be allowed in the theatre. Mr Wayburn, the producer, has a method of teaching dancing which is peculiarly his own. Every movement is taught separately and one step has apparently no connection with the other until the moment comes for assembling them. Every step has a name of its own and Mr Ned Wayburn's repertoire includes some 600 of these. The secrets of mechanical effects must also be jealously guarded . .

Wayburn was given carte blanche with the show's production and for the first time a director's name appeared among the author's credits while the programme gave additional credit for

> All the 'effects' incidental to the performance, 'colour schemes', 'stage lighting', 'properties', 'groupings', 'evolutions', 'dances' etc. invented by Ned Wayburn.

But when the first night came, the efforts of Messrs de Courville, Wallace, Wayburn and Leoncavallo were quickly seen to amount to nothing but a total and utter failure:

. . it had apparently been thought that noise and colour might be mistaken for musical comedy if only the noise was sufficiently loud and the music sufficiently glaring . . (*Times*)

The end of the entertainment was marked by a noisy demonstration from the audience and de Courville strode angrily on to the stage to hurl at the protesters a mock apology 'if I have offended any blasé people who do not like to see something new'. At this the sounds of disapproval only increased as *Are You There?* sank justifiably into the slough of its own pretensions.

The papers did not spare any of it:

. . one leaves the house without any definite idea or clear conception as to what the play is all about. The music, except in one or two rare instances, is peculiarly lacking in distinction and the author would appear to have excercised his ingenuity rather in dodging a story than telling one. Never, surely, has such a formless, go-as-you-please production seen the light in these Islands and the pity of it all is that such an evidently vast amount of time and money has been spent with such unsatisfactory results. To put it bluntly *Are You There?* is over-produced. (*Stage*)

The lack of any quality indeed is so painfully evident that to have produced the piece at all can only be regarded as an expensive blunder. In the opening scene–a telephone exchange–that service is ineptly satirised. Mr Albert de Courville, the author of the book, labours hard to be funny when he writes an interlude where Mr Lawrence Grossmith has to clown in a telephone box with a telephone book the while Miss Shirley Kellogg as a 'Hullo Girl' is supposed to be reading from a novelette. One feels considerable pity for both actor and actress and commiseration may also be extended to Mr Billy Arlington who has come all the way from America to act a character endowed with fun of the forcible, feeble kind . . . . Miss Carmen Turia as a burlesque lady desperado of the Italian brand scores by sheer energy and her capital voice is heard to advantage. The one number that stands out in Leoncavallo's music is 'Roses Red and White' sung with unquestionable success by Miss Shirley Kellogg whose voice falls pleasantly on the ear until she forces it quite unreasonably. Miss Veronica Brady introduces a number, 'Not Now', not by Leoncavallo–but it is difficult to understand the reason why. Mr Alec Fraser who sings pleasantly must lose his self-consciousness before we can accept him as a stage lover. The staging of the second act with its central staircase has brilliancy and elegance but there is nothing original about it and it was scarcely necessary to seek the aid of an American stage-manager to produce it. (*Era*)

Are You There? was an awful mistake from beginning to end. De Courville had failed dismally both as a writer and a producer of musical comedy; Leoncavallo had failed to emulate the success, theatrical and financial, of Lehár, which he had supposed rather too easy; Wayburn had failed to grasp the different requirements of the British public and its light musical theatre; and none of the artists, imported or native, had come out of the affair with any credit.

De Courville and Wayburn consoled themselves with the revue *Hullo, Tango!* which replaced *Hullo, Ragtime!* at the Hippodrome. Back in a field which they understood, they scored another tidy success with a show which would keep London dancing for more than a year to come. Some of *Are You There?* resurfaced the following year as *Hullo, Everybody* at the Finsbury Park Empire. The music had been enlivened by some new numbers from G. H. Clutsam, the Australian composer of *A Summer Night*, and William Neale, and the 'new' telephone piece moved briefly into the natural habitat of its creator for one final fling.

The provincial year produced nothing except a follow up to *The Girl in the Picture* written for and by Miss Isa Bowman with music by William Neale. Entitled *Little Miss Ragtime*, it had members of a theatrical company posing as hotel guests to impress the wealthy Little Miss Ragtime from America and performing, on the way, as many up-to-date revue type numbers as could fairly be squeezed in. It toured in repertoire with *Florodora* and theatres were allowed to choose six nights of either or half a week of each. *Lucky Miss Chance*, produced at Pontefract in January, proved more mischance than lucky and folded after strenuous attempts to get bookings had achieved only a hesitant tour around Maidenhead, Worthing, Deal and Margate for a few nights apiece.

The supply of pieces to the provincial theatres had in no way decreased, but it was noticeable now that it was largely the touring companies of the successful West End hits which occupied the best dates to the exclusion of almost everything else. At the height of the 1913 season there were multiple companies of *The Arcadians*, *The Girl in the Taxi*, *The Girl on the Film*, *The Sunshine Girl*, *The Quaker Girl*, *A Waltz Dream*, and *Oh! Oh! Delphine* touring alongside *The Dancing Mistress*, *The Count of Luxembourg*, *The Girl in the Train*, *Princess Caprice* and such older pieces as *The Catch of the Season*, *La Poupée* and even *A Trip to Chinatown* and *The Lady Slavey* as well as such regulars as *Somebody's Sweetheart* and *Miss Lancashire Ltd*, sole survivors of the hardy provincial musicals of former years.

There was still plenty of room for the straight play and, if anything, dramatic companies seemed to be on the increase, but a new phenomenon had arisen which was moving into the theatres from the beaches and the pier – the concert party. Names like Andie Caine's Entertainers, the Busy Bees, Cantabs, Carltonians, Cigarettes, Corinthians, Excelsiors, Gaieties, Gay Cadets, Gay Bohemians, Gay Gondoliers, Gay Sparks, Gay Lieutenants, Gems, Lyrics, Mad Hatters, Vivandières, Mexicans, Merry Monarchs, Oysters, Phantoms, Nomads, Nobodies, West End Dandies, Whimsicals, Stingarees, Scarlet Pierrots, So and Sos, Somebodies, Vagabond Players, Poppies, Queer Quakers, Rangers and many, many others cropped up in theatrical dates – some near and some not so near the sea. They dealt in sub-revue material, with some of the better of them attempting to cover the same areas used by H. G. Pélissier's famous *Follies*, and they filled some of the space left by the provincial musical which seemed now to be a thing of the past.

1913

0380 **THE PEARL GIRL** a musical comedy in three acts by Basil Hood. Music by Howard Talbot and Hugo Felix. Produced at the Shaftesbury Theatre under the management of Robert Courtneidge 25 September, 1913 for a run of 254 performances closing 15 May, 1914.

Duke of Trent . . . . Harry Welchman/Robert MacLachlan
Robert Jaffray . . . . Jack Hulbert
Mr Jecks . . . . Lauri de Frece
Mr Muggeridge . . . . Edgar Stanmore
Mr Banbury . . . . Duncan Tovey
Mr Poulter . . . . Sebastian Smith
Mr Hopkins . . . . Harry Ray
Byles . . . . Alfred Lester
Lord George Matlock . . . . Reginald Sharland/Jack Lang
Captain Cunningham . . . . T. Bryce-Wilson
Mr Pringle . . . . H. V. Tollemache
James Ogilvie . . . . Rix Curtis
Higgins . . . . George Elton
Ernest . . . . Reginald Andrews
William . . . . Frank Haylett
Duchess of Trent . . . . Dorothea Temple
Lady Betty Biddulph . . . . Cicely Courtneidge
Lady Catherine Wheeler . . . . Sadrene Storri
Madame Alvarez . . . . Marjorie Maxwell
Miss Mabel Cheyne-Walker . . . . Joan Hay/Grace Wilson
Mrs Baxter-Browne . . . . Ada Blanche
Miss Beresford . . . . Violet Crompton
Miss Fitzroy . . . . Violet Blythe
Miranda Peploe . . . . Iris Hoey/Fay Compton/Marie Blanche

Dir: Robert Courtneidge; md: Arthur Wood; ch: Willie Warde & Espinosa; sc: R. C. McCleery and Conrad Tritschler; cos: Reville & Rossiter, Davies, Jamieson & Wood, Phillips & Son, Herbert Norris, Morris Angel &c.

0381 **THE GIRL FROM UTAH** a musical play in two acts by James T. Tanner. Dialogue in collaboration with Paul Rubens. Lyrics by Adrian Ross, Percy Greenbank and Paul Rubens. Music by Paul Rubens and Sidney Jones. Produced at the Adelphi Theatre under the management of George Edwardes 18 October, 1913 for a run of 195 performances closing 9 May, 1914.

Lord Amersham . . . . Alfred de Manby
Policeman PR38 . . . . George Cooper/Albert Sims/H. B. Davey
Colonel Oldham-Pryce . . . . Douglas Marrs
Page . . . . Michael Matthews
Commissionaire . . . . David Hallam/Hallam Bentley
Detective Shooter . . . . F. W. Russell
Lord Orpington . . . . Harold Latham

Archie Tooth . . . . William Bainbridge
Douglas Noel . . . . Harry R. Drummond
Bobbie Longshot . . . . Sidney Laine
Sandy Blair . . . . Joseph Coyne
Trimmit. . . . . Edmund Payne (Victor Gouriet)/Horace Mills
Una Trance . . . . Ina Claire
Clancy. Gracie Leigh
Lady Amersham . . . . Bella Graves
Miss Mona West . . . . Heather Featherstone
Miss Sylvia Paget. . . . . Gertrude White
Miss Lydia Savile. . . . . Dorothy Devere
Miss Alma Cavendish. . . . . Kitty Kent
Miss Violet Vesey. . . . . Isobel Elsom/Rosie Campbell
Miss Rosie Jocelyn . . . . Queenie Vincent
Waitress . . . . Gladys Kurton
Lady Muriel Chepstowe . . . . Cynthia Murray
Hon Miss St Aubyn . . . . Valerie Richards
Lady Mary Nowell . . . . Helen Rae
Mrs Ponsonby. . . . . Beatrice Guiver
Dora Manners. . . . . Phyllis Dare
Lady Diana Trelawny . . . . Claire Lynch/Peggy Nadine

Dir: J. A. E. Malone; md: Carl Kiefert; ch: Willie Warde and Will Bishop; sc: Alfred Terraine, Ryan, Hawes Craven and Joseph Harker

Produced at the Knickerbocker Theatre, New York, under the management of Charles Frohman 24 August, 1914 for a run of 120 performances. Additional numbers by Jerome Kern. Alfred de Manby (LORD), Frank Markham (PC), George Grundy (COL), Robert Slattery (PAGE), William Francis Jr (COMM), Walter Gilbert (SHOOT), George Wharton (ORP), Frank Snyder (TOOTH), William Hobart (NOEL), Winship Fink (BOB), Donald Brian (SANDY), Joseph Cawthorn (TRIMPEL), Julia Sanderson (UNA), Renee Reel (CLANCY), Queenie Vassar (LADY), Clara Eckstrom (MONA), Mabel Gibson (SY), Dorothy Dumont (LY), Helen Allen (ALMA), Dolly Wilmot (VI), Gene Cole (RO), Anita McCloskey (MU), Mabel Landers (StA), Pauline Hendrix (MARY), Lillian Clifford (PONS), Eleanor Henry (DORA), Katherine Murray (FLAPPER) with Louise Worthington, Edith Barr, Paula Langdon, Beth Belle, Belle Irving, Nettie Hamilton, Marie Francis, Louise Ward, Leona Francis, Edward C. Yeager, William W. Fink, Lester Ostrander, A. Von Bereghy, Frank Ratcliffe, Charles Naldrett, William Coan. Dir: James Darling; md: Theodore Stearns; cos: Schneider-Anderson Co, Dazian, Bendel

0382 **ARE YOU THERE?** a musical play by Albert de Courville. Lyrics by Edgar Wallace. Music by Ruggiero Leoncavallo. Produced at the Prince of Wales Theatre under the management of Albert de Courville 1 November, 1913 for a run of 23 performances closing 23 November, 1913.

Percy Pellett. . . . . Lawrence Grossmith
Gordon Grey . . . . Alec Fraser
Antonio . . . . Eric Roper
Bertie Carlton . . . . Lawford Davidson
Commissionaire . . . . Alec Johnstone
Viscount Guineas . . . . Francis E. Vane
Carlo . . . . William Thomas
Casino customer. . . . . Harold Treadway
Another customer . . . . Ronald Graham
Gregory Lester . . . . Billy Arlington
Miss Bing . . . . Veronica Brady
Mafalda Malatesta . . . . Carmen Turia
Maud Waring . . . . Dorothy Fane
Winifred Miller . . . . Madge Melbourne
Miss Norah Hammersmith . . . . Winifred West
Miss Gladys Kensington . . . . Marjorie Dunbar
Miss London Wall . . . . Helen Beltramo

Miss Gerrard . . . . Violet Leicester
Miss Mayfair . . . . Olive Horner
Miss Wimbledon . . . . Sophie Fox
Miss Hopp . . . . Cissie Moore
Loafer . . . . Arthur Bourne
Keepers . . . . Ernest Shannon and Harry Dench
Mr Record . . . . Lawford Davidson
Mr Nott-Wright . . . . Eric Roper
Grand Vizier . . . . Alec Johnstone
Sylvia Lester . . . . Shirley Kellogg

with Dorothy O'Neil, Winifred Izard, Irene Millard, Marcia Willard, Marjorie Dunbar, Mirabel Hillier, Winifred West, Frances Finlay, Evie Hampton, Poppy Clifford, Pat Bevan, Edith Fraser, Marguerite Edgeley, Esme Manette, Violette Leicester, Poppy McNally, Gypsy Gordon, Nora Browne, Olive Horner, Flora Hayden, May Dodson, Amy Broadwood, Marie Burnand, Lola Campbell, Sophie Fox, Cissie Moore, Audrey Thorpe, Helen Beltramo, Zara Castille, Marie Leonard, Hettie Bullen, Cynthia Holland, Doris Woodger, Victor Wright, Jack Killick, Charles Tudhall, Malcolm Mortimer, Stanley Dalton, Gerald George, Walter Heal, Frederick Hawkins, Herbert Fenwick, John Boys, Ernest Shannon.

Dir/ch: Ned Wayburn; md: Julian Jones; sc: Alfred Terraine and E. H. Ryan; cos: Callcott Soeurs, Margaine Lacroix, Zimmerman, Michard Soeurs, Hubert Fenn, Maison Landolff, Pope & Bradley, Morris Angel, Lucile Ltd &c.

0383 **LITTLE MISS RAGTIME** a musical comedy in two acts by Isa Bowman. Music by William Neale. Produced at the Theatre Royal, Harrogate, under the management of Isa Bowman 24 July, 1913 and toured in repertoire with *Florodora*.

Teddy Walkover . . . . Alf Passmore
George Mashwell . . . . Frank Green
Harry Weston . . . . Frank Barclay
K. Ragtime . . . . Joseph R. Tate/George Fairhurst
J. Jacoby . . . . Ernest Foster/W. Nixon
François . . . . George Russell
George Wise . . . . Claude Farrow
Fred Knowal . . . . Percy Pope
Ernest Cleaver . . . . H. Rinaldo
Betty Barlow . . . . Dulcie Delmar/May Warden
Connie Gardiner . . . . Dora McCaskey/Mora Greaves
Miss Swankfirst . . . . Essie Compton
Bridget Magee . . . . Kitty Kirwan
Peggy . . . . Lillie Ellis/Irene Warden
Lallie . . . . Nellie McCaskey
Suzette . . . . Marie Jermaine
Marjie . . . . Winnie New
Mrs Drummedout . . . . Mollie Cuthbert
Mary Johnson . . . . May Warden/Lillie Ellis
Lady Pat . . . . May Compton
Hon. Miss Porter . . . . R. T. Mack
Miss Hathaway . . . . M. Richardson
Little Miss Ragtime . . . . Isa Bowman/Claire St Claire
add John Willie Binns . . . . Fred Rayne
Pauline Vardon . . . . Isa Bowman

Md: William Neale

LUCKY MISS CHANCE a musical play in three acts by W. T. Ivory and Kenneth Morrison. Produced at the Alexandra Theatre, Pontefract, under the management of Ivory & Morrison 13 January, 1913 and toured.

Professor Tootle . . . . Gus Danby
Dickie Avery . . . . Frank Lester
Captain Filibert . . . . Dudley Middleton

Basil Strong . . . . Charles Shepley
Rhino Burns . . . . Victor V. Norreys
Pimple. . . . . Edmund Richardson
Old Moore . . . . Freean Rode
Stella Fleece. . . . . Amy Abercrombie
Winnie Wynsom . . . . Phyllis Spalding
Marion Bright. . . . . Maudie Sheila
Virginia Creeper . . . . Minnie Best
Honey Suckle . . . . Cissie Best
Rosie Budd . . . . Madge Best
Lily White . . . . Clara Best
Delia Chance . . . . Geraldine Verner

Md: Raymunde Lancaster; sc: W. B. Robertson

1914

The early weeks of 1914 saw the musical theatre in London bubbling along nicely, in spite of the proliferating revues which crowded into every West End and suburban music hall and attracted the public in numbers which the halls had not seen in years.

The Girl from Utah at the Adelphi and *The Pearl Girl* at the Shaftesbury were established as successful musicals from the British stable, while *The Marriage Market* was proving itself one of the most attractive of the continental imports of recent years at Daly's. The Gaiety was dark, as *The Girl on the Film* had closed down before Christmas to be transferred with its English cast to Broadway, but a new Paul Rubens musical was in preparation to open in February and George Edwardes, in spite of ill health, was busily buying up the rights to new continental pieces with which to stock the Gaiety, Daly's and the Adelphi which, rumour had it, were about to be brought together into one large entertainment company under Edwardes' name.

Jean Gilbert seemed to be the most popular composer of the moment amongst managers. Edwardes laid out £1,000 in advance for the rights of his *Püppchen*, something less for *The Tango Princess* and also approached him for a new piece to be specially written for London. Robert Courtneidge announced a London production of *Die Kino-Königin (The Cinema Star)*; *Autoliebchen* was in preparation at the New Theatre for Durrant Swan under the title of *The Joy-Ride Lady*; and Michael Faraday had booked *Mademoiselle Tralala* for the Lyric where *The Girl in the Taxi* had made Gilbert's English reputation.

While other managers stuck to the 'safety' of the prolific and popular Gilbert, Edwardes, typically, also looked further afield. He secured the rights of Emmerich Kálmán's *Der Ziegeunerprimas*, (a New York hit under the title *Sari*) with the Adelphi in mind, together with several other less obvious continental pieces and also, unlike his competitors, retained his faith in British writers. Paul Rubens, George Grossmith, Percy Greenbank and Co. all figured in his plans for the three major theatres under his control. 1914 showed promise of being a busy and interesting year in the musical theatre, if biased towards continental shows. As it turned out, it was nothing of the sort. When the declaration of war intervened in August, throwing theatrical plans into a turmoil along with everything else in the civilised world, the musical theatre in London was already at one of its lowest periods in memory. Five of the year's six new pieces had already closed in failure, including the sole British piece, *After the Girl*, which J. A. E. Malone had produced 'for George Edwardes' at the Gaiety.

It was done 'for' Edwardes because 'The Guv'nor' had been too unwell to take the production in hand himself. Illness, convalescence and trips to healthy places at home and abroad to try to recoup his strength meant that Edwardes had little time or energy to devote to the physical production of the new Gaiety show. George Grossmith, one of

Edwardes' most trusted helpers, was away in America with *The Girl on the Film* and had, in any case, managerial thoughts of his own, and so the whole burden of the production of *After the Girl* fell on Malone, now a member of the Gaiety Board of Directors as well as Edwardes' confidant and the stager of all the theatre's shows. He, in turn, left the writing of the show almost entirely to Paul Rubens who had done well for the theatre with *The Sunshine Girl*, and devoted himself to assembling a cast of new faces to replace the usual favourites deployed either in different theatres or on the American trip.

The result was what Rubens called, with an eye to the latest style, 'a revusical comedy', a show in six scenes (set in five picturesque European cities and a Custom House) with a plot of minimal proportions which allowed for the most colourful songs and costumes possible. *The Times* remarked:

> The effect of revue upon musical comedy was bound to be felt sooner or later. The general trend of musical comedy was towards looser technique, the provision of a greater amount of variety with less and less of plot. (We are not referring of course to Mr Edwardes' productions of comic opera, but to musical comedies only). Then came revue which merely did not trouble about plot at all and has lately all but dispensed even with the compère and commère. Revue in fact did what musical comedy had never dared do; and musical comedy, seeing itself confronted by its own logical conclusion was bound either to pull the strings of its technique tighter or let them dangle still looser. Mr George Edwardes has chosen, for this once at any rate, to let them slip a little more, and when Mr Paul Rubens calls his new piece a revusical comedy he tells the truth . . .

The plot which set the evening's entertainment in action concerned Cincinnati heiress Miss Doris Pitt, her family and a young man. While coming from Brussels to meet her parents in Paris, Doris meets a young man on Amiens station. The young man is good enough to find her lost suitcase and Doris asks him to lunch with her parents. But Papa is livid at the thought of a young man after his daughter, sends Freddie packing and decides that another term of school will be necessary to teach Doris discretion. Doris has no intention of going back to school and heads instead for Amsterdam with her family and, eventually, a whole lot of other people in pursuit. Amsterdam is succeeded by Buda-Pesth and then by Berlin where Doris ends up working as a cabaret singer before all is finally resolved in the ballroom of the Carlton Hotel, London.

The settings gave the designers all the opportunities that could be desired. Ryan, Craven, Terraine and the Harkers all had a hand in creating the splendid scenes for the show; there were reams of glorious costumes from the now famous Lucile of Hanover Square, the Michard Soeurs, B. J. Simmons of Covent Garden and so forth; and Malone's impeccable direction ensured that everything looked as good as was humanly possible. Rubens had done a perfectly adequate job with both the framework and the 'items' with which the evening was enlivened, and the first night response from all concerned was satisfying:

> A new musical play conceived in a new manner with a wealth of dainty costumes, a tastefully blended colour scheme, pointed dialogue and neat lyrics and merry and lilting harmonies – all these eminently desirable qualities go to ensure the emphatic success of *After the Girl* . . (*Stage*)
>
> The piece contains all that goes to make up a successful musical play – bright, catchy music, the most up-to-date and beautiful costumes worn by the prettiest women that the stage can show us . . . the mounting and dressing of the

> piece were artistic and lavish . . . Mr Paul Rubens has composed some remarkable, happy, inspired melodies and the lyrics are neatly written (*Era*)
>
> Mr Rubens wanted to romp without restriction and he romps through five towns and a Custom house in chase of a madcap girl who does not want to go back to school. On the whole he romps very jollily . . . the piece gets several of its characters into plenty of ridiculous situations, it is full of those very light familiar catchy 'jingles' which Mr Rubens . . turns out so quickly and merrily [and] there are many spirited and ingenious dances . . (*Times*)

The happiest of his songs was a graceful duet for Doris and her Freddie called 'Waiting for the Moon to Shine':

> No-one must guess that we are really friendly, that would never do
> Well, I'll pretend I'm a perfect stranger when I meet with you
> If there are people there then I'll simply cut you dead
> I'll give a vacant stare then and turn away my head.
> If someone meets us with our noses in the air
> And someone asks us what on earth we're doing there
> We'll say politely 'As the afternoon's so fine
> We're simply waitin', waitin' for the moon to shine . . .

There was an attractive ballad for Freddie called 'Wonderful Eyes' and a tuneful if lyrically unoriginal piece for Doris called 'Keep on Walking'. One step-out chorus girl sang how 'You Can Do Anything you Like if you Have Money', another contributed a 'Lovely Budapest' piece and a third sang about 'The Danube'. The low comic (in a show where, by Gaiety standards, there was little low comedy) sang about 'Amsterd 'Eath and Amsterdam':

> Amsterd 'Eath to Amsterdam
> Is a nice long way
> Yet both of these
> Are quite 'the cheese'
> As the cockneys say . .

with some success.

After the Girl was by no means the best show the Gaiety had produced but it was a fair enough piece which ought to have had some degree of success had it not had to compete with genuine revue in the halls. It also lacked popular Gaiety names in its cast list. It had been difficult enough to persuade Gaiety audiences to accept the break-up of the Gertie Millar-Connie Ediss-Edmund Payne team even in favour of such accepted stars as Phyllis Dare. To persuade them to come to 'their' theatre for an entertainment which was not in the habitual mould performed by a cast lacking all their favourites was a task which even Edwardes would have found difficult. Malone and his associates were the ones who had to try.

It was not that the cast was bad. Isobel Elsom in her first lead role as Doris was perfectly charming; Mabel Sealby in the comical maid part confirmed her *Sunshine Girl* success; Bonita and Lew Hearn, lifted from revue, were joined by two other talented Americans, Clifton Crawford – a more vocally endowed version of Joe Coyne – as Freddie and Muriel Hudson, with the oversized Mlle Caumont doing her best in the shadow of Connie Ediss to take the low comedy prize. But they were not Gaiety and, strange as it may sound, that mattered.

After the Girl never took off. In an attempt to bolster the humour of the piece Willie Stephens, who had been given the 'Teddy Payne part' after having previously understudied the star comic, was dismissed and music hall comedian Will Evans was brought in at considerable expense to take over. Malone even went to the extent of offering £250 per week to George Graves to get him into the part but Graves was not interested. He was right, for *After the Girl* lasted only three and a half months and the Gaiety had to record a genuine flop. It was quickly followed by the first of the Jean Gilbert pieces as *The Joy-Ride Lady* went under after an identical run of 105 performances and then *Mademoiselle Tralala* which ran them a sad triple dead-heat.

To fill the Gaiety, Malone brought in a ready-made replacement; a completely imported company with the entire production of *Adèle* from New York's Longacre Theatre where it had had a successful run of nearly 200 performances. *Adèle*, a charming French piece with a score by Jean Briquet, was decidedly less attractive in its American incarnation and proved anathema to London and most particularly to the Gaiety. It lasted not even three weeks and the theatre was closed to await better times, a new show and, hopefully, the recovery and return of George Edwardes.

A week after the opening of *Adèle* another American company hit town with a most unlikely offering. Sam Bernard had made a huge success with the character of 'Piggy' Hoggenheimer in *The Girl from Kays* in America. Following his original triumph in the Broadway version of the London show he had had *The Rich Mr Hoggenheimer* written to allow him to appear again as the same character and, in March of 1914, he appeared in a new revamping of *The Girl from Kays* at New York's Shubert Theatre. This time the piece was called *The Belle of Bond Street*. Owen Hall got no mention on the programme. Lyricist Harold Atteridge took a book credit and Monckton and Caryll's score was unrecognisably filled out with American ditties including the famous 'Who Paid the Rent for Mrs Rip van Winkle (when Rip van Winkle was away)'.

The raison d'être of the exercise was Bernard who took over the stage completely to give London his version of the role made so famous twelve years previously by Willie Edouin. He did not succeed. Most of the public and critics admitted that he was clever and funny, but the show was not going to succeed. Some, like *The Times*, regarded it as bad but no worse than *The Girl from Kays* (which was grossly unfair), others took the opposite attitude:

> Twelve-year-old memories of *The Girl from Kays* are of a gay and bright entertainment with a certain sense of form and an artistic handling in which Mr Owen Hall's audacious wit was no less apparent than Mr George Edwardes' tasteful and brilliant producing art. *The Belle of Bond Street* is a collection of inconsequent and noisy humours – a crude medley of which ragtime songs and dances, gags, show lady exhibitions overdressed and underdressed and American 'stunts' in general are the chief ingredients. (*Stage*)

Alongside Bernard, Ina Claire did impersonations of such folk as Ethel Levey and Harry Lauder and sang a pretty coon song ('Oh, you Moon'), and Mabel Sealby did her best with the remnants of the role Kate Cutler had once played so charmingly, for the forty nights which *The Belle of Bond Street* managed to last before folding its tents and departing.

So, by the end of July *After the Girl*, *The Joy-Ride Lady*, *Mademoiselle Tralala*, *Adèle* and *The Belle of Bond Street* had been and gone, and August was seen in only by a revival of *The Belle of New York* at the Lyceum and Robert Courtneidge's production of *The Cinema Star* (*Kino-Königin*) which showed signs of doing rather better than Gilbert's other pieces. Daly's, the Gaiety and the Adelphi all awaited new shows and George Edwardes languished in the Palace Hotel at Bad Nauheim. There was a rumour of a Grossmith production called *The Bing Boys are Here* for the Gaiety, then of another called *Tonight's the Night*. Rubens was at work on a new libretto to be set by 'a German composer'. Then war was declared, 'The Guv'nor' was still in Germany, and his theatrical plans were in ruin. Everything Germanic was anathema. Jean Gilbert was German and *Püppchen* and *The Tango Princess* could no longer be considered. The commissions given to German composers were off. Kálmán's *Sari* was off. Courtneidge removed *The Cinema Star* which was showing signs of becoming a real success and sent it on the road where the thought of boycotting German-written music had not yet taken hold.

Revivals of older pieces were hurriedly staged to fill the gaps. *The Chocolate Soldier* did not take on, but *A Country Girl* at Daly's proved an excellent choice and *The Earl and the Girl* was successful enough at the Aldwych to warrant a transfer to the Lyric when its first home was needed for pantomine. *Miss Hook of Holland* played a season at its original home at the Prince of Wales, and producers started to pull themselves together. Paul Rubens went to work on his own book for the new Edwardes show and provided in addition the music which was to have been foreign. He did it with such speed that the show was ready early enough to be opened out of town while *The Country Girl* revival ran to the end of its course.

Betty opened at the Prince's, Manchester, on Christmas Eve 1914 and was received with enormous approval. Britain was not going to see a proper new Viennese or German musical for a good while. It needed genuine successes of its own and *Betty*, from the same theatre where *The Sultan of Mocha* had grown up nearly half a century previously, sent out a strong ray of hope for the theatrical future.

It would be a future in a very different world – a Britain where the standards and values which had seen the country triumphantly through the greatest period of its history would be questioned and gradually eroded, where the form of civilisation which had been the basis of so many great institutions of daily life would be broken down and made into something else. Such relatively unimportant things as the light musical theatrical entertainment would, as such things do, change with it. It would be a world without George Edwardes who had only months to live, and without his kind of entertainment; without Charles Frohman, drowned in May 1915 on the *Lusitania*, Teddy Payne, already gone in July of 1914, or William Hamilton Codrington Nation, the wonderful dilettante. The light musical theatre in Britain had reached a watershed. Four years of a war like no one had ever known could bring anything and only one thing was certain – that 'anything' would assuredly be something different.

1914

0384 **AFTER THE GIRL** a revusical comedy in two acts and six scenes by Paul Rubens. Lyrics by Percy Greenbank and Paul Rubens. Music by Paul Rubens. Produced at the Gaiety Theatre under the management of George Edwardes 7 February, 1914. A second edition staged 25 April, 1914. Closed 22 May, 1914 after a run of 105 performances.

Mr Pitt . . . . Lew Hearn/Shaun Glenville
Mr Clayton . . . . Frederick Volpe
Bill Dabsley . . . . Willie Stephens/Will Evans
Count Cleves . . . . Guy Le Feuvre
Hon. Eddie Stone . . . . W. Cecil
Maurice . . . . Austin Camp
Customs Officers . . . . H. Jones, J. Redmond, M. Raven
Gendarmes . . . . Joseph Grande, Fred Raynham
House decorators . . . . Albert Gater, J. Delaney
Captain Valda . . . . George Grundy
Marton . . . . M. Ewart
Franz . . . . R. Richards
M. Hammermeyer . . . . W. Levaux
Hans Schmidt . . . . S. Penton
Freddy Charlston . . . . Clifford Crawford
Doris . . . . Isobel Elsom/Emmy Wehlen
Emma . . . . Mabel Sealby
Mrs Pitt . . . . Mlle Caumont
Bijou . . . . Bonita
Fay . . . . Muriel Hudson/Gwendoline Brogden
Betty . . . . Maggie Jarvis
Julita . . . . Margaret Paul
Ninette . . . . Ethel Lawson
Miss Hoyt . . . . F. Hadley
Thekla . . . . Joan Penrose
Martha . . . . M. Tomlins
Gaga . . . . David Rose
Googoo . . . . Minnie Kioski
Norah . . . . Dot Temple
Aranka . . . . E. Mackay
Paula . . . . Barbara Dunbar
Margit . . . . Florence Reade

Dir: J. A. E. Malone; md: Gustav Wanda; ch: Willie Warde and Will Bishop; sc: T. E. Ryan, Alfred Craven, Alfred Terraine, Joseph & Phil Harker; cos: Comelli, Lucile Ltd, Doeuillet Ltd &c.

0385 **MISS LAMB OF CANTERBURY** a musical comedy in three acts by T. C. Mac and Henry L. Osmond. Lyrics by Sylvester Stuart. Produced at Woolwich under the management of Henry L. Osmond 25 May, 1914 and toured.

Major Blarney O'Neale . . . . Henry L. Osmond

George Goodman . . . . Sylvester Stuart
Jeremiah Stoney. . . . . Percy Foreman
Ezekiah Stoney . . . . W. Ridley
Thomas Twickenham. . . . . Tom Solly
Mr Groaner . . . . Harry Brace
Mr Outosight . . . . Albert Allmark
Mr Fly . . . . Leslie Haslam
Hilda Marston . . . . Dorothy Barron
Miss Eureka Gamoney . . . . Vera Vivian
Grace Gampney. . . . . Hilda Playfair
Clara O'Neale . . . . Ethel Clyde

Md: T. C. Parsons

270a **THE BELLE OF BOND STREET** a musical play in three acts, a revised version of *The Girl from Kays*. Originally produced at the Shubert Theatre, New York, 30 March, 1914. Produced at the Adelphi Theatre 8 June, 1914 for a run of 40 performances closing 17 July, 1914.

Max Hoggenheimer. . . . . Sam Bernard
Harry Gordon. . . . . Martin Brown
Hon. Percy Fitzthistle . . . . Percy Ames
Theodore Quench, Q.C. . . . . Jere McAuliffe
Mr Chalmers . . . . Walter Leveaux
Joseph. . . . . Grafton Williams
Jack Richley. . . . . Sammy Lee
James . . . . Douglas Marrs
Pepper. . . . . Leslie Dawson
Nora Chalmers . . . . Mabel Sealby
Ellen. . . . . Ruby Norton
Mrs Chalmers. . . . . Rita Presano
Miss Slender . . . . Carol Orr
Winnie Harborough. . . . . Ina Claire

Dir: Julian Alfred; md: Gustav Wanda; cos: Lucile, Zyrot & Cie.

Appendix I: Printed music

This list has been compiled from the author's collection and the catalogues of the British Library, London, the Library of Congress, Washington, and the performing Arts Research Center of New York Public Library at Lincoln Center. It includes vocal scores, where printed, and in other cases those single numbers known to exist in print. Vocal scores, particularly in the 1890s and 1900s, went through many editions in which the changing contents of the shows were reflected in long appendices and, in consequence, they vary considerably. Foreign editions are listed only where no British publication is known.

Windsor Castle	Vocal score (Metzler)
The Contrabandista	Vocal score (Boosey)
The Chieftain	Vocal score (Boosey)
Aladdin II	Vocal score (Metzler)
Cinderella the Younger	French language vocal score under the title *Javotte* (E. & A. Girod)
Thespis	Cousin Robin (Little Maid of Arcadee) (Cramer)
Babil and Bijou	Faces in the Fire/To Her who Owns my Heart's Devotion/River of Life March/Spring, gentle Spring/Pages' Chorus/Of Lovers We have Heard/ Gondola Song (Hawkes)
The Black Crook	Nobody Knows as I Know/Where can my little Brother Be (Enoch), The Love Birds Kiss (Klein)
Whittington	Vocal score (Cramer)
Cattarina	Chorus of Ministers/It Is so like the Men/There Is Hope within our Breast (Boosey)
The Sultan of Mocha	Vocal score (Enoch)
Tower of London	Brown October/Who would not Be a Soldier/ I Told my Love (Enoch)
Pom	'Twixt their mossy Banks/Ah! when I Remember (J. Williams)
Princess Toto	Vocal score (Metzler)
Don Quixote	Vocal score (Duff & Stewart)
Nell Gwynne	If I Were but the Morning Light/The broken Tryst/Her Heart/Oh Cupid Is a Madcap/Well I Know my Love Loves Me (Metzler)
The Lying Dutchman	'All the music' (Charles Sheard)
The Sorcerer	Vocal score (Metzler)
H.M.S. Pinafore	Vocal score (Metzler)
The Lancashire Witches	Vocal score (Forsyth Bros)
Celia	Earlier version published as *Sylvia* (q.v.) (Metzler)
The Pirates of Penzance	Vocal score (Chappell)

Billee Taylor	Vocal score (J. Williams)
Patience	Vocal score (Chappell)
Claud Duval	Vocal score (J. Williams)
Lord Bateman	Vocal score (J. Williams)
Les Manteaux Noirs	Vocal score (Cramer)
The Vicar of Bray	Vocal score (J. Williams)
The Captain of the Guard	Libretto published by J. Williams
Rip Van Winkle	Vocal score (Chappell)
Melita	Vocal score (W. D. Cubitt)
Iolanthe	Vocal score (Chappell)
Cymbia	Vocal score (J. Williams)
The Merry Duchess	Love's Memories/Love's Messenger/The Captive Bird (Chappell). A vocal score is said to have been published in America.
Estrella	Vocal score (W. A. Pond & Co., USA)
Virginia and Paul	Vocal score (Chappell)
Princess Ida	Vocal score (Chappell)
Nell Gwynne	Vocal score (Metzler)
Dick	Vocal score (Ch. Jefferys)
Polly	Vocal score (Ascherberg)
The Mikado	Vocal score (Chappell)
Erminie	Vocal score (J. Williams)
The Vicar of Wide-Awake-Field	Vocal score (J. Williams)
Little Jack Sheppard	Vocal selection (J. Williams)
The Lily of Léoville	Vocal score (Ch. Jefferys)
The Palace of Pearl	The Gipsy/A Babe was I/The Minstrel's Song/Oh, Bird of Love (J. Williams)
Glamour	Vocal score (Wm. Marshall)
Dorothy	Vocal score (Chappell)
Rhoda	Vocal score (Cramer)
Indiana	Vocal score (Boosey); The plain Potato (Boosey)
Alice in Wonderland	Vocal score (Ascherberg, Hopwood & Crew)
Monte Cristo Jr	Piano score/Ballyhooley/I'm a Jolly little Chap all Round/Je Suis un grand Detective (Ch. Jefferys)
Ruddigore	Vocal score (Chappell)
Mynheer Jan	Vocal score (J. Williams)
Miss Esmeralda	Vocal score (Ascherberg)
Gipsy Gabriel	Vocal score (J. Williams)
Frankenstein	Vocal score (Ascherberg)
The Punch Bowl	Vocal score (Agate)
Carina	Vocal score (Enoch)
The Yeomen of the Guard	Vocal score (Chappell)
Faust up-to-Date	Vocal score; He Knew It/Suit the Action to the Words/I Was there as Well/McCarthy's Widow (Ascherberg); Another/Enniscorthy (Hopwood & Crew)
Doris	Vocal score (Chappell)
Lancelot the Lovely	Merlin the Prophet/The Man with the mashing Eye/Excalibur/If Briton to Briton be True/Who's that a-calling (Ch. Jefferys)
Mignonette	Vocal score (Cramer)
Ruy Blas and the Blasé Roué	Vocal score; Don't Know/In Dreamland/The Crossing Sweeper's Love (Ascherberg)
La Prima Donna	Vocal score (Ch. Jefferys)
The New Corsican Brothers	Vocal score (Cramer)
The Red Hussar	Vocal score (Metzler)
The Gondoliers	Vocal score (Chappell)
Paola	Vocal selection (W. A. Pond, USA)
Tra-La-La Tosca	Vocal score (J. Williams)

Marjorie	Vocal score (Hopwood & Crew)
Captain Thérèse	Vocal score (Hopwood & Crew)
Carmen up-to-Data	Vocal score; How to Mesmerise 'Em/One who Is Life to Me/Told by the Cards (Ascherberg)
The Rose and the Ring	Vocal score (Ascherberg)
Joan of Arc	Vocal score; Jack the Dandy-oh! (Ascherberg)
The Nautch Girl	Vocal score (Chappell)
Cinder-Ellen up too Late	Vocal score (Ascherberg)
The Mountebanks	Vocal score (Chappell)
Blue-Eyed Susan	Vocal score (Ascherberg)
Haste to the Wedding	Vocal score (Chappell)
Cigarette	Vocal score (Leonard/Rbt. Cocks)
Haddon Hall	Vocal score (Chappell)
In Town	Vocal score (J. Williams)
La Rosière	Some music published by Alfred Hays and Ascherberg
The Magic Opal	Vocal score (J. Williams)
The Golden Web	Vocal score (Chappell)
Morocco Bound	Vocal score (J. Williams)
Jane Annie	Vocal score (Chappell)
A Modern Don Quixote	After the Ball Parody (Francis, Day & Hunter)
The Lady Slavey	Vocal score (Chappell)
Utopia (Limited)	Vocal score (Chappell)
Little Christopher Columbus	Vocal score (Hopwood & Crew)
A Gaiety Girl	Vocal score (Hopwood & Crew)
Miami	Vocal score advertised by Ascherberg
Don Juan	Vocal score (Ascherberg)
Go-Bang	Vocal score (J. Williams)
King Kodak	Vocal score (Hopwood & Crew)
The Gay Parisienne	Vocal score (Chappell)
The Queen of Brilliants	Excerpts from the Vienna score published by J. Weinberger (Vienna)
His Excellency	Vocal score (J. Williams)
The Shop Girl	Vocal score (Hopwood & Crew); My shy Love/The Shop Girl/These Days and those Days/If only You Knew/The Guards' Brigade/Is it Fair?/Popperty Pop/Jockeys' Dance (Darewski)
An Artist's Model	Vocal score (Hopwood & Crew)
Gentleman Joe	Vocal score (Ascherberg)
Dandy Dick Whittington	Vocal score (Chappell)
All Abroad	Vocal score (Willcocks)
The New Barmaid	Vocal score (Hopwood & Crew)
The Bric à Brac Will	Vocal score (Willcocks)
Shamus O'Brien	Vocal score (Boosey)
The Grand Duke	Vocal score (Chappell)
The French Maid	Vocal score (Ascherberg)
Lord Tom Noddy	Vocal score (Ascherberg)
Biarritz	Vocal score (Francis, Day & Hunter)
My Girl	Vocal score (J. Williams)
The Geisha	Vocal score (Hopwood & Crew)
On the March	Vocal score (Ascherberg)
Newmarket	Cockalorum (Francis, Day & Hunter)
Monte Carlo	Vocal score (Hopwood & Crew)
The White Silk Dress	Vocal score (Hopwood & Crew)
The Belle of Cairo	Vocal score (Chappell)
The Black Squire	Vocal score (J. Williams)
The Circus Girl	Vocal score (Chappell)
His Majesty	Vocal score (J. Williams)
The Ballet Girl	Vocal score (Enoch)
The Yashmak	Vocal score (Francis, Day & Hunter)

The Land of Nod	Vocal score (Reynolds)
The Maid of Athens	The Socialistic Club of Tipperary/I Am so Careful/If you Please (Hopwood & Crew)
Regina B.A.	Vocal score (Ascherberg)
Kitty	Vocal score (C. Cary)
Dandy Dan the Lifeguardsman	Vocal score (Ascherberg)
The Transit of Venus	Vocal score (Ascherberg)
The Dandy Fifth	Vocal score
Bilberry of Tilbury	I Haven't Got my Sea Legs Yet/Lady of Love/ When the Roses are in Bloom (Feldman)
A Runaway Girl	Vocal score (Chappell)
The Beauty Stone	Vocal score (Chappell)
A Greek Slave	Vocal score (Chappell)
Orlando Dando	Vocal score (Ascherberg)
Her Royal Highness	Vocal score (Ascherberg)
Milord Sir Smith	Where do I come In?/She's never Been in Pantomime Before (Francis, Day & Hunter), Love me a little, Sue (Ch. Sheard)
Little Miss Nobody	Vocal score (Hopwood & Crew)
The Lucky Star	Vocal score (Chappell)
Great Caesar	Vocal score (Keith, Prowse)
A Chinese Honeymoon	Vocal score (Hopwood & Crew)
San Toy	Vocal score (Keith, Prowse)
Florodora	Vocal score (Francis, Day & Hunter)
The Rose of Persia	Vocal score (Chappell)
The Messenger Boy	Vocal score (Chappell)
H.M.S. Irresponsible	Various numbers published
Kitty Grey	Vocal score (Ascherberg)
The Wonder Worker	Vocal score (Hammond)
The Gay Pretenders	Vocal score (Keith, Prowse)
The Thirty Thieves	Vocal score (Boosey)
The Ladies' Paradise	Bobbing/Fiddle dee Dee/The Dreamland Dimple/When a Man's in Love/The Social Polkarette/Le Petit Caporal/Gustave Gigot's Band (USA)
The Emerald Isle	Vocal score (Chappell)
The Silver Slipper	Vocal score (Francis, Day & Hunter)
The Toreador	Vocal score (Chappell)
The Gay Cadets	Love and I, A Pair of Eyes, Moon! Moon!, The topical Topper (Keith, Prowse)
Bluebell in Fairyland	Vocal score (Francis, Day & Hunter)
A Country Girl	Vocal score (Chappell)
Naughty Nancy	Vocal score (Hopwood & Crew)
Merrie England	Vocal score (Chappell)
Three Little Maids	Vocal score (Chappell)
An English Daisy	'Songs published'
My Lady Molly	Vocal score (Keith, Prowse)
The Girl from Kays	Vocal score (Chappell)
The Water Babies	Vocal score (Metzler)
A Princess of Kensington	Vocal score (Chappell)
The Medal and the Maid	Vocal score (Keith, Prowse)
The School Girl	Vocal score (Francis, Day & Hunter)
Percy, the Ladykiller	Vocal score (Keith, Prowse)
Amorelle	Vocal score (Hopwood & Crew)
The Duchess of Dantzic	Vocal score (Chappell)
The Orchid	Vocal score (Chappell)
The Earl and the Girl	Vocal score (Chappell)
The Cherry Girl	Vocal score (Chappell)
Alice Through the Looking Glass	Vocal score (Hopwood & Crew)

Little Hans Andersen	Vocal score (Ascherberg)
The Lovebirds	Vocal score (Keith, Prowse)
The Blue Moon	Vocal score (Chappell)
The Cingalee	Vocal score (Chappell)
Sergeant Brue	Vocal score (Hopwood & Crew)
The Catch of the Season	Vocal score (Francis, Day & Hunter)
Lady Madcap	Vocal score (Chappell)
The Talk of the Town	Vocal score (Ascherberg, Hopwood & Crew)
The Spring Chicken	Vocal score (Chappell)
The White Chrysanthemum	Vocal score (Chappell)
Mr Popple (of Ippleton)	Vocal score (Chappell)
The Little Cherub	Vocal score (Chappell)
The Beauty of Bath	Vocal score (Ascherberg, Hopwood & Crew)
The Scottish Bluebells	Sweet Bluebell/Sing just one Song (Paterson & Sons)
The Belle of Mayfair	Vocal score (Francis, Day & Hunter)
The Dairymaids	Vocal score (Chappell)
The Girl Behind the Counter	Vocal score (Chappell)
See See	Vocal score (Keith, Prowse)
Amasis	Vocal score (Metzler)
The New Aladdin	Vocal score (Chappell)
The Vicar of Wakefield	Vocal score (Boosey)
Nelly Neil	Vocal score (Chappell)
Miss Hook of Holland	Vocal score (Chappell)
My Darling	Vocal score (Ascherberg, Hopwood & Crew)
Tom Jones	Vocal score (Chappell)
Lady Tatters	Vocal score (Francis, Day & Hunter)
The Girls of Gottenberg	Vocal score (Chappell)
The Maid and the Motorman	Meet me at Twilight (Ascherberg, Hopwood & Crew)/When little Maid is Wooed (Bosworth)/ Little Miss Moon (Price & Reynolds)/ Any Time you're Passing By (Francis, Day & Hunter)
The Three Kisses	Life's a Song/Neapolitan Boat Song (Chappell)
The Gay Gordons	Vocal score (Ascherberg, Hopwood & Crew)
My Mimosa Maid	Vocal score (Chappell)
Butterflies	Vocal score (Ascherberg, Hopwood & Crew)
Havana	Vocal score (Chappell)
King of Cadonia	Vocal score (Keith, Prowse)
The Hon'ble Phil	Sixteen separate numbers advertised by Ascherberg, Hopwood & Crew; Vesuvius (Francis, Day & Hunter)
The Belle of Brittany	Vocal score (Keith, Prowse)
The Antelope	All along the River/The Antelope/The Drums of the Fore and Aft/The Little Drummer/Little Pickings of the Trade/Mari/Rat-a-tat/Won't You? (Chappell)
Pinkie and the Fairies	Vocal score (Chappell)
Our Miss Gibbs	Vocal score (Chappell)
The Dashing Little Duke	Vocal score (Ascherberg, Hopwood & Crew)
A Persian Princess	Vocal score (Keith, Prowse)
The Arcadians	Vocal score (Chappell)
Dear Little Denmark	Vocal score (Chappell)
The Mountaineers	Vocal score (Ascherberg, Hopwood & Crew)
Fallen Fairies	Vocal score (Chappell)
The Balkan Princess	Vocal score (Chappell)
The Islander	Vocal score (Metzler)
The Quaker Girl	Vocal score (Chappell)
Peggy	Vocal score (Chappell)
The Mousmé	Vocal score (Chappell)

Bonita	Vocal score (Keith, Prowse)
The Sunshine Girl	Vocal score (Chappell)
The Dancing Mistress	Vocal score (Chappell)
The Pearl Girl	Vocal score (Chappell)
The Girl from Utah	Vocal score (Chappell)
Are You There?	Roseway (Enoch)
After the Girl	Vocal score (Chappell)
The Black Rover	Vocal score (London Music Publishing Co)
Paul Jones	Vocal score (Hopwood & Crew)
The Old Guard	Vocal score (Enoch)
The Devil's Deputy	Vocal gems (Harms, USA)
Pot Pourri	Vocal score (Boosey)
La Cigale	Vocal score (Chappell)
Ma Mie Rosette	Vocal score (Boosey)
The Slim Princess	Vocal score (Chappell, USA)
Victorian	Vocal score (J. Williams)
Nemesis	Vocal selection (J. Williams)
Jack in the Box	Sweet Italy (Willcocks)
Castles in Spain	Come, my Sweetheart to Me, Is it you?, The Kingdom of Love, Tom the Piper's Son (Keith, Prowse)

The following short pieces are known to have been published. In some cases both script and score are printed together, in others only the music was published, or, frequently, only the play for which would-be performers were then obliged to hire manuscript music from the publisher. These last are marked *

1860	*Out of Sight*	Berridge
1865	*Widows Bewitched*	Metzleq
	Constance	Metzler
	Castle Grim	Metzler
	Felix	Metzler (three songs)
1866	*Love's Limit*	Metzler
	Sylvia	Metzler
1867	*Cox and Box*	Boosey
1869	*Ages Ago*	Boosey
	No Cards	J. Williams
1871	*A Sensation(al) Novel*	J. Williams
1872	*Charity Begins at Home*	J. Williams
	My Aunt's Secret	Boosey
1872	*Happy Arcadia*	J. Williams
	Very Catching	J. Williams
1873	*The Three Tenants*	J. Williams
1875	*Trial by Jury*	Chappell
	The Zoo	Cramer
	Eyes and No Eyes	J. Williams
1877	*Our Dolls' House (Our Toys)*	J. Williams
1878	*The Spectre Knight*	Metzler
	*An Artful Automaton**	J. Williams
	*A Tremendous Mystery**	J. Williams
	Cups and Saucers	J. Williams/S. French
	After All	Metzler
1879	*A Dress Rehearsal*	Boosey
	*£100 Reward**	J. Williams
	A Pirates' Home	Duff & Stewart
	M. D.	Cramer
1880	*Castle Botherem**	J. Williams
	*A Flying Visit**	J. Williams
	*A Merry Christmas**	J. Williams

	Prisoners at the Bar	Patey & Willis
1881	*All at Sea**	J. Williams
	*Cherry Tree Farm**	J. Williams
	*Many Happy Returns**	J. Williams
	*A Bright Idea**	J. Williams
	Quid Pro Quo	J. Williams
	Quite an Adventure	Chappell
1882	*Mr Guffin's Elopement*	'The Speaker's Eye' (Hopwood & Crew)
	An Adamless Eden	Boosey
	*Head of The Poll**	J. Williams
	*Nobody's Fault**	J. Williams
	*A Strange Host**	J. Williams
	His Only Coat	J. Williams
	A Simple Sweep	J. Williams
1883	*A Treasure Trove**	J. Williams
	A Moss Rose Rent	J. Williams
1884	*A Double Event**	J. Williams
	*A Terrible Fright**	J. Williams
	*A Peculiar Case**	J. Williams
	Old Knockles	J. Williams
1885	*A Pretty Bequest**	J. Williams
1886	*A United Pair**	J. Williams
1887	*The Naturalist**	J. Williams
	Tally Ho!	J. Williams
	Jubilation	Willcocks
1889	*A Capital Joke*	Ascherberg
	The Verger	J. Williams
	Tuppins & Co (Jealousy)	J. Williams
	Penelope	Ascherberg
	Pickwick	Boosey
1890	*His Last Chance*	Ascherberg
	The Tiger	Hopwood & Crew
	Domestic Economy	Enoch
1891	*A Pantomime Rehearsal*	Ascherberg
	Love and Law	Boosey
	The 15th of October	L. Bathlot, Paris
1892	*The Wooden Spoon*	Boosey
	The Composer	Mathias & Strickland (3 songs/libretto)
1893	*Box B*	J. Williams
	The Venetian Singer	Boosey
1896	*Weather or No*	J. Williams
1897	*Old Sarah*	J. Williams
1901	*Ib and Little Christina*	Chappell
1902	*The Knights of the Road*	Metzler
	The Willow Pattern	Chappell
1908	*A Welsh Sunset*	Metzler
1910	*A Summer Night*	Chappell

Appendix II: Recorded music

compiled by Ian Bevan

Commercial recording (and reproduction) of sound became a practical proposition in the 1890s. Thomas Alva Edison took out his first recording patent in the U.S.A. in December, 1877, and in England in April, 1878. The first commercial recordings were made in America, on cylinder by Edison in 1889 and on disc by Emile Berliner in 1894. In 1897 The Gramophone Company (from 1901 The Gramophone & Typewriter Co.) was formed in England to market Berliner's records, and in 1898 they began recording in London at a studio in Maiden Lane where H. Scott Russell recorded 'Jack's the Boy' from *The Geisha* and 'Take a Pair of sparkling Eyes' from *The Gondoliers* on August 19, 1898 and Syria Lamonte recorded 'A Geisha's Life' from *The Geisha* on August 28, 1898. From this time onwards, the recording of artists and music from British musicals was consistent, and a remarkable number of 'original cast' recordings exist from many pre-1914 shows – notably from *San Toy* (1899), *Florodora* (1899), *Three Little Maids* (1902), *The Girl from Kays* (1902), *The Cingalee* (1904), *Our Miss Gibbs* (1909), *The Arcadians* (1909), *The Quaker Girl* (1910), *Peggy* (1911) and *The Mousmé* (1911). Sadly, only a few of these early recordings have been re-assembled under their show title and made available in LP form, although many individual songs have been included in various compilation albums.

This selected discography has been compiled from contemporary record catalogues (including reprints by the City of London Phonograph and Gramophone Society and others), programmes and magazines, the British Sound Archive, the published discographies of John R. Bennett, Brian Rust and David Hummel, and the private collections of the compiler, Rexton S. Bunnett, Peter D. Parker and others. It cannot pretend to be a complete listing of every recording ever made of every song from British musicals. It is hoped to list every recording which is still accessible (albeit in specialist collections) and which might be assumed to reflect the theatrical intentions of the composer. As such, it gives preference to original cast performances. Where no such recordings are known to exist, and other contemporary or near-contemporary recordings do exist, these have been listed as the only way of hearing recorded versions of these particular songs although they may be in medley form or even in brass or dance band arrangements.

Duplicate or 'cover' versions are listed in some detail for pre-1920 shows to afford the maximum chance of finding still existing copies, but they are listed in less detail after that date and many dance band and 'popular' versions in the '30s and '40s are not included. Once LP original cast albums become common in the late 1940s and early '50s, the listing of single records becomes much more selective and singles are not listed if the material is also on an album. Soundtracks of film and television versions, and foreign-language cast albums, are listed for their unusual interest. The Gilbert and

Sullivan works, the most recorded of all British musicals, form a special case. The five main series of recordings have been listed in full, together with early single recordings and certain 'rogue' recordings such as *The Black Mikado* and the American television version with Groucho Marx as Ko-Ko, but only a few of the numerous 'highlights', 'selections', etc., most of which have been assembled from the basic HMV and Decca studio cast recordings. Throughout, only professional recordings which have been commercially released are listed. Composers' demonstration records, private tapes, and pirate recordings have been excluded. Cassettes and cartridges which exist alongside LPs are not separately noted, and at the time of compiling there has been no significant issue of British show music on compact disc. Serial numbers are British release numbers unless otherwise noted and are followed (in brackets) by the year of recording where this is known with reasonable certainty. For convenient comparison with recording dates, the year of the show's first London production is given after its title.

OC = original cast	RC = replacement cast	SC = studio cast
RevC = revival cast	RR = re-released	Orch = orchestral
Inst = instrumental	LP = album at $33\frac{1}{3}$ rpm	45 = single at 45 rpm

Ber = Berliner; Bru = Brunswick; Col = UK Columbia; Col US = American Columbia; Dec = Decca; EB = Edison Bell; Fav = Favourite; G&T = Gramophone & Typewriter Co.; GC = Gramophone Company; MFP = Music for Pleasure; Par = Parlophone; RZon = Regal Zonophone; Vic = US Victor; WRC = World Record Club; Zon = Zonophone

— **Cox and Box** (1866/7)

SC LP LK4404/SKL4140 (rel. 1961) (sixth side of *The Gondoliers* recording)
SC LP BASF BUK17 25138–1, RR many times incl. Pye NSPH15
SC LP Dec TXS128 (rel. 1978)
Orch Selection (Band of H.M. Coldstream Guards) HMVC 1050

0003 **The Contrabandista/The Chieftain** (1867/1894)

RevC Recorded as *The Chieftain* in a new version with libretto and revised lyrics by D. J. Eden, produced in 1978 and recorded by the Sawston Village College Operatic Society with the orchestral parts reconstructed from the original Sullivan scores. Rare Recorded Editions SRRE 181/2 (1978)

— **Trial by Jury** (1875)

SC HMV D1469–72, D7117–20, D7507–10 (1928), RR HMV ALP1294 (1955), RR WRC SHB641/2, RR Pearl GEMM148
SC Dec AK2248–51 (78 rpm) (1949)/LP LK4001 (rel. 1950)
SC LP HMV DW/SXDW3034 (1958)
SC LP Dec LK/SKL4579 (rel. 1964)
SC LP BASF BUK17 25138–1
SC LP Dec TXS113 (rel. 1975)
RevC 'When I, good Friends, was called to the Bar' (Walter Passmore with chorus) Col 371 (1912)
RevC 'When I, good Friends, Was Called to the Bar' (C.H. Workman) RR Pearl GEMM135
SC 'When I, good Friends, Was Called to the Bar' (Sullivan Operatic Party) HMV 4402

SC 'When I, good Friends, Was Called to the Bar' (Peter Dawson) G&T 4402 (1906), RR LP HMV ED 29.0422.1
Orch Selection (Band of H.M. Coldstream Guards) HMV 0127

— **The Zoo** (1875)
RevC LP (Fulham Light Operatic Society) Rare Recorded Editions SRRE134 (1972)
SC LP Dec TXS128 (1978)

0023 **The Sorcerer** (1877)
SC HMV B8054–9, B7018–23 (1933) abridged
SC LP Dec LK4070/1 (1953)
SC LP Dec LK/SKL4825/6 (rel. 1966)
RevC 'My Name is John Wellington Wells' (Walter Passmore) Ber 2455 (1900), RR LP HMV ED 29.0422.1
RevC 'My Name is John Wellington Wells' (C. H. Workman) RR Pearl GEMM135
RevC 'Time Was when Love and I' (Henry Lytton) G&T 2–2103 (1902), RR 'The Art of the Savoyard' Pearl GEMM119, RR Pearl GEMM197, RR LP HMV ED 29.0422.1
SC 'Time Was when Love and I' (Dalton Baker) Odeon 0577/57616
SC 'Time Was when Love and I' (Frederick Ranalow) EB Winner 2414
SC Vocal Gems (Victor Light Opera Co) Vic 36147 (USA)
Orch Selection (Band of H.M. Coldstream Guards) HMV 0309

0025 **H.M.S. Pinafore** (1878)
SC The following Gramophone Company recordings were made and released in 1908. Unlike earlier G&T recordings of *The Mikado* and *The Yeomen of the Guard*, these catalogue serial numbers were substantially in sequence with libretto sequence, indicating that they were conceived and issued as a set. See notes for *The Mikado* regarding their HMV listing.

GC 4469	RR HMV B435	'For I'm Called little Buttercup' (Amy Augarde)
GC 04032	RR HMV C513	'A Maiden fair to See' (Ernest Pike)
GC 4470	RR HMV B436	'I Am the Captain of the Pinafore' (Thorpe Bates)
GC 4471	RR HMV B435	'Sorry her Lot who Loves too Well' (Eleanor Jones-Hudson)
GC 4472		'Over the bright blue Sea' (Sullivan Operatic Party)
GC 4473		'Now Give three Cheers' ('When I Was a Lad') (Alan Turner)
GC 4474		'A British Tar' (Sullivan Operatic Party)
GC 4457	RR HMV B438	'Refrain, audacious Tar' (Eleanor Jones-Hudson, Ernest Pike)
GC 04033		'Messmates Ahoy!' (Sullivan Operatic Party)
GC 04034		'This very Night with bated Breath' (Sullivan Operatic Party)
GC 4475	RR HMV B436	'Fair Moon, to thee I Sing' (Thorpe Bates)
GC 4476	RR HMV B439	'Things Are seldom what they Seem' (Amy Augarde, Thorpe Bates)

GC 04035 RR HMV C513 'The Hours Creep on Apace' (Eleanor Jones-Hudson)
GC 4477 RR HMV B439 'Never Mind the why and Wherefore' (Amy Augarde, Thorpe Bates, Alan Turner)
GC 4478 RR HMV B440 'Kind Captain, I've important Information' (Peter Dawson, Thorpe Bates)
GC 4479 'In uttering a Reprobation' (Alan Turner)
GC 4480 RR HMV B441 'Farewell, my Own' (Sullivan Operatic Party)
GC 4481 RR HMV B441 'Oh Joy, oh Rapture' (Sullivan Operatic Party)

SC Overture/opening chorus/4 solos/2 duets/octet/Act 1 finale/selection from Act 11. Sterling cyls 940/948 and 950/951 (1907), RR Pathé discs 8067, 8068, 1387, 1378
SC Odeon 0437/0446 (1908)
SC HMV D724/31 (1924)
SC HMV D1844/52, D7230/38, D7511/19 (1930), RR HMV ALP1293/4 (1955), MFP2070
SC Dec AK2261/8 (78 rpm) (1949)/LK4002/3 (LP) (rel. 1950), RR Dec ACL/SCL 1054/5
SC LP HMV DW/SXDW3034 (1958)
SC LP Dec 4334/5 and SKL 4081/2 (1960)
SC LP Dec OPFS1/2 (1971)
SC LP (excerpts) RCA Reader's Digest RDS461
SC LP BASF BUK 17 25136–5, RR many times incl. Pye NSPH14
RevC 'When I Was a Lad' (C. H. Workman) RR Pearl GEMM135
RevC 'When I Was a Lad' (Walter Passmore) Col 326 (1912)
SC Vocal Gems (Victor Light Opera Co) VIC 31782 and 35386 (USA)
Orch Selection (The British Military Band) Zon 1127
SC 'Things Are seldom what they Seem' (Winifred Marwood, Montague Borwell) Ber 4016 (1899)
SC The Nightingale . . . a Maiden fair to See' (Walter Hyde) Odeon 44872 (1908), RR LP HMV ED 29.0422.1

0029 **The Pirates of Penzance** (1880)

SC HMV D504/14 (1921)
SC HMV D1678/88, D7101/11, D7730/40 (1929), RR Pearl GEMM 171/2
SC HMV B3846/51, B7006/11, (1931) abridged, RR MFP 2143 (1971)
SC Dec AK2315/25 (78 rpm) (1950)/LK4004/5 (LP) (1951), RR Dec DPA 3051/2
SC LP Dec LK4249/50 and SKL 4038/9 (1958)
SC LP HMV DW/SXDW3041 (released 1961)
SC LP RCA Reader's Digest RDS460 (1963)
SC LP RCA Vic S6007A/B (USA) (1963)
SC LP BASF BUK 25135–7, RR Pye NSPH14
SC LP Highlights WRC T125
RevC LP Elektra VE–601 (USA) (1981)
OC 'I Am a Pirate King' (Richard Temple) G&T 2–2928 (1904), RR Pearl 'The Art of the Savoyard' GEMM118
RevC 'Poor wandering One!' (Isabel Jay) Ber 3214 (1900), G&T 3258 (1904), G&T 3567. RR 'Singing Actresses' WRC SH433 (1982), RR 'The Art of the Savoyard' Pearl GEMM118, RR LP HMV ED 29.0422.1

RevC 'I Am the very Model of a modern Major-General' (C. H. Workman) Odeon 66654 (c. 1910), RR 'The Art of the Savoyard' Pearl GEMM120 and also on Pearl GEMM135
RevC 'When a Felon's not Engaged' (Walter Passmore) Col 1866 (1912?), RR LP HMV ED 29.0422.1
RevC 'Sighing softly to the River' (C. H. Workman) Odeon 113000 (c. 1910), RR 'The Art of the Savoyard' Pearl GEMM120 and also on Pearl GEMM135
SC 'Pour, oh Pour' (Sullivan Operatic Party) G&T 4434
SC 'I Am the very Model' (Sullivan Operatic Party) G&T 4463
SC 'With cat-like Tread' (Sullivan Operatic Party) G&T 4435
SC 'When the Foeman Bares his Steel' (Sullivan Operatic Party) G&T 3–2846
SC 'I Am a Pirate King' (Louis Breeze) Ber 2427 (1900)
SC Vocal Gems (Victor Light Opera Co) Vic 31808 (USA)
SC Selection (Savoy Light Opera Singers & Players) EB Winner 4964
Orch Selection (Zonophone Military Band) Zon 40001
Orch Selection (Band of H.M. Coldstream Guards) HMV 2–206, HMV 0131

0033 **Patience** (1881)

SC HMV D563/71 (1922)
SC HMV D1909/18, D7272/81, D7844/53 (1930)
SC LP Dec LK4047/8 (1952), RR ACL/SCL 1174/5
SC LP HMV DW/SXDW3031 (1959)
SC LP Dec LK4414/5 and SKL4146/7 (1961)
SC LP RCA Reader's Digest RDS462
RevC 'Twenty love-sick Maidens We' (Savoy Opera Chorus) Ber 4526 (1900)
RevC 'If you're anxious for to Shine' (Walter Passmore) Ber 2454 (1900), RR 'The Art of the Savoyard' Pearl GEMM120, RR LP HMV ED 29.0422.1
RevC 'If you're anxious for to Shine' (Walter Passmore) Col 2534 (1913)
RevC 'If you're anxious for to Shine' (C. H. Workman) RR Pearl GEMM135
RevC 'When I Go out of Door' (Walter Passmore, Robert Howe) Col 2534 (1913)
SC 'Prithee, pretty Maiden' (Winifred Marwood, Montague Borwell) Ber 4014, Zon 12895 (1898), RR LP HMV ED 29.0422.1
SC 'If you want a Receipt' (Peter Dawson) HMV D564, RR Pearl GEMM 200
Orch 'I Hear a soft Voice' (Zonophone Military Band) Zon 40006
Orch Selection (Band of H.M. Coldstream Guards) HMV 0176

0042 **Rip Van Winkle** (1882) (French title: **Rip**)

SC 'True Love from o'er the Sea' (The Letter Song) (Winifred Hare) EB 6878
SC 'Oh, where's my Girl?' (John M. Hay) Zon 12810
FRevC 'Le Rêve' (M. Soulacroix) (in French) French Ber 32854
FRevC 'Vive la Paresse' (M. Soulacroix) (in French) French Ber 32855
FSC 'Vive la Paresse' (M. Bru) (in French) French Ber 32575
FSC 'Romance des Enfants' (M. Bru) (in French) French Ber 32582
FSC 'Vive la Paresse' (M. Piccaluga) (in French) Pathé 0670
FSC LP (in French) EMI-Pathé 2C057–12899 (1958), RR 1979

0044 **Iolanthe** (1882)

SC HMV D632/41 (1923)
SC HMV D1785/95, D7190/7200, D7708/18 (1930)

SC LP Dec LK4044/5 (1952), RR Dec ACL/SCL 1128/9
SC LP HMV DW/SXDW3047, SXLP30112/3 (1959)
SC LP Dec LK4378/9 and SKL4119/20 (1960)
SC LP RCA Reader's Digest RDS461
SC Dec SKL 5188/9 (rel. 1974)
SC LP BASF BUK 17 25137–3, RR Pye NSPH11
RevC LP Highlights (Sadlers Wells, 1st recording after expiry of G&S copyright) HMV (1962)
RevC 'When you're lying Awake' (Walter Passmore) Col 354 (1912)
RevC 'When you're lying Awake' (C. H. Workman) Col 66653, RR 'The Art of the Savoyard' Pearl GEMM120, RR Pearl GEMM135
RevC 'None shall Part Us' (Henry Lytton, Louie Henri) G&T 4161 (1902), RR 'The Art of the Savoyard' Pearl GEMM119, RR 'The Art of Henry Lytton' Pearl GEMM197, RR LP HMV ED 29.0422.1
RevC 'The Law Is the true Embodiment' (C. H. Workman), Odeon 113001 (1911), RR LP Pearl GEMM 135, RR LP HMV ED 29.0422.1
RevC "When I Went to the Bar' (C. H. Workman), Odeon 113002 (1911), RR LP Pearl GEMM 135, RR LP HMV ED 29.0422.1
SC 'Sentry's Song' (Harry Dearth) Sterling Cyl 450 (1906)
SC 'Sentry's Song' (Norman Francis) EB Winner 2410
SC 'Sentry's Song' (Sturley Chutter) Zon 12865
SC 'Sentry's Song' (Eric Farr) Zon X225
SC Entrance and March of Peers 04007 (Sullivan Operatic Party) G&T
SC 'If you Go In' (Sullivan Operatic Party) G&T 4430
SC 'When Britain really Ruled the Waves' (Sullivan Operatic Party) G&T 4429
SC Selection (Savoy Light Opera Singers & Players) E B Winner 4942/3
Orch Selection (Band of H.M. Coldstream Guards) G&T 0101

0050 **Princess Ida** (1884)

SC HMV D977/86 (1925)
SC HMV DB4016/25, DB7271/80 (1932)
SC LP Dec LK4092/3 (1955)
SC LP Dec LK/SKL 4708/9 (1965)
RevC 'Would you Know the kind of Maid' (H. Scott Russell) Ber 2973 (1900), RR LP Pearl GEMM 118, RR LP HMV ED 29.0422.1
RevC 'If you Give me your Attention' (C. H. Workman) Col 66651, RR 'The Art of the Savoyard' Pearl GEMM120, RR Pearl GEMM135
RevC 'If you Give me your Attention' (Henry Lytton) HMV D979, RR 'The Art the Savoyard' Pearl GEMM119
RevC 'Whene'er I Spoke sarcastic Joke' (Henry Lytton) HMV D985, RR 'The Art of the Savoyard' Pearl GEMM119
RevC 'Whene'er I Spoke sarcastic Joke' (C.H. Workman), RR Pearl GEMM135
Orch Selection (Band of H.M. Coldstream Guards) HMV C283

0057 **The Mikado** (1885)

SC The following G&T recordings, made in September/October 1906 and released in 1907, constitute the first extended recording of the score of a British musical. Despite there being one 12″ record with sixteen 10″ records, they were advertised in Savoy programmes of 1907 and 1908 as a set. 'His Master's Voice' became the company's accepted trademark title in August,

1910, and the records were listed under their original G&T serial numbers in HMV's numerical catalogue of 1911. Some of the titles were subsequently re-released on HMV double-sided records and allotted new serial numbers. The recordings are listed here in libretto sequence.

G&T 4606	'If you Want to Know who we Are' (Sullivan Operatic Party)
G&T 02073 RR HMV D242	'A wandering Minstrel I' (John Harrison)
G&T 2491 RR HMV B429	'Our great Mikado' (Stanley Kirkby and the Sullivan Operatic Party)
G&T 4403	'Behold the Lord High Executioner' (Sullivan Operatic Party)
G&T 4407	'Three little Maids' (Sullivan Operatic Party)
G&T 4411	'So please you, Sir' (Sullivan Operatic Party)
G&T 4414 RR HMV B430	'Were you not to Ko-Ko Plighted' (Ernest Pike, Eleanor Jones-Hudson)
G&T 3363	'The Sun, whose Rays' (Eleanor Jones-Hudson)
G&T 4605	'Brightly Dawns our wedding Day' (Sullivan Operatic Party)
G&T 4408	'Here's a How-de-do!' (Sullivan Operatic Party)
G&T 4412 RR HMV B427	'Miya Sama' (Amy Augarde, Peter Dawson and the Sullivan Operatic Party)
G&T 3-2476	'A more humane Mikado' (Peter Dawson and chorus)
G&T 4409	'The Criminal Cried' (Peter Dawson, Amy Augarde)
G&T 4607	'See how the Fates' (Sullivan Operatic Party)
G&T 4410	'The Flowers that Bloom in the Spring' (Stanley Kirkby and the Sullivan Operatic Party)
G&T 3-2493 RR HMV B429	'On a Tree by a River' (Stanley Kirkby and the Sullivan Operatic Party)
G&T 4413 RR HMV B430	'There is Beauty in the Bellow of the Blast' (Amy Augarde, Peter Dawson)

SC	Odeon 0425–0436 (1908), RR Pearl GEMM198
SC	HMV D2/12 (1918)
SC	HMV D1172/82, D7000/10, D7697/7707 (1926), RR Pearl GEMM137/8
SC	Col DB321/6 (circa 1928)
SC	HMV DB4038/48, DB8105/15 (1936), RR HMV ALP1255/6 (1955), RR MFP 2038
SC	Dec AK2388/98 (78 rpm) and LK4010/1 (LP) (1950), RR HMV ACL/SCL 1014/5
SC	LP HMV ALP1485/6, DW/SXDW3019 (1956)
SC	LP Dec LK4251/2 and SKL4006/7 (1958)
SC	LP RCA Reader's Digest RDS460 (1963)
RevC	LP HMV CSD 1458/9 (1962)
SC	LP BASF BUK 17 51071 (also BUK 17 25107–1) (1972), RR HMV ESDW 1077183 Pye NSPH13
SC	LP Dec SKL5158/9 (1973)

SC LP Highlights WRC T119 (1958)
SC Vocal Gems (Victor Light Opera Co.) Vic 31789/31881/35551/35796 (USA)
SC Selection (Savoy Light Opera Singers & Players) EB Winner 4948/9
OC 'A more humane Mikado' (Richard Temple) G&T 2–2767 (1902), RR 'The Art of the Savoyard' Pearl GEMM118, RR LP HMV ED 29.0422.1
RevC 'Behold the Lord High Executioner!'/'As some Day it may Happen' (Walter Passmore, chorus) Odeon A206 (1908), 'As some Day it may Happen' RR Pearl GEMM120
RevC Trio ('I Am so Proud') (Walter Passmore, Harry Dearth, Harry Thornton) Odeon A274 (1908)
RevC 'The Criminal Cried as he Dropped him Down' (Walter Passmore, Ada Florence, Harry Dearth) Odeon A293 (1908)
RevC 'The Flowers that Bloom in the Spring' (Walter Passmore, Harry Thornton, Walter Hyde, Elsa Sinclair)/'See how the Fates' (Walter Passmore, Harry Thornton, Harry Dearth, Elsa Sinclair) Odeon A305 (1908)
RevC 'On a Tree by a River' (Walter Passmore) Odeon 0435 (1908), Col 326 (1912), RR LP HMV ED 29.0422.1
RevC 'On a Tree by a River' (C. H. Workman) Odeon 66655 (c. 1910), RR 'The Art of the Savoyard' Pearl GEMM120, RR Pearl GEMM135
RevC 'Here's a How-de-do!' (Walter Passmore, Hilda Francis, Edward James)/'The Criminal Cried as he Dropped him Down' (Walter Passmore, Carrie Herwin, Robert Howe, chorus) Col 387 (1913)
SC 'The Madrigal'/'The Flowers that Bloom in the Spring'/'There is Beauty in the Bellow of the Blast'/'Were you not to Ko-Ko Plighted' (Elda May, Amy Augarde, Robert Carr, Wilfrid Virgo) EB Winner 2436/7 (c. 1912)
SC 'Three little Maids' (May Davis, Enid Dickens, K. Jones) Ber 4023 (1898), 4023–x (1899)
SC 'A Wandering Minstrel I' (Webster Booth) HMV C3261
Orch Selection I, II, III (Band of H.M. Coldstream Guards) HMV 2–201/2/3
Orch Selection (Ed Isler's Orchestra) EB cyl (1890)
Orch Selection (The British Military Band) Zon 688
Inst 'Brightly Dawns our wedding Day' (W. A. Fransella's flute quartet) Ber 8017, 9153 (1898)
TV TV soundtrack Col OS–2022 (USA) (1960)
Film Film soundtrack 'The Cool Mikado' Par PMC–1194 (1963)
Radio Radio soundtrack 'The Hot Mikado' extracts from New York 1939 stage production, on 'Stars Over Broadway' Star-Tone 214 (USA)
OC LP 'The Black Mikado' (London) Transatlantic TRA300 (1975)
OC LP 'The Black Mikado' (South Africa) RPM 1111 (1976)

0059 **Erminie** (1885)

SC 'Lullaby' (Helen Jenyngs) Ber 397 (recorded USA 1895)
SC 'Lullaby' (unidentified artist) Col cyl XP 6604, Col 658
SC Vocal Gems (Victor Light Opera Co.) Vic 31818, 35451 (USA) (1915), RR HMV 04520 (UK)
SC Medley (New York Light Opera Co.) Edison 80689
SC Medley (Columbia Light Opera Co.) Col US A–5243 (1911)
Orch Selection (Ed Isler's Orchestra) Edison cyl (1890)
Orch Selection (Columbia Orchestra) Col cyl 32337, Col 1626

0072 **Dorothy** (1886)

SC 'Queen of my Heart' (Tom Bryce) Ber 2941 (1900)

SC 'Queen of my Heart' (Arthur Grover) EB 13391, Homophone 660
SC 'Queen of my Heart' (Stanley Kirkby) G&T 3–2509, Fav 456–65310
SC 'Queen of my Heart' (Ian Colquhoun) Nicole 5170, Zon 12797
SC 'Queen of my Heart' (Ivor Foster) Odeon X47–72535
SC 'Queen of my Heart' (Tom Burke) Zon 121
SC 'Queen of my Heart' (Charles Tree) Pathé 531
SC 'Queen of my Heart' (Thorpe Bates) Pathé 5651
SC 'Queen of my Heart' (Stanley Kirkby as Charles Holland) Zon X42145
SC 'Queen of my Heart' (Jack Sherwood) Beka 641/41724
SC 'Queen of my Heart'/'With such a dainty Dame' (Alfred Heather) Pathé 541
SC Medley (Light Opera Co.) HMV C–515 (1911)
Orch 'Queen of my Heart' (Band of H. M. Grenadier Guards) Ber 61 (1899)
Orch 'Be wise in Time' (Band of H. M. Grenadier Guards) Ber 59 (1899)
Orch 'Graceful Dance' (Band of H. M. Grenadier Guards) Ber 60 (1899)
Orch 'Graceful Dance' (London Concert Orchestra) EB cyl 289

0076 **Monte Cristo Jr** (1886)

SC 'Ballyhooley' (Alfred Hurley) EB Winner 2138 (rel. 1912)

0077 **Ruddigore** (1887)

SC HMV D878/86 (1924)
SC HMV DB4005/13, DB7096/7104, DB7522/30 (1931)
SC Dec AK2426/34 (78 rpm) (1950), LK4027/8 (LP) (1951), RR ACL/SCL 1193/4 (1965)
SC LP Dec LK/SKL 4504/5 (1962)
SC LP HMV DW/SXDW3029 (1968)

0088 **The Yeomen of the Guard** (1888)

SC The following G&T recordings were made in 1906/7 and released in 1907. See note for *The Mikado* regarding their HMV listing. The recordings are listed here in libretto sequence.

G&T 3703 RR HMV B404	'When our gallant Norman Foes' (Florence Venning)
G&T 4423 RR HMV B405	'Alas! I Waver to and Fro' (Florence Venning, Ernest Pike, Peter Dawson)
G&T 3-2848 RR HMV B409	'Is Life a Boon' (Ernest Pike)
G&T 4609	'Here's a Man of Jollity' (Sullivan Operatic Party)
G&T 4415 RR HMV B406	'I Have a Song to Sing, O!' (Eleanor Jones-Hudson, Stanley Kirkby)
G&T 4422 RR HMV B408	'How Say you, Maiden' (Eleanor Jones-Hudson, Peter Dawson, Stanley Kirkby)
G&T 3698 RR HMV B407	''Tis Done! I Am a Bride!' (Eleanor Jones-Hudson)
G&T 3699 RR HMV B407	'Were I thy Bride' (Eleanor Jones-Hudson)
G&T 4416	'To thy fraternal Care' (Sullivan Operatic Party)
G&T 4421 RR HMV B408	'Hereupon we're both Agreed' (Peter Dawson, Stanley Kirkby)
G&T 3-2847 RR HMV B409	'Free from his Fetters Grim' (Ernest Pike)
G&T 4424	'Strange Adventure!' (Sullivan Operatic Party)

	G&T 4610	'Like a Ghost his Vigil Keeping' (Sullivan Operatic Party)
	G&T 4426	'A Man who would Woo a fair Maid' (Sullivan Operatic Party)
	G&T 4425	'When a Wooer Goes A-wooing' (Sullivan Operatic Party)
	G&T 4420 RR HMV B403	'Rapture, Rapture' (Florence Venning, Peter Dawson)
	G&T 04500	Finale (Sullivan Operatic Party)

SC HMV D481/5 and D496/501 (1920) (NB serial numbers D486/495 are nothing to do with 'The Yeomen' set)
SC HMV D1549/59, D7055/65, D7719/29 (1929)
SC HMV B3799/3804, B7000/05 (10" abridged) (1931)
SC Dec AK2415/25 (78 rpm) (1950)/LK2029/30 (LP, rel. 1951)
SC LP HMV DW/SXDW3033 (1958)
SC LP Dec LK/SKL 4624/5 (1964)
RevC 'Is Life a Boon'/'Free from his Fetters Grim' (Robert Evett) respectively Odeon 44603 and 44604, coupled on Odeon A-307 (1907), RR Odeon 0241, RR 'The Art of the Savoyard' Pearl GEMM119
RevC 'Like a Ghost his Vigil Keeping' (Walter Passmore, Robert Howe)/'I Have a Song to Sing, O!' (Walter Passmore, Hilda Francis) Col 354 (1912) 'I Have a Song to Sing, O!' RR LP Pearl GEMM120; 'Like a Ghost' RR LP HMV ED 29.0422.1
RevC 'A Private Buffoon' (Walter Passmore) RR Pearl GEMM120
RevC 'I Have a Song to Sing, O!' (C. H. Workman, Elsie Spain), 'I've a Jibe and a Joke' (C. H. Workman), 'A private Buffoon' (C. H. Workman) all RR Pearl GEMM135; 'A private Buffoon' RR LP HMV ED 29.0422.1
SC 'Strange Adventure' (Violet Essex, Miss Blanchard, John Roberts, Harry Thornton) Beka 390 (1910)
SC 'Strange Adventure'/'When a Wooer Goes A-wooing' (London Opera Quartette) Col 338
SC 'Were I thy Bride' (Eleanor Jones-Hudson) G&T 3699 (1907), RR LP HMV 29.0422.1
SC Selection (Savoy Light Opera Singers & Players) EB Winner 4947
Orch Overture (Bohemian Orchestra) HMV0547
Orch Selection (Band of H.M. Coldstream Guards) HMV 0184 and HMV0218

0089 **Faust Up-To-Date** (1888)

Orch 'Pas de Quatre' (Garde Republicaine) Zon 120001

0091 **Doris** (1889)

OC 'So Fare thee Well' (I've Sought the Brake and Bracken') (Ben Davies) G&T GC 2–2781 (1902)
SC 'So Fare thee Well' (Wilfrid Hudson) EB 4922, EB Winner 5170
SC 'So Fare thee Well' (John Harrison) Ber 02141 (1908)
SC 'So Fare thee Well' (Wills Page) G&T 2–2336
SC 'So Fare thee Well' (Maurice d'Oisley) Col D1335
SC 'So Fare thee Well' (Walter Hyde), Odeon 0226, 57595, 0717, 66888
SC 'So Fare thee Well' (Arthur Edwards) Zon 42164, EB 6234
SC 'So Fare thee Well' (Herbert Emlyn) Zon 12896, Col 25221
SC 'So Fare thee Well' (Elliston Webb) Col cyl 200 361
SC 'So Fare thee Well' (Gerald O'Brien) EB Winner 3454

0101 **The Gondoliers** (1889)

The following G&T titles were absorbed by HMV and are listed in the HMV numerical catalogue for 1911. (The titles are shown in libretto sequence)

G&T4614 'Chorus of Men' (Sullivan Operatic Party)
G&T4462 'In Enterprise of martial Kind' (Sullivan Operatic Party)
G&T3679 'When a merry Maiden Marries' (Sullivan Operatic Party)
G&T4427 'Then One of Us will be a Queen' (Sullivan Operatic Party)
G&T4615 'Dance a Cachucha' (Sullivan Operatic Party)
G&T4445 'In contemplative Fashion' (Sullivan Operatic Party)
G&T4444 'I Am a Courtier grave and Serious' (Sullivan Operatic Party)

SC HMV D36/46 (1919)
SC HMV D1334/45, D7011/22, D7520/31 (1927), RR Pearl GEMM141/2
SC HMV B3866/71, B7012/17 (1931) (abridged)
SC Dec AK2403/14 (78 rpm) (1950), LP LK4015/6 (1951), RR ACL/SCL 1151/2
SC LP HMV ALP1504/5 DW/SXDW3027 (1957)
SC LP Dec LK4402/4 and SKL4138/40 (with 'Cox and Box' on sixth side) (1961)
SC LP RCA Reader's Digest RSD462 (1963)
SC LP Highlights WRC T129 (1908)
RevC 'In Enterprise of martial Kind' (C. H. Workman) RR Pearl GEMM135
RevC 'I Stole the Prince' (C. H. Workman) RR Pearl GEMM135
RevC 'Take a Pair of sparkling Eyes' (John Coates) G&T HMV3–2910 (1907), Col D1411, RR LP Pearl GEMM118, RR LP HMV ED 29.0422.1
RevC 'Take a Pair of sparkling Eyes' (H. Scott Russell) Ber 2006 (1898)
SC 'Take a Pair of sparkling Eyes' (Robert Curtis) Zon X42017
SC 'Take a Pair of sparkling Eyes' (Arthur Edwards) Zon X42259
SC 'Take a Pair of sparkling Eyes' (Wilson Pembroke) EB Winner 2016
SC 'Take a Pair of sparkling Eyes' (Gerald O'Brien) EB Winner 3454
SC 'Take a Pair of sparkling Eyes' (Wilfrid Hudson) EB Winner 5170
SC 'Take a Pair of sparkling Eyes' (Webster Booth) HMV c3261
SC 'When a merry Maiden Marries' (Syria Lamonte) GC E3018 (1898), RR LP HMV ED 29.0422.1
SC 'Then One of Us will be a Queen' (Miss Blanchard, John Roberts, Harry Thornton, Violet Essex) Beka 390 (1910)
SC Selection (Savoy Light Opera Singers & Players) EB Winner 4944/5
Orch Selection/Gavotte (Zonophone Military Band) Zon 40005
Orch Selection (Band of H. M. Coldstream Guards) HMV C1273

0122 **Cigarette** (1892)

SC 'Oh, how I Love Thee' (Walter Hyde) Odeon 0221, 66205

0123 **Haddon Hall** (1892)

RevC LP (Cheam Operatic Society with Southern Festival Orchestra) Pearl SHE566/7 (1982)
SC 'When the budding Bloom' (Perceval Allen, Alice Lakin, John Harrison, Robert Radford) G&T 04051 (1909)
Orch Selection (Band of H. M. Coldstream Guards) HMV 0328 (1911) HMV 0183

0133 **The Lady Slavey** (1894)

SC 'In Friendship's Name' (Arthur Grover) EB 6480, EB 13404, G&T 3–2270

SC 'In Friendship's Name' (Hamilton Hill) Zon X42105
SC 'In Friendship's Name' (Sullivan Operatic Party) HMV 4428

0134 **Utopia (Limited)** (1893)

RevC LP (Blue Hill Troupe of New York) Basingstoke T1001 (USA) (1955)
RevC LP (Lyric Theatre Company of Washington, DC) private label H8-OP-8180/3 (two records) (USA) (1957)
RevC LP (Lyric Theatre Company of Washington, DC) private label R4RM 4950/5 (three records) (USA) (1963), RR Pearl SHEZ 505/7 (UK) (1972)
SC LP Dec LK/SKL 4579 (excerpts) (1964)
SC LP Dec SKL 5225/6 (rel. 1976)
RevC 'A Tenor, all Singers Above' (H. Scott Russell) Ber 2971 (1900), RR 'The Art of the Savoyard' Pearl GEMM118, RR LP HMV ED 29.0422.1
RevC 'First you're Born' (C. H. Workman) Odeon A143062, RR Pearl 'The Art of the Savoyard' GEMM120 and Pearl 'C. H. Workman' GEMM135
RevC 'Some seven Men Form an Association' (C. H. Workman), RR Pearl 'C. H. Workman' GEMM135

0136 **A Gaiety Girl** (1893, revived 1899)

OC 'Sunshine Above' (Louis Bradfield) Ber 2911 (1900)
SC 'Sunshine Above' (Ian Colquhoun) Ber 2711 (1899), Zon X1091
SC 'Sunshine Above' (Ian Foster) Odeon 0808, 143817
SC 'Sunshine Above' (George Harrison) EB 5883
SC 'Private Tommy Atkins' (Ian Colquhoun) Ber 2743 (1899)
Orch Selection (Band of H. M. Grenadier Guards) Ber 48 (1899)

0146 **The Gay Parisienne** (1896)

OC 'Sister Mary Jane's Top Note' (Louie Freear) G&T 3413 (1902)
SC 'Sister Mary Jane's Top Note' (S. H. Dudley) G&T GC2–2729 (1902)
SC 'Sister Mary Jane's Top Note' (Alma Jones) EB 5070

0151 **The Shop Girl** (1894)

OC Her golden Hair was Hanging down her Back' (Seymour Hicks) HMV C–2432 (1932)
RC 'Lousiana Lou' (Ellaline Terriss) G&T 3441 (1903)
RC 'Lousiana Lou' (in 'Gaiety Medley') (Ellaline Terriss) G&T 03006, G&T 3457 (1903)
RC 'I Want yer, ma Honey' (Ellaline Terriss) G&T 03000 (1903)
RC 'I Want yer, ma Honey'/'Lousiana Lou' (Ellaline Terriss) HMV C–2432 (1932)
SC 'Lousiana Lou' (Louis Bradfield) Ber 2525 (1901)
SC 'Lousiana Lou' (Alma Jones) EB 5041, Zon 594
SC 'I Want yer, ma Honey' (Burt Shepard) Ber 2261 (1898)
SC 'I Want yer, ma Honey' (Louis Bradfield) Ber 2530 (1901)
SC 'I Want yer, ma Honey' (Yvette Guilbert) G&T 3736 (1907)
SC 'I Want yer, ma Honey' (Alma Jones) EB 5043
SC 'Her golden Hair was Hanging down her Back' (Harry Taylor) Ber 2859 (1900)
SC 'Her golden Hair was Hanging down her Back' (George J. Gaskin) Ber 938 recorded USA 1896
SC 'Over the Hills' (Alma Jones) EB 5043

	Inst	'Lousiana Lou' (Leslie Stuart, piano) Ber 5516 (1899)
	Orch	'Her golden Hair . . .'/'Over the Hills' (Grenadier Guards Band) Ber 63 (1899)
	Orch	'Brown of Colorado'/Japanese Dance/'I Am the Johnny who Trots them Round' (Grenadier Guards Band) Ber 64 (1899)
	Orch	Perambulator Duet/'Superfluous Relations' (Grenadier Guards Band) Ber 65 (1899)
	Orch	'She'll now be a Lady' (Grenadier Guards Band) Ber 66 (1899)
	SC	Vocal Gems (Light Opera Company) HMV 04533
0151	**The Shop Girl** (1920 revival)	
	OC	'My shy Love' (Thorpe Bates, Nancie Lovat)/'If you only Knew' (Thorpe Bates) Col F-1048 (1920)
	OC	'Not a little Bit'/'You Know how much I Love You' (Evelyn Laye, Roy Royston) Col F–1049 (1920)
	OC	'The Guards' Brigade'/'The Shop Girl' (Evelyn Laye) Col F–1050, Col F–1052 (1920)
	OC	'Is it Fair?'/'The popular Poplar Sweetstuff Shop (Popperty-Pop)' (Alfred Lester) Col F–1053 (1920)
	OC	'Over the Hills' (Nancie Lovat) Col F–1052 (1920)
	OC	'Brown of Colorado' (Leonard Mackay)/'Love on the Japanese Plan' (Roy Royston, Mamie Watson) Col F–1051 (1920)
	Orch	Selection (Gaiety Theatre Orchestra) Col 822 (1920)
0155	**An Artist's Model** (1895)	
	OC	'Laughing Song' (Maurice Farkoa) Ber 1302 (1896), Ber 2128 (1898), Ber 32651 (1899)
	OC	'Le Fou Rire' (Maurice Farkoa) (in French) Ber 2125 (1898), Ber 32111 (1899), Ber 32654 (1899), G&T GC3–2261, Zon X2282, HMV E–325 (1905)
	SC	'Is Love a Dream' (Conway Dixon) Zon 12870
	Orch	Selection (Band of H. M. Grenadier Guards) Ber 49/50/51 (1899)
0161	**Shamus O'Brien** (1896)	
	OC	'Ochone! When I Used to be Young' (Joseph O' Mara) G&T GC2–2567 (1901)
	SC	'The Song of the Banshee' (Muriel Terry) Pathé 579
	SC	'Where Is the Man?' (Edith Kirkwood) Pathé 5193
	Orch	Overture (conducted by the composer, Sir Charles Stanford) HMV 2–0699, D–192 (1916)
	Orch	Overture (Hallé Orchestra conducted by Sir Hamilton Harty) Col D1428
0162	**The Grand Duke** (1896)	
	RevC	LP (Lyric Theatre of Washington, DC) private label (USA) two records (1962)
	RevC	LP (Cheam Operatic Society with Southern Festival Orchestra) Pearl SHE516/7 (1974)
	SC	Dec SKL5239/40 (rel. 1976)
0164	**The French Maid** (1897)	
	SC	'Twin Duet' (Stanley Kirkby, Ernest Pike) G&T 4309 (1904)
	SC	'Twin Duet' (Stanley Kirkby, George Baker) Pathé 200
	SC	'Twin Duet' (Harry Bluff) Fav 475 (1912)

	Orch	Medley No. 1 (Seventh Regiment Band) Ber 85
	Orch	Medley No. 2 (Seventh Regiment Band) Ber 86
0168	**The Geisha** (1896)	
	OC	'The Jewel of Asia' (Marie Tempest) Ber 3229 (1901), RR 'Singing Actresses' WRC SH 433 (1982) and on '40 years of English Musical Comedy' Rococo 4007 (Canada)
	RC	'Jack's the Boy' (Conway Dixon, OC understudy) Zon C–2291 (1903)
	RC	'Star of my Soul' (Conway Dixon, OC understudy) Zon 12871
	RevC	'Jack's the Boy' (H. Scott Russell) Ber 2005 (1898), Ber 2005–X (1899), Ber 2983 (1900)
	RevC	'Star of my Soul' (Robert Evett) Odeon A–140, Odeon 0240, Odeon 44632 (1907)
	SC	'The Jewel of Asia' (Syria Lamonte) Ber 3012 (1898)
	SC	'The Jewel of Asia' (Eric Farr) EB 5251
	SC	'Jack's the Boy' (Louis Breeze) Ber 2278 (1901)
	SC	'Jack's the Boy' (Ian Colquhoun) Ber 2721 (1899)
	SC	'Jack's the Boy' (George Baker) Pathé 8847
	SC	'Jack's the Boy' (Stephen Burdock) Ariel 4216, Grammavox D83–2175
	SC	'Jack's the Boy' (Eric Farr) Zon X–2291, EB 5278
	SC	'Jack's the Boy' (Robert Howe) EB Winner 2689
	SC	'Star of my Soul' (George Baker) HMV B3546
	SC	'Star of my Soul' (Tom Bryce) Ber 2187 (1898)
	SC	'Star of my Soul' (Wills Page) Ber 2199 (1898) Ber 2964
	SC	'Star of my Soul' (Robert Michaelis) HMV 02293 (1910)
	SC	'Star of my Soul' (Bantock Pierpoint) Pathé 192
	SC	'Star of my Soul' (Louis Breeze) G&T 2–2553 (1902)
	SC	'Star of my Soul' (Ivor Foster) Odeon 0660, Odeon 66659
	SC	'Star of my Soul' (Jack Sherwood) Beka 641–4172
	SC	'Star of my Soul' (Alan Turner) Sterling Cyl 645 (1906)
	SC	'Star of my Soul' (Eric Farr) EB 5243
	SC	'Star of my Soul' (William Howard) EB 5413
	SC	'Star of my Soul' (Walter Hyde) Zon X–42642
	SC	'Chin Chin Chinaman' (S. H. Dudley) G&T 2–2165, GC2–2696 Ber 1011 (USA)
	SC	'Chin Chin Chinaman' (Ewald Bruckner) (in German) Ber 42603
	SC	'Chin Chin Chinaman' (Stanley Kirkby) G&T 3–2492
	SC	'Chin Chin Chinaman' (Dan W. Quinn) Ber 525 (recorded USA 1896)
	SC	'Chin Chin Chinaman' (Will Terry) Zon X–42532
	SC	'Chin Chin Chinaman' (Harry Bluff) EB 5601
	SC	'The Amorous Goldfish' (Virginia Perry) Col 5020
	SC	'The Amorous Goldfish' (Syria Lamonte) Ber 3020 (1898)
	SC	'The Amorous Goldfish' (Edith Trew) Fav 452–66124
	SC	'The Amorous Goldfish' (Alma Jones) EB 5061
	SC	'The Amorous Goldfish' (Herr Gialdini, whistler) Zon Z29589
	SC	'The Interfering Parrot' (Denise Orme) G&T 3655 (1906) B–442
	SC	'The Interfering Parrot' (Harry Bluff) EB 5613
	SC	'Chon Kina' (Denise Orme) G&T 3665 (1906)
	SC	'Chon Kina' (Beatrice Hart) Ber 3079 (1899)
	SC	'A Geisha's Life' (Syria Lamonte) Ber 3000 (1898)

SC 'I Can't Refrain from Laughing' (Clara Evelyn) HMV 3935, HMV B–480 (1912)
SS 'Love, Could I only Tell Thee' (Harrison Brockbank) Ber 2016 (1898)
SC 'Love, Could I only Tell Thee' (Thorpe Bates) Pathé 5580
SC 'Love, Could I only Tell Thee' (Albert Goodwin) Zon X–42070
SC 'Kissing Duet' (Denise Orme as May Loveday, Stanley Kirkby as Walter Miller) Zon X–44054, Zon 524 (1906)
SC 'Kissing Duet' (Winifred Hare, Stanley Kirkby) EB 6929
SC 'Toy Duet' (Winifred Marwood, Montague Borwell) Ber 4017 (1898)
SC 'Pearl of the radiant Eastern Sea' (Finale Act I) (John M. Hay) Zon X–2293
GSC LP 'Die Geisha' (in German) Dec LW5049 (UK)
GSC 'Goldfischlied' (Anna Müller) (in German) Ber 43157
GSC 'Goldfischlied' (Phylla Siegmann-Wolff) (in German) Ber 43139
GSC 'Mimosa Walzer' (Phylla Siegmann-Wolff) (in German) Ber 43140
GSC 'Lach Arie' (Marie Halton) (in German) Ber 73164
ISC LP 'La Geisha' (in Italian) Fonit-Cetra LPS27 (1974)
ISC LP 'La Geisha' (in Italian) EDM 4020
SC Vocal Gems (Savoy Light Opera Singers and Players) EB Winner L5305
SC Vocal Gems (Light Opera Company) HMV C–2144
SC Vocal Gems, Vocalian Broadcast 5030
SC Medley (Columbia Light Opera Company) Col DX–256 (1930)
Orch 'The Interfering Parrot' and 'A Geisha's Life' (Grenadier Guards Band) Ber 8 (1899)
Orch 'Chin Chin Chinaman' (Grenadier Guards Band) Ber 9 (1899)
Orch 'Oh, what Will they Do with Molly?' and 'Star of my Soul' (Grenadier Guards Band) Ber 55 (1899)
Orch 'On Service' (Grenadier Guards Band) Ber 56 (1899)
Orch 'A Geisha's Life' and 'Chon-Kina' (Royal Artillery Band) Ber 78 (1899)
Orch Selection (British Military Band) Zon 681
Orch Selection (Silver Stars Band) Regal G–8189
Orch Pot-pourri (Seidler's Military Band, Berlin) Zon X–20516
Orch Selection (Band of H. M. Coldstream Guards) HMV2–216/7

0180 **The Circus Girl** (1896)
OC 'A simple little String' (Ellaline Terriss) G&T GC–3440 (1903)
OC 'The Way to Treat a Lady' (Connie Ediss) Ber 3162 (1900), G&T GC–3445
USOC 'A simple little String' (Virginia Earle) BER 1776 (Recorded USA)
RC 'She May not Be that Kind of Girl at All' (Louis Bradfield) Ber 2910
SC 'A simple little String' (Alma Jones) EB 5045
SC 'A simple little String' (Harry Bluff) EB 5623
SC 'She never Did the same Thing Twice' (Dan W. Quinn) Ber 1731
SC 'She never Did the same Thing Twice' (Russel Hunting) EB 5755
Orch Selection (Seventh Regiment Band) Ber 87
Orch Selections I and II (Grenadier Guards Band) Ber 21 and 27 (1898)

0207 **The Dandy Fifth** (1898)
RC 'The Toast of the Dandy Fifth' (H. Scott Russell) Ber 2264 (1898)

0209 **A Runaway Girl** (1898)
OC 'Society' (Connie Ediss) Ber 3159 (1900) RR 'Forty Years of English Musical

	Comedy' Rococo 4007 (Canada), G&T 3268 (1901), EB 6483
OC	'The Boy Guessed Right'/'No one in the World' (Ellaline Terriss) in 'Gaiety Medley' G&T 03006, G&T 3268, G&T 3457 (1903)
OC	'I Thought it my Business to Say So' (Connie Ediss) Ber 3156 (1900)
OC	'Not the sort of a Girl I Care About' (Louis Bradfield) Ber 2939 (1900)
SC	'Not the sort of a Girl I Care About' (Harry Bluff) EB 5598
SC	'The Singing Girl' (Syria Lamonte) Ber 3016 (1898)
SC	'Soldiers in the Park' (Syria Lamonte) Ber 3011 (1898)
SC	'Soldiers in the Park' (Mrs G.) Ber 3063
SC	'Soldiers in the Park' (Beatrice Hart, chorus) Ber 3080 (1899)
SC	'Soldiers in the Park' (Alma Jones) EB 5044
SC	'Soldiers in the Park' (Georgia Glee Singers) Ber 4107 (1899)
Orch	'Soldiers in the Park' (Hotel Cecil Orchestra) Zon 1113
Orch	'Soldiers in the Park' (Band of H. M. Grenadier Guards) Ber 24 (1899)
SC	'Sea-girt Land of my Home' (Tom Bryce) Ber 2332 (1899)
SC	'No one in the World like you' (Winifred Marwood, Montague Borwell) Ber 4015–X (1898)
SC	'The Man from Cooks' (Fred Dixon) G&T 2–2042 (1982)
SC	'Society' (Florence Venning) Col cyl 200 362
SC	'The Boy Guessed Right' (S. H. Dudley) G&T 2–2750 (1902)
SC	'The Boy Guessed Right' (Harry Bluff) EB 5602
SC	'The Piccaninnies' (Harry Bluff) EB 5604
SC	'Society' (Harry Bluff) EB 5605
SC	'Not the sort of Girl I Care About' (Alf Gordon) Col cyl 200 189
SC	Vocal Gems (Victor Light Opera Co.) Vic 31845 (USA) (1911)
Orch	Selection (The British Military Band) Zon 687

0210 **The Beauty Stone** (1898)

RevC	LP (The Prince Consort conducted by David Lyle) Pearl SHE579/80 (1983)

0211 **A Greek Slave** (1898)

OC	'Saturnalia' (H. Scott Russell with chorus) Ber 2338 (1899)
OC	'The Revels' (H. Scott Russell) Ber 2959 (1900)
OC	'The Girl of my Heart' (H. Scott Russell) Ber 2984 (1900)
RC	'The golden Isle' (Maud Boyd) Ber 3182 (1899)
RC	'Freedom' (Conway Dixon) Ber 2962 (1900)
SC	'Freedom' (Ian Colquhoun) Ber 2714 (1899), Zon 12796
SC	'All Is Fair' (Winifred Marwood, Montague Borwell) Ber 4110 (1899)
SC	'The Girl of my Heart' (Stanley Kirkby) G&T 3–2135 (1904)
SC	'The Girl of my Heart' (Louis Breeze) Ber 2925 (1900)
SC	'I'm a naughty Girl' (Beatrice Hart) Ber 3078 (1899)
Orch	'Whirligig Trio' Ber 14, 'The golden Isle' Ber 15, 'Duet' Ber 18, 'The Girl of my Heart' Ber 28, all by Band of H. M. Grenadier Guards (1899)

0219 **Milord Sir Smith** (1898)

OC	'Love Me just a little, Sue' (Ada Reeve) Ber 3206 (1900), Pathé 50065

0229 **A Chinese Honeymoon** (1901)

OC	'I Want to be a Lidy' (Louie Freear) G&T 3412 (1902 and 1903), Pathé 50033

RC 'I Want to be a Lidy' (Hilda Trevalyan) Pathé 50025
RC 'The twiddley Bits' (Hilda Trevalyan) Pathé 50026
RC 'Martha Spanks the grand Pianner' (Hilda Trevalyan) Pathé 50029
RC 'The à la Girl' (Marie Dainton) G&T 3409, Pathé 50030, G&T 3317 (1902)
RC 'Sweet little Sing-Sing' (Marie Dainton) G&T 3416 (1902), Pathé 50033
RC 'Mandie of Ohio' (Marie Dainton) Pathé 50031
SC 'I Want to be a Lidy' (Alma Jones) EB 5083
SC 'I Want to be a Lidy' (W. H. Berry) Col cyl 200 731
SC 'The twiddley Bits' (Alma Jones) EB 5082
SC 'The twiddley Bits' (W. H. Berry) Col cyl 200 746
SC 'Martha Spanks the grand Pianner' (Alma Jones) EB 5085
SC 'The à la Girl' (Alma Jones) EB 5081
SC 'The à la Girl' (Elsie Steadman) Zon 12847, EB 5989
SC 'The à la Girl' (W. H. Berry) Col 25014 (1903), Zon 587
SC 'Daisy with the Dimple on her Chin' (Alma Jones) EB 5084
SC 'Daisy with the Dimple on her Chin' (Florence de Vere) G&T 3299, G&T 3308 (1902)
SC 'That happy Land' (Owen Way) Zon 1064
SC 'That happy Land' (W. H. Berry) Col cyl 200 591
SC 'A paper Fan' (Florence de Vere) G&T 3298 (1902)
SC 'Egypt' (Stanley Kirkby) G&T 2121 (1904), G&T 2–2491 (1904)
SC 'Egypt' (Stanley Kirkby as Charles Holland) Zon X–42255, Zon 42317
SC 'Egypt' (May Beatty) Sterling cyl 751 (1908)
SC 'Roses red and White' (Alma Jones, Eric Farr) EB 5545

0230 **San Toy** (1899)

OC 'The One in the World' (H. Scott Russell) Ber 2960 (1900)
OC 'Love has Come from Lotus Land' (H. Scott Russell) Ber 1985 (1900)
OC 'When you Are Wed to Me' (H. Scott Russell with RC Louie Collier) Ber 4082–X (1900)
OC 'The little China Maid' (H. Scott Russell with RC Louie Collier) Ber 4078 (1900)
OC 'I Mean to Introduce it into China' (Daly's Theatre Chorus) Ber 4518 (1900)
OC 'Chinee Soje-Man' (Huntley Wright) Ber 2946
OC 'The Moon' (Maude Marsden with Daly's Theatre Chorus) Ber 520 (1900)
RC 'The Emperor's Own' (Louis Bradfield with Daly's Theatre Chorus) Ber 4519 (1900)
RevC 'Love has Come from Lotus Land' (Conway Dixon) Zon X–2290
SC 'The One in the World' (Louis Henry) Ber 2907 (1900)
SC 'The Little China Maid' (Miss Fowler, Reginald Kenneth) Ber 4120
SC 'The Little China Maid' (Florence de Vere, William Paull) Ber 4049
SC 'The Little China Maid' (Maude Marsden, Louis Henry) Ber 4069 (1900)
SC 'I Mean to Introduce it into China' (Harry Bluff) EB 5686
SC 'Chinee Soje-Man' (Fred Dixon) G&T 2–2047, G&T 2–2571 (1901)
SC 'Chinee Soje-Man' (Harry Bluff) EB 5646
SC 'The Moon' (Maude Marsden) Ber 4520, Ber 5520 (1900)
SC 'Rhoda and her Pagoda' (Maude Marsden) Ber 4517 (1900)
SC 'Rhoda and her Pagoda' (Alma Jones) Zon 591, EB 5047
SC 'Sons of the Motherland' (William Paull) G&T 2–2631
SC 'Sons of the Motherland' (Leo Stormont) Col 25334, Pathé 60280, Col cyl 200 484

SC 'Sons of the Motherland' (R. Lloyd Morgan) EB 12832
SC 'Sons of the Motherland' (Eric Farr) EB 5320
SC 'Sons of the Motherland' (Ian Colquhoun) Zon X–2309 (1902)
SC 'A.B.C.' (Maude Marsden, Louis Henry) Ber 4071 (1900)
SC 'Pletty Little Chinee' (Maude Marsden, Louis Henry) Ber 4070 (1900)
SC 'Samee Gamee' (Maude Marsden, Louis Henry) Ber 4068 (1900)
SC 'Samee Gamee' (Fred Dixon) G&T 2–2048, G&T 2–2572 (1901)
SC 'Six little Wives' (Harry Bluff) EB 5676
Orch Selections I, II, III, IV (London Regimental Band) EB cyls 136/7/8/9
Orch Selection (British Military Band) Zon X–262
Orch Selection (Municipal Concert Band) Ber 97/104/105/106

0231 **Florodora** (1899)

OC 'I've an Inkling' (Ada Reeve, accompanist Paul Rubens) Ber 3211 (1900)
OC 'Tact' (Ada Reeve, accompanist Paul Rubens) Ber 3210 (1900)
OC 'Willie Was a gay Boy' (Kate Cutler) Ber 3205 (1900)
OC 'Whistling' (Kate Cutler) Ber 3204 (1900)
OC 'The Queen of the Philippine Islands' (Evie Greene) Pathé 941
OC 'The Queen of the Philippine Islands' (Ada Reeve) Ber 3209 (1900), RR 'Singing Actresses' WRC SH433
OC 'Tell me, pretty Maiden' (Lyric Theatre Chorus with Leslie Stuart, piano) Ber 4524 (1900)
OCUS 'Tell me, pretty Maiden' (three members of the original New York sextette, with male chorus) Col cyl 31604, Col 6471, Col A–485, Marconi 0376 (1902)
OC 'Galloping' (Kate Cutler with Louis Bradfield RC) Ber 4119 (1900), 4119–X
OC 'Opening Chorus' (Lyric Theatre chorus with Leslie Stuart, piano) Ber 4523 (1900)
RC 'I Want to Be a Military Man' (Louis Bradfield) Ber 4521 (1900), Ber 4521–X, Zon X–2289 (1903), EB 5426
RC 'Phrenology' (Louis Bradfield) Ber 4522 (1900)
RC 'He Loves me, he Loves me Not' (Florence St John) Ber 3200 (1900)
RC 'The Shade of the Palm' (Sydney Barraclough) Ber 2932 (1900)
SC 'I've an Inkling' (Harry Bluff) EB 5642
SC 'Tact' (Harry Bluff) EB 5643
SC 'Whistling' (S. H. Dudley) G&T 2–2694
SC 'Tell me, pretty Maiden' (Stanley Kirkby, Mabel Medrow) Ber 4300
SC 'Tell me, pretty Maiden' (Alma Jones, Eric Farr) EB 5548
SC 'Tell me, pretty Maiden' (Victor Light Opera Co.) Vic 16061 (USA)
BC 'The Shade of the Palm' (Stanley Kirkby as Charles Holland) Zon X–42146
SC 'The Shade of the Palm' (Edgar Coyle) Col 25259, Col cyl 200751
SC 'The Shade of the Palm' (Leonard Russell) Nicole 5442
SC 'The Shade of the Palm' (Arthur Grover) Sterling cyl 300 (1906)
SC 'The Shade of the Palm' (Eric Farr) EB 5291
SC 'When I Leave Town' (Alma Jones) EB 5054
SC Vocal Gems (HMV Light Opera Co.) HMV C–2253 (1931)
SC Vocal Gems (Victor Light Opera Co.) Vic 31817 (USA) (1911) HMV 04519, Vic 35451 (USA)
SC Vocal Gems (Light Opera Co.) HMV 04534, HMV C–516 (1913)
SC Vocal Medley (Columbia Light Opera Co.) Col A–5326 (1911), Col A–6158 (1920), Col DX–126 (1930)
SC Vocal Medley (Brunswick Light Opera Co.) Bru 20021

Orch 'I've an Inkling'/'The Shade of the Palm' (Municipal Military Band) Ber 109
Orch Selections I, II, III (London Regimental Band) EB cyls 143/4/5
Orch Selection (Band of H. M. Coldstream Guards) HMV C-407 (1911)
Orch Selection (British Military Band) Zon 682
Orch Selection (Hotel Cecil Orchestra) Zon X–342

0232 **The Rose of Persia** (1899)

RevC LP (Believed to be St Albans' Operatic Society) Rare Recorded Editions SRRE 152/3 (1963)
SC 'The small street Arab' (C. H. Workman) Odeon 0851 (1912), RR 'The Art of the Savoyard' Pearl GEMM120, and on Pearl GEMM135
SC 'Drinking Song' ('I Care not if the Cup I Hold') (H. Scott Russell) Ber 2963 (1900)
SC 'Drinking Song' (Alfred Heather) Pathé 215
SC 'Drinking Song' (John M. Hay) Zon 12808
SC 'Drinking Song' (Harry Dearth) Sterling cyl 357 (1906)
SC 'Drinking Song' (Vincent Hands) Grammavox 085–2168
SC 'Drinking Song' (Albert Pearce) EB 5138
SC 'Drinking Song' (Walter Glynne) HMV B–4045
SC 'Drinking Song' (Webster Booth) HMV B–9999 (1950)
Orch Selections I, II, III (London Regimental Band) EB cyls 140/141/142

0233 **The Messenger Boy** (1900)

OC 'Comme çi, comme Ça' (Connie Ediss) Ber 3161 (1900)
OC 'In the Wash' (Connie Ediss) Ber 3160, Ber 3160–X (1900)
OC 'They're all after Pott' (Fred Wright Jr) G&T 3–2039 (1904)
SC 'They're all after Pott' (Herbert Darnley) Ber 2965
SC 'They're all after Pott' (Harry Taylor) Ber 2870 (1900), Ber 2870X
SC 'When the Boys Come Home once More' (H. Scott Russell) Ber 2974 (1900)
SC 'When the Boys Come Home once More' (Eric Farr) Ber 2877 (1900)
SC 'When the Boys Come Home once More' (Florence Venning) Col cyl 200 615
SC 'When the Boys Come Home once More' (Alma Jones) EB 5051
SC 'In the Wash' (Alma Jones) EB 5049
SC 'Comme çi, comme Ça' (Alma Jones) EB 5050
SC 'Maisie' (Alma Jones) EB 5048
SC 'Maisie' (Florence Venning) Col cyl 200 281
SC 'Maisie' (Ernest Chester) Col cyl 200 146
SC 'The Messenger Boy' (Herbert Darnley) Ber 2457 (1900)
SC 'The Messenger Boy' (Fred Dixon) G&T 2–2578 (1901)
SC 'Hooker Pasha' (Harry Taylor) Ber 2872 (1900), Ber 2872X
Orch 'They're all after Pott'/'Bradshaw's Guide' (Municipal Concert Band) Ber 99 (1900)
Orch 'The Messenger Boy'/'Mary, Mary, quite Contrary' (Municipal Concert Band) Ber 100 (1900)
Orch 'Comme çi, comme Ça'/'Mummies' (Municipal Concert Band) Ber 102 (1900)
Orch 'Maisie'/'Up the Nile' (Municipal Concert Band) Ber 103 (1900)
Orch Selections I, II, III, IV (London Regimental Band) EB cyls 146/147/148/149

0236 **H.M.S. Irresponsible** (1901)

OC 'Topsy-Turvy' (Arthur Roberts) G&T 3–2272 (1905)

SC 'Topsy-Turvy' (Louis Bradfield) Ber 2101 (1901) G&T 2–2679 (1902), Pathé 60765
SC 'La, la, la' (Florence Schuberth) G&T 3241 (1902)
SC 'La, la, la' (Maud Mortimer) Zon 12852

0237 **Kitty Grey** (1901)

OC 'The Powder Puff' (Evie Greene) G&T 3410 (1902), Zon X–43055, RR 'Singing Actresses' WRC SH433
OC 'Kitty Grey' (Maurice Farkoa) G&T 2–2528 (1901)
OC 'Trust Me' (Ethel Sydney) G&T 3429 (1902)
RC 'The Powder Puff' (Ada Reeve) Pathé 50063
SC 'Just Seventeen' (Alma Jones) EB 5089
SC 'Kitty's not Built that Way' (Alma Jones) EB 5090
SC 'Walking Home with Angeline' (Stanley Kirkby as Charles Holland) Zon X–42290
SC 'Walking Home with Angeline' (Stanley Kirkby) EB6587
SC 'Walking Home with Angeline' (Florrie Forde) Sterling cyl 172 (1905)

0244 **The Emerald Isle** (1901)

RevC LP (The Prince Consort) Pearl SHE 574/5 (1982)
SC 'The Age in which we're Living' (Harry Bluff) EB 5697
Orch Selection (Band of H.M. Coldstream Guards) HMV C415, RR RRE 169
Orch Selection (British Military Band) Zon 679

0246 **The Silver Slipper** (1901)

OC 'Good Behaviour' (Connie Ediss) G&T 3266 (1901)
OC 'Class' (Connie Ediss) G&T 3267 (1901), EB 6484
OC 'The Detrimental Man' (Louis Bradfield) G&T 2433 (1901) Zon X–42057
OC 'A Happy Day' (Louis Bradfield) G&T 2414 (1901), Zon X–42058
OC 'Clytie' (Louis Bradfield) Col 25155 (1903)
SC 'Good Behaviour' (Harry Bluff) EB 5682
SC 'Class' (Alma Jones) EB 5079
SC 'Class' (Harry Bluff) EB 5681
SC 'Class' (Elsie Steadman) Zon 12851
SC 'Two Eyes of Blue' (Albert Pearce) Ber 2–2069, (1902) G&T 2–2618, EB 5136
SC 'Two Eyes of Blue' (Louis Breeze) G&T 2–2040 (1901)
SC 'Two Eyes of Blue' (Harry McDonough) G&T 2–2720 (1902)
Orch Selection (Band of H.M. Scots Guards) G&T 01 (1903)
Orch 'Come little Girl and Tell me Truly' (Municipal Military Band) Ber 303

0249 **The Toreador** (1901)

OC 'Keep off the Grass' (Gertie Millar) recorded 1939 RR 'Forty Years of English Musical Comedy' Rococo 4007 (Canada)
RC 'Maud' (Connie Ediss) G&T 3447 (1903)
RC 'The Language of the Flowers' (Ethel Sydney) G&T 3432 (1903)
SC 'Keep off the Grass' (W. H. Berry) Col cyl 200 459
SC 'Keep off the Grass' (Fred Dixon) G&T 2–2281 (1903)
SC 'Keep off the Grass' (Harry Bluff) EB 5736
SC 'Maud' (Alma Jones) Zon 5901, EB 5078
SC 'Maud' (Will Deller) G&T 2–2254 (1902)

SC	'Maud' (W. H. Berry) Col cyl 200 495
SC	'Maud' (Harry Bluff) EB 5680
SC	'The Language of the Flowers' (Ernest Chester) Col cyl XP200 561
SC	'Everybody's awfully good to Me' (Henry Lytton) G&T 2–2110 (1902), RR 'The Art of Henry Lytton' Pearl GEMM197
SC	'Everybody's awfully good to Me' (W. H. Berry) Col cyl 200 551
SC	'Everybody's awfully good to Me' (Louis Bradfield) Zon 12866
SC	'Everybody's awfully good to Me' (Harry Bluff) EB 5721
SC	'When I Marry Amelia' (Louis Bradfield) Zon 12861
SC	'When I Marry Amelia' (W. H. Berry) Col cyl 200 557 Col 25009
SC	'When I Marry Amelia' (Harry Bluff) EB 5734
SC	'When I Marry Amelia' (Henry Lytton) G&T 2–2112 (1902), RR 'The Art of Henry Lytton' Pearl GEMM197
SC	'Archie' (W. H. Berry) Col cyl 200 550
SC	'Archie' (Harry Bluff) EB 5735
SC	'Archie' (Henry Lytton) G&T 2–2137 (1902), RR 'The Art of Henry Lytton' Pearl GEMM197
SC	'Archie' (Louis Bradfield) Zon 12860
SC	'I'm Romantic' (Harry Bluff) EB 5737
SC	'Captivating Cora' (W. H. Berry) Col cyl 200 667 Col 25009 (1903)
SC	'My Toreador' (Lena Maitland) G&T 3439 (1903)
SC	'Toreador's song'/'España' (Columbia Light Opera Co.) Col 9896
Orch	'The Language of the Flowers' (Municipal Military Band) Ber 300
Orch	'Keep off the Grass'/'Away to España' (Municipal Military Band) Ber 301
Orch	'The Toreador Song' (Municipal Military Band) Ber 304
Orch	Selection (British Military Band) Zon X 264

0255 **Bluebell in Fairyland** (1901)

OC	'The Honeysuckle and the Bee'/'Only a Penny, Sir' (Ellaline Terriss) HMV C–2432 (1932)
SC	'The Honeysuckle and the Bee' (Alma Jones) Zon 1092
SC	'The Honeysuckle and the Bee' (Maurice Farkoa, in French) Ber 32112 (1899)
SC	'Dreamland' (Arthur Grover) EB 13456
SC	'Dreamland' (Albert Pearce) Zon 1075
SC	'The Sunflower and the Sun' (Alma Jones) Zon 593
Orch	'The Honeysuckle and the Bee' (Musical Avolos) Zon 46750

0257 **A Country Girl** (1902)

OC	'Try again Johnnie' (Evie Greene) G&T 3411 (1902), RR 'Singing Actresses' WRC SH433, RR 'Forty Years of English Musical Comedy' Rococo 4007 (Canada)
OC	'Not the little Boy she Knew' (Evie Greene) G&T 3419 (1902), Zon 43056, RR as 'There Went a country Girl one Day' in 'Singing Actresses' WRC SH433
OC	'Me and Mrs Brown' (Huntley Wright) EB 6171
RC	'Me and Mrs Brown' (Roland Henry) Zon X 2352
RC	'Yo Ho, little Girls, Yo Ho' (Roland Henry) Zon 12932
RC	'The pink Hungarian Band' (Roland Henry) Zon X 2353
RC	'Coo' (Isabel Jay) G&T 3530 (1904)

RevC 'Me and Mrs Brown' (W. H. Berry) Col cyl 200 575
RevC 'Yo Ho, little Girls, Yo Ho' (W. H. Berry) Col cyl 200 744 Col 25080 (1903)
RevC 'Peace, Peace' (W. H. Berry) Col cyl 200 745, Col 25081
SC 'Try again, Johnnie' (Florence Venning) Col cyl 200 585
SC 'Try again, Johnnie' (Florence de Vere) Ber 3242 (1902)
SC 'Try again, Johnnie' (Harry Bluff) EB 5726
SC 'Try again, Johnnie' (Jane Eyre) Nicole 5420
SC 'Me and Mrs Brown' (Harry Bluff) EB 5738
SC 'Me and Mrs Brown' (Henry Lytton) G&T 2–2136 (1902), RR 'The Art of Henry Lytton' Pearl GEMM197
SC 'Coo' (Margaret Parker) EB 6135
SC 'Coo' (Florence de Vere) Ber 3242
SC 'Yo Ho, little Girls, Yo Ho' (Harry Bluff) EB 5721
SC 'Peace, Peace' (Harry Bluff) EB 5732
SC 'Peace, Peace' (Albert Pearce) EB 5120
SC 'Peace, Peace' (Henry Lytton) G&T 2–2111 (1902), RR 'The Art of Henry Lytton' Pearl GEMM197
SC 'Two little Chicks' (Henry Lytton, Louie Henri) G&T 4062 (1902), G&T 4244, RR 'The Art of Henry Lytton' Pearl GEMM197
SC 'Two little Chicks' (Florence Venning, Edgar Coyle) Col 25352
SC 'Two little Chicks' (Elsie Steadman, Harry Bluff) EB 5998
SC 'Quarrelling' (Elsie Steadman, Harry Bluff) EB 5999
SC 'Quarrelling' (Henry Lytton, Louie Henri) G&T 4084 (1902) G&T 5245, RR 'The Art of Henry Lytton' Pearl GEMM197
SC 'In the King's Name, Stand!' (William Howard) EB 5405
SC 'In the King's Name, Stand!' (William Paull) G&T 2–2096 (1902)
SC 'The Sailor's Life' (William Paull) G&T 2–2115 (1902)
SC 'The Sailor's Life' (William Howard) EB 5406
SC 'Molly the Marchioness' (Florence de Vere) Ber 3311 (1902)
SC 'Molly the Marchioness' (Harry Bluff) EB 5739
SC 'Molly the Marchioness' (Elsie Steadman) Zon 12850
SC 'Under the Deodar' (Florence Venning) Col cyl 202 586 Col 25139
SC 'Under the Deodar' (Jane Eyre) Nicole 5416
SC 'Under the Deodar' (Louie Henri) Ber 3247 (1902)
SC 'My own little Girl' (Albert Pearce) EB 5133
SC 'My own little Girl' (William Howard) EB 5407
SC 'Boy and Girl' (Margaret Parker, Albert Pearce) EB 6159
SC 'Boy and Girl' (Amy Evans, Francis Ludlow) Pathé 586
SC 'Boy and Girl' (Florence de Vere, William Paull) G&T 4061 (1902)
SC 'There's plenty of Love in the World' (Bessie Jones as Aimee Maxwell) HMV B–649
SC 'The Language of Love' (Annie Purcell) Pathé 50183
SC Vocal Gems (Victor Light Opera Co.) Vic 31838 (USA)
SC Vocal Gems (Columbia Light Opera Co.) Col DX–73
Orch Selection (Municipal Military Band) Ber 309
Orch Selection II (Municipal Military Band) Ber 311
Orch Selection (Band of H.M. Coldstream Guards) HMV C–416
Orch Selection (Band of the Royal Air Force) Re MX–10
Orch Selection (London Theatre Orchestra) Col DX–45

0258 **Naughty Nancy** (1902)

SC	'You Are my World' (John M. Hay) Zon X–2667

0260 **Merrie England** (1902)

SC	Conducted by Mr Edward German HMV D19 to 28 (1918)
SC	Conducted by Sir Edward German Col DB–478 to 483 (1931)
SC	LP Sadlers Wells revised version HMV CLP 1376/7, CSD 1311/2 (1960), RR EMI-Double Up DUO 121
OC	'The Yeomen of England' (Henry Lytton) G&T 2–2654 (1902), RR 'The Art of Henry Lytton' Pearl GEMM197
OC	'King Neptune Sat on his lonely Throne' (Walter Passmore) Col 371 (1912)
OC	'The big brass Band' (Walter Passmore, Robert Howe SC) Col 252
OC	'The English Rose' (Robert Evett) Odeon 44189 (1906)
OC	'Imagination' (Henry Lytton) G&T 2–2125 (1902), RR 'The Art of Henry Lytton' Pearl GEMM197
OC	'Imagination' (Walter Passmore) Col 2521 (1913)
SC	'Love Is Meant to Make us Glad' (BBC Revue Chorus and Theatre Orchestra) Dec K844
SC	'Come to Arcadie' (Dora Labette, Hubert Eisdel) Col 9346
SC	'The Yeomen of England' (Howard Roberts) Homochord 4302, Homophone 716
SC	'The Yeomen of England' (Ian Colquhoun) Zon X2336
SC	'The Yeomen of England' (Albert Pearce) EB 5922
SC	'The Yeomen of England' (Kennerly Rumford) Col L–1008
SC	'The Yeomen of England' (Francis Ludlow) Pathé 198
SC	'The Yeomen of England' (Herbert Heyner) EB Winner 2868
SC	'The Yeomen of England' (Dennis Noble) HMV C3490
SC	'The Yeomen of England' (Oscar Natzke) Par R2723
SC	'The Yeomen of England' (Peter Dawson) HMV B3111, RR HMV G. 7EG8093
SC	'Long Live Elizabeth' (Chorus and Massed Bands) HMV B8601
SC	'Long Live Elizabeth' (Charles Williams, Concert Orchestra and Chorus) Col 371
SC	'O, peaceful England' (Gladys Ripley and Chorus) HMV C3490
SC	'O, peaceful England' (Essie Ackland and Chorus) HMV B8537
SC	'The Queen of May Is Crowned Today' (BBC Revue Chorus and Theatre Orchestra) Dec K844
SC	'The English Rose' (Webster Booth) HMV B8947
SC	'The English Rose' (D. Lloyd) Col DB 2109
SC	'The English Rose' (Walter Midgley) Col DB1899
SC	'The English Rose' (Richard Tauber) Par RO20402 (1938), RR LP Par Odeon PMC 7163
RevC	'The English Rose' (Joseph Hislop) HMV C2729
SC	'The English Rose' (Walter Glynne) HMV B2633
SC	'The English Rose' (Wilfrid Hudson) EB Winner 4922
SC	'Who Shall Say that Love Is Cruel' (Waltz song) (H. Esserman) HMV B3372
SC	'Who Shall Say that Love Is Cruel' (Gwen Catley) HMV B 1–0058
SC	Selection (Light Opera Chorus) HMV C2106, C9893
SC	Vocal Excerpts (Savoy Light Opera Singers & Players) EB Winner L5148
SC	'Love Is Meant to Make us Glad' (Rosina Buckman) Pathé 4302

SC 'Love Is Meant to Make us Glad' (Margaret Cooper) G&T 3820 (1909)
SC 'O, peaceful England' (Kirkby Lunn) Pathé 50003
SC 'In England, merrie England' (Perceval Allen, Alice Lakin, John Harrison, Robert Radford) HMV 04047 (1909), RR HMV D292
Orch Selections I & II (London Regimental Band) G&T 104/5 (1903)
Orch Selection (New Mayfair Orchestra) HMV BD746
Orch Selection (New Symphony Orchestra) HMV C2196
Orch Selection (Band of H. M. Grenadier Guards) Col 9607
Orch Selection (Band of H. M. Scots Guards) EB Winner 3414

0261 **Three Little Maids** (1902)

OC 'Girls, Girls, Girls' (George Carroll) G&T 2–2224 (1902), G&T 2–2773
OC 'The Golf Scene' (George Carroll, G. P. Huntley) G&T 1233 (1902), G&T 1372 (1907), HMV B–402 (1907), RR HMV 1372
OC 'Algy's simply awf'lly good at Algebra' (G. P. Huntley) G&T 2–2762 (1902)
OC 'A real town Lady' (Hilda Moody) Pathé 50040
OC 'She Was a Miller's Daughter' (Hilda Moody) Pathé 50041/2/3
OC 'The Fishes in the Sea' (Hilda Moody) Pathé 50044
OC 'Sal' (Madge Crichton) G&T 3425 (1902)
OC 'Men' (Madge Crichton) G&T 3426 (1902)
OC 'Something sweet about Me' (Madge Crichton) G&T 3427 (1902)
RC 'Men' (Ada Reeve) Pathé 50064
SC 'Algy's simply awf'lly good at Algebra' (Harry Bluff) EB 5731
SC 'She Was a Miller's Daughter' (J. H. Scotland) EB 5016
SC 'She Was a Miller's Daughter' (Stanley Kirkby) EB 6774
SC 'She Was a Miller's Daughter' (Florence Venning) Col cyl 200 613
SC 'She Was a Miller's Daughter' (Florence de Vere) G&T 3309, G&T 3041
SC 'She Was a Miller's Daughter' (Elsie Steadman) Zon 12848
SC 'Sal' (J. H. Scotland) EB 5015
SC 'Golf' (Fred Allandale) Fav 229–1–67015
SC 'Men' (J. H. Scotland) EB 5017
SC 'The Girl you Love' (Edgar Coyle) Col cyl 200 787, Col 25101
SC 'Men' (Elsie Steadman) Zon 12849, EB 5981
SC 'Men' (Florence Venning) Col cyl 200 614
SC 'What's a Maid to Do?' (Florence de Vere) G&T 3310 G&T 3400 (1902)
SC 'What's a Maid to Do?' (Alma Jones) EB 5018
Orch Selection (French Military Band) Ber 326
Orch Selection (Earls Court Exhibition Band) Zon 40003

0266 **My Lady Molly** (1903)

OC 'There's a little Maid I Know' (Walter Hyde) Odeon 0222, Odeon 44890, Odeon 0782 (1907)
SC 'Ballinasloe' (Herbert Darnley) G&T 2–2366 (1904)
SC 'At my Lady's Feet' (Arthur Grover) G&T 2–2877 (1903), EB 6016
SC 'At my Lady's Feet' (George Sherwood) Zon 42035
SC 'At my Lady's Feet' (Edgar Coyle) Nicole 5371
SC 'To you, Sir Miles' (Edgar Coyle) Col cyl 200 768
Orch Selections I & II (London Regimental Band) G&T 010 and 021 (1903)
Orch Selection (British Military Band) Zon X 2326

0270 **The Girl from Kays** (1902)

OC 'The Customers at Kays' (Louis Bradfield) G&T 2–2931 (1903), Col 25156, Zon X–2285
OC 'Mr Hoggenheimer' (Louis Bradfield) G&T 2–2932 (1903)
OC 'Glass, Glass' (Louis Bradfield) G&T 2–2946 (1903)
OC 'A little Thing like That' (Louis Bradfield) G&T 02033 (1903)
OC 'I Don't Care' (Louis Bradfield) G&T 02041 (1903), Col 25157, Zon X 2284, EB 6087
OC 'Matilda and the Builder' (Louis Bradfield) Col 25152, Zon X-2283 (1903), EB 6088
OC 'A high old Time' (Louis Bradfield) Col 25160 (1903)
OC * 'The Philosopher' (Louis Bradfield) G&T 2–2999 (1903)
OC * 'Remorse' (Louis Bradfield) G&T 02042 (1903)
OC * 'Mr Mosenstein' (Louis Bradfield) Col 25151 (1903), Pathé 60762, EB 6086
SC 'I don't Care' (R. Lloyd Morgan) Nicole 5348
SC 'Semi-Detached' (Henry Lytton, Louie Henri) G&T 4243 (1903), G&T GC–4295 (1903)
SC 'Make it Up' (Henry Lytton, Louie Henri) G&T 4336, G&T 4295 (1903), RR 'The Art of Henry Lytton' Pearl GEMM197
Orch Selection (London Regimental Band) G&T 09 (1903)

0272 **A Princess of Kensington** (1903)

OC 'He was a simple Sailorman' (Henry Lytton) Zon X 42329
OC 'Four jolly Sailormen' (Savoy Theatre Male Quartet, not named but almost certainly Henry Lytton, Powis Pinder, Rudolph Lewis and Charles Childerstone) G&T 04000 (1903), RR 'The Art of Henry Lytton' Pearl GEMM197
SC 'Four jolly Sailormen' (Kennerly Rumford) Monarch 02200 (1909)
SC 'Four jolly Sailormen' (Morlais Morgan) EB 2262
SC 'Four jolly Sailormen' (Robert Howe) Homochord H449
SC 'Four jolly Sailormen' (Keith Falkner) HMV B–3658 (1930)
SC 'Four jolly Sailormen' (Thorpe Bates) G&T 3–2952 (1908), HMV B–314
SC 'Four jolly Sailormen' (Oscar Natzke) Par R2723
SC 'A Sprig of Rosemarie' (Randall Jackson) Nicole 5295
SC 'Where Haven Lies' (Walter Glynne) HMV B4096

0274 **The Medal and the Maid** (1903)

SC 'In my Curriculum' (Louis Bradfield) G&T 3–2064, Col 25231 (1903)
SC 'The Frills upon the Petticoat' (Louis Bradfield) Zon X42046 (1903)
SC 'The Lady Wasn't Taking any Fruit' (Louis Bradfield) G&T 3–2000 (1903)
SC 'Vanderdecken' (Louis Bradfield) G&T 2–2948 (1903)
SC 'Publicity' (Louis Bradfield) G&T 3–2030 (1903)
SC 'The Philosophic Brigand' (Louis Bradfield) G&T 2–2999 (1903)
SC 'Any sort of a Girl' (Louis Bradfield) G&T 2–2975 (1903)
SC 'Click Went the Kodak' (Louis Bradfield) Col 25230 (1903)
SC 'Who'll Buy my Flowers?' (Sylvia Sablanc) Pathé 50048

0275 **The School Girl** (1903)

SC 'My little Canoe' (Louis Bradfield) G&T 2–2925, Col 25153 (1903)

* these songs labelled as from '*The Girl from Kays*'

SC 'The Needle in the Haystack' (Louis Bradfield), G&T 3–2055 (1903), Col 25154, Pathé 60761, EB 6094
SC 'The Needle in the Haystack' (R. Lloyd Morgan) EB 12981
SC 'Belinda on the Line' (R. Lloyd Morgan) Col 25648 (1903), Odeon 2592
SC 'My little Canoe' (Edgar Coyle) Nicole 5368
SC 'My little Canoe' (Annie Purcell) Pathé 50184

0280 **The Duchess of Dantzic** (1903)

SC 'Gentlemen of France' (Stanley Kirkby) G&T 3–2159, G&T 3–2523
SC 'Gentlemen of France' (Dalton Baker) Odeon 0577/57623
SC Vocal Gems (Light Opera Co.) HMV 04535 (1913)
SC Vocal Gems (Light Opera Co.) HMV C-2262 (1931)
Orch Selection (Band of H.M. Coldstream Guards) G&T 2–96/97
Orch Selection (The Meny's Hungarian Orchestra) Col 25537
Orch Selections (The London Military Band) Col cyls 200 940/941/942

0281 **The Orchid** (1903)

OC 'Bunny at the Bun Shop' (Fred Wright Jr) Col 25203 (1903), G&T 3–2044 (1904)
OC 'Little Mary' (Fred Wright Jr) G&T 3–2022 (1904)
OC 'Liza Ann' (Fred Wright Jr) G&T 3–2023 (1904)
OC 'The Emperor of Sahara' (Fred Wright Jr) G&T 3–2038 (1904)
SC 'Little Mary' (W. H. Berry) Col 25481 (1904) Col cyl 200 937
SC 'Bedelia' (W. H. Berry) Col cyl 200 904
SC 'Bedelia' (Hamilton Hill) G&T 3–2070 (1904)
SC 'Bedelia' (Joe O'Gorman) G&T 2–2435 (1904)
SC 'Bedelia' (Lloyd Morgan) Nicole 5543
SC 'Bedelia' (Harry Bluff) EB 6285
SC 'Bedelia' (Charles Foster) Zon X42069
SC 'Little Mary' (Lloyd Morgan) Nicole 5544
SC 'Little Mary' (Mabel Medrow) G&T 3521 (1904)
SC 'Little Mary' (Ernest Shand) Col 25517
SC 'Cordelia Malone' (Mike Magee) G&T 3–2344
SC 'Cordelia Malone' (Walter Miller) Zon 42271
SC 'Come along with Me' (Elsie Steadman) G&T 3375 (1905)
Orch Selections (Zonophone Military Band) Zon X40011 and X40016

0282 **The Earl and the Girl** (1903)

OC 'My cosy corner Girl' (Henry Lytton) G&T 3–2072 (1904), G&T 2–2462, RR 'The Art of Henry Lytton' Pearl GEMM197
OC 'By the Shores of the Mediterranean' (Henry Lytton) G&T 3–2079, G&T 2–2463 (1904), RR 'The Art of Henry Lytton' Pearl GEMM197
SC 'My cosy corner Girl' (Nora Guy) Pathé 50194
SC 'My cosy corner Girl' (Stanley Kirkby) G&T 3–2149 (1904), EB 6353
SC 'My cosy corner Girl' (Lloyd Morgan) Nicole 5345
SC 'My cosy corner Girl' (Stanley Kirkby as Charles Holland) Col cyl 200 972, Col 25615, Zon X42078
SC 'Sammy' (Louie Pounds) Pathé 50160
SC 'Sammy' (Lloyd Morgan) Nicole 5542
SC 'Sammy' (Mabel Medrow) G&T 3562 (1904)

SC 'Sammy' (Florence de Vere) G&T 3522 (1904), Zon X43061
SC 'Sammy' (Hamilton Hill) Zon 42104
SC 'Sammy' (Arthur Pearce) EB 6258
SC 'Sammy' (Wilson Hallett) Zon 42102
SC 'Sammy' (Georgia Glee Singers) Zon 44003
SC 'In Zanzibar' (Peter Dawson) EB 6509
SC 'In Zanzibar' (Wilson Hallett) Zon X42071
SC 'In Zanzibar' (Florence de Vere) G&T 3352, G&T 3525 (1904)
SC 'In Zanzibar' (Stanley Kirkby) G&T 3–2136 (1904)
Orch Waltz (Meny's White Viennese Band) G&T 082 (1906)
Orch Selections 1 & 2 (Imperial Guards Band) Zon A-120 (1913)
Orch Selection (London Regimental Band) Zon X40068

0283 **The Cherry Girl** (1903)
SC 'Little yellow Bird' (Florence de Vere) G&T 3526 (1904)
SC 'Little yellow Bird' (Lloyd Morgan) Col 25609, Col cyl 200 959
SC 'Little yellow Bird' (Stanley Kirkby) EB 6263
SC 'Pansy' (George Sherwin) Zon X42068
SC 'Pansy' (Ernest Pike as Herbert Payne) Sterling cyl 1108
SC 'Navajo' (Florrie Forde) Zon X43088
SC 'Navajo' (Peter Dawson) EB 6398
SC 'Navajo' (George Atkinson) Zon 42154
SC 'Navajo' (Stanley Kirkby as Charles Holland) Zon X42143
SC 'By the Sycamore Tree' (Miss Morgan as Helen Haydn) G&T 3361 (1904)
Orch 'Miss Innocent' (The Bohemian Band) EB cyl 683
Orch Selection (London Regimental Band) Zon X40069

0286 **The Lovebirds** (1904)
'Sammy' (see *The Earl and the Girl*)

0287 **The Blue Moon** (1905)
SC 'Burmah Girl' (Morgan Williams) Fav 1–69062 (1905)
SC 'Burmah Girl' (Arthur Grover) Sterling cyl 369 (1906)
SC 'She Didn't know' (Will Terry) Zon X42480 (1906)
SC 'Mother' (Will Terry) Zon X42479 (1906), Sterling cyl 586 (1906)
SC 'The Crocodile' (Will Terry) Sterling cyl 391 (1906)
SC 'Mother' (Alf Gordon) Pathé 308, Pathé 60559
SC 'The Crocodile' (Alf Gordon) Pathé 309, Pathé 1192, 60560
Orch Selection (Band of H.M. Coldstream Guards) Zon X40154/5/6 (1906)
Orch Selection (Band of H.M. Scots Guards) Pathé 18, 1015

0289 **The Cingalee** (1904)
OC 'My Heart's at your Feet' (Isabel Jay) G&T 3527 (1904), G&T GC-3566 (1904), RR 'Singing Actresses' WRC SH433
OC 'You and I' (Isabel Jay) G&T 3523 (1904)
OC 'You and I' (Isabel Jay, Louis Bradfield), G&T 4373 (1905), RR 'Singing Actresses' WRC SH433
OC 'The Ladies' (Louis Bradfield) G&T 3–2589 (1905), Zon X42284
OC 'Four little Girls of Ceylon' (Louis Bradfield) G&T 3–2244 (1905)

OC 'A Marriage Has Been Arranged' (Isabel Jay, Louis Bradfield) G&T 4372 (1905)
OC 'The wonderful English Pot' (Huntley Wright) EB 6332
OC 'What's the Matter with Chan' (Huntley Wright) EB 6337
SC 'My dear little Cingalee' (Stanley Kirkby) G&T 3–2110 (1904), EB 6320
SC 'My dear little Cingalee' (Stanley Kirkby as Charles Holland) Zon X42080
SC 'Pearl of sweet Ceylon' (Stanley Kirkby as Charles Holland) Zon X42079
SC 'Pearl of sweet Ceylon' (Stanley Kirkby) EB 6321
SC 'Monkey Duet' (Stanley Kirkby, Mabel Medrow) G&T 4299 (1904)
SC 'The Cinnamon Tree' (Jane Eyre) Nicole 5570
SC 'The Cinnamon Tree' (Eva Stephens) Fav 1–66032
SC 'You and I' (Jane Eyre) Nicole 5569
SC 'You and I' (Amy Evans, Francis Ludlow) Pathé 586
SC 'Sloe Eyes' (Robert Dennant) Sterling cyl 518 (1906)
SC 'Make a Fuss of Me' (Harry Bluff) EB 6412
Orch 'Pearl of sweet Ceylon'/'Tea, Tea' (London Regimental Band) Zon 40009
Orch 'The Cinnamon Tree' (London Regimental Band) Zon 40010
Orch Selections 1, 2 and 3 (London Regimental Band) Zon X40022/40025/40031
Orch Finale (London Regimental Band) Zon 40070

0295 **Sergeant Brue** (1904)

OC 'Under a Panama' (Olive Morrell) Pathé 50220 (1904)
OC 'The sweetest Girl in Dixie' (Olive Morrell) Pathé 50221 (1904)
SC 'The sweetest Girl in Dixie' (Stanley Kirkby) G&T 2–2489 (1904), G&T 3–2119 (1904), EB 6404
SC 'The sweetest Girl in Dixie' (Stanley Kirkby as Charles Holland) Zon 42113, Zon X42088
SC 'So Did Eve' (Stanley Kirkby) EB 6418
SC 'So Did Eve' (Burt Shepard) G&T 3–2511 (1904)
SC 'So Did Eve' (Charles Foster) Zon X42153
SC 'Under a Panama' (Stanley Kirkby) G&T 3–2120 (1904)
SC 'Under a Panama' (Stanley Kirkby as Charles Holland), Zon 42117
SC 'Under a Panama' (Mabel Medrow) EB 6430
SC 'Put me in my little Cell' (George Atkinson) Zon X42414
SC 'If I Built the World for You' (Arthur Graves) Pathé 871

0298 **The Catch of the Season** (1904)

RC 'My Rainbow' (Phyllis Dare) G&T 3675 (1906)
SC 'Cigarette' (Stanley Kirkby) G&T 3–2176 (1904), EB 6460
SC 'Cigarette' (Violet Essex) Pilot/Polyphon 5651 (1912)
SC 'Cigarette' (Arthur Grover) EB 13211
SC 'The Church Parade' (Stanley Kirkby) EB 6488
SC 'The Church Parade' (Stanley Kirkby as Charles Holland) Zon X42200
SC 'The Church Parade' (Stanley Kirkby as Walter Miller) G&T 3–2199 (1905), G&T 3–2555
SC 'The Church Parade' (Lloyd Morgan) EB 13226
SC 'The Church Parade' (Alfred Gordon) Nicole 5735
SC 'A wise old Owl' (Stanley Kirkby as Walter Miller) G&T 3–2210 (1905), EB 6492
SC 'A wise old Owl' (Vesta Tilley) Pathé 50211

SC 'A quaint old Bird' (Stanley Kirkby) G&T 3–2551 (1904)
SC 'A quaint old Bird' (Harry Bluff) EB 6552
SC 'My singing Bird' (Stanley Kirkby) EB 6459
SC 'Teasing' (Ernest Pike as Herbert Payne) G&T 3–2211 (1905)
SC 'Teasing' (Arthur Edwards) Zon X42227
SC 'Teasing' (Peter Hampton) EB 6506
SC 'Teasing' (Walter Malone) Zon 42270
SC 'Come down from that big Fig Tree' (Stanley Kirkby as Walter Miller) Zon X42357
SC 'The Gondolier' (Albert Pearce) EB 6403
SC 'Molly O'Halloran' (Stanley Kirkby) EB 6523
SC 'Sombrero' (Stanley Kirkby) EB 6731
SC 'Butterfly' (Albert Pearce) EB 6553
SC 'Butterfly' (Arthur Leonard) EB 6581
Orch 'The Church Parade' (London Regimental Band) EB Winner 2239
Orch 'The Church Parade' (Band of H.M. Scots Guards) EB Winner 4751

0302 **Lady Madcap** (1904)
OC 'I Like you in Velvet' (Maurice Farkoa) G&T 3–2254 (1905), HMV 4–2016, HMV B–453 (1908), Pathé 6945 (1 10)
OC 'Do I Like Love?' (Maurice Farkoa) G&T 3–2255 (1905)
OC 'My Portuguese Princess' (Maurice Farkoa, Delia Mason) G&T 4374 (1905)
SC 'I Like you in Velvet' (Arthur Grover) EB 13242
SC 'I Like you in Velvet' (Robert Dennant) Sterling cyl 254 (1906)
SC 'It's a Way we Have in the Army' (Edgar Coyle as George Preston) G&T 3–2372 (1905), Zon 42264

0304 **The Talk of the Town** (1905)
OC 'For You' (Robert Evett) Odeon 44192 (1906)
OC 'Bombay on the Nile' (Walter Passmore) Nicole 5741 (1905)
OC 'If I Were a Vanderbilt' (Walter Passmore) Nicole D–565, Nicole D–5739 (1905)
OC 'Me and my little Brood' (Walter Passmore) Nicole D–565, Nicole D–5739 (1905)
SC 'Just for the Sake of Society' (Stanley Kirkby) G&T 3–2588 (1905)
SC 'My little Laplander' (Stanley Kirkby) G&T 3–2590, G&T 3–2232, EB6615
SC 'My little Laplander' (Edgar Coyle) EB 13275
SC 'Pepita Maguire' (Stanley Kirkby) G&T 3–2591 (1905)
SC 'Pepita Maguire' (Stanley Kirkby as Charles Holland) Zon X42281 X42221
SC 'My Ellaline' (Albert Pearce) G&T 2–2082

0309 **The Spring Chicken** (1905)
Orch Selection (Black Diamonds Band as Home Guards Band) Zon 323 (1910)

0313 **The White Chrysanthemum** (1905)
OC 'O wandering Breeze' (Isabel Jay) Fav 1–66016 (1906)
OC 'Mammy's Piccaninny' (Marie George) Fav 1–66027 (1906)
Orch Selections I & II (London Regiment) Zon X4012 and 4013

0314 **Mr Popple (of Ippleton)** (1905)

OC	'Rabbits' (G. P. Huntley) G&T 1371 (1907), HMV B–394
OC	'Just Because' (Denise Orme) G&T 3644 (1906)

0316 **The Beauty of Bath** (1906)

OC	'Au Revoir, my little Hyacinth' (Phyllis Dare) G&T 3671 (1906)
SC	'Au Revoir, my little Hyacinth' (Ernest Pike as Herbert Payne) Sterling cyl 730 (1906)
SC	'Au Revoir, my little Hyacinth' (Stanley Kirkby) EB 10070

0318 **The Belle of Mayfair** (1906)

RC	'Where you Go, will I Go' (Phyllis Dare) G&T GC–3672 (1906)
SC	'Montezuma' (Stanley Kirkby) G&T 3–2459 (1906)
Orch	Selection (Clark's Concert Orchestra) Zon X40160

0319 **The Dairymaids** (1906)

SC	'The Sea Serpent' (Stanley Kirkby) G&T 3–2761 (1906)
SC	'The Sandow Girl' (Carrie Tubb) G&T 3668 (1906)
SC	'Hullo, little Stranger' (Carrie Tubb) G&T 3669 (1906)
SC	'Dreamland' (Arthur Grover) EB 13504
Orch	Selections 1, 2 & 3 (Band of H.M. Coldstream Guards) G&T (1906)

0320 **The Girl Behind the Counter** (1906)

OC	'If there Hadn't Been an Apple on the Tree' (Fred Allandale) Fav 1–67001 (1906)
OC	'Enid' (Fred Allandale) Fav 1–65030 (1906)
OC	'I Mean to Marry a Man' (Isabel Jay) Fav 1–66015 (1906)
OC	'Won't you Buy?' (Isabel Jay with E. Gordon Cleather – not OC) Fav 1–69003 (1906), Ar 579
SC	'If there Hadn't Been an Apple on the Tree' (Harry Bluff) EB 6913
Orch	Selection (Band of H.M. Coldstream Guards as London Volunteer Brigade) Zon X–04145 (1906)

0323 **Amasis** (1906)

OC	'Little Princess, Look Up' (Ruth Vincent) Col 6003, Col 132 (1907)
SC	'Little Princess, Look Up' (Margaret Cooper) Pathé 268
SC	'Little Princess, Look Up' (Violet Essex) Pop P–338, Imp 905
Orch	Selection (Band of H.M. Scots Guards) Pathé 63/64 (1906)

0324 **The New Aladdin** (1906)

SC	'Dougal' (Peter Dawson as Hector Grant) Zon X–42558 (1907)
Orch	Selection (Band of H.M. Scots Guards) Pathé 62/63 (1906)

0325 **The Vicar of Wakefield** (1906)

SC	'There Are Birds in the Valley' (Reed Miller) Pathé 5505
SC	'There Are Birds in the Valley' (Walter Hyde) Odeon 0397/57636

0328 **Miss Hook of Holland** (1907)

SC	'Little Miss Wooden Shoes' (Ruby Gray) Beka 40171
SC	'A pink Petty from Peter' (Ruby Gray) Beka 40174
SC	Vocal Gems (Zonophone Light Opera Co.) Zon 5662

SC Vocal Gems (Light Opera Co.) HMV C–1989 (1930)
Orch Selection (Band of H.M. Coldstream Guards) HMV 0111

0329 **My Darling** (1907)

SC 'The shady Side of Bond Street' (Stanley Kirkby as Walter Miller) G&T GC3–2885 (1907)
SC 'Hats off to the King' (George Baker) Pathé 8847

0330 **Tom Jones** (1907)

OC 'For Tonight' (Ruth Vincent) Col 6009, Col 132 (1907)
RC 'West Country Lad' (Harry Welchman) Col DB–783, DB–754 (1932)
SC 'For Tonight' (Florence Smithson) HMV 3917, B–444 (1912), RR 'Singing Actresses' WRC SH433
SC 'For Tonight' (Violet Essex) Pilot/Polyphon 5628 (1912)
SC 'For Tonight' (Rosina Buckman) Pathé 63, 2091
SC 'For Tonight' (Edith Trew) Fav 415.66114
SC 'For Tonight' (Anne Ziegler) HMV B9241
SC 'For Tonight' (Carrie Lanceley) Grammavox D30–2058
SC 'On a January Morning' (Keith Falkner) HMV B–3658 (1930)
SC 'On a January Morning' (David Brazell) Pathé 991
SC 'West Country Lad' (David Brazell) Pathé 991
SC 'On a January Morning'/'West Country Lad' (Ivor Foster) Odeon 0623, 66624, 66643
SC LP Highlights EMI–Odeon CSD 3628 (1967)
Orch Dances (Symphony Orchestra conducted by Edward German) HMV 2–579 and E–28 (1917)
Orch Selection (New Symphony Orchestra) HMV C–2442 (1931)

0333 **Lady Tatters** (1907)

SC 'Captive am I' (Ivor Foster) Odeon 44927
SC 'Boot, Saddle, to Horse and to Duty' (Ivor Foster) Odeon 66127
These two titles RR Odeon 0256

0334 **The Girls of Gottenberg** (1907)

SC 'The Girls of Gottenberg' (Billy Williams) Homophone 384
Orch Selection (Band of H.M. Coldstream Guards) G&T 0126 (1907)
Orch Selection (Band of H.M. King's Colonials) Pathé 8080

0338 **The Three Kisses** (1907)

SC 'Life's a Song' (Mabel Green) Pathé 896/78962 (1911)

0340 **The Gay Gordons** (1907)

OC 'Humpty and Dumpty' (Ellaline Terriss) G&T 3741 (1907), HMV 3741
OC 'Everybody's fond of Me' (Ellaline Terriss) G&T 3742 (1907)
SC 'Humpty and Dumpty' (H. Payne) Zon X42720

0342 **My Mimosa Maid** (1908)

Orch Selection (Band of H.M. Coldstream Guards) GC 0169 (1908)

0344 **Havana** (1908)

OC 'Zara' (Jessie Broughton) Col 26461 (1908)

SC Vocal Gems (Victor Light Opera Co.) Vic 31744 (USA) (1909)
Orch Selection (Band of H.M. King's Colonials) Pathé 8079

0348 **King of Cadonia** (1908)
Orch Selection (Black Diamonds Band) GC 0190 (1908)

0350 **The Belle of Brittany** (1908)
SC Vocal Gems (Victor Light Opera Co.) Vic 31765 (USA), HMV 04504 (1909)

0353 **Our Miss Gibbs** (1909)
OC 'Moonstruck' (Gertie Millar) HMV 03215 (1910), RR HMV C–530 (1910), RR WRC SH186
OC 'In Yorkshire' (Gertie Millar) HMV 03214 (1910), RR HMV C–529 (1910), RR WRC SH186
OC 'Yip! I-addy! I-ay!' (George Grossmith Jr) HMV 02219 (1910), RR HMV C–569, Jumbo A–415 (1909), RR WRC SH186
OC 'Bertie the Bounder' (George Grossmith Jr) HMV 02255 (1910), RR HMV C–568, Jumbo A–520 (1910), RR WRC SH186
OC 'Angelina' (George Grossmith Jr) HMV 02253, Jumbo A–520 (1910)
OC 'Ou-la-la' (George Grossmith Jr) HMV 02285, Jumbo A–569, Ar 1838 (1910)
SC 'Our Farm' (W. H. Berry) HMV 4–2111 (1910)
SC 'Mary'/'In Yorkshire' (Violet Essex) Beka 359 (1910)
SC 'Bertie the Bounder' (Jack Charman) Pathé 8292
SC 'My Yorkshire Lassie' (Stewart Gardner as Thomas Franklin) GC4–2032 (1909)
SC 'Moonstruck' (Eleanor Jones-Hudson as Marion Jerome) GC 3824 (1909)
SC 'Mary' (Eleanor Jones-Hudson as Marion Jerome) HMV GC 3825 (1909)
SC 'In Yorkshire' (Eleanor Jones-Hudson as Marion Jerome) GC 3826 (1909)
SC 'Our Farm' (Eleanor Jones-Hudson as Marion Jerome, Charles Handy) GC 2–4005 (1909)
SC 'Moonstruck' (Freda Matthews) Indestructible 7014
SC 'Mary' (Ethel Williams, Jack Charman) Indestructible 7023
SC 'In Yorkshire' (Lottie Berg) Indestructible 7003
SC 'Yip! I-addy! I-ay!' (Blanche Ring) G&T GC 3817 (1909)
SC 'Yip! I-addy! I-ay!' (Harry Fay)/'Mary' (Yoland Noble, Ernest Wilson) Col 1143
SC Vocal Gems (Victor Light Opera Co.) Vic 31802 (USA) (1910)
SC Gems (Bohemian Orchestra & chorus) GC 0598 (1909)
Orch 'Yip! I-addy! I-ay!'/'Bertie the Bounder' (Black Diamonds Band) HMV 2–471 (1910)
Orch Selection (Reginald Burston and the London Coliseum Orchestra) Dec MW–274 (1944)
Orch Selection (Imperial Orchestra) EB Winner 2040

0354 **The Dashing Little Duke** (1909)
SC 'Nobody Cares for Me' (Eleanor Jones-Hudson as Marion Jerome) GC 3828 (1909)
SC 'Five Little Pigs' (Eleanor Jones-Hudson as Marion Jerome) GC 3829 (1909)
SC 'Love and Pride' (Eleanor Jones-Hudson as Marion Jerome) GC 3823 (1909)
SC 'Lisette' (Ernest Pike as Herbert Payne) GC 4–2038 (1909)
SC 'A good Story' (Ernest Pike as Herbert Payne, Stewart Gardner as Clarence Franklin) GC 2–4004 (1909)

Orch Selection (Black Diamonds Band) GC 0191/2 (1909)

0355 **A Persian Princess** (1909)

SC 'Land of Heart's Content' (Eleanor Jones-Hudson as Marion Jerome) GC 3827 (1909)
SC 'Juniper Tree' (Eleanor Jones-Hudson as Marion Jerome) GC 3830 (1909)
SC 'Cupid's Caravan' (Harold Wilde as Horatio Germaine) GC 4–2037 (1909)

0356 **The Arcadians** (1909)

OC 'Bring me a Rose' (Phyllis Dare) HMV 03190 (1910)
OC 'The Girl with a Brogue' (Phyllis Dare) HMV 03191 (1910), RR HMV C–524
OC 'The Pipes of Pan'/'Arcady Is ever Young' (Florence Smithson) Col 542 (1915)
OC 'Come back to Arcady'/'Light Is my Heart' (Florence Smithson) Col 543 (1915)
OC 'My Motter' (Alfred Lester) Col 544 (1915), RR 'Forty Years of English Musical Comedy' Rococo 4007 (Canada)
SC 'Charming Weather'/'Half-past Two' (Violet Essex, Harry Thornton) Fav 289, John Bull B–29 (1910)
SC 'The Pipes of Pan' (Violet Essex) Pilot–Polyphon 5651 (1912)
SC 'The Pipes of Pan'/'Arcady Is ever Young' (Winnie Melville) HMV 3285 (1929)
SC 'The Pipes of Pan' (Eleanor Jones-Hudson as Marion Jerome) HMV 3832, RR B480
SC 'The Pipes of Pan' (Elsie Fox-Bennett) Jumbo A25088
SC 'Light Is my Heart' (Caroline Hatchard) Pathé 844
SC 'My Motter' (Harry Carlton) Gramophone Concert Record GC 4–2057
SC 'My Motter' (Harry Fay) Indestructible 7013
SC 'Charming Weather' (Mabel Mayhew, Irving Gillette)/'The Girl with a Brogue' (Ada Jones) Col 1577
SC 'Sweet Simplicitas' (Charles Handy) GC 4–2036 (1909)
SC 'Arcady is ever Young' (Elsie Fox-Bennett) Jumbo A25125
SC 'Bring Me a Rose' (Phyllis Drew) Indestructible 7042
SC Vocal Gems (Anne Welch, Morton Colyer, Victor Conway) Dec K–564
SC Vocal Gems (Victor Light Opera Co.) Vic 31775 (USA)
SC Gems (Bohemian Orchestra and Chorus) HMV 0596
SC Medley (Light Opera Co.) HMV C–1684 (1929)
SC LP (studio cast album) Col TWO 233 (1968)
SC LP (studio cast album) MFP 1323 (1969)
Orch Selections I & II (Band of H.M. Coldstream Guards) HMV 0203 and 0209
Orch Overture (Arthur Wood and his Orchestra) Col DX–573

0363 **The Balkan Princess** (1910)

SC 'A hard Life' (Albert Whelan) Jumbo 504 (1910)
SC 'Wonderful World' (Annie Bartle) Indestructible 7002
SC 'Love and Laughter' (Mabel Green) Pathé 896
SC 'Oh, You dear delightful Women' (Jack Charman, Ida Hamilton) Indestructible 7012
Orch 'Valse' (Leslie Jeffries and the Grand Hotel Orchestra, Eastbourne) Par R–1887 (1934)
SC Vocal Gems (Light Opera Co.) HMV 04507 (1910)
SC Vocal Gems (Victor Light Opera Co.) Vic 31821 (USA)

0366 **The Islander** (1910)

SC 'I Feel so Lonely' (Albert Whelan) Jumbo A–91
SC 'The Caledonian Chiel' (Dugas Cratur) Pathé 8553

0369 **The Quaker Girl** (1910)

OC 'Come to the Ball' (George Carvey) HMV 02298 (1910), RR WRC SH186
OC 'I'm a married Man' (Joseph Coyne) HMV 02369 (1911), RR WRC SH186
OC 'A Quaker Girl' (Gertie Millar) HMV 03216, C–529 (1910)
OC 'Tony from America' (Gertie Millar) HMV 03242, C–530 (1911)
OC 'The little grey Bonnet' (Gertie Millar) HMV 03260 (1911) (All three Gertie Millar titles RR WRC SH186)
OC 'Come to the Ball' (Gracie Leigh) HMV 03298
SC 'A Quaker Girl' (Elsie Fox-Bennett) Jumbo A25126
SC 'Ah, Oui!'/'O Time, Time' (Violet Essex) Beka 411 (1911)
SC 'Wonderful'/'The bad Boy and the good Girl' (Violet Essex, Stanley Kirkby) Beka 410 (1911)
SC 'O Time, Time' (Dorothy Dayne) HMV 03229 (1911)
SC 'Come to the Ball' (Stanley Kirkby) Col Rena 1615
SC 'Just like Father Used to Do' (Harry Fay as Harry Carlton) HMV 4–2112, B–446 (1910)
SC 'Take a step' (Doris Cowan, George Baker) HMV B–487
SC 'Come to the Ball' (Ralph Errol)/Selection (Prince's Orchestra) Col Rena 303
SC Vocal Gems (Victor Light Opera Co.) Vic 31847, 35410 (USA)
SC Vocal Gems (Columbia Light Opera Co.) Col Rena 336 (1912), US Col A–5388
SC Vocal Gems (Light Opera Co.) HMV C–2015 (1930)
SC Vocal Gems (Columbia Light Opera Co.) Col DX–413 (1932)
Orch Selection (Band of H.M. Coldstream Guards) HMV 0312
Orch Selections I and II (Band of H.M. Coldstream Guards) HMV 0352/3
Orch 'Quaker Girl Waltz' (Iff's Orchestra) HMV 0651
Orch Selection (Imperial Orchestra) EB Winner 2040

0370 **Peggy** (1911)

OC 'Mr Edison' (George Grossmith) HMV 02345 (1911), RR 'Forty Years of English Musical Comedy' Rococo 4007 (Canada)
OC 'Ladies, Beware!' (Phyllis Dare) HMV 03230 (1911)
OC 'You're the one Man I'm Looking For' (Phyllis Dare, George Grossmith) HMV 04083 (1911)
OC 'Which he Didn't Expect from a Lady' (Connie Ediss) HMV 03251 (1911)
OC 'I Like to 'ave a little Bit On' (Connie Ediss) HMV 02352 (1911)
OC 'Whistle and the Girls Come Round' (Robert Hale) HMV 02344 (1911)
OC 'The Lass with the Lasso' (Olive May) HMV 03231 (1911)
OC 'I Beg your Pardon' (George Grossmith, Edmund Payne) HMV 04082, C–567 (1911)
OC 'Don't Forget you're a Lady' (George Grossmith) HMV 02316 (1911)
SC 'Whistle and the Girls Come Round' (Jack Charman) Pathé 8422
SC Vocal Gems (Light Opera Co.) HMV 04517/8

0373 **The Mousmé** (1911)

OC 'The little Japanese Mama' (Cicely Courtneidge) HMV 3892 B–444 (1911),

		RR 'Singing Actresses' WRC SH433
	OC	'Honourable Jappy Bride' (Cicely Courtneidge) HMV 3894 (1911), RR 'Singing Actresses' WRC SH433
	OC	'Oh Dear! little Jappy Girls' (Cicely Courtneidge) HMV 3904 (1911), RR 'Singing Actresses' WRC SH433
	OC	'I Know nothing of Life' (Florence Smithson) HMV 3893 B–444 (1911), RR 'Singing Actresses' WRC SH433
	OC	'The Temple Bell' (Florence Smithson) HMV 03256, C–532 (1911), RR 'Singing Actresses' WRC SH433
	OC	'My Samisen' (Florence Smithson) HMV 03254, C–531 (1911), RR 'Forty Years of English Musical Comedy' Rococo 4007 (Canada)
	OC	'The Corner of my Eye' (George Hestor) HMV 02353 (1911)
	OC	'In Toki-oki-o' (Dan Rolyat) HMV 4–2159 (1911)
	SC	'Memories' (George Baker, Carrie Herwin) Pathé 5218
	SC	'Memories' (Charles Holland, Mary Reed)/'The Corner of my Eye' (Charles Holland) Col 1900
	SC	Vocal Gems (Light Opera Co.) HMV 04521/2/3 (1911)
	Orch	Selection (The Mayfair Orchestra) HMV 0675
	Orch	Overture (The Mayfair Orchestra) HMV 0676
	Orch	Overture (Arthur Wood and his Orchestra) Col DX–573
0376	**The Sunshine Girl** (1912)	
	OC	'Here's to Love' (Violet Essex) Pilot/Polyphon 5628 (1912)
	OC	'Little Girl, Little Girl' (George Grossmith) HMV 02404, C–577 (1912)
	OC	'The other Chap' (George Grossmith) HMV 02406 (1912)
	SC	'Brighton' (Eva Vine) Pathé 79870
	SC	'I've Been to the Durbar' (Eva Vine) Pathé 79871
	SC	'You can't Play every Instrument in the Band' (Joseph Cawthorn) Vic 70098 (USA)
	SC	Vocal Gems (Light Opera Co.) Part I HMV 04529, C–522; Part II HMV 04530 (1912)
	SC	Vocal Gems (Victor Light Opera Co.), Vic 31889, Vic 35444 (USA), HMV 04576 (1913)
	Orch	Selection (Band of H.M. Coldstream Guards) HMV C–198
	Orch	Selection (Imperial Symphony Orchestra) Pathé 8641
	Orch	Selection (Royal Court Orchestra) EB Winner 2270
0379	**The Dancing Mistress** (1912)	
	SC	Vocal Gems (Light Opera Co.) HMV 04561 C–520 (1913)
	Orch	Selection (The Mayfair Orchestra) HMV C–275 (1913)
0381	**The Girl from Utah** (1913)	
	SC	Vocal Gems (Victor Light Opera Co.) Vic 35404 (USA) (1914), Vic 12413 (USA) (1938)
	SC	Vocal Gems (Chappell Light Opera Co.) Chappell A–1 (1913)
	Orch	Selection (The Royal Guards Band) EB Winner 2601
0382	**Are you There?** (1913)	
	OC	'Roseway' (Shirley Kellogg) HMV 03357 C–524 (1913)
0384	**After the Girl** (1914)	
	SC	Vocal Gems (Chappell Light Opera Co.) Chappell A–2 (1914)

Index

This index includes all people involved in musical theatre mentioned in the text. It also includes the following people listed in the production details: composers, authors, librettists, lyricists, producers, directors and musical directors.

All musical show titles are indexed (except for titles which were, for various reasons, dropped at an early stage) and the 'code numbers' of the important shows are given in square brackets. The pages on which their production details occur are shown in bold.

London theatres and those in the provinces are included, as are newspapers, magazines and journals mentioned or quoted from in the text.

CHARTERHOUSE LIBRARY
023041